SHEPARD'S
ACTS AND CASES
BY
POPULAR NAMES

FEDERAL AND STATE

A compilation of popular names by which federal and
state acts and cases have been referred to or cited
together with an identification of each act
in terms of its constitutional or statutory
references and each case in terms of
the volume and page reference
where the text of the decision
may be found.

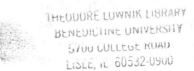
FIFTH EDITION - 1999, PART 1

SHEPARD'S
555 Middle Creek Parkway
Colorado Springs, CO 80921-3622
1-800-899-6000

EDITORIAL STAFF
Shepard's Acts and Cases by Popular Names

Team Leader: LEE A. HENRY

Editorial Staff Members: CAROL SUE ANDERSEN, BRADLEY W. BAECKER, B.M. HANSON, THOMAS M. HENNEMAN, GLORIA S. LIKNESS, PETER J. PASQUALE, JEANNE SAMPLE-MCNEIL

Editor: CHERYL L. ROSS

Editorial Quality Assurance Coordinator: CHRISTOPHER J. WEST

Publisher, Specialized Citations: LISA M. PETERSON, J.D.

**To reach Shepard's call 1-800-899-6000
or visit our homepage at http://www.shepards.com.**

TABLE OF CONTENTS

PART 1

PAGE

Preface - iv

Abbreviations—Acts - v-vi

Abbreviations—Cases - vii

Federal and State Acts Cited by Popular Name - - - - - - - - - - - - - - - - 1

PREFACE

Shepard's Acts and Cases by Popular Names is a reference tool that provides citation information for statutes and cases that are commonly referred to by popular name.

Federal and state acts are listed alphabetically and can be located by name (e.g., Pine Creek Scenic Rivers Act or Pilot Records Improvement Act of 1996). Shepard's Acts and Cases by Popular Names also provides a quick indexing system for locating a citation or list of citations from several states–including federal statutes–dealing with a specific topic (e.g., Lemon Law or Water Conservation). These indexes also include citations to Constitutional provisions (e.g., Equal Suffrage Amendment).

Where a particular case is known only by its popular name, the alphabetical indexes found in these volumes can be used to locate the needed citation to the case (e.g., Miranda).

SUPPLEMENTATION

Shepard's Acts and Cases by Popular Names consists of the 1999 bound volume (Parts 1–3) and the current issue of the soft-covered cumulative supplement. Cumulative supplements are published bimonthly in February, April, June, August, October and December. Supplementation is cumulative, therefore, only the most recent supplement needs to be retained and used with the bound volume. From time to time, as the accumulation of citations necessitates, a cumulative supplement will be permanently bound. Each supplement-cover provides the necessary information as to "What Your Library Should Contain." Always consult these supplement covers before discarding any soft-covered supplements or bound volumes.

ORGANIZATION

Shepard's Acts and Cases by Popular Names contains two divisions. Acts, i.e., federal and state statutory and constitutional materials, are listed alphabetically by popular name in the first division. Cases are listed alphabetically by popular name in the second division. Please consult the tables of abbreviations used in the division for Federal and State cases cited by Popular Names to identify the citing references that appear in these bound volumes.

Citations to federal statutes include the United States Code title and section numbers wherever this information is available. Sometimes a law is merely cited by the date on which it was enacted. The citation format contained in these volumes for federal statutes includes a citation to the date a law was enacted, the Public sequential number and Congressional Session that enacted the law, a Statutes at Large citation, and the citation to the U.S. Code where this information is available.

Parallel citations, cases that are published in more than one reporter, are included for the widely available reports (e.g., U.S., S. Ct., and L. Ed. citations for the United States Supreme Court decisions; official and regional reporter citations for state-court decisions in jurisdictions that publish a separate state official report).

CITATIONS RESEARCH

After identifying a case or statute in Shepard's Acts and Cases by Popular Names, ascertain its status as authority and locate additional cases dealing with similar issues by consulting the pertinent Shepard's Citations.

SHEPARD'S

ABBREVIATIONS—ACTS

Adm.–Administrative

AG–Agriculture

Ala.–Alabama

Am.–Amended

Amend.–Amendment

Ann.–Annotated

Appx.–Appendix

Ariz.–Arizona

Ark.–Arkansas

Art.–Article

Aug.–August

BO–Business Occupations and
    Professions

BR–Business Regulation

CA–Corporations and Associations

Cal.–California

Ch[s].–Chapter[s]

Civ.–Civil

CJ–Courts and Judicial Proceedings

CL–Commercial Law

Cl[s].–Clause[s]

Colo.–Colorado

Comp.–Compiled

Conn.–Connecticut

Consol.–Consolidated

Const.–Constitution

Crim.–Criminal

C.S.–Called Session

D.C.–District of Columbia

Dec.–December

Del.–Delaware

Div.–Division

ED–Education

EN–Environment

ET–Estates and Trusts

Ex.–Extra

Ex. Sess.–Extra Session

Feb.–February

Fla.–Florida

FI–Financial Institutions

FL–Family Law

Ga.–Georgia

G.A.–General Assembly

Gen.–General

H.B.–House Bill

Haw.–Hawaii

HE–Health-Environmental

HG–Health-General

HO–Health-Occupation

H.R.–House Reports

Ida.–Idaho

Ill.–Illinois

IN–Insurance Law

Ind.–Indiana

Init. Meas.–Initiative Measure

Jan.–January

Kan.–Kansas

Ky.–Kentucky

La.–Louisiana

L.B.–Legislative Bill

LE–Labor and Employment

Leg.–Legislature

Mass.–Massachusetts

Md.–Maryland

Me.–Maine

Mich.–Michigan

Minn.–Minnesota

Miss.–Mississippi

Mo.–Missouri

Mont.–Montana

N.C.–North Carolina

N.D.–North Dakota

Neb.–Nebraska

Nev.–Nevada

N.H.–New Hampshire

N.J.–New Jersey

N.M.–New Mexico

No.–Number

Nov.–November

NR–Natural Resources

nt[s].–note[s]

N.Y.–New York

Oct.–October
Okla.–Oklahoma
Ore.–Oregon
p[p].–page[s]
Pa.–Pennsylvania
Pamph. Laws–Pamphlet Laws
P.L.–Public Law
PP–State Personnel and Pension
prec.–preceding
Proc.–Procedure
P.R.–Puerto Rico
Rev.–Revised
R.I.–Rhode Island
RP–Real Property
§[§]–Section[s]
S.B.–Senate Bill
S.C.–South Carolina
S.D.–South Dakota
SF–State Finance & Procurement
SG–State Government
Sept.–September
Sess.–Session

Sp.–Special
Sp. Sess.–Special Session
S.R.–Senate Reports
Stat.–Statutes or United States
    Statutes at Large
Subd.–Subdivision
Subsec.–Subsection
Supp.–Supplement
Tenn.–Tennessee
Tex.–Texas
TG–Tax-General
TP–Tax Property
TR–Transportation
Unconsol.–Unconsolidated
U.S.–United States
Va.–Virginia
Vol[s].–Volume[s]
Vt.–Vermont
Wash.–Washington
Wis.–Wisconsin
W. Va.–West Virginia
Wyo.–Wyoming

ABBREVIATIONS—CASES

The following abbreviations are used to identify the citing references that appear in this bound volume:

A.–Atlantic Reporter

A.2d–Atlantic Reporter, Second Series

Abb. N. Cas.–Abbott's New Cases, New York

Abb. Pr.–Abbott's Practice Reports, New York

Abb. Pr. (n.s.)–Abbott's Practice Reports, New Series, New York

Abs. (n.s.)–Abstracts, New Series (Treasury Decisions)

A.D.–Appellate Division Reports (New York Supreme Court)

A.D.2d–Appellate Division Reports, Second Series (New York Supreme Court)

Ala.–Alabama Reports

Ala. App.–Alabama Appellate Courts Reports

Alaska–Alaska Reports

Alaska Fed.–Alaska Federal Reports

Allen–Allen's Massachusetts Reports

Am. B.R. (n.s.)–American Bankruptcy Reports, New Series

A.M.C.–American Maritime Cases

App. D.C.–Appeal Cases, District of Columbia

Ariz.–Arizona Reports

Ariz. App.–Arizona Appeals Reports

Ark.–Arkansas Reports

Ark. App.–Arkansas Appellate Reports

Bailey–Bailey's South Carolina Law Reports

Barb.–Barbour's Supreme Court Reports, New York

Baxt.–Baxter's Tennessee Reports

B.C.R.–Baltimore City Reports

Bosw.–Bosworth's Superior Court Reports, New York

Boyce–Boyce's Reports, Delaware

B.R.–Bankruptcy Reporter

Bradf.–Bradford's Surrogate Reports, New York

Brewst.–Brewster's Reports, Pennsylvania

B.T.A.–Reports of the United States Board of Tax Appeals

Cal.–California Supreme Court Reports

Cal. 2d–California Supreme Court Reports, Second Series

Cal. 3d–California Supreme Court Reports, Third Series

Cal. 3d S.–California Supreme Court Reports, Third Series (Special Tribunal Supplement)

Cal. 4th–California Supreme Court Reports, Fourth Series

Cal. App.–California Appellate Reports

Cal. App. 2d–California Appellate Reports, Second Series

Cal. App. 3d–California Appellate Reports, Third Series

Cal. App. 3d S.–California Appellate Reports, Third Series Supplement

Cal. App. 4th–California Appellate Reports, Fourth Series

Cal. App. 4th S.–California Appellate Reports, Fourth Series Supplement

Cal. Comp. Cas.–California Compensation Cases

Cal. R. Com.–Opinions and Orders of the Railroad Commission of California

Cal. Rptr.–California Reporter

Cal. Rptr. 2d–California Reporter, Second Series

C.C.A.–Circuit Court of Appeals Reports

C.C.P.A.–United States Court of Customs and Patent Appeals Reports

C.D.–Decisions of the Commissioner of Patents

Civ. P. Rep.–Civil Procedure Reports, New York

Clark–Clark's Pennsylvania Law Journal Reports

Code Rep.–Code Reporter, New York

Colo.–Colorado Reports

Colo. App.–Colorado Court of Appeals Reports

Conn.–Connecticut Reports

Conn. App.–Connecticut Appellate Reports

Conn. Cir. Ct.–Connecticut Circuit Court Reports

Conn. Supp.–Connecticut Supplement

Cow.–Cowen's Common Law Reports, New York

Ct. Cl.–Court of Claims Reports, United States

Ct. Cust.–Court of Customs Appeals Reports, United States

Ct. Int'l Trade–United States Court of International Trade Reports

Cust. Ct.–Customs Court Reports, United States

Cush.–Cushing Massachusetts Reports

Dakota–Dakota Reports

Daly–Daly's Common Pleas Reports, New York

D.C.–District of Columbia Reports

D.C.H.–Reports of the United States District Court of Hawaii

Del.–Delaware Reports

Del. Ch.–Delaware Chancery Reports

Denio–Denio's Common Law Reports, New York

Dep't Rep.–State Department Reports, New York

Duer–Duer's Superior Court Reports, New York

E.D.R.–Education Department Reports, New York

Edm. Sel. Cas.–Edmond's Select Cases, New York

F.–Federal Reporter

F.2d–Federal Reporter, Second Series

F.3d–Federal Reporter, Third Series

F. Cas.–Federal Cases

F.C.C.–Federal Communications Commission Reports

F.C.C.2d–Federal Communications Commission Reports, Second Series

F. Supp.–Federal Supplement

F. Supp. 2d–Federal Supplement, Second Series

F.T.C.–Federal Trade Commission Decisions

Fla.–Florida Reports

Fla. Supp.–Florida Supplement

Fla. Supp. 2d–Florida Supplement, Second Series

F.P.C.–Federal Power Commission Reports

F.R.D.–Federal Rules Decisions

G. & J.–Gill and Johnson Reports, Maryland

Ga.–Georgia Reports

Ga. App.–Georgia Appeals Reports

Gen. Appraisers–United States General Appraisers

Gratt.–Grattan Virginia Reports

Gray–Gray Massachusetts Reports

Harr.–Harrington Delaware Reports

H.H.–Hayward and Hazleton's Reports, United States

Haw.–Hawaii Reports

Haw. App.–Hawaii Appellate Reports

Heisk.–Heiskell Tennessee Reports

Hill–Hill's Common Law Reports, New York

Hopk. Ch.–Hopkins' Chancery Reports

Houst.–Houston Reports, Delaware

How. Pr.–Howard's Practice Reports, New York

Hun–Hun's Supreme Court Reports, New York

I.C.–Interstate Commerce Reports

I.C.C.–Interstate Commerce Commission Reports

Idaho–Idaho Reports

Ill. Dec.–Illinois Decisions

Ill.–Illinois Reports

Ill. 2d–Illinois Reports, Second Series

Ill. App.–Illinois Appellate Court Reports

Ill. App. 2d–Illinois Appellate Court Reports, Second Series

Ill. App. 3d–Illinois Appellate Court Reports, Third Series

Ill. Cir. Ct.–Illinois Circuit Court Reports

Ill. Ct. Cl.–Illinois Court of Claims Reports

Ind.–Indiana Reports

Ind. App.–Indiana Court of Appeals Reports (Indiana Appellate Court Reports before 1972)

Interior Dec.–Decisions of the Department of the Interior

Iowa–Iowa Reports

Johns.–Johnson's Common Law Reports, New York

Johns. Ch.–Johnson's Chancery Reports, New York

Jones & S.–Jones and Spencer's Superior Court Reports, New York

Kan.–Kansas Reports

Kan. App.–Kansas Court of Appeals Reports

Kan. App. 2d–Kansas Court of Appeals Reports, Second Series

Keyes–Keyes' Reports, New York

Ky. Law Rep.–Kentucky Law Reporter

Ky.–Kentucky Reports

La.–Louisiana Reports

La. Ann.–Louisiana Annual Reports

La. App.–Louisiana Court of Appeals Reports

L. Ed.–Lawyer's Edition, United States Supreme Court Reports

L. Ed. 2d–Lawyer's Edition, United States Supreme Court Reports, Second Series

Leigh–Leigh Virginia Reports

Mart. (n.s.)–Martin Louisiana Reports, New Series (Louisiana Term Reports)

Mart. (o.s.)–Martin Louisiana Reports, Old Series (Louisiana Term Reports)

Marv.–Marvel Delaware Reports

Mass. App. Ct.–Massachusetts Appeals
  Court Reports
Mass. App. Div.–Appellate Division
  Reports Massachusetts
Mass.–Massachusetts Reports
McGrath–McGrath's Mandamus Cases,
  Michigan
M.C.C.–Interstate Commerce Commission
  Reports, Motor Carrier Cases
Md.–Maryland Reports
Md. App.–Maryland Appellate Reports
Me.–Maine Reports
Met.–Metcalf Massachusetts Reports
Mich.–Michigan Reports
Mich. App.–Michigan Appeals Reports
Mills–Mills' Surrogate's Court Reports,
  New York
Minn.–Minnesota Reports
Minor–Minor Alabama Reports
Misc.–New York Miscellaneous Reports
Misc. 2d–New York Miscellaneous Reports,
  Second Series
Miss.–Mississippi Reports
M.J.–Military Justice Reporter
Mo.–Missouri Reports
Mo. App.–Missouri Appeals Reports
Mont.–Montana Reports
N.C.–North Carolina Supreme Court Reports
N.C. App.–North Carolina Court of Appeals
  Reports
N.D.–North Dakota Reports
N.E.–North Eastern Reporter
N.E.2d–North Eastern Reporter, Second
  Series
Neb.–Nebraska Reports
Nev.–Nevada Reports
N.H.–New Hampshire Reports
N.J.–New Jersey Reports
N.J. Eq.–New Jersey Equity Reports
N.J.L.–New Jersey Law Reports
N.J. Misc.–New Jersey Miscellaneous
  Reports
N.J. Super.–New Jersey Superior Court
  Reports
N.L.R.B.–Decisions and Orders of the
  National Labor Relations Board
N.M.–New Mexico Reports
N.W.–North Western Reporter
N.W.2d–North Western Reporter, Second
  Series
N.Y.–New York Reports
N.Y.2d–New York Reports, Second Series

N.Y. Crim.–New York Criminal Reports
N.Y. St. Rep.–New York State Reporter
N.Y. Super. Ct.–New York Superior Court
  Reports
N.Y.S.–New York Supplement
N.Y.S.2d–New York Supplement, Second
  Series
Off. Gaz. Pat. Office–Official Gazette of the
  United States Patent Office
Ohio–Ohio Reports
Ohio Law Abs.–Ohio Law Abstract
Ohio App.–Ohio Appellate Reports
Ohio App. 2d–Ohio Appellate Reports,
  Second Series
Ohio App. 3d–Ohio Appellate Reports,
  Third Series
Ohio C.C. (n.s.)–Ohio Circuit Court Reports,
  New Series
Ohio Cir. Dec.–Ohio Circuit Decisions
Ohio Dec.–Ohio Decisions
Ohio Dec. Reprint–Ohio Decisions, Reprint
Ohio F. Des.–Ohio Federal Decisions
Ohio Law Rep.–Ohio Law Reporter
Ohio Misc.–Ohio Miscellaneous
Ohio Misc. 2d–Ohio Miscellaneous,
  Second Series
Ohio N.P. (n.s.)–Ohio Nisi Prius Reports,
  New Series
Ohio Op.–Ohio Opinions
Ohio Op. 2d–Ohio Opinions, Second Series
Ohio Op. 3d–Ohio Opinions, Third Series
Ohio St.–Ohio State Reports
Ohio St. 2d–Ohio State Reports, Second Series
Ohio St. 3d–Ohio State Reports, Third Series
Okla.–Oklahoma Reports
Okla. Crim.–Oklahoma Criminal Reports
Ore.–Oregon Reports
Ore. App.–Oregon Reports, Court of Appeals
P.–Pacific Reporter
P.2d–Pacific Reporter, Second Series
Pa.–Pennsylvania State Reports
Paige Ch.–Paige's Chancery Reports,
  New York
Park.–Parker's Criminal Reports, New York
Pa. Commw.–Pennsylvania Commonwealth
  Court Reports
Pa. D. & C.–Pennsylvania District and
  County Reports
Pa. D. & C.2d–Pennsylvania District and
  County Reports, Second Series
Pa. D. & C.3d–Pennsylvania District and
  County Reports, Third Series

Pa. D. & C.4th–Pennsylvania District and County Reports, Fourth Series

Pa. L.J. Rep.–Pennsylvania Law Journal Reports

Pa. Super.–Pennsylvania Superior Court Reports

Pelt.–Peltier's Decisions, Parish at Orleans, Louisiana

Penne.–Pennewill Delaware Reports

Phila.–Philadelphia Reports

Pick.–Pickering Massachusetts Reports

Pub. Lands Dec.–Public Lands Decisions

Quincy–Quincy's Massachusetts Reports

Reappr. Dec.–Reappraisement Decisions

Redf.–Redfield's Surrogates Reports, New York

R.I.–Rhode Island Reports

Sandf.–Sandford's Superior Court Reports, New York

Sandf. Ch.–Sandford's Chancery Reports, New York

S. Ct.–Supreme Court Reporter

S.C.–South Carolina Reports

S.C. Eq.–South Carolina Equity Reports

S.C.L.–South Carolina Law Reports

S.D.–South Dakota Reports

S.D.C. (n.s.)–Supreme Court, District of Columbia Reports, New Series

S.E.–South Eastern Reporter

S.E.2d–South Eastern Reporter, Second Series

S.E.C.–Securities and Exchange Commission Decisions and Reports

Serg. & Rawle–Sergeant and Rawle Pennsylvania State Reports

Silv.–Silvernail's Supreme Court Reports, New York

So.–Southern Reporter

So. 2d–Southern Reporter, Second Series

Stew.–Stewart Alabama Reports

S.W.–South Western Reporter

S.W.2d–South Western Reporter, Second Series

T.B. Mon.–Kentucky Reports, T.B. Monroe

T.C.–Tax Court Reports of the United States Tax Court

Tenn.–Tennessee Reports

Tenn. App.–Tennessee Appeals Reports

Tenn. Crim. App.–Tennessee Criminal Appeals Reports

Tex.–Texas Reports

Tex. Civ. App.–Texas Civil Appeals Reports

Tex. Crim.–Texas Criminal Reports

Thomp. & Cook's–Thompson and Cook's Supreme Court Reports, New York

Treas. Dec.–United States Treasury Decisions

U.S.–United States Reports

U.S. App. D.C.–United States Court of Appeals Reports

U.S.L.W.–United States Law Week

U.S.P.Q.–United States Patents Quarterly

Utah–Utah Reports

Utah 2d–Utah Reports, Second Series

Va.–Virginia Reports

Va. App.–Virginia Court of Appeals Reports

Va. Cir. Ct.–Virginia Circuit Court Opinions

Vt.–Vermont Reports

Wash.–Washington Reports

Wash. App.–Washing Appellate Reports

Wash. 2d–Washington Reports, Second Series

Wend.–Wendell's Common Law Reports, New York

Wheel. Crim. Cas.–Wheeler's Criminal Cases, New York

Wis.–Wisconsin Reports

Wis. 2d–Wisconsin Reports, Second Series

Wkly. L. Bull.–Weekly Law Bulletin, Ohio

W.L.J.–Western Law Journal, Ohio

W. Va.–West Virginia Reports

Wyo.–Wyoming Reports

Yates Sel. Cas.–Yates' Select Cases, New York

FEDERAL AND STATE ACTS
CITED BY POPULAR NAMES

A – G

A

A B C Act (Alcoholic Beverage Control)
Ala. Code 1975, § 28-3-1 et seq.
Cal. Business and Professions Code § 23000
et seq.
N.C. Gen. Stat. 1943, § 18B-100 et seq.

A. B. C. Fair Trade Act (Alcoholic Beverages)
Cal. Business and Professions Code § 23000
et seq.

A B C Store Act
N.C. Gen. Stat. 1943, §§ 18B-800 to
18B-807

AAA Farm Relief and Inflation Act
May 12, 1933, Ch. 25, 48 Stat. 31, 7 U.S.
Code §§ 601 to 604, 607 to 620; 12 U.S.
Code §§ 347, 462b, 636, 723, 771, 781,
810, 992, 993, 1016 to 1019; 31 U.S. Code
§§ 462, 821 to 823

Aaron Sahli Child Boating Safety Act
Minn. Laws 1996, Ch. 396

Abaca Production Act
Aug. 10, 1950, Ch. 673, 64 Stat. 435, 50 U.S.
Code §§ 541 to 546

Abandoned and Derelict Vessels Act
Alaska Stat. 1962, § 30.30.010 et seq.

Abandoned and Unclaimed Property Disposition Act
N.D. Cent. Code, 47-30-01 et seq.
Pa. Purdon's Stat., Title 72, § 1301.1 et seq.

Abandoned Animals Act
La. Rev. Stat. Ann., 3:2451 et seq.

Abandoned Automobile Act (Houston County)
Ala. Code 1975, 32-13-1 et seq.

Abandoned Barge Act of 1992
Nov. 4, 1992, P.L. 102-587, 46 U.S. Code
§ 4701 nt.

Abandoned Cemeteries Act (Hickerson-Whitlock)
Ky. Rev. Stat. 1971, 381.720 et seq.

Abandoned Children Prevention Act
Ill. Rev. Stat. 1991, Ch. 23, §§ 2358 to 90,
2359

Abandoned Cultural Properties Act
N.M. Stat. Ann., 18-10-1 et seq.
Tenn. Public Acts 1984, Ch. 802

Abandoned Families Act
D.C. Code 1967, § 22-903 et seq.

Abandoned Hardrock Mine Reclamation Act
Ida. Code 1947, 47-1702 et seq.

Abandoned Horse Act
N.M. Laws 1927, Ch. 146
Utah Code Ann. 1953, 47-2-1 et seq.

Abandoned Housing Rehabilitation Act
Ill. Comp. Stat. 1992, Ch. 310, § 50/1 et seq.

Abandoned Iceboxes Act
Mont. Code Ann., 45-8-113
Pa. Cons. Stat., Title 18, § 65.02

Abandoned Infants Assistance Act Amendments of 1991
Dec. 12, 1991, P.L. 102-236, 42 U.S. Code
§ 670 nt.

Abandoned Infants Assistance Act of 1988
Oct. 18, 1988, P.L. 100-505, 102 Stat. 2533,
42 U.S. Code § 670 nt.
Dec. 12, 1991, P.L. 102-236, 42 U.S. Code
§ 670 nt.
Oct. 3, 1996, P.L. 104-235, 42 U.S. Code
§ 670 nt.

Abandoned Landfills Construction Activity Prohibition Act
Ga. Code Ann., 8-6-1 et seq.

Abandoned Military Reservations Acts
July 5, 1884, Ch. 214, 23 Stat. 103, 43 U.S.
Code § 1073 et seq.
Aug. 23, 1894, Ch. 314, 28 Stat. 491
Continued

July 3, 1916, Ch. 217, 39 Stat. 342

Abandoned Mine Drainage Control Act
Md. Ann. Code 1974, Art. NR, § 7-601 et seq.

Abandoned Mine Lands and Reclamation Act
W. Va. Code 1966, § 22-3-1 et seq.

Abandoned Mine Reclamation Act
Ida. Code 1947, 47-1701 et seq.
Okla. Stat. Ann., Title 45, § 740.1 et seq.

Abandoned Mine Reclamation Act of 1990
Nov. 5, 1990, P.L. 101-508, 30 U.S. Code § 1201 nt.

Abandoned Mine Subsidence Assistance Act
Pa. Purdon's Stat., Title 52, § 3351 et seq.

Abandoned Mined Lands and Water Reclamation Act
Ill. Comp. Stat. 1992, Ch. 20, § 1920/1.01

Abandoned Mined Lands Reclamation Act
Ill. Rev. Stat. 1979, Ch. 98 1/2, § 4601 et seq.
N.M. Stat. Ann., 69-25B-1 et seq.
Okla. Stat. Ann., Title 45, § 740.1 et seq.
W. Va. Code 1966, § 20-6C-1 et seq.

Abandoned Mobile Home Act
Ill. Comp. Stat. 1992, Ch. 210, § 117/5 et seq.

Abandoned Oilfield Waste Site Law
La. Rev. Stat. Ann., 30:71 et seq.

Abandoned or Unclaimed Money and Other Liquid Assets Act
P.R. Acts 1989, No. 36

Abandoned Property Act
Ark. Stat. 1947, 50-601 et seq.
Cal. Code of Civil Procedure § 1500 et seq.
Conn. Gen. Stat. Ann., § 50-1 et seq.
Del. Code of 1974, Title 12, § 1130 et seq.
Ky. Rev. Stat. 1971, 393.010 et seq.
Mass. Gen. Laws Ann., 200A:1 et seq.
Mich. Comp. Laws Ann., 567.11 et seq.
N.Y. Consol. Laws, Ch. 1
Ore. Rev. Stat., 98.302 et seq.

R.I. Gen. Laws 1956, 34-44-1 et seq.

Abandoned Property Act (Bank Deposits)
Pa. 1872 Pamph. Laws 62, No. 49

Abandoned Property Act (Corporations)
Utah Code Ann. 1953, 78-44-12 et seq.

Abandoned Property Collection Act
March 12, 1863, Ch. 120, 12 Stat. 820

Abandoned Property Disposition Act
Va. Code 1950, § 55.210.1 et seq.

Abandoned Refrigerator Act
Cal. Penal Code § 402b
Ill. Comp. Stat. 1992, Ch. 720, §§ 505/0.01, 505/1
N.D. Cent. Code, 38-14.2-01 et seq.

Abandoned Shaft Law
Cal. Health and Safety Code § 2 4400 et seq.

Abandoned Shipwreck Act of 1987
April 28, 1988, P.L. 100-298, 102 Stat. 432, 43 U.S. Code §§ 2101 et seq., 2101 nt.

Abandoned Surface Mine Reclamation Act
N.D. Cent. Code, 38-14.2-01 et seq.

Abandoned Vehicle Act
Ind. Code Ann., 9-9-1.1-1 et seq.
Tex. Rev. Civ. Stat., Art. 4477-9a, § 5.01 et seq.

Abandoned Vessels Disposition Act
Haw. Rev. Stat. Ann., § 267A-1 et seq.
N.J. Stat. Ann., 12:7C-7 et seq.

Abandoned Well Act
Mich. Comp. Laws Ann., 750.493b
W. Va. Code 1966, § 22B-5-1 et seq.

Abandonment Act
Ga. Code Ann., 19-10-1, 19-10-2
Md. Ann. Code 1974, Art. FL, 310-201
N.C. Gen. Stat. 1943, § 14-322 et seq.
Wis. Stat. Ann., 767.08

Abandonment Act (Children)
N.Y. Penal Law 1965 (Consol. Laws Ch. 40)
§ 260.00

Abandonment Act (Spouse or Child)
Ga. Code Ann., 19-10-1, 19-10-2

Abandonment Act (Wells)
Ill. Rev. Stat. 1991, Ch. 96 1/2, § 5200 et seq.

Abandonment and Nonsupport Act
Mont. Rev. Code 1947, 94-301 et seq.
R.I. Gen. Laws 1956, 11-2-1 et seq.

Abandonment of Actions Act
La. Code of Civil Procedure, Art. 561

Abatement Act
Ill. Rev. Stat. 1991, Ch. 1, § 1 et seq.
Miss. Code Ann. 1972, § 11-7-25 et seq.
N.J. Stat. Ann., Superseded Vol., 2:26-4 to
2:26-26
Ohio Rev. Code 1953, 2311.21

Abatement Act (Asbestos)
Minn. Stat. Ann., 326.71 et seq.

Abatement Act (Drug)
Ark. Code 1987, 16-105-401 et seq.

Abatement Act (Nuisance)
N.Y. Adm. Code '85, § 7-702

Abatement Act (Prostitution)
Minn. Stat. Ann., 617.33 et seq.

Abatement Act (Public Lands)
Miss. Code Ann. 1972, § 29-1-117

Abatement and Injunction Act
Ill. Rev. Stat. 1991, Ch. 100 1/2 §§ 1 to 29

Abatement of Taxes Act
Pa. Purdon's Stat., Title 72, § 5571.1 et seq.

**Abatement Projects Administration Fund
Act (Water Pollution)**
Mass. Gen. Laws Ann., 21:27a, 29:2w

Abbeville Community Improvement Act
La. Acts 1969, No. 171

ABC Campaign Against Illiteracy Act
P.R. Laws Ann. 1954, Title 18, § 418 et seq.

Abduction Act
Mo. Rev. Stat. 1969, 559.290
Ore. Rev. Stat., 163.640
Wash. Rev. Code Ann., 9A.40.010 et seq.

**Abele Act (Municipal Water Front
Development)**
Ohio Rev. Code 1953, 721.11

Abele Act (Standard Time)
Ohio Rev. Code 1953, 1.04

Abington Town Offices Project Loan Act
Mass. Acts 1957, Ch. 237

Able Seamen Act
July 8, 1941, Ch. 279, 55 Stat. 579, 46 U.S.
Code § 672-2

**Abolishment of Doctrine of Worthier Title
Act**
Ill. Rev. Stat. 1991, Ch. 30, § 187.9 et seq.

Abolishment of Private Seal Act
Ill. Rev. Stat. 1991, Ch. 30, §§ 153a.9, 153b

Abolishment of Rule in Shelley's Case Act
Ill. Rev. Stat. 1991, Ch. 30, § 185.9 et seq.

Abolition Act (Death Penalty)
Tenn. Code Ann., 39-2405, 39-13-203

**Abolition of Slavery Acts (District of
Columbia)**
April 16, 1862, Ch. 54, 12 Stat. 376
July 12, 1862, Ch. 155, 12 Stat. 538

Abolition of Slavery Acts (Territories)
June 19, 1862, Ch. 112, 12 Stat. 432

Abortion Act
Ala. Code 1975, § 13A-13-7
Cal. Penal Code § 274 et seq.
Colo. Rev. Stat., 40-2-50 et seq.
Continued

D.C. Code 1973, § 22-201
Ga. Official Code Ann., 16-12-140 et seq.
Kan. Stat. Ann., 21-3407
Mass. Gen. Laws Ann., 272:19 et seq.
Mich. Comp. Laws Ann., 710.21 et seq.
Minn. Stat. Ann., 617.20 et seq.
N.C. Gen. Stat. 1943, § 14-44 et seq.
N.H. Rev. Stat. 1955, 585:12 et seq.
N.J. Stat. Ann., 2A:87-1
Ohio Rev. Code 1953, 2919.11 et seq.
Okla. Stat. Ann., Title 21, § 861 et seq.
Ore. Rev. Stat., 435.405 et seq.
S.C. Code Ann. 1976, § 44-41-10 et seq.
S.D. Codified Laws 1967, 34-23A-1 et seq.
Va. Code 1950, § 18.2-71 et seq.
Wis. Stat. Ann., 940.04

Abortion Act (Parental Notice of)
Del. Code of 1974, Title 24, § 1780 et seq.
Ill. Comp. Stat. 1992, Ch. 720, § 70/1 et seq.
Mont. Code Ann., 50-20-201 et seq.

Abortion Act (Therapeutic)
Cal. Health and Safety Code § 25950 et seq.

Abortion Ban Act (Partial-Birth)
Ala. Code 1975, § 13A-13-40 et seq.
Ariz. Rev. Stat. Ann., § 13-3603.01
Ark. Code 1987, 5-61-201 to 5-61-204
Ill. Comp. Stat. 1992, Ch. 720, § 513/1 et seq.
Miss. Code Ann. 1972, §§ 41-41-71 to 41-41-73

Abortion Control Act
Mont. Code Ann., 50-20-101 et seq.
N.D. Cent. Code, 14-02.1-01 et seq.
Pa. Cons. Stat. Title 18, § 3201 et seq.

Abortion Facility Reporting and Licensing Act
Tex. Health and Safety Code, § 245.001 et seq.

Abortion Information Act (Alternatives to)
R.I. Gen. Laws 1956, 23-4.13-1 et seq.

Abortion Parental Consent Act
Ill. Rev. Stat. 1991, Ch. 38, § 81-51 et seq.

Abortion Performance Act
S.D. Codified Laws 1967, 34-23A-1 et seq.

Abortion Performance Refusal Act
Ill. Comp. Stat. 1992, Ch. 745, §§ 30/0.01, 30/1
Ill. Rev. Stat. 1991, Ch. 111 1/2, §§ 5200, 5201

Abortion Prevention and Family Responsibility Act
Wis. Stat. Ann., 46.24, 46.245, 46.93, 940.13, 940.15, 943.145

Abortion Procedures Act
Cal. Health and Safety Code § 25270 et seq.
Mass. Gen. Laws Ann., 112.121 et seq.

Abortion Reform Act
N.Y. Penal Law 1965 (Consol. Laws Ch. 40) § 125.00 et seq.

Above Ground Petroleum Storage Act
Cal. Health and Safety Code § 25270 et seq.

Aboveground and Underground Storage Tank Trust Fund Act
Ala. Code 1975, § 22-35-1 et seq.

Aboveground Tank Regulation Act
Okla. Stat. 1981, Title 17, § 401 et seq.

Abraham Lincoln Birthplace National Historic Site Acts
July 17, 1916, Ch. 247, 39 Stat. 385, 16 U.S. Code §§ 211 et seq.
Feb. 11, 1929, Ch. 176, 45 Stat. 1162
March 2, 1934, Ch. 38, 48 Stat. 389
Aug. 11, 1939, Ch. 686, 53 Stat. 1405
May 27, 1949, Ch. 149, 63 Stat. 140
Sept. 8, 1959, P.L. 86-231, 73 Stat. 466

Abrams-Alldredge Act (Insurance Department)
Ind. Laws 1919, Ch. 48, p. 109

Abrams-McCray Act (Insurance)
Ind. Code Ann., 27-2-4-1

Absence as Evidence of Death Act
Wis. Stat. Ann., 813.22 et seq.

Absence as Evidence of Death and Absentees' Property Act
See also Uniform Absence as Evidence of Death and Absentees' Property Act
Md. Ann. Code 1974, Art. CJ, § 3-102
Tenn. Code Ann., 30-3-101 et seq.
Wis. Stat. Ann., 813.22 et seq.

Absence on Military Duty Act (Public Officers and Employees')
N.Y. Military Law (Consol. Laws Ch. 36) §§ 242, 243

Absent Defendant Act
Fla. Stat. Ann., 95.051

Absent Persons Act
Md. Ann. Code 1974, Art CJ, § 3-101 et seq.

Absent Voter Precinct Act
N.M. Stat. Ann., 1-6-19 et seq.

Absentee Balloting Procedures Law
Miss. Code Ann. 1972, § 23-15-621 et seq.

Absentee-Early Voting Act
N.M. Stat. Ann., 1-6A-1 et seq.

Absentee Motorist Act
Ohio Rev. Code 1953, 2703.20

Absentee Voter Act
Miss. Code Ann. 1972, § 23-15-711 et seq.

Absentee Voters Act
Ark. Code Ann. 1987, 3-901 et seq.
Cal. Elections Code 1976, § 1000 et seq.
Colo. Rev. Stat., 1-8-101 et seq.
Conn. Gen. Stat. Ann., § 9-134 et seq.
Del. Code of 1974, Title 15, § 5501 et seq.
Ill. Rev. Stat. 1991, Ch. 46, § 19-1 et seq.
Ind. Code Ann., 3-11-4-1 et seq.
Iowa Code Ann., 53.1 et seq.
Kan. Stat. Ann., 25-1119 et seq.
Ky. Rev. Stat. 1971, 117.085 et seq.
La. Rev. Stat. Ann., 18:1301 et seq.
Mass. Gen. Laws Ann., 54:86 et seq.
Md. Ann. Code 1957, Art. 33, § 27-1 et seq.
Me. Rev. Stat. Ann. 1964, Title 21, § 1251 et seq., Title 21A, § 751 et seq.
Mich. Comp. Laws Ann., 168.758 et seq.
Minn. Stat. Ann., 203B.01 et seq.
Miss. Code Ann. 1972, § 23-9-601 et seq.
Mo. Rev. Stat., 115.275
Mont. Code Ann., 13-13-201 et seq.
N.C. Gen. Stat. 1943, § 163-226 et seq.
N.D. Cent. Code, 16.1-07-01 et seq.
Neb. Rev. Stat. 1943, 32-801 et seq.
Nev. Rev. Stat. 1979 Reprint, 293.310 et seq.
N.H. Rev. Stat. 1955, 60:1 et seq.
N.J. Stat. Ann., 19:57-1 et seq.
N.M. Stat. Ann., 1-6-1 et seq.
N.Y. Election Law 1976 (Consol. Laws Ch. 17) § 8-400 et seq.
Ohio Rev. Code 1953, 3509.01 et seq.
Okla. Stat. Ann., Title 26, § 14-101 et seq.
Ore. Rev. Stat., 253.010 et seq.
Pa. Purdon's Stat., Title 25, § 3146.1 et seq.
R.I. Gen. Laws 1956, 17-20-1 et seq.
S.C. Code Ann. 1976, § 7-15-10 et seq.
S.D. Codified Laws 1967, 12-19-1 et seq.
Tenn. Code Ann., 2-6-101 et seq.
Tex. Election Code, Art. 82.001 et seq.
Va. Code 1950, § 24.1-227 et seq.
Vt. Stat. Ann., Title 17, § 2531 et seq.
Wash. Rev. Code Ann., 29.36.010 et seq.
Wis. Stat. Ann., 6.85 et seq.
W. Va. Code 1966, § 3-3-1 et seq.
Wyo. Stat. Ann., § 22-9-101 et seq.

Absentee Voters Registration Act
Fla. Stat. Ann., 97.063, 97.064, 97.065, 101.692

Absentee Voting Act (Armed Services)
Miss. Code Ann. 1972, § 23-15-671 et seq.

Absentee Voting Act (Servicemen)
Md. Ann. Code 1957, Art. 33, § 3-7 et seq.
Miss. Code Ann. 1972, § 23-15-711 et seq.
Wash. Rev. Code Ann., 29.39.010 et seq.
Wyo. Stat. 1957, § 22-242 et seq.

Absentees' Estates Act
Mich. Comp. Laws Ann., 705.1 et seq.
R.I. Gen. Laws 1956, 33-20-1 et seq.

Absentees' Property Act
Md. Ann. Code 1974, Art. CJ, § 3-101 et seq.
Wis. Stat. Ann., 813.22 et seq.

Abshire-Kelly Salinity Control Barrier Act
Cal. Statutes 1953, Ch. 1104, p. 2601
Cal. Statutes 1957, Ch. 2092, p. 3717

Abshire-Maloney-John McCarthy-Murdy-J. Howard Williams Bill (Average Annual Earnings)
Cal. Labor Code §§ 4452, 4453, 4455, 4460, 4702

Absolute Escheat Act
N.J. Stat. Ann., 46:30B-6 et seq., 46:30B-19 et seq.

Absolute Ownership Act (Water)
S.D. Code 1939, 61.0101

Abstract and Title Insurance Law
Ind. Code Ann., 27-7-3-1 et seq.

Abstract, Conceptually-Oriented Mathematics Program Act
Cal. Education Code 1976, § 54680 et seq.

Abstracters Act
Neb. Rev. Stat. 1943, 76-535 et seq.

Abstracters' Bond Act
Neb. Rev. Stat. 1943, 76-501 et seq.
N.M. Stat. Ann., 47-4-1 et seq.
Okla. Stat. 1981, Title 74, § 227.10

Abstracters License Act
Ark. Code Ann. 1987, 17-11-101 et seq.
Kan. Stat. Ann., 58-2801 et seq.
Minn. Stat. Ann., 386.61 et seq.
Mont. Code Ann., 37-52-301 et seq.
N.D. Cent. Code, 43-01-01 et seq.
Okla. Stat. Ann., Title 74, § 227.10 et seq.
S.D. Codified Laws 1967, 36-13-1 et seq.

Abstracters' Lien Act
N.M. Stat. Ann., 48-4-1 et seq.

Abuse Act (Domestic)
S.C. Code Ann. 1976, § 16-25-10 et seq.

Abuse and Neglect Act
N.M. Stat. Ann., 32A-4-1 et seq.

Abuse and Neglect Act (Child)
Wash. Rev. Code 1983, 26.44.010 et seq.

Abuse and Neglect Act (Resident)
N.M. Stat. Ann., 30-47-1 et seq.

Abuse and Neglect Child Prevention Act
Ala. Code 1975, § 26-16-1 et seq.
Ga. Code Ann., 19-14-1 et seq.

Abuse Counselor Certification Act
La. Rev. Stat. Ann., 37:3371 et seq.

Abuse Hotline Act (Welfare)
Kan. Stat. Ann., 39-760

Abuse of Children Act
Iowa Code Ann., 232.67 et seq., 235A.1 et seq.

Abuse of Elderly Persons Act
Mass. Gen. Laws Ann., 19A:14 et seq.

Abuse of Elders Demonstration Project Act
Ill. Rev. Stat. 1991, Ch. 23, § 6500 et seq.

Abuse of Personal Identity Act
Utah Code Ann. 1953, 45-3-1 et seq.

Abuse Prevention Act
Ore. Rev. Stat., 107.700 et seq.

Abuse Prevention Act (Child)
Okla. Stat. 1981, Title 63, § 1-227 et seq.

Abuse Prevention Act (Elder and Developmentally Disabled)
Mont. Code Ann., 53-5-501 et seq.

Abuse Prevention Act (Elder)
Mont. Code Ann., 52-3-80 et seq.
Ore. Rev. Stat., 124.005 et seq.

Abuse Prevention and Treatment Act (Substance)
Me. Rev. Stat. Ann. 1964, Title 5, § 20001 et seq.

Abuse Protection Act
Pa. Cons. Stat., Title 23, § 6101 et seq.

Abuse Reporting Act (Domestic)
Okla. Stat. 1981, Title 22, § 40.5, 40.6

Abuse Resistance Education Act (Drug)
Fla. Stat. Ann., 233.0661 et seq.

Abuse Services Oversight Act
Tex. Health and Safety Code, § 468.001 et seq.

Abused and Neglected Child Reporting Act
Ill. Comp. Stat. 1992, Ch. 325, § 5/1 et seq.

Abused and Neglected Children's Confidentiality and Disclosure of Records Act
D.C. Code Ann., §§ 6-2126, 6-2127

Abused and Neglected Long-Term Care Facility Residents Reporting Act
Ill. Comp. Stat. 1992, Ch. 210, § 30/1 et seq.

Abused, Neglected or Exploited Disabled Adult Act
N.C. Gen. Stat. 1943, §§ 108A-99 to 108A-111

Abutting Property Law
Tenn. Code Ann., 7-32-101 et seq.

Academic Achievement Act (Assessment of)
Cal. Education Code 1976, § 60600 et seq.

Academic and Health Education Loan Act
Cal. Education Code 1976, § 69300 et seq.

Academic and Vocational Integration Development Program
Wash. Rev. Code Ann., 28A.630.880

Academic Assistance Act (Early Childhood Development)
S.C. Code Ann. 1976, § 59-139-05 et seq.

Academic Degree Act
Ill. Comp. Stat. 1992, Ch. 110, § 1010/0.01 et seq.

Academic Excellence Act
Minn. Stat. Ann., 121.612

Academic Freedom and Religious Liberty Act (Nation's Capital)
D.C. Code Ann., § 1-2520

Academic Medicine Act (Excellence in)
Ill. Comp. Stat. 1992, Ch. 30, § 775/1 et seq.

Academic Plagiarism Act
Ill. Comp. Stat. 1992, Ch. 110, §§ 5/0.01, 5/1

Academic Research Facilities Modernization Act of 1988
Oct. 31, 1988, P.L. 100-570, 42 U.S. Code § 1861 nt.

Academic Scholars Act (State Regents')
Okla. Stat. 1981, Title 70, § 2401 et seq.

Academic Schools Act (Private)
Pa. Purdon's Stat., Title 24, § 6701 et seq.

Academic Volunteer and Mentor Service Act
Cal. Government Code § 96100 et seq.

Academically Talented Education Act
Mich. Comp. Laws Ann., 388.1091 et seq.

Academies Act
Cal. Education Code 1976, §§ 21100 et seq., 26201

Acadia National Park Acts
Feb. 26, 1919, Ch. 45, 40 Stat. 1178, 16 U.S. Code § 341 et seq.
Jan. 19, 1929, Ch. 77, 45 Stat. 1083
May 23, 1930, Ch. 315, 46 Stat. 377
Dec. 22, 1944, Ch. 674, 58 Stat. 914
Sept. 7, 1949, Ch. 541, 63 Stat. 691
July 24, 1956, Ch. 667, 70 Stat. 597
Oct. 3, 1966, P.L. 89-615, 80 Stat. 866
March 4, 1968, P.L. 90-262, 82 Stat. 40
March 12, 1968, P.L. 90-265, 82 Stat. 46

Accelerated Capacity and Transportation Improvements of the Nineties Bond Act
N.Y. Transportation Law (Consol. Laws Ch. 61a) § 450 et seq.

Acceptance of Credit Cards Act (Local Governmental)
Ill. Comp. Stat. 1992, Ch. 50, § 345/1 et seq.

Acceptance of National Employment System Act
Cal. Statutes 1935, Ch. 258, p. 943

Access Act (Employee Health Care)
Fla. Stat. Ann., 627.6699

Access Act (Guide Dog)
Ill. Rev. Stat. 1991, Ch. 38, § 65-1

Access Act (Health Care)
Wash. Rev. Code 1983, 70.47.900

Access Act (Health Insurance Coverage)
Wash. Rev. Code 1983, 48.41.010 et seq.

Access Act (Maternity Care)
Wash. Rev. Code 1983, 74.09.760

Access Act (Pharmacy)
Del. Code of 1974, Title 18, § 7301 et seq.

Access by Children to Tobacco Products Act (Prevention)
Fla. Laws 1992, Ch. 285

Access Facilities Act (Highways)
Wyo. Stat. Ann., § 24-6-101 et seq.

Access for Infants and Mothers Program Law
Cal. Insurance Code, § 12695 et seq.

Access for the Disabled Act
N.Y. Executive Law (Consol. Laws Ch. 18) § 374a, Subd. 4
N.Y. Public Buildings Law (Consol. Laws Ch. 43) § 50 et seq.

Access Improvement Fund Act
Tenn. Code Ann., 54-2-201 et seq.

Access Law (Freedom of)
Me. Rev. Stat. Ann. 1964, Title 1, § 401 et seq.

Access Road Maintenances Act (Cemetery)
Tenn. Public Acts 1993, Ch. 352

Access Roads Act
Alaska Stat. 1962, § 19.30.010 et seq.

Access System Act (Telecommunications)
Fla. Stat. Ann., 427.701 et seq.

Access to Civil Justice Act
May 26, 1994, P.L. 103-259, 108 Stat. 694
N.C. Gen. Stat. 1943, §§ 7A-474.1 to 7A-474.4

Access to Emergency Medical Care Act
S.C. Code Ann. 1976, § 38-71-1510 et seq.

Access to Food and Nutrition Act
Mont. Laws 1991, Ch. 569

Access to Health Care Act
Fla. Stat. Ann., 776.1115

Access to Health Care Act (Women's)
Ala. Code 1975, § 27-49-1 et seq.
Ga. Code Ann., 33-24-58

Access to Higher Education Act
Mo. Rev. Stat 1986, 166.200 et seq., 173.053, 173.262

Access to Insurance Requirements Plan Act
Ga. Code Ann., 33-33-1 et seq.

Access to Justice Act (Equal)
Fla. Stat. Ann., 57.111

Access to Medical Treatment Act
Ga. Code Ann., 43-34-42.1

Access to Parking for Handicapped Persons Act
Ark. Code Ann. 1987, 27-15-301 et seq.

Access to Psychologists and Optometrists Act
D.C. Code Ann., § 35-517

Access to Public Records Act
N.H. Rev. Stat. 1955, 91-A:1 et seq.

Access to Public Records Sunshine Law
Vt. Stat. Ann., Title 1, § 315 et seq.

Access to Tobacco Act (Prevention of Youth)
Miss. Laws 1994, Ch. 486

Access 2000 Act (Higher Education)
Fla. Laws 1995, Ch. 243, §§ 10 to 20

Accessibility Act (Architectural Barriers)
Ark. Code 1987, 20-14-601 et seq.

Accessibility Capital Improvement Grant Act (School Building)
Minn. Laws 1993, Ch. 373, §§ 20 to 22

Accession Act (Personal Property)
Cal. Civil Code § 1025 et seq.

Accession Act (Real Property)
Cal. Civil Code § 1013 et seq.

Accessories Act (Criminal)
Wash. Rev. Code Ann., 9A.08.020 et seq.

Accessory After the Fact Act
Ariz. Rev. Stat. Ann., § 13-2510 et seq.
Ark. Code Ann. 1987, 5-54-105
Ill. Rev. Stat. 1991, Ch. 38, § 31-5
Mont. Code Ann., 45-7-303
Utah Code Ann. 1953, 76-1-45

Accident Act (Motor Vehicle)
R.I. Gen. Laws 1956, 31-26-1 et seq.

Accident and Health Filing Reform Act
Pa. Purdon's Stat., Title 40, § 3801 et seq.

Accident and Health Insurance Act
Ark. Code Ann. 1987, 23-85-102 et seq., 23-60-101 et seq.
Cal. Insurance Code § 10320 et seq.
Fla. Stat. Ann., 627.601 et seq.
Mich. Comp. Laws Ann., 500.3400 et seq.
Minn. Stat. Ann., 62A.01 et seq.
Mo. Rev. Stat., 376.770 et seq.
Ohio Rev. Code 1953, 3923.01 et seq.

Okla. Stat. Ann., Title 36, § 4401 et seq.

Accident and Health Insurance Act (Credit)
Vt. Stat. Ann., Title 8, § 4101 et seq.

Accident and Health Insurance Agents Act
Fla. Stat. Ann., 626.826

Accident and Health Insurance Minimum Standards Act (Individual)
Iowa Code Ann., 514D.1 et seq.

Accident and Life and Health Insurance Policy Language Simplification Act
N.D. Cent. Code, 26.1-36-13 et seq.

Accident and Sickness Act (Individual)
Iowa Code Ann., 514A.1 et seq.

Accident and Sickness and Medicare Supplement Insurance Minimum Standards Act
Neb. Rev. Stat. 1943, 44-3601 et seq.

Accident and Sickness Insurance Act (Minimum Standards)
Pa. Purdon's Stat., Title 40, § 776.1 et seq.
Va. Code 1950, § 38.2-3516 et seq.
W. Va. Code 1966, § 33-28-1 et seq.

Accident and Sickness Policy Provisions Act (Individual)
Ind. Code Ann., 27-8-5-2

Accident Compensation Act (Employees')
Nev. Rev. Stat. 1957, 41.140 et seq.

Accident Fault Determination Act (Public Utility)
N.J. Stat. Ann., 48:2-21.4 et seq.

Accident Fund Act
Md. Ann. Code 1974, Art. LE, §§ 10-104, 10-117 et seq.

Accident, Health and Life Guaranty Act
Cal. Insurance Code, Art. 21.28E

Accident Indemnification Corporation Law (Uninsured Motorists)
N.Y. Insurance Law 1984 (Consol. Laws Ch. 28) § 5201 et seq.

Accident Insurance Act
La. Rev. Stat. Ann., 22:211 et seq.

Accident Insurance Act (Omnibus Coverage)
Wis. Stat. 1975, 204.30, Subsec. 3

Accident, Life and Health Insurance Broker Act
Okla. Stat. Ann., Title 36, § 1461 et seq.

Accident, Life, and Health Insurance Guaranty Association Act
S.C. Code Ann. 1976, § 38-29-10 et seq.

Accident, Life Insurance and Health Insurance Act (Credit)
Mass. Gen. Laws Ann., 167F:2, 175:110, 175:117C, 175:133, 175:177, 175:184, 255:12G, 255B:10, 255C:14A, 255D:1 to 255D:11, 255D:26

Accident Prevention Act (Overhead Power Line)
Kan. Stat. Ann., 66-1701 et seq.

Accident Reparations Act (Standard Auto)
Colo. Rev. Stat., 10-4-701 et seq.

Accident Reporting Act (Motor Vehicles)
Alaska Stat. 1962, § 28.35.080 et seq.
Mont. Code Ann., 61-7-101 et seq.
N.D. Cent. Code, 39-08-04 et seq.

Accident Reports Act
N.J. Stat. Ann., 34:15-96 to 34:15-102
Pa. Cons. Stat., Title 75, § 3746

Accident Reports Acts (Railroads)
March 3, 1901, Ch. 866, 31 Stat. 1446 (See 45 U.S. Code §§ 38, 39, 41, 42)
May 6, 1910, Ch. 208, 36 Stat. 350, 45 U.S. Code §§ 38 to 43
Feb. 17, 1911, Ch. 103, 36 Stat. 916, 45 U.S. Code §§ 32 to 34
April 22, 1940, Ch. 124, 54 Stat. 148, 45 U.S. Code §§ 32 to 34
Aug. 14, 1957, P.L. 85-135, 71 Stat. 352, 45 U.S. Code § 34
Sept. 13, 1960, P.L. 86-762, 74 Stat. 903, 45 U.S. Code §§ 38, 42, 43

Jan. 3, 1975, P.L. 93-633, 88 Stat. 2166, 45 U.S. Code § 39
June 22, 1988, P.L. 100-342, 102 Stat. 633, 45 U.S. Code §§ 38 to 40, 43
Sept. 3, 1992, P.L. 102-365, 45 U.S. Code §§ 39, 43

Accident, Sickness and Life Insurance Guaranty Association Act
Va. Code 1950, § 38.2-1700 et seq.

Accident, Sickness and Life Insurance Policy Readability Act
Neb. Rev. Stat. 1943, 44-3401 et seq.

Accidental and Sickness and Life Insurance Policy Language Simplification Act
W. Va. Code 1966, § 33-29-1 et seq.

Accidental Failure of Suit Act
Conn. Gen. Stat. Ann., § 52-592

Accidental Release Prevention and Risk Management Planning Act
Fla. Stat. Ann., 252.934 to 252.945

Accommodations Act (Antidiscrimination)
Minn. Stat. Ann., 363.03

Accommodations Tax Act
Mont. Code Ann., 15-65-101 et seq.
S.C. Code Ann. 1976, §§ 12-35-30 et seq., 12-35-710 et seq.

Accommodations Tax Act (Local)
S.C. Code Ann. 1976, §§ 6-1-500 to 6-1-560

Accomplices Act
N.Y. Criminal Procedure Law (Consol. Laws Ch. 11A) § 60.22
Tex. Penal Code § 7.01 et seq.

Accord and Satisfaction Act
Cal. Civil Code § 1521 et seq.

Account Act (Judicial Retirement)
Wash. Rev. Code 1983, 2.14.010 et seq.

Account Act (Medical Savings)
Colo. Rev. Stat., 39-22-504.5 to 39-22-504.9

Account Book Act (Evidence)
Fla. Stat. Ann., 817.21
Mo. Rev. Stat., 490.650

**Account Program and College Savings Bond
Act (Tuition)**
Pa. 1992 Pamph. Laws, No. 11

Accountability Act (Educational Funding)
Fla. Stat. Ann., 236.685

Accountability Act (Government)
Mont. Code Ann., 2-11-101 et seq.

Accountability Act (Governmental)
Del. Code of 1974, Title 29, § 10501 et seq.

Accountability Act (Litigation)
Miss. Code Ann. 1972, § 11-55-1 et seq.

Accountability Act (Persistent Offender)
N.J. Stat. Ann., 2C:43-7.1 et seq.
Wash. Rev. Code Ann., 9.94A.392

**Accountability and Adequate Education
Program Act**
Miss. Code Ann. 1972, § 37-151-1 et seq.

**Accountability and Reform Act
(Government)**
S.C. Code Ann. 1976, §§ 2-47-50 et seq.,
8-1-15 et seq., 11-35-310

**Accountability Funding for Excellence
Program (School)**
Md. Ann. Code 1974, Art. ED, § 5-206

**Accountability in Curriculum, Educational
Materials and Testing Act**
N.C. Laws 1991, Ch. 778

Accountability Statute (Crimes)
Ill. Rev. Stat. 1991, Ch. 38, § 5-1 et seq.

**Accountable Pipeline Safety and
Partnership Act of 1996**
Oct. 12, 1996, P.L. 104-304, 49 U.S. Code
§ 60101 nt.

Accountancy Act
Ala. Code 1975, § 34-1-1 et seq.

Ark. Code Ann. 1987, 17-12-101 et seq.
Cal. Business and Professions Code § 5000 et
seq.
Colo. Rev. Stat., 12-2-101 et seq.
Fla. Stat. Ann., 473.301 et seq.
Ga. Code Ann., 43-3-1 et seq.
Haw. Rev. Stat. Ann., § 466-1 et seq.
Ida. Code 1947, 54-201 et seq.
Ind. Code Ann., 25-2.1-1-1 et seq.
Iowa Code Ann., 116.1 et seq.
Mich. Comp. Laws Ann., 338.2101 et seq.
Miss. Code Ann. 1972, § 73-33-1 et seq.
N.D. Laws 1993, Ch. 417
Neb. Rev. Stat. 1943, 1-105.01 et seq.
N.H. Rev. Stat. 1955, 309-B:1 et seq.
Okla. Stat. Ann., Title 59, § 15.1 et seq.
Pa. Purdon's. Stat., Title 63, § 9.1 et seq.
P.R. Laws Ann. 1954, Title 20, § 771 et seq.
R.I. Gen. Laws 1956, 5-3.1-1 et seq.
S.D. Codified Laws 1967, 36-20A-1 et seq.
Tenn. Code Ann., 62-1-101 et seq.
Wash. Rev. Code Ann., 18.04.015 et seq.

Accountancy Act (Public)
See Public Accountants Act
N.M. Stat. Ann., 61-28A-1 et seq.

Accountancy Board Act
D.C. Code Ann., § 2-103

Accountancy Corporations Act
Cal. Business and Professions Code § 5150 et
seq.
S.D. Codified Laws 1967, 47-13B-1 et seq.

Accountant-Client Privilege Act
Pa. Purdon's Stat., Title 63, § 9.11a

Accountants Act
Ill. Rev. Stat. 1991, Ch. 111, § 5500.01
Mich. Comp. Laws Ann., 338.2101 et seq.
N.H. Rev. Stat. 1955, 309-A:1 et seq.
S.C. Code Ann. 1976, § 40-1-10 et seq.
Vt. Stat. Ann., Title 26, § 1 et seq.

Accountants Act (Public)
N.C. Gen. Stat. 1943, § 93-1 et seq.

Accountants Privilege Act
Fla. Stat. Ann., 473.316
Ill. Rev. Stat. 1991, Ch. 111, § 5533

Accountants' Registration Act
Mass. Gen. Laws Ann., 112:87A et seq.

Accounting Act
Ky. Rev. Stat. 1971, 46.010 et seq.

Accounting Act (County)
Mich. Comp. Laws Ann., 750.485
N.J. Stat. Ann., 45:2B-1 et seq.

Accounting Act (Local Government)
Colo. Rev. Stat., 29-1-501 et seq.

Accounting and Auditing Act of 1950
Sept. 12, 1950, Ch. 946, 64 Stat. 834, 31 U.S. Code §§ 65 to 67
Aug. 20, 1964, P.L. 88-454, 78 Stat. 551, 31 U.S. Code § 67
Oct. 7, 1977, P.L. 95-125, 31 U.S. Code § 67
July 21, 1978, P.L. 95-320, 31 U.S. Code § 67; 18 U.S. Code § 1906
Nov. 10, 1978, P.L. 95-630, 31 U.S. Code § 67

Accounting and Auditing Practices for Community Agencies
See Uniform Accounting and Auditing Practices for Community Agencies Act

Accounting and Budgeting Procedures Law
Tenn. Private Acts 1979, Ch. 49

Accounting and Fiscal Responsibility Account Act (State)
Mich. Comp. Laws Ann., 18.1495 et seq.

Accounting by Railroads Acts
June 29, 1906, Ch. 3591, 34 Stat. 593, 49 U.S. Code § 20

Accounting Corporations Law (Professional)
La. Rev. Stat. Ann., 12:1011 et seq.

Accounting, Financial Reporting and Budget Accountability Reform Act
N.Y. Laws 1981, Chs. 405, 957

Accounting of Public Funds Act
Ill. Rev. Stat. 1991, Ch. 102, § 19.9 et seq.

Accounting Practice Act
Wis. Stat. Ann., 442.01 et seq.

Accounting Procedures Law
Ark. Stat. 1947, 13-301 et seq.
Nev. Rev. Stat. 1979 Reprint, 353.291 et seq.

Accounting Project Act
Tex. General and Special Laws 1991, Ch. 4

Accounting Project Act (Statewide)
Tex. Rev. Civ. Stat., Art. 4348f

Accounting Simplification Acts (Meter Readings)
April 27, 1937, Ch. 143, 50 Stat. 119, 31 U.S. Code § 668a
April 26, 1939, Ch. 103, 53 Stat. 624, 31 U.S. Code § 668a

Accounting System Act (State and County)
Mich. Comp. Laws Ann., 21.41 et seq.

Accounting Systems Act (Local Government)
Ill. Rev. Stat. 1991, Ch. 15, § 600 et seq.

Accounts and Notes Receivable Abatement Act
Ark. Code Ann. 1987, 19-2-301 et seq.

Accounts Receivable Act
Ala. Code 1958, Title 39, § 207 et seq.
Ariz. Rev. Stat. Ann., § 47-9101 et seq.
Cal. Civil Code § 3017 et seq.
Colo. Rev. Stat., 11-2-1 et seq.
Fla. Stat. 1965, 524.01 et seq.
Ida. Code 1947, 28-9-101 et seq.
Ill. Rev. Stat. 1991, Ch. 17, §§ 5101, 5102
La. Rev. Stat. Ann., 9:3101 et seq.
Mich. Comp. Laws 1948, 691.901 et seq., 600.5401 et seq.
Miss. Code 1942, § 243-01 et seq.
Mo. Rev. Stat. 1959, 410.010 et seq.
N.H. Rev. Stat. 1955, 382-A:9-101 et seq.
Ohio Rev. Code 1953, 1309.01 et seq.

Pa. 1941 Pamph. Laws 606, No. 255
P.R. Laws Ann. 1954, Title 10, § 581 et seq.
R.I. Gen. Laws 1956, 6-15-2
Tenn. Public Acts 1959, Ch. 114
Wash. Rev. Code Ann., 62A.9-101 et seq.
Wis. Stat. 1963, 241.28
Wyo. Stat. 1957, § 34-272 et seq.

Accounts Receivable Assignment Act
N.C. Gen. Stat. 1943, § 44-77 et seq.

Accounts Receivable Financing Act
Tex. Business and Commerce Code, § 9.101 et seq.

Accounts Receivable Management Act
Cal. Government Code § 16580 et seq.

Accreditation Act (Asbestos Workers)
Mich. Comp. Laws Ann., 338.3401 et seq.

Accreditation Act (Insurance)
R.I. Gen. Laws 1956, 27-51-1 et seq.

Accreditation Act (Schools)
Neb. Rev. Stat. 1943, 79-1247.02

Accreditation and Certification Act (Asbestos Abatement)
Miss. Code Ann. 1972, § 37-138-1 et seq.

Accreditation and Certification Act (Asbestos Occupations)
Pa. Purdon's Stat., Title 63, § 2101 et seq.

Accreditation and Regulation Act (Asbestos Contractor)
Tenn. Code Ann., 62-41-101 et seq.

Accreditation of Child-Care Facilities and Child-Placing Agencies Act
Tex. Human Resources Code, § 42.101 et seq.

Accrediting and Licensing Act (Nursing Home)
Wis. Stat. Ann., 50.01

Accretion Act
N.D. Cent. Code, 47-06-05

Accumulated Earnings Tax Act
P.R. Laws Ann. 1954, Title 13, § 3102

Accumulation Act
Pa. 1931 Pamph. Laws 29, No. 27

Accumulations Act (Estates)
Minn. Stat. Ann., 500.17

Accused as Witness Act
N.H. Rev. Stat. 1955, 516:31
N.M. Stat. Ann. 1953, 41-12-19

Accused Persons Rendition Act
See Uniform Rendition of Accused Persons Act

Acequia and Community Ditch Fund Act
N.M. Stat. Ann., 73-2A-1 et seq.

ACES Act (Arts Create Excellent Schools Program)
N.J. Stat. Ann., 18A:54G-1 et seq.

ACF Compact (Apalachicola-Chattahoochee-Flint River Basin)
Ala. Code 1975, § 33-19-1
Ga. Code Ann., 12-10-100 et seq.

Achievement Program Act (Mathematics, Engineering and Science)
Cal. Education Code 1976, § 8600 et seq.

Acid Deposition Act
Cal. Health and Safety Code § 39900 et seq.
N.Y. Environmental Conservation Law 1972 (Consol. Laws Ch. 43B) § 19-0901 et seq.

Acid Deposition Control Act (State)
N.Y. Tax Law (Consol. Laws Ch. 60) §§ 208, Subd. 9, 612, Subd. h,

Acid or Caustic Alkali Act
Vt. Stat. Ann. 1959, Title 9, § 2821 et seq.
Wis. Stat. Ann., 100.37

Acid Precipitation Act of 1980
June 30, 1980, P.L. 96-294, 42 U.S. Code § 8901 nt., 42 U.S. Code § 8901 et seq.

Acid Rain Act
N.Y. Environmental Conservation Law
(Consol. Laws Ch. 43B) § 19-0901 et seq.

Acid Rain Control Act
N.H. Rev. Stat. 1955, 125-D-1 et seq.

Acid Transportation Act (Carriage by Sea)
Aug. 2, 1882, Ch. 374, 22 Stat. 189 (See 18
U.S. Code § 2278)
June 25, 1948, Ch. 645, § 17, 62 Stat. 862
Aug. 26, 1983, P.L. 98-89, sect4(b), 97 Stat.
599

Acidity Protection Act (Atmospheric)
Cal. Health and Safety Code § 39900 et seq.

Acker-Paterson Milk Marketing Act
Mich. Public Acts 1941, No. 369

Ackerman Act (Yellow Dog Contract)
Ohio Rev. Code 1953, 4113.02

Ackia Battleground National Monument Act
Aug. 27, 1935, Ch. 755, 49 Stat. 897, 16 U.S.
Code §§ 450r to 450t

Acknowledgment Act
Ariz. Rev. Stat. Ann., § 33-511 et seq.

Acknowledgment of Parentage Act
Mich. Comp. Laws Ann., 722.1001 et seq.

Acknowledgment Short Forms Act
Fla. Stat. Ann., 695.25

Acknowledgment Validation Act
Ill. Comp. Stat. 1992, Ch. 765, § 25/1 et seq.

Acknowledgments Act
See also Uniform Acknowledgments Act
R.I. Gen. Laws 1956, 34-12-1 et seq.
Tenn. Code Ann., 66-22-101 et seq.
Wash. Rev. Code Ann., 64.08.010 et seq.
W. Va. Code 1966, § 39-1-1 et seq.

Acknowledgments Act (Armed Forces)
Conn. Gen. Stat. Ann., § 27-137

Acknowledgments Act (Foreign)
La. Rev. Stat. Ann., 35:551 et seq.
Tenn. Code Ann., 66-22-104

Acknowledgments and Notarial Act
R.I. Gen. Laws 1956, 34-12-1 et seq.

Acknowledgments Recognition Act
See Uniform Recognition of Acknowledgments Act

Acquired Immune Deficiency Syndrome (AIDS) Housing Act
Miss. Code Ann. 1972, § 43-33-717

Acquired Immune Deficiency Syndrome Act (Home and Community-Based Services for Persons with Health Complexes Related to AIDS)
Colo. Rev. Stat., 26-4-641 et seq.

Acquired Immune Deficiency Syndrome Assistance Act
N.J. Stat. Ann., 26:5C-1 et seq.

Acquired Immune Deficiency Syndrome Research Confidentiality Act
Cal. Health and Safety Code § 199.30 et seq.

Acquisition Act (Emergency Archaeological Property)
Fla. Stat. 1989, 253.027

Acquisition Act (Property Rights)
Mich. Comp. Laws Ann., 3.251 et seq.

Acquisition and Improvement Act
Cal. Statutes 1925, Ch. 419, p. 849

Acquisition of Property for Transportation Purposes Act
Ga. Code Ann., 32-3-1 et seq.

Acquisition Policies Law (Real Property)
Miss. Code Ann. 1972, § 43-37-1 et seq.

Acquisition Procedures and Street and Alley Closing Act
D.C. Code Ann., § 7-411 et seq.

Acquisitions and Condemnation of Land Act
S.C. Code Ann. 1976, § 5-31-410 et seq.

Acres for Wildlife Act
La. Rev. Stat. Ann., 56:191 et seq.

Act Against Discrimination
Kan. Stat. Ann., 44-1001 et seq.

Act Against Organized Crime
P.R. Laws Ann. 1954, Title 25, § 971 et seq.

Act and Intent Act (Crimes)
Ga. Code Ann., 16-1-4

ACT Compact (Alabama-Coosa-Tallapoosa River Basin)
Ala. Code 1975, § 33-18-1
Ga. Code Ann., 12-10-110 et seq.

Act Concerning Cosmetology
Mich. Comp. Laws Ann., 338.751 et seq.

Act Concerning the Support of Children of Parents not Married to Each Other
N.C. Gen. Stat. 1943, § 49-1 et seq.

Act Controlling the Sale and Possession of Cannabis (Marijuana) and Peyote
Me. Rev. Stat. Ann. 1964, Title 17A, § 1101 et seq.

Act Creating the Altamaha River Basin Commission
Ga. Code Ann., 12-5-420 et seq.

Act Creating the Eaton-Putnam County Charter Commission
Ga. Laws 1972, p. 2665

Act Creating the Public School Employees Retirement System
Ga. Code Ann., 47-4-1 et seq.

Act Creating the Superior Court Judges Retirement System
Ga. Code Ann., 47-9-1 et seq.

Act Fixing Basis of Participation by Secured Creditors in Insolvent Estates
N.Y. Debtor and Creditor Law (Consol. Laws Ch. 12) § 30 et seq.

Act for a Constitutional Government for Puerto Rico
P.R. Acts 1951, 13th Sp. Sess., No. 1

Act for a State Register of Critical Areas
Me. Rev. Stat. Ann. 1964, Title 5, § 3310 et seq.

Act for Capital Punishment
S.C. Code Ann. 1976, § 16-3-20 et seq.

Act for Coordination of Efforts for Prevention of Adolescent Pregnancy and Sexually Transmitted Diseases
Okla. Stat. Ann., Title 63, § 1-235 et seq.

Act for Coordination of Special Services to Children and Youth
Okla. Stat. 1981, Title 10, § 601.41 et seq.

Act for Development of Employment and Industrial Resources
Tex. Gov. Code, § 481.001 et seq.

Act for Development of Employment, Industrial and Health Resources
Tex. Rev. Civ. Stat., Art. 5190.1

Act for Extradition of Persons of Unsound Mind
See Uniform Act for Extradition of Persons of Unsound Mind

Act for International Development
See also Foreign Assistance Act Of 1961
June 5, 1950, Ch. 220, 64 Stat. 204
Oct. 10, 1951, Ch. 479, 65 Stat. 586
June 20, 1952, Ch. 449, 66 Stat. 150
July 16, 1953, Ch. 195, 67 Stat. 161

Act for International Development of 1961
See Foreign Assistance Act Of 1961

Act for Judicial Review and Civil Enforcement of Agency Actions
Kan. Stat. Ann., 77-601 et seq.

Act for Obtaining a Guardian or Conservator, or Both

Kan. Stat. Ann., 59-3001 et seq.

Act for Obtaining Treatment for a Mentally Ill Person

Kan. Stat. Ann., 59-2901 et seq.

Act for Out of State Parolee Supervision (Uniform)

See Uniform Act for Out of State Parolee Supervision

Act for Reform in Emerging New Democracies and Support and Help for Improved Partnership with Russia, Ukraine, and Other New Independent States (Friendship Act)

Dec. 17, 1993, P.L. 103-199, 22 U.S. Code § 5801 nt.

Act for Simplification of Fiduciary Security Transfers (Uniform)

See Uniform Act for Simplification of Fiduciary Security Transfers

Act for Tax Simplification and Equalization

N.D. Laws 1965, Ch. 386

Act for the Cadastration, Classification and Assessment of Property

P.R. Laws Ann. 1954, Title 13 § 431 et seq.

Act for the Certification of Operators of Treatment Plants for Drinking Water and Used Water

P.R. Laws Ann. 1954, Title 20, § 2801 et seq.

Act for the Conservation, Development and Use of Water Resources

P.R. Laws Ann. 1954, Title 12, § 1501 et seq.

Act for the Development of the Coffee Industry

P.R. Laws Ann. 1954, Title 5, § 321 et seq.

Act for the Management of Motor Vehicles

S.C. Code Ann. 1976, § 1-11-220 et seq.

Act for the Prevention and Punishment of Crimes Against Internationally Protected Persons

Oct. 8, 1976, P.L. 94-467, 90 Stat. 1997, 18 U.S. Code §§ 11, 112, 878, 970, 1116, 1201

Act for the Prevention and Punishment of the Crime of Hostage-Taking

Oct. 12, 1984, P.L. 98-473, 18 U.S. Code §§ 1201 nt., 1203

Act for the Promotion and Development of Agricultural Markets

P.R. Laws Ann. 1954, Title 5, § 101 et seq.

Act for the Promotion of Agricultural Development

P.R. Laws Ann. 1954, Title 5, § 1551 et seq.

Act for the Protection and Preservation of the Caves, Caverns or Sinkholes of Puerto Rico

P.R. Laws Ann. 1954, Title 12, § 1143 et seq.

Act for the Protection, Conservation and Study of the Underwater Archaeological Sites and Resources

P.R. Laws Ann. 1954, Title 18, § 1501 et seq.

Act for the Regulation and Inspection of Farm Markets

P.R. Laws Ann. 1954, Title 5, § 121 et seq.

Act for the Regulation and Integral Development of the Puerto Rico Artisanry

P.R. Laws Ann. 1954, Title 18, § 1205 et seq.

Act for the Regulation of Credit Life Insurance and Credit Accident and Health Insurance

D.C. Code 1973, § 35-1001 et seq.
N.M. Stat. Ann., 59A-25-1 et seq.

Act for the Simplification of Fiduciary Security Transfers

See Uniform Act for the Simplification of Fiduciary Security Transfers

Act for Voting by New or Former Residents in Presidential Elections

Neb. Rev. Stat. 1943, 32-1301.01 et seq.

Act Governing Secured Creditors' Dividends in Liquidation Proceedings

See Uniform Act Governing Secured Creditors' Dividends in Liquidation Proceedings

Act Making It Legal for a Student Living in One School District to Attend School in Another School District Under Specified Conditions

Ark. Code Ann. 1987, 6-18-204 et seq.

Act of Attainder

N.Y. Laws 1779, 3rd Sess., Ch. 25

Act of Cession (Fort Leavenworth)

Kan. Stat. Ann., 27-104

Act of Descents

Ky. Rev. Stat. 1971, 391.010 et seq.

Act of Maine's Elderly

Me. Rev. Stat. Ann. 1964, Title 22, § 5101 et seq.

Act of the Caribbean Economic Development Corporation

P.R. Laws Ann. 1954, Title 23, § 261 et seq.

Act of the Office of Construction Officer, Attached to the Urban Renewal and Housing Administration (Construction Officer)

P.R. Laws Ann. 1954, Title 17, § 501 et seq.

Act of the University of Puerto Rico

P.R. Laws Ann. 1954, Title 18, § 601 et seq.

Act on Aging

D.C. Code Ann., § 6-2201 et seq.

Ill. Rev. Stat. 1991, Ch. 23, § 6101 et seq.

Act on Blood Tests to Determine Paternity

See Uniform Act on Blood Tests to Determine Paternity

Act on Claims and Suits Against the Commonwealth

P.R. Laws Ann. 1954, Title 32, § 3077 et seq.

Act on Fresh Pursuit (Uniform)

See Uniform Act on Fresh Pursuit

Act on Interstate Fresh Pursuit

S.D. Codified Laws 1967, 23A-3-9 et seq.

Act on the Aging (Illinois)

Ill. Comp. Stat. 1992, Ch. 20, § 105/1 et seq.

Act on the Aging (Kansas)

Kan. Stat. Ann., 75-5901 et seq.

Act on Transfers of Funds Abroad

P.R. Laws Ann. 1954, Title 7, § 1401 et seq.

Act Prohibiting Unjust Discrimination in Employment Because of Age

Alaska Stat. 1962, § 18.80.060 et seq.

Neb. Rev. Stat. 1943, 48-1006 et seq.

Act Providing for the Review, Continuation, Reestablishment or Termination of Regulation Agencies

Ga. Code Ann.,43-2-1 et seq.

Act Regarding Liability for Persons Responding to Oil Spills

Ala. Code 1975, § 6-5-332.2

Act Regulating and Supervising the Sale of Securities

W. Va. Code 1966, § 32-1-101 et seq.

Act Regulating Nonprofit Hospital Service and Indemnity Plans

N.M. Stat. Ann., 59A-47-1 et seq.

Act Regulating Public Warehouses For, and Buyers of, Agricultural Seeds

Mont. Rev. Code 1947, 3-301 et seq.

Act Regulating Traffic on Highways

See Uniform Act Regulating Traffic on Highways

Act Relating to Children Born Out of Wedlock

Jan. 11, 1951, Ch. 1225, 64 Stat. 1240

Act to Authorize the Acquisition of Property for Management, Construction and Maintenance of Rights-of-Way by the State Highway Department in Advance of Present Need

Ga. Code Ann., 32-3-1

Act to Authorize the Additional Lottery System

P.R. Acts 1989, No. 10

Act to Authorize the United States to Participate in Chapter II of the Patent Cooperation Treaty

Nov. 6, 1986, P.L. 99-616, 35 U.S. Code § 351 nt.

Act to Create the Corporation for the Development and Administration of the Marine, Lacustrine and Fluvial Resources

P.R. Laws Ann. 1954, Title 12, § 1351 et seq.

Act to Create the Governor's Advisory Committee for the Restoration, Preservation and Improvement of La Fortaleza

P.R. Laws Ann. 1954, Title 3, § 18 et seq.

Act to Deter Criminal Activity

N.J. Stat. Ann., 52:17B-151 et seq.

Act to Eliminate Civic Unemployment in Puerto Rico

P.R. Laws Ann. 1954, Title 28, § 661 et seq.

Act to Establish a Down-Payment System for Government Purveyors of Goods and Services

P.R. Acts 1989, Second Session, No. 25

Act to Establish Minimum Procedural Requirements for the Suspension of Essential Public Services

P.R. Laws Ann. 1954, Title 27, § 1301 et seq.

Act to Establish the Wage Subsidy Program for Eligible Farmers

P.R. Acts 1989, No. 46

Act to Implement the Maine Indian Claims Settlement

Me. Rev. Stat. Ann. 1964, Title 30, § 6201 et seq.

Act to Preserve the Habitability of Rental Units Subject to Notice to Vacate

D.C. Code Ann., § 5-525 et seq.

Act to Prevent Pollution from Ships

Oct. 21, 1980, P.L. 96-478, 33 U.S. Code § 1901 et seq.

Dec. 29, 1987, P.L. 100-220, 33 U.S. Code § 1901 et seq.

Dec. 12, 1989, P.L. 101-225, 33 U.S. Code §§ 1905, 1907

Aug. 18, 1990, P.L. 101-380, 33 U.S. Code § 1908

Dec. 19, 1991, P.L. 102-241, 33 U.S. Code § 1906

Nov. 30, 1993, P.L. 103-160, 33 U.S. Code §§ 1901, 1902

Dec. 8, 1993, P.L. 103-182, 33 U.S. Code § 1908

Sept. 23, 1996, P.L. 104-201, 33 U.S. Code § 1902

Oct. 2, 1996, P.L. 104-227, 33 U.S. Code §§ 1901 to 1903, 1905, 1907, 1908

Oct. 17, 1998, P.L. 105-261, 33 U.S. Code § 1902

Act to Prevent the Perpetration of Certain Fraudulent Practices by Photographers within the State of North Carolina

N.C. Gen. Stat. 1943, § 66-59 et seq.

Act to Prevent Unfair Cigarette Sales in Kentucky

Ky. Rev. Stat. 1971, 365.260 et seq.

Act to Promote the Elimination of the Cattle Fever Tick; to Prevent its Propagation and Spread and to Eradicate it

P.R. Laws Ann. 1954, Title 5, § 741 et seq.

Act to Promote the State Use System of Industries in the Public Welfare Institutions

R.I. Gen. Laws 1956, 13-7-1 et seq.

Act to Protect Motor Vehicle Buyers
P.R. Laws Ann. 1954, Title 23, § 1021 et seq.

Act to Protect the Insignia of the Olympic Movement and to Grant the Puerto Rico Olympic Committee Exclusive Rights Thereon
P.R. Acts 1987, No. 71

Act to Protect the Insignias of the San Blas Marathon and the Exclusive Rights for Commercial Advertisements in Radio and Television Transmissions of the Activities of the Marathon on the Island
P.R. Laws Ann. 1954, Title 15, § 551a et seq.

Act to Protect the Purity of Drinking Water
P.R. Laws Ann. 1954, Title 12, § 1551 et seq.

Act to Provide Certain Deductions for Deed Recordation Taxes and Motor Vehicle Fees and for the Accelerated Payment of Taxes on Insurance Premium Receipts
D.C. Code Ann., §§ 47-1803.3, 47-2606

Act to Provide for the Reorganization of School Districts
N.D. Cent. Code, 15-53.1-08 et seq.
Wyo. Stat. 1957, § 21-224 et seq.

Act to Regulate Contracting between the Government and Private Interests for the Administration and Operation of Government Health Facilities
P.R. Laws Ann. 1954, Title 24, § 338 et seq.

Act to Regulate Public Conduct on Public Passenger Vehicles
D.C. Code Ann., § 44-223 et seq.

Act to Regulate the Business of Public Parking Areas for Motor Vehicles
P.R. Laws Ann. 1954, Title 23, § 805 et seq.

Act to Regulate the Commercial Application of Insecticides and/or Economic Poisons in Puerto Rico
P.R. Laws Ann. 1954, Title 10, § 976 et seq.

Act to Regulate the Health Service Administrators' Profession
P.R. Laws Ann. 1954, Title 20, § 2351 et seq.

Act to Regulate the Hemodialysis Technologist's Profession
P.R. Laws Ann. 1954, Title 20, § 2901 et seq.

Act to Regulate the Marketing of Meat in Puerto Rico
P.R. Laws Ann. 1954, Title 10, § 241 et seq.

Act to Regulate the Operation of Mobile Sales Businesses
P.R. Laws Ann. 1954, Title 10, § 2001 et seq.

Act to Regulate the Operations of Business Establishments
P.R. Acts 1989, First Special Session, No. 1

Act to Regulate the Practice of Nursing in the Commonwealth of Puerto Rico
P.R. Laws Ann. 1954, Title 20, § 203 et seq.

Act to Regulate the Practice of the Profession of Psychology in Puerto Rico
P.R. Laws Ann. 1954, Title 20, § 3201 et seq.

Act to Regulate the Practice of the Profession of Speech-Language Pathology, Audiology, and Speech-Language Therapy in Puerto Rico
P.R. Laws Ann. 1954, Title 20, § 3101 et seq.

Act to Regulate the Practice of Veterinary Medicine
P.R. Laws Ann. 1954, Title 20, § 2951 et seq.

Act to Regulate the Profession of Chemist in Puerto Rico
P.R. Acts 1983, No. 97

Act to Regulate the Profession of Health Educators in Puerto Rico
P.R. Laws Ann. 1954, Title 20, § 2550 et seq.

Act to Regulate the Profession of Medical Technology in Puerto Rico
P.R. Laws Ann. 1954, Title 20, § 281 et seq.

Act to Regulate the Profession of Rehabilitation Counseling
P.R. Laws Ann. 1954, Title 20, § 2651 et seq.

Act to Regulate the Respiratory Care Practice in Puerto Rico
P.R. Laws Ann. 1954, Title 20, § 3401 et seq.

Act to Regulate the Sale of Drafts
P.R. Laws Ann. 1954, Title 10, § 111 et seq.

Act to Regulate the Sale on the Island of Real Estate Located Outside Puerto Rico
P.R. Acts 1980, No. 145

Act to Regulate the Teaching Practice Program of the Department of Education of Puerto Rico
P.R. Acts 1989, No. 79

Act to Secure Rendition of Prisoners as Witnesses in Criminal Proceedings
See Uniform Act to Secure Rendition of Prisoners as Witnesses in Criminal Proceedings

Act to Secure the Attendance of Witness from Without a State in Criminal Proceedings
See also Uniform Act to Secure the Attendance of Witnesses from Without a State in Criminal Proceedings
Oct. 18, 1962, P.L. 87-845, 76A Stat. 1, 6 U.S. Code § 4331 et seq. (Canal Zone)
Ala. Code 1975, 12-21-280 et seq.
Ind. Code Ann., 35-37-5-1 et seq.
Kan. Stat. Ann., 22-4201 et seq.
Md. Ann. Code 1974, Art. CJ, § 9-301 et seq.
Mont. Code Ann., 46-15-111 et seq.
N.D. Cent. Code, 31-03-25 et seq.
Wis. Stat. Ann., 976.02

Act to Secure the Attendance of Witnesses from Within or Without a State in Criminal Proceedings
N.Y. Criminal Procedure Law (Consol. Laws Ch. 11A) § 640.10
Pa. Cons. Stat., Title 42, § 5961 et seq.
P.R. Laws Ann. 1954, Title 34, § 1471 et seq.

Act to Transfer the Rice Corporation, Inc., and the Vegetable Corporation, Inc. to the Land Authority of Puerto Rico
P.R. Acts 1985, No. 10

Action Report Act (Governor's Bill)
Ill. Rev. Stat. 1991, Ch. 63, § 330 et seq.

Action to Establish Title Act
La. Code of Civil Procedure, Art. 3651

Actionable Words Act
Miss. Code Ann. 1972, § 95-1-1
Va. Code 1950, § 8.01-45

Actions By or Against Unincorporated Organizations or Associations
Ga. Code Ann., 9-2-24 et seq.

Actions for Recovery of Real Property Act
Cal. Code of Civil Procedure § 315 et seq.

Actions Saving Statute
Ky. Rev. Stat. 1971, 413.270

Actions to Enforce Payment Act
Ill. Comp. Stat. 1992, Ch. 815, § 115/0.01 et seq.
Ill. Rev. Stat. 1991, Ch. 17, § 605.9 et seq.

Activity Act (Forestry)
Miss. Laws 1994, Ch. 647

Activity Bond Act (Private)
N.M. Stat. Ann., 60-20-1 et seq.

Activity Bond Allocation Act (Private)
Kan. Stat. Ann., 74-5058 et seq.

Activity Development Authority Act (Pueblo Depot)
Colo. Rev. Stat., 29-23-101 et seq.

Activity Law (Nuclear Waste)
Me. Rev. Stat. Ann. 1964, Title 38, § 1451 et seq.

Actuarial Note Act
N.C. Gen. Stat. 1943, §§ 120-112 to 120-114

Actuarial Note Act (Legislative)
N.C. Gen. Stat. 1943, § 120-112 et seq.

Acupuncture Act
Ga. Code Ann., 43-3A-1 et seq.
Haw. Rev. Stat. Ann., § 436E-1 et seq.

Md. Ann. Code 1974, Art. HO, § 1A-101 et
seq.

**Acupuncture and Oriental Medicine
Practice Act**
N.M. Stat. Ann., 61-14A-1 et seq.

Acupuncture Licensing Act
Cal. Business and Professions Code §§ 4925,
4927, 4935, 4938
Utah Code Ann. 1953, 58-12-57 et seq.

Acupuncture Practice Act
Ill. Comp. Stat. 1992, Ch. 225, § 2/1 et seq.
Mont. Code Ann., 37-13-101 et seq.
N.M. Stat. Ann., 61-14A-1 et seq.

Acupuncture Registration Act
Pa. Purdon's Stat., Title 63, § 1801 et seq.

**Acworth Area Convention and Visitors
Bureau Authority Act**
Ga. Laws 1997, p. 3793

Acworth Lake Authority Act
Ga. Laws 1951, p. 265

Ad Valorem Tax Act
Ohio Rev. Code 1953, 5711.01 et seq.
Okla. Stat. Ann., Title 68, § 2801 et seq.

Ad Valorem Tax Act (Copper Production)
N.M. Stat. Ann., 7-39-1 et seq.

Ad Valorem Tax Act, 1958 (Motor Vehicle)
Miss. Code Ann. 1972, § 27-55-1 et seq.

Ad Valorem Tax Code
Okla. Stat. Ann., Title 68, § 2801 et seq.

Ad Valorem Tax Law (Private Care)
Mo. Rev. Stat., 137.1000 to 137.1030

ADA Flat Grant Law (Schools)
Ind. Code Ann., 21-3-4.5-1 et seq.

Adair Act (Intoxicating Liquors)
Ohio Rev. Code 1953, 4399.01 et seq.

Adak Reuse Authority Act
Alaska Stat. 1962, § 30.17.010 et seq.

ADAMHA Reorganization Act
July 10, 1992, P.L. 102-321, 42 U.S. Code
§ 201 nt.
Aug. 26, 1992, P.L. 102-352, 42 U.S. Code
§§ 290aa nt., 290cc-21, 290cc-28,
290cc-30, 300x nt.

**Adams Act (Agricultural Experiment
Stations)**
See Agricultural Experiment Stations Act
March 16, 1906, Ch. 951, 34 Stat. 63

**Adams-Bates-Slenker Act (Taxation-Public
Utilities)**
Ind. Burns' 1933, 64-410 to 64-712

Adams County Act (Boundaries)
Colo. Rev. Stat., 30-5-102

Adams National Historical Park Act of 1998
Nov. 2, 1998, P.L. 105-342, 112 Stat. 3200,
16 U.S. Code § 410eee nt.

Adams Tax Law
Del. Laws 1974 Vol. 20, Part 2, p. 334, Ch.
381; Vol. 21, p. 40, Ch. 24

Adamson Act (Eight Hour Day)
See Hours Of Service Acts (Railroads)
Sept. 3, 5, 1916, Ch. 436, 39 Stat. 721

Add On Act (Installment Sales)
Cal. Civil Code § 1808.1 et seq.
Ill. Rev. Stat. 1965, Ch. 121 1/2, § 250

Added Assessments Act
N.J. Stat. Ann., 54:4-63.1 et seq.

**Addict Rehabilitation and Civil
Commitment Act**
Cal. Welfare and Institutions Code § 3000 et
seq.

Addiction Act (Narcotics)
Mo. Rev. Stat. 1978, 195.010 et seq.
Tex. Health and Safety Code, § 481.001 et
seq.
Wis. Stat. Ann., 161.02, Subsec. 3

Addiction Services Department Organic Act
P.R. Laws Ann. 1954, Title 3, § 401 et seq.

Additional Employer Specific Skills Training Grant Program
N.Y. Education Law 1947 (Consol. Laws Ch. 16) § 3032

Additional House Office Building Act
April 22, 1955, Ch. 26, 69 Stat. 41, 40 U.S. Code § 175, nt.

Additional Judgeship Act
See Judgeship Act (Additional Judges)

Additional Lottery System Act
P.R. Acts 1989, No. 10

Additional State School Building Aid Act
N.J. Stat. Ann.,18A:58-33.22 et seq.

Additional Supplemental Local Government Sales and Use Tax Act
N.C. Gen. Stat. 1943, § 105-495 et seq.

Additional Teachers' Salary Act Amendments
D.C. Laws 1977, No. 2-1

Additional Transfer Inheritance Tax Act
Pa. Purdon's Stat., Title 72, § 2303

Additional Unemployment Compensation Benefits Act
Haw. Rev. Stat. Ann., § 385-1 et seq.

Additional Urgent Deficiency Appropriations Act of 1941
May 24, 1941, Ch. 132, 55 Stat. 199, 42 U.S. Code § 1523 nt.

Additions to Trusts Act
S.C. Code Ann. 1976, Superseded Vols., § 21-33-10 et seq.

Additions to Trusts Act (Testamentary)
Me. Rev. Stat. Ann. 1964, Title 18-A, § 2-511

Address Disclosure Act (Mail Order)
R.I. Gen. Laws 1956, 6-40-1 et seq.

Adequate Facilities Tax Act (Spring Hill)
Tenn. Private Acts 1988, Ch. 173

Adequate Program for Education Act
Ga. Code Ann. 20-2-130 et seq.

Adequate Water Service Law
Cal. Public Utilities Code § 8201 et seq.

Adirondack Mountain Authority Act
N.Y. Public Authority Law (Consol. Laws Ch. 43A) § 100 et seq.

Adirondack Park Act
N.Y. Environmental Conservation Law (Consol. Laws, Ch. 43B) § 9-101

Adirondack Park Agency Act
N.Y. Executive Law 1951 (Consol. Laws Ch. 18) § 800 et seq.

Adjacent Landowner Excavation Protection Act
Ill. Comp. Stat. 1992, Ch. 765, §§ 140/0.01, 140/1

Adjacent Property Improvement Law
Tenn. Code Ann., 7-32-101 et seq.

Adjoining District Act
Ill. Rev. Stat. 1953, Ch. 42, § 219 et seq.

Adjudicating Act (Water Rights)
Colo. Rev. Stat., 148-9-1 et seq.

Adjudication Act (Parking Offenses)
N.J. Stat. Ann., 39:4-139.2 et seq.

Adjusted Compensation Act
See World War Adjusted Compensation Act

Adjusted Compensation Act (Soldiers)
Kan. Gen. Stat. 1949, 73-101 et seq.

Adjusted Compensation Act (Veterans)
Minn. Stat. Ann., 197.80 et seq.

Adjusted Compensation Payment Act
Jan. 27, 1936, Ch. 32, 49 Stat. 1099
Aug. 14, 1937, Ch. 628, 50 Stat. 641

Adjusted Gross Income Tax Act
Ind. Code Ann., 6-3-1-1 et seq.

Adjuster Law (Insurance)
Me. Rev. Stat. Ann. 1964, Title 24-A, § 1851 et seq.

Adjusters' Licensing Act (Public)
N.J. Stat. Ann., 17:22B-1 et seq.

Adjustment Act (Dollar)
S.C. Code Ann. 1976, § 37-1-109 et seq.

Adjustment Act (Irrigation Projects)
May 25, 1926, Ch. 383, 44 Stat. 647, 43 U.S. Code §§ 423 to 423g
April 23, 1930, Ch. 205, 46 Stat. 249
July 11, 1956, Ch. 563, § 1, 70 Stat. 524

Adjustment Act (Railroad Land Grants)
March 3, 1887, Ch. 376, 24 Stat. 556, 43 U.S. Code §§ 894 to 899
Feb. 12, 1896, Ch. 18, 29 Stat. 6, 43 U.S. Code § 897

Adjustment and Conservation Act (Agriculture)
Colo. Rev. Stat., 35-3-101 et seq.
Ga. Code Ann., 2-6-1 et seq.

Adjustment Center for the Blind Act
Miss. Code Ann. 1972, § 43-3-1 et seq.

Adjustment of Assets and Liabilities Act (Municipal)
Wis. Stat. 1975, 66.03

Adjustment to Lawful Resident Status of Certain Nationals of Countries for Which Extended Voluntary Departure Has Been Made Available
Dec. 22, 1987, P.L. 100-202, 8 U.S. Code § 1255a nt.

Adjustor and Private Investigator Act
Cal. Business and Professions Code § 7500 et seq.

Administration (Consumer Act)
Wis. Stat. Ann., 426.101 et seq.

Administration (Consumer Credit Code)
Iowa Code Ann., 537.6101 et seq.

Me. Rev. Stat. Ann. 1964, Title 9-A, § 6.101 et seq.

Administration (Consumer Protection Code)
S.C. Code Ann. 1976, § 37-6-101 et seq.

Administration (Revised Uniform Consumer Credit Code)
See Revised Uniform Consumer Credit Code—Administration

Administration (Uniform Consumer Credit Code)
See Uniform Consumer Credit Code—Administration

Administration Act
Ind. Code Ann., 4-13-1-1 et seq.

Administration Act (Agricultural Development)
P.R. Laws Ann. 1954, Title 5, § 1831 et seq.

Administration Act (Agricultural Services)
P.R. Laws Ann. 1954, Title 5, § 31 et seq.

Administration Act (College of Agriculture, Cornell University)
N.Y. Education Law 1947 (Consol. Laws Ch. 16) § 5712

Administration Act (Court)
Tex. Government Code, § 74.001 et seq.

Administration Act (Employment Security)
Nev. Rev. Stat. 1979 Reprint, 612.205 et seq.

Administration Act (Estates)
Mo. Rev. Stat., 473.010 et seq.
Ohio Rev. Code 1953, 2113.01 et seq.
Tenn. Code Ann., 30-1-101 et seq.
Wis. Stat. Ann., 851.001

Administration Act (General Services)
N.J. Stat. Ann., 52:18A-178 et seq.

Administration Act (Motor Vehicle)
N.M. Stat. Ann., 66-1-1 et seq.

Administration Act (Optional Forms of Municipal)
Mass. Gen. Laws Ann., 43C:1 et seq.

Administration Act (Rural Finance)
Minn. Stat. Ann., 41B.01 et seq.

Administration Act (Workers' Compensation)
N.M. Stat. Ann., 52-5-1.1 et seq.

Administration and Finance Act (Property Assessment)
Fla. Stat. Ann., 195.0011 et seq.

Administration Code Act
Mich. Comp. Laws 1948, 24.71 et seq.

Administration Department Act
Mich. Comp. Laws Ann., 18.1 et seq.
N.C. Gen. Stat. 1943, §§ 143-334 to 143-345.8

Administration Exempt Estate Act
Neb. Rev. Stat. 1943, 30-24,127, 30-24,128

Administration of Charitable Trust Act
Md. Ann. Code 1974, Art ET, § 14-301 et seq.

Administration of Child Welfare Law
Miss. Code Ann. 1972, § 43-15-1 et seq.

Administration of County Highway Department Act
Ind. Code Ann., 8-17-3-1 et seq.

Administration of Estates Act
Ill. Rev. Stat. 1991, Ch. 110 1/2, § 1-1 et seq.

Administration of Estates Act (Ancillary)
Mont. Code Ann., 72-4-402

Administration of Estates Act (Independent)
Cal. Probate Code § 10400 et seq.

Administration of Oaths, Public Assistance Technical Clarification, and Police Service and Fire Service Schedule Approval Act
D.C. Code Ann., §§ 1-338.1, 3-205.52

Administration of Taxes on Petroleum Products Law
Tenn. Code Ann., 67-3-101 et seq.

Administration of Taxing Laws Act
Ga. Code Ann., 48-2-1 et seq.

Administration of the Insurance Laws Act
Wis. Stat. Ann., 601.01 et seq.

Administration of the Receivership of the Savings and Loan Labor Bank
P.R. Laws Ann. 1954, Title 7, § 851 et seq.

Administration Reorganization Act
Tenn. Code Ann., 4-3-101 et seq.

Administrative Adjudication Act
Ind. Code Ann., 4-22-2-3 et seq.

Administrative Agencies Act
Neb. Rev. Stat. 1943, 84-901 et seq.

Administrative Agencies Judicial Review Act
Mich. Comp. Laws Ann., 24.301 et seq.
N.C. Gen. Stat. 1943, § 150B-43 et seq.

Administrative Agencies Uniform Practice Act
N.D. Cent. Code, 28-32-01 et seq.

Administrative Agency Law
Pa. Cons. Stat., Title 2, §§ 103 et seq., 501 et seq.

Administrative and Executive Departments Act
Haw. Rev. Stat. Ann., § 226-1 et seq.

Administrative Appeals Act
Ohio Rev. Code 1953, 2506.01 et seq.

Administrative Assistants Acts (Executive Departments)
April 3, 1939, Ch. 36, 53 Stat. 565 (See 3 U.S. Code § 106)
June 25, 1948, Ch. 644, 62 Stat. 672, 3 U.S. Code § 106
Oct. 15, 1949, Ch. 695, 63 Stat. 880, 3 U.S. Code § 106

Nov. 2, 1978, P.L. 95-570, § 1(a), 92 Stat. 2446

Administrative Board Act (State)
Mich. Comp. Laws Ann., 17.1 et seq.

Administrative Building Council Act
Ind. Code Ann., 4-26-3-1 et seq.

Administrative Code
Colo. Rev. Stat., 24-2-101 et seq.

Ind. Code Ann., 2-6-1.5-2, 4-22-8-1 et seq.

La. Acts 1940, No. 47

Me. Rev. Stat. Ann. 1964, Title 5, § 8002 et seq.

Neb. Rev. Stat. 1943, 84-901 et seq.

Ohio Laws Vol. 109, p. 105

Pa. Purdon's Stat., Title 71, §§ 1 et seq., 51 et seq.

R.I. Public Laws 1939, January Session, Ch. 660

Tex. Rev. Civ. Stat., Art. 6252-13b

Wash. Rev. Code Ann., 43.17.010 et seq.

Administrative Code (City of New York)
N.Y. Adm. Code 1985, § 1-101 et seq.

N.Y. Laws 1937, Ex. Sess., Ch. 929

Administrative Code Act
Ill. Comp. Stat. 1992, Ch. 20, § 5/1

Administrative Conference Act
Aug. 30, 1964, P.L. 88-499, 78 Stat. 615 (See 5 U.S. Code §§ 571 to 576)

Sept. 6, 1966, P.L. 89-554, 80 Stat. 632

Dec. 24, 1969, P.L. 91-164, 83 Stat. 446

Oct. 21, 1972, P.L. 52-526, 86 Stat. 446

June 13, 1978, P.L. 920526, § 1(a), 92 Stat. 317

Sept. 13, 1982, P.L. 97-258, § 3(a)(1), 96 Stat. 1062

Oct. 15, 1982, P.L. 97-330, 96 Stat. 1618

Oct. 14, 1986, P.L. 99-470, 100 Stat. 1198

Oct. 12, 1990, P.L. 101-422, 104 Stat. 910

Aug. 26, 1992, P.L. 102-354, 106 Stat. 944

Oct. 9, 1992, P.L. 102-403, 106 Stat. 1968

Administrative Department Act
N.C. Gen. Stat. 1943, § 143-334 et seq.

Administrative Determination of Overpayments Act
Utah Code Ann. 1953, 62A-11-201 et seq.

Administrative Dispute Resolution Act
Nov. 15, 1990, P.L. 101-552, 5 U.S. Code §§ 556, 581 et seq.; 9 U.S. Code § 10; 28 U.S. Code § 2672; 31 U.S. Code § 3711

Aug. 26, 1992, P.L. 102-354, 5 U.S. Code § 571 nt.

Oct. 19, 1996, P.L. 104-320, 5 U.S. Code §§ prec. 500, 556, 571 nt., 572 to 583; 9 U.S. Code § 10; 28 U.S. Code § 2672; 29 U.S. Code § 173; 31 U.S. Code § 3711; 41 U.S. Code §§ 605, 607

Administrative Dispute Resolution Act of 1996
Oct. 19, 1996, P.L. 104-320, 5 U.S. Code § 571 nt.

Administrative Expenses Act of 1946
Aug. 2, 1946, Ch. 774, 60 Stat. 806 (See 5 U.S. Code §§ 302, 503, 3109, 5703, 5722, 5724, 5730, 5731, 7903; 19 U.S. Code § 1645; See 28 U.S. Code § 1823; 31 U.S. Code §§ 529, 638a; 41 U.S. Code §§ 5, 5a; 44 U.S. Code § 321)

Sept. 23, 1950, Ch. 1010, 64 Stat. 985 (See 5 U.S. Code §§ 5722, 5724)

Aug. 31, 1954, Ch. 1155, 68 Stat. 1008 (See 5 U.S. Code §§ 5728, 5729)

July 28, 1955, Ch. 424, 69 Stat. 394 (See 5 U.S. Code § 5703)

Feb. 12, 1958, P.L. 85-326, 72 Stat. 14 (See 5 U.S. Code § 5724)

Aug. 25, 1958, P.L. 85-749, 72 Stat. 843 (See 5 U.S. Code § 5723)

Sept. 2, 1958, P.L. 85-858, 72 Stat. 1274 (See 5 U.S. Code § 5728)

July 5, 1960, P.L. 86-587, 74 Stat. 327 (See 5 U.S. Code § 5723)

Sept. 6, 1960, P.L. 86-707, 74 Stat. 796 (See 5 U.S. Code §§ 5724, 5726, 5727, 5913)

Aug. 14, 1961, P.L. 87-139, 75 Stat. 339 (See 5 U.S. Code § 5703; 22 U.S. Code §§ 287o, 287q)

Aug. 30, 1961, P.L. 87-172, 75 Stat. 409 (See 5 U.S. Code § 5722)

Oct. 9, 1962, P.L. 87-776, 76 Stat. 777 (See 5 U.S. Code § 5724)

Continued

Oct. 16, 1963, P.L. 88-146, 77 Stat. 252 (See
5 U.S. Code § 5723)

Feb. 5, 1964, P.L. 88-266, 78 Stat. 8 (See 5
U.S. Code § 5721)

July 21, 1966, P.L. 89-516, 80 Stat. 323 (See
5 U.S. Code §§ 5724, 5724a, 5726)

Administrative Hearing Commission Act
Mo. Rev. Stat., 621.015 et seq.

Administrative Judicial Districts Act
Tex. Gov. Code, § 74.041 et seq.

Administrative Judicial Review Act
Ind. Code Ann., 4-21.5-5-1 et seq.

Administrative Office Act (Courts)
Ill. Rev. Stat. 1963, Ch. 37, § 23e et seq.
Md. Ann. Code 1974, Art. CJ, § 13-101 et
seq.

**Administrative Office of the United States
Courts Personnel Act of 1990**
Oct. 30, 1990, P.L. 101-474, 28 U.S. Code
§ 602 nt.

Administrative Orders Review Act
Dec. 29, 1950, Ch. 1189, 64 Stat. 1129 (See
28 U.S. Code §§ 41, 43, 2341 to 2352)
Aug. 30, 1954, Ch. 1073, 68 Stat. 961 (See
28 U.S. Code §§ 2341, 2342)
Aug. 28, 1958, P.L. 85-791, 72 Stat. 951 (See
28 U.S. Code §§ 2346, 2347)

Administrative Organization Act
Colo. Rev. Stat., 24-1-101 et seq.

Administrative Procedure Act
See also Uniform Administrative Procedure
Act
June 11, 1946, Ch. 324, 60 Stat. 237 (See 5
U.S. Code §§ 551 to 559, 701 to 706, 1305,
3105, 3344, 4301, 5335, 5362, 7521)
Aug. 8, 1946, Ch. 870, 60 Stat. 918 (See 5
U.S. Code §§ 551, 701)
Aug. 10, 1946, Ch. 951, 60 Stat. 993 (See 5
U.S. Code §§ 551, 701)
March 31, 1947, Ch. 30, 61 Stat. 37 (See 5
U.S. Code §§ 551, 701)
June 30, 1947, Ch. 163, 61 Stat. 201 (See 5
U.S. Code §§ 551, 701)

March 30, 1948, Ch. 164, 62 Stat. 99 (See 5
U.S. Code §§ 551, 701)
July 4, 1966, P.L. 89-487, 80 Stat. 250 (See 5
U.S. Code § 552)
Sept. 6, 1966, P.L. 89-554, § 8(a), 80 Stat.
632
June 5, 1967, P.L. 90-23, § 1, 81 Stat. 54
Sept. 11, 1967, P.L. 90-23, § 1, 81 Stat. 54
Oct. 22, 1968, P.L. 90-623, § 1(1), 82 Stat.
1312
Nov. 21, 1974, P.L. 93-502, 88 Stat. 1561
Dec. 31, 1975, P.L. 94-183, 89 Stat. 1057
Sept. 13, 1976, P.L. 94-409, 90 Stat. 1241
Oct. 21, 1976, P.L. 94-574, 90 Stat. 2721
March 27, 1978, P.L. 95-251, 92 Stat. 183
Oct. 13, 1978, P.L. 95-454, 92 Stat. 1134,
1221, 1224, 1225
Dec. 21, 1982, P.L. 97-375, 96 Stat. 1821
Jan. 12, 1983, P.L. 97-452, 96 Stat. 2478
Oct. 15, 1984, P.L. 98-477, 98 Stat. 2211
Oct. 19, 1984, P.L. 98-497, 98 Stat. 2292
Nov. 8, 1984, P.L. 98-620, 98 Stat. 3357
Oct. 27, 1986, P.L. 99-570, 100 Stat. 3207-48
Oct. 18, 1988, P.L. 100-503, 102 Stat. 2507
Nov. 5, 1990, P.L. 101-508, 104 Stat.
1388-334
Nov. 15, 1990, P.L. 101-552, 104 Stat. 2737
Aug. 10, 1993, P.L. 103-66, 107 Stat. 611
July 5, 1994, P.L. 103-272, 108 Stat. 1373
Alaska Stat. 1962, § 44.62.010 et seq.
Cal. Government Code § 11340 et seq.
Colo. Rev. Stat., 24-4-101 et seq.
Fla. Stat. Ann., 120.50 et seq.
Haw. Rev. Stat. Ann., § 91-1 et seq.
Ill. Comp. Stat. 1992, Ch. 5, § 100/1-1
Ind. Code Ann., 4-22-2-1 et seq.
Iowa Code Ann., 17A.1101 et seq.
Kan. Stat. Ann., 77-501 et seq.
Ky. Rev. Stat. 1971, 13A.010 et seq.
Mass. Gen. Laws Ann., 30A:1 et seq.
Minn. Stat. Ann., 14.01 et seq.
Miss. Code Ann. 1972, § 25-43-1 et seq.
N.C. Gen. Stat. 1943, § 150B-1 et seq.
N.H. Rev. Stat. 1955, 541-A:1 et seq.
N.J. Stat. Ann., 52:14B-1 et seq.
N.M. Stat. Ann., 12-8-1 et seq.
Ohio Rev. Code 1953, 119.01 et seq.

Okla. Stat. Ann., Title 75, § 250 et seq.
S.C. Code Ann. 1976, § 1-23-10 et seq.
Tex. Government Code, § 2001.001 et seq.
Utah Code Ann. 1953, 63-46b-0.5 et seq.
Va. Code 1950, § 9-6.14:1 et seq.
Wash. Rev. Code Ann., 34.05.010 et seq.
Wis. Stat. Ann., 227.01 et seq.

Administrative Procedure Act (State Higher Education)
Wash. Rev. Code Ann., 28B.19.010 et seq.

Administrative Procedure Act Amendments Act
D.C. Code 1973, § 1-1501 et seq.

Administrative Procedure Act for the Establishment and Enforcement of Child Support
Colo. Rev. Stat., 26-13.5-101 et seq.

Administrative Procedure and Texas Register Act
Tex. Rev. Stat., Art. 6252-13a

Administrative Procedure Technical Amendments Act of 1991
Aug. 26, 1992, P.L. 102-354, 5 U.S. Code § 561 nt.

Administrative Procedures Reform Act
R.I. Gen. Laws 1956, 42-35-1 et seq.

Administrative Process for Child Support Act
Ky. Rev. Stat. 1971, 405.400 et seq.

Administrative Purchasing Act
Alaska Stat. 1962, § 36.30.005 et seq.

Administrative Regulation Act
Ind. Code Ann., 4-22-2-1 et seq.

Administrative Regulation Review Act
Wyo. Stat. Ann., § 28-9-101 et seq.

Administrative Reorganization Act
Ky. Rev. Stat. 1971, 12.010 et seq.
Miss. Code Ann. 1972, § 7-13-1 et seq.

Administrative Review Act
Ariz. Rev. Stat. Ann., § 12-901 et seq.
Ill. Comp. Stat. 1992, Ch. 735, § 5/3-101 et seq.

Administrative Rule Making Act
Ind. Code Ann., 4-22-2-1 et seq.
Mich. Comp. Laws 1948, 24.71 et seq.
Utah Code Ann. 1953, 63-46a-1 et seq.

Administrative Rules Act (Registration)
N.C. Gen. Stat. 1943, § 150B-58 et seq.

Administrative Rules and Procedures Reform Act
Tenn. Public Acts 1986, Ch. 738

Administrative Rules and Regulations Filing Act
Kan. Stat. Ann., 77-415 et seq.

Administrative School District Act
Ore. Rev. Stat., 330.505 et seq.

Administrative Services Act
Utah Code Ann. 1953, 53-1-201 et seq.

Administrative Services Code
Utah Code Ann. 1953, 63A-1-101 et seq.

Administrative Simplification Act (Health Care)
Minn. Stat. Ann., 62J.50 to 62J.61

Administrative Supervision Model Act (Insurance)
Minn. Stat. Ann., 60G.01 et seq.

Administrative Supervision of Insurers Act
S.C. Code Ann. 1976, § 38-26-10 et seq.

Administrative Traffic Checkpoint Act
Utah Code Ann. 1953, 77-23-101 et seq.

Administrative Trust Act
Neb. Rev. Stat. 1943, 30-2801 et seq.

Administrator Act (Third Party)
Neb. Laws 1992, L.B. 1006, §§ 76 to 91
Okla. Stat. Ann., Title 36, § 1441 et seq.

Administrator and Professional Teacher Act
Mo. Rev. Stat., 168.400 et seq.

Administrators Act
Md. Ann. Code 1974, Art. ET, § 7-101 et seq.
Wash. Rev. Code Ann., 11.36.010, 11.48.010 et seq.

Administrators and Executors Act
Del. Code of 1974, Title 12, § 1501 et seq.

Administrator's Licensing and Disciplinary Act (Nursing Home)
Ill. Rev. Stat. 1991, Ch. 111, § 3651 et seq.

Administrators Licensure Act (Insurance)
Pa. Purdon's Stat., Title 40, § 324.1 et seq.

Administrators Licensure Act (Nursing Home)
Pa. Purdon's Stat., Title 63, § 1101 et seq.
Tex. Rev. Civ. Stat., Art. 4442d

Admiralty Act
Aug. 30, 1954, Ch. 1076, 68 Stat. 968, 46 U.S. Code § 752
Aug. 6, 1981, P.L. 97-31, 95 Stat. 155, 46 Appx. U.S. Code §§ 743, 747, 749 to 752

Admiralty Bond Act
Aug. 4, 1790, Ch. 35, 1 Stat. 176 (See 28 U.S. Code § 2464)

Admiralty Interlocutory Decrees Appeals Act
June 25, 1948, Ch. 646, 62 Stat. 869, 28 U.S. Code §§ 1292, 2107
May 24, 1949, Ch. 139, 63 Stat. 104, 28 U.S. Code § 2107
Sept. 2, 1958, P.L. 85-919, 72 Stat. 1770, 28 U.S. Code § 1292

Admiralty Island National Monument Land Management Act of 1990
Aug. 17, 1990, P.L. 101-378, 104 Stat. 468

Admiralty Jurisdiction Extension Act
June 19, 1948, Ch. 526, 62 Stat. 496, 46 U.S. Code § 740

Admiralty Rules Enabling Act
June 25, 1948, Ch. 646, 62 Stat. 869, 28 U.S. Code § 2073
May 24, 1949, Ch. 139, 63 Stat. 104, 28 U.S. Code § 2073
May 10, 1950, Ch. 174, 64 Stat. 158, 28 U.S. Code § 2073

Admissibility of Business Entries Act
Conn. Gen. Stat. Ann., § 52-180

Admission Procedures Act (Mental Hospital)
Okla. Stat. Ann., Title 43A, § 5-301 et seq.

Admission Testing Act
N.Y. Education Law 1947 (Consol. Laws Ch. 16) § 340 et seq.

Admission to Bar Act
Wash. Rev. Code Ann., 2.48.010 et seq.

Admissions Tax Act
Md. Ann. Code 1974, Art. TG, § 4-101 et seq.
Ohio Laws Vol. 115, p. 657
S.C. Code Ann. 1976, § 12-21-2410 et seq.
Tex. Tax Code, § 21.01 et seq.

Admissions Tax Acts
Oct. 3, 1917, Ch. 63, 40 Stat. 318
Feb. 24, 1919, Ch. 18, 40 Stat. 1120
Nov. 23, 1921, Ch. 136, 42 Stat. 289
June 2, 1924, Ch. 234, 43 Stat. 320
Feb. 10, 1939, Ch. 2, 53 Stat. 189
June 25, 1940, Ch. 419, 54 Stat. 523
Sept. 20, 1941, Ch. 412, 55 Stat. 706
July 23, 1942, Ch. 521, 56 Stat. 703
Oct. 21, 1942, Ch. 619, 56 Stat. 981

Adolescent Alcohol and Drug Treatment Recovery Program
Cal. Health and Safety Code § 11759 et seq.

Adolescent Family Life Act
Cal. Health and Safety Code § 309.100 et seq.

Adolescent Family Life Program
Ill. Comp. Stat. 1992, Ch. 20, § 301/35-10

Adolescent Pregnancy Prevention Act
S.C. Code Ann. 1976, § 44-122-10 et seq.

Adolescent Pregnancy Prevention and Services Act
N.Y. Social Services Law (Consol. Laws Ch. 55) § 465 et seq.

Adolescent Tobacco-Use Prevention Act
N.Y. Public Health Law 1953 (Consol. Laws Ch. 45) § 13991 nt.

Adolescent Treatment Hospital Act
N.M. Stat. Ann., 23-9-1 et seq.

Adopt a Beach Act
N.J. Laws 1992, Ch. 213

Adopt-A-Highway Act
Ill. Comp. Stat. 1992, Ch. 605, § 120/1 et seq.

Adopted Children's Instruments Act
Ill. Rev. Stat. 1991, Ch. 40, §§ 1651.9, 1652

Adopted Persons' Change of Name Act
N.C. Gen. Stat. 1943, §§ 48-29, 48-36

Adoption Act
See also Uniform Adoption Act (Revised)
Ala. Code 1975, §§ 26-10-1 et seq., 26-10A-1 et seq.
Alaska Stat. 1962, § 25.23.010 et seq.
Ariz. Rev. Stat. Ann., § 8-101 et seq.
Ark. Stat. 1947, § 56-201 et seq.
Cal. Civil Code § 221 et seq.
Colo. Rev. Stat., 19-5-201 et seq.
Conn. Gen. Stat. Ann., § 45a-706 et seq.
D.C. Code 1973, § 16-301 et seq.
Del. Code of 1974, Title 13, § 901 et seq.
Fla. Stat. Ann., 63.012 et seq.
Ga. Code Ann., 19-8-1 et seq.
Haw. Rev. Stat. Ann., § 578-1 et seq.
Ida. Code 1947, 16-1501 et seq.
Ill. Comp. Stat. 1992, Ch. 750, § 50/0.01 et seq.
Ind. Code Ann., 31-3-1-1 et seq.
Iowa Code Ann., 600.1 et seq.
Kan. Stat. Ann., 59-2101 et seq.
Ky. Rev. Stat. 1971, 199.470 et seq.
La. Rev. Stat. Ann., 9:421 et seq.
Mass. Gen. Laws Ann., 210:1 et seq.
Md. Ann. Code 1974, Art. FL, § 5-301 et seq.
Me. Rev. Stat. Ann. 1964, Title 18-A, § 9-101 et seq.
Mich. Comp. Laws Ann., 710.21 et seq.
Minn. Stat. Ann., 259.21 et seq.
Miss. Code Ann. 1972, § 93-17-1 et seq.
Mo. Rev. Stat., 453.005 et seq.
Mont. Code Ann., 42-1-101 et seq.
N.C. Gen. Stat. 1943, § 48-1 et seq.
N.D. Cent. Code, (Superseded Vol.), 14-11-01 et seq.
Neb. Rev. Stat. 1943, 43-101 et seq.
Nev. Rev. Stat. 1979 Reprint, 127.005 et seq.
N.H. Rev. Stat. 1955, 170-B:1 et seq.
N.J. Stat. Ann., 9:3-17 et seq.
N.M. Stat. Ann., 32A-5-1 et seq.
N.M. Stat. Ann., 40-7-29 et seq.
N.Y. Domestic Relations Law (Consol. Laws Ch. 14) § 109 et seq.
Okla. Stat. Ann., Title 10, § 60.1 et seq.
Ore. Rev. Stat., 109.305 et seq.
Pa. Cons. Stat., Title 23, § 2101 et seq.
R.I. Gen. Laws 1956, 15-7-1 et seq.
S.C. Code Ann. 1976, §§ 15-45-10 et seq., 20-1-1646 et seq., 20-7-1646 et seq.
S.D. Codified Laws 1967, 25-6-1 et seq.
Tenn. Code Ann., § 36-1-101 et seq.
Tex. Family Code, § 16.01 et seq.
Utah Code Ann. 1953, 78-30-1 et seq.
Va. Code 1950, § 63.1-220 et seq.
Vt. Stat. Ann., Title 15, § 431 et seq.
Wash. Rev. Code Ann., 26.33.010 et seq.
Wis. Stat. Ann., 48.81 et seq.
W. Va. Code 1966, § 48-4-1 et seq.
Wyo. Stat. Ann., § 1-22-101 et seq.

Adoption Act (Adult)
N.J. Stat. Ann., 2A:22-1 et seq.
N.M. Stat. Ann., 40-14-1 et seq.

Adoption Act (Black Market)
N.Y. Penal Law 1909 (Consol. Laws Ch. 40) § 487a

Adoption Act (Confidential)
Me. Rev. Stat. Ann. 1964, Title 19, § 534

Adoption Act (Contest of)
Ill. Comp. Stat. 1992, Ch. 750, §§ 55/0.01, 55/1

Adoption Act (Subsidized)
Mont. Code Ann., 52-2-501 et seq.

Adoption and Foster Care Services Act
Mich. Comp. Laws Ann., 722.951 et seq.

Adoption and Medical Assistance Compact
Okla. Stat. Ann., Title 10, § 61 et seq.

Adoption and Medical Assistance Interstate Compact Act
See Interstate Compact on Adoption and Medical Assistance

Adoption and Relinquishment Act
Kan. Stat. Ann., 59-2111 et seq.

Adoption and Safe Families Act of 1997
Nov. 19, 1997, P.L. 105-89, 42 U.S. Code § 1305 nt.

Adoption Assistance and Child Welfare Act of 1980
June 17, 1980, P.L. 96-272, 42 U.S. Code §§ 670 et seq., 1305 nt.
Dec. 28, 1980, P.L. 96-611, 94 Stat. 3574, 42 U.S. Code § 672 nt.
Oct. 11, 1983, P.L. 98-118, 97 Stat. 803, 42 U.S. Code § 672 nt.
Nov. 8, 1984, P.L. 98-617, 98 Stat. 3297, 42 U.S. Code § 672 nt.
April 7, 1986, P.L. 99-272, 42 U.S. Code § 672 nt.
Dec. 22, 1987, P.L. 100-203, 42 U.S. Code § 672 nt.

Adoption Assistance Compact
Me. Rev. Stat. Ann. 1964, Title 22, § 4171 et seq.

Adoption Assistance Interstate Compact
See Interstate Compact on Adoption Assistance

Adoption Compensation Prohibition Act
Ill. Comp. Stat. 1992, Ch. 720, § 525/0.01 et seq.

Adoption Confidentiality Act
Miss. Code Ann. 1972, § 93-17-201 et seq.

Adoption Cooperative Exchange Act
Pa. Cons. Stat., Title 23, § 255 et seq.

Adoption Facilitation Act (Step-Parents)
D.C. Code 1973, § 16-308

Adoption Information Act
Cal. Civil Code § 2245 et seq.

Adoption of the Code of Laws
S.C. Code Ann. 1976, § 2-7-45 et seq.

Adoption Opportunities Act
Pa. Purdon's Stat., Title 62, § 771 et seq.

Adoption Preplacement Program Act (Independent)
Cal. Civil Code §§ 221.5, 226.5, 226.51
Cal. Health and Safety Code § 1522.4

Adoption Revision Act
Fla. Stat. 1983, 63.022, 63.032, 63.062, 63.092, 63.097, 63.102, 63.112, 63.122, 63.162, 63.172, 63.207, 63.212

Adoption Subsidy Act
Md. Ann. Code 1974, Art. FL, § 5-401 et seq.
Me. Rev. Stat. Ann. 1964, Title 19, § 541 et seq.

Adoption Supplemental Benefits Act
Miss. Code Ann. 1972, § 93-17-51 et seq.
S.C. Code Ann. 1976, §§ 15-45-310 et seq., 20-7-1900 et seq.

Adoption Support Act
Kan. Stat. Ann., 38-319 et seq.

Adoption Support Demonstration Act
Wash. Rev. Code Ann., 74.13.100 et seq.

Adoption Tax Credit Act (Special Needs)
Mo. Rev. Stat., 135.325 et seq.

Adoptions Act (Contest of)
Ill. Rev. Stat. 1991, Ch. 40, §§ 1600, 1601

Adult Abuse, Neglect and Exploitation Act
Ida. Code 1947, 39-5301 et seq.

Adult Adoption Act
Fla. Stat. 1965, 72.34 et seq.
N.J. Rev. Stat. 1937, 2A:22-1 et seq.
N.M. Stat. Ann., 40-14-1 et seq.
Tex. Family Code, § 16.51 et seq.

Adult and Youth Offender Education and Crime Prevention Act
Cal. Government Code § 12811
Cal. Penal Code § 5000

Adult Authority Law
Cal. Penal Code § 5075 et seq.

Adult Basic and Literacy Education Act
Pa. Purdon's Stat., Title 24, § 6401 et seq.

Adult Care Home Licensure Act
Kan. Stat. Ann., 39-923 et seq.

Adult Community Corrections Act
Wyo. Stat. Ann., § 7-18-101 et seq.

Adult Companion Home Certification Act
Okla. Stat. Ann., Title 56, § 530.1 et seq.

Adult Congregate Living Facilities Act
Fla. Stat. Ann., 400.401 et seq.

Adult Contributory Act (Delinquents)
N.Y. Penal Law 1965 (Consol. Laws Ch. 40) § 260.10, Subd. 2

Adult Day Care Act
Okla. Stat. 1981, Title 63, § 1-871 et seq.
Tex. Human Resources, § 103.001 et seq.

Adult Day Care Center License Act
Pa. 1959 Pamph. Laws 1353, No. 466

Adult Day Care Centers Act
Fla. Stat. Ann., 400.55 et seq.

Adult Day Health Care Act
Cal. Health and Safety Code § 1570 et seq.

Adult Day Health Medi-Cal Law
Cal. Welfare and Institutions Code § 14520 et seq.

Adult Day Services Act
Cal. Welfare and Institutions Code § 9770 et seq.

Adult Delinquency Act
Colo. Rev. Stat., 22-8-14

Adult Education Act
July 22, 1987, P.L. 100-77, 20 U.S. Code §§ 1205, 1207a
April 28, 1988, P.L. 100-297, 102 Stat. 302, 20 U.S. Code §§ 1201 et seq., 1201 nt., 1211a
Aug. 23, 1988, P.L. 100-418, 102 Stat. 1474
Nov. 16, 1990, P.L. 101-589, 20 U.S. Code § 1201a
April 9, 1991, P.L. 102-26, 20 U.S. Code § 1211b
July 25, 1991, P.L. 102-73, 20 U.S. Code §§ 1201a, 1201b, 1203a, 1205, 1205a, 1206a, 1207a, 1208, 1208aa, prec. 1209, 1209, 1211, 1211b, 1213c
Sept. 7, 1992, P.L. 102-367, 20 U.S. Code § 1205a
Oct. 20, 1994, P.L. 103-382, 20 U.S. Code §§ 1203a, 1206a, 1213c
Dec. 21, 1995, P.L. 104-66, 20 U.S. Code § 1203a
Aug. 7, 1998, P.L. 105-220, 20 U.S. Code §§ 1201 to 1209, 1211 to 1211b, 1213 to 1213c
Ark. Code Ann. 1987, 6-16-301 et seq.
Ore. Rev. Stat., 336.145, 339.145
R.I. Gen. Laws 1956, 16-63-1 et seq.

Adult Education Act of 1966
Nov. 3, 1966, P.L. 89-750, 80 Stat. 1216, 20 U.S. Code §§ 1201 to 1213
Jan. 2, 1968, P.L. 90-247, 81 Stat. 815, 20 U.S. Code §§ 1203 to 1206, 1213
Oct. 16, 1968, P.L. 90-576, 82 Stat. 1095, 20 U.S. Code § 1202
April 13, 1970, P.L. 91-230, 84 Stat. 159, 20 U.S. Code §§ 1201 to 1211
Dec. 30, 1970, P.L. 91-600, 84 Stat. 1669, 20 U.S. Code §§ 1204, 1211
Continued

May 3, 1973, P.L. 93-29, 87 Stat. 59, 20 U.S. Code §§ 1208a, 1209 to 1211

Sept. 24, 1977, P.L. 95-112, 20 U.S. Code §§ 1208a, 1209 et seq.

Nov. 1, 1978, P.L. 95-561, 20 U.S. Code §§ 1201 et seq.

Oct. 19, 1984, P.L. 98-511, 20 U.S. Code §§ 1202 et seq., 1211a

Adult Education Amendments of 1988

April 28, 1988, P.L. 100-297, 102 Stat. 302, 20 U.S. Code §§ 1201 et seq., 1201 nt.

May 11, 1989, P.L. 101-26, 20 U.S. Code § 1201a

Adult Education and Family Literacy Act

Aug. 7, 1998, P.L. 105-220, 20 U.S. Code § 9201 nt.

Oct. 21, 1998, P.L. 105-277, 20 U.S. Code §§ 9202 to 9204, 9211, 9212, 9225, 9253, 9273

Oct. 31, 1998, P.L. 105-332, 20 U.S. Code §§ 9224, 9276

Adult Education Reporting Act

Ill. Comp. Stat. 1992, Ch. 105, § 410/0.01 et seq.

Adult Entertainment Facilities Act

Ill. Comp. Stat. 1992, Ch. 55, § 5/5-1097.5; Ch. 65, § 5/11-5-1.5

Adult Family-Care Home Act

Fla. Stat. Ann., 400.616 et seq.

Adult Foster Care Facility Licensing Act

Mich. Comp. Laws Ann., 400.701 et seq.

Adult Foster Family Care Act

Mont. Code Ann., 52-3-301 et seq.

Adult Foster Home Care Act

Fla. Stat. Ann., 400.616 et seq.

Adult General Education Act

Fla. Stat. Ann., 228.072

Adult Health Care Consent Act

S.C. Code Ann. 1976, § 44-66-10 et seq.

Adult Health Care Decisions Act

Minn. Stat. Ann., 145B.01 et seq.

Adult In-Home Care Act

N.H. Rev. Stat. 1955, 161-F:71 et seq.

Adult Indian Vocational Training Act

Aug. 3, 1956, Ch. 930, 70 Stat. 986, 25 U.S. Code §§ 309, 309a

Sept. 22, 1961, P.L. 87-273, 75 Stat. 571, 25 U.S. Code § 309a

Dec. 23, 1963, P.L. 88-230, 77 Stat. 471, 25 U.S. Code §§ 309, 309a

Adult Literacy Act

Colo. Rev. Stat., 22-10-101 et seq.

Fla. Laws 1991, Ch. 84-336

Ore. Rev. Stat., 344.760 et seq.

Adult Mental Health Act (Comprehensive)

Minn. Stat. Ann., 245.461 et seq.

Adult Offender Special Act

Ga. Code 1933, 77-365 et seq.

Adult Offenders Act

Mont. Code Ann., 53-30-101 et seq.

Adult-Oriented Establishment Registration Act

Tenn. Code Ann., 7-51-1101 et seq.

Adult Parole and Mandatory Supervision Act

Tex. Code of Criminal Procedure, Art. 42.18

Adult Probation Act

Conn. Gen. Stat. Ann., § 54-103a et seq.

Pa. Cons. Stat., Title 42, § 9722 et seq.

Adult Probation, Parole, and Mandatory Supervision Law

Tex. Code of Criminal Procedure 1965, Arts. 42.12, 42.18

Adult Protection Act

N.C. Gen. Stat. 1943, §§ 108A-99 to 108A-111

Tenn. Code Ann., 71-6-101 et seq.

Adult Protection Act (Omnibus)

S.C. Code Ann. 1976, § 43-35-5 et seq.

Adult Protective Services Act
Ala. Code 1975, § 38-9-1 et seq.
Ariz. Rev. Stat. Ann., §§ 46-451, 46-452
Fla. Stat. Ann., 415.101 et seq.
Ky. Rev. Stat. 1971, 209.010 et seq.
Me. Rev. Stat. Ann. 1964, Title 22, § 3470 et seq.
Miss. Code Ann. 1972, § 43-45-1 et seq.
Neb. Rev. Stat. 1943, 32-827 et seq.
N.J. Stat. Ann., 52:27D-406 et seq.
N.M. Stat. Ann., 27-7-14 et seq.
N.Y. Social Services Law (Consol. Laws Ch. 52) §§ 473a, 473b
Wyo. Stat. Ann., § 35-20-101 et seq.

Adult Residential Care Licensing Law
La. Rev. Stat. Ann., 40:2151 et seq.

Adult Rights Act
Ala. Acts 1975, No. 126

Adulterated Butter Act
See Oleomargarine Acts

Adulterated Drug Act
Mich. Comp. Laws Ann., 750.16 et seq.

Adulterated Food Act
Ind. Code Ann., 16-1-29-1 et seq.
Iowa Code Ann., 190.1 et seq.

Adulterated Food, Drug and Cosmetic Act
Wash. Rev. Code Ann., 69.04.001 et seq.

Adulterated or Mishandled Foods Act
Tenn. Code Ann., 53-1-101 et seq.

Adulterated Seeds Act
Aug. 24, 1912, Ch. 382, 37 Stat. 506 (See 7 U.S. Code §§ 1581 to 1584, 1592, 1596)

Adulteration Act
D.C. Code Ann., § 31-1025
N.Y. Agriculture and Markets Law (Consol. Laws Ch. 69) § 198 et seq.
Ohio Rev. Code 1953, 3715.01 et seq.
Tenn. Code Ann. 1955, 52-101 et seq.
Utah Code Ann. 1953, 4-20-8

Adulteration Act (Agricultural Feeds)
Wis. Stat. Ann., 94.72, Subsec. 14, Subd. b

Adulteration Act (Food)
N.Y. Agriculture and Markets Law (Consol. Laws Ch. 69) § 198 et seq.
Utah Code Ann. 1953, 4-5-7

Adulteration and Food Acts
Ohio Rev. Code 1953, 3715.01 et seq.

Adultery Act
Cal. Penal Code §§ 269a, 269b
Wash. Rev. Code 1974, 9.79.110
Wis. Stat. Ann., 944.16

Adults Act (Zollie M. Maunard, Sr., Education for Handicapped)
Fla. Stat. Ann., 228.0727

Adults Mental Retardation Act (Public Guardianship)
Minn. Stat. Ann., 252A.01 et seq.

Adults Protective Services Act (Older)
Pa. Purdon's Stat., Title 35, § 10225.101 et seq.

Advance Directives for Health Care Act
N.J. Stat. Ann., 26:2H-53 et seq.
Pa. Cons. Stat., Title 20, § 5401 et seq.

Advance Fee Act (Real Estate Brokers)
Conn. Gen. Stat. Ann., § 20-320

Advance Funding Authority Act
Iowa Code Ann., 442.1 et seq.

Advance Loan Law
N.J. Stat. Ann., 17:9A-59.1 et seq.

Advance Pay and Allotment Act of 1961
Sept. 26, 1961, P.L. 87-304, 75 Stat. 662 (See 5 U.S. Code §§ 5521 to 5527)
June 24, 1965, P.L. 89-47, 79 Stat. 171 (See 5 U.S. Code § 5521)
Sept. 6, 1966, P.L. 89-554, 80 Stat. 632

Advance Refinancing and Refunding Bond Act
Ore. Rev. Stat., 288.605 et seq.

Advance Refunding Law
Fla. Stat. Ann., 132.33 et seq.

Advanced Additional Leave Act
Utah Code Ann. 1953, Miscellaneous Superseded Code Provisions, 4-20-8

Advanced Database System Act
Tex. Tax Code, §§ 111.0035, 111.0036

Advanced Emergency Medical Technician Practices Act
Mich. Comp. Laws Ann., 338.1901 et seq.

Advanced Life Support Act
D.C. Code, §§ 2-1344, 1-1211, 1-319

Advanced Registered Nurse Practitioner Student Scholarship Program
Kan. Stat. Ann., 74-32,131 et seq.

Advanced Technology Initiative Act
Miss. Code Ann. 1972, § 57-54-1 et seq.

Advancement Act
Md. Ann. Code 1974, Art. ET, § 3-106

Advancement and Allotment of Pay in Emergency Evacuation Act
See Advance Pay and Allotment Act of 1961

Advancement District Act (Economic)
N.M. Stat. Ann., 6-19-1 et seq.

Advancement of Science and Technology Act
Okla. Stat. Ann., Title 74, § 5060.1 et seq.

Adverse Claim Act (Bank Deposits)
Miss. Code Ann. 1972, § 81-5-67
N.Y. Banking Law (Consol. Laws Ch. 2) §§ 134, 171, 239, 310
S.D. Codified Laws 1967, 51-15-2

Adverse Claims to Deposit Accounts Act
Ill. Comp. Stat. 1992, Ch. 205, § 700/1 et seq.

Adverse Examination Act
Wis. Stat. 1971, 885.14

Adverse Interest Act
Pa. Purdon's Stat., Title 71, § 776.1 et seq.

Adverse Mineral Claims Act
Alaska Comp. Laws Ann. 1949, § 47-3-41 et seq.

Adverse Party Act
Cal. Code of Civil Procedure § 2055
Ill. Rev. Stat. 1991, Ch. 110, § 2-1102
Mass. Gen. Laws Ann., 233:22
Mich. Comp. Laws Ann., 600.2161
N.J. Stat. Ann., 2A:81-11
Ohio Rev. Code 1953, 2317.07

Adverse Party Witness Act
Ida. Code 1947, 9-1206
Md. Ann. Code 1974, Art. CJ, § 9-113 et seq.
Mo. Rev. Stat., 491.030

Adverse Possession Act
Ala. Code 1975, § 6-5-200
Alaska Stat. 1962, § 09.25.050
Cal. Civil Code § 1007
Cal. Code of Civil Procedure § 322 et seq.
Colo. Rev. Stat., 38-41-101 et seq.
Fla. Stat. 1983, 95.12 et seq.
Ga. Code Ann., 44-5-160 et seq.
Ida. Code 1947, 5-207 et seq.
Ill. Rev. Stat. 1981, Ch. 83, § 101 et seq.
Ind. Code Ann., 32-1-20-1
Miss. Code Ann. 1972, § 15-1-13
Mont. Code Ann., 70-19-401 et seq.
N.D. Cent. Code, 28-01-04 et seq.
Neb. Rev. Stat. 1943, 25-202
R.I. Gen. Laws 1956, 34-7-1
S.D. Codified Laws 1967, 15-3-15 et seq.
Tenn. Code Ann., 28-2-101 et seq.
Tex. Civil Practice and Remedies Code, § 16.001 et seq.
Utah Code Ann. 1953, 78-12-5 et seq.
Vt. Stat. Ann., Title 12, § 501
Wash. Rev. Code Ann., 7.28.010 et seq.
Wis. Stat. Ann., 893.24 et seq.

Adverse Witness Act
Conn. Gen. Stat. Ann., § 52-178
Haw. Rev. Stat. Ann., § 621-27
N.J. Stat. Ann., 2A:81-11
Ohio Rev. Code 1953, 2317.07
Okla. Stat. Ann., Title 12, § 2501

Advertisement Act (Fraud)
Minn. Stat. Ann., 325F.67

Advertisement for Strike Workers Act
Ill. Comp. Stat. 1992, Ch. 820, § 25/0.01 et seq.

Advertisement of Proposed Ad Valorem Tax Increases Act
Miss. General Laws 1994, Ch. 414

Advertising Act (Citrus Fruits)
Fla. Stat. Ann., 601.15

Advertising Act (Deceptive)
Ill. Rev. Stat. 1991, Ch. 121 1/2, § 157.21a et seq.

Advertising Act (Eye Exam)
Ill. Rev. Stat. 1991, Ch. 121 1/2, § 340 et seq.

Advertising Act (Gasoline Price)
Ill. Rev. Stat. 1991, Ch. 121 1/2, § 860 et seq.

Advertising Act (Legal Matters)
Ind. Code Ann., 5-3-1-1 et seq.

Advertising Act (Newspaper)
Pa. Cons. Stat., Title 45, § 101 et seq.

Advertising Act (Ophthalmic)
Ill. Rev. Stat. 1991, Ch. 121 1/2, § 349 et seq.

Advertising Act (Outdoor)
Mass. Gen. Laws Ann., 93:29 et seq.
Vt. Stat. Ann., Title 9, § 3621 et seq.

Advertising Act (Public Purchases)
March 2, 1861, Ch. 84, 12 Stat. 220, 41 U.S. Code § 5
Aug. 2, 1946, Ch. 744, 60 Stat. 809, 41 U.S. Code § 5
June 30, 1949, Ch. 288, 63 Stat. 400, 41 U.S. Code § 5
Sept. 5, 1950, Ch. 849, 64 Stat. 583, 41 U.S. Code § 5
Aug. 28, 1958, P.L. 85-800, 72 Stat. 967, 41 U.S. Code § 5
July 25, 1974, P.L. 93-356, 88 Stat. 390
Dec. 1, 1983, P.L. 98-191, 97 Stat. 1332

Advertising Act (Unsolicited Telefacsimile)
Tenn. Code Ann., 47-18-1601 et seq.

Advertising Commission Law
Neb. Laws 1939, Ch. 130

Advertising Control Act (Highways)
Okla. Stat. 1981, Title 69, § 1271 et seq.
S.C. Code Ann. 1976, § 57-25-110 et seq.

Advertising Control Act (Outdoor)
N.C. Gen. Stat. 1943, § 136-126 et seq.

Advertising Fund Act (State)
Mich. Comp. Laws Ann., 2.101 et seq.

Advertising Loans to Bankrupts Act
Ill. Rev. Stat. 1991, Ch. 121 1/2, § 157.24 et seq.

Advertising of Prizes Law (Promotional)
Wash. Rev. Code 1983, 19.170.010 et seq.

Advertising Rate Act (Legal)
Ill. Rev. Stat. 1991, Ch. 100, §§ 10.9, 11

Advisory Board Act (East Asia Development)
Ill. Rev. Stat. 1991, Ch. 127, §§ 3451, 3460

Advisory Board Act (Juvenile Court)
Ga. Code 1933, 24-2434

Advisory Board Act (Township)
Ind. Code 1976, 17-4-28-1 et seq.

Advisory Board Carp River Forge Act
Mich. Comp. Laws Ann., 399.71 et seq.

Advisory Board on Transportation Act
P.R. Acts 1980, 9th Sp. Sess., No. 16

Advisory Commission on Intergovernmental Relations Act of 1959

Sept. 24, 1959, P.L. 86-380, 73 Stat. 703, 42 U.S. Code §§ 4271 to 4278

Aug. 14, 1964, P.L. 88-426, 78 Stat. 429, 42 U.S. Code § 4276

Nov. 2, 1966, P.L. 89-733, 80 Stat. 1162, 42 U.S. Code §§ 4273, 4276, 4277, 4279

Advisory Commission on Internet Privacy Act

Ill. Comp. Stat. 1992, Ch. 20, § 3902/1 et seq.

Advisory Committee on Intergovernmental Relations Act of 1959

Sept. 24, 1959, P.L. 86-380, 73 Stat. 703, 42 U.S. Code §§ 4271 to 4278

Aug. 14, 1964, P.L. 88-426, 78 Stat. 429, 42 U.S. Code § 4276

Nov. 2, 1966, P.L. 89-733, 80 Stat. 1162, 42 U.S. Code §§ 4273, 4276, 4277, 4279

Advisory Committee to the Grade A Milk Program Act

Ark. Code Ann. 1987, 20-59-501 et seq.

Advisory Council Act (Anti-Crime)

Ill. Comp. Stat. 1992, Ch. 20, § 3910/0.01 et seq.

Advisory Council Act (Crime Victim and Witness)

Minn. Stat. Ann., 611A.70, 611A.71

Advisory Council for Nuclear Act

S.C. Code Ann. 1976, § 13-7-810 et seq.

Advisory Council on California Indian Policy Act of 1992

Oct. 14, 1992, P.L. 102-416, 25 U.S. Code § 651 nt.

Feb. 12, 1996, P.L. 104-109, 25 U.S. Code § 651 nt.

Oct. 27, 1998, P.L. 105-294, 25 U.S. Code § 651 nt.

Advisory Council on California Indian Policy Extension Act of 1998

Oct. 27, 1998, P.L. 105-294, 112 Stat. 2818, 25 U.S. Code § 651 nt.

Advisory Council on Intergovernmental Relations Act

Fla. Stat. Ann., 163.701 et seq.

Advisory Defense Committee Acts

Neb. Rev. Stat. 1943, 81-829.36 et seq.

Advisory Judicial Council Act

Tex. Gov. Code, § 71.001 et seq.

Advisory Neighborhood Commissions Act

D.C. Code Ann., § 1-251 et seq.

Advisory Neighborhood Commissions Additional Notice Act

D.C. Code, §§ 1-261, 1-264

Advisory Neighborhood Councils Act

D.C. Code 1973, §§ 1-252 et seq., 1-1441, 1-1443, 1-1462

Advisory Opinion Act

Ala. Code 1975, § 12-2-10 et seq.

Advisory Referendum Act

N.M. Stat. Ann., 22-4A-1 et seq.

Advocacy and Guardianship Act

Ill. Rev. Stat. 1991, Ch. 91 1/2, § 701 et seq.

Advocacy and Protection for Developmentally Disabled Persons Act

Ill. Rev. Stat. 1991, Ch. 91 1/2, §§ 1150, 1151

Advocacy and Protection for Mentally Ill Persons Act

Ill. Rev. Stat. 1991, Ch. 91 1/2, § 1350 et seq.

Advocacy Center Act (Children's)

Ill. Comp. Stat. 1992, Ch. 55, § 80/1 et seq.

Ill. Rev. Stat. 1991, Ch. 23, § 1801 et seq.

Advocate Act (Consumer)

S.C. Code Ann. 1976, § 37-6-601 et seq.

Advocate Law (Victim)

Pa. Purdon's Stat., Title 71, § 2301 et seq.

AECA

See Arms Export Control Act

Aerial Exhibitors Safety Act
Ill. Comp. Stat. 1992, Ch. 720, § 530/0.01 et seq.

Aerial Photography Act
Mich. Comp. Laws Ann., 321.151 et seq.

Aerial Transportation Law
Iowa Code Ann., 328.1 et seq.

Aeronautical Administration Act
Ida. Code 1947, 21-131 et seq.

Aeronautical Regulatory Act
R.I. Gen. Laws 1956, 1-4-1 et seq.
S.C. Code Ann. 1976, § 55-5-10 et seq.
Utah Code Ann. 1953, 2-1-1 et seq.

Aeronautics Act
See also Uniform Aeronautics Act
Cal. Public Utilities Code § 21001 et seq.
Ill. Comp. Stat. 1992, Ch. 620, § 5/1 et seq.
Me. Rev. Stat. Ann. 1964, Title 6, § 1 et seq.
Mont. Code Ann., 67-1-201 et seq.
Vt. Stat. Ann., Title 5, § 201 et seq.

Aeronautics Act (State)
Vt. Stat. Ann., Title 5, § 201 et seq.

Aeronautics and Space Administration Authorization Act
See National Aeronautics and Space Administration Authorization Act

Aeronautics Commission Act
Cal. Statutes 1947, Ch. 1379, p. 2927
Ind. Code Ann., 8-21-1-1 et seq.
Okla. Stat. Ann., Title 3, § 81 et seq.
Tenn. Code Ann., 42-2-101 et seq.
Tex. Rev. Civ. Stat., Art. 46c-1 et seq.
Wash. Rev. Code Ann., 47.68.010 et seq.
W. Va. Code 1966, § 29-2A-1 et seq.

Aeronautics Department Act
Ala. Code 1975, § 4-2-1 et seq.
Del. Code of 1974, Title 2, § 101 et seq.
Ida. Code 1947, 21-101 et seq.
Minn. Stat. Ann., 360.011 et seq.
Neb. Rev. Stat. 1943, 3-101 et seq.

Vt. Stat. Ann., Title 5, § 1 et seq.

Aeronautics Fund and Appropriation Act
Minn. Stat. Ann., 360.301 et seq.

Aeronautics Regulation Act
Wash. Rev. Code Ann., 14.16.010 et seq.

Aeronautics Regulatory Act
Mont. Code Ann., 67-1-101 et seq.

Aerosol Act (Hazardous)
La. Rev. Stat. Ann., 40:1057 et seq.

Aerospace Development Corporation Act
Alaska Laws 1991, Ch. 88
Alaska Laws 1995, Ch. 88

Aerospace Job Retention Act
Cal. Health and Safety Code § 33320.6

AFDC Act
N.C. Gen. Stat. 1943, §§ 108A-27 to 108A-39

AFDC Recipient Work Incentive Act
N.M. Stat. Ann., 27-2-37 et seq.

Affairs of the Elderly Act (Office for)
P.R. Laws Ann. 1954, Title 3, § 1951 et seq.

Affidavit of Completion Law
Cal. Government Code §§ 34080, 34081

Affidavit of Possession Act (Real Estate Claims)
Iowa Code Ann., 614.17

Affidavit of Prejudice Act
Ore. Rev. Stat., 14.260

Affirmations and Oaths Act
Ill. Rev. Stat. 1991, Ch. 101, § 0.01 et seq.
Wash. Rev. Code Ann., 5.28.010 et seq.

Affirmative Action Clarifying Act
D.C. Code Ann., § 1-514

Affirmative Action in District Government Employment Act
D.C. Code Ann., § 1-507 et seq.

Afflicted Adults Act (Indigent)
Mich. Comp. Laws 1948, 404.101 et seq.

Afflicted Children Act
Mich. Comp. Laws Ann., 722.301 et seq.

Affordable Basic Health Care Act
Cal. Labor Code § 2100 et seq.

Affordable Housing Act
See Cranston-Gonzalez National Affordable Housing Act
Conn. Gen. Stat. Ann., § 8-38 et seq.
Fla. Stat. Ann., 420.601 et seq.
Ill. Comp. Stat. 1992, Ch. 310, § 65/1 et seq.
Ky. Rev. Stat. 1971, 198A.700c et seq.
Neb. Rev. Stat. 1943, 58-701 to 58-711
N.J. Stat. Ann., 40:55D-100 et seq.
Pa. 1992 Pamph. Laws, No. 172
Wash. Laws 1989, 143.185A.010 et seq.
Wash. Rev. Code 1983, 43.185A.900

Affordable Housing Act (William E. Sadowski)
Fla. Laws 1992, Ch. 317

Affordable Housing Funds Act (Optional County)
Pa. Purdon's Stat., Title 35, § 1690.1 et seq.

Affordable Housing Opportunity Act
R.I. Gen. Laws 1956, 42-11.2-1 et seq.

Affordable Housing Ownership Act (Cooperative)
Me. Rev. Stat. Ann. 1964, Title 13, § 1741 et seq.

Affordable Housing Partnership Act
Me. Rev. Stat. Ann. 1964, Title 30-A, § 5001 et seq.

Affordable Housing Planning and Community Assistance Act
Fla. Stat. Ann., 420.601 et seq.

Affordable Housing Preservation Act
R.I. Gen. Laws 1956, 34-45-1 et seq.

Affordable Housing Programs Assistance Bond Act
N.J. Stat. Ann., 18A:70-21 et seq.

Affordable Neighborhood Housing Tax Credit Act
Ark. Code 1987, 15-5-1301 et seq.

Affordable Residential Housing Act of Pawtucket
R.I. Public Laws 1991, Ch. 454

Affordable Residential Housing and Historic Building Preservation Act
R.I. Gen. Laws 1956, 44-4.2-1 et seq.

Afforestation and Economic Diversification Act
Mo. Rev. Stat. 1978, 252.300
Mo. Rev. Stat., 252.300

A.F.I.S. Policy Council Act
Mich. Comp. Laws Ann., 28.151 et seq.

Africa: Seeds of Hope Act of 1998
Nov. 13, 1998, P.L. 105-385, 112 Stat. 3460, 7 U.S. Code § 1691 nt.

African American History Landmark Theme Study Act
Aug. 17, 1991, P.L. 102-98, 16 U.S. Code § 1a-5

African Conflict Resolution Act
Oct. 19, 1994, P.L. 103-381, 22 U.S. Code § 2151 nt.

African Development Bank Act
Aug. 13, 1981, P.L. 97-35, 22 U.S. Code § 290i et seq.
Dec. 22, 1987, P.L. 100-202, 22 U.S. Code § 190i-10
Dec. 19, 1989, P.L. 101-240, 22 U.S. Code § 290i-3
Nov. 5, 1990, P.L. 101-513, 22 U.S. Code §§ 290i-1, 290l to 290l-7

African Development Foundation Act
Aug. 8, 1985, P.L. 99-83, 22 U.S. Code §§ 290h-8, 290h-9

Nov. 21, 1989, P.L. 101-167, 22 U.S. Code
§§ 290h-5, 290h-9

African Development Fund Act
Oct. 3, 1977, P.L. 95-118, 22 U.S. Code
§ 290q-10

June 3, 1980, P.L. 96-259, 22 U.S. Code
§ 290g-11

Nov. 30, 1983, P.L. 98-181, 22 U.S. Code
§ 290g-12

Oct. 1, 1988, P.L. 100-461, 22 U.S. Code
§ 290g-14

Dec. 19, 1989, P.L. 101-240, 22 U.S. Code
§ 290g-2

April 1, 1992, P.L. 102-266, 22 U.S. Code
§ 290g-15

African Elephant Conservation Act
Oct. 23, 1992, P.L. 102-440, 16 U.S. Code
§ 4245

Aug. 5, 1998, P.L. 105-217, 16 U.S. Code
§ 4245

African Elephant Conservation Reauthorization Act of 1998
Aug. 5, 1998, P.L. 105-217, 16 U.S. Code
§ 4201 nt.

African Famine Relief and Recovery Act of 1985
April 2, 1985, P.L. 99-8, 22 U.S. Code
§§ 2292q, 2292q nt.

Africatown, U. S. A. Act
Ala. Code 1975, 41-10-230

Afro-American History Repository Act
Fla. Stat. 1983, 241.477

After Acquired Property Act
Wis. Stat. Ann., 238.03

After Acquired Title Act
Ark. Code Ann. 1987, 18-12-601

Okla. Stat. Ann., Title 16, § 17

After-Born Children Act
Del. Code of 1974, Title 12, § 301 et seq.

N.C. Gen. Stat. 1943, § 31-5.5

N.Y. Estates, Powers and Trusts Law
(Consol. Laws Ch. 17B) § 5-3.2

After-School Child Care Programs (Latchkey Children)
N.Y. Education Law 1947 (Consol. Laws Ch.
16) § 414, Subd. 1

N.Y. Social Services Law (Consol. Laws Ch.
55) § 410c, Subd. 5

After School Opportunity Fund Program
Md. Ann. Code 1974, Governor-Executive
and Administrative Departments, §§ 6-801
to 6-807

Aftermarket Crash Parts Act
Fla. Stat. Ann., 501.30 et seq.

Mich. Comp. Laws Ann., 257.1361 et seq.

Utah Code Ann. 1953, 13-20a-101 et seq.

Aftermarket Crash Parts Regulation Act
Okla. Stat. Ann., Title 15, § 951 et seq.

Age Act (Discrimination in Employment)
Neb. Rev. Stat. 1943, 48-1001 et seq.

Age Act (Unjust Discrimination in Employment)
Neb. Rev. Stat. 1943, 48-1001 et seq.

Age Antidiscrimination Act
Tex. Rev. Civ. Stat., Art. 5221k

Age Discrimination Act
Alaska Stat. 1962, § 18.80.060et seq.

Ind. Code Ann., 22-9-2-1 et seq.

Mass. Gen. Laws Ann., 149:24A et seq.,
151B:4

N.Y. Executive Law 1951 (Consol. Laws Ch.
18) § 296 et seq.

Pa. Purdon's Stat., Title 43, § 955

Age Discrimination Act (Employment)
Fla. Stat. Ann., 112.044

Kan. Stat. Ann., 44-1111 et seq.

La. Rev. Stat. Ann., 23:893

Neb. Rev. Stat. 1943, 48-1001 et seq.

R.I. Gen. Laws 1956, 28-5-1 et seq.

Age Discrimination Act of 1975
Nov. 28, 1975, P.L. 94-135, 89 Stat. 728, 42
U.S. Code §§ 6101 et seq.
Continued

July 11, 1977, P.L. 95-65, 42 U.S. Code
§ 6106

Oct. 18, 1978, P.L. 95-478, 42 U.S. Code
§ 6101 et seq.

April 7, 1986, P.L. 99-272, 42 U.S. Code
§ 6101

March 22, 1988, P.L. 100-259, 102 Stat. 30,
42 U.S. Code § 6107

Oct. 20, 1994, P.L. 103-382, 42 U.S. Code
§ 6107

Oct. 21, 1998, P.L. 105-277, 42 U.S. Code
§ 6103

Age Discrimination Claims Assistance Act of 1988

April 7, 1988, P.L. 100-283, 29 U.S. Code
§ 626 nt.

Nov. 3, 1990, P.L. 101-504, 29 U.S. Code
§ 626 nt.

Age Discrimination Claims Assistance Amendments of 1990

Nov. 3, 1990, P.L. 101-504, 29 U.S. Code
§ 626 nt.

Age Discrimination in Employment Act

Kan. Stat. Ann., 44-1111 et seq.

Age Discrimination in Employment Act Amendments of 1978

April 6, 1978, P.L. 95-256, 29 U.S. Code
§§ 621 nt., 623 et seq.

Age Discrimination in Employment Act of 1967

Dec. 15, 1967, P.L. 90-202, 81 Stat. 602, 29
U.S. Code §§ 621 to 634

April 8, 1974, P.L. 93-259, 88 Stat. 74, 29
U.S. Code §§ 621 nt., 630, 633a, 634

April 6, 1978, P.L. 95-256, 29 U.S. Code
§ 623 et seq.

July 18, 1984, P.L. 98-369, 98 Stat. 1063, 29
U.S. Code §§ 623, 623 nt.

Oct. 9, 1984, P.L. 98-459, 98 Stat. 1792, 29
U.S. Code §§ 623, 630, 631, 631 nt.

April 7, 1986, P.L. 99-272, 29 U.S. Code
§§ 623, 631

Oct. 21, 1986, P.L. 99-509, 29 U.S. Code
§ 623

Oct. 31, 1986, P.L. 99-592, 29 U.S. Code
§§ 623, 623 nt., 630, 631, 631 nt.

Dec. 19, 1989, P.L. 101-239, 29 U.S. Code
§§ 623, 631

Oct. 16, 1990, P.L. 101-433, 29 U.S. Code
§§ 623, 623 nt., 626, 630

Nov. 5, 1990, P.L. 101-521, 29 U.S. Code
§ 623

Nov. 21, 1991, P.L. 102-166, 29 U.S. Code
§ 626

Jan. 23, 1995, P.L. 104-1, 29 U.S. Code
§ 633a

Sept. 30, 1996, P.L. 104-208, 29 U.S. Code
§ 623

Aug. 7, 1998, P.L. 105-220, 29 U.S. Code
§ 633a

Oct. 7, 1998, P.L. 105-244, 29 U.S. Code
§ 623

Age Discrimination in Employment Amendments of 1986

Oct. 31, 1986, P.L. 99-592, 29 U.S. Code
§ 621 nt.

Sept. 30, 1996, P.L. 104-208, 29 U.S. Code
§ 623 nt.

Age Discrimination in Employment Amendments of 1996

Sept. 30, 1996, P.L. 104-208, Title I, § 119,
29 U.S. Code § 621 nt.

Age Law (Pensions)

See Service Pension Acts

Age of Consent Act

Colo. Rev. Stat., 40-2-25
Kan. Gen. Stat. 21-3502, 21-3503
Ky. Rev. Stat. 1971, 510.040 et seq.
Tenn. Code Ann., 39-13-506

Age of Consent Act (Rape)

Miss. Code Ann. 1972, § 97-3-67

Age of Consent to Marriage Act

D.C. Code 1973, § 30-103

Age of Majority Act

D.C. Laws 1976, No. 1-75
Ga. Code Ann., 39-1-1
Iowa Code Ann., 599.1
Ky. Rev. Stat. 1971, 2.015
Mich. Comp. Laws Ann., 722.51 et seq.
Wis. Laws 1971, Ch. 213

Age of Majority Act Amendment
D.C. Code Ann., §§ 12-302, 28:1-103, 29-346

Age of Responsibility Act
Wash. Rev. Code Ann., 9A.04.050

Aged and Disabled Hearing Aid Assistance Act
N.J. Stat. Ann., 30:4D-36 et seq.

Aged Persons Protective Services Act
Mont. Code Ann., 53-5-201 et seq.

Agencies Coming Together for Children and Youth at Risk Act
Utah Code Ann. 1995, 63-75-1 et seq.

Agency Act (Employment)
Mont. Code Ann. 1987, 39-5-101 et seq.

Agency Act (Housing Finance)
Vt. Stat. Ann., Title 10, § 381 et seq.

Agency Act (Municipal and Rural Electrification Cooperative)
Me. Rev. Stat. Ann. 1964, Title 35-A, § 4101 et seq.

Agency Budget Sunset Act
Fla. Stat. Ann., 11.61 et seq.

Agency for Employment Act
S.C. Code Ann. 1976, § 41-25-10 et seq.

Agency for Health Care Policy and Research Reauthorization Act of 1992
Oct. 13, 1992, P.L. 102-410, 42 U.S. Code §§ 201 nt., 299, 299a, 299a-1, 299a-2, 299a-2 nt., 299b, 299b-1, 299b-1 nt., 299b-2, 299b-2 nt., 299b- 3, 299c, 299c-1, 299c-2, 299c-3, 299c-5, 300w-9

Agency Law
Ky. Rev. Stat. 1971, 13.080 et seq.

Agency Leasing Act (State)
La. Rev. Stat. Ann., 30:152.

Agency Licensing Act (Nurse)
Ill. Rev. Stat. 1991, Ch. 111, § 951 et seq.

Agency Procedure Act
Wis. Stat. Ann., 227.01 et seq.

Agency Productivity and Employee Incentive Act
Miss. General Laws 1999, H.B. 406

Agency Regulation Act (Collection)
La. Rev. Stat. Ann., 9:3576.1

Agency Relations in Real Estate Transactions Act
La. Rev. Stat. Ann., 9:3891 to 9:3899

Agency Review Act
Miss. Code Ann. 1972, § 5-9-1 et seq.

Agency Termination Act
N.J. Stat. Ann., 17:22-6.14a

Agenda for Cost-Effectiveness in Education Act
Ill. Comp. Stat. 1992, Ch. 105, § 225/0.01 et seq.

Agent and Broker Law (General Lines Insurance)
Me. Rev. Stat. Ann. 1964, Title 24-A, § 1601 et seq.

Agent and Broker Law (Life Insurance)
Me. Rev. Stat. Ann. 1964, Title 24-A, § 1671 et seq.

Agent Licensing Procedures Law (Insurance)
Fla. Stat. Ann., 626.011 et seq.

Agent Orange Act
Minn. Stat. Ann., 196.19 et seq.
N.J. Laws 1979, Ch. 443
N.Y. Civil Practice Laws and Rules (Consol. Laws Ch. 8) § 214b

Agent Orange Act of 1991
Feb. 6, 1991, P.L. 102-4, 38 U.S. Code §§ 101 nt., 241 nt.
Aug. 14, 1991, P.L. 102-86, 38 U.S. Code §§ 1116 nt., 1154 nt., prec. 301, 313, 316, 316 nt., 354, 354 nt., 610

Agent Orange Award Exemption Act
Mich. Comp. Laws Ann., 35.1071, 35.1072

Agent Orange Information and Assistance Act
Minn. Stat. Ann., 196.19 et seq.
S.C. Code Ann. 1976, § 44-40-10 et seq.

Agent Orange Study Act
Ill. Rev. Stat. 1983, Ch. 126 1/2, § 101 et seq.

Agents Act (Executive)
Mass. Gen. Laws Ann., 3:39 et seq.

Agents Act (Managing General)
Iowa Code Ann., 510.1A et seq.

Agents and Factors Act
Md. Ann. Code 1974, Art. CL, § 11-801 et seq.

Agents and Proxies Act (Health Care)
N.Y. Public Health Law 1953 (Consol. Laws Ch. 45) § 2980 et seq.

Agents, Brokers and Solicitors License Act
Ill. Rev. Stat. 1991, Ch. 73, § 1065.37-1 et seq.

Agents Licensing Act (Insurance)
Tenn. Code Ann., 56-6-101 et seq.
Utah Code Ann. 1953, 31a-23-101 et seq.

Agents Qualifications License Law for Agents of Legal Reserve Life Insurance Companies
Tex. Insurance Code, Art. 21.07-1

Agents Regulation Act (Sports)
Va. Code 1950, §§ 18.2-501.1 to 18.2-501.5

Aggravated Assault Act
Okla. Stat. Ann., Title 21, § 646
Tex. Penal Code, § 22.01 et seq.
Va. Code 1950, § 18.2-51 et seq.

Aggravated Battery Act
Wis. Stat. Ann., 940.19

Aggravated Child Abuse Bill Act
Tenn. Code Ann., 39-4-401

Aggregate Quarry and Pit Safety Act
Tex. Natural Resources Code, § 133.001 et seq.

Aging Act
D.C. Code 1973, § 6-2201 et seq.
Ill. Rev. Stat. 1991, Ch. 23, § 6101 et seq.
Kan. Stat. Ann., 75-5901 et seq.

Aging Act (Burton)
Cal. Welfare and Institutions Code § 9000 et seq.

Aging Aircraft Safety Act of 1991
Oct. 28, 1991, P.L. 102-143, 49 U.S. Code Appx. § 1421 nt.

Aging Services Act (Community)
Neb. Rev. Stat. 1943, 81-2201 et seq.

Agister Lien Act
Miss. Code Ann. 1972, § 85-7-101 et seq.
Wash. Rev. Code Ann., 60.56.010 et seq.
Wyo. Stat. Ann., § 29-7-101 et seq.

Agnew-Hart Act (Bookmaking)
N.Y. Penal Law 1909 (Consol. Laws Ch. 40) § 225.05

Agnos Child Support Standards Act
Cal. Civil Code § 4720 et seq.

Agreed Upon Value Act
Del. Code of 1953, Title 18, § 1102

Agreement Act (Consumer Lease-Purchase)
Kan. Stat. Ann., 50-680 et seq.

Agreement Act (Rental-Purchase)
Mich. Comp. Laws Ann., 445.951 et seq.

Agreement Act (Wholesale Licensee)
Me. Rev. Stat. Ann. 1964, Title 28-A, § 1454 et seq.

Agreement on Detainers Act
See Interstate Agreement on Detainers Act

Agreement on Detainers Compact Act
See Interstate Agreement on Detainers Act

Agreement on Qualification of Educational Personnel Act
Ala. Code 1975, 16-23A-1 et seq.
Haw. Rev. Stat. § 315-1 et seq.
Ky. Rev. Stat. 1971, 161.124
Mont. Code Ann., 20-4-121 et seq.
N.C. Gen. Stat. 1943, § 115C-349

Agreement on Qualification of Educational Personnel Act (Interstate)
See Interstate Agreement on Qualification of Educational Personnel Act

Agreement on Qualifications of Educational Personnel Act
Iowa Code Ann., 272A.1 et seq.

Agreements Law (Rental-Purchase)
Minn. Stat. Ann., 325F.84 et seq.

Agri-Business Development Authority Act
S.D. Codified Laws 1967, 1-16C-1 et seq.

Agribusiness Council Act
Miss. Code Ann. 1972, § 69-41-1 et seq.

Agricultural Act of 1948
July 3, 1948, Ch. 827, 62 Stat. 1247, 7 U.S. Code §§ 602, 608c, 612c, 624, 672, 1301, 1301a, and others; 15 U.S. Code § 713a-8 nt.; 16 U.S. Code § 590h
June 10, 1949, Ch. 191, 63 Stat. 169, 7 U.S. Code § 1282 nt.

Agricultural Act of 1948-1980
Ala. Code 1975, § 2-1-1 et seq.
Cal. Statutes 1933, Ch. 25, p. 60
Okla. Stat. Ann., Title 2, § 1-1 et seq.
Utah Code Ann. 1953, 4-1-1 et seq.
Wyo. Stat. Ann., § 11-7-118 et seq.

Agricultural Act of 1949
Oct. 31, 1949, Ch. 792, 63 Stat. 1051, 7 U.S. Code §§ 612c, 1301, 1322, 1328, 1343 to 1345, 1353 to 1356, 1421 to 1431, 1441, 1446 to 1449; 12 U.S. Code §§ 1134c, 1134j, 15 U.S. Code § 713a-4
July 12, 1951, Ch. 223, 65 Stat. 119, 7 U.S. Code §§ 1461, 1462 to 1468; See 26 U.S. Code §§ 3121, 7701; 42 U.S. Code § 410

July 17, 1952, Ch. 933, 66 Stat. 759, 7 U.S. Code §§ 1432, 1441
Aug. 8, 1953, Ch. 391, 67 Stat. 500, 7 U.S. Code § 1461 nt.
March 16, 1954, Ch. 98, 68 Stat. 28, 7 U.S. Code § 1461
July 10, 1954, Ch. 469, 68 Stat. 458, 7 U.S. Code §§ 1427, 1431
July 29, 1954, Ch. 643, 68 Stat. 583, 7 U.S. Code § 1427
Aug. 28, 1954, Ch. 1041, 68 Stat. 899, 7 U.S. Code §§ 397, 1421, 1428, 1441, 1446
Aug. 9, 1955, Ch. 679, 69 Stat. 615, 7 U.S. Code §§ 1461 nt., 1462, 1463
Jan. 28, 1956, Ch. 14, 70 Stat. 6, 7 U.S. Code § 1427
April 2, 1956, Ch. 159, 70 Stat. 87, 7 U.S. Code § 1446
May 28, 1956, Ch. 327, 70 Stat. 203, 7 U.S. Code §§ 1431, 1446d
April 25, 1957, P.L. 85-28, 71 Stat. 27, 7 U.S. Code § 1441
July 2, 1958, P.L. 85-483, 72 Stat. 286, 7 U.S. Code § 1431
July 2, 1958, P.L. 85-497, 72 Stat. 296, 7 U.S. Code § 1441
Aug. 27, 1958, P.L. 85-779, 72 Stat. 934, 7 U.S. Code § 1461 nt.
Aug. 28, 1958, P.L. 85-835, 72 Stat. 988, 7 U.S. Code §§ 1423, 1425, 1441, 1443, 1444, 1446, 1446a
July 24, 1959, P.L. 86-108, 73 Stat. 250, 7 U.S. Code § 1431
Feb. 20, 1960, P.L. 86-389, 74 Stat. 6, 7 U.S. Code § 1445
Sept. 14, 1960, P.L. 86-783, 74 Stat. 1021, 7 U.S. Code § 1461 nt.
Sept. 16, 1960, P.L. 86-799, 74 Stat. 1054, 7 U.S. Code § 1446
March 22, 1961, P.L. 87-5, 75 Stat. 6, 7 U.S. Code § 1441 nt.
Aug. 7, 1961, P.L. 87-127., 75 Stat. 293, 7 U.S. Code § 1427
Aug. 8, 1961, P.L. 87-128, 75 Stat. 301, 7 U.S. Code §§ 1441 nt., 1446a
Oct. 3, 1961, P.L. 87-345, 75 Stat. 761, 7 U.S. Code §§ 1461 nt., 1462 to 1468
March 30, 1962, P.L. 87-425, 76 Stat. 50, 7 U.S. Code § 1441 nt.
Continued

43

June 25, 1962, P.L. 87-495, 76 Stat. 109, 7 U.S. Code § 1446a

Sept. 27, 1962, P.L. 87-703, 76 Stat. 611, 7 U.S. Code §§ 1427, 1431, 1441, nts., 1445a

May 20, 1963, P.L. 88-26, 77 Stat. 44, 7 U.S. Code § 1441 nt.

Dec. 13, 1963, P.L. 88-203, 77 Stat. 363, 7 U.S. Code § 1461 nt.

April 11, 1964, P.L. 88-297, 78 Stat. 174, 7 U.S. Code §§ 1421, 1427, 1441 nt., 1444, 1445a

Aug. 31, 1964, P.L. 88-529, 78 Stat. 736, 7 U.S. Code § 1446a

Sept. 11, 1964, P.L. 88-585, 78 Stat. 927, 7 U.S. Code §§ 1427, 1433

Oct. 8, 1964, P.L. 88-638, 78 Stat. 1038, 7 U.S. Code § 1431

April 16, 1965, P.L. 89-12, 79 Stat. 72, 7 U.S. Code § 1445

Aug. 6, 1965, P.L. 89-112, 79 Stat. 446, 7 U.S. Code §§ 1441 nt., 1444

Nov. 3, 1965, P.L. 89-321, 79 Stat. 1188, 7 U.S. Code §§ 1423, 1441 nt., 1445a

June 17, 1966, P.L. 89-451, 7 U.S. Code §§ 1441 nt., 1444

Nov. 11, 1966, P.L. 89-808, 80 Stat. 1538, 7 U.S. Code §§ 1427, 1431, 1446a-1, 1701 nt.

Nov. 16, 1967, P.L. 90-140, 81 Stat. 464, 7 U.S. Code § 1446a

Aug. 11, 1968, P.L. 90-475, 82 Stat. 702, 7 U.S. Code §§ 1427, 1441

Oct. 11, 1968, P.L. 90-559, 82 Stat. 996, 7 U.S. Code §§ 1427, 1428, 1441 nt., 1444, 1445a

April 17, 1970, P.L. 91-233, 84 Stat. 199, 7 U.S. Code § 1431

Nov. 30, 1970, P.L. 91-524, 84 Stat. 1361, 7 U.S. Code §§ 1427, 1428, 1441, 1444, 1445a, 1446, 1446a

April 14, 1971, P.L. 92-10, 85 Stat. 27, 7 U.S. Code § 1445

Aug. 10, 1973, P.L. 93-86, 87 Stat. 224, 7 U.S. Code § 1445a

Oct. 18, 1973, P.L. 93-125, 87 Stat. 450, 7 U.S. Code §§ 1444, 1445a

Dec. 29, 1973, P.L. 93-225, 87 Stat. 942, 7 U.S. Code § 1146

Dec. 29, 1973, P.L. 93-228, 87 Stat. 944, 7 U.S. Code §§ 1441 nt., 1445a

Sept. 29, 1977, P.L. 95-113, 7 U.S. Code §§ 1421 nt., 1446 et seq.

Nov. 8, 1977, P.L. 95-156, 7 U.S. Code § 1307 nt.

May 15, 1978, P.L. 95-279, 7 U.S. Code §§ 1444, 1445g

Nov. 28, 1979, P.L. 96-127, 7 U.S. Code § 1446

Dec. 31, 1979, P.L. 96-176, 7 U.S. Code § 1441

March 18, 1980, P.L. 96-213, 7 U.S. Code §§ 1441 et seq.

April 11, 1980, P.L. 96-234, 7 U.S. Code § 1445e

July 20, 1982, P.L. 97-218, 7 U.S. Code §§ 1445, 1445 nt., 1445-1 nt., 1445-2, 1445-2 nt.

Sept. 8, 1982, P.L. 97-253, 7 U.S. Code §§ 1431, 1441, 1444d, 1445b-1, 1445b-1 nt., 1445b-2, 1445b-2 nt., 1446, 1446 nt.

Jan. 12, 1983, P.L. 97-446, 7 U.S. Code § 1444

Nov. 29, 1983, P.L. 98-180, 7 U.S. Code §§ 1445, 1445-1, 1445-2, 1446

April 10, 1984, P.L. 98-258, 7 U.S. Code §§ 1431, 1441, 1444, 1444d, 1445b-1

Aug. 8, 1985, P.L. 99-83, 7 U.S. Code § 1431

Oct. 1, 1985, P.L. 99-114, 7 U.S. Code §§ 1444, 1446

Nov. 15, 1985, P.L. 99-157, 7 U.S. Code § 1446

Dec. 13, 1985, P.L. 99-182, 7 U.S. Code § 1446

Dec. 23, 1985, P.L. 99-198, 7 U.S. Code §§ 1385 nt., 1421 to1428, 1431 to 1433c nt., 1441 to 1446, 1461 nt.

Feb. 27, 1986, P.L. 99-253, 7 U.S. Code §§ 1444e, 1445b-3, 1464

March 20, 1986, P.L. 99-260, 7 U.S. Code §§ 1431, 1441-1, 1444-1, 1444e, 1445-b, 1446, 1446 nt. 1464, 1466

April 7, 1986, P.L. 99-272, 7 U.S. Code §§ 1445, 1445 nt., 1445- 1,1445-1 nt., 1445-2, 1445-2 nt.

July 2, 1986, P.L. 99-349, 7 U.S. Code § 1441-1 nt.

Oct. 18, 1986, P.L. 99-500, 7 U.S. Code §§ 1444, 1445

Oct. 30, 1986, P.L. 99-591, 7 U.S. Code §§ 1444, 1445, 1445c-2, 1445-1

Nov. 10, 1986, P.L. 99-641, 7 U.S. Code §§ 1444, 1445b-3, 1445c-2

May 27, 1987, P.L. 100-45, 7 U.S. Code
§§ 1441-1, 1444-1, 1444e, 1445b-3, 1446

Dec. 22, 1987, P.L. 100-202, 7 U.S. Code
§ 1446

Dec. 22, 1987, P.L. 100-203, 7 U.S. Code
§§ 1423, 1431, 1444 et seq., 1445 et seq.,
1446 nt.

April 4, 1988, P.L. 100-277, 7 U.S. Code
§ 1431

April 4, 1988, P.L. 100-283, 29 U.S. Code
§ 626 nt.

June 14, 1988, P.L. 100-331, 102 Stat. 602, 7
U.S. Code § 1444

Aug. 11, 1988, P.L. 100-387, 102 Stat. 925, 7
U.S. Code §§ 1427, 1433, 1444e nt., 1445e,
1445e nt., 1446, 1463, 1464, 1464 nt., prec.
1471, 1471 to 1471j

Aug. 23, 1988, P.L. 100-418, 102 Stat. 1163,
7 U.S. Code §§ 1431, 1444

Oct. 1, 1988, P.L. 100-460, 102 Stat. 2263, 7
U.S. Code §§ 1425, 1425 nt., 1425a

Nov. 23, 1988, P.L. 100-707, 7 U.S. Code
§§ 1421, 1427

Aug. 14, 1989, P.L. 101-81, 7 U.S. Code
§§ 1464, 1464 nt., 1463, 1463 nt.

Aug. 14, 1989, P.L. 101-82, 7 U.S. Code
§§ 1464, 1464 nt., 1471d, 1471e

Dec. 12, 1989, P.L. 101-220, 7 U.S. Code
§§ 1444e, 1466 nt.

Dec. 19, 1989, P.L. 101-239, 7 U.S. Code
§§ 1433d, 1444e, 1445b- 2, 1446, 1464

Nov. 5, 1990, P.L. 101-508, 7 U.S. Code
§§ 1441-2, 1444-2, 1444f, 1445, 1445b-3a,
1445c-3, 1445j, 1446, 1446e, 1446g, 1446h

Nov. 28, 1990, P.L. 101-624, 7 U.S. Code
§ 1421 et seq. generally

June 13, 1991, P.L. 102-54, 7 U.S. Code
§ 1446a

Dec. 13, 1991, P.L. 102-237, 7 U.S. Code
§§ 1425, 1426, 1433e, 1441-2, 1444-2,
1444f, 1445b-3a, 1445c-2, 1445c-3, 1445e,
1445j, 1446, 1446a, 1446e, 1446f, 1446g,
1463, 1464

May 20, 1992, P.L. 102-289, 7 U.S. Code
§ 1431

Aug. 10, 1993, P.L. 103-66, 7 U.S. Code
§§ 1441-2, 1444-2, 1444f, 1445, 1445-1,
1445-2, 1445b-3a, 1445c-3, 1445j, 1446e,
1446f, 1446g, 1446h, 1463, 1465, 1469

May 6, 1994, P.L. 103-247, 7 U.S. Code
§§ 1441-2, 1444f, 1446e, 1446g

Aug. 23, 1994, P.L. 103-306, 7 U.S. Code
§ 1431

Oct. 13, 1994, 103-354, 7 U.S. Code
§§ 1433e, 1433f, 1441-2, 1445b-3a, 1446i

Dec. 8, 1994, P.L. 103-465, 7 U.S. Code
§§ 1442, 1445

April 4, 1996, P.L. 104-127, 7 U.S. Code
§§ 1426, 1431, 1433f, 1441, 1441-2, 1441f,
1445b-3a, 1445c-3, 1445h, 1445j, 1446e,
1446g, 1446h

Aug. 20, 1996, P.L. 104-188, 7 U.S. Code
§ 1444-2

Agricultural Act of 1954

Aug. 28, 1954, Ch. 1041, 68 Stat. 897, 7 U.S.
Code §§ 1741 to 1747

April 2, 1956, Ch. 159, 70 Stat. 87, 7 U.S.
Code § 397

Aug. 3, 1956, Ch. 950, 70 Stat. 1034, 7 U.S.
Code § 1766

Aug. 4, 1965, P.L. 89-106, 79 Stat. 431, 7
U.S. Code § 1762

Oct. 1, 1976, P.L. 94-449, 90 Stat. 1500

Oct. 21, 1978, P.L. 95-501, 92 Stat. 1688

July 30, 1979, P.L. 96-41, 93 Stat. 324

Nov. 28, 1990, P.L. 101-624, 7 U.S. Code
§§ 1748, 1749

Dec. 13, 1991, P.L. 102-237, 7 U.S. Code
§ 1748

April 4, 1996, P.L. 104-127, 7 U.S. Code
§ 1748

Agricultural Act of 1956

May 28, 1956, Ch. 327, 70 Stat. 188, 7 U.S.
Code §§ 1301, 1334, 1342, 1344, 1353,
1359, 1377, 1380a to 1380p, 1381, 1431,
1442, 1446d and others; 16 U.S. Code
§§ 568e, 568f

April 7, 1958, P.L. 85-369, 72 Stat. 81, 7
U.S. Code § 1802

Aug. 28, 1958, P.L. 85-829, 72 Stat. 986, 16
U.S. Code § 568g

Sept. 6, 1958, P.L. 85-931, 72 Stat. 1791, 7
U.S. Code § 1856

Sept. 21, 1959, P.L. 86-341, 73 Stat. 611, 7
U.S. Code § 1856

June 19, 1962, P.L. 87-488, 76 Stat. 104, 7
U.S. Code § 1854

Oct. 11, 1962, P.L. 87-793, 76 Stat. 849, 7
§ 1857
Continued

July 1, 1978, P.L. 95-313, 16 U.S. Code § 568e.

Nov. 28, 1990, P.L. 101-624, 7 U.S. Code § 1851

Dec. 8, 1994, P.L. 103-465, 7 U.S. Code §§ 1852, 1853, 1854

April 4, 1996, P.L. 104-127, 7 U.S. Code §§ 1748, 1851, 1852, 1857

Oct. 11, 1996, P.L. 104-295, 7 U.S. Code § 1854

Agricultural Act of 1958

Aug. 28, 1958, P.L. 85-835, 72 Stat. 988, 7 U.S. Code §§ 1301b nt., 1313, 1334, 1342, 1344, 1347, 1353, 1358, 1378, 1423, and others

Agricultural Act of 1961

Aug. 8, 1961, P.L. 87-128, 75 Stat. 294, 5 U.S. Code § 577; 7 U.S. Code §§ 602, 608a, 608c, 608e-1, 1013a, 1282 nt., 1334 to 1336, 1340, and others; 16 U.S. Code § 590p

March 3, 1962, P.L. 87-410, 76 Stat. 19, 7 U.S. Code § 1334 nt.

May 15, 1962, P.L. 87-451, 76 Stat. 70, 7 U.S. Code § 1334 nt.

Sept. 27, 1962, P.L. 87-703, 76 Stat. 631

Oct. 11, 1962, P.L. 87-798, 76 Stat. 908

Oct. 15, 1962, P.L. 87-832, 76 Stat. 958

Oct. 15, 1962, P.L. 89-240, 79 Stat. 931

May 24, 1966, P.L. 89-429, 80 Stat. 167

Sept. 19, 1966 P.L. 89-586, 80 Stat. 809

Oct. 8, 1966, P.L. 89-633, 80 Stat. 879

Nov. 6, 1966, P.L. 89-796, 80 Stat. 1318

Aug. 15, 1968, P.L. 90-488, 82 Stat. 770

Nov. 30, 1970, P.L. 91-524, 84 Stat. 1383

Dec. 31, 1970, P.L. 91-620, 84 Stat. 1862

Oct. 5, 1971, P.L. 92-133, 85 Stat. 364

Nov. 24, 1971, P.L. 92-173, 85 Stat. 491

Aug. 16, 1972, P.L. 92-385, 86 Stat. 557

Aug. 30, 1972, P.L. 92-419, 86 Stat. 657

April 20, 1973, P.L. 93-24, 87 Stat. 24

Aug. 10, 1973, P.L. 93-86, 87 Stat. 237

June 16, 1975, P.L. 94-35, 89 Stat. 214

Aug. 5, 1975, P.L. 94-68, 89 Stat. 381

Aug. 4, 1977, P.L. 95089, 91 Stat. 561

Sept. 29, 1977, P.L. 95-113, 91 Stat. 1011

Aug. 4, 1978, P.L. 95-334, 92 Stat. 420

July 2, 1980, P.L. 96-302, 94 Stat. 841

Sept. 24, 1980, P.L. 96-355, 94 Stat. 1174

Sept. 25, 1980, P.L. 94 Stat. 1187

Oct. 13, 1980, P.L.96-438, 94 Stat. 871

Aug. 13, 1981, P.L.97-35, 95 Stat. 368

Dec. 22, 1981, P.L.97-98, 95 Stat. 1346

April 10, 1984, P.L. 98-258, 98 Stat. 138

Dec. 23, 1985, P.L. 99-198, 99 Stat. 1518

Oct. 18, 1986, P.L. 99-500, 100 Stat. 3341-372

Nov. 28, 1990, P.L. 101-624, 104 Stat. 3817

Oct. 28, 1992, P.L. 102-554, 106 Stat. 4142

Nov. 1, 1993, P.L.103-129, 107 Stat. 1366

May 11, 1994, P.L. 103-248, 108 Stat. 619

Nov. 2, 1994, P.L.103-437, 108 Stat. 4582

Agricultural Act of 1964

April 11, 1964, P.L. 88-297, 78 Stat. 173, 7 U.S. Code §§ 1301, 1334, 1336, 1339, 1344, 1348 to 1350, 1376, 1377, and others

Nov. 3, 1965, P.L. 89-321, 79 Stat. 1203, 7 U.S. Code §§ 1339 nt., 1379c nt., 1427 nt.

Oct. 11, 1968, P.L. 90-559, 82 Stat. 996, 7 U.S. Code §§ 1339, 1350, 1379b, 1379c nt., 1427, 1441 nt., 1444, 1445a

Agricultural Act of 1970

Nov. 30, 1970, P.L. 91-524, 84 Stat. 1358, 7 U.S. Code §§ 450j, 450l, 608c, 1305, 1307 and others; 16 U.S. Code §§ 590p, 590q-2; 42 U.S. Code § 3122

Aug. 30, 1972, P.L. 92-419, 86 Stat. 674, 42 U.S. Code § 3122

Aug. 10, 1973, P.L. 93-86, 87 Stat. 221, 7 U.S. Code §§ 428b, 450j, 450l, 608c, 612c-2, 612c-3, 1282a, 1301, 1305 to 1307, 1334a-1, 1342a, 1344b, 1350, 1374, 1379b, 1379c, 1379g, 1427a, 1428, 1434, 1441a, 1444, 1445a, 1446, 1446a, 1703, 1736c, 1736e, 1782, 1787, 1925, 1926, 1932, 2012, 2119, 2651,2654; 16 U.S. Code §§ 1501 to 1510

Oct. 18, 1973, P.L. 93-125, 87 Stat. 450, 7 U.S. Code § 1703

Sept. 29, 1977, P.L. 95-113, 7 U.S. Code §§ 1307, 608c nt. et seq.; 16 U.S. Code § 1505.

Nov. 8, 1977, P.L. 95-156, 7 U.S. Code § 1307 nt.

July 1, 1978, P.L. 95-313, 16 U.S. Code §§ 1509, 1510

Jan. 11, 1983, P.L. 97-444, 7 U.S. Code § 612c-3

Dec. 23, 1985, P.L. 99-198, 16 U.S. Code § 1501

Nov. 23, 1988, P.L. 100-707, 7 U.S. Code § 1427a

Nov. 28, 1990, P.L. 101-624, 7 U.S. Code §§ 612c-3, 612c-3 nt.

Oct. 5, 1994, P.L. 103-337, 7 U.S. Code § 1427a

April 4, 1996, P.L. 104-127, 16 U.S. Code §§ 1501 et seq.

Agricultural Act of 1980

Dec. 3, 1980, P.L. 96-494, 7 U.S. Code § 4001 nt.

April 4, 1996, P.L. 104-127, 7 U.S. Code § 1736f-1

Nov. 13, 1998, P.L. 105-385, 7 U.S. Code §§ 1736f-1 nt., 1736f-1

Agricultural Adjustment Act

May 12, 1933, Ch. 25, 48 Stat. 31, 7 U.S. Code §§ 601 to 605, 607 to 623

Jan. 25, 1940, Ch. 13, 54 Stat. 17, 7 U.S. Code § 624

Feb. 10, 1942, Ch. 52, 56 Stat. 85, 7 U.S. Code § 608c

Aug. 1, 1947, Ch. 425, 61 Stat. 707, 7 U.S. Code §§ 602, 608c, 610

July 3, 1948, Ch. 827, 62 Stat. 1248, 7 U.S. Code §§ 602, 608c, 624

June 29, 1949, Ch. 273, 63 Stat. 282, 7 U.S. Code § 608c

June 28, 1950, Ch. 381, 64 Stat. 261, 7 U.S. Code § 624

June 16, 1951, Ch. 141, 65 Stat. 75, 7 U.S. Code § 624

Aug. 7, 1953, Ch. 348, 67 Stat. 472, 7 U.S. Code § 624

Aug. 31, 1954, Ch. 1172, 68 Stat. 1047, 7 U.S. Code § 608e-1

Aug. 8, 1961, P.L. 87-128, 75 Stat. 303, 7 U.S. Code §§ 602, 608a, 608c, 608e-1

Sept. 27, 1962, P.L. 87-703, 76 Stat. 632, 7 U.S. Code § 608c

Nov. 3, 1965, P.L. 89-321, 79 Stat. 1187, 7 U.S. Code § 608c

Nov. 8, 1965, P.L. 89-330, 79 Stat. 1270, 7 U.S. Code §§ 602, 608c

Feb. 20, 1970, P.L. 91-196, 84 Stat. 14, 7 U.S. Code § 608c

June 25, 1970, P.L. 91-292, 84 Stat. 333, 7 U.S. Code §§ 602, 608c

July 18, 1970, P.L. 91-341, 84 Stat. 438, 7 U.S. Code § 608c

July 31, 1970, P.L. 91-363, 84 Stat. 687, 7 U.S. Code § 608c

Aug. 18, 1970, P.L. 91-384, 84 Stat. 827, 7 U.S. Code § 608c

Nov. 25, 1970, P.L. 91-522, 84 Stat. 1357, 7 U.S. Code § 608c

Nov. 30, 1970, P.L. 91-524, 84 Stat. 1359, 7 U.S. Code § 608c

Jan. 11, 1971, P.L. 91-670, 84 Stat. 2040, 7 U.S. Code §§ 608c, 608e to 1

Aug. 13, 1971, P.L. 92-120, 85 Stat. 340, 7 U.S. Code § 608c

Feb. 15, 1972, P.L. 92-233, 85 Stat. 340, 7 U.S. Code § 608c

Oct. 6, 1972, P.L. 92-466, 86 Stat. 780, 7 U.S. Code § 608c

Dec. 29, 1973, P.L. 93-230, 87 Stat. 945, 7 U.S. Code § 608c

Sept. 29, 1977, P.L. 95-113, 7 U.S. Code § 608e-1

May 15, 1978, P.L. 95-279, 7 U.S. Code § 608c

Nov. 6, 1978, P.L. 95-598, 7 U.S. Code § 623

Oct. 14, 1982, P.L. 97-312, 7 U.S. Code § 608e-1

Nov. 29, 1983, P.L. 98-171, 7 U.S. Code § 608c

Dec. 23, 1985, P.L. 99-198, 7 U.S. Code §§ 608c, 608c nt., 608d

Dec. 12, 1989, P.L. 101-220, 7 U.S. Code § 608b

April 4, 1996, P.L. 104-127, 7 U.S. Code § 1736f-1

Nov. 13, 1998, P.L. 105-385, 7 U.S. Code §§ 1736f-1 nt., 1736f-1

Cal. Statutes 1933, Ch. 1029, p. 2619

Wash. Laws 1933, Extra Session, Ch. 7

Agricultural Adjustment Act of 1933

Dec. 22, 1987, P.L. 100-203, 7 U.S. Code § 608c

Agricultural Adjustment Act of 1937

June 3, 1937, Ch. 296, 50 Stat. 246, 7 U.S. Code §§ 601, 602, 608a to 608e, 610, 612, 614, 624, 671 to 674

Nov. 29, 1983, P.L. 98-180, 7 U.S. Code § 608c

Agricultural Adjustment Act of 1938

Feb. 16, 1938, Ch. 30, 52 Stat. 31, 7 U.S. Code §§ 612c, 1281 to 1407, 1501 to 1504, 1505 to 1519; 16 U.S. Code §§ 590h, 590o

March 26, 1938, Ch. 54, 52 Stat. 120, 7 U.S. Code § 1312

April 7, 1938, Ch. 107, 52 Stat. 202, 7 U.S. Code §§ 1301 (b) (13) (A), 1301 (b) (13) (B), 1301 (b) (13) (E), 1313 (a), 1313 (e), 1328, and others; 16 U.S. Code § 590h (c) (5), 590h (c) (6), 590h (g), 590o

April 13, 1938, Ch. 143, 52 Stat. 215, 7 U.S. Code § 608c

May 31, 1938, Ch. 292, 52 Stat. 586, 7 U.S. Code §§ 1313 (e), 1313 (f), 1344 (h)

June 20, 1938, Ch. 518, 52 Stat. 775, 7 U.S. Code § 1333

June 6, 1940, Ch. 237, 54 Stat. 232, 7 U.S. Code § 1335

June 13, 1940, Ch. 360, 54 Stat. 392, 7 U.S. Code §§ 1301, 1312, 1313, 1314, 1373

Nov. 22, 1940, Ch. 914, 54 Stat. 12.09, 7 U.S. Code §§ 1301, 1312

Nov. 25, 1940, Ch. 917, 54 Stat. 1211, 7 U.S. Code § 1301

April 3, 1941, Ch. 39, 55 Stat. 88, 7 U.S. Code §§ 1357 to 1359

May 26, 1941, Ch. 133, 55 Stat. 203, 7 U.S. Code §§ 1330, 1340

Dec. 26, 1941, Ch. 636, 55 Stat. 872, 7 U.S. Code §§ 1330 (12), 1340 (12)

Jan. 31, 1942, Ch. 32, 56 Stat. 41, 7 U.S. Code § 1392

Feb. 6, 1942, Ch. 44, 56 Stat. 51, 7 U.S. Code §§ 1313 (h), 1334 (d), 1344 (j)

Feb. 28, 1942, Ch. 123, 56 Stat. 121, 7 U.S. Code § 1312 (a)

July 9, 1942, Ch. 497, 56 Stat. 653, 7 U.S. Code §§ 1358 (d), 1359 (b) (d), 1301 (b) (13) (B)

April 29, 1943, Ch. 80, 57 Stat. 69, 7 U.S. Code § 1313

March 31, 1944, Ch. 149, 58 Stat. 136, 7 U.S. Code §§ 1312 nt., 1313 nt.

Feb. 19, 1946, Ch. 31, 60 Stat. 21, 7 U.S. Code § 1314, 1314 nt.

July 26, 1946, Ch. 677, 60 Stat. 705, 7 U.S. Code § 1358

Aug. 1, 1947, Ch. 445, 61 Stat. 721, 7 U.S. Code §§ 1358, 1359

July 3, 1948, Ch. 827, 62 Stat. 1250, 7 U.S. Code §§ 1301, 1302, 1312, 1322, 1328, 1333, 1335, and others

Aug. 29, 1949, Ch. 518, 63 Stat. 670, 7 U.S. Code §§ 1301, 1301b, 1330, 1334 nt., 1340, 1342 to 1348, 1358, 1362, 1374

Oct. 31, 1949, Ch. 792, 63 Stat. 1051, 7 U.S. Code §§ 1301, 1322, 1328, 1343 to 1345, 1353, 1355, 1421 nt.

March 31, 1950, Ch. 81, 64 Stat. 40, 7 U.S. Code §§ 1344, 1358, 1358 nt., 1359, 1363 nt., 1431 nt., 1450, 1450 nt.

June 16, 1950, Ch. 268, 64 Stat. 232, 7 U.S. Code § 1353

April 12, 1951, Ch. 28, 65 Stat. 29, 7 U.S. Code §§ 1358, 1359, 1363

Oct. 17, 1951, Ch. 511, 65 Stat. 422, 7 U.S. Code § 1313

July 17, 1952, Ch. 933, 66 Stat. 758, 7 U.S. Code §§ 1301, 1347

June 22, 1954, Ch. 339, 68 Stat. 270, 7 U.S. Code § 1314

Aug. 28, 1954, Ch. 1041, 68 Stat. 897, 7 U.S. Code §§ 1301, 1327 to 1330, 1332, 1334, 1334a, 1335, 1340, 1344, 1348, 1371, 1374, 1421

Aug. 30, 1954, Ch. 1076, 68 Stat. 966, 7 U.S. Code § 1292

Feb. 19, 1955, Ch. 8, 69 Stat. 9, 7 U.S. Code § 1334

March 31, 1955, Ch. 21, 69 Stat. 24, 7 U.S. Code §§ 1313, 1314

April 30, 1955, Chs. 29, 30, 69 Stat. 45, 7 U.S. Code § 1353

May 5, 1955, Ch. 31, 69 Stat. 46, 7 U.S. Code § 1353

Aug. 9, 1955, Ch. 639, 69 Stat. 557, 7 U.S. Code § 1312

Aug. 9, 1955, Ch. 648, 69 Stat. 576, 7 U.S. Code § 1352

Aug. 9, 1955, Ch. 652, 69 Stat. 578, 7 U.S. Code § 1353

Aug. 11, 1955, Ch. 789, 69 Stat. 670, 7 U.S. Code § 1313

Aug. 11, 1955, Ch. 799, 69 Stat. 684, 7 U.S. Code § 1313

March 16, 1956, Ch. 86, 70 Stat. 50, 7 U.S. Code § 1334

May 28, 1956, Ch. 327, 70 Stat. 203, 7 U.S. Code §§ 1301, prec. 1331, 1334, 1342, 1344, 1353, 1359, 1377, 1380a to 1380p, prec. 1381

June 22, 1956, Ch. 427, 70 Stat. 330, 7 U.S. Code § 1312

Aug. 3, 1956, Ch. 950, 70 Stat. 1034, 7 U.S. Code § 1392

Aug. 7, 1956, Ch. 1030, 70 Stat. 1117, 7 U.S. Code § 1334

April 2, 1957, P.L. 85-13, 71 Stat. 10, 7 U.S. Code § 1334

July 10, 1957, P.L. 85-92, 71 Stat. 284, 7 U.S. Code § 1301

Aug. 13, 1957, P.L. 85-127, 71 Stat. 344, 7 U.S. Code § 1359

Aug. 28, 1957, P.L. 85-203, 71 Stat. 477, 7 U.S. Code §§ 1334, 1335

Sept. 2, 1957, P.L. 85-266, 71 Stat. 592, 7 U.S. Code § 1337

April 4, 1958, P.L. 85-366, 72 Stat. 78, 7 U.S. Code § 1334

May 1, 1958, P.L. 85-390, 72 Stat. 101, 7 U.S. Code § 1334

June 4, 1958, P.L. 85-443, 72 Stat. 177, 7 U.S. Code §§ 1353, 1356

June 11, 1958, P.L. 85-456, 72 Stat. 186, 7 U.S. Code § 1344

July 2, 1958, P.L. 85-489, 72 Stat. 291, 7 U.S. Code § 1313

Aug. 21, 1958, P.L. 85-705, 72 Stat. 703, 7 U.S. Code § 1314a

Aug. 21, 1958, P.L. 85-717, 72 Stat. 709, 7 U.S. Code §§ 1358, 1359

Aug. 28, 1958, P.L. 85-835, 72 Stat. 989, 7 U.S. Code §§ 1301b nt., 1313, 1334, 1342, 1344, 1347, 1353, 1358, 1378

Aug. 18, 1959, P.L. 86-172, 73 Stat. 393, 7 U.S. Code §§ 1344, 1377

Sept. 21, 1959, P.L. 86-341, 73 Stat. 611, 7 U.S. Code § 1347

Feb. 20, 1960, P.L. 86-385, 74 Stat. 4, 7 U.S. Code § 1334

Feb. 20, 1960, P.L. 86-389, 74 Stat. 6, 7 U.S. Code § 1441

April 4, 1960, P.L. 86-408, 74 Stat. 15, 7 U.S. Code § 1354

April 9, 1960, P.L. 86-419, 74 Stat. 39, 7 U.S. Code § 1334

April 9, 1960, P.L. 86-423, 74 Stat. 41, 7 U.S. Code § 1378

June 11, 1960, P.L. 86-507, 74 Stat. 200, 7 U.S. Code §§ 1365, 1373

June 30, 1960, P.L. 86-553, 74 Stat. 258, 7 U.S. Code § 1374

June 30, 1960, P.L. 86-566, 74 Stat. 295, 7 U.S. Code § 1347

May 16, 1961, P.L. 87-33, 75 Stat. 78, 7 U.S. Code § 1378

May 20, 1961, P.L. 87-37, 75 Stat. 84, 7 U.S. Code § 1344

July 25, 1961, P.L. 87-104, 75 Stat. 220, 7 U.S. Code § 1336

Aug. 8, 1961, P.L. 87-128, 75 Stat. 296, 7 U.S. Code §§ 1334 to 1336

Sept. 6, 1961, P.L. 87-200, 75 Stat. 469, 7 U.S. Code § 1314b

Oct. 4, 1961, P.L. 87-357, 75 Stat. 778, 7 U.S. Code § 1334

March 6, 1962, P.L. 87-412, 76 Stat. 20, 7 U.S. Code § 1353

April 27, 1962, P.L. 87-446, 76 Stat. 64, 7 U.S. Code § 1344

July 10, 1962, P.L. 87-530, 76 Stat. 151, 7 U.S. Code § 1314b

July 19, 1962, P.L. 87-540, 76 Stat. 170, 7 U.S. Code § 1336

Sept. 27, 1962, P.L. 87-703, 76 Stat. 618, 7 U.S. Code §§ 1301, 1301 nt., 1331 to 1334, 1334b to 1337, 1339, 1371, 1379a to 1379j, 1385

Oct. 15, 1962, P.L. 87-824, 76 Stat. 947, 7 U.S. Code § 1314b

April 26, 1963, P.L. 88-12, 77 Stat. 13, 7 U.S. Code § 1344

July 17, 1963, P.L. 88-64, 77 Stat. 79, 7 U.S. Code § 1334

July 19, 1963, P.L. 88-68, 77 Stat. 81, 7 U.S. Code § 1314b

July 30, 1963, P.L. 88-80, 77 Stat. 114, 7 U.S. Code § 1314b

Jan. 28, 1964, P.L. 88-261, 78 Stat. 6, 7 U.S. Code § 1353

Continued

April 11, 1964, P.L. 88-297, 78 Stat. 173, 7
U.S. Code §§ 1301, 1334, 1336, 1339,
1344, 1348 to 1350, 1376, 1377, 1379b to
1379d, 1385

Aug. 20, 1964, P.L. 88-469, 78 Stat. 581, 7
U.S. Code § 1314b

April 16, 1965, P.L. 89-12, 79 Stat. 66, 7
U.S. Code §§ 1313, 1314c

May 27, 1965, P.L. 89-29, 79 Stat. 118, 7
U.S. Code § 1314b

July 24, 1965, P.L. 89-82, 79 Stat. 258, 7
U.S. Code § 1336

Aug. 6, 1965, P.L. 89-112, 79 Stat. 447, 7
U.S. Code § 1379c

Nov. 3, 1965, P.L. 89-321, 79 Stat. 1192, 7
U.S. Code §§ 1301, 1314b, 1332 to 1335,
1339, 1340, 1344b, 1346, and others

June 17, 1966, P.L. 89-451, 80 Stat. 202, 7
U.S. Code § 1379c

June 24, 1966, P.L. 89-471, 80 Stat. 220, 7
U.S. Code § 1314b

March 29, 1967, P.L. 90-6, 81 Stat. 6, 7 U.S.
Code § 1314b

July 7, 1967, P.L. 90-51, 81 Stat. 120, 7 U.S.
Code § 1314d

July 7, 1967, P.L. 90-52, 81 Stat. 121, 7 U.S.
Code § 1314b

Oct. 11, 1967, P.L. 90-106, 81 Stat. 275, 7
U.S. Code § 1313

Dec. 14, 1967, P.L. 90-191, 81 Stat. 578, 7
U.S. Code § 1356

Dec. 18, 1967, P.L. 90-211, 81 Stat. 658, 7
U.S. Code § 1358a

Jan. 2, 1968, P.L. 90-243, 81 Stat. 781, 7 U.S.
Code § 1334

July 5, 1968, P.L. 90-387, 82 Stat. 293, 7
U.S. Code § 1314d

Aug. 11, 1968, P.L. 90-475, 82 Stat. 701, 7
U.S. Code § 1347

Oct. 11, 1968, P.L. 90-559, 82 Stat. 996, 7
U.S. Code §§ 1314b, 1332, 1339, 1344,
1346, 1350, 1353, 1359 nt., 1379b, 1379c
nt.; 16 U.S. Code § 590p

Nov. 21, 1969, P.L. 91-122, 83 Stat. 213, 7
U.S. Code § 1358a

March 31, 1970, P.L. 91-220, 84 Stat. 86, 7
U.S. Code § 1334

June 19, 1970, P.L. 91-284, 84 Stat. 314, 7
U.S. Code §§ 1314b, 1314c

July 23, 1970, P.L. 91-348, 84 Stat. 448, 7
U.S. Code § 1336

Oct. 15, 1970, P.L. 91-455, 84 Stat. 969, 7
U.S. Code § 1336

Nov. 30, 1970, P.L. 91-524, 84 Stat. 1362, 7
U.S. Code §§ 1342a, 1344b, 1350, 1378,
1379, 1379b to 1379e, 1385

Dec. 22, 1970, P.L. 91-568, 84 Stat. 1499, 7
U.S. Code § 1358a

April 14, 1971, P.L. 92-10, 85 Stat. 23, 7
U.S. Code §§ 1314e, 1378

Aug. 3, 1971, P.L. 92-62, 85 Stat. 163, 7 U.S.
Code § 1358

Oct. 23, 1971, P.L. 92-144, 85 Stat. 393, 7
U.S. Code § 1314d

June 6, 1972, P.L. 92-311, 86 Stat. 215, 7
U.S. Code § 1314b

July 26, 1972, P.L. 92-354, 86 Stat. 499, 7
U.S. Code § 1378

April 27, 1973, P.L. 93-27, 87 Stat. 27, 7
U.S. Code § 1353

July 10, 1973, P.L. 93-68, 87 Stat. 161, 7
U.S. Code § 1336

Aug. 1, 1973, P.L. 93-80, 87 Stat. 178, 7 U.S.
Code § 1314b

Aug. 10, 1973, P.L. 93-86, 87 Stat. 225, 7
U.S. Code §§ 1379b, 1379c, 1379g

Sept. 3, 1974, P.L. 93-411, 88 Stat. 1089, 7
U.S. Code § 1314f

July 25, 1975, P.L. 94-61, 89 Stat. 302, 7
U.S. Code § 1301

June 17, 1977, P.L. 95-48, 7 U.S. Code
§ 1336

June 25, 1977, P.L. 95-54, 7 U.S. Code
§ 1314b

Sept. 29, 1977, P.L. 95-113, 7 U.S. Code
§§ 1281, 1379d nt. et seq.

Nov. 4, 1978, P.L. 95-592, 7 U.S. Code
§ 1314f

July 7, 1979, P.L. 96-31, 7 U.S. Code
§§ 1539, 1539 nt.

Nov. 16, 1979, P.L. 96-113, 7 U.S. Code
§ 1372

July 20, 1982, P.L. 97-218, 7 U.S. Code
§§ 1301, 1314, 1314 nt., 1314-1, 1314b,
1314b-1, 1314b-2, 1314c, 1314e

Nov. 29, 1983, P.L. 98-180, 7 U.S. Code
§§ 1314b to 1314e

July 11, 1985, P.L. 99-63, 7 U.S. Code
§ 1336

Nov. 15, 1985, P.L. 99-157, 7 U.S. Code
§§ 1343, 1358, 1445, 1445-2

Dec. 13, 1985, P.L. 99-182, 7 U.S. Code
§ 1314c

Dec. 23, 1985, P.L. 99-198, 7 U.S. Code
§§ 1301, 1331 to 1336, 1336 nt., 1338 nt.,
1340 nt., 1342 nt., 1358 to 1359, 1373 to
1388

Jan. 30, 1986, P.L. 99-241, 7 U.S. Code
§§ 1314c, 1314e

April 7, 1986, P.L. 99-272, 7 U.S. Code
§§ 1301, 1312, 1314c, 1314c nt., 1314e,
1314e nt., 1314h, 1314h nt., 1372, 1372 nt.

Dec. 22, 1987, P.L. 100-203, 7 U.S. Code
§§ 1314b, 1314c

Aug. 11, 1988, P.L. 100-387, 102 Stat. 948, 7
U.S. Code §§ 1314e, 1358a, 1358a nt.

Aug. 23, 1988, P.L. 100-418, 102 Stat. 1407,
7 U.S. Code §§ 608c, 608e

Aug. 14, 1989, P.L. 101-82, 7 U.S. Code
§§ 1359, 1359 nt.

Oct. 30, 1989, P.L. 101-134, 7 U.S. Code
§§ 1314b, 1314c, 1314e

April 10, 1990, P.L. 101-270, 7 U.S. Code
§ 1332 nt.

Nov. 15, 1990, P.L. 101-577, 7 U.S. Code
§§ 1314e, 1379

Nov. 28, 1990, P.L. 101-624, 7 U.S. Code
§§ 1358-1, 1358b, 1358c, 1359a, 1359aa-
1359jj, 1373, 1373 nt., 1374

Dec. 13, 1991, P.L. 102-237, 7 U.S. Code
§§ 1314e, 1358, 1358-1 1358b, 1359,
1359a, 1359aa-1359ii, 1374, 1379

Oct. 27, 1992, P.L. 102-535, 7 U.S. Code
§ 1359ff

Oct. 28, 1992, P.L. 102-566, 7 U.S. Code
§ 1341d

Aug. 10, 1993, P.L. 103-66, 7 U.S. Code
§§ 1314c, 1314e, 1314i, 1358-1, 1359a,
1359bb

Dec. 8, 1993, P.L. 103-182, 7 U.S. Code
§ 1359a nt.

Nov. 2, 1994, P.L. 103-437, 7 U.S. Code
§ 1314c

Dec. 8, 1994, P.L. 103-465, 7 U.S. Code
§§ 624, 1314i, 1359a

Dec. 29, 1995, P.L. 104-88, 7 U.S. Code
§ 1291

April 4, 1996, P.L. 104-127, 7 U.S. Code
§§ 1344, 1358-1, 1358b, 1358c, 1359a,
1373, 1377

Agricultural Adjustment Act of 1980

March 18, 1980, P.L. 96-213, 7 U.S. Code
§§ 1421 nt., 1441 et seq.

Agricultural Administration Act

Ariz. Rev. Stat. Ann., § 3-101 et seq.

Agricultural Advisory Board Act (Department of Environmental Resources)

Pa. 1993 Pamph. Laws, No. 11

Agricultural Aid and Trade Missions Act

Aug. 23, 1988, P.L. 100-418, 102 Stat. 1411

Nov. 28, 1990, P.L. 101-624, 104 Stat. 3663,
7 U.S. Code § 1736bb-6

April 4, 1996, P.L. 104-127, 7 U.S. Code
§§ 1691 nt., 1736bb et seq.

Agricultural Ammonia Law

Ind. Code Ann., 15-3-2-1 et seq.

Agricultural and Consumer Protection Act of 1973

Dec. 22, 1981, P.L. 97-98, 95 Stat. 1292, 7
U.S. Code § 612c nt.

Agricultural and Forestal Districts Act (Local)

Va. Code 1950, § 15.1-1513.1 et seq.

Agricultural and Forestry Activity Act

Miss. Code Ann. 1972, § 49-33-1 et seq.

Agricultural and Forestry Residue Utilization Act

Cal. Public Resources Code § 25630 et seq.

Agricultural and Industrial Board Act

Miss. Code Ann. 1972, § 57-1-1 et seq.

Agricultural and Industrial Development Commission Act

Tenn. Code Ann., 4-14-101 et seq.

Agricultural and Industrial Finance Authority Act

N.M. Stat. Ann., 58-24-1 et seq.

Agricultural and Industrial Relief Commission Act
Fla. Stat. 1953, 420.01 et seq.

Agricultural and Mechanical College Housing Authority Act
Okla. Stat. Ann., Title 70, § 3401 et seq.

Agricultural and Mechanics Colleges Acts
July 2, 1862, Ch. 130, 12 Stat. 503, 7 U.S. Code §§ 301 to 305, 307, 308
July 23, 1866, Ch. 209, 14 Stat. 208, 7 U.S. Code § 305
March 3, 1873, Ch. 281, 17 Stat. 559, 7 U.S. Code § 305
March 3, 1883, Ch. 102, 22 Stat. 484, 7 U.S. Code § 304
Aug. 30, 1890, Ch. 841, 26 Stat. 417, 7 U.S. Code §§ 321 to 326, 328
March 4, 1907, Ch. 2907, 34 Stat. 1281, 7 U.S. Code § 322
April 13, 1926, Ch. 130, 44 Stat. 247, 7 U.S. Code § 304
June 29, 1935, Ch. 338, 49 Stat. 436, 7 U.S. Code § 329
June 12, 1952, Ch. 419, 66 Stat. 135, 7 U.S. Code § 329
July 14, 1960, P.L. 86-658, 74 Stat. 525, 7 U.S. Code § 329

Agricultural and Rural Youth Development Act
Pa. 1991 Pamph. Laws, No. 33

Agricultural and Small Business Development Loan Act
Mo. Rev. Stat. 1986, 348.005 et seq.

Agricultural and Technical Institute Building Loan Act (Essex)
Mass. Acts 1963, Ch. 516

Agricultural and Wildlife Damage Prevention Act
Utah Code Ann. 1953, 4-23-1 et seq.

Agricultural Appropriation Act of 1940
See Department Of Agriculture Appropriation Acts And Farm Credit Administration Appropriation Acts

Agricultural Area Security Act
Pa. Purdon's Stat., Title 3, § 901 et seq.

Agricultural Areas Conservation and Protection Act
Ill. Comp. Stat. 1992, Ch. 505, § 5/1 et seq.

Agricultural Association Act
Miss. Code Ann. 1972, § 79-17-1 et seq.

Agricultural Association Corporate Income Tax Act (Cooperative)
Pa. Purdon's Stat., Title 72, § 3420-21

Agricultural Association Corporate Net Income Tax Act
Pa. Purdon's Stat., Title 72, § 7401 et seq.

Agricultural Association Law (Cooperative)
Pa. Cons. Stat., Title 15, § 7501 et seq.

Agricultural Authority Act
Wis. Laws 1937, Special Session, Ch. 4

Agricultural Aviation Licensing Act
Miss. Code Ann. 1972, § 69-21-101 et seq.

Agricultural Biotechnology Act
Okla. Stat. 1981, Title 2, § 2011

Agricultural Bonded Warehouse Law
Iowa Code Ann., 203C.1 et seq.

Agricultural Center Board Law
Ala. Code 1975, § 2-6-1 et seq.

Agricultural Chemical Act
Kan. Stat. Ann., 2-2201 et seq.
Okla. Stat. Ann., Title 2, § 3-61 et seq.

Agricultural Chemical Control Act
Ore. Rev. Stat., 573.005 et seq.

Agricultural Chemical Ground Water Protection Act
Mont. Code Ann., 80-15-101 et seq.

Agricultural Chemical Response and Reimbursement Law
Minn. Stat. Ann., 18E.01 et seq.

Agricultural Code
   Okla. Stat. Ann., Title 2, § 1-1 et seq.

Agricultural College Acts
   See Agricultural And Mechanical Colleges
   Acts

Agricultural College and School of Mines Act (Land Grant)
   Alaska Comp. Laws Ann. 1949, § 47-2-21 et seq.

Agricultural Commodities Act
   Cal. Food and Agricultural Code 1967, § 58651 et seq.

Agricultural Commodities Authority Act
   Ga. Code 1933, 5-2601 et seq.

Agricultural Commodities Controls Act
   Minn. Stat. Ann., 17.90 et seq.

Agricultural Commodities Dealers Act
   Me. Rev. Stat. Ann. 1964, Title 7, § 451 et seq.

Agricultural Commodities Development Act
   Del. Code of 1974, Title 3, § 701 et seq.

Agricultural Commodities Marketing Act
   Fla. Stat. Ann., 573.101 et seq.
   La. Rev. Stat. Ann., 3:711 et seq.
   Me. Rev. Stat. Ann. 1964, Title 7, § 421 et seq.
   Mich. Comp. Laws Ann., 290.651 et seq.
   Pa. Cons. Stat., Title 5, § 4501 et seq.
   Pa. Purdon's Stat., Title 3, § 1001 et seq.
   S.C. Code Ann. 1976, § 46-17-10 et seq.
   Utah Code Ann. 1953, Miscellaneous Superseded Code Provisions, 5-5-1 et seq.

Agricultural Commodities Promotion Act
   Ga. Code Ann., 2-8-1 et seq.
   Minn. Stat. Ann., 17.51 et seq.
   Tenn. Code Ann., 43-29-101 et seq.

Agricultural Commodities Sales Promotion Act
   Ga. Code 1933, 5-2901a et seq.

Agricultural Commodity-Based Plastics Development Act
   Ill. Rev. Stat. 1991, Ch. 5, § 2601 et seq.

Agricultural Commodity Commission Act
   N.M. Stat. Ann., 76-21-1 et seq.

Agricultural Commodity Dealer and Warehouse Law
   La. Rev. Stat. Ann., 3:3401 et seq.

Agricultural Commodity Insurance Act
   Mich. Comp. Laws Ann., 285.211 et seq.

Agricultural Competitiveness and Trade Act of 1988
   Aug. 23, 1988, P.L. 100-418, 102 Stat. 1388, 7 U.S. Code § 5201 nt.

Agricultural Conservation Act
   N.D. Cent. Code, 4-23-01 et seq.
   N.Y. Consol. Laws, Ch. 9A
   Wash. Rev. Code Ann., 15-68-010 et seq.

Agricultural Conservation and Adjustment Act
   Colo. Rev. Stat., 35-3-101 et seq.
   Del. Code of 1974, Title 7, § 3701
   Ga. Code Ann., 2-6-1 et seq.
   N.D. Cent. Code, 4-23-01 et seq.
   N.Y. Agricultural Conservation and Adjustment Law (Consol. Laws, Ch. 9A) § 1 et seq.
   Pa. Purdon's Stat., Title 73, §§ 392.1 et seq., 541
   S.D. Code 1939, 4.0401 et seq.
   Tenn. Code Ann., 43-14-101701 et seq.
   Va. Code 1950, § 3-17 et seq.
   Wash. Rev. Code Ann., 15.67.010 et seq.

Agricultural Conservation Plans Act
   Wash. Rev. Code Ann., 15.67.010 et seq.

Agricultural Consultants Licensing Act
   Ark. Code Ann. 1987, No. 609

Agricultural Cooperative Marketing Act
   Mo. Rev. Stat., 274.010 et seq.

**Agricultural Cooperative Marketing
Associations Law**
Miss. Code Ann. 1972, § 79-19-1 et seq.

Agricultural Cooperatives Act
Ill. Comp. Stat. 1992, Ch. 805, § 315/1 et seq.

Agricultural Cooperatives Associations Act
Fla. Stat. Ann., 618.01 et seq.
Haw. Rev. Stat. Ann., § 421-1 et seq.
Ind. Code Ann., 15-7-1-1 et seq.
Me. Rev. Stat. Ann. 1964, Title 13, § 1771 et
seq.
N.J. Stat. Ann., 4:13-1 et seq.
Ohio Rev. Code 1953, 1729.01 et seq.
Utah Code Ann. 1953, 3-1-1 et seq.
Va. Code 1950, § 13.1-312 et seq.
Wash. Rev. Code Ann., 24.32.010 et seq.
W. Va. Code 1966, § 19-4-1 et seq.

Agricultural Credit Act of 1978
Aug. 4, 1978, P.L. 95-334, 7 U.S. Code
§§ 1921 nt., 1922 et seq., 2201 et seq., 2908
July 2, 1986, P.L. 99-349, 100 Stat. 710
Aug. 14, 1989, P.L. 101-82, 16 U.S. Code
§§ 2202, 2202 nt.
April 4, 1996, P.L. 104-127, 16 U.S. Code
§ 2203

Agricultural Credit Act of 1987
Jan. 6, 1987, P.L. 100-233, 7 U.S. Code
§§ 5101 to 5106; 12 U.S. Code 2001 et seq.
Nov. 28, 1990, P.L. 101-624, 7 U.S. Code
§§ 1985 nt., 5106
Oct. 28, 1992, P.L. 102-552, 12 U.S. Code
§ 2011 nt.
Oct. 28, 1992, P.L. 102-554, 7 U.S. Code
§ 5102
Oct. 13, 1994, P.L. 103-354, 7 U.S. Code
§ 5101, et seq.

Agricultural Credit Association Act
Pa. Purdon's Stat., Title 15, § 12201 et seq.

Agricultural Credit Corporations Act
March 3, 1932, Ch. 70, 47 Stat. 60, 12 U.S.
Code §§ 1401 to 1404

**Agricultural Credit Improvement Act of
1992**
Oct. 28, 1992, P.L. 102-554, 7 U.S. Code
§ 1921 nt.

**Agricultural Credit Technical Corrections
Act of 1988**
Sept. 17, 1988, P.L. 100-399, 102 Stat. 989, 7
U.S. Code §§ 1988, 5101, 5103; 12 U.S.
Code §§ 1202 nt., generally 1201 et seq.; 31
U.S. Code § 9105

Agricultural Credits Act of 1923
March 4, 1923, Ch. 252, 42 Stat. 1461, 12
U.S. Code §§ 1151, 1161 to 1163, 1171 to
1172, 1181 to 1182, 1191, 1201 to 1202, and
others
Sept. 9, 1959, P.L. 86-251, 73 Stat. 488, 12
U.S. Code § 10

**Agricultural Crop Consultants Act
(Independent)**
Ga. Code Ann., 43-21A-1 et seq.

Agricultural Debt Relief Act
See Frazier-Lemke Farm Mortgage Act

**Agricultural Departments Consolidation
Act**
Wis. Stat. Ann., 93.01 et seq.

Agricultural Development Act
Iowa Code Ann., 175.1 et seq.
Minn. Stat. Ann., 41C.01 et seq.
N.C. Gen. Stat. 1943, § 106-580 et seq.
N.D. Cent. Code, 4-36-01 et seq.
Pa. Purdon's Stat., Title 3, § 1301 et seq.
Tenn. Code Ann., 4-31-102 to 4-31-104,
4-31-201 et seq.
Tex. Agri. Code, § 57.001 et seq.

**Agricultural Development Administration
Act**
P.R. Laws Ann. 1954, Title 5, § 1831 et seq.

Agricultural Development Agency Act
Ark. Stat. 1947, 77-2301 et seq.

Agricultural Development and Trade Act of 1990

Nov. 28, 1990, P.L. 101-624, 7 U.S. Code §§ 624 nt., 958, 1691 nt., 1761, 3293, 5622 nt., 5694 nt.; 22 U.S. Code § 2151x-2; 46 U.S. Code Appx. §§ 1241q to 1241v

Oct. 24, 1992, P.L. 102-511, 7 U.S. Code § 5622 nt.

Agricultural Development Authority Act

Ala. Code 1975, 2-3A-1 et seq.

Colo. Rev. Stat., 35-75-101 et seq.

Va. Code 1950, § 3.1-27.1 et seq.

Agricultural Development Corporation Act

Ind. Code Ann., 15-7-5-1 et seq.

Neb. Rev. Stat. 1943, 2-4101 et seq.

P.R. Laws Ann. 1954, Title 5, § 1801 et seq.

Agricultural Development Promotion Act

P.R. Laws Ann. 1954, Title 5, § 1551 et seq.

Agricultural District and Farmland Preservation Act

Tenn. Code Ann., 43-34-101 et seq.

Agricultural Districts Act

N.Y. Agriculture and Markets Law (Consol. Laws Ch. 69) § 300 et seq.

Agricultural Economic Development Act

Fla. Stat. Ann., 570.247

Agricultural Employees Act (Workmen's Compensation)

Pa. Purdon's Stat., Title 77, § 463

Agricultural Employment Relations Act

Ariz. Rev. Stat. Ann., § 23-1381 et seq.

Agricultural Employment Retraining Act

Okla. Stat. Ann., Title 2, § 2001 et seq.

Agricultural Enabling Act

Wash. Rev. Code 1983, 15.65.010 et seq.

Agricultural Enabling Amendments Act of 1961

Aug. 8, 1961, P.L. 87-128, 75 Stat. 295, 7 U.S. Code §§ 602, 608a, 608c, 608e-1, 1334 to 1336, 1340, 1441, nt., 1782, 1911 to 1913; 16 U.S. Code § 590p

March 3, 1962, P.L. 87-410, 76 Stat. 19, 7 U.S. Code § 1334 nt.

Agricultural Entries Act

Alaska Comp. Laws Ann. 1949, §§ 47-2-56, 47-2-57

Agricultural Entry Acts

July 17, 1914, Ch. 142, 38 Stat. 509, 30 U.S. Code §§ 121 to 123

March 4, 1933, Ch. 278, 47 Stat. 1570, 30 U.S. Code § 124

Agricultural Equipment Dealership Act

Kan. Stat. Ann., 16-1201 et seq.

Minn. Stat. Ann., 325E.061 et seq.

Agricultural Ethanol Production Law

La. Rev. Stat. Ann., 3:3701 et seq.

Agricultural Experiment Stations Acts

March 2, 1887, Ch. 314, 24 Stat. 440, 7 U.S. Code §§ 361a to 361i

Feb. 1, 1888, Ch. 5, 25 Stat. 32

June 7, 1888, Ch. 373, 25 Stat. 176

March 2, 1889, Ch. 373, 25 Stat. 840

March 16, 1906, Ch. 951, 34 Stat. 63 (See 7 U.S. Code §§ 361c to 361e, 361g, 361i)

Feb. 24, 1925, Ch. 308, 43 Stat. 971 (See 7 U.S. Code §§ 361c to 361e, 361g, 361i)

Aug. 11, 1955, Ch. 790, 69 Stat. 671, 7 U.S. Code §§ 361a to 361i

June 29, 1960, P.L. 96-533, 74 Stat. 249, 7 U.S. Code § 361g

Agricultural Experimental Station Act (University of Illinois)

Ill. Rev. Stat. 1991, Ch. 144, §§ 60.9, 61

Agricultural Exposition Authority Act

Ga. Code Ann., 12-3-470 et seq.

Agricultural Extension Act

Iowa Code Ann., 176A.1 et seq.

Agricultural Extension Council Act (Escambia County)
Fla. Special Laws 1947, Ch. 24501

Agricultural Extension Work Acts
May 8, 1914, Ch. 79, 38 Stat. 372, 7 U.S. Code §§ 341 to 348
May 22, 1928, Ch. 687, 45 Stat. 711 (See 7 U.S. Code §§ 341 to 343, 344 to 348)
March 10, 1930, Ch. 73, 46 Stat. 83 (See 7 U.S. Code §§ 341 to 343, 344 to 348)
June 26, 1953, Ch. 157, 67 Stat. 83, 7 U.S. Code §§ 341 to 343, 344 to 346, 348
Aug. 11, 1955, Ch. 798, 69 Stat. 684, 7 U.S. Code §§ 347a, 348
Oct. 5, 1962, P.L. 87-749, 76 Stat. 745, 7 U.S. Code §§ 342, 343, 344, 345, 346, 347a, 349
June 30, 1982, P.L. 96-294, 7 U.S. Code §§ 341, 342 Dec. 23, 1985, P.L. 99-198, 7 U.S. Code §§ 342, 343, 343 nt.

Agricultural Facilities Finance Act
N.C. Gen. Stat. 1943, § 122B-1

Agricultural Fair Act
Ill. Comp. Stat. 1992, Ch. 30, § 120/1 et seq.
Neb. Rev. Stat. 1943, 2-201 et seq.
Pa. Purdon's Stat., Title 3, § 1501 et seq.

Agricultural Fair Practices Act of 1967
April 16, 1968, P.L. 90-288, 82 Stat. 93, 7 U.S. Code §§ 2301 to 2306

Agricultural Fair Trade Act
Utah Code Ann. 1953, 4-8-1 et seq.

Agricultural Feed Law
Neb. Rev. Stat. 1943, 81-2.147 et seq.

Agricultural Feeds Adulteration Act
Wis. Stat. Ann., 94.72, Subsec. 14, Subd. b

Agricultural Finance Act
La. Rev. Stat. Ann., 3:261 et seq.
N.C. Gen. Stat. 1943, § 122D-1 et seq.
Tex. Agriculture Code, § 58.001 et seq.

Agricultural Finance Corporation Act
Ky. Rev. Stat. 1971, 247.940 et seq.

Agricultural Financial and Family Counseling Act
Tenn. Public Acts 1986, Ch. 848

Agricultural Foreign Investment Disclosure Act
Ark. Code Ann. 1987, 2-3-101 et seq.
Ill. Comp. Stat. 1992, Ch. 765, § 50/1 et seq.

Agricultural Foreign Investment Disclosure Act of 1978
Oct. 14, 1978, P.L. 95-460, 7 U.S. Code §§ 3501 et seq.
Dec. 21, 1995, P.L. 104-66, 7 U.S. Code § 3504
Nov. 10, 1998, P.L. 105-362, 7 U.S. Code § 3504

Agricultural, Forest and Open Space Land Act
Tenn. Code Ann., 11-14-201, 11-15-107, 11-15-108, 67-5-1001 et seq.

Agricultural Gasoline Refund Law
Tenn. Code Ann., 67-3-301 et seq.

Agricultural Grain Marketing Compact (Interstate)
See Interstate Compact on Agricultural Grain Marketing Act

Agricultural Growing Media Act
Ga. Code Ann., 2-12-100 et seq.

Agricultural Improvement District Act
Ariz. Rev. Stat. Ann., § 48-2301 et seq.

Agricultural Improvement Societies Act
Ind. Code Ann., 15-1-10-1 et seq.

Agricultural Industry Finance Act
Iowa Code Ann., 15E.201 to 15E.212

Agricultural Industry Law
Iowa Code Ann., 159.1 et seq.

Agricultural Investment Disclosure Act
Va. Code 1950, § 3.1-22.22 et seq.

Agricultural Labor Act
Ida. Code 1947, 22-4101 et seq.

Agricultural Labor Relations Act
Cal. Labor Code § 1140 et seq.

Agricultural Laborers' Right to Work Law
La. Rev. Stat. Ann., 23:881 et seq.

Agricultural Land Interest Act
Me. Rev. Stat. Ann. 1964, Title 7, § 31 et seq.

Agricultural Land Ownership Act
Ill. Comp. Stat. 1992, Ch. 765, § 55/0.01 et seq.
Ill. Rev. Stat. 1991, Ch. 5, § 2100 et seq.

Agricultural Land Stewardship Program Act
Cal. Public Resources Code § 10299 et seq.

Agricultural Land Tax Credit Act
Iowa Code Ann., 426.1 et seq.

Agricultural Lands Preservation Act
Del. Code of 1974, Title 3, § 901 et seq.

Agricultural Law Resource and Reference Center Act
Pa. 1998 Pamph. Laws, No. 11

Agricultural Lien Act
Va. Code 1950, § 43-44 et seq.

Agricultural Lime Act
Ore. Rev. Stat., 633.330

Agricultural Liming Materials Act
Ala. Code 1975, § 2-23-1 et seq.
Ark. Code Ann. 1987, 2-19-301 et seq.
Del. Code of 1974, Title 3, § 1901 et seq.
Ga. Code Ann., 2-12-40 et seq.
Kan. Stat. Ann., 2-2901 et seq.
La. Rev. Stat. Ann., 3:1361 et seq.
Me. Rev. Stat. Ann. 1964, Title 7, § 761 et seq.
Minn. Stat. Ann., 18C.530 et seq.
Miss. Code Ann. 1972, § 69-39-1 et seq.
Mo. Rev. Stat., 266.500 et seq.
Neb. Rev. Stat. 1943, 2-4301 et seq.
N.H. Rev. Stat. 1955, 431:22 et seq., 431:23 et seq.
N.J. Stat. Ann., 4:9-21.1 et seq.

Okla. Stat. Ann., Title 2, § 1451 et seq.
Pa. Purdon's Stat., Title 3, § 132-1 et seq.
R.I. Gen. Laws 1956, 2-21-1 et seq.
S.C. Code Ann. 1976, § 46-26-10 et seq.
Tenn. Code Ann., 43-11-201 et seq.
Va. Code 1950, § 3.1-126.1 et seq.

Agricultural Liming Materials and Landplaster Act
N.C. Gen. Stat. 1943, § 106-92.1 et seq.

Agricultural Linked Deposit Program
Okla. Stat. Ann., Title 2, § 1761 et seq.

Agricultural Loan Act
Alaska Stat. 1962, § 03.10.010 et seq.
P.R. Laws Ann. 1954, Title 5, § 164 et seq.

Agricultural Loan Authority Act
Mont. Code Ann., 80-12-101 et seq.

Agricultural Market Development Act
N.M. Stat. Ann., 76-20-1 et seq.

Agricultural Market Transition Act
April 4, 1996, P.L. 104-127, Title I, 7 U.S. Code §§ 7201 et seq.
Nov. 18, 1997, P.L. 105-86, 7 U.S. Code § 7236
Aug. 12, 1998, P.L. 105-228, 7 U.S. Code § 7212
Oct. 21, 1998, P.L. 105-277, 7 U.S. Code §§ 7236, 7237, 7333

Agricultural Marketing Act
June 15, 1929, Ch. 24, 46 Stat. 11, 12 U.S. Code §§ 1141 to 1141j
March 4, 1931, Ch. 520, 46 Stat. 1550, 12 U.S. Code § 1141j
June 16, 1933, Ch. 98, 48 Stat. 262, 12 U.S. Code §§ 1141c, 1141d, 1141e, 1141f, 1141j
June 3, 1935, Ch. 164, 49 Stat. 316, 12 U.S. Code §§ 1141e, 1141f, 1141j
Aug. 19, 1937, Ch. 704, 50 Stat. 704, 12 U.S. Code §§ 1141b, 1141d, 1141f
Aug. 30, 1954, Ch. 1076, 68 Stat. 968, 12 U.S. Code § 1141i
Aug. 11, 1955, Ch. 785, 69 Stat. 662, 12 U.S. Code § 1141f
June 25, 1962, P.L. 87-494, 76 Stat. 109, 12 U.S. Code § 1141d
Continued

Aug. 2, 1966, P.L. 89-525, 80 Stat. 334, 12 U.S. Code § 1141f

Ala. Code 1975, § 2-10-20 et seq.

Colo. Rev. Stat., 35-28-101 et seq.

Haw. Rev. Stat. Ann., § 163-1 et seq.

Ore. Rev. Stat., 576.006 et seq.

Tex. Agriculture Code, § 104.001 et seq.

Wis. Stat. Ann., 96.01 et seq.

Wyo. Stat. Ann., § 11-35-101 et seq.

Agricultural Marketing Act of 1946

Aug. 14, 1946, Ch. 966, 60 Stat. 1087, 7 U.S. Code §§ 1621 to 1627

Aug. 30, 1954, Ch. 1076, 68 Stat. 966, 7 U.S. Code § 1624

Aug. 9, 1955, Ch. 632, 69 Stat. 553, 7 U.S. Code § 1622

June 23, 1972, P.L. 92-318, 86 Stat. 351, 7 U.S. Code § 1626

Sept. 29, 1977, P.L. 95-113, 7 U.S. Code § 1622

Aug. 28, 1984, P.L. 98-403, 7 U.S. Code § 1622

Oct. 4, 1984, P.L. 98-443, 98 Stat. 1708, 7 U.S. Code § 1622

Oct. 21, 1998, P.L. 105-277, 7 U.S. Code § 1622

Agricultural Marketing Agreement Act of 1937

June 3, 1937, Ch. 296, 50 Stat. 246, 7 U.S. Code §§ 601, 602, 608a, 608c, 610, 612, 671, 672, 673, 674

Aug. 5, 1937, Ch. 567, 50 Stat. 563, 7 U.S. Code § 608c

Jan. 25, 1940, Ch. 13, 54 Stat. 17, 7 U.S. Code § 624

Aug. 1, 1947, Ch. 425, 61 Stat. 721, 7 U.S. Code §§ 602, 608c, 610

July 3, 1948, Ch. 827, 62 Stat. 1248, 7 U.S. Code §§ 602, 608c, 624, 672

Aug. 28, 1954, Ch. 1041, 68 Stat. 906, 7 U.S. Code §§ 602, 608c, 608e-1

Aug. 31, 1954, Ch. 1172, 68 Stat. 1047, 7 U.S. Code § 608e-1

Nov. 3, 1965, P.L. 89-321, 79 Stat. 1187, 7 U.S. Code § 608c

Nov. 8, 1965, P.L. 89-330, 79 Stat. 1270, 7 U.S. Code §§ 602, 608c

June 25, 1970, P.L. 91-292, 84 Stat. 333, 7 U.S. Code §§ 602, 608c

July 31, 1970, P.L. 91-363, 84 Stat. 687, 7 U.S. Code § 608c

Aug. 18, 1970, P.L. 91-384, 84 Stat. 827, 7 U.S. Code § 608c

Nov. 25, 1970, P.L. 91-522, 84 Stat. 1357, 7 U.S. Code § 608c

Aug. 13, 1971, P.L. 92-120, 85 Stat. 340, 7 U.S. Code § 608c

Feb. 15, 1972, P.L. 92-233, 86 Stat. 39, 7 U.S. Code § 608c

Oct. 6, 1972, P.L. 92-466, 86 Stat. 780, 7 U.S. Code § 608c

Aug. 10, 1973, P.L. 93-86, 87 Stat. 222, 7 U.S. Code § 608c

Sept. 29, 1977, P.L. 95-113, 7 U.S. Code § 608e-1

May 15, 1978, P.L. 95-279, 7 U.S. Code § 608c

Oct. 13, 1982, P.L. 97-312, 7 U.S. Code § 608e-1

Dec. 23, 1985, P.L. 99-198, 7 U.S. Code §§ 608c, 608c nt.

Nov. 28, 1990, P.L. 101-624, 7 U.S. Code § 608c

Agricultural Marketing Agreements Act

Cal. Statutes 1935, p. 1856

N.Y. Agriculture and Markets Law (Consol. Laws Ch. 69) § 258k et seq.

Agricultural Marketing and Bargaining Act

Me. Rev. Stat. Ann. 1964, Title 13, § 1953 et seq.

Mich. Comp. Laws Ann., 290.701 et seq.

Minn. Stat. Ann., 17.691 et seq.

Agricultural Marketing and Unfair Practices Act

Wash. Rev. Code Ann., 15.83.005 et seq., 15.83.900

Agricultural Marketing Research Act

Ind. Code Ann., 15-4-2-1 et seq.

Agricultural Markets Promotion and Development Act

P.R. Laws Ann. 1954, Title 5, § 101 et seq.

Agricultural Minerals Act
Ariz. Laws 1947, Ch. 136
Cal. Food and Agricultural Code 1967,
§ 14501 et seq.

Agricultural Nonpoint Financial Assistance Act
Ala. Code 1975, § 22-38-1 et seq.

Agricultural Nuisance Protection Act
Ariz. Rev. Stat. Ann., §§ 3-1051, 3-1061

Agricultural Pest Districts Act
Wash. Rev. Code Ann., 17.12.010 et seq.

Agricultural Pests and Diseases Act
Wash. Rev. Code Ann., 15.08.010 et seq.

Agricultural Policy Act
Cal. Food and Agricultural Code § 801 et seq.

Agricultural Preserve Demonstration Program Act
N.J. Stat. Ann., 4:1B-1 et seq.

Agricultural Preserves Act (Metropolitan)
Minn. Stat. Ann., 473H.01 et seq.

Agricultural Produce Dealers Law
Cal. Food and Agricultural Code 1967,
§§ 52001, 56101 et seq., 60011 et seq.

Agricultural Producer Pool Act (Beginning)
Okla. Stat. Ann., Title 74, § 5063.21 et seq.

Agricultural Producers' Marketing Law
Cal. Food and Agricultural Code 1967,
§ 59501 et seq.

Agricultural Production Input Law
Tenn. Public Acts 1986, Ch. 922

Agricultural Products and Seeds Act
Nev. Rev. Stat. 1979 Reprint, 587.015 et seq.

Agricultural Products Dealers' Act
S.C. Code Ann. 1976, § 46-41-10 et seq.
Utah Code Ann. 1953, 4-7-1 et seq.

Agricultural Products Grading Act
Ark. Code Ann. 1987, 2-20-101 et seq.

Agricultural Products Marketing Act
Cal. Agricultural Code §§ 3050 et seq.,
58601
Cal. Statutes 1935, p. 1032
Cal. Statutes 1943, p. 2060
Neb. Rev. Stat. 1943, 2-3801 et seq.

Agricultural Products Marketing and Industry Program Act
Miss. Code Ann. 1972, § 69-1-101 et seq.

Agricultural Products Processing Development Law
La. Rev. Stat. Ann., 3:446.1 et seq.

Agricultural Products Tax Law
Ky. Rev. Stat. 1971, 132.200

Agricultural Program Reporting and Recordkeeping Improvement Act of 1990
Nov. 28, 1990, P.L. 101-624, 7 U.S. Code
§ 1421 nt.

Agricultural Programs Adjustment Act of 1984
April 10, 1984, P.L. 98-258, 7 U.S. Code
§ 1421 nt.
Dec. 23, 1985, P.L. 99-198, 7 U.S. Code
§ 1981 nt.

Agricultural Promotion and Development Administration Act
P.R. Laws Ann. 1954, Title 5, § 1851 et seq.

Agricultural Promotion Programs Act of 1990
Nov. 28, 1990, P.L. 101-624, 7 U.S. Code
§ 2278 nt., 6001 nt.

Agricultural Promotional Campaign Act
Fla. Stat. Ann., 571.21 et seq.

Agricultural Property Tax Act
Minn. Stat. Ann., 273.111

Agricultural Prorate Act
Ariz. Rev. Stat. Ann., § 3-401 et seq.
Continued

Cal. Food and Agricultural Code 1967,
§§ 59513 et seq., 59641 et seq.

Agricultural Protective Act
Tex. Agriculture Code, § 101.001 et seq.

Agricultural Reconciliation Act of 1987
Dec. 22, 1987, P.L. 100-203, 7 U.S. Code
§ 1421 nt.

Agricultural Reconciliation Act of 1989
Dec. 19, 1989, P.L. 101-239, 7 U.S. Code
§ 1421 nt.

Agricultural Reconciliation Act of 1990
Nov. 5, 1990, P.L. 101-508, 7 U.S. Code
§ 1421 nt.

Agricultural Reconciliation Act of 1993
Aug. 10, 1993, P.L. 103-66, 7 U.S. Code
§ 1421 nt.

Agricultural Research Act
June 29, 1935, Ch. 338, 49 Stat. 438, 7 U.S.
Code § 329 (See 7 U.S. Code §§ 341 to 343,
344 to 348)
June 6, 1945, Ch. 175, 59 Stat. 231 (See 7
U.S. Code §§ 341 to 343, 344 to 348)
June 12, 1952, Ch. 419, 66 Stat. 135, 7 U.S.
Code § 329
July 14, 1960, P.L. 86-658, 74 Stat. 525, 7
U.S. Code § 329
Mich. Comp. Laws Ann., 390.161

**Agricultural Research, Development and
Promotion Act of 1970**
N.J. Stat. Ann., 4:10-43 et seq.

**Agricultural Research, Extension, and
Education Reform Act of 1998**
June 23, 1998, P.L. 105-185, 7 U.S. Code
§ 7601 nt.
Oct. 21, 1998, P.L. 105-277, 7 U.S. Code
§ 7621

Agricultural Revitalization Authority Act
Neb. Rev. Stat. 1943, 2-4701 et seq.

**Agricultural School Building Loan Act
(Essex County)**
Mass. Acts 1961, Ch. 387

**Agricultural School Loan Act (Bristol
County)**
Mass. Acts 1958, Ch. 248

**Agricultural School Poultry Plant Loan Act
(Bristol County)**
Mass. Acts 1963, Ch. 603

**Agricultural Science and Institute of Food
Supplemental Retirement Act**
Fla. Stat. Ann., 121.40

Agricultural Seed Growers Registration Act
Tex. Agriculture Code, § 101.001 et seq.

Agricultural Seed Warehousemen Act
Mont. Rev. Code 1947, 3-301 et seq.

Agricultural Seeds Act
Ind. Code Ann., 15-4-1-1 et seq.
Iowa Code Ann., 199.1 et seq.
Kan. Stat. Ann., 2-1415 et seq.
Mich. Comp. Laws Ann., 286.701 et seq.
Mont. Code Ann., 80-5-101 et seq.
Nev. Rev. Stat. 1979 Reprint, 587.015 et seq.
Ohio Rev. Code 1953, 907.01 et seq.
S.C. Code Ann. 1976, § 46-21-10 et seq.
Tex. Agriculture Code, § 61.001 et seq.
Wash. Rev. Code Ann., 15.49.005 et seq.

Agricultural Services Administration Act
P.R. Laws Ann. 1954, Title 5, § 31 et seq.

Agricultural Statistics Act
Ill. Comp. Stat. 1992, Ch. 505, § 15/0.01 et
seq.
Ill. Rev. Stat. 1991, Ch. 5, § 90a.9 et seq.

**Agricultural Subterminal Facilities Act of
1980**
Sept. 25, 1980, P.L. 96-358, 7 U.S. Code
§ 3701 nt.

Agricultural Trade Act of 1978
Oct. 21, 1978, P.L. 95-501, 5 U.S. Code
§ 5314; 7 U.S. Code §§ 612c-3 nt., 1707a et
seq., 1761, 1761 nt., 1762 et seq., 2211a,
2211a nt.;19 U.S. Code § 2431 nt.

Nov. 28, 1990, P.L. 101-624, 7 U.S. Code §§ 612c-3 nt., 1707b to 1707d, 1761 nt., 1765b-1, 2211a, 2211a nt., 5601 et seq. generally, 5711 to 5713; 19 U.S. Code § 2431 nt.

Dec. 13, 1991, P.L. 102-237, 7 U.S. Code §§ 5603, prec. 5621, 5622 to 5624, 5651, 5664, 5676, 5695, 5711, 5712

Oct. 24, 1992, P.L. 102-511, 7 U.S. Code §§ 5602, 5621, 5622, 5651

Aug. 10, 1993, P.L. 103-66, 7 U.S. Code §§ 1421 nt., 1445b-3a nt., 5623, 5641

Dec. 8, 1994, P.L. 103-465, 7 U.S. Code §§ 5651, 5623

April 4, 1996, P.L. 104-127, 7 U.S. Code §§ 5602, 5603, 5606, 5621 to 5623, 5641, 5651, 5661, 5662, 5664, 5674, 5677, 5693, 5711, 5713, prec. 5721, 5721 to 5723

Agricultural Trade and Export Policy Commission Act

Aug. 30, 1984, P.L. 98-412, 7 U.S. Code § 1691 nt.

Agricultural Trade Development and Assistance Act of 1954

July 10, 1954, Ch. 469, 68 Stat. 454, 7 U.S. Code §§ 1427, 1431, 1691 et seq., 1701 to 1709, 1721 to 1724

April 25, 1955, Ch. 27, 69 Stat. 44, 7 U.S. Code § 1702

Aug. 12, 1955, Ch. 624, 69 Stat. 721, 7 U.S. Code §§ 1703, 1706

May 28, 1956, Ch. 327, 70 Stat. 201, 7 U.S. Code §§ 1703, 1721, 1723

July 18, 1956, Ch. 627, 70 Stat. 564, 7 U.S. Code § 1704

Aug. 3, 1956, Ch. 933, 70 Stat. 988, 7 U.S. Code §§ 1703, 1704, 1721

Aug. 13, 1957, P.L. 85-128, 71 Stat. 345, 7 U.S. Code §§ 1693, 1703, 1704, 1704a, 1709, 1723, 1724

June 30, 1958, P.L. 85-477, 72 Stat. 275, 7 U.S. Code § 1704

Sept. 6, 1958, P.L. 85-931, 72 Stat. 1790, 7 U.S. Code §§ 1692, 1701, 1703, 1704, 1709, 1724

Sept. 21, 1959, P.L. 86-341, 73 Stat. 606, 7 U.S. Code §§ 1431c, 1694 to 1697, 1703, 1704, 1709, 1723, 1724, 1731 to 1736

May 14, 1960, P.L. 86-472, 74 Stat. 140, 7 U.S. Code §§ 1722, 1723

May 4, 1961, P.L. 87-28, 75 Stat. 64, 7 U.S. Code § 1703

Aug. 8, 1961, P.L. 87-128, 75 Stat. 306, 7 U.S. Code §§ 1701, 1703, 1704, 1706, 1709, 1723, 1724

Sept. 4, 1961, P.L. 87-195, 75 Stat. 463, 7 U.S. Code § 1704

Sept. 27, 1962, P.L. 87-703, 203, 76 Stat. 610, 7 U.S. Code §§ 1697, 1731 to 1733, 1735, 1736

Oct. 18, 1962, P.L. 87-839, 76 Stat. 1074, 7 U.S. Code § 1704

Dec. 16, 1963, P.L. 88-205, 77 Stat. 390, 7 U.S. Code §§ 1701, 1705, 1706, 1722

Oct. 8, 1964, P.L. 88-638, 78 Stat. 1035, 7 U.S. Code §§ 1693, 1701 to 1704, 1707 to 1709, 1723, 1724, 1733

Aug. 4, 1965, P.L. 89-106, 79 Stat. 432, 7 U.S. Code § 1704

Sept. 6, 1965, P.L. 89-171, 79 Stat. 662, 7 U.S. Code § 1707

Nov. 11, 1966, P.L. 89-808, 80 Stat. 1526, 7 U.S. Code §§ 1691, 1701 to 1710, 1721 to 1725, 1731 to 1736d

July 29, 1968, P.L. 90-436, 82 Stat. 450, 7 U.S. Code §§ 1692, 1702 to 1704, 1736a, 1736c

Nov. 30, 1970, P.L. 91-524, 84 Stat. 1379, 7 U.S. Code §§ 1704, 1736c

July 1, 1971, P.L. 92-42, 85 Stat. 99, 7 U.S. Code § 1732

Aug. 10, 1973, P.L. 93-86, 87 Stat. 237, 7 U.S. Code §§ 1703, 1736a, 1736e

Dec. 20, 1975, P.L. 94-161, 89 Stat. 849, 7 U.S. Code §§ 1691, 1691a, 1703, 1704, 1706, 1709, 1711, 1721, 1726, 1736a, 1736b, 1736f

Aug. 3, 1977, P.L. 95-88, 7 U.S. Code §§ 1427 et seq.

Sept. 29, 1977, P.L. 95-113, 7 U.S. Code §§ 1702, 1715 et seq.

Aug. 14, 1979, P.L. 96-53, 7 U.S. Code §§ 1703, 1704, 1722, 1726, 1727, 1727a, 1727b, 1727d to 1727f, 1731, 1734, 1736g

Sept. 29, 1979, 7 U.S. Code § 1732

Oct. 12, 1984, P.L. 98-473, 7 U.S. Code § 1723

Nov. 8, 1984, P.L. 98-623, 7 U.S. Code §§ 1707, 1732

Aug. 8, 1985, P.L. 99-83, 7 U.S. Code §§ 1721, 1722, 1727a, 1736b

Continued

Nov. 13, 1985, P.L. 99-151

Dec. 23, 1985, P.L. 99-198, 7 U.S. Code §§ 1691, 1701 to 1709, 1721 to 1727g

Aug. 23, 1988, P.L. 100-418, 102 Stat. 1346, 7 U.S. Code §§ 1704, 1708 Oct. 31, 1988, P.L. 100-576, 7 U.S. Code §§ 1727, 1727 nt.

Nov. 5, 1990, P.L. 101-508, 7 U.S. Code §§ 1722, 1736, 1736a

Nov. 28, 1990, P.L. 101-624, 7 U.S. Code §§ 1691, 1691 nt., 1691a, 1701 to 1705, 1721 to 1727e, 1731 to 1736g-1, 1737 to 1738m

Dec. 13, 1991, P.L. 102-237, 7 U.S. Code §§ 1733, 1736, 1736a, 1736c, 1736d, 1736e, 1737, 1738b, 1738c, 1738e, 1738f, 1738i, 1738k, 1738m, 1738n

Oct. 27, 1992, P.L. 102-532, 7 U.S. Code §§ 1738m, 1738n to 1738r

Oct. 28, 1992, P.L. 102-549, 7 U.S. Code § 1738i

Dec. 21, 1995, P.L. 104-66, 7 U.S. Code § 1736a

April 4, 1996, P.L. 104-127, 7 U.S. Code §§ 1691a, 1701 to 1705, 1722 to 1725, 1726a, 1727e, 1731 to 1734, 1736, 1736a to 1736d, 1736f, 1736g, 1736g-2, 1736g-3, 1737

Agricultural Trade Suspension Adjustment Act of 1980

Dec. 3, 1980, P.L. 96-494, 7 U.S. Code § 4001 nt.

April 4, 1996, P.L. 104-127, 7 U.S. Code § 4001

Nov. 13, 1998, P.L. 105-385, 7 U.S. Code § 4001

Agricultural Unbonded Warehouse Law

Iowa Code 1962, 544.1 et seq.

Agricultural Unemployment Compensation Act

Haw. Rev. Stat. Ann., § 383-9 et seq.

Agricultural Viability Act

Me. Rev. Stat. Ann. 1964, Title 7, § 311 et seq.

Agricultural Warehouse Act

Cal. Food and Agricultural Code 1967, § 54601 et seq.

N.C. Gen. Stat. 1943, § 106-429.1 et seq.

Agricultural Warehouse, Commodity Dealer, and Grain Standards Act

Mont. Code Ann., 80-4-401 et seq.

Agricultural Water Conservation and Management Act

Cal. Water Code § 10520 et seq.

Agricultural Water Management Planning Act

Cal. Water Code § 10800 et seq.

Agricultural Water Requirements Act

N.M. Laws 1967, Ch. 220

Agricultural Water Suppliers Efficient Water Management Practices Act

Cal. Water Code § 10900 et seq.

Agricultural Worker Safety Act

Fla. Stat. Ann., 487.201 et seq.

Agriculture Act (Sustainable)

Ill. Rev. Stat. 1991, Ch. 5, § 2651 et seq.

Pa. Purdon's Stat., Title 3, § 2101 et seq.

Agriculture and Business Development Authority Act

S.D. Laws 1986, Ch. 16, § 2 et seq.

Agriculture and Commerce Reorganization Act

Miss. Code Ann. 1972, § 69-1-201 et seq.

Agriculture and Consumer Protection Act of 1973

Aug. 10, 1973, P.L. 93-86, 87 Stat. 221, 7 U.S. Code §§ 135b nt., 428b, 450j, 450l, 608c, 612c nt., 612c-2, 612c-3, 624 nt., 1282a, 1301, 1305 to 1307, 1330 to 1334 nt., 1334a-1, 1335 nt., 1336 nt., 1338 nt., 1339 nt., 1342 nt., 1342a nt., 1343 nt., 1344 nt., 1344b, 1345 nt., 1346 nt., 1350, 1374, 1377 to 1379 nt., 1379c, 1379d nt., 1379g, 1385 nt., 1427 nt., 1427a, 1428, 1434, 1441 nt., 1441a, 1444, 1445a, 1446, 1446a, 1446d nt., 1703, 1736c, 1736e, 1782, 1787, 1925, 1926, 1932, 2012, 2014, 2016, 2019, 2025, 2026, 2119, 2651, 2654; 13U.S. Code § 142 nt.; 16 U.S. Code §§ 1501 to 1510; 45 U.S. Code § 71 nt.

Oct. 18, 1973, P.L. 93-125, 87 Stat. 450, 7 U.S. Code §§ 608c nt., 624 nt.

July 12, 1974, P.L. 93-347, 88 Stat. 340, 7 U.S. Code § 612c nt.

Sept. 29, 1977, P.L. 95-113, 7 U.S. Code §§ 1427a, 612c nt. et seq.; 16 U.S. Code § 1505

July 1, 1978, P.L. 95-313, 16 U.S. Code §§ 1509, 1510

Dec. 23, 1985, P.L. 99-198, 7 U.S. Code § 612c nt.

Nov. 28, 1990, P.L. 101-624, 7 U.S. Code §§ 612c nt.

Dec. 13, 1991, P.L. 102-237, 7 U.S. Code § 612c nt.

April 4, 1996, P.L. 104-127, 7 U.S. Code § 612c nt.

Aug. 22, 1996, P.L. 104-193, 7 U.S. Code § 612c nt.

Agriculture and Food Act of 1981

Dec. 22, 1981, P.L. 97-98, 7 U.S. Code § 1281 nt.

Aug. 30, 1984, P.L. 98-412, 7 U.S. Code § 1691 nt.

Dec. 23, 1985, P.L. 99-198, 7 U.S. Code §§ 608c nt., 1431e, 1736j, 1736m, 2242a, 4102, 4110

Nov. 14, 1986, P.L. 99-661, 7 U.S. Code § 1431e nt.

Jan. 8, 1988, P.L. 100-237, 7 U.S. Code § 1431e

Nov. 28, 1990, P.L. 101-624, 7 U.S. Code §§ 608c nt., 1431e, 1736i to 1736k, 1736n, 2242a, 4102, 4110; 16 U.S. Code §§ 3459, 3461

Dec. 13, 1991, P.L. 102-237, 7 U.S. Code § 1431e

Aug. 10, 1993, P.L. 103-66, 7 U.S. Code § 608c nt.

Dec. 21, 1995, P.L. 104-66, 16 U.S. Code § 3415 et seq.

April 4, 1996, P.L. 104-127, 7 U.S. Code §§ 1431e, 1736m, 1736n; 16 U.S. Code §§ 3401, 3411 to 3414, 3416 to 3418, 3420, 3431 to 3436, 3441 to 3445, 3461

Agriculture and Industrial Branch Rail Line Revitalization Act

Neb. Rev. Stat. 1943, 74-1401 et seq.

Agriculture and Markets Law

N.Y. Consol. Laws, Ch. 69

Agriculture and Water Policy Coordination Act

Nov. 28, 1990, P.L. 101-624, 7 U.S. Code §§ 5501 to 5505

Agriculture Center and Horse Park Authority

Fla. Stat. Ann., 570.952

Agriculture Code

Pa. Purdon's Stat., Title 3, § 101 et seq.

Agriculture, Conservation, and Trade Act of 1990

Oct. 13, 1994, P.L. 103-354, 7 U.S. Code § 1926-1

Agriculture Cooperative Marketing Act

Miss. Code Ann. 1972, § 79-19-1 et seq.

Agriculture Department Act

Colo. Rev. Stat., 35-1-101 et seq.

Agriculture Education Loan Forgiveness Act

Pa. Purdon's Stat., Title 24, § 5198.1 et seq.

Agriculture-Environmental and Consumer Protection Appropriation Act of 1972

Aug. 10, 1971, P.L. 92-73, 85 Stat. 183, 7 U.S. Code §§ 411b, 435, 1623a, 2254; 15 U.S. Code § 713a-10; 16 U.S. Code §§ 590e-1, 590e-2; 21 U.S. Code § 129

Agriculture-Environmental and Consumer Protection Appropriation Acts

Aug. 22, 1972, P.L. 92-399, 86 Stat. 593, 7 U.S. Code §§ 411b, 435, 1623a, 2254; 15 U.S. Code § 713a-10; 16 U.S. Code §§ 590e-1, 590e-2; 21 U.S. Code § 129

Oct. 24, 1973, P.L. 93-135, 87 Stat. 468, 7 U.S. Code §§ 411b, 435, 1623a, 2254; 15 U.S. Code § 713a-10; 16 U.S. Code §§ 590e-1, 590e-2; 21 U.S. Code § 129

Agriculture Export Relief Act of 1998

July 14, 1998, P.L. 105-194, 22 U.S. Code § 2751 nt.

Agriculture Fertilizing System
Okla. Stat. Ann., Title 68, § 1358 et seq.

Agriculture Foreign Market Development Export Incentive Program Act
Cal. Food and Agricultural Code 1967, § 58551 et seq.

Agriculture Gas Users Act
April 4, 1996, P.L. 104-127, 110 Stat. 888, Titles 1 to 9
Tex. Utilities Code, § 123.021 et seq.

Agriculture-Linked Investment Program
Pa. Purdon's Stat., Title 3, § 1721 et seq.

Agriculture Programs Act (Production)
Ill. Rev. Stat. 1991, Ch. 5, § 2550 et seq.

Agriculture Regulatory Act
April 4, 1940, Ch. 75, 54 Stat. 81, 7 U.S. Code §§ 450c to 450g

Agriculture Retention and Development Act
N.J. Stat. Ann., 4:1C-11 et seq.

Agriculture, Rural Development, and Related Agencies Appropriations Act, 1979
Oct. 11, 1978, P.L. 95-448, 91 Stat. 821

Agriculture, Rural Development, and Related Agencies Appropriations Act, 1980
Nov, 9, 1979, P.L. 96-108, 93 Stat. 821

Agriculture, Rural Development, and Related Agencies Appropriations Act, 1981
Dec. 15, 1980, P.L. 96-528, 94 Stat. 3095
Sept. 13, 1982, P.L. 97-258, 96 Stat. 1068

Agriculture, Rural Development, and Related Agencies Appropriations Act, 1982
Dec. 23, 1981, P.L. 97-103, 95 Stat. 1467

Agriculture, Rural Development, and Related Agencies Appropriations Act, 1983
Dec. 18, 1982, P.L. 97-370, 96 Stat. 1787

Aug. 22, 1986, P.L. 99-386, 100 Stat. 823

Agriculture, Rural Development, and Related Agencies Appropriations Act, 1986
Dec. 19, 1985, P.L. 99-190, 99 Stat. 1185
Dec. 22, 1987, P.L. 100-202, 101 Stat. 1329-433

Agriculture, Rural Development, and Related Agencies Appropriations Act, 1987
Oct. 18, 1986, P.L. 99-500, 100 Stat. 3341
Oct. 30, 1986, P.L. 99-591, 100 Stat. 3341
May 27, 1987, P.L. 100-45, 100 Stat. 321, 323

Agriculture, Rural Development, Food and Drug Administration, and Related Agencies Appropriations Act, 1992
Oct. 28, 1991, P.L. 102-142, 105 Stat. 878
April 4, 1996, P.L. 104-127, 7 U.S. Code § 2272a

Agriculture, Rural Development, Food and Drug Administration, and Related Agencies Appropriations Act, 1993
Aug. 14, 1992, P.L. 102-341, 7 U.S. Code §§ 612c nt., 1623a, 1981a nt., 2209b, 2254, 4201, 4201 nt.; 12 U.S. Code § 2278a-3 nt.; 16 U.S. Code §§ 590e-1, 590e-2; 20 U.S. Code § 191 nt.; 21 U.S. Code § 129; 42 U.S. Code §§ 1776a, 1776b
Sept. 23, 1992, P.L. 102-368, 106 Stat. 1130

Agriculture, Rural Development, Food and Drug Administration, and Related Agencies Appropriations Act, 1994
Oct. 21, 1993, P.L. 103-111, 107 Stat. 1046

Agriculture, Rural Development, Food and Drug Administration, and Related Agencies Appropriations Act, 1995
Sept. 30, 1994, P.L. 103-330, 108 Stat. 2435

Agriculture, Rural Development, Food and Drug Administration, and Related Agencies Appropriations Act, 1996
Oct. 21, 1995, P.L. 104-37, 109 Stat. 299

Agriculture, Rural Development, Food and Drug Administration, and Related Agencies Appropriations Act, 1997
Aug. 6, 1996, P.L. 104-180, 110 Stat. 1569

Agriculture, Rural Development, Food and Drug Administration, and Related Agencies Appropriations Act, 1998
Nov. 18, 1997, P.L. 105-86, 111 Stat. 2079

Agriculture, Rural Development, Food and Drug Administration, and Related Agencies Appropriations Act, 1999
Oct. 21, 1998, P.L. 105-277, 101(b), 112 Stat. 2681

Agriculture Society Act (County)
Neb. Rev. Stat. 1943, 2-250 to 2-273

Agro-Industry Act (Puerto Rican Purebred Paso Fino Horse)
P.R. Laws Ann. 1954, Title 5, § 2001 et seq.

Ahearn Law (Teachers' Salaries)
N.Y. Laws 1899, Ch. 417

AHERA
See Asbestos Hazard Emergency Response Act of 1986

Aid Act (Dependent Children)
Mass. Gen. Laws Ann., 118:1 et seq.

Aid Act (Military)
Mass. Gen. Laws Ann., 115:1 et seq.

Aid Act (Mutual)
Fla. Stat. Ann., 23.12 et seq.

Aid Act (School)
Vt. Stat. Ann., Title 16, § 3469

Aid and Services to Needy Families with Children Law
Tenn. Code Ann., 71-3-101 et seq.

Aid for Hearing Act
S.C. Code Ann. 1976, § 40-25-10 et seq.

Aid for the Adoption of Children Act
Cal. Welfare and Institutions Code § 16115 et seq.

Aid for Urban Environmental Concerns Act
N.J. Stat. Ann., 13:1H-8 et seq.

Aid Highway Act
See Federal Aid Highway Acts

Aid in an Emergency Act (Interstate Compact Mutual Military)
Conn. Gen. Stat. Ann., § 27-38

Aid the Endangered Act
Vt. Stat. Ann., Title 12, § 519

Aid to Aviation Channeling Act (Federal)
Ind. Code Ann., 8-21-8-1

Aid to Cities Act (Streets)
Cal. Streets and Highways Code § 1680 et seq.

Aid to Dependent Children Act
June 14, 1944, Ch. 257, 58 Stat. 277
Alaska Stat. 1962, § 47.25.310 et seq.
Cal. Welfare and Institutions Code § 11200 et seq.
Colo. Rev. Stat., 26-2-101 et seq.
D.C. Code Ann., § 3-201.1 et seq.
Ga. Code Ann., 49-4-100 et seq.
Ill. Rev. Stat. 1965, Ch. 23, § 601 et seq.
Iowa Code Ann., 239.1 et seq.
Ky. Rev. Stat. 1971, 205.010 et seq.
Mass. Gen. Laws Ann., 118:1 et seq.
Me. Rev. Stat. Ann. 1964, Title 22, § 3741 et seq.
Minn. Stat. Ann., 256.72 et seq.
Mo. Rev. Stat., 208.040 et seq.
N.C. Gen. Stat. 1943, § 108A-27 et seq.
N.D. Cent. Code, 50-09-01 et seq.
Nev. Rev. Stat. 1979 Reprint, 425.010 et seq.
Ohio Rev. Code 1953, 5107.01 et seq.
R.I. Gen. Laws 1956, 40-6-4 et seq.
Tenn. Code Ann., 71-3-101 et seq.
Wash. Rev. Code Ann., 74.12.010 et seq.

Aid to Disabled Persons Act
Iowa Code 1973, 241A.1 et seq.

Aid to Education Act
Mich. Comp. Laws 1948, 388.611 et seq.

Aid to Families with Dependent Children Act
Cal. Welfare and Institutions Code § 11350 et seq.
N.C. Gen. Stat. 1943, §§ 108A-27 to 108A-39

Aid to Indigent Defendants Act
Kan. Stat. Ann., 22-4501 et seq.

Aid to Indigent Tuberculars Act
Colo. Rev. Stat., 119-2-1 et seq.

Aid to Law Enforcement and Victims of and Witnesses to Crimes Assistance Act
Colo. Rev. Stat., 24-4.2-101 et seq.

Aid to Needy Blind Law
Cal. Welfare and Institutions Code § 3000 et seq.

Aid to Needy Children Law
Cal. Welfare and Institutions Code § 11200 et seq.

Aid to Subdivisions Act
S.C. Code Ann. 1976, § 6-27-10 et seq.

Aid to the Blind Act
Ariz. Rev. Stat. Ann., § 46-281 et seq.
Cal. Welfare and Institution Code § 12500 et seq.
Colo. Rev. Stat., 16-2-1 et seq.
Colo. Rev. Stat., 26-2-120 et seq.
Del. Code of 1974, Title 31, § 2301 et seq.
Ga. Code Ann., 49-4-50 et seq.
Ill. Rev. Stat. 1991, Ch. 23, § 3-1 et seq.
Iowa Code 1973, 241.1 et seq.
Ky. Rev. Stat. 1971, Superseded Vols., 207.020 et seq.
Mo. Rev. Stat., 209.210 et seq.
Neb. Rev. Stat. 1943, 68-401 et seq.
N.Y. Social Services Law (Consol. Laws Ch. 55) §§ 283, 300 et seq.

Ore. Rev. Stat., 412.005 et seq.
R.I. Gen. Laws 1956, 40-9-1 et seq.
Tenn. Code Ann., 71-4-101 et seq.
Wash. Rev. Code Ann., 74.18.010 et seq.

Aid to the Disabled Act
Colo. Rev. Stat., 26-2-101 et seq.
Ga. Code Ann., 49-4-80 et seq.
Neb. Rev. Stat. 1943, 68-1001 et seq.
Tenn. Code Ann., 71-4-1101 et seq.

Aid to the Permanently and Totally Disabled Act
Alaska Stat. 1962, § 47.25.790 et seq.

Aid, Trade, and Competitiveness Act of 1992
Oct. 28, 1992, P.L. 102-549, 22 U.S. Code § 2421a

Aider and Abettor Act
June 25, 1948, Ch. 645, 62 Stat. 684, 18 U.S. Code § 2
Oct. 31, 1951, Ch. 655, 65 Stat. 717, 18 U.S. Code § 2

Aiding Escape Act
Ill. Rev. Stat. 1991, Ch. 38, § 31-7

AIDS Amendments of 1988
Nov. 4, 1988, P.L. 100-607, 42 U.S. Code §§ 201 nt., 300cc et seq., 300aaa et seq.

AIDS Assistance Act
N.J. Stat. Ann., 26:5C-1

AIDS Confidentiality Act
Ill. Comp. Stat. 1992, Ch. 410, § 305/1 et seq.

AIDS Housing Opportunity Act
Nov. 28, 1990, P.L. 101-625, 42 U.S. Code §§ 12901 to 12912

AIDS Prevention Act
Mont. Code Ann., 50-16-1000 et seq.
Mont. Laws 1989, Ch. 614

AIDS Registry Act
Ill. Comp. Stat. 1992, Ch. 410, § 310/1 et seq.

AIDS Research Confidentiality Act
Cal. Health and Safety Code § 199.30 et seq.

Aigler-Ball Act (Corporations)
Ohio Rev. Code 1953, 1701.01 et seq.

Aikin-Gilmer Act (School Administration)
Tex. Education Code, § 11.01 et seq.

Aikin-Gilmer Act (Teachers' Retirement)
Tex. Education Code, § 3.01 et seq.

Air Act (Clean Indoor)
Fla. Stat. Ann., 386.201 et seq.
Me. Rev. Stat. Ann. 1964, Title 22, § 1578
Neb. Rev. Stat. 1943, 2-3101 et seq.
Wash. Rev. Code 1983, 70.160.010 et seq.

Air and Surface Transportation Act (Northeast Georgia)
Ga. Laws 1991, p. 4596

Air and Surface Transportation Commission Act (Middle Georgia)
Ga. Laws 1990, p. 5170

Air and Water Pollution Control Act
Ark. Code Ann. 1987, 8-4-101 et seq.
Fla. Stat. Ann., 403.011 et seq.
Miss. Code Ann. 1972, § 49-17-1 et seq.

Air and Water Pollution Control Act (Lake County)
Fla. Special Laws 1967, Ch. 67-1608

Air and Water Pollution Control Act (Orange County)
Fla. Special Laws 1967, Ch. 67-1830

Air and Water Pollution Control Act (Seminole County)
Fla. Special Laws 1967, Ch. 67-2084

Air and Water Pollution Control Tax Refund Act
Neb. Rev. Stat. 1943, 77-27, 149 et seq.

Air and Water Quality Reporting Act
N.C. Gen. Stat. 1943, § 143-215.63 et seq.

Air and Water Resources Act
N.C. Gen. Stat. 1943, §§ 143-211 to 143-215.73

Air Base Act
See Wilcox Air Base Act

Air Brakes Act (Railroads)
March 2, 1903, Ch. 976, 32 Stat. 943, 45 U.S. Code § 9
April 11, 1958, P.L. 85-375, 72 Stat. 86, 45 U.S. Code § 9
July 5, 1994, P.L. 103-272, 108 Stat. 1379

Air Cargo Airport Authority Act
N.C. Gen. Stat. 1943, § 63A-1 et seq.

Air Carrier Access Act of 1986
Oct. 2, 1986, P.L. 99-435, 49 Appx. U.S. Code § 1301 nt.

Air Carrier Economic Regulation Act
June 23, 1938, Ch. 601, 52 Stat. 987 (See 49 U.S. Code §§ 1371 to 1386)
July 2, 1940, Ch. 526, 54 Stat. 735 (See 49 U.S. Code § 1375)
May 16, 1942, Ch. 318, 56 Stat. 301 (See 49 U.S. Code § 1382)
June 23, 1952, Ch. 485, 66 Stat. 286 (See 49 U.S. Code § 1375)
July 14, 1952, Ch. 740, 66 Stat. 628 (See 49 U.S. Code § 1381)
May 19, 1955, Ch. 41, 69 Stat. 49 (See 49 U.S. Code § 1371)
July 20, 1956, Ch. 650, 70 Stat. 591 (See 49 U.S. Code § 1371)
Aug. 1, 1956, Ch. 816, 70 Stat. 784 (See 49 U.S. Code § 1373)
Aug. 26, 1957, P.L. 85-166, 71 Stat. 415 (See 49 U.S. Code § 1371)
April 9, 1958, P.L. 85-373, 72 Stat. 84 (See 49 U.S. Code § 1386)

Air Carriers Act
Ida. Code 1947, 61-1101 et seq.
Ill. Rev. Stat. 1989, Ch. 15 1/2, § 501 et seq.
R.I. Gen. Laws 1956, 39-11-1 et seq.

Air Commerce Act
Ala. Code 1975, § 37-9-1 et seq.
Alaska Stat. 1962, Replaced Titles, § 02.05.010 et seq.
Ark. Code Ann. 1987, 23-14-101 et seq.
Ida. Code 1947, 21-301 et seq.
Continued

Vt. Stat. Ann., Title 5, §§ 301 et seq., 71 et seq.

Air Commerce Act of 1926

May 20, 1926, Ch. 344, 44 Stat. 568 (See 49 U.S. Code §§ 1301, 1472, 1473, 1507 to 1509)

Aug. 5, 1950, Ch. 591, 64 Stat. 414 (See 49 U.S. Code §§ 1472, 1473, 1509)

Oct. 11, 1951, Ch. 495, 65 Stat. 407 (See 49 U.S. Code § 1509)

Aug. 8, 1953, Ch. 379, 67 Stat. 489 (See 49 U.S. Code § 1508)

June 16, 1982, P.L. 97-195, 96 Stat. 115

Air Conditioning and Refrigeration Contractor License Law

Tex. Rev. Civ. Stat., Art. 8861

Air Conditioning Contractor License Law

Tex. Rev. Civ. Stat., Art. 8861

Air Conditioning, Heating and Ventilation Act

Mont. Code Ann. 1979, 37-70-101 et seq.

Air Conditioning, Refrigeration, Heating and Ventilation Contractors Act

Md. Ann. Code 1974, Art. BR, § 9A-601 et seq.

Air Conditioning, Ventilation, and Heating Contractors' Act

Ky. Acts 1994, Ch. 59, §§ 1 to 21

Air Conservation Act

Mo. Rev. Stat., 643.010 et seq.

Utah Code Ann. 1953, 19-2-101 et seq., 26-13-1 et seq.

Air Contamination Control Act

P.R. Laws Ann. 1954, Title 24, § 341 et seq.

Air Control Act

La. Rev. Stat. Ann., 40:2201 et seq.

Air Corps Act

July 2, 1926, Ch. 721, 44 Stat. 780

Oct. 12, 1949, Ch. 681, 63 Stat. 839

Aug. 10, 1956, Ch. 1041, 70A Stat. 641

Air Emissions Bubble Rule-Generic

Fla. Stat. Ann., 403.08735

Air Engineering Development Center Act of 1949

Oct. 27, 1949, Ch. 766, 63 Stat. 937, 50 U.S. Code §§ 521, 521 nt., 522 to 524

Sept. 21, 1950, Ch. 969, 64 Stat. 895, 50 U.S. Code § 524

Air Engineering Duty Act

June 5, 1935, Ch. 175, 49 Stat. 323

Air Force Academy Act

April 1, 1954, Ch. 127, 68 Stat. 47 (See 10 U.S. Code §§ 541, 8075, 9331, 9331 nt.)

Aug. 3, 1956, Ch. 939, 70 Stat. 1018 (See 10 U.S. Code § 9331 nt.)

Aug. 30, 1957, P.L. 85-241, 71 Stat. 559, 10 U.S. Code § 9331 nt.

Aug. 20, 1958, P.L. 85-685, 72 Stat. 659, 10 U.S. Code § 9331 nt.

June 27, 1961, P.L. 87-57, 75 Stat. 108, 10 U.S. Code § 9331 nt.

July 21, 1968, P.L. 90-408, 82 Stat. 385, 10 U.S. Code § 9331 nt.

Air Force Base Retrocession Law (Chanute)

Ill. Comp. Stat. 1992, Ch. 5, § 537/5-1 et seq.

Air Force Headquarters Act

May 12, 1939, Ch. 127, 53 Stat. 740 (See 10 U.S. Code §§ 3961, 3962, 3991)

Air Force Organization Act of 1951

Sept. 19, 1951, Ch. 407, 65 Stat. 326

April 1, 1954, Ch. 127, 68 Stat. 48

Aug. 3, 1954, Ch. 652, 68 Stat. 649

Aug. 9, 1955, Ch. 654, 69 Stat. 579

Air Licensing Act

Alaska Stat. 1962, § 02.35.010 et seq.

La. Rev. Stat. Ann., 2:1 et seq.

Me. Rev. Stat. Ann. 1964, Title 6, § 44

N.D. Cent. Code, 2-05-01 et seq.

Tenn. Code Ann., 42-2-101 et seq.

Air Mail Acts

Feb. 2, 1925, Ch. 128, 43 Stat. 805 (See 39 U.S. Code § 5401 et seq.)

Feb. 21, 1925, Ch. 283, 43 Stat. 960
June 3, 1926, Ch. 460, 44 Stat. 692
March 8, 1928, Ch. 149, 45 Stat. 248
May 17, 1928, Ch. 603, 45 Stat. 594
March 2, 1929, Ch. 478, 45 Stat. 1450
April 29, 1930, Ch. 223, 46 Stat. 259
March 27, 1934, Ch. 100, 48 Stat. 508
June 12, 1934, Ch. 466, 48 Stat. 933
June 19, 1934, Ch. 652, 48 Stat. 1102
June 26, 1934, Ch. 762, 48 Stat. 1243
Aug. 14, 1935, Ch. 530, 49 Stat. 614
Aug. 24, 1935, Ch. 638, 49 Stat. 744
Aug. 20, 1937, Ch. 718, 50 Stat. 725
Jan. 14, 1938, Ch. 9, 52 Stat. 6
April 15, 1938, Ch. 157, 52 Stat. 218
June 23, 1938, Ch. 601, 52 Stat. 997
July 6, 1945, Ch. 274, 59 Stat. 451
Aug. 14, 1946, Ch. 963, 60 Stat. 1062
June 23, 1948, Ch. 607, 62 Stat. 576
June 29, 1948, Ch. 717, 62 Stat. 1097
July 3, 1948, Ch. 830, 62 Stat. 1261
Aug. 30, 1949, Ch. 523, 63 Stat. 680
May 27, 1958, P.L. 85-426, 72 Stat. 138
Aug. 23, 1958, P.L. 85-726, 72 Stat. 808

Air Navigation Act
Cal. Public Utilities Code § 21401 et seq.
Conn. Gen. Stat. Ann., § 15-34

Air Pollution Act
R.I. Gen. Laws 1956, 23-23-1 et seq.
Tex. Health and Safety Code, § 382.001 et seq.

Air Pollution Act (Rees-Richard)
Ariz. Rev. Stat. Ann., § 49-448 et seq.
Cal. Health and Safety Code § 426.5
Me. Rev. Stat. Ann. 1964, Title 38, § 581 et seq.
Nev. Rev. Stat. 1979 Reprint, 445.401 et seq.
N.H. Rev. Stat. 1955, 125-C:1 et seq.

Air Pollution Agreements Act (Interstate)
Pa. Purdon's Stat., Title 35, § 4101 et seq.

Air Pollution and Traffic Congestion Control Act
N.J. Stat. Ann., 27:26A-1 et seq.

Air Pollution Compact
See Interstate Compact on Air Pollution Act

Air Pollution Compact Act
Ohio Rev. Code 1953, 3723.01 et seq.
W. Va. Code 1966, § 29-1G-1 et seq.

Air Pollution Compact Act (Ohio-Kentucky)
Ohio Rev. Code 1953, 3723.04 et seq.

Air Pollution Compact Act (Ohio-West Virginia)
Ohio Rev. Code 1953, 3723.04 et seq.

Air Pollution Control Act
See also Clean Air Act
July 14, 1955, Ch. 360, 69 Stat. 322, 42 U.S. Code §§ 1857 to 1857f
Sept. 22, 1959, P.L. 86-365, 73 Stat. 646, 42 U.S. Code §§ 1857d, 1857g
Ala. Code 1975, § 22-28-1 et seq.
Cal. Health and Safety Code §§ 24198 et seq., 40000 et seq.
Colo. Rev. Stat. 25-7-101 et seq.
Conn. Gen. Stat. Ann., § 22a-170 et seq.
Del. Code of 1953, Title 16, § 1601 et seq.
Fla. Stat. 1983, 403-011 et seq.
Haw. Rev. Stat. Ann., § 342B-1 et seq.
Ida. Code 1947, 32-2901 et seq.
Ill. Rev. Stat. 1991, Ch. 111 1/2, § 1008 et seq.
Ind. Code Ann., 13-1-1-1 et seq.
Iowa Code Ann., 455B.131 et seq.
Kan. Stat. Ann., 65-3001 et seq.
Ky. Rev. Stat. 1971, 77.005 et seq.
Mich. Comp. Laws Ann., 336.11 et seq.
Mo. Rev. Stat., 643.010 et seq.
N.D. Cent. Code, 23-25-01 et seq.
N.J. Stat. Ann., 26:2C-1 et seq.
N.M. Stat. Ann., 74-2-1 et seq.
N.Y. Environmental Conservation Law 1972 (Consol. Law Ch. 43B) § 19-0101 et seq.
Ore. Rev. Stat., 468.275 et seq.
Pa. Purdon's Stat., Title 35, § 4001 et seq.
R.I. Gen. Laws 1956, 23-25-1 et seq.
S.D. Codified Laws 1967, 34A-1-1 et seq.
Utah Code Ann. 1953, 19-2-101 et seq.
Vt. Stat. Ann., Title 10, § 551 et seq.

Air Pollution Control Act (Bay Area)
Cal. Health and Safety Code §§ 24345, 40200 et seq.

Air Pollution Control Act (Rees-Richard)
Ariz. Rev. Stat. Ann., § 36-770 et seq.
D.C. Code Ann., § 6-901 et seq.
Me. Rev. Stat. Ann. 1964, Title 38, § 581 et seq.
N.H. Rev. Stat. 1955, 125-C:1 et seq.
Ohio Rev. Code 1953, 3704.01 et seq.
Tenn. Code Ann., 68-201-101 et seq.
Va. Code 1950, § 10-17.9:1 et seq.
Wis. Stat. Ann., 144.30 et seq.
W. Va. Code 1966, § 29-1G-1 et seq.

Air Pollution Control Code (New York City)
N.Y. City Adm. Code 85, § 24-101 et seq.

Air Pollution Control Compact (Illinois-Indiana)
Ind. Code Ann., 13-5-7-1 et seq.

Air Pollution Control Compact (Mid-Atlantic States)
N.Y. Environmental Conservation Law 1972 (Consol. Laws Ch. 43B) § 21-1501 et seq.

Air Pollution Control Compact (Mid-Atlantic)
Conn. Gen. Stat. §§ 22a-166, 22a-167 et seq.
N.J. Stat. Ann., 32:29-1 et seq.

Air Pollution Control Compact Act
Conn. Gen. Stat. Ann., §§ 22a-166, 22a-167

Air Pollution Control District Law (San Joaquin Valley)
Cal. Statutes 1959, Ch. 1915, p. 4486

Air Pollution Control Facilities Tax Exemption Act
Mich. Comp. Laws Ann., 336.1 et seq.

Air Pollution Emergency Control Act
N.J. Stat. Ann., 26:2C-26 et seq.

Air Pollution Episode Control Act
R.I. Gen. Laws 1956, 23-23.1 et seq.

Air Pollution Permit Streamlining Act
Cal. Health and Safety Code § 42320 et seq.

Air Pollution Prevention and Control Act
Colo. Rev. Stat., 25-7-101 et seq.

Air Quality Act
Nov. 21, 1967, P.L. 90-148, 81 Stat. 485, 42 U.S. Code §§ 1857 to 1857l
Tenn. Code Ann., 68-201-101 et seq.
Wyo. Stat. 1957, § 35-487 et seq.

Air Quality Amendment No. 2 Relating to the Sulfur Content of Fuels
D.C. Laws 1976, No. 1-54

Air Quality Amendment No. 4 Relating to the Sulfur Content of Fuels
D.C. Laws 1977, No. 1-125

Air Quality Compact (Kansas-Missouri)
Mo. Rev. Stat. 1978, 643.600 et seq.

Air Quality Conservation Act
Kan. Stat. Ann., 65-3001 et seq.

Air Quality Control Act
Colo. Rev. Stat., 25-7-101 et seq.
Kan. Stat. Ann., 65-3001 et seq.
Md. Ann. Code 1974, Art. EN, § 2-102 et seq.
N.M. Stat. Ann., 74-2-1 et seq.

Air Quality Control Amendment
D.C. Laws 1978, No. 2-77

Air Quality Control Regulations Amendments
D.C. Laws 1975, No. 1-13
D.C. Laws 1977, Nos. 1-94, 1-119

Air Quality Management Act
Cal. Health and Safety Code § 40400 et seq.

Air Quality Management Act (Lewis-Presley)
Cal. Health and Safety Code § 40400 et seq.

Air Quality Management Act (Pinellas County)
Fla. Special Laws 1978, Ch. 601

Air Raid Attack Act
Jan. 27, 1942, Ch. 20, 56 Stat. 19

Air Raid Precautions Act
Kan. Laws 1943, Ch. 205
Pa. Purdon's Stat., Title 35, § 2001 et seq.
Tenn. Code Ann., 58-2-101 et seq.
Wash. Laws 1943, Ch. 241

Air Resources Act
Cal. Health and Safety Code § 39000 et seq.

Air Resources Act-Air and Water Resources Act
N.C. Gen. Stat. 1943, § 143-211 et seq.

Air Rifle Act
Ill. Comp. Stat. 1992, Ch. 720, § 535/0.01 et seq.

Air Rights Act (Local Government)
Ill. Rev. Stat. 1991, Ch. 85, § 1060 et seq.

Air Safety and Hazardous Zoning Act
N.J. Stat. Ann., 6:1-80 et seq.

Air Safety Board Act
June 23, 1938, Ch. 601, 52 Stat. 1012 (See 49 U.S. Code § 1441)
Aug. 23, 1958, P.L. 85-726, 72 Stat. 806

Air Service Building Commission Act
Ala. General Acts 1931, p. 402, No. 347

Air Terminal Act
N.J. Stat. Ann., 32:1-35.1 et seq.

Air Toxics "Hot Spots" Information and Assessment Act
Cal. Health and Safety Code §§ 44300 et seq., 44306 et seq., 44320 et seq., 44340 et seq., 44360 et seq., 44380 et seq.

Air Traffic Management system Performance Improvement Act of 1996
Oct. 9, 1996, P.L. 104-264, Title II, 49 U.S. Code § 40101 nt.

Air Transport Labor Act
See Railroad Labor Act

Air Transportation Act
Ga. Code Ann., 50-19-20 et seq.

Air Transportation and Service Act
Ala. Acts 1982, 3d Sp., p. 389

Air Transportation Development Act
Ala. Acts 1986, No. 214

Air Washington Act (Clean)
Wash. Rev. Code 1983, 70.94.440

Airbag Safety and Anti-Theft Act
N.Y. Insurance Law 1984 (Consol. Laws Ch. 28) §§ 3411, 3412
N.Y. Vehicle and Traffic Law 1959 (Consol. Laws Ch. 71) §§ 119b, 301, 398d, 415a, 415c, 603, 605

Airborne Hunting Act
N.M. Stat. Ann., 17-3-43 et seq.

Aircraft Act
Fla. Stat. Ann., 332.001 et seq.
Mich. Comp. Laws Ann., 259.1 et seq.

Aircraft Act (Navigation)
Cal. Statutes 1929, p. 1874

Aircraft Act (Registration and Licenses)
Cal. Statutes 1921, p. 1421

Aircraft Act (State)
N.M. Stat. Ann., 15-9-1 et seq.

Aircraft Boarding with Weapon Act
Ill. Rev. Stat. 1991, Ch. 38, § 84-0.1 et seq.

Aircraft Contracts Act
March 5, 1940, Ch. 44, 54 Stat. 45

Aircraft Crash Parts Act
Ill. Comp. Stat. 1992, Ch. 720, §§ 205/0.01, 205/1

Aircraft Damage Reporting Act
Cal. Public Utilities Code §§ 24450, 24451

Aircraft Development Act
June 30, 1938, Ch. 852, 52 Stat. 1255, 50 U.S. Code § 95

Aircraft Equipment Settlement Leases Act of 1993
March 17, 1993, P.L. 103-7, 11 U.S. Code § 1110 nt.

Aircraft Excise Tax Act
Wash. Rev. Code Ann., 82.48.010 et seq.

Aircraft Financial Responsibility Act
See also Uniform Aircraft Financial Responsibility Act
Ind. Code Ann., 8-21-3-1 et seq.

Aircraft Gas Tax Act
Mich. Comp. Laws Ann., 259.203

Aircraft Landing and Taking Off Restrictions Act
Ill. Comp. Stat. 1992, Ch. 620, § 15/0.01 et seq.

Aircraft License Act
Tex. Rev. Civ. Stat., Art. 46f-2

Aircraft License Excise Tax Act
Ind. Code Ann., 6-6-6.5-1 et seq.

Aircraft Lien Act
Cal. Code of Civil Procedure § 1208.61 et seq.

Aircraft Maintenance and Engine Repair Facilities State Financing Act
Minn. Stat. Ann., 116R.01 et seq.

Aircraft Motor Vehicle Registration Law
Fla. Stat. 1983, 330.06 et seq.

Aircraft Noise Attenuation Act (Metropolitan Area)
Minn. Stat. Ann., 473.192

Aircraft Parts Secrecy Act
July 13, 1939, Ch. 265, 53 Stat. 1000 (See 10 U.S. Code §§ 2301, 2303 to 2305)

Aircraft Pool Act
Miss. Code 1942, § 4061-51 et seq.
Tex. Rev. Civ. Stat., Art. 4413(34b)

Aircraft Pooling Act (State)
Tex. Government Code, § 2205.001 et seq.

Aircraft Prize Act
June 24, 1941, Ch. 232, 55 Stat. 261 (See 10 U.S. Code § 7651)

Aircraft Protection Act
Tex. Penal Code, § 28.01 et seq.

Aircraft Registration Act
June 23, 1938, Ch. 601, 52 Stat. 1005 (See 49 U.S. Code §§ 1401 to 1403)
June 16, 1948, Ch. 482, 62 Stat. 470 (See 49 U.S. Code § 1404)
June 19, 1948, Ch. 523, 62 Stat. 494 (See 49 U.S. Code § 1403)
Aug. 23, 1958, P.L. 85-726, 72 Stat. 806
N.J. Stat. Ann., 6:1-63 et seq.
N.M. Stat. Ann., 64-4-1 et seq.

Aircraft Registration and License Tax Act
Ohio Rev. Code 1953, 4561.17 et seq.

Aircraft Regulation Act
Va. Code 1950, § 5.1-1 et seq.

Aircraft Rescue Act
Cal. Public Utilities Code § 21500 et seq.

Aircraft Restriction Act (Military Emergency)
Ill. Rev. Stat. 1991, Ch. 15 1/2, § 178.9 et seq.

Aircraft Sabotage Act
Oct. 12, 1984, P.L. 98-473, 18 U.S. Code §§ 31, 31 nt., 32
July 5, 1994, P.L. 103-272, 108 Stat. 1379

Aircraft Sales and Use Tax Act
Va. Code 1950, § 58.1-1500 et seq.

Aircraft Service Act (Nonresident)
Pa. 1935 Pamph. Laws 130, No. 53

Aircraft Theft Act
Fla. Stat. 1973, 814.01 et seq.

Aircraft Title Recordation Act
Minn. Laws 1953, Ch. 721

Aircraft Transportation Brokers Act
Cal. Public Utilities Code § 24001 et seq.

Airfield and Armory Site Act (Park District)
Ill. Rev. Stat. 1991, Ch. 105, § 327a.1 et seq.

Airline Authority Act
Neb. Rev. Stat. 1943, 3-801 et seq.

Airline Deregulation Act of 1978
Oct. 24, 1978, P.L. 95-504, 49 U.S. Code
§§ 1301, 1301 nt., 1302 et seq.
Feb. 15, 1980, P.L. 96-192, 49 U.S. Code
§ 1341 nt.
Jan. 12, 1983, P.L. 97-449, 96 Stat. 2444
July 5, 1994, P.L. 103-272, 108 Stat. 1379
Oct. 31, 1994, P.L. 103-429, 49 U.S. Code
Appx. § 1301 nt.

Airlines Flight Property Tax Act
Mont. Code Ann., 15-23-401 et seq.

Airplane Dealers' Tax Act
N.M. Stat. Ann. 1953, 72-9-1

Airplane Guest Act
Ill. Rev. Stat. 1975, Ch. 15 1/2, § 22.83

Airport Access Road Act (University)
Ill. Rev. Stat. 1991, Ch. 144, §§ 78b, 78c

Airport Act
Ind. Code Ann., 8-22-1-1 et seq.

Airport Act (East St. Louis)
Ill. Rev. Stat. 1991, Ch. 15 1/2, §§ 260, 261

Airport Act (Municipal)
See Municipal Airports Act

Airport Act (University of Illinois)
Ill. Rev. Stat. 1991, Ch. 144, § 78.9 et seq.

Airport and Airway Development Act Amendments of 1976
July 12, 1976, P.L. 94-353, 90 Stat. 871
Sept. 3, 1982, P.L. 97-248, 96 Stat. 697
Jan. 12, 1983, P.L. 97-449, 96 Stat. 2443
July 5, 1994, P.L. 103-272, 108 Stat. 1379

Airport and Airway Development Act of 1970
May 21, 1970, P.L. 91-258, 84 Stat. 219, 49
U.S. Code §§ 1701 et seq., 1701 nt., 1711 to 1727
Nov. 27, 1971, P.L. 92-174, 85 Stat. 491, 49
U.S. Code §§ 1711 to 1715, 1717
June 18, 1973, P.L. 93-44, 87 Stat. 88, 49
U.S. Code §§ 1711, 1712, 1714, 1716, 1717
Feb. 18, 1980, P.L. 96-193, 49 U.S. Code
§ 1711 et seq.
April 7, 1986, P.L. 99-272, 49 U.S. Code
Appx. § 1741
Oct. 22, 1986, P.L. 99-514, 49 U.S. Code
Appx., § 1741
July 5, 1994, P.L. 103-272, 108 Stat. 1379

Airport and Airway Improvement Act of 1982
Sept. 3, 1982, P.L. 97-248, 49 U.S. Code
§ 2201 et seq.
Oct. 2, 1982, P.L. 97-276, 49 U.S. Code
§ 2207
Jan. 6, 1983, P.L. 97-424, 49 U.S. Code
§§ 2204, 2205, 2206
Dec. 30, 1987, P.L. 100-223, 49 U.S. Code
Appx. §§ 2226, 2227
Aug. 14, 1988, P.L. 100-393, 102 Stat. 971
Nov. 3, 1988, P.L. 100-591, 49 U.S. Code
Appx. § 2205
Aug. 4, 1989, P.L. 101-71, 49 U.S. Code
Appx. § 2212
May 4, 1990, P.L. 101-281, 49 U.S. Code
Appx. § 2210
Nov. 5, 1990, P.L. 101-508, 49 U.S. Code
Appx. §§ 2201 to 2207, 2227
Oct. 31, 1992, P.L. 102-581, 49 U.S. Code
Appx. §§ 2201 to 2212, 2226c, 2227
May 26, 1994, P.L. 103-260, 49 U.S. Code
Appx. §§ 2204, 2206, 2207, 2212

Airport and Airway Revenue Act of 1970

May 21, 1970, P.L. 91-258, 84 Stat. 236, 26 U.S. Code §§ 39, 874, 4041, 4082, 4261 to 4263, 4271, and others; 49 U.S. Code § 1742

Feb. 18, 1980, P.L. 96-193, 49 U.S. Code § 1742

July 1, 1980, P.L. 96-298, 42 U.S. Code § 1742

Airport and Airway Revenue Act of 1987

Dec. 30, 1987, P.L. 100-223, 26 U.S. Code §§ 1 nt., 4041, 4261, 4271, 9502, 6427

Airport and Airway Safety and Capacity Expansion Act of 1987

Dec. 30, 1987, P.L. 100-223, 49 U.S. Code Appx. § 2201 et seq.

Nov. 5, 1990, P.L. 101-508, 104 Stat. 1388-370

Oct. 31, 1992, P.L. 102-581, 49 U.S. Code Appx. § 2204 nt.

Airport and Airway Safety, Capacity, Noise Improvement, and Intermodal Transportation Act of 1992

Oct. 31, 1992, P.L. 102-581, 49 U.S. Code Appx. § 2201 nt.

April 7, 1993, P.L. 103-13, 49 U.S. Code Appx. § 1371 nt.

Airport and Airway Trust Fund Tax Reinstatement Act of 1997

Feb. 28, 1997, P.L. 105-2, 26 U.S. Code § 1 nt.

Airport and Airways Improvement Act of 1989

Dec. 15, 1989, P.L. 101-236, 49 U.S. Code Appx. § 2210

Airport and Landing Field Act (Counties)

Ill. Rev. Stat. 1991, Ch. 15 1/2, § 68.90 et seq.

Airport and Maritime Plant Quarantine Inspection and Plant Protection Act

Cal. Food and Agriculture Code 1967, § 5350 et seq.

Airport and Riverport Financing Act (Multicounty)

Ark. Acts 1991, No. 738

Airport and Waterfront Commission Act

N.Y. Unconsolidated Laws, § 9801 et seq.

Airport Approaches Zoning Law

Cal. Government Code § 50485 et seq.

Airport Authorities Act

Ill. Comp. Stat. 1992, Ch. 70, § 5/0.01 et seq.

Miss. Code Ann. 1972, § 61-3-1 et seq.

Airport Authorities Act (Cities)

Neb. Rev. Stat. 1943, 3-501 et seq.

Airport Authorities Act (Interstate)

Ill. Rev. Stat. 1991, Ch. 15 1/2, § 250 et seq.

Airport Authorities Act (Joint)

Neb. Rev. Stat. 1943, 3-701 et seq.

Airport Authority Act (Albany County)

N.Y. Public Authorities Law (Consol. Laws Ch. 43A) § 2776 et seq.

Airport Authority Act (Blue Ridge)

Va. Acts 1964, Ch. 25, § 1 et seq.

Airport Authority Act (Boca Raton)

Fla. Special Laws 1982, Ch. 82-259

Airport Authority Act (Brazos County)

Tex. Laws 61st Leg. 1969, p. 1161, Ch. 374

Airport Authority Act (Calhoun-Gordon County)

Ga. Laws 1971, p. 2861

Airport Authority Act (Columbia County)

Ga. Laws 1975, p. 4559

Airport Authority Act (Columbus County)

N.C. Laws 1995, Ch. 134

Airport Authority Act (Community)

Mich. Comp. Laws Ann., 259.621 et seq.

Airport Authority Act (County)

W. Va. Code 1966, § 8-29A-1 et seq.

Airport Authority Act (Cuthbert-Randolph)
Ga. Laws 1971, p. 2837

Airport Authority Act (Dawson-Terrell County)
Ga. Laws 1997, p. 3696

Airport Authority Act (Duluth)
Minn. Laws 1969, Ch. 577

Airport Authority Act (Dunnellon)
Fla. Laws 1981, Ch. 81-436

Airport Authority Act (Folkston-Charlton County)
Ga. Laws 1970, p. 3253

Airport Authority Act (Forsyth County)
Ga. Laws 1978, p. 3490

Airport Authority Act (Fort Pierce)
Fla. Special Laws 1961, Ch. 61-2754

Airport Authority Act (Franklin-Hart)
Ga. Laws 1996, p. 3927

Airport Authority Act (Grayson County)
Tex. Laws 62nd Leg., 1971, p. 1087, Ch. 237

Airport Authority Act (Greene County)
Ga. Laws 1978, p. 3223

Airport Authority Act (Gwinnett County)
Ga. Laws 1971, p. 3668

Airport Authority Act (Harris County)
Ga. Laws 1984, p. 5239

Airport Authority Act (Howard County)
Tex. Laws 60th Leg., 1967, p. 964, Ch. 425

Airport Authority Act (Jackson County)
Ga. Laws 1964, Ex. Sess., p. 2260

Airport Authority Act (Kankakee River Valley Area)
Ill. Rev. Stat. 1991, Ch. 15 1/2, § 701 et seq.

Airport Authority Act (Lander County)
Nev. Stat. 1983, Ch. 458, p. 1208

Airport Authority Act (Liberty)
N.Y. Public Authorities Law (Consol. Laws Ch. 43A) § 1725 et seq.

Airport Authority Act (Madison-Morgan County)
Ga. Laws 1965, p. 2687

Airport Authority Act (Manatee County)
Fla. Laws 1984, Ch. 84-472

Airport Authority Act (Meriwether County)
Ga. Laws 1997, p. 3640

Airport Authority Act (Metropolitan)
Tenn. Code Ann., 42-4-101 et seq.

Airport Authority Act (Monroe County)
N.Y. Public Authorities Law (Consol. Laws Ch. 43A) § 2750 et seq.

Airport Authority Act (Mountain Resorts)
Me. Rev. Stat. Ann. 1964, Title 10, § 7001 et seq.

Airport Authority Act (New York City)
N.Y. Public Authorities Law (Consol. Laws Ch. 43A) § 1444 et seq.

Airport Authority Act (Newman-Coweta County)
Ga. Laws 1965, p. 2041

Airport Authority Act (North Central Texas)
Tex. Laws 60th Leg., 1967, p. 6, Ch. 6

Airport Authority Act (Orange County)
Tex. Laws 60th Leg., 1967, p. 1993, Ch. 739

Airport Authority Act (Paulding County)
Ga. Laws 1972, p. 3645

Airport Authority Act (Peachtree City)
Ga. Laws 1984, p. 4935

Airport Authority Act (Perry-Fort Valley)
Ga. Laws 1971, p. 2589

Airport Authority Act (Public)
Colo. Rev. Stat., 41-3-101 et seq.

Airport Authority Act (Rabun County)
Ga. Laws 1975, p. 3003

Airport Authority Act (Saint Marys)
Ga. Laws 1964, p. 2438

Airport Authority Act (Sanford)
Fla. Special Laws 1971, Ch. 71-924

Airport Authority Act (Sarasota-Manatee)
Fla. Laws 1991, Ch. 358
Fla. Special Laws 1977, Ch. 77-651

Airport Authority Act (Sebring)
Fla. Special Laws 1967, Ch. 67-2070

Airport Authority Act (Southside Regional at Blackstone)
Va. Acts 1992, Ch. 371

Airport Authority Act (St. Louis Metropolitan Area)
Ill. Rev. Stat. 1983, Ch. 15 1/2, § 301 et seq.

Airport Authority Act (Telfair-Wheeler)
Ga. Laws 1998, H.B. 1908

Airport Authority Act (Thomaston-Upson County)
Ga. Laws 1988, Ch. 4225

Airport Authority Act (Toccoa-Stephens County)
Ga. Laws 1961, p. 2423

Airport Authority Act (Troup County)
Ga. Laws 1977, p. 3387

Airport Authority Act (Tweed-New Haven)
Conn. Public Acts 1997, No. 271

Airport Authority Act (Washoe County)
Nev. Statutes 1977, Ch. 474, p. 968

Airport Authority Act (West Georgia)
Ga. Laws 1968, p. 2769

Airport Authority Ordinance (Dalton)
Ga. Laws 1988, Ch. 5201

Airport Commission Act
Ark. Code Ann. 1987, 14-359-101 et seq.

Airport Commission Act (Capital Region)
Va. Acts 1980, Ch. 380

Airport Commission Act (Roanoke)
Va. Acts 1986, Ch. 140

Airport Commission Compact
N.J. Stat. Ann., 32:23-150 et seq.
N.Y. Unconsolidated Laws § 9961 et seq.

Airport Development Acceleration Act
June 18, 1973, P.L. 93-44, 87 Stat. 88, 49
U.S. Code §§ 1513, 1711, 1712, 1714, 1716, 1717

Airport Development Act
N.C. Gen. Stat. 1943, §§ 63-65 to 63-72

Airport Development and Assistance Act
Fla. Stat. Ann., 332.003 et seq.

Airport Development Authority Law
Ga. Code Ann., 6-4-1 et seq.

Airport Development Bond Act
W. Va. Code 1966, § 13-2D-1 et seq.

Airport District Act
Cal. Public Utilities Code § 22001 et seq.

Airport District Act (South Brevard)
Fla. Special Laws 1969, Ch. 69-880

Airport District Act of 1963 (Titusville-Cocoa)
Fla. Special Laws 1963, Ch. 63-1143

Airport Districts Act (Special)
N.C. Gen. Stat. 1943, § 63-78 et seq.

Airport Funds Act (Federal)
Utah Code Ann. 1953, 2-3-1 et seq.

Airport Hazards Zoning Elimination Act
Ill. Rev. Stat. 1991, Ch. 15 1/2, § 48.100 et seq.

Airport Improvement Loan Act (Logan)
Mass. Acts 1951, Ch. 733
Mass. Acts 1957, Chs. 484, 712

Airport Improvement Program Temporary Extension Act of 1994
May 26, 1994, P.L. 103-260, 26 U.S. Code § 9502; 49 U.S. Code Appx. §§ 1348 nt., 2201 nt., 2204, 2206, 2207, 2212
Oct. 31, 1994, P.L. 103-429, 49 U.S. Code Appx. § 2204

Airport Industrial City Study Act
Tenn. Public Acts 1972, Ch. 745

Airport Law
Fla. Stat. Ann., 332.12

Airport Law (County)
Ill. Comp. Stat. 1992, Ch. 620, § 45/1 et seq.

Airport Licensing Law
Fla. Stat. 1965, 330.27 et seq.

Airport Loan Act
Tenn. Code Ann., 4-31-601 et seq.

Airport Loan Act (Dukes County)
Mass. Acts 1952, Ch. 429
Mass. Acts 1957, Ch. 201
Mass. Acts 1958, Ch. 504

Airport Loan Act (Municipalities)
Mass. Acts 1941, Ch. 24

Airport Noise and Capacity Act of 1990
Nov. 5, 1990, P.L. 101-508, 49 U.S. Code Appx. §§ 2151 nt., 2151 to 2158
Oct. 31, 1992, P.L. 102-581, 49 U.S. Code Appx. §§ 2153, 2158

Airport Parking Tax Act
Mich. Comp. Laws Ann., 207.371 et seq.

Airport Protection and Development Policy Act
Cal. Public Utilities Code § 21605

Airport Relocation Act
Haw. Rev. Stat. § 261-31 et seq.

Airport Revenue Protection Act of 1996
Oct. 9, 1996, P.L. 104-264, Title VIII, 49 U.S. Code § 40101 nt.

Airport Safety Act
N.J. Stat. Ann.,6:1-89 et seq.

Airport Site Act (Park District)
Ill. Rev. Stat. 1991, Ch. 105, § 327c1.1 et seq.

Airport Traffic Control Act (Sarasota-Manatee)
Fla. Special Laws 1967, Ch. 67-2053

Airport Transportation Security Act of 1974
Aug. 5, 1974, P.L. 93-366, 88 Stat. 415, 49 U.S. Code §§ 1301, 1356, 1357, 1472, 1511, 1515

Airport Zoning Act
Ala. Code 1975, § 4-6-1 et seq.
Alaska Stat. 1962, § 02.25.010 et seq.
Ark. Code Ann. 1987, 14-363-201 et seq.
Cal. Government Code §§ 26027, 26028
Fla. Stat. Ann., 333.01 et seq.
Ga. Code 1933, 11-401 et seq.
Haw. Rev. Stat. § 262-1 et seq.
Ida. Code 1947, 21-501 et seq.
Ill. Comp. Stat. 1992, Ch. 620, § 25/1 et seq.
Iowa Code Ann., 329.1 et seq.
Kan. Stat. Ann., 3-701 et seq.
Ky. Rev. Stat. 1971, 183.861 et seq.
La. Rev. Stat. Ann., 2:381 et seq.
Mass. Gen. Laws Ann., 90:40A et seq.
Md. Ann. Code 1974, Art. TR, § 5-501 et seq.
Me. Rev. Stat. Ann. 1964, Title 6, § 241 et seq.
Mich. Comp. Laws Ann., 259.431 et seq.
Minn. Stat. Ann., 360.061 et seq.
Miss. Code Ann. 1972, § 61-7-1 et seq.
Mont. Code Ann., 67-6-101 et seq.
N.C. Gen. Stat. 1943, § 63-30 et seq.
N.D. Cent. Code, 2-04-01 et seq.
Neb. Rev. Stat. 1943, 3-301 et seq.
Nev. Rev. Stat. 1979 Reprint, 497.010 et seq.
N.H. Rev. Stat. 1955, 424:1 et seq.
Continued

N.M. Stat. Ann., 3-39-16 et seq.

Okla. Stat. Ann., Title 3, § 100 et seq.

Ore. Rev. Stat., 836.400 et seq.

Pa. Cons. Stat., Title 74, § 5912 et seq.

P.R. Laws Ann. 1954, Title 23, § 191 et seq.

R.I. Gen. Laws 1956, 1-3-1 et seq.

S.D. Codified Laws 1967, 50-10-1 et seq.

Tex. Local Government Code, § 241.001 et seq.

Utah Code Ann. 1953, 2-4-1 et seq.

Vt. Stat. Ann., Title 5, § 1001 et seq.

Wash. Rev. Code Ann., 14.12.010 et seq.

Airport Zoning Act (Park District)

Ill. Rev. Stat. 1989, Ch. 105, § 327c1.9 et seq.

Vt. Stat. Ann., Title 5, § 1001 et seq.

Airports Act (Counties)

Fla. Laws 1937, Ch. 17708

Ill. Rev. Stat. 1991, Ch. 15 1/2, § 104 et seq.

Airports Act (Federal)

Alaska Stat. 1962, § 02.15.060 et seq.

Del. Code of 1974, Title 2, § 901 et seq.

Fla. Stat. Ann., 332.01 et seq.

Ga. Code Ann., 6-3-1 et seq.

Ind. Code Ann., 19-6-1-1 et seq.

Iowa Code Ann., 330.1 et seq.

La. Rev. Stat. Ann., 2:81 et seq.

Minn. Stat. Ann., 360.031 et seq.

N.J. Stat. Ann., 32:1-35.1 et seq.

N.M. Stat. Ann., 3-39-1 et seq.

N.Y. General Municipal Law (Consol. Laws Ch. 24) § 350 et seq.

S.C. Code Ann. 1976, § 55-9-10 et seq.

Tenn. Code Ann.,42-5-101

Utah Code Ann. 1953, 2-2-1 et seq.

Va. Code 1950, §§ 5.1-47, 5.1-48

Wash. Rev. Code Ann., 14.08.010 et seq.

Airports Act (Joint)

Ill. Rev. Stat. 1991, Ch. 15 1/2, § 600 et seq.

Airports Act (Municipal)

See Municipal Airports Act

Tex. Rev. Civ. Stat., Art. 46d-1 et seq.

Vt. Stat. Ann., Title 5, § 601 et seq.

Airports Act (Revised)

Neb. Rev. Stat. 1943, 3-201 et seq.

Airports Act (State)

Nev. Rev. Stat. 1979 Reprint, 494.010 et seq.

Airports Acts

See also Federal Airport Act

May 24, 1928, Ch. 728, 45 Stat. 728, 49 U.S. Code §§ 211 to 214

March 4, 1929, Ch. 713, 45 Stat. 1698

June 23, 1938, Ch. 601, 52 Stat. 1027, 49 U.S. Code § 212

Aug. 16, 1941, Ch. 354, 55 Stat. 621, 49 U.S. Code § 211

March 18, 1950, Ch. 72, 64 Stat. 27, 16 U.S. Code §§ 7a to 7e; 49 U.S. Code §§ 1102, 1108

Aug. 23, 1958, P.L. 85-726, 72 Stat. 806, 16 U.S. Code § 7a; 49 U.S. Code § 212

Airports Commission Act (Metropolitan)

Minn. Stat. Ann., 473.601 et seq.

Airspace Act

Ariz. Rev. Stat. Ann., § 28-1702 et seq.

Del. Code of 1974, Title 2, §§ 302, 303

Ind. Code Ann., 8-21-4-3

Mo. Rev. Stat., 305.020 et seq.

N.D. Cent. Code, 2-03-01 et seq.

Nev. Rev. Stat. 1979 Reprint, 493.030 et seq.

Okla. Stat. Ann., Title 60, § 801 et seq.

S.C. Code Ann. 1976, § 55-3-10 et seq.

Vt. Stat. Ann., Title 5, § 141 et seq.

Wis. Stat. Ann., 114.03

Airways Modernization Act of 1957

Aug. 14, 1957, P.L. 85-133, 71 Stat. 349

Ak-Chin Water Use Amendments of 1992

Oct. 24, 1992, P.L. 102-497, 106 Stat. 3258

Alabama-Coosa-Tallapoosa River Basin Compact

Ala. Code 1975, § 33-18-1

Ga. Code Ann., 12-10-110 et seq.

Alabama-Georgia-Mississippi-Louisiana Rapid Rail Transit Compact
Ga. Code Ann., 46-9-300

Alabama-Mississippi Railroad Authority Compact
Miss. Code Ann. 1972, § 77-9-531 et seq.

Alachua County and Municipality Tax Assessment and Tax Collection Act
Fla. Special Laws 1967, Ch. 67-1075

Alachua County Charter
Fla. Special Laws 1976, Ch. 76-322

Alachua County Subdivision Road and Bridge Act
Fla. Special Laws 1953, Ch. 28872

Alameda County Flood Control and Water Conservation District Act
Cal. Statutes 1949, Ch. 1275, p. 2240
Cal. Water Code, Appendix, § 55-1 et seq.

Alameda-Santa Clara-San Benito Water Authority Act
Cal. Statutes 1955, Ch. 1289, p. 2349

Alan Pattee Scholarship Act (Surviving Child of Policeman or Fireman)
Cal. Education Code 1959, §§ 23060, 23762, 68120

Alan Short Development Centers for the Handicapped Act
Cal. Education Code 1976, § 56800 et seq.

Alarm Company Act
Cal. Business and Professions Code § 7590 et seq.

Alarm Contractors Licensing Act
Tenn. Code Ann., 62-32-301 et seq.

Alarm Industry Act
Okla. Stat. 1981, Title 59, § 1800.1 et seq.

Alarm Systems Licensing Act
Ark. Code Ann. 1987, 17-13-101 et seq.
N.C. Gen. Stat. 1943, § 74D-1 et seq.

Alaska Agricultural Experiment Stations Acts
Feb. 23, 1929, Ch. 299, 45 Stat. 1256 (See 7 U.S. Code § 361a)
June 20, 1936, Ch. 631, 49 Stat. 1553 (See 7 U.S. Code § 361a)
Oct. 27, 1949, Ch. 768, 63 Stat. 939 (See 7 U.S. Code §§ 341 to 343, 344 to 348)
Aug. 29, 1950, Ch. 820, 64 Stat. 563 (See 7 U.S. Code § 361a)

Alaska Centennial Act of 1966
March 26, 1966, P.L. 89-375, 80 Stat. 82

Alaska Civil Code
June 6, 1900, Ch. 786, 31 Stat. 494

Alaska Claims Settlement Act
Jan. 2, 1976, P.L. 94-204, 89 Stat. 1145, 43 U.S. Code §§ 1615, 1616, 1620, 1621, 1625 to 1627

Alaska Coal Lands Act
Oct. 20, 1914, Ch. 330, 38 Stat. 741
June 6, 1934, Ch. 405, 48 Stat. 909
Alaska Comp. Laws Ann. 1949, §§ 47-2-56, 47-2-57, 47-2-141 et seq.

Alaska Communications Disposal Act
Nov. 14, 1967, P.L. 90-135, 81 Stat. 441, 40 U.S. Code §§ 771, 781 to 786, 791, 792

Alaska Criminal Code
March 3, 1899, Ch. 429, 30 Stat. 1253

Alaska Federal-Civilization Energy Efficiency Swap Act of 1980
Dec. 22, 1980, P.L. 96-571, 40 U.S. Code § 795 nt.
Nov. 2, 1994, P.L. 103-437, 40 U.S. Code § 795d
Nov. 10, 1998, P.L. 105-362, 40 U.S. Code § 795d

Alaska Fisheries Act
June 6, 1924, Ch. 272, 43 Stat. 464
June 18, 1926, Ch. 621, 44 Stat. 752
Aug. 2, 1937, Ch. 556, 50 Stat. 557
Aug. 14, 1937, Ch. 622, 50 Stat. 639
April 7, 1938, Ch. 110, 52 Stat. 208

Alaska Five Acre Homestead Act
March 3, 1927, Ch. 323, 44 Stat. 1364

Alaska Fur Farming Act
July 3, 1926, Ch. 745, 44 Stat. 821

Alaska Game Laws
June 7, 1902, Ch. 1037, 32 Stat. 327
May 11, 1908, Ch. 162, 35 Stat. 102
Jan. 13, 1925, Ch. 75, 43 Stat. 739
July 1, 1943, Ch. 183, 57 Stat. 301
July 24, 1947, Ch. 307, 61 Stat. 415
April 20, 1949, Ch. 81, 63 Stat. 56
July 23, 1953, Ch. 238, 67 Stat. 185

Alaska Government Act
Aug. 24, 1912, Ch. 387, 37 Stat. 512
April 18, 1940, Ch. 105, 54 Stat. 111

Alaska Housing Act
April 23, 1949, Ch. 89, 63 Stat. 57
July 14, 1952, Ch. 723, 66 Stat. 603

Alaska Hydroelectric Power Development Act
Oct. 22, 1976, P.L. 94-587, 90 Stat. 2946, 42 U.S. Code § 1962d-14a

Alaska Industrial School Act
Feb. 25, 1925, Ch. 320, 43 Stat. 978

Alaska International Highway Commission Act
May 31, 1938, Ch. 299, 52 Stat. 590
June 11, 1940, Ch. 303, 54 Stat. 262

Alaska International Rail and Highway Commission Act
Aug. 1, 1956, Ch. 840, 70 Stat. 888
April 20, 1957, P.L. 85-16, 71 Stat. 14
Aug. 8, 1958, P.L. 85-601, 72 Stat. 524
July 6, 1959, P.L. 86-78, 73 Stat. 161

Alaska Land Status Technical Corrections Act of 1992
Oct. 14, 1992, P.L. 102-415, 43 U.S. Code § 1601 nt.

Alaska Liquor Repeal Act
April 13, 1934, Ch. 119, 48 Stat. 583

Alaska Livestock Grazing Act
March 4, 1927, Ch. 513, 44 Stat. 1452, 42 U.S. Code § 316 et seq.
July 18, 1968, P.L. 90-403, 82 Stat. 358

Alaska Mental Health Enabling Act
July 28, 1956, Ch. 772, 70 Stat. 709, 42 U.S. Code §§ 273, 274

Alaska Military Code
Dec. 31, 1941, Ch. 644, 55 Stat. 879

Alaska Miner's Labor Lien Act
June 25, 1910, Ch. 422, 36 Stat. 848

Alaska National Interest Lands Conservation Act
Dec. 2, 1980, P.L. 96-487, 16 U.S. Code § 3101 nt.
Dec. 12, 1982, P.L. 97-394, 16 U.S. Code § 3142
Nov. 8, 1984, P.L. 98-620, 16 U.S. Code § 3117
Jan. 9, 1986, P.L. 99-235
March 19, 1986, P.L. 99-258, 42 U.S. Code § 1631
Nov. 10, 1986, P.L. 99-644, 43 U.S. Code § 1631.
Dec. 22, 1987, P.L. 100-203, 16 U.S. Code § 3148
Feb. 3, 1988, P.L. 100-241, 43 U.S. Code § 1636
Aug. 16, 1988, P.L. 100-395, 102 Stat. 979, 16 U.S. Code § 3192; 43 U.S. Code § 1631
Nov. 18, 1988, P.L. 100-689, 16 U.S. Code § 3198
Aug. 17, 1990, P.L. 101-378, 16 U.S. Code § 1132 nt.
Aug. 18, 1990, P.L. 101-380, 16 U.S. Code § 3145; 43 U.S. Code § 1642
Nov. 28, 1990, P.L. 101-626, 16 U.S. Code §§ 539d, 539e, 1132 nt.
Oct. 14, 1992, P.L. 102-415, 16 U.S. Code § 3198; 43 U.S. Code § 1634
Nov. 2, 1994, P.L. 103-437, 16 U.S. Code §§ 539e, 3116, 3203
Nov. 2, 1995, P.L. 104-42, 109 Stat. 355
Nov. 12, 1996, P.L. 104-333, 16 U.S. Code §§ 410hh, 1132 nt.

Nov. 14, 1997, P.L. 105-83, 16 U.S. Code §§ 3102, 3111, 3113 to 3115, 3117, 3124, 3125

Oct. 21, 1998, P.L. 105-277, 16 U.S. Code § 3115

Oct. 31, 1998, P.L. 105-333, 16 U.S. Code § 3197; 43 U.S. Code §§ 1634, 1636

Alaska Native Claims Settlement Act

Dec. 18, 1971, P.L. 92-203, 85 Stat. 688, 43 § 1601 nt.

Jan. 2, 1976, P.L. 94-204, 43 U.S. Code § 1604 et seq.

Nov. 15, 1977, P.L. 95-178, 43 U.S. Code § 1628

Sept. 25, 1985, P.L. 99-96, 43 U.S. Code §§ 1629, 1629a

Feb. 3, 1988, P.L. 100-241, 43 U.S. Code § 1629b-e

Aug. 17, 1990, P.L. 101-378, 43 U.S. Code 1629c

Dec. 10, 1991, P.L. 102-201, 43 U.S. Code § 1629c

Oct. 14, 1992, P.L. 102-415, 43 U.S. Code §§ 1606, 1617, 1620, 1621, 1626

Nov. 2, 1994, P.L. 103-437, 43 U.S. Code § 1629

May 18, 1995, P.L. 104-10, 43 U.S. Code §§ 1606, 1607

Nov. 2, 1995, P.L. 104-42, 43 U.S. Code §§ 1606, 1613, 1621, 1629f

Oct. 21, 1998, P.L. 105-276, 43 U.S. Code § 1629g

Oct. 31, 1998, P.L. 105-333, 43 U.S. Code §§ 1606, 1611, 1621, 1626, 1629e

Alaska Native Claims Settlement Act Amendments of 1987

Feb. 3, 1988, P.L. 100-241, 43 U.S. Code § 1601 nt.

Alaska Native Culture and Arts Development Act

May 4, 1994, P.L. 103-239, 20 U.S. Code § 4401 nt.

Alaska Native Educational Equity, Support and Assistance Act

April 11, 1965, P.L. 89-10, as added Oct. 20, 1994, P.L. 103-382, 108 Stat. 3805, 20 U.S. Code § 7931 et seq.

Alaska Natural Gas Transportation Act of 1976

Oct. 22, 1976, P.L. 94-586, 15 U.S. Code § 719 et seq.

Nov. 8, 1984, P.L. 98-620, 15 U.S. Code § 719h

Oct. 24, 1992, P.L. 102-486, 15 U.S. Code § 719e

Alaska Omnibus Act

June 25, 1959, P.L. 86-70, 73 Stat. 141, 1 U.S. Code § 1 nt.; 7 U.S. Code §§ 101, 1837; 10 U.S. Code §§ 101, 802, 2662; 12 U.S. Code §§ 144, 221, 466, 1422, 1466, 1706d, 1707, 1713, 1715d, 1736, 1747l, 1748, 1748e; 14 U.S. Code § 634; 15 U.S. Code §§ 77b, 78c, 80a-2, 80a-6, 80b-2; 16 U.S. Code §§ 590h, 590q, 607, 668, 669g-1, 777k; 18 U.S. Code §§ 1385, 4208 nt., 5024; 20 U.S. Code §§ 14, 15i, 15jj, 15ggg, 16 nt., 238, 244, 403, 442, 588, 645; 21 U.S. Code §§ 149, 188k; 23 U.S. Code §§ 101, 103, 104, 116, 120; 26 U.S. Code §§ 2202, 3121, 3306, 4221, 4233, 4262, 4502, 4774, 7621, 7653, 7701; 28 U.S. Code § 81A; 29 U.S. Code § 41; 31 U.S. Code §§ 444, 448b; 32 U.S. Code § 101; 33 U.S. Code §§ 466d, 466j; 38 U.S. Code §§ 903, 2007; 40 U.S. Code §§ 472, 522; 41 U.S. Code § 10c; 42 U.S. Code §§ 201, 273 nt., 274, 291i, 402, 410, 724, 1301, 1651, 1701, 1704, 1711; 44 U.S. Code §§ 183, 308; 48 U.S. Code prec. § 21 nt.; 49 U.S. Code § 1324 nt.; 50 U.S. Code Appx. §§ 466, 2285

May 27, 1964, P.L. 88-311, 78 Stat. 201, 48 U.S. Code prec. § 21 nt.

Aug. 19, 1964, P.L. 88-451, 78 Stat. 505, 48 U.S. Code prec. § 21 nt.

May 25, 1967, P.L. 90-19, 81 Stat. 24, 48 U.S. Code prec. § 21 nt.

July 31, 1970, P.L. 91-367, 84 Stat. 691, 48 U.S. Code prec. § 21 nt.

Sept. 13, 1982, P.L. 97-258, 96 Stat. 1068

Jan. 12, 1983, P.L. 97-449, 96 Stat. 2439

July 5, 1994, P.L. 103-272, 108 Stat. 1379

Alaska Power Administration Asset Sale and Termination Act

Nov. 28, 1995, P.L. 104-58, Title I, 42 U.S. Code § 7152 nt.

Alaska Prohibition Act
Feb. 14, 1917, Ch. 53, 39 Stat. 903

Alaska Public Works Act
Aug. 24, 1949, Ch. 504, 63 Stat. 627
July 15, 1954, Ch. 510, 68 Stat. 483
Aug. 30, 1957, P.L. 85-233, 71 Stat. 515
Dec. 23, 1963, P.L. 88-229, 77 Stat. 471

Alaska Railroad Acts
March 12, 1914, Ch. 37, 38 Stat. 305
Nov. 18, 1921, Ch. 128, 42 Stat. 221
April 10, 1926, Ch. 114, 44 Stat. 239
March 29, 1940, Ch. 74, 54 Stat. 80, 16 U.S.
Code § 353a
Aug. 4, 1955, Ch. 554, 69 Stat. 494
Oct. 21, 1976, P.L. 94-579, 90 Stat. 2792
Oct. 10, 1980, P.L. 96-423, 94 Stat. 1817
Jan. 14, 1983, P.L. 97-468, 96 Stat. 2577

Alaska Railroad Retirement Act
June 29, 1936, Ch. 859, 49 Stat. 2017

Alaska Railroad Transfer Act of 1982
Jan. 14, 1983, P.L. 97-468, 96 Stat. 2556, 45
U.S. Code § 1201 et seq.
Nov. 8, 1984, P.L. 98-620, 98 Stat. 3361
Jan. 8, 1988, P.L. 100-238, 45 U.S. Code
§ 1206
March 30, 1994, P.L. 103-226, 45 U.S. Code
§ 1206
Dec. 29, 1995, P.L. 104-88, 45 U.S. Code
§ 1207

Alaska Relief of Indigent Act
March 3, 1913, Ch. 109, 37 Stat. 728

Alaska Right of Way Act
May 14, 1898, Ch. 299, 30 Stat. 409

Alaska Road and Trail Act
Jan. 27, 1905, Ch. 277, 33 Stat. 616

Alaska Salmon Fisheries Act
March 2, 1889, Ch. 415, 25 Stat. 1009
June 26, 1906, Ch. 3547, 34 Stat. 478
June 6, 1924, Ch. 272, 43 Stat. 465
Feb. 28, 1929, Ch. 365, 45 Stat. 1349
April 16, 1934, Ch. 146, 48 Stat. 594

July 2, 1940, Ch. 514, 54 Stat. 723
March 16, 1955, Ch. 12, 69 Stat. 12

Alaska Special Peace Officers Act
March 3, 1909, Ch. 266, 35 Stat. 837

Alaska Statehood Bill
July 7, 1958, P.L. 85-508, 72 Stat. 339, 48
U.S. Code prec. § 21 nt.
Aug. 18, 1959, P.L. 86-173, 73 Stat. 395, 48
U.S. Code prec. § 21 nt.
Oct. 8, 1963, P.L. 88-135, 77 Stat. 223, 48
U.S. Code prec. § 21 nt.
March 25, 1964, P.L. 88-289, 78 Stat. 168,
48 U.S. Code prec. § 21 nt.
Nov. 2, 1966, P.L. 89-702, 80 Stat. 1098, 48
U.S. Code prec. § 21 nt.

Alaska Trust Act
Alaska Stat. 1962, § 13.36.105 et seq.

Alaskan Airports Act
May 28, 1948, Ch. 354, 62 Stat. 277
Oct. 10, 1951, Ch. 457, 65 Stat. 371
Oct. 31, 1951, Ch. 654, 65 Stat. 707
Aug. 23, 1958, P.L. 85-726, 72 Stat. 807

Alaskan Native Townsite Act of 1926
May 25, 1926, Ch. 379, 44 Stat. 629

Alatorre-Dymally Bilingual Services Act
Cal. Government Code § 7290 et seq.

**Alatorre-Zenovich-Dunlap-Berman
Agricultural Labor Relations Act**
Cal. Labor Code § 1140 et seq.

Albany Business Rent Control Law
N.Y. Laws 1948, Ch. 679

Albany City Court Act
N.Y. Laws 1914, Ch. 368

Albany County Airport Authority Act
N.Y. Public Authorities Law (Consol. Laws
Ch. 42) § 2776 et seq.

**Albany Light, Heat and Power Authority
Act**
N.Y. Public Authorities Law (Consol. Laws
Ch. 43A) § 1025 et seq.

Albany Municipal Water Finance Authority Act

N.Y. Public Authorities Law (Consol. Laws Ch. 43A) § 1115 et seq.

Albany Parking Authority Act

N.Y. Public Authorities Law (Consol. Laws Ch. 43A) § 1493a et seq.

Albany Port District Act

N.Y. Laws 1925, Ch. 192

Albany Regional Market Authority Act

N.Y. Public Authorities Law (Consol. Laws Ch. 43A) § 850 et seq.

Albany Traffic Court Act

N.Y. Laws 1937, Ch. 135

Albany Water Board Act

N.Y. Public Authorities Law (Consol. Laws Ch. 43A) §§ 1116, 1118

Albemarle Historic Tour Highway Act

N.C. Laws 1975, Ch. 567

Albert C. Smith Egg Act

Ky. Rev. Stat. 1971, 260.600 et seq.

Albert Einstein Distinguished Educator Fellowship Act of 1994

Oct. 20, 1994, P.L. 103-382, 42 U.S. Code §§ 7382 nt., 7382 et seq.

Albert Law (Disorderly Houses)

Neb. Laws 1911, Ch. 3

Alcohol Abuse Control Act

Pa. Purdon's Stat., Title 71, § 1690.101 et seq.

Alcohol Abuse, Drug Abuse, and Mental Health Amendments of 1984

Oct. 19, 1984, P.L. 98-509, 98 Stat. 2353

Alcohol Abuse Education and Prevention Act

Cal. Health and Safety Code § 11802
Cal. Vehicle Code 1959, § 23196

Alcohol Abuse Prevention Act

Tenn. Code Ann., 33-8-501 et seq.

Alcohol and Drug Abuse Act

Ind. Code Ann., 16-13-6.1-1 et seq.
Md. Ann. Code 1974, Art. HG, § 8-101 et seq.

Alcohol and Drug Abuse Amendments of 1983

April 26, 1983, P.L. 98-24, 97 Stat. 175
Oct. 19, 1984, P.L. 98-509, 98 Stat. 2364

Alcohol and Drug Abuse Amendments of 1986

Oct. 27, 1986, P.L. 99-570, 42 U.S. Code § 201 nt.
Nov. 28, 1990, P.L. 101-630, 104 Stat. 4567
Oct. 29, 1992, P.L. 102-573, 106 Stat. 4562

Alcohol and Drug Abuse Commitment Act

S.C. Code Ann. 1976, § 44-52-10 et seq.

Alcohol and Drug Abuse Education Act

Dec. 3, 1970, P.L. 91-527, 84 Stat. 1385
Sept. 21, 1974, P.L. 93-422, 88 Stat. 1154, 21 U.S. Code §§ 1001 to 1004, 1007
Oct. 17, 1979, P.L. 96-88, 21 U.S. Code § 1004
Aug. 13, 1982, P.L. 97-35, 95 Stat. 480

Alcohol and Drug Abuse Education Act Amendments of 1974

Sept. 21, 1974, P.L. 930422, 88 Stat. 1154

Alcohol and Drug Abuse Education Amendments of 1978

Aug. 4, 1978, P.L. 95-336, 20 U.S. Code §§ 1070e-1, 1070e-1 nt.; 21 U.S. Code §§ 1001, 1001 nt., 1002, 1007; 38 U.S. Code § 246

Alcohol and Drug Abuse Policy Board Act

Okla. Stat. Ann., Title 74, § 30 et seq.

Alcohol and Drug Abuse Prevention and Life Skills Education Act

Okla. Stat. Ann., Title 70, § 1210.229-1 et seq.

Alcohol and Drug Abuse Services Act
Okla. Stat. 1981, Title 43A, § 3-401 et seq.
Tex. Rev. Civ. Stat., Art. 5561c-2

Alcohol and Drug Affected Mothers and Infants Act
Cal. Health and Safety Code § 11757.50 et seq.

Alcohol and Drug-Free Workplace Act (Private Employer)
Ida. Code 1947, 72-1701 et seq.

Alcohol and Drug Treatment Act
Tenn. Code Ann., 33-8-101

Alcohol and Drug Treatment Recovery Program (Adolescent)
Cal. Health and Safety Code § 11759 et seq.

Alcohol and Other Drug Abuse Counselor Registration Act
Kan. Stat. Ann., 65-6601 et seq.

Alcohol and Other Drug Abuse Prevention, Intervention and Treatment Law
Ky. Rev. Stat. 1971, 222.001 et seq.

Alcohol and Other Drug Abuse Professional Practice Act
N.H. Rev. Stat. 1955, 330-C:1 et seq.

Alcohol and Other Drug Services Act (Hal S. Marchman)
Fla. Stat. Ann., 397.301 et seq.

Alcohol and Substance Abuse Services Oversight Act
Tex. Health and Safety Code, § 468.001 et seq.

Alcohol Beverage Licensing Code
Ala. Code 1975, § 28-3A-1 et seq.

Alcohol Blending Act
Neb. Rev. Stat. 1943, 66-317, 66-401 Subd. 2

Alcohol Boating Safety Act
Miss. Code Ann. 1972, § 59-23-1 et seq.
R.I. Gen. Laws 1956, 46-22.2-1 et seq.

Alcohol, Drug Abuse, and Mental Health Services Act
Fla. Stat. Ann., 394.65 et seq.

Alcohol, Drug Abuse, Developmental Disabilities and Mental Health Act
Wis. Stat. Ann., 51.001 et seq.

Alcohol, Drugs and Substance Abuse in Schools Act (Comprehensive Action against)
La. Rev. Stat. Ann., 17:402 et seq.

Alcohol Permit Act
Okla. Stat. Ann., Title 37, § 50.1 et seq.

Alcohol Plants Transfer Act
July 2, 1948, Ch. 818, 62 Stat. 1234, 7 U.S. Code §§ 439 to 439e

Alcohol Purchase Age Law
N.Y. Alcoholic Beverage Law (Consol. Laws Ch. 3B), §§ 65 Subd. 1, 65a, 65b Subd. 1
N.Y. General Obligations Law (Consol. Laws Ch. 24A), § 11-100 Subd. 6
N.Y. Penal Law 1965 (Consol. Laws Ch. 40), § 260-20 Subd. 4

Alcohol Sales Act (Druggists)
S.C. Code Ann. 1976, § 61-11-10 et seq.

Alcohol Server Education Act
N.M. Stat. Ann., 60-6D-1 et seq.

Alcohol Server Responsibility and Training Act
Tenn. Code Ann., 57-3-701 to 57-3-710

Alcohol Services Act
Okla. Stat. Ann., Title 63, § 2100 et seq.

Alcohol Tax Incentive and Administration Act
Mont. Code Ann., 15-70-501 et seq.

Alcohol Tests Act (Driver's Consent)
N.M. Stat. Ann., 66-8-105 et seq.
Utah Code Ann. 1953, 41-6-44.10

Alcohol Traffic Safety Programs

Oct. 25, 1982, P.L. 97-364, 23 U.S. Code § 408

Alcohol/Drug Intervention and Prevention Act (Teen)

Utah Code Ann. 1953, 62A-8-202 et seq.

Alcoholic and Narcotic Addict Rehabilitation Act

Oct. 15, 1968, P.L. 90-574, 82 Stat. 1006, 42 U.S. Code §§ 2688e to 2688q, 2697a

Alcoholic Beverage Act

Ariz. Rev. Stat. Ann., § 4-101 et seq.

Fla. Stat. Ann., 561.01 et seq.

Ind. Code Ann., 7.1-1-1-1 et seq.

Iowa Code Ann., 123.1 et seq.

Md. Ann. Code 1957, Art. 2B

Mont. Code Ann.,16-1-101 et seq.

N.D. Cent. Code, 5-01-01 et seq.

N.H. Rev. Stat. 1955, 175:1 et seq.

N.M. Stat. Ann., 60-3A-1 et seq.

Okla. Stat. Ann., Title 37, § 501

P.R. Laws Ann. 1954, Title 13, § 6001 et seq.

Vt. Stat. Ann., Title 7, § 1 et seq.

Alcoholic Beverage Code

Mont. Code Ann. 1987, 16-1-101 to 16-6-331

Alcoholic Beverage Control Act (New Hanover County)

N.C. Public Laws 1935, Ch. 418

Alcoholic Beverage Excise Tax Act

N.M. Stat. Ann., 7-17-1 et seq.

Alcoholic Beverage Server Fair Liability Act (Licensed)

N.J. Stat. Ann., 2A:22A-1 et seq.

Alcoholic Beverage Tax Act

Cal. Revenue and Taxation Code § 32001 et seq.

Ky. Rev. Stat. 1971, 243.010 et seq.

N.J. Stat. Ann., 54:41-1 to 54:47-7

S.C. Code Ann. 1976, § 12-33-10 et seq.

Alcoholic Beverage Tax Bill of Rights

Cal. Revenue and Taxation Code § 32460 et seq.

Alcoholic Beverage Tax Law

Cal. Revenue and Taxation Code § 32001 et seq.

Alcoholic Beverage Wholesale Sales Tax Act

N.J. Stat. Ann., 54:32C-1 et seq.

Alcoholic Beverages Advertising and Display Act

Miss. Code Ann. 1972, § 67-1-85

Alcoholic Beverages Control Act

Ala. Code 1975, § 28-3-1 et seq.

Alaska Stat. 1962, § 04.06.010 et seq.

Ark. Code Ann. 1987, 3-1-101 et seq.

Cal. Business and Professions Code § 23000 et seq.

Colo. Rev. Stat., 12-47-101 et seq.

D.C. Code 1973, § 25-101 et seq.

Del. Code of 1974, Title 4, § 101 et seq.

Ga. Code Ann., 3-1-1 et seq.

Haw. Rev. Stat. Ann., § 281-1 et seq.

Ida. Code 1947, 23-101 et seq.

Iowa Code Ann., 123.1 et seq.

Kan. Stat. Ann., 41-101 et seq.

Ky. Rev. Stat. 1971, 241.010 et seq.

La. Rev. Stat. Ann., 26:1 et seq.

Mass. Gen. Laws Ann., 138:1 et seq.

Me. Rev. Stat. Ann. 1964, Title 28A, § 1 et seq.

Mich. Comp. Laws Ann., 436.1 et seq.

Minn. Stat. Ann., 340A.101 et seq.

Miss. Code Ann. 1972, 67-1-1 et seq.

Mo. Rev. Stat., 311.010 et seq.

N.C. Gen. Stat. 1943, § 18B-100 et seq.

Neb. Rev. Stat. 1943, 53-101 et seq.

Nev. Rev. Stat. 1979 Reprint, 369.010 et seq.

N.J. Stat. Ann., 33:1-3 et seq.

N.Y. Consol. Laws, Ch. 3B

Ohio Rev. Code 1953, 4301.01 et seq.

Okla. Stat. Ann., Title 37, § 501 et seq.

Ore. Rev. Stat., 471.005 et seq.

Pa. Purdon's Stat., Title 47, § 1-101 et seq.

R.I. Gen. Laws 1956, 3-1-1 et seq.

Continued

S.C. Code Ann. 1976, § 61-6-10 et seq.
S.D. Codified Laws 1967, 35-1-1 et seq.
Tenn. Code Ann., 57-1-101 et seq.
Tex. Alcoholic Beverage Code, § 1.01 et seq.
Utah Code Ann. 1953, 32A-1-101 et seq.
Va. Code 1950, § 4-1 et seq.
Wash. Rev. Code Ann., 66.04.010 et seq.
Wis. Stat. Ann., 125.01 et seq.
W. Va. Code 1966, § 60-1-1 et seq.
Wyo. Stat. Ann., § 12-1-101 et seq.

Alcoholic Beverages Tax Act
S.C. Code Ann. 1976, § 12-33-10 et seq.

Alcoholic Content of Blood Chemical Test Act
S.C. Code Ann. 1976, § 56-5-2950

Alcoholic Fair Trade Act
Ill. Rev. Stat. 1977, Ch. 43, § 196 et seq.

Alcoholic Habit Act
Pa. Purdon's Stat., Title 50, § 2101 et seq.

Alcoholic Liquor Control Act
Ill. Rev. Stat. 1991, Ch. 43, § 93.9 et seq.

Alcoholic Liquor Sale by Individual Drink Act
Ore. Rev. Stat., 472.010 et seq.

Alcoholic Liquors Minimum Price Act
Conn. Gen. Stat. Ann., § 30-64 et seq.

Alcoholic Rehabilitation Act of 1968
Oct. 15, 1968, P.L. 90-574, 82 Stat. 1006, 42
    U.S. Code §§ 2688e to 2688j
March 13, 1970, P.L. 91-211, 84 Stat. 57
Dec. 31, 1970, P.L. 91-616, 84 Stat. 1851
June 18, 1973, P.L. 93-45, 87 Stat. 94
May 14, 1974, P.L. 93-282, 88 Stat. 137
July 29, 1975, P.L. 94-63, 89 Stat. 352

Alcoholic Sales Act
Ind. Code 1971, 7-2-1-1 et seq.

Alcoholic Study Commission Act
Ky. Acts 1952, Ch. 32

Alcoholics Act
Wash. Rev. Code Ann., 70.96A.010 et seq.

Alcoholics Rehabilitation Act
D.C. Code Ann., § 24-521 et seq.

Alcoholism Act
Neb. Rev. Stat. 1943, 83-158.01 et seq.
N.M. Stat. Ann. 1953, 46-12-1 et seq.

Alcoholism Act (McAteer)
Cal. Health and Safety Code § 427 et seq.

Alcoholism and Alcohol Abuse Prevention, Control and Treatment Act
Miss. Code Ann. 1972, § 40-30-1 et seq.

Alcoholism and Alcohol Abuse Prevention, Screening and Treatment Act
N.M. Stat. Ann., 43-3-8 et seq.

Alcoholism and Drug Abuse Act of 1973
Me. Rev. Stat. Ann. 1964, Title 22, § 7101 et seq.

Alcoholism And Drug Abuse Division Act
Neb. Rev. Stat. 1943, 83-158.01 et seq.

Alcoholism and Drug Addiction Treatment and Support Act
Wash. Rev. Code, 1989, 74.50.010 et seq.

Alcoholism and Intoxication Act
Md. Ann. Code 1974, Art. HG, § 8-101 et seq.

Alcoholism and Intoxication Treatment Act
See also Uniform Alcoholism and
    Intoxication Treatment Act
Conn. Gen. Stat. Ann., § 17-155k et seq.
Ill. Rev. Stat. 1983, Ch. 91 1/2, § 501 et seq.
Iowa Code Ann., 125.1 et seq.
Me. Rev. Stat. Ann. 1964, Title 22, § 1361 et seq.

Alcoholism and Other Drug Abuse and Dependency Act
Ill. Comp. Stat. 1992, Ch. 20, § 301/1-1 et seq.

Alcoholism and Other Drug Addiction Intervenor and Reporting Immunity Law
Ill. Comp. Stat. 1992, Ch. 745, § 35/1 et seq.

Alcoholism and Substance Abuse Act
Ill. Rev. Stat. 1987, Ch. 111 1/2, § 6301 et seq.
N.Y. Mental Hygiene Law 1977 (Consol. Laws Ch. 27) § 19.01 et seq.

Alcoholism and Substance Abuse Services Consolidation Act
N.Y. Laws 1992, Ch. 223

Alcoholism Commission Act
Ida. Laws 1965, Ch. 184
N.M. Stat. Ann. 1953, 46-12-1 et seq.

Alcoholism Control Act
Md. Ann. Code 1974, Art. HG, § 8-101 et seq.

Alcoholism Prevention, Control and Treatment Act
Fla. Stat. Ann., 396.012 et seq.
Miss. Code Ann. 1972, § 41-30-1 et seq.

Alcoholism Treatment Act
Ga. Code Ann., 37-8-1 et seq.
N.M. Stat. Ann., 43-3-1 et seq.

Alcoholism Treatment and Detoxification Act (Community)
N.M. Stat. Ann., 43-3-1 et seq.

Alcoholism Treatment and Rehabilitation
Ky. Rev. Stat. 1971, 222.011 et seq.
Mass. Gen. Laws Ann., 111B:1 et seq.
N.J. Stat. Ann., 26:2B-7 et seq.

Alcoholism Treatment Licensing Act
Ill. Rev. Stat. 1987, Ch. 111 1/2, § 2301 et seq.

Alcovy Shores Water and Sewerage Authority Act
Ga. Laws 1979, p. 3177

Aldene Plan Act (Railroad Transportation)
N.J. Stat. Ann., 48:12A-17 et seq.

Aldermanic Reapportionment Act (New York City)
N.Y. Laws 1921, Ch. 670

Aldrich Act (Currency)
March 4, 1907, Ch. 2913, 34 Stat. 1289, 12 U.S. Code §§ 90, 178; 31 U.S. Code §§ 403, 429

Aldrich-Vreeland Act (National Currency Associations)
May 30, 1908, Ch. 229, 35 Stat. 546, 12 U.S. Code § 104

Ale, Beer, Porter, and Wine Act
S.C. Code Ann. 1976, 61-9-10 et seq.

Aledo Civic Center Act
Ill. Comp. Stat. 1992, Ch. 70, § 220/1 et seq.

Aledo Civic Center Law
Ill. Rev. Stat. 1985, Ch. 85, § 4501 et seq.

Aledo, Normal, Mason County, Jasper County, Brownstown Park District, Jo Daviess County, Milford, Sheldon, Katherine Dunham, and Oak Park Civil Centers Act
Ill. Rev. Stat. 1991, Ch. 85, § 4500 et seq.

Aleutian and Pribilof Islands Restitution Act
Aug. 10, 1988, P.L. 100-383, 102 Stat. 911, 50 U.S. Code Appx. §§ 1989c to 1989c-8
Oct. 22, 1994, P.L. 103-402, 50 U.S. Code Appx. § 1989c-4

Aleutian Trade Act of 1990
Nov. 16, 1990, P.L. 101-595, 46 U.S. Code §§ 2101, 2101 nt., 2102, 3302, 4104, 4502, 4502 nt., 5102, 5115, 7306 nt., prec. 8101, 8103 to 8105, 8702, 12109, 12501, 12503, 12505, 14102, 31308

Aleutian World War II National Historic Areas Act of 1996
Nov. 12, 1996, P.L. 104-333, § 513, 16 U.S. Code § 461 nt.

Alexander Road Law
Ark. Acts 1915, p. 1400, No. 338

Alexandria and Bogalusa, Louisiana, Redevelopment Agency Act
La. Acts 1972, No. 673

Alexandria Parking Authorities Act
Va. Acts 1956, Ch. 406
Va. Acts 1958, Ch. 348

Alexandria Port Commission Act
Va. Acts 1962, Ch. 392

Alfalfa Leaf-Cutting Bee Act
Mont. Code Ann., 80-6-1101 et seq.
Wyo. Stat. Ann., § 11-7-201 et seq.

Alfalfa Seed Industry Act
Ida. Code 1947, 22-4201 et seq.
Mont. Code Ann., 80-11-301 et seq.

Alfred, Almond, Hornellsville Sewer Authority Project Act
N.Y. Public Authorities Law (Consol. Laws Ch. 43A) § 1147 et seq.

Alfred E. Alquist Earthquake Act
Cal. Health and Safety Code § 15000 et seq.

Alfred E. Alquist Hospital Facility Seismic Safety Act
Cal. Health and Safety Code § 15000 et seq.

Alfred P. Murrah Federal Building Commemorative Coin Act
Okla. Stat. Ann., Title 25, § 93.2

Alibi Act
Ariz. Rules of Criminal Procedure 1973, Rule 15.2
Ind. Code Ann., 35-36-4-1 et seq.
Kan. Stat. Ann., 22-3218
Minn. Stat. 1978, 630.14
Mont. Code Ann., 46-15-322 et seq.
N.J. Rules Governing the Courts 1969, Rule 3:11
N.Y. Criminal Procedure Law (Consol. Laws Ch. 11A) § 250.20
Ohio Rev. Code 1953, 2945.58
Okla. Stat. Ann., Title 22, § 585
Utah Code Ann. 1953, 77-14-2

Alibi Defense Act
Iowa Rules of Criminal Procedure, Rule 10

Alibi Notice Act
Wis. Stat. Ann., 971.23, Subsec. 8

Alien Agency Act
Aug. 6, 1939, Ch. 521, 53 Stat. 1244

Alien Contract Labor Act
Ill. Rev. Stat. 1991, Ch. 6, § 0.01 et seq.

Alien Contract Labor Laws
Feb. 26, 1885, Ch. 164, 23 Stat. 332
March 3, 1891, Ch. 551, 26 Stat. 1084
March 3, 1903, Ch. 1012, 32 Stat. 1214
Feb. 20, 1907, Ch. 1134, 34 Stat. 898
Feb. 5, 1917, Ch. 29, 39 Stat. 875

Alien Enemies Acts
June 25, 1798, Ch. 58, 1 Stat. 570
July 6, 1798, Ch. 66, 1 Stat. 577
July 6, 1812, Ch. 130, 2 Stat. 781

Alien Firearms Law
Pa. Purdon's Stat., Title 34, § 1311.1001 et seq.

Alien Fishing Act
Alaska Stat. 1962, §§ 16.05.905, 16.05.910

Alien Immigration Acts
See Immigration Acts

Alien Labor Law (Governmental Departments)
Cal. Labor Code § 1940 et seq.

Alien Labor Law (Public Works)
Cal. Labor Code § 1850 et seq.

Alien Land Act
Ariz. Rev. Stat. Ann., § 33-1201 et seq.
Ark. Acts 1925, p. 726, No. 249
Cal. Statutes 1913, Ch. 113, p. 206
Ida. Code 1947, 24-101 et seq.
Mont. Rev. Code 1947, 67-1001 et seq.
Ore. Code 1930, § 19-101 et seq.
Pa. Purdon's Stat., Title 68, § 22

Tex. Property Code, § 5.005
Wash. Rev. Code Ann., 64.16.005 et seq.
Wis. Stat. Ann., 710.01
W. Va. Code 1966, § 36-1-21
Wyo. Stat. Ann., § 34-15-101 et seq.

Alien Land Holding Law
Neb. Rev. Stat. 1943, 76-402 et seq.

Alien Poll Tax Act
Cal. Statutes 1921, Ch. 424, p. 613

Alien Property Act
N.C. Gen. Stat. 1943, § 64-1 et seq.

Alien Reciprocal Inheritance Act
N.C. Gen. Stat. 1943, §§ 64-3 to 64-5

Alien Registration Act
Pa. Purdon's Stat., Title 35, § 1801 et seq.

Alien Registration Act, 1940
June 28, 1940, Ch. 439, 54 Stat. 670 (See 8
U.S. Code §§ 1101, 1182, 1201, 1251,
1254, 1301 to 1306, 1351) 18 U.S. Code
§§ 9 to 13
June 25, 1948, Ch. 645, 62 Stat. 862
Sept. 23, 1950, Ch. 1024, 64 Stat. 1012 (See
8 U.S. Code §§ 1304, 1305)
June 27, 1952, Ch. 477, 66 Stat. 279

**Alien Species Prevention and Enforcement
Act of 1992**
Oct. 6, 1992, P.L. 102-393, 39 U.S. Code
§§ prec. 3001, 3015, 3015 nt.

Alien Veterans Act
June 21, 1939, Ch. 234, 53 Stat. 851

Alien Visa Act
June 20, 1941, Ch. 209, 55 Stat. 252

Alienation of Affections Act
Ill. Comp. Stat. 1992, Ch. 740, § 5/0.01 et
seq.

**Aliens' Real Estate Ownership Acts
(Territories)**
March 3, 1887, Ch. 340, 24 Stat. 476, 48 U.S.
Code §§ 1501 to 1508

March 2, 1897, Ch. 363, 29 Stat. 618, 48 U.S.
Code §§ 1501 to 1508

Aliens Reciprocal Inheritance Act
N.C. Gen. Stat. 1943, § 64-3 et seq.
Ore. Rev. Stat., 111.070

Alimony Act
Ala. Code 1975, §§ 30-2-50 to 30-2-53
Ga. Code Ann., 19-6-1 et seq.
Ky. Rev. Stat. 1971, Superseded Vols.,
403.080
Mich. Comp. Laws Ann., 552.23 et seq.
N.C. Gen. Stat. 1943, § 50-16.1 et seq.
N.J. Stat. Ann., 2A:34-23
Okla. Stat. Ann., Title 43, § 121

Alimony Act (Modification)
Ga. Code Ann., 19-6-18 et seq.

Alimony and Divorce Act
Colo. Rev. Stat., 11-4-101 et seq.

Alimony and Property Act (Divorce)
Kan. Gen. Stat. 60-1610

Alimony Enforcement Act
Mich. Comp. Laws Ann., 552.27

Alimony without Divorce Act
N.C. Gen. Stat. 1943, § 50-16.1

All Fallen Officers Career Criminal Act
Fla. Stat. Ann., 775.084 to 775.0843,
790.235

All Goods Act (Installment Sales)
Ind. Code Ann., 24-5-2-26
Kan. Laws 1958, Ch. 9
Neb. Rev. Stat. 1943, 45-334 et seq.

All-Inclusive Care for the Elderly Act
Ill. Comp. Stat. 1992, Ch. 320, § 40/1 et seq.
Ill. Rev. Stat. 1991, Ch. 23, § 6901 et seq.

All Industry Rate Act (Casualty Insurance)
Ark. Code Ann. 1987, 23-67-101 et seq.

All-Terrain Vehicle and Snowmobile Law
Pa. Cons. Stat., Title 75, § 7701 et seq.

All-Terrain Vehicle Safety Act
Ill. Rev. Stat. 1991, Ch. 95 1/2, § 1201-1 et seq.

All Writs Act
March 3, 1911, Ch. 231, 36 Stat. 1156 (See 28 U.S. Code § 1651)

Alldredge-Abrams Act (Insurance Department)
Ind. Laws 1919, Ch. 48, p. 109

Allegheny County Court Act
Pa. Purdon's Stat., Title 17, § 621 et seq.

Allegheny County Juvenile Court Law
Pa. Purdon's Stat., Title 11, § 269-1 et seq.

Allen Act (Street Railway Valuations)
N.J. Laws 1920, p. 860, Ch. 351

Allen Cable, Evans Law (State Board of Education-Negro Member)
Ind. Laws 1939, Ch. 82, p. 474

Allen-Cologne Act (Mistreatment of Children)
Cal. Penal Code §§ 11110, 11161.5

Allen-Nunan Act (Milk Control)
N.Y. Agriculture and Markets Law (Consol. Laws Ch. 69) § 258k et seq.

Allen-Rogers Act (Milk Control)
N.Y. Agriculture and Markets Law (Consol. Laws Ch. 69) § 258k et seq.

Allen Short Development Centers for the Handicapped Act of 1974
Cal. Education Code 1976 § 56800 et seq.

Alley and Street Closing Act
D.C. Code Ann., § 7-411 et seq.

Alley and Street Closing and Acquisition Procedures Act
D.C. Code Ann., § 7-411 et seq.

Alley Dwelling Act
D.C. Code Ann., § 5-101 et seq.

Allied Health Care Professional Assistance Law
Ill. Comp. Stat. 1992, Ch. 110, § 905/2001 et seq.

Allied Health Professions Personal Training Act of 1966
Nov. 3, 1966, P.L. 89-751, 80 Stat. 1222, 12 U.S. Code § 1717; 42 U.S. Code §§ 293e, 294a to 294d, 294h-1 to 294h-5, 296, 297c to 297f, 298c, 298c-1 to 298c-8

Allied Health Student Loan for Service Act
N.M. Stat. Ann., 21-22C-1 et seq.

Alligator Market Development Act
La. Rev. Stat. Ann., 3:599 et seq.

Alligator Point Water Resources Act
Fla. Special Laws 1963, Ch. 63-1350

Allison Shipping Act (Intoxicating Liquors)
Tex. General Laws 33rd Leg., 1913, p. 125, Ch. 67

Allocation Act (Income Tax)
Ore. Rev. Stat., 314.280

Allocation Act (Net Income)
Minn. Stat. Ann., 290.20

Allocation Act (Private Activity Bond)
Kan. Stat. Ann., 74-5058 et seq.

Allocation Act (Volume Cap)
Utah Code Ann. 1953, 9-4-501 et seq.

Allocation for Art for Public Facilities Act
R.I. Gen. Laws 1956, 42-75.2-1 et seq.

Allocation of Liability Act (Controlled)
Mont. Code Ann., 75-10-742 et seq.

Allocation or Apportionment of Income Act
S.C. Code Ann. 1976, § 12-7-1110 et seq.

Allocation Plan for Private Activity Bonds and Student Loan Bonds Act
Tenn. Code Ann., 13-29-101 et seq.

Allocation System Act
Ga. Code Ann., 36-82-180 et seq.

Allopathic and Osteopathic Health Care Discrimination Act
Ill. Comp. Stat. 1992, Ch. 225, § 62/1

Allopathic Medical and Surgical Licensure and Supervision Act
Okla. Stat. Ann., Title 59, § 480 et seq.

Allowances, Costs and Fees Act
W. Va. Code 1966, § 59-1-1 et seq.

Alpharetta Community Improvement District Act
Ga. Laws 1992, p. 5842

Alpine County Water Agency Act
Cal. Water Code, Appendix, § 102-1 et seq.

Alpine Lakes Area Management Act of 1976
July 12, 1976, P.L. 94-357, 16 U.S. Code § 1132 et seq.

Alquist-Campbell Community College Finance Act
Cal. Education Code 1976, § 84720 et seq.

Alquist-Cobey Flood Plain Management Act
Cal. Water Code § 8400 et seq.

Alquist-Ingalls Act (Transportation)
Cal. Statutes 1977, Ch. 1106

Alquist-Klehs Tax Conformity Act
Cal. Revenue and Taxation Code §§ 6051, 6201 et seq.
Cal. Statutes 1991, Ch. 117

Alquist Open Presidential Primary Act
Cal. Election Code 1976, § 6300 et seq.

Alquist-Priolo Earthquake Fault Zoning Act
Cal. Public Resources Code § 2621 et seq.

Alquist-Priolo Geologic Hazards Zones Act
Cal. Public Resources Code § 2621 et seq.

Alquist-Warren State Energy Resources Conservation and Development Act
Cal. Public Resources Code § 25000 et seq.

Altamaha River Basin Commission Act
Ga. Code Ann., 12-5-420 et seq.

Altered and Stolen Property Act (Motor Vehicle Chop Shop)
Okla. Stat. Ann., Title 47, § 1501 et seq.

Altered Motor Vehicle Chop Shop and Stolen Property Act
R.I. Gen. Laws 1956, 31-48-1 et seq.

Alternate Fuels Act
Ill. Comp. Stat. 1992, Ch. 425, § 120/1-1 et seq.

Alternate Jurors Act
N.J. Stat. Ann., 2A:74-2
N.Y. Criminal Procedure Law (Consol. Laws Ch. 11A) § 270.30 et seq.
Okla. Stat. Ann., Title 22, § 601a

Alternative Agricultural Research and Commercialization Act of 1990
Nov. 28, 1990, P.L. 101-624, 7 U.S. Code §§ 5901 to 5908
Dec. 13, 1991, P.L. 102-237, 7 U.S. Code §§ 5902, 5907

Alternative and Reverse Annuity Mortgage Loan Act
Iowa Code Ann., 528.1 et seq.

Alternative County Government Act
N.Y. Alternative County Government Law § 1 et seq.

Alternative Custody Act (Personal Property)
N.J. Stat. Ann., 2A:37-29 et seq.

Alternative Dispute Resolution Act
Utah Code Ann. 1953, 78-31b-11 et seq.

Alternative Dispute Resolution Act (Court-Connected)
Ga. Code Ann., 15-23-1 et seq.

Alternative Dispute Resolution Act of 1998
Oct. 30, 1998, P.L. 105-315, 112 Stat. 2993,
28 U.S. Code § 1 nt.

Alternative Dispute Resolution Providers Certification Act
Utah Code Ann. 1953, 58-39a-1 et seq.

Alternative Drainage District Act
Ark. Code Ann. 1987, 14-121-101 et seq.

Alternative Education Act
Mo. Rev. Stat. 1978, 167.320

Alternative Energy Source Financing Authority Act
Cal. Public Resources Code § 26000 et seq.

Alternative Form County Government Act
Ohio Rev. Code 1953, 302.14 et seq.

Alternative Fuel Conversion Act
N.M. Stat. Ann., 13-1B-1 et seq.

Alternative Fuel Tax Act
Neb. Rev. Stat. 1943, 66-684
N.M. Stat. Ann., 7-16B-1 et seq.

Alternative Fuels Conversion Act
Okla. Stat. 1981, Title 74, § 130.1 et seq.

Alternative Fuels Loan Program
Kan. Stat. Ann., 75-37,116

Alternative Fuels Technician Certification Act
Okla. Stat. 1981, Title 74, § 130.11 et seq.

Alternative Health Care Delivery Act
Ill. Comp. Stat. 1992, Ch. 210, § 3/1 et seq.

Alternative Incarceration Act (Special)
Mich. Comp. Laws Ann., 798.11 et seq.

Alternative Local Government Sales and Use Tax Act
N.C. Gen. Stat. 1943, § 105-488 et seq.

Alternative Mortgage Transaction Parity Act of 1982
Oct. 15, 1982, P.L. 97-320, 12 U.S. Code §§ 3801 nt., 3801 et seq.
Nov. 30, 1983, P.L. 98-181, 12 U.S. Code § 3804
Aug. 9, 1989, P.L. 101-73, 12 U.S. Code §§ 3801, 3802

Alternative Motor Fuels Act of 1988
Oct. 24, 1992, P.L. 102-486, 42 U.S. Code § 6374 nt.

Alternative Motor Fuels Act of 1988 Oct. 14, 1988, P.L. 100-494, 42 U.S. Code § 6201 nt.

Alternative Procedure for Dispute Resolution Act
N.J. Stat. Ann., 2A:23A-1 et seq.

Alternative Protest Pilot Project
Cal. Public Contract Code § 12125 et seq.

Alternative Receivership Act
R.I. Gen. Laws 1956, 19-15.1-1 et seq.

Alternative Routes to Teacher Certification and Licensure Act of 1992
July 23, 1992, P.L. 102-325, 20 U.S. Code §§ 1108 to 1108g

Alternative Salary Policies For Teachers Act
Colo. Rev. Stat., 22-66-101 et seq.

Alternative Sentencing Job Training Act
Ill. Comp. Stat. 1992, Ch. 730, § 170/1 et seq.

Alternative Service Act
Ark. Code Ann. 1987, 16-93-501 et seq., 16-93-601, 12-27-104

Alternative Work Schedule Act (State Employees')
R.I. Gen. Laws 1956, 36-3.1-1 et seq.

Alternatives to Abortion Information Act
R.I. Gen. Laws 1956, 23-4.13-1 et seq.

Alternatives to Long-term Nursing Home Care Act
Colo. Rev. Stat., 26-4.5-101 et seq.

Alternatives to Long-term Nursing Home Care for the Developmentally Disabled and Mentally Ill Act
Colo. Rev. Stat., 26-4.5-201 et seq.

Altman Act (Banks)
N.J. Stat. Ann., 1937, 17:9A-224

Alton Lake Heritage Parkway Corridor Act
Ill. Comp. Stat. 1992, Ch. 20, § 3905/1001 et seq.

Alviso Nuevo Development Corporation Act
Cal. Statutes 1972, Ch. 1096, p. 2057

Alzheimer's Day Care-Resource Center Pilot Project Act
Cal. Health and Safety Code § 1568.10 et seq.

Alzheimer's Disease and Related Dementias Research Act of 1992
Nov. 10, 1998, P.L. 105-362, 42 U.S. Code §§ 11211, 11212

Alzheimer's Disease and Related Dementias Services Research Act of 1986
Nov. 14, 1986, P.L. 99-660, 42 U.S. Code § 11201 nt.
Nov. 4, 1988, P.L. 100-607, 42 U.S. Code §§ 285e et seq., 11231 et seq.

Alzheimers Disease and Related Dementias Services Research Act of 1992
June 13, 1991, P.L. 102-54, 42 U.S. Code §§ 11211, 11261
Oct. 24, 1992, P.L. 102-507, 42 U.S. Code §§ 11201, 11201 nt., 11211, 11212, 11221, 11223, 11251, 11253, 11261, 11263, 11292, 11294
Dec. 2, 1993, P.L. 103-171, 42 U.S. Code §§ 11211, 11221

Alzheimer's Disease and Related Disorders Act
S.C. Code Ann. 1976, § 44-36-1 et seq.

Alzheimer's Disease Assistance Act
Ill. Comp. Stat. 1992, Ch. 410, § 405/1 et seq.

Alzheimer's Disease Initiative
Fla. Stat. Ann., 430.501 et seq.

Alzheimer's Disease Institute Act (Duffy)
Cal. Health and Safety Code § 1310 et seq.

Alzheimer's Disease Research Act
Ill. Comp. Stat. 1992, Ch. 410, § 410/1 et seq.

Alzheimer's Disease Research, Training, and Education Amendments of 1992
Oct. 24, 1992, P.L. 102-507, 42 U.S. Code § 11201 nt.

Alzheimer's Patients Pilot Program Act
Tex. Human Resources Code, § 32.0246

Alzheimer's Special Care Disclosure Act
Ill. Comp. Stat. 1992, Ch. 210, § 4/1 et seq.
Neb. Rev. Stat. 1943, 71-516.01 et seq.
S.C. Code Ann. 1976, §§ 44-36-510, 44-36-520

Amador County Water Agency Act
Cal. Water Code, Appendix, § 95-1 et seq.

Amateur Athletics Authority Act (Conyers-Rockdale)
Ga. Laws 1999, S.B. 209

Amateur Sports Act of 1978
Nov. 8, 1978, P.L. 95-606, 36 U.S. Code §§ 371, 371 nt., 372 et seq.

Amateur Sports Law (Sunday)
Me. Rev. Stat. Ann. 1964, Title 17, § 3205

Amber Hegerman Child Protection Act of 1996
Sept. 30, 1996, P.L. 104-208, Title I, § 121(7), 18 U.S. Code § 2241 nt.

Ambulance Authority Act (Richmond)
Va. Acts 1991, Ch. 431

Ambulance District Law
Mo. Rev. Stat., 190.005 et seq.

Ambulance Emergency Service Act
W. Va. Code 1966, § 7-15-1 et seq.

Ambulance Licensing Act (Municipal)
Ark. Code Ann. 1987, 14-266-101 et seq.

Ambulance Regulation Act
Conn. Gen. Stat. Ann., § 19a-175 et seq.

Ambulance Service District Act (Rural)
Okla. Stat. Ann., Title 19, § 1201 et seq.

Ambulance Service, Rescue Squad and Fire Company Assistance Act (Volunteer)
Pa. Purdon's Stat., Title 72, § 3943.1 et seq.

Ambulance Services Law
N.D. Cent. Code, 23-27-01 et seq.

Ambulance Services Law (Regional)
Ill. Rev. Stat. 1991, Ch. 111 1/2, § 8301 et seq.

Ambulance Standards Act
N.M. Stat. Ann., 65-6-1 et seq.

Ambulance Workers' Benefit Law (Volunteer)
N.Y. Volunteer Firemen's Benefit Law (Consol. Laws Ch. 64B)

Ambulatory Surgical Centers Licensing Act
La. Rev. Stat. Ann., 40:2131 et seq.
Tex. Health and Safety Code § 243.001 et seq.

Ambulatory Surgical Facility Act
Utah Code Ann. 1953, Miscellaneous Superseded Code Provisions, 26-32-1 et seq.

Ambulatory Surgical Facility Licensure Act
N.C. Gen. Stat. 1943, § 131E-145 et seq.

Ambulatory Surgical Treatment Center Act
Ill. Comp. Stat. 1992, Ch. 210, § 5/1 et seq.

Ambulatory Surgical Treatment Center Licensure Act
D.C. Code Ann., § 32-1301 et seq.

Amended Bear River Compact Act
Utah Code Ann. 1953, 73-16-3 et seq.

Amended Eligibility Requirements for AFDC by Reason of the Unemployment of the Father Act
D.C. Code Ann., § 1-319

Amended Unincorporated Business Franchise Tax Revision Act
D.C. Code Ann., §§ 47-1803.3, 47-1808.4

Amendment No. 74 Enabling Act
Mar. 29, 1996, P.L. 104-121, 110 Stat. 847, Titles 1, 2
Ark. Code 1987, 26-80-101 et seq.

Amendment to the Interstate Compact on Juveniles
Ala. Acts 1986, No. 419

Amendments and Jeofails Act
Ill. Laws 1965, p. 3344
Ill. Laws 1980, P.A. 80-742, § 1
Ill. Rev. Stat. 1975, Ch. 7

Amendments of 1973 to Federal Law Relating to Explosives
Jan. 4, 1975, P.L. 93-639, 88 Stat. 2217

America the Beautiful Act of 1990
Nov. 28, 1990, P.L. 101-624,16 U.S. Code § 2101 nt.

American Aid to Poland Act of 1988
Aug. 23, 1988, P.L. 100-418, 102 Stat. 1356, 7 U.S. Code § 1421 nt.
Nov. 5, 1990, P.L. 101-513, 7 U.S. Code § 1431 nt.
Aug. 23, 1994, P.L. 103-306, 7 U.S. Code § 1431 nt.

American Antiques Preservation Act
See National Monument Act (Preservation of Antiquities)

American Arts Gold Medallion Act
Nov. 10, 1978, P.L. 95-630, 92 Stat. 3679, 31 U.S. Code § 5111 nt.

American Automobile Labeling Act
Oct. 20, 1972, P.L. 92-513, 106 Stat. 1556
(See 49 U.S. Code §§ 32304, 32309)
July 5, 1994, P.L. 103-272, 108 Stat. 1379

American Bankers Association Bank Collections Code
Okla. Stat. Ann., Title 6, § 901 et seq.
Wis. Stat. Ann., 710.01

American Battlefield Protection Act of 1996
Nov. 12, 1996, P.L. 104-333, § 604, 16 U.S.
Code § 469k

American Bicentennial Celebration Act
Ill. Rev. Stat. 1975, Ch. 85, § 1776 et seq.

American Competitiveness and Workforce Improvement Act of 1998
Oct. 21, 1998, P.L. 105-277, Division C,
Title IV, 112 Stat. 2681, 8 U.S. Code
§ 1101 nt.

American Conservation and Youth Service Corps Act of 1990
Nov. 16, 1990, P.L. 101-610, 42 U.S. Code
§§ 12501 nt., 12541 to 12556

American Fire Act
March 3, 1851, Ch. 43, 9 Stat. 635, 466 U.S.
Code § 182

American Fisheries Act
Oct. 21, 1998, P.L. 105-277, Division C,
Title II, 112 Stat. 2681, 46 U.S. Code
§ 2101 nt.

American Fisheries Promotion Act
Dec. 22, 1980, P.L. 96-561, 16 U.S. Code
§ 1801 nt.
July 12, 1983, P.L. 98-44, 97 Stat. 216
Oct. 19, 1984, P.L. 98-498, 98 Stat. 2310

American Folklife Preservation Act
Jan. 2, 1976, P.L. 94-201, 89 Stat. 1129, 20
U.S. Code § 2101 et seq.
April 17, 1978, P.L. 95-259, 20 U.S. Code
§§ 2103, 2107
Aug. 21, 1984, P.L. 98-392, 20 U.S. Code
§ 2107

Sept. 26, 1989, P.L. 101-99, 20 U.S. Code
§ 2107
Oct. 6, 1992, P.L. 102-399, 20 U.S. Code
§ 2107
Oct. 8, 1993, P.L. 103-101, 20 U.S. Code
§ 2107
Oct. 21, 1998, P.L. 105-275, 20 U.S. Code
§§ 2103, 2106, 2107

American Friendship Treaty
Haw. Session Laws 1850, p. 208, Dec. 20,
1849

American Heart Month Act
Dec. 30, 1963, P.L. 88-254, 77 Stat. 843 (See
36 U.S. Code § 101)

American History Month Act
Ill. Comp. Stat. 1992, Ch. 5, § 490/5

American Indian Agricultural Resource Management Act
Dec. 3, 1993, P.L. 103-177, 25 U.S. Code
§§ 3701 nt., 3701 et seq., 3711 et seq., 3731
et seq., 3741 et seq.
Nov. 2, 1994, P.L. 103-435, 25 U.S. Code
§§ 3715, 3746

American Indian, Alaska Native, and Native Hawaiian Culture and Art Development Act
Oct. 17, 1986, P.L. 99-498, 100 Stat. 1600,
20 U.S. Code §§ 4401 et seq.
Nov. 5, 1987, P.L. 100-153, 101 Stat. 887
Nov. 29, 1990, P.L. 101-644, 20 U.S. Code
§§ 4414, 4417, 4421, 4424, 4425, 4451
July 23, 1992, P.L. 102-325, 20 U.S. Code
§§ 4412, 4414, 4416, 4417, 4418, 4421 to
4426

American Indian Arts and Crafts Sales Act
Neb. Rev. Stat. 1943, 69-1801 et seq.
Okla. Stat. Ann., Title 78, § 71 et seq.

American Indian Education Act
Minn. Stat. Ann., 126.45 et seq.

American Indian Language and Culture Education Act
Minn. Stat. Ann., 126.45 et seq.

American Indian Religious Freedom Act

Aug. 11, 1978, P.L. 95-341, 42 U.S. Code §§ 1996, 1996 nt.

Oct. 6, 1994, P.L. 103-344, 42 U.S. Code § 1996a

American Indian Religious Freedom Act Amendments of 1994

Oct. 6, 1994, P.L. 103-344, 42 U.S. Code § 1996 nt.

American Indian Trust Fund Management Reform Act of 1994

Oct. 25, 1994, P.L. 103-412, 25 U.S. Code § 4001 nt.

Feb. 12, 1996, P.L. 104-109, 25 U.S. Code §§ 4043, 4046

American Legion Acts

Sept. 16, 1919, Ch. 59, 41 Stat. 284, 36 U.S. Code §§ 41 to 51

Oct. 29, 1942, Ch. 633, 56 Stat. 1012, 36 U.S. Code §§ 43, 45

July 9, 1946, Ch. 546, 60 Stat. 524, 36 U.S. Code § 45

Dec. 28, 1950, Ch. 1177, 64 Stat. 1122, 36 U.S. Code § 45

June 26, 1953, Ch. 153, 67 Stat. 82, 36 U.S. Code §§ 44, 48

July 26, 1955, Ch. 386, 67 Stat. 379, 36 U.S. Code §§ 43, 45

Sept. 1, 1966, P.L. 89-550, 80 Stat. 371, 36 U.S. Code §§ 43, 45

American-Mexican Boundary Treaty Act of 1972

Oct. 25, 1972, P.L. 92-549, 86 Stat. 1161, 19 U.S. Code § 1322; 22 U.S. Code §§ 277d-34 to 277d-42

American-Mexican Chamizal Convention Act of 1964

April 29, 1964, P.L. 88-300, 78 Stat. 184, 22 U.S. Code §§ 277d- 17 to 277d-25

April 30, 1994, P.L. 103-236, 22 U.S. Code § 277d-18

American-Mexican Treaty Act of 1950

Sept. 13, 1950, Ch. 948, 64 Stat. 846, 22 U.S. Code §§ 277d-1 to 277d-9

Aug. 19, 1964, P.L. 88-448, 78 Stat. 494, 22 U.S. Code § 277d-3

Aug. 17, 1977, P.L. 95-105, 22 U.S. Code § 277d-3

Oct. 28, 1991, P.L. 102-138, 105 Stat. 676

American National Red Cross Acts

June 6, 1900, Ch. 784, 31 Stat. 277

Jan. 5, 1905, Ch. 23, 33 Stat. 599, 36 U.S. Code §§ 1, 1 nt., 2, 3, 5, 6, 8. (See 18 U.S. Code §§ 1, 706, 917)

June 23, 1910, Ch. 372, 36 Stat. 604, 36 U.S. Code § 9. (See 18 U.S. Code §§ 1, 706, 917.)

Dec. 10, 1912, Ch. 1, 37 Stat. 647, 36 U.S. Code § 5

Feb. 27, 1917, Ch. 137, 39 Stat. 946, 36 U.S. Code § 6

May 29, 1920, Ch. 214, 41 Stat. 659, 36 U.S. Code § 7

March 3, 1921, Ch. 131, 41 Stat. 1354, 36 U.S. Code § 5

May 8, 1947, Ch. 50, 61 Stat. 80, 36 U.S. Code §§ 1 nt., 2, 3, 4a, 5, 9

July 17, 1953, Ch. 222, 67 Stat. 178, 36 U.S. Code §§ 3, 6, 7

American National Red Cross Headquarters Act

Feb. 7, 1930, Ch. 42, 46 Stat. 66, 36 U.S. Code § 13

American Printing House for the Blind Amendments of 1988

Nov. 7, 1988, P.L. 100-630, 20 U.S. Code § 101 nt.

American Revolution Bicentennial Celebration Act

N.J. Stat. Ann., Superseded Vol., 52:9P-1 et seq.

American Revolution Bicentennial Commission Act

Conn. Gen. Stat. Ann., § 10-321h et seq.

Ind. Code Ann., 4-23-7.5-1 et seq.

American River Act (Development)

Cal. Statutes 1927, p. 954

Cal. Statutes 1929, p. 184

Cal. Statutes 1931, p. 2291

American River Act (Flood Control District)
Cal. Statutes 1927, p. 1596

American River Flood Control District Act
Cal. Water Code, Appendix, § 37-1 et seq.

American River Parkway Preservation Act (Urban)
Cal. Public Resources Code § 5840 et seq.

American Samoa Labor Standards Amendments of 1956
Aug. 8, 1956, Ch. 1035, 70 Stat. 1118, 29 U.S. Code §§ 206, 213, 216

American Society of International Law Headquarters Act
Aug. 25, 1959, P.L. 86-208, 73 Stat. 431, 36 U.S. Code § 344 nt.

American Society of International Law Incorporation Act
Sept. 20, 1950, Ch. 958, 64 Stat. 869, 36 U.S. Code §§ 341 to 352

American Technology Preeminence Act of 1991
Feb. 14, 1992, P.L. 102-245, 15 U.S. Code § 3701 nt.
Aug. 3, 1992, P.L. 102-329, 15 U.S. Code §§ 1453, 1453 nt.

American University Incorporation Amendments Act of 1990
Oct. 31, 1990, P.L. 101-480, 104 Stat. 1160

American War Mothers Incorporation Act
Feb. 24, 1925, Ch. 308, 43 Stat. 966, 36 U.S. Code §§ 91 to 104
Sept. 26, 1942, Ch. 563, 56 Stat. 758, 36 U.S. Code § 97
June 26, 1953, Ch. 152, 67 Stat. 81, 36 U.S. Code §§ 97, 98
April 12, 1974, P.L. 93-267, 88 Stat. 85, 36 U.S. Code § 97

Americans with Disabilities Accessibility Implementation Act
Fla. Stat. Ann., 553.501 et seq.

Americans with Disabilities Act of 1990
July 26, 1990, P.L. 101-336, 42 U.S. Code § 12101 nt.
Nov. 21, 1991, P.L. 102-166, 42 U.S. Code §§ 12111, 12112, 12209
Jan. 23, 1995, P.L. 104-1, 42 U.S. Code § 12209
Nov. 28, 1995, P.L. 104-59, 42 U.S. Code § 12186
Oct. 11, 1996, P.L. 104-287, 42 U.S. Code § 12161

Americus Merit System Act
Ga. Laws 1951, p. 2007

Americus Retirement System Act
Ga. Laws 1950, p. 2230

Amherst School Loan Act
Mass. Acts 1949, Ch. 9

Amnesty Act (Tax Delinquency)
La. Acts 1985, No. 301

Amnesty Act (Tax Penalty)
Ark. Acts 1997, No. 1001

Amnesty Acts (Removal of Disabilities under Fourteenth Amendment)
May 22, 1872, Ch. 193, 17 Stat. 142
June 6, 1898, Ch. 389, 30 Stat. 432

Amnesty Proclamations
Dec. 8, 1863, No.11, 13 Stat. 737
May 29, 1865, No.37, 13 Stat. 758
Dec. 25, 1868, No.15, 15 Stat. 711

Amnesty Program Act (Property Tax)
Ga. Code Ann., 48-16A-1 et seq.

Amphetamine Drug Act
Ky. Rev. Stat. 1971, 217.720 et seq.

Amsterdam City Court Act
N.Y. Laws 1955, Ch. 406

Amsterdam Parking Authority Act
N.Y. Public Authorities Law (Consol. Laws Ch. 43A) § 1400 et seq.

Amtrak Authorization and Development Act
Oct. 27, 1992, P.L. 102-533, 45 U.S. Code § 501 nt.
July 5, 1994, P.L. 103-272, 108 Stat. 1379
Oct. 31, 1994, P.L. 103-429, 45 U.S. Code §§ 650d, 650e

Amtrak Improvement Act of 1973
Nov. 3, 1973, P.L. 93-146, 87 Stat. 548, 45 U.S. Code §§ 502, 543, 545, 546, 548, 561 to 564, 601, 602, 641

Amtrak Improvement Act of 1974
Oct. 28, 1974, P.L. 93-496, 88 Stat. 1526, 5 U.S. Code § 5313, 26 U.S. Code § 250; 45 U.S. Code §§ 501 nt., 544, 545, 563, 564, 701, 602, 641, 644

Amtrak Improvement Act of 1975
May 26, 1975, P.L. 94-25, 89 Stat. 90, 45 U.S. Code §§ 501 nt., 543, 545, 548

Amtrak Improvement Act of 1976
Oct. 19, 1976, P.L. 94-555, 45 U.S. Code § 501 et seq.

Amtrak Improvement Act of 1978
Oct. 5, 1978, P.L. 95-421, 92 Stat. 923
Sept. 29, 1979, P.L. 96-73, 45 U.S. Code § 521 nt.
July 5, 1994, P.L. 103-272, 108 Stat. 1379

Amtrak Improvement Act of 1981
Aug. 13, 1981, P.L. 97-35, 45 U.S. Code § 501 nt.
July 5, 1994, P.L. 103-272, 108 Stat. 1379

Amtrak Reauthorization Act of 1985
April 7, 1986, P.L. 99-272, 45 U.S. Code § 501 nt.
July 5, 1994, P.L. 103-272, 108 Stat. 1379

Amtrak Reauthorization and Improvement Act of 1990
July 6, 1990, P.L. 101-322, 45 U.S. Code § 501 nt.
July 5, 1994, P.L. 103-272, 108 Stat. 1379

Amtrak Reform and Accountability Act of 1997
Dec. 2, 1997, P.L. 105-134, 49 U.S. Code § 20101 nt.

Amtrak Reorganization Act of 1979
Sept. 29, 1979, P.L. 96-73, 45 U.S. Code §§ 501, 501 nt., 501a, 502, 521, 545 et seq.
July 5, 1994, P.L. 103-272, 108 Stat. 1379
Oct. 11, 1996, P.L. 104-287, 45 U.S. Code § 564

Amusement and Carnival Games Act
Okla. Stat. Ann., Title 3A, § 501 et seq.

Amusement and Carnival Rides Safety Act
Ill. Rev. Stat. 1991, Ch. 111 1/2, § 4051 et seq.

Amusement-Carnival Safety Act
Ill. Comp. Stat. 1992, Ch. 430, § 85/2 et seq.

Amusement Device and Redemption Machine Tax Act (Coin-Operated)
Ill. Comp. Stat. 1992, Ch. 35, § 510/1 et seq.

Amusement Device Safety Act
N.C. Gen. Stat. 1943, § 95-111.1 et seq.

Amusement Device Tax Act
Neb. Rev. Stat. 1943, 77-3001 et seq.

Amusement Devices Licensing Act
S.C. Code Ann. 1976, § 12-21-2720
Tenn. Code Ann., Superseded Vol., 67-4203, Item 75 et seq.

Amusement Games Licensing Act
N.J. Stat. Ann., 5:8-100 et seq.

Amusement License Law
Iowa Code 1954, 361.1 et seq.

Amusement Revenue Act (Emergency)
Miss. Code Ann. 1972, § 27-11-1 et seq.

Amusement Ride Act
Neb. Rev. Stat. 48-1801 et seq.

Amusement Ride and Attraction Safety Insurance Act

Ark. Code Ann. 1987, 23-89-501 et seq.

Fla. Stat. 1983, 546.001 et seq.

Ill. Rev. Stat. 1983, Ch. 38, § 50-11 et seq.

Tenn. Public Acts 1984, Ch. 586

Amusement Ride Inspection Act

Pa. Purdon's Stat., Title 4, § 401 et seq.

Amusement Ride Safety Inspection and Insurance Act

Del. Code of 1974, Title 16, § 6401 et seq.

Md. Ann. Code 1974, Art. BR, § 3-201 et seq.

N.Y. Laws 1947, Ch. 278, § 1, Subd. d

Pa. 1935 Pamph. Laws 429, No. 183

R.I. Gen. Laws 1956, 23-34-1 et seq.

Tex. Insurance Code, Art. 21.60

Amusement Rider Safety and Liability Act

Pa. Purdon's Stat., Title 4, § 501 et seq.

Amusement Rides and Amusement Attractions Safety Act

W. Va. Code 1966, § 21-10-1 et seq.

Amusement Rides Safety Act

Cal. Labor Code § 7900 et seq.

Ga. Code Ann., 34-12-1 et seq.

La. Rev. Stat. Ann., 40:1484.1 et seq.

Okla. Stat. Ann., Title 40, § 460 et seq.

R.I. Gen. Laws 1956, 23-34.1-1 et seq.

S.C. Code Ann. 1976, § 41-18-10 et seq.

Amusement Tax Act

Md. Ann. Code 1974, Art. TG, § 4-101 et seq.

Amvets Incorporation Act

July 23, 1947, Ch. 298, 61 Stat. 403, 36 U.S. Code §§ 67 to 67s

Dec. 28, 1950, Ch. 1178, 64 Stat. 1122, 36 U.S. Code § 67e

July 26, 1955, Ch. 383, 69 Stat. 375, 36 U.S. Code § 67e

Sept. 14, 1966, P.L. 89-576, 80 Stat. 772, 36 U.S. Code § 67e

June 13, 1991, P.L. 102-54, 105 Stat. 278

Amy Somers Volunteers at Food Banks Act

Aug. 7, 1998, P.L. 105-221, 29 U.S. Code § 201 nt.

An Act Concerning the Support of Children of Parents Not Married to Each Other

N.C. Gen. Stat. 1943, § 49-1

An Act to Implement the Maine Indian Claims Settlement

Me. Rev. Stat. Ann. 1964, Title 30, § 6201

An Act to Prevent the Perpetuation of Certain Fraudulent Practices by Photographers within the State of North Carolina

N.C. Gen. Stat. 1943, § 66-59

An Act to Provide for the Display of the Code of Ethics for Government Service

Aug. 6, 1996, P.L. 104-179, 5 U.S. Code § 7301 nt.

Anabolic Steroids Act

S.C. Code Ann. 1976, § 44-53-10 et seq.

Anabolic Steroids Control Act of 1990

Nov. 29, 1990, P.L. 101-647, 21 U.S. Code §§ 333a, 801 nt., 802 nt., 829 nt.

S.C. Code Ann. 1976, § 44-53-10 et seq.

Anadromous Fish Conservation Act

Oct. 30, 1965, P.L. 89-304, 79 Stat. 1125, 16 U.S. Code §§ 757a to 757f

May 14, 1970, P.L. 91-249, 84 Stat. 214, 16 U.S. Code §§ 757a, 757d

Nov. 16, 1979, P.L. 96-118, 16 U.S. Code §§ 757a, 757a nt., 757b, 757d, 757g

Jan. 12, 1983, P.L. 97-453, 16 U.S. Code §§ 757a, 757d, 757g

Oct. 31, 1984, P.L. 98-613, 16 U.S. Code § 757g

Oct. 1, 1986, P.L. 99-432, 16 U.S. Code § 757g

Nov. 14, 1986, P.L. 99-659, 16 U.S. Code § 757d

Nov. 3, 1988, P.L. 100-589, 16 U.S. Code § 757g

Nov. 28, 1990, P.L. 101-627, 16 U.S. Code § 757d

Continued

Oct. 17, 1991, P.L. 102-130, 16 U.S. Code § 757g

Oct. 11, 1996, P.L. 104-297, 16 U.S. Code § 757d

Dec. 16, 1997, P.L. 105-146, 16 U.S. Code § 757g

Anaerobic Manure Digesters Act
Pa. Purdon's Stat., Title 3, § 2001 et seq.

Analytical-Biochemical-Biological Laboratory Act
Pa. Purdon's Stat., Title 35, § 2151 et seq.

Anarchist Exclusion Acts
Oct. 16, 1918, Ch. 186, 40 Stat. 1012 (See 8 U.S. Code § 1182)

June 5, 1920, Ch. 251, 41 Stat. 1008 (See 8 U.S. Code § 1182)

June 27, 1952, Ch. 477, 66 Stat. 279

Anarchy Act
Vt. Stat. Ann., Title 13, § 3405 et seq.

Anarchy and Criminal Syndicalism Act
Mich. Comp. Laws Ann., 750.46 et seq.

Anatomical Act
Ind. Code Ann., 4-26-3-1 et seq.
Pa. Purdon's Stat., Title 35, § 1091 et seq.

Anatomical Gift Act
See also Uniform Anatomical Gift Act
Ark. Code Ann. 1987, 20-17-601, 20-17-609 et seq.
Mass. Gen. Laws Ann., 113:8 et seq.
P.R. Laws Ann. 1954, Title 18, § 731 et seq.

Anatomical Science Promotion Act
D.C. Code Ann., § 2-1401 et seq.

Ancestral Property Act
Tenn. Code Ann., Superseded Vol., 31-101

Anchorage Grounds Act
Sept. 15, 1922, Ch. 313, 42 Stat. 844, 33 U.S. Code § 472

Anchoring of Mobile Homes Act
Ala. Code 1975, § 24-5-30 et seq.

Ancient Documents Act
La. Rev. Stat. Ann., 13:3728 et seq.

Ancient Mortgage Act
N.Y. Real Property Actions and Proceedings Law (Consol. Laws Ch. 81) § 1931 et seq.

Ancillary Administration of Estates Act
See also Ancillary Administration of Estates Act
See Uniform Ancillary Administration of Estates Act
Oct. 31, 1998, P.L. 105-333, 112 Stat. 3129
Mont. Code Ann., 72-4-402

Ancillary Probate of Foreign Wills Act
Tenn. Code Ann., 32-5-101 et seq.

ANCSA Land Bank Protection Act of 1998
Oct. 31, 1998, P.L. 105-333, 112 Stat. 3136, 43 U.S. Code § 1601 nt.

Andal-Boatwright-Johnston-Baker Delta Protection Act
Cal. Public Resources Code § 29700 et seq.

Andean Trade Preference Act
Dec. 4, 1991, P.L. 102-182, 19 U.S. Code § 3201 et seq.
Dec. 8, 1994, P.L. 103-465, 19 U.S. Code §§ 3202, 3203
Aug. 20, 1996, P.L. 104-188, 19 U.S. Code § 3202

Anderson Act (Prohibition)
Ore. Code 1930, §§ 15-101 to 15-163

Anderson County Road Act
Tenn. Private Acts 1963, Ch. 232

Anderson-Goemaere Wetland Protection Act
Mich. Comp. Laws Ann., 281.701 et seq.

Anderson-Myer State Aid Act
Ky. Rev. Stat. 1962, 166.160, 166.170

Anderson-Price Atomic Energy Damages Act
See Atomic Energy Act Of 1954

Anderson-Rockwell Environmental Protection Act
Mich. Comp. Laws Ann., 691.1201 et seq.

Andrew Johnson Homestead National Monument Act
Aug. 29, 1935, Ch. 801, 49 Stat. 958, 16 U.S. Code §§ 450o to 450q

Andrews-Dayton Act (Campaign Expenses)
Fla. Stat. Ann., 99.061

Andrews Draft Act Amendment
See Selective Training and Service Act of 1940

Andrus-Brannan Levee Maintenance District Act
Cal. Statutes 1967, Ch. 910, p. 2362

Anemia Control Act (Equine Infectious)
Ill. Rev. Stat. 1991, Ch. 8, § 951 et seq.

Anglo-Irish Agreement Support Act of 1986
Sept. 19, 1986, P.L. 99-415, 100 Stat. 947

Anhydrous Ammonia Facilities Safety Act
Mont. Code Ann., 80-10-501 et seq.

Anhydrous Ammonia Fertilizer and Equipment Law
La. Rev. Stat. Ann., 3:1351 et seq.

Anhydrous Ammonia Storage and Equipment Act
Tenn. Code Ann., 43-11-301 et seq.

ANILCA
See Alaska National Interest Lands Conservation Act

Animal Act
Ill. Rev. Stat. 1991, Ch. 1, § 2901-45

Animal and Poultry By-Products Disposal Act of 1964
Miss. Code Ann. 1972, § 41-51-1 et seq.

Animal Brand Act
Okla. Stat. Ann., Title 2, § 4-1 et seq.

Animal Brands and Marks Act
Wash. Rev. Code Ann., 16.57.010 et seq.

Animal Cancer Research Act
Oct. 17, 1980, P.L. 96-469, 7 U.S. Code § 3901 nt.

Animal Canned Food Act
Va. Code 1950, § 3.1-885 et seq.

Animal Care and Facilities Act (Pet)
Colo. Rev. Stat., 35-80-101 to 35-80-117

Animal Care Facilities Act
Mo. Laws 1992, S.B. No. 626, §§ 1 to 6

Animal Control Act
D.C. Code Ann., § 6-1001 et seq.
Ill. Comp. Stat. 1992, Ch. 510, § 5/1 et seq.

Animal Cruelty Act
See Cruelty to Animals Act

Animal Dealer Act
Kan. Stat. Ann., 47-1701 et seq.

Animal Disease Control Cooperation Act of 1947
Feb. 28, 1947, Ch. 8, 61 Stat. 7, 21 U.S. Code § 114b et seq.
Aug. 3, 1956, Ch. 950, 70 Stat. 1033
June 29, 1960, P.L. 86-533, 74 Stat. 249
July 27, 1966, P.L. 89-521, 80 Stat. 330
Nov. 5, 1971, P.L. 92-152, 85 Stat. 418
March 15, 1976, P.L. 94-231, 90 Stat. 216
March 15, 1990, P.L. 101-255, 21 U.S. Code § 114b nt.
Nov. 28, 1990, P.L. 101-624, 104 Stat. 4068

Animal Disease Laboratories Act
Ill. Comp. Stat. 1992, Ch. 510, §§ 10/0.01, 10/1

Animal Diseases Act
R.I. Gen. Laws 1956, 4-4-1 et seq.
Wash. Rev. Code Ann., 16.36.005 et seq., 16.38.010 et seq., 16.44.020 et seq.

Animal Diseases Act (Foreign)
Okla. Stat. Ann., Title 2, § 6-131 et seq.

Animal Diseases, Hog Cholera Control and Eradication Act
Neb. Rev. Stat. 1943, 54-1513 et seq.

Animal Disposal Act
Ind. Code Ann., 15-2.1-16-1 et seq.

Animal Drug Amendments of 1968
July 13, 1968, P.L. 90-399, 82 Stat. 342, 21 U.S. Code §§ 321, 331, 342, 351, 352, 357, 360b, 381, 392

Animal Drug Availability Act of 1996
Oct. 9, 1996, P.L. 104-250, 21 U.S. Code § 301 nt.
Fla. Stat. Ann., 828.40 et seq.

Animal Enterprise Protection Act of 1992
Aug. 26, 1992, P.L. 102-346, 18 U.S. Code §§ 43, 43 nt.

Animal Euthanasia Act
S.C. Code Ann. 1976, § 47-3-410 et seq.

Animal Experiments Law
N.Y. Public Health Law 1953 (Consol. Laws Ch. 45) § 504 et seq.

Animal Facilities Protection Act
Okla. Stat. Ann., Title 21, § 1680 et seq.

Animal Fighting Act
Fla. Stat. Ann., 828.122

Animal Fighting and Baiting Act
S.C. Code Ann. 1976, § 16-27-10 et seq.

Animal Gastroenteritis Act
Ill. Comp. Stat. 1992, Ch. 510, § 15/0.01 et seq.
Ill. Rev. Stat. 1991, Ch. 8, § 202.9 et seq.

Animal Health Law
Iowa Code Ann., 163.1 et seq.

Animal Importation Act
Ga. Code Ann.,4-11-11 et seq.
Neb. Rev. Stat. 1943, 54-784.01 et seq.

Animal Importation Permit and Health Certificate Act
Mont. Code Ann., 81-2-701 et seq.

Animal Industry Act
May 29, 1884, Ch. 60, 23 Stat. 31, 7 U.S. Code § 391; 21 U.S. Code §§ 112 to 115, 117, 118, 119, 120, 130
May 31, 1920, Ch. 217, 41 Stat. 699
June 28, 1926, Ch. 700, 44 Stat. 774
Feb. 7, 1928, Ch. 30, 45 Stat. 59
Oct. 30, 1951, Ch. 637, 65 Stat. 394
Aug. 8, 1953, Ch. 381, 67 Stat. 493
Aug. 3, 1956, Ch. 950, 70 Stat. 1032
July 31, 1958, P.L. 85-573, 72 Stat. 454, 21 U.S. Code § 113a
July 2, 1962, P.L. 87-518, 76 Stat. 131
Oct. 9, 1962, P.L. 87-763, 76 Stat. 762
Oct. 10, 1978, P.L. 95-439, 92 Stat. 1061
Jan. 12, 1983, P.L. 97-461, 96 Stat. 2524
Nov. 28, 1990, P.L. 101-624, 104 Stat. 3733
Iowa Code Ann., 159.1 et seq.
Mich. Comp. Laws Ann., 287.2 et seq., 287.701 et seq.

Animal Inspection Act
N.Y. Agriculture and Markets Law (Consol. Laws Ch. 69), § 72 et seq.

Animal Intended for Food Act
Ill. Rev. Stat. 1991, Ch. 8, § 105.90 et seq.

Animal Medicinal Drug Use Clarification Act of 1994
Oct. 22, 1994, P.L. 103-396, 21 U.S. Code § 301 nt.

Animal Nutrient Products Law (Bulk Dry)
Iowa Code Ann., 200A.1 to 200A.15

Animal Owner Responsibility Act (Elmore County)
Ala. Acts 1995, p. 789, No. 387

Animal Protection Act
Colo. Rev. Stat., 35-42-101 et seq.
Ga. Code Ann., 4-11-1 et seq.
P.R. Laws Ann. 1954, Title 5, § 1651 et seq.

Animal Quarantine Act
Ark. Code Ann. 1987, 2-40-102 et seq.
Wash. Rev. Code Ann., 16.36.005 et seq.
W. Va. Code 1966, § 19-9-1 et seq.

Animal Quarantine Acts
See Cattle Contagious Diseases Act

Animal Registration under False Pretenses Act
Ill. Comp. Stat. 1992, Ch. 720, § 210/0.01 et seq.

Animal Remedies Act
S.D. Codified Laws 1967, 39-18-1 et seq.
Va. Code 1950, § 3.1-829 et seq.
Wash. Rev. Code Ann., 15.52.010 et seq.

Animal Research and Production Facilities Protection Act
Ill. Comp. Stat. 1992, Ch. 720, § 215/1 et seq.
Mo. Laws 1992, S.B. No. 498

Animal Research or Exhibiting Facilities Protection Act
Miss. Code Ann. 1972, § 69-29-301 et seq.

Animal Treatment Biological Products Act
P.R. Laws Ann. 1954, Title 5, § 821 et seq.

Animal Trespassing Act
S.D. Codified Laws 1967, 40-28-4 et seq.

Animal Trespassing Law
Iowa Code Ann., 169B.1 et seq.

Animal Virus, Serum, Toxin, Antitoxin Act
March 4, 1913, Ch. 145, 37 Stat. 828, 21 U.S. Code §§ 151 to 158

Animal Welfare Act
Dec. 24, 1970, 84 Stat. 1560, 7 U.S. Code §§ 2131 to 2147, 2149, 2150, 2155
Dec. 31, 1970, P.L. 91-611, 84 Stat. 1829, 10 U.S. Code § 3013
Oct. 4, 1984, P.L. 98-443, 98 Stat. 1708, 7 U.S. Code § 2145
Dec. 23, 1985, P.L. 99-198, 7 U.S. Code §§ 2131 nt., 2132, 2143 to 2146, 2149, 2157

Nov. 28, 1990, P.L. 101-624, 7 U.S. Code §§ 2146, 2158, 2159
Dec. 13, 1991, P.L. 102-237, 7 U.S. Code § 2158
Dec. 21, 1995, P.L. 104-66, 7 U.S. Code § 2155
Dec. 29, 1995, P.L. 104-88, 7 U.S. Code § 2145
Ill. Comp. Stat. 1992, Ch. 225, § 605/1 et seq.
Me. Rev. Stat. Ann. 1964, Title 17, § 3901 et seq.
N.C. Gen. Stat. 1943, § 19A-20 et seq.
Va. Code 1950, § 3.1-796.39 et seq.
Vt. Stat. Ann., Title 20, § 3901 et seq.

Animal Welfare Act of 1970
Dec. 24, 1970, P.L. 91-579, 84 Stat. 1560, 7 U.S. Code §§ 2131 et seq.

Animal Welfare Board Act
Me. Rev. Stat. Ann. 1964, Title 7, § 3901 et seq., Title 17, § 1011 et seq.

Animals Fund Act (Testing)
Neb. Rev. Stat. 1943, 59-701.01 et seq.

Animals Intended for Food Act
Ill. Comp. Stat. 1992, Ch. 410, § 605/0.01 et seq.

Animals Running-at-Large Act
Ill. Comp. Stat. Ch. 510, § 55/1 et seq.
Wash. Rev. Code Ann., 9.08.020, 16.12.010 et seq.

Animas-La Plata Project Compact Act
Colo. Rev. Stat., 37-64-101

Ann Kravitz Kids Voting Act
Fla. Laws 1992, Ch. 134

Anna Veterans Home Act
Ill. Rev. Stat. 1991, Ch. 126 1/2, § 700 et seq.

Annexation Act
Ariz. Rev. Stat. Ann., § 9-471
Colo. Rev. Stat., 31-12-101 et seq.
Ill. Rev. Stat. 1991, Ch. 24, § 7-1-16
Ind. Code Ann., 18-5-10-19 et seq.
Ky. Rev. Stat. 1971, 81A.010 et seq.
Mich. Comp. Laws Ann., 117.6 et seq.
Continued

Miss. Code Ann. 1972, § 21-1-27 et seq.

Mo. Rev. Stat., 71.015

N.D. Cent. Code, 40-51.2-01 et seq.

Nev. Rev. Stat. 1979 Reprint, 268.570 et seq., 318.256 et seq. 474.325 et seq., 539.708 et seq.

N.M. Stat. Ann., 3-7-1

Ohio Rev. Code 1953, 709.01 et seq.

S.C. Code Ann. 1976, § 5-3-10 et seq.

S.D. Codified Laws 1967, 9-4-1 et seq.

Tex. Local Gov. Code, § 43.001 et seq.

Wash. Rev. Code Ann., 35.13.010 et seq.

Wis. Stat. Ann., 66-021 et seq.

Annexation Act (Baltimore City)

Md. Laws 1918, Ch. 82

Annexation Act (Barren Island)

N.Y. Laws 1802, Ch. 28

Annexation Act (Charlotte)

N.Y. Laws 1915, Ch. 359, § 4 et seq.

Annexation Act (Cities and Towns)

Wash. Rev. Code Ann., 35.10.203 et seq.

Annexation Act (Improvement Districts)

Ark. Code Ann. 1987, 14-88-503

Annexation Act (Municipalities)

Alaska Stat. 1962, § 29.06.040 et seq.

Cal. Government Code §§ 35100 et seq., 56650 et seq.

Iowa Code Ann., 368.4 et seq.

Md. Ann. 1957, Art. 23A, § 19

Mich. Comp. Laws Ann., 117.6 et seq.

Mo. Rev. Stat., 71.015

N.C. Gen. Stat. 1943, § 160A-29 et seq.

N.D. Cent. Code, 40-51.2-01 et seq.

N.J. Stat. Ann.,40A:7-1 et seq.

N.M. Stat. Ann., 3-7-1

N.Y. General Municipal Law (Consol. Laws Ch. 24) § 700 et seq.

Ohio Rev. Code 1953, 709.01 et seq.

Pa. Purdon's Stat., Title 53, § 67501 et seq.

Tenn. Code Ann., 6-51-101 et seq.

Tex. Local Gov. Code, § 43.001 et seq.

Va. Code 1950, § 15.1-1032 et seq.

Annexation Act (School Districts)

Mo. Rev. Stat., 162.441

Annexation Act (Township)

Ill. Rev. Stat. 1991, Ch. 139, § 126.90 et seq.

Annexation Act (Westchester County)

N.Y. Laws 1895, Ch. 934

Annexation and Consolidation Act (School)

Okla. Stat. 1981, Title 70, § 7-201 et seq.

Annexation and Consolidation Incentive Plan (Voluntary)

Mont. Code Ann., 20-6-401 et seq.

Annexation and Incorporation Act (Towns)

Ind. Burns' 1933, 48-101 et seq.

Annexation and School Consolidation Act

Okla. Stat. Ann., Title 70, § 7-201 et seq.

Annexation of Enclosed Territory Act

Cal. Government Code § 56650.5 et seq.

Annexation of Uninhabited Territory Act

Cal. Government Code § 57026 et seq.

Annexation or Contraction Act (Municipal)

Fla. Stat. Ann., 171.011 et seq.

Annexation Treaty

S.C. Codified Laws of 1904, p. 243

Annie Plummer Act

Ga. Code Ann., 20-2-142

Annotated Act (Statutes)

Vt. Stat. Ann., Title 3, § 51 et seq.

Annual and Sick Leave Act of 1951

Oct. 30, 1951, Ch. 631, 65 Stat. 679 (See 5 U.S. Code §§ 6301 to 6305, 6307, 6309 to 6311)

July 2, 1953, Ch. 178, 67 Stat. 136 (See 5 U.S. Code §§ 5508, 6301, 6302, 6304, 6305, 6308)

Aug. 18, 1959, P.L. 86-168, 73 Stat. 389 (See 5 U.S. Code §§ 6306, 6308)

Sept. 6, 1960, P.L. 86-707, 74 Stat. 799 (See 5 U.S. Code §§ 6301, 6303 to 6305, 6310)

Aug. 19, 1964, P.L. 88-448, 78 Stat. 487 (See 5 U.S. Code § 6303)
Aug. 21, 1964, P.L. 88-471, 78 Stat. 583 (See 5 U.S. Code §§ 6301, 6307, 6308)

Annual Capital Improvement Acts
Del. Laws Vol. 55, p. 519, Ch. 167
Del. Laws Vol. 55, p. 1416, Ch. 429
Del. Laws Vol. 56, p. 496, Ch. 121
Del. Laws Vol. 56, p. 1852, Ch. 469
Del. Laws Vol. 57, p. 26, Ch. 18
Del. Laws Vol. 57, p. 178, Ch. 106
Del. Laws Vol. 57, p. 915, Ch. 299
Del. Laws Vol. 57, p. 2093, Ch. 736
Del. Laws Vol. 58, p. 1071, Ch. 347
Del. Laws Vol. 59, p. 744, Ch. 223
Del. Laws Vol. 60, Chs. 271, 691
Del. Laws Vol. 61, Chs. 376, 408

Annual Franchise Tax Act
Mo. Rev. Stat., 147.010 et seq.

Annual Report Act (Tax Expenditure)
Miss. Code Ann. 1972, §§ 57-13-45, 57-13-47

Annual Sessions Act
Ala. Acts 1975, 2d Sp. Sess., p. 115

Annual Vault Charge Enabling Act
N.Y. Unconsolidated Laws, § 9445

Annualized Income Installment Act
Mass. Gen. Laws Ann., 62B:13, 62B:14

Annuities Act
Wash. Rev. Code Ann., 48.23.140 et seq.

Annuities Act (Variable)
Neb. Rev. Stat. 1943, 44-2201 et seq.

Annuity and Benefit Fund Act (Municipal Employees, Officers, and Officials)
Ill. Rev. Stat. 1991, Ch. 108 1/2, § 8-101 et seq.

Annuity and Benefit Fund Act (Policemen)
Ga. Code Ann.,47-17-1 et seq.
Ill. Rev. Stat. 1991, Ch. 108 1/2, § 5-101 et seq.

Annuity and Benefit Fund Act (Sanitary Districts)
Ill. Rev. Stat. 1991, Ch. 108 1/2, § 13-101 et seq.

Annuity and Benefit Fund Civil Service Act (Park)
Ill. Rev. Stat. 1991, Ch. 24 1/2, § 113.9 et seq.

Annuity and Insurance Act (Police)
S.C. Code Ann. 1962, § 61-301 et seq.

Annuity and Life Insurance Policyholders Protection Act
Okla. Stat. Ann., Title 6, § 4031 et seq.

Annuity Exemption Act (Charitable Gift)
Pa. Purdon's Stat., Title 10, § 361 et seq.

Annulment Act (Marriage)
Cal. Civil Code §§ 82 et seq., 4425 et seq.
Colo. Rev. Stat., 46-3-1 et seq.
Conn. Gen. Stat. Ann., 46b-40
Del. Code of 1974, Title 13, § 1501 et seq.
Ga. Code Ann., 19-4-1 et seq.
Mich. Comp. Laws Ann., 552.3, 552.34 et seq.
Miss. Code Ann. 1972, § 93-7-1 et seq.
Mont. Code Ann., 1991, 40-1-402
N.D. Cent. Code, 14-04-01 et seq.
N.Y. Domestic Relations Law (Consol. Laws Ch. 14) § 140 et seq.
Ohio Rev. Code 1953, 3105.31 et seq.
Pa. Cons. Stat., Title 23, § 3101

Annunzio-Wylie Anti-Money Laundering Act
Oct. 28, 1992, P.L. 102-550, 12 U.S. Code § 1811 nt.
Sept. 13, 1994, P.L. 103-322, 108 Stat. 2149
Sept. 23, 1994, P.L. 103-325, 108 Stat. 2254

Antacrtic Marine Living Resources Convention Act of 1984
Nov. 8, 1984, P.L. 98-623, 98 Stat. 3398, 16 U.S. Code § 2431 et seq.

Antarctic Conservation Act of 1978
Oct. 28, 1978, P.L. 95-541, 16 U.S. Code §§ 2401, 2401 nt., 2402 et seq.; 22 U.S. Code §§ 1971, 1971 nt.
Oct. 2, 1996, P.L. 104-227, 16 U.S. Code §§ 2401 to 2403, 2403a, 2404, 2405, 2413

Antarctic Protection Act of 1990
Nov. 16, 1990, P.L. 101-594, 16 U.S. Code §§ 2461 nt., 2461 to 2466
Oct. 2, 1996, P.L. 104-227, 16 U.S. Code §§ 2463, 2464, 2466

Antarctic Science, Tourism, and Conversation Act of 1996
Oct. 2, 1996, P.L. 104-227, 16 U.S. Code § 2401 nt.

Ante-Mortem Probate Act
Ark. Code Ann. 1987, 28-40-201 et seq.
N.D. Cent. Code, 30.1-08.1-01 et seq.
Ohio Rev. Code 1953, 2107.081 et seq.

Antelope Valley-East Kern Water Agency Act
Cal. Statutes 1959, Ch. 2146, p. 5114, § 49 et seq.

Antenuptial Agreements Act
N.C. Gen. Stat. 1943, §§ 39-18, 52-11

Antenuptial Contract Act
Ark. Code Ann. 1987, 9-11-402, 9-11-404 et seq.
Mass. Gen. Laws Ann., 209:25
Mo. Rev. Stat., 474.120 et seq.

Antenuptial Physical Examination Act
Mich. Comp. Laws Ann., 551.151 et seq.

Anthracite Coal Mine Act
Pa. Purdon's Stat., Title 52, § 70-101 et seq.

Anthracite Coal Mine Act (Child Labor)
Pa. Purdon's Stat., Title 52, § 31 et seq.

Anthracite Coal Reconstruction Transportation Appropriation Act
Pa. 1939 Pamph. Laws 1113, No. 393

Anthracite Mine Safety Act
Pa. 1891 Pamph. Laws 176, No. 177

Anthracite Mine Water Control Act
July 15, 1955, Ch. 369, 69 Stat. 352, 30 U.S. Code §§ 571 to 576
Oct. 15, 1962, P.L. 87-818, 76 Stat. 934, 30 U.S. Code §§ 571, 572, 575

Anthracite Standards Law
Pa. Purdon's Stat., Title 73, § 261 et seq.

Anthracite Strip Mining and Conservation Act
Pa. Purdon's Stat., Title 52, § 681.1 et seq.

Anthropological Research Act
April 10, 1928, Ch. 335, 45 Stat. 413, 20 U.S. Code §§ 69, 70
Aug. 22, 1949, Ch. 494, 63 Stat. 623, 20 U.S. Code § 69

Anti A S C A P Act (Musical Compositions)
Mont. Laws 1939, Ch. 123

Anti-Apartheid Act
Ore. Rev. Stat., 293.830 et seq.

Anti-Arson Act of 1982
Oct. 12, 1982, P.L. 97-298, 18 U.S. Code §§ 841 nt., 844

Anti Arson Application Law
Pa. Purdon's Stat., Title 40, § 1615.1 et seq.

Anti-Assignment Act
July 29, 1846, Ch. 66, 9 Stat. 41, 31 U.S. Code § 203
Feb. 26, 1853, Ch. 81, 10 Stat. 170, 31 U.S. Code § 203
May 27, 1908, Ch. 206, 35 Stat. 411, 31 U.S. Code § 203
Oct. 9, 1940, Ch. 779, 54 Stat. 1029, 31 U.S. Code § 203
May 15, 1951, Ch. 75, 65 Stat. 41, 31 U.S. Code § 203

Anti-Beer Act
See National Prohibition Acts

Anti-Bid Rigging Act
Pa. Cons. Stat., Title 62, § 4501 et seq.

Anti-bid-Rigging Act
Pa. Purdon's Stat., Title 73, § 1611 et seq.

Anti Birth Control Act
Conn. Gen. Stat. Ann., § 53-32

Anti Black Market Act
Wis. Laws 1943, Ch. 550

Anti-Blacklisting Act
Me. Rev. Stat. Ann. 1964, Title 17, § 401

Anti-Boycott Certification Act (International)
Ill. Comp. Stat. 1992, Ch. 30, § 582/1

Anti Bucket Shop Act
Ga. Code Ann., 13-9-6

Anti-Car Theft Act of 1992
Oct. 25, 1992, P.L. 102-519, 15 U.S. Code § 1901 nt.

Anti-Car Theft Improvements Act of 1996
July 2, 1996, P.L. 104-152, 49 U.S. Code § 30101 nt.
Nov. 20, 1997, P.L. 105-102, 49 U.S. Code §§ 30501, 30502, 30503, 30504

Anti Cattle Rustling Act
Ala. Code 1975, § 2-15-40 et seq.

Anti Chain Store Act
Fla. Stat. 1965, 204.01 et seq.

Anti-Child Pornography Act (Polanco-Ferguson)
Cal. Penal Code § 311.11

Anti-Cigarette Law
Iowa Code Ann., 453A.2, 453A.3

Anti Closed Shop Act
Ark. Code Ann. 1987, 11-3-301 et seq.
N.C. Gen. Stat. 1943, § 95-78 et seq.
N.D. Cent. Code, 34-01-14
N.H. Rev. Stat. 1955, 275:1

Tenn. Code Ann., 50-1-201 et seq.
Tex. Rev. Civ. Stat., Art. 5207a

Anti-Copying act (Boat Hull)
N.C. Gen. Stat. 1943, § 75A-27 et seq.

Anti-Crime Advisory Council Act
Ill. Comp. Stat. 1992, Ch. 20, § 3910/0.01 et seq.

Anti Crime Comic Books Act
Ohio Rev. Code 1953, 2903.10

Anti-Darwinism Act
Ark. Stat. 1947, 80-1627, 80-1628

Anti Daylight Saving Time Act
Ky. Rev. Stat. 1962, 2.160

Anti Deceptive Practices and False Advertising Act
Wis. Stat. Ann., 100.18

Anti-Deficiency Act
Feb. 27, 1906, Ch. 510, 34 Stat. 49, 31 U.S. Code § 665
Sept. 6, 1950, Ch. 896, 64 Stat. 765, 31 U.S. Code § 665
July 22, 1974, P.L. 93-344, 88 Stat. 332, 31 U.S. Code § 665
Sept. 13, 1982, P.L. 97-258, 96 Stat. 1068

Anti Department Store Act
Mo. Laws 1899, p. 72

Anti-Discrimination Act (Morbid Obesity)
Ga. Code Ann., 33-24-59.1

Anti-Discrimination Act (Public Housing)
Vt. Stat. Ann., Title 9, § 4500 et seq.

Anti-Discrimination Laws (Publicly-Aided Housing)
N.Y. Civil Rights Law (Consol. Laws Ch. 6), § 18a et seq.

Anti-Drug Abuse Act of 1986
Oct. 27, 1986, P.L. 99-570, 21 U.S. Code § 801
July 11, 1987, P.L. 100-71, 101 Stat. 438
Continued

Oct. 23, 1987, P.L. 100-138, 20 U.S. Code § 4601 nt.

Nov. 18, 1988, P.L. 100-690, 16 U.S. Code §§ 1 nt., 559e; 21 U.S. Code §§ 801 nt., 857; 22 U.S. Code § 2291-1; 43 U.S. Code § 2 nt.; 46 U.S. Code Appx. § 1902 nt.

April 18, 1990, P.L. 101-272, 104 Stat. 137

Nov. 28, 1990, P.L. 101-630, 104 Stat. 4567

Nov. 29, 1990, P.L. 101-647, 21 U.S. Code §§ 801 nt., 857, 857 nt.

Oct. 28, 1991, P.L. 105 Stat. 959

Oct. 29, 1991, P.L. 106 Stat. 4582

July 5, 1994, P.L. 103-272, 108 Stat. 1379

Nov. 2, 1994, P.L. 103-437, 48 U.S. Code § 1494a

Nov. 2, 1994, P.L. 103-447, 108 Stat. 4595

Oct. 19, 1996, P.L. 104-316, 19 U.S. Code § 2081

Anti-Drug Abuse Act of 1988

Nov. 18, 1988, P.L. 100-690, 21 U.S. Code § 1501 nt.

Nov. 5, 1990, P.L. 101-509, 5 U.S. Code §§ 4521 nt., 5541 nt.

Nov. 5, 1990, P.L. 101-510, 21 U.S. Code § 1502a

Nov. 28, 1990, P.L. 101-625, 42 U.S. Code § 11908

Nov. 29, 1990, P.L. 101-647, 21 U.S. Code §§ 333a, 801 nt., 857, 857nt., 844a, 1509; 26 U.S. Code §§ 6103 nt., 7608 nt.; 42 U.S. Code § 10601 nt.

Oct. 18, 1991, P.L. 102-132, 42 U.S. Code §§ 11801, 11805, 11806, 11823

Oct. 6, 1992, P.L. 102-393, 21 U.S. Code § 1509

Oct. 28, 1992, P.L. 102-550, 42 U.S. Code §§ 11902 to 11904, 11909

Sept. 21, 1993, P.L. 103-82, 42 U.S. Code § 11851

July 5, 1994, P.L. 103-272, 49 U.S. Code § 10530

Oct. 20, 1994, P.L. 103-382, 42 U.S. Code § 11841

Dec. 21, 1995, P.L. 104-66, 21 U.S. Code § 848 nt.; 49 U.S. Code § 45302 nt.

Feb. 10, 1996, P.L. 104-106, 10 U.S. Code § 9441 nt.

July 30, 1996, P.L. 104-168, 26 U.S. Code § 7608 nt.

Oct. 7, 1998, P.L. 105-244, 42 U.S. Code § 11851

Oct. 21, 1998, P.L. 105-276, 42 U.S. Code §§ 11901 to 11909

Oct. 27, 1998, P.L. 105-285, 42 U.S. Code § 11841

Anti-Drug Abuse Amendments Act of 1988

Nov. 18, 1988. P.L. 100-690, 21 U.S. Code § 801 nt.

Aug. 16, 1989, P.L. 101-93, 42 U.S. Code §§ 242c, 295g-7, 300x-1a, 300x-4, 300x-4a, 300x-9a nt., 300x-11 nt., 11841, 11842

Nov. 21, 1989, P.L. 101-162, 21 U.S. Code § 881 nt.; 42 U.S. Code § 10713

Dec. 7, 1989, P.L. 101-204, 42 U.S. Code §§ 5671, 5751, 5777, 11803, 11825, 11842, 11851

Anti-Drug Commission Act (Athens-Clarke County)

Ga. Laws 1991, p. 4792

Anti-Drug Commission Act (Griffin-Spaulding Act)

Ga. Laws 1988, p. 4053

Anti-Drug Commission Act (Marietta-Cobb County)

Ga. Laws 1991, p. 4233

Anti-Drug Commission Act (Savannah-Chatham County)

Ga. Laws 1990, p. 4059

Anti-Drug Diversion Act

Okla. Stat. 1981, Title 63, § 2-309A et seq.

Anti-Drug Profiteering Act

N.J. Stat. Ann., 2C:35A-1 et seq.

Anti-Dumping Act, 1921

May 27, 1921, Ch. 14, 42 Stat. 11, 19 U.S. Code §§ 160 to 171

Sept. 1, 1954, Ch. 1213, 68 Stat. 1136

Aug. 14, 1958, P.L. 85-630, 72 Stat. 583, 19 U.S. Code §§ 160, 161, 164, 165, 168, 169, 170a, 171

June 2, 1970, P.L. 91-271, 84 Stat. 292, 19 U.S. Code §§ 161, 167 to 169

July 26, 1979, P.L. 96-39, 19 U.S. Code §§ 160 to 173 were repealed

Anti-Economic Discrimination Act of 1994
April 30, 1994, P.L. 103-236, 22 U.S. Code
§§ 2679c, 2679c nt., 2751 nt.
Oct. 21, 1998, P.L. 105-277, 22 U.S. Code
§ 2679

Anti-Eviction Act
N.J. Stat. Ann., 2A:18-61.1 et seq.

Anti-Featherbedding Law (Railroad)
Cal. Labor Code § 6900 et seq.

Anti Fish Trap Act
Alaska Stat. 1962, § 16.10.060 et seq.

Anti-Freeze Act
Neb. Rev. Stat. 1943, 81-2, 186 et seq.

Anti-Gag Law
Aug. 24, 1912, Ch. 389, 37 Stat. 555

Anti-Gambling Act (District of Columbia)
May 16, 1908, Ch. 172, 35 Stat. 163

Anti-Gin Act
Miss. Code Ann. 1972, § 75-41-1 et seq.

Anti-Gridlock Act
Cal. Vehicle Code 1959, § 22526

Anti-Harassment Act
Wash. Rev. Code 1983, 9A.46.900 et seq.

Anti-Hazing Law
Del. Code of 1974, Title 14, § 9301 et seq.
W. Va. Code 1966, § 18-16-1 et seq.

Anti Heart Balm Act
Cal. Civil Code § 43.5
Ill. Rev. Stat. 1991, Ch. 40, § 1900 et seq.
N.Y. Civil Rights Law (Consol. Laws Ch. 6)
§ 80a
Pa. Purdon's Stat., Title 48, § 170 et seq.

Anti-Heroin Act
June 7, 1924, Ch. 352, 43 Stat. 657, 21 U.S.
Code § 173

Anti-Immunity Act (Trusts and Interstate Commerce)
June 30, 1906, Ch. 3920, 34 Stat. 798, 49
U.S. Code § 48

Anti-Incommunicado Detention Act
Wash. Rev. Code Ann., 9.33.020, Subd. 5

Anti Injunction Act
Ariz. Rev. Stat. Ann., § 12-1808
Colo. Rev. Stat., 8-3-118
Ind. Code Ann., 22-6-1-1 et seq.
Kan. Stat. Ann., 60-904
Mass. Gen. Laws Ann., 214:6
Minn. Stat. Ann., 185.01 et seq.
N.M. Stat. Ann., 50-3-1 et seq.

Anti-Injunction Act (Labor Disputes)
Conn. Gen. Stat. Ann., § 31-112 et seq.
Haw. Rev. Stat. § 380-1 et seq.
Ida. Code 1947, 44-701 et seq.
La. Rev. Stat. Ann., 23:841 et seq.
Md. Ann. Code 1957, Art. 100, § 63 et seq.
Md. Ann. Code 1974, Art. LE, § 4-301 et seq.
Me. Rev. Stat. Ann. 1964, Title 26, § 5
Mich. Comp. Laws Ann., 423.13 et seq.
N.D. Cent. Code, 34-08-01 et seq.
N.J. Stat. Ann., 2A:15-51 et seq.
N.Y. Labor Law (Consol. Laws Ch. 31)
§ 807
Ore. Rev. Stat., 662.040 et seq.
Pa. Purdon's Stat., Title 43, § 206a et seq.
R.I. Gen. Laws 1956, 28-10-1 et seq.
Utah Code Ann. 1953, 34-19-1 et seq.
Wash. Rev. Code , 49.32.011 et seq.
Wis. Stat. Ann., 103.51 et seq.
Wyo. Stat. Ann., § 27-7-103

Anti-Injunction Law
March 23, 1932, Ch. 90, 47 Stat. 70, 29 U.S.
Code §§ 101 to 115

Anti Insurrection Act
Ga. Code Ann., 16-11-2, 16-11-3

Anti Intimidation and Defacing of Public or Private Property Criminal Penalty Act
D.C. Code Ann., §§ 22-3112.1 to 22-3112.4

Anti-Intoxication Act
D.C. Code 1973, § 25-128

Anti Japanese Act
Ark. Stat. 1947, 50-302 et seq.
Del. Laws Vol. 32, p. 616, Ch. 188

Anti Japanese Land Act
Cal. Statutes 1913, Ch. 113, p. 206
Cal. Statutes 1919, p. 1

Anti-Kickback Act (Labor Disputes)
Me. Rev. Stat. Ann. 1964, Title 26, § 629

Anti-Kickback Act of 1986
Oct. 13, 1994, P.L. 103-355, 41 U.S. Code
§§ 57, 58
Feb. 10, 1996, P.L. 104-106, 41 U.S. Code
§ 57

Anti-Kickback Acts
June 13, 1934, Ch. 482, 48 Stat. 948, 40 U.S.
Code §§ 276b, 276c
March 8, 1946, Ch. 80, 60 Stat. 37, 41 U.S.
Code §§ 51 to 54
Sept. 2, 1960, P.L. 86-695, 74 Stat. 740, 41
U.S. Code §§ 51 to 54

Anti-Kickback Enforcement Act of 1986
Nov. 7, 1986, P.L. 99-634, 42 U.S. Code
§§ 51 nt., 51 to 58

Anti-Klan Act
La. Rev. Stat. Ann., 12:501 et seq.

Anti Labor Injunction Act
Ill. Rev. Stat. 1991, Ch. 48, § 2a

Anti-Liars License Act
Ky. Rev. Stat. 1971, 329.010 et seq.

Anti-Lobbying Act
See Federal Regulation Of Lobbying Act
July 11, 1919, Ch. 6, 41 Stat. 68 (See 18 U.S.
Code § 1913)

Anti-Lottery Act
Sept. 19, 1890, Ch. 908, 26 Stat. 465

Anti-lottery Act
See also Gambling and Gaming Acts
Haw. Rev. Stat. Ann., § 712-1220

Anti-Merger Act
Dec. 29, 1950, Ch. 1184, 64 Stat. 1125, 15
U.S. Code §§ 18, 21

Anti Minors Mendicancy Act
Pa. Cons. Stat., Title 18, § 6301

Anti-Moiety Act (Informers)
June 22, 1874, Ch. 391, 18 Stat. 186, 19 U.S.
Code §§ 494, 535, 537

Anti Morewitz Act (Maritime Bonds)
Va. Code 1950, § 8.01-538

Anti-Motor Vehicle Hijacking Act
Ga. Laws 1994, p. 1625

Anti-Motor Vehicle Theft Act
S.C. Code Ann. 1976, § 56-19-810 et seq.

Anti Muskopf Act
Cal. Civil Code § 22.3

Anti N A A C P Act
Va. Code 1950, § 18.1-372 et seq.

Anti-Narcotic Act
See Narcotics Acts

Anti-Obscenity Act (Deddeh-Polanco)
Cal. Penal Code § 311 et seq.

Anti-Pass Acts
June 29, 1906, Ch. 3591, 34 Stat. 584, 49
U.S. Code § 1
April 13, 1908, Ch. 143, 35 Stat. 60, 49 U.S.
Code § 1
June 18, 1910, Ch. 309, 36 Stat. 546, 49 U.S.
Code § 1
Oct. 17, 1978, P.L. 950473, 92 Stat. 1467

Anti-Peonage Act
March 2, 1867, Ch. 187, 14 Stat. 546, 42 U.S.
Code § 1994 (See 18 U.S. Code § 1581)

Anti-picketing Act
Haw. Rev. Stat. Ann., §§ 379A-1, 379A-2

Anti-Piracy Act
N.J. Stat. Ann., 2C:21-21 et seq.

Anti-Pollution Bond Act
Ill. Comp. Stat. 1992, Ch. 30, § 405/1 et seq.

Anti-Pollution Bond Fund Transfer Act
Ill. Comp. Stat. 1992, Ch. 30, § 410/0.01 et seq.

Anti-Polygamy Acts
July 1, 1862, Ch. 126, 12 Stat. 501
March 22, 1882, Ch. 47, 22 Stat. 30
March 3, 1887, Ch. 397, 24 Stat. 635

Anti Price Discrimination Act
Ida. Code 1947, 48-201 et seq.
Minn. Stat. Ann., 325D.01 et seq.
Mont. Rev. Code 1947, 51-101 et seq.
Okla. Stat. Ann., Title 79, § 81 et seq.
Ore. Rev. Stat., 646.010 et seq.
Va. Code 1950, § 59-1 et seq.

Anti-Racketeering Act
June 18, 1934, Ch. 569, 48 Stat. 979 (See 18 U.S. Code § 1951)
July 3, 1946, Ch. 537, 60 Stat. 420, 15 U.S. Code § 17 nt.; 29 U.S. Code §§ 52, 101, 151 nt.

Anti-Rebate Act (Insurance)
Ore. Rev. Stat., 736.620
Pa. Purdon's Stat., Title 40, §§ 275, 276
Wis. Stat. Ann., 628.33

Anti-Rebate Act (Railroads)
Feb. 19, 1903, Ch. 708, 32 Stat. 847, 49 U.S. Code §§ 41 to 43
June 29, 1906, Ch. 3591, 34 Stat. 587, 49 U.S. Code § 41

Anti Red Law
N.Y. Civil Service Law 1958 (Consol. Laws Ch. 7) § 105

Anti-Reviver Act (Repeals)
Feb. 25, 1871, Ch. 71, 16 Stat. 431 (See 1 U.S. Code § 108)
July 30, 1947, Ch. 388, 61 Stat. 633, 1 U.S. Code § 108

Anti-Secrecy Act (Departmental Information)
See also Housekeeping Acts
Aug. 12, 1958, P.L. 85-619, 72 Stat. 547 (See 5 U.S. Code § 301)

Anti-Sedition Act
Ga. Code Ann., 16-11-1 et seq.
Mich. Comp. Laws Ann., 752.321 et seq.
Pa. Purdon's Stat., Title 18, § 4207

Anti-Sex Discriminatory Language Act
D.C. Laws 1976, No. 1-87

Anti-Skullduggery Act
Tenn. Code Ann., 2-5-101

Anti-SLAPP Law (Strategic Lawsuits Against Public Participation)
Mass. Gen. Laws Ann., 231:59H

Anti-Smuggling Act
Aug. 5, 1935, Ch. 438, 49 Stat. 517 (See 14 U.S. Code § 638) 19 U.S. Code §§ 170, 483, 1401, 1432a, 1434, 1436, 1441, 1581, 1584 to 1587, 1591, 1592, 1601a, 1615, 1619, 1621, 1701 to 1711; 46 U.S. Code §§ 60, 91, 106, 277, 288, 319, 325
June 30, 1955, Ch. 258, 69 Stat. 242, 19 U.S. Code § 1709

Anti-Snob Zoning Law
Mass. Gen. Laws Ann., 40B:20 et seq.

Anti-Stalking Act
Mass. Gen. Laws Ann., 265:43
Mich. Comp. Laws Ann., 600.2954 et seq.
N.Y. Penal Law 1965 (Consol. Laws Ch. 40) §§ 120.13, 120.14, 240.25, 240.26

Anti Stock Fraud Law
N.Y. General Business Law (Consol. Laws Ch. 20) § 352 et seq.

Anti-Street Crimes Act
Cal. Penal Code §§ 12025, 12031

Anti-Strike Act
See War Labor Disputes Act

Anti-Strike Act (Public Employees)
Mich. Comp. Laws Ann., 423.201 et seq.
Minn. Stat. 1969, 179.50 et seq.
Pa. Purdon's Stat., Title 43, § 215.1 et seq.

Anti-Strikebreaking Act
June 24, 1936, Ch. 746, 49 Stat. 1899 (See 18 U.S. Code § 1231)
June 29, 1938, Ch. 813, 52 Stat. 1242 (See 18 U.S. Code § 1231)
June 25, 1948, Ch. 645, 62 Stat. 862

Anti-Subversive Activities Act
Oct. 17, 1940, Ch. 897, 54 Stat. 1201 (See 18 U.S. Code § 2386)

Anti Subversive Control Act
Mass. Gen. Laws Ann., 264:16 et seq.

Anti-Tampering Act
Fla. Stat. Ann., 501.001

Anti Terrorism Act
N.M. Stat. Ann., 30-20A-1 et seq.

Anti Terrorism Act (Motor Vehicles)
Ga. Code Ann., 35-3-60 et seq.
N.M. Stat. Ann., 30-20A-1 et seq.

Anti-Terrorism Act of 1987
Dec. 22, 1987, P.L. 100-204, 22 U.S. Code §§ prec. 5201, 5201 to 5203, 5201 nt.

Anti-Terrorism and Arms Export Amendments Act of 1989
Dec. 12, 1989, P.L. 101-222, 22 U.S. Code § 2151 nt.

Anti-Terrorism Provisions
Mont. Code Ann., 45-8-107 to 45-8-109

Anti-Theft and Airbag Safety Act
N.Y. Insurance Law 1984 (Consol. Laws Ch. 28) §§ 3411, 3412
N.Y. Vehicle and Traffic Law 1959 (Consol. Laws Ch. 71) §§ 119b, 301, 398d, 415a, 415c, 603, 605

Anti Trade Restraint Act
Mo. Rev. Stat., 416.011 et seq.

Anti Trading Stamp Act
Iowa Code 1975, 553.15 et seq.
Ky. Acts 1922, Ch. 131
Wyo. Stat. Ann., § 40-16-101 et seq.

Anti-Trust Act (Monopolies and Unfair Trade Practices)
Ariz. Rev. Stat. Ann., § 44-1401 et seq.

Anti-Trust Acts
July 2, 1890, Ch. 647, 26 Stat. 209, 15 U.S. Code §§ 1 to 7
Oct. 15, 1914, Ch. 323, 38 Stat. 730, 15 U.S. Code §§ 12 to 27, 44 (See 18 U.S. Code §§ 402, 3285, 3691) 29 U.S. Code § 52
Aug. 17, 1937, Ch. 690, 50 Stat. 693, 15 U.S. Code § 1
July 7, 1955, Ch. 281, 69 Stat. 282, 15 U.S. Code §§ 1 to 3

Anti Trust and Pooling Act
Ky. Acts 1889-90 (Public) Ch. 1621

Anti-Trust Improvements Act
Sept. 30, 1976, P.L. 94-435, 15 U.S. Code § 1311 et seq.

Anti-Uniform Act
N.Y. Military Law (Consol. Laws Ch. 36), § 238

Anti Usury Injunction Act
Tex. Rev. Civ. Stat., Art. 5069-1.01 et seq.

Anti-Vandalism Act
N.Y. Laws 1991, Ch. 133

Anti-Violent Crime Act
Alaska Laws 1992, Ch. 79

Anti-Wire Tapping Act
N.Y. Penal Laws 1965 (Consol. Laws Ch. 40), § 250.00 et seq.

Anti Yellow Dog Act
Ariz. Rev. Stat. Ann., § 23-1341
Cal. Labor Code § 921
Kan. Laws 1903, Ch. 222
N.J. Stat. Ann., 34:12-2 to 34:12-4

Antiabortion Act
  Okla. Stat. Ann., Title 21, § 861 et seq.

Antiaddiction Act (Narcotics)
  Ky. Rev. Stat. 1971, 218A.010 et seq.

Antiadvertising Liquor Law
  Ala. Code 1975, § 28-3-16

Antialien Land Law
  Wash. Rev. Code Ann., 64.16.010 et seq.

Antiambulance Chasing Act
  N.D. Cent. Code, 9-08-08, 9-08-09
  Neb. Laws 1921, Ch. 171

Antianarchy Act
  Mass. Gen. Laws Ann., 264:11
  N.Y. Penal Law 1965 (Consol. Laws Ch. 40)
    § 240.15

Antibarratry Act
  S.C. Code Ann. 1976, § 16-17-10 et seq.

Antibetting Act
  Ky. Rev. Stat. 1971, 372.010 et seq.

Antibias Act
  N.Y. Executive Law 1951 (Consol. Laws Ch.
    18) § 296

Antibias Act (Employment)
  Ill. Rev. Stat. 1991, Ch. 68, § 2-101

Antibias Act (Housing)
  N.J. Stat. Ann., 10:5-1 et seq.

Antiblacklisting Act
  Ala. Code 1975, § 13A-11-123
  Ariz. Const. 1910, Art. 18, § 9
  Ark. Code Ann. 1987, 11-3-202
  Cal. Labor Code § 1050 et seq.
  Colo. Rev. Stat., 8-2-110, 8-2-111
  Ind. Code Ann., 22-5-3-1, 22-5-3-2
  Iowa Code Ann., 730.1 et seq.
  Kan. Stat. Ann., 44-117 et seq.
  Me. Rev. Stat. Ann. 1964, Title 17, § 401
  Minn. Stat. Ann., 179.60
  Mo. Rev. Stat. 1969, 559.390

  Mont. Code Ann., 39-2-803
  N.C. Gen. Stat. 1943, §§ 14-355, 14-356
  N.D. Cent. Code, 34-01-07
  Nev. Rev. Stat. 1979 Reprint, 613.210
  N.M. Stat. Ann., 30-13-3
  N.Y. Labor Law (Consol. Laws Ch. 31)
    § 704, Subds. 2, 9
  Okla. Stat. Ann., Title 40, §§ 172, 173
  Ore. Rev. Stat., 659.230
  Tex. Rev. Civ. Stat., Art. 5196 et seq.
  Utah Code Ann. 1953, 34-24-1, 34-24-2
  Va. Code 1950, § 40.1-27
  Wash. Rev. Code Ann., 49.44.010
  Wis. Stat. Ann., 111.06, Subsec. 1, Subd. k

Antibookmaking Act
  Fla. Stat. Ann., 849.01 et seq.
  Tex. Penal Code, § 47.01 et seq.

Antiboycott Act
  Ala. Code 1975, § 13A-11-122

Antibucketing Law
  Colo. Rev. Stat., 11-53-101 et seq.

Antibugging Act (Wiretapping)
  Nev. Rev. Stat. Ann., 200.610 et seq.

Antibusing Law
  N.C. Gen. Stat. 1943, § 115-176 et seq.

Antibypass Act (Highways)
  Wyo. Stat. Ann., §§ 24-7-101, 24-7-102

Anticigarette Act
  Ind. Code Ann., 35-1-105-1, 35-1-105-2,
    35-14-2-1, 35-14-7-1 et seq.
  Tenn. Acts 1901, Ch. 86

Anticoercion Act (Automobile Dealers)
  Ark. Code Ann. 1987, 4-75-401 et seq.
  Cal. Business and Professions Code
    §§ 18400 to 18413

Anticoercion Act (Labor)
  Colo. Rev. Stat., 8-2-101 et seq.

Anticoercion Act (Loan Insurance)
  Pa. Cons. Stat., Title 18, § 7309 et seq.

Anticombination Act (Monopolies)
Mo. Rev. Stat., 416.011 et seq.

Anticommunism Act
Ark. Acts 1943, p. 465, No. 221
Ind. Code Ann., 35-26-2-1 et seq.
Mass. Gen. Laws Ann., 264:16 et seq.

Anticompact Act (Insurance Companies)
Ga. Code Ann.,33-6-5
Iowa Code Ann., 515.131 et seq.
Mo. Rev. Stat., 416.290
Ore. Rev. Stat., 746.160
Wash. Rev. Code Ann., 48.30.020

Anticonspiracy Act
Mich. Comp. Laws Ann., 750.151 et seq.

Anticontraceptive Act
Conn. Gen. Stat. Ann., § 53-32
Mass. Gen. Laws Ann., 272:20, 272:21

Anticorporate Farming Act
N.D. Cent. Code, 10-06-01 et seq.

Anticorruption Act
N.D. Cent. Code, 54-03-21

Anticounterfeiting Consumer Protection Act of 1996
July 2, 1996, P.L. 104-153, 18 U.S. Code § 2311 nt.

Antideficiency Act
Cal. Code of Civil Procedure § 580a et seq.

Antideficiency Judgment Act
N.C. Gen. Stat. 1943, § 45-21.38
Tex. Rules of Civil Procedure, Rule 309

Antidilution Act (Trademarks)
Conn. Gen. Stat. Ann., § 35-11a et seq.
Ga. Code Ann., 10-1-451
Ill. Rev. Stat. 1991, Ch. 140, § 22
Mass. Gen. Laws Ann., 110B:11
N.Y. General Business Law (Consol. Laws Ch. 20) § 368d

Antidilution Act (Unfair Competition)
Mass. Gen. Laws Ann., 110B:12 et seq.

Antidiscrimination Act
Alaska Stat. 1962, § 18.80.200 et seq.
Colo. Rev. Stat., 24-34-401 et seq.
Conn. Gen. Stat. Ann., § 46a-64
Ida. Code 1947, 18-7301 et seq.
Ind. Code Ann., 22-9-1-1 et seq.
Iowa Code Ann., 601A.6 et seq.
Mo. Laws 1937, p. 536
Neb. Rev. Stat. 1943, 48-214
N.J. Stat. Ann., 10:1-1 et seq., 10:5-1 et seq.
N.Y. Executive Law 1951 (Consol. Laws Ch. 18) § 290 et seq.
Okla. Stat. Ann., Title 25, § 1101 et seq.
Ore. Rev. Stat., 30.670 et seq.
Pa. Purdon's Stat., Title 43, § 951 et seq.
Utah Code Ann. 1953, 34-35-1 et seq.
Wyo. Stat. Ann., § 40-4-101 et seq.

Antidiscrimination Act (Civil Rights)
Cal. Civil Code § 51 et seq.
Minn. Stat. Ann., 363.01 et seq.
N.H. Rev. Stat. 1955, 354-A:1 et seq.

Antidiscrimination Act (Employment)
Del. Code of 1974, Title 19, § 710 et seq.
Haw. Rev. Stat. § 378-1 et seq.
Mass. Gen. Laws Ann., 149:24A et seq., 151B:1 et seq.
Ohio Rev. Code 1953, 4112.01 et seq.
Ore. Rev. Stat., 659.010 et seq.
R.I. Gen. Laws 1956, 28-5-1 et seq.
Vt. Stat. Ann., Title 21, § 495 et seq.
Wash. Rev. Code Ann., 49.60.010 et seq.

Antidiscrimination Act (Housing)
Colo. Rev. Stat., 24-34-501 et seq.
Mass. Gen. Laws Ann., 151B:1 et seq.
Ore. Rev. Stat., 659.031, 659.033
Wash. Rev. Code Ann., 49.60.222

Antidiscrimination Act (Insurance)
Ala. Code 1975, § 27-12-11
Fla. Stat. Ann., 849.01 et seq.
Iowa Code Ann., 507B.3 et seq.
Miss. Code Ann. 1972, § 83-7-3
N.C. Gen. Stat. 1943, § 58-58-35

Antidiscrimination Act (Labor)
Ind. Burns' 1933 Repl., 40-2301 et seq.
Neb. Rev. Stat. 1943, 48-214 et seq.
N.H. Rev. Stat. 1955, 275:36 et seq.
N.M. Stat. Ann., 28-1-7 et seq.
Wis. Stat. Ann., 111.31 et seq.

Antidiscrimination Act (Private Employment)
Cal. Labor Code § 1410 et seq.
Conn. Gen. Stat. Ann., § 46a-51 et seq.
Ill. Rev. Stat. 1985, Ch. 68, § 2-101 et seq.
Kan. Stat. Ann., 44-1001 et seq.
Mich. Comp. Laws Ann., 423.301 et seq.
Mo. Rev. Stat., 213.055 et seq.

Antidiscrimination Act (Private Hospitals)
Ill. Rev. Stat. 1991, Ch. 120, § 500.7

Antidiscrimination Act (Private Housing)
N.Y. Private Housing Finance Law (Consol. Laws Ch. 44B) § 602

Antidiscrimination Act (Private Schools)
Ill. Rev. Stat. 1991, Ch. 144, § 151
Ore. Rev. Stat., 345.240

Antidiscrimination Act (Privately Owned Public Accommodations)
Cal. Civil Code § 51

Antidiscrimination Act (Public Accommodations)
Colo. Rev. Stat., 24-34-601 et seq.
Ill. Rev. Stat. 1991, Ch. 68, § 5-101 et seq.
Kan. Stat. Ann., 21-4003
Md. Ann. Code 1957, Art. 49B, § 11 et seq.
Me. Rev. Stat. Ann. 1964, Title 17, § 1301
Mich. Comp. Laws Ann., 750.146, 750.147
Minn. Stat. 1980, 327.09
Mont. Code Ann., 49-1-102
N.D. Cent. Code, 12.1-14-04
Neb. Rev. Stat. 1943, 20-132 et seq.
N.H. Rev. Stat. 1955, 354-A:8
N.J. Stat. Ann., 10:1-3
N.M. Stat. Ann. 1953, 49-8-1 et seq.
Ohio Rev. Code 1953, 2901.35
Ore. Rev. Stat., 30.670 et seq.

Pa. Cons. Stat., Title 18, § 7323
R.I. Gen. Laws 1956, 11-24-1 et seq.
S.D. Codified Laws 1967, 20-12-1 et seq.
Wis. Stat. Ann., 942.04

Antidiscrimination Act (Public Employment)
Ariz. Rev. Stat. Ann., § 41-1461 et seq.

Antidiscrimination Act (Race)
Miss. Code Ann. 1972, § 25-9-149

Antidiscrimination Act (Schools)
Mass. Gen. Laws Ann., 76:5, 151C:1 et seq.

Antidiscrimination Act (State Employment)
Okla. Stat. Ann., Title 74, § 951 et seq.

Antidiscrimination Act (Wages)
Ill. Rev. Stat. 1991, Ch. 48, § 4a et seq.

Antidiscrimination Law (Unfair Trade Practices)
Cal. Business and Professions Code § 17000 et seq.

Antidueling Act
Ky. Rev. Stat. 1971, 437.030
Miss. Code Ann. 1972, § 97-39-1 et seq.
Va. Code 1950, § 18-57 et seq.
W. Va. Code 1966, § 61-2-18 et seq.

Antiduplication Law (Public Utility Construction)
Colo. Rev. Stat., 40-5-101 et seq.

Antiencumbrance Act (Fire Insurance)
Tex. Insurance Code, Art. 5.37

Antietam Battlefield Site Acts
May 14, 1940, Ch. 191 54 Stat. 212, 16 U.S. Code § 430nn
April 22, 1960, P.L. 86-438, 74 Stat. 79, 16 U.S. Code § 430oo

Antievolution Act
Ark. Stat. 1947, 80-1627, 80-1628
Tenn. Code Ann., Superseded Vol., 49-1922

Antifeatherbedding Act (Railroad)
Ariz. Rev. Stat. Ann., § 40-886.01

Antifee Law
Tenn. Code Ann., 8-22-101 et seq.

Antifelon Act (Labor Organizations)
N.J. Stat. Ann., 32:23-80

Antifencing Act
Fla. Stat. Ann., 812.005 et seq.

Antiflirting Act
N.C. Gen. Stat. 1943, § 14-274

Antiforfeiture Act
S.D. Codified Laws 1967, 21-9-11

Antifraud Act (Securities)
N.J. Stat. Ann., 49:3-47 et seq.

Antifreeze Act (Motor Vehicle)
Fla. Stat. Ann., 501.91 et seq.
Iowa Code Ann., 208A.1 et seq.
Miss. Code Ann. 1972, § 75-56-1 et seq.
N.C. Gen. Stat. 1943, § 106-579.1 et seq.
N.D. Cent. Code, 19-16.1-01 et seq.
Neb. Rev. Stat. 1943, 81-2,186 et seq.
Nev. Rev. Stat. 1979 Reprint, 590.340 et seq.
N.M. Stat. Ann. 1953, 64-32-1 et seq.
Okla. Stat. Ann., Title 47, § 461 et seq.
S.C. Code Ann. 1976, § 39-51-10 et seq.

Antifreeze Law
Colo. Rev. Stat., 8-20-101 et seq.

Antigambling Act
Ark. Code Ann. 1987, 5-39-101 et seq.
Cal. Penal Code § 330 et seq.
D.C. Code 1973, § 22-1501 et seq.
Del. Code of 1974, Title 11, § 1401 et seq.
Fla. Stat. Ann., 849.01 et seq.
Ida. Code 1947, 18-3801 et seq.
Ind. Code Ann., 35-25-1-1 et seq.
Ky. Rev. Stat. 1971, Superseded Vols., 436.200 et seq.
Ky. Rev. Stat. 1971, 372.010 et seq.
Ohio Rev. Code 1953, 2915.01 et seq.
Tenn. Code Ann., 39-17-501 et seq.
Tex. Penal Code, § 47.01 et seq.
Wis. Stat. Ann., 945.01 et seq.

Antigangster Act
N.J. Stat. Ann., 2:136-1 et seq.

Antigossip Law
Ky. Rev. Stat. 1971, Superseded Vols., 435.300

Antiharassment Act
Wash. Rev. Code Ann., 9A.46.010 et seq., 10.14.010 et seq.

Antihate Act
Ill. Rev. Stat. 1991, Ch. 38, § 12-7.1
Ind. Code Ann., 35-15-1-1 et seq.

Antihazing Law
Pa. Purdon's Stat., Title 24, § 5351 et seq.

Antihijacking Act of 1974
Aug. 5, 1974, P.L. 93-366, 88 Stat. 409, 49 U.S. Code §§ 1301, 1471 to 1473, 1487, 1514, 1515

Antihitchhiking Law
Wash. Rev. Code Ann., 46.61.255

Antijaywalkers Act
Wis. Stat. Ann., 346.25

Antikickback Act
Ill. Rev. Stat. 1991, Ch. 48, § 216a et seq.
Me. Rev. Stat. Ann. 1964, Title 26, § 629
Okla. Stat. Ann., Title 74, § 3401 et seq.
Wash. Rev. Code Ann., 49.52.050 et seq.

Antikickback Act (Gifts by Subcontractors)
Miss. Code Ann. 1972, § 97-11-53

Antilapse Act (Devises and Legacies)
Ala. Code 1975, § 43-8-224
Ark. Code Ann. 1987, 28-26-104
Cal. Probate Code § 92
Colo. Rev. Stat., 15-11-605 et seq.
Conn. Gen. Stat. Ann., § 45a-441 et seq.
Del. Code of 1974, Title 12, § 2313
Fla. Stat. Ann., 732.603 et seq.
Ga. Code Ann.,53-2-90, 53-2-104
Ida. Code 1947, 15-2-501 et seq.
Ill. Rev. Stat. 1991, Ch. 110 1/2, § 4-11

Ind. Code Ann., 29-1-6-1, Subd. g
Iowa Code Ann., 633.273
Kan. Stat. Ann., 59-614
Ky. Rev. Stat. 1971, 394.400
Mass. Gen. Laws Ann., 191:22
Md. Ann. Code 1974, Art. ET, § 4-401 et seq.
Me. Rev. Stat. Ann. 1964, Title 18A, § 2-605
Mich. Comp. Laws Ann., 700.134
Minn. Stat. Ann., 525.203
Mo. Rev. Stat., 474.460
Mont. Rev. Code 1987, 72-2-512
N.C. Gen. Stat. 1943, § 31-42 et seq.
Neb. Rev. Stat. 1943, 30-2343
Nev. Rev. Stat. 1979 Reprint, 133.200
N.H. Rev. Stat. 1955, 551:12
N.J. Stat. Ann., 33:3-35
N.Y. Estates, Powers and Trusts Law
  (Consol. Laws Ch. 17B) § 3-3.3
Ohio Rev. Code 1953, 2107.52
Okla. Stat. Ann., Title 84, § 142
Ore. Rev. Stat., 112.395
Pa. Purdon's Stat., Title 20, § 2514
R.I. Gen. Laws 1956, 33-6-19
S.C. Code Ann. 1976, Superseded Vols.
  § 21-7-470
S.D. Codified Laws 1967, 29-6-8
Tenn. Code Ann., 32-3-105
Tex. Probate Code, § 68
Va. Code 1950, § 64.1
Wash. Rev. Code Ann., 11.12.110 et seq.
Wis. Stat. Ann., 853.27
W. Va. Code 1966, § 41-3-3

Antiliquor Law
Ky. Acts 1922, Ch. 33

Antilittering Act
Tex. Rev. Civ. Stat., Art. 4477-9a, §§ 2.04,
  4.01 et seq.

Antilittering Act (Highways)
Wis. Stat. Ann., 60.70, 86.07, 346.94 Subsec.
  7

Antilittering Laws
Miss. Code Ann. 1972, §§ 49-1-13, 49-1-44,
  97-15-29, 97-15-31, 97-27-9

Antiloafing Act
N.J. Stat. Ann., 34:14-1 to 34:14-11

Antilobbying Act
Mass. Gen. Laws Ann., 3:39 et seq.
Ohio Rev. Code 1953, 101.70 et seq.

Antilottery Act
Ala. Code 1975, § 13A-12-20 et seq.
Md. Ann. Code 1957, Art. 27, § 356 et seq.
N.J. Stat. Ann., 2C:37-2 et seq.
N.Y. Penal Law 1965 (Consol. Laws Ch. 40)
  § 225.00 et seq.
Va. Code 1950, § 18.2-325 et seq.

Antilynching Act
Cal. Penal Code §§ 405a, 405b
Ind. Code Ann., 35-1-77-3 et seq., 35-27-1-1
  et seq.
Va. Code 1950, § 18.2-38 et seq.

Antimacing Act
Pa. Purdon's Stat., Title 25, §§ 2374, 2375

Antimask Act
Ind. Code 1971, 35-1-77-2
La. Rev. Stat. Ann., 14:313
Tex. Penal Code 1925, Arts. 454a to 454g

**Antimerging Law (New York City Teacher
  Lists)**
N.Y. Laws 1912, Ch. 455

**Antimicrobial Regulation Technical
  Corrections Act of 1998**
Oct. 30, 1998, P.L. 105-324, 112 Stat. 3035,
  21 U.S. Code § 301 nt.

Antimiscegenation Act
Ala. Code 1958, Title 14, §§ 360, 361
Cal. Civil Code §§ 60, 69
Fla. Stat. Ann., 626.9541
Ga. Code 1933, 53-106
Ky. Rev. Stat. 1971, 402.020
La. Rev. Stat. Ann., 9:201, 14:79
N.C. Gen. Stat. 1943, § 14-181
Va. Code 1950, § 20-50 et seq.

Antimixing Act
La. Rev. Stat. Ann., 33:4558.1 et seq.

Antimonopoly Act
Fla. Stat. Ann., 542.01 et seq.
Ill. Rev. Stat. 1963, Ch. 121 1/2, § 301 et seq.
Ind. Code Ann., 24-1-1-1 et seq.
La. Rev. Stat. Ann., 51:121 et seq.
Mass. Gen. Laws Ann., 93:1 et seq.
Mich. Comp. Laws Ann., 445.722 et seq.
Mo. Rev. Stat., 416.011 et seq.
Mont. Code Ann., 30-14-201 et seq.
N.C. Gen. Stat. 1943, § 75-1 et seq.
N.M. Stat. Ann., 57-1-1 et seq.
N.Y. General Business Law (Consol. Laws Ch. 20) § 340 et seq.
P.R. Laws Ann. 1954, Title 10, § 257 et seq.
Tex. Business and Commerce Code, § 15.01 et seq.
Va. Code 1950, § 59.1-9.1 et seq.

Antimonopoly Financing Law (Motor Vehicles)
Colo. Rev. Stat., 12-6-201 et seq.

Antimonopoly Law (Transportation of Oil)
Cal. Statutes 1913, p. 523

Antinarcotics Act
Alaska Stat. 1962, § 11.71.010 et seq.
Ark. Code Ann. 1987, 20-64-201 et seq.
Cal. Health and Safety Code §§ 11018 et seq., 1100 et seq.
Ind. Code 1971, 35-24-1-1 et seq.
N.Y. Public Health Law 1953 (Consol. Laws Ch. 45) § 3300 et seq.
Pa. Purdon's Stat., Title 35, § 780.101 et seq.

Antinepotism Act
Ariz. Rev. Stat. Ann., § 38-481
Fla. Stat. Ann., 112.3135
Ida. Code 1947, 59-701, 59-702
Mont. Code Ann., 2-2-301 et seq.
Nev. Rev. Stat. 1979 Reprint, 281.210
N.M. Stat. Ann., 10-1-10
Tex. Rev. Civ. Stat., Art. 5996i
Utah Code Ann. 1953, 52-3-1 et seq.

Antinuisance Act (Sarasota County)
Fla. Special Laws 1953, Ch. 29527

Antiobscenity Act
Cal. Penal Code § 311
Conn. Gen. Stat. Ann., § 53a-193 et seq.
La. Rev. Stat. Ann., 14:106
Mich. Comp. Laws Ann., 750.343 et seq.
S.C. Code Ann. 1976, § 16-15-150 et seq.

Antiparamilitary Training Act
Fla. Stat. Ann., 790.29

Antipass Act (Public Utilities)
Tex. Rev. Civ. Stat., Art. 4005a et seq.

Antipass Act (Railroads)
Neb. Rev. Stat. 1943, 74-815 et seq.

Antipicketing Act
Ala. Acts 1921, Sp. Sess., p. 31
Ariz. Rev. Stat. Ann., § 23-1321 et seq.
Colo. Rev. Stat., 8-3-108, Subd. 2
Ga. Code Ann., 34-6-5
Mich. Comp. Laws Ann., 423.9f
Ore. Laws 1939, Ch. 2
Va. Code 1950, § 40.1-53
Wis. Stat. Ann., 103.535

Antipicketing Act (Public Places)
Miss. Code Ann. 1972, § 97-7-63

Antipicketing Act (Residence)
Conn. Gen. Stat. Ann., § 31-120

Antipirating Act (Public Utilities)
Ida. Code 1947, 61-332 et seq.

Antipollution Act
Pa. Purdon's Stat., Title 35, § 691.1 et seq.

Antipollution Act (Miller)
Cal. Harbors and Navigation Code § 293

Antipollution Bond Act
Ill. Rev. Stat. 1991, Ch. 127, § 451 et seq.

Antipreference Act (Assignments)
Mo. Rev. Stat., 426.010

Antiprivity Act
Va. Code 1950, § 8.2-318

Antiprivity Act (Sales)
Ark. Code Ann. 1987, 4-2-318

Antiprivity Act (Warranties)
Ark. Code Ann. 1987, 85-2-318.1
Ga. Code Ann., 11-2-318

Antiprostitution Act
Fla. Stat. Ann., 796.01 et seq.

Antipumping Law (Mineral Springs)
N.Y. Public Lands Law (Consol. Laws Ch. 46) § 90 et seq.

Antique Boiler Law
Pa. Purdon's Stat., Title 35, § 1330.1 et seq.

Antiquities Act
Fla. Stat. Ann., 267.011 et seq.
Miss. Code Ann. 1972, § 39-7-1 et seq.
Mont. Code Ann., 22-3-421 et seq.
R.I. Gen. Laws 1956, 42-45.1-1 et seq.
Tex. Natural Resources Code, § 191.001 et seq.
Va. Code 1950, § 10.1-900 et seq.

Antirabies Act
N.C. Gen. Stat. 1943, § 130A-184 et seq.
Tenn. Code Ann., 68-8-101 et seq.

Antirabies Act (Hamilton County)
Tenn. Private Acts 1967, Ch. 440

Antirebate and Discrimination Act
Ohio Rev. Code 1953, 3933.01

Antireviver Act (Repeals)
N.D. Cent. Code, 1-02-16

Antirevocation Law (Estates)
Ala. Code 1975, § 43-8-137

Antisaloon Law
Tex. Alcoholic Beverage Code, §§ 25.09, 69.12, 71.04

Antisaloon Territory Act
Ill. Laws 1907, p. 297

Antiscalper Act
Ill. Rev. Stat. 1991, Ch. 114, § 104.9 et seq.

Antiscalping Act (Railroad Tickets)
Ore. Rev. Stat., 760.425

Antiscreen Act
Ky. Acts 1916, Ch. 14

Antiscreen Act (Mines)
Ohio Laws Vol. 104, p. 181, § 6

Antisecrecy Act
Ind. Code Ann., 5-14-1.5-1 et seq.

Antisecrecy Act (Local Legislative Meetings)
Cal. Government Code § 54950 et seq.

Antisecrecy Act (State Offices)
Wis. Stat. Ann., 19.81 et seq.

Antisecret Organization Law
N.Y. Civil Rights Law (Consol. Laws Ch. 6) § 53 et seq.

Antisegregation Act
Ill. Rev. Stat. 1991, Ch. 122, § 10-22.5
N.Y. Executive Law 1951 (Consol. Laws Ch. 18) § 296

Antisegregation Act (Schools)
R.I. Gen. Laws 1956, 16-38-1

Antishipping Law (Liquors)
Ala. Code 1975, § 28-4-120 et seq.

Antishoplifting Act
Ill. Rev. Stat. 1991, Ch. 38, § 16A-1 et seq.

Antiskyjacking Law
Miss. Code Ann. 1972, § 97-25-55

Antislot Machine Act
Ind. Code Ann., 35-25-4-1 et seq.
Md. Ann. Code 1957, Art. 27, § 264B
Minn. Stat. Ann., 349.30 et seq.
N.C. Gen. Stat. 1943, § 14-304 et seq.

Antismog Law
Cal. Health and Safety Code § 39000 et seq.

Antisolicitation Act (Attorneys)
Ohio Rev. Code 1953, 4705.08
Va. Code 1950, § 54.1-3939 et seq.

Antistrike Act
Ark. Code Ann. 1987, 11-3-401 et seq.
Colo. Rev. Stat., 8-1-126 et seq.
Wis. Stat. Ann., 111.01 et seq.

Antistrike Act (Public Utilities)
Mo. Rev. Stat., 295.010 et seq.
N.J. Stat. Ann., 34:13B-1 et seq.
Pa. Purdon's Stat., Title 43, § 213.1 et seq.
Wis. Stat. Ann., 111.50 et seq., 111.62

Antistrikebreaking Act
Utah Code Ann. 1953, 34-19-1 et seq.

Antisubsidence Act
Cal. Public Resources Code § 3315 et seq.

Antisubversion Act
Kan. Stat. Ann., 21-3803
La. Rev. Stat. Ann., 14:358 et seq.
Ohio Rev. Code 1953, 2921.21 et seq.

Antisweating Act
Ky. Rev. Stat. 1971, 422.110

Antisyphilis Act (Blood Tests)
N.Y. Domestic Relations Law (Consol. Laws Ch. 14) § 13a
N.Y. Public Health Law 1953 (Consol. Laws Ch. 45) § 2308

Antitechnicality Act (Insurance)
Tex. Insurance Code, Art. 6.14

Antiterrorism Act
Mich. Comp. Laws Ann., 750.352

Antiterrorism Act of 1990
Nov. 5, 1990, P.L. 101-519, 18 U.S. Code §§ 2331, 2231 nt., 2332 et seq.
April 10, 1991, P.L. 102-27, 105 Stat. 155

Antiterrorism and Effective Death Penalty Act of 1996
April 24, 1996, P.L. 104-132, 18 U.S. Code § 1 nt.
Sept. 30, 1996, P.L. 104-208, 8 U.S. Code §§ 1105a, 1182, 1225, 1252, 1252a
Oct. 11, 1996, P.L. 104-294, 18 U.S. Code §§ 2332, 3663; 28 U.S. Code § prec. 2201
Nov. 26, 1997, P.L. 105-119, 42 U.S. Code § 10602 nt.

Antiterroristic Training Act
Ga. Code Ann., 16-11-150 et seq.

Antitheft Act (Motor Vehicles)
Conn. Gen. Stat. Ann., § 14-196 et seq.
Del. Code of 1974, Title 21, § 2301 et seq.
Ida. Code 1947, 49-401 et seq.
Ill. Rev. Stat. 1991, Ch. 95 1/2, § 4-100 et seq.
Iowa Code Ann., 321.72 et seq.
Mich. Comp. Laws Ann., 257.252 et seq.
N.D. Cent. Code, 39-05-01 et seq.
N.H. Rev. Stat. 1955, 262:1 et seq.
N.M. Stat. Ann. 1953, 64-9-1 et seq.
Okla. Stat. Ann., Title 47, § 4-101 et seq.
S.C. Code Ann. 1976, § 56-19-810 et seq.
Utah Code Ann. 1953, 41-1-105 et seq.
Vt. Stat. Ann., Title 23, § 2001 et seq.
W. Va. Code 1966, § 17A-8-1 et seq.

Antitheft and Brand Act (Livestock)
Utah Code Ann. 1953, 4-24-1 et seq.

Antitheft and Certificate of Title Act
Ala. Code 1975, § 32-8-1 et seq.

Antitheft and Motor Vehicle Certificate of Title Act
Me. Rev. Stat. Ann. 1964, Title 29-A, § 601 et seq.

Antitipping Act
Ill. Rev. Stat. 1961, Ch. 38, § 551 et seq.

Antitipping Law (Fiduciary Officers)
Iowa Code Ann., 722.2

Antitrespass Act
  Ga. Code Ann., 16-7-21
  S.D. Codified Laws 1967, 41-9-1 et seq.

Antitrust Act
  Ala. Code 1975, § 8-10-1 et seq.
  Ark. Code Ann. 1987, 4-75-309 et seq.
  Cal. Business and Professions Code § 16700
    et seq.
  Colo. Rev. Stat., 6-4-101 et seq.
  Conn. Gen. Stat. Ann., § 35-24 et seq.
  Del. Code of 1974, Title 6, § 2101 et seq.
  Fla. Stat. Ann., 542.15 et seq.
  Haw. Rev. Stat. § 480-1 et seq.
  Ida. Code 1947, 48-101 et seq.
  Ill. Comp. Stat. 1992, Ch. 740, § 10/1 et seq.
  Ind. Code Ann., 24-1-1-1 et seq.
  Iowa Code Ann., 553.1 et seq.
  Kan. Stat. Ann., 50-101 et seq.
  La. Rev. Stat. Ann., 51:121 et seq.
  Mass. Gen. Laws Ann., 93:1 et seq.
  Md. Ann. Code 1974, Art. CL, § 11-201 et
    seq.
  Me. Rev. Stat. Ann. 1964, Title 10, § 1101 et
    seq.
  Mich. Comp. Laws Ann., 445.701 et seq.,
    445.722 et seq.
  Minn. Stat. Ann., 325D.49 et seq.
  Miss. Code Ann. 1972, § 75-21-1 et seq.
  Mo. Rev. Stat., 416.011 et seq.
  Mont. Rev. Code 1947, 94-1104 et seq.
  N.C. Gen. Stat. 1943, § 75-1 et seq.
  Neb. Rev. Stat. 1943, 44-360
  N.H. Rev. Stat. 1955, 356:1 et seq.
  N.J. Stat. Ann., 56:9-1 et seq.
  N.M. Stat. Ann., 57-1-1.1 et seq.
  N.Y. General Business Law (Consol. Laws
    Ch. 20) § 340 et seq.
  Ohio Rev. Code 1953, 1331.01 et seq.
  Okla. Stat. Ann., Title 79, § 1 et seq.
  P.R. Laws Ann. 1954, Title 10, § 257 et seq.
  R.I. Gen. Laws 1956, 6-36-1 et seq.
  S.C. Code Ann. 1976, § 39-3-10 et seq.
  Tenn. Code Ann., 47-25-101 et seq.
  Tex. Business and Commerce Code, § 15.01
    et seq.
  Utah Code Ann. 1953, 76-10-911 et seq.

  Va. Code 1950, § 59.1-9.1 et seq.
  Wash. Const. 1889, Art. 12, § 22
  Wis. Stat. Ann., 133.01 et seq.
  W. Va. Code 1966, § 47-18-1 et seq.

Antitrust Act (Commodities)
  Neb. Rev. Stat. 1943, 59-101 et seq.

Antitrust Act (Insurance Rates)
  Neb. Rev. Stat. 1943, 44-360 et seq.

Antitrust Act (Junkin)
  Neb. Rev. Stat. 1943, 59-801 et seq.

Antitrust Act (Uniform)
  Ariz. Rev. Stat. Ann., § 44-1401 et seq.

Antitrust Amendments Act of 1990
  Nov. 16, 1990, P.L. 101-588, 15 U.S. Code
    § 1 nt.

Antitrust and Free Enterprise Act
  Tex. Business and Commerce Code, § 15.01
    et seq.

Antitrust Civil Process Act
  Sept. 19, 1962, P.L. 87-664, 76 Stat. 548, 15
    U.S. Code §§ 1311 to 1314; 18 U.S. Code
    § 1505
  Sept. 12, 1980, P.L. 96-349, 15 U.S. Code
    § 1311 et seq.
  Nov. 2, 1994, P.L. 103-438, 15 U.S. Code
    §§ 1311, 1312

**Antitrust Exemption Act (Local
  Government)**
  Ill. Rev. Stat. 1991, Ch. 85, §§ 2900, 2901

**Antitrust Procedural Improvements Act of
  1980**
  Sept. 12, 1980, P.L. 96-349, 15 U.S. Code
    §§ 1311 et seq., 1311 nt.

Antitrust Reform Act
  Mich. Comp. Laws Ann., 445.771 et seq.

**Antitrust/Consumer Protection Improve-
  ments Act**
  Wash. Rev. Code Ann., 19.86.090, et seq.

Antiuniform Act
N.Y. Military Law (Consol. Laws Ch. 36) § 238a

Antivandalism Act (Minors)
N.C. Gen. Stat. 1943, § 1-538.1

Antiviolence Act (Strikes)
Ark. Code Ann. 1987, 11-3-401 et seq.

Antiwagering Act
Ky. Rev. Stat. 1971, Superseded Vols., 436.190 et seq.

Antiwiretapping Act
N.Y. Penal Law 1965 (Consol. Laws Ch. 40) § 145.20
Pa. Cons. Stat., Title 18, § 5701

Apalachicola Bay Area Protection Act
Fla. Stat. Ann., 380.0555

Apalachicola-Chattahoochee-Flint River Basin Compact
Ala. Code 1975, § 33-19-1
Ga. Code Ann., 12-10-100 et seq.

Apartment Fire Instruction Act
Ill. Comp. Stat. 1992, Ch. 425, § 5/0.01 et seq.

Apartment Ownership Act
Ala. Code 1975, § 35-8-1 et seq.
Ga. Code 1933, 85-1601b et seq.
Kan. Stat. Ann., 58-3101 et seq.
Minn. Stat. Ann., 515.01 et seq.
Ore. Rev. Stat., 100.100 et seq.

Apex Project, Nevada Land Transfer and Authorization Act of 1989
July 31, 1989, P.L. 101-67, 103 Stat. 168

Apiaries and Bees Act
Ill. Comp. Stat. 1992, Ch. 510, § 20/1 et seq.

Apiary Act
Ark. Stat. 1947, 78-1725 et seq.
Ky. Rev. Stat. 1971, 252.170 et seq.
Mich. Comp. Laws Ann., 286.1 et seq.
Neb. Rev. Stat. 1943, 81-2,165-01 et seq.

Okla. Stat. Ann., Title 2, § 3-100 et seq.
R.I. Gen. Laws 1956, 4-12-1 et seq.
Tenn. Code Ann., 44-15-201 et seq.
Vt. Stat. Ann., Title 6, § 3001 et seq.
Wash. Rev. Code Ann., 15.60.005 et seq.
W. Va. Code 1966, § 19-13-1 et seq.

Apiary Inspection Act
Cal. Food and Agricultural Code 1967, § 29001 et seq.
Kan. Stat. Ann., 2-411 et seq.
Ore. Rev. Stat., 602.010 et seq.
Vt. Stat. Ann., Title 6, § 3021 et seq.

Apiary Protection Act
Cal. Food and Agricultural Code 1967, § 29000 et seq.

Apiculture Act
Mo. Rev. Stat., 264.011 et seq.
R.I. Gen. Laws 1956, 4-12-1 et seq.
Wyo. Stat. Ann., § 11-7-130 et seq.

Apothecary Act
Me. Rev. Stat. Ann. 1964, Title 32, § 2801 et seq.

Appalachian Forest Act (Forest Conservation)
See Conservation Act (Navigable Waters)

Appalachian Regional Development Act
March 9, 1965, P.L. 89-4, 79 Stat. 5, 40 U.S. Code § 461; 40 U.S. Code Appx. §§ 1, 2, 101 to 108, 201 to 206, 211 to 214, 221 to 224, 301 to 304, 401 to 405
Oct. 15, 1966, P.L. 89-670, 80 Stat. 942, 943, 40 U.S. Code Appx. §§ 201, 206
Oct. 11, 1967, P.L. 90-103, 81 Stat. 257, 40 U.S. Code Appx. §§ 102, 105, 106, 109, 201 to 207, 211, 212, 214, 221, 223, 224, 302, 303, 401, 403
Aug. 1, 1968, P.L. 90-448, 82 Stat. 502, 40 U.S. Code Appx. § 207
Nov. 25, 1969, P.L. 91-123, 83 Stat. 214, 40 U.S. Code Appx. §§ 105, 201, 205, 207, 214, 302, 401, 403, 405
May 21, 1970, P.L. 91-258, 84 Stat. 235, 40 U.S. Code Appx. § 214

Aug. 5, 1971, P.L. 92-65, 85 Stat. 168, 40 U.S. Code Appx. §§ 105, 106, 201, 202, 205, 207, 208, 211, 214, 302, 401, 405

Dec. 31, 1975, P.L. 94-188, 89 Stat. 1079, 40 Appx. U.S. Code §§ 2 nt., 31 nt., 32, 101, 102, 105 to 107, 201, 202, 205, 207, 211, 214, 223 to 225, 302, 303, 320, 401, 405

Nov. 18, 1977, P.L. 95-193, 40 U.S. Code Appx. § 202

Nov. 6, 1978, P.L. 95-599, 40 U.S. Code Appx. §§ 201, 201 nt.

Oct. 19, 1984, P.L. 98-524, 40 U.S. Code Appx. § 113

Nov. 1, 1985, P.L. 99-141, 40 U.S. Code Appx. § 401 nt.

Md. Ann. Code 1957, Art. 41A, § 6-401 et seq.

Appalachian Regional Development Act of 1965

Oct. 17, 1990, P.L. 101-434, 40 U.S. Code Appx. § 403

Dec. 18, 1991, P.L. 102-240, 40 U.S. Code Appx. § 403

Nov. 2, 1994, P.L. 103-437, 40 U.S. Code Appx. § 403

Sept. 30, 1996, P.L. 104-208, 40 U.S. Code Appx. § 214

June 9, 1998, P.L. 105-178, 40 U.S. Code Appx. §§ 201, 403, 405, 405 nt.

Aug. 7, 1998, P.L. 105-220, 40 U.S. Code Appx. § 211

Oct. 31, 1998, P.L. 105-332, 40 U.S. Code Appx. § 214

Nov. 13, 1998, P.L. 105-393, 40 U.S. Code Appx. §§ 2, 101, 105, 106, 202 to 208, 211 to 214, 224, 226, 302, 401, 405

Appalachian Regional Development Reform Act of 1998

Nov. 13, 1998, P.L. 105-393, Title II, 112 Stat. 3618, 40 U.S. Code Appx. § 1 nt.

Appalachian States Low-Level Radioactive Waste Compact Act

W. Va. Code 1966, § 29-1H-1 et seq.

Appalachian States Low-Level Radioactive Waste Compact Consent Act

May 19, 1988, P.L. 100-319, 102 Stat. 471, 42 U.S. Code § 2021d nt.

Appalachian Trail Act

Pa. Purdon's Stat., Title 64, § 801 et seq.

Appalachian Trails System Act

N.C. Gen. Stat. 1943, § 113A-72 et seq.

Apparel Industry Revitalization Act

Cal. Government Code § 15317

Appeal Act

Ariz. Rev. Stat. Ann., § 12-2101 et seq.
Fla. Stat. Ann., 59.04 et seq.
Kan. Stat. Ann., 60-2101 et seq.
W. Va. Code 1966, § 58-1-1 et seq.

Appeal Bond Act

Pa. Purdon's Stat., Title 12, § 1133 et seq.

Appeal Bond Act (Municipal Courts)

Colo. Rev. Stat., 139-36-1 et seq.

Appeals Act (Civil)

Wash. Rev. Code Ann., 4.88.010 et seq.

Appeals Act (Criminal)

Wash. Rev. Code Ann., 10.73.010 et seq.

Appeals Board (State Comprehensive Plan)

R.I. Gen. Laws 1956, 45-22.3-1 et seq.

Appeals Court Law

S.C. Code Ann. 1976, § 8-21-300 et seq.

Appeals from Registrars of Property Act

P.R. Laws Ann. 1954, Title 30, § 2271 et seq.

Appearance Bond Act

Wash. Rev. Code Ann., 10.19.040 et seq.

Appellate Court Act

Ill. Comp. Stat. 1992, Ch. 705, § 25/0.01 et seq.

Appellate Court Efficiency Act

Tenn. Public Acts 1989, Ch. 147

Appellate Court Improvements Act

Tenn. Public Acts 1992, Ch. 952

Appellate Court Jurisdiction Act of 1970
Pa. Purdon's Stat., Title 17, § 211.101 et seq.

Appellate Court Law Clerk and Secretary Act
Ill. Comp. Stat. 1992, Ch. 705, § 30/01.0 et seq.

Appellate Courts Act
Ill. Rev. Stat. 1991, Ch. 37, § 24m et seq.

Appellate Defender Act
Mich. Comp. Laws Ann., 780.711 et seq.
Mont. Laws 1991, Ch. 781, §§ 1, 3 to 5

Appellate Defender Act (State)
Ill. Rev. Stat. 1991, Ch. 38, § 208-1 et seq.

Appellate Defense Commission Act
S.C. Code Ann. 1976, § 17-4-10 et seq.

Appellate Practice Act
Ga. Code Ann., 5-6-30 et seq.

Appellate Procedure (Rules)
Mont. Code Ann. 1987, Title 25, Ch. 21

Appellate Procedure Act
Ark. Code Ann. 1987, 16-67-310, 16-67-315 et seq.
N.M. Stat. Ann., 39-3-1 et seq.
Ohio Rev. Code 1953, 2505.01 et seq.

Appellate Prosecutor's Act
Ill. Rev. Stat. 1991, Ch. 14, § 201 et seq.

Appellate Review Act
Ohio Rev. Code 1953, 2505.01 et seq.

Apple Act
Kan. Laws 1933, Ch. 1
Mich. Comp. Laws Ann., 290.51 et seq.

Apple Advertising Commission Act
Wash. Rev. Code Ann., 15.24.010 et seq.

Apple and Peach Marketing Act
Ill. Comp. Stat. 1992, Ch. 505, § 20/1 et seq.

Apple Commission Act
N.M. Stat. Ann., 76-23-1 et seq.

Apple Grading Act
Mass. Gen. Laws Ann., 94:101 et seq.
Md. Ann. Code 1974, Art. AG, § 10-801 et seq.
Me. Rev. Stat. Ann. 1964, Title 7, § 531 et seq.
Mich. Comp. Laws 1948, 290.81 et seq.
N.Y. Agriculture and Markets Law (Consol. Laws Ch. 69) § 158 et seq.
Wash. Rev. Code Ann., 15.17.100

Apple Industry Promotion and Tax Act
N.J. Stat. Ann., 54:47D-1 et seq.

Apple Industry Regulation Act
Wash. Laws 1939, Ch. 224

Apple Marketing Act
Pa. Purdon's Stat., Title 3, § 1001 et seq.

Apple Merchandising Act
Mo. Rev. Stat., 265.010 et seq.

Apple Packing Law
N.Y. Agriculture and Markets Law (Consol. Laws Ch. 69) § 157 et seq.

Apple Standard Law
Cal. Food and Agricultural Code 1967, §§ 43801 et seq., 75501

Apple Storage Act
Colo. Rev. Stat., 35-23.5-101 et seq.

Apple Tax Act
Mich. Comp. Laws Ann., 290.59

Appliance and Electronic Repair Dealer Registration Law
Cal. Business and Professions Code § 9800 et seq.

Appliance Efficiency Standards Act
Mass. Gen. Laws Ann., 25B:1 et seq.

Appliance Tag Act
Ill. Comp. Stat. 1992, Ch. 720, § 220/0.01 et seq.

Application of Pesticides Act
Tenn. Code Ann., 62-21-101 et seq.

Applications Insurance Implementation Act
D.C. Code Ann., § 5-301 et seq.

Appling Water Authority Act
Ga. Laws 1975, p. 2605
Iowa Code Ann., 41.1, 41.2

Appointing Authority Act (General Assembly)
Ill. Rev. Stat. 1991, Ch. 85, § 40 et seq.

Appointive Registry Act
Cal. Government Code §§ 1750.5, 12033 et seq.

Appointment Act (Vacant State Offices)
Ohio Rev. Code 1953, 3.03

Appointment of Commissioners Act
Ky. Rev. Stat. 1971, 7.110

Appointment of Commissioners Act (Uniform State Laws)
Okla. Stat. Ann., Title 74, § 471 et seq.

Appointments Act (Gender Balanced)
Ill. Rev. Stat. 1991, Ch. 127, § 4301 et seq.

Appointments Act (General Assembly)
Ill. Rev. Stat. 1991, Ch. 63, §§ 160, 161

Appointments and Nominations Act (Judicial)
Vt. Stat. Ann., Title 4, § 601 et seq.

Appomattox Court House National Historical Park Acts
June 18, 1930, Ch. 520, 46 Stat. 777, 16 U.S. Code §§ 450b, 450d
Aug. 13, 1935, Ch. 520, 49 Stat. 613, 16 U.S. Code §§ 450b, 450d, 450e
July 17, 1953, Ch. 227, 67 Stat. 181, 16 U.S. Code § 450d-1
April 15, 1954, Ch. 142, 68 Stat. 54, 16 U.S. Code § 450e.

Apportionment Act (Assembly Districts)
Cal. Government Code §§ 490, 491

Apportionment Act (Congress)
Fla. Stat. Ann., 8.01
Tenn. Code Ann., 2-16-103

Apportionment Act (Congressional Districts)
Cal. Government Code § 470
Ind. Code Ann., 3-3-1-1, 3-3-2-1, 3-3-2-2
Mich. Comp. Laws 1948, 3.11 et seq.

Apportionment Act (Congressional)
Ill. Rev. Stat. 1991, Ch. 46, § 156F.1 et seq.

Apportionment Act (Corporate Income Tax)
Ga. Code Ann., 48-7-31

Apportionment Act (County Boards of Supervisors)
Mich. Comp. Laws Ann., 46.401 et seq.

Apportionment Act (District Courts)
Tex. Gov. Code, § 24.101 et seq.

Apportionment Act (Educational)
N.M. Stat. Ann., 22-3-1 et seq.

Apportionment Act (Elections)
Md. Ann. Code 1957, Art. 33, §§ 22-1, 22-2

Apportionment Act (Estate Tax)
Mass. Gen. Laws Ann., 65A:5

Apportionment Act (Estate Taxes)
Conn. Gen. Stat. Ann., § 12-400 et seq.
Fla. Stat. Ann., 733.817
Mass. Gen. Laws Ann., 65A:5
Md. Ann. Code 1974, Art. ET, § 11-109
Neb. Rev. Stat. 1943, 77-2108
Nev. Rev. Stat. 1979 Reprint, 150.290 et seq.
N.J. Rev. Stat. 1937, 54:33-1 et seq.
N.Y. Estates, Powers and Trusts Law (Consol. Laws Ch. 17B) § 2-1.8
Okla. Stat. 1961, Title 58, § 2001 et seq.
Pa. 1937 Pamph. Laws 2762, No. 565
Pa. 1951 Pamph. Laws 1405, No. 338
R.I. Gen. Laws 1956, 44-23.1 et seq.
Va. Code 1950, § 64.1-160 et seq.
Wash. Rev. Code Ann., 83.110.010 et seq.

Apportionment Act (Federal and State)
N.Y. Estate, Powers and Trust Law (Consol. Laws Ch. 17B) § 2-1.8

Apportionment Act (Income Tax)
Ore. Rev. Stat., 314.280

Apportionment Act (Judicial Districts)
Pa. 1931 Pamph. Laws 167, No. 106

Apportionment Act (Legislative)
Ala. Code 1975, §§ 29-1-1, 29-1-2
Cal. Elections Code 1976, § 30000 et seq.
Colo. Rev. Stat., 63-1-1 et seq.
Fla. Stat. Ann., 8.01, 10.001 et seq.
Ga. Code Ann., 28-1-1 et seq.
Ida. Code 1947, 67-201 et seq.
Ill. Rev. Stat. 1991, Ch. 46, § 158-1 et seq.
Ind. Code Ann., 2-1-1.2-1 et seq.
Iowa Code Ann., 41.1, 41.2
Kan. Stat. Ann., 4-101 et seq.
Ky. Rev. Stat. 1971, Superseded Vols., 6.010, 6.030
Mich. Comp. Laws Ann., 4.11 et seq.
Minn. Stat. Ann., 2.021 et seq.
Miss. Code Ann. 1972, §§ 5-1-1, 5-1-3
Mo. Rev. Stat. 1969, 128.204 et seq.
Mont. Code Ann., 5-1-101 et seq.
N.C. Gen. Stat. 1943, §§ 120-1, 120-2
N.D. Cent. Code, 54-03-01.5
Neb. Rev. Stat. 1943, 5-101.01 et seq., 32-1501 et seq.
N.J. Stat. Ann., 52:10-3 et seq.
N.M. Stat. Ann. 1953, 2-7-14 et seq., 2-9-13 et seq.
N.Y. Laws 1802, Ch. 79
N.Y. Laws 1808, Ch. 90
N.Y. Laws 1822, Ch. 209
N.Y. Laws 1826, Ch. 289
N.Y. Laws 1836, Ch. 436
N.Y. Laws 1846, Ch. 94
N.Y. Laws 1857, Ch. 339
N.Y. Laws 1866, Ch. 805
N.Y. Laws 1879, Ch. 208
N.Y. Laws 1892, Ch. 397
N.Y. Laws 1906, Ch. 431
N.Y. Laws 1907, Ch. 727
N.Y. Laws 1916, Ch. 373
N.Y. Laws 1917, Ch. 798
N.Y. Stat. Law (Consol. Laws Ch. 57) § 120 et seq.
Okla. Stat. Ann., Title 14, §§ 79 et seq., 80.1 et seq., 111 et seq., 116 et seq.
Pa. Purdon's Stat., Title 25, §§ 2201, 2215, 2216
R.I. Gen. Laws 1956, 22-2-1 et seq.
S.C. Code Ann. 1976, § 2-1-10 et seq.
S.D. Codified Laws 1967, 2-2-14 et seq.
Tenn. Code Ann., 3-1-101 et seq.
Tex. Rev. Civ. Stat., Art. 1936 et seq.
Utah Code Ann. 1953, Miscellaneous Superseded Code Provisions, 36-1-11 et seq.
Va. Code 1950, § 24.1-12.3
Vt. Stat. Ann., Title 17, § 1881
Wash. Rev. Code Ann., 44.07B.001 et seq.
Wis. Stat. Ann., 4.001 et seq.
W. Va. Code 1966, §§ 1-2-1, 1-2-2
Wyo. Stat. Ann., § 28-2-101 et seq.

Apportionment Act (Occupational Disease)
Mich. Comp. Laws 1948, 417.9

Apportionment Act (Public Regulation Commission)
N.M. Stat. Ann., 8-7-1 to 8-7-10

Apportionment Act (Representatives)
Okla. Stat. Ann., Title 14, § 116 et seq.

Apportionment Act (Senate)
Kan. Stat. Ann., 4-4,101 et seq.
S.C. Code Ann. 1976, § 2-1-60

Apportionment Act (Senatorial Districts)
Cal. Government Code § 480
Tex. Rev. Civ. Stat., Art. 193a et seq.

Apportionment Act (State Senate)
Okla. Stat. Ann., Title 14, § 180.1 et seq.

Apportionment Act (Succession Taxes)
Del. Code of 1974, Title 12, § 2901 et seq.

Apportionment Act (Workmen's Compensation)
Cal. Labor Code § 4663

Miss. Code Ann. 1972, § 71-3-7

Apportionment Acts
Jan. 16, 1901, Ch. 93, 31 Stat. 733
Aug. 8, 1911, Ch. 5, 37 Stat. 13, 2 U.S. Code §§ 2a, 5
June 18, 1929, Ch. 28, 46 Stat. 26, 2 U.S. Code § 2a (See 13 U.S. Code §§ 2, 5 to 9, 21, 23, 41, 42, 141, 146, 214) 42 U.S. Code § 244a
April 25, 1940, Ch. 152, 54 Stat. 162, 2 U.S. Code § 2a
Okla. Stat. Ann., Title 14, § 102 et seq.

Apportionment Law (Special Assessment)
Ill. Comp. Stat. 1992, Ch. 35, § 200/28-1 et seq.

Apportionment of Estate Tax Act
Vt. Stat. Ann., Title 32, § 7301 et seq.

Apportionment of House of Representatives
S.C. Code Ann. 1976, § 2-1-10 et seq.

Apportionment of Receipts and Expenses Act
Conn. Gen. Stat. Ann., § 45-110 et seq.

Apportionment of Senate Act
S.C. Code Ann. 1976, § 2-1-60 et seq.

Apportionment or Allocation of Income Act
S.C. Code Ann. 1976, § 12-7-1110 et seq.

Apportionment Statute (Death Tax)
La. Rev. Stat. Ann., 9:2431 et seq.

Appraisal Act (Corporate Merger)
N.Y. Business Corporations Law 1961 (Consol. Laws Ch. 4) §§ 623, 901 et seq.

Appraisal Act (Dissenting Stockholders)
Tenn. Code Ann. 1955, 48-909

Appraisal Act (Lancaster-Montoya)
Cal. Civil Code § 1922 et seq.

Appraisal Act (Stock)
Del. Code of 1974, Title 8, § 262

Appraisal Right Act
N.C. Gen. Stat. 1943, § 55-113, Subsec. e

Appraisal Rights Act (Shareholders)
Tex. Business Corporation Act, § 1.01 et seq.

Appraiser Act (Certified Real Estate)
Wash. Rev. Code Ann., 18.140.005 et seq.

Appraiser Act (Motor Vehicle Physical Damage)
Pa. Purdon's Stat., Title 63, § 851 et seq.

Appraiser Act (Real Estate)
Ala. Code 1975, § 34-27A-1 et seq.
Wash. Rev. Code Ann., 18.140.900 et seq.

Appraiser Certification and Voluntary Appraisal Standards Law
Iowa Code Ann., 117B.1 et seq.

Appraiser Licensing Act (Real Estate)
Ill. Comp. Stat. 1992, Ch. 225, § 457/1 et seq.

Appraiser Licensing and Certification Act
Tex. Rev. Civ. Stat., Art. 6573a.2

Appraiser Licensing and Certification Act (Real Estate)
Ga. Code Ann., 43-39A-1 et seq.
Miss. Code Ann. 1972, § 73-34-1 et seq.

Appraiser Registration, License, and Certification Act (Real Estate)
S.C. Code Ann. 1976, § 40-60-60 et seq.

Appraisers' Act (Canal Lands)
N.Y. Canal Law (Consol. Laws Ch. 5) § 40

Appraisers Act (Real Estate)
Ala. Code 1975, § 34-27A-1
N.J. Stat. Ann., 45:14F-1 et seq.
Okla. Stat. 1981, Title 59, § 858-700 et seq.

Apprec.iation Loan Law (Shared)
Cal. Civil Code § 1917 et seq.

Apprentice and Training Act (Public Works)
N.M. Stat. Ann., 13-4D-1 et seq.

Apprentice Labor Standards Act
Cal. Labor Code § 3070 et seq.

Apprenticeship Act
    D.C. Code 1973, § 36-401 et seq.
    Fla. Stat. Ann., 446.011 et seq.
    La. Rev. Stat. Ann., 23:381 et seq.
    Md. Ann. Code 1957, Art. 89, § 50 et seq.
    Me. Rev. Stat. Ann. 1964, Title 26, § 1001 et seq.
    Nev. Rev. Stat. 1979 Reprint, 610.010 et seq.
    Ore. Rev. Stat., 660.002 et seq.
    Pa. Purdon's Stat., Title 43, § 90.1 et seq.
    S.C. Code Ann. 1976, § 41-21-10 et seq.
    Tex. Rev. Civ. Stat., Art. 201 et seq.
    Wash. Rev. Code Ann., 49.04.010 et seq.

Apprenticeship Assistance Act
    N.M. Stat. Ann., 21-19A-1 et seq.

Appropriate Patient Care Act
    Ga. Code Ann., 33-24-70 et seq.

Appropriation Act
    N.M. Laws 1992, Ch. 94

Appropriation Act (Education)
    N.M. Laws 1995, Ch. 13

Appropriation Act (Federal Augmentation)
    Pa. 1979 Pamph. Laws 665, No. 10-A
    Pa. 1980 Pamph. Laws 1445, No. 23-A

Appropriation Act (Federal Supplemental)
    Pa. 1978 Pamph. Laws 1664, No. 62-A

Appropriation Act (General 1992)
    Pa. 1992 Pamph. Laws, No. 8A

Appropriation Act (General)
    Fla. Stat. Ann., 216.053, 216.178
    N.M. Laws 1994, Ch. 6
    N.M. Laws 1995, Ch. 30
    Vt. Acts 1969, No. 300

Appropriation Act (Permanent Improvements)
    N.C. Laws 1947, Ch. 662
    N.C. Laws 1949, Ch. 1248
    N.C. Laws 1951, Ch. 995
    N.C. Laws 1953, Ch. 873

Appropriation Act (Second Supplemental)
    Pa. 1979 Pamph. Laws 595, No. 2A

Appropriation Act (Supplemental)
    Pa. 1979 Pamph. Laws 587, No. 1-A

Appropriation Act (Surface Waters)
    Nev. Rev. Stat. 1979 Reprint, 533.010 et seq.

Appropriation Act (Underground Waters)
    Nev. Rev. Stat. 1979 Reprint, 534.010 et seq.

Appropriation Act, 1995
    Ida. Code 1947, 67-3531

Appropriation Budget Act (Educational)
    Ala. Acts 1978, p. 1616

Appropriation, Budgeting, and Receipt of Federal Moneys Act
    R.I. Gen. Laws 1956, 42-41-1 et seq.

Appropriation of 1978 Surplus Act
    Vt. Acts 1979, No. 72

Appropriation Reversion Law
    Cal. Government Code § 16304

Appropriations Act (Capital Improvement)
    N.C. Laws 1985, Ch. 480
    N.C. Laws 1987, Ch. 795
    N.C. Laws 1989, Ch. 754
    N.C. Laws 1990, Ch. 1074

Appropriations Act (Capital Improvements)
    N.C. Laws 1992, Ch. 1044

Appropriations Act (Current Operations)
    N.C. Laws 1992, Ch. 900

Appropriations Act (General)
    Haw. Session Laws 1993, Act 289
    Mont. Laws 1995, Ch. 593

Appropriations Act (Judiciary)
    Haw. Session Laws 1993, Act 277

Appropriations Allotment Act
    Mich. Comp. Laws Ann., 21.11

Appropriations and Budget Revenue Act
N.C. Laws 1991, Ch. 689

Appropriations and Expenditures Review Act
Neb. Rev. Stat. 1943, 50-701.01 et seq.

Appropriations and Expenditures Review Act of 1977
Neb. Rev. Stat. 1943, 50-701.01 et seq.

Appropriations Limitation Act
N.J. Stat. Ann., 52:9H-24 et seq.

APRICOT (A Prototype Realistically Innovative Community of Today) Act
Fla. Laws 1994, Ch. 153

Aptitude Tests for Standardized Testing Act
N.Y. Education Law 1947 (Consol. Laws Ch. 16) § 340 et seq.

Aquaculture Act
Colo. Rev. Stat., 35-24.5-101 et seq.
Del. Code of 1974, Title 3, § 401 et seq.
Miss. Code Ann. 1972, § 79-22-1 et seq.
Utah Code Ann. 1953, 4-37-101 et seq.

Aquaculture Development Act
Cal. Public Resources Code § 825 et seq.
Ga. Code Ann., 2-15-1 et seq., 27-4-251 et seq.
Ill. Comp. Stat. 1992, Ch. 20, § 215/1 et seq.
Minn. Stat. Ann., 17.46 et seq.
N.J. Stat. Ann., 4:27-1 et seq.

Aquaculture Policy Act
Fla. Stat. Ann., 597.001 et seq.
Tenn. Code Ann., 43-33-101 et seq.

Aquaculture Promotion Act
Cal. Fish and Game Code 1957, §§ 1123.5, 15000 et seq.

Aquarium and Museum Act (Park District)
Ill. Rev. Stat. 1991, Ch. 105, § 325h et seq.

Aquatic Life Act
Tex. Health and Safety Code, § 436.001 et seq.

Aquatic Life and Fish Code
Ill. Rev. Stat. 1991, Ch. 56, § 1.1 et seq.

Aquatic Nuisance Control Act
Mich. Comp. Laws Ann., 323.221 et seq.

Aquatic Nuisance Species Prevention and Control Act
Cal. Fish and Game Code 1967, § 6430 et seq.

Aquatic Plant Control Act (Nonindigenous)
Ala. Code 1975, § 9-20-1 et seq.

Aquatic Preserve Act
Fla. Stat. Ann., 258.35 et seq.
Iowa Code Ann., 280A.1 et seq.

Aquatic Products Marketing Act
Miss. Code Ann. 1972, § 79-21-1 et seq.

Aquatic Resources Act
Haw. Rev. Stat. Ann., § 187A-1 et seq.

Aquatic Weed Control Act
Fla. Stat. Ann., 369.20
N.C. Gen. Stat. 1943, §§ 113A-220 to 113A-227

Aqueduct Act (City of New York)
N.Y. Laws 1883, Ch. 490

Aqueduct and Sewer Act of Puerto Rico
P.R. Laws Ann. 1954, Title 22, § 141 et seq.

Aqueduct Commission Act (Florida Keys)
Fla. Special Laws 1941, Ch. 21230

Aqueduct District Act (Florida Keys)
Fla. Special Laws 1953, Ch. 29301

Arbitration
July 30, 1947, Ch. 392, 61 Stat. 669, 9 U.S. Code §§ 1 to 14
Oct. 31, 1951, Ch. 655, 65 Stat. 715, 9 U.S. Code § 7
Sept. 3, 1954, Ch. 1263, 68 Stat. 1233, 9 U.S. Code § 4
July 31, 1970, P.L. 91-368, 84 Stat. 692, 9 U.S. Code §§ 201 to 208

Arbitration Act

See also Uniform Arbitration Act

Alaska Stat. 1962, § 09.43.010 et seq.

Cal. Code of Civil Procedure § 1280 et seq.

Colo. Rev. Stat., 13-22-201 et seq.

Conn. Gen. Stat. Ann., § 52-408 et seq.

D.C. Code Ann., § 16-4301 et seq.

Del. Code of 1974, Title 10, § 5701 et seq.

Fla. Stat. Ann., 682.01 et seq.

Ga. Code Ann., 9-9-1 et seq.

Ida. Code 1947, 7-901 et seq.

Ill. Rev. Stat. 1991, Ch. 10, § 101 et seq.

Ind. Code Ann., 34-4-1-1 et seq., 34-4-2-1 et seq.

Iowa Code Ann., 679A.1 et seq.

Kan. Stat. Ann., 5-201 et seq., 5-401 et seq.

Ky. Rev. Stat. 1971, 417.010 et seq.

La. Rev. Stat. Ann., 9:4201 et seq.

Mass. Gen. Laws Ann., 251:1 et seq.

Md. Ann. Code 1974, Art. CJ, § 3-201 et seq.

Me. Rev. Stat. Ann. 1964, Title 14, § 5927 et seq.

Mich. Comp. Laws Ann., 600.5001 et seq.

Minn. Stat. Ann., 572.08 et seq.

Miss. Code Ann. 1972, § 11-15-1 et seq.

Mo. Rev. Stat., 435.350 et seq.

Mont. Code Ann., 27-5-101 et seq.

N.C. Gen. Stat. 1943, § 1-567.1 et seq.

N.D. Cent. Code, 32-29.2-01 et seq.

Neb. Rev. Stat. 1943, 25-2103 et seq.

Nev. Rev. Stat. Ann., 38.015 et seq.

N.H. Rev. Stat. 1955, 542:1 et seq.

N.J. Rev. Stat. 1937, 2A:24-1 et seq.

N.M. Stat. Ann., 44-7-1 et seq.

N.Y. Civil Practice Law and Rules (Consol. Laws Ch. 8) § 7501 et seq.

Ohio Rev. Code 1953, 2711.01 et seq.

Okla. Stat. Ann., Title 12, § 801 et seq.

Ore. Rev. Stat., 33.210 et seq.

Pa. Cons. Stat., Title 42, § 7361 et seq.

P.R. Laws Ann. 1954, Title 32, § 3201 et seq.

S.C. Code Ann. 1976, § 15-47-10 et seq.

Tenn. Code Ann. 1955, 23-501 et seq.

Tex. Rev. Civ. Stats., Art. 224 et seq.

Utah Code Ann. 1953, 78-31a-1 et seq.

Va. Code 1950, § 8.01-577 et seq.

Vt. Stat. Ann., Title 12, § 5651 et seq.

Wash. Rev. Code Ann., 7.04.010 et seq.

Wis. Stat. Ann., 788.01 et seq.

W. Va. Code 1966, § 55-10-1 et seq.

Wyo. Stat. Ann., § 1-36-101 et seq.

Arbitration Act (911 Employees)

R.I. Gen. Laws 1956, 28-9.6-1 et seq.

Arbitration Act (Commercial)

N.C. Gen. Stat. 1943, § 1-567.1

Arbitration Act (Construction)

Miss. Code Ann. 1972, § 11-15-101 et seq.

Arbitration Act (Contracts and Controversies)

Cal. Code of Civil Procedure § 1281 et seq.

Arbitration Act (Creation of Board)

Pa. Purdon's Stat., Title 72, § 4651.1 et seq.

Arbitration Act (Death Taxes)

W. Va. Code 1966, § 11-11B-1 et seq.

Arbitration Act (Employee)

Ill. Rev. Stat. 1991, Ch. 10, § 18.9 et seq.

Arbitration Act (Fire Fighters)

Me. Rev. Stat. Ann. 1964, Title 26, § 965 et seq.

R.I. Gen. Laws 1956, 28-9.1-1 et seq.

Arbitration Act (General)

R.I. Gen. Laws 1956, 10-3-1 et seq.

Tex. Rev. Civ. Stat., Art. 224 et seq.

Arbitration Act (Health Care)

Ill. Rev. Stat. 1991, Ch. 10, § 201 et seq.

Arbitration Act (Labor Disputes)

June 1, 1898, Ch. 370, 30 Stat. 424

July 15, 1913, Ch. 6, 38 Stat. 103

Ala. Code 1975, § 25-7-50 et seq.

Alaska Laws 1913, Ch. 70

Ark. Code Ann. 1987, 11-2-108, 11-2-109, 16-108-101 et seq., 16-108-201 et seq.

Ind. Code Ann., 22-6-2-1 et seq.

Mass. Gen. Laws Ann., 150:1 et seq., 150C:1 et seq.

Md. Ann. Code 1974, Art. LE, § 4-101 et seq.
Mo. Rev. Stat., 295.080,
Mont. Code Ann., 41-901 et seq.
N.C. Gen. Stat. 1943, § 95-36.1 et seq.
Nev. Rev. Stat. 1979 Reprint, 614.010 et seq.
Ohio Rev. Code 1953, 4129.01 et seq.
R.I. Gen. Laws 1956, 28-9-1 et seq.
S.C. Code Ann. 1976, § 41-17-10 et seq.
Tex. Rev. Civ. Stat., Art. 239 et seq.
Utah Code Ann. 1953, 78-31a-1 et seq.
Vt. Stat. Ann., Title 21, § 521 et seq.
Wash. Rev. Code Ann., 49.08.010 et seq.

Arbitration Act (Labor)
Mass. Gen. Laws Ann., 150c:1 et seq.
Mont. Code Ann. 1947, 41-901 et seq.

Arbitration Act (Mandatory)
Colo. Rev. Stat., 13-22-401 et seq.

Arbitration Act (Maritime Transactions)
See United States Arbitration Act
Sept. 7, 1950, Ch. 908, 64 Stat. 780

Arbitration Act (Medical Malpractice)
Mich. Comp. Laws Ann., 600.5040 et seq.

Arbitration Act (Municipal Employees)
R.I. Gen. Laws 1956, 28-9.4-1 et seq.

Arbitration Act (Policemen and Firemen Labor Disputes)
Pa. Purdon's Stat., Title 43, § 217.1 et seq.

Arbitration Act (Public Utilities)
Fla. Stat. Ann., 453.01 et seq.
Wis. Stat. Ann., 111.50 et seq.

Arbitration Act (Public Works)
R.I. Gen. Laws 1956, 37-16-1 et seq.

Arbitration Act (School Teachers)
R.I. Gen. Laws 1956, 28-9.3-1 et seq.

Arbitration Act (State Police)
R.I. Gen. Laws 1956, 28-9.5-1 et seq.

Arbitration Act (Water)
Mont. Code Ann. 1947, 41-901 et seq.

Arbitration Acts
S.C. Code Ann. 1976, § 15-48-10 et seq.

Arbitration and Award Act
Haw. Rev. Stat. Ann., § 658-1 et seq.

Arbitration and Compromise of Death Taxes Act
Conn. Gen. Stat. Ann., § 12-371 et seq.
Mass. Gen. Laws Ann., 65B:1 et seq.
S.C. Code Ann. 1976, § 12-16-20 et seq.
Va. Code 1950, § 58.1-920 et seq.
Vt. Stat. Ann., Title 32, § 7101 et seq.

Arbitration and Mediation Act
Conn. Gen. Stat. Ann., § 31-91 et seq.
La. Rev. Stat. Ann., 23:861 et seq.

Arbitration Code for Construction Contracts
Ga. Code Ann., 9-9-80 et seq.

Arbitration Law (Firefighters and Policemen)
Mich. Comp. Laws, 1979, 423.231 et seq.
Okla. Stat. Ann., Title 11, § 51-101 et seq.

Arbitration, Mediation, and Conciliation Act (International)
Haw. Rev. Stat. Ann., § 658D-1 et seq.

Arbitration of Death Taxes Act (Interstate)
See Uniform Act on Interstate Arbitration of Death Taxes

Arbitration of Death Taxes, Interstate Compact
Cal. Revenue and Taxation Code §§ 13820 et seq., 14195
Me. Rev. Stat. Ann. 1964, Title 36, § 3911 et seq.

Arbor and Bird Act
Ill. Comp. Stat. 1992, Ch. 5, § 490/10

Arcadia Revenue Financing Act
Fla. Special Laws 1941, Ch. 21102

Archaeological and Paleontological Resources Protection Act
Ill. Comp. Stat. 1992, Ch. 20, § 3425/0.01 et seq.

Archaeological Exploration Act
S.D. Codified Laws 1967, 1-20-17 et seq.

Archaeological Property Acquisition Act (Emergency)
Fla. Stat. Ann., 253.027

Archaeological Record Program
N.C. Gen. Stat. 1943, § 70-46 et seq.

Archaeological Resources Act
Md. Ann. Code 1974, Art. NR, § 2-305 et seq.

Archaeological Resources Protection Act
N.C. Gen. Stat. 1943, § 70-10 et seq.

Archaeological Resources Protection Act of 1979
Oct. 31, 1979, P.L. 96-95, 16 U.S. Code §§ 470aa, 470aa nt., 477bb et seq.
Oct. 28, 1988, P.L. 100-555, 16 U.S. Code § 470mm
Nov. 2, 1994, P.L. 103-437, 16 U.S. Code § 470ii

Archaeology Act
Minn. Stat. Ann., 138.31 et seq.

Archer-Roberson Act
Ala. Code 1975, § 33-5-50 et seq.

Arches National Park Expansion Act of 1998
Oct. 30, 1998, P.L. 105-329, 112 Stat. 3060, 16 U.S. Code § 272 nt.

Archie Craft Act
Ky. Rev. Stat. 1962, 152.410 et seq.

Archie-Hudson and Cunneen Postsecondary Education Technology Revenue Bond Act
Cal. Education Code 1976, § 67359.10 et seq.

Archie-Hudson and Cunneen School Technology Revenue Bond Act
Cal. Education Code 1976, § 17860 et seq.

Architect and Engineer Selection Act
N.M. Stat. Ann., 13-1-119 et seq.

Architect-Engineers Act (Banks)
June 30, 1949, c. 288, Title 9, §§ 901 to 904

Architect-Engineers Act (Brooks)
P.R. Laws Ann. 1954, Title 20, § 711 et seq.

Architect of the Capitol Human Resources Act
July 22, 1994, P.L. 103-283, 40 U.S. Code § 166b-7
Jan. 23, 1995, P.L. 104-1, 40 U.S. Code § 166b-7

Architect Registration and Licensing Act (Landscape)
Ida. Code 1947, 54-3001 et seq.

Architects Act
Ala. Code 1975, § 34-2-1 et seq.
Ark. Code Ann. 1987, 17-14-101 et seq.
Cal. Business and Professions Code § 5500 et seq.
Colo. Rev. Stat., 12-4-101 et seq.
Del. Code of 1974, Title 24, § 301 et seq.
Ill. Rev. Stat. 1987, Ch. 111, § 1201 et seq.
Ind. Code Ann., 25-4-1-1 et seq.
Md. Ann. Code 1974, Art. BO, § 3-101 et seq.
Mich. Comp. Laws Ann., 338.551 et seq.
N.D. Cent. Code, 43-03-01 et seq.
Nev. Rev. Stat. 1979 Reprint, 623.010 et seq.
N.H. Rev. Stat. 1955, 310:28 et seq.
Ore. Rev. Stat., 671.010 et seq.
R.I. Gen. Laws 1956, 5-1-1 et seq.
S.C. Code Ann. 1976, § 40-3-10 et seq.
Vt. Stat. Ann., Title 26, § 121 et seq.
Wash. Rev. Code Ann., 18.08.150 et seq.

Architects Act (Landscape)
N.M. Stat. Ann., 61-24B-1 et seq.
S.C. Code Ann. 1976, § 40-28-10 et seq.

Architects, Engineers, Land Surveyors, and Landscape Architects Registration Act
Alaska Stat. 1962, § 08.48.011 et seq.

Architects Licensing Act
Ark. Code Ann. 1987, 71-301 et seq.
Iowa Code Ann., 118.1 et seq.
Md. Ann. Code 1957, Art. 43, § 515 et seq.
Mich. Comp. Laws Ann., 338.551 et seq.
N.C. Gen. Stat. 1943, § 83A-1 et seq.
N.D. Cent. Code, 43-03-01 et seq.
N.H. Rev. Stat. 1955, 310:28 et seq.
N.J. Stat. Ann., 45:3-1 to 45:3-16
N.M. Stat. Ann., 61-15-1 et seq.
Pa. Purdon's Stat., Title 63, § 34.1 et seq.
Utah Code Ann. 1953, 58-3-1 et seq.
W. Va. Code 1966, § 30-12-1 et seq.
Wyo. Stat. Ann., § 33-4-101 et seq.

Architects Licensing Act (Landscape)
Utah Code Ann. 1953, 58-53-1 et seq.

Architects Practice Act
Cal. Business and Professions Code § 5501 et seq.

Architects' Registration Act
D.C. Code Ann., § 2-201 et seq.
Ky. Rev. Stat. 1971, 323.010 et seq.
Mass. Gen. Laws Ann., 112:60A et seq.
Pa. Purdon's Stat., Title 63, § 34.1 et seq.

Architects' Registration Acts
Dec. 13, 1924, Ch. 9, 43 Stat. 713
May 29, 1928, Ch. 861, 45 Stat. 950

Architectural Act
N.M. Stat. Ann., 61-15-1 et seq.
Okla. Stat. Ann., Title 59, § 45.1 et seq.
Ore. Code 1930, §§ 68-301 to 68-315

Architectural and Engineering Services Act
Md. Ann. Code 1974, Art. SF, §§ 11-166 et seq., 13-301 et seq.

Architectural and Engineering Services Act (Transportation)
Md. Ann. Code 1974, Art. SF, § 13-303 et seq.

Architectural Barriers Accessibility Act
Ark. Code 1987, 20-14-601 et seq.

Architectural Barriers Act of 1968
Aug. 12, 1968, P.L. 90-480, 82 Stat. 718, 42 U.S. Code §§ 4151 to 4156
March 5, 1970, P.L. 91-205, 84 Stat. 49, 42 U.S. Code § 4151

Architectural Engineer Corporation Law
La. Rev. Stat. Ann., 12:1171 et seq.

Architectural, Engineering, and Land Surveying Qualifications Based Section Act
Ill. Comp. Stat. 1992, Ch. 30, § 535/1 et seq.

Architectural, Engineering and Land Surveying Services Procurement Act
Wyo. Stat. Ann., § 9-2-1027 et seq.

Architectural Works Copyright Protection Act
Dec. 1, 1990, P.L. 101-650, 17 U.S. Code §§ 101 et seq. generally, 301

Architecture-Engineering Internship Act
Ill. Comp. Stat. 1992, Ch. 110, § 910/1 et seq.

Architecture Practice Act
Cal. Business and Professions Code § 5500 et seq.
Ga. Code Ann., 43-4-1 et seq.
Ga. Code 1933, 84-301 et seq.
Ill. Comp. Stat. 1992, Ch. 225, § 305/1 et seq.
Mont. Code Ann., 37-65-101 et seq.
Tex. Rev. Civ. Stat., Art. 249a

Archives Act
Cal. Government Code § 12220 et seq.
Minn. Stat. 1969, 138.161 et seq.
S.C. Code Ann. 1976, § 60-11-10 et seq.

Archives and Historical Records Act
R.I. Gen. Laws 1956, 42-8.1-1 et seq.

Archives and History Act
Fla. Stat. Ann., 267.011 et seq.
N.C. Gen. Stat. 1943, 121-1 et seq.

Archives and Records Act
Okla. Stat. Ann., Title 67, § 305 et seq.

Archives and Records Management Act
Me. Rev. Stat. Ann. 1964, Title 5, § 91 et seq.
Miss. Code Ann. 1972, § 25-59-1 et seq.
N.H. Rev. Stat. 1955, 5:25 et seq.

Archives and Records Service and Information Practices Act
Utah Code Ann. 1953, 63-2-901 et seq.

Archives Partnership Trust Act (New York State)
N.Y. Arts and Cultural Affairs Law (Consol. Laws Ch. 11C) § 57.05
N.Y. Laws 1992, Ch. 758

Arctic Research and Policy Act of 1984
July 31, 1984, P.L. 98-373, 15 U.S. Code §§ 1401 et seq., 1401 nt.
Nov. 16, 1990, P.L. 101-609, 15 U.S. Code §§ 4102, 4103, 4105, 4107
Dec. 17, 1993, P.L. 103-199, 15 U.S. Code § 4101

Area College Center Act
Pa. Purdon's Stat., Title 24, § 2501.1 et seq.

Area Development Act
Va. Code 1950, § 15.1-1400 et seq.

Area Development Act (East St. Louis)
Ill. Rev. Stat. 1991, Ch. 85, § 5501 et seq.

Area Education District Act
Ore. Rev. Stat., 341.025 et seq.

Area of Critical State Concern Restoration Trust Fund Act
Fla. Stat. Ann., 380.0558, 573.101 et seq.

Area of State Act
Mich. Comp. Laws Ann., 2.1, 2.2

Area Plan Act (Bovine Tuberculosis)
S.D. Codified Laws 1967, 40-6-2 et seq.

Area Planning and Development Act
Ky. Rev. Stat. 1971, Superseded Vols., 147A.010 et seq.

Area Planning Departments Act
Ind. Code Ann., 18-7-4-1 et seq.

Area Redevelopment Act
May 1, 1961, P.L. 87-27, 75 Stat. 47, 15 U.S. Code § 696; 40 U.S. Code § 461; 42 U.S. Code §§ 1464, 2501 to 2525
Aug. 14, 1964, P.L. 88-426, 78 Stat. 425, 42 U.S. Code § 2502
June 30, 1965, P.L. 89-55, 79 Stat. 195, 42 U.S. Code § 2525
Minn. Stat. 1986, 472.01 et seq.

Area Redevelopment Assistance Act
N.J. Stat. Ann., 13:1B-15.13 et seq.

Area Redevelopment Finance Act
Ga. Code 1933, 40-2127 et seq.

Area Vocational Schools and Community Colleges Act
Iowa Code Ann., 280a.1 et seq.

Areias-Chandler-Connelly Rice Straw Burning Reduction Act
Cal. Health and Safety Code § 41865

Areias-Robbins Credit Card Full Disclosure Act
Cal. Civil Code § 1748.10 et seq.

Areias-Robbins Retail Installment Account Full Disclosure Act
Cal. Civil Code §§ 1810.20, 1810.21

Areias-Stirling Contractors State License Board Enforcement Act
Cal. Business and Professions Code §§ 7019, 7020, 7065.3, 7091

Arid Land Act
Oct. 2, 1888, Ch. 1069, 25 Stat. 526, 43 U.S. Code § 662

Arid Lands Reclamation Act
Wash. Rev. Code Ann., 79.48.010 et seq.

Arizona-California Boundary Compact
Ariz. Laws 1963, Ch. 77

Arizona-California Reciprocal Hunting and Fishing Licenses Act
Cal. Fish and Game Code 1957, § 375

Arizona Desert Wilderness Act of 1990
Nov. 28, 1990, P.L. 101-628, 16 U.S. Code §§ 1a-5 nt., 1a-9-1a- 13, 410ee, 460ddd et seq., 463, 1132 nt.

Arizona-Idaho Conservation Act of 1988
Nov. 18, 1988, P.L. 100-696, 16 U.S. Code § 460xx nt.
May 25, 1990, P.L. 101-302, 40 U.S. Code 188a-1, 188a-2
Nov. 28, 1990, P.L. 101-628, 104 Stat. 4501
Nov. 2, 1994, P.L. 103-437, 16 U.S. Code § 460xx-5
Aug. 20, 1996, P.L. 104-186, 40 U.S. Code §§ 188a, 188c
Nov. 12, 1996, P.L. 104-333, 16 U.S. Code § 431 nt.

Arizona-Nevada Boundary Compact
Ariz. Laws 1960, Ch. 69

Arizona Wilderness Act of 1984
Aug. 28, 1984, P.L. 98-406, 16 U.S. Code §§ 1132 nt., 1274
Oct. 19, 1984, P.L. 98-508, 16 U.S. Code § 1132 nt.
Nov. 28, 1990, P.L. 101-628, 16 U.S. Code § 1132 nt.

Arizona Wilderness Land Title Resolution Act of 1994
Oct. 14, 1994, P.L. 103-365, 16 U.S. Code § 1132 nt.

Arizonans with Disabilities Act
Ariz. Rev. Stat. Ann., § 41-1492 et seq.

Arkansas-Idaho Land Exchange Act of 1992
Nov. 2, 1992, P.L. 102-584, 16 U.S. Code § 668dd nt.

Arkansas-Mississippi Great River Bridge Construction Compact
Miss. Code Ann. 1972, § 65-25-121 et seq.

Arkansas-Oklahoma-Kansas River Basin Compact
Okla. Stat. 1981, Title 82, § 1401 et seq.

Arkansas River Basin Compact (Arkansas-Oklahoma)
Ark. Code Ann. 1987, 15-23-401
Okla. Stat. Ann., Title 82, § 1421 et seq.

Arkansas River Basin Compact (Kansas-Oklahoma)
Okla. Stat. Ann., Title 82, §§ 1421, 1422

Arkansas River Compact Act
Colo. Rev. Stat., 37-69-101 et seq.

Arkansas River Recreational Act
Colo. Rev. Stat., 33-12.5-101 et seq.

Arkansas Wild and Scenic Rivers Act of 1992
April 22, 1992, P.L. 102-275, 16 U.S. Code § 1271 nt.

ARKids First Program Act
Ark. Code 1987, 20-77-601 et seq.

Armament Conference Resolution
July 12, 1921, Ch. 44, 42 Stat. 141

Armament Retooling and Manufacturing Support Act of 1992
Oct. 23, 1992, P.L. 102-484, 10 U.S. Code § 2501 nt.
Oct. 5, 1994, P.L. 103-337, 10 U.S. Code § 2501 nt.
Sept. 23, 1996, P.L. 104-201, 10 U.S. Code § 2501 nt.
Oct. 17, 1998, P.L. 105-261, 10 U.S. Code § 2501 nt.

Armed Career Criminal Act of 1984
Oct. 12, 1984, P.L. 98-473, 18 U.S. Code Appx. § 1201 nt.

Armed Forces
Aug. 10, 1956, Ch. 1041, 70A Stat. 1, 10 U.S. Code §§ 1 to 9840
May 31, 1957, P.L. 85-43, 71 Stat. 44, 10 U.S. Code § 7230
Continued

June 1, 1957, P.L. 85-44, 71 Stat. 45, 10 U.S. Code § 2633

June 17, 1957, P.L. 85-56, 71 Stat. 160, 10 U.S. Code §§ 1218 to 1220, 6159, 6160

Aug. 2, 1957, P.L. 85-117, 71 Stat. 313, 10 U.S. Code §§ 807, 858, 4308, 4333, 4382 nt.

Aug. 21, 1957, P.L. 85-155, 71 Stat. 375, 10 U.S. Code §§ 3069, 3070, 3206, 3207, 3288, 3291, 3296, 3297, 3298, 3299, 3304, 3305, 3888, 3915, 3916, and others

Aug. 28, 1957, P.L. 85-182, 71 Stat. 463, 10 U.S. Code § 9342 nt.

Aug. 29, 1957, P.L. 85-215, 71 Stat. 489, 10 U.S. Code § 2231

Aug. 30, 1957, P.L. 85-241, 71 Stat. 555, 10 U.S. Code §§ 4774, 7574, 9774, 9331 nt.

Sept. 2, 1957, P.L. 85-263, 71 Stat. 589, 10 U.S. Code § 4594

Feb. 28, 1958, P.L. 85-337, 72 Stat. 29, 10 U.S. Code §§ 2661, 2671

March 28, 1958, P.L. 85-355, 72 Stat. 66, 10 U.S. Code § 773

May 20, 1958, P.L. 85-422, 72 Stat. 129, 10 U.S. Code §§ 1401, 1405, 3888, 3927, 3991, 5083, 5201, 5233, 6151, 6325, 6326, and others

June 30, 1958, P.L. 85-477, 72 Stat. 275, 10 U.S. Code § 712

July 29, 1958, P.L. 85-568, 72 Stat. 432, 10 U.S. Code §§ 2302, 2303

July 31, 1958, P.L. 85-577, 72 Stat. 455, 10 U.S. Code §§ prec. 1581, 1585

July 31, 1958, P.L. 85-578, 72 Stat. 456, 10 U.S. Code § 6911

Aug. 1, 1958, P.L. 85-583, 72 Stat. 480, 10 U.S. Code §§ 6327, 6330 to 6332

Aug. 1, 1958, P.L. 85-588, 72 Stat. 488, 10 U.S. Code § 6018

Aug. 6, 1958, P.L. 85-599, 72 Stat. 516, 10 U.S. Code §§ 141, 143, 171, 716, 2351 nt., 3013, 3015, 3032, 3034, 3035, 5034, 5081, 5085, 5201, 5202, 8013, 8032, 8034, 8035, 8074

Aug. 6, 1958, P.L. 85-600, 72 Stat. 522, 10 U.S. Code §§ 3075, 3204, 3205, 3283, 3296, 3883, 3886, and others

Aug. 8, 1958, P.L. 85-603, 72 Stat. 526, 10 U.S. Code §§ 3258, 3448, 8258, 8448

Aug. 20, 1958, P.L. 85-685, 72 Stat. 659, 10 U.S. Code §§ 2233, 2233a, 9331 nt.

Aug. 21, 1958, P.L. 85-704, 72 Stat. 702, 10 U.S. Code § 1331

Aug. 21, 1958, P.L. 85-716, 72 Stat. 708, 10 U.S. Code § 1482

Aug. 21, 1958, P.L. 85-723, 72 Stat. 711, 10 U.S. Code § 4331

Aug. 23, 1958, P.L. 85-729, 72 Stat. 813, 10 U.S. Code § 2733

Aug. 25, 1958, P.L. 85-747, 72 Stat. 839, 10 U.S. Code § 7299

Aug. 28, 1958, P.L. 85-800, 72 Stat. 967, 10 U.S. Code §§ 2304, 2307, 2310, 2311

Sept. 2, 1958, P.L. 85-857, 72 Stat. 1266, 10 U.S. Code §§ 1441, 1553, 1554, 6160

Sept. 2, 1958, P.L. 85-861, 72 Stat. 1437, 10 U.S. Code §§ 101, 122, 123, 268 to 272, 275, 279, 280, 311, 511, 516, 560, 591 to 593, 651, and others

March 23, 1959, P.L. 86-4, 73 Stat. 13

May 29, 1959, P.L. 86-36, 73 Stat. 63, 10 U.S. Code § 1581

June 23, 1959, P.L. 86-55, 73 Stat. 89, 10 U.S. Code § 7227

June 25, 1959, P.L. 85-70, 73 Stat. 142, 10 U.S. Code §§ 101, 802, 2662

Aug. 7, 1959, P.L. 86-140, 73 Stat. 288, 10 U.S. Code § 6031

Aug. 7, 1959, P.L. 86-142, 73 Stat. 289, 10 U.S. Code § 1038

Aug. 10, 1959, P.L. 86-149, 73 Stat. 321, 10 U.S. Code §§ 2674 nt., 4774, 7574, 9774

Aug. 11, 1959, P.L. 86-155, 73 Stat. 333, 10 U.S. Code §§ 5701 nt., 6387

Aug. 14, 1959, P.L. 86-156, 73 Stat. 338, 10 U.S. Code § 2481

Aug. 14, 1959, P.L. 86-160, 73 Stat. 358, 10 U.S. Code § 1036

Aug. 18, 1959, P.L. 86-174, 73 Stat. 395, 10 U.S. Code §§ 5131, 5154

Aug. 25, 1959, P.L. 86-197, 73 Stat. 425, 10 U.S. Code §§ 1332, 3683, 3926, 6324, 8683, 8926

Aug. 29, 1959, P.L. 86-211, 73 Stat. 436, 10 U.S. Code § 1441

Sept. 1, 1959, P.L. 86-223, 73 Stat. 453, 10 U.S. Code § 2734

Sept. 23, 1959, P.L. 86-377, 73 Stat. 701, 10 U.S. Code §§ 1581, 1582

April 8, 1960, P.L. 86-411, 74 Stat. 16, 10 U.S. Code § 2734

May 13, 1960, P.L. 86-454, 74 Stat. 103, 10 U.S. Code § 5145

June 8, 1960, P.L. 86-500, 74 Stat. 186, 10 U.S. Code § 2662

June 11, 1960, P.L. 86-511, 74 Stat. 207, 10 U.S. Code § 6161

June 29, 1960, P.L. 86-533, 74 Stat. 246, 10 U.S. Code § 1552

June 30, 1960, P.L. 86-558, 74 Stat. 263, 10 U.S. Code § 6387

June 30, 1960, P.L. 86-559, 74 Stat. 264, 10 U.S. Code §§ 123, 269, 274, 281, 1006, 1007, 1374, 1402, 3212, 3352, 3353, 3360, 3362 to 3364, 3366, and others

July 5, 1960, P.L. 86-582, 74 Stat. 320, 10 U.S. Code §§ 3744, 6248, 8744

July 5, 1960, P.L. 86-585, 74 Stat. 325, 10 U.S. Code § 1586

July 5, 1960, P.L. 86-589, 74 Stat. 329, 10 U.S. Code § 936

July 6, 1960, P.L. 86-593, 74 Stat. 331, 10 U.S. Code §§ 8742, 8744, 8745, 8747, 8748, 8750

July 7, 1960, P.L. 86-601, 74 Stat. 338, 10 U.S. Code §§ 807 nt., 858 nt., 4308 nt., 4382 nt.

July 7, 1960, P.L. 86-603, 74 Stat. 357, 10 U.S. Code §§ 1004, 3080, 8080

July 12, 1960, P.L. 86-616, 74 Stat. 386, 10 U.S. Code §§ 1431 nt., 3297, 3300, 3303, 3781 to 3787, 3791 to 3797, 3913, 5701 nt., 6382, 6383, 6384, 6401, 6402, 8297, 8300, 8303, 8781 to 8787, 8791 to 8797, 8913

July 12, 1960, P.L. 86-624, 74 Stat. 411, 10 U.S. Code §§ 101, 802, 2662, 4744

July 12, 1960, P.L. 86-633, 74 Stat. 468, 10 U.S. Code § 858a

July 12, 1960, P.L. 86-641, 74 Stat. 473, 10 U.S. Code § 2771

Sept. 8, 1960, P.L. 86-726, 74 Stat. 855, 10 U.S. Code § 2386

Aug. 3, 1961, P.L. 87-123, 75 Stat. 263, 10 U.S. Code §§ 5001, 5204, 5409, 5443, 5448, 5589, 5703, 5706, 5707, 5709, 5751, 5765, 5769, 5775, 5776, 6374, 6376 to 6378

Aug. 17, 1961, P.L. 87-142, 75 Stat. 364, 10 U.S. Code § 3579

Aug. 17, 1961, P.L. 87-143, 75 Stat. 364, 10 U.S. Code §§ 3253, 8253

Aug. 25, 1961, P.L. 87-165, 75 Stat. 401, 10 U.S. Code § 1039

Sept. 8, 1961, P.L. 87-212, 75 Stat. 488, 10 U.S. Code § 2736

Sept. 26, 1961, P.L. 87-304, 75 Stat. 665, 10 U.S. Code §§ 3689, 8689

Oct. 4, 1961, P.L. 87-367, 75 Stat. 790, 10 U.S. Code § 1581

Oct. 4, 1961, P.L. 87-378, 75 Stat. 807, 10 U.S. Code §§ 270, 3261, 8261

Oct. 4, 1961, P.L. 87-381, 75 Stat. 810, 10 U.S. Code §§ 1431, 1434, 1436, 1444, 1445, 1446

Oct. 4, 1961, P.L. 87-385, 75 Stat. 814, 10 U.S. Code § 923a

June 8, 1962, P.L. 87-480, 76 Stat. 94, 10 U.S. Code § 2773

June 28, 1962, P.L. 87-509, 76 Stat. 121, 10 U.S. Code §§ 680, 1167, 3303, 6382, 6383, 6384, 6401, 8303

July 10, 1962, P.L. 87-533, 76 Stat. 154, 10 U.S. Code §§ 7391 to 7394

July 27, 1962, P.L. 87-554, 76 Stat. 239, 10 U.S. Code §§ 2233a, 2677, 4774, 7574, 9774

July 27, 1962, P.L. 87-555, 76 Stat. 244, 10 U.S. Code § 2603

Aug. 24, 1962, P.L. 87-599, 76 Stat. 401, 10 U.S. Code §§ 7422, 7430

Sept. 7, 1962, P.L. 87-648, 76 Stat. 447, 10 U.S. Code § 815

Sept. 7, 1962, P.L. 87-649, 76 Stat. 492, 10 U.S. Code §§ 101, 142, 517, 555, 564, 701 to 704, 1166, 1167, 1293, 1305, 1405, 3068 to 3071, 3263, 3536, 3687, 4338, and others

Sept. 7, 1962, P.L. 87-651, 76 Stat. 506, 10 U.S. Code §§ 124 to 126, 131 to 137, 141, 280, 674, 687, 717, 718, 802, 1006, 1163, 1168, 1201 to 1203, and others

Sept. 10, 1962, P.L. 87-653, 76 Stat. 528, 10 U.S. Code §§ 2304, 2306, 2310, 2311

Sept. 14, 1962, P.L. 87-663, 76 Stat. 547, 10 U.S. Code §§ 4342, 6954, 6958, 9342

Oct. 5, 1962, P.L. 87-751, 76 Stat. 748, 10 U.S. Code § 501

Oct. 9, 1962, P.L. 87-769, 76 Stat. 767, 10 U.S. Code § 2736

Oct. 9, 1962, P.L. 87-777, 76 Stat. 777, 10 U.S. Code § 6112

Oct. 11, 1962, P.L. 87-793, 76 Stat. 863, 10 U.S. Code § 1581

Continued

Oct. 11, 1962, P.L. 87-796, 76 Stat. 904, 10 U.S. Code §§ 7421 to 7424, 7428, 7430 to 7435, 7438

July 25, 1963, P.L. 88-77, 77 Stat. 93, 10 U.S. Code §§ 3741, 3742, 3746, 6241, 6242, 6244, 8741, 8742, 8746

Sept. 3, 1963, P.L. 88-110, 77 Stat. 135, 10 U.S. Code §§ 270, 511

Oct. 2, 1963, P.L. 88-132, 77 Stat. 213, 10 U.S. Code §§ 1401a, 1402, 3991, 6151, 6323, 6325 to 6327, 6381, 6383, 6390, 6394, 6396, 6398 to 6400, 6483, 8991

Nov. 7, 1963, P.L. 88-174, 77 Stat. 325, 10 U.S. Code §§ 2674, 2681, 2682, 4774, 7574, 9774

Dec. 3, 1963, P.L. 88-236, 77 Stat. 474, 10 U.S. Code §§ 510, 591

March 3, 1964, P.L. 88-276, 78 Stat. 148, 10 U.S. Code §§ 4342, 4343, 4348, 6954, 6956, 6959, 9342, 9343, 9348

Aug. 14, 1964, P.L. 88-426, 78 Stat. 422, 10 U.S. Code §§ 137, 867, 3012, 3013, 5031, 5033, 8012, 8013

Aug. 14, 1964, P.L. 88-431, 78 Stat. 439, 10 U.S. Code § 2634

Aug. 14, 1964, P.L. 88-436, 78 Stat. 443, 10 U.S. Code § 7394

Oct. 3, 1964, P.L. 88-620, 78 Stat. 999, 10 U.S. Code § 3383

Oct. 8, 1964, P.L. 88-636, 78 Stat. 1034, 10 U.S. Code § 1332

Oct. 13, 1964, P.L. 88-647, 78 Stat. 1063, 10 U.S. Code §§ 1475, 1478, 1481, 2031, 2101 to 2111, 3201, 4348, 5404, 5504, 5652b, 6023, 6387, 6959, 8201, 9348

June 11, 1965, P.L. 89-37, 79 Stat. 129, 10 U.S. Code § 8074

June 28, 1965, P.L. 89-51, 79 Stat. 173, 10 U.S. Code §§ 2107, 2109

July 7, 1965, P.L. 89-67, 79 Stat. 212, 10 U.S. Code §§ 4802, 4803, 7622, 7623, 9802, 9803

July 30, 1965, P.L. 89-101, 79 Stat. 425, 10 U.S. Code § 2634

Aug. 21, 1965, P.L. 89-132, 79 Stat. 547, 10 U.S. Code §§ 1040, 1401, 1401a

Aug. 28, 1965, P.L. 89-140, 79 Stat. 579, 10 U.S. Code § 1040

Aug. 28, 1965, P.L. 89-143, 79 Stat. 581, 10 U.S. Code § 2575

Aug. 28, 1965, P.L. 89-150, 79 Stat. 585, 10 U.S. Code § 1485

Aug. 28, 1965, P.L. 89-151, 79 Stat. 586, 10 U.S. Code § 701

Sept. 1, 1965, P.L. 89-160, 79 Stat. 615, 10 U.S. Code § 2002

Sept. 8, 1965, P.L. 89-172, 79 Stat. 662, 10 U.S. Code § 8373

Sept. 15, 1965, P.L. 89-185, 79 Stat. 789, 10 U.S. Code § 2732

Sept. 16, 1965, P.L. 89-188, 79 Stat. 819, 10 U.S. Code § 2674

Sept. 22, 1965, P.L. 89-198, 79 Stat. 830, 10 U.S. Code § 1124

Oct. 19, 1965, P.L. 89-264, 79 Stat. 989, 10 U.S. Code § 1085

Oct. 19, 1965, P.L. 89-266, 79 Stat. 990, 10 U.S. Code § 7541a

Oct. 20, 1965, P.L. 89-275, 79 Stat. 1010, 10 U.S. Code § 5899

Oct. 22, 1965, P.L. 89-288, 79 Stat. 1050, 10 U.S. Code §§ 3036, 3962, 5133, 5137, 8036, 8962

July 13, 1966, P.L. 89-501, 80 Stat. 278, 10 U.S. Code § 125

Aug. 11, 1966, P.L. 89-529, 80 Stat. 339, 10 U.S. Code § 1125

Aug. 11, 1966, P.L. 89-534, 80 Stat. 345, 10 U.S. Code § 1124

Aug. 11, 1966, P.L. 89-536, 80 Stat. 346, 10 U.S. Code § 7043

Aug. 14, 1966, P.L. 89-538, 30 Stat. 347, 10 U.S. Code § 1035

Sept. 12, 1966, P.L. 89-568, 80 Stat. 756, 10 U.S. Code § 2674

Sept. 24, 1966, P.L. 89-603, 80 Stat. 846, 10 U.S. Code §§ 3068, 3210

Sept. 27, 1966, P.L. 89-607, 80 Stat. 850, 10 U.S. Code §§ 2310, 2313

Sept. 30, 1966, P.L. 89-609, 80 Stat. 852, 10 U.S. Code §§ 3069, 3070, 3291, 3915, 5140, 5510, 5773, 5776, and others

Sept. 30, 1966, P.L. 89-614, 80 Stat. 862, 10 U.S. Code §§ 1071 to 1074, 1076 to 1079, 1082, 1084, 1086, 1087

Oct. 13, 1966, P.L. 89-650, 80 Stat. 896, 10 U.S. Code §§ 4342, 6954, 9342

Oct. 14, 1966, P.L. 89-652, 80 Stat. 902, 10 U.S. Code §§ 1331, 1406

Oct. 15, 1966, P.L. 89-670, 80 Stat. 948, 10 U.S. Code § 801

Oct. 15, 1966, P.L. 89-683, 80 Stat. 960, 10 U.S. Code § 719

Oct. 15, 1966, P.L. 89-690, 80 Stat. 1016, 10 U.S. Code §§ 1571 to 1577

Oct. 19, 1966, P.L. 89-696, 80 Stat. 1056, 10 U.S. Code § 2389

Nov. 2, 1966, P.L. 89-718, 80 Stat. 1115, 10 U.S. Code §§ 123, 173, 564, 687, 717, 1072, 1073, 1124, 1126, 1164, and others

Nov. 2, 1966, P.L. 89-731, 80 Stat. 1160, 10 U.S. Code §§ 5443, 5902

Nov. 2, 1966, P.L. 89-735, 80 Stat. 1163, 10 U.S. Code § 703

June 5, 1967, P.L. 90-22, 81 Stat. 53, 10 U.S. Code §§ 3034, 5081, 5201, 8034

June 30, 1967, P.L. 90-40, 81 Stat. 105, 10 U.S. Code § 673a

Sept. 11, 1967, P.L. 90-83, 81 Stat. 220, 10 U.S. Code §§ 280, 1586, 2031, 8851

Oct. 21, 1967, P.L. 90-110, 81 Stat. 310, 10 U.S. Code §§ 5221, 5222

Nov. 3, 1967, P.L. 90-122, 81 Stat. 361, 10 U.S. Code § 1035

Nov. 8, 1967, P.L. 90-130, 81 Stat. 374, 10 U.S. Code §§ 123, 510, 591, 1006, 1164, 1263, 1405, 3069 to 3071, and others

Dec. 1, 1967, P.L. 90-168, 81 Stat. 521, 10 U.S. Code §§ 136, 175, 262, 264, 268, 269, 270, 511, and others

Dec. 8, 1967, P.L. 90-179, 81 Stat. 545, 10 U.S. Code §§ 801, 806, 815, 827, 865, 936, 5148, 5149, 5404, 5508, and others

Dec. 16, 1967, P.L. 90-207, 81 Stat. 652, 10 U.S. Code §§ 1401, 1401a, 1402, 1436, 3991, 6326, 6330, 8991

Dec. 28, 1967, P.L. 90-228, 81 Stat. 745, 10 U.S. Code §§ 3202, 5793, 8202

Jan. 2, 1968, P.L. 90-235, 77 Stat. 753, 10 U.S. Code §§ 101, 501 to 509, 518, 519, 671a, 671b, 711a, 747, 749, 771a, 971, and others

Jan. 2, 1968, P.L. 90-245, 81 Stat. 782, 10 U.S. Code § 701

March 16, 1968, P.L. 90-268, 82 Stat. 49, 10 U.S. Code §§ 2304, 2305

June 4, 1968, P.L. 90-329, 82 Stat. 170, 10 U.S. Code §§ 711a, 3064, 3067, 3210, 3296, 3579, 4624

June 5, 1968, P.L. 90-330, 82 Stat. 170, 10 U.S. Code § 703

June 15, 1968, P.L. 90-340, 82 Stat. 178, 10 U.S. Code § 867

July 5, 1968, P.L. 90-374, 82 Stat. 283, 10 U.S. Code §§ 4342, 6954, 6956, 9342

July 5, 1968, P.L. 90-377, 82 Stat. 287, 10 U.S. Code §§ 951 to 954

July 5, 1968, P.L. 90-378, 82 Stat. 289, 10 U.S. Code §§ 2306, 2310, 2311

July 5, 1968, P.L. 90-386, 82 Stat. 293, 10 U.S. Code §§ 5406 to 5408, 5442, 5447, 5587

Aug. 13, 1968, P.L. 90-485, 82 Stat. 751, 10 U.S. Code §§ 1331, 1431, 1434 to 1437, 1446

Aug. 13, 1968, P.L. 90-486, 82 Stat. 760, 10 U.S. Code §§ 3848, 3851, 8848, 8851

Aug. 23, 1968, P.L. 90-496, 82 Stat. 841, 10 U.S. Code § 336

Sept. 11, 1968, P.L. 90-497, 82 Stat. 847, 10 U.S. Code § 335

Sept. 20, 1968, P.L. 90-500, 82 Stat. 851, 10 U.S. Code §§ 2304, 2576

Sept. 20, 1968, P.L. 90-502, 82 Stat. 852, 10 U.S. Code § 6388

Sept. 25, 1968, P.L. 90-512, 82 Stat. 863, 10 U.S. Code § 2306

Sept. 26, 1968, P.L. 90-521, 82 Stat. 874, 10 U.S. Code §§ 2734, 2734a, 2736

Sept. 26, 1968, P.L. 90-522, 82 Stat. 875, 10 U.S. Code § 2733

Sept. 26, 1968, P.L. 90-525, 82 Stat. 877, 10 U.S. Code § 2733

Oct. 22, 1968, P.L. 90-623, 82 Stat. 1314, 10 U.S. Code §§ 101, 510, 815, 1124, 3534, 4342, 5149, 6483, 6954, 9342

Oct. 24, 1968, P.L. 90-632, 82 Stat. 1335, 10 U.S. Code §§ 801, 806, 816, 818 to 820, 825, 827, 829, 835, 837 to 842, 845, 849, 851, 852, 854, 857, 865 to 871, 873, 936

May 2, 1969, P.L. 91-11, 83 Stat. 8, 10 U.S. Code § 5202

Nov. 19, 1969, P.L. 91-121, 83 Stat. 206, 10 U.S. Code §§ 136, 264

Dec. 5, 1969, P.L. 91-142, 83 Stat. 312, 10 U.S. Code §§ 4774, 7574, 9774

Dec. 30, 1969, P.L. 91-179, 83 Stat. 837, 10 U.S. Code § 1401a

Feb. 24, 1970, P.L. 91-197, 84 Stat. 15, 10 U.S. Code § 6222

Feb. 26, 1970, P.L. 91-198, 84 Stat. 15, 10 U.S. Code §§ 5942, 6024

Continued

Feb. 26, 1970, P.L. 91-199, 84 Stat. 16, 10 U.S. Code §§ 5701, 5893

Feb. 26, 1970, P.L. 91-200, 84 Stat. 16, 10 U.S. Code § 1035

June 12, 1970, P.L. 91-278, 84 Stat. 306, 10 U.S. Code § 2002

July 2, 1970, P.L. 91-302, 84 Stat. 368, 10 U.S. Code § 703

July 8, 1970, P.L. 91-312, 84 Stat. 412, 10 U.S. Code §§ 2733, 2734

Sept. 1, 1970, P.L. 91-392, 84 Stat. 834, 10 U.S. Code § 716

Sept. 1, 1970, P.L. 91-393, 84 Stat. 835, 10 U.S. Code §§ 4776, 9776

Sept. 1, 1970, P.L. 91-397, 84 Stat. 837, 10 U.S. Code § 1482

Sept. 22, 1970, P.L. 91-405, 84 Stat. 852, 10 U.S. Code §§ 4342, 6954, 9342

Oct. 21, 1970, P.L. 91-481, 84 Stat. 1081, 10 U.S. Code § 1088

Oct. 21, 1970, P.L. 91-482, 84 Stat. 1082, 10 U.S. Code § 6159 nt.

Oct. 22, 1970, P.L. 91-487, 84 Stat. 1086, 10 U.S. Code § 1482

Oct. 22, 1970, P.L. 91-491, 84 Stat. 1089, 10 U.S. Code § 5769

Oct. 26, 1970, P.L. 91-511, 84 Stat. 1224, 10 U.S. Code §§ 2674, 2675, 2683

Dec. 24, 1970, P.L. 91-582, 84 Stat. 1574, 10 U.S. Code § 6388

Dec. 24, 1970, P.L. 91-588, 84 Stat. 1584, 10 U.S. Code § 1441

Dec. 31, 1970, P.L. 91-603, 84 Stat. 1674, 10 U.S. Code § 2604

Dec. 31, 1970, P.L. 91-611, 84 Stat. 1829, 10 U.S. Code § 3013

July 29, 1971, P.L. 92-58, 85 Stat. 157, 10 U.S. Code § 1079

Sept. 28, 1971, P.L. 92-129, 85 Stat. 361, 10 U.S. Code §§ 593, 3447, 5597, 5787, 5791, 5912, 8447

Oct. 27, 1971, P.L. 92-145, 85 Stat. 408, 10 U.S. Code §§ 4774, 7574, 9774

Nov. 17, 1971, P.L. 92-156, 85 Stat. 425, 10 U.S. Code § 270

Nov. 24, 1971, P.L. 92-166, 85 Stat. 487, 10 U.S. Code § 2107

Nov. 24, 1971, P.L. 92-168, 85 Stat. 489, 10 U.S. Code § 2003

Dec. 22, 1971, P.L. 92-215, 85 Stat. 777, 10 U.S. Code § 136

March 10, 1972, P.L. 92-249, 86 Stat. 62, 10 U.S. Code § 2544

Aug. 7, 1972, P.L. 92-365, 86 Stat. 505, 10 U.S. Code §§ 4342, 6954, 9342

Aug. 29, 1972, P.L. 92-413, 86 Stat. 649, 10 U.S. Code § 2735

Aug. 29, 1972, P.L. 92-417, 86 Stat. 654, 10 U.S. Code §§ 4802, 4804, 7365, 7622, 9802, 9804

Sept. 21, 1972, P.L. 92-425, 86 Stat. 706, 10 U.S. Code §§ 1435 to 1442, 1444 to 1455

Sept. 21, 1972, P.L. 92-426, 86 Stat. 713, 10 U.S. Code §§ 2112 to 2117, 2120 to 2127

Oct. 2, 1972, P.L. 92-453, 86 Stat. 758, 10 U.S. Code § 2774

Oct. 2, 1972, P.L. 92-455, 86 Stat. 761, 10 U.S. Code § 1401

Oct. 9, 1972, P.L. 92-481, 86 Stat. 795, 10 U.S. Code § 703

Oct. 13, 1972, P.L. 92-492, 86 Stat. 810, 10 U.S. Code § 101

Oct. 25, 1972, P.L. 92-545, 86 Stat. 1154, 10 U.S. Code §§ 2662, 2683

Oct. 25, 1972, P.L. 92-559, 86 Stat. 1173, 10 U.S. Code § 5457

Oct. 25, 1972, P.L. 92-561, 86 Stat. 1175, 10 U.S. Code §§ 3202, 8202 nt.

Oct. 27, 1972, P.L. 92-596, 86 Stat. 1317, 10 U.S. Code §§ 134 to 136, 171, 701

July 9, 1973, P.L. 93-64, 87 Stat. 447, 10 U.S. Code § 1173

Nov. 16, 1973, P.L. 93-155, 87 Stat. 607, 10 U.S. Code § 673

Nov. 29, 1973, P.L. 93-165, 87 Stat. 660, 10 U.S. Code § 2031

Nov. 29, 1973, P.L. 93-166, 87 Stat. 677, 10 U.S. Code §§ 2674, 2676, 2684, 4774, 9774

Nov. 29, 1973, P.L. 93-169, 87 Stat. 689, 10 U.S. Code §§ 4301, 9301

Nov. 29, 1973, P.L. 93-171, 87 Stat. 690, 10 U.S. Code §§ 4343, 6954, 6956, 6958, 9342, 9343

May 14, 1974, P.L. 93-283, 88 Stat. 141, 10 U.S. Code § 2683

May 24, 1974, P.L. 93-290, 88 Stat. 173, 10 U.S. Code § 505

July 8, 1974, P.L. 93-336, 88 Stat. 291, 10 U.S. Code §§ 2733, 2734

July 25, 1974, P.L. 93-356, 88 Stat. 390, 10 U.S. Code § 2304

Aug. 5, 1974, P.L. 93-365, 88 Stat. 405, 10 U.S. Code § 7307

Oct. 7, 1975, P.L. 94-106, 89 Stat. 537, 10 U.S. Code §§ 138, 139, 140, 511, 675, 1401a, 2233a, 2662, 2667, 2672a, 2674, 2675, 4324, 6954, 9324

Armed Forces Absentee Voting Act
See Soldier's Vote Act

Armed Forces Acknowledgments Act
Conn. Gen. Stat. Ann., § 27-137

Armed Forces Damages Settlement Act
Jan. 2, 1942, Ch. 645, 55 Stat. 880 (See 10 U.S. Code §§ 2734, 2735)

April 22, 1943, Ch. 67, 57 Stat. 66 (See 10 U.S. Code §§ 2734, 2735)

Armed Forces Enlisted Personnel Bonus Revision Act of 1974
May 10, 1974, P.L. 93-277, 88 Stat. 119, 37 U.S. Code §§ 308, 308a

Armed Forces Immigration Adjustment Act of 1991
Oct. 1, 1991, P.L. 102-110, 8 U.S. Code § 1101 nt.

Armed Forces Leave Act of 1946
Aug. 9, 1946, Ch. 931, 60 Stat. 963 (See 37 U.S. Code § 501 et seq.)

July 26, 1947, Ch. 344, 61 Stat. 510

Aug. 4, 1947, Ch. 475, 61 Stat. 748

June 19, 1948, Ch. 541, 62 Stat. 506

April 26, 1950, Ch. 105, 64 Stat. 88

June 2, 1950, Ch. 217, 64 Stat. 194

Sept. 23, 1950, Ch. 998, 64 Stat. 978

July 24, 1956, Ch. 682, 70 Stat. 625

Aug. 10, 1956, Ch. 1041, 70A Stat. 630

May 20, 1958, P.L. 85-422, 72 Stat. 129

June 29, 1960, P.L. 86-533, 74 Stat. 247

Armed Forces Regular Officer Augmentation Act of 1956
July 20, 1956, Ch. 646, 70 Stat. 582

Armed Forces Reserve Act of 1952
July 9, 1952, Ch. 608, 66 Stat. 481

Sept. 3, 1954, Ch. 1257, 68 Stat. 1189

Aug. 9, 1955, Ch. 665, 69 Stat. 598

April 23, 1956, Ch. 209, 70 Stat. 115

July 30, 1956, Ch. 789, 70 Stat. 729

Sept. 2, 1958, P.L. 85-857, 72 Stat. 1266

July 17, 1959, P.L. 86-96, 73 Stat. 221

Sept. 21, 1959, P.L. 86-324, 73 Stat. 596

June 28, 1962, P.L. 87-509, 76 Stat. 120

Armed Forces Retirement Home Act of 1991
Nov. 5, 1990, P.L. 101-510, 10 U.S. Code §§ 1089, 2575, 2772, 2272 nt., 4621, 4624, 4712, 4713, 9624, 9712, 9713; 24 U.S. Code §§ 6a, 21a, 21b, 22 to 25, 41 to 43, 44b, 45, 46, 46a, 46b, 48 to 50, 54, 59, 401, 401 nt., 411 et seq. generally; 31 U.S. Code § 1321; 37 U.S. Code § 1007; 44 U.S. Code § 906

Oct. 23, 1992, P.L. 102-484, 24 U.S. Code § 421

Nov. 30, 1993, P.L. 103-160, 24 U.S. Code §§ 411, 413, 415, 420, 401 nt.

Sept. 23, 1996, P.L. 104-201, 24 U.S. Code §§ 415, 417, 421, 422

Oct. 19, 1996, P.L. 104-316, 24 U.S. Code § 420

Oct. 17, 1998, P.L. 105-261, 24 U.S. Code §§ 417, 418

Armed Forces Voluntary Recruitment Act of 1945
Oct. 6, 1945, Ch. 393, 59 Stat. 538

Armed Forces Voting Act
R.I. Gen. Laws 1956, 17-20.1-1 et seq.

Armed Occupation Acts (Florida)
Aug. 4, 1842, Ch. 122, 5 Stat. 502

June 15, 1844, Ch. 71, 5 Stat. 671

July 1, 1848, Ch. 90, 9 Stat. 243

Armed Robbery Act
Ky. Rev. Stat. 1971, 511.020, 511.030, 515.020

Armed Services Absentee Voting Act
Miss. Code Ann. 1972, § 23-15-671 et seq.

N.H. Rev. Stat. 1955, 657:1 et seq.

Armed Services Procurement Act of 1947

Feb. 19, 1948, Ch. 65, 62 Stat. 21 (See 10 U.S. Code §§ 2202, 2301 to 2314, 2381, 2383)

Oct. 31, 1951, Ch. 652, 65 Stat. 700 (See 10 U.S. Code §§ 2306 to 2613)

Aug. 9, 1955, Ch. 628, 69 Stat. 551 (See 10 U.S. Code § 2305)

Armed Services Rights Act (Public Employee)

Ill. Rev. Stat. 1991, Ch. 126 1/2, § 801 et seq.

Armistice Day Act

May 13, 1938, Ch. 210, 52 Stat. 351 (See 5 U.S. Code § 6103)

Armored Car Carrier Act

N.Y. General Business Law (Consol. Laws Ch. 20) § 89aaa et seq.

Armored Car Guard Act

N.Y. General Business Law (Consol. Laws Ch. 20) § 89ooo et seq.

Armored Car Industry Reciprocity Act of 1993

July 28, 1993, P.L. 103-55, 15 U.S. Code §§ 5901 nt., 5901 to 5904

Dec. 29, 1995, P.L. 104-88, 15 U.S. Code § 5904

Oct. 27, 1998, P.L. 105-287, 15 U.S. Code § 5902

Armored Car Reciprocity Amendments of 1998

Oct. 27, 1998, P.L. 105-287, 112 Stat. 2776, 15 U.S. Code § 5901 nt.

Armories Land Act

Ill. Rev. Stat. 1991, Ch. 129, § 310.9 et seq.

Armory Act

N.C. Gen. Stat. 1943, § 127A-161 et seq.

Tenn. Code Ann., 58-1-501 et seq.

Armory Act (Salem)

Ore. Laws 1959, Ch. 590

Armory and Airfield Site Act (Park District)

Ill. Rev. Stat. 1991, Ch. 105, § 327a.1 et seq.

Armory and Emergency Relief Facilities Act

Ida. Code 1947, 46-720 et seq.

Armory Board Act

D.C. Code Ann., § 2-301 et seq.

Ill. Rev. Stat. 1985, Ch. 129, § 223 et seq.

N.M. Stat. Ann., 20-7-1 et seq.

Utah Code Ann. 1953, 39-2-1 et seq.

Armory Board Amendment Act

D.C. Code Ann., §§ 2-306, 2-307, 2-325

Armory Commission Act

Ky. Rev. Stat. 1971, 36.070 et seq.

N.C. Gen. Stat. 1943, § 127A-161 et seq.

Armory Construction Act

Ida. Code 1947, 46-706 et seq.

Armory Construction Act (National Guard)

Ky. Rev. Stat. 1971, 36.082

Arms Control and Disarmament Act

Sept. 26, 1961, P.L. 87-297, 75 Stat. 631, 22 U.S. Code §§ 2551, 2552, 2561 to 2566, 2571 to 2575

Nov. 26, 1963, P.L. 88-186, 77 Stat. 341, 22 U.S. Code §§ 2571, 2573, 2585, 2589

Aug. 14, 1964, P.L. 88-426, 78 Stat. 424, 22 U.S. Code §§ 2562 to 2564

Aug. 19, 1964, P.L. 88-448, 78 Stat. 490, 22 U.S. Code § 2584

May 27, 1965, P.L. 89-27, 79 Stat. 118, 22 U.S. Code § 2589

May 23, 1968, P.L. 90-314, 82 Stat. 129, 22 U.S. Code § 2589

May 12, 1970, P.L. 91-246, 84 Stat. 207, 22 U.S. Code § 2589

July 13, 1972, P.L. 92-352, 86 Stat. 494, 22 U.S. Code § 2589

Nov. 29, 1975, P.L. 94-141, 89 Stat. 757, 22 U.S. Code §§ 2551, 2562, 2571 et seq., 2585, 2589, 2590

Aug. 17, 1977, P.L. 95-108, 22 U.S. Code § 2567 et seq.

Aug. 8, 1978, P.L. 95-338, 22 U.S. Code §§ 2576, 2589, 2589 nt.

Sept. 21, 1979, P.L. 96-66, 22 U.S. Code §§ 2562, 2563, 2589, 2589 nt.

Oct. 15, 1982, P.L. 97-339, 22 U.S. Code
§§ 2551 nt., 2571, 2585, 2589

Dec. 2, 1983, P.L. 98-202, 22 U.S. Code
§§ 2562, 2567, 2568, 2589

Aug. 16, 1985, P.L. 99-93, 22 U.S. Code
§§ 2589, 2592

Oct. 27, 1986, P.L. 99-550, 22 U.S. Code
§ 2588

Dec. 24, 1987, P.L. 100-213, 22 U.S. Code
§§ 2578, 2579, 2589, 2592, 2593

Dec. 11, 1989, P.L. 101-216, 22 U.S. Code
§§ 2563, 2567, 2588, 2589, 2595 to 2595c

Dec. 12, 1991, P.L. 102-228, 22 U.S. Code
§§ 2581, 2589, 2595, 2595b-1, 2595c

Dec. 17, 1993, P.L. 103-199, 22 U.S. Code
§§ 2578, 2591, 2592, 2595, 2799c, 2799d

April 30, 1994, P.L. 103-236, 22 U.S. Code
§§ 2551, 2562, 2565 et seq., 2571 et seq.,
2579, 2581, 2585, 2589 et seq., 2591

Oct. 21, 1998, P.L. 105-277, 22 U.S. Code
§§ 2551, 2552, 2561 to 2568, 2571 to 2579,
2581, 2582, 2583 to 2588, 2591, 2593,
2593a to 2593d, 2595, 2595a, 2595b,
2595b-1, 2595c

**Arms Control and Disarmament
Amendments Act of 1987**

Dec. 24, 1987, P.L. 100-213, 22 U.S. Code
§ 2551 nt.

**Arms Control and Disarmament
Amendments Act of 1989**

Dec. 11, 1989, P.L. 101-216, 22 U.S. Code
§ 2551 nt.

**Arms Control and Nonproliferation Act of
1964**

April 30, 1994, P.L. 103-236, 22 U.S. Code
§ 2551

Arms Export Control Act

Oct. 22, 1968, P.L. 90-629, 22 U.S. Code
§§ 2341 nt., 2344, 2382, 2392, 2394, 2403,
2751 et seq.

Jan. 12, 1971, P.L. 910672, 85 Stat. 2053, 22
U.S. Code §§ 2751, 2753, 2771, 2773

Aug. 4, 1977, P.L. 95-92, 22 U.S. Code
§ 2753 et seq.

Aug. 17, 1977, P.L. 95-105, 22 U.S. Code
§ 2755

Sept. 29, 1979, P.L. 96-72, 22 U.S. Code
§ 2778

Oct. 29, 1979, P.L. 96-92, 22 U.S. Code
§§ 2753, 2761, 2765, 2767, 2768, 2771,
2773, 2776, 2792, 2794

Dec. 16, 1980, P.L. 96-533, 94 Stat. 3131, 22
U.S. Code §§ 2753, 2761, 2762, 2764,
2765, 2769, 2771, 2776 to 2779, 2791,
2794

Dec. 29, 1981, P.L. 97-113, 22 U.S. Code
§§ 2751, 2752, 2753, 2754, 2756, 2761,
2765, 2768, 2771, 2776, 2778, 2792, 2795,
2795a, 2795b, 2796 to 2796c

Dec. 29, 1982, P.L. 97-392, 22 U.S. Code
§§ 2761, 2770, 2791

Nov. 14, 1983, P.L. 98-151, 22 U.S. Code
§ 2771

Oct. 19, 1984, P.L. 98-525

July 12, 1985, P.L. 99-64, 22 U.S. Code
§ 2778

Aug. 8, 1985, P.L. 99-83, 22 U.S. Code
§§ 2752, 2753, 2761, 2763 to 2767, 2771,
2776, 2778, 2791, 2792, 2794, 2795

Oct. 30, 1985, P.L. 99-139, 22 U.S. Code
§§ 2795, 2795 nt.

Nov. 8, 1985, P.L. 99-145, 22 U.S. Code
§§ 2752, 2753, 2767, 2791

Feb. 12, 1986, P.L. 99-247, 22 U.S. Code
§§ 2753, 2776, 2796

Aug. 27, 1986, P.L. 99-399, 22 U.S. Code
§ 2780

Oct. 18, 1986, P.L. 99-500, 22 U.S. Code
§ 2796

Oct. 30, 1986, P.L. 99-591, 22 U.S. Code
§ 2796

Nov. 14, 1986, P.L. 99-661, 22 U.S. Code
§ 2767

July 11, 1987, P.L. 100-71, 22 U.S. Code
§ 2764

Sept. 26, 1987, P.L. 95-384, 92 Stat. 739, 22
U.S. Code §§ 2751, 2761, 2762, 2765,
2766, 2771, 2776

Dec. 22, 1987, P.L. 100-202, 22 U.S. Code
§§ 2761, 2763, 2778, 2796

Dec. 22, 1987, P.L. 100-204, 22 U.S. Code
§ 2278

Sept. 29, 1988, P.L. 100-456, 102 Stat. 2037,
22 U.S. Code §§ 2761, 2796d

Oct. 1, 1988, P.L. 100-461, 22 U.S. Code
§§ 2753, 2796

Nov. 21, 1989, P.L. 101-165, 22 U.S. Code
§§ 2761, 2770, 2792

Continued

Nov. 21, 1989, P.L. 101-167, 22 U.S. Code § 2796

Dec. 12, 1989, P.L. 101-222, 22 U.S. Code §§ 2753, 2776, 2778, 2780

Dec. 13, 1989, P.L. 101-231, 22 U.S. Code § 2795

Nov. 5, 1990, P.L. 101-510, 22 U.S. Code § 2797 et seq. generally

Nov. 5, 1990, P.L. 101-513, 22 U.S. Code §§ 2763, 2771, 2796

April 6, 1991, P.L. 102-25, 22 U.S. Code §§ 2761, 2796d

Oct. 28, 1991, P.L. 102-138, 22 U.S. Code §§ 2780, 2797b, 2797c, prec. 2798, 2798

Dec. 4, 1991, P.L. 102-182, 22 U.S. Code § 2798

Dec. 12, 1991, P.L. 102-228, 22 U.S. Code §§ 2799 to 2799d

April 1, 1992, P.L. 102-266, 22 U.S. Code § 2796

Oct. 6, 1992, P.L. 102-391, 22 U.S. Code § 2796

Oct. 21, 1992, P.L. 102-429, 22 U.S. Code § 2772

Oct. 23, 1992, P.L. 102-484, 22 U.S. Code §§ 2761, 2767

Nov. 2, 1992, P.L. 102-583, 106 Stat. 4935

Sept. 30, 1993, P.L. 103-87, 22 U.S. Code § 2796

April 30, 1994, P.L. 103-236, 22 U.S. Code §§ 2753, 2755, 2761, 2776, 2778, 2779a, 2780, 2791, 2796 et seq., 2799aa et seq.

Aug. 23, 1994, P.L. 103-306, 22 U.S. Code § 2796

Nov. 2, 1994, P.L. 103-437, 22 U.S. Code §§ 2755, 2766, 2776

Feb. 10, 1996, P.L. 104-106, 22 U.S. Code §§ 2761, 2768, 2797b

Feb. 12, 1996, P.L. 104-107, 22 U.S. Code §§ 2762, 2796

April 24, 1996, P.L. 104-132, 22 U.S. Code § 2781

July 21, 1996, P.L. 104-164, 22 U.S. Code §§ 2761, 2753, 2761, 2763, 2765, 2771, 2776, 2778, prec. 2785, 2785, 2794, 2795, 2795b, 2796, 2796a, 2796b, 2796d

Sept. 23, 1996, P.L. 104-201, 22 U.S. Code §§ 2761, 2776

Nov. 26, 1997, P.L. 105-118, 22 U.S. Code §§ 2765, 2796

July 14, 1998, P.L. 105-194, 22 U.S. Code § 2799aa-1

Oct. 21, 1998, P.L. 105-277, 22 U.S. Code §§ 2776, 2796

Arms Sale Resolution
May 28, 1934, Ch. 365, 48 Stat. 811

Armstrong Act (Anti-Segregation)
Ill. Rev. Stat. 1991, Ch. 122, § 10-21.3

Armstrong Act (Regina Mae)
Fla. Stat. Ann., 777.04 et seq.

Armstrong-Higbie Act (Highways)
N.Y. Laws 1898, Ch. 115

Armstrong-Snyder Act (Liquor Control)
Pa. 1923 Pamph. Laws 34, No. 25

Army Air Base Act
Aug. 12, 1935, Ch. 511, 49 Stat. 610 (See 10 U.S. Code §§ 9773, 9774)

Army and Air Force Authorization Act of 1949
July 10, 1950, Ch. 454, 64 Stat. 321

Army and Air Force Vitalization and Retirement Equalization Act of 1948
June 29, 1948, Ch. 708, 62 Stat. 1081
Sept. 7, 1949, Ch. 547, 63 Stat. 693
July 12, 1952, Ch. 698, 66 Stat. 590
Aug. 9, 1955, Ch. 654, 69 Stat. 579
May 31, 1956, Ch. 348, 70 Stat. 222
June 20, 1956, Ch. 412, 70 Stat. 297
July 24, 1956, Ch. 677, 70 Stat. 623

Army at Polls (Army Appropriation Act)
May 4, 1880, Ch. 81, 21 Stat. 113

Army Aviation Cadet Act
June 3, 1941, Ch. 165, 55 Stat. 239
June 3, 1941, Ch. 167, 55 Stat. 241
July 8, 1942, Ch. 493, 56 Stat. 649
March 31, 1955, Ch. 20, 69 Stat. 22

Army Clothing-Equipage Act
Feb. 13, 1941, Ch. 6, 55 Stat. 7

Army Experimental Test Act
July 15, 1939, Ch. 283, 53 Stat. 1042, 50 U.S. Code § 89

Army-Foreign Service Act
July 15, 1939, Ch. 289, 53 Stat. 1045 (See 10 U.S. Code §§ 3544, 8544)

Army Housing Act
Sept. 24, 1940, Ch. 726, 54 Stat. 958

Army Medical Department Act
April 23, 1908, Ch. 150, 35 Stat. 66 (See 10 U.S. Code §§ 3289, 3302, 8289, 8302)

Army National Guard Combat Readiness Reform Act of 1992
Oct. 23, 1992, P.L. 102-484, 10 U.S. Code § 3077 nt.
Nov. 30, 1993, P.L. 103-160, 10 U.S. Code § 3077
Oct. 5, 1994, P.L. 103-337, 10 U.S. Code § 3077 nt.
Feb. 10, 1996, P.L. 104-106, 10 U.S. Code § 10105 nt.

Army-Navy Medical Services Corps Act of 1947
Aug. 4, 1947, Ch. 459, 61 Stat. 734
June 19, 1948, Ch. 547, 62 Stat. 533
March 23, 1954, Ch. 103, 68 Stat. 30
Aug. 23, 1954, Ch. 822, 68 Stat. 763

Army-Navy Nurses Act of 1947
April 16, 1947, Ch. 38, 61 Stat. 41
May 16, 1950, Ch. 186, 64 Stat. 160
July 9, 1952, Ch. 608, 66 Stat. 506
May 27, 1953, Ch. 71, 67 Stat. 36
Aug. 4, 1955, Ch. 551, 69 Stat. 492
Aug. 4, 1955, Ch. 555, 69 Stat. 494
Aug. 9, 1955, Ch. 654, 69 Stat. 579

Army-Navy Pay Act
March 7, 1942, Ch. 166, 56 Stat. 143
July 9, 1952, Ch. 608, 66 Stat. 508

Army-Navy-Public Health Service Medical Officer Procurement Act of 1947
Aug. 5, 1947, Ch. 494, 61 Stat. 776
April 30, 1956, Ch. 223, 70 Stat. 119

July 24, 1956, Ch. 675, 70 Stat. 608

Army-Navy Unification Act
See National Security Act Of 1947

Army Nurse and Medical Specialist Act
Aug. 21, 1957, P.L. 85-155, 71 Stat. 375, 10 U.S. Code §§ 3069, 3070, 3201, 3206, 3207, and others

Army Organization Act of 1950
June 28, 1950, Ch. 383, 64 Stat. 263
Sept. 19, 1951, Ch. 407, 65 Stat. 333
Aug. 3, 1954, Ch. 652, 68 Stat. 649, 10 U.S. Code §§ 101, 3001, 3011 to 3013, 3017, 3062, 4532
Aug. 21, 1954, Ch. 783, 68 Stat. 759 (See 10 U.S. Code §§ 3072, 3209, 3210)
Aug. 9, 1955, Ch. 654, 69 Stat. 579 (See 10 U.S. Code §§ 3067, 3070)

Army Posts Construction Act
June 29, 1940, Ch. 461, 54 Stat. 704

Army Promotion Act
July 31, 1935, Ch. 422, 49 Stat. 504 (See 10 U.S. Code §§ 3294, 3296, 3911, 3991, 8911, 8991)
June 13, 1940, Ch. 344, 54 Stat. 379 (See 10 U.S. Code §§ 3296, 3911, 3991, 8911, 8991)

Army Reorganization Acts
Feb. 2, 1901, Ch. 192, 31 Stat. 748
April 25, 1914, Ch. 71, 38 Stat. 347
June 3, 1916, Ch. 134, 39 Stat. 166
April 17, 1918, Ch. 56, 40 Stat. 531
June 4, 1920, Ch. 227, 41 Stat. 765
Sept. 22, 1922, Ch. 423, 42 Stat. 1033.
June 28, 1930, Ch. 711, 46 Stat. 828
April 25, 1938, Ch. 171, 52 Stat. 221
April 3, 1939, Ch. 35, 53 Stat. 555
March 15, 1940, Ch. 60, 54 Stat. 52
March 15, 1940, Ch. 61, 54 Stat. 53
May 14, 1940, Ch. 194, 54 Stat. 213
May 14, 1940, Ch. 195, 54 Stat. 214
May 15, 1940, Ch. 203, 54 Stat. 217
June 28, 1940, Ch. 440, 54 Stat. 676
June 29, 1940, Ch. 462, 54 Stat. 705
July 2, 1940, Ch. 508, 54 Stat. 712
Continued

July 2, 1940, Ch. 519, 54 Stat. 726
Oct. 4, 1940, Ch. 742, 54 Stat. 963
Oct. 14, 1940, Ch. 858, 54 Stat. 1116
Oct. 14, 1940, Ch. 875, 54 Stat. 1134
Oct. 21, 1940, Ch. 904, 54 Stat. 1206
May 13, 1941, Ch. 113, 55 Stat. 189
May 28, 1941, Ch. 134, 55 Stat. 206
May 31, 1941, Ch. 157, 55 Stat. 236
July 29, 1941, Ch. 326, 55 Stat. 606
Aug. 18, 1941, Ch. 363, 55 Stat. 628
March 27, 1942, Ch. 199, 56 Stat. 177
May 14, 1942, Ch. 312, 56 Stat. 282
June 6, 1942, Ch. 382, 56 Stat. 328
Oct. 1, 1942, Ch. 570, 56 Stat. 762
July 12, 1943, Ch. 216, 57 Stat. 430
June 26, 1944, Ch. 279, 58 Stat. 359
June 9, 1945, Ch. 181, 59 Stat. 235
June 29, 1945, Ch. 197, 59 Stat. 263
June 28, 1947, Ch. 162, 61 Stat. 192
June 30, 1947, Ch. 184, 61 Stat. 214
July 1, 1947, Ch. 192, 61 Stat. 239
March 25, 1948, Ch. 157, 62 Stat. 87
June 19, 1948, Ch. 501, 62 Stat. 477
June 24, 1948, Ch. 625, 62 Stat. 643
March 16, 1950, Ch. 60, 64 Stat. 19
Sept. 27, 1950, Ch. 1058, 64 Stat. 1072
Sept. 15, 1951, Ch. 402, 65 Stat. 323
Aug. 27, 1954, Ch. 1014, 68 Stat. 880

Army Reserve and Retired Personnel Service Law of 1940
See National Guard Mobilization Act of 1940

Army Reserve-National Guard Equity Reimbursement Act
Dec. 17, 1997, P.L. 105-152, 111 Stat. 2688

Army Vitalization Act
See Army Reorganization Acts

Arnold-Bee-Kennick Act (Youth Authority)
Cal. Welfare and Institutions Code § 1820 et seq.

Arnold-Kennick Juvenile Court Law
Cal. Welfare and Institutions Code §§ 200 et seq., 500 et seq.

Aroostook Band of Micmacs Settlement Act
Nov. 26, 1991, P.L. 102-171, 25 U.S. Code § 1721 nt.

Arraignment Act
Minn. Stat. 1978, 630.01 et seq.
Wash. Rev. Code Ann., 10.40.050 et seq.

Arrangement Act (Employer Welfare)
Fla. Stat. Ann., 624.436 et seq.

Arrearage Act (City of Brooklyn)
N.Y. Laws 1883, Ch. 114

Arrearage Liens Act (Child Support)
S.C. Code Ann. 1976, § 20-7-1295

Arrears Act (Civil War Pensions)
See Pension Acts

Arrest Act (Criminal)
Cal. Penal Code § 813 et seq.
N.Y. Criminal Procedure Law (Consol. Laws Ch. 11A) § 140.25
S.C. Code Ann. 1976, § 17-13-10 et seq.

Arrest and Bail Act (Civil Actions)
S.C. Code Ann. 1976, § 15-17-20 et seq.
S.D. Codified Laws 1967, 15-22-1 et seq.

Arrest and Conviction of Out of State Murderers Act
Ill. Comp. Stat. 1992, Ch. 725, §§ 110/0.01, 110/1

Arrest Facilitation Act
March 22, 1934, Ch. 73, 48 Stat. 454 (See 18 U.S. Code §§ 752, 755, 3042, 3183, 3187)
June 6, 1934, Ch. 408, 48 Stat. 910 (See 18 U.S. Code § 3059)

Arrest, Process, Searches, and Seizures Act
S.C. Code Ann. 1976, § 17-13-10 et seq.

Arrest Record Information Act
N.M. Stat. Ann., 29-10-1 et seq.

Arrest Ticket Act
See Uniform Arrest Ticket Act

Arrest Without Warrant Act
  D.C. Code Ann., §§ 23-581, 23-582
  Iowa Code Ann., 804.6 et seq.
  N.Y. Criminal Procedure Law (Consol. Laws Ch. 11A) § 140.10 et seq.

Arrested Narcotic Addict Commitment Act
  N.Y. Mental Hygiene Law 1977 (Consol. Laws Ch. 27) § 23.07 et seq.

Arrests Act
  Cal. Penal Code § 811 et seq.
  Del. Code of 1974, Title 11, § 1901 et seq.
  La. Code of Criminal Procedure 1966, Art. 201 et seq.
  Mass. Gen. Laws Ann., 276.21 et seq.
  Mich. Comp. Laws Ann., 764.1 et seq.
  Mont. Code Ann., 46-6-101 et seq.
  N.C. Gen. Stat. 1943, § 15A-401
  N.H. Rev. Stat. 1955, 594:1 et seq.
  N.Y. Criminal Procedure Law (Consol. Laws Ch. 11A) § 120.10 et seq.
  R.I. Gen. Laws 1956, 12-7-1 et seq.
  S.C. Code Ann. 1976, § 17-13-10 et seq.
  S.D. Codified Laws 1967, 15-22-1 et seq.
  Wash. Rev. Code Ann., 10.31.030 et seq.
  Wis. Stat. Ann., 968.07

Arroyo Flood Control Act
  N.M. Stat. Ann., 72-16-1 et seq.

Arroyo Seco Parklands Preservation Law
  Cal. Public Resources Code § 8650 et seq.

Arsenical Spray Act
  Fla. Stat. Ann., 601.92 et seq.

Arson Act
  Cal. Penal Code § 447a et seq.
  Iowa Code Ann., 712.1 et seq.
  Mich. Comp. Laws Ann., 750.71 et seq.
  Mont. Code Ann., 45-6-102, 45-6-103
  N.H. Rev. Stat. 1955, 634:1 et seq.
  Ohio Rev. Code 1953, 2909.01 et seq.
  Ore. Rev. Stat., 164.305 et seq.
  Wash. Rev. Code Ann., 9A.48.010 et seq.

Arson and Fires Act
  R.I. Gen. Laws 1956, 11-4-1 et seq.

Arson and Theft Reporting Immunity Act
  Okla. Stat. Ann., Title 36, § 6301 et seq.

Arson Information Reporting Act (Fraudulent Claims)
  Colo. Rev. Stat., 10-4-1001 et seq.

Arson Information Reporting-Immunity Act
  Colo. Rev. Stat., 10-4-1001 et seq.
  R.I. Gen. Laws 1956, 27-8.1-1 et seq.

Arson Lab Construction Fund
  July 3, 1996, P.L. 104-155, 110 Stat. 1392, §§ 1 to 8
  Miss. General Laws 1996, Ch. 341, p. 117

Arson Prevention Act of 1994
  May 19, 1994, P.L. 103-254, 15 U.S. Code §§ 2201 nt., 2216, 2220, 2221, 2227, 2228

Arson Reporting Immunity Act
  Ark. Code Ann. 1987, 12-13-301 et seq.
  D.C. Code Ann., § 4-317
  Kan. Stat. Ann., 31-401 et seq.
  Me. Rev. Stat. Ann. 1964, Title 25, § 2411 et seq.
  Minn. Stat. Ann., 299F.052 et seq.
  Neb. Rev. Stat. 1943, 81-5, 115 et seq.
  N.M. Stat. Ann., 41-8-1 et seq.
  Okla. Stat. Ann., Title 36, § 6301 et seq.
  Pa. Purdon's Stat., Title 40, § 1610.1 et seq.
  S.C. Code Ann. 1976, § 23-41-10 et seq.
  Va. Code 1950, § 27-85.3 et seq.
  Wash. Rev. Code Ann., 48.50.010 et seq.
  Wyo. Stat. Ann., § 6-3-108 et seq.

Art Acceptance Act
  N.M. Stat. Ann., 7-7-15 et seq.

Art Act (Percent for)
  Me. Rev. Stat. Ann. 1964, Title 27, § 451 et seq.

Art and Artifacts Indemnity Act
  Dec. 20, 1985, P.L. 99-194, 20 U.S. Code §§ 971, 972, 974

Art Auction House Act
Ill. Comp. Stat. 1992, Ch. 225, § 405/0.01 et
 seq.

Art Collection Act
Neb. Rev. Stat. 1943, 82-401 et seq.

Art Commission and Town Plan Act
N.J. Laws 1910, p. 154

Art Consignment Act
Ga. Code Ann., 10-1-521 to 10-1-529
Ill. Comp. Stat. 1992, Ch. 815, § 320/0.01 et
 seq.

Art in Public Places Act
Cal. Government Code § 15813 et seq.
Mich. Comp. Laws Ann., 18.71 et seq.
N.M. Stat. Ann., 13-4A-1 et seq.

Art in State Buildings Program Act
Ga. Code Ann., 8-5-1 et seq.
N.C. Gen. Stat. 1943, § 143-408.1 et seq.

Art Multiple Sales Act
Mich. Comp. Laws Ann., 442.351 et seq.

Art Percent Act
Mont. Code Ann., 22-2-401 et seq.

Art Preservation Act
Cal. Civil Code § 987

Arterial Highway Act
Ky. Rev. Stat. 1971, Superseded Vols.,
 93.880 et seq.

Arterial Stop Act
Wis. Stat. Ann., 346.46

Arterial Trafficway Act
Kan. Laws 1929, Ch. 132

Artesian Conservancy District Act
N.M. Stat. Ann., 73-1-1 et seq.

Artesian Well Act
N.M. Stat. Ann., 72-13-1 et seq.
S.D. Codified Laws 1967, 46-6-1 et seq.
Wis. Laws 1901, Ch. 354

Artesian Well Law (County)
S.D. Codified Laws 1967, 46-6-1

Artesian Well Law (State)
S.D. Codified Laws 1967, 46-6-1

Artesian Well Law (Township)
S.D. Codified Laws 1967, 46-1-1

**Arthritis, Diabetes, and Digestive Disease
 Amendments of 1976**
Nov. 9, 1978, P.L. 95-622, 42 U.S. Code
 § 289a nt.

Articles for the Government of the Navy
See Uniform Code Of Military Justice

Articles of War
See Uniform Code Of Military Justice

Articles of War Act (Fugitive Slaves)
March 13, 1862, Ch. 40, 12 Stat. 354

Artificial Insemination Act
N.C. Gen. Stat. 1943, § 90-187.10

Artificial Reef Act (Terrebonne Parish)
La. Rev. Stat. Ann., 56:2021 et seq.

Artificial Tanning Device Operation Act
Colo. Rev. Stat., 25-5-1001 et seq.

**Artisanry Regulation and Integral
 Development Act**
P.R. Laws Ann. 1954, Title 18, § 1205 et seq.

Artisans' Lien Act
Miss. Code Ann. 1972, § 85-7-101
Neb. Rev. Stat. 1943, 52-201 et seq.
Tenn. Code Ann., 66-14-101 et seq.
Tex. Property Code, § 58.001 et seq.

Artistic Contracts by Minors Act
Ill. Comp. Stat. 1992, Ch. 820, § 20/0.01 et
 seq.

Artistic Excellence Act (Regional Centers)
N.J. Stat. Ann., 52:16A-26.1 et seq.

Artistic Variety Company Act
P.R. Laws Ann. 1954, Title 23, § 691 et seq.

Artists' Authorship Rights Act
La. Rev. Stat. Ann., 51:2151 et seq.
N.Y. Laws 1991, Ch. 994

Artists' Consignment Act
Ark. Code Ann. 1987, 4-73-201 et seq.
N.M. Stat. Ann., 56-11-1 et seq.
Tenn. Code Ann., 47-25-1001 et seq.
Tex. Rev. Civ. Stat., Art. 9018

Artists-Gallery Relations Act
Cal. Civil Code § 1738 et seq.

Artists' Rights Act
N.J. Stat. Ann., 2A:24A-1 et seq.

Arts Act
Cal. Government Code § 8750 et seq.

Arts and Artifacts Indemnity Act
Dec. 20, 1975, P.L. 94-158, 89 Stat. 844, 20 U.S. Code § 971 et seq.
Nov. 5, 1990, P.L. 101-512, 20 U.S. Code § 974
Oct. 21, 1998, P.L. 105-277, 20 U.S. Code § 974

Arts and Crafts Loan Fund Act
Ky. Rev. Stat. 1962, 152.410 et seq.

Arts and Crafts Sales Act (Indian)
N.M. Stat. Ann., 30-33-1 et seq.

Arts and Cultural Affairs Law
N.Y. Arts and Cultural Affairs Law (Consol. Laws, Ch. 11C) § 1 et seq.

Arts and Culture Development Administration Act
P.R. Laws Ann. 1954, Title 18, § 1159 et seq.

Arts and Humanities Act
Ark. Code Ann. 1987, 13-8-101 et seq.
Colo. Rev. Stat., 23-9-101 et seq.
Okla. Stat. Ann., Title 53, § 161 et seq.

Arts and Humanities Act of 1980
Dec. 4, 1980, P.L. 96-496, 20 U.S. Code § 951 nt.

Arts and Humanities Commission Act
D.C. Code Ann., § 31-2001 et seq.
Ida. Code 1947, 67-5601 et seq.

Arts and Humanities Council Act
Mass. Gen. Laws Ann., 15:40 et seq.

Arts Commission Act
Kan. Stat. Ann., 74-5202 et seq.
S.C. Code Ann. 1976, § 60-15-10 et seq.

Arts Council Act
Ill. Comp. Stat. 1992, Ch. 20, § 3915/0.01 et seq.
Wyo. Stat. Ann., § 9-2-901 et seq.

Arts Create Excellent Schools (ACES) Program Act
N.J. Stat. Ann., 18A:54G et seq.

Arts, Humanities, and Cultural Affairs Act of 1976
Oct. 8, 1976, P.L. 94-462, 20 U.S. Code §§ 951 et seq.

Arts, Humanities, and Museums Amendments of 1985
Dec. 20, 1985, P.L. 99-194, 20 U.S. Code §§ 951 et seq., 951 nt.

Arts, Humanities, and Museums Amendments of 1990
Nov. 5, 1990, P.L. 101-512, 20 U.S. Code § 951 nt.

Artworks Consignment Act
N.C. Gen. Stat. 1943, §§ 25C-1 to 25C-5
N.J. Stat. Ann., 12A:2-329 et seq.
Pa. Purdon's Stat., Title 73, § 2121 et seq.

Asa E. Matthews Act (St. Joseph Superior Court)
Ind. Burns' 1933, 4-1801 et seq.

Asbestos Abatement Accreditation and Certification Act
Miss. Code Ann. 1972, § 37-138-1 et seq.

Asbestos Abatement Act
Ill. Comp. Stat. 1992, Ch. 105, § 105/1 et seq.
Minn. Stat. Ann., 326.71 et seq.
Continued

149

R.I. Gen. Laws 1956, 23-24.5-1 et seq.

Asbestos Abatement Act (Commercial and Public Building)

Ill. Comp. Stat. 1992, Ch. 225, § 207/1 et seq.

Asbestos Abatement Act (School)

La. Rev. Stat. Ann., 30:1150.41 et seq.

Asbestos Abatement Authority Act

Ill. Comp. Stat. 1992, Ch. 20, § 3120/0.01 et seq.

Asbestos Abatement Contractors Licensing Act

Mich. Comp. Laws Ann., 338.3101 et seq.

Asbestos Abatement Finance Act

Ill. Comp. Stat. 1992, Ch. 20, § 3510/0.01 et seq.

Asbestos Contractor Accreditation Act

Ala. Code 1975, § 22-39-1 et seq.

Asbestos Contractor Accreditation and Regulation Act

Tenn. Code Ann., 62-41-101 et seq.

Asbestos Control Act

Mont. Code Ann., 75-2-500 et seq.

Neb. Rev. Stat. 1943, 71-6317 et seq.

Okla. Stat. Ann., Title 40, §§ 450 to 454

Asbestos Detection Program (Educational Facilities)

La. Rev. Stat. Ann., 17:3701

Asbestos Hazard Elimination Act

Miss. Code Ann. 1972, § 37-137-1 et seq.

Asbestos Hazard Emergency Response Act of 1986

Oct. 22, 1986, P.L. 99-519, 15 U.S. Code § 2601 nt.

July 18, 1988, P.L. 100-368, 102 Stat. 833, 20 U.S. Code § 4014

Nov. 28, 1990, P.L. 101-637, 20 U.S. Code § 4022

Dec. 21, 1995, P.L. 104-66, 20 U.S. Code § 4022

Asbestos Health Protection Act

Tex. Rev. Civ. Stat., Art. 4477-3a

Asbestos Information Act of 1988

Oct. 31, 1988, P.L. 100-577, 15 U.S. Code § 2607 nt.

Asbestos NESHAP Act

Va. Code 1950, § 40.1-51.20 et seq.

Asbestos Occupations Accreditation and Certification Act

Pa. Purdon's Stat., Title 63, § 2101 et seq.

Asbestos Safety Act

Ga. Code Ann., 12-12-1 et seq.

Asbestos Safety Act (School)

N.Y. Education Law 1947 (Consol. Laws, Ch. 16) § 430 et seq.

Asbestos School Hazard Abatement Act of 1984

Aug. 11, 1984, P.L. 98-377, 20 U.S. Code §§ 4011 et seq., 4011 nt.

Oct. 22, 1986, P.L. 99-519, 20 U.S. Code §§ 4014, 4021

July 18, 1988, P.L. 100-368, 102 Stat. 833, 20 U.S. Code § 4021

Nov. 28, 1990, P.L. 101-637, 20 U.S. Code §§ 4011, 4011 nt., 4012 to 4017, 4020, 4021

Oct. 20, 1994, P.L. 103-382, 20 U.S. Code § 4020

Asbestos School Hazard Abatement Reauthorization Act of 1990

Nov. 28, 1990, P.L. 101-637, 20 U.S. Code § 4011 nt.

Asbestos Workers Accreditation Act

Mich. Comp. Laws Ann., 338.3401 et seq.

Asbestosis and Silicosis Act

N.J. Stat. Ann., Superseded Vol., 34:15-35.1 et seq.

ASCAP Act

Fla. Stat. 1975, 543.19 et seq.

Ascertainment of Principal and Income Act
Conn. Gen. Stat. Ann., § 45-110 et seq.
§ 45-110 et seq.

Ascherman Act (Psychopathic Offenders)
Ohio Rev. Code 1953, 2947.24 et seq.

Asexualization Statutes
Cal. Penal Code §§ 645, 2670
Cal. Welfare and Institutions Code § 6624

Ash Disposal Act (Special Incinerator)
Wash. Rev. Code, 1989, 70.138.010 et seq.

Ash Pan Act (Railroads)
May 30, 1908, Ch. 225, 35 Stat. 476, 45 U.S.
Code §§ 17 to 21
Tex. Rev. Civ. Stat., Art. 6381

Ashby Act (Waterway Development)
Ky. Rev. Stat. 1971, 182.300 et seq.

**Ashby, Nichols, Hahn, Frymeier, Hale,
Render Act (Mosquito Control)**
Ky. Rev. Stat. 1971, 249.510 et seq.

**Asheville Classified Employees Civil Service
Act**
N.C. Laws 1951, Ch. 1000

**Asheville Police and Firemen's Civil Service
Act**
N.C. Laws 1947, Ch. 83

Ashurst-Sumners Act
June 6, 1934, Ch. 406, 48 Stat. 909 (See 4
U.S. Code § 111)

**Ashurst-Sumners Act (Shipment in
Interstate Commerce of Convict Made
Goods)**
July 24, 1935, Ch. 412, 49 Stat. 494

Asia Foundation Act
Nov. 22, 1983, P.L. 98-164, 22 U.S. Code
§§ 4401 to 4403, 4401 nt.
Aug. 16, 1985, P.L. 99-93, 22 U.S. Code
§ 4403
Dec. 22, 1987, P.L. 100-204, 22 U.S. Code
§ 4403

Feb. 16, 1990, P.L. 101-246, 22 U.S. Code
§ 4403
Oct. 21, 1998, P.L. 105-277, 22 U.S. Code
§ 4403

Asian Development Bank Act
March 16, 1966, P.L. 89-369, 80 Stat. 71, 22
U.S. Code §§ 285 to 285h
March 10, 1972, P.L. 92-245, 86 Stat. 57, 22
U.S. Code §§ 285l to 285p
Dec. 17, 1973, P.L. 93-189, 87 Stat. 732, 22
U.S. Code § 285a.
Dec. 22, 1974, P.L. 93-537, 88 Stat. 1735, 22
U.S. Code §§ 285q, 285r
Oct. 3, 1977, P.L. 95-118, 22 U.S. Code
§§ 285s, 285t
June 3, 1980, P.L. 96-259, 22 U.S. Code
§§ 285u, 285v
Oct. 17, 1980, P.L. 96-465, 94 Stat. 2160, 22
U.S. Code § 285a
Aug. 13, 1981, P.L. 97-35, 95 Stat. 744, 22
U.S. Code §§ 285s, 285t, 285u, 285w
Nov. 30, 1983, P.L. 98-181, 22 U.S. Code
§§ 285x, 285y
Dec. 22, 1987, P.L. 100-202, 22 U.S. Code
§ 285z
Dec. 19, 1989, P.L. 101-240, 22 U.S. Code
§ 285b
April 1, 1992, P.L. 102-266, 22 U.S. Code
§ 285aa

Asian Elephant Conservation Act of 1997
Nov. 19, 1997, P.L. 105-96, 16 U.S. Code
§ 4261 nt.

Asparagus Industry Promotion and Tax Act
N.J. Stat. Ann., 54:47C-1 et seq.

Assateague Island National Seashore Act
Sept. 21, 1965, P.L. 89-195, 79 Stat. 824, 16
U.S. Code §§ 459f to 459f-10
July 10, 1992, P.L. 102-320, 16 U.S. Code
§§ 459f-1, 459f-5

Assault Act
Mont. Code Ann., 45-5-201 et seq.
N.Y. Penal Law 1965 (Consol. Laws Ch. 40)
§ 120.00 et seq.
S.C. Code Ann. 1976, § 16-3-651 et seq.
Wash. Rev. Code Ann., 9A.36.011 et seq.

Assault Act (Second Degree)
N.Y. Penal Laws 1965 (Consol. Laws Ch. 40) § 120.05

Assault and Battery Act
Ala. Code 1975, § 13A-6-20 et seq.
Cal. Penal Code § 240 et seq.
Me. Rev. Stat. Ann. 1964, Title 17A, § 207 et seq.
P.R. Laws Ann. 1954, Title 33, § 821 et seq.
Tex. Penal Code, § 22.01 et seq.

Assault Prevention and Crisis Services Act (Sexual)
Tex. Health and Safety Code, § 44.001 et seq.
Tex. Rev. Civ. Stat., Art. 4447z

Assault Weapons Control Act (Roberti-Roos)
Cal. Penal Code § 12275 et seq.

Assessment Act
Ind. Code Ann., 6-1.1-4-1 et seq.
Ore. Rev. Stat., 308.005 et seq.
Pa. Purdon's Stat., Title 53, § 7101 et seq.
W. Va. Code 1966, § 11-3-1 et seq.

Assessment Act (Demand Reduction)
Ala. Code 1975, § 13A-12-280
Ala. Code 1975, § 13A-27A-1 et seq.

Assessment Act (Environmental Quality)
Cal. Health and Safety § 25570 et seq.

Assessment Act (Farmland)
Utah Code Ann. 1953, 59-2-501 et seq.

Assessment Act (Fourth to Eighth Class Counties)
Pa. Purdon's Stat., Title 72, § 5453.101 et seq.

Assessment Act (General County)
Pa. Purdon's Stat., Title 72, § 5020-1 et seq.

Assessment Act (Hail Associations)
Neb. Rev. Stat. 1943, 44-813 et seq.

Assessment Act (Health Care Provider)
R.I. Gen. Laws 1956, 44-50-1 et seq.

Assessment Act (Improvements)
Iowa Code Ann., 384.37 et seq.

Assessment Act (Nursing Facility Provider)
R.I. Gen. Laws 1956, 44-51-1 et seq.

Assessment Act (Outpatient Health Care Facility)
R.I. Gen. Laws 1956, 44-52-1 et seq.

Assessment Act (Private Property)
Mont. Code Ann., 2-10-101 et seq.

Assessment Act (Public Improvements)
Ala. Code 1975, § 11-48-1 et seq.

Assessment Act (Reduction)
Ala. Code 1975, § 13A-12-280 et seq.
Mont. Code Ann., 2-10-101 et seq.

Assessment Act (Taxation)
Fla. Stat. Ann., 193.011 et seq.
Md. Ann. Code 1974, Art. TG, § 13-401 et seq.
Tenn. Code Ann., 9-2-101 et seq.

Assessment Act (Third Class Counties)
Pa. Purdon's Stat., Title 72, § 5342 et seq.

Assessment and Control Act (Chronic Disease Prevention)
N.H. Rev. Stat. 1955, 141-B:1 et seq.

Assessment Apportionment Law (Special)
Ill. Comp. Stat. 1992, Ch. 35, § 200/28-1 et seq.

Assessment Benefiting State Property Laws (Special)
Ill. Comp. Stat. 1992, Ch. 35, § 200/29-1 et seq.

Assessment Bond Act (Hillsborough County)
Fla. Special Laws 1927, Ch. 12867

Assessment Bond Refunding Act
Cal. Statutes 1933, pp. 1915, 1940

Assessment Company Act (Insurance)
Ind. Code Ann., 27-8-1-1 et seq.

Assessment Insurance Act
Ill. Rev. Stat. 1987, Ch. 73, § 983 et seq.

Assessment Insurance Act (Reciprocal)
Ky. Rev. Stat. 1971, 304.27-010 et seq.

Assessment Life Insurance Act
Iowa Code Ann., 510.1 et seq.

Assessment of Academic Achievement Act
Cal. Education Code 1976, § 60600 et seq.

Assessment of Basic Skills Program Act
S.C. Code Ann. 1976, 59-30-10 et seq.

Assessment of Performance and Educational Accountability Act
Miss. Code Ann. 1972, § 37-3-46 et seq.

Assessment of Primary Forest Product Act
N.C. Gen. Stat. 1943, § 113A-189 et seq.

Assessment of Property Act
P.R. Laws Ann. 1954, Title 13, § 431 et seq.

Assessment of Proposed Accident and Sickness Insurance Coverage Act
Ga. Code Ann., 33-24-60 et seq.

Assessment Readjustment Bond Act
Cal. Statutes 1933, p. 1948
Cal. Statutes 1935, Ch. 393, p. 1420

Assessment Reform Law (1966)
Cal. Statutes 1966, 1st. Ex. Sess., Ch. 147, p. 648

Assessments Act (Public Utilities)
Wash. Rev. Code Ann., 84.12.200 et seq.

Assessors' Act (Dorchester County)
S.C. Code Ann. 1962, § 65-1811

Assessor's Certification Act
Pa. Purdon's Stat., Title 72, § 5010.1 et seq.

Assessor's Law (County)
Iowa Code Ann., 441.1 et seq.

Assessors Registration and Professional Certification Act
Tex. Rev. Civ. Stat., Art. 8885

Asset Conservation, Lender Liability, and Deposit Insurance Protection Act of 1996
Sept. 30, 1996, P.L. 104-208, Subtitle E, 42 U.S. Code § 9601 nt.

Asset Forfeiture Amendments Act of 1988
Nov. 18, 1988, P.L. 100-690, 21 U.S. Code § 801 nt.
Sept. 13, 1994, P.L. 103-322, 21 U.S. Code § 1509
Oct. 21, 1998, P.L. 105-277, 21 U.S. Code § 1509

Asset Management Board Act
Mass. Gen. Laws Ann., 7B:1 et seq.

Asset Protection Act
N.C. Gen. Stat. 1943, § 58-410 et seq.
Tex. Insurance Code, Art. 21.39A

Asset Seizure and Forfeiture Act
Kan. Stat. Ann., 60-4101 et seq.

Assets for Independence Act
Oct. 27, 1998, P.L. 105-285, Title IV, 112 Stat. 2759, 42 U.S. Code § 604 nt.

Assigned Appellate Judges Salary Act
Ill. Comp. Stat. 1992, Ch. 5, § 295/0.01 et seq.

Assigned Risk Act
Cal. Insurance Code § 11620 et seq.
N.C. Gen. Stat. 1943, § 20-279.21

Assigned Risk Plan (Motor Vehicle Insurance)
N.Y. Insurance Law 1984 (Consol. Laws Ch. 29) § 5301 et seq.

Assigned Risk Pool Law (Workers' Compensation)
N.M. Stat. Ann., 59A-33-1 et seq.

Assigned Risks Law (Motor Vehicle)
N.M. Stat. Ann., 59A-32-1 et seq.

Assignment Act
Ga. Code Ann., 18-2-41 et seq.
N.J. Stat. Ann., 2A:19-1 et seq.
N.Y. Debtor and Creditor Law (Consol.
Laws Ch. 12) § 2 et seq.
Ohio Rev. Code 1953, 1313.01 et seq.
Ore. Laws 1878, p. 36
Tenn. Code Ann., 47-13-101 et seq.

Assignment Act (Insolvency)
Pa. Purdon's Stat., Title 39, § 1 et seq.
S.C. Code Ann. 1976, § 27-25-10 et seq.

Assignment Act (Pupils)
La. Rev. Stat. Ann., 17:81.1
Miss. Code Ann. 1972, § 37-15-13 et seq.
Tenn. Code Ann., 49-6-3102 et seq.

Assignment Act (Schools)
Fla. Stat. Ann., 230.232

Assignment Act (Workmen's Compensation)
S.C. Code Ann. 1976, § 42-9-360 et seq.

Assignment for Benefit of Creditors Act
Cal. Civil Code § 3448 et seq.
Mich. Comp. Laws Ann., 600.5201 et seq.
Mont. Code Ann., 31-2-201 et seq.
N.M. Stat. Ann., 56-9-1 et seq.
N.Y. Debtor and Creditor Law (Consol.
Laws Ch. 12) § 2 et seq.
R.I. Gen. Laws 1956, 10-4-1 et seq.
S.D. Codified Laws 1967, 54-9-1 et seq.
Tenn. Code Ann., 47-13-101 et seq.
Tex. Business and Commerce Code, § 23.01
et seq.
Vt. Stat. Ann., Title 9, § 2151 et seq.
Wash. Rev. Code Ann., 7.08.010 et seq.

Assignment of Accounts Receivable Act
Ala. Code 1958, Title 39, § 207 et seq.
Ariz. Rev. Stat. Ann., § 47-9101 et seq.
Cal. Civil Code § 3017 et seq.
Colo. Rev. Stat., 11-2-1 et seq.
Fla. Stat. 1965, 524.01 et seq.
Ida. Code 1947, 28-9-101 et seq.
Ill. Rev. Stat. 1961, Ch. 17, §§ 5101, 5102

Ind. Burns' 1933, 19-2101
La. Rev. Stat. Ann., 9:3101 et seq.
Me. Public Laws 1945, Ch. 100
Mich. Comp. Laws 1948, 600.5401
Mo. Rev. Stat. 1959, 410.010 et seq.
N.C. Gen. Stat. 1943, § 44-77 et seq.
N.H. Rev. Stat. 1955, 333:1 et seq.
Ohio Rev. Code 1953, 1309.01 et seq.
Okla. Stat. 1961, Title 15, § 631 et seq.
P.R. Laws Ann. 1954, Title 10, § 581 et seq.
Tenn. Public Acts 1959, Ch. 114
Tex. Business and Commerce Code, § 9.101
et seq.
Va. Code 1950, §§ 11-5 to 11-7
Wash. Rev. Code Ann., 62A.9-101 et seq.

Assignment of Claims Act of 1940
Oct. 9, 1940, Ch. 779, 54 Stat. 1029, 31 U.S.
Code § 203; 41 U.S. Code § 15
May 15, 1951, Ch. 75, 65 Stat. 41, 15 U.S.
Code § 203; 41 U.S. Code § 15

Assignment of Dower Act
Mass. Gen. Laws Ann., 189:1 et seq.

Assignment of Future Wages Act
R.I. Gen. Laws 1956, 28-15-1 et seq.

Assignment of Mortgage Act
Fla. Stat. Ann., 701.02

Assignment of Pupils Act
N.C. Gen. Stat. 1943, § 115C-366 et seq.

Assignment of Wages Act
Ill. Rev. Stat. 1985, Ch. 48, § 39.01 et seq.
Mass. Gen. Laws Ann., 154:1 et seq.
Wash. Rev. Code Ann., 49.48.090 et seq.

Assignment or Purchase of Wages Act
N.J. Stat. Ann., 34:11-25

Assignments for Benefits of Creditors Act (General)
N.Y. Debtor and Creditor Law (Consol.
Laws Ch. 12) § 2 et seq.

Assignments to Magistrates Act
Ill. Rev. Stat. 1969, Ch. 37, § 621 et seq.

Assimilative Crimes Act
June 6, 1940, Ch. 241, 54 Stat. 234 (See 18 U.S. Code § 13)

Assistance Act
Pa. Purdon's Stat., Title 62, § 1971 et seq.

Assistance Act (Acquired Immune Deficiency Syndrome)
N.J. Stat. Ann., 26:5c-1 et seq.

Assistance Act (Early Childhood)
Wash. Rev. Code 1983, 28A.215.900

Assistance Act (Economic Development and Manufacturing)
Conn. Gen. Stat. Ann., § 32-220 et seq.

Assistance Act (Family Insurance)
Tenn. Code Ann., 68-1-115, 4-3-1404, 50-7-304

Assistance Act (Handicapped and Elderly Security)
Fla. Stat. Ann., 426.001 et seq.

Assistance Act (Institutional Grants)
Pa. Purdon's Stat., Title 24, § 5181 et seq.

Assistance Act (Inventors)
Ark. Acts 1992, No. 707
Okla. Stat. 1981, Title 74, § 5064.1 et seq.

Assistance Act (Local Government Transportation)
Fla. Stat. Ann., 335.20

Assistance Act (Old Age)
Ga. Code Ann., 49-4-30 et seq.
Me. Rev. Stat. Ann. 1964, Title 22, § 3172 et seq.
Neb. Rev. Stat. 1943, 68-214 et seq., 68-1001 et seq.
S.C. Code Ann. 1976, § 43-21-10 et seq.

Assistance Act (Paupers)
Me. Rev. Stat. Ann. 1964, Title 22, § 4307 et seq.

Assistance Act (Physicians for Rural Areas)
Ga. Code Ann., 31-34-1 et seq.

Assistance Act (Public)
N.M. Stat. Ann., 27-2-1 et seq.

Assistance Act (Small and Minority Business)
Fla. Stat. Ann., 288.702 et seq.

Assistance Act (Small Business)
Miss. Code Ann. 1972, § 57-10-501 et seq.

Assistance Act (Small Water Systems)
Pa. Purdon's Stat., Title 35, § 724.1 et seq.

Assistance Act (Student Financial)
Tex. Education Code, Art. 56.001 et seq.

Assistance Act (Tactical Incident)
Mont. Laws 1989, Ch. 455

Assistance Act (Tuition)
Tex. Education Code, § 56.101

Assistance Act for Victims of Rape and Sex Offenses
N.C. Gen. Stat. 1943, § 143B-480.1 et seq.

Assistance and Development Act (Airport)
Fla. Stat. Ann., 332.003 et seq.

Assistance and Homeless Housing Program
N.Y. Social Services Law (Consol. Laws Ch. 55) § 41 et seq.

Assistance and Preservation Act (Railroad)
Me. Rev. Stat. Ann. 1964, Title 23, § 7101 et seq.

Assistance and Preservation Act (State Railroad)
Me. Rev. Stat. Ann. 1964, Title 23, § 7101 et seq.
N.Y. State Finance Law 1940 (Consol. Laws Ch. 56) § 92 1

Assistance Compact (Emergency Management)
Del. Code of 1974, Title 20, § 3401 et seq.

Assistance Corporation Act (Community Economic Development)
Mass. Gen. Laws Ann., 40H:1 et seq.

Assistance Corporation Act (Local Government)
N.Y. Public Authorities Law (Consol. Laws Ch. 43A) § 3231 et seq.

Assistance Department Act (Transitional)
Mass. Gen. Laws Ann., 18:1 et seq.

Assistance for Individuals with Disabilities Act (Technology Related)
Ga. Code Ann., 30-9-1 et seq.

Assistance for Old Age Act
S.C. Code Ann. 1976, § 43-21-10 et seq.

Assistance for the Aged Act (Medical)
Ga. Code Ann., 49-4-120 et seq.

Assistance for the Medically Indigent Act
S.C. Code Ann. 1976, § 44-6-135 et seq.

Assistance Fund for Enterprise Act
Cal. Financial Code § 32000 et seq.

Assistance Grants Program Act
Tex. Education Code, § 56.010 et seq.

Assistance Law (Port Development)
Minn. Stat. Ann., 457A.01 et seq.

Assistance Plan (Insurance)
Mont. Laws 1986 Sp. Sess., Ch. 11, § 1 et seq.

Assistance Program (Temporary)
Alaska Stat. 1962, § 47.27.900

Assistance Program Act (Rail Service)
Kan. Stat. Ann., 75-5040 et seq.

Assistance Program for Persons with Disabilities Act (Personal)
Ga. Code Ann., 30-6-1 et seq.

Assistance to Dependent Children Act
Ariz. Rev. Stat. Ann., § 46-291 et seq.

Assistance to Homeless Families Act
Haw. Rev. Stat. Ann., § 358D-1 et seq.

Assistance to Indigent Veterans Act
Ill. Comp. Stat. 1992, Ch. 330, § 45/0.01 et seq.

Assistance to Needy Blind Act
Ariz. Rev. Stat. Ann., § 46-281 et seq.

Assistance to the Elderly (Pharmaceutical)
R.I. Gen. Laws 1956, 42-66.2-1 et seq.

Assistance to the Families of the Working Poor Act
N.J. Laws 1971, Ch. 209

Assistance to Victims of and Witnesses to Crimes and Aid to Law Enforcement Act
Colo. Rev. Stat., 24-4.2-101 et seq.

Assistant Licensing Act (Physician)
Tex. Gen. Laws 1993, Ch. 214

Assistant Practices Act (Immigration)
Wash. Rev. Code 1983, 19.154.010 et seq.

Assisted Housing Preservation Act
Md. Ann. Code 1957, Art. 83B, § 9-101 et seq.
Md. Ann. Code 1974, Department of Housing and Community Development, § 9-101 et seq.

Assisted Living Facilities Act
Fla. Stat. Ann., 400.401 et seq.

Assisted Living Facility and Residential Care Licensing Act
R.I. Gen. Laws 1956, 23-17.4-1 et seq.

Assisted Suicide Funding Restriction Act
Mo. Laws 1999, H.B. No. 511

Assisted Suicide Funding Restriction Act of 1997
April 30, 1997, P.L. 105-12, 42 U.S. Code § 14401 nt.

Assistive Devices Lemon Law
Nov. 13, 1998, P.L. 105-394, 112 Stat. 3627, Titles 1 to 4
N.M. Stat. Ann., 57-27-1 to 57-27-5
Okla. Stat. Ann., Title 15, § 910 et seq.

Assistive Technology Act of 1998
Nov. 13, 1998, P.L. 105-394, 112 Stat. 3627,
29 U.S. Code § 3001 nt.

Assistive Technology Device Warranty Act
Fla. Stat. Ann., 427.801 et seq.

Assistive Technology Evaluation and Training Centers Act
Ill. Comp. Stat. 1992, Ch. 20, § 1320/1 et seq.

Assistive Technology Regulation Act
Neb. Rev. Stat. 1943, 69-2601 to 69-2619

Assistive Technology Warranty Act
Haw. Rev. Stat. Ann., § 481K-1 et seq.
Ida. Code 1947, 48-1401 et seq.

Associate Counselor, Professional Counselor, and Marital and Family Therapist Licensing Act
S.C. Code Ann. 1976, § 40-75-10 et seq.

Associate Judges Act
Ill. Comp. Stat. 1992, Ch. 705, § 45/2 et seq.

Associate Justices Act (Municipal)
Mich. Comp. Laws Ann., 730.321 et seq.

Association Act (Cooperative)
Tex. Rev. Civ. Stat., Art. 1396-50.01
Wis. Stat. Ann., 185.01 et seq.

Association Act (Insurance Guaranty)
N.H. Rev. Stat. 1955, 404-B:1 et seq.

Association Act (Joint Underwriting)
Minn. Stat. Ann., 62I.01 et seq.

Association Act (Life and Health Insurance Guaranty)
N.H. Rev. Stat. 1955, 404-D:1 et seq.

Association Act (Property and Casualty Insurance Guaranty)
Vt. Stat. Ann., Title 8, § 3611 et seq.

Association Act (Property Owners')
Ga. Code Ann., 44-3-220 et seq.

Association Act (Savings)
Miss. Code Ann. 1972, § 81-12-1 et seq.

Association for the Prevention of Cruelty to Animals Act
D.C. Code Ann., § 32-901 et seq.

Association of Warranty of All Kinds of Insurance Except Life, Disability and Health Act
P.R. Laws Ann. 1954, Title 26, § 3801 et seq.

Association of Warranty of Life, Disability and Health Insurance Act
P.R. Laws Ann. 1954, Title 26, § 3901 et seq.

Associations, Organizations and Agents Act
Md. Ann. Code 1974, Art. CJ, § 5-406

Assumed Business Name Act
Ida. Code 1947, 53-501 et seq.
Ill. Comp. Stat. 1992, Ch. 805, § 405/0.01 et seq.
N.C. Gen. Stat. 1943, § 66-68 et seq.

Assumed Business Names and Mercantile Partnerships Act
Ind. Code Ann., 23-15-1-1 et seq.
Me. Rev. Stat. Ann. 1964, Title 31, § 1 et seq.
Ore. Rev. Stat., 648.005 et seq.

Assumed Name Act
Mich. Comp. Laws Ann., 445.1 et seq.
N.J. Rev. Stat. 1937, 56:1-2
Pa. Cons. Stat., Title 54, § 301 et seq.
R.I. Gen. Laws 1956, 6-1-1 et seq.
Tex. Business and Commerce Code, § 36.10 et seq.
Utah Code Ann. 1953, 42-2-5 et seq.
Va. Code 1950, § 59.1-69 et seq.

Assumed Risk Act (Railroad Employees)
Tex. Rev. Civ. Stat., Art. 6437

Assumption Act (State Debts)
Aug. 4, 1790, Ch. 34, 1 Stat. 138

Assumption Reinsurance Act
Neb. Rev. Stat. 1943, 44-6201 et seq.

Assured Clear Distance Act
Iowa Code Ann., 321.285
Mich. Comp. Laws Ann., 257.627
Ohio Rev. Code 1953, 4511.21
Okla. Stat. 1961, Title 47, § 121.3
Pa. 1929 Pamph. Laws 905, No. 403, § 1002, Subd. a

At Risk and Minority Student Scholarship Act
Ida. Code 1947, 33-4601 et seq.

Athens Civil Service Act
Ga. Laws 1918, p. 528

Athens-Clarke County Anti-Drug Commission Act
Ga. Laws 1991, p. 4792

Athens-Clarke County Charter Commission Act
Ga. Laws 1981, p. 3065

Athens-Clarke County Public Facilities Authority Act
Ga. Laws 1996, p. 3746

Athens Public Facilities Authority Act
Ga. Laws 1960, p. 2531

Athlete Agents Regulatory Act
Ala. Code 1975, § 8-26-1 et seq.
Ga. Code Ann., 43-4A-1 et seq.

Athlete and Child Performer Protection Act
Fla. Stat. Ann., 743.08 to 743.095

Athletes Agents Registration Act
Iowa Code Ann., 9A.1 et seq.
Wash. Rev. Code 1983, 18.175.010 et seq.

Athletic Agent Registration Act
Pa. Cons. Stat., Title 5, § 3101 et seq.

Athletic Association Compliance Enforcement Procedures Act (Collegiate)
Fla. Stat. Ann., 240.5339 et seq.
Ill. Comp. Stat. 1992, Ch. 110, § 25/1 et seq.
Ill. Rev. Stat. 1991, Ch. 144, § 2901 et seq.

Athletic Association Procedures Act (Collegiate)
Neb. Rev. Stat. 1943, 85-1201 et seq.

Athletic Code
Pa. Purdon's Stat., Title 4, § 31.101 et seq.

Athletic Commission Act
Cal. Business and Professions Code § 18600 et seq.
N.D. Cent. Code, 53-01-02 et seq.
N.Y. Laws 1920, Ch. 912
S.D. Codified Laws 1967, 42-6-1 et seq.
Utah Code Ann. 1953, 58-48-1 et seq.

Athletic Commission Law (State)
N.Y. Unconsolidated Laws, § 8901 et seq.

Athletic Contests Bribery Act
D.C. Code 1973, § 22-1513

Athletic Exhibition Registration Act
Ill. Rev. Stat. 1979, Ch. 111, § 1401 et seq.

Athletic Exhibitions Act
Ill. Rev. Stat. 1991, Ch. 85, § 1201 et seq.

Athletic Field Loan Act (Wilmington)
Mass. Acts 1955, Ch. 200

Athletic Organization Act (Interscholastic)
Ill. Rev. Stat. 1991, Ch. 122, §§ 1820, 1821

Athletic Trainers Act
La. Rev. Stat. Ann., 37:3301 et seq.
Mo. Rev. Stat., 334.700 et seq.
N.D. Laws 1984, Ch. 490
N.M. Stat. Ann., 61-14D-1 et seq.
Okla. Stat. Ann., Title 59, § 525 et seq.
S.C. Code Ann. 1976, § 44-75-10 et seq.

Athletic Trainers Licensure Act
Ala. Code 1975, § 34-40-1 et seq.
Miss. Code Ann. 1972, § 73-55-1 et seq.

Athletic Trainers Practice Act
Ill. Comp. Stat. 1992, Ch. 225, § 5/1 et seq.
N.M. Stat. Ann., 61-14D-1 to 61-14D-19

Athletic Trainers Registration Act
Kan. Stat. Ann., 65-6901 et seq.

Athletic Training Practice Act
N.J. Stat. Ann., 45:9-37.35 et seq.

Athletics Eligibility Act (Interscholastic)
Ill. Rev. Stat. 1987, Ch. 122, § 1801.01 et seq.

Atlanta and Fulton County Recreation Authority Act
Ga. Laws 1960, p. 2810

Atlanta Charters
Ga. Laws 1973, p. 2188

Atlanta Community Improvement District Act
Ga. Laws 1991, p. 3653

Atlanta Group Insurance Board Authority Act
Ga. Laws 1979, p. 4037

Atlanta Market for Georgia Farm Products Authority Act
Ga. Laws 1988, p. 4947

Atlanta Municipal Court Act
Ga. Laws 1913, p. 145

Atlanta Rapid Transit Authority Act
Ga. Laws 1965, p. 2243

Atlanta Urban Enterprise Zone Act
Ga. Laws 1988, p. 4164

Atlantic Avenue Improvement Act
N.Y. Laws 1897, Ch. 499

Atlantic City Charter
N.J. Laws 1980, Ch. 1

Atlantic City Convention Center Authority Act
N.J. Stat. Ann., 52:27H-29 et seq.

Atlantic Coastal Fisheries Cooperative Management Act
Dec. 20, 1993, P.L. 103-206, 16 U.S. Code §§ 5101 nt., 5101 et seq.
Oct. 11, 1996, P.L. 104-297, 16 U.S. Code §§ 5102, 5103, 5107a, 5107b, 5108

Atlantic Fisheries Act
May 4, 1942, Ch. 283, 56 Stat. 267

Atlantic Salmon Compact (Connecticut River)
Mass. Acts 1981, Ch. 716
Vt. Stat. Ann., Title 10, § 4651 et seq.

Atlantic Salmon Compact Act
Conn. Gen. Stat. Ann., § 26-302
N.H. Rev. Stat. 1955, 213-A:1 et seq.
Vt. Stat. Ann., Title 10, § 4651 et seq.

Atlantic Salmon Convention Act of 1982
Dec. 29, 1982, P.L. 97-389, 16 U.S. Code § 3601 et seq.

Atlantic States Marine Fisheries Compact
Conn. Gen. Stat. 1983, § 26-295
Ga. Code Ann., 27-4-210 et seq.
Md. Ann. Code 1974, Art. NR, § 4-301 et seq.
Me. Rev. Stat. Ann. 1964, Title 12, § 4601 et seq.
N.C. Gen. Stat. 1943, § 113-252 et seq.
N.H. Rev. Stat. 1955, 213:1 et seq.
R.I. Gen. Laws 1956, 20-8-1 et seq.
Va. Code 1950, § 28.1-202

Atlantic Striped Bass Conservation Act
Oct. 31, 1985, P.L. 98-613, 16 U.S. Code § 1851 nt.
Oct. 1, 1986, P.L. 99-432, 16 U.S. Code § 1851 nt.
Nov. 3, 1988, P.L. 100-589, 16 U.S. Code § 1851 nt.
Oct. 17, 1991, P.L. 102-130, 16 U.S. Code § 1851 nt.
Dec. 20, 1993, P.L. 103-206, 16 U.S. Code § 1851 nt.
Dec. 16, 1997, P.L. 105-146, 16 U.S. Code § 1851 nt.

Atlantic Striped Bass Conservation Act Amendments of 1997

Dec. 16, 1997, P.L. 105-146, 16 U.S. Code § 1851 nt.

Atlantic Tunas Convention Act of 1975

May 26, 1977, P.L. 95-33, 16 U.S. Code § 971

Sept. 4, 1980, P.L. 96-339, 16 U.S. Code § 971b et seq.

Nov. 14, 1986, P.L. 99-659, 16 U.S. Code § 971h

Nov. 28, 1990, P.L. 101-627, 16 U.S. Code §§ 971a, 971a nt., 971b, 971b-1, 971d, 971h

Nov. 3, 1995, P.L. 104-43, Title III, 16 U.S. Code § 971 et seq.

Nov. 13, 1998, P.L. 105-384, 16 U.S. Code §§ 971, 971 nt., 971c, 971d, 971h, 971j, 971k

Atlantic Tunas Convention Authorization Act of 1995

Nov. 3, 1995, P.L. 104-43, Title 111, 16 U.S. Code § 971 nt.

Atlantic Water and Sewerage Authority Act

Ga. Laws 1998, H.B. 1898

ATM Safety Act

N.Y. Banking Law (Consol. Laws Ch. 2) § 75a et seq.

ATM Security Act

Ill. Comp. Stat. 1992, Ch. 205, § 695/1 et seq.

Atmospheric Acidity Protection Act

Cal. Health and Safety Code § 39900 et seq.

Atoka Agreement (Indians)

June 28, 1898, Ch. 517, 30 Stat. 495

Atomic Code

Fla. Stat. Ann., 404.011 et seq.

Atomic Energy Act

Feb. 10, 1996, P.L. 104-106, 42 U.S. Code § 2153

Me. Rev. Stat. Ann. 1964, Title 10, § 51 et seq., Title 22, § 671

N.H. Rev. Stat. 1955, 162-B:1 et seq.

N.Y. Commerce Law (Consol. Laws Ch. 7A) §§ 2, 50, 100, 102 et seq.

Tenn. Code Ann., 68-202-101 et seq.

Atomic Energy Act of 1946

Aug. 1, 1946, Ch. 724, 60 Stat. 755

July 3, 1948, Ch. 828, 62 Stat. 1259

Oct. 11, 1949, Ch. 673, 63 Stat. 762

Sept. 23, 1950, Ch. 1000, 64 Stat. 979

Oct. 30, 1951, Ch. 633, 65 Stat. 692

April 5, 1952, Ch. 159, 66 Stat. 43

July 17, 1953, Ch. 228, 67 Stat. 181

July 31, 1953, Chs. 283, 284, 67 Stat. 240

Aug. 13, 1953, Ch. 432, 67 Stat. 575

Aug. 13, 1954, Ch. 730, 68 Stat. 715

Aug. 30, 1954, Ch. 1073, 68 Stat. 919

Atomic Energy Act of 1954

Aug. 30, 1954, Ch. 1073, 68 Stat. 919, 42 U.S. Code §§ 2011 nts., 2011 to 2104, 2015 to 2020, 2031 to 2038, 2051 to 2053, 2061 to 2064, 2071 to 2077, and others

Aug. 9, 1955, Ch. 697, 69 Stat. 630, 42 U.S. Code § 2031

July 14, 1956, Ch. 608, 70 Stat. 553, 42 U.S. Code § 2201

Aug. 6, 1956, Ch. 1015, 70 Stat. 1069, 42 U.S. Code §§ 2014, 2051, 2131, 2133, 2163, 2201, 2232, 2278a, 2278b, 2279, 2280, 2281

April 12, 1957, P.L. 85-14, 71 Stat. 11, 42 U.S. Code § 2153 nt.

July 3, 1957, P.L. 85-79, 71 Stat. 274, 42 U.S. Code §§ 2017, 2078

Aug. 21, 1957, P.L. 85-162, 71 Stat. 410, 42 U.S. Code § 2201

Aug. 28, 1957, P.L. 85-177, 71 Stat. 455, 42 U.S. Code § 2074

Sept. 2, 1957, P.L. 85-256, 71 Stat. 576, 42 U.S. Code §§ 2012, 2014, 2039, 2073, 2210, 2232, 2239

Sept. 4, 1957, P.L. 85-287, 71 Stat. 612, 42 U.S. Code §§ 2032, 2034, 2035, 2201

July 2, 1958, P.L. 85-479, 72 Stat. 276, 42 U.S. Code §§ 2121, 2122, 2153, 2164

July 7, 1958, P.L. 85-507, 72 Stat. 337, 42 U.S. Code § 2201

Aug. 8, 1958, P.L. 85-602, 72 Stat. 525, 42 U.S. Code §§ 2014, 2210

Aug. 19, 1958, P.L. 85-681, 72 Stat. 632, 42 U.S. Code §§ 2073, 2098, 2153, 2165, 2201, 2206

Aug. 23, 1958, P.L. 85-744, 72 Stat. 837, 42 U.S. Code § 2210

June 11, 1959, P.L. 86-43, 73 Stat. 73, 42 U.S. Code § 2016

June 23, 1959, P.L. 86-50, 73 Stat. 87, 42 U.S. Code § 2183

Sept. 21, 1959, P.L. 86-300, 73 Stat. 574, 42 U.S. Code §§ 2201, 2203

Sept. 23, 1959, P.L. 86-373, 73 Stat. 688, 42 U.S. Code §§ 2021, 2138

Sept. 6, 1961, P.L. 87-206, 75 Stat. 476, 42 U.S. Code §§ 2014, 2074, 2163, 2165, 2181, 2182, 2187, 2188, 2201, 2207, 2210, 2240, 2252

Aug. 29, 1962, P.L. 87-615, 76 Stat. 409, 42 U.S. Code §§ 2014, 2017, 2139, 2165, 2182, 2201, 2210, 2232, 2239, 2241

Oct. 11, 1962, P.L. 87-793, 76 Stat. 864, 42 U.S. Code § 2201

July 22, 1963, P.L. 88-72, 77 Stat. 88, 42 U.S. Code § 2017

March 26, 1964, P.L. 88-294, 78 Stat. 172, 42 U.S. Code § 2252

Aug. 1, 1964, P.L. 88-394, 78 Stat. 376, 42 U.S. Code §§ 2183, 2210

Aug. 14, 1964, P.L. 88-426, 78 Stat. 423, 42 U.S. Code §§ 2032, 2034, 2035, 2037, 2038

Aug. 19, 1964, P.L. 88-448, 78 Stat. 490, 42 U.S. Code § 2038

Aug. 26, 1964, P.L. 88-489, 78 Stat. 602, 42 U.S. Code §§ 2012, 2013, 2073 to 2078, 2135, 2153, 2201, 2221, 2233, 2234

Aug. 24, 1965, P.L. 89-135, 79 Stat. 551, 42 U.S. Code § 2018

Sept. 29, 1965, P.L. 89-210, 79 Stat. 855, 42 U.S. Code § 2210

Oct. 13, 1966, P.L. 89-645, 80 Stat. 891, 42 U.S. Code §§ 2014, 2139, 2210

Dec. 14, 1967, P.L. 90-190, 81 Stat. 577, 42 U.S. Code §§ 2035, 2038, 2053, 2061, 2073, 2201, 2273

Dec. 24, 1969, P.L. 91-161, 83 Stat. 444, 42 U.S. Code §§ 2183, 2271 to 2276, 2282

Oct. 15, 1970, P.L. 91-452, 84 Stat. 930, 42 U.S. Code § 2201

Dec. 19, 1970, P.L. 91-560, 84 Stat. 1472, 42 U.S. Code §§ 2051, 2076, 2132 to 2135, 2201, 2232, 2241

Aug. 11, 1971, P.L. 92-84, 85 Stat. 307, 42 U.S. Code §§ 2051, 2053

June 16, 1972, P.L. 92-314, 86 Stat. 227, 42 U.S. Code § 2201

May 10, 1974, P.L. 93-276, 88 Stat. 119, 42 U.S. Code § 2187

Aug. 17, 1974, P.L. 93-377, 88 Stat. 473, 42 U.S. Code §§ 2074, 2077, 2111, 2153, 2183, 2201

Dec. 31, 1975, P.L. 94-197, 89 Stat. 1111, 42 U.S. Code §§ 2014, 2210

Sept. 20, 1977, P.L. 95-110, 2 U.S. Code 190j; 42 U.S. Code §§ 2258, 2259 et seq.; 31 U.S. Code § 1302

Dec. 13, 1977, P.L. 95-209, 42 U.S. Code § 2039

Nov. 6, 1978, P.L. 95-601, 42 U.S. Code § 2210a

Nov. 8, 1978, P.L. 95-604, 42 U.S. Code §§ 2014, 2021, 2022, 2111, 2113, 2114, 2201

Nov. 9, 1979, P.L. 96-106, 42 U.S. Code § 2113

June 30, 1980, P.L. 96-295, 42 U.S. Code § 2133 et seq.

Jan. 4, 1983, P.L. 97-415, 42 U.S. Code §§ 2021, 2022, 2077, 2114, 2168, 2210, 2239, 2239 nt., 2242, 2284

July 12, 1985, P.L. 99-64, 42 U.S. Code § 2153

Aug. 27, 1986, P.L. 99-399, 42 U.S. Code §§ 2160b, 2160c, 2169

Nov. 14, 1986, P.L. 99-661, 42 U.S. Code §§ 2037, 2201

Aug. 20, 1988, P.L. 100-408, 102 Stat. 1066, 42 U.S. Code §§ 2014, 2210, 2273, 2282a

Sept. 29, 1988, P.L. 100-456, 102 Stat. 2076, 42 U.S. Code §§ prec. 2286, 2286 to 2286i

Nov. 29, 1989, P.L. 101-189, 42 U.S. Code § 2121

Nov. 5, 1990, P.L. 101-510, 42 U.S. Code § 2286b

Nov. 15, 1990, P.L. 101-575, 42 U.S. Code §§ 2014, 2061, 2201, 2243, 2284

Nov. 29, 1990, P.L. 101-647, 42 U.S. Code § 2271

Dec. 5, 1991, P.L. 102-190, 42 U.S. Code §§ 2286a, 2286b, 2286g

Oct. 23, 1992, P.L. 102-484, 42 U.S. Code § 2162

Continued

Oct. 24, 1992, P.L. 102-486, 42 U.S. Code §§ prec. 2011, 2011 et seq., 2111 et seq., 2201 et seq., 2297 et. seq.

Nov. 30, 1993, P.L. 103-160, 42 U.S. Code §§ 2122a, 2286h-1, 2286i

April 30, 1994, P.L. 103-236, 42 U.S. Code § 2160c

Oct. 5, 1994, P.L. 103-337, 42 U.S. Code §§ 2153 nt., 2164

Nov. 2, 1994, P.L. 103-437, 42 U.S. Code §§ 2014, 2071, 2074, 2078, 2091, 2153, 2155, 2157, 2158, 2159, 2160, 2204, 2242

April 26, 1996, P.L. 104-134, 42 U.S. Code §§ 2014, 2239, 2243, 2259, 2282, 2297 nt., 2297f, 2297f-1

Nov. 18, 1997, P.L. 105-85, 42 U.S. Code § 2016

Oct. 21, 1998, P.L. 105-277, 42 U.S. Code §§ 2077, 2139, 2141, 2153, 2155, 2160

Nov. 10, 1998, P.L. 105-362, 42 U.S. Code §§ 2039, 2210, 2297f

Nov. 13, 1998, P.L. 105-388, 42 U.S. Code § 2297g-1

Atomic Energy Act of 1955

Nov. 2, 1994, P.L. 103-437, 42 U.S. Code § 2349

Atomic Energy and Radiation Control Act

S.C. Code Ann. 1976, § 13-7-10 et seq.

Atomic Energy and Space Development Law

N.Y. Executive Law 1951 (Consol. Laws Ch. 18) § 463 et seq.

Atomic Energy Authority Act

Ky. Rev. Stat. 1971, Superseded Vols., 152.510 et seq.

Atomic Energy Commission Act

Mass. Gen. Laws Ann., 6:85 et seq.

R.I. Gen. Laws 1956, 42-27-1 et seq.

Atomic Energy Commission Appropriation Acts

Aug. 28, 1957, P.L. 85-175, 71 Stat. 450

Aug. 18, 1959, P.L. 86-164, 73 Stat. 363

Atomic Energy Community Act of 1955

Aug. 4, 1955, Ch. 543, 69 Stat. 471, 12 U.S. Code § 1715n; 20 U.S. Code § 243; 42 U.S. Code §§ 2301 to 2315, 2321 to 2326, 2331 to 2333, 2341 to 2347, 2361 to 2366, 2371 to 2375, 2381, 2386, 2391 to 2394

July 25, 1956, Ch. 731, 70 Stat. 653, 42 U.S. Code §§ 2326, 2362, 2310 to 2312

Aug. 21, 1957, P.L. 85-162, 71 Stat. 410, 42 U.S. Code § 2325

Aug. 30, 1961, P.L. 87-174, 75 Stat. 409, 42 U.S. Code § 2343

Sept. 28, 1962, P.L. 87-719, 76 Stat. 664, 42 U.S. Code §§ 2304, 2312, 2322, 2326, 2331, 2342, 2343, 2345, 2347, 2348, 2362 to 2364, 2372, 2375, 2381, 2383

Aug. 1, 1964, P.L. 88-394, 78 Stat. 376, 42 U.S. Code § 2349

May 25, 1967, P.L. 90-19, 81 Stat. 23, 42 U.S. Code §§ 2322, 2362

Dec. 14, 1967, P.L. 90-190, 81 Stat. 575, 42 U.S. Code §§ 2312, 2348, 2391, 2394

Dec. 31, 1975, P.L. 94.-187, 89 Stat. 1077, 42 U.S. Code §§ 2391 to 2394

Sept. 20, 1977, P.L. 95-110, 42 U.S. Code § 2315

Feb. 25, 1978, P.L. 95-238, 42 U.S. Code §§ 2391, 2394

Nov. 14, 1986, P.L. 99-661, 42 U.S. Code § 2394

Feb. 10, 1996, P.L. 104-106, 42 U.S. Code §§ 2372, 2383, 2391, 2394

Atomic Energy Development and Radiation Control Law

Pa. Purdon's Stat., Title 35, § 7110.101 et seq.

Atomic Energy Development Law

Cal. Health and Safety Code § 25700 et seq.

Atomic Energy, Nuclear Energy Development and Radiation Control Act

Kan. Stat. Ann., 48-1601 et seq.

Atomic Research and Development Act

N.Y. Public Authorities Law (Consol. Laws Ch. 43A) § 1850 et seq.

Atomic Testing Liability Act
Nov. 5, 1990, P.L. 101-510, 42 U.S. Code § 2212

Atomic Weapons and Special Nuclear Materials Rewards Act
Aug. 17, 1974, P.L. 93-377, 88 Stat. 472, 50 U.S. Code §§ 47a, 47b, 47d, 47e
Sept. 30, 1996, P.L. 104-208, 50 U.S. Code § 47c

Atomic Weapons Rewards Act
July 15, 1955 Ch. 372, 69 Stat. 365, 50 U.S. Code §§ 47a to 47f
Aug. 17, 1974, P.L. 93-377, 88 Stat. 472, 50 U.S. Code §§ 47a, 47b, 47d, 47e

Attachment Act
Ala. Code 1975, § 6-6-30 et seq.
Alaska Stat. 1962, § 09.40.010 et seq.
Ark. Code Ann. 1987, 16-110-101 et seq.
Cal. Code of Civil Procedure § 483.010 et seq.
Conn. Gen. Stat. Ann., § 52-279 et seq.
Del. Code of 1974, Title 10, § 3501 et seq.
Fla. Stat. 1983, 76.01 et seq.
Ga. Code Ann., 18-3-1 et seq.
Haw. Rev. Stat. Ann., § 651-1 et seq.
Ida. Code 1947, 8-501 et seq.
Ill. Rev. Stat. 1991, Ch. 110, § 4-101 et seq.
Ky. Rev. Stat. 1971, Superseded Vols., 425.185 et seq.
La. Code of Civil Procedure 1960, Art. 3541 et seq.
Md. Ann. Code 1974, Art. CJ, § 3-301 et seq.
Me. Rev. Stat. Ann. 1964, Title 14, 4101 et seq.
Mich. Comp. Laws Ann., 600.4001 et seq.
Miss. Code Ann. 1972, § 11-33-1 et seq.
Mo. Rev. Stat., 521.010 et seq.
Mont. Code Ann., 27-18-101 et seq.
N.C. Gen. Stat. 1943, §§ 1-440.1 et seq.
N.D. Cent. Code, 32-08.1-01 et seq.
Neb. Rev. Stat. 1943, 25-1001 et seq.
N.H. Rev. Stat. 1955, 511:1 et seq.
N.J. Stat. Ann., 2A:26-1 et seq.
N.M. Stat. Ann., 42-9-1 et seq.

N.Y. Civil Practice Law and Rules (Consol. Laws Ch. 8) § 6201 et seq.
Ohio Rev. Code 1953, 2715.01 et seq.
Okla. Stat. Ann., Title 12, § 1151 et seq.
Ore. Rev. Stat., 29.110 et seq.
R.I. Gen. Laws 1956, 10-5-1 et seq.
S.C. Code Ann. 1976, § 15-19-10 et seq.
S.D. Codified Laws 1967, 21-17A-1 et seq.
Tenn. Code Ann., 29-6-101 et seq.
Wash. Rev. Code Ann., 6.25.010 et seq.
W. Va. Code 1966, § 38-7-1 et seq.

Attachment Act (Chose in Action)
Ark. Code Ann. 1987, 16-110-121

Attachment Act (Motor Vehicle)
S.C. Code Ann. 1976, § 29-15-20 et seq.

Attachment Act (Procedure on Execution)
Pa. Cons. Stat., Title 42, § 5529 et seq.

Attachment Act (Purchase Money)
S.C. Code Ann. 1976, § 15-19-510 et seq.

Attachment and Garnishment Act
Colo. Rev. Stat., 79-9-1 et seq.
Okla. Stat. 1981, Title 12, § 1171 et seq.
Wyo. Stat. Ann., § 1-15-101 et seq.

Attachments against Debtors Act
Miss. Code Ann. 1972, § 11-33-1 et seq.

Attempt Act (Crimes)
Cal. Penal Code § 663 et seq.
Ill. Rev. Stat. 1991, Ch. 38, § 8-4
Wis. Stat. Ann., 939.32

Attempted Abortion Act
Tenn. Code Ann., 39-15-20

Attempts to Kill Act
Okla. Stat. Ann., Title 21, § 651 et seq.

Attendance Act (Compulsory)
Conn. Gen. Stat. Ann., § 10-184 et seq.

Attendance Act (Schools)
Ala. Code 1975, § 16-28-1 et seq.
Ky. Rev. Stat. 1971, 159.010 et seq.
Continued

Me. Rev. Stat. Ann. 1964, Title 20A, § 5001 et seq.

Miss. Code Ann. 1972, § 37-13-91

Attendance and Leave Policy Act
Ark. Code Ann. 1987, 21-4-201 et seq.

Attendance Area Act (School Transportation)
Wis. Stat. Ann., 121.54

Attendance of Foreign Witnesses Law
S.D. Codified Laws 1967, 23-40-14 et seq.

Attendance of Witness in Criminal Proceedings Act
Tenn. Code Ann., 40-17-201 et seq.

Attendance of Witnesses Act
Ind. Code Ann., 35-37-5-1 et seq.
Pa. Cons. Stat., Title 42, § 5961 et seq.
Tenn. Code Ann., 24-2-101 et seq.

Attendance of Witnesses from Within or Without a State in Criminal Proceedings Act
See Uniform Act to Secure the Attendance of Witnesses from Within or Without a State in Criminal Proceedings

Attendance of Witnesses from Without a State in Criminal Proceedings Act
See also Uniform Act to Secure the Attendance of Witnesses from Without a State in Criminal Proceedings
Kan. Stat. Ann., 22-4201 et seq.
Neb. Rev. Stat. 1943, 29-1906 et seq.
R.I. Gen. Laws 1956, 12-16-1 et seq.

Attendant Allowance Adjustment Act
Nov. 7, 1990, P.L. 101-534, 5 U.S. Code §§ 8101 nt., 8111, 8111 nt.

Attendant Care Services Act
Pa. Purdon's Stat., Title 62, § 3051 et seq.

Attendant Services Act (Personal)
N.J. Stat. Ann., 30:4G-13 et seq.

Attested Account Act
Ohio Rev. Code 1953, 1311.26 et seq.

Attorney-Client Privilege Act
Cal. Code of Civil Procedure § 1881, Subd. 2
N.Y. Civil Practice Law and Rules (Consol. Laws Ch. 8) § 4503
Ohio Rev. Code 1953, 2317.02, Subd. A
Pa. Cons. Stat., Title 42, § 5928

Attorney General Act
Ill. Comp. Stat. 1992, Ch. 15, § 205/0.01 et seq.
Ore. Rev. Stat., 180.010 et seq.

Attorney General Career Service Act
Utah Code Ann. 1953, 67-5-6 et seq.

Attorney Unauthorized Compensation Law
Tex. Government Code, § 84.001 et seq.

Attorneys Act
Ill. Comp. Stat., Ch. 710, § 205/0.01 et seq.
La. Rev. Stat. Ann., 37:211 et seq.
Mich. Comp. Laws 1970, 600.901 et seq.
Mont. Code Ann., 37-61-101 et seq.
N.H. Rev. Stat. 1955, 311:1 et seq.
Pa. Purdon's Stat., Title 71, § 732-101 et seq.

Attorneys Act (Commonwealth)
Pa. Purdon's Stat., Title 71, § 732-101 et seq.

Attorneys' Antisolicitation Act
Ohio Rev. Code 1953, 4705.08

Attorneys' Appearance Act (State Bodies)
N.Y. Executive Law 1951 (Consol. Laws Ch. 18) § 168

Attorneys Cummings Act
Tenn. Code Ann., Superseded Vol., 29-110

Attorneys Fees in Wage Actions Act
Ill. Comp. Stat. 1992, Ch. 705, § 225/0.01 et seq.

Attorneys-General Retirement Act
Tenn. Code Ann. 1955, 8-618 et seq.

Attorneys Lien Act
Alaska Stat. 1962, § 34.35.430
Ark. Code Ann. 1987, 16-22-301 et seq.
Colo. Rev. Stat., 12-5-119, 12-5-120

Ill. Comp. Stat. 1992, Ch. 770, §§ 5/0.01, 5/1
Ind. Code Ann., 33-1-3-1
Mass. Gen. Laws Ann., 221:50 to 221:50B
Mo. Rev. Stat., 484.130 et seq.
Mont. Code Ann., 37-61-420, 484.130, 484.140
Neb. Rev. Stat. 1943, 7-108
N.J. Stat. Ann., 2A:13-5
N.Y. Judiciary Law (Consol. Laws Ch. 30) § 475
Okla. Stat. Ann., Title 5, § 6 et seq.
Ore. Rev. Stat., 87.430 et seq.
Pa. 1915 Pamph. Laws 261, No. 154
R.I. Gen. Laws 1956, 9-3-1 et seq.
S.D. Codified Laws 1967, 16-18-21
Wash. Rev. Code Ann., 60.40.010 et seq.
Wis. Stat. Ann., 757.36 et seq.

Attorneys' Professional Corporation Act
Minn. Stat. Ann., 319A.01 et seq.

Attorneys' Professional Service Corporations Act
S.D. Codified Laws 1967, 47-13A-1 et seq.

Attorneys Unauthorized Practice Act
Wis. Stat. Ann., 757.30

AU-Inclusive Program (Elderly Care Act)
Colo. Rev. Stat., 26-16-101 et seq.

Auburn Industrial Development Authority Act
N.Y. Public Authorities Law (Consol. Laws Ch. 43A) § 2300 et seq.

Auburn School Loan Act
Mass. Acts 1952, Ch. 328

Auburndale Urban Renewal Law
Fla. Special Laws 1961, Ch. 61-1687

Auction Act
Neb. Laws 1955, Ch. 266

Auction Act (Livestock)
Ore. Rev. Stat., 599.205 et seq.

Auction Act (Public)
Mont. Code Ann., 30-11-501 et seq.

Auction License Act
Cal. Business and Professions Code § 5700 et seq.
S.D. Codified Laws 1967, 37-14-1 et seq.

Auction Livestock Market Development Act
Neb. Rev. Stat. 1943, 54-1157 et seq.

Auction Market Act (Livestock)
Okla. Stat. Ann., Title 2, § 9-130 et seq.

Auction Sales Act (Jewelry and Appliances)
Wash. Rev. Code Ann., 18.12.010 et seq.

Auction Sales Act (Livestock)
Okla. Stat. Ann., Title 4, § 361 et seq.

Auction Sales Sign Act
Ill. Comp. Stat. 1992, Ch. 720, § 225/0.01 et seq.

Auctioneer and Auction Licensing Act
Cal. Business and Professions Code § 5700 et seq.
Ind. Code Ann., 25-6.1-1-1 et seq.
Pa. Purdon's Stat., Title 63, § 734.1 et seq.

Auctioneer Recovery Fund
S.C. Code Ann. 1976, § 40-6-200 et seq.

Auctioneer Registration Act
Wash. Rev. Code, 1989, 18.11.050 et seq.

Auctioneers Act
Ky. Rev. Stat. 1971, 330.010 et seq.
Mich. Comp. Laws Ann., 446.26 et seq.
Mont. Code Ann., 30-11-501 et seq.
Ore. Rev. Stat., 698.510 et seq.
Pa. Purdon's Stat., Title 63, § 701 et seq.
R.I. Gen. Laws 1956, 5-58-1 et seq.

Auctioneer's License Act
Ida. Code 1947, 54-1301 et seq.
Miss. Code Ann. 1972, § 73-4-1 et seq.

Auctioneers' License Act
Ala. Code 1975, § 34-4-1 et seq.
Ark. Code Ann. 1987, 17-15-102 et seq.
La. Rev. Stat. Ann., 37:3101 et seq.
Va. Code 1950, § 54.1-600 et seq.
Continued

Vt. Stat. Ann. 1959, Title 32, § 7601 et seq.

Auctioneers Recovery Act
Va. Code 1950, § 54-824.22 et seq.

Auctioneers' Registration and Certification Act
Va. Code 1950, § 54.1-600 et seq.

Auctioneers Regulation Act
N.H. Rev. Stat. 1955, 311-B:1 et seq.

Auctions Act
Iowa Code 1981, 546A.1 et seq.
Ky. Rev. Stat. 1971, 330.010 et seq.
La. Rev. Stat. Ann., 37:3101 et seq.
Mich. Comp. Laws 1970, 446.51 et seq.
N.H. Rev. Stat. 1955, 311-B:1 et seq.
Va. Code 1950, § 54.1-600 et seq.
Vt. Stat. Ann., Title 32, § 7601 et seq.
Wash. Rev. Code Ann., 18.11.050 et seq.

Audio-Visual Deposition Act
Va. Code 1950, § 8.01-412.2 et seq.

Audiologists Act
Md. Ann. Code 1974, Art. HO, § 2-101 et seq.

Audiologists and Speech Pathologists Licensure Act
Ark. Code Ann. 1987, 17-97-101 et seq.
Cal. Business and Professions Code § 2530 et seq.
Ga. Code Ann., 43-44-1 et seq.
Me. Rev. Stat. Ann. 1964, Title 32, § 6001 et seq.
Okla. Stat. Ann., Title 59, § 1601 et seq.
S.C. Code Ann. 1976, § 40-67-10 et seq.
Tenn. Code Ann., 63-17-101 et seq.
Utah Code Ann. 1953, 58-41-1 et seq.
Wyo. Stat. Ann., § 33-33-101 et seq.

Audiologists, Hearing Aid Dealers, and Speech-Language Pathologists Act
Md. Ann. Code 1974, Art. HO, § 2-101 et seq.

Audiology and Speech Language Pathology Practice Act
Ill. Rev. Stat. 1991, Ch. 111, § 7901 et seq.
N.M. Stat. Ann., 61-14B-1 et seq.

Audit Act
Haw. Rev. Stat. § 40-1 et seq.
Ill. Rev. Stat. 1981, Ch. 15, § 301-1 et seq.
Iowa Code Ann., 11.24 et seq.
N.M. Stat. Ann., 12-6-1 et seq.

Audit Act (Governmental Account)
Ill. Rev. Stat. 1991, Ch. 85, § 700 et seq.

Audit Act (Local Government)
Colo. Rev. Stat., 29-1-601 et seq.

Audit Act (Municipal)
Ore. Rev. Stat., 297.010 et seq.

Audit Act (Single)
Mass. Gen. Laws Ann., 44:40

Audit Act (State Park)
Ill. Rev. Stat. 1991, Ch. 105, §§ 489.9, 490

Audit Law (County)
Ark. Code Ann. 1987, 10-4-202 et seq., 10-4-216, 10-4-217

Audit Law (School)
Okla. Stat. 1981, Title 70, § 22-101 et seq.

Audit Privilege Act (Environmental, Health and Safety)
Tex. Rev. Civ. Stat., Art. 4447cc et seq.

Audited Financial Reports Law
La. Rev. Stat. Ann., 22:331 et seq., 22:1321 et seq.

Auditing Act (Internal)
Tex. Government Code, § 2102.001 et seq.
Tex. Rev. Civ. Stat., Art. 6252-5d

Auditing Act (Municipal)
Conn. Gen. Stat. Ann., § 7-391 et seq.
Ill. Rev. Stat. 1991, Ch. 24, § 8-8-1 et seq.

Auditor Act (County)
Ohio Rev. Code 1953, 319.01 et seq.

Auditorily Impaired, Learning Disabled, and Visually Impaired Students Act
N.J. Stat. Ann., 18A:72H-1 et seq.

Auditorium Act (Municipal)
N.M. Stat. Ann., 5-3-1 et seq.

Auditorium Authorities Law
Pa. Purdon's Stat., Title 53, §§ 1371 et seq., 23841 et seq.

Auditors Act
Ga. Code Ann., 9-7-1 et seq.
Mass. Gen. Laws Ann., 221:53 et seq.

Auditor's Agent Act
Ky. Acts 1881-82 (Public) Ch. 1304

Augusta City Charter
Ga. Laws 1947, p. 320

Augusta Employees' Pension Fund Act
Ga. Laws 1945, p. 813

Augusta Firemen's Pension Act
Ga. Laws 1925, p. 867

Augusta Officers' and Employees' Tenure Act
Ga. Laws 1937-38 Ex. Sess., p. 938

Augusta Pension Act
Ga. Laws 1945, p. 813

Augusta Pension Act (Firemen)
Ga. Laws 1925, p. 867

Augusta-Richmond County Building Authority Act
Ga. Laws 1952, p. 338

Augusta-Richmond County Charter Commission Act
Ga. Laws 1974, p. 2324

Augusta-Richmond County Coliseum Authority Act
Ga. Laws 1973, p. 3042

Augusta-Richmond County Transportation Act
Ga. Laws 1970, p. 3208

Augusta Tenure Act (Employees and Officers)
Ga. Laws 1937-38 Ex. Sess., p. 938

Augustus F. Hawkins Human Services Reauthorization Act of 1990
Nov. 3, 1990, P.L. 101-501, 42 U.S. Code § 9801 nt.

Augustus F. Hawkins-Robert T. Stafford Elementary and Secondary School Amendments of 1988
May 18, 1994, P.L. 103-252, 42 U.S. Code §§ 9801 nt., 9881 nt.
Oct. 20, 1994, P.L. 103-382, 20 U.S. Code §§ 4901 to 4909
Dec. 21, 1995, P.L. 104-66, 20 U.S. Code § 7451 nt.

Augustus F. Hawkins-Robert T. Stafford Elementary and Secondary School Improvement Amendments of 1988
April 28, 1988, P.L. 100-297, 102 Stat. 130, 20 U.S. Code § 2701 nt.
April 28, 1988, P.L. 100-297, 102 Stat. 274, 20 U.S. Code §§ 3281 et seq.
June 27, 1988, P.L. 100-351, 102 Stat. 661, 20 U.S. Code §§ 2701 nt.
Sept. 9, 1988, P.L. 100-427, 102 Stat. 1612, 25 U.S. Code §§ 17, 2001 nt., 2016a

Aujeszky's Disease Act
Iowa Code 1989, 166C.1 et seq.

Aumend Act (Marriage Licenses)
Ohio Laws Vol. 114, p. 93

Aurora Charter
Nev. Statutes 1864, Ch. 74, p. 110

Aurora Civic Center Act
Ill. Comp. Stat. 1992, Ch. 70, § 225/1 et seq.

Austin Act (Attorneys to Act as Notary Public)
N.Y. Executive Law (Consol. Laws Ch. 18) § 130 et seq.

Austin Charter
Nev. Statutes 1865, Ch. 77, p. 243

Austin Liquor Act
Tenn. Code Ann., 57-3-101 et seq.

Austin-Wicks Act (Public Housing Discrimination)
N.Y. Civil Rights Law (Consol. Laws Ch. 6) § 18a et seq.

Australian Ballot Act
Alaska Stat. 1962, § 15.15.030 et seq.
Colo. Rev. Stat. Replaced Vols., 1-4-207 et seq.
Ga. Code Ann.,21-2-580 et seq.
Ill. Rev. Stat. 1991, Ch. 46, § 16-1 et seq.
Ind. Code Ann., 3-11-8-1 et seq.
Kan. Gen. Stat. 25-106, 25-301 to 25-311, 25-601 to 25-605, 25-608
Md. Ann. Code 1957, Art. 33, § 14-1
Minn. Stat. 1982, 205.04
Mont. Code Ann., 23-1101 et seq.
N.C. Gen. Stat. 1943, §§ 163-135 to 163-155
N.D. Laws 1891, Ch. 66
Neb. Rev. Stat. 1943, 32-417 et seq.
Ohio Rev. Code 1953, 3505.01 et seq.
Ore. Rev. Stat., 249.354 et seq.
S.D. Codified Laws 1967, 12-16-1 et seq.
Tenn. Code Ann., 2-7-101 et seq.
Wis. Stat. Ann., 5.51 et seq.

Austro-Hungarian Friendship Treaty
Haw. Session Laws 1876, p. 166, June 2, 1876

Authorities Act (Sports)
Tenn. Code Ann., 7-67-101 et seq.

Authorities Act for Large Municipalities (Urban Residential Finance)
Ga. Code Ann., 36-41-1 et seq.

Authorities Law (Downtown Development)
Colo. Rev. Stat., 31-25-801 et seq.

Authority Act (Beef Council)
Colo. Rev. Stat., 35-57-101 et seq.

Authority Act (County Water)
Cal. Water Code, Appendix, § 45-1 et seq.

Authority Act (Economic Growth)
Mich. Comp. Laws Ann., 207.801 et seq.

Authority Act (Equestrian Center)
Conn. Public Acts 1995, No. 231

Authority Act (Finance)
N.M. Stat. Ann., 6-21-1 et seq.
Tex. Rev. Civ. Stat., Art. 601c

Authority Act (Health Care)
Okla. Stat. Ann., Title 63, § 5004 et seq.

Authority Act (Housing and Finance)
Colo. Rev. Stat., 29-4-701 et seq.

Authority Act (Postsecondary Educational Facilities)
Ala. Code 1975, § 10-4-701 et seq.

Authority Act (Sheep and Wool)
Colo. Rev. Stat., 35-57.5-101 et seq.

Authority Act (Sports)
Utah Code Ann. 1953, 9-1-301 et seq.

Authority Act for Private Nonprofit Institutions of Higher Learning (Educational Facilities)
Miss. Code Ann. 1972, § 37-104-1 et seq.

Authority Reconstruction Act (Fair and Exposition)
Ill. Comp. Stat. 1992, Ch. 70, § 215/1 et seq.

Authority to Construct—Capital Improvement Act
N.C. Laws 1965, Ch. 944

Authorization Act (County Hospital)
N.M. Stat. Ann., 4-48B-1 et seq.

Authorization for Use of Military Force Against Iraq Resolution
Jan. 14, 1991, P.L. 102-1, 50 U.S. Code § 1541 nt.

Authorized Corporation Protection Act
Tenn. Code Ann., 48-30-101 et seq.

Authorized Insurers Process Act
N.C. Gen. Stat. 1943, § 58-16-35

Authorship Rights Act
La. Rev. Stat. Ann., 51:2131 et seq.
N.Y. Laws 1991, Ch. 994

Autism Act
Me. Rev. Stat. Ann. 1964, Title 34-B, § 6001
et seq.

**Autism and Pervasive Developmental
Disorders Act**
Tex. Human Resources Code, § 114.001 et
seq.

**Autism and Pervasive Developmental
Disorders Act (Interagency Council on)**
Tex. Human Resources Code, § 114.001 et
seq.

Autistic Child Development Act
N.J. Laws 1980, Ch. 76

Auto Accident Reparation Act
Colo. Rev. Stat., 10-4-701 et seq.

Auto Body Repair Study Act
Cal. Business and Professions Code
§ 9889.60 et seq.

Auto Buses Act
N.J. Stat. Ann., 48:4-1 to 48:4-55

Auto Camp Register Law
Cal. Health and Safety Code § 18720 et seq.

Auto Camps Act
Colo. Rev. Stat., 43-5-201 et seq.

Auto Court, Resort and Motel Act
Cal. Health and Safety Code § 18500 et seq.

Auto Dealership Act
Wis. Stat. Ann., 218.01 et seq.

Auto Insurance Nondiscrimination Law
Cal. Insurance Code § 11628

Auto License Act
Ohio Rev. Code 1953, 4503.01 et seq.

Auto Pricing Law
See Automobile Information Disclosure Act

Auto Repair Fraud Prevention Act
Del. Code of 1974, Title 6, § 4901A et seq.

Auto Testing Law
Ark. Pope's Digest 1937, §§ 6793 to 6798

Auto Theft Act
Colo. Rev. Stat., 42-5-101 et seq.
Fla. Stat. 1973, 814.01 et seq.
Mich. Comp. Laws Ann., 257.252 et seq.

Auto Tourist Camps Act
Colo. Rev. Stat., 43-5-201 et seq.

Auto Transportation Act
Fla. Stat. 1983, 323.01 et seq.

Auto Transportation Companies Act
Ida. Code 1947, 61-801 et seq.
Wash. Rev. Code Ann., 81.68.010 et seq.

Auto Truck Transportation Act
Cal. Statutes 1917, Ch. 213, p. 330

Automated Data Processing Act
N.M. Stat. Ann., 15-1-1 et seq.

**Automated Fingerprint Identification
System Policy Council Act**
Mich. Comp. Laws Ann., 2.151 et seq.

**Automated Motor Vehicle Registration
Code**
Ky. Rev. Stat. 1971, 186A.010, 186A.020

Automated Teller Machine Safety Act
N.Y. Banking Law (Consol. Laws Ch. 2)
§ 75a et seq.

Automated Teller Machine Security Act
Ill. Comp. Stat. 1992, Ch. 205, § 695/1 et seq.

Automated Voter Records System Act
N.M. Stat. Ann., 1-5-1 et seq.

Automatic Appeal Act (Death Sentence)
Ala. Code 1975, § 12-22-150

Automatic Appeal Law
Ore. Rev. Stat., 138.410 et seq.

Automatic Bell-Ringer Act (Locomotives)
Ind. Code 1971, 8-8-6-1, 8-8-6-2

Automatic Continuance Act
Fla. Stat. Ann., 11.111

Automatic Coupler Act (Amendment)
See also Safety Appliance Acts (Interstate
Commerce)
March 2, 1903, Ch. 976, 32 Stat. 943, 45 U.S.
Code §§ 8 to 10

Automatic Coupler Act (Interstate Commerce)
See also Safety Appliance Acts (Interstate
Commerce)
March 2, 1893, Ch. 196, 27 Stat. 531, 45 U.S.
Code §§ 1 to 7

Automatic Coupler Act (Railroads)
Ohio Rev. Code 1953, 4963.09

Automatic Couplers Act
Mich. Comp. Laws Ann., 469.181 et seq.

Automatic Fire Door Act
Ohio Rev. Code 1953, 4963.22

Automatic Telephone Dialers Act
Ill. Comp. Stat. 1992, Ch. 815, § 305/1 et seq.

Automobile Accident Reporting Act
N.D. Cent. Code, 39-08-04 et seq.

Automobile Accident Social Protection Act
P.R. Laws Ann. 1954, Title 9, § 2051 et seq.

Automobile Act
Md. Ann. Code 1974, Art. TR, § 11-101 et
seq.
Mo. Rev. Stat., 301.010 et seq.
Pa. Cons. Stat., Title 75, § 101 et seq.
Tenn. Code Ann. 1955, 59-101 et seq.

Automobile and Pickup Truck Acquisition Act
Ark. Code Ann. 1987, 22-8-201 et seq.

Automobile and Traffic Act
P.R. Laws Ann. 1954, Title 9, § 171 et seq.

Automobile Banditry Act
Ind. Code Ann., 35-12-2-1

Automobile Certificate of Title Act
Tenn. Code Ann., 55-3-101 et seq.
Utah Code Ann. 1953, 41-1a-501 et seq.
Wash. Rev. Code Ann., 46.12.005 et seq.

Automobile Club Services Act
Kan. Stat. Ann., 40-2501 et seq.
Mass. Gen. Laws Ann., 174B:1 et seq.
Miss. Code Ann. 1972, § 83-11-201 et seq.
Tex. Rev. Civ. Stat., Art. 1528d

Automobile Company Operators Association Act
Pa. 1921 Pamph. Laws 442, No. 215

Automobile Compulsory Insurance Act
Mass. Gen. Laws Ann., 90:34A et seq.,
175:113A et seq.

Automobile Consent Act (Driving)
Iowa Code Ann., 321.493

Automobile Dealer Tag Permit Act
Miss. Code Ann. 1972, § 27-19-301 et seq.

Automobile Dealers' and Salesmens' Licensing Act
Ohio Rev. Code 1953, 4517.01 et seq.

Automobile Dealers' Anti-Coercion Act
Ark. Code Ann. 1987, 4-75-401 et seq.
Cal. Business and Professions Code
§§ 18400 to 18413
Minn. Stat. 1980, 325.15 et seq., 325D.17 et
seq.

Automobile Dealers' Day in Court Act
Aug. 8, 1956, Ch. 1038, 70 Stat. 1125, 15
U.S. Code §§ 1221 to 1225

Automobile Dealers Day in Court Act
Ga. Code Ann., 10-1-630, 10-1-631

Automobile Dealers' License Act
Colo. Rev. Stat., 12-6-101 et seq.
N.C. Gen. Stat. 1943, § 20-285 et seq.
Wash. Rev. Code Ann., 46.70.005 et seq.

Automobile Driver's License Act
N.C. Gen. Stat. 1943, § 20-5 et seq.

Automobile Equipment Law
Wash. Rev. Code Ann., 46.37.005 et seq.

Automobile Excise Tax Act
Wash. Rev. Code Ann., 82.44.010 et seq.

Automobile Fair Insurance Reform Act
N.J. Stat. Ann., 17:33B-1 et seq.

Automobile Fair Trade Act
Kan. Stat. Ann., 8-601 et seq.

Automobile Finance Act
Mich. Comp. Laws Ann., 492.101 et seq.

Automobile Financial Responsibility Act
D.C. Code 1973, § 40-417 et seq.
Fla. Stat. Ann., 324.011 et seq.
Mich. Comp. Laws Ann., 257.501 et seq.
Minn. Stat. Ann., 65B.001 et seq.
N.Y. Vehicle and Traffic Law 1986 (Consol. Laws Ch. 71) § 330 et seq.
Tenn. Code Ann., 55-12-101 et seq.

Automobile Franchise Act
Cal. Vehicle Code 1959, § 3060 et seq.
Utah Code Ann. 1953, 13-14-1 et seq.
Wyo. Stat. Ann., § 40-15-101 et seq.

Automobile Fuel Efficiency Act of 1980
Oct. 10, 1980, P.L. 96-425, 15 U.S. Code § 1901 nt.

Automobile Full Insurance Availability Act
N.J. Stat. Ann.,17:30E-1 et seq.

Automobile Graveyard Act
Ark. Code Ann. 1987, 27-74-406 et seq.
Ark. Stat. 1947, 76-129 et seq.

Automobile Guest Act
Ala. Code 1975, § 32-1-2
Ark. Stat. 1947, 75-913 et seq.
Cal. Vehicle Code 1959, § 17158
Colo. Rev. Stat., 42-9-101
Conn. Public Acts 1991, p. 4404, Ch. 308
Del. Code of 1974, Title 21, § 6101
Fla. Stat. 1965, 320.59
Ida. Code 1947, 49-1401, 49-1402
Ill. Rev. Stat. 1991, Ch. 95 1/2, §§ 10-201, 10-202
Ind. Code Ann., 9-3-3-1, 9-3-3-2
Iowa Code 1983, 321.494
Kan. Laws 1931, Ch. 81
Mich. Comp. Laws Ann., 257.401
Mont. Code. Ann. 1991, 32-1113 et seq.
N.D. Cent. Code, (Superseded Vol.) 39-15-01 et seq.
Neb. Rev. Stat. 1943, 39-6, 191
Nev. Rev. Stat. 1979 Reprint, Replaced Pages, 41.180
N.M. Stat. Ann. 1953, 64-24-1, 64-24-2
Ohio Rev. 1953, 4515.02
Ore. Rev. Stat., 30.115
S.C. Code Ann. 1976, § 15-1-290 et seq.
S.D. Codified Laws 1967, 32-34-1, 32-34-2
Tex. Civil Practice and Remedies Code, § 72.001 et seq.
Utah Code Ann. 1953, Miscellaneous Superseded Code Provisions, 41-9-1, 41-9-2
Va. Code 1950, § 8.01-63
Vt. Acts 1929, No. 78
Wash. Rev. Code Ann., 46.08.070 et seq.
Wyo. Stat. Ann. Replacement Titles, § 31-5-1116

Automobile Homicide Act
N.Y. Penal Law 1965 (Consol. Laws Ch. 40) §§ 125.10, 125.15, Subd. 1
Utah Code Ann. 1953, 76-5-207

Automobile Host and Guest Act
Wash. Rev. Code Ann., 46.08.070 et seq.

Automobile Information Disclosure Act
July 7, 1958, P.L. 85-506, 72 Stat. 325, 15 U.S. Code §§ 1231, 1232, 1233
Continued

July 28, 1972, P.L. 92-359, 86 Stat. 502, 15
U.S. Code § 1231

Automobile Injury Reparations Act
Iowa Code 1973, 515D.1 et seq.
Kan. Stat. Ann., 40-3101 et seq.

Automobile Inspection Law
Wash. Rev. Code Ann., 46.32.010 et seq.

Automobile Insurance Act
N.H. Rev. Stat. 1955, 268:1 et seq.

Automobile Insurance Act (Mandatory)
Alaska Stat. 1962, § 28.22.001 et seq.

**Automobile Insurance Cancellation Control
Act**
Iowa Code Ann., 515D.1 et seq.
Me. Rev. Stat. Ann. 1964, Title 24-A, § 2911
et seq.

**Automobile Insurance Freedom of Choice
and Cost Containment Act**
N.J. Stat. Ann., 17:28-1.1 et seq.

Automobile Insurance Law (No.Fault)
N.Y. Insurance Law 1984 (Consol. Laws Ch.
28) § 5101 et seq.

Automobile Insurance Plan Act
Vt. Stat. Ann., Title 8, § 4241 et seq.

Automobile Insurance Reform Act
N.J. Stat. Ann., 17:29A-33 et seq.
S.C. Code Ann. 1976, § 38-77-1 et seq.

Automobile Insurance Reparations Act
N.J. Rev. Stat. 1937, 39:6A-1 et seq.
N.Y. Insurance Law (Consol. Laws Ch. 28)
§ 5101 et seq.

Automobile Insurers' Direct Action Act
Wis. Stat. 1973, 260.11

Automobile Larceny Act
Wash. Rev. Code Ann., 9A.56.070

Automobile Law
Cal. Vehicle Code 1959, § 1 et seq.

Automobile Lemon Law
Ga. Code Ann.,10-1-640 et seq.
Pa. 1984 Pamph. Laws 150 No. 28

**Automobile Liability Act (Financial
Responsibility)**
Kan. Laws 1939, Ch. 86
Ky. Rev. Stat. 1971, 187.290 et seq.

Automobile Liability Security Act
Haw. Rev. Stat. Ann., § 287-1 et seq.
Pa. 1933 Pamph. Laws 553, No. 110
Wash. Rev. Code, 46.29.010 et seq.

Automobile License Act
Ark. Code Ann. 1987, 27-14-1001 et seq.
Ind. Code Ann., 9-1-4-1 et seq.
Me. Rev. Stat. Ann. 1964, Title 29, § 101 et
seq.
Wash. Rev. Code Ann., 46.16.006 et seq.

Automobile License Fee Law
Cal. Revenue and Taxation Code § 10701 et
seq.

Automobile Lien Act
Fla. Stat. Ann., 319.27

Automobile Lien Filing Act
Ark. Code Ann. 1987, 27-14-801 et seq.

Automobile Manslaughter Act
Md. Ann. Code 1957, Art. 27, § 388

Automobile Manufacturers' License Act
N.C. Gen. Stat. 1943, § 20-285 et seq.

Automobile National Heritage Area Act
Nov. 6, 1998, P.L. 105-355, Title I, 112 Stat.
3247, 16 U.S. Code § 461 nt.

Automobile No-Fault Insurance Act
Utah Code Ann. 1953, 31A-22-301 et seq.

Automobile Nuisance Act
Kan. Stat. Ann., 41-805

Automobile Operator's License Act
Md. Ann. Code 1974, Art. TR, § 16-101 et
seq.

Wash. Rev. Code Ann., 46.20.011 et seq.

Automobile Owner's Liability Act
Ga. Code 1933, 68-301

Automobile Parking District Act
Cal. Statutes 1941, pp. 1312, 2802

Automobile Parking Law
Wash. Rev. Code Ann., 46.61.575 et seq.

Automobile Registration Act
Ark. Code Ann. 1987, 27-24-201 et seq.
Ga. Code Ann.,40-2-1 et seq.
Kan. Stat. Ann., 8-126 et seq.
Mich. Comp. Laws Ann., 257.201 et seq., 257.801 et seq.
Minn. Stat. Ann., 168.011 et seq.
Ore. Rev. Stat., 481.103 et seq., 803.010
Tenn. Code Ann., 55-3-101 et seq.
Tex. Rev. Civ. Stat., Arts. 6675a-1 et seq.
Va. Code 1950, § 46.1-41 et seq.

Automobile Rental Act
Conn. Gen. Stat. Ann., § 14-154a

Automobile Rental Excise Tax Act
Iowa Code Ann., 422C.1 et seq.

Automobile Renting Occupation and Use Tax Act
Ill. Comp. Stat. 1992, Ch. 55, §§ 5/5-1032, 5/5-1033

Automobile Renting Occupation Tax Act (County)
Ill. Rev. Stat. 1991, Ch. 34, § 5-1032

Automobile Renting Occupation Tax Act (Municipal)
Ill. Rev. Stat. 1991, Ch. 24, § 8-11-7

Automobile Renting Use Tax Act (County)
Ill. Rev. Stat. 1991, Ch. 34, § 5-1033

Automobile Renting Use Tax Act (Municipal)
Ill. Rev. Stat. 1991, Ch. 24, § 8-11-8

Automobile Repair Act
Cal. Business and Professions Code § 9880 et seq.

Automobile Repair Facilities Act
Va. Code 1950, § 59.1-207.1 et seq.

Automobile Reparations Reform Act
Fla. Stat. Ann., 627.730 et seq.
N.J. Stat. Ann., 39:6A-1 et seq.
S.C. Code Ann. 1976, Superseded Vols., § 56-11-10 et seq.

Automobile Retirement Act
La. Rev. Stat. Ann., 30:2064

Automobile Right of Way Act
Md. Ann. Code 1974, Art. TR, § 21-401 et seq.

Automobile Sales Act
N.J. Stat. Ann., 39:10-1 et seq.

Automobile Sales Finance Act
Cal. Civil Code § 2981 et seq.

Automobile Salesmen's License Act
N.C. Gen. Stat. 1943, § 20-285 et seq.

Automobile Seat Belt Law
N.Y. Vehicle and Traffic Law 1959 (Consol. Laws Ch. 69) § 1229c

Automobile Seat Belt Usage Act (Passenger)
N.J. Laws 1984, Ch. 179

Automobile Services Act
La. Rev. Stat. Ann., 22:1401 et seq., 22:1751 et seq.

Automobile Speed Act
Ohio Rev. Code 1953, 4511.21
Wash. Rev. Code Ann., 46.61.400 et seq.

Automobile Tax Act
June 25, 1940, Ch. 419, 54 Stat. 522 (See 26 U.S. Code §§ 4061 to 4063, 6416(c))
Neb. Rev. Stat. 1943, 60-101 et seq.
Tenn. Code Ann., 55-4-101 et seq.

Automobile Teenage Protection Act
Ga. Code Ann., 40-5-63, 40-6-255

Automobile Theft Prevention Act
Pa. Purdon's Stat., Title 40, § 3601 et seq.

Automobile Title Registration Act
Fla. Stat. Ann., 320.01 et seq.
La. Rev. Stat. Ann. 1950, 32:701 et seq.

Automobile Transportation Company Act
Ky. Rev. Stat. 1971, 281.010 et seq.

Automobile Use Vicarious Liability Law
N.Y. Vehicle and Traffic Law 1959 (Consol.
Laws Ch. 71) § 388

Automobile Wreckers Act
Wash. Rev. Code Ann., 46.80.005 et seq.

Automobiles Title Act
Neb. Rev. Stat. 1943, 60-101 et seq.

Automotive Consumer Notification Act
Cal. Civil Code §§ 1793.23, 1793.24

Automotive Dismantlers and Parts Recycler Act
Okla. Stat. Ann., Title 47, § 591.1 et seq.

Automotive Products Trade Act of 1965
Oct. 21, 1965, P.L. 89-283, 79 Stat. 1016, 19
U.S. Code §§ 1202, 2001, 2011 to 2015,
2021 to 2024, 2031 to 2033
Nov. 6, 1978, P.L. 95-598, 19 U.S. Code
§ 2022
Aug. 23, 1988, P.L. 100-418, 102 Stat. 1157,
19 U.S. Code § 2011

Automotive Propulsion Research and Development Act of 1978
Feb. 25, 1978, P.L. 95-238, 15 U.S. Code
§ 2701 et seq.
Nov. 2, 1994, P.L. 103-437, 15 U.S. Code
§ 2703
Dec. 21, 1995, P.L. 104-66, 15 U.S. Code
§ 2704

Automotive Repair Act
Cal. Business and Professions Code § 9880 et
seq.

Ill. Comp. Stat. 1992, Ch. 815, § 306/1 et seq.

Automotive Transportation Act
Ore. Rev. Stat., 767.005 et seq.

Autonomy Act
Aug. 29, 1916, Ch. 416, 39 Stat. 545

Autopsy Act
Ill. Comp. Stat. 1992, Ch. 410, § 505/0.01 et
seq.
P.R. Laws Ann. 1954, Title 24, § 731a et seq.
Tenn. Code Ann., 38-7-101 et seq.

Auxiliary Services Act
Mich. Comp. Laws Ann., 340.622

Auxiliary Street Opening Bond Act
Cal. Streets and Highways Code § 4500 et
seq.

Availability Act (Health Care)
Colo. Rev. Stat., 13-64-101 et seq.

Availability and Simplification of Bank Credit Act
Pa. 1994 Pamph. Laws, No. 167

Average Annual Earnings (Abshire-Maloney-John McCarthy-Murdy-J. Howard Williams Bill)
Cal. Labor Code §§ 4452, 4453, 4455, 4460,
4702

Average Rate Law
N.J. Stat. Ann., 54:29A-13 to 54:29-20

Aviation Act
Ky. Rev. Stat. 1971, 183.010 et seq.
N.M. Stat. Ann., 64-1-11 et seq.
Pa. 1984 Pamph. Laws No. 164
Va. Code 1950, § 5.1-1 et seq.

Aviation Authority Act
Iowa Code Ann., 330A.1 et seq.
Va. Code 1950, § 5.1-1 et seq.

Aviation Authority Act (Greater Orlando)
Fla. Special Laws 1957, Ch. 57-1658
Fla. Special Laws 1975, Ch. 75-464

Aviation Authority Act (Hernando County)
Fla. Special Laws 1965, Ch. 65-1623

Aviation Authority Special Purpose Facilities Revenue Bond Law (Hillsborough County)
Fla. Special Laws 1961, Ch. 61-2261

Aviation Cadet Act of 1942
Oct. 25, 1943, Ch. 275, 57 Stat. 574

Aviation Career Incentive Act of 1974
May 31, 1974, P.L. 93-294, 88 Stat. 177, 37 U.S. Code §§ 301, 301a

Aviation Code
Pa. Cons. Stat., Title 74, § 5101 et seq.

Aviation Commission Act
Ala. General Acts 1943, p. 205
Md. Ann. Code 1974, Art. TR, § 5-101 et seq.
Okla. Stat. Ann., Title 3, § 72 et seq.

Aviation Day Act
May 11, 1939, Ch. 123, 53 Stat. 739, 36 U.S. Code § 151

Aviation Development Act
Pa. Cons. Stat., Title 74, § 6101 et seq.

Aviation Disaster Family Assistance Act of 1996
Oct. 9, 1996, P.L. 104-264, Title VII, 49 U.S. Code § 40101 nt.

Aviation Districts Act
Ill. Rev. Stat. 1943, Ch. 15 1/2, § 23 et seq.

Aviation Drug-Trafficking Control Act
Oct. 19, 1984, P.L. 98-499, 49 U.S. Code Appx. § 1301 nt.

Aviation Education Program Act
Cal. Education Code 1959, §§ 8401 et seq., 78270, 33115 et seq.

Aviation Guest Act
Ill. Rev. Stat. 1975, Ch. 15 1/2, § 22.83

Aviation Hall of Fame Act
Ga. Code Ann., 50-12-70 et seq.

Aviation Insurance Reauthorization Act of 1997
Dec. 2, 1997, P.L. 105-137, 49 U.S. Code § 40101 nt.

Aviation Medical Assistance Act of 1998
April 24, 1998, P.L. 105-170, 49 U.S. Code § 44701 nt.

Aviation Pilots Act
Nov. 5, 1941, Ch. 468, 55 Stat. 759 (See 10 U.S. Code § 6915; 14 U.S. Code §§ 758a, 759a)

Aviation Safety and Capacity Expansion Act of 1990
Nov. 5, 1990, P.L. 101-508, 49 U.S. Code Appx. §§ 106, 2201 nt., 2226a to 2226c
Oct. 31, 1992, P.L. 102-581, 49 U.S. Code Appx. § 2226b

Aviation Safety and Noise Abatement Act of 1979
Feb. 18, 1980, P.L. 96-193, 49 U.S. Code §§ 2101 nt., 2101 et seq.
Dec. 30, 1987, P.L. 100-223, 49 U.S. Code Appx. §§ 2101, 2104
Oct. 28, 1991, P.L. 102-143, 49 U.S. Code Appx. § 2104
Aug. 23, 1994, P.L. 103-305, 49 U.S. Code Appx. § 1348 nt.

Aviation Safety Commission Act of 1986
Oct. 18, 1986, P.L. 99-500, 49 U.S. Code § 106 nt.
Oct. 30, 1986, P.L. 99-591, 49 U.S. Code § 106 nt.

Aviation Safety Research Act of 1988
Nov. 3, 1988, P.L. 100-591, 49 U.S. Code Appx. § 1301 nt.

Aviation Security Improvement Act of 1990
Nov. 16, 1990, P.L. 101-604, 22 U.S. Code §§ 5501 to 5513; 49 U.S. Code § 106; 49 U.S. Code Appx. §§ 1301 nt., 1652b, 1652b nt.

Aviation Service Act
July 18, 1914, Ch. 186, 38 Stat. 514

Avifaunal Emblem Law
Cal. Government Code § 423

Avocado, Mango and Lime Sales Law
Fla. Stat. Ann., 570.55

Award Exemption Act (Agent Orange)
Mich. Comp. Laws Ann., 35.1071, 35.1072

Award for Excellence in Education Program Act
Wash. Rev. Code 1983, 28A.625.010 et seq.

Award for Excellence in Teacher Preparation Act
Wash. Rev. Code 1983, 28A.625.350 et seq.

Award Program Act (State Scholarship)
Neb. Rev. Stat. 1943, 85-980 et seq.

Award Restoration Act (Student Assistance)
Tenn. Code Ann., 49-4-801 et seq.

Awards and Decorations Act
Okla. Stat. 1981, Title 44 § 195.1 et seq.

Awareness and Compliance Act (Selective Service Registration)
Mo. Laws 1999, H.B. No. 415

Awareness of Consumers Contracts Act
Cal. Civil Code § 1799.200 et seq.

Axle-Mile Tax Act
Ohio Rev. Code 1953, 5728.01 et seq.

Axle Weight Act
Ga. Code Ann., 32-6-20 et seq.

Ayala-Baca Economic Development Act
Cal. Statutes 1993, 1st Ex. Sess., Ch. 1

Ayala-Mojonnier Electronic Home Detention Act
Cal. Penal Code § 1203.016

Ayala-Monteith-Johannessen Mandate Relief and Reform Act
Cal. Government Code §§ 17526, 17553 et seq.
Cal. Revenue and Taxation Code § 2246

Ayer Sewer Loan Act
Mass. Acts 1949, Ch. 300
Mass. Acts 1960, Ch. 167

B

B-Girl Act
Alaska Stat. 1962, § 04.15.090
Cal. Business and Professions Code § 25657
Fla. Stat. 1965, 562.131

Babcock Amendment (Taxation of Motor Vehicles)
Minn. Const. 1857, Art. 16, § 9

Babcock Test Act
Ky. Rev. Stat. 1971, 260.775 et seq.

Baby Bonds
See Savings Bond Act

Baby Brokers Act
D.C. Code Ann., § 32-1001 et seq.

Baby Chicks and Eggs Acts
Iowa Code Ann., 168.1 et seq.
S.C. Code Ann. 1976, § 39-39-10 et seq.

Baby Doe Amendment
Oct. 9, 1984, P.L. 98-457, 42 U.S. Code §§ 5101 nt., 5102, 5102 nt., 5103, 5103 nt.

Baby Doe Provision
Mont. Code Ann., 41-3-102

Baby Richard Law
Ill. Comp. Stat. 1992, Ch. 750, § 50/1 et seq.

Baby Wagner Act (Labor Relations)
Conn. Gen. Stat. Ann., § 31-101 et seq.
Mass. Gen. Laws Ann., 150A:1 et seq.
Pa. Purdon's Stat., Title 43, § 211.1 et seq.
R.I. Gen. Laws 1956, 28-7-1 et seq.
Utah Code Ann. 1953, 34-19-1 et seq.
Va. Code 1950, § 8.4-101 et seq.
Wis. Stat. Ann., 111.01 et seq.

Baca-Ayala Economic Development Act
Cal. Statutes 1993, 1st Ex. Sess., Ch. 2

Baca Location No. 1 Land Acquisition and Study Act of 1990
Nov. 15, 1990, P.L. 101-556, 104 Stat. 2762

Baccalaureate Assistance Law for Registered Nurses
Ill. Comp. Stat. 1992, Ch. 110, § 915/1 et seq.

Baccalaureate Bond Act
Ore. Rev. Stat., 286.700 et seq.

Baccalaureate Education Savings for Tennessee Act
Tenn. Code Ann., 49-7-901 et seq.

Baccalaureate Education System Trust Act
Tenn. Code Ann., 49-7-801 to 49-7-806
Tenn. Public Acts 1991, Ch. 281

Baccalaureate Savings Act
Ill. Comp. Stat. 1992, Ch. 110, § 920/1 et seq.

Bach-Juett-Daniels Act (Counties-Leases)
Ky. Acts 1940, Ch. 44

Bach-Scheben Act (Needy Blind)
Ky. Rev. Stat. 1971, Superseded Vols., 207.010 et seq.

Bacharach Act (Salaries of Customs Employees)
May 29, 1928, Ch. 865, 45 Stat. 955

Back Pay Act
March 30, 1966, P.L. 89-380, 80 Stat. 94

Back Tax Act (Realty)
Mo. Rev. Stat., 140.010 et seq.

Back Tax Law
Ark. Stat. 1947, 84-4001 et seq.

Backbone Grant Act (Texas Pacific Railroad)
March 3, 1871, Ch. 122, 16 Stat. 573

Background Check Act (Health Care Worker)
Ill. Comp. Stat. 1992, Ch. 225, § 46/1 et seq.

Background Check Act (Kari Koskinen Manager)
Minn. Stat. Ann., 299C.66 et seq.

Background Check System Act (Instant Criminal)
Colo. Rev. Stat., 12-26.5-101 et seq.

Bacon-Davis Act (Wage Rates)
See Davis-Bacon Act

Bad Check Act (Hotels)
La. Rev. Stat. Ann., 21:21

Bad Check Acts
Ala. Code 1975, § 13A-9-13.1 et seq.
Cal. Penal Code § 476a
Colo. Rev. Stat., 18-5-205
Conn. Gen. Stat. Ann., § 53a-128
D.C. Code 1973, § 22-1410
Ida. Code 1947, 18-3106
Iowa Code Ann., 714.1
Kan. Stat. Ann., 21-3707 et seq.
La. Rev. Stat. Ann., 14:71
Mich. Comp. Laws Ann., 750.131 et seq.
Minn. Stat. Ann., 609.535
Miss. Code Ann. 1972, §§ 11-7-12, 97-19-1 et seq.
Mo. Rev. Stat., 570.120
Mont. Code Ann., 45-6-316
N.C. Gen. Stat. 1943, §§ 14-106 to 14-107.1
Neb. Rev. Stat. 1943, 28-611
Nev. Rev. Stat. 1973 Reprint, 205.130
N.H. Rev. Stat. 1955, 507:7
N.M. Stat. Ann., 30-36-1 et seq.
R.I. Gen. Laws 1956, 19-19-2 et seq.
S.C. Code Ann. 1976, § 34-11-60 et seq.
S.D. Codified Laws 1967, 22-41-1 et seq.
Tenn. Code Ann., 39-14-121 et seq.
Tex. Penal Code, § 31.06
Va. Code 1950, § 18.2-181 et seq.
Vt. Stat. Ann., Title 9, § 2311 et seq.
Wash. Rev. Code Ann., 9A.56.060
W. Va. Code 1966, § 61-3-39 et seq.
Wyo. Stat. Ann., § 6-3-701 et seq.

Bad Check Law (District of Columbia)
July 1, 1922, Ch. 273, 42 Stat. 820

Bad Faith Act (Insurance Companies)
Ga. Code Ann., 33-4-6

Badham-Marks Environmental Protection and Research Act
Cal. Health and Safety Code §§ 39069 to 39074
Cal. Vehicle Code 1959, § 5100 et seq.

Baer-Martin Act (Alcoholic Study Commission)
Ky. Acts 1952, Ch. 32

Baggage Act
Ark. Stat. 1947, 23-10-209 et seq.

Bagley-Burton-Moscone Citizens' Income Security Act for Aged, Blind and Disabled Californians
Cal. Welfare and Institutions Code § 12000 et seq.

Bagley-Nejedly-Z'berg Suisun Marsh Preservation Act
Cal. Fish and Game Code 1957, § 1850 et seq.

Bail Act (Criminal)
S.C. Code Ann. 1976, § 17-15-110 et seq.

Bail Act (Fugitives)
Colo. Rev. Stat., 16-19-116 et seq.

Bail Act (Quasi-Criminal and Misdemeanor)
Ill. Rev. Stat. 1991, Ch. 16, § 80 et seq.

Bail Agency Act (District of Columbia)
D.C. Code Ann., § 23-1301 et seq.

Bail and Arrest Act (Civil Actions)
S.C. Code Ann. 1976, § 15-17-10 et seq.
S.D. Codified Laws 1967, 15-22-1 et seq.

Bail and Recognizance Reform Act
N.H. Rev. Stat. 1955, 597:1 et seq.

Bail and Recognizances Act
S.C. Code Ann. 1976, § 17-15-10 et seq.

Bail Approval Commissioner Act
Pa. Cons. Stat., Title 42, § 5702 et seq.

Bail Bond Act
Ill. Rev. Stat. 1979, Ch. 16, § 51 et seq.
Tex. Code of Criminal Procedure, Art. 17.01 et seq.
Wash. Rev. Code Ann., 10.19.040 et seq.

Bail Bond False Statement Act
Ill. Comp. Stat. 1992, Ch. 720, §§ 540/0.01, 540/1

Bail Bond Procedure Act (State and Municipal Traffic)
Okla. Stat. Ann., Title 22, § 1115 et seq.

Bail Bond Regulation Law
Cal. Insurance Code § 1800 et seq.

Bail Bondsmen Licensing Law
N.M. Stat. Ann., 59A-51-1 et seq.

Bail Bondsmen Qualification Law
Fla. Stat. 1983, 648.25 et seq.

Bail Bondsmens Act
Ind. Code Ann., 27-10-1-1 et seq.
Nev. Rev. Stat. 1979 Reprint, 697.010 et seq.

Bail Code
Ind. Code Ann., 27-10-1-1 et seq.
Me. Rev. Stat. Ann. 1964, Title 15, § 1001 et seq.
Mich. Comp. Laws Ann., 765.1 et seq.

Bail Commissioners Act
Ill. Rev. Stat. 1991, Ch. 73, § 1091.9 et seq.

Bail Deposit Act (Traffic Offenses or Misdemeanors)
Mich. Comp. Laws Ann., 780.61 et seq.

Bail in Civil Cases Act
Ill. Rev. Stat. 1961, Ch. 16, §§ 1 to 25

Bail Procedure Act
Conn. Gen. Stat. Ann., § 54-63a et seq.

Bail Reform Act
Ala. Code 1975, § 15-13-100 et seq.
Mass. Acts 1966, Ch. 681
Tenn. Code Ann., 40-11-101 et seq.

Bail Reform Act of 1966
June 22, 1966, P.L. 89-465, 80 Stat. 214, 18 U.S. Code §§ 3041, 3141 to 3143, 3146 to 3152, 3568

Bail Reform Act of 1984
Oct. 12, 1984, P.L. 98-473, 18 U.S. Code § 3141 nt.

Bailee Embezzlement Act
Kan. Stat. Ann., 21-547

Bailee's Lien Act
Ohio Rev. Code 1953, 1333.41

Bailey Merchant Marine Act
June 29, 1940, Ch. 442, 54 Stat. 684, 46 U.S. Code § 1242a

Bailiff Act
Haw. Rev. Stat. Ann., § 606-14

Bailment Act
Pa. 1947 Pamph. Laws 1140, No. 477
S.C. Code Ann. 1976, Superseded Vols. § 27-23-80

Bailment Insurance Act
Ill. Comp. Stat. 1992, Ch. 765, § 1015/0.01 et seq.

Bailor Responsibility Act (Motor Vehicle)
Conn. Gen. Stat. 1958, § 14-154a

Bait Advertising Acts
Ga. Code Ann., 10-1-420 et seq.
Miss. Code Ann. 1972, § 75-24-5

Bait and Switch Act
Miss. Code Ann. 1972, § 75-24-5

Bait Shrimp Act
Ala. Code 1975, § 9-12-55 et seq.

Bait Shrimp Law (Duval County)
Fla. Special Laws 1970, Ch. 70-678

Baiting and Fighting Act (Animal)
S.C. Code Ann. 1976, § 16-27-10 et seq.

Baker Act (Banking)
Ohio Laws Vol. 115, p. 121

Baker Act (Mental Health)
Fla. Stat. 1983, 394.451 et seq.

**Baker-Andall-Boatwright-Johnston Delta
Protection Act**
Cal. Public Resources Code § 29700 et seq.

Baker Ballot Act
Pa. 1893 Pamph. Laws 419, No. 318

**Baker County Development Commission
Act**
Fla. Special Laws 1957, Ch. 57-1129

**Baker-Katz-Kopp-Campbell Transpor-
tation Blueprint for Twenty-First
Century**
Cal. Statutes 1989, Ch. 106

**Baker-Kopp-Katz Transportation Blueprint
for Twenty-First Century**
Cal. Statutes 1989, Ch. 105

**Baker-Metcalf Act (Discrimination in
Housing Accommodations)**
N.Y. Civil Rights Law (Consol. Laws Ch. 6)
§ 18b, Subd. 3
N.Y. Executive Law 1951 (Consol. Laws Ch.
18) §§ 292, Subd. 12, 296, Subd. 5

Baker's Descent Law
Neb. Laws 1889, Ch. 57

**Bakersfield Metropolitan Transit District
Act**
Cal. Public Utilities Code § 101000 et seq.

Bakery Act
Pa. Purdon's Stat., Title 43, § 403 et seq.
Wash. Rev. Code Ann., 69.12.010 et seq.
Wis. Stat. 1985, 97.36, 97.40.

Bakery Sanitation Law
Cal. Health and Safety Code § 28190 et seq.

Balanced Budget Act of 1997
Aug. 5, 1997, P.L. 105-33, 111 Stat. 251

Aug. 5, 1997, P.L. 105-34, 42 U.S. Code
§§ 254c-2, 5701 nt.
Nov. 13, 1997, P.L. 105-78, 26 U.S. Code
§ 5701 nt.
Nov. 19, 1997, P.L. 105-100, 40 U.S. Code
§§ 138, 1396b, 1396d, 1397dd, 1397ee,
1397jj
Nov. 26, 1997, P.L. 105-119, 47 U.S. Code
§ 254 nt.
July 16, 1998, P.L. 105-200, 42 U.S. Code
§ 608 nt.
Oct. 21, 1998, P.L. 105-277, 26 U.S. Code
§§ 3121, 3121 nt.; 42 U.S. Code §§ 410,
1395fff nt.

**Balanced Budget and Emergency Deficit
Control Act of 1985**
Dec. 12, 1985, P.L. 99-177, 2 U.S. Code
§§ 602, 621 nt., 622, 631 et seq., 651 et seq.,
901 et seq., 921, 922; 31 U.S. Code
§§ 1104, 1105, 1106, 1109; 42 U.S. Code
§ 911
July 7, 1986, P.L. 99-366, 2 U.S. Code § 902
nt.
Aug. 10, 1987, P.L. 100-86, 2 U.S. Code
§§ 905, 906
Sept. 29, 1987, P.L. 100-119, 2 U.S. Code
§§ 901 et seq., 901 nt.
Dec. 22, 1987, P.L. 100-203, 2 U.S. Code
§ 901
Aug. 9, 1989, P.L. 101-73, 2 U.S. Code
§§ 905, 906
Dec. 12, 1989, P.L. 101-220, 2 U.S. Code
§ 905
Nov. 5, 1990, P.L. 101-508, 2 U.S. Code
§§ 601, 900 to 907, 900 nt. 907a to 907d,
Nov. 5, 1990, P.L. 101-509, 2 U.S. Code
§ 906
June 13, 1991, P.L. 102-54, 2 U.S. Code
§ 905
Oct. 24, 1992, P.L. 102-486, 2 U.S. Code
§ 905
Oct. 29, 1992, P.L. 102-572, 2 U.S. Code
§ 905
Aug. 10, 1993, P.L. 103-66, 2 U.S. Code
§§ 900 to 907 et seq. nts., 901, 902, 904
Sept. 30, 1993, P.L. 103-87, 2 U.S. Code
§ 901
Aug. 23, 1994, P.L. 103-306, 2 U.S. Code
§ 901

Sept. 13, 1994, P.L. 103-322, 2 U.S. Code §§ 901a, 904

Oct. 13, 1994, P.L. 103-354, 2 U.S. Code §§ 901, 902

March 29, 1996, P.L. 104-121, 2 U.S. Code § 901

Aug. 22, 1996, P.L. 104-193, 2 U.S. Code §§ 901, 905, 906

Sept. 30, 1996, P.L. 104-208, 2 U.S. Code §§ 901, 905

Oct. 19, 1996, P.L. 104-316, 2 U.S. Code § 904

Aug. 5, 1997, P.L. 105-33, 2 U.S. Code §§ 900, 900 nt., 901, 901a , 902, 905 to 908, 922

Nov. 19, 1997, P.L. 105-89, 2 U.S. Code § 901

June 9, 1998, P.L. 105-178, 2 U.S. Code §§ 900, 901

Balanced Budget and Emergency Deficit Control Reaffirmation Act of 1987

Sept. 29, 1987, P.L. 100-119, 2 U.S. Code §§ 622, 632, 642, 684, 687, 901 et. seq.; 31 U.S. Code §§ 1105, 3101; 42 U.S. Code §§ 1306-8 nt., 1395ww nt.

Dec. 22, 1987, P.L. 100-203, 42 U.S. Code § 1395ww nt.

Balanced Budget Downpayment Act, I

Jan. 26, 1996, P.L. 104-99, 110 Stat. 26

April 26, 1996, P.L. 104-134, 12 U.S. Code § 1710 nt.

Sept. 26, 1996, P.L. 104-204, 42 U.S. Code §§ 1437a nt., 1710 nt.

Aug. 5, 1997, P.L. 105-33, 12 U.S. Code § 1710 nt.

Oct. 27, 1997, P.L. 105-65, 42 U.S. Code §§ 1437a nt., 1437f nt.

Oct. 21, 1998, P.L. 105-276, 42 U.S. Code §§ 1437 nt., 1437d nt.

Balanced Budget Note Act

Ill. Comp. Stat. 1992, Ch. 25, § 80/1 et seq.

Balanced Growth Policy Act

N.C. Gen. Stat. 1943, § 143-506.6 et seq.

Balanced Treatment for Creation—Science and Evolution—Science Act

Ark. Stat. 1947, 80-1663 et seq.

La. Rev. Stat. Ann., 17:286.1 et seq.

Balancing Agriculture with Industry Act

Miss. Code Ann. 1972, § 57-1-1 et seq.

Bald Eagle Protection Act

June 8, 1940, Ch. 278, 54 Stat. 250, 16 U.S. Code §§ 668, 668 nt., 668a to 668d

Oct. 24, 1962, P.L. 87-884, 76 Stat. 1246, 16 U.S. Code §§ 668, 668a

Bald Mountain Water and Sewer Authority Act

Ga. Laws 1983, p. 4466

Baldwin Amendment

Aug. 28, 1965, P.L. 89-139, 23 U.S. Code § 402(a)

Baldwin-Steele Act (Workmen's Death Benefits)

Mich. Comp. Laws 1948, 412.8

Ball Act (Rents in District of Columbia)

Oct. 22, 1919, Ch. 80, 41 Stat. 298

Aug. 24, 1921, Ch. 91, 42 Stat. 200

May 22, 1922, Ch. 197, 42 Stat. 543

Ball-Aigler Act (Corporations)

Ohio Rev. Code 1953, 1701.01 et seq.

Ballistic Knife Prohibition Act of 1986

Oct. 27, 1986, P.L. 99-570, 15 U.S. Code § 1241 nt.

Nov. 18, 1988, P.L. 100-690, 15 U.S. Code § 1245

Ballistic Missile Defense Act of 1995

Feb. 10, 1996, P.L. 104-106, Division A, Title II, Subtitle C, 10 U.S. Code § 2431 nt.

Nov. 18, 1997, P.L. 105-85, 10 U.S. Code § 2431 nt.

Balloon Dart Game Permit Act

Ill. Rev. Stat. 1991, Ch, 111 1/2, § 4091-1 et seq.

Balloon Mortgage Act

Fla. Stat. 1965, 697.05

Balloon Payment Act
S.C. Code Ann. 1976, §§ 37-2-405 et seq.,
37-3-402 et seq.

Balloon Payments Act
N.C. Gen. Stat. 1943, § 25A-34

Ballot Acts
Ala. Code 1975, § 17-8-1 et seq.
Alaska Stat. 1962, § 15.15.030
Colo. Stat. Ann. 1935, Ch. 59, § 197 et seq.
Ga. Code Ann., 21-2-280 et seq.
Ill. Rev. Stat. 1991, Ch. 46, § 16-1 et seq.
Md. Ann. Code 1957, Art. 33, § 16-1 et seq.
Mich. Comp. Laws Ann., 168.684 et seq.
Mont. Code Ann., 13-12-201 et seq.
Neb. Rev. Stat. 1943, 32-501 et seq.
Nev. Rev. Stat. 1979 Reprint, 293.256 et seq.
N.H. Rev. Stat. 1955, 59:2 et seq.
Vt. Stat. Ann., Title 17, § 2471 et seq.
Wash. Rev. Code Ann., 29.30.010 et seq.

Ballot Law Commission Act
Mass. Gen. Laws Ann., 55B:1 et seq.
N.H. Rev. Stat. 1955, 665:1 et seq.

Ballot Paper Purchase Law
Cal. Elections Code 1961, § 10004

Ballot Positioning Act
N.M. Stat. Ann., 1-10A-1 et seq.

Ballot Recount Act
Mich. Comp. Laws Ann., 168.861 et seq.

Ballot Reform Act
N.Y. Laws 1890, Ch. 262
Pa. 1891 Pamph. Laws 349, No. 289
Pa. 1893 Pamph. Laws 419, Ch. 318
Pa. 1913 Pamph. Laws 1001, No. 457

Balloting Procedures Act (Absentees)
Miss. Code Ann. 1972, § 23-15-621 et seq.

Balm Act (Heart)
Fla. Stat. Ann., 771.04 et seq.
Me. Rev. Stat. Ann. 1964, Title 14, § 854

Baltimore City Annexation Act
Md. Laws 1918, Ch. 82

Baltimore City Juvenile Court Act
Md. Laws 1943, Ch. 818, § 1

Baltimore City Port Development Act
Md. Laws 1951, Ch. 200

Baltimore City Tax Sale Act
Md. Laws 1941, Ch. 540

Baltimore County Parking Authority Act
Md. Laws 1951, Ch. 345

Baltimore County Zoning Enabling Act
Md. Laws 1941, Ch. 247

Bancroft Bonding Act (Municipal Improvements)
Ore. Rev. Stat. 1953, 223.205 et seq.

Bandelier National Monument Administrative Improvement and Watershed Protection Act of 1998
Nov. 12, 1998, P.L. 105-376, 112 Stat. 3388,
16 U.S. Code § 431 nt.

Banding and Confederating Act
Ky. Rev. Stat. 1971, 506.040 et seq.

Bangladesh Disaster Assistance Act of 1988
Oct. 31, 1988, P.L. 100-576, 7 U.S. Code
§ 1691 nt.

Bang's Disease Act
N.C. Gen. Stat. 1943, §§ 106-388 to 106-398

Bang's Disease Control Act
Ill. Rev. Stat. 1991, Ch. 8. § 134 et seq.
Mo. Rev. Stat., 267.011 et seq.
Neb. Rev. Stat. 1943, 54-1367 et seq.
N.Y. Agriculture and Markets Law (Consol.
Laws Ch. 69) § 90
Ohio Rev. Code 1953, 941.21 et seq.
Okla. Stat. 1981, Title 2, § 6-91 et seq.
Ore. Laws 1939, Ch. 503
Va. Code 1950, § 3.1-749 et seq.

Bank Acquisition and Bank Holding Company Act
Conn. Gen. Stat. Ann., § 36-418 et seq.

Bank Act
Cal. Statutes 1909, p. 87
Haw. Rev. Stat. Ann., § 412:5-100 et seq.
Mich. Comp. Laws 1948, 487.23 et seq.
Mont. Code Ann., 32-1-101 et seq.
Neb. Rev. Stat. 1943, 8-101 et seq.
Nev. Rev. Stat. 1979 Reprint, 657.005 et seq.
Ore. Rev. Stat., 706.005 et seq.
S.C. Code Ann. 1976, § 34-3-10 et seq.

Bank Act (Consumer Credit)
Me. Rev. Stat. Ann. 1964, Title 35-A, § 2901 et seq.
N.M. Stat. Ann., 58-1A-1 et seq.

Bank Act (Development)
Miss. Code Ann. 1972, § 31-25-1 et seq.

Bank Act (Rural Bond)
Ill. Rev. Stat. 1991, Ch. 17, § 7201-1 et seq.

Bank Act (Savings)
La. Rev. Stat. Ann., 6:1131 et seq.

Bank Act (Service Resource)
P.R. Laws Ann. 1954, Title 10, § 2221 et seq.

Bank Adverse Claims Act
Miss. Code Ann. 1972, § 81-5-67

Bank Agency Act (International)
Ga. Code Ann., 7-1-710 et seq.

Bank and Corporation Franchise Tax Act
Cal. Revenue and Taxation Code § 23101 et seq.

Bank and Corporation Tax Fairness, Simplification, and Conformity Act
Cal. Business and Professions Code § 23438
Cal. Revenue and Taxation Code § 17087.5 et seq.

Bank and Corporation Tax Law
Cal. Revenue and Taxation Code § 23001 et seq.

Bank and Trust Company Act
Conn. Gen. Stat. Ann., § 36-53 et seq.

Bank and Trust Company Insurance Powers Act
Del. Laws, Vol. 67, Ch. 223

Bank Branch Act
N.C. Gen. Stat. 1943, § 53-62
N.J. Rev. Stat. 1937, 17:9A-19 et seq.

Bank Branching Act (Interstate)
Miss. Code Ann. 1972, § 81-23-1 et seq.

Bank Bribery Amendments Act of 1985
Aug. 4, 1986, P.L. 99-370, 18 U.S. Code §§ 201 nt., 215, 215 nt.

Bank Checks Act
Ind. Burns' 1933, 18-2501 to 18-2517

Bank Collection Code
Ida. Code 1947, 28-4-101 et seq.
Ill. Rev. Stat. 1991, Ch. 26, § 4-101 et seq.
Ind. Burns' 1933, 18-2501 to 18-2517
Ky. Rev. Stat. 1971, 355.4-101 et seq.
Md. Ann. Code 1974, Art. CL, 4-201 et seq.
Mich. Comp. Laws 1948, 487.601 et seq.
Mo. Rev. Stat. 1959, 402.010 et seq.
N.J. Stat. 12A:4-101
N.M. Stat. Ann. 1953, 48-9-1 et seq.
N.Y. Negotiable Instruments Law (Consol. Laws Ch. 38) § 350 et seq.
Okla. Stat. 1961, Title 6, § 118 et seq.
Ore. Rev. Stat. 1953, 74.1010 et seq.
Pa. 1931 Pamph. Laws 568, No. 198
S.C. Code Ann. 1976, § 36-4-101 et seq.
Tex. Rev. Civ. Stat., Art. 342.701 et seq.
Wash. Rev. Code Ann., 62A.4101 et seq.
W. Va. Acts 1931, Ch. 15
Wyo. Stat. 1957, § 13-111 et seq.

Bank Collections Law (Provisional Credit)
N.J. Stat Ann., Superseded Vol., 12A:4-106, 12A:4-107, 12A:4-212, 12A:4-213, 12A:4-301

Bank Conservation Act
March 9, 1933, Ch. 1, 48 Stat. 2, 12 U.S. Code §§ 201 to 211
May 20, 1933, Ch. 34, 48 Stat. 72, 12 U.S. Code § 207
Sept. 3, 1954, Ch. 1263, 68 Stat. 1234, 12 U.S. Code § 209
Aug. 9, 1989, P.L. 101-73, 12 U.S. Code §§ 202 to 209, 211
Dec. 19, 1991, P.L. 102-242, 12 U.S. Code § 203
N.H. Rev. Stat. 1955, 396:5 et seq.

Bank Conservator Act
Ohio Rev. Code 1953, 1113.02
R.I. Gen. Laws 1956, 19-16-1 et seq.
Vt. Stat. Ann., Title 8, § 1601 et seq.

Bank Consolidation Act
N.H. Rev. Stat. 1955, 388:1 et seq.

Bank Control Act (State Board)
S.C. Code Ann. 1976, § 34-1-10 et seq.

Bank Customer Dispute Resolution Act
Tenn. Code Ann., 45-1-301 et seq.

Bank Deferred Posting Act
Colo. Rev. Stat. 1963, 14-8-4

Bank Deposit Insurance Act
See Federal Deposit Insurance Act
Mich. Comp. Laws 1948, 487.15, 487.125 et seq.

Bank Deposit Joint Tenancy Act
Cal. Financial Code § 852
Haw. Rev. Stat. Ann., § 403-134
Mich. Comp. Laws Ann., 487.703
Mo. Rev. Stat., 362.470
Wash. Rev. Code Ann., 64.28.030

Bank Depositors Guaranty Act
Kan. Laws 1909, Ch. 61
Neb. Laws 1909, Ch. 10, §§ 44 to 47
Okla. Stat. 1988, Title 6, § 812 et seq.
Tex. Rev. Civ. Stat., Art. 342-701 et seq.

Bank Depository Act
Neb. Rev. Stat. 1943, 77-2301 et seq.
Okla. Stat. 1961, Title 6, § 118 et seq.

Bank Deposits Act
D.C. Code 1973, § 26-201

Bank Deposits Adverse Claim Act
S.D. Codified Laws 1967, 51-15-2

Bank Deposits and Collections (Uniform Commercial Code)
See Uniform Commercial Code-Bank Deposits and Collections

Bank Deposits and Collections Act
See Uniform Commercial Code-Bank Deposits and Collections

Bank Deposits Tax Act
R.I. Gen. Laws 1956, 44-15-1 et seq.

Bank Dissolution Law (Voluntary)
Cal. Statutes 1891, p. 271

Bank Electronic Funds Act
Colo. Rev. Stat., 11-6.5-101 et seq.

Bank Enterprise Act of 1991
Dec. 19, 1991, P.L. 102-242, 12 U.S. Code § 1811 nt.
Oct. 28, 1992, P.L. 102-550, 12 U.S. Code § 1834a
Sept. 23, 1994, P.L. 103-325, 12 U.S. Code § 1834a
Sept. 30, 1996, P.L. 104-208, 12 U.S. Code §§ 1834, 1841

Bank Examiners Education Foundation Act
Ill. Comp. Stat. 1992, Ch. 20, § 3210/2

Bank Excise Tax Act
Haw. Rev. Stat. Ann., § 241-1 et seq.

Bank Export Services Act
Oct. 8, 1982, P.L. 290, 12 U.S. Code §§ 1841 nt., 1843 nt.

Bank Extraordinary Situation Closing Act
Cal. Financial Code § 3600 et seq.

Bank for Economic Cooperation and Development in the Middle East and North Africa Act

Sept. 30, 1996, P.L. 104-208, Title VII, 22 U.S. Code § 290o nt.

Bank Franchise Tax Act

Va. Code 1950, § 58.1-1200 et seq.

Bank Guaranty Act

Kan. Laws 1909, Ch. 61

Bank Guaranty Fund Act

S.D. Laws 1915, Ch. 102, Art. 3

Wash. Laws 1917, Ch. 81

Bank Holding Company Act

Ark. Stat. 1947, 23-32-301 et seq.

Ill. Comp. Stat. 1992, Ch. 205, § 10/1 et seq.

Ind. Code Ann., 28-2-14-1 et seq., 28-2-15-1 et seq.

La. Rev. Stat. Ann., 6:1001 et seq.

Me. Rev. Stat. Ann. 1964, Title 9-B, § 1011 et seq.

N.C. Gen. Stat. 1943, § 53-225

Neb. Rev. Stat. 1943, 8-1201 et seq.

Okla. Stat. 1981, Title 6, § 502

Pa. Purdon's Stat., Title 7, § 115

S.C. Code Ann. 1976, § 34-24-10 et seq.

Bank Holding Company Act Amendments of 1970

Dec. 31, 1970, P.L. 91-607, 84 Stat. 1760, 12 U.S. Code §§ 1841 to 1843, 1849, 1850, 1971 to 1978; 31 U.S. Code §§ 317e nt., 324, 324b, 324c, 391, 405a-1 nt.

Nov. 10, 1978, P.L. 95-630, 12 U.S. Code § 1972

March 7, 1979, P.L. 96-2, 31 U.S. Code § 317e nt.

Aug. 9, 1989, P.L. 101-73, 12 U.S. Code § 1972

Dec. 19, 1991, P.L. 102-242, 12 U.S. Code § 1972

Sept. 30, 1996, P.L. 104-208, 12 U.S. Code § 1972

Bank Holding Company Act of 1956

May 9, 1956, Ch. 240, 70 Stat. 133, 12 U.S. Code §§ 1841 nt., 1841, 1842, 1843, 1844, 1845, 1846, 1847, 1848

Aug. 28, 1958, P.L. 85-791, 72 Stat. 951, 12 U.S. Code § 1848

July 1, 1966, P.L. 89-485, 80 Stat. 236, 12 U.S. Code §§ 1841, 1842, 1843, 1848, 1849

Dec. 31, 1970, P.L. 91-607, 84 Stat. 1760, 12 U.S. Code §§ 1841 to 1843, 1849, 1850, 1971 to 1978

Nov. 16, 1977, P.L. 95-188, 12 U.S. Code § 1841 et seq.

Nov. 10, 1978, P.L. 95-630, 12 U.S. Code §§ 1843, 1844, 1847

March 31, 1980, P.L. 96-221, 12 U.S. Code §§ 1842, 1843

Oct. 8, 1982, P.L. 97-290, 12 U.S. Code §§ 1843, 1843 nt.

Oct. 15, 1982, P.L. 97-320, 12 U.S. Code §§ 1841 to 1843, 1847

Jan. 12, 1983, P.L. 97-457, 12 U.S. Code § 1843

Aug. 10, 1987, P.L. 100-86, 12 U.S. Code §§ 1841 to 1843, 1849

Aug. 23, 1988, P.L. 100-418, 102 Stat. 1385, 12 U.S. Code § 1843

Aug. 9, 1989, P.L. 101-73, 12 U.S. Code §§ 1841 to 1843, 1847

Dec. 19, 1991, P.L. 102-242, 12 U.S. Code §§ 1842, 1843, 3101

Sept. 23, 1994, P.L. 103-325, 12 U.S. Code §§ 1842, 1843, 1849

Sept. 29, 1994, P.L. 103-328, 12 U.S. Code §§ 1841, 1842, 1846

Sept. 30, 1996, P.L. 104-208, 12 U.S. Code §§ 1841, 1843

Bank Holding Company Act of 1966

Nov. 16, 1977, P.L. 95-188, 12 U.S. Code § 1849

Bank Holding Company and Bank Acquisition Act

Conn. Gen. Stat. Ann., § 36-418 et seq.

Bank Holding Company Subsidiary Trust Company Formation Act

Ark. Code Ann. 1987, 23-32-1901 et seq.

Bank Holiday Act
Minn. Laws 1933, Ch. 56

Bank Holiday and Promissory Note Act
Ill. Rev. Stat. 1991, Ch. 17, § 600 et seq.

Bank Incorporation Act
Vt. Stat. Ann. Title 8, § 551 et seq.

Bank Installment Loan Act
Iowa Code 1989, 524.906 et seq.
N.M. Stat. Ann., 58-7-1 et seq.

Bank Intangible Tax Act
Ind. Code Ann., 6-5-1-1-1 et seq.

Bank Liquidation Act
N.H. Rev. Stat. 1955, 395:1 et seq.
R.I. Gen. Laws 1956, 19-17-1 et seq.

Bank Merger Act
Haw. Rev. Stat. Ann., § 404-1 et seq.
Me. Rev. Stat. Ann. 1964, Title 9-B, § 351 et seq.
N.Y. Banking Law (Consol. Laws Ch. 2) § 600 et seq.
Ore. Rev. Stat. 1953, 711.005 et seq.

Bank Merger Acts
See also Federal Deposit Insurnace Act
May 13, 1960, P.L. 86-463, 74 Stat. 129, 12 U.S. Code § 1828
Feb. 21, 1966, P.L. 89-356, 80 Stat. 7, 12 U.S. Code §§ 1828, 1828 nts.

Bank Moratorium Act
Neb. Laws 1933, Ch. 17
Pa. 1933 Pamph. Laws 9, No. 6

Bank Nt. and Redemption Act
July 12, 1870, Ch. 252, 16 Stat. 251

Bank of North Dakota Act
N.D. Cent. Code, 6-09-01 et seq.

Bank Officers and Employees Stock Option Plan Act
N.J. Rev. Stat. 1937, 17:9A-27.50 et seq.

Bank Official Loan Act
June 16, 1933, Ch. 89, 48 Stat. 182, 12 U.S. Code § 375a

Bank Organization Act
Ark. Stat. 1987, 23-32-201 et seq.

Bank Parity Act
Nov. 26, 1997, P.L. 105-121, 111 Stat. 2528
Cal. Financial Code §§ 753, 857, 1757, 1935, 3359, 3371 to 3373
N.J. Stat. Ann., 17:13B-1 et seq.

Bank Posting Deadline Act
Ind. Code Ann., 26-1-4-301 et seq.

Bank Privacy Act
Tenn. Code Ann. 1955, Superseded Vols., 45-2601 et seq.

Bank Protection Act
July 7, 1968, P.L. 90-389, 82 Stat. 294, 12 U.S. Code §§ 1729, 1881 to 1884
Aug. 9, 1989, P.L. 101-73, 12 U.S. Code §§ 1881, 1882
N.Y. Banking Law (Consol. Laws Ch. 2) §§ 134, 171, Subd. 3, 239

Bank Protection Act (Joint Accounts)
Conn. Gen. Stat. Ann., § 36-3
Ill. Rev. Stat. 1991, Ch. 76, § 2
Wis. Stat. Ann., 705.01 et seq.

Bank Protection Act (Minors)
N.Y. Banking Law (Consol. Laws Ch. 2) § 134

Bank Receivership Act
R.I. Gen. Laws 1956, 19-15-1 et seq.
Vt. Stat. Ann., Title 8, § 1651 et seq.

Bank Records Retention Act
S.C. Code Ann. 1976, § 34-3-510 et seq.

Bank Reorganization Act
Minn. Laws 1933, Ch. 55
N.H. Rev. Stat. 1955, 396:11
S.D. Codified Laws 1967, 51-26-1 et seq.
Vt. Stat. Ann., Title 8, § 1701 et seq.

Bank Representative Office Act (Foreign)
Ill. Rev. Stat. 1991, Ch. 17, § 2851 et seq.

Bank Robbery Act
May 18, 1934, Ch. 304, 48 Stat. 783 (See 18 U.S. Code §§ 2113, 3231)
Aug. 23, 1935, Ch. 614, 49 Stat. 720 (See 18 U.S. Code § 2113)
Aug. 24, 1937, Ch. 747, 50 Stat. 749 (See 18 U.S. Code § 2113)
June 29, 1940, Ch. 455, 54 Stat. 695 (See 18 U.S. Code § 2113)
Ind. Code Ann., 35-13-5-1

Bank Savings Guaranty Act (Industrial)
Colo. Rev. Stat., 11-22-201 et seq.

Bank Secrecy Act
Oct. 26, 1970, P.L. 91-508, 12 U.S. Code §§ 1730d, 1829b, 1951 to 1959; 18 U.S. Code § 6002; 31 U.S. Code §§ 321, 5311 to 5314, 5316 to 5322

Bank Securities Powers Act
Del. Code of 1974, Title 5, § 101 et seq.

Bank Service Corporation Act
Oct. 23, 1962, P.L. 87-856, 12 U.S. Code §§ 1861 to 1865
Nov. 10, 1978, P.L. 95-630, 12 U.S. Code § 1865
Oct. 15, 1982, P.L. 97-320, 12 U.S. Code §§ 1861 to 1867
Jan. 12, 1983, P.L. 97-457, 12 U.S. Code §§ 1861, 1864, 1867
Sept. 23, 1994, P.L. 103-325, 12 U.S. Code § 1865
Sept. 30, 1996, P.L. 104-208, 12 U.S. Code §§ 1861 to 1867
Fla. Stat. 1983, 662.01 et seq.

Bank Shares Tax Act
Ga. Code 1933, 92-2406
Pa. Purdon's Stat., Title 72, § 7701 et seq.

Bank Slander Act
Wash. Rev. Code Ann., 9.58.100

Bank Stabilization Act
Iowa Code Ann., 524.224 et seq.

Wash. Rev. Code Ann., 30.56.010 et seq.

Bank Stock Tax Act
N.J. Stat. Ann., 54:9-1 to 54:9-18
Wash. Rev. Code 1951, 84.40.270 et seq.

Bank Stockholders Double Liability Act
Miss. Code Ann. 1972, § 81-5-27
Okla. Stat. 1981, Title 6, § 805

Bank Stockholders' Liability Act
Cal. Financial Code § 3135
Mich. Comp. Laws 1948, 487.59
Tenn. Code Ann. 45-2-1401
Vt. Stat. Ann., Title 8, § 855
Wash. Rev. Code Ann., 30.12.140 et seq.

Bank Structure Act
Tenn. Code Ann., 45-2-1401 et seq.
Tenn. Code Ann., 45-619 et seq.

Bank Tax Act
Ill. Rev. Stat. 1981, Ch. 120, §§ 557, 558
Mo. Rev. Stat., 148.010 et seq.
Mont. Code Ann., 15-24-501 et seq.
Ohio Laws Vol. 50, p. 135, § 19 et seq.
R.I. Gen. Laws 1956, 44-14-1 et seq.

Bankers' Amendment (Negotiable Instruments)
Minn. Stat. 1961, 335.052, Subd. 3

Bankers and Brokers Act (Mortgage)
Pa. Purdon's Stat., Title 63, § 456.01

Bankers' Embezzlement Act
Ind. Burns' 1933, 10-1714

Bankers' Lien Act
Cal. Civil Code § 3054
Okla. Stat. 1971, Title 42, § 32

Bankers' Relief Act (Taxation)
Mont. Rev. Code 1947, 84-303 et seq.

Bankhead Cotton-Control Act
See Cotton Control Act

Bankhead-Jones Act

June 29, 1935, Ch. 338, 49 Stat. 436, 7 U.S. Code §§ 343c, 343d, 427 to 427g

Sept. 21, 1944, Ch. 412, 58 Stat. 735, 7 U.S. Code § 427d

June 6, 1945, Ch. 175, 59 Stat. 231, 7 U.S. Code §§ 343c, 343d-1

Aug. 14, 1946, Ch. 966, 60 Stat. 1082, 7 U.S. Code §§ 427, 427h to 427j

July 31, 1947, Ch. 412, 61 Stat. 694, 7 U.S. Code § 427j

July 28, 1954, Ch. 591, 68 Stat. 574, 7 U.S. Code § 427i

Aug. 30, 1954, Ch. 1076, 68 Stat. 966, 7 U.S. Code §§ 427j, 1624

July 14, 1960, P.L. 86-658, 74 Stat. 525, 7 U.S. Code § 329

Mich. Comp. Laws Ann., 390.161

Bankhead-Jones Farm Tenant Act

See Consolidated Farmers Home Administration Act Of 1961

July 22, 1937, Ch. 517, 50 Stat. 522, 7 U.S. Code §§ 1010 to 1012

July 28, 1942, Ch. 531, 56 Stat. 725, 7 U.S. Code § 1011

Aug. 14, 1946, Ch. 964, 60 Stat. 1064

July 26, 1947, Ch. 339, 61 Stat. 493

June 19, 1948, Ch. 551, 62 Stat. 534

April 20, 1950, Ch. 94, 64 Stat. 73

Aug. 23, 1951, Ch. 144, 65 Stat. 75

June 30, 1953, Ch. 174, 67 Stat. 132

July 22, 1954, Ch. 562, 68 Stat. 525

Aug. 30, 1954, Ch. 1076, 68 Stat. 966

Aug. 9, 1955, Ch. 633, 69 Stat. 553

Aug. 1, 1956, Ch. 829, 70 Stat. 801

Aug. 3, 1956, Ch. 950, 70 Stat. 1034

Aug. 25, 1958, P.L. 85-748, 72 Stat. 840

Sept. 2, 1958, P.L. 85-857, 72 Stat. 1265

Sept. 21, 1959, P.L. 86-332, 73 Stat. 599, 7 U.S. Code § 1006d

March 29, 1961, P.L. 87-8, 75 Stat. 17, 7 U.S. Code § 1007

Aug. 8, 1961, P.L. 87-128, 75 Stat. 318, 4 U.S. Code § 1013a

Sept. 27, 1962, P.L. 87-703, 76 Stat. 607, 7 U.S. Code §§ 1010, 1011

Aug. 31, 1964, P.L. 88-537, 78 Stat. 745, 7 U.S. Code § 1011

Nov. 8, 1966, P.L. 89-796, 80 Stat. 1478, 7 U.S. Code §§ 1010, 1011

July 18, 1970, P.L. 91-343, 84 Stat. 439, 7 U.S. Code § 1011

Aug. 30, 1972, P.L. 92-419, 86 Stat. 669, 7 U.S. Code §§ 1010a, 1011

Sept. 29, 1977, P.L. 95-113, 7 U.S. Code § 1011

July 2, 1986, P.L. 99-349, 100 Stat. 735

Nov. 2, 1994, P.L. 103-437, 7 U.S. Code § 1011

April 4, 1996, P.L. 104-127, 7 U.S. Code § 1011

Banking Act

Ala. Code 1975, § 11-22-101 et seq.

Colo. Rev. Stat., 11-22-101 et seq.

Ill. Comp. Stat. 1992, Ch. 205, § 5/1 et seq.

Tex. Finance Code, § 31.001 et seq.

Wis. Stat. Ann., 221.0101 et seq.

Banking Act (Private)

Pa. Purdon's Stat., Title 7, § 1901 et seq.

Banking Act (Reciprocal)

Fla. Stat. Ann., 658.295

Banking Act (Regional Reciprocal)

Ark. Code 1987, 23-32-1801 et seq.

Tenn. Code Ann., 45-18-101 et seq.

Banking Act (Resource Mitigation)

Colo. Rev. Stat., 37-85.5-101 et seq.

Banking Act of 1933

June 16, 1933, Ch. 89, 48 Stat. 162

May 18, 1953, Ch. 59, 67 Stat. 27, 12 U.S. Code § 64a

Sept. 8, 1959, P.L. 86-230, 73 Stat. 466, 12 U.S. Code § 378

July 1, 1966, P.L. 89-485, 80 Stat. 242, 12 U.S. Code § 221a

Aug. 1, 1968, P.L. 90-448, 82 Stat. 543, 12 U.S. Code § 378a

Sept. 17, 1978, P.L. 95-369, 12 U.S. Code § 378

Banking Act of 1935

Aug. 23, 1935, Ch. 614, 49 Stat. 684, 11 U.S. Code § 101; 15 U.S. Code §§ 19, 19a

May 25, 1948, Ch. 334, 62 Stat. 265, 12 U.S. Code § 371

March 31, 1980, P.L. 96-221, 12 U.S. Code § 51b-1

Banking Acts

Ala. Code 1975, 5-1A-1 et seq.

Alaska Stat. 1962, § 06.05.005 et seq.

Ariz. Rev. Stat. Ann., § 6-101 et seq.

Ark. Stat. 1947, 23-31-201 et seq.

Cal. Financial Code § 99 et seq.

Conn. Gen. Stat. Ann., § 36-1 et seq.

D.C. Code 1973, § 26-101 et seq.

Fla. Stat. 1983, 658.1101 et seq.

Ga. Code Ann., 7-1-1 et seq.

Haw. Rev. Stat. Ann., § 403-1 et seq.

Ida. Code 1947, 26-101 et seq.

Ind. Code Ann., 28-1-1-1 et seq.

Iowa Code Ann., 524.101 et seq.

Kan. Stat. Ann., 9-701 et seq.

Ky. Rev. Stat. 1971, 287.010 et seq.

La. Rev. Stat. Ann., 6:1 et seq.

Mass. Gen. Laws 1990, 167:1 et seq.

Md. Ann. Code 1974, Art. FI, § 1-101 et seq.

Mich. Comp. Laws Ann., 487.301 et seq.

Minn. Stat. Ann., 48.01 et seq.

Miss. Code Ann. 1972, § 81-1-1 et seq.

Mo. Rev. Stat., 362.010 et seq.

Mont. Code Ann., 32-1-101 et seq.

N.C. Gen. Stat. 1943, § 53-1 et seq.

Nev. Rev. Stat. 1979 Reprint, 657.005 et seq.

N.J. Stat. Ann., 17:1-1 et seq.

N.M. Stat. Ann., 58-1-1 et seq.

N.Y. Banking Code (Consol. Laws, Ch. 2) § 1 et seq.

N.Y. Laws 1984, Ch. 360

Ohio Rev. Code 1953, 1101.01 et seq.

Okla. Stat. 1981, Title 6, § 101 et seq.

Ore. Rev. Stat. 1953, 706.005 et seq.

Pa. Purdon's Stat., Title 7, § 101 et seq.

Pa. Purdon's Stat., Title 71, § 733-1 et seq.

P.R. Laws Ann. 1954, Title 7, § 1 et seq.

R.I. Gen. Laws 1956, 19-1-1 et seq.

S.C. Code Ann. 1976, § 34-3-10 et seq.

S.D. Codified Laws 1967, 51-5-1 et seq.

Tenn. Code Ann., 45-1-101 et seq.

Va. Code 1950, § 6.1-1 et seq.

Vt. Stat. Ann. 1959, Title 8, § 1 et seq.

Wash. Rev. Code Ann., 30.04.010 et seq.

W. Va. Code 1966, § 31A-1-1 et seq.

Banking Acts (Emergency)

Md. Laws 1933, Ch. 46

Me. Rev. Stat. Ann. 1964, Title 9-B, §§ 151, 152

Mich. Public Acts 1933, No. 32

Banking Acts (International)

N.C. Gen. Stat. 1943, § 53-232.1 et seq.

Banking Acts (Interstate)

Del. Code of 1974, Title 5, § 841 et seq.

S.C. Code Ann. 1976, § 34-24-10 et seq.

Banking Affiliates Act of 1982

Oct. 15, 1982, P.L. 97-320, 12 U.S. Code §§ 226 nt., 371c, 375b, 1820, 1972

Banking and Branching Efficiency Act

S.C. Code Ann. 1976, § 34-25-10 et seq.

Banking and Financial Corporation Tax Act

N.M. Stat. Ann., 7-2A-1 et seq.

Banking and Insurance Act (Department of)

N.J. Stat. Ann., 17:1-13 et seq.

Banking and Related Programs Authorization Adjustment Act

Aug. 13, 1981, P.L. 97-35, 12 U.S. Code §§ 635 nt.

Banking Center Regulatory Act

P.R. Laws Ann. 1954, Title 7, § 231 et seq.

Banking Center Regulatory Act (International)

P.R. Acts 1989, No. 52

Banking Code

Ark. Code 1987, 23-45-101 et seq.

Banking Corporations and Bank Agencies Act (International)

Ga. Code Ann., 7-7-710 et seq.

Banking Department Act
N.J. Stat. Ann., 17:1 B-1 et seq.
Pa. 1895 Pamph. Laws 4, No. 3
Pa. 1919 Pamph. Laws 209, No. 130

Banking Department Reorganization Act
Tenn. Public Acts 1973, Ch. 294

Banking Department Self-Support and Administration Act
Tex. Rev. Civ. Stat., Arts. 342-101A, 342-112, 342-112A, 342-210 et seq.

Banking Development Act (Foreign)
Del. Code of 1974, Title 5, §§ 101, 907, 936, 1101
Del. Code of 1974, Title 6, § 2307
Del. Code of 1974, Title 30, § 1903
Del. Laws Vol. 65, p. 856, Ch. 444

Banking Emergencies Act
Ill. Comp. Stat. 1992, Ch. 205, § 610/0.01 et seq.

Banking Industry and Financial Services Act
Dec. 29, 1995, 104-88, 109 Stat. 943, Title 3, Subtitle A
Del. Laws Vol. 71, Ch. 25

Banking Mercantile Act
N.M. Stat. Ann. 1953, 48-14-1 et seq.

Banking Oversight and Change of Control Act
N.J. Stat. Ann., 17:9A-373 et seq.

Banking Practices Validation Act
Ill. Rev. Stat. 1991, Ch. 17, § 301 et seq.

Banking Reform Act
Ala. Code 1975, § 5-1A-1 et seq.

Bankruptcy Act
Conn. Gen. Stat. 1983, § 45-159
Haw. Session Laws 1884, Ch. 35

Bankruptcy Act, Amendments of 1938
See Chandler Act, Bankruptcy Revision

Bankruptcy Act, Amendments of 1939
See Chandler Rail Bankruptcy Act

Bankruptcy Acts
April 4, 1800, Ch. 19, 2 Stat. 19
Aug. 19, 1841, Ch. 9, 5 Stat. 440
March 2, 1867, Ch. 176, 14 Stat. 517
June 22, 1874, Ch. 390, 18 Stat. 178
July 1, 1898, Ch. 541, 30 Stat. 544, 11 U.S. Code §§ 1, 11, 21 to 35, 41 to 55, 61 to 81, 91 to 96, 101 to 112
Feb. 5, 1903, Ch. 487, 32 Stat. 797, 11 U.S. Code §§ 11, 21, 22, 32, 35, 41, 44, 46, 68, 75, 76, 93, 96, 104, 105, 107, 110 to 112
June 15, 1906, Ch. 3333, 34 Stat. 267, 11 U.S. Code § 104
June 25, 1910, Ch. 412, 36 Stat. 838, 11 U.S. Code §§ 11, 22, 30, 32, 46, 75, 76, 94 to 96, 107, 112
March 2, 1917, Ch. 153, 39 Stat. 999, 11 U.S. Code § 35
Jan. 7, 1922, Ch. 22, 42 Stat. 354, 11 U.S. Code § 35
March 3, 1933, Ch. 204, 47 Stat. 1467, 11 U.S. Code §§ 101a, 201 to 205
May 24, 1934, Ch. 345, 48 Stat. 798
June 7, 1934, Ch. 424, 48 Stat. 912, 11 U.S. Code §§ 76a, 103, 103a, 107, 202, 202a, 203, 203a, 204, 205a, 206, 207
June 28, 1934, Ch. 869, 48 Stat. 1289, 11 U.S. Code § 203
May 15, 1935, Ch. 114, 49 Stat. 246, 11 U.S. Code §§ 22, 203
March 4, 1940, Ch. 39, 54 Stat. 40, 11 U.S. Code § 203
March 4, 1940, Ch. 41, 54 Stat. 44, 11 U.S. Code § 403
June 28, 1940, Ch. 438, 54 Stat. 667, 11 U.S. Code §§ 401, 403
July 1, 1940, Ch. 500, 54 Stat. 709, 11 U.S. Code §§ 670, 796, 922
Aug. 22, 1940, Ch. 686, 54 Stat. 835, 11 U.S. Code §§ 72, 107
June 22, 1942, Ch. 434, 56 Stat. 377
Oct. 16, 1942, Ch. 610, 56 Stat. 787, 11 U.S. Code §§ 1200 to 1255
March 11, 1944, Ch. 87, 58 Stat. 113, 11 U.S. Code § 203

June 3, 1946, Ch. 280, 60 Stat. 230, 11 U.S. Code § 203

June 28, 1946, Ch. 512, 60 Stat. 323, 11 U.S. Code §§ 1, 62, 62 nts., 63, 65, 65 nt., 67, 68, 71, 79, 80, 81, 102, 104, 112, 517, 1024, 1033, 1059

July 1, 1946, Ch. 532, 60 Stat. 409, 11 U.S. Code §§ 401 to 403

June 30, 1947, Ch. 182, 61 Stat. 213, 11 U.S. Code § 63

April 21, 1948, Ch. 225, 62 Stat. 198, 11 U.S. Code § 203

May 24, 1949, Ch. 139, 63 Stat. 107, 11 U.S. Code §§ 32, 104

March 18, 1950, Ch. 70, 64 Stat. 24, 11 U.S. Code §§ 96, 110

Sept. 19, 1950, Ch. 954, 64 Stat. 866, 11 U.S. Code § 71

Dec. 20, 1950, Ch. 1138, 64 Stat. 1113, 11 U.S. Code § 1 nt.

Dec. 29, 1950, Ch. 1193, 64 Stat. 1134, 11 U.S. Code § 1006

May 16, 1951, Ch. 81, 65 Stat. 42, 11 U.S. Code § 62

May 16, 1951, Ch. 82, 65 Stat. 42, 11 U.S. Code § 91

July 3, 1951, Ch. 205, 65 Stat. 114, 11 U.S. Code § 94

Oct. 24, 1951, Ch. 543, 65 Stat. 606, 11 U.S. Code §§ 205, 205 nt.

July 7, 1952, Ch. 579, 66 Stat. 420, 11 U.S. Code §§ 1, 11, 21, 25, 29, 32, 41, 44, 47, 48, 55, 67, 70, 93, 94, 95, 101, 102, 103, 104, 105, 107, 109, 110, 624, 629, 638, 665, 724, 728, 737, 738, 755, 766, 767, 769, 771, 776, 781, 824, 859, 872, 873, 881, 886, 1024, 1044, 1056, 1060, 1061, 1066, 1069

July 7, 1952, Ch. 580, 66 Stat. 438, 11 U.S. Code § 68

Aug. 5, 1953, Ch. 327, 67 Stat. 366, 11 U.S. Code § 63

May 10, 1956, Ch. 257, 70 Stat. 151, 11 U.S. Code § 68

May 28, 1956, Ch. 330, 70 Stat. 216, 11 U.S. Code § 76

July 30, 1956, Ch. 784, 70 Stat. 725, 11 U.S. Code § 104

Aug. 1, 1956, Ch. 819, 70 Stat. 785, 11 U.S. Code § 106

Aug. 2, 1956, Ch. 893, 70 Stat. 955, 11 U.S. Code § 94

Sept. 2, 1957, P.L. 85-275, 71 Stat. 599, 11 U.S. Code §§ 32, 94

Sept. 4, 1957, P.L. 85-295, 71 Stat. 617, 11 U.S. Code § 516

July 11, 1958, P.L. 85-515, 72 Stat. 357, 11 U.S. Code § 205

Aug. 23, 1958, P.L. 85-732, 72 Stat. 820, 11 U.S. Code §§ 723, 731, 734 to 737, 763, 776, 787

Aug. 28, 1958, P.L. 85-824, 72 Stat. 984, 11 U.S. Code § 205

May 13, 1959, P.L. 86-24, 73 Stat. 24, 11 U.S. Code §§ 1006, 1059

June 23, 1959, P.L. 86-49, 73 Stat. 80, 11 U.S. Code § 67

June 23, 1959, P.L. 86-64, 73 Stat. 109, 11 U.S. Code §§ 1, 41, 45, 731, 1031

July 28, 1959, P.L. 86-110, 73 Stat. 259, 11 U.S. Code §§ 68, 79, 104, 112, 1024, 1033, 1059

Aug. 7, 1959, P.L. 86-144, 73 Stat. 296, 11 U.S. Code §§ 62, 71

Sept. 21, 1959, P.L. 86-293, 73 Stat. 571, 11 U.S. Code § 41

June 11, 1960, P.L. 86-504, 74 Stat. 198, 11 U.S. Code §§ 76, 532

June 12, 1960, P.L. 86-519, 74 Stat. 217, 11 U.S. Code § 93

July 12, 1960, P.L. 86-621, 74 Stat. 408, 11 U.S. Code §§ 32, 35

July 12, 1960, P.L. 86-631, 74 Stat. 466, 11 U.S. Code §§ 94, 1078

July 14, 1960, P.L. 86-662, 74 Stat. 528, 11 U.S. Code § 67

Sept. 19, 1962, P.L. 87-677, 76 Stat. 559, 11 U.S. Code § 68

Sept. 25, 1962, P.L. 87-681, 76 Stat. 570, 11 U.S. Code §§ 11, 44 , 76, 93, 94, 95, 104, 110, 205, 560, 647, 665, 793

May 8, 1963, P.L. 88-16, 77 Stat. 14, 11 U.S. Code § 75

May 8, 1963, P.L. 88-17, 77 Stat. 14, 11 U.S. Code § 96

Nov. 13, 1963, P.L. 88-175, 77 Stat. 330, 11 U.S. Code §§ 734, 755a, 767, 769

Aug. 14, 1964, P.L. 88-426, 78 Stat. 434, 11 U.S. Code § 68

Sept. 2, 1965, P.L. 89-166, 79 Stat. 646, 11 U.S. Code § 32

May 10, 1966, P.L. 89-414, 80 Stat. 135, 11 U.S. Code § 67

Continued

July 5, 1966, P.L. 89-495, 80 Stat. 268, 11 U.S. Code §§ 1, 104, 107, 110

July 5, 1966, P.L. 89-496, 80 Stat. 270, 11 U.S. Code §§ 11, 35, 104

Nov. 3, 1966, P.L. 89-754, 80 Stat. 1278, 11 U.S. Code § 663

Nov. 28, 1967, P.L. 90-156, 81 Stat. 510, 11 U.S. Code §§ 734, 755a, 767, 769

Nov. 28, 1967, P.L. 90-157, 81 Stat. 511, 11 U.S. Code §§ 104, 638, 778, 883

Nov. 28, 1967, P.L. 90-158, 81 Stat. 516, 11 U.S. Code §§ 737 to 739

Nov. 28, 1967, P.L. 90-161, 81 Stat. 518, 11 U.S. Code §§ 68, 80

Oct. 17, 1968, P.L. 90-586, 82 Stat. 1149, 11 U.S. Code § 516

Oct. 15, 1970, P.L. 91-452, 84 Stat. 929, 11 U.S. Code § 25

Oct. 19, 1970, P.L. 91-467, 84 Stat. 990, 11 U.S. Code §§ 11, 32, 33, 35, 66, 94

June 6, 1972, P.L. 92-310, 86 Stat. 205, 11 U.S. Code § 78

Dec. 27, 1973, P.L. 93-200, 87 Stat. 838, 11 U.S. Code § 68

Aug. 14, 1979, P.L. 96-56, 11 U.S. Code § 35 nt.

Bankruptcy Amendments and Federal Judgeship Act of 1984

July 10, 1984, P.L. 98-354, 5 U.S. Code §§ 8331 et seq.; 11 U.S. Code §§ 101 et seq., 303, 321 et seq., 341 et seq., 501 et seq., 701 et seq., 1101 et seq., 1301 et seq., 1501 et seq.; 28 U.S. Code §§ 151 nt., 151 to 158, 1334, 1408 to 1412, 1452

June 19, 1986, P.L. 99-336, 5 U.S. Code §§ 8706, 8706 nt., 8714a to 8714c

Oct. 27, 1986, P.L. 99-554, 28 U.S. Code § 152 nt.

Oct. 19, 1996, P.L. 104-317, 28 U.S. Code § 152 nt.

Bankruptcy Court Judgments (Uniform Federal Lien Registration Act)

Md. Ann. Code 1974, Art. RP, § 3-401 et seq.

Bankruptcy Extension Act

See Municipal Bankruptcy Extension Act

Bankruptcy Judges, United States Trustees, and Family Farmer Bankruptcy Act of 1986

Oct. 27, 1986, P.L. 99-554, 28 U.S. Code § 581 nt.

Dec. 1, 1990, P.L. 101-650, 11 U.S. Code § 3077 nt.; 28 U.S. Code § 581 nt.

Aug. 6, 1993, P.L. 103-65, 11 U.S. Code §§ 1201 et seq. nts., 1221 et seq. nts.; 28 U.S. Code § 581 nt.

Bankruptcy Judgeship Act of 1992

Aug. 26, 1992, P.L. 102-361, 28 U.S. Code § 1 nt.

Oct. 19, 1996, P.L. 104-317, 28 U.S. Code § 152 nt.

Bankruptcy Reform Act of 1994

Oct. 22, 1994, P.L. 103-394, 11 U.S. Code § 101 nt.

Bankruptcy Tax Act

Cal. Statutes 1982, Ch. 278

Bankruptcy Tax Act of 1980

Dec. 24, 1980, P.L. 96-589, 26 U.S. Code § 1 nt.

Banks Act (Savings)

N.C. Gen. Stat. 1943, § 54C-1 et seq.

Banks and Savings Banks Officers' and Employees' Retirement and Benefit Act

N.J. Stat. Ann., 17:9A-27.3 et seq.

Banks and Trust Companies Act (Commissioner of)

Ill. Comp. Stat. 1992, Ch. 20, § 3201/1 et seq.

Banks and Trust Companies Commissioner Act

Ill. Rev. Stat. 1991, Ch. 17, § 451

Bannack Act (Arraignment)

Mont. Rev. Code 1947, 94-7810

Bannack Act (County Relief)

Mont. Rev. Code 1947, 71-101 et seq.

Bar Acts

Ala. Code 1975, § 34-3-40 et seq.

Alaska Stat. 1962, § 08.08.010 et seq.

Cal. Business and Professions Code § 6000 et seq.

Ga. Code Ann., 15-19-30 et seq.

Mich. Comp. Laws Ann., 600.901 et seq.

Miss. Code Ann. 1972, § 73-3-101 et seq.

N.C. Gen. Stat. 1943, § 84-15 et seq.

Nev. Rev. Stat. 1979 Reprint, 7.275, 7.285

N.M. Stat. Ann., 36-2-1 et seq.

Okla. Laws 1929, Special Session, p. 376

Ore. Rev. Stat. 1953, 9.005 et seq.

Tex. Gov. Code, § 81.001 et seq.

Va. Code 1950, § 54.1-3909 et seq.

Wash. Rev. Code Ann., 2.48.010 et seq.

Bar Admission Act
Md. Ann. Code 1974, Art. BO, § 10-206 et seq.

Bar Association Incorporation Act
N.Y. Laws 1871, Ch. 819

Bar Association Law
Miss. Code Ann. 1972, § 73-3-101 et seq.

Bar Board Act
N.D. Cent. Code, 27-11-06 et seq.

Bar Dues Act
Ky. Rev. Stat. 1971, Superseded Vols., 30.170

Bar Exam Statute
Miss. Code Ann. 1972, § 73-3-2 et seq.

Bar Examination Rule Making Act
Ga. Code Ann., 15-19-3

Bar Integration Act
Ky. Rev. Stat. 1971, Superseded Vols., 30.170

Bar-Maid Act
Pa. Purdon's Stat., Title 47, § 4-493, Subd. 25

Bar Order Act (Equity Cases)
Ga. Code Ann., 23-2-97

Bar Organization Act (Attorneys)
Utah Code Ann. 1953, 78-51-1 et seq.

Bar Standards Act of 1954
Miss. Code Ann. 1972, § 73-3-1 et seq.

Bar, Tavern, and Restaurant Wage Protection Act
Mont. Code Ann., 39-3-601 et seq.

Barber and Beautician Act
Ky. Rev. Stat. 1971, 317.410 et seq.
Me. Rev. Stat. Ann. 1964, Title 32, § 351 et seq.

Barber and Cosmetologist Act
Colo. Rev. Stat., 12-8-101 et seq.
Ill. Rev. Stat. 1991, Ch. 111 § 1701 et seq.

Barber and Cosmetologist Licensing Act
Me. Rev. Stat. Ann. 1964, Title 32, § 14201 et seq.
Utah Code Ann. 1953, 58-11-1 et seq.

Barber and Dry Cleaning Act
Ala. General Acts 1935, p. 746, No. 316

Barber, Cosmetology and Nail Technology Act
Ill. Comp. Stat. 1992, Ch. 225, § 410/1-1 et seq.

Barbering and Cosmetology Act
Cal. Business and Professions Code § 7301 et seq.

Barbering and Cosmetology Licensure Act
Me. Rev. Stat. Ann. 1964, Title 32, § 14201 et seq.

Barbers Acts
Ala. Code 1975, § 34-5-1 et seq.
Ariz. Rev. Stat. Ann., § 32-301 et seq.
Ark. Stat. 1947, 17-18-301
Cal. Business and Professions Code § 6500 et seq.
D.C. Code Ann., § 2-401 et seq.
Fla. Stat. Ann., 476.014 et seq.
Ga. Code Ann., 43-7-1 et seq.
Ida. Code 1947, 54-501 et seq.
Ind. Code Ann., 25-7-1-1 et seq.
Iowa Code Ann., 158.1 et seq.
Kan. Stat. Ann., 65-1808 et seq.
Continued

Ky. Rev. Stat. 1971, 317.410 et seq.

La. Rev. Stat. Ann., 37:341 et seq.

Mass. Gen. Laws 1990, 112:87F et seq.

Md. Ann. Code 1974, Art. BO, § 4-102 et seq.

Me. Rev. Stat. Ann. 1964, Title 32, § 301 et seq.

Mich. Comp. Laws 1948, 338.601 et seq.

Minn. Stat. Ann., 154.01 et seq.

Miss. Code Ann. 1972, § 73-5-1 et seq.

Mo. Rev. Stat., 328.010 et seq.

Mont. Code Ann., 37-30-101 et seq.

N.C. Gen. Stat. 1943, § 86A-1 et seq.

N.D. Cent. Code, 43-04-01 et seq.

Neb. Rev. Stat. 1943, 71-201 et seq.

N.H. Rev. Stat. 1955, 313-A:1 et seq.

N.J. Stat. Ann., 45:5B-1 et seq.

N.M. Stat. Ann., 61-17-1 et seq.

N.Y. General Business Law (Consol. Laws Ch. 20) § 430 et seq.

Ohio Rev. Code 1953, 4709.01 et seq.

Okla. Stat. 1981, Title 59, § 61 et seq.

Ore. Rev. Stat. 1953, 690.005 et seq.

R.I. Gen. Laws 1956, 5-27-1 et seq.

S.C. Code Ann. 1976, § 40-7-10 et seq.

S.D. Codified Laws 1967, 36-14-1 et seq.

Tex. Rev. Civ. Stat., Art. 8402 et seq.

Vt. Stat. Ann., Title 26, § 261 et seq.

Wash. Rev. Code Ann., 18.16.010 et seq.

Wyo. Stat. Ann., § 33-7-101 et seq.

Barbers and Cosmetologists Act
N.M. Stat. Ann., 61-17A-1 et seq.

Barbers' Board Act
N.M. Stat. Ann., 61-17-1 et seq.

Barbers License Act
Cal. Business and Professions Code § 6546 et seq.
Mich. Comp. Laws 1979, 338.1601 et seq.
Pa. Purdon's Stat., Title 63, § 551 et seq.
Wis. Stat. 1985, 457.01 et seq.

Barbers, Manicurists, and Cosmetologists Act
Wash. Rev. Code Ann., 18-16-010 et seq.

Barber's Price and Hour Act
Utah Code Ann. 1953, Miscellaneous Superseded Code Provisions, 13-3-1 et seq.

Barbers' Price Fixing Act
N.M. Stat. Ann. 1953, 67-14-25 et seq.
Ore. Laws 1945, Ch. 198

Barbers Sanitary Act
Okla. Stat. Ann., Title 59, § 77

Barbers Unfair Trade Practices Act
Okla. Stat. 1981, Title 59, § 92 et seq.

Barbershop Act
Kan. Stat. Ann., 65-1823 et seq.
Pa. Purdon's Stat., Title 63, § 551 et seq.

Barbiturate Act
Fla. Stat. Ann., 893.01 et seq.
Ky. Rev. Stat. 1962, 217.461 et seq.
Ohio Rev. Code 1953, 3719.23 et seq.
Tex. Health and Safety Code, § 481.001 et seq.

Barbiturate and Benzedrine Act
Ark. Stat. 1947, 82-956.1 et seq.

Barbiturate and Central Nervous System Stimulant Act
La. Acts 1952, No. 296
R.I. Gen. Laws 1956, 21-28-1.01 et seq.

Barbiturate and Stimulant Drugs Act
N.C. Gen. Stat. 1943, § 90-86 et seq.

Barbiturates and Other Dangerous Drugs Act
P.R. Laws Ann. 1954, Title 24, § 930 et seq.

Barbiturates Sale Act
Wash. Rev. Code Ann., 69.40.060 et seq.

Barbituric Acid and Stimulant Control Act
Miss. Code Ann. 1972, § 41-29-117 et seq.

Barbour County Condominium Act
Ala. Acts 1973, p. 1787

Barbour Espionage Act
See Espionage Act

Barbour Fight Film Act
June 29, 1940, Ch. 443, 54 Stat. 686, 15 U.S. Code § 1001

Bard Law (Historical Places)
N.Y. General Municipal Law (Consol. Laws Ch. 24) § 96-a

Bargaining Act (Public Employee Collective)
Ore. Rev. Stat., 243.650 et seq.

Bargaining Act (Public Employee)
Nov. 4, 1992, P.L. 102-587, 106 Stat. 5039, § 5301
N.M. Stat. Ann., 10-70-1 et seq.

Barge Canal Act
N.Y. Laws 1903, Ch. 147

Barge Canal Terminal Act
N.Y. Laws 1911, Ch. 746

Barkley-Cole Trust Indenture Act of 1939
See Trust Indenture Act Of 1939

Barkley-Norris Resolution (T. V. Authority)
April 4, 1938, Ch. 61, 52 Stat. 154

Barnes Act (Electric Railroad Fares)
N.Y. Laws 1905, Ch. 358

Barnes Act (High Schools)
Kan. Laws 1905, Ch. 397

Barnes Act (Labor Unions)
Mass. Acts 1946, Ch. 618

Barnes Act (Railroad Employees)
N.Y. Railroad Law (Consol. Laws Ch. 49) § 64

Barnes-Wright Study Act
Tex. Education Code § 11.15

Barnett Act (Fees-Justice of Peace)
Mo. Laws 1891, p. 138, No. 2, § 26

Barnstable County Jail Loan Act
Mass. Acts 1959, Ch. 482

Barnstable County Probate Court and Registry of Deeds Loan Act
Mass. Acts 1952, Ch. 472

Barnstable County Shore Protection Loan Act
Mass. Acts 1953, Ch. 98
Mass. Acts 1957, Ch. 518

Barr-Walker Act
Pa. Cons. Stat., Title 42, § 9721 et seq.

Barratry Act
Ark. Stat. 1947, 5-3-201 et seq.
Cal. Penal Code §§ 158, 159
Ill. Rev. Stat. 1991, Ch. 13, § 21
Miss. Code Ann. 1972, § 97-9-11 et seq.
N.Y. Penal Law 1909 (Consol. Laws Ch. 40) § 320 et seq.
Ohio Rev. Code 1953, 2917.43
S.C. Code Ann. 1976, § 16-17-10 et seq.
Tex. Penal Code, § 38.12
Va. Code 1950, § 18.2-451 et seq.
Wash. Rev. Code Ann., 9.12.010 et seq.

Barren Island Annexation Act
N.Y. Laws 1802, Ch. 28

Barrett Act (Assessments)
Ind. Code 1976, 18-6-5-1 et seq.

Barrett Act (Streets)
Ind. Code 1976, 19-8-16-1 et seq.

Barrett-Bean Act (Post Roads)
Ore. Code 1930, §§ 44-401 to 44-412

Barrett Law (Municipal and County)
Ind. Code Ann., 36-9-18-1 et seq.

Barrier Free Design Act
S.C. Code Ann. 1976, § 10-5-240 et seq.

Barrier Pillar Act
Pa. 1891 Pamph. Laws 1976, No. 177, Art. 3, § 10

Barrington Charter Validation Act
R.I. Public Laws 1959, Ch. 34

Barrow County Water and Sewerage Authority Act
Ga. Laws 1991, p. 4444

Barrow Gas Field Transfer Act of 1984
July 17, 1984, P.L. 98-366, 42 U.S. Code §§ 6502, 6504, 6504 nt.

Barry Goldwater Scholarship and Excellence in Education Act
Nov. 14, 1986, P.L. 99-661, 20 U.S. Code § 4701 nt.
Dec. 5, 1991, P.L. 102-190, 20 U.S. Code §§ 4703, 4707, 4709
Oct. 23, 1992, P.L. 102-484, 20 U.S. Code § 4707
Nov. 30, 1993, P.L. 103-160, 20 U.S. Code §§ 4703, 4710
Oct. 7, 1998, P.L. 105-244, 20 U.S. Code § 4702

Barry Keene Underground Storage Tank Cleanup Trust Fund Act
Cal. Health and Safety Code § 25299.10 et seq.

Bartholomew Act (Canals)
N.Y. Canal Law (Consol. Laws Ch. 5) § 62

Bartlett Act (Three Mile Fishery Jurisdiction)
May 20, 1964, P.L. 88-308, 16 U.S. Code §§ 1081 to 1085
July 26, 1968, P.L. 90-427, 16 U.S. Code § 1081
Oct. 17, 1968, P.L. 90-578, 16 U.S. Code § 1083
Oct. 27, 1970, P.L. 91-514, 16 U.S. Code §§ 1082, 1083, 1086
Jan. 2, 1974, P.L. 93-242, 16 U.S. Code § 1085

Bartlett Act (Twelve Mile Fishery Jurisdiction)
Oct. 14, 1966, P.L. 89-658, 16 U.S. Code §§ 1091 to 1094

Bartlett-Strange Act (Parks)
Ky. Rev. Stat. 1962, 148.110 et seq.

Bartley-Fox Gun Control Law
Mass. Gen. Laws Ann., 269:10

Base Closure Community Redevelopment and Homeless Assistance Act of 1994
Oct. 25, 1994, P.L. 103-421, 42 U.S. Code § 11301 nt.

Base Load Renewable Resource Facilities Electricity Purchase Act
R.I. Gen. Laws 1956, 39-22-1 et seq.

Baseball Bribery Act
Wash. Rev. Code Ann., 67.04.010 et seq.

Baseball Contracts with Minors Act
Wash. Rev. Code Ann., 67.04.090 et seq.

Baseball Facility Liability Act
Ill. Comp. Stat. 1992, Ch. 745, § 38/1 et seq.

Baseball Spectator Safety Act
Colo. Rev. Stat., 13-21-120

Baseball Stadium Bond Act
N.J. Laws 1991, Chs. 275, 276

Basic and Literacy Education Act (Adult)
Pa. Purdon's Stat., Title 24, § 6401 et seq.

Basic Assistance for Industry and Trade Act
W. Va. Code 1966, § 5C-1-1 et seq.

Basic Bathroom Standards Act
Ga. Code Ann., 30-3-2, 30-3-3.1

Basic Education Act
Ore. Laws 1985, Ch. 831, § 1 et seq.
Wash. Rev. Code Ann., 28A.58.750 et seq.

Basic Health Insurance Coverage Law (Voluntary)
Miss. Code Ann. 1972, § 83-61-1 et seq.

Basic Health Insurance Plan
Ga. Code Ann., 33-51-1 et seq.
La. Rev. Stat. Ann., 22:244 et seq.

Basic Juvenile Court Act
Wash. Rev. Code Ann., 13.04.005 et seq.

Basic Literacy Act
Colo. Rev. Stat., 22-53-601 et seq.

Basic Reading Act (Miller-Unruh)
Cal. Education Code 1976, § 54100 et seq.

Basic Safety Act (Employers' Liability)
Ore. Rev. Stat. 1953, 654.305 et seq.

Basic School Support Fund Act
Ore. Rev. Stat. 1953, 327.006 et seq.

Basic Science Acts
Ala. Code 1958, Title 46, § 257 (26) et seq.
Ariz. Laws 1936, 1st Sp. Sess. c. 9
Ark. Stat. 1947, 72-101 et seq.
Colo. Stat. Ann. 1935, Ch. 109, § 51 et seq.
Fla. Stat. 1967, 456.01 et seq.
Iowa Code 1973, 146.1 et seq.
Kan. Laws 1937, Ch. 278
Kan. Laws 1957, Ch. 344
Mich. Comp. Laws Ann., 338.1 et seq.
Minn. Stat. Ann., 120.101
Neb. Laws 1927, Ch. 164
Nev. Rev. Stat. 1979 Reprint, Replaced
Pages, 629.010 et seq.
N.M. Stat. Ann. 1953, Superseded Vol.,
67-1-1 et seq.
Okla. Stat. 1971, Title 59, § 701 et seq.
Ore. Rev. Stat. 1953, 676.010 et seq.
R.I. Gen. Laws 1956, 5-28-1 et seq.
S.D. Codified Laws 1967, 36-3-1.1 et seq.
Tenn. Code Ann., Superseded Vol., 63-201
et seq.
Tex. Rev. Civ. Stat., Art. 4590c
Wash. Rev. Code Ann., 43.74.005 et seq.

Basic Skills Assessment Program Act
S.C. Code Ann. 1976, § 59-30-10 et seq.

Basic Speed Act
Ore. Rev. Stat., 811.100 et seq.

Basic Speed Act (Highways)
Cal. Vehicle Code 1959, § 22350

Basin Compact Act (Great Lakes)
Ill. Rev. Stat. 1991, Ch. 127, § 192.01 et seq.

Basin Improvement Loan Act (Charles River)
Mass. Acts 1957, Ch. 646
Mass. Acts 1962, Ch. 550

Baskets, Boxes, Containers, Carts and Cases Act
Fla. Stat. Ann. 506.501 et seq.

Bass Act (Striped)
N.J. Stat. Ann., 23:5-43 et seq.

Bass-Brooks Medical Training Act
Tex. Education Code, § 73.051 et seq.

Bastardy Act
Ala. Code 1975, § 26-12-1 et seq.
Ariz. Rev. Stat. Ann., § 12-841 et seq.
Colo. Rev. Stat. Replaced Vols., 19-6-101 et
seq.
Conn. Gen. Stat. Ann., § 46b-160 et seq.
D.C. Code 1973, § 16-2341 et seq.
Fla. Stat. 1983, 742.011 et seq.
Ga. Code Ann., 19-7-40 et seq.
Haw. Rev. Stat. Ann., § 579-1 et seq.
Ill. Rev. Stat. 1991, Ch. 40, § 2501 et seq.
Ind. Code 1976, 31-4-1-1 et seq.
Iowa Code Ann., 675.1 et seq.
Kan. Stat. Ann., 38-1101 et seq.
Ky. Rev. Stat. 1971, 406.011 et seq.
Md. Ann. Code 1957, Art. 16, § 66A et seq.
Mich. Comp. Laws Ann., 722.711 et seq.
Minn. Stat. 1969, 257.18 et seq.
Miss. Code Ann. 1972, § 93-9-1 et seq.
Mont. Code Ann., 40-6-101 et seq.
N.C. Gen. Stat. 1943, § 49-1 et seq.
N.D. Cent. Code, 14-17-01 et seq.
Neb. Rev. Stat. 1943, 13-101 et seq.
N.H. Rev. Stat. 1955, 168-A:1 et seq.
N.J. Stat. Ann., 9:17-1 et seq.
N.M. Stat. Ann., 40-11-1 et seq.
N.Y. Family Court Act, § 511 et seq.
Ohio Rev. Code 1953, 3111.01 et seq.
Okla. Stat. 1981, Title 10, § 71 et seq.
Pa. Cons. Stat., Title 42, § 7604 et seq.
Continued

R.I. Gen. Laws 1956, 15-8-1 et seq.
S.C. Code Ann. 1962, § 20-305 et seq.
S.D. Codified Laws 1967, 25-8-1 et seq.
Tenn. Code Ann., 36-2-101 et seq.
Utah Code Ann. 1953, 77-60-1 et seq.
Va. Code 1950, § 20-61.1
Vt. Stat. Ann., Title 15, § 331 et seq.
Wash. Rev. Code Ann., 26.26.010 et seq.

Bateman Act (Public Expenditures)
N.M. Stat. Ann., 6-6-11 et seq.

Bateman Act (School Aid)
N.J. Stat. Ann., 18A:7A-3, 18A:7A-7,
18A:7A-11, 18A:7A-17, 18A:7A-18,
18A:7A-28

Bates Act (Home Rule Cities—Taxation)
Mich. Comp. Laws Ann., 117.3, 117.5

Bates-Edwards Act (Utility Pensions)
Ky. Rev. Stat. 1971, 96.180

Bates-McLinn Reciprocal Tax Act
Ind. Code 1976, 6-2-2-1 et seq.

Bates Revenue Act
D.C. Code Ann., § 47-1801.1 et seq.

**Bates-Slenker-Adams Act (Taxation—
Public Utilities)**
Ind. Burns' 1933, 64-710, 64-712

Bates Teachers' Salary Act
D.C. Code Ann., § 31-1101 et seq.

Bates-Warinner Act (Alcoholic Beverages)
Ky. Rev. Stat. 1971, 244.195

Bathing Act (Public)
Pa. Purdon's Stat., Title 35, § 672 et seq.

Bathing Beach and Swimming Pool Act
Ill. Rev. Stat. 1991, Ch. 111 1/2, § 1201 et
seq.

Bathing Resort Safety Law
Cal. Health and Safety Code § 24050 et seq.

**Baton Rouge City-Parish Community
Improvement Act**
La. Act 1968, No. 224

Battered Child Act
Kan. Stat. Ann., 38-716 et seq.
Ohio Rev. Code 1953, 2151.421

Battered Child Protection Law
N.Y. Family Court Act, § 1011 et seq.
N.Y. Penal Law 1965 (Consol. Laws Ch. 40)
§ 260.10
N.Y. Social Services Law (Consol. Laws Ch.
55) § 411 et seq.

Battered Wives Act
Iowa Code Ann., 236.1 et seq.

Battered Wives Syndrome
N.Y. Family Court Act, § 812 et seq.

Battered Women's Protection Act
Cal. Health and Safety Code § 300.5

Battered Women's Testimony Act of 1992
Oct. 27, 1992, P.L. 102-527, 42 U.S. Code
§ 10702 nt.

Battery and Assault Law
See Assault and Battery Act

Battery Management Act (Dry Cell)
Cal. Public Resources Code § 15000 et seq.

Battery Park City Authority Act
N.Y. Public Authorities Law (Consol. Laws
Ch. 43A) § 1970 et seq.

Battle Act
See Mutual Defense Assistance Control Act
Of 1951

Battle Act (Quieting Title)
N.C. Gen. Stat. 1943, § 41-10

Battle Flags Act (Memorials Commission)
Ind. Code Ann., 10-7-2-6

Battleship Overhaul Act
July 25, 1939, Ch. 348, 53 Stat. 1079

Battleship U S S North Carolina Act
N.C. Gen. Stat. 1943, § 143-360 et seq.

Bauer Act (Rapid Transit Commission)
Ohio Rev. Code 1953, 747.01 et seq.

Bauer-Maloney Act (Taxation)
Ky. Rev. Stat. 1971, 132.200

Baumes Law (Persistant Felony Offenders)
N.Y. Criminal Procedure Law (Consol. Laws
Ch. 11A) § 400.15 et seq.
N.Y. Penal Law 1965 (Consol. Laws Ch. 40)
§ 70.10

**Baumes Law (Punishment Two or More
Convictions)**
Fla. Stat. 1969, 775.084 et seq.

Bawdy-House Act
N.Y. Real Property Actions and Proceedings
Law (Consol. Laws Ch. 81) § 715 et seq.
Tex. Penal Code, § 43.03

**BAWI (Balancing Agriculture with Industry
Act)**
Miss. Code Ann. 1972, § 57-1-1 et seq.

Baxley Street Improvement Act
Ga. Laws 1927, p. 902

Baxter Act (Taxation)
Ohio Laws Vol. 112, p. 542

Bay Area Air Pollution Control Law
Cal. Health and Safety Code §§ 24345,
40200 et seq.

Bay Area Assault Act
Cal. Penal Code, § 240 et seq.

**Bay Area County Traffic and Transpor-
tation Funding Act**
Cal. Public Utilities Code § 131000 et seq.

Bay Area Sewage Services Agency Law
Cal. Water Code § 16000 et seq.

**Bay Area Transportation Study
Commission Act**
Cal. Government Code § 66500 et seq.

Bay County Natural Gas Utility Act
Fla. Special Laws 1967, Ch. 67-1103

Bay County Revenue Bond Act
Fla. Special Laws 1951, Ch. 51-27397

Bay County Shrimp Net Restriction Act
Fla. Special Laws 1973, Ch. 73-404

**Bay County Solid Waste Disposal and
Resource Recovery Act**
Fla. Special Laws 1983, Ch. 83-370

Bay Park Library Services Act
N.Y. Laws 1998, Ch. 216

Bay State Skills Corporations Act
Mass. Gen. Laws Ann., 40I:1 et seq.

Bayh-Dole Act
Dec. 12, 1980, P.L. 96-517, 35 U.S. Code
§§ 200 to 212
Nov. 8, 1984, P.L. 98-620, 35 U.S. Code
§§ 201 to 203, 206 to 208, 210, 212
Oct. 20, 1986, P.L. 99-502, 35 U.S. Code
§ 210

**Beach Access Preservation and
Enhancement, Dune Protection and
Coastal Erosion Management Plan**
Tex. Gen. Laws 1991, Ch. 295

Beach and Shore Preservation Act
Fla. Stat. 1983, 161.011 et seq.

Beach Commission Law
N.J. Stat. Ann., 40:55A-1 to 40:55A-12

Beach Development Act
R.I. Public Laws 1958, Ch. 177

Beach Erosion Control Districts Act
N.J. Stat. Ann., 40:68-27 et seq.

Beach Erosion Facilities Construction Act
Del. Laws Vol. 56, p. 1823, Ch. 459

**Beach Erosion Loan Act (Metropolitan
District)**
Mass. Acts 1956, Ch. 736

Beach, Park, Recreational and Historical Facilities Bond Act (Cameron-Unruh)
Cal. Public Resources Code § 5096.1 et seq.

Beach Preservation Act
Del. Code of 1974, Title 7, § 6801 et seq.

Beach Preservation Act (St. Lucie County)
Fla. Special Laws 1961, Ch. 61-2755

Beaches and Harbors Bond Act
N.J. Laws 1977, Ch. 208

Beacon-Davis Act (Little)
N.M. Stat. Ann., 13-4-11 et seq.

Beadleston Act (Handicapped Children)
N.J. Stat. Ann., 18A:46-2 et seq.

Beadleston Act (School Attendance)
N.J. Stat. Ann., 18A:38-1 et seq.

Bean-Barrett Act (Post Roads)
Ore. Code 1930, § 44-401 et seq.

Bean Industry Promotion Act
N.D. Cent. Code, 4-10.3-01 et seq.

Beano Act
Mass. Gen. Laws 1990, 271:22B

Bear River Compact Act
Ida. Code 1947, 42-3501 et seq.
Wyo. Stat. Ann., §§ 41-12-101, 41-12-102

Bear River Compact Act (Amended)
Utah Code Ann. 1953, 73-16-3

Bear River Development Act
Utah Code Ann. 1953, 73-26-101 et seq.

Bear River-Yuba Basin Authority Act
Cal. Statutes 1959, Ch. 2131, p. 5032

Beard Act (Fireworks)
Ohio Rev. Code 1953, 3743.27 et seq.

Beatty Fireworks Act
Ky. Rev. Stat. 1971, 227.700 et seq.

Beatty Memorial Hospital Act
Ind. Code 1976, 16-14-20-1 et seq.

Beatty, Williamson, Love Act (Trucks)
Ky. Rev. Stat. 1971, 189.340

Beauchamp Act (Local Fairs)
Ky. Rev. Stat. 1971, 247.220

Beauchamp-Montgomery-Keck Super Highway Act
Ky. Rev. Stat. 1971, 177.390 et seq.

Beaufort County Law Enforcement Officers' Association Act
N.C. Laws 1967, Ch. 627

Beaufort County Peace Officers' Relief Act
N.C. Laws 1949, Ch. 678

Beautician Act
Ky. Rev. Stat. 1971, 317A.010 et seq.

Beautician and Barber Act
Ky. Rev. Stat. 1971, 317.410 et seq.

Beautification Act (Bicentennial)
Tenn. Code Ann., 54-5-1201 et seq.

Beautification Act (Highway)
Kan. Stat. Ann., 68-2201 et seq.

Beautification and Litter Control Act
N.M. Stat. Ann., 67-16-1 et seq.

Beauty Culture Act
Ariz. Rev. Stat. Ann., § 32-501 et seq.
Fla. Stat. Ann., 477.011 et seq.
Ill. Rev. Stat. 1983, Ch. 111, § 1801 et seq.
Ind. Code Ann., 25-8-2-1 et seq.
Md. Ann. Code 1974, Art. BO, § 5-101 et seq.
Minn. Stat. 1980, 155.01 et seq.
N.J. Stat. 45:5B-1 et seq.
Pa. Purdon's Stat., Title 63, § 507 et seq.
Tex. Rev. Civ. Stat., Art. 8451a
Wash. Rev. Code Ann., 18.16.010 et seq.

Beauty Operators Practice Act
Ill. Rev. Stat. 1991, Ch. 111, § 1703-1 et seq.

Beauty Shop Act
Okla. Stat. 1981, Title 59, § 199.1 et seq.

Beaver Control Act
Colo. Rev. Stat., 33-22-101 et seq.

Becca Too Bill
Wash. Rev. Code Ann., 13.32A.010 et seq.

Bechtold Act (License Revocation)
N.Y. Vehicle and Traffic Law 1959 (Consol. Laws Ch. 71) § 510

Beck-Harrison Act (State Planning Commission)
Ala. Code 1940, Title 55, § 368 et seq.

Bed and Breakfast Act
Ill. Comp. Stat. 1992, Ch. 50, § 820/1 et seq.
S.C. Code Ann. 1976, § 45-4-10 et seq.

Bed and Breakfast Establishment Inspection Act
Tenn. Code Ann., 68-14-501 et seq.

Bed Tax Act
Mont. Code Ann., 15-65-101 et seq.

Bedding Act
Ind. Code Ann., 16-1-33-1, 16-9-4-1 et seq.
N.J. Rev. Stat. 1937, 26:10-1 to 26:10-18
N.Y. General Business Law (Consol. Laws Ch. 20) § 383 et seq.
Okla. Stat. 1981, Title 63, § 1-1001 et seq.
Va. Code 1950, § 32.1-212 et seq.

Bedding Act (Sterilization)
Colo. Rev. Stat., 25-5-301 et seq.

Bedding and Furniture Label Law
Mass. Gen. Laws Ann., 94:270 et seq.

Bedding and Upholstered Furniture Act
La. Rev. Stat. Ann., 51:915 et seq.

Bedding and Upholstery Act
Ore. Rev. Stat. 1953, 433.405 et seq.
Pa. Purdon's Stat., Title 35, § 972 et seq.

Bedding Inspection Act
Fla. Stat. 1983, 556.011 et seq.
Ohio Rev. Code 1953, 3713.01 et seq.

Bedding Label Act
Fla. Stat. 1991, 501.145

Bedding Manufacture and Sale Act
Ore. Rev. Stat. 1953, 433.405 et seq.

Bedding Regulation Act
Okla. Stat. Ann., Title 63, § 1-1001.1 et seq.

Bedding, Upholstered Furniture and Quilted Clothing Inspection Act
Utah Code Ann. 1953, 4-10-1 et seq.

Bee Acts
Colo. Rev. Stat., 35-25-101 et seq.
Fla. Stat. 1983, 586.01 et seq.
N.M. Stat. Ann., 76-9-1 et seq.
Ore. Rev. Stat. 1953, 602.010 et seq.
Tenn. Code Ann., 44-15-101 et seq.

Bee and Honey Act
N.C. Gen. Stat. 1943, § 106-634 et seq.

Bee Groundwater Conservation District Act
Tex. General Laws 1997, Ch. 678

Bee Inspection Act
Kan. Stat. Ann., 2-411 et seq.
S.D. Codified Laws 1967, 38-18-1 et seq.
Utah Code Ann. 1953, 4-11-1 et seq.

Bee-Kennick-Arnold Act (Youth Authority)
Cal. Welfare and Institutions Code § 1821 et seq.

Bee Law
Pa. Cons. Stat., Title 3, § 2101 et seq.

Bee Management Act
Mont. Code Ann., 80-6-1101 et seq.

Beef Check-Off Act
W. Va. Code 1966, § 19-2F-1 et seq.

Beef Commission Act
Wash. Rev. Code Ann., 16.67.010 et seq.

Beef Council Act
Cal. Food and Agriculture Code 1967,
§ 64501 et seq.
N.M. Stat. Ann., 77-2A-1 et seq.

Beef Council Authority Act
Colo. Rev. Stat., 35-57-101 et seq.

Beef Industry Commission Act
Mich. Comp. Laws Ann., 287.601 et seq.

Beef Industry Development Act
Neb. Rev. Stat. 1943, 54-2101 et seq.

Beef Market Development Act
Ill. Comp. Stat. 1992, Ch. 505, § 25/1 et seq.

Beef Promotion Act
Ala. Code 1975, § 2-8-1 et seq.
N.D. Cent. Code, 4-34-01 et seq.
Okla. Stat. 1981, Title 2, § 1604 et seq.
Utah Code Ann. 1953, 41-21-1 et seq.

Beef Promotion and Research Act of 1985
Dec. 23, 1985, P.L. 99-198, 7 U.S. Code
§§ 2901 et seq., 2901 nt.

Beef Research and Information Act
May 28, 1976, P.L. 94-292, 7 U.S. Code
§ 2901 et seq.
Aug. 4, 1978, P.L. 95-334, 7 U.S. Code
§ 2908
Dec. 23, 1985, P.L. 99-198, 7 U.S. Code
§ 2901 et seq.

Beef Research and Marketing Act
Mont. Code Ann. 1987, 81-8-801 et seq.

Beef Slough Act
Wis. General Laws 1872, Ch. 105

Beekeepers Act
N.D. Cent. Code, 4-12.3 et seq.

Beekeepers Commission Act
Ill. Rev. Stat. 1991, Ch. 8, § 126.9 et seq.

Beer Act (Nonintoxicating)
W. Va. Code 1966, § 11-16-1 et seq.

Beer Acts
Colo. Rev. Stat., 12-46-101 et seq.
Fla. Stat. 1983, 561.01 et seq.
Ida. Code 1947, 23-1001 et seq.
Mich. Comp. Laws Ann., 436.1 et seq.
Minn. Stat. Ann., 340A.101 et seq.
Mont. Code Ann., 16-1-101 et seq.
N.D. Cent. Code, 5-01-01 et seq.
N.J. Laws 1933, Ch. 85
N.Y. Alcoholic Beverage Control Law
(Consol. Laws Ch. 3B) § 50 et seq.
Okla. Stat. 1981, Title 37, § 163.1 et seq.
S.C. Code Ann. 1976, 61-9-10 et seq.
S.D. Codified Laws 1967, 35-1-1 et seq.

Beer Advertising Prohibition Act
Ohio Rev. Code 1953, 4301.211

Beer, Ale, Porter, and Wine Act
S.C. Code Ann. 1976, § 61-9-10 et seq.

Beer and Liquor Control Act
Iowa Code Ann., 123.1 et seq.

Beer and Malt Liquor Law
Iowa Code Ann., 123.122 et seq.

Beer and Wine Act
Miss. Code Ann. 1972, § 67-3-1 et seq.
S.C. Code Ann. 1976, § 61-9-10 et seq.

Beer and Wine Local Option Act
N.C. Gen. Stat. 1943, § 18A-52 et seq.

Beer Consumers Sales Tax Act (Nyberg)
Ark. Acts 1939, p. 758, No. 310

Beer Control Act
Tex. Alcoholic Beverage Code, § 1.01 et seq.

Beer-Dance Hall Act
Okla. Stat. 1971, Title 37, § 211 et seq.

Beer Franchise Act
Va. Code 1950, § 4-118.3 et seq.

Beer Franchise Fair Dealing Act
Md. Ann. Code 1957, Art. 2B, § 203A et seq.
Va. Code 1950, § 4-118.3 et seq.

Beer Industry Fair Dealing Act
Ill. Comp. Stat. 1992, Ch. 815, § 720/1 et seq.
Miss. Code Ann. 1972, § 67-7-1 et seq.
R.I. Gen. Laws 1956, 3-13-1 et seq.

Beer Inspection Act
Mo. Laws 1899, p. 228

Beer License Act
Ga. Code Ann., 3-5-1 et seq.
La. Rev. Stat. Ann., 26:271 et seq.
Neb. Rev. Stat. 1943, 53-142 et seq.
Wis. Stat. Ann., 125.25 et seq.

Beer, Light Wine and Other Alcoholic Beverages Law
Miss. Code Ann. 1972, § 67-3-1 et seq.

Beer Tax Act
Ga. Code Ann., 3-5-60, 3-5-61
Okla. Stat. 1981, Title 37, § 163.1 et seq.
Tenn. Code Ann., 57-5-101 et seq.

Beer Tax Act (Wholesale)
Tenn. Code Ann., 57-6-101 et seq.

Beer, Wine and Liquor Control Act
Iowa Code Ann., 123.1 et seq.

Beer-Wine Revenue Act
March 22, 1933, Ch. 4, 48 Stat. 16

Bees and Apiaries Act
Ill. Comp. Stat. 1992, Ch. 510, § 20/1 et seq.

Beginning Agricultural Producer Pool Act
Okla. Stat. Ann., Title 74, § 5063.21 et seq.

Beginning-Teacher Incentive Program (Jack O'Connell)
Cal. Education Code 1976, § 45023.4

Behavior Disordered and Hearing Impaired Children Services Act
Ill. Rev. Stat. 1991, Ch. 23, §§ 3404.9, 3405

Behavior Disordered/Hearing Impaired Children Interagency Board Act
Ill. Rev. Stat. 1991, Ch. 23, § 6701 et seq.

Bejack Law (Emancipation Act)
Tenn. Code Ann., 36-3-504

Belchertown School Building Loan Act
Mass. Acts 1951, Ch. 628

Bell and Whistle Act (Railroads)
Ark. Stat. 1947, 23-12-410
Miss. Code Ann. 1972, § 77-9-225
Neb. Rev. Stat. 1943, 74-573

Bell Ringing Act
Mo. Rev. Stat., 389.990

Belle Fourche River Compact Act
S.D. Codified Laws 1967, 46A-17-1, 46A-17-2 et seq.
Wyo. Stat. Ann., § 41-12-201 et seq.

Belmont-De Villier Improvement Board Act
Fla. Special Laws 1975, Ch. 75-483

Belotti-Christensen Act (Logging Trucks)
Cal. Vehicle Code 1959, § 35552

Below Cost Sales Act
Ga. Code Ann., 10-1-250 et seq.

Ben Franklin/IRC Partnership Act
Pa. 1993 Pamph. Laws, No. 64

Ben Hill County and Fitzgerald Development Authority Act
Ga. Laws 1963, p. 2003

Bendixen Act (Railroad Passenger Rates)
Minn. Stat. Ann., 218.021

Beneficial Interest Disclosure Act (Land Trust)
Ill. Rev. Stat. 1991, Ch. 148, § 70 et seq.

Beneficial Societies Act
Pa. Purdon's Stat., Title 40, § 1141-101 et seq.

Beneficial Use Tax Act
Tenn. Code Ann., 67-4-1501 et seq.

Beneficiary Contract Act (Third Party)
Ill. Rev. Stat. 1991, Ch. 110 1/2, § 400 et seq.

Benefit Act (Automobile Owners' Liability)
Ga. Code 1933, 68-301

Benefit Act (Disability)
N.Y. Worker's Compensation Law (Consol.
Laws Ch. 67) § 200 et seq.
P.R. Laws Ann. 1954, Title 11, § 201 et seq.

**Benefit and Annuity Fund Act (Peace
Officers)**
Ga. Code Ann., 47-17-1 et seq.

Benefit Assessment Act
Cal. Government Code § 54701 et seq.

Benefit Contribution Act (Employee)
Ill. Rev. Stat. 1991, Ch. 48, § 39v.9 et seq.

Benefit Corporation Act
Ariz. Laws 1937, Ch. 36

Benefit District Reimbursement Act
Kan. Laws 1941, Ch. 318

Benefit Fund Act (County Employees)
Ill. Rev. Stat. 1991, Ch. 108 1/2, § 9-101 et
seq.

Benefit Insurance Corporation Act
Ariz. Laws 1943, Ch. 95

Benefit Insurance Incontestability Act
Ariz. Rev. Stat. Ann., § 20-937, Subd. 3

Benefit Insurance Stock Corporation Act
Ariz. Laws 1947, Ch. 138

Benefit Road Act
Mo. Rev. Stat., 233.170 et seq.

Benefit Rule Act (Foreign Inheritance)
Md. Ann. Code 1974, Art. ET, § 9-108
Ohio Rev. Code 1953, 2113.81

Benefit Rule Act (Inheritance)
Conn. Gen. Stat. Ann., § 45a-449
Mass. Gen. Laws Ann., 206:27B
N.J. Stat. Ann., 3B:23-22
R.I. Gen. Laws 1956, 33-13-13
Wis. Stat. 1969, 318.06

Benefit Societies Act (Fraternal)
Ariz. Rev. Stat. Ann., § 20-861 et seq.
Pa. 1992 Pamph. Laws, No. 134

Benefit Society Act (Fraternal)
Ga. Code Ann., 33-15-1 et seq.

Benefits Act (Dental Care)
Miss. Code Ann. 1972, § 83-51-1 et seq.

**Benefits Act (Group Disability Insurance
Coordination)**
Mich. Comp. Laws Ann., 550.251

Benefits Act (State Employees Flexible)
Okla. Stat. Ann., Title 74, § 1341 et seq.

Benefits Act (State Employees)
Okla. Stat. Ann., Title 74, § 1362 et seq.

Benefits Protection Act (Private Pension)
Minn. Stat. Ann., 181B.01 et seq.

Benevolent Associations Act
N.D. Cent. Code, 26-25-01 et seq.

Benevolent Corporation Act
Ark. Stat. 1947, 4-28-201 et seq.
S.D. Codified Laws 1967, 47-22-1 et seq.

Benevolent Orders Law
N.Y. Benevolent Orders Law (Consol. Laws
Ch. 3) § 1 et seq.

**Benevolent Religious and Charitable
Associations Act**
Mo. Rev. Stat., 352.010 et seq.

**Benjamin Franklin National Memorial
Commemorative Medal and Fire Service
Bill of Rights Act**
Oct. 12, 1992, P.L. 102-406, 31 U.S. Code
§ 5111 nt.

**Bennett Act (Maximum Debt of Persons to
Banks)**
Ky. Rev. Stat. 1971, 287.280, 287.290

**Bennett, Randall and Stacey Shareholder
Equity Act**
Mich. Comp. Laws Ann., 450.1790 et seq.

Benning Road Widening Act
May 16, 1908, Ch. 172, 35 Stat. 163

Bense Act (Water Supply)
Ohio Rev. Code 1953, 6111.09 et seq.

Bentley-Smyer Act (War Emergency Council)
Ala. General Acts 1943, p. 169, No. 185

Bently Act (Presidential Electors)
Ala. Code 1975, § 17-19-7

Benton Civic Center Law
Ill. Comp. Stat. 1992, Ch. 70, § 230/1-1 et seq.

Benzedrine and Barbiturate Act
Ark. Stat. 1947, 82-956.1 et seq.

Benzie-LaFramboise-Carpenter-MacKay Act (Game Bag Limit)
Mich. Comp. Laws Ann., 312.12

Benzine Container Act
Mich. Comp. Laws Ann., 750.502

Bequests and Trust Interests Act (Distributions in Kind)
Mich. Comp. Laws Ann., 700.216

Bergen County Sewer Authority Act
N.J. Stat. Ann., 40:14B-1 et seq.

Bergeson Act (Teacher Credentialing)
Cal. Education Code 1976, § 44200 et seq.

Bergeson-Costa-Robbins-Nielsen County Revenue Stabilization Act
Cal. Government Code § 16265 et seq.

Bergeson Fire District Law
Cal. Health and Safety Code § 13800 et seq.

Bergeson-Peace Infrastructure and Economic Development Bank Act
Cal. Government Code § 63000 et seq.

Berkshire County Court House Loan Act
Mass. Acts 1954, Ch. 571

Berkshire District Court Building Loan Act
Mass. Acts 1962, Ch. 185

Berman-Alatorre-Zenovich-Dunlap Agricultural Labor Relations Act of 1975
Cal. Labor Code § 1140 et seq.

Berne Convention Implementation Act of 1988
Oct. 31, 1988, P.L. 100-568, 17 U.S. Code § 101 nt.

Berrien County Tax Commissioner Act
Ga. Laws 1931, p. 390

Berryhill Total Compensation Act
Cal. Statutes 1974, Ch. 374

Bert J. Harris, Jr., Private Property Rights Protection Act
Fla. Stat. Ann., 70.001 et seq.

Bertie County Law Enforcement Officers' Relief Act
N.C. Laws 1953, Ch. 897

Bessemer Court Act
Ala. Local Acts 1919, p. 62

Bessesen Act (Initiative Petitions)
N.D. Laws 1911, Ch. 93
N.D. Laws 1913, Ch. 101

Best and Brightest Scholarship Act
R.I. Gen. Laws 1956, 16-37-1 et seq.

Best Evidence Act
Ore. Rev. Stat. 1953, 41.360

Best Management Practices Act (Forest)
S.C. Code Ann. 1976, §§ 48-36-10 to 48-36-30

Best School Facilities Act
Miss. General Laws 1990, Ch. 588, §§ 42 to 71, p. 914

Bethel Island Municipal Improvement District Act
Cal. Statutes 1960, 1st Ex. Sess., Ch. 22

Bethpage Park Authority Act
N.Y. Public Authorities Law (Consol. Laws Ch. 43A) § 200 et seq.

Betterment Act
Ark. Stat. 1947, 18-60-213 et seq.
Mo. Rev. Stat., 524.160
N.C. Gen. Stat. 1943, § 1-340 et seq.
Pa. Purdon's Stat., Title 72, § 5875
S.C. Code Ann. 1976, § 27-27-10 et seq.

Betterment Act (Improvements)
Tex. Property Code, § 22.021 et seq.

Betterment Act (Real Estate)
Utah Code Ann. 1953, 57-6-1 et seq.

Betterment Act (Real Property Improvements)
Wash. Rev. Code Ann., 7.28.160 et seq.

Betterment Act (Real Property)
S.C. Code Ann. 1976, § 27-27-10 et seq.

Betterment and Improvement Act
Haw. Rev. Stat. Ann., § 70-111

Betterments Act (Lands)
Me. Rev. Stat. Ann. 1964, Title 14, § 6956 et seq.

Betting Act (Elections)
Mont. Code Ann. 1978, 13-35-212

Betting Act (Pari-Mutuel)
R.I. Gen. Laws 1956, 41-4-1 et seq.

Betting Act (Prohibition)
Tex. Penal Code, § 47.01 et seq.

Betting Act (Racing)
Mont. Rev. Code 1947, 94-2425 et seq.

Beverage Act (3.2)
Fla. Stat. Ann., 561.01 et seq.
Va. Code 1950, § 4-99 et seq.

Beverage Act (Alcoholic)
N.M. Stat. Ann., 60-3A-1 et seq.

Beverage Act (Malt)
Ga. Code Ann., 3-5-1 et seq.

Beverage Act (Nonalcoholic)
Okla. Stat. Ann., Title 37, § 163.1 et seq.
Ore. Rev. Stat. 1953, 635.015 et seq.

Beverage Act (Soft Drinks)
La. Rev. Stat. Ann., 40:711 et seq.

Beverage Container Act
La. Rev. Stat. Ann., 40:681 et seq.
N.M. Stat. Ann., 57-20-1 et seq.

Beverage Container Recycling and Litter Reduction Act
Cal. Public Resources Code § 14500 et seq.

Beverage Container Recycling and Litter Reduction Incentive Act
Ga. Code Ann., 12-17-1 et seq.

Beverage Control Act
Ala. Code 1975, § 28-3-101 et seq.
N.C. Gen. Stat. 1943, § 18B-100 et seq.
S.C. Code Ann. 1976, § 61-3-10 et seq.

Beverage Control Act (Alcoholic)
Iowa Code Ann., 123.1 et seq.
Okla. Stat. Ann., Title 37, § 501 et seq.

Beverage Distribution Act (Nonintoxicating)
Okla. Stat. Ann., Title 37, § 1163.18A et seq.

Beverage Inspection Act
N.D. Cent. Code, 19-08-01 et seq.

Beverage License Law
Pa. 1933 Pamph. Laws 252, No. 91
Pa. 1935 Pamph. Laws 1217, No. 398
Pa. 1937 Pamph. Laws 1827, No. 372

Beverage Tax Act
Pa. Purdon's Stat., Title 47, § 103 et seq.
Pa. Purdon's Stat., Title 72, § 9001 et seq.
S.C. Code Ann. 1976, § 12-33-10 et seq.

Beverage Tax Act (Sealed Bottles)
Ohio Rev. Code 1953, 4307.01 et seq.

Beverage Tax Acts
Oct. 3, 1917, Ch. 63, 40 Stat. 308
Feb. 24, 1919, Ch. 18, 40 Stat. 1105, 19 U.S. Code § 460
Nov. 23, 1921, Ch. 136, 42 Stat. 285

Beverage Tax Law (Alcoholic)
Cal. Revenue and Taxation Code § 32001 et seq.

Beverages Act (Alcoholic)
P.R. Laws Ann. 1954, Title 13, § 6001 et seq.

Beverages and Liquor Control Act
Ga. Code Ann., 3-3-1 et seq.

Beverly Chapman Act
Fla. Stat. Ann., 338.155

Beverly-Killean Limited Liability Company Act
Cal. Corporations Code § 17000

Beverly-Murray Small Business Bridge Loan Program
Cal. Statutes 1992, Ch. 61

Beverly Public Parking Loan Act
Mass. Acts 1963, Ch. 139

Beverly School Loan Act
Mass. Acts 1950, Ch. 642

Beverly-Song Consumer Warranty Act
Cal. Civil Code § 1790 et seq.

Beverly-Song Credit Card Act
Cal. Civil Code § 1747 et seq.

Bexar County Road and Bridge Act
Tex. Special Laws 42nd Leg., 1931, p. 259, Ch. 137

Bi-State Development Agency Act
Ill. Comp. Stat. 1992, Ch. 45, § 105/0.01 et seq.
Ill. Rev. Stat. 1991, Ch. 127, § 63s et seq.

Bi-State Development Compact Act
Ill. Comp. Stat. 1992, Ch. 45, § 100/0.01 et seq.

Ill. Rev. Stat. 1991, Ch. 127, § 63r et seq.

Bi-State Development Powers Act
Ill. Rev. Stat. 1991, Ch. 127, § 63s-8.9 et seq.

Bi-State Regional Planning Compact Act
N.Y. Laws 1965, Ch. 413

Bi-State Transit Safety Act
Ill. Comp. Stat. 1992, Ch. 45, § 111/1 et seq.

Bias Crimes Information and Documentation Act
Ga. Code Ann., 35-3-120 to 35-3-124

Bibb County Water and Sewerage Authority Act
Ga. Laws 1966, p. 2737

Bible Reading Act
Ala. Code 1958, Title 52, § 542 et seq.
Del. Code of 1974, Title 14, § 4101
N.J. Stat. Ann., Superseded Vol., 18:14-77
Tenn. Code Ann., 49-5-201

Bible Reading Act (Public Schools)
Ida. Code 1947, 33-1604
Me. Rev. Stat. Ann. 1964, Title 20, § 1223
Pa. Purdon's Stat., Title 24, § 15-1516

Bicentennial Beautification Act
Tenn. Code Ann., 54-5-1201 et seq.

Bicentennial Celebration Act (American Revolution)
N.J. Stat. Ann., 52:9P-1 et seq.

Bicentennial Commission Act
Fla. Stat. 1983, 13.997 et seq.
Haw. Session Laws 1970, Act 98
Ill. Rev. Stat. 1977, Ch. 127, § 214.21 et seq.
N.J. Laws 1969, Ch. 126
Pa. Purdon's Stat., Title 71, § 1047.11 et seq.
S.D. Codified Laws 1967, Superseded Vol., 1-18A-1 et seq.

Bicentennial Grant-in-Aid Act
N.M. Stat. Ann., 11-5-1 et seq.

Bicentennial of the Constitution Coins Act
Oct. 29, 1986, P.L. 99-582, 31 U.S. Code
§ 5112 nt.

Bicentennial of the United States Congress Commemorative Coin Act
Nov. 17, 1988, P.L. 100-673, 102 Stat. 3992

Bicycle Act
Mich. Comp. Laws Ann., 257.657
R.I. Gen. Laws 1956, 31-19-1 et seq.

Bicycle and Bikeway Act
N.C. Gen. Stat. 1943, § 136-71.6 et seq.

Bicycle Operation and Equipment Act
Wash. Rev. Code Ann., 46.61.750 et seq.

Bicycle Pathways Act
Nev. Rev. Stat. 1979 Reprint, 407.211 et seq.

Bicycle Racing Act
N.M. Stat. Ann., 60-2D-1

Bicycle Regulation Act
N.H. Rev. Stat. 1955, 265.143 et seq.

Bicycle Safety Act
Ga. Code Ann., 40-6-290 et seq.

Bicycle Safety Act (Brad Hudson)
Ala. Code 1975, § 32-5A-280 et seq.

Bicycle Safety Act (Child)
Tenn. Code Ann., 55-52-101 et seq.
W. Va. Code 1966, § 17C-11A-1 et seq.

Bicycle Traffic Act
Mont. Code Ann., 61-8-601 et seq.

Bicycle Trail Act
Mont. Code Ann., 60-3-301 et seq.

Bicycle Transportation Act
Cal. Streets and Highways Code § 890 et seq.

Bicyclist Protection Act
Cal. Vehicle Code 1959, §§ 2900, 21202, 21208, 21212, 21750, 39002, 39012

Bid Act (Public Contracts)
Mass. Gen. Laws Ann., 149:44A et seq.

Bid Act (State Purchases)
Alaska Stat. 1962, § 37.05.220 et seq.

Bid Act (Territorial Purchases)
Alaska Stat. 1962, § 37.05.230 et seq.

Bid Disclosure Act (Public)
Fla. Stat. 1991, 218.80

Bid Law (Public)
La. Rev. Stat. Ann., 38:2181 et seq., 38:2211 et seq.

Bid Listing Act
Cal. Government Code §§ 4103, 4104

BIDCO Act
Alaska Stat. 1962, § 10.13.010 et seq.
Mich. Com. Laws 1979, 487.1101 et seq.
Tenn. Code Ann., 45-8-201 et seq.

Bidders' Prequalification Act
Ore. Rev. Stat. 1953, 279.011 et seq.

Bidding Act (Competitive)
Mass. Gen. Laws Ann., 29:8A et seq.

Bidding Act (Municipal Contracts)
N.J. Stat. Ann., 40A:11-4 et seq.

Bidding Act (Public Competitive)
Okla. Stat. 1981, Title 61, § 101 et seq.

Bidding Act (Public)
N.Y. General Municipal Law (Consol. Laws Ch. 24) § 103

Bidding Law (Blind)
Mont. Code Ann., 30-14-301 et seq.

Biddle—Strong Act
Ala. Code 1975, § 36-21-2

Biennial Budget Act (Municipal)
Wash. Rev. Code Ann., 35A.34.020 et seq.

Biennial Election Act
Kan. Stat. Ann., 25-101

Big Bill-Fiscal Year 1993 Omnibus Appropriations Act
Vt. Acts 1992, No. 245

Big Bill-Fiscal Year 1995 Appropriations Act
Vt. Acts 1993, No. 210

Big Bill-Fiscal Year 1998 Appropriations Act
Vt. Acts 1997, No. 61

Big Bill-Omnibus Appropriations Act
Vt. Acts 1991, No. 50

Big Blue River Compact
Kan. Stat. Ann., 82a-529

Big Brothers (Big Sisters of America)
Nov. 11, 1977, P.L. 95-167, 36 U.S. Code §§ 881, 883, 885, 887, 895, 896, 1101

Big Cypress Conservation Act
Fla. Stat. 1983, 380.055

Big Cypress National Preserve Addition Act
April 29, 1988, P.L. 100-301, 102 Stat. 443, 16 U.S. Code §§ 698f , 698f nt., 698h, 698j

Big Horn Mountains Water Agency Law
Cal. Water Code, Appendix, § 112-1 et seq.

Big Kincaid Creek Reservoir Act
Ill. Comp. Stat. 1992, Ch. 615, § 80/0.01 et seq.

Big Mac Laws
N.Y. Public Authorities Law (Consol. Laws Ch. 42) §§ 3001 et seq., 3030 et seq.

Big River-Wood River Reservoir Site Acquisition Act
R.I. Public Laws 1962, Ch. 91
R.I. Public Laws 1964, Ch. 133

Big Thicket National Preserve Addition Act of 1993
July 1, 1993, P.L. 103-46, 16 U.S. Code §§ 698 nt., 698, 698e

Bigamy Act
Cal. Penal Code §§ 281 to 283
Colo. Rev. Stat., 18-6-201, 18-6-202
Ga. Code Ann., 16-6-20, 16-6-21
Md. Ann. Code 1957, Art. 27, § 18
Mont. Code Ann., 45-5-611, 45-5-612
Nev. Rev. Stat. 1979 Reprint, 201.160 et seq.
N.J. Rev. Stat. 2C:24-1
Ohio Rev. Code 1953, 2919.01
R.I. Gen. Laws 1956, 11-6-1
Wash. Rev. Code Ann., 9A.64.010
Wis. Stat. Ann., 944.01
W. Va. Code 1966, § 61-8-1

Bigamy Act (Divorce)
Okla. Stat. Ann., Title 43, § 123
Okla. Stat. 1981, Title 12, § 1280

Bighorn Canyon National Recreation Area Act
Oct. 15, 1966, P.L. 89-664, 80 Stat. 913, 16 U.S. Code §§ 460t to 460t-4

Bighorn Mountains Water Agency Law
Cal. Water Code Appendix, § 112-1 et seq.

Bikeway Act
Cal. Streets and Highways Code § 2370 et seq.
Ill. Comp. Stat. 1992, Ch. 605, § 30/0.01 et seq.

Bilingual and Bicultural Education Act
Cal. Education Code 1976, §§ 52160 et seq., 52178.1 et seq.

Bilingual-Bicultural Education Act (Chacon-Moscone)
Cal. Education Code 1976, § 52160 et seq.

Bilingual-Crosscultural Teacher Preparation and Training Act
Cal. Education Code 1976, §§ 52163 et seq., 52178 et seq.

Bilingual Education Act
Jan. 2, 1968, P.L. 90-247, 81 Stat. 816, 20 U.S. Code §§ 880b to 880b-6
Nov. 1, 1978, P.L. 95-561, 20 U.S. Code § 3221 et seq.
Continued

Oct. 19, 1984, P.L. 98-511, 20 U.S. Code § 3221 et seq.

April 28, 1988, P.L. 100-297, 102 Stat. 274, 20 U.S. Code §§ 3281 et seq., 3306 et seq., 3341

Bilingual Education Acts

Cal. Education Code 1976, §§ 51200 et seq., 52160 et seq.

Ill. Rev. Stat. 1991, Ch. 122, § 14C-1 et seq.

Mass. Gen. Laws Ann., 71A:1 et seq.

Minn. Stat. 1978, 126.31 et seq.

R.I. Gen. Laws 1956, 16-54-1 et seq.

Bilingual Education Improvement and Reform Act

Cal. Statutes 1980, Ch. 1339

Bilingual Instruction Act

N.M. Stat. Ann. 1953, 77-21-1 et seq.

Bilingual Instruction Act (Transitional)

Wash. Rev. Code Ann., 28A.58.800 et seq.

Bilingual Multi-Cultural Education Act

N.M. Stat. Ann., 22-23-1 et seq.

Bilingual Services Act

Cal. Government Code § 7290 et seq.

Bilingual Translation Services Act

D.C. Code Ann., § 1-2342 et seq.

Bill Emerson Humanitarian Trust Act of 1998

Nov. 13, 1998, P.L. 105-385, Subtitle B, 112 Stat. 3465, 7 U.S. Code § 1691 nt.

Bill for Religious Liberty

Va. Code 1950, §§ 57-1, 57-2

Bill Introduction and Duplication Act

Ill. Comp. Stat. 1992, Ch. 25, § 35/0.01 et seq.

Bill King Annual Sessions Act

Ala. Acts 1975, 2d Sp. Sess., p. 115

Bill of Abominations (Tariff)

May 19, 1828, Ch. 55, 4 Stat. 270

Bill of Exceptions Act

Ky. Civil Code of Practice 1932, §§ 333 to 339

Wash. Rev. Code Ann., 4.80.010 et seq.

Bill of Human Rights

Wis. Stat. Ann., 66.433

Bill of Lading Act (Carriage of Goods by Sea)

See Limited Liability Acts (Shipping)

Bill of Lading Act (Interstate and Foreign Commerce)

Aug. 29, 1916, Ch. 415, 39 Stat. 538, 49 U.S. Code §§ 81 to 124

Bill of Rights (Bradley-Burns)

Cal. Revenue and Taxation Code § 7221 et seq.

Bill of Rights (Children's)

Ill. Comp. Stat. 1992, Ch. 725, § 115/1 et seq.

N.Y. Family Court Act, § 1011 et seq.

Bill of Rights (Crime Victims')

Ga. Code Ann., 17-17-1 et seq.

Bill of Rights (Drunk Driving Victims)

N.J. Stat. Ann., 39:4-50.9 et seq.

Bill of Rights (Emergency Telephone Users')

Cal. Revenue and Taxation Code § 41160 et seq.

Bill of Rights (Energy Resources Surcharge)

Cal. Revenue and Taxation Code § 40200 et seq.

Bill of Rights (Home Protection)

Cal. Penal Code § 198.5

Bill of Rights (Mental Patients')

N.Y. Mental Hygiene Law 1972 (Consol. Laws Ch. 27) § 33.02

Bill of Rights (Mobile Home Tenant)

N.Y. Real Property Law (Consol. Laws Ch. 50) § 233

Bill of Rights (Nursing Home Patients')
N.Y. Public Health Law 1953 (Consol. Laws Ch. 45) § 2803c

Bill of Rights (Pain Patient's)
Cal. Health and Safety Code § 124960 et seq.

Bill of Rights (Patients')
Mass. Gen. Laws Ann., 111.70E

Bill of Rights (Policeman's)
Fla. Stat. Ann., 112.532 et seq.

Bill of Rights (Taxpayers')
Ariz. Rev. Stat. Ann., § 42-139 et seq.
Ark. Code 1987, 26-18-801 et seq.
Colo. Const. Art. 10, § 20
Fla. Stat. Ann., 213.015
Ga. Code Ann., 48-1-8
Ill. Rev. Stat. 1991, Ch. 120, § 2301 et seq.
Kan. Stat. Ann., 79-3268
Minn. Stat. Ann., 270.0602 et seq.
Mont. Code Ann., 15-1-221 to 15-1-223
Ore. Rev. Stat., 305.860 et seq.
Pa. Purdon's Stat., Title 72, § 3310-101 et seq.
S.C. Code Ann. 1976, § 12-54-710 et seq.
S.C. Code Ann. 1976, § 12-58-10 et seq.
Va. Code 1950, § 58.1-1845

Bill of Rights (Underground Storage Tank Maintenance Fee)
Cal. Revenue and Taxation Code § 50156 et seq.

Bill of Rights (Utility Consumers')
N.Y. Public Service Law (Consol. Laws Ch. 48) § 30 et seq.

Bill of Rights (Veterans')
P.R. Laws Ann. 1954, Title 29, § 761

Bill of Rights (Victims)
Cal. Const. 1979, Art. 1, § 28

Bill of Rights Act (Alcoholic Beverage Tax)
Cal. Revenue and Taxation Code § 32460 et seq.

Bill of Rights Act (Crime Victims')
N.Y. Executive Law 1951 (Consol. Laws Ch. 18) § 640 et seq.

Bill of Rights Act (Educational Records)
R.I. Gen. Laws 1956, 16-71-1 et seq.

Bill of Rights Act (Gasoline Dealer)
Wash. Rev. Code Ann., 19.120.010 et seq.

Bill of Rights Act (Victim's)
R.I. Gen. Laws 1956, 12-28-1 et seq.
Tenn. Code Ann., 40-38-101 et seq.
Wyo. Stat. Ann., § 1-40-201 et seq.

Bill of Rights and Responsibilities (Patients')
Fla. Stat. Ann., 381.026, 381.0261

Bill of Rights and Service Quality Standards of Persons with Mental Retardation, Developmental Disabilities, Brain Injury, or Chronic Mental Illness
Iowa Code Ann., 225C.25 et seq.

Bill of Rights Cigarette and Tobacco Products Tax Act
Cal. Revenue and Taxation Code § 30458 et seq.

Bill of Rights Commission Act
Haw. Session Laws 1923, Act 86

Bill of Rights Declaration
N.Y. Civil Rights Law (Consol. Laws Ch. 6) § 2 et seq.

Bill of Rights for Campus Sexual Assault Victim's
N.J. Stat. Ann., 18A:61E-1 et seq.

Bill of Rights for Child Victims and Witnesses
Del. Code of 1974, Title 11, § 5131 et seq.

Bill of Rights for Children Act
Ill. Rev. Stat. 1991, Ch. 38, § 1351 et seq.

Bill of Rights for Displaced Defense Workers
Conn. Public Acts 1994, May Special Session No. 2, § 192

Bill of Rights for Employment and Training Services for New York State Veterans
N.Y. Laws 1994, Ch. 553

Bill of Rights for Persons with Developmental Disabilities and Traumatic Brain Injury
Ala. Code 1975, § 38-9C-1 et seq.

Bill of Rights for Residents of Long-Term Care Facilities
Ga. Code Ann., 31-8-100 et seq.
Mont. Code Ann., 50-5-1101 et seq.
S.C. Code Ann. 1976, § 44-81-10 et seq.

Bill of Rights for Solid Waste Disposal Site Cleanup and Maintenance
Cal. Revenue and Taxation Code § 45856 et seq.

Bill of Rights for the Handicapped Act
S.C. Code Ann. 1976, § 43-33-510 et seq.

Bill of Rights for Victims and Witnesses of Violent Crime Act
Ill. Rev. Stat. 1991, Ch. 38, § 1401 et seq.

Bill of Rights for Victims of Crime Act
Kan. Stat. Ann., 74-73333
Ore. Rev. Stat., 147.405

Bill of Rights Hazardous Substances Tax Act
Cal. Health and Safety Code § 43511 et seq.

Bill of Rights of Developmentally Disabled Person
Fla. Stat. Ann., 393.13

Bill of Rights of Retarded Persons
Fla. Stat. 1983, 393.13, 393.14

Bill of Rights Use Fuel Tax Law
Cal. Revenue and Taxation Code § 9260 et seq.

Bill of Sale Act (Motor Vehicles)
Ohio Rev. Code 1953, 4505.03 et seq.

Bill Payers, Proraters and Check Sellers Law
Cal. Financial Code § 12000 et seq.

Bill Synopsis Act
Ill. Comp. Stat. 1992, Ch. 25, §§ 30/0.01, 30/1

Billboard Act
Cal. Business and Professions Code § 5200 et seq.
Ill. Rev. Stat. 1991, Ch. 121, § 501 et seq.
Ky. Rev. Stat. 1971, 177.830 et seq.
N.J. Stat. Ann., 54:40-50 et seq.
N.Y. Parks, Recreation and Historic Preservation Law (Consol. Laws Ch. 37B) § 13.07
Ohio Rev. Code 1953, 5516.01 et seq.
Vt. Stat. Ann., Title 9, § 3621 et seq.
Vt. Stat. Ann., Title 10, § 481 et seq.

Billboard Act (Parks)
N.Y. Parks and Recreation Law (Consol. Laws Ch. 36B) § 13.07

Billboard Control Act
Conn. Gen. Stat. 1958, § 21-50
Iowa Code Ann., 306C.10 et seq.
Ore. Rev. Stat. 1953, 377.715 et seq.

Billboard Regulation and Control Act
Tenn. Code Ann., 54-21-101 et seq.

Billboard Regulatory Act
Ind. Code Ann., 8-12-2-1 et seq.
Mass. Gen. Laws 1990, 93:29 et seq.

Billiard Table Act
Mo. Rev. Stat., 318.010 et seq.

Billing Act (Revolving Charge)
Ill. Rev. Stat. 1991, Ch. 17, § 5100 et seq.

Billing and Electronic Data Exchange Act
See Uniform Billing and Electronic Data Exchange Act

Bills of Exchange Act
Ill. Rev. Stat. 1991, Ch. 26, § 101 et seq.
Tenn. Code 1932, § 7450 et seq.
Wash. Rev. Code Ann., 62A.3-101 et seq.

Bills of Lading Acts

See also Uniform Commercial Code Documents of Title

Ala. Code 1958, Title 48, § 356 et seq.

Alaska Laws 1913, Ch. 59

Ariz. Laws 1921, Ch. 48

Ark. Stat. 1947, 68-1101 et seq.

Cal. Civil Code § 2126 et seq.

Del. Code of 1974, Title 6, § 301 et seq.

Ida. Code 1947, 62-601 et seq.

Ill. Rev. Stat. 1961, Ch. 27, § 2 et seq.

Ind. Code Ann., 26-1-7-101

Iowa Code Ann., 554.7301 et seq.

La. Acts 1912, No. 94

Mass. Gen. Laws Ann., 106:7-301 et seq.

Md. Ann. Code 1974, Art. CL, § 7-301

Me. Rev. Stat. Ann. 1964, Title 11, § 7-101 et seq.

Mich. Comp. Laws Ann., 440.3101 et seq.

Minn. Stat. 1961, 228.01 et seq.

Mo. Rev. Stat. 1959, 407.010 et seq.

Mont. Rev. Code 1947, 8-501 et seq.

N.C. Gen. Stat. 1943, § 21-1 et seq.

Nev. Rev. Stat. Ann., 104.7101 et seq.

N.H. Rev. Stat.,Superseded Volume, 334:1 et seq.

N.J. Stat. Ann., 48:20-1 to 48:20-54

N.M. Stat. Ann. 1953, 50-12-1 et seq.

N.Y. General Business Law (Consol. Law Ch. 20) § 90 et seq.

N.Y. Uniform Commercial Code (Consol. Laws Ch. 38) § 7-101 et seq.

Ohio Rev. Code 1953, 4965.01 et seq.

Okla. Stat. 1961, Title 12A, § 7-301 et seq.

Pa. 1911 Pamph. Laws 838

R.I. Gen. Laws 1956, Superseded Vol., 6-24-1 et seq.

S.C. Code Ann. 1976, § 36-7-101 et seq.

Tex. Business and Commerce Code, § 7.301 et seq.

Tex. Penal Code 1925, Art. 1674 et seq.

Vt. Stat. Ann., Title 9A, § 7-301 et seq.

Wash. Rev. Code Ann., 62A.7-101 et seq.

Wis. Stat. Ann., 407.301 et seq.

Wyo. Stat. Ann., § 34-16-101 et seq.

Bills of Sale Act

Md. Ann. Code 1974, Art. RP, § 7-106 et seq.

Wash. Rev. Code Ann., 62A.2-401 et seq.

Billy Marsh Act

Ala. Acts 1997, 1st Sp. Sess., No. 949

Binding Element Enforcement Act

Ky. Rev. Stat. 1971, 100.401 to 100.419

Bindweed Law

Okla. Stat. 1971, Title 2, § 3-221 et seq.

Bingham Cooperative Marketing Act

Ky. Rev. Stat. 1962, 272.100 et seq.

Bingham Police Bill (New York City)

N.Y. Laws 1907, Ch. 160

Binghamton City Court Act

N.Y. Laws 1931, Ch. 482

N.Y. Laws 1950, Ch. 370

Binghamton Parking Authority Act

N.Y. Public Authorities Law (Consol. Laws Ch. 43A) § 1599 et seq.

Binghamton Water Act

N.Y. Laws 1867, Ch. 780

Bingo Act (City of Jasper)

Ala. Acts 1992, p. 1185, No. 573

Bingo Acts

Ala. Acts 1991, p. 942

Ala. Acts 1991, p. 1378, No. 710

Alaska Stat. 1962, § 05.15.010 et seq.

Conn. Gen. Stat. 1958, § 7-169

Ga. Code Ann., 16-12-50 et seq.

Kan. Stat. Ann., 79-4701 et seq.

Neb. Rev. Stat. 1943, 9-201 et seq.

Okla. Stat. 1981, Title 21, § 995.1 et seq.

Pa. Purdon's Stat., Title 10, § 301 et seq.

R.I. Gen. Laws 1956, 11-19-30 et seq.

S.C. Code Ann. 1976, § 12-21-3310 et seq.

Bingo and Keno Licensing Law (Charitable Raffles)

La. Rev. Stat. Ann., 33:4861.1 et seq.

Bingo and Lottery Control Act
Neb. Rev. Stat. 1943, 9-201 et seq.

Bingo and Pickle Card Regulatory Act
Neb. Rev. Stat. 1943, 9-201 et seq.

Bingo and Raffles Acts
Colo. Rev. Stat., 12-9-101 et seq.
Mont. Code Ann. 1987, 23-5-401 et seq.
N.M. Stat. Ann., 60-2B-1 et seq.

Bingo Control Act
N.Y. Executive Law 1951 (Consol. Laws Ch. 18) § 430 et seq.
Wis. Stat. Ann., 163.02 et seq.

Bingo Enabling Act
Tex. Rev. Civ. Stat., Art. 179d

Bingo Law (Charitable)
Miss. Code Ann. 1972, § 97-33-50 et seq.

Bingo License and Tax Act
Ill. Comp. Stat. 1992, Ch. 230, § 25/1 et seq.

Bingo Licensing Act
Ky. Acts 1970, Ch. 60
La. Rev. Stat. Ann., 33:4861.1 et seq.
Mich. Comp. Laws Ann., 432.102 et seq.
N.J. Stat. Ann., 5:8-24 et seq.
N.Y. General Municipal Law (Consol. Laws Ch. 24) § 475 et seq.

Bingo Licensing Law (New York City)
N.Y. City Adm. Code '85, N.Y. Adm. Code, § 20-338 et seq.

Bingo Tax Act
S.C. Code Ann. 1976, §§ 35-3-100 to 35-3-108

Bio-Analytical Laboratory and Laboratory Directors Act
N.J. Stat. 1937, 45:9-42.1 et seq.

Biologic Products Institute Transfer Act
Mich. Comp. Laws Ann., 333.26331 et seq.

Biological Diversity Conservation Act
Mich. Comp. Laws Ann., 299.231 et seq.

Biological Organism Act
N.C. Gen. Stat. 1943, § 106-65.42 et seq.

Biological Residue Act
Tenn. Code Ann., 53-7-301 et seq.

Biological Weapons Anti-Terrorism Act of 1989
May 22, 1990, P.L. 101-298, 18 U.S. Code prec. 1, prec. 175, 175, 175 nt., 176 to 178, 2516

Biologicals Permit Act
Ga. Code Ann., 4-9-1 et seq.

Biologics Act
N.C. Gen. Stat. 1943, § 106-707 et seq.

Biomass Energy and Alcohol Fuels Act of 1980
June 30, 1980, P.L. 96-294, 42 U.S. Code §§ 8801 et seq., 8801 nt.
April 16, 1985, P.L. 99-24, 42 U.S. Code § 8821
April 7, 1986, P.L. 99-272, 42 U.S. Code § 8821
Aug. 22, 1986, P.L. 99-386, 5 U.S. Code § 3104; 42 U.S. Code § 8818
Oct. 18, 1986, P.L. 99-500, 42 U.S. Code § 8821
Oct. 20, 1986, P.L. 99-591, 42 U.S. Code § 8821

Biomaterials Access Assurance Act of 1998
Aug. 13, 1998, P.L. 105-230, 21 U.S. Code § 1601 nt.

Biomedical and Social Research Act
Fla. Stat. Ann., 402.105

Biomedical Research and Research Training Amendments of 1978
Nov. 9, 1978, P.L. 95-622, 42 U.S. Code §§ 201 nt., 241, 248, 277, 280b, 281 et seq., 4541, 4573, 4585

Biomedical Research Extension Act of 1977
Aug. 1, 1977, P.L. 95-83, 42 U.S. Code §§ 201 nt., 280b et seq.

Biotechnology Act (Agricultural)
Okla. Stat. Ann., Title 2, § 2011

Biotechnology and High Technology Industry Promotion Act
N.J. Stat. Ann., 52:9X-9.1 et seq.

Biotechnology Sector Development Act
Ill. Comp. Stat. 1992, Ch. 20, § 230/1

Bipartisan Personnel System Act
Ind. Code 1982, 8-13-1.5-1 et seq.

Bird Act
Ill. Rev. Stat. 1991, Ch. 1, § 2901-10

Bird and Animal Import Law
Cal. Fish and Game Code 1957, § 2116 et seq.

Bird and Arbor Day Act
Ill. Comp. Stat. 1992, Ch. 5, § 490/10
Ill. Rev. Stat. 1991, Ch. 1, § 3051-10

Bird Dealers Licensing Act
Ga. Code Ann., 4-10-1 et seq.
Miss. Code Ann. 1972, § 75-40-101 et seq.

Bird Preserve Land Acquisition Act
Ill. Comp. Stat. 1992, Ch. 5, §§ 580/0.01, 580/1

Bird Shooting Act
Ill. Rev. Stat. 1989, Ch. 8, § 111.01 et seq.

Birmingham City Act (Boundaries)
Ala. General Acts 1949, p. 472, No. 325

Birth and Death Registration Act
Ill. Rev. Stat. 1991, Ch. 111 1/2, § 73-1 et seq.

Birth Center Licensure Act
Fla. Stat. Ann., 383.30 et seq.

Birth Certificate Act
Tex. Health and Safety Code, § 192.001 et seq.
Wash. Rev. Code Ann., 70.58.070 et seq.

Birth Control Act
Conn. Gen. Stat. 1958, § 53-32
Mass. Gen. Laws Ann., 272:21
Miss. Code Ann. 1972, § 41-42-1 et seq.
N.Y. Education Law 1947 (Consol. Laws Ch. 16) § 6811

Birth Control and Family Planning Act
Wyo. Stat. Ann., § 35-14-101 et seq.

Birth Control Services to Minors Act
Ill. Comp. Stat. 1992, Ch. 325, §§ 10/0.01, 10/1

Birth Defect Prevention Act
Cal. Food and Agricultural Code 1967, § 13121 et seq.

Birth Defects Prevention Act of 1998
April 21, 1998, P.L. 105-168, 42 U.S. Code § 201 nt.

Birth Defects Treatment Program Act
Del. Code of 1974, Title 16, § 201 et seq.

Birth Related Neurological Injury Compensation Act
Va. Code 1950, § 38.2-5000 et seq.

Birthing Center Licensure Act
Fla. Stat. Ann., 383.30 et seq.
S.C. Code Ann. 1976, § 44-89-10 et seq.
Tex. Health and Safety Code, § 244.001 et seq.

Births, Deaths and Vital Statistics Act
N.J. Stat. Ann., 26:8-1 et seq.

Births Delayed Registration Act
Mich. Comp. Laws Ann., 333.2827
Neb. Rev. Stat. 1943, 71-617 et seq.

Biscayne National Park Act
June 28, 1980, P.L. 96-297, 16 U.S. Code §§ 410gg to 410gg-5

Bischoff-Munshaw Act (Emergency Foreclosure)
Mich. Public Acts 1933, No. 98

Bishop Act (Intoxicating Liquor)
N.J. Laws 1906, p. 199, Ch. 114

Bishop Act (State Budget)
Mich. Comp. Laws Ann., 21.1 et seq.

Bishop Act (Teachers Retirement)
Ky. Rev. Stat. 1971, Superseded Vols.,
161.715

Bisti/De-Na-Zin Wilderness Expansion and Fossil Forest Protection Act
Nov. 12, 1996, P.L. 104-333, § 1022, 110
Stat. 4211

Bituminous Coal Act of 1937
April 26, 1937, Ch. 127, 50 Stat. 72
April 11, 1941, Ch. 64, 55 Stat. 134
April 24, 1943, Ch. 68, 57 Stat. 68
May 21, 1943, Ch. 97, 57 Stat. 82

Bituminous Coal Conservation Act
See Guffey-Snyder Coal Act

Bituminous Coal Fair Competition Law
Colo. Stat. Ann. 1935, Ch. 110, § 167(1) et
seq.

Bituminous Coal Mine Act
Pa. Purdon's Stat., Title 52, § 701-101 et seq.

Bituminous Coal Reconstruction Transportation Appropriation Act
Pa. 1939 Pamph. Laws 1115, No. 394

Bituminous Mine Subsidence and Land Conservation Act
Pa. Purdon's Stat., Title 52, § 1406.1 et seq.

Bituminous Strip Mining Act
Pa. Purdon's Stat., Title 52, § 1396.1 et seq.

Black Act (Commission Government)
Ida. Laws 1911, Ch. 82

Black Act (Tax Payment Loan)
Ore. Rev. Stat. 1953, 82.140

Black Bass Act
May 20, 1926, Ch. 346, 44 Stat. 576, 16 U.S.
Code §§ 851, 852

July 2, 1930, Ch. 801, 46 Stat. 845, 16 U.S.
Code §§ 851 to 856
July 30, 1947, Ch. 348, 61 Stat. 517, 16 U.S.
Code §§ 851 to 855
July 16, 1952, Ch. 911, 66 Stat. 736, 16 U.S.
Code §§ 851 to 852b, 854, 856
Aug. 25, 1959, P.L. 86-207, 72 Stat. 430, 16
U.S. Code § 855
Dec. 5, 1969, P.L. 91-135, 83 Stat. 281, 16
U.S. Code §§ 851, 852 , 852a, 852d

Black Bass Conservation and Management Act
Cal. Fish and Game Code 1957, § 1740 et
seq.

Black-Connery Fair Labor Standards Act
See Fair Labor Standards Act of 1938

Black List Act (Liquor Sales)
Ohio Rev. Code 1953, 4399.01

Black Lung Benefits Act
Dec. 30, 1969, P.L. 91-173, 83 Stat. 792, 30
U.S. Code § 901 et seq.
March 1, 1978, P.L. 95-239, 92 Stat. 105, 30
U.S. Code § 901 et seq.
Sept. 28, 1984, P.L. 98-426, 30 U.S. Code
§ 932
Nov. 5, 1990, P.L. 101-509, 30 U.S. Code
§ 938
Dec. 21, 1995, P.L. 104-66, 30 U.S. Code
§ 936

Black Lung Benefits Act of 1972
May 19, 1972, P.L. 92-303, 86 Stat. 150, 30
U.S. Code §§ 901, 902, 921 to 924, 931 to
934, 935 to 940, 951

Black Lung Benefits Amendments of 1981
Dec. 29, 1981, P.L. 97-119, 30 U.S. Code
§ 801 nt.

Black Lung Benefits Reform Act of 1977
March 19, 1978, P.L. 95-239, 30 U.S. Code
§§ 801 nt., 901 nt., 902 et seq., 4121 nt.; 29
U.S. Code § 675 nt.

Black Lung Benefits Revenue Act of 1977
Feb. 10, 1978, P.L. 95-227, 26 U.S. Code
§§ 192, 501, 4121 et seq., 4940 et seq.;
6104 et seq., 30 U.S. Code § 934, 934 nt.

April 1, 1980, P.L. 96-222, 26 U.S. Code
§ 6503 et seq.

Black Lung Benefits Revenue Act of 1981
Dec. 29, 1981, P.L. 97-119, 26 U.S. Code § 1
nt.

Black Market Act
Cal. Penal Code §§ 540 to 543
Wis. Laws 1943, Ch. 550

Black Market Act (Adoption)
N.Y. Penal Law 1909 (Consol. Laws Ch. 40)
§ 487a

Black Market Adoption Act
N.C. Gen. Stat. 1943, §§ 48-37, 48-38

Black-McKellar Act
See Air Mail Acts
June 12, 1934, Ch. 466, 48 Stat. 933

Black Sox Scandal Act
Ohio Rev. Code 1953, 3773.15

Blackboard Act (Railroad Station)
Ind. Code 1971, 8-2-26-1, 8-2-26-2

Blacklist Trade Law
Ill. Comp. Stat. 1992, Ch. 775, § 15/1 et seq.

Blacklisting Act
Ala. Code 1975, § 13A-11-123
Ariz. Const. 1910, Art. 18 § 9
Ark. Stat. 1947, 11-3-202
Cal. Labor Code § 1050 et seq.
Ind. Code Ann., 22-5-3-1, 22-5-3-2
Iowa Code Ann., 730.1 et seq.
Kan. Stat. Ann., 44-117 et seq.
Me. Rev. Stat. Ann. 1964, Title 17, § 401
Minn. Stat. Ann., 179.60
Mo. Rev. Stat. 1969, 559.390
Mont. Code Ann., 39-2-801 et seq.
N.C. Gen. Stat. 1943, § 14-355
N.D. Cent. Code, 34-01-07
Nev. Rev. Stat. 1979 Reprint, 613.210
N.M. Stat. Ann., 30-13-3
N.Y. Labor Law (Consol. Laws Ch. 31)
§ 704, Subds. 2, 9
Okla. Stat. 1981, Title 40, §§ 172, 173

Ore. Rev. Stat. 1953, 659.230
Tex. Rev. Civ. Stat., Art. 5196 et seq.
Utah Code Ann. 1953, 34-24-1, 34-24-2
Va. Code 1950, § 40.1-27
Wash. Rev. Code Ann., 49.44.010
Wis. Stat. Ann., 111.06, Subsec. 1, Subd. k;
134.02

Blackmail Act
Conn. Gen. Stat. 1958, § 53a-192
Iowa Code Ann., 711.4
Mont. Code Ann., 45-5-203
N.H. Rev. Stat. 1955, 637.5
R.I. Gen. Laws 1956, 11-42-2
Wash. Rev. Code Ann., 9A.56.110 et seq.

Blackout Act (District of Columbia)
D.C. Code 1973, § 6-1501 et seq.

Blackstone Valley Sewer District Act
R.I. Gen. Laws 1956, 46-21-1 et seq.

Blackwell Act (Divorce)
N.J. Stat. Ann., 2A:34-2

Blaine Amendment
N.Y. Const., Art. 11, § 3

**Blake, Robinson and Vance Act (Soil
Conservation)**
Ky. Rev. Stat. 1971, 261.010 et seq.

**Blake, Swope, Moore and Howard Act
(Elections)**
Ky. Acts 1944. Ch. 5

Bland-Allison Act (Coinage of Silver)
See Coinage Act (Silver Dollar)

Bland Change of Masters Act
May 31, 1939, Ch. 159, 53 Stat. 794, 46 U.S.
Code § 276

Bland Merchant Marine Act
Aug. 4, 1939, Ch. 417, 53 Stat. 1182, 46 U.S.
Code §§ 822, 845, 1111, 1126, 1152, 1160,
1173, 1174, 1177, 1195, 1196, 1204, 1228,
1274
May 2, 1941, Ch. 84, 55 Stat. 148

Bland Ship Requisitioning Act
See Ship Seizure Bill

Bland War-Risk Insurance Act
See Merchant Marine Act, 1936

Blanford-Rose Long Term Policy Act
Ky. Rev. Stat. 1971, 7B.010c et seq.

Blanket Act
Vt. Stat. Ann., Title 13, § 203

Blanket Disability Insurance Act
Ida. Code 1947, 41-2201 et seq.
Wyo. Stat. Ann., § 26-19-101 et seq.

Blanket Health Insurance Law
Ky. Rev. Stat. 1971, 304.18-010 et seq.
Me. Rev. Stat. Ann. 1964, Title 24-A, § 2801 et seq.
Nev. Rev. Stat. 1979 Reprint, 689B.010 et seq.

Blanket Mill Tax Levy Act
Neb. Laws 1949, Ch. 250

Blasphemy Act
Conn. Gen. Stat. 1958, § 53-242
Mass. Gen. Laws Ann., 271:36

Blasting Standards Act
Ga. Code Ann., 25-8-1 et seq.
Tenn. Code Ann., 68-105-101 et seq.

Bleckley Act (Practice in Courts of Review)
Ga. Code 1933, 6-805, 6-912, 6-913, 6-1609, 19-404

Blending Act (Alcohol)
Neb. Rev. Stat. 1943, 66-401

Blight Elimination and Slum Clearance Act
Wis. Stat. Ann., 66.431

Blighted Area Act
Ark. Stat. 1947, 14-169-601 et seq.
N.J. Rev. Stat. 1943, 40:55-21.1
Wis. Stat. Ann., 66.43

Blighted Areas Redevelopment Act
Ill. Comp. Stat. 1992, Ch. 315, § 5/1 et seq.
S.C. Code Ann. 1976, Superseded Vols., § 31-7-10 et seq.

Blighted Areas Rehabilitation Act
Mich. Comp. Laws Ann., 125.71 et seq.

Blighted Vacant Areas Development Act
Ill. Comp. Stat. 1992, Ch. 315, § 10/1 et seq.

Blind Act (Services)
Mont. Code Ann., 53-7-301 et seq.

Blind Aid Act
See Aid to the Blind Act

Blind and Deaf Children Education Act
Kan. Stat. Ann., 72-853 et seq.

Blind and Deaf School Building Act
Ga. Code Ann., 32-2801a

Blind and Deaf Schools Act (State)
Wash. Rev. Code Ann., 72.40.010 et seq.

Blind and Disabled Old Age Assistance Law
N.Y. Social Services Law (Consol. Laws Ch. 55) § 207 et seq.

Blind and Otherwise Incapacitated Persons Right-of-Way Act
D.C. Laws 1977, No. 1-121

Blind Bidding Law
Mont. Code Ann., 30-14-301 et seq.

Blind Intersection Law
Cal. Vehicle Code 1959, § 22352, Subd. a

Blind Law
N.Y. Social Services Law (Consol. Laws Ch. 55) § 300 et seq.

Blind Made Products and Services Act
Okla. Stat. 1971, Title 7, § 101 et seq.

Blind or Deaf School Transportation Act
Ill. Rev. Stat. 1991, Ch. 23, §§ 1209.9, 1210

Blind Pensions Act
Mo. Rev. Stat., 209.030 et seq.
Ore. Rev. Stat. 1953, 412.005 et seq.
Pa. 1933 Ex. Pamph. Laws 246, No. 61
Pa. 1965 Pamph. Laws, Nos. 400, 204

Blind Persons' Literacy Rights and Education Act
Fla. Stat. Ann., 233.0561
Ga. Code Ann., 30-7-1 et seq.
La. Rev. Stat. Ann., 17:1981 et seq.
Miss. Code Ann. 1972, §§ 37-23-191 to 37-23-203
S.C. Code Ann. 1976, § 59-34-10 et seq.
Utah Code Ann. 1953, 53A-25a-101 et seq.

Blind Persons Operating Vending Facilities Act
Ill. Comp. Stat. 1992, Ch. 20, § 2420/0.01

Blind Relief Act
Ohio Rev. Code 1953, 5151.01 et seq.

Blind Students' Education Law
Cal. Education Code 1959, § 10651

Blind Tiger Act (Intoxicating Liquor)
Ark. Stat. 1947, 48-1001 et seq.
Ga. Code 1933, 58-110 et seq.
Ind. Laws 1907, Ch. 16, p. 27 § 1
La. Rev. Stat. Ann., 26:711 et seq.

Blind Vocational Rehabilitation Act
Miss. Code Ann. 1972, § 37-33-51 et seq.
Tenn. Code Ann., 71-4-601 et seq.
Tex. Human Resources Code, § 91.051 et seq.

Blindness Prevention Act (Infants)
Okla. Stat. 1981, Title 63, § 1-509 et seq.

Block Grant Entitlement Program Act (Community Development)
Pa. Purdon's Stat., Title 35, § 1751 et seq.

Block Grant Program Act (Community Services)
Cal. Government Code § 12725 et seq.

Block Signal, Resolution (Railroads)
June 30, 1906, No. 46, 34 Stat. 838, 45 U.S. Code § 35

Blockade of Southern Ports Proclamation (Civil War)
April 19, 1861, No. 4, 12 Stat. 1258

Blood Alcohol Level Act
Utah Code Ann. 1953, 41-6-44.10

Blood-Alcohol Test Act (Intoxicated Drivers)
Neb. Rev. Stat. 1943, 39-669.08

Blood and Organ Transaction Liability Act
Ill. Comp. Stat. 1992, Ch. 745, § 40/0.01 et seq.

Blood Bank Act
Okla. Stat. 1981, Title 63, § 2161 et seq.
Pa. Purdon's Stat., Title 35, § 6501 et seq.

Blood Bank and Clinical Laboratory Act
Ill. Comp. Stat. 1992, Ch. 210, § 25/1-101 et seq.

Blood Donation Act
Ill. Comp. Stat. 1992, Ch. 210, §§ 15/0.01, 15/1

Blood Exchange Act
Okla. Stat. Ann., Title 63, § 2161 et seq.

Blood Grouping Act
Pa. 1951 Pamph. Laws 402, No. 92

Blood Grouping Test Act
Mass. Gen. Laws Ann., 273:12A

Blood Labeling Act
Fla. Stat. Ann., 381.0041, 381.698
Ga. Code Ann., 31-24-1 et seq.
Ill. Rev. Stat. 1991, Ch. 111 1/2, § 620-1 et seq.

Blood Safety Act
Cal. Health and Safety Code § 1645
N.J. Stat. Ann., 26:2A-13 et seq.

Blood Shield Law
Mich. Comp. Laws Ann., 333.9121

Blood Test Act
N.Y. Civil Practices Laws and Rules
(Consol. Laws Ch. 8) § 3121
N.Y. Family Court Act § 532
Wis. Stat. Ann., 885.23

Blood Test Act (Implied Consent)
Ga. Code Ann., 40-5-55
Kan. Stat. Ann., 8-1001 et seq.
Me. Rev. Stat. Ann. 1964, Title 29, § 1312
Neb. Rev. Stat. 1943, 39-669.08
S.D. Codified Laws 1967, 32-23-10 et seq.
Vt. Stat. Ann., Title 23, § 12.02 et seq.

Blood Test Act (Pregnancy)
Mich. Comp. Laws Ann., 329.153
Okla. Stat. 1981, Title 63, § 1-515 et seq.

Blood Test Act (Premarital)
Ala. Code 1975, §§ 22-16-5, 22-16-6
Cal. Civil Code § 4300 et seq.
Colo. Rev. Stat., 14-2-106
Okla. Stat. 1981, Title 43, § 31 et seq.
Va. Code 1950, § 20-1 et seq.

Blood Test Act (Prenatal)
Conn. Gen. Stat. 1958, § 19a-90

Blood Tests to Determine Paternity Act
See Uniform Act on Blood Tests to
Determine Paternity Act
Conn. Gen. Stat. 1958, § 46b-168
Mich. Comp. Laws Ann., 722.716
Utah Code Ann. 1953, 78-25-18 et seq.

Blood Transfusion Act
Feb. 9, 1927, Ch. 91, 44 Stat. 1066, 24 U.S.
Code § 30
June 2, 1939, Ch. 173, 53 Stat. 803, 24 U.S.
Code § 30
July 30, 1941, Ch. 332, 55 Stat. 609, 24 U.S.
Code § 30
Fla. Stat. 1983, 381.698

Bloody Bill Act (Suits against Revenue Officers)
See Force Act (Suits Against Revenue
Officers)

Bloomington Civic Center Authority Act
Ill. Comp. Stat. 1992, Ch. 70, § 235/1 et seq.

Blowpost Act
Ga. Code Ann., 46-8-190

Blue Book Act
Cal. Government Code §§ 13606, 13607

Blue Cross Act
Mich. Comp. Laws Ann., 550.501 et seq.

Blue-Eyed Nurses Act
Mont. Code Ann., 39-32-101 et seq.

Blue Laws (Sunday)
Ala. Code 1975, § 13A-12-1 et seq.
Ark. Code 1982, 5-60-119 et seq.
Ark. Stat. 1947, 41-3805 et seq.
Conn. Gen. Stat. 1958, § 53-300a et seq.
Fla. Stat. 1967, 855.01 et seq.
Iowa Code 1954, 729.1
Kan. Gen. Stat. 1949, 21-952 et seq.
Ky. Rev. Stat. 1971, 436.160
Mass. Gen. Laws Ann., 136.1 et seq.
Md. Ann. Code 1957, Art. 2B, § 90 et seq.
Md. Ann. Code 1957, Art. 27, § 492 et seq.
Md. Ann. Code 1974, Art. NR, §§ 4-1008,
Subd. a, 10-410, Subd. a
Me. Rev. Stat. Ann. 1964, Title 17, § 3201 et
seq.
Minn. Stat. Ann., 340A.504
N.C. Gen. Stat. 1943, § 14-346.2
N.J. Stat. Ann., 2A:171-1 et seq.
N.M. Stat. Ann., 60-6A-4
N.Y. General Business Law (Consol. Laws
Ch. 20) § 2 et seq.
Okla. Stat. Ann., Title 21, § 907 et seq.
Pa. April 22, 1794, 3 Sm. L. 177, Ch. 1746
Pa. 1705, 1 Sm. L. 25, Ch. 119
S.C. Code Ann. 1976, § 53-1-10 et seq.
Tenn. Code Ann., 6-32-208
Tex. Penal Code 1925, Art. 283 et seq.

Va. Code 1950, § 18.2-341 et seq.

Vt. Stat. Ann., Title 13, § 3301 et seq.

Wash. Rev. Code Ann., 9.76.010 et seq.

Blue Ribbon Jury Law

N.Y. Judiciary Law (Consol. Laws Ch. 30) § 749aa

Blue Ridge Airport Authority Act

Va. Acts 1964, Ch. 25

Va. Acts 1996, Ch. 465

Blue Ridge Parkway Acts

June 30, 1936, Ch. 883, 49 Stat. 2041, 16 U.S. Code § 460a-2

June 8, 1940, Ch. 277, 54 Stat. 250, 16 U.S. Code §§ 460a-1 to 460a-3

May 13, 1952, Ch. 263, 66 Stat. 69, 16 U.S. Code § 460a-4

June 30, 1961, P.L. 87-76, 75 Stat. 196, 16 U.S. Code § 460a-5

Oct. 9, 1968, P.L. 90-555, 82 Stat. 967, 16 U.S. Code §§ 460a-6 to 460a-11

Blue River Basin Compact Act

Neb. Laws 1971, L. B. 609

Blue Shield Act

Mich. Comp. Laws Ann., 550.301 et seq.

Minn. Stat. 1969, 159.01 et seq.

Blue Shield Regulatory Act

Pa. Cons. Stat., Title 40, § 6101 et seq.

Blue Sky Act

Miss. Code Ann. 1972, § 75-71-101 et seq.

Blue Sky Acts

Ala. Code 1975, § 8-6-1 et seq.

Alaska Stat. 1962, § 45.55.010 et seq.

Ariz. Rev. Stat. Ann., § 44-1801 et seq.

Ark. Stat. 1947, 23-42-507 et seq.

Cal. Corporations Code § 25000 et seq.

Colo. Rev. Stat., 11-51-101 et seq.

Conn. Gen. Stat. 1958, § 36-470 et seq.

Fla. Stat. Ann., 517.011 et seq.

Ga. Code Ann., 10-5-1 et seq.

Haw. Rev. Stat. Ann., § 485-1 et seq.

Ida. Code 1947, 30-1401 et seq.

Ill. Rev. Stat. 1991, Ch. 121 1/2, § 137.1 et seq.

Ind. Code 1976, 23-2-1-1 et seq.

Iowa Code Ann., 502.101 et seq.

Kan. Stat. Ann., 17-1252 et seq.

Ky. Rev. Stat. 1971, 292.310 et seq.

La. Rev. Stat. Ann., 51:701 et seq.

Mass. Gen. Laws Ann., 110A:1 et seq.

Md. Ann. Code 1974, Art. CA, § 11-101 et seq.

Me. Rev. Stat. Ann. 1964, Title 32, § 10101 et seq.

Mich. Comp. Laws Ann., 451.501 et seq.

Minn. Stat. Ann., 80A.01 et seq.

Miss. Code Ann. 1972, § 75-71-1 et seq.

Mo. Rev. Stat., 409.101 et seq.

Mont. Code Ann., 30-10-101 et seq.

N.C. Gen. Stat. 1943, § 78A-1 et seq.

N.D. Cent. Code, 10-04-01 et seq.

Neb. Rev. Stat. 1943, 8-1101 et seq.

Nev. Rev. Stat. 1979 Reprint, 90.010 et seq.

N.H. Rev. Stat. 1955, 421-B:1 et seq.

N.J. Rev. Stat. 1937, 49:3-47 et seq.

N.M. Stat. Ann., 58-13B-1 et seq.

N.Y. General Business Law (Consol. Laws Ch. 20) § 352 et seq.

Ohio Rev. Code 1953, 1707.01 et seq.

Okla. Stat. Ann., Title 71, § 1 et seq.

Ore. Rev. Stat. 1953, 59.005 et seq.

Pa. Purdon's Stat., Title 70, § 31 et seq.

R.I. Gen. Laws 1956, 7-11-1 et seq.

S.C. Code Ann. 1976, § 35-1-10 et seq.

S.D. Codified Laws 1967, 47-31-1 et seq.

Tenn. Code Ann., 48-2-101 et seq.

Tex. Rev. Civ. Stat., Art. 581-1 et seq.

Utah Code Ann. 1953, 61-1-1 et seq.

Va. Code 1950, § 13.1-501 et seq.

Vt. Stat. Ann., Title 9, § 4201 et seq.

Wash. Rev. Code 1983, 21.20.005 et seq.

Wis. Stat. Ann., § 551.01 et seq.

W. Va. Code 1966, § 32-1-101 et seq.

Wyo. Stat. Ann., § 17-4-101 et seq.

Blue Star Mothers of America Act

July 14, 1960, P.L. 86-653, 74 Stat. 515, 36 U.S. Code §§ 941 to 958

Blue Waters Ditch Flood Control Act
Ill. Comp. Stat. 1992, Ch. 615, § 85/0.01 et seq.

Blueberry Tax Act
Me. Rev. Stat. Ann. 1964, Title 36, § 4301 et seq.

Bluegrass State Skills Corporation Act
Ky. Rev. Stat. 1971, 157.710 et seq.

Bluff Recession and Setback Act
Pa. Purdon's Stat., Title 32, § 5201 et seq.

Boar-Bull Act
Kan. Stat. Ann., 47-105

Board Act (Animal Welfare)
Me. Rev. Stat. Ann. 1964, Title 7, § 3901 et seq.

Board Act (Medical Disciplinary)
Wash. Rev. Code 1983, 18.72.010 et seq.

Board Act (Statewide Emergency Telecommunications)
Mass. Gen. Laws Ann., 6A:18B et seq.

Board and Home Care Licensing Law
La. Rev. Stat. Ann., 40:2151 et seq.

Board and Home Care Registration
Ill. Comp. Stat. 1992, Ch. 225, § 7/1 et seq.

Board and Lodging Home Registration Act
Tex. Human Resources Code, § 105.001 et seq.

Board Certified Social Work Practice Act
La. Rev. Stat. Ann., 37:2701 et seq.

Board for International Broadcasting Act of 1973
Oct. 19, 1973, P.L. 93-129, 87 Stat. 456, 22 U.S. Code §§ 2871 to 2877
Aug. 28, 1974, P.L. 93-392, 88 Stat. 781, 22 U.S. Code § 2877
Oct. 6, 1975, P.L. 94-104, 89 Stat. 508 to 510, 22 U.S. Code §§ 2370, 2877
Aug. 17, 1977, P.L. 95-105, 22 U.S. Code § 2871 et seq.

Aug. 15, 1979, P.L. 96-60, 22 U.S. Code §§ 2877, 2879
Aug. 24, 1982, P.L. 97-241, 22 U.S. Code §§ 2871 nt., 2872, 2877, 2880
Nov. 22, 1983, P.L. 98-164, 22 U.S. Code §§ 2877, 2881, 2882
Aug. 16, 1985, P.L. 99-93, 22 U.S. Code §§ 2871, 2875, 2877, 2883
July 2, 1986, P.L. 99-349, 100 Stat. 718
Dec. 22, 1987, P.L. 100-204, 22 U.S. Code § 2877
Feb. 16, 1990, P.L. 101-246, 22 U.S. Code §§ 2871, 2877
Oct. 28, 1991, P.L. 102-138, 22 U.S. Code § 2877
April 30, 1994, P.L. 103-236, 22 U.S. Code § 2873

Board for International Broadcasting Authorization Act, Fiscal Years 1982 and 1983
Aug. 24, 1982, P.L. 97-241, 22 U.S. Code §§ 2871 nt., 2872, 2877, 2880

Board for International Broadcasting Authorization Act, Fiscal Years 1984 and 1985
Nov. 22, 1983, P.L. 98-164, 22 U.S. Code § 2871 nt.
Dec. 17, 1993, P.L. 103-199, 107 Stat. 2323

Board of Accounts Retirement Act (State)
Ind. Code Ann., 4-26-3-1 et seq.

Board of Adjustment Act
Ala. Code 1975, § 41-9-60 et seq.

Board of Administration Act
Fla. Stat. 1983, 344.01 et seq.

Board of Arbitration Act
Pa. Purdon's Stat., Title 72, § 4651.1 et seq.

Board of Barber Examiners Act
Okla. Stat. Ann., Title 59, § 61 et seq.

Board of Censors Act (Motion Pictures)
Pa. 1915 Pamph. Laws 534, No. 239

Board of Charities Act
D.C. Code Ann., § 3-101 et seq.

Board of Claims Act
Ky. Rev. Stat. 1971, 44.070 et seq.
Tenn. Code Ann., 9-8-101 et seq.

Board of Control Act
Tex. Rev. Civ. Stat., Art. 601b

Board of Control Act (State Homes for the Aged)
Colo. Rev. Stat. 1963, 133-1-1 et seq.

Board of Economic Development Act
Ill. Rev. Stat. 1991, Ch. 127, § 200-1 et seq.

Board of Education Act
D.C. Code 1973, § 31-101 et seq.
La. Rev. Stat. Ann., 17:1 et seq.
Okla. Stat. Ann., Title 70, § 3-101 et seq.

Board of Education Act (County)
Ind. Code Ann., 20-2-1-1 et seq.

Board of Education Bond Act
Del. Laws Vol. 53, p. 864, Ch. 334

Board of Education Leasing Authority Act
D.C. Code Ann., §§ 31-201, 31-201.1, 31-201.2

Board of Education School Seal Act
D.C. Code Ann., § 31-119

Board of Election Commissioners Annuity and Benefit Fund Act
Ill. Rev. Stat. 1959, Ch. 46, § 496 et seq.

Board of Elections and Ethics Additional Compensation Act
D.C. Code Ann., § 1-1304

Board of Examiners of Architects Act
Pa. Purdon's Stat., Title 63, § 34.1 et seq.

Board of Financial Institutions Act
S.C. Code Ann. 1976, § 34-1-10 et seq.

Board of Govenors Act
Ill. Rev. Stat. 1991, Ch. 144, § 1000 et seq.

Board of Governors of State Colleges and Universities Revenue Bond Act
Ill. Comp. Stat. 1992, Ch. 110, § 610/1 et seq.

Board of Health Act
Kan. Stat. Ann., 65-101 et seq.
N.J. Rev. Stat. Ann., 26:1A-1 et seq.

Board of Higher Education Act
Ill. Comp. Stat. 1992, Ch. 110, § 205/0.01 et seq.
N.D. Cent. Code, 15-10-01 et seq.

Board of Medical Education and Licensure Act
Pa. 1929 Pamph. Laws 177, No. 175, § 412

Board of Mineral Development Act
Tex. Rev. Civ. Stat., Art. 5241c

Board of Parole Act
Pa. Purdon's Stat., Title 61, § 331.1 et seq.

Board of Parole Amendment Act
D.C. Code Ann., § 24-201.1 et seq.

Board of Pharmacy Act
D.C. Code Ann., § 2-2001 et seq.

Board of Public Utilities Act
Mo. Rev. Stat. 1969, 91.330 et seq.

Board of Public Utility Commissioners Act
N.J. Rev. Stat. 1937, 48:2-1 et seq.

Board of Public Welfare Act
D.C. Code 1973, § 3-101 et seq.

Board of Regents Revenue Bond Act
Ariz. Rev. Stat. Ann., § 15-782 et seq.
Ill. Comp. Stat. 1992, Ch. 110, § 710/1 et seq.
S.D. Codified Laws 1967, 13-51A-1 et seq.

Board of Review Act
Ohio Rev. Code 1953, 4743.01 et seq.

Board of Sponsors Act (Governor's Scholars)
Ill. Rev. Stat. 1991, Ch. 127, § 63b130 et seq.

Board of Supervisors Law
Ky. Rev. Stat. 1971, 133.020 et seq.

Board of Survey Act
Mass. Gen. Laws Ann., 41:73 et seq.

Board of Tax Adjustment Act (County)
Ind. Code Ann., 6-1.1-29-1 et seq.

Board of Tourism Commissioners Act
N.Y. Laws 1977, Ch. 357, § 2

Board of Trade Act
N.Y. Not-For-Profit Corporation Law
(Consol. Laws Ch. 35) § 1410

Board of Vehicles Act
Pa. Purdon's Stat. Title 63, § 818.1 et seq.

Board of Veterans' Appeals Administrative Procedures Improvement Act of 1994
July 1, 1994, P.L. 103-271, 38 U.S. Code
§§ 101 nt., 1315, 1506, 7101, 7102, 7103,
7104, 7107, 7110

Board of Viewers Act
Pa. 1911 Pamph. Laws 1123

Board Termination Act (Service Recognition)
Ill. Rev. Stat. 1991, Ch. 126 1/2, §§ 62m, 63

Boarding Aircraft with Weapon Act
Ill. Rev. Stat. 1991, Ch. 38, § 84-0.1 et seq.

Boarding and Foster Homes for Children Act
Alaska Stat. 1962, § 47.35.010 et seq.

Boarding and Rooming House Act
N.J. Stat. Ann., 55:13B-1 et seq.

Boarding Home Act
Neb. Rev. Stat. 1943, 71-5901 et seq.

Boarding Home Act (Children)
Mich. Comp. Laws Ann., 750.144

Boarding Home License Law (Aged)
Cal. Welfare and Institutions Code § 16200
et seq.

Boarding Home Licensure Act
N.M. Stat. Ann. 1953, 60-1-3.1 et seq.

Boarding House Life Safety Improvement Act
N.J. Stat. Ann., 55:14K-13 et seq.

Boardinghouses, Restaurants, Hotels and Motels Act
S.C. Code Ann. 1976, § 45-1-10 et seq.

Boards of Cooperative Educational Services Act
Colo. Rev. Stat., 22-5-101 et seq.
Wyo. Stat. Ann., § 21-20-101 et seq.

Boardwalk Act
N.J. Stat. Ann., 40:179-78 to 40:179-125

Boat Act
Md. Ann. Code 1974, Art. NR, § 8-701 et
seq.
Neb. Rev. Stat. 1943, 37-1201 et seq.
Nev. Rev. Stat. 1979 Reprint, 488.015 et seq.
N.J. Stat. Ann., 12:7-34.36 et seq.
N.M. Stat. Ann., 66-12-1 et seq.

Boat Act (State)
Neb. Rev. Stat. 1943, 37-1274

Boat and Fish Code
Pa. Cons. Stat., Title 30, § 101 et seq.

Boat and Fish Funds Capital Budget Act
Pa. 1986 Pamph. Laws, No. 95
Pa. 1990 Pamph. Laws, No. 15

Boat and Motor Excise Tax Act
Okla. Stat. Ann., Title 63, § 828 et seq.

Boat and Vessel Act
Ohio Rev. Code 1953, 4585.01 et seq.

Boat Hull Anti-Copying Act
N.C. Gen. Stat. 1943, § 75A-27 et seq.

Boat Industry Loan Guarantee Fund Act
N.J. Stat. Ann., 34:1B-7.28 et seq.

Boat Lien Act
Ore. Rev. Stat. 1953, 783.010 et seq.

Boat Operation Act
Mich. Comp. Laws Ann., 281.571 et seq.

Boat or Boat Motor Theft Act
Fla. Stat. 1973, 814.01 et seq.

Boat Ownership Certificate Act
N.J. Stat. Ann., 12:7-16.1 et seq.

Boat Registration Act
Ala. Code 1975, § 33-5-1 et seq.
Mich. Comp. Laws Ann., 281.801 et seq.

Boat Registration and Safety Act
Del. Code of 1974, Title 23, § 2111 et seq.
Fla. Stat. 1983, 327.01 et seq.
Ill. Comp. Stat. 1992, Ch. 625, § 45/1-1 et seq.
Ill. Rev. Stat. 1991, Ch. 95 1/2, § 311-1 et seq.

Boat Regulation Act
N.J. Stat. Ann., 12.7-34.1 et seq., 12.7-44 et seq., 12.7B-1 et seq.

Boat Safety Act
Conn. Gen. Stat. 1958, § 15-121 et seq.
Ga. Code Ann., 52-7-1 et seq.
Tenn. Code Ann., 69-10-201 et seq.

Boat Safety Act (Charter)
Wash. Rev. Code Ann., 88.04.005 et seq.

Boat Titling Act
See Uniform Boat Titling Act

Boaters Lien Law
Cal. Harbors and Navigation Code § 500 et seq.

Boating Act
Cal. Harbor and Navigation Code §§ 76.3, 80.6, 656 et seq.
Haw. Rev. Stat. Ann., § 267-1 et seq.
Ida. Code 1947, 49-3201 et seq.
Ind. Code Ann., 14-1-1-1 et seq.
Ky. Rev. Stat. 1971, 235.010 et seq.

Me. Rev. Stat. Ann. 1964, Title 12, § 2061 et seq.
Miss. Code Ann. 1972, § 59-21-1 et seq.
Ore. Rev. Stat. 1953, 830.005 et seq.
S.C. Code Ann. 1976, § 50-21-10 et seq.
Tenn. Public Acts 1959, Ch. 212
Utah Code Ann. 1953, 73-18-1 et seq.

Boating Act Fund Act
Ill. Rev. Stat. 1991, Ch. 95 1/2, §§ 320-1, 320-2

Boating and Water Safety Act
N.C. Gen. Stat. 1943, § 75A-1 et seq.

Boating Safety Act (Alcohol)
R.I. Gen. Laws 1956, 46-22.2-1 et seq.

Boating Safety Reform Act
Ala. Code 1975, § 33-5-50 et seq.

Boating Safety Regulation Act
Okla. Stat. Ann., Title 63, § 4200 et seq.

Boatwright-Eaves Parole Review Act
Cal. Penal Code § 3041.2

Boatwright-Johnston-Baker-Andall Delta Protection Act
Cal. Public Resources Code § 29700 et seq.

Boatyard and Marina Storage Act
Me. Rev. Stat. Ann. 1964, Title 10, § 1381 et seq.

Bob Hill Youthful Offender Act
Ala. Code 1975, § 15-19-1 et seq.

Bobbie Green McDowell Gift of Life Act
Ala. Code 1975, §§ 22-19-70 to 22-19-74

Boccia Act (Rents)
N.Y. Laws 1940, Ch. 440

Boden Act (Motor Vehicles)
Ohio Laws Vol. 113, p. 283

Bodie Protection Act of 1994
Oct. 31, 1994, P.L. 103-433, 108 Stat. 4509

Bodine Act (School Corporations Annexation)
Ind. Code Ann., 20-4-4-1 et seq.

Body Execution Act
Colo. Rev. Stat., 13-59-101 et seq.

Body Gift Act
Ill. Rev. Stat. 1967, Ch. 3, § 42a

Bodywork/Massage Practitioner Act (Professional)
Del. Code of 1974, Title 24, § 5301 et seq.

Boesche's Division Retrocession Act
Ill. Comp. Stat. 1992, Ch. 5, §§ 55-/0.01, 550/1

Boesel Act (Railroads)
Ohio Laws Vol. 69, p. 84

Bogalusa and Alexandria, Louisiana, Redevelopment Agency Act
La. Acts 1972, No. 673

Bogardus Act (Indigent War Veterans)
Ill. Rev. Stat. 1991, Ch. 23, § 3080 et seq.

Boggs Act
Nov. 2, 1951, Ch. 666, 65 Stat. 767, 21 U.S. Code § 174

Bogus Check Act
Okla. Stat. 1981, Title 21, § 1541.1
S.C. Code Ann. 1976, § 34-11-60 et seq.

Boiler Act
Mich. Comp. Laws Ann., 408.751 et seq.
Pa. Purdon's Stat., Title 35, § 1301 et seq.

Boiler and Elevator Safety Law
Haw. Rev. Stat. Ann., § 397-1 et seq.

Boiler and Pressure Vessel Repairer Regulation Act
Ill. Comp. Stat. 1992, Ch. 225, § 203/1 et seq.

Boiler and Pressure Vessel Safety Act
See also Uniform Boiler and Pressure Vessel Safety Act
Ga. Code Ann., 34-11-1 et seq.

Ill. Comp. Stat. 1992, Ch. 430, § 75/1 et seq.
Ill. Rev. Stat. 1991, Ch. 111 1/2, § 3201 et seq.
Ky. Rev. Stat. 1971, 236.005 et seq.
Md. Ann. Code 1957, Art. 48, § 167 et seq.
Miss. Code Ann. 1972, § 45-23-1 et seq.
Mo. Rev. Stat., 650.200 et seq.
Okla. Stat. 1981, Title 40, § 141.1 et seq.
R.I. Gen. Laws 1956, 28-25-1 et seq.
Va. Code 1950, § 40.1-51.5 et seq.

Boiler and Unfired Pressure Vessel Act
Pa. 1998 Pamph. Laws, No. 85

Boiler Erectors and Repairers Act
Tenn. Code Ann., 68-122-201 et seq.

Boiler Inspection Act
Ark. Stat. 1947, 20-23-202 et seq.
Cal. Labor Code § 7680 et seq.
D.C. Code Ann., § 1-1001 et seq.
Ind. Code Ann., 22-15-6-1 et seq.
Iowa Code Ann., 89.1 et seq.
Mass. Gen. Laws Ann., 146:5 et seq.
Minn. Stat. Ann., 183.375 et seq.
Miss. Code Ann. 1972, § 71-1-51
Mont. Code Ann., 50-74-201 et seq.
Neb. Rev. Stat. 1943, 48-719 et seq.
Okla. Stat. 1981, Title 40, § 141 et seq.
Tex. Health and Safety Code, § 755.001 et seq.
Utah Code Ann. 1953, 35-7-5 et seq.
Vt. Stat. Ann., Title 21, § 241 et seq.

Boiler Inspection Acts (Railroads)
Feb. 17, 1911, Ch. 103, 36 Stat. 913, 45 U.S. Code §§ 22 to 29, 31 to 34
March 4, 1915, Ch. 169, 38 Stat. 1192, 45 U.S. Code § 30
June 26, 1918, Ch. 105, 40 Stat. 616
June 7, 1924, Ch. 355, 43 Stat. 659, 45 U.S. Code §§ 22 to 27
April 22, 1940, Ch. 124, 54 Stat. 148, 45 U.S. Code §§ 24 to 34
May 27, 1947, Ch. 85, 61 Stat. 120, 45 U.S. Code §§ 24, 24 nts., 25, 26
Aug. 14, 1957, P.L. 85-135, 71 Stat. 352, 45 U.S. Code § 34

July 8, 1976, P.L. 94-348, 90 Stat. 818, 45
U.S. Code § 34
June 22, 1988, P.L. 100-342, 102 Stat. 632,
45 U.S. Code §§ 22 to 24, 28, 29, 32, 34

Boiler Regulation Act
Wash. Rev. Code Ann., 70.79.010 et seq.

Boiler Rules Act
Md. Ann. Code 1957, Art. 48, § 167 et seq.

Boiler Safety Act
Fla. Stat. Ann., 554.1011 et seq.
Kan. Stat. Ann., 44-913 et seq.
Ky. Rev. Stat. 1971, 236.005 et seq.
S.D. Codified Laws 1967, 34-29A-1 et seq.

Boilers and Pressure Vessels Act
Me. Rev. Stat. Ann. 1964, Title 26, § 141 et
seq.

Boilers and Unfired Vessels Act
Me. Rev. Stat. Ann. 1964, Title 26, § 171 et
seq.
N.H. Rev. Stat. 1955, 157-A:1 et seq.
Ore. Rev. Stat. 1953, 480.510 et seq.

Bolita Act
P.R. Laws Ann. 1954, Title 33, § 1247 et seq.

Boll Weevil Control Act
Tex. Agriculture Code, § 74.001 et seq.

Boll Weevil Eradication Act
See also Uniform Boll Weevil Eradication
Act
Ark. Acts 1992, No. 710
Fla. Stat. Ann., 593.101 et seq.
Ga. Code Ann., 2-7-150 et seq.
Miss. Code Ann. 1972, § 69-37-1 et seq.
Okla. Stat. Ann., Title 2, §§ 3-50.1 to 3-50.20
S.C. Code Ann. 1976, § 46-10-10 et seq.

Bollworm Act
Tex. Agriculture Code, § 74.051 et seq.

Bolton Act (Taxation)
Ohio Rev. Code 1953, 5713.22 et seq.

Bomb Threats Act
Oct. 15, 1970, P.L. 91-452, 18 U.S. Code
§ 844(e)

Bombing Act
Miss. Code Ann. 1972, § 97-37-25

**Bombing Remembrance Day Act
(Oklahoma City)**
Okla. Stat. Ann., Title 25, § 90.9

Bond Act
Kan. Stat. Ann., 10-101 et seq.
N.J. Stat. Ann., 2A:44-143 et seq.
Ohio Rev. Code 1953, 133.01 et seq.

Bond Act (Anti-Pollution)
Ill. Comp. Stat. 1992, Ch. 30, § 405/1 et seq.

Bond Act (Chester County)
S.C. Acts 1948, p. 2504, No. 951

Bond Act (City)
Nev. Rev. Stat. 1979 Reprint, 268.672 et seq.

Bond Act (Clean Water)
Cal. Water Code §§ 13985 et seq., 13999 et
seq.

Bond Act (College Savings)
Wash. Rev. Code Ann., 28B.106.005 et seq.

Bond Act (Contractors)
Ga. Code Ann., 13-10-1
Mich. Comp. Laws Ann., 570.101 et seq.

**Bond Act (County Correction Facility
Capital Expenditure and Juvenile
Facility)**
Cal. Penal Code § 4496.50 et seq.

**Bond Act (County Courthouse Facility
Capital Expenditure)**
Cal. Government Code § 23800 et seq.

Bond Act (County)
Nev. Rev. Stat. 1979 Reprint, 244A.011 et
seq.

Bond Act (Dormitory Revenue)
Cal. Statutes 1947, Ch. 1027, p. 2289

Bond Act (Earthquake Safety and Housing Rehabilitation)
Cal. Government Code § 8878.15 et seq.

Bond Act (Earthquake Safety and Public Buildings Rehabilitation)
Cal. Government Code § 8878.50 et seq.

Bond Act (Emergency Relief)
Wash. Laws 1933, Ch. 65

Bond Act (Employer as Lessee)
Ill. Rev. Stat. 1991, Ch. 48, § 39f-1 et seq.

Bond Act (Environmental Quality)
N.Y. Environmental Conservation Law 1972 (Consol. Laws Ch. 43B), §§ 49-0201 et seq., 51-0101 et seq., 52-0101 et seq., 54-0101 et seq.
N.Y. State Finance Law 1940 (Consol. Laws Ch. 56) § 61

Bond Act (Fiscal Court-Roads)
Ky. Rev. Stat. 1971, 178.010 et seq.

Bond Act (Green Acres, Clean Water, Farmland, and Historic Preservation)
N.J. Laws 1992, Ch. 88

Bond Act (Greenville County)
S.C. Acts 1926, p. 1534, No. 782

Bond Act (Health Science Facilities Construction Program)
Cal. Statutes 1971, Ch. 665, p. 1315

Bond Act (High Educational Facilities)
Cal. Education Code 1976, §§ 67330 et seq., 67345 et seq., 67350 et seq., 67358 et seq.

Bond Act (Highway)
Neb. Rev. Stat. 1943, 39-2201 et seq.
S.C. Code Ann. 1976, § 57-11-210 et seq.

Bond Act (Housing)
Cal. Health and Safety Code § 53500 et seq.

Bond Act (Improvement Bonds)
Cal. Streets and Highways Code § 8500 et seq.

Bond Act (Industrial Project)
Ill. Rev. Stat. 1991, Ch. 24, § 11-74-1 et seq.

Bond Act (Jobs for the New)
N.Y. Laws 1992, Ch. 649

Bond Act (Juvenile Facility Capital Expenditure)
Cal. Penal Code § 4496.50 et seq.

Bond Act (Library Construction and Renovation)
Cal. Education Code 1976, § 19950 et seq.

Bond Act (Mental Institutions)
Ill. Rev. Stat. 1991, Ch. 127, § 313.9 et seq.
N.C. Laws 1953, Ch. 1148

Bond Act (Municipal Improvements)
Cal. Statutes 1901, Ch. 32, p. 27
Nev. Rev. Stat. 1967 Reprint, Replaced Pages, 350.260 et seq.

Bond Act (Municipal Revenue)
Mont. Rev. Code 1947, 11-2401 et seq.

Bond Act (Municipal)
Ala. Code 1975, § 11-81-1 et seq.
Mich. Comp. Laws Ann., 131.1 et seq.
Nev. Rev. Stat. 1979 Reprint, 350.010 et seq.
N.H. Rev. Stat. 1955, 33:1 et seq.
N.J. Rev. Stat. 1937, 40A:2-1 et seq.
S.C. Code Ann. 1976, § 5-21-210 et seq.
Utah Code Ann. 1953, 11-14-1 et seq.
Vt. Stat. Ann., Title 24, § 1751 et seq.
Wash. Rev. Code Ann., 39.44.010 et seq.

Bond Act (New Prison Construction)
Cal. Penal Code §§ 7420 et seq., 7440 et seq.

Bond Act (Passenger Rail and Clean Air)
Cal. Streets and Highways Code §§ 2701 et seq., 2701.05 et seq., 2701.10 et seq.

Bond Act (Paving)
S.C. Code Ann. 1976, § 5-21-610 et seq.

Bond Act (Peace)
Mont. Rev. Code 1947, 94-5101 et seq.

Bond Act (Permanent Improvements)
   N.C. Laws 1953, Ch. 1149

Bond Act (Private Activity)
   Ga. Code Ann., 36-82-182 et seq.
   N.M. Stat. Ann., 6-20-1 et seq.
   Va. Code 1950, § 15.1-1399.1 et seq.

Bond Act (Public Construction)
   Ill. Rev. Stat. 1991, Ch. 29, § 14.9 et seq.

Bond Act (Public Contract)
   Md. Ann. Code 1957, Art. 90 § 11
   Md. Ann. Code 1974, Art. RP, § 9-113

Bond Act (Public Officers)
   March 2, 1895, Ch. 177, 28 Stat. 807, 6 U.S.
      Code §§ 1 to 3
   Wash. Rev. Code 1983, 42.08.005 et seq.

Bond Act (Public Works)
   N.J. Stat. Ann., 2A:44-143 et seq.

Bond Act (Rail Preservation)
   N.Y. Transportation Law (Consol. Laws Ch.
      61a) § 6

Bond Act (Revenue)
   Ga. Code Ann., 36-82-60 et seq.
   Mich. Comp. Laws Ann., 141.101 et seq.
   N.C. Gen. Stat. 1943, § 160-413 et seq.
   N.C. Public Laws 1935, Ch. 473
   Neb. Rev. Stat. 1943, 18-1614 et seq.
   P.R. Laws Ann. 1954, Title 21, § 661 et seq.

Bond Act (Safe Drinking Water)
   Cal. Water Code §§ 13810 et seq., 14000 et
      seq.

Bond Act (School Construction)
   Ill. Rev. Stat. 1981, Ch. 122, § 1201 et seq.

Bond Act (School Facilities)
   Cal. Education Code 1976, §§ 17650 et seq.,
      17645 et seq.

Bond Act (Secondary Roads)
   N.C. Laws 1949, Ch. 1250

Bond Act (Senior Center)
   Cal. Welfare and Institutions Code § 9450 et
      seq.

Bond Act (Sewerage Facilities)
   Md. Ann. Code 1974, Art. EN, § 9-801 et
      seq.

Bond Act (State Bonds)
   Fla. Stat. 1983, 215.57 et seq.

Bond Act (State Construction Program)
   Cal. Statutes 1962, 1st Ex. Sess., Ch. 23,
      p. 193

Bond Act (State Refunding)
   N.C. Gen. Stat. 1943, § 142-29.1 et seq.

Bond Act (State School Building Aid)
   Cal. Education Code 1976, § 17000 et seq.

Bond Act (Street Improvements)
   Cal. Streets and Highways Code § 7000 et
      seq.

Bond Act (Street Opening)
   Cal. Streets and Highways Code § 4500 et
      seq.

Bond Act (Super Collider)
   Cal. Government Code § 8790.50 et seq.

Bond Act (Surety)
   See Surety Bond Act

Bond Act (Township Library)
   Ill. Rev. Stat. 1991, Ch. 81, § 45.9 et seq.

Bond Act (Veterans')
   Cal. Military and Veterans Code §§ 993 et
      seq., 995.01 et seq., 996.87 et seq., 996.87
      et seq., 996 et seq., 998.041 et seq., 998.063
      et seq., 998.074 et seq.

Bond Act (Water Resources)
   Cal. Water Code § 15000 et seq.
   N.J. Laws 1975, Ch. 202

Bond Act (Youth Center and Youth Shelter)
   Cal. Welfare and Institutions Code § 2000 et
      seq.

Bond Allocation Act (Private Activity)
Ark. Code Ann. 1987, 15-5-501 et seq.
Ill. Rev. Stat. 1991, Ch. 17 § 6851 et seq.
Kan. Stat. Ann., 74-5058 et seq.
Miss. Code Ann. 1972, § 31-23-53
Mont. Code Ann., 17-5-1201 et seq.
N.Y. General Municipal Law (Consol. Laws Ch. 24) § 850 nt.
N.Y. Laws 1990, Ch. 47
N.Y. Laws 1991, Ch. 43
N.Y. Laws 1992, Ch. 60
N.Y. Laws 1994, Ch. 44
N.Y. Laws 1995, Ch. 127
Okla. Stat. Ann., Title 62, § 695.21 et seq.

Bond Allocation Act (Tax Exempt)
Pa. Purdon's Stat., Title 73, § 397.1 et seq.

Bond Allocation Plan Act (Private Activity and Student Loan)
Tenn. Code Ann., 13-29-101 et seq.

Bond and Capital Improvements Act (Fiscal Year 1996)
Del. Laws Vol. 70, Ch. 210

Bond and Capital Improvements Act (Fiscal Year 1997)
Del. Laws Vol. 70, Ch. 473

Bond and Compensation Act (Persian Gulf Conflict Veterans')
Pa. 1992 Pamph. Laws, No. 106

Bond and Coupon Collection Law
Cal. Government Code § 16311

Bond and Coupon Registration Law
Cal. Statutes 1935, p. 994

Bond and License Act (Citrus Fruits)
Fla. Stat. 1983, 601.55 et seq.

Bond and Lien Collateral Act
Ariz. Rev. Stat. Ann., § 30-191 et seq.

Bond and Minibond Procedure Act (Boston)
Mass. Acts 1983, Ch. 643

Bond and Mortgage Act
N.J. Stat. Ann., 2A:50-1 et seq.

Bond and Tax Act (Municipal Federal Grant)
Ill. Rev. Stat. 1991, Ch. 24, § 808.01 et seq.

Bond and Undertaking Law
Cal. Code of Civil Procedure § 995.010 et seq.

Bond and Warrant Act
N.J. Stat. Ann., Superseded Vol., 2:27-266 to 2:27-277, 22:1-13
Tex. Rev. Civ. Stat., Art. 2368a

Bond Anticipation Note Act
Colo. Rev. Stat., 29-14-101 et seq.
Wyo. Stat. Ann., § 16-5-401 et seq.

Bond Approval Act (County Official)
Ill. Comp. Stat. 1992, Ch. 55, §§ 60/0.01, 60/1

Bond Assumption Act (Highways)
Tex. Rev. Civ. Stat., Arts. 6674q-1 et seq.

Bond Authorization Act
Ill. Comp. Stat. 1992, Ch. 30, § 305/0.01 et seq.

Bond Authorization Act (Educational Institution)
Ill. Rev. Stat. 1991, Ch. 127, § 306.9 et seq.

Bond Authorization Act (Omnibus)
La. Acts 1994, No. 16

Bond Bank Authority Act (Municipal)
Alaska Stat. 1962, § 44.85.005 et seq.

Bond Bank Law (Municipal)
Vt. Stat. Ann., Title 24, § 4551 et seq.

Bond Bill 1971 (Capital Improvements)
Del. Laws Vol. 57, p. 2093, Ch. 736

Bond Ceiling Allocation Act (Private Activity)
Colo. Rev. Stat., 24-32-1701 et seq.

Bond Certification Law
Cal. Water Code § 20000 et seq.

Bond Compromise Law (Municipal)
Cal. Statutes 1903, p. 164

Bond Curative Act (Municipalities)
Wis. Stat. Ann., 67.02

Bond Election Act
N.M. Stat. Ann., 6-15-23 et seq.

Bond for Deed Act
La. Rev. Stat. Ann., 9:2941 et seq.

Bond Fund Transfer Act (Anti-Pollution)
Ill. Comp. Stat. 1992, Ch. 30, §§ 410/0.01, 410/1
Ill. Rev. Stat. 1991, Ch. 127, §§ 463.9, 464

Bond Guarantors Protection Law
Cal. Government Code § 5100 et seq.

Bond Investment Act
Ohio Rev. Code 1953, 3949.01 et seq.

Bond Investment Act (Building Authority)
Ill. Comp. Stat. 1992, Ch. 20, § 3115/1 et seq.

Bond Investment Act (General Obligation)
Ill. Rev. Stat. 1991, Ch. 127, § 330 et seq.

Bond Issue Act (Roads)
Ill. Rev. Stat. 1981, Ch. 121, § 6-510 et seq.

Bond Issue Acts (Federal Aid Roads)
Ill. Rev. Stat. 1957, Ch. 121, §§ 266 et seq., 281a et seq.

Bond Issue Proceeds Act
Okla. Stat. 1981, Title 62, § 571 et seq.

Bond Law (Public Works Contractors' Surety)
Me. Rev. Stat. Ann. 1964, Title 14, § 871 et seq.

Bond Law (Teeter Plan)
Cal. Government Code § 54773

Bond Limitation Act
See Second Liberty Bond Act
Kan. Stat. Ann., 10-306 et seq.

Bond Money Refund Act (Township)
Ill. Rev. Stat. 1991, Ch. 139, § 160.90 et seq.

Bond Oversight and Reform Act
Okla. Stat. Ann., Title 62, § 695.1 et seq.

Bond Payment Act
Ill. Rev. Stat. 1991, Ch. 103, § 15.9 et seq.

Bond Plan Enabling Act (Industrial Locations)
Ala. Code 1975, § 11-54-20 et seq.

Bond Procedures Act
Tex. Rev. Civ. Stat., Art. 717k-6

Bond Purchase Clause (Sundry Civil Appropriation Act)
March 3, 1881, Ch. 133, 21 Stat. 457, 31 U.S. Code § 741

Bond Refinancing Act
Miss. Code Ann. 1972, § 31-27-7 et seq.

Bond Refinancing Act (Revenue)
Ark. Stat. 1947, 14-231-101 et seq.
W. Va. Code 1966, § 13-2A-1 et seq.

Bond Refunding Act
Ark. Pope's Digest 1937, §§ 11237 to 11367

Bond Refunding Act (Municipal)
Mich. Comp. Laws Ann., 136.1 et seq.

Bond Refunding Act (Revenue)
W. Va. Code 1966, § 13-2E-1 et seq.

Bond Refunding and Special Assessment Law
Cal. Government Code § 59100 et seq.

Bond Refunding Trust Act (Municipal)
Conn. Gen. Stat. Ann., § 3-76a et seq.
Conn. Gen. Stat. 1958, § 3-76a et seq.

Bond Registration Act
Kan. Stat. Ann., 10-620 et seq.
Continued

Mo. Rev. Stat., 108.240 et seq.

Tex. Rev. Civ. Stat., Art. 715b

Bond Registration Act (Municipal)

Kan. Stat. Ann., 10-601 et seq.

N.C. Gen. Stat. 1943, § 160-406 et seq.

Vt. Stat. Ann., Title 24, § 1881 et seq.

Bond Replacement Act

Ill. Comp. Stat. 1992, Ch. 30, § 315/1 et seq.

Ill. Rev. Stat. 1991, Ch. 17, § 6701 et seq.

Bond Retirement Fund Act

Okla. Stat. 1961, Title 62, § 217.1 et seq.

Bond Revenue Act (State)

Va. Code 1950, § 33.1-267 et seq.

Bond Sinking Fund Law

Cal. Statutes 1943, Ch. 611, p. 2225

Bond Supervision Act (Municipal)

Colo. Rev. Stat., 11-59-101 et seq.

Bond Surrender Act

Okla. Stat. 1981, Title 62, § 341 et seq.

Bond Trust Fund Act

Nev. Rev. Stat. 1979 Reprint, Replaced Pages, 282.230 et seq.

Bond Validating Act

Fla. Stat. 1983, 75.01 et seq.

Ida. Laws 1935, 1st Ex. Sess., Ch. 3

Ida. Laws 1937, Ch. 232

Miss. Code Ann. 1972, § 31-13-1 et seq.

Mont. Code Ann., 17-5-201 et seq., Laws 1935, 1st Ex. Sess., Ch. 3

Mont. Laws 1973, Ch. 145

Mont. Laws 1974, Ch. 68

Mont. Rev. Code 1947, 79-2001 et seq.

N.C. Public Laws 1939, Ch. 117

N.D. Cent. Code, 21-08-01 et seq., 21-09-01 et seq.

Utah Code Ann. 1953, 11-30-1 et seq.

Wyo. Session Laws 1935, Ch. 102

Bond Validation and Education Ballot Act

Ill. Rev. Stat. 1991, Ch. 122, §§ 407.35h, 407.36

Bond Validation Laws (County or City)

Cal. Statutes 1933, Ch. 17, p. 42

Cal. Statutes 1935, Ch. 90, p. 441

Cal. Statutes 1935, Ch. 115, p. 465

Bond Validation Laws (Flood Control District)

Cal. Statutes 1933, Ch. 120, p. 574

Cal. Statutes 1935, Ch. 116, p. 466

Bond Validation Laws (Municipal Improvement Districts)

Cal. Statutes 1925, Ch. 212, p. 363.

Cal. Statutes 1927, Ch. 450, p. 772

Cal. Statutes 1933, Ch. 759, p. 2002

Bond Validation Laws (Municipal)

Cal. Statutes 1911, Ch. 83, p. 95

Cal. Statutes 1913, Ch. 183, p. 329

Cal. Statutes 1915, Ch. 33, p. 41

Cal. Statutes 1921, Ch. 146, p. 146

Cal. Statutes 1927, Ch. 9, p. 6

Cal. Statutes 1929, Ch. 10, p. 16

Cal. Statutes 1931, Ch. 429, p. 983

Cal. Statutes 1933, Ch. 18, p. 44

Cal. Statutes 1935, Ch. 93, p. 444

Bond Validation Laws (School and Junior College Districts)

Cal. Statutes 1933, Ch. 19, p. 45

Cal. Statutes 1935, Ch. 13, p. 70

Cal. Statutes 1935, Ch. 21, p. 83

Cal. Statutes 1935, Ch. 114, p. 464

Bond Validation Procedures Law

La. Rev. Stat. Ann., 13:5121 et seq.

Bond Validity Act (Local Government)

Ill. Rev. Stat. 1991, Ch. 85, §§ 860, 861

Bond Volume Cap Allocation Act (Private Activity)

N.J. Stat. Ann., 49:2A-1 et seq.

Bonded Warehouse Act

Ida. Code 1947, 69-201 et seq.

N.H. Rev. Stat. 1955, 348:1 et seq.

Bonded Warehouse Law (Agricultural Products)
Iowa Code Ann., 543.1 et seq.

Bonded Warehouse Law (Agricultural)
Iowa Code Ann., 203C.1 et seq.

Bonded Weighmaster's Law
Miss. Code Ann. 1972, § 75-27-301 et seq.

Bondholders Committee Act
Mich. Comp. Laws 1948, 451.351 et seq.

Bonding Act
Alaska Stat. 1962, § 37.15.010 et seq.
N.J. Rev. Stat. 1937, 40A:2-1 et seq.

Bonding Act (Bancroft)
Ore. Rev. Stat. 1953, 223.205 et seq.

Bonding Act (Highways)
Ore. Rev. Stat. 1953, 367.105 et seq.

Bonding Act (Milk Dealers)
Me. Rev. Stat. Ann. 1964, Title 7, § 2911 et seq.

Bonding Act (Public Works)
Fla. Stat. 1983, 255.05

Bonding Act (Salem)
Ore. Laws 1935, Sp. Sess., Ch. 25

Bonding Act (Schools)
Ore. Rev. Stat. 1953, 328.205 et seq.

Bonding Act (State Employee)
Tex. Government Code, § 653.001 et seq.

Bonding Assistance Program (Small Business)
La. Rev. Stat. Ann., 51:1121 et seq.

Bonding Fund Act
N.D. Cent. Code, 26.1-21-01 et seq.
Neb. Laws 1935, Ch. 23

Bonds for Refunding Act (Special Obligations)
S.C. Code Ann. 1976, § 11-15-600 et seq.

Bondsmen Act
N.H. Rev. Stat. 1955, 598-A:1 et seq.

Bondsmen Act (Professional)
Nev. Rev. Stat. 1979 Reprint, 697.010 et seq.

Bone Copyright Amendment
See Copyright Acts

Bone-Dry Act
Ala. Code 1975, § 28-4-1 et seq.
Ark. Acts 1917, p. 41, No. 13
Ga. Code Ann., 3-10-1 et seq.
Kan. Laws 1917, Ch. 215
Ky. Acts 1922, Ch. 33
Mo. Laws 1919, p. 408, No. 2
Mo. Rev. Stat., 311.110 et seq.
N.D. Laws 1917, Ch. 136
N.Y. Laws 1917, Ch. 814
Okla. Stat. 1981, Title 37, § 501 et seq.
Ore. Code 1930, § 15-101 et seq.
Tenn. Code Ann., 39-6-906 et seq.
Wash. Laws 1917, Ch. 19

Bone Marrow Donor Act
S.C. Code Ann. 1976, § 44-43-60 et seq.

Bone Mass Measurement Coverage Act
Ga. Code Ann., 31-15A-1 et seq.

Bone Power Act
Wash. Rev. Code Ann., 54.04.020 et seq.

Bonine-Patterson Act (Unemployment Compensation)
Mich. Comp. Laws Ann., 421.3 et seq.

Bonine-Tripp Act (Labor Disputes)
Mich. Comp. Laws Ann., 423.9 et seq.

Bonn-Walsh Act (Air Pollution Control)
Ky. Rev. Stat. 1971, 77.005 et seq.

Bonner Act
See Federal Boating Act Of 1958

Bonner Act (Salaries)
Ala. Code 1975, § 12-17-191

Bonner Anti-Shipping Law (Liquors)
Ala. Code 1975, § 28-4-120 et seq.

Bonneville Project Act
Aug. 20, 1937, Ch. 720, 50 Stat. 720, 16 U.S. Code §§ 832 to 832l
March 6, 1940, Ch. 47, 54 Stat. 47, 16 U.S. Code §§ 832a, 832c
July 26, 1946, Ch. 673, 60 Stat. 701, 16 U.S. Code § 832k

Bonus Act
See World War Adjusted Compensation Act
Ill. Rev. Stat. 1939, Ch. 126 1/2, § 1 et seq.
Iowa Code 1977, 35A.1 et seq.
N.D. Cent. Code, 37-25-01 et seq.
N.J. Stat. Ann., Superseded Vol., 38:15-1 to 38:15-5
N.Y. Laws 1920, Ch. 872
N.Y. Laws 1921, Chs. 315, 344
Pa. Cons. Stat., Title 51, § 101 et seq.

Bonus Act (Armed Forces)
N.Y. Laws 1947, Ch. 547

Bonus Act (Capital Stock)
Pa. 1899 Pamph. Laws 189, No. 120

Bonus Act (Educational)
Wis. Stat. Ann., 45.396

Bonus Act (Korean War Veterans)
Ind. Code 1976, 10-5-16-1 et seq.
Mich. Comp. Laws Ann., 35.971 et seq.

Bonus Act (Korean War/World War II)
Mont. Rev. Code 1947, 84-5606 et seq.

Bonus Act (Prisoner of War)
Ill. Rev. Stat. 1991, Ch. 126 1/2, § 57.60 et seq.

Bonus Act (Soldiers)
Minn. Laws 1919, Extra Session, Ch. 49

Bonus Act (Veterans')
Ind. Code 1976, 10-5-14-1 et seq.
Ky. Rev. Stat. 1971, 40.005 et seq.
Mass. Acts 1945, Ch. 731
Mont. Rev. Code 1947, 84-5606 et seq.

R.I. Public Laws 1946, January Session, Ch. 1721
R.I. Public Laws 1955, Ch. 3608
Vt. Stat. Ann., Title 20, § 1544
Wash. Rev. Code Ann., 73.32.020 et seq., 73.33.010 et seq.

Bonus Act (Vietnam Conflict)
Conn. Gen. Stat. 1958, § 27-140a et seq.
R.I. Public Laws 1976, Ch. 81
S.D. Codified Laws 1967, 33-17-16 et seq.

Bonus Act (War of 1812)
Pa. 1868 Pamph. Laws 47, No. 14

Bonus Act (World War I)
Ore. Rev. Stat. 1953, 407.510 et seq.

Bonus Act (World War II Veterans)
Mich. Comp. Laws Ann., 35.921 et seq.
Ore. Rev. Stat. 1953, 407.310 et seq.

Bonus Extension Act (War)
Ill. Rev. Stat. 1991, Ch. 126 1/2, § 57.70 et seq.

Bonus Fund Act (Soldiers)
Mass. Acts 1924, Ch. 480

Bonus Loan Law
Ore. Rev. Stat. 1953, 407.075 et seq.

Bonus Payment Act of 1936
See Adjusted Compensation Payment Act

Bonus Tax Act (Foreign Corporations)
Pa. Purdon's Stat., Title 72, § 1851 et seq.

Bonus Tax Law (Veterans)
N.J. Stat. Ann., 54:10C-1 et seq.

Book Account Act
Colo. Rev. Stat., 13-90-103 et seq.
Ill. Rev. Stat. 1991, Ch. 110, § 8-401

Book Burning Act
Wash. Rev. Code Ann., 7.42.010 et seq.

Book Debt Law
Tenn. Code Ann., 24-7-101 et seq.

Book Labeling Act
Ala. Code 1958, Title 52, §§ 433(6a),
433(6b)

Book Loan Act (Textbooks)
N.Y. Education Law 1947 (Consol. Laws Ch.
16) § 701

Book Postage Act
June 30, 1942, Ch. 459, 56 Stat. 462

Bookmaking Acts
Cal. Penal Code § 337a
Fla. Stat. 1983, 365.01 et seq.
N.J. Stat. Ann., 2C:37-1 et seq.
N.Y. Penal Law 1965 (Consol. Laws Ch. 40)
§ 225.050 et seq.
Okla. Stat. 1981, Title 21, § 991 et seq.
R.I. Gen. Laws 1956, 11-19-14
Tex. Penal Code, § 47.01 et seq.
Wash. Rev. Code Ann., 9.46.0213

Bookmarking Act (Accounts Receivable)
N.D. Cent. Code, 9-11-08, 9-11-09
Pa. 1941 Pamph. Laws 606, No. 255

Boom Act (Logging)
W. Va. Code 1966, § 31-3-1 et seq.

Boom Companies Act
Wash. Rev. Code Ann., 76.28.010 et seq.

Boot Camp Act
Ark. Code Ann. 1987, 12-28-701 et seq.

Boot Camp Act (Motivational)
Pa. Purdon's Stat., Title 61, § 1121 et seq.

Boot Camp Incarceration Act
Del. Code of 1974, Title 11, § 6701 et seq.

Booth Act (California School Lands)
March 1, 1877, Ch. 81, 19 Stat. 267

Bootleg Coal Law
N.Y. Agriculture and Markets Law (Consol.
Laws Ch. 69) § 197h

Borah Act
Aug. 25, 1937, Ch. 777, 50 Stat. 810 (See 18
U.S. Code § 155)

Borah Resolution (Armament Conference)
July 12, 1921, Ch. 45, 42 Stat. 141

Border Act
N.M. Stat. Ann., 12-13-1 et seq.

Border Development Act
N.M. Stat. Ann., 58-27-1 et seq.

Border Smog Reduction Act of 1998
Oct. 27, 1998, P.L. 105-286, 112 Stat. 2773,
42 U.S. Code § 7401 nt.

Border State School Interstate Compact Act
Ill. Comp. Stat. 1992, Ch. 45, § 95/0.01 et
seq.

Borland Amendment (District of Columbia Improvements)
July 21, 1914, Ch. 191, 38 Stat. 524

Borland Amendment (Improvements)
D.C. Code Ann., §§ 1-502, 7-612, 8-107

Borough Act
N.J. Stat. Ann., 40A:60-1 et seq.
Pa. Purdon's Stat., Title 53, § 45101 et seq.

Borough Civil Service Act
Pa. Purdon's Stat., Title 53, § 46101 et seq.

Borough Incorporation Act
Alaska Stat. 1962, § 29.05.031

Borough, Town and Township Permanent Registration Act
Pa. Purdon's Stat., Title 25, § 951-1 et seq.

Borough Zoning Enabling Act
Pa. Purdon's Stat., Title 53, § 10101 et seq.

Borrowers Act
Cal. Civil Code, 3081.1 et seq.

Borrowing Act (Foreign Limitations)
Tex. Civil Practice & Remedies Code,
§ 16.06 et seq.
Continued

Tex. Rev. Civ. Stat., Art. 5530

Borrowing Act (Limitations)
Cal. Code of Civil Procedure § 361
Colo. Rev. Stat., 13-80-116
Del. Code of 1974, Title 10, § 8120
Fla. Stat. 1983, 95.10
Ill. Rev. Stat. 1991, Ch. 110, § 13-210
Ind. Code Ann., 34-1-2-6
Ky. Rev. Stat. 1971, 413.320
La. Civil Code, Art. 3532
Mich. Comp. Laws Ann., 600.5861
Minn. Stat. 1976, 541.14
Miss. Code Ann. 1972, § 15-1-65
Mo. Rev. Stat. 1978, 516.190
N.C. Gen. Stat. 1943, § 1-21
N.Y. Civil Practice and Rules (Consol. Laws Ch. 8) § 202
Ohio Rev. Code 1953, 2305.20
Pa. Cons. Stat., Title 42, § 5521

Borrowing Act (Municipal)
Pa. 1941 Pamph. Laws 159, No. 87
Wis. Stat. Ann., 67.01 et seq.

Borrowing Act (Short-Term)
Ky. Rev. Stat. 1971, 65.7701 et seq.

Borrowing Statute (Limitations)
Okla. Stat. Ann., Title 12, § 104 et seq.

Bossier City, Louisiana, Redevelopment Agency Act
La. Acts 1972, No. 90

Boston Bond and Minibond Procedure Act
Mass. Acts 1983, Ch. 643

Boston, Brighton & Watertown Incinerator Loan Act
Mass. Acts 1954, Ch. 523

Boston Building Act
Mass. Acts 1907, Ch. 550
Mass. Acts 1938, Ch. 479

Boston Elevated Railway Public Control Act
Mass. Special Acts 1918, Ch. 159

Boston Extraordinary Repairs Loan Act
Mass. Acts 1955, Ch. 364
Mass. Acts 1958, Ch. 668

Boston Funding Loan Act
Mass. Acts 1957, Ch. 717

Boston Municipal Auditorium Loan Act
Mass. Acts 1957, Ch. 718

Boston National Historical Park Act of 1974
Nov. 10, 1978, P.L. 95-625, 16 U.S. Code §§ 410z nt., 410z-1

Boston Parking Facilities Loan Act
Mass. Acts 1951, Ch. 625

Boston Public Facilities Department Act
Mass. Acts 1966, Ch. 642

Boston Public Health Act
Mass. Gen. Laws Ann., 111 Appendix :2-1 et seq.

Boston Railroad Holding Company Dissolution Act
Mass. Acts 1946, Ch. 518

Boston Retirement Act
Mass. Acts 1922, Ch. 521

Boston Terminal Act
Mass. Acts 1896, Ch. 516

Boston Water and Sewer Reorganization Act
Mass. Acts 1977, Ch. 436

Boston Zoning Act
Mass. Acts 1924, Ch. 488

Boswell Amendment (Registration of Electors)
Ala. Const. 1901, Amend. 55

Botanic Gardens Act (Forest Preserve)
Ill. Rev. Stat. 1991, Ch. 96 1/2, § 6700 et seq.

Bottle Act
N.J. Stat. Ann., 56:3-14 to 56:3-34

N.Y. Environmental Conservation Law 1972
(Consol. Laws Ch. 43B) § 27-1001 et seq.

Bottle Ban Act
Vt. Stat. Ann., Title 10, § 1521 et seq.

Bottle Bill
Mass. Gen. Laws Ann., 64H:6, 94:321 et seq.

Bottle Bill Act (Deposit)
Iowa Code Ann., 455C.1 et seq.

Bottle Club Act
Mich. Comp. Laws Ann., 436.26c

Bottle Refund Law
Ore. Rev. Stat., 459A.700 et seq.

Bottled Water Act
Fla. Stat. Ann., 500.457
Ill. Comp. Stat. 1992, Ch. 815, §§ 310/0.01,
310/1
Ill. Rev. Stat. 1991, Ch. 111 1/2, §§ 121.100,
121.110
Pa. Purdon's Stat., Title 35, § 721.1 et seq.

Bottlemark Act
W. Va. Code 1966, § 47-3-1 et seq.

Bottlers Act
Tenn. Acts 1909, Ch. 446

Bottling Act
Mo. Laws 1885, p. 151

Bottling Act (Trademarks)
N.Y. General Business Law (Consol. Laws,
Ch. 20) § 360

Boulder Canyon Project Act
Dec. 21, 1928, Ch. 42, 45 Stat. 1057, 43 U.S.
Code §§ 617 to 617t
March 6, 1946, Ch. 58, 60 Stat. 36, 43 U.S.
Code § 617h
Nov. 6, 1978, P.L. 95-598, 43 U.S. Code
§ 617p
Aug. 17, 1984, P.L. 98-381, 43 U.S. Code
§§ 617a, 617b

Boulder Canyon Project Adjustment Act
July 19, 1940, Ch. 643, 54 Stat. 774, 43 U.S.
Code §§ 618 to 618o
April 30, 1947, Ch. 46, 61 Stat. 56, 43 U.S.
Code §§ 618, 618a, 618h, 618i, 618n
May 14, 1948, Ch. 292, 62 Stat. 235, 43 U.S.
Code § 618a
June 1, 1948, Ch. 364, 62 Stat. 284, 43 U.S.
Code § 618a
Aug. 17, 1984, P.L. 98-381, 43 U.S. Code
§§ 618, 618a, 618e, 618k

Boulder City Act of 1958
Sept. 2, 1958, P.L. 85-900, 72 Stat. 1726, 12
U.S. Code § 1715n; 43 U.S. Code § 617u nt.

Boulevard District Act
Cal. Streets and Highways Code § 26000 et
seq.

Boulevard Stop Act
Mass. Gen. Laws Ann., 89:9
Md. Ann. Code 1974, Art. TR, §§ 21-401 to
21-404.1

Boundaries Act
D.C. Code Ann., §§ 1-1306, 1-1308
Haw. Rev. Stat. Ann., § 664-1 et seq.
Tenn. Code Ann., 16-11-106
Wash. Rev. Code Ann., 58.04.010 et seq.

Boundary Act (City)
Kan. Stat. Ann., 12-517 et seq.

Boundary Act (Grant Park)
Ill. Rev. Stat. 1991, Ch. 105, § 800 et seq.

Boundary Act (Queens)
N.Y. Laws 1928, Ch. 802

Boundary Act (School Districts)
Mo. Rev. Stat. 1959, 165.294

Boundary Extension Act
La. Civil Code, Art. 663

Boundary Line Act
Cal. Statutes 1911, Ch. 496, p. 1018

Boundry Act
Nov. 21, 1990, P.L. 101-622. 16 U.S. Code § 668dd nt.

Bounties Act (Ground Hog)
Ill. Rev. Stat. 1989, Ch. 8, § 120 et seq.

Bounty Act
Alaska Stat. 1962, § 16.35.050 et seq.
Mont. Code Ann., 81-7-101 et seq.
Pa. 1864 Pamph. Laws 85, No. 88

Bounty Act (County)
Tenn. Code Ann., 38-11-201

Bounty Act (Wild Animals)
Colo. Rev. Stat., 35-40-107 et seq.
Iowa Code Ann., 350.1 et seq.
Ore. Rev. Stat. 1953, 610.205 et seq.

Bouse Act (Illegal Search Evidence)
Md. Ann. Code 1957, Superseded Vol., Art. 35, § 5

Bovidae and Cervidae Tuberculosis Eradication Act
Ill. Comp. Stat. 1992, Ch. 510, § 35/1 et seq.

Bovine Brucellosis Act
Cal. Food and Agricultural Code 1967, § 10301 et seq.
Iowa Code Ann., 164.1 et seq.
Neb. Rev. Stat. 1943, 54-1367 et seq.

Bovine Brucellosis Eradication Act
Ill. Comp. Stat. 1992, Ch. 510, § 30/1 et seq.

Bovine Tuberculosis Act
Cal. Food and Agricultural Code 1967, § 9901 et seq.
Iowa Code Ann., 165.1 et seq.
Ohio Rev. Code 1953, 941.51 et seq.
S.D. Codified Laws 1967, 40-61 et seq.

Bovine Tuberculosis and Brucellosis Act
N.D. Cent. Code, 36-15-01 et seq.

Bovine Tuberculosis Control Act
S.D. Codified Laws 1967, 40-61 et seq.

Bovine Tuberculosis Eradication Act
Ill. Rev. Stat. 1991, Ch. 8 § 87 et seq.

Bowdre Township Civic Center Act
Ill. Comp. Stat. 1992, Ch. 70, § 305/3-1 et seq.

Bowdre Township Civic Center Law
Ill. Rev. Stat. 1991, Ch. 85, § 6351 et seq.

Bowdre Township, Marengo, and Crystal Lake Civic Centers Act
Ill. Rev. Stat. 1991, Ch. 85, § 6250 et seq.

Bowman Act (Claims)
March 3, 1883, Ch. 116, 22 Stat. 485

Bowman-McCauley-Traxler-Law-McNeely Lottery Act
Mich. Comp. Laws Ann., 432.1 et seq.

Bowman-Traxler-McCauley-Law Bingo Act
Mich. Comp. Laws Ann., 432.102 et seq.

Boxes, Containers, Carts, Cases and Baskets Act
Fla. Stat. Ann., 506.501 et seq.

Boxing Act
Cal. Business and Professions Code § 18600 et seq.
Ky. Rev. Stat. 1971, 229.011 et seq.
Me. Rev. Stat. Ann. 1964, Title 8, § 101 et seq., Title 32, § 13501 et seq.
Mich. Comp. Laws Ann., 431.101 et seq.
N.Y. Unconsolidated Laws, § 8901 et seq.
Pa. Cons. Stat., Title 5, § 1901 et seq.
Pa. Purdon's Stat., Title 4, § 31.501 et seq.
Wash. Rev. Code Ann., 67.08.001 et seq.

Boxing and Wrestling Act
Cal. Business and Professions Code § 18600 et seq.
Colo. Rev. Stat., 12-10-101 et seq.
Ill. Rev. Stat. 1991, Ch. 111, § 5001 et seq.
Tex. Rev. Civ. Stat., Art. 8501-1

Boxing and Wrestling Commission Act
D.C. Code Ann., § 2-601 et seq.

Boxing and Wrestling Commission Amendment Act
D.C. Code 1973, § 2-601 et seq.

Boxing and Wrestling Commission Nominee Confirmation Procedure Act
D.C. Code Ann., § 2-604

Boxing Commission Act
Ind. Code Ann., 25-9-1-1 et seq.
Mont. Rev. Code 1947, 82-301 et seq.
N.Y. Laws 1920, Ch. 912
N.Y. Laws 1921, Ch. 714
Okla. Stat. 1971, Title 3A, § 1 et seq.
Ore. Rev. Stat. 1953, 463.010 et seq.

Boxing Licensing Act (Professional)
Okla. Stat. Ann., Title 3A, § 500 et seq.

Boxing, Sparring and Wrestling Act
Kan. Stat. Ann., 21-1801 et seq.

Boxwell Act (Common Schools)
Ohio Laws Vol. 89, p. 123

Boycott Act
Mo. Rev. Stat., 416.030
Tex. Business and Commerce Code, § 15.01 et seq.

Boycotting and Picketing Act
Ala. Code 1975, § 13A-11-122

Boykin Act
Ga. Code Ann., 13-9-3 et seq.

Boykin Merchant Marine Act
June 6, 1939, Ch. 186, 53 Stat. 810, 46 U.S. Code § 1159

Boylan Bill (New York City Employees' Retirement Law)
N.Y. City Adm. Code '85 § 13-101 et seq.

Boylan-Town Act (Drugs)
N.Y. Laws 1914, Ch. 363

Boyle Act (Tax Districts)
Tenn. Acts 1905, Ch. 345

Boyle Act (Taxation)
Ohio Rev. Code 1953, 5721.01 et seq.

Boylston Water District Loan Act
Mass. Acts 1951, Ch. 421
Mass. Acts 1955, Ch. 537

Boynton Act (Workmen's Compensation)
Cal. Insurance Code § 11770 et seq.

Boys' and Girls' Homes Act
N.J. Stat. Ann., 30:4-156 et seq.

Brad Hudson Bicycle Safety Act
Ala. Code 1975, § 32-5A-280 et seq.

Bradenton Civic Center Revenue Bond Act
Fla. Special Laws 1951, Ch. 51-27412

Bradenton Downtown Development Authority Law
Fla. Special Laws 1974, Ch. 74-425

Bradenton Waterfront Development Act
Fla. Special Laws 1963, Ch. 63-1129

Bradford Act (Labor Department)
Ala. Code 1975, § 25-7-1 et seq.

Bradford-Cole Act (Blind Persons)
Ala. Gen. Acts 1943, p. 8, No. 6

Bradford County Historical Board of Trustees Act
Fla. Special Laws 1973, Ch. 73-408

Bradford County Recreation and Water Conservation and Control Act
Fla. Special Laws 1967, Ch. 67-1130

Bradford County Reference Act
Pa. 1869 Pamph. Laws 725, No. 698

Bradley-Burns Bill of Rights
Cal. Revenue and Taxation Code § 7221 et seq.

Bradley-Burns Uniform Local Sales and Use Tax Law
Cal. Revenue and Taxation Code § 7200 et seq.

Brady Handgun Violence Prevention Act
Nov. 30, 1993, P.L. 103-159, 18 U.S. Code §§ 921 nt., 921 et seq. , 42 U.S. Code § 3759
Sept. 13, 1994, P.L. 103-322, 18 U.S. Code § 922 nt.
Oct. 11, 1996, P.L. 104-294, 18 U.S. Code § 922 nt.

Brady-Jared Teen Driver Safety Act
Cal. Vehicle Code 1959, § 12814.6

Braille Literacy Act
N.M. Stat. Ann., 22-15-21 et seq.

Brain Death Act
See Uniform Brain Death Act

Braintree Electric Light Loan Act
Mass. Acts 1957, Ch. 674

Brake Act
Mo. Rev. Stat., 307.170

Brake Equipment Act
Ohio Rev. Code 1953, 4513.20

Brake-Stout-DeLano Act (Unemployment Compensation)
Mich. Comp. Laws Ann., 421.1 et seq.

Branch Banking Acts
Ill. Rev. Stat. 1991, Ch. 17 § 3406
Mich. Comp. Laws 1948, 487.34a
Mont. Code Ann., 32-1-372
N.C. Gen. Stat. 1943, § 53-62
N.J. Stat. Ann., 17:9A-19 et seq.
N.M. Stat. Ann., 58-5-2 et seq.
Ore. Rev. Stat., 714.030 et seq.
Utah Code Ann. 1953, 7-1-708 et seq.
Wash. Rev. Code Ann., 30.40.010 et seq.
Wis. Stat. Ann., 221.04, Subsec. 1, Subd. f

Branch Rail Line Revitalization Act
Neb. Rev. Stat. 1943, 74-1401 et seq.

Branching by Merger Act (Interstate)
Neb. Rev. Stat. 1943, 8-2101 to 8-2108

Brand Act
Ida. Code 1947, 25-1101 et seq.
Ill. Comp. Stat. 1992, Ch. 510, § 40/1 et seq.
La. Rev. Stat. Ann., 3:731 et seq.
N.M. Stat. Ann., 77-9-1 et seq.

Brand Act (Livestock)
Colo. Rev. Stat., 35-43-101 et seq.
Kan. Stat. Ann., 47-414 et seq.
La. Rev. Stat. Ann., 3:731 et seq.
Mont. Code Ann., 81-3-101 et seq.
N.D. Cent. Code, 36-09-01 et seq.
Neb. Rev. Stat. 1943, 54-101 et seq.
Okla. Stat. 1981, Title 2, § 4-1 et seq.
S.D. Codified Laws 1967, 40-18-1 et seq.
Wash. Rev. Code Ann., 9.16.010 et seq.

Brand and Antitheft Act (Livestock)
Utah Code Ann. 1953, 4-24-1 et seq.

Brand Inspection Act
Ida. Code 1947, 25-1101 et seq.
Ore. Rev. Stat. 1953, 604.005 et seq.

Branding Iron Act (Election Registration)
Kan. Stat. Ann., 25-3301 et seq.

Brandon Act
Ga. Code Ann., 31-17A-4

Brandy Law (Native)
Ark. Stat. 1947, 3-6-101 et seq.

Brandy Thurmond Act
Okla. Stat. Ann., Title 21, § 1287.1

Brandywine River Valley Compact Act
Pa. Purdon's Stat., Title 32, § 818 et seq.

Brandywine Scenic Rivers Act
Pa. Purdon's Stat., Title 32, § 820.101 et seq.

Brannan-Andrus Levee Maintenance District Act
Cal. Statutes 1967, Ch. 910, p. 2362

Brantley County Development Authority Act
Ga. Laws 1968, p. 3488

Brazoria County Pilots Licensing and Regulatory Act

Tex. Transportation Code, § 68.001 et seq.

Brazos County, Texas, Airport Authority Act

Tex. Laws 61st Leg. 1969, p. 1161, Ch. 374

Brazos River Act (Conservation and Reclamation)

Tex. General and Special Laws 43rd Leg., 1934, 4th C.S., p. 3, Ch. 3

Tex. General and Special Laws 44th Leg., 1935, 1st C.S., p. 1527, Ch. 368

Tex. Local and Special Laws 41st Leg., 1929, 2nd C.S., p. 22, Ch. 13

Breach of Peace Act

Ala. Code 1975, § 13A-11-7

Conn. Gen. Stat. Ann., § 53A-181

La. Rev. Stat. Ann., 14:103

Miss. Code Ann. 1972, § 97-35-13 et seq.

Breach of Promise Abolition Act

N.H. Rev. Stat. 1955, 508:11

Breach of Promise Act

Ill. Comp. Stat. 1992, Ch. 740, § 15/0.01 et seq.

Mich. Comp. Laws Ann., 551.301 et seq.

Wis. Stat. Ann., § 768.01 et seq.

Breachy Animals Act

Wash. Rev. Code Ann., 16.60.075

Bread Act (Hearth Baked)

Ill. Rev. Stat. 1991, Ch. 56 1/2, § 288.9 et seq.

Bread and Corn Meal Enrichment Act

N.C. Gen. Stat. 1943, § 106-219.1 et seq.

Bread and Flour Act

N.M. Stat. Ann., 25-5-1 et seq.

Bread Content Act

Wash. Rev. Code Ann., 69.08.010 et seq.

Bread, Flour and Corn Meal Enrichment Act

Ala. Code 1975, § 20-1-70 et seq.

Bread Law

Iowa Code Ann., 210.19 et seq.

Bread Standard Weight Law

Neb. Laws 1931, Ch. 162

Wash. Rev. Code Ann., 19.92.100

Breaker Law (Circuit)

Mont. Code Ann., 15-30-171 et seq.

Breaking Act (Arrest)

N.Y. Criminal Procedure Law (Consol. Laws Ch. 11A) §§ 140.15, Subd. 4, 140.25(3)

Breaking and Entering Act

N.C. Gen. Stat. 1943, § 14-54

Breaks Interstate Park Compact (Virginia and Kentucky)

Ky. Rev. Stat. 1971, 148.220

Breast and Cervical Cancer Mortality Prevention Act

Aug. 10, 1990, P.L. 101-354, 42 U.S. Code § 201 nt.

W. Va. Code 1966, § 16-33-1 et seq.

Breast Cancer Act

Aug. 13, 1997, P.L. 105-41, 111 Stat. 1119

Ark. Code 1987, 20-15-1301 et seq., 26-57-211, 26-57-236, 26-57-1101 et seq.

Okla. Stat. Ann., Title 74, § 3315 et seq.

Breast Cancer Patient Care Act

Also known as Mastectomy Patient Care Act

Ga. Code Ann., 33-24-70 et seq.

Breast Cancer Patient Protection Act

Cal. Health and Safety Code § 1367.635

Cal. Insurance Code § 10123.86

Breast Cancer Screening Act

Ala. Code 1975, § 22-13-50 et seq.

Breathalyzer Act

Tex. Rev. Civ. Stat., Art. 6701l-5

Brees Act (Absentees on Military Duty)
N.Y. Military Law (Consol. Laws Ch. 36)
§ 243 et seq.

Bremen Friendship Treaty (1851)
Haw. Session Laws 1855, p. 61, March 27,
1854

Brendon Maguire Act
Cal. Elections Code 1976, § 6490.3

**Brennan-Speno Act (Public Moneys;
Transportation)**
N.Y. Education Law 1947 (Consol. Laws Ch.
16) § 3635

Bretton Woods Agreements Act
July 31, 1945, Ch. 339, 59 Stat. 512, 22 U.S.
Code §§ 286 to 286k; 31 U.S. Code § 822a
April 3, 1948, Ch. 169, 62 Stat. 141, 22 U.S.
Code § 286b
June 29, 1949, Ch. 276, 60 Stat. 298, 22 U.S.
Code § 286k-1
Aug. 9, 1954, Ch. 660, 68 Stat. 677, 22 U.S.
Code § 286b
June 17, 1959, P.L. 86-48, 73 Stat. 80, 22
U.S. Code §§ 286e, 286e-1
June 19, 1962, P.L. 87-490, 76 Stat. 105, 22
U.S. Code §§ 286e, 286e-2, 286e-3
Nov. 13, 1963, P.L. 88-178, 77 Stat. 334, 22
U.S. Code § 286e-1a
June 2, 1965, P.L. 89-31, 79 Stat. 119, 22
U.S. Code § 286e-1b
Aug. 14, 1965, P.L. 89-126, 79 Stat. 519, 22
U.S. Code §§ 286b, 286c, 286e-4
Dec. 30, 1970, P.L. 91-599, 84 Stat. 1657, 22
U.S. Code §§ 286e-1c, 286e-1d
Aug. 15, 1973, P.L. 93-94, 87 Stat. 314, 22
U.S. Code § 286a
Oct. 19, 1976, P.L. 94-564, 22 U.S. Code
§ 286a et seq.
Oct. 3, 1977, P.L. 95-118, 22 U.S. Code
§ 286e-H
Oct. 28, 1977, P.L. 95-147, 22 U.S. Code
§§ 286c, 286k
Nov. 30, 1983, P.L. 98-181, 22 U.S. Code
§§ 286b to 286c, 286e-li , 286e-2, 286y,
286z, 286aa to 287gg
Oct. 18, 1986, P.L. 99-500, 22 U.S. Code
§ 286gg

Oct. 30, 1986, P.L. 99-591, 22 U.S. Code
§ 286gg
Dec. 22, 1987, P.L. 100-202, 22 U.S. Code
§ 296e-5a
Oct. 1, 1988, P.L. 100-461, 22 U.S. Code
§ 286e-1k
Dec. 19, 1989, P.L. 101-240, 22 U.S. Code
§§ 286b, 286b-2, 286e-9 , 286e-12, 286k-1,
286kk, 286s
Oct. 24, 1992, P.L. 102-511, 22 U.S. Code
§§ 286e-1l, 286e-5b, 286e-13, 286ll,
286mm
Nov. 23, 1993, P.L. 103-149, 22 U.S. Code
§ 286aa
Oct. 21, 1998, P.L. 105-277, 22 U.S. Code
§§ 286e-1m, 286e-2
June 25, 1999, P.L. 106-36, 22 U.S. Code
§ 286gg.

**Brevard County and Municipality Tax
Collection Act**
Fla. Special Laws 1961, Ch. 61-1917

Brevard County Cemetery Act
Fla. Special Laws 1967, Ch. 67-1185

Brevard County Erosion District Act
Fla. Special Laws 1970, Ch. 70-603

Brevard County Expressway Authority Act
Fla. Stat. 1983, 348.216 et seq.

Brevard County Public Works Act
Fla. Special Laws 1967, Ch. 67-1145

Brevard County Re-registration Act
Fla. Laws 1949, Ch. 25453

Brevard County Solid Waste Disposal Act
Fla. Special Laws 1967, Ch. 67-1146

**Brevard County Water and Navigation
Control Act**
Fla. Special Laws 1963, Ch. 63-1145

Brevard County Water District Act
Fla. Special Laws 1951, Ch. 27419

Brewers Act
Pa. 1897 Pamph. Laws 176, No. 144

Brewpub Act
Ala. Code 1975, § 28-4A-1 et seq.

Brewster Water Loan Act
Mass. Acts 1965, Ch. 552

Bribery Act (Commercial)
La. Rev. Stat. Ann., 14:73
N.Y. Penal Law 1965 (Consol. Laws Ch. 40)
§§ 180.00, 180.05
Wash. Rev. Code Ann., 49.44.020

Bribery Act (Elections)
Wis. Stat. Ann., 12.11

Bribery Act (Public Officials)
Wis. Stat. Ann., 946.10 et seq.

Bribery Acts
Conn. Gen. Stat. Ann., § 53a-146 et seq.
Fla. Stat. 1983, 838.014 et seq.
Ind. Code Ann., 35-44-1-1
Iowa Code Ann., 722.1 et seq.
La. Rev. Stat. Ann., 14:73
Md. Ann. Code 1957, Art. 27, § 23
Mich. Comp. Laws Ann., 750.117 et seq.
Mont. Code Ann., 45-7-101 et seq.
Neb. Rev. Stat. 1943, 28-917 et seq.
Nev. Rev. Stat. 1979 Reprint, 199.010 et seq.
N.H. Rev. Stat. 1955, 640:1 et seq.
N.Y. Penal Law 1965 (Consol. Laws Ch. 40)
§§ 180.00 et seq., 200.00 et seq.
R.I. Gen. Laws 1956, 11-7-1 et seq.
Tex. Penal Code, § 36.01
Vt. Stat. Ann., Title 13, § 1101 et seq.
Wash. Rev. Code Ann., 9A.68.010 et seq.
Wis. Stat. Ann., 134.05

Bribery and Corrupt Practices Act
W. Va. Code 1966, § 61-5A-1 et seq.

Bridge Act
March 23, 1906, Ch. 1130, 34 Stat. 84, 33
U.S. Code §§ 491 to 498
Oct. 15, 1982, P.L. 97-322, Title I, 33 U.S.
Code §§ 491, 495
April 2, 1987, P.L. 100-17, 33 U.S. Code
§§ 494, 508

Bridge Act (Condemnation of Toll Bridges)
Pa. Purdon's Stat., Title 36, § 3141.21

Bridge Act (County)
Neb. Rev. Stat. 1943, 39-835 et seq.

Bridge Act (Defective)
Ga. Code Ann., 32-4-70

Bridge Act (Delaware River)
Pa. Purdon's Stat., Title 36, § 3421 et seq.

Bridge Act (Interstate)
Neb. Rev. Stat. 1943, 39-891 et seq.
Wis. Stat. Ann., 84.12

Bridge Act (Self Liquidating)
N.J. Stat. Ann., 27:19-26 et seq.

Bridge Act (State Aid)
Me. Rev. Stat. Ann. 1964, Title 23, § 451 et
seq.

Bridge Act (Street Railroad)
Ill. Rev. Stat. 1991, Ch. 131 1/4, §§ 4.9, 5

Bridge Acts
Ky. Rev. Stat. 1971, 180.010 et seq.
Mich. Comp. Laws Ann., 254.1 et seq.
Mo. Rev. Stat., 234.010 et seq.
S.D. Codified Laws 1967, 31-14-1 et seq.
Wis. Stat. Ann., 84.11

Bridge and Ferry Authorities Act
La. Rev. Stat. Ann., 48:1091 et seq.

Bridge and Highway Authority Act
Pa. Purdon's Stat., Title 36, § 3601 et seq.

Bridge and Highway District Law
Cal. Streets and Highways Code § 27000 et
seq.

Bridge and Railroad Capital Budget
Supplemental Act for 1991-1992
Pa. 1992 Pamph. Laws, No. 143

Bridge and Road Act (Alachua County
Subdivision)
Fla. Special Laws 1953, Ch. 28872

Bridge and Tunnel Authority Act (Triborough)
N.Y. Public Authorities Law (Consol. Laws Ch. 43A) § 550 et seq.

Bridge and Tunnel Revenue Bond Act (Woodrow Wilson)
Md. Ann. Code 1974, Art. TR, § 10-301 et seq.

Bridge and Tunnel Unification Act (New York-New Jersey)
N.Y. Laws 1931, Ch. 47
N.Y. Unconsolidated Laws, § 6501 et seq.

Bridge and Turnpike Authority Act
R.I. Gen. Laws 1956, 24-12-1 et seq.

Bridge Authority Act
N.Y. Public Authorities Law (Consol. Laws Ch. 43A) § 525 et seq.

Bridge Authority Act (Buffalo and Fort Erie)
N.Y. Laws 1933, Ch. 824

Bridge Authority Act (Mackinac)
Mich. Comp. Laws Ann., 254.301 et seq.

Bridge Authority Act (Nassau County)
N.Y. Public Authorities Law (Consol. Laws Ch. 43A) § 651 et seq.

Bridge Authority Act (Ogdensburg)
N.Y. Public Authorities Law (Consol. Laws Ch. 43A) § 700 et seq.

Bridge Authority Act (Toll)
Mont. Rev. Code 1947, 32-1901 et seq.

Bridge Building Authority Act
Ga. Code 1933, 95-2301 et seq.

Bridge Commission Act
Ala. Code 1958, Title 23, § 97 et seq.
Ky. Rev. Stat. 1971, 181.010 et seq.
Ohio Rev. Code 1953, 5593.01 et seq.

Bridge Commission Act (Illinois-Missouri)
Ill. Rev. Stat. 1991, Ch. 127, § 63s-24.9 et seq.

Bridge Commission Act (Lake Champlain)
N.Y. Laws 1927, Ch. 321

Bridge Commission Act (Missouri-Illinois-Jefferson-Monroe)
Ill. Rev. Stat. 1991, Ch. 127, § 63s-34.9 et seq.

Bridge Commission Act (State)
Mich. Comp. Laws Ann., 254.151 et seq.

Bridge Commission Compact (Lake Champlain)
Vt. Stat. Ann., Title 19, § 1711

Bridge Commissioners Act (Illinois-Indiana)
Ill. Rev. Stat. 1991, Ch. 121, § 420 et seq.

Bridge Compact (Portsmouth-Kittery)
N.H. Stat. 1955, 234:43 et seq.

Bridge Compact Act (Illinois-Indiana)
Ill. Rev. Stat. 1991, Ch. 121, § 410 et seq.

Bridge Compact Act (Illinois-Missouri)
Ill. Rev. Stat. 1991, Ch. 127, § 63s-20 et seq.

Bridge Compact Act (Missouri-Illinois-Jefferson-Monroe)
Ill. Rev. Stat. 1991, Ch. 127, § 63s-30.9 et seq.

Bridge Companies Act
N.J. Stat. Ann., 48:5-18

Bridge Construction Act
Ill. Comp. Stat. 1992, Ch. 605, §§ 105/0.01, 105/1

Bridge Construction Compact Act
La. Rev. Stat. Ann., 48:1107

Bridge Corporation Act
Ala. General Acts 1927, p. 278

Bridge Corporations Act (Toll)
Okla. Stat. 1961, Title 18, § 191 et seq.

Bridge District Act
Wash. Rev. Code Ann., 47.56.010

Bridge District of Palm Beach Act
Fla. Laws 1935, Ch. 16837

Bridge Grant Program Act
Tenn. Code Ann., 54-4-501 et seq.

Bridge Improvement Act (County)
Okla. Stat. Ann., Title 69, § 657

Bridge Load Limit Act
N.C. Gen. Stat. 1943, § 136-72

Bridge Loan Program (Beverly-Murray Small Business)
Cal. Statutes 1992, Ch. 61

Bridge Pier Protection Act
Ill. Comp. Stat. 1992, Ch. 605, §§ 110/1, 110/1.1
Ill. Rev. Stat. 1991, Ch. 121, §§ 193a, 193a.1

Bridge Reconstruction and Replacement Act
Cal. Streets and Highways Code § 2400 et seq.

Bridge Rehabilitation and Improvement and Railroad Right-of-Way Preservation Bond Act
N.J. Laws 1991, Ch. 180

Bridge Rehabilitation and Improvement Bond Act
N.J. Laws 1983, Ch. 363

Bridge Revenue Bond Act
La. Rev. Stat. Ann., 48:851 et seq.
N.C. Gen. Stat. 1943, § 136-89.31 et seq.

Bridge Revenue Bond Act (Escambia County)
Fla. Special Laws 1941, Ch. 21216

Bridge Revenue Bond Act (Mississippi River)
Miss. Code Ann. 1972, § 65-25-1 et seq.

Bridge Revenue Bond Act (Pearl River)
Miss. Code Ann. 1972, § 65-23-301 et seq.

Bridges, Ferries and Highways Act
S.C. Code Ann. 1976, § 57-1-10 et seq.

Bridgford Act (Irrigation Districts)
Cal. Water Code § 20500 et seq.

Briggs Act (Mental Condition of Prisoners)
Mass. Gen. Laws 1990, 123:15 et seq.

Brighton, Watertown & Boston Incinerator Loan Act
Mass. Acts 1954, Ch. 523

Brine Development Act
Okla. Stat. Ann., Title 17, § 500 et seq.

Bring Our Children Home Act
N.J. Stat. Ann., 30:4C-66 et seq.

Brisbane County Water District Act
Cal. Water Code, Appendix, § 57-1 et seq.

Bristol Bay Act (Alaska Fisheries)
Alaska Comp. Laws Ann. 1949, § 39-2-4

Bristol County Agricultural School Loan Act
Mass. Acts 1958, Ch. 248

Bristol County Agricultural School Poultry Plant Loan Act
Mass. Acts 1963, Ch. 603

Bristol County Court House Loan Act
Mass. Acts 1958, Ch. 505
Mass. Acts 1970, Ch. 482

Bristol County Jail and House of Correction Loan Act
Mass. Acts 1953, Ch. 419

Bristol County T. B. Hospital Loan Act
Mass. Acts 1953, Ch. 131

Bristol County Water Authority Act
R.I. Public Laws 1981, Ch. 102

Bristol County Water Supply Act
R.I. Gen. Laws 1956, 45-15.5-1 et seq.

Bristol Merger Act
Tenn. Private Acts 1921, Ch. 967

Bristol Parking Authority Act
Va. Acts 1968, Ch. 555

British Friendship Treaty
Haw. Session Laws 1858-59, p. 467, May 6, 1852
Haw. Statute Laws Vol. 2, p. 100, March 26, 1846

Broad Brook Watershed Project Act
Mass. Acts 1963, Ch. 563

Broadcast Defamation Acts
Ariz. Rev. Stat. Ann., § 12-652
Cal. Civil Code § 48.5
Colo. Rev. Stat., 13-21-106
Fla. Stat. 1983, 770.01 et seq.
Ga. Code Ann., 51-5-10
Ind. Code Ann., 34-4-14-1, 34-4-14-2
Kan. Gen. Stat. 1949, 60-746a
Ky. Rev. Stat. 1971, 411.061, 411.062
La. Rev. Stat. Ann., 45:1351 et seq.
Md. Ann. Code 1974, Art. CJ, § 3-503 et seq.
Mich. Comp. Laws Ann., 484.331, 484.332
Minn. Stat. Ann., 544.043
N.C. Gen. Stat. 1943, § 99-1 et seq.
Neb. Rev. Stat. 1943, 86-601 et seq.
N.M. Stat. Ann., 42-7-6 et seq.
Ore. Rev. Stat. 1953, 30.150 et seq.
S.D. Codified Laws 1967, 20-11-6
Tenn. Code Ann., 29-24-104
W. Va. Code 1966, § 55-7-14
Wyo. Stat. Ann., § 1-29-101 et seq.

Broadcasting Council Act (Public)
Kan. Stat. Ann., 75-4912 et seq.

Broadcasting Liability Act
Wash. Rev. Code Ann., 19.64.010 et seq.

Broadened Ownership Act
Md. Ann. Code 1957, Art. 83A, § 1-206
Md. Ann. Code 1974, Department of Business and Economic Development, § 2-106

Brock-Gilbert Election Law
Ky. Stat. 1936, §§ 1468, 1472, 1481 et seq.

Brockton Departmental Equipment Loan Act
Mass. Acts 1956, Ch. 273

Brockton Sewer Loan Act
Mass. Acts 1961, Ch. 453

Brockton Water Loan Act
Mass. Acts 1953, Ch. 147

Broker and Agent Law (General Lines Insurance)
Me. Rev. Stat. Ann. 1964, Title 24-1, § 1601 et seq.

Broker and Agent Law (Life Insurance)
Me. Rev. Stat. Ann. 1964, Title 24-A, § 1671 et seq.

Broker and Life and Health Agent Law
Me. Rev. Stat. Ann. 1964, Title 22, § 2081 et seq.

Broker Controlled Insurer Act
La. Rev. Stat. Ann., 22:1210.1 et seq.
N.M. Stat. Ann., 59A-12C-1 et seq.
Wyo. Stat. Ann., § 26-45-101 et seq.

Broker Practices Act (Mortgage)
Wash. Rev. Code Ann., 19.146.005 et seq.

Brokerage Act
Wis. Stat. Ann., 240.10

Brokerage and Lenders Act (Mortgage)
Fla. Stat. Ann., 494.001 et seq.

Brokerage and Mortgage Lending Act
Fla. Stat. Ann., 494.001 et seq.

Brokerage Relationship Disclosure Act
Fla. Stat. Ann., 475.2701 to 475.2801

Brokerage Relationships in Real Estate Transactions Act
Ga. Code Ann., 10-5A-1 et seq.
Ill. Comp. Stat. 1992, Ch. 225, § 455/38.1 et seq.
Kan. Stat. Ann., 58-30,101 et seq.

Brokerage Representation Act (Real Estate)
Ida. Code 1947, 54-2060 et seq.

Brokers Act (Aircraft Transportation)
Cal. Public Utilities Code § 24001 et seq.

Brokers' Act (Real Estate)
See Real Estate Brokers Act

Brokers Act (Wages)
Mont. Code Ann., 31-1-301 et seq.

Brokers Agents and Solicitors License Act
Ill. Rev. Stat. 1991, Ch. 73, § 1065.37-1 et
seq.

Brokers Licensing Act (Real Estate)
Cal. Business and Professions Code § 10150
et seq.
Mich. Comp. Laws Ann., 451.201 et seq.
N.J. Stat. Ann., 45:15-1 et seq.
Ohio Rev. Code 1953, 4735.01 et seq.
Pa. 1907 Pamph. Laws 175, No. 139

Brokers Real Estate Act
Ill. Rev. Stat. 1991, Ch. 111, § 5801 et seq.
S.C. Code Ann. 1976, § 40-57-10 et seq.

Bronx County Act (Erection)
N.Y. Laws 1912, Ch. 548

Bronx River Parkway Act
N.Y. Laws 1907, Ch. 594

Bronx River Parkway Extension Act
N.Y. Laws 1925, Ch. 197

Bronx Valley Sewer Act
N.Y. Laws 1905, Ch. 646
N.Y. Laws 1907, Ch. 747

Bronzan-Mojonnier Act (Mental Health)
Cal. Statutes 1985, Ch. 1286

Bronzan, Wright, and McCorquodale Act
Cal. Welfare and Institutions Code § 5800 et
seq.

Brook Clearance Loan Act (Stoneham)
Mass. Acts 1959, Ch. 404

Mass. Acts 1960, Ch. 105

**Brook-Coudert Act (Employment of
Minors)**
N.Y. Labor Law (Consol. Laws Ch. 31)
§ 170 et seq.

Brook Improvement Loan Act (Dedham)
Mass. Acts 1956, Ch. 446

Brookfield School Building Loan Act
Mass. Acts 1950, Ch. 676

Brookhart Act
July 3, 1930, Ch. 850, 46 Stat. 1003

Brookhart-Looreen Law (Sinking Fund)
Iowa Code 1985, 453.9

Brookline Act (Precinct Voting)
Mass. Acts 1921, Ch. 36

Brooklyn Arrearage Act
N.Y. Laws 1883, Ch. 114

Brooklyn Bridge Authorization Act
March 3, 1869, Ch. 139, 15 Stat. 336

Brooklyn Common School Act
N.Y. Laws 1850, Ch. 143

Brooklyn Sports Center Authority Act
N.Y. Public Authority Law (Consol. Laws
Ch. 43A) § 1700 et seq.

Brooks Architect-Engineers Act
June 30, 1949, Ch. 288, 40 U.S. Code § 541
nt.

Brooks Automatic Data Processing Act
June 30, 1949, Ch. 288, 40 U.S. Code § 759

Brooks-Bass Medical Training Act
Tex. Education Code, § 73.051 et seq.

Brooks-Coleman Act (Street Railways)
Minn. Stat. 1961, 220.01 et seq.

Brooks High License Law (Liquor)
Pa. 1887 Pamph. Laws 108, No. 53

Brooks Study Act
Tex. Rev. Civ. Stat. 1925, Art. 2654-1g

Brooksville Urban Renewal Law
Fla. Special Laws 1969, Ch. 69-884

Broome County Resource Recovery Agency Act
N.Y. Public Authorities Law (Consol. Laws Ch. 43A) § 2047a et seq.

Broome County Sports Center Authority Act
N.Y. Public Authorities Law (Consol. Laws, Ch. 43A) § 2050 et seq.

Broughton Act (Sale of Public Utility Franchises)
Cal. Public Utilities Code § 6001 et seq.

Broward County Area Planning Board Act
Fla. Special Laws 1959, Ch. 59-1154
Fla. Special Laws 1972, Ch. 72-497

Broward County Cemetary Act
Fla. Laws, 1967, Ch. 67-1185

Broward County Electronic Data Processing Act
Fla. Special Laws 1969, Ch. 69-904

Broward County Erosion District Act
Fla. Special Laws 1961, Ch. 61-1967

Broward County Erosion Prevention District Act
Fla. Special Laws 1959, Ch. 59-1159

Broward County Expressway Authority Act
Fla. Stat. Ann., 348.24 et seq.

Broward County Human Rights Act
Fla. Laws 1991, Ch. 359

Broward County Natural Resource Protection Act
Fla. Laws 1991, Ch. 355

Broward County Permanent Registration Act
Fla. Laws 1947, Ch. 24216

Broward County Transportation Authority Law
Fla. Special Laws 1969, Ch. 69-907

Broward County Waste Collection and Disposal System Act
Fla. Special Laws 1963, Ch. 63-1172

Broward County Water and Sewer Act
Fla. Special Laws 1963, Ch. 63-1181

Brown Act (Local Legislative Meetings)
Cal. Government Code § 54950 et seq.

Brown Act (Public Meetings of Local Public Agencies)
Cal. Government Code § 54950 et seq.

Brown Bag Network Act
Cal. Welfare and Institutions Code § 9600 et seq.

Brown-Bagging Act (Alcoholic Liquors)
N.C. Gen. Stat. 1943, §§ 18B-301, 18B-1001
S.C. Code Ann. 1976, § 61-5-20

Brown-Joseph F. Martin Act (Agricultural Research)
Mich. Comp. Laws Ann., 390.161

Brown-Lea Natural Gas Act
See Natural Gas Act

Brown-Lodge Bill
July 7, 1947, Ch. 207, 61 Stat. 246
Dec. 31, 1948, Ch. 837, 62 Stat. 1292

Brown Lung Act
S.C. Code Ann. 1976, § 42-11-60

Brown-McNeely Insurance Fund Act
Mich. Comp. Laws Ann., 500.2500 et seq.

Brown-Meyers-Millias Act (Public Employees Organizations)
Cal. Government Code § 3500 et seq.

Brown Municipal Court Act
Wis. Laws 1951, Ch. 383

Brown-Presley Trial Court Funding Act
Cal. Government Code § 77000 et seq.

Brown-Rodda-Moretti-Lewis Child Development Act
Cal. Education Code 1976, § 8200 et seq.

Brown Sharkey-Isaacs Act (Discrimination)
N.Y. City Adm. Code '38, Ch. 1, § D1-1-0

Brown-Simpson Act (Teachers' Tenure)
Ala. Code 1975, § 16-24-1 et seq.

Brown-Song Family Physician Training Act
Cal. Education Code 1976, § 69270 et seq.

Brown-Stevens Act
May 6, 1910, Ch. 202, 36 Stat. 348
Dec. 30, 1916, Ch. 10, 39 Stat. 865

Brownfield Redevelopment Financing Act
Mich. Comp. Laws Ann., 125.2651 et seq.

Brownfields Redevelopment Act
Fla. Stat. Ann., 376.77 to 376.85

Brownfields Voluntary Cleanup and Redevelopment Act
Miss. Code Ann. 1972, § 49-35-1 et seq.

Brownfields Voluntary Redevelopment Act
Okla. Stat. Ann., Title 27A, § 2-15-101 et seq.

Brownstone Park District Civic Center Act
Ill. Comp. Stat. 1992, Ch. 70, § 220/5-1 et seq.

Brownstown Park District, Jo Daviess County, Milford, Sheldon, Katherine Dunham, Oak Park, Aledo, Normal, Mason County, and Jasper County Civic Centers Act
Ill. Rev. Stat. 1991, Ch. 85, § 4500 et seq.

Brownsville Wetlands Policy Act of 1994
April 11, 1994, P.L. 103-232, 108 Stat. 338

Brucellosis Act (Bovine)
Iowa Code Ann., 164.1 et seq.
N.C. Gen. Stat. 1943, § 106-388 et seq.

Neb. Rev. Stat. 1943, 54-1367 et seq.

Brucellosis and Pseudorabies Control and Eradication Act (Service)
Mich. Comp. Laws Ann., 287.801 et seq.

Brucellosis Control Act
S.D. Codified Laws 1967, 40-7-1 et seq.
Vt. Acts 1949, No. 111

Brucellosis Eradication Act (Bovine)
Ill. Comp. Stat. 1992, Ch. 510, § 30/1 et seq.

Brucellosis Eradication and Control Act
Utah Code Ann. 1953, Miscellaneous Superseded Code Provisions, 4-28-1 et seq.

Brucellosis Vaccination Program Act
Ark. Stat. 1947, 2-40-502 et seq.

Brumbaugh Act (Labor Relations)
Pa. Purdon's Stat., Title 43, § 601 et seq.

Brundidge Primary Election Law
Ark. Stat. 1947, 3-204 et seq.

Brunner-Stonier Act (Local Taxes)
Pa. 1947 Pamph. Laws 1145, No. 481

Brunswick County Peace Officers' Relief Act
N.C. Laws 1957, Ch. 1077

Brunswick-Glynn County Charter Commission Act
Ga. Laws 1968, p. 2914
Ga. Laws 1979, p. 3378

Brunswick-New Hanover Maritime Commission Act
N.C. Laws 1965, Ch. 1097

Brunswick Port Authority Act
Ga. Laws 1945, p. 1023

Brush Disposal Act
Aug. 11, 1916, Ch. 313, 39 Stat. 462, 16 U.S. Code § 490
April 24, 1950, Ch. 97, 64 Stat. 84, 16 U.S. Code § 490

Brussels Convention (Postal Union)
N.Y. Local Laws 1973, Town of Brut

Bryan Primary Law
Fla. Laws 1913, Ch. 6469

Bryson Act
July 19, 1952, Ch. 950, 66 Stat. 792, 15 U.S. Code § 1071; 35 U.S. Code §§ 1 to 293

Bubble Law
Colo. Rev. Stat., 13-21-106.7, 18-9-122

Bubble Rule-Generic Air Emissions
Fla. Stat. Ann., 553.990 et seq.

Buchanan County Housing Development Corporation Act
Va. Acts 1982, Ch. 524

Buck Act
Oct. 9, 1940, Ch. 787, 54 Stat. 1059 (See 4 U.S. Code §§ 105 to 110)

Buck Act (Deer and Bear)
N.Y. Environmental Conservation Law 1972 (Consol. Laws Ch. 43B) § 11-0907

Bucket Shop Act
Cal. Corporations Code § 29000 et seq.
D.C. Code 1973, § 22-1509 et seq.
Ga. Code Ann., 13-9-3 et seq.
Ind. Code 1976, 35-18-9-1 et seq.
Kan. Stat. Ann., 50-121 et seq.
Mich. Comp. Laws Ann., 750.126 et seq.
Mo. Rev. Stat. 1969, 563.450 et seq.
N.C. Gen. Stat. 1943, § 16-3 et seq.
N.H. Rev. Stat. 1955, 294-B:1 et seq.
Ohio Rev. Code 1953, 2915.31 et seq.
R.I. Gen. Laws 1956, 6-17-1 et seq.
Tex. Rev. Civ. Stat., Art. 8651 et seq.
Vt. Stat. Ann., Title 13, § 2171 et seq.
Wash. Rev. Code Ann., 9.47.080 et seq.

Buckley Act (Unemployment Relief Tax)
N.Y. Laws 1933, 1st Ex. Sess., Ch. 815

Buckley Amendment
See Family Educational Rights and Privacy Act of 1974

Buckman Act (State University)
Fla. Stat. 1965, 239.01 et seq.

Buckman-Ford-DeMarcus College Scholarship Act
Ky. Rev. Stat. 1971, 164.740 et seq.

Buckwheat Flour Act
Mich. Comp. Laws Ann., 289.501 et seq.

Budd and William Bell Prevention and Protection Act
Fla. Stat. Ann., 39.001 et seq.

Budd-Deacon Act (Mortgage Foreclosure)
N.J. Rev. Stat. 1937, 2A:50-1 et seq.
N.Y. Laws 1981, Ch. 405

Budget Accountability Act
Ga. Code Ann., 28-5-25

Budget Act
Ariz. Rev. Stat. Ann., § 35-101 et seq.
Cal. Statutes 1945, Ch. 664, p. 1188
Cal. Statutes 1947, Ch. 486, p. 1390
Cal. Statutes 1948, Ch. 23, p. 34
Cal. Statutes 1949, Ch. 700, p. 1201
Cal. Statutes 1950, Ch. 2, p. 255
Cal. Statutes 1951, Ch. 1020, p. 2649
Cal. Statutes 1952, Ch. 3, p. 4
Cal. Statutes 1953, Ch. 971, p. 2348
Cal. Statutes 1954, Ch. 1, p. 3
Cal. Statutes 1955, Ch. 777, p. 1267
Cal. Statutes 1956, Ch. 1, p. 3
Cal. Statutes 1957, Ch. 600, p. 1694
Cal. Statutes 1958, 2nd Ex. Sess., Ch. 1, p. 465
Cal. Statutes 1959, Ch. 1300, p. 3455
Cal. Statutes 1960, Ch. 11
Cal. Statutes 1961, Ch. 888
Cal. Statutes 1962, 2nd Ex. Sess., Ch. 1, p. 425
Cal. Statutes 1963, Ch. 1050, p. 2349
Cal. Statutes 1964, 2nd Ex. Sess., Ch. 2, p. 712
Cal. Statutes 1965, Ch. 757, p. 2181
Cal. Statutes 1966, 2nd Ex. Sess., Ch. 2
Cal. Statutes 1967, Ch. 500, p. 1703

Cal. Statutes 1968, Ch. 430, p. 895
Cal. Statutes 1969, Ch. 355, p. 732
Cal. Statutes 1970, Ch. 303, p. 581
Cal. Statutes 1971, Ch. 266, p. 424
Cal. Statutes 1972, Ch. 156, p. 210
Cal. Statutes 1973, Ch. 129, p. 199
Cal. Statutes 1974, Ch. 375
Cal. Statutes 1975, Ch. 176
Cal. Statutes 1976, Ch. 320, p. 636
Cal. Statutes 1977, Ch. 219, p. 757
Cal. Statutes 1979, Ch. 259
Cal. Statutes 1980, Ch. 510, p. 1069
Cal. Statutes 1981, Ch. 99, p. 223
Cal. Statutes 1982, Ch. 326
Cal. Statutes 1983, Ch. 324
Cal. Statutes 1984, Ch. 258
Cal. Statutes 1985, Ch. 111
Cal. Statutes 1986, Ch. 186
Cal. Statutes 1987, Ch. 135
Cal. Statutes 1989, Ch. 93
Cal. Statutes 1991, Ch. 118
Ga. Code Ann., 45-12-70 et seq.
Haw. Rev. Stat. Ann., § 37-61 et seq.
Ida. Code 1947, 67-3501 et seq.
Kan. Stat. Ann., 79-2925 et seq.
La. Rev. Stat. Ann., 39:1 et seq.
Md. Ann. Code 1957, Art. 15A
Mont. Code Ann., 17-7-101 et seq.
N.C. Gen. Stat. 1943, §§ 143-1 to 143-34.7
Neb. Rev. Stat. 1943, 13-501 et seq.
Nev. Rev. Stat. 1979 Reprint, 353.150 et seq.
N.M. Stat. Ann., 6-3-1 et seq.
Okla. Stat. 1981, Title 62, § 41.1 et seq.
Pa. 1991 Pamph. Laws, No. 34
P.R. Laws Ann. 1954, Title 23, § 81 et seq.
Tenn. Code Ann., 5-22-101 et seq.
Tex. Rev. Civ. Stat., Art. 689a-1 et seq.
Wash. Laws 1959, Extra Session, Chs. 11, 12, 13

Budget Act (Capital)
Pa. 1995 Pamph. Laws, No. 38

Budget Act (County)
Cal. Government Code § 29000 et seq.
Miss. Code Ann. 1972, § 19-11-1 et seq.
Mo. Rev. Stat. 50.525 et seq.

Mont. Rev. Code 1947, 16-1901 et seq.
Neb. Rev. Stat. 1943, 23-901 et seq.
N.M. Stat. Ann., 6-6-1 et seq.
Ohio Rev. Code 1953, 5705.27 et seq.
S.D. Codified Laws 1967, 7-21-1 et seq.
Tex. Local Government Code, § 111.004 et seq.
Wash. Rev. Code Ann., 36.40.010 et seq.
Wyo. Session Laws 1939, Ch. 87

Budget Act (Dyer County)
Tenn. Private Acts 1972, Ch. 319

Budget Act (Emergency Medical Service District)
Okla. Stat. Ann., Title 19, § 1701 et seq.

Budget Act (Executive)
See Executive Budget Act

Budget Act (Fire Protection District)
Okla. Stat. Ann., Title 19, § 901.31 et seq.

Budget Act (Highway Supplement)
Pa. 1990 Pamph. Laws, No. 218

Budget Act (Licensing Agency)
La. Rev. Stat. Ann., 39:1331 et seq.

Budget Act (Local Governments)
Colo. Rev. Stat., 29-1-101 et seq.
Nev. Rev. Stat. 1979 Reprint, 354.470 et seq.
Ore. Rev. Stat. 1953, 294.305 et seq.

Budget Act (Maury County)
Tenn. Private Acts 1963, Ch. 233

Budget Act (Municipal Biennial)
Wash. Rev. Code Ann., 35A.34.020 et seq.

Budget Act (Municipal)
See Municipal Budget Act

Budget Act (School)
Fla. Stat. 1971, 237.05 et seq.
Ill. Rev. Stat. 1991, Ch. 122, § 42 et seq.
Mont. Rev. Code 1947, 75-6701 et seq.
N.M. Stat. Ann., 22-8-1 et seq.

Budget Act (State)
Ind. Code Ann., 4-12-1-12 et seq.
Mich. Comp. Laws Ann., 21.1 et seq.
Miss. Code Ann. 1972, § 27-103-1 et seq.
N.D. Cent. Code, 54-44.1-01 et seq.
N.H. Rev. Stat. 1955, 9:1 et seq.
N.J. Stat. Ann., 52:27B-10 et seq.
R.I. Gen. Laws 1956, 35-3-1 et seq.
S.D. Codified Laws 1967, 4-7-1 et seq.
Wash. Rev. Code Ann., 43.88.010 et seq.
Wyo. Stat. 1957, § 9-504 et seq.

Budget Act (Thomson)
Wis. Stat. 1991, 65.90

Budget Act for Cities Over Three Hundred Thousand Population
Wash. Rev. Code Ann., 35.32A.010 et seq.

Budget Act of the City of Troy (Cash Basis)
N.Y. Laws 1949, Ch. 668

Budget Act of the County of Erie
N.Y. Laws 1944, Ch. 383

Budget Act of the County of Essex (Cash Basis)
N.Y. Laws 1946, Ch. 883

Budget Act of 1996
Cal. Statutes 1996, Ch. 162

Budget Act of 1997
Cal. Statutes 1997, Chs. 282, 928

Budget Adjustment Act
Vt. Acts 1977, Nos. 22, 126
Vt. Acts 1979, Nos. 13, 247
Vt. Acts 1982, No. 116
Vt. Acts 1983, Nos. 9, 253
Vt. Acts 1984, No. 97
Vt. Acts 1986, No. 102
Vt. Acts 1987, No. 3
Vt. Acts 1988, No. 125
Vt. Acts 1989, No. 22
Vt. Acts 1991, Nos. 3, 5, 22, 185

Budget Adjustment Act-Fiscal Year 1994
Vt. Acts 1993, No. 140

Budget Adjustment Act for Fiscal Year 1985 (First and Second)
Vt. Acts 1983, No. 253
Vt. Acts 1985, No. 5

Budget Administration Act (Judicial)
Ga. Laws 1998, H.R. 1617

Budget Agency Law
Ind. Code Ann., 4-12-1-1 et seq.

Budget Amendment (Modern)
W. Va. Acts 1968, Ch. 15

Budget and Accounting Act
Mich. Comp. Laws 1979, 141.421 et seq.
Tenn. Private Acts 1979, Ch. 49
Wash. Rev. Code Ann., 43.88.010 et seq.

Budget and Accounting Act of 1921
June 10, 1921, Ch. 18, 42 Stat. 20, 31 U.S. Code §§ 1, 2, 11, 13 to 24, 41 to 44, 46 to 50, 52 to 57
Sept. 12, 1950, Ch. 946, 64 Stat. 832, 31 U.S. Code §§ 2, 11, 14, 16, 22 to 24
July 28, 1953, Ch. 256, 67 Stat. 229, 31 U.S. Code § 43
Aug. 1, 1956, Ch. 814, 70 Stat. 782, 31 U.S. Code §§ 11, 24
Aug. 25, 1958, P.L. 85-759, 72 Stat. 852, 31 U.S. Code § 11
July 13, 1959, P.L. 86-87, 73 Stat. 197, 31 U.S. Code § 43b
July 26, 1966, P.L. 89-520, 80 Stat. 329, 31 U.S. Code §§ 43, 43b
Oct. 26, 1970, P.L. 91-510, 84 Stat. 1169, 31 U.S. Code § 11
March 2, 1974, P.L. 93-250, 88 Stat. 11, 31 U.S. Code § 16
July 12, 1974, P.L. 93-344, 88 Stat. 323, 31 U.S. Code § 11
Oct. 25, 1978, P.L. 95-512, 31 U.S. Code §§ 1 nt., 43, 43b, 43c
April 3, 1980, P.L. 96-226, 31 U.S. Code §§ 42 et seq.

FEDERAL AND STATE ACTS CITED BY POPULAR NAME   **Bud**

Budget and Accounting Procedures Act of 1950

Sept. 12, 1950, Ch. 946, 64 Stat. 832, 16 U.S. Code § 452; 24 U.S. Code § 278; 31 U.S. Code §§ 2, 11, 14, 16, 18a, 18b, 22 to 24, 65 to 67, 581 to 581c, 624, 719, 847

Aug. 1, 1956, Ch. 814, 70 Stat. 782, 31 U.S. Code §§ 18c, 65a, 66a

Oct. 27, 1972, P.L. 92-599, 86 Stat. 1325, 31 U.S. Code § 581c-1

March 8, 1973, P.L. 93-9, 87 Stat. 7, 31 U.S. Code § 581c-1

Nov. 4, 1978, P.L. 95-595, 31 U.S. Code § 68 et seq.

April 3, 1980, P.L. 96-226, 31 U.S. Code § 67

Budget and Appropriations Revenue Act
N.C. Laws 1991, Ch. 689

Budget and Control Law (Municipalities)
Iowa Code 1983, 24.1 et seq.

Budget and Financial Administration Act
Ky. Rev. Stat. 1971, 42.010 et seq.

Budget and Financial Control Act
Ala. Code 1975, § 41-4-80 et seq.
Iowa Code Ann., 8.1 et seq.

Budget and Financial Control Act (Counties)
Ala. Code 1975, § 11-8-1 et seq.

Budget and Fiscal Control Act (Local Government)
N.C. Gen. Stat. 1943, § 159-7 et seq.

Budget and Management Act
Mich. Comp. Laws Ann., 18.1101 et seq.

Budget and Management Office Organic Act
P.R. Laws Ann. 1954, Title 23, § 101 et seq.

Budget Appropriation Act
Del. Laws Vol. 52, p. 127, Ch. 57

Budget Bureau Organic Act
P.R. Laws Ann. 1954, Title 23, § 1 et seq.

Budget Commission Act (County)
Fla. Laws 1931, Ch. 14678
Ky. Rev. Stat. 1971, 68.210 et seq.

Budget Commission Act (State)
Ky. Rev. Stat. 1971, 42.010 et seq.

Budget Committee Act
Ind. Code Ann., 4-12-1-1 et seq.
Wash. Rev. Code Ann., 44.28.010 et seq.

Budget Control Act
Ark. Stat. 1947, 13-301 et seq.
Miss. Code 1942, § 9108
Ore. Rev. Stat. 1953, 291.232 et seq.
W. Va. Acts 1933, 1st Ex. Sess., Ch. 56

Budget Director Act
Wash. Rev. Code Ann., 43.41.030 et seq.

Budget Efficiency and Conservation Act
Fla. Stat. Ann., 366.80 et seq.

Budget Enforcement Act
Nov. 5, 1990, P.L. 101-508, 2 U.S. Code § 900 nt.
Aug. 5, 1997, P.L. 105-33, 2 U.S. Code § 900 nt.

Budget Limit Act (Political Subdivision)
Neb. Rev. Stat. 1943, 77-3412 et seq.

Budget Management Act
Ala. Code 1975, § 41-19-1 et seq.

Budget Management Improvement Act
Ala. Code 1975, § 41-19-3

Budget Reduction Act for Fiscal Year 1992
Vt. Acts 1991, No. 144

Budget Reduction Act for Fiscal Year 1993
Vt. Acts 1993, No. 25

Budget Reform Act
Miss. Code Ann. 1972, § 27-103-201 et seq.

Budget Relief Act (Penitentiary)
Ark. Pope's Digest 1937, §§ 12757 to 12767

253

Budget Relief Act (State Departments)
Ark. Acts 1933, p. 13, No. 5

Budget Revenue Act
N.C. Gen. Stat. 1943, § 105-1 et seq.

Budget Sunset Act (Agency)
Fla. Stat. Ann., 11.61

Budgetary Control Law
Ark. Stat. 1947, 13-301 et seq.
Miss. Code 1942, § 9108

Budgetary Efficiency Act
D.C. Code Ann., §§ 47-119, 47-3406,
47-3406.1

Budgetary Procedures Act
Utah Code Ann. 1953, 63-38-1 et seq.

**Budgeting and Planning Act (Capital
Facilities)**
Fla. Stat. Ann., 216.015 et seq.

**Budgeting, Appropriation, and Receipt of
Federal Moneys Act**
R.I. Gen. Laws 1956, 42-41-1 et seq.

Budgeting Law (Local Option)
Tenn. Code Ann., 5-12-201 et seq.

**Buffalo and Fort Erie Public Bridge
Authority Act**
N.Y. Laws 1933, Ch. 824

Buffalo Municipal Housing Authority Act
N.Y. Public Housing Law (Consol. Laws Ch.
44A) § 403 et seq.

**Buffalo Municipal Water Finance Authority
Act**
N.Y. Public Authorities Law (Consol. Laws
Ch. 43A) § 1048a et seq.

Buffalo Park Act
N.Y. Laws 1869, Ch. 165

Buffalo River Improvement Act
N.Y. Laws 1957, Ch. 493

Buffalo Sewer Authority Act
N.Y. Public Authorities Law (Consol. Laws
Ch. 43A) § 1175 et seq.

Buffalo Terminal Commission Act
N.Y. Laws 1911, Ch. 842

Build Illinois Act
Ill. Comp. Stat. 1992, Ch. 30, § 750/1-1 et
seq.

Build Illinois Bond Act
Ill. Comp. Stat. 1992, Ch. 30, § 425/1 et seq.

Builders Licensing Act
Mich. Comp. Laws Ann., 338.1501 et seq.

Builders' Lien Act
La. Rev. Stat. Ann., 9:4801 et seq.

**Builders' Registration and New Home
Warranty Act**
N.J. Stat. Ann. 46:3B-1 et seq.

Building Act
Colo. Rev. Stat., 9-1-101 et seq.
Fla. Stat. 1983, 553.70 et seq.
Iowa Code Ann., 103A.1 et seq.
Mass. Gen. Laws Ann., 143:1 et seq.
Minn. Stat. Ann., 16B.59 et seq.
Mont. Code Ann., 50-60-203
N.C. Gen. Stat. 1943, § 143-138 et seq.
N.D. Cent. Code, 54-21.3-01 et seq.
N.H. Rev. Stat. 1955, 47:22 et seq.
N.J. Stat. Ann., 52:27D-119 et seq.
N.M. Stat. Ann. 1953, 67-35-1 et seq.
N.Y. Executive Law 1951 (Consol. Laws Ch.
18) § 370 et seq.
Ohio Rev. Code 1953, 3781.01 et seq.
Ore. Rev. Stat. 1953, 276.010 et seq.
Wash. Rev. Code Ann., 19.27.010 et seq.

Building Act (Boston)
Mass. Acts 1907, Ch. 550

Building Act (Safety Regulations)
Neb. Rev. Stat. 1943, 48-401 et seq.

Building Aid Act (State School)
Cal. Education Code 1976, §§ 16000 et seq., 16400 et seq.

Building Alteration Loan Act (Gardner)
Mass. Acts 1955, Ch. 53

Building and Facilities Act
Fla. Stat. Ann., 255.501 et seq.

Building and Housing Codes (Statewide)
Md. Ann. Code 1957, Art. 83B, § 6-101 et seq.

Building and Loan Acts
Ga. Code 1933, 16-401 et seq.
La. Rev. Stat. Ann., 6:721 et seq.
Mich. Comp. Laws Ann., 491.102 et seq.
Neb. Rev. Stat. 1943, 8-301 et seq.
Pa. Purdon's Stat., Title 7, § 6020-1 et seq.
Va. Code 1950, § 6-140 et seq.

Building and Loan Association Act (Capital Stock)
N.M. Stat. Ann., 58-10-4 et seq.

Building and Loan Association Acts
Cal. Financial Code § 5000 et seq.
Colo. Rev. Stat., 11-40-101 et seq.
Ga. Code Ann., 7-1-770 et seq.
Ind. Code Ann., 28-1-21-1 et seq.
Iowa Code Ann., 534.1 et seq.
Minn. Stat. 1967, 51.01 et seq.
Mont. Code Ann., 32-2-101 et seq.
N.D. Cent. Code, 7-01-01 et seq.
N.H. Rev. Stat. 1955, 393:1 et seq.
N.J. Stat. Ann., 17:12B-1 et seq.
N.M. Stat. Ann., 58-10-1 et seq.
Ohio Rev. Code 1953, 1151.01 et seq.
Ore. Rev. Stat. 1953, 722.002 et seq.
R.I. Gen. Laws 1956, 19-22-1 to 19-23-15
S.C. Code Ann. 1976, Superseded Vols., § 34-25-10 et seq.
Tex. Rev. Civ. Stat., Art. 852a et seq.
Vt. Stat. Ann., Title 8, § 1831 et seq.
W. Va. Code 1966, § 31-6-1 et seq.

Building and Loan Association Supervision Law
Okla. Stat. 1971, Title 18, § 311 et seq.

Building and Loan Association Tax Act
N.M. Stat. Ann., 7-2A-1 et seq.

Building and Loan Commissioner Law
Cal. Financial Code § 5200 et seq.

Building and Loan Deed Valuation Act
Ill. Comp. Stat. 1992, Ch. 765, §§ 110/0.01, 110/1

Building and Loan Intangibles Tax Act
Ind. Code 1982, 6-5-8-1 et seq.

Building and Loan Mortgage Release Act
Ill. Comp. Stat. 1992, Ch. 765, § 105/0.01 et seq.

Building and Loan Receivership Fee Act
Ill. Comp. Stat. 1992, Ch. 705, §§ 230/0.01, 230/1

Building and Loan Tax Act
Pa. 1897 Pamph. Laws 178, No. 147

Building and Local Grant Act (Health Department)
Ark. Code 1987, 20-7-201 et seq.

Building and Mobile Home Act (Industrialized)
Md. Ann. Code 1957, Art. 41B, § 6-201 et seq.

Building Association Act (University)
Mass. Acts 1958, Ch. 603

Building Associations Act
D.C. Code Ann., § 26-501 et seq.

Building Authority Act
Ga. Code Ann., 50-9-1 et seq.
Ida. Code 1947, 67-6401 et seq.
Ill. Comp. Stat. 1992, Ch. 20, § 3110/0.01 et seq.

Building Authority Act (Augusta-Richmond County)
Ga. Laws 1952, p. 338

Building Authority Act (Bridges)
Ga. Code 1933, 95-2301 et seq.

Building Authority Act (County)
Ind. Code 1976, 19-8-4-1 et seq.
Mich. Comp. Laws Ann., 123.951 et seq.

Building Authority Act (Hospital)
Ga. Code Ann., 31-7-20 et seq.

Building Authority Act (Industrial)
Me. Rev. Stat. Ann. 1964, Title 10, § 701 et seq.

Building Authority Act (Markets)
Ga. Code Ann., 2-10-1 et seq.

Building Authority Act (Penal)
Ga. Code Ann., 42-3-1 et seq.

Building Authority Act (School)
Ga. Code Ann., 20-2-550 et seq.

Building Authority Act (State Office)
Ga. Code Ann., 50-9-1 et seq.

Building Authority Act (State Public School)
Pa. Purdon's Stat., Title 14, § 791.1 et seq.

Building Authority Act (University System)
Ga. Code Ann., 20-3-150 et seq.

Building Authority Act (Vocational Trade School)
Ga. Code Ann., 20-2-554

Building Authority Bond Investment Act
Ill. Comp. Stat. 1992, Ch. 20, § 3115/1 et seq.

Building Bond and College Savings Bond Act
Okla. Stat. Ann., Title 62, § 57.300 et seq.

Building Code (City of New York)
N.Y. Adm. Code '85, § 27-101 et seq.
N.Y. City Adm. Code '38, Ch. 26, § C26-1.0 et seq.

Building Code (School)
S.C. Code Ann. 1976, § 59-23-10 et seq.

Building Code (Second Amendment)
D.C. Laws 1977, No. 2-18

Building Code (Second Class Cities)
Pa. Purdon's Stat., Title 53, § 25081 et seq.

Building Code Act
Fla. Stat. Ann., 553.70 et seq.
Iowa Code Ann., 103A.1 et seq.
N.C. Gen. Stat. 1943, §§ 143-128 to 143-135.5
Wash. Rev. Code Ann., 19.27.010 et seq.

Building Code Act (Commission)
Cal. Health and Safety Code, § 18900 et seq.

Building Code Act (County)
Colo. Rev. Stat., 30-28-201 et seq.
Mich. Comp. Laws Ann., 125.251 et seq.

Building Code Act (New Castle County)
Del. Code of 1974, Title 16, § 3801 et seq.

Building Code Act (Township)
Mich. Comp. Laws Ann., 125.351 et seq.

Building Code Advisory Act
Ida. Code 1947, 39-4101 et seq.

Building Code Authority Act (Muscogee County)
Ga. Laws 1951, p. 2729

Building Code for Cities of the First Class
Pa. 1929 Pamph. Laws 1063, No. 413

Building Code Violation Notice Posting Act
Ill. Comp. Stat. 1992, Ch. 50, § 810/0.01 et seq.
N.J. Stat. Ann. 52:18A-78.1 et seq.
Ore. Rev. Stat. 1953, 276.800 et seq.
S.D. Codified Laws 1967, 5-12-1 et seq.

Building Commission Act
Ala. Code 1975, § 41-9-140 et seq.
Ill. Comp. Stat. 1992, Ch. 20, § 3918/1 et seq.

Building Construction Act
Cal. Health and Safety Code § 19100 et seq.
Neb. Rev. Stat. 1943, 71-6401 et seq.

Building Construction Administration Act
Tex. Rev. Civ. Stat., Art. 601b, § 5.01 et seq.

Building Contract Act
La. Civil Code, Art. 2756 et seq.

Building Contract Act (Privileges)
La. Rev. Stat. Ann., 9:4801 et seq.

Building Contractors Law (Residential)
Minn. Stat. Ann., 326.83 et seq.

Building Corporations Law
N.Y. Laws 1853, Ch. 117

Building Design Services Act
N.J. Stat. Ann., 45:4B-1 et seq.

Building Egress Act
D.C. Code Ann., § 5-518 et seq.

Building Energy Conservation Act
Mont. Code Ann., 90-4-601 et seq.
Pa. Purdon's Stat., Title 35, § 7201.101 et seq.

Building Energy Efficiency Rating Act
Fla. Stat. Ann., 553.990 et seq.

Building Energy Efficiency Standard Act
S.C. Code Ann. 1976, § 6-10-10 et seq.

Building Fund Act (Cumulative)
Ind. Code Ann., 21-2-6-1 et seq.

Building Inspection Act
Vt. Stat. Ann., Title 24, § 3101 et seq.

Building Law Violation Ownership Disclosure Act
Ill. Comp. Stat. 1992, Ch. 765, § 425/0.01 et seq.

Building Lines Act
D.C. Code 1973, § 5-201 et seq.

Building, Loan and Homestead Association Act
Ill. Rev. Stat. 1991, Ch. 17, § 3600 et seq.

Building-Loan Association Act
R.I. Gen. Laws 1956, 19-22-1 et seq.

Building Maintenance Regulation Act
P.R. Laws Ann. 1954, Title 17, § 601 et seq.

Building Officials and Inspectors Registration Act
Mich. Comp. Laws Ann., 338.2301 et seq.

Building or Homestead Association Act
Md. Ann. Code 1974, Art. CA, § 6-222 et seq.

Building Ownership Act (State)
Utah Code Ann. 1953, 63-9a-1 et seq.

Building Permit Act
N.J. Stat. Ann., 40:550-3

Building Renewal Act (Deferred)
Neb. Rev. Stat. 1943, 81-173

Building Restrictions Act
D.C. Code 1973, § 5-413 et seq.

Building Safety Act
Ga. Laws 1947, p. 1452

Building Safety Law (Industrialized)
Va. Code 1950, § 36-70 et seq.

Building Standards Law
Cal. Health and Safety Code § 18901 et seq.

Building Unit Ownership Act
N.M. Stat. Ann., 47-7-1 et seq.

Buildings, Zoning and City Planning Act
Okla. Stat. 1981, Title 11, § 43-101 et seq.

Bulgarian Declaration of War
June 5, 1942, Ch. 323, 56 Stat. 307, 50 U.S. Code Appx. prec. § 1 nt.

Bulk Commodities Transportation Act
N.J. Stat. Ann., 39:5E-1 et seq.

Bulk Dry Animal Nutrient Products Law
Iowa Code Ann., 200A.1 to 200A.15

Bulk Grain Act
Ill. Comp. Stat. 1992, Ch. 610, § 110/0.01 et seq.

Bulk Grain Storage Act
Nev. Rev. Stat. 1957, 103.010 et seq.

Bulk Grain Storage Laws (Private)
Cal. Civil Code § 1880 et seq.

Bulk Milk Tank Operators Licensing Act
Ill. Rev. Stat. 1981, Ch. 111, § 1001 et seq.

Bulk Mortgage Act
Mich. Comp. Laws 1948, 442.51 et seq.

Bulk Mortgage Act (Chattels)
N.Y. Uniform Commercial Code (Consol. Laws, Ch. 38) § 9-101 et seq.

Bulk Sales (Uniform Commercial Code)
See Uniform Commercial Code-Bulk Sales

Bulk Sales Act
June 16, 1998, P.L. 105-181, 112 Stat. 512
Ala. Code 1958, Title 20, § 10
Alaska Comp. Laws Ann. 1949, § 29-3-1 et seq.
Ariz. Laws 1909, Ch. 47
Ark. Stat. 1947, 68-1501 et seq.
Cal. Civil Code § 3440.1
Cal. Commercial Code § 6101 et seq.
Colo. Rev. Stat. 1963, 18-1-1 et seq.
Conn. Gen. Stat. Ann., § 42a-6-101 et seq.
Del. Code of 1953, Title 6, § 2101 et seq.
Fla. Stat. 1965, 726.02 et seq.
Ga. Code Ann., 11-6-101 et seq.
Ida. Code 1947, 28-6-101 et seq.
Ill. Rev. Stat. 1961, Ch. 121 1/2, § 78 et seq.
Ind. Burns' 1933, 33-201 et seq.
Iowa Code Ann., 554.6101 et seq.
Kan. Laws 1915, Ch. 369
La. Rev. Stat. Ann., 9:2961 et seq.
Md. Ann. Code 1974, Art. CL, § 6-101
Me. Rev. Stat. Ann. 1964, Title 10, §§ 1301, 1302

Mich. Comp. Laws Ann., 440.6101 et seq.
Minn. Stat. 1961, 513.18
Miss. Code 1942, §§ 274, 276 et seq.
Mo. Rev. Stat. 1959, 427.010 et seq.
Mont. Rev. Code 1947, 18-201 et seq.
N.C. Gen. Stat. 1943, § 39-23
Nev. Rev. Stat. Ann., 104.6101 et seq.
N.H. Rev. Stat. 1955, 340:1 et seq.
N.J. Stat. Ann., 12A:6-101 et seq.
N.M. Stat. Ann., 55-6-101 et seq.
N.Y. Uniform Commercial Code (Consol. Laws, Ch. 38) § 6-101 et seq.
Okla. Stat. Ann., Title 68, § 501 et seq.
Ore. Rev. Stat. 1953, 79.1010 et seq.
Pa. 1905 Pamph. Laws 62, No. 44
Pa. 1919 Pamph. Laws 262, No. 141
P.R. Laws Ann. 1954, Title 10, §§ 61, 62
R.I. Public Laws 1909, Ch. 387
S.C. Code Ann. 1976, § 36-6-101 et seq.
S.D. Code 1939, 54.0301 et seq.
Tenn. Code 1932, §§ 7283 to 7285
Tex. Business and Commerce Code, § 6.103 et seq.
Va. Acts 1964, Ch. 219
Vt. Stat. Ann., Title 9, §§ 1631, 1632
Wash. Rev. Code Ann., 62A.6-101 et seq.
Wis. Stat. Ann., 406.101 et seq.
W. Va. Code 1966, Miscellaneous Superseded Code Provisions, § 46-6-101 et seq.
Wyo. Stat. 1957, § 34-236 et seq.

Bulk Transfer Act
Mass. Gen. Laws Ann., 106:6-101 et seq.
Pa. Cons. Stat., Title 13, § 6101 et seq.

Bulk Transfers Acts (Uniform Commercial Code)
See Uniform Commercial Code-Bulk Transfers

Bulkhead Act
Fla. Stat. 1983, 253.1221 et seq.

Bulkhead Transfers (Uniform Commercial Code)
Fla. Stat. Ann., 676.101 et seq.

Bull-Boar Act
Kan. Stat. Ann., 47-105

Bull Leasing Act
Ill. Rev. Stat. 1991, Ch. 8, § 250 et seq.

Bullard-Milliken Worker Safety Act
Mich. Comp. Laws Ann., 408.1002 et seq.

Bullard-Plawecki Employee Right to Know Act
Mich. Comp. Laws Ann., 423.501 et seq.

Buller-Duffey Act (Highways)
Ind. Laws 1919, Ch. 53, p. 119

Bulletproof Vest Partnership Grant Act of 1998
June 16, 1998, P.L. 105-181, 42 U.S. Code § 3711 nt.

Bullitt Act (First Class Cities)
Pa. 1885 Pamph. Laws 37, No. 33

Bully Law
Ga. Code Ann., 16-5-90

Bunco Act
Mont. Code Ann., 23-5-106

Bungee Jumping Act
Mass. Gen. Laws Ann., 22:11B, 149:129D

Bungee Jumping Safety Act (Commercial)
W. Va. Code 1966, § 21-12-1 et seq.

Burbank Trust Fund Act (Orphans)
Ore. Rev. Stat. 1953, 418.675 et seq.

Burchill Law (Trust Forclosures)
N.Y. Real Property Law (Consol. Laws Ch. 50) § 119 et seq.

Bureau for the Blind Act
Ill. Comp. Stat. 1992, Ch. 20, § 2410/1 et seq.

Bureau of Corporations Act
Feb. 14, 1903, Ch. 552, 32 Stat. 827

Bureau of Identification Act
N.J. Stat. Ann., 53:1-12 et seq.

Bureau of Investigation Act
Colo. Rev. Stat., 24-32-401 et seq.
Okla. Stat. 1981, Title 74, § 150.1 et seq.

Bureau of Investigation Nomenclature Act
Ga. Code Ann., 35-3-100 to 35-3-108

Bureau of Marine Inspection and Navigation Act
May 27, 1936, Ch. 463, 49 Stat. 1380, 46 U.S. Code §§ 239, 369, 373, 374a, 382b, 417 to 419

Bureau of Mines Acts
May 16, 1910, Ch. 240, 36 Stat. 369
Feb. 25, 1913, Ch. 72, 37 Stat. 681, 30 U.S. Code §§ 1, 3, 5 to 7

Bureau of Professional and Occupational Affairs Fee Act
Pa. Purdon's Stat., Title 63, § 1401-101 et seq.

Bureau of Standards Act
March 3, 1901, Ch. 872, 31 Stat. 1449, 15 U.S. Code §§ 203, 271 to 278
July 22, 1950, Ch. 486, 64 Stat. 373, 15 U.S. Code §§ 272, 278a to 278c
Aug. 3, 1956, Ch. 906, 70 Stat. 959, 15 U.S. Code §§ 275a, 276, 278a to 278c
June 22, 1972, P.L. 92-317, 86 Stat. 235, 15 U.S. Code §§ 272, 273, 278d, 278e, 278h

Bureau of the Budget Act
Ill. Comp. Stat. 1992, Ch. 20, § 3005/0.01 et seq.
Ill. Rev. Stat. 1991, Ch. 127, § 410 et seq.

Bureau of Workmen's Compensation Act
Pa. 1915 Pamph. Laws 758, No. 339

Bureau of Workshop and Factory Inspection Act
Tenn. Code Ann., Superseded Vol., 50-101

Burgess-Glasscock Act (Water Uses)
Tex. Water Code, § 11.021 et seq.

Burglar Alarm Security Certification Act
Utah Code Ann. 1953, 13-18-1 et seq.

Burglar Alarm System Businesses Regulation Act
S.C. Code Ann. 1976, § 40-79-10 et seq.

Burglary Act
Ala. Code 1975, § 13A-7-5 et seq.
Alaska Stat. 1962, § 11.46.300 et seq.
Cal. Penal Code § 459 et seq.
Del. Code of 1974, Title 11, § 824 et seq.
Ga. Code Ann., 16-7-1
Ill. Rev. Stat. 1991, Ch. 38, §§ 19-1, 19-2
Ind. Code Ann., 35-43-2-1
Kan. Stat. Ann., 21-3715 et seq.
Md. Ann. Code 1957, Art. 27, § 28 et seq.
Mich. Comp. Laws Ann., 750.110 et seq.
Mont. Code Ann., 45-6-201 et seq.
N.C. Gen. Stat. 1943, § 14-51 et seq.
Neb. Rev. Stat. 1943, 28-507 et seq.
N.H. Rev. Stat. 1955, 635:1 et seq.
N.Y. Penal Law 1965 (Consol. Laws Ch. 40) § 140.00 et seq.
Ohio Rev. Code 1953, 2911.11 et seq.
Pa. Cons. Stat., Title 18, § 3502
R.I. Gen. Laws 1956, 11-8-1 et seq.
Vt. Stat. Ann., Title 13, § 1201 et seq.
Wash. Rev. Code Ann., 9A.52.010 et seq.
Wyo. Stat. Ann., § 6-3-301 et seq.

Burglary, Robbery and Housebreaking Act
S.C. Code Ann. 1976, § 16-11-310 et seq.

Burglary Tools Act
N.C. Gen. Stat. 1943, § 14-55

Burial Association Act
Ark. Stat. 1947, 23-78-101 et seq.
Ky. Rev. Stat. 1971, 303.100 et seq.
Neb. Laws 1931, Ch. 25
Okla. Stat. 1981, Title 8, § 201 et seq.

Burial Association Rate Board Act
Tex. Insurance Code, Art. 14.37 et seq.

Burial Insurance Act
Colo. Rev. Stat., 10-15-101 et seq.
Ill. Rev. Stat. 1991, Ch. 73, § 767.5 et seq.
Tenn. Code Ann., 56-34-101 et seq.

Burial Lot Perpetual Trust Act
Ill. Comp. Stat. 1992, Ch. 760, § 90/0.01 et seq.

Burial of Dead Bodies Act
Ill. Comp. Stat. 1992, Ch. 410, §§ 5/1, 5/2

Burial on Sunday or Holiday Act
Also known as Burial Rights Act
Ill. Comp. Stat. 1992, Ch. 820, § 135.0.01 et seq.

Burial Places Act (Conveyance to County)
Ill. Rev. Stat. 1991, Ch. 21, §§ 0.01, 1

Burial Places Act (Veterans)
Ill. Rev. Stat. 1991, Ch. 21, § 59.9 et seq.

Burial Plot Act (Wallace-Dickey Memorial)
Ill. Rev. Stat. 1991, Ch. 21, §§ 65.9, 66

Burial Pre-Need Sale Act
Neb. Rev. Stat. 1943, 12-1101 et seq.

Burial Site and Human Skeletal Remains Protection Act
Mont. Laws 1991, Ch. 748, §§ 1 to 10, 13

Burial Sites Preservation Act (Unmarked)
Kan. Stat. Ann., 75-2741 et seq.

Burke Act (Indians)
May 8, 1906, Ch. 2348, 34 Stat. 182, 25 U.S. Code § 349

Burke Act (Milk Marketing)
Ohio Rev. Code 1953, 917.01 et seq.

Burke County Economic Development Authority Act
Ga. Laws 1991, p. 4120

Burke County Project Financing Community Improvement Districts Act
Ga. Laws 1991, p. 4136

Burke-Roberts Employers' Liability Act
La. Rev. Stat. Ann., 23:1021 et seq.

Burke-Rowell-Smith Martin-Hittle Act (Occupational Disease)
Mich. Comp. Laws 1948, 417.1 et seq.

Burke-Wadsworth Act
See Selective Training And Service Act Of 1940

Burlington County Transfer of Development Rights Demonstration Act
N.J. Stat. Ann., 40:55D-113 et seq.

Burnet County Court Act
Tex. Government Code, §§ 25.0291, 25.0292

Burnett Act (Marriage Licenses)
Ky. Rev. Stat. 1971, 402.080

Burning Act (Prescribed)
Ala. Code 1975, § 9-13-210, 9-13-270 to 9-13-274
Fla. Stat. Ann., 590.026
Ga. Code Ann., 12-6-145 et seq.

Burning Bed Act (Prescribed)
Miss. Code Ann. 1972, § 49-19-301 et seq.

Burnley-McCann Act (Pay of Election Officers)
Ky. Rev. Stat. 1971, Superseded Vols., 116.140

Burnley, Morgan and McCallum Act (Circuit Court Districts)
Ky. Rev. Stat. 1971, Superseded Vols., 23.040 et seq.
Ky. Rev. Stat. 1971, 23A.020

Burns-Bradley Uniform Local Sales and Use Tax Law
Cal. Revenue and Taxation Code § 7200 et seq.

Burns-Collier Act of 1961 (Business and Transportation Agency)
Cal. Government Code § 13975 et seq.

Burns-Collier Highway Act
Cal. Streets and Highways Code § 2000 et seq.

Burns-Diggs-Hailwood-Dunckel Act (Civil Rights)
Mich. Comp. Laws Ann., 750.146 et seq.

Burns-Porter Act (Water Resources Development Bond Act)
Cal. Water Code § 12930 et seq.

Burnt, Damaged and Destroyed Records and Documents Act
Cal. Code of Civil Procedure § 1855a
Cal. Evidence Code § 1601,

Burnt Records Act
Ill. Rev. Stat. 1991, Ch. 116, § 4.9 et seq.

Burnt Timber Act
March 4, 1913, Ch. 165, 37 Stat. 1015, 16 U.S. Code §§ 614, 615
July 3, 1916, Ch. 779, 44 Stat. 890, 16 U.S. Code §§ 614, 615

Burr Act (Water Supply)
N.Y. Laws 1896, Ch. 942

Burton Act (San Francisco Harbor)
Cal. Statutes 1968, Ch. 1333, p. 2544

Burton Act for the Aging
Cal. Welfare and Institutions Code § 9000 et seq.

Burton-Grunsky Open Meeting Act
Cal. Government Code § 9027 et seq.

Burton-Hill Hospital Survey and Construction Act
See Hospital Survey And Construction Act

Burton Law (Control and Regulation of Waters of Niagara Falls)
June 29, 1906, Ch. 3621, 34 Stat. 626

Burton-Levering Act (Defense Production)
Cal. Statutes 1950, 3rd Ex. Sess., Ch. 33, p. 58, § 11
Cal. Statutes 1959, Ch. 99, p. 1951

Burton-Miller Act (Needy Children)
Cal. Welfare and Institutions Code § 11200 et seq.

Burton-Moscone-Bagley Citizens' Income Security Act for Aged, Blind and Disabled Californians
Cal. Welfare and institutions Code § 12000 et seq.

Burton-Rattigan Act (Medical Aid)
Cal. Welfare and Institutions Code § 14500 et seq.

Burton-Rattigan Act (Medical Assistance for Aged)
Cal. Welfare and Institutions Code § 4700 et seq.

Burton-Stull Vietnam Veterans Employment Act
Cal. Government Code § 7280 et seq.

Bus Act
Alaska Stat. 1962, Replaced Titles, § 42.15.011 et seq.
N.C. Gen. Stat. 1943, Superseded Vol., § 62-121.43 et seq.
S.C. Code Ann. 1976, § 58-23-10 et seq.

Bus and Rail Passenger Safety Act
Ga. Code Ann., 16-12-121 et seq.
N.M. Stat. 1978, 30-7-10 et seq.
Okla. Stat. Ann., Title 21, § 1901 et seq.
Utah Code Ann. 1953, 76-10-1501 et seq.

Bus and Truck Act
Mo. Rev. Stat., 390.011 et seq.

Bus and Truck Transportation Act
Wis. Stat. Ann., 194.01 et seq.

Bus License Act
Ohio Rev. Code 1953, 4921.01 et seq.

Bus Motor Fuel Tax Compact Act
N.H. Rev. Stat. 1955, 260:66

Bus Passenger Safety Act
Okla. Stat. Ann., Title 21, § 1901 et seq.

Bus Regulatory Reform Act
N.C. Laws 1985, Ch. 676

Bus Regulatory Reform Act of 1982
Sept. 20, 1982, P.L. 97-261, 49 U.S. Code § 10101 nt.
Oct. 11, 1996, P.L. 104-287, 49 U.S. Code § 10935 nt.

Bus Safety Act (School)
Alaska Stat. 1962, Replaced Titles, § 28.05.104

Bus Safety Compliance Act
N.J. Stat. Ann., 48:4-2.1c et seq.

Bus Safety Inspection Act
D.C. Laws 1976, No. 1-60

Bus Segregation Act
Tex. Penal Code 1925, Art. 1661.1

Bus Taxation Proration Agreement Act
N.H. Rev. Stat. 1955, 261:49 et seq.
Pa. Cons. Stat., Title 75, § 8101 et seq.
Vt. Stat. Ann., Title 23, § 561 et seq.

Bus Taxation Proration and Reciprocity Agreement
Me. Rev. Stat. Ann. 1964, Title 36, § 1492 et seq.

Bus Taxation Proration and Reciprocity Agreement Act
Conn. Gen. Stat. Ann., § 14-365 et seq.
Me. Rev. Stat. Ann. 1964, Title 29, § 431 et seq.

Bus Ticket Brokers Act
Tex. Rev. Civ. Stat., Art. 911d

Bus Transportation Act
Tex. Rev. Civ. Stat., Art. 911a

Busby-Fouts Act (Highways)
Ohio Laws Vol. 108, p. 478

Buses Act (School)
S.C. Code Ann. 1976, § 59-67-710 et seq.

Bush Act (Foreign Corporations)
Kan. Laws 1907, Ch. 140, § 13 et seq.

Bush Oyster Act
Wash. Laws 1895, Ch. 24

Bushy Lake Preservation Act
Cal. Public Resources Code § 5830 et seq.

Business Act (Public Livestock Marketing)
Ala. Code 1975, § 2-15-115

Business Activities Tax Act
Mich. Comp. Laws 1948, 205.551 et seq.

Business Alliance for Training and Employment Act
N.J. Stat. Ann., 34:15B-1 et seq.

Business and Agriculture Development Authority Act
S.D. Laws 1986, Ch. 16 § 32 et seq.

Business and Commerce Code
Tex. Business Corporation Act, Art. 1.01 et seq.

Business and Economic Development Act
Cal. Government Code § 15310 et seq.
D.C. Code Ann., § 1-2201 et seq.
Utah Code Ann. 1953, 9-2-201 et seq.

Business and Financial Tax Law (New York City)
N.Y. City Adm. Code '38, Ch. 46, § B46-1.0 et seq.

Business and Industrial Development Act
N.D. Cent. Code, 54-34-01 et seq.

Business and Industrial Development Corporation Act
Alaska Stat. 1962, § 10.10.010 et seq.
Cal. Financial Code § 31000 et seq.
Conn. Public Acts 1993, No. 382, §§ 56 to 66
Ida. Code 1947, 26-2701 et seq.
La. Rev. Stat. Ann., 51:2386 et seq.
Mich. Comp. Laws Ann., 487.1101 et seq.

Business and Industrial Training Act
Mich. Comp. Laws Ann., 421.221 et seq.

Business and Licensing System Act
Del. Code of 1974, Title 29, § 10301 et seq.

Business and Occupations Tax Act
Wash. Rev. Code Ann., 82.04.010 et seq.
W. Va. Code 1966, § 11-13-1 et seq.

Business and Parking Improvement Area Law
Cal. Streets and Highways Code §§ 36500 et seq., 36520 et seq., 36540 et seq., 36550, 36551

Business and Parking Improvement District Act
Utah Code Ann. 1953, 17A-3-401 et seq.

Business and Professions Code
Cal. Statutes 1937, Ch. 399, p. 1229

Business and Public Records as Evidence Act
Colo. Rev. Stat., 13-26-101 et seq.
Me. Rev. Stat. Ann. 1964, Title 16, § 451 et seq.
Okla. Stat. Ann., Title 12, § 521 et seq.
Va. Code 1950, § 8.01-391
Vt. Stat. Ann., Title 12, § 1701

Business and Public Records as Evidence Act (Photographic Copies)
See Uniform Photographic Copies of Business and Public Records as Evidence Act

Business and Severance Privilege Tax Act
W. Va. Code 1966, § 11-13A-1 et seq.

Business Assistance Act (Small and Minority)
Fla. Stat. Ann., 288.702 et seq.

Business Assistance and Regulatory Reform Act
Ill. Comp. Stat. 1992, Ch. 20, § 608/1 et seq.

Business Association Act (Minority and Women's)
Ore. Rev. Stat., 200.005 et seq.

Business Brokers Act
Ill. Comp. Stat. 1992, Ch. 815, § 307/10-1 et seq.

Business Certificate Act
Mass. Gen. Laws 1990, 110:5

Business Chance Broker Act
Mich. Comp. Laws Ann., 451.201 et seq.
Ore. Rev. Stat. 1953, 696.610 et seq.

Business Clean Air Assistance Act (Small)
Mich. Comp. Laws Ann., 336.121 et seq.

Business Combination Act
Ida. Code 1947, 30-1701 et seq.
Ky. Rev. Stat. 1971, 271B.12-200
R.I. Gen. Laws 1956, 7-5.2-1 et seq.
Tenn. Code Ann., 48-35-101 et seq.

Business Combination Law
Tex. Business Corporation Act, Art. 13.01 et seq.

Business Coordination Act
Fla. Stat. Ann., 606.01 et seq.
Wash. Rev. Code Ann., 43.31.870 et seq.

Business Coordination Procedures Act
Mich. Comp. Laws Ann., 445.11 et seq.

Business Corporation Act
See also Uniform Business Corporation Act
Ala. Code 1975, § 10-2B-1.01 et seq.
Alaska Stat. 1962, Replaced Titles, § 10.05.003 et seq.
Ariz. Rev. Stat. Ann., § 10-120 et seq.
Ark. Stat. 1947, 4-26-101 et seq.
Colo. Rev. Stat., 7-101-101 et seq.
Conn. Public Acts 1994, No. 186
D.C. Code Ann., § 29-301 et seq.
Fla. Stat. Ann., 607.0101 et seq.
Ga. Code Ann., 14-2-101 et seq.
Haw. Rev. Stat. Ann., § 415-1 et seq.
Ida. Code 1947, 30-1-1 et seq.
Ill. Comp. Stat. 1992, Ch. 805, § 5/1.01 et seq.
Ind. Code Ann., 23-1-17-1 et seq.
Iowa Code Ann., 490.101 et seq.

Ky. Rev. Stat. 1971, 271B.1-010 et seq.
La. Rev. Stat. Ann., 12:1 et seq.
Mass. Gen. Laws Ann., 156:1 et seq.
Me. Rev. Stat. Ann. 1964, Title 13-A, § 101 et seq.
Mich. Comp. Laws Ann., 450.1101 et seq.
Minn. Stat. Ann., 302A.001 et seq.
Miss. Code Ann. 1972, § 79-4-1.01 et seq.
Mo. Rev. Stat., 351.010 et seq.
Mont. Code Ann., 35-1-112 et seq.
N.C. Gen. Stat. 1943, § 55-1-01 et seq.
N.D. Cent. Code, 10-19.1-01 et seq.
Neb. Rev. Stat. 1943, 21-2001 et seq.
Nev. Rev. Stat. 1979 Reprint, 78.010 et seq.
N.H. Rev. Stat. 1955, 293-A:1.01 et seq.
N.J. Stat. Ann., 14A:1-1 et seq.
N.M. Stat. Ann., 53-11-1 et seq.
N.Y. Consol. Laws, Ch. 4
Okla. Stat. Ann., Title 18, § 901 et seq.
Ore. Rev. Stat., 60.001 et seq.
Pa. Cons. Stat., Title 15, § 1101 et seq.
R.I. Gen. Laws 1956, 7-1, 1-1 et seq.
S.C. Code Ann. 1976, § 33-1-101 et seq.
S.D. Codified Laws 1967, 47-2-1 et seq.
Tenn. Public Acts 1986, Ch. 887
Tex. Business Corporation Act, Art. 1.01 et seq.
Utah Code Ann. 1953, 16-10A-101 et seq.
Va. Code 1950, § 13.1-1 et seq.
Vt. Stat. Ann., Title 11A, § 1.01 et seq.
Wash. Rev. Code Ann., 23B.01.010 et seq.
Wis. Stat. Ann., 180.0101 et seq.
Wyo. Stat. Ann., § 17-1-101 et seq.

Business Corporation Act (Revised)
Utah Code Ann. 1953, 16-10a-101 et seq.

Business Corporation Act Amendments of 1963 (District of Columbia)
D.C. Code 1973, § 29-303 et seq.

Business Corporation Law (Small)
Cal. Corporation Code § 14000 et seq.

Business Corporation Tax Act
N.Y. Tax Law (Consol. Laws Ch. 60) § 208 et seq.
R.I. Gen. Laws 1956, 44-11-1 et seq.

Business Damage Act (Eminent Domain)
Fla. Stat. Ann., 73.012, Subsec. 3

Business Development Act (Large)
Ill. Rev. Stat. 1987, Ch. 127, § 141.164

Business Development Act (Small)
Ill. Rev. Stat. 1987, Ch. 127, § 2709.1 et seq.
Ore. Rev. Stat., 285.500 et seq.

Business Development Compliance Act (Minority)
R.I. Gen. Laws 1956, 37-21-1 et seq.

Business Development Corporation Act
Ariz. Rev. Stat. Ann., § 10-951 et seq.
Colo. Rev. Stat., 7-48-101 et seq.
Ga. Code Ann., 7-1-740 et seq.
Ky. Rev. Stat. 1971, 155.001 et seq.
Miss. Code Ann. 1972, § 79-5-1 et seq.
N.C. Gen. Stat. 1943, § 53A-1 et seq.
Neb. Rev. Stat. 1943, 21-2101 et seq.
N.H. Laws 1951, Ch. 328
N.J. Stat. Ann., 17:52-1 et seq.
N.M. Stat. Ann., 53-7-18 et seq.
N.Y. Banking Law (Consol. Laws Ch. 2) § 210 et seq.
Okla. Stat. 1981, Title 18, § 901 et seq.
S.C. Code Ann. 1976, § 33-37-10 et seq.
W. Va. Code 1966, § 31-14-1 et seq.

Business Development Corporation Act (County)
S.C. Code Ann. 1976, § 33-39-10 et seq.

Business Development Credit Corporation Law
Pa. Purdon's Stat., Title 15, § 2701 et seq.
S.D. Codified Laws 1967, 47-10-1 et seq.

Business Development Finance Act
Iowa Code Ann., 15E.131 et seq.

Business Development Partnership Act
Neb. Rev. Stat. 1943, 81-1272 et seq.

Business Economic Development Act (Minority)
Ark. Acts 1991, No. 698

Business Economic Support Act
Ill. Comp. Stat. 1992, Ch. 30, § 760/1 et seq.

Business Energy Improvement Program
N.C. Gen. Stat. 1943, § 143B-472.30

Business Enterprise Act (Minority and Women's)
La. Rev. Stat. Ann., 36:1951 et seq.

Business Enterprise Act (Minority)
Miss. Code Ann. 1972, § 57-69-1 et seq.

Business Enterprise Assistance Act (Minority)
Okla. Stat. Ann., Title 74, § 85.45 et seq.

Business Enterprise for Minorities, Females and Persons with Disabilities Act
Ill. Comp. Stat. 1992, Ch. 30, § 575/0.01 et seq.

Business Entries Act (Evidence)
Tex. Rules of Criminal Evidence, Rule 902

Business Entries Admissibility Act
Conn. Gen. Stat. Ann., § 52-180

Business Entry Act
Mich. Comp. Laws Ann., 600.2146
N.D. Cent. Code, 31-08-01
Pa. Purdon's Stat., Title 73, § 393.1 et seq.

Business Establishment Name Act
S.C. Code Ann. 1976, § 39-13-10 et seq.

Business Establishments Act (Equal Rights)
Cal. Civil Code §§ 51, 52

Business Expansion Support Act
Ga. Code Ann., 48-7-40.1 et seq.

Business Financing Act (Small)
Miss. Code Ann. 1972, § 57-10-201 et seq.

Business Flexibility Act
Ind. Code Ann., 23-18-1-1 et seq.

Business Franchise Registration Act
W. Va. Code 1966, § 11-12-1 et seq.

Business Franchise Tax Act
W. Va. Code 1966, § 11-23-1 et seq.

Business Improvement District Act
Ark. Stat. 1947, 14-184-101 et seq.
Colo. Rev. Stat., 31-25-1201 et seq.
Ga. Code Ann., 36-43-1 et seq.
Ida. Code 1947, 50-2601 et seq.
Kan. Stat. Ann., 12-1781 et seq.
Miss. Code Ann. 1972, §§ 21-43-101 to
21-43-133
Mont. Code Ann., 7-12-1100 et seq.
Neb. Rev. Stat. 1943, 19-4015 et seq.
N.M. Stat. Ann., 3-63-1 et seq.
N.Y. General Municipal Law (Consol. Laws
Ch. 23) § 980 et seq.
Pa. Cons. Stat., Title 53, § 5401 et seq.
Pa. Purdon's Stat., Title 53, § 1551 et seq.
W. Va. Code 1966, § 8-13A-1 et seq.

Business Incentive Loan Act
N.J. Stat. Ann., 52:270-71 et seq.

Business Incubation Act
Mich. Comp. Laws Ann., 125.1571 et seq.

Business Incubation Program Act
Cal. Government Code §§ 15339.1 to
15339.3

Business Incubator Assistance Act
Miss. Laws 1999, H.B. 233

Business Incubators (Small)
Mo. Rev. Stat. 1978, 620.495

Business Infrastructure Development Act
Pa. Purdon Stat., Title 73, § 393.1 et seq.

Business Investment Act
Miss. Code Ann. 1972, § 57-61-1 et seq.

**Business Investment and Jobs Expansion
Tax Credit Act**
W. Va. Code 1966, § 11-13C-1 et seq.

Business License Act
Alaska Stat. 1962, § 43.70.010 et seq.
Kan. Laws 1957, Ch. 96

Business License Center Act
Wash. Rev. Code Ann., 19.02.010 et seq.

Business License Information Act
Cal. Government Code § 15366 et seq.

Business Licensing Coordination Act
Mont. Code Ann., 30-16-101 et seq.

**Business Methods Inquiry Act (Executive
Departments)**
June 25, 1910, Ch. 384, 36 Stat. 703

Business Names Act
Me. Rev. Stat. Ann. 1964, Title 31, § 1 et seq.
N.J. Stat. Ann., 56:1-1 to 56:1-7

Business Names Act (Assumed)
Ida. Code 1947, 53-501 et seq.
Ill. Comp. Stat. 1992, Ch. 805, § 405/0.01 et
seq.

Business Names Registration Act
Mass. Gen. Laws 1990, 110:5
Vt. Stat. Ann., Title 11, § 1621 et seq.

Business Opportunities Sales Act
Ky. Rev. Stat. 1971, 367.801 et seq.
N.C. Gen. Stat. 1943, § 66-94 et seq.
S.C. Code Ann. 1976, 39-57-10 et seq.
Va. Code 1950, § 59.1-262 et seq.

Business Opportunity Act
Tex. Business and Commerce Code,
§ 41.001

Business Opportunity Act (Handicapper)
Mich. Comp. Laws Ann., 450.791 et seq.

**Business Opportunity Development Reform
Act of 1988**
Nov. 15, 1988, P.L. 100-656, 15 U.S. Code
§ 631 nt.
June 15, 1989, P.L. 101-37, 15 U.S. Code
§§ 631 nt., 633, 633 nt., 636, 636nt., 637 nt.,
644 nt.
Nov. 5, 1990, P.L. 101-515, 15 U.S. Code
§ 637 nt.
Nov. 15, 1990, P.L. 101-574, 15 U.S. Code
§§ 636 nt., 637 nt.

June 13, 1991, P.L. 102-54, 15 U.S. Code § 644 nt.

Sept. 4, 1992, P.L. 102-366, 15 U.S. Code § 636 nt.

Oct. 22, 1994, P.L. 103-403, 15 U.S. Code § 637 nt.

Business Opportunity Development Reform Act Technical Corrections Act

June 15, 1989, P.L. 101-37, 15 U.S. Code § 631 nt.

Business Opportunity Disclosure Act

Utah Code Ann. 1953, 13-15-1 et seq.

Business Opportunity Fraud Act

Wash. Rev. Code Ann., 19.110.010 et seq.

Business Opportunity Investment Act

Conn. Gen. Stat. Ann., § 36-503 et seq.

Business Opportunity Law (Brokers and Salesmen)

Cal. Business and Professions Code § 10250 et seq.

Business Opportunity Purchasers Protection Act

Ohio Rev. Code 1953, 1334.01 et seq.

Business Opportunity Sales Act

Ill. Comp. Stat. 1992, Ch. 815, § 602/5-1 et seq.

Md. Ann. Code 1974, Art. BR, § 14-129 et seq.

Okla. Stat. Ann., Title 71, § 801 et seq.

Business Ownership Act (Women's)

Cal. Government Code § 15365.40 et seq.

Ill. Comp. Stat. 1992, Ch. 20, § 705/1

Business Ownership Succession and Employee Ownership (Center for)

Ill. Comp. Stat. 1992, Ch. 20, § 609/1 et seq.

Business Personal Property Tax Act

N.J. Stat. Ann., 54:11A-1 et seq.

Business Practice Regulation and Consumer Protection Act

Mass. Gen. Laws 1990, 93A:1 et seq.

Business Practices Act (Personal Sports Mobile)

Me. Rev. Stat. Ann. 1964, Title 10, § 1241 et seq.

Business Producer Controlled Property and Casualty Insurance Act

Iowa Code Ann., 510A.1 et seq.

Business Profits Tax Act

N.H. Rev. Stat. 1955, 77-A:1 et seq.

Ore. Laws 1973, Ch. 17, §§ 36 to 47

Business Records Act

June 20, 1936, Ch. 640, 49 Stat. 1561 (See 28 U.S. Code § 1732)

Ala. Code 1975, § 12-21-42 et seq.

Wis. Stat. Ann., 908.03

Business Records Act (Photographic Copies)

Ala. Code 1975, § 12-21-44

Haw. Rev. Stat. 1968, § 622-4

Business Records Admissibility in Evidence Act

Md. Ann. Code 1974, Art. CJ, § 10-101 et seq.

Business Records as Evidence Act

See also Uniform Business Records as Evidence Act

Ariz. Rev. Stat. Ann., § 12-2262

Ark. Stat. 1947, 28-928 et seq.

Cal. Code of Civil Procedure § 1953e et seq.

Conn. Gen Stat. 1983, § 52-180 et seq.

Del. Code of 1974, Title 10, § 4309

Fla. Stat. Ann., 90.803(6)

Ga. Code Ann., 24-3-14

Haw. Rev. Stat. Ann., § 622-5

Ida. Code 1947, 9-413 et seq.

Kan. Stat. Ann., 60-460, Subd. m

Md. Ann. Code 1974, Art. CJ, § 10-101

Minn. Stat. Ann., 600.02 et seq.

Mo. Rev. Stat., 490.660 et seq.

N.D. Cent. Code, 31-08-01 et seq.

Neb. Rev. Stat. 1943, 25-12,114 et seq.

N.H. Rev. Stat. 1955, 521:1

N.J. Stat. Ann., 2A:82-34 et seq.

N.M. Stat. Ann. 1953, 20-2-12

Continued

N.Y. Civ. Prac. Laws and Rules (Consol. Laws Ch. 8) Rule 4518

Ohio Rev. Code 1953, 2317.40 et seq.

Ore. Rev. Stat. 1953, 44.550 et seq.

Pa. Cons. Stat., Title 42, §§ 6108, 6109

S.C. Code Ann. 1976, § 19-5-510

S.D. Codified Laws 1967, 19-16-10

Vt. Stat. Ann., Title 12, § 1700

Wash. Rev. Code Ann., 5.45.010 et seq.

Wyo. Stat. 1957, § 1-170 et seq.

Business Records as Evidence Act (Photographic Copies)
Iowa Code Ann., 622.30

Md. Ann. Code 1974, CJ, 10-102

Wash. Rev. Code Ann., 5.46.010 et seq.

Business Records Photographic Copies as Evidence Act
See Uniform Photographic Copies of Business and Public Records as Evidence Act

Business Records Preservation Act
Md. Ann. Code 1974, Art. BR, § 1-307 et seq.

N.H. Rev. Stat. 1955, 337-A:1 et seq.

Okla. Stat. 1981, Title 67, § 251 et seq.

Business Records Preservation Act (Private)
Okla. Stat. Ann., Title 67, § 251 et seq.

Business Records Shop Book Act
N.Y. Civil Practice Laws and Rules (Consol. Laws Ch. 8) Rule 4518

Business Registration Act
Ill. Rev. Stat. 1991, Ch. 96, § 3m et seq.

Business Registration and Licensing System Act
Del. Code of 1974, Title 29, § 10301 et seq.

Business Registration Tax Act
W. Va. Code, § 11-12-1 et seq.

Business Regulation Act (Equipment)
Neb. Rev. Stat. 1943, 87-701 et seq.

Business Regulation Act (Escrow)
Mont. Laws 1985, Ch. 651

Business Regulation Act (Motor Vehicle)
Utah Code Ann. 1953, 41-3-101 et seq.

Business Relocation Mission Private Partnership Act
N.J. Stat. Ann., 34:1B-88 et seq.

Business Rent Control Law (Albany)
N.Y. Laws 1948, Ch. 679

Business Rent Stabilization Law
N.Y. Laws 1945, Ch. 314

Business Research and Development Act
Minn. Stat. 1949, 362.07 et seq.

Business Retention Act
N.J. Stat. Ann., 54:4-1.13 et seq.

Business Schools Act
Ill. Rev. Stat. 1991, Ch. 144, § 136 et seq.

Pa. Purdon's Stat., Title 24, § 2751 et seq.

Business Security Act (Convenience)
Fla. Stat. Ann., 812.1701 et seq.

Business Sign Act
Miss. Code Ann. 1972, § 15-3-7

Business Space Rent Control Law
N.Y. Laws 1945, Ch. 314

N.Y. Laws 1949, Ch. 535

N.Y. Laws 1950, Ch. 326

N.Y. Laws 1951, Ch. 430

N.Y. Laws 1952, Ch. 417

Business Take-Over Act
Ill. Rev. Stat. 1981, Ch. 121 1/2, § 137.51 et seq.

Ind. Code Ann., 23-2-3.1-1 et seq.

Miss. Code Ann. 1972, § 75-72-101 et seq.

Business Tax Act
Conn. Gen. Stat. Ann., § 12-610 et seq.

Mich. Comp. Laws Ann., 208.1 et seq.

Tenn. Code Ann., 67-4-701 et seq.

Business Tax Act (Corporations)
Conn. Gen. Stat. Ann., § 12-213 et seq.

Iowa Code Ann., 422.32 et seq.

Business Tax Act (First Class School Districts)

Pa. Purdon's Stat., Title 24, § 584.1 et seq.

Business Tax Reform Act (First Class City)

Pa. Purdon's Stat., Title 53, § 16181 et seq.

Business Tax Reform and Rate Reduction Act

N.Y. Environmental Conservation Law 1972 (Consol. Laws Ch. 43B), §§ 17-0707, 19-0309

N.Y. Laws 1987, Ch. 817

N.Y. Tax Law (Consol. Laws Ch. 60) §§ 5, 181, 208, 209, 209B, 210, 211, 290, 606, 612, 658, 1081, 1083, 1085, 1087, 1452 to 1455, 1462, 1503, 1510, 1512, 1515

Business Tender Offer Law

Miss. Code Ann. 1972, § 75-72-101 et seq.

Business Transacted with Broker Controlled Insurer Act

Ida. Code 1947, 47-1701 et seq.

Kan. Stat. Ann., 40-37a01 et seq.

La. Rev. Stat. Ann., 22:1210.1 et seq.

Mass. Gen. Laws Ann., 175:174F to 175:174K

Me. Rev. Stat. Ann. 1964, Title 24-A, § 6401 et seq.

Business Transacted with Broker Controlled Property and Casualty Insurer Act

Wash. Rev. Code Ann., 48.97.900

Business Transacted with Producer Controlled Insurer Act

Cal. Insurance Code § 1216 et seq.

Minn. Stat. Ann., 60J.06 et seq.

Miss. Code Ann. 1972, § 83-59-1 et seq.

Okla. Stat. Ann., Title 36, § 1671 et seq.

Business Transacted with Producer Controlled Property and Casualty Insurer Act

Ga. Code Ann., 33-48-1 et seq.

Minn. Stat. Ann., 60J.01 et seq.

Business Transacted with Producer Controlled Property or Casualty Insurer Act

Ala. Code 1975, § 27-6B-1 et seq.

Fla. Stat. Ann., 626.7491

Ky. Rev. Stat. 1971, 304.3-400c et seq.

R.I. Gen. Laws 1956, 27-48-1 et seq.

W. Va. Code 1966, § 33-36-1 et seq.

Business Trust Act

Del. Code of 1974, Title 12, § 3815 et seq.

Ind. Code Ann., 23-5-1-1 et seq.

Kan. Stat. Ann., 17-2027 et seq.

Ohio Code 1953, 1746.01 et seq.

Business Under Assumed Name Act

N.C. Gen. Stat. 1943, § 66-68 et seq.

Business Use of Military Terms Act

Ill. Comp. Stat. 1992, Ch. 720, § 230/0.01 et seq.

Business with Foreign Corporations Act

N.Y. Business Corporations Law 1961 (Consol. Laws Ch. 4) § 1301 et seq.

Busing Law

N.C. Gen. Stat. 1943, § 115-176 et seq.

Butler Act (Antievolution)

Tenn. Code Ann., Superseded Vol., 49-1922

Butler Act (Riparian)

Fla. Stat. 1969, 271.01 et seq.

Butler Act (Tax Extension)

Ill. Rev. Stat. 1991, Ch. 120, § 643a

Butter Act (Assessment Equalization)

Ill. Rev. Stat. 1991, Ch. 120, § 627 et seq.

Butter and Cheese Factories Act

Ill. Comp. Stat. 1992, Ch. 410, § 610/0.01 et seq.

Ill. Rev. Stat. 1991, Ch. 5, § 42.9 et seq.

Butter Grading Act

Mich. Comp. Laws Ann., 288.211 et seq.

Butter Standard Act
March 4, 1923, Ch. 268, 42 Stat. 1500, 21 U.S. Code § 6

Butterfat Tax Act
S.D. Codified Laws 1967, 40-31-1 et seq.

Butterine and Ice Cream Factories Act (Sanitary Standards)
Ill. Rev. Stat. 1971, Ch. 48, § 53 et seq.

Button Act (Military Service)
Ill. Rev. Stat. 1991, Ch. 126 1/2, §§ 44.9, 45

Butts County, City of Flovilla, City of Jackson, and City of Jenkinsburg Water and Sewer Authority Act
Ga. Laws 1986, p. 5457

Butts County Water Authority Act
Ga. Laws 1971, p. 3568

Buy American Act
March 3, 1933, Ch. 212, 47 Stat. 1520, 41 U.S. Code §§ 10a to 10c
June 25, 1959, P.L. 86-70, 73 Stat. 151, 41 U.S. Code § 10c
July 12, 1960, P.L. 86-624, 74 Stat. 419, 41 U.S. Code § 10c
Aug. 23, 1988, P.L. 100-418, 102 Stat. 1545, 1552
Oct. 13, 1994, P.L. 103-355, 41 U.S. Code §§ 10a, 10a nt., 10b-1
Cal. Government Code § 4300 et seq.
N.J. Stat. Ann. 52:32-1 et seq.
Tenn. Code Ann., 54-5-135

Buy American Act of 1988
Aug. 23, 1988, P.L. 100-418, 102 Stat. 1545, 41 U.S. Code § 10a nt.
Mo. Rev. Stat., 34.350 et seq.

Buy-American Motor Vehicle Act
Pa. Purdon's Stat., Title 73, § 1891 et seq.

Buy American Steel Act
Md. Ann. Code 1974, Art. SF, § 17-301 et seq.

Buy Indian Act
June 25, 1910, Ch. 431, 25 U.S. Code § 47
Nov. 2, 1994, P.L. 103-435, 25 U.S. Code § 47

Buy Massachusetts Program Act
Mass. Gen. Laws Ann., 23A:10A

Buyback Disclosure Act (Motor Vehicle)
Utah Code Ann. 1953, 41-3-406 et seq.

Buyer Property Protection Act
Del. Code of 1974, Title 6, § 2570 et seq.

Buyer Protection Act
Kan. Stat. Ann., 50-623 et seq.

Buyer Protection Act (Farm Implement)
Ill. Rev. Stat. 1991, Ch. 5, § 1551 et seq.

Buyer Protection Act (New Vehicle)
Ill. Rev. Stat. 1991, Ch. 121 1/2, § 1201 et seq.

Buyers Club Law
Mo. Rev. Stat. 1978, 407.670 et seq.

Buying Services Act
Fla. Stat. Ann., 559.3901 et seq.
Ga. Code Ann., 10-1-590 et seq.

Buzzo Act (Throwing Incendiary Substance on Highway)
Cal. Vehicle Code 1959, § 23111

By-Products Disposal Act (Animals)
Miss. Code Ann. 1972, § 41-51-1 et seq.

Byfield Water District Loan Act
Mass. Acts 1954, Ch. 470
Mass. Acts 1956, Ch. 251

Bypass Act (Highways)
Wyo. Stat. Ann., §§ 24-7-101, 24-7-102

Byrne Act
Cal. Water Code § 65000 et seq.

Byrne Act (Water Facilities)
Cal. Water Code § 12950 et seq.

Byrne Act (Water Project Costs for Local Government Services)
Cal. Water Code § 12950 et seq.

Byrne-Killgrew Act (Unemployment Insurance)
N.Y. Labor Act (Consol. Laws Ch. 31) § 500 et seq.

Byrne-Porter Act
Cal. Water Code § 12930 et seq.

Byrnes Act (Transporting Strikebreakers)
June 24, 1936, Ch. 746, 49 Stat. 1899 (See 18 U.S. Code § 1231)

Byrnes-Cochran Reorganization Act
Fla. Special Laws 1983, Ch. 83-370
Wyo. Stat. Ann., § 41-12-201 et seq.

Byssinosis Act
S.C. Code Ann. 1976, § 42-11-60 et seq.

C

C Corporation Income Tax Act
Colo. Rev. Stat., 39-22-301 et seq.

Cab Liability Insurance Act
D.C. Code 1973, §§ 40-1714 to 40-1716

Cabaret Tax Law (County)
Wash. Rev. Code Ann., 36.38.010 et seq.

Cabbage Standardization and Inspection Act
Tex. Rev. Civ. Stat., Art. 118c-2

Cable Act (Naturalization and Citizenship of Married Women)
See Married Women's Citizenship Act

Cable, Allen, Evans Law (State Board of Education-Negro Member)
Ind. Laws 1939, Ch. 82, p. 474

Cable Communications Policy Act of 1984
Oct. 30, 1984, P.L. 98-549, 47 U.S. Code § 609 nt.

Cable Communications Systems Law
Haw. Rev. Stat. Ann., § 440G-1 et seq.

Cable Fair Competition Act (Local Government)
Ga. Code Ann., 36-89-1 et seq.

Cable Subscriber Privacy Protection Act
N.J. Stat. Ann., 48:5A-54 et seq.

Cable System and Geothermal Development Permitting Act
Haw. Rev. Stat. Ann., § 196D-1

Cable Television Act
Haw. Rev. Stat. Ann., § 440G-1 et seq.
N.J. Stat. Ann., 48:5A-1 et seq.
S.C. Code Ann. 1976, § 58-12-10 et seq.
S.D. Codified Laws 1967, 9-35-16 et seq.
Tenn. Code Ann., 7-59-101 et seq.

Cable Television Act (Municipal)
N.M. Stat. Ann., 3-23A-1 et seq.

Cable Television and Video Provider Customer Service and Information Act
Cal. Government Code § 53054 et seq.

Cable Television Commission Act
D.C. Code Ann., § 43-1801 et seq.
N.Y. Executive Law 1951 (Consol. Laws Ch. 18) § 811 et seq.

Cable Television Communications Systems Act
Haw. Rev. Stat. Ann., § 440G-1 et seq.

Cable Television Consumer Protection and Competition Act of 1992
Oct. 5, 1992, P.L. 102-385, 47 U.S. Code §§ 325 nt., 521 nt., 531 nt., 543 nt., 554 nt., 609 nt.

Cable Television Development Act
Cal. Statutes 1982, Ch. 679

Cable Television Programming Decency Act
Utah Code Ann. 1953, 76-10-1229 et seq.

Cable Television Reform Act
Vt. Stat. Ann., Title 30 §§ 501 to 515

Cable Television Service Theft Act
S.C. Code Ann. 1976, § 16-11-810 et seq.

Cable Television Services Act (Tenants Rights to)
Pa. Purdon's Stat., Title 68, § 250.501-B et seq.
W. Va. Code 1966, § 5-18A-1 et seq.

Cable Television Systems Act
W. Va. Code 1966 § 5-18-1 et seq.

Cache La Poudre River Corridor Act
Oct. 19, 1996, P.L. 104-323, 16 U.S. Code § 461 nt.

Cadastration, Classification, and Assessment of Property Act
P.R. Laws Ann. 1954, Title 13, § 431 et seq.

Cadaver Act
Ill. Comp. Stat. 1992, Ch. 410, § 510/0.01 et seq.

Caddo Lake Compact Act
La. Acts 1979, No. 367
Tex. Water Code, § 47.001 et seq.

Caddo Parish Zoning Act
La. Rev. Stat. Ann., 33:140.1 et seq.

Cadet Corps Act (Law Enforcement Youth)
N.M. Stat. Ann., 29-7B-1 et seq.

Cadet Corps Termination Act
D.C. Code 1973, § 31-1103 et seq.

Cafeteria Plan Act
N.M. Stat. Ann., 10-7-14 et seq.

Cafeteria Plan-Retirement Systems Act
S.C. Code Ann. 1976, §§ 9-1-60 et seq.,
12-7-775 et seq.

Cal-COBRA (Continuation Benefits Replacement Act)
Cal. Health and Safety Code § 1366.20 et seq.
Cal. Insurance Code § 10128.50 et seq.

Cal-First Home Buyers Act
Cal. Health and Safety Code § 52500 et seq.

Calder Act (Daylight Saving)
March 19, 1918, Ch. 24, 40 Stat. 450, 15 U.S. Code §§ 261 to 263
Aug. 20, 1919, Ch. 51, 41 Stat. 280

Caldera, Weggeland, and Killea California Interstate Banking and Branching Act
Cal. Statutes 1995, Ch. 480

Calderon-Sher Safe Drinking Water Act
Cal. Health and Safety Code §§ 116300, 116355, 116360, 116365, 116370, 116470

Calhoun County Civil Service Act
Ala. General Acts 1951, p. 363, No. 138

Calhoun County Commissioners Act
Ala. Local Acts 1939, p. 252, No. 420

Calhoun County Hospital District Act
Tex. Rev. Civ. Stat., Art. 4494q

Calhoun-Gordon County Airport Authority Act
Ga. Laws 1971, p. 2861

Calhoun Recreation Authority Act
Ga. Laws 1992, p. 6750

Caliente Charter
Nev. Statutes 1971, Ch. 31, p. 55

California-Arizona Boundary Compact
Ariz. Laws 1963, Ch. 77

California-Arizona Reciprocal Hunting and Fishing Licenses Act
Cal. Fish and Game Code 1957, § 375

California Bay-Delta Environmental Enhancement and Water Security Act
Sept. 30, 1996, P.L. 104-208, Title I, 110 Stat. 3009

California Desert Protection Act of 1994
Oct. 31, 1994, P.L. 103-433, 16 U.S. Code § 410aaa nt.

California Military Lands Withdrawal and Overflights Act of 1994
Oct. 31, 1994, P.L. 103-433, 16 U.S. Code § 410aaa-82 nt.

California NAFTA Conformity Act
Cal. Vehicle Code 1959, §§ 2418, 2418.1

California-Nevada Interstate Compact Act (Water Apportionment)
Cal. Water Code §§ 5975, 5976
Nev. Rev. Stat. 1979 Reprint, 538.600 et seq.

California-Nevada Super Speed Ground Transportation Act
Cal. Statutes 1988, Ch. 149
Cal. Statutes 1992, Ch. 27

California Pioneers' Monument Law
Cal. Public Resources Code § 5101 et seq.

California State Prohibition of Female Genital Mutilation Act
Cal. Health and Safety Code § 124170
Cal. Penal Code § 273.4

California State University Contract Law
Cal. Public Contract Code § 10700 et seq.

California Wilderness Act of 1984
Sept. 28, 1984, P.L. 98-425, 98 Stat. 1619, 6
U.S. Code §§ 46 nt. , 80 nt., 543 et seq.,
1132 nt., 1274
June 19, 1992, P.L. 102-301, 106 Stat. 244
Nov. 2, 1994, P.L. 103-437, 16 U.S. Code
§ 543

California Work Opportunity and Responsibility to Kids Act (CalWORKS)
Cal. Welfare and Institutions Code § 11200
et seq.

Call Before You Dig Act (Rosemary Elebash)
Ala. Acts 1995, p. 922, No. 489

Callahan Act (Foreign Agencies)
Mich. Comp. Laws Ann., 14.201 et seq.

Callan Law (Hit and Run Driving)
N.Y. Vehicle and Traffic Law 1959 (Consol.
Laws Ch. 71) § 600 et seq.

Cambean Basin Projects Financing Authority Act
P.R. Acts 1989, First Special Session, No. 9

Cambodian Genocide Justice Act
April 30, 1994, 22 U.S. Code § 2656 nt.

Cambridge Hospital Loan Act
Mass. Acts 1960, Ch. 292

Cambridge School Loan Act
Mass. Acts 1952, Ch. 571

Camden County Public Service Authority Act
Ga. Laws 1990, p. 4273

Cameras in the Courtroom Law
N.Y. Judiciary Law (Consol. Laws Ch. 30)
§ 218

Cameron-Unruh Beach, Park, Recreational and Historical Facilities Bond Act
Cal. Public Resources Code § 5096.1 et seq.

Cameron-Unruh Park and Recreation Bond Act
Cal. Public Resources Code §§ 5095.1 et
seq., 5096.1. et seq.

Cammack Law (Local Option)
Ky. Rev. Stat. 1942, 242.210
Ky. Rev. Stat. 1971, 242.030

Camp Act (Youth)
Md. Ann. Code 1974, Art. HG, § 14-401 et
seq.

Camp Resort and Timeshare Act
Utah Code Ann. 1953, 57-19-1 et seq.

Camp Sanitation Law
Cal. Labor Code § 2410 et seq.

Camp W.G. Williams Land Exchange Act of 1989
Nov. 28, 1990, P.L. 101-628, 104 Stat. 4499

Campaign Act (Election)
Mass. Gen. Laws Ann., 55:1 et seq.

Campaign Act (Public Financing)
Ky. Rev. Stat. 1971, 121A.010c et seq.

Campaign Act (State Employee Combined Charitable)
Ala. Code 1975, § 36-1A-1

Campaign Communications Reform Act
Feb. 7, 1972, P.L. 92-225, 86 Stat. 3, 47 U.S.
Code §§ 312, 315, 801 to 805

Campaign Contribution Limits Act
Tenn. Code Ann., 2-10-301 to 2-10-310

Campaign Contribution Limits without Taxpayer Financing Amendments to the Political Reform Act
Cal. Government Code § 85101 et seq.

Campaign Contributions Act
S.D. Codified Laws 1967, 12-25-1 et seq.

Campaign Contributions and Expenditures Reporting Act
N.J. Stat. Ann., 19:44A-1 et seq.

Okla. Stat. Ann., Title 26, § 15-101 et seq.
R.I. Gen. Laws 1956, 17-25-1 et seq.

Campaign Disclosure Act
Cal. Elections Code 1976, § 11500 et seq.

Campaign Disclosure Act (Election)
Mass. Gen. Laws Ann., 55:1 et seq.

Campaign Disclosure—Income Tax Check-off Act
Iowa Code Ann., 56.1 et seq.

Campaign Expenses Publicity Act
See Federal Corrupt Practices Acts

Campaign Fair Practices Act
N.J. Stat. Ann., 19:34-64 et seq.

Campaign Fairness Act (Judicial)
Tex. Election Code, 1985, § 253.151 et seq.

Campaign Finance Act
Conn. Gen. Stat. Ann., § 9-333 et seq.
Kan. Stat. Ann., 25-4142 et seq.
Md. Ann. Code 1957, Art. 33, § 31-1 et seq.
Mich. Comp. Laws Ann., 169.201 et seq.
Okla. Stat. Ann., Title 26, § 18-101 et seq.
Vt. Stat. Ann., Title 17, § 2801 et seq.

Campaign Finance Act (City of New York)
N.Y. Adm. Code 1985, § 3-701 et seq.

Campaign Finance Limitation Act
Neb. Rev. Stat. 1943, 32-1601 et seq.

Campaign Finance Reform Act (Labor and Employer)
Ga. Laws 1998, S.B. 497

Campaign Finance Reform and Conflict of Interest Act
D.C. Code Ann., § 1-1401 et seq.

Campaign Financing Disclosure Act
Del. Code of 1974, Title 15, §§ 8001 et seq., 8040 et seq.
Ga. Code Ann., 21-5-1 et seq.
La. Rev. Stat. Ann., 18:1481 et seq.
Mo. Rev. Stat., 130.011 et seq.
Tenn. Code Ann., 2-10-101 et seq.

Campaign Fund Act
Mont. Code Ann., 13-37-301 et seq.

Campaign Fund Act (Election)
Cal. Revenue and Taxation Code § 18701 et seq.

Campaign Practices Act
Minn. Stat. Ann., 210A.01 et seq.

Campaign Practices Act (Fair)
Ala. Code 1975, § 17-22A-1 et seq.
Wash. Laws 1993, Ch. 2

Campaign Reform Act
Colo. Rev. Stat., 1-45-101 et seq.

Campaign Reform Act (Congressional)
Minn. Stat. Ann., 10A.40 et seq.

Campaign Reform, Government Accountability and Ethics Act
S.C. Code Ann. 1976, § 8-13-100 et seq.

Campaign Reporting Act
N.M. Stat. Ann., 1-19-25 et seq.
Wash. Rev. Code 1951, 29.83.010 et seq.

Campaign Reporting and Disclosure Act
Tex. Election Code, § 251.001 et seq.

Campaign Spending Limits Act
Cal. Government Code § 85100 et seq.

Campaigns, Elections and Procedures Law
N.Y. Election Law 1949 (Consol. Laws Ch. 17) § 465 et seq.

Campbell-Alquist Community College Finance Act
Cal. Education Code 1976, § 84720 et seq.

Campbell-Baker-Katz-Kopp Transportation Blueprint for the Twenty-First Century
Cal. Statutes 1991, Ch. 106

Campbell County Road Act
Tenn. Private Acts 1947, Ch. 159

Campbell-Martin-Estes Act
Ala. Code 1975, §§ 32-6-150, 32-6-156

Campbell-Moretti-Deukmejian Drug Abuse Treatment Act
Cal. Statutes 1972, Ch. 1255, p. 2464

Campbell-Torres-Cortese Natural Disaster Assistance Act Amendments
Cal. Government Code, § 8680.3

Camper Tax Act
Neb. Rev. Stat. 1943, 60-1801 et seq.

Campground Licensing and Recreation Area Act
Ill. Comp. Stat. 1992, Ch. 210, § 95/1 et seq.

Campground Membership Act
Minn. Stat. Ann., 82A.01 et seq.
Neb. Rev. Stat. 1943, 76-2101 et seq.
N.Y. General Business Law (Consol. Laws Ch. 20) § 650 et seq.

Camping Act (Membership)
N.C. Gen. Stat. 1943, § 66-220 et seq.

Camping Membership Resort Act
Tex. Property Code, § 222.001

Campus Demonstration Policy Act
Ill. Comp. Stat. 1992, Ch. 110, § 10/0.01 et seq.

Campus Disorder Act
Ohio Rev. Code 1953, 3345.21 et seq.

Campus Financing Act (Centennial)
N.C. Gen. Stat. 1943, § 116-198.31 et seq.

Campus Incentive Program
S.C. Code Ann. 1976, § 59-21-1210 et seq.

Campus Police Act (Private College)
Ill. Rev. Stat. 1991, Ch. 144, §§ 1950, 1951

Campus Rideshare and Clean Fuel Act (Harvey)
Cal. Public Resources Code § 25620 et seq.

Campus Safety Act (Kristin Smart)
Cal. Education Code 1976, § 67381

Campus Security Act
Ill. Comp. Stat. 1992, Ch. 110, § 12/1 et seq.
Okla. Stat. Ann., Title 74, § 360.15 et seq.

Campus Sexual Assault Victim's Bill of Rights Act
N.J. Stat. Ann., 18A:61E-1 et seq.

Canada-United States Interparliamentary Group Act
June 11, 1959, P.L. 86-42, 73 Stat. 72, 22 U.S. Code §§ 276d to 276g

Canadian Boundary Act
June 13, 1902, Ch. 1079, 32 Stat. 373

Canadian-Maine Legislative Advisory Commission Act
Me. Rev. Stat. Ann. 1964, Title 3, § 221 et seq.

Canadian Reciprocity Act
July 26, 1911, Ch. 3, 37 Stat. 4

Canadian River Compact Act
N.M. Stat. Ann., 72-15-2
Okla. Stat. Ann., Title 82, § 526.1 et seq.
Tex. Water Code, § 43.001 et seq.

Canadian River Project Prepayment Act
Oct. 30, 1998, P.L. 105-316, 112 Stat. 2999, 43 U.S. Code § 600b nt.

Canal Act
N.J. Stat. Ann., 48:6-14 et seq.
N.Y. Consol. Laws, Ch. 5
Ohio Rev. Code 1953, 307.67

Canal Act (Panama and Isthmian)
See Panama and Isthmian Canal Act

Canal Act of 1890
Aug. 30, 1890, Ch. 837, 26 Stat. 391, 43 U.S. Code § 945

Canal Acts
See Panama Canal Acts

Canal Authority Act
Fla. Stat. Ann., 374.011 et seq.

Canal Construction Act (Corporation)
Ill. Rev. Stat. 1991, Ch. 32, § 367.9 et seq.

Canal Development Act (Illinois and Michigan)
Ill. Rev. Stat. 1991, Ch. 19, § 37.10 et seq.

Canal Land Use Act (Illinois and Michigan)
Ill. Rev. Stat. 1991, Ch. 19, § 37.01 et seq.

Canal Management Act (Illinois and Michigan)
Ill. Rev. Stat. 1991, Ch. 19, § 0.01 et seq.

Canal Place Preservation and Development Authority Act
Md. Ann. Code 1974, Art. FI, § 13-1001 et seq.

Canal Protection Act (Illinois and Michigan)
Ill. Rev. Stat. 1991, Ch. 19, § 29.9 et seq.

Canal Referendum Act
N.Y. Laws 1903, Ch. 147

Canal State Park Act (Illinois and Michigan)
Ill. Rev. Stat. 1991, Ch. 105, § 491.01 et seq.

Canal Tolls Repeal Act
June 15, 1914, Ch. 106, 38 Stat. 385

Canal Zone Code
June 19, 1934, Ch. 667, 48 Stat. 1122
June 13, 1940, Ch. 358, 54 Stat. 387
July 29, 1942, Ch. 536, 56 Stat. 726
Oct. 1, 1942, Ch. 574, 56 Stat. 763
July 1, 1944, Ch. 366, 58 Stat. 676
July 2, 1945, Ch. 220, 59 Stat. 312
Aug. 4, 1947, Ch. 470, 61 Stat. 743
June 29, 1948, Ch. 706, 62 Stat. 1166
Aug. 10, 1949, Ch. 415, 63 Stat. 593
Aug. 12, 1949, Ch. 422, 63 Stat. 600
Sept. 26, 1950, Ch. 1049, 64 Stat. 1038
Oct. 24, 1951, Ch. 557, 65 Stat. 635
Aug. 23, 1954, Ch. 839, 68 Stat. 773

Oct. 18, 1962, P.L. 87-845, 76A Stat. 1, 18 U.S. Code §§ 14, 4210 ; 22 U.S. Code § 1934; 24 U.S. Code § 196; 28 U.S. Code §§ 414 , 547, 1404, 1406; 50 U.S. Code §§ 191a, 191b, 858

Canal Zone Government Act
April 28, 1904, Ch. 1758, 33 Stat. 429
Sept. 21, 1922, Ch. 370, 42 Stat. 1004

Canales Act (Conservation and Reclamation Districts)
Tex. Water Code, § 56.011 et seq.

Canals and Waterways Act
Ill. Rev. Stat. 1981, Ch. 19

Cancellation Control Act
Me. Rev. Stat. Ann. 1964, Title 24-A, § 2911 et seq. (Automobile Insurance)
Me. Rev. Stat. Ann. 1964, Title 24-A, § 3048 et seq. (Property Insurance)

Cancellation Control Act (Automobile Insurance)
Me. Rev. Stat. Ann. 1964, Title 24-A, § 2911 et seq.

Cancellation Control Act (Property Insurance)
Me. Rev. Stat. Ann. 1964, Title 24-A, § 3048 et seq.

Cancellation of Commercial Risk Insurance Act
Tenn. Public Acts 1986, Ch. 656

Cancer Act
Cal. Health and Safety Code § 1700 et seq.
Pa. Purdon's Stat., Title 35, § 5601 et seq.

Cancer Act of 1971
See National Cancer Act Of 1971

Cancer Control Act
Tex. Health and Safety Code, § 82.001 et seq.

Cancer Control and Research Act
Fla. Stat. Ann., 240.5121

Cancer Control, Prevention and Research Act
Del. Code of 1974, Title 16, § 3201 et seq.
Fla. Stat. Ann., 385.201
N.J. Stat. Ann., 52:9U-1 et seq.
Pa. Purdon's Stat., Title 35, § 5631 et seq.
W. Va. Code 1966, § 16-5A-1 et seq.

Cancer Incidence Reporting Act
Tex. Health and Saftey Code, § 82.001 et seq.

Cancer Institute Corporation Act (Roswell Park)
N.Y. Public Authorities Law (Consol. Laws Ch. 43A) § 3550 et seq.

Cancer Prevention and Control Act (Breast and Cervical)
W. Va. Code 1966 § 16-33-1 et seq.

Cancer Protection Act (Police Officer's)
Cal. Labor Code § 3212.1

Cancer Registries Amendment Act
Oct. 24, 1992, P.L. 102-515, 42 U.S. Code § 201 nt.

Cancer Registry Act
Miss. Code Ann., § 41-91-1 et seq.

Cancer Registry Act (Central)
S.C. Code Ann. 1976, § 44-35-10 et seq.

Cancer Registry Act (Statewide)
Ala. Code 1975, § 22-13-30 et seq.

Cancer Reporting System Act
Tenn. Code Ann., 68-1-1001 et seq.

Cancer Research Act
Cal. Health and Safety Code § 104175 et seq.

Cancer Research Improvement Act

Cancer Therapeutic Research Act
Fla. Stat. 1983, 402.36

Cancer Treatment Act (Experimental)
Ill. Rev. Stat. 1991, Ch. 111 1/2, § 6001 et seq.

Candidates Law (Ghost)
S.C. Code Ann. 1976, § 7-11-50 et seq.

Cane Pole Tax Repeal Act
Fla. Stat. Ann., 372.57

Cane River Creole National Historic Park and National Heritage Area Act
Nov. 2, 1994, P.L. 103-449, 16 U.S. Code §§ 410ccc nt., 410ccc et seq.

Cannabis and Controlled Substances Act
Ill. Comp. Stat. 1992, Ch. 35, § 520/1 et seq.

Cannabis and Controlled Substances Tort Claims Act
Ill. Comp. Stat. 1992, Ch. 740, § 20/1 et seq.

Cannabis Control Act
Ill. Comp. Stat. 1992, Ch. 720, § 550/1 et seq.

Canned Animal Food Act
Va. Code 1950, § 3.1-885 et seq.

Canned Foods Standards Law (Fruits and Vegetables)
Cal. Food and Agricultural Code 1967, §§ 41301 et seq., 42501 et seq.

Cannella Environmental Farming Act
Cal. Food and Agricultural Code § 560 et seq.

Cannery Inspection Act
Cal. Statutes 1925, p. 931

Canning Factory Act
Mich. Comp. Laws Ann., 289.121 et seq.

Canning Inspection Act (Sardines)
Me. Rev. Stat. Ann. 1964, Title 32, § 4151 et seq.

Cannon Municipal Bankruptcy Act
See Bankruptcy Acts

Canola and Rapseed Research, Promotion, and Consumer Information Act
April 4, 1996, P.L. 104-127, Title V, Subtitle C, 7 U.S. Code § 7401 nt.

Cantor Act (Railroad Franchise)
N.Y. Laws 1886, Ch. 65

Canvas or Cotton Duck Act
Ill. Rev. Stat. 1991, Ch. 147, § 44.9 et seq.

Canyonlands National Park Act
Sept. 12, 1964, P.L. 88-590, 78 Stat. 934, 16 U.S. Code §§ 271 to 271d

Cape Cod National Seashore Act
Aug. 7, 1961, P.L. 87-126, 75 Stat. 284, 16 U.S. Code §§ 459b to 459b-8

Cape Coral Health Facilities Authority Law
Fla. Special Laws 1975, Ch. 75-354

Cape Coral Seawall Assessment Act
Fla. Special Laws 1976, Ch. 76-342

Cape Lookout National Seashore Act
March 10, 1966, P.L. 89-366, 80 Stat. 33, 16 U.S. Code §§ 459g to 459g-6

Cape May County Ferry Act
N.J. Stat. Ann., Superseded Volume, B2:13A-6

Cape May-Lewes Ferry Act
N.J. Stat. Ann., 27:12B-27 et seq.

Capias Act
N.J. Stat. Ann., 2A:15-41 et seq.

Capital Access Act
Utah Code Ann. 1953, 9-2-1301 et seq.

Capital Access Program Act
Tex. Government Code, § 481.401 et seq.

Capital Act (Financial)
Conn. Gen. Stat. Ann., § 32-11a et seq.

Capital Act (Innovation)
Conn. Gen. Stat. Ann., § 32-32 et seq.

Capital Act (Risk-Based)
N.M. Stat. Ann., 59A-5A-1 et seq.

Capital and Surplus Act (Dynamic)
N.J. Stat. Ann., 17B:18-67 et seq.

Capital Budget Act
Ill. Comp. Stat. 1992, Ch. 20, § 3010/0.01 et seq.
Pa. 1968 Pamph. Laws 560, No. 218
Pa. 1969 Pamph. Laws 310, No. 133
Pa. 1970 Pamph. Laws 38, No. 16
Pa. 1970 Pamph. Laws 229, No. 94
Pa. 1971 Pamph. Laws 538, No. 140
Pa. 1971 Pamph. Laws 686, No. 185
Pa. 1971 Pamph. Laws 761, No. 188
Pa. 1972 Pamph. Laws 721, No. 167
Pa. 1972 Pamph. Laws 911, No. 217
Pa. 1972 Pamph. Laws 1235, No. 275
Pa. 1973 Pamph. Laws 56, No. 24
Pa. 1973 Pamph. Laws 95, No. 42
Pa. 1974 Pamph. Laws 727, No. 245
Pa. 1974 Pamph. Laws 1068, No. 346
Pa. 1974 Pamph. Laws 1081, No. 349
Pa. 1974 Pamph. Laws 1160, No. 369
Pa. 1976 Pamph. Laws 101, No. 44
Pa. 1976 Pamph. Laws 155
Pa. 1976 Pamph. Laws 857, No. 154
Pa. 1978 Pamph. Laws 69, No. 34
Pa. 1978 Pamph. Laws 822, No. 161
Pa. 1980 Pamph. Laws 7, No. 5
Pa. 1984 Pamph. Laws 583, No. 117
Pa. 1986 Pamph. Laws 1, No. 1
Pa. 1986 Pamph. Laws 542, No. 94 (Game Fund)
Pa. 1986 Pamph. Laws 543, No. 95 (Boat and Fish Funds)
Pa. 1986 Pamph. Laws 563, No. 99
Pa. 1986 Pamph. Laws 1285, No. 118
Pa. 1986 Pamph. Laws 1407, No. 124
Pa. 1988 Pamph. Laws 851, No. 113
Pa. 1988 Pamph. Laws 842, No. 111
Pa. 1988 Pamph. Laws 962, No. 114
Pa. 1990 Pamph. Laws 10, No. 5 (Game Fund)
Pa. 1990 Pamph. Laws 73, No. 15 (Boat and Fish Funds)
Pa. 1990 Pamph. Laws 350, No. 80
Pa. 1990 Pamph. Laws 632, No. 162 (Fish Fund Hatchery Improvement)
Pa. 1990 Pamph. Laws 1399, No. 218 (Highway Supplement)
Pa. 1991 Pamph. Laws 329, No. 34
Pa. 1991 Pamph. Laws 190, No. 26
Continued

Pa. 1991 Pamph. Laws 320, No. 54
Pa. 1991 Pamph. Laws 578, No. 59
Pa. 1992 Pamph. Laws 1127, No. 147
Pa. 1993 Pamph. Laws 134, No. 31
Pa. 1994 Pamph. Laws 344, No. 50
Pa. 1995 Pamph. Laws 269, No. 38
Pa. 1997 Pamph. Laws 193, No. 21

Capital Budget Act for 1992-1993 (Game Fund)
Pa. 1992, Pamph. Laws 1374, No. 171
Pa. 1995 Pamph. Laws 252, No. 32

Capital Budget Project Itemization Act
Pa. 1990 Pamph. Laws 1472, No. 223
Pa. 1992 Pamph. Laws 1694, No. 188
Pa. 1994 Pamph. Laws 444, No. 74
Pa. 1996 Pamph. Laws 921, No. 148

Capital Budget Project Itemization Act for 1994-1995 (First Supplemental)
Pa. 1994 Pamph. Laws 962, No. 136

Capital Budget Supplement (Highway-Railroad and Highway Bridge)
Pa. 1992 Pamph. Laws 894, No. 143
Pa. 1994 Pamph. Laws 1074, No. 147

Capital Building Authority Act
N.C. Gen. Stat. 1943, § 129-40 et seq.

Capital City Incorporation Act
Alaska Stat. 1962, § 29.18.510 et seq.

Capital City Planning Commission Act
Ill. Comp. Stat. 1992, Ch. 20, § 3920/0.01 et seq.

Capital City Railroad Relocation Authority Act
Ill. Comp. Stat. 1992, Ch. 70, § 1910/1 et seq.

Capital City Redevelopment Corporation Act
N.J. Stat. Ann., 52:9Q-9 et seq.

Capital Companies Tax Credit Program Act
La. Rev. Stat. Ann., 51:1921 et seq.

Capital Company Act
Mont. Code Ann., 90-8-101 et seq.
W. Va. Code 1966 § 5E-1-1 et seq.

Capital Company Act (Certified)
Fla. Stat., 288.99
Mo. Rev. Stat. Ann., 135.500 to 135.529

Capital Complex Centennial Commission Act
Okla. Stat. Ann., Title 73, § 98 et seq.

Capital Complex Master Plan Act
Mont. Code Ann., 2-17-801 et seq.

Capital Construction Assistance Program (School District)
Colo. Rev. Stat., 22-43.7-101 et seq.

Capital Construction Budget Act
Mont. Laws 1971, p. 1791

Capital Corporation Act (Development)
Okla. Stat. Ann., Title 74, § 5086.1 et seq.

Capital Corporation Act (Seed)
Iowa Code 1995, 15E.81 et seq.

Capital Corporation and Partnership Act
S.C. Code Ann. 1976, § 41-44-10 et seq.

Capital Debt Service Fund Act of the City of Buffalo
N.Y. Laws 1977, Ch. 12

Capital Depository Act (Foreign)
Mont. Code Ann., 15-31-801 et seq.

Capital Development Board Act
Ill. Comp. Stat. 1992, Ch. 20, § 3105/1 et seq.

Capital Development Bond Act
Ill. Comp. Stat. 1992, Ch. 30, § 420/1 et seq.

Capital District Transportation Act
N.Y. Public Authorities Law (Consol. Laws Ch. 43A) § 1300 et seq.

Capital Expansion Act
  Neb. Rev. Stat. 1943, 72-1269 et seq.

Capital Expansion Act (State Investments)
  Neb. Rev. Stat. 1943, 72-1261 et seq.

Capital Facilities Debt Enabling Act
  Pa. Purdon's Stat., Title 72, § 1601-A et seq.

Capital Facilities Legislative Bond Act of 1991
  N.C. Laws 1991, Ch. 760

Capital Facilities Planning and Budgeting Act
  Fla. Stat. 1989, 216.015 et seq.

Capital Felony Expense Act
  Ga. Code Ann., 17-11-20 et seq.

Capital Finance Assistance Act (Public School)
  N.J. Stat. Ann., 34:1B-7.20 et seq.

Capital for Life or Health Insurers Act (Risk-Based)
  Ariz. Rev. Stat. Ann., § 20-488 et seq.

Capital Formation Act
  Okla. Stat. Ann., Title 74, § 5085.1 et seq.

Capital Funding Act (Primary Care)
  N.M. Stat. Ann., 24-1C-1 et seq.

Capital Gains Act (Income Tax)
  Ore. Rev. Stat., 316.002 et seq.

Capital Gains and Other Unearned Income Tax Act
  N.J. Stat. Ann., 54A:5-1 et seq.

Capital Highway District Act
  S.C. Acts 1927, p. 1023, No. 521

Capital Improvement Act
  See also Annual Capital Improvement Act
  Del. Laws Vol. 54, p. 1182, Ch. 384
  Del. Laws Vol. 55, p. 519, Ch. 167
  Haw. Session Laws 1982, Act 263
  Haw. Session Laws 1983, Act 283

  N.C. Laws 1959, Ch. 1039

Capital Improvement Act (Municipal Government)
  Ala. Acts 1986, No. 234

Capital Improvement Act (Public Schools)
  N.M. Stat. Ann., 22-25-1 et seq.

Capital Improvement Appropriation Acts
  N.C. Laws 1963, Ch. 684
  N.C. Laws 1965, Ch. 916
  N.C. Laws 1967, Ch. 1108
  N.C. Laws 1969, Ch. 755
  N.C. Laws 1971, Ch. 693
  N.C. Laws 1973, Ch. 523
  N.C. Laws 1974, Ch. 1202
  N.C. Laws 1975, Ch. 874
  N.C. Laws 1977, Ch. 681
  N.C. Laws 1979, Ch. 731
  N.C. Laws 1983, Ch. 757
  N.C. Laws 1985, Ch. 480
  N.C. Laws 1990, Ch. 1074
  N.C. Laws 1991, Ch. 754
  N.C. Laws 1991, Ch. 795
  N.C. Laws 1991, Ch. 860

Capital Improvement - Authority to Construct Act of 1965
  N.C. Laws 1965, Ch. 944

Capital Improvement Bonds Act
  N.C. Laws 1961, Ch. 951
  S.C. Code Ann. 1976, §§ 4-29-10 et seq., 59-107-10 et seq., 59-115-80 et seq.

Capital Improvement Grant Act (Desegregation)
  Minn. Stat. Ann., 124C.55 et seq.

Capital Improvement Grant Act (School Building Accessibility)
  Minn. Laws 1993, Ch. 373, §§ 20 to 22

Capital Improvement Law (Municipal)
  Pa. Purdon's Stat., Title 53, § 10501-A et seq.

Capital Improvement Legislative Bond Act
  N.C. Laws 1961, Ch. 951
  Continued

N.C. Laws 1963, Ch. 838
N.C. Laws 1965, Ch. 915
N.C. Laws 1971, Ch. 722
N.C. Laws 1971, Ch. 1240
N.C. Laws 1991, Ch. 1048

Capital Improvement Planning Process Act (Local and Regional)
Okla. Stat. Ann., Title 62, § 910 et seq.

Capital Improvement Revenue Bond Act (Local Government)
Ark. Code Ann. 1987, 14-164-401 et seq.

Capital Improvement Voted Bond Act
N.C. Laws 1961, Ch. 1037

Capital Improvements Appropriations Act
N.C. Laws 1992, Ch. 1044

Capital Investment Act
Okla. Stat. Ann., Title 74, § 5061.11 et seq.

Capital Investment Act (Venture)
N.M. Stat. Ann., 7-20-1 et seq.

Capital Investment Incentive Program
Cal. Government Code § 51298 et seq.

Capital Issues Law (Securities)
N.C. Gen. Stat. 1943, § 78A-1 et seq.

Capital Law (Risk-Based)
Oct. 11, 1996, P.L. 104-290, 110 Stat. 3416, Title 1
Ill. Comp. Stat. 1992, Ch. 215, § 5/35A-1 et seq.

Capital Loan Fund Act
Pa. Purdon's Stat., Title 73, § 394.1 et seq.

Capital Markets Efficiency Act of 1996
Oct. 11, 1996, P.L. 104-290, Title I, 15 U.S. Code § 78a nt.

Capital Outlay Act (Public School)
N.M. Stat. Ann., 22-24-1 et seq.

Capital Outlay Loan Act
Mass. Acts 1950, Ch. 795
Mass. Acts 1951, Ch.756

Mass. Acts 1952, Ch. 604
Mass. Acts 1954, Ch. 471
Mass. Acts 1955, Ch. 738
Mass. Acts 1956, Ch. 711
Mass. Acts 1961, Ch. 544, § 6
Mass. Acts 1965, Ch. 791

Capital Outlay Loan Act (Emergency)
Mass. Acts 1957, Ch. 485

Capital Park Extension Act
Pa. 1943 Pamph. Laws 818, No. 346

Capital Program Act
N.M. Stat. Ann., 15-3-21 et seq.

Capital Project Itemization Act
Pa. 1990, P.L. No. 117

Capital Project Loan Fund Act (Local Government)
Pa. Purdon's Stat., Title 53, § 6781-1 et seq.
Pa. 1990 Pamph. Laws, No. 210

Capital Project Sales Tax Act
S.C. Code Ann. 1976, §§ 4-10-300 to 4-10-370

Capital Projects Bond Act
N.M. Laws 1988, Special Session, Ch. 1

Capital Projects General Obligation Bond Act
N.M. Laws 1992, Ch. 103
N.M. Laws 1994, Ch. 142
N.M. Laws 1996, Ch. 13

Capital Projects General Obligations Bond Act
N.M. Laws 1990, Ch. 133

Capital Punishment Act
Md. Ann. Code 1957, Art. 27, § 71 et seq.
N.C. Gen. Stat. 1943, § 15A-2000 et seq.
S.C. Code Ann. 1976, § 16-3-20 et seq.

Capital Region Airport Commission Act
Va. Acts 1980, Ch. 380

Capital Reserve Act (County)
N.C. Gen. Stat. 1943, § 153-142.1 et seq.

Capital Reserve Act (Municipal)
N.C. Gen. Stat. 1943, § 160-425 et seq.

Capital Reserve Act of the City of Durham
N.C. Laws 1955, Ch. 1091

Capital Resource Company Act
Mass. Acts 1977, Ch. 816, §§ 1 to 20

Capital Square Preservation Council Act
Va. Code 1950, §§ 9-304.1 to 9-304.6

Capital Stock Act
Pa. Purdon's Stat., Title 15, § 615 et seq.

Capital Stock Association Act
La. Rev. Stat. Ann., 6:937 et seq.

Capital Stock Building and Loan Association Act
N.M. Stat. Ann. 1953, 48-15-26 et seq.

Capital Stock Tax Act
Fla. Stat. 1971, 608.33 et seq.
N.J. Stat. Ann., 54:12-1 et seq.
Pa. Purdon's Stat., Title 72, § 1601 et seq.

Capital Stock Tax Act (Banks)
Pa. Purdon's Stat., Title 72, § 7701 et seq.

Capital Stock Tax Act (Foreign Corporations)
La. Rev. Stat. Ann., 47:2611 et seq.

Capital Unitary Review Act
Pa. Cons. Stat., Title 42, § 9570 et seq.

Capitation Tax Act
Nev. Rev. Stat. 1957, 363.010 et seq.

Capitol City Planning Commission Act
Ill. Rev. Stat. 1991, Ch. 123, § 30.9 et seq.

Capitol Expansion Act
N.M. Stat. Ann. 1953, 6-2-14 et seq.

Capitol Expenditure Bond Act for County Correctional Facilities
Cal. Penal Code, § 4475 et seq.

Capitol Grounds Act
S.D. Codified Laws 1967, 5-15-1 et seq.

Capitol Police Retirement Act
Oct. 15, 1990, P.L. 101-428, 5 U.S. Code § 8331 nt.

Capitol Punishment Act
Ga. Laws 1973, p. 159

Capitol View Protection Act
Cal. Government Code § 8162.5 et seq.

Capper-Cramton Act (District of Columbia, Park and Playground System)
D.C. Code Ann., § 8-101 et seq.

Capper-Ketcham Act
May 22, 1928, Ch. 687, 45 Stat. 711, 7 U.S. Code §§ 343a, 343b
N.M. Stat. Ann., 76-2-3

Capper-Lenroot-Anderson Act (Agricultural Credits)
See Agricultural Credits Act Of 1923

Capper-Tincher Act (Grain Futures)
See Grain Futures Act

Capper-Volstead Act
See Co-Operative Marketing Associations Act

Capping and Running Acts (Attorneys)
Va. Code 1950, § 54.1-3939

Captive Insurance Company Act
Colo. Rev. Stat., 10-6-101 et seq.
Ga. Code Ann., 33-41-1 et seq.
Tenn. Code Ann., 56-13-101 et seq.
Va. Code 1950, § 38.2-1100 et seq.

Car Carrier Act (Armored)
N.Y. General Business Law (Consol. Laws Ch. 20) § 89aaa et seq.

Car Dispatchers Act (State Automobiles)
Iowa Code Ann., 18.114 et seq.

Car Guard Act (Armored)
N.Y. General Business Law (Consol. Laws Ch. 20) § 89ooo et seq.

Car Key Act
W. Va. Code 1966, § 17C-14-1

Car Pooling Act
S.C. Code Ann. 1976, § 58-23-10 et seq.

Car Pricing Law
See Automobile Information Disclosure Act

Car Rental Act
Conn. Gen. Stat. Ann., § 14-154a

Car Rental and Collision Damage Waiver Act
Iowa Code Ann., 516D.1 et seq.

Car Service Act
May 29, 1917, Ch. 23, 40 Stat. 101, 49 U.S. Code § 1

Car Supply Law (Railroads)
Neb. Rev. Stat. 1943, 74-503 et seq.

Car Titles Act
Miss. Code Ann., § 63-21-1 et seq.

Caravan Act (Motor Vehicles)
Cal. Statutes 1937, p. 2253
Ida. Code 1947, 49-1101 et seq.
Wash. Rev. Code Ann., 46.76.010 et seq.

Caravan Tax Act (Motor Vehicles)
N.M. Stat. Ann., 66-6-2

Carbon Dioxide Act
N.M. Stat. 1978, 19-10A-1 et seq.

Carbon Hill National Fish Hatchery Conveyance Act
Oct. 1, 1996, P.L. 104-213, 110 Stat. 3016

Carbonated Beverages Act
Pa. 1925 Pamph. Laws 730, No. 399

Carbondale Civic Center Law
Ill. Comp. Stat. 1992, Ch. 70, § 325/2 et seq.

Carbondale, Riverside, Matteson, Ottawa, Illinois Valley, Waukegan, Pontiac and Randolph County Civic Centers Act
Ill. Rev. Stat. 1991, Ch. 85, § 7000-1 et seq.

Carcinogens Control Act
Cal. Health and Safety Code § 24200 et seq.

Carcinogens Control Act (Occupational)
Cal. Labor Code § 9000 et seq.

Card Games Act
Mont. Code Ann., 23-5-301 et seq.

Cardiac Rehabilitation Certification Program Act
N.C. Gen. Stat. 1943, § 131E-165 et seq.

Cardiovascular Center Corporation Act (Puerto Rico and the Caribbean)
P.R. Laws Ann. 1954, Title 24, § 343 et seq.

Care Access Act (Health)
Wash. Rev. Code Ann., 70.47.010

Care Access Act (Maternity)
Wash. Rev. Code Ann., 74.09.760 et seq.

Care Aide Training Act (Long Term)
Ark. Code Ann. 1987, 20-10-701 et seq.

Care and Custody of the Insane Act
Alaska Stat. 1962, § 47.30.010 et seq.

Care and Treatment of the Developmentally Disabled Act
Colo. Rev. Stat., 27-10.5-101 et seq.

Care for Police Survivors Act of 1998
June 16, 1998, P.L. 105-180, 42 U.S. Code § 3711 nt.

Care for the Elderly Act (All-Inclusive)
Ill. Comp. Stat. 1992, Ch. 320, § 40/1 et seq.

Care Health Insurance Program
Colo. Rev. Stat., 10-21-101 et seq.

Care Insurance Act (Long-Term)
Mo. Laws 1990, S.B. No. 765, §§ 1 to 8

Care Plan Act (Managed)
Neb. Rev. Stat. 1943, 68-1048 et seq.

Care Provider Income Tax Act (Health)
Neb. Rev. Stat. 1943, 77-4801 et seq.

Care Provider Registration and Disclosure Act (Continuing)
Pa. Purdon's Stat., Title 40, § 3201 et seq.

Care Purchasing Cooperative Act (Health)
Fla. Stat. Ann., 408.001

Care Reform Act (Long-Term)
Mont. Code Ann., 53-6-601 et seq.

Career Act
N.Y. Civil Service Law (Consol. Laws Ch. 7), § 130 et seq.

Career Compensation Act of 1949
Oct. 12, 1949, Ch. 681, 63 Stat. 802, 14 U.S. Code §§ 239 nt., 309; (See 37 U.S. Code § 201 et seq.) 42 U.S. Code §§ 209, 210 to 212, 215, 216
May 10, 1950, Ch., 175, 64 Stat. 158
Sept. 8, 1950, Ch. 922, 64 Stat. 794
Oct. 26, 1951, Ch. 580, 65 Stat. 653
May 19, 1952, Ch. 310, 66 Stat. 79
June 25, 1952, Ch. 459, 66 Stat. 156
July 9, 1952, Ch. 608, 66 Stat. 494
June 29, 1953, Ch. 158, 67 Stat. 89
May 29, 1954, Ch. 249, 68 Stat. 167
July 16, 1954, Ch. 535, 68 Stat. 488
March 31, 1955, Ch. 20, 69 Stat. 18
June 30, 1955, Ch. 250, 69 Stat. 225
July 12, 1955, Ch. 325, 69 Stat. 294
Aug. 5, 1955, Ch. 571, 69 Stat. 532
Aug. 5, 1955, Ch. 579, 69 Stat. 538
Aug. 11, 1955, Ch. 806, 69 Stat. 691
April 23, 1956, Ch. 208, 70 Stat. 114
April 30, 1956, Ch. 223, 70 Stat. 121
June 13, 1956, Ch. 383, 70 Stat. 275
June 25, 1956, Ch. 445, 70 Stat. 338
July 24, 1956, Ch. 686, 70 Stat. 628
Aug. 10, 1956, Ch. 1041, 70A Stat. 627
Aug. 28, 1957, P.L. 85-208, 71 Stat. 484
Sept. 2, 1957, P.L. 85-272, 71 Stat. 597
March 17, 1958, P.L. 85-347, 72 Stat. 37
May 20, 1958, P.L. 85-422, 72 Stat. 122
Sept. 2, 1958, P.L. 85-861, 72 Stat. 1556
March 23, 1959, P.L. 86-4, 73 Stat. 13
June 30, 1960, P.L. 86-559, 74 Stat. 282
July 12, 1960, P.L. 86-635, 74 Stat. 469
July 12, 1960, P.L. 86-637, 74 Stat. 471
July 12, 1960, P.L. 86-638, 74 Stat. 471
July 25, 1961, P.L. 87-103, 75 Stat. 219
Aug. 17, 1961, P.L. 87-140, 75 Stat. 341
Aug. 17, 1961, P.L. 87-145, 75 Stat. 382
Aug. 25, 1961, P.L. 87-164, 75 Stat. 401
Sept. 14, 1961, P.L. 87-233, 75 Stat. 507
Oct. 4, 1961, P.L. 87-374, 75 Stat. 804

Career Criminal Act (Officer Evelyn Gort and All Fallen Officers)
Fla. Stat., 775.084 to 775.0843, 790.235

Career Criminal Punishment Act
Cal. Statutes 1986, Ch. 85

Career Criminals Amendment Act of 1986
Oct. 27, 1986, P.L. 99-570, 18 U.S. Code § 921 nt.

Career Development Act (High Risk Youth)
Ill. Rev. Stat. 1991, Ch. 23, §§ 6550, 6551

Career Education Act
Colo. Rev. Stat., 22-8-101 et seq.
Fla. Stat. Ann., 229.601
Ky. Rev. Stat. 1971, Superseded Vols., 158.505 et seq.
Mich. Comp. Laws Ann., 388.1311 et seq.

Career Education Incentive Act
Dec. 13, 1977, P.L. 95-207, 20 U.S. Code §§ 2601, 2601 nt., 2602 et seq.
Aug. 6, 1979, P.L. 96-46, 20 U.S. Code §§ 1221h, 2603

Career Employee Act
Tenn. Public Acts 1986, Ch. 869

Career Incentive Act of 1955
March 31, 1955, Ch. 20, 69 Stat. 18 (See 10 U.S. Code § 6912; See 37 U.S. Code § 201 et seq.)

Career Ladder Programs
Ariz. Rev. Stat. Ann., §§ 15-918.01 to 15-918.03

Career System Act (Highway Department)
Pa. Purdon's Stat., Title 71, § 741.3 et seq.

Career Teacher Act
Minn. Stat. Ann., 124C.26 et seq., 129B.41 et seq.

Caregiver Grant Program
Va. Code 1950, § 63.1-331 et seq.

Caregiver Support Act (Family)
Ga. Code Ann., 49-6-70 et seq.
Pa. Purdon's Stat. Title 62, § 3061 et seq.

Caregivers Criminal History Screening Act
N.M. Stat. Ann., 29-17-2 to 29-17-5

Careless Driving Act
N.J. Stat. Ann., 39:4-97

Carey Act
Colo. Rev. Stat., 36-3-101 et seq.

Carey Act (Emergency Poor Relief)
Ohio Rev. Code 1953, 5113.01 et seq.

Carey Act (Irrigation)
Aug. 18, 1894, Ch. 301, 28 Stat. 422, 43 U.S. Code § 641

Carey Act (Soldiers' Home)
Aug. 18, 1894, Ch. 301, 28 Stat. 372

Carey Land Act (Reclamation)
Mont. Rev. Code 1947, 81-2101 et seq.

Cargo Preference Laws
March 26, 1934, Ch. 90, 48 Stat. 500, 46 Appx. § 1241-1
Aug. 26, 1954, Ch. 936, 68 Stat. 832, 46 U.S. Code § 1241

Caribbean and Puerto Rico Cardiovascular Center Corporation Act
P.R. Laws Ann. 1954, Title 24, § 343 et seq.

Caribbean Basin Economic Recovery Act
Aug. 5, 1983, P.L. 98-67, 19 U.S. Code §§ 1202, 1319 nt., 2251 nt., 2582, 2701 to 2706; 26 U.S. Code §§ 274, 7652; 33 U.S. Code § 1311 nt.
Oct. 30, 1984, P.L. 98-573, 19 U.S. Code § 2703
Oct. 22, 1986, P.L. 99-514, 19 U.S. Code §§ 2703, 2703 nt.
Oct. 27, 1986, P.L. 99-570, 19 U.S. Code § 2702
Aug. 23, 1988, P.L. 100-418, 102 Stat. 1159, 19 U.S. Code §§ 2702, 2703
Aug. 20, 1990, P.L. 101-382, 19 U.S. Code §§ 2702, 2703, 2706
Dec. 8, 1993, P.L. 103-182, 19 U.S. Code § 2707
Dec. 8, 1994, P.L. 103-465, 19 U.S. Code §§ 2702, 2703
Aug. 20, 1996, P.L. 104-188, 19 U.S. Code § 2702
Oct. 11, 1996, P.L. 104-295, 19 U.S. Code § 2707

Caribbean Basin Economic Recovery Expansion Act of 1990
Aug. 20, 1990, P.L. 101-382, 19 U.S. Code § 2701 nt.

Caribbean Basin Projects Financing Authority Act
P.R. Acts 1989, First Special Session, No. 9

Caribbean Economic Development Corporation Act
P.R. Laws Ann. 1954, Title 23, § 261 et seq.

Carjacking Act
Mass. Gen. Laws Ann., 265:2A
Miss. Code Ann., § 97-3-113 et seq.
Pa. Cons. Stat., Title 18, § 702

Carjacking Correction Act of 1996
Oct. 1, 1996, P.L. 104-217, 18 U.S. Code § 2111 nt.

Carl Albert Public Internship Program
Okla. Stat. Ann., Title 74, § 840-3.2 et seq.

Carl D. Perkins Vocational and Applied Technology Education Act

Dec. 18, 1983, P.L. 88-210, 20 U.S. Code § 2301 et seq.

Oct. 19, 1984, P.L. 98-524, 20 U.S. Code §§ 2301 nt., 2301 et seq. .

Nov. 22, 1985, 99-159, 20 U.S. Code §§ 2301 nt., 2311, 2311 nt., 2312, 2322, 2323, 2333, 2361 to 2363, 2383, 2392, 2417, 2464, 2471

July 8, 1986, P.L. 99-350, 20 U.S. Code § 2311

Dec. 22, 1987, P.L. 100-202, 20 U.S. Code § 2332

April 28, 1988, P.L. 100-297, 102 Stat. 324, 20 U.S. Code §§ 2331 , 2332

Aug. 23, 1988, P.L. 100-418, 102 Stat. 1508, 20 U.S. Code §§ 2302 , 2341, prec. 2371, 2393

Sept. 25, 1990, P.L. 101-392, 20 U.S. Code § 2301 et. seq. generally, 2401 et. seq. generally

Oct. 30, 1990, P.L. 101-476, 20 U.S. Code § 1400 nt.

Aug. 17, 1991, P.L. 102-103, 20 U.S. Code §§ 2312, 2313

Sept. 7, 1992, P.L. 102-367, 20 U.S. Code § 2322

Dec. 20, 1993, P.L. 103-208, 20 U.S. Code §§ 2311a, 2341a

March 31, 1994, P.L. 103-227, 20 U.S. Code §§ 2421, 2422

Oct. 20, 1994, P.L. 103-382, 20 U.S. Code §§ 2311a, 2321, 2323, 2325, 2341, 2341a, 2404, 2420, 2466a, 2471

Dec. 21, 1995, P.L. 104-66, 20 U.S. Code §§ 2396h, 2441

Aug. 22, 1996, P.L. 104-193, 20 U.S. Code §§ 2341, 2341a, 2471

Oct. 7, 1998, P.L. 105-244, 20 U.S. Code § 2394e

Oct. 31, 1998, P.L. 105-332, 20 U.S. Code §§ 2301, 2301 nt., 2302 to 2307, 2311, 2311a, 2312, 2313, prec. 2321, 2321 to 2328, 2331, 2335, 2335a, 2335b, prec. 2341, 2341 to 2344, 2341a to 2341c, prec. 2351, 2351 to 2355, 2361 to 2363, prec. 2371, 2371 to 2377, 2381 to 2383, prec. 2391, 2391 to 2398, 2394a to 2394e, 2396 nt., 2396a to 2396I, 2396m, 2397 nt., 2397a to 2397h, 2401 to 2404, prec. 2411, 2411 to 2415, 2416 to 2420, 2420a, 2421 to 2424, 2441, 2451, 2461, 2463, 2466, 2466a to 2466e, 2468a to 2468e, 2471

Carl D. Perkins Vocational and Applied Technology Education Act Amendments of 1990

Sept. 25, 1990, P.L. 101-392, 20 U.S. Code § 2301 nt.

Dec. 21, 1995, P.L. 104-66, 20 U.S. Code § 2303

Carl D. Perkins Vocational and Applied Technology Education Amendments of 1998

Oct. 31, 1998, P.L. 105-332, 112 Stat. 3076, 20 U.S. Code § 2301 nt.

Carl D. Perkins Vocational Education Act

See Carl D. Perkins Vocational And Applied Technology Education Act

Carlin Act (Larceny from Interstate Carriers)

Feb. 13, 1913, Ch. 50, 37 Stat. 670 (See 18 U.S. Code §§ 659, 660, 2117)

Carlin Charter

Nev. Statutes 1971, Ch. 344, p. 603

Carlisle Act (Internal Revenue)

May 28, 1880, Ch. 108, 21 Stat. 148, 19 U.S. Code §§ 468, 469

Carlisle Act (Spirits Regauging)

Aug. 27, 1894, Ch. 349, 28 Stat. 509

Carlsbad Caverns National Park Act

May 14, 1930, Ch. 272, 46 Stat. 279, 16 U.S. Code §§ 407 to 407c

Dec. 30, 1963, P.L. 88-249, 77 Stat. 818, 16 U.S. Code §§ 407e to 407h

Carlucci Hunter Safety Act
Fla. Stat. Ann., 372.5717

Carlucci Uniform Firearms Act
Fla. Stat. Ann., 790.33

Carmack Amendment to Hepburn Act (Interstate Commerce)
June 29, 1906, Ch. 3591, 34 Stat. 595, 49 U.S. Code § 20 (11, 12)

Carmichael Act (Electric System Bonds)
Ala. Code 1975, § 11-81-200 et seq.

Carnal Knowledge Act
Minn. Stat. 1965, 617.02
Ohio Rev. Code 1953, 2907.04 et seq.
Utah Code Ann. 1953, 76-53-19
Wash. Rev. Code Ann., 9A.44.010 et seq.

Carnival-Amusement Safety Act
Ill. Comp. Stat. 1992, Ch. 430, § 85/2 et seq.

Carnival and Amusement Rides Safety Act
Ga. Code Ann., 34-12-1 et seq.
Mich. Comp. Laws Ann., 408.651 et seq.
N.J. Stat. Ann., 5:3-31 et seq.

Carnival Games and Amusement Act
Okla. Stat. Ann., Title 3A, § 501 et seq.

Carnival Regulation Act
Ill. Comp. Stat. 1992, Ch. 225, § 201/0.01 et seq.

Carnival Ride Insurance Act
N.M. Stat. Ann., 57-25-1 et seq.

Carp River Forge Advisory Board Act
Mich. Comp. Laws Ann., 399.71 et seq.

Carpenter Act (Public Utilities)
Ohio Rev. Code 1953, 4901.19, 4909.17 et seq.

Carpenter-Katz Small Business Equal Access to Justice Act
Cal. Code of Civil Procedure § 1028.5

Carpenter-MacKay-Benzie-LaFramboise Act (Game Bag Limit)
Mich. Comp. Laws 1970, 312.12

Carpenter-Presley-Tanner Hazardous Substance Account Act
Cal. Health and Safety Code § 25300 et seq.

Carr-Owen State Parks Development Act
Ala. Code 1975, §§ 40-25-2, 40-25-23

Carrel Act (Mass Transportation)
Cal. Streets and Highways Code § 149

Carrell Memorial Tunnel and Mine Safety Act
Cal. Labor Code § 7950 et seq.

Carrell-Mulford Air Resources Act
Cal. Health and Safety Code § 39000 et seq.

Carriage of Goods by Sea Act
April 16, 1936, Ch. 229, 49 Stat. 1207, 46 U.S. Code §§ 1300 to 1315

Carrier Corporation Privilege Tax Act
W. Va. Code 1966, § 11-12A-1 et seq.

Carrier Incentive Act (Motorcoach)
Ark. Acts 1997, No. 1187

Carrier, Racing, Hobby, and Show Pigeon Act
Ill. Comp. Stat. 1992, Ch. 510, § 45/1 et seq.

Carrier Safety Act (Motor Vehicle)
N.M. Stat. Ann., 65-3-1 et seq.

Carrier Segregation Act
S.C. Code Ann. 1962, § 58-1491 et seq.

Carriers Act (Auto Transportation)
Wash. Rev. Code Ann., 81.68.010 et seq.

Carriers' Act (Carriage of Goods by Sea)
See Limited Liability Acts (Shipping)

Carriers Act (City)
Cal. Public Utilities Code, § 3901 et seq.

Carriers Act (Commercial)
Colo. Rev. Stat., 40-12-101 et seq.

Carriers Act (Common)
Wash. Rev. Code Ann., 81.28.010 et seq.

Carriers Act (Highway)
Cal. Public Utilities Code § 3501 et seq.

Carriers Act (Household Goods)
Cal. Public Utilities Code § 5101 et seq.

Carriers Act (Motor Vehicles)
Me. Rev. Stat. Ann. 1964, Title 35, § 1501 et seq.
N.C. Gen. Stat. 1943, § 62-259 et seq.
S.C. Code Ann. 1976, § 58-23-10 et seq.
Wash. Rev. Code Ann., 81.80.010 et seq.

Carriers and Employees Tax Act
Aug. 29, 1935, Ch. 813, 49 Stat. 974

Carriers' City Tax Exemption Law
Cal. Public Utilities Code §§ 4301, 4302.

Carrier's Lien Law
Iowa Code 1962, 575.1 et seq.

Carriers Taxing Act of 1937
June 29, 1937, Ch. 405, 50 Stat. 435

Carroll County Civil Service Act
Ga. Laws 1979, p. 4335

Carroll County Purchasing Law
Tenn. Private Acts 1975, Ch. 23
Tenn. Private Acts 1977, Ch. 68

Carroll-Goulette-Heath Act (Liquor Purchases by Minors)
Mich. Comp. Laws Ann., 750.141c

Carrying Concealed Weapons Act
D.C. Code 1973, §§ 22-3204, 22-3205
N.D. Cent. Code, 62.1-04-01 et seq.
Ohio Rev. Code 1953, 2923.12

Carson City Charter
Nev. Statutues 1969, Ch. 213. p. 85

Carter Act (Alaska Civil Code)
See Alaska Civil Code

Carter County Massage Registration Act
Tenn. Private Acts 1978, Ch. 276

Carter-Tackett Act (Jailers)
Ky. Acts 1936, 4th Sp. Sess., Ch. 14

Cartman Licensing Act (New York City)
N.Y. City Adm. Code '85, § 20-248

Carts, Cases, Baskets, Boxes, and Containers Act
Fla. Stat. Ann., 506.501 et seq.

Cartway Act
N.C. Gen. Stat. 1943, § 136-69

Cartwright Anti-Trust Act
Cal. Business and Professions Code § 16700 et seq.

Cartwrights Act
Ill. Rev. Stat. 1985, Ch. 30, § 40

Case Act (Savings and Loan)
Md. Ann. Code 1974, Art. FI, § 9-102 et seq.

Case Garnishment Act
Ill. Rev. Stat. 1991, Ch. 110, § 12-701 et seq.

Case-Jarvis Act (Home Rule Cities—Territorial Changes)
Mich. Comp. Laws Ann., 117.9

Case-Root-Jarvis-Mosier Act (Fresh Fruit)
Mich. Comp. Laws Ann., 286.341 et seq.

Case-Zablocki Act
Dec. 22, 1987, P.L. 100-204, 1 U.S. Code § 112b nt.

Casey Act (Chattel Loans)
Mo. Laws 1913, p. 545

Cash Basis Act
Kan. Stat. Ann., 10-1101 et seq.
Tenn. Code Ann., 9-11-101 et seq.

Cash Basis Act (Municipalities)
Minn. Stat. 1967, 471.1 et seq.

Cash Basis Budget Act of the City of Troy
N.Y. Laws 1949, Ch. 668

Cash Basis Budget Act of the County of Essex
N.Y. Laws 1946, Ch. 883

Cash Consumer Protection Act
Pa. Purdon's Stat., Title 73, § 204-1 et seq.

Cash Deposit Act (Bail)
Ill. Rev. Stat. 1991, Ch. 38, § 110-7

Cash Discount Act
July 27, 1981, P.L. 97-25, 15 U.S. Code
§ 1601 nt.

Cash Exchange Act (Federal—State)
Utah Code Ann. 1953, 67-4-2 et seq.

Cash Management Act
Okla. Laws 1991, Ch. 194

Cash Management Act (Short-Term)
N.M. Stat. Ann., 6-12A-1 to 6-12A-15

Cash Management Improvement Act Amendments of 1992
Nov. 4, 1992, P.L. 102-589, 31 U.S. Code
§ 6501 nt.

Cash Management Improvement Act of 1990
Oct. 24, 1990, P.L. 101-453, 31 U.S. Code
§ 6501 nt.
Nov. 4, 1992, P.L. 102-589, 31 U.S. Code
§ 3335 nt.
Oct. 19, 1996, P.L. 104-316, 31 U.S. Code
§ 6503 nt.

Cash Sickness Benefits Law
N.Y. Workmen's Compensation Law
(Consol. Laws Ch. 67) § 200 et seq.

Cash Sickness Compensation Act
R.I. Gen. Laws 1956, 28-39-1 et seq.

Cash Wage Act
Pa. Purdon's Stat., Title 43, § 251 et seq.

Cashman Act (Railroad Freight Rates)
Minn. Stat. Ann., 218.041 et seq.

Casimir Pulaski Holiday Act
Ill. Comp. Stat. 1992, Ch. 5, § 490/20

Casino Control Act
N.J. Stat. Ann., 5:12-1 et seq.

Casino Interest Registration Act
Mich. Comp. Laws Ann., 432.271 to 432.278

Cass Act (Highways)
Ohio Laws, 106, p. 574

Castaic Lake Water Agency Law
Cal. Statutes 1962, 1st Ex Sess., Ch. 28, p.
208
Cal. Statutes 1970, Ch. 443, p. 873

Casual Deficit Act
Ill. Rev. Stat. 1991, Ch. 120, § 405H et seq.

Casual Employment Act
N.J. Stat. Ann., 34:15-36

Casualty and Property Insurance Guaranty Act
See Property and Casualty Insurance
Guaranty Act

Casualty and Property Insurance Rate and Form Act
Neb. Rev. Stat. 1943, 44-5001 et seq.

Casualty and Property Policy Language Simplification Act
Mont. Code Ann., 33-15-333 et seq.

Casualty and Surety Rate Regulatory Act
Ga. Code Ann., 33-9-1 et seq.
Mass. Gen. Laws Ann., 175A:1 et seq.
Minn. Stat. 1967, 70.35 et seq.
Mo. Rev. Stat., 379.420 et seq.
Pa. Purdon's Stat., Title 40, § 1181 et seq.

Casualty Guarantee Association Act
Mich. Comp. Laws Ann., 500.7901 et seq.

Casualty Insurance Act
Ill. Rev. Stat. 1991, Ch. 73, § 990 et seq.
Mich. Comp. Laws Ann., 500.3004 et seq.
Miss. Code Ann., § 83-3-101 et seq.

Casualty Insurance and Property Data Reporting Act
Neb. Rev. Stat. 1943, 44-4601 et seq.

Casualty Insurance Guaranty Association Act
Utah Code Ann. 1953, 31A-28-201 et seq.

Casualty Insurance Policy Simplification Act
Ark. Code Ann. 1987, 23-80-301 et seq.

Casualty Insurer Act (Business Transacted with Broker-Controlled Property)
Wash. Laws 1993, Ch. 462, §§ 16 to 21

Casualty Insurer Act (Business Transacted with Producer Controlled Property)
Fla. Stat. Ann., 626.7491
Ky. Rev. Stat. 1977, 304.3-400c et seq.
Neb. Laws 1992, L.B. 1006, §§ 68 to 75
W. Va. Code 1966 § 33-36-1 et seq.

Casualty Insurer and Business Transacted with Producer Controlled Property Act
Ga. Code Ann., 33-48-1 et seq.
Iowa Code Ann., 510A.1 et seq.
Minn. Stat. Ann., 60J.01 et seq.

Casualty Rating Act (Automobile Insurance)
Va. Code 1950, § 38-247 et seq.

Casualty Rating Act (Insurance)
Mich. Comp. Laws Ann., 500.2400 et seq.
Miss. Code Ann., § 83-3-101 et seq.
Okla. Stat. Ann., Title 36, § 901 et seq.
Wis. Stat. 1975, 204.37 et seq.

Casualty Underwriting Association Act (Commercial)
Md. Ann. Code 1957, Art. 48A, § 598 et seq.

Caswell County Peace Officers' Relief Act
N.C. Laws 1963, Ch. 274

Cat and Dog Humane Death Act
Tenn. Code Ann., 44-17-301 et seq.

Cat and Dog Sterilization Act
Okla. Stat. Ann., Title 4, § 499 et seq.

Catastrophe Prevention Act (Toxic)
N.J. Stat. Ann., 13:1k-19 et seq.

Catastrophe Property Insurance Pool Act
Tex. Insurance Code, Art. 21.49

Catastrophic Deaths Certification Act
P.R. Laws Ann. 1954, Title 24, § 1311 et seq.

Catastrophic Health Care Expense Program
N.Y. Social Services Law (Consol. Laws Ch. 55) § 369a et seq.

Catastrophic Health Expense Protection Act
Minn. Stat. Ann., 62E.51 et seq.

Catastrophic Health Insurance Coverage Act
Colo. Rev. Stat., 10-16-114 to 10-16-117

Catastrophic Health Insurance Plan ("CHIP") Act
R.I. Gen. Laws 1956, 42-62-1 et seq.

Catawba Indian Claims Settlement Act
S.C. Code Ann. 1976, § 27-16-10 et seq.

Catawba Indian Tribe of South Carolina Land Claims Settlement Act of 1993
Oct. 27, 1993, P.L. 103-116, 25 U.S. Code §§ 941 nt., 941 et seq.

Catawba Valley Natural Gas Authority Act
N.C. Laws 1955, Ch. 1267

Catch All Act (Statute of Limitations)
Ohio Rev. Code 1953, 2305.09, Subd. D

Cater Act (Municipal Industrial Development)
Ala. Code 1975, § 11-54-80 et seq.

Cater-Wallace Act (Industrial Development Board)
Ala. Code 1975, § 11-54-80 et seq.

Cates-Gulledge Banking Reform Act
Ala. Code 1975, § 5-1A-1 et seq.

Catfish Marketing Act
Ark. Code Ann. 1987, 20-61-201 et seq.

Catfish Marketing and Consumer Act
Ala. Code 1975, § 2-11-30 et seq.

Catfish Marketing Law
Miss. Code Ann., § 69-7-601 et seq.

Catfish Processor Fair Practices Act
Ark. Code Ann. 1987, 2-6-101 et seq.
Miss. Code Ann., § 69-7-651 et seq.

Catholic School Bus Act
N.Y. Education Law 1947 (Consol. Laws Ch. 16) §§ 1807, 1907, 2021, 3635

Catlin Act (Political Contributions)
Wis. Stat. 1989, 11.26

Catlin Antipicketing Act
Wis. Stat. 1989, 103.535

Catoosa County Public Works Authority Act
Ga. Laws 1998, H.B. 1734

Cattle Act (Texas)
Kan. Stat. Ann., 47-607

Cattle and Beef Promotion Act
Ala. Code 1975, § 2-8-1 et seq.

Cattle Brand Act
Tex. Agriculture Code, § 144.001 et seq.

Cattle Contagious Diseases Act
Ind. Burns' 1933, 16-701 et seq.

Cattle Contagious Diseases Acts
Aug. 30, 1890, Ch. 839, 26 Stat. 416, 21 U.S. Code § 102
Feb. 2, 1903, Ch. 349, 32 Stat. 791, 21 U.S. Code §§ 111 to 113, 120 to 122

March 3, 1905, Ch. 1496, 33 Stat. 1264 (See 18 U.S. Code § 111) 21 U.S. Code §§ 123 to 127
March 4, 1913, Ch. 145, 37 Stat. 831, 21 U.S. Code §§ 151 to 153

Cattle Dipping Act
La. Rev. Stat. Ann., 3:2171 et seq.

Cattle Fever Tick Eradication Act
P.R. Laws Ann. 1954, Title 5, § 741 et seq.

Cattle Guard Act
Kan. Stat. Ann., 66-224 et seq.
Ky. Rev. Stat. 1971, 256.150

Cattle Inspection Act
March 3, 1891, Ch. 555, 26 Stat. 1089

Cattle Restraint Law (Railroads)
Iowa Code Ann., 327G.1 et seq.

Cattle Testing Act
Minn. Stat. Ann., 35.245 et seq.

Cattle Theft Act
La. Rev. Stat. Ann., 14:67.1

Cattle Theft Protection Act
Cal. Statutes 1917, p. 1237

Cattle Tick Act
Fla. Stat. Ann., 585.24 et seq.

Caucus Law (Primaries)
S.D. Laws 1905, Ch. 107

Caustic Alkali or Acid Act
Colo. Stat. Ann. 1935, Ch. 58 § 61 et seq.
Del. Code of 1974, Title 16, § 2301 et seq.
Vt. Stat. Ann., Title 9, § 2821 et seq.
Wis. Stat. 1989, 100.37

Caustic Poison Act
See Federal Caustic Poison Act

Caustic Poisons Act
Miss. Code Ann., § 41-29-1 et seq.
N.Y. Agriculture and Markets Law (Consol. Laws Ch. 9) § 170 et seq.
Wash. Rev. Code Ann., 69.36.010 et seq.

W. Va. Code 1931, Miscellaneous
Superseded Code Provisions, § 16-8-1 et
seq.

Cave Conservation Act
Mont. Code Ann., 23-2-901 et seq.

Cave Creek Canyon Protection Act of 1993
Aug. 2, 1993, P.L. 103-56, 107 Stat. 278

Cave in Rock Township Civic Center Law
Ill. Comp. Stat. 1992, Ch. 720, § 240/1001 et
seq.

Cave Protection Act
Ga. Code Ann., 12-4-140 et seq.
Ill. Comp. Stat. 1992, Ch. 525, § 5/1 et seq.
N.C. Gen. Stat. 1943, § 14-159.20
Pa. Purdon's Stat., Title 32, § 5601 et seq.
Tex. Natural Resources Code, § 201.001 et
seq.

Cave Resources Act
Mo. Rev. Stat., 578.200 et seq.

Caves, Caverns or Sinkholes Act (Protection and Preservation)
P.R. Laws Ann. 1954, Title 12, § 1143 et seq.

Cayuga and Seneca Canal Act
N.Y. Laws 1909, Ch. 391

Cayuga County Water and Sewer Authority Act
N.Y. Public Authorities Law (Consol. Laws
Ch. 43A) § 1199aaaa et seq.

C.C.C. Act
June 28, 1937, Ch. 383, 50 Stat. 319
June 13, 1940, Ch. 348, 54 Stat. 383
Oct. 21, 1940, Ch. 906, 54 Stat. 1206

C.C.C. Extension Act
Aug. 7, 1939, Ch. 553, 53 Stat. 1253

Cedar River Watershed Land Exchange Act of 1992
Oct. 23, 1992, P.L. 102-453, 106 Stat. 2258

Cedar Rust Act
Neb. Laws 1929, Ch. 2

Va. Code 1950, § 3.1-158 et seq.
W. Va. Code 1931, Miscellaneous
Superseded Code Provisions, § 19-12-13 et
seq.

Celery and Sweet Corn Marketing Act
Fla. Stat. Ann., 573.01 et seq.

Celler Act (Liquor Prescriptions)
March 31, 1933, Ch. 18, 48 Stat. 23

Celler Anti-Merger Act
See Anti-Merger Act

Celler-Hennings Act of 1958
Aug. 25, 1958, P.L. 85-752, 72 Stat. 845, 18
U.S. Code §§ 4208, 4209; 28 U.S. Code
§ 334

Celler-Kefauver Act
See Anti-Merger Act

Cellular and Cordless Radio Telephone Privacy Act
Cal. Penal Code § 632.5

Cellular Radio Telephone Privacy Act
Cal. Statutes 1985, Ch. 909

Cellular Telephone Services Act
N.M. Stat. Ann., 63-9B-1 et seq.

Cement Commission Act
S.D. Codified Laws 1967, 5-17-1 et seq.

Cement Producers' License Tax Act
Mont. Code Ann., 15-59-101 et seq.

Cemeteries Perpetual Care Fund Act
Okla. Stat. Ann., Title 8, § 161 et seq.

Cemeteries, Private and Community Mausoleum and Columbarium Law
Cal. Health and Safety Code, § 9501 et seq.

Cemetery Access Road Maintenance Act
Tenn. Public Acts 1993, Ch. 352

Cemetery Act
Ark. Stat. 1947, 82-426.1 et seq.
Cal. Business and Professions Code § 9600 et
seq.
Continued

Cal. Health and Safety Code § 8100 et seq.

Fla. Stat. Ann., 497.001 et seq.

Ga. Code Ann., 44-3-130 et seq.

Ind. Code Ann., 23-14-1-1 et seq.

Ky. Rev. Stat. 1971, Superseded Vols.,
307.100 et seq.

Mass. Gen. Laws Ann., 114:1 et seq.

Md. Ann. Code 1974, Art. BR, § 5-1001 et
seq.

Mich. Comp. Laws Ann., 456.521 et seq.

Miss. Code Ann., § 41-43-31 et seq.

Mont. Code Ann., 35-20-101 et seq.

N.C. Gen. Stat. 1943, § 65-46 et seq.

N.H. Rev. Stat. 1955, 289:1 et seq.

N.J. Stat. Ann., 8A:3-5, 8A:3-7, 8A:3-13

R.I. Gen. Laws 1956, 23-18-1 et seq.

S.C. Code Ann. 1972, § 39-55-15 et seq.

Tenn. Code Ann., 46-1-101 et seq.

Tex. Health and Safety Code, § 711.001 et
seq.

Vt. Stat. Ann., Title 18, § 5301 et seq.

Cemetery Act (Brokers)

Cal. Business and Professions Code, §§ 9600
et seq., 9676

Cemetery Act (Broward Country)

Fla. Special Laws 1967, Ch. 67-1185

Cemetery Act (City)

Mich. Comp. Laws Ann., 128.11 et seq.

Cemetery Act (Endowed Care)

N.M. Stat. Ann., 58-17-1 et seq.

Cemetery Act (Joint)

Ill. Rev. Stat. 1991, Ch. 21, § 21.9 et seq.

Wash. Rev. Code Ann., 68.04.020 et seq.

Wis. Stat. 1989, 157.061 et seq.

Cemetery Act (National)

Ill. Rev. Stat. 1991, Ch. 21, §§ 64.90, 65

Cemetery Act (Public Districts)

Cal. Health and Safety Code § 8890 et seq.

Cemetery Act (Removal)

Cal. Health and Safety Code § 7600 et seq.

Cemetery Act (Rural)

Mich. Comp. Laws Ann., 456.101 et seq.

Cemetery Act (Shelby County)

Tenn. Private Acts 1925, Ch. 405

Cemetery Act (Township)

Ill. Rev. Stat. 1991, Ch. 21, § 3.9 et seq.

**Cemetery Act for Perpetually Maintained
Cemeteries**

Ark. Code Ann. 1987, 20-17-1001 et seq.

Cemetery and Funeral Services Act

Fla. Stat. Ann., 497.001 et seq.

Cemetery and Grave Restoration Act

Ill. Rev. Stat. 1991, Ch. 21, § 60.9 et seq.

**Cemetery Association Land Not Used for
Burial Act**

Ill. Rev. Stat. 1991, Ch. 21, § 7.9 et seq.

Cemetery Associations Act

Ill. Comp. Stat. 1992, Ch. 805, § 320/0.01 et
seq.

Cemetery Care Act

Ill. Comp. Stat. 1992, Ch. 760, § 100/1 et seq.

Cemetery Care Act (County)

Ill. Rev. Stat. 1991, Ch. 21, § 21y et seq.

**Cemetery Company Land Not Used for
Burial Act**

Ill. Comp. Stat. 1992, Ch. 765, §§ 810/0.01,
810/1

Cemetery Corporations Act

Mich. Comp. Laws Ann., 456.1 et seq.

N.Y. Not-for-Profit Corporation Law
(Consol. Laws Ch. 35) § 1401

**Cemetery District Permanent Care and
Improvement Fund Act**

Mont. Code Ann., 7-35-2131 et seq.

Cemetery Districts Act

Mont. Code Ann., 7-35-2101 et seq.

Neb. Rev. Stat. 1943, 12-909 et seq.

Wash. Rev. Code Ann., 68.52.090 et seq.

Cemetery Endowed Care Fund Law
Mo. Rev. Stat., 214.270 et seq.

Cemetery Land Ownership and Transfer Act
Ill. Comp. Stat. 1992, Ch. 765, § 820/0.01 et seq.

Cemetery Maintenance District Act
Ida. Code 1947, 27-101 et seq.
Utah Code Ann. 1953, 8-1-1 et seq.

Cemetery Maintenance District Law
Ill. Comp. Stat. 1992, Ch. 70, § 105/1 et seq.

Cemetery Merchandise and Services Act
Tenn. Code Ann., 46-2-401 et seq.

Cemetery Merchandise Trust Act
Okla. Stat. Ann., Title 8, § 301 et seq.

Cemetery Perpetual Trust Authorization Act
Ill. Comp. Stat. 1992, Ch. 760, § 95/0.01 et seq.

Cemetery Preservation and Consumer Protection Act
Fla. Stat., 497.005 et seq.

Cemetery Protection Act
Ill. Comp. Stat. 1992, Ch. 765, § 835/0.01 et seq.

Cemetery Regulation Act
Mich. Comp. Laws Ann., 456.521 et seq.

Cemetery Removal Act
Ill. Comp. Stat. 1992, Ch. 765, §§ 830/0.01, 830/1

Cemetery Sales Act (Pre-Need)
Ill. Rev. Stat. 1991, Ch. 21, § 201 et seq.

Censorship Act
Mich. Comp. Laws 1948, 750.343
Ohio Rev. Code 1953, 2907.31 et seq.

Censorship Act (Motion Pictures)
Fla. Stat. Ann., 521.01 et seq., 847.011 et seq.

Kan. Laws 1917, Ch. 308
La. Rev. Stat. Ann., 4:301 et seq., 9:5521 et seq.
Md. Ann. Code 1957, Art. 66A, § 1 et seq.
N.Y. Education Law 1947 (Consol. Laws Ch. 16) § 120 et seq.
Ohio Rev. Code 1953, 2907.31 et seq.
Pa. Cons. Stat., Title 18 § 5903
Va. Code 1950, § 2.1-1 et seq.

Census Act (Municipal)
Ala. Code 1975, § 11-47-90 et seq.

Census Acts
Aug. 31, 1954, Ch. 1158, 68 Stat. 1012, 13 U.S. Code §§ 1 to 241; 42 U.S. Code § 244a
Aug. 28, 1957, P.L. 85-207, 71 Stat. 481, 13 U.S. Code §§ 3, 6, 8, 12, 13, 26, 131, 141, 142, 161, 191, 193, 195, 221 to 224, 241
Sept. 13, 1960, P.L. 86-769, 74 Stat. 911, 13 U.S. Code §§ 22 to 24
June 19, 1962, P.L. 87-489, 76 Stat. 104, 13 U.S. Code § 14
Oct. 15, 1962, P.L. 87-813, 76 Stat. 922, 13 U.S. Code § 9
Oct. 15, 1962, P.L. 87-826, 76 Stat. 951, 13 U.S. Code §§ 301 to 307
Aug. 19, 1964, P.L. 88-448, 78 Stat. 492, 13 U.S. Code § 23
Aug. 31, 1964, P.L. 88-530, 78 Stat. 737, 13 U.S. Code § 25
Aug. 31, 1964, P.L. 88-532, 78 Stat. 737, 13 U.S. Code § 131
Aug. 31, 1964, P.L. 88-535, 78 Stat. 744, 13 U.S. Code § 24
Oct. 15, 1971, P.L. 92-143, 85 Stat. 393, 13 U.S. Code § 43
June 30, 1972, P.L. 92-331, 86 Stat. 400, 13 U.S. Code §§ 42, 45
R.I. Gen. Laws 1956, 42-25-1 et seq.

Census Address List Improvement Act of 1994
Oct. 31, 1994, P.L. 103-430, 13 U.S. Code § 1 nt.

Census of Agriculture Act of 1997
Nov. 21, 1997, P.L. 105-113, 7 U.S. Code § 2201 nt.

Centennial Campus Financing Act
N.C. Gen. Stat. 1943, § 116-198.31 et seq.

Centennial Commission Act
Colo. Laws 1957, p. 771, Ch. 251
W. Va. Acts 1959, Ch. 175

Centennial Commission Act (Capital Complex)
Okla. Stat. Ann., Title 73, § 98 et seq.

Centennial of Flight Commemoration Act
Nov. 13, 1998, P.L. 105-389, 112 Stat. 3486, 36 U.S. Code § 143 nt.

Centennial Partnership Act
Wash. Laws 1984, Ch. 231

Centennial Road Act
Mo. Rev. Stat., 226.010 et seq.

Center Authority of Glenn Falls Act
N.Y. Public Authorities Law (Consol. Laws Ch. 43A) § 1930

Center for Business Ownership Succession and Employee Ownership Act
Ill. Comp. Stat. 1992, Ch. 20, § 609/1 et seq.

Center for Cultural and Technical Interchange Between East and West Act of 1960
May 14, 1960, P.L. 86-472, 74 Stat. 141, 22 U.S. Code §§ 2054 to 2057

Center for Cultural and Technical Interchange between North and South Act of 1990
Nov. 5, 1990, P.L. 101-513, 22 U.S. Code § 2075

Center for Forensic Psychiatry Act
Mich. Comp. Laws Ann., 767.27a

Center for the Advancement of Science and Technology Act
Okla. Stat. Ann., Title 74, § 5060.1 et seq.

Center for Voluntary Action Act
Wash. Rev. Code Ann., 43.150.010 et seq.

Center for Volunteerism and Citizens Service Act
Wash. Rev. Code Ann., 43.150.020

Centers for Excellence Act
Utah Code Ann. 1953, 63-62-1 et seq.

Centers of Artistic Excellence Act (Regional)
N.J. Stat. Ann. 52:16A-26.1 et seq.

Central Bering Sea Fisheries Enforcement Act of 1992
Nov. 2, 1992, P.L. 102-582, 16 U.S. Code § 1823 nt.
Nov. 3, 1995, P.L. 104-43, 16 U.S. Code § 1823 nt.

Central Business District Redevelopment Act
Okla. Stat. Ann., Title 11, § 40-101 et seq.

Central Business Improvement District Act
Ark. Code Ann. 1987, 14-184-101 et seq.
Tenn. Code Ann., 7-84-101 et seq., 7-84-501 et seq.

Central Cancer Registry Act
S.C. Code Ann. 1976, § 44-35-10 et seq.

Central City Neighborhood Development Board Act (Orlando)
Fla. Special Laws 1971, Ch. 71-810

Central Colorado River Authority Act
Tex. General Laws 44th Leg., 1935, p. 777, Ch. 338

Central Data Processing Authority Act
Miss. Code Ann., § 25-53-1 et seq.

Central Delta Water Agency Act
Cal. Water Code, Appendix, § 117-1.1 et seq.

Central Disability Resource Directory Act
Mich. Comp. Laws Ann., 395.321 et seq.

Central Falls Minimum Standards Housing Act
R.I. Public Laws 1958, Ch. 56

Central Filing of Effective Financing Statement Act

Colo. Rev. Stat., 4-9.5-101 et seq.

Central Florida Commuter Rail Authority Act

Fla. Stat. Ann., 343.61 et seq.

Central Florida Regional Transportation Authority Act

Fla. Stat. Ann., 343.61 et seq.

Central Idaho Wilderness Act of 1980

July 23, 1980, P.L. 96-312, 16 U.S. Code § 1132 nt.

Nov. 8, 1984, P.L. 98-620, 16 U.S. Code § 3168

Central Intelligence Agency Act of 1949

June 20, 1949, Ch. 227, 63 Stat. 208, 50 U.S. Code §§ 403a to 403j

Aug. 16, 1950, Ch. 719, 64 Stat. 450, 50 U.S. Code § 403i

June 26, 1951, Ch. 151, 65 Stat. 89, 50 U.S. Code § 403f

July 7, 1958, P.L. 85-507, 72 Stat. 337, 50 U.S. Code §§ 403a nts., 403e to 403h, 403j

Sept. 6, 1960, P.L. 86-707, 74 Stat. 795, 798, 800, 801, 50 U.S. Code §§ 403a, 403e

Aug. 19, 1964, P.L. 88-448, 78 Stat. 494, 50 U.S. Code § 403f

Sept. 27, 1982, P.L. 97-269, 50 U.S. Code § 403 nt.

Dec. 9, 1983, P.L. 98-215, 50 U.S. Code § 403f

Oct. 12, 1984, P.L. 98-473

Oct. 27, 1986, P.L. 99-569, 50 U.S. Code §§ 403n, 403p

Dec. 2, 1987, P.L. 100-178, 50 U.S. Code § 403 nt.

Nov. 30, 1989, P.L. 101-193, 50 U.S. Code §§ 403q, 403r, 403s

Oct. 24, 1992, P.L. 102-496, 50 U.S. Code §§ 403n, 403q to 403s

Dec. 3, 1993, P.L. 103-178. 50 U.S. Code §§ 403f, 403g, 403p, 403s

Oct. 14, 1994, P.L. 103-359, 50 U.S. Code §§ 403e, 403q

Jan. 6, 1996, P.L. 104-93, 50 U.S. Code § 403q

Feb. 10, 1996, P.L. 104-106, 50 U.S. Code § 403c nt.

Sept. 30, 1996, P.L. 104-208, 50 U.S. Code § 403h

Oct. 11, 1996, P.L. 104-293, 50 U.S. Code § 403t

Nov. 20, 1997, P.L. 105-107, 50 U.S. Code §§ 403f, 403q, 403o, 403u

Oct. 20, 1998, P.L. 105-272, 50 U.S. Code §§ 403f, 403g, 403q

Central Intelligence Agency Information Act

Oct. 15, 1984, P.L. 98-477, 5 U.S. Code § 522a; 50 U.S. Code §§ 401nt, 431, 431 nt., 432, 432 nt.

Central Intelligence Agency Retirement Act

Aug. 14, 1991, P.L. 102-88, 50 U.S. Code § 403 nts.

Oct. 24, 1992, P.L. 102-496, 50 U.S. Code §§ 2001 et seq., 2001 nt., prec. 2111, 2111 et seq.

Aug. 10, 1993, P.L. 103-66, 50 U.S. Code § 2143

Dec. 3, 1993, P.L. 103-178, 50 U.S. Code §§ 2001, 2011, 2021, 2031, 2032, 2034, 2035, 2051, 2052, 2054, 2071, 2094, 2095, 2131, 2154

Aug. 5, 1997, P.L. 105-33, 50 U.S. Code § 2082

Oct. 20, 1998, P.L. 105-272, 50 U.S. Code § 2011

Central Intelligence Agency Retirement Act of 1964

Oct. 13, 1964, P.L. 88-643, 78 Stat. 1043, 50 U.S. Code § 403 nt.

Sept. 30, 1968, P.L. 90-539, 82 Stat. 902, 50 U.S. Code § 403 nt.

Dec. 30, 1969, P.L. 91-185, 83 Stat. 847, 50 U.S. Code § 403 nt.

Dec. 31, 1970, P.L. 91-626, 84 Stat. 1872 to 1874, 50 U.S. Code § 403 nts.

Oct. 17, 1976, P.L. 94-522, 50 U.S. Code § 403 et seq.

June 16, 1978, P.L. 95-295, 16 U.S. Code § 758e et seq.

Sept. 27, 1982, P.L. 97-269, 50 U.S. Code § 503 nt.

Dec. 4, 1985, P.L. 99-169, 50 U.S. Code § 403 nt.

Continued

June 6, 1986, P.L. 99-335, 50 U.S. Code
§ 403 nt.

Oct. 27, 1986, P.L. 99-569, 50 U.S. Code
§ 403 nt.

Dec. 2, 1987, P.L. 100-178, 50 U.S. Code
§ 403 nt.

Nov. 30, 1989, P.L. 101-193, 50 U.S. Code
§ 403 nt.

**Central Intelligence Agency Retirement Act
of 1964 for Certain Employees**

See Central Intelligence Agency Retirement
Act

**Central Intelligence Agency Spouses'
Retirement Equity Act of 1982**

Sept. 27, 1982, P.L. 97-269, 50 U.S. Code
§ 403 nt.

**Central Intelligence Agency Voluntary
Separation Pay Act**

June 8, 1993, P.L. 103-36, 50 U.S. Code
§§ 403-4 nt., 2001 nt., 2053

Jan. 6, 1996, P.L. 104-93, 50 U.S. Code
§ 403-4 nt.

Oct. 11, 1996, P.L. 104-293, 50 U.S. Code
§ 403-4 nt.

**Central Interstate Low-Level Radioactive
Waste Compact Act**

Jan. 15, 1986, P.L. 99-240, 99 Stat. 1863

Ark. Code Ann. 1987, 8-8-202 et seq.

Kan. Stat. Ann., 65-34a01

La. Rev. Stat. Ann., 30:1117 et seq.

Neb. Laws 1983, L.B. 200

Okla. Stat. Ann., Title 63, § 1-2101 et seq.

**Central Midwest Interstate Low-Level
Radioactive Waste Compact**

Jan. 15, 1986, P.L. 99-240, 99 Stat. 1880

Ill. Comp. Stat. 1992, Ch. 45, §§ 140/0.01,
140/1

Ky. Rev. Stat., 211.859

**Central Midwest Interstate Low-Level
Radioactive Waste Compact
Amendments Consent Act of 1994**

Nov. 2, 1994, P.L. 103-439, 42 U.S. Code
§ 2021d nt.

**Central Nervous System Stimulant
Barbiturate and Hallucinogenic Drug
Act**

La. Acts 1952, No. 96

R.I. Gen. Laws 1956, 21-28-1.01 et seq.

Central Nevada Resource Development Act

Nev. Statutes 1969, Ch. 615, p. 1180

**Central New York Regional Market
Authority Act**

N.Y. Public Authorities Law (Consol. Laws
Ch. 43A) § 825 et seq.

**Central New York Regional Transportation
Authority Act**

N.Y. Public Authorities Law (Consol. Laws
Ch. 43A) § 1325 et seq.

Central Pinellas Transit Authority Law

Fla. Special Laws 1970, Ch. 70-907

Central Purchasing Act

Ala. Code 1975, § 41-4-110 et seq.

Okla. Stat. Ann., Title 74, § 85.1 et seq.

Central Railroad Tax Act

Ill. Comp. Stat. 1992, Ch. 35, §§ 605/1,
605/18, 605/22

Ill. Rev. Stat. 1991, Ch. 120, § 372.90 et seq.

Central Register for Missing Children

Mass. Gen. Laws Ann., 22A:1 et seq.

Central Registry Act

Ill. Rev. Stat. 1975, Ch. 40, § 21.3 (Divorces)

Ill. Rev. Stat. 1991, Ch. 40, §§ 210, 211
(Marriages)

Central Statistical Act

July 25, 1935, Ch. 416, 49 Stat. 498

Central Utah Project Completion Act

Oct. 30, 1992, P.L. 102-575, 106 Stat. 4605

Central Valley Project Improvement Act

Oct. 30, 1992, P.L. 102-575, 106 Stat. 4706

Central Valley Project Law

Cal. Water Code § 11100 et seq.

Central, Western, and South Pacific Fisheries Development Act
Sept. 29, 1972, P.L. 92-444, 86 Stat. 744, 16 U.S. Code § 758a nt.
April 21, 1976, P.L. 94-273, 90 Stat. 375, 16 U.S. Code § 758a nt.
July 6, 1976, P.L. 94-343, 90 Stat. 809, 16 U.S. Code §§ 758e, 758e-1, 758e-1a, 758e-2 to 758e-5
Jan. 12, 1983, P.L. 97-453, 16 U.S. Code § 758e-5
Oct. 19, 1984, P.L. 98-498, 16 U.S. Code § 758e
Aug. 22, 1986, P.L. 99-386, 16 U.S. Code § 758e-2
Nov. 14, 1986, P.L. 99-659, 16 U.S. Code § 758e-5
Nov. 28, 1990, P.L. 101-627, 16 U.S. Code § 758e-5

Centralized Support Registry Act
Okla. Stat. Ann., Title 43, § 410 et seq.

Centre East Civic Center Act
Dec. 11, 1980, P.L. 96-510, 94 Stat. 2767
Ill. Comp. Stat. 1992, Ch. 70, § 270/5-1 et seq.

CERCLA
See Comprehensive Environmental Response, Compensation, and Liability Act of 1980

Cereal Malt Beverage Act
Kan. Stat. Ann., 41-2701 et seq.

Cereal Malt Beverages and Malt Products Tax Act
Kan. Stat. Ann., 79-3817 et seq.

Cerebral Palsy Act
Ga. Code 1933, 99-1801 et seq.

Certificate Act (Revenue)
Ga. Code Ann., 36-82-60 et seq.
La. Rev.Stat. Ann., 17:2131 et seq.

Certificate-holders' Relief Act (State School Lands)
Cal. Statutes 1941, p. 2484

Certificate of Approval Holder and Maine Wholesale Licensee Agreement Act
Me. Rev. Stat. Ann. 1964, Title 28-A, § 1451 et seq.

Certificate of Approval Holder and Wholesale Licensee Agreement Act
Me. Rev. Stat. Ann. 1964, Title 28-A, § 1451 et seq.

Certificate of Competency Act (Miners)
Okla. Stat. Ann., Title 45, § 391 et seq.

Certificate of Judgment Act
Ohio Rev. Code 1953, 2329.02

Certificate of Legal Questions Act
Me. Rev. Stat. Ann. 1964, Title 4, § 57

Certificate of Need Act
D.C. Code 1973, § 32-302 et seq.
Ky. Rev. Stat. 1971, 216B.015 et seq.
Me. Rev. Stat. Ann. 1964 Title 22, § 301 et seq.
Minn. Stat. 1982, 145.832 et seq.
Mo. Rev. Stat., 197.300 et seq.
Neb. Rev. Stat. 1943, 71-5801 et seq.
N.M. Stat. Laws 1978, 24-3A-1 et seq.
Okla. Stat. Ann., Title 63, § 1-850 et seq.
S.D. Codified Laws 1967, 34-7A-1 et seq.

Certificate of Need Act (Psychiatric and Chemical Dependency)
Okla. Stat. Ann., Title 63, § 1-880.1 et seq.

Certificate of Obligation Act
Tex. Local Government Code, § 271.041 et seq.

Certificate of Origin Act (Motor Vehicles)
Colo. Rev. Stat., 42-6-111

Certificate of Public Necessity Act
Colo. Rev. Stat., 25-3-501 et seq.

Certificate of Title Act (Motor Vehicle)
See Motor Vehicle Certificate of Title Act
Colo. Rev. Stat., 42-6-101 to 42-6-143

Certificate of Title and Anti-Theft Act (Motor Vehicles)
See Motor Vehicle Certificate of Title and Anti-Theft Act

Certificate Plan Act
Tex. Rev. Civ. Stat. 1925, Art. 342-1101 et seq.

Certificate Procedure Act (Federal Court Local Law)
Wash. Rev. Code Ann., 2.60.010

Certificate Training Program Act (County Officials)
Tenn. Code Ann., 5-1-301 et seq.

Certificated Carrier Law
Iowa Code Ann., 325.1 et seq.

Certificated Carrier Tax Law
Iowa Code 1966, 326.1 et seq.

Certificated Personnel Performance Evaluation Act
Colo. Rev. Stat., 22-9-101 et seq.

Certificated Staff Performance Incentive Act
Cal. Education Code 1976, § 44650 et seq.

Certificates of Delinquency Act (Taxation)
Wash. Rev. Code Ann., 84.64.010 et seq.

Certificates of Public Convenience and Necessity Act
Miss. Code Ann., § 77-3-1 et seq.

Certification Act (Appeals)
W. Va. Code 1966, § 58-5-2

Certification Act (Catastrophic Deaths)
P.R. Laws Ann. 1954, Title 24, § 1311 et seq.

Certification Act (Electric Transmission Line)
Mich. Comp. Laws Ann., 460.561 et seq.

Certification Act (Food Employee)
Pa. Purdon's Stat., Title 3, § 6501 et seq.

Certification Act (Lead)
Pa. Purdon's Stat., Title 35, § 5901 et seq.

Certification Act (Liabilities)
Mass. Gen. Laws Ann., 78:22 et seq.

Certification Act (Librarians)
Mass. Gen. Laws Ann., 78:22

Certification Act (Private Occupational)
Conn. Gen. Stat. Ann., § 10-7a et seq.

Certification Act (Radiologic Technologist)
Fla. Stat. Ann., 468.3001 et seq.
Wash. Rev. Code Ann., 18.84.010 et seq.

Certification Act (State Law)
Fla. Stat. 1983, 25.031

Certification Act (Therapeutic Recreation Personnel)
N.C. Gen. Stat. 1943, § 90C-1 et seq.

Certification Act (Utility Operators)
N.M. Stat. Ann., 61-33-1 et seq.

Certification Act (Water and Wastewater Operators)
Fla. Stat. Ann., 468.540 et seq.

Certification and Licensing Act (Appraiser)
Tex. Rev. Civ. Stat., Art. 6573a.2

Certification and Licensing Act (Psychologists')
Tex. Rev. Civ. Stat., Art. 4512c

Certification and Licensing Act (Real Estate Appraiser)
Miss. Gen. Laws 1990, Ch. 576, p. 872
W. Va. Code 1966 § 37-14-1 et seq.

Certification Compact (Interstate)
Conn. Gen. Stat. Ann., § 10-146-C et seq.

Certification, License and Real Estate Appraiser Registration Act
S.C. Code Ann. 1976, § 40-60-10 et seq.

Certification of Psychologists Act
Kan. Stat. Ann., 74-5301 et seq.

Certification of Questions of Law Act
See Uniform Certification of Questions of Law Act

Certification of Real Estate Appraisers Act
Pa. Purdon's Stat., Title 63, § 457.1 et seq.

Certification of Teachers Act
Colo. Rev. Stat., 22-60-101 et seq.
Ill. Rev. Stat. 1991, Ch. 122, § 21-1 et seq.

Certification of Water and Wastewater Treatment Plant Operators and Laboratory Analysts Act
Ga. Code Ann., 43-51-1 et seq.

Certified Capital Company Act
Fla. Stat., 288.99
Ind. Code Ann., 27-14-1-1 et seq.

Certified Capital Company Law
Mo. Rev. Stat. Ann., 135.500 to 135.529

Certified Cottonseed Law
Cal. Agricultural Code 1933, §§ 931 et seq., 52851 et seq.

Certified Farm Land Act
Mich. Public Acts 1923, No. 292

Certified Industrial Hygienist Title Protection Act
Neb. Rev. Stat. 1943, 71-8001 to 71-8008

Certified Interior Designers Act
Md. Ann. Code 1974, Art. BO, § 8-101 et seq.

Certified Master Teacher Law
Cal. Education Code 1976, § 44490 et seq.

Certified Nurse Midwifery Practice Act
Neb. Laws 1984, L.B. 761, §§ 1 to 28
Neb. Rev. Stat. 1943, 71-1738 et seq.

Certified Process Server Act
Cal. Business and Professions Code § 22350 et seq.
Fla. Stat. 1983, 48.25 et seq.

Certified Professional Midwifery Act
Ga. Code Ann., 31-26-1 et seq.

Certified Public Accountant Education Minority Assistance Program
Fla. Stat., 473.3065

Certified Public Accountants Act
Cal. Business and Professions Code §§ 5000 et seq., 5090 et seq.
D.C. Code Ann., § 2-107 et seq.
Ind. Code Ann., 25-2-1-1 et seq.
Mich. Comp. Laws Ann., 339.701 et seq.
N.Y. Education Law 1947 (Consol. Laws Ch. 16) § 7401 et seq.
Okla. Stat. Ann., Title 59, § 15.1 et seq.
Pa. Purdon's Stat., Title 63, § 9.1 et seq.
Utah Code Ann. 1953, 58-26-1 et seq.
W. Va. Code 1966, § 30-9-1 et seq.
Wyo. Stat. Ann., § 33-3-101 et seq.

Certified Public Accountants Professional Corporation Act
Minn. Stat. Ann., 319A.01 et seq.

Certified Public Weigher Law
Ga. Code Ann., 10-2-40 et seq.
Tenn. Code Ann., 47-26-801 et seq.

Certified Real Estate Appraisers Act
Ida. Code 1947, 54-4101 et seq.
La. Rev. Stat. Ann., 37:3391 et seq.
Okla. Stat. Ann., Title 59, § 858-700 et seq.
Tenn. Code Ann., 62-39-101 et seq.
Wash. Rev. Code Ann., 18.140.900 et seq.
Wash. Rev. Code 1989, 140.005 et seq.
Wyo. Stat. Ann., § 33-39-101 et seq.

Certified School Personnel Act
N.M. Stat. Ann., 22-10-1 et seq.

Certified School to Career Program
Iowa Code 1983, 15.361 to 15.367

Certified Seed Act
Fla. Stat. Ann., 575.01 et seq.
Kan. Stat. Ann., 2-1429 et seq.
La. Rev. Stat. Ann., 3:1431 et seq.
Continued

Me. Rev. Stat. Ann. 1964, Title 7, § 2101 et seq.

Okla. Stat. Ann., Title 2, § 788.1 et seq.

Pa. Purdon's Stat., Title 3, § 291 et seq.

Certified Shorthand Reporters Act

Ida. Code 1947, 54-3101 et seq.

Ill. Comp. Stat. 1992, Ch. 225, § 415/1 et seq.

Nev. Rev. Stat. 1973 Reprint, 656.010 et seq.

Certified Stress Analyst Act

La. Rev. Stat. Ann., 37:2861 et seq.

Certified Territory Law (Unincorporated Area)

Pa. Cons. Stat., Title 15, § 7351 et seq.

Certiorari Act

Mont. Code Ann., 27-25-101 et seq.

N.J. Stat. Ann., Superseded Vol., 2:81-1 et seq.

P.R. Laws Ann. 1954, Title 32, § 3491 et seq.

Wash. Rev. Code Ann., 7.16.010 et seq.

Cervical and Breast Cancer Prevention and Control Act

W. Va. Code 1966 § 16-33-1 et seq.

Cession Act

Ga. Code Ann., 50-2-22 et seq.

Ind. Code Ann., 4-21-1-1, 4-21-1-2

N.C. Laws 1789, Ch. 3

Cession Act (District of Columbia)

Md. Laws 1791, Ch. 45, § 2

Cession Act (Federal Enclaves)

Va. Code 1950, §§ 7.1-12, 7.1-18.1 et seq.

Cession Act (Federal Lands)

S.C. Code Ann. 1976, § 3-1-110 et seq.

Cessions Act (Jurisdiction)

Ohio Rev. Code 1953, 159.04 et seq.

CFTC Reauthorization Act of 1995

April 21, 1995, P.L. 104-9, 7 U.S. Code § 1 nt.

Chacoan Outliers Protection Act of 1995

May 18, 1995, P.L. 104-11, 16 U.S. Code § 410ii nt.

Chacon-Moscone Bilingual-Bicultural Education Act

Cal. Education Code 1959, § 5767 et seq.

Cal. Education Code 1977, § 52160 et seq.

Chacon-Zenovich-Moscone Housing and Home Finance Act

Cal. Health and Safety Code § 50000 et seq.

Chain Dam Hydroelectric Facility Leasing Act

Pa. Purdon's Stat., Title 32, § 629.1 et seq.

Chain O Lakes—Fox River Waterway Management Agency Act

Ill. Rev. Stat. 1991, Ch. 19, § 1201 et seq.

Chain of Rocks Retrocession Act

Ill. Comp. Stat. 1992, Ch. 5, §§ 565/0.01, 565/1

Chain Store Act

See Robinson-Patman Price Discrimination Act

Colo. Rev. Stat., 12-49-101 et seq.

Fla. Stat. 1965, 204.01 et seq.

Ind. Burns' 1965 Repl., 42-301 et seq.

Chain Store License Fee Act

Md. Ann. Code 1974, Art. BR, § 17-1805

Chain Store Liquor License Act

N.J. Stat. Ann., 33:1-12.31 et seq.

Chain Store Tax Act

Ala. Code 1975, § 40-12-310 et seq.

Ida. Code 1947, Superseded Vol., 63-2401 et seq.

Iowa Code 1979, 424.1 et seq.

La. Rev. Stat. Ann., 47:10 et seq.

Mich. Comp. Laws 1948, 205.401 et seq.

Mont. Code Ann. 1989, 15-57-101 et seq.

S.C. Code Ann. 1976, § 12-35-310 et seq.

Tex. Taxation-General 1959, Art. 17.01 et seq.

W. Va. Code 1966, § 11-13A-1 et seq.

Challenge Act (Voter Registration)
La. Rev. Stat. Ann., 18:196

Challenge Grant Program for the Gifted
Fla. Stat. Ann., 236.1225

Challenge Grants Act (Rhode Island)
R.I. Gen. Laws 1956, 16-72-1 et seq.

Challenge to Secondary School Pupils Act
Kan. Stat. Ann., 72-11a01 et seq.

Chamberlain-Ferris Act
June 9, 1916, Ch. 137, 39 Stat. 218

Chambers County-Cedar Bayou Navigation District Act
Tex. General and Special Laws 1997, Ch. 589

Champaign Land Cession Act
Ill. Comp. Stat. 1992, Ch. 5, §§ 525/0.01, 525/01
Ill. Rev. Stat. 1991, Ch. 1, §§ 3850, 3851

Champerty and Maintenance Act
Ky. Rev. Stat. 1971, 372.060 et seq.
Miss. Code Ann., § 97-9-11 et seq.
Okla. Stat. Ann., Title 21, § 547 et seq.
Tenn. Code Ann., 66-4-201 et seq.
Tex. Penal Code, § 38.12

Champlain Basin Compact
N.Y. Environmental Conservation Law 1972 (Consol. Laws Ch. 43B) § 21-1101 et seq.
Vt. Stat. Ann., Title 10, § 181 et seq.

Chancellor-Sheriff Jury Act
N.J. Stat. Ann., 2A:68-1, 2A:68-11, 2A:68-13, 2A:69-4, 2A:70-1 et seq., 2A:71-1 et seq., 2A:71-7, 2A:71-9, 2A:71-14, 2A:72-1, 2A:73-1, 2A:28-1

Chancellors Act (University)
Ill. Rev. Stat. 1991, Ch. 144, §§ 5m, 6

Chancery Act
Fla. Stat. 1965, 62.01 et seq.
Ill. Rev. Stat. 1985, Ch. 110, § 355 et seq.
Md. Ann. Code 1957, Art. 16

Miss. Code Ann., § 9-5-3 et seq.
N.J. Stat. Ann., 3B:1-2 et seq.
Ohio Laws Vol. 22, p. 75

Chancery Attachment Act
Miss. Code Ann., § 11-31-1 et seq.

Chandler Act, Bankruptcy Revision
June 22, 1938, Ch. 575, 52 Stat. 840

Chandler-Connelly-Areias Rice Straw Burning Reduction Act
Cal. Health and Safety Code § 41865

Chandler Rail Bankruptcy Act
July 28, 1939, Ch. 393, 53 Stat. 1134

Change in Bank Control Act of 1978
Nov. 10, 1978, P.L. 95-630, 12 U.S. Code § 1817

Change in Savings and Loan Control Act of 1978
Nov. 10, 1978, P.L. 95-630, 12 U.S. Code § 1730

Change of Corporate Limits Act
S.C. Code Ann. 1976, § 5-3-10 et seq.

Change of Grade Act
Cal. Streets and Highways Code § 8000 et seq.
Kan. Laws 1903, Ch. 122, § 156

Change of Name Act
N.C. Gen. Stat. 1943, §§ 48-29, 48-36
Okla. Stat. Ann., Title 12, § 1631 et seq.
Tex. Family Code, § 32.01 et seq.
Vt. Stat. Ann., Title 15, § 811 et seq.
Wash. Rev. Code Ann., 4.24.130
W. Va. Code 1966, § 48-5-1 et seq.

Change of Venue Act
Fla. Stat. Ann., 47.011 et seq.
Ill. Rev. Stat. 1991, Ch. 110, § 2-101 et seq.
Ind. Code Ann., 34-1-13-1 et seq.
Miss. Code Ann., § 11-11-51 et seq.
N.C. Gen. Stat. 1943, § 1-83
Tex. Rules of Civil Procedure as am. 1984, Rules 255 to 261
Continued

Vt. Stat. Ann., Title 13, § 4631 et seq.
Wash. Rev. Code Ann., 4.12.030

Change of Venue Act (Criminal)
Miss. Code Ann., § 99-15-35 et seq.
Wash. Rev. Code Ann., 10.25.070 et seq.

Change Ticket Act
Ark. Code Ann. 1987, 4-17-102 et seq.

Channel Encroachment Act (Floodways)
Conn. Gen. Stat. Ann., § 22a-342 et seq.
Ill. Rev. Stat. 1991, Ch. 19, § 70 et seq.
Ind. Code Ann., 13-2-22-1 et seq.
Iowa Code Ann., 455.275 et seq.
Ky. Rev. Stat. 1962, 104.390 et seq.
Md. Ann. Code 1974, Art. NR, § 8-803 et
seq.

Channel Encroachment Act (Waterways)
Mass. Gen. Laws Ann., 91:12A
N.J. Stat. Ann., 58:16A-52, 58:16A-55

Channeling Act (Airports)
Ind. Code Ann., 8-21-8-1

Chanute Air Force Base Retrocession Law
Ill. Comp. Stat. 1992, Ch. 5, § 537/5-1 et seq.

Chaplains Day Act
Ill. Comp. Stat. 1992, Ch. 5, § 490/20

Chapman Act (Beverly)
Fla. Stat. Ann., 338.155

**Chappie-Gregorio Off-Highway Gas Tax
Act**
Cal. Revenue and Taxation Code §§ 8101,
8352, 8352.6
Cal. Statutes 1972, Ch. 1382, p. 2870
Cal. Statutes 1972, Ch. 1405, p. 2928

**Chappie James Most Promising Teacher
Scholarship Act**
Fla. Stat. Ann., 240.4068

**Chappie-Z'berg Off-Highway Motor
Vehicle Act**
Cal. Vehicle Code § 38000 et seq.

Charge Account Act (Revolving)
S.C. Code Ann. 1976, § 37-2-207 et seq.

Chariho Regional School District Act
R.I. Public Laws 1958, Ch. 55, § 20
R.I. Public Laws 1992, Ch. 479

**Charitable and Religious Risk Pooling Trust
Act**
Ill. Rev. Stat. 1991, Ch. 148, § 201 et seq.

**Charitable Assistance and Food Bank Act of
1987**
Jan. 5, 1988, P.L. 100-232, 7 U.S. Code
§§ 2011 nt., 2014, 2014 nt.
Aug. 22, 1996, P.L. 104-193, 7 U.S. Code
§ 612c nt.

Charitable Bingo Law
Miss. Code Ann., § 97-33-50 et seq.

**Charitable Campaign Act (Public
Employees)**
P.R. Laws Ann. 1954, Title 3, § 2051 et seq.

**Charitable Campaign Act (State Employee
Combined)**
Ala. Code 1975, § 36-1A-1 et seq.

Charitable Contribution Act
Del. Code of 1974, Title 12, § 3710

**Charitable Contribution Act (State
Employee)**
Okla. Stat. Ann., Title 74, § 7001 et seq.

**Charitable Contributions Act (Corpora-
tions)**
Ind. Code Ann., 23-15-5-1

Charitable Corporations Act
Mass. Gen. Laws Ann., 180:1 et seq.
Nev. Rev. Stat. Ann., 81.550 et seq.
Ore. Rev. Stat. 1953, 61.005 et seq.

**Charitable Donation Antitrust Immunity
Act of 1997**
July 3, 1997, P.L. 105-26, 15 U.S. Code § 1
nt.

Charitable Fund Raising Act (Public Employees)
N.J. Stat. Ann., 52:14-15.9cl et seq.

Charitable Funds Solicitation Act
See Solicitation of Charitable Funds Act

Charitable Gift Annuity Act
Neb. Rev. Stat. 1943, 59-1801 to 59-1803

Charitable Gift Annuity Antitrust Relief Act of 1995
Dec. 8, 1995, P.L. 104-63, 15 U.S. Code §§ 1 nt., 37, 37a
July 3, 1997, P.L. 105-26, 15 U.S. Code §§ 37, 37a

Charitable Gift Annuity Exemption Act
Pa. Purdon's Stat., Title 10, § 361 et seq.

Charitable Health Care Services Act
Ky. Rev. Stat. 1971, 216.940 to 216.944

Charitable Hospitals Act (Labor Relations)
Minn. Stat. Ann., 179.35 et seq.

Charitable Immunity Act
N.J. Stat. Ann., 2A:53A-7 et seq.
S.C. Code Ann. 1976, § 15-3-530 et seq.

Charitable Immunity and Liability Act
Tex. Civil Practice and Remedies Code, § 84.001 et seq.

Charitable Instruments Act
Pa. Purdon's Stat., Title 10, § 201 et seq.

Charitable Organization Reform Act
Mo. Rev. Stat., 407.450 et seq.
Pa. Purdon's Stat., Title 10, § 161.1 et seq.

Charitable Organizations and Solicitations Act
Kan. Stat. Ann., 17-1759 et seq.
Mich. Comp. Laws Ann., 400.271 et seq.

Charitable Purposes Act (Solicitation of Funds)
Pa. Purdon's Stat., Title 10, § 162.1 et seq.

Charitable Raffle and Gambling Enabling Act
Tex. Rev. Civ. Stat., Art. 179f

Charitable Raffle Boards and Games Act
W. Va. Code 1966, § 47-23-1 et seq.

Charitable Raffles, Bingo and Keno Licensing Law
La. Rev. Stat. Ann., 33:4861.1 et seq.

Charitable Registration and Investigation Act
N.J. Stat. Ann., 45:17A-18 et seq.

Charitable Remainder Trusts Administration Act
Ill. Rev. Stat. 1991, Ch. 32, §§ 200.9, 201
N.C. Gen. Stat. 1943, § 36A-59.1

Charitable Solicitation Reform Act
Tenn. Code Ann., 48-3-501, 48-3-503 to 48-3-507, 48-3-509, 48-3-511 to 48-3-514, 48-3-518, 48-3-520

Charitable Solicitations Act
See Solicitation of Charitable Funds Act
Md. Ann. Code 1974, Art. BR, § 6-701 et seq.

Charitable Trust and Solicitation Act
Ore. Rev. Stat., 128.801

Charitable Trust Tax Law Conformance Act
Ill. Comp. Stat. 1992, Ch. 760, § 60/0.01 et seq.

Charitable Trustees Powers Act
Mich. Comp. Laws 1948, 14.271 et seq.

Charitable Trusts Act
Cal. Government Code § 12580 et seq.
Fla. Stat. 1973, 691.10 et seq.
Ga. Code Ann., 53-12-90 et seq.
Ill. Comp. Stat. 1992, Ch. 760, § 55/1 et seq.
La. Rev. Stat. Ann., 9:2271 et seq.
Mass. Gen. Laws Ann., 12:8 et seq.
Md. Ann. Code 1974, Art. ET, § 14-302
Mich. Comp. Laws Ann., 554.351 et seq.
Minn. Stat. 1986, 501.12
Continued

N.C. Gen. Stat. 1943, § 36A-53
Nev. Rev. Stat. 1973 Reprint, 163.420 et seq.
N.H. Rev. Stat. 1955, 7:19 et seq.
N.J. Stat. Ann., 3B:11-8 et seq.
N.Y. Estates, Powers and Trusts Law
  (Consol. Laws Ch. 17B) § 8-1.1 et seq.
Ohio Rev. Code 1953, 1719.01 et seq.
R.I. Gen. Laws 1956, 18-9-1 et seq.
Utah Code Ann. 1953, 59-18-101 et seq.
Wis. Stat. 1989, 701.10

**Charitable Trusts and Trustees Act
(Supervision of)**
Minn. Stat. Ann., 501B.33 et seq.

**Charitable Trusts and Trustees Supervision
Act**
Minn. Stat. Ann., 501.71 et seq.

Charitable Trusts and Uses Act
N.Y. Estates, Powers, and Trusts Law
  (Consol. Laws Ch. 17B), § 8-1.1 et seq.

Charitable Trusts, Devises and Bequests Act
Vt. Stat. Ann., Title 14, § 2328

Charitable Use of Gifts to State Act
Ill. Rev. Stat. 1991, Ch. 23, §§ 4000, 4001

Charitable Uses Act
Conn. Gen. Stat. Ann., § 47-2
N.Y. Estates, Powers and Trusts Law
  (Consol. Laws Ch. 17B) § 8-1.1

Charitable—Fraternal Solicitation Act
Del. Code of 1974, Title 6, § 2591 et seq.

Charities Act
Pa. 1855 Pamph. Laws 328, No. 347

Charities and Corrections Act
N.J. Stat. Ann., 30:1B-21

Charities and Public Welfare Act
Ill. Rev. Stat. 1991, Ch. 23

Charity Act (Racing Profits)
Fla. Stat. Ann., 550.03

Charity Begins at Home Act
Iowa Code Ann., 633.266

Charity Games Act
Ill. Comp. Stat. 1992, Ch. 230, § 30/1 et seq.
Okla. Stat. Ann., Title 3A, § 401 et seq.

**Charity Games Advertising Clarification
Act of 1988**
Nov. 7, 1988, P.L. 100-625, 18 U.S. Code
  § 1301 nt.

Charity Hospital Act (State)
Miss. Code Ann., § 41-11-1 et seq.

Charity Limitation Act
Cal. Probate Code § 40 et seq.

Charlemont School Addition Loan Act
Mass. Acts 1948, Ch. 212

Charles Brown Fish and Game Act
Cal. Fish and Game Code 1957, § 1 et seq.

**Charles Brown Fish and Game Reorgani-
zation Act**
Cal. Statutes 1951, Ch. 715, p. 1979

Charles County Freedom of Information Act
Md. Ann. Code 1957, Art. 24, § 5-101

**Charles Lazzaretto Peace Officer Widows
and Widowers Protection Act**
Cal. Government Code § 823

Charles River Basin Improvement Loan Act
Mass. Acts 1957, Ch. 646
Mass. Acts 1962, Ch. 550

Charles River Flood Control Act
Mass. Acts 1955, Ch. 768

Charleston County School Budget Act
S.C. Code Ann. 1962, § 21-1662

Charlestown Charter Validation Act
R.I. Public Laws 1991, Ch. 15

**Charlie Mack Overstreet Brain or Spinal
Cord Injuries Act**
Fla. Stat., 413.465 et seq.

Charlotte Annexation Act
N.Y. Laws 1915, Ch. 359, § 4 et seq.

Charlotte Firefighters' Retirement System Act
N.C. Laws 1991, Ch. 506

Charlton Mobile Home Parks and Trailer Camps Law
N.Y. Local Laws 1969, Town of Charlton, p. 990

Charter Act
Pa. Purdon's Stat., Title 53, § 22181 et seq.
Wis. Stat. 1989, 62.01 et seq.

Charter Act (County)
Mich. Comp. Laws Ann., 45.501 et seq.
N.Y. Municipal Home Rule Law (Consol. Laws Ch. 36A) § 1 et seq.

Charter Act (First Class Cities)
Pa. Purdon's Stat., Title 53, § 12101 et seq.

Charter Act (First Class Corporations)
Pa. 1923 Pamph. Laws 246, No. 160

Charter Act (Home Rule)
Pa. Purdon's Stat., Title 53, § 13101 et seq.

Charter Act (Livestock Market)
La. Rev. Stat. Ann., 3:661 et seq.

Charter Act (Municipal Corporations)
Md. Ann. Code 1957, Art. 23B

Charter Amendments Procedures Act
D.C. Laws 1977, No. 2-15

Charter and Livery Boat Safety Act
Mich. Comp. Laws Ann., 281.571 et seq.

Charter Boat Safety Act
Cal. Harbors and Navigation Code § 773 et seq.
Wash. Rev. Code Ann., 88.04.005 et seq.

Charter Commission Act
Ga. Laws 1969, p. 3571 (Muscogee County)
Ga. Laws 1974, p. 2324 (Augusta-Richmond County)
Ga. Laws 1983, p. 3590 (Tifton-Tift County)

Ga. Laws 1986, p. 3609 (Lakeland-Lanier County)
Ga. Laws 1988, p. 3899 (Conyers-Rockdale County)
Ga. Laws 1991, p. 4297 (Douglasville-Douglas County)

Charter Day Act
Pa. Purdon's Stat., Title 44, § 28

Charter Expense Law
Cal. Government Code § 34091

Charter for Alachua County
Fla. Special Laws 1976, Ch. 76-322

Charter for the Unified Government of Gainesville and Alachua County
Fla. Special Laws 1975, Ch. 75-376

Charter Law (County)
N.Y. Municipal Home Rule Law (Consol. Laws Ch. 36A) § 30 et seq.

Charter Municipality Tax Act
N.M. Laws 1971, Ch. 208

Charter of Chautauqua County
N.Y. Local Laws 1973, County of Chautauqua, p. 946

Charter of Elkton
Tenn. Private Acts 1972, Ch. 296

Charter of Geneva City
N.Y. Local Laws 1973, City of Geneva, p. 69

Charter of Montville Township
N.J. Laws 1974, Ch. 95

Charter of Pensacola-Escambia
Fla. Special Laws 1970, Ch. 70-681

Charter of Rensselaer County
N.Y. Local Laws 1972, County of Rensselaer, p. 777

Charter of Rossville
Tenn. Private Acts 1972, Ch. 289

Charter of Suffolk County
N.Y. Laws 1958, Ch. 278

Charter of Tampa—Hillsborough County
Fla. Special Laws 1970, Ch. 70-724

Charter of the City of Jacksonville
Fla. Special Laws 1967, Ch. 67-1320

Charter of the City of Kingston
Tenn. Private Acts 1972, Ch. 298

Charter of the City of Port Jervis
N.Y. Local Laws 1973, City of Port Jervis, p. 636

Charter of the City of Raleigh
N.C. Laws 1949, Ch. 1184

Charter of the Consolidated Government of the City of Fort Pierce and St. Lucie County
Fla. Special Laws 1972, Ch. 72-543

Charter of the Consolidated Government of the City of Tallahassee and Leon County
Fla. Special Laws 1971, Ch. 71-747, 1973, Ch. 73-628

Charter of the Government of Tallahassee and Leon County
Fla. Special Laws 1976, Ch. 76-492

Charter of the Town of Liberty
N.C. Laws 1991, Ch. 579
N.C. Private Laws 1889, Ch. 16
N.C. Public Local Laws 1939, Ch. 514

Charter of Trimble
Tenn. Private Acts 1974, Ch. 62

Charter-Party Carriers Act
Cal. Public Utilities Code § 5351 et seq.

Charter Procedures Act (County)
Mass. Gen. Laws Ann., 34A:1 et seq.

Charter School Expansion Act of 1998
Oct. 22, 1998, P.L. 105-278, 112 Stat. 2682, 20 U.S. Code § 6301 nt.

Charter School Program Act
N.J. Stat. Ann., 180A:36A-1 et seq.

Charter Schools Act
Cal. Education Code 1976, § 47600 et seq.
Colo. Rev. Stat., 22-30.5-101 et seq.
Del. Code of 1974, Title 14, § 501 et seq.
Ga. Code Ann., 20-2-2060 et seq.
Ill. Comp. Stat. 1992, Ch. 105, § 5/27A-1 et seq.
N.M. Stat. Ann., 22-8A-1 et seq.
N.Y. Education Law 1947 (Consol. Laws Ch. 16) §§ 2850 to 2857
Pa. Purdon's Stat., Title 24, § 17-1701 et seq.
S.C. Code Ann. 1976, § 59-40-10 et seq.

Charter Township Act
Mich. Comp. Laws Ann., 42.1 et seq.

Charter Water Authority Act
Mich. Comp. Laws Ann., 121.1 et seq.

Chatham Area Transit Authority Act
Ga. Laws 1986, p. 5082

Chatham County Community Improvement District Act
Ga. Laws 1994, p. 4931

Chatham County Employee-Management Cooperation Act
Ga. Laws 1968, p. 2953

Chatham County Pension Act
Ga. Laws 1937, p. 1273

Chatham County Recreation Authority Act
Ga. Laws 1995, p. 4281

Chatham Local Option Law
N.J. Laws 1871, (Sp. Sess.) p. 1470 Ch. 560

Chatham-Savannah Authority for the Homeless Act
Ga. Laws 1991, p. 4701

Chatham-Savannah County Anti-Drug Commission Act
Ga. Laws 1990, p. 4059

Chatham-Savannah Youth Futures Authority Act
Ga. Laws 1988, p. 3743

Chatsworth-Murray County Water and Sewage Authority Act
Ga. Laws 1991, p. 3779

Chattahoochee National Forest Protection Act of 1991
Dec. 11, 1991, P.L. 102-217, 16 U.S. Code § 460ggg nt.
Nov. 2, 1994, P.L. 103-437, 16 U.S. Code § 460ggg-3

Chattahoochee River Basin Act
Ga. Code Ann., 12-5-400 et seq.

Chattahoochie Compact Act
Ala. Code 1975, § 41-9-311

Chattanooga Metropolitan Improvement Act
Tenn. Private Acts 1927, Ch. 457

Chattanooga Planning Act
Tenn. Private Acts 1923, Ch. 397

Chattanooga Transit Authority Act
Tenn. Private Acts 1967, Ch. 460

Chattel Lien Act
Wash. Rev. Code Ann., 60.08.010 et seq.

Chattel Lien Act (Farm Chattels)
Va. Code 1950, § 43-44 et seq.

Chattel Loan Law
Iowa Code 1966, 536.1 et seq.
Neb. Rev. Stat. 1943, 45-459 et seq.

Chattel Mortgage Act
See also Uniform Commercial Code-Secured Transactions
Colo. Rev. Stat., 13-15-101 et seq.
Conn. Gen. Stat. Ann., § 42a-9-101 et seq.
Ind. Burns' 1964 Repl., 51-501 et seq.
Ky. Rev. Stat. 1953, 382.600 et seq.
La. Rev. Stat. Ann., 9:5351 et seq.
Md. Ann. Code 1974, Art. CL, § 9-301 et seq.
Me. Rev. Stat. Ann. 1964, Title 11, § 9-101 et seq.
Mo. Rev. Stat. 1959, 443.450 et seq.

Mont. Code Ann. 1947, 52-301 et seq.
N.H. Rev. Stat. 1955, Superseded Vols. 360:1 et seq.
N.Y. Uniform Commercial Code (Consol. Laws, Ch. 38) § 9-101 et seq.
Ohio Rev. Code 1953, 1309.01 et seq.
Okla. Stat. 1961, Title 12A, § 9-101 et seq.
Pa. 1945 Pamph.Laws 1358, No. 434
R.I. Gen. Laws 1956, 6A-9-101 et seq.
Utah Code Ann. 1953, 70A-9-101 et seq.
Vt. Acts 1878, No. 51
Wash. Rev. Code Ann., 62A.9-203 et seq.
Wyo. Stat. 1957 § 32-242 et seq.

Chattel Mortgage Act (Secured Transactions)
N.Y. Uniform Commercial Code (Consol. Laws Ch. 38), § 9-101 et seq.

Chattel Mortgage Deficiency Judgment Act
Mich. Comp. Laws 1948, 566.401 et seq.

Chattel Mortgage Filing Act
Wis. Stat. 1989, 409.401 et seq.

Chattel Mortgage Foreclosure Act
Mich. Comp. Laws 1948, 440.9501 et seq.

Chattel Mortgage Inventory Act
Colo. Rev. Stat. 1963, 21-2-1 et seq.

Chattel Mortgage Recording Act
Ala. Code 1958, Title 47, § 110 et seq.
Cal. Civil Code § 2955 et seq.
Colo. Rev. Stat. 1963, 21-1-1 et seq.
Conn. Gen. Stat. 1983, § 49-93 et seq.
Ill. Rev. Stat. 1961, Ch. 95, § 1 et seq.
Kan. Stat. Ann., 58-301 et seq.
Md. Ann. Code 1957, Art. 95B, § 9-301 et seq.
Md. Ann. Code 1957, Superseded Vol., Art. 21, § 52 et seq.
Me. Rev. Stat. 1954, Ch. 178. § 1 et seq.
Mich. Comp. Laws Ann., 440.9401
Minn. Stat. 1963, 511.01 et seq.
Mo. Rev. Stat. 1959, 443.450 et seq.
Mont. Rev. Code 1947, 52-301 et seq.
N.C. Gen. Stat. 1943, § 47-20
Continued

N.H. Rev. Stat. 1955, Superseded Vol., 360:1 et seq.

N.J. Stat. Ann., 46:28-1 to 46:28-14

N.Y. Lien Law (Consol. Laws Ch. 33) § 230 et seq.

N.Y. Uniform Commercial Code (Consol. Laws, Ch. 38) § 9-101 et seq.

Ohio Rev. Code 1953, 1319.01 et seq.

Okla. Stat. 1961, Title 19, § 290 et seq.

Okla. Stat. 1961, Title 46, § 57 et seq.

P.R. Laws Ann. 1954, Title 30, § 1871 et seq.

R.I. Gen. Laws 1956, 34-24-1 et seq.

S.D. Codified Laws, 57A-9-101 to 57A-9-507

Tenn. Code Ann., Superseded Vol., 64-901

Tex. Business and Commerce Code, § 9.201 et seq.

Utah Code Ann. 1953, 9-1-1 et seq.

Vt. Acts 1878, No. 51

Wash. Rev. Code 1951, 61.04.010 et seq.

Wyo. Stat. 1957, § 34-242 et seq.

Chattel Mortgage Registration Act
Neb. Rev. Stat. 1943, Superseded Vol., 36-301 et seq.

Okla. Stat. Ann., Title 46, § 57 et seq.

Chattel Mortgages Floor Plan Act
Okla. Stat. 1961, Title 46, § 91 et seq.

Chattel Mortgages Registry Act
Ark. Sales 1947, 6-201

Chattel Security Act
Ill. Rev. Stat. 1991, Ch. 26, § 9-101 et seq.

Chauffeur Protection Act
Ill. Comp. Stat. 1992, Ch. 625, § 20/0.01 et seq.

Chauffeurs' and Operators' License Act (Motor Vehicles)
Mich. Comp. Laws Ann., 257.301 et seq.

N.M. Stat. Ann. 1953, 64-13-31 et seq.

R.I. Gen. Laws 1956, 31-10-1 et seq.

Tenn. Code Ann., 55-7-101 et seq.

Utah Code Ann. 1953, 41-2-201 et seq.

Va. Code 1950, § 46.1-348 et seq.

W. Va. Code 1966, § 17B-1-1 et seq.

Wyo. Stat. Ann., § 31-7-101 et seq.

Chauffeur's License Act
Ariz. Rev. Stat. Ann., § 28-401 et seq.

Ida. Code 1947, 49-301 et seq.

Ind. Code Ann., 9-1-4-26 et seq.

Okla. Stat. Ann., Title 47, § 6-101 et seq.

Wis. Stat. 1987, 343.125, 343.126

Chauffeurs' Social Security Act
P.R. Laws Ann. 1954, Title 29, § 681 et seq.

Chautauqua County Charter
N.Y. Local Laws 1973, County of Chautauqua, p. 946

Chautauqua Navigation Commission Act
N.Y. Laws 1950, Ch. 780

Cheaha Wilderness Act
Jan. 3, 1983, P.L. 97-411, 16 U.S. Code § 1132

Check Act
S.C. Code Ann. 1976, § 34-11-60 et seq.

Check Casher Licensing Act
Pa. 1998 Pamph. Laws, No. 22

Check Cashers Act
Miss. Code Ann., §§ 75-67-501 to 75-67-539

Check Casher's Fee Act
Cal. Statutes 1992, Ch. 1043

Check Casher's Regulatory Act
N.J. Stat. Ann., 17:15A-30 et seq.

Check Cashiers Licensing Act
Mass. Gen. Laws Ann., 169A:1 to 169A:13

Check Cashing Act
Ill. Comp. Stat. 1992, Ch. 815, § 315/0.01 et seq.

N.J. Stat. Ann., 17:15A-1 et seq.

Check Cashing and Foreign Currency Exchange Act
Fla. Stat. Ann., 560.301 to 560.310

Me. Rev. Stat. Ann. 1964, Title 32, § 6131 et seq.

Check-Off Act (Beef)
W. Va. Code 1966, § 19-2F-1 et seq.

Check Printer and Check Number Act
Ill. Comp. Stat. 1992, Ch. 205, § 690/1 et seq.

Check Sale Act
Ala. Code 1975, 8-7-1 et seq.
Ark. Code Ann. 1987, 23-41-101 et seq.
Ga. Code Ann., 7-1-680 et seq.
La. Rev. Stat. Ann., 6:1031 et seq.
Mo. Rev. Stat., 361.700 et seq.
N.D. Cent. Code, 51-17-01 et seq.
Neb. Rev. Stat. 1943, 8-1001 et seq.
N.J. Stat. Ann., 17:15B-1 et seq.
R.I. Gen. Laws 1956, 19-27-1 et seq.
Tex. Rev. Civ. Stat., Art. 489d
Wis. Stat. 1989, 217.01 et seq.

Check Sellers and Cashers Act
Cal. Financial Code § 12000 et seq.

Check Sellers, Bill Payers and Proraters Law
Cal. Financial Code § 12000 et seq.

Checkoff Act (Union Dues)
Iowa Code Ann., 731.5
Tex. Rev. Civ. Stat., Art. 5154e

Checks Act (Sales)
Neb. Rev. Stat. 1943, 8-1001 et seq.

Cheese and Butter Factories Act
Ill. Rev. Stat. 1991, Ch. 5, § 42.9 et seq.

Chehalis River Basin Fishery Resources Study and Restoration Act of 1990
Oct. 24, 1990, P.L. 101-452, 104 Stat. 1054

Chelsea Municipal Hospital Loan Act
Mass. Acts 1958, Ch. 670

Chelsea School Loan Act
Mass. Acts 1952, Ch. 528

Chemical and Biological Weapons Control and Warfare Elimination Act of 1991
Oct. 28, 1991, P.L. 102-138, 22 U.S. Code §§ 5601 to 5603, 5601 nt.

Dec. 4, 1991, P.L. 102-182, 22 U.S. Code § 5601 et seq.

Chemical Dependency and Mental Health Insurance Act
Mo. Rev. Stat. Ann., 376.825 to 376.833

Chemical Dependency and Psychiatric Facility Certificate of Need Act
Okla. Stat. Ann., Title 63, § 1-871 et seq.

Chemical Dependency Plan
Mont. Code Ann., 53-24-204

Chemical Dependency Professional Act
R.I. Gen. Laws 1956, 5-69-1 et seq.

Chemical Diversion and Trafficking Act of 1988
Nov. 18, 1988, P.L. 100-690, 21 U.S. Code § 801 nt.

Chemical Ground Water Protection Act (Agricultural)
Mont. Code Ann., 80-15-101 et seq.

Chemical Laboratory Authorization Act
Miss. Code Ann., § 57-21-1 et seq.

Chemical Plant and Oil Refinery Safety Preparedness Act
Cal. Government Code § 51020 et seq.

Chemical Purchasing Act
R.I. Gen. Laws 1956, 42-110-1 et seq.

Chemical Release Reporting Act (Toxic)
Tex. Health and Safety Code, § 370.001 et seq.

Chemical Response and Reimbursement Law (Agricultural)
Minn. Stat. Ann., 18E.01 et seq.

Chemical Right to Know Act (Public Employees')
Ark. Acts 1991, No. 556

Chemical Safety Act
Ill. Rev. Stat. 1991, Ch. 111 1/2, § 951 et seq.

Chemical Safety Information, Site Security and Fuels Regulatory Relief Act

Aug. 5, 1999, P.L. 106-40, 113 Stat. 207, 42 U.S. Code § 7401 nt.

Chemical Test for Intoxication of Drivers Act

Ala. Code 1975, § 32-5-190 et seq.

Ariz. Rev. Stat. Ann., § 28-692

Colo. Rev. Stat., 42-4-1202

Conn. Gen. Stat. Ann., § 14-227a

Ga. Code Ann., 40-5-55

Haw. Rev. Stat. Ann., § 291-5

Ida. Code 1947, 18-8002

Ill. Rev. Stat. 1991, Ch. 95 1/2, § 11-500 et seq.

Ind. Code Ann., 9-4-1-39.1

Iowa Code 1985, 321B.1 et seq.

Kan. Stat. Ann., 8-1001 et seq.

Ky. Rev. Stat. 1971, 189.520

Mass. Gen. Laws Ann., 90:24

Md. Ann. Code 1974, Art. CJ, § 10-302 et seq.

Me. Rev. Stat. Ann. 1964, Title 29, § 1312

Mich. Comp. Laws Ann., 257.625a

Minn. Stat. Ann., 169.123

Mo. Rev. Stat., 577.020 et seq.

Mont. Code Ann., 61-8-401 et seq.

N.C. Gen. Stat. 1943, § 2-139.1 et seq.

N.D. Cent. Code 39-20-01 et seq.

Neb. Rev. Stat. 1943, 39-669.07 et seq.

Nev. Rev. Stat. 1979 Reprint, 484.381 et seq.

N.H. Rev. Stat. 1955, 265:89

N.J. Stat. Ann., 39:4-50.1 et seq.

N.M. Stat. Ann., 66-8-103 et seq.

N.Y. Vehicle and Traffic Law 1959 (Consol. Laws Ch. 71) § 1192

Okla. Stat. Ann., Title 47, § 751 et seq.

Ore. Rev. Stat., 487.805 et seq.

R.I. Gen. Laws 1956, 31-27-2.1, 31-27-3

S.C. Code Ann. 1976, § 56-5-2950

S.D. Codified Laws 1967, 32-23-7 et seq.

Chemical Weapons Act

Ind. Code Ann., 35-23-6-1 et seq.

Chemical Weapons Convention Implementation Act of 1998

Oct. 21, 1998, P.L. 105-277, Division I, 112 Stat. 2681, 22 U.S. Code § 6701 nt.

Chemical Weapons Destruction Limitation Act

Ala. Code 1975, § 33-1-5

Chemigation Act

Colo. Rev. Stat., 35-11-101 et seq.

Neb. Rev. Stat. 1943, 46-1101 et seq.

Chemigation Safety Law

Kan. Stat. Ann., 2-3301 et seq.

Chemist Regulation Act

P.R. Laws Ann. 1954, Title 20 § 471 et seq.

Cherokee Agreement Act

July 1, 1902, Ch. 1375, 32 Stat. 716

Cherokee County Community Improvement Districts Act

Ga. Laws 1998, H.B. 1748

Cherokee County Parks and Recreation Authority Act

Ga. Laws 1995, p. 4223

Cherokee County Supply Act

S.C. Acts 1945, p. 745, No. 274

Cherokee Leasing Act

Dec. 23, 1985, P.L. 99-221, 25 U.S. Code §§ 415 nt., 450i; 26 U.S . Code § 3121; 42 U.S. Code § 410

Cherry Act

Mich. Comp. Laws Ann., 290.501 et seq.

Cherry Commission Act

Ida. Code 1947, 22-3701 et seq.

Cherry Fruit Fly Act

Mich. Comp. Laws Ann., 286.81 et seq.

Cherry Pest Act

Mich. Comp. Laws Ann., 286.81 et seq.

Chesapeake and Ohio Canal Development Act

Jan. 8, 1971, P.L. 91-664, 84 Stat. 1978, 16 U.S. Code §§ 410y to 410y-6

July 3, 1990, P.L. 101-320, 16 U.S. Code § 410y-4

Nov. 2, 1994, P.L. 103-437, 16 U.S. Code § 410y-1

Chesapeake Bay Bridge and Tunnel Revenue Bond Act

Va. Code 1950, § 33.1-253

Chesapeake Bay Initiative Act of 1998

Oct. 30, 1998, P.L. 105-312, Title V, 112 Stat. 2961, 16 U.S. Code § 461 nt.

Chesapeake Bay Preservation Act

Neb. Laws 1986, L.B. 284

Va. Code 1950, § 10-313 et seq.

Chesapeake Bay Research Coordination Act of 1980

Oct. 15, 1980, P.L. 96-460, 16 U.S. Code § 3001 nt.

Chesapeake Bay Revenue Bond Act

Va. Acts 1956, Ch. 714

Chester County Bond Act

S.C. Acts 1948, p. 2504, No. 951

Cheyenne River Compact Act

S.D. Codified Laws 1967, 46-31-1, 46-31-2

Wyo. Stat. 1957, §§ 41-503, 41-504

Chicago Amendment

Ill. Const. 1870, Art. 4, § 34

Chicago Budget Act

Ill. Rev. Stat. 1953, Ch. 24, §§ 22-1, 22-2

Chicago Community Schools Study Commission Act

Ill. Comp. Stat. 1992, Ch. 105, § 215/0.01 et seq.

Chicago Delinquent Special Assessment Act

Ill. Comp. Stat. 1992, Ch. 65, § 65/7 et seq.

Chicago Drainage District Act

Ill. Comp. Stat. 1992, Ch. 70, § 615/0.01 et seq.

Chicago Land Cession Act

Ill. Comp. Stat. 1992, Ch. 5, §§ 515/0.01, 515/2

Chicago Learning Zone Implementation Law

Ill. Comp. Stat. 1992, Ch. 105, § 5/34-8.6 et seq.

Chicago Medical Center Act

Ill. Rev. Stat. 1991, Ch. 111 1/2, § 5000 et seq.

Chicago Municipal Court Act

Ill. Rev. Stat. 1963, Ch. 37, § 356 et seq.

Chicago Out-Patient Clinic Act

Ill. Comp. Stat. 1992, Ch. 20, §§ 2315/0.01, 2315/1

Chicago Park and City Exchange of Functions Act

Ill. Comp. Stat. 1992, Ch. 70, § 1545/0.01 et seq.

Chicago Park Debt Assumption Act of 1935

Ill. Rev. Stat. 1991, Ch. 105, § 333.28s

Chicago Park District Act

Ill. Comp. Stat. 1992, Ch. 70, § 1505/0.01 et seq.

Chicago Park District Bond Acts

Ill. Comp. Stat. 1992, Ch. 70, §§ 1520/0.01 et seq., 1525/0.01 et seq.

Chicago Park District Corporate Note Act

Ill. Comp. Stat. 1992, Ch. 70, § 1530/0.01 et seq.

Chicago Park District Debt Assumption Act

Ill. Comp. Stat. 1992, Ch. 70, § 1515/0.01 et seq.

Chicago Park District Judgment Indebtedness Bond Act

Ill. Comp. Stat. 1992, Ch. 70, §§ 1540/0.01, 1540/1

Chicago Park District Street Car Line Act
Ill. Comp. Stat. 1992, Ch. 70, § 1535/0.01 et seq.

Chicago Park District Working Cash Fund Act
Ill. Comp. Stat. 1992, Ch. 70, § 1510/0.01 et seq.

Chicago Public Library Act
Ill. Comp. Stat. 1992, Ch. 75, § 20/0.01 et seq.

Chicago Sanitary District Act
Ill. Rev. Stat. 1981, Ch. 42, § 320 et seq.

Chicago Sanitary District Enlargement (1st) Act
Ill. Rev. Stat. 1991, Ch. 42, §§ 360.9, 361

Chicago Sanitary District Enlargement (2nd A) Act
Ill. Rev. Stat. 1989, Ch. 42, § 361.01 et seq.

Chicago Sanitary District Enlargement (2nd B) Act
Ill. Rev. Stat. 1989, Ch. 42, §§ 372m, 373

Chicago Sanitary District Enlargement (3rd) Act
Ill. Rev. Stat. 1989, Ch. 42, §§ 374.9, 375

Chicago Sanitary District Enlargement (4th) Act
Ill. Rev. Stat. 1989, Ch. 42, §§ 376.9, 377

Chicago Sanitary District Enlargement (5th) Act
Ill. Rev. Stat. 1989, Ch. 42, §§ 378.9, 379

Chicago Sanitary District Enlargement (6th) Act
Ill. Rev. Stat. 1989, Ch. 42, §§ 380.9, 380a

Chicago Sanitary District Enlargement (7th) Act
Ill. Rev. Stat. 1989, Ch. 42, §§ 380b.9, 380c

Chicago Sanitary District Enlargement (8th) Act
Ill. Rev. Stat. 1989, Ch. 42, §§ 380c.9, 380d

Chicago Sanitary District Enlargement (9th) Act
Ill. Rev. Stat. 1989, Ch. 42, §§ 380e.9, 380f

Chicago Sanitary District Enlargement (10th) Act
Ill. Rev. Stat. 1989, Ch. 42, §§ 380f.9, 380g

Chicago Sanitary District Enlargement (11th) Act
Ill. Rev. Stat. 1989, Ch. 42, §§ 380g.9, 380h

Chicago Sanitary District Enlargement (12th) Act
Ill. Rev. Stat. 1989, Ch. 42, §§ 380h.9, 380i

Chicago Sanitary District Enlargement (13th) Act
Ill. Rev. Stat. 1989, Ch. 42, §§ 380i.9, 380j

Chicago Sanitary District Enlargement (14th) Act
Ill. Rev. Stat. 1989, Ch. 42, §§ 380j.9, 380k

Chicago Sanitary District Enlargement (15th) Act
Ill. Rev. Stat. 1989, Ch. 42, §§ 380k.9, 380l

Chicago Sanitary District Enlargement (16th) Act
Ill. Rev. Stat. 1989, Ch. 42, §§ 380l.9, 380m

Chicago Sanitary District Enlargement (17th) Act
Ill. Rev. Stat. 1989, Ch. 42, §§ 380m.9, 380n

Chicago Sanitary District Enlargement (18th) Act
Ill. Rev. Stat. 1989, Ch. 42, §§ 380n.9, 380o

Chicago Sanitary District Enlargement (19th) Act
Ill. Rev. Stat. 1989, Ch. 42, §§ 380o.9, 380p

Chicago Sanitary District Enlargement (20th) Act
Ill. Rev. Stat. 1989, Ch. 42, §§ 380p.9, 380q

Chicago Sanitary District Enlargement (21st) Act
Ill. Rev. Stat. 1989, Ch. 42, §§ 380q.9, 380r

Chicago Sanitary District Enlargement (22nd) Act
Ill. Rev. Stat. 1989, Ch. 42, §§ 380r.9, 380s

Chicago Sanitary District Enlargement (23rd) Act
Ill. Rev. Stat. 1989, Ch. 42, §§ 380s.9, 380t

Chicago Sanitary District Enlargement (24th) Act
Ill. Rev. Stat. 1989, Ch. 42, §§ 380t.9, 380u

Chicago Sanitary District Enlargement (25th) Act
Ill. Rev. Stat. 1989, Ch. 42, §§ 380u.9, 380v

Chicago Sanitary District Enlargement (26th) Act
Ill. Rev. Stat. 1989, Ch. 42, §§ 380v.9, 380w

Chicago Sanitary District Enlargement (27th) Act
Ill. Rev. Stat. 1989, Ch. 42, §§ 380w.9, 380x

Chicago Sanitary District Enlargement (28th) Act
Ill. Rev. Stat. 1989, Ch. 42, §§ 380x.9, 380y

Chicago Sanitary District Enlargement (29th) Act
Ill. Rev. Stat. 1989, Ch. 42, §§ 380y.9, 380z

Chicago Sanitary District Enlargement (30th) Act
Ill. Rev. Stat. 1989, Ch. 42, §§ 380z.9, 380z1

Chicago Sanitary District Enlargement (31st) Act
Ill. Rev. Stat. 1989, Ch. 42, §§ 380z1.9, 380z2

Chicago Sanitary District Enlargement (32nd) Act
Ill. Rev. Stat. 1989, Ch. 42, §§ 380z2.9, 380z3

Chicago Sanitary District Enlargement (33rd) Act
Ill. Rev. Stat. 1989, Ch. 42, §§ 380z3.9, 380z4

Chicago Sanitary District Enlargement (34th) Act
Ill. Rev. Stat. 1989, Ch. 42, §§ 380z4.9, 380z5

Chicago Sanitary District Enlargement (35th) Act
Ill. Rev. Stat. 1989, Ch. 42, §§ 380z5.9, 380z6

Chicago Sanitary District Enlargement (36th) Act
Ill. Rev. Stat. 1989, Ch. 42, §§ 380z6.9, 380z7

Chicago Sanitary District Enlargement (37th) Act
Ill. Rev. Stat. 1989, Ch. 42, §§ 380z7.9, 380z8

Chicago Sanitary District Enlargement (38th) Act
Ill. Rev. Stat. 1989, Ch. 42, §§ 380z8.9, 380z9

Chicago Sanitary District Enlargement (39th) Act
Ill. Rev. Stat. 1989, Ch. 42, §§ 380z9.9, 380z10

Chicago Sanitary District Enlargement (40th) Act
Ill. Rev. Stat. 1989, Ch. 42, §§ 38z10.9, 380z11

Chicago Sanitary District Enlargement (41st) Act
Ill. Rev. Stat. 1989, Ch. 42, §§ 380z11.9, 380z12

Chicago Sanitary District Enlargement (42nd) Act
Ill. Rev. Stat. 1989, Ch. 42, §§ 380z12.9, 380z13

Chicago Sanitary District Enlargement (43rd) Act
Ill. Rev. Stat. 1989, Ch. 42, §§ 380z13.9, 380z14

Chicago Sanitary District Enlargement (44th) Act

Ill. Rev. Stat. 1989, Ch. 42, §§ 380z14.9, 380z15

Chicago Sanitary District Enlargement (45th) Act

Ill. Rev. Stat. 1989, Ch. 42, §§ 380z16.9, 380z17

Chicago Sanitary District Enlargement (46th) Act

Ill. Rev. Stat. 1989, Ch. 42, §§ 380z17.9, 380z18

Chicago Sanitary District Enlargement (47th) Act

Ill. Rev. Stat. 1989, Ch. 42, §§ 380z18.9, 380z19

Chicago Sanitary District Enlargement (48th) Act

Ill. Rev. Stat. 1989, Ch. 42, §§ 380z19.9, 380z20

Chicago Sanitary District Enlargement (49th) Act

Ill. Rev. Stat. 1989, Ch. 42, §§ 380z20.9, 380z21

Chicago Sanitary District Enlargement (50th) Act

Ill. Rev. Stat. 1989, Ch. 42, §§ 380z21.9, 380z22

Chicago Sanitary District Enlargement (51st) Act

Ill. Rev. Stat. 1989, Ch. 42, §§ 380z22.9, 380z23

Chicago Sanitary District Enlargement (52nd) Act

Ill. Rev. Stat. 1989, Ch. 42, §§ 380z23.9, 380z24

Chicago Sanitary District Enlargement (53rd) Act

Ill. Rev. Stat. 1989, Ch. 42, §§ 380z24.9, 380z25

Chicago Sanitary District Enlargement (54th) Act

Ill. Rev. Stat. 1989, Ch. 42, §§ 380z25.9, 380z26

Chicago Sanitary District Enlargement (55th) Act

Ill. Rev. Stat. 1989, Ch. 42, §§ 380z26.9, 380z27

Chicago Sanitary District Enlargement (56th) Act

Ill. Rev. Stat. 1989, Ch. 42, §§ 380z27.9, 380z28

Chicago Sanitary District Enlargement (57th) Act

Ill. Rev. Stat. 1989, Ch. 42, §§ 380z28.9, 380z29

Chicago Sanitary District Enlargement (58th) Act

Ill. Rev. Stat. 1989, Ch. 42, §§ 380z29.9, 380z30

Chicago Sanitary District Enlargement (59th) Act

Ill. Rev. Stat. 1989, Ch. 42, §§ 380z30.9, 380z31

Chicago Sanitary District Enlargement (60th) Act

Ill. Rev. Stat. 1989, Ch. 42, §§ 380z31.9, 380z32

Chicago Sanitary District Enlargement (61st) Act

Ill. Rev. Stat. 1989, Ch. 42, §§ 380z32.9, 380z33

Chicago Sanitary District Enlargement (62nd) Act

Ill. Rev. Stat. 1989, Ch. 42, §§ 380z34.9, 380z35

Chicago Sanitary District Enlargement (63rd) Act

Ill. Rev. Stat. 1989, Ch. 42, §§ 380z35.9, 380z36

Chicago Sanitary District Enlargement (64th) Act

Ill. Rev. Stat. 1989, Ch. 42, §§ 380z36.9, 380z37

Chicago Sanitary District Enlargement (65th) Act

Ill. Rev. Stat. 1989, Ch. 42, §§ 380z37.9, 380z38

Chicago Sanitary District Enlargement (66th) Act

Ill. Rev. Stat. 1989, Ch. 42, §§ 380z38.9, 380z39

Chicago Sanitary District Enlargement (67th) Act

Ill. Rev. Stat. 1989, Ch. 42, §§ 380z39.9, 380z40

Chicago Sanitary District Enlargement (68th) Act

Ill. Rev. Stat. 1989, Ch. 42, §§ 380z40.9, 380z41

Chicago Sanitary District Enlargement (69th) Act

Ill. Rev. Stat. 1989, Ch. 42, § 380z41.9 et seq.

Chicago Sanitary District Enlargement (70th) Act

Ill. Rev. Stat. 1989, Ch. 42, §§ 380z44.9, 380z45

Chicago Sanitary District Enlargement (71st) Act

Ill. Rev. Stat. 1989, Ch. 42, § 380z45.9 et seq.

Chicago Sanitary District Enlargement (72nd) Act

Ill. Rev. Stat. 1989, Ch. 42, §§ 380z47.9, 380z48

Chicago Sanitary District Enlargement (73rd) Act

Ill. Rev. Stat. 1989, Ch. 42, §§ 380z48.9, 380z49

Chicago Sanitary District Enlargement (74th) Act

Ill. Rev. Stat. 1989, Ch. 42, § 380z49.9 et seq.

Chicago Sanitary District Enlargement (75th) Act

Ill. Rev. Stat. 1989, Ch. 42, §§ 380z52.9, 380z53

Chicago Sanitary District Enlargement (76th) Act

Ill. Rev. Stat. 1989, Ch. 42, §§ 380z53.9, 380z54

Chicago Sanitary District Enlargement (77th) Act

Ill. Rev. Stat. 1989, Ch. 42, §§ 380z54.9, 380z55

Chicago Sanitary District Enlargement (78th) Act

Ill. Rev. Stat. 1989, Ch. 42, §§ 380z55.9, 380z56

Chicago Sanitary District Enlargement (79th) Act

Ill. Rev. Stat. 1989, Ch. 42, § 380z56.9 et seq.

Chicago Sanitary District Enlargement (80th) Act

Ill. Rev. Stat. 1989, Ch. 42, §§ 380z58.9, 380z59

Chicago Sanitary District Enlargement (81st) Act

Ill. Rev. Stat. 1989, Ch. 42, §§ 380z59.9, 380z60

Chicago Sanitary District Enlargement (82nd) Act

Ill. Rev. Stat. 1989, Ch. 42, §§ 380z60.9, 380z61

Chicago Sanitary District Enlargement (84th) Act

Ill. Rev. Stat. 1989, Ch. 42, § 380z62.9 et seq.

Chicago Sanitary District Navigable Streams Act
Ill. Rev. Stat. 1989, Ch. 42, § 350m et seq.

Chicago Sanitary District Obstruction Removal Act
Ill. Rev. Stat. 1989, Ch. 42, § 372.9 et seq.

Chicago Sanitary District Police Powers Act
Ill. Rev. Stat. 1989, Ch. 42, §§ 359.9, 360

Chicago Sanitary District, Purchasing Act
Ill. Comp. Stat. 1992, Ch. 70, § 2605/11.1 et seq.

Chicago Sanitary District Sewer Contract Act
Ill. Rev. Stat. 1989, Ch. 42, §§ 380z99, 381

Chicago Sanitary District Water Power Act
Ill. Rev. Stat. 1989, Ch. 42, § 369.9 et seq.

Chicago South and Melrose Park Civic Center Act
Ill. Comp. Stat. 1992, Ch. 70, § 245/0.01 et seq.

Chicago South Civic Center Law
Ill. Comp. Stat. 1992, Ch. 70, § 245/1-1 et seq.

Chicago State University Law
Ill. Comp. Stat. 1992, Ch. 110, § 660/5-1 et seq.

Chicago State University Revenue Bond Law
Ill. Comp. Stat. 1992, Ch. 110, § 661/6-1 et seq.

Chicago Submerged Lands Act
Ill. Comp. Stat. 1992, Ch. 70, §§ 1550/0.01, 1550/1, 1555/1, 1555/1.1

Chicago U.S. Courthouse Cession Act
Ill. Comp. Stat. 1992, Ch. 5, §§ 530/0.01, 530/1

Chicago World's Fair—1992 Authority Act
Ill. Rev. Stat. 1983, Ch. 127, § 2101.01 et seq.

Chichester Act (Deficiency Judgments)
Ala. General Acts 1935, p. 184

Chicopee Falls Flood Protection Loan Act
Mass. Acts 1962, Ch. 552

Chicopee Stream Clearance Loan Act
Mass. Acts 1960, Ch. 636

Chicopee Swimming Pool Loan Act
Mass. Acts 1962, Ch. 428

Chicopee Woods Area Park Commission Act
Ga. Laws 1988, p. 3783

Chief Financial Officers Act of 1990
Nov. 15, 1990, P.L. 101-576, 5 U.S. Code §§ 5313 to 5315; 31 U.S. Code §§ 501 et seq., 901, et seq., 1105, 3501 et seq. generally, 9105, 9106

Chief Judge Act (Atlanta Judicial Circuit)
Ga. Laws 1963, p. 646

Child Abandomnent Act
Ga. Code Ann., 19-10-1, 19-10-2

Child Abandonment Act
Ala. Code 1975, § 13A-13-5

Child Abduction Act
Ill. Rev. Stat. 1991, Ch. 38, § 10-5

Child Abuse Accountability Act
Oct. 14, 1994, P.L. 103-358, 5 U.S. Code § 8331 nt.

Child Abuse Act
Ala. Code 1975, § 26-15-1 et seq.
Cal. Welfare and Institutions Code § 18950 et seq.
Ind. Code Ann., 31-6-11-1 et seq.
Iowa Code Ann., 232.67 et seq., 235A.1 et seq.
Kan. Stat. Ann., 38-716 et seq.
Mo. Rev. Stat., 210.110 et seq.
N.D. Cent. Code 50-25.1-01 et seq.
N.J. Stat. Ann., 9:6-8.8 et seq.
Ohio Rev. Code 1953, 2151.421
S.D. Comp. Laws, 26-10-10 et seq.

Vt. Stat. Ann., Title 33, § 4911 et seq.

Child Abuse Act (Trust Fund for the Prevention of)

Minn. Stat. Ann., 299A.20 et seq.

Child Abuse Act of 1990

Oct. 30, 1998, P.L. 105-314, 42 U.S. Code § 13032

Child Abuse Amendments of 1984

Oct. 9, 1984, P.L. 98-457, 98 Stat. 1749, 42 U.S. Code §§ 5101 et seq., 5111 to 5113, 5115, 10401 et seq.

Child Abuse and Neglect Prevention Act

Ala. Code 1975, § 26-16-1 et seq.

Ark. Code Ann. 1987, 9-30-101 et seq.

Cal. Welfare and Institutions Code § 18950 et seq.

D.C. Code Ann., § 6-2101 et seq.

Ga. Code Ann., 19-14-1 et seq.

Mich. Comp. Laws Ann., 722.601 et seq.

N.Y. Criminal Procedure Law (Consol. Laws Ch. 11A), § 190.25

N.Y. Education Law 1947 (Consol. Laws Ch. 16), §§ 4212, 4314, 4358, 4403

N.Y. Executive Law 1951 (Consol. Laws Ch. 18), §§ 501, 510a, 532d

N.Y. Family Court Act, §§ 1012, 1024

N.Y. Laws 1985, Chs. 676, 677

N.Y. Mental Hygiene Law 1972 (Consol. Laws Ch. 27), §§ 29.29, 45.07

N.Y. Social Services Law (Consol. Laws Ch. 55), §§ 34a, 37b, 376, 377, 390, 390b, 412, 413, 415, 417, 421 et seq., 425, 426, 460c, 462

Ohio Rev. Code 1953, 3109.13 to 3109.18

Okla. Stat. Ann., Title 63, § 1-227 et seq.

Wash. Rev. Code Ann., 26.44.010 et seq.

Child Abuse and Neglect Reporting Act

Cal. Penal Code § 11164 et seq.

Ill. Rev. Stat. 1991, Ch. 23, § 2051 et seq.

Child Abuse and Neglect Task Force Act

N.J. Stat. Ann., 9:6-8.74 et seq.

Child Abuse, Domestic Violence, Adoption and Family Services Act of 1992

May 28, 1992, P.L. 102-295, 42 U.S. Code § 5101 nt.

Dec. 2, 1993, P.L. 103-171, 42 U.S. Code § 5106a

Child Abuse Evidence Law

Miss. Code Ann., § 13-1-401 et seq.

Child Abuse Prevention Act

Cal. Welfare and Institutions Code § 18950 et seq.

Child Abuse Prevention, Adoption, and Family Services Act of 1988

April 25, 1988, P.L. 100-294, 42 U.S. Code §§ 5101 et seq., 5101 nt.

Child Abuse Prevention and Treatment Act

April 24, 1978, P.L. 95-266, 42 U.S. Code § 5101 et seq.

Oct. 9, 1984, P.L. 98-457, 98 Stat. 1749, 42 U.S. Code § 5101 et seq.

Aug. 27, 1986, P.L. 99-401, 42 U.S. Code §§ 5103, 5105

Sept. 28, 1987, P.L. 100-117, 42 U.S. Code § 5103

April 25, 1988, P.L. 100-294, 42 U.S. Code §§ 5101, 5101 nt., 5102 to 5106h

Oct. 25, 1989, P.L. 101-126, 42 U.S. Code § 5101 et seq.

Dec. 12, 1989, P.L. 101-226, 42 U.S. Code § 5106a-1

Nov. 29, 1990, P.L. 101-645, 42 U.S. Code §§ 5118 to 5118e

Nov. 4, 1992, P.L. 102-586, 42 U.S. Code § 5106a

May 18, 1994, P.L. 103-252, 42 U.S. Code §§ 5106a-1, 5116 et seq.

Oct. 3, 1996, P.L. 104-235, 42 U.S. Code §§ 5101 nt., 5101 to 5106, 5106a to 5106d, 5106f to 5106i, prec. 5116, 5116, 5116a to 5116i, 5118 to 5118e

Child Abuse Prevention and Treatment Act (Comprehensive)

N.J. Stat. Ann., 9:6-8.83 et seq.

Child Abuse Prevention and Treatment Act Amendments of 1996

Oct. 3, 1996, P.L. 104-235, 42 U.S. Code § 5101 nt.

Child Abuse Prevention and Treatment and Adoption Reform Act of 1978

April 24, 1978, P.L. 95-266, 42 U.S. Code §§ 5101, 5101 nt. et seq.

Oct. 9, 1984, P.L. 98-457, 98 Stat. 1755, 42 U.S. Code §§ 5111 to 5113, 5115

April 25, 1988, P.L. 100-294, 42 U.S. Code §§ 5113, 5115

May 28, 1992, P.L. 012-295, 42 U.S. Code §§ 5111, 5112, 5113, 5115

Oct. 3, 1996, P.L. 104-235, 42 U.S. Code §§ 5111, 5113, 5115

Child Abuse Prevention Challenge Grants Reauthorization Act of 1989

Oct. 25, 1989, P.L. 101-126, 42 U.S. Code § 5101 nt.

Child Abuse Prevention Coordinating Council Act

Cal. Welfare and Institutions Code § 18980 et seq.

Child Abuse Prevention Training Act

Cal. Welfare and Institutions Code § 18975 et seq.

Fla. Stat. Ann., 415.5015

Child Abuse Protection and Treatment Act

May 28, 1992, P.L. 102-295, 42 U.S. Code §§ 5101 nt., 5102, 5105, 5106, 5106a, 5106a-1, 5106c, 5106f-1, 5106h, 5116, 5116c, 5116d, 5116e

Child Abuse Reporting and Prevention Act

Okla. Stat. Ann., Title 10, § 7101 et seq.

Child Abuse Reporting Law

N.C. Gen. Stat. 1943, § 7A-542 et seq.

Child Abuse Victims' Rights Act of 1986

Oct. 18, 1986, P.L. 99-500, 18 U.S. Code § 2251 nt.

Oct. 30, 1986, P.L. 99-591, 18 U.S. Code § 2251 nt.

Child Adoption Act

Ga. Code Ann., 19-8-1 et seq.

Child Aid Act

Cal. Welfare and Institutions Code § 1500 et seq.

Colo. Rev. Stat. 1963, 22-11-1 et seq.

R.I. Gen. Laws 1956, 40-6-7

Child and Family Services and Child Protection Act

Me. Rev. Stat. Ann. 1964, Title 22, § 4001 et seq.

Child and Family Services Resources Act

Miss. Code Ann., § 43-1-59

Child and Maternal Health Plan Act (County)

N.M. Stat. Ann., 24-1B-1 et seq.

Child and Maternal Nutrition Act

Minn. Stat. Ann., 145.891 et seq.

Child and Sex Offender Registration Act

Ark. Code 1987, 12-12-901 et seq.

Child Bicycle Safety Act

Tenn. Code Ann., 55-52-101 et seq.

W. Va. Code 1966, § 17C-11A-1 et seq.

Child Boating Safety Act (Aaron Sahli)

Minn. Laws 1996, Ch. 396

Child Care Act

Ala. Code 1975, § 38-7-1 et seq.

Colo. Rev. Stat., 26-6-101 et seq.

Ill. Comp. Stat. 1992, Ch. 225, § 10/1 et seq.

Mont. Code Ann., 52-2-701 et seq.

Child Care Act (Illegitimates)

Cal. Penal Code § 270

Child Care Act (Intergenerational)

Cal. Education Code 1976, § 8475 et seq.

Child Care Affordability Scholarship Assistance Fund Act

Mass. Gen. Laws Ann., 28A:5A

Child Care and Development Block Grant Act Amendments of 1992

Nov. 4, 1992, P.L. 102-586, 42 U.S. Code §§ 9858h, 9858n, 9858q

Child Care and Development Block Grant Act of 1990

Nov. 5, 1990, P.L. 101-508, 42 U.S. Code §§ 9801 nt., 9858 to 9858p

April 10, 1991, P.L. 102-27, 42 U.S. Code § 9858h

Oct. 7, 1992, P.L. 102-401, 42 U.S. Code § 9858n

Aug. 5, 1997, P.L. 105-33, 42 U.S. Code §§ 9858c, 9858i, 9858j, 9858m, 9858n

Oct. 7, 1998, P.L. 105-244, 42 U.S. Code § 9877

Child Care and Development Block Grant Amendments of 1996

Aug. 22, 1996, P.L. 104-193, 42 U.S. Code § 9801 nt.

Child Care and Development Services Act

Cal. Education Code 1976, § 8200 et seq.

Child Care and Employment Act

Cal. Education Code 1976, § 8420 et seq.

Child Care Center Act (McBride)

Cal. Education Code 1959, § 8200 et seq.

Child Care Center Regulatory Act (Prescribed)

Tenn. Public Acts 1992, Ch. 1030

Child Care Certification Act

Wyo. Stat. Ann., § 14-4-101 et seq.

Child Care Development Act

Mo. Rev. Stat., 660.500 et seq.

Child Care Facilities Financing Act

Cal. Health and Safety Code § 1499 et seq.

Child Care Facilities Licensing Act

Okla. Stat. Ann., Title 10, § 401 et seq.

Child Care Facility and Child Placing Agency Licensing Act

La. Rev. Stat. Ann., 46:1401 et seq.

Child Care Initiative Act

S.C. Acts 1989, p. 623, No. 189, Part 2, § 43

Child Care License Act

Ark. Code Ann. 1987, 20-78-201 et seq.

Ida. Code 1947, 39-1101 et seq.

Md. Ann. Code 1974, Art. FL, § 5-501 et seq.

Miss. Code Ann., § 43-20-1 et seq.

N.J. Stat. Ann., 30:1-25 et seq., 30:5B-1 et seq.

Okla. Stat. Ann., Title 10, § 401 et seq.

Tex. Human Resources Code, § 42.001 et seq.

Child Care Partnership Act

Fla. Stat. Ann., 409.178

Child Care Program (School-Age)

N.Y. Education Law 1947 (Consol. Laws Ch. 16) § 414, Subd. 1

N.Y. Social Services Law (Consol. Laws Ch. 55) § 410c, Subd. 5

Child Care Provider Registration Act

Cal. Health and Safety Code § 1596.60 et seq.

Child Care Registration Law

La. Rev. Stat. Ann., 46:1441 et seq.

Child Care Services Act (Miller)

Cal. Welfare and Institutions Code § 10811

Child Care Services Act (State Agency Employees)

Ill. Rev. Stat. 1991, Ch. 127 § 3001 et seq.

Child Care Support Act (Senior Citizens)

Ill. Rev. Stat. 1991, Ch. 23. § 7001 et seq.

Child-Care Training Center Pilot Programs Act

Tex. Labor Code, § 302.003

Child Civil Rights Act of 1964

March 22, 1988, P.L. 100-259, 102 Stat. 31, 42 U.S. Code § 2000d-4a

Child Curfew Act
Ill. Comp. Stat. 1992, Ch. 720, § 555/0.01 et seq.
Ill. Rev. Stat. 1991, Ch. 23, § 2370.9 et seq.
Tenn. Code Ann., 39-17-1601 et seq.

Child Custody Act
Mich. Comp. Laws Ann., 722.21 et seq.
N.C. Gen. Stat. 1943, § 50-13.1 et seq.
Okla. Stat. Ann., Title 10, § 25 et seq.

Child Custody Jurisdiction Act
See Uniform Child Custody Jurisdiction Act

Child Custody Jurisdiction and Enforcement Act
See Uniform Child Custody Jurisdiction and Enforcement Act

Child Day Care Center Act
Conn. Gen. Stat. Ann., § 19a-77 et seq.

Child Day Care Facilities Act
Cal. Health and Safety Code § 1596.70 et seq.
S.C. Code Ann. 1976, § 20-7-2700 et seq.

Child Day Care License Act
Pa. 1959 Pamph. Laws 1395, No. 494

Child Death Act
Wash. Rev. Code Ann., 4.24.010

Child Death Review Board Act
Okla. Stat. Ann., Title 10, § 1150 et seq.

Child Death Review Team Act
Ill. Comp. Stat. 1992, Ch. 20, § 515/1

Child Delinquency Act
Colo. Rev. Stat., 19-7-101 et seq.
Ky. Rev. Stat. 1971, 600.010 et seq.
Tex. Family Code, § 51.01 et seq.

Child Desertion Act
Iowa Code Ann., 726.3
Ky. Rev. Stat. 1971, 530.040, 530.050

Child Development Act
Cal. Education Code 1976, § 8200 et seq.

Tenn. Code Ann., 37-3-101 et seq.

Child Development Act (Gifted)
N.J. Laws 1979, Ch. 192

Child Development Assistance Act
Iowa Code Ann., 256A.1 et seq.

Child Development Associate Scholarship Assistance Act of 1985
Sept. 30, 1986, P.L. 99-425, 42 U.S. Code § 10901 nt.
Nov. 3, 1990, P.L. 101-501, 42 U.S. Code §§ 10902, 10903, 10905
May 18, 1994, P.L. 103-252, 42 U.S. Code § 10905

Child Development Facilities Regulation Amendment Act
D.C. Code Ann., § 1-319

Child Development Reform Act
Cal. Statutes 1985, Ch. 1278

Child Development Teacher and Supervisor Grant Program
Cal. Education Code 1976, § 69620 et seq.

Child Development Teacher Scholarship Act
Ill. Comp. Stat. 1992, Ch. 110, § 922/1 et seq.

Child Exploitation and Pornography Prevention Act (Computer)
Fla. Stat. Ann., 847.0135

Child Exploitation Prevention and Computer Pornography Act
Ga. Code Ann., 16-12-100.2

Child Exploitation Protection Act
Ark. Code Ann. 1987, 5-27-301 et seq.

Child Fatality Review and Prevention Act
S.C. Acts 1993, p. 1263, No. 164
Tenn. Code Ann., 68-142-101 to 68-142-104

Child Health Act
N.M. Stat. Ann., 27-12-1 to 27-12-7

Child Health Associate Law
Colo. Rev. Stat., 12-31-101 et seq.

Child Health Assurance Act
Fla. Stat. 1983, 626.6416 et seq.

Child Health Insurance Reform Act
Okla. Stat. Ann., Title 36, § 3201 et seq.

Child Health Insurance Reform Plan
Mo. Rev. Stat., 376.801

Child Hearing Test Act
Ill. Rev. Stat. 1991, Ch. 23, § 2331 et seq.

Child Identification and Protection Act
Mich. Comp. Laws Ann., 722.771 et seq.

Child Immunization Act
Miss. Code Ann., §§ 41-88-1, 41-88-3

Child in Need of Aid Act
Alaska Stat. 1962, § 47.10.010 et seq.

Child Insurance Health Reform Act
Okla. Stat. Ann., Title 36, § 3201 et seq.

Child Labor Act
Ala. Code 1975, § 25-8-1 et seq.
Ariz. Rev. Stat. Ann., § 23-231 et seq.
Ark. Code Ann. 1987, 11-6-104 et seq.
Cal. Labor Code §§ 1285 et seq., 1290 to 1308
Colo. Rev. Stat., 8-12-101 et seq.
D.C. Code Ann., § 36-501 et seq.
Del. Code of 1974, Title 19, § 501 et seq.
Fla. Stat. Ann., 450.001 et seq.
Ga. Code Ann., 39-2-1 et seq.
Haw. Rev. Stat. Ann., § 390-1 et seq.
Ida. Code 1947, 44-1301 et seq.
Ill. Comp. Stat. 1992, Ch. 820, § 205/1 et seq.
Ind. Code Ann., 20-8.1-4-1 et seq.
Iowa Code Ann., 92.1 et seq.
Kan. Stat. Ann., 38-601 et seq.
Ky. Rev. Stat. 1971, 339.210 et seq.
La. Rev. Stat. Ann., 23:151 et seq.
Mass. Gen. Laws Ann., 149:56 et seq.
Md. Ann. Code 1974, Art. LE, § 3-201 et seq.
Me. Rev. Stat. Ann. 1964, Title 26, § 771 et seq.
Mich. Comp. Laws Ann., 409.1 et seq.

Minn. Stat. Ann., 181A.01 et seq.
Miss. Code Ann., § 71-1-17 et seq.
Mo. Rev. Stat., 294.011 et seq.
Mont. Code Ann., 41-2-101 et seq.
N.D. Cent. Code, 34-07-01 et seq.
Neb. Rev. Stat. 1943, 48-302 et seq.
N.H. Rev. Stat. 1955, 276A:1 et seq.
N.J. Stat. Ann., 34:2-21.1 et seq.
N.M. Stat. Ann., 50-6-1 et seq.
N.Y. Labor Law (Consol. Laws Ch. 31) § 130 et seq.
Ohio Rev. Code 4109.01 et seq.
Okla. Stat. Ann., Title 40, § 71 et seq.
Ore. Rev. Stat., 653.305 et seq.
Pa. Purdon's Stat., Title 43, § 41 et seq.
P.R. Laws Ann. 1954, Title 29, § 431 et seq.
R.I. Gen. Laws 1956, 28-3-1 et seq.
S.C. Code Ann. 1976, § 41-13-10
S.D. Codified Laws 1967, 60-12-1 et seq.
Tenn. Code Ann., 50-5-101 et seq.
Tex. Rev. Civ. Stat., Art. 5181.1
Utah Code Ann. 1953, 34-23-1 et seq.
Va. Code 1950, § 40.1-78 et seq.
Vt. Stat. Ann., Title 21, § 431 et seq.
Wash. Rev. Code Ann., 26.28.060, 26.28.070, 49.12.005 et seq.
Wis. Stat. 1989, 103.64 et seq.
W. Va. Code 1966, § 21-6-1 et seq.
Wyo. Stat. Ann., § 27-6-107 et seq.

Child Labor Act (Anthracite Coal Mines)
Pa. Purdon's Stat., Title 52, § 31 et seq.

Child Labor Amendments of 1976
D.C. Code Ann., § 36-501 et seq.

Child Labor Law (District of Columbia)
May 28, 1908, Ch. 209, 35 Stat. 420
Sept. 1, 1916, Ch. 432, 39 Stat. 675

Child Labor Standards Act
Mont. Code Ann., 41-2-102 et seq.

Child Labor Tax Act
Cal. Business and Professions Code § 17801 et seq.

Child Labor Tax Acts
Feb. 24, 1919, Ch. 18, 40 Stat. 1138
Continued

Nov. 23, 1921, Ch. 136, 42 Stat. 306

Child Marriage, and Family Counselors Act
Cal. Business and Professions Code, 4980 et seq.

Child Medical Support Act
Ariz. Rev. Stat. Ann., § 12-2481 et seq.

Child Molestation Law
Cal. Penal Law § 647a
Fla. Stat. Ann., 794.011 et seq.

Child Mortality Prevention Act (Fetal Infant)
Mont. Code Ann., 50-19-401 et seq.

Child Neglect Act
Ill. Rev. Stat. 1965, Ch. 23 § 2001 et seq.
N.Y. Code of Criminal Procedure, § 913a et seq.

Child Nutrition Act
Alaska Stat. 1962, Replaced Titles, § 14.52.010 et seq.
Cal. Education Code 1976, § 49530 et seq.

Child Nutrition Act of 1966
Oct. 11, 1966, P.L. 89-642, 80 Stat. 885, 42 U.S. Code §§ 1771 to 1785
May 8, 1968, P.L. 90-302, 82 Stat. 119, 42 U.S. Code §§ 1773, 1776
May 14, 1970, P.L. 91-248, 84 Stat. 208, 42 U.S. Code §§ 1773, 1774, 1776, 1779
June 30, 1970, P.L. 91-295, 84 Stat. 336, 42 U.S. Code § 1772
June 30, 1971, P.L. 92-32, 85 Stat. 85, 42 U.S. Code § 1773
Sept. 26, 1972, P.L. 92-433, 86 Stat. 724, 42 U.S. Code §§ 1773, 1774, 1779, 1786
Nov. 7, 1973, P.L. 93-150, 87 Stat. 562, 42 U.S. Code §§ 1772, 1773, 1786
Jan. 31, 1974, P.L. 93-247, 88 Stat. 5, 42 U.S. Code §§ 5101 to 5106
June 30, 1974, P.L. 93-326, 88 Stat. 287, 42 U.S. Code §§ 1774, 1786
July 12, 1974, P.L. 93-347, 88 Stat. 341, 42 U.S. Code § 1772
May 28, 1975, P.L. 94-28, 89 Stat. 96, 42 U.S. Code § 1786
Nov. 10, 1977, P.L. 95-166, 42 U.S. Code § 1771 et seq.

Nov. 1, 1978, P.L. 95-561, 42 U.S. Code §§ 1773, 1789
Nov. 10, 1978, P.L. 95-627, 42 U.S. Code §§ 1772 to 1774, 1776, 1784, 1786
Nov. 9, 1979, P.L. 96-108, 42 U.S. Code § 1786
July 2, 1986, P.L. 99-349, 100 Stat. 711
Oct. 18, 1986, P.L. 99-500, 42 U.S. Code §§ 1772 nt., 1772, 1773nt., 1773, 1776, 1784, 1786, 1786 nt., 1788, 1789
Oct. 30, 1986, P.L. 99-591, 42 U.S. Code §§ 1772 nt., 1772, 1773 nt., 1773, 1776, 1784, 1786, 1786 nt., 1788, 1789
Nov. 14, 1986, P.L. 99-661, 42 U.S. Code §§ 1772, 1772 nt., 1773, 1773 nt., 1766 nt., 1766 nt., 1776, 1784, 1786, 1786 nt., 1788, 1789
July 11, 1987, P.L. 100-71, 42 U.S. Code §§ 1784, 1786
Jan. 8, 1988, P.L. 100-237, 42 U.S. Code § 1786
June 28, 1988, P.L. 100-356, 102 Stat. 669, 42 U.S. Code § 1786
Sept. 19, 1988, P.L.100-435, 102 Stat. 1657, 42 U.S. Code §§ 1773, 1786
Nov. 18, 1988, P.L. 100-690 42 U.S. Code, § 1786
Nov. 10, 1989, P.L. 101-147, 42 U.S. Code §§ 1722, 1773, 1776, 1776 nt., 1779, 1783, 1784, 1786, 1786 nts., 1788
July 12, 1990, P.L. 101-330, 42 U.S. Code § 1786
July 7, 1992, P.L. 102-314, 42 U.S. Code § 1786
Aug. 14, 1992, P.L. 102-342, 42 U.S. Code §§ 1786, 1790
Oct. 24, 1992, P.L. 102-512, 42 U.S. Code §§ 1776, 1786
Nov. 2, 1994, P.L. 103-448, 42 U.S. Code §§ 1773, 1776, 1786, 1779, 1788
Dec. 21, 1995, P.L. 104-66, 42 U.S. Code § 1786
Aug. 22, 1996, P.L. 104-193, 42 U.S. Code §§ 1772, 1773, 1776, 1779, 1780, 1784 to 1788
Oct. 31, 1998, P.L. 105-336, 42 U.S. Code §§ 1773, 1776, 1784, 1786, 1788
Nov. 10, 1998, P.L. 105-362, 42 U.S. Code § 1786

Child Nutrition Act of 1974
Cal. Education Code § 49530 et seq.

Child Nutrition Amendments of 1978
Nov. 10, 1978, P.L. 95-627, 42 U.S. Code
§ 1755 et seq.

Child Nutrition Amendments of 1986
Nov. 14, 1986, P.L. 99-661, 42 U.S. Code
§ 1751 nt.
Nov. 10, 1989, P.L. 101-147, 42 U.S. Code
§§ 1758, 1760, 1762a, 1772, 1773, 1786

Child Nutrition Amendments of 1992
Aug. 14, 1992, P.L. 102-342, 42 U.S. Code
§ 1751 nt.
Oct. 31, 1998, P.L. 105-336, 42 U.S. Code
§ 1769 nt.

**Child Nutrition and WIC Reauthorization
Act of 1989**
Nov. 10, 1989, P.L. 101-147, 42 U.S. Code
§§ 1751 nt.

Child Nutrition Facilities Act
Cal. Education Code 1959, §§ 10702, 11872,
11921 et seq., 11930 et seq., 16710, 17314,
17315, 17459 et seq.

Child Online Protection Act
Oct. 21, 1998, P.L. 105-277, Division C,
Title XIV, 112 Stat. 2681, 47 U.S. Code
§ 609 nt.

Child Passenger Protection Act
Ark. Code Ann. 1987, 27-34-101 et seq.
Cal. Vehicle Code 1959, § 27350 et seq.
Ill. Comp. Stat. 1992, Ch. 625, § 25/1 et seq.
Kan. Stat. Ann., 8-1343 et seq.

Child Passenger Restraint Act
Ill. Rev. Stat. 1991, Ch. 95 1/2, § 1101 et seq.

Child Performer and Athlete Protection Act
Fla. Stat., 743.08 to 743.095

**Child Physical and Sexual Abuse Victim
Protection Act**
Ala. Code 1975, § 15-25-30 et seq.

Child Placement Agency Act
Ark. Code Ann. 1987, 9-28-401 et seq.
Iowa Code Ann., 238.1 et seq.
N.D. Cent. Code, 50-12-01 et seq.
N.M. Ann. 1978, 40-7A-1 et seq.
R.I. Gen. Laws 1956, 42-73-1 et seq.

Child Placement Compact Act
Ala. Code 1975, 44-2-20 et seq.
Ariz. Rev. Stat., § 8-548 et seq.
Colo. Rev. Stat., 24-60-1801 et seq.
Conn. Gen. Stat. Ann., 17-81a et seq.
D.C. Code Ann., § 32-1001 et seq.
Kan. Stat. Ann., 38-1501 et seq.
Ky. Rev. Stat. 1971, 208A.300
La. Rev. Stat. Ann., 46:1700 et seq.
Me. Rev. Stat. Ann. 1964, Title 22, § 4191 et
seq.
Minn. Stat. Ann., 257.40 et seq.
N.C. Gen. Stat. 1943, § 110-57.1 et seq.
N.D. Cent. Code, 14-13-01 et seq.
Neb. Rev. Stat. 1943, 39-669.07 et seq.
N.H. Rev. Stat. 1955, 170-A:1 et seq.
Okla. Stat. Ann., Title 10, § 571 et seq.
Pa. Purdon's Stat., Title 62, § 746 et seq.
R.I. Gen. Laws 1956, 42-73-1 et seq.
S.D. Codified Laws 1967, 26-13-1 et seq.
Vt. Stat. Ann., Title 33, § 5901 et seq.
Wash. Rev. Code Ann., 26.34.010 et seq.
Wis. Stat. 1989, 48.988, 48.989
Wyo. Stat. Ann., § 14-5-101 et seq.

Child Placement Review Act
N.J. Stat. Ann., 30:4C-50 et seq.

**Child Placing Agency and Child Care
Facility Licensing Act**
La. Rev. Stat. Ann., 46:1401 et seq.

Child Pornography Law
S.C. Code Ann. 1976, § 16-3-80 et seq.

Child Pornography Prevention Act
Neb. Rev. Stat. 1943, 28-1463.01 et seq.

Child Pornography Prevention Act of 1996
Sept. 30, 1996, P.L. 104-208, Title I, § 121,
18 U.S. Code § 2251 nt.

Child Protection Act

Ala. Acts 1984, p. 442

Conn. Gen. Stat. Ann., § 21a-335 et seq.

Ga. Code Ann., 16-5-70, 16-6-3 to 16-6-5, 16-12-100, Subd. g.

Haw. Rev. Stat. Ann., § 587-1 et seq.

Ida. Code 1947, 16-1601 et seq.

Ill. Rev. Stat. 1991, Ch. 23, § 2211 et seq.

Kan. Stat. Ann., 60-3101 et seq.

Me. Rev. Stat. Ann. 1964, Title 22, § 4001 et seq.

Mich. Comp. Laws Ann., 722.553 et seq.

Mich. Comp. Laws Ann., 722.621 et seq.

N.H. Rev. Stat. 1955, 169-C:1 et seq.

P.R. Laws Ann. 1954, Title 8 § 401 et seq.

S.C. Code Ann. 1976, § 20-7-480 et seq.

Wyo. Stat. Ann., § 14-3-101 et seq.

Child Protection Act (Philipps—Reeves In-Home)

Cal. Health and Safety Code § 1597-80 et seq.

Child Protection Act of 1966

Nov. 3, 1966, P.L. 89-756, 80 Stat. 1303, 15 U.S. Code §§ 1261 to 1265, 1273

May 14, 1970, P.L. 91-248, 84 Stat. 208, 42 U.S. Code §§ 1773, 1774, 1776, 1779

June 30, 1970, P.L. 91-295, 84 Stat. 336, 42 U.S. Code § 1772

Child Protection Act of 1966 to 1984

Colo. Rev. Stat., 19-3-301 et seq., 19-10-101 et seq.

La. Rev. Stat. Ann., 15:587.1

Child Protection Act of 1984

May 21, 1984, P.L. 98-292, 18 U.S. Code §§ 2251, 2251 nt., 2252 to 2254

Child Protection and Family Preservation Reform Act

Ga. Code Ann., 49-5-200 et seq.

Child Protection and Obscenity Enforcement Act

Fla. Stat. Ann., 847.001, 847.012, 847.013, 847.0145, 847.0147

Child Protection and Obscenity Enforcement Act of 1988

Nov. 18, 1988, P.L. 100-690, 18 U.S. Code § 2251 nt.

Child Protection and Toy Safety Act of 1969

Nov. 6, 1969, P.L. 91-113, 83 Stat. 187, 15 U.S. Code §§ 401 nt., 1261, 1262, 1274

Child Protection from Domestic Violence Act

Del. Code of 1974, Title 13, § 701A et seq.

Child Protection Law (Battered)

N.Y. Family Court Act, § 1011 et seq.

N.Y. Penal Law 1965 (Consol. Laws Ch. 40) 260.10

N.Y. Social Services Law (Consol. Laws Ch. 55) § 411 et seq.

Child Protection Orders Act

Mo. Laws 1991, H.B. No. 598

Child Protection Reform Act

S.C. Laws 1996, p. 2731, No. 450

Child Protection Restoration and Penalties Enhancement Act of 1990

Nov. 29, 1990, P.L. 101-647, 18 U.S. Code §§ 1460, 2243, 2251 nt., 2252, 2257, 2257 nt.; 28 U.S. Code § 994 nt.

Child Protective Investigator and Child Welfare Specialist Certification Act

Ill. Comp. Stat. 1992, Ch. 225, § 420/1 et seq.

Child Protective Services Act

Cal. Welfare and Institutions Code § 16500 et seq.

N.Y. Social Services Law (Consol. Laws Ch. 55) § 411 et seq.

Pa. Cons. Stat., Title 23, § 6301 et seq.

W. Va. Code 1966 § 49-6D-1 et seq.

Child Protective Services Reform Act (Elisa's Law)

N.Y. Domestic Relations Law (Consol. Laws Ch. 14) § 240

N.Y. Family Court Act, § 651a

N.Y. Mental Hygiene Law 1972 (Consol. Laws Ch. 27) § 45.07

N.Y. Social Services Law (Consol. Laws Ch. 55) §§ 20, 372, 409a, 422, 422a, 424, 424a, 424c

Child Reporting Act (Abused and Neglected)
Ill. Comp. Stat. 1992, Ch. 325, § 5/1 et seq.

Child Reporting Act (Missing)
Ida. Code 1947, 18-4507 et seq.

Child Residential Home Notification Act
Miss. Code Ann., § 43-16-1 et seq.

Child Restraint Act
D.C. Code Ann., § 40-1201 et seq.
S.C. Code Ann. 1976, § 20-7-10 et seq.
Wyo. Stat. Ann., § 31-5-1301 et seq.

Child Restraint Law (Seat Belts)
N.Y. Vehicle and Traffic Law 1959 (Consol. Laws Ch. 71) § 1229c

Child Safety Act
Tenn. Code Ann., 55-9-602, 55-9-611

Child Safety Protection Act
June 16, 1994, P.L. 103-267, 15 U.S. Code §§ 1261 nt., 1278, 1278 nt., 2004 nt., 6001 et seq.

Child Safety Reform Act (Lance's Law)
Cal. Penal Code §§ 11165.12, 11166.9, 11167.5, 11169, 11170, 11170.5

Child Safety School Zone Act
Del. Code of 1974, Title 11, § 1112

Child Safety Transportation Act
N.Y. Education Law 1947 (Consol. Laws Ch. 16) §§ 3635, 3635b
N.Y. Transportation Law (Consol. Laws Ch. 61A) § 14

Child Sex Offender and Murderer Community Notification Law
Ill. Comp. Stat. 1992, Ch. 730, § 152/101 et seq.

Child Sex Offender Registration Act
Ark. Code Ann. 1987, 12-12-901 et seq.
Ill. Rev. Stat. 1991, Ch. 38, 221 et seq.

Child Sexual Abuse and Pornography Act of 1986
Nov. 7, 1986, P.L. 99-628, 18 U.S. Code § 2251 nt.

Child Sexual Abuse Prevention Act
Cal. Penal Code § 288
Ill. Comp. Stat. 1992, Ch. 325, § 15.0.01 et seq.

Child Sexual Abuse Victim Protection Act
Ala. Code 1975, § 15-25-30 et seq.

Child Support Act
Ala. Code 1975, § 38-10-1 et seq.
Ariz. Rev. Stat. Ann., § 12-2458
Ga. Code Ann. 19-6-17 et seq.
Mo. Rev. Stat., 454.010 et seq.
R.I. Gen. Laws 1956, 15-9-1 et seq.

Child Support Act (Expedited)
Ill. Rev. Stat. 1991, Ch. 40, § 2701 et seq.

Child Support Act (Office of)
Mich. Comp. Laws Ann., 400.231 et seq.

Child Support Act (Special)
P.R. Laws Ann. 1954, Title 8, § 501 et seq.

Child Support Administrative Process Act
Ky. Rev. Stat. 1971, 405.400 et seq.

Child Support and Maintenance Act
Miss. Code Ann., § 9-11-101 et seq.

Child Support Arrearage Liens Act
S.C. Code Ann. 1976, § 20-7-1295

Child Support Collection Reform Act
N.J. Stat. Ann., 2A:17-56.27 et seq.

Child Support Delinquency Reporting Act
Cal. Civil Code §§ 4750, 4751

Child Support Delinquency Reporting Law
Cal. Family Code §§ 4700, 4701

Child Support Enforcement Act
Colo. Rev. Stat., 26-13-101 et seq.
Mont. Code Ann., 40-5-401 et seq.
Continued

N.Y. Civil Practice Laws and Rules (Consol. Laws Ch. 8) §§ 5241, 5242, 5252

N.Y. Domestic Relations Law (Consol. Laws Ch. 14) §§ 37a, 236, 240, 244, 245

N.Y. Family Court Act §§ 117, 424, 433, 435, 439, 439a, 440, 448, 451, 460, 510a, 517, 522

N.Y. Social Services Law (Consol. Laws Ch. 55) §§ 111b, 111c, 111f, 111k, 111m, 111n

N.Y. Tax Law (Consol. Laws Ch. 60) § 171c

N.Y. Worker's Compensation Law (Consol. Laws Ch. 67) §§ 33, 218

Tenn. Public Acts 1985, Ch. 477

Wyo. Stat. Ann., § 20-6-101 et seq.

Child Support Enforcement Amendments of 1984

Aug. 16, 1984, P.L. 98-378, 26 U.S. Code §§ 6103, 6402, 7213; 42 U.S. Code §§ 602, 602 nt., 603, 606, 651 et seq., 664, 666, 667, 671, 1305 nt., 1315, 1396a

Oct. 13, 1988, P.L. 100-485, 102 Stat. 2393, 42 U.S. Code § 606 nt.

Dec. 19, 1989, P.L. 101-239, 42 U.S. Code § 606 nt.

Child Support Enforcement Improvements Act

Tex. Laws 69th Leg., 1986, p. 30, Ch. 10

Child Support Enforcement Procedures Act

Colo. Rev. Stat., 14-14-101 et seq.

Child Support Hearing Officer Act

N.M. Stat. Ann., 40-4B-1 et seq.

Child Support Income Deduction Act of 1981

Mont. Code Ann., 40-5-301 et seq.

Child Support Income Tax Setoff Act

Miss. Code Ann., § 27-7-501 et seq.

Child Support Income Withholding Act

Neb. Rev. Stat. 1943, 43-1601 et seq.

Child Support Information Act

Ill. Comp. Stat. 1992, Ch. 5, § 405/1 et seq.

Child Support Performance and Incentive Act of 1998

July 16, 1998, P.L. 105-200, 42 U.S. Code § 1305 nt.

Oct. 28, 1998, P.L. 105-306, 42 U.S. Code § 652 nt.

Child Support Program Improvement Act

N.J. Stat. Ann., 2A:17-56.7a et seq.

Child Support Recovery Act

Ga. Code Ann. 19-11-1 et seq.

Ky. Rev. Stat. 1971, 205.712 et seq.

Child Support Recovery Act of 1992

Oct. 25, 1992, P.L. 102-521, 18 U.S. Code § 228 nt.

Child Support Reform Act

Ala. Code 1975, § 30-3-190 et seq.

Child Support Security Act

Cal. Civil Code §§ 4700, 4710, 4750

Cal. Unemployment Insurance, § 1255.7

Child Support Security Deposit Act

R.I. Gen. Laws 1956, 15-19-1 et seq.

Child Support Standards Act

N.Y. Domestic Relations Laws (Consol. Laws, Ch. 14) § 240 et seq.

N.Y. Family Court Act §§ 413, 434, 440, 513

N.Y. Judiciary Law (Consol. Laws Ch. 30) § 216

N.Y. Social Services Law (Consol. Laws Ch. 55) §§ 111b,

Child Testing Act (Newborn)

Pa. Purdon's Stat., Title 35, § 621 et seq.

Child Victim Witness Pilot and Demonstration Programs

Cal. Penal Code § 14000 et seq.

Child Victim Witness Protection Act

Cal. Penal Code § 14150 et seq.

Mo. Rev. Stat., 491.675

Child Victims and Witnesses Bill of Rights

Del. Code 1974, Title 11, § 5131 et seq.

Child Victims of Criminal Sexual Offenses Privacy Act
Ill. Rev. Stat. 1991, Ch. 38, § 1451 et seq.

Child Vision and Hearing Test Act
Ill. Comp. Stat. 1992, Ch. 410, § 205/1 et seq.

Child Visitation Registry Act
Okla. Stat. Ann., Title 43, § 420

Child Welfare Act
Ind. Code Ann., 31-6-1-1 et seq.
Iowa Code Ann., 235.1 et seq.
N.C. Gen. Stat. 1943, § 110-1 et seq.
N.D. Cent. Code 50-09-01 et seq.
N.J. Stat. Ann., 9:11-9, 9:17-1
Ore. Rev. Stat., 418.001 et seq.
S.D. Codified Laws 1967, 26-6-1 et seq.
Tex. Human Resources Code, § 41.001 et seq.
Vt. Stat. Ann., Title 33, § 2751 et seq.
W. Va. Code 1966, § 49-1-1 et seq.

Child Welfare Act (Administration)
Miss. Code Ann., § 43-15-5 et seq.

Child Welfare Act (Homes)
Ohio Rev. Code 1953, 5153.01 et seq.

Child Welfare Agencies Act
Wash. Rev. Code Ann., 74.15.010 et seq.

Child Welfare Agency Licensing Act
Ark. Acts 1997, No. 1041

Child Welfare Reform Act
N.Y. Social Services Law (Consol. Laws Ch. 55) § 409 et seq.

Child Welfare Reform Act (Preventive Services)
N.Y. Social Services Law (Consol. Laws Ch. 55) §§ 22, 153d, 153e, 358a, 358b, 372b, 372c, 372e, 383, 387, 398b, 407, 409d et seq., 442

Child Welfare Sanitarium Act (Park)
Ill. Rev. Stat. 1989, Ch. 105, §§ 327v9, 327w

Child Welfare Services Act
Vt. Stat. Ann., Title 33, § 4901 et seq.

Child Welfare Specialist and Child Protective Investigator Certification Act
Ill. Comp. Stat. 1992, Ch. 225, § 420/1 et seq.

Child Witness Trauma Reduction Act
Ill. Comp. Stat. 1992, Ch. 705, §§ 80/0.01, 80/1

Childhood Assistance Act (Early)
Wash. Rev. Code 1983, 28A.215.900

Childhood Education Professional Loan Forgiveness Act
Pa. 1993 Pamph. Laws No. 73

Childhood Immunization Coverage Act
Tex. Insurance Code, § 21.53F

Childhood Immunization Insurance Act
Pa. Purdon's Stat., Title 40, § 3501 et seq.

Childhood Lead Poisoning Act
Minn. Stat. Ann., 144.9501 et seq.

Childhood Lead Poisoning Prevention Act
Cal. Health and Safety Code §§ 309.7, 372 et seq.
Del. Code of 1974, Title 16, § 2601 et seq.
Neb. Rev. Stat. 1943, 71-2513 et seq.

Childhood Vaccine Act
Neb. Rev. Stat. 1943, 71-526 et seq.

Children Aid Act (Dependent)
Nev. Rev. Stat. 1979 Reprint, 425.010 et seq.

Children and Families Act
Ore. Rev. Stat., 417.300 et seq.

Children and Families Act (Policy Council for)
Ga. Code Ann., 49-5-250 to 49-5-264

Children and Family Community Protection Act
Ill. Comp. Stat. 1992, Ch. 705, § 80/1

Children and Family Services Act
Ill. Comp. Stat. 1992, Ch. 20, § 505/1 et seq.
Wash. Rev. Code Ann., 74.14A.010 et seq.

Children and Family Trust Fund Act
N.Y. Executive Law (Consol. Laws, Ch. 18) § 171 et seq.

Children and Family Trust Fund Act (William B. Hoyt Memorial)
N.Y. Social Services Law (Consol. Laws Ch. 55) § 481a et seq.

Children and Juvenile Facility Criminal Records Screening Act
N.M. Stat. Ann., 32A-15-1 to 32A-15-4

Children and Pregnant Womens' Health Care Act
R.I. Gen. Laws 1956, 42-12.3-1 et seq.

Children and Youth Act
Ga. Code Ann., 49-5-1 et seq.

Children and Youth Act (Houston County Commission on)
Ga. Laws 1998, S.B. 373

Children and Youth Advocacy Council Act
N.C. Gen. Stat. 1943, § 143B-414 et seq.

Children and Youth At-Risk Act (Coordinated Services)
Utah Code Ann. 1953, 63-75-1 et seq.

Children and Youth Services Act (Community)
Ore. Rev. Stat., 417.400 et seq.

Children Born Out of Wedlock Act
D.C. Code 1973, § 16-2341 et seq.
Ind. Code Ann., 31-9-6.1-1 et seq.

Children Born Out of Wedlock Act (Inheritance)
Ind. Code Ann., 29-1-2-7

Children First Act
La. Rev. Stat. Ann., 17:3871 et seq.

Children First Program
Ala. Acts 1998, No. 382

Children in Need of Supervision and Delinquent Children Act
Tex. Family Code, Art. 51.01 et seq.

Children of Deceased Veterans Act
Ill. Comp. Stat. 1992, Ch. 330, §§ 105/0.01, 105/1

Children Placement Compact Act
See Interstate Compact on Placement of Children Act

Children Public Support Act
Utah Code Ann. 1953, 62A-11-301 et seq.

Children Resource Center Act (Emergency Medical Services for)
Okla. Stat. Ann., Title 63, § 1-706.10 et seq.

Children Services Act (Hearing Impaired and Behavior Disordered)
Ill. Rev. Stat. 1991, Ch. 23, §§ 3404.9, 3405

Children with Disabilities and Family Service System Act
Neb. Rev. Stat. 1943, 79-3901 et seq.

Children with Disabilities Temporary Care Reauthorization Act of 1989
Oct. 25, 1989, P.L. 101-127, 42 U.S. Code § 5117 nt.

Children, Youth and Families Act (Dublin-Laurens County)
Ga. Laws 1998, H.B. 1763

Children, Youth and Families Department Act
N.M. Stat. Ann., 9-2A-1 et seq.

Children's Act for Clean Indoor Air
Tenn. Code Ann., 39-17-1601 et seq.

Children's Advocacy Center Act
Ill. Comp. Stat. 1992, Ch. 55, § 80/1 et seq.

Children's Agency Licensing Act
Okla. Stat. Ann., Title 10, § 401 et seq.

Children's Aid Act
Ga. Code Ann., 49-4-100 et seq.
Minn. Stat. Ann., 256.72 et seq.
N.C. Gen. Stat. 1943, § 108-38 et seq.

Children's Bicycle Helmet Safety Act of 1994
June 16, 1994, P.L. 103-267, 15 U.S. Code §§ 6001 nt., 6001 et seq.

Children's Bill of Rights
Ill. Comp. Stat. 1992, Ch. 725, § 115/1 et seq.
N.Y. Family Court Act, § 1011 et seq.

Children's Bureau Act
April 9, 1912, Ch. 73, 37 Stat. 79

Children's Center Construction Act
Cal. Education Code 1976, § 16260 et seq.

Children's Civil Commitment and Mental Health Treatment Act
Cal. Welfare and Institutions Code § 5585 et seq.

Children's Code
Colo. Rev. Stat., 19-1-101 et seq.
Kan. Stat. Ann., 38-1501 et seq.
La. Acts 1991, No. 235
N.M. Stat. Ann., 32A-1-1 et seq.
Okla. Stat. Ann., Title 10, § 7001-1.1 et seq.
S.C. Code Ann. 1976, § 20-7-10 et seq.
Wis. Stat. 1989, 48.01 et seq.

Children's Code Records and Information Act
Colo. Rev. Stat., 19-1-301 to 19-1-311

Children's Community Mental Health Act
N.C. Laws 1973, Ch. 584

Children's Court Act
Okla. Stat. 1961, Title 20, § 91.1 et seq.

Children's Court Act of the City of New York
N.Y. Laws 1924, Ch. 254

Children's Court Act of the State of New York
N.Y. Laws 1930, Ch. 393

Childrens Court of Conciliation Law
Cal. Code of Civil Procedure § 1740 et seq.

Children's Crusade for Higher Education Act
R.I. Gen. Laws 1956, 16-70-1 et seq.

Childrens Custody Act
Mich. Comp. Laws 1948, 722.541

Children's Early Investment Act
Fla. Stat. Ann., 411.23

Children's Educational Act (Exceptional)
Colo. Rev. Stat., 22-20-101 et seq.

Children's Emancipation Act
Ga. Code Ann., 19-9-3

Children's Emergency Medical Services Act
S.C. Code Ann. 1976, § 44-61-300 et seq.

Children's Firearm Accident Prevention Act
Cal. Penal Code §§ 12035, 12071

Children's Health Care Act
Miss. Code Ann., § 41-86-1 et seq.
Pa. Purdon's Stat., Title 62, § 5001.101 et seq.

Children's Health Care Plan
N.H. Rev. Stat. 1955, 167:66

Children's Health Care Trust Fund Act
Miss. Laws 1999, H.B. 69

Children's Health Insurance Program Act
Ill. Comp. Stat. 1992, Ch. 215, § 106/1 et seq.
Miss. Code Ann., § 41-86-1 et seq.

Children's Health Plan Act
Colo. Rev. Stat., 26-17-101 et seq.

Children's Healthy Start Support Services Act
Cal. Education Code 1976 § 8800 et seq.

Children's Hospital Act
N.J. Stat. Ann., 26:2H-1 et seq., 26:2H-18c et seq.

Children's Internet Protection Act
Cal. Education Code 1976, §§ 48980, 51870.5

Children's Justice Act
Aug. 27, 1986, P.L. 99-401, 42 U.S. Code §§ 290dd-3, 290ee-3, 5101, 5101 nts., 5103, 5105, 10601, 10603, 10603a

Children's Justice and Assistance Act of 1986
Aug. 27, 1986, P.L. 99-401, 42 U.S. Code § 5101 nt.

Children's Medical Services Act
Fla. Stat. 1983, 391.011 et seq.

Children's Mental Health Act (Comprehensive)
Minn. Stat. Ann., 245.487 et seq.

Children's Mental Health and Developmental Disabilities Act
N.M. Stat. Ann., 32A-6-1 et seq.

Children's Mental Health Integrated Fund
Minn. Stat. Ann., 245.491 to 245.496

Children's Mental Health Services Act
Cal. Welfare and Institutions Code §§ 5565.10 et seq., 5850 et seq.
Cal. Welfare and Institutions Code § 5850 et seq.

Children's Nutrition Assistance Act of 1992
Oct. 24, 1992, P.L. 102-512, 42 U.S. Code § 1771 nt.

Children's Ombudsman Act
Mich. Comp. Laws Ann., 722.921 et seq.

Children's Online Privacy Protection Act of 1998
Oct. 21, 1998, P.L. 105-277, Division C, Title XIII, 112 Stat. 2681, 15 U.S. Code § 6501 nt.

Children's Placement Compact Act
Ky. Rev. Stat. 1971, 615.030, 615.040
S.C. Code Ann. 1976, § 20-7-1980 et seq.

Children's Poison Protection Act
Cal. Health and Safety Code § 30050 et seq.

Children's Preventive Health Care Act
Ark. Code 1987, 23-79-141

Children's Program Act (Uninsured)
Ark. Code Ann. 1987, 20-77-601 et seq.

Children's School-based Early Mental Health Intervention and Prevention Services Act
Cal. Welfare and Institutions Code § 4370 et seq.

Children's Services Act
Cal. Health and Safety Code § 248 et seq.

Children's Services Act (Interim)
Me. Rev. Stat. Ann. 1964, Title 22, § 3711 et seq.

Children's Services Act (Mental Health)
Cal. Welfare and Institutions Code § 5850 et seq.

Children's Services Commission Act
Tenn. Code Ann., 37-3-101 et seq.

Children's Services Department Act (Counties)
Tenn. Code Ann., 37-2-201 et seq.

Children's Shelter Care Act
N.M. Stat. Ann., 32A-9-1 to 32A-9-7
Tenn. Code Ann., 37-3-101 et seq.

Children's Support Act (Unmarried Parents)
N.C. Gen. Stat. 1943, § 49-1 et seq.

Children's Surgical Institute Act
Ill. Rev. Stat. 1991, Ch. 23, § 2200 et seq.

Children's Television Act of 1990
Oct. 18, 1990, P.L. 101-437, 47 U.S. Code § 609 nt.

Aug. 26, 1992, P.L. 102-356, 47 U.S. Code § 303b

Oct. 25, 1994, P.L. 103-414, 47 U.S. Code § 303b

Childrens Trust Fund Act

Colo. Rev. Stat., 19-3.5-101 et seq.

Del. Code of 1974, Title 31, § 401 et seq.

La. Rev. Stat. Ann., 46:2401 et seq.

Miss. Code Ann., § 93-21-301 et seq.

N.J. Stat. Ann., 9:6A-1 et seq., 54A-9-25.4, 54A-9-25.5

N.M. Stat. Ann., 24-19-1 et seq.

Pa. Purdon's Stat., Title 11, § 2231 et seq.

Wyo. Stat. Ann., § 14-8-101 et seq.

Children's Vision Screening Act

Tex. Health and Safety Code, § 36.001 et seq.

China Affairs Council Act

Ill. Comp. Stat. 1992, Ch. 625, § 15/1

China Aid Act

Feb. 7, 1942, Ch. 47, 56 Stat. 82

China Aid Act of 1948

April 3, 1948, Ch. 169, 62 Stat. 158

China Appropriation Act

Feb. 12, 1942, Ch. 71, 56 Stat. 89

China Area Aid Act of 1950

June 5, 1950, Ch. 220, 64 Stat. 202

China Trade Act (Corporations Act)

June 6, 1932, Ch. 209, 47 Stat. 232

China Trade Acts

Sept. 19, 1922, Ch. 346, 42 Stat. 849, 15 U.S. Code §§ 141 to 162

Feb. 26, 1925, Ch. 345, 43 Stat. 995 to 997, 15 U.S. Code §§ 144, 146, 147, 149, 150, 160, 162

Oct. 15, 1970, P.L. 91-452, 84 Stat. 929, 15 U.S. Code § 155

Chinese Restriction Act

Haw. Session Laws 1887, Sp. Sess., Ch. 28

Chinese Student Protection Act of 1992

Oct. 9, 1992, P.L. 102-404, 8 U.S. Code § 1255 nt.

Chino Basin Production Assessment Law

Cal. Water Code § 72140 et seq.

Chipley Revenue Financing Act

Fla. Special Laws 1941, Ch. 21145

Chiropody Act

Mass. Gen. Laws Ann., 112:13 et seq.

Okla. Stat. Ann., Title 59, § 136 et seq.

Vt. Stat. Ann., Title 26, § 321 et seq.

Chiropractic Act

Ala. Code 1975, § 34-24-230 et seq.

Ariz. Rev. Stat. Ann., § 32-901 et seq.

Ark. Code Ann. 1987, 17-81-101 et seq.

Cal. Business and Professions Code, Appendix

Fla. Stat. Ann., 460.401 et seq.

Ga. Code Ann., 43-9-1 et seq.

Ida. Code 1947, 54-701 et seq.

Ill. Rev. Stat. 1991, Ch. 111, § 4801 et seq.

Ind. Code Ann., 25-10-1-1 et seq.

Iowa Code Ann., 151.1 et seq.

Ky. Rev. Stat. 1971, 312.015 et seq.

Mass. Gen. Laws Ann., 112:89 et seq.

Md. Ann. Code 1974, Art. HO, §§ 3-101 et seq., 16-101 et seq.

Mich. Comp. Laws Ann., 338.301 et seq.

Mont. Code Ann., 37-6-101 et seq.

N.D. Cent. Code, 43-05-01 et seq.

Nev. Rev. Stat. 1979 Reprint, 635.010 et seq.

N.H. Rev. Stat. 1955, 315:1 et seq.

N.J. Stat. Ann., 45:9-41.1 et seq.

N.M. Stat. Ann., 61-4-1 et seq.

Ore. Rev. Stat., 684.010 et seq.

Pa. Purdon's Stat., Title 63, §§ 42.1 et seq., 601 et seq., 625.101 et seq.

P.R. Laws Ann. 1954, Title 20, § 151 et seq.

R.I. Gen Laws 1956, 5-29-1 et seq.

S.C. Code Ann. 1976, §§ 40-9-10 et seq., 40-51-10 et seq., 59-103-120 et seq.

Tex. Rev. Civ. Stat., Art. 4512b, 4567 et seq.

Vt. Stat. Ann., Title 26, § 321 et seq.

Vt. Stat. Ann., Title 26, § 421 et seq.

Continued

Wash. Rev. Code Ann., 18.22.003 et seq., 18.25.003 et seq.

Wis. Stat. 1989, 448.01 et seq.

W. Va. Code 1966, § 30-11-1 et seq.

Wyo. Stat. Ann., § 33-10-101 et seq.

Chiropractic Amendments Act
Ala. Code 1975, § 34-24-120 et seq.

Chiropractic Board Act
N.J. Stat. Ann., 45:9-41.17 et seq.

Chiropractic Corporations Act
Cal. Business and Professions Code § 1050 et seq.
La. Rev. Stat. Ann., 12:1051 et seq.
Minn. Stat. Ann., 319A.01 et seq.
S.D. Codified Laws 1967, 47-11A-1 et seq.

Chiropractic Improvements Act
Utah Code Ann. 1953, 58-12-50 et seq.

Chiropractic Legal Panel Act
Mont. Code Ann., 27-12-101 et seq.

Chiropractic Practice Act
Okla. Stat. Ann., Title 59, § 161.1 et seq.

Chiropractor's Lien Act
Mont. Code Ann., 71-3-1111 et seq.

Chittenden County Circumferential Highway Act
Vt. Acts 1985, No. 185

Chloroflourocarbon Reduction and Recycling Act (Comprehensive)
Minn. Stat. Ann., 116.731 et seq.

Chlorofluorocarbon Reduction and Recycling Act
Minn. Stat. Ann., 116.70 et seq.

Choctaw-Chickasaw Supplemental Agreement.
July 1, 1902, Ch. 1362, 32 Stat. 641, 16 U.S. Code § 151

Choice for Customers of Electric Cooperatives Act (Electricity Generation)
Pa. Cons. Stat., Title 66, § 2801 et seq.

Choice in Education Act
Wash. Init. Meas. No. 173, § 2, prec. Wash. Rev. Code Ann., 28A.01.010

Choice in Public Housing Management Act
Oct. 21, 1998, P.L. 105-276, 42 U.S. Code § 1437w

Choice in Public Housing Management Act of 1991
Oct. 28, 1992, P.L. 102-550, 42 U.S. Code § 1437w

Choice of Forum Act
Neb. Rev. Stat. 1943, 25-413 et seq.
N.H. Rev. Stat. 1955, 508-A:1 et seq.

Choice of Law and Forum Act
Ill. Comp. Stat. 1992, Ch. 735, § 105/5-1 et seq.

Choke-Saving Methods Act
Ill. Comp. Stat. 1992, Ch. 410, § 10/1 et seq.
Ind. Code Ann., 16-1-41-1 et seq.

Cholera Control Act
Neb. Rev. Stat. 1943, 54-1513 et seq.

Cholesterol Screening Center Licensure Act
Fla. Stat. Ann., 483.601 et seq.

Chop Shop, Stolen and Altered Property Act (Motor Vehicle)
Ga. Code Ann., 16-8-80 et seq.
Miss. Code Ann., § 63-25-1 et seq.
N.Y. Penal Law 1965 (Consol. Laws Ch. 40) §§ 170.70, 170.71
Okla. Stat. Ann., Title 47, § 1501 et seq.
S.C. Code of Law 1976, § 56-29-10 et seq.

Chop Shop Stolen Motor Vehicle and Altered Property Act
R.I. Gen. Laws 1956, 31-48-1 et seq.

Chowan-Perquimans County Peace Officers' Relief Act
N.C. Laws 1963, Ch. 86

Christa McAuliffe Ambassador for Education Act
Fla. Stat. Ann., 231.6255

Christensen-Belotti Act (Logging Trucks)
Cal. Vehicle Code 1959, § 35552

Christmas Tree Act
Me. Rev. Stat. Ann. 1964, Title 12, § 8841 et seq.

Christmas Tree Regulation Act
Colo. Rev. Stat., 23-30-401 et seq.

Christopher Columbus Fellowship Act
May 13, 1992, P.L. 102-281, 20 U.S. Code §§ 5701 to 5708; 5701 nt.

Christopher Columbus Quincentenary Jubilee Act
Aug. 8, 1984, P.L. 98-375
Aug. 18, 1987, P.L. 100-94, 101 Stat. 700
Me. Rev. Stat. Ann. 1964, Title 32, § 4401 et seq.

Christopher Columbus Quincentenery Coin Act
May 13, 1992, P.L. 102-281, 31 U.S. Code § 5112 nt.

Chronic Alcoholics Act
N.C. Gen. Stat. 1943, § 122-65.6 et seq.
Wash. Rev. Code Ann., 70.96A.010 et seq.

Chronic Disabilities Act (Community Trust)
N.J. Stat. Ann., 3B:11-19 et seq.

Chronic Disease Prevention, Assessment, and Control Act
N.H. Rev. Stat. 1955, 141-B:1 et seq.

Chronic Diseases Act
Fla. Stat. Ann., 385.101 et seq.

Chronically Ill and Disabled Children's Services Act
Tex. Health and Safety Code, § 35.001 et seq.

Chrysler Corporation Loan Guarantee Act of 1979
Jan. 7, 1980, P.L. 96-185, 15 U.S. Code §§ 631 nt., 1861 et seq., 2003, 2512

Church Arson Prevention Act of 1996
July 3, 1996, P.L. 104-155, 18 U.S. Code § 241 nt.

Churches, Religious Societies and Religious Organizations Act
Ind. Code 1971, 23-11-1-1 et seq.

Churchill Downs Authority Act
Ky. Rev. Stat. 1971, 58.500 et seq.

CIARDS Technical Corrections Act of 1992
Oct. 24, 1992, P.L. 102-496, 50 U.S. Code § 2001 nt.

Cigar and Cigarette Tax Act
Ark. Stat. 1947, 84-4212 et seq.
Del. Code of 1974, Title 30, § 5301 et seq.
Ga. Code Ann., 48-11-1 et seq.

Cigarette Act
Iowa Code Ann., 98.1 et seq.

Cigarette Act (Minors)
Okla. Stat. Ann., Title 21, § 1241 et seq.

Cigarette and Tobacco License Act
Neb. Rev. Stat. 1943, 28-1418 et seq.

Cigarette and Tobacco Products Sales Act
Okla. Stat. Ann., Title 68, § 326 et seq.

Cigarette and Tobacco Products Tax Bill of Rights
Cal. Revenue and Taxation Code § 30458 et seq.

Cigarette and Tobacco Tax Health Protection Act
Cal. Revenue and Taxation Code § 30121 et seq.

Cigarette, Cigarette Papers and Snuff Tax Act
N.D. Cent. Code 57-36-01 et seq.

Cigarette Excise Act
Mass. Gen. Laws Ann., 64C:1 et seq.

Cigarette Excise Stamp Act
Mass. Gen. Laws Ann., 64C:29 et seq.

Cigarette Fair Trade Act
Ind. Code Ann., 24-3-2-1 et seq.
N.M. Stat. Ann., 57-2-1 et seq.

Cigarette Health Warning Act
Ill. Comp. Stat. 1992, Ch. 410, § 85/1 et seq.

Cigarette Marketing Standards Act
N.Y. Tax Law (Consol. Laws Ch. 60) § 483 et seq.

Cigarette or Tobacco Products License Act
Md. Ann. Code 1957, Art. 56, § 65 et seq.
Ohio Rev. Code 1953, 5743.01 et seq.
Vt. Stat. Ann., Title 32, § 7771 et seq.

Cigarette Prohibitions Act
Ark. Acts 1907, p. 653, No. 280
Ohio Rev. Code 1953, 5743.41 et seq.

Cigarette Safety Act of 1984
Oct. 30, 1984, P.L. 98-567, 15 U.S. Code § 2054 nt.

Cigarette Sales Act
See also Unfair Cigarette and Tobacco Products Sales Act
Mont. Code Ann., 16-10-101 et seq.

Cigarette Sales Below Cost Act
Md. Ann. Code 1974, Art. CL, § 11-501 et seq.
Va. Code 1950, § 59.1-285 et seq.

Cigarette Sales Below Cost Act (Unfair)
Wash. Rev. Code Ann., 19.91.010 et seq.

Cigarette Tax Act
Alaska Stat. 1962, § 43.50.010 et seq.
Ark. Stat. 1947, 84-2301 et seq.
Cal. Revenue and Taxation Code § 30001 et seq.
D.C. Code Ann., § 47-2401 et seq.
Del. Code of 1974, Title 30, § 5301 et seq.
Fla. Stat. Ann., 210.01 et seq.
Ida. Code 1947, 63-2501 et seq.
Ill. Comp. Stat. 1992, Ch. 35, § 130/1 et seq.
Ill. Rev. Stat. 1991, Ch. 120, § 453.1 et seq.
Ind. Code Ann., 6-7-1-1 et seq.

Kan. Stat. Ann., 79-3301 et seq.
Ky. Rev. Stat. 1971, 138.130 et seq.
Mich. Comp. Laws Ann., 205.501 et seq.
Minn. Stat. Ann., 297.01 et seq.
Minn. Stat. Ann., 297.21 et seq.
Mo. Rev. Stat., 149.011 et seq.
Mont. Code Ann., 16-11-101 et seq.
Neb. Rev. Stat. 1943, 77-2601 et seq.
Nev. Rev. Stat. 1979 Reprint, 370.001 et seq.
N.J. Rev. Stat. 1937, 54:40A-1 et seq.
N.M. Stat. Ann., 7-12-1 et seq.
N.Y. Tax Law (Consol. Laws Ch. 60) § 470 et seq.
Ohio Rev. Code 1953, 5743.01 et seq.
Okla. Stat. Ann., Title 68, § 301 et seq.
Ore. Rev. Stat., 323.005 et seq.
Pa. Purdon's Stat., Title 72, § 8201 et seq.
R.I. Gen Laws 1956, 44-20-1 et seq.
S.D. Codified Laws 1967, 10-50-1 et seq.
Tex. Tax Code, § 154.001 et seq.
Utah Code Ann. 1953, 59-14-204 et seq.
Vt. Stat. Ann., Title 32, § 7771 et seq.
Wash. Rev. Code Ann., 82.24.010 et seq.
W. Va. Code 1966, § 11-17-1 et seq.

Cigarette Tax Restriction Act (Home Rule)
Ill. Comp. Stat. 1992, Ch. 35, § 140/l
Ill. Rev. Stat. 1991, Ch. 120, §§ 453.110, 453.111

Cigarette Unfair Sales Act
Conn. Gen. Stat. Ann., § 12-326a et seq.
Del. Code of 1974, Title 6, § 2601 et seq.
Ore. Laws 1951, Ch. 540

Cigarette Use and Storage Tax Act
Ohio Rev. Code 1953, 5743.31 et seq.

Cigarette Use Tax Act
Ill. Comp. Stat. 1992, Ch. 35, § 135/1 et seq.

Cigeratte Tax Law
Okla. Stat. Ann., Title 68, § 301 et seq.

Cihak-Montgomery-Romana Act (Charter Townships)
Mich. Comp. Laws Ann., 42.1 et seq.

Cilano Law (Wage Assignments)
N.Y. Personal Property Law (Consol. Laws Ch. 41) § 46

Circuit Apportionment Act (Cook County)
Ill. Rev. Stat. 1991, Ch. 37, § 901 et seq.

Circuit Breaker Law
Mont. Code Ann., 15-30-171 to 15-30-179

Circuit Breaker Tax Credit Act (Real Property Tax)
N.Y. Tax Law (Consol. Laws Ch. 60) § 606, Subd. e

Circuit Court Act
Conn. Gen. Stat. Ann., § 51-248 et seq.
Miss. Code Ann., § 9-7-1 et seq.
Utah Code Ann. 1953, 78-4-1 et seq.

Circuit Court Clerk Regulation Act
Ill. Comp. Stat. 1992, Ch. 705, § 110/0.01 et seq.

Circuit Court Clerks' Salary Act
Ky. Rev. Stat. 1971, 23A.010 et seq.
Mich. Comp. Laws 1948, 600.579 et seq.

Circuit Court Districts Act
Ky. Rev. Stat. 1971, 23A.010 et seq.

Circuit Court Drainage Act
Mo. Rev. Stat., 242.010 et seq.

Circuit Court Family Counseling Services Act
Mich. Comp. Laws Ann., 551.331 et seq.

Circuit Court Judges Travel Expense Act
Ill. Comp. Stat. 1992, Ch. 5, §§ 300/0.01, 300/1 et seq.

Circuit Court Marriage Counseling Service Act
Mich. Comp. Laws Ann., 551.331 et seq.

Circuit Court of Appeals Act
March 3, 1891, Ch. 517, 26 Stat. 826 (See 28 U.S. Code §§ 43, 44, 46, 604, 711, 713, 961, 962, 2101, 2106, 2107)

Circuit Courts Act
Ill. Comp. Stat. 1992, Ch. 705, § 35/0.01 et seq.

Circuit Judges Act
Ky. Rev. Stat. 1971, Superseded Vols., 21.305 et seq.

Circuit Judges' Retirement Act
Fla. Stat. Ann., 123.01 et seq.
Ky. Rev. Stat. 1971, 21.345 et seq.

Circuit Probation Officers Act
Ga. Code Ann., 42-8-25 et seq.

Circumferential Highway Act (Chittenden County)
Vt. Acts 1985, No. 185

Cities Act (Division Into Classes)
Pa. Purdon's Stat., Title 53, § 101 et seq.

Cities Airport Authorities Act
Neb. Rev. Stat. 1943, 3-514 et seq.

Cities and Towns Act
Colo. Rev. Stat., 31-1-101 et seq.
Ind. Code Ann., 36-3-1-1 et seq.
Wash. Rev. Code Ann., 35.01.010 et seq.

Cities and Towns Housing Act
Iowa Code Ann., 403A.1 et seq.

Cities and Towns Incorporation Act
Ind. Code 1976, 18-1-1-1 et seq.

Cities and Towns Validating Act
Tex. Local Gov. Code, § 43.903

Cities and Villages Act (Revised)
Ill. Rev. Stat. 1991, Ch. 24, § 21-0.1 et seq.

Cities Annexation Act
Wis. Stat. 1989, 66.021 et seq.

Cities of First and Second Class and Villages Industrial Areas
Neb. Rev. Stat. 1943, 19-2501 et seq.

Cities of First and Second Class Combined Improvement Act
Neb. Rev. Stat. 1943, 19-2408 et seq.

Cities of First Class Firemen's Pension Law
Neb. Rev. Stat. 1943, 35-201 et seq.

Cities of First Class Zoning Act
Neb. Rev. Stat. 1943, 19-901 et seq.

Cities of Primary, First and Second Classes and Villages
Neb. Rev. Stat. 1943, 19-1401 et seq.

Cities of Second Class Zoning Act
Neb. Rev. Stat. 1943, 19-901 et seq.

Cities of the First Class Intergovernmental Cooperation Authority Act
Pa. Purdon's Stat., Title 53, § 12720.101 et seq.

Citizen Complaint Act
Cal. Government Code §§ 8330 to 8332

Citizen Preference Act (Employment)
N.J. Stat. Ann.,34:9-1, 34:9-2

Citizen Review Board Pilot Program Act (Local)
Mont. Code Ann., 41-3-1001 et seq.

Citizen Substitute Care Review Act
N.M. Stat. Ann., 27-1-5 et seq., 32-7-1 et seq.
N.M. Stat. Ann., 32A-8-1 et seq.

Citizen's Advisory Board Act (Juvenile Courts)
Okla. Stat. 1961 Title 20, § 849

Citizens Aide Act
Iowa Code Ann., 2C.1 et seq.

Citizens Arrest Act
N.C. Gen. Stat. 1943, §§ 15A-404, 15A-405

Citizens Constitutional Rights and Dignity Act (Mentally Retarded)
D.C. Code Ann., § 6-1901 et seq.

Citizens Dispute Settlement Act
Fla. Stat. Ann., 44.201

Citizens' Income Security Act for Aged, Blind, and Disabled Californians
Cal. Welfare and Institutions Code § 12000 et seq.

Citizens Investigating Official (Ombudsman) Act
P.R. Laws Ann. 1954, Title 3, § 531 et seq.

Citizen's Job Protection Act
Conn. Gen. Stat. Ann., § 31-48a

Citizens' Public Assistance Act
Wash. Rev. Code Ann., 74.04.005 et seq., 74.08.025 et seq.

Citizens' Rights Act (Foreign States)
July 27, 1868, Ch. 249, 15 Stat. 223

Citizens' Security Act
Wash. Rev. Code Ann., 74.04.005 et seq., 74.08.025 et seq.

Citizens Self-Defense Act (Law Abiding)
S.C. Code Ann. 1976, § 23-31-205 et seq.

Citizens Utility Board Act
Ill. Comp. Stat. 1992, Ch. 220, § 10/1 et seq.
Wis. Stat. 1989, 199.01 et seq.

Citizenship Acts
March 2, 1907, Ch. 2534, 34 Stat. 1228
July 2, 1940, Ch. 509, 54 Stat. 715

Citizenship Day Act
Ill. Comp. Stat. 1992, Ch. 5, § 490/25

Citron Flood Compact Act
June 8, 1936, Ch. 542, 49 Stat. 1490, 33 U.S. Code § 567a

Citrus Advertising Act
Fla. Stat. Ann., 601.15

Citrus Code
Fla. Stat 1991, 601.01 et seq.

Citrus Commission Act
Tex. Rev. Civ. Stat., Art. 118d

Citrus County Hospital Act
Fla. Special Laws 1949, Ch. 25728

Citrus County Hospital Act (First Amendment)
Fla. Laws 1970, CH. 70-101

Citrus County Recreation and Water Conservation and Control Act
Fla. Special Laws 1967, Ch. 67-1205

Citrus Dealers Act
Tex. Agriculture Code, § 102.001 et seq.

Citrus Fruit Bond and License Act
Fla. Stat. Ann., 601.55 et seq.

Citrus Fruit Coloring Act
Tex. Agriculture Code, § 95.001 et seq.

Citrus Fruit Growers Act
Tex. Agriculture Code, § 102.001 et seq.

Citrus Fruit Inspection and Grading Act
Tex. Agriculture Code, § 93.001 et seq.

Citrus Fruit Labeling Act
Fla. Stat. Ann., 601.9905 et seq.

Citrus Fruit Regulatory Act
Ga. Code 1933, 5-632 et seq.

Citrus Fruit Standardization Act
Ariz. Rev. Stat. Ann., § 3-441 et seq.

Citrus Marketing Act
Fla. Stat. Ann., 600.011 et seq.
Tex. Agriculture Code, § 102.151 et seq.

Citrus Maturity Act
Fla. Stat. Ann., 601.9910

Citrus Pest District Control Act
Cal. Food and Agriculture Code 1967, § 8401 et seq.

Citrus Stabilization Act
Fla. Stat. Ann., 601.152, 601.154

Citrus, Stone and Pome Fruit Pest District Control Law
Cal. Food and Agriculture Code 1967, § 8401 et seq.

Citrus White Fly Prevention Law
Cal. Food and Agricultural Code 1967, § 5901 et seq.

City Act (Onondaga)
N.Y. Laws 1864, Ch. 366

City Act (Third Class)
Pa. Purdon's Stat., Title 53, § 35101 et seq.

City and County Consolidation Act
N.M. Stat. Ann. 1953, Superseded Vol., 14-12-1 et seq.

City and County Economic Development Grant Authorization Act
Ark. Code Ann. 1987, 14-173-101 et seq.

City and County Jails Act
Wash. Rev. Code Ann., 70.48.170 et seq.

City and County Lottery Act
Neb. Rev. Stat. 1943, 9-601 et seq.

City and County Ordinance Publication Law
Cal. Government Code §§ 50021, 50022

City and Park Exchange of Functions Act (Chicago)
Ill. Rev. Stat. 1991, Ch. 105, § 333.50 et seq.

City and School District Relief Act (Emergency)
N.Y. Unconsolidated Law, § 9471 et seq.

City and Town Development Act
Conn. Gen. Stat. Ann., § 7-480 et seq.

City and Town Street, Alley and Other Public Improvement Act
Ind. Code Ann., 19-8-16-1 et seq.

City and Village Planning Act
Mich. Comp. Laws Ann., 125.31 et seq.

City and Village Zoning Act
Mich. Comp. Laws Ann., 125.581 et seq.
Mich. Comp. Laws Ann., 125.593 et seq.

City Bond Act
Nev. Rev. Stat. 1979 Reprint, 268.672 et seq.

City Bond Validation Law
Cal. Statutes 1933, Ch. 17, p. 42
Cal. Statutes 1935, Ch. 90, p. 441
Cal. Statutes 1935, Ch. 115, p. 465

City Boundary Act
Kan. Stat. Ann., 12-517 et seq.

City Budget Act
Mont. Code Ann., 7-6-4201 et seq.
N.D. Cent. Code 40-40-01 et seq.
Wash. Rev. Code Ann., 35.32A.010 et seq.,
    35.33.011 et seq.

City Business Improvement District Act
Ga. Code Ann., 36-43-1 et seq.
N.Y. General City Law (Consol. Laws Ch.
    21) § 24a et seq.

City Carriers Act
Cal. Public Utilities Code § 3901 et seq.

City Carriers' Act (Property)
Cal. Statutes 1935, p. 1057

City Cemetery Act
Mich. Comp. Laws Ann., 128.11 et seq.

**City Center Authority Act (Saratoga
Springs)**
N.Y. Public Authorities Law (Consol. Laws
    Ch. 43A) § 2490a et seq.

City Charter Act (Augusta)
Ga. Laws 1947, p. 320

City Charters Local Option, Enabling Act
N.H. Rev. Stat. 1955, 49-B:1 et seq.

City Civil Service Act
Ill. Rev. Stat. 1991, Ch. 24, § 10-1-1 et seq.
La. Constitution 1974, Art. 10
La. Rev. Stat. Ann., 33:2391 et seq.

City Claims Act
Wash. Rev. Code Ann., 35.31.010 et seq.

City Cleanliness Act
Kan. Laws 1913, Ch. 107

City Code
Iowa Code Ann., 362.1 et seq.

City Code (Third Class)
Pa. Purdon's Stat., Title 53, § 35101 et seq.

City Commission Act
N.J. Stat. Ann., 40:70-1 to 40:78-5

City-County Act
Ore. Rev. Stat., 199.705 et seq.

City-County Act (Consolidation)
N.C. Gen. Stat. 1943, § 160B-1 et seq.
Tenn. Code Ann., 7-1-101 et seq.

City-County Building Act
N.M. Stat. Ann., 5-5-1 et seq.

City-County Consolidation Act
N.C. Gen. Stat. 1943, § 160B-1 et seq.

City-County Free Public Library Act
N.Y. Laws 1953, Ch. 768

City-County Library Act
Okla. Stat. Ann., Title 65, § 151 et seq.

City-County Park and Recreation Act
Okla. Stat. Ann., Title 19, § 1001 et seq.

City-County Planning Act
Mont. Code Ann., 76-1-101 et seq.

City-County Planning and Zoning Act
Okla. Stat. Ann., Title 19, § 863.1 et seq.

City-County Relief Tax Law
Nev. Rev. Stat. 1979 Reprint, 377.010 et seq.

**City-County Tourist Meeting and
    Entertainment Facilities Assistance Law**
Ark. Code Ann. 1987, 14-171-201 et seq.

City Court Act
Ill. Rev. Stat. 1963, Ch. 37, § 333 et seq.
La. Rev. Stat. Ann., 13:1871 et seq.
N.Y. Laws 1964, Ch. 497
N.Y. Uniform City Court Act, § 101 et seq.
Okla. Stat. 1961, Title 11, § 831 et seq.

City Court Act (Albany)
N.Y. Laws 1914, Ch. 368

City Court Act (Amsterdam)
N.Y. Laws 1955, Ch. 406

City Court Act (Binghamton)
N.Y. Laws 1931, Ch. 482
N.Y. Laws 1950, Ch. 370

City Court Act (Buffalo)
N.Y. Laws 1909, Ch. 570

City Court Act (Corning)
N.Y. Laws 1905, Ch. 142, § 86 et seq.

City Court Act (Cortland)
N.Y. Laws 1935, Ch. 423

City Court Act (Dublin)
Ga. Laws 1900, p. 117

City Court Act (Glens Falls)
N.Y. Laws 1961, Ch. 425

City Court Act (Hornell)
N.Y. Laws 1932, Ch. 434

City Court Act (Ithaca)
N.Y. Laws 1931, Ch. 415

City Court Act (Jamestown)
N.Y. Laws 1923, Ch. 666

City Court Act (Jefferson)
Ga. Laws 1903, p. 138

City Court Act (Kingston)
N.Y. Laws 1952, Ch. 813

City Court Act (Little Falls)
N.Y. Laws 1945, Ch. 544

City Court Act (Mechanicville)
N.Y. Laws 1955, Ch. 798

City Court Act (Middletown)
N.Y. Laws 1955, Ch. 730

City Court Act (Mount Vernon)
N.Y. Laws 1922, Ch. 490, § 173 et seq.

City Court Act (New Rochelle)
N.Y. Laws 1931, Ch. 499

City Court Act (New York)
N.Y. Laws 1926, Ch. 539

City Court Act (Newburgh)
N.Y. Laws 1948, Ch. 569

City Court Act (Niagara Falls)
N.Y. Laws 1957, Ch. 994

City Court Act (North Tonawanda)
N.Y. Laws 1942, Ch. 907

City Court Act (Norwich)
N.Y. Laws 1952, Ch. 812

City Court Act (Oswego)
N.Y. Laws 1933, Ch. 747

City Court Act (Port Jervis)
N.Y. Laws 1958, Ch. 270

City Court Act (Rochester)
N.Y. Laws 1918, Ch. 495, § 10
N.Y. Laws 1950, Ch. 771

City Court Act (Rome)
N.Y. Laws 1954, Ch. 579

City Court Act (Schenectady)
N.Y. Laws 1927, Ch. 393

City Court Act (Syracuse)
N.Y. Laws 1962, Ch. 513

City Court Act (Tonawanda)
N.Y. Laws 1942, Ch. 906

City Court Act (Troy)
N.Y. Laws 1939, Ch. 881

City Court Act (Utica)
N.Y. Laws 1882, Ch. 103
N.Y. Laws 1966, Ch. 443

City Court Act (White Plains)
N.Y. Laws 1915, Ch. 356, §§ 239 to 256
N.Y. Laws 1944, Ch. 783

City Court Act (Yonkers)
N.Y. Laws 1893, Ch. 416

City Court Act of Kansas City
Kan. Laws 1927, Ch. 180

City Court Act of Wichita
Kan. Laws 1899, Ch. 130

City Court of Polk County Juvenile Law
Ga. Laws 1947, p. 1245

City Court Practice Act (Schenectady)
N.Y. Laws 1927, Ch. 393

City Depository Act
Tex. Local Gov. Code, § 105.001 et seq.
Wash. Rev. Code Ann., 35.38.010 et seq.

City Economic Development Revenue Bond Law
Nev. Rev. Stat. 1979 Reprint, 268.512 et seq.

City Election Act
Ill. Rev. Stat. 1991, Ch. 46, § 6-2 et seq.

City Election Validation Act
Ill. Rev. Stat. 1991, Ch. 46, §§ 700, 701

City Eminent Domain Law
Wash. Rev. Code Ann., 8.12.010 et seq.

City Employees' Retirement Law (Third Class Cities)
Pa. Purdon's Stat., Title 53, § 39371 et seq.

City Employees' Retirement System Law
Wash. Rev. Code Ann., 41.44.010 et seq.

City Government Bill—Cities of the First Class
Ky. Rev. Stat. 1971, Superseded Volume, 83.010 et seq.

City Government Law (Optional)
N.Y. Laws 1914, Ch. 444

City Health Board Act
Wash. Rev. Code Ann., 70.05.005 et seq.

City Home Rule Act
Mich. Comp. Laws Ann., 117.1 et seq.
N.Y. Consol. Laws, Ch. 76

City Home Rule Law
N.Y. Municipal Home Rule (Consol. Laws Ch. 36A) § 1 et seq.

City Housing Codes Act
Colo. Rev. Stat., 29-4-101 et seq.
Iowa Code Ann., 364.17

City Income Tax Act
Mich. Comp. Laws Ann., 141.501 et seq.

City Income Tax Surcharge Act
N.Y. Tax Law (Consol. Laws Ch. 60) § 1320 et seq.

City Local Improvements Act
Wash. Rev. Code Ann., 35.43.010 et seq.

City Local Option Law
N.Y. Alcoholic Beverage Control Law(Consol. Laws Ch. 3B) § 140 et seq.

City Manager Act
Ala. Code 1975, § 11-43-20 et seq.
Alaska Stat. 1962, § 29.20.460 et seq.
Ark. Code Ann. 1987, 14-47-101 et seq.
Cal. Government Code § 34851 et seq.
Ill. Rev. Stat. 1991, Ch. 24, § 5-1-1 et seq.
Kan. Stat. Ann., 12-1001 et seq.
Ky. Rev. Stat. 1971, 83A.150
N.J. Stat. Ann., 40:79-1 et seq.
S.D. Codified Laws 1967, 9-10-1 et seq.
Tenn. Code Ann., 6-18-101 et seq.
Tex. Local Gov. Code, § 25.001 et seq.
Wash. Rev. Code Ann., 35.18.005 et seq.

City Manager Enabling Act
Ark. Code 1987, 14-61-101 et seq.

City Manager Enabling Act—Cities of Second, Third and Fourth Classes
Ky. Rev. Stat. 1971, Superseded Vols., 89.390 et seq.

City Merger or Consolidation Act
Ky. Rev. Stat. 1971, 81.410 et seq.

City Motor Vehicle Racing Act
Mich. Comp. Laws Ann., 257.1701 et seq.

City of Abbeville Community Improvement Act
La. Acts 1969, No. 171

City of Alabaster, Shelby County, Alabama, Civil Service System Act
Ala. Acts. 1993, p. 555, No. 358

City of Albany Parking Authority Act
N.Y. Public Authorities Law (Consol. Laws Ch. 43A) § 1493-a et seq.

City of Arcadia, Florida Revenue Financing Act of 1941
Fla. Special Laws 1941, Ch. 21102

City of Atlanta and Fulton County Recreation Authority Act
Ga. Laws 1960, p. 2810

City of Atlanta Group Insurance Board Authority Act
Ga. Laws 1979, p. 4037

City of Binghamton Parking Authority Act
N.Y. Public Authorities Law (Consol. Laws Ch. 43A), § 1599a et seq.

City of Boston Bond and Minibond Procedure Act
Mass. Acts 1983, Ch. 643

City of Cape Coral Health Facilities Authority Law
Fla. Special Laws 1975, Ch. 75-354

City of Chipley, Florida Revenue Financing Act of 1941
Fla. Special Laws 1941, Ch. 21145

City of Cohoes Parking Authority Act
N.Y. Public Authorities Law (Consol. Laws Ch. 43A), § 1599a et seq.

City of Dalton Airport Authority Ordinance
Ga. Laws 1988, p. 5201

City of Dalton Public Safety Commission Ordinance
Ga. Laws 1992, p. 7205

City of Dalton Street Improvement Act
Ga. Laws 1991, p. 5309

City of Daytona Beach Local Improvement Act
Fla. Laws 1967, Ch. 67-1277

City of Decatur Parking Authority Act
Ga. Laws 1968, p. 2892

City of Decatur Tax Deferral for Elderly Act
Ga. Laws 1991, p. 3985

City of Gatlinburg Development Impact Fee Act
Tenn. Private Acts 1990, Ch. 167

City of Helena, Shelby County, Alabama, Civil Service System Act
Ala. Acts 1992, p. 442, No. 201

City of Jasper Bingo Act
Ala. Acts 1992, p. 1185, No. 573

City of Lafayette Community Improvement Act
La. Acts 1968, No. 484

City of Lakeland Hospital Revenue Bond Act
Fla. Special Laws 1970, Ch. 70-775

City of Lilburn Merit System Act
Ga. Laws 1975, p. 4819

City of Long Beach Parking Authority Act
N.Y. Public Authorities Law (Consol. Laws Ch. 43A) § 1599aaaa et seq.

City of Mount Vernon Parking Authority Act
N.Y. Public Authorities Law (Consol. Law Ch. 43A), § 1599a et seq.

City of Naples Airport Authority Act
Fla. Special Laws 1969, Ch. 69-1326

City of New Rochelle Parking Authority Act
N.Y. Public Authorities Law (Consol. Laws Ch. 43A), § 1597a et seq.

City of Niagara Falls Hotel Room Occupancy Tax Law
N.Y. Local Laws 1973, City of Niagara Falls p. 586

City of Niagara Falls Parking Authority Act
N.Y. Public Authorities Law (Consol. Law Ch. 43A), § 1599 et seq.

City of North Tonawanda Parking Authority Act
N.Y. Public Authorities Law (Consol. Laws Ch. 43A), § 1601 et seq.

City of Pearson, Georgia Industrial Authority Act
Ga. Laws 1969, p. 2905

City of Peekskill Civic Center Authority Act
N.Y. Public Authorities Law (Consol. Laws Ch. 43A) § 2070 et seq.

City of Pelham, Shelby County, Alabama, Civil Service System Act
Ala. Acts 1991, p. 186

City of Poughkeepsie Parking Authority Act
N.Y. Public Authorities Law (Consol. Laws Ch. 43A) § 1598 et seq.

City of Rome Parking Authority Act
N.Y. Public Authority Law (Consol. Laws Ch. 43A) § 1470 et seq.

City of Sarasota Erosion Control Act
Fla. Special Laws 1969, Ch. 69-1571, § 3

City of Schenectady Parking Authority Act
N.Y. Public Authorities Law (Consol. Laws Ch. 43A), § 1599a et seq.

City of Wilmington Employees' Retirement Act
Del. Laws Vol. 46, p. 637, Ch. 237

City of Yonkers Educational Construction Fund Act
N.Y. Education Law 1947 (Consol. Laws Ch. 16) § 475 et seq.

City of Yonkers Financial Emergency Act
N.Y. Laws 1984, Ch. 103, § 2

City of Yonkers Parking Authority Act
N.Y. Public Authorities Law (Consol. Laws Ch. 43A), § 1596a et seq.

City Ordinance Violation Law
Ind. Code Ann., 18-5-12.5-1 et seq.

City Park Act (First Class)
Ind. Code Ann., 36-10-2-2 et seq.

City Park Act (Second Class)
Ind. Code Ann., 36-10-7-1 et seq.

City Personal Income Tax Act
N.Y. Tax Law (Consol. Laws Ch. 60) § 1300 et seq.

City Planning Act
Ark. Stat. 1947, 19-2811 et seq.
Okla. Stat. Ann., Title 11, § 47-101 et seq.
Ore. Rev. Stat., 227.010 et seq.
S.D. Codified Laws 1967, 11-6-1 et seq.

City Planning and Zoning Act
Ky. Rev. Stat. 1971, 100.11 et seq.

City Planning and Zoning Act—Cities of the First Class
Ky. Rev. Stat. 1962, 100.031 et seq.

City Planning and Zoning Act—Cities of the Second Class
Ky. Rev. Stat. 1962, 100.320 et seq.

City Planning Board Act
Mont. Code Ann., 76-1-101 et seq.

City Planning Commission Act
Ill. Rev. Stat. 1991, Ch. 24, § 11-12-4 et seq.

Ind. Code Ann., 18-7-5-1 et seq.
Wash. Rev. Code Ann., 35.63.010 et seq.

City Powers Act
N.Y. General City Law (Consol. Laws Ch. 21), § 19 et seq.

City Primary Act
Ore. General Laws 1901, p. 317

City Property Tax Alternatives Act
Ida. Code 1947, 50-1043 et seq.

City Rent and Rehabilitation Law (New York)
N.Y. City Admin. Code 1985, § 26-401 et seq.

City Retired Employees' Pension Law
S.D. Codified Laws 1967, 9-16-1 et seq.

City Sale or Lease of Land for Cemeteries Act
Ill. Rev. Stat. 1991, Ch. 21, §§ 6h, 7

City Sales Tax Act
Miss. Code Ann., § 27-65-95

City Sales Tax Act (Transportation)
Mo. Rev. Stat. 1978, 94.500 et seq.

City School Districts Act
N.Y. Education Law 1947 (Consol. Laws Ch. 16) § 2501 et seq.

City School Plan Act
Wis. Stat. 1989, 120.40 et seq.

City Sewerage System Act
Wash. Rev. Code Ann., 35.67.010 et seq.

City Sidewalks Act
Wash. Rev. Code Ann., 35.68.010 et seq.

City Sinking Fund Act
Ind. Code Ann., 18-1-5-1 et seq.

City Tax Enabling Act
Pa. 1947 Pamph. Laws 1145, No. 481

City Tax Exemption Act (Motor Carriers')
Cal. Public Utilities Code § 4301 et seq.

City University Construction Fund Act
N.Y. Education Law 1947 (Consol. Laws Ch. 16) § 6270 et seq.

City University of New York and the State University of New York Retirement Incentive Act
N.Y. Laws 1992, Ch. 494 §§ 1 to 14

City Utility Tax Law
Miss. Code Ann., § 21-33-201 et seq.

City Utility Users Tax Act
Mich. Comp. Laws Ann., 141.801 et seq., 141.1151 et seq.

City Utility Users Tax Ordinance
See Uniform City Utility Users Tax Ordinance

City, Village and Municipal Corporation Ground Water Permit Act
Neb. Rev. Stat. 1943, 46-638 et seq.

City Water Supply Act
N.Y. Laws 1905, Ch. 724

City Zoning Act
Ill. Rev. Stat. 1991, Ch. 24, § 11-13-1 et seq.
Kan. Stat. Ann., 12-715b et seq.
N.D. Cent. Code 40-47-01 et seq.
Tex. Local Gov. Code, § 211.001 et seq.

Civic Auditorium and Sports Arena Act
Utah Code Ann. 1953, Miscellaneous Superseded Code Provisions 17-12-4

Civic Center Act
Cal. Education Code 1976, § 40040 et seq.
Ore. Rev. Stat., 332.810

Civic Center Act (Aledo, Normal, Mason County, Jasper County, Brownstone Park District, Jo Daviess County, Milford, Sheldon, Katherine Dunham, and Oak Park)
Ill. Comp. Stat. 1992, Ch. 70, § 220/1 et seq.

Civic Center Act (Aurora)
Ill. Comp. Stat. 1992, Ch. 70, § 225/1 et seq.

Civic Center Act (Benton)
Ill. Comp. Stat. 1992, Ch. 70, § 230/1-1 et seq.

Civic Center Act (Brownstone Park District)
Ill. Comp. Stat. 1992, Ch. 70, § 220/5-1 et seq.

Civic Center Act (Carbondale)
Ill. Comp. Stat. 1992, Ch. 70, § 325/2 et seq.

Civic Center Act (Cave in Rock Township)
Ill. Comp. Stat. 1992, Ch. 720, § 240/1001 et seq.

Civic Center Act (Centre East)
Ill. Comp. Stat. 1992, Ch. 70, § 270/1 et seq.

Civic Center Act (Chicago South)
Ill. Comp. Stat. 1992, Ch. 70, § 245/1-1 et seq.

Civic Center Act (Collinsville)
Ill. Comp. Stat. 1992, Ch. 70, § 250/1

Civic Center Act (Columbia)
Ill. Comp. Stat. 1992, Ch. 70, § 255/2001 et seq.

Civic Center Act (Crystal Lake)
Ill. Comp. Stat. 1992, Ch. 70, § 305/2-1 et seq.

Civic Center Act (Decatur and Vermilion County)
Ill. Comp. Stat. 1992, Ch. 70, § 265/1 et seq.

Civic Center Act (Dupage County)
Ill. Rev. Stat. 1991, Ch. 85, § 3401 et seq.

Civic Center Act (Elgin)
Ill. Rev. Stat. 1991, Ch. 85, § 3601 et seq.

Civic Center Act (International)
Ill. Rev. Stat. 1985, Ch. 85, § 3901 et seq.

Civic Center Act (Metropolitan)
Ill. Rev. Stat. 1991, Ch. 85, § 1361 et seq.

Civic Center Act (Milford)
Ill. Rev. Stat. 1991, Ch. 85, § 5101 et seq.

Civic Center Act (Orland Park)
Ill. Rev. Stat. 1991, Ch. 85, § 3701 et seq.

Civic Center Act (Peoria)
Ill. Rev. Stat. 1991, Ch. 85, § 1441 et seq.

Civic Center Act (River Forest)
Ill. Rev. Stat. 1991, Ch. 85, § 3301 et seq.

Civic Center Act (Rockford)
Ill. Rev. Stat. 1991, Ch. 85, § 1331 et seq.

Civic Center Act (School Property)
Cal. Education Code 1976, §§ 40048 et seq., 82537 et seq.

Civic Center Act (Sheldon)
Ill. Rev. Stat. 1991, Ch. 85, § 5201 et seq.

Civic Center Act (Sterling)
Ill. Rev. Stat. 1991, Ch. 85, § 3501 et seq.

Civic Center Authority Act
Tex. Local Government Code, § 281.001 et seq.

Civic Center Authority Act (Bloomington)
Ill. Comp. Stat. 1992, Ch. 70, § 235/1 et seq.
Ill. Rev. Stat. 1991, Ch. 85, § 1581-1 et seq.

Civic Center Authority Act (DeKalb County)
Ga. Laws 1996, p. 4216

Civic Center Authority Act (Peekskill)
N.Y. Public Authorities Laws (Consol. Laws Ch. 43A) § 2070 et seq.

Civic Center Authority Law (Pekin)
Ill. Rev. Stat. 1991, Ch. 85, § 3201 et seq.

Civic Center Authority Law (Quad City)
Ill. Rev. Stat. 1991, Ch. 85, § 3101 et seq.

Civic Center Code
Ill. Comp. Stat. 1992, Ch. 70, § 200/1-1 et seq.

Civic Center Law (Aledo)
Ill. Rev. Stat. 1991, Ch. 85, § 4501 et seq.

Civic Center Law (Benton)
Ill. Rev. Stat. 1991, Ch. 85, § 6601 et seq.

Civic Center Law (Bowdre Township)
Ill. Rev. Stat. 1991, Ch. 85, § 6351 et seq.

Civic Center Law (Forest Park)
Ill. Rev. Stat. 1991, Ch. 85, § 7401 et seq.

Civic Center Law (Illinois Valley)
Ill. Rev. Stat. 1991, Ch. 85, § 7006-2 et seq.

Civic Center Law (Jasper County)
Ill. Rev. Stat. 1991, Ch. 85, § 4801 et seq.

Civic Center Law (Jo Daviess County)
Ill. Rev. Stat. 1991, Ch. 85, § 5001 et seq.

Civic Center Law (Marengo)
Ill. Rev. Stat. 1991, Ch. 85, § 6251 et seq.

Civic Center Law (Mason County)
Ill. Rev. Stat. 1991, Ch. 85, § 4701 et seq.

Civic Center Law (Matteson)
Ill. Rev. Stat. 1991, Ch. 85, § 7004-1 et seq.

Civic Center Law (Maywood)
Ill. Rev. Stat. 1991, Ch. 85, § 6905-1 et seq.

Civic Center Law (Melrose Park)
Ill. Rev. Stat. 1991, Ch. 85, § 6702-1 et seq.

Civic Center Law (Normal)
Ill. Rev. Stat. 1991, Ch. 85, § 4601 et seq.

Civic Center Law (Oak Park)
Ill. Rev. Stat. 1991, Ch. 85, § 5401 et seq.

Civic Center Law (Ottawa)
Ill. Rev. Stat. 1991, Ch. 85, § 7005-1 et seq.

Civic Center Law (Pontiac)
Ill. Rev. Stat. 1991, Ch. 85, § 7008-1 et seq.

Civic Center Law (Randolph County)
Ill. Rev. Stat. 1991, Ch. 85, §§ 6901-1 et seq.,
7001-1 et seq.

Civic Center Law (Riverside)
Ill. Rev. Stat. 1991, Ch. 85, § 7003-1 et seq.

Civic Center Law (Salem)
Ill. Rev. Stat. 1991, Ch. 85, § 7101 et seq.

Civic Center Law (Waukegan)
Ill. Rev. Stat. 1991, Ch. 85, § 7007-1 et seq.

Civic Center Law (West Frankfurt)
Ill. Rev. Stat. 1991, Ch. 85, § 6101 et seq.

Civic Center Support Act (Metropolitan)
Ill. Rev. Stat. 1991, Ch. 85, § 1391 et seq.

Civic Centers Act (Aledo, Normal, Mason County, Jasper County, Brownstown Park District, Jo Daviess County, Milford, Sheldon, Katherine Dunham, and Oak Park)
Ill. Rev. Stat. 1991, Ch. 85, § 4500 et seq.

Civic Centers Act (Chicago South and Melrose Park)
Ill. Rev. Stat. 1991, Ch. 85, § 6701 et seq.

Civic Centers Act (DuPage County, Sterling, Elgin, Orland Park, Centre East, and Schuamburg International)
Ill. Rev. Stat. 1991, Ch. 85, § 3400 et seq.

Civic Centers Act (Herrin, Jefferson County, and Quincy)
Ill. Rev. Stat. 1991, Ch. 85, § 2700 et seq.

Civic Centers Act (Marengo, Crystal Lake, and Bowdre Township)
Ill. Rev. Stat. 1991, Ch. 85, § 6250 et seq.

Civic Centers Act (Quad City and Pekin)
Ill. Rev. Stat. 1991, Ch. 85, § 3100 et seq.

Civic Centers Act (Randolph County, Carbondale, Riverside, Matteson, Ottawa, Illinois Valley, Waukegan, and Pontiac)
Ill. Rev. Stat. 1991, Ch. 85, § 7000-1 et seq.

Civic Unemployment Elimination Act
P.R. Laws Ann. 1954, Title 28, § 661 et seq.

Civil Action Competency Act
Wash. Rev. Code Ann., 5.60.020 et seq.

Civil Activities National Defense Appropriation Act, 1941
June 26, 1940, Ch. 430, 54 Stat. 599
April 5, 1941, Ch. 41, 55 Stat. 129

Civil Administrative Code Act
Ill. Comp. Stat. 1992, Ch. 20, § 5/1

Civil Aeronautics Act of 1938
June 23, 1938, Ch. 601, 52 Stat. 973 (See 49 U.S. Code §§ 1301 to 1542)
July 2, 1940, Ch. 526, 54 Stat. 735 (See 49 U.S. Code § 1375)
May 16, 1942, Ch. 318, 56 Stat. 300 (See 49 U.S. Code §§ 1382, 1483)
Aug. 8, 1946, Ch. 911, 60 Stat. 944 (See 49 U.S. Code § 1463)
Aug. 4, 1947, Ch. 471, 61 Stat. 743 (See 49 U.S. Code § 1483)
June 16, 1948, Ch. 482, 62 Stat. 470 (See 49 U.S. Code § 1404)
June 19, 1948, Ch. 523, 62 Stat. 493 (See 49 U.S. Code §§ 1301, 1403)
June 29, 1948, Ch. 713, 62 Stat. 1093 (See 49 U.S. Code §§ 1344, 1348)
July 1, 1948, Ch. 792, 62 Stat. 1216 (See 49 U.S. Code §§ 1344, 1348, 1354, 1421)
July 26, 1949, Ch. 362, 63 Stat. 480 (See 49 U.S. Code § 1472)
Aug. 30, 1949, Ch. 520, 63 Stat. 678
Aug. 3, 1950, Ch. 517, 64 Stat. 395 (See 49 U.S. Code § 1472)
Aug. 8, 1950, Ch. 643, 64 Stat. 417 (See 49 U.S. Code §§ 1353, 1354)
Sept. 9, 1950, Ch. 938, 64 Stat. 825 (See 49 U.S. Code §§ 1521 to 1523)
Sept. 29, 1950, Ch. 1107, 64 Stat. 1079 (See 49 U.S. Code § 1355)
June 14, 1951, Ch. 123, 65 Stat. 65 (See 49 U.S. Code §§ 1301, 1531 to 1541)
Oct. 11, 1951, Ch. 495, 65 Stat. 407 (See 49 U.S. Code § 1430)
June 28, 1952, Ch. 485, 66 Stat. 286 (See 49 U.S. Code § 1375)
July 14, 1952, Ch. 740, 66 Stat. 628 (See 49 U.S. Code §§ 1301, 1381, 1472)
May 19, 1955, Ch. 41, 69 Stat. 49 (See 49 U.S. Code § 1371)
July 20, 1956, Ch. 650, 70 Stat. 591 (See 49 U.S. Code § 1371)
July 20, 1956, Ch. 655, 70 Stat. 594 (See 49 U.S. Code § 1542)
Aug. 1, 1956, Ch. 816, 70 Stat. 784 (See 49 U.S. Code § 1373)
Aug. 26, 1957, P.L. 85-166, 71 Stat. 415 (See 49 U.S. Code § 1371)
April 9, 1958, P.L. 85-373, 72 Stat. 84 (See 49 U.S. Code § 1376)
July 7, 1958, P.L. 85-507, 72 Stat. 337 (See 49 U.S. Code §§ 1353 , 1354, 1463)
Aug. 28, 1958, P.L. 85-791, 72 Stat. 947 (See 49 U.S. Code § 646)

Civil Aeronautics Board Sunset Act of 1984
Oct. 4, 1984, P.L. 98-443, 98 Stat. 1703, 49 U.S. Code Appx. § 1301 nt. .
Sept. 30, 1988, P.L. 100-457, 102 Stat. 2155, 49 U.S. Code Appx. §§ 1551, 1553
Oct. 31, 1994, P.L. 103-429, 49 U.S. Code Appx. § 1371 nt.

Civil Air Patrol Members, Paramedics, Firemen, Law Enforcement Officers, and Civil Defense Workers Compensation Act
Ill. Rev. Stat. 1991, Ch. 48, § 281 et seq.

Civil and Equal Rights Enforcement Act
Ill. Comp. Stat. 1992, Ch. 15, §§ 210/0.01, 210/1

Civil and Professional Engineers Act
Cal. Business and Professions Code § 6700 et seq.

Civil Appeals Act
Minn. Stat. 1971, 605.001 et seq.
Wash. Rev. Code 1951, 4.88.010 et seq.

Civil Arrest and Bail Act
S.C. Code Ann. 1976, § 15-17-10 et seq.

Civil Claims Court Act
Fla. Laws 1949. Ch. 25574

Civil Code
Mo. Rev. Stat., 506.010 et seq.
P.R. Laws Ann. 1954, Title 31, § 1 et seq.

Civil Commitment Act (Mentally Ill)
Ohio Rev. Code 1953, 5123.71 et seq.

Civil Commitment and Addict Rehabilitation Act
Cal. Welfare and Institutions Code § 3000 et seq.

Civil Commitment and Mental Health Treatment Act (Children's)
Cal. Welfare and Institutions Code § 5585 et seq.

Civil Commitment Law
N.Y. Mental Hygiene Law 1972 (Consol. Laws Ch. 27), § 9.01 et seq.

Civil Commitment of Habitual Sexual Offenders Act
Ida. Code 1947, 66-1401 et seq.

Civil Contempt Act
Mont. Code Ann., 3-1-501 et seq.

Civil Contempt Imprisonment Limitation Act
D.C. Code Ann., §§ 11-721, 11-741, 11-944

Civil Court Act
Wis. Laws 1909, Ch. 549

Civil Court Act (Milwaukee County)
Wis. Laws 1951, Ch. 168

Civil Court Act (New York City)
N.Y. Laws 1962, Ch. 693

Civil Courts Act (Counties)
N.C. Gen. Stat. 1943, §§ 7-308 et seq.

Civil Damage Act
Ark. Stat. 1879, p. 33, No. 31, §§ 10 to 14
Mass. Gen. Laws Ann., 138:69 et seq.
Miss. Code Ann., § 67-1-83(i)
Ohio Rev. Code 1953, 4399.01

Civil Damage Act (Dram Shops)
Ill. Rev. Stat. 1991, Ch. 43, § 135
Minn. Stat. Ann., 340A.801

Civil Damage Act (Illegal Liquor Sale)
Conn. Gen. Stat. 1958, § 30-102
Del. Code of 1953, Title 4, § 716

Iowa Code Ann., 123.92 et seq.
N.D. Cent. Code 5-01-06
Pa. 1854 Pamph. Laws 663, No. 648
R.I. Gen. Laws 1956, 3-11-1
Wis. Stat. 1975, 176.35
W. Va. Code 1931, Miscellaneous Superseded Code Provisions, § 60-3-22

Civil Damage Act (Intoxicating Liquor)
Ala. Code 1975, § 6-5-71
Ind. Laws 1875, Special Session, Ch. 13, p. 55, § 20
Ind. Laws 1917, Ch. 4, p. 15, § 32
Ind. Laws 1925, Ch. 48, p. 144, § 38
Kan. Laws 1881, Ch. 128, § 15
Kan. Laws 1915, Ch. 233
Me. Rev. Stat. Ann. 1964, Title 17, § 2002
Mich. Comp. Laws Ann., 436.22
Minn. Stat. Ann., 340.95
N.C. Gen. Stat. 1943, § 14-332
Nev. Rev. Stat. 1967 Reprint, Replaced Pages, 202.070
N.J. Laws 1921, Ch. 103, § 55
N.Y. General Obligations Law (Consol. Laws Ch. 24A) § 11-101 et seq.
S.D. Codified Laws 1967, 35-5-7, 35-5-7.1
S.D. Laws 1897, Ch. 72, § 16
Vt. Stat. Ann., Title 7, § 501
Wash. Rev. Code 1951, 71.08.080
Wyo. Stat. Ann., § 12-5-502

Civil Death Act
Alaska Stat. 1962, § 33.30.320 et seq.
Ariz. Rev. Stat. Ann., § 13-904
Cal. Penal Code § 2601
Ida. Code 1947, 18-311
Ind. Code Ann., 3-1-21-4
Kan. Stat. Ann., 21-4615
Minn. Stat. 1961, 610.34
Miss. Code Ann., §§ 99-19-35, 99-19-37
Mo. Rev. Stat. 1969, 222.010
Mont. Rev. Code 1947, 94-4721
N.Y. Civil Rights Law (Consol. Laws Ch. 6) § 79a
Ore. General Laws 1864 (In Deady's Laws 1866), p. 441, § 702
Vt. Stat. Ann., Title 13, § 7005

Civil Death Act (Convicts)
N.D. Cent. Code 12.1-33-01
R.I. Gen. Laws 1956, 13-6-1

Civil Death Act (Life Sentence)
Utah Code Ann. 1953, Miscellaneous
Superseded Code Provisions, 76-1-37

Civil Death Act (Wills)
Ala. Code 1958, Title 61, § 3

Civil Defense Act
Ark. Stat. 1947, 11-1901 et seq., 11-1916 et
seq., 11-1934 et seq.
Colo. Rev. Stat., 28-3-101 et seq.
Ill. Rev. Stat. 1973, Ch. 127, § 269 et seq.
Ind. Laws 1949, Ch. 275, p. 1016
Ky. Rev. Stat. 1971, 39.400 et seq.
Me. Rev. Stat. Ann. 1964, Title 37-B, § 701
et seq.
Miss. Code Ann., §§ 33-15-7, 33-15-9
Ohio Rev. Code 1953, 5915.01 et seq.
Okla. Stat. Ann., Title 63, § 664 et seq.
P.R. Laws Ann. 1954, Title 25, § 130 et seq.
S.C. Code Ann. 1976, Superseded Vols.,
§ 25-5-10 et seq.
S.D. Codified Laws 1967, 33-15-1 et seq.
Wis. Stat. 1989, 166.01 et seq.

Civil Defense Act (State Council)
Pa. Cons. Stat., Title 35 § 7101 et seq.

**Civil Defense and Disaster Compact
(Interstate)**
Me. Rev. Stat. Ann. 1964, Title 37-B, § 902
et seq.

Civil Defense and Disaster Compact Act
See also Interstate Civil Defense and Disaster
Compact Act
Conn. Gen. Stat. Ann., § 28-23
Kan. Stat. Ann., 48-3201 et seq.
Me. Rev. Stat. Ann. 1964, Title 37-B, § 902
et seq.
Mont. Code Ann., 10-3-206
Nev. Rev. Stat. Ann., 415.010
Wash. Rev. Code Ann., 38.52.090

**Civil Defense and Disaster Compacts Act
(Interstate)**
S.C. Code Ann. 1976, § 25-9-20 et seq.

Civil Defense and Disaster Law
Ala. Code 1975, § 31-9-1 et seq.
Alaska Stat. 1962, § 26.23.130 et seq.
Ariz. Rev. Stat. Ann., § 26-301 et seq.
Ark. Code Ann. 1987, 11-1934 et seq.
Cal. Military and Veterans Code § 1500 et
seq.
Colo. Rev. Stat., 28-2-101 et seq.
Del. Code of 1974, Title 20, § 3101 et seq.
Fla. Stat. 1977, 252.31 et seq.
Ga. Code Ann., 38-3-1 et seq.
Ida. Code 1947, 46-1001 et seq.
Ind. Code Ann., 10-4-1-1 et seq.
Iowa Code Ann., 29C.1 et seq.
Kan. Stat. Ann., 48-904 et seq.
Md. Ann. Code 1957, Art. 16A, § 1 et seq.
Mich. Comp. Laws Ann., 30.401 et seq.
Minn. Stat. Ann., 12.01 et seq.
Miss. Code Ann., § 33-15-1 et seq.
Mont. Rev. Code 1947, 77-2301 et seq.
N.C. Gen. Stat. 1943, § 166A-1 et seq.
Neb. Rev. Stat. 1943, 81-829.36 et seq.
Nev. Rev. Stat. 1979 Reprint, 414.020 et seq.
N.H. Rev. Stat. 1955, 107:1 et seq.
N.J. Stat. Ann., App. A:9-33 et seq.
N.Y. Executive Law 1951, (Consol. Laws,
Ch. 18) § 20 et seq.
Okla. Stat. Ann., Title 63, § 680 et seq.
Ore. Rev. Stat., 401.015 et seq.
P.R. Laws Ann. 1954, Title 25, § 171 et seq.
S.C. Code Ann. 1962, § 44-301 et seq.
S.D. Codified Laws 1967, 33-15-1 et seq.
Wash. Rev. Code Ann., 38.52.005 et seq.
Wis. Stat. 1991, 166.01 et seq.
Wyo. Stat. Ann., § 19-5-101 et seq.

Civil Defense and Disaster Preparedness Act
Md. Ann. Code 1957, Art. 16A, § 1 et seq.

Civil Defense and Emergency Act
Haw. Rev. Stat. Ann., § 128-1 et seq.

Civil Defense and Emergency Resources Management Act
Okla. Stat. Ann., Title 63, § 683.1 et seq.

Civil Defense and Public Safety Act
Me. Rev. Stat. Ann. 1964, Title 37-B, § 701 et seq.

Civil Defense Compact Act (Interstate)
See Interstate Civil Defense Compact Act

Civil Defense Disaster Compact Act
S.C. Code Ann. 1976, § 25-9-20
Vt. Stat. Ann., Title 20, § 81 et seq.

Civil Defense Emergency Interim Legislative Succession Act
Okla. Stat. 1971, Title 63, § 686.1 et seq.

Civil Defense Emergency Interim Relocation Act
Okla. Stat. Ann., Title 63, § 687.1 et seq.

Civil Defense Emergency Interim Succession Act
Vt. Stat. Ann., Title 20 § 181 et seq.

Civil Defense Interstate Compact Act
N.H. Rev. Stat 1955, 108:1 et seq.

Civil Defense Law
N.Y. Unconsolidated Law § 9101 et seq.

Civil Defense Liability Act
Colo. Rev. Stat., 24-32-2301 et seq.
Colo. Rev. Stat., 24-33.5-901 et seq.

Civil Defense Loan Act
Mass. Acts 1950, Ch. 639

Civil Defense Shelter Incentive Act
Okla. Stat. Ann., Title 63, § 688.1 et seq.

Civil Defense Workers, Civil Air Patrol Members, Paramdeics, Firemen, and Law Enforcement Officers Compensation Act
Ill. Rev. Stat. 1991, Ch. 48, § 281 et seq.

Civil Discovery Act
Cal. Code of Civil Procedure § 2016 et seq.

Civil Disqualifications Act (Judges)
Mont. Code Ann. 1979, 3-1-801

Civil Divisions Act (Nassau County)
N.Y. Laws 1939, Ch. 273

Civil Emergency Preparedness Act
Me. Rev. Stat. Ann. 1964, Title 37-B, § 701 et seq.
N.M. Stat. Ann., 12-10-1 et seq.

Civil Enforcement and Judicial Review of Agency Actions Act
Kan. Stat. Ann., 77-601 et seq.

Civil Engineering Act
Cal. Business and Professions Code, § 6700 et seq.
La. Rev. Stat. Ann., 37:681 et seq.

Civil Functions Appropriation Acts
June 25, 1948, Ch. 655, 62 Stat. 1019, 24 U.S. Code §§ 45 nt., 290; 42 U.S. Code § 6b
Oct. 13, 1949, Ch. 688, 63 Stat. 845, 24 U.S. Code § 290; 41 U.S. Code § 6b
Sept. 6, 1950, Ch. 896, 64 Stat. 724, 24 U.S. Code § 290; 33 U.S. Code § 574; 41 U.S. Code § 6b
Oct. 24, 1951, Ch. 556, 65 Stat. 616, 24 U.S. Code § 290; 41 U.S. Code § 6b
July 11, 1952, Ch. 669, 66 Stat. 579, 24 U.S. Code § 290; 41 U.S. Code § 6b
July 27, 1953, Ch. 245, 67 Stat. 202, 24 U.S. Code § 290; 33 U.S. Code §§ 576, 701b-10; 41 U.S. Code § 6b
June 30, 1954, Ch. 425, 68 Stat. 334, 41 U.S. Code § 6b

Civil Government Act
Alaska Comp. Laws Ann. 1949, § 2-1-1 et seq.

Civil Jurisdiction Act
Ark. Code Ann. 1987, 16-17-701 et seq.

Civil Justice Act (Access to)
N.C. Gen. Stat. 1943, §§ 7A-474.1 to 7A-474.4

Civil Justice Reform Act of 1990

Dec. 1, 1990, P.L. 101-650, 28 U.S. Code §§ 1 nt., 471 to 482

Oct. 29, 1992, P.L. 102-572, 28 U.S. Code § 471 nt.

Oct. 25, 1994, P.L. 103-420, 28 U.S. Code § 471 nt.

Oct. 3, 1995, P.L. 104-33, 28 U.S. Code § 471 nt.

Oct. 19, 1996, P.L. 104-317, 28 U.S. Code § 471 nt.

Oct. 6, 1997, P.L. 105-53, 28 U.S. Code § 471 nt.

Civil Liabilities Act (Intoxication)

Okla. Stat. 1951, Title 37, § 121

Civil Liability Act (Motor Vehicles)

Md. Ann. Code 1957, Art. 16A, § 1 et seq.

Mich. Comp. Laws Ann., 257.401 et seq. .

Civil Liability for Support Act

See Uniform Civil Liability for Support Act

Civil Liability Reform Act (Willie L. Brown Jr.-Bill Lockyer)

Cal. Statutes 1987, Ch. 1498, p. 5777

Civil Libel Act

Ala. Code 1975, § 6-5-180 et seq.

Civil Liberties Act Amendments of 1992

Sept. 27, 1992, P.L. 102-371, 50 U.S. Code Appx. § 1989b nt.

Civil Liberties Act of 1988

Aug. 10, 1988, P.L. 100-383, 102 Stat. 903, 50 U.S. Code Appx. §§ 1989b to 1989b-8

Nov. 21, 1989, P.L. 101-162, 50 U.S. Code Appx. §§ 1989b-4, 1989b-9

Sept. 27, 1992, P.L. 102-371, 50 U.S. Code Appx. §§ 1989b-3, 1989b-4, 1989b-4 nt., 1989b-7, 1989b-9

Civil Limitations Act

N.C. Gen. Stat. 1943, § 1-15 et seq.

Civil Litter Act

Minn. Stat. Ann., 169.421

Civil Mediation Act

Minn. Stat. Ann., 572.31 et seq.

Civil Nonsuit Act

N.C. Gen. Stat. 1943, § 1-183

Civil Obedience Act

April 11, 1968, P.L. 90-284, 82 Stat. 90, 18 U.S. Code §§ 231 to 233

Civil Practice and Procedure Act

Alaska Stat. 1962, § 09.05.010 et seq.

Ark. Code Ann. 1987, 16-55-101 et seq.

Ga. Code Ann., 9-11-1 et seq.

Ida. Code 1947, 5-201 et seq.

Ind. Code Ann., 34-5-1-1 et seq.

Kan. Stat. Ann., 60-101 et seq.

Mich. Comp. Laws Ann., 600.101 et seq.

Mo. Rev. Stat. 1978, 506.010 et seq.

N.C. Gen Stat. 1943, § 1-1 et seq.

Neb. Rev. Stat. 1943, 25-101 et seq.

Nev. Rev. Stat. 1979 Reprint, 10.010 et seq.

Okla. Stat. Ann., Title 12

S.C. Code Ann. 1976, § 15-1-10 et seq.

S.D. Codified Laws 1967, 15-1-1 et seq.

Wash. Rev. Code Ann., 4.04.010 et seq.

Civil Preparedness Act

N.C. Gen. Stat. 1943, § 166A-1 et seq.

Civil Procedural Support Law

Pa. Cons. Stat., Title 42, § 6769 et seq.

Civil Procedure Act

Okla. Stat 1991, Title 12

Civil Procedure Act (Courts of Limited Jurisdiction)

Kan. Stat. Ann., 61-1601 et seq.

Civil Procedure Code

Ill. Comp. Stat. 1992, Ch. 735, § 5/1-101 et seq.

Civil Procedure Code for Limited Actions Act

Kan. Stat. Ann., 61-1601 et seq.

Civil Proceedings Act (Dragonetti)
  Pa. Cons. Stat., Title 42, § 8351 et seq.

Civil Process Law
  Miss. Code Ann., § 13-3-1 et seq.

Civil Protection Act
  Tex. Gov. Code, § 418.001 et seq.

Civil Recovery for Retail Theft Act
  Me. Rev. Stat. Ann. 1964, Title 14, § 8301 et seq.

Civil Relief Act (Soldiers and Sailors)
  See Soldiers' And Sailors' Civil Relief Acts Of 1918 and 1940
  Wis. Stat. 1989, 45.53

Civil Remedies Act
  Fla. Stat., 624.155

Civil Remedies and Procedure Act
  Ala. Code 1958, Title 7, § 1 et seq.

Civil Remedies for Criminal Practices Act
  Fla. Stat. Ann., 772.101 et seq.

Civil Responsibility Act (Motor Vehicles)
  Cal. Vehicle Code 1959, § 17100 et seq. (State and Governmental Agencies)
  Cal. Vehicle Code 1959, § 17150 et seq. (Private Owners)

Civil Restitution Lien and Crime Victims' Remedy Act
  Fla. Laws 1994, Ch. 342
  Fla. Stat., 960.29 et seq.

Civil Rights Act
  July 31, 1861, c. 33, 12 Stat. 284
  Apr. 9, 1866, c. 31, 14 Stat. 27
  May 31, 1870, c. 114, 16 Stat. 140
  Feb. 28, 1871, c. 99, 16 Stat. 433
  Apr. 20, 1871, c. 22, 17 Stat. 13
  Mar. 1, 1875, c. 114, 18 Stat. 235
  Alaska Stat. 1962, § 18.80.200 et seq.
  Ariz. Rev. Stat. Ann., § 41-1401 et seq.
  Cal. Civil Code § 51 et seq.
  Cal. Labor Code, § 1419
  Colo. Rev. Stat., 24-34-501 et seq.

  Conn. Gen Stat. 1983, § 46a-58 et seq.
  Del. Code of 1974, Title 24, § 1501
  Fla. Stat. Ann., 760.01 et seq.
  Ida. Code 1947, 18-7301 et seq.
  Ill. Rev. Stat. 1991, Ch. 68
  Ind. Code Ann., 22-9-1-1 et seq.
  Iowa Code Ann., 729.1 et seq.
  Kan. Stat. Ann., 21-4003
  Ky. Rev. Stat. 1971, 344.010 et seq.
  La. Rev. Stat. Ann., 13:4791 et seq.
  Me. Rev. Stat. Ann. 1964, Title 5, § 4681 et seq.
  Me. Rev. Stat. 1964, Title 17, § 1301-A et seq.
  Mich. Comp. Laws Ann., 37.2101 et seq., 750.146 et seq.
  Minn. Stat. Ann., 363.03
  Mont. Code Ann., 49-2-101 et seq.
  N.D. Cent. Code 12.1-14-04, 12.1-14-05
  Neb. Rev. Stat. 1943, 20-125 et seq.
  N.H. Rev. Stat. 1955, 35-A:1 et seq.
  N.J. Stat. Ann., 10:1-1 et seq.
  N.M. Stat. Ann., 28-1-1 et seq.
  N.Y. Consol. Laws, Ch. 6
  Ohio Rev. Code 1953, 4112.01 et seq.
  Ore. Rev. Stat., 30.670 et seq.
  Pa. Purdon's Stat., Title 18, § 4654
  P.R. Laws Ann. 1954, Title 1, § 13 et seq.
  S.D. Comp. Laws 1967, 20-12-1 et seq.
  Tenn. Code Ann., 4-21-801 et seq.
  Utah Code Ann. 1953, 34-35-1 et seq.
  Vt. Stat. Ann., Title 13, § 1451 et seq.
  Wash. Rev. Code Ann., 9.91.010
  Wis. Stat. 1987, 942.04
  Wyo. Stat. Ann., § 6-9-102

Civil Rights Act (Public Accomodations)
  See Public Accommodations Act (Civil Rights)

Civil Rights Act (Tom Bane)
  Cal. Statutes 1987, Ch. 1277

Civil Rights Act (Unruh)
  Cal. Civil Code § 51 et seq.

Civil Rights Act for Handicapped Persons
  La. Rev. Stat. Ann., 46:2251 et seq.
  Continued

353

Mich. Comp. Laws Ann., 37.1101 et seq.

Civil Rights Act of 1957

Sept. 9, 1957, P.L. 85-315, 71 Stat. 634 (See 5 U.S. Code § 5315(19)) 28 U.S. Code §§ 1343, 1861; 42 U.S. Code §§ 1971, 1975, 1975a , 1975b, 1975c, 1975d, 1975e, 1995

Sept. 28, 1959, P.L. 86-383, 73 Stat. 724, 42 U.S. Code § 1975c

May 6, 1960, P.L. 86-449, 74 Stat. 89, 42 U.S. Code §§ 1971, 1975d

Sept. 21, 1961, P.L. 87-264, 75 Stat. 559, 42 U.S. Code § 1975c

Oct. 17, 1963, P.L. 88-152, 77 Stat. 271, 42 U.S. Code § 1975c

July 2, 1964, P.L. 88-352, 78 Stat. 249, 42 U.S. Code §§ 1975a to 1975d

Dec. 14, 1967, P.L. 90-198, 81 Stat. 582, 42 U.S. Code §§ 1975c, 1975e

Nov. 25, 1970, P.L. 91-521, 84 Stat. 1356, 42 U.S. Code §§ 1975a, 1975b, 1975d, 1975e

Aug. 4, 1971, P.L. 92-64, 85 Stat. 166, 42 U.S. Code § 1975e

Oct. 14, 1972, P.L. 92-496, 86 Stat. 813, 42 U.S. Code §§ 1975a to 1975e

Oct. 6, 1979, P.L. 96-81, 42 U.S. Code §§ 1975c, 1975e

Civil Rights Act of 1960

May 6, 1960, P.L. 86-449, 74 Stat. 86, 18 U.S. Code §§ 837, 1074, 1509; 20 U.S. Code §§ 241, 640; 42 U.S. Code §§ 1971, 1974 to 1974e, 1975d

Civil Rights Act of 1964

July 2, 1964, P.L. 88-352, 78 Stat. 241, 28 U.S. Code § 1447; 42 U.S. Code §§ 1971, 1975a to 1975d, 2000a to 2000h-6

March 27, 1978, P.L. 95-251, 42 U.S. Code § 2000e-4

Oct. 31, 1978, P.L. 95-555, 42 U.S. Code §§ 2000e, 2000e nt.

Nov. 6, 1978, P.L. 95-598, 42 U.S. Code § 2000e

Nov. 9, 1978, P.L. 95-624, 42 U.S. Code § 2000g

Feb. 15, 1980, P.L. 96-191, 42 U.S. Code § 2000e-16

March 22, 1988, P.L. 100-259, 102 Stat. 31, 42 U.S. Code § 2000d-4a

Nov. 21, 1991, P.L. 102-166, 42 U.S. Code §§ 2000e, 2000e-1, 2000e-2, 2000e-4, 2000e-5, 2000e-16

Oct. 14, 1992, P.L. 102-411, 42 U.S. Code § 2000e-4

Oct. 20, 1994, P.L. 103-382, 42 U.S. Code § 2000d-4a

Jan. 23, 1995, P.L. 104-1, 42 U.S. Code § 2000e-16

Dec. 21, 1995, P.L. 104-66, 42 U.S. Code § 2000e-4

Aug. 7, 1998, P.L. 105-220, 42 U.S. Code § 2000e-16

Civil Rights Act of 1968

April 11, 1968, P.L. 90-284, 82 Stat. 73, 18 U.S. Code §§ 231 to 233, 241, 242, 245, 1153, 2101, 2102; 25 U.S. Code §§ 1301 to 1303, 1311, 1312, 1321 to 1326, 1331, 1341; 42 U.S. Code §§ 1973j, 3533, 3535, 3601 to 3619, 3631

April 12, 1974, P.L. 93-265, 88 Stat. 84, 25 U.S. Code § 1341

Oct. 11, 1996, P.L. 104-294, 42 U.S. Code § 3631

Civil Rights Act of 1991

Nov. 21, 1991, P.L. 102-166, 42 U.S. Code § 1981 nt.

Civil Rights Acts

April 9, 1866, Ch. 31, 14 Stat. 27, 8 U.S. Code §§ 1, 42, 49 to 55; 42 U.S. Code § 1982

May 31, 1870, Ch. 114, 16 Stat. 140, 8 U.S. Code §§ 31, 41, 49 to 53, 55, 135; 42 U.S. Code § 1981

Feb. 28, 1871, Ch. 99, 16 Stat. 433

April 20, 1871, Ch. 22, 17 Stat. 13, 8 U.S. Code §§ 43, 48, 242; 42 U.S. Code §§ 1983, 1985, 1986; 50 U.S. Code § 203

March 1, 1875, Ch. 114, 18 Stat. 336

Civil Rights Attorney's Fees Awards Act of 1976

Oct. 19, 1976, P.L. 94-559, 42 U.S. Code § 1988 et seq.

Civil Rights Commission Amendments Act of 1994

Oct. 25, 1994, P.L. 103-419, 42 U.S. Code §§ 1975 nt., 1975 et seq.

Civil Rights Commission Authorization Act of 1976

May 27, 1976, P.L. 94-292, 42 U.S. Code § 1975e et seq.

Civil Rights Commission Authorization Act of 1977

Oct. 13, 1977, P.L. 95-132, 42 U.S. Code §§ 1975 nt., 1975e

Civil Rights Commission Authorization Act of 1979

Oct. 6, 1979, P.L. 96-81, 42 U.S. Code §§ 1975 nt., 1975c, 1975e

Civil Rights Commission Authorization Act of 1980

Oct. 13, 1980, P.L. 96-447, 42 U.S. Code § 1975 nt.

Civil Rights Commission Reauthorization Act of 1989

Nov. 28, 1989, P.L. 101-180, 42 U.S. Code § 1975 nt.

Civil Rights of Institutionalized Persons Act

May 23, 1980, P.L. 96-247, 42 U.S. Code § 1997 et seq.

Sept. 8, 1982, P.L. 97-256, 42 U.S. Code §§ 1997b, 1997f

Sept. 13, 1994, P.L. 103-322, 42 U.S. Code § 1997e

April 26, 1996, P.L. 104-134, 42 U.S. Code §§ 1997a, 1997b, 1997c , 1997e, 1997f, 1997h

Civil Rights Remedies for Gender-Motivated Violence Act

Sept. 13, 1994, P.L. 103-322, 28 U.S. Code § 1445; 42 U.S. Code §§ 1988, 13701 nt., 13981

Civil Rights Restoration Act

Wash. Rev. Code Ann., 9-96-010 et seq.

Civil Rights Restoration Act of 1987

March 22, 1988, P.L. 100-259, 102 Stat. 28, 20 U.S. Code §§ 1681 nt., 1687, 1687 nt., 1688, 1688 nt.; 29 U.S. Code §§ 705, 794; 42 U.S. Code §§ 2000d-4a, 6107

Civil Service Act

Jan. 16, 1883, Ch. 27, 22 Stat. 403 (See 5 U.S. Code §§ 1101 to 1105, 1301 to 1303, 1307, 1308, 2102, 2951, 3302 to 3306, 3318, 3321, 3361, 5706, 7152, 7153, 7321, 7322, 7352; (See 18 U.S. Code §§ 1, 371, 1917) 40 U.S. Code § 42

July 26, 1937, Ch. 522, 50 Stat. 533 (See 5 U.S. Code § 7152)

June 10, 1948, Ch. 434, 62 Stat. 351 (See 5 U.S. Code § 7153)

Cal. Government Code § 18500 et seq.

Colo. Rev. Stat. 1963, 26-5-1 et seq.

Fla. Laws 1935, Ch. 16867

Haw. Rev. Stat. Ann., § 76-11 et seq.

Ill. Rev. Stat. 1955, Ch. 24 1/2, § 1 et seq. 73, Title 10

Iowa Code Ann., 400.1 et seq.

Kan. Stat. Ann., 75-2925 et seq., 75-2961

La. Const. 1974, Art. 10

La. Rev. Stat. Ann., 33:2391 et seq.

Mass. Gen. Laws Ann., 31:1 et seq.

Md. Ann. Code 1957, Art. 64A

Me. Rev. Stat. Ann. 1964, Title 5, § 7039 et seq.

Mich. Public Acts 1937, No. 346

Minn. Stat. Ann., 43A.01 et seq.

Minn. Stat. 1980, 43.001 et seq.

Mont. Rev. Code 1947, 59-1201 et seq.

Neb. Rev. Stat. 1943, 19-1825 et seq.

N.H. Rev. Stat. 1955, 21-I:48 et seq.

N.J. Stat. Ann., 11:2A-1 et seq.

N.Y. Consol. Laws, Ch. 7

Ohio Rev. Code 1953, 124.01 et seq.

Ore. Rev. Stat., 240.005 et seq.

Pa. Purdon's Stat., Title 71, § 741.1 et seq.

P.R. Laws Ann. 1954, Title 3, § 1301 et seq.

R.I. Gen. Laws 1956, 36-3-1 et seq.

Tenn. Code Ann., 8-30-101 et seq.

Tenn. Code Ann. 1955, 8-3001 et seq.

Vt. Stat. Ann., Title 3, § 301 et seq.

Wash. Rev. Code Ann., 41.06.010 et seq.

Wis. Stat. 1989, 230.05

W. Va. Code 1966, § 29-6-1 et seq.

Civil Service Act (Ashville)

N.C. Laws 1947, Ch. 83

Continued

N.C. Laws 1951, Ch. 1000

Civil Service Act (Athens)
Ga. Laws 1918, p. 528

Civil Service Act (Boroughs)
Pa. Purdon's Stat., Title 53, § 46101 et seq.

Civil Service Act (Calhoun County)
Ala. General Acts 1951, p. 363, No. 138

Civil Service Act (Carroll County)
Ga. Laws 1979, 4335

Civil Service Act (Chicago Sanitary District)
Ill. Rev. Stat. 1991, Ch. 42, § 323.2 et seq.

Civil Service Act (Cities)
Ill. Rev. Stat. 1991, Ch. 24, § 10-1-1 et seq.
Iowa Code 1983, 400.1 et seq.
Ky. Rev. Stat. 1971, 90.110 et seq.
La. Const. 1974, Art. 10
La. Rev. Stat. Ann., 33:2391 et seq.
N.D. Cent. Code, 40-44-01 et seq.
Ore. Rev. Stat., 242.010 et seq.

Civil Service Act (Classified)
N.Y. Civil Services Law (Consol. Laws Ch. 7), § 40 et seq.

Civil Service Act (Counties)
Ala. Code 1958, Title 12, § 133 et seq.
Ill. Rev. Stat. 1939, Ch. 34, § 64, Subds. 10 et seq.
Mich. Comp. Laws Ann., 38.401 et seq.
Ore. Rev. Stat., 241.002 et seq.
Wis. Stat. 1989, 59.07, Subsec. 20

Civil Service Act (County and City)
Wis. Stat. 1989, 63.01 et seq.

Civil Service Act (County Schools)
Ga. Laws 1937, p. 879

Civil Service Act (County Sheriffs)
Tenn. Code Ann., 8-8-401 et seq.

Civil Service Act (Custodians)
Ore. Rev. Stat., 242.310 et seq.

Civil Service Act (Daytona Beach)
Fla. Special Laws 1943, Ch. 22253

Civil Service Act (De Kalb County)
Ga. Laws 1951, p. 3226

Civil Service Act (Deputy Sheriffs)
W. Va. Code 1966, § 7-14-1 et seq.

Civil Service Act (Douglas County)
Ga. Laws 1967, p. 2579

Civil Service Act (Escambia County)
Fla. Special Laws 1951, Ch. 27537

Civil Service Act (Firemen and Policemen)
La. Rev. Stat. Ann., 33:2471 et seq.
Mich. Comp. Laws Ann., 38.501 et seq.
Minn. Stat. Ann., 420.01 et seq.
Mo. Rev. Stat. 1969, 85.360 et seq.
Pa. Purdon's Stat., Title 53, § 39861 et seq.
Tex. Local Gov. Code, § 143.001 et seq.
Wash. Rev. Code Ann., 41.08.010 et seq.
Wyo. Stat. Ann., § 15-5-101 et seq.

Civil Service Act (First Class Cities)
Pa. Cons. Stat., Title 42, § 4322

Civil Service Act (Forsyth County)
Ga. Laws 1978, p. 3572

Civil Service Act (Fulton County)
Ga. Laws 1943, p. 971

Civil Service Act (Gainesville)
Ga. Laws 1960, p. 2240

Civil Service Act (Hall County)
Ga. Laws 1967, p. 2556

Civil Service Act (Highway Patrol)
Utah Code Ann. 1953, 27-11-1 et seq.

Civil Service Act (Hillsborough County)
Fla. Special Laws 1951, Ch. 27601

Civil Service Act (Hollywood)
Fla. Special Laws 1965, Ch. 65-1689

Civil Service Act (Jackson)
Tenn. Private Acts 1949, Ch. 156

Civil Service Act (Jefferson County)
Ala. Code 1958, App., § 645 et seq.

Civil Service Act (Larger Counties)
Fla. Laws 1955, Ch. 30255

Civil Service Act (Marietta)
Ga. Laws 1952, p. 2246, § 7 et seq.

Civil Service Act (Miami Beach)
Fla. Special Laws 1937, Ch. 18696

Civil Service Act (Mobile County)
Ala. Local Acts 1939, p. 298

Civil Service Act (Municipal)
Ark. Code Ann. 1987, 14-49-102 et seq.
Minn. Stat. Ann., 44.01 et seq.
Miss. Code Ann., §§ 21-31-1 et seq.,
21-31-51 et seq.

Civil Service Act (Municipalities)
Conn. Gen. Stat. Ann., § 7-407 et seq.
Neb. Rev. Stat. 1943, 19-801 et seq.

Civil Service Act (Paid Fire Departments)
W. Va. Code 1966, § 8-15-11 et seq.

Civil Service Act (Panama City)
Fla. Special Laws 1941, Ch. 21476

Civil Service Act (Park Annuity and Benefit Fund)
Ill. Rev. Stat. 1989, Ch. 24 1/2, § 113.9 et seq.

Civil Service Act (Park System)
Ill. Rev. Stat. 1991, Ch. 24 1/2, § 77m et seq.

Civil Service Act (Paulding County)
Ga. Laws 1980, p. 3119

Civil Service Act (Police Departments)
Minn. Stat. Ann., 419.01 et seq.
Pa. Purdon's Stat., Title 53, § 53251 et seq.
Wash. Rev. Code Ann., 41.12.010 et seq.
W. Va. Code 1966, § 8-14-6 et seq.

Civil Service Act (Raleigh)
N.C. Laws 1981, Ch. 241

Civil Service Act (Ramsey County)
Minn. Laws 1941, Ch. 513

Civil Service Act (Savannah)
Ga. Laws 1947, p. 938

Civil Service Act (Second Class Cities)
Pa. Purdon's Stat., Title 53, § 23431 et seq.

Civil Service Act (Shelby County)
Ala. Acts 1993, No. 664

Civil Service Act (Spartanburg)
S.C. Code Ann. 1962, § 47-800.51

Civil Service Act (St. Petersburg)
Fla. Special Laws 1937, Ch. 18890

Civil Service Act (State Universities)
Ill. Rev. Stat. 1991, Ch. 24 1/2, § 38b.01 et seq.

Civil Service Act (Sylacauga)
Ala. Acts 1951, p. 763

Civil Service Act (Third Class Cities)
Pa. Purdon's Stat., Title 53, § 35901 et seq.

Civil Service Act (University)
Ill. Rev. Stat. 1991, Ch. 24 1/2, § 38b.01 et seq.

Civil Service Act (Veterans' Preference)
Pa. Cons. Stat., Title 51, § 7101 et seq.

Civil Service Act of Dothan
Ala. Local Acts 1947, p. 196, No. 273

Civil Service Board Act (Duval County)
Fla. Special Laws 1943, Ch. 22263

Civil Service Commission Act
Pa. Purdon's Stat., Title 71, § 741.1 et seq.

Civil Service Commission Act (Municipalities)
Ark. Stat. 1947, 19-1601 et seq.

Civil Service Commission Procedures Improvement Act
Tenn. Code Ann., 8-30-101 et seq.

Civil Service Due Process Amendments
Aug. 17, 1990, P.L. 101-376, 5 U.S. Code §§ 4303, 4303 nt., 7501 nt., 7511, 7701

Civil Service Enabling Act (Municipal Employees)
Cal. Statutes 1935, Ch. 48, p. 380

Civil Service Enabling Law (County)
Cal. Government Code § 31100 et seq.

Civil Service Examination in State of Domicile Act
July 2, 1909, Ch. 2, 36 Stat. 3 (See 5 U.S. Code §§ 3305, 3306)

Civil Service Law (City)
La. Rev. Stat. Ann., 33:2392 et seq.

Civil Service Merit System Act
Okla. Stat. Ann., Title 74, § 801 et seq.

Civil Service Miscellaneous Amendments Act of 1983
March 2, 1984, P.L. 98-224, 5 U.S. Code §§ 1101 nt., 1304, 3323, 4108, 4109, 7104, 7108

Civil Service Position Classification Act
Tex. Rev. Civ. Stat., Art. 6252-11

Civil Service Reform Act of 1978
Oct. 13, 1978, P.L. 95-454, 5 U.S. Code §§ 1101 nt., 1201 et seq.

Civil Service Retirement Act Amendments of 1966
July 18, 1966, P.L. 89-504, 80 Stat. 300 (See 5 U.S. Code §§ 8332 , 8336, 8339 to 8341)

Civil Service Retirement Act of 1930
May 29, 1930, Ch. 349, 46 Stat. 468 (See 5 U.S. Code §§ 1308, 2102, 2107, 3323, 8331 to 8348)
Aug. 4, 1939, Ch. 426, 53 Stat. 1200
Jan. 24, 1942, Ch. 16, 56 Stat. 13
June 26, 1944, Ch. 274, 58 Stat. 326

June 26, 1944, Ch. 276, 58 Stat. 334
June 28, 1944, Ch. 295, 58 Stat. 425
Dec. 19, 1944, Ch. 606, 58 Stat. 815
Dec. 23, 1944, Ch. 726, 58 Stat. 926
Dec. 23, 1944, Ch. 728, 58 Stat. 927
Nov. 9, 1945, Ch. 456, 59 Stat. 577
Dec. 21, 1945, Ch. 584, 59 Stat. 621
July 24, 1946, Ch. 608, 60 Stat. 658
July 24, 1946, Ch. 612, 60 Stat. 659
July 27, 1946, Ch. 682, 60 Stat. 705
July 27, 1946, Ch. 684, 60 Stat. 706
Aug. 2, 1946, Ch. 753, 60 Stat. 850
Aug. 8, 1946, Ch. 908, 60 Stat. 939
July 11, 1947, Ch. 219, 61 Stat. 307
July 30, 1947, Ch. 353, 61 Stat. 521
Jan. 26, 1948, Ch. 17, 62 Stat. 5
Feb. 28, 1948, Ch. 84, 62 Stat. 48
June 19, 1948, Ch. 538, 62 Stat. 504
June 25, 1948, Ch. 636, 62 Stat. 670
July 2, 1948, Ch. 807, 62 Stat. 1221
June 10, 1949, Ch. 194, 63 Stat. 170
June 24, 1949, Ch. 240, 63 Stat. 266
July 21, 1949, Ch. 356, 63 Stat. 475
Aug. 2, 1949, Ch. 381, 63 Stat. 490
Aug. 8, 1949, Ch. 404, 63 Stat. 577
Aug. 16, 1949, Ch. 443, 63 Stat. 609
Sept. 30, 1949, Ch. 588, 63 Stat. 699
Oct. 5, 1949, Ch. 602, 63 Stat. 704
Oct. 19, 1949, Ch. 698, 63 Stat. 884
June 14, 1950, Ch. 240, 64 Stat. 214
July 6, 1950, Ch. 449, 64 Stat. 320
Sept. 26, 1950, Ch. 1049, 64 Stat. 1038
Dec. 28, 1950, Ch. 1174, 64 Stat. 1120
July 16, 1952, Ch. 880, 66 Stat. 722
April 4, 1953, Ch. 19, 67 Stat. 22
July 23, 1953, Ch. 239, 67 Stat. 186
March 6, 1954, Ch. 59, 68 Stat. 21
Aug. 31, 1954, Ch. 1148, 68 Stat. 1004
Aug. 31, 1954, Ch. 1165, 68 Stat. 1043
Aug. 11, 1955, Ch. 807, 69 Stat. 692
June 4, 1956, Ch. 357, 70 Stat. 242

Civil Service Retirement Act of 1930, Renumbered July 31, 1956
May 29, 1930, Ch. 349, as renumbered July 31, 1956, Ch. 804, 70 Stat. 743 (See 5 U.S. Code §§ 1308, 3323, 8331 to 8348)

Aug. 1, 1956, Ch. 837, 70 Stat. 877 (See 5 U.S. Code § 8332)

June 17, 1957, P.L. 85-56, 71 Stat. 157 (See 5 U.S. Code § 8332)

June 29, 1957, P.L. 85-65, 71 Stat. 209 (See 5 U.S. Code § 8334)

Aug. 14, 1958, P.L. 85-661, 72 Stat. 614 (See 5 U.S. Code § 8343)

Aug. 27, 1958, P.L. 85-772, 72 Stat. 930 (See 5 U.S. Code §§ 8333 , 8334, 8341)

Sept. 2, 1958, P.L. 85-857, 72 Stat. 1264 (See 5 U.S. Code § 8332)

Sept. 21, 1959, P.L. 86-306, 73 Stat. 583 (See 5 U.S. Code § 8332)

April 8, 1960, P.L. 86-415, 74 Stat. 35 (See 5 U.S. Code § 8331)

July 1, 1960, P.L. 86-568, 74 Stat. 302 (See 5 U.S. Code §§ 8331, 8332, 8347)

July 7, 1960, P.L. 86-604, 74 Stat. 358 (See 5 U.S. Code §§ 8331, 8336, 8338, 8339, 8344)

July 12, 1960, P.L. 86-622, 74 Stat. 409 (See 5 U.S. Code §§ 8336 , 8338, 8339, 8342, 8344)

Sept. 6, 1960, P.L. 86-713, 74 Stat. 813 (See 5 U.S. Code §§ 8341 , 8345)

Sept. 14, 1961, P.L. 87-233, 75 Stat. 507 (See 5 U.S. Code § 8331)

Sept. 22, 1961, P.L. 87-293, 75 Stat. 623 (See 5 U.S. Code § 8332)

Oct. 4, 1961, P.L. 87-350, 75 Stat. 770 (See 5 U.S. Code §§ 8332, 8337, 8339, 8342, 8344, 8348)

Oct. 11, 1962, P.L. 87-793, 76 Stat. 869 (See 5 U.S. Code §§ 8331 , 8339 to 8341)

Feb. 7, 1964, P.L. 88-267, 78 Stat. 8 (See 5 U.S. Code §§ 8331, 8335)

Sept. 27, 1965, P.L. 89-205, 79 Stat. 840 (See 5 U.S. Code §§ 8331, 8340, 8348)

Nov. 1, 1965, P.L. 89-314, 79 Stat. 1162 (See 5 U.S. Code § 8340)

March 23, 1966, P.L. 89-373, 80 Stat. 78 (See 5 U.S. Code § 8342)

March 30, 1966, P.L. 89-378, 80 Stat. 93 (See 5 U.S. Code § 8344)

April 25, 1966, P.L. 89-407, 80 Stat. 131 (See 5 U.S. Code §§ 8341, 8342)

July 18, 1966, P.L. 89-504, 80 Stat. 300 (See 5 U.S. Code §§ 8332 , 8336, 8339 to 8341)

Sept. 26, 1966, P.L. 80-604, 80 Stat. 846 (See 5 U.S. Code §§ 2107, 8331, 8347)

Nov. 2, 1966, P.L. 89-702, 80 Stat. 1096 (See 5 U.S. Code § 8334)

Civil Service Retirement Acts

See Civil Service Retirement Act of 1930 and Civil Service Retirement Act of 1930, Renumbered July 31, 1956

May 22, 1920, Ch. 195, 41 Stat. 614 (See 5 U.S. Code §§ 1308, 2102, 2107, 3323, 8331 to 8348)

Feb. 14, 1922, Ch. 51, 42 Stat. 364

March 27, 1922, Ch. 116, 42 Stat. 470

June 17, 1922, Ch. 222, 42 Stat. 651

Sept. 22, 1922, Ch. 428, 42 Stat. 1047

July 3, 1926, Ch. 801, 44 Stat. 904

Civil Service Retirement Acts Amendments of 1956

July 31, 1956, Ch. 804, 70 Stat. 743 (See 5 U.S. Code §§ 1308, 3323, 8331 to 8348)

July 7, 1960, P.L. 86-604, 74 Stat. 359

Civil Service Retirement Amendments of 1969

Oct. 20, 1969, P.L. 91-93, 83 Stat. 136, 5 U.S. Code §§ 1308, 8331, 8331 nt., 8333, 8334, 8339 to 8341, 8348

Civil Service Retirement Spouse Equity Act of 1984

Nov. 8, 1984, P.L. 98-615, 5 U.S. Code prec. §§ 5401 to 5410, 5384, 5401, 8331, 8339, 8341, 8342, 8345, 8901 to 8903, 8905, 8907

Feb. 27, 1986, P.L. 99-251, 5 U.S. Code § 8341 nt.

Oct. 27, 1986, P.L. 99-549, 100 Stat. 3139

Jan. 8, 1988, P.L. 100-238, 5 U.S. Code § 8341 nt.

Civil Service System Act

Ga. Laws 1967, p. 2556

Civil Service System Act (City of Alabaster, Shelby County, Alabama)

Ala. Acts 1993, No. 358

Civil Service System Act (City of Helena, Shelby County, Alabama)

Ala. Acts 1992, p. 442, No. 201

Civil Service System Act (City of Pelham, Shelby County, Alabama)
Ala. Acts 1991, p. 186

Civil Service System Act (Phoenix City)
Ala. Local Acts 1947, p. 14, No. 15

Civil Service System Act (Tuscaloosa)
Ala. Local Acts 1947, p. 174

Civil Space Employee Testing Act of 1991
Dec. 9, 1991, P.L. 102-195, 42 U.S. Code § 2473c

Civil War Battlefield Commemorative Coin Act of 1992
Oct. 5, 1992, P.L. 102-379, 31 U.S. Code § 5112 nt.

Civil War Claims Act
July 4, 1864, Ch. 239, 13 Stat. 381

Civil War Sites Study Act of 1990
Nov. 28, 1990, P.L. 101-628, 16 U.S. Code § 1a-5 nt.
Nov. 2, 1994, P.L. 103-437, 16 U.S. Code § 1a-9

Civil Works Administration Act
June 16, 1933, Ch. 90, 48 Stat. 200

Civil Works—Emergency Relief Act
Feb. 15, 1934, Ch. 13, 48 Stat. 351

Civilian Conservation Corps Act
Mich. Comp. Laws Ann., 409.301 et seq.

Civilian Conservation Corps Reforestation Relief Act
March 31, 1933, Ch. 17, 48 Stat. 22

Civilian Defense Act
Me. Public Laws 1942, Special Session, Ch. 305
Mich. Comp. Laws Ann., 30.1 et seq.
N.M. Stat. Ann. 1953, 9-13-1 et seq.

Civilian Defense Act of 1943
S.D. Laws 1943, Ch. 151

Civilian Defense Council Act
Miss. Code Ann., §§ 33-15-7, 33-15-9

Civilian Pilot Training Act
June 27, 1939, Ch. 244, 53 Stat. 855
July 24, 1942, Ch. 522, 56 Stat. 704
June 10, 1943, Ch. 121, 57 Stat. 150

Clabaugh Act (Subversive Activities)
Ill. Rev. Stat. 1985, Ch. 144, §§ 48.7n, 48.8

Claiborne Pell Institute for International Relations and Public Policy Act
Oct. 19, 1996, P.L. 104-319, Title III, 110 Stat. 3867

Claim Act (Bank Deposits)
S.D. Codified Laws 1967, 51-15-2

Claim Act (Health Care False)
Wash. Rev. Code 1983, 48.80.010 et seq.

Claim and Delivery Act
Cal. Code of Civil Procedure § 509 et seq.
Wash. Rev. Code Ann., 7.64.010 et seq.

Claim and Judgment Fund Act (Motor Vehicles)
Md. Rules of Procedure, Rule BW5 et seq.

Claim Statutes, Damages
Cal. Government Code § 1980 et seq. (Public Officers)
Cal. Government Code § 16041 et seq. (State)
Cal. Statutes 1931, p. 2475 (Cities and Counties)
Cal. Water Code § 22727 et seq. (Irrigation Districts)

Claimants Act
Okla. Stat. Ann., Title 12, § 1481 et seq.

Claims Act
Pa. Purdon's Stat., Title 72, § 4651-1 et seq.
Tenn. Code Ann., 30-2-306 et seq.

Claims Act (Cities and Towns)
Wash. Rev. Code Ann., 35.31.010 et seq.

Claims Act (Counties)
Wash. Rev. Code Ann., 36.45.010 et seq.

Claims Act (Estates)
Colo. Rev. Stat., 15-12-805
Ohio Rev. Code 1953, 2117.06 et seq.
Ore. Rev. Stat., 116.505 et seq.
Wash. Rev. Code Ann., 11.40.010 et seq.

Claims Act (Governmental Tort)
Ore. Rev. Stat., 30.260 et seq.

Claims Act (Health Care False)
Conn. Gen. Stat. Ann., § 53-440 et seq.

Claims Act (Probate)
Minn. Stat. Ann., 524.3-104

Claims Act (Small)
Me. Rev. Stat. Ann. 1964, Title 14, § 7481 et seq.

Claims Act (Townships)
Wash. Rev. Code Ann., 45.52.010 et seq.

Claims Against Counties Act
Mich. Comp. Laws Ann., 46.71 et seq.

Claims Against the State Act
Alaska Stat. 1962, § 09.50.250 et seq.
Cal. Government Code §§ 810 et seq., 950 et seq.
Tenn. Code Ann., 30-2-306 et seq.

Claims and Suits Against the Commonwealth Act
P.R. Laws Ann. 1954, Title 32, § 3077 et seq.

Claims Classification Act (Probate)
Ill. Rev. Stat. 1991, Ch. 110 1/2, § 18-10

Claims Commission Act
Conn. Gen. Stat. Ann., § 4-141 et seq.

Claims Court Act
W. Va. Code 1966, § 14-2-1 et seq.

Claims Limitation Act (Foreign)
Okla. Stat. Ann., Title 12, § 104 et seq.

Claims Preference for Wages Act
Ill. Rev. Stat. 1991, Ch. 82, § 62.9 et seq.

Claims Resolution Act (Insurance)
Okla. Stat. 1981, Title 36, § 1251 et seq.

Claims Settlement Implementation Act (Indian)
Me. Rev. Stat. Ann. 1964, Title 30, § 6201 et seq.

Clam and Oyster Act
N.J. Stat. Ann., 58:24-1, et seq.

Clam River Watershed Project Act
Mass. Acts 1963, Ch. 563

Clandestine Drug Lab Act
Utah Code Ann. 1953, 58-37d-1 et seq.

Clark Act (Bridge Revenue Bonds)
Ky. Rev. Stat. 1971, 180.110 et seq.

Clark Act (Third Class Cities)
Pa. 1913 Pamph. Laws 568, No. 367

Clark Amendment (Angolan Assistance Limitation)
June 30, 1976, P.L. 94-329, 22 U.S. Code § 2293 nt.

Clark County SD No. 1 Sewerage Consolidation Law
Nev. Statutes 1979, Ch. 447, p. 646

Clark-Parsons Consumer Protection Law
Ala. Code 1975, § 8-19-1 et seq.

Clark Toll Bridge Act
Ky. Rev. Stat. 1971, 180.010 et seq.

Clarke-Athens County Charter Commission Act
Ga. Laws 1991, p. 3065

Clarke-McNary Act (Reforestation)-
June 7, 1924, Ch. 348, 43 Stat. 653, 16 U.S. Code §§ 471, 505, 515, 564 to 570
Sept. 21, 1944, Ch. 412, 58 Stat. 736, 16 U.S. Code § 565
Continued

Oct. 26, 1949, Ch. 735, 63 Stat. 909, 16 U.S. Code §§ 567, 568

May 5, 1972, P.L. 92-288, 86 Stat. 134, 16 U.S. Code § 566

Clarks Fork Wild and Scenic River Designation Act of 1990
Nov. 28, 1990, P.L. 101-628, 16 U.S. Code § 1271 nt.

Clarksburg Sewerage Loan Act
Mass. Acts 1951, Ch. 668

Clarksburg Water Loan Act
Mass. Acts 1951, Ch. 651

Clason Naturalization Act
July 2, 1940, Ch. 512, 54 Stat. 715

Class Action Act
Ill. Rev. Stat. 1991, Ch. 110, § 2-801 et seq.

Class Action Rule
N.D. Rules of Civil Procedure, 1957 as amended 1974, Rule 23

Class Doctrine Act
Tenn. Code Ann., 32-3-104

Class Representation Act
Ark. Stat. 1947, 27-809

Class Size Reduction Act (Morgan-Hart)
Cal. Education Code 1976, § 52080 et seq.

Class X Felonies Act
Tenn. Code Ann., 39-1-701 et seq.

Classification Act
Miss. Code Ann., § 25-9-101 et seq.
N.D. Laws 1917, Ch. 59
N.D. Laws 1919, Ch. 220
N.J. Stat. Ann., 40A:6-4

Classification Act (Civil Service)
Tex. Rev. Civ. Stat., Art. 6252-11

Classification Act (Corporate Directors)
Pa. 1933 Pamph. Laws 364, No. 106, § 403

Classification Act (Municipal Corporations)
Cal. Statutes 1883, p. 24

Classification Act (Position)
Tex. Government Code, § 654.001 et seq.

Classification Act (State Highways)
Cal. Streets and Highways Code § 230 et seq.

Classification Act (Taxation)
Minn. Stat. Ann., 273.13
Mont. Code Ann., 15-6-101 et seq.

Classification Act Amendments of 1962
Oct. 11, 1962, P.L. 87-793, 76 Stat. 843 (See 5 U.S. Code §§ 5108 , 5332 to 5337) 7 U.S. Code § 1857; 10 U.S. Code § 3535 nt.; 16 U.S. Code § 742b; 42 U.S. Code § 2521

Classification Act of 1923
March 4, 1923, Ch. 265, 42 Stat. 1488
Nov. 26, 1940, Ch. 919, 54 Stat. 1215
June 30, 1942, Ch. 212, 59 Stat. 298 to 300
Aug. 1, 1942, Ch. 543, 56 Stat. 733
May 24, 1946, Ch. 270, 60 Stat. 216

Classification Act of 1949
Oct. 28, 1949, Ch. 782, 63 Stat. 954 (See 5 U.S. Code §§ 305, 5101 to 5108, 5110 to 5113, 5115, 5332 to 5334, 5341, 5342, 5504, 5509, 7154) 12 U.S. Code § 1138f
June 16, 1950, Ch. 269, 64 Stat. 232 (See 5 U.S. Code § 5102)
Sept. 26, 1950, Ch. 1049, 64 Stat. 1038 (See 5 U.S. Code § 5102)
Sept. 30, 1950, Ch. 1123, 64 Stat. 1100 (See 5 U.S. Code §§ 5335, 5336)
Oct. 24, 1951, Ch. 554, 65 Stat. 612 (See 5 U.S. Code §§ 5332, 5335)
Sept. 1, 1954, Ch. 1208, 68 Stat. 1105 (See 5 U.S. Code §§ 305, 5102 to 5104, 5108, 5115, 5332 to 5336, 5338, 5341, 5342)
June 19, 1956, Ch. 402, 70 Stat. 291 (See 5 U.S. Code §§ 5337, 5338)
July 31, 1956, Ch. 804, 70 Stat. 740 (See 5 U.S. Code § 1113)
June 17, 1957, P.L. 85-56, 71 Stat. 159 (See 5 U.S. Code § 5102)
Aug. 14, 1957, P.L. 85-136, 71 Stat. 352 (See 5 U.S. Code § 5108)

May 29, 1958, P.L. 85-432, 72 Stat. 151 (See 5 U.S. Code § 5334)

June 20, 1958, P.L. 85-462, 72 Stat. 203 (See 5 U.S. Code §§ 3324 , 5104, 5108, 5332)

July 25, 1958, P.L. 85-550, 72 Stat. 411 (See 5 U.S. Code § 5102)

Aug. 23, 1958, P.L. 85-735, 72 Stat. 830 (See 5 U.S. Code § 5337)

Sept. 2, 1958, P.L. 85-857, 72 Stat. 1266 (See 5 U.S. Code § 5102)

May 29, 1959, P.L. 86-36, 73 Stat. 63 (See 5 U.S. Code § 5102)

July 17, 1959, P.L. 86-91, 73 Stat. 213 (See 5 U.S. Code § 5102)

July 31, 1959, P.L. 86-122, 73 Stat. 268 (See 5 U.S. Code § 5334)

Sept. 23, 1959, P.L. 86-370, 73 Stat. 650 (See 5 U.S. Code §§ 5102, 5108)

Sept. 23, 1959, P.L. 86-377, 73 Stat. 700 (See 5 U.S. Code § 5108)

July 1, 1960, P.L. 86-568, 74 Stat. 298 (See 5 U.S. Code §§ 5108, 5332)

Sept. 13, 1960, P.L. 86-768, 74 Stat. 910 (See 5 U.S. Code § 3324)

Sept. 13, 1960, P.L. 86-769, 74 Stat. 912 (See 5 U.S. Code § 5102)

Sept. 21, 1961, P.L. 87-270, 75 Stat. 567 (See 5 U.S. Code § 5337)

Sept. 26, 1961, P.L. 87-322, 75 Stat. 685 (See 5 U.S. Code § 5108)

Oct. 4, 1961, P.L. 87-367, 75 Stat. 786 (See 5 U.S. Code § 5108)

Oct. 11, 1962, P.L. 87-793, 76 Stat. 843 (See 5 U.S. Code §§ 5108 , 5332 to 5337)

Aug. 14, 1964, P.L. 88-426, 78 Stat. 400 (See 5 U.S. Code §§ 5108 , 5332, 5333)

Oct. 29, 1965, P.L. 89-301, 79 Stat. 1111 (See 5 U.S. Code §§ 5332, 5335)

June 9, 1966, P.L. 89-444, 80 Stat. 198 (See 5 U.S. Code § 5102)

July 18, 1966, P.L. 89-504, 80 Stat. 288 (See 5 U.S. Code §§ 5332 , 5333)

July 19, 1966, P.L. 89-512, 80 Stat. 318 (See 5 U.S. Code § 5545)

Classification and Compensation Act
Ark. Code Ann. 1987, 21-5-201 et seq.

Classification and Pay Plan
Mont. Code Ann., 2-18-201 to 2-18-305

Classification and Salary Act (Cities)
Ind. Code Ann., 36-3-6-2 et seq.

Classification Plan Act
Vt. Stat. Ann., Title 3, § 310 et seq.

Classification Tax Act (Intangibles)
Ga. Code Ann., 48-6-20 et seq.

Classification—Alternatives to Incarceration Act
N.Y. Correction Law (Consol. Laws Ch. 43), §§ 485, 500, 500b, 500c, 500g
N.Y. Executive Law 1951 (Consol. Laws Ch. 18), § 261 et seq.

Classified Civil Service Act
Colo. Rev. Stat., 24-50-101 et seq.
N.Y. Civil Services Law (Consol. Laws Ch. 7), § 40 et seq.

Classified Commercial Driver's License Act
See also Uniform Classified Commercial Driver's License Act
R.I. Gen. Laws 1956, 31-10.3-1 et seq.

Classified Employees Civil Service Act of the City of Asheville
N.C. Laws 1951, Ch. 1000

Classified Information Procedures Act
Oct. 15, 1980, P.L. 96-456, 18 U.S. Code Appx. § 16
Nov. 18, 1988, P.L. 100-690, 18 U.S. Code Appx. § 14

Classified Service Act
N.Y. Civil Service Law 1958 (Consol. Laws Ch. 7) §§ 10, 11a, 23 et seq.

Classified Service Salary Act
Colo. Rev. Stat., 24-50-101 et seq.

Classified Tax List Act
Ohio Rev. Code 1953, 319.34

CLAST and Other Skills Act (Robert H. McCabe)
Fla. Laws 1995, Ch. 411

Claude Pepper Young Americans Act of 1990

Nov. 3, 1990, P.L. 101-501, 42 U.S. Code §§ 12301 nt., 12301, 12302, 12311 to 12315, 12331 to 12340

Sept. 21, 1993, P.L. 103-82, 42 U.S. Code § 12312

May 18, 1994, P.L. 103-252, 42 U.S. Code §§ 12314, 12339, 12340, 12353, 12355

Clay County Development Authority

Fla. Special Laws 1957, Ch. 57-1226

Clay Mine Act

Ky. Rev. Stat. 1948, 354.010 et seq.

Clayton Act

Oct. 15, 1914, Ch. 323, 38 Stat. 730, 15 U.S. Code §§ 12 to 27, 44; 29 U.S. Code § 52

Dec. 29, 1950, Ch. 1184, 64 Stat. 1125, 15 U.S. Code §§ 18, 21

July 7, 1955, Ch. 283, 69 Stat. 282, 15 U.S. Code §§ 15a, 15b, 16

July 23, 1959, P.L. 86-107, 73 Stat. 243, 15 U.S. Code § 21

Sept. 12, 1980, P.L. 96-349, 15 U.S. Code § 15 et seq.

Dec. 29, 1982, P.L. 97-393, 15 U.S. Code § 15

Oct. 4, 1984, P.L. 98-443, 98 Stat. 1708, 15 U.S. Code §§ 18, 21

Aug. 9, 1989, P.L. 101-73, 15 U.S. Code § 18a

Nov. 16, 1990, P.L. 101-588, 15 U.S. Code §§ 15a, 19, 20

Dec. 17, 1993, P.L. 103-203, 15 U.S. Code § 19

Dec. 29, 1995, P.L. 104-88, 15 U.S. Code §§ 18, 21, 26

Feb. 8, 1996, P.L. 104-104, 15 U.S. Code § 18

Oct. 27, 1998, P.L. 105-297, 15 U.S. Code § 27a

Clayton County Community Improvement Districts Act

Ga. Laws 1992, p. 5698

Clayton County Tax Commissioner Clerk-Bond-Salary Act

Ga. Laws 1941, p. 824

Clayton-Rabun County Water and Sewer Authority Act

Ga. Laws 1992, p. 6403

Clean Air Act

July 14, 1955, Ch. 360, as added Dec. 17, 1963, P.L. 88-206, 42 U.S. Code § 7401 et seq.

Dec. 17, 1963, P.L. 88-206, 77 Stat. 392, 42 U.S. Code §§ 1857 to 1857l

Oct. 20, 1965, P.L. 89-272, 79 Stat. 992, 42 U.S. Code §§ 1857 to 1857f, 1857g to 1857l

Oct. 15, 1966, P.L. 89-675, 80 Stat. 954, 42 U.S. Code §§ 1857c, 1857l

Nov. 21, 1967, P.L. 90-148, 81 Stat. 485, 42 U.S. Code §§ 1857 to 1857l

Dec. 5, 1969, P.L. 91-137, 83 Stat. 283, 42 U.S. Code § 1857b-1

Dec. 31, 1970, P.L. 91-604, 84 Stat. 1676, 42 U.S. Code §§ 1857a, 1857b, 1857b-1, 1857c to 1857c-9, 1857d, and others

Nov. 18, 1971, P.L. 92-157, 85 Stat. 464, 42 U.S. Code §§ 1857c-6 , 1857c-8, 1857f-6c, 1857h-5

April 9, 1973, P.L. 93-15, 87 Stat. 11, 42 U.S. Code §§ 1857b-1, 1857f-6e, 1857l

June 22, 1974, P.L. 93-319, 88 Stat. 248, 42 U.S. Code 1857b-1, 1857c-5, 1857c-8 to 1857c-10, 1857d-1, 1857f-1, 1857f-6e, 1857f-6f, 1857f-7, 1857h-5, 1857l

Aug. 7, 1977, P.L. 95-95, 42 U.S. Code § 7403 et seq.

Nov. 16, 1977, P.L. 95-190, 42 U.S. Code § 7410 et seq.

July 2, 1980, P.L. 96-300, 42 U.S. Code § 7623 et seq.

Dec. 8, 1983, P.L. 98-213, 42 U.S. Code §§ 7625a, 7625-1, 7226

Nov. 15, 1990, P.L. 101-549, 29 U.S. Code § 655 nt.; 42 U.S. Code §§ 6921 nt., 7171 nt., 7401 et seq. generally, 7501 et seq. generally, 7601 et seq. generally

Dec. 4, 1991, P.L. 102-187, 42 U.S. Code § 7412

Nov. 2, 1994, P.L. 103-437, 42 U.S. Code § 7625-1

Nov. 28, 1995, P.L. 104-59, 42 U.S. Code § 7506

Dec. 23, 1995, P.L. 104-70, 42 U.S. Code § 7511a

Oct. 9, 1996, P.L. 104-260, 42 U.S. Code § 7506

Oct. 9, 1996, P.L. 104-264, 42 U.S. Code § 7571

Oct. 21, 1998, P.L. 105-277, 42 U.S. Code § 7671c

Oct. 27, 1998, P.L. 105-286, 42 U.S. Code § 7511b

Nov. 10, 1998, P.L. 105-362, 42 U.S. Code §§ 7408, 7412

Aug. 5, 1999, P.L. 106-40, 42 U.S. Code § 7412

Cal. Statutes 1988, Ch. 1568

Mont. Code Ann., 75-2-101 et seq.

Okla. Stat. Ann., Title 27A, § 2-5-101 et seq.

Okla. Stat. Ann., Title 63, § 1-1801 et seq.

R.I. Gen. Laws 1956, 23-23-1 et seq.

S.D. Codified Laws 1967, 34A-1-1 et seq.

Tex. Health and Safety Code, § 382.001 et seq.

Wash. Rev. Code Ann., 70.94.011 et seq.

Clean Air Act Amendments of 1966

Oct. 15, 1966, P.L. 89-675, 80 Stat. 954, 42 U.S. Code §§ 1857c, 1857l

Clean Air Act Amendments of 1970

Dec. 31, 1970, P.L. 91-604, 84 Stat. 1676, 42 U.S. Code §§ 215 nt., 1857 nt., 1857a, 1857b, 1857b-1, 1857c to 1857c-9, 1857d, 1857d-1, 1857e, and others; 49 U.S. Code §§ 1421, 1430; 50 U.S. Code Appx. § 456

Clean Air Act Amendments of 1977

Aug. 7, 1977, P.L. 95-95, 15 U.S. Code § 792 nt.; 42 U.S. Code §§ 4362, 7401 et seq.

Nov. 16, 1977, P.L. 95-190, 42 U.S. Code §§ 7401 nt., 7413, 7502 nt., 7521

Dec. 21, 1982, P.L. 97-375, 42 U.S. Code § 7551

Clean Air Act Amendments of 1990

Oct. 19, 1996, P.L. 104-316, 42 U.S. Code § 7612 nt.

Clean Air and Passenger Rail Act of 1990, 1994

Cal. Streets and Highways Code §§ 2701 to 2701.02, 2701.05 to 2701.08, 2701.10 to 2701.23

Cal. Streets and Highways Code §§ 2703 to 2703.02, 2703.05 to 2703.08, 2703.10 to 2703.22

Clean Air and Passenger Rail Bond Act

Cal. Streets and Highways Code §§ 2702 to 2702.02, 2702.05 to 2702.08, 2702.10 to 2702.22

Clean Air and Passenger Rail Bond Act of 1990

Cal. Streets and Highways Code § 2701 et seq.

Clean Air and Passenger Rail Bond Act of 1992

Cal. Streets and Highways Code § 2702 et seq.

Clean Air and Passenger Rail Bond Act of 1994

Cal. Streets and Highways Code § 2703 et seq.

Clean Air and Transportation Improvement Act

Cal. Public Utilities Code § 99600 et seq.

Clean Air and Transportation Improvement Bond Act

Cal. Public Utilities Code § 99690 et seq.

Clean Air Assistance Act (Small Business)

Mich. Comp. Laws Ann., 336.121 et seq.

Clean Air Compliance Act

N.Y. Environmental Conservation Law 1972 (Consol. Laws Ch. 43B) § 19-0311 nt.

Clean Air Financing Act

Tex. Health and Safety Code, § 383.001 et seq.

Clean Air, Jobs, and Transportation Efficiency Act

Cal. Public Utilities Code §§ 99385 et seq., 99399 et seq.

Clean Air Mandate Act (Federal)
N.J. Stat. Ann., 39:8-41 et seq.

Clean Air Washington Act
Wash. Rev. Code 1983, 70.94.440

Clean Air—Clean Water Bond Act
N.Y. Environmental Conservation Law 1972 (Consol. Laws Ch. 43B) § 56-0101 et seq.

Clean and Green, Farmland and Forest Land Assessment Act
Pa. Purdon's Stat., Title 72, § 5490.1 et seq.

Clean and Safe Neighborhoods Act
N.J. Stat. Ann., 52:27D-118.1 et seq.

Clean Communities and Recycling Act
N.J. Stat. Ann., 13:1E-92 et seq.

Clean Election Act
Me. Rev. Stat. Ann. 1964, Title 21-A, § 1121 et seq.
Va. Code 1950, §§ 24.2-941 to 24.2-955, 58.1-344.2

Clean Election Law
Ky. Rev. Stat. 1971, Superseded Vols., 117.600 et seq.

Clean Food Transport Act
Cal. Public Utilities Code §§ 215.6, 215.7, 1071.5, 3558, 3587, 3588, 3595, 3595.5, 4848.5
Cal. Vehicle Code 1959, § 34516

Clean Fuel and Campus Rideshare Act (Harvey)
Cal. Public Resources Code § 25620 et seq.

Clean Fuels Act
Cal. Public Resources Code §§ 25675, 25676

Clean Fuels Conversion Program Act
Utah Code Ann. 1953, 9-1-701 et seq.

Clean Glass Recycling Act
Cal. Public Resources Code § 70000 et seq.

Clean Hands Doctrine
Mont. Code Ann., 27-1-416

Clean Highways Act
N.M. Stat. Ann., 67-15-1 et seq.

Clean Indoor Air Act
Cal. Health and Safety Code § 25940 et seq.
Fla. Stat. Ann., 386.201 et seq.
Ill. Comp. Stat. 1992, Ch. 705, § 105/0.01 et seq.
Ind. Code Ann., 13-1-13-1 et seq.
Iowa Code Ann., 142B.1 et seq.
Me. Rev. Stat. Ann. 1964, Title 22, § 1578
Mich. Comp. Laws Ann., 333.12616
Minn. Stat. Ann., 144.411 et seq.
Mont. Code Ann., 50-40-101 et seq.
Neb. Rev. Stat. 1943, 71-5701 et seq.
N.M. Stat. Ann., 24-16-1 et seq.
N.Y. Adm. Code '85, § 17-501 et seq.
Pa. Purdon's Stat., Title 35, § 1230.1
S.C. Code Ann. 1976, § 44-95-10 et seq.
Wash. Rev. Code 1983, 70.160.010 et seq.

Clean Indoor Air Act (Smoking)
Neb. Rev. Stat. 1943, 2-3101 et seq.

Clean Michigan Fund Act
Mich. Comp. Laws Ann., 324.19101 et seq.

Clean Ocean Act
N.J. Stat. Ann., 58:10-23.25 et seq.

Clean Ocean and Shore Trust Committee Act (COAST)
N.J. Stat. Ann., 32:34-1 et seq.

Clean Ocean Education Act
N.J. Stat. Ann., 58:10A-52 et seq.

Clean Outdoor Air Act
Fla. Stat. Ann., 325.201 et seq.

Clean Public Elevator Air Act
Ill. Comp. Stat. 1992, Ch. 720, § 560/1 et seq.

Clean Rivers Act
Tex. General And Special Laws 1991, Ch. 294

Clean Streams Law
Pa. Purdon's Stat., Title 35, § 691.1 et seq.

Clean Vessel Act
Fla. Laws 1994, Ch. 241

Clean Vessel Act of 1992
Nov. 4, 1992, P.L. 102-587, 33 U.S. Code § 1322 nt.

Clean Water Act
See Federal Water Pollution Control Act
Mass. Gen. Laws Ann., 21:26 et seq.
Mo. Rev. Stat. 1978, 644.006 et seq.
Mo. Rev. Stat., 644.006 et seq.
Tenn. Code Ann., 69-3-101 et seq.

Clean Water Act of 1977
Dec. 27, 1977, P.L. 95-217, 33 U.S. Code §§ 1251 nt., 1254 et seq. .
Dec. 16, 1979, P.L. 96-148, 33 U.S. Code § 1284 nt.

Clean Water and Water Conservation Bond Law
Cal. Water Code § 13955 et seq.

Clean Water and Water Reclamation Bond Law
Cal. Water Code § 14050 et seq.

Clean Water Assistance Act (State)
Mich. Comp. Laws Ann., 323.451 et seq.

Clean Water Bond Act
Cal. Water Code §§ 13970 et seq., 13985 et seq., 13999 et seq.
N.C. Laws 1971, Ch. 909
N.C. Laws 1977, Ch. 677
N.C. Laws 1991, Ch. 993
N.J. Laws 1976, Ch. 92

Clean Water Council Act
N.J. Stat. Ann., 58:25-11 et seq.

Clean Water, Farmland, Green Acres and Historic Preservation Bond Act
N.J. Laws 1992, Ch. 88

Clean Water Infrastructure Act (Comprehensive)
R.I. Gen. Laws 1956, 46-15.6-1 et seq.

Clean Water Partnership Law
Minn. Stat. Ann., 103F.701 et seq.
Minn. Stat. 1986, 103F.701 et seq.

Clean Water Restoration Act of 1966
Nov. 3, 1966, P.L. 89-753, 80 Stat. 1246, 33 U.S. Code §§ 431 to 437, 466a, 466c-1 to 466e, 466g, 466j, 466l to 466n

Clean Water Revolving Loan and Grant Act
N.C. Gen. Stat. 1943, § 159G-1 et seq.

Clean Water Trust Fund Act (Petroleum)
Ida. Code 1947, 41-4901 et seq.

Clean Water—Clean Air Bond Act
N.Y. Environmental Conservation Law 1972 (Consol. Laws Ch. 43B) § 56-0101 et seq.

Clean Waters Commission Act
Neb. Laws 1967, Ch. 436

Cleaner Control Act (Sewage System)
Pa. Purdon's Stat., Title 35, § 770.1 et seq.

Cleaners and Dyers Act
Cal. Health and Safety Code § 13201 et seq.
Mich. Comp. Laws Ann., 29.201 et seq.

Cleaners, Dyers and Pressers Act
Fla. Laws 1937, Ch. 17894
Okla. Stat. Ann., Title 59, § 741 et seq.

Cleanup Act (Hazardous Sites)
Pa. Purdon's Stat., Title 35, § 6020.101 et seq.

Cleanup Act (Hazardous Substances)
Del. Code of 1974, Title 7, § 9101 et seq.

Cleanup Act (Petroleum Tank Release)
Minn. Stat. Ann., 115C.01 et seq.

Clear Creek County, Colorado, Public Lands Transfer Act of 1993
May 19, 1994, P.L. 103-253, 108 Stat. 674

Clear Distance Act (Motor Vehicles)
Mich. Comp. Laws Ann., 257.627
Ohio Rev. Code 1953, 4511.21

CLEAR Project (Community Law Enforcement and Recovery)
Cal. Penal Code § 14000 et seq.

Clearance Act
Mo. Rev. Stat., 389.580 et seq.

Clearing Corporation Deposit Act
N.J. Stat. Ann., 3B:20-26 et seq.

Clearing House Act (Gambling)
Ohio Rev. Code 1953, 2915.111

Clearing House Act (Self-Help)
Ill. Rev. Stat. 1991, Ch. 127, §§ 3350, 3351

Clearwater Downtown Development Board Act
Fla. Special Laws 1970, Ch. 70-635

Clemency Act (Executive)
Mont. Code Ann., 46-23-101 et seq.

Clerget Wine Law
Ark. Code Ann. 1987, 3-5-401 et seq.

Clerk Regulation Act (Circuit Court)
Ill. Comp. Stat. 1992, Ch. 705, § 110/0.01 et seq.

Clerk's Book Act
La. Code Civil Procedure Art. 4972

Clerk's Fee Act (Superior Court)
N.C. Gen. Stat. 1943, § 7A-101 et seq.

Clerks of Courts Act
Ill. Comp. Stat. 1992, Ch. 705, § 105/0.01 et seq.

Cleveland County School Act
N.C. Public-Local Laws 1935, Ch. 559

Cleveland-Melton Act (Horticulture)
Ky. Rev. Stat. 1971, 247.060

Cleveland Reservoir Loan Act
Mass. Acts 1962, Ch. 405

Clewiston Revenue Bond Act
Fla. Special Laws 1961, Ch. 61-2018

Client-Patient Protection Act
S.C. Code Ann. 1976, § 43-30-10 et seq.

Client Rights for Mentally Retarded in Community Residences
R.I. Gen. Laws 1956, 40.1-22.1-1 et seq.

Client Services Act (Forensic)
Fla. Stat. Ann., 916.10 et seq.

Clifton Park Water Authority Act
N.Y. Public Authorities Law (Consol. Laws Ch. 43A) § 1120 et seq.

Cline, Lowman, Rayburn, Lyon, Hayes Act (Workmen's Compensation)
Ky. Rev. Stat. 1971, 342.121, 342.185, 342.315, 342.316

Clinger-Cohen Act of 1996
Nov. 18, 1997, P.L. 105-85, 40 U.S. Code §§ 1492, 1501

Clinic Act (Prepaid Health)
Fla. Stat. Ann., 641.40 et seq.

Clinic Corporation Act
Conn. Gen. Stat. Ann., § 33-180 et seq.

Clinic Permit Act
Cal. Health and Safety Code § 1210 et seq.

Clinical Autopsies Act
P.R. Laws Ann. 1954, Title 18, § 731a et seq.

Clinical Health Services Act
D.C. Code Ann., § 32-119.1 et seq.

Clinical Laboratories Certification Act
Neb. Rev. Stat. 1943, 71-6801 et seq.

Clinical Laboratories Improvement Act of 1967
Dec. 5, 1967, P.L. 90-174, 81 Stat. 536, 42 U.S. Code § 263a

Clinical Laboratory Act
Ariz. Rev. Stat. Ann., § 36-451 et seq.
Cal. Business and Professions Code § 1200 et seq.
Fla. Stat. Ann., 483.011 et seq.

Ga. Code Ann., 31-22-1 et seq.

Pa. Purdon's Stat., Title 35, § 2151 et seq.

Clinical Laboratory and Blood Bank Act
Ill. Comp. Stat. 1992, Ch. 210, § 25/1-101 et seq.

Clinical Laboratory Improvement Act
N.J. Stat. Ann., 45:9-42.26 et seq.

Clinical Laboratory Improvement Amendments of 1988
Oct. 31, 1988, P.L. 100-578, 42 U.S. Code § 201 nt.

Clinical Laboratory Personnel Law
La. Rev. Stat. Ann., 37:1311 et seq.

Clinical Laboratory Registration Act
Ill. Rev. Stat. 1991, Ch. 111, § 621-101 et seq.

Clinical Laboratory Science Practice Act
Mont. Code Ann., 37-34-101 to 37-34-308
R.I. Gen. Laws 1956, 23-16.3-1 et seq.

Clinical Nurse Specialist—Nurse Practitioner Certification Act
N.J. Laws 1991, Ch. 377

Clinical Nurse Specialists Act
Cal. Business and Professions Code § 2838 et seq.

Clinical Professional Counselor Licensing Act
Ill. Comp. Stat. 1992, Ch. 225, § 107/1 et seq.

Clinical Profusionist Licensure Act
Mo. Laws 1997, S.B. No. 141, §§ 15 to 35

Clinical Psychologist Lien Act
Ill. Comp. Stat. 1992, Ch. 770, § 10/0.01 et seq.

Clinical Psychologists Licensing Act
Ill. Comp. Stat. 1992, Ch. 225, § 15/1 et seq.

Clinical Social Work and Social Work Practice Act
Ill. Comp. Stat. 1992, Ch. 225, § 20/1 et seq.

Clinical Thermometer Act
Mich. Comp. Laws Ann., 750.469

Clinton Avenue Courtyard Act
N.Y. Laws 1899, Ch. 257

Clinton-Huron Metropolitan Authority Act
Mich. Comp. Laws Ann., 119.51 et seq.

Clinton-Newberry Natural Gas Authority Act
S.C. Acts 1952, p. 1958, No. 789

Clinton Sewage Loan Act
Mass. Acts 1954, Ch. 462

Cloon-Girrbach-Goulette Act (City Charter Amendments—Primaries)
Mich. Comp. Laws Ann., 117.21

Close Corporation Act
Del. Code of 1974, Title 8, § 341 et seq.
Fla. Stat. 1975, 608.70 et seq.
Ill. Rev. Stat. 1991, Ch. 32, § 1201 et seq.
Md. Ann. Code 1974, Art. CA, § 4-101 et seq.
Mont. Code Ann., 35-9-101 et seq.
Tex. Business Corporation Act. Art. 12.01 et seq.

Close Pursuit Act
See also Uniform Act on Close Pursuit
Mont. Code Ann., 46-6-411
N.Y. Criminal Procedure Law (Consol. Laws Ch. 11A) § 140.55
R.I. Gen. Laws 1956, 12-8-1 et seq.
Wis. Stat. 1989, 976.04

Closed Range Act
Mo. Rev. Stat., 270.010 et seq.

Closed Shop Act
Mich. Comp. Laws Ann., 423.14
N.C. Gen. Stat. 1943, § 95-78 et seq.
N.D. Cent. Code 34-01-14

Closed Shop Labor Act (Prohibition)
Tex. Rev. Civ. Stat., Art. 5207a

Closeup Act
Tex. Rev. Civ. Stat., Art. 4413(32f)

Closing Act
P.R. Laws Ann. 1954, Title 33, § 2201

Closing Act (Plant)
Mass. Gen. Laws Ann., 151A:71A et seq.

Closing Out Sales Act
N.C. Gen. Stat. 1943, § 66-76 et seq.
R.I. Gen. Laws 1956, 6-14-1 et seq.

Closing Partnership Business Act
Ind. Code Ann., 23-4-3-1 et seq.

Cloud on Title Act
Ga. Code Ann., 23-3-42

Club Act
N.Y. Benevolent Orders Law (Consol. Laws Ch. 3)

Club Act (Discriminatory)
Ill. Rev. Stat. 1991, Ch. 68, § 100 et seq.

Club and Drinking Establishment Act
Kan. Stat. Ann., 41-2601 et seq.

Clyde Randolph Ketchum Act
Wash. Rev. Code 1989, 43.20A.720

Co-Depositor Act
Mich. Comp. Laws Ann., 487.703

Coach Law
Ky. Rev. Stat. 1962, 276.440, 276.990

Coachella District Merger Law
Cal. Water Code § 33100 et seq.

Coachella Valley Intermodal Transportation Authority Act
Cal. Public Utilities Code § 141000 et seq.

Coal Act
Ill. Rev. Stat. 1991, Ch. 29, § 35.9 et seq.
Ohio Rev. Code 1953, 1327.21 et seq.

Coal and Energy Development Bond Act
Ill. Comp. Stat. 1992, Ch. 20, § 1110/1 et seq.

Coal and Food Commission Act
Ind. Laws 1920, Special Session, Ch. 44, p. 143

Coal and Gas Resource Coordination Act
Pa. Purdon's Stat., Title 58, § 501 et seq.

Coal and Oil Resolutions (Railroads)
March 7, 1906, No. 8, 34 Stat. 823
March 21, 1906, No. 11, 34 Stat. 824

Coal Commission Acts
Sept. 22, 1922, Ch. 412, 42 Stat. 1023
March 4, 1923, Ch. 248, 42 Stat. 1446

Coal Conservation Act
See Guffey-Snyder Coal Act
Mont. Code Ann. 1979, 82-3-101 et seq.

Coal Conservation Act (Strip Mined)
Mont. Code Ann. 1979, 82-3-101 et seq.

Coal Cooperative Marketing Association Law
Tenn. Code Ann., 59-13-101 et seq.

Coal Development and Energy Conservation Act
Ill. Comp. Stat. 1992, Ch. 20, § 1105/13.1 et seq.

Coal Gasification Generation Act
Cal. Public Resources Code § 25650 et seq.

Coal Industry Retiree Health Benefit Act of 1992
Oct. 24, 1992, P.L. 102-486, 26 U.S. Code § 1 nt.

Coal Industry Seizure Act
Va. Code 1950, § 45.1-145 et seq.

Coal Lands Act
March 3, 1873, Ch. 279, 17 Stat. 607
Alaska Comp. Laws Ann. 1949, §§ 47-2-56, 47-2-57, 47-2-141 et seq.

Coal Lands Lease Act
Wash. Rev. Code Ann., 79.01.652 et seq.

Coal Leasing Practices Act
N.D. Cent. Code 38-17-01 et seq.

Coal Mine Act (Anthracite)
Pa. Purdon's Stat., Title 52, § 70-101 et seq.

Coal Mine Act (Bituminous)
Pa. Purdon's Stat., Title 52, § 701-101 et seq.

Coal Mine Inspection Act
Wyo. Stat. Ann., § 30-2-201 et seq.

Coal Mine Land Regulation Act
Ill. Rev. Stat. 1991, Ch. 96 1/2, § 3801 et seq.

Coal Mine Medical Emergencies Act
Ill. Comp. Stat. 1992, Ch. 410, § 15/1 et seq.

Coal Mine Safety Act
Ala. Code 1975, § 25-9-1 et seq.
Va. Code 1950, § 45.1-1 et seq.

Coal Mine Sealing Act
Pa. Purdon's Stat., Title 52, § 28.1 et seq.

Coal Miners Memorial Day Act
Ill. Comp. Stat. 1992, Ch. 5, § 490/30

Coal Mines Act
Mich. Comp. Laws Ann., 425.1 et seq.

Coal Mining Act
Colo. Rev. Stat., 34-20-101 et seq.
Ga. Laws 1984, p. 398
Ill. Comp. Stat. 1992, Ch. 225, § 705/1.01 et seq.
Mont. Code Ann., 50-73-101 et seq.
Mont. Code Ann. 1947, 50-401 to 50-531
Okla. Stat. Ann., Title 45, § 1 et seq.
Wash. Rev. Code Ann., 78.40.010 et seq.
Wyo. Stat. Ann., § 30-2-101 et seq.

Coal Mining Act (Surface)
Mo. Rev. Stat., 444.800 et seq.

Coal Mining and Petroleum Act
Pa. Purdon's Stat., Title 58, § 601.101 et seq.

Coal Mining and Reclamation Act (Surface)
W. Va. Code 1966, § 22A-3-1 et seq.

Coal Mining and Reclamation Law
Miss. Code Ann., § 53-9-1 et seq.

Coal Mining Regulatory and Reclamation Act
Mass. Gen. Laws Ann., 21B:1 et seq.

Coal Mining, Surface Land Conservation and Reclamation Act
Ill. Comp. Stat. 1992, Ch. 225, § 720/1.01 et seq.

Coal Notice Act
Pa. Purdon's Stat., Title 52, § 1551 et seq.

Coal Preference Act
Iowa Code Ann., 73.6 et seq.

Coal Processing Act (County)
Ill. Rev. Stat. 1991, Ch. 96 1/2, § 4000 et seq.

Coal Production Incentive Act
Okla. Stat. Ann., Title 68, §§ 2357.10, 2357.11

Coal Products Commission Transfer Act
Ill. Comp. Stat. 1992, Ch. 20, §§ 1910/0.01, 1910/1

Coal Reclamation Act
Okla. Stat. Ann., Title 45, § 742 et seq.

Coal Refuse Disposal Control Act
Pa. Purdon's Stat., Title 52, § 30.51 et seq.
W. Va. Code 1966, §§ 20-6C-1 et seq, 30.51 et seq.

Coal Research Act
Ky. Rev. Stat. 1971, 152A.210

Coal Resources Development and Renewable Energy Efficiency Law
Ill. Comp. Stat. 1992, Ch. 20, § 687/6-1 et seq.

Coal Severance Tax Act
Mont. Code Ann., 15-35-101 et seq.
N.D. Cent. Code, 57-61-01 et seq.

Coal Stripping Act
Pa. Purdon's Stat., Title 52, § 1471 et seq.

Coal Surface Mining Act
N.M. Stat. Ann., 69-25A-1 et seq.
Tenn. Code Ann., 59-8-401 et seq.

Coal Surface Mining Control and Reclamation Act
Va. Code 1950, § 45.1-226 et seq.

Coal Surface Mining Reclamation Act
Ala. Code 1975, § 9-16-1 et seq.

Coal Technology Development Assistance Act
Ill. Comp. Stat. 1992, Ch. 30, § 730/1 et seq.

Coalbed Methane Gas Well Plugging Fund Act
Ala. Code 1975, § 9-17-130 et seq.

Coast and Geodetic Survey Act
Ill. Comp. Stat. 1992, Ch. 765, § 230/0.01 et seq.

Coast and Geodetic Survey Commissioned Officers' Act of 1948
June 3, 1948, Ch. 390, 62 Stat. 297, 33 U.S. Code §§ 852a, 852b, 853a to 853r, 854a, 864d
June 21, 1955, Ch. 172, 69 Stat. 169, 33 U.S. Code §§ 853e (a), 853i (a)
Sept. 8, 1980, P.L. 96-342, 33 U.S. Code § 853o
Oct. 19, 1984, P.L. 98-498, 33 U.S. Code § 853h
Nov. 8, 1985, P.L. 99-145, 33 U.S. Code § 853u
July 1, 1986, P.L. 99-348, 33 U.S. Code § 853o
June 13, 1991, P.L. 102-54, 33 U.S. Code § 853h
Nov. 18, 1997, P.L. 105-85, 33 U.S. Code § 853h
Nov. 13, 1998, P.L. 105-384, 33 U.S. Code §§ 853a, 853u

Coast and Geodetic Survey Commissioned Officers' Act of 1961
Sept. 14, 1961, P.L. 87-233, 75 Stat. 506, 33 U.S. Code §§ 851a nt., 852a nt., 852b nt., 853a, 853e, 853j-1, 853k, 853l, 853s, 853t, 854a nt.

Coast Guard
Aug. 4, 1949, Ch. 393, 63 Stat. 496, 14 U.S. Code §§ 1 to 894
Sept. 27, 1949, Ch. 586, 63 Stat. 698, 14 U.S. Code § 433
Aug. 3, 1950, Ch. 536, 64 Stat. 406, 14 U.S. Code §§ 89, 93, 145, 233, 234, 239 to 243, 309 to 313, 351, 357, 359 to 362, 367, 423, 431, 485, 490 , 562 to 564, 639, 751, 755
Sept. 23, 1950, Ch. 996, 64 Stat. 978, 14 U.S. Code § 434
Sept. 26, 1950, Ch. 1049, 64 Stat. 1038, 14 U.S. Code § 91
June 22, 1951, Ch. 150, 65 Stat. 89, 14 U.S. Code § 81
May 29, 1954, Ch. 249, 68 Stat. 167, 14 U.S. Code § 230
June 8, 1955, Ch. 136, 69 Stat. 88, 14 U.S. Code § 370
June 15, 1955, Ch. 142, 69 Stat. 134, 14 U.S. Code § 640
Aug. 4, 1955, Ch. 553, 69 Stat. 493, 14 U.S. Code § 232
Aug. 9, 1955, Ch. 650, 69 Stat. 577, 14 U.S. Code §§ 432, 511
Aug. 9, 1955, Ch. 684, 69 Stat. 620, 14 U.S. Code §§ 247, 248
June 4, 1956, Ch. 351, 70 Stat. 226, 14 U.S. Code § 85
July 20, 1956, Ch. 647, 70 Stat. 588, 14 U.S. Code §§ 42, 439
July 24, 1956, Ch. 692, 70 Stat. 631, 14 U.S. Code § 367
Aug. 3, 1956, Ch. 926, 70 Stat. 981, 14 U.S. Code § 760
Aug. 7, 1956, Ch. 1023, 70 Stat. 1077, 14 U.S. Code § 650
Aug. 10, 1956, Ch. 1041, 70A Stat. 620, 14 U.S. Code §§ 41, 350, 351, 435 to 438, 462a, 471a, 492a, 494, 497, 510, 751a, 752a, 753a, 758a, 759a, 762
Aug. 14, 1957, P.L. 85-144, 71 Stat. 366, 14 U.S. Code §§ 243, 313a
Aug. 16, 1957, P.L. 85-149, 71 Stat. 369, 14 U.S. Code § 755
May 20, 1958, P.L. 85-422, 72 Stat. 132, 14 U.S. Code § 423
Aug. 23, 1958, P.L. 85-726, 72 Stat. 808, 14 U.S. Code §§ 81, 82, 90

Aug. 23, 1958, P.L. 85-738, 72 Stat. 832, 14 U.S. Code §§ 490, 645

Sept. 2, 1958, P.L. 85-861, 72 Stat. 1547, 14 U.S. Code §§ 435 nt., 440, 770 to 795

June 25, 1959, P.L. 86-70, 73 Stat. 143, 14 U.S. Code § 634

Aug. 14, 1959, P.L. 86-159, 73 Stat. 357, 14 U.S. Code § 654

Sept. 21, 1959, P.L. 86-309, 73 Stat. 585, 14 U.S. Code § 432

May 14, 1960, P.L. 86-474, 74 Stat. 144, 14 U.S. Code §§ 41, 42, 44, 46, 47, 186 to 191, 222, 247, 365, 462

June 29, 1960, P.L. 86-533, 74 Stat. 245, 14 U.S. Code §§ 646, 647

June 30, 1960, P.L. 86-559, 74 Stat. 280, 14 U.S. Code §§ 772, 773, 787a

Oct. 5, 1961, P.L. 87-396, 75 Stat. 827, 14 U.S. Code §§ 2, 94

June 28, 1962, P.L. 87-509, 76 Stat. 121, 14 U.S. Code § 437

July 10, 1962, P.L. 87-526, 76 Stat. 141, 14 U.S. Code §§ 461, 496, 655

Sept. 7, 1962, P.L. 87-649, 76 Stat. 495, 14 U.S. Code §§ 462a, 485, 755, 758a

Sept. 27, 1962, P.L. 87-704, 76 Stat. 632, 14 U.S. Code § 763

June 21, 1963, P.L. 88-45, 77 Stat. 68, 14 U.S. Code § 656

July 25, 1963, P.L. 88-77, 77 Stat. 95, 14 U.S. Code § 491

Sept. 6, 1963, P.L. 88-114, 77 Stat. 144, 14 U.S. Code § 357

Sept. 24, 1963, P.L. 88-130, 77 Stat. 174, 14 U.S. Code §§ 41a, 42, 44, 46, 47, 190, 211 to 214, 251 to 262, 271 to 277, 281 to 294, 321 to 327 , 331 to 335, 433, 759a, 791

Oct. 2, 1963, P.L. 88-132, 77 Stat. 214, 14 U.S. Code § 423

March 3, 1964, P.L. 88-276, 78 Stat. 153, 14 U.S. Code § 182

Sept. 15, 1965, P.L. 89-185, 79 Stat. 789, 14 U.S. Code § 490

Sept. 17, 1965, P.L. 89-189, 79 Stat. 820, 14 U.S. Code § 336

Sept. 17, 1965, P.L. 89-191, 79 Stat. 822, 14 U.S. Code § 86

Sept. 25, 1965, P.L. 89-200, 79 Stat. 834, 14 U.S. Code § 755

June 9, 1966, P.L. 89-444, 80 Stat. 195, 14 U.S. Code §§ 4, 42, 44, 46, 47, 182, 186, 190, 211, 214, 253, 256, 258, 332, 334, 371 to 373, 438, 654, 755, 771

Oct. 14, 1966, P.L. 89-662, 80 Stat. 912, 14 U.S. Code §§ 81, 82

Nov. 2, 1966, P.L. 89-718, 80 Stat. 1124, 14 U.S. Code § 461

Sept. 11, 1967, P.L. 90-83, 81 Stat. 220, 14 U.S. Code § 461

July 5, 1968, P.L. 90-377, 82 Stat. 288, 14 U.S. Code § 509

July 5, 1968, P.L. 90-385, 82 Stat. 293, 14 U.S. Code § 42

June 12, 1970, P.L. 91-278, 84 Stat. 304, 14 U.S. Code §§ 2, 41a, 88, 182, 190, 195, 271, 332, 432, 475, 650, 657

Sept. 18, 1970, P.L. 91-402, 84 Stat. 838, 14 U.S. Code §§ 762, 770, 772, 774, 775, 780 to 782, 784, 787, 790, 791, 796 to 798

Sept. 28, 1971, P.L. 92-129, 85 Stat. 362, 14 U.S. Code § 275

July 10, 1972, P.L. 92-343, 86 Stat. 450, 14 U.S. Code § 475

Aug. 29, 1972, P.L. 92-417, 86 Stat. 655, 14 U.S. Code § 646

Oct. 2, 1972, P.L. 92-451, 86 Stat. 755, 14 U.S. Code §§ 41, 42, 44, 47, 50, 51, 287, 290

Oct. 2, 1972, P.L. 92-455, 86 Stat. 761, 14 U.S. Code § 423

Oct. 9, 1972, P.L. 92-479, 86 Stat. 794, 14 U.S. Code § 764

July 9, 1973, P.L. 93-65, 87 Stat. 151, 14 U.S. Code § 475

Dec. 5, 1973, P.L. 93-174, 87 Stat. 692, 14 U.S. Code §§ 41a, 42, 755, 771, 775, 780, 787, 796

May 14, 1974, P.L. 93-283, 88 Stat. 139, 14 U.S. Code §§ 83, 85, 86, 214, 283, 285, 288, 656, 658, 780, 785, 832

Coast Guard Act

Jan. 28, 1915, Ch. 20, 38 Stat. 800

Coast Guard Appropriation Act, 1947

July 12, 1946, Ch. 569, 60 Stat. 531

Coast Guard Authorization Act of 1982

Oct. 15, 1982, P.L. 97-322, 14 U.S. Code §§ 81, 81 nt., 475

Coast Guard Authorization Act of 1984
Oct. 30, 1984, P.L. 98-557, 98 Stat. 2860
May 15, 1985, P.L. 99-36, 46 U.S. Code
prec. § 3101, §§ 3102, 3102 nt.
Nov. 8, 1985, P.L. 99-145, 14 U.S. Code § 89
nt.
Oct. 19, 1996, P.L. 104-324, 14 U.S. Code
§ 88 nt.

Coast Guard Authorization Act of 1986
Nov. 10, 1986, P.L. 99-640, 100 Stat. p. 3345

Coast Guard Authorization Act of 1988
Dec. 21, 1995, P.L. 104-66, 10 U.S. Code
§ 2304 nt.

Coast Guard Authorization Act of 1989
Dec. 12, 1989, P.L. 101-225, 103 Stat. 1908
Nov. 16, 1990, P.L. 101-595, 104 Stat. 2990

Coast Guard Authorization Act of 1991
Dec. 19, 1991, P.L. 102-241, 105 Stat. 2208
Nov. 30, 1993, P.L. 103-160, 37 U.S. Code
§ 406 nt.

Coast Guard Authorization Act of 1992
Nov. 4, 1992, P.L. 102-587, 106 Stat. 5068

Coast Guard Authorization Act of 1993
Dec. 20, 1993, P.L. 103-206, 107 Stat. 2419

Coast Guard Authorization Act of 1996
Oct. 19, 1996, P.L. 104-324, 110 Stat. 3901

Coast Guard Authorization Act of 1998
Nov. 13, 1998, P.L. 105-383, 112 Stat. 3411

**Coast Guard Auxiliary and Reserve Act of
1941**
Feb. 19, 1941, Ch. 8, 55 Stat. 9
July 11, 1941, Ch. 290, 55 Stat. 584
June 6, 1942, Ch. 385, 56 Stat. 329
Oct. 26, 1942, Ch. 628, 56 Stat. 990
Nov. 23, 1942, Ch. 639, 56 Stat. 1020
Dec. 23, 1943, Ch. 378, 57 Stat. 609
Sept. 27, 1944, Ch. 428, 58 Stat. 754
Sept. 30, 1944, Ch. 449, 58 Stat. 756
Sept. 30, 1944, Ch. 453, 58 Stat. 759

Coast Guard Cutter Act
July 15, 1941, Ch. 302, 55 Stat. 597

Coast Guard Defense Act
June 2, 1939, Ch. 167, 53 Stat. 797

Coast Guard Omnibus Act of 1990
Nov. 16, 1990, P.L. 101-595, 14 U.S. Code
§§ 194, 633, 667, 668; 15 U.S. Code § 313
nt.; 33 U.S. Code §§ 59d, 59aa; 46 U.S.
Code §§ 3302, 8103 nt., 8502, 13101 to
13103, 13105, 13108, 14301

Coast Guard Personnel Act
May 24, 1939, Ch. 148, 53 Stat. 756 (See 14
U.S. Code §§ 47, 48)

Coast Guard Regulatory Reform Act of 1996
Oct. 19, 1996, P.L. 104-324, Title VI, 46
U.S. Code § 2101 nt.

Coast Guard Reserve Act
June 23, 1939, Ch. 243, 53 Stat. 854

Coast Guard Retirement Act
May 24, 1939, Ch. 146, 53 Stat. 755 (See 14
U.S. Code §§ 355, 357, 358 to 360, 423,
633)

Coast Life Support District Act
Cal. Statutes 1986, Ch. 375

Coast Survey Ship Act
June 2, 1939, Ch. 172, 53 Stat. 803

Coastal Act
Cal. Public Resources Code § 30000 et seq.

Coastal Area Facility Review Act
N.J. Stat. Ann., 13:19-1 et seq.

Coastal Area Management Act
N.C. Gen. Stat. 1943, § 113A-100 et seq.

Coastal Barrier Improvement Act of 1990
Nov. 16, 1990, P.L. 101-591, 12 U.S. Code
§ 1441a-3; 16 U.S. Code §§ 3501 nt., 3503
nt.

Coastal Barrier Resources Act
Oct. 18, 1982, P.L. 97-348, 16 U.S. Code §§ 3501 nt., 3501 et seq.
Dec. 31, 1982, P.L. 97-396, 16 U.S. Code § 3503
April 7, 1986, P.L. 99-272, 16 U.S. Code § 3502
Nov. 23, 1988, P.L. 100-707, 16 U.S. Code §§ 3501, 3502, 3505
Nov. 16, 1990, P.L. 101-591, 16 U.S. Code §§ 3502 to 3506, 3510

Coastal Conservancy Act
Cal. Public Resources Code § 31000 et seq.

Coastal Conveyance Act
Fla. Stat. Ann., 376.011 et seq.
Me. Rev. Stat. Ann. 1964, Title 38, § 541 et seq.

Coastal Coordination Act
Tex. Natural Resources Code, § 33.201 et seq.

Coastal Erosion, Beach Access Preservation and Enhancement, and Dune Protection Coastal Management Plan
Tex. General and Special Laws 1991, Ch. 295

Coastal Erosion Coastal Management Plan
Tex. General and Special Laws 1991, Ch. 295

Coastal Erosion Law
Tex. Natural Resources Code, § 33.601 et seq.

Coastal Erosion Management Act
N.Y. Environmental Conservation Law 1972 (Consol. Laws Ch. 43B) 34-0101 et seq., 70-0107, 70-0117

Coastal Facilities Improvement Act
Mass. Gen. Laws Ann., 21F:1 et seq.

Coastal Facilities Review Act
Md. Ann. Code 1974, Art. NR, § 6-501 et seq.

Coastal Fisheries Act
Ga. Code Ann., 12-2-1, 12-2-24, 27-1-4
Me. Rev. Stat. Ann. 1964, Title 12, § 6001 et seq.
S.C. Code Ann. 1976, § 50-17-10 et seq.

Coastal Highway Act
S.C. Acts 1926, p. 1492, No. 756

Coastal Highway District Act
Ga. Laws 1924, p. 307

Coastal Management Act
Conn. Gen. Stat. Ann., § 22a-90 et seq.
Fla. Stat. Ann., 380.20 et seq.
Ga. Code Ann., 12-5-320 et seq.

Coastal Management Plan for Beach Access, Preservation and Enhancement, Dune Protection, and Coastal Erosion
Tex. General and Special Laws 1991, Ch. 295

Coastal Management Plan for State-Owned Coastal Wetlands
Tex. Parks and Wildlife Code, § 14.001

Coastal Mapping Act
Fla. Stat. 1983, 177.25 et seq.

Coastal Marshlands Protection Act
Ga. Code Ann., 12-5-280 et seq.

Coastal Public Lands Management Act
Tex. Natural Resources Code, § 33.001 et seq.

Coastal Resources and Energy Assistance Act
Cal. Public Resources Code § 35000 et seq.

Coastal Resources Management Act
La. Rev. Stat. Ann., 49:213.1 et seq.

Coastal Sanctuary Act
Cal. Public Resources Code § 6250 et seq.

Coastal Scenic Highway Authority Act
Ga. Laws 1947, p. 1480

Coastal, State, and Urban Park Bond Act
Cal. Public Resources Code § 5096.111 et
seq.

Coastal Tidelands and Wetlands Act
S.C. Code Ann. 1976, § 48-39-270 et seq.

Coastal Turnpike Act
Va. Code 1950, § 58-341

Coastal Waters Protection Act
Wash. Rev. Code Ann., 90.48.370 et seq.

Coastal Waterways Act
Tex. Transportation Code, § 51.001 et seq.

Coastal Wetland Acquisition Act
Tex. Natural Resources Code, § 33.231 et
seq.

Coastal Wetlands Act
N.J. Stat. Ann., 13:9A-1 et seq.

Coastal Wetlands Alteration Act
Me. Rev. Stat. Ann. 1964, Title 38, § 480-A
et seq.

**Coastal Wetlands Conservation and
Restoration Act**
La. Rev. Stat. Ann., 49:214.1 et seq.

**Coastal Wetlands Planning, Protection and
Restoration Act**
Nov. 29, 1990, P.L. 101-646, 16 U.S. Code
§ 3951 et seq.
Dec. 11, 1991, P.L. 102-212, 16 U.S. Code
§ 3954
Oct. 12, 1996, P.L. 104-303, 16 U.S. Code
§ 3952

Coastal Wetlands Protection Act
Miss. Code Ann., § 49-27-1 et seq.

Coastal Zone Act
Del. Code of 1974, Title 7, § 7001 et seq.

**Coastal Zone Act Reauthorization
Amendments of 1990**
Nov. 5, 1990, P.L. 101-508, 16 U.S. Code
§ 1451 nt.

Nov. 4, 1992, P.L. 102-587, 16 U.S. Code
§§ 1452, 1453, 1455a, 1455b, 1456, 1456a

Coastal Zone Conservation Act
Cal. Public Resources Code § 27000 et seq.

Coastal Zone Management Act
Haw. Rev. Stat. Ann., § 205A-1 et seq.

**Coastal Zone Management Act
Amendments of 1976**
Dec. 28, 1977, P.L. 95-219, 15 U.S. Code
§ 1511a
April 7, 1986, P.L. 99-272, 16 U.S. Code
§ 1451 nt.

Coastal Zone Management Act of 1972
Oct. 27, 1972, P.L. 92-583, 86 Stat. 1280, 16
U.S. Code §§ 1451 to 1464
Sept. 18, 1978, P.L. 95-372, 16 U.S. Code
§§ 1456, 1456a, 1464
April 7, 1986, P.L. 99-272, 16 U.S. Code
§ 1455
Nov. 7, 1986, P.L. 99-626, 16 U.S. Code
§§ 1456a nt., 1464
Nov. 5, 1990, P.L. 101-508, 16 U.S. Code
§§ 1451 to 1455, 1455a, 1456, 1456a to
1456c, 1458, 1460, 1461, 1464
Nov. 4, 1992, P.L. 102-587, 16 U.S. Code
§§ 1454, 1455, 1455b, 1456a, 1456b, 1458,
1461
June 3, 1996, P.L. 104-150, 16 U.S. Code
§§ 1454, 1455a, 1456a, 1456b, 1461, 1464,
1465

**Coastal Zone Management Improvement
Act of 1980**
Oct. 17, 1980, P.L. 96-464, 16 U.S. Code
§ 1451 nt.
Nov. 8, 1984, P.L. 98-620, 16 U.S. Code
§ 1463a

**Coastal Zone Management Reauthorization
Act of 1985**
April 7, 1986, P.L. 99-272, 16 U.S. Code
§ 1451 nt.

Coastal Zone Protection Act
Fla. Stat. Ann., 161.52 et seq.

Coastal Zone Protection Act of 1996
June 3, 1996, P.L. 104-150, 16 U.S. Code
§ 1451 nt.

Coasting Act
N.H. Rev. Stat. 1955, Superseded Volume,
570:13

Coastwise Load Line Act, 1935
Aug. 27, 1935, Ch. 747, 49 Stat. 888, 46 U.S.
Code §§ 88 to 88i
Oct. 30, 1984, P.L. 98-577, 46 U.S. Code
Appx. §§ 88, 88a

**Coats Human Services Reauthorization Act
of 1998**
See Communities Opportunities, Accountability, And Training And Educational
Services Act Of 1998

Cobb Act (Cherokee Law and Equity Court)
Ala. Local Acts 1943, p. 81, No. 163

**Cobb County Community Improvement
Districts Act**
Ga. Laws 1985, p. 4009

Cobb County-Marietta Water Authority Act
Ga. Laws 1951, p. 497

Cobb County Parking Authority Act
Ga. Laws 1957, p. 2744

Cobb County Planning Commission Act
Ga. Laws 1943, p. 902

Cobb County Recreation Authority Act
Ga. Laws 1958, p. 2004

Cobb County Stadium Authority Act
Ga. Laws 1984, p. 4727

Cobb County Zoning and Planning Act
Ga. Laws 1956, p. 2006

**Cobb-Marietta County Anti-Drug
Commission Act**
Ga. Laws 1991, p. 4233

Cobern Act (Alcoholic Beverages)
Ky. Rev. Stat. 1971, 242.230, 242.990

Cobey-Alquist Flood Plain Management Act
Cal. Water Code § 8400 et seq.

**Cobey-Porter Federal Water Project
Recreation Act**
Cal. Public Resources Code § 5094 et seq.

Cobey-Porter Saline Water Conversion Law
Cal. Water Code § 12945et seq.

Cobey-Song Evidence Act
Cal. Statutes 1965, Ch. 299, p. 1297

Cobey Work Furlough Law
Cal. Penal Code § 1208

COBRA
See Consolidated Omnibus Budget Reconciliation Act of 1985

Cocaine Baby Reporting Act
Minn. Stat. Ann., 626.5562

Cochran-Hull Act
July 8, 1932, Ch. 467, 47 Stat. 649 (See 18
U.S. Code §§ 876, 877, 3239)

Cochran-Patterson Acts
June 22, 1932, Ch. 271, 47 Stat. 326 (See 18
U.S. Code §§ 10, 1201)
May 18, 1934, Ch. 301, 48 Stat. 781 (See 18
U.S. Code §§ 10, 1201)

Cocoa-Titusville Airport District Act
Fla. Special Laws 1963, Ch. 63-1143

Cocoa Urban Renewal Law
Fla. Special Laws 1961, Ch. 2020

C.O.D. Statute
Ky. Rev. Stat. 1971, 242.270

Code Commission Law
Cal. Government Code § 10300 et seq.

Code Construction Act
Tex. Government Code, § 311.001 et seq.

**Code Enforcement Board Act (Local
Government)**
Ky. Rev. Stat. 1971, 65.8801 to 65.8839

Code for Mobile Homes and Recreational Vehicles
Neb. Rev. Stat. 1973, 71-4601 et seq.

Code for the Anchoring of Mobile Homes
Ala. Code 1975, § 24-5-30 et seq.

Code for the Enforcement of County Codes and Resolutions
Kan. Stat. Ann., 19-4701 et seq.

Code of Civil Procedure
Alaska Stat. 1962, § 09.05.010 et seq.
Ill. Comp. Stat. 1992, Ch. 735, § 5/1-101 et seq.
Kan. Stat. Ann., 60-101 et seq.
Mo. Rev. Stat., 506.010 et seq.
Mont. Code Ann., 3-1-101 et seq.
Okla. Stat. Ann., Title 12, § 1 et seq.
P.R. Laws Ann. 1954, Title 32, § 1 et seq.

Code of Civil Procedure for Limited Actions
Kan. Stat. Ann., 61-1601 et seq.

Code of Conduct for State Employees, Officers and Officials
Del. Code of 1974, Title 29, § 5801 et seq.

Code of Construction and Installation Standards for Mobile Homes
N.Y. Executive Law 1951 (Consol. Laws Ch. 18) § 400aa et seq.

Code of Criminal Justice
N.J. Stat. Ann., 2C:1-1 et seq.

Code of Criminal Procedure
Alaska Stat. 1962, § 12.05.010 et seq.
Colo. Rev. Stat., 16-1-101 et seq.
Ill. Comp. Stat. 1992, Ch. 725, § 5/100-1 et seq.
Iowa Code Ann., 801.1 et seq.
Kan. Stat. Ann., 22-2101 et seq.
La. Rev. Stat. Ann., 15:21 et seq.
Mich. Comp. Laws Ann., 760.1 et seq.
Mont. Code Ann., 46-1-101 et seq.
Okla. Stat. Ann., Title 22, § 1
Pa. 1860 Pamph. Laws 382, No. 374

P.R. Laws Ann. 1954, Title 34, Appendix 2 Rule 1 et seq.
S.D. Codified Laws 1967, 23A-1-1 et seq.
Tex. Code of Criminal Procedure, Art. 1.01 et seq.
Utah Code Ann. 1953, 77-1-1 et seq.

Code of Escheats
Mich. Comp. Laws Ann., 567.11 et seq.

Code of Ethics
La. Rev. Stat. Ann., 42:1101 et seq.
Mass. Acts 1961, Ch. 610

Code of Ethics (Executive Branch)
Ky. Rev. Stat. 1971, 11A.001 et seq.

Code of Ethics (Legislative)
Pa. Purdon's Stat., Title 46, § 143.1 et seq.

Code of Ethics (Public Officers)
N.Y. Public Officers Law (Consol. Laws Ch. 47) § 74

Code of Ethics (Public Official)
Ala. Code 1975, 32-25-1 et seq.

Code of Ethics for Public Officers and Employees
Fla. Stat., 112.311 et seq.

Code of Ethics for State Officials and Employees
Okla. Stat. Ann., Title 74, § 1401 et seq.

Code of Fair Campaign Practices
Mont. Code Ann., 13-35-301 et seq.

Code of Fair Practices
Mont. Code Ann., 49-3-101 et seq.

Code of Financial Institutions
Haw. Rev. Stat. Ann., § 412:1-100 et seq.

Code of Juvenile Justice
N.J. Stat. Ann., 2A:4A-20 et seq.

Code of Juvenile Procedure
La. Acts 1978, No. 172

Code of Legislative Ethics
 Ky. Rev. Stat. 1971, 6.601 to 6.849

Code of Military Justice
 Colo. Rev. Stat., 28-3.1-101 et seq.
 Conn. Gen. Stat. Ann., § 27-141 et seq.
 Ga. Code Ann., 38-2-320 et seq.
 Haw. Rev. Stat. Ann., § 124A-1 et seq.
 Ida. Code 1947, 46-1101 et seq.
 Iowa Code Ann., 29B.1 et seq.
 Kan. Stat. Ann., 48-2101 et seq.
 Ky. Rev. Stat. 1971, 35.010 et seq.
 La. Rev. Stat. Ann., 29:101 et seq.
 Me. Rev. Stat. Ann. 1964, Title 37-B § 401 et
  seq.
 Mich. Comp. Laws Ann., 32.301 et seq.
 Mich. Comp. Laws 1970, 32.1001 et seq.
 Miss. Code Ann., §§ 33-13-1, 33-13-303,
  33-9-1, 33-3-11 et seq.
 Neb. Rev. Stat. 1943, 55-401 et seq.
 Nev. Rev. Stat. 1979 Reprint, 412.196 et seq.
 N.H. Rev. Stat. 1955, 110-B:39 et seq.
 N.M. Stat. Ann., 20-11-1 et seq.
 N.Y. Military Law (Consol. Laws Ch. 36)
  § 130.1 et seq.
 Ohio Rev. Code 1953, 5924.01 et seq.
 Okla. Stat. Ann., Title 44, § 2101 et seq.
 Pa. Cons. Stat., Title 51, § 5100 et seq.
 R.I. Gen. Laws 1956, 30-13-1 et seq.
 S.C. Code Ann. 1976, § 25-1-2410 et seq.
 Tex. Government Code, § 432.001 et seq.
 Utah Code Ann. 1953, 39-6-1 et seq.
 Wash. Rev. Code Ann., 38.38.004 et seq.
 Wis. Laws 1969, Ch. 20, § 10
 W. Va. Code 1966 § 15-1E-1 et seq.

Code of Municipal Government
 Minn. Stat. Ann., 412.015 et seq.

Code of Penal Procedure
 Pa. 1860 Pamph. Laws 427, No. 375

Code of Procedure for Municipal Courts
 Kan. Stat. Ann., 12-4101 et seq.

Code of Public Instruction Act
 Wash. Rev. Code Ann., 28A.01.010 et seq.

Code of Public Transportation
 Ga. Code Ann., 32-1-1 et seq.

Code Revision Act
 Ore. Rev. Stat., 174.510 et seq.

Code Revision Fund
 Ark. Code Ann. 1987, 1-2-303, 1-2-304

**Codes and Records Act (Municipal
 Adoption)**
 Ill. Rev. Stat. 1991, Ch. 85, § 1000 et seq.

Codes Enforcement Act
 Fla. Special Laws 1977, Ch. 617

Codification Act (District of Columbia)
 D.C. Code 1973, § 1-1601 et seq.

Codification Act (School Laws)
 Ky. Rev. Stat. 1971, 158.010 et seq.

Codification Amendment Act
 D.C. Code Ann., § 1-1602

Coercive Picketing Act
 Neb. Rev. Stat. 1943, 28-1317 et seq.

Coffee Adulteration Act
 P.R. Laws Ann. 1954, Title 24, § 821 et seq.

Coffee Industry Development Act
 P.R. Laws Ann. 1954, Title 5, § 321 et seq.

Coffee Insurance Act
 P.R. Laws Ann. 1954, Title 5, § 290 et seq.

Cogeneration Act
 Ala. Code 1975, § 37-12-1 et seq.
 Ga. Code Ann., 46-3-50 et seq.

Coggins Tests Act
 S.C. Code Ann. 1976, § 47-13-1310 et seq.,
  § 47-13-1370 et seq.

Cognovit Note Act
 Ind. Code Ann., 34-2-26-1

Cohabitation Act
 Fla. Stat. Ann., 798.01, 798.02

Cohasset Sewerage Loan Act
Mass. Acts 1962, Ch. 65

Cohoes Parking Authority Act
N.Y. Public Authorities Law (Consol. Laws
Ch. 43A) § 1599a et seq.

Coin Machines Tax Act
Tex. Taxation-General 1595, Art. 13.01 et
seq.

**Coin-Operated Amusement Device and
Redemption Machine Tax Act**
Ill. Comp. Stat. 1992, Ch. 35, § 510/1 et seq.

**Coin Operated Amusement Device Control
Act**
Ida. Laws 1945, Ch. 112
Ida. Laws 1947, Ch. 151

Coin-Operated Amusement Device Tax Act
Ill. Rev. Stat. 1991, Ch. 120, § 481b.1 et seq.

Coin Processor Licensing Act
N.Y. General Business Law (Consol. Laws
Ch. 20) § 418 et seq.

Coin Purchase Act
March 17, 1862, Ch. 45, 12 Stat. 370

Coin Slug Act
Ill. Comp. Stat. 1992, Ch. 720, §§ 235/1,
235/1a
Ill. Rev. Stat. 1991, Ch. 134, §§ 16.3, 16.3a

Coinage Act (Silver Dollar)
Feb. 28, 1878, Ch. 20, 20 Stat. 25, 31 U.S.
Code §§ 316, 405, 458

Coinage Act of 1873
Feb. 12, 1873, Ch. 131, 17 Stat. 424

Coinage Act of 1890 (Silver Dollar)
Nov. 1, 1893, Ch. 8, 28 Stat. 4, 31 U.S. Code
§ 311

Coinage Act of 1965
July 23, 1965, P.L. 89-81, 79 Stat. 254, 18
U.S. Code §§ 337, 485; 31 U.S. Code
§§ 283, 294, 301 to 304, 317c, 324, and
others

Dec. 31, 1970, P.L. 91-607, 84 Stat. 1768, 31
U.S. Code § 391

Colasacco Law (Parole or Warrant Office)
N.Y. Executive Law (Consol. Laws Ch. 18)
§ 259f, Subd. 4

Cold Check Act
Ky. Rev. Stat. 1971, 514.040
Miss. Code Ann., §§ 11-7-12, 97-19-55 et
seq.
Ohio Rev. Code 1953, 2913.11
Tenn. Code Ann., 39-14-121 et seq., 1115.23

Cold Spring Sewer Rent Law
N.Y. Local Laws 1972, Village of Cold
Spring, p. 3138

Cold Spring Sewer Use Law
N.Y. Local Laws 1972, Village of Cold
Spring, p. 3122

Cold Spring Zoning Law
N.Y. Local Laws 1967, Village of Cold
Spring, p. 2128

Cold Storage Act
Cal. Health and Safety Code § 28110 et seq.
Ill. Rev. Stat. 1991, Ch. 56 1/2, § 80 et seq.
Md. Ann. Code 1974, Art. HG, § 21-501 et
seq.
Neb. Laws 1913, Ch. 90
N.H. Rev. Stat. 1955, 145:1 et seq.
N.J. Stat. Ann., 24:9-17 et seq.
Ohio Rev. Code 1953, 915.01 et seq.
Ore. Rev. Stat., 628.210 et seq.
Pa. Purdon's Stat., Title 31, § 963 et seq.
Tenn. Code Ann., 53-9-101 et seq.
Wis. Stat. 1989, 99.01 et seq.

Cold Storage Act (Intoxicating Liquors)
Tex. Penal Code 1911, Arts. 151 to 154
Tex. Rev. Civ. Stat., 1911, Arts. 7480-7482

Cold Storage Egg Act
Fla. Stat. Ann., 583.01 et seq.

Cold Storage Locker Plants Act
Ind. Code Ann., 16-1-22-1 et seq.
Iowa Code Ann., 172.1 et seq.

Cold Storage Plants Law
Iowa Code Ann., 171.1 et seq.

Cold Storage Warehouse Act
Ind. Code Ann., 16-1-21-1 et seq.

Cole-Bradford Act (Blind Persons)
Ala. General Acts 1943, p. 8, No. 6

Coleman Act (Housing)
Ala. Code 1975, § 24-1-20 et seq.

Coleman-Brooks Act (Street Railway)
Minn. Stat. 1961, 220.01 et seq.

Coleman Emergency Act (Taxes)
Tenn. Public Acts 1933, Ch. 7

Coliseum Authority Act (Augusta-Richmond County)
Ga. Laws 1973, p. 3042

Coliseum Authority Act (De Kalb County)
Ga. Laws 1969, p. 2567

Coliseum Authority and Urban Area Trade Mart Act
Ala. Acts 1975, No. 932

Collapsed Structures Law (Town of Putnam Valley)
N.Y. Local Laws 1967, Town of Putnam Valley, p. 186

Collateral Act (Public Funds)
Tex. Government Code, § 2257.001 et seq.
Tex. Rev. Civ. Stat., Art. 2529d

Collateral Inheritance Tax Act
Mo. Rev. Stat., 145.009 et seq.
N.Y. Laws 1885, Ch. 483
N.Y. Laws 1887, Ch. 713
Pa. Purdon's Stat., Title 72, § 2301 et seq.
Tenn. Code Ann., 67-8-301 et seq.

Collateral Loan Act
Wis. Stat. 1971, 138.07

Collateral Pool for Public Deposits Act
Tenn. Code Ann., 9-4-501 et seq.

Collateral Protection Act
Ill. Comp. Stat. 1992, Ch. 815, § 180/1 et seq.

Collateral Security Act
March 9, 1933, Ch. 1, 48 Stat. 6, 12 U.S. Code §§ 347b, 347c, 347d, 445

Collateralization of Public Deposits Act
R.I. Gen. Laws 1956, 35-10.1-1 et seq.

Collecting Agencies Act
P.R. Laws Ann. 1954, Title 981 et seq.

Collection Act (Art)
Neb. Rev. Stat. 1943, 82-401

Collection Act (Garbage)
N.M. Stat. Ann., 4-56-1 et seq.

Collection Act (Land Tax)
Mo. Rev. Stat., 141.210 et seq.

Collection Agency Act
Cal. Business and Professions Code § 6850 et seq.
Conn. Gen. Stat. Ann., § 42-127 et seq.
Ida. Code 1947, 26-2223A et seq.
Ill. Comp. Stat. 1992, Ch. 225, § 425/1 et seq.
Mass. Gen. Laws Ann., 93:24 et seq.
Mich. Comp. Laws Ann., 445.201 et seq.
N.D. Cent. Code, 13-05-01 et seq.
Neb. Rev. Stat. 1943, 45-601 et seq.
N.J. Rev. Stat. 1937, 45:18-1 et seq.
N.M. Stat. Ann., 61-18-1 et seq.
Ore. Rev. Stat. 1989, 697.005 et seq.
Pa. Cons. Stat., Title 18, § 7311
P.R. Laws Ann. 1954, Title 10, § 981 et seq.
Tenn. Code Ann., 62-20-101 et seq.
Wash. Rev. Code Ann., 19.16.100 et seq.
Wis. Stat. 1989, 218.04
W. Va. Code 1966, § 47-16-1 et seq.

Collection Agency Licensing Act
Md. Ann. Code 1974, Art. BR, § 7-501 et seq.

Collection Agency Regulation Act
La. Rev. Stat. Ann., 9:3576.1 et seq.

Collection and Disposal of Waste Act
Ind. Code Ann., 36-9-31-1 et seq.

Collection and Payment Law (Wage)
Md. Ann. Code 1974, Art. LE, § 3-501 et seq.

Collection and Wage Payment Act
Kan. Stat. Ann., 44-313 et seq.

Collection Code (Banks)
N.Y. Negotiable Instruments Laws (Consol.
Laws Ch. 38) § 350 et seq.
Tex. Bus. and Comm. Code, § 4.101 et seq.

**Collection, Management and Recycling of
Used Oil Act**
Tex. Health and Safety Code, § 371.001 et
seq.

Collection of Duties Act (Civil War)
July 13, 1861, Ch. 3, 12 Stat. 255

**Collection of Personal Property Tax Act
(Limitation)**
Ill. Rev. Stat. 1991, Ch. 120, §§ 2201, 2202

Collection of Rent by Distraint Act
S.C. Code Ann. 1976, § 27-39-210 et seq.

**Collection of Wages Act (Reciprocal
Agreement)**
Mont. Code Ann., 39-3-301 et seq.

Collection Practices Act
Mich. Comp. Laws Ann., 445.211 et seq.
N.Y. General Business Law (Consol. Laws
Ch. 20) § 600 et seq.

Collection Practices Act (Commercial)
Fla. Stat. Ann., 559.541 et seq.

Collection Practices Act (Consumer)
Fla. Stat. Ann., 559.551 et seq.

Collection Practices Act (Fair Debt)
Me. Rev. Stat. Ann. 1964, Title 32, § 11001
et seq.

Collection Procedures Law (Fee)
Cal. Revenue and Taxation Code § 55001 et
seq.

Collection Reform Act (Child Support)
N.J. Stat. Ann., 2A:17-56.27 et seq.

Collection Suit Act (Tax)
Ill. Comp. Stat. 1992, Ch. 35, §§ 705/1 to
705/3

Collections Act (Magistrates)
Pa. Purdon's Stat., Title 42, § 1107

**Collective Bargaining Act (Municipal
Employees)**
Conn. Gen. Stat. Ann., § 7-467 et seq.

Collective Bargaining Act (New York City)
N.Y. City Adm. Code '85, § 12-310 et seq.

**Collective Bargaining Act (Palm Beach
County Firefighters)**
Fla. Special Laws 1970, Ch. 1004

**Collective Bargaining Act (Public
Employees)**
Haw. Rev. Stat. Ann., § 89-1 et seq.
Mont. Code Ann., 39-31-101 et seq.
Neb. Rev. Stat. 1943, 81-1369 et seq.
N.Y. General Obligations Law (Consol.
Laws Ch. 24A) §§ 1-203 Subd., 9, 5-301
Ore. Rev. Stat., 243.650 et seq.
Vt. Stat. Ann., Title 21, § 1721 et seq.
Wash. Rev. Code Ann., 41.56.010 et seq.

**Collective Bargaining Successor Employer
Act**
Ill. Comp. Stat. 1992, Ch. 820, § 10/0.01 et
seq.

Collective Negotiations Act
Kan. Stat. Ann., 72-5413 et seq.

Collective Trademarks Act
Conn. Gen. Stat. Ann., § 35-18a et seq.

Collector Road Construction Act
Utah Code Ann. 1953, Miscellaneous
Superseded Code Provisions 27-13-1

College Act (Community and Technical)
Wash. Rev. Code Ann., 28B.50.010 et seq.

College and Trade School Authority Act
Ala. Acts 1963, p. 259

College and Tuition Account Program Savings Bond Act
Pa. 1992 Pamph. Laws, No. 11

College and University Employees Insurance Benefits Act
See Uniform College and University Employees Insurance Benefits Act

College and University Equipment Financing Act
Miss. Code Ann., § 37-101-419 et seq.

College and University Security Information Act
Del. Code of 1974, Title 14, § 9001 et seq.
Pa. Purdon's Stat., Title 24, § 2502-1 et seq.
Tenn. Code Ann., 49-7-2201 et seq.

College Auxiliary Organization Act (Public)
N.J. Stat. Ann., 18A:64-26 et seq.

College Building Authority Act
Va. Code 1950, § 23-30.23 et seq.

College Center Act
Pa. Purdon's Stat., Title 24, § 2501.1 et seq.

College Choice Tuition Savings Program Act (New York State)
N.Y. Education Law 1947 (Consol. Laws Ch. 16) § 695 et seq.

College Contract Act
Cal. Education Code 1976, § 90100 et seq.
N.J. Stat. Ann., 18A:64-52 et seq.

College District Tax Act
N.M. Stat. Ann., 21-2A-1 to 21-2A-10

College Districting Act
N.M. Stat. Ann. 1953, 73-39-1 et seq.

College Housing Amendment of 1955
Aug. 11, 1956, Ch. 783, 70 Stat. 646, 12 U.S. Code § 1749

College Maintenance Act (Two Years)
N.M. Stat. Ann., 21-27-4, 21-27-5

College of Law Act (Regents)
Ill. Rev. Stat. 1991, Ch. 144, §§ 330, 331

College of Medical Technologists Act
P.R. Laws Ann. 1954, Title 20, § 2151 et seq.

College of Physicians and Surgeons Act
P.R. Laws Ann. 1954, Title 20, § 72 et seq.

College of Technology Act
Kan. Stat. Ann., 76-205 et seq.
Pa. Purdon's Stat., Title 24, § 2510.501 et seq.

College Opportunity Act
Ga. Code Ann., 20-3-600 et seq.
Tex. Rev. Civ. Stat., Art. 717a

College Registration Act
Miss. Code Ann., § 75-60-1 et seq.

College Reorganization Act
N.J. Stat. Ann., 18A:64A-50 et seq.

College Revenue Bond Act
Cal. Education Code 1976, § 90010 et seq.

College Savings Bond Act
Ark. Code 1987, 6-62-701 et seq.
Wash. Laws 1988, Ch. 125
Wash. Rev. Code Ann., 28B.106.005 et seq.

College Savings Bond and Building Bond Act
Okla. Stat. Ann., Title 62, § 57.300 et seq.

College Savings Bond and Tuition Account Program Act
Pa. Purdon's Stat., Title 24, § 6901.101 et seq.
Pa. 1992 Pamph. Laws, No. 11

College Student Aid Commission Act
Iowa Code Ann., 261.1 et seq.

College Student Immunization Act
Ill. Comp. Stat. 1992, Ch. 110, § 20/0.01 et seq.

College Student Loan Authority Act
Mass. Gen. Laws Ann., 15C:1 et seq.

College Tenure Act (State and County)
N.J. Stat. Ann., 18A:60-6 et seq.

College Trustees Act (Nonresident)
Ill. Rev. Stat. 1991, Ch. 144, § 6.9 et seq.

Colleges Scholarship Assistance Act
Va. Code 1950, § 23-38.45 et seq.

Collegiate Athletic Association Compliance Enforcement Procedures Act
Fla. Stat. Ann., 240.5339 et seq.
Ill. Comp. Stat. 1992, Ch. 110, § 25/1 et seq.

Collegiate Athletic Association Procedures Act
Neb. Rev. Stat. 1943, 85-1201 et seq.

Collegiate License Plates Act
Mont. Code Ann., 61-3-461 et seq.

Colleton County Library Commission Act
S.C. Code Ann. 1962, § 42-361 et seq.

Collier Act (School Districts)
Cal. Education Code 1959, §§ 41200, 84200

Collier-Burns Act (Highway Transportation Agency)
Cal. Government Code § 13975 et seq.

Collier-Burns Highway Act
Cal. Streets and Highways Code § 2000 et seq.

Collier County Water District Conservation Act
Fla. Special Laws 1961, Ch. 2037

Collier-Foran Act
Cal. Streets and Highways Code § 135.3 et seq.

Collier-Foran Act (Relocation Assistance)
Cal. Government Code § 15950 et seq.

Collier-Keene State Hostel Facilities Act
Cal. Public Resources Code § 5050 et seq.

Collier-Miller Act
Cal. Unemployment Insurance Code § 3501 et seq.

Collier Park Preservation Fund Act
Cal. Public Resources Code § 5010

Collier-Porter Act (Vehicles)
Cal. Vehicle Code 1959, § 35551

Collier-Unruh Local Transportation Development Act
Cal. Revenue and Taxation Code § 7351
Cal. Statutes 1963, Ch. 1852, p. 3805

Collier-Z'berg Act (Highway Beautification)
Cal. Business and Professions Code § 5208 et seq.

Collier-Z'berg Act (Outdoor Advertising)
Cal. Statutes 1964, 1st Ex. Sess., Ch. 128, p. 393

Collier-Z'berg Park Bond Act
Cal. Public Resources Code § 5096.71 et seq.

Collier-Z'berg State Seashore Act
Cal. Public Resources Code §§ 5001.5, 5001.6

Collins Amendment
Ark. Const. 1874, Amend. 29

Collinsville Civic Center Act
Ill. Comp. Stat. 1992, Ch. 70, § 250/1

Collision Damage Waiver Act
Iowa Code Ann., 516C.1 et seq.
Kan. Stat. Ann., 50-654 et seq.
La. Rev. Stat. Ann., 22:2091.1 et seq.
Va. Code 1950, § 59.1-207.15 et seq.

Cologne-Allen Act (Mistreatment of Children)
Cal. Penal Code §§ 11110, 11161.5

Cologne-Porter Water Quality Control Act
Cal. Water Code § 13000 et seq.

Colonie Town Park Law
N.Y. Local Laws 1967, Town of Colonie, p. 1456

Color Additive Amendments of 1960
July 12, 1960, P.L. 86-618, 74 Stat. 397, 21 U.S. Code §§ 321, 331, 333, 342, 343, 346, 351, 352, 361, 362, 371, 376

Color of Title Acts
Dec. 22, 1928, Ch. 47, 45 Stat. 1069, 43 U.S. Code §§ 1068, 1068a
July 28, 1953, Ch. 254, 67 Stat. 227, 43 U.S. Code §§ 1068, 1068a
Oct. 25, 1988, P.L. 100-529, 102 Stat. 2650
N.C. Gen. Stat. 1943, §§ 1-38, 98-8
N.D. Cent. Code 47-06-03
Tenn. Code Ann., 28-2-101
Wash. Rev. Code Ann., 7.28.070 et seq.

Colorado River Basin Compact
Utah Code Ann. 1953, 73-13-9 et seq.

Colorado River Basin Project Act
Sept. 30, 1968, P.L. 90-537, 82 Stat. 885, 43 U.S. Code §§ 616aa-1, 620, 620a, 620a-1, 620a-2, 620c-1, 620d-1, 620k nt., 1501, 1511 to 1514, 521 to 1528, 1541 to 1544, 1551 to 1556
June 24, 1974, P.L. 93-320, 88 Stat. 273, 43 U.S. Code § 1543
Aug. 17, 1984, P.L. 98-381, 43 U.S. Code § 1543

Colorado River Basin Salinity Control Act
June 24, 1974, P.L. 93-320, 88 Stat. 266, 43 U.S. Code §§ 620d, 1543, 1571 to 1578, 1591 to 1599
July 28, 1995, P.L. 104-20, 43 U.S. Code §§ 1592, 1595, 1598
April 4, 1996, P.L. 104-127, 43 U.S. Code §§ 1592, 1595

Colorado River Board Act
Cal. Water Code § 12500 et seq.

Colorado River Commission Act
Nev. Rev. Stat. 1979 Reprint, 538.041 et seq.

Colorado River Commission Validation Act
Nev. Statutes 1967, Ch. 259, pp. 761, 762

Colorado River Compact Act
Cal. Statutes 1923, p. 1530
Colo. Rev. Stat., 37-61-101 et seq.
N.M. Stat. Ann., 72-15-5
Wyo. Stat. Ann., §§ 41-12-301, 41-12-302

Colorado River Floodway Protection Act
Oct. 8, 1986, P.L. 99-450, 43 U.S. Code §§ 1600 nt., 1600a et seq. .
Nov. 2, 1994, P.L. 103-437, 43 U.S. Code § 1600a
Nov. 10, 1998, P.L. 105-362, 43 U.S. Code § 1600c

Colorado River Jurisdiction Compact Act
Ariz. Rev. Stat. Ann., § 37-620.11

Colorado River Limitation Act
Cal. Statutes 1929, Ch. 16, p. 38

Colorado River Storage Project Act
April 11, 1956, Ch. 203, 70 Stat. 105, 43 U.S. Code §§ 620a to 620o
June 13, 1962, P.L. 87-483, 76 Stat. 102, 43 U.S. Code §§ 620, 620a, 620d, 620f
Sept. 2, 1964, P.L. 88-568, 78 Stat. 852, 43 U.S. Code §§ 620, 620a
Sept. 30, 1968, P.L. 90-537, 82 Stat. 896, 43 U.S. Code §§ 620, 620a
June 24, 1974, P.L. 93-320, 88 Stat. 273, 43 U.S. Code § 620d
Oct. 30, 1984, P.L. 98-569, 43 U.S. Code §§ 620d, 1595

Colorado River Toll Bridge Compact
Cal. Streets and Highways Code § 31460 et seq.

Colorado River Upper Basin Compact
Colo. Rev. Stat., 37-62-101 et seq.

Colorado Self-Sufficiency and Employment Act
Colo. Rev. Stat., 26-2-901 et seq.

Colorado Ute Indian Water Rights Settlement Act of 1988
Nov. 3, 1988, P.L. 100-585, 102 Stat. 2973

Colorado Wilderness Act of 1993
Aug. 13, 1993, P.L. 103-77, 16 U.S. Code §§ 539i nt., 539j nt., 1132

Coloring Act (Grain)
Ill. Rev. Stat. 1991, Ch. 5, § 210 et seq.

Colquitt Act (Tax Delinquents)
Tex. Rev. Civ. Stat., Art. 7342
Tex. Rules of Civil Procedure 1984, Rule 117a

Columbarium-Mausoleum Act
Mont. Code Ann., 35-21-101 et seq.
Wash. Rev. Code Ann., 43.49.010 et seq.

Columbia Basin Commission Act
Wash. Rev. Code Ann., 43.49.010 et seq.

Columbia Basin Project Act
March 10, 1943, Ch. 14, 57 Stat. 14, 16 U.S. Code §§ 835 to 835c- 5
Sept. 26, 1950, Ch. 1048, 64 Stat. 1037, 16 U.S. Code §§ 835a, 835b, 835c
Sept. 27, 1950, Ch. 1060, 64 Stat. 1074, 16 U.S. Code § 835c-3
Sept. 2, 1957, P.L. 85-264, 71 Stat. 590, 16 U.S. Code §§ 835a, 835c
Oct. 1, 1962, P.L. 87-728, 76 Stat. 678, 16 U.S. Code §§ 835c, 835c-1, 835c-2, 835c-4

Columbia Civic Center Act
Ill. Comp. Stat. 1992, Ch. 70, § 255/2001 et seq.

Columbia County Airport Authority Act
Ga. Laws 1975, p. 4559

Columbia Interstate Compact
Ida. Code 1947, 42-3503
Mont. Rev. Code 1947, 89-3201 et seq.
Nev. Rev. Stat. 1979 Reprint, 538.530 et seq.
Utah Code Ann. 1953, 73-19-6 et seq.

Columbia-Richland County Study Commission Act
S.C. Acts 1971, p. 1682, No. 832

Columbia River Gorge Compact Act
Wash. Rev. Code 1989, 43.97.015 et seq.

Columbia River Gorge National Scenic Area Act
Nov. 17, 1986, P.L. 99-663, 16 U.S. Code § 544 nt.
Nov. 2, 1994, P.L. 103-437, 16 U.S. Code § 544b
Dec. 21, 1995, P.L. 104-66, 16 U.S. Code § 544g
Oct. 21, 1998, P.L. 105-277, 16 U.S. Code § 544b

Columbia River Sanctuary Act
Wash. Rev. Code Ann., 75.20.110 et seq.

Columbus County Airport Authority Act
N.C. Laws 1995, Ch. 134

Columbus County Peace Officers' Relief Act
N.C. Laws 1957, Ch. 422

Columbus Countywide Government Charter
Ga. Laws 1971, Ex. Sess., p. 2007

Columbus Holiday Act
Ill. Comp. Stat. 1992, Ch. 5, § 490/35

Columbus-Muscogee Board of Commissioners Act
Ga. Laws 1962, p. 2166

Colusa Basin Drainage District Act
Cal. Water Code, Appendix, § 127-1 et seq.

Colusa County Flood Control and Water Conservation District Act
Cal. Statutes 1983, Ch. 926

Colville Indian Reservation Criminal Jurisdiction Retrocession Act
Wash. Rev. Code 1989, 37.12.100 et seq.

Comanche, Kiowa, and Apache Tribes Act
June 6, 1900, Ch. 813, 31 Stat. 672

Combat Duty Pay Act of 1952
July 10, 1952, Ch. 630, 66 Stat. 538

Combating Proliferation of Weapons of Mass Destruction Act of 1996
Oct. 11, 1996, P.L. 104-293, Title VII, 50 U.S. Code § 2301 nt.
Oct. 21, 1998, P.L. 105-277, 50 U.S. Code § 2351 nt.

Combination and Service Sharing Incentives Law (Local Government)
Minn. Stat. Ann., 465.80 et seq.

Combinations and Conspiracies Act
See Anti-Trust Acts

Combinations Pools and Trust Law
Iowa Code 1975, 553.1 et seq.

Combined Charitable Campaign Act (State Employee)
Ala. Code 1975, 36-1A-1

Combined Improvement Act
Neb. Rev. Stat. 1943, 19-2408 et seq.

Combined Improvement Act (Cities of First and Second Class and Villages)
Neb. Rev. Stat. 1943, 19-2408 et seq.

Combined Old-Age Survivors, and Disability Insurance Income Tax Reporting Amendments of 1975
Jan. 2, 1976, P.L. 94-202, 89 Stat. 1137, 26 U.S. Code § 6103; 42 U.S. Code §§ 401, 403, 418, 424a, 430, 432

Combined Sewer Overflow Abatement and Storm Water Management Bond Act
N.J. Laws 1991, Ch. 181

Combines, Trusts and Pools Act
Ill. Rev. Stat. 1959, Ch. 121 1/2, § 301 et seq.

Combining Revisory Act of 1978 (Second)
Ill. Laws 1978, P.A. 80-4194

Combining Revisory Act of 1978, 1980
Ill. Laws 1977, p. 2978
Ill. Laws 1978, P.A. 80-1364
Ill. Laws 1979, P.A. 81-1050
Ill. Laws 1980, P.A. 81-1509, Art. 1

Combining Revisory Article of 1979
Ill. Laws 1979, P.A. 81-1050

Combustible and Flammable Liquids Act
Pa. 1998 Pamph. Laws, No. 15

Come-Back Act (Habitual Criminals)
Va. Code 1950, § 53-296

Comfort Station Act (Township)
Ill. Rev. Stat. 1991, Ch. 139, § 160d9 et seq.

Comic Book Act
Md. Laws 1955, Ch. 720
Ohio Rev. Code 1953, 2903.10
Pa. Cons. Stat., Title 18, § 5903
Wash. Rev. Code 1979, 19.18.010 et seq.

Comity Act (Statute of Limitations)
Mo. Rev. Stat., 516.190

Command of Army Clause
March 2, 1867, Ch. 170, 14 Stat. 486

Commemoration Authority Act
Colo. Laws 1956, p. 199, Ch. 106

Commemoration of First Reading of United States Constitution to 1787 General Assembly of Pennsylvania Act
Pa. 1991 Pamph. Laws, No. 19

Commemoration of Pennsylvania Ratification of United States Constitution Act
Pa. 1991 Pamph. Laws, No. 7

Commemorative Works Act
Nov. 14, 1986, P.L. 99-652, 40 U.S. Code § 1001 et seq., 1001 nt.

Commerce Act
Conn. Gen. Stat. Ann., § 32-1a
Pa. Purdon's Stat., Title 71, § 1709-1 et seq.
P.R. Laws Ann. 1954, Title 10, § 1001 et seq.

Commerce and Industry Department Act
N.M. Stat. Ann., 9-2-1 et seq.

Commerce and Labor Act
See Department of Commerce and Labor Act

Commerce Commission Act
Ill. Rev. Stat. 1991, Ch. 111 2/3, § 1-101 et seq.
Iowa Code Ann., 474.1 et seq.

Commerce Court Act
June 18, 1910, Ch. 309, 36 Stat. 539

Commerce Department Act
N.J. Stat. Ann., 52:27H-1 et seq.
Okla. Stat. Ann., Title 74 § 5003.1 et seq.

Commerce Under-Secretary Act
June 5, 1939, Ch. 180, 53 Stat. 808, 15 U.S. Code §§ 1502, 1503

Commercial Air Pilots Act
April 29, 1942, Ch. 266, 56 Stat. 265

Commercial and Industrial Authority Law
Pa. Purdon's Stat., Title 73, § 371 et seq.

Commercial and Industrial Development Bond Act
W. Va. Code 1966, § 13-2C-1 et seq.

Commercial and Industrial Revenue Bond Act
N.M. Stat. Ann., 3-31-1 et seq.

Commercial and Public Building Asbestos Abatement Act
Ill. Comp. Stat. 1992, Ch. 225, § 207/1 et seq.

Commercial Arbitration Act
N.C. Gen. Stat. 1943, § 1-567.1 et seq.
Wis. Stat. 1989, 788.01 et seq.

Commercial Arbitration Act (International)
Ill. Comp. Stat. 1992, Ch. 710, § 30/1-1 et seq.
Md. Ann. Code 1974, Art. CJ, § 3-2B-01 et seq.

Commercial Arbitration Act (UNCITRAL Model Law on International)
Conn. Gen. Stat. Ann., § 50a-100 et seq.

Commercial Arbitration and Conciliation Act (International)
Ore. Laws 1991, Ch. 405

Commercial Banking Law
N.C. Gen. Stat. 1943, § 53-1 et seq.

Commercial Bribery Act
Conn. Gen. Stat. Ann., §§ 53a-160, 53a-161
Iowa Code Ann., 722.1 et seq.
La. Rev. Stat. Ann., 14:73
Mass. Gen. Laws Ann., 271:39
Mich. Comp. Laws Ann., 750.125
Nev. Rev. Stat. 1979 Reprint, 207.295
N.J. Stat. Ann., 2C:21-10
N.Y. Penal Law 1965 (Consol. Laws Ch. 40) §§ 180.00, 180.05
R.I. Gen. Laws 1956, 11-7-1 et seq.
Wash. Rev. Code Ann., 49.44.060, 49.44.070
Wis. Stat. 1989, 134.05

Commercial Bungee Jumping Safety Act
W. Va. Code 1966, § 21-12-1 et seq.

Commercial Carrier Act
Colo. Rev. Stat., 40-12-101 et seq.

Commercial Casualty Underwriting Association Act
Md. Ann. Code 1957, Art. 48A, §§ 598 to 607

Commercial Chicks Act
Neb. Rev. Stat. 1943, 69-1001 et seq.

Commercial Code
See Uniform Commercial Code-Commercial Development Company Act

Commercial Collection Practices Act
Fla. Stat. Ann., 559.541 et seq.

Commercial Development Company Act
P.R. Laws Ann. 1954, Title 23, § 251 et seq.

Commercial Dispute Arbitration and Conciliation Act (International)
Cal. Code of Civil Procedure § 1297.11 et seq.

Commercial Driver License Act
N.J. Stat. Ann., 39:3-10.9 et seq.

Commercial Driver Training Schools Act
Utah Code Ann. 1953, 53-3-501 et seq.

Commercial Driver's License Act
See also Uniform Commercial Driver's License Act
Ark. Code Ann. 1987, 27-23-101 et seq.
Colo. Rev. Stat., 42-2-501 et seq.
Ga. Code Ann., 40-5-140 et seq.
Md. Ann. Code 1974, Art. TR, § 16-801 et seq.
Me. Rev. Stat. Ann. 1964, Title 29, § 631 et seq.
Miss. Code Ann., § 63-1-73 et seq.
Mo. Rev. Stat., 302.700 et seq.
N.C. Gen. Stat. 1943, §§ 20-37.10 to 20-37.23
N.J. Stat. Ann., 39:3-10.9 to 39:3-10.30
N.M. Stat. Ann., 66-5-52 et seq.
Pa. Cons. Stat., Title 75, § 1601 et seq.
S.C. Code Ann. 1976, § 56-1-2010 et seq.
Tex. Transportation Code, § 522.001 et seq.
Utah Code Ann. 1953, 41-2-701 et seq.
Va. Code 1950, § 46.2-341.1 et seq.
Wash. Rev. Code Ann., 46.25.001 et seq.
Wyo. Stat. Ann., § 31-17-101 et seq.

Commercial Driving Instruction Licensure Act
Me. Rev. Stat. Ann. 1964, Title 32, § 9501 et seq.

Commercial Establishments Safety Inspection and Education Act
Ill. Rev. Stat. 1991, Ch. 48, § 59.01 et seq.

Commercial Feed Act
Ala. Code 1975, § 2-21-16 et seq.
Cal. Food and Agricultural Code 1967, § 14901 et seq.
Colo. Rev. Stat., 35-60-101 et seq.
Del. Code of 1974, Title 3, § 1701 et seq.
Fla. Stat. 1983, 580.011 et seq.
Ida. Code 1947, 25-2715 et seq.
Ill. Comp. Stat. 1992, Ch. 505, § 30/1 et seq.
Ind. Code Ann., 15-5-13-1 et seq.
Iowa Code Ann., 198.1 et seq.
Ky. Rev. Stat. 1971, 250.491 et seq.
La. Rev. Stat. Ann., 3:1891 et seq.
Mass. Gen. Laws Ann., 128:51 et seq.
Md. Ann. Code 1974, Art. AG, § 6-101 et seq.
Me. Rev. Stat. Ann. 1964, Title 7, § 711 et seq.
Mich. Comp. Laws Ann., 287.521 et seq.
Minn. Stat. Ann., 25.31 et seq.
Miss. Code Ann., § 75-45-151 et seq.
Mo. Rev. Stat., 266.152 et seq.
Mont. Code Ann., 80-9-101 et seq.
N.C. Gen. Stat. 1943, § 106-284.30 et seq.
N.D. Cent. Code 19-13.1-01 et seq.
N.H. Rev. Stat. 1955, 435:17 et seq.
N.J. Stat. Ann., 4:4-20.1 et seq.
N.M. Stat. Ann., 76-19-1 et seq.
Okla. Stat. Ann., Title 2, § 8-41.1 et seq.
Ore. Rev. Stat., 633.006 et seq.
Pa. Cons. Stat., Title 3, § 5101 et seq.
R.I. Gen. Laws 1956, 4-2-1 et seq.
S.C. Code Ann. 1976, § 46-27-10 et seq.
S.D. Codified Laws 1967, 39-14-39 et seq.
Tenn. Code Ann., 44-6-101 et seq.
Vt. Stat. Ann., Title 6, §§ 291 et seq., 321 et seq.
Wash. Rev. Code Ann., 15.53.901 et seq.

Commercial Feed Control Act
Tex. Agriculture Code, § 141.002 et seq.

Commercial Feed for Domestic Animals Act
P.R. Laws Ann. 1954, Title 5, § 554 et seq.

Commercial Fertilizer Act
Cal. Food and Agricultural Code 1967, §§ 14501 et seq., 14516, 14522 et seq.
Colo. Rev. Stat., 35-12-101 et seq.
Fla. Stat. Ann., 576.011 et seq.
Ga. Code Ann., 2-12-1 et seq.
Ida. Code 1947, 22-601 et seq.
Ind. Code Ann., 15-3-3-1 et seq.
Md. Ann. Code 1974, Art. AG, § 6-201 et seq.
Me. Rev. Stat. Ann. 1964, Title 7, § 741 et seq.
Continued

Mich. Comp. Laws Ann., 286.751 et seq.

Miss. Code Ann., § 75-47-1 et seq.

Mont. Code Ann., 80-10-101 et seq.

N.C. Gen. Stat. 1943, § 106-655 et seq.

N.M. Stat. Ann., 76-11-1 et seq.

R.I. Gen. Laws 1956, 2-7-1 et seq.

S.D. Codified Laws 1967, 38-19-1 et seq.

Tenn. Code Ann., 43-11-101 et seq.

Tex. Agriculture Code, § 63.001 et seq.

Utah Code Ann. 1953, 4-13-1 et seq.

Wash. Rev. Code Ann., 15.54.270 et seq.

Wis. Stat. 1989, 94.72

W. Va. Code 1966, § 19-14-1 et seq.

Wyo. Stat. Ann., § 11-13-101 et seq.

Commercial Fertilizer and Soil Conditioner Act

Del. Code of 1974, Title 3, § 2101 et seq.

Neb. Rev. Stat. 1943, 81.2, 162.22 et seq.

N.J. Stat. Ann., 4:9-15.1 et seq.

Commercial Fertilizer, Soil Conditioner, Plant Amendment, and Agricultural Liming Material Act

Colo. Rev. Stat., 35-12-101 et seq.

Commercial Finance Lenders Law

Cal. Financial Code § 26000 et seq.

Commercial Fisheries Act

S.C. Code Ann. 1976, § 50-17-10 et seq.

Commercial Fisheries Act (Alaska)

Alaska Comp. Laws Ann. 1949, § 39-2-13 et seq.

Commercial Fisheries and Marine Fisheries Management Act

N.J. Stat. Ann., 23:2B-1 et seq.

Commercial Fisheries Investigation Law

Cal. Fish and Game Code 1957, § 8010 et seq.

Commercial Fisheries Research and Redevelopment Act

May 20, 1964, P.L. 88-309, 78 Stat. 197, 16 U.S. Code §§ 742c, 779 to 779f

Oct. 4, 1968, P.L. 90-551, 82 Stat. 957, 16 U.S. Code § 779b

Oct. 27, 1972, P.L. 92-590, 86 Stat. 1303, 16 U.S. Code § 779b

Oct. 12, 1976, P.L. 94-485, 16 U.S. Code § 779 et seq.

June 22, 1977, P.L. 95-53, 16 U.S. Code § 779b

June 5, 1980, P.L. 96-262, 16 U.S. Code § 779b

Dec. 29, 1982, P.L. 97-389, 16 U.S. Code § 779b

Nov. 14, 1986, P.L. 99-659, 16 U.S. Code §§ 779 nt., 779 to 779f

Commercial Fishermen and Dealers License Act

Tex. Parks and Wildlife Code, § 47.001 et seq.

Commercial Fishermen's Hull Insurance Protection and Indemnity Club Act

N.C. Gen. Stat. 1943, § 58-340.1 et seq.

Commercial Fishing Act

La. Rev. Stat. Ann., 56:311 et seq.

Mich. Comp. Laws Ann., 308.1 et seq.

Commercial Fishing and Fisheries Act

Ore. Rev. Stat., 506.001 et seq.

Commercial Fishing Industry Vessel Act

July 17, 1984, P.L. 98-364, 46 U.S. Code §§ 2101 nt., 3301, 3302, 3304, 3306, 3702, 4501 et seq., 7111, 7301, 7306, 7312, 8102, 8104, 8701, 8702 , 10101, 11108, 11109, 12101

May 15, 1985, P.L. 99-36, 46 U.S. Code § 3302 nt.

Commercial Fishing Industry Vessel Anti-Reflagging Act of 1987

Jan. 11, 1988, P.L. 100-239, 46 U.S. Code §§ 8103, 8103 nt., 8701 et seq., 12101 et seq.

Oct. 21, 1998, P.L. 105-277, 46 U.S. Code § 12102 nt.

Commercial Fishing Industry Vessel Safety Act of 1988

Sept. 9, 1988, P.L. 100-424, 46 U.S. Code §§ prec. 2101, 2101, 2101 nt., prec. 3101, 3102, 3701, 4101, 4101, prec. 4501, 4501, 4501 nt., 4502, 4502 nt., 4503 to 4508, 4508 nt., prec. 6101, 6103, 6104, 7101 nt., prec. 10601, 10601 to 10603; 46 Appx. 531 to 534

Commercial Fishing License Act

Alaska Stat. 1962, § 16.05.440 et seq.

Commercial Fishing Loan Act

Alaska Stat. 1962, § 16.10.300 et seq.

Commercial Forest Reserve Act

Mich. Comp. Laws Ann., 320.301 et seq.

Commercial Fur Act

La. Rev. Stat. Ann., 56:251 et seq.

Commercial Hazardous Waste Management Facility Siting Act

W. Va. Code 1966, § 22C-5-1 et seq.

Commercial Insurance Deregulation Act

N.J. Stat. Ann., 17:29AA-1 et seq.

Commercial Laws

See Uniform Commercial Code

Commercial Motor Vehicle Safety Act

Cal. Public Utilities Code § 3557

Commercial Motor Vehicle Safety Act of 1986

Oct. 27, 1986, P.L. 99-570, 49 U.S. Code Appx. § 2701 nt.

April 2, 1987, P.L. 100-17, 49 U.S. Code Appx. § 2716

Oct. 28, 1991, P.L. 102-143, 49 U.S. Code Appx. § 2717

Dec. 18, 1991, P.L. 102-240, 49 U.S. Code Appx. §§ 2708, 2716, 2717

Commercial Motor Vehicle Safety Standards Act

Tex. Transportation Code § 644.001 et seq.

Commercial Paper (Uniform Commercial Code)

See Uniform Commercial Code-Commercial Paper

Commercial Paper Act

Mass. Gen. Laws Ann., 106:3-101 et seq.

Pa. Cons. Stat., Title 13, § 3101 et seq.

Commercial Pesticide Applicator's Act

Colo. Rev. Stat., 35-10-101 et seq.

Commercial Print Copyright Act

July 31, 1939, Ch. 396, 53 Stat. 1142 (See 17 U.S. Code §§ 5, 6, 25)

Commercial Propagation of Quail and Pheasant Act

Okla. Stat. 1971, Title 29, § 751 et seq.

Commercial Property Investment Act

Cal. Civil Code § 1954.25 et seq.

Commercial Public Assembly Act

Vt. Stat. Ann., Title 20, § 4501 et seq.

Commercial Quail Act

Miss. Code Ann., § 49-13-1 et seq.

Commercial Real Estate Broker Lien Act

Ill. Comp. Stat. 1992, Ch. 770, § 15/1 et seq.

Pa. 1998 Pamph. Laws, No. 34

Commercial Real Property Rental Control Act

Cal. Civil Code § 1954.25 et seq.

Commercial Redevelopment Act

Mich. Comp. Laws Ann., 207.651 et seq.

Commercial Refuse Collection License Law

N.Y. Local Laws 1971, County of Yates, p. 970

Commercial Relocation of Trespassing Vehicles Law

Ill. Comp. Stat. 1992, Ch. 625, § 5/18a-100 et seq.

Commercial Renewal and Redevelopment Act
Ill. Rev. Stat. 1991, Ch. 24, § 11-74.2-1 et seq.

Commercial Rent Control Act
Haw. Session Laws 1945, Act 69

Commercial Rent or Occupancy Tax Law (New York City)
N.Y. Laws 1963, Ch. 257

Commercial Self-Insurance Fund Act
Fla. Stat. Ann., 624.460 et seq.

Commercial Space Act of 1998
Oct. 28, 1998, P.L. 105-303, 112 Stat. 2843, 42 U.S. Code § 14701 nt.

Commercial Space Launch Act
Oct. 30, 1984, P.L. 98-575, 49 U.S. Code Appx. §§ 2601 nt., 2601 et seq.
Dec. 5, 1985, P.L. 99-170, 49 U.S. Code Appx. § 2623
Nov. 15, 1988, P.L. 100-657, 49 U.S. Code Appx. §§ 2603, 2614, 2615
Nov. 17, 1988, P.L. 100-685, 49 U.S. Code Appx. § 2623
Nov. 16, 1990, P.L. 101-611, 49 U.S. Code Appx. §§ 2601, 2602, 2604, 2614, 2623
Dec. 9, 1991, P.L. 102-195, 49 U.S. Code Appx. § 2623
Nov. 4, 1992, P.L. 102-588, 49 U.S. Code Appx. §§ 2615, 2623

Commercial Space Launch Act Amendments of 1988
Nov. 15, 1988, P.L. 100-657, 49 U.S. Code Appx. § 2601 nt.

Commercial Space Rent Control Laws
N.Y. Laws 1945, Ch. 3
N.Y. Laws 1945, Ch. 315
N.Y. Laws 1949, Ch. 534
N.Y. Laws 1950, Ch. 327
N.Y. Laws 1951, Ch. 431
N.Y. Laws 1952, Ch. 416

Commercial Transportation Law
Ill. Comp. Stat. 1992, Ch. 625, § 5/18a-1101 et seq.

Commercial Travelers Act
N.J. Stat. Ann., 45:24-1 to 45:24-13

Commercial Travelers and Solicitors Licensing Law (Monroe County)
N.Y. Local Laws 1972, County of Monroe, p. 721

Commercial Trout License Act
Mich. Comp. Laws 1948, 308.101 et seq.

Commercial Vehicle Act
Wyo. Stat. Ann., § 37-8-101 et seq.

Commercial Vehicles Gross Weight Restrictions Law (Town of Hempstead)
N.Y. Local Laws 1966, Town of Hempstead, p. 1061

Commercial Waterway Districts Act
Wash. Rev. Code 1951, 91.04.010 et seq.

Commercial Weight-Loss Practices Act
Fla. Stat. Ann., 501.057 et seq.

Comminuted Meat Act
Mich. Comp. Laws Ann., 289.581 et seq.

Commission Act (Ballot Law)
Mass. Gen. Laws Ann., 55B:1 et seq.

Commission Act (Distance Learning)
N.H. Rev. Stat. 1955, 70:1 et seq.

Commission Act (Financing and Investment)
Ga. Code Ann., 50-17-20 et seq.

Commission Act (Historical)
Mass. Gen. Laws Ann., 9:26 et seq.

Commission Act (Investigation)
N.Y. Unconsolidated Law, § 7501 et seq.

Commission Act (Motor Vehicle Dealers)
Pa. 1937 Pamph. Laws 2465, No. 461

Commission Act (Motor Vehicle)
La. Rev. Stat. Ann., 32:1251

Commission Act (Port of Pittsburgh)
Pa. Purdon's Stat., Title 55, §§ 698.1 et seq., 698.21 et seq.

Commission Act (Real Estate)
Mo. Rev. Stat., 339.010 et seq.

Commission City Bond Law
Nev. Rev. Stat. 1979, Reprint, 267.250 et seq.

Commission City Law
Iowa Code Ann., 372.5

Commission Compact (Lake Champlain Bridge)
Vt. Stat. Ann., Title 19, § 1711

Commission for Arts Act
S.C. Code Ann. 1976, § 60-15-10 et seq.

Commission for Children and Families Act (Hall County)
Ga. Laws 1999, p. 1474

Commission for Higher Education (Mid-Carolina)
S.C. Code Ann. 1976, § 59-108-10 et seq.

Commission for Higher Education Act
S.C. Code Ann. 1976, § 59-103-5 et seq.

Commission for Higher Education Facilities Act (State)
Me. Rev. Stat. Ann. 1964, Title 20-A, § 10501 et seq.

Commission for the Blind Act
N.M. Stat. Ann., 28-7-15 et seq.

Commission for the National Bicentennial Celebration
Ga. Code Ann., 50-12-1 et seq.

Commission for Women Act
D.C. Code Ann., § 2-801 et seq.
Md. Ann. Code 1957, Art. 49C, § 1 et seq.

Commission Form of Government Act (Knox County)
Tenn. Private Act 1937, Ch. 183

Commission Form of Government Act (Municipal)
Ala. Code 1975, § 11-44-1 et seq.
Ida. Laws 1911, Ch. 82
Ill. Rev. Stat. 1991, Ch. 24, § 4-1-1 et seq.
Kan. Stat. Ann., 13-1501 et seq.
Mo. Rev. Stat. 1969, 75.010 et seq.
N.J. Stat. Ann., 40:70-1 et seq.
S.C. Code Ann. 1962, § 47-481 et seq.
Wash. Rev. Code Ann., 35.17.010 et seq.

Commission Form of Government Act-Cities of the Fifth and Sixth Class
Ky. Rev. Stat. 1971, Superseded Vols., 89.300 et seq.

Commission Form of Government Act-Cities of the Second to Fourth Class
Ky. Rev. Stat. 1971, Superseded Vols., 89.030 et seq.

Commission Governed Cities Act
S.D. Codified Laws 1967, 9-9-1 et seq.

Commission Law (Youth)
La. Rev. Stat. Ann., 46:271 et seq.

Commission Merchants Act
D.C. Code 1973, § 22-1208 et seq.
Mo. Rev. Stat. 1969, 412.010 et seq.
Ohio Rev. Code 1953, 4711.01 et seq.
Tex. Rev. Civ. Stat., Art. 1274 et seq.
Wash. Rev. Code Ann., 20.01.010 et seq.

Commission of Appellate Defense Act
S.C. Code Ann. 1976, § 17-4-10 et seq.

Commission of Investigation Act
N.Y. Laws 1958, Ch. 989
N.Y. Unconsolidated Laws § 7501 et seq.

Commission on Alcoholism Act
Ida. Code 1947, 67-3108 et seq.

Commission on Children and Youth Act
Tenn. Code Ann., 37-3-101 et seq.

Commission on Community Services Act
Ill. Comp. Stat. 1992, Ch. 15, § 105/0.01 et seq.

Commission on Delinquency Prevention Act
Ill. Rev. Stat. 1985, Ch. 23, § 2701 et seq.

Commission on Human Rights Act
Tex. Rev. Civ. Stat. Art. 5221K

Commission on Interstate Cooperation
Me. Rev. Stat. Ann., Title 3, § 201 et seq.

Commission on Mental Health and Developmental Disabilities Act
Ill. Rev. Stat. 1983, Ch. 91 1/2, § 100-101 et seq.

Commission on Mobile Home Act
Mich. Comp. Laws Ann., 125.2301 et seq.

Commission on National and Community Service Act
Utah Code Ann. 1953, 9-1-801 et seq.

Commission on Security and Cooperation in Europe
March 27, 1985, P.L. 99-7, 22 U.S. Code §§ 3003, 3007, 3008

Commission on State Growth Policy Act
Ga. Code Ann., 50-12-130 et seq.

Commission on the Advancement of Women and Minorities in Science Engineering, and Technology Development Act
Oct. 14, 1998, P.L. 105-255, 112 Stat. 1889, 42 U.S. Code § 1885a nt.

Commission on the Aging Act
Iowa Code 1985, 249B.1 et seq.
Tenn. Code Ann., 71-2-101 et seq.

Commission on the Arts and Humanities Act
D.C. Code Ann., § 31-2001 et seq.

Commission on the Status of Women Act
Ga. Code Ann., 50-12-80 et seq.
Md. Ann. Code 1957, Art. 49C, § 1 et seq.

Commission on Wartime Relocation and Internment of Civilians Act
July 31, 1980, P.L. 96-317, 50 U.S. Code Appx. § 1981 nt.
Dec. 21, 1982, P.L. 97-377, 50 U.S. Code Appx. § 1981 nt.

Commission on Workfare Act
La. Rev. Stat. Ann., 23:1851 et seq.

Commission to Preserve the Peace Act
Ala. Acts 1963, p. 380, No. 3

Commission Transfer Act (Coal Products)
Ill. Comp. Stat. 1992, Ch. 20, §§ 1910/0.01, 1910/1

Commissioned Law Enforcement and Custodial Officer Supplemental Retirement Benefit Act
Tex. Rev. Civ. Stat. 1974, Art. 6228f-1

Commissioners Act (Calhoun County)
Ala. Local Acts 1939, p. 252, No. 420

Commissioners Act (Columbus-Muscogee)
Ga. Laws 1962, p. 2166

Commissioners Act (Supreme Court)
Mo. Rev. Stat. 1969, 477.083 et seq.

Commissioners' Additional Powers Act
D.C. Code 1973, § 1-337 et seq.

Commissioners' Appointment Act
Ky. Rev. Stat. 1971, 7.110

Commissioner's Office Act (Financial Institutions)
P.R. Laws Ann. 1954, Title 7, § 2001 et seq.

Commissioners on Uniform State Laws Acts
Okla. Stat. Ann., Title 74, § 471 et seq.

Commissioners Powers Act
D.C. Code Ann., § 1-337 et seq.

Commissioner's Practice Act (Public Utilities)
Ore. Rev. Stat., 756.505 et seq.

Commissions and Councils Code (State)
Utah Code Ann. 1953, 63C-1-101 et seq.

Commissions for Local Planning Act
S.C. Code Ann. 1976, § 6-7-310 et seq.

Commitment Act
Minn. Stat. Ann., 253B.01 et seq.

Commitment Act (Mentally Ill)
Ala. Code 1975, § 22-52-1 et seq.
Ga. Code Ann., 37-3-40 et seq.
Mass. Gen. Laws Ann., 123:5 et seq.
Md. Ann. Code 1957, Art. 59, § 1 et seq.
N.M. Stat. Ann. 1953, 34-2-1 et seq.
Ohio Rev. Code 1953, 5125.01 et seq.
S.C. Code Ann. 1976, § 44-23-10
Va. Code 1950, § 37.1-63 et seq.

Commitment Procedure Act
S.C. Code Ann. 1976, § 44-23-10

Committee Act (Forest Fire Emergency)
Ga. Code 1933, 43-244 et seq.

Committee and Study Commission Act
N.C. Gen. Stat. 1943, § 120-180 et seq.

Committee and Study Commission Act on Aging
N.C. Gen. Stat. 1943, § 120-180 et seq.

Committee for Public Counsel Services Act
Mass. Gen. Laws Ann., 211D:1 et seq.

Committee for the Coordination of Police Services to Elderly Persons Law
La. Rev. Stat. Ann., 15:1231 to 15:1236

Committee on Purchases of Blind-Made Products and Service Act
Okla. Stat. 1971, Title 7, § 101 et seq.

Committee to Fight Crime Act
P.R. Laws Ann. 1954, Title 25, § 901 et seq.

Committees and Study Commissions Act
N.C. Laws 1991, Ch. 873

Commodities Act
Me. Rev. Stat. Ann. 1964, Title 32, § 11201 et seq.
N.D. Cent. Code, 51-23-01 et seq.
Pa. 1913 Pamph. Laws 965, No. 445

Commodities Authority Act (Agriculture)
Ga. Code Ann., 2-8-1 et seq.

Commodities Controls Act (Agricultural)
Minn. Stat. Ann., 17.90 et seq.

Commodities Development Act (Agricultural)
Del. Code of 1974, Title 3, § 701 et seq.

Commodities Enforcement Act
Miss. Code Ann., § 75-89-1 et seq.

Commodities Marketing Act (Agricultural)
Pa. Cons. Stat., Title 5, § 4501 et seq.

Commodities Marketing Law
La. Rev. Stat. Ann., 3:552.1 et seq.

Commodities Surplus Food Distribution Act
Mich. Comp. Laws Ann., 400.181 et seq.

Commodity Act
Cal. Corporations Code § 29500 et seq.

Commodity Clause of Railroad Rate Act
June 29, 1906, Ch. 3591, 34 Stat. 584, 49 U.S. Code § 1[8]

Commodity Code
Cal. Corporations Code § 29500 et seq.
Colo. Rev. Stat. 11-53-101
Ida. Code 1947, 30-1501 et seq.
Me. Rev. Stat. Ann. 1964, Title 32, § 11201 et seq.
Neb. Rev. Stat. 1943, 8-1701 et seq.
N.M. Stat. Ann., 58-13A-1 et seq.
S.C. Code Ann. 1976, § 33-73-10

Commodity Commission Act
Ore. Rev. Stat., 576.051 et seq.

Commodity Credit Corporation Act

Aug. 9, 1940, Ch. 649, 54 Stat. 782, 15 U.S. Code § 713a-4

April 12, 1945, Ch. 54, 59 Stat. 50, 15 U.S. Code §§ 713a-1, 713a-4

Commodity Credit Corporation Charter Act

June 29, 1948, Ch. 704, 62 Stat. 1070, 15 U.S. Code §§ 714 to 714o

June 7, 1949, Ch. 175, 63 Stat. 154, 15 U.S. Code §§ 714, 714b, 714g, 714h, 714m

June 28, 1950, Ch. 381, 64 Stat. 261, 15 U.S. Code § 714b

March 20, 1954, Ch. 102, 68 Stat. 30, 15 U.S. Code § 714b

Aug. 31, 1954, Ch. 1172, 68 Stat. 1047, 15 U.S. Code § 714b

May 23, 1955, Ch. 46, 69 Stat. 65, 15 U.S. Code § 714p

Aug. 1, 1956, Ch. 815, 70 Stat. 783, 15 U.S. Code §§ 713a-4, 714b, 714m

Nov. 5, 1966, P.L. 89-758, 80 Stat. 1307, 15 U.S. Code § 714b

June 6, 1972, P.L. 92-310, 86 Stat. 206, 15 U.S. Code § 714h

Sept. 29, 1977, P.L. 95-113, 15 U.S. Code §§ 714b, 714b nt.

May 15, 1978, P.L. 95-279, 15 U.S. Code § 714b

July 30, 1979, P.L. 96-41, 15 U.S. Code § 714b

April 11, 1980, P.L. 96-234, 15 U.S. Code § 714b

Nov. 8, 1984, P.L. 98-623, 15 U.S. Code § 741c

Dec. 23, 1985, P.L. 99-198, 15 U.S. Code § 714b

March 20, 1986, P.L. 99-260, 15 U.S. Code § 714b

Dec. 22, 1987, P.L. 100-202, 15 U.S. Code § 714b

April 4, 1996, P.L. 104-127, 15 U.S. Code §§ 714b, 714c, 714i, 714k

June 23, 1998, P.L. 105-185, 15 U.S. Code § 714b

Oct. 21, 1998, P.L. 105-277, 15 U.S. Code § 714b

Commodity Dealer Act

Ida. Code 1947, 69-501 et seq.

Commodity Dealer and Warehouse Law

Tenn. Code Ann., 43-32-101 et seq.

Commodity Dealer, Warehouse, and Grain Standards Act (Agricultural)

Mont. Code Ann., 80-4-401 et seq.

Commodity Disbursement Act

Ill. Rev. Stat. 1991, Ch. 127, § 176a9 et seq.

Commodity Distribution Reform Act and WIC Amendments of 1987

Jan. 8, 1988, P.L. 100-237, 7 U.S. Code §§ 612c nt., 1431e; 42 U.S. Code § 1769, 1786

Nov. 28, 1990, P.L. 101-624, 7 U.S. Code § 612c nts.

Aug. 14, 1992, P.L. 102-342, 42 U.S. Code § 612c nt.

Nov. 2, 1994, P.L. 103-448, 7 U.S. Code § 612c nt.

Oct. 31, 1998, P.L. 105-336, 7 U.S. Code § 612c nt.

Commodity Exchange Act

Sept. 21, 1922, Ch. 369, 42 Stat. 998, 7 U.S. Code §§ 1 to 17

June 15, 1936, Ch. 545, 49 Stat. 1491

April 7, 1938, Ch. 108, 52 Stat. 205, 7 U.S. Code § 2

Dec. 19, 1947 Ch. 523, 61 Stat. 941, 7 U.S. Code § 12-1

Aug. 28, 1954, Ch. 1041, 68 Stat. 913, 7 U.S. Code § 2

June 16, 1955, Ch. 151, 69 Stat. 160, 7 U.S. Code § 15

July 26, 1955, Ch. 382, 69 Stat. 375, 7 U.S. Code § 2

July 24, 1956, Ch. 690, 70 Stat. 630, 7 U.S. Code § 6a

Aug. 28, 1958, P.L. 85-791, 72 Stat. 944, 7 U.S. Code §§ 8, 9

June 11, 1960, P.L. 86-507, 74 Stat. 200, 7 U.S. Code § 9

Feb. 19, 1968, P.L. 90-258, 82 Stat. 26, 7 U.S. Code §§ 2, 6a, 6b , 6d, 6f, 6g, 6i, 7 to 9, 12 to 12b, 13, 13a to 13c, 17b

July 23, 1968, P.L. 90-418, 82 Stat. 413, 7 U.S. Code § 2

Oct. 15, 1970, P.L. 91-452, 84 Stat. 928, 7 U.S. Code § 15

Nov. 6, 1978, P.L. 95-598, 7 U.S. Code § 24

Jan. 11, 1983, P.L. 97-444, 7 U.S. Code §§ 2, 4, 6a, 6m to 6p, 12a, 13, 16, 21, 23, 25, 26

Nov. 10, 1986, P.L. 99-641, 7 U.S. Code §§ 2a, 6b, 6c, 7a, 13, 13a-1, 14 to 16, 21, 23

Oct. 28, 1992, P.L. 102-546, 7 U.S. Code § 1 et seq.

April 21, 1995, P.L. 104-9, 7 U.S. Code § 16

Commodity Futures Trading Commission Act of 1974

April 16, 1975, P.L. 94-16, 89 Stat. 77, 7 U.S. Code §§ 4a nt., 6j, 18

Commodity Handler Act

Colo. Rev. Stat., 12-16-201 et seq.

Commodity Indemnity Account Program

Ida. Code 1947, 69-255 et seq.

Commodity Indemnity and Public Warehouse Act

N.M. Stat. Ann., 58-13A-1 et seq.

Okla. Stat. Ann., Title 2, § 9-20 et seq.

Commodity Insurance Act (Agricultural)

Mich. Comp. Laws Ann., 285.211 et seq.

Commodity Marketing Law (Agriculture)

La. Rev. Stat. Ann., 3:711 et seq.

Commodity, Options, or Stock Transaction Tax Exemption Act

Ill. Rev. Stat. 1991, Ch. 121 1/2, § 1000 et seq.

Commodity Producer Indemnity Law

Tenn. Code Ann., 43-32-201 et seq.

Commodity Promotion, Research, and Information Act of 1996

April 4, 1996, P.L. 104-127, Title V, Subtitle B, 7 U.S. Code § 7401 nt.

Commodity Rate Act

Minn. Stat. 1953, 218.41 et seq.

Commodore Bill

April 9, 1943, Ch. 38, 57 Stat. 60 (See 10 U.S. Code §§ 5501, 5597, 5787) 14 U.S. Code 351 §§ 435 to 438; 42 U.S. Code § 212

Common Carrier Act

Colo. Rev. Stat., 40-9-101 et seq.

Ga. Code Ann., 46-1-1 et seq., 46-6-1 et seq., 46-7-1 et seq.

Ind. Code Ann., 8-2-7-1 et seq.

Kan. Stat. Ann., 66-237 et seq.

Mont. Rev. Code 1947, 8-701 et seq.

N.D. Cent. Code, 8-07-01 et seq.

Utah Code Ann. 1953, 54-6-1 et seq.

Common Carrier Act (Express Companies)

Ill. Laws 1911, p. 464

Common Carrier by Pipeline Law

Ill. Comp. Stat. 1992, Ch. 220, § 5/15-100 et seq.

Common Carrier Liability Act

Ill. Comp. Stat. 1992, Ch. 740, § 25/0.01 et seq.

Common Carriers Death Act

N.M. Stat. Ann., 41-2-4

Common Carrier's Financial Responsibility Act

Wis. Stat. 1989, 194.41 et seq.

Common Carrier's Lien Law

Iowa Code 1962, 575.1 et seq.

Common Carriers Rate Act

Wash. Rev. Code Ann., 81.28.010 et seq.

Common Carriers Rebate Act

Wash. Rev. Code Ann., 81.28.210 et seq.

Common Day of Rest Act

Ga. Code Ann., 10-1-570 et seq.

Mass. Gen. Laws Ann., 136:1 et seq.

Vt. Stat. Ann., Title 13, § 3351 et seq.

Common Disaster Act

Mass. Gen. Laws Ann., 190A:1 et seq.

Common Drunk Act
Ill. Rev. Stat. 1991, Ch. 30, § 312.1

Common Gamblers Act
Ohio Rev. Code 1953, 2915.14
Ore. Rev. Stat., 167.117 et seq.

Common Interest Development Act
Cal. Statutes 1985, Ch. 874, Title 6

**Common Interest Development Act
(Davis-Stirling)**
Cal. Civil Code § 1350 et seq.

**Common Interest Development Open
Meetings Act**
Cal. Civil Code § 1363.05

Common Interest Ownership Act
See also Uniform Common Interest
Ownership Act
Colo. Rev. Stat., 38-33.3-101 et seq.
Conn. Gen. Stat. Ann., § 47-200
Conn. Public Acts 1991, No. 474
W. Va. Code 1966, § 36B-1-101 et seq.

Common Law Act
Ill. Comp. Stat. 1992, Ch. 5, §§ 50/0.01, 50/1

Common Law Adoption Act
Ill. Rev. Stat. 1991, Ch. 1, §§ 800, 801
Mo. Rev. Stat., 1.010

Common Law Ejectment Act
Fla. Stat. Ann., 66.011

Common Law Marriage Act
Miss. Code Ann., §§ 93-1-5, 93-1-13

Common Law Reception Act
Ala. Code 1975, § 1-3-1

Common Pleas Court Act
Del. Code of 1974, Title 10, § 1301 et seq.
Mich. Comp. Laws Ann., 728.1 et seq.
Ohio Rev. Code 1953, 2301.01 et seq.

Common Pleas Prothonotaries Fee Act
Pa. Purdon's Stat., Title 17, § 1596.1 et seq.

Common Purchaser Act
La. Rev. Stat. Ann., 30:41 et seq.

Common Purchaser Act (Oil)
Tex. Natural Resources Code, § 111.001 et
seq.

Common Retirement Fund Act
N.Y. Retirement and Social Security Law
(Consol. Laws Ch. 51A) § 420 et seq.

Common School Act
Ky. Rev. Stat. 1971, 156.010 et seq.
Pa. 1857 Pamph. Laws 587, No. 620

Common School Act (Brooklyn)
N.Y. Laws 1850, Ch. 143

Common School Capital Improvement Act
Okla. Stat. Ann., Title 70, § 18-151 et seq.

Common Sense Indictment Law
Tex. Code of Criminal Procedure, Art. 21.14
et seq.

Common Thief Act
Md. Ann. Code 1957, Art. 27, § 558

Common Towel Law
Cal. Health and Safety Code § 3800 et seq.

Common Trust Act
Mont. Code Ann., 32-1-701 et seq.

Common Trust Fund Act
Ill. Comp. Stat. 1992, Ch. 760, § 45/1 et seq.
R.I. Gen. Laws 1956, 18-5-1 et seq.
S.D. Codified Laws 1967, 55-6-1 et seq.

Commonwealth Attorneys Act
Pa. Purdon's Stat., Title 71, § 732-101 et seq.

Commonwealth Board Health Act
P.R. Laws Ann. 1954, Title 24, § 301 et seq.

Commonwealth Court Act
Pa. Cons. Stat., Title 42, § 561 et seq.

Commonwealth Defense Act
Mass. Acts 1917, Ch. 342

Commonwealth Emergency Defense Act
Mass. Acts 1941, Ch. 719

Commonwealth Employees Association Act
P.R. Laws Ann. 1954, Title 3, § 862 et seq.

Commonwealth Highways Administration, Maintenance, and Policing Act
P.R. Laws Ann. 1954, Title 9, § 2101 et seq.

Commonwealth Procurement Act
Pa. Cons. Stat., Title 62, § 101 et seq.

Commonwealth Property Recovery Act
Pa. Purdon's Stat., Title 71, § 826.1 et seq.

Commonwealth Venture Fund Act
Ky. Rev. Stat. 1971, 155.400 et seq.

Communicable Disease Act
D.C. Code Ann., § 6-117 et seq.

Communicable Disease Control Act
Oct. 16, 1970, P.L. 91-464, 84 Stat. 988, 42 U.S. Code § 247b
Sept. 30, 1972, P.L. 92-449, 86 Stat. 748, 42 U.S. Code §§ 247b, 247c, 300
Utah Code Ann. 1953, 26-6-1 et seq.

Communicable Disease Prevention Act
Ill. Comp. Stat. 1992, Ch. 410, § 315/0.01 et seq.

Communicable Disease Prevention and Control Act
Tex. Health and Safety Code, § 81.001 et seq.

Communicable Disease Report Act
Ill. Comp. Stat. 1992, Ch. 745, §§ 45/0.01, 45/1

Communicable Disease Segregation Act
Ill. Rev. Stat. 1965, Ch. 23, § 3461 et seq.

Communication Act (Hazard)
Tex. Health and Safety Code, § 502.001 et seq.

Communication Authority Act
P.R. Laws Ann. 1954, Title 27, § 291 et seq.

Communication, Complacency, Privilege Act
Wyo. Stat. 1957, § 1-140

Communication Disorders and Special Senses Act
Tex. Health and Safety Code, § 36.001 et seq.

Communication District Act (Emergency)
Tex. Health and Safety Code, § 772.201 et seq.

Communication Services for the Deaf Act (Telephone)
Fla. Stat. Ann., 427.501 et seq.

Communications Act
Cal. Statutes 1947, Ch. 1071, p. 2472

Communications Act (Emergency)
Ark. Acts 1991, No. 554

Communications Act (Privacy)
Minn. Stat. Ann., 626A.01 et seq.

Communications Act (Privileged)
Colo. Rev. Stat., 13-90-107

Communications Act Amendments, 1952
July 16, 1952, Ch. 879, 66 Stat. 711, 18 U.S. Code prec. §§ 1341, 1343; 47 U.S. Code §§ 153, 154, 155, 307, 308, 310, 311, 312, 315, 316 , 319, 402, 405, 409, 410

Communications Act Amendments, 1960
Sept. 13, 1960, P.L. 86-752, 74 Stat. 889, 47 U.S. Code §§ 154, 307, 309, 311 to 313, 317, 319, 405, 503, 504, 508, 509

Communications Act of 1934
June 19, 1934, Ch. 652, 48 Stat. 1064, 15 U.S. Code § 21; 47 U.S. Code §§ 35, 151 to 155, 201 to 221, 301 to 329, 401 to 416, 501 to 505, 601 to 609
March 29, 1937, Ch. 58, 50 Stat. 56, 47 U.S. Code § 318
May 20, 1937, Ch. 229, 50 Stat. 189, 46 U.S. Code § 484 nt.; 47 U.S. Code §§ 151, 153, 154, 303, 321, 322, 329, 351 to 362, 402, 504
Continued

March 18, 1940, Ch. 66, 54 Stat. 54, 46 U.S. Code §§ 484 to 487 nt.; 47 U.S. Code § 602

June 25, 1940, Ch. 422, 54 Stat. 570, 47 U.S. Code § 210

March 23, 1941, Ch. 24, 55 Stat. 46, 47 U.S. Code § 154

March 6, 1943, Ch. 10, 57 Stat. 5, 47 U.S. Code §§ 3, 214, 222

June 22, 1943, Ch. 137, 57 Stat. 161, 47 U.S. Code § 353 (b)

April 16, 1946, Ch. 138, 60 Stat. 89, 47 U.S. Code § 506

May 24, 1949, Ch. 139, 63 Stat. 108, 47 U.S. Code § 402

Sept. 26, 1950, Ch. 1049, 64 Stat. 1038, 47 U.S. Code § 352

Oct. 24, 1951, Ch. 553, 65 Stat. 611, 47 U.S. Code § 606

July 16, 1952, Ch. 879, 66 Stat. 711, 18 U.S. Code § 1343; 47 U.S. Code §§ 153 to 155, 307 to 312, 315, 316, 319, 402, 405, 409, 410

March 23, 1954, Ch. 104, 68 Stat. 30, 47 U.S. Code § 501

March 26, 1954, Ch. 110, 68 Stat. 35, 47 U.S. Code § 309

March 26, 1954, Ch. 111, 68 Stat. 35, 47 U.S. Code § 319

April 27, 1954, Ch. 175, 68 Stat. 63, 47 U.S. Code §§ 152, 153, 221

Aug. 13, 1954, Ch. 729, 68 Stat. 704, 47 U.S. Code §§ 153, 351, 352, 353, 353a, 354, 354a, 355, 356, 357, 358, 359, 360, 361, 362

Aug. 13, 1954, Ch. 735, 68 Stat. 729, 47 U.S. Code §§ 153, 154, 504, 507

Jan. 20, 1956, Ch. 1, 70 Stat. 3, 47 U.S. Code § 309

Aug. 2, 1956, Ch. 874, 70 Stat. 931, 47 U.S. Code §§ 212, 219, 221, 410

Aug. 6, 1956, Ch. 973, 70 Stat. 1047, 47 U.S. Code §§ 153, 381 to 386, 504

Aug. 28, 1958, P.L. 85-791, 72 Stat. 945, 47 U.S. Code § 402

Aug. 28, 1958, P.L. 85-817, 72 Stat. 981, 47 U.S. Code §§ 303, 310

Sept. 14, 1959, P.L. 86-274, 73 Stat. 557, 47 U.S. Code § 315

June 29, 1960, P.L. 86-533, 74 Stat. 249, 47 U.S. Code § 154

July 7, 1960, P.L. 86-609, 74 Stat. 363, 47 U.S. Code §§ 318, 319

July 12, 1960, P.L. 86-619, 74 Stat. 407, 47 U.S. Code § 154

July 12, 1960, P.L. 86-624, 74 Stat. 421, 47 U.S. Code § 222

Sept. 13, 1960, P.L. 86-751, 74 Stat. 888, 47 U.S. Code § 202

Sept. 13, 1960, P.L. 86-752, 74 Stat. 889, 47 U.S. Code §§ 154, 307, 309, 311 to 313, 317, 319, 405, 503

Aug. 31, 1961, P.L. 87-192, 75 Stat. 420, 47 U.S. Code §§ 155, 405, 409

April 27, 1962, P.L. 87-439, 76 Stat. 58, 47 U.S. Code § 307

April 27, 1962, P.L. 87-444, 76 Stat. 63, 47 U.S. Code §§ 219, 308, 319

April 27, 1962, P.L. 87-445, 76 Stat. 64, 47 U.S. Code § 303

May 1, 1962, P.L. 87-447, 76 Stat. 64, 47 U.S. Code §§ 390 to 397

May 11, 1962, P.L. 87-448, 76 Stat. 68, 47 U.S. Code §§ 504, 510

July 10, 1962, P.L. 87-529, 76 Stat. 150, 47 U.S. Code §§ 303, 330

Oct. 11, 1962, P.L. 87-795, 76 Stat. 903, 47 U.S. Code § 305

Oct. 15, 1962, P.L. 87-811, 76 Stat. 922, 47 U.S. Code § 360

May 14, 1964, P.L. 88-306, 78 Stat. 193, 47 U.S. Code § 309

May 14, 1964, P.L. 88-307, 78 Stat. 194, 47 U.S. Code § 309

May 28, 1964, P.L. 88-313, 78 Stat. 202, 47 U.S. Code §§ 303, 310

Aug. 22, 1964, P.L. 88-487, 78 Stat. 602, 47 U.S. Code § 303

Aug. 13, 1965, P.L. 89-121, 79 Stat. 511, 47 U.S. Code §§ 153, 351 to 355, 357, 359

Oct. 19, 1965, P.L. 89-268, 79 Stat. 990, 47 U.S. Code § 303

Nov. 7, 1967, P.L. 90-129, 81 Stat. 365, 47 U.S. Code §§ 390 to 399

April 26, 1968, P.L. 90-294, 82 Stat. 108, 47 U.S. Code § 396

May 3, 1968, P.L. 90-299, 82 Stat. 112, 47 U.S. Code §§ 153, 223

July 5, 1968, P.L. 90-379, 82 Stat. 290, 47 U.S. Code § 302a

Oct. 27, 1969, P.L. 91-97, 83 Stat. 146, 47 U.S. Code §§ 391, 396

Oct. 7, 1970, P.L. 91-437, 84 Stat. 888, 47 U.S. Code § 396

Oct. 15, 1970, P.L. 91-452, 84 Stat. 930, 47 U.S. Code § 409

Aug. 10, 1971, P.L. 92-81, 85 Stat. 302, 47 U.S. Code §§ 303, 310

Sept. 30, 1971, P.L. 92-131, 85 Stat. 363, 47 U.S. Code § 410

Feb. 7, 1972, P.L. 92-225, 86 Stat. 4, 47 U.S. Code §§ 312, 315

Aug. 29, 1972, P.L. 92-411, 86 Stat. 643, 47 U.S. Code §§ 391, 396

Aug. 6, 1973, P.L. 93-84, 87 Stat. 219, 47 U.S. Code §§ 391, 396, 399

Sept. 14, 1973, P.L. 93-107, 87 Stat. 350, 47 U.S. Code § 331

Dec. 31, 1975, P.L. 94-192, 89 Stat. 1099, 47 U.S. Code §§ 396, 397

Feb. 21, 1978, P.L. 95-224, 47 U.S. Code §§ 152, 152 nt., 224, 503 et seq., 609 nt.

Nov. 2, 1978, P.L. 95-567, 47 U.S. Code § 390 et seq.

Sept. 13, 1982, P.L. 97-259, 47 U.S. Code §§ 153 to 155, 224, 301 to 304, 311, 402, 503, 510, 605

Dec. 8, 1983, P.L. 98-214, 47 U.S. Code §§ 154, 156, 157, 223, 310, 316, 396, 503

Oct. 30, 1984, P.L. 98-549, 47 U.S. Code §§ 521, 522, 531 to 533, 541 to 547, 551 to 559, 605

Nov. 8, 1984, P.L. 98-620, 47 U.S. Code § 402

April 7, 1986, P.L. 99-272, 47 U.S. Code §§ 154 to 156, 158, 158 nt., 391, 393, 396

June 6, 1986, P.L. 99-334, 47 U.S. Code § 154

April 28, 1988, P.L. 100-297, 102 Stat. 424, 47 U.S. Code § 223

Aug. 16, 1988, P.L. 100-394, 102 Stat. 976, 47 U.S. Code § 610

Nov. 3, 1988, P.L. 100-594, 47 U.S. Code §§ 154 to 156, 156 nt., 158, 204, 208, 405

Nov. 7, 1988, P.L. 100-626, 47 U.S. Code §§ 391, 396, 396 nt., 398, 399, 605

Nov. 16, 1988, P.L. 100-667, 47 U.S. Code §§ 605, 612, 613

Nov. 18, 1988, P.L. 100-690, 47 U.S. Code § 223

Nov. 21, 1989, P.L. 101-166, 47 U.S. Code §§ 152, 223

Dec. 19, 1989, P.L. 101-239, 47 U.S. Code §§ 158, 202, 203, 205, 214, 219, 220, 362, 386, 503

Sept. 28, 1990, P.L. 101-396, 47 U.S. Code §§ 154, 156, 203, 303, 310, 333, 503

Oct. 15, 1990, P.L. 101-431, 47 U.S. Code §§ 303, 330

Oct. 17, 1990, P.L. 101-435, 47 U.S. Code § 226

Oct. 18, 1990, P.L. 101-437, 47 U.S. Code §§ 393A[(394)], 394, prec. 395, prec. 396, prec. 397, 397

Nov. 15, 1990, P.L. 101-555, 47 U.S. Code § 226

Dec. 20, 1991, P.L. 102-243, 47 U.S. Code §§ 152, 227, 331

Aug. 26, 1992, P.L. 102-356, 47 U.S. Code §§ 391, 393, 396

Oct. 5, 1992, P.L. 102-385, 47 U.S. Code §§ 325, 332, 334, 335, 522, 532 to 537, 541 to 544, 544a, 546, 548, 551 to 555, 555a, 558

Oct. 27, 1992, P.L. 102-538, 47 U.S. Code §§ 154, 158, 204, 226, 303, 304, 308, 318, 319, 394, 503

Oct. 28, 1992, P.L. 102-556, 47 U.S. Code §§ 227, 228, 302a

Aug. 10, 1993, P.L. 103-66, 47 U.S. Code §§ 152, 153, 156, 158, 159, 309, 332

Oct. 27, 1993, P.L. 103-121, 47 U.S. Code § 159

Oct. 25, 1994, P.L. 103-414, 47 U.S. Code §§ 154, 155, 157, 158, 159, 212, 213, 214, 220, 222, 223, 224, 226 et seq., 308, 309, 328, 331, 356, 381 et seq., 410, 413, 533, 544, 554, 602, 604, 605, 610, 612, 613

Dec. 8, 1994, P.L. 103-465, 47 U.S. Code § 309

Dec. 21, 1995, P.L. 104-66, 47 U.S. Code §§ 154, 393a

Feb. 8, 1996, P.L. 104-104, 47 U.S. Code § 151 et seq.

Sept. 30, 1996, P.L. 104-208, 47 U.S. Code § 254

Oct. 19, 1996, P.L. 104-316, 47 U.S. Code § 397

Aug. 5, 1997, P.L. 105-33, 47 U.S. Code §§ 153, 303, 309, 337

Continued

Dec. 1, 1997, P.L. 105-125, 47 U.S. Code § 214

Oct. 21, 1998, P.L. 105-277, 47 U.S. Code §§ 223, 230, 231, 309

Communications Amendments Act of 1982
Sept. 13, 1982, P.L. 97-259, 47 U.S. Code § 609 nt.

Communications and Information Management Act
N.M. Stat. Ann., 15-1-1 et seq.

Communications Assistance for Law Enforcement Act
Oct. 25, 1994, P.L. 103-414, 47 U.S. Code §§ 1001 nt., 1001 et seq.

Oct. 19, 1996, P.L. 104-316, 47 U.S. Code § 1010

Communications Authority Act
P.R. Laws Ann. 1954, Title 27, § 291

Communications Consumer Privacy Act
Conn. Gen. Stat. Ann., § 53-420 et seq.
Ill. Comp. Stat. 1992, Ch. 720, § 110/1 et seq.

Communications Decency Act of 1996
Feb. 8, 1996, P.L. 104-104, Title V, 47 U.S. Code § 609 nt.

Communications Fraud Act
Fla. Stat. Ann., 817.034
Ga. Code Ann., 10-1-901 et seq.

Communications Interception Act
Utah Code Ann. 1953, 77-23a-1 et seq.

Communications Joint Board Act
See Federal-State Communications Joint Board Act

Communications Satellite Act of 1962
Aug. 31, 1962, P.L. 87-624, 76 Stat. 419, 47 U.S. Code §§ 701, 702, 721, 731 to 735, 741 to 744

March 12, 1969, P.L. 91-3, 83 Stat. 4, 47 U.S. Code § 733

Nov. 1, 1978, P.L. 95-564, 47 U.S. Code §§ 751, 751 nt., 752 et seq.

Jan. 3, 1983, P.L. 97-410, 47 U.S. Code § 734

Oct. 25, 1994, P.L. 103-414, 47 U.S. Code §§ 721, 731, 732, 733, 734, 744, 751, 752, 754, 755, 756, 757

Dec. 21, 1995, P.L. 104-66, 47 U.S. Code § 744

Communications Security Act
Ida. Code 1947, 18-6701 et seq.

Communications Systems Act (Cable Television)
Haw. Rev. Stat. Ann., § 440G-1 et seq.

Communist Act
Mass. Gen. Laws Ann., 264:16 et seq.

Communist Control Act
Ala. Code 1958, Title 14, § 97(1) et seq.
Ariz. Rev. Stat. Ann., §§ 16-805, 16-806, 38-231, 38-233
La. Rev. Stat. Ann., 14:358 et seq.
Mich. Comp. Laws Ann., 752.321 et seq.
Tex. Rev. Civ. Stat., Art. 6889-3
Wyo. Stat. Ann., § 19-5-114 et seq.

Communist Control Act of 1954
Aug. 24, 1954, Ch. 886, 68 Stat. 775, 50 U.S. Code §§ 782, 784, 785, 789, 790 to 793, 841 to 844

Communist Propaganda Control Act
La. Rev. Stat. Ann., 14:390 et seq.

Communist Registration Act
Ark. Code Ann. 1987, 5-51-404 et seq.
N.M. Stat. Ann., 12-4-1 et seq.

Communist Teachers Act (Dilworth)
Cal. Education Code 1976, § 7000 et seq.

Communities Act (Safe and Secure)
N.J. Stat. Ann., 52:17B-159 et seq.

Communities Action Program Act (Industrial)
Pa. Purdon's Stat., Title 73, § 399.51 et seq.

Communities Opportunities, Accountability, and Training and Educational Services Act of 1998
Oct. 27, 1998, P.L. 105-285, 112 Stat. 2702, 42 U.S. Code § 9801 nt.

Communities Trust Act
Fla. Stat. Ann., 380.501 et seq.

Community Act (Planned)
Ore. Rev. Stat., 94.550 et seq.

Community Action Act
N.M. Stat. Ann., 27-8-1 et seq.
Va. Code 1950, § 2.1-587 et seq.

Community Action Agency Act
N.J. Stat. Ann., 52:27D-395 et seq.

Community Action Partnership Act
N.C. Gen. Stat. 1943, §§ 108B-21, 113.28.21 et seq.

Community Action Program Act
Ark. Stat. 1947, 83-1101 et seq.

Community Administration Act
Tex. Probate Code, § 155 et seq.

Community Affairs and Planning Act
Okla. Stat. 1971, Title 74, § 1501 et seq.

Community Affairs Demonstration Grant Act
N.J. Rev. Stat. 1937, 52:27D-59 et seq.

Community Affairs Department Act
Conn. Gen. Stat. Ann., § 8-201 et seq.

Community Affairs in the United States Act (Puerto Rican)
P.R. Acts 1989, No. 58

Community Aging Services Act
Neb. Rev. Stat. 1943, 81-2201 et seq.

Community Airport Authority Act
Mich. Comp. Laws Ann., 259.621 et seq.

Community Alcohol, Drug Abuse, and Mental Health Services Act
Fla. Stat. Ann., 394.65 et seq.

Community Alcoholism Treatment and Detoxification Act
N.M. Stat. Ann., 43-3-1 et seq.

Community and Economic Improvement Act
Pa. 1998 Pamph. Laws, No. 174

Community and Employee Hazardous Chemical Information Act
Mont. Code Ann., 50-78-101 et seq.
Mont. Laws 1985, Ch. 641

Community and Home-Based Services for Mentally Ill Person and Persons with Developmental Disabilities Act
Colo. Rev. Stat., 26-4.5-201 et seq.

Community and Home-Based Services for Persons with Developmental Disabilities Act
Colo. Rev. Stat., 26-4-621 et seq.

Community and Home-Based Services for Persons with Health Complexes Related to Acquired Immune Deficiency Syndrome Act
Colo. Rev. Stat., 26-4-641 et seq.

Community and Home-Based Services for the Elderly, Blind, and Disabled Act
Colo. Rev. Stat., 26-4-601 et seq.

Community and Migrant Health Centers Amendments of 1988
Aug. 10, 1988, P.L. 100-386, 102 Stat. 919, 42 U.S. Code §§ 201 nt., 254b, 254b nt., 254c

Community and Private Mausoleum and Columbarium Law
Cal. Health and Safety Code § 9501 et seq.

Community and Rural Development Loan Program
Iowa Code Ann., 15.281 et seq.

Community and Technical College Act
Wash. Rev. Code Ann., 28B.50.010 et seq.

Community and Urban Forestry Act
Mont. Code Ann., 77-5-401 et seq.

Community and Worker Right to Know Act
N.J. Stat. Ann., 34:5A-1 et seq.
Pa. Pardons. Stat., Title 35, § 7301 et seq.
Wash. Rev. Code Ann., 49.70.010 et seq.

Community Antenna Television System Act
Nev. Rev. Stat. 1979 Reprint, 711.020 et seq.

Community Assistance Act
N.M. Stat. 1978, 11-6-1 et seq.

Community Assistance Act (Leasehold)
N.M. Stat. Ann., 6-6A-1 et seq.

Community Assistance and Affordable Housing Planning Act
Fla. Stat. Ann., 420.601 et seq.

Community-Based Facilities and Public Purpose Buildings Construction Bond Act
N.J. Laws 1991, Ch. 184

Community-Based Health Care Program Law
La. Rev. Stat. Ann., 40:2194

Community Based Planning Act
Minn. Laws 1997, Ch. 202, §§ 1 to 13

Community Building Act (Townships)
Ill. Rev. Stat. 1991, Ch. 139, § 151.9 et seq.

Community Building Complex Committee of Boone County Law
Ill. Comp. Stat. 1992, Ch. 70, § 260/1-1 et seq.

Community Cable Television Law
N.Y. Local Laws 1969, Town of New Castle, p. 1698

Community Care Facilities Act
Cal. Health and Safety Code § 1500 et seq.

Community Care for Disabled Adults Act
Fla. Stat. Ann., 410.601 et seq.

Community Care for the Elderly Act
Fla. Stat., 430.201 et seq.

Community Children and Youth Services Act
Ore. Rev. Stat., 417.400 et seq.

Community Code
Ida. Code 1947, 30-1501 et seq.

Community College Act
Alaska Stat. 1962, § 14.40.560 et seq.
Ill. Rev. Stat. 1991, Ch. 122, § 101-1 et seq.
Iowa Code Ann., 280A.1 et seq.
Kan. Stat. Ann., 71-120 et seq.
Kan. Stat. Ann., 71-701 et seq.
Mass. Gen. Laws Ann., 15:27 et seq.
Mich. Comp. Laws Ann., 389.1 et seq.
N.C. Gen. Stat. 1943, § 116-47 et seq.
N.M. Stat. Ann., 21-13-1 et seq.
Ore. Rev. Stat., 341.005 et seq.
Pa. Purdon's Stat., Title 24, § 19-1901-A
Wash. Rev. Code Ann., 28B.50.010 et seq.
Wyo. Stat. Ann., § 21-18-201 et seq.

Community College and Occupational Education Act
Colo. Rev. Stat., 23-60-101 et seq.

Community College Construction Act
Cal. Education Code 1976, § 81800 et seq.

Community College Construction Program Bond Act
Cal. Statutes 1971, Ch. 937, p. 1835, §§ 1 to 10

Community College District Act
Mich. Comp. Laws 1948, 390.871 et seq.

Community College Election Act
Kan. Stat. Ann., 71-1401 et seq.

Community College Emergency Finance Act
Cal. Education Code 1976, § 84900 et seq.

Community College Facility Construction Law
Cal. Education Code 1959, § 25546.01 et seq.

Community College Finance Act
Cal. Education Code 1976, § 84720 et seq.

Community College Part-Time Faculty Office Hours Program
Cal. Education Code 1976, § 87880 et seq.

Community College Revenue Bond Act
Cal. Education Code 1976, § 81900 et seq.

Community Confinement Act
R.I. Gen. Laws 1956, 42-56-20.2

Community Consolidated School District Act
Ill. Rev. Stat. 1991, Ch. 122, § 11A-1 et seq.

Community Convention and Tourism Marketing Act
Mich. Comp. Laws Ann., 141.871 et seq.

Community Correctional Facilities and Programs Act
Neb. Rev. Stat. 1943, 47-601 et seq.

Community Correctional Treatment Act (Substance Abuse)
Cal. Penal Code § 6240 et seq.

Community Corrections Act
Kan. Stat. Ann., 75-5290 et seq.
Mich. Comp. Laws Ann., 791.401 et seq.
Mont. Code Ann., 53-30-301 et seq.
N.M. Stat. Ann., 33-9-1 et seq.
Ore. Rev. Stat., 423.550 et seq.
Tenn. Code Ann., 40-36-101 et seq.

Community Corrections Act (Juvenile)
N.M. Stat. Ann., 33-9A-1 et seq.

Community Corrections Incentive Act
S.C. Code Ann. 1976, § 2-48-10 et seq.

Community Corrections Partnership Act
Fla. Stat. Ann., 948.50 et seq.

Community Court Act
Pa. Cons. Stat., Title 42, § 1101 et seq.

Community Cultural Grants Program Act
Iowa Code 1985, 7A-51 et seq.

Community Currency Exchange Act
Ill. Rev. Stat. 1991, Ch. 17 § 4801.01 et seq.
Wis. Stat. 1989, 218.05

Community Development Act
D.C. Code Ann., § 5-901 et seq.
La. Rev. Stat. Ann., 33:7601 et seq.
Miss. Code Ann., § 43-35-501 et seq.
Mo. Rev. Stat., 251.150 et seq.
Mont. Code Ann., 7-2-4701 et seq.
Neb. Rev. Stat. 1943, 18-2101 et seq.
N.M. Stat. Ann., 3-60-1 et seq.
S.C. Code Ann. 1976, § 31-10-10 et seq.
Tex. Local Government Code, § 373.001 et seq.
Vt. Stat. Ann., Title 10, § 681 et seq.

Community Development Act (Economic Impact Zone)
S.C. Code Ann. 1976, § 12-14-10 et seq.

Community Development Act (Planned)
Mont. Code Ann., 7-2-4701 et seq.

Community Development Act (Rural)
Iowa Code 1983, 387.1 et seq.

Community Development Assistance Act
Neb. Rev. Stat. 1943, 13-201 et seq.

Community Development Authority Act
W. Va. Code 1966, § 31-19-1 et seq.
Wyo. Stat. Ann., § 9-7-101 et seq.

Community Development Banking and Financial Institutions Act of 1994
Sept. 23, 1994, P.L. 103-325, 12 U.S. Code § 4701 nt.

Community Development Block Grant Entitlement Program for Nonurban Counties and Certain Other Municipalities Act
Pa. Purdon's Stat., Title 35, § 1751 et seq.

Community Development Block Grant Program Act (Small Cities)
Fla. Stat. Ann., 290.0401 et seq.

Community Development Bond Act
N.J. Laws 1991, Ch. 486

Community Development Corporation Act (Enterprise)
Mich. Comp. Laws Ann., 125.2601 et seq.

Community Development Corporation Support and Assistance Program Act
Fla. Stat. Ann., 290.0301 et seq.

Community Development Corporations Act
N.Y. Private Housing Finance Law (Consol. Laws Ch. 44B) § 250 et seq.

Community Development Credit Union Revolving Loan Fund Transfer Act
Nov. 8, 1986, P.L. 99-609, 42 U.S. Code § 9822 nt.

Community Development District Act
Fla. Stat. Ann., 190.001 et seq.

Community Development Finance Authority Act
N.H. Rev. Stat. 1955, 162-L:1 et seq.

Community Development Finance Corporation Act
Ill. Comp. Stat. 1992, Ch. 315, § 15/1 et seq.
Mass. Gen. Laws Ann., 40F:1 et seq.

Community Development Law (Urban Renewal)
Neb. Rev. Stat. 1943, 18-2101 et seq.

Community Development Program Law
Nev. Rev. Stat. 1979 Reprint, 268.745 et seq.

Community Development Research and Training Act
Pa. Purdon's Stat., Title 53, § 9501 et seq.

Community Dispute Resolution Act
Mich. Comp. Laws Ann., 691.1551 et seq.

Community Ditch and Acequia Fund Act
N.M. Stat. Ann., 73-2A-1 et seq.

Community Ditches or Acequias Act
N.M. Stat. Ann., 73-2-3, 73-2-11 et seq.

Community Diversion Pilot Project Act (Long-Term Care)
Fla. Stat., 430.702

Community Economic Betterment Program
Iowa Code Ann., 15.315 et seq.

Community Economic Development Act of 1981
Aug. 13, 1981, P.L. 97-35, 42 U.S. Code § 9801 nt.
Oct. 18, 1986, P.L. 99-500, 100 Stat. 3377
Oct. 30, 1986, P.L. 99-591, 100 Stat. 3377
Nov. 28, 1990, P.L. 101-624, 42 U.S. Code §§ 9812, 9817
Oct. 21, 1998, P.L. 105-277, 42 U.S. Code § 9806
Oct. 27, 1998, P.L. 105-285, 42 U.S. Code §§ 9803, 9804

Community Economic Development Assistance Act
Mass. Gen. Laws Ann., 40H:1 et seq.

Community Economic Development Assistance Corporation Act
Mass. Gen. Laws Ann., 40H:1 et seq.

Community Economic Opportunity Act
S.C. Code Ann. 1976, § 43-45-10

Community Economic Recovery Program Act
Pa. Purdon's Stat., Title 73, § 399.1 et seq.

Community Education Act
Fla. Stat. Ann., 228.071
Iowa Code Ann., 276.1 et seq.
S.C. Code Ann. 1976, § 59-44-10 et seq.

Community Education and Development Act
Ga. Code Ann., 50-8-140 et seq.

Community Education Employment Center Act of 1990

Sept. 25, 1990, P.L. 101-392, 20 U.S. Code § 2396 nt.

Community Emergency Drought Relief Act of 1977

May 23, 1977, P.L. 95-31, 42 U.S. Code §§ 3121 nt., 5184 nt.

Community Emergency Response Hazardous Substances Protection Act

Minn. Stat. Ann., 299F.091 et seq.

Community Energy Authority Act

Cal. Government Code § 52000 et seq.

Community Environmental Response Facilitation Act

Oct. 19, 1992, P.L. 102-426, 42 U.S. Code §§ 9601 nt., 9620, 9620 nt.

Community Facilities Act

Cal. Government Code § 53311 et seq.
Cal. Health and Safety Code § 4600 et seq.

Community Facilities for Mentally Retarded Act

R.I. Public Laws 1966, Ch. 170

Community Facilities Law

Cal. Health and Safety Code § 4600 et seq.

Community Facilities Project Guarantee Fund Act

N.Y. Laws 1969, Ch. 1013, § 14
N.Y. Unconsolidated Law § 8721 et seq.

Community Food Garden Act

Ill. Comp. Stat. 1992, Ch. 20, § 3923/1 et seq.

Community Forest Law

Fla. Stat. Ann., 591.15 et seq.

Community Forestry and Shade Tree Assistance Act

N.J. Stat. Ann., 13:1L-17.1 et seq.

Community Gardening Act

Tenn. Code Ann., 43-24-101 et seq.

Community Gardening Pilot Program Act

Fla. Stat. Ann., 570.60

Community Hazardous Chemical Information Act

Mont. Code Ann., 39-30-101 et seq.

Community Health Agency Act

Tenn. Code Ann., 68-2-1101 et seq.

Community Health Care Act

Neb. Rev. Stat. 1943, 71-7501 et seq.

Community Health Center Facilities Loan Insurance Law

Cal. Health and Safety Code § 436.70 et seq.

Community Health Management Information System Act

Iowa Code 1995, 144C.1 et seq.
Tenn. Code Ann., 63-6-228

Community Health Services Act

Cal. Welfare and Institutions Code § 5000 et seq.
Minn. Stat. 1986, 145.911 et seq.

Community Health Services and Facilities Act of 1961

Oct. 5, 1961, P.L. 87-395, 75 Stat. 824, 42 U.S. Code §§ 246, 247a, 291i, 291n, 291s, 291t, 291w, 292c to 292g

Community High School Act

Ill. Rev. Stat. 1991, Ch. 122, § 12-1 et seq.
Kan. Laws 1923, Ch. 187

Community Homes for Developmentally Disabled Persons Location Act

Ark. Code Ann. 1987, 20-48-601 et seq.

Community Homes for Disabled Persons Location Act

Tex. Human Resources Code, § 123.001 et seq.

Community Hospital Act

Mich. Comp. Laws Ann., 331.1 et seq.

Community Hospital Education Act

Fla. Stat. Ann., 381.0403

Community Human Services Act
Wyo. Stat. Ann., § 35-1-611 et seq.

Community Improvement Act
Fla. Stat. Ann., 220.183
W. Va. Code 1966 § 16-13B-1 et seq.

Community Improvement Act (Abbeville)
La. Acts 1969, No. 171

Community Improvement Act (Baton Rouge)
La. Acts 1968, No. 224

Community Improvement Act (Lafayette)
La. Acts 1968, No. 484

Community Improvement Act (New Iberia and Zachary)
La. Acts 1972, No. 32

Community Improvement Act (New Orleans)
La. Acts 1968, No. 170

Community Improvement District Act (Atlanta)
Ga. Laws 1986, p. 4175
Ga. Laws 1991, p. 3653

Community Improvement District Act (Cobb County)
Ga. Laws 1985, p. 4009

Community Improvement District Act (Douglas County)
Ga. Laws 1991, p. 3709

Community Improvement District Act (Fulton County)
Ga. Laws 1991, p. 5460

Community Improvement District Act (Henry County)
Ga. Laws 1985, p. 4946

Community Improvement District Act (Johns Creek)
Ga. Laws 1990, p. 4665

Community Improvement District Act (Lenox Park)
Ga. Laws 1988, p. 4582

Community Improvement Districts Act (Alpharetta)
Ga. Laws 1992, p. 5842

Community Improvement Districts Act (Burke County)
Ga. Laws 1991, p. 4136

Community Improvement Districts Act (Chatham County)
Ga. Laws 1994, p. 4931

Community Improvement Districts Act (Cherokee County)
Ga. Laws 1998, H.B. 1748

Community Improvement Districts Act (Clayton County)
Ga. Laws 1992, p. 5698

Community Improvement Districts Act (Dahlonega)
Ga. Laws 1991, p. 4649

Community Improvement Districts Act (DeKalb County)
Ga. Laws 1998, S.B. 598

Community Improvement Volunteer Act of 1994
Sept. 30, 1996, P.L. 104-208, 40 U.S. Code § 276d-3

Community Infrastructure Authority Act
W. Va. Code 1966 § 31-19-1 et seq.

Community Integrated Living Arrangements Licensure and Certification Act
Ill. Comp. Stat. 1992, Ch. 210, § 135/1 et seq.

Community Integrated Service Network Act
Minn. Stat. 1986, 62N.01 to 62N.24

Community Investment Corporation Demonstration Act
Oct. 28, 1992, P.L. 102-550, 42 U.S. Code § 5305 nt.

Community Investment Recovery Act
Ill. Comp. Stat. 1992, Ch. 740, §§ 30/1, 30/5

Community Junior College Act
Okla. Stat. Ann., Title 70, § 4401 et seq.

Community Justice and Probation Act
Ill. Laws 1985, P.A. 84-823

Community Juvenile Justice System Act
Fla. Stat. Ann., 39.025 et seq.

Community Juvenile Services Act
Ore. Rev. Stat., 417.400 et seq.

Community Land Chest Law
Cal. Health and Safety Code § 35100

Community Land Grant Act
N.M. Stat. Ann., 49-1-1 et seq.

Community Law Enforcement and Recovery Demonstration Project (CLEAR)
Cal. Penal Code § 14000 et seq.

Community Living Facilities Licensing Act
Ill. Comp. Stat. 1992, Ch. 210, § 35/1 et seq.

Community Mental Health Act
Fla. Stat. Ann., 394.65 et seq.

Community Mental Health Acts
Ill. Comp. Stat. 1992, Ch. 405, § 20/0.01 et seq.

Community Mental Health Centers Act
Oct. 31, 1963, P.L. 88-164, 77 Stat. 290, 42 U.S. Code §§ 2681 to 2687
June 24, 1967, P.L. 90-31, 81 Stat. 79, 42 U.S. Code §§ 2681, 2687, 2688a, 2688d
Oct. 15, 1968, P.L. 90-574, 82 Stat. 1006, 42 U.S. Code §§ 2688e to 2688q, 3442 nt.
March 13, 1970, P.L. 91-211, 84 Stat. 54, 42 U.S. Code §§ 2681, 2682, 2687, 2688, 2688a, 2688d, 2688f to 2688h, 2688j-1, 2688k, 2688l, 2688o, 2688r to 2688v, 2691, 2697b
June 30, 1970, P.L. 91-296, 84 Stat. 352, 42 U.S. Code § 2688

Oct. 27, 1970, P.L. 91-513, 84 Stat. 1238, 42 U.S. Code §§ 2688k to 2688o, 2688r
Dec. 31, 1970, P.L. 91-616, 84 Stat. 1851, 42 U.S. Code §§ 2688h, 2688j-2, 2688t
March 21, 1972, P.L. 92-255, 86 Stat. 76, 42 U.S. Code §§ 2684, 2688a, 2688k, 2688n-1, 2688t
June 18, 1973, P.L. 93-45, 87 Stat. 94, 42 U.S. Code §§ 2681, 2687, 2688a, 2688d, 2688j-1, 2688j-2, 2688l, 2688l-1, 2688-1, 2688o, 2688u
Aug. 1, 1977, P.L. 95-83, 42 U.S. Code § 2689a et seq.
Nov. 9, 1978, P.L. 95-622, 42 U.S. Code §§ 2689 et seq., 4588
Oct. 4, 1979, P.L. 96-79, 42 U.S. Code § 2689t
Ida. Code 1947, 39-3101 et seq.

Community Mental Health Centers Amendments of 1970
March 13, 1970, P.L. 91-211, 84 Stat. 54, 42 U.S. Code §§ 2681, 2682, 2687 to 2688a, 2688d, 2688e nt., 2688f to 2688h, 2688j-1 to 2688l, 2688o, 2688r to 2688v, 2691, 2693, 2697b
Oct. 30, 1970, P.L. 91-515, 84 Stat. 1308, 42 U.S. Code § 2688 nt.

Community Mental Health Centers Assistance Act
Kan. Stat. Ann., 65-4431 et seq.

Community Mental Health Centers Construction Act
Wis. Stat. 1989, 140.65 et seq.

Community Mental Health Centers Extension Act of 1978
Nov. 9, 1978, P.L. 95-622, 42 U.S. Code §§ 246, 2689 et seq., 4588
July 10, 1979, P.L. 96-32, 42 U.S. Code §§ 2689 nt., 2689b, 2689b nt., 2689e

Community Mental Health Equity Funding Act
Ill. Comp. Stat. 1992, Ch. 405, § 70/1 et seq.

Community Mental Health Facilities Loan Insurance Law
Cal. Health and Safety Code § 436.30 et seq.

Community Mental Health Program Act
Mich. Comp. Laws Ann., 330.1200 et seq.

Community Mental Health Service System Act
Ill. Rev. Stat. 1991, Ch. 91 1/2, § 1601 et seq.

Community Mental Health Services Act
Alaska Stat. 1962, § 47.30.520 et seq.
Cal. Welfare and Institutions Code § 5000 et seq.
Fla. Stat. Ann., 394.65 et seq.
Minn. Stat. 1984, 245.61 et seq.
Neb. Rev. Stat. 1943, 71-5001 et seq.
Nev. Rev. Stat. 1979 Reprint, 436.110 et seq.
N.M. Stat. Ann., 23-7-2 et seq.
N.Y. Mental Hygiene Law 1972 (Consol. Laws Ch. 27) § 41.01 et seq.
Okla. Stat. Ann., Title 43A, § 613 et seq.
Utah Code Ann. 1953, 26-17-6 et seq.
Vt. Stat. Ann., Title 18, § 8901 et seq.
Wash. Rev. Code Ann., 71.24.011 et seq.

Community Mental Health Services Act (Short-Doyle Act)
Cal. Welfare and Institutions Code § 9000 et seq.

Community Mental Health Services and Mental Retardation Services Companies Law
N.Y. Mental Hygiene Law 1977 (Consol. Laws Ch. 27) § 75.01 et seq.

Community Mental Health Task Force Act
Ill. Comp. Stat. 1992, Ch. 405, § 60/0.01 et seq.

Community Mental Retardation Facilities Assistance Act
Kan. Stat. Ann., 65-4411 et seq.

Community Notification Act
Ala. Code 1975, §§ 15-20-1, 15-20-20 et seq.

Community Outreach Partnership Act of 1992
Oct. 28, 1992, P.L. 102-550, 42 U.S. Code § 5307 nt.

Community Parkland Act of 1986
Cal. Public Resources Code § 5700 et seq.

Community Penalties Act
N.C. Gen. Stat. 1943, § 143B-500 et seq.

Community Planning Act
Tenn. Code Ann., 13-3-201 et seq.

Community Policing and Mentoring for School Safety Program
Cal. Education Code 1976, § 49350 et seq.

Community Property Act
Alaska Stat. 1962, § 34.75.010 et seq.
Ariz. Rev. Stat. Ann., § 25-211 et seq.
Cal. Civil Code § 5110 et seq.
Haw. Rev. Stat. Ann., § 510-2 et seq.
La. Rev. Stat. Ann., 9:2801 et seq.
Mich. Comp. Laws Ann., 557.201 et seq.
Nev. Rev. Stat. 1979 Reprint, 123.220 et seq.
N.M. Stat. Ann., 40-3-6 et seq.
Okla. Stat. Ann., Title 43, § 215
Ore. Laws 1943, Ch. 440
Ore. Laws 1947, Ch. 525
Pa. 1947 Pamph. Laws 1423, No. 550
Tex. Family Code, § 5.01 et seq.
Wash. Rev. Code Ann., 26.16.030 et seq.

Community Property Disposition Act
Ark. Code Ann. 1987, 28-12-101 et seq.

Community Property Disposition at Death Act
Haw. Rev. Stat. Ann., § 510-21 et seq.

Community Property Disposition Rights at Death Act
Wyo. Stat. Ann., § 2-7-720 et seq.

Community Property Law
Neb. Rev. Stat. 1943, 42-603 et seq.

Community Property Law (New)
Cal. Statutes 1973, Ch. 987, p. 1897
Cal. Statutes 1974, Ch. 1206

Community Property Rights at Death Act
Conn. Gen. Stat. Ann., § 45a-458 et seq.

Community Property Rights at Death Act (Disposition of)

See also Uniform Disposition of Community Property Rights at Death Act

Conn. Gen. Stat. Ann., § 45-298a et seq.

Community Property Rights Disposition at Death Act

See Uniform Disposition of Community Property Rights of Death Act

Community Protection Act (Children and Family)

Ill. Comp. Stat. 1992, Ch. 705, § 80/1

Community Public Health Services Act

Neb. Laws 1992, L.B. 1019, §§ 101 to 121

Community Punishment and Corrections Act

Ala. Code 1975, § 15-18-170 et seq.

Community Recreation Act

Cal. Education Code 1976, § 10900 et seq.

Community Redevelopment Act

Cal. Health and Safety Code § 33000 et seq.
Fla. Stat. Ann., 163.330 et seq.
Nev. Rev. Stat. 1979 Reprint, 279.382 et seq.
R.I. Gen. Laws 1956, 45-31-1 et seq.
Utah Code Ann. 1953, 11-15-1 et seq.

Community Redevelopment Financial Assistance and Disaster Project Law

Cal. Health and Safety Code § 34000 et seq.

Community Redevelopment Financing Act

Ark. Code Ann. 1987, 14-168-201 et seq.
Wash. Rev. Code Ann., 39.88.010 et seq.

Community Rehabilitation Districts Law

Cal. Government Code § 53370 et seq.

Community Reinvestment Act

N.Y. Banking Law (Consol. Laws Ch. 4) § 28b
W. Va. Code 1966 § 31A-8B-1 et seq.

Community Reinvestment Act of 1977

Oct. 12, 1977, P.L. 95-128, 12 U.S. Code §§ 2901 et seq., 2901 nt.
Aug. 9, 1989, P.L. 101-73, 12 U.S. Code §§ 2902, 2906
Dec. 12, 1991, P.L. 102-233, 12 U.S. Code § 2907
Dec. 19, 1991, P.L. 102-242, 12 U.S. Code § 2906
Oct. 28, 1992, P.L. 102-550, 12 U.S. Code §§ 2903, 2907
Sept. 29, 1994, P.L. 103-328, 12 U.S. Code § 2906

Community Reinvestment Fund Act

Md. Ann. Code 1974, Department of Housing and Community Development, § 10-101 et seq.

Community Residence Facilities Licensure Act

D.C. Code Ann., § 32-1301 et seq.

Community Residence Location Planning Act

Ill. Rev. Stat. 1989, Ch. 91 1/2, § 921 et seq.

Community Residential Alternative Licensing Act

Ill. Comp. Stat. 1992, Ch. 210, § 140/1 et seq.

Community Residential Living Act (Disabled Persons)

Okla. Stat. Ann., Title 60, § 860 et seq.

Community Resource Act

Kan. Stat. Ann., 74-5021 et seq.

Community Right to Know Act

Ga. Code Ann., 12-17-1 et seq.
Me. Rev. Stat. Ann. 1964, Title 22, § 1696-A et seq.
N.Y. Adm. Code '85, § 24-701 et seq.
Tex. Health and Safety Code, § 483.001 et seq.
W. Va. Code 1966, § 16-31-1 et seq.

Community Right to Know Act (Hazardous Substances)

Me. Rev. Stat. Ann. 1964, Title 22, § 1696-A et seq.
Continued

R.I. Gen. Laws 1956, 23-24.4-1 et seq.

Community Right-to-Know Act (Nonmanu-facturing Facility)

Tex. Health and Safety Code, § 507.001

Community Right-to-Know Act (Public Employee)

Tex. Health and Safety Code, § 506.001 et seq.

Community Right to Know and Emergency Planning Act

Ariz. Rev. Stat. Ann., § 26-341 et seq.

Haw. Session Laws 1993, Act 300

Ill. Rev. Stat. 1991, Ch. 111 1/2, § 7701 et seq.

Kan. Stat. Ann., 65-5701 et seq.

Neb. Rev. Stat. 1943, 81-15,191 to 81-15,235

Community Right to Know and Protection Act

Ore. Laws 1985, Ch. 726, § 1 et seq.

Ore. Rev. Stat., 457.307 et seq.

Community Risk Pooling Act (Condominium and Common Interest)

Ill. Comp. Stat. 1992, Ch. 765, § 605/12.1

Community Sales Act

Mo. Rev. Stat., 277.010 et seq.

Community Sales Act (Livestock)

Ill. Rev. Stat. 1991, Ch. 121 1/2, § 208 et seq.

Okla. Stat. Ann., Title 2, § 9-131 et seq.

Community Scholarship Mobilization Act

Oct. 7, 1998, P.L. 105-244, 112 Stat. 1810, 20 U.S. Code § 1070 nt.

Community School District Act

Me. Rev. Stat. Ann. 1964, Title 20-A § 1601 et seq.

Community School Partnership Act

Oct. 20, 1994, P.L. 103-382, 20 U.S. Code § 1070 nt.

Oct. 21, 1998, P.L. 105-277, 20 U.S. Code § 1070 nt.

Community Schools Act

Ala. Code 1975, § 16-63-1 et seq.

Fla. Stat. 1971, 228.162

N.C. Gen. Stat. 1943, § 115C-203 et seq.

Community Schools and Comprehensive Community Education Act of 1978

Nov. 1, 1978, P.L. 95-561, 20 U.S. Code § 3281 et seq.

Community Schools Study Commission Act (Chicago)

Ill. Comp. Stat. 1992, Ch. 105, § 215/0.01 et seq.

Community Schools Youth Services and Supervision Grant Program Act of 1994

Sept. 13, 1994, P.L. 103-322, 42 U.S. Code § 13791

Oct. 7, 1998, P.L. 105-244, 42 U.S. Code § 13791

Community Senior Citizens Centers and Services Companies Law

N.Y. Private Housing Finance Law (Consol.Laws Ch. 44B) § 350 et seq.

Community Service Act

Ill. Comp. Stat. 1992, Ch. 405, § 30/1 et seq.

Mont. Code Ann., 90-14-101 et seq.

Pa. Purdon's Stat., Title 62, § 2981 et seq.

Community Service Act (Probation)

Fla. Stat. Ann., 228.0716

Ill. Rev. Stat. 1991, Ch. 38, §§ 204a, 204a-1

Community Service Corps Program Act

Mich. Public Acts 1983, No. 259, §§ 25 to 35

Community Service Employment Act (Older Worker)

Ark. Stat. 1947, 81-1501 et seq.

Community Service Employment for Older Workers Act

Ark. Code Ann. 1987, 20-80-201 et seq.

Community Service Restitution Act

Miss. Code Ann., § 99-20-1 et seq.

Community Services Act
 Me. Rev. Stat. Ann. 1964, Title 5, § 3511 et
 seq.
 Pa. Purdon's Stat., Title 62, § 2981 et seq.

Community Services Act (Commission on)
 Ill. Comp. Stat. 1992, Ch. 15, § 105/0.01 et
 seq.

Community Services Act (Developmental
 Disabilities)
 N.M. Stat. 1978, 43-1A-1 et seq.

Community Services Act (Mental Health)
 Ill. Rev. Stat. 1991, Ch. 91 1/2, § 901 et seq.

Community Services Act (Youth)
 Okla. Stat. Ann., Title 70, § 11-108 et seq.

Community Services Act for the Mentally
 Retarded
 Ga. Code Ann., 37-5-1 et seq.

Community Services and Developmental
 Disabilities Prevention Act
 Fla. Stat., 393.061 et seq.

Community Services and Rural Electric
 Cooperative Act
 Tenn. Code Ann., 65-26-101 et seq.

Community Services Block Grant Act
 Aug. 13, 1981, P.L. 97-35, 42 U.S. Code
 § 9901 nt.
 Sept. 30, 1982, P.L. 97-274, 42 U.S. Code
 § 9911
 May 21, 1984, P.L. 98-288, 42 U.S. Code
 §§ 9902, 9912
 Oct. 30, 1984, P.L. 98-558, 42 U.S. Code
 §§ 9901 to 9910a
 Sept. 30, 1986, P.L. 99-425, 42 U.S. Code
 § 9901 et seq.
 Nov. 3, 1990, P.L. 101-501, 42 U.S. Code
 §§ 9901 to 9904, 9905a, 9910, 9910a, 9911
 Nov. 28, 1990, P.L. 101-624, 42 U.S. Code
 § 9904
 Oct. 6, 1993, P.L. 103-94, 42 U.S. Code
 § 9904
 Dec. 2, 1993, P.L. 103-171, 42 U.S. Code
 §§ 9902, 9903, 9909, 9910, 9910a, 9911

 Oct. 7, 1998, P.L. 105-244, 42 U.S. Code
 § 9910c
 Oct. 27, 1998, P.L. 105 to 285, 42 U.S. Code
 §§ prec. 9901, 9901, 9901 nt., 9902 to 9905,
 9905a, 9906 to 9910, 9910a to 9910d, 9911
 to 9924, 9925, 9926

Community Services Block Grant
 Amendments of 1994
 May 18, 1994, P.L. 103-252, 42 U.S. Code
 §§ 9901 nt., 9901, 9903, 9904, 9910 et seq.

Community Services Block Grant Program
 Act
 Cal. Government Code § 12725 et seq.
 Fla. Laws 1982, Ch. 82-228

Community Services District Act
 Cal. Government Code § 61000 et seq.
 N.M. Stat. Ann., 4-54-1 et seq.

Community Services Extension
 Amendments
 Aug. 5, 1965, P.L. 89-109, 79 Stat. 435, 42
 U.S. Code §§ 242h, 246, 247a, 247b

Community Services Program Act
 Kan. Stat. Ann., 79-32,194 et seq.

Community Sewer Construction Assistance
 Act (Small)
 Fla. Stat. Ann., 403.1838

Community Slum Clearance and Redevel-
 opment Act
 Ky. Rev. Stat. 1971, 99.330 et seq.

Community Social Service Centers Act
 Okla. Stat. Ann., Title 63, § 2051 et seq.

Community Social Services Act
 Minn. Stat. Ann., 256E.01 et seq.

Community Strategic Planning Assistance
 Act
 Kan. Stat. Ann., 74-5092 et seq.

Community Support Systems for Mentally
 Deficient and Mentally Ill Persons Act
 Ill. Comp. Stat. 1992, Ch. 405, § 35/1 et seq.

Community-Supported Living Arrangement Services for Persons with Developmental Disabilities Act
Colo. Rev. Stat., 26-4-651 et seq.

Community System Act (Juvenile Justice)
Fla. Stat. Ann., 39.025 et seq.

Community Trust for Persons with Severe Chronic Disabilities Act
Iowa Code Ann., 458A.1 et seq.
N.C. Gen. Stat. 1943, § 36A-59.10 et seq.
N.J. Stat. Ann., 3B:11-19 et seq.

Community Unit School District Act
Ill. Rev. Stat. 1991, Ch. 122, § 11A-1 et seq.

Community Urban Renewal and Redevelopment Act
Ky. Rev. Stat. 1971, 99.330 et seq.

Community Water Facility Loan Act
N.D. Cent. Code, 6-09.5-01

Community Workfare Experience Act
Okla. Stat. Ann., Title 56, § 501 et seq.

Community Youth Development Act
Okla. Stat. 1981, Title 10, § 601.61 et seq.

Communter Relief Act (Santa Clara County)
Cal. Statutes 1984, § Ch. 446

Commutation Act (Sentences)
N.Y. Executive Law (Consol. Laws, Ch. 18) § 259c
Pa. Purdon's Stat., Title 61, § 271 et seq.

Commutation Clause of Homestead Act
May 20, 1862, Ch. 75, 12 Stat. 393

Commute Options Act (Employee)
Del. Code of 1974, Title 2, § 1901 et seq.
Ill. Laws 1992, P.A. 87-1275

Commuter and Intercity Transit Right of Way Preservation Act
Cal. Government Code § 67410 et seq.

Commuter and Intercity Transit Right-of-Way Preservation Act
Cal. Government Code §§ 67410, 67421, 67460 et seq.
Cal. Streets and Highways Code § 164.57

Commuter Rail Authority Act (Central Florida)
Fla. Stat. Ann., 343.61 et seq.

Commuter Rail Authority Act (Tampa Bay)
Fla. Stat. Ann., 343.71 et seq.

Commuter Rail Authority Act (Tri-County)
Fla. Stat. Ann., 343.51 et seq.

Commuter Tax Act (City Earnings Tax on Nonresidents)
N.Y. Model Local Law § 1 et seq.; Gen. City Law (Consol. Laws Ch. 21) § 25m

Commuter Transit Corporation Act
R.I. Gen. Laws 1956, 42-64.2-1 et seq.

Commuters Income Tax Act
N.J. Stat. Ann., 54:8A-1 et seq.

Compact Act (Instate Civil Defense and Disaster)
Mont. Code Ann. 1983, 10-3-206

Compact Act (New York and New Jersey Waterfront Commission)
N.J. Stat. Ann., 32:1-1 et seq., 32:23-1 et seq.

Compact Act (Yellowstone River)
Mont. Code Ann., 85-20-101

Compact Act for Education
Mass. Acts 1967, Ch. 453

Compact Act for Western Regional Cooperation in Higher Education
Ariz. Rev. Stat. Ann., § 15-1741 et seq.

Compact Agreement on Detainers
W. Va. Code 1966, § 62-14-1

Compact Enabling Act (Interstate Library)
Vt. Stat. Ann., Title 22, § 21 et seq.

Compact for Driver License
Mont. Code Ann., 61-5-401 et seq.

Compact for Education
Ky. Rev. Stat. 1971, 156.710
N.D. Cent. Code, 15-64-01, 15-64-02
R.I. Gen. Laws 1956, 16-47-1

Compact for Education Act
See Education Compact Act

Compact for Falls of the Ohio Interstate Bank
Ind. Code Ann., 14-6-24-1 et seq.

Compact for Interstate Qualification of Educational Personnel
Utah Code Ann. 1953, 53A-6-201 et seq.

Compact for Jurisdiction on the Colorado River (Interstate)
Ariz. Rev. Stat. Ann., § 37-620.11

Compact for Juveniles Act
Fla. Stat. Ann., 39.51 et seq.
Miss. Code Ann., § 43-25-1 et seq.

Compact for Mental Health (Interstate)
Cal. Welfare and Institutions Code § 1300
Me. Rev. Stat. Ann. 1964, Title 34B, § 9001 et seq.

Compact for Motor Vehicle Safety Equipment (Interstate)
Vt. Stat. Ann., Title 23, § 1801 et seq.

Compact for Out-of-State Parolee Supervision
N.Y. Executive Law 1977 (Consol. Laws Ch. 18) § 259m

Compact for State and Federal Membership in the Connecticut River Atlantic Salmon Commission
Vt. Stat. Ann., Title 10, § 4651 et seq.

Compact for the Conservation and Utilization of Natural Energy and Water Resources Act
Tex. Natural Resources Code, § 142.001 et seq.

Compact for the Supervision of Parolees and Probationers (Interstate)
Mont. Code Ann., 46-23-1102

Compact for the Supervision of Parolees and Probationers Act
Ariz. Rev. Stat. Ann., § 31-461 et seq.

Compact of Free Association Act of 1985
Jan. 14, 1986, P.L. 99-239, 48 U.S. Code § 1821 nt.
July 18, 1988, P.L. 100-369, 102 Stat. 387, 48 U.S. Code § 1681 nt.

Compact of 1958 (Potomac River)
Md. Ann. Code 1974, Art. NR, § 4-306

Compact on Adoption and Medical Assistance
Okla. Stat. Ann., Title 10, § 61 et seq.

Compact on Adoption Assistance (Interstate)
Ind. Code Ann., 31-3-5-1 et seq.

Compact on Agricultural Grain Marketing (Interstate)
See Interstate Compact on Agricultural Grain Marketing Act

Compact on Air Pollution
Ky. Rev. Stat. 1971, 224.18-200

Compact on Air Pollution Act
See Interstate Compact on Air Pollution

Compact on Air Pollution Act (Ohio-Kentucky)
Ohio Rev. Code 1953, 3723.04 et seq.

Compact on Air Pollution Act (Ohio-West Virginia)
Ohio Rev. Code 1953, 3723.01 et seq.

Compact on Education
Kan. Stat. Ann., 72-6011 et seq.

Compact on Historic Chattahoochee Act
Ala. Code 1975, 41-9-311

Compact on Industrialized—Modular Buildings (Interstate)
Minn. Stat. Ann., 16B.75

Compact on Interstate High Speed Intercity Rail Passenger Network Act
Pa. Purdon's Stat., Title 55, § 671

Compact on Juveniles
See Uniform Interstate Compact on Juveniles

Compact on Juveniles Act (Interstate)
Ala. Code 1975, 44-2-20 et seq.
Cal. Welfare and Institutions Code, § 1300
Conn. Gen. Stat. Ann., § 46b-151 et seq.
D.C. Code Ann., § 32-1101 et seq.
Del. Code of 1974, Title 31, § 5201 et seq.
Ill. Rev. Stat. 1991, Ch. 23, § 2590 et seq.
Ind. Code Ann., 31-6-10-1 et seq.
Ky. Rev. Stat. 1971, 615.010 et seq.
Mont. Code Ann., 41-6-101 et seq.
Tex. Family Code, § 25.01 et seq.
Utah Code Ann. 1953, 55-12-1 et seq.
Va. Code 1950, § 16.1-323 et seq.
Vt. Stat. Ann., Title 33, § 5701
Wyo. Stat. Ann., § 14-6-101 et seq.

Compact on Kansas-Missouri Flood Prevention and Control
Mo. Rev. Stat. 1991, 70.327

Compact on Libraries (Interstate)
Mont. Code Ann. 1987, 22-1-601, 22-1-602

Compact on Low-Level Radioactive Waste (Midwest Interstate)
Ind. Code Ann., 13-5-9-1 et seq.

Compact on Low-Level Radioactive Waste Management Act (Northwest Interstate)
Ida. Code 1947, 39-3025

Compact on Mental Health Act
D.C. Code 1981, § 6-1801 et seq.
Ky. Rev. Stat. 1971, 210.520
Mo. Rev. Stat., 630.810 et seq.
Mont. Code Ann., 53-22-101 et seq.
Ohio Rev. Code 1953, 5119.50

Compact on Mental Health Act (Interstate)
See Interstate Compact on Mental Health Act

Compact on Mentally Disordered Offenders Act (Interstate)
See Interstate Compact on Mentally Disordered Offenders Act

Compact on Placement of Children Act
Ala. Code 1975, 44-2-20 et seq.
Ariz. Rev. Stat. Ann., § 8-548 et seq.
Colo. Rev. Stat., 24-60-1801 et seq.
Conn. Gen. Stat. 1983, § 17-175 et seq.
Fla. Stat. Ann., 409.401 et seq.
Ga. Code Ann., 39-4-1 et seq.
Ida. Code 1947, 16-2101 et seq.
Ill. Rev. Stat. 1991, Ch. 23, § 2600 et seq.
Kan. Stat. Ann., 38-1201 et seq.
Ky. Rev. Stat. 1971, 600.010 et seq., 615.030
Md. Ann. Code 1974, Art. FL, § 5-601 et seq.
Me. Rev. Stat. Ann. 1964, Title 22, § 491 et seq.
Mont. Code Ann., 41-4-101 et seq.
N.C. Gen. Stat. 1943, §§ 96-1 et seq., 110-57.1 et seq.
Ohio Rev. Code 1953, 5103.20 et seq.
Ore. Rev. Stat., 417.200 et seq.
S.C. Code Ann. 1976, § 20-7-1980 et seq.
Utah Code Ann. 1953, 62A-4-301 et seq.
Wash. Rev. Code Ann., 26.34.010 et seq.
Wis. Stat. 1989, 48.988, 48.989
Wyo. Stat. Ann., § 14-5-101 et seq.

Compact on Placement of Children Act (Interstate)
See Interstate Compact on Placement of Children Act

Compact on Potomac Highlands Airport Authority Act
Md. Ann. Code 1974, Art. TR, § 10-103

Compact on Radiological Health Protection Act
Conn. Gen. Stat. Ann., §§ 22a-159, 22a-160
Mass. Acts 1967, Ch. 801
N.H. Rev. Stat. 1955, 125-B:1 et seq.

Compact on Vehicle Equipment Safety Act
Md. Ann. Code 1974, Art. TR, § 22-503

Compact to Conserve Oil and Gas Act
See also Interstate Compact to Conserve Oil and Gas Act
Cal. Public Resources Code, § 3275 et seq.
S.C. Code Ann. 1976, § 48-41-10
Tex. Natural Resources Code, § 90.001 et seq.
Va. Code 1950, §§ 45.1-381, 45.1-382

Compact to Conserve Oil and Gas Act (Interstate)
N.Y. Environmental Conservation Law (Consol. Laws Ch. 43B) § 23-2101 et seq.

Compacts for Nonresident Traffic Violators
S.C. Code Ann. 1976, § 56-25-10 et seq.

Companion Animal and Pet Welfare Act
Minn. Stat. Ann., 346.35 et seq.

Company Act (Limited Liability)
Conn. Public Acts 1993, p. 730, No. 267
Fla. Stat. Ann., 608.401 et seq.

Company Police Act
N.C. Gen. Stat. 1943, § 74E-1 et seq.

Company Registration Act (Employee Leasing)
Utah Code 1953, 16-14-1 et seq.

Comparative Negligence Act
Ark. Code Ann. 1987, 16-64-122 et seq., 21-5-201
Colo. Rev. Stat., 13-21-111
Fla. Stat. Ann., 440.39, 769.03
Kan. Stat. Ann., 60-258a et seq.
Mass. Gen. Laws Ann., 231:85
Minn. Stat. Ann., 604.01
Miss. Code Ann., § 11-7-15
N.D. Cent. Code, 9-10-07
Neb. Rev. Stat. 1943, 25-1151
N.Y. Civil Practice Laws and Rules (Consol. Laws Ch. 8) § 1411 et seq.
Ohio Rev. Code 1953, 2315.19
Okla. Stat. Ann., Title 23, §§ 12, 13

Pa. Cons. Stat., Title 42, § 7102
S.D. Codified Laws 1967, 20-9-2
Tex. Civil Practice and Remedies Code, § 33.001 et seq.
Utah Code Ann. 1953, 78-27-37 et seq.
Wis. Stat. 1989, 895.045

Comparative Negligence Act (Employer-Employee)
Ohio Rev. Code 1953, 4113.07

Comparative Negligence Act (General Tort)
Ga. Code Ann., 51-11-7 et seq.

Comparative Negligence Act (Railroad)
See Railroad Comparative Negligence Act

Comparative Negligence Statute
N.Y. Civil Practice Laws and Rules (Consol. Laws Ch. 8) § 1411 et seq.

Compensable Occupational Disease Act
N.J. Stat. Ann., 34:15-30 to 34:15-35

Compensated Emancipation Resolution
April 10, 1862, No. 26, 12 Stat. 617
Feb. 24, 1992, P.L. 102-247, 48 U.S. Code § 1681 nt.
July 29, 1998, P.L. 105-209, 48 U.S. Code § 1903

Compensating Tax Act
Ark. Code Ann. 1987, 26-53-101 et seq.
Haw. Rev. Laws 1955, § 118-1 et seq.
Kan. Stat. Ann., 79-3701 et seq.
Miss. Code Ann., § 27-67-1 et seq.
N.M. Stat. Ann. 1953, 72-17-1 et seq.
Wash. Rev. Code Ann., 82.12.010 et seq.

Compensating Use Tax Act
Mo. Rev. Stat., 144.600 et seq.
N.C. Gen. Stat. 1943, §§ 105-164.1 to 105-164.44C
N.Y. City Adm. Code '38, Ch. 41, § M46-15.0 et seq.

Compensation Act (Crime Victims')
Miss. Code Ann., § 99-41-1 et seq.
Tex. Code of Criminal Procedure, Art. 56.31 et seq.

Compensation Act (Crime Victims)
Mass. Gen. Laws Ann., 258A:1 et seq.
W. Va. Code 1966, § 14-2A-1 et seq.

Compensation Act (Unemployment)
Tex. Rev. Civ. Stat., Art. 5221b-22b

Compensation Act (Workers')
See Workers' Compensation Act

Compensation Act for Victims of Violent Crimes
D.C. Code Ann., § 3-401 et seq.

Compensation and Bond Act (Persian Gulf Conflict Veteran's)
Pa. 1992 Pamph. Laws, No. 106

Compensation and Classification Act
Ark. Code Ann. 1987, 12-58-201, 16-64-122 et seq.

Compensation and Dividends Tax Act
Haw. Rev. Laws 1955, § 120-1et seq.

Compensation Board Act (Crime Victim's)
Pa. Purdon's Stat., Title 71, § 180-7 et seq.

Compensation Competition Rating Act (Workers)
Me. Rev. Stat. Ann. 1964, Title 24-A, § 2361 et seq.

Compensation Cost Containment Act (Workers')
Colo. Rev. Stat., 8-14.5-101 et seq.

Compensation, Employment and Dismissal Act (Teacher)
Colo. Rev. Stat., 22-63-101 et seq.

Compensation for Crime Victims Act
Wyo. Stat. Ann., § 1-40-101 et seq.

Compensation Funds for Patients Act
S.C. Code Ann. 1976, § 38-79-410 et seq.

Compensation Insurance Law (Regulation)
Cal. Insurance Code § 11690 et seq.

Compensation Law for Crime Victims
N.Y. Executive Law 1951 (Consol. Laws Ch. 18) § 620 et seq.

Compensation Pilot Program Act (State Treasurer's Bank)
Ill. Rev. Stat. 1991, Ch. 130, § 201 et seq.

Compensation Presumption Statute
Mass. Gen. Laws Ann., 152:7A

Compensation Prohibition Act (Adoption)
Ill. Comp. Stat. 1992, Ch. 720, § 525/0.01 et seq.

Compensation Review Act
Ill. Comp. Stat. 1992, Ch. 25, § 120/1 et seq.

Compensatory Education Act
Fla. Stat. Ann., 236.088

Compensatory or Remedial, or Both, Education Act
La. Rev. Stat. Ann., 17:394 et seq.

Competence Determinations Act (Due Process)
Cal. Civil Code § 39
Cal. Probate Code §§ 810 to 814, 1801, 1881, 3201, 3204, 3208

Competency Act (Accused as Witness)
N.H. Rev. Stat. 1955, 516:31
N.M. Stat. Ann. 1953, 41-12-19
S.D. Codified Laws 1967, 23-44-1
Wash. Rev. Code Ann., 5.60.010 et seq.
Wis. Stat. 1971, 885.13

Competency Act (Civil Action)
Wash. Rev. Code Ann., 5.60.020

Competency Act (Criminal Defendants)
Cal. Penal Code, § 1323
Del. Code of 1974, Title 11, § 3501
Haw. Rev. Stat. Ann., § 621-15
Minn. Stat. Ann., 611.11
N.C. Gen. Stat. 1943, § 8-54
N.J. Stat. Ann., 2A:81-8
Va. Code 1950, § 19.2-268
Wash. Rev. Code Ann., 10.52.040

W. Va. Code 1966, § 57-3-6

Competency Act (Defendant Witness)
Ala. Code 1975, § 12-21-220
Ark. Code Ann. 1987, 46-43-501
N.D. Cent. Code 29-21-11
Okla. Stat. Ann., Title 22, § 701

Competency Act (Parties as Witnesses)
Mich. Comp. Laws Ann., 600.2159

Competency Act (Witnesses)
Ariz. Rev. Stat. Ann. 1956, §§ 12-2201,
   12-2202
Ark. Code Ann. 1987, 80-5801 et seq.
Conn. Gen. Stat. 1977, § 54-84
Del. Code of 1974, Title 10, § 4302 et seq.
Ida. Code 1947, 9-201
Ind. Code Ann., 34-1-14-4
Iowa Code Ann., 622.1 et seq.
Mass. Gen. Laws Ann., 233:20
Mich. Comp. Laws Ann., 600.2166
Mo. Rev. Stat., 491.010 et seq.
Mont. Rev. Code 1947, 94-8801 et seq.
Ohio Rev. Code 1953, 2945.42 et seq.
Utah Code Ann. 1953, 78-24-2
Va. Code 1950, § 8.01-396 et seq.

Competency Based Education Act
Ark. Code Ann. 1987, 6-15-401 et seq.

Competency of Witnesses Act
S.C. Code Ann. 1976, § 19-11-10 et seq.

Competition Act (Motion Picture Theatre)
Wash. Rev. Code Ann., 19.58.010 et seq.

Competition Act (Unfair)
Mass. Gen. Laws Ann., 93:14E et seq.

Competition Development and Telecommunications Act
Ga. Code Ann., 46-5-160- to 46-5-174

Competition in Contracting Act of 1984
July 18, 1984, P.L. 98-369, 98 Stat. 1175, 41
   U.S. Code § 251 nt.
Nov. 8, 1985, P.L. 99-145, 10 U.S. Code
   § 2304 nt.

Competition Law
Iowa Code Ann., 553.1 et seq.

Competitive Bidding Act
Cal. Government Code § 13402 et seq.
Mass. Gen. Laws Ann., 29:8A et seq.
N.J. Stat. Ann., 40A:11-4

Competitive Bidding Act (Cities andTowns)
Wyo. Stat. Ann., § 15-1-113

Competitive Bidding Act (Highways)
Tex. Rev. Civ. Stat., Art. 6674h

Competitive Bidding Act (Public Service)
Ohio Rev. Code 1953, 735.05 et seq.

Competitive Bidding Act (Public)
Minn. Stat. Ann., 16B.07
Okla. Stat. Ann., Title 61, § 101 et seq.

Competitive Equality Banking Act of 1987
Aug. 10, 1987, P.L. 100-86, 2 U.S. Code
   §§ 905, 906; 12 U.S. Code §§ 24, 226 nt.,
   248a, 248a nt., 371c-1, 481, 619, 619 nt.,
   1430, 1436, 1437 nt., 1439-1, 1441 to
   1442a, 1464 to 1468, 1725 to 1730, 1730
   nt., 1730a, 1730h, 1730i, 1751 et seq., 1811
   nt., 1813 et seq.; 12 U.S. Code §§ 24, 226
   nt., 371c-1, 619, 619 nt., 846, 1430, 1730,
   1730a, 1730a nt., 1813, 1828, 1831, 1832,
   1841 nt., 1841 to 1843; 15 U.S. Code §§ 45,
   46, 57a; 31 U.S. Code §§ 3328, 3328 nt.,
   3334, 3702, 3712, 9101, 9105
Aug. 10, 1987, P.L. 100-86, 12 U.S. Code
   §§ 24, 226
Oct. 28, 1992, P.L. 102-550, 12 U.S. Code
   § 3806

Competitive Negotiation Act (Consultants)
Neb. Rev. Stat. 1943, 81-1701

Competitive Negotiations Act (Institute of Phosphate Research)
Fla. Stat., 378.102

Competitive Negotiations Act (Professional Consultants)
Fla. Stat. Ann., 287.055

Competitive Scholarship Act
N.J. Stat. Ann., 18A:71-7.2, 18A:71-7.3

Competitive, Special, and Facilities Research Grant Act
Dec. 13, 1991, P.L. 102-237, 7 U.S. Code § 450i
April 4, 1996, P.L. 104-127, 7 U.S. Code § 450i
June 23, 1998, P.L. 105-185, 7 U.S. Code § 450i

Competitiveness, Education and Jobs Bond Act
N.J. Laws 1988, Ch. 78

Competitiveness Policy Council Act
Aug. 23, 1988, P.L. 100-418, 102 Stat. 1454, 15 U.S. Code § 4801 nt.
Dec. 19, 1995, P.L. 104-65, 15 U.S. Code § 4804

Complacency, Privilege, Communication Act
Wyo. Stat. 1957, § 1-140

Complementary and Alternative Health Care Freedom of Access Act
Ga. Code Ann., 31-43-1 et seq.

Complete Supplementation Act (Pensioners)
P.R. Acts 1988, No. 39

Compliance Act (Health Care Professional)
S.C. Code Ann. 1976, § 44-30-10 et seq.

Compliance Act (Reapportionment)
Vt. Stat. Ann., Title 17, § 1891 et seq.

Compliance Enforcement Procedure Act (Collegiate Athletic Association)
Fla. Stat. Ann., 240.5339 et seq.

Compliance Review Act
S.C. Code Ann. 1976, § 1-22-10 et seq.

Composite Reports as Evidence Act
Neb. Rev. Stat. 1943, 25-12, 119 et seq.
Ohio Rev. Code 1953, 2317.36 et seq.
S.D. Codified Laws 1967, 19-15-5 to 19-15-8

Compounding of Felony Act
Tex. Penal Code, § 38.06

Comprehensive Action Against Alcohol, Drugs and Substance Abuse in Schools Act
La. Rev. Stat. Ann., 17:402 et seq.

Comprehensive Adult Mental Health Act
Minn. Stat. Ann., 245.461 et seq.

Comprehensive Alcohol Abuse and Alcoholism Prevention, Treatment, and Rehabilitation Act Amendments of 1979
Jan. 2, 1980, P.L. 96-180, 42 U.S. Code §§ 218, 4541, 4541 nt., 4551 to 4553, 4561, 4571 to 4573, 4576, 4578, 4585, 4587, 4588, 4594

Comprehensive Alcohol Abuse and Alcoholism Prevention, Treatment, and Rehabilitation Act of 1970
Dec. 31, 1970, P.L. 91-616, 84 Stat. 1848, 42 U.S. Code §§ 218, 246, 2688h, 2688j-2, 2688t, 4551, 4552, and others
Oct. 25, 1972, P.L. 92-554, 86 Stat. 1167, 42 U.S. Code § 4571
May 14, 1974, P.L. 93-282, 88 Stat. 126, 42 U.S. Code §§ 4541, 4542, 4551 to 4553, 4571, 4574, 4577, 4581, 4582
Aug. 1, 1977, P.L. 95-83, 42 U.S. Code § 4572 et seq.
Nov. 9, 1978, P.L. 95-622, 42 U.S. Code §§ 4541, 4573, 4585
Oct. 4, 1979, P.L. 96-79, 42 U.S. Code § 4573
Jan. 2, 1980, P.L. 96-180, 42 U.S. Code §§ 4541, 4541 nt., 4551 to 4553, 4561, 4571 to 4573, 4576 to 4578, 4585, 4587, 4588, 4594

Comprehensive Alcohol Abuse, Drug Abuse, and Mental Health Amendments Act of 1988
Nov. 18, 1988, P.L. 100-690, 42 U.S. Code § 201 nt.
Oct. 30, 1990, P.L. 101-476, 20 U.S. Code § 1400 nt.

Comprehensive Alcohol and Drug Treatment Act

Tenn. Code Ann., 33-8-101 et seq.

Comprehensive Alcoholism and Alcohol Abuse Prevention, Control and Treatment Act

Miss. Code Ann., § 41-30-1 et seq.

Comprehensive Alcoholism Prevention, Control and Treatment Act

Fla. Stat. Ann., 396.012 et seq.

Tenn. Public Acts 1972, Ch. 857

Comprehensive Anti-Apartheid Act of 1986

Oct. 2, 1986, P.L. 99-440, 22 U.S. Code § 5001 nt.

Nov. 7, 1986, P.L. 99-631, 100 Stat. p. 3515, 22 U.S. Code §§ 5001, 5012 to 5016, 5019, 5034, 5035, 5039, 5053, 5056, 5059, 5062 to 5064, 5067 to 5072, 5081, 5082, 5091, 5092, 5095, 5100, 5101, 5112

Aug. 23, 1988, P.L. 100-418, 102 Stat. 1158, 22 U.S. Code § 5059

Dec. 4, 1991, P.L. 102-182, 22 U.S. Code § 5100

Nov. 23, 1993, P.L. 103-149, 22 U.S. Code §§ 2346d nt., 5002 et seq.

Comprehensive Automobile Insurance Reparations Act

N.Y. Insurance Law (Consol. Laws Ch. 28) § 5101 et seq.

Comprehensive Child Abuse Prevention and Treatment Act

N.J. Stat. Ann., 9:6-8.83 et seq.

Comprehensive Child and Adolescent Mental Health Services Act

Fla. Stat., 394.490 to 394.497

Comprehensive Child Development Act

April 28, 1988, P.L. 100-297, 102 Stat. 325, 42 U.S. Code § 9881 et seq.

Nov. 3, 1990, P.L. 101-501, 42 U.S. Code § 9887

Oct. 7, 1991, P.L. 102-119, 42 U.S. Code § 9886

May 18, 1994, P.L. 103-252, 42 U.S. Code §§ 9881 to 9887

Oct. 20, 1994, P.L. 103-382, 42 U.S. Code § 9886

Comprehensive Child Development Centers Act of 1988

April 28, 1988, P.L. 100-297, 102 Stat. 325, 42 U.S. Code § 9801 nt.

May 18, 1994, P.L. 103-252, 42 U.S. Code §§ 9801 nt., 9881 nt.

Comprehensive Children's Mental Health Act

Minn. Stat. Ann., 245.487 et seq.

Comprehensive Chlorofluorocarbon Reduction and Recycling Act

Minn. Stat. Ann., 116.70 et seq.

Comprehensive Clean Water Infrastructure Act

R.I. Gen. Laws 1956, 46-15.6-1 et seq.

Comprehensive Community Mental Health Services Act

Neb. Rev. Stat. 1943, 71-5001 et seq.

Comprehensive Computer Data Access and Fraud Act

Cal. Penal Code § 502

Cal. Welfare and Institutions Code §§ 653.1, 653.5

Comprehensive Conflict of Interests Act

Va. Code 1950, § 2.1-599 et seq.

Comprehensive Correction Improvement Act

Tenn. Public Acts 1985 Ex. Sess., Ch. 5

Comprehensive Court Enforcement Program Act

Fla. Laws 1998, Ch. 247, §§ 1 to 5

Comprehensive Crime Control Act of 1984

Oct. 12, 1984, P.L. 98-473, 18 U.S. Code § 1 nt.

Dec. 26, 1985, P.L. 99-217, 18 U.S. Code § 3551 nt.

Oct. 27, 1986, P.L. 99-570, 21 U.S. Code §§ 841, 845, 848, 960

Nov. 10, 1986, P.L. 99-646, 18 U.S. Code § 3551 nt.

Continued

Nov. 14, 1986, P.L. 99-651, 18 U.S. Code
§ 3006A

Dec. 7, 1987, P.L. 100-182, 18 U.S. Code
§§ 3551 nt., 3553 nt.

**Comprehensive Criminal—Juvenile Justice
Information System Act**

R.I. Gen. Laws 1956, 42-108-1 et seq.

Comprehensive Curative Act

Neb. Rev. Stat. 1943, 76-258 et seq.

**Comprehensive Drug Abuse Prevention Act
of 1978**

Oct. 27, 1986, P.L. 99-570, 21 U.S. Code
§ 881

**Comprehensive Drug Abuse Prevention and
Control Act**

Fla. Stat. Ann., 893.01 et seq.

**Comprehensive Drug Abuse Prevention and
Control Act of 1970**

Oct. 27, 1970, P.L. 91-513, 84 Stat. 1236, 18
U.S. Code §§ 1114, 1952, 4251; 21 U.S.
Code §§ 198a, 321, 333, 334, 360, 372, and
others; 26 U.S. Code §§ 4901, 4905, 6808,
7012, 7103, and others; 31 U.S. Code
§§ 529e to 529f; 40 U.S. Code § 304m; 42
U.S. Code §§ 3411, 3509; 46 U.S. Code
§ 239a; 49 U.S. Code § 787

May 14, 1971, P.L. 92-13, 85 Stat. 37, 21
U.S. Code § 801 nt.

Nov. 10, 1978, P.L. 95-633, 21 U.S. Code
§§ 881, 965

Oct. 12, 1984, P.L. 98-473, 21 U.S. Code
§§ 821, 824, 851, 854, 881

Oct. 27, 1986, P.L. 99-570, 21 U.S. Code
§ 881

Nov. 10, 1986, P.L. 99-646, 21 U.S. Code
§ 881

Nov. 18, 1988, P.L. 100-690, 102 Stat. 4316

Sept. 13, 1994, P.L. 103-322, 21 U.S. Code
§ 841

Nov. 2, 1994, P.L. 103-437, 42 U.S. Code
§ 3509

Nov. 10, 1998, P.L. 105-362, 42 U.S. Code
§ 3509

**Comprehensive Drug Abuse Prevention and
Control Act of 1975**

Oct. 27, 1986, P.L. 99-570, 21 U.S. Code
§ 853

Comprehensive Drug Control Act

Mo. Rev. Stat., 195.005 et seq.

Comprehensive Drug Reform Act

N.J. Stat. Ann., 2A:4A-26, 2C:5-2, 2C:20-2,
2C:35-1 et seq., 2C:36-1 et seq., 2C:36A-1,
2C:39-7, 2C:41-1, 2C:43-1 et seq., 2C:43-6,
2C:43-7, 2C:43-12, 2C:44-2, 2C:52-5,
2C:64-2, 24:21-22 et seq., 24:21-29,
24:21-36

Comprehensive Economic Development Act

Fla. Laws 1990, Ch. 201

Comprehensive Education Reform Act

Tenn. Code Ann., 49-5-5001 et seq.

**Comprehensive Educational Improvement
and Financing Act**

N.J. Stat. Ann., 18A:7F-1 et seq.

Comprehensive Educational Planning Act

Colo. Rev. Stat., 22-6-101 et seq.

Comprehensive Election Act

Mo. Rev. Stat., 115.001 et seq.

**Comprehensive Emergency Management
Act**

Utah Code Ann. 1953, 53-2-101 et seq.

**Comprehensive Employment and Training
Act Amendments of 1977**

June 15, 1977, P.L. 95-44, 29 U.S. Code
§§ 801 nt., 802 et seq.

**Comprehensive Employment and Training
Act Amendments of 1978**

Oct. 27, 1978, P.L. 95-524, 29 U.S. Code
§§ 173, 175a, 186, 801 et seq.

Comprehensive Employment Training Act of 1973

Dec. 28, 1973, P.L. 93-203, 87 Stat. 839, 18 U.S. Code § 665; 29 U.S. Code §§ 801, 802, 811 to 822, 841 to 851, 871 to 875, 881 to 885, 911 to 929, 951 to 956, 981 to 992; 42 U.S. Code § 2571 nt.

June 3, 1977, P.L. 95-40, 29 U.S. Code § 817 et seq.

June 15, 1977, P.L. 95-44, 29 U.S. Code § 802 et seq.

Aug. 5, 1977, P.L. 95-93, 29 U.S. Code § 802 et seq.

Oct. 27, 1978, P.L. 95-524, 29 U.S. Code § 801 et seq.

Oct. 17, 1979, P.L. 96-88, 29 U.S. Code §§ 821, 829, 873, 879, 882, 914, 952

Sept. 8, 1980, P.L. 96-341, 29 U.S. Code § 941a

Comprehensive Enforcement Program Fund Act

N.J. Stat. Ann., 2B:19-1 et seq.

Comprehensive Environmental Cleanup and Responsibilities Act

Mont. Code Ann., 75-10-701 et seq.

Comprehensive Environmental Response, Compensation, and Liability Act of 1980

Dec. 11, 1980, P.L. 96-510, 42 U.S. Code § 9601 nt.

Oct. 17, 1986, P.L. 99-499, 42 U.S. Code §§ 9601 to 9609, 9611 to 9614, 9616 to 9626, 9631, 9651, 9653, 9656 to 9661, 9671 to 9675

Nov. 23, 1988, P.L. 100-707, 42 U.S. Code § 9601

Nov. 9, 1989, P.L. 101-144, 42 U.S. Code § 9611

Nov. 5, 1990, P.L. 101-508, 42 U.S. Code § 9611

Nov. 15, 1990, P.L. 101-584, 42 U.S. Code § 9619

Oct. 19, 1992, P.L. 102-426, 42 U.S. Code § 9620

Oct. 23, 1992, P.L. 102-484, 42 U.S. Code § 9619

Oct. 27, 1992, P.L. 102-531, 42 U.S. Code § 9604

Oct. 31, 1994, P.L. 103-429, 42 U.S. Code §§ 9601, 9607

Feb. 10, 1996, P.L. 104-106, 42 U.S. Code § 9620

Sept. 23, 1996, P.L. 104-201, 42 U.S. Code § 9620

Sept. 30, 1996, P.L. 104-208, 42 U.S. Code §§ 9601, 9607

Oct. 11, 1996, P.L. 104-287, 42 U.S. Code §§ 9601, 9607

Oct. 21, 1998, P.L. 105-276, 42 U.S. Code § 9619

Mont. Code Ann., 75-10-601 et seq.

Wyo. Stat. Ann., § 34-8-101 et seq.

Comprehensive Family Planning Act

Fla. Stat. Ann., 381.0051

Comprehensive Forfeiture Act of 1984

Oct. 12, 1984, P.L. 98-473, 18 U.S. Code § 1961 nt.

Comprehensive Health Association Act

Fla. Stat. Ann., 627.648 et seq.

Comprehensive Health Education Act

Cal. Education Code 1976, § 51880 et seq.

Colo. Rev. Stat., 22-25-101 et seq.

S.C. Code Ann. 1976, § 59-32-5 et seq.

Comprehensive Health Education and Critical Health Problems Act

Ill. Comp. Stat. 1992, Ch. 105, § 110/1 et seq.

Comprehensive Health Education and Substance Abuse Prevention Act

Fla. Stat. Ann., 233.067

Comprehensive Health Insurance Act

Minn. Stat. Ann., 62E.01 et seq.

Comprehensive Health Insurance Plan Act

Ill. Comp. Stat. 1992, Ch. 215, § 105/1 et seq.

Comprehensive Health Insurance Pool Act

Ark. Code 1987, 23-60-101 et seq.

Neb. Rev. Stat. 1943, 44-4201 et seq.

N.M. Stat. Ann., 59A-54-1 et seq.

Tenn. Public Acts 1986, Ch. 870

Utah Code Ann. 1953, 31A-29-101 et seq.

Comprehensive Health Insurance Risk Pool Association Act
Miss. Code Ann., § 83-9-201 et seq.

Comprehensive Health Manpower Training Act of 1971
Nov. 18, 1971, P.L. 92-157, 85 Stat. 431, 42 U.S. Code § 292b nt.
Nov. 16, 1990, P.L. 101-597, 42 U.S. Code § 3505d

Comprehensive Health Planning Act
Ill. Rev. Stat. 1987, Ch. 111 1/2, § 1071 et seq.
S.C. Code Ann. 1976, § 44-5-10 et seq.
Tenn. Code Ann., 68-11-101 et seq.

Comprehensive Health Planning and Public Health Services
Nov. 3, 1966, P.L. 89-749, 80 Stat. 1180, 42 U.S. Code §§ 242g, 243, 246, 247a nt.

Comprehensive Intoxication and Alcoholism Control Act
Md. Ann. Code 1974, Art. HG, § 8-101 et seq.

Comprehensive Kindergarten Act
Ala. Code 1975, § 16-13-52

Comprehensive Local Water Management Act
Minn. Laws 1985, 1st Sp. Ch. 2
Minn. Stat. 1986, 103B.301 et seq.
Minn. Stat. 1988, 110B.01 et seq.

Comprehensive Mass Transportation Study Commission Act
Ind. Laws 1971, P.L. 487

Comprehensive Medical Malpractice Reform Act
Fla. Stat. Ann., 95.11, 627.351, 627.357, 725.01, 768.41, 768.47, 768.48

Comprehensive Mental Health Act
Minn. Stat. Ann., 245.461 et seq.

Comprehensive Mental Health Services for the Deaf and Hearing Impaired Act
Okla. Stat. 1981, Title 43A, § 3-501 et seq.

Comprehensive Methamphetamine Control Act of 1996
Oct. 3, 1996, P.L. 104-237, 21 U.S. Code § 801 nt.

Comprehensive Multimedia Waste Minimization Act
Miss. Code Ann., § 49-31-1 et seq.

Comprehensive Municipal Solid Waste Management, Resource Recovery, and Conservation Act
Tex. Health and Safety Code, § 363.001 et seq.

Comprehensive Older Americans Act Amendments of 1978
Oct. 18, 1978, P.L. 95-478, 42 U.S. Code §§ 1975c nt., 3001 et seq., 5001, 5011, 5012, 5082, 6101 et seq.
Oct. 9, 1984, P.L. 98-459, 98 Stat. 1792, 42 U.S. Code § 3045 nt.

Comprehensive Petroleum Underground Storage Tank Fund Act
Iowa Code Ann., 455G.1 et seq.

Comprehensive Plan Appeals Board
R.I. Gen. Laws 1956, 45-22.3-1 et seq.

Comprehensive Planning Act
Fla. Stat. Ann., 23.011 et seq.

Comprehensive Planning Act (Local Government)
Fla. Stat. Ann., 163.3161 et seq.

Comprehensive Planning Act (Seminole County)
Fla. Special Laws 1974, Ch. 612

Comprehensive Planning Act (State)
Fla. Stat. Ann., 186.001 et seq.

Comprehensive Planning and Land Development Regulation Act
Fla. Stat. Ann., 163.3161 et seq.

Comprehensive Planning and Land Use Regulation Act
Me. Rev. Stat. Ann. 1964, Title 30-A, § 4311 et seq.

R.I. Gen. Laws 1956, 45-22.2-1 et seq.

Comprehensive Planning Enabling Act (Local Government)

S.C. Code Ann. 1976, § 6-29-310 et seq.

Comprehensive Real Estate Appraisal Act

Neb. Rev. Stat. 1943, 77-1301 et seq.

Comprehensive Regulated Medical Waste Management Act

N.J. Stat. Ann., 13:1E-48.1 et seq.

Comprehensive School Act

Ga. Code Ann., 20-2-1 et seq.

Comprehensive Small Business Act

Miss. Code Ann., § 57-10-151 et seq.

Comprehensive Smokeless Tobacco Health Education Act of 1986

Feb. 27, 1986, P.L. 99-252, 15 U.S. Code § 4401 nt.

Comprehensive Smoking Education Act

Oct. 12, 1984, P.L. 98-474, 15 U.S. Code §§ 1331 nt., 1331 et seq. .

Aug. 16, 1985, P.L. 99-92, 15 U.S. Code § 1341

Oct. 27, 1992, P.L. 102-531, 15 U.S. Code § 1341

Comprehensive Solar Energy Act

Ill. Comp. Stat. 1992, Ch. 30, § 725 et seq.

Comprehensive Solid Waste Management Act

Ga. Code Ann., 12-8-20 et seq.

Comprehensive State Insurance Plan Act

Mont. Code Ann., 2-9-201 et seq.

Comprehensive State Insurance Plan and Torts Claim Act

Mont. Code Ann., 2-9-101 to 2-9-318 et seq.

Comprehensive Substance Abuse Administrative Act

R.I. Gen. Laws 1956, 42-7.1-1 et seq.

Comprehensive Thrift and Bank Fraud Prosecution and Taxpayer Recover Act of 1990

Nov. 29, 1990, P.L. 101-647, 11 U.S. Code §§ 101, 365, 507, 522, 523; 18 U.S. Code §§ 20, 212, 213, 215, 225, 648, 655 to 657, 981, 982, 1001 nt., 1004 to 1007, 1014, 1030, 1032, 1341, 1343 to 1345, 1517, 1657, 1818 nt., 1906, 1956, 2113, 2516, 3289, 3293, 3293 nt., 3663; 28 U.S. Code §§ 509 nt., 522 nt., 604, 994 nt.

Comprehensive Youth Services Act

Cal. Welfare and Institutions Code § 18220 et seq.

Comprehensive Zoning Law (Village of Greenwood Lake)

N.Y. Local Laws 1964, Village of Greenwood Lake, p. 912

Compressed Air Law

N.J. Stat. Ann., Superseded Vols., 34:3-1 to 34:3-23

Compressed Fuel Tax Act

Neb. Rev. Stat. 1943, 66-697 et seq.

Compromise Act (Misdemeanors)

Ariz. Rev. Stat. Ann., § 13-3981

Compromise and Arbitration of Death Taxes

S.C. Code Ann. 1976, § 12-16-20 et seq.

Compromise and Arbitration of Death Taxes Act (Interstate)

Cal. Revenue and Taxation Code § 13801 et seq.

Conn. Gen. Stat. Ann., § 12-371 et seq.

Neb. Rev. Stat. 1943, 77-3315 et seq.

Va. Code 1950, 58.1-920 et seq.

Vt. Stat. Ann., Title 32, § 7201 et seq.

W. Va. Code 1966, § 11-11A-1 et seq.

Compromise of Death Taxes Act (Interstate)

See Uniform Interstate Compromise of Death Taxes Act

Compromise of 1820 (Missouri)

March 6, 1820, Ch. 22, 3 Stat. 545

Continued

March 2, 1821, No. 1, 3 Stat. 645

Compromise of 1850 (California)
Sept. 9, 1850, Ch. 50, 9 Stat. 452

Compromise of 1850 (Fugitives from Justice)
Sept. 18, 1850, Ch. 55, 9 Stat. 462

Compromise of 1850 (Slave Trade in District of Columbia)
Sept. 20, 1850, Ch. 63, 9 Stat. 467

Compromise of 1850 (Texas and New Mexico)
Sept. 9, 1850, Ch. 49, 9 Stat. 446

Compromise of 1850 (Utah)
Sept. 9, 1850, Ch. 51, 9 Stat. 453

Comptroller Act (Greenville County)
S.C. Acts 1930, p. 1244, No. 729

Comptroller Act (State)
Ill. Rev. Stat. 1991, Ch. 15, § 201 et seq.

Comptroller General Annuity Adjustment Act of 1978
Oct. 25, 1978, P.L. 95-512, 31 U.S. Code §§ 1 nt., 43, 43b, 43c

Comptrollers Merit Employment Code
Ill. Comp. Stat. 1992, Ch. 30, § 725/1 et seq.

Comptrollers Records Act
Ill. Comp. Stat. 1992, Ch. 15, § 415/0.01 et seq.

Compulsion of Evidence Act
Also known as the Immunity Statute
N.Y. Criminal Procedure Law (Consol. Laws Ch. 11A) § 50.10 et seq.

Compulsive Gaming Prevention Act
Mich. Comp. Laws Ann., 432.251 to 432.256

Compulsory Arbitration Act
Mich. Comp. Laws Ann., 423.231 et seq.
Pa. Cons. Stat., Title 42, §§ 7361, 7362

Compulsory Arbitration Act (Public Utilities)
Mo. Rev. Stat., 295.010 et seq.
Wis. Stat. 1989, 111.50 et seq.

Compulsory Assignment Risk Law
Cal. Insurance Code § 11620 et seq.

Compulsory Attendance Act
Conn. Gen. Stat. Ann., § 10-184 et seq.
Mont. Code Ann., 20-5-101 et seq.
N.Y. Education Law 1947 (Consol. Laws Ch. 16) § 3202

Compulsory Automobile Insurance Act
N.H. Rev. Stat. 1955, 264:1 et seq.
N.Y. Vehicle and Traffic Law 1959 (Consol. Laws Ch. 71) § 310 et seq.

Compulsory Commitment Act (Criminal Insane)
Ga. Code Ann., 17-7-131
Mich. Comp. Laws 1948, 766.15c

Compulsory Commitment Act (Insane Persons)
Colo. Rev. Stat., 27-10-101 et seq.

Compulsory Counterclaim Act
Ark. Rules of Civil Procedure 1979, Rule 13
Ark. Stat. 1947, 27-1121
Mo. Rev. Stat., 509.420 et seq.

Compulsory Dividend Act
N.M. Stat. Ann. 1953, 51-3-16

Compulsory Education Act
Alaska Stat. 1962, § 14.30.010 et seq.
D.C. Code Ann., § 31-401 et seq.
Ill. Rev. Stat. 1943, Ch. 122, § 298 et seq.
Neb. Rev. Stat. 1943, 79-201 et seq.
N.J. Stat. Ann., 18A:38-25
Ore. Rev. Stat., 339.005 et seq.
S.D. Codified Laws 1967, 13-27-1 et seq.
Tex. Education Code, § 21.032 et seq.

Compulsory Eugenic Sterilization Act
Neb. Rev. Stat. 1943, Superseded Vol., 83-501 et seq.

Compulsory Financial Responsibility Act (Motor Vehicles)
Cal. Vehicle Code 1959, § 16000 et seq.

Compulsory Housing Integration Act
N.J. Stat. Ann., 10:5-1 et seq.

Compulsory Immunization Act
La. Rev. Stat. Ann., 17:170

Compulsory Insurance Act
N.J. Stat. Ann., 34:15-70 et seq.

Compulsory Insurance Act (Motor Vehicles)
Conn. Gen. Stat. Ann., § 14-112 et seq.
Mass. Gen. Laws Ann., 90:34A et seq., 175:113A et seq.
N.C. Gen. Stat. 1943, § 20-309 et seq.
N.Y. Vehicle and Traffic Law (Consol. Laws Ch. 71) § 310 et seq.

Compulsory Joinder Act
Mo. Rev. Stat., 507.030

Compulsory Liability Insurance Act
Haw. Rev. Stat. Ann., § 287-1 et seq.

Compulsory Liability Security Act
Mass. Gen. Laws Ann., 90:34A et seq.

Compulsory Meat Inspection Act
N.C. Gen. Stat. 1943, § 106-549.15 et seq.
Ore. Rev. Stat., 619.010 et seq.

Compulsory Motor Vehicle Inspection Act
N.Y. Vehicle and Traffic Law 1959 (Consol. Laws Ch. 71) § 301 et seq.

Compulsory No-Fault Motor Vehicle Insurance Act
D.C. Code Ann., § 35-2101 et seq.

Compulsory Pilotage Act
N.C. Gen. Stat. 1943, §§ 76-13, 76-33, 76-69
Tex. Transportation Code, § 61.001 et seq.

Compulsory Pleading Law
Ark. Rules of Civil Procedure 1979, Rule 8
Ark. Stat. 1947, 27-1121

Compulsory Pooling Act (Oil and Gas)
Ala. Code 1975, § 9-17-1 et seq.
Miss. Code Ann., § 53-3-7
Tex. Natural Resources Code, § 102.001 et seq.
Wyo. Stat. Ann., § 30-5-109

Compulsory Poultry Inspection Act
N.C. Gen. Stat. 1943, § 106-549.49 et seq.

Compulsory Presidential Primaries Act
P.R. Laws Ann. 1954, Title 16, § 1321 et seq.

Compulsory Primary Act
Ark. Stat. 1947, 3-201.1 et seq.

Compulsory Reporting of Automobile Accident Law
N.D. Cent. Code 39-08-04 et seq.

Compulsory Retirement Age Act
W. Va. Acts 1965, Ch. 131

Compulsory Retirement for Judges Act
Ill. Comp. Stat. 1992, Ch. 705, §§ 55/0.01, 55/1

Compulsory School Age Act
Ohio Rev. Code 1953, 3321.01

Compulsory School Attendance Act
Ala. Code 1975, § 16-28-1 et seq.
Ariz. Rev. Stat. Ann., § 15-802
Ark. Stat. 1947, 80-1502
Cal. Education Code 1976, § 4820 et seq.
Colo. Rev. Stat., 22-33-104
Conn. Gen. Stat. Ann., § 10-184 et seq.
D.C. Code Ann., § 31-401 et seq.
Fla. Stat. Ann., 232.01 et seq.
Ga. Code Ann., 20-2-690 et seq.
Haw. Rev. Stat. Ann., § 298-9
Ida. Code 1947, 33-201 et seq.
Ill. Rev. Stat. 1991, Ch. 122, § 26-1 et seq.
Ind. Code Ann., 20-8.1-3-1 et seq.
Iowa Code Ann., 299.1 et seq.
Kan. Stat. Ann., 72-1111
Ky. Rev. Stat. 1971, 159.010 et seq.
La. Rev. Stat. Ann., 17:221 et seq.
Mass. Gen. Laws Ann., 76:1 et seq.
Continued

Md. Ann. Code 1974, Art. ED, § 7-301 et seq.

Me. Rev. Stat. Ann., Title 20-A, § 5001 et seq.

Mich. Comp. Laws Ann., 340.731 et seq.

Minn. Stat. 1957, 120.10

Miss. Code Ann., § 37-13-91

Mo. Rev. Stat., 167.031 et seq.

N.C. Gen. Stat. 1943, § 115C-378 et seq.

N.D. Cent. Code, 15-34.1-01 et seq.

Neb. Rev. Stat. 1943, 79-201 et seq.

N.H. Rev. Stat. 1955, 193:1 et seq.

N.J. Stat. Ann., 18A:38-25 et seq.

N.M. Stat. Ann., 22-12-1 et seq.

N.Y. Education Law 1947 (Consol. Laws Ch. 16) § 3204 et seq.

Ohio Rev. Code 1953, 3321.01 et seq.

Okla. Const. 1907, Art. 13, § 4

Ore. Rev. Stat., 339.010 et seq.

Pa. Purdon's Stat., Title 24, § 13-1301 et seq.

R.I. Gen. Laws 1956, 16-19-1 et seq.

S.C. Code Ann. 1976, § 59-65-10 et seq.

S.D. Codified Laws 1967, 13-27-1 et seq.

Tenn. Code Ann., 49-6-3001 et seq.

Tex. Education Code, § 21.032 et seq.

Va. Code 1950, § 22.1-254 et seq.

Vt. Stat. Ann., Title 16, § 1121 et seq.

Wash. Rev. Code Ann., 28A.27.010 et seq.

Wis. Stat. 1989, 118.15

W. Va. Code 1966, § 18-8-1 et seq.

Compulsory School Law
Miss. Code 1942, § 6509 et seq.

Compulsory School Law (Blind and Deaf)
Ark. Stat. 1947, 80-2401 et seq.
Ark. Stat. 1987, 6-43-105 et seq.

Compulsory Sterilization Act
Cal. Welfare and Institutions Code § 6624

Compulsory Testimony Act (Interstate Commerce)
See Immunity Acts (Trusts and Interstate Commerce)

Compulsory Tuberculosis Control Act
Ky. Rev. Stat. 1962, 214.330 et seq.

Compulsory Unitization Act (Oil and Gas)
Ala. Code 1975, § 9-17-80 et seq.
Alaska Stat. 1962, § 31.05.110 et seq.
Ariz. Rev. Stat. Ann., § 27-531 et seq.
Ark. Code Ann. 1987, 15-72-301 et seq., 15-72-323
Cal. Public Resources Code, § 3315 et seq.
Colo. Rev. Stat., 34-60-118
Fla. Stat. Ann., 377.25
Ga. Code Ann., 12-4-40 et seq.
Kan. Stat. Ann., 55-1301 et seq.
La. Rev. Stat. Ann., 30:9 et seq.
Mich. Comp. Laws Ann., 319.351 et seq.
Miss. Code Ann., § 53-3-7
Neb. Rev. Stat. 1943, 57-910 et seq.
Nev. Rev. Stat. 1957 ed., 97.010 et seq.
N.Y. Environmental Conservation Law 1972, (Consol. Laws Ch. 43B) § 23-0901
Ohio Rev. Code 1953, 1509.27, 1509.28
Okla. Stat. Ann., Title 52, § 287.1 et seq.
Ore. Rev. Stat., 520.260
S.D. Codified Laws 1967, 45-9-20 et seq.

Compulsory Vaccination Act
Mass. Gen. Laws Ann., 111:181 et seq.
Pa. 1895 Pamph. Laws 203, No. 124, § 12

Compulsory Voting Machine Act
N.M. Stat. Ann. 1953, 3-9-1 et seq.

Compulsory Witness Act (Reciprocal Provisions)
S.D. Codified Laws 1967, 23-40-1 et seq.

Compulsory Work Act
Md. Ann. Code 1957, Art. 89, § 3

Computer Abuse Amendments Act of 1994
Sept. 13, 1994, P.L. 103-322, 18 U.S. Code §§ 1001 nt., 1030

Computer Chip Copyright Law
See Semi Conductor Chip Protection Act of 1984

Computer Crime and Abuse Act
W. Va. Code 1966, § 61-3C-1 et seq.

Computer Crime Prevention Act

Ill. Comp. Stat. 1992, Ch. 720, § 5/16D-1 et seq.

Computer Crimes Act

Ala. Code 1975, § 13A-8.100

Fla. Stat. Ann., 815.01 et seq.

Ga. Code Ann., 16-9-90 et seq.

Minn. Stat. Ann., 609.87 et seq.

Miss. Code Ann., § 97-45-1 et seq.

Neb. Rev. Stat. 1943, 28-1341 et seq.

N.M. Stat. Ann., 30-45-1 et seq.

Okla. Stat. Ann., Title 21, § 1951 et seq.

S.C. Code Ann. 1976, § 16-16-10 et seq.

Tenn. Code Ann., 39-3-1401 et seq.

Utah Code Ann. 1953, 76-6-701 et seq.

Va. Code 1950, § 18.2-152.1 et seq.

Computer Data Access and Fraud Act (Comprehensive)

Cal. Penal Code § 502

Computer Fraud Act

N.Y. Local Laws 1972, Town of Oyster Bay, p. 2489

Computer Fund and Abuse Act of 1986

Oct. 16, 1986, P.L. 99-474, 18 U.S. Code § 1001 nt.

Computer Maintenance Competition Assurance Act

Oct. 28, 1998, P.L. 105-304, Title III, 112 Stat. 2886, 17 U.S. Code § 101 nt.

Computer Matching and Privacy Protection Act Amendments of 1989

July 19, 1989, P.L. 101-56, 5 U.S. Code § 552a nt.

Computer Matching and Privacy Protection Act of 1988

July 19, 1989, P.L. 101-56, 5 U.S. Code § 552a nt.

Computer Matching and Privacy Protection Act of 1990

Nov. 5, 1990, P.L. 101-508 5 U.S. Code §§ 552a, 552a nt.

Computer Pornography and Child Exploitation Prevention Act

Fla. Stat. Ann., 847.0135

Ga. Code Ann., 16-12-100.2

Computer Recycling for Education and Technological Enhancement Act

N.Y. Education Law 1947 (Consol. Laws Ch. 16) § 318

N.Y. State Finance Law 1940 (Consol. Laws Ch. 56) §§ 167, 168

Computer Resource Center Law

Pa. Purdon's Stat., Title 24, § 6001 et seq.

Computer Security Act of 1987

Jan. 8, 1988, P.L. 100-235, 15 U.S. Code §§ 271 nt., 272, 278g-3, 278g-4, 278h; 40 U.S. Code § 759, 759 nt.

Feb. 10, 1996, P.L. 104-106, 40 U.S. Code § 759 nt.

Nov. 18, 1997, P.L. 105-85, 40 U.S. Code § 1441 nt.

Computer Software Rental Amendments Act of 1990

Dec. 1, 1990, P.L. 101-650, 17 U.S. Code §§ 101 nt., 109, 109 nt. , 205 nt.

Dec. 8, 1994, P.L. 103-465, 17 U.S. Code § 109 nt.

Computer Systems Protection Act

Ga. Code Ann., 16-9-90 et seq.

Computerization Act (Statute)

Ill. Rev. Stat. 1991, Ch. 63, § 150 et seq.

Comstock Act

March 3, 1873, Ch. 158, 17 Stat. 599 (See 18 U.S. Code § 1461)

Comstock Act (Obscenity)

N.Y. Penal Law 1965, (Consol. Laws Ch. 40), § 235.00 et seq.

Comstock Historic District Act

Nev. Rev. Stat. 1979 Reprint, 384.010 et seq.

Concealed Handguns Licensing Act

Tex. Government Code, § 411.171 et seq.

Concealed Weapon Act
Utah Code Ann. 1953, 53-5-701 et seq.

Concealed Weapons Act
Cal. Penal Code § 12000 et seq.
D.C. Code Ann., §§ 22-3204, 22-3205
Ill. Rev. Stat. 1985, Ch. 38, § 24-1
Iowa Code Ann., 724.4, 724.5
Kan. Stat. Ann., 21-4201
Md. Ann. Code 1957, Art. 27, § 36
Mich. Comp. Laws Ann., 750.227
Mont. Code Ann., 45-8-315 et seq.
N.C. Gen. Stat. 1943, § 14-269
N.D. Cent. Code, 62-03-01 et seq.
N.H. Rev. Stat. 1955, 159:4 et seq.
N.J. Stat. Ann. 1937, 2A:63-1 et seq.
Ohio Rev. Code 1953, 2923.12
R.I. Gen. Laws 1956, 11-47-35 et seq.

Concealment of Evidence Act
Alaska Stat. 1962, § 11.56.610 et seq.

Concealment of Treason Act
Ga. Code 1933, 26-804

Concentration Act
Feb. 17, 1922, Ch. 55, 42 Stat. 375

Conception and Venereal Disease Prevention Device Act
Ore. Rev. Stat. 1983, 435.010 et seq.

Concession Regulation Act (Public Facilities)
Pa. Purdon's Stat., Title 69, § 2501 et seq.

Conciliation Act
Mont. Code Ann., 40-3-101 et seq.
N.D. Laws 1921, Ch. 38

Conciliation Act (Labor Disputes)
Mass. Gen. Laws Ann., 150:1 et seq.
Ore. Rev. Stat., 662.405 et seq.

Conciliation and Arbitration Act
Ill. Rev. Stat. 1991, Ch. 10, § 18.9 et seq.

Conciliation, Arbitration and Mediation Act
Haw. Rev. Stat. Ann., § 658D-1

Conciliation, Arbitration and Mediation Act (International)
Haw. Rev. Stat. Ann., § 658D-1 et seq.

Conciliation Court Act (Duluth)
Minn. Laws 1927, Ch. 17

Conciliation Court Law
Neb. Rev. Stat. 1943, 42-802 et seq.

Conciliation Court Law (Family)
Cal. Code of Civil Procedure § 1730 et seq.
Cal. Family Code § 1800 et seq.

Conciliation Department Act
Okla. Stat. 1961, Title 20, § 91.1 et seq.

Concilliation of Industrial Disputes Act
S.C. Code Ann. 1976, § 41-17-10 et seq.

Concubinage Act
Ark. Stat. 1947, Superseded Vol., 41-806 et seq.

Concursus Act
La. Code of Civil Procedure Art. 4651 et seq.

Condemnation Act
Iowa Code Ann., 6A.1 et seq.

Condemnation Act (Corporation)
Mo. Rev. Stat., 523.010 et seq.

Condemnation Act (Eminent Domain)
Ind. Code Ann., 32-11-1-1 et seq.

Condemnation Act (Federal)
Va. Code 1950, § 25-56 et seq.

Condemnation Act (General)
Ala. Code 1975, § 18-1-1 et seq.
Ariz. Rev. Stat. Ann., § 12-1111 et seq.
Cal. Code of Civil Procedure, §§ 1230.010 et seq., 1237
Colo. Rev. Stat., 38-1-101 et seq.
Conn. Gen. Stat. 1983, § 48-1 et seq.
D.C. Code Ann., § 16-1301 et seq.
Del. Code of 1974, Title 10, § 6101 et seq.
Fla. Stat. 1983, 73.012 et seq.
Ga. Code Ann., 22-1-1 et seq.

Ida. Code 1947, 7-701 et seq.

Ill. Rev. Stat. 1991, Ch. 110, § 7-101 et seq.

Ind. Code Ann., 32-11-1-1 et seq.

Iowa Code Ann., 471.1 et seq.

Kan. Stat. Ann., 26-101 et seq.

Ky. Rev. Stat. 1971, 416.010 et seq.

La. Civil Code, Art. 2626 et seq.

Mass. Gen. Laws Ann., 79:1 et seq.

Md. Ann. Code 1974, Art. RP, § 12-101 et seq.

Mich. Comp. Laws Ann., 213.21 et seq.

N.C. Gen. Stat. 1943, § 40A-1 et seq.

N.D. Cent. Code 32-15-01 et seq.

Nev. Rev. Stat. 1979 Reprint, 37.009 et seq.

N.J. Stat. Ann., 20:3-1 et seq.

N.Y. Consol. Laws, Ch. 73

Ohio Rev. Code 1953, 163.01 et seq.

Okla. Stat. Ann., Title 27

Ore. Rev. Stat., 281.010 et seq.

Pa. Purdon's Stat., Title 26, § 1-101 et seq.

P.R. Laws Ann. 1954, Title 32, § 2901 et seq.

S.C. Code Ann. 1976, § 5-31-410 et seq.

S.D. Codified Laws 1967, 21-35-1 et seq.

Tex. Property Code, § 21.011 et seq.

Utah Code Ann. 1953, 78-34-1 et seq.

Va. Code 1950, § 25-46.1 et seq.

Wis. Stat. 1989, 32.01 et seq.

W. Va. Code 1966, § 54-1-1 et seq.

Wyo. Stat. Ann., § 1-26-101 et seq.

Condemnation Act (Government)
Ga. Code Ann., 22-2-130 et seq.

Condemnation Act (Highways)
Me. Rev. Stat. Ann. 1964, Title 23, § 3021
Mich. Comp. Laws Ann., 213.171 et seq.
Mo. Rev. Stat. 1964, Title 23, § 3021 et seq.
Va. Code 1950, § 33.1-89 et seq.
Vt. Stat. Ann., Title 19, § 221 et seq.

Condemnation Act (Inverse)
N.M. Stat. Ann., 42-1-23

Condemnation Act (Lands for Public Uses)
Aug. 1, 1888, Ch. 728, 25 Stat. 357, 40 U.S. Code § 257

Condemnation Act (Municipalities)
Tenn. Code Ann., 7-31-107 et seq.

Condemnation Act (Natural Gas)
Ark. Code Ann. 1987, 15-72-601 et seq.

Condemnation Act (Power Companies)
Mich. Comp. Laws Ann., 486.252a et seq.

Condemnation Act (Public Parks)
Va. Code 1950, § 33.1-89 et seq.

Condemnation Act (Railroads)
Md. Ann. Code 1957, Art. 23, § 193 et seq.
Mich. Comp. Laws Ann., 464.15 et seq.

Condemnation Act (School Land)
Me. Rev. Stat. Ann. 1964, Title 20-A, § 16101 et seq.

Condemnation Act (State Agencies)
Mich. Comp. Laws Ann., 213.21 et seq.
Tenn. Code Ann., 29-16-101 et seq.

Condemnation and Acquisitions of Land Act
S.C. Code Ann. 1976, § 5-31-410 et seq.

Condemnation-Eminent Domain Proceedings before a Special Master Act
Ga. Code Ann., 22-2-107

Condemnation Procedure Act
Iowa Code Ann., 6B.1 et seq.
Iowa Code Ann., 472.1 et seq.
Mich. Comp. Laws Ann., 213.51 et seq.
Ore. Rev. Stat., 35.205 et seq.

Condemnation Procedures Act (Eminent Domain)
Mich. Comp. Laws Ann., 213.51 et seq.

Condemned Cannon Act
May 22, 1896, Ch. 230, 29 Stat. 133

Condit-Mello-McClintock Tax Rebate Act
Cal. Revenue and Taxation Code § 17070 et seq.

Condit-Nolan Public Participation in Parole Act
Cal. Penal Code § 3043.5

Conditional Release Program Act
Fla. Stat. 1983, 947.1405 et seq.

Conditional Sales Act
Alaska Comp. Laws Ann. 1949, § 29-2-1 et seq.
Cal. Civil Code, §§ 2980.5 et seq., 2980
Del. Code of 1953, Title 6, § 901 et seq.
Ga. Code 1933, 67-1401 et seq.
Haw. Rev. Laws 1955, § 201-1 et seq.
Ida. Code 1947, 64-801 et seq.
Ind. Burns' 1961 Repl., 58-801 et seq.
Kan. Stat. Ann., 1949, 58-314 et seq.
Md. Ann. Code 1957, Superseded Vol., Art. 21, § 66
Me. Rev. Stat. Ann. 1964, Title 11, § 9-101 et seq.
Minn. Stat. Ann., 336.9-101 et seq.
Mont. Rev. Code 1947, 74-201 et seq.
Neb. Rev. Stat. 1943, Superseded Vol., 69-301 et seq., UCC 9-101 et seq.
N.H. Rev. Stat. 1955, Superseded Vols., 361:1 et seq.
N.J. Stat. Ann., 12A:9-101
N.Y. Uniform Commercial Code (Consol. Laws, Ch. 38) § 9-101 et seq.
Ohio Rev. Code 1953, 1319.11 et seq.
Pa. 1925 Pamph. Laws 603, No. 325
P.R. Laws Ann. 1954, Title 10, § 31 et seq.
S.D. Code 1939, 54.0201 et seq.
Tenn. Code Ann., Superseded Vol., 47-1301 et seq.
Utah Code Ann. 1953, Miscellaneous Superseded Code Provisions, 15-1-2a
Va. Code 1950, § 55-88 et seq.
Vt. Acts 1870, No. 63, § 1
Vt. Acts 1884, No. 93
Wash. Rev. Code 1951, 62A.9-101 et seq.
Wis. Stat. 1963, 122.01 et seq.
W. Va. Code 1966, § 46-2-101 et seq.
Wyo. Stat. 1957, § 34-239 et seq.

Conditional Sales Act (Uniform)
Ariz. Laws 1919, Ch. 40

Conditional Sales Filing Act
Wash. Rev. Code 1951, 62A.9-110 et seq.

Conditional Sales of Vehicles Act
Nev. Rev. Stat. 1979 Reprint, 108.270

Conditional Sales Protection Act
Ill. Comp. Stat. 1992, Ch. 720, §§ 240/0.01, 240/1

Conditional Sales Recording Act
Md. Ann. Code 1974, Art. CL, § 9-301 et seq.
Me. Rev. Stat. Ann. 1964, Title 11, § 9-401
Okla. Stat. 1961, Title 60, § 318

Conditioned Air Contractors Act
Ga. Official Code Ann., 43-14-1 et seq.

Conditioner and Plant Growth Substance Act
Pa. Purdon's Stat., Title 3, § 68.1 et seq.

Condominium Act
See also Uniform Condominium Act
Alaska Stat. 1962, § 34.07.010 et seq.
Ariz. Rev. Stat. Ann., § 33-1201 et seq.
Ark. Code Ann. 1987, 18-13-101 et seq.
Cal. Civil Code § 1350 et seq.
Conn. Gen. Stat. Ann., § 47-68a et seq.
D.C. Code Ann., §§ 45-1701 et seq., 45-1801 et seq.
Fla. Stat. Ann., 718.101 et seq.
Ga. Code Ann., 44-3-70 et seq.
Haw. Rev. Stat. Ann., § 514A-1 et seq.
Ida. Code 1947, 55-1501 et seq.
Ill. Rev. Stat. 1991, Ch. 30, § 301 et seq.
Ind. Code Ann., 32-1-6-1 et seq.
Iowa Code Ann., 499.1 et seq., 499B.1 et seq.
Ky. Rev. Stat. 1971, 381.805 et seq., 381.810 et seq.
La. Rev. Stat. Ann., 9:1121.101 et seq.
Mass. Gen. Laws Ann., 183A:1 et seq.
Md. Ann. Code 1974, Art. RP, § 11-101 et seq.
Me. Rev. Stat. Ann. 1964, Title 33, § 1601-101 et seq.
Mich. Comp. Laws Ann., 559.1 et seq., 559.101 et seq.

Minn. Stat. Ann., 515.01 et seq., 515A.1-101 et seq.

Miss. Code Ann., § 89-9-1 et seq.

Mo. Rev. Stat., 448.1-101 et seq.

Mont. Code Ann., 70-23-101 et seq.

N.C. Gen. Stat. 1943, § 47C-1-101 et seq.

N.D. Cent. Code 47-04.1-01 et seq.

Neb. Rev. Stat. 1943, 76-825 et seq.

N.H. Rev. Stat. 1955, 356-B:1 et seq.

N.J. Stat. Ann., 46:8A-1 et seq.

N.M. Stat. Ann., 47-7A-1 et seq.

N.Y. Real Property Law (Consol. Laws Ch. 50) § 339d et seq.

Ohio Rev. Code 1953, 5311.01 et seq.

Okla. Stat. Ann., Title 60, § 501 et seq.

Ore. Rev. Stat., 100.005 et seq.

Pa. Cons. Stat., Title 68, § 3101 et seq.

P.R. Laws Ann. 1954, Title 31, § 1291 et seq.

R.I. Gen. Laws 1956, 34-36.1-1.01 et seq.

S.C. Code Ann. 1976, § 27-31-10 et seq.

S.D. Codified Laws 1967, 43-15-1 et seq.

Tenn. Code Ann., 66-27-101 et seq.

Utah Code Ann. 1953, 57-8-1 et seq.

Va. Code 1950, §§ 55-79.1 et seq., 55-79.39 et seq.

Wash. Rev. Code Ann., 64.32.010 et seq.

Wis. Stat. 1989, 703.01 et seq.

W. Va. Code 1966, § 36B-1-101 et seq.

Wyo. Stat. Ann., § 34-20-101 et seq.

Condominium Act (Barbour County)
Ala. Acts 1973, p. 1787

Condominium Act Amendment
D.C. Code Ann., § 45-1802 et seq.

Condominium and Common Interest Community Risk Pooling Trust Act
Ill. Comp. Stat. 1992, Ch. 765, § 605/12.1

Condominium and Cooperative Abuse Relief Act of 1980
Oct. 8, 1980, P.L. 96-399, 15 U.S. Code § 3601 nt.

Condominium Ownership Act
Ala. Code 1975, § 35-8-1 et seq.
Colo. Rev. Stat., 38-33-101 et seq.
R.I. Gen. Laws 1956, 34-36-1 et seq.

Vt. Stat. Ann., Title 27, § 1301 et seq.

Wis. Stat. 1989, 703.01 et seq.

Wyo. Stat. Ann., § 34-20-101 et seq.

Condominium Property Act
Haw. Rev. Stat. Ann., §§ 196D-1 et seq., 514A-1 et seq.
Ill. Comp. Stat. 1992, Ch. 765, § 605/1 et seq.
Mo. Rev. Stat., 448.005 et seq.
Neb. Rev. Stat. 1943, 76-801 et seq.

Condon Act (Public Works Contracts)
N.Y. Public Works Law (Consol. Laws Ch. 75) § 14

Condon-Wadlin Act (Strikes by Public Employees)
N.Y. Civil Service Law 1967 (Consol. Laws Ch. 7) § 210

Conduit Act (Income Tax)
Ore. Rev. Stat. 1953, 316.815, Subd. 3

Confectionery Act
Wash. Rev. Code Ann., 69.20.005 et seq.

Confederate Pension Act
Ala. Code 1975, § 31-8-1 et seq.
Ark. Stat. 1947, 11-1349
Ky. Rev. Stat. 1971, 206.010 et seq.
Okla. Stat. 1961, Title 72, § 131 et seq.

Confederate Pension Note Act
Ark. Pope's Digest 1937, §§ 10670 to 10672

Confederated Tribes of the Colville Reservation Grand Coulee Dam Settlement Act
Nov. 2, 1994, P.L. 103-436, 108 Stat. 4577

Confederating and Banding Act
Ky. Rev. Stat. 1971, 506.040 et seq.

Conference and Activities Leave Act (School and Day Care)
La. Rev. Stat. Ann., 23:1015 et seq.

Conference Center Commission Act (Hotel Roanoke)
Va. Acts 1991, Ch. 440

Conference of State Legislatures Act
Ill. Rev. Stat. 1991, Ch. 63, §§ 122.9, 123

Confessions Act
Tex. Code of Criminal Procedure, Arts.
38.21, 38.22
Wash. Rev. Code Ann., 10.58.030

Confidence Game Act
Ill. Rev. Stat. 1991, Ch. 38, §§ 256, 257
Mo. Rev. Stat. 1969, 561.450
Mont. Code Ann. 1985, 23-5-106
Okla. Stat. Ann., Title 21, § 1541.1 et seq.

Confidential Adoption Act
Me. Rev. Stat. Ann. 1964, Title 19, § 534
Miss. Code Ann., § 93-17-201 et seq.

Confidential Communications Act
Wyo. Stat. Ann., § 1-12-101

Confidential Communications for Sexual Assault Act
Utah Code Ann. 1953, 78-3C-1 et seq.

Confidential Materials Act
N.M. Stat. Ann., 14-3A-1, 14-3A-2

Confidential Report Act
Iowa Code Ann., 321.266 et seq.

Confidential Research Information Act
Mich. Comp. Laws Ann., 390.1551 et seq.

Confidentiality Act (Data Processing)
Ill. Rev. Stat. 1991, Ch. 127, § 2900 et seq.

Confidentiality Act (Media)
Mont. Code Ann., 26-1-901 et seq.

Confidentiality and Disclosure of Records on Abused and Neglected Children Act
D.C. Code Ann., §§ 6-2126, 6-2127

Confidentiality of Health Care Information Act
R.I. Gen. Laws 1956, 5-37.3-1 et seq.

Confidentiality of HIV-Related Information Act
Pa. Purdon's Stat., Title 35, § 7601 et seq.

Confidentiality of Medical Information Act
Cal. Civil Code § 56 et seq.

Confined Voter Law
Neb. Rev. Stat. 1943, 32-1241

Confinement Act (Insanity Plea)
Wis. Stat. 1967, 957.13

Confinement Facilities Health Act
Ky. Rev. Stat. 1971, 211.920 et seq.

Confirmation Act (Drainage and Irrigation Districts)
Cal. Statutes 1889, Ch. 178, p. 212
Ore. Rev. Stat., 548.105 et seq.

Confirmation Act (Tax Titles)
Ark. Code Ann. 1987, 18-60-601 et seq.

Confirmation Act of 1852
Tex. General Laws 4th Leg., 1851-52, p. 63, Ch. 71

Confirmatory Act (Tennessee Boundary)
N.C. Laws 1821, Ch. 41

Confiscation Acts (Civil War)
Aug. 6, 1861, Ch. 60, 12 Stat. 319
July 17, 1862, Ch. 195, 12 Stat. 589

Confiscation and Seizure Act (Liquor)
Tenn. Code Ann., 57-9-201 et seq.

Conflict of Interest Act
N.M. Stat. Ann., 10-16-1 et seq.

Conflict of Interest Act (Judges)
N.H. Rev. Stat. 1955, 492:1 et seq.

Conflict of Interest Act (Justice of Peace)
N.M. Stat. Ann. 1953, 36-20-2

Conflict of Interest Disclosure Act (Physicians')
Tenn. Code Ann., 63-6-501 et seq.

Conflict of Interest Law
N.J. Stat. Ann., 52:13D-12 et seq.

Conflict of Interests and Disclosure Act (Governmental)
Cal. Government Code § 3601 et seq.

Conflict of Jurisdictions Model Law
Conn. Gen. Stat. Ann., § 50a-200 et seq.

Conflict of Laws Act
Ga. Code Ann., 1-3-9, 1-3-10

Conflict of Laws—Limitations Act
See also Uniform Conflict of Laws—Limitations Act
Colo. Rev. Stat., 13-82-101 et seq.
Mont. Laws 1991, Ch. 293, § 1 et seq.
Ore. Rev. Stat., 12.410 et seq.
Wash. Rev. Code Ann., 4.18.010 et seq.

Conflict Resolution and Peace Studies Act
N.J. Stat. Ann., 18A:3A-3 et seq.

Conflicts of Interest Act
Ariz. Rev. Stat. Ann., § 38-501 et seq.
Cal. Government Code § 3600 et seq.
Mass. Gen. Laws 1984, 268A:1 et seq.
Md. Ann. Code 1957, Art. 40A § 3-101 et seq.
N.J. Stat. Ann., 52:13D-12
N.M. Stat. Ann., 10-16-1 et seq.
Va. Code 1950, § 2.1-347 et seq.
Wash. Rev. Code Ann., 42.18.010 et seq.

Conflicts of Interest Act (Criminal)
Mass. Gen. Laws Ann., 268A:3, 268A:4, 268A:17

Conflicts of Interest and Disclosure Amendments Act
D.C. Code Ann., §§ 1-1461, 1-1462

Conformity Act
See Practice Conformity Act
Ill. Rev. Stat. 1991, Ch. 110, § 1108

Conformity Act (Judgments)
N.C. Gen. Stat. 1943, § 1-237

Conformity Act (Prohibition)
N.C. Gen. Stat. 1943, § 18B-100 et seq.

Conformity Income Tax Act
Kan. Stat. Ann., 79-32,109 et seq.

Congaree Swamp National Monument Expansion and Wilderness Act
Oct. 24, 1988, P.L. 100-524, 102 Stat. 2606

Congregate Adult Living Facilities Act
Fla. Stat. Ann., 400.401 et seq.

Congregate Housing Services Act
N.J. Stat. Ann., 52:27D-182 et seq.

Congregate Housing Services Act of 1978
Oct. 31, 1978, P.L. 95-557, 42 U.S. Code §§ 1437e, 8001 et seq.
Nov. 30, 1983, P.L. 98-181, 42 U.S. Code §§ 8007, 8010
Oct. 17, 1984, P.L. 98-479, 42 U.S. Code § 8010
Feb. 5, 1988, P.L. 100-242, 42 U.S. Code §§ 8007, 8010

Congregate Services Act
N.H. Rev. Stat. 1955, 161-F:34 et seq.

Congressional Accountability Act of 1995
Jan. 23, 1995, P.L. 104-1, 2 U.S. Code § 1301 nt.
Nov. 19, 1995, P.L. 104-53, 2 U.S. Code § 1371
Oct. 21, 1998, P.L. 105-275, 2 U.S. Code § 1436

Congressional Act
Tex. Rev. Civ. Stat., Art. 197a

Congressional Apportionment Act
Fla. Stat. Ann., 8.001 et seq.
Ill. Rev. Stat. 1991, Ch. 46, § 156f.2 et seq.
Mich. Comp. Laws Ann., 3.51
Tex. Rev. Civ. Stat., Art. 197g

Congressional Award Act
Nov. 16, 1979, P.L. 96-114, 2 U.S. Code §§ 801 et seq., 801 nt.

Continued

Nov. 25, 1985, P.L. 99-161, 2 U.S. Code
§§ 802, 803, 806, 807, 808

Nov. 17, 1988, P.L. 100-674, 2 U.S. Code
§§ 802, 803, 806, 808

Nov. 6, 1990, P.L. 101-525, 2 U.S. Code
§§ 802, 803, 806 to 808, 808 nt.

Oct. 23, 1992, P.L. 102-457, 2 U.S. Code
§§ 804, 808

Sept. 30, 1994, P.L. 103-329, 2 U.S. Code
§ 802

Sept. 30, 1996, P.L. 104-208, 2 U.S. Code
§§ 804, 808

Congressional Award Act Amendments Act of 1988

Nov. 17, 1988, P.L. 100-674, 2 U.S. Code
§ 801 nt.

Congressional Award Act Amendments of 1992

Oct. 23, 1992, P.L. 102-457, 2 U.S. Code
§ 801 nt.

Congressional Award Amendments of 1985

Nov. 25, 1985, P.L. 99-161, 2 U.S. Code
§§ 801 nt., 802, 803, 806 , 807, 808

Congressional Award Amendments of 1990

Nov. 6, 1990, P.L. 101-525, 2 U.S. Code
§ 801 nt.

Congressional Budget Act of 1974

July 12, 1974, P.L. 93-344, 1 U.S. Code
§ 105; 2 U.S. Code §§ 109a-1 nt., 190a-3,
190b, 190d, 601 to 603, 621 to 623, 631 to
642, 651 to 653, 661; 31 U.S. Code §§ 702,
717, 719, 731, 1102, 1104 to 1106, 1108 to
1110, 1112, 1113, 1512, 1552

Oct. 27, 1978, P.L. 95-523, 2 U.S. Code
§§ 632, 636

Dec. 23, 1981, P.L. 97-108, 2 U.S. Code
§ 653

Dec. 12, 1985, P.L. 99-177, 2 U.S. Code
§§ 602, 621 nt., 631 et seq., 651 to 656, 661

Sept. 29, 1987, P.L. 100-119, 2 U.S. Code
§§ 632, 635, 636, 642

April 28, 1988, P.L. 100-297, 20 U.S. Code
§§ 2701 et seq., 2701 nt.

Aug. 23, 1988, P.L. 100-418, 2 U.S. Code
§ 632

Nov. 5, 1990, P.L. 101-508, 2 U.S. Code
§§ 601, 621 nt., 622, 632 to 634, 636, 637,
639, 641 to 644, 651, 652, 665 nt., 665 to
665e

Aug. 10, 1993, P.L. 103-66, 2 U.S. Code
§§ 665, 665 nt.

Sept. 13, 1994, P.L. 103-322, 2 U.S. Code
§ 665a

Aug. 20, 1996, P.L. 104-186, 2 U.S. Code
§ 602

Aug. 22, 1996, P.L. 104-193, 2 U.S. Code
§ 665e

Aug. 5, 1997, P.L. 105-33, 2 U.S. Code
§§ 601, 602, 621 nt., 631 to 636, 639, 641 to
645, 645a, 651 to 656, 665 to 665e

Nov. 19, 1997, P.L. 105-89, 2 U.S. Code
§ 645

Congressional Budget and Impoundment Control Act of 1974

July 12, 1974, P.L. 93-344, 1 U.S. Code
§ 105; 2 U.S. Code §§ 190a-1, 190a-3,
190b, 190d, nt., 601 et seq.; 31 U.S. Code
§§ 702, 717, 719, 731, 1102, 1104 to 1106,
1108 to 1110, 1112, 1113, 1512, 1552

July 12, 1974, P.L. 93-344, 2 U.S. Code
§ 621 nt.

Sept. 20, 1977, P.L. 95-110, 31 U.S. Code
§ 1302

Dec. 12, 1985, P.L. 99-177, 2 U.S. Code
§ 622

Sept. 29, 1987, P.L. 100-119, 2 U.S. Code
§ 662

Nov. 5, 1990, P.L. 101-508, 2 U.S. Code
§§ 602, 621 nt., 622, 631 to 633, 635, 641,
642

March 22, 1995, P.L. 104-4, 2 U.S. Code
§§ 602, 632, 653, 658 et seq.

March 29, 1996, P.L. 104-121, 2 U.S. Code
§ 665e

April 9, 1996, P.L. 104-130, 2 U.S. Code
§§ 621 nt., prec. 691, 691, 691a to 691f

Aug. 5, 1997, P.L. 105-33, 2 U.S. Code
§§ 622, 691a, 691c, 691e

Congressional Campaign Reform Act

Minn. Stat. Ann., 10A.40 et seq.

Congressional Committees Witness Immunity Act
June 25, 1948, Ch. 645, 62 Stat. 833, 18 U.S. Code § 3486
Aug. 20, 1954, Ch. 769, 68 Stat. 745, 18 U.S. Code § 3486

Congressional District Act for the State of New Jersey (1982)
N.J. Stat. Ann. 19:46-4, 19:46-5

Congressional Districting Act
Cal. Elections Code 1976, § 30030
Conn. Gen. Stat. Ann., § 9-9
Ill. Rev. Stat. 1991, Ch. 46, § 156f.1 et seq.
N.H. Rev. Stat. 1955, 63:1 et seq.
N.J. Stat. Ann. 19:46-4, 19:46-5
N.Y. State Law (Consol. Laws Ch. 57) § 111
Tenn. Code Ann., 2-16-103

Congressional Merit Scholarships in Mathematics, Science, and Engineering Education
Aug. 11, 1984, P.L. 98-377, 20 U.S. Code §§ 3931 et seq., 3931 nt.

Congressional Operations Appropriation Act, 1978
Aug. 5, 1977, P.L. 95-94, 2 U.S. Code § 31a-1 et seq.

Congressional Operations Appropriation Act, 1984
July 13, 1983, P.L. 98-51, 2 U.S. Code §§ 59d, 60j-4, 65d, 68-3, 74a-5, 84-1, 88b-5, 136c, 142g, 276a, 276b, 288n, 333a; 5 U.S. Code §§ 5318 nt., 8332, 8332 nt.; 40 U.S. Code § 206a-9
Aug. 22, 1984, P.L. 98-396

Congressional Operations Appropriations Act, 1989
Oct. 1, 1988, P.L. 100-458, 102 Stat. 2176
Nov. 21, 1989, P.L. 101-163, 103 Stat. 1043
Aug. 20, 1996, P.L. 104-186, 2 U.S. Code §§ 74a-5, 333a

Congressional Operations Appropriations Act, 1990
Nov. 21, 1989, P.L. 101-163, 103 Stat. 1041

Congressional Operations Appropriations Act, 1991
Aug. 14, 1991, P.L. 102-90, 2 U.S. Code § 61g-6a

Congressional Operations Appropriations Act, 1992
Aug. 14, 1991, P.L. 102-90, 105 Stat. 461

Congressional Operations Appropriations Act, 1993
Oct. 6, 1992, P.L. 102-392, 106 Stat. 1716

Congressional Operations Appropriations Act, 1995
July 22, 1994, P.L. 103-283, 108 Stat. 1423

Congressional Operations Appropriations Act, 1996
Nov. 19, 1995, P.L. 104-53, Title I, 109 Stat. 514

Congressional Operations Appropriations Act, 1998
Oct. 7, 1997, P.L. 105-55, Title I, 111 Stat. 1177

Congressional Reapportionment Act
Ga. Code Ann., 21-2-4
Ind. Code Ann., 3-3-1.1-1 et seq.
Ky. Rev. Stat. 1971, Superseded Vols., 120.070
Miss. Code Ann., § 23-5-223
Okla. Stat. Ann., Title 14, § 5
Tex. Rev. Civ. Stat., Art. 197g

Congressional Redistricting Act
Miss. Code Ann., § 23-5-223
Mo. Rev. Stat., 128.204 et seq.
Okla. Stat. Ann., Title 14, § 5.1 et seq.
Va. Code 1950, § 24.1-4.3

Congressional Reports Elimination Act of 1986
Aug. 22, 1986, P.L. 99-386, 100 Stat. 821, 5 U.S. Code §§ 3104, 5114, 7701; 12 U.S. Code §§ 1701z-4, 1701z-5; 15 U.S. Code § 713a-10; 16 U.S. Code §§ 758e-2, 1821; 18 U.S. Code § 2101; 20 U.S. Code §§ 1017, 1119c-2, 1125, 1453; 26 U.S. Code § 6103; 33 U.S. Code § 1106; 42 U.S. Code §§ 1883, 5906, 8818, 9210; 50 U.S. Code Appx. § 1746

Congressional Representatives Act
Ala. Code 1958, Title 17, § 426(1) et seq.

Congressional Term Limitations Act
Me. Rev. Stat. Ann. 1964, Title 21-A, §§ 421 et seq., 641 et seq.

Conley-Kelly-Jackson Act (Zoning and Planning)
Ky. Rev. Stat. 1962, 100.850 et seq.

Conley-Swope Act (Atomic Energy)
Ky. Rev. Stat. 1962, 152.510 et seq.

Connally "Hot Oil" Act
See Hot Oil Act

Connally-Carillo Act
Tex. Education Code, § 56.001 et seq.

Connally-Smith Anti-Strike Act
See War Labor Disputes Act

Connected Title Statute
Wash. Rev. Code Ann., 7.28.050

Connecticut Coastal Protection Act of 1990
Oct. 19, 1990, P.L. 101-443, 16 U.S. Code § 668dd nt.

Connecticut-New York Railroad Passenger Transportation Compact Act
Conn. Gen. Stat. Ann., § 16-343
Mass. Acts 1991, Ch. 716
Vt. Stat. Ann., Title 10, § 4651 et seq.

Connecticut River Atlantic Salmon Compact
Mass. Acts 1991, Ch. 716
N.H. Rev. Stat. 1955, 487:1 et seq.

Vt. Stat. Ann., Title 10, § 4651 et seq.

Connecticut River Flood Control Compact Act
Conn. Gen. Stat. 1983, § 25-99
N.H. Rev. Stat. 1955, 484:1 et seq.
Vt. Stat. Ann., Title 10, § 1151 et seq.

Connecting Link Road Act
Fla. Stat. Ann., 335.04
Ind. Code Ann., 19-8-22-1 et seq.

Connelly-Areias-Chandler Rice Straw Burning Reduction Act
Cal. Health and Safety Code § 41865

Connor Act (Land Contracts Registration)
N.C. Gen. Stat. 1943, § 47-18

Conrail Privatization Act
Oct. 21, 1986, P.L. 99-509, 45 U.S. Code § 1301
Dec. 29, 1995, P.L. 104-88, 45 U.S. Code § 1344

Conscientious Employee Protection Act
N.J. Stat. Ann., 34:19-1 et seq.

Conscious Suffering Act
Mass. Gen. Laws Ann., 229:6 et seq.

Conscription Acts
See Selective Draft Acts

Consent Act (Actions Against State)
Cal. Government Code § 905.2

Consent Act (Adult Health Care)
S.C. Code Ann. 1976, § 44-66-10 et seq.

Consent Act (Contracts)
La. Civil Code, Art. 1819

Consent Act (Federal Acquisition of Land)
W. Va. Code 1966, § 1-1-3

Consent Act (Implied)
N.M. Stat. Ann., 66-8-105
N.Y. Vehicle and Traffic Law 1959 (Consol. Laws Ch. 71) § 1194
Ore. Rev. Stat. 1953, 801.010 et seq.

Vt. Stat. Ann., Title 23, § 1202 et seq.

Consent Act (Medical)
Ga. Code Ann., 31-9-1 et seq.

Consent by Minors to Medical Treatment Act
Ill. Comp. Stat. 1992, Ch. 410, § 210/0.01 et seq.

Consent Law (Medical)
Fla. Stat. Ann., 766.103

Consent to Medical Treatment Act
Tex. Health and Safety Code, § 313.001 et seq.

Consenting Adults Act
Cal. Education Code 1959, § 12912
Cal. Evidence Code §§ 972, 985
Cal. Penal Code §§ 220, 286, 286.5, 287, 288a, 290

Conservance Act
Ohio Rev. Code 1953, 6101.01 et seq.

Conservancy Act (Floods)
Colo. Rev. Stat., 37-1-101 et seq.

Conservancy Act (San Joaquin River)
Cal. Public Resources Code § 32500 et seq.

Conservancy Act (Water)
Colo. Rev. Stat., 37-45-101 et seq.
Ind. Code Ann., 19-3-2-1 et seq.
N.M. Stat. Ann., 73-14-1 et seq.
Okla. Stat. Ann., Title 82, § 531 et seq.

Conservancy District Act
Mont. Code Ann., 85-9-101 et seq.
S.D. Codified Laws 1967, 46A-17-1 et seq.

Conservancy District Act (River)
Ill. Rev. Stat. 1991, Ch. 42, § 383 et seq.

Conservancy District Act (Water)
Okla. Stat. Ann., Title 82, § 541 et seq.

Conservancy District-Reclamation Contract Act
N.M. Stat. Ann., 73-18-1 et seq.

Conservancy Water Act
Utah Code Ann. 1953, 17A-2-1402

Conservation Act
Ind. Code Ann., 14-2-1-1 et seq.
La. Rev. Stat. Ann., 30:1 et seq.
Me. Rev. Stat. Ann. 1964, Title 38, § 541 et seq.
N.Y. Consol. Laws, Ch. 65
Okla. Stat. Ann., Title 82, § 531 et seq.
Wis. Stat. 1989, 23.09

Conservation Act (Agriculture)
Pa. 1937 Pamph. Laws 2688, No. 541

Conservation Act (Bituminous Coal)
Pa. Purdon's Stat., Title 52, § 1396.1 et seq.

Conservation Act (Cave)
Mont. Code Ann., 23-2-901 et seq.

Conservation Act (Endangered Species)
Neb. Rev. Stat. 1943, 37-430

Conservation Act (Energy)
N.C. Laws 1977, Ch. 792

Conservation Act (Fish and Wildlife)
Ind. Code Ann., 14-2-1-1 et seq.

Conservation Act (Forests)
Mont. Rev. Code 1947, 28-101 et seq.
N.H. Rev. Stat. 1955, 79:1 et seq.

Conservation Act (Gas and Oil)
Miss. Code Ann., § 53-1-1 et seq.

Conservation Act (Gas)
Okla. Stat. Ann., Title 52, § 231 et seq.

Conservation Act (Geothermal Resources)
N.M. Stat. Ann., 71-5-1 et seq.

Conservation Act (Grass)
Mont. Rev. Code 1947, 46-2301 et seq.

Conservation Act (Metallic Minerals)
Iowa Code Ann., 458A.1 et seq.

Conservation Act (Minerals, Oil, Gas)
La. Rev. Stat. Ann., 30:1 et seq.

Conservation Act (Minerals)
Miss. Code Ann., § 53-1-1 et seq.

Conservation Act (Navigable Waters)
March 1, 1911, Ch. 186, 36 Stat. 961, 16 U.S.
Code §§ 480, 500, 513 to 519, 521, 552,
563

**Conservation Act (Nongame and
Endangered Species)**
Colo. Rev. Stat., 33-8-101 et seq.
Kan. Stat. Ann., 32-957 et seq., 32-1009 et
seq., 32-1033
Miss. Code Ann., § 49-5-101 et seq.

Conservation Act (Oil and Gas)
See Oil and Gas Conservation Act

Conservation Act (Oil)
N.M. Stat. Ann., 70-2-2 et seq.

Conservation Act (Riparian Habitat)
Cal. Fish and Game 1957, 1385 et seq.

Conservation Act (Soil)
La. Rev. Stat. Ann., 3:1201 et seq.
Mass. Gen. Laws Ann., 1288.1 et seq.
N.H. Rev. Stat. 1955, 432:1 et seq.
R.I. Gen. Laws 1956, 2-4-1 et seq.
Vt. Stat. Ann., Title 10, § 701 et seq.

Conservation Act (State Lands)
Minn. Stat. Ann., 84.01 et seq.

Conservation Act (Water)
Cal. Water Code, Appendix, § 34-1 et seq.
Colo. Rev. Stat., 37-60-101 et seq.

Conservation Act (Wetland)
Minn. Laws 1991, Ch. 354

Conservation Act (Wild Birds, Game)
La. Rev. Stat. Ann., 56:101 et seq.

Conservation Act (Wild Plant)
Ill. Rev. Stat. 1991, Ch. 5, § 230 et seq.

Conservation Act (Wildlife)
Cal. Statutes 1947, Ch. 1325, p. 2881

Conservation Acts (Food)
See Food Conservation Acts

Conservation Air Act
Utah Code Ann. 1953, 19-2-101 et seq.

Conservation Amendment
Tex. Const. 1876, Art. 16, § 59

**Conservation and Adjustment Act
(Agriculture)**
Colo. Rev. Stat., 35-3-101 et seq.
Ga. Code Ann., 2-6-1 et seq.

Conservation and Assistance Act (Energy)
Pa. Purdon's Stat., Title 62, § 3011 et seq.

Conservation and Efficiency Act (Budget)
Fla. Stat. Ann., 366.80 et seq.

Conservation and Facade Easement Act
Ga. Code Ann., 44-10-1 et seq.

**Conservation and Historic Preservation
Agreements Act**
N.C. Gen. Stat. 1943, § 121-34 et seq.

**Conservation and Historic Preservation
Easement Act**
Mich. Comp. Laws Ann., 399.251 et seq.

Conservation and Housing Trust Fund Act
R.I. Gen. Laws 1956, 42-113-1 et seq.
Vt. Stat. Ann., Title 10, § 301 et seq.

Conservation and Landscaping Act (Water)
Cal. Government Code § 65591 et seq.

**Conservation and Management of
Recreational Fisheries Act**
S.C. Code Ann. 1976, § 50-20-10 et seq.

**Conservation and Management Planning
Act (Trout and Steelhead)**
Cal. Fish and Game Code 1957, § 1725 et
seq.

Conservation and Natural Resources Act
Pa. Purdon's Stat., Title 71, § 1340.101 et seq.

Conservation and Planning Act
Cal. Government Code, § 65000 et seq.

Conservation and Planning Act (Pacific Northwest Electric Power)
Wash. Rev. Code Ann., 43.52A.010 et seq.

Conservation and Preservation Easements Act
Del. Code of 1974, Title 7, § 6901 et seq.
Neb. Rev. Stat. 1943, 76-2, 111 et seq.
W. Va. Code 1966, § 20-12-1 et seq.

Conservation and Protection Act (Agricultural Areas)
Ill. Comp. Stat. 1992, Ch. 505, § 5/1 et seq.
Ill. Rev. Stat. 1991, Ch. 5, § 1001 et seq.

Conservation and Reclamation Act (Surface Coal Mining Land)
Ill. Rev. Stat. 1991, Ch. 96 1/2, § 7901.01 et seq.

Conservation and Recreation Act
Fla. Stat. Ann., 375.011 et seq.

Conservation and Relocation Act (Mined-Land)
Kan. Stat. Ann., 49-401 et seq.

Conservation and Service Corps Act (Youth)
Mass. Gen. Laws Ann., 78A:1 to 78A:7

Conservation and Underground Natural Gas Storage Act
Tex. Natural Resources Code, § 91.171 et seq.

Conservation and Utilization of Natural Energy and Water Resources Compact Act
Tex. Natural Resources Code, § 142.001 et seq.

Conservation and Waterway Development Act
Me. Rev. Stat. Ann. 1964, Title 38, § 630 et seq.

Conservation Bond Law (Water)
Cal. Water Code § 12879 et seq.

Conservation Commission Act
Mich. Comp. Laws Ann., 299.1 et seq.
N.Y. Local Laws 1970, Town of Perinton, p. 2285

Conservation Commission Act (Soil)
Utah Code Ann. 1953, 4-18-1

Conservation Commission and Tax Supervising Act
Ore. Rev. Stat., 295.605 et seq.

Conservation Compact Act
Wyo. Stat. Ann., § 30-5-201 et seq.

Conservation Corporation Act
Neb. Rev. Stat. 1943, 2-4201 et seq.

Conservation Corps Act
Cal. Public Resources Code § 14000 et seq.
Fla. Stat. Ann., 369.105
Mich. Comp. Laws Ann., 409.301 et seq.
Pa. Purdon's Stat., Title 32, § 5501 et seq.

Conservation Corps Act (Youth)
Ga. Code Ann., 12-11-1 et seq.

Conservation Department Act
Ala. Code 1975, § 9-2-1 et seq.

Conservation, Development and Use of Water Resources Act
P.R. Laws Ann. 1954, Title 12, § 1501 et seq.

Conservation District Act
Ill. Comp. Stat. 1992, Ch. 70, § 410/1 et seq.
Kan. Stat. Ann., 2-1901 et seq.
Miss. Code Ann., § 69-27-1 et seq.
Mont. Code Ann., 76-15-301 et seq.
Nev. Rev. Stat. 1979, Reprint, 548.010 et seq.
N.H. Rev. Stat. 1955, 430-B:1 et seq.

Continued

N.M. Stat. Ann., 73-20-25 et seq.
Okla. Stat. Ann., Title 27A, § 3-1-101 et seq.
Pa. Purdon's Stat., Title 3, § 849 et seq.
S.D. Codified Laws 1967, 38-8-1 et seq.
Wash. Rev. Code Ann., 89.08.005 et seq.
Wyo. Stat. Ann., § 11-16-101 et seq.

Conservation District Act (Kings River)
Cal. Statutes 1951, Ch. 931, p. 2463
Cal. Water Code, Appendix, § 59-1 et seq.

Conservation District Act (Manasota Key)
Fla. Special Laws 1971, Ch. 71-904

Conservation District Act (North Casey Key)
Fla. Special Laws 1970, Ch. 70-937

Conservation District Act (Oil and Gas)
Ill. Rev. Stat. 1991, Ch. 96 1/2, § 7101 et seq.

Conservation District Act (Soil and Water)
Minn. Stat. 1986, 103C.005 et seq.

Conservation District Act (Water)
Cal. Water Code § 74000 et seq.

Conservation District Organization Valuation Act
Ill. Comp. Stat. 1992, Ch. 70, §§ 415/0.01, 415/1

Conservation Districts Act
Ark. Code Ann. 1987, 14-125-101 et seq.
Cal. Statutes 1919, p. 559
Colo. Rev. Stat., 37-45-101 et seq.
N.H. Rev. Stat. 1955, 432:8 et seq.

Conservation Districts Act (Forests)
Md. Ann. Code 1974, Art. NR, § 5-601 et seq.

Conservation Districts Act (Natural Resource)
N.M. Stat. Ann., 73-20-25 et seq.

Conservation Districts Act (Soil and Water)
Me. Rev. Stat. Ann. 1964, Title 12, § 1 et seq.
Mont. Rev. Code 1947, 76-101 et seq.
S.C. Code Ann. 1976, § 48-9-10 et seq.

Conservation Districts Act (Soil)
Md. Ann. Code 1974, Art. AG, § 8-101 et seq.
Mo. Rev. Stat., 278.060 et seq.
Utah Code Ann. 1953, 4-18-1 et seq.
W. Va. Code 1966, § 19-21A-1 et seq.

Conservation Easement Act
See also Uniform Conservation Easement Act
Ark. Code Ann. 1987, 15-20-401 et seq.
Minn. Stat. Ann., 84C.01 et seq.
S.C. Code Ann. 1976, § 27-8-10 et seq.
Tenn. Code Ann., 66-9-301 et seq.
Wis. Stat. 1989, 700.40

Conservation Easement Law
N.Y. Local Laws 1972, Town of Perinton, p. 2550

Conservation Education Act
Ill. Comp. Stat. 1992, Ch. 105, § 415/0.01 et seq.

Conservation Education School Act
Ill. Rev. Stat. 1969, Ch. 127, § 63b51 et seq.

Conservation Enhancement Act
Ill. Comp. Stat. 1992, Ch. 505, § 35/1-1 et seq.

Conservation Foundation Act
Ill. Comp. Stat. 1992, Ch. 20, § 880/1

Conservation Law (Air)
Mo. Rev. Stat. 1978, 643.010 et seq.

Conservation of Oil and Gas Compact Act (Interstate)
Ill. Rev. Stat. 1991, Ch. 96 1/2, § 5300 et seq.

Conservation Planning Act (Natural Community)
Cal. Fish and Game Code 1957, 2800 et seq.

Conservation Program Improvements Act
Nov. 28, 1990, P.L. 101-624, 7 U.S. Code §§ 136a nt., 136i-1, 450i, 3130, 5401 to 5403, 5506, 5822; 16 U.S. Code § 3801 nt.

Conservation Projects Act (Water)
Cal. Water Code § 11950 et seq.

Conservation Ranger Act
Ga. Code Ann., 27-1-16 et seq.

Conservation Restriction and Historic Preservation Restriction Act
N.J. Stat. Ann., 13:8B-1 et seq.

Conservation Rights Act (Real Property)
Ill. Rev. Stat. 1991, Ch. 30, § 400 et seq.

Conservation Schools Act (Garrigus-Lagomarsino)
Cal. Education Code 1976, § 1790 et seq.
Tex. Health & Safety Code, § 363.001 et seq.

Conservation Service Reform Act of 1986
Aug. 28, 1986, P.L. 99-412, 42 U.S. Code § 8201 nt.

Conservation Servitude Act
La. Rev. Stat. Ann., 9:1271 et seq.

Conservation, Solid Waste Management, and Resource Recovery Act (Municipal)
Tex. Health and Safety Code, § 363.001 et seq.

Conservation Standards Act (Energy)
Fla. Stat. Ann., 553.951 et seq.

Conservator Act
Ill. Rev. Stat. 1991, Ch. 110 1/2, § 11a-1 et seq.
Neb. Rev. Stat. 1943, 30-2601 et seq.
N.H. Rev. Stat. 1955, 464:A:13 et seq.

Conservator Act (Insurance)
Tex. Insurance Code, Art. 21.28

Conservatorship Act
Cal. Probate Code § 1701 et seq.

Conservatorship and Guardianship Act
Okla. Stat. Ann., Title 30, § 1-101 et seq.

Consignment Act
Wis. Stat. 1963, 241.26

Consignment Act (Artists)
Tex. Rev. Civ. Stat., Art. 9018

Consignment of Art Act
Ga. Code Ann., 10-1-521 to 10-1-529
Ill. Comp. Stat. 1992, Ch. 815, § 320/0.01 et seq.

Consignment Sales Act
Utah Code Ann. 1953, 41-3-801 et seq.

Consolidated Budget Reconciliation Act of 1985
See Consolidated Omnibus Budget Reconciliation Act of 1985

Consolidated City-County Act
N.C. Gen. Stat. 1943, 160B-1 et seq.
Tenn. Code Ann., 34-4-201 et seq.

Consolidated Court Act
Ala. Code 1975, § 12-11-30 et seq.

Consolidated Election Law
Cal. Elections Code 1976, § 23300 et seq.

Consolidated Farm and Rural Development Act
Aug. 8, 1961, P.L. 87-128, 7 U.S. Code § 1921 et seq.
Aug. 30, 1972, P.L. 92-419, 86 Stat. 657, 7 U.S. Code §§ 1924 to 1927, 1929, 1929a, 1931 to 1933, 1941 to 1943, 1947, 1981, 1983, 1985, 1991, 1992
April 20, 1973, P.L. 93-24, 87 Stat. 24, 7 U.S. Code §§ 1961, 1964, 1968
Aug. 10, 1973, P.L. 93-86, 87 Stat. 237, 7 U.S. Code §§ 1925, 1926, 1932
June 16, 1975, P.L. 94-35, 89 Stat. 214, 7 U.S. Code § 1992
Aug. 4, 1977, P.L. 95-89, 7 U.S. Code § 1964
Sept. 29, 1977, P.L. 95-113, 7 U.S. Code §§ 1929, 1929a
Aug. 4, 1978, P.L. 95-334, 7 U.S. Code §§ 1921 et seq., 1921 nt.
July 2, 1980, P.L. 96-302, 7 U.S. Code § 1961 et seq.
April 10, 1984, P.L. 98-258, 7 U.S. Code §§ 1943, 1946, 1961, 1964, 1981b, 1986, 1994

Continued

Dec. 23, 1985, P.L. 99-198, 7 U.S. Code §§ 1922, 1926, 1927, 1941 to 1942, 1961 to 2000

Aug. 28, 1986, P.L. 99-409, 7 U.S. Code § 1932

Oct. 18, 1986, P.L. 99-500, 7 U.S. Code § 1929a

Oct. 21, 1986, P.L. 99-509, 7 U.S. Code § 1929a

Oct. 30, 1986, P.L. 99-591, 7 U.S. Code § 1929a

Dec. 22, 1987, P.L. 100-203, 7 U.S. Code § 1932

Jan. 6, 1988, P.L. 100-233, 7 U.S. Code §§ 1926 nt., 1927, 1927a, 1927a nt., 1981, 1981d, 1981e, 1982, 1983b, 1983c, 1985, 1988, 1989 nt., 1991, 1997, 1999 nt., 1999, 2000, 2001 to 2005, 2001 nt.

Aug. 11, 1988, P.L. 100-387, 102 Stat. 948, 7 U.S. Code § 1961 nt.

Nov. 23, 1988, P.L. 100-707, 7 U.S. Code §§ 1961, 1964

Aug. 44, 1989, P.L. 101-82, 7 U.S. Code §§ 1926a, 1926a nt.

Nov. 5, 1990, P.L. 101-508, 7 U.S. Code §§ 1994, 1999

Nov. 28, 1990, P.L. 101-624, 7 U.S. Code § 1924 et seq. generally

Dec. 13, 1991, P.L. 102-237, 7 U.S. Code §§ 1924, 1926, 1932, 1942, 1981, 1983, 1985, 1994, 2000, 2001, 2006e, 2006f, 2008, 2008a, 2008b

Oct. 28, 1992, P.L. 102-552, 7 U.S. Code §§ 1926, 1927, 1932, 1934, 1981e, 2000

Oct. 28, 1993, P.L. 102-554, 7 U.S. Code §§ 1925, 1926c, 1929, 1932, 1935, 1936, 1948, 1949, 1981d, 1982, 1983, 1983a, 1985, 1989, 1991, 1994, 2003

Nov. 1, 1993, P.L. 103-129, 7 U.S. Code §§ 1926, 2006f, 2008e

May 11, 1994, P.L. 103-248, 7 U.S. Code § 1981

Sept. 29, 1994, P.L. 103-328, 7 U.S. Code § 1927

Oct. 13, 1994, P.L. 103-354, 7 U.S. Code §§ 1926, 1982, 1983, 1983b, 2006, 2006f, 2008f

Nov. 2, 1994, P.L. 103-437, 7 U.S. Code § 1993

Feb. 10, 1996, P.L. 104-105, 7 U.S. Code § 1999

April 4, 1996, P.L. 104-127, 7 U.S. Code §§ 1922 to 1924, 1926, 1926b, 1926d, 1927 to 1929, 1929a, 1931, 1932, 1934, 1936, 1941, 1942, 1945 to 1949, 2003, 2006e, 2006f, 2008, 2008a to 2008c, 2008g to 2008j, prec. 2009, 2009, 2009a et seq.

Nov. 21, 1997, P.L. 105-113, 7 U.S. Code § 1991

Oct. 21, 1998, P.L. 105-277, 7 U.S. Code §§ 1922, 1925, 1926d, 1941, 1943, 1964, 2001, 2006a, 2008h

Nov. 10, 1998, P.L. 105-362, 7 U.S. Code § 1988

May 21, 1999, P.L. 106-31, 7 U.S. Code §§ 1989, 2001

Consolidated Farmers Home Administration Act

S.C. Code Ann. 1976, § 33-35-10 et seq.

Consolidated Farmers Home Administration Act of 1961

Aug. 8, 1961, P.L. 87-128, 75 Stat. 307, 7 U.S. Code §§ 1013a, 1921 to 1929, 1941 to 1946, 1961 to 1967, 1981 to 1990

Sept. 27, 1962, P.L. 87-703, 76 Stat. 631, 7 U.S. Code §§ 1923, 1926, 1929, 1942, 1991

Oct. 11, 1962, P.L. 87-798, 76 Stat. 908, 7 U.S. Code § 1928

Oct. 15, 1962, P.L. 87-832, 76 Stat. 958, 7 U.S. Code § 1961

Oct. 7, 1965, P.L. 89-240, 79 Stat. 931, 7 U.S. Code §§ 1926, 1928, 1929

May 24, 1966, P.L. 89-429, 80 Stat. 167, 7 U.S. Code § 1988

Sept. 19, 1966, P.L. 89-586, 80 Stat. 809, 7 U.S. Code § 1991

Oct. 8, 1966 P.L. 89-633, 80 Stat. 879, 7 U.S. Code § 1929

Nov. 6, 1966, P.L. 89-769, 80 Stat. 1318, 7 U.S. Code § 1926

Aug. 15, 1968, P.L. 90-488, 82 Stat. 770, 7 U.S. Code §§ 1923, 1924, 1926, 1928, 1929, 1942, 1943, 1946, 1981, 1983

Nov. 30, 1970, P.L. 91-524, 84 Stat. 1383, 7 U.S. Code §§ 1926, 1930

Dec. 31, 1970, P.L. 91-620, 84 Stat. 1862, 7 U.S. Code §§ 1922, 1925, 1983

Oct. 5, 1971, P.L. 92-133, 85 Stat. 364, 7 U.S. Code § 1928

Nov. 24, 1971, P.L. 92-173, 85 Stat. 491, 7 U.S. Code § 1968

Aug. 16, 1972, P.L. 92-385, 86 Stat. 557, 7 U.S. Code § 1969

Aug. 30, 1972, P.L. 92-419, 86 Stat. 657, 7 U.S. Code §§ 1924 to 1927, 1929, 1929a, 1931 to 1933, 1941 to 1943, 1947, 1981, 1983, 1985

Consolidated Federal Funds Report Act of 1982

Oct. 15, 1982, P.L. 97-326, 31 U.S. Code § 6102 nt.

Consolidated Federal Funds Report Amendments of 1985

Oct. 27, 1986, P.L. 99-547, 31 U.S. Code § 6201 nt.

Consolidated First-Class Cities and Counties Act

Ind. Code Ann., 36-3-1-1 et seq.

Consolidated Food Licensing Act

Minn. Stat. Ann., 28A.01 et seq.

Consolidated Judicial Retirement Act

N.C. Gen. Stat. 1943, § 135-50 et seq.

Consolidated Law Enforcement Act

Kan. Stat. Ann., 19-4468 et seq.

Consolidated Local Improvements Law

Nev. Rev. Stat. 1979 Reprint, 271.010 et seq.

Consolidated Municipal Service Act

N.J. Stat. Ann., 40:48B-1 et seq.

Consolidated Omnibus Budget Reconciliation Act of 1965

Oct. 31, 1994, P.L. 103-432, 42 U.S. Code § 1395y nt.

Consolidated Omnibus Budget Reconciliation Act of 1985

April 7, 1986, P.L. 99-272, 100 Stat. 82

May 23, 1986, P.L. 320, 20 U.S. Code §§ 1078, 1078 nt.

July 2, 1986, P.L. 99-349, 15 U.S. Code § 636 nt.

Oct. 21, 1986, P.L. 99-509, 19 U.S. Code § 58c; 38 U.S. Code § 4109; 42 U.S. Code §§ 1301 nt., 1320c-3 nt., 1396a nt., 1396b nt., 1396d nt., 1396n nt.

Oct. 22, 1986, P.L. 99-514, 19 U.S. Code §§ 58c, 58c nt., 403 nt.; 26 U.S. Code § 57 nt.; 42 U.S. Code §§ 603 nt., 1301, 1395u, 1395cc nt., 1395ww nt., 1395yy nt., 1396b nt.

Sept. 29, 1987, P.L. 100-119, 101 Stat. 784

Dec. 22, 1987, P.L. 100-203, 19 U.S. Code §§ 58, 58c, 2071 nt.; 42 U.S. Code §§ 1395ww, nt., 1396r-3, 2213

Aug. 23, 1988, P.L. 100-418, 102 Stat. 1156, 19 U.S. Code § 58c

Oct. 13, 1988, P.L. 100-485, 102 Stat. 2425, 42 U.S. Code § 603nt.

Nov. 10, 1988, P.L. 100-647, 42 U.S. Code § 1395ww nt.

Dec. 19, 1989, P.L. 101-239, 42 U.S. Code §§ 1395b-1 nt., 2213

Aug. 20, 1990, P.L. 101-382, 19 U.S. Code § 58c

Nov. 5, 1990, P.L. 101-508, 2 U.S. Code § 644; 19 U.S. Code § 58c; 42 U.S. Code §§ 1395b-1 nt., 1395y nt., 1395ww nt., 1396b nt., 2213, 8791 nt.

April 9, 1991, P.L. 102-26, 105 Stat. 125

Aug. 10, 1993, P.L. 103-66, 19 U.S. Code § 58c; 42 U.S. Code § 1395b-1 nt.

Dec. 8, 1993, P.L. 103-182, 19 U.S. Code § 58c

Nov. 2, 1994, P.L. 103-437, 15 U.S. Code § 1530

Dec. 8, 1994, P.L. 103-465, 19 U.S. Code § 58c

Dec. 21, 1995, P.L. 104-66, 31 U.S. Code § 6701 nt.

Oct. 8, 1996, P.L. 104-240, 42 U.S. Code § 1396b nt.

Oct. 11, 1996, P.L. 104-295, 19 U.S. Code § 58c

Aug. 5, 1997, P.L. 105-33, 42 U.S. Code § 1395b-1 nt.

Dec. 16, 1997, P.L. 105-150, 19 U.S. Code § 58c

June 25, 1999, P.L. 106-36, 19 U.S. Code § 58c

Consolidated Omnibus Budget Reconciliation Act of 1990
Nov. 10, 1998, P.L. 105-362, 42 U.S. Code § 1395b nt.

Consolidated Procurement Code
S.C. Code Ann. 1976, § 11-35-10 et seq.

Consolidated Public Utility System Improvement District Law
Ark. Code Ann. 1987, 14-217-101 et seq.

Consolidated Refugee Education Assistance Act
Aug. 13, 1981, P.L. 97-35, 8 U.S. Code § 1522 nt.

Consolidated School Act
Mo. Rev. Stat. 1969, 162.671 et seq.

Consolidated School District Act
Ill. Rev. Stat. 1991, Ch. 122, § 11A-1 et seq.
S.D. Code 1939, 15.2601 et seq.

Consolidated Sewer Districts Act
Vt. Stat. Ann., Title 24, § 3671 et seq.

Consolidated Water District Law (Mesa)
Cal. Water Code, Appendix, § 33200 et seq.

Consolidated Weights and Measures Act
Pa. Cons. Stat., Title 3, § 4101 et seq.

Consolidation Act (Agricultural Departments)
Wis. Stat. 1989, 93.01 et seq.

Consolidation Act (Cities)
Pa. Purdon's Stat., Title 53, § 221 et seq.

Consolidation Act (City and County)
N.M. Stat. Ann. 1953, Superseded Vol., 14-12-1 et seq.

Consolidation Act (City of New York)
N.Y. Laws 1882, Ch. 410

Consolidation Act (Contiguous Territory)
Wis. Stat. 1989, 66.02

Consolidation Act (Corporations)
Colo. Rev. Stat., 7-7-101 et seq.
Pa. Purdon's Stat., Title 15, § 421 et seq.

Consolidation Act (County Clerk)
Okla. Stat. Ann., Title 19, § 225

Consolidation Act (Funds)
Utah Code Ann. 1953, 51-5-1 et seq.

Consolidation Act (Municipal Corporation)
Cal. Government Code, § 35900

Consolidation Act (Philadelphia)
Pa. Purdon's Stat., Title 53, § 16251 et seq.

Consolidation Act (Railroads)
Pa. Purdon's Stat., Title 15, § 4254 et seq.

Consolidation Act (San Francisco)
Cal. Statutes 1856, Ch. 125, p. 145

Consolidation Act (Schools)
Ind. Code Ann., 20-4-5-1 et seq.

Consolidation Act (Stanislaus County Court Services)
Cal. Statutes 1992, Ch. 181

Consolidation Act (Township)
Ill. Rev. Stat. 1991, Ch. 139, § 140m et seq.

Consolidation Act (Trials)
Ala. Code 1958, Title 7, § 221

Consolidation and Annexation Act (School)
Okla. Stat. Ann., Title 70, § 7-201 et seq.

Consolidation and Annexation Incentive Plan (Voluntary)
Mont. Code Ann., 20-6-401 et seq.

Consolidation and Coordination Law (McElhanon-Dudley)
Ark. Stat. 1947, 84-1701 et seq.

Consolidation-Durham County
N.C. Laws 1974, Ch. 989

Consolidation Enabling Act (Metropolitan Areas)
N.C. Laws 1973, Ch. 574
Tenn. Code Ann., 7-1-101 et seq.

Consolidation of Government Bureaus Act
July 3, 1930, Ch. 863, 46 Stat. 1016

Consolidation of Municipalities Act
Mich. Comp. Laws Ann., 123.1001 et seq.

Consolidation or City Merger Act
Ky. Rev. Stat. 1971, 81.410 et seq.

Consolidation or Merger Act (Municipal)
Pa. Cons. Stat., Title 53, § 731 et seq.

Consortium Act (Sea Grant)
S.C. Code Ann. 1976, § 48-45-10 et seq.

Consortium for Educational Opportunities Act
Ill. Comp. Stat. 1992, Ch. 110, § 930/1 et seq.

Conspiracies Act (Civil War)
July 31, 1861, Ch. 33, 12 Stat. 284

Conspiracies in Restraint of Trade Act
Tex. Business and Commerce Code, § 15.01 et seq.

Conspiracy Act
Cal. Penal Code § 182 et seq.
Fla. Stat. Ann., 448.045, 777.04
Haw. Rev. Stat. Ann., § 705-520 et seq.
Ill. Rev. Stat. 1991, Ch. 38, § 8-2 et seq.
Iowa Code Ann., 706.1 et seq.
Ky. Rev. Stat. 1971, Superseded Vols., 437.110
La. Rev. Stat. Ann., 14:26
Mich. Comp. Laws Ann., 750.151 et seq.
Mo. Rev. Stat. 1969, 556.120, 556.130
Okla. Stat. Ann., Title 21, § 421 et seq.
Ore. Rev. Stat., 161.450 et seq.
S.C. Code Ann. 1976, § 16-17-410
Vt. Stat. Ann., Title 13, § 1404 et seq.

Conspiracy Act (Defrauding State or County)
Ga. Code Ann., 16-10-21, 16-10-22

Conspiracy Act (Monopolies)
N.Y. General Business Law (Consol. Laws Ch. 20) § 340 et seq.

Conspiracy Act (Offenses Against U.S.)
March 4, 1909, Ch. 321, 35 Stat. 1096
Sept. 27, 1944, Ch. 425, 58 Stat. 752
June 25, 1948, Ch. 645, 62 Stat. 701, 18 U.S. Code § 371

Constables Act
N.J. Stat. Ann., 40A:9-120 et seq.
Wash. Rev. Code Ann., 45.12.080, 45.12.18, 45.16.035
W. Va. Code 1966, Miscellaneous Superseded Provisions, § 50-1-1 et seq.

Constables and Justices Act
Ill. Rev. Stat. 1991, Ch. 79

Constables Fee Bill Act
Pa. Purdon's Stat., Title 13, § 61 et seq.

Constables Law Enforcement Training Act
Neb. Rev. Stat. 1943, 81-1401 et seq.
Tenn. Code Ann., 39-12-103 et seq.
Vt. Stat. Ann., Title 13, § 1401 et seq.
Wash. Rev. Code Ann., 9A.28.040 et seq.

Constituent Services Act
D.C. Code Ann., § 1-1443 et seq.

Constitution Amendment Act (U.S.)
Ill. Rev. Stat. 1991, Ch. 1, §§ 300, 301

Constitution Heritage Act of 1988
Sept. 16, 1988, P.L. 100-433, 102 Stat. 1640, 16 U.S. Code §§ 407aa to 407ee

Constitutional Amendment Act
Ill. Comp. Stat. 1992, Ch. 5, § 20/0.01 et seq.

Constitutional Amendment Resolution
March 2, 1861, No. 13, 12 Stat. 251

Constitutional Amendments Publications Board Act
Ga. Code Ann., 5-12-100, 50-12-101

Constitutional Convention Act
Ida. Code 1947, 34-2216 et seq.
Ill. Comp. Stat. 1992, Ch. 5, § 25/0.01 et seq.
Ky. Acts 1879-80 (Public) Ch. 30
Vt. Acts 1969, No. 74

Constitutional Convention Election Expense Act
Ill. Comp. Stat. 1992, Ch. 50, §§ 435/0.01, 435/1

Constitutional Convention Enabling Act
Mont. Laws 1971, Ch. 296

Constitutional Convention Lobbyists Registration Act
Ill. Comp. Stat. 1992, Ch. 5, § 30/1 et seq.

Constitutional Government Act
P.R. Acts 1951, 13th Sp. Sess., No. 1

Constitutional Qualification Enforcement Law
Cal. Government Code §§ 1364 to 1366

Constitutionally Based Educational Claims Act
Ida. Code 1947, 6-2201 et seq.

Construction Act (Bridge)
Ill. Rev. Stat. 1991, Ch. 121, §§ 191, 192

Construction Act (Building)
Neb. Rev. Stat. 1943, 71-6401 et seq.

Construction Act (County Industrial Sewer)
Neb. Rev. Stat. 1943, 23-3601 et seq.

Construction Act (Hospitals)
S.C. Code Ann. 1976, § 44-7-110 et seq.

Construction Act (Navy)
See Naval Construction Act

Construction Act (Private Well)
Va. Code 1950, § 32.1-176.1 et seq.

Construction Act (Sidewalk)
Utah Code Ann. 1953, 27-14-1 et seq.

Construction Act (State Museum)
Ill. Rev. Stat. 1991, Ch. 127, §§ 59.01, 59.1

Construction Activity Prohibition on Abandoned Landfills Act
Ga. Code Ann., 8-6-1 et seq.

Construction Aid Law of 1968 (Urban School)
Cal. Education Code 1976, § 17300 et seq.

Construction and Employment Act
Cal. Statutes 1946, 1st Ex. Sess., Ch. 20, p. 30

Construction and Hospital Survey Act
Neb. Rev. Stat. 1943, 71-2001 et seq.

Construction and Maintenance Regulations for the Town of Louisville
N.Y. Local Laws 1970, Town of Louisville, p. 2042

Construction and Planning Act (Public Building)
Okla. Stat. Ann., Title 61, § 201 et seq.

Construction and Safety Standards Act (Manufactured Housing)
W. Va. Code 1966, § 21-9-1 et seq.

Construction and Survey Act (Hospitals)
Wis. Stat. 1991, 50.20 et seq.

Construction and Survey Act (Medical Facilities)
Kan. Stat. Ann., 65-411 et seq.

Construction Arbitration Act
Miss. Code Ann., § 11-15-101 et seq.

Construction Bidding for Public Projects Act
Colo. Rev. Stat., 24-92-101 et seq.

Construction Bidding for State-Funded Local Projects Act
Colo. Rev. Stat., 29-1-701 et seq.

Construction Bond Act
D.C. Code 1967, §§ 1-1104 to 1-1108

Construction Bond Act (Correctional Facilities)
N.J. Laws 1991, Ch. 178

Construction Bond Act (New Prison)
Cal. Penal Code § 7420 et seq.

Construction Bond Act for Higher Education Facilities
N.J. Laws 1979, Ch. 206

Construction Code
See Uniform State Construction Code

Construction Code (Uniform)
La. Rev. Stat. Ann., 40:1725 et seq.

Construction Code Act
Mich. Comp. Laws Ann., 125.1501 et seq.
N.J. Stat. Ann., 52:27D-119 et seq.

Construction Contract Act (Privileges)
La. Rev. Stat. Ann., 9:4801 et seq.

Construction Contract Indemnification for Negligence Act
Ill. Comp. Stat. 1992, Ch. 740, § 35/0.01 et seq.

Construction Contract Prompt Payment Law
Fla. Stat. Ann., 715.12

Construction Contractor's Licensing Act
Alaska Stat. 1962, § 08.18.010 et seq.

Construction Contractors Registration Act
Ore. Rev. Stat., 701.005 et seq.

Construction Control Law
Nev. Rev. Stat. 1979, 627.010 et seq.

Construction Disclosure Act (Hazardous Substances)
Ill. Rev. Stat. 1991, Ch. 29, §§ 1001, 1002

Construction Equipment Identification Defacement Act
Ill. Comp. Stat. 1992, Ch. 720, §§ 245/0.01, 245/1

Construction Equipment, Motor Vehicle and Farm Machinery Franchise Practices Act
Ga. Code 1933, 84-6601 et seq.

Construction Evaluation Act
Ill. Comp. Stat. 1992, Ch. 20, § 3015/1 et seq.

Construction, Farm, and Industrial Equipment Fair Dealership Law
Ill. Rev. Stat. 1991, Ch. 5, § 1501 et seq.

Construction Financing Act (University of Illinois)
Ill. Rev. Stat. 1991, Ch. 144, § 67.9 et seq.

Construction Fund Act (City University)
N.Y. Education Law 1947 (Consol. Laws Ch. 16) § 6270 et seq.

Construction Grant Anticipation Note Act (Public Entry)
La. Rev. Stat. Ann., 39:1801

Construction Impact Fee Act (Spring Hill)
Tenn. Private Acts 1988, Ch. 176

Construction Industries Licensing Act
N.M. Stat. Ann., 60-13-1 et seq.

Construction Industry Lien Act
Wash. Rev. Code Ann., 60.04.010 et seq.

Construction Inspectors Act
Cal. Business and Professions Code § 9100 et seq.

Construction Lien Act
Fla. Stat. Ann., 713.001 et seq.
Mich. Comp. Laws Ann., 570.1101 et seq.
Neb. Rev. Stat. 1943, 52-125 et seq.
Ore. Rev. Stat., 87.001 et seq.
Wis. Stat. 1989, 779.01 et seq.

Construction Lien Law
N.J. Stat. Ann., 2A:44A-1 et seq.

Construction Loan Act
Md. Laws 1960, Ch. 86

Construction Management Education Sponsorship Act
Cal. Business and Professions Code § 7139 et seq.

Construction Management Licensure Act
Ida. Code 1947, 54-4501 et seq.

Construction Mortgage Act (Priority)
Ohio Rev. Code 1953, 1311.14

Construction of Hospital and Medical Facilities Act
Alaska Stat. 1962, § 18.20.140 et seq.

Construction of Statutes Act
Ill. Rev. Stat. 1991, Ch. 1, § 1001 et seq.
Pa. Cons. Stat., Title 1, § 1501 et seq.

Construction Officer, Act of the Office of Construction Officer, Attached to the Urban Renewal and Housing Administration
P.R. Laws Ann. 1954, Title 17, § 501 et seq.

Construction Program Bond Act
Cal. Statutes 1955, Ch. 1709, p. 3142
Cal. Statutes 1958, 1st Ex. Sess., Ch. 88, p. 320

Construction Prompt Payment Act
Del. Code of 1974, Title 6, § 3501 et seq.

Construction Safety Act
Mich. Comp. Laws Ann., 408.711 et seq.
N.J. Stat. Ann., 34:5-166 et seq.

Construction Trade Licensing Act
Utah Code Ann. 1953, 58-55-1 et seq.

Construction Trades Licensing Act
Utah Code Ann. 1953, 58-55-101 et seq.

Construction Workers' Fringe Benefit Security Act
N.J. Stat. Ann., 34:11A-1 et seq.

Constructive Service Act
Fla. Stat. Ann., 49.011 et seq.
Kan. Stat. Ann., 60-307

Constructive Youth Act
Fla. Stat. Ann., 230.23165

Consular Corps License Plates Act
Ga. Code Ann., 40-2-64

Consular Reorganization Acts
April 5, 1906 Ch. 1366, 34 Stat. 99, 22 U.S. Code §§ 9, 54, 57, 84, 98, 99, 100, 106, 107
May 11, 1908, Ch. 161, 35 Stat. 101
Feb. 5, 1915, Ch. 23, 38 Stat. 805

Consultant Continuing Education Act (Insurance Producer)
Mont. Code Ann., 33-17-1201 to 33-17-1207

Consultant Law (Insurance)
Me. Rev. Stat. Ann. 1964, Title 24-A, § 1801 et seq.

Consultants Competetive Negotiation Act (Professional)
Fla. Stat. Ann., 278.055

Consultants Competitive Negotiation Act
Fla. Stat. Ann., 287.055
Neb. Rev. Stat. 1943, 81-1702 et seq.

Consultants' Competitive Negotiation Act
Fla. Stat. Ann., 287.055

Consumer Access to Eye Care Act
N.J. Stat. Ann., 40:48-1.1 et seq.

Consumer Access to Vision Care Act
Wash. Rev. Code Ann., 18.195.900

Consumer Act
Wis. Stat. 1989, 421.101 et seq., 422.101 et seq. (Consumer Credit Transactions), 423.101 et seq. (Consumer Approval Transactions and Advertising), 424.101 et seq. (Insurance), 425.101 et seq. (Remedies and Penalties), 427.101 et seq. (Debt Collection)
Wis. Stat. 1991, 426.101 et seq. (Administration)

Consumer Advocate Act
S.C. Code Ann. 1976, § 37-6-601 et seq.

Consumer Affairs Act
Cal. Business and Professions Code § 300 et seq.
N.J. Stat. Ann., 52:17B-118 et seq.
S.D. Codified Laws 1967, 37-23-4 et seq.

Consumer Affairs Department Organic Act
P.R. Laws Ann. 1954, Title 3, § 341 et seq.

Consumer Approval Transactions and Advertising (Consumer Act)
Wis. Stat. 1989, 423.101 et seq.

Consumer Assistance Plan (Health Maintenance Organization)
Fla. Stat. Ann., 631.811 et seq.

Consumer Checking Account Equity Act of 1980
March 31, 1980, P.L. 96-221, 12 U.S. Code §§ 226 nt., 371a

Consumer Collection Practices Act
Fla. Stat. Ann., 559.551 et seq.

Consumer Contract Act (Plain Language)
Pa. Purdon's Stat., Title 73, § 2201 et seq.

Consumer Contract Awareness Act
Cal. Civil Code § 1799.200 et seq.

Consumer Contracts Plain Language Law
N.J. Stat. Ann., 59:12-1 et seq.

Consumer Cooperative Act
Mich. Comp. Laws Ann., 450.3100 et seq.

Consumer Cooperative Association Law
R.I. Gen. Laws 1956, 7-8-1 et seq.

Consumer Cooperative Corporation Law
Cal. Corporations Code § 12200 et seq.

Consumer Cooperatives Act
Md. Ann. Code 1974, § 5-5A-01 et seq.
Me. Rev. Stat. Ann. 1964, Title 13, § 1501 et seq.

Consumer Council Act
Mont. Code Ann., 69-1-201 et seq.

Consumer Credit Act (Interest)
Mo. Rev. Stat., 408.100 et seq.

Consumer Credit Act (Small Loans)
Mo. Rev. Stat. 1978, 367.100

Consumer Credit and Protection Act
D.C. Code Ann., § 28-3801 et seq.
W. Va. Code 1966, § 46A-1-101 et seq

Consumer Credit Bank Act
Del. Code of 1974, Title 5, § 1001 et seq.
N.M. Stat. Ann., 58-1A-1 et seq.

Consumer Credit Code
See also Uniform Consumer Credit Code
Ark. Code Ann. 1987, 4-87-101 et seq.
La. Rev. Stat. Ann., 9:3510 et seq.
Okla. Stat. Ann., Title 14A, § 1-101 et seq.
Tex. Finance Code, § 301.001 et seq.
Tex. Rev. Civ. Stat., Art. 5069-1.01 et seq.
Utah Code Ann. 1953, 70C-1-101 et seq.
Va. Code 1950, § 6.1-352 et seq.
Wyo. Stat. Ann., § 40-14-101 et seq.

Consumer Credit Code—Administration
See Uniform Consumer Credit Code—Administration

Consumer Credit Code—Credit Service Organizations
See Uniform Consumer Credit Code—Administration

Consumer Credit Code—Deferred Presentment
See Uniform Consumer Credit Code—Deferred Presentment

Consumer Credit Code—Finance Charges and Related Provisions
See Uniform Consumer Credit Code—Administration
See Uniform Consumer Credit Code—Finance Charges and Related Provisions

Consumer Credit Code—Insurance
See Uniform Consumer Credit Code—Administration

Consumer Credit Code—Regulation of Agreements and Practices

See Uniform Consumer Credit Code—Regulation of Agreements and Practices

Consumer Credit Code—Regulations of Agreements and Practices

See Uniform Consumer Credit Code—Administration

Consumer Credit Code—Remedies and Penalties

See Uniform Consumer Credit Code—Remedies and Penalties

Consumer Credit Code—Rental Purchase Agreements

See Uniform Consumer Credit Code—Rental Purchase Agreements

Consumer Credit Code—Truth-in-Lending

Me. Rev. Stat. Ann. 1964, Title 9-A, §§ 8-101 et seq., 7-101

Consumer Credit Cost Disclosure Act

Mass. Gen. Laws Ann., 140D:1 et seq.

Consumer Credit Counseling Corporation Act

Ill. Comp. Stat. 1992, Ch. 805, § 140/1 et seq.

Consumer Credit Insurance Model Act

Del. Code of 1974, Title 18, § 3701 et seq.

Consumer Credit Interest Rate and Nonprofit Housing Developments' Water and Sanitary Sewer Service Rate Charges Reduction Amendments Clarification Act

D.C. Code Ann., § 43-1522 et seq.

Consumer Credit Protection Act

May 29, 1968, P.L. 90-321, 82 Stat. 146, 15 U.S. Code §§ 1601 to 1613, 1631 to 1641, 1661 to 1665, 1671 to 1677; 18 U.S. Code §§ 891 to 896

Oct. 26, 1970, P.L. 91-508, 84 Stat. 1128, 15 U.S. Code §§ 1681 to 1681t

June 30, 1972, P.L. 92-321, 86 Stat. 382

May 23, 1977, P.L. 95-30, 15 U.S. Code § 1673 et seq.

Sept. 20, 1977, P.L. 95-109, 15 U.S. Code §§ 1601 nt., 1692 et seq.

Nov. 6, 1978, P.L. 95-598, 15 U.S. Code § 1673

Nov. 10, 1978, P.L. 95-630, 15 U.S. Code §§ 1601 nt., 1693 et seq. .

Oct. 4, 1984, P.L. 98-443, 98 Stat. 1708, 15 U.S. Code §§ 1607, 1681s, 1691c, 1692l

Oct. 25, 1988, P.L. 100-533, 15 U.S. Code § 1691b

Sept. 30, 1996, P.L. 104-208, 15 U.S. Code §§ prec. 1679, 1679, 1679a to 1679j

Oct. 11, 1996, P.L. 104-287, 15 U.S. Code § 16930

Consumer Credit Reporting Act

Cal. Civil Code § 1750 et seq.

Consumer Credit Reporting Agencies Act

Cal. Civil Code § 1785.1 et seq.

Consumer Credit Reporting Reform Act of 1996

Sept. 30, 1996, P.L. 104-208, Subtitle D, Chapter 1, 15 U.S. Code § 1601 nt.

Consumer Credit Transactions (Consumer Act)

Wis. Stat. 1989, 422.101 et seq.

Consumer Debt Collection Act

Md. Ann. Code 1974, Art. CL, § 14-201 et seq.

Consumer Deposit Account Act

Ill. Comp. Stat. 1992, Ch. 205, § 605/0.01 et seq.

Consumer Deposit Security Act

Ill. Comp. Stat. 1992, Ch. 815, § 165/1 et seq.

Consumer Disclosure of Prizes and Gifts Act

Okla. Stat. Ann., Title 21, § 996.1 et seq.

Consumer Discount Company Act

Pa. Purdon's Stat., Title 7, § 6201 et seq.

Consumer Education and Free Enterprise Act

Fla. Stat. Ann., 233.0641

Consumer Finance Act
Ala. Code 1975, § 5-19-1 et seq.
Colo. Rev. Stat., 5-3-101 et seq.
Fla. Stat. Ann., 516.001 et seq.
Ida. Code 1947, 26-2027 et seq.
Ill. Rev. Stat. 1981, Ch. 74, § 19 et seq.
Ill. Rev. Stat. 1991, Ch. 17, § 5601 et seq.
Md. Ann. Code 1974, Art. CL § 14-101 et
   seq.
Mich. Comp. Laws Ann., 493.1 et seq.
Mo. Rev. Stat., 408.100 et seq.
N.C. Gen. Stat. 1943, § 53-164 et seq.
N.D. Cent. Code 13-03.1-01 et seq.
Ore. Rev. Stat., 725.010 et seq.
S.C. Code Ann. 1976, § 34-29-10 et seq.
S.D. Codified Laws 1967, 54-4-1 et seq.,
   54-6-1 et seq.
Va. Code 1950, § 6.1-244 et seq.
Wash. Rev. Code Ann., 31.08.010 et seq.

Consumer Finance Lenders Law
Cal. Financial Code § 24000 et seq.

Consumer Financial Services Act
Mich. Comp. Laws Ann., 487.2051 et seq.

Consumer Fraud Act
Iowa Code Ann., 714.16
N.J. Stat. Ann., 56:8-1 et seq.
Vt. Stat. Ann. 1959, Title 9, § 2451 et seq.

**Consumer Fraud and Deceptive Business
Practices Act**
Ill. Comp. Stat. 1992, Ch. 815, § 505/1 et seq.
Ky. Rev. Stat. 1971, 288.410 et seq.

Consumer Funds Transfer Facilities Act
Utah Code Ann. 1953, 7-16-1 et seq.

Consumer Goods Pricing Act of 1975
Dec. 12, 1975, P.L. 94-145, 89 Stat. 801, 15
   U.S. Code § 1 et seq.

Consumer Goods Rental Protection Act
W. Va. Code § 46B-1-1 et seq.

Consumer Goods Repair Board Act
D.C. Code Ann., §§ 2-3903, 28-3905

**Consumer Home Mortgage Assistance Act of
1974**
Aug. 22, 1974, P.L. 93-383, 12 U.S. Code
   § 1464 nt.

Consumer Housing Cooperatives Act
Mich. Comp. Laws Ann., 125.1471 et seq.

**Consumer Information Act (Mercury
Emissions)**
Minn. Stat. Ann., 116.925

Consumer Installment Loan Act
D.C. Code Ann., § 28-3818
Ill. Comp. Stat. 1992, Ch. 205, § 670/1 et seq.

Consumer Lease Act (Motor Vehicle)
Wis. Stat. Ann., 429.101 et seq.

Consumer Lease-Purchase Agreement Act
Kan. Stat. Ann., 50-680 et seq.

Consumer Leasing Act of 1976
March 23, 1976, P.L. 94-240, 15 U.S. Code
   § 1601 et seq.

Consumer Legal Remedies Act
Cal. Civil Code § 1750 et seq.

Consumer Loan Act
Ind. Code 1971, 28-7-2-1 et seq.
Kan. Laws 1955, Ch. 135
Ky. Rev. Stat. 1971, 288.410 et seq.
Md. Ann. Code 1974, Art. CL, § 12-301 et
   seq.
Mont. Code Ann., 32-5-101 et seq.
N.J. Stat. Ann., 17:10-1 et seq.
Wash. Rev. Code 1989, 31.04.005 et seq.

Consumer Loan Act (Market Rate)
N.J. Stat. Ann., 17:12B-155

Consumer Loan Act-Licensing Provisions
Md. Ann. Code 1974, Art. FI, § 11-201 et
   seq.

Consumer Loan Broker Act
Miss. Code Ann., § 81-19-1 et seq.

Consumer Notification Act (Automotive)
Cal. Civil Code §§ 1793.23, 1793.24

Consumer-Patient Radiation Health and Safety Act of 1981
Aug. 13, 1981, P.L. 97-35, 42 U.S. Code § 10001 et seq.
June 13, 1991, P.L. 102-54, 42 U.S. Code §§ 10004, 10007
Dec. 21, 1995, P.L. 104-66, 42 U.S. Code § 10006

Consumer Privacy Act (Communications)
Ill. Comp. Stat. 1992, Ch. 720, § 110/1 et seq.

Consumer Privacy Act (Video)
N.Y. General Business Law (Consol. Laws Ch. 20) § 670 et seq.

Consumer Product Promotion Fair Practices Act (Mail and Telephone)
Ark. Acts 1991, No. 680

Consumer Product Safety Act
Oct. 27, 1972, P.L. 92-573, 86 Stat. 1207, 5 U.S. Code §§ 5314, 5315; 15 U.S. Code §§ 2051 to 2081
July 11, 1978, P.L. 95-319, 15 U.S. Code §§ 2068, 2082
Nov. 10, 1978, P.L. 95-631, 15 U.S. Code §§ 2053, 2056, 2058, 2067 to 2069, 2076
Jan. 4, 1983, P.L. 97-414, 15 U.S. Code §§ 2055, 2060, 2064, 2068 , 2080
Nov. 16, 1990, P.L. 101-608, 15 U.S. Code § 2053 et seq. generally
Nov. 2, 1994, P.L. 103-437, 15 U.S. Code § 2081
Mont. Code Ann., 50-30-101 et seq.

Consumer Product Safety Act of 1975
Mont. Code Ann., 50-30-101 et seq.

Consumer Product Safety Amendments of 1981
Aug. 13, 1981, P.L. 97-35, 15 U.S. Code § 2051 nt.

Consumer Product Safety Improvement Act of 1990
Nov. 16, 1990, P.L. 101-608, 15 U.S. Code §§ 2051 nt., 2054 nt., 2076 nt.

Consumer Products Guaranty Act
Md. Ann. Code 1974, Art. CL, § 14-401 et seq.

Consumer Protection Act
Colo. Rev. Stat., 6-1-101 et seq.
Ida. Code 1947, 48-601 et seq.
Kan. Stat. Ann., 50-623 et seq.
Ky. Rev. Stat. 1971, 367.110 et seq.
La. Rev. Stat. Ann., 51:1401 et seq.
Md. Ann. Code 1974, Art. CL, § 13-101 et seq.
Mich. Comp. Laws Ann., 445.901 et seq.
Miss. Code Ann., § 75-24-1 et seq.
Mont. Code Ann., 30-14-101 et seq.
Neb. Rev. Stat. 1943, 59-1601 et seq.
N.H. Rev. Stat. 1955, 358-A:1 et seq.
N.Y. Adm. Code '85, Ch. 20, § 20-700 et seq.
Okla. Stat. Ann., Title 15, § 751 et seq.
S.D. Codified Laws 1967, 37-24-1 et seq.
Tenn. Code Ann., 47-18-101 et seq.
Va. Code 1950, § 59.1-196 et seq.
Wash. Rev. Code Ann., 19.86.010 et seq.
Wyo. Stat. Ann., § 40-12-101 et seq.

Consumer Protection Act (Communications)
Conn. Gen. Stat. Ann., § 53-420 et seq.

Consumer Protection Act (DeceptiveTrade Practices)
Ala. Code 1975, § 8-19-1 et seq.

Consumer Protection Act (Health Spa)
Ark. Code Ann. 1987, 4-94-108 et seq.

Consumer Protection Act (Hillsborough County)
Fla. Special Laws 1975, Ch. 75-394

Consumer Protection Act (Insurance Sales)
Ark. Code 1987, 23-66-601 et seq.
Ida. Code 1947, 41-5701 et seq.
W. Va. Code 1966, § 33-11A-1 et seq.

Consumer Protection Act (Kosher Food)
N.J. Stat. Ann., 56:8-61 et seq.

Consumer Protection Act (Land Development)
Ore. Rev. Stat., 94.029, 92.500 et seq., 92.990, 696.300

Consumer Protection Act (Packaged Commodities)
Conn. Gen. Stat. Ann., § 42-115g et seq.

Consumer Protection Act (Pasco County)
Fla. Special Laws 1974, Ch. 74-573

Consumer Protection Act (Pay-Per-Call Services)
Ill. Rev. Stat. 1991, Ch. 134, § 151 et seq.

Consumer Protection Act (Pinellas County)
Fla. Special Laws 1973, Ch. 602, 1976, Ch. 76-471

Consumer Protection Act (Tanner)
Cal. Civil Code § 1793.22

Consumer Protection Act (Telecommunications)
Fla. Stat., 364.601 to 364.604

Consumer Protection Act (Travel Promotion)
Ill. Rev. Stat. 1991, Ch. 121 1/2, § 1851 et seq.

Consumer Protection Act (Unfair Trade Practices)
Fla. Stat. Ann., 501.201 et seq.

Consumer Protection Act Relative to the Sale of Insurance by Banks
Mass. Gen. Laws Ann., 167F.2A, 175.209 to 175.211, 178A.4, 183.68

Consumer Protection and Banking Deregulation Act (Omnibus)
N.Y. General Business Law (Consol. Laws Ch. 20) § 520c

Consumer Protection and Regulation of Business Practice Act
Mass. Gen. Laws Ann., 93A:1 et seq.

Consumer Protection and Truth in Construction Act
Tenn. Code Ann., 66-11-201 et seq.

Consumer Protection and Unfair Trade Practices Act
See Unfair Trade Practices and Consumer Protection Act

Consumer Protection Code
S.C. Code Ann. 1976, § 37-1-101 et seq.

Consumer Protection Code Revision Act
S.C. Code Ann. 1976, §§ 37-1-109, 37-1-201 et seq.

Consumer Protection Code—Administration
S.C. Code Ann. 1976, § 37-6-101 et seq.

Consumer Protection Code—Credit Sales
S.C. Code Ann. 1976, § 37-2-101 et seq.

Consumer Protection Code—Insurance
S.C. Code Ann. 1976, § 37-4-101 et seq.

Consumer Protection Code—Loans
S.C. Code Ann. 1976, § 37-3-101 et seq.

Consumer Protection Code—Remedies and Penalties
S.C. Code Ann. 1976, § 37-5-101 et seq.

Consumer Protection Law (Observant)
N.Y. General Business Law (Consol. Laws Ch. 20) § 349a

Consumer Protection Leasing Act
N.J. Stat. Ann., 56:12-60 et seq.

Consumer Protection Procedures Act
D.C. Code Ann., § 28-3901 et seq.

Consumer Protection Warranty Extension Act
Tenn. Code Ann., 47-18-1401 et seq.

Consumer Rental Purchases Agreement Act
Iowa Code Ann., 537.3601 et seq.
Neb. Rev. Stat. 1943, 69-2101 et seq.

455

Consumer Reporting Employment Clarification Act of 1998
Nov. 2, 1998, P.L. 105-347, 112 Stat. 3208, 15 U.S. Code § 1601 nt.

Consumer Sales Practices Act
Kan. Stat. Ann., 50-623 et seq.
Ohio Rev. Code 1953, 1345.01 et seq.
Utah Code Ann. 1953, 13-11-1 et seq.

Consumer Sales Tax Act
W. Va. Code 1966, § 11-15-1 et seq.

Consumer Services Act
Fla. Stat. Ann., 570.542 et seq.

Consumer Services Office Information Act
Ill. Rev. Stat. 1991, Ch. 127, § 1600 et seq.

Consumer Telemarketing Protection Act
La. Rev. Stat. Ann., 45:810 et seq.

Consumer Transmission of Money Act
D.C. Code Ann., § 47-3101 et seq.

Consumer Unit Pricing Act
Fla. Stat. Ann., 501.135

Consumer Utilities Rate Advocacy Division Act
Ark. Acts 1983, p. 2469, First Ex. No. 39

Consumer Warranty Act
Cal. Civil Code § 1790 et seq.

Consumer—Antitrust Protection Improvement Act
Wash. Rev. Code Ann., 19.86.090 et seq.

Consumers Agency and Disclosure Act (Real Estate)
Ala. Code 1975, §§ 34-27-8, 34-27-80 et seq.

Consumer's Cooperative Act
Me. Rev. Stat. Ann. 1964, Title 13, § 1501 et seq.

Consumers' Council Act
R.I. Gen. Laws 1956, 42-42-1 et seq.

Consumers Disclosure of Prizes and Gifts Act
Okla. Stat. Ann., Title 21, § 996.1 et seq.

Consumers Legal Remedies Act
Cal. Civil Code § 1750 et seq.

Consumers Power Districts Law
S.D. Codified Laws 1967, 49-35-1 et seq.

Consumers Rights Act (Mental Health)
Ala. Code 1975, § 22-56-1 et seq.

Consumers' Sales and Use Tax Act
Ga. Code Ann., 48-8-1 et seq.

Consumers Sales Tax Act
N.Y. Local Laws 1954, Buffalo, No. 2
Okla. Stat. Ann., Title 68, § 1350 et seq.
Pa. 1953 Pamph. Laws 389, No. 86
W. Va. Code 1931, Ch. 11, Art. 15

Consumers' Utility Counsel Act
Ga. Code Ann., 46-10-1 et seq.

Consumption Tax Law
Haw. Rev. Stat. Ann., § 238-1 et seq.

Contact Lens Dispenser Act
N.J. Stat. Ann., 52:17B-41.1 et seq.

Contact Lens Prescription Act
Tex. Rev. Civ. Stat., Art. 4552-A

Contact Lens Seller Registration Act (Nonresident)
Cal. Business and Professions Code § 2546 et seq.

Contagious Disease Prevention Act
D.C. Code Ann., § 6-117 et seq.

Container Act (Milk Products)
Mass. Gen. Laws Ann., 110:21 et seq.

Container Coding Act (Plastic)
Neb. Laws 1993, L.B. 63, § 1

Container Label Obliteration Act
Ill. Comp. Stat. 1992, Ch. 720, § 565/0.01 et seq.

Container Trade Mark Act
Ill. Rev. Stat. 1991, Ch. 140, § 121 et seq.

Containers, Carts, Cases, Baskets, and Boxes Act
Fla. Stat. Ann., 506.501 et seq.

Containment Act (Hospital Cost)
Cal. Health and Safety Code §§ 436.4, 436.490 to 436.492, 443.22, 15047.5, 15049.5, 15057, 15071

Contempt Act
Mich. Comp. Laws Ann., 600.1701 et seq.
N.C. Gen. Stat. 1943, § 5A-11 et seq.
Ore. Rev. Stat. 1989, 33.010 et seq.
P.R. Laws Ann. 1954, Title 33, § 517 et seq.
Va. Code 1950, § 16.1-69.24
Wis. Stat. 1989, 785.01 et seq.

Contempt Act (Civil)
Mont. Code Ann., 3-1-501 et seq.
Wash. Rev. Code Ann., 7.21.010 et seq.

Contempt Act (Criminal)
Mont. Code Ann., 45-7-309
Wash. Rev. Code Ann., 9.92.040

Contest of Adoption Act
Ill. Comp. Stat. 1992, Ch. 750, §§ 55/0.01, 55/1

Contested Elections Act
Mo. Rev. Stat., 115.526 et seq.

Contests and Gift Giveaway Act
Tex. Rev. Civ. Stat., Art. 5069-17.01

Contiguous Cities Merger Act
Ky. Rev. Stat. 1971, 81.410 et seq.

Continental Scientific Drilling and Exploration Act
Sept. 22, 1988, P.L. 100-441, 102 Stat. 1760, 43 U.S. Code § 31 nt.

Contingency Fund Act
Del. Laws Vol. 50, p. 1211, Ch. 518

Contingent Claims Act (Estates)
Ohio Rev. Code 1953, 2117.37 et seq.

Contingent Remainder Act
Ill. Comp. Stat. 1992, Ch. 765, §§ 340/0.01, 340/1
Iowa Code Ann., 557.7, 557.8
Mass. Gen. Laws Ann., 184:2, 184:3

Continuation of Business Act
Ill. Rev. Stat. 1991, Ch. 110 1/2, § 19-6

Continuing Care Act
N.M. Stat. Ann., 24-17-1

Continuing-Care Disclosure Act
Ida. Code 1947, 67-2750 et seq.

Continuing Care Facility Disclosure and Rehabilitation Act
Minn. Stat. Ann., 80D.01 et seq.
Tex. Health and Safety Code, § 246.001 et seq.

Continuing Care Facility Registration Act
Minn. Stat. Ann., 80D.03

Continuing Care Provider Registration and Disclosure Act
La. Rev. Stat. Ann., 51:2171 et seq.
Pa. Purdon's Stat., Title 40, § 3201 et seq.

Continuing Care Provider Regulation Act
Ark. Code Ann. 1987, 23-93-101 et seq.

Continuing Care Retirement Community Act
S.C. Code Ann. 1976, § 37-11-10 et seq.

Continuing Care Retirement Community Provider Registration Act
Ore. Rev. Stat., 101.010 et seq.

Continuing Care Retirement Community Regulation and Financial Disclosure Act
N.J. Stat. Ann., 52:27D-330 et seq.

Continuing Contract Act (Teachers)
Kan. Stat. Ann., 72-5410 et seq.
Tenn. Code Ann., 49-5-409

Continuing Drug Enterprises Act of 1986
Oct. 27, 1986, P.L. 99-570, 21 U.S. Code
§ 801 nt.

Continuing Education Act
Iowa Code Ann., 258A.1 et seq.

Continuing Garnishment Act
La. Rev. Stat. Ann., 13:3921 et seq.

Continuing Pharmaceutical Education Act
N.J. Stat. Ann., 45:14-11.2 et seq.

Continuity Act (Corporations)
Del. Code of 1974, Title 8, § 278

Continuity Act (Dissolved Corporations)
Mass. Gen. Laws Ann., 155:51

Continuity in Government Act
Mont. Code Ann., 10-3-601 et seq.

Continuity of Government Act
Wash. Rev. Code Ann., 42.14.010 et seq.

**Continuous Benefits Replacement Act
(Cal-COBRA)**
Cal. Health and Safety Code § 1366.20 et
seq.
Cal. Insurance Code § 10128.50 et seq.

Continuous Contract Act (Teachers)
Wis. Stat. 1989, 118.21 et seq.

**Contra Costa County Court Services
Consolidation Act**
Cal. Government Code § 26625 et seq.

**Contra Costa County Flood Control and
Water Conservation District Act**
Cal. Water Code, Appendix, § 63-1 et seq.

Contra Costa County Storm Drainage Act
Cal. Water Code, Appendix, § 69-1 et seq.

Contra Costa County Water Agency Act
Cal. Water Code, Appendix, § 80-1 et seq.

Contraband Forfeiture Act
Colo. Rev. Stat., 16-13-501 et seq.
Fla. Stat. Ann., 932.701 et seq.

W. Va. Code 1966, § 60A-7-701 et seq.

Contraband Seizure Act
Aug. 9, 1939, Ch. 618, 53 Stat. 1291, 49 U.S.
Code §§ 781 to 788
Aug. 1, 1956, Ch. 852, 70 Stat. 911, 49 U.S.
Code § 789

Contraband Transportation Act
Fla. Stat. Ann., 943.41 et seq.

Contraceptive Act
Conn. Gen. Stat. Ann., § 53-32

Contraceptives and Prophylactic Act
Ore. Rev. Stat., 435.010 et seq.

Contract and Grant Management Act
Tex. Government Code, § 783.001

**Contract and Property Emancipation
Statute (Married Women)**
Iowa Code Ann., 597.1 et seq.

Contract Carrier Act
N.Y. Public Service Law, (Consol. Laws, Ch.
48) § 160 et seq.
Ohio Rev. Code 1953, 4923.02 et seq.

Contract-Carrier Vehicle Act
Ind. Code Ann., 8-2-7-1 et seq.

**Contract Deposit and Maintenance Laws of
the Town of Ramapo**
N.Y. Local Laws 1967, Town of Ramapo,
pp. 1911, 1915

Contract Disputes Act of 1978
Nov. 1, 1978, P.L. 95-563, 41 U.S. Code
§§ 601 et seq., 601 nt.
Nov. 8, 1985, P.L. 99-145, 10 U.S. Code
§ 2324
Nov. 5, 1990, P.L. 101-509, 41 U.S. Code
§ 607
Nov. 15, 1990, P.L. 101-552, 41 U.S. Code
§§ 605, 607
Oct. 29, 1992, P.L. 102-572, 41 U.S. Code
§ 605
Oct. 13, 1994, P.L. 103-355, 41 U.S. Code
§§ 605, 607, 608, 609

Feb. 10, 1996, P.L. 104-106, 41 U.S. Code §§ 601, 605, 612

Oct. 19, 1996, P.L. 104-320, 41 U.S. Code § 605

Nov. 18, 1997, P.L. 105-85, 41 U.S. Code § 605

Contract Forfeiture Act (Real Estate)

Wash. Rev. Code Ann., 61.30.010 et seq.

Contract Fraud Act (Public)

Ill. Rev. Stat. 1991, Ch. 127, § 132.50 et seq.

Contract Labor Act

Haw. Session Laws 1850, p. 170, June 21, 1850, § 22 et seq.

Contract Labor Laws

See Alien Contract Labor Laws

Contract Law (Variable)

N.M. Stat. Ann., 59A-20-30

Contract Lien Act

Md. Ann. Code 1974, Art. RP, § 14-201 et seq.

Contract Motor Carrier Act

Kan. Stat. Ann., 66-1, 112a et seq.

Contract Preference Act (Target Area)

Cal. Government Code § 4530 et seq.

Contract Prompt Payment Law (Construction)

Fla. Laws 1992, Ch. 286

Contract Sentencing Act

Tenn. Code Ann., 40-34-101 et seq.

Contract Services for Drug Dependent Federal Offenders Act of 1978

Oct. 27, 1978, P.L. 95-537, 18 U.S. Code §§ 3651, 3651 nt., 4255, 4255 nt.

Oct. 27, 1986, P.L. 99-570, 18 U.S. Code § 4255 nt.

Oct. 12, 1990, P.L. 101-421, 18 U.S. Code § 3672 nt.

Contract Services for Drug Dependent Federal Offenders Authorization Act of 1983

March 20, 1984, P.L. 98-236, 18 U.S. Code § 4255 nt.

Contract Settlement Act of 1944

July 1, 1944, Ch. 358, 58 Stat. 649 (See 18 U.S. Code § 3287) 41 U.S. Code § 101 et seq.

July 28, 1953, Ch. 253, 67 Stat. 226, 41 U.S. Code § 114

June 28, 1954, Ch. 403, 68 Stat. 300, 41 U.S. Code § 117

Oct. 19, 1996, P.L. 104-316, 41 U.S. Code §§ 116, 118

Contract Statute of Limitations

N.Y. Civil Practice Laws and Rules (Consol. Laws Ch. 8) § 213

Contract Termination Act

Cal. Code of Civil Procedure § 875 et seq.

Ill. Rev. Stat. 1991, Ch. 70, § 300 et seq.

Contract with America Advancement Act of 1996

March 29, 1996, P.L. 104-121, 5 U.S. Code § 601 nt.

Aug. 22, 1996, P.L. 104-193, 42 U.S. Code § 401 nt.

Aug. 5, 1997, P.L. 105-33, 42 U.S. Code § 1382 nt.

Contract Work Hours and Safety Standards Act

Aug. 13, 1962, P.L. 87-581, 76 Stat. 357, 40 U.S. Code §§ 327 to 332

Aug. 9, 1969, P.L. 91-54, 83 Stat. 96, 40 U.S. Code § 333

Nov. 8, 1985, P.L. 99-145, 40 U.S. Code § 328

Oct. 13, 1994, P.L. 103-355, 40 U.S. Code §§ 329, 333, 334

Contracting and Enabling Act (Private Prison)

W. Va. Code 1966 § 25-5-1 et seq.

Contracting Regulations between Government and Private Interests for the Administration and Operation of Government Health Facilities Act
P.R. Laws Ann. 1954, Title 24, § 338 et seq.

Contractor and Subcontractor Payment Act
Pa. Purdon's Stat., Title 73, § 501 et seq.

Contractor Certification Act (Landscape Irrigation)
N.J. Stat. Ann., 45:5AA-1 to 45:5AA-3

Contractor Development Act (Highway)
Kan. Stat. Ann., 68-440 et seq.

Contractor Indemnification Act (Response Action)
Ill. Rev. Stat. 1991, Ch. 111 1/2, § 7201 et seq.

Contractor License Law (Air Conditioning and Refrigeration)
Tex. Rev. Civ. Stat., Art. 8861

Contractor Licensing Act
W. Va. Code 1966, § 21-11-1 et seq.

Contractor Registration Act
Neb. Rev. Stat. 1943, 48-2101 et seq.

Contractor Transaction Recovery Act
Va. Code 1950, § 54.1-1118 et seq.

Contractor-Under Act
Mich. Comp. Laws 1948, 411.10
Tex. Rev. Civ. Stat., Art. 8307, § 6

Contractor-Under Act (Workmen's Compensation)
Ga. Code Ann., 34-9-8

Contractor Unified License and Permit Bond Act
Ill. Comp. Stat. 1992, Ch. 50, § 830/1 et seq.

Contractors Act
S.C. Code Ann. 1976, § 40-11-10 et seq.
Va. Code 1950, § 54.1-1100 et seq.

Contractors Act (Electrical)
N.M. Stat. Ann. 1953, 67-19-1 et seq.

Contractors Act (Farm Labor)
Neb. Rev. Stat. 1943, 48-1701 et seq.

Contractors Act (Residential Building)
Minn. Stat. Ann., 326.83 et seq.

Contractors Act (Warm Air Heating)
Ga. Code Ann., 43-14-1 et seq.

Contractors Bond Act
D.C. Code Ann., §§ 1-1104 to 1-1108
Ga. Code Ann., 13-10-1, 13-10-21, 13-10-22
Mich. Comp. Laws Ann., 570.101 et seq.
N.J. Rev. Stat. 1937, 2A:44-143 et seq.
Ohio Rev. Code 1953, 153.04 et seq.
Utah Code Ann. 1953, 14-2-1, 14-2-2
Wash. Rev. Code Ann., 39.08.010 et seq.

Contractors' Bond Act (MacGregor)
Tex. Rev. Civ. Stat., Art. 5160

Contractors Indemnification Act (Hazardous Substance Response Action)
N.J. Laws 1991, Ch. 373, 39:7-2

Contractors License Act
Ariz. Rev. Stat. Ann., § 32-1101 et seq.
Ark. Code Ann. 1987, 17-22-101, 17-22-102
Cal. Business and Professions Code § 7000 et seq.
Nev. Rev. Stat. 1973 Reprint, 624.230 et seq.
Tenn. Code Ann., 62-6-101 et seq.
Utah Code Ann. 1953, Miscellaneous Superseded Code Provision, 58-23-1 et seq.

Contractors License Act (Plumbing)
Ida. Code 1947, 54-2601 et seq.

Contractors Licensing Act
N.M. Stat. Ann. 1953, 67-16-1 et seq.
Utah Code Ann. 1953, 58-55-1 et seq.

Contractors' Licensing Act (Public Works)
Nev. Rev. Stat. Ann. 33.010 et seq.

Contractors' Licensing and Water Well Standards Act
Neb. Rev. Stat. 1943, 46-1201 et seq.

Contractors Registration Act
Wash. Rev. Code Ann., 18.27.010 et seq.

Contractors' Relief Act
Ind. Laws 1919, Ch. 93, p. 475

Contractors' State License Board Enforcement Act (Stirling-Areias)
Cal. Business and Professions Code §§ 7019, 7020, 7065.3, 7091

Contractors State License Law
Cal. Business and Profession Code, § 7000 et seq.

Contractors' Surety Bond Law (Public Works)
Me. Rev. Stat. Ann. 1964, Title 14, § 871 et seq.

Contracts Act
Mont. Code Ann., 28-2-101 et seq.

Contracts by Minors Act (Artistic)
Ill. Comp. Stat. 1992, Ch. 820, § 20/0.01 et seq.

Contracts Treble Damage Law
Tenn. Code Ann., 47-50-109

Contractual Arbitration Act
Pa. Cons. Stat., Title 42, § 7301 et seq.

Contractual Liability Act
N.J. Stat. Ann., 59:13-1 et seq.

Contributing to Delinquency Act
Ill. Rev. Stat. 1991, Ch. 23, § 2360a et seq.
Ky. Rev. Stat. 1971, Superseded Vols., 208.020

Contribution Among Joint Tortfeasors Act
Del. Code of 1974, Title 10, § 6301 et seq.
Ga. Code Ann., 51-12-32
Ill. Rev. Stat. 1991, Ch. 70, § 301 et seq.
Mass. Gen. Laws Ann., 231B:1 et seq.
Md. Ann. Code 1957, Art. 50, § 16 et seq.

Contribution Among Tort-Feasors Act
See also Uniform Contribution Among Tort-Feasors Act
Cal. Code of Civil Procedure § 875 et seq.
N.Y. Civil Practice Laws and Rules (Consol. Laws Ch. 8) § 1401 et seq.

Contributory Delinquent Children Law
Colo. Rev. Stat., 19-7-101 et seq.

Contributory Negligence Act
Miss. Code Ann., § 11-7-15
N.H. Rev. Stat. 1955, 507:7a
Wis. Stat. 1989, 895.045

Contributory Negligence Act (Damages)
Ark. Stat. 1947, 27-1730.1, 27-1730.2

Contributory Negligence Statute (Railroads)
Ark. Code Ann. 1987, 23-12-904

Contributory Retirement Act
Me. Rev. Stat. Ann. 1964, Title 5, § 17001 et seq.

Contributory Retirement Act (Employees')
Me. Rev. Stat. Ann. 1964, Title 5, § 17001 et seq.

Contributory Retirement Act (Public Employees)
Mass. Gen. Laws Ann., 32:1 et seq.
Mass. Gen. Laws 1984, 32:1 et seq.

Control Act (Asbestos)
Okla. Stat. Ann., Title 40, §§ 450 to 454

Control Act (Gun)
Mass. Gen. Laws Ann., 140:121 et seq.

Control Act (Plant Pest)
Mass. Gen. Laws Ann., 128:16 et seq.

Control Act (Radiation)
Utah Code Ann. 1953, 19-3-101 et seq.

Control Act (Radon)
Mont. Code Ann., 75-3-601 et seq.

Control Act (Sewage System Cleaner)
Pa. 1992 Pamph. Laws, No. 41

Control Act (Structural Pest)
Okla. Stat. Ann., Title 2, § 3-171 et seq.

Control and Assessment Act (Chronic Disease Prevention)
N.H. Rev. Stat. 1955, 141-B:1 et seq.

Control and Disclosure & Political Contributions and Expenditures
Okla. Stat. Ann., Title 63, § 1-2001 et seq.

Control and Prevention Act (Hazardous Substances Spill)
Tex. Water Code, § 26.261 et seq.

Control and Procedures Act (Revenue)
Utah Code Ann. 1953, 63-38a-101 et seq.

Control and Research Act (Cancer)
Fla. Stat. Ann., 240.5121

Control of Money Laundering in Financial Institutions Act
Fla. Stat. Ann., 655.50

Control of Money Laundering in Money Transmitters Act
Fla. Stat. Ann., 560.123

Control of Paperwork Amendments of 1978
Nov. 1, 1978, P.L. 95-561, 20 U.S. Code §§ 1221-3, 1221-3 nt., 1221e-1, 1231g

Control of Profits of Organized Crime Act
Cal. Penal Code § 186 et seq.

Control of Sexually Transmissable Disease Act
Fla. Stat. Ann., 384.21 et seq.

Control of Wild Animals and Pests in Counties Act
Ida. Code 1947, 25-2601 et seq.

Control Radiation Act
Utah Code Ann. 1953, 19-3-101 et seq.

Control Share Acquisition Act
Ida. Code 1947, 30-1601 et seq.
N.C. Gen. Stat. 1943, § 55-9A-01 et seq.
Tenn. Code Ann., 48-35-301 et seq.
Utah Code Ann. 1953, 61-6-1 et seq.

Control Share Act
Miss. Code Ann., § 79-27-1 et seq.
Ore. Rev. Stat., 60.801 et seq.

Controlled Access Highway Act
Ala. Code 1975, § 23-3-1 et seq.
Ark. Code Ann. 1987, 27-68-101 et seq.
Del. Code of 1974, Title 17, § 171 et seq.
Fla. Stat. Ann., 338.01 et seq.
Ga. Code Ann., 40-6-50, 40-6-51
Ind. Code Ann., 8-11-1-1 et seq.
Iowa Code Ann., 306A.1 et seq.
Kan. Stat. Ann., 68-1901 et seq.
Ky. Rev. Stat. 1971, 177.220 et seq., 177.990
La. Rev. Stat. Ann., 48:301 et seq.
Mich. Comp. Laws Ann., 252.51 et seq.
Miss. Code Ann., § 65-5-1 et seq.
Mont. Rev. Code 1947, 32-2001 et seq.
N.H. Rev. Stat. 1955, 236:1 et seq.
Ohio Rev. Code 1953, 5537.04
Pa. Purdon's Stat., Title 36, § 2391.1 et seq.
S.C. Code Ann. 1976, § 57-5-1010 et seq.
S.D. Codified Laws 1967, 31-8-1 et seq.
Tenn. Code Ann., 54-16-101 et seq.
Utah Code Ann. 1953, 27-12-111 et seq.
Vt. Stat. Ann., Title 19, § 1701 et seq.
Wash. Rev. Code Ann., 47.52.001 et seq.
W. Va. Code 1966, § 17-4-39 et seq.
Wyo. Stat. Ann., § 24-6-101 et seq.

Controlled Allocation of Liability Act
Mont. Code Ann., 75-10-742 et seq.

Controlled Atmosphere Storage Act
N.J. Stat. Ann., 4:10-26 et seq.

Controlled Atmosphere Storage of Apples Act
Colo. Rev. Stat., 35-23.5-101 et seq.

Controlled Dangerous Substances Act
See Uniform Controlled Substances Act

N.H. Rev. Stat. 1955, 318-B:1 et seq.

Vt. Stat. Ann., Title 18, § 4201 et seq.

Controlled Dangerous Substances Registry Act

N.J. Stat. Ann., 26:2G-17 et seq.

Controlled Drug Act

N.H. Rev. Stat. 1955, 318-B:1 et seq.

Controlled Industrial Waste Disposal Act

Okla. Stat. Ann., Title 63, §§ 2262, 1-2001 et seq.

Controlled Industrial Waste Fund Act

Okla. Stat. Ann., Title 63, § 1-2015 et seq.

Controlled Insurer Act (Broker)

Kan. Stat. Ann., 40-37a01 et seq.

Wyo. Stat. Ann., § 26-45-101 et seq.

Controlled Insurer Act (Business Transacted with Producer)

Miss. Code Ann., § 83-59-1 et seq.

Controlled Property and Casualty Insurers Act (Business Transacted with Producer)

Ariz. Rev. Stat. Ann., § 36-2501 et seq.

Ga. Code Ann., 33-48-1 et seq.

La. Rev. Stat. Ann., 40:961 et seq.

Md. Ann. Code 1957, Art. 27, § 276 et seq.

Minn. Stat. Ann., 152.01 et seq.

N.J. Stat. Ann., 24:21-1 et seq.

Controlled Substance Analogue Enforcement Act of 1986

Oct. 27, 1986, P.L. 99-570, 21 U.S. Code § 801 nt.

Controlled Substance and Cannabis Nuisance Act

Ill. Comp. Stat. 1992, Ch. 740, § 40/0.01 et seq.

Controlled Substance and Marijuana Tax Act

S.C. Code Ann. 1976, § 12-21-5010 et seq.

Controlled Substance, Drug, Device and Cosmetic Act

Pa. Purdon's Stat., Title 35, § 780-101 et seq.

Controlled Substance Precursor Act

Utah Code Ann. 1953, 58-37c-1 et seq.

Controlled Substance Prescription Act

Tenn. Code Ann., 53-10-301 et seq.

Controlled Substance Registrant Protection Act of 1984

May 31, 1984, P.L. 98-305, 18 U.S. Code § 2118, 2118 nt.

Controlled Substance Tax Act

N.M. Stat. Ann., 7-18A-1 et seq.

Controlled Substances Act

See also Uniform Controlled Substances Act

Oct. 27, 1970, P.L. 91-513, 84 Stat. 1242, 18 U.S. Code §§ 1114, 1952; 21 U.S. Code §§ 321, 331, 333, 334, 360, 372, 381, 801 to 803, 811, 812, 821 to 829, 841 to 851, 871 to 886, 901 to 904; 42 U.S. Code § 242

May 14, 1974, P.L. 93-281, 88 Stat. 124, 21 U.S. Code §§ 802, 823, 824, 827

Oct. 18, 1977, P.L. 95-137, 21 U.S. Code §§ 904, 803

Nov. 10, 1978, P.L. 95-633, 21 U.S. Code §§ 802, 811, 812, 823, 827, 830, 841, 842, 872

Nov. 30, 1979, P.L. 96-132, 21 U.S. Code §§ 802, 878, 881, 883, 886, 904

Jan. 4, 1983, P.L. 97-414, 21 U.S. Code § 904

Oct. 27, 1986, P.L. 99-570, 21 U.S. Code §§ 802, 812, 813, 841, 843, 844, 845, 845a, 845b, 848, 856, 873, 878, 881, 960

Nov. 10, 1986, P.L. 99-646, 21 U.S. Code §§ 802, 812, 845a, 873, 878

Aug. 18, 1987. P.L. 100-93, 21 U.S. Code § 824

Nov. 18, 1988, P.L. 100-690, 21 U.S. Code §§ 802, 813, 830, 841 to 846, 848, 858, 872, 876, 881, 881 nt., 881-1, 884, 886, 963

Nov. 29, 1989, P.L. 101-189, 21 U.S. Code § 881

Nov. 29, 1990, P.L. 101-647, 18 U.S. Code § 2254; 21 U.S. Code §§ 802, 812, 841, 844, 844a, 845, 845a, 845b, 853a, 859 to 863, 880, 881, 881a, 881-1, 888, 889

Dec. 17, 1991, P.L. 102-239, 21 U.S. Code § 881

Continued

Dec. 17, 1993, P.L. 103-200, 21 U.S. Code §§ 802, 814, 822, 823, 824, 830, 843, 880

Sept. 13, 1994, P.L. 103-322, 21 U.S. Code §§ 802, 848, 849, 860

April 24, 1996, P.L. 104-132, 21 U.S. Code § 848

Sept. 23, 1996, P.L. 104-201, 21 U.S. Code § 890

Oct. 3, 1996, P.L. 104-237, 21 U.S. Code §§ 802, 814, 830, 841 to 844, 853, 881

Oct. 11, 1996, P.L. 104-294, 21 U.S. Code § 802

Oct. 13, 1996, P.L. 104-305, 21 U.S. Code § 841

Nov. 21, 1997, P.L. 105-115, 21 U.S. Code § 802

Oct. 21, 1998, P.L. 105-277, 21 U.S. Code §§ 841, 842

Controlled Substances Act (Cannabis and)

Ill. Comp. Stat. 1992, Ch. 35, § 520/1 et seq.

Controlled Substances Act (Drugs)

Miss. Code Ann., § 41-29-101 et seq.

Controlled Substances Act (Imitation and Counterfeit)

Colo. Rev. Stat., 18-18-419 to 18-18-424

Iowa Code Ann., 124A.1 et seq.

Controlled Substances Act (Imitation)

Ala. Code 1975, § 20-2-140 et seq.

Cal. Health and Safety Code § 1670 et seq.

Iowa Code Ann., 204A.1 et seq.

Utah Code Ann. 1953, 58-37b-1 et seq.

Controlled Substances Act (Licensing of)

Colo. Rev. Stat., 12-22-301 et seq.

Controlled Substances Act (Narcotics)

Iowa Code Ann., 204.101 et seq.

Controlled Substances Act (Regulation of Precursors to)

Haw. Rev. Stat. Ann., §§ 329-1 to 329-91

Controlled Substances Act (Regulation of Precursors)

Haw. Rev. Stat. Ann., § 329-81 et seq.

Controlled Substances and Dangerous Drugs Act

S.C. Code Ann. 1976, § 44-53-110 et seq.

Controlled Substances and Legend Drug Research Act

Tenn. Code Ann., 53-14-101 et seq.

Controlled Substances and Marijuana Taxation Act

R.I. Gen. Laws 1956, 44-49-1 et seq.

Controlled Substances Import and Export Act

Oct. 27, 1970, P.L. 91-513, 84 Stat. 1285, 21 U.S. Code §§ 171 nt., 198a, 951 to 966; 26 U.S. Code §§ 4901, 4905, 6808, 7012, 7103, 7326, 7607, 7609, 7641, 7651, 7655; 28 U.S. Code § 2901; 31 U.S. Code §§ 529d to 529f; 40 U.S. Code § 304m; 42 U.S. Code § 3411; 46 U.S. Code § 239a; 49 U.S. Code § 787

Nov. 10, 1978, P.L. 95-633, 21 U.S. Code §§ 952, 953

Oct. 12, 1984, P.L. 98-473, 21 U.S. Code § 960

Oct. 27, 1986, P.L. 99-570, 21 U.S. Code § 960

Aug. 23, 1988, P.L. 100-418, 21 U.S. Code § 951

Nov. 18, 1988, P.L. 100-690, 21 U.S. Code §§ 960, 961, 971

Nov. 29, 1990, P.L. 101-647, 21 U.S. Code § 960

Dec. 17, 1993, P.L. 103-200, 21 U.S. Code §§ 957, 958, 960, 971

Oct. 3, 1996, P.L. 104-237, 21 U.S. Code §§ 959, 960

Oct. 13, 1996, P.L. 104-305, 21 U.S. Code §§ 844, 959, 960

Oct. 21, 1998, P.L. 105-277, 21 U.S. Code §§ 956, 960

Nov. 6, 1998, P.L. 105-357, 21 U.S. Code § 956

Controlled Substances Import and Export Penalties Enhancement Act of 1986

Oct. 27, 1986, P.L. 99-570, 21 U.S. Code §§ 801 nt., 853, 958 to 960

Controlled Substances Monitoring Act
W. Va. Code 1966, § 60A-9-1 et seq.

Controlled Substances Penalties Amendments Act of 1984
Oct. 12, 1984, P.L. 98-473, 21 U.S. Code § 801 nt.

Controlled Substances Tax Act
Mass. Gen. Laws Ann., 64K:1 to 64K:14

Controlled Substances Tax Act (Cannabis and)
Ill. Comp. Stat. 1992, Ch. 35, § 520/1 et seq.

Controlled Substances Tax Act (Marijuana)
S.C. Code Ann. 1976 § 12-21-5010 et seq.

Controlled Substances Therapeutic Research Act
Ala. Code 1975, § 20-2-110 et seq.
Fla. Stat. Ann., 402.36
Ga. Code Ann., 43-34-120 et seq.
Mass. Gen. Laws Ann., 94D:1 et seq.
N.J. Stat. Ann., 26:2L-1 et seq.
N.M. Stat. Ann., 26-2A-1 et seq.
N.Y. Public Health Law 1953 (Consol. Laws Ch. 45) §§ 3397a to 3399g
S.C. Code Ann. 1976, § 44-53-610 et seq.
Tenn. Code Ann., 68-52-101 et seq.
Wash. Rev. Code Ann., 69.51.010 et seq.

Controlled Substances Tort Claims Act (Cannabis and)
Ill. Comp. Stat. 1992, Ch. 740, § 20/1 et seq.

Controlled Substances Trafficking Prohibition Act
Oct. 21, 1998, P.L. 105-277, Division C, Title VIII, Subtitle G, 21 U.S. Code § 801 nt.
Nov. 10, 1998, P.L. 105-357, 112 Stat. 3271, 21 U.S. Code § 801 nt.

Controllers Act (Counties)
Pa. Purdon's Stat., Title 16, § 7351 et seq.

Controlling Agents Act
Ky. Rev. Stat. 1971, 304.3-500 to 304.3-570

Controls Act (Agricultural Commodities)
Minn. Stat. Ann., 17.90 et seq.

Controversies and Provisional Legal Status Act
P.R. Laws Ann. 1954, Title 32, § 2871 et seq.

Convalescent Colony Law
Cal. Health and Safety Code § 24380 et seq.

Convalescent Statutes Act (Mental Patients)
N.M. Stat. Ann. 1953, 34-2-11

Convenience Business Security Act
Fla. Stat. Ann., 812.1701 et seq.

Convenience Store Security Act
Fla. Stat. Ann., 812.171 et seq.

Convenience Warehouse Act
Ga. Code Ann., 10-4-190 et seq.

Convention and Tourism Marketing Act
Mich. Comp. Laws Ann., 141.881 et seq.

Convention and Visitors Bureau Authority Act (Acworth Area)
Ga. Laws 1997, p. 3793

Convention and Visitors Bureau Authority Act (Conyers)
Ga. Laws 1999, S.B. 206

Convention and Visitors Bureau Authority Act (Kingsland Area)
Ga. Laws 1991, p. 4101

Convention and Visitors Bureau Authority Act (Perry Area)
Ga. Laws 1990, p. 3542

Convention and Visitors Bureau Authority Act (Richmond Hill Area)
Ga. Laws 1996, p. 4442

Convention and Visitors Bureau Authority Act (Thomasville)
Ga. Laws 1991 Ex. Sess., p. 434

Convention Center Authority Act
Conn. Gen. Stat. Ann., § 32-185 et seq.
Continued

Pa. Purdon's Stat., Title 53, § 16201 et seq.
R.I. Gen. Laws 1956, 42-99-1 et seq.

Convention Center Authority Act (Lower Fairfield County)
Conn. Gen. Stat. Ann., § 32-200 et seq.

Convention Center Authority Act (Newman)
Ga. Laws 1999, p. 222

Convention Center Authority Act (Third Class County)
Pa. Purdon's Stat., Title 16, § 13101 et seq.

Convention Center Operating Corporation Act
N.Y. Public Authorities Law (Consol. Laws Ch. 43A) § 2560 et seq.

Convention Development Tax Act
Fla. Stat. Ann., 212.0305

Convention Facilities Act
Ala. Code 1975, § 11-100-1 et seq.

Convention Facility and Tourism Promotion Tax Act
Mich. Comp. Laws Ann., 436.141

Convention Facility Development Act (State)
Mich. Comp. Laws Ann., 207.621 et seq.

Convention of Physical Protection of Nuclear Material Implementation Act of 1982
Oct. 18, 1982, P.L. 97-351, 18 U.S. Code §§ 831, 831 nt.

Convention on Cultural Property Implementation Act
Jan. 12, 1983, P.L. 97-446, 19 U.S. Code §§ 2601 et seq., 2601 nt. .
Dec. 22, 1987, P.L. 100-204, 19 U.S. Code §§ 2605, 2605 nt.

Convention on the Settlement of Investment Disputes Act of 1966
Aug. 11, 1966, P.L. 89-532, 80 Stat. 344, 22 U.S. Code §§ 1650, 1650a

Convention or Tourism Marketing Act (Community)
Mich. Comp. Laws Ann., 141.871 et seq.

Convention Promotion Act
Ill. Rev. Stat. 1991, Ch. 24, § 8-3-13

Convention, Sports Facility, Meeting and Tourism Act (State and Local Government)
Mo. Rev. Stat. 1978, 70.840 et seq.

Conventional Forces in Europe Treaty Implementation Act of 1991
Dec. 12, 1991, P.L. 102-228, 22 U.S. Code § 2751 nt.
April 30, 1994, P.L. 103-236, 22 U.S. Code § 2551 nt.

Conventional Home Loan Assistance and Protection Act
Minn. Stat. Ann., 47.20, 47.21

Conventional Interest Law
Tenn. Public Acts 1869-70, 1st Sess., Ch. 69

Conversion Act (Defense)
Cal. Government Code § 15346

Conversion Act (Home Equity)
Fla. Stat. Ann., 697.20 et seq.

Conversion Disclosure and Home Heating System Act
N.Y. General Business Law (Consol. Laws Ch. 20) § 778aa

Conversion Mortgage Act (Home Equity)
Tenn. Code Ann., 47-30-101 et seq.

Conversion of Utilities Law (Underground)
Ida. Code 1947, 50-2501 et seq.
Mont. Code Ann., 69-4-301 et seq.

Conversion Program Act (Clean Fuels)
Utah Code Ann. 1953, 9-1-701 et seq.

Converted Dwelling Act
N.Y. Multiple Dwelling Law 1946 (Consol. Laws Ch. 61A) § 170 et seq.

Conveyance Act (Park Commissioners Federal Government)
Ill. Rev. Stat. 1991, Ch. 105, §§ 325a., 325b

Conveyance Law (Real Estate)
Cal. Civil Code § 1091 et seq.

Conveyance of Burial Places to County Act
Ill. Comp. Stat. 1992, Ch. 765, §§ 805/0.01, 805/1
Ill. Rev. Stat. 1991, Ch. 21, §§ 0.01, 1

Conveyances Act
Fla. Stat. Ann., 689.01 et seq.
Ill. Comp. Stat. 1992, Ch. 765, § 5/0.01 et seq.
Ky. Rev. Stat. 1971, 382.010 et seq.
Md. Ann. Code 1974, Art. RP, § 3-101 et seq.
Mich. Comp. Laws Ann., 565.1 et seq.
Mo. Rev. Stat., 442.010 et seq.
Neb. Rev. Stat. 1943, 76-201 et seq.
Nev. Rev. Stat. 1979 Reprint, 111.105 et seq.
N.H. Rev. Stat. 1955, 477:1 et seq.
N.J. Stat. Ann., 46:3-1 et seq.
Ohio Rev. Code 1953, 5301.01 et seq.
Okla. Stat. Ann., Title 16, § 1 et seq.
R.I. Gen. Laws 1956, 34-11-1 et seq.
Tex. Property Code, § 5.001 et seq.
Va. Code 1950, § 55-1 et seq.
Vt. Stat. Ann., Title 27, § 301 et seq.
Wash. Rev. Code Ann., 64.04.010 et seq.

Conveyances Act (Short Forms)
N.M. Stat. Ann., 47-1-27 et seq.

Conveyances Recording Act
Colo. Rev. Stat., 38-35-101 et seq.
Haw. Rev. Stat. Ann., § 502-1 et seq.
Ky. Rev. Stat. 1971, 382.080 et seq.
Mich. Comp. Laws Ann., 565.29
Minn. Stat. Ann., 507.01 et seq.
Utah Code Ann. 1953, 57-3-1 et seq.

Conveyances Tax Act
Haw. Rev. Stat. Ann., § 247-1 et seq.
Wash. Rev. Code Ann., 82.20.005 et seq.

Conveyancing Act
W. Va. Code 1966, § 36-1-1 et seq.

Conveyancing and Recording Act
Colo. Rev. Stat., 38-35-109 et seq.

Convict Labor Act
N.H. Rev. Stat. 1955, 619:20 et seq.
Wash. Rev. Code Ann., 72.64.010 et seq.

Convict Lime Grinding Act
Va. Code 1950, § 53-75.1 et seq.

Convict-Made Goods Act
Oct. 14, 1940, Ch. 872, 54 Stat. 1134 (See 18 U.S. Code § 1761)

Convict-Made Goods Sale Act
Wash. Rev. Code 1979, 19.20.010 et seq.

Convicted Persons Status Act
Haw. Rev. Stat. Ann., § 831-1 et seq.
N.H. Rev. Stat. 1955, 607-A:1 et seq.

Convicted Sex Offender Act
Neb. Rev. Stat. 1943, 29-2922 et seq.

Conviction Information Act
See Uniform Conviction Information Act

Convicts' Civil Death Act
R.I. Gen. Laws 1956, 13-6-1

Convicts Road Camp Law
Cal. Penal Code § 2760 et seq.

Conway Act (Municipal Liability)
N.Y. General Municipal Law (Consol. Laws Ch. 24) §§ 50a, 50b et seq.

Conway Town Hall Building Loan Act
Mass. Acts 1950, Ch. 722

Conyers Convention and Visitors Bureau Authority Act
Ga. Laws 1999, S.B. 206

Conyers-Rockdale Amateur Athletic Authority Act
Ga. Laws 1999, S.B. 209

Conyers-Rockdale-Big Haynes Impoundment Authority Act
Ga. Laws 1991, p. 5053

Conyers-Rockdale County Charter Commission Act
Ga. Laws 1988, p. 3899

Cook County Board of Review Districts Act
Ill. Comp. Stat. 1992, Ch. 10, § 105/1 et seq.

Cook County Circuit Apportionment Act
Ill. Comp. Stat. 1992, Ch. 705, § 50/1 et seq.

Cook County Forest Preserve District Act
Ill. Comp. Stat. 1992, Ch. 70, § 810/0.01 et seq.

Cook County Secretary of State Buildings Act
Ill. Rev. Stat. 1991, Ch. 124, § 11.9 et seq.

Cooley Tobacco Act
See Agricultural Adjustment Act of 1938

Coolie Trade Prohibition Act
Feb. 19, 1862, Ch. 27, 12 Stat. 340

Cooling-Off Act (Divorce)
Ill. Rev. Stat. 1991, Ch. 40, § 401 et seq.

Coon Dog Act
Tenn. Code Ann., 70-4-122

Cooper Act (Oil and Gas Interstate Compact)
Mich. Comp. Laws Ann., 319.301 et seq.

Cooper-Hawes Act (Convict Made Goods)
Jan. 19, 1929, Ch. 79, 45 Stat. 1084, 49 U.S. Code § 60

Cooper-Howard-Hilton Act (Pari-Mutuel Betting)
Ky. Rev. Stat. 1971, 47.012, 137.190, 138.510 et seq.

Cooperation Act (Government)
Fla. Stat. Ann., 164.101 et seq.

Cooperation Act (Health Care)
S.C. Code Ann. 1976, § 44-7-500 et seq.

Cooperation Act (Housing)
Fla. Stat. Ann., 422.01 et seq.

Cooperation Act (Interagency)
Tex. Government Code, § 771.001 et seq.

Cooperation Act (Local Governmental)
Wis. Stat. 1989, 66.30

Cooperation and Hospital Efficiency Act
Colo. Rev. Stat., 24-32-2701 et seq.

Cooperation Commission Act (Interstate)
Mass. Gen. Laws 1984, 9:21 et seq.

Cooperative Act
Colo. Rev. Stat., 7-56-101 to 7-56-901
Ill. Comp. Stat. 1992, Ch. 805, § 310/1 et seq.

Cooperative Act (Electric)
Vt. Stat. Ann., Title 30, § 3001 et seq.

Cooperative Act (Health Care)
Minn. Stat. Ann., 62R.01 et seq.

Cooperative Act (Telephone)
S.C. Code Ann. 1976, § 33-46-10 et seq.

Cooperative Affordable Housing Ownership Act
Me. Rev. Stat. Ann. 1964, Title 13, § 1741 et seq.

Cooperative Agency Act (Municipal and Rural Electrification)
Me. Rev. Stat. Ann. 1964, Title 35-A, § 4101 et seq.

Cooperative Agreement Act (State Department of Health Services)
Cal. Health and Safety Code § 38070

Cooperative Agricultural Association Corporate Income Tax Act
Pa. Purdon's Stat., Title 72, § 3420-21

Cooperative Agricultural Association Corporate Net Income Tax Act
Pa. Purdon's Stat., Title 72, § 3420-21 et seq.

Cooperative Agricultural Association Law
Pa. Cons. Stat., Title 15, § 7501 et seq.

Cooperative Agricultural Marketing Associations Act (Nonprofit)
Cal. Corporations Code § 14550 et seq.

Cooperative Aquatic Products Marketing Act
Miss. Code Ann., § 79-21-1 et seq.

Cooperative Association Act (Agricultural)
Haw. Rev. Stat. Ann., § 421-1 et seq.
Me. Rev. Stat. Ann. 1964, Title 13, § 1771 et seq.
N.J. Stat. Ann., 4:13-1 et seq.
Utah Code Ann. 1953, 3-1-1 et seq.
Wash. Rev. Code Ann., 24.32.010 et seq.
W. Va. Code 1966, § 19-4-1 et seq

Cooperative Association and Nonprofit Corporation Act
Utah Code Ann. 1953, 16-6-18 et seq.

Cooperative Associations Act
Ark. Code Ann. 1987, 4-30-102, 4-30-105
Colo. Rev. Stat. 1963, 30-2-1 et seq.
D.C. Code Ann., § 29-1101 et seq.
Fla. Stat. Ann., 719.101 et seq.
Ill. Rev. Stat. 1991, Ch. 32, § 305 et seq.
Iowa Code Ann., 497.1 et seq.
Md. Ann. Code 1974, Art. CA, § 5-501 et seq.
Me. Rev. Stat. Ann. 1964, Title 13, § 1501 et seq.
Mich. Comp. Laws Ann., 500.6400 et seq.
Miss. Code Ann., § 79-17-1 et seq.
Mont. Code Ann., 35-15-101 et seq.
N.D. Cent. Code, 10-15-01 et seq.
N.M. Stat. Ann., 53-4-1 et seq.
P.R. Laws Ann. 1954, Title 5, § 881 et seq.
S.C. Code Ann. 1976, § 33-45-10 et seq.
Tex. Rev. Civ. Stat., Art. 1396-50.01
Wis. Stat., 185.01 et seq.

Cooperative Associations Act (Nonprofit)
Ga. Code Ann., 2-10-80 et seq.

Cooperative Bank Act
P.R. Laws Ann. 1954, Title 7, § 751 et seq.

Cooperative Companies Act
Mo. Rev. Stat., 357.010 et seq.

Cooperative Conversion Moratorium Act
D.C. Laws 1976, No. 1-71

Cooperative Corporation Act (Rural Electrification)
Ark. Code Ann. 1987, 23-18-301 et seq.

Cooperative Corporations Act
Alaska Stat. 1962, § 10.15.005 et seq.
Cal. Corporations Code § 12200 et seq.
Fla. Stat. Ann., 719.604 et seq.
Mass. Gen. Laws 1984, 157:1 et seq.
N.Y. Consol. Laws, Ch. 77
Okla. Stat. Ann., Title 18, § 421 et seq.
Ore. Rev. Stat. 1953, 62.005 et seq.
S.D. Codified Laws 1967, 47-15-1 et seq.
Tex. Rev. Civ. Stat., Art. 1396-50.01
Va. Code 1950, § 13.1-301 et seq.
Vt. Stat. Ann., Title 11, § 1081 et seq.
Wash. Rev. Code Ann., 23.86.010 et seq.
Wis. Stat. 1989, 185.01 et seq.

Cooperative Corporations Act (Employee)
Ala. Acts 1997, 1st Sp. Sess., No. 949
Me. Rev. Stat. Ann. 1964, Title 13, § 1971 et seq.
Wash. Rev. Code 1989, 23.78.010 et seq.

Cooperative Corporations Act (Worker)
Conn. Gen. Stat. Ann., § 33-418f

Cooperative Credit Union Act
S.C. Code Ann. 1976, § 34-27-10 et seq.

Cooperative Development Administration Act
P.R. Laws Ann. 1954, Title 5, § 931 et seq.

Cooperative Development and Operations of Juvenile Detention Facilities Act
Ark. Code Ann. 1987, 12-41-801 et seq.

Cooperative Development Company Act
P.R. Laws Ann. 1954, Title 5, § 981 et seq.

Cooperative Economic Development Law
La. Rev. Stat. Ann., 33:9020 et seq.

Cooperative Educational Services Boards Act
Ga. Code Ann., 20-2-200 et seq.
Wyo. Stat. Ann., § 21-20-101 et seq.

Cooperative Emergency Revenue Act
Ida. Laws 1935, First Extra Session, Ch. 12

Cooperative Emergency Revenue Fund Treasury Anticipation Note Act
Ida. Laws 1935, First Extra Session, Ch. 16

Cooperative Enabling Act (Rural Electrification)
Me. Rev. Stat. Ann. 1964, Title 35A, § 2801 et seq.

Cooperative Extension Service Act
Colo. Rev. Stat., 23-34-101 et seq.

Cooperative Farm Forestry Act
May 18, 1937, Ch. 226, 50 Stat. 188, 16 U.S. Code § 568b

Cooperative Forest Management Act
Aug. 25, 1950, Ch. 781, 64 Stat. 473, 16 U.S. Code §§ 568c, 568d
Sept. 25, 1962, P.L. 87-680, 76 Stat. 569, 16 U.S. Code § 568d
May 5, 1972, P.L. 92-288, 86 Stat. 134, 16 U.S. Code §§ 568c, 568d

Cooperative Forest Management Services Act
Wash. Rev. Code Ann., 76.52.010 et seq.

Cooperative Forestry Assistance Act of 1978
July 1, 1978, P.L. 95-313, 16 U.S. Code §§ 2101 et seq., 2101 nt.
Aug. 23, 1988, P.L. 100-418, 102 Stat. 1400, 16 U.S. Code § 2112

Nov. 5, 1990, P.L. 101-515, 16 U.S. Code §§ 2101, 2109
Nov. 28, 1990, P.L. 101-624, 7 U.S. Code §§ 2651 to 2654; 16 U.S. Code §§ 564 to 567, 594-1 et seq. generally, 1509, 1510, 1606, 2101 to 2112
Dec. 13, 1991, P.L. 102-237, 16 U.S. Code §§ 2103a, 2103c, 2105, 2106
April 4, 1996, P.L. 104-127, 16 U.S. Code §§ 2103, 2103c

Cooperative Grazing Association Act
N.D. Cent. Code 36-08-01 et seq.

Cooperative Housing Act
Iowa Code Ann., 499A.1 et seq.

Cooperative Housing Corporation Act
La. Rev. Stat. Ann., 12:499.1 et seq.
Mass. Gen. Laws Ann., 157B:1 et seq.
Md. Ann. Code 1974, Art. CA, § 5-6B-01 et seq.

Cooperative Housing Corporations Act
Mass. Gen. Laws Ann., 157B:1 et seq.

Cooperative Housing Ownership Act
Vt. Stat. Ann., Title 11, §§ 1250 et seq., 1581 et seq.

Cooperative Identity and Protection Act
Mich. Comp. Laws Ann., 445.51 et seq.

Cooperative Industrial Development Act
Tenn. Code Ann., 4-14-101 et seq.

Cooperative Insurance Company Act
Mich. Comp. Laws Ann., 500.6400 et seq.

Cooperative Law
Minn. Stat. Ann., 308A.001 et seq.

Cooperative Law (Electric)
La. Rev. Stat. Ann., 12:401 et seq.

Cooperative Life Insurance Association Act
Utah Code Ann. 1953, Miscellaneous Superseded Code Provisions, § 31-32-1 et seq.

Cooperative Livestock and Poultry Raising Law

Miss. Code Ann., § 79-19-1 et seq.

Cooperative Marketing Act

July 2, 1926, Ch. 725, 44 Stat. 802, 7 U.S. Code §§ 451 to 457

Ariz. Rev. Stat. Ann., § 10-701 et seq.

Ark. Code Ann. 1987, 2-2-401 et seq.

Colo. Rev. Stat., 7-56-101 et seq.

Ga. Code Ann., 2-10-80 et seq.

Ida. Code 1947, 22-2601 et seq.

Kan. Stat. Ann., 17-1601 et seq.

Ky. Rev. Stat. 1971, 272.010 et seq.

La. Rev. Stat. Ann., 3:121 et seq.

Minn. Stat. 1988, 308.51 et seq.

Mont. Code Ann. 1987, 35-17-101 et seq.

Neb. Rev. Stat. 1943, 21-1401 et seq.

Ore. Rev. Stat., 62.005 et seq.

S.C. Code Ann. 1976, § 33-47-10 et seq.

S.D. Code 1939, 4.1601 et seq.

Tenn. Code Ann., 43-16-101 et seq.

Tex. Agriculture Code, § 52.001 et seq.

Va. Code 1950, § 13.1-312 et seq.

Vt. Ann., Title 11, § 991 et seq.

Wis. Stat. 1989, 93.075 et seq.

Cooperative Marketing Act (Agricultural)

Ind. Code Ann., 15-7-1-1 et seq.

Miss. Code Ann., § 79-19-1 et seq.

Ohio Rev. Code 1953, 1729.01 et seq.

Cooperative Marketing Act (Real Estate)

Utah Code Ann. 1953, 57-23-6 et seq.

Cooperative Marketing Association Act

N.C. Gen. Stat. 1943, § 54-129 et seq.

N.H. Rev. Stat. 1955, 301:1 et seq.

N.M. Stat. Ann., 76-12-1 et seq.

Okla. Stat. Ann., Title 2, § 361 et seq.

Cooperative Marketing Association Act (Agricultural)

Cal. Food and Agricultural Code 1967, § 54031 et seq.

Cooperative Marketing Associations Act

Feb. 18, 1922, Ch. 57, 42 Stat. 388, 7 U.S. Code §§ 291, 292

Cooperative Public Facilities Financing Act

Tenn. Public Acts 1988, Ch. 1022

Cooperative Recording Act

N.J. Stat. Ann., 46:8D-1 et seq.

Cooperative Regulation Act

D.C. Code 1973, § 5-1301 et seq.

Cooperative Research Act

April 11, 1965, P.L. 89-10, 79 Stat. 44, 20 U.S. Code §§ 331 to 332b

Nov. 3, 1966, P.L. 89-750, 80 Stat. 1202, 20 U.S. Code §§ 331a, 332a, 332b

Jan. 2, 1968, P.L. 90-247, 81 Stat. 820, 20 U.S. Code § 331a

April 13, 1970, P.L. 91-230, 84 Stat. 193, 20 U.S. Code §§ 331a, 332a

Cooperative Return of Parole and Probation Violators Act

Colo. Rev. Stat., 17-2-301 et seq.

Cooperative Savings and Credit Unions Act

P.R. Acts 1989, First Special Session, No. 6

Cooperative Savings and Credit Unions Act (Shares and Deposits Insurance Corporation)

P.R. Acts 1989, First Special Session, No. 5

Cooperative Sea Food Marketing Law

La. Rev. Stat. Ann., 12:441 et seq.

Cooperative Secondary Facilities Grant Act

Minn. Stat. Ann., 124.491 et seq.

Cooperative Services Boards Act

Colo. Rev. Stat., 22-5-101 et seq.

Cooperative Societies Act

Kan. Stat. Ann., 17-1501 et seq.

Cooperative Take-Over Act

Wis. Stat., 552.01 et seq.

Cooperative Teacher Education Act
Colo. Rev. Stat., 22-62-101 et seq.
Wyo. Stat. Ann., § 21-21-101 et seq.

Cooperative Telephone Corporation Act
Ky. Rev. Stat. 1971, 279.310 et seq.

Cooperative Telephone District Law
Ore. Rev. Stat., 262.010 et seq.

Cooperative Threat Reduction Act of 1993
Nov. 30, 1993, P.L. 103-160, 22 U.S. Code
§§ 5951 nt., 5951 et seq.
Oct. 5, 1994, P.L. 103-337, 22 U.S. Code
§ 5956

Cooperative Utilities Act
Wyo. Stat. Ann., § 17-20-101 et seq.

Cooperative Work Study Program Act
Ill. Comp. Stat. 1992, Ch. 110, § 225/1 et seq.

Cooperatives Act (Agricultural)
Ill. Comp. Stat. 1992, Ch. 805, § 315/1 et seq.

Cooperatives Act (Consumer)
Me. Rev. Stat. Ann. 1964 Title 13, § 1501 et
seq.

Coordinate System Act
Ill. Comp. Stat. 1992, Ch. 765, § 225/1 et seq.
Me. Rev. Stat. Ann. 1964, Title 33, § 801 et
seq.
S.C. Code Ann. 1976, § 27-2-10 et seq.

Coordinate System Law (Surveys and Maps)
Cal. Public Resources Code, § 8801 et seq.

**Coordinated Public Transportation
Assistance Act (Elderly and Disabled)**
Kan. Stat. Ann., 75-5032 et seq.

**Coordinated Public Transportation
Assistance Act (Elderly and
Handicapped)**
Kan. Stat. Ann., 75-5032 et seq.

**Coordinated Services for At-Risk Children
and Youth Act**
Utah Code Ann. 1953, 63-75-1 et seq.

Coordinated Transit Districts Act
Kan. Stat. Ann., 75-5-51 et seq.

**Coordinating Commission on
Post-Secondary Education**
Neb. Rev. Stat. 1943, 85-1401 et seq.

**Coordinating Committee on Transportation
Act**
Ill. Comp. Stat. 1992, Ch. 20, § 3925/1 et seq.

Coordinating Council Act (Interagency)
Ill. Rev. Stat. 1991, Ch. 127, § 3831 et seq.

**Coordinating Human Service and Volunteer
Transportation Barrier Removal Act**
N.C. Gen. Stat. 1943, § 62-289.1 et seq.

Coordination Act (Job Training)
Utah Code Ann. 1953, 9-2-1101 et seq.

Coordination of Benefits Act
Mich. Comp. Laws Ann., 550.251 et seq.

**Coordination of Benefits Act (Group
Disability Insurance)**
Mich. Comp. Laws Ann., 550.251

**Coordination of Federally Aided State
Programs Act**
S.D. Codified Laws 1967, 4-8B-1 et seq.

Coordination of Information Act
Colo. Rev. Stat., 24-1-136

**Coordination of Services for Older
Oklahomans Act**
Okla. Stat. Ann., Title 56, § 3001

**Coordination of Special Services to Children
and Youth Act**
Okla. Stat. 1981, Title 10, § 601.41 et seq.

**Coordination Procedures Act (Environ-
mental)**
Wash. Rev. Code 1983, 90.62.010 et seq.

Coordination Zone Act (Intergovernmental)
Del. Code of 1974, Title 9, § 2675 et seq.

Coos, Lower Umpqua, and Siuslaw Restoration Act
Oct. 17, 1984, P.L. 98-481, 25 U.S. Code §§ 714, 714a to 714f, 714 nt.
Oct. 14, 1998, P.L. 105-256, 25 U.S. Code § 714e

Coosa Water Authority Act
Ga. Laws 1972, p. 3926

Copartnership for the New Housing Operation (Public and Private Sector)
P.R. Laws Ann. 1954, Title 17, § 891 et seq.

Cope and Norris Act
Ala. Acts 1991, p. 1479, No. 758

Copeland Anti-Racketeering Act
See Anti-Racketeering Act

Copeland Firearms Act
See Federal Firearms Act

Copeland-Guffey-Gibson Ship Subsidy Act
See Merchant Marine Act, 1936

Copeland Pure Food and Drugs Act
See Food, Drug, and Cosmetic Act

Copies of Legislative Materials Act
Ill. Rev. Stat. 1991, Ch. 63, §§ 800, 801

Coppell Municipal Courts of Record Act
Tex. Government Code, § 30.01441

Copper Production Ad Valorem Tax Act
N.M. Stat. Ann., 7-39-1 et seq.

Copper Purchase Registration Law
Ill. Comp. Stat. 1992, Ch. 815, § 325/1 et seq.

Copps-Tracy Act (Vocational Rehabilitation)
Ohio Laws Vol. 109, p. 310

Copyright Act
Haw. Rev. Stat. 482C-1 et seq.
N.D. Cent. Code, 47-21-01 et seq.
N.M. Stat. Ann., 57-4-1 et seq.
Wash. Rev. Code 1991, 19.24.010 et seq.

Copyright Acts
June 18, 1874, Ch. 301, 18 Stat. 79 (See 17 U.S. Code § 19)
March 3, 1891, Ch. 565, 26 Stat. 1106
Jan. 7, 1904, Ch. 2, 33 Stat. 4
March 4, 1909, Ch. 320, 35 Stat. 1075 (See 17 U.S. Code §§ 1 to 215)
Aug. 24, 1912, Ch. 356, 37 Stat. 488 (See 17 U.S. Code §§ 5, 12, 101)
March 2, 1913, Ch. 97, 37 Stat. 724 (See 17 U.S. Code § 209)
March 28, 1914, Ch. 47, 38 Stat. 311 (See 17 U.S. Code § 13)
Dec. 18, 1919, Ch. 11, 41 Stat. 368 (See 17 U.S. Code § 22)
March 15, 1940, Ch. 57, 54 Stat. 51 (See 17 U.S. Code § 24)
April 11, 1940, Ch. 81, 54 Stat. 106 (See 17 U.S. Code § 109)

Copyright Amendments Act of 1992
June 26, 1992, P.L. 102-307, 17 U.S. Code § 101 nt.
Oct. 27, 1998, P.L. 105-298, 17 U.S. Code §§ 101 nt., 304 nt.

Copyright Enforcement Act (Music Licensing and)
Ida. Code 1947, 48-1301 et seq.

Copyright Fees and Technical Amendments Act of 1989
July 3, 1990, P.L. 101-318, 17 U.S. Code § 101 nt.

Copyright Remedy Clarification Act
Nov. 15, 1990, P.L. 101-553, 17 U.S. Code §§ 101 nt., 501, 501 nt., 511, 910, 911

Copyright Renewal Act of 1992
June 26, 1992, P.L. 102-307, 17 U.S. Code §§ 101, 101 nt., 304, 304 nt., 408, 409, 708

Copyright Royalty Collection Practices Act
Ark. Code 1987, 4-76-101 et seq.
Tex. Rev. Civ. Stat., Art. 851-D

Copyright Royalty Tribunal Reform Act of 1993

Oct. 15, 1971, P.L. 92-140, 17 U.S. Code §§ 1, 5, 19, 20, 26, 101

Dec. 31, 1974, P.L. 93-573, 17 U.S. Code § 104

Oct. 19, 1976, P.L. 94-553, 17 U.S. Code §§ 101 et seq., 201 to 205, 301 to 305, 401 et seq., 501 et seq., 601 to 603, 701 et seq., 801 et seq.

Aug. 5, 1977, P.L. 95-94, 17 U.S. Code §§ 203, 708

Nov. 6, 1978, P.L. 95-598, 17 U.S. Code § 201

Dec. 12, 1980, P.L. 96-517, 17 U.S. Code §§ 101, 117

May 24, 1982, P.L. 97-180, 17 U.S. Code § 506

July 13, 1982, P.L. 97-215, 17 U.S. Code § 601

Oct. 25, 1982, P.L. 97-366, 17 U.S. Code §§ 110, 708

Oct. 4, 1984, P.L. 98-450, 17 U.S. Code §§ 109, 115

Nov. 8, 1984, P.L. 98-620, 17 U.S. Code §§ 901 et seq., 901 nt.

Aug. 27, 1986, P.L. 99-397, 17 U.S. Code §§ 111, 801

Nov. 9, 1987, P.L. 100-159, 17 U.S. Code §§ 902, 914

Oct. 31, 1988, P.L. 100-568, 17 U.S. Code §§ 101, 104, 116, 116A, 205, 301, 401 et seq., 411, 501, 504, 801

Nov. 5, 1988, P.L. 100-617, 17 U.S. Code § 109

Nov. 16, 1988, P.L. 100-667, 17 U.S. Code §§ 111, 119, 501, 801, 804

Nov. 19, 1988, P.L. 100-702, 17 U.S. Code § 912

Nov. 15, 1990, P.L. 101-553, 17 U.S. Code §§ 501, 511, 910, 911

Dec. 1, 1990, P.L. 101-650, 17 U.S. Code §§ 101, 102, 106, 106A, 107, 109, 113, 120, 301, 411, 412, 501, 506

June 28, 1991, P.L. 102-64, 17 U.S. Code § 914

June 26, 1992, P.L. 102-307, 17 U.S. Code §§ 108, 304, 408, 409, 708

Oct. 24, 1992, P.L. 102-492, 17 U.S. Code § 107

Oct. 28, 1992, P.L. 102-563, 17 U.S. Code §§ 101, 801, 804, 912, 1001 to 1010

Dec. 8, 1993, P.L. 103-182, 17 U.S. Code § 104A

Dec. 17, 1993, P.L. 103-198, 17 U.S. Code §§ 101, 111, 116, 118, 119, 801, 802, 803, 805 et seq., 1004, 1005, 1006, 1010

Copyright Royalty Tribunal Reform and Miscellaneous Pay Act of 1989

July 3, 1990, P.L. 101-319, 17 U.S. Code § 101 nt.

Copyright Users Protection Act

Wyo. Stat. Ann., § 40-13-101 et seq.

Copyrights

July 30, 1947, Ch. 391, 61 Stat. 652, 17 U.S. Code §§ 1 to 215

April 27, 1948, Ch. 236, 62 Stat. 202, 17 U.S. Code §§ 211, 215

June 25, 1948, Ch. 646, 62 Stat. 992, 17 U.S. Code § 101

June 3, 1949, Ch. 171, 63 Stat. 153, 17 U.S. Code §§ 16, 22, 23, 215

Oct. 31, 1951, Ch. 655, 65 Stat. 716, 17 U.S. Code §§ 3, 8, 112, 114

July 17, 1952, Ch. 923, 66 Stat. 752, 17 U.S. Code § 1

April 13, 1954, Ch. 137, 68 Stat. 52, 17 U.S. Code § 216

Aug. 31, 1954, Ch. 1161, 68 Stat. 1030, 17 U.S. Code §§ 9, 16, 19

March 29, 1956, Ch. 109, 70 Stat. 63, 17 U.S. Code § 13

Sept. 7, 1957, P.L. 85-313, 71 Stat. 633, 17 U.S. Code § 115

Sept. 7, 1962, P.L. 87-646, 76 Stat. 446, 17 U.S. Code § 8

Oct. 27, 1965, P.L. 89-297, 79 Stat. 1072, 17 U.S. Code §§ 211, 215

Aug. 12, 1970, P.L. 91-375, 84 Stat. 777, 17 U.S. Code § 8

Coquille Restoration Act

June 28, 1989, P.L. 101-42, 25 U.S. Code §§ 715 et seq., 715 nt.

Sept. 30, 1996, P.L. 104-208, 25 U.S. Code § 715c

Coral Gables Local Improvement Act
Fla. Special Laws 1949, Ch. 25742

Coral Gables Sewer Financing Act
Fla. Special Laws 1949, Ch. 25743

Coral Keys Restoration Trust Fund Act
Fla. Laws 1986, Ch. 202, § 1

Coram Nobis Act
Ill. Rev. Stat. 1991, Ch. 110, § 2-1401
Miss. Code Ann., § 99-35-145

Cordless and Cellular Radio Telephone Privacy Act
Cal. Penal Code § 632.5

Core-Street Act (Congressional Districts)
Ind. Laws 1931, Ch. 113, p. 447

Corlett Act (Insolvency Court)
Ohio Laws Vol. 114, p. 44

Corn and Wheat Marketing Quota Act of 1941
See Agricultural Adjustment Act of 1938

Corn Borer Act
Ky. Rev. Stat. 1971, Superseded Vols., 249.210 et seq., 249.990
Mich. Comp. Laws 1948, 286.301 et seq.

Corn Marketing Act
Ill. Comp. Stat. 1992, Ch. 505, § 40/1 et seq.

Corn Meal Enrichment Act
N.C. Gen. Stat. 1943, § 106-219.1 et seq.

Corn Resources Act
Neb. Rev. Stat. 1943, 2-3601 et seq.

Corn Seed Law (Hybrid)
Iowa Code Ann., 199.5

Corneal Transplant Act
Ill. Comp. Stat. 1992, Ch. 755, § 55/1 et seq.

Cornell University New York State Waste Management Institute Act
N.Y. Environmental Conservation Law 1972 (Consol. Laws Ch. 43B) § 27-0403 nt.

Corner Perpetuation and Filing Act
Ida. Code 1947, 55-1601 et seq.
Nev. Rev. Stat. 1979 Reprint, 329.030 et seq.
Okla. Stat. Ann., Title 65, § 3-116 et seq.
Wyo. Stat. Ann., § 36-11-101 et seq.

Corner Perpetuation and Filing Law
Ida. Code 1947, 55-1601 et seq.

Corner Recordation Act
Mich. Comp. Laws Ann., 54.201 et seq.
Mont. Code Ann., 70-22-101 et seq.

Corning City Court Act
N.Y. Laws 1905, Ch. 142, § 86 et seq.

Corning National Fish Hatchery Conveyance Act
Sept. 6, 1995, P.L. 104-23, 109 Stat. 261

Cornshellers Act
Iowa Code Ann., 571.1 et seq.

Cornshellers' Lien Act
Iowa Code Ann., 571.1 et seq.

Coronado National Trail Study Act of 1988
Oct. 28, 1988, P.L. 100-559, 16 U.S. Code § 1241 nt.

Coroner Reorganization Act
Miss. Code Ann., § 19-21-101 et seq.

Coroners Act
Ill. Rev. Stat. 1991, Ch. 31
Ind. Code Ann., 36-2-14-1 et seq.
Kan. Stat. Ann., 22a-201 et seq.
Ky. Rev. Stat. 1971, 72.400 et seq.
Me. Rev. Stat. Ann. 1964, Title 22, § 3021 et seq.
Mo. Rev. Stat., 58.010 et seq.
N.D. Cent. Code 11-19-01 et seq.
N.J. Rev. Stat. 40:40-1 et seq.

Coroners and Inquests Act
Mo. Rev. Stat. 1978, 58.010 et seq.

Coroner's Training Council Act
Ga. Code Ann., 45-16-60 et seq.

Coroners Warrant Act
Conn. Gen. Stat. Ann., § 19a-400 et seq.

Corporate and Unincorporated Business Franchise Surtax Act
D.C. Code Ann., §§ 47-1807.2, 47-1808.3

Corporate Authorities Act (Cities and Villages)
Ill. Rev. Stat. 1991, Ch. 24, § 11-1-1 et seq.

Corporate Bankruptcy Act
June 7, 1934, Ch. 424, 48 Stat. 912, 11 U.S. Code §§ 76a, 103, 103a, 107, 203, 203a, 204, 205a, 206, 207

Corporate Charter Reinstatement Act
Mich. Comp. Laws Ann., 450.431 et seq.

Corporate Code
Fla. Stat. Ann., 607.0101 et seq.

Corporate Criminal Liability Act
Cal. Penal Code § 387

Corporate Deadlock Act
N.J. Stat. Ann., 14A:12-7
Ore. Rev. Stat., 57.595

Corporate Directors Classification Act
Pa. 1933 Pamph. Laws 364, No. 106, § 403

Corporate Dissolution Act
Mont. Code. Ann. 1989, 35-1

Corporate Dissolution Act (Deadlock)
Wis. Stat. 1987, 180.771, Subsec. 1, Subd. a

Corporate Donations Act
N.J. Stat. Ann., 14A:3-4

Corporate Excess Tax Act
Minn. Laws 1885, Ch. 78

Corporate Exemption Act (Usury)
N.Y. General Obligations Law (Consol. Laws Ch. 24A) § 5-521

Corporate Farming Law
N.D. Cent. Code 10-06-01 et seq.

Corporate Fiduciary Act
Ill. Comp. Stat. 1992, Ch. 205, § 620/1-1 et seq.

Corporate Franchise Tax Act
Ark. Code Ann. 1987, 26-54-101 et seq.
Miss. Code Ann., § 27-13-1 et seq.
Okla. Stat. Ann., Title 68, § 644.1 et seq.

Corporate Governance Parity Act
Cal. Corporations Code § 318

Corporate Income and Franchise Tax Act
N.M. Stat. Ann., 7-2A-1 et seq.

Corporate Income Tax Act
Del. Code of 1974, Title 30, § 1901 et seq.
Fla. Stat. Ann., 719.101 et seq.
N.M. Stat. Ann., 7-2A-1 et seq.

Corporate Income Tax Reform Act
Ala. Acts 1985, p. 517

Corporate Insolvency Act
N.J. Stat. Ann., 14A:14-1 et seq.

Corporate License Tax Credit Act
Mont. Code Ann., 15-31-124 et seq.

Corporate Limits Act
S.C. Code of Law 1976, § 5-3-10 et seq.

Corporate Loan Act
Ill. Rev. Stat. 1991, Ch. 32, § 1401 et seq.

Corporate Loans Tax Act
Pa. 1935 Pamph. Laws 414, No. 182, § 19

Corporate Merger Appraisal Act
N.Y. Business Corporations Law 1961 (Consol. Laws Ch. 4) §§ 623, 901 et seq.

Corporate Name Act
Mich. Comp. Laws Ann., 450.1211
Ore. Rev. Stat., 57.045

Corporate Net Income Tax Act
Pa. Purdon's Stat., Title 72, § 7401a et seq.

Corporate Notes Act (Sanitary District)
Ill. Rev. Stat. 1991, Ch. 42, § 319.30 et seq.

Corporate Officers Act (Trap)
N.J. Stat. Ann., Superseded Vol., 14:8-16

Corporate Officers Indemnification Act
N.C. Gen. Stat. 1943, §§ 55-19 to 55-21

Corporate Reorganization Act
June 22, 1938, Ch. 575, 52 Stat. 883, 11 U.S. Code § 501 et seq.

Corporate Reports Act
N.M. Stat. Ann., 53-5-1 et seq.

Corporate Sale and Merger Act
Ohio Rev. Code 1953, 1701.74 et seq.

Corporate Securities Law
Cal. Corporations Code § 25000 et seq.

Corporate Shareholders Security for Expenses Act
Cal. Corporations Code § 800

Corporate Stock Transfer Act
Ind. Burns' 1960 Repl., 25-701 et seq.

Corporate Stockholder's Voting Act
Ga. Code Ann., 14-2-720 et seq.

Corporate Surety Act
Aug. 13, 1894, Ch. 282, 28 Stat. 279, 6 U.S. Code §§ 6 to 13

Corporate Surplus Return Act
Me. Rev. Stat. Ann. 1964, Title 36, § 6501 et seq.

Corporate Takeover Act
Ida. Code 1947, 30-1501 et seq.
Md. Ann. Code 1974, Art. CA, § 11-901 et seq.
Neb. Rev. Stat. 1943, 21-2418 et seq.
N.Y. Business Corporations Law 1961 (Consol. Laws Ch. 4) §§ 513 Subd. e, 912, 1600 et seq.
S.C. Code Ann. 1976, § 33-1-101 et seq.
Wis. Stat. Ann., 552.01 et seq.

Corporate Tax Act
Ga. Code Ann., 48-7-31

Corporation Act
Ark. Code Ann. 1987, 4-26-101 et seq.
Colo. Rev. Stat., 7-1-101 et seq.
Del. Code of 1974, Title 8, § 101 et seq.
Ida. Code 30-1-1 et seq.
Ill. Rev. Stat. 1991, Ch. 32, § 1.01 et seq.
Ind. Code Ann., 23-1-17-1 et seq.
Iowa Code Ann., 491.1 et seq.
Ky. Rev. Stat. 1971, 217B.1-010 et seq.
Mich. Comp. Laws Ann., 450.1101 et seq.
Minn. Stat. Ann., 300.01 et seq.
Miss. Code Ann., § 79-4-1.01 et seq.
N.D. Cent. Code, 10-19.1-01 et seq.
Okla. Stat. 1981, Title 18, § 1001 et seq.
Ore. Rev. Stat., 60.001 et seq.
Pa. Cons. Stat., Title 15, § 1101 et seq.
Tex. Rev. Civ. Stat., Art. 1301-1.01 et seq.
Wash. Rev. Code Ann., 23A.04.010 et seq., 23B.01.010 et seq.
Wis. Stat. 1989, 180.0101 et seq.
W. Va. Code 1966, § 31-1-1 et seq.

Corporation Act (Business and Industrial Development)
Ida. Code 1947, 26-2701 et seq.
La. Rev. Stat. Ann., 51:2386 et seq.

Corporation Act (Business Development)
Miss. Code Ann., § 79-5-1 et seq.
N.C. Gen. Stat. 1943, § 53A-1 et seq.

Corporation Act (Business)
See also Uniform Business Corporation Act
Ala. Code 1975, § 10-2A-1 et seq.
Alaska Stat. 1962, Replaced Titles, § 10.05.003 et seq.
Ariz. Rev. Stat. Ann., § 10-002 et seq.
Ark. Code Ann. 1987, 64-101 et seq.
Cal. Corporations Code § 100 et seq.
D.C. Code 1973, § 29-101 et seq.
Fla. Stat. 1977, 607.001 et seq.
Ga. Code Ann., 14-2-101 et seq.
Haw. Rev. Stat. Ann., § 416-1 et seq.
Ida. Code 1947, 30-101 et seq.
Continued

477

Ind. Code Ann., 23-1-1-1 et seq.

Kan. Stat. Ann., 17-6001 et seq.

Ky. Rev. Stat. 1971, 271A.005 et seq.

La. Rev. Stat. Ann., 12:1 et seq.

Mass. Gen. Laws Ann., 156:1 et seq., 156B:1 et seq.

Md. Ann. Code 1974, Art. CA, § 1-101 et seq.

Me. Rev. Stat. Ann. 1964, Title 13A, § 101 et seq.

Mich. Comp. Laws Ann., 450.1 et seq.

Minn. Stat. Ann., 300.01 et seq.

Miss. Code Ann., § 79-3-1 et seq.

Mo. Rev. Stat., 351.010 et seq.

Mont. Rev. Code 1947, 15-652 et seq.

N.C. Gen. Stat. 1943, § 55-1-01 et seq.

N.D. Cent. Code 10-19-01 et seq.

Neb. Rev. Stat. 1943, 21-2001 et seq.

Nev. Rev. Stat. 1979 Reprint, 78.010 et seq.

N.H. Rev. Stat. 1955, 293-A:1 et seq.

N.J. Stat. Ann., 14A:1-1 et seq.

N.M. Stat. Ann., 53-11-1 et seq.

N.Y. Consol. Laws, Ch. 23

Ohio Rev. Code 1953, 1701.01 et seq.

Okla. Stat. Ann., Title 18

Ore. Rev. Stat., 57.002 et seq.

Pa. Purdon's Stat., Title 15, §§ 1001 et seq., 3001 et seq.

P.R. Laws Ann. 1954, Title 14, § 1101 et seq.

R.I. Gen. Laws 1956, 7-1.1-1 et seq.

S.C. Code Ann. 1976, § 33-1-101 et seq.

S.D. Comp. Laws. 1967, 47-1-1 et seq.

Tenn. Code Ann., 48-1-101 et seq.

Utah Code Ann. 1953, 16-4-4 et seq.

Va. Code 1950, § 13.1-1 et seq.

Vt. Stat. Ann., Title 11A, § 1.01 et seq.

Wash. Rev. Code Ann., 23B.01.010

W. Va. Code 1966, § 31-1-1 et seq.

Wyo. Stat. Ann., § 17-1-101 et seq.

Corporation Act (Cultural Education Facilities Finance)
Tex. Rev. Civ. Stat., Act. 1528m

Corporation Act (Dental Service)
N.J. Stat. Ann., 17:48C-1 et seq.
S.D. Codified Laws 1967, 47-12-1 et seq.

Corporation Act (Development Capital)
Okla. Stat. Ann., Title 74, § 5086.1 et seq.

Corporation Act (Electric Co-operative)
Neb. Rev. Stat. 1943, 70-701 et seq.

Corporation Act (Electric Membership)
N.C. Gen. Stat. 1943, § 117-6 et seq.

Corporation Act (Export Finance)
Fla. Stat. Ann., 288.771 et seq.

Corporation Act (Facilities Development)
N.Y. Unconsolidated Law, § 4401 et seq.

Corporation Act (Foreign)
Colo. Rev. Stat., 7-5-110
Md. Ann. Code 1974, Art. CA, § 1-101 et seq.
N.H. Rev. Stat. 1955, 293-A:112
R.I. Gen. Laws 1956, 7-1.1-99 et seq.
S.D. Codified Laws 1967, 47-8-1 et seq.

Corporation Act (General)
Okla. Stat. Ann., Title 18, § 1002 et seq.

Corporation Act (German School Educational)
Ill. Rev. Stat. 1991, Ch. 32, §§ 199.90, 199a

Corporation Act (Healthy Kids)
Fla. Stat. Ann., 624.91 et seq.

Corporation Act (Hospital Service)
N.H. Rev. Stat. 1955, 419:1 et seq.

Corporation Act (Industrial Development)
Ark. Acts 1989, No. 660

Corporation Act (John Dempsey Hospital Finance)
Conn. Gen. Stat. Ann., § 10a-250 et seq.

Corporation Act (Medical Service)
N.H. Rev. Stat. 1955,420:1 et seq.

Corporation Act (Municipal)
Ala. Code 1975, 11-40-1 et seq.
Alaska Stat. 1962, § 29.03.010 et seq.
N.C. Gen. Stat. 1943, § 160A-1 et seq.

Corporation Act (Musical Arts)
P.R. Laws Ann. 1954, Title 18, § 1165 et seq.

Corporation Act (Non-Profit)
See Nonprofit Corporation Act

Corporation Act (Nonprofit Miscellaneous and Mutual)
Wash. Rev. Code Ann., 24.06.005

Corporation Act (Nonprofit)
S.C. Code Ann. 1976, § 33-31-101 et seq.

Corporation Act (Nonstock)
Conn. Gen. Stat. Ann., § 33-419 et seq.
Wis. Stat. 1989, 181.01 et seq.

Corporation Act (Professional Service)
N.D. Cent. Code, 10-31-01 et seq.
N.J. Stat. Ann., 14A:17-1 et seq.

Corporation Act (Professional)
Ariz. Rev. Stat. Ann., § 10-2201 et seq.

Corporation Act (Public Facility)
Tex. Rev. Civ. Stat., Art. 717s

Corporation Act (Religious)
Md. Ann. Code 1974, Art. CA, § 5-301 et seq.

Corporation Act (Rural Rehabilitation)
Ill. Rev. Stat. 1991, Ch. 127, § 42a2.9 et seq.

Corporation Act (Stock)
Conn. Gen. Stat. Ann., 33-282 et seq.
Md. Ann. Code 1974, Art. CA, § 1-101 et seq.

Corporation Act (Survival)
Md. Ann. Code 1974, Art. CA, § 3-408 et seq.

Corporation Act (Technology Development)
Mass. Gen. Laws 1984, 40G:1 et seq.

Corporation Act (Transportation)
Mo. Rev. Stat. 1978, 238.300

Corporation Act (Turnpike)
Wis. Stat. 1989, 182.30 et seq.

Corporation and Bank Tax Law
Cal. Revenue and Taxation Code, § 23001 et seq.

Corporation Annual Franchise Tax Act
Mo. Rev. Stat., 147.010 et seq.

Corporation Bureau and UCC Fee Law
Pa. Cons. Stat., Title 15, § 151 et seq.

Corporation Business Activities Reporting Act
N.J. Stat. Ann., 14A:13-14 et seq.

Corporation Business Tax Act
Conn. Gen. Stat. Ann., § 12-213 et seq.
N.J. Stat. Ann., 54:10A-1 et seq.

Corporation Canal Construction Act
Ill. Comp. Stat. 1992, Ch. 805, § 25/0.01 et seq.

Corporation Capital Stock Tax Act
Pa. Purdon's Stat., Title 72, § 7601 et seq.

Corporation Charter Act
Ga. Code 1933, 22-1801 et seq.

Corporation Charter Amendment Act
Pa. Purdon's Stat., Title 15, § 3160 et seq.

Corporation Code
Cal. Statutes 1947, § Ch. 1038, p. 2309

Corporation Commission Act
Ariz. Rev. Stat. Ann. 1956, § 10-002 et seq.
Ark. Code Ann. 1987, 23-2-101 et seq.
Kan. Stat. Ann., 66-101 et seq.

Corporation Condemnation Act
Mo. Rev. Stat., 523.010 et seq.

Corporation Continuity Act
Mass. Gen. Laws Ann., 155:51

Corporation Court Act
Tex. Code of Criminal Procedure, Art. 45.01 et seq.
Tex. Government Code, § 29.001 et seq.

Corporation Development Act
Mont. Code Ann., 32-4-101 et seq.

Corporation Directors Act
Mich. Comp. Laws Ann., 450.1501

Corporation Dissolution Act
Del. Code of 1974, Title 8, § 251 et seq.
Ill. Rev. Stat. 1991, Ch. 32, § 189h et seq.
Mass. Gen. Laws Ann., 155:50 et seq.
Minn. Stat. 1978, 301.46 et seq.
Mont. Code Ann., 35-1-901 et seq.
N.J. Rev. Stat. Ann., 14A:12-1 et seq.
W. Va. Code 1966, § 31-1-39 et seq.

Corporation Dissolution Act (Religious, Educational or Charitable)
Ill. Rev. Stat. 1991, Ch. 32, §§ 200.9, 201

Corporation Dividend Act
Colo. Rev. Stat., 7-5-110

Corporation Division Act (Administration)
Cal. Corporations Code, § 25600 et seq.

Corporation Eminent Domain Law
Wash. Rev. Code Ann., 8.20.010 et seq.

Corporation Employees' Lien Act
Ind. Code Ann., 32-8-24-1 et seq.

Corporation Excise Tax Act
Mass. Gen. Laws Ann., 63:30 et seq.
Ore. Rev. Stat., 317.005 et seq.
Tenn. Code Ann., 67-4-801 et seq.

Corporation Fee Act
Ind. Code Ann., 23-1-18-3

Corporation for Change Act
Kan. Stat. Ann., 38-1801 et seq.

Corporation for the Administration of the Receivership of the Savings and Loans Labor Bank Act
P.R. Acts 1979, No. 24

Corporation for the Development and Administration of the Marine, Lacustrine and Fluvial Resources Act
P.R. Laws Ann. 1954, Title 12, § 1351 et seq.

Corporation for the Promotion of Rifle Practice and Firearms Safety Act
Feb. 10, 1996, P.L. 104-106, Division A, Title XVI, 36 U.S. Code § 5501 nt.
Sept. 23, 1996, P.L. 104-201, 36 U.S. Code §§ 5505, 5506, 5509

Corporation Franchise and Privilege Fee Act
Mich. Comp. Laws Ann., 450.2060 et seq.

Corporation Franchise Tax Act
Cal. Revenue and Taxation Code § 23183 et seq.
Ga. Code Ann., 48-5-420 et seq.
Ga. Code 1933, 92-2401 et seq.
La. Rev. Stat. Ann., 47:601 et seq.
Md. Ann. Code 1974, Art. TG, § 8-101 et seq.
Miss. Code Ann., § 27-31-1 et seq.
Mo. Rev. Stat., 147.010 et seq.
N.J. Stat. Ann., 54:10A-1 et seq.
Okla. Stat. Ann., Title 68, § 1201 et seq.
Pa. Purdon's Stat., Title 72, § 7601 et seq.
R.I. Gen. Laws 1956, 44-12-1 et seq.
Utah Code Ann. 1953, 59-7-101 et seq.

Corporation Gift Act
Md. Ann. Code 1971, CA, § 2-103 et seq.

Corporation Income Tax Act
Cal. Revenue and Taxation Code § 23501 et seq.
Del. Code of 1974, Title 30, § 1901 et seq.
La. Rev. Stat. Ann., 47:287.2 et seq.
Mass. Gen. Laws Ann., 63C:1 et seq.
Mont. Code Ann., 15-31-401 et seq.
N.C. Gen. Stat. 1943, § 105-130 et seq.
N.J. Stat. Ann., 54:10E-1 et seq.
N.Y. Tax Law (Consol. Laws Ch. 60) § 208 et seq.
Ore. Rev. Stat., 318.010 et seq.
Pa. Purdon's Stat., Title 72, § 7401 et seq.
W. Va. Code 1966, § 11-24-1 et seq.

Corporation Law
Neb. Rev. Stat. 1943, 21-2001 et seq.

Corporation Law (Professional)
Mass. Gen. Laws Ann., 156A:1 et seq.

Corporation Law (Small Business)
Cal. Corporation Code § 14000 et seq.

Corporation Law for State Banks and Trust Companies
Del. Code of 1974, Title 5, § 701 et seq.

Corporation Laws Act (Miscellaneous)
Tex. Rev. Civ. Stat., Art. 1302-1.01 et seq.

Corporation License Act
Cal. Corporations Code § 5900 et seq.

Corporation License Fee Act
Wash. Rev. Code Ann., 23A.040.010 et seq.

Corporation License Tax Act
Ky. Rev. Stat. 1971, 136.070 et seq.
Mont. Code Ann., 15-31-101 et seq.

Corporation Merger Act
Conn. Gen. Stat. Ann., § 33-364 et seq.
Del. Code of 1974, Title 8, § 251 et seq.
Md. Ann. Code 1974, Art. CA, § 3-101 et seq.
Mo. Rev. Stat., 351.410 et seq.
Nev. Rev. Stat. 1979 Reprint, 78.450 et seq.
N.J. Stat. Ann., 14A:10-1 et seq.
N.Y. Business Corporation Law 1961 (Consol. Laws Ch. 4) § 901 et seq.
Ohio Rev. Code 1953, 1701.78 et seq.
S.C. Code Ann. 1976, § 33-11-101 et seq.
Tenn. Code Ann. 1955, 48-517 et seq.
Tex. Business Corporation Act, Art. 5.01 et seq.

Corporation Net Income Tax Act
W. Va. Code 1966, § 11-24-1 et seq.

Corporation Not for Profit Act
Colo. Stat. Ann. 1935, Ch. 41 § 1172 et seq.
Ill. Rev. Stat. 1991, Ch. 32, § 101.01

Corporation Not-for-Profit Code
Pa. Cons. Stat., Title 15, § 5101 et seq.

Corporation Occupation Tax Lien Act
Neb. Rev. Stat. 1943, 21-312, 21-323

Corporation of Foreign Bondholders Act, 1933
May 27, 1933, Ch. 38, 48 Stat. 92, 15 U.S. Code §§ 77bb to 77mm

Corporation Practice of Law Prohibition Act
Ill. Comp. Stat. 1992, Ch. 705, § 220/0.01 et seq.

Corporation Priviledge Tax Act (Carrier)
W. Va. Code 1966, § 11-12A-1 et seq.

Corporation Program (Local Development)
La. Rev. Stat. Ann., 51:2381 et seq.

Corporation Property and Borrowing Powers Act (Fraternal)
Ill. Rev. Stat. 1991, Ch. 32, §§ 388.9, 389

Corporation Property Tax Act
Mich. Comp. Laws Ann., 211.5, 211.11

Corporation Registration Act
Mo. Rev. Stat., 351.120 et seq.

Corporation Registration Act (Foreign)
N.Y. Business Corporations Law 1961 (Consol. Laws Ch. 4) § 1301 et seq.

Corporation Resident Agent Act
Neb. Rev. Stat. 1943, 21-20,112 et seq.

Corporation Short Merger Act
N.Y. Business Corporation Laws (Consol. Laws, Ch. 4) § 901 et seq.

Corporation Takeover Bid Disclosure Law
N.J. Stat. Ann., 49:5-1 et seq.

Corporation Tax Act
Aug. 5, 1909, Ch. 6, 36 Stat. 112
Fla. Stat. 1971, 608.33 et seq.
Iowa Code Ann., 422.32 et seq.
Continued

N.Y. Tax Law (Consol. Laws Ch. 60) § 180 et seq.

Vt. Stat. Ann., Title 32, § 8101 et seq.

Corporation Voting Trust Act
S.C. Code Ann. 1976, Superseded Vols., § 33-11-160

Corporations Abandoned Property Act
Utah Code Ann. 1953, 78-44-12 et seq.

Corporations Act
Vt. Stat. Ann., Title 11, § 1201 et seq.

Corporations Act (Bay State Skills)
Mass. Gen. Laws Ann., 40I:1 et seq.

Corporations Act (Business and Industrial Development)
Mich. Comp. Laws Ann., 487.1101 et seq.

Corporations Act (Co-operative Housing)
Mass. Gen. Laws Ann., 157:1 et seq., 157B:1 et seq.

Corporations Act (Cooperative)
Cal. Corporations Code § 12200 et seq.
Okla. Stat. Ann., Title 59, § 328.1 et seq.

Corporations Act (Employee Cooperative)
Wash. Rev. Code Ann., 23.78.010 et seq.

Corporations Act (Foreign)
Mass. Gen. Laws Ann., 181:1 et seq.
Vt. Stat. Ann., Title 11, § 1201 et seq.

Corporations Act (Professional Architectural Corporations)
La. Rev. Stat. Ann., 12:1086 et seq.

Corporations Act (Special Charter Not for Profit)
Ill. Rev. Stat. 1991, Ch. 32, § 197.9 et seq.

Corporations Act (Worker Cooperative)
Conn. Gen. Stat. Ann., § 33-418f

Corporations and Labor Unions Campaign Finance Act
D.C. Code Ann., § 1-1441 et seq.

Corporations Charitable Contributions Act
Ind. Code Ann., 23-15-5-1

Corporations Code
Alaska Stat. 1962, § 10.06.005 et seq.

Corporations Compact (Interstate)
Mont. Code Ann., 46-19-401 et seq.

Corporations Dissolution Act
Ill. Rev. Stat. 1991, Ch. 32, § 189h et seq.

Corporations for Profit Act
Ind. Code Ann., 23-1-2-1 et seq.

Corporations Long Arm Act
Ind. Code Ann., 23-1-24-4

Corporations Merger Act (Nonstock)
Wis. Stat. 1989, 181.42 et seq.

Corporations Not for Profit Act
Ill. Rev. Stat. 1991, Ch. 32, § 101.01
Ind. Code Ann., 23-7-1.1-1 et seq.

Corporations Qualification Act (Foreign)
W. Va. Code 1966, § 31-1-49 et seq.

Corporations' Subchapter S
Mont. Code Ann., 15-31-201 et seq.

Corps Act (Firefighters)
P.R. Laws Ann. 1954, Title 25, § 331 et seq.

Corps of Volunteers in the Service of Puerto Rico Act
P.R. Laws Ann. 1954, Title 18, § 1411 et seq.

Corpse Disposal Law
Cal. Health and Safety Code § 7200 et seq.

Corpus Christi Pilots Licensing and Regulatory Act (Port of)
Tex. Transportation Code, § 70.001 et seq.

Correction Authority Act (Youth)
Mass. Gen. Laws Ann., 120:1 et seq.

Correction Compact Act (Interstate)
Ohio Rev. Code 1953, 5120.50

Correction Department Act
Ind. Code Ann., 11-8-1-1 et seq.
N.C. Gen. Stat. 1943, § 143B-260 et seq.

Correction Education and Demonstration Project Act of 1978
Nov. 1, 1978, P.L. 95-561, 20 U.S. Code §§ 3031 to 3034

Correction Officers Health and Safety Act of 1998
Nov. 12, 1998, P.L. 105-370, 112 Stat. 3374, 18 U.S. Code § 4001 nt.

Correctional Administration Organic Act
P.R. Laws Ann. 1954, Title 4, § 1101 et seq.

Correctional and Penal Code
Ida. Code 1947, 20-101 et seq.

Correctional Budget and Impact Note Act
Ill. Comp. Stat. 1992, Ch. 25, § 70/1 et seq.

Correctional Education Program Act
Colo. Rev. Stat., 17-32-101 et seq.

Correctional Facilities Act (Regional)
Ill. Rev. Stat. 1991, Ch. 5, § 2203-1 et seq.

Correctional Facilities and Jail Authority Act
W. Va. Code, § 31-20-1 et seq.

Correctional Facilities and Programs Act (Community)
Neb. Rev. Stat. 1943, 47-601 et seq.

Correctional Facilities Bond Act
Va. Acts 1977, Ch. 651

Correctional Facilities Construction Bond Act
N.J. Laws 1987, Ch. 178

Correctional Facility Act
Cal. Penal Code § 6200 et seq.
Miss. Code Ann., § 47-5-1 et seq.

Correctional Facility Act (Regional)
Mont. Code Ann., 53-30-501 et seq.

Correctional Facility and Jail Authority Act
W. Va. Code 1966, § 31-20-1 et seq.

Correctional Facility Capital Expenditure Bond Act (County)
Cal. Penal Code § 4475 et seq.

Correctional Facility Moratorium Act (Private)
Ill. Rev. Stat. 1991, Ch. 38, § 1581 et seq.

Correctional Facility Reimbursement Act
Mich. Comp. Laws Ann., 800.401 et seq.

Correctional Facility Siting Act (State Private)
Ida. Code 1947, 20-801 et seq.

Correctional House Law
Tenn. Code Ann., 41-3-101 et seq.

Correctional Incentive Time Act
Ala. Code 1975, § 14-9-40 et seq.

Correctional Industries Act
Colo. Rev. Stat., 17-24-101 et seq.
Ga. Code Ann., 42-10-1 et seq.
Ida. Code 1947, 20-401 et seq.
Mich. Comp. Laws Ann., 800.321 et seq.
Utah Code Ann. 1953, 64-13a-1 et seq.

Correctional Industry Act of 1965
Colo. Rev. Stat., 27-25-101 et seq.

Correctional Institutions and New Prisons Construction Bond Act
Cal. Penal Code § 7100

Correctional Officers' Training Act
Mich. Comp. Laws Ann., 791.501 et seq.

Correctional Organization Act
Fla. Stat. Ann., 20.04, 20.315, 921.231, 944.024, 945.025

Correctional Privatization Commission Act
Fla. Stat. Ann., 957.01 et seq.

Correctional Reform Act
Fla. Stat. Ann., 253.037, 921.005, 921.187, 944.01, 944.05, 944.096, 944.275, 947.16, 947.1746, 947.175, 947.23, 948.001 et seq., 951.23

Correctional Rehabilitation Study Act of 1965
Sept. 10, 1965, P.L. 89-178, 79 Stat. 676, 29 U.S. Code § 42 nt.

Corrections Act
Iowa Code Ann., 901.1 et seq.
Kan. Stat. Ann., 76-3001 et seq.
Mich. Comp. Laws Ann., 791.201 et seq.
Miss. Code Ann., § 47-5-1 et seq.
Neb. Rev. Stat. 1943, 83-170 et seq.
N.Y. Consol. Laws, Ch. 43
Okla. Stat. Ann., Title 57, § 501 et seq.

Corrections Act (Drug-Free)
Fla. Stat. Ann., 944.471 et seq.

Corrections and Criminal Rehabilitation Department Act
N.M. Stat. 1978, 9-3-1 et seq.

Corrections and Punishment Act (Community)
Ala. Code 1975, § 15-18-170

Corrections and Secure Facilities Capital Budget Project Itemization Act
Pa. 1995 Pamph. Laws, Special Session, Nos. 1, 19

Corrections and Treatment Act (Prisons and Prisoners)
Neb. Rev. Stat. 1943, 83-170 et seq.

Corrections Compact (Intrastate)
Wash. Rev. Code Ann., 72.76.005

Corrections Compact (New England Interstate)
Me. Rev. Stat. Ann. 1964, Title 34-A, § 9201 et seq.

Corrections Compact Act
Fla. Stat. Ann., 941.55 et seq.
Ida. Code 1947, 20-701 et seq.

Minn. Stat. Ann., 241.28 et seq.
N.C. Gen. Stat. 1943, §§ 148-119, 148-120
Ore. Rev. Stat., 421.245 et seq.
Pa. Purdon's Stat., Title 61, § 1061 et seq.
S.C. Code Ann. 1976, § 24-11-10 et seq.
Utah Code Ann. 1953, 77-63a-1 et seq.
Vt. Stat. Ann., Title 28, § 1601 et seq.

Corrections Compact Act (Interstate)
See Interstate Corrections Compact Act
Iowa Code Ann., 913.1 et seq.
Mich. Comp. Laws Ann., 3.981 et seq.

Corrections Compact Act (National)
N.H. Rev. Stat. 1955, 622-B:1 et seq.

Corrections Compact Act (New England Interstate)
Conn. Gen. Stat. Ann., § 18-102 et seq.
Me. Rev. Stat. Ann. 1964, Title 34-A, § 9401 et seq.
N.H. Rev. Stat. 1955, 622-A:1 et seq.
R.I. Gen. Laws 1956, 13-11-1 et seq.
Vt. Stat. Ann., Title 28, § 1401 et seq.
Wash. Rev. Code Ann., 72.76.900

Corrections Compact Act (Western Interstate)
See Western Interstate Corrections Compact Act

Corrections Cooperative Endeavors and Private Management Act
Ark. Code Ann. 1987, 12-50-101 et seq.

Corrections Department Act
N.J. Stat. Ann., 30:1B-1 et seq.
N.M. Stat. Ann., 9-3-1 et seq.

Corrections Department Act (Counties)
Ill. Rev. Stat. 1987, Ch. 125, § 201 et seq.

Corrections Equality Act
Fla. Stat. Ann., 944.24

Corrections Equality Act (County)
Fla. Stat. Ann., 951.175

Corrections Incentive Act (Community)
S.C. Code Ann. 1976, § 2-48-10 et seq.

Corrections Industries Act
N.M. Stat. Ann., 33-8-1 et seq.

Corrections Law (Community)
Ore. Rev. Stat., 423.550 et seq.

Corrections Mental Health Act
Fla. Stat. Ann., 945.40 et seq.

Corrections Partnership Act (Cummunity)
Fla. Stat. Ann., 948.50 et seq.

Corrections Private Management Act
La. Rev. Stat. Ann., 39:1800.1 et seq.

Corrections Reform Act
Wash. Rev. Code Ann., 72.09.010 et seq.

Correspondence Schools Act
Mass. Gen. Laws Ann., 75C:1 et seq.

Corridor of Economic Significance Act (Intermodal)
Cal. Streets and Highways Code §§ 2190, 2191

Corridors of Opportunity and Development Act
Ill. Comp. Stat. 1992, Ch. 20, § 610/1 et seq.

Corrigan-Devine Act (Employee's Fitness)
Ohio Rev. Code 1953, 124.35

Corroboration Act (Accomplices)
Tex. Code of Criminal Procedure, Art. 38.14

Corrupt and Bribery Practices Act
W. Va. Code 1966, § 61-5A-1 et seq.

Corrupt and Racketeer Influenced Organizations Act
N.D. Cent. Code, 12.1-06.1-01 et seq.

Corrupt Organizations Act
Pa. Cons. Stat., Title 18, § 911 et seq.

Corrupt Organizations and Racketeer-Influenced Act
Del. Code of 1974, Title 11, § 1501 et seq.
Fla. Stat. Ann., 895.01 et seq.
Ga. Code Ann., 16-14-1 et seq.

Corrupt Organizations and Racketeering Activities Act (CORA)
Conn. Gen. Stat. Ann., § 53-393 et seq.

Corrupt Organizations Prevention Act
Okla. Stat. Ann., Title 22, § 1401 et seq.

Corrupt Practices Act
Ala. Code 1975, § 17-22-1 et seq.
Ark. Code Ann. 1987, 7-9-105, 5-52-101 et seq.
Colo. Rev. Stat., 1-13-101 et seq.
Conn. Gen. Stat. Ann., § 9-333 et seq.
Fla. Stat. 1971, 99.161
Ill. Rev. Stat. 1991, Ch. 102, § 0.01 et seq.
Ind. Code Ann., 3-1-30-1 et seq.
Kan. Stat. Ann., 25-2407 et seq.
Ky. Rev. Stat. 1971, 521.015 et seq.
Mass. Gen. Laws Ann., 55:1 et seq.
Md. Ann. Code 1957, Art. 33, § 24-1 et seq.
Mich. Comp. Laws Ann., 168.901 et seq., 168.931 et seq.
Minn. Stat. 1949, 211.01 et seq.
Miss. Code Ann., § 23-3-1 et seq.
Mo. Rev. Stat. 1969, 129.010 et seq.
Mont. Code Ann., 13-37-225 et seq.
N.C. Gen. Stat. 1943, § 163-269 et seq.
N.D. Cent. Code 16.1-10-01 et seq.
Neb. Rev. Stat. 1943, 32-1201 et seq.
Nev. Rev. Stat. Ann., 294A.001 et seq.
N.J. Laws 1911, p. 329
N.Y. Election Law 1976 (Consol. Laws Ch. 17) § 14-100 et seq.
Ohio Rev. Code 1953, 3517.08 et seq.
Okla. Stat. Ann., Title 21, § 181 et seq.
Ore. Rev. Stat., 260.005 et seq.
Pa. 1906 Ex. Pamph. Laws 78, No. 17
S.D. Codified Laws 1967, 12-25-1 et seq.
Tenn. Code Ann., 2-19-101 et seq.
Tex. Election Code, § 31.035
Va. Code 1950, § 24-440 et seq.
Wis. Stat. 1989, 12.01 et seq.
Wyo. Stat. 1957, § 22-346 et seq.

Corrupt Practices Act (Elections)
Alaska Stat. 1962, §§ 15.55.010 et seq., 15.56.010 et seq.
Continued

Utah Code Ann. 1953, 20-14-1 et seq.

Corrupt Practices Act, 1925
See Federal Corrupt Practices Acts

Cortese-Knox Local Government Reorganization Act
Cal. Government Code § 56000 et seq.

Cosmetic Act
Alaska Stat. 1962, § 17.20.010 et seq.
Cal. Health and Safety Code § 26001 et seq.
Haw. Rev. Stat. Ann., § 328-1 et seq.
Iowa Code Ann., 203A.1 et seq.
N.C. Gen. Stat. 1943, § 106-120 et seq.
N.H. Rev. Stat. 1955, 146:1 et seq.
Ore. Rev. Stat. 1981, 690.005 et seq.

Cosmetic Act (Food and Drug)
Ark. Stat. 1987, 20-56-201 et seq.

Cosmetic and Drug Act
Ga. Code Ann., 26-3-1 et seq.

Cosmetic and Food Act
S.C. Code Ann. 1976, § 39-25-10 et seq.

Cosmetic and Hazardous Substance Labeling Act
Vt. Stat. Ann., Title 18, § 4051 et seq.

Cosmetic Art Act
N.C. Gen. Stat. 1943, § 88-1 et seq.

Cosmetic, Drug and Device Act
Ill. Rev. Stat. 1965, Ch. 111 1/2, § 401 et seq.
Iowa Code Ann., 203B.1 et seq.
N.M. Stat. Ann., 26-1-1 et seq.
Pa. Purdon's Stat., Title 35, § 780-101 et seq.

Cosmetic, Drug and Food Act
Conn. Gen. Stat. Ann., § 21a-91 et seq.

Cosmetic, Food and Drug Act
See Food, Drug and Cosmetic Act

Cosmetic, Food and Drug Law
Cal. Health and Safety Code § 26000 et seq.

Cosmetic, Food, Drug and Device Salvage Act
Tex. Health and Safety Code, § 432.001 et seq.

Cosmetic Implant Act
Cal. Statutes 1992, Ch. 1140

Cosmetic Therapy Act
La. Rev. Stat. Ann., 37:491 et seq.
Ore. Rev. Stat. 1953, 691.010 et seq.

Cosmetologist and Barber Act
Colo. Rev. Stat., 12-8-101 et seq.

Cosmetologist and Barber Licensing Act
Utah Code Ann. 1953, 58-11-1 et seq.

Cosmetologists Act
Ky. Rev. Stat. 1971, 317A.010 et seq.
Md. Ann. Code 1974, Art. BO, § 5-101 et seq.

Cosmetologists and Barbers Act
N.M. Stat. Ann., 61-17A-1 et seq.

Cosmetologists and Hairdressers Act
S.C. Code Ann. 1976, § 40-13-10 et seq.

Cosmetologists, Barbers and Manicurists Act
Wash. Rev. Code Ann., 18.16.010 et seq.

Cosmetology Act
Ala. Code 1975, § 34-7-1 et seq.
Ark. Code Ann. 1987, 17-23-101 et seq.
Cal. Business and Professions Code § 7300 et seq.
Colo. Rev. Stat., 12-8-101 et seq.
D.C. Code Ann., § 2-901 et seq.
Fla. Stat. Ann., 477.011 et seq.
Ida. Code 1947, 54-801 et seq.
Ill. Comp. Stat. 1992, Ch. 225, § 410/1-1 et seq.
Iowa Code Ann., 157.1 et seq.
Kan. Stat. Ann., 65-1901 et seq.
La. Rev. Stat. Ann., 37:491 et seq.
Me. Rev. Stat. Ann. 1964, Title 32, § 1551 et seq.
Mich. Comp. Laws Ann., 338.751 et seq.

Mont. Code Ann., 37-31-101 et seq.
N.D. Cent. Code, 43-11-01 et seq.
Neb. Rev. Stat. 1943, 71-340 et seq.
Nev. Rev. Stat. 1979 Reprint, 644.020 et seq.
N.M. Stat. Ann., 61-19A-1 et seq.
Ohio Rev. Code 1953, 4713.01 et seq.
Okla. Stat. Ann., Title 59, § 199.1 et seq.
S.D. Codified Laws 1967, 36-15-1 et seq.
Tenn. Public Acts 1986, Ch. 817
Tex. Rev. Civ. Stat., Art. 8451a
Vt. Stat. Ann., Title 26, § 561 et seq.
Wis. Stat. 1989, 454.01 et seq.
Wyo. Stat. Ann., § 33-12-119 et seq.

Cosmetology and Barbering Act
Cal. Business and Professions Code § 7301 et seq.

Cosmetology and Barbering Law
N.H. Rev. Stat. 1955, 313-A:1 et seq.

Cosmetology and Barbering Licensure Act
Me. Rev. Stat. Ann. 1964, Title 32, § 14201 et seq.

Cosmetology and Cosmetologists Act
S.C. Code Ann. 1976, § 40-13-10 et seq.

Cosmetology and Hairstyling Act
N.J. Stat. Ann., 45:5B-1 et seq.

Cosmetology, Barber and Nail Technology Act
Ill. Comp. Stat. 1992, Ch. 225, § 410/1-1 et seq.

Cosmetology, Esthetics and Barber Act
Ill. Rev. Stat. 1991, Ch. 111, 1701-1 et seq.

Cost Containment Act (Health Care)
Pa. Purdon's Stat., Title 35, § 449.1 et seq.

Cost Containment Commission Act
Colo. Rev. Stat., 24-40.5-101 et seq.

Cost-Effectiveness in Education Act (Agenda for)
Ill. Comp. Stat. 1992, Ch. 105, § 225/0.01 et seq.

Cost-Effectiveness in Education Agenda Act
Ill. Rev. Stat. 1991, Ch. 122, § 1950 et seq.

Cost-Efficiency and Inmate Responsibility Omnibus Act (Department of Corrections)
Wash. Rev. Code Ann., 72.09.450 et seq.

Cost of Energy Act
N.Y. Energy Law (Consol. Laws Ch. 17A) § 17-101 et seq.

Cost of Higher Education Review Act of 1997
June 12, 1997, P.L. 105-18, Title IV, 111 Stat. 207

Cost of Living Salary Increase Act (State Employees)
W. Va. Code 1966, § 5-5-1 et seq.

Cost Recovery Act (Police Search)
Ill. Rev. Stat. 1991, Ch. 70, §§ 850, 851

Costa-Isenberg Water Transfer Act
Cal. Water Code § 470 et seq.

Costa-Keene-Seymour Commercial Property Investment Act
Cal. Civil Code § 1954.25 et seq.

Costa-Marks Housing Bond Allocation Act
Cal. Health and Safety Code § 50171 et seq.

Costa-Marks Mortgage Bond and Credit Certificate Act
Cal. Health and Safety Code § 50173 et seq.

Costa-McCorquodale-Keene Distressed County Assistance Act
Cal. Statutes 1986, Ch. 1146

Costa Mesa District Merger Law
Cal. Water Code § 33200 et seq.

Costa Rail Transportation Improvement Act
Cal. Streets and Highways Code §§ 2701 et seq., 2701.05 et seq., 2701.10 et seq., 2702 et seq., 2702.05 et seq., 2702.08, 2702.10 et seq., 2703 et seq., 2703.05 et seq., 2703.10 et seq.

Costa-Robbins-Nielson-Bergeson County Revenue Stabilization Act
Cal. Government Code § 16265 et seq.

Costilla Creek Compact Act
N.M. Stat. Ann., 72-15-10

Costs Act
Alaska Stat. 1962, § 09.60.010 et seq.
Ill. Rev. Stat. 1991, Ch. 33
Mich. Comp. Laws Ann., 600.2401
Mont. Code Ann., 25-10-101 et seq.
N.H. Rev. Stat. 1955, 525:1 et seq.
N.J. Stat. Ann., 2A:15-59 et seq.
R.I. Gen. Laws 1956, 9-22-1 et seq.
Wash. Rev. Code Ann., 4.84.010 et seq.

Costs, Fees and Allowances Act
W. Va. Code 1966, § 59-1-1 et seq.

Costs Savings Act (Public)
Tenn. Code Ann., 68-11-1201 et seq.

Cotton Arbitration Act
Tenn. Code Ann., 29-5-201 et seq.

Cotton Boll Weevil Control Act
N.M. Laws 1996, Ch. 77

Cotton Classers Act
Tex. Agriculture Code, § 112.001 et seq.

Cotton Classification Act
April 13, 1937, Ch. 75, 50 Stat. 62, 7 U.S. Code §§ 473a to 473c

Cotton Classing Fees Act of 1991
See Uniform Cotton Classing Fees Act of 1991

Cotton Control Act
April 21, 1934, Ch. 157, 48 Stat. 598, 7 U.S. Code § 724

Cotton District Act
N.M. Stat. Ann., 76-18-1 et seq.

Cotton Duck or Canvas Act
Ill. Comp. Stat. 1992, Ch. 815, § 330/0.01 et seq.

Cotton Factor Act
Tenn. Code Ann., 66-12-108

Cotton Futures Acts, United States
See United States Cotton Futures Acts

Cotton Gin Act
Okla. Stat. Ann., Title 17, § 41 et seq.

Cotton Ginning and Handling Act
N.M. Stat. Ann., 76-14-1 et seq.

Cotton Pest Control Districts Act
Ariz. Rev. Stat. Ann., § 48-1301 et seq.

Cotton Pests Abatement District Act
Cal. Food and Agriculture Code 1967, § 6051 et seq

Cotton Reports Act
May 27, 1912, Ch. 135, 37 Stat. 118, 7 U.S. Code § 476

Cotton Research and Promotion Act
July 13, 1966, P.L. 89-502, 80 Stat. 279, 7 U.S. Code §§ 2101 to 2118
Oct. 15, 1970, P.L. 91-452, 84 Stat. 929, 7 U.S. Code § 2115
Nov. 28, 1990, P.L. 101-624, 7 U.S. Code §§ 2101, 2101 nt., 2106 to 2110, 2116
Dec. 13, 1991, P.L. 102-237, 7 U.S. Code §§ 2106, 2107, 2109, 2110

Cotton Research and Promotion Act Amendments of 1990
Nov. 28, 1990, P.L. 101-624, 7 U.S. Code § 2101 nts.

Cotton Research Laboratory Act
Tex. Agriculture Code, § 42.001 et seq.

Cotton Road Law
Ark. Pope's Digest 1937, § 7062 et seq.

Cotton Standards Act
See United States Cotton Standards Act

Cotton Statistics Acts
July 22, 1912, Ch. 249, 37 Stat. 198
April 2, 1924, Ch. 80, 43 Stat. 31

Cotton Statistics and Estimates Act

March 3, 1927, Ch. 337, 44 Stat. 1372, 7 U.S. Code §§ 471 to 473, 474 to 476

April 13, 1937, Ch. 75, 50 Stat. 62, 7 U.S. Code §§ 473a to 473c

April 7, 1941, Ch. 42, 55 Stat. 131, 7 U.S. Code § 473d

July 5, 1960, P.L. 86-588, 74 Stat. 328, 7 U.S. Code §§ 473c-1 to 473c-3

Aug. 28, 1984, P.L. 98-403, 7 U.S. Code §§ 473a, 473a nt.

Aug. 10, 1987, P.L. 100-108, 7 U.S. Code §§ 473a, 473a nt.

Dec. 13, 1991, P.L. 102-237, 7 U.S. Code § 473a

April 4, 1996, P.L. 104-127, 7 U.S. Code §§ 473a, 474

Cotton-Tobacco-Potato Lien Act

March 2, 1936, Ch. 112, 49 Stat. 1155

Cotton-Tobacco-Potato Repeal Act

Feb. 10, 1936, Ch. 42, 49 Stat. 1106

Cotton Warehouse Act

N.C. Gen. Stat. 1943, § 106-451.6 et seq.

Cotty Act (Tax Assessments)

Mo. Rev. Stat., 137.035 et seq.

Coudert Act (Subway Loitering)

N.Y. Penal Law 1965 (Consol. Laws Ch. 40) § 240.35, Subd. 7

Coudert Bill (School Transportation)

N.Y. Education Law 1947 (Consol. Laws Ch. 16) §§ 1807, 1809, 2503, 3635

Coudert-Brook Act (Employment of Minors)

N.Y. Labor Law, (Consol. Laws Ch. 31) § 170 et seq.

Coudert-Jarema Law (Demolition of Elevated Railroad)

N.Y. Laws 1942, Ch. 580

Coudert-Mitchell Laws (Action for Corporate Misconduct)

N.Y. Business Corporations Law 1961 (Consol. Laws Ch. 4) §§ 626, 706, 720

Coudert-Mitchell Laws (Security for Expenses in Derivative Action)

N.Y. Business Corporations Law 1961 (Consol. Laws Ch. 4) §§ 627, 7206

Coulee Dam Community Act of 1957

Aug. 30, 1957, P.L. 85-240, 71 Stat. 524, 12 U.S. Code § 1715n; 16 U.S . Code § 835c nt.

Council for the Arts Act

Ga. Code Ann., 50-12-20 et seq.

Council Manager Act

Ala. Code 1958, App., § 1504 et seq.

Ala. Code 1975, § 11-43A-1 et seq.

Council-Manager Act

Ala. Code 1975, § 11-43A-70 et seq.

Council-Manager Act (Hamilton County)

Tenn. Private Acts 1941, Ch. 156

Council-Manager Form of Government Act

S.C. Code Ann. 1976, § 5-13-10 et seq.

Council-Manager Form of Municipal Government Act

S.C. Code Ann. 1976, § 5-13-10 et seq.

Council-Mayor Act of 1971, 1973

Ala. Code 1958, App. §§ 1123(38c) et seq., 1247(216a) et seq.

Council of Defense Act

Ill. Rev. Stat. 1949, Ch. 127, § 63j et seq.

S.C. Code Ann. 1976, § 25-9-10 et seq.

Council of Defense Act (State)

Del. Laws Vol. 43, p. 1173, Ch. 285

Council on Autism and Pervasive Developmental Disorders Act (Interagency)

Tex. Human Resources Code, § 114.001 et seq.

Council on Libraries Act

Okla. Stat. 1971, Title 65, § 501 et seq.

Council on Maternal Infant and Child Health Act (State)
S.C. Code Ann. 1976, § 20-7-5410 et seq.

Council on State Goals and Policy Act
N.C. Gen. Stat. 1943, § 143-476 et seq.

Council on the Arts Act
Wyo. Stat. Ann., § 9-2-901 et seq.

Council on the Deaf and Hard of Hearing Act
Ida. Code 1947, 67-7301 et seq.

Council on Vocational Education Act
Ill. Comp. Stat. 1992, Ch. 105, § 420/0.01 et seq.

Council on Wage and Price Stability Act
Aug. 24, 1974, P.L. 93-387, 88 Stat. 750, 12 U.S. Code § 1904 nt.
Aug. 9, 1975, P.L. 94-78, 89 Stat. 411, 112 U.S. Code § 1904 nt.
Oct. 6, 1977, P.L. 95-121, 12 U.S. Code § 1904 nt.
May 10, 1979, P.L. 96-10, 12 U.S. Code § 1904 nt.

Council on Women's Economic Development and Training Act
Mo. Rev. Stat., 186.005 et seq.

Council on Youth Act
Nev. Rev. Stat. 1979 Reprint, 233D.020 et seq.

Counseling and Therapy Practice Act
N.M. Stat. Ann., 61-9A-1 et seq.

Counselor Certification Act
La. Rev. Stat. Ann., 37:3371 et seq.

Counselor Certification Act (Fee-Based Practicing Pastoral)
N.C. Gen. Stat. 1943, § 90-350 et seq.

Counselor Confidentiality Act (Victim)
Ala. Acts 1991, p. 1040 No. 598
N.M. Stat. Ann., 31-25-1 et seq.

Counselor Licensing Act (Mental Health)
La. Rev. Stat. Ann., 37:1101 et seq.

Counselor Licensing Act (Professional)
Utah Code Ann. 1953, 58-60-401 et seq.

Counselor Registration Act (Alcohol and Other Drug Abuse)
Kan. Stat. Ann., 65-6601 et seq.

Counselors Act
Okla. Stat. 1981, Title 59, § 1901 et seq.

Counselors Omnibus Credentialing Act
Wash. Rev. Code Ann., 18.19.010 et seq.

Counselors Registration Act (Professional)
Kan. Stat. Ann., 65-5801 et seq.

Counter-Drug Activities Compact (National Guard Mutual Assistance)
Ala. Code 1975, §§ 31-11-1, 31-11-2
Miss. Code Ann., §§ 33-7-501, 33-7-503
S.C. Code Ann. 1976, §§ 1-3-490, 1-3-491
Va. Code 1950, § 44-75.1:1

Counterclaim Act
Miss. Code Ann., § 11-7-69

Countercyclical Construction Industry Jobs Program for Special School Manitenance Act
Fla. Laws 1979, Ch. 79-583

Counterfeit Access Device and Computer Fraud and Abuse Act of 1984
Oct. 12, 1984, P.L. 98-473, 18 U.S. Code § 1001 nt.

Counterfeit and Imitation Controlled Substances Act
Colo. Rev. Stat., 18-18-419 to 18-18-424
Iowa Code 1983, 124A.1 et seq.

Counterfeit Deterrence Act of 1992
Oct. 28, 1992, P.L. 102-550, 18 U.S. Code § 471 nt.

Counterfeit Drugs Act
S.C. Code Ann. 1976, § 44-53-110 et seq.

Counterfeit Trademark Act
Ill. Comp. Stat. 1992, Ch. 765, § 1040/0.01 et seq.

Counterfeiting and Forgery Act
R.I. Gen. Laws 1956, 11-17-1 et seq.

Counterfeiting Law
Wash. Rev. Code Ann., 9.16.030

Counties and Municipalities Hydroelectric Power Development Revenue Bond Law
Ark. Code Ann. 1987, 14-204-101 et seq.

Counties Code
Ill. Comp. Stat. 1992, Ch. 55, § 5/1-1-1 et seq.

Counties Fiscal Procedures Act
Utah Code Ann. 1953, 17-36-1 et seq.

Counties Health Act
Ga. Code Ann., 31-3-1 et seq., 31-5-1 et seq.

Counties or Road Districts General Bond Act
S.C. Acts 1926, p. 1001, No. 559

Counties Recreation Districts Act
Wash. Rev. Code Ann., 36.69.010

Counties-Sales and Use Tax Act
Tex. Tax Code, § 323.001 et seq.

Country Road Improvement Act
Okla. Stat. Ann., Title 69, § 685 et seq.

Country Warehouse Act
Ind. Burns' 1961 Repl., 67-501 et seq.

County Accounting Act
Ark. Code Ann. 1987, 14-25-101 et seq.
Mich. Comp. Laws Ann., 750.485

County Act
Haw. Rev. Stat. Ann., § 61-1 et seq.
N.Y. Consol. Laws, Ch. 11
Pa. Purdon's Stat., Title 16, § 101 et seq.
Wash. Rev. Code Ann., 36.01.010 et seq.

County Administration Act
Fla. Stat. 1983, 125.70 et seq.

County Administration Act (School System)
Iowa Code 1973, 273.1 et seq.

County Affordable Housing Funds Act (Optional)
Pa. 1992 Pamph. Laws, No. 137

County Agricultural Extension Law
Iowa Code Ann., 176A.1 et seq.

County Agricultural School Loan Act (Norfolk County)
Mass. Acts 1956, Ch. 372

County Agriculture Society Act
Neb. Rev. Stat. 1943, 2-250 to 2-273

County Aid Act (Streets)
Cal. Streets and Highways Code § 1680 et seq.

County Aid Road Act
Mo. Rev. Stat., 231.440 et seq.

County Air and Water Pollution Control Act (Broward)
Fla. Laws 1963, Ch. 63-1080

County Airport Authority Act
Ga. Laws 1977, p. 1136
W. Va. Code 1966, § 8-29A-1 et seq.

County Airport Authority Act (Gwinnett)
Ga. Laws 1971, p. 3668

County Airport Law
Ill. Comp. Stat. 1992, Ch. 620, § 45/1 et seq.

County Airports Act
Fla. Stat. Ann., 332.001 et seq.
Ill. Rev. Stat. 1991, Ch. 15 1/2, § 104 et seq.
Neb. Rev. Stat. 1943, 3-601 et seq.

County and City Civil Service Act
Wis. Stat. 1989, 63.01 et seq.

County and City Economic Development Grant Authorization Act
Ark. Code Ann. 1987, 14-173-101 et seq.

County and City Jails Act
Wash. Rev. Code Ann., 70.48.020 et seq.

County and City Lottery Act
Neb. Rev. Stat. 1943, 9-601 et seq.

County and District High School Act
Ore. Rev. Stat. 1953, 335.005 et seq.

County and District Road Bond Act
Tex. Rev. Civ. Stat., Art. 6702-1, § 4.411 et seq.

County and Municipal Barrett Law
Ind. Code Ann., 36-9-18-1 et seq.

County and Municipal Corporations Deposit Act
Cal. Statutes 1933, p. 642

County and Municipal Employees Grievance Procedure Act
S.C. Code Ann. 1976, § 8-17-110 et seq.

County and Municipal Fireworks Act
Utah Code Ann. 1953, 11-3-1 et seq.

County and Municipal Gasoline Tax Act
N.M. Stat. Ann., 7-24A-1 et seq.

County and Municipal Home Rule Act
S.C. Code Ann. 1976, §§ 4-9-10 et seq., 5-5-10 et seq.

County and Municipal Housing and Redevelopment Law
S.D. Codified Laws 1967, 11-7-1 et seq.

County and Municipal Industrial Development Bonds Act
Okla. Stat. Ann., Title 62, § 800 et seq.

County and Municipal Investigations Law
N.J. Stat. Ann., 2A:67A-1 et seq.

County and Municipal Planning for Future Development Act
Fla. Stat. 1983, 163.160 et seq.

County and Municipal Police Pension Plan Act
Del. Code of 1974, Title 11, § 8801 et seq.

County and Municipal Sewerage Act
N.J. Stat. Ann., 40A:26A-1 et seq.

County and Municipal Solid Waste Disposal Act
Ark. Code Ann. 1987, 14-233-101 et seq.

County and Municipal Water Supply Act
N.J. Stat. Ann., 40A:31-1 et seq.

County and Municipality Development Revenue Bond Act
Colo. Rev. Stat., 29-3-101 et seq.

County and Regional Housing Commission Act
Ky. Rev. Stat. 1971, 80.310 et seq.

County Apportionment Act
Mich. Comp. Laws Ann., 46.401 et seq.

County Artesian Well Law
S.D. Code 1939, 61.0601 et seq.

County Assessment Act
Pa. Purdon's Stat., Title 72, § 5020-1 et seq.

County Assessment Act (Fourth to Eighth Class)
Pa. Purdon's Stat., Title 72, § 5453.101 et seq.

County Assessors Act
Iowa Code Ann., 441.1 et seq.

County Assessors Act (Dorchester)
S.C. Code Ann. 1962, § 65-1811

County Assistance Act
Cal. Statutes 1986, Ch. 1146

County Audit Law
Ark. Code Ann. 1987, 10-4-202 et seq.,
10-4-216, 10-4-217
Ohio Rev. Code 1953, 319.01 et seq.

County Auditing Law
Ill. Comp. Stat. 1992, Ch. 55, § 5/6-31001 et
seq.

**County Automobile Renting Occupation
Tax Act**
Ill. Comp. Stat. 1992, Ch. 55, §§ 5/5-1032,
5/5-1033

County Board Act
N.J. Stat. Ann., 54:1-36, 54:2-35, 54:3-1 to
54:3-31
Wis. Stat. 1981, 59.03 et seq.

County Board of Education Act
Ida. Laws 1947, Ch. 275
Ind. Code Ann., 20-2-1-1 et seq.

County Board of School Trustees Act
Ill. Rev. Stat. 1991, Ch. 122, § 6-1 et seq.

County Board of Tax Adjustment Act
Ind. Code Ann., 6-1.1-29-1 et seq.

County Bond Act
Ala. Code 1975, 11-18-80 et seq.
Miss. Code Ann., § 19-9-1 et seq.
Nev. Rev. Stat. 1979 Reprint, 244A.011 et
seq.
S.C. Code Ann. 1976, § 4-15-10 et seq.
S.D. Codified Laws 1967, 7-24-1 et seq.
Wash. Rev. Code Ann., 36.67.030 et seq.

County Bond Act (Chester)
S.C. Acts 1948, p. 2504, No. 951

County Bond Road Act
Mo. Laws 1907, p. 411

County Bond Validation Laws
Cal. Statutes 1933, Ch. 17, p. 42
Cal. Statutes 1935, Ch. 90, p. 441
Cal. Statutes 1935, Ch. 115, p. 465

County Boundary Act (Alteration)
Cal. Statutes 1941, p. 1801

County Boundary Commission Act
Cal. Government Code § 58850 et seq.

County Bounty Act
Tenn. Code Ann., 38-11-201 et seq.

County Bridge Act
Neb. Rev. Stat. 1943, 39-835 et seq.

County Bridge Improvement Act
Okla. Stat. Ann., Title 69, § 657 et seq.

County Budget Act
Ala. Code 1975, § 11-8-1 et seq.
Cal. Government Code § 29040 et seq.
Ida. Code 1947, 31-1601 et seq.
Ill. Rev. Stat. 1991, Ch. 34, § 6-1001 et seq.
Miss. Code Ann., § 19-11-1 et seq.
Mo. Rev. Stat., 50.525 et seq.
Mont. Code Ann., 7-6-2301 et seq.
Neb. Rev. Stat. 1943, 23-901 et seq.
N.M. Stat. Ann., 6-6-1 et seq.
Ohio Rev. Code 1953, 5705.27 et seq.
Okla. Stat. Ann., Title 19, § 1401 et seq.
S.D. Codified Laws 1967, 7-21-1 et seq.
Tenn. Code Ann., 5-22-101 et seq.
Tex. Local Gov. Code, § 111.001 et seq.
Wash. Rev. Code Ann., 36.40.010 et seq.
Wyo. Session Laws 1939, Ch. 87

County Budget Commission Act
Fla. Laws 1931, Ch. 14678
Ky. Rev. Stat. 1971, 68.210 et seq.

County Budgeting Act (Rutherford County)
Tenn. Private Acts 1975, Ch. 82, § 1

County Building Authority Act
Ga. Laws 1980, p. 4488
Ind. Code Ann., 19-8-4-1 et seq.
Mich. Comp. Laws Ann., 123.951 et seq.
Tex. Local Government Code, § 293.001 et
seq.

County Building Code Act
Colo. Rev. Stat., 30-28-201 et seq.
Continued

Mich. Comp. Laws Ann., 125.251 et seq.

County Business Development Corporation Act
S.C. Code Ann. 1976, § 33-39-10 et seq.

County Cabaret Tax Law
Wash. Rev. Code Ann., 36.38.010 et seq.

County Canvassers Act (Elections)
Mich. Comp. Laws Ann., 168.821 et seq.

County Capital Improvement Trust Fund Financing Act
Colo. Rev. Stat., 30-26-501 et seq.

County Capital Reserve Act
N.C. Gen. Stat. 1943, § 153-142.1 et seq.

County Care for Mentally Retarded and Developmentally Disabled Persons Act
Ill. Comp. Stat. 1992, Ch. 55, § 105/0.01 et seq.

County Cemetery Care Act
Ill. Comp. Stat. 1992, Ch. 55, § 65/0.01 et seq.

County Charter Commission Act
Ga. Laws 1999, H.B. 896

County Charter Commission Act (Griffin-Spalding)
Ga. Laws 1991, p. 3802

County Charter Law
N.Y. Municipal Home Rule Law (Consol. Laws Ch. 36A) § 30 et seq.

County Charter Law (Optional)
Fla. Stat. Ann., 125.80 et seq.
N.J. Stat. Ann., 40:41A-1 et seq.

County Charter Procedures Act (Fitzgerald-Ben Hill)
Mass. Gen. Laws Ann., 34A:1 et seq.

County Children's Court Act
N.Y. Laws 1922, Ch. 547

County-City Act
Ore. Rev. Stat., 199.705 et seq.

County-City Consolidation Act
N.C. Gen. Stat. 1943, § 160B-1 et seq.
Tenn. Code Ann., 7-1-101 et seq.

County-City Relief Tax Law
Nev. Rev. Stat. 1979 Reprint, 377.010 et seq.

County Civil Court Act (Milwaukee)
Wis. Laws 1951, Ch. 168

County Civil Courts Act
N.C. Gen. Stat. 1943, § 7-308 et seq.

County Civil Service Act
Ala. Code 1958, Title 12, § 133 et seq.
Ill. Rev. Stat. 1939, Ch. 34, § 64, Subd. 10 et seq.
Mich. Comp. Laws Ann., 38.401 et seq.
Ore. Rev. Stat., 241.002 et seq.

County Civil Service Enabling Act
Cal. Government Code § 31100 et seq.

County Claims Act
Wash. Rev. Code Ann., 36.45.010 et seq.

County Classification Act
Wash. Rev. Code Ann., 36.13.010 et seq.

County Coal Processing Act
Ill. Comp. Stat. 1992, Ch. 55, § 100/0.01 et seq.

County Code (Second Class)
Pa. Purdon's Stat., Title 16, § 3101 et seq.

County College Bond Act
N.J. Stat. Ann., 18A:64A-1 et seq.

County College Contracts Act
N.J. Stat. Ann., 18A:64A-25.1 et seq.

County Commission Drainage Act
Mo. Rev. Stat., 243.010 et seq.

County Commissioners Act
Colo. Rev. Stat., 30-10-301 et seq.
Wash. Rev. Code Ann., 36.32.005 et seq.

County Conference Center and Tourism Authority Act (Valdosta and Lowndes)
Ga. Laws 1999, H.B. 899

County Controllers Act
Pa. Purdon's Stat., Title 16, § 7351 et seq.

County Cooperative Extension Law
Ill. Comp. Stat. 1992, Ch. 505, § 45/1 et seq.

County Coroner's Act
N.D. Cent. Code 11-19-01 et seq.

County Correctional Facility Capital Expenditure and Juvenile Facility Bond Act
Cal. Penal Code § 4496.50 et seq.

County Correctional Facility Capital Expenditure Bond Act
Cal. Penal Code § 4475 et seq.

County Correctional Facility Gross Receipts Tax Act
N.M. Stat. Ann., 7-20F-1 et seq.

County Correctional Incentives Act
Tenn. Code Ann., 41-8-101 et seq.

County Correctional Policy Act
N.J. Stat. Ann., 30:8-16.3 et seq.

County Corrections Equality Act
Fla. Stat. Ann., 951.175
Fla. Stat., 951.175

County Council Act
Ind. Code Ann., 17-1-24-1 et seq.

County Council Act (Lindsay)
Md. Ann. Code 1957, Art. 25A, § 2

County Court Act
Colo. Rev. Stat. 1963, 37-5-1 et seq.
Ill. Rev. Stat. 1963, Ch. 37, § 171 et seq.
Minn. Stat. Ann., 487.01 et seq.
Miss. Code Ann., § 9-9-1 et seq.
Ohio Rev. Code 1953, 1907.011 et seq.

County Court Act (Portage)
Wis. Laws 1891, Ch. 357

County Court Act (Wood)
Wis. Laws 1951, Ch. 197

County Court Condemnation Act
Ark. Code Ann. 1987, 14-298-101 et seq.

County Court House Loan Act (Bristol)
Mass. Acts 1970, Ch. 482

County Court Procedure Act
S.D. Codified Laws 1967, 15-31-1 et seq.

County Court Unification Act
Cal. Government Code § 70200 et seq.

County Courthouse Building Commission Act
Okla. Stat. Ann., Title 19, § 771 et seq.

County Courthouse Facility Capital Expenditure Bond Act
Cal. Government Code § 23800 et seq.

County Courts Trial Commissioner Act
Ky. Rev. Stat. 1971, Superseded Vols., 25.280

County Criminal Courts Act
N.C. Gen. Stat. 1943, § 7-384 et seq.

County Debt Act
Ky. Rev. Stat. 1971, 66.280 et seq.

County Debt Limit Act
Wash. Rev. Code Ann., 36.67.010 et seq.

County Department of Children's Services Act
Tenn. Code Ann., 37-2-201 et seq.

County Department of Corrections Act
Ill. Comp. Stat. 1992, Ch. 55, § 5/3-15001 et seq.

County Department of Solid Waste Management Act
Mich. Comp. Laws Ann., 45.581 et seq.

County Depository Act
Ark. Code Ann. 1987, 19-8-105 et seq.
Mo. Rev. Stat., 110.130 et seq.
Ohio Rev. Code 1953, 323.61 et seq.
Okla. Stat. Ann., Title 19, § 112 et seq.
Ore. Rev. Stat. 1953, 295.005 et seq.
Tex. Local Government Code, § 116.021
Wash. Rev. Code Ann., 36.48.010 et seq.

County Detectives and County Investigators Act (Revision of 1951)
N.J. Stat. Ann., 2A:157-1 et seq.

County Detention Home Act
Ill. Comp. Stat. 1992, Ch. 55, § 75/1 et seq.

County Development District Act
Tex. Local Government Code, § 383.001 et seq.

County District Law
Ky. Rev. Stat. 1971, 160.010 et seq.

County Ditch Act
Ohio Rev. Code 1953, 6131.01 et seq.

County Drainage Act
Neb. Rev. Stat. 1943, 31-901 et seq.

County Drainage District Act
Cal. Water Code § 56000 et seq.

County Economic Development Project Area Property Tax Allocation Act
Ill. Comp. Stat. 1992, Ch. 55, § 90/1 et seq.

County Economic Development Project Area Tax Increment Allocation Act
Ill. Rev. Stat. 1991, Ch. 34, § 8001 et seq.

County Economic Development Revenue Bond Law
Nev. Rev. Stat. 1979 Reprint, 244A.669 et seq.

County Election Books Act
Fla. Laws 1935, Ch. 17399

County Eminent Domain Law
Wash. Rev. Code Ann., 8.08.010 et seq.

County Employees and Officers Annuity and Benefit Fund Act
Ill. Rev. Stat. 1991, Ch. 108 1/2, § 9-101 et seq.

County Employees Benefit Fund Act
Ill. Rev. Stat. 1961, Ch. 34, § 1601 et seq.
Ill. Rev. Stat. 1991, Ch. 108 1/2, § 9-101 et seq.

County Employees Retirement Act
Cal. Government Code § 31450 et seq.
Ky. Rev. Stat. 1971, 78.510 et seq.
Mich. Comp. Laws 1948, 46.12a
Neb. Rev. Stat. 1943, 23-2301 et seq., 23-2331 et seq.
N.J. Rev. Stat. 1937, 43:10-1 et seq.

County Employees Retirement Act (Fifth to Eighth Class)
Pa. Purdon's Stat., Title 16, § 11621 et seq.

County Enabling Act (Bonds)
Ark. Stat. 1947, 13-1202 et seq.

County Enabling Act (Initiative and Referendum)
Ark. Stat. 1947, 2-301 et seq.

County Engineer Act
Cal. Statutes 1919, Ch. 625, p. 1290

County Engineer Act (Henderson)
Ala. Code 1975, § 11-6-1 et seq.

County Engineers and Highway Superintendent Liability Act
Ill. Comp. Stat. 1992, Ch. 745, § 15/0.01 et seq.

County Environmental Health Act
N.J. Stat. Ann., 26:3A2-1 et seq.

County Environmental Services Gross Receipts Tax Act
N.M. Stat. Ann., 7-20B-1 et seq.

County Executive Act
Ill. Rev. Stat. 1991, Ch. 34, § 2-5001 et seq.

County Expenditures Law
Iowa Code Ann., 331.901

County Express Powers Act
Md. Ann. Code 1957, Art. 25A, § 5 et seq.

County Fair Act
Mont. Code Ann., 7-21-3401 et seq.
Neb. Rev. Stat. 1943, 2-201 et seq.

County Finance Act
N.C. Gen. Stat. 1943, § 159-7 et seq.

County Financial Control Act
Ala. Code 1975, § 11-8-1 et seq.

County Financial Management System Act
Tenn. Code Ann., 5-21-101 et seq.

County Fire Insurance Act
Ill. Rev. Stat. 1935, Ch. 73, § 15 et seq.

County Fire Protection District Law
Cal. Health and Safety Code § 14400 et seq.

County Fire Service Retirement Law
Cal. Government Code § 32200 et seq.

County Fiscal Control Act
N.C. Gen. Stat. 1943, § 159-7 et seq.

County Fiscal Procedure Act
Tenn. Code Ann., 5-13-101 et seq.

County Fiscal Procedure Law (Rutherford County)
Tenn. Private Acts 1975, Ch. 82, § 2

County Fish Hatcheries Law
Cal. Fish and Game Code 1957, § 1150

County Fishing Season Act (Newberry)
S.C. Acts 1933, p. 387, No. 282

County Flood Control Act
Wash. Rev. Code Ann., 86.12.010 et seq.

County Flood Control Financing Law
N.J. Stat. Ann., 40:14-16

County Food Distribution Authorities Law
N.J. Stat. Ann., 40:37D-1, et seq.

County Forestry Act
Ky. Rev. Stat. 1971, 149.010 et seq.
Wis. Stat. 1989, 28.10, 28.11

County Free Library Act
Cal. Education Code 1976, § 19100 et seq.

County Funds Daily Deposit Act
N.C. Gen. Stat. 1943, § 153.135

County Funds Deposit Law
Cal. Statutes 1933, Ch. 189, p. 642

County Government Act
Ark. Code Ann. 1987, 14-14-101 et seq.
Cal. Political Code, § 4000 et seq.
Colo. Rev. Stat., 30-11-101 et seq.
Nev. Rev. Stat. 1979 Reprint, 244.010 et seq.
N.Y. Laws 1936, Ch. 879
S.C. Code Ann. 1976, § 4-9-10 et seq.

County Government Act (Alternative Form)
Ohio Rev. Code 1953, 302.14 et seq.

County Government Act (Optional Forms of)
Ida. Code 1947, 31-5001 et seq.

County Government Act (York)
S.C. Code Ann. 1962, § 14-3601 et seq.

County Government Capital Improvement Act
Ala. Acts 1986, No. 206

County Government Reorganization Act
Miss. Code Ann., § 19-2-1 et seq.

County Grazing Act
Ore. Code 1930, §§ 20-2101 to 20-2111

County Gross Receipts Tax Act
N.M. Stat. Ann., 7-20-1 et seq.

County Health Board Act
Wash. Rev. Code Ann., 70.05.005 et seq.

County Health Care Gross Receipts Tax Act
N.M. Stat. Ann., 7-20D-1 et seq.

County Herd Act
Kan. Stat. Ann., 47-301 et seq.

County High School Act
Tenn. Code Ann., 49-6-401 et seq.

County High School Building Fund
Fla. Laws 1947, Ch. 24224

County High School Fund Act
Ore. Code 1930, §§ 35-4001 to 35-4008

County High School Tuition Fund Act
Ore. Code 1930, §§ 35-4101 to 35-4113

County Highway Aid Act
Cal. Statutes 1945, pp. 1751, 1834
Miss. Code Ann., § 65-11-1 et seq.

County Highway Assessment Act
Fla. Laws 1925, Ch. 10140

County Highway Commission Law
Cal. Streets and Highways Code § 1220 et seq.

County Highway Maintenance Act
Ind. Code Ann., 8-17-3-1 et seq.

County Highway Protection Loan Act (Dukes)
Mass. Acts 1954, Ch. 215

County Highways Enabling Act
Minn. Stat. Ann., 163.01 et seq.

County Historic Preservation Act
Ill. Comp. Stat. 1992, Ch. 55, § 5/5-30001 et seq.

County Historical Commission Act
N.J. Stat. Ann., 40:33B-1 et seq.

County Historical Museum District Act
Ill. Rev. Stat. 1987, Ch. 34, § 6601 et seq.

County Historical Research Act
Ill. Comp. Stat. 1992, Ch. 55, § 95/0.01 et seq.

County Home Act
Ill. Rev. Stat. 1985, Ch. 34, § 5361 et seq.
Ind. Code Ann., 12-4-3-1 et seq.

County Home Rule Act
Colo. Rev. Stat., 30-35-101 et seq.
Ga. Laws 1947, p. 1501
Iowa Code Ann., 331.101 et seq.
Mich. Comp. Laws Ann., 45.501 et seq.
Tex. Local Government Code, § 71.035
Wis. Stat. 1989, 59.001 et seq.

County Home Rule Amendment
Tex. Const. 1876, Art. 9, § 3

County Home Rule Charter Act
Okla. Stat. Ann., Title 19, § 8.1 et seq.

County Homesite Land Act
Wash. Rev. Code Ann., 36.59.300 et seq.

County Horse Racing Facility Bond Act
Neb. Rev. Stat. 1943, 23-389 et seq.

County Hospital Authority Act
N.M. Stat. Ann., 4-48B-5 et seq.
Tex. Health and Safety Code, § 264.001 et seq.

County Hospital Loan Act (Plymouth)
Mass. Acts 1939, Ch. 262

County Hospitals Act
Ill. Comp. Stat. 1992, Ch. 55, § 5/5-37001 et seq.
Ind. Code Ann., 16-12.1-1-1 et seq.
Mich. Comp. Laws Ann., 331.151 et seq.
Mo. Rev. Stat., 205.160 et seq.
N.C. Gen. Stat. 1943, § 131-28.1 et seq.
Ohio Rev. Code 1953, 339.01 et seq.
Tex. Health and Safety Code, § 263.021

County Hospitals Act (Building Authorities)
Ind. Code Ann., 16-12-1-1 et seq.

County Hospitals Governing Commission Act
Ill. Rev. Stat. 1991, Ch. 34, § 5011 et seq.

County Housing Authorities Act
Mont. Code Ann., 7-15-2101 et seq.

County Housing Authorities and Cooperation Law
Ida. Code 1947, 31-4201 et seq.

County Hunting Season Act (Newberry)
S.C. Acts 1933, p. 387, No. 282

County Improvement Authorities Law
N.J. Stat. Ann., 40:37A-44 et seq.

County Improvement District Act
Ariz. Rev. Stat. Ann., § 11-701 et seq.
N.M. Stat. Ann., 4-55A-1 et seq.
Utah Code Ann. 1953, 17-3-201 et seq.

County Improvements Act
Cal. Statutes 1921, Ch. 872, p. 1658
Nev. Rev. Stat. 1979 Reprint, Replaced Pages, 244A.067 et seq.
N.M. Stat. Ann., 4-55-1 et seq.

County Industrial Development Corporation Act
Ark. Acts 1989, No. 660

County Industrial Farm and Road Camp Act
Cal. Penal Code § 4100 et seq.

County Industrial Farm, Workhouse, and Reformatory Act
Pa. 1917 Pamph. Laws 1151, No. 399

County Industrial Revenue Bond Act
N.M. Stat. Ann., 4-59-1 et seq.

County Industrial Sewer Construction Act
Neb. Rev. Stat. 1943, 23-3601 et seq.

County Insect Abatement Act
Ore. Rev. Stat., 452.210 et seq.

County Institution District Law
Pa. Purdon's Stat., Title 62, § 2201 et seq.

County Intermediate Punishment Act
Pa. Purdon's Stat., Title 61, § 1101 et seq.

County Jail Act
Cal. Penal Code § 4000 et seq.
Ill. Comp. Stat. 1992, Ch. 730, § 125/0.01 et seq.

County Jail and House of Correction Loan Act (Bristol)
Mass. Acts 1953, Ch. 419

County Jail Capital Expenditure Bond Act
Cal. Penal Code §§ 387, 4400 et seq., 4450 et seq.

County Jail Farm Barn Loan Act (Worcester)
Mass. Acts 1970, Ch. 266

County Jail Good Behavior Allowance Act
Ill. Comp. Stat. 1992, Ch. 730, § 130/1 et seq.

County Jail Loan Act (Barnstable)
Mass. Acts 1959, Ch. 482

County Jail Overcrowding Act
Mich. Comp. Laws Ann., 801.51 et seq.

County Jail Revenue Bond Act
Ark. Code Ann. 1987, 12-41-601 et seq.

County Johnson Grass Control and Eradication Act
Ark. Code Ann. 1987, 2-16-501 et seq.

County Judges Act
Ky. Rev. Stat. 1971, Supersedes Vols., 25.260, 64.230, 453.030

County Judges Minimum Salary Act
Tenn. Code Ann., Superseded Vol., 8-2414 et seq.
Tenn. Public Acts 1957, Ch. 172, §§ 1, 4

County Land Administration and Management Law
S.D. Codified Laws 1967, 7-31-1 et seq.

County Land Use Development and Management Act
Utah Code Ann. 1953, 17-27-101 et seq.

County Law Library Act
Ark. Code Ann. 1987, 16-23-101 et seq.
Ky. Rev. Stat. 1971, 57.300 et seq.

County Leadership Act
Ga. Code Ann., 36-20-1 et seq.

County Leasing Act
Ky. Rev. Stat. 1971, 56.220

County Libraries Act
See Uniform County Libraries Act
N.J. Stat. Ann., 40:33-1 et seq.
S.D. Codified Laws 1967, 14-3-1 et seq.

County Library Commission Act (Colleton)
S.C. Code Ann. 1962, § 42-361 et seq.

County Library District Act
Ohio Rev. Code 1953, 3375.19 et seq.

County Library Reorganization Law
N.J. Stat. Ann., 40:33-13.2d et seq.

County License Act (Vendors)
Colo. Rev. Stat., 12-51-101 et seq.

County Line Road Act
Ind. Code Ann., 8-17-11-1 et seq.

County Linked Deposit Program
W. Va. Code 1966, § 7-19-1 et seq.

County Local Option Gross Receipts Taxes Act
N.M. Stat. Ann., 7-20E-2 et seq.

County Local Optional Secondary Highway Reorganization Act
Ida. Code 1947, 40-2701 et seq.

County Manager Act
Neb. Laws 1933, Ch. 35

County Mass Transit Authority Act
Tex. Transportation Code, § 457.001 et seq.

County Maternal and Child Health Plan Act
N.M. Stat. Ann., 24-1B-1 et seq.

County Medical Examiners Act
Mich. Comp. Laws Ann., 52.201 et seq.

County Memorial Commission Act (Florence)
S.C. Acts 1946, p. 2102, No. 711

County Memorial Hospital Act
Wyo. Stat. Ann., § 18-8-101 et seq.

County Mental Health Clinic Act
Ind. Code Ann., 16-16-1-1 et seq.

County Microfilm Act
Kan. Stat. Ann., 19-250 et seq.

County Mineral Lands Lease Act
Wash. Rev. Code Ann., 78.16.010 et seq.

County Monition Law (New Castle County)
Del. Code of 1974, Title 9, § 8721 et seq.

County Mosquito Control Act
Fla. Stat. Ann., 388.011 et seq.

County Motor Vehicle Fuel Tax Act
Nev. Rev. Stat. 1979 Reprint, 373.010 et seq.

County-Municipal Court Act
N.C. Gen. Stat. 1943, § 7-240 et seq.

County Museums Act
Mont. Code Ann., 7-16-2201 et seq.

County Mutual Fire Insurance Act
Cal. Insurance Code § 5050 et seq.

County Mutual Insurance Act
Mo. Rev. Stat., 380.011 et seq.

County Mutual Reinsurance Company Law
Cal. Insurance Code § 7080 et seq.

County Nursing Home Act
Ill. Rev. Stat. 1987, Ch. 34, § 5361 et seq.

County of Essex Solid Waste Management Authority Act
N.Y. Public Authorities Law (Consol. Laws Ch. 43A) § 2051a et seq.

County of Franklin Solid Waste Management Authority Act
N.Y. Public Authorities Law (Consol. Laws Ch. 43A) § 2051a et seq.

County of Hillsborough Aviation Authority Act
Fla. Special Laws 1945, Ch. 23339

County of Origin Act (Water)
Cal. Water Code § 10505

County Officer Property Sale Act
Ill. Comp. Stat. 1992, Ch. 55, § 55/0.01 et seq.
Ill. Rev. Stat. 1991, Ch. 102, § 4.01 et seq.

County Officers Act
Wash. Rev. Code Ann., 36.16.010 et seq.

County Officers and Employees Disclosure Act
Utah Code Ann. 1953, 17-16a-1 et seq.

County Officers and Employees Retirement Act
Fla. Stat. Ann., 122.01 et seq.

County Officers Cash Difference Fund Act
Cal. Government Code § 29370 et seq.

County Officers Fee Act
Wash. Rev. Code Ann., 36.18.010 et seq.

County Officers' Fees and Salaries Act
Ind. Code Ann., 36-3-6-2 et seq.

County Officers Minimum Salary Act
Tenn. Code Ann., 8-24-104 et seq.

County Officers Office-Hour Act
Nev. Rev. Stat. 1979 Reprint, 245.040

County Officers Salary Act
Mich. Comp. Laws Ann., 45.401 et seq.
N.D. Cent. Code 11-10-10 et seq.

Okla. Stat. 1961, Title 19, § 179.13 et seq.
Wash. Rev. Code Ann., 36.17.010 et seq.

County Officers Salary Act (Eighth Class)
Pa. Purdon's Stat., Title 16, § 1555

County Official Bond Approval Act
Ill. Comp. Stat. 1992, Ch. 55, §§ 60/0.01; 60/1

County Officials Certificate Training Program Act
Tenn. Code Ann., 5-1-301 et seq.

County Oil Lands Lease Act
Wash. Rev. Code Ann., 78.16.010 et seq.

County Option Act (Liquor)
Minn. Stat. 1963, 340.25, et seq.

County Option Dumping Ground Act
Mo. Rev. Stat., 64.460 et seq.

County Option Kitchen and Table Wine Act
Ida. Code 1947, 23-1301 et seq.

County Park Abandonment Act
Cal. Government Code § 25580 et seq.

County Park Act
Ark. Code Ann. 1987, 14-270-101 et seq.
N.J. Rev. Stat. 1937, 40:37-1 et seq.

County Patrol Act
Ky. Rev. Stat. 1971, 70.150 et seq.

County Paving Act
Ark. Acts 1927, p. 1169, No. 359

County Peace Officer and Fire Service Retirement Plan
Cal. Government Code § 33000

County Peace Officers' Retirement Law
Cal. Government Code § 31900 et seq.

County Peddlers Act
Wash. Rev. Code Ann., 36.71.010 et seq.

County Pension Act
Ga. Laws 1937, p. 738
Continued

501

Mich. Comp. Laws Ann., 46.12a
Nev. Rev. Stat. Ann., 286.015 et seq.
Pa. Purdon's Stat., Title 16, § 11651 et seq.

County Personal Property Tax Act
Pa. Purdon's Stat., Title 72, § 4821 et seq.

County Personnel Management Act
Utah Code Ann. 1953, 17-33-1 et seq.

County Plan Commission Act
Ind. Code Ann., 18-7-5-1 et seq.

County Planning Act
Colo. Rev. Stat., 30-28-101 et seq.
Mich. Comp. Laws Ann., 125.101 et seq.
N.J. Stat. Ann., 40:27-1 et seq.
S.C. Code Ann. 1976, § 4-27-10 et seq.

County Planning and Zoning Act
Ariz. Rev. Stat. Ann., § 11-801 et seq.
Mo. Rev. Stat., 64.010 et seq.
Mont. Code Ann., 76-2-101 et seq.
S.D. Codified Laws 1967, 11-2-1 et seq.

County Planning Board Act
Ark. Code Ann. 1987, 14-17-203 et seq.

County Police Departments Act
Ill. Rev. Stat. 1987, Ch. 125, § 51 et seq.

County Pollution Control Revenue Bond Act
N.M. Stat. Ann., § 4-60-1 et seq.

County Poor Relief Fund Act
N.D. Cent. Code 50-03-01 et seq.

County Power Pumping District Act
Cal. Water Code § 55000 et seq.

County Predator Control Act
N.M. Stat. Ann., 77-15-6 et seq.

County Primary Act
Ore. General Laws 1901, p. 400

County Primary Road Improvement Act
Okla. Stat. Ann., Title 69, § 670 et seq.

County Printing Act
Mont. Code Ann., 7-5-2401 et seq.

County Printing Commission Act
Mont. Code Ann. 1947, 16-1225 et seq.

County Prison Inmate Care and Custody Reimbursement Act
Colo. Rev. Stat., 17-26-201 et seq.

County Probate Court and Registry of Deeds Loan Act (Barnstable)
Mass. Acts 1952, Ch. 472

County Probation and Parole Officers' Firearm Education and Training Law
Pa. Purdon's Stat., Title 61, § 332.1 et seq.

County Public Health Departments Act
Ill. Rev. Stat. 1987, Ch. 111 1/2, § 20c et seq.

County Public Improvement Act
Mich. Comp. Laws Ann., 46.171 et seq.

County Public Improvement District Act
Colo. Rev. Stat., 30-20-501 et seq.

County Public Works Act
Fla. Laws 1967, Ch. 67-664, 1968 Extra Session, Ch. 68-74
Mich. Comp. Laws Ann., 123.731 et seq.

County Public Works Projects and Post War Aid Act
Tenn. Code Ann., 5-11-101 et seq.

County Purchasing Act
Ga. Laws 1941, p. 408
Neb. Rev. Stat. 1943, 23-3101 et seq.
Tenn. Code Ann., 5-14-201 et seq.
Tex. Local Government Code, § 262.021 et seq.

County Purchasing Act (Carroll County)
Tenn. Private Acts 1975, Ch. 23

County Purchasing Act (Sumner County)
Tenn. Private Acts 1975, Ch. 6

County Purchasing Agent Act
Mich. Comp. Laws Ann., 45.81 et seq.

County Quarantine Act
N.C. Gen. Stat. 1943, § 130A-145 et seq.

County Recorders' Courts Act
Ark. Code Ann. 1987, 14-17-203 et seq.
N.C. Gen. Stat. 1943, §§ 7-218, 7A-109 et seq.

County Records Act
Me. Rev. Stat. Ann. 1964, Title 30, § 551 et seq.

County Recovery and Post War Aid Act
Tenn. Code Ann., 5-11-101 et seq.

County Recreation and Water Conservation and Control Act
Fla. Laws 1965, Ch. 65-1099

County Recreation Authority Act (First Class)
N.J. Rev. Stat. 1937, 40:37B-1 et seq.

County Recreation District Act
Wash. Rev. Code Ann., 36.69.010 et seq.

County Recreational System Act
Mo. Rev. Stat. Ann., 67.781 et seq.

County Redistricting Act
N.D. Cent. Code, 11-07-01 et seq.

County Reform Act
Ind. Code Ann., 17-1-24-1 et seq.

County Regional Justice Facilities Financing Act
Cal. Government Code § 26299.000 et seq.

County Registration Act (Tulsa)
Okla. Stat. 1971, Title 26, § 101 et seq.

County Registry of Deeds Loan Act (Plymouth)
Mass. Acts 1952, Ch. 475

County Reimbursement Act
Kan. Laws 1933, Ch. 164

County Relief Act (Bannack)
Mont. Rev. Code 1947, 71-101 et seq.

County Removal Act (Arrests)
Pa. 1899 Pamph. Laws 173, No. 114

County Retailers Occupation Tax Act
Ill. Rev. Stat. 1987, Ch. 34, § 409.1

County Retirement Act (Fifth Class)
Pa. Purdon's Stat., Title 16, § 11621 et seq.

County Retirement Act (Fourth Class)
Pa. Purdon's Stat., Title 16, § 11561 et seq.

County Revenue Stabilization Act
Cal. Government Code § 16265 et seq.

County Road Act
Mich. Comp. Laws Ann., 224.1 et seq.
Neb. Rev. Stat. 1943, 39-1401 et seq.
N.Y. Laws 1890, Ch. 555
Ore. General Laws 1905, Ch. 230
Pa. 1911 Pamph. Laws 244

County Road and Bridge Act
Tex. Rev. Civ. Stat. 1974, Art. 6702-1 et seq.

County Road Bond Act (York)
S.C. Acts 1955, p. 1493, No. 604

County Road Bonding Act
Ore. Rev. Stat., 370.010 et seq.

County Road Camp Act (Joint)
Cal. Penal Code § 4200 et seq.

County Road Facilities Improvement Act (Tuolumne)
Cal. Public Utilities Code § 150000 et seq.

County Road Improvement Act
Okla. Stat. 1981, Title 69, § 685 et seq.

County Road Improvement Districts Act
Wash. Rev. Code Ann., 36.88.010 et seq.

County Road Law (Optional)
Tex. Rev. Civ. Stat., Art. 6702-1, § 3.201 et seq.

County Road Law of Dickson County
Tenn. Private Acts 1985, Ch. 53

County Road Superintendent Act (Kershaw)
S.C. Code Ann. 1952, § 33-1729 et seq.

County Road Vacation Act
Wash. Rev. Code Ann., 36.87.010 et seq.

County Rural Highway System Act
Kan. Stat. Ann., 68-591 et seq.

County Rural Police Act (Kershaw)
S.C. Code Ann. 1952, § 53-561 et seq.

County Rural Zoning Act
Ohio Rev. Code 1953, 303.01 et seq.

County Rural Zoning Enabling Act
Mich. Comp. Laws Ann., 125.201 et seq.

County Salary Act
Minn. Stat. 1963, 382.187 et seq.
N.M. Stat. Ann., 4-44-1 et seq.
Ohio Rev. Code 1953, 325.01 et seq.

County Sales and Use Tax Act
Tex. Tax Code, § 323.001 et seq.

County Sales Tax Act
Ark. Code Ann. 1987, 26-74-307 et seq.
Mo. Rev. Stat., 67.500 et seq.
N.M. Stat. Ann., 7-21-1 et seq.

County Sanatorium Act
Mich. Comp. Laws Ann., 332.151 et seq.

County Sanitation District Act
Cal. Health and Safety Code § 4700 et seq.

County School Act
Ore. Rev. Stat., 333.005 et seq.

County School Budget Act (Charleston)
S.C. Code Ann. 1962, § 21-1662

County School Committee Act
Wis. Stat. 1965, 40.02 et seq.

County School District Act
Mich. Comp. Laws Ann., 340.291a et seq.

County School Library Act
Ore. Code 1930, § 35-4433 et seq.

County School Superintendent Act
Ore. Code 1930, §§ 35-501 to 35-509

County School System Act
Iowa Code 1973, 273.1 et seq.

County Seat Municipal Court Act
Ark. Code Ann. 1987, 16-17-301 et seq.

County Seat Removal Act
Nev. Rev. Stat. 1979 Reprint, 243.460 et seq.

County Service Act
Tenn. Code Ann., 5-1-114

County Service Area Act
Cal. Government Code § 25210.1 et seq.
Utah Code Ann. 1953, 17A-2-401 et seq.

County Service District Act
N.C. Gen. Stat. 1943, § 153A-300 et seq.

County Service Occupation Tax Act
Ill. Rev. Stat. 1987, Ch. 34, § 409.2

County Service Occupation Tax Act (Home Rule)
Ill. Rev. Stat. 1987, Ch. 34, § 303a-2

County Sewage and Waste Water Law
Nev. Rev. Stat. 1979 Reprint, Replaced Pages, 244A.455 et seq.

County Sewer Act (New Castle)
Del. Code of 1974, Title 9, § 2201 et seq.

County Sewerage Financing Law
N.J. Stat. Ann., 40:23-19.1 et seq.

County Shelter Care and Detention Home Act
Ill. Rev. Stat. 1991, Ch. 23, § 2681 et seq.

County Sheriff's Civil Service Act
Tenn. Code Ann., 8-8-401 et seq.

County Shore Protection Loan Act
Mass. Acts 1951, Ch. 396
Mass. Acts 1952, Ch. 531
Mass. Acts 1953, Ch. 98

Mass. Acts 1955, Ch. 381
Mass. Acts 1957, Ch. 518

County Solid Waste Control Act
Tex. Health and Safety Code, § 364.001 et seq.

County Solid Waste Disposal Financing Law
N.J. Stat. Ann., 40:6A-31.1 et seq.

County Solid Waste Management Act
Minn. Stat. Ann., 400.01 et seq.

County Special Service Districts Act
N.D. Cent. Code, 11-28.1-01 et seq.

County Statistics Commission Act
Wash. Laws 1945, Ch. 258

County Subdivision Control Act
Ala. Code 1975, § 11-3-11
Ill. Rev. Stat. 1991, Ch. 34, § 5-1041 et seq.
Mo. Rev. Stat., 64.580
Wash. Rev. Code Ann., 58.17.010 et seq.

County Subway Act
Ohio Rev. Code 1953, 307.201

County Supervising Auditor Act (Spartanburg)
S.C. Acts 1923, p. 842, No. 497

County Supplementary Service Occupation Tax Act
Ill. Rev. Stat. 1987, Ch. 34, § 409.2a

County Supplementary Use Tax Act
Ill. Rev. Stat. 1987, Ch. 34, § 409.10a

County Surplus Fund Investment Law
Cal. Government Code § 53601 et seq.

County Surveyors Act
Ill. Comp. Stat. 1992, Ch. 55, §§ 125/0.01, 125/1
Ill. Rev. Stat. 1991, Ch. 133, §§ 4.9, 5

County Tax Discount Act (Dillon)
S.C. Code Ann. 1962, § 65-1989

County TB Hospital Loan Act (Bristol)
Mass. Acts 1953, Ch. 131

County Teachers' Aid Fund Act
Ida. Laws 1944, 2nd Ex. Sess., Ch. 7

County Traffic and Transportation Funding Act (Bay Area)
Cal. Public Utilities Code § 130000 et seq.

County Transactions and Use Tax for Library Programs
Cal. Revenue and Taxation Code § 7286.59

County Transportation Authorities Act
N.J. Stat. Ann., 40:35B-1 et seq.

County Transportation Commissions Act
Cal. Public Utilities Code § 130000 et seq.

County Treasurer Act
Ill. Rev. Stat. 1991, Ch. 34, § 3-10001 et seq.

County Treasurer's Tax Sales Act
Pa. Purdon's Stat., Title 72, § 5971a et seq.

County Tuberculosis Hospitals Act
Ill. Rev. Stat. 1991, Ch. 34, § 5-23001 et seq.
Ind. Code Ann., 16-11-1-1 et seq.
Mo. Rev. Stat., 205.380 et seq.

County Turnpike Authority Act
Ky. Rev. Stat. 1971, Superseded Vols., 175A.010 et seq.

County Unification Commission Act (Cumming-Forsyth)
Ga. Laws 1991, p. 3611

County Uniform Road Law
Tenn. Code Ann., 54-7-101 et seq.

County Unit Act (Schools)
Neb. Laws 1915, Ch. 233
Ore. Rev. Stat., 333.005 et seq.
W. Va. Acts 1933, 1st Ex. Sess., Ch. 8

County Unit Law (Alcoholic Beverage-Local Option)
Ky. Rev. Stat. 1971, 242.030,

County Unit Road Act
Ind. Code Ann., 8-17-1-1 et seq.

County Unit Vote Act
Ga. Code 1933, 34-3212 et seq.

County Use and Sales Tax Act
Tex. Tax Code, § 323.001 et seq.

County Use Tax Act
Ill. Rev. Stat. 1987, Ch. 34, § 409.10

County Use Tax Act (Home Rule)
Ill. Rev. Stat. 1987, Ch. 34, § 303a-3

County Validation Act (Home Rule)
N.M. Stat. Ann., 4-37-10 et seq.

County War Memorial Act
Ind. Code Ann., 10-7-1-1 et seq.

County Water and Sewer District Act
Fla. Stat. Ann., 153.50 et seq.

County Water Authority Act
Cal. Statutes 1943, Ch. 545, p. 2090
Cal. Water Code, Appendix, § 45-1 et seq.

County Water Districts Act
Cal. Water Code § 30000 et seq.
Mont. Code Ann., 7-13-2201 et seq.

County Water Supply Authority Act
Pa. Purdon's Stat., Title 16, § 12901 et seq.

County Water Supply Financing Law
N.J. Stat. Ann., 40:14C-1 et seq.

County Water System and Sanitary Sewer Financing Act
Fla. Stat. Ann., 153.01 et seq.

County Waterworks District Act
Cal. Water Code § 55000 et seq.

County Waterworks Districts Securities Commission Law
Cal. Water Code § 20200 et seq.

County Weed Control Act
Mont. Code Ann., 7-22-2101 et seq.

County Welfare Board Law
Cal. Welfare and Institutions Code § 17000 et seq.

County Welfare Per Capita Cost Limitation Act
N.J. Stat. Ann., 44:14-1 et seq.

County-Wide Stock Law
Ark. Pope's Digest 1937, § 335 et seq.

County Workhouse Law
Tenn. Code Ann., 41-2-101 et seq.

County Wrap-Around Services Pilot Project
Cal. Welfare and Institutions Code § 18250 et seq.

County Zoning Act
Ill. Rev. Stat. 1991, Ch. 34, § 5-120001 et seq.
Iowa Code Ann., 335.1 et seq., 358A.1 et seq.
Kan. Stat. Ann., 19-2901 et seq.
Miss. Code Ann., § 17-1-1 et seq.
S.C. Code Ann. 1976, § 4-27-10 et seq.
Tenn. Code Ann., 13-7-101 et seq.
Utah Code Ann. 1953, 17-27-1 et seq.
Wash. Rev. Code Ann., 36.70.010 et seq.
Wis. Stat. 1989, 59.97
Wyo. Stat. Ann., § 18-5-201 et seq.

County Zoning Act (New Castle)
Del. Code of 1974, Title 9, § 2601 et seq.

County Zoning and Planning Act
Okla. Stat. Ann., Title 19, § 863.1 et seq.

County Zoning Enabling Act
Colo. Rev. Stat., 30-28-101 et seq.

Coupon Sales Promotion Act
Tenn. Code Ann., 47-25-801 et seq.

Court Act (Allegheny County)
Pa. Purdon's Stat., Title 17, § 621 et seq.

Court Act (Common Pleas)
Ohio Rev. Code 1953, 2301.01 et seq.

Court Act (District)
N.Y. Uniform District Act, § 101 et seq.

Court Act (Franklin County)
Ala. Local Acts 1923, p. 272

Court Act (Justice)
N.Y. Uniform Justice Court Act, § 101 et seq.

Court Act (Juvenile)
Ga. Code Ann., 15-11-1 et seq.
Minn. Stat. Ann., 260.011 et seq.
Mont. Rev. Code 1947, 10-601 et seq.

Court Act (Municipal)
Minn. Stat. Ann., 488A.01 et seq.
Mont. Rev. Code 1947, 11-1701 et seq.
N.H. Rev. Stat. 1955, 502:1 et seq.
Ohio Rev. Code 1953, 1901.01 et seq.

Court Act (Police)
Mont. Rev. Code 1947, 11-1601 et seq.

Court Administration Act
Tex. Government Code, § 74.001 et seq.

Court Administrative Office Act
Md. Ann. Code 1974, Art. CJ, § 13-101 et seq.

Court Administrator Act
Ill. Rev. Stat. 1963, Ch. 37, § 23e et seq.
Mich. Comp. Laws 1948, 692.701 et seq.
N.J. Rev. Stat. 1937, 2A:12-1 et seq.
Utah Code Ann. 1953, 78-3-18 et seq.
Wash. Rev. Code Ann., 2.56.010 et seq.

Court and Practice Act
R.I. Gen. Laws 1956, 8-1-1 et seq.

Court Commissioners Act
Mo. Rev. Stat., 477.083 et seq.
Wash. Rev. Code Ann., 2.24.010 et seq.

Court-Connected Alternative Dispute Resolution Act
Ga. Code Ann., 15-23-1 et seq.

Court Contempt Act
Ohio Rev. Code 1953, 2705.01 et seq.

Court Costs and Sheriff Fees Transfer Act
Ill. Comp. Stat. 1992, Ch. 55, § 40/0.01 et seq.

Court Enforcement Program Act (Comprehensive)
Fla. Laws 1998, Ch. 247, §§ 1 to 5

Court Facilities Authority Act
Me. Rev. Stat. Ann. 1964, Title 4, § 1601 et seq.

Court House Act (Suffolk County)
Mass. Acts 1935, Ch. 474

Court House Addition Act (Dukes County)
Mass. Acts 1953, Ch. 88

Court House Commission Act (Morgan County)
Ala. Local Acts 1927, p. 249

Court House Construction Act
D.C. Code 1961, § 11-103 et seq.

Court House Loan Act (Berkshire County)
Mass. Acts 1954, Ch. 571

Court House Loan Act (Bristol County)
Mass. Acts 1958, Ch. 505
Mass. Acts 1970, Ch. 482

Court House Loan Act (Essex County)
Mass. Acts 1963, Ch. 140

Court House Loan Act (Hampden County)
Mass. Acts 1961, Ch. 358
Mass. Acts 1962, Ch. 539

Court House Loan Act (Middlesex County)
Mass. Acts 1952, Ch. 491
Mass. Acts 1967, Ch. 542

Court House Loan Act (Norfolk County)
Mass. Acts 1949, Ch. 590

Court House Loan Act (Plymouth County)
Mass. Acts 1961, Ch. 336

Court House Loan Act (Worcester County)
Mass. Acts 1932, Ch. 98

Court Improvement Act
Wash. Rev. Code Ann., 3.30.010 et seq.

Court Interpreter Act (Foreign Language)
Ill. Comp. Stat. 1992, Ch. 705, § 78/1 et seq.

Court Interpreter Amendments Act of 1988
Nov. 19, 1988, P.L. 100-702, 28 U.S. Code
§ 1 nt.

Court Interpreters Act
Oct. 28, 1978, P.L. 95-539, 28 U.S. Code
§§ 1 nt., 602, 602 nt., 603, 604, 1827, 1828
N.M. Stat. Ann., 38-10-1 et seq.

**Court Jurisdiction and Procedure Act
(Uniform Parish)**
La. Rev. Stat. Ann., 13:1441 et seq.

Court Law (Conciliation)
Neb. Rev. Stat. 1943, 42-801 et seq.

Court-Martial Law (National Guard)
Ark. Code Ann. 1987, 12-60-102 et seq.

Court of Appeals Act
Ark. Code Ann. 1987, 16-12-101 et seq.
D.C. Code 1973, §§ 11-301 et seq., 11-701 et
seq.
Ida. Code 1947, 1-2401 et seq.
Mich. Comp. Laws Ann., 600.301 et seq.
S.C. Code Ann. 1976, § 8-21-300 et seq.

Court of Appeals Reorganization Act
Tenn. Code Ann., 16-4-101 et seq.

Court of Claims Act
Ill. Comp. Stat. 1992, Ch. 705, § 505/24 et
seq.
Mich. Comp. Laws Ann., 600.6401 et seq.
N.Y. Laws 1939, Ch. 860
W. Va. Code 1966, § 14-2-1 et seq.

Court of Claims Review Act
May 22, 1939, Ch. 140, 53 Stat. 752 (See 28
U.S. Code § 1255)

Court of Customs Appeals Act
Aug. 5, 1909, Ch. 6, 36 Stat. 105 (See 28
U.S. Code §§ 211 to 213, 215, 293, 296,
452, 456, 604, 831 to 834, 956, 957, 1256,
1541, 1542, 1926, 2601, 2071)

**Court of Federal Claims Technical and
Procedural Improvements Act of 1992**
Oct. 29, 1992, P.L. 102-572, 28 U.S. Code
§ 1 nt.

Court of Industrial Relations Act
Kan. Stat. Ann., 44-601 et seq.
Neb. Rev. Stat. 1943, 48-801.01 et seq.

Court of Inquiry Act
Ky. Rev. Stat. 1971, Superseded Vols.,
25.150
Tex. Code of Crim. Prod., Art. 52.01 et seq.

Court of Private Land Claims Act
March 3, 1891, Ch. 539, 26 Stat. 854

**Court of Veterans Appeals Judges
Retirement Act**
Aug. 16, 1989, P.L. 101-94, 38 U.S. Code
§§ 101 nt., 4096 to 4098

Court of Visitation Act
Kan. Laws 1898, Sp. Sess., Ch. 28

Court Proctor Act
Aug. 7, 1939, Ch. 501, 53 Stat. 1223

**Court Realignment and Efficiency Act
(Trial)**
Cal. Statutes 1991, Ch. 90

Court Records Restoration Act
Ill. Comp. Stat. 1992, Ch. 705, § 85/0.01 et
seq.

Court Reform Act
N.C. Gen. Stat. 1943, § 7A-1 et seq.

Court Reform Act (General Sessions)
Tenn. Public Acts 1993, Ch. 241

Court Reform and Criminal Procedure Act
D.C. Code Ann., §§ 11-101 to 23-1504

Court Reform and Revision Act
Mo. Laws 1978, p. 696

Court Register Act
S.C. Code Ann. 1976, § 14-3-940 et seq.

Court Reorganization Act
D.C. Code 1973, §§ 11-101 to 16-3901
Kan. Laws 1975, Ch. 178
Mass. Acts 1978, Ch. 478
Wis. Laws 1959, Ch. 315

Court Reporter Fair Labor Amendments of 1995
Sept. 6, 1995, P.L. 104-26, 29 U.S. Code §§ 201 nt., 207

Court Reporter Transcript Act
Ill. Comp. Stat. 1992, Ch. 705, § 75/0.01 et seq.

Court Reporters Act
Ga. Code Ann., 15-14-20 et seq.
Ill. Comp. Stat. 1992, Ch. 705, § 70/1 et seq.
Tex. Gov. Code §§ 51.601, 52.041

Court Reporting Practice Act
Wash. Rev. Code Ann., 18.145.005 et seq.

Court Reports Act (Official)
Ill. Rev. Stat. 1991, Ch. 37, § 640 et seq.

Court Review Act
Ind. Code Ann., 4-22-2-3 et seq.

Court Rules Enabling Act
Minn. Stat. Ann., 480.05
Utah Code Ann. 1953, 78-2-4

Court Services Consolidation Act (Stanislaus County)
Cal. Statutes 1992, Ch. 181

Court Statistics Act
Ill. Comp. Stat. 1992, Ch. 705, §§ 125/0.01, 125/1

Courtesy Patrol Act
Colo. Rev. Stat., 43-5-101 et seq.

Courthouse Cession Act (Chicago U.S.)
Ill. Rev. Stat. 1991, Ch. 1, § 3900 et seq.

Courtney's Law
Cal. Penal Code §§ 191.5, 1192.8
Cal. Vehicle Code 1959, § 20001

Courts Act
Alaska Comp. Laws Ann. 1949, § 4-2-7, 66-16-20

Courts and Judicial Procedure Act
La. Rev. Stat. Ann., 13:1 et seq.

Courts of Limited Jurisdiction Compensation Act
Ga. Code Ann., 15-22-1 et seq.

Covenant Marriage Act
Ga. Code Ann., 19-3-80 et seq.

Covenants of Warranty Act
Ill. Comp. Stat. 1992, Ch. 765, §§ 20/0.01, 20/1

Coventry Act
N.C. Gen. Stat. 1943, §§ 14-30, 14-30d

Coverage Access Act (Health Insurance)
Wash. Rev. Code Ann., 48.41.010 et seq.

Covering-in Act
June 20, 1874, Ch. 328, 18 Stat. 110, 31 U.S. Code § 713

Covert Act (Highways)
Mich. Comp. Laws 1948, 247.415 et seq.

Cow Creek Band of Umpqua Tribe of Indians Distribution of Judgment Funds Act of 1987
Oct. 26, 1987, P.L. 100-139, 25 U.S. Code §§ 712, 712 nt., 712a to 712c

Cow Creek Band of Umpqua Tribe of Indians Recognition Act
Oct. 26, 1987, P.L. 100-139, 25 U.S. Code §§ 712a to 712c
Sept. 27, 1988, P.L. 100-446, 25 U.S. Code §§ 152 nt., 712c
Continued

509

Oct. 14, 1998, P.L. 105-256, 25 U.S. Code
§ 712e

Cow Creek Band of Umpqua Tribe of Oregon
Dec. 29, 1982, P.L. 97-391, 25 U.S. Code
§§ 712 et seq., 712 nt.

Coweta County-Newman Airport Authority Act
Ga. Laws 1965, p. 2041

Coweta County Pension and Retirement Pay Act
Ga. Laws 1949, p. 30

Cox-Phillips Act (Labor Injunctions)
Mass. Gen. Laws Ann., 214:6

Cox Pipe Line Act
Tex. Rev. Civ. Stat. 1974, Art. 6050 et seq.

Coyote Bounty Act
Alaska Stat. 1962, § 16.35.050 et seq.

CPA Law
Pa. Purdon's Stat., Title 63, § 91.1 et seq.

Crab Act
Md. Ann. Code 1974, Art. NR, § 4-801 et seq.

Crab Meat Act
Tex. Health and Safety Code, § 436.041 et seq.

Crab Orchard Retrocession Act
Ill. Comp. Stat. 1992, Ch. 5, §§ 555/0.01, 555/1

Crabbe Act, First (Prohibition Enforcement)
Ohio Laws Vol. 108, p. 388

Crabbe Act, Second (Prohibition Enforcement)
Ohio Laws Vol. 108, p. 1182

Crack House Abatement Act
Alaska Stat. 1962, § 29.35.125

Craft Act
Ky. Rev. Stat. 1962, 152.410 et seq.

Craft Act (Public Improvements)
Ala. Code 1958, Title 62, § 89 et seq.

Crafts and Arts Sales Act (Indian)
N.M. Stat. Ann., 30-33-1 et seq.

Craig Dickinson Act
Fla. Stat., 232.425

Craig Emergency Act (Taxes)
Tenn. Acts 1933, Ch. 22

Cramer-Daniels School Act
Ohio Laws Vol. 122, p. 534

Cramer-Gillen Act (Habitual Criminals)
Ohio Rev. Code 1953, 2929.11 et seq.

Cranberry Act
Wis. Stat. 1989, 94.26 et seq.

Crane and Hoisting Equipment Operators Licensing Act (Hazardous Waste)
Ill. Rev. Stat. 1991, Ch. 111, § 7701 et seq.

Crane-Fox-Lance Act (Urban Development)
N.J. Stat. Ann., 40:55C-40 et seq.

Cranston-Gonzalez National Affordable Housing Act
Nov. 28, 1990, P.L. 101-625, 12 U.S. Code §§ 1701q nt., 1701z-1 nt., 1701z-6 nt., 1713 nt., 4101 nt., 4125; 42 U.S. Code §§ 1437a nt. et seq. generally, 1437aa nt., 1490o nt., 5302 nt. et seq. generally, 7714a, 8011 to 8013, 8107 nt., 11301 nt., 11361 nt., 11391 nt., 11399 nt., 11403 nt., 11403h nt., 12712 to 12714, 11903a, 12701 to 12711
April 10, 1991, P.L. 102-27, 42 U.S. Code §§ 8013, 11403h nt.
Oct. 28, 1991, P.L. 102-139, 12 U.S. Code § 1701g; 42 U.S. Code § 1437d
Dec. 12, 1991, P.L. 102-229, 42 U.S. Code §§ 12704, 12747
Dec. 12, 1991, P.L. 102-230, 42 U.S. Code §§ 12704, 12747
Dec. 17, 1991, P.L. 102-238, 42 U.S. Code § 1437f nt.

Dec. 19, 1991, P.L. 102-242, 12 U.S. Code
§ 1713 nt.

April 21, 1992, P.L. 102-273, 42 U.S. Code
§ 12747

Oct. 6, 1992, P.L. 102-389, 42 U.S. Code
§§ 11903a, 12747

Oct. 24, 1992, P.L. 102-486, 42 U.S. Code
§§ 12704, 12709, 12712 nt.

Oct. 28, 1992, P.L. 102-550, 12 U.S. Code
§§ 1701q, 1701z-6 nt., 4101 nt., 4125; 42
U.S. Code §§ 1437d nt., 1437t nt.,
1437aaa-2, 5306 nt., 8011, 8011 nt., 8012,
8013, 11301 nt., 11361 nt., 11903a, 12704,
12705, 12710, 12724, 12742, 12745,
12746, 12746 nt., 12747, 12748, 12750,
12771 to 12774, 12782, 12784, 12810,
12852, 12857, 12859, 12870, 12871,
12876, 12891, 12892, 12894, 12896, prec.
12899, 12899, 12899a to 12899i, 12901,
12905 to 12910

Oct. 27, 1993, P.L. 103-120, 42 U.S. Code
§ 12724

March 31, 1994, P.L. 103-227, 42 U.S. Code
§ 11903a

April 11, 1994, P.L. 103-233, 42 U.S. Code
§§ 12704, 12744, 12745 , 12750, 12833,
12838, 12840, 12893

Oct. 20, 1994, P.L. 103-382, 42 U.S. Code
§ 12899f

Dec. 21, 1995, P.L. 104-66, 42 U.S. Code
§§ 1437f, 12880

Jan. 26, 1996, P.L. 104-99, 42 U.S. Code
§§ 1437f nt., 12714

Sept. 26, 1996, P.L. 104-204, 42 U.S. Code
§§ 5306 nt., 12832

Oct. 26, 1996, P.L. 104-330, 12 U.S. Code
§ 1701z-6 nt.; 42 U.S. Code §§ 11903a,
12747, 12838, 12899i

Oct. 27, 1997, P.L. 105-65, 42 U.S. Code
§ 12747

Oct. 7, 1998, P.L. 105-244, 42 U.S. Code
§ 12899f

Oct. 21, 1998, P.L. 105-276, 12 U.S. Code
§ 1701z-6 nt.; 42 U.S. Code §§ 1437a-1,
1437c nt., 1437f nt., 1437g nt., 1437t nt.,
11903a, 12705, 12742, 12744, 12745,
12899d, 12899h-1, 12910

Oct. 21, 1998, P.L. 105-277, 42 U.S. Code
§§ 12899c, 12899e

Cranston 2000 Corporation Act
R.I. Gen. Laws 1956, 42-64.8-1 et seq.

Crash Parts Act (Aftermarket)
Fla. Stat. Ann., 501.30 et seq.
Okla. Stat. Ann., Title 15, § 951 et seq.
Utah Code Ann. 1953, 13-20a-101 et seq.

Crash Parts Act (Aircraft)
Ill. Comp. Stat. 1992, Ch. 720, §§ 205/0.01,
205/1
Ill. Rev. Stat. 1991, Ch. 15 1/2, §§ 200, 201

Crawfish Market Development Act
La. Rev. Stat. Ann., 3:445.1 et seq.

Crawford Amendment (Claims)
See Omnibus Claims Act

Crawford-Feld Act (Fair Trade)
N.Y. General Business Law (Consol. Laws
Ch. 20) § 369a et seq.

**Crawford National Fish Hatchery
Conveyance Act**
Oct. 1, 1996, P.L. 104-215, 110 Stat. 3018

Crawford-Webb Act (Apportionment)
Ala. Acts 1962, Sp. Sess., p. 121

Cream and Milk Act
Kan. Stat. Ann., 65-701 et seq.

Cream Grading Law
Iowa Code Ann., 195.1 et seq.

Creameries and Dairies Act
Miss. Code Ann., § 75-31-1 et seq.

Creamery and Testers' License Act
Ind. Code Ann., 15-6-1-1 et seq.

**Creation of Jobs by Stimulating Small
Business Growth Act**
Ark. Code Ann. 1987, 15-4-401 et seq.

Crecelius Act
Ky. Acts 1908, Ch. 8

**Credentialed Out-of-State Teacher
Recruitment and Retention Act**
Cal. Education Code 1976, §§ 44205,
44205.5

Credentialing Act
Kan. Stat. Ann., 65-5001 et seq.

Credentialing Verification Act (Health Care Professional)
Neb. Rev. Stat. 1943, 44-7001 to 44-7013

Credentiality Act for Counselors (Omnibus)
Wash. Rev. Code 1989, 18.19.010 et seq.

Credit Accident and Health Insurance Act
R.I. Gen. Laws 1956, 27-31-1 et seq.

Credit Accident, Credit Life Insurance and Health Insurance Act
Mass. Gen. Laws Ann., 167F:2, 175:110, 175:117C, 175:133, 175:177, 175:184, 255:12G, 255B:10, 255C:14A, 255D:1 to 255D:11, 255D:26

Credit Act (Filmmaker's)
N.M. Stat. Ann., 7-9B-1 et seq.

Credit Act (Rural)
Minn. Stat. 1971, 41.51 et seq.

Credit Agreements Act
Ill. Comp. Stat. 1992, Ch. 815, § 160/0.01 et seq.

Credit and Debit Card Crime Act
Ky. Rev. Stat. 1971, 434.550 et seq.

Credit Card Act
Ala. Code 1975, § 15-14A-1 et seq.
Cal. Civil Code § 1747 et seq.
Fla. Stat. Ann., 817.481
Ill. Rev. Stat. 1991, Ch. 12, § 6000 et seq.
N.M. Stat. Ann., 56-4-1 et seq.

Credit Card Act (Lender)
Iowa Code Ann., 536C.1 et seq.

Credit Card and Credit Card Bank Act
Ga. Code Ann., 7-5-1 et seq.

Credit Card and Debit Card Act
Ill. Comp. Stat. 1992, Ch. 720, § 250/1 et seq.

Credit Card Bank Act
Fla. Stat. Ann., 658.995

Credit Card Crime Act
Alaska Stat. 1962, § 11.46.290 et seq.
Ariz. Rev. Stat. Ann., § 13-2101 et seq.
Ark. Code Ann. 1987, 5-37-207
Fla. Stat. Ann., 817.57 et seq.
Haw. Rev. Stat. Ann., § 708-8100 et seq.
Ill. Rev. Stat. 1991, Ch. 17, § 6100 et seq.
Ky. Rev. Stat. 1971, 434.550 et seq.
La. Rev. Stat. Ann., 14:67.3
Miss. Code Ann., § 97-19-5 et seq.
N.C. Gen. Stat. 1943, § 14-113.8 et seq.
Okla. Stat. Ann., Title 21, § 1550.21 et seq.
R.I. Gen. Laws 1956, 11-49-1 et seq.
Tenn. Code Ann., 39-3-501 et seq.
Tex. Penal Code, § 32.31

Credit Card Disclosure Act
Cal. Civil Code § 1748.10 et seq.
Minn. Stat. Ann., 325G.40 et seq.

Credit Card Fraud Act of 1984
Oct. 12, 1984, P.L. 98-473, 18 U.S. Code § 1001 nt.

Credit Card Insurance Act
N.C. Gen. Stat. 1943, § 58-3-145

Credit Card Issuance Act
Ill. Comp. Stat. 1992, Ch. 815, § 140/0.01 et seq.

Credit Card Liability Act
Ill. Comp. Stat. 1992, Ch. 815, § 145/0.01 et seq.

Credit Charges Act
Mo. Rev. Stat., 408.250 et seq.

Credit Code
Ida. Code 1947, 28-41-101 et seq., 28-42-101 et seq. (Finance Charges and Related Provisions), 28-43-101 et seq. (Regulation of Agreements and Practices), 28-44-101 et seq. (Insurance in Regulated Consumer Credit Transactions), 28-45-101 et seq. (Remedies and Penalties), 28-46-101 et seq. (Administration)

Credit Control Act
Dec. 23, 1969, P.L. 91-151, 83 Stat. 376, 12 U.S. Code §§ 1901 to 1909

Credit Corporation Act (Small Business Development)
Colo. Rev. Stat., 11-36-101 et seq.

Credit Data Reporting Act
N.Y. General Business Law (Consol. Laws Ch. 20) § 369a et seq.

Credit Denial Disclosure Act
Cal. Civil Code § 1787.1 et seq.

Credit Disability Insurance Act
Mont. Code Ann., 33-21-101 et seq.

Credit Disclosure Act
Wash. Rev. Code Ann., 63.14.010 et seq.

Credit Enhancement Act (Economic Development)
Ark. Acts 1989, No. 945

Credit Enhancement Act (Local Government)
Ill. Rev. Stat. 1991, Ch. 85, § 4301 et seq.

Credit Enhancement Reserve Fund Act
Okla. Stat. Ann., Title 74, § 5063.1 et seq.

Credit Financing Institutions Licensing Act
Mo. Rev. Stat., 364.010 et seq.

Credit for Reinsurance Act
Iowa Code Ann., 521B.1 et seq.
Okla. Stat. Ann., Title 36, § 5121 et seq.

Credit Institutions Tax Act
Mo. Rev. Stat., 148.120 et seq.

Credit Insurance Act
Colo. Rev. Stat., 10-10-101 et seq.
Mich. Comp. Laws Ann., 550.601 et seq.
S.D. Code Supp. 1960, 31-36A01 et seq.

Credit Law (Tax)
Wash. Rev. Code 1983, 82.04.440 et seq.

Credit Life and Disability Insurance Act
P.R. Laws Ann. 1954, Title 26 § 1801 et seq.

Credit Life and Health Insurance Act
Nev. Rev. Stat. 1979 Reprint, 690A.010 et seq.

Credit Life Insurance Act
R.I. Gen. Laws 1956, 27-30-1 et seq.
Tenn. Code Ann., 45-5-305, 56-2-114, 56-5-501, 56-7-901 et seq.

Credit Life Insurance and Credit Accident and Health Insurance Act
Conn. Gen. Stat. Ann., § 38a-645 et seq.
D.C. Code Ann., § 35-1001 et seq.
Ill. Rev. Stat. 1991, Ch. 73, § 767.51 et seq.
Ind. Code Ann., 27-8-4-1 et seq.
Mass. Gen. Laws 1984, 167F:2, 175:110, 175:117C, 175:133, 175:177, 175:184, 255:12G, 255B:10, 255C:14A, 255D:1 to 255D:11, 255D:26
Me. Rev. Stat. Ann. 1964, Title 24-A, § 2851 et seq.
N.D. Cent. Code, 26.1-37-01 et seq.
Neb. Rev. Stat. 1943, 44-1701 et seq.
N.H. Rev. Stat. 1955, 408-A:1 et seq.
N.J. Stat. Ann., 17B:29-1 et seq.
Ohio Rev. Code 1953, 3918.01 et seq.
Ore. Rev. Stat., 743.371 et seq.
Pa. Purdon's Stat., Title 40, § 1007.1 et seq.
S.D. Code Supp. 1960, 31.36A01 et seq.
S.D. Codified Laws 1967, 58-19-1 et seq.
Tex. Insurance Code, Art. 3.53
Utah Code Ann. 1953, Miscellaneous Superseded Code Provisions, 31-34-1 et seq.
Va. Code 1950, § 38.2-3700 et seq.
Vt. Stat. Ann., Title 8, § 4101 et seq.
Wash. Rev. Code Ann., 48.34.010 et seq.

Credit Life Insurance and Credit Accident and Sickness Insurance Act
Ga. Code Ann., 33-31-1 et seq.

Credit Life Insurance and Credit Disability Insurance Act
Alaska Stat. 1962, § 21.57.010 et seq.
Ariz. Rev. Stat. Ann., § 20-1601 et seq.
Continued

Ark. Code Ann. 1987, 23-87-101, 23-87-105

Cal. Insurance Code § 779.1 et seq.

Fla. Stat. Ann., 627.676 et seq.

Haw. Rev. Stat. Ann., § 431:10B-101 et seq.

Ida. Code 1947, 41-2301 et seq.

Miss. Code Ann., § 83-53-1 et seq.

Mont. Code Ann., 33-21-101 et seq.

Credit Life Insurance and Credit Health Insurance Regulatory Act

N.M. Stat. Ann., 59A-25-1 et seq.

P.R. Laws Ann. 1954, Title 26, § 1801 et seq.

Wyo. Stat. Ann., § 26-21-101 et seq.

Credit Life Insurance Regulation Act

Mont. Code Ann., 33-21-101 et seq.

Credit Provisions

Md. Ann. Code 1974, Art. CL, § 12-201 et seq. (Small Loan Law)

Md. Ann. Code 1974, Art. CL, § 12-301 et seq. (Consumer Loan Law)

Md. Ann. Code 1974, Art. CL, § 12-401 et seq. (Secondary Mortgage Loan Law)

Credit Reform Act

Mich. Comp. Laws Ann., 445.1851 et seq.

Credit Regulation Act

Mass. Gen. Laws Ann., 140D:1 et seq.

Credit Repair Services Act

N.C. Gen. Stat. 1943, §§ 66-220 to 66-226

Credit Reporting Act

N.H. Rev. Stat. 1955, 359-BL1 et seq.

Credit Reporting Agencies Act

Cal. Civil Code § 1785.1 et seq.

Credit Reporting Disclosure Act

Ark. Code Ann. 1987, 4-93-101 et seq.

Ark. Code 1987, 4-93-101 et seq.

Credit Sales (Consumer Protection Code)

S.C. Code Ann. 1976, § 37-2-101 et seq.

Credit Sales (Uniform Commercial Credit Code)

Ida. Code 1947, 28-32-101 et seq.

Wyo. Stat. Ann., § 40-14-201 et seq.

Credit Sales (Uniform Consumer Credit Code)

See Uniform Consumer Credit Code—Credit Sales

Credit Sales Act

Haw. Rev. Stat. Ann., § 476-1 et seq.

Mo. Rev. Stat., 408.250 et seq.

Credit Sales Act (Unruh)

Cal. Civil Code § 1801 et seq.

Credit Services Act

Cal. Civil Code § 1789.10 et seq.

Mich. Comp. Laws Ann., 445.1701 et seq.

N.H. Rev. Stat. 1955, 359-D:1 et seq.

Pa. 1992 Pamph. Laws, No. 150

Credit Services Businesses Act

Md. Ann. Code 1974, Art. CL, § 14-1901 et seq.

Tenn. Code Ann., 47-18-1001 et seq.

Credit Services Organizations Act

Ark. Code Ann. 1987, 4-91-101 et seq.

Colo. Rev. Stat., 12-14.5-101 et seq.

Ill. Comp. Stat. 1992, Ch. 815, § 605/1 et seq.

La. Rev. Stat. Ann., 9:3573.1 et seq.

Minn. Stat. Ann., 332.52 et seq.

Neb. Rev. Stat. 1943, 45-801 et seq.

Okla. Stat. Ann., Title 24, § 131 et seq.

Utah Code Ann. 1953, 13-21-1 et seq.

Wash. Rev. Code Ann., 19.134.010 et seq.

Credit Services Protection Act

Mich. Comp. Laws Ann., 445.1821 et seq.

Credit Simplification Act

S.C. Code Ann. 1976, § 29-3-40 et seq.

Credit Title

Tex. Rev. Civ. Stat., Art. 5069-1B.001 et seq.

Credit Transfer Act

Ga. Laws 1953 (Nov.-Dec. Sess.), p. 3000

Credit Union Act

See Federal Credit Union Act

Ala. Code 1975, § 5-17-1 et seq.

Ariz. Rev. Stat. Ann., § 6-501 et seq.

Cal. Financial Code § 14000 et seq.

D.C. Code Ann., § 26-601 et seq.

Fla. Stat. Ann., 657.001 et seq.

Ga. Code Ann., 7-1-630 et seq.

Haw. Rev. Stat. Ann., § 412:10-100 et seq.

Ida. Code 1947, 26-2101 et seq.

Ill. Comp. Stat. 1992, Ch. 205, § 305/1 et seq.

Ill. Rev. Stat. 1991, Ch. 17, § 4401 et seq.

Ind. Code Ann., 28-7-1-0.5 et seq.

Kan. Stat. Ann., 17-2201 et seq.

Ky. Rev. Stat. 1971, 290.005 et seq.

La. Rev. Stat. Ann., 6:641 et seq.

Mass. Gen. Laws Ann., 171:1 et seq.

Md. Ann. Code 1974, Art. FI, § 6-101 et seq.

Me. Rev. Stat. Ann. 1964, Title 9-B, § 811 et seq.

Mich. Comp. Laws Ann., 490.1 et seq.

Miss. Code Ann., § 81-13-1 et seq.

Mo. Rev. Stat., 370.010 et seq.

Mont. Code Ann., 32-3-101 et seq.

N.C. Gen. Stat. 1943, § 54-109.1 et seq.

N.D. Cent. Code, 6-06-01 et seq.

Neb. Rev. Stat. 1943, 21-1701 to 21-17,116

Neb. Rev. Stat. 1943, 21-1760 et seq.

N.H. Rev. Stat. 1955, 394-B:1 et seq.

N.J. Stat. Ann., 17:13-79 et seq.

N.M. Stat. Ann., 58-11-1 et seq.

Ohio Rev. Code 1953, 1733.01 et seq.

Ore. Rev. Stat., 723.002 et seq.

Pa. Cons. Stat., Title 17, § 101 et seq.

P.R. Laws Ann. 1954, Title 7, § 1101 et seq.

R.I. Gen. Laws 1956, 19-21-1 et seq.

S.C. Code Ann. 1976, § 34-27-10 et seq., 34-26-100 et seq.

Tenn. Code Ann., 45-4-101 et seq.

Tex. Finance Code, § 121.001 et seq.

Tex. Rev. Civ. Stat., Art. 2461-1.01 et seq.

Utah Code Ann. 1953, 7-9-1 et seq.

Va. Code 1950, § 6.1-225.1 et seq.

Vt. Stat. Ann., Title 8, § 2051 et seq.

Wash. Rev. Code Ann., 31.12.005 et seq.

Credit Union Amendments of 1987
Aug. 10, 1987, P.L. 100-86, 12 U.S. Code §§ 1751 nt., 1757, 1761a , 1761b, 1764, 1766, 1767, 1772c, 1786, 1787, 1788; 15 U.S. Code §§ 45 , 46, 57a

Credit Union Guaranty Corporation Act
Fla. Stat. Ann., 657.25 et seq.

Credit Union Membership Access Act
Aug. 7, 1998, P.L. 105-219, 12 U.S. Code § 1751 nt.

Credit Union Protection Law
Mo. Rev. Stat. 1978, 407.430 et seq.

Credit Union Safe Deposit Boxes Act
N.M. Stat. Ann., 58-11A-1 et seq.

Credit Union Share Guaranty Association Act
Wash. Rev. Code Ann., 31.12A.005 et seq.

Credit Union Share Insurance Corporation Act
N.M. Stat. Ann., 58-12-1 et seq.
Va. Code 1950, § 6.1-226.1 et seq.

Credit Unions and Cooperative Savings Act
P.R. Acts 1989, First Special Session, No. 6

Creditors Assignment Act
Mont. Code Ann., 31-2-201 et seq.
N.M. Stat. Ann., 56-9-1 et seq.

Creditor's Bill Act
Mich. Comp. Laws 1948, 634.1 et seq.

Creditors' Dividends in Liquidation Proceedings
N.Y. Debtor and Creditor Law (Consol. Laws Ch. 12) § 30 et seq.

Creditors' Rights Act
Cal. Civil Code §§ 5116, 5125, 5127

Creek Original Agreement
March 1, 1901, Ch. 676, 31 Stat. 861

Creek Supplemental Agreement
June 30, 1902, Ch. 1323, 32 Stat. 500

Creen-McNitt Act (Emergency Banking)
Mich. Public Acts 1933, No. 32

Cremation Act (Safe)
S.C. Code Ann. 1976, § 32-8-300 et seq.

Crematory Act
N.C. Gen. Stat. 1943, § 90-210.40 et seq.

Crematory Regulation Act
Ill. Comp. Stat. 1992, Ch. 410, § 18/1 et seq.

Crenshaw 1st Act
Ala. Acts 1996, p. 947, No. 604

Crestline-Lake Arrowhead Water Agency Act
Cal. Statutes 1962, 1st Ex. Sess., Ch. 40, p. 278
Cal. Water Code, Appendix, § 104-1 et seq.

Crib Safety Act
Colo. Rev. Stat., 13-21-105.5
Wash. Rev. Code Ann., 70.111.900

Crime Act (Anti-Violent)
Alaska Laws 1992, Ch. 79

Crime Against Nature Act
Tenn. Code Ann., 39-13-501

Crime Awareness and Campus Security Act of 1990
Nov. 8, 1990, P.L. 101-542, 20 U.S. Code §§ 1001 nt., 1092 nt.

Crime Bill
See Violent Crime Control And Law Enforcement Act Of 1994

Crime Classification Act
Utah Code Ann. 1953, 76-1-101 et seq.

Crime Classification Act (Omnibus)
S.C. Code Ann. 1976, § 16-1-10 et seq.

Crime Comic Book Prohibition Act
Md. Laws 1955, Ch. 720
Ohio Rev. Code 1953, 2903.10

Crime Commission Act
Ill. Rev. Stat. 1969, Ch. 38, § 203-13
Pa. Purdon's Stat., Title 71, § 1190.1 et seq.

Crime Compact Act (Interstate)
See Interstate Crime Compact Act

Crime Control Act
Fla. Stat., 921.0001 et seq.

Crime Control Act (Organized)
Colo. Rev. Stat., 18-17-101 et seq.
N.Y. Civil Practice Laws and Rules (Consol. Laws Ch. 8) § 1353 et seq.
N.Y. Criminal Procedure Law (Consol. Laws Ch. 11A) §§ 40.20, 40.50, 200.40, 200.65, 210.40, 300.10, 310.50, 450.10, 450.20
N.Y. Penal Law 1965 (Consol. Laws Ch. 40) §§ 105.35, 460.00 et seq.

Crime Control Act of 1973
Aug. 6, 1973, P.L. 93-83, 87 Stat. 197, 5 U.S. Code §§ 5108, 5314 to 5316; 40 U.S. Code § 484; 42 U.S. Code §§ 3334, 3701, 3711, 3721 to 3725, 3731 to 3738, 3741 to 3747, 3750, 3750a to 3750d, 3751 to 3771, 3791 to 3793, 3795

Crime Control Act of 1976
Oct. 15, 1976, P.L. 94-503, 42 U.S. Code § 3701 et seq.

Crime Control Act of 1990
Nov. 29, 1990, P.L. 101-647, 18 U.S. Code § 1 nt.
Dec. 5, 1991, P.L. 102-190, 42 U.S. Code § 13041
Nov. 4, 1992, P.L. 102-586, 42 U.S. Code §§ 13051, 13051 nt., 13052 to 13055
Oct. 21, 1998, P.L. 105-277, 28 U.S. Code § 509 nt.
Nov. 10, 1998, P.L. 105-362, 12 U.S. Code § 4211

Crime Control Acts
May 18, 1934, Ch. 299, 48 Stat. 780 (See 18 U.S. Code §§ 111, 1114, 2231)
May 18, 1934, Ch. 300, 48 Stat. 781 (See 18 U.S. Code §§ 875, 3239)
May 18, 1934, Ch. 301, 48 Stat. 781 (See 18 U.S. Code §§ 10, 1201)

May 18, 1934, Ch. 302, 48 Stat. 782 (See 18 U.S. Code § 1201)

May 18, 1934, Ch. 303, 48 Stat. 782 (See 18 U.S. Code §§ 752, 1792)

May 18, 1934, Ch. 304, 48 Stat. 783 (See 18 U.S. Code §§ 2113, 3231)

Crime Control and Prevention Districts Act
Tex. Rev. Civ. Stat., Art. 2370c-4

Crime Fighting Committee Act
P.R. Laws Ann. 1954, Title 25, § 901 et seq.

Crime Identification Technology Act of 1998
Oct. 9, 1998, P.L. 105-251, Title I, 112 Stat. 1871, 42 U.S. Code § 14601 nt.

Crime Insurance Act
Cal. Insurance Code § 10101 et seq.

Crime Investigating Commission Act
Ill. Rev. Stat. 1969, Ch. 38, § 203-1 et seq.

Crime Law (White Collar)
Tenn. Code Ann., 40-3-201

Crime Prevention Act (Domestic Violence)
Ida. Code 1947, 39-6301 et seq.

Crime Prevention Act (Neighborhood Preservation)
N.Y. Executive Law 1951 (Consol. Laws Ch. 18) § 846a et seq.

Crime Prevention Act (Neighborhood)
R.I. Gen. Laws 1956, 42-96-1 et seq.

Crime Prevention and Control Act
Fla. Laws 1991, Ch. 243

Crime Prevention Compact Act
June 6, 1934, Ch. 406, 48 Stat. 909 (See 4 U.S. Code § 111)

April 8, 1952, Ch. 162, 66 Stat. 45, 18 U.S. Code §§ 5023 to 5026

April 8, 1952, Ch. 164, 66 Stat. 46, 18 U.S. Code § 2113

May 8, 1952, Ch. 246, 66 Stat. 67, 18 U.S. Code § 1716

May 9, 1952, Ch. 253, 66 Stat. 68, 18 U.S. Code § 5003

May 15, 1952, Ch. 289, 66 Stat. 72, 18 U.S. Code § 4284

May 23, 1952, Ch. 327, 66 Stat. 92, 18 U.S. Code § 711

July 1, 1952, Ch. 535, 66 Stat. 314, 18 U.S. Code § 1708

July 3, 1952, Ch. 547, 66 Stat. 321, 18 U.S. Code § 709

July 3, 1952, Ch. 553, 66 Stat. 325, 18 U.S. Code § 1699

July 3, 1952, Ch. 570, 66 Stat. 333, 18 U.S. Code §§ 794 nt., 2151, 2153, 2154, 2388 nt.

July 12, 1952, Ch. 695, 66 Stat. 589, 18 U.S. Code § 7

Crime Prevention Consortium Act (Youth)
Ill. Comp. Stat. 1992, Ch. 110, § 125/1 et seq.

Crime Prevention in Schools Act
La. Rev. Stat. Ann., 17:13.1

Crime Profits Act
W. Va. Code 1966, § 14-2B-1 et seq.

Crime Punishment Act
Wash. Rev. Code. 1989, 31.12A.005 et seq.

Crime Report Act (School)
S.C. Code Ann. 1976, § 59-63-310 et seq.

Crime Stoppers Commission Act
N.M. Stat. Ann., 29-12-1 et seq.

Crime Victim and Witness Advisory Council Act
Minn. Stat. Ann., 611A.70, 611A.71

Crime Victim Ombudsman Act
Minn. Stat. Ann., 611A.72 et seq.

Crime Victim Restitution Program
Cal. Penal Code §§ 1202.4, 11225
Cal. Welfare and Institutions Code §§ 656.2, 729.6, 729.7

Crime Victims' Act (Fair Treatment Standards for)
Also known as the Crime Victims' Bill of Rights
N.Y. Executive Law 1951 (Consol. Laws Ch. 18) § 640 et seq.

Crime Victims Act (Rights of)
Utah Code Ann. 1953, 77-38-1 et seq.

Crime Victims' and Witnesses' Bill of Rights Act
N.M. Stat. Ann., 31-24-1 et seq.

Crime Victims' Bill of Rights
Ga. Code Ann., 17-17-1 et seq.

Crime Victim's Bill of Rights Act
Mich. Comp. Laws Ann., 780.751
N.J. Stat. Ann., 52:4B-34 et seq.
Ore. Rev. Stat., 147.405

Crime Victims' Compensation Act
Ala. Code 1975, § 15-23-1
Ill. Comp. Stat. 1992, Ch. 740, § 45/1 et seq.
Miss. Code Ann., § 99-41-1 et seq.
Tex. Code of Criminal Procedure, Art. 56.31 et seq.
W. Va. Code 1966, § 14-2A-1 et seq.

Crime Victims Compensation Act
Ala. Code 1975, § 15-23-1
Cal. Government Code § 13959 et seq.
Colo. Rev. Stat., 24-4.1-100.1 et seq.
D.C. Code Ann., § 3-401 et seq.
Ida. Code 1947, 72-1001 et seq.
Ind. Code 1982, 16-7-3.6-1 et seq.
Ky. Rev. Stat. 1971, 346.010 et seq.
Mass. Gen. Laws Ann., 258A:1 et seq.
Mont. Code Ann., 53-9-101 et seq.
N.C. Gen. Stat. 1943, § 15B-1 et seq.
N.Y. Executive Law 1951 (Consol. Laws Ch. 18) § 620 et seq.
Okla. Stat. Ann., Title 21, § 142.1 et seq.
W. Va. Code 1966 § 14-2A-1 et seq.
Wyo. Stat. Ann., § 1-40-101 et seq.

Crime Victims Compensation Act (Murrah)
Okla. Stat. Ann., Title 21, § 142.31 et seq.

Crime Victim's Compensation Board Act
Pa. Purdon's Stat., Title 71, § 180-7 et seq.

Crime Victims' Court Attendance Act
Ala. Code 1975, § 15-14-50 et seq.

Crime Victims' Escrow Account Act
Miss. Code Ann., § 99-38-1 et seq.

Crime Victims Protection Act
Fla. Laws 1995, Ch. 207

Crime Victims' Remedy and Civil Restitution Lien Act
Fla. Laws 1994, Ch. 342

Crime Victim's Reparations Act
See also Uniform Crime Victims Reparations Act
Minn. Stat. Ann., 611A.51 et seq.
Mont. Code Ann., 53-9-101 et seq.
Neb. Rev. Stat. 1943, 81-1801 et seq.
N.M. Stat. Ann., 31-22-1 et seq.
S.D. Codified Laws 1967, 15-8-11 et seq.
Tenn. Code Ann., 29-11-101 et seq.
Utah Code Ann. 1953, 63-63-1 et seq.
W. Va. Code 1966, § 14-2A-1 et seq.

Crime Victim's Rights Act
Alaska Stat. 1962, § 12.61.010 et seq.
Mich. Comp. Laws Ann., 780.751 et seq.

Crime Victims Trial Attendance Act
Cal. Penal Code § 1102.6

Crime Victims With Disabilities Awareness Act
Oct. 27, 1998, P.L. 105-301, 112 Stat. 2838, 42 U.S. Code § 3732 nt.

Crimes Act
Kan. Stat. Ann., 21-3101 et seq.
La. Acts 1805, Ch. 4, p. 36

Crimes Against Household Members Act
N.M. Stat. Ann., 30-3-10 et seq.

Crimes and Criminal Procedure
June 25, 1948, Ch. 645, 62 Stat. 683, 18 U.S. Code §§ 1 to 5037
May 24, 1949, Ch. 139, 63 Stat. 89
Aug. 2, 1949, Ch. 383, 63 Stat. 491, 18 U.S. Code §§ 3654, 3654 nt.
Sept. 7, 1949, Ch. 535, 63 Stat. 686, 18 U.S. Code §§ 4244, 4244 nt., 4245 to 4248

Oct. 15, 1949, Ch. 695, 63 Stat. 881, 18 U.S. Code § 4041

May 10, 1950, Ch. 174, 64 Stat. 158, 18 U.S. Code § 3771

May 27, 1950, Ch. 214, 64 Stat. 194, 18 U.S. Code § 1462

Aug. 3, 1950, Ch. 516, 64 Stat. 394, 18 U.S. Code § 2113

Aug. 4, 1950, Ch. 578, 64 Stat. 413, 18 U.S. Code § 705

Aug. 16, 1950, Ch. 722, 64 Stat. 451, 18 U.S. Code § 1305

Aug. 25, 1950, Ch. 784, 64 Stat. 475, 18 U.S. Code § 612

Sept. 21, 1950, Ch. 967, 64 Stat. 894, 18 U.S. Code §§ 220, 709, 709 nt.

Sept. 23, 1950, Ch. 1024, 64 Stat. 1003, 18 U.S. Code §§ 792 nt., 793, 1507

Sept. 28, 1950, Ch. 1092, 64 Stat. 1077, 18 U.S. Code § 710

Sept. 30, 1950, Ch. 1115, 64 Stat. 1085, 18 U.S. Code §§ 4201, 4201 nt., 5002, 5005 to 5024

Jan. 10, 1951, Ch. 1221, 64 Stat. 1239, 18 U.S. Code §§ 3052, 3107

June 29, 1951, Ch. 176, 65 Stat. 98, 18 U.S. Code § 4164

June 30, 1951, Ch. 194, 65 Stat. 107, 18 U.S. Code § 3291

July 16, 1951, Ch. 226, 65 Stat. 121, 18 U.S. Code §§ 331, 475, 489, 3056

July 31, 1951, Ch. 277, 65 Stat. 150, 18 U.S. Code § 4202

Sept. 13, 1951, Ch. 380, 65 Stat. 320, 18 U.S. Code § 215

Sept. 25, 1951, Ch. 413, 65 Stat. 336, 18 U.S. Code § 1724

Oct. 24, 1951, Ch. 546, 65 Stat. 609, 18 U.S. Code § 3619

Oct. 31, 1951, Ch. 655, 65 Stat. 717, 18 U.S. Code §§ 2, 431, 443, 603, 610, 658, 708, 709, 798, 872, 1012, 1020, 1114, 1302, 3113, 4122, 4124

June 27, 1952, Ch. 477, 66 Stat. 275, 18 U.S. Code §§ 1114, 1429, 1546

July 18, 1952, Ch. 879, 66 Stat. 722, 18 U.S. Code § 1343

June 30, 1953, Ch. 175, 67 Stat. 133, 18 U.S. Code §§ 794 nt., 798, 2152, 2153, 2154, 2157, 2388 nt., 2391

Aug. 5, 1953, Ch. 325, 67 Stat. 366, 18 U.S. Code § 14

Aug. 15, 1953, Ch. 502, 67 Stat. 586, 18 U.S. Code prec. § 1151

Aug. 15, 1953, Ch. 505, 67 Stat. 588, 18 U.S. Code prec. § 1151

Aug. 15, 1953, Ch. 506, 67 Stat. 590, 18 U.S. Code § 1157

May 6, 1954, Ch. 181, 68 Stat. 76, 18 U.S. Code § 1020

June 4, 1954, Ch. 261, 68 Stat. 170, 18 U.S. Code § 836

Aug. 2, 1954, Ch. 649, 68 Stat. 609, 18 U.S. Code § 709

Aug. 20, 1954, Ch. 769, 68 Stat. 745, 18 U.S. Code § 3486

Aug. 20, 1954, Ch. 771, 68 Stat. 747, 18 U.S. Code § 1071

Aug. 20, 1954, Ch. 772, 68 Stat. 747, 18 U.S. Code § 3146

Aug. 24, 1954, Ch. 890, 68 Stat. 782, 18 U.S. Code § 545

Aug. 24, 1954, Ch. 910, 68 Stat. 795, 18 U.S. Code § 1162

Aug. 27, 1954, Ch. 1008, 68 Stat. 867, 18 U.S. Code § 709

Aug. 31, 1954, Ch. 1143, 68 Stat. 999, 18 U.S. Code § 3056

Sept. 1, 1954, Ch. 1213, 68 Stat. 1141, 18 U.S. Code § 545

Sept. 1, 1954, Ch. 1214, 68 Stat. 1145, 18 U.S. Code § 3282

Sept. 3, 1954, Ch. 1261, 68 Stat. 1216, 18 U.S. Code §§ 794, 2151, 2153, 2154, 2155, 2156

Sept. 3, 1954, Ch. 1263, 68 Stat. 1239, 18 U.S. Code § 3620

June 1, 1955, Ch. 115, 69 Stat. 80, 18 U.S. Code § 871

June 28, 1955, Ch. 190, 69 Stat. 183, 18 U.S. Code §§ 1461, 1465

June 30, 1955, Ch. 258, 69 Stat. 242, 18 U.S. Code §§ 542, 544, 545

July 7, 1955, Ch. 282, 69 Stat. 282, 18 U.S. Code § 4004

April 6, 1956, Ch. 177, 70 Stat. 100, 18 U.S. Code § 1073

May 28, 1956, Ch. 331, 70 Stat. 216, 18 U.S. Code § 752

Continued

519

July 9, 1956, Ch. 519, 70 Stat. 507, 18 U.S. Code § 2314

July 11, 1956, Ch. 561, 70 Stat. 523, 18 U.S. Code § 1343

July 14, 1956, Ch. 595, 70 Stat. 538, 18 U.S. Code §§ 31 to 35

July 18, 1956, Ch. 629, 70 Stat. 572, 18 U.S. Code §§ 1401 to 1407

July 24, 1956, Ch. 678, 70 Stat. 623, 18 U.S. Code §§ 2384, 2385

July 26, 1956, Ch. 741, 70 Stat. 667, 18 U.S. Code §§ 658, 1014

July 28, 1956, Ch. 773, 70 Stat. 714, 18 U.S. Code §§ 657, 1006

Aug. 1, 1956, Ch. 818, 70 Stat. 784, 18 U.S. Code § 1721

Aug. 1, 1956, Ch. 822, 70 Stat. 793, 18 U.S. Code § 1163

Aug. 1, 1956, Ch. 825, 70 Stat. 797, 18 U.S. Code §§ 41, 46

Aug. 2, 1956, Ch. 879, 70 Stat. 935, 18 U.S. Code § 1508

Aug. 6, 1956, Ch. 971, 70 Stat. 1043, 18 U.S. Code § 1201

Aug. 10, 1956, Ch. 1041, 70A Stat. 626, 18 U.S. Code § 1385

July 10, 1957, P.L. 85-86, 71 Stat. 277, 18 U.S. Code § 1157

Sept. 2, 1957, P.L. 85-268, 71 Stat. 594, 18 U.S. Code § 1716

Sept. 2, 1957, P.L. 85-269, 71 Stat. 595, 18 U.S. Code § 3500

June 20, 1958, P.L. 85-463, 72 Stat. 216, 18 U.S. Code § 3651

July 7, 1958, P.L. 85-508, 72 Stat. 348, 18 U.S. Code §§ 3241, 3401, 3771, 3772

July 29, 1958, P.L. 85-568, 72 Stat. 434, 18 U.S. Code §§ 799, 1114

Aug. 6, 1958, P.L. 85-595, 72 Stat. 512, 18 U.S. Code § 3237

Aug. 8, 1958, P.L. 85-615, 72 Stat. 545, 18 U.S. Code § 1162

Aug. 12, 1958, P.L. 85-623, 72 Stat. 562, 18 U.S. Code § 1716

Aug. 21, 1958, P.L. 85-699, 72 Stat. 698, 18 U.S. Code §§ 217, 218, 221, 657, 1006, 1014

Aug. 23, 1958, P.L. 85-741, 72 Stat. 834, 18 U.S. Code § 3651

Aug. 25, 1958, P.L. 85-752, 72 Stat. 845, 18 U.S. Code §§ 4208, 4209

Aug. 28, 1958, P.L. 85-796, 72 Stat. 962, 18 U.S. Code §§ 1461, 1462

Sept. 2, 1958, P.L. 85-921, 72 Stat. 1771, 18 U.S. Code §§ 15, 504

Sept. 6, 1958, P.L. 85-928, 72 Stat. 1783, 18 U.S. Code § 4201

March 18, 1959, P.L. 86-3, 73 Stat. 11, 18 U.S. Code §§ 3771, 3772

June 25, 1959, P.L. 86-70, 73 Stat. 144, 18 U.S. Code §§ 1385, 5024

Sept. 8, 1959, P.L. 86-234, 73 Stat. 470, 18 U.S. Code § 47

Sept. 14, 1959, P.L. 86-256, 73 Stat. 518, 18 U.S. Code § 4083

Sept. 14, 1959, P.L. 86-259, 73 Stat. 546, 18 U.S. Code § 4161

Sept. 21, 1959, P.L. 86-291, 73 Stat. 570, 18 U.S. Code § 712

Sept. 22, 1959, P.L. 86-354, 73 Stat. 639, 18 U.S. Code § 2113

May 6, 1960, P.L. 86-449, 74 Stat. 86, 18 U.S. Code §§ 837, 1074, 1509

June 12, 1960, P.L. 86-519, 74 Stat. 217, 18 U.S. Code § 152

July 12, 1960, P.L. 86-624, 74 Stat. 413, 18 U.S. Code §§ 1401, 5024

July 12, 1960, P.L. 86-634, 74 Stat. 469, 18 U.S. Code §§ 1164, 1165

Sept. 2, 1960, P.L. 86-691, 74 Stat. 738, 18 U.S. Code § 3568

Sept. 2, 1960, P.L. 86-701, 74 Stat. 753, 18 U.S. Code § 152

Sept. 2, 1960, P.L. 86-702, 74 Stat. 753, 18 U.S. Code § 42, 53

Sept. 6, 1960, P.L. 86-710, 74 Stat. 808, 18 U.S. Code §§ 831 to 835

Sept. 13, 1961, P.L. 87-216, 75 Stat. 491, 18 U.S. Code §§ 1081, 1084

Sept. 13, 1961, P.L. 87-218, 75 Stat. 492, 18 U.S. Code §§ 1302, 1953

Sept. 13, 1961, P.L. 87-228, 75 Stat. 498, 18 U.S. Code § 1952

Sept. 26, 1961, P.L. 87-299, 75 Stat. 648, 18 U.S. Code § 3282

Sept. 26, 1961, P.L. 87-306, 75 Stat. 669, 18 U.S. Code § 1362

Sept. 26, 1961, P.L. 87-317, 75 Stat. 681, 18 U.S. Code § 4126

Oct. 3, 1961, P.L. 87-336, 75 Stat. 750, 18 U.S. Code § 5021

Oct. 3, 1961, P.L. 87-338, 75 Stat. 751, 18 U.S. Code § 35

Oct. 4, 1961, P.L. 87-353, 75 Stat. 774, 18 U.S. Code § 433, 493, 657, 658, 1006, 1014

Oct. 4, 1961, P.L. 87-367, 75 Stat. 793, 18 U.S. Code § 4201

Oct. 4, 1961, P.L. 87-368, 75 Stat. 795, 18 U.S. Code § 1073

Oct. 4, 1961, P.L. 87-371, 75 Stat. 802, 18 U.S. Code §§ 2311, 2314, 2315

March 20, 1962, P.L. 87-420, 76 Stat. 41, 18 U.S. Code §§ 664, 1027, 1954

March 31, 1962, P.L. 87-428, 76 Stat. 52, 18 U.S. Code § 5034

June 19, 1962, P.L. 87-486, 76 Stat. 103, 18 U.S. Code § 2385

July 2, 1962, P.L. 87-518, 76 Stat. 132, 18 U.S. Code § 1114

Sept. 19, 1962, P.L. 87-664, 76 Stat. 551, 18 U.S. Code § 1505

Sept. 19, 1962, P.L. 87-665, 76 Stat. 552, 18 U.S. Code § 4163

Sept. 19, 1962, P.L. 87-667, 76 Stat. 555, 18 U.S. Code § 491

Sept. 19, 1962, P.L. 87-672, 76 Stat. 557, 18 U.S. Code § 4281

Oct. 9, 1962, P.L. 87-773, 76 Stat. 775, 18 U.S. Code § 2318

Oct. 10, 1962, P.L. 87-791, 76 Stat. 809, 18 U.S. Code § 3056

Oct. 18, 1962, P.L. 87-845, 76A Stat. 698, 18 U.S. Code §§ 14, 4210

Oct. 23, 1962, P.L. 87-849, 76 Stat. 1119, 18 U.S. Code §§ 201 to 218

May 23, 1963, P.L. 88-27, 77 Stat. 48, 18 U.S. Code § 3238

Oct. 16, 1963, P.L. 88-139, 77 Stat. 248, 18 U.S. Code §§ 3288, 3289

Dec. 30, 1963, P.L. 88-251, 77 Stat. 834, 18 U.S. Code §§ 751, 752

June 6, 1964, P.L. 88-316, 78 Stat. 203, 18 U.S. Code § 224

July 2, 1964, P.L. 88-353, 78 Stat. 269, 18 U.S. Code § 1014

Aug. 20, 1964, P.L. 88-455, 78 Stat. 552, 18 U.S. Code § 3006A

Aug. 27, 1964, P.L. 88-493, 78 Stat. 610, 18 U.S. Code § 112

Aug. 30, 1964, P.L. 88-520, 78 Stat. 699, 18 U.S. Code §§ 3288, 3289

Oct. 3, 1964, P.L. 88-619, 78 Stat. 995, 18 U.S. Code §§ 1621, 3491

July 7, 1965, P.L. 89-64, 79 Stat. 210, 18 U.S. Code § 35

July 7, 1965, P.L. 89-68, 79 Stat. 212, 18 U.S. Code § 1952

July 15, 1965, P.L. 89-74, 79 Stat. 234, 18 U.S. Code § 1114

July 23, 1965, P.L. 89-81, 79 Stat. 257, 18 U.S. Code §§ 337, 485

July 27, 1965, P.L. 89-95, 79 Stat. 285, 18 U.S. Code § 831

Aug. 28, 1965, P.L. 89-141, 79 Stat. 580, 18 U.S. Code §§ 1751, 3486

Sept. 10, 1965, P.L. 89-176, 79 Stat. 674, 18 U.S. Code §§ 751, 752, 4082

Sept. 15, 1965, P.L. 89-186, 79 Stat. 791, 18 U.S. Code § 3056

Sept. 29, 1965, P.L. 89-218, 79 Stat. 890, 18 U.S. Code § 3056

Oct. 19, 1965, P.L. 89-267, 79 Stat. 990, 18 U.S. Code § 5003

June 22, 1966, P.L. 89-465, 80 Stat. 214, 18 U.S. Code §§ 3041, 3141 to 3143, 3146 to 3152, 3568

July 4, 1966, P.L. 89-486, 80 Stat. 248, 18 U.S. Code §§ 219, 613

Sept. 6, 1966, P.L. 89-554, 80 Stat. 608, 18 U.S. Code §§ 292, 1916 to 1923, 4010, 4011

Oct. 14, 1966, P.L. 89-654, 80 Stat. 904, 18 U.S. Code §§ 659, 2111

Oct. 15, 1966, P.L. 89-670, 80 Stat. 948, 18 U.S. Code § 1020

Nov. 2, 1966, P.L. 89-707, 80 Stat. 1100, 18 U.S. Code §§ 1153, 3242

Nov. 2, 1966, P.L. 89-713, 80 Stat. 1108, 18 U.S. Code § 3237

Nov. 11, 1966, P.L. 89-807, 80 Stat. 1525, 18 U.S. Code § 713

May 25, 1967, P.L. 90-19, 81 Stat. 27, 18 U.S. Code §§ 493, 657, 709, 1006, 1010, 1012

Nov. 3, 1967, P.L. 90-123, 81 Stat. 362, 18 U.S. Code § 1510

Dec. 15, 1967, P.L. 90-203, 81 Stat. 611, 18 U.S. Code § 1306

Dec. 27, 1967, P.L. 90-226, 81 Stat. 741, 18 U.S. Code §§ 4122, 5024, 5025

Continued

April 11, 1968, P.L. 90-284, 82 Stat. 73, 18 U.S. Code §§ 231 to 233, 241, 242, 245, 1153, 2101, 2102

May 29, 1968, P.L. 90-321, 82 Stat. 159, 18 U.S. Code §§ 891 to 896

June 19, 1968, P.L. 90-351, 82 Stat. 210, 18 U.S. Code §§ 921 to 928, 2510 to 2520, 3103a, 3501, 3502, 3731

June 20, 1968, P.L. 90-353, 82 Stat. 240, 18 U.S. Code § 504

June 22, 1968, P.L. 90-357, 82 Stat. 248, 18 U.S. Code § 14

July 1, 1968, P.L. 90-371, 82 Stat. 280, 18 U.S. Code § 4042

July 5, 1968, P.L. 90-381, 82 Stat. 291, 18 U.S. Code § 700

July 21, 1968, P.L. 90-413, 82 Stat. 396, 18 U.S. Code § 1730

Aug. 1, 1968, P.L. 90-448, 82 Stat. 545, 18 U.S. Code § 709

Aug. 2, 1968, P.L. 90-449, 82 Stat. 611, 18 U.S. Code § 1114

Sept. 26, 1968, P.L. 90-518, 82 Stat. 872, 18 U.S. Code § 1263

Sept. 28, 1968, P.L. 90-535, 82 Stat. 885, 18 U.S. Code § 2314

Oct. 12, 1968, P.L. 90-560, 82 Stat. 997, 18 U.S. Code §§ 1716A, 3061

Oct. 17, 1968, P.L. 90-578, 82 Stat. 115, 18 U.S. Code §§ 202, 3006A, 3041, 3043, 3045, 3060, 3102, 3116, 3184, 3191, 3195, 3401, 3402, 3569, 3771

Oct. 21, 1968, P.L. 90-608, 82 Stat. 1198, 18 U.S. Code § 3056

Oct. 22, 1968, P.L. 90-618, 82 Stat. 1214, 18 U.S. Code §§ 921 to 928

Dec. 5, 1969, P.L. 91-135, 83 Stat. 279, 18 U.S. Code §§ 43, 44, 3054, 3112

July 17, 1970, P.L. 91-339, 84 Stat. 437, 18 U.S. Code §§ 5014, 5020

July 29, 1970, P.L. 91-358, 84 Stat. 654, 18 U.S. Code §§ 2511, 2518, 2520

Aug. 12, 1970, P.L. 91-375, 84 Stat. 777, 18 U.S. Code §§ 12, 440 , 441, 500, 501, 612, 876, 877, 1114, 1303, 1341, 1342, 1463, 1696, 1699, 1703, 1704, 1707, 1709 to 1713, 1715 to 1718, 1721 to 1725, 1729, 1730, 1733, 1735 to 1737, 3061

Sept. 22, 1970, P.L. 91-405, 84 Stat. 853, 18 U.S. Code §§ 201, 203, 204, 591, 594, 595

Sept. 25, 1970, P.L. 91-419, 84 Stat. 870, 18 U.S. Code § 714; 31 U.S. Code §§ 488b, 488b-1, 488b-2

Oct. 14, 1970, P.L. 91-447, 84 Stat. 916, 18 U.S. Code § 3006A

Oct. 14, 1970, P.L. 91-448, 84 Stat. 920, 18 U.S. Code § 501

Oct. 15, 1970, P.L. 91-452, 84 Stat. 923, 18 U.S. Code §§ 3331 to 3334, 3500, 6001 to 6005

Oct. 19, 1970, P.L. 91-468, 84 Stat. 1016, 18 U.S. Code §§ 493, 657, 709, 1006, 1014, 2113

Oct. 22, 1970, P.L. 91-492, 84 Stat. 1090, 18 U.S. Code §§ 3651, 4203

Oct. 27, 1970, P.L. 91-513, 84 Stat. 1282, 18 U.S. Code §§ 1114, 1952

Nov. 25, 1970, P.L. 91-523, 84 Stat. 1358, 18 U.S. Code § 1162

Dec. 29, 1970, P.L. 91-596, 84 Stat. 1607, 18 U.S. Code § 1114

Dec. 31, 1970, P.L. 91-609, 84 Stat. 1815, 18 U.S. Code § 1014

Jan. 2, 1971, P.L. 91-644, 84 Stat. 1889, 18 U.S. Code §§ 351, 924, 1752, 2516, 3731

Jan. 5, 1971, P.L. 91-651, 84 Stat. 1940, 18 U.S. Code §§ 713, 3056

Jan. 8, 1971, P.L. 91-662, 84 Stat. 1973, 18 U.S. Code §§ 552, 1461, 1462

Sept. 25, 1971, P.L. 92-128, 85 Stat. 347, 18 U.S. Code § 2

Dec. 15, 1971, P.L. 92-191, 85 Stat. 647, 18 U.S. Code § 1716

Feb. 7, 1972, P.L. 92-225, 86 Stat. 8, 18 U.S. Code §§ 591, 600, 608, 610, 611

May 11, 1972, P.L. 92-293, 86 Stat. 136, 18 U.S. Code §§ 3651, 4203

July 11, 1972, P.L. 92-347, 86 Stat. 461, 18 U.S. Code § 715

Sept. 16, 1972, P.L. 92-420, 86 Stat. 677, 18 U.S. Code § 4251

Sept. 23, 1972, P.L. 92-430, 86 Stat. 722, 18 U.S. Code § 500

Oct. 24, 1972, P.L. 92-539, 86 Stat. 1070, 18 U.S. Code §§ 112, 970, 1116, 1117, 1201

Nov. 3, 1973, P.L. 93-147, 87 Stat. 554, 18 U.S. Code § 712

Dec. 28, 1973, P.L. 93-203, 87 Stat. 881, 18 U.S. Code § 665

Dec. 28, 1973, P.L. 93-209, 87 Stat. 907, 18 U.S. Code § 4082

June 22, 1974, P.L. 93-318, 88 Stat. 245, 18 U.S. Code §§ 711, 711a

Sept. 3, 1974, P.L. 93-412, 88 Stat. 1093, 18 U.S. Code § 3006A

Sept. 7, 1974, P.L. 93-415, 88 Stat. 1133, 18 U.S. Code §§ 4351 to 4353, 5031 to 5042

Crimes and Punishments Act
Nev. Rev. Stat. 1979 Reprint, 193.010 et seq.
N.J. Stat. Ann., 2C:1-1 et seq.
Wash. Rev. Code Ann., 9.92.010 et seq.
W. Va. Code 1966, 61-1-1 et seq.

Crimes Compensation Act
Fla. Stat. Ann., 960.01 et seq.

Crimes Reporting Act (Hate)
Fla. Stat. Ann., 877.19

Crimes Statistics Act (Hate)
Utah Code Ann. 1953, 77-26-3 et seq.

Crimes Victims Act
Mont. Code Ann., 53-9-101 et seq.

Crimestoppers Act (Livestock)
Mont. Code Ann., 81-6-301 et seq.

Criminal Abortion Act
Ore. Rev. Stat. 1953, 163.060

Criminal Accessories Act
Wash. Rev. Code 1951, 9.01.040, 9.01.060

Criminal Act (Habitual)
Neb. Rev. Stat. 1943, 29-2222
Vt. Stat. Ann., Title 13, § 11

Criminal Activity Forfeiture Act (CAFA)
Mo. Rev. Stat., 513.600 et seq.

Criminal Addiction Act (Narcotics)
Tex. Penal Code 1925, Art. 725c
Wis. Stat. 1969, 161.02, Subsec. 3

Criminal Alibi Defense Act
Iowa Rules of Criminal Procedure, Rule 10

Criminal Anarchy Act
La. Rev. Stat. Ann., 14:115

N.Y. Penal Law 1965 (Consol. Laws Ch. 40) § 240.15
Wash. Rev. Code Ann., 9.05.010 et seq.

Criminal Anarchy and Communism Act
Fla. Stat. Ann., 876.01 et seq.

Criminal Appeals Act
March 2, 1907, Ch. 2564, 34 Stat. 1246 (See 18 U.S. Code § 3731)
Ill. Rev. Stat. 1991, Ch. 110A, § 601 et seq.
Ohio Rev. Code 1953, 2953.02 et seq.
Wash. Rev. Code 1951, 10.73.010 et seq.

Criminal Arrest Act
S.C. Code Ann. 1976, § 17-13-10 et seq.

Criminal Arson Act
Iowa Code Ann., 712.1 et seq.

Criminal Attempt Act
Cal. Penal Code § 663 et seq.
Ore. Rev. Stat. 1953, 161.090

Criminal Background Check System Act (Instant)
Colo. Rev. Stat., 12-26.5-101 et seq.

Criminal Bail Act
S.C. Code Ann. 1976, § 17-15-110 et seq.

Criminal Bail Bond Act
Ill. Rev. Stat. 1991, Ch. 16, § 51 et seq.

Criminal Cases Disposition on the Merits Act
Okla. Stat. Ann., Title 22, § 1145.1 et seq.

Criminal Code
March 4, 1909, Ch. 321, 35 Stat. 1088 (See 18 U.S. Code Chs. 1 to 15)
Ala. Code 1975, § 13A-1-1 et seq.
Alaska Stat. 1962, § 11.16.100 et seq.
Ariz. Rev.Stat., § 13-101 et seq.
Ark. Code Ann. 1987, 5-1-101 et seq.
Colo. Rev. Stat., 18-1-101 et seq.
Del. Code of 1974, Title 11, § 101 et seq.
Fla. Stat. Ann., 775.01 et seq.
Ga. Code Ann., 16-1-1 et seq.
Ill. Comp. Stat. 1992, Ch. 720, § 5/1-1 et seq.
Continued

Iowa Code Ann., 701.1 et seq.

Kan. Stat. Ann., 21-3101 et seq.

Ky. Rev. Stat. 1971, 431.005 et seq.

La. Rev. Stat. Ann., 14:1 et seq.

Me. Rev. Stat. Ann. 1964, Title 17-A.1 et seq.

Mich. Comp. Laws Ann., 750.1 et seq.

Minn. Stat. Ann., 609.01 et seq.

Mo. Rev. Stat., 556.011 et seq.

Mont. Code Ann., 45-1-101 et seq.

N.D. Cent. Code 12.1-01-01 et seq.

Neb. Rev. Stat. 1943, 28-101 et seq.

N.H. Rev. Stat. 1955, 625:1 et seq.

N.M. Stat. Ann., 30-1-1 et seq.

Ohio Rev. Code 1953, 2901.01 et seq.

Ore. Rev. Stat., 161.005 et seq.

Pa. Cons. Stat., Title 18, § 101 et seq.

Utah Code Ann. 1953, 76-1-101 et seq.

Wash. Rev. Code Ann., 9A.04.010 et seq.

Wis. Stat. 1989, 939.01 et seq.

Wyo. Stat. Ann., § 6-1-101 et seq.

Criminal Code Amendments

June 25, 1910, Ch. 431, 36 Stat. 857 (See 18 U.S. Code §§ 1853, 1856)

March 4, 1921, Ch. 172, 41 Stat. 1444 (See 18 U.S. Code §§ 831 to 835)

March 28, 1940, Ch. 73, 54 Stat. 80 (See 18 U.S. Code § 1382)

April 30, 1940, Ch. 164, 54 Stat. 171 (See 18 U.S. Code § 1024)

June 6, 1940, Ch. 241, 54 Stat. 234 (See 18 U.S. Code § 13)

June 11, 1940, Ch. 323, 54 Stat. 304 (See 18 U.S. Code § 7)

April 1, 1944, Ch. 151, 58 Stat. 149 (See 18 U.S. Code § 491)

Sept. 27, 1944, Ch. 425, 58 Stat. 752 (See 18 U.S. Code § 371)

June 8, 1945, Ch. 178, 59 Stat. 234 (See 18 U.S. Code §§ 371, 1503, 1505)

Criminal Compromise Act

Ore. Rev. Stat., 135.703 et seq.

Criminal Confessions Act

Wash. Rev. Code Ann., 10.58.030

Criminal Conspiracy Act

Iowa Code Ann., 706.1

Criminal Contempt Act

Ala. Code 1975, § 12-1-10

Mont. Code Ann., 45-7-309

N.Y. Penal Law 1965 (Consol. Laws Ch. 40) § 215.50 et seq.

Criminal Conversation Act

Ill. Comp. Stat. 1992, Ch. 740, § 50/0.01 et seq.

Criminal Convictions Record Act

Cal. Evidence Code §§ 452.5, 1280, 1500.5

Cal. Government Code §§ 69844.5, 71280.5

Criminal Court Act (New York City)

N.Y. Laws 1962, Ch. 697

Criminal Court of Record Act (Municipal)

Okla. Stat. Ann., Title 11, § 28-101 et seq.

Criminal Courts Act (Counties)

N.C. Gen. Stat. 1943, § 7-384 et seq.

Criminal Courts Act (Magistrates)

Ohio Rev. Code 1953, 2931.01 et seq.

Criminal Damage to Property Act

Wis. Stat. 1989, 943.01 et seq.

Criminal Defamation Act

La. Rev. Stat. Ann., 14:47 et seq.

Criminal Discovery Act

Conn. Gen. Stat. Ann., § 54-86a

Neb. Rev. Stat. 1943, 29-1912 et seq.

Wash. Rev. Code Ann., 10.37.030

Criminal Discovery Code

Okla. Stat. Ann., Title 22, § 2001 et seq.

Criminal Disqualification Act (Judges)

Mont. Code Ann. 1983, 3-1-802

Criminal Enterprise and Racketeering Influences Act

Utah Code Ann. 1953, 76-10-1601 et seq.

Criminal Evidence Act
Pa. 1911 Pamph. Laws 20

Criminal Extradition Act
See also Uniform Criminal Extradition Act

Criminal Fine Enforcement Act of 1984
Oct. 30, 1984, P.L. 98-596, 18 U.S. Code §§ 1 nt., 3565, 3579, 3611, 3622, 3651, 3655, 4209

Criminal Fine Improvements Act of 1987
Dec. 11, 1987, P.L. 100-185, 18 U.S. Code §§ 1 nt., 18, 19, 3013, 3559, 3571 to 3573, 3611, 3611 nt., 3612, 3663; 28 U.S. Code § 604

Criminal Forfeiture Act (Omnibus)
Haw. Rev. Stat. Ann., § 712A-1 et seq.

Criminal Fraud Act
Vt. Stat. Ann., Title 13, § 2001 et seq.

Criminal History and Intelligence Disclosure Act
Iowa Code Ann., 692.1 et seq.

Criminal History Record Information Act
Me. Rev. Stat. Ann. 1964, Title 16, § 611 et seq.
Pa. Cons. Stat., Title 18, § 9101 et seq.

Criminal History Record Information Act (Sex Offense)
Miss. Code Ann., § 45-27-3 et seq.

Criminal History Records Act
Nev. Rev. Stat. 1979, 179A.010 et seq.

Criminal History Screening Act (Caregivers)
N.M. Stat. Ann., 29-17-2 to 29-17-5

Criminal Identification Act
Ill. Comp. Stat. 1992, Ch. 20, § 2630/0.01 et seq.
Mich. Comp. Laws Ann., 28.241 et seq.
Mo. Rev. Stat., 222.040 et seq.
Utah Code Ann. 1953, 53-5-201 et seq.

Criminal Identification and Investigation Bureau Law
Cal. Penal Code § 11000 et seq.

Criminal Immunity Act
Wash. Rev. Code Ann., 10.52.090

Criminal Injuries Compensation Act
Haw. Rev. Stat. Ann., § 351-1 et seq.
Md. Ann. Code 1957, Art. 26A, § 1 et seq.
N.J. Stat. Ann., 52:4B-1 et seq.
R.I. Gen. Laws 1956, 12-25-1 et seq.
Tenn. Code Ann., 29-13-101 et seq.

Criminal Insanity Act
Ala. Code 1975, § 15-16-1 et seq.
Cal. Penal Code § 1367 et seq.
Colo. Rev. Stat., 16-8-101 et seq.
Ill. Rev. Stat. 1991, Ch. 38, § 1005-21-2 et seq.
Ohio Rev. Code 1953, 2945.37 et seq.
Wash. Rev. Code Ann., 10.77.010 et seq.

Criminal Interstate Rendition Act
Mass. Gen. Laws Ann., 276:11 et seq.

Criminal Investigator Retirement Act
Wyo. Stat. Ann., § 9-3-601 et seq.

Criminal Investigatory Act
Wash. Rev. Code Ann., 10.27.010 et seq.

Criminal Judicial Courts Act
N.J. Stat. Ann., 2A:7-1 et seq.

Criminal Jurisdiction Retrocession Act (Colville Indian Reservation)
Wash. Rev. Code 1989, 37.12.100 et seq.

Criminal Jurisprudence Act (Attorneys)
Ill. Rev. Stat. 1991, Ch. 13, § 20 et seq.

Criminal Justice Act
D.C. Code 1973, § 11-2601 et seq.
Ga. Code Ann., 17-12-1 et seq.
N.J. Stat. Ann., 52:17B-87
S.C. Code Ann. 1976, § 23-4-10 et seq.

Criminal Justice Act Authorization Extension Act
D.C. Code 1973, § 11-2608 et seq.

Criminal Justice Act of 1964
Aug. 20, 1964, P.L. 88-455, 78 Stat. 552, 18 U.S. Code § 3006A

Criminal Justice Act Revision of 1984
Oct. 12, 1984, P.L. 98-473, 18 U.S. Code §§ 3006A nt., 3006A

Criminal Justice Act Revision of 1986
Nov. 14, 1986, P.L. 99-651, 18 U.S. Code § 3006a nt.

Criminal Justice Centers Act
Ark. Code Ann. 1987, 12-41-201 et seq.

Criminal Justice Code
Ga. Code Ann., 17-12-1 et seq.
N.J. Stat. Ann., 2C:1-1 et seq.

Criminal Justice Coordinating Council Act
Ga. Code Ann., 35-6A-1 et seq.

Criminal Justice Council Act
Fla. Stat. Ann., 23.152, 23.153

Criminal Justice Department Act
N.M. Stat. Ann., 9-3-1 et seq.

Criminal Justice Improvements Act
S.C. Acts 1986, p. 2955, No. 462

Criminal Justice Information Act
Colo. Rev. Stat., 16-20.5-101 et seq.
Ill. Comp. Stat. 1992, Ch. 20, § 3930/1 et seq.
Md. Ann. Code 1957, Art. 27, § 742 et seq.
Mont. Code Ann., 44-5-101 et seq.
P.R. Laws Ann. 1954, Title 4, § 531 et seq.
Wash. Rev. Code Ann., 10.98.010 et seq.

Criminal Justice Planning and Coordination Act
Ga. Code Ann., 35-6A-1 et seq.

Criminal Justice School Act
N.J. Stat. Ann., 18A:65-55.1, 18A:65-55.2

Criminal Justice Supervisory Board Act
D.C. Code Ann., § 2-1101 et seq.

Criminal Justice Training Council Act
Vt. Stat. Ann., Title 20, § 2351 et seq.

Criminal Law and Procedure Technical Amendments Act of 1986
Nov. 10, 1986, P.L. 99-646, 18 U.S. Code § 1 nt.
Dec. 11, 1987, P.L. 100-185, 18 U.S. Code § 18
Nov. 18, 1988, P.L. 100-690, 18 U.S. Code §§ 18, 1961, 4217
Sept. 13, 1994, P.L. 103-322, 18 U.S. Code § 201

Criminal Law Enforcement Department Act
Fla. Stat. Ann., 943.01 et seq.

Criminal Law Magistrates Act (El Paso)
Tex. Laws 70th Leg., 1991, p. 3382, Ch. 317

Criminal Libel Act
Ala. Code 1975, § 13A-11-160 et seq.
Cal. Penal Code § 248 et seq.
Ga. Code Ann., 16-11-40
Ill. Rev. Stat. 1985, Ch. 38, §§ 27-1, 27-2
Ind. Code Ann., 34-4-13-1
La. Rev. Stat. Ann., 14:47 et seq.
Mo. Rev. Stat. 1969, 559.410 et seq.
Mont. Code Ann., 45-8-212
N.Y. Penal Law 1909 (Consol. Laws Ch. 40) § 1340 et seq.

Criminal Limitation of Actions
Okla. Stat. Ann., Title 22, § 151 et seq.

Criminal Limitations Act
See Statute of Limitations (Criminal)

Criminal Mischief Act
Ala. Code 1975, § 13A-7-20 et seq.
La. Rev. Stat. Ann., 14:59

Criminal Neglect Act
N.J. Stat. Ann., 9:6-1 et seq.

Criminal Neglect of Family Act
La. Rev. Stat. Ann., 14:74, 14:75

Criminal Non-Support Act
Kan. Stat. Ann., 21-3605
Mo. Rev. Stat. 1969, 559.410

Criminal Nonsuit Act
N.C. Gen. Stat. 1943, § 15-173

Criminal Nuisance Act
See Nuisance Act (Criminal)

Criminal Offender Employment Act
N.M. Stat. Ann., 28-2-1 et seq.

Criminal Offender Record Information System Act
Mass. Gen. Laws Ann., 6:167 et seq.

Criminal Offender Treatment Act
Haw. Session Laws 1998, Act 152

Criminal Penalties Act (Minimum)
Md. Ann. Code 1957, Art. 27, § 643

Criminal Pleadings Act
Mass. Gen. Laws Ann., 277:1 et seq.

Criminal Practice Act
Haw. Rev. Stat. Ann., §§ 805-1 et seq., 806-1 et seq.

Criminal Practices Act (Civil Remedies for)
Fla. Stat. Ann., 772.101 et seq.

Criminal Procedure Act
Cal. Penal Code § 681 et seq.
Colo. Rev. Stat., 16-1-101 et seq.
D.C. Code 1973, § 23-101 et seq.
Fla. Stat. Ann., 900.01 et seq.
Ga. Code Ann., 17-1-1 et seq.
Ida. Code 1947, 19-101 et seq.
Ind. Code Ann., 35-32-1-1 et seq.
Iowa Code Ann., 801.1 et seq.
La. Rev. Stat. Ann., 15:21 et seq.
Mich. Comp. Laws Ann., 760.1 et seq.
Mont. Code Ann., 46-1-101 et seq.
N.C. Gen. Stat. 1943, § 15A-101 et seq.
N.D. Cent. Code, 29-01-01 et seq.
Nev. Rev. Stat. 1979 Reprint, 169.015 et seq.
N.H. Rev. Stat. 1955, 592-A:1 et seq.
N.J. Stat. Ann., 2A:152-1 et seq.
N.M. Stat. Ann., 31-1-1 et seq.
Okla. Stat. Ann., Title 22, § 1 et seq.
Pa. Cons. Stat., Title 42
S.D. Codified Laws 1967, 23A-1-1 et seq.
Tenn. Code Ann., 40-1-101 et seq.
Utah Code Ann. 1953, 77-1-1 et seq.
Wash. Rev. Code Ann., 10.01.030 et seq.
Wis. Stat. 1989, 967.01 et seq.
W. Va. Code 1966, § 62-1-1 et seq.

Criminal Procedure Act (Appeals)
Ohio Rev. Code 1953, 2953.02 et seq.

Criminal Procedure Code
Ill. Comp. Stat. 1992, Ch. 725, § 5/100-1 et seq.

Criminal Procedure Reform Act
Ark. Code Ann. 1987, 16-85-210

Criminal Proceeding Interpreter Act
Ill. Comp. Stat. 1992, Ch. 725, § 140/0.01 et seq.

Criminal Proceedings Act
N.H. Rev. Stat. 1955, 613-A:1 et seq.

Criminal Proceedings Act (Rendition of Prisoners as Witnesses in)
Me. Rev. Stat. Ann. 1964, Title 15, § 1464 et seq.

Criminal Profiteering Act
Wash. Rev. Code Ann., 9A.82.001 et seq.

Criminal Punishment Code
Fla. Stat., 921.002 et seq.

Criminal Recklessness Act (Motor Vehicles)
Minn. Stat. Ann., 169.13

Criminal Records Privacy Act
Wash. Rev. Code Ann., 10.97.010 et seq.

Criminal Records Screening Act (Childrens' and Juvenile Facility)
N.M. Stat. Ann., 32-9-1 et seq.

Criminal Responsibility Act (Mental Illness)
Mo. Rev. Stat., 552.010 et seq.

Criminal Responsibility and Post Trial Disposition Act
See Uniform Criminal Responsibility and Post Disposition Act

Criminal Rewards Act
Wash. Rev. Code Ann., 10.85.030 et seq.

Criminal Royalties Distribution Act
R.I. Gen. Laws 1956, 12-25.1-1 et seq.

Criminal Sentencing Act
Colo. Rev. Stat., 16-16-101 et seq.
N.M. Stat. Ann., 31-18-12 et seq.

Criminal Sentencing Reform Act
Tenn. Code Ann., 40-35-101 et seq.

Criminal Severance Act
Tex. Code of Criminal Procedure, Art. 38.06

Criminal Sexual Deviant Statute
Ind. Code Ann., 35-42-4-2 et seq.

Criminal Sexual Offenses Child Victims Privacy Act
Ill. Rev. Stat. 1991, Ch. 38, § 1451 et seq.

Criminal Sexual Psychopaths Act
See also Sexual Psychopaths Act
Iowa Code 1977, 225A.1 et seq.

Criminal Slander Act
Ind. Code Ann., 35-13-6-1

Criminal Statistics Act
See also Uniform Criminal Statistics Act
Cal. Penal Code § 13000 et seq.
N.Y. Correction Law (Consol. Laws Ch. 43) §§ 29 Subd. 1, 618
N.Y. Criminal Procedure Law (Consol. Laws Ch. 11A) § 160.10 et seq.
N.Y. Executive Law 1951 (Consol. Laws Ch. 18) § 837
S.D. Codified Laws 1967, 23-6-1 et seq.

Criminal Statute of Limitations Act
D.C. Code Ann., § 23-113
Haw. Rev. Stat. 1968, § 721-1 et seq.

Criminal Street Gang Prevention Act
Fla. Stat., 874.01 et seq.

Criminal Syndicalism Act
See Syndicalism Act

Criminal Trespass Act
Ala. Code 1975, § 13A-7-2 et seq.
Cal. Penal Code § 602
Del. Code of 1974, Title 11, § 829 et seq.
Fla. Stat. Ann., 806.13
Ga. Code Ann., 16-7-21
Ill. Rev. Stat. 1991, Ch. 38, §§ 21-2, 21-3
Ind. Code Ann., 35-43-2-2
La. Rev. Stat. Ann., 14:63 et seq.
Md. Ann. Code 1957, Art. 27, § 577
Ohio Rev. Code 1953, 2911.21
S.C. Code Ann. 1976, § 16-1, 1-510 et seq.
Wash. Rev. Code Ann., 9A.52.070 et seq.

Criminal Trials Act (Three Term)
Ind. Code Ann., 35-1-27-1

Criminal Venue Act
N.H. Rev. Stat. 1955, 602:1

Criminal Victims' Asset Discovery Act
Ill. Comp. Stat. 1992, Ch. 725, § 145/1 et seq.

Criminal Victims' Escrow Account Act
Ill. Rev. Stat. 1991, Ch. 70, § 401 et seq.

Criminal Victims Protection Act of 1990
Nov. 15, 1990, P.L. 101-581, 11 U.S. Code §§ 101 nt., 523, 523 nt., 1328
Nov. 29, 1990, P.L. 101-647, 11 U.S. Code §§ 101 nt., 523, 523 nt., 1328

Criminal—Juvenile Comprehensive Justice Information System Act
R.I. Gen. Laws 1956, 42-108-1 et seq.

Crippled Children Services Act
Cal. Health and Safety Code § 248 et seq.
Ill. Comp. Stat. 1992, Ch. 110, § 345/0.01 et seq.
Kan. Stat. Ann., 65-5a01 et seq.
Mich. Comp. Laws Ann., 722.201 et seq.
Okla. Stat. 1971, Title 10, § 172.17 et seq.

Tex. Health and Safety Code, § 35.001

Wash. Rev. Code Ann., 13.20A.635 et seq.

Crisp Act (Process)

N.C. Public Laws 1919, Ch. 304, § 1

Critical Agricultural Materials Act

Nov. 4, 1978, P.L. 95-592, 7 U.S. Code §§ 178, 178 nt., 178a et seq., 1314f

May 16, 1984, P.L. 98-284, 7 U.S. Code §§ 178 nt., 178a et seq.

Dec. 23, 1985, P.L. 99-198, 7 U.S. Code § 178c

Nov. 28, 1990, P.L. 101-624, 7 U.S. Code § 178n

Dec. 13, 1991, P.L. 102-237, 7 U.S. Code §§ 178c, 178i

April 4, 1996, P.L. 104-127, 7 U.S. Code §§ 178b, 178n

June 23, 1998, P.L. 105-185, 7 U.S. Code § 178n

Critical Areas Act

Minn. Stat. Ann., 116G.01 et seq.

Critical Areas State Register Act

Me. Rev. Stat. Ann. 1964, Title 5, § 3310 et seq.

Critical Health Problems and Comprehensive Health Education Act

Ill. Comp. Stat. 1992, Ch. 105, § 110/1 et seq.

Critical Health Problems Education Act

Mich. Comp. Laws Ann., 388.381 et seq.

Critical Health Problems Reporting Act

Mich. Comp. Laws Ann., 325.71 et seq.

N.H. Rev. Stat. 1955, 141-A:1 et seq.

Critical Incident Stress Debriefing Act

Neb. Rev. Stat. 1943, 71-7101 et seq.

Critical Needs for Tribal Development Act

July 23, 1992, P.L. 102-325, 25 U.S. Code §§ 3321 to 3325

Critical State Concern Restoration Trust Fund Act

Fla. Stat. Ann., 380.0558

Critical Teacher Shortage Act

Miss. Code Ann., § 37-159-1 et seq.

Crop Credit Act

Wash. Rev. Code Ann., 31.16.020 et seq.

Crop Lien Act

Fla. Stat. 1965, 700.01 et seq.

Tenn. Code Ann., 66-12-101 et seq.

Wash. Rev. Code Ann., 60.11.010 et seq.

Crop Loan Act

Feb. 23, 1934, Ch. 23, 48 Stat. 354

Crop Loan and Sugar Appropriation Act

See Sugar Act Of 1937

Crop Mortgage Act

Md. Ann. Code 1974, Art. CL, § 9-101 et seq.

N.D. Cent. Code 35-05-01 et seq.

N.J. Rev. Stat. 1937, 12A:9-109 to 12A:9-507

Ohio Rev. Code 1953, 1309.07, 1309.15, 1309.44

Crop Pest Act

Iowa Code Ann., 177A.1 et seq.

Crop Pledge Act

La. Rev. Stat. Ann., 9:4341 et seq.

Crop Pooling Act

Ky. Rev. Stat. 1971, 272.010 et seq.

Crop Security Interest Act

Ill. Comp. Stat. 1992, Ch. 810, § 15/0.01 et seq.

Crops Fund Act (Emerging)

Ga. Code Ann., 2-8A-1 et seq.

Cross Appeal Act

Kan. Stat. Ann., 60-2103, Subd. h

Cross Claim Act

N.Y. Civil Practice Law and Rules (Consol. Laws Ch. 8) §§ 3011, 3019

Cross Complaint Act
Cal. Code of Civil Procedure § 435

Cross-Country Skiing Act
Ida. Code 1947, 49-3101 et seq.

Cross County Parkway Authority Act (Westchester County)
N.Y. Public Authorities Law (Consol. Laws Ch. 43A) § 300 et seq.

Cross Declaration Act
Tenn. Code Ann., Superseded Vol., 20-1007

Cross Examination Act (Opposite Party)
La. Code of Civil Procedure Arts. 1436, 1634
Mich. Comp. Laws Ann., 600.2161

Cross of Valor Act (Prisoners of War)
Okla. Stat. Ann., Title 72, § 50.21 et seq.

Crosser Act (Referendum)
Ohio Rev. Code 1953, 731.28 et seq.

Crosser-Wheeler Railroad Unemployment Insurance Act
See Railroad Unemployment Insurance Act

Crossing Act
N.J. Rev. Stat. 1937, 48:12-83

Crossing Act (Highways)
N.H. Rev. Stat. 1955, 265:30

Crossing Act (Railroad)
See Railroad Crossing Act

Crossing Elimination Act (Buffalo)
N.Y. Laws 1923, Ch. 231

Crossing Elimination Act (City of New York)
N.Y. Laws 1928, Ch. 677

Crossing Elimination Act (Outside Cities of New York, Buffalo and Syracuse)
N.Y. Laws 1928, Ch. 678

Crossing Elimination Act (Syracuse)
N.Y. Laws 1926, Ch. 439

Crossing Guard Maintenance District Act
Cal. Government Code § 55530 et seq.

Crossing Signal Law (Railroads)
S.C. Code Ann. 1976, §§ 58-15-910, 58-17-1390, 58-17-3380 et seq.

Crow Boundary Settlement Act of 1994
Nov. 2, 1994, P.L. 103-435, 25 U.S. Code § 1776d
Nov. 2, 1994, P.L. 103-444, 25 U.S. Code §§ 1776 nt., 1776 et seq.
Feb. 12, 1996, P.L. 104-109, 25 U.S. Code §§ 1776c, 1776g, 1776h

Crow Creek Sioux Tribe Infrastructure Development Trust Fund Act of 1996
Oct. 1, 1996, P.L. 104-223, 110 Stat. 3026

Crowner's Quest Act (Coroners)
Ark. Code Ann. 1987, 16-83-102 et seq.

Crude Oil and Natural Gas Production Incentive Act
N.M. Laws 1995, Ch. 15, §§ 1 to 6

Crude Oil Windfall Profit Tax Act of 1980
April 2, 1980, P.L. 96-223, 26 U.S. Code §§ 1 nt., 4986 et seq.
Oct. 25, 1982, P.L. 97-362, 26 U.S. Code § 336 nt.

Cruelty to Animals Act
See Livestock Transportation Act
Ariz. Rev. Stat. Ann., § 13-2910
Cal. Penal Code § 597
Colo. Rev. Stat., 18-9-201 et seq.
Ga. Code Ann., 16-12-4 et seq.
Me. Rev. Stat. Ann. 1964, Title 17-A, §§ 510, 1051
Mich. Comp. Laws Ann., 752.21 et seq.
Miss. Code Ann., § 97-41-1 et seq.
Mont. Code Ann., 45-8-211
N.H. Rev. Stat. 1955, 105:14 et seq.
N.J. Stat. Ann., 4:22-15 et seq.
N.M. Stat. Ann., 30-18-1 et seq.
Pa. Cons. Stat., Title 18, § 5511
R.I. Gen. Laws 1956, 4-1-1 et seq.
R.I. General Statutes 1872, Ch. 86

Tex. Health and Safety Code, § 821.001 et
seq.
Vt. Stat. Ann., Title 13, § 401 et seq.
Wash. Rev. Code Ann., 16.52.010 et seq.

Cruelty to Children and Animals Act
Fla. Stat. Ann., 828.02 et seq.

**Cruelty to Domestic Animals and Domestic
Animal Control Act**
Ga. Laws 1979, p. 516

**Crystal Lake, Bowdre Township, and
Marengo Civic Centers Act**
Ill. Rev. Stat. 1991, Ch. 85, § 6250 et seq.

Crystal Lake Civic Center Act
Ill. Comp. Stat. 1992, Ch. 70, § 305/2-1 et
seq.

Crystal Waters Act
Minn. Stat. 1971, 116.15

CSRS
See Civil Service Retirement Spouse Equity
Act of 1984

Cuban Democracy Act of 1992
Oct. 23, 1992, P.L. 102-484, 22 U.S. Code
§ 6001 et seq.
March 12, 1996, P.L. 104-114, 22 U.S. Code
§§ 6003 to 6005

Cuban Freedom Act
Fla. Stat., 288.851 et seq.

Cuban Independence Resolution
April 20, 1898, No. 24, 30 Stat. 738

**Cuban Liberty and Democratic Solidarity
(LIBERTAD) Act of 1996**
March 12, 1996, P.L. 104-114, 22 U.S. Code
§ 6021 nt.
Oct. 21, 1998, P.L. 105-277, 22 U.S. Code
§ 6037

Cuban Political Prisoners and Immigrants
Dec. 22, 1987, P.L. 100-202, 8 U.S. Code
§ 1201 nt.

Cuban Refugee Adjustment Act
Nov. 2, 1966, P.L. 89-732, 8 U.S. Code
§ 1255 nt.

Culebra Conservation and Development Act
P.R. Laws Ann. 1954, Title 21, § 890 et seq.

Cull Act
Md. Ann. Code 1974, Art. NR, § 4-1015

Cullen Earthquake Act
Cal. Code of Civil Procedure § 751.50 et seq.

Cullom Act (Interstate Commerce)
Feb. 4, 1887, Ch. 104, 24 Stat. 379, 49 U.S.
Code §§ 1 to 15, 16, 17 to 19, 20, 21, 22

Culpable Negligence Act
Fla. Stat. Ann., 784.05
Miss. Code Ann., § 97-3-47

Culpeper Parking Authority Act
Va. Acts 1976, Ch. 584

Cultivable Public Lands Sales Law
Cal. Public Resources Code § 7351 et seq.

Cultural Affairs and Arts Law
N.Y. Consol. Laws, Ch. 11c

Cultural Affairs Office Act
N.M. Stat. Ann., 9-6-7 et seq.

**Cultural and Educational Facilities
Authority Act**
Colo. Rev. Stat., 23-15-101 et seq.

Cultural and Scientific Facilities District Act
Colo. Rev. Stat., 32-13-101 et seq.

Cultural Arts Commission Act
R.I. Gen. Laws 1956, 16-46.1 et seq.

Cultural Basin Act
Tex. Government Code, § 781.001 et seq.

**Cultural Center and Historic Preservations
Bond Act**
N.J. Laws 1991, Ch. 265

Cultural Education Facilities Finance Corporation Act
Tex. Government Code, § 782.001 et seq.

Cultural Endeavors Act (Fund for Financing)
P.R. Laws Ann. 1954, Title 18, § 1701 et seq.

Cultural Properties Act
N.M. Stat. Ann., 18-6-1 et seq.

Cultural Properties Act (Abandoned)
N.M. Stat. Ann., 18-10-1 et seq.

Cultural Properties Preservation Easement Act
N.M. Stat. Ann., 47-12A-1 et seq.

Cultural Properties Protection Act
N.M. Stat. Ann., 18-6A-1 et seq.

Cultural Resources Act
N.Y. General Municipal Law (Consol. Laws Ch. 24) § 301 et seq.

Culture Act (Safety)
Mont. Code Ann., 39-71-1501 et seq.

Culture Development and Arts Administration Act
P.R. Laws Ann. 1954, Title 18 § 1159 et seq.

Cumberland Gap National Historical Park Act
June 11, 1940, Ch. 304, 54 Stat. 262, 16 U.S. Code §§ 261 to 264
May 26, 1943, Ch. 103, 57 Stat. 85, 16 U.S. Code §§ 261, 262
July 26, 1961, P.L. 87-111, 75 Stat. 224, 16 U.S. Code § 265

Cumberland Island National Seashore Act
Oct. 23, 1972, P.L. 92-536, 16 U.S. Code §§ 459i to 459i-9

Cumbres and Toltec Scenic Railroad Act
N.M. Stat. Ann., 16-5-1 et seq.

Cumbres and Toltec Scenic Railroad Compact Act
Colo. Rev. Stat., 24-60-1701, 24-60-1702

Cumming-Forsyth County Unification Commission Act
Ga. Laws 1991, p. 3611

Cummings Act (Attorneys)
Tenn. Code Ann., Superseded Vol., 29-110
Tenn. Public Acts 1955, Ch. 54

Cummins Acts
March 4, 1915, Ch. 176, 38 Stat. 1196, 49 U.S. Code § 20 (11)
Feb. 28, 1920, Ch. 91, 41 Stat. 456, 40 U.S. Code § 316; 49 U.S. Code §§ 1 to 6, 10 to 18, 19a 20, 20a, 26, 27, 71 to 74, 76 to 80, 141, 142

Cumulative Building Fund Act
Ind. Code Ann., 21-2-6-1 et seq.

Cumulative Sureties Statute
Ky. Rev. Stat. 1971, 134.230, 134.260, 134.280

Cunningham-Shell Tidelands Act
Cal. Statutes 1955, Ch. 1724, p. 3165

Curative Act
Neb. Rev. Stat. 1943, 76-258 et seq.

Curative Act (Deeds and Other Instruments)
Wyo. Stat. Ann., § 34-8-101 et seq.

Curative Act (Defective Conveyances)
Md. Ann. Code 1974, Art. RP, § 4-109

Curative Act (School Reorganization)
Kan. Stat. Ann., 72-5629

Curative Act (Tax Proceedings)
Cal. Statutes 1943, Ch. 458, p. 1993
Cal. Statutes 1945, Ch. 1134, p. 2176

Curators for Veterans Act
Kan. Stat. Ann., 73-501 et seq.

Curatorship of the Property of Absent Persons Act
La. Rev. Stat. Ann., 3:4101 et seq.

Curfew Act
Fla. Stat. Ann., 870.045

Mass. Gen. Laws Ann., 40:37A et seq.
N.H. Rev. Stat. 1955, 31:43a et seq.
Vt. Stat. Ann., Title 24, § 2151

Curfew Act (Child)
Ill. Rev. Stat. 1991, Ch. 23, § 2370.9 et seq.

Currency Act
See National Currency Act

Currency Act (Legal Tender Nts.)
May 31, 1878, Ch. 146, 20 Stat. 87, 31 U.S.
Code § 404

Currency Acts
June 3, 1864, Ch. 106, 13 Stat. 99
June 20, 1874, Ch. 343, 18 Stat. 123, 12 U.S.
Code §§ 38, 105, 121, 123, 126, 131, 176;
31 U.S. Code § 402
July 12, 1882, Ch. 290, 22 Stat. 162, 12 U.S.
Code §§ 146, 177, 178; 31 U.S. Code § 429
March 14, 1900, Ch. 41, 31 Stat. 45, 12 U.S.
Code §§ 51, 101, 177, 178, 542; 31 U.S.
Code §§ 146, 313, 314, 320, 406, 408, 410,
411, 429, 455, 751
May 30, 1908, Ch. 229, 35 Stat. 546, 12 U.S.
Code § 104

**Currency and Foreign Transactions
Reporting Act**
Oct. 26, 1970, P.L. 91-508, 84 Stat. 1118, 31
U.S. Code §§ 1051 to 1062, 1081 to 1083,
1101 to 1105, 1121, 1122

Currency Exchange Act
Ill. Comp. Stat. 1992, Ch. 205, § 405/0.01 et
seq.
Ind. Code Ann., 28-8-3-1 et seq.
Md. Ann. Code 1957, Art. 11, § 207 et seq.
Wis. Stat. 1989, 218.05

Currency Reduction Suspension Act
Feb. 4, 1868, Ch. 6, 15 Stat. 34

Currency Reporting Act
Ill. Comp. Stat. 1992, Ch. 205, § 685/1 et seq.

**Currency Transaction and Money
Laundering Reporting Act**
Utah Code Ann. 1953, 76-10-1901 et seq.

Current Income Tax Payment Act
Ga. Code Ann., 48-7-100 et seq.

Current Operations Appropriations Act
Ga. Laws 1991, Ch. 738
N.C. Laws 1985, Ch. 479
N.C. Laws 1990, Ch. 1066
N.C. Laws 1991, Chs. 500, 738
N.C. Laws 1992, Ch. 900

**Current Revenue Project Itemization Act
(Keystone Recreation Park and
Conservation Fund)**
Pa. 1995 Pamph. Laws, No. 56

Current Tax Payment Act of 1943
June 9, 1943, Ch. 120, 57 Stat. 126

Currituck Act (Racing)
N.C. Laws 1949, Ch. 541

Curt Flood Act of 1998
Oct. 27, 1998, P.L. 105-297, 112 Stat. 2824,
15 U.S. Code § 1 nt.

Curtailment Act (Oil)
Okla. Stat. Ann., Title 52, § 271 et seq.

Curtesy Act
Ark. Stat. 1947, 61-228
N.H. Rev. Stat. 1955, 560:3
N.J. Stat. Ann., 3B:28-1 et seq.
Wis. Stat. 1969, 233.23

Curtis Act (Five Civilized Tribes)
April 26, 1906, Ch. 1876, 34 Stat. 137

Curtis Act (Indians in Indian Territory)
June 28, 1898, Ch. 517, 30 Stat. 495

Curtis Act (Reclamation and Irrigation)
Feb. 13, 1911, Ch. 49, 36 Stat. 902, 43 U.S.
Code § 468

Curtsey Dower and Jointure Act
Va. Code 1950, § 64.1-19 et seq.

Curve Act (Road Crossing)
Ala. Code 1975, § 37-2-81

Custodial Account for Livestock Sellers Act
Ga. Code Ann., 4-6-20 et seq.

Custodial Accounts Act (University Employees)
Ill. Rev. Stat. 1991, Ch. 144, § 1700 et seq.

Custodial Act
Del. Code of 1974, Title 12, § 1188

Custodial Escheat Act
N.J. Stat. Ann., 2A:37-29 et seq.

Custodial Pay Act
Aug. 1, 1942, Ch. 543, 56 Stat. 733

Custodial Trust Act
See Uniform Custodial Trust Act

Custodian Act (Gifts to Minors)
Conn. Gen. Stat. Ann., § 45-101 et seq.

Custodian Law (Personal)
Mo. Rev. Stat. 1978, 404.410 et seq.

Custodians' Civil Service Law
Ore. Rev. Stat., 242.310 et seq.

Custody Act (Children)
Mich. Comp. Laws Ann., 722.21 et seq.
Okla. Stat. Ann., Title 10, § 25 et seq.
S.D. Codified Laws 1967, 25-4-45

Custody Act (Long-Term Foster Care)
N.J. Stat. Ann., 30:4C-26.10 et seq.

Custody and Grandparents Visitation Act
Pa. Purdon's Stat., Title 23, § 1001 et seq.

Custody and Support Act (Children)
N.C. Gen. Stat. 1943, § 50-13.1 et seq.

Custody Assistance Act (Relative)
Minn. Stat. 1986, 257.85

Custody Release and Bail Reform Act
Tenn. Code Ann., 40-11-101 et seq.

Custom Home Protection Act
Md. Ann. Code 1974, Art. RP, § 10-504 et seq.

Customer Choice and Competition Act (Electricity Generation)
Pa. Cons. Stat., Title 66. § 2801 et seq.

Customer Choice and Rate Relief Law (Electric Service)
Ill. Comp. Stat. 1992, Ch. 220, § 5/16-101 et seq.

Customer Service Act (Telecommunications)
Cal. Public Utilities Code § 2895 et seq.

Customer Service Act (Video)
Cal. Government Code § 53088 et seq.

Customer Service and Information Act (Cable Television and Video Provider)
Cal. Government Code § 53054 et seq.

Customized Job Training Act
Pa. Purdon's Stat., Title 24, § 6201 et seq.

Customized Training Act
Colo. Rev. Stat., 23-60-306

Customs Administration Acts
June 10, 1890, Ch. 407, 26 Stat. 131
Aug. 5, 1909, Ch. 6, 36 Stat. 91
Sept. 21, 1922, Ch. 356, 42 Stat. 948, 19 U.S. Code §§ 5, 257, 258, 261; 31 U.S. Code §§ 521, 549; 46 U.S. Code §§ 58, 321, 333
June 17, 1930, Ch. 497, 46 Stat. 708, 19 U.S. Code §§ 1401, 1402
June 25, 1938, Ch. 679, 52 Stat. 1077, 19 U.S. Code §§ 1304, 1308, 1309, 1314, 1315, 1317, 1321, 1401, 1402, 1451, 1459, 1460, 1467, 1484, 1485, 1491, 1499, 1501, 1516, 1520, 1524, 1528, 1553, 1557, 1558, 1559, 1562, 1563, 1598, 1603, 1607, 1609, 1613, 1623, 1653a, 1709; 46 U.S. Code § 331

Customs Administrative Act of 1970
June 2, 1970, P.L. 91-271, 84 Stat. 282, 19 U.S. Code §§ 2, 6, 32, 58, 66, 81, 81c, 151, 161, 167 to 169, 261, 267, 282, 293, 341, and others

Customs and Trade Act of 1990

Aug. 20, 1990, P.L. 101-382, 19 U.S. Code § 2101 nt.

Nov. 5, 1990, P.L. 101-508, 19 U.S. Code §§ 58c nt., 1613b nt., 2082

Dec. 8, 1993, P.L. 103-182, 19 U.S. Code § 2083

Nov. 2, 1994, P.L. 103-437, 16 U.S. Code § 620i

Dec. 8, 1994, P.L. 103-465, 19 U.S. Code § 1466 nt.

Oct. 11, 1996, P.L. 104-295, 19 U.S. Code §§ 1466 nt., 1553 nt.

Customs Bureau Act

March 3, 1927, Ch. 348, 44 Stat. 1381, 19 U.S. Code §§ 13, 52, 2071 to 2073; 2 U.S. Code § 163

Customs Court Act

See Court Of Customs Appeals Act

Customs Courts Act of 1970

June 2, 1970, P.L. 91-271, 84 Stat. 274, 28 U.S. Code §§ 253 to 257, 1541, 1582, 2601, 2602, 2631 to 2634, 2639

Customs Courts Act of 1980

Oct. 10, 1980, P.L. 96-417, 28 U.S. Code § 1 nt.

Customs Employees Salaries Act

May 29, 1928, Ch. 865, 45 Stat. 955, 19 U.S. Code §§ 6a to 6d

Customs Enforcement Act of 1986

Oct. 27, 1986, P.L. 99-570, 19 U.S. Code § 1654 nt.

Customs Procedural Reform and Simplification Act of 1978

Jan. 12, 1983, P.L. 97-456, 19 U.S. Code § 2075

Oct. 30, 1984, P.L. 98-573, 19 U.S. Code § 1330

April 7, 1986, P.L. 99-272, 19 U.S. Code § 2075

Oct. 21, 1986, P.L. 99-509, 19 U.S. Code § 2075

Oct. 27, 1986, P.L. 99-570, 100 Stat. 3299

Dec. 22, 1987, P.L. 100-203, 19 U.S. Code § 2075

Nov. 18, 1988, P.L. 100-690, 19 U.S. Code § 2075

Dec. 7, 1989, P.L. 101-207, 19 U.S. Code § 2075

Aug. 20, 1990, P.L. 101-382, 19 U.S. Code § 2075

Customs Reorganization Act

Aug. 24, 1912, Ch. 355, 37 Stat. 434, 16 U.S. Code §§ 421, 451; 19 U.S. Code §§ 31, 44, 55, 57, 58; 20 U.S. Code § 84; 24 U.S. Code §§ 171, 282; 31 U.S. Code § 177; 40 U.S. Code §§ 68, 280; 44 U.S. Code §§ 40, 283

Customs Simplification Act of 1953

Aug. 8, 1953, Ch. 397, 67 Stat. 407, 19 U.S. Code §§ 258, 258 nt., 1304, 1308, 1309, 1313, and others

Customs Simplification Act of 1954

Sept. 1, 1954, Ch. 1213, 68 Stat. 1136, 18 U.S. Code § 545; 19 U.S. Code §§ 160, 161, 1301a, 1332 nt., 1441, 1451, 1581, 1595a, 1605, 1607, 1610, 1612; 46 U.S. Code § 91; 48 U.S. Code §§ 1421e, 1644

Aug. 2, 1956, Ch. 894, 70 Stat. 955, 19 U.S. Code § 1332 nt.

May 19, 1958, P.L. 85-418, 72 Stat. 120, 19 U.S. Code § 1332 nt.

Customs Simplification Act of 1956

Aug. 2, 1956, Ch. 887, 70 Stat. 943, 19 U.S. Code §§ 2 nt., 160 nt., 1336, 1351 nt., 1401a, 1402, 1500, 1583; 31 U.S. Code §§ 372, 711

Cut-Over and Wild Land Tax Exemption Act

Mich. Comp. Laws Ann., 211.561 et seq.

Cuthbert-Randolph Airport Authority Act

Ga. Laws 1971, p. 2837

Cuyahoga County Jury Act

Ohio Laws Vol. 74, p. 218

Cy Pres Act

Ala. Code 1975, § 35-4-251

Cal. Civil Code § 715.5

Ida. Code 1947, 55-111

Continued

La. Rev. Stat. Ann., 9:2331 et seq.

Mass. Gen. Laws Ann., 214:3, Subd. 10

Md. Ann. Code 1974, Art. ET, § 14-302 et seq.

Me. Rev. Stat. Ann. 1964, Title 33, § 101 et seq.

Mo. Rev. Stat., 442.555

N.Y. Estates, Powers and Trusts Law (Consol. Laws Ch. 17B) § 8-1.1

Ohio Rev. Code 1953, 2131.08

Pa. 1855 Pamph. Laws 328, No. 347

Va. Code 1950, §§ 55-31, 55-32

Vt. Stat. Ann., Title 14, § 2328

Cycle Rider Safety Training Act

Ill. Comp. Stat. 1992, Ch. 625, § 35/1 et seq.

Czechoslovakian Claims Settlement Act

Aug. 8, 1958, P.L. 85-604, 72 Stat. 527, 22 U.S. Code §§ 1641c, 1641j, 1642 to 1642p

Czechoslovakian Claims Settlement Act of 1981

Dec. 29, 1981, P.L. 97-127, 22 U.S. Code prec. § 1642 nt.

D

D. A. R. E. (Drug Abuse Resistance Education) Act
Fla. Stat. Ann., 233.0661 et seq.
Mont. Code Ann., 15-30-158, 44-2-701 et seq.

Dade County Port Authority Act
Fla. Laws 1945, Ch. 22963

Dade County Registration Act
Fla. Laws 1945, Ch. 22971

Dade County Water Authority Act
Ga. Laws 1958, p. 3260

Dahlonega Community Improvement Districts Act
Ga. Laws 1991, p. 4649

Daily Deposit Act (County Funds)
N.C. Gen. Stat. 1943, § 153-135

Daily Living Centers for Older Adult Licensing Act
Pa. Purdon's Stat., Title 62, § 1511.1 et seq.

Dairies and Creameries Act
Miss. Code Ann. 1972, § 75-31-1 et seq.

Dairy Act
Cal. Food and Agricultural Code 1967, §§ 32501, 61301 et seq.
Ga. Code Ann., 26-2-230
Ill. Rev. Stat. 1981, Ch. 56 1/2, § 221 et seq.
Kan. Stat. Ann., 65-701 et seq.
Md. Ann. Code 1974, Art. HG, 321-401 et seq.
Minn. Stat. Ann., 32.01 et seq.
N.M. Stat. Ann., 25-7-1 et seq.
Okla. Stat. Ann., Title 2, § 7-1 et seq.
S.C. Code Ann. 1976, § 39-33-10 et seq.
Tenn. Code Ann., 53-3-101 et seq.

Dairy and Food Act
Ore. Rev. Stat. 1953, 616.005 et seq.

Dairy and Food Inspection Act
Mich. Comp. Laws Ann., 289.35 et seq.

Dairy and Tobacco Adjustment Act of 1983
Nov. 29, 1983, P.L. 98-180, 7 U.S. Code § 1421 nt.
Dec. 23, 1985, P.L. 99-198, 7 U.S. Code § 511r
Aug. 11, 1988, P.L. 100-387, 102 Stat. 932, 7 U.S. Code § 1427 nt.
Nov. 5, 1990, P.L. 101-508, 7 U.S. Code § 511r

Dairy Council of California Act
Cal. Food and Agricultural Code 1967, § 64001 et seq.

Dairy Establishment Sanitation Act
N.M. Stat. Ann., 25-7B-1 et seq.

Dairy, Farm and Business Emergency Assistance Act
Wis. Laws 1983, Act 92

Dairy Farm Stabilization Act
Me. Rev. Stat. Ann. 1964, Title 36, § 4541 et seq.

Dairy, Food and Drug Act
Wis. Stat. Ann., 97.01 et seq.

Dairy Industry Act
Iowa Laws 1939 (48th G. A.), Ch. 90

Dairy Industry Advisory Board Act
Cal. Food and Agricultural Code 1967, § 64001 et seq.

Dairy Industry Commission Act
Vt. Acts 1953, No. 249

Dairy Industry Development Act
Neb. Laws 1992, L.B. 275

Dairy Industry Indemnity Act
N.M. Stat. Ann., 77-6-1 et seq.

Dairy Industry Marketing Act
S.D. Codified Laws 1967, 37-3-8 et seq.

Dairy Industry Promotion Act
La. Rev. Stat. Ann., 3:557.1 et seq.
Tenn. Public Acts 1984, Ch. 948

Dairy Industry Regulation Act
Mont. Code Ann., 81-21-101 et seq.

Dairy Industry Stabilization Act
Ark. Acts 1967, p. 650, No. 306
S.C. Code Ann. 1976, Superseded Vols.,
§ 39-33-1010 et seq.

Dairy Industry Trade Practices Act
Neb. Rev. Stat. 1943, 81-263.37 et seq.

Dairy Industry Unfair Trade Practices Act
Minn. Stat. Ann., 32A.01 et seq.

Dairy Inspection Act
Ga. Code 1933, 42-501 et seq.

Dairy License Act
Vt. Stat. Ann., Title 6, § 2721 et seq.
Wyo. Stat. Ann., § 35-7-513

Dairy Market Testing and Milk Manufacturing Law
Mo. Rev. Stat., 196.520 et seq.

Dairy Marketing Act
Wyo. Stat. Ann., § 11-36-101 et seq.

Dairy Practices Act
Kan. Stat. Ann., 50-501 et seq.

Dairy Pricing Interstate Compact (Northeast)
Vt. Stat. Ann., Title 6, § 1801 et seq.

Dairy Product Act
N.M. Stat. Ann., 25-7A-1 et seq.

Dairy Production Act
Tenn. Code Ann., 53-3-101 et seq.

Dairy Production Stabilization Act of 1983
Nov. 29, 1983, P.L. 98-180, Title I, 7 U.S. Code § 1421 nt.
Dec. 23, 1985, P.L. 99-198, 7 U.S. Code § 4531 et seq.

April 4, 1996, P.L. 104-127, 7 U.S. Code § 4504

Dairy Products Act
Colo. Rev. Stat., 35-24-101 et seq.
Iowa Code Ann., 192.5 et seq.
Mich. Comp. Laws Ann., 288.21 et seq.
Mont. Code Ann., 81-22-101 et seq.
N.J. Rev. Stat. 1937, 24:10-57.1 et seq.
Wash. Rev. Code Ann., 15.32.010 et seq.

Dairy Products Act (Discrimination in Buying)
S.D. Codified Laws 1967, 37-3-1 et seq.

Dairy Products Act (Filled)
See Filled Dairy Products Act

Dairy Products Act (Licenses)
S.D. Codified Laws 1967, 40-32-1 et seq.

Dairy Products Commission Act
Wash. Rev. Code Ann., 15.44.010 et seq.

Dairy Products Dealers Act
Okla. Stat. Ann., Title 2, § 7-321 et seq.

Dairy Products Marketing Act
Iowa Code Ann., 192A.1 et seq.

Dairy Products Plant Act
Ore. Rev. Stat. 1953, 621.151 et seq.

Dairy Products Promotion Act
N.D. Cent. Code, 4-27-01 et seq.

Dairy Products Regulation Act
N.D. Cent. Code, 4-30-01 et seq.

Dairy Promotion Act
Ala. Code 1975, § 2-13-110 et seq.
Minn. Stat. 1980, 32B.01 et seq.
Miss. Code Ann. 1972, § 69-35-1 et seq.
N.Y. Agriculture and Markets Law (Consol. Laws Ch. 69) § 258aa
Utah Code Ann. 1953, 4-22-2 et seq.

Dairy Statistics Act
Ill. Comp. Stat. 1992, Ch. 505, § 50/0.01 et seq.
Ill. Rev. Stat. 1991, Ch. 5, § 90h.9 et seq.

Dairy Trade Practices Act
Wis. Stat. Ann., 100.201

Dakota Interstate Low-Level Radioactive Waste Management Compact Act
N.D. Cent. Code, 23-20.5-01 et seq.

Dale Bumpers Wilderness Resources Protection Act
Oct. 7, 1998, P.L. 105-245, 112 Stat. 1858

D'Alesandro Repatriation Act
See Citizenship Acts

Dallas County Road Act
Tex. Laws 52nd Leg., 1951, p. 563, Ch. 328

Dalton Airport Authority Ordinance
Ga. Laws 1988, p. 5201

Dalton City Limits Extension Act
Ga. Laws 1946, p. 477, No. 2

Dalton Police and Fire Department Organization Act
Ga. Laws 1945, p. 593

Dalton Police and Firemen Pension Act
Ga. Laws 1945, p. 593, § 15 et seq.

Dalton Street Improvement Act
Ga. Laws 1923, p. 593
Ga. Laws 1991, p. 5309

Dalworthington Gardens Municipal Courts of Record Act
Tex. Government Code, § 30.01371 et seq.

Dam Act
Cal. Water Code § 6000 et seq.
N.H. Rev. Stat. 1955, 482:1 et seq.
Vt. Stat. Ann., Title 10, § 1081 et seq.

Dam Act (McHenry County)
Ill. Rev. Stat. 1991, Ch. 19, § 1350 et seq.

Dam Acts
June 21, 1906, Ch. 3508, 34 Stat. 386
June 23, 1910, Ch. 360, 36 Stat. 593, 33 U.S. Code Ch. 9 nt.

Dam Authority Act (Grand River)
Okla. Stat. Ann., Title 82, § 861 et seq.

Dam Construction Act
Ida. Code 1947, 42-1710 et seq.
Mich. Comp. Laws Ann., 281.131 et seq.

Dam Control Act
W. Va. Code 1966, § 20-5D-1 et seq.

Dam Control and Safety Act
W. Va. Code 1966, § 2-14-1 et seq.

Dam Loan Act (Mystic River)
Mass. Acts 1957, Ch. 647

Dam Registration, Abandonment and Water Level Act
Me. Rev. Stat. Ann. 1964, Title 38, § 815 et seq.

Dam Safety Act
Haw. Rev. Stat. Ann., § 179D-1 et seq.
Mich. Comp. Laws Ann., 281.1301 et seq.
Mont. Code Ann., 85-15-105 et seq.
N.C. Gen. Stat. 1943, § 143-215.23 et seq.
Okla. Stat. Ann., Title 82, § 110.1 et seq.

Dam Safety and Encroachment Act
Pa. Purdon's Stat., Title 32, § 693.1 et seq.

Dam Supervision Act
Cal. Water Code § 6000 et seq.

Dam Use Act (Water)
Ill. Rev. Stat. 1991, Ch. 96 1/2, §§ 8150, 8151

Damage Act (Railroads)
S.D. Codified Laws 1967, 49-26-5 et seq.

Damage Act (Treble Contracts)
Tenn. Code Ann., 47-50-109

Damage Disclosure Act (Motor Vehicle)
S.C. Code Ann. 1976, §§ 56-32-10, 56-32-20

Damage Limitation Act (Wrongful Death)
Colo. Rev. Stat., 13-21-201 et seq.

Damage Prevention Act (Underground Utility)
Kan. Stat. Ann., 66-1801 et seq.

Damage Prevention Act (UnderGround)
N.C. Gen. Stat. 1943, § 87-100 et seq.

Damage Prevention and Safety Act (Underground Facility)
Fla. Stat. Ann., 556.101 et seq.

Damage Prevention and Safety Act (Underground Utility)
Del. Code of 1974, Title 26, § 801 et seq.

Damage Waiver Act (Collision)
Kan. Stat. Ann., 50-654 et seq.

Damaged and Destroyed Records and Documents Act
Cal. Evidence Code § 1601

Damages Act
Cal. Civil Code § 3281 et seq.
Mass. Gen. Laws Ann., 138:69 et seq.
Mo. Rev. Stat., 537.010 et seq.
Mont. Code Ann., 27-1-201 et seq.
S.D. Codified Laws 1967, 21-3-1 et seq.

Damages Act (Escaped Inmate)
Ill. Rev. Stat. 1991, Ch. 23, §§ 4040, 4041

Damages by Mobs and Riots Act (Liability)
N.Y. General Municipal Law (Consol. Laws Ch. 24) § 71

Dams Act
Vt. Stat. Ann., Title 10, § 1081 et seq.

Dams Act (General)
Cal. Water Code § 6000 et seq.

Dams and Reservoirs Safety Act
S.C. Code Ann. 1976, § 49-11-110 et seq.

Dams, Mills and Electric Power Act
Mo. Rev. Stat., 236.010 et seq.

Dance Hall Act
Minn. Stat. 1988, 624.42 et seq.

Ore. Rev. Stat. 1953, 464.110 et seq.
S.D. Codified Laws 1967, 42-4-1 et seq.
Wash. Rev. Code Ann., 67.12.021 et seq.

Dance Hall-Beer Act
Okla. Stat. 1971, Title 37, § 211 et seq.

Dance Studio Act
Cal. Civil Code § 1812.80 et seq.
Fla. Stat. Ann., 501.143
Ill. Comp. Stat. 1992, Ch. 815, § 610/1 et seq.
Ill. Rev. Stat. 1991, Ch. 29, § 50-1 et seq.

Dangerous Animals Act
Ill. Comp. Stat. 1992, Ch. 815, § 610/1 et seq.
Ill. Rev. Stat. 1991, Ch. 8, § 240 et seq.

Dangerous Cargo Act
Oct. 9, 1940, Ch. 777, 54 Stat. 1023 (See 18 U.S. Code §§ 831 to 835) 46 U.S. Code §§ 170 to 170b, 391a, 402, 414, 463a

Dangerous Dog Control Act
Ga. Code Ann., 4-8-20 et seq.

Dangerous Drug Act
Tex. Health and Safety Code, § 483.001 et seq.

Dangerous Drug Act for the District of Columbia
July 24, 1956, Ch. 676, 70 Stat. 622, 42 U.S. Code §§ 257, 260, 260a

Dangerous Drug Diversion Control Act of 1984
Oct. 12, 1984, P.L. 98-473, 21 U.S. Code § 801 nt.

Dangerous Drug Tax Act
Mont. Laws 1987, Ch. 563, § 1 et seq.

Dangerous Drugs Act
Cal. Business and Professions Code § 4211 et seq.
Colo. Rev. Stat., 12-22-401 et seq.
D.C. Code 1973, § 33-501 et seq.
Ga. Code Ann., 16-13-70 et seq.
Ill. Rev. Stat. 1983, Ch. 91 1/2, § 120.1 et seq.
Ind. Code Ann., 16-6-8-1 et seq.

Ky. Rev. Stat. 1971, Superseded Vols.,
217.721 et seq.
Md. Ann. Code 1957, Art. 27, § 307 et seq.
Mich. Comp. Laws Ann., 333.7101 et seq.,
333.7401 et seq.
Mont. Code Ann., 45-9-101 et seq.
N.M. Stat. Ann. 1953, 54-6-20 et seq.
Ohio Rev. Code 1953, 4729.50 et seq.
Pa. 1955 Pamph. Laws 913, No. 281
P.R. Laws Ann. 1954, Title 24, § 930 et seq.
S.C. Code Ann. 1976, § 44-53-110 et seq.
Va. Code 1950, § 54-440 et seq.
Wis. Stat. Ann., 161.001 et seq.

Dangerous Drugs Therapeutic Research Act
Colo. Rev. Stat. 25-5-901 et seq.
N.J. Stat. Ann. 26:2L-1 et seq.

Dangerous Machinery Law
Ky. Rev. Stat. 1962, 338.011 et seq.

Dangerous Occupation Act
Ind. Code 1971, 22-11-4-1 et seq.

Dangerous Persons Act (Sexually)
Ill. Rev. Stat. 1991, Ch. 38, § 105 et seq.

Dangerous Substances Act
P.R. Laws Ann. 1954, Title 24, § 2701 et seq.

Dangerous Substances Act (Controlled)
La. Rev. Stat. Ann., 40:961 et seq.
Md. Ann. Code 1957, Art. 27, § 276 et seq.
N.J. Stat. Ann., 24:21-1 et seq.

Dangerous Substances Registry Act
N.J. Stat. Ann. 1937, 2C:35

**Dangerous Substances Therapeutic
Research Act**
N.J. Stat. Ann., 26:2L-I et seq.

Dangerous Weapons Act
D.C. Code 1973, § 22-3201 et seq.
Okla. Stat. Ann., Title 21, § 645
Wash. Rev. Code Ann., 9.41.250
W. Va. Code 1966, § 61-7-1 et seq.

Dangerous Weapons Control Act
Cal. Penal Code § 12000 et seq.

Dangs Act (Taxes)
Wis. Stat. Ann., 74.03

Daniels-Bach-Juett Act (Counties—Leases)
Ky. Acts 1940, Ch. 44

Daniels-Cramer School Act
Ohio Rev. Code 1953, 3313.48, 3317.01 et
seq.

Danish Friendship Treaty (1846)
Haw. Statutes Laws Vol. 2, p. 103, Oct. 19,
1846

Danish West Indies Acquisition Act
See Virgin Islands Acquisition Act

**Dante B. Fascell North-South Center Act of
1991**
Oct. 28, 1991, P.L. 102-138, 22 U.S. Code
§ 2075

**Dante Fascell Biscayne National Park
Visitor Center Designation Act**
Oct. 29, 1998, P.L. 105-307, 112 Stat. 2931,
16 U.S. Code § 410gg nt.

Danvers School Loan Act
Mass. Acts 1949, Ch. 523

**Dare County Law Enforcement Officers'
Relief Act**
N.C. Laws 1963, Ch. 411

Dartmouth Rechartering Act
N.H. Laws 1816, June Session Ch. 35

Dartsmouth Water Loan Act
Mass. Acts 1955, Ch. 22

**Data and Information Technology
Resources Act (Security)**
Fla. Stat. Ann., 282.318

**Data Communications Act (Intergovern-
mental)**
Neb. Rev. Stat. 1943, 81-2301 et seq.

Data Facility Act (Federal)
Mich. Comp. Laws Ann., 3.951

Data Processing Act
Ind. Code Ann., 4-13-6-1 et seq.

Data Processing Act (Law Enforcement Agency)
N.M. Stat. Ann., 15-1-1 et seq.

Data Processing Authority Act
Miss. Code Ann. 1972, § 25-53-1 et seq.

Data Processing Confidentiality Act
Ill. Comp. Stat. 1992, Ch. 30, § 585/0.01 et seq.
Ill. Rev. Stat. 1991, Ch. 127, § 2900 et seq.

Data Processing Planning and Management Act
Okla. Stat. Ann., Title 62, § 41.5a et seq.

Database and Databank Act (DNA)
Me. Rev. Stat. Ann. 1964, Title 25, § 1571 et seq.
N.J. Stat. Ann., 53:1-20.17 et seq.

Database Commission Act (Medical)
N.C. Gen. Stat. 1943, § 131E-210 et seq.

Dating Referral Services Act
Ill. Comp. Stat. 1992, Ch. 815, § 615/1 et seq.

Dating Service Act
Ga. Code Ann., 10-1-1000 et seq.

D.A.V. Motor Vehicle Registration Certificate and Identification Tag Act
D.C. Code Ann., § 40-103

Dave Elder Public Employees' System Member Home Loan Program Act
Cal. Government Code § 20215

Dave Elder State Teachers' Retirement System Home Loan Program Act
Cal. Education Code 1976, § 22360

David A. DeBolt Teacher Shortage Scholarship Program
Ill. Comp. Stat. 1992, Ch. 110, § 947/52

David L. Boren National Security Education Act of 1991
Dec. 4, 1991, P.L. 102-183, 50 U.S. Code § 1901 et seq.
Oct. 24, 1992, P.L. 102-496, 50 U.S. Code §§ 1901 to 1904
Nov. 30, 1993, P.L. 103-160, 50 U.S. Code § 1904
Sept. 23, 1996, P.L. 104-201, 50 U.S. Code §§ 1902, 1903, 1906, 1908
Oct. 7, 1998, P.L. 105-244, 50 U.S. Code § 1908
Oct. 20, 1998, P.L. 105-272, 50 U.S. Code §§ 1901 to 1903, 1906

Davidson County Act (General Sessions Court)
Tenn. Private Acts 1937, Ch. 12

Davidson County Jury Commission Act
Tenn. Acts 1901, Ch. 124

Davidson County Pension Act
Tenn. Private Acts 1943, Ch. 274

Davidson, Travis, May and Overbey Act (State Colleges)
Ky. Rev. Stat. 1971, 164.290, 164.310

Davis Act (Teachers' Salaries)
N.Y. Laws 1900, Ch. 751

Davis-Areias Truth in Sentencing Act
Cal. Penal Code § 1191.3

Davis-Bacon Act
March 3, 1921, Ch. 411, 46 Stat. 1494, 40 U.S. Code § 276a
Aug. 30, 1935, Ch. 825, 49 Stat. 1011, 40 U.S. Code §§ 276a to 276a-5
July 12, 1960, P.L. 86-624, 74 Stat. 418, 40 U.S. Code § 276a
July 2, 1964, P.L. 88-349, 78 Stat. 238, 40 U.S. Code § 276a
Mont. Code Ann., 18-2-401 et seq.

Davis-Beacon Act (Little)
N.M. Stat. Ann., 13-4-11 et seq.

Davis-Dolwing Act (Water Projects)
Cal. Water Code § 11900 et seq.

Davis-Garamendi Senior Citizens Housing Assistance Act
Cal. Health and Safety Code § 51450 et seq.

Davis-Grisham Missing Children Act
Cal. Education Code 1976, § 40048
Cal. Statutes 1986, Ch. 249

Davis-Grunsky Act (State Financial Assistance for Local Water Projects)
Cal. Water Code § 12880 et seq.

Davis-Lyon Act (Merger or Consolidation of Cities)
Ky. Rev. Stat. 1971, 81.410 et seq.

Davis-Stirling Common Interest Development Act
Cal. Civil Code § 1350 et seq.

Davis Strang Act
Ala. Code 1975, 41-9-708 et seq.

Dawes Act (Indians)
See Indian General Allotment Act

Dawes Act (Marriage with Indian Women)
Aug. 9, 1888, Ch. 818, 25 Stat. 392, 25 U.S. Code §§ 181 to 183

Dawson-Terrell County Airport Authority Act
Ga. Laws 1997, p. 3696

Day Act
Ky. Rev. Stat. 1962, 158.020, 158.990

Day Care Act (Adult)
Okla. Stat. Ann., Title 63, § 1-871 et seq.
Pa. 1959 Pamph. Laws 1353, No. 466
Tex. Human Resources Code § 103.001 et seq.

Day Care Facilities Act (Child)
S.C. Code Ann. 1976, § 20-7-2700 et seq.

Day Care Home Act (Family)
R.I. Gen. Laws 1956, 42-72.1-1 et seq.

Day Care License Act (Children)
Pa. 1959 Pamph. Laws 1395, No. 494

Day Care Policy Act
D.C. Code Ann., § 3-301 et seq.

Day Care Provider Registration Act
N.J. Stat. Ann., 30:5B-16 et seq.

Day Child Care Program Act (Extended)
Mo. Rev. Stat. 1978, 167.290 et seq.

Day in Court (Automobile Dealers)
Ga. Code Ann., 10-1-630, 10-1-631

Day of Rest Act
Cal. Labor Code § 550 et seq.
Ga. Code Ann., 10-1-570 et seq.
Mass. Gen. Laws Ann., 136:1 et seq.
N.Y. Labor Law (Consol. Laws Ch. 31) § 161
Vt. Stat. Ann., Title 13, § 3351 et seq.
Wis. Stat. Ann., 103.85

Daylight Saving Time Act
Cal. Government Code § 6807-1 et seq.
Colo. Rev. Stat. 2-4-109
D.C. Code 1973, 2711
Iowa Code Ann., 122A.1, 122A.2
Mass. Gen. Laws Ann., 4:10
Md. Ann. Code 1957, Art. 94, § 3
N.Y. General Construction Law (Consol. Laws Ch. 22) § 52

Daylight Savings Acts
See Standard Time Acts
See War Time Act

Dayton-Andrews Act (Campaign Expenses)
Fla. Stat. 1971, 99.161

Dayton Aviation Heritage Preservation Act of 1992
Oct. 16, 1992, P.L. 102-419, 16 U.S. Code § 410ww et seq.
Nov. 12, 1996, P.L. 104-333, 16 U.S. Code § 410ww-21

Daytona Beach Civil Service Act
Fla. Special Laws 1943, Ch. 22253

Daytona Beach Downtown Improvement Authority Act
Fla. Special Laws 1972, Ch. 72-520

Daytona Beach Local Improvement Act
Fla. Special Laws 1945, Ch. 23236, 1967
Fla. Special Laws 1967, Ch. 67-1277

Daytona Beach Sewer Revenue Bond Act
Fla. Special Laws 1945, Ch. 23240

Daytona Beach Urban Renewal Law
Fla. Laws 1961, Ch. 61-2067

Daytona Beach Utilities Revenue Bond Act
Fla. Special Laws 1945, Ch. 23242

Daytona Beach-Volusia County Improvement Authority Act
Fla. Special Laws 1951, Ch. 27963

Daytona Beach Water Revenue Bond Act
Fla. Special Laws 1945, Ch. 23237

D.C. General Hospital Commission Act
D.C. Code Ann., § 32-201 et seq.

D.C. Register Publication Act
D.C. Code Ann., § 1-1505

De Kalb County Civil Service Act
Ga. Laws 1951, p. 3226

De Kalb County Coliseum Authority Act
Ga. Laws 1969, p. 2567

De Kalb County Merit System Act
Ga. Laws 1956, p. 3111

De Kalb County Oglethorpe Housing Development Authority Act
Ga. Laws 1974, p. 2591
Ga. Laws 1975, p. 3053

De Kalb County Pension Act
Ga. Laws 1953 (Nov.-Dec. Sess.), p. 3198

De Kalb County Planning Commission Act
Ga. Laws 1956, p. 3332

De Kalb County Road Act
Tenn. Private Acts 1931, Ch. 558

De Novo Statute
N.D. Cent. Code, 28-27-32

De Villier-Belmont Improvement Board Act
Fla. Special Laws 1975, Ch. 75-483

Dead Agent Act (Witnesses)
Wis. Stat. Ann., 885.17

Dead Animal Act
Pa. Purdon's Stat., Title 31, § 501 et seq.

Dead Animal Disposal Act
Ga. Code Ann., 4-5-1 et seq.
Ill. Rev. Stat. 1991, Ch. 8, § 149.1 et seq.
Ind. Code Ann., 15-2.1-16-1 et seq.
Iowa Code Ann., 167.1 et seq.
Mich. Comp. Laws Ann., 287.231 et seq.
Mo. Rev. Stat., 269.010 et seq.
Wash. Rev. Code Ann., 16.68.010 et seq.

Dead Animals Disposal Act
Ill. Comp. Stat. 1992, Ch. 225, § 610/1.1 et seq.

Dead Bodies Act (Burial of)
Ill. Comp. Stat. 1992, Ch. 410, §§ 5/1, 5/2

Dead Body Disposal Law
Iowa Code 1966, 141.1 et seq.

Dead Head Act
N.M. Stat. Ann., 30-23-2

Dead Head Act (Public Pay Roll)
La. Rev. Stat. Ann., 14:138

Dead Man's Act
Ala. Code 1975, § 12-21-163
Ariz. Rev. Stat. Ann., § 12-2251
Ark. Const. 1874, Schedule, § 2
Cal. Evidence Code § 1261
Colo. Rev. Stat., 13-90-102 et seq.
Conn. Gen. Stat. Ann., § 52-172
Del. Code of 1974, Title 10, § 4302
Fla. Stat. Ann., 90.05

Ga. Code Ann., 24-9-1 et seq.

Ida. Code 1947, 9-202

Ill. Comp. Stat. 1992, Ch. 735, § 5/8-201

Ill. Rev. Stat. 1991, Ch. 110, § 8-201

Ind. Code Ann., 34-1-14-6

Iowa Code Ann., 622.4, 622.5

Kan. Gen. Stat. 1949, 60-2804

Ky. Rev. Stat. 1971, 421.210

La. Rev. Stat. Ann., 13:3721, 13:3722

Mass. Gen. Laws Ann., 233:65

Md. Ann. Code 1974, Art. CJ, § 9-116 et seq.

Me. Rev. Stat. Ann. 1964, Title 16, § 1

Mich. Comp. Laws Ann., 600.2166

Minn. Stat. 1986, 595.04

Miss. Code Ann. 1972, § 13-1-7

Mo. Rev. Stat., 491.010

Mont. Rev. Code 1947, 93-701-3, Subd. 3

N.C. Gen. Stat. 1943, § 8C-1 Rule 601,c

N.D. Cent. Code, 31-01-03

N.D. Rules of Evidence, Rule 601

Neb. Rev. Stat. 1943, 25-1202

Nev. Rev. Stat. 1979 Reprint, 48.064

N.H. Rev. Stat. 1955, 516:25, 516:26

N.J. Rev. Stat. 1937, 2A:81-2

N.M. Stat. Ann. 1953, 20-2-5

N.Y. Civil Practice Law and Rules (Consol. Laws Ch. 8) § 4519

Ohio Rev. Code 1953, 2317.03

Okla. Stat. Ann., Title 12, § 2501

Ore. Rev. Stat. 1953, 41.850

R.I. Gen. Laws 1956, 9-19-9, 9-19-10

S.C. Code Ann. 1976, § 19-11-10 et seq.

S.D. Codified Laws 1967, 19-16-34

Tenn. Code Ann., 24-1-203

Tex. Rev. Civ. Stat., Art. 3716

Tex. Rules of Civ. Evid., Rule 601(b)

Utah Code Ann. 1953, 78-24-2,

Va. Code 1950, § 8.01-397

Vt. Stat. Ann., Title 12, § 1602 et seq.

Wash. Rev. Code Ann., 5.60.030

Wis. Stat. Ann., 885.16

W. Va. Code, § 57-3-1

Wyo. Stat. 1957, § 1-140

Dead Man's Act (Evidence)
Cal. Code of Civil Procedure § 1880 Subd. 3
Cal. Evidence Code § 667

N.C. Gen. Stat. 1943, § 8C-1 Rule 601, c

N.M. Stat. Ann. 1953, 20-2-5 et seq.

Ore. Rev. Stat. 1953, 41.850

Pa. Cons. Stat., Title 42, § 5930

R.I. Gen. Laws 1956, 6-19-9, 9-19-10

S.C. Code Ann. 1976, § 19-11-10 et seq.

Wis. Stat. Ann., 885.16

Deadbeat Parents Punishment Act of 1998
June 24, 1998, P.L. 105-187, 18 U.S. Code § 228 nt.

Deadlock Act (Corporate Dissolution)
N.Y. Business Corporations Law 1961 (Consol. Laws Ch. 4) § 1104 et seq.
Ore. Rev. Stat., 60.621

Deadlock Act (Corporations)
Ind. Code Ann., 23-1-47-1
Ky. Rev. Stat. 1971, Superseded Vol., 271.570
Minn. Stat. Ann., 302A.751
Mo. Rev. Stat., 351.485
N.J. Stat. Ann., 14A:12-7
N.Y. Business Corporation Law (Consol. Laws Ch. 4) § 1104
Ore. Rev. Stat. 1953, 57.595
Pa. 1933 Pamph. Laws 364, No. 106, § 1107
Wis. Stat. Ann., 180.771, Subsec. 1, Subd. a

Deadly Weapons Act
Cal. Penal Code § 12000 et seq.
Ill. Rev. Stat. 1991, Ch. 38, § 24-1 et seq.
Ky. Rev. Stat. 1971, 527.010 et seq.
Wash. Rev. Code Ann., 9.41.010 et seq.

Deadman-Jenema Act (Reforestation Fund)
Mich. Comp. Laws Ann., 320.71

Deaf and Blind School Building Act
Ga. Code Ann., 32-2801a

Deaf and Blind Schools Act (State)
Wash. Rev. Code Ann., 72.40.010 et seq.

Deaf and Hard of Hearing Commission Act
Ill. Comp. Stat. 1992, Ch. 20, § 3932/1 et seq.

Deaf and Hard of Hearing Services Act
Minn. Stat. Ann., 256C.21 to 256C.27

Deaf Interpreter Act
Mich. Comp. Laws Ann., 393.501 et seq.
N.M. Stat. Ann., 38-9-1 et seq.

Deaf or Blind School Transportation Act
Ill. Rev. Stat. 1991, Ch. 23, §§ 1209.9, 1210

Deafness Act (Division on)
Mich. Comp. Laws Ann., § 408.201 et seq.

Dealer Act (Multiline Heavy Equipment)
Ga. Code Ann., 10-1-730 et seq.

Dealer Bill of Rights Act (Gasoline)
Wash. Rev. Code, 1989, 19.120.010 et seq.

Dealer Financing Act
Utah Code Ann. 1953, 41-4-1 et seq.

Dealer Licensing Act (Motor Vehicles)
Colo. Rev. Stat., 12-6-101 et seq.
La. Rev. Stat. Ann., 32:1251 et seq.
Va. Code 1950, § 46.1-515 et seq.
Wash. Rev. Code Ann., 46.70.005 et seq.

Dealer Licensing and Livestock Market Agency Act
Minn. Stat. Ann., 17A.01 et seq.

Dealer-Manufacturer Licensing Act (Motor Vehicles)
Tenn. Code Ann., 55-17-101 et seq.

Dealer Reserve Income Adjustment Act of 1960
May 13, 1960, P.L. 86-459, 74 Stat. 124, 26 U.S. Code § 481 nt.

Dealer Tag Permit Law
See Uniform Dealer Tag Permit Law

Dealers Act (Produce)
See Produce Dealers Act

Dealers and Distributors Franchising Practices Act (Motor Vehicle)
Vt. Stat. Ann., Title 9, § 4083 et seq.

Dealers and Manufacturers Act (Farm Equipment)
Fla. Stat. Ann., 686.40 et seq.

Dealers and Warehousemen of Agricultural Products Act
Colo. Rev. Stat., 12-16-101.1 et seq.

Dealers' Chattel Mortgage Act
Colo. Rev. Stat. 1963, 21-2-1 et seq.
N.Y. Uniform Commercial Code (Consol. Law Ch. 38), § 9-101 et seq.

Dealers Commission Law (Motor Vehicles)
Pa. 1937 Pamph. Laws 2465, No. 461

Dealers Franchise Act (Motorcycle)
Wash. Rev. Code 1983, 46.94.001 et seq.

Dealers in Used Motor Vehicle Parts Registration Act
Ga. Code 1933, 84-4601 et seq.

Dealers' Licensing Act (Bird)
Ga. Code Ann., 4-10-1 et seq.

Dealers Registration Act (Motor Vehicles)
Kan. Stat. Ann., 8-2401 et seq.

Dealership Act (Agricultural Equipment)
Kan. Stat. Ann., 16-1201 et seq.
Minn. Stat. Ann., 325E.061 et seq.

Dealership Act (Motor Vehicles)
La. Rev. Stat. Ann., 32:1251

Dealership Act (Outdoor Power Equipment)
Kan. Stat. Ann., 16-1301 et seq.

Dean Act (Intoxicating Liquors)
Tex. Alcoholic Beverage Code, 101 et seq.
Tex. Penal Code 1925, Art. 666 et seq.

DeArmond Act (Miami and Erie Canal Partial Abandonment)
Ohio Laws Vol. 114, p. 546

Death Act
Alaska Stat. 1962, Replaced Titles, § 13.20.340
Ariz. Rev. Stat. Ann., § 12-611 et seq.
Colo. Stat. Ann. 1935, Ch. 50, §§ 2, 3
Conn. Gen. Stat. Ann., § 52-555
D.C. Code Ann., § 16-2701 et seq.

Haw. Rev. Stat. Ann., § 663-3
Ida. Code 1947, 5-310, 5-311
Mass. Gen Laws 1990, 229:1 et seq.
Mich. Comp. Laws Ann., 600.2922
Miss. Code Ann. 1972, § 11-7-13
Ore. Rev. Stat., 30.020
P.R. Laws Ann. 1954 Title 32, §§ 255, 311
W. Va. Code 1966, §§ 55-7-5, 55-7-6

Death Act (Absentee)
N.J. Stat. Ann. 3B:27-1 et seq.

Death Act (Brain)
Mont. Code Ann., 50-22-101

Death Act (Civil Rights)
Mo. Rev. Stat. 1978, 222.010
N.Y. Civil Rights Law (Consol. Laws Ch. 6) § 79a
N.Y. Estates, Powers, and Trusts Law (Consol. Laws Ch. 17B) § 5-4.1
Vt. Stat. Ann. 1959, Title 13, § 1451

Death Act (Civil)
Miss. Code Ann., §§ 99-19-35, 99-19-37

Death Act (Common Carriers)
N.M. Stat. Ann., 41-2-4

Death Act (Damages)
Iowa Code Ann., 613.15
Pa. Cons. Stat., Title 42, § 8301

Death Act (Dignified)
Mich. Comp. Laws Ann., 333.5651 et seq.

Death Act (Simultaneous)
See Uniform Simultaneous Death Act

Death Act (Survival of Actions)
Del. Code of 1974, Title 10, § 3701 et seq.
Ohio Rev. Code 1953, 2125.01 et seq.
Pa. Cons. Stat., Title 20, § 3371 et seq.
P.R. Laws Ann. 1954, Title 32, § 255
S.C. Code Ann. 1976, § 15-51-10 et seq.

Death Act (Wrongful)
See Wrongful Death Act

Death After Judgment Act
Okla. Stat. 1961, Title 12, § 1081

Death and Birth Registration Act
Ill. Rev. Stat. 1991, Ch. 111 1/2, § 73-1 et seq.

Death Benefit Act (Workmen's Compensation)
Ohio Rev. Code 1953, 4123.59 et seq.
Okla. Stat. Ann., Title 85, § 3.1 et seq.

Death Benefits Act
N.C. Gen. Stat. 1943, §§ 143-166.1 to 143-166.7

Death Certification in Cases of Catastrophic Events Act
P.R. Laws Ann. 1954, Title 24, § 1311 et seq.

Death Claim Act
Ind. Code Ann., 34-1-1-2

Death Gamble Act (Teachers' Retirement)
N.Y. Adm. City Code 1985, § 13-543

Death in Line of Duty Compensation Act
Ill. Rev. Stat. 1991, Ch. 48, § 281 et seq.

Death Investigation Act
Ga. Code Ann., 45-16-20 et seq.

Death of Minors Act
Fla. Stat. 1971, 768.03

Death on the High Seas Act
March 30, 1920, Ch. 111, 41 Stat. 537, 46 U.S. Code §§ 761 to 768

Death Penalty Act
Ill. Rev. Stat. 1991, Ch. 38, § 9-1
N.Y. Penal Law 1965 (Consol. Laws Ch. 40) §§ 125.30, 1045, 1045a
S.C. Code Ann. 1976, § 16-3-20 et seq.

Death Penalty Act (Effective)
Ark. Code 1987, 16-91-201 et seq.
S.C. Code Ann. 1976, §§ 16-3-21, 17-25-380, 17-27-130, 17-27-150, 17-27-160

Death Penalty Habeas Corpus Reform Act
Ga. Code Ann., 9-14-44 et seq., 15-1-9.1

Death Registration Law
Cal. Health and Safety Code § 10200 et seq.

Death Review Board Act (Child)
Okla. Stat. Ann., Title 10, § 1150 et seq.

Death Review Team Act (Child)
Ill. Comp. Stat. 1992, Ch. 20, § 515/1

Death Statute (Wrongful)
Cal. Code of Civil Procedure § 377 et seq.

Death Tax Act
Cal. Revenue and Taxation Code § 13301 et seq.
Ill. Rev. Stat. 1991, Ch. 120, § 405A-1 et seq.
Iowa Code Ann., 450.1 et seq.
Mass. Gen. Laws Ann., 65B:1 et seq.
Mich. Comp. Laws Ann., 205.201 et seq.
Miss. Code Ann. 1972, § 27-9-1 et seq.
Mont. Code Ann., 72-16-301 et seq.
N.H. Rev. Stat. 1955, 86:6 et seq.

Death Tax Apportionment Statute
La. Rev. Stat. Ann., 9:2431 et seq.

Death Taxes Act (Interstate)
Conn. Gen. Stat., § 12-371 et seq.

Death Taxes Compromise Act
Cal. Revenue and Taxation Code § 13801 et seq.

Death Taxes Compromise and Arbitration Act (Interstate)
Va. Code 1950 § 58.1-920 et seq.

Death Taxes Interstate Arbitration Act
See also Uniform Interstate Arbitration of Death Taxes Act
Cal. Revenue and Taxation Code § 13820 et seq.
Md. Ann. Code 1974, Art. TG, § 7-104 et seq.
Me. Rev. Stat. Ann. 1964, Title 36, § 3911 et seq.
Vt. Stat. Ann., Title 32, § 7101 et seq.

Death Taxes Interstate Compromise Act
See also Uniform Interstate Arbitration of Death Taxes Act
Md. Ann. Code 1974, Art. TG, § 7-118 et seq.
Me. Rev. Stat. Ann. 1964, Title 36, § 3981 et seq.
Vt. Stat. Ann., Title 32, § 7201 et seq.

Death Transfer Tax Act
Pa. Purdon's Stat., Title 72, § 2301 et seq.

Death With Dignity Act
Ark. Code Ann. 1987, 20-17-201 et seq.
Cal. Civil Code § 2525 et seq.
Del. Code of 1974, Title 16, § 2501 et seq.
Kan. Stat. Ann., 65-28,101 et seq.
Mich. Comp. Laws Ann., 333.5651 et seq.
N.M. Stat. Ann., 24-7-1 et seq.
Ore. Rev. Stat. 1953, 127.800 et seq.
S.C. Code Ann. 1976, § 44-77-10 et seq.

Deathbed Gift Act
Cal. Probate Code § 1050
Pa. 1855 Pamph. Laws 328, No. 347. § 11

Debate Transcript Act
Ill. Comp. Stat. 1992, Ch. 25, § 100/0.01 et seq.
Ill. Rev. Stat. 1991, Ch. 63, § 200 et seq.

Debenture Acts (Highway Treasury Anticipation)
Mont. Laws 1939, p. 743
Mont. Laws 1943, Ch. 217
Mont. Laws 1945, Ch. 39

Debit Card and Credit Card Act
Ill. Rev. Stat. 1981, Ch. 17, § 5901 et seq.

Debit Card Crime Act
Tenn. Code Ann., 39-3601 et seq.

Debris Damsite Title Law
Cal. Statutes 1901, Ch. 118, p. 282

Debt Act (Counties)
Ky. Rev. Stat. 1971, 66.280 et seq.

Debt Act (Income Tax Setoff for Child Support)
Miss. Code Ann., § 27-7-501 et seq.

Debt Act (Income Tax Setoff for Student Loans)
Miss. Code Ann., § 27-7-701 et seq.

Debt Adjusters Act
Conn. Gen. Stat. 36-364 et seq.
Kan. Stat. Ann., 21-4402
N.D. Cent. Code, 13-06-01 et seq.
N.H. Rev. Stat. 1955, 399-D:1 et seq.
N.J. Stat. Ann., 2C:21-19 et seq.

Debt Collection (Consumer Act)
Fla. Stat. 1981, 427.101 et seq.

Debt Collection Act
Minn. Stat. Ann., 16D.01 et seq.

Debt Collection Act (Setoff)
S.C. Code Ann. 1976, §§ 12-54-410 et seq., 12-56-10 et seq.

Debt Collection Improvement Act of 1996
April 26, 1996, P.L. 104-134, 31 U.S. Code § 3701 nt.

Debt Collection Procedures Act
Iowa Code Ann., 537.7101 et seq.
Me. Rev. Stat. Ann. 1964, Title 32, § 11001 et seq.
N.Y. General Business Law (Consol. Laws Ch. 20) 600 et seq.
Tex. Rev. Civ. Stat. 1974, Art. 5069-11.01 et seq.
Va. Code 1950, § 2.1-726 et seq.

Debt Default Act
See Johnson Debt Default Act

Debt Enabling Act (Capital Facilities)
Pa. Purdon's Stat., Title 72, § 1601A et seq.

Debt Funding Law
Tenn. Code Ann., 9-9-101 et seq.

Debt Impact Note Act
Ill. Rev. Stat. 1991, Ch. 63, § 42.71 et seq.

Debt Limit Act (Counties)
Wash. Rev. Code Ann., 36.67.010 et seq.

Debt Limit Act (Municipal Corporations)
Wash. Rev. Code Ann., 39.36.010 et seq.

Debt Limitation Act
See also National Debt Limitation Act
Ill. Rev. Stat. 1991, Ch. 85, § 851 et seq

Debt Limitation Act (Local Government)
Ill. Rev. Stat. 1991, Ch. 85, § 850 et seq.

Debt Limitation Law (Special Assessments)
Cal. Streets and Highways Code § 2900 et seq.

Debt Management Act
Ariz. Rev. Stat. Ann., § 6-701 et seq.
Mich. Comp. Laws Ann., 451.411 et seq.
Neb. Rev. Stat. 1943, 69-1201 et seq.
W. Va. Code, § 12-6A-1 et seq.

Debt Management Act (Public Corporation)
R.I. Gen. Laws 1956, 35-18-1 et seq.

Debt Management Act of 1983
W. Va. Code 1966, § 12-6A-1 et seq.

Debt Offering Act (Local Government)
Ill. Rev. Stat. 1991, Ch. 85, § 840 et seq.

Debt Policy Law and Procedures Act (State)
La. Rev. Stat. Ann., 39:1361 et seq.

Debt Pooling Act
Ohio Rev. Code 1953, 4710.01 et seq.

Debt Readjustment Act (Municipal Corporations)
Wash. Rev. Code Ann., 39.64.005 et seq.

Debt Refinancing Act
Tenn. Code Ann., 9-9-103 et seq.

Debt Service Aid Law
Minn. Stat. 1980, 475A.01 et seq.

Debtor and Creditor Law
N.Y. Consol. Laws, Ch. 12

Debtors Act (Fraudulent)
Ga. Code Ann., 18-2-20 et seq.

Debtors Exemption Act
Pa. Cons. Stat., Title 42, § 8121 et seq.

Decatur and Vermilion County Civic Center Act
Ill. Comp. Stat. 1992, Ch. 70, § 265/1 et seq.

Decatur and Vermillion Civic Centers Act
Ill. Rev. Stat. 1991, Ch. 85, § 1551 et seq.

Decatur County Emergency Communications Service District Act
Ga. Laws 1990, p. 3982

Decatur Parking Authority Act
Ga. Laws 1968, p. 2892

Decatur Tax Deferral for Elderly Act
Ga. Laws 1991, p. 3985

Deceased Person's Statute
W. Va. Code 1966, § 57-3-1

Deceased Veterans Act (Children of)
Ill. Comp. Stat. 1992, Ch. 330, §§ 105/0.01, 105/1

Decedents' Estates Act
Ind. Code Ann., 29-1-1-1 et seq.
Mich. Comp. Laws Ann., 702.1 et seq.
N.Y. Consol. Laws, Ch. 13

Decedents' Estates Act (Fiduciaries)
Pa. 1917 Pamph. Laws 447, No. 193

Decedents' Estates and Fiduciary Relations Act
D.C. Code 1973, § 18-101 et seq.

Decedents' Estates Nonclaim Act
Haw. Rev. Stat. Ann., § 560:3-801 et seq.

Decedents' Estates Reciprocity Act
Wis. Stat. Ann., 72.11, Subsec. 2

Decennial Census Improvement Act of 1991
Oct. 24, 1991, P.L. 102-135, 13 U.S. Code § 141 nt.

Deception and Truth Examiners Licensing Act
Neb. Rev. Stat. 1943, 81-1901

Deception Detection Act
Ky. Rev. Stat. 1971, 329.010 et seq.

Deception Detection Examiners Act
Utah Code Ann. 1953, 34-37-1 et seq.
Utah Code Ann. 1953, 53-5-301 et seq.

Deceptive Advertising Act
Ill. Rev. Stat. 1991, Ch. 121 1/2, § 157.21a et seq.

Deceptive and Unfair Trade Practices Act
Fla. Stat. Ann., 501.201 et seq.

Deceptive Business Practices Act
Pa. Cons. Stat., Title 18, § 4107

Deceptive Mailings Prevention Act of 1990
Nov. 6, 1990, P.L. 101-524, 39 U.S. Code §§ 413, 3001 nt., 3001, 3005

Deceptive or Misleading Advertisements Act
Mich. Comp. Laws Ann., 445.801 et seq.
Neb. Laws 1913, Ch. 104

Deceptive Practices Act
Ill. Comp. Stat. 1992, Ch. 815, § 505/1 et seq.

Deceptive Sale of Gold and Silver Act
Ill. Rev. Stat. 1991, Ch. 121 1/2, § 157.16 et seq.

Deceptive Trade Practices Act
See also Uniform Deceptive Trade Practices Act
Ala. Code 1975, § 8-19-1 et seq.
Conn. Gen. Stat. 1983, § 42-115c et seq.
Del. Code of 1974, Title 6, § 2531 et seq.
Fla. Stat. 1971, 817.69 et seq.
Ga. Code Ann., 10-1-370 et seq.
Haw. Rev. Stat. Ann., § 481A-1 et seq.
Ida. Laws 1965, Ch. 293
Ill. Rev. Stat. 1991, Ch. 121 1/2, § 311 et seq.
Ind. Code Ann., 24-5-0.5-1 et seq.
Me. Rev. Stat. Ann. 1964, Title 10, § 1211
Minn. Stat. Ann., 325D.43 et seq.

Neb. Rev. Stat. 1943, 87-301 et seq.

N.M. Stat. Ann., 57-12-1 et seq.

Okla. Stat. Ann., Title 78, § 51 et seq.

Ore. Rev. Stat. 1953, 646.605 et seq.

R.I. Gen. Laws 1956, 6-13.1-1 et seq.

S.D. Codified Laws 1967, 37-24-1 et seq.

Tex. Business and Commerce Code, § 17.41 et seq.

Decisions Act (Health Care)
See Uniform Health Care Decisions Act

Declaration for Mental Health Treatment Act
Ida. Code 1947, 66-601 et seq.

Declaration of Death Act
N.J. Stat. Ann., 26:6A-1 et seq.

Declaration of Paternity Act (Voluntary)
Utah Code Ann. 1953, 78-45e-1 et seq.

Declaration of Rights Act (Hawaiian Citizens)
Haw. Session Laws 1925, Act 222

Declaration of Sheep Ownership Act
Wyo. Stat. 1957, § 11-466 et seq.

Declaration of Taking Act
Feb. 26, 1931, Ch. 307, 46 Stat. 1421, 40 U.S. Code §§ 258a, 258e

Declaration of War against Great Britain
June 18, 1812, Ch. 102, 2 Stat. 755

Declaration of War against Spain
April 25, 1898, Ch. 189, 30 Stat. 364

Declaration Terminating War with Germany and Austria-Hungary
July 2, 1921, Ch. 40, 42 Stat. 105

Declaratory Judgment Act
June 14, 1934, Ch. 512, 48 Stat. 955 (See 28 U.S. Code §§ 2201, 2202)

Declaratory Judgments Act
See also Uniform Declaratory Judgments Act
Alaska Stat. 1962, § 22.10.020, Subd. b
Cal. Code of Civil Procedure § 1060 et seq.

Conn. Gen. Stat. Ann., § 52-29

Haw. Rev. Stat. Ann., § 632-1 et seq.

Kan. Stat. Ann., 60-1701 et seq.

Ky. Rev. Stat. 1971, 418.040 et seq.

Mich. Comp. Laws 1948, 691.501 et seq.

Mont. Code Ann., 27-8-101 et seq.

N.H. Rev. Stat. 1955, 491:22

N.Y. Civil Practice Law and Rules (Consol. Laws Ch. 8) § 3001

Declaratory Judgments Act (Bond Issues)
Wash. Rev. Code Ann., 7.25.010 et seq.

Declaratory Judgments Act (Validity of Rules)
Mo. Rev. Stat., 536.050

Declaratory Procedure Act
Mass. Gen. Laws Ann., 231A:1 et seq.

Decommissioning Act (Nuclear Facility)
Cal. Public Utilities Code § 8321 et seq.

Decommissioning Financing Act (Nuclear)
Me. Rev. Stat. Ann. 1964, Title 35-A, § 4351 et seq.

Decorations and Awards Act
Okla. Stat. Ann., Title 44, § 195.1 et seq.

Decrees, Executions and Judgments Act
Ill. Rev. Stat. 1991, Ch. 110, § 12-101 et seq.

Deddeh-Mills Transit Development Act
Cal. Public Utilities Code § 120000 et seq.

Deddeh-Polanco Anti-Obscenity Act
Cal. Penal Code § 311 et seq.

Deddeh Transportation Bond Act
Cal. Streets and Highways Code § 2700 et seq.

Deddeh Transportation Improvement and Reform Act
Cal. Government Code § 14524.15
Cal. Streets and Highways Code §§ 163, 2600

Deddens Act (Water Pollution Control)
Ohio Rev. Code 1953, 6111.01 et seq.

Dedham Brook Improvement Loan Act
Mass. Acts 1956, Ch. 446

Dedicated Research Investment Act
La. Rev. Stat. Ann., 51:2201 et seq.

Dedicated Reserve Tax Act
Tex. Taxation-General 1959, Art. 3.11

Dedication Act
Wash. Rev. Code Ann., 58.17.010 et seq.

Deed of Trust Act
N.M. Stat. Ann., 48-10-1 et seq.

Deed Validation Act (Building and Loan)
Ill. Rev. Stat. 1991, Ch. 17, §§ 3642.9, 3643

Deed Valuation Act (Building and Loan)
Ill. Comp. Stat. 1992, Ch. 765, §§ 110/0.01,
110/1

Deeds Act
Mich. Comp. Laws Ann., 565.1 et seq.
Ohio Rev. Code 1953, 5301.01 et seq.
Wash. Rev. Code Ann., 64.04.010

Deeds Act (Short Form)
Me. Rev. Stat. Ann. 1964, Title 33, § 761 et
seq.

Deeds Tax Act
Wash. Rev. Code Ann., 82.20.005 et seq.,
82.32.010 et seq.

Deep Drilling Act (Gas and Oil)
Ga. Code Ann., 12-4-40 et seq.

**Deep Seabed Hard Mineral Removal Tax
Act of 1979**
June 28, 1980, P.L. 96-283, 26 U.S. Code § 1
nt., 26 U.S. Code § 4495 et seq.

Deep Seabed Hard Mineral Resources Act
June 28, 1980, P.L. 96-283, 30 U.S. Code
§§ 1401 et seq., 1401 nt.
Jan. 4, 1983, P.L. 97-416, 30 U.S. Code
§ 1470
Nov. 28, 1989, P.L. 101-178, 30 U.S. Code
§ 1470

**Deep Seabed Hard Mineral Resources,
Reauthorization Act of 1986**
Oct. 21, 1986, P.L. 99-507, 30 U.S. Code
§§ 1401 nt., 1470

Deepwater Port Act Amendments of 1984
Sept. 25, 1984, P.L. 98-419, 33 U.S. Code
§§ 1501 nt., 1502 to 1504, 1506, 1507,
1517, 1518, 1518 nt.

Deepwater Port Act of 1974
Jan. 3, 1975, P.L. 93-627, 33 U.S. Code
§§ 1501 to 1524, 1501 nt.; 43 U.S. Code
§ 1333
June 1, 1977, P.L. 95-36, 33 U.S. Code
§ 1524
Sept. 25, 1984, P.L. 98-419, 33 U.S. Code
§§ 1501 nt., 1502 to 1504, 1506, 1507,
1517, 1518 nt.
Aug. 18, 1990, P.L. 101-380, 26 U.S. Code
§ 9509 nt., 33 U.S. Code §§ 1503, 1514,
1517
Dec. 21, 1995, P.L. 104-66, 33 U.S. Code
§ 1519
Oct. 19, 1996, P.L. 104-324, 33 U.S. Code
§§ 1501 to 1504, 1506, 1507, 1509

Deepwater Port Authority Act
Tex. Water Code, § 19.001 et seq.

Deepwater Port Modernization Act
Oct. 19, 1996, P.L. 104-324, Title V, 33 U.S.
Code § 1501 nt.

Deepwater Port Procedures Act
Tex. Transportation Code, § 52.001 et seq.

Deepwater Port Siting Act
Md. Ann. Code 1974, Art. NR, § 3-601 et
seq.

Deer Hunting Regulation Law
Cal. Fish and Game Code 1957, § 4300 et
seq.

Defaced Bond Duplication Law
Cal. Statutes 1907, p. 53

**Defacing and Anti Intimidation of Public or
Private Property Criminal Penalty Act**
D.C. Code Ann., § 22-3112.1 et seq.

Defamation Act
Ala. Code 1975, § 6-5-180 et seq.
La. Rev. Stat. Ann., 14:47 et seq.
Miss. Code Ann. 1972, § 95-1-1
Mont. Code Ann., 27-1-801 et seq.
Okla. Stat. Ann., Title 12, § 1441 et seq.

Defamation Act (Race)
Ill. Rev. Stat. 1961, Ch. 38, § 471

Defamation and Libel Act
Ala. Code 1975, § 13A-11-160et seq.

Defamation by Radio Act
Ariz. Rev. Stat. Ann., § 12-652
Cal. Civil Code § 48.5
Colo. Rev. Stat., 13-21-106
Fla. Stat. Ann., 770.03, 770.04
Ga. Code Ann., 51-5-10
Ida. Code 1947, 6-706 et seq.
Ind. Code Ann., 34-4-14-1, 34-4-14-2
Kan. Gen. Stat. 1949, 60-746a
Ky. Rev. Stat. 1971, 411.061, 411.062
La. Rev. Stat. Ann., 45:1351 et seq.
Mass. Gen. Laws Ann., 231:91A
Md. Ann. Code 1974, Art. CJ, §§ 3-503 et
seq.
Mich. Comp. Laws Ann., 484.331, 484.332
Minn. Stat. Ann., 544.043
Miss. Code Ann. 1972, § 95-1-3
Mont. Code Ann., 27-1-811 et seq.
N.C. Gen. Stat. 1943, § 99-1 et seq.
Neb. Rev. Code 1943, 86-601 et seq.
Nev. Rev. Stat. 1979 Reprint, 41.340 et seq.
N.M. Stat. Ann., 41-7-6
Ohio Rev. Code 1953, 2739.03
Ore. Rev. Stat. 1953, 30.150 et seq.
S.D. Codified Laws 1967, 20-11-6
Tenn. Code Ann., 29-24-104
W. Va. Code 1966, § 55-7-14
Wyo. Stat. Ann., § 1-29-101 et seq.

Defamation Retraction Act
Ore. Rev. Stat. 1953, 30.155 et seq.

Default Act (Educational Loan)
Ill. Rev. Stat. 1991, Ch. 127, § 3550 et seq.

Default Affirmance Act
Cal. Penal Code § 1253

Default Judgment Act
Ga. Code 1933, 110-401 et seq.
Ind. Code Ann., 34-5-1-1
Wash. Rev. Code Ann., 12.20.020

Defaulting Purchasers' Redemption Law (Public Lands)
Cal. Public Resources Code § 7907

Defeasance Act (Deeds)
Pa. Purdon's Stat., Title 21, § 951 et seq.

Defeasance Act (Mortgages)
Ala. Code 1975, § 35-10-26

Defeasance of Debt Law (Local Government)
Ill. Rev. Stat. 1991, Ch. 85, § 4400 et seq.

Defective Assistive Device Act
Okla. Stat. Ann., Title 15, § 9101 et seq.

Defective Bond Repayment Act (Forest Preserve District)
Ill. Rev. Stat. 1991, Ch. 96 1/2, § 6500 et seq.

Defective Bridge Act
Ga. Code Ann., 32-4-70

Defective Conveyances Act
Md. Ann. Code 1974, Art. RP, § 4-109

Defective Delinquents Act
Mass. Gen. Laws 1932, Ch. 123, § 113 et seq.
Md. Ann. Code 1957, Art. 31B
Pa. Purdon's Stat., Title 61, § 541-1 et seq.

Defective Delinquents Act (Recommitment)
Mass. Acts 1953, Ch. 645

Defective Highway Act
Conn. Gen. Stat. Ann., 13a-149

Defective or Psychopathic Delinquents Act
Cal. Welfare and Institutions Code § 7050 et seq.

Defective Windshield Act
Cal. Vehicle Code 1959, § 26710

Defendant as Witness Act (Criminal)
Cal. Penal Code § 1323
N.D. Cent. Code, 29-21-11

Defendant Witness Competency Act
Okla. Stat. Ann., Title 22, § 701

Defender Act
Colo. Rev. Stat., 21-1-101 et seq.

Defense Acquisition Improvement Act
See Department of Defense Appropriations
Act, Title X and Department of Defense
Appropriations Act, Title IX

Defense Acquisition Improvement Act of 1986
Oct. 18, 1986, P.L. 99-500, 10 U.S. Code
§ 2301 nt.
Oct. 30, 1986, P.L. 99-591, 10 U.S. Code
§ 2301 nt.
Nov. 14, 1986, P.L. 99-661, 10 U.S. Code
§ 101 nt.
Dec. 4, 1987, P.L. 100-180, 15 U.S. Code
§ 632 nt.
July 19, 1988, P.L. 100-370, 102 Stat. 843,
10 U.S. Code § 113 nt.
Feb. 10, 1996, P.L. 104-106, 10 U.S. Code
§ 2326 nt.

Defense Acquisition Workforce Improvement Act
Nov. 5, 1990, P.L. 101-510, 10 U.S. Code
§ 1701 et seq. generally
April 6, 1991, P.L. 102-25, 10 U.S. Code
§§ 1701 nt., 1705 nt., 1721 nt., 1724 nt.,
1733 nt.
Oct. 2, 1992, P.L. 102-378, 5 U.S. Code
§§ prec. 5301, 5380, 5532, 8344, 3468

Defense Act
See also National Defense Act
Fla. Stat. Ann., 250.01 et seq.
Haw. Sessions Law 1941, Sp. Sess., Act 24
Mass. Acts 1917, Ch. 342
Utah Code Ann. 1953, 63-5-1 et seq.

Defense Act (Civil)
See also Civil Defense Act
Fla. Stat. 1973, 252.01 et seq.
Me. Public Laws 1942, Special Session, Ch.
305
Mich. Comp. Laws Ann., 30.261 et seq.
Mont. Code Ann. 1947, 77-1801 et seq.
P.R. Laws Ann. 1954, Title 25, § 130 et seq.

Defense Act (Indigents)
S.C. Code Ann. 1976, § 17-3-10 et seq.

Defense Act (Poison Pill)
Feb. 12, 1994, P.L. 103-211, 108 Stat. 41,
Title 4, § 410
Oct. 13, 1994, P.L. 103-355, 108 Stat. 3350,
Title 5, § 5002
N.Y. Business Corporation Law (Consol.
Laws Ch. 4) § 505, Subd. a

Defense Acts (Emergency)
R.I. Public Laws 1942, Ch. 1150
R.I. Public Laws 1950, Ch. 2641

Defense Against Weapons of Mass Destruction Act of 1996
Sept. 23, 1996, P.L. 104-201, Title XIV, 50
U.S. Code § 2301 nt.
Oct. 17, 1998, P.L. 105-261, 50 U.S. Code
§§ 2332, 2351, 2354, 2363

Defense Against Weapons of Mass Destruction Act of 1998
Oct. 17, 1998, P.L. 105-261, Title XIV, 112
Stat. 2167, 50 U.S. Code § 2301 nt.

Defense Aid Appropriation Acts
June 30, 1944, Ch. 324, 58 Stat. 628
July 5, 1945, Ch. 271, 59 Stat. 429

Defense Aid Supplemental Appropriation Acts
March 27, 1941, Ch. 30, 55 Stat. 53
Oct. 28, 1941, Ch. 460, 55 Stat. 745, 22 U.S.
Code §§ 421, 422
June 14, 1943, Ch. 122, 57 Stat. 152, 22 U.S.
Code § 423

Defense Amortization Act
See Internal Revenue Code

Defense and Disaster Compact (Civil)

Me. Rev. Stat. Ann. 1964, Title 37-B, § 902 et seq.

Defense and Security Act

Cal. Military and Veterans Code § 550 et seq.

Defense Appropriation Acts

Sept. 6, 1950, Ch. 896, 64 Stat. 730, 31 U.S. Code § 649a

Oct. 18, 1951, Ch. 512, 65 Stat. 423

Defense Authorization Amendments and Base Closure and Realignment Act

Oct. 24, 1988, P.L. 100-526, 10 U.S. Code § 2687 nt.

Dec. 5, 1991, P.L. 102-190, 10 U.S. Code § 2687 nt.

Oct. 23, 1992, P.L. 102-484, 10 U.S. Code § 2687 nt.

Nov. 30, 1993, P.L. 103-160, 10 U.S. Code § 2687 nt.

Oct. 5, 1994, P.L. 103-337, 10 U.S. Code § 2687 nt.

Feb. 10, 1996, P.L. 104-106, 10 U.S. Code § 2687 nt.

Sept. 23, 1996, P.L. 104-201, 10 U.S. Code § 2687 nt.

Nov. 18, 1997, P.L. 105-85, 10 U.S. Code § 2687 nt.

Defense Base Act

Aug. 16, 1941, Ch. 357, 55 Stat. 622, 42 U.S. Code §§ 1651 to 1654

Dec. 2, 1942, Ch. 668, 56 Stat. 1035, 42 U.S. Code § 1651

June 30, 1953, Ch. 176, 67 Stat. 135, 42 U.S. Code § 1651

June 30, 1958, P.L. 85-477, 72 Stat. 272, 42 U.S. Code § 1651

June 25, 1959, P.L. 86-70, 73 Stat. 150, 42 U.S. Code § 1651

July 24, 1959, P.L. 86-108, 73 Stat. 257, 42 U.S. Code § 1651

Sept. 4, 1961, P.L. 87-195, 75 Stat. 463, 42 U.S. Code § 1651

Defense Base Closure and Realignment Act of 1990

Nov. 5, 1990, P.L. 101-510, 10 U.S. Code §§ 2687, 2687 nt.

Dec. 5, 1991, P.L. 102-190, 10 U.S. Code § 2687 nt.

Oct. 23, 1992, P.L. 102-484, 10 U.S. Code § 2687 nt.

Nov. 30, 1993, P.L. 103-160, 10 U.S. Code § 2687 nt.

Oct. 5, 1994, P.L. 103-337, 10 U.S. Code § 2687 nt.

Oct. 25, 1994, P.L. 103-421, 10 U.S. Code § 2687 nt.

Feb. 10, 1996, P.L. 104-106, 10 U.S. Code § 2687 nt.

Defense Cataloging and Standardization Act

July 1, 1952, Ch. 539, 66 Stat. 318 (See 10 U.S. Code §§ 2451 to 2456)

Defense Civil Preparedness Act

R.I. Gen. Laws 1956, 30-15-1 et seq.

Defense Contract Bond Act

April 29, 1941, Ch. 81, 55 Stat. 147, 40 U.S. Code § 270e

Defense Contract Employment Discrimination Act

Ill. Rev. Stat. 1991, Ch. 29, § 24a.1 et seq.

Defense Conversion Act

Cal. Government Code § 15346

Defense Conversion and Technology Act

N.M. Stat. Ann., 9-15-37 et seq.

Defense Conversion, Reinvestment, and Transition Assistance Act of 1992

Oct. 23, 1992, P.L. 102-484, 10 U.S. Code § 2491 nt.

Nov. 30, 1993, P.L. 103-160, 10 U.S. Code §§ 2391 nt., 2501 nt.

Oct. 5, 1994, P.L. 103-337, 5 U.S. Code §§ 3502 nt., 8348 nt.; 10 U.S. Code §§ 1143 nt., 2501 nt.

Nov. 18, 1997, P.L. 105-85, 5 U.S. Code § 8348 nt.

Defense Conversion, Reinvestment, and Transition Assistance Amendments of 1993

Nov. 30, 1993, P.L. 103-160, 10 U.S. Code § 2491 nt.

Defense Conversion, Reinvestment, and Transition Assistance Amendments of 1994

Oct. 5, 1994, P.L. 103-337, 10 U.S. Code § 2491 nt.

Defense Council Act

Fla. Laws 1941, Ch. 20213
Mich. Comp. Laws Ann., 30.221 et seq.
Pa. Cons. Stat., Title 35, § 7101 et seq.
S.C. Code Ann. 1976, § 25-9-10 et seq.
Wash. Rev. Code Ann., 38.48.050

Defense Department Overseas Teachers Pay and Personnel Practices Act

July 17, 1959, P.L. 89-91, 73 Stat. 213 (See 5 U.S. Code §§ 5102, 5334, 5541, 6301, 8331, 8701) 20 U.S. Code §§ 901 to 907
Sept. 23, 1959, P.L. 86-370, 73 Stat. 652, 20 U.S. Code § 903
Aug. 30, 1961, P.L. 87-172, 75 Stat. 409, 5 U.S. Code § 905
Aug. 19, 1964, P.L. 88-448, 78 Stat. 492, 20 U.S. Code § 907
April 14, 1966, P.L. 89-391, 80 Stat. 117, 20 U.S. Code §§ 902, 903
July 18, 1984, P.L. 98-369, 98 Stat. 1059
Oct. 31, 1994, P.L. 103-425, 20 U.S. Code § 904
Sept. 23, 1996, P.L. 104-201, 20 U.S. Code §§ 901, 903

Defense Dependents' Education Act of 1978

Nov. 1, 1978, P.L. 95-561, 20 U.S. Code §§ 921 et seq., 921 nt.; 37 U.S. Code § 429
Oct. 17, 1979, P.L. 96-88. 20 U.S. Code §§ 928, 929
Nov. 8, 1985, P.L. 99-145, 20 U.S. Code §§ 921, 923, 928, 929
Nov. 29, 1989, P.L. 101-189, 20 U.S. Code §§ 923, 932
Nov. 5, 1990, P.L. 101-510, 20 U.S. Code §§ 926, 932; 37 U.S. Code § 429

Oct. 7, 1991, P.L. 102-119, 20 U.S. Code § 927
Oct. 23, 1992, P.L. 102-484, 20 U.S. Code § 921
Nov. 30, 1993, P.L. 103-160, 20 U.S. Code § 926
Oct. 17, 1998, P.L. 105-261, 20 U.S. Code § 926

Defense Drug Interdiction Assistance Act

Oct. 27, 1986, P.L. 99-570, 10 U.S. Code § 371 nt.
Feb. 10, 1996, P.L. 104-106, 10 U.S. Code § 9441 nt.

Defense Economic Adjustment, Diversification, Conversion, and Stabilization Act of 1990

Nov. 5, 1990, P.L. 101-510, 10 U.S. Code §§ 2391, 2391 nt.
Dec. 5, 1991, P.L. 102-190, 10 U.S. Code § 2391 nt.
Oct. 23, 1992, P.L. 102-484, 10 U.S. Code § 2391 nt.

Defense Economic Readjustment Zone Act

Tex. Government Code, § 2310.001 et seq.

Defense Eight-Hour Day Act

Oct. 10, 1940, Ch. 838, 54 Stat. 1092, 40 U.S. Code § 326 nt.

Defense Emergency Act

N.Y. Laws 1951, Ch. 784
N.Y. Unconsolidated Law § 9101 et seq.

Defense Entry and Departure Act

June 21, 1941, Ch. 210, 55 Stat. 252, 22 U.S. Code §§ 223, 225, 226, 226a, 226b

Defense for the Indigent Act

Okla. Stat. Ann., Title 22, § 1355 et seq.

Defense Force Act (State)

Colo. Rev. Stat., 28-4-101 et seq.
Haw. Rev. Stat. Ann., § 122A-1 et seq.
Wis. Stat. Ann., 21.025

Defense Forces Act

Colo. Laws 1941, p. 570, Ch. 172
Mont. Rev. Code 1947, 7-1201 et seq.

Defense Guard Act
Tex. Government Code, § 431.051 et seq.

Defense Highway Act of 1941
Nov. 19, 1941, Ch. 474, 55 Stat. 765
July 2, 1942, Ch. 474, 56 Stat. 562
July 13, 1943, Ch. 236, 57 Stat. 560
April 4, 1944, Ch. 164, 58 Stat. 189

Defense Housing Act
Md. Ann. Code 1957, Art. 44A, 1-601 et seq.
Mich. Comp. Laws Ann., 125.711 et seq.

Defense Housing Act of 1942
Jan. 21, 1942, Ch. 14, 56 Stat. 11, 42 U.S.
Code §§ 1521, 1522, 1523, 1524, 1534,
1544, 1545, 1546, 1549, 1552
June 23, 1945, Ch. 192, 59 Stat. 260, 42 U.S.
Code §§ 1571 to 1573

Defense Housing and Community Facilities and Services Act of 1951
Sept. 1, 1951, Ch. 378, 65 Stat. 293, 12 U.S.
Code §§ 371, 1430, 1701a-1, 1701g
1701g-1 to 1701g-3, and others; 42 U.S.
Code §§ 1507, 1584, 1585, 1589a 1589b,
1591, 1591 nts., 1591a to 1591c, 1592 to
1592o, 1593 to 1593e; 50 U.S. Code Appx.
§§ 2135, 2136
July 14, 1952, Ch. 723, 66 Stat. 602, 42 U.S.
Code §§ 1422, 1423, 1592a, 1592l
June 30, 1953, Ch. 170, 67 Stat. 125, 42 U.S.
Code §§ 1591, 1591c, 1592d, 1592n
June 29, 1954, Ch. 410, 68 Stat. 320, 42 U.S.
Code § 1591
Aug. 2, 1954, Ch. 649, 68 Stat. 609, 42 U.S.
Code § 1591c
June 30, 1955, Ch. 251, 69 Stat. 225, 42 U.S.
Code § 1591c
Aug. 11, 1956, Ch. 783, 70 Stat. 637, 42 U.S.
Code § 1591c
June 13, 1991, P.L. 102-54, 42 U.S. Code
§§ 1592a, 1592n

Defense Housing Appropriation Act
Oct. 14, 1940, Ch. 857, 54 Stat. 1115, 42
U.S. Code Ch. 9 nt.
April 29, 1941, Ch. 80, 55 Stat. 147, 42 U.S.
Code §§ 1521, 1523

June 28, 1941, Ch. 260, 55 Stat. 361, 42 U.S.
Code §§ 1521, 1523, 1531 to 1534, 1541,
1542 to 1551
July 7, 1943, Ch. 196, 57 Stat. 387, 42 U.S.
Code §§ 1523, 1543, 1553
July 15, 1943, Ch. 240, 57 Stat. 565, 42 U.S.
Code § 1534, 1534 nt.

Defense Housing Insurance Act
See National Housing Act

Defense Impacted Region Assistance Act
Tex. Laws 69th Leg., 1985, p. 263, Ch. 69,
Art. 1, §§ 1 to 4

Defense Industrial Reserve Act
Nov. 14, 1986, P.L. 99-661, 50 U.S. Code
§ 453
Nov. 5, 1990, P.L. 101-510, 50 U.S. Code
§ 454
Oct. 23, 1992, P.L. 102-484, 10 U.S. Code
§ 2535; 50 U.S. Code §§ 451 to 453

Defense Loan Act
Mass. Acts 1941, Ch. 487

Defense of Indigents Act
Ga. Code Ann., 17-12-30 et seq.
Ga. Laws 1967, p. 3014
S.C. Code Ann. 1976, § 17-3-10 et seq.

Defense of Marriage Act
Sept. 21, 1996, P.L. 104-199, 1 U.S. Code § 1
nt.

Defense Officer Personnel Management Act
Dec. 12, 1980, P.L. 96-513, 10 U.S. Code
§ 101 nt.
Oct. 19, 1984, P.L. 98-525, 10 U.S. Code
§ 611 nt.
Sept. 29, 1988, P.L. 100-456, 102 Stat. 1267,
10 U.S. Code § 611 nt.

Defense Officer Personnel Management Act Technical Corrections Act
July 10, 1981, P.L. 97-22, 10 U.S. Code
§ 101 nt.

Defense Patents Act
June 16, 1942, Ch. 415, 56 Stat. 370

Defense Procurement Improvement Act of 1985

Nov. 8, 1985, P.L. 99-145, 10 U.S. Code §§ 139 nt., 139c, 1621 to 1624, 2301 nt., 2304, 2305a, 2306, 2307 nt., 2313, 2320, 2323, 2324, 2397, 2397a 2411 to 2415; 18 U.S. Code § 287 nt.; 31 U.S. Code § 3729 nt.; 40 U.S. Code § 759; 41 U.S. Code §§ 253, 418a; 50 U.S. Code Appx. § 2168

Oct. 18, 1986, P.L. 99-500, 10 U.S. Code §§ 2305 nt., 2397a nt.

Oct. 30, 1986, P.L. 99-591, 10 U.S. Code §§ 2304 nt., 2397a nt.

April 21, 1987, P.L. 100-26, 10 U.S. Code § 2431 nt.

July 19, 1988, P.L. 100-370, 102 Stat. 843, 10 U.S. Code §§ 2304 nt., 2307 nt., 2324 nt.

Defense Procurement Reform Act of 1984

Oct. 12, 1984, P.L. 98-473, 42 U.S. Code §§ 3796 to 3796b, 3796 nt.

Oct. 19, 1984, P.L. 98-525, 10 U.S. Code § 2301 nt.

April 21, 1987, P.L. 100-26, 10 U.S. Code § 2432 nt.

July 19, 1988, P.L. 100-370, 102 Stat. 848, 10 U.S. Code § 2432 nt.

Defense Production Act (Levering-Burton)

Cal. Statutes 1950, 3rd Ex. Sess., Ch. 33, p. 58, § 11

Cal. Statutes 1959, Ch. 99, p. 1951

Defense Production Act Amendments of 1980

June 30, 1980, P.L. 96-294, 50 U.S. Code Appx. § 2601 et seq., 2061 nt.

Defense Production Act Amendments of 1984

April 17, 1984, P.L. 98-265, 50 U.S. Code Appx. §§ 2061, 2061 nt., 2066, 2091, 2092, 2093, 2099

Defense Production Act Amendments of 1986

Oct. 3, 1986, P.L. 99-441, 50 U.S. Code Appx. § 2061 nt.

Defense Production Act Amendments of 1992

Oct. 28, 1992, P.L. 102-558, 50 U.S. Code Appx. § 2061 nt.

Defense Production Act Amendments of 1995

Dec. 18, 1995, P.L. 104-64, 50 U.S. Code Appx. § 2061 nt.

Defense Production Act Extension Amendments of 1977

June 1, 1977, P.L. 95-37, 50 U.S. Code Appx. §§ 2061 nt., 2166

Defense Production Act Extension and Amendments of 1991

Aug. 17, 1991, P.L. 102-99, 50 U.S. Code Appx. § 2061 nt.

Defense Production Act of 1950

Sept. 8, 1950, Ch. 932, 64 Stat. 798, 50 U.S. Code Appx. §§ 2061, 2062, 2071 to 2073, 2081, 2091 to 2094, 2101 to 2110, 2121 to 2123, 2131 to 2135, 2151 to 2166

June 30, 1951, Ch. 198, 65 Stat. 110, 50 U.S. Code Appx. § 2166

July 31, 1951, Ch. 275, 65 Stat. 132, 50 U.S. Code Appx. §§ 2071, 2072, 2074, 2081, 2093, 2094, 2102, 2103, 2105, 2109, 2122, 2123, 2131, 2133, 2135, 2151, 2153, 2154, 2155, 2156, 2160, 2163a, 2164 to 2166

Sept. 1, 1951, Ch. 378, 65 Stat. 313, 50 U.S. Code Appx. §§ 2135, 2136

June 30, 1952, Ch. 530, 66 Stat. 296, 50 U.S. Code Appx. §§ 2071, 2074, 2092, 2102, 2103, 2107, 2108, 2111, 2112, 2113, 2137, 2155, 2157, 2158, 2162, 2163a, 2166

April 30, 1953, Ch. 31, 67 Stat. 25, 50 U.S. Code Appx. § 1894a

June 30, 1953, Ch. 170, 67 Stat. 126, 50 U.S. Code Appx. § 2166

June 30, 1953, Ch. 171, 67 Stat. 129, 50 U.S. Code Appx. §§ 2062, 2071, 2091, 2093, 2151, 2152, 2155, 2163, 2166

June 30, 1955, Ch. 251, 69 Stat. 225, 50 U.S. Code Appx. § 2166

Aug. 9, 1955, Ch. 655, 69 Stat. 580, 50 U.S. Code Appx. §§ 2062, 2062 nt., 2093, 2151, 2158, 2160, 2162, 2166

June 29, 1956, Ch. 474, 70 Stat. 408, 50 U.S. Code Appx. §§ 2062, 2093, 2162, 2162 nt., 2166

June 28, 1958, P.L. 85-471, 72 Stat. 241, 50 U.S. Code Appx. § 2166

June 30, 1960, P.L. 86-560, 74 Stat. 282, 50 U.S. Code Appx. §§ 2094, 2166

Sept. 26, 1961, P.L. 87-305, 75 Stat. 667, 50 U.S. Code Appx. § 2158

June 28, 1962, P.L. 87-505, 76 Stat. 112, 50 U.S. Code Appx. § 2166

June 30, 1964, P.L. 88-343, 78 Stat. 235, 50 U.S. Code Appx. §§ 2093, 2094, 2166

June 30, 1966, P.L. 89-482, 80 Stat. 235, 50 U.S. Code Appx. §§ 2162, 2166

July 1, 1968, P.L. 90-370, 82 Stat. 279, 50 U.S. Code Appx. §§ 2162, 2166, 2167

Dec. 23, 1969, P.L. 91-151, 83 Stat. 376, 50 U.S. Code Appx. § 2158

June 30, 1970, P.L. 91-300, 84 Stat. 367, 50 U.S. Code Appx. § 2166

Aug. 1, 1970, P.L. 91-371, 84 Stat. 694, 50 U.S. Code Appx. § 2166

Aug. 15, 1970, P.L. 91-379, 84 Stat. 796, 50 U.S. Code Appx. §§ 2091, 2152, 2166, 2168

Oct. 15, 1970, P.L. 91-452, 84 Stat. 931, 50 U.S. Code Appx. § 2155

May 18, 1971, P.L. 92-15, 85 Stat. 38, 50 U.S. Code Appx. § 2166

June 30, 1972, P.L. 92-325, 50 U.S. Code Appx. §§ 2093, 2166

Nov. 16, 1973, P.L. 93-155, 87 Stat. 615, 50 U.S. Code Appx. § 2092

June 30, 1974, P.L. 93-323, 88 Stat. 280, 50 U.S. Code Appx. § 2166

Aug. 7, 1974, P.L. 93-367, 88 Stat. 419, 50 U.S. Code Appx. § 2166

Sept. 30, 1974, P.L. 93-426, 88 Stat. 1167, 50 U.S. Code Appx. §§ 2094, 2161, 2166

March 21, 1975, P.L. 94-9, 89 Stat. 15, 50 U.S. Code Appx. § 2169

June 28, 1975, P.L. 94-42, 89 Stat. 232, 15 U.S. Code § 1026; 50 U.S. Code Appx. § 2166

Oct. 1, 1975, P.L. 94-100, 89 Stat. 483, 50 U.S. Code Appx. § 2166

Dec. 16, 1975, P.L. 94-152, 89 Stat. 810, 50 U.S. Code Appx. §§ 2061, 2158, 2158A, 2160, 2162, 2166, 2168, 2169

Dec. 22, 1975, P.L. 94-163, 89 Stat. 871, 50 U.S. Code Appx. §§ 2071, 2158 nt.

June 1, 1977, P.L. 95-37, 50 U.S. Code Appx. § 2166

July 30, 1979, P.L. 96-41, 50 U.S. Code Appx. § 2093

Sept. 29, 1979, P.L. 96-77, 50 U.S. Code Appx. § 2166

Jan. 28, 1980, P.L. 96-188, 50 U.S. Code Appx. § 2166

April 3, 1980, P.L. 96-225, 50 U.S. Code Appx. § 2166

May 26, 1980, P.L. 96-250, 50 U.S. Code Appx. § 2166

Oct. 15, 1982, P.L. 97-336, 50 U.S. Code Appx. § 2166

Nov. 30, 1983, P.L. 98-181, 50 U.S. Code Appx. § 2166

April 17, 1984, P.L. 98-265, 50 U.S. Code Appx. §§ 2061, 2066, 2091, 2092, 2093, 2099

Nov. 8, 1985, P.L. 99-145, 50 U.S. Code Appx. § 2168

Oct. 3, 1986, P.L. 99-441, 50 U.S. Code Appx. §§ 2099, 2161, 2166

Nov. 14, 1986, P.L. 99-661, 50 U.S. Code Appx. § 2168

Aug. 23, 1988, P.L. 100-418, 102 Stat. 1425, 50 U.S. Code Appx. § 2170

Nov. 17, 1988, P.L. 100-679, 50 U.S. Code Appx. § 2168

Nov. 3, 1989, P.L. 101-137, 50 U.S. Code Appx. §§ 2161, 2166

Aug. 9, 1990, P.L. 101-351, 50 U.S. Code Appx. § 2166

Oct. 4, 1990, P.L. 101-407, 50 U.S. Code Appx. § 2166

Oct. 6, 1990, P.L. 101-411, 50 U.S. Code Appx. § 2166

Aug. 17, 1991, P.L. 102-99, 50 U.S. Code Appx. §§ 2071, 2158, 2158a, 2161, 2166

Dec. 6, 1991, P.L. 102-193, 50 U.S. Code Appx. § 2166

Oct. 23, 1992, P.L. 102-484, 50 U.S. Code Appx. § 2170

Oct. 28, 1992, P.L. 102-558, 50 U.S. Code Appx. §§ 2062, 2074, 2077, 2078, 2091 to 2094, 2097, 2099, 2099a, 2151 to 2155, 2159 to 2162, 2165 to 2167, 2169 to 2171

Oct. 14, 1994, P.L. 103-359, 50 U.S. Code Appx. § 2170

Continued

Dec. 18, 1995, P.L. 104-64, 50 U.S. Code
Appx. §§ 2161, 2166
Oct. 17, 1998, P.L. 105-261, 50 U.S. Code
Appx. §§ 2161, 2166

Defense Public Works Act
See Defense Housing Appropriation Act
La. Rev. Stat. Ann., 53: 151, 53:152
R.I. Public Laws 1942, Ch. 1203

Defense Technical Correction Act of 1987
April 21, 1987, P.L. 100-26, 10 U.S. Code
§ 101 nt.

Defense Training School Act
Cal. Business and Professions Code § 16500
et seq.

Defense Workers Housing Act
Oct. 1, 1942, Ch. 572, 56 Stat. 763, 42 U.S.
Code § 1523

Deferral Act (Homestead Property Tax)
Fla. Stat. Ann., 197.242 et seq.

Deferred Building Renewal Act
Neb. Rev. Stat. 1943, 81-173 et seq.

Deferred Compensation Act
N.M. Stat. Ann., 10-7A-1 et seq.
S.C. Code Ann. 1976, § 8-23-10 et seq.

**Deferred Compensation Continuing
Appropriation Act**
Ill. Rev. Stat. 1991, Ch. 108 1/2, §§ 100, 101

**Deferred Compensation Plan Act
(Government Employees)**
Fla. Stat. Ann., 112.215
Miss. Code Ann. 1972, § 25-14-1 et seq.
Tenn. Code Ann., 8-25-101 et seq.
Va. Code 1950, § 51-111.67:14 et seq.

Deferred Posting Act (Banks)
Ark. Stat. 1947, 67-544 et seq.
Colo. Rev. Stat. 1963, 14-8-4
Ind. Burns' 1933, 18-2518 et seq.
Neb. Laws 1949, Ch. 183
Ohio Rev. Code 1953, 1304.01 et seq.
Okla. Stat. 1961, Title 6, § 119.1 et seq.
Tenn. Public Acts 1951, Ch. 96

Deferred Presentment Act
Ga. Code Ann., 7-9-1 et seq.

Deferred Presentment Services Act
Ala. Acts 1999, H.B. 104

Deferred Sentence Act
Wash. Rev. Code Ann., 9.95.210 et seq.

Defiance of Teachers Act
Ky. Rev. Stat. 1971, 158.150

Deficiency Appropriation Acts
June 29, 1950, Ch. 405, 64 Stat. 275
June 9, 1964, P.L. 88-317, 78 Stat. 204
Aug. 20, 1996, P.L. 104-186, 2 U.S. Code
§ 40a

Deficiency Judgment Act
Cal. Code of Civil Procedure § 580a et seq.
La. Rev. Stat. Ann., 13:4106 et seq.
N.C. Gen. Stat. 1943, § 45-21.38
Neb. Rev. Stat. 1943, 25-2139 et seq.
N.Y. Real Property Actions and Proceedings
Law (Consol. Laws Ch. 81) § 137
N.Y. Real Property Actions and Proceedings
Law (Consol. Laws Ch. 81) § 1371

Deficiency Judgment Act (Enforcement)
Ohio Rev. Code 1953, 2329.08

Deficiency Judgment Act (Mortgages)
Ala. General Acts 1935, p. 184, No. 146
Mich. Comp. Laws 1948, 566.401 et seq.
Pa. Cons. Stat., Title 42, § 8103

Deficit Act (Casual)
Ill. Rev. Stat. 1991, Ch. 120, § 405H et seq.

Deficit Reduction Act (Emergency)
D.C. Code Ann., §§ 1-242, 31-104.1, 47-321

Deficit Reduction Act (Fiscal Year 1995)
Vt. Acts 1995, No. 74

Deficit Reduction Act of 1984
July 18, 1984, P.L. 98-369, 98 Stat. 494, 26
U.S. Code § 1 nt.

Nov. 8, 1984, P.L. 98-617, 42 U.S. Code §§ 1395f, 1395h nt., 1395n, 1395u 1395x, 1395mm nt., 1396a, 1396b

May 24, 1985, P.L. 99-44, 26 U.S. Code §§ 274 nt., 6653, 6653 nt. , 6695

April 7, 1986, P.L. 99-272, 26 U.S. Code § 861 nt.; 42 U.S. Code § 1395ww nt.

Oct. 18, 1986, P.L. 99-500, 40 U.S. Code § 759 nt.

Oct. 21, 1986, P.L. 99-509, 42 U.S. Code §§ 1396h nt., 1395ww nt.

Oct. 22, 1986, P.L. 99-514, 42 U.S. Code §§ 410 nt., 602 nt., 602

Oct. 30, 1986, P.L. 99-591, 40 U.S. Code § 759 nt.

Aug. 18, 1987, P.L. 100-93, 42 U.S. Code § 1396a nt.

Oct. 16, 1987, P.L. 100-136, 38 U.S. Code § 1816 nt.

Dec. 21, 1987, P.L. 100-198, 38 U.S. Code § 1816 nt.

Dec. 22, 1987, P.L. 100-203, 42 U.S. Code §§ 602 nt., 6103, 6402 and nt., 7213; 31 U.S. Code § 3720A

July 1, 1988, P.L. 100-360, 102 Stat. 773, 42 U.S. Code §§ 1395mm , 1395mm nt.

Oct. 13, 1988, P.L. 100-485, 26 U.S. Code § 6402 nt.

Dec. 19, 1989, P.L. 101-239, 42 U.S. Code §§ 1395h nt., 1395mm

Nov. 5, 1990, P.L. 101-508, 104 Stat. 1388-118, 1388-559

Nov. 15, 1991, P.L. 102-164, 26 U.S. Code § 6402 nt.

Oct. 31, 1994, P.L. 103-432, 42 U.S. Code § 1395h

Definite Sentence Act
Ill. Rev. Stat. 1991, Ch. 38, § 1005-8-1

Degradable Plastic Act
Ill. Rev. Stat. 1991, Ch. 111 1/2, § 7901 et seq.

Degradable Products Act
Neb. Rev. Stat. 1943, 69-2001 et seq.

Degree of Murder Act
Pa. Cons. Stat., Title 18, § 1102, 2501 et seq.

DeKalb County Civic Center Authority Act
Ga. Laws 1996, p. 4216

DeKalb County Community Improvement District Act
Ga. Laws 1998, S.B. 598

DeKalb County Special Services Tax Districts Act
Ga. Laws 1982, p. 4396

Del Norte County Flood Control District Act
Cal. Statutes 1955, Ch. 166, p. 613
Cal. Water Code, Appendix, § 72-1 et seq.

Delaney Amendment.
See Food Additives Amendment of 1958

DeLange, Geake, Cherry, Murphy Wage Record Conversion Act
Mich. Comp. Laws Ann., 421.1 et seq.

DeLano-Brake-Stout Act (Unemployment Compensation)
Mich. Comp. Laws Ann., 421.1 et seq.

Delaware and Lehigh Navigation Canal National Heritage Corridor Act of 1988
Nov. 18, 1988, P.L. 100-692, 16 U.S. Code § 461 nt.
Nov. 6, 1998, P.L. 105-355, 16 U.S. Code § 461 nt.

Delaware and Raritan Canal State Park Law
N.J. Stat. Ann., 13:13A-1 et seq.

Delaware-New Jersey Compact
Del. Code of 1974, Title 17, § 1701 et seq.
N.J. Stat. Ann., 32:11E-1 et seq.

Delaware River Act
Pa. Purdon's Stat., Title 55, §§ 401,402

Delaware River Basin Compact Act
Del. Code of 1974, Title 7, § 6501
N.J. Stat. Ann., 32:11D-1 et seq.
N.Y. Environmental Conservation Law 1972 (Consol. Laws Ch. 43B) § 21-0701 et seq.
Pa. Purdon's Stat., Title 32, § 815.101

Delaware River Basin Water Commission Compact Act
N.J. Stat. Ann., 32:110-1 et seq.

Delaware River Bridge Act
Pa. Purdon's Stat., Title 36, § 3211 et seq.

Delaware River Bridge Companies Act
N.J. Stat. Ann., 48:5-13 to 48:5-25

Delaware River Extension Act (Pennsylvania Turnpike)
Pa. Purdon's Stat., Title 36, § 658.1 et seq.

Delaware Valley Urban Area Compact
N.J. Stat. Ann., 32:27-1 et seq.
Pa. Purdon's Stat., Title 73, § 701

Delaware Water Gap National Recreation Area Act
Sept. 1, 1965, P.L. 89-158, 79 Stat. 618, 16 U.S. Code §§ 460o to 460o-7
Oct. 27, 1972, P.L. 92-575, 86 Stat. 1250, 16 U.S. Code §§ 460o-1, 460o-7

Delay Act (Insurance Claims)
Ark. Code Ann. 1987, § 23-79-208

Delay Penalty Act (Insurers)
Tenn. Code Ann., 56-7-105

Delayed Births Registration Act
Mich. Comp. Laws Ann., 333.2827 et seq.
Neb. Rev. Stat. 1943, 71-617 et seq.

Delayed Deposit Services Licensing Act
Iowa Code 1983, 533D.1 et seq.
Neb. Rev. Stat. 1943, 45-901 et seq.

Delayed Sentencing Program for Young Adults
Okla. Stat. Ann., Title 22, § 996 et seq.

Delegate Act
D.C. Code Ann., §§ 1-401, 1-402

Delegate Act (Alaska)
Alaska Comp. Laws Ann. 1949, §§ 3-1-1 et seq., 38-7-1 et seq.

Deleterious Substances Act (Oil and Gas)
Okla. Stat. Ann., Title 52, § 139 et seq.

Delinquency Act
Md. Ann. Code 1974, Art. CJ, § 3-801
N.M. Stat. Ann., 32A-2-1 et seq.
S.D. Codified Laws 1967, 26-8-1 et seq.

Delinquency Prevention Act
Fla. Stat. Ann., 959.31

Delinquency Prevention Commission Act
Ill. Rev. Stat. 1983, Ch. 26, § 2701 et seq.

Delinquency Prevention Program and Juvenile Justice Act
P.R. Laws Ann. 1954, Title 3, § 1631 et seq.

Delinquency Reporting Law (Child Support)
Cal. Family Code § 4700 et seq.

Delinquent and Neglected Children Act
Mo. Rev. Stat., 211.011 et seq.

Delinquent Assessment Acquisition and Sale Act
Cal. Government Code § 53860 et seq.

Delinquent Child Act
Colo. Rev. Stat., 19-8-101 et seq.
Ill. Rev. Stat. 1991, Ch. 37, § 801-1 et seq.
Ind. Code Ann., 31-6-1-1 et seq.
Iowa Code 1983, 232.1 et seq.
Ky. Rev. Stat. 1971, 208.010 et seq.
Mass. Gen. Laws Ann., 119:52 et seq.
Mont. Rev. Code 1947, 10-601 et seq.
N.H. Rev. Stat. 1955, 517:1 et seq.
N.Y. Penal Law 1965 (Consol. Laws Ch. 40) § 260.10
P.R. Laws Ann. 1954, Title 34, § 2001 et seq.
Tex. Family Code, § 51.01 et seq.

Delinquent Child Contributory Law
Colo. Rev. Stat. 19-7-101 et seq.

Delinquent Children and Children in Need of Supervision Act
Tex. Family Code, Art. 51.01 et seq.

Delinquent Railroad Tax Adjustment Law
N.J. Stat. Ann., App. A:4-7.1 to App.
A:4-7.13

Delinquent Special Assessment Act (Chicago)
Ill. Comp. Stat. 1992, Ch. 65, § 65/7 et seq.

Delinquent Special Assessment Act (Cities)
Ill. Rev. Stat. 1991, Ch. 24, § 808.37h et seq.

Delinquent Special Assessment Act (Municipalities)
Ill. Rev. Stat. 1989, Ch. 24, § 866g1 et seq.

Delinquent Tax Abatement Acts
Pa. Purdon's Stat., Title 72, § 5567.1 et seq.

Delinquent Tax Act
Kan. Stat. Ann., 79-2101 et seq.
Nev. Rev. Stat. 1979 Reprint, 361.480 et seq.
N.J. Stat. Ann., 54:4-104
Tenn. Code Ann., 67-5-2001 et seq.
Tex. Rev. Civ. Stat., Art. 7319 et seq.

Delinquent Tax Enforcement Act
See Uniform Delinquent Tax Enforcement
Act
N.Y. Real Property Tax Law (Consol. Laws.
Ch. 50A) § 1100 et seq.
Pa. Purdon's Stat., Title 72, §§ 5860.101,
5971a et seq.

Delinquent Taxes Act (Installment Payment)
Mich. Comp. Laws Ann., 211.301 et seq.

Delinquent Tenant Act
Fla. Stat. Ann., 83.05

Delinquents Act (Defective)
Md. Ann. Code 1957, Art. 31B

Delivery and Claim Act
Wash. Rev. Code Ann., 7.64.010 et seq.

Delivery Guarantee Act (Food Products)
N.M. Stat. Ann., 57-24-1 et seq.

Delray Beach Downtown Development Authority Act
Fla. Special Laws 1971, Ch. 71-604

Delta Development Act
Oct. 1, 1988, P.L. 100-460, 102 Stat. 2246,
42 U.S. Code § 3121 nt.

Delta Economic Compact (Tri-State)
La. Rev. Stat. Ann., 51:1021 to 51:1024

Delta Flood Protection Act
Cal. Water Code §§ 12300, 12301, 12310 et
seq., 12912.5, 12986, 12987, 12987.5,
12992, 12993

Delta Levees Act
Cal. Water Code § 12225 et seq.

Delta Protection Act (Johnston-Baker-Andall-Boatwright)
Also known as Sacramento-San Joaquin
Delta Protection Act
Cal. Public Resources Code § 29700 et seq.

Delta Water Agency Act of 1968
Cal. Statutes 1968, Ch. 419, p. 860

Demand Act (Speedy Trial)
Ga. Code Ann., 17-7-170

Demand Reduction Assessment Act
Ala. Code 1975, § 13A-12-280
Ala. Code 1975, § 13A-27A-1 et seq.

DeMarcus-Buckman-Ford College Scholarship Act
Ky. Rev. Stat. 1971, 164.740 et seq.

Dementia Education and Training Act
Ala. Code 1975, § 22-50-70 et seq.

Democracy Act (Labor Unions)
Minn. Stat. Ann., 179.18 et seq.

Demonstration Cities and Metropolitan Development Act of 1966

Nov. 3, 1966, P.L. 89-754, 80 Stat. 1255, 11 U.S. Code § 663; 12 U.S. Code §§ 24, 371, 1432, 1438, 1701d-3 nt., 1701q nt., 1702, 1709, 1715c , 1715e, and others; 15 U.S. Code §§ 77ddd, 637; 16 U.S. Code § 470b-1; 40 U.S. Code § 461; 42 U.S. Code §§ 1416, 1421b, 1453, 1455, 1456, 1460, 1463, and others

June 19, 1968, P.L. 90-351, 82 Stat. 208, 42 U.S. Code § 3334

Aug. 1, 1968, P.L. 90-448, 82 Stat. 531, 42 U.S. Code §§ 3331, 3332, 3335, 3336, 3338, 3311, 3356, 3372

Dec. 5, 1969, P.L. 91-142, 83 Stat. 313, 42 U.S. Code § 3374

Dec. 24, 1969, P.L. 91-152, 83 Stat. 390, 42 U.S. Code §§ 3311, 3356, 3371, 3372

May 21, 1970, P.L. 91-258, 84 Stat. 235, 42 U.S. Code § 3338

Oct. 26, 1970, P.L. 91-511, 84 Stat. 1225, 42 U.S. Code § 3374

Dec. 31, 1970, P.L. 91-609, 84 Stat. 1780, 42 U.S. Code §§ 3311, 3356

July 1, 1972, P.L. 92-335, 86 Stat. 405, 42 U.S. Code § 3311

Oct. 2, 1973, P.L. 93-117, 87 Stat. 422, 42 U.S. Code § 3311

Nov. 29, 1973, P.L. 93-166, 87 Stat. 679, 42 U.S. Code § 3374

Oct. 31, 1978, P.L. 95-557, 42 U.S. Code § 3371

Nov. 5, 1990, P.L. 101-510, 42 U.S. Code § 3374

Dec. 5, 1991, P.L. 102-190, 42 U.S. Code § 3374

Oct. 23, 1992, P.L. 102-484, 42 U.S. Code § 3374

Oct. 5, 1994, P.L. 103-337, 42 U.S. Code § 3374

Sept. 30, 1996, P.L. 104-208, 42 U.S. Code § 3338

Demonstration for Human Services Project Act

S.C. Code Ann. 1976, § 1-25-10 et seq.

Demonstration of Restructuring in Public Education Act

Cal. Education Code 1976, § 58900 et seq.

Demonstration Project Act (Magnetic Levitation)

Fla. Stat. Ann., 341.401 et seq.

Demonstration Resource Centers Act (Hispanic Women's)

N.J. Laws 1991, Ch. 378

Demonstration Scholarship Act

Cal. Education Code 1976, § 58000 et seq.

Demonstration Scholarship Program Authorization Act

Conn. Gen. Stat. Ann., § 10-239a et seq.

Demonstrations Policy Act (Campus)

Ill. Comp. Stat. 1992, Ch. 110, § 10/0.01 et seq.

Dempsey Act (Franchise Tax)

Ohio Rev. Code 1953, 5733.01 et seq.

Dempsey J. Barron, W.D. Childers and Joe Kershaw Cane Pole Tax Repeal Act

Fla. Stat. Ann., 372.57

Demurrage Act (Railroads)

Minn. Laws, 1907, Ch. 23

Demurrer to Evidence Act (Criminal)

N.C. Gen. Stat. 1943, § 15-173

Demutualization Act (Insurers)

Neb. Rev. Stat. 1943, 44-6101 et seq.

Denali Commission Act of 1998

Oct. 21, 1998, P.L. 105-277, Division C, Title III, 112 Stat. 2681, 42 U.S . Code § 3121 nt.

May 21, 1999, P.L. 106-31, 42 U.S. Code § 3121 nt.

Denatured Alcohol Acts

June 7, 1906, Ch. 3047, 34 Stat. 217
Oct. 3, 1913, Ch. 16, 38 Stat. 199
Oct. 3, 1917, Ch. 63, 40 Stat. 309
Feb. 24, 1919, Ch. 18, 40 Stat. 1107

Oct. 28, 1919, Ch. 85, 41 Stat. 319

Denial of Rights Act
Wis. Stat. Ann., 942.04

Dennis Golf Course Loan Act
Mass. Acts 1963, Ch. 599

Dense Smoke Act
Mo. Rev. Stat., 71.760

Densely Populated Municipalities Act (State Aid)
N.J. Stat Ann., 52:27D-384 et seq.

Dent Act
March 2, 1919, Ch. 94, 40 Stat. 1272

Dental Act
Okla. Stat. Ann., Title 59, § 328.1 et seq.

Dental and Medical Education Act
N.J. Stat. Ann., 18A:64G-1 et seq.

Dental and Medical Service Corporation Act (Nonprofit)
Pa. Cons. Stat., Title 40, § 6101 et seq.

Dental Anesthesia Act
Neb. Rev. Stat. 1943, 71-193.22 et seq.

Dental Auxiliaries Act
N.J. Stat. Ann. 45:6-48 et seq.

Dental Care Act
Colo. Rev. Stat., 25-21-101 et seq.

Dental Care Act (State Employees)
Cal. Government Code § 22950 et seq.

Dental Care Benefits Act
Miss. Code Ann., § 83-51-1 et seq.

Dental College Act
N.J. Stat. Ann., 18A:64C-1 et seq.

Dental Corporation Act
Ark. Code Ann. 1987, 4-29-401 et seq.
Cal. Business and Professions Code § 1800 et seq.
La. Rev. Stat. Ann., 12:981 et seq.

N.J. Stat. Ann., 17:48C-1 et seq.
S.D. Codified Laws 1967, 47-12-1 et seq.

Dental Disciplinary Board Act
Wash. Rev. Code Ann., 18.32.500 et seq.

Dental Freedom of Choice Act (Employees)
Ill. Rev. Stat. 1991, Ch. 32, § 690.71 et seq.

Dental Health Act
Me. Rev. Stat. Ann. 1964, Title 22, § 2091 et seq.

Dental, Health and Life Insurance Act (State Employees)
Okla. Stat. Ann., Title 74, § 1301 et seq.

Dental Health Care Act
N.M. Stat. Ann., 61-5A-1 et seq.

Dental Health Education Act
Me. Rev. Stat. Ann. 1964, Title 22, § 2121 et seq.

Dental Hygiene Division Law
Cal. Health and Safety Code § 350 et seq.

Dental Hygienist Act
Ind. Code Ann., 25-13-1-1 et seq.
N.C. Gen. Stat. 1943, § 90-221 et seq.
N.D. Cent. Code, 43-20-01 et seq.
N.M. Stat. Ann., 61-5-11 et seq.

Dental Inspection Law
Ore. Rev. Stat. 1953, 336.375 et seq.

Dental Inspection Law (School Pupils)
Ore. Rev. Stat. 1953, 336.380 et seq.

Dental Mediation Act
Okla. Stat. Ann., Title 59, § 328.60 et seq.

Dental Peer Review Protection Act
N.C. Gen. Stat. 1943, § 90-48.7 et seq.

Dental Plan Act (Prepaid)
N.M. Stat. 1978, 59A-48-1 et seq.
Okla. Stat. Ann., Title 36, § 6141 et seq.

Dental Plan Organization Act
Del. Code of 1974, Title 18, § 3801 et seq.
Continued

N.J. Stat. Ann. 17:48D-1 et seq.

Dental Practice Act
Ala. Code 1975, § 34-9-1 et seq.
Alaska Stat. 1962, § 08.36.010 et seq.
Ariz. Rev. Stat. Ann., § 32-1201 et seq.
Ark. Code Ann. 1987, 17-82-101 et seq.
Cal. Business and Professions Code § 1600 et seq.
Colo. Rev. Stat., 12-35-101 et seq.
Conn. Gen. Stat. Ann., 20-103a et seq.
D.C. Code Ann., § 2-1201 et seq.
Del. Code of 1974, Title 24, § 1121 et seq.
Fla. Stat. Ann., 466.001 et seq.
Ga. Code Ann., 43-11-1 et seq.
Haw. Rev. Stat. Ann., § 448-1 et seq.
Ida. Code 1947, 54-901 et seq.
Ill. Rev. Stat. 1991, Ch. 111, § 2301 et seq.
Ind. Code Ann., 25-14-1-1 et seq.
Iowa Code 1983, 153.13 et seq.
Kan. Stat. Ann., 65-1421 et seq.
Ky. Rev. Stat. 1971, 313.010 et seq.
La. Rev. Stat. Ann., 37:751 et seq.
Mass. Gen. Laws Ann., 112:43 et seq.
Md. Ann. Code 1974, Art. HO, § 4-101 et seq.
Me. Rev. Stat. Ann. 1964, Title 32, § 1061 et seq.
Mich. Comp. Laws Ann., 333.16601 et seq.
Minn. Stat. Ann., 150A.01 et seq.
Miss. Code Ann. 1972, § 73-9-1 et seq.
Mo. Rev. Stat., 332.011 et seq.
Mont. Code Ann., 37-4-101 et seq.
N.C. Gen. Stat. 1943, § 90-22 et seq.
N.D. Cent. Code, 43-28-01 et seq.
Nev. Rev. Stat. 1979 Reprint, 631.005 et seq.
N.H. Rev. Stat. 1955, 317-A:1 et seq.
N.J. Rev. Stat. 1937, 45:6-1 et seq.
N.M. Stat. Ann., 61-5-1 et seq.
N.Y. Education Law 1947 (Consol. Laws Ch. 16) § 6600 et seq.
Ohio Rev. Code 1953, 4715.01 et seq.
Okla. Stat. Ann., Title 59, § 328.1 et seq.
Ore. Rev. Stat., 679.010 et seq.
Pa. Purdon's Stat., Title 63, § 120 et seq.
P.R. Laws Ann. 1954, Title 20, § 81 et seq.
R.I. Gen. Laws 1956, 5-31-1 et seq.
S.C. Code Ann. 1976, § 40-15-10 et seq.
S.D. Codified Laws 1967, 36-6-1 et seq.
Tenn. Code Ann., 63-5-101 et seq.
Tex. Rev. Civ. Stat., Art. 4543 et seq.
Vt. Stat. Ann., Title 26, § 721 et seq.
Wash. Rev. Code Ann., 18.32.005 et seq.
Wis. Stat. Ann., 447.01 et seq.
W. Va. Code 1966, § 30-4-1 et seq.
Wyo. Stat. Ann., § 33-15-101 et seq.

Dental Professional Corporation Act
Ind. Code Ann., 23-1-1.5-1-8 et seq.
Minn. Stat. Ann., 319A.01 et seq.

Dental Program Act (Public Health)
Fla. Stat. Ann., 381.0052

Dental Service Corporation Act
Ala. Code 1975, § 22-21-360 et seq.
Kan. Stat. Ann., 40-19a01 et seq.
Miss. Code Ann. 1972, § 83-43-1 et seq.
N.D. Cent. Code, 26.1-17-01 et seq.
N.J. Stat. Ann., 17:48C-1 et seq.
Okla. Stat. Ann., Title 36, § 2671 et seq.
S.D. Codified Laws 1967, 58-39-1 et seq.

Dental Service Corporation Act (Nonprofit)
Kan. Stat. Ann., 40-19a01 et seq.
Pa. Cons. Stat., Title 40, § 6101 et seq.

Dental Service Plan Act
Ill. Rev. Stat. 1991, Ch. 32, § 690.1 et seq.
Tenn. Code Ann., 56-30-101 et seq.

Dental Student Grant Act
Ill. Rev. Stat. 1991, Ch. 144, § 1501 et seq.

Dental Surgery Act
Ill. Rev. Stat. 1991, Ch. 111, § 2301 et seq.

Dentist Good Samaritan Law
N.Y. Education Law 1947 (Consol. Laws Ch. 16) § 6611, Subd. 6

Dentist-Physician Loan Redemption Program Act
N.J. Stat. Ann. 18A:72D-1 et seq.

Dentists and Dental Hygienists Act
Utah Code Ann. 1953, 58-7-1 et seq.

Dentists' Lien Act

Ill. Rev. Stat. 1991, Ch. 82, § 120 et seq.

Mont. Code Ann., 71-3-1111 et seq.

Denturists Act

Wash. Rev. Code Ann., 18.30.005 et seq.

Denver Metropolitan Major League Baseball Stadium District Act

Colo. Rev. Stat., 32-14-101 et seq.

Department of Addiction Services Organic Act

P.R. Laws Ann. 1954, Title 3, § 401 et seq.

Department of Administration Act

Ind. Code Ann., 4-13-1-1 et seq.

Kan. Stat. Ann., 75-3701 et seq.

Mich. Comp. Laws Ann., 18.1 et seq.

Mont. Code Ann., 2-15-1001 et seq.

N.C. Gen. Stat. 1943, § 143-334 et seq.

Department of Agriculture Act

May 15, 1862, Ch. 72, 12 Stat. 387

Feb. 9, 1889, Ch. 122, 25 Stat. 659, 21 U.S. Code § 119

Colo. Rev. Stat., 35-1-101 et seq.

N.J. Stat. Ann., 4:1-1 et seq.

Ore. Rev. Stat. 1953, 561.005 et seq.

Department of Agriculture and Commerce Act

P.R. Laws Ann. 1954, Title 3, § 351 et seq.

Department of Agriculture and Commerce Reorganization Act

Miss. Code Ann., § 69-1-201 et seq.

Department of Agriculture and Farm Credit Administration Appropriation Acts

June 25, 1954, Ch. 409, 68 Stat. 304, 7 U.S. Code §§ 411b, 428, 453, 1506b, 1623a, 1630, 2254; 12 U.S. Code §§ 1020a-2, 1020c-1, 1023a, 1131a-1; 15 U.S. Code § 713a-10; 16 U.S. Code §§ 571, 571b, 579, 581a-2, 590e-1, 590e-2; 21 U.S. Code § 129

Jan. 25, 1955, Ch. 3, 69 Stat. 5, 15 U.S. Code § 713a-10

May 23, 1955, Ch. 43, 69 Stat. 51, 7 U.S. Code §§ 411b, 428, 435, 1506b, 1623a, 1630, 2254; 12 U.S. Code §§ 1020a-2, 1020c-1, 1023a, 1131a-1; 15 U.S. Code § 713a-10; 16 U.S. Code §§ 590e-1, 590e-2; 21 U.S. Code § 129; 33 U.S. Code § 701f-3

May 19, 1956, Ch. 313, 70 Stat. 162, 15 U.S. Code § 713a-10

June 4, 1956, Ch. 355, 70 Stat. 229, 7 U.S. Code §§ 411b, 428, 435, 1506b, 1623a, 1630, 2254; 12 U.S. Code §§ 1020a-2, 1020c-1, 1023a, 1131a-1; 15 U.S. Code § 713a-10; 16 U.S. Code §§ 590e-1, 590e-2; 21 U.S. Code § 129

June 13, 1958, P.L. 85-459, 72 Stat. 188, 7 U.S. Code §§ 411b, 435, 1623a, 1831a, 2254; 12 U.S. Code §§ 1020a-3, 1023a; 15 U.S. Code § 713a-10; 16 U.S. Code §§ 590e-1, 509e-2; 21 U.S. Code § 129

May 20, 1959, P.L. 86-30, 73 Stat. 36, 15 U.S. Code § 713a-10

July 8, 1959, P.L. 86-80, 73 Stat. 167, 7 U.S. Code §§ 411b, 435, 1623a, 2254; 12 U.S. Code § 1020a-3; 15 U.S. Code § 713a-10; 16 U.S. Code §§ 590e-1, 590e-2; 21 U.S. Code § 129

April 13, 1960, P.L. 86-424, 74 Stat. 42, 15 U.S. Code § 713a-10

June 29, 1960, P.L. 86-532, 74 Stat. 232, 7 U.S. Code §§ 411b, 435, 1623a, 2254; 12 U.S. Code § 1020a-3; 15 U.S. Code § 713a-10; 16 U.S. Code §§ 590e-1, 590e-2; 21 U.S. Code § 129

Aug. 2, 1967, P.L. 85-118, 71 Stat. 329, 7 U.S. Code §§ 411b, 435 , 1623a, 2254; 12 U.S. Code §§ 1020a-3, 1023a; 15 U.S. Code § 5713a-10; 16 U.S. Code §§ 590e-1, 590e-2; 21 U.S. Code § 129

April 4, 1996, P.L. 104-127, 7 U.S. Code § 1831a

Department of Agriculture and Related Agencies Appropriation Acts

July 26, 1961, P.L. 87-112, 75 Stat. 225, 7 U.S. Code §§ 411b, 435, 1623a, 2254; 12 U.S. Code § 1020a-3; 15 U.S. Code § 713a-10; 16 U.S. Code §§ 590e-1, 590e-2; 21 U.S. Code § 129

Oct. 24, 1962, P.L. 87-879, 76 Stat. 1203, 7 U.S. Code §§ 411b, 435, 1623a, 2254; 15 U.S. Code § 713a-10; 16 U.S. Code §§ 590e-1, 590e-2; 21 U.S. Code § 129

Continued

Dec. 30, 1963, P.L. 88-250, 77 Stat. 820, 7 U.S. Code §§ 411b, 435, 450a, 1623a, 2254; 15 U.S. Code 713a-10; 16 U.S. Code §§ 590e-1, 590e-2; 21 U.S. Code § 129

Sept. 2, 1964, P.L. 88-573, 78 Stat. 862, 7 U.S. Code §§ 411b, 435, 1623a, 2254; 15 U.S. Code § 713a-10; 16 U.S. Code §§ 590e-1, 590e-2; 21 U.S. Code § 129

Nov. 2, 1965, P.L. 89-316, 79 Stat. 1165, 7 U.S. Code §§ 411b, 435, 1623a, 2254; 15 U.S. Code § 713a-10; 16 U.S. Code §§ 590e-1, 590e-2; 21 U.S. Code § 129

Sept. 7, 1966, P.L. 89-556, 80 Stat. 704, 7 U.S. Code §§ 411b, 435, 1623a, 2254; 15 U.S. Code § 713a-10; 16 U.S. Code §§ 590e-1, 590e-2; 21 U.S. Code § 129

Oct. 24, 1967, P.L. 90-113, 81 Stat. 319, 7 U.S. Code §§ 411b, 435, 1623a, 2254; 15 U.S. Code § 713a-10; 16 U.S. Code §§ 590e-1, 590e-2; 21 U.S. Code § 129

Aug. 8, 1968, P.L. 90-463, 82 Stat. 639, 7 U.S. Code §§ 411b, 435 , 1623a, 2254; 15 U.S. Code § 713a-10; 16 U.S. Code §§ 590e-1, 590e-2; 21 U.S. Code § 129; 42 U.S. Code § 1474a

Nov. 26, 1969, P.L. 91-127, 83 Stat. 244, 7 U.S. Code §§ 411b, 435, 1623a, 2254; 15 U.S. Code § 713a-10; 16 U.S. Code §§ 590e-1, 590e-2; 21 U.S. Code § 129

Dec. 22, 1970, P.L. 91-566, 84 Stat. 1480, 7 U.S. Code §§ 411b, 435, 1623a, 2254; 15 U.S. Code § 713a-10; 16 U.S. Code §§ 590e-1, 590e-2; 21 U.S. Code § 129; 33 U.S. Code § 701f-3

Department of Agriculture Appropriation Act, 1952

June 30, 1978, P.L. 95-307, 16 U.S. Code § 581a-1

Department of Agriculture Appropriation Acts

June 4, 1936, Ch. 489, 49 Stat. 1421, 7 U.S. Code §§ 204, 228a, 231, 367, 414, 415a, 419, 2231, 2232, 2237; 15 U.S. Code § 319; 21 U.S. Code § 129

June 29, 1937, Ch. 404, 50 Stat. 395, 7 U.S. Code §§ 204, 228a, 231, 367, 414, 415a, 419, 2231, 2232; 15 U.S. Code §§ 319, 322; 16 U.S. Code §§ 590i-1, 715k-2; 21 U.S. Code § 129

June 16, 1938, Ch. 464, 52 Stat. 711, 7 U.S. Code §§ 204, 228a, 231, 367, 414, 415a, 419, 1381a, 1404a, 1404b, 2231, 2232; 15 U.S. Code §§ 319, 322; 16 U.S. Code §§ 590h-1, 590i-1, 715k-2; 21 U.S. Code § 129

June 30, 1939, Ch. 253, 53 Stat. 939, 7 U.S. Code §§ 204, 228a, 231, 367, 411b, 414, 415e, 419, 612c, 2231, 2232; 15 U.S. Code §§ 319, 322; 16 U.S. Code §§ 501a, 578, 590i-1, 715k-2; 21 U.S. Code § 129

June 25, 1940, Ch. 421, 54 Stat. 532, 7 U.S. Code §§ 204, 228a, 231, 367, 411b, 414, 415e, 419, 428, 612c nt., 1179 nt., 2231, 2232; 12 U.S. Code § 1020n-1; 15 U.S. Code §§ 319, 322, 609g, 609h; 16 U.S. Code §§ 501a, 571a, 578, 579, 590h nt., 590i-1; 21 U.S. Code § 129

July 1, 1941, Ch. 267, 55 Stat. 408, 7 U.S. Code §§ 204, 228a, 231, 367, 411b, 414, 415e 419, 428, 612c nt., 1007a, 2231, 2232; 12 U.S. Code § 1020n-1; 15 U.S. Code §§ 609l, 609m, 609n; 16 U.S. Code §§ 501a, 571a, 578a, 579, 580, 590h nt., 590i-1; 21 U.S. Code § 129

Dec. 22, 1941, Ch. 611, 55 Stat. 850, 16 U.S. Code § 590h nt.

July 22, 1942, Ch. 516, 56 Stat. 664, 7 U.S. Code prec. § 141 nt., §§ 204, 228a, 231 nt., 367, 395, 411b, 414, 415e, 419, 428, 2231, 2232, 2244, 2251; 12 U.S. Code §§ 1020n-1, 1756a; 15 U.S. Code §§ 609s, 609t, 609u; 16 U.S. Code §§ 501a, 571a, 578a, 579, 580 590i-1, 590h nt.; 21 U.S. Code § 129

July 12, 1943, Ch. 215, 57 Stat. 392, 7 U.S. Code §§ 174, 204, 228a, 367, 395, 411b, 414, 415e, 419, 428, 2231, 2232, 2235; 12 U.S. Code § 952a; 15 U.S. Code §§ 609v, 609w; 16 U.S. Code §§ 501a, 571a, 578a, 579, 580, 590h nt.; 21 U.S. Code § 129; 40 U.S. Code § 435

June 28, 1944, Ch. 296, 58 Stat. 420, 7 U.S. Code §§ 161a, 174, 228a, 283, 367, 395, 411b, 414, 415e, 419, 428, 429, 1001 nt., 2231, 2232, 2235; 12 U.S. Code § 832; 15 U.S. Code §§ 609v, 609w, 609x; 16 U.S. Code §§ 501a, 571a, 578a, 579, 580, 581, 590e-1, 590h nt.; 21 U.S. Code § 129; 40 U.S. Code § 435

May 5, 1945, Ch. 109, 59 Stat. 136, 7 U.S. Code §§ 174, 367, 411b, 414, 419, 428, 1001 nt., 2254; 15 U.S. Code §§ 609v, 609y; 16 U.S. Code §§ 571a, 571b, 579, 590e-1; 21 U.S. Code § 129; 40 U.S. Code § 435

June 22, 1946, Ch. 445, 60 Stat. 270, 7 U.S. Code §§ 367, 411b, 414, 428, 1001 nt., 2254; 15 U.S. Code §§ 609a-1, 609z; 16 U.S. Code §§ 571a, 571b, 579, 590e-1; 21 U.S. Code § 129; 40 U.S. Code § 435

July 30, 1947, Ch. 356, 61 Stat. 523, 7 U.S. Code §§ 367, 411b, 414, 428, 435, 612c nt., 903, 1032, 1506a, 1506a nt., 2254; 15 U.S. Code §§ 713a-10, 713a-10 nt.; 16 U.S. Code §§ 571a, 571b, 579, 590e-1; 21 U.S. Code §§ 97 to 97d, 129; 42 U.S. Code § 1752 nt.

June 19, 1948, Ch. 543, 62 Stat. 507, 7 U.S. Code §§ 367, 411b, 414, 428, 435, 2254; 16 U.S. Code §§ 571a, 571b, 579, 590e-1; 21 U.S. Code § 129

June 29, 1949, Ch. 280, 63 Stat. 324, 7 U.S. Code §§ 128, 367, 411b, 414, 435, 438 nt., 440, 2254; 12 U.S. Code §§ 1020a-2, 1020c-1, 1023a, 1131a-1; 15 U.S. Code § 713a-10; 16 U.S. Code §§ 553, 571a, 571b, 579, 580b, 590e-1

Sept. 6, 1950, Ch. 896, 64 Stat. 657, 7 U.S. Code §§ 367, 414, 435, 2236, 2254; 12 U.S. Code §§ 1020a-2, 1020c-1, 1023a, 1131a-1; 15 U.S . Code § 713a-10; 16 U.S. Code §§ 571a, 571b, 579, 590e-1; 21 U.S. Code § 129

Aug. 31, 1951, Ch. 374, 65 Stat. 293, 7 U.S. Code §§ 414, 414a, 435, 567, 2226, 2254; 12 U.S. Code §§ 1020a-2, 1020c-1, 1023a, 1131a-1 ; 15 U.S. Code § 713a-10; 16 U.S. Code §§ 571a, 571b, 579, 581a-1, 590e-1; 21 U.S. Code §§ 99, 129

July 5, 1952, Ch. 574, 66 Stat. 355, 7 U.S. Code §§ 51a-1, 367, 411b, 414, 428, 435, 2254; 12 U.S. Code §§ 1020a-2, 1020c-1, 1023a, 1131a-1; 15 U.S. Code § 713a-10; 16 U.S. Code §§ 571a, 571b, 579, 581a-2, 590e-1, 590e-2, 590g-1, 590g-2; 21 U.S. Code § 129

July 28, 1953, Ch. 251, 67 Stat. 225, 7 U.S. Code §§ 367, 411b, 414, 428, 435, 2254; 12 U.S. Code §§ 1020a-2, 1020c-1, 1023a, 1131a-1; 15 U.S. Code § 713a-10; 16 U.S. Code §§ 571a, 571b, 579, 581a-2, 590e-1, 590e-2, 590g-1; 21 U.S. Code § 129

Aug. 4, 1965, P.L., 89-106, 79 Stat. 432, 7 U.S. Code § 2263

Department of Agriculture Organic Act of 1944

Sept. 21, 1944, Ch. 412, 58 Stat. 734, 7 U.S. Code §§ 57a, 147a, 228a, 228a nt., 283, 343c-1, 395, 395 nt., 415e, 427d, 429 to 431, 431 nt., 432, 903 to 905, 915, 1605; 12 U.S. Code §§ 832, 833, 1020a-1, 2231, 2232, 2244, 2249, 2250, 2252, 2255 to 2258; 16 U.S. Code §§ 500, 501, 526, 527, 554b, 554c, 559a, 565, 567 nt., 572a, 579a, 580, 580a, 590f, 590h, 590q-1; 21 U.S. Code § 114a, 114a nt.

Dec. 23, 1944, Ch. 725, 58 Stat. 925, 7 U.S. Code § 904

June 29, 1948, Ch. 703, 62 Stat. 1070, 7 U.S. Code § 904

June 17, 1949, Ch. 220, 63 Stat. 200, 7 U.S. Code § 147a

Aug. 4, 1950, Ch. 579, 64 Stat. 413, 7 U.S. Code § 429

Aug. 11, 1955, Ch. 785, 69 Stat. 665, 12 U.S. Code § 832

July 26, 1956, Ch. 741, 70 Stat. 667, 12 U.S. Code § 832

May 23, 1957, P.L. 85-36, 71 Stat. 35, 7 U.S. Code § 147a

Oct. 6, 1970, P.L. 91-435, 84 Stat. 888, 16 U.S. Code § 579a

Nov. 28, 1990, P.L. 101-624, 7 U.S. Code § 147a

Oct. 13, 1994, P.L. 103-354, 7 U.S. Code § 915

Department of Agriculture Organic Act of 1956

Aug. 3, 1956, Ch. 950, 70 Stat. 1032, 7 U.S. Code §§ 428a, 1004, 1040, 1392, 1516, 1766, 2228, 2229, 2233; 16 U.S. Code §§ 579b, 590h-4, 590k, 590n; 21 U.S. Code §§ 114a, 114c

Oct. 23, 1962, P.L. 87-869, 76 Stat. 1157, 16 U.S. Code § 579b

April 4, 1996, P.L. 104-127, 16 U.S. Code § 590h-4

Department of Agriculture Registration, License and Permit Act

Ga. Code Ann., 2-5-1 et seq.

Department of Agriculture Reorganization Act of 1994

Oct. 13, 1994, P.L. 103-354, 7 U.S. Code § 6901 nt.

April 4, 1996, P.L. 104-127, 7 U.S. Code §§ 6911, 6932, 6933, 6941, 6942, 6943, 6962

June 23, 1998, P.L. 105-185, 7 U.S. Code § 6920

Department of Air Transportation and Service Act

Ala. Acts 1982, 3d Sp., p. 389

Department of Arkansas State Police Communications Equipment Leasing Act

Ark. Code Ann. 1987, 12-8-301 et seq.

Department of Arkansas State Police Headquarters Facility and Wireless Data Equipment Financing Act

Ark. Acts 1997, No. 1057

Department of Automated Data Processing Act

N.M. Stat. Ann., 15-1-1 et seq.

Department of Banking and Insurance Act

N.J. Stat. Ann., 17:1-1 et seq., 45:15-5 et seq.

N.J. Stat. Ann., 17:1-13 et seq.

Department of Banking Code

Pa. Purdon's Stat., Title 71, § 733-1 et seq.

Department of Banking Reorganization Act

Tenn. Public Acts 1973, Ch. 294

Department of Central Management Services Executive Order Implementation Act

Ill. Laws 1982, P.A. 82-789

Department of Children's Services Act of 1979

Tenn. Code Ann., 37-2-201

Department of Commerce Act

Mass. Gen. Laws Ann., 23A:1 et seq.

Okla. Stat. Ann., Title 74, § 5003.1 et seq.

Department of Commerce and Economic Development Act

N.J. Stat. Ann., 52:27H-1 et seq.

Department of Commerce and Industry Act

N.M. Stat. Ann., 9-15-1 et seq.

Department of Commerce and Labor Act

Feb. 14, 1903, Ch. 552, 32 Stat. 825, 15 U.S. Code §§ 1501, 1504, 1510 to 1519; 16 U.S. Code § 631; 29 U.S. Code § 557; 40 U.S. Code § 483

Department of Commerce and Related Agencies Appropriation Acts

June 30, 1955, Ch. 253, 69 Stat. 226, 15 U.S. Code §§ 285 nt., 327 nt., 329; 23 U.S. Code §§ 13a nt., 23 nt., 57; 33 U.S. Code §§ 851, 872; 41 U.S. Code § 6b; 46 U.S. Code §§ 1241b, 1241b nt., 1242-1; 50 U.S. Code Appx. § 1738b

Aug. 4, 1955, Ch. 541, 69 Stat. 452

May 19, 1956, Ch. 313, 70 Stat. 162, 46 U.S. Code § 1241b

June 20, 1956, Ch. 415, 70 Stat. 314, 15 U.S. Code §§ 285 nt., 327 nt., 329, 633 nt.; 33 U.S. Code §§ 851, 872; 41 U.S. Code § 6b; 46 U.S. Code §§ 1241b, 1242-1; 50 U.S. Code Appx. § 1738b

June 13, 1957, P.L. 85-52, 71 Stat. 70, 15 U.S. Code §§ 285 nt., 327 nt., 329; 33 U.S. Code §§ 851, 872; 41 U.S. Code § 6b; 46 U.S. Code §§ 1177a, 1242-1; 50 U.S. Code Appx. § 1738b

March 28, 1958, P.L. 85-352, 72 Stat. 52, 41 U.S. Code § 6b

June 25, 1958, P.L. 85-469, 72 Stat. 226, 15 U.S. Code §§ 278e nt., 285, 327 nt., 329; 33 U.S. Code §§ 851, 872; 41 U.S. Code § 6b; 46 U.S. Code §§ 1242-1, 1280; 49 U.S. Code §§ 1322 nt., 1343 nt.; 50 U.S. Code Appx. § 1738b

July 13, 1959, P.L. 86-88, 73 Stat. 201, 15 U.S. Code §§ 278e nt. , 327 nt., 329, 633 nt.; 33 U.S. Code §§ 851, 872; 41 U.S. Code § 6b; 50 U.S. Code Appx. 1738b

May 13, 1960, P.L. 86-451, 74 Stat. 93, 15 U.S. Code §§ 278e nt., 327 nt., 329 nt., 633 nt.; 33 U.S. Code §§ 851 nt., 872 nt.; 41 U.S. Code § 6b; 50 U.S. Code Appx. § 1738b

Oct. 4, 1961, P.L. 87-367, 75 Stat. 787, 49 U.S. Code § 1322 nt.

Department of Commerce and Related Agencies Appropriations Act, 1996

April 26, 1996, P.L. 104-134, Title II, 110 Stat. 1321-23

Department of Commerce and Related Agencies Appropriations Act, 1997

Sept. 30, 1996, P.L. 104-208, Title II, 110 Stat. 3009

Department of Commerce and Related Agencies Appropriations Act, 1998

Nov. 26, 1997, P.L. 105-119, Title II, 111 Stat. 2471

Department of Commerce and Related Agencies Appropriations Act, 1999

Oct. 21, 1998, P.L. 105-277, 101(b), Title II, 112 Stat. 2681

Department of Commerce Appropriation Acts

June 29, 1939, Ch. 248, 53 Stat. 885, 15 U.S. Code §§ 197f, 198; 33 U.S. Code § 851

May 14, 1940, Ch. 189, 54 Stat. 192, 33 U.S. Code § 851

June 28, 1941, Ch. 258, 55 Stat. 277, 15 U.S. Code §§ 319, 322; 33 U.S. Code § 851

July 2, 1942, Ch. 472, 56 Stat. 489, 15 U.S. Code §§ 319, 322; 33 U.S. Code § 851

July 1, 1943, Ch. 182, 57 Stat. 290, 15 U.S. Code §§ 319, 322, 323; 33 U.S. Code § 851

June 28, 1944, Ch. 294, 58 Stat. 414, 5 U.S. Code § 607; 15 U.S. Code §§ 319, 324

May 21, 1945, Ch. 129, 59 Stat. 196, 15 U.S. Code §§ 319, 324, 1509; 33 U.S. Code § 872

July 5, 1946, Ch. 541, 60 Stat. 465, 15 U.S. Code §§ 319, 324; 33 U.S. Code § 872

July 9, 1947, Ch. 211, 61 Stat. 294, 15 U.S. Code §§ 319, 324; 33 U.S. Code §§ 851, 872

June 3, 1948, Ch. 400, 62 Stat. 321, 15 U.S. Code §§ 319, 324; 33 U.S. Code §§ 851, 872

July 20, 1949, Ch. 354, 63 Stat. 462, 15 U.S. Code §§ 283, 284, 327 nt., 329; 33 U.S. Code §§ 851, 872

Sept. 6, 1950, Ch. 896, 64 Stat. 620, 15 U.S. Code §§ 283, 284, 327 nt., 329; 33 U.S. Code §§ 851, 872

Oct. 22, 1951, Ch. 533, 65 Stat. 585, 15 U.S. Code §§ 284, 327 nt., 329, 1153a; 33 U.S. Code §§ 851, 872

July 10, 1952, Ch. 651, 66 Stat. 560, 15 U.S. Code §§ 327 nt., 329 nt.; 33 U.S. Code §§ 851, 872

Aug. 5, 1953, Ch. 328, 67 Stat. 384, 15 U.S. Code §§ 327 nt., 329; 33 U.S. Code §§ 851, 872; 46 U.S. Code § 1242-1; 50 U.S. Code Appx. . § 1738b

July 2, 1954, Ch. 456, 68 Stat. 422, 5 U.S. Code §§ 133z-15 nt., 591 nt., 592a-3; 15 U.S. Code §§ 327 nt., 329; 23 U.S. Code § 57; 46 U.S. Code § 1242-1; 50 U.S. Code Appx. § 1738b

Oct. 18, 1962, P.L. 87-843, 76 Stat. 1089, 15 U.S. Code § 278e nt.; 31 U.S. Code § 25; 33 U.S. Code § 851; 50 U.S. Code Appx. § 1738b

Dec. 30, 1963, P.L. 88-245, 77 Stat. 784, 15 U.S. Code § 278e nt.; 33 U.S. Code § 851; 50 U.S. Code Appx. § 1738b

Aug. 31, 1964, P.L. 88-527, 78 Stat. 720, 15 U.S. Code § 278e nt.; 33 U.S. Code § 851; 50 U.S. Code Appx. § 1738b

Sept. 2, 1965, P.L. 89-164, 79 Stat. 636, 15 U.S. Code § 278e nt.; 33 U.S. Code § 851; 50 U.S. Code Appx. § 738b

Nov. 8, 1966, P.L. 89-797, 80 Stat. 1488, 50 U.S. Code Appx. § 1738b

Nov. 8, 1967, P.L. 90-133, 81 Stat. 419, 50 U.S. Code Appx. § 1738b

Aug. 9, 1968, P.L. 90-470, 82 Stat. 682, 50 U.S. Code Appx. § 1738b

Dec. 24, 1969, P.L. 91-153, 83 Stat. 412, 50 U.S. Code Appx. § 1738b

Oct. 21, 1970, P.L. 91-472, 84 Stat. 1048, 50 U.S. Code Appx. § 1738b

Aug. 10, 1971, P.L. 92-77, 85 Stat. 260, 50 U.S. Code Appx. § 1738b

Oct. 25, 1972, P.L. 92-544, 86 Stat. 1118, 50 U.S. Code Appx. § 1736b

Nov. 27, 1973, P.L. 93-162, 87 Stat. 649, 50 U.S. Code Appx. § 1738b

Oct. 2, 1975, P.L. 94-121, 89 Stat. 622, 50 U.S. Code Appx. § 1738b

July 12, 1976, P.L. 94-352, 49 U.S. Code § 1701 et seq.

Continued

Dec. 13, 1985, P.L. 99-180, 33 U.S. Code
§ 851
Oct. 18, 1986, P.L. 99-500, 100 Stat. 3386
Oct. 30, 1986, P.L. 99-591, 100 Stat. 3386
Dec. 22, 1987, P.L. 100-202, 101 Stat. 1329
Oct. 1, 1988, P.L. 100-459, 102 Stat. 2192
Nov. 21, 1989, P.L. 101-162, 103 Stat. 988

Department of Commerce Appropriations Act, 1991
Nov. 5, 1990, P.L. 101-515, 13 U.S. Code
§ 23 nt., 19 U.S. Code § 2171 nt., 33 U.S.
Code §§ 851, 2706 nt.

Department of Commerce Appropriations Act, 1992
Oct. 28, 1991, P.L. 102-140, 105 Stat. 799

Department of Commerce Appropriations Act, 1993
Oct. 6, 1992, P.L. 102-395, 106 Stat. 1848

Department of Commerce Appropriations Act, 1994
Oct. 27, 1993, P.L. 103-121, 107 Stat. 1169

Department of Commerce, Justice, and State, the Judiciary and Related Agencies Appropriations Act, 1988
Oct. 28, 1991, P.L. 102-138, 105 Stat. 665

Department of Commerce, Justice, and State, the Judiciary, and Related Agencies Appropriations Act, 1999
May 21, 1999, P.L. 106-31, 16 U.S. Code
§ 1851 nt.

Department of Commerce Organic Act
P.R. Laws Ann. 1954, Title 3 § 431 et seq.

Department of Community Affairs Act
N.J. Stat. Ann., 52:27D-1 et seq.

Department of Community Affairs Demonstration Grant Act
N.J. Stat. Ann. 1937, 52:27D-59 et seq.

Department of Conservation and Economic Development Act
N.J. Rev. Stat. 1937, 13:1B-1 et seq.

Department of Consumer Affairs Organic Act
P.R. Laws Ann. 1954, Title 3, § 341 et seq.

Department of Correction Cost-Efficiency and Inmate Responsibility Omnibus Act
Wash. Rev. Code Ann., 72.09.450 et seq.

Department of Corrections Act
Ariz. Rev. Stat. Ann., § 41-1601 et seq.
Ind. Code Ann., 11-8-1-1 et seq.
Mich. Comp. Laws Ann., 791.201 et seq.
N.C. Gen. Stat. 1943, § 143B-260 et seq.
N.J. Stat. Ann., 30:1B-1 et seq.
N.M. Stat. Ann., 9-3-1 et seq.

Department of Corrections Act (County)
Ill. Comp. Stat. 1992, Ch. 55, § 5/3-15001 et seq.

Department of Corrections Volunteer Program Act
Miss. Code Ann. 1972, § 47-5-201 et seq.

Department of Defense Act
N.J. Stat. Ann., 38A:3-1 et seq.

Department of Defense Act of 1948
N.J. Stat. Ann., 38:14B-1 et seq.

Department of Defense Appropriation Acts
Oct. 18, 1951, Ch. 512, 65 Stat. 423, 31 U.S. Code § 649a
July 10, 1952, Ch. 630, 66 Stat. 517, 31 U.S. Code § 649a; 40 U.S. Code § 483a; 50 U.S. Code Appx. §§ 2351 to 2356
April 16, 1953, Ch. 25, 67 Stat. 23
Aug. 1, 1953, Ch. 305, 67 Stat. 336, 10 U.S. Code § 2210; 31 U.S. Code §§ 493a, 634b, 649a, 649b, 650a to 650c; 40 U.S. Code § 483a; 50 U.S. Code § 65
June 30, 1954, Ch. 432, 68 Stat. 337, 31 U.S. Code § 649a; 37 U.S. Code § 237a; 40 U.S. Code § 483a
July 13, 1955, Ch. 358, 69 Stat. 301, 31 U.S. Code §§ 529i, 649a; 40 U.S. Code § 483a
July 2, 1956, Ch. 488, 70 Stat. 455, 31 U.S. Code § 649a; 40 U.S. Code § 483a

Aug. 2, 1957, P.L. 85-117, 71 Stat. 312, 10 U.S. Code §§ 807, 858 , 4308, 4333, 4382 nt.; 24 U.S. Code § 21a nt.; 31 U.S. Code § 649a; 32 U.S. Code § 709 nt.; 40 U.S. Code § 483a

Aug. 22, 1958, P.L. 85-724, 72 Stat. 711, 10 U.S. Code §§ 807 nt. , 858 nt., 4308 nt., 4333 nt., 4382 nt.; 31 U.S. Code § 649a; 32 U.S. Code § 709 nt.; 40 U.S. Code § 483

May 20, 1959, P.L. 86-30, 73 Stat. 38

Aug. 18, 1959, P.L. 86-166, 73 Stat. 366, 10 U.S. Code §§ 807 nt., 858 nt., 4308 nt., 4382 nt.; 31 U.S. Code § 649a; 32 U.S. Code § 709 nts.; 40 U.S. Code § 483a

July 7, 1960, P.L. 86-601, 74 Stat. 338, 10 U.S. Code §§ 807 nt., 858 nt., 4308 nt., 4382 nt.; 31 U.S. Code § 649a; 32 U.S. Code § 709 nts.; 40 U.S. Code § 483a

Aug. 17, 1961, P.L. 87-144, 75 Stat. 365, 10 U.S. Code §§ 807 nt. , 858 nt., 4308 nt., 4382 nt.; 31 U.S. Code § 649a; 32 U.S. Code § 709 nts.; 40 U.S. Code § 483a

Aug. 9, 1962, P.L. 87-577, 76 Stat. 318, 10 U.S. Code §§ 807 nt., 858 nt., 4308 nt., 4382 nt.; 31 U.S. Code § 649a; 32 U.S. Code § 709 nt.; 40 U.S. Code § 483a

Oct. 17, 1963, P.L. 88-149, 77 Stat. 254, 31 U.S. Code § 649a; 40 U.S. Code § 483a

Aug. 19, 1964, P.L. 88-446, 78 Stat. 465, 10 U.S. Code §§ 807 nt. , 858 nt., 4308 nt., 4382 nt.; 31 U.S. Code § 649a; 32 U.S. Code § 709 nts.; 40 U.S. Code § 483a

Sept. 29, 1965, P.L. 89-213, 79 Stat. 880, 10 U.S. Code §§ 807 nt., 858 nt., 2103, 4308 nt.; 31 U.S. Code § 649a; 32 U.S. Code § 709 nts.; 40 U.S. Code § 483a

Oct. 15, 1966, P.L. 89-687, 80 Stat. 980, 10 U.S. Code §§ 263 nt., 807 nt., 858 nt., 2103 nt., 4303 nt.; 31 U.S. Code §§ 649a; 32 U.S. Code § 709 nts.; 40 U.S. Code § 483a; 41 U.S. Code § 11

Sept. 29, 1967, P.L. 90-96, 81 Stat. 231, 31 U.S. Code §§ 649a, 700, 700a; 40 U.S. Code § 483a; 50 U.S. Code § 100a

Oct. 17, 1968, P.L. 90-580, 82 Stat. 1120, 5 U.S. Code § 3101 nt.; 31 U.S. Code §§ 649a 700, 700a; 32 U.S. Code § 709 nt.; 40 U.S. Code § 483a; 50 U.S. Code § 100a

Dec. 29, 1969, P.L. 91-171, 83 Stat. 469, 10 U.S. Code §§ 807 nt., 858 nt., 2103 nt., 4308 nt.; 31 U.S. Code §§ 649a, 700, 700a; 40 U.S. Code § 483a; 50 U.S. Code § 100a

Jan. 11, 1971, P.L. 91-668, 84 Stat. 2020, 10 U.S. Code §§ 807 nt., 858 nt., 2103 nt., 4308 nt.; 31 U.S. Code §§ 649a, 700, 700a; 40 U.S. Code § 483a; 50 U.S. Code § 100a

Dec. 18, 1971, P.L. 92-204, 85 Stat. 716, 31 U.S. Code §§ 649a, 700, 700a; 40 U.S. Code § 483a

Oct. 26, 1972, P.L. 92-570, 86 Stat. 1204, 31 U.S. Code §§ 649a, 700, 700a; 40 U.S. Code § 483a; 50 U.S. Code § 100a

Jan. 2, 1974, P.L. 93-238, 87 Stat. 1026, 10 U.S. Code §§ 807 nt., 858 nt., 2103 nt., 4308 nt.; 31 U.S. Code §§ 649a, 700, 700a; 40 U.S. Code § 483a; 50 U.S. Code § 100a

Aug. 5, 1974, P.L. 93-365, 88 Stat. 399, 10 U.S. Code §§ 138 nt., 4314, 7291 nt., 7307; 50 U.S. Code Appx. § 2403-1

Oct. 7, 1975, P.L. 94-106, 89 Stat. 531, 10 U.S. Code §§ 133 nt., 138, 139, 140, 511, 675, 1401a, 2004 nt., 2304 nt., 4342, 6954, 6956, 7291 nt., 9342; 37 U.S. Code § 1009 nt.; 50 U.S. Code § 1511 nt.; 50 U.S. Code Appx. §§ 454, 456

Feb. 9, 1976, P.L. 94-212, 37 U.S. Code § 1006 et seq.

Sept. 21, 1977, P.L. 95-111, 10 U.S. Code

§§ 807 nt., 858 nt., 2103 nt., 2304 nt.; 31 U.S. Code §§ 649a, 700, 700a; 40 U.S. Code § 483a; 50 U.S. Code § 100a

Dec. 21, 1979, P.L. 96-154, 10 U.S. Code §§ 807 nt., 858 nt., 2103 nt., 2208 nt.; 31 U.S. Code §§ 649a, 700, 700a; 40 U.S. Code § 483a; 50 U.S. Code § 100a

Dec. 8, 1983, P.L. 98-212, 10 U.S. Code §§ 138 nt., 483a, 802 nt., 858 nt., 1584 nt., 2103, 2304 nt., 2807 nt.

Oct. 12, 1984, P.L. 98-473

Oct. 19, 1984, P.L. 98-525, 10 U.S. Code § 2304 nt.

Nov. 8, 1985, P.L. 99-145, 5 U.S. Code § 5102; 10 U.S. Code §§ 133 nt., 517, 523, 524, 555, 597, 1201 et seq., 1447 nt., 2301 nt., 3848, 3852, 4348, 5101, 5442, 5444, 6959, 7572, 9314, 9348; 14 U.S. Code § 41; 22 U.S. Code §§ 1928 nt., 592a; 33 U.S. Code § 853u

Dec. 19, 1985, P.L. 99-190, 10 U.S. Code §§ 138 nt., 139 nt., 1584 nt., 2324, 2324 nt., 2553 nt., 7572 nt.; 37 U.S. Code § 403 nt.; 40 U.S. Code § 483a; 42 U.S. Code § 2464a

May 31, 1986, P.L. 99-331, 100 Stat. 510

Continued

July 1, 1986, P.L. 99-348, 10 U.S. Code § 6330 nt.

July 2, 1986, P.L. 99-349, 100 Stat. 719

Oct. 18, 1986, P.L. 99-500, 100 Stat. 3522

Oct. 30, 1986, P.L. 99-591, 100 Stat. 3522

Nov. 14, 1986, P.L. 99-661, 100 Stat. 3967, 3972

April 21, 1987, P.L. 100-26, 10 U.S. Code §§ 1466, 1621 nt., 2326, 2365, 2437 nt.; 37 U.S. Code § 1014 nt.

July 11, 1987, P.L. 100-71, 101 Stat. 397

Dec. 22, 1987, P.L. 100-202, 10 U.S. Code § 114 nt.

Dec. 22, 1987, P.L. 100-202, 101 Stat. 1329

July 19, 1988, P.L. 100-370, 10 U.S. Code § 2304 nt.

July 19, 1988, P.L. 100-370, 102 Stat. 849, 10 U.S. Code § 114 nt.; 40 U.S. Code § 483a

July 19, 1988, P.L. 100-370, 102 Stat. 851, 10 U.S. Code § 113 nt.

July 19, 1988, P.L. 100-370, 102 Stat. 851, 10 U.S. Code § 114 nt.

Aug. 23, 1988, P.L. 100-418, 102 Stat. 1370

Sept. 29, 1988, P.L. 100-456, 102 Stat. 2053, 10 U.S. Code § 194 nt.

Oct. 1, 1988, P.L. 100-463, 102 Stat. 2270-60

Oct. 24, 1988, P.L. 100-526, 102 Stat. 2624

Nov. 21, 1989, P.L. 101-165, 103 Stat. 1112

Nov. 21, 1989, P.L. 101-165, 103 Stat. 1146

Nov. 5, 1990, P.L. 101-510, 10 U.S. Code §§ 1584 nt., 2241 nt.

Department of Defense Appropriation Authorization Act of 1974

Nov. 16, 1973, P.L. 93-155, 87 Stat. 605, 10 U.S. Code §§ 131 nts., 138, 139, 673, 1448 nt., 2004, 2307, 2635; 15 U.S. Code § 751 nt.; 22 U.S. Code § 1928 nt.; 50 U.S. Code §§ 451 to 455, 1431; 50 U.S. Code Appx. §§ 468, 2092

Department of Defense Appropriation Authorization Act, 1975

Sept. 8, 1982, P.L. 97-252, 10 U.S. Code § 2451 nt.

July 19, 1988, P.L. 100-370, 10 U.S. Code § 2301 nt.

Department of Defense Appropriation Authorization Act, 1976

Nov. 9, 1979, P.L. 96-107, 10 U.S. Code § 139 nt.

Sept. 8, 1982, P.L. 97-252, 10 U.S. Code §§ 133 nt., 139 nt.

Nov. 8, 1984, P.L. 98-620, 10 U.S. Code § 2304 nt.

Department of Defense Appropriation Authorization Act, 1977

July 14, 1976, P.L. 94-361, 46 U.S. Code § 1126-1

Department of Defense Appropriation Authorization Act, 1978

July 30, 1977, P.L. 95-79, 10 U.S. Code § 131 et seq.; 32 U.S. Code §§ 105, 708; 50 U.S. Code § 1520; 50 U.S. Code Appx. § 462 nt.

Nov. 9, 1979, P.L. 96-107, 10 U.S. Code § 131 nt.

Sept. 8, 1980, P.L. 96-342, 10 U.S. Code § 131 nt.

Dec. 21, 1982, P.L. 97-275, 50 U.S. Code § 1520

July 19, 1988, P.L. 100-370, 102 Stat. 840, 10 U.S. Code § 523

Department of Defense Appropriation Authorization Act, 1979

Oct. 20, 1978, P.L. 95-485, 10 U.S. Code §§ 141, 264, 269, 271, 505, 511, 2132, 2135, 3209, 3215, 3220, 3283, 3296, 3297, 3311, 3363, 3364, 3383, 3818, 3848; 37 U.S. Code §§ 302, 302 nt., 303 et seq.

Sept. 8, 1980, P.L. 96-343, 37 U.S. Code § 305a, 305a nt.

July 19, 1988, P.L. 100-370, 102 Stat. 851, 10 U.S. Code § 2304 nt.

Department of Defense Appropriations Act, Fiscal Year 1989

April 30, 1994, P.L. 103-236, 10 U.S. Code § 113 nt.

Department of Defense Appropriations Act, 1983

Feb. 10, 1996, P.L. 104-106, 10 U.S. Code § 114 nt.

Department of Defense Appropriations Act, 1987

Oct. 23, 1992, P.L. 102-484, 10 U.S. Code § 167 nt.

Department of Defense Appropriations Act, 1989

Feb. 10, 1996, P.L. 104-106, 10 U.S. Code § 113 nt.

Department of Defense Appropriations Act, 1990

Nov. 5, 1990, P.L. 101-510, 10 U.S. Code §§ 114 nt., 1056, 1593 nt., 2241 nt., 2341 nt.
Nov. 5, 1990, P.L. 101-511, 16 U.S. Code § 396f nt.
Dec. 17, 1993, P.L. 103-204, 16 U.S. Code § 396f

Department of Defense Appropriations Act, 1991

Nov. 5, 1990, P.L. 101-511, 104 Stat. 1856
April 6, 1991, P.L. 102-25, 105 Stat. 87
April 10, 1991, P.L. 102-27, 105 Stat. 140
Oct. 9, 1991, P.L. 102-124, 25 U.S. Code § 1301 nt.
Nov. 26, 1991, P.L. 102-172, 50 U.S. Code §§ 98e nt., 401 nt.

Department of Defense Appropriations Act, 1992

Nov. 26, 1991, P.L. 102-172, 105 Stat. 1150
Oct. 23, 1992, P.L. 102-484, 106 Stat. 2353
Oct. 6, 1993, P.L. 102-396, 10 U.S. Code §§ 113 nt., 114 nt., 166, 221 nt., 401 nt., 1175 nt., 1584 nt., 2218, 2218 nt., 2341 nt., 2441 nt., 2488 nt., 2687 nt., 2774 nt.; 16 U.S. Code § 4107; 21 U.S. Code § 873 nt.; 25 U.S. Code § 1621d; 28 U.S. Code § 118; 32 U.S. Code § 112; 41 U.S. Code § 10b-2; 42 U.S. Code §§ 11701, 11701 nt., 11702 to 11714; 50 U.S. Code § 1705
Feb. 10, 1996, P.L. 104-106, 10 U.S. Code § 2208 nt.
Oct. 21, 1998, P.L. 105-277, 37 U.S. Code § 301b nt.

Department of Defense Appropriations Act, 1993

Oct. 6, 1992, P.L. 102-396, 106 Stat. 1876
July 2, 1993, P.L. 103-50, 107 Stat. 241

Nov. 11, 1993, P.L. 103-139, 10 U.S. Code § 2241 nt.

Department of Defense Appropriations Act, 1995

Sept. 30, 1994, P.L. 103-335, 108 Stat. 2599
April 10, 1995, P.L. 104-6, 10 U.S. Code § 1174a nt.

Department of Defense Appropriations Act, 1996

Dec. 1, 1995, P.L. 104-61, 109 Stat. 636

Department of Defense Appropriations Act, 1997

Sept. 30, 1996, P.L. 104-208, Title I to Title VII, 110 Stat. 3009
Oct. 21, 1998, P.L. 105-277, 10 U.S. Code § 113 nt.

Department of Defense Appropriations Act, 1998

Oct. 8, 1997, P.L. 105-56, 111 Stat. 1203

Department of Defense Appropriations Act, 1999

Oct. 17, 1998, P.L. 105-262, 112 Stat. 2279

Department of Defense Appropriations Authorization Act, 1975

Dec. 17, 1993, P.L. 103-199, 50 U.S. Code Appx. § 2403-1 nt.

Department of Defense Appropriations Authorization Act, 1976

Nov. 5, 1990, P.L. 101-510, 10 U.S. Code § 7291 nt.

Department of Defense Appropriations Authorization Act, 1978

Nov. 18, 1997, P.L. 105-85, 50 U.S. Code § 1520
Oct. 21, 1998, P.L. 105-277, 50 U.S. Code § 1520

Department of Defense Authorization Act for Fiscal Year 1991

Oct. 23, 1992, P.L. 102-484, 10 U.S. Code § 2430 nt.

Department of Defense Authorization Act for Fiscal Years 1988 and 1989

Feb. 10, 1996, P.L. 104-106, 10 U.S. Code § 2431 nt.

Department of Defense Authorization Act, 1980

Nov. 9, 1979, P.L. 96-107, 5 U.S. Code §§ 5315, 5316; 10 U.S. Code §§ 131 nt., 136, 138, 138 nt., 139 nt., 511, 651, 686, 976, 2112, 2114, 2115, 2121, 2121 nt., 2131, 2131 nt., 2304 nt., 2358 nt., 2359, 2359 nt., 2388 nt., 33013, 3218, 3855, 5034, 5457, 5458, 8013, 8218, 8855; 22 U.S. Code § 287c nt.; 37 U.S. Code §§ 309, 309 nt., 313, 405, 405 nt., 406; 50 U.S. Code Appx. §§ 451, 451 nt., 2260

Department of Defense Authorization Act, 1981

Sept. 8, 1982, P.L. 97-252, 10 U.S. Code §§ 520 nt., 2031 nt., 2304 nt.

Oct. 19, 1984, P.L. 98-525, 10 U.S. Code §§ 520 nt., 2141 nt.

Nov. 8, 1985, P.L. 99-145, 10 U.S. Code §§ 520 nt., 2141 nt., 2304 nt.

Nov. 14, 1986, P.L. 99-661, 10 U.S. Code § 2304 nt.

July 19, 1988, P.L. 100-370, 102 Stat. 854, 10 U.S. Code § 2304 nt.

Department of Defense Authorization Act, 1982

Nov. 8, 1985, P.L. 99-145

Nov. 14, 1986, P.L. 99-661, 100 Stat. p. 3827

Dec. 4, 1987, P.L. 100-180, 101 Stat. 1036

Nov. 29, 1989, P.L. 101-189, 10 U.S. Code § 2407 nt.

Department of Defense Authorization Act, 1983

Sept. 8, 1982, P.L. 97-252, 5 U.S. Code § 5315; 10 U.S. Code §§ 138, 138 nt., 503, 520 nt., 525 nt., 1072, 1401, 2031 nt.; 20 U.S. Code § 3442; 38 U.S. Code § 2021 nt.; 50 U.S. Code Appx. §§ 462, 462 nt.

Oct. 1, 1986, P.L. 99-433, 10 U.S. Code § 133 nt.

Department of Defense Authorization Act, 1984

Oct. 30, 1984, P.L. 98-557, 42 U.S. Code § 248d

Nov. 8, 1985, P.L. 99-145, 10 U.S. Code §§ 133 nt., 139c nt., 3360 nt.

Nov. 14, 1986, P.L. 99-661, 10 U.S. Code § 1052 nt.; 42 U.S. Code § 248d

Dec. 4, 1987, P.L. 100-180, 101 Stat. 1134

Sept. 29, 1988, P.L. 100-456, 102 Stat. 1988, 42 U.S. Code § 248d

Nov. 5, 1990, P.L. 101-510, 42 U.S. Code § 248d

April 6, 1991, P.L. 102-25, 42 U.S. Code § 248d

Oct. 23, 1992, P.L. 102-484, 10 U.S. Code § 3360 nt.

May 31, 1993, P.L. 103-35, 10 U.S. Code § 2452 nt.

Nov. 11, 1993, P.L. 103-139, 107 Stat. 1418

Nov. 30, 1993, P.L. 103-160, 10 U.S. Code § 248d

Feb. 10, 1996, P.L. 104-106, 10 U.S. Code § 3360 nt.; 42 U.S. Code § 248d

Sept. 23, 1996, P.L. 104-201, 42 U.S. Code § 248d

Department of Defense Authorization Act, 1985

Oct. 19, 1984, P.L. 98-525

Nov. 8, 1985, P.L. 99-145, 10 U.S. Code § 2304 nt.; 22 U.S. Code § 1928 nt.; 37 U.S. Code §§ 403a, 1451 nt.; 46 U.S. Code Appx. § 1120 nt.; 50 U.S. Code §§ 98d nt., 98h nt.

April 7, 1986, P.L. 99-272, 100 Stat. 101

Sept. 30, 1986, P.L. 99-426, 46 U.S. Code Appx. 1120 nt.

Oct. 18, 1986, P.L. 99-500, 10 U.S. Code § 2301 nt.

Oct. 30, 1986, P.L. 99-591, 10 U.S. Code § 2301 nt.

Nov. 14, 1986, P.L. 99-661, 100 Stat. pp. 3831, 3875, 3935; 10 U.S. Code §§ 1072 nt., 2301 nt., 8251 nt.; 37 U.S. Code §§ 403 nt., 403a nt.

June 1, 1987, P.L. 100-48, 38 U.S. Code § 101 nt.

Dec. 4, 1987, P.L. 100-180, 10 U.S. Code § 2431 nt.

March 29, 1988, P.L. 100-271, 102 Stat. 45, 10 U.S. Code § 1072 nt.

Sept. 29, 1988, P.L. 199-456, 102 Stat. 1974, 10 U.S. Code §§ 1072 nt., 8251 nt.

Oct. 31, 1988, P.L. 100-569, 22 U.S. Code § 4609

Nov. 29, 1989, P.L. 101-189, 22 U.S. Code § 1928 nt.

Nov. 5, 1990, P.L. 101-510, 22 U.S. Code § 1928 nt.

Dec. 5, 1991, P.L. 102-190, 22 U.S. Code § 1928 nt.

Nov. 30, 1993, P.L. 103-160, 22 U.S. Code § 1928 nt.

Oct. 5, 1994, P.L. 103-337, 22 U.S. Code § 1928 nt.

Feb. 10, 1996, P.L. 104-106, 22 U.S. Code § 1928 nt.

Department of Defense Authorization Act, 1986

Nov. 8, 1985, P.L. 99-145, 99 Stat. 583 et seq.

Dec. 10, 1985, P.L. 99-173

Dec. 19, 1985, P.L. 99-190, 99 Stat. 1217

July 1, 1986, P.L. 99-348, 100 Stat. 705

Nov. 14, 1986, P.L. 99-661, 10 U.S. Code §§ 113 nt., 2304 nt., 3851; 22 U.S. Code §§ 2752 nt., 2752, 2753, 2767, 2791; 37 U.S. Code § 302b nt.; 50 U.S. Code § 89d nt.; 100 Stat. pp. 3836, 3842, 3856, 3901, 4000

Dec. 4, 1987, P.L. 100-180, 10 U.S. Code § 2413; 37 U.S. Code § 431 nt.

Sept. 29, 1988, P.L. 100-456, 102 Stat. 1934, 50 U.S. Code § 1521

Nov. 29, 1989, P.L. 101-189, 10 U.S. Code §§ 113 nt., 2407 nt.

Nov. 5, 1990, P.L. 101-510, 10 U.S. Code §§ 113 nt., 2304 nt.; 37 U.S. Code §§ 406, 406 nt.

Dec. 5, 1991, P.L. 102-190, 24 U.S. Code § 43 nt.; 50 U.S. Code § 1521

Oct. 23, 1992, P.L. 102-484, 50 U.S. Code § 1521

Nov. 30, 1993, P.L. 103-160, 42 U.S. Code § 2391 nt.; 50 U.S. Code § 1521

Dec. 17, 1993, P.L. 103-199, 22 U.S. Code § 2592a

Oct. 5, 1994, P.L. 103-337, 50 U.S. Code § 1521

Feb. 10, 1996, P.L. 104-106, 10 U.S. Code § 2431 nt.; 50 U.S. Code § 1521

Sept. 23, 1996, P.L. 104-201, 50 U.S. Code § 1521

Oct. 17, 1998, P.L. 105-261, 50 U.S. Code § 1521

Department of Defense Authorization Act, 1987

Nov. 14, 1986, P.L. 99-661, 100 Stat. p. 3816

April 21, 1987, P.L. 100-26, 26 U.S. Code §§ 1006 nt., 1408, 1450, 2007, 2364

July 19, 1988, P.L. 100-370, 102 Stat. 854, 10 U.S. Code § 2394 nt.

Nov. 5, 1990, P.L. 101-510, 10 U.S. Code § 2301 nt.

Department of Defense Authorization Act, 1988

Sept. 29, 1988, P.L. 100-456, 102 Stat. 2032, 22 U.S. Code §§ 2592a, 2592a nt.

Department of Defense Civilian Intelligence Personnel Policy Act of 1996

Sept. 23, 1996, P.L. 104-201, Title XVI, Subtitle B, 10 U.S. Code § 1601 nt.

Department of Defense Reorganization Act of 1958

Aug. 6, 1958, P.L. 85-599, 72 Stat. 514, 10 U.S. Code §§ 141, 143 , 171, 716, 2351 nt., 3013, 3015, 3032, 3034, 3035, 5034, 5081, 5085, 5201, 5202, 8013, 8032, 8034, 8035, 8074; 50 U.S. Code § 401

Department of Defense Supplemental Appropriation Authorization Act, 1979

June 27, 1979, P.L. 96-29, 10 U.S. Code § 139 nt.

Department of Defense Supplemental Appropriations Authorization Act, 1974

July 19, 1988, P.L. 100-370, 102 Stat. 840, 10 U.S. Code § 520 nt.

Department of Economic and Community Development Act

Tenn. Public Acts 1972, Ch. 852

Department of Education Act

Colo. Rev. Stat., 22-2-101 et seq.

**Department of Education Appropriation
Act, 1985**

Nov. 8, 1984, P.L. 98-619, 12 U.S. Code
§ 1749a

**Department of Education Appropriation
Act, 1986**

Dec. 12, 1985, P.L. 99-178, 12 U.S. Code
§ 1749a; 20 U.S. Code §§ 170a nt., 170b-3
nt.

**Department of Education Appropriation
Act, 1988**

Dec. 22, 1987, P.L. 100-202, 101 Stat. 1329

**Department of Education Appropriation
Act, 1989**

Sept. 20, 1988, P.L. 100-436, 102 Stat. 1708,
42 U.S. Code § 285g nt.

**Department of Education Appropriation
Act, 1990**

Nov. 21, 1989, P.L. 101-166, 103 Stat. 1179

**Department of Education Appropriations
Act, 1991**

April 10, 1991, P.L. 102-27, 105 Stat. 144
Oct. 20, 1994, P.L. 103-382, 108 Stat. 4026

**Department of Education Appropriations
Act, 1992**

Nov. 26, 1991, P.L. 102-170, 105 Stat. 1128

**Department of Education Appropriations
Act, 1993**

Oct. 6, 1992, P.L. 102-394, 20 U.S. Code
§ 1141 nt.

**Department of Education Appropriations
Act, 1994**

Oct. 21, 1993, P.L. 103-112, 107 Stat. 1100

**Department of Education Appropriations
Act, 1995**

Sept. 30, 1994, P.L. 103-333, 108 Stat. 2562

**Department of Education Appropriations
Act, 1996**

April 26, 1996, P.L. 104-134, Title III, 110
Stat. 1321-229

**Department of Education Appropriations
Act, 1997**

Sept. 30, 1996, P.L. 104-208, Title III, 110
Stat. 3009

**Department of Education Appropriations
Act, 1998**

Nov. 13, 1997, P.L. 105-78, Title III, 111
Stat. 1496

**Department of Education Appropriations
Act, 1999**

Oct. 21, 1998, P.L. 105-277, 101(f), Title III,
112 Stat. 2681

Department of Education Organization Act

Oct. 17, 1979, P.L. 96-88, 3 U.S. Code § 19;
5 U.S. Code §§ 101, 5312, 5314 to 5316; 5
U.S. Code Appx.; 20 U.S. Code §§ 928,
929, 1102, 1102 nt., 2390, 2711, 3012,
3401, 3401 nt., 3402 et seq.; 21 U.S. Code
§ 1004; 29 U.S. Code §§ 761, 794c, 821,
829, 873, 879, 882, 914, 952

Sept. 8, 1982, P.L. 97-252, 20 U.S. Code
§ 3442

Oct. 19, 1984, P.L. 98-511, 20 U.S. Code
§§ 1221e, 1221e-1, 3414, 3473

Nov. 8, 1985, P.L. 99-145, 20 U.S. Code
§§ 3412, 3418, 3442, 3461 , 3474

Sept. 25, 1990, P.L. 101-392, 20 U.S. Code
§§ 3423, 3423a, 3424

Oct. 30, 1990, P.L. 101-476, 20 U.S. Code
§§ 1400 nt., 3404, 3412

July 25, 1991, P.L. 102-73, 20 U.S. Code
§ 3412

Aug. 17, 1991, P.L. 102-103, 20 U.S. Code
§ 3412

July 23, 1992, P.L. 102-325, 20 U.S. Code
§ 3412

March 31, 1994, P.L. 103-227, 20 U.S. Code
§§ 3412, 3419, 3425, 3462

Sept. 13, 1994, P.L. 103-322, 20 U.S. Code
§ 3423a

Oct. 20, 1994, P.L. 103-382, 20 U.S. Code
§§ 3414, 3419 et seq., 3443 et seq.

Dec. 21, 1995, P.L. 104-66, 20 U.S. Code
§ 3463

Sept. 30, 1996, P.L. 104-208, 20 U.S. Code
§§ 3441, 3473

Oct. 7, 1998, P.L. 105-244, 20 U.S. Code
§ 3426

Oct. 21, 1998, P.L. 105-277, 20 U.S. Code
§ 3443

Department of Education Teaching Practice Act

P.R. Acts 1993, No. 79

Department of Education Trust Fund Act

Neb. Rev. Stat. 1943, 79-1345

Department of Educational Finance and Cultural Affairs Act

N.M. Laws 1977, Ch. 246, § 1 et seq.

N.M. Stat. Ann., 9-4-1 et seq.

Department of Elderly Affairs Act

Also known as the Pepper Act

Fla. Stat. Ann., 430.01 et seq.

Department of Employment Law

Ore. Rev. Stat. 1953, 657.005 et seq.

Department of Energy Act

Ky. Rev. Stat. 1971, 152A.011 et seq.

N.J. Stat. Ann. 52:27F-1 et seq.

Department of Energy Act of 1978 Civilian Application

Feb. 25, 1978, P.L. 95-238, 15 U.S. Code
§§ 2506 et seq., 2701 et seq.; 22 U.S. Code
§§ 2429 nt., 3224a; 30 U.S. Code § 1121 et
seq.; 42 U.S. Code §§ 2391 et seq., 2451,
5556a, 5821 nt., 5905 et seq., 7125a et seq.

Nov. 2, 1994, P.L. 103-437, 22 U.S. Code
§ 3224a

Dec. 21, 1995, P.L. 104-66, 22 U.S. Code
§ 2429 nt.

Department of Energy and Minerals Act

N.M. Stat. 1978, 9-5-1 et seq.

Department of Energy Metal Casting Competitiveness Research Act of 1990

Oct. 15, 1990, P.L. 101-425, 15 U.S. Code
§§ 5301 to 5309

Oct. 24, 1992, P.L. 102-486, 15 U.S. Code
§ 5307

Department of Energy National Security and Military Applications of Nuclear Energy Authorization Act of 1979

Oct. 24, 1978, P.L. 95-509, 42 U.S. Code
§§ 7235, 7271, 7271 nt.

Department of Energy National Security and Military Applications of Nuclear Energy Authorization Act of 1980

Dec. 29, 1979, P.L. 96-164, 42 U.S. Code
§§ 7272, 7273

Department of Energy National Security and Military Applications of Nuclear Energy Authorization Act of 1985

Oct. 19, 1984, P.L. 98-525, 42 U.S. Code
§§ 2212, 7158 nt.

Nov. 5, 1990, P.L. 101-510, 42 U.S. Code
§ 2212

Department of Energy National Security and Military Applications of Nuclear Energy Authorization Act of 1986

Nov. 8, 1985, P.L. 99-145

Nov. 14, 1986, P.L. 99-661, 100 Stat. p. 4063

Dec. 4, 1987, P.L. 100-180, 42 U.S. Code
§ 7256a

Department of Energy National Security and Military Applications of Nuclear Energy Authorization Act of 1987

Nov. 14, 1986, P.L. 99-661, 100 Stat. p. 4055

Dec. 4, 1987, P.L. 100-180, 42 U.S. Code
§ 7261a

Department of Energy National Security and Military Applications of Nuclear Energy Authorization Act of 1988

Dec. 4, 4987, P.L. 100-180, 101 Stat. 1231

Department of Energy Organization Act

Aug. 4, 1977, P.L. 95-91, 3 U.S. Code § 19; 5
U.S. Code § 101 et seq.; 7 U.S. Code
§ 916; 15 U.S. Code § 766 et seq.; 42 U.S.
Code §§ 2201 nt., 7101 et seq.

Nov. 9, 1978, P.L. 95-620, 42 U.S. Code
§ 7193

Nov. 9, 1978, P.L. 95-621, 42 U.S. Code
§ 7255

April 3, 1980, P.L. 96-226, 42 U.S. Code
§ 7138

Continued

Dec. 21, 1982, P.L. 97-375, 42 U.S. Code § 7138

Oct. 21, 1986, P.L. 99-509, 42 U.S. Code § 7135

Oct. 18, 1988, P.L. 100-504, 42 U.S. Code § 7138

Oct. 25, 1988, P.L. 100-531, 42 U.S. Code §§ 7270a, 7270b

April 11, 1990, P.L. 101-271, 42 U.S. Code § 7171

Nov. 5, 1990, P.L. 101-510, 42 U.S. Code §§ 7112, 7213 nt., 7214 nt., 7215 nt., 7216 nt., 7217 nt., 7218 nt.

Aug. 14, 1991, P.L. 102-88, 42 U.S. Code § 7231

Oct. 24, 1992, P.L. 102-486, 42 U.S. Code § 7135

Nov. 1, 1993, P.L. 103-160, 42 U.S. Code §§ 7211 et seq., 7256

Oct. 5, 1994, P.L. 103-337, 42 U.S. Code § 7143

Nov. 28, 1995, P.L. 104-58, 42 U.S. Code § 7152

Dec. 21, 1995, P.L. 104-66, 42 U.S. Code § 7267

Feb. 10, 1996, P.L. 104-106, 10 U.S. Code §§ 2397, 2397a, 2397b, 2397c; 42 U.S. Code §§ prec. 7211, 7211, 7212, 7218

July 18, 1997, P.L. 105-28, 42 U.S. Code §§ 7191, 7234

Oct. 7, 1998, P.L. 105-245, 42 U.S. Code § 7139

Department of Energy Science Education Enhancement Act

Nov. 5, 1990, P.L. 101-510, 42 U.S. Code §§ 7381, 7381 nt., 7381 et seq. generally

Oct. 7, 1998, P.L. 105-245, 42 U.S. Code §§ 7381d, 7381e

Department of Energy Standardization Act of 1997

July 18, 1997, P.L. 105-28, 42 U.S. Code § 7101 nt.

Department of Environment Act

N.M. Stat. Ann., 9-7A-1 et seq.

Department of Environmental Protection Act

N.J. Stat. Ann. 13:1D-1 et seq.

Department of Environmental Resources Agricultural Advisory Board Act

Pa. 1993 Pamph. Laws, No. 11

Department of Finance Act

Ala. Code 1975, § 41-4-1 et seq.

Department of Finance Act (Syracuse)

N.Y. Laws 1905, Ch. 681

Department of Finance and Administration Act

N.M. Stat. Ann., 9-6-1 et seq.

Department of General Services Act

Tenn. Public Acts 1972, Ch. 543

Department of Health Act

N.J. Stat. Ann., 26:1A-2 et seq.

Department of Health and Environment Act

N.M. Stat. Ann., 9-7-1 et seq.

Department of Health and Human Services Appropriation Act, 1986

Dec. 12, 1985, P.L. 98-178, 24 U.S. Code §§ 168b, 170a; 42 U.S. Code §§ 210 nt., 1383 nt.

Department of Health and Human Services Appropriations Act of 1993

Oct. 6, 1992, P.L. 102-394, 106 Stat. 1813

Department of Health and Human Services Appropriations Act, 1988

Dec. 22, 1987, P.L. 100-202, 101 Stat. 1329

June 10, 1993, P.L. 103-43, 42 U.S. Code § 286

Department of Health and Human Services Appropriations Act, 1989

Sept. 20, 1988, P.L. 100-436, 102 Stat. 1701, 20 U.S. Code § 1070a

Department of Health and Human Services Appropriations Act, 1990

Nov. 21, 1989, P.L. 101-166, 103 Stat. 1166

Department of Health and Human Services Appropriations Act, 1992

Nov. 26, 1991, P.L. 102-170, 105 Stat. 1114

Department of Health and Human Services Appropriations Act, 1994

Oct. 21, 1993, P.L. 103-112, 107 Stat. 1089

Department of Health and Human Services Appropriations Act, 1995

Sept. 30, 1994, P.L. 103-333, 108 Stat. 2549

Department of Health and Human Services Appropriations Act, 1996

April 26, 1996, P.L. 104-134, Title II, 110 Stat. 1321-221

Department of Health and Human Services Appropriations Act, 1997

Sept. 30, 1996, P.L. 104-208, Title II, 110 Stat. 3009

Aug. 5, 1997, P.L. 105-33, 42 U.S. Code §§ 652, 653

Department of Health and Human Services Appropriations Act, 1998

Nov. 13, 1997, P.L. 105-78, Title II, 111 Stat. 1477

Department of Health and Human Services Appropriations Act, 1999

Oct. 21, 1998, P.L. 105-277, 101(f), Title II, 112 Stat. 2681

Department of Health and Urban Development; Space, Science, Veterans and Certain Other Independent Agencies Appropriation Act

Aug. 10, 1971, P.L. 92-78, 85 Stat. 271, 12 U.S. Code § 1428a nt.

Department of Health Building Act

Ark. Acts 1965, No. 469

Department of Health Education Act

N.M. Stat. Ann., 24-3B-1 et seq.

Department of Health, Education, and Welfare Appropriation Acts

July 31, 1953, Ch. 296, 67 Stat. 257, 42 U.S. Code §§ 212c, 214a, 703a, 704a, 3508; 43 U.S. Code § 617v

July 2, 1954, Ch. 457, 68 Stat. 437, 42 U.S. Code §§ 703a, 704a, 3508

Aug. 1, 1955, Ch. 437, 69 Stat. 401, 29 U.S. Code § 34; 42 U.S. Code §§ 210, 421 nt., 703a, 704a, 3508

June 29, 1956, Ch. 477, 70 Stat. 430, 42 U.S. Code §§ 210, 421 nt., 702 nt., 703a, 704a, 3508

June 29, 1957, P.L. 85-67, 71 Stat. 214, 42 U.S. Code §§ 290, 421 nt., 702 nt., 703a, 704a, 3506, 3508

Aug. 1, 1958, P.L. 85-580, 72 Stat. 461, 42 U.S. Code §§ 267, 421 nt., 702 nt., 703a, 704a, 3508

Aug. 14, 1959, P.L. 86-158, 73 Stat. 343, 20 U.S. Code § 612; 42 U.S. Code §§ 227a, 291-1, 291v, 421 nt., 702 nt., 703a, 704a, 3508

Sept. 2, 1960, P.L. 86-703, 74 Stat. 760, 42 U.S. Code §§ 210, 227a, 246a, 421 nt., 702 nt., 703a, 704a, 905, 3508

Sept. 22, 1961, P.L. 87-290, 75 Stat. 594, 42 U.S. Code §§ 227a, 290, 421 nt., 702 nt., 703a, 704a, 3508

Sept. 22, 1961, P.L. 87-290, 75 Stat. 603, 42 U.S. Code § 290

Aug. 14, 1962, P.L. 87-582, 76 Stat. 366, 42 U.S. Code §§ 227a, 421 nt., 702 nt., 703a, 704a, 3508

Oct. 11, 1963, P.L. 88-136, 77 Stat. 229, 42 U.S. Code §§ 227a, 703a, 704a, 3508

Sept. 19, 1964, P.L. 88-605, 78 Stat. 963, 42 U.S. Code §§ 227a, 421 nt., 702 nt., 703a, 704a, 3508

Aug. 31, 1965, P.L. 89-156, 79 Stat. 609, 42 U.S. Code §§ 227a, 421 nt., 702 nt., 703a, 704a, 3508

Nov. 7, 1966, P.L. 89-787, 80 Stat. 1382, 42 U.S. Code §§ 227a, 421 nt., 702 nt., 703a, 704a, 3508

Nov. 8, 1967, P.L. 90-132, 81 Stat. 390, 42 U.S. Code §§ 227a, 421 nt., 702 nt., 703a, 704a, 3508

Oct. 11, 1968, P.L. 90-557, 82 Stat. 974, 42 U.S. Code §§ 421 nt., 703 nt., 704a, 3508

March 5, 1970, P.L. 91-204, 84 Stat. 27, 42 U.S. Code §§ 421 nt., 703 nt., 704a, 3508

Jan. 11, 1971, P.L. 91-677, 84 Stat. 2005, 42 U.S. Code §§ 291j-7 nt., 421 nt., 703 nt., 704a, 3508, 3510

Aug. 10, 1971, P.L. 92-80, 85 Stat. 290, 42 U.S. Code §§ 704a, 905a, 3508

Continued

Dec. 18, 1973, P.L. 93-192, 87 Stat. 759, 42 U.S. Code §§ 421 nt., 3508

Oct. 17, 1975, P.L. 94-116, 89 Stat. 581, 12 U.S. Code § 1428a; 36 U.S. Code §§ 121b, 122, 122a

Department of Health Services Cooperative Agreement Act (State)
Cal. Health and Safety Code § 38070

Department of Highways Act
Colo. Rev. Stat., 43-1-101 et seq.

Department of Highways Career System Act
Pa. Purdon's Stat., Title 71, § 741.3 et seq.

Department of Highways Organization Act
N.M. Stat. Ann., 67-1-1 et seq., 67-2-4, 67-3-7, 67-3-8, 67-3-23

Department of Housing and Urban Development Act
Sept. 9, 1965, P.L. 89-174, 79 Stat. 667, 3 U.S. Code § 19 (See 5 U.S. Code §§ 101, 5312, 5314 to 5316) 12 U.S. Code § 1723; 42 U.S. Code §§ 1451, 3531 to 3537

Sept. 11, 1967, P.L. 90-83, 81 Stat. 233, 42 U.S. Code §§ 3532 to 3534

April 11, 1968, P.L. 90-284, 82 Stat. 84, 42 U.S. Code §§ 3533, 3535

Aug. 1, 1968, P.L. 90-448, 82 Stat. 544, 42 U.S. Code §§ 3533, 3534, 3535

Dec. 31, 1970, P.L. 91-609, 84 Stat. 1775, 42 U.S. Code §§ 3533, 3535

Oct. 12, 1977, P.L. 95-128, 42 U.S. Code § 4533

Oct. 31, 1978, P.L. 95-557, 42 U.S. Code § 3535

February 5, 1988, P.L. 100-242, 42 U.S. Code §§ 3532, 3535

Dec. 15, 1989, P.L. 101-235, 42 U.S. Code §§ 3533, 3535, 3537a, 3537b

Nov. 5, 1990, P.L. 101-509, 42 U.S. Code § 3533

Nov. 15, 1990, P.L. 101-576, 42 U.S. Code § 3533

Nov. 28, 1990, P.L. 101-625, 42 U.S. Code § 3535

Oct. 28, 1992, P.L. 102-550, 42 U.S. Code §§ 3533, 3535, 3537b, 3537c

April 11, 1994, P.L. 103-233, 42 U.S. Code § 3535

Dec. 19, 1995, P.L. 104-65, 42 U.S. Code § 3537b

Nov. 10, 1998, P.L. 105-362, 42 U.S. Code § 3535

Department of Housing and Urban Development Independent Agencies Appropriation Act of 1985
July 17, 1984, P.L. 98-371, 12 U.S. Code §§ 1428a nt., 1701q nt., 1721 nt., 1723e nt.; 31 U.S. Code § 1305; 36 U.S. Code §§ 121b, 122, 122a

Aug. 15, 1985, P.L. 99-88, 99 Stat. 331

Dec. 22, 1987, P.L. 100-202, 42 U.S. Code § 1437o

Department of Housing and Urban Development Independent Agencies Appropriation Act, 1984
Nov. 30, 1983, P.L. 98-181, 12 U.S. Code § 1701q nt.

Aug. 22, 1984, P.L. 98-396

Oct. 12, 1984, P.L. 98-473

Department of Housing and Urban Development Independent Agencies Appropriations Act, 1986
Nov. 25, 1985, P.L. 99-160, 12 U.S. Code §§ 1428a nt., 1701q nt.; 36 U.S. Code §§ 121b, 122, 122a; 42 U.S. Code §§ 1437, 1887

Department of Housing and Urban Development Independent Agencies Appropriations Act, 1989
Aug. 19, 1988, P.L. 100-404, 102 Stat. 1014

Sept. 28, 1994, P.L. 103-327, 42 U.S. Code § 2467

Department of Housing and Urban Development Reform Act of 1989
Dec. 15, 1989, P.L. 101-235, 42 U.S. Code § 3531 nt.

Nov. 28, 1990, P.L. 101-625, 12 U.S. Code § 1715z-1a; 42 U.S. Code § 5306 nt.

Oct. 28, 1992, P.L. 102-550, 12 U.S. Code § 1715z-1a nt.; 42 U.S. Code § 1437aa nt.

Department of Housing and Urban Development (Independent Agencies Appropriations Act, 1988

Dec. 22, 1987, P.L. 100-202, 101 Stat. 1329

Department of Housing and Urban Development; Space, Science, Veterans, and Certain Other Independent Agencies Appropriation Acts, 1973

Aug. 14, 1972, P.L. 92-383, 86 Stat. 540, 42 U.S. Code § 4413a

Oct. 26, 1973, P.L. 93-137, 87 Stat. 491, 12 U.S. Code § 1428a

Sept. 6, 1974, P.L. 93-414, 88 Stat. 1095, 12 U.S. Code § 1428a; 36 U.S. Code §§ 121b to 122a

Nov. 23, 1988, P.L. 100-707, 42 U.S. Code § 3539

Department of Housing Organic Act

P.R. Laws Ann. 1954, Title 3, § 441 et seq.

Department of Human Resources Hospital Facilities Finance Act

N.C. Gen. Stat. 1943, § 131-138 et seq.

Department of Human Services Act

Ill. Comp. Stat. 1992, Ch. 20, § 1305/1-1 et seq.

N.M. Stat. Ann., 9-8-1 et seq.

Department of Human Services, Division of Economic Assistance Act

N.J. Stat. Ann., 30:4B-1 et seq.

Department of Insurance Act

N.J. Stat. Ann., 17:1C-1 et seq.

Department of Interior Airports Act

March 18, 1950, Ch. 72, 64 Stat. 27, 16 U.S. Code §§ 7a to 7e; 49 U.S. Code §§ 1102, 1108

Aug. 23, 1958, P.L. 85-726, 72 Stat. 807, 16 U.S. Code §§ 7a to 7e; 49 U.S. Code §§ 1102, 1108

May 21, 1970, P.L. 91-258, 84 Stat. 235, 16 U.S. Code § 7a

Department of Interior and Related Agencies Appropriations Act, 1988

Dec. 22, 1987, P.L. 100-202, 101 Stat. 1329

Department of Interior and Related Agencies Appropriations Act, 1990

Oct. 23, 1989, P.L. 101-121, 103 Stat. 701

Department of Justice Act

Iowa Code 1983, 13.1 et seq.

N.M. Stat. Ann., 8-5-1 et seq.

Ore. Rev. Stat. 1953, 180.210 et seq.

Department of Justice and Related Agencies Appropriations Act, 1992

Oct. 28, 1991, P.L. 102-140, 105 Stat. 782

Department of Justice and Related Agencies Appropriations Act, 1993

Oct. 6, 1992, P.L. 102-395, 106 Stat. 1828

Department of Justice and Related Agencies Appropriations Act, 1994

Oct. 27, 1993, P.L. 103-121, 107 Stat. 1153

Department of Justice Appropriation Acts

June 29, 1939, Ch. 248, 53 Stat. 885, 41 U.S. Code § 6a

May 14, 1940, Ch. 189, 54 Stat. 200

June 28, 1941, Ch. 258, 55 Stat. 289 (See 28 U.S. Code §§ 533, 534, 536)

July 2, 1942, Ch. 472, 56 Stat. 481 (See 28 U.S. Code §§ 533, 534, 536)

July 1, 1943, Ch. 182, 57 Stat. 282, 3 U.S. Code § 53 (See 28 U.S. Code §§ 533, 534, 536)

June 28, 1944, Ch. 294, 58 Stat. 407, 3 U.S. Code § 53 nt. (See 28 U.S. Code §§ 533, 534, 536)

May 21, 1945, Ch. 129, 59 Stat. 181, 3 U.S. Code § 53 (See 28 U.S. Code §§ 533, 534, 536)

July 5, 1946, Ch. 541, 60 Stat. 458, 3 U.S. Code § 53 nt. (See 28 U.S. Code §§ 533, 534, 536)

July 9, 1947, Ch. 211, 61 Stat. 289, 3 U.S. Code § 201 nt. (See 28 U.S. Code §§ 533, 534, 536)

June 3, 1948, Ch. 400, 62 Stat. 316 (See 28 U.S. Code §§ 533, 534, 536)

July 20, 1949, Ch. 354, 63 Stat. 457, 3 U.S. Code § 201 nt. (See 28 U.S . Code §§ 533, 534, 536) 50 U.S. Code Appx. § 6b

Continued

583

Sept. 6, 1950, Ch. 896, 64 Stat. 615, 3 U.S. Code § 201 nt. (See 28 U.S . Code §§ 533, 534, 536) 50 U.S. Code Appx. § 6b

Oct. 22, 1951, Ch. 533, 65 Stat. 582, 3 U.S. Code § 201 nt. (See 28 U.S . Code §§ 533, 534, 536) 50 U.S. Code Appx. § 6b

July 10, 1952, Ch. 651, 66 Stat. 556 (See 28 U.S. Code §§ 533, 534, 536) 43 U.S. Code § 666; 50 U.S. Code Appx. § 6b

Aug. 5, 1953, Ch. 328, 67 Stat. 376 (See 28 U.S. Code §§ 533, 534, 536) 28 U.S. Code §§ 508 nt., 533, 534, 536; 50 U.S. Code Appx. § 6b

July 2, 1954, Ch. 456, 68 Stat. 419, 28 U.S. Code §§ 508 nt., 533, 534, 536; 50 U.S. Code Appx. § 6b

July 7, 1955, Ch. 279, 69 Stat. 270, 8 U.S. Code § 1553; 18 U.S. Code § 4041 nt. (See 28 U.S. Code §§ 533, 534, 536) 50 U.S. Code Appx. § 6b

June 20, 1956, Ch. 414, 70 Stat. 306, 8 U.S. Code § 1553 (See 28 U.S. Code §§ 533, 534, 536) 50 U.S. Code Appx. § 6b

June 11, 1957, P.L. 85-49, 71 Stat. 60 (See 28 U.S. Code §§ 533, 534, 536; 50 U.S. Code Appx. § 6b)

June 30, 1958, P.L. 85-474, 72 Stat. 249 (See 28 U.S. Code §§ 533 , 534, 536; 50 U.S. Code Appx. § 6b)

Aug. 31, 1960, P.L. 86-678, 74 Stat. 561 (See 28 U.S. Code §§ 533 , 534, 536; 42 U.S. Code § 250a; 50 U.S. Code Appx. § 6b)

Sept. 21, 1961, P.L. 87-264, 75 Stat. 550 (See 28 U.S. Code §§ 533, 534, 536; 42 U.S. Code § 250a; 50 U.S. Code Appx. § 6b)

Oct. 11, 1962, P.L. 87-793, 76 Stat. 850, 5 U.S. Code § 298a

Oct. 18, 1962, P.L. 87-843, 76 Stat. 1085 (See 28 U.S. Code §§ 533, 534, 536; 42 U.S. Code § 250a; 50 U.S. Code Appx. § 6b)

Dec. 30, 1963, P.L. 88-245, 77 Stat. 781 (See 28 U.S. Code §§ 533 , 534, 536; 42 U.S. Code § 250a; 50 U.S. Code Appx. § 6b)

Aug. 31, 1964, P.L. 88-527, 78 Stat. 716 (See 28 U.S. Code §§ 533 , 534, 536; 42 U.S. Code § 250a; 50 U.S. Code Appx. § 6b)

Sept. 2, 1965, P.L. 89-164, 79 Stat. 628 (See 28 U.S. Code §§ 533, 534, 536; 42 U.S. Code § 250a; 50 U.S. Code Appx. § 6b)

Nov. 8, 1966, P.L. 89-797, 80 Stat. 1484, 50 U.S. Code Appx. § 6b

Aug. 9, 1968, P.L. 90-470, 82 Stat. 673, 42 U.S. Code § 250a; 50 U.S. Code Appx. § 6b

Dec. 24, 1969, P.L. 91-153, 83 Stat. 408, 42 U.S. Code § 250a

Oct. 21, 1970, P.L. 91-472, 84 Stat. 1045, 42 U.S. Code § 250a

Aug. 10, 1971, P.L. 92-77, 85 Stat. 253, 42 U.S. Code § 250a

Oct. 25, 1972, P.L. 92-544, 86 Stat. 1114, 42 U.S. Code § 250a

Nov. 27, 1973, P.L. 93-162, 87 Stat. 643, 42 U.S. Code § 250a

Oct. 21, 1975, P.L. 94-121, 89 Stat. 617, 42 U.S. Code § 250a

Dec. 13, 1985, P.L. 99-180, 18 U.S. Code § 3525 nt.; 23 U.S. Code § 114 nt.; 28 U.S. Code § 533 nt.; 42 U.S. Code § 250a

Oct. 18, 1986, P.L. 99-500, 100 Stat. 3399

Oct. 30, 1986, P.L. 99-591, 100 Stat. 3399

July 11, 1987, P.L. 100-71, 101 Stat. 472

Dec. 22, 1987, P.L. 100-202, 101 Stat. 1329

Oct. 1, 1988, P.L. 100-459, 102 Stat. 2203

Oct. 24, 1988, P.L. 100-525, 8 U.S. Code §§ 1222, 1223, 1356

Nov. 21, 1989, P.L. 101-162, 103 Stat. 995

Department of Justice Appropriation Authorization Act, Fiscal Year 1979

Nov. 9, 1978, P.L. 95-624, 5 U.S. Code § 5108; 8 U.S. Code § 1255 nt.; 18 U.S. Code § 351 nt., 4001 nt., 4121 nt.; 22 U.S. Code § 263a; 28 U.S. Code § 519 nt.; 42 U.S. Code § 2000g, 4002

Department of Justice Appropriation Authorization Act, Fiscal Year 1980

Nov. 30, 1979, P.L. 96-132, 5 U.S. Code §§ 5315, 5924; 8 U.S. Code § 1551 nt.; 21 U.S. Code §§ 802, 878, 881, 883, 886, 904; 28 U.S. Code §§ 509 nt., 519 nt.; 42 U.S. Code § 3731 nt.

Department of Justice Appropriations Act, 1989

Dec. 12, 1991, P.L. 102-232, 8 U.S. Code § 1356

Department of Justice Appropriations Act, 1990

Dec. 12, 1991, P.L. 102-232, 8 U.S. Code § 1356

Department of Justice Appropriations Act, 1991

Nov. 5, 1990, P.L. 110-515, 28 U.S. Code §§ 533 nt., 534 nt., 42 U.S. Code § 250a

Dec. 12, 1991, P.L. 102-232, 8 U.S. Code § 1356

Department of Justice Appropriations Act, 1996

April 26, 1996, P.L. 104-134, Title I, 110 Stat. 1321

Department of Justice Appropriations Act, 1997

Sept. 30, 1996, P.L. 104-208, Title I, 110 Stat. 3009

Department of Justice Appropriations Act, 1998

Nov. 26, 1997, P.L. 105-119, Title I, 111 Stat. 2440

Department of Justice Appropriations Act, 1999

Oct. 21, 1998, P.L. 105-277, 101(b), Title I, 112 Stat. 2681

Department of Justice Assets Forfeiture Fund Amendments Act of 1986

Oct. 27, 1986, P.L. 99-570, 28 U.S. Code § 1 nt.

Department of Labor Acts

June 13, 1888, Ch. 389, 25 Stat. 182, 29 U.S. Code §§ 1, 3, 4, 6

March 4, 1913, Ch. 141, 37 Stat. 736, 5 U.S. Code §§ 611, 612, 615 to 622

Department of Labor, and Health, Education, and Welfare, and Related Agencies Appropriation Act, 1970

March 5, 1970, P.L. 91-204, 84 Stat. 23, 29 U.S. Code § 564; 39 U.S. Code § 4152 nt.; 42 U.S. Code §§ 421 nt., 703 nt., 704a, 2702 nt., 3508

Department of Labor and Health, Education and Welfare Appropriation Act of 1976

Jan. 28, 1976, P.L. 94-206, 42 U.S. Code § 201 et seq.

Department of Labor, and Health, Education, and Welfare Appropriation Act, 1971

Jan. 11, 1971, P.L. 91-667, 84 Stat. 2001, 39 U.S. Code § 3202 nt.; 42 U.S. Code §§ 291j-7 nt., 421 nt., 703 nt., 704a, 3508, 3510

Department of Labor and Industry Act

N.J. Stat. Ann., 34:1A-1 et seq.

Department of Labor Appropriation Acts

June 29, 1939, Ch. 249, 53 Stat. 924, 42 U.S. Code § 704a

June 26, 1940, Ch. 428, 54 Stat. 574, 42 U.S. Code § 704a

July 1, 1941, Ch. 269, 55 Stat. 466, 42 U.S. Code § 704a

July 2, 1942, Ch. 475, 56 Stat. 565, 42 U.S. Code § 704a

July 12, 1943, Ch. 221, 57 Stat. 494

June 28, 1944, Ch. 302, 58 Stat. 550, 42 U.S. Code § 704a

July 3, 1945, Ch. 263, 59 Stat. 361, 42 U.S. Code §§ 703a, 704a

July 26, 1946, Ch. 672, 60 Stat. 679, 29 U.S. Code §§ 49c nt., 49c -2 to 49c-5

July 8, 1947, Ch. 210, 61 Stat. 261, 42 U.S. Code §§ 1915, 1916

June 14, 1948, Ch. 465, 62 Stat. 394

June 29, 1949, Ch. 275, 63 Stat. 283

Sept. 6, 1950, Ch. 896, 64 Stat. 642, 29 U.S. Code §§ 49d nt.

Aug. 31, 1951, Ch. 373, 65 Stat. 293

July 5, 1952, Ch. 575, 66 Stat. 358

July 31, 1953, Ch. 296, 67 Stat. 248

July 2, 1954, Ch. 457, 68 Stat. 434

Aug. 1, 1955, Ch. 437, 69 Stat. 397

June 29, 1956, Ch. 477, 70 Stat. 424

June 29, 1957, P.L. 85-67, 71 Stat. 210, 29 U.S. Code § 563

Aug. 1, 1958, P.L. 85-580, 72 Stat. 457, 7 U.S. Code § 1462 nt.

Aug. 14, 1959, P.L. 86-158, 73 Stat. 339, 7 U.S. Code § 1462 nt.

Sept. 2, 1960, P.L. 86-703, 74 Stat. 755, 29 U.S. Code § 563

Sept. 22, 1961, P.L. 87-290, 75 Stat. 589, 39 U.S. Code § 3202 nt.

Continued

585

Aug. 14, 1962, P.L. 87-582, 76 Stat. 361, 39 U.S. Code § 3202 nt.; 42 U.S. Code § 1101 nt.

Oct. 11, 1963, P.L. 88-136, 77 Stat. 224

Sept. 19, 1964, P.L. 88-605, 78 Stat. 959, 39 U.S. Code § 3202 nt.

Aug. 31, 1965, P.L. 89-156, 79 Stat. 592, 39 U.S. Code § 3202 nt.

Nov. 7, 1966, P.L. 89-787, 80 Stat. 1378, 39 U.S. Code § 3202 nt.

Nov. 8, 1967, P.L. 90-132, 81 Stat. 386, 39 U.S. Code § 3202 nt.

Oct. 11, 1968, P.L. 90-557, 82 Stat. 970, 39 U.S. Code § 3202 nt.

March 5, 1970, P.L. 91-204, 84 Stat. 23, 29 U.S. Code § 564, 39 U.S. Code § 3202 nt.

Jan. 11, 1971, P.L. 91-667, 84 Stat. 2001, 39 U.S. Code § 3202 nt.

Aug. 10, 1971, P.L. 92-80, 85 Stat. 287, 39 U.S. Code § 3202 nt.

Jan. 28, 1976, P.L. 94-206, 42 U.S. Code § 201 et seq.

Dec. 12, 1985, P.L. 99-178, 30 U.S. Code § 962

Dec. 22, 1987, P.L. 100-202, 30 U.S. Code § 962

Sept. 20, 1988, P.L. 100-436, 102 Stat. 1687, 24 U.S. Code §§ 168b, 170a; 42 U.S. Code §§ 210 nt., 1383 nt.

Nov. 21, 1989, P.L. 101-166, 103 Stat. 1159

Department of Labor Appropriations Act, 1991

April 10, 1991, P.L. 102-27, 105 Stat. 142

Department of Labor Appropriations Act, 1992

Nov. 26, 1991, P.L. 102-170, 105 Stat. 1107

Department of Labor Appropriations Act, 1993

Oct. 6, 1992, P.L. 102-394, 106 Stat. 1799

Department of Labor Appropriations Act, 1994

Oct. 21, 1993, P.L. 103-112, 107 Stat. 1082

Department of Labor Appropriations Act, 1995

Sept. 30, 1994, P.L. 103-333, 108 Stat. 2539

Department of Labor Appropriations Act, 1996

April 26, 1996, P.L. 104-134, Title I, 110 Stat. 1321-211

Department of Labor Appropriations Act, 1997

Sept. 30, 1996, P.L. 104-208, Title I, 110 Stat. 3009

Department of Labor Appropriations Act, 1998

Nov. 13, 1997, P.L. 105-78, Title I, 111 Stat. 1467

Department of Labor Appropriations Act, 1999

Oct. 21, 1998, P.L. 105-277, 101(f), Title I, 112 Stat. 2681

Department of Labor Executive Level Conforming Amendments of 1986

Nov. 6, 1986, P.L. 99-619, 29 U.S. Code § 551 nt.

Department of Labor, Health and Human Services, and Education, and Related Agencies Appropriations Act, 1994

Oct. 21, 1993, P.L. 103-112, 107 Stat. 1082

Department of Labor, Health and Human Services, and Education, and Related Agencies Appropriations Act, 1995

Sept. 30, 1994, P.L. 103-333, 108 Stat. 2539

Department of Labor, Health and Human Services, and Education, and Related Agencies Appropriations Act, 1997

Nov. 13, 1997, P.L. 105-78, 5 U.S. Code § 5597 nt.

Department of Labor, Health and Human Services, and Education, and Related Agencies Appropriations Act, 1998

Nov. 13, 1997, P.L. 105-78, 111 Stat. 1467

Oct. 21, 1998, P.L. 105-277, 101(g), 112 Stat. 2681

Department of Labor Organic Act

P.R. Laws Ann. 1954, Title 3, § 304 et seq.

Department of Law Act
N.J. Stat. Ann., 52:17A-1 et seq.

Department of Law and Public Safety Act
N.J. Stat. Ann., 52:17B-1 et seq.

Department of Law Enforcement Act
Fla. Stat. Ann., 943.01 et seq.

Department of Local Affairs Act
N.C. Gen. Stat. 1943, § 143-320 et seq.

Department of Mental Health and Developmental Disabilities Act
Ill. Rev. Stat. 1991, Ch. 91 1/2, § 100-0.1 et seq.

Department of Military and Veterans Affairs Act
N.C. Gen. Stat. 1943, § 165-1 et seq.

Department of Natural Resources Act
Ga. Code Ann., 12-2-1 et seq.
Ill. Comp. Stat. 1992, Ch. 20, § 801/1-1 et seq.
N.M. Stat. Ann., 9-5A-1 et seq.

Department of Natural Resources Organic Act
P.R. Laws Ann. 1954, Title 3, § 151 et seq.

Department of Parole Reorganization Act
Colo. Rev. Stat., 17-2-101 et seq.

Department of Public Advocate Act
N.J. Stat. Ann., 52:27E-1 et seq.

Department of Public Health Act
Ill. Rev. Stat. 1991, Ch. 111 1/2, § 21.1 et seq.

Department of Public Health Reorganization Act
Colo. Rev. Stat., 25-1-101 et seq.

Department of Public Safety Act
Ariz. Rev. Stat. Ann., § 41-1701 et seq.
Ga. Code Ann., 35-2-1 et seq.

Department of Public Safety Building Act
Ark. Acts 1977, p. 1199, No. 490

Department of Public Safety Nomenclature Act
Oct. 29, 1992, P.L. 102-568, 106 Stat. 4320, Title 1
Ga. Code Ann., 35-2-80 to 35-2-88

Department of Public Safety Reorganization Act
W. Va. Code 1966, § 15-2-1 et seq.

Department of Public Utilities Act
N.J. Stat. Ann., 48:2-1 et seq.

Department of Public Works Act
La. Rev. Stat. Ann., 38:1 et seq.

Department of Public Works Reorganization Act
Mass. Gen. Laws Ann., 16:1 et seq.

Department of Revenue Act
Ind. Code Ann., 6-8-3-1 et seq.
Mich. Comp. Laws Ann., 205.1 et seq.

Department of Revenue Sunshine Act
Ill. Rev. Stat. 1991, Ch. 127, § 2001 et seq.

Department of Social Services Organic Act
P.R. Laws Ann. 1954, Title 3 § 211 et seq.

Department of Standards and Purchases Law
Tenn. Code Ann., 12-3-201 et seq.

Department of State Act
N.J. Stat. Ann. 52:16A-1 et seq.

Department of State and Related Agencies Appropriations Act, 1992
Oct. 28, 1991, P.L. 102-140, 105 Stat. 816

Department of State and Related Agencies Appropriations Act, 1993
Oct. 6, 1992, P.L. 102-395, 106 Stat. 1864

Department of State and Related Agencies Appropriations Act, 1994
Oct. 27, 1993, P.L. 103-121, 107 Stat. 1185

Department of State and Related Agencies Appropriations Act, 1996

April 26, 1996, P.L. 104-134, Title IV, 110 Stat. 1321-36

Department of State and Related Agencies Appropriations Act, 1997

Sept. 30, 1996, P.L. 104-208, Title IV, 110 Stat. 3009

Department of State and Related Agencies Appropriations Act, 1998

Nov. 26, 1997, P.L. 105-119, Title IV, 111 Stat. 2494

Department of State and Related Agencies Appropriations Act, 1999

Oct. 21, 1998, P.L. 105-277, 101(b), Title IV, 112 Stat. 2681

Department of State Appropriation Act of 1937

Oct. 21, 1998, P.L. 105-277, 22 U.S. Code § 2661

Department of State Appropriation Acts

June 29, 1939, Ch. 248, 53 Stat. 885, 22 U.S. Code § 294a

May 14, 1940, Ch. 189, 54 Stat. 181, 22 U.S. Code §§ 130a, 130b, 266a nt., 268a, 269a, 269b, 274, 275, 276, 277, 278, 278b, 294a, 2663

June 28, 1941, Ch. 258, 55 Stat. 265, 22 U.S. Code §§ 130a, 130b, 136, 269a, 269b, 274, 275 nt., 276 nt., 277, 278, 278b, 2663; 41 U.S. Code § 6a nt.; 49 U.S. Code § 231

July 2, 1942, Ch. 472, 56 Stat. 468, 22 U.S. Code §§ 41, 130a, 130b, 136, 275 nt., 276 nt., 278b, 2663; 41 U.S. Code § 6a nt.

July 1, 1943, Ch. 182, 57 Stat. 271, 22 U.S. Code §§ 41, 130a, 130b, 136, 275, 276, 278b, 2663; 41 U.S. Code § 6a

June 28, 1944, Ch. 294, 58 Stat. 395, 22 U.S. Code §§ 41, 130a, 130b, 136, 269a nt., 269b nt., 274 nt., 275 nt., 276 nt., 277 nt., 278 nt., 278b, 2663; 41 U.S. Code § 6a nt.

May 21, 1945, Ch. 129, 59 Stat. 169, 22 U.S. Code §§ 41, 130a, 130b, 136, 269a nt., 269b nt., 274 nt., 275 nt., 276 nt., 277 nt., 278 nt., 2663; 41 U.S. Code § 6a nt.

July 5, 1946, Ch. 541, 60 Stat. 446, 22 U.S. Code §§ 41, 269a nt., 269b nt., 274 nt., 275 nt., 276 nt., 277 nt., 278 nt., 901 nt., 909 nt., 1140, 2663; 31 U.S. Code §§ 107a, 665 nt.; 41 U.S. Code § 6a nt.

July 9, 1947, Ch. 211, 61 Stat. 279, 22 U.S. Code §§ 269a nt., 269b nt., 274 nt., 275 nt., 276 nt., 277 nt., 278 nt., 295a nt., 2669; 31 U.S. Code §§ 107a, 665 nt.; 41 U.S. Code § 6a nt.

June 3, 1948, Ch. 400, 62 Stat. 305, 22 U.S. Code §§ 269a, 269b, 277, 278, 280b, 280i, 287e, 287r, 295a nts., 2669; 31 U.S. Code §§ 107a, 665 nt.; 41 U.S. Code § 6a nt., 269b nt., 275 nt., 276 nt., 277 nt., 278 nt., 280b nt., 280i nt., 287e nt., 287r nt., 295a nt., 297a, 2669; 31 U.S. Code §§ 107a, 534 nt., 665 nt.; 41 U.S. Code § 6a nt.

Sept. 6, 1950, Ch. 896, 64 Stat. 609, 22 U.S. Code §§ 269a, 269b, 275, 276, 277, 278, 280b, 281i, 287e nts., 287f, 287r nt., 297a, 2669; 31 U.S. Code §§ 107a, 543 nt., 665 nt.; 41 U.S. Code § 6a nt.

Oct. 22, 1951, Ch. 533, 65 Stat. 575, 22 U.S. Code §§ 269a nt., 269b nt., 275 nt., 276 nt., 277 nt., 278 nt., 280b nt., 280i nt., 287e nt., 287f, 287r nt., 297a, 2669; 31 U.S. Code §§ 107a, 543 nt., 685 nt.; 41 U.S. Code § 6a nt.

July 10, 1952, Ch. 651, 66 Stat. 549, 22 U.S. Code §§ 262b, 269a, 269b, 269e, 275, 276, 277, 278, 280b, 280i, 287e, 287r, 297a, 1480, 2669; 31 U.S. Code §§ 107a, 543 nt., 665 nt.; 41 U.S. Code § 6a nt.

Aug. 5, 1953, Ch. 328, 67 Stat. 367, 22 U.S. Code §§ 269a, 269b nts., 269e, 275 nt., 276, 277, 278, 280b, 280i, 287, 287e, 287r nts., 1480, 2669; 31 U.S. Code §§ 107a, 543 nt.; 41 U.S. Code § 6a nt.

July 2, 1954, Ch. 456, 68 Stat. 413, 22 U.S. Code §§ 269a nt., 269b, nt., 269e, 276 nt., 277 nt., 280b nt., 280i nt., 287 nt., 287e nt., 287r nt., 1480, 2669; 31 U.S. Code §§ 107a, 543 nt.; 41 U.S. Code § 6a nt.

July 7, 1955, Ch. 279, 69 Stat. 264, 22 U.S. Code §§ 269a nt., 269b nt., 269e, 275 nt., 276 nt., 277 nt., 280b nt., 280i nt., 287 nt., 287e nt., 287r nt., 1480, 2669; 31 U.S. Code §§ 107a, 543 nt.; 41 U.S. Code § 6a nt.

June 20, 1956, Ch. 414, 70 Stat. 299, 22 U.S. Code §§ 269a, 269b, 275, 276, 280b, 280i, 287e, 287r nt., 269e, 277 nt., 277d-12, 287 nt., 1480, 2669; 31 U.S. Code §§ 107a, 543 nt.; 41 U.S. Code § 6a nt.

June 11, 1957, P.L. 85-49, 71 Stat. 55, 22 U.S. Code §§ 269a, 269b, 275, 276, 277, 280b, 280i, 287, 287e, 287r, 1136 nts.

June 30, 1958, P.L. 85-474, 72 Stat. 244, 22 U.S. Code §§ 269a, 269b, 275, 276, nts., 276c, 277, 280b, 280i, 287, 287e, 287r, 1136 nts.

July 13, 1959, P.L. 86-84, 73 Stat. 182, 22 U.S. Code §§ 269a, 269b, 275, 276, 277, 280b, 280i, 287, 287e, 287r, 1136 nts.

Aug. 31, 1960, P.L. 86-678, 74 Stat. 555, 22 U.S. Code §§ 269a nt., 269b nt., 275 to 277 nts., 280b nt., 280i nt., 287 nt., 287e nt., 287r nt., 1136 nt.

Sept. 21, 1961, P.L. 87-264, 75 Stat. 545, 22 U.S. Code §§ 269a, 269b, 275, 276, 277, 280b, 280i, 287, 287e, 287r nts.

Oct. 18, 1962, P.L. 87-843, 76 Stat. 1080, 22 U.S. Code §§ 269a, 269b, 275, 276, 277, 280b, 280i, 287, 287e, 287r nts.

Dec. 30, 1963, P.L. 88-245, 77 Stat. 776, 22 U.S. Code §§ 269a, 269b, 275, 276, 277, 280b, 280i, 287, 287e, 287r nts.

Aug. 31, 1964, P.L. 88-527, 78 Stat. 711, 22 U.S. Code §§ 269a, 269b, 275, 276, 277, 280b, 280i, 287, 287e, 287r nts.

Sept. 2, 1965, P.L. 89-164, 79 Stat. 625, 22 U.S. Code §§ 269a nt., 269b nt., 275 nt., 276 nt., 277 nt., 280b nt., 280i nt., 287 nt., 287e nt., 287r nt.

Nov. 8, 1966, P.L. 89-797, 80 Stat. 1479, 22 U.S. Code §§ 269a, 269b, 275 to 277, 280b, 280i, 287, 287e, 287r nts.

Nov. 8, 1967, P.L. 90-133, 81 Stat. 411, 22 U.S. Code §§ 269a nt., 269b nt., 275 nt., 276 nt., 277 nt., 280b nt., 280i nt., 287 nt., 287e nt., 287r nt.

Aug. 9, 1968, P.L. 90-470, 62 Stat. 667, 22 U.S. Code §§ 269a nt., 269b nt., 275 nt., 276 nt., 277 nt., 280b nt., 280i nt., 287 nt., 287e nt., 287r nt.

Dec. 24, 1969, P.L. 91-153, 83 Stat. 403, 22 U.S. Code §§ 269a, 269b, 275 to 277, 280b, 280i, 287, 287e, 287r nts.

Oct. 21, 1970, P.L. 91-472, 84 Stat. 1040, 22 U.S. Code §§ 269a nt., 269b nt., 269f nt., 269g-1 nt., 269h nt., 272a nt., 273 to 277 nts., 279a nt., 280b nt., 280i nt., 280k nt., 287 nt., 287e nt., 287r nt., 290b nt., 1896b nt., 1928 nt., 1928b nt., 2673 nt.

Aug. 10, 1971, P.L. 92-77, 85 Stat. 247, 22 U.S. Code §§ 269a nt., 269b nt., 269f nt., 269g-1 nt., and others

Oct. 25, 1972, P.L. 92-544, 86 Stat. 1109, 22 U.S. Code §§ 269a, 269b, 269f, 269g-1, 269n, 269n nt.

Oct. 21, 1975, P.L. 94-121, 89 Stat. 617, 22 U.S. Code §§ 269a, 269b, 269f, 269g-1, 269h, 272a, 273 et seq., 279a, 279b, 280i, 280k, 287r, 290b, 1896b, 1928, 1928b, 2673

Dec. 13, 1985, P.L. 99-180, 22 U.S. Code § 296a nt.

Oct. 18, 1986, P.L. 99-500, 100 Stat. 3402

Oct. 30, 1986, P.L. 99-591, 100 Stat. 3402

July 11, 1987, P.L. 100-71, 22 U.S. Code § 269 nt.

Dec. 22, 1987, P.L. 100-202, 101 Stat. 1329

Dec. 22, 1987, P.L. 100-204, 22 U.S. Code § 2661

Oct. 1, 1988, P.L. 100-459, 102 Stat. 2207, 22 U.S. Code § 276 nt.

Oct. 1, 1988, P.L. 100-459, 102 Stat. 2209

Nov. 21, 1989, P.L. 101-162, 103 Stat. 1006

Department of State Appropriations Act, 1988

Nov. 5, 1990, P.L. 101-515, 22 U.S. Code § 276 nt.

Department of State Appropriations Act, 1989

April 30, 1994, P.L. 103-236, 108 Stat. 408

Department of State Appropriations Act, 1991

Nov. 5, 1990, P.L. 101-515, 22 U.S. Code §§ 269a nt., 276i

Department of State Appropriations Authorization Act of 1973

Aug. 16, 1985, P.L. 99-93, 22 U.S. Code § 2685

April 30, 1994, P.L. 103-236, 22 U.S. Code § 2655a

Continued

Aug. 23, 1994, P.L. 103-306, 108 Stat. 1632

Department of State Authorization Act, Fiscal Years 1980 and 1981

Aug. 15, 1979, P.L. 96-60, 5 U.S. Code § 1304; 16 U.S. Code § 916 nt.; 22 U.S. Code §§ 287c nt., 288f-2, 889, 889 nt., 1434, 1461, 1469, 1469 nt., 1471, 1474, 1475, 1477, 1731 nt., 2454, 2456, 2456 nt., 2458, 2458a, 2691, 2696, 2696 nt., 2871 nt., 2877, 2879, 3007, 3401

Department of State Authorization Act, Fiscal Years 1982 and 1983

Aug. 24, 1982, P.L. 97-241, 18 U.S. Code § 203 nt.; 22 U.S. Code §§ 214, 217a, 217a nt., 269g-1, 273, 280k, 287e, 287e nt., 287r nt., 1477b, 2458 nt., 2651 nt., 2656 nt., 2679a, 2680a, 2696, 2705, 2877, 3927, 3962, 4024, 4054

Nov. 22, 1983, P.L. 98-164, 22 U.S. Code § 2656 nt.

Dec. 17, 1993, P.L. 103-199, 22 U.S. Code § 2458 nt.

April 30, 1994, P.L. 103-236, 22 U.S. Code § 2656 nt.

Department of State Authorization Act, Fiscal Years 1984 and 1985

Aug. 16, 985, P.L. 99-93, 22 U.S. Code §§ 287 nt., 287e nt.

Nov. 22, 1983, P.L. 98-164, 5 U.S. Code §§ 5314, 5315, 5928, 5944; 8 U.S. Code § 1522; 22 U.S. Code §§ 269f, 287 nt., 287b nt., 287e nt., 287q, 288f-1, 290f, 302, 1928e, 2151, 2291, 2346a nt., 2384, 2651 nt., 2653, 2656, nt., 2671, 2675, 2691 nt., 2706, 2707, 3311, 3361, 3902, 3968, 3982, 4021, 4086, 4153, 4154; 50 U.S. Code § 1546a

Dec. 22, 1987, P.L. 100-204, 22 U.S. Code §§ 287 nt., 287b nt., 287e

Oct. 1, 1988, P.L. 100-459, 102 Stat. 2207

Nov. 5, 1990, P.L. 101-515, 22 U.S. Code § 276 nt.

April 30, 1994, P.L. 103-236, 22 U.S. Code §§ 287b nt., 2460 nt., 3982 nt.

Department of State Basic Authorizations Act of 1956

See State Department Basic Authorities Act Of 1956

Department of State Special Agents Retirement Act of 1998

Nov. 13, 1998, P.L. 105-382, 112 Stat. 3406, 22 U.S. Code § 3901 nt.

Department of Taxation and Revenue Act

N.M. Stat. Ann., 9-11-1 et seq.

Department of the Interior and Related Agencies Appropriation Acts

June 16, 1955, Ch. 147, 69 Stat. 141, 16 U.S. Code §§ 556a, 557b, 560a, 571a, 581a-2; 25 U.S. Code § 372-1; 43 U.S. Code §§ 50, 775; 48 U.S. Code §§ 1401f, 1423l, 1434, 1435, 1436, 1440, 1470a

June 13, 1956, Ch. 380, 70 Stat. 273, 16 U.S. Code §§ 556a, 560a, 571a, 581a-2; 25 U.S. Code § 372-1; 43 U.S. Code §§ 50, 775, 1468; 48 U.S. Code 1401f, 1423l, 1434, 1435, 1436, 1440, 1470a

July 1, 1957, P.L. 85-77, 71 Stat. 257, 16 U.S. Code §§ 560a, 571a; 25 U.S. Code § 372-1; 43 U.S. Code §§ 50, 775; 48 U.S. Code §§ 1401f, 1423l, 1434, 1435, 1436, 1440, 1470a

June 4, 1958, P.L. 85-439, 72 Stat. 155, 16 U.S. Code §§ 560a, 571b; 25 U.S. Code § 372-1; 43 U.S. Code §§ 50, 775; 48 U.S. Code §§ 1401f, 1423l, 1434, 1435, 1436, 1440, 1470a

June 23, 1959, P.L. 86-60, 73 Stat. 92, 16 U.S. Code § 560a; 25 U.S. Code § 372-1; 43 U.S. Code §§ 50, 775; 48 U.S. Code §§ 1401f, 1423l, 1470a, 1665, 1682, 1683, 1687

June 23, 1959, P.L. 86-60, 73 Stat. 98, 25 U.S. Code § 372-1; 43 U.S. Code §§ 50, 775; 48 U.S. Code §§ 1401f, 1423l

May 13, 1960, P.L. 86-455, 74 Stat. 104, 16 U.S. Code § 560a; 25 U.S. Code § 372-1; 43 U.S. Code §§ 50, 775; 48 U.S. Code §§ 1401f, 1423l, 1470a, 1665, 1682, 1683, 1687

Aug. 3, 1961, P.L. 87-122, 75 Stat. 246, 16 U.S. Code § 506a; 25 U.S. Code § 372-1; 43 U.S. Code § 50; 48 U.S. Code §§ 1401f, 1423l, 1470a, 1665, 1682, 1683, 1687

Aug. 9, 1962, P.L. 87-578, 76 Stat. 335, 16 U.S. Code § 560a; 25 U.S. Code § 372-1; 43 U.S. Code § 50; 48 U.S. Code §§ 1401f, 1423l, 1470a, 1665, 1682, 1683, 1687

July 26, 1963, P.L. 88-79, 77 Stat. 96, 16 U.S. Code § 560a; 25 U.S. Code § 372-1; 43 U.S. Code § 50; 48 U.S. Code §§ 1401f, 1423l, 1470a, 1665, 1682, 1683, 1687

July 7, 1964, P.L. 88-356, 78 Stat. 273, 16 U.S. Code § 560a; 25 U.S. Code § 372-1; 43 U.S. Code § 50; 48 U.S. Code §§ 1401f, 1423l, 1470a, 1665, 1682, 1683, 1687

June 28, 1965, P.L. 89-52, 79 Stat. 174, 16 U.S. Code § 560a; 25 U.S. Code § 372-1; 43 U.S. Code § 50; 48 U.S. Code §§ 1401f, 1423l, 1470a, 1665, 1682, 1683, 1687

May 31, 1966, P.L. 89-435, 80 Stat. 170, 16 U.S. Code § 560a; 25 U.S. Code § 372-1; 43 U.S. Code § 50; 48 U.S. Code §§ 1401f, 1423l, 1470a, 1665, 1682, 1683, 1687

June 24, 1967, P.L. 90-28, 81 Stat. 59, 16 U.S. Code § 560a; 25 U.S. Code § 372-1; 43 U.S. Code § 50; 48 U.S. Code §§ 1401f, 1423l, 1470a, 1665, 1682, 1683, 1687

July 26, 1968, P.L. 90-425, 82 Stat. 425, 16 U.S. Code § 560a; 43 U.S. Code § 50; 48 U.S. Code §§ 1401f, 1423l, 1470a, 1665, 1682, 1683, 1687

Oct. 29, 1969, P.L. 91-98, 83 Stat. 147, 16 U.S. Code § 560a; 43 U.S. Code § 50; 48 U.S. Code §§ 1401f, 1423l, 1470a, 1665, 1682, 1683, 1687

July 31, 1970, P.L. 91-361, 84 Stat. 673, 16 U.S. Code § 560a; 43 U.S. Code 50; 48 U.S. Code §§ 1401f, 1423l, 1470a, 1665, 1682, 1683, 1687

Aug. 10, 1971, P.L. 92-76, 85 Stat. 229, 16 U.S. Code § 560a; 43 U.S. Code § 50; 48 U.S. Code §§ 1401f, 1423l, 1470a, 1665, 1682, 1683, 1687

Nov. 27, 1979, P.L. 96-126, 16 U.S. Code § 20b nt.; 42 U.S. Code § 5915 nt.; 43 U.S. Code § 1752 nt.; 50 U.S. Code Appx. § 2406 nt.

Oct. 12, 1984, P.L. 98-473, 20 U.S. Code § 76 h

Oct. 18, 1986, P.L. 99-500, 100 Stat. 3629

Oct. 30, 1986, P.L. 99-591, 100 Stat. 3629

Department of the Interior and Related Agencies Appropriations Act, 1991

Nov. 5, 1990, P.L. 101-512, 5 U.S. Code § 5315; 10 U.S. Code § 7422 nt.; 14 U.S. Code §§ 1682, 1683; 16 U.S. Code §§ 18f-1, 20b, 431 nt., 441 nt., 459f-1, 460l-10a nt., 460yy-1 nt., 554d, 935 nt., 1132 nt., 1166, 6832; 25 U.S. Code 450f nt., 1681, 1773d nt.; 30 U.S. Code § 1211 nt.; 31 U.S. Code §§ 1352, 6305 nt.; 43 U.S. Code §§ 50, 50-1, 50a, 1338a, 1735 nt., 1752 nt.; 48 U.S. Code §§ 1401f, 1423l, 1469b 1665

Oct. 28, 1992, P.L. 102-552, 16 U.S. Code § 3832

Department of the Interior and Related Agencies Appropriations Act, 1992

Nov. 13, 1991, P.L. 102-154, 105 Stat. 1037

Department of the Interior and Related Agencies Appropriations Act, 1993

Oct. 5, 1992, P.L. 102-381, 106 Stat. 1374

Department of the Interior and Related Agencies Appropriations Act, 1994

Nov. 8, 1993, P.L. 103-138, 107 Stat. 1379

Department of the Interior and Related Agencies Appropriations Act, 1995

Sept. 30, 1994, P.L. 103-332, 108 Stat. 2499

Department of the Interior and Related Agencies Appropriations Act, 1996

April 26, 1996, P.L. 104-134, 110 Stat. 1321-156

Department of the Interior and Related Agencies Appropriations Act, 1997

Sept. 30, 1996, P.L. 104-208, 110 Stat. 3009

Oct. 21, 1998, P.L. 105-277, 16 U.S. Code § 1011

Department of the Interior and Related Agencies Appropriations Act, 1998

Nov. 14, 1997, P.L. 105-83, 111 Stat. 1543

Oct. 21, 1998, P.L. 105-277, 25 U.S. Code § 2717 nt.

Oct. 21, 1998, P.L. 105-277, 101(f), 112 Stat. 2681

Department of the Interior and Related Agencies Appropriations Act, 1999

May 21, 1999, P. L. 106-31, 16 U.S. Code /sect 410hh-4 nt., 544b, 1374.

May 21, 1999, P.L. 106-31, 16 U.S. Code §§ 410hh-4 nt., 544b, 1374

Department of the Navy Appropriation Act, 1949

June 24, 1948, Ch. 617, 62 Stat. 584

Department of the Treasury Act

N.J. Stat. Ann. 52:18A-1 et seq.

Department of Transportation Act

N.M. Stat. Ann., 9-11-4, 67-3-70 et seq.

Utah Code Ann. 1953, 63-49-1 et seq.

Department of Transportation Acts

Oct. 15, 1966, P.L. 89-670, 80 Stat. 931, 3 U.S. Code § 19; 5 U.S. Code §§ 101, 5312 to 5317; 10 U.S. Code § 801; 15 U.S. Code § 1404; 18 U.S. Code § 1020; 23 U.S. Code § 401 nt.; 29 U.S. Code § 213; 33 U.S. Code §§ 981, 1102; 40 U.S. Code Appx. §§ 201, 206; 42 U.S. Code § 1376; 49 U.S. Code §§ 312, 1651 to 1659; 50 U.S . Code § 123

Sept. 11, 1967, P.L. 90-83, 81 Stat. 224, 49 U.S. Code § 1652

Oct. 23, 1967, P.L. 90-112, 81 Stat. 311, 14 U.S. Code § 92 nt.; 20 U.S. Code § 241 nt.

Aug. 8, 1968, P.L. 90-464, 82 Stat. 654, 14 U.S. Code § 92 nt.; 20 U.S . Code § 241 nt.

Aug. 23, 1968, P.L. 90-495, 82 Stat. 824, 49 U.S. Code § 1653

March 27, 1978, P.L. 95-251, 49 U.S. Code §§ 1655h, 1657

Nov. 8, 1978, P.L. 95-607, 49 U.S. Code § 1654

Sept. 29, 1979, P.L. 96-73, 49 U.S. Code § 1653

May 30, 1980, P.L. 96-254, 49 U.S. Code § 1657

April 7, 1986, P.L. 99-272, 49 U.S. Code Appx. § 1654

April 2, 1987, P.L. 100-17, 49 U.S. Code Appx. § 1655

Dec. 11, 1989, P.L. 101-213, 49 U.S. Code Appx. § 1654

Sept. 3, 1992, P.L. 102-365, 49 U.S. Code Appx. § 1654

Oct. 11, 1996, P.L. 104-287, 5 U.S. Code § 101 nt.

Department of Transportation and Related Agencies Appropriation Acts

Dec. 26, 1969, P.L. 91-168, 83 Stat. 454, 14 U.S. Code § 92 nt.; 20 U.S. Code § 241 nt.

Aug. 10, 1971, P.L. 92-74, 85 Stat. 201, 14 U.S. Code § 92 nt.; 20 U.S . Code § 241 nt.; 49 U.S. Code § 305a

Aug. 22, 1972, P.L. 92-398, 86 Stat. 580, 49 U.S. Code § 305a

Aug. 16, 1973, P.L. 93-98, 87 Stat. 329, 14 U.S. Code § 92 nt.; 20 U.S . Code § 241 nt.; 49 U.S. Code § 305a

Aug. 28, 1974, P.L. 93-391, 88 Stat. 769, 14 U.S. Code § 92 nt.; 20 U.S. Code § 241 nt.; 49 U.S. Code § 305a

Nov. 24, 1975, P.L. 94-134, 22 U.S. Code §§ 155 et seq.

Nov. 24, 1975, P.L. 94-134, 89 Stat. 695, 14 U.S. Code § 92 nt.; 20 U.S. Code § 241; 22 U.S. Code § 155 nt.; 49 U.S. Code § 305a

Oct. 12, 1984, P.L. 98-473, 98 Stat. 1944

Dec. 19, 1985, P.L. 99-190, 10 U.S. Code § 2304 nt.; 14 U.S. Code § 92 nt.; 20 U.S. Code § 241 nt.; 23 U.S. Code §§ 104 nt., 119, 125 nt.; 33 U.S. Code § 1571a; 45 U.S. Code §§ 711, 851 nt.; 49 U.S. Code § 10344 nt.; 49 U.S. Code Appx. §§ 1324 nt., 1519, 1604, 1607a nt., 1614, 1617

Dec. 22, 1987, P: L. 100-202, 101 Stat. 1329

Sept. 30, 1988, P.L. 100-457, 102 Stat. 2157

Nov. 21, 1989, P.L. 101-164, 103 Stat. 1069

Department of Transportation and Related Agencies Appropriations Act, 1987

Nov. 23, 1993, P.L. 103-149, 22 U.S. Code § 5056a

Department of Transportation and Related Agencies Appropriations Act, 1988

Oct. 28, 1991, P.L. 102-143, 105 Stat. 950

Department of Transportation and Related Agencies Appropriations Act, 1991

Nov. 5, 1990, P.L. 101-516, 10 U.S. Code § 2403 nt.; 14 U.S. Code § 92 nt.; 20 U.S. Code § 241 nt.; 23 U.S. Code §§ 104, 104 nt., 154 nt., 410; 40 U.S. Code § 817 nt.; 41 U.S. Code § 10b nt.; 49 U.S. Code § 10344 nt.; 49 U.S. Code Appx. §§ 1324 nt., 1354a, 1617nt., 2205 nt., 2212 nt.

April 10, 1991, P.L. 102-27, 23 U.S. Code § 104 nt.

Oct. 28, 1991, P.L. 102-143, 23 U.S. Code §§ prec. 101, 104, 104 nt.

Department of Transportation and Related Agencies Appropriations Act, 1992

Oct. 28, 1991, P.L. 102-143, 105 Stat. 917

Dec. 18, 1991, P.L. 102-240, 105 Stat. 2130

Oct. 6, 1992, P.L. 102-388, 106 Stat. 1555

Department of Transportation and Related Agencies Appropriations Act, 1993

Oct. 6, 1992, P.L. 102-388, 106 Stat. 1520

Department of Transportation and Related Agencies Appropriations Act, 1994

Oct. 27, 1993, P.L. 103-122, 107 Stat. 1198

Feb. 12, 1994, P.L. 103-211, 23 U.S. Code § 104 nt.

Oct. 31, 1994, P.L. 103-430, 40 U.S. Code Appx. § 2205 nt.

Department of Transportation and Related Agencies Appropriations Act, 1995

Sept. 30, 1994, P.L. 103-331, 108 Stat. 2471

Nov. 28, 1995, P.L. 104-59, 23 U.S. Code § 104 nt.

Oct. 11, 1996, P.L. 104-287, 49 U.S. Code § 44502 nt.

Department of Transportation and Related Agencies Appropriations Act, 1996

Nov. 15, 1995, P.L. 104-50, 109 Stat. 436

Nov. 20, 1997, P.L. 105-102, 49 U.S. Code § 5302

Oct. 31, 1998, P.L. 105-339, 49 U.S. Code § 106 nt.

Department of Transportation and Related Agencies Appropriations Act, 1997

Sept. 30, 1996, P.L. 104-205, 110 Stat. 2951

Department of Transportation and Related Agencies Appropriations Act, 1998

Oct. 27, 1997, P.L. 105-66, 111 Stat. 1425

Department of Transportation and Related Agencies Appropriations Act, 1999

Oct. 21, 1998, P.L. 105-277, 101(h), 112 Stat. 2681

Department of Veterans Affairs Act

Oct. 25, 1988, P.L. 100-527, 102 Stat. 2635

Aug. 16, 1989, P.L. 101-94, 38 U.S. Code § 201 nt.

Nov. 15, 1990, P.L. 101-576, 38 U.S. Code § 201 nt.

Aug. 6, 1991, P.L. 102-83, 38 U.S. Code § 201 nt.

Ill. Rev. Stat. 1991, Ch. 126 1/2, § 65.9 et seq.

Department of Veterans Affairs and Housing, and Urban Development, and Independent Agencies Appropriations Act, 1990

May 25, 1990, P.L. 101-302, 33 U.S. Code § 1384 nt.

Dec. 12, 1991, P.L. 102-229, 105 Stat. 1711

Department of Veterans Affairs and Housing and Urban Development, and Independent Agencies Appropriations Act, 1996

Oct. 27, 1997, P.L. 105-65, 42 U.S. Code § 1437f nt.

Oct. 21, 1998, P.L. 105-276, 42 U.S. Code §§ 1437f nt., 1437l nt.

Department of Veterans Affairs and Housing and Urban Development, and Independent Agencies Appropriations Act, 1997

Oct. 21, 1998, P.L. 105-276, 12 U.S. Code § 1715z-11a

Department of Veterans Affairs and Housing and Urban Development, and Independent Agencies Appropriations Act, 1998

Oct. 27, 1997, P.L. 105-65, 111 Stat. 1344

Oct. 21, 1998, P.L. 105-276, 12 U.S. Code § 1715w

Continued

Nov. 3, 1998, P.L. 105-354, 36 U.S. Code
Appx. §§ 121b, 122, 122a

Department of Veterans Affairs Codification Act

Aug. 6, 1991, P.L. 102-83, 38 U.S. Code
§ 101 nt.

Department of Veterans Affairs Health-Care Personnel Act of 1991

May 7, 1991, P.L. 102-40, 38 U.S. Code
§ 101 nt.

Department of Veterans Affairs Health Care Personnel Incentive Act of 1998

Nov. 11, 1998, P.L. 105-368, Title VIII, 112
Stat. 3352, 38 U.S. Code § 101 nt.

Department of Veterans Affairs Labor Relations Improvement Act of 1991

May 7, 1991, P.L. 102-40, 38 U.S. Code
§§ 101 nt., 7421 to 7423, 7461 to 7464

Department of Veterans Affairs Nurse Pay Act of 1990

Aug. 15, 1990, P.L. 101-366, 38 U.S. Code
§ 101 nt.

Nov. 2, 1994, P.L. 103-452, 38 U.S. Code
§ 1720C

Department of Veterans Affairs Physician and Retention Act of 1991

May 7, 1991, P.L. 102-40, 38 U.S. Code
§§ 101 nt., 7431 to 7440

Department of Water Resources Act

N.C. Gen. Stat. 1943, § 143-350 et seq.

Departmental Equipment Loan Act (Brockton)

Mass. Acts 1956, Ch. 273

Departmental Supplies Acts

Jan. 27, 1894, Ch. 22, 28 Stat. 33

April 21, 1894, Ch. 61, 28 Stat. 58, 62

Departments of Commerce, Justice and State, The Judiciary, and Related Agencies Appropriation Act, 1985

Aug. 30, 1984, P.L. 98-411, 22 U.S. Code
§§ 269a nt., 1465e, 2873 nt.; 23 U.S. Code
§§ 114 nt., 604 nt.; 28 U.S. Code § 533 nt.;
33 U.S. Code § 851; 42 U.S. Code §§ 250a,
3796, 3796a, 3796b; 50 Appx. 2406 nt.

Departments of Commerce, Justice and State, the Judiciary, and Related Agencies Appropriation Act, 1986

Dec. 13, 1985, P.L. 99-180, 18 U.S. Code
§ 3525; 22 U.S. Code § 269a nt.; 23 U.S.
Code 114 nt.; 28 U.S. Code §§ 533 nt., 604
nt.; 33 U.S. Code § 851; 42 U.S. Code
§ 250a

June 17, 1988, P.L. 100-340, 102 Stat. 622

Aug. 14, 1988, P.L. 100-393, 102 Stat. 974

Departments of Commerce, Justice, and State, the Judiciary, and Related Agencies Appropriation Act, 1987

Oct. 18, 1986, P.L. 99-500, 100 Stat. 3424

Oct. 30, 1986, P.L. 99-591, 100 Stat. 3424

July 11, 1987, P.L. 100-71, 8 U.S. Code
§ 1356

Departments of Commerce, Justice, and State, the Judiciary, and Related Agencies Appropriations Act, 1988

Dec. 22, 1987, P.L. 100-202, 101 Stat. 1329

Sept. 30, 1996, P.L. 104-208, 8 U.S. Code
§ 1201 nt.

Oct. 21, 1998, P.L. 105-277, 22 U.S. Code
§ 276 nt.

Departments of Commerce, Justice, and State, the Judiciary, and Related Agencies Appropriations Act, 1989

Oct. 1, 1988, P.L. 100-459, 102 Stat. 2228

Dec. 1, 1990, P.L. 101-650, 28 U.S. Code
§ 533 nt.

Aug. 26, 1992, P.L. 102-356, 47 U.S. Code
§ 303 nt.

Departments of Commerce, Justice, and State, the Judiciary, and Related Agencies Appropriations Act, 1990

Nov. 21, 1989, P.L. 101-162, 103 Stat. 988

May 25, 1990, P.L. 101-302, 15 U.S. Code
§ 18a nt.

Departments of Commerce, Justice, and State, the Judiciary, and Related Agencies Appropriations Act, 1991
Nov. 5, 1990, P.L. 101-515, 15 U.S. Code
§ 77f nt.; 42 U.S. Code § 2996f nt.

Departments of Commerce, Justice, and State, the Judiciary, and Related Agencies Appropriations Act, 1992
Oct. 28, 1991, P.L. 102-140, 105 Stat. 782
Nov. 13, 1991, P.L. 102-154, 105 Stat. 1013
July 22, 1992, P.L. 102-302, 106 Stat. 249

Departments of Commerce, Justice, and State, the Judiciary, and Related Agencies Appropriations Act, 1993
Oct. 6, 1992, P.L. 102-395, 106 Stat. 1875
Nov. 26, 1997, P.L. 105-119, 8 U.S. Code
§§ 1153 nt., 1440 nt.
Nov. 10, 1998, P.L. 105-362, 21 U.S. Code
§ 886a

Departments of Commerce, Justice, and State, the Judiciary, and Related Agencies Appropriations Act, 1994
Oct. 27, 1993, P.L. 103-121, 107 Stat. 1153

Departments of Commerce, Justice, and State, the Judiciary, and Related Agencies Appropriations Act, 1995
Aug. 26, 1994, P.L. 103-317, 108 Stat. 1724
Nov. 26, 1997, P.L. 105-119, 8 U.S. Code
§ 1182 nt.

Departments of Commerce, Justice, and State, the Judiciary, and Related Agencies Appropriations Act, 1996
April 26, 1996, P.L. 104-134, 110 Stat. 1321

Departments of Commerce, Justice, and State, the Judiciary, and Related Agencies Appropriations Act, 1997
Sept. 30, 1996, P.L. 104-208, 110 Stat. 3009

Departments of Commerce, Justice, and State, the Judiciary, and Related Agencies Appropriations Act, 1998
Nov. 26, 1997, P.L. 105-119, 111 Stat. 2440

Departments of Commerce, Justice, and State, the Judiciary, and Related Agencies Appropriations Act, 1999
Oct. 21, 1998, P.L. 105-277, 101(c), 112 Stat. 2681

Departments of Commerce, Justice, State, the Judiciary, and Related Agencies Appropriation Act, 1985
April 2, 1987, P.L. 100-17, 23 U.S. Code
§ 114 nt.

Departments of Labor, and Health, Education, and Welfare, and Related Agencies Appropriation Acts
Aug. 1, 1955, Ch. 437, 69 Stat. 397, 29 U.S. Code § 34 nt.; 42 U.S. Code §§ 210, 421 nt., 703a, 704a, 3508; 45 U.S. Code § 355a
Aug. 10, 1971, P.L. 92-80, 85 Stat. 285, 39 U.S. Code § 3202 nt.; 42 U.S. Code §§ 421 nt., 704a, 905a, 3508

Departments of Labor, and Health, Education and Welfare Appropriation Acts
July 31, 1953, Ch. 296, 67 Stat. 260, 42 U.S. Code §§ 212c, 214a, 703a, 704a, 3508; 43 U.S. Code § 617v
July 2, 1954, Ch. 457, 68 Stat. 434, 42 U.S. Code §§ 703a, 704a, 3508
June 29, 1956, Ch. 477, 70 Stat. 423, 42 U.S. Code §§ 210, 421 nt., 702 nt., 703a, 704a, 3508; 45 U.S. Code § 355a
June 29, 1957, P.L. 85-67, 71 Stat. 210, 29 U.S. Code § 562; 42 U.S. Code §§ 290, 421 nt., 702 nt., 703a, 704a, 3506, 3508
Aug. 1, 1958, P.L. 85-580, 72 Stat. 457, 7 U.S. Code § 1462 nt.; 42 U.S. Code §§ 267, 421 nt., 702 nt., 703a, 704a, 3508
Aug. 14, 1959, P.L. 86-158, 73 Stat. 339, 7 U.S. Code § 1462 nt.; 20 U.S. Code § 612; 42 U.S. Code §§ 227a, 291n-1, 291v, 421 nt., 702 nt., 703a, 704a, 3508
Sept. 2, 1960, P.L. 86-703, 74 Stat. 755, 7 U.S. Code § 1462 nt.; 29 U.S. Code § 562; 42 U.S. Code §§ 210, 227a, 246a, 421 nt., 702 nt. , 703a, 704a, 905, 3508
Sept. 22, 1961, P.L. 87-290, 75 Stat. 589, 39 U.S. Code § 3202 nt.; 42 U.S. Code §§ 227a 290, 421 nt., 702 nt., 703a, 740a, 3508
Continued

Aug. 14, 1962, P.L. 87-582, 76 Stat. 361, 39 U.S. Code § 3202 nt.; 42 U.S. Code §§ 227a, 421 nt., 702 nt., 703a, 704a, 1101 nt., 3508

Oct. 11, 1963, P.L. 88-136, 77 Stat. 224, 42 U.S. Code §§ 227a, 703a, 704a, 3508

Sept. 19, 1964, P.L. 88-605, 78 Stat. 959, 39 U.S. Code § 3202 nt.; 42 U.S. Code §§ 227a, 421 nt., 702 nt., 703a, 704a, 3508

Aug. 31, 1965, P.L. 89-156, 79 Stat. 611, 39 U.S. Code § 3202 nt.; 42 U.S. Code §§ 227a, 421 nt., 702 nt., 703a, 704a, 3508

Nov. 7, 1966, P.L. 89-787, 80 Stat. 1378, 39 U.S. Code § 3202 nt.; 42 U.S. Code §§ 227a, 421 nt., 702 nt., 703a, 704a, 3508

Nov. 8, 1967, P.L. 90-132, 81 Stat. 386, 39 U.S. Code § 3202 nt.; 42 U.S. Code §§ 227a, 421 nt., 702 nt., 703a, 704a, 3508

Oct. 11, 1968, P.L. 90-557, 82 Stat. 969, 39 U.S. Code § 3202 nt.; 42 U.S. Code §§ 421 nt., 703 nt., 704a, 3508

Jan. 11, 1971, P.L. 91-667, 84 Stat. 2001, 39 U.S. Code § 3202 nt.; 42 U.S. Code §§ 291j-7 nt., 421 nt., 703 nt., 704a, 3508, 3510

Jan. 11, 1971, P.L. 91-667, 84 Stat. 2001, 42 U.S. Code §§ 704a, 350a, 3510

Departments of Labor, and Health, Education, and Welfare Supplemental Appropriation Act, 1966

Sept. 23, 1965, P.L. 89-199, 79 Stat. 831

Departments of Labor, Health and Human Services, and Education and Related Agencies Appropriation Acts

Nov. 8, 1984, P.L. 98-619, 98 Stat. 3305

Dec. 12, 1985, P.L. 99-178, 12 U.S. Code § 1749a; 20 U.S. Code §§ 1070a nt., 1070b-3 nt., 24 U.S. Code § 68b, 170a; 30 U.S. Code § 962; 42 U.S. Code §§ 210 nt., 1383 nt.

Dec. 22, 1987, P.L. 100-202, 101 Stat. 1329

Sept. 20, 1988, P.L. 100-436, 102 Stat. 1716

Nov. 21, 1989, P.L. 101-166, 103 Stat. 1159

Departments of Labor, Health and Human Services, and Education, and Related Agencies Appropriations Act, 1991

Nov. 5, 1990, P.L. 101-517, 20 U.S. Code § 1070a nt.; 30 U.S. Code § 962; 42 U.S. Code § 1383 nt.

Departments of Labor, Health and Human Services, and Education, and Related Agencies Appropriations Act, 1992

Nov. 26, 1991, P.L. 102-170, 105 Stat. 1107

Departments of Labor, Health and Human Services, and Education, and Related Agencies Appropriations Act, 1993

Oct. 6, 1992, P.L. 102-394, 106 Stat. 1827

Departments of Labor, Health and Human Services, and Education, and Related Agencies Appropriations Act, 1996

April 26, 1996, P.L. 104-134, 110 Stat. 1321-211

Departments of Labor, Health and Human Services, and Education, and Related Agencies Appropriations Act, 1997

Sept. 30, 1996, P.L. 104-208, 110 Stat. 3009

Departments of State and Justice, the Judiciary, and Related Agencies Appropriation Acts

July 7, 1955, Ch. 279, 69 Stat. 264, 8 U.S. Code § 1553; 18 U.S. Code § 4041 nt.; 22 U.S. Code §§ 269a nt., 269b nt., 269e, 275 nt., 276 nt., 277 nt., 280b nt., 280i nt., 287 nt., 287e nt., 287r nt., 1461a, 1461b, 1461c, 1480, 2669 (See 28 U.S. Code §§ 533, 534, 536) 31 U.S. Code §§ 107a, 543 nt.; 41 U.S. Code § 6a nt.; 50 U.S. Code Appx. § 6b

June 20, 1956, Ch. 414, 70 Stat. 299, 8 U.S. Code § 1553; 22 U.S. Code §§ 269a, 269b, 275, 276, 280b, 280i, 287e, 287r nts., 269e, 277 nt., 277d-12, 287 nt., 1461a to 1461c 1480, 2669; 28 U.S. Code §§ 533, 534, 536, 604 nt.; 31 U.S. Code §§ 107a, 543 nt.; 41 U.S. Code § 6a nt.; 42 U.S. Code § 250a; 50 U.S. Code Appx. § 6b

June 11, 1957, P.L. 85-49, 71 Stat. 55, 22 U.S. Code §§ 269a, 269b, 275, 276, 280b, 280i, 287, 287e, 287r, 1136 nts., 1461a to 1461c; 28 U.S. Code §§ 533, 534, 536, 604 nt.; 42 U.S. Code § 250a; Title 50 U.S. Code Appx. § 6b

June 30, 1958, P.L. 85-474, 72 Stat. 244, 22 U.S. Code §§ 269a, 269b, 275, 276 nts., 276c, 277, 280b, 280i, 287, 287e, 287r, 1136 nts., 1461a to 1461c; 28 U.S. Code §§ 533, 534, 536, 604 nt.; 42 U.S. Code § 250a; 50 U.S. Code Appx. § 6b

July 13, 1959, P.L. 86-84, 73 Stat. 182, 22 U.S. Code §§ 269a, 269b, 275, 276, 277, 280b, 280i, 287, 287e, 287r, 1136 nts., 1461a, 1461b, 1461c; 28 U.S. Code §§ 533, 534, 536, 604 nt.; 42 U.S. Code § 250a; 50 U.S. Code Appx. § 6b

Aug. 31, 1960, P.L. 86-678, 74 Stat. 555, 22 U.S. Code §§ 269a nt., 269b nt., 275 to 277 nts., 280b nt., 280i nt., 287 nt., 287e nt., 287r nt. , 1136 nt., 1461a to 1461c; 28 U.S. Code §§ 533, 534, 536, 604 nt.; 42 U.S. Code § 250a, 50 U.S. Code Appx. § 6b

Sept. 21, 1961, P.L. 87-264, 75 Stat. 545, 22 U.S. Code §§ 269a, 269b, 275 to 277, 280b, 280i, 287, 287e, 287r nts., 1461b, 1461c; 28 U.S. Code §§ 533, 534, 536, 604 nt.; 42 U.S. Code §§ 250a, 1975c; 50 U.S. Code Appx. § 6b

Departments of State, Justice, and Commerce Appropriation Acts

July 1, 1943, Ch. 182, 57 Stat. 271, 3 U.S. Code § 53; 15 U.S. Code §§ 319, 322, 324; 22 U.S. Code §§ 41, 136, 269a, 269b, 274, 275 nt., 276 nt., 278, 278b, 279, 2663 (See 28 U.S. Code §§ 533, 534, 536) 33 U.S. Code § 851; 41 U.S. Code § 6a nt.

June 28, 1944, Ch. 294, 58 Stat. 395, 3 U.S. Code § 53; 15 U.S. Code §§ 319, 324, 1509, 1521; 22 U.S. Code §§ 41, 136, 269a nt., 269b nt., 274 to 277 nts., 278 (See 28 U.S. Code §§ 533, 534, 536) 33 U.S. Code § 851; 41 U.S. Code § 6a nt.

Departments of State, Justice, and Commerce, the Judiciary, and Related Agencies Appropriation Acts

Oct. 11, 1962, P.L. 87-793, 76 Stat. 850, 5 U.S. Code § 298a

Oct. 18, 1962, P.L. 87-843, 76 Stat. 1080, 15 U.S. Code §§ 278e, 633 nts.; 22 U.S. Code §§ 269a, 269b, 275, 276, 277, 280b, 280i, 287, 287e, 287r nts., 1461b, 1461c; 28 U.S. Code §§ 533, 534, 536, 604 nt.; 31 U.S. Code § 25; 33 U.S. Code § 851; 36 §§ 121b, 122, 122a; 42 U.S. Code § 250a; 50 U.S. Code Appx. §§ 6b, 1738b

Dec. 30, 1963, P.L. 88-245, 77 Stat. 776, 15 U.S. Code §§ 278e, 633 nt.; 22 U.S. Code §§ 269a, 269b, 275, 276, 277, 280b, 280i, 287, 287e, 287r nts., 1461b, 1461c; 28 U.S. Code §§ 533, 534, 536, 604 nt.; 33 U.S. Code § 851; 36 U.S. Code §§ 121b, 122, 122a; 42 U.S. Code § 250a; 50 U.S. Code Appx. §§ 6b, 1738b

Aug. 31, 1964, P.L. 88-527, 78 Stat. 711, 15 U.S. Code § 278e nt.; 22 U.S. Code §§ 269a, 269b, 275, 276, 277, 280b, 280i, 287, 287e, 287r nts., 1461b, 1461c; 28 U.S. Code §§ 533, 534, 536, 604 nt.; 33 U.S. Code § 851; 36 U.S. Code §§ 121b, 122, 122a; 42 U.S. Code § 250a; 50 U.S. Code Appx. §§ 6b, 1738b

Sept. 2, 1965, P.L. 89-164, 79 Stat. 645, 15 U.S. Code § 278e nt.; 22 U.S. Code §§ 269a nt., 269b nt., 275 nt., 276 nt., 277 nt., 280b nt., 280i nt., 287 nt., 287e nt., 287r nt.; 28 U.S. Code § 604 nt.; 33 U.S. Code § 851; 50 U.S. Code Appx. §§ 6b, 738b

Nov. 8, 1966, P.L. 89-797, 80 Stat. 1479, 22 U.S. Code §§ 269a, 269b, 275 to 277, 280i, 287, 278e, 287r nts., 1461b, 1461c; 28 U.S. Code § 604 nt.; 36 U.S. Code §§ 121b, 122, 122a; 50 U.S. Code Appx. §§ 6b, 1738b

Nov. 8, 1967, P.L. 90-133, 81 Stat. 410, 22 U.S. Code §§ 269a nt. , 269b nt., 275 nt., 276 nt., 277 nt., 280b nt., 280i nt., 287 nt., 287e nt., 287r nt., 1461b, 1461c; 28 U.S. Code § 604 nt.; 36 U.S. Code §§ 121b, 122, 122a; 42 U.S. Code § 250a; 50 U.S. Code Appx. §§ 6b 1738b

Aug. 9, 1968, P.L. 90-470, 82 Stat. 667, 22 U.S. Code §§ 269a nt. , 269b nt., 275 nt., 276 nt., 277 nt., 280b nt., 280i nt., 287 nt., 287e nt., 287r nt., 1761b 1461c; 28 U.S. Code § 604 nt.; 36 U.S. Code §§ 121b to 122a; 42 U.S. Code § 250a; 50 U.S. Code Appx. §§ 6b, 1738b

Dec. 24, 1969, P.L. 91-153, 83 Stat. 403, 22 U.S. Code §§ 269a, 269b, 275 to 277, 280b, 280i, 287, 287e, 287r nts.; 1461b; 28 U.S. Code § 604 nt.; 36 U.S. Code §§ 121b, 122, 122a; 42 U.S. Code § 250a; 50 U.S. Code Appx. § 1738b

Continued

Oct. 21, 1970, P.L. 91-472, 84 Stat. 1040, 22 U.S. Code §§ 269a nt., 269b nt., 269f nt., 269g-1 nt., 269h nt., 272a nt., 273 to 277 nts., 22, §§ 269a, 269b, 275 to 277, 280b, 280i, 287, nt., 287e nt., 287r nt., 290b nt., 1461b nt., 1896b nt., 1928 nt., 1928b nt., 2673 nt.; 28 U.S. Code § 604 nt., 36 U.S. Code §§ 121b nt., 122 nt., 122a nt., 42 U.S. Code § 250a nt., 50 U.S. Code Appx. § 1738b

Aug. 10, 1971, P.L. 92-77, 85 Stat. 245, 22 U.S. Code §§ 269a nt. , 269b nt., 269f nt., 269g-1 nt. and others; 28 U.S. Code § 604 nt.; 36 U.S . Code § 121b to 122a; 42 U.S. Code § 250a; 50 U.S. Code Appx. § 1738b

Oct. 25, 1972, P.L. 92-544, 86 Stat. 1109, 22 U.S. Code §§ 269a, 269b, 269f, 269g-1, 269h, 272a, 273 to 277, 279a, 280b, and other sections; 28 U.S. Code § 604 and nt.; 36 U.S. Code §§ 121b, 122, 122a; 42 U.S. Code § 250a; 50 U.S. Code Appx. § 1738b

Departments of State, Justice, Commerce, and the Judiciary Appropriation Act, 1947

July 5, 1946, Ch. 541, 60 Stat. 541, 3 U.S. Code § 53 nt.; 15 U.S. Code §§ 319, 324; 22 USC §§ 269a nt., 269b nt., 274 nt., 275 nt., 276 nt., 277 nt., 278 nt., 901 nt., 909 nt., 1140, 2663 (See 28 U.S. Code §§ 533, 534, 536) 31 U.S. Code §§ 107a, 665 nt.; 33 U.S. Code §§ 851, 872; 41 U.S. Code § 6a nt.

July 9, 1947, Ch. 211, 61 Stat. 279, 3 U.S. Code § 201 nt.; 15 U.S. Code §§ 319, 324; 22 U.S. Code §§ 269a nt., 269b nt., 274 nt. , 275 nt., 276 nt., 277 nt., 278 nt., 295a nt., 2669 (See 28 U.S. Code §§ 533, 534, 536) 31 U.S. Code §§ 107a, 665 nt.; 33 U.S. Code §§ 851, 872; 41 U.S. Code § 6a nt.

June 3, 1948, Ch. 400, 62 Stat. 305, 15 U.S. Code §§ 319, 324; 22 U.S. Code §§ 269a, 269b, 275, 276, 277, 278, 280b, 280i, 287e, 287r, 295a nts., 2669 (See 28 U.S. Code §§ 533, 534, 536) 31 U.S. Code §§ 107a, 665 nt.; 33 U.S. Code §§ 851, 872; 41 U.S. Code § 6a nt.

July 20, 1949, Ch. 354, 63 Stat. 447, 3 U.S. Code § 201 nt.; 15 U.S. Code §§ 283, 284, 327 nt., 329; 22 U.S. Code §§ 269a nt., 269b nt., 275 nt., 276 nt., 277 nt., 278 nt., 280b nt., 280i nt., 287e nt., 287r nt., 295a nt., 297a, 2669 (See 28 U.S. Code §§ 533, 534, 536) 31 U.S. Code §§ 107a, 543, nt., 665 nt.; 33 U.S. Code §§ 851, 872; 41 U.S. Code § 6a nt.; 50 U.S. Code Appx. § 6b

Sept. 6, 1950, Ch. 896, 64 Stat. 609, 3 U.S. Code § 201 nt.; 15 U.S. Code §§ 283, 284, 327 nt., 329; 22 U.S. Code §§ 269a, 269b, 275, 276, 277, 278, 280b, 280i, 287e nt., 287f, 287r nt., 297a, 2669 (See 28 U.S. Code §§ 533, 534, 536) 31 U.S. Code §§ 107a, 543 nt., 665 nt.; 33 U.S. Code §§ 851, 872; 41 U.S. Code § 6a nt.; 46 U.S. Code § 1241 nt.; Title 50 U.S. Code Appx. § 6b

Oct. 22, 1951, Ch. 533, 65 Stat. 575, 3 U.S. Code § 201 nt.; 15 U.S. Code §§ 284, 327 nt., 329, 1153a; 22 U.S. Code §§ 262b, 269a nt., 269b nt., 275 nt., 276 nt., 277 nt., 278 nt., 280b nt., 280i nt., 287e nt. , 287f, 287r nt., 297a, 2669 (See 28 U.S. Code §§ 533, 534, 536) 31 U.S. Code §§ 107a, 543 nt., 665 nt.; 33 U.S. Code §§ 851, 872 ; 41 U.S. Code § 6a nt.; 50 U.S. Code Appx. § 6b

July 10, 1952, Ch. 651, 66 Stat. 549, 15 U.S. Code §§ 327 nt., 329 nt.; 22 U.S. Code §§ 262b, 269a, 269b, 269e, 275, 276, 277, 278, 280b, 280i, 287e, 287r, 297a, 1480, 2669 (See 28 U.S. Code §§ 533, 534, 536) 31 U.S. Code §§ 107a, 543 nt., 665 nt.; 33 U.S. Code §§ 851, 872; 41 U.S. Code § 6a nt.; 43 U.S. Code § 666; 50 U.S. Code Appx. § 6b

Aug. 5, 1953, Ch. 328, 67 Stat. 385, 15 U.S. Code §§ 327 nt., 329; 22 U.S. Code §§ 269a, 269b nts., 269e, 275, 276, 277, 278, 280b, 280I, 287, 287e, 287r nts., 1480, 2669; 28 U.S. Code §§ 508 nt., 533, 534, 536; 31 U.S. Code §§ 107a, 543 nt.; 33 U.S. Code §§ 851, 872; 41 U.S. Code § 6a nt.; 46 U.S. Code § 1242-1; 50 U.S. Code Appx. §§ 6b, 1738b

July 2, 1954, Ch. 456, 68 Stat. 413, 15 U.S. Code §§ 327 nt., 329; 22 U.S. Code §§ 269a nt., 269b nt., 269e, 276 nt., 277 nt., 280b nt., 280i nt., 287 nt., 287e nt., 287r nt., 1461a, 1461b, 1480, 2669; 23 U.S. Code § 57; 28 U.S. Code §§ 508 nt., 533, 534, 536; 31 U.S. Code §§ 107a, 543 nt.; 33 U.S. Code §§ 851, 872; 41 U.S. Code § 6a nt.; 46 U.S. Code § 1242-1; 50 U.S. Code Appx. §§ 6b, 1738b

Departments of State, Justice, Commerce, the Judiciary, and the Federal Loan Agency Appropriation Act, 1946

May 21, 1945, Ch. 129, 59 Stat. 169, 3 U.S. Code § 53; 15 U.S. Code §§ 319, 324; 22 U.S. Code §§ 41, 136, 269a nt., 269b nt., 274 nt., 275 nt., 276 nt., 277 nt., 278 nt., 2663 (See 28 U.S. Code §§ 533 , 534, 536) 33 U.S. Code §§ 851, 872; 41 U.S. Code § 6a nt.

Departments of Veterans Affairs and Housing and Urban Development, and Independent Agencies Appropriations Act, 1990

Nov. 9, 1989, P.L. 101-144, 103 Stat. 839

Departments of Veterans Affairs and Housing and Urban Development, and Independent Agencies Appropriations Act, 1991

Nov. 5, 1990, P.L. 101-507, 104 Stat. 1351

Departments of Veterans Affairs and Housing and Urban Development, and Independent Agencies Appropriations Act, 1992

Oct. 28, 1991, P.L. 102-139, 105 Stat. 736

Dec. 12, 1991, P.L. 102-229, 38 U.S. Code § 1722A

Departments of Veterans Affairs and Housing and Urban Development, and Independent Agencies Appropriations Act, 1993

Oct. 6, 1992, P.L. 102-389, 106 Stat. 1571

Oct. 27, 1993, P.L. 103-120, 107 Stat. 1152

Departments of Veterans Affairs and Housing and Urban Development, and Independent Agencies Appropriations Act, 1994

Oct. 27, 1993, P.L. 103-124, 107 Stat. 1275

Departments of Veterans Affairs and Housing and Urban Development, and Independent Agencies Appropriations Act, 1995

Sept. 28, 1994, P.L. 103-327, 108 Stat. 2298

Departments of Veterans Affairs and Housing and Urban Development, and Independent Agencies Appropriations Act, 1996

April 26, 1996, P.L. 104-134, 110 Stat. 1321-257

Sept. 26, 1996, P.L. 104-204, 42 U.S. Code §§ 1437f nt., 1437l nt. .

Departments of Veterans Affairs and Housing and Urban Development, and Independent Agencies Appropriations Act, 1997

June 12, 1997, P.L. 105-18, 42 U.S. Code 1437f nt.

Oct. 27, 1997, P.L. 105-65, 12 U.S. Code § 1715z-11a; 42 U.S. Code § 1437f nt.

Departments of Veterans Affairs and Housing and Urban Development, and Independent Agencies Appropriations Act, 1999

Oct. 21, 1998, P.L. 105-276, Titles I, II, III, IV, VI, 112 Stat. 2461, 2469, 2492, 2507, 2670

Oct. 21, 1998, P.L. 105-277, 12 U.S. Code § 1454

Dependency and Indemnity Compensation Reform Act of 1992

Oct. 29, 1992, P.L. 102-568, 38 U.S. Code § 101 nt.

Dependency Plan (Chemical)

Mont. Code Ann., 53-24-204

Dependency-Producing Drugs Act

Conn. Gen. Stat. Ann., § 21a-240 et seq.

Dependent and Neglected Children Act

Colo. Rev. Stat. 1963, 22-1-1

Fla. Stat. Ann., 39.40 et seq.

Ill. Rev. Stat. 1991, Ch. 40, § 2501 et seq.

Ind. Code Ann., 31-6-1-1 et seq.

Iowa Code Ann., 232.61 et seq.

Kan. Stat. Ann., 38-824, 38-825

Ky. Rev. Stat. 1971, 199.011 et seq., 208.010 et seq.

N.M. Stat. Ann., 32-1-1 et seq.

Ohio Rev. Code 1953, 5107.02 et seq.

S.C. Code Ann. 1976, § 20-7-110 et seq.

Tex. Family Code, § 15.01 et seq.

Utah Code Ann. 1953, 62A-11-301 et seq.

W. Va. Code 1966, § 48A-1-1 et seq.

Wyo. Stat. Ann., § 14-3-201 et seq.

Dependent Children Aid Act

Ariz. Rev. Stat. Ann., § 46-291 et seq.

Colo. Rev. Stat. 1963, 22-11-1 et seq.

Ga. Code Ann., 49-4-100 et seq.

Ill. Rev. Stat. 1965, Ch. 37, § 601 et seq.

Mass. Gen. Laws Ann., 118:1 et seq.

Wash. Rev. Code Ann., 74.12.010 et seq.

Dependent Children Scholarship Act

Mass. Gen. Laws Ann., 118:1 et seq.

Mich. Comp. Laws Ann., 400.56

Minn. Stat. Ann., 256.72 et seq.

N.C. Gen. Stat. 1943, § 108A-27 et seq.

Nev. Rev. Stat. 1979 Reprint, 425.260 et seq.

Tenn. Code Ann., 49-4-704, 3201 et seq.

Dependent Mothers Act

Utah Code Ann. 1953, 17-13-1 et seq.

Dependent, Neglected and Delinquent Children Act.

Ill. Rev. Stat. 1991, Ch. 23, § 801-1 et seq.

Dependent Pension Act

See Invalid Pension Acts

Dependents Act (Transfer of)

Conn. Gen. Stat. Ann., § 17-293

Dependents Assistance Act of 1950

Sept. 8, 1950, Ch. 922, 64 Stat. 794, 50 U.S. Code Appx. §§ 2201 to 2216

March 23, 1953, Ch. 8, 67 Stat. 6, 50 U.S. Code Appx. § 2216

June 30, 1955, Ch. 250, 69 Stat. 224, 50 U.S. Code Appx. § 2216

July 24, 1956, Ch. 697, 70 Stat. 634, 50 U.S. Code Appx. § 2213a

March 23, 1959, P.L. 86-4, 73 Stat. 13, 50 U.S. Code Appx. § 2216

July 10, 1962, P.L. 87-531, 76 Stat. 152, 50 U.S. Code Appx. §§ 2203, 2207, 2208

Sept. 7, 1962, P.L. 87-649, 76 Stat. 496, 50 U.S. Code Appx. §§ 2201 to 2204

March 28, 1963, P.L. 88-2, 77 Stat. 4, 50 U.S. Code Appx. § 2216

June 30, 1967, P.L. 90-40, 81 Stat. 105, 50 U.S. Code Appx. § 2216

Dec. 16, 1967, P.L. 90-207, 81 Stat. 654, 50 U.S. Code Appx. § 2203

Sept. 28, 1971, P.L. 92-129, 85 Stat. 355, 50 U.S. Code Appx. §§ 2203, 2204, 2207, 2216

Dependents' Medical Care Act

June 7, 1956, Ch. 374, 70 Stat. 250, 24 U.S. Code § 35 nt.; 42 U.S. Code § 253 nt. (See 10 U.S. Code §§ 1071 to 1085)

Dependents' Support Act

Conn. Gen. Stat. Ann., § 46b-215

Iowa Code Ann., 252A.1 et seq.

Mo. Rev. Stat., 454.010 et seq.

Ohio Rev. Code 1953, 3115.01 et seq.

Deployment Act (Technology)

Conn. Public Acts 1993, No. 382, §§ 30 to 38

Deportation Act

May 10, 1920, Ch. 174, 41 Stat. 593

Deportation Act (Welfare Cases)

Ind. Code Ann., 16-14-10-6

Deposit Account Act (Consumer)

Ill. Comp. Stat. 1992, Ch. 205, § 605/0.01 et seq.

Deposit Account Contract Act
Conn. Gen. Stat. Ann., § 36-27a et seq.

Deposit Accounts Act (Adverse Claims to)
Ill. Comp. Stat. 1992, Ch. 205, § 700/1 et seq.

Deposit Act (Fee)
Ill. Rev. Stat. 1991, Ch. 85, § 720 et seq.

Deposit Act (Insurance Companies)
N.M. Stat. Ann. 1953, 58-5-4

Deposit Act (Linked)
Iowa Code Ann., 12.31 et seq.

Deposit Act (Student Educational Enhancement)
Me. Rev. Stat. Ann. 1964, Title 20-A, § 12601 et seq.

Deposit By Trustee Act
Mich. Comp. Laws Ann., 487.702

Deposit in Two Names Act
Mo. Rev. Stat., 362.470

Deposit Insurance Act
N.M. Stat. Ann., 58-2-1 et seq.

Deposit Insurance Corporation Act
Pa. Purdon's Stat., Title 7, § 6451 et seq.

Deposit Insurance Extension Act
Aug. 23, 1935, Ch. 614, 49 Stat. 684 (See 12 U.S. Code §§ 1811 to 1831)

Deposit Insurance Flexibility Act
Oct. 15, 1982, P.L. 97-320, 12 U.S. Code § 1811 nt.

Deposit Insurance Funds Act of 1996
Sept. 30, 1996, P.L. 104-208, 12 U.S. Code § 1811 nt.

Deposit Law (County Funds)
Cal. Government Code § 53630 et seq.

Deposit Law (State Funds)
Cal. Government Code § 16300 et seq.
Ill. Rev. Stat. 1991, Ch. 130, § 19m et seq.

Deposit of Public Funds Act
Ill. Rev. Stat. 1991, Ch. 102, § 33.9 et seq.

Deposit of State Moneys Act
Ill. Rev. Stat. 1991, Ch. 130, § 19m et seq.

Deposit Program (Agricultural Linked)
Okla. Stat. Ann., Title 2, § 1761 et seq.

Deposit Program Act (Linked)
Ark. Acts 1991, Nos. 671, 682

Deposit Protection Act (Governmental Units)
N.J. Stat. Ann., 17:9-41 et seq.

Deposit Protection Act (Public)
Colo. Rev. Stat., 11-10.5-101 et seq.

Deposit Security Act (Consumer)
Ill. Comp. Stat. 1992, Ch. 815, § 165/1 et seq.

Deposit Security Act (Public Funds)
Neb. Laws 1996, L.B. 1274

Deposition and Discovery Act
Ala. Code 1958, Title 7, § 457 et seq.
Cal. Code of Civil Procedure § 2016 et seq.
Ga. Code Ann., 9-11-26 et seq.
La. Rev. Stat. Ann., 13:3821, 13:3822

Deposition Recording Act
Me. Rev. Stat. Ann. 1964, Title 16, § 551 et seq.

Depositions Act (Civil)
Conn. Gen. Stat. Ann., § 52-148a et seq.
Iowa Code 1977, 781.10 et seq.
Kan. Stat. Ann., 60-226 et seq.
Mich. Comp. Laws 1948, 617.6 et seq.
N.C. Gen. Stat. 1943, § 8-74 et seq.
N.H. Rev. Stat. 1955, 517:1 et seq.
Ohio Civ. Rule 30 et seq.
Ohio Rev. Code 1953, 2319.05 et seq.
R.I. Gen. Laws 1956, 9-18-1 et seq.
Tenn. Code Ann., 24-9-101 et seq.
Tex. Rev. Civ. Stat., Art. 3740 et seq.
Tex. Rules of Civil Procedure as Am. 1984, Rule 187 et seq.
Continued

Vt. Acts 1957, No. 217
Wash. Rev. Code Ann., 10.16.160, Rules of Court, Rule 26 et seq.
W. Va. Code 1966, § 57-4-1 et seq.

Depositions Act (Criminal)
Iowa Code Ann., 624.1, 813.2
Tex. Code of Criminal Procedure, Art. 39.01 et seq.

Depositions Act (Foreign)
See Foreign Depositions Act

Depositories Act (Public Funds)
Mich. Comp. Laws Ann., 129.11 et seq.

Depositors Economic Protection Act
R.I. Gen. Laws 1956, 42-116-1 et seq.

Depositors' Final Settlement Fund Act
Neb. Laws 1930, Ex. Sess., Ch. 6

Depositors' Guaranty Fund Act
Kan. Laws 1909, Ch. 61
N.D. Laws 1917, Ch. 126
N.D. Laws 1923, Ch. 200
Neb. Laws 1909, Ch. 10, §§ 44-47
Okla. Stat. 1961, Title 6, § 404 et seq.
S.D. Laws 1915, Ch. 102, Art. 3
Tex. Rev. Civ. Stat. 1925, Arts. 437, 440-449

Depository Act
Alaska Stat. 1962, §§ 37.10.050, 37.10.060
Ariz. Rev. Stat. Ann., § 35-321 et seq.
Ark. Code Ann. 1987, 13-801 et seq.
D.C. Code Ann., § 47-341 et seq.
Ida. Code 1947, 57-101 et seq.
Ind. Code Ann., 5-13-5-1 et seq.
Kan. Stat. Ann., 9-1401 et seq.
Neb. Rev. Stat. 1943, 30-103.01 et seq.
Ohio Rev. Code 1953, 135.01 et seq.
Tenn. Code Ann., 9-5-101 et seq., 45-2-806
Wis. Stat. Ann., 34.01 et seq.
Wyo. Stat. Ann., § 9-4-801 et seq.

Depository Act (Banks)
Okla. Stat. 1961, Title 12A, § 4-105 et seq.

Depository Act (Counties)
Ark. Code. Ann. 19-8-105 et seq.
Mo. Rev. Stat., 110.130 et seq.
Ohio Rev. Code 1953, 323.61 et seq.
Okla. Stat. 1971, Title 19, § 112 et seq.
Ore. Rev. Stat. 1953, 295.410 et seq.
Tex. Local Government Code, § 116.021
Wash. Rev. Code Ann., 36.48.010 et seq.

Depository Act (Fiduciaries)
Fla. Stat. 1965, 69.031

Depository Act (Municipal)
Mont. Code Ann., 7-6-201 et seq
Tex. Local Government Code, § 105.002 et seq.
Wash. Rev. Code Ann., 35.38.010 et seq.

Depository Act (Public Funds)
Utah Code Ann. 1953, 51-7-1 et seq.

Depository Act (Schools)
Minn. Stat. 1953, 124.05
Ohio Rev. Code 1953, 3313.51

Depository Act (State)
Mo. Rev. Stat., 110.070 et seq.
Nev. Rev. Stat. 1979 Reprint, 356.005 et seq.
Ore. Rev. Stat. 1953, 295.005 et seq.
Tex. Rev. Civ. Stat., Art. 2525 et seq.
Wash. Rev. Code Ann., 43.85.070 et seq.

Depository and Farm Warehouse Act
Ind. Code 1971, 26-3-6-1 et seq.

Depository Corporation Sale, Merger, and Conversion Law
Cal. Financial Code § 4800 et seq.

Depository Institution-GSE Affiliation Act of 1998
Oct. 21, 1998, P.L. 105-277, Division H, 112 Stat. 2681, 12 U.S. Code § 1811 nt.

Depository Institution Guaranty Corporation Act
Neb. Rev. Stat. 1943, 21-17, 127 et seq.

Depository Institution Management Interlocks Act

Oct. 15, 1982, P.L. 97-320, 12 U.S. Code §§ 3204, 3208

Nov. 30, 1983, P.L. 98-181, 12 U.S. Code § 3202

Nov. 10, 1988, P.L. 100-650, 12 U.S. Code §§ 3201, 3204, 3205

Aug. 9, 1989, P.L. 101-73, 12 U.S. Code §§ 3204, 3206

Sept. 13, 1994, P.L. 103-325, 12 U.S. Code §§ 3205, 3207

Sept. 30, 1996, P.L. 104-208, 12 U.S. Code §§ 3203, 3205, 3207

Depository Institutions Act (Interstate)

N.M. Stat. Ann., 58-26-1 et seq.

Depository Institutions Deregulation Act of 1980

March 31, 1980, P.L. 96-221, 12 U.S. Code §§ 3501 et seq., 3501 nt.

Oct. 15, 1982, P.L. 97-320, 12 U.S. Code § 3503

Jan. 12, 1983, P.L. 97-457, 12 U.S. Code § 3503

Aug. 9, 1989, P.L. 101-73; 12 U.S. Code § 3507

Depository Institutions Deregulation and Monetary Control Act of 1980

March 31, 1980, P.L. 96-221, 12 U.S. Code §§ 226 nt., 248, 461

Oct. 15, 1982, P.L. 97-320, 12 U.S. Code §§ 191 nt., 216a et seq.

Depository Institutions Disaster Relief Act of 1992

Oct. 23, 1992, P.L. 102-485, 12 U.S. Code § 1811 nt.

Depository Institutions Disaster Relief Act of 1993

Aug. 12, 1993, P.L. 103-76, 12 U.S. Code §§ 1811 nt., 1828 nt., 1831o nt., 4008 nt.

Depository Institutions Disaster Relief Act of 1997

June 12, 1997, P.L. 105-18, Title V, 12 U.S. Code § 1811 nt.

Depository Library Act of 1962

Aug. 9, 1962, P.L. 87-579, 76 Stat. 352, 44 U.S. Code §§ 81a to 81c, 82, 83, 84, 84a 85, 86, 87, 92

Deposits and Shares Insurance Fund for Savings and Credit Unions Act

P.R. Laws Ann. 1954, Title 7 § 1151 et seq.

Deposits Regulation Act

June 23, 1836, Ch. 115, 5 Stat. 52

Depredation Act (Indians)

March 3, 1891, Ch. 538, 26 Stat. 851

Depredation Act (Timber)

March 3, 1859, Ch. 78, 11 Stat. 408

Depressant and Stimulant Drug Control Act

N.Y. Penal Law 1965, (Consol. Law Ch. 40) § 220.00 et seq., 220.31 et seq.

N.Y. Public Health Law (Consol. Laws Ch. 45) § 3370 et seq.

Depressed Areas Redevelopment Act

Haw. Rev. Stat. Ann., § 208-1 et seq.

Depressed Rural Centers Aid Act

N.J. Stat. Ann. 52:27D-162 et seq.

Deputy Chief of Staff Act

July 14, 1939, Ch. 269, 53 Stat. 1002 (See 10 U.S. Code § 3031)

Deputy Sheriff Act (Junior)

Ill. Rev. Stat. 1991, Ch. 125, § 90 et seq.

Deputy Sheriffs' Civil Service Act

W. Va. Code 1966, § 7-14-1 et seq.

Deputy Sheriffs' Education and Training Act

Pa. Purdon's Stat., Title 71, § 2101 et seq.

Deputy Sheriffs' Tort Liability Act

W. Va. Code 1966, § 7-14A-1 et seq.

Derailing Switch Law

Cal. Public Utilities Code § 7601 et seq.

Deregulation Law
N.Y. Laws 1984, Ch. 360

Derelict and Abandoned Vessels Act
Alaska Stat. 1962, § 30.30.010 et seq.

Derenzinski-Geerlings Job Development Authority Act
Mich. Comp. Laws Ann., 125.1701 et seq.

DeRidder Louisiana Redevelopment Agency Act
La. Acts 1968, No. 439

Derivative Action Act
Del. Code of 1974, Title 8, § 327

Dernham-Doyle Act (Hunting Licenses and Permits)
Mich. Comp. Laws Ann., 314.7 et seq.

Derogatory Statements about Banks Act
Ill. Rev. Stat. 1991, Ch. 17, § 900 et seq.

Des Act
Ill. Rev. Stat. 1991, Ch. 111 1/2, § 4501 et seq.

DES Education and Research Amendments of 1992
Oct. 13, 1992, P.L. 102-409, 42 U.S. Code § 201 nt.

DES Information Law
Pa. Purdon's Stat., Title 35, § 6211 et seq.

Des Plaines and Illinois Rivers Act
Ill. Rev. Stat. 1989, Ch. 19, § 40.9 et seq.

DES Public Information and Education Act
Pa. Purdon's Stat., Title 35, § 6211 et seq.

Descent and Distribution Act
Ala. Code 1975, § 43-8-40 et seq.
Alaska Stat. 1962, § 13.11.005 et seq.
Ariz. Rev. Stat. Ann., § 14-2101 et seq.
Ark. Code Ann. 1987, 28-10-101 et seq.
Colo. Rev. Stat., 15-11-101 et seq.
D.C. Code Ann., § 19-301 et seq.
Del. Code of 1974, Title 12, § 501 et seq.

Fla. Stat. Ann., 732.101 et seq.
Ga. Code Ann., 53-4-1 et seq.
Haw. Rev. Stat. Ann., § 532-1 et seq.
Ill. Rev. Stat. 1991, Ch. 110 1/2, § 2-1 et seq.
Ind. Code Ann., 29-1-2-1 et seq.
Iowa Code Ann., 633.210 et seq.
Kan. Stat. Ann., 59-501 et seq.
Ky. Rev. Stat. 1971, 391.010 et seq.
La. Civil Code, Art. 886 et seq.
Mass. Gen. Laws Ann., 190:1 et seq.
Md. Ann. Code 1974, Art. ET, § 3-101 et seq.
Me. Rev. Stat. Ann. 1964, Title 18-A, § 1002-102 et seq.
Mich. Comp. Laws Ann., 702.80 et seq.
Minn. Stat. Ann., 525.13 et seq.
Miss. Code Ann. 1972, § 91-1-1 et seq.
Mo. Rev. Stat., 474.010 et seq.
Mont. Code Ann., 72-2-101 et seq., 72-3-901 et seq.
N.C. Gen. Stat. 1943, § 29-1 et seq.
N.D. Cent. Code, 30.1-04-01 et seq.
Neb. Rev. Stat. 1943, 30-103.01 et seq.
N.H. Rev. Stat. 1955, 561:1 et seq.
N.J. Stat. Ann. 3B:5-1 et seq.
N.M. Stat. Ann. 1953, 29-1-1 et seq.
N.Y. Estates, Powers and Trusts Law (Consol. Laws Ch. 17B) § 4-1.1 et seq.
Ohio Rev. Code 1953, 2105.01 et seq.
Okla. Stat. Ann., Title 84, § 211 et seq.
Ore. Rev. Stat. 1953, 111.005 et seq.
Pa. Cons. Stat., Title 20, § 2101 et seq.
R.I. Gen. Laws 1956, 33-1-1 et seq.
S.C. Code Ann. 1976, Superseded Vols., § 21-3-10 et seq.
Tenn. Code Ann., 31-1-101 et seq.
Tex. Probate Code, § 37 et seq.
Va. Code 1950, § 64.1-1 et seq.
Vt. Stat. Ann., Title 14, § 551
Wash. Rev. Code Ann., 11.04.015 et seq.
Wis. Stat. Ann., 852.01 et seq.
W. Va. Code 1966, § 42-1-1 et seq.
Wyo. Stat. Ann., § 2-4-101 et seq.

Descent of Homestead Act
Fla. Stat. Ann., 732.401

Desecration of the Flag Act
Ill. Rev. Stat. 1991, Ch. 1 § 3350 et seq.

Desegregation Capital Improvement Grant Act
Minn. Stat. Ann., 124C.55 et seq.

Desert Land Acts
March 3, 1877, Ch. 107, 19 Stat. 377, 43 U.S. Code §§ 321 to 323
March 26, 1908, Ch. 103, 35 Stat. 48

Desert Land Board Act
Ore. Rev. Stat. 1953, 555.010 et seq.

Desert Native Plants Act
Cal. Food and Agricultural Code 1967, §§ 70500 et seq., § 80001
Cal. Food and Agricultural Code 1967, § 80001 et seq.

Desert Water Agency Act
Cal. Water Code, Appendix, § 100-1 et seq.

Desert Water Agency Law
Cal. Statutes 1961, Ch. 1069

Desertion Act
Md. Ann. Code 1974, Art. FL, § 10-201 et seq.

Desertion Act (Children)
Iowa Code 1983, 726.3

Desertion Act (Navy and Marine Corps)
Aug. 14, 1888, Ch. 890, 25 Stat. 442

Desertion Act (Wife and Children)
Iowa Code 1983, 726.3
Md. Ann. Code 1974, Art. FL, § 10-201 et seq.
Mont. Rev. Code 1947, 94-301 et seq.
R.I. Gen. Laws 1956, 11-2-1 et seq.

Desertion and Nonsupport Act
See also Uniform Desertion and Nonsupport Act
Colo. Rev. Stat., 14-6-101 et seq.
Ida. Code 1947, 18-401 et seq.
Iowa Code Ann., 252A.1 et seq., 726.5
Kan. Stat. Ann., 21-3605
La. Rev. Stat. Ann., 14:74, 14:75

Md. Ann. Code 1974, Art. FL, § 10-201 et seq.
Mich. Comp. Laws Ann., 750.161 et seq.
Mo. Rev. Stat., 568.040
N.C. Gen. Stat. 1943, § 14-322 et seq.
Pa. Cons. Stat., Title 42, § 6741 et seq.
Tenn. Code Ann., 39-15-101, 39-15-104
Tex. Penal Code, § 25.05

Desertion and Nonsupport Act (Criminal)
Pa. Cons. Stat., Title 18, § 4322

Design Services Act (Building)
N.J. Stat. Ann., 45:4B-1 et seq.

Designer Selection Board Act
Minn. Stat. Ann., 16B.33

Desmond Act (Sacramento State College)
Cal. Statutes 1949, Ch. 406, p. 748

Desmond Act (Sanity Proceedings)
N.Y. Criminal Procedure Law (Consol. Laws, Ch. 11A) § 730.10 et seq.

Desmond Act (Wage Kick-Back)
N.Y. Labor Law (Consol. Laws, Ch. 31) § 198b

Desmond Plumage Act (Fishing Lures)
N.Y. Environmental Conservation Law (Consol. Laws, Ch. 43B) § 11-729 et seq.

Desmond-Todd Act (Marriage Licenses)
N.Y. Domestic Relations Law (Consol. Laws, Ch. 14) § 13 et seq.

DeSoto Expedition Trail Commission Act of 1990
Nov. 16, 1990, P.L. 101-607, 16 U.S. Code § 1244 nt.

DeSoto National Memorial Act
March 11, 1948, Ch. 109, 62 Stat. 78, 16 U.S. Code §§ 450dd, 450dd -1
Sept. 8, 1960, P.L. 86-728, 74 Stat. 856, 16 U.S. Code § 450dd

DeSoto National Trail Study Act of 1987
Dec. 11, 1987, P.L. 100-187, 16 U.S. Code § 1241 nt., 1244

DeSoto Trail Commission Act
Miss. Code Ann. 1972, § 39-5-101 et seq.

Destroyed Court Records Law
Cal. Code of Civil Procedure § 1953 et seq.

Destroyed Land Records Relief Law
Cal. Code of Civil Procedure § 751.01 et seq.

Destroyed or Lost Wills Act
N.Y. Surrogate Procedure Act (Consol. Laws, Ch. 54A) § 1407

Destroyed Public Records Act
Ill. Rev. Stat. 1991, Ch. 116, § 4.9 et seq.

Destroyed Tax Records Law
Cal. Revenue and Taxation Code § 4838

Destruction Limitation Act (Chemical Weapons)
Ala. Code 1975, § 33-1-5

Destruction of Indebtedness Certificates Act
Ill. Rev. Stat. 1991, Ch. 130, § 19c9 et seq.

Destruction of Landmarks Act
Mo. Rev. Stat. 1969, 560.530

Destruction of Public Records Law
N.J. Stat. Ann. 47:3-15 et seq.

Destruction of Records Act (Interstate Commerce)
Feb. 25, 1909, Ch. 193, 35 Stat. 649, 49 U.S. Code § 20

Destruction of War Material Act
April 20, 1918, Ch. 59, 40 Stat. 533, 50 U.S. Code §§ 101 to 103

Detainer Act (Real Estate)
Colo. Rev. Stat., 13-40-101 et seq.

Detainer and Forcible Entry Act
Ohio Rev. Code 1953, 1923.01 et seq.
Wash. Rev. Code Ann., 59.12.010 et seq.

Detainers Act
Pa. Cons. Stat., Title 42, § 9101 et seq.

Detainers Agreement Act
See Interstate Agreement on Detainers Act

Detainers Disposition Act (Mandatory)
See Uniform Mandatory Disposition of Detainers Act

Detection Examiners Act (Deception)
Utah Code Ann. 1953, 53-5-301 et seq.

Detection of Deception Examiners Act
Ill. Rev. Stat. 1991, Ch. 111, § 2400 et seq.

Detective Act
Cal. Business and Professions Code § 7500 et seq.
Ind. Code Ann., 25-30-1-1 et seq.
Mich. Comp. Laws Ann., 338.821 et seq.
Pa. Purdon's Stat., Title 22, § 11 et seq.
P.R. Laws Ann. 1954, Title 25, § 285 et seq.

Detective Agencies and Detectives Law
Wash. Rev. Code Ann., 18.165.010 et seq.

Detectives and Detective Agencies Act
Ill. Rev. Stat. 1991, Ch. 111, § 2651 et seq.
N.D. Cent. Code, 43-30-01 et seq.

Detectives and Private Investigators Act
Cal. Business and Professions Code § 7512 et seq.

Detention Act
R.I. Gen. Laws 1956, 12-7-1 et seq.

Detention Act (Arrest)
Mo. Rev. Stat. 1978, 544.170

Detention Act (Suspects)
Del. Code of 1974, Title 11, § 1902

Detention and Commitment Act (Insane)
Ohio Rev. Code 1953, 5122.11 et seq.

Detention Facilities Cooperative Development and Operations Act (Juvenile)
Ark. Code Ann. 1987, 12-41-801 et seq.

Detention Home and Shelter Care Act (County)
Ill. Rev. Stat. 1991, Ch. 23, § 2681 et seq.

Detention Homes Act
Ga. Code Ann., 42-4-30 et seq.

Detention of Insane Act
D.C. Code 1973, § 21-521 et seq.

Determinate Sentence Law
Cal. Statutes 1976, Ch. 1139
La. Code of Crim. Proc. 1966, Art. 879

Determination of Death Act
See also Uniform Determination of Death Act
See also Uniform Determination of Death Law
Cal. Health and Safety Code § 7180 et seq.
Mich. Comp. Laws Ann., 333.1031 et seq.
Mont. Code Ann., 50-22-101
Tenn. Code Ann., 68-3-501
Utah Code Ann. 1953, 26-34-1 et seq.

Determination of Heirship Act
Ohio Rev. Code 1953, 2123.01 et seq.

Detinue Act
Va. Code 1950, § 8.01-121

Detoxification Act
N.M. Stat. Ann., 43-2-1 et seq.

Detoxification Act (Transportation of Intoxicated Person)
N.M. Stat. Ann., 43-2-18 et seq.

Detoxification and Treatment Act (Community Alcoholism)
N.M. Stat. Ann., 43-3-1 et seq.

Detroit Recorder's Court Act
Mich. Comp. Laws Ann., 726.1 et seq.

Deukmejian-Campbell-Moretti Drug Abuse Treatment Act
Cal. Statutes 1972, Ch. 1255, p. 2464

Deukmejian-Gonsalves-Petris Senior Citizens Property Tax Assistance Law
Cal. Revenue and Taxation Code § 20501 et seq.

Deukmejian-Moretti Act (Crime Council)
Cal. Penal Code § 13800 et seq.

Devaney Law (Anti-Red)
N.Y. Civil Service Law 1958 (Consol. Laws Ch. 7) § 105

Development Account Act (Individual)
Kan. Stat. Ann., 79-32,117h

Development Act (Agricultural)
Iowa Code Ann., 175.1 et seq.

Development Act (Aquaculture)
Ill. Comp. Stat. 1992, Ch. 20, § 215/1 et seq.

Development Act (Biotechnology)
Ill. Comp. Stat. 1992, Ch. 20, § 230/1 et seq.

Development Act (Export Trade)
Miss. Code Ann., § 57-57-1 et seq.

Development Act (Human Resource)
Fla. Laws 1994, Ch. 319, §§ 4 to 6

Development Act (Local)
Okla. Stat. Ann., Title 62, § 850 et seq.

Development Act (Trauma Systems)
Neb. Rev. Stat. 1943, 71-5166 et seq.

Development Act (Water Resources)
Miss. Code Ann., § 51-3-1 et seq.

Development Agency Act (Bi-State)
Ill. Comp. Stat. 1992, Ch. 45, § 105/0.01 et seq.

Development Agreement Act (Local Government)
S.C. Code Ann. 1976, § 6-31-10 et seq.

Development and Airport Protection Policy Act
Cal. Public Utilities Code § 21605

Development and Assistance Act (Airport)
Fla. Stat. Ann., 332.003 et seq.

Development and Assistance Act (Micro-Business)
N.J. Stat. Ann., 34:1B-70 et seq.

Development and Education Act (Community)
Ga. Code Ann., 50-8-170 et seq.

Development and Growth Act
Ga. Code Ann., 12-5-41, 20-2-553, 32-5-24, 32-10-4, 45-12-170

Development and Industrial Facilities Act
Utah Code Ann. 1953, 11-17-1 et seq.

Development and Industrial Loan Act (New Bedford)
Mass. Acts 1949, Ch. 736

Development and Manufacturing Assistance Act (Economic)
Conn. Gen. Stat. Ann., § 32-220 et seq.

Development and Marketing Act (Salmon)
Cal. Food and Agricultural Code 1967, § 76501 et seq.

Development and Opportunity Act
Ill. Rev. Stat. 1991, Ch. 127, § 3401 et seq.

Development and Planning Act
Vt. Stat. Ann., Title 24, § 4301 et seq.

Development and Radiation Control Act (Atomic Energy, Nuclear Energy)
Kan. Stat. Ann., 48-1601 et seq.

Development and Reclamation Grants Program Act
Mont. Code Ann., 90-2-1101 et seq.

Development and Recreation Act
Okla. Stat. Ann., Title 74, § 1901 et seq.

Development and Renewal Authority Act (Savannah)
Ga. Laws 1992, p. 6764

Development and Research Act
Miss. Code Ann. 1972, § 57-13-1 et seq.

Development and Research Act (Trucking Industry)
Okla. Stat. Ann., Title 47, § 1161 et seq.

Development and Research Corporation Law (Urban)
N.Y. Unconsolidated Law, § 6301 et seq.

Development and Research Incentives Act
Okla. Stat. Ann., Title 68, § 54001 et seq.

Development and Training Act (Manpower)
Miss. Code Ann., § 37-31-101 et seq.

Development Assistance Act (Coal Technology)
Ill. Comp. Stat. 1992, Ch. 30, § 730/1 et seq.

Development Assistance Act (Community)
Neb. Rev. Stat. 1943, 13-201 et seq.

Development Assistance Corporation Act (Community Economic)
Mass. Gen. Laws Ann., 4014:1 et seq.

Development Assistance Law (Port)
Minn. Stat. Ann., 457A.01 et seq.

Development Authorities Act (Industrial)
Ga. Code Ann., 36-62-1 et seq.

Development Authorities Law (Resource Recovery)
Ga. Code Ann., 36-63-1 et seq.

Development Authority Act
Ga. Code Ann., 50-10-1 et seq.
Ill. Rev. Stat. 1987, Ch. 85, § 6151 et seq.
Pa. Purdon's Stat., Title 73, § 301 et seq.

Development Authority Act (Agriculture and Business)
S.D. Laws 1986, Ch. 16, § 2 et seq.

Development Authority Act (Brantley County)
Ga. Laws 1968, p. 3488

Development Authority Act (Clay County)
Fla. Special Laws 1957, Ch. 57-1226

Development Authority Act (Elbert County)
Ga. Laws 1991, p. 3587

Development Authority Act (Emanuel County)
Ga. Laws 1965, p. 2770

Development Authority Act (Fort Lauderdale)
Fla. Special Laws 1969, Ch. 69-1056

Development Authority Act (Greater Arizona)
Ariz. Rev. Stat. Ann., §§ 41-1554 et seq., 42-1341, 43-206

Development Authority Act (Green County)
Ga. Laws 1963, p. 3005

Development Authority Act (Henry County)
Ga. Laws 1967, p. 2291

Development Authority Act (Historic Rome)
N.Y. Public Authorities Law (Consol. Laws Ch. 43A) § 1900 et seq.

Development Authority Act (International)
Ariz. Rev. Stat. Ann., § 41-1553 et seq.

Development Authority Act (Monroe County)
Fla. Special Laws 1963, Ch. 63-1658

Development Authority Act (Municipal Utilities)
Wis. Laws 1937, Ch. 334

Development Authority Act (Pueblo Depot)
Colo. Rev. Stat., 29-23-101 et seq.

Development Authority Act (Putman County)
Fla. Special Laws 1961, Ch. 61-2727

Development Authority Act (Schley County)
Ga. Laws 1967, p. 2795

Development Authority Act (Small Business)
Neb. Laws 1984, L.B. 1117

Development Authority Act (South Cobb)
Ga. Laws 1982, p. 3772

Development Authority Act (Upper Savannah River)
Ga. Code Ann., 12-3-400 et seq.

Development Authority Act (Washington County)
Fla. Special Laws 1961, Ch. 61-2988

Development Authority and Canal Place Preservation Act
Md. Ann. Code 1974, Art. FI, § 13-1001 et seq.

Development Authority Law (Airport)
Ga. Code Ann., 6-4-1 et seq.

Development Authority Law (Tri-County River Valley)
Ill. Rev. Stat. 1991, Ch. 85, § 7501 et seq.

Development Authority of the North Country Act
N.Y. Public Authorities Law (Consol. Law Ch. 43A) § 2701 et seq.

Development Bank Act
Miss. Code Ann., § 31-25-1 et seq.
P.R. Laws Ann. 1954, Title 7, § 611 et seq.

Development Board Act (Capital)
Ill. Comp. Stat. 1992, Ch. 20, § 3105/1 et seq.

Development Bond Act (Capital)
Ill. Comp. Stat. 1992, Ch. 30, § 420/1 et seq.

Development Bond Act (Coal and Energy)
Ill. Comp. Stat. 1992, Ch. 20, § 1110/1 et seq.

Development Capital Corporation Act
Okla. Stat. Ann., Title 74, § 5086.1 et seq.

Development Centers for the Handicapped Act
Cal. Education Code 1976, § 56800 et seq.

Development Commission Act (Baker County)
Fla. Special Laws 1957, Ch. 57-1129

Development Compact Act (Bi-State)
Ill. Comp. Stat. 1992, Ch. 45, § 100/0.01 et seq.

Development Control Act
Me. Rev. Stat. Ann. 1964, Title 38, § 481 et seq.

Development Corporation Act
Mont. Code Ann., 32-4-101 et seq.
Tex. Rev. Civ. Stat. 1974, Art. 5190.6

Development Corporation Act (Aerospace)
Alaska Laws 1991, Ch. 88

Development Corporation Act (Alviso Nuevo)
Cal. Statutes 1972, Ch. 1096, p. 2057

Development Corporation Act (Business and Industrial)
Conn. Public Acts 1993, No. 382, §§ 56 to 66
La. Rev. Stat. Ann., 51:2386 et seq.

Development Corporation Act (Empowerment Zone)
Mich. Comp. Laws Ann., 125.2561 et seq.

Development Corporations Act (Industrial and Economic)
Okla. Stat. Ann., Title 74, § 1351 et seq.

Development Council Act
R.I. Gen. Laws 1956, 42-63-1 et seq.

Development Council Act (Hardwoods)
Pa. Purdon's Stat., Title 73, § 399.21 et seq.

Development Credit Corporations Act
Mich. Comp. Laws 1948, 487.831 et seq.
Mont. Code Ann., 32-4-101 et seq.
N.M. Stat. Ann., 53-7-1 et seq.
Tenn. Code Ann., 48-3-101 et seq.

Development Credit Corporations Act (Business)
N.M. Stat. Ann., 53-7-18 et seq.

Development Department Act
Del. Code of 1974, Title 29, § 8631 et seq.

Development Department Act (Economic)
N.M. Stat. Ann., 9-15-1 et seq.

Development Disabilities Assistance and Bill of Rights Act
Oct. 31, 1963, P.L. 88-164, 42 U.S. Code 6000 et seq.
Oct. 4, 1975, P.L. 94-103, 42 U.S. Code §§ 295-295e, 2661, 2678 to 2678d, 6001 et seq.
April 22, 1976, P.L. 94-278, 42 U.S. Code § 6001 nt.
Nov. 6, 1978, P.L. 95-602, 42 U.S. Code §§ 6000 et seq., 6031 to 6033, 6061 et seq., 6081
Feb. 21, 1984, P.L. 98-221, 42 U.S. Code §§ 6001, 6012, 6033, 6061, 6081
Aug. 15, 1985, P.L. 99-91, 42 U.S. Code § 6022
Oct. 29, 1987, P.L. 100-146, 42 U.S. Code §§ 6000, 6000 nt., 6001, 6006, 6021 et seq., 6042, 6061 et seq., 6081 to 6083
Oct. 7, 1991, P.L. 102-119, 42 U.S. Code §§ 6022, 6024
April 6, 1994, P.L. 103-230, 42 U.S. Code § 6000 et seq.
Aug. 6, 1996, P.L. 104-183, 42 U.S. Code §§ 6030, 6043, 6066, 6083
April 30, 1997, P.L. 105-12, 42 U.S. Code §§ 6022, 6042, 6062, 6082

Development District Act
Tenn. Code Ann., 13-14-101 et seq.

Development District Act (Local)
Pa. Purdon's Stat., Title 73, § 801 et seq.

Development District Act (Transportation)
Mo. Rev. Stat. 1978, 238.200

Development District and Tourism Improvement Act
N.J. Stat. Ann., 40:54D-1 et seq.

Development District Correction Act
Tenn. Code Ann., 41-1-701 et seq.

Development Fees Act
N.M. Stat. Ann., 5-8-1 et seq.

Development Finance Act
Ky. Rev. Stat. 1971, 154.001 et seq.
La. Rev. Stat. Ann., 51:2553 et seq.

Development Finance Act (Business)
Iowa Code Ann., 15E.131 et seq.

Development Finance Act (Small Enterprise)
Miss. Code Ann., § 57-71-1 et seq.

Development Finance Authority Act
Ark. Code Ann. 1987, 15-5-101 et seq.
Ill. Rev. Stat. 1991, Ch. 48, § 850.01 et seq.
Kan. Stat. Ann., 74-8901
Okla. Stat. Ann., Title 74, § 5062.1 et seq.

Development Finance Authority Act (Community)
N.H. Rev. Stat. 1955, 162-L:1 et seq.

Development Finance Authority Small Business Act
Ark. Code 1987, 15-5-701 et seq.

Development Finance Corporation Act
Ark. Code Ann. 1987, 15-4-901 et seq.
Fla. Stat. Ann., 288.9602 et seq.
Mo. Rev. Stat., 371.010 et seq.

Development Finance Fund Act
Neb. Rev. Stat. 1943, 76-1801 et seq.

Development Financing Act (Industrial)
Fla. Stat. Ann., 159.44 et seq.

Development Financing Act (Local)
Mich. Comp. Laws Ann., 125.2151 et seq.

Development Financing Law (Economic)
Pa. Purdon's Stat., Title 73, § 371 et seq.

Development Fund Act (Human Services)
Pa. Purdon's Stat., Title 62, § 3101 et seq.

Development Impact Fee Act
Ga. Code Ann., 36-71-1 et seq.

Ida. Code 1947, 67-8201 et seq.

Development Incentive Act
N.M. Stat. Ann., 3-64-1 et seq.

Development Innovation Act (Economic)
Okla. Stat. Ann., Title 74, § 5009.1 et seq.

Development of Economic Fund for Jobs Act
S.C. Code Ann. 1976, § 41-43-10 et seq.

Development of Employment, Health Industrial Resources Act
Tex. Government Code § 481.001 et seq.

Development Permitting Act (Geothermal and Cable System)
Haw. Rev. Stat. Ann., § 196D-1 et seq.
Haw. Rev. Stat. Ann., § 196D-1 et seq.

Development Planning Act (Transit Village)
Cal. Government Code § 65460 et seq.

Development, Planning and Research Act
S.C. Code Ann. 1976, § 13-3-10 et seq.

Development Program Act (Rural Economic)
Pa. Purdon's Stat., Title 73, § 392.101 et seq.

Development Projects Act (Industrial)
S.C. Code Ann. 1976, § 4-29-10 et seq.

Development, Research, and Planning Act
Minn. Stat. 1988, 126.81
S.C. Code Ann. 1976, § 13-3-10 et seq.

Development Revenue Bond Act (County and Municipality)
Colo. Rev. Stat., 29-3-101 et seq.

Development Review Enabling Act (Land and Subdivision)
R.I. Gen. Laws 1956, 45-23-25 et seq.

Development Rights Bank Act (State Transfer of)
N.J. Stat. Ann., 4:1C-49 et seq.

Development Services Act
Utah Code Ann. 1953, 63-33-1 et seq.

Development Services Act (Invention)
Okla. Stat. Ann., Title 15, § 680 et seq.

Development Services Act (Inventory)
Iowa Code Ann., 523G.1 et seq.

Development Training Act
N.M. Stat. Ann., 21-19-1 et seq.

Development Water Bonding Law
Mont. Code Ann., 90-2-101 et seq.

Development Zone Act (Job)
Vt. Stat. Ann., Title 10, § 691 et seq.

Developmental Disabilities Act
Md. Ann. Code 1974, Art. HG, § 7-1001 et seq.
N.M. Stat. Ann., 28-16A-1 et seq.
R.I. Gen. Laws 1956, 40.1-22-1 et seq.
Tenn. Public Acts 1992, Ch. 535

Developmental Disabilities Act (Community-Supported Living Arrangement Services)
Colo. Rev. Stat., 26-4-651 et seq.

Developmental Disabilities Act (Group Homes for Persons with)
Okla. Stat. Ann., Title 63, § 1-818.1 et seq.

Developmental Disabilities and Juvenile Research Institutes Act (University of Illinois)
Ill. Rev. Stat. 1991, Ch. 144, § 2650 et seq.

Developmental Disabilities and Mental Health Act
Ill. Rev. Stat. 1991, Ch. 91 1/2, § 1-100 et seq.
N.M. Stat. Ann., 43-1-2 et seq.

Developmental Disabilities and Mental Health Confidentiality Act
Ill. Rev. Stat. 1991, Ch. 91 1/2, § 801 et seq.

Developmental Disabilities and Mental Health Department Act
Ill. Rev. Stat. 1991, Ch. 91 1/2, § 100-0.1 et seq.

Developmental Disabilities and Mental Retardation Act
La. Rev. Stat. Ann., 28:380 et seq.
Md. Ann. Code 1974, Art. HG, § 7-101 et seq.
N.Y. Mental Hygiene Law 1977 (Consol. Laws Ch. 27) § 1301 et seq

Developmental Disabilities and Mentally Ill Persons Home and Community-Based Services Act
Colo. Rev. Stat., 26-4.5-201 et seq.

Developmental Disabilities Assistance and Bill of Rights Act Amendments of 1987
Oct. 29, 1987, P.L. 100-146, 42 U.S. Code §§ 6000, 6000 nt., 6001 , 6006, 6021 et seq., 6042, 6061 et seq., 6081 to 6083
Oct. 30, 1990, P.L. 101-476, 20 U.S. Code § 1400 nt.

Developmental Disabilities Assistance and Bill of Rights Act Amendments of 1994
April 6, 1994, P.L. 103-230, 42 U.S. Code §§ 6000 nt.

Developmental Disabilities Assistance and Bill of Rights Act Amendments of 1996
Aug. 6, 1996, P.L. 104-183, 42 U.S. Code § 6000 nt.

Developmental Disabilities Assistance and Bill of Rights Act of 1990
Oct. 31, 1990, P.L. 101-496, 42 U.S. Code §§ 6000 nt., 6000 et seq. generally

Developmental Disabilities Community Services Act
N.M. Stat. Ann., 28-16-1 et seq.

Developmental Disabilities Division Act
N.J. Stat. Ann. 55:13B-3 et seq.

Developmental Disabilities In-Home Financial Assistance Act
Ida. Code 1947, 39-5101 et seq.

Developmental Disabilities Law (Planning Council)
Ill. Rev. Stat. 1991, Ch. 91 1/2, § 1951 et seq.

Developmental Disabilities Prevention and Community Services Act
Fla. Stat. Ann., 393.061 et seq.

Developmental Disabilities Reform Act
Kan. Stat. Ann., 39-1801

Developmental Disabilities Services Act
Cal. Health and Safety Code § 38000 et seq.
Neb. Rev. Stat. 1943, 83-1201 et seq.
S.D. Codified Laws 1967, 27B-1-2, 27B-1-3 et seq.

Developmental Disabilities Services and Facilities Act
Ida. Code 1947, 39-4601 et seq.
Mont. Code Ann., 53-20-201 et seq.

Developmental Disabilities Services and Facilities Construction Act
Oct. 31, 1963, P.L. 88-164, 77 Stat. 282, 42 U.S. Code §§ 295 to 295e, 2661 to 2665, 2671 to 2677
Dec. 4, 1967, P.L. 90-170, 81 Stat. 527, 42 U.S. Code §§ 266, 2665, 2671, 2672, 2674, 2677 to 2678d
Oct. 30, 1970, P.L. 91-517, 84 Stat. 1316, 42 U.S. Code §§ 2661 to 2666, 2670 to 2677c
Nov. 18, 1971, P.L. 92-157, 85 Stat. 464, 42 U.S. Code § 2676
June 18, 1973, P.L. 93-45, 87 Stat. 95, 42 U.S. Code §§ 2661a, 2671, 2677
Nov. 6, 1978, P.L. 95-602, 42 U.S. Code §§ 6000 et seq., 6031 to 6033, 6061 et seq., 6081

Developmental Disabilities Services and Facilities Construction Amendments of 1970
Oct. 30, 1970, P.L. 91-517, 84 Stat. 1316, 42 U.S. Code §§ 2661 to 2666, 2670 to 2677c, 2691, 2693 to 2696

Developmental Disabilities Services Law
Cal. Welfare and Institutions Code § 4500 et seq.

Developmental Disabilities Waiting List Reduction and Human Services Facilities Construction Bond Act
N.J. Laws 1994, Ch. 108

Developmental Disability and Mental Disability Services Act
Ill. Rev. Stat. 1991, Ch. 91 1/2, § 1801-1 et seq.

Developmental Disability Prevention Act
Ill. Rev. Stat. 1991, Ch. 111 1/2, § 2100 et seq.

Developmental Research School Act
Okla. Stat. Ann., Title 70, § 1210.571 et seq.

Developmental Research School Act (Sidney Martin)
Fla. Stat. Ann., 228.053

Developmentally Disabled Abuse Prevention Act
Mont. Code Ann., 53-5-501 et seq.

Developmentally Disabled Act
Colo. Rev. Stat., 27-10.5-101 et seq.

Developmentally Disabled and Mentally Ill Long-term Nursing Home Care Alternatives Act
Colo. Rev. Stat., 26-4.5-201 et seq.

Developmentally Disabled and Mentally Retarded Persons' Act (County Care)
Ill. Rev. Stat. 1991, Ch. 91 1/2, § 200 et seq.

Developmentally Disabled Assistance and Bill of Rights Act
See Developmental Disabilities Assistance and Bill Of Rights Act

Developmentally Disabled or Physically Handicapped Persons Act (Group Homes)
Okla. Stat. Ann., Title 63, § 1-818.1 et seq.

Developmentally Disabled Persons (Bill of Rights)
Fla. Stat. Ann., 393.13

Developmentally Disabled Persons Community Homes Location Act
Ark. Code Ann. 1987, 20-48-601

Developmentally Disabled Persons in Community Residences Rights Act
R.I. Gen. Laws 1956, 40.1-22.1-1 et seq.

Developmentally Disabled Persons' Protection and Advocacy Act
Ill. Rev. Stat. 1991, Ch. 91 1/2, §§ 1150, 1151

Developmentally Disabled Persons' Rights Act
R.I. Gen. Laws 1956, 40.1-26-1 et seq.

Developmentally Disabled Rights Act
N.J. Stat. Ann. 30:6D-1 et seq.

Developmentally or Physically Disabled Persons Community Residential Living Act
Okla. Stat. Ann., Title 60, § 860 et seq.

Device, Cosmetic and Drug Act
N.M. Stat. Ann., 26-1-1 et seq.

Device, Cosmetic, Food and Drug Salvage Act
Tex. Health and Safety Code, § 432.001 et seq.
Tex. Rev. Civ. Stat. 1974, Art. 4476-5e

Device, Drug, and Cosmetic Act
Ill. Rev. Stat. 1965, Ch. 111 1/2, § 401 et seq.
Iowa Code Ann., 203B.1 et seq.
Pa. Purdon's Stat., Title 35, § 780-101 et seq.

Devine Act (Antisubversion)
Ohio Rev. Code 1953, 2921.21 et seq.

Devine-Corrigan Act (Employee's FitAct (Shoalwater Bay Indian Tribe)
Ohio Rev. Code 1953, 124.35

Devisee or Legatee Act (Premature Death)
Ohio Rev. Code 1953, 2107.52

Dewey Law (Joinder of Offenses)
N.Y. Criminal Procedure Law (Consol. Laws, Ch. 54A) § 1407

Dewey Law (Lesser Included Offense)
N.Y. Criminal Procedure Law (Consol. Laws Ch. 11A) § 220.20

Di Constanzo Act (Commercial Rent Control)
N.Y. Laws 1945, Ch. 314

Diagnostic and Animal Health Act
Pa. Purdon's Stat., Title 3, § 430.1 et seq.

Diagnostic Center Act
Mich. Comp. Laws Ann., 330.21

Diagnostic X-Ray Facility Act
Okla. Stat. Ann., Title 63, §§ 1-1501.1 to 1-1505

Dick Acts (Militia)
Jan. 21, 1903, Ch. 196, 32 Stat. 775
May 27, 1908, Ch. 204, 35 Stat. 399

Dickey Act (Water Quality)
Cal. Water Code § 13000 et seq.

Dickey-Freiberg Act (Narcotics)
N.Y. Laws 1927, Ch. 672

Dickey-Wallace Burial Plot Act
Ill. Rev. Stat. 1991, Ch. 21, §§ 65.9, 66

Dickey Water Pollution Act
Cal. Water Code § 13000 et seq.

Dickson County Highway Act
Tenn. Private Acts 1919, Ch. 161

Dickson County Road Law
Tenn. Code Ann., 63-25-101 et seq.
Tenn. Private Acts 1985, Ch. 53

Dickson Mounds State Memorial Act
Ill. Rev. Stat. 1989, Ch. 105, §§ 4681.9, 468m

Dickstein Alien Officials Act
See Immigration Act of 1924

Die and Tool Lien Act
Ill. Rev. Stat. 1991, Ch. 82, § 350 et seq.

Diehl-Porter Act (Port Districts Report)
Mich. Comp. Laws 1948, 120.24b

Dies and Molds Ownership Transfer Act
Ill. Comp. Stat. 1992, Ch. 765, § 1053/1 et
seq.

Diesel Fuel and Motor Fuel Use Tax Act
Fla. Stat. Ann., 207.001 et seq.

Diesel Fuel Tax Act
Ala. Code 1975, § 40-17-1 et seq.
Mich. Comp. Laws Ann., 207.121 et seq.
Neb. Rev. Stat. 1943, 66-650 et seq.
Tex. Tax. Code, § 153.201 et seq.
Vt. Stat. Ann., Title 23, § 3001 et seq.

Dietary Manager Practice Act
R.I. Gen. Laws 1956, 5-64.1-1 et seq.

Dietary Supplement Act of 1992
Oct. 29, 1992, P.L. 102-571, 21 U.S. Code
§§ 301 nt., 343 nt., 343-1 nt.

**Dietary Supplement Health and Education
Act of 1994**
Oct. 25, 1994, P.L. 103-417, 21 U.S. Code
§ 301 nt.

Dietetics and Nutrition Practice Act
Ala. Code 1975, § 34-34A-1 et seq.
Fla. Stat. Ann., 468.501 et seq.
La. Rev. Stat. Ann., 37:3081 et seq.
N.C. Gen. Stat. 1943, § 90-350 et seq.
N.M. Stat. Ann., 61-7A-1 et seq.

Dietetics and Nutrition Services Practice Act
Ill. Rev. Stat. 1991, Ch. 111, § 8401-5 et seq.

Dietetics Practice Act
Ark. Code Ann. 1987, 17-100-101 et seq.
Ga. Code Ann., 43-11A-1 et seq.
Miss. Code Ann., § 73-10-1 et seq.

**Diethylstilbestrol Public Information and
Education Act**
Pa. Purdon's Stat., Title 35, § 6211 et seq.

Dieticians Licensing Act
Ga. Code Ann., 43-11A-1 et seq.

Kan. Stat. Ann., 65-5901 et seq.
Md. Ann. Code 1974, Art. HO, 5-101 et seq.
Okla. Stat. Ann., Title 59, § 1721 et seq.
Utah Code Ann. 1953, 58-49-1 et seq.

Dietitian—Nutritionist Act
R.I. Gen. Laws 1956, 5-64-1 et seq.

Dietitian—Nutritionist Act (Licensed)
R.I. Gen. Laws 1956, 5-64-1 et seq.

**Diggs-Hailwood-Dunckel-Burns Act (Civil
Rights)**
Mich. Comp. Laws Ann., 750.146 et seq.

Dighton Water District Loan Act
Mass. Acts 1967, Ch. 500

**Digital High School Education Technology
Grant Act**
Cal. Education Code 1976, § 52250 et seq.

Digital Millenium Copyright Act
Oct. 28, 1998, P.L. 105-304, 112 Stat. 2860,
17 U.S. Code § 101 nt.

**Digital Performance Right in Sound
Recordings Act of 1995**
Nov. 1, 1995, P.L. 104-39, 17 U.S. Code
§ 101 nt.
Nov. 13, 1997, P.L. 105-80, 17 U.S. Code
§ 115

Digital Signature Act
Miss. Code Ann., § 26-63-1 et seq.
N.H. Rev. Stat. 1955, 294-D:1 et seq.

**Digital Signature Act (Financial Institu-
tions)**
Ill. Comp. Stat. 1992, Ch. 205, § 705/1 et seq.

Dignified Death Act
Mich. Comp. Laws Ann., 333.5651 et seq.

Diking Code
Ore. Rev. Stat. 1953, 549.510 et seq.,
551.010 et seq.

Diking District Levy Act
Wash. Rev. Code Ann., 85.18.005 et seq.

Diking District Reorganization Act
Wash. Rev. Code Ann., 85.20.010 et seq.

Diking Districts Act
Ore. Rev. Stat. 1953, 551.010 et seq.
Wash. Rev. Code Ann., 85.05.010 et seq.

Diking Improvement District Act
Wash. Rev. Code Ann., 85.08.010 et seq.

Diking Improvement District Maintenance Act
Wash. Rev. Code Ann., 85.16.010 et seq.

Diking Intercounty District Act
Wash. Rev. Code Ann., 85.24.010 et seq.

Dill-Crosser Railway Labor Act
See Railway Labor Act

Dill-Rayburn Communications Act
See Communications Acts

Dillon Act (Alcoholic Liquors)
Ark. Code Ann. 1987, 3-7-102 et seq.

Dillon County Tax Discount Act
S.C. Code Ann. 1962, § 65-1989

Dills-Bronzan Winegrowers Joint Commission Act
Cal. Food and Agricultural Code 1967, § 74001 et seq.

Dills-Nejedly-Z'berg Solid Waste Management and Resource Recovery Act
Cal. Government Code § 66700 et seq.

Dills-Regan Act (Narcotics)
Cal. Health and Safety Code § 11500 et seq.

Dilution Act (Trademarks)
Ill. Rev. Stat. 1991, Ch. 140, § 22
Mass. Gen. Laws Ann., 110B:12

Dilworth Act (Communist Teachers)
Cal. Education Code 1976, § 7000 et seq.

Dingell-Johnson Enabling Act (Fish Restoration)
Mich. Comp. Laws Ann., 300.151

Dingell-Johnson Fish Restoration Act
See Fish Restoration and Management Projects Act

Dingley Act (Shipping)
June 26, 1884, Ch. 121, 23 Stat. 53, 46 U.S. Code §§ 47, 101, 121, 189, 221, 541, 572, 573, 599, 658, 670, 679, 682 to 685, 703

Dingley Act (Tariff)
July 24, 1897, Ch. 11, 30 Stat. 151

Diploma Privilege Act (Attorneys)
Ida. Code 1947, 3-101

Diplomatic Relations Act
Sept. 30, 1978, P.L. 95-393, 22 U.S. Code §§ 254a to 254e; 28 U.S . Code §§ 1251, 1351, 1364
Aug. 24, 1982, P.L. 97-241, 22 U.S. Code §§ 254a to 254c
Nov. 22, 1983, P.L. 98-164, 22 U.S. Code § 254e

Diplomatic Security Act
Aug. 27, 1986, P.L. 99-399, 5 U.S. Code § 5315; 22 U.S. Code §§ 2652, 4801 nt., 4801 to 4806, 4821 to 4823, 4831 to 4835, 4851 to 4862
Dec. 22, 1987, P.L. 100-204, 22 U.S. Code §§ 4831, 4834, 4851, 4861
Feb. 16, 1990, P.L. 101-246, 22 U.S. Code §§ 4801, 4802, 4852

Dire Emergency Supplemental Appropriations Act, 1988
Aug. 14, 1988, P.L. 100-393, 102 Stat. 975

Dire Emergency Supplemental Appropriations Act, 1992, for Disaster Assistance to Meet Urgent Needs Because of Calamities Such as those which Occurred in Los Angeles and Chicago
June 22, 1992, P.L. 102-302, 106 Stat. 254

Dire Emergency Supplemental Appropriations Act, 1992, Including Dire Emergency Supplemental Appropriations and Transfers for Relief from the Effects of Natural Disasters, for Other Urgent Needs and for the Dire Emergency Supplemental Appropriations and Transfers for Relief From the Effects of Natural Disasters, for Other Urgent Needs, and for Incremental Cost of "Operation Desert Shield—Desert Storm" Act of 1992

Dec. 12, 1991, P.L. 102-229, 105 Stat. 1701

Sept. 23, 1992, P.L. 102-368, 7 U.S. Code § 1421 nt.

Dire Emergency Supplemental Appropriations and Transfers, Urgent Supplemental, and Correcting Enrollment Errors Act of 1989

Nov. 9, 1989, P.L. 101-144, 103 Stat. 853

Nov. 23, 1993, P.L. 103-149, 22 U.S. Code § 5117

Dire Emergency Supplemental Appropriations for Consequences of Operation Dessert Shield—Desert Storm, Food Stamps, Unemployment. Compensation Administration, Veterans Compensation and Pensions, and Other Urgent Needs Act of 1991

April 10, 1991, P.L. 102-27, 105 Stat. 160

Dire Emergency Supplemental Appropriations From Contributions of Foreign Governments and—or Interests for Humanitarian Assistance to Refugees and Displaced Persons in and around Iraq as a Result of the Recent Invasion of Kuwait and for Peacekeeping Activities and Other Urgent Needs Act of 1991

June 13, 1991, P.L. 102-55, 105 Stat. 290

Direct Action Act (Insurance)

Ark. Code Ann. 1987, 23-79-210

Iowa Code 1983, 516.1 et seq.

La. Rev. Stat. Ann., 22:655

N.Y. Insurance Law (Consol. Laws. Ch. 28) § 3420

P.R. Laws Ann. 1954, Title 26, §§ 2001, 2003

Wis. Stat. 1973. 260.1

Direct Action Act (Liability Insurance)

R.I. Gen. Laws 1956, 27-7-1

Direct Appeal Act

Wyo. Session Laws 1917, Ch. 32

Direct Deposit Act (State Employee and Retiree)

Fla. Stat. Ann., 17.075, 17.076, 216.331

Direct Deposit Act (State Employees)

Okla. Stat. Ann., Title 74, § 292.10 et seq.

Direct Deposit of Public Funds Act

Fla. Stat. Ann., 215.85

Direct-Entry Midwifery Licensing Act

Mont. Code Ann., 37-27-101 et seq.

Mont. Laws 1991, Ch. 550, §§ 1 to 4, 6 to 23

Direct Inheritance Tax Act

Ohio Laws Vol. 97, p. 398

Pa. Purdon's Stat., Title 72, § 2301 et seq.

Direct Liability Act (Insurance)

Wis. Stat. 1975, 204.30, Subsec. 4

Direct Lien Act

Cal. Code of Civil Procedure § 1185.1, Subd. a

Direct Loans to Industry Act

June 19, 1934, Ch. 653, 48 Stat. 1105

Direct Pay Permit Implementation Act

Ill. Comp. Stat. 1992, Ch. 35, §§ 160/1, 160/5

Direct Payment in Lieu of Tax Act

D.C. Code Ann., §§ 47-1002, 47-1007, 47-1010

Direct Primary Elections Act

Ariz. Rev. Stat. Ann., § 16-201 et seq.

Cal. Elections Code 1976, § 2550 et seq.

Mich. Comp. Laws Ann., 168.531 et seq.

Mont. Code Ann., 13-10-301 et seq.

N.Y. Laws 1913, Ex. Sess., Ch. 820

Ore. Rev. Stat. 1953, 249.011 et seq.

Pa. 1906 Ex. Pamph. Laws 36, No. 10

Pa. 1913 Pamph. Laws 719, No. 400

Continued

Utah Code Ann. 1953, 20-3-1 et seq.

Direct Primary Law
Cal. Elections Code 1976, § 6400 et seq.

Direct Property Tax Act
Ind. Code Ann., 6-1.1-1-1 et seq.

Direct Service Act
N.M. Stat. Ann., 38-1-16

Direct Service Act (Nonresidents)
Wash. Rev. Code Ann., 4.28.185

Direct Service Contracts Reform Act
Cal. Health and Safety Code § 38000 et seq.

Direct Tax Act (Insurrectionary Districts)
June 7, 1862, Ch. 98, 12 Stat. 422

Direct Vehicle Loan Company Act
La. Rev. Stat. Ann., 6:970 et seq.

Directed Verdict Act
La. Code of Crim. Proc. 1966, Art. 778
Mich. Comp. Laws 1948, 691.691 et seq.

Directive Act (Living Will)
Ky. Acts 1994, Ch. 235, §§ 1 to 12

Director of Budget Act
Wash. Rev. Code Ann., 43.41.030 et seq.

Directors Act (Corporations)
Mich. Comp. Laws Ann., 450.1501
Okla. Stat. Ann., Title 18, § 1.34 et seq.

Directory of New Hires Act (State)
N.M. Stat. Ann., 50-13-1 to 50-13-4

Dirksen Memorial Highway Act
Ill. Rev. Stat. 1991, Ch. 121, §§ 388, 389

Dirt Roads Act
Conn. Gen. Stat. Ann., § 13-56 et seq.

Disabilities Accessibility Implementation Act (Americans with)
Ariz. Rev. Stat. Ann., § 41-1492 et seq.
Fla. Stat. Ann., 553.501 et seq.

Disabilities Act (Community Trust)
N.J. State. Ann., 3B:11-19 et seq.

Disabilities Act (Division of Developmental)
N.J. Stat. Ann., 30:60-23 et seq.

Disabilities Act (Home and Community-based Services)
Colo. Rev. Stat., 26-4-621 et seq.

Disabilities Act (Infants and Toddlers)
S.C. Code Ann. 1976, § 44-7-2510 et seq.

Disabilities Act (Personal Assistance Program)
Ga. Code Ann., 30-6-1 et seq.

Disabilities Act (Screening for Learning—Language)
Wash. Rev. Code Ann., 28A.155.110 et seq.

Disabilities Services Act (Developmental)
Neb. Rev. Stat. 1943, 83-1201 et seq.

Disability Act
N.Y. Workmen's Compensation Law (Consol. Laws Ch. 67)

Disability Act (Public Employee)
Ill. Rev. Stat. 1991, Ch. 70, §§ 90.9, 91

Disability Agent Act
Fla. Stat. Ann., 626.826 et seq.

Disability and Life Insurance Guaranty Association Act
Ala. Code 1975, § 27-44-1 et seq.
Ark. Code Ann. 1987, 23-96-101 et seq.
Haw. Rev. Stat. Ann., § 431:16-101 et seq.
Utah Code Ann. 1953, 31A-28-101 et seq.
Wash. Rev. Code Ann., 48.32A.010 et seq.

Disability and Life Insurance Policy Language Simplification Act
Ark. Code Ann. 1987, 23-80-201 et seq.
Mont. Code Ann., 33-15-321 et seq.

Disability Assistance Act
Wash. Rev. Code 1979, 74.10.010 et seq.

Disability Benefit Act
N.J. Stat. Ann., 43:21-25 et seq.
N.Y. Worker's Compensation Law (Consol. Laws Ch. 67) § 200 et seq.
P.R. Laws Ann. 1954, Title 11, § 201 et seq.

Disability Benefits Act (Unemployment Compensation)
Cal. Unemployment Insurance Code § 2601 et seq.

Disability Benefits Act (Workmen's Compensation)
Kan. Stat. Ann., 44-510 et seq.
N.Y. Workmen's Compensation Law (Consol. Laws, Ch. 67) § 200 et seq.
P.R. Laws Ann. 1954, Title 11, § 201 et seq.

Disability Compensation Act
Mich. Comp. Laws Ann., 418.101 et seq.
Utah Code Ann. 1953, 35-2-1 et seq.

Disability Compensation Act (Policemen and Firemen)
Pa. Purdon's Stat., Title 53, §§ 637 et seq.

Disability Fund Investment Law (Central Office Building)
Cal. Unemployment Insurance Code § 3125 et seq.

Disability Income Plan of North Carolina
N.C. Gen. Stat. 1943, § 135-100

Disability Insurance Act (Temporary)
R.I. Gen. Laws 1956, 28-39-1 et seq.
Wash. Rev. Code Ann., 48.20.002 et seq.

Disability Insurance Hospital Benefit Act (Jesse Mayo)
Cal. Unemployment Insurance code § 2800 et seq.

Disability Insurance Policy Provisions Act
Mich. Comp. Laws Ann., 500.3400 et seq.

Disability Pension Act
See Invalid Pension Acts

Disability Policy Provision Act
Wyo. Stat. Ann., § 26-18-101 et seq.

Disability Policy Provision Law
Wyo. Stat. Ann., § 26-18-101 et seq.

Disability Program Act (State Employees)
Okla. Stat. Ann., Title 74, § 1331 et seq.

Disability Resource Directory Act (Central)
Mich. Comp. Laws Ann., 395.321 et seq.

Disabled Adult Act (Abused, Neglected or Exploited)
N.C. Gen. Stat. 1943, §§ 108A-99 to 108A-111

Disabled Adult Protection Act
N.C. Gen. Stat. 1943, § 108A-99 et seq.

Disabled Adults Community Care Act
Fla. Stat. Ann., 410.601 et seq.

Disabled Adults, Elder Persons, and Vulnerable Adults Protection Act
Ga. Code Ann., 30-5-1 et seq.

Disabled Adults Guardianship Act
Ill. Rev. Stat. 1991, Ch. 110 1/2, § 11a-1 et seq.

Disabled Adults Personal Attendant Care Program Act
Ga. Code Ann., 30-6-1 et seq.

Disabled Adults Protective Services Act
Mont. Code Ann., 52-3-201 et seq.

Disabled American Veterans Acts
June 17, 1932, Ch. 268, 47 Stat. 320, 36 U.S. Code §§ 90a to 90k
July 15, 1942, Ch. 505, 56 Stat. 659, 36 U.S. Code §§ 90a, 90c, 90e, 90f, 90h to 90j
Dec. 18, 1967, P.L. 90-208, 81 Stat. 655, 36 U.S. Code § 90i

Disabled and Aged Hearing Aid Assistance Act
N.J. Stat. Ann., 30:40-36 et seq.

Disabled and Senior Citizens Protected Tenancy Act
N.J. Stat. Ann. 2A:18-61.22 et seq.

Disabled Children and Chronically Ill Services Act
Tex. Health and Safety Code, § 35.001 et seq.

Disabled Militarymen Money Act
Ill. Rev. Stat. 1989, Ch. 130, § 17.9 et seq.

Disabled Parking Standards and Enforcement Act
N.M. Stat. Ann., 66-7-352.1 et seq.

Disabled Persons Act
See also Uniform Duties to Disabled Persons Actons Act
Ohio Rev. Code 1953, 2305.41 et seq.

Disabled Persons Aid Act
Colo. Rev. Stat. 26-3-101
Ga. Code Ann., 49-4-80 et seq.

Disabled Persons and Family Support Act
Neb. Rev. Stat. 1943, 68-1501 et seq.

Disabled Persons Community Residential Living Act
Okla. Stat. Ann., Title 60, § 860 et seq.

Disabled Persons Investigating Offical Act
P.R. Laws Ann. 1954, Title 3, § 532 et seq.

Disabled Persons License Plates Act
Ga. Code Ann., 40-2-72

Disabled Persons Limited Guardianship Proceedings Act
Tenn. Code Ann., 34-12-101 et seq.

Disabled Persons Location Act (Community Homes)
Tex. Human Resources Code, § 123.001 et seq.

Disabled Persons Rehabilitation Act
Ill. Rev. Stat. 1991, Ch. 23, § 3429 et seq.

Disabled Persons Special Identification-Registration-Parking Regulations Act
Ark. Stat. 1947, 75-266.19 et seq.

Disabled Persons Tax Relief Act
Ill. Rev. Stat. 1991, Ch. 67 1/2, § 401 et seq.

Disabled Physician Law
Ida. Code 1947, 54-1831 et seq.
Miss. Code Ann. 1972, § 73-25-51 et seq.

Disabled Resident and Senior Citizen Transportation Assistance Act
N.J. Stat. Ann., 27:25-25 et seq.

Disabled Soldiers Home Land Cession Act
Ill. Rev. Stat. 1989, Ch. 1, §§ 3700, 3701

Disabled Students Act (Higher Education Services for Visually and Auditorily Impaired)
N.J. Stat. Ann., 18A:72H-1 et seq.

Disabled Veterans' and Servicemen's Automobile Assistance Act of 1970
Jan. 11, 1971, P.L. 91-666, 84 Stat. 1998, 38 U.S. Code §§ 1901 to 1903

Disabled Veterans Employment Act
Okla. Stat. Ann., Title 72, § 401 et seq.

Disabled Veterans Exemption Act
D.C. Code Ann., § 40-104, Subd.f

Disabled Veterans' Housing Act
Ill. Rev. Stat. 1991, Ch. 126 1/2, § 57.90 et seq.

Disabled Voters Act
Minn. Stat. 1957, 207.01 et seq.
Neb. Rev. Stat. 1943, 32-801 et seq.

Disadvantaged Minority Health Improvement Act of 1990
Nov. 6, 1990, P.L. 101-527, 42 U.S. Code §§ 201 nt., 300u-6 nt.

Disagreement Act (Jury)
Mich. Comp. Laws Ann., 730.520

Disarmament Conference Resolution
July 12, 1921, Ch. 44, 42 Stat. 141

Disaster Act
Cal. Government Code § 8550 et seq.

Cal. Military and Veterans Code § 1500 et seq.
La. Rev. Stat. Ann., 29:701 et seq.
Mass. Gen. Laws Ann., 190A:1 et seq.
Mont. Code Ann., 10-3-101 et seq.
N.D. Cent. Code, 37-17.1-01 et seq.
Tex. Government Code, § 418.001 et seq.
Tex. Rev. Civ. Stat., Art. 6889-7

Disaster Agency and Emergency Services Act
Ill. Rev. Stat. 1987, Ch. 127, § 1101 et seq.

Disaster and Civil Defense Act
Neb. Rev. Stat. 1943, 81-829.36 et seq.
Wyo. Stat. Ann., § 19-5-101 et seq.

Disaster and Civil Defense Compact (Interstate)
Me. Rev. Stat. Ann. 1964, Title 37-B, § 902 et seq.

Disaster and Civil Defense Compact Act
See also Interstate Civil Defense and Disaster Compact Act
Alaska Stat. 1962, § 26.23.130
Conn. Gen. Stat. Ann., § 28-23
La. Rev. Stat. Ann., 29:715
Me. Rev. Stat. Ann. 1964, Title 37-B § 902 et seq.
W. Va. Code 1966, § 15-5-22

Disaster and Civil Defense Preparedness Act
Md. Ann. Code 1957, Art. 16A, § 1 et seq.

Disaster and Emergency Assistance Act
La. Rev. Stat. Ann., 29:721 et seq.

Disaster and Emergency Management Act
Ind. Code Ann., 10-4-1-1 et seq.

Disaster and Emergency Management Compact Act
Ky. Rev. Stat. 1971, 39.450 et seq.

Disaster and Emergency Services Law
Va. Code 1950, § 44-146.13 et seq.

Disaster Assistance Act
Miss. Code Ann., § 33-15-301 et seq.

Disaster Assistance Act of 1988
Aug. 11, 1988, P.L. 100-387, 102 Stat. 924, 7 U.S. Code § 1421 nt.
Aug. 14, 1989, P.L. 101-82, 7 U.S. Code § 1421 nt.; 16 U.S. Code § 2203 nt.
Dec. 19, 1989, P.L. 101-239, 7 U.S. Code § 1421 nt.
Nov. 28, 1990, P.L. 101-624, 7 U.S. Code § 1464 nt.
Dec. 13, 1991, P.L. 102-237, 7 U.S. Code § 1464 nt.

Disaster Assistance Act of 1989
Aug. 14, 1989, P.L. 101-82, 7 U.S. Code § 1421 nt.
Oct. 30, 1989, P.L. 101-134, 7 U.S. Code § 1421 nt.
Dec. 12, 1989, P.L. 101-220, 7 U.S. Code §§ 1421 nt., 1426 nt., 1429a nt.
Nov. 28, 1990, P.L. 101-624, 7 U.S. Code § 1421 nt.
Dec. 13, 1991, P.L. 102-237, 7 U.S. Code § 1421 nt.

Disaster Assistance to Meet the Present Emergencies Arising from the Consequences of Hurricane Andrew, Typhoon Omar, Hurricane Iniki and Other Natural Disasters, and Additional Assistance to Distressed Communities
Sept. 23, 1992, P.L. 102-368, 106 Stat. 1117
Oct. 6, 1992, P.L. 102-389, 106 Stat. 1604

Disaster Compact Act (Interstate)
See Interstate Disaster Compact Act

Disaster Control Act
N.J. Stat. Ann., App. A:9-30 et seq.

Disaster Emergency Act
Colo. Rev. Stat., 24-32-2101 et seq.

Disaster Law (Flooding)
Miss. Code Ann., § 27-107-151 et seq.

Disaster Loan Act
April 17, 1936, Ch. 234, 49 Stat. 1232, 12 U.S. Code § 1703; 15 U.S. Code § 605k

Disaster Loan Corporation Act
Feb. 11, 1937, Ch. 10, 50 Stat. 19

Disaster Location Act

N.M. Stat. Ann., 12-11-19 et seq.

Disaster Preparedness Act

Fla. Stat. Ann., 252.31 et seq.

Ida. Code 1947, 46-1001 et seq.

Disaster Project Law

Cal. Health and Safety Code § 34000 et seq.

Disaster Recovery Reconstruction Act

Cal. Government Code § 8877.1 et seq.

Disaster Relief Act

Ill. Rev. Stat. 1991, Ch. 127, § 293 et seq.

Mont. Laws 1949, Ch. 29

Disaster Relief Act Amendments of 1980

Dec. 22, 1980, P.L. 96-568, 42 U.S. Code § 5121 nt.

Disaster Relief Act of 1970

Dec. 31, 1970, P.L. 91-606, 84 Stat. 1744, 7 U.S. Code § 1926; 12 U.S. Code §§ 1706c, 1709, 1715l; 20 U.S. Code §§ 241-1, 646, 758; 26 U.S. Code §§ 165, 5064, 5708; 38 U.S. Code § 1820; 40 U.S. Code § 461; 42 U.S. Code §§ 4401, 4402, 4411 to 4420, 4431 to 4436, 4451 to 4462, 4481 to 4484

Dec. 18, 1971, P.L. 92-209, 85 Stat. 743, 42 U.S. Code § 4485

Aug. 18, 1972, P.L. 92-385, 86 Stat. 559, 42 U.S. Code § 4451

March 7, 1974, P.L. 93-251, 88 Stat. 24, 42 U.S. Code § 4482

Oct. 13, 1994, P.L. 103-354, 7 U.S. Code § 912a

Disaster Relief Act of 1974

See Robert T. Stafford Disaster Relief and Emergency Assistance Act

May 22, 1974, P.L. 93-288, 88 Stat. 143, 12 U.S. Code §§ 1706c, 1709, 1715l; 20 U.S. Code §§ 241-1, 646, 758; 26 U.S. Code §§ 165, 5064, 5708; 31 U.S. Code § 1264; 38 U.S. Code § 1820; 40 U.S. Code § 461; 42 U.S. Code §§ 3231 to 3236; 4401 nts. 5121, 5122, 5131, 5132, 5141 to 5158, 5171 to 5184, 5186 to 5189, 5201, 5202; 48 U.S. Code § 1681 nt.

June 20, 1977, P.L. 95-51, 42 U.S. Code § 5202

July 2, 1986, P.L. 99-349, 7 U.S. Code § 1441-1 nt.

Disaster Relief Acts

Nov. 6, 1966, P.L. 89-769, 80 Stat. 1316, 7 U.S. Code § 1926; 12 U.S. Code § 1715l; 15 U.S. Code § 636; 20 U.S. Code § 758; 38 U.S. Code § 1820

Oct. 1, 1969, P.L. 91-79, 83 Stat. 125

Disaster Relief and Civil Defense Act

Ida. Laws 1955, Ch. 269

Disaster Relief and Emergency Assistance Act

See Robert T. Stafford Disaster Relief And Emergency Assistance Act

Disaster Relief and Emergency Assistance Amendments of 1988

Nov. 23, 1988, P.L. 100-707, 42 U.S. Code § 5121 nt.

Disaster Relief Fund Act

Tenn. Code Ann., 58-2-501 et seq.

Disaster Response and Recovery Act

Utah Code Ann. 1953, 63-5a-1 et seq.

Disaster Service Volunteer Leave Act

Ala. Code 1975, § 36-1-9

Del. Code of 1974, Title 29, § 6001 et seq.

Fla. Stat. Ann., 110.120

Kan. Stat. Ann., 75-5546 et seq.

R.I. Gen. Laws 1956, 28-49-1 et seq.

Disaster Succession Act

N.M. Stat. Ann., 12-11-1 et seq.

Disbarment Act

Cal. Business and Professions Code § 6078 et seq., § 6100 et

Md. Ann. Code 1957, Art. 10, § 13 et seq.

Mont. Code Ann., 37-61-301 et seq.

N.H. Rev. Stat. 1955, 311:8

Ohio Rev. Code 1953, 4705.02

Tex. Government Code § 81.001 et seq.

Wash. Rev. Code Ann., 2.48.010 et seq.

Disbursing Officers' Relief Act
Aug. 1, 1947, Ch. 441, 61 Stat. 720, 31 U.S. Code § 82a-1
Aug. 9, 1955, Ch. 694, 69 Stat. 626, 31 U.S. Code § 82a-1

Disc Sign Act
N.Y. Railroad Law (Consol. Laws Ch. 49) § 53a

Discharge from Employment Act (Wrongful)
Mont. Code Ann., 39-2-901 et seq.

Discharge Notification Act
N.Y. Environmental Conservation Law 1972 (Consol. Laws Ch. 43B) § 17-0815a

Discharge of Hazardous Wastes Good Samaritan Law
N.Y. Environmental Conservation Law 1972 (Consol. Laws Ch. 43B) § 27-1321

Disciplinary Act (Health Professions)
Wash. Rev. Code Ann., 18.130.010 et seq.

Disciplinary Act (Inmates)
Cal. Penal Code § 2933

Disciplinary Act (Medicaid)
S.C. Code Ann. 1976, § 40-47-200 et seq.

Disciplinary Board Act (Medical)
Wash. Rev. Code Ann., 18.72.010 et seq.

Disciplinary Powers Act (Attorneys)
Ala. Code 1975, § 34-3-80 et seq.

Discipline Act (Student)
Neb. Rev. Stat. 1943, 79-4,170 to 79-4,205

Discipline Procedures Act (Peace Officer)
Minn. Stat. Ann., 626.89

Disclaimer Act
Colo. Rev. Stat. 1963, 153-5-43
Minn. Stat. Ann., 525.532
Neb. Rev. Stat. 1943, 30-129 et seq.

Disclaimer of Property Interests Act
See also Uniform Disclaimer of Property Interests Act
Haw. Rev. Stat. Ann., § 522-1 et seq.
Md. Ann. Code 1974, Art. ET, § 9-201 et seq.
Vt. Stat. Ann., Title 14, § 1951 et seq.

Disclaimer of Transfers by Will, Intestacy or Appointment Act
See also Uniform Disclaimer of Transfers by Will, Intestacy or Appointment Act
N.C. Gen. Stat. 1943, § 31B-1 et seq.

Disclaimer of Transfers under Nontestamentary Instruments Act
See also Uniform Disclaimer of Transfers under Nontestamentary Instruments Act
Ill. Rev. Stat. 1991, Ch. 30, §§ 210, 211
N.D. Cent. Code, 47-11.1-01 et seq.
Ore. Rev. Stat., 105.625 et seq.

Disclosure Act
Conn. Gen. Stat. Ann., § 52-197

Disclosure Act (County Officers and Employees)
Utah Code Ann. 1953, 17-16a-1 et seq.

Disclosure Act (Credit Card)
Minn. Stat. Ann., 325G.40 et seq.

Disclosure Act (Credit Reporting)
Ark. Code Ann. 1987, 4-93-101 et seq.
Ark. Code 1987, 4-93-101 et seq.

Disclosure Act (Finance Charges)
N.H. Rev. Stat. 1955, 399-B:1 et seq.

Disclosure Act (Financial Institutions)
Ill. Rev. Stat. 1991, Ch. 17, §§ 360.2, 503
Wash. Rev. Code 1979, 19.106.010 et seq.

Disclosure Act (Fine Prints)
Ill. Rev. Stat. 1991, Ch. 121 1/2, § 360 et seq.

Disclosure Act (Fraternal Benefit Funds)
Cal. Insurance Code § 11130 et seq.

Disclosure Act (Health Insurance)
Cal. Insurance Code § 10600 et seq.

Disclosure Act (Invention Development Services)
Neb. Rev. Stat. 1943, 87-601 et seq.

Disclosure Act (Land Sales)
N.H. Rev. Stat. 1955, 356-A:1 et seq.

Disclosure Act (Mine Subsidence)
Ill. Rev. Stat. 1991, Ch. 30, § 1001 et seq.

Disclosure Act (Motor Vehicle Buyback)
Utah Code Ann. 1953, 41-3-406 et seq.

Disclosure Act (Motor Vehicle Lease)
Fla. Stat. Ann., 521.001 et seq.

Disclosure Act (Political Action)
Utah Code Ann. 1953, 20-14a-1 et seq.

Disclosure Act (Political Issues)
Utah Code Ann. 1953, 20-14b-1 et seq.

Disclosure Act (Property Condition)
Ida. Code 1947, 55-2501 et seq.

Disclosure Act (Real Estate)
N.M. Stat. Ann., 47-13-1 et seq.

Disclosure Act (Take-Over)
Okla. Stat. Ann., Title 71, § 451 et seq.

Disclosure Act (Welfare Funds)
Cal. Insurance Code § 10640 et seq.
Mass. Gen. Laws Ann., 151D:1 et seq.

Disclosure Act for Public Initiatives, Referendums and Measures Referred to Voters by the General Assembly
Ark. Code Ann. 1987, 7-9-401 et seq.
Ark. Code 1987, 7-9-401 et seq.

Disclosure and Campaign Financing Act
Del. Code of 1974, Title 15, § 8040 et seq.

Disclosure and Regulation Act (Lobbyist)
Utah Code Ann. 1953, 36-11-101 et seq.

Disclosure and Rehabilitation Act (Continuing Care Facility)
Tex. Health and Safety Code, § 246.001 et seq.

Disclosure and Reporting Act (Public Retirement System)
N.Y. Retirement and Social Security Law (Consol. Laws Ch. 51A) § 150 et seq.

Disclosure of Association Act (Teachers)
Ark. Stat. 1947, 80-1229 et seq.

Disclosure of Cost of Energy Act
N.Y. Energy Law (Consol. Laws Ch. 17A) § 17-101 et seq.

Disclosure of Material Insurance Transactions Act
Neb. Rev. Stat. 1943, 44-6301 et seq.

Disclosure of Material Transactions Act
Ala. Code 1975, § 27-2A-1 et seq.
Iowa Code 1995, 521D.1 et seq.
Mont. Code Ann., 33-3-701 et seq.

Disclosure of Offenses against Children Act
Ill. Rev. Stat. 1991, Ch. 23, §§ 2240, 2241

Disclosure of Prizes and Gifts Act (Consumer)
Okla. Stat. Ann., Title 21, § 996.1 et seq.

Disclosure of Prizes and Gifts Act (Consumers)
Okla. Stat. Ann., Title 21, § 996.1 et seq.

Disconnection Act (Land)
Ill. Rev. Stat. 1991, Ch. 24, § 7-3-1 et seq.

Discount for Safe Drivers Act
S.C. Code Ann. 1976, § 38-73-760 et seq.

Discount Loan Law
Wis. Stat. Ann., 138.09

Discovery Act
Ark. Code Ann. 1987, 16-44-115 et seq.
Kan. Stat. Ann., 60-226 et seq.
La. Code of Civil Procedure 1960, Art. 1421 et seq.
Mich. Comp. Laws 1948, 634.1 et seq.
Miss. Code Ann. 1972, § 13-1-201 et seq.
Mo. Rev. Stat., 492.080 et seq.
Neb. Rev. Stat. 1943, 25-1267.01 et seq.

N.Y. Civil Practice Law and Rules (Consol. Laws Ch. 8) § 3120

Okla. Stat. Ann., Title 12, §§ 3201, 3224 et seq.

R.I. Gen. Laws 1956, 9-19-23

R.I. Rules of Civil Procedure 1965, Rule 34

S.C. Code Ann. 1976, § 19-13-10 et seq.

Wash. Rev. Code Ann., 10.37.035

Wis. Stat. Ann., 804.01 et seq.

Wis. Stat. 1973, 269.57

Discovery Act (Criminal)
See Criminal Discovery Act

Discovery Act (Depositions)
N.Y. Civil Practice Law and Rules (Consol. Laws, Ch. 8) § 3101 et seq.

Discovery Act (Pre-Trial Examination)
N.C. Rules of Civil Procedure, Rules 26 et seq.

Discovery and Deposition Act
See Deposition and Discovery Act

Discovery and Investigation Act
La. Rev. Stat. Ann., 13:4861 et seq.

Discovery Code (Criminal)
Okla. Stat. Ann., Title 22, § 2001 et seq.

Discovery Law (Employee Welfare Funds)
N.Y. Insurance Law 1984 (Consol. Laws Ch. 28) § 4401 et seq.

Discovery Law (Reciprocal)
N.Y. Criminal Procedure Law (Consol. Laws Ch. 11A) § 240.10 et seq.

Discovery Shaft Act (Mining Claims)
Colo. Rev. Stat., 34-43-101 et seq.

Discretionary Appeal Act
Tenn. Code Ann., 27-3-105

Discretionary Trust Act
Md. Ann. Code 1974, Art. ET, § 14-401 et seq.

Discrimination Act
Kan. Stat. Ann., 44-1001 et seq.

Mass. Gen. Laws Ann., 149:24A et seq.

Mont. Rev. Code 1947, 64-301 et seq.

N.H. Rev. Stat. 1955, 354-A:1 et seq.

N.J. Rev. Stat. 1937, 10:5-1 et seq.

Okla. Stat. Ann., Title 25, § 1101 et seq.

Vt. Stat. Ann., Title 13, § 1451 et seq.

Wash. Rev. Code Ann., 49.60.010 et seq.

Wis. Stat. Ann., 111.31 et seq.

Discrimination Act (Civil Rights)
Minn. Stat. Ann., 363.01 et seq.

Discrimination Act (Defense Contract Employment)
Ill. Rev. Stat. 1991, Ch. 29, § 24a.1 et seq.

Discrimination Act (Employment)
Conn. Gen. Stat. Ann., 46a-51 et seq.
Wis. Stat. Ann., 111.31 et seq.

Discrimination Act (Genetic)
Minn. Stat. 1986, 72A.139

Discrimination Act (Housing)
Cal. Health and Safety Code § 35700 et seq.
Wash. Rev. Code Ann., 49.60.222 et seq.

Discrimination Act (Osteopathic and Allopathic Health Care)
Ill. Comp. Stat. 1992, Ch. 225, § 62/1

Discrimination Act (Private Dwellings)
N.Y. City Adm. Code, 38, Ch. 1, § D1-1.0

Discrimination Act (Public Accommodations)
Vt. Stat. Ann., Title 13, § 1451 et seq.
Wis. Stat. 1987, 942.04

Discrimination Act (Public Works Employment)
Ill. Rev. Stat. 1991, Ch. 29, § 16.9 et seq.

Discrimination Act (Sex)
Neb. Rev. Stat. 1943, 48-1219 et seq.

Discrimination Act (State Employment)
Okla. Stat. Ann., Title 74, § 951 et seq.

Discrimination against Subjects of Abuse in Health Benefits Plans Act (Unfair)
R.I. Gen. Laws 1956, 27-60-1 et seq.

Discrimination in Employment Act (Age)
Kan. Stat. Ann., 44-1111 et seq.

Discrimination in Employment Because of Age Act
Alaska Stat. 1962, § 18.80.220 et seq.
Neb. Rev. Stat. 1943, 48-1001 et seq.

Discrimination in Housing Act
Mass. Gen. Laws Ann., 151B:1 et seq.

Discrimination in Housing Act (Metcalf-Baker)
N.Y. Civil Rights Law (Consol. Laws Ch. 6) § 18b, Subd. 3

Discrimination in Sale of Real Estate Act
Ill. Rev. Stat. 1991, Ch. 38, § 70-50 et seq.

Discrimination in Selling Act
N.M. Stat. Ann., 60-8A-13 et seq.

Discrimination Law (School)
Mass. Gen. Laws Ann., 76:5, 151C:1 et seq.

Discriminatory Club Act
Ill. Rev. Stat. 1991, Ch. 68, § 100 et seq.

Discriminatory Employment Practices Act
Mo. Rev. Stat., 213.055 et seq.

Disease Act (Cattle)
Neb. Rev. Stat. 1943, 54-1331 et seq.

Disease Act (Domestic Animals)
Neb. Rev. Stat. 1943, 54-701 et seq.

Disease Act (Occupational)
Ga. Code Ann., 34-9-280 et seq.

Disease Assistance Act (Alzheimer's)
Ill. Comp. Stat. 1992, Ch. 410, § 405/1 et seq.

Disease Control Act (Poultry)
Neb. Rev. Stat. 1943, 2-3001 et seq.

Disease Control Act (Seed Potatoes)
Mont. Laws 1989, Ch. 610

Disease Law (Occupational)
Me. Rev. Stat. Ann., Title 39-A, §§ 601 to 615

Disease Prevention Act (Communicable)
Ill. Comp. Stat. 1992, Ch. 410, § 315/0.01 et seq.

Disease Prevention Act (Livestock)
Ga. Code Ann., 4-4-1 et seq.

Disease Prevention and Control Act (Communicable)
Tex. Health and Safety Code, § 81.001 et seq.

Disease Prevention and Control Law
Pa. Purdon's Stat., Title 35, § 521.1 et seq.

Disease Prevention, Assessment and Control Act (Chronic)
N.H. Rev. Stat. 1955, 141-B:1 et seq.

Disease Report Act (Communicable)
Ill. Comp. Stat. 1992, Ch. 745, §§ 45/0.01, 45/1

Disease Research Act (Alzheimer's)
Ill. Comp. Stat. 1992, Ch. 410, § 410/1 et seq.

Diseased Animals Act
Ill. Rev. Stat. 1991, Ch. 8, § 168 et seq.
Neb. Rev. Stat. 1943, 54-701 et seq.
N.Y. Agriculture and Markets Law (Consol. Laws Ch.) § 72 et seq.
W. Va. Code 1966, § 19-9-1 et seq.

Diseases Act (Infections)
S.C. Code Ann. 1976, § 44-29-10 et seq.

Diseases Act (Occupational)
S.C. Code Ann. 1976, § 42-11-60 et seq.

Disentailing Act
Ohio Rev. Code 1953, 5303.21

Disguised Persons Act
Wash. Rev. Code Ann., 9.27.090, 9.27.100

Dishonored Check Fees Act
Ariz. Rev. Stat. Ann., § 44-6851 et seq.

Dislocated Worker Training Assistance Act
Pa. Purdon's Stat., Title 43, § 690a.1 et seq.

Disloyal Persons Payments Resolution
March 2, 1867, No. 46, 14 Stat. 571

Disloyalty Act
Haw. Rev. Stat. 1968, § 733-1 et seq.
Tex. Penal Code, § 42.09
Tex. Penal Code 1925, Arts. 153 to 156

Dismissal Act (Actions)
Ala. Code 1975, § 36-26-100 et seq.
Ga. Code Ann., 9-2-60
Okla. Stat. Ann., Title 12, § 683 et seq.
R.I. Gen. Laws 1956, 9-8-3 et seq.

Dismissal and Nonsuit Act
Wash. Rev. Code Ann., 4.56.120

Dismissal, Compensation, and Employment Act (Teacher)
Colo. Rev. Stat., 72-63-101 et seq.

Disorderly Conduct Act
Conn. Gen. Stat. Ann., § 53a-182
D.C. Code 1973, § 22-1107
Del. Code of 1974, Title 11, § 1301
Ill. Rev. Stat. 1991, Ch. 38, § 26-1 et seq.
Md. Ann. Code 1957, Art. 27, § 123 et seq.
Miss. Code Ann., §§ 97-35-3, 97-35-5, 97-35-15
N.Y. Code of Criminal Procedure § 899 et seq.
N.Y. Penal Law 1965 (Consol. Laws Ch. 40) § 240.20
Pa. 1939 Pamph. Laws 872, No. 375, § 406
Wis. Stat. Ann., 947.01

Disorderly Houses Law
Mich. Comp. Laws Ann., 750.167, 750.168
Neb. Laws 1911, Ch. 63
N.J. Stat. Ann. 2A:169-3, 2C:52-3, 2C:52-9 to 2C:52-11

Disparities Act (Fiscal)
Minn. Stat. Ann., 473F.01 et seq.

Dispatcher Training Act (Radio)
N.M. Stat. Ann., 29-7A-1 et seq.

Dispensary Act (Alcohol Sales)
S.C. Code Ann. 1976, § 61-11-10 et seq.

Dispensing Act (Nursing)
S.C. Code Ann. 1976, § 40-33-30 et seq.

Dispensing Opticians Act
Cal. Business and Professions Code § 2550 et seq.
Nev. Rev. Stat. 1979, Reprint, 637.010 et seq.

Displaced Defense Workers' Bill of Rights
Conn. Public Acts 1994, May Special Session No. 2, § 192

Displaced Homemaker Emergency Loan Act
Cal. Government Code § 8256 et seq.
Cal. Unemployment Insurance Code § 16000 et seq.

Displaced Homemakers Act
Ark. Stat. 1947, 81-630 et seq.
Cal. Government Code § 7320 et seq.
Colo. Rev. Stat., 8-15.5-101 et seq.
Ida. Code 1947, 39-5001 et seq.
Ill. Rev. Stat. 1991, Ch. 23, § 3451 et seq.
Iowa Code 1983, 241.1 et seq.
Ky. Rev. Stat. 1971. 195.120 et seq.
La. Rev. Stat. Ann., 46:1983 et seq., 46:1991 et seq.
Mass. Gen. Laws Ann., 23:11P et seq., 40I:7A
Me. Rev. Stat. Ann. 1964, Title 26, § 1601 et seq.
Mich. Comp. Laws Ann., 421.101 et seq.
Mont. Code Ann., 39-7-301 et seq.
N.D. Cent. Code, 14-06.1-01 et seq.
Neb. Rev. Stat. 1943, 48-1301 et seq.
N.J. Stat. Ann. 52:27D-43.18 et seq.
N.M. Stat. 1978, 28-3-7 et seq.
N.Y. Labor Law (Consol. Laws Ch. 31) § 825 et seq.
Continued

Okla. Stat. Ann., Title 70, § 14-113 et seq.

R.I. Gen. Laws 1956, 16-27.1-1 et seq.

Tex. Rev. Civ. Stat. 1974, Art. 695m

Wash. Rev. Code Ann., 28B.04.010 et seq.

Wis. Stat. Ann., 38.04, Subsec. 13

Displaced Homemakers Self-Sufficiency Assistance Act

Nov. 15, 1990, P.L. 101-554, 29 U.S. Code §§ 2301 to 2314

Aug. 7, 1998, P.L. 105-220, 29 U.S. Code §§ 2301, 2301 nt., 2302 to 2314

Displaced Person Relocation Act

Ill. Rev. Stat. 1991, Ch. 67 1/2, § 107 et seq.

Displaced Persons Act of 1948

June 25, 1948, Ch. 647, 62 Stat. 1009

June 16, 1950, Ch. 262, 64 Stat. 219

June 28, 1951, Ch. 167, 65 Stat. 65

June 27, 1952, Ch. 477, 66 Stat. 277

Displaced Worker Education and Training Act

Cal. Unemployment Insurance Code § 9950 et seq.

Display Act (Drivers' Licenses)

Ga. Code Ann., 40-5-29

Ky. Rev. Stat. 1971, 186.510

Display of Offensive Sexual Material Law (Public)

N.Y. Penal Law 1965 (Consol. Laws Ch. 40) §§ 245.10, 245.11

Disposal Act (Dead Animals)

Ga. Code Ann., 4-5-1 et seq.

Ga. Code 1933, 62-2101 et seq.

Disposal Act (Low-Level Radioactive Waste)

Me. Rev. Stat. Ann. 1964, Title 38, § 1481 et seq.

Disposal Act (Solid Waste)

Mass. Gen. Laws Ann., 16.18 et seq.

Disposal Act (Special Incinerator Ash)

Wash. Rev. Code Ann., 70.138.010 et seq.

Disposal Act (Waste Pesticide)

Miss. Code Ann., § 69-23-301 et seq.

Disposal and Codisposal Site Cleanup Program Law (Solid Waste)

Cal. Public Resources Code § 48020 et seq.

Disposal and Transportation of Radioactive Waste Act

S.C. Code Ann. 1976, § 48-48-10 et seq.

Disposal District Act (Garbage, Waste and Trash)

Colo. Rev. Stat., 30-20-201 et seq.

Disposal of Low-Level Radioactive Waste Act

Me. Rev. Stat. Ann. 1964, Title 38, § 1481 et seq.

Neb. Stat. 1943, 81-1578 et seq.

Disposal Projects Act (Sanitation)

Iowa Code 1971, 406.1 et seq.

Disposal Site Hazard Reduction Act (Solid Waste)

Cal. Public Resources Code § 46000 et seq.

Disposal Well Act

Tex. Water Code, § 27.001 et seq.

Disposition of Abandoned and Unclaimed Property Act

Md. Ann. Code 1974, Art. CL, § 17-101 et seq.

N.D. Cent. Code, 47-30-01 et seq.

Pa. Purdon's Stat., Title 72, § 1301.1 et seq.

Disposition of Abandoned Vessels Law

N.J. Stat. Ann., 12:7C-7 et seq.

Disposition of Affairs Act (Five Civilized Tribes)

April 26, 1906, Ch. 1876, 34 Stat. 137

Disposition of Community Property Rights at Death Act

See also Uniform Disposition of Community Property Rights at Death Act

Conn. Gen. Stat. 1983, § 45-298a et seq.

Mont. Laws 1991, Ch. 395

N.C. Gen. Stat. 1943, § 31C-1 et seq.

Disposition of Criminal Cases on the Merits Act
Okla. Stat. Ann., Title 22, § 1145.1 et seq.

Disposition of Detainers Act
See also Uniform Mandatory Disposition of Detainers Act
Colo. Rev. Stat., 16-14-101 et seq.
Ida. Laws 1969, Ch. 131
Kan. Stat. Ann., 22-4301 et seq.
N.D. Cent. Code, 29-33-01 et seq.
N.H. Rev. Stat. 1955, 606-A:1 et seq.

Disposition of Intrastate Detainer Act (Prison Inmates)
Wis. Stat. Ann., 971.111

Disposition of Museum Property Act
Ill. Comp. Stat. 1992, Ch. 765, § 1033/1 et seq.

Disposition of Personal Property Landlord and Tenant Act
Fla. Stat. Ann., 715.10 et seq.
Neb. Rev. Stat. 1943, 69-2301 et seq.

Disposition of Property Act (Law Enforcement)
Ill. Rev. Stat. 1991, Ch. 141, § 140 et seq.

Disposition of Traffic Infractions Act
Fla. Stat. Ann., 318.11 et seq.

Disposition of Unclaimed Property Act
See also Uniform Disposition of Unclaimed Property Act
Tex. Property Code, § 72.001 et seq.

Dispossession Act (Tenants)
N.J. Stat. Ann., 2A:18-53 et seq.

Dispossessory Proceeding Act
Ga. Code Ann., 44-7-50 et seq.

Dispute Reduction Act (International)
Colo. Rev. Stat., 13-22-501 et seq.

Dispute Resolution Act
Feb. 12, 1980, P.L. 96-190, 28 U.S. Code Appx.
Colo. Rev. Stat., 13-22-301 et seq.
Kan. Stat. Ann., 5-501 et seq.
Okla. Stat. Ann., Title 12, § 1801 et seq.

Dispute Resolution Act (Alternative)
Utah Code Ann. 1953, 78-31b-11 et seq.

Dispute Resolution Act (Environmental and Land Use)
Fla. Stat. Ann., 70.51

Dispute Resolution Act (Governmental)
Tex. Government Code, § 2008.001 et seq.

Disqualification Act (Criminal Defendants)
Ga. Code Ann., 24-9-20
Ga. Code 1933, 38-416

Disqualification Act (Electors)
Fla. Stat. Ann., 97.041

Disqualification Act (Executors and Administrators)
Wash. Rev. Code Ann., 11.36.010

Disqualification Act (Judges)
Mont. Code Ann., 3-1-801
Ohio Rev. Code 1953, 2701.03

Disqualification Act (Jurors)
Mo. Rev. Stat., 494.190

Disqualification Act (Witnesses)
Ala. Code 1975, § 12-21-162

Dissemination, Security, and Privacy of Criminal History Information Act
Neb. Rev. Stat. 1943, 29-3501 et seq.

Dissent from Will Act
N.C. Gen. Stat. 1943, § 30-1 et seq.

Dissenting Shareholders' Appraisal Act
Wash. Rev. Code Ann., 23A.24.030 et seq.

Dissolution Act (Corporations)
See Corporation Dissolution Act

Dissolution Act (Insurers)
Ill. Rev. Stat. 1981, Ch. 73, § 799 et seq.

Dissolution, Invalidity, and Marriage Records Act
Ill. Rev. Stat. 1991, Ch. 40, § 900 et seq.

Dissolution of Marriage Act
See Marriage Dissolution Act

Dissolutions of Marriage and Trusts Act
Ill. Rev. Stat. 1991, Ch. 138, §§ 300, 301

Distance Learning and Telemedicine Act
Ga. Code Ann., 50-5-190 et seq.

Distance Learning Commission Act
N.H. Rev. Stat. 1955, 70:1 et seq.

Distance Tariff Act (Railroads)
Minn. Stat. 1953, 218.41 et seq.

Distilled Liquor Control Act
Ore. Rev. Stat. 1953, 472.010 et seq.

Distilled Spirits and Wine Fair Trade Act
Ky. Rev. Stat. 1971, 244.380 to 244.470

Distilled Spirits Distribution Act
Ga. Code Ann., 3-4-150 et seq.

Distilled Spirits Tax Act
Ky. Rev. Stat. 1962, 243.680 et seq.

Distilled Spirits Tax Revision Act of 1979
July 26, 1979, P.L. 96-39, 26 U.S. Code §§ 1 nt., 5001 et seq., 5001 nt.

Distillers Act
Mo. Laws 1909, p. 654
Pa. 1893 Pamph. Laws 474, No. 344

Distillery Bonded Warehouse Certificate Act
Pa. 1939 Pamph. Laws 764, No. 348

Distinctive Color Act (Traffic Officers)
Cal. Vehicle Code 1959, § 40800

Distinguished Service Medal Act
Tex. Rev. Civ. Stat., Art. 6144h

Distraint Act
Del. Code of 1953, Title 25, § 6101
S.C. Code Ann. 1976, § 27-39-270

Distraint Act (Rent Collection)
S.C. Code Ann. 1976, § 27-39-210

Distraint Act (Rent)
Haw. Session Laws 1864-65, p. 25, Jan. 10, 1865

Distraint Act for Collection of Rent
S.C. Code Ann. 1976, § 27-39-210 et seq.

Distress Act
N.J. Stat. Ann., 2A:33-1 et seq.

Distress for Rent Act
Md. Ann. Code 1974, Art. RP, § 8-301 et seq.

Distress Merchandise Sales Act (Mecklenburg County)
N.C. Laws 1955, Ch. 1375

Distress Sales Act
N.M. Stat. Ann., 57-10-1 et seq.

Distressed Areas Economic Revitalization Act
R.I. Gen. Laws 1956, 42-64.3-1 et seq.

Distressed City Law (Financially)
Ill. Rev. Stat. 1991, Ch. 24, § 8-12-1 et seq.

Distressed County Assistance Act (Costa-McCorquodale-Keene)
Cal. Statutes 1986, Ch. 1146

Distressed Food Act
S.D. Codified Laws 1967, 34-5-9 et seq.

Distressed Industry Task Force Act
Mo. Rev. Stat., 620.520 et seq.

Distributable Aid Bond Act (Municipal)
Mich. Comp. Laws Ann., 141.1021 et seq.

Distributing and Importing Corporation Act
P.R. Laws Ann. 1954, Title 23, § 761 et seq.

Distribution Act
Ala. Code 1975, 43-8-40 et seq.
Md. Ann. Code 1974, Art. ET, § 9-101 et seq.
Mich. Comp. Laws Ann., 702.93 et seq.,
    700.155 et seq.
Mont. Code Ann., 72-3-901 et seq.
N.C. Gen. Stat. 1943, § 29-1 et seq.
N.H. Rev. Stat. 1955, 561:1 et seq.

Distribution Act (Estates)
Ala. Code 1975, § 43-8-40 et seq.
Conn. Gen. Stat. Ann., § 45-272 et seq.
Mich. Comp. Laws Ann., 702.93 et seq.
N.J. Stat. Ann. 3B:5-1 et seq.
Pa. 1832-33 Pamph. Laws 315, No. 143
R.I. Gen. Laws 1956, 33-1-10

Distribution Act (Food Stamp)
Mich. Comp. Laws Ann., 400.751 et seq.

Distribution Act (Motor Fuel)
Mich. Comp. Laws Ann., 445.1801 et seq.

Distribution Act (School Funds)
Ind. Code Ann., 21-3-1.6-1 et seq.

**Distribution Act of 1841 (Public Lands
    Proceeds)**
See State Selection Acts (Public Lands)

Distribution and Descent Act
See Descent and Distribution Act

Distribution and Sales Act (Motor Vehicles)
Okla. Stat. 1971, Title 47, § 561 et seq.

Distribution Cooperatives Act
Va. Code 1950, § 56-209 et seq.

**Distributions in Kind Act (Bequests and
    Trust Interests)**
Mich. Comp. Laws Ann., 700.215, 700.216

Distributive Act
Wash. Rev. Code Ann., 11.04.015 et seq.

**Distributor-Supplier Equity Agreement Act
    (Wholesale)**
Wash. Rev. Code 1983, 31.12.005 et seq.

**Distributors and Dealers Franchising
    Practices Act (Motor Vehicle)**
Vt. Stat. Ann., Title 32, § 5931 et seq.

Distributor's Gasoline License Tax Act
Mont. Code Ann., 15-70-201 et seq.

**Distributorship and Franchis Investment
    Regulations Act**
R.I. Gen. Laws 1956, 19-28-1 et seq.

Distributorship Disclosure Act
N.H. Rev. Stat. 1955, 358-E:1 et seq.

District Act
N.Y. Laws 1926, Ch. 470

District Act (Public Library)
Ill. Laws 1992, P.A. 87-1277

District Agricultural Association Act
Cal. Food and Agricultural Code 1967,
    §§ 3851 et seq., 3901.5

**District Alteration and Election Data
    Reporting Act**
Pa. Purdon's Stat., Title 25, § 3601 et seq.

**District Assessment Act (Public
    Improvement)**
Tex. Government Code, § 372.001 et seq.

**District Attorney Personnel and
    Compensation Act**
N.M. Stat. Ann., 36-1A-1 et seq.

District Attorneys General Fiscal Affairs Act
Tenn. Public Acts 1986, Ch. 766

District Attorneys Retirement Act
Ga. Code Ann., 47-13-1 et seq.

District Authority Act (Savannah)
Ga. Laws 1951, p. 190

District Boundaries Commission Law
Cal. Statutes 1949, Ch. 920, p. 1684

District Boundary Procedure Act
Ore. Rev. Stat., 198.705 et seq.

District Budgets Act
Cal. Government Code § 29190 et seq.

District Cooperative Extension Service Act
Ky. Rev. Stat. 1971, 164.605 et seq.

District Court Act
Alaska Comp. Laws Ann. 1949, § 53-1-1
Me. Rev. Stat. Ann. 1964, Title 4, § 151 et
seq.
N.H. Rev. Stat. 1955, 502-A:1 et seq.
N.J. Stat. Ann., 2A:18-1 et seq.
N.Y. Uniform District Court Act, § 101 et
seq.
Vt. Stat. Ann., Title 4, § 436 et seq.

District Court Act (Milwaukee)
Wis. Laws 1899, Ch. 218

District Court Act (Nassau County)
N.Y. Laws 1939, Ch. 274

District Court Act (Suffolk County)
N.Y. Laws 1962, Ch. 811

District Court Apportionment Act
Tex. Government Code, § 24.01

**District Court Building Loan Act
(Berkshire)**
Mass. Acts 1962, Ch. 185

District Court Civil Procedure Act
Wash. Rev. Code Ann., 12.04.010 et seq.

District Court Conciliation Department Act
Okla. Stat. 1961, Title 20, § 951 et seq.

**District Court of Somerville Court House
Loan Act**
Mass. Acts 1963, Ch. 519

District Court Reorganization Act
Mass. Gen. Laws Ann., 218:6 et seq.
Mich. Comp. Laws Ann., 600.8101 et seq.

District Court Rules (Uniform)
Mont. Code Ann., Title 25, Ch. 19

District Courts Remand Act
Mass. Gen. Laws Ann., 231:102C

District Dissolution Act
Cal. Government Code §§ 56038, 58300 et
seq.

District Election Act
Cal. Elections Code 1976, § 23500 et seq.

District Enabling Act
Ariz. Rev. Stat. Ann., § 48-171 et seq.

District Enabling Act (Municipal Electric)
Me. Rev. Stat. Ann. 1964, Title 35-A, § 3901
et seq.

District Health Department Act
Ky. Rev. Stat. 1971, 212.810 et seq.

**District Heights Urban Renewal Authority
for Slum Clearance Act**
Md. Laws 1999, Ch. 413

District Improvement Act
Ariz. Rev. Stat. Ann., § 11-701 et seq.
Ore. Rev. Stat. 1953, 554.010 et seq.

District Investigation Act
Cal. Government Code § 58500 et seq.

District Law (General)
N.Y. Unconsolidated Law, § 5651 et seq.

District Library Establishment Act
Mich. Comp. Laws Ann., 397.171 et seq.

District Library Financing Act
Mich. Comp. Laws Ann., 397.281 et seq.

**District of Columbia Act for the Regulation
of Credit Life Insurance and Credit
Accident and Health Insurance**
Sept. 25, 1962, P.L. 87-686, 76 Stat. 580

**District of Columbia Administrative
Procedure Act**
Oct. 21, 1968, P.L. 90-586, 82 Stat. 1203
July 29, 1970, P.L. 91-358, 84 Stat. 582

District of Columbia Air Pollution Control Act
July 30, 1968, P.L. 90-440, 82 Stat. 458

District of Columbia Alcoholic Beverage Control Act
Jan. 24, 1934, Ch. 4, 48 Stat. 319
April 26, 1950, Ch. 106, 64 Stat. 88
March 31, 1956, Ch. 154, 70 Stat. 81
July 29, 1970, P.L. 91-358, 84 Stat. 572
Dec. 8, 1970, P.L. 91-535, 84 Stat. 1393
Jan. 5, 1971, P.L. 91-650, 84 Stat. 1940

District of Columbia Alcoholic Rehabilitation Act of 1967
Aug. 3, 1968, P.L. 90-452, 82 Stat. 618

District of Columbia Alley Dwelling Act
June 12, 1934, Ch. 465, 48 Stat. 930
June 8, 1944, Ch. 238, 58 Stat. 271
Aug. 2, 1946, Ch. 736, 60 Stat. 801
April 4, 1960, P.L. 86-400, 74 Stat. 12
July 29, 1970, P.L. 91-358, 84 Stat. 587

District of Columbia Anatomical Gift Act
May 26, 1970, P.L. 91-268, 84 Stat. 266

District of Columbia Appropriation Act, 1990
Oct. 1, 1991, P.L. 102-111, 105 Stat. 570
Oct. 5, 1992, P.L. 102-382, 106 Stat. 1434

District of Columbia Appropriation Act, 1992
Oct. 1, 1991, P.L. 102-111, 105 Stat. 571
Oct. 5, 1992, P.L. 102-382, 106 Stat. 1446

District of Columbia Appropriation Acts
July 15, 1939, Ch. 281, 53 Stat. 1033
June 12, 1940, Ch. 333, 54 Stat. 307
July 1, 1941, Ch. 271, 55 Stat. 499
June 27, 1942, Ch. 452, 56 Stat. 435
July 1, 1943, Ch. 184, 57 Stat. 324
June 28, 1944, Ch. 300, 58 Stat. 509
June 30, 1945, Ch. 209, 59 Stat. 271
July 21, 1945, Ch. 321, 59 Stat. 500
July 9, 1946, Ch. 544, 60 Stat. 518.
July 25, 1947, Ch. 324, 61 Stat. 425
July 19, 1948, Ch. 555, 62 Stat. 537
June 29, 1949, Ch. 279, 63 Stat. 303
July 18, 1950, Ch. 467, 64 Stat. 347
Aug. 3, 1951, Ch. 292, 65 Stat. 167
July 5, 1952, Ch. 576, 66 Stat. 374
July 31, 1953, Ch. 299, 67 Stat. 278
July 1, 1954, Ch. 449, 68 Stat. 386
July 5, 1955, Ch. 272, 69 Stat. 246
June 29, 1956, Ch. 479, 70 Stat. 439
June 27, 1957, P.L. 85-61, 71 Stat. 192
Aug. 6, 1958, P.L. 85-594, 72 Stat. 498
July 23, 1959, P.L. 86-104, 73 Stat. 225
April 8, 1960, P.L. 86-412, 74 Stat. 17
Sept. 21, 1961, P.L. 87-265, 75 Stat. 560
Oct. 23, 1962, P.L. 87-867, 76 Stat. 1150
Dec. 30, 1963, P.L. 88-252, 77 Stat. 835
Aug. 22, 1964, P.L. 88-479, 78 Stat. 588
July 16, 1965, P.L. 89-75, 79 Stat. 236
Nov. 2, 1966, P.L. 89-743, 80 Stat. 1174
Nov. 13, 1967, P.L. 90-134, 81 Stat. 435
Aug. 10, 1968, P.L. 90-473, 82 Stat. 694
Dec. 24, 1969, P.L. 91-155, 83 Stat. 428
June 30, 1970, P.L. 91-297, 84 Stat. 367
July 16, 1970, P.L. 91-337, 84 Stat. 432
Oct. 18, 1986, P.L. 99-500, 100 Stat. 3536
Oct. 30, 1986, P.L. 99-591, 100 Stat. 3536
July 11, 1987, P.L. 100-71, 101 Stat. 474
Dec. 22, 1987, P.L. 100-202, 101 Stat. 1329
Oct. 1, 1988, P.L. 100-462, 102 Stat. 2269-17
Nov. 21, 1989, P.L. 101-168, 103 Stat. 1282
Nov. 21, 1989, P.L. 101-168, 103 Stat. 1284

District of Columbia Appropriations Act, 1991
Nov. 5, 1990, P.L. 101-518, 104 Stat. 2224
Oct. 1, 1991, P.L. 102-111, 105 Stat. 572-574

District of Columbia Appropriations Act, 1993
Oct. 5, 1992, P.L. 102-382, 106 Stat. 1422

District of Columbia Appropriations Act, 1994
Oct. 29, 1993, P.L. 103-127, 107 Stat. 1336

District of Columbia Appropriations Act, 1995
Sept. 30, 1994, P.L. 103-334, 108 Stat. 2576
April 17, 1995, P.L. 104-8, 109 Stat. 109

District of Columbia Appropriations Act, 1996
April 26, 1996, P.L. 104-134, Title I, 110 Stat. 1321-77

District of Columbia Appropriations Act, 1997
D.C. Code Ann., § 1-601.1 et seq.

District of Columbia Appropriations Act, 1998
Nov. 19, 1997, P.L. 105-100, Title I, 111 Stat. 2160

District of Columbia Appropriations Act, 1999
Oct. 21, 1998, P.L. 105-277, 101(d), 112 Stat. 2681

District of Columbia Bail Agency Act
July 26, 1966, P.L. 89-519, 80 Stat. 327
April 15, 1970, P.L. 91-232, 84 Stat. 199
July 29, 1970, P.L. 91-358, 84 Stat. 654

District of Columbia Barber Act
June 7, 1938, Ch. 322, 52 Stat. 620

District of Columbia Blackout Act
Dec. 26, 1941, Ch. 625, 55 Stat. 858

District of Columbia Boiler Inspection Act
July 25, 1936, Ch. 802, 49 Stat. 1917
July 29, 1970, P.L. 91-358, 84 Stat. 570

District of Columbia Bond Financing Improvements Act of 1997
Aug. 5, 1997, P.L. 105-33, Title XI, Subtitle F, 111 Stat. 768

District of Columbia Budgetary Efficiency Act of 1991
Aug. 17, 1991, P.L. 102-102, 105 Stat. 495

District of Columbia Business Corporation Act
June 8, 1954, Ch. 269, 68 Stat. 177
July 29, 1970, P.L. 91-358, 84 Stat. 582

District of Columbia Certified Public Accountancy Act of 1966
Sept. 16, 1966, P.L. 89-578, 80 Stat. 785

April 22, 1968, P.L. 90-292, 82 Stat. 101

District of Columbia Cession Act
Md. Laws 1791, Ch. 45, § 2

District of Columbia Charitable Solicitation Act
July 10, 1957, P.L. 85-87, 71 Stat. 278
July 29, 1970, P.L. 91-358, 84 Stat. 571

District of Columbia Civil Contempt Imprisonment Limitation Act of 1989
Sept. 23, 1989, P.L. 101-97, 103 Stat. 633

District of Columbia Claims Act
June 16, 1880, Ch. 243, 21 Stat. 284

District of Columbia Code
March 3, 1901, Ch. 854, 31 Stat. 1189
June 30, 1902, Ch. 1329, 32 Stat. 520
April 19, 1920, Ch. 153, 41 Stat. 555
June 12, 1940, Ch. 339, 54 Stat. 347
Oct. 28, 1986, P.L. 99-573, 100 Stat. 3228
Jan. 8, 1988, P.L. 100-238, 101 Stat. 1745
Nov. 21, 1989, P.L. 101-168, 103 Stat. 1283

District of Columbia Convention Center and Sports Arena Authorization Act of 1995
Sept. 6, 1995, P.L. 104-28, 109 Stat. 267

District of Columbia Cooperative Association Act
June 19, 1940, Ch. 397, 54 Stat. 480

District of Columbia Court Reform and Criminal Procedure Act of 1970
July 29, 1970, P.L. 91-358, 84 Stat. 570
Oct. 28, 1986, P.L. 99-573, 100 Stat. 3234

District of Columbia Court Reorganization Act of 1970
July 29, 1970, P.L. 91-358, 84 Stat. 570

District of Columbia Courts and Justice Technical Corrections Act of 1998
Oct. 20, 1998, P.L. 105-274, 112 Stat. 2419, 5 U.S. Code § 8401 nt.

District of Columbia Credit Unions Act
June 23, 1932, Ch. 272, 47 Stat. 326
April 28, 1950, Ch. 119, 64 Stat. 90

District of Columbia Dangerous Weapons Act
July 8, 1932, Ch. 465, 47 Stat. 650

District of Columbia Death Act
Feb. 17, 1885, Ch. 126, 23 Stat. 307

District of Columbia Delegate Act
Sept. 22, 1970, P.L. 91-405, 84 Stat. 848
Aug. 20, 1996, P.L. 104-186, 2 U.S. Code § 25b

District of Columbia Election Act
April 22, 1968, P.L. 90-292, 82 Stat. 101

District of Columbia Emergency Deficit Reduction Act of 1991
Aug. 17, 1991, P.L. 102-106, 105 Stat. 539

District of Columbia Emergency Highway Relief Act
Aug. 4, 1995, P.L. 104-21, 109 Stat. 257

District of Columbia Emergency Rent Act
Dec. 2, 1941, Ch. 553, 55 Stat. 788
April 19, 1949, Ch. 73, 63 Stat. 48
June 30, 1951, Ch. 192, 65 Stat. 98

District of Columbia Federal Payment Authorization and Borrowing Authority Act of 1967
Nov. 3, 1967, P.L. 90-120, 81 Stat. 339

District of Columbia Financial Responsi-bility and Management Assistance Act of 1995
April 17, 1995, P.L. 104-8, 109 Stat. 97

District of Columbia Fire and Casualty Acts
Oct. 9, 1940, Ch. 792, 54 Stat. 1063
April 22, 1944, Ch. 173, 58 Stat. 192
July 29, 1970, P.L. 91-358, 84 Stat. 575, 589

District of Columbia Government Comprehensive Merit Personnel Act of 1978
Nov. 21, 1989, P.L. 101-168, 103 Stat. 1277

District of Columbia Horizontal Property Act
Dec. 21, 1963, P.L. 88-218, 77 Stat. 449

July 29, 1970, P.L. 91-358, 84 Stat. 571

District of Columbia Hospital Treatment for Drug Addicts Act
June 24, 1953, Ch. 149, 67 Stat. 77
July 24, 1956, Ch. 676, 70 Stat. 609
July 29, 1970, P.L. 91-358, 84 Stat. 572

District of Columbia Hospitalization of the Mentally Ill Act
Sept. 15, 1964, P.L. 88-597, 78 Stat. 944

District of Columbia Income and Franchise Tax Act of 1947
July 16, 1947, Ch. 259, 61 Stat. 328
May 3, 1948, Ch. 246, 62 Stat. 206
June 30, 1970, P.L. 91-297, 84 Stat. 366
July 29, 1970, P.L. 91-358, 84 Stat. 573
Jan. 5, 1971, P.L. 91-650, 84 Stat. 1933

District of Columbia Income Tax Act
July 26, 1939, Ch. 367, 53 Stat. 1085
July 29, 1970, P.L. 91-358, 84 Stat. 573

District of Columbia Inspector General Improvement Act of 1997
March 25, 1997, P.L. 105-7, 111 Stat. 14
D.C. Code Ann., § 1-610.6

District of Columbia Insurance Placement Act
July 29, 1970, P.L. 91-358, 84 Stat. 583

District of Columbia Judges Retirement Act of 1964
Oct. 13, 1964, P.L. 88-644, 78 Stat. 1055

District of Columbia Judicial Efficiency and Improvement Act of 1986
Oct. 28, 1986, P.L. 99-573, 100 Stat. 3228

District of Columbia Judiciary and Judicial Procedure
Dec. 23, 1963, P.L. 88-241, 77 Stat. 478

District of Columbia Jury System Act
Nov. 14, 1986, P.L. 99-650, 100 Stat. p. 3635

District of Columbia Justice Reform Act of 1994
Aug. 23, 1994, P.L. 103-303, 108 Stat. 1564

District of Columbia Juvenile Fraternal Act
May 29, 1928, Ch. 862, 45 Stat. 953

District of Columbia Law Enforcement Act of 1953
Aug. 16, 1954, Ch. 737, 68 Stat. 730
July 29, 1970, P.L. 91-358, 84 Stat. 575

District of Columbia Legal Aid Act
July 29, 1970, P.L. 91-358, 84 Stat. 657

District of Columbia Life Insurance Act
June 19, 1934, Ch. 672, 48 Stat. 1125
July 2, 1940, Ch. 518, 54 Stat. 726
Oct. 3, 1962, P.L. 87-738, 76 Stat. 711
Oct. 3, 1962, P.L. 87-740, 76 Stat. 715
July 29, 1970, P.L. 91-358, 84 Stat. 572

District of Columbia Management Reform Act of 1997
Aug. 5, 1997, P.L. 105-33, Title XI, Subtitle B, 111 Stat. 731

District of Columbia Management Restoration Act of 1999
March 5, 1999, P.L. 106-1, 113 Stat. 3

District of Columbia Materialmen's Act
Feb. 28, 1899, Ch. 218, 30 Stat. 906

District of Columbia Medical and Dental Manpower Act of 1970
Jan. 5, 1971, P.L. 91-650, 84 Stat. 1934

District of Columbia Medical Facilities Construction Act of 1968
Aug. 3, 1968, P.L. 90-457, 82 Stat. 631

District of Columbia Mental Health Program Assistance Act of 1991
Oct. 31, 1991, P.L. 102-150, 24 U.S. Code § 225 nt.

District of Columbia Merger Act
Jan. 14, 1933, Ch. 10, 47 Stat. 752

District of Columbia Metropolitan Police Relief Association Incorporation Act
July 5, 1962, P.L. 87-523, 76 Stat. 135

District of Columbia Minimum Wage Act
Sept. 19, 1918, Ch. 174, 40 Stat. 960
Oct. 14, 1941, Ch. 438, 55 Stat. 738
Jan. 5, 1971, P.L. 91-650, 84 Stat. 1938

District of Columbia Motor Vehicle Safety Responsibility Act
May 25, 1954, Ch. 222, 68 Stat. 120
July 29, 1970, P.L. 91-358, 84 Stat. 583

District of Columbia Nonprofit Corporation Act
Aug. 6, 1962, P.L. 87-569, 76 Stat. 265
July 29, 1970, P.L. 91-358, 84 Stat. 589

District of Columbia Organic Act
June 11, 1878, Ch. 180, 20 Stat. 102

District of Columbia Physical Therapists Practice Act
July 29, 1970, P.L. 91-358, 84 Stat. 585

District of Columbia Police and Firemen's Salary Acts
Aug. 31, 1954, Ch. 1146, 68 Stat. 1000
Aug. 5, 1955, Ch. 570, 69 Stat. 530
July 24, 1956, Ch. 680, 70 Stat. 624
July 18, 1958, P.L. 85-533, 72 Stat. 378
Aug. 1, 1958, P.L. 85-584, 72 Stat. 485
Nov. 13, 1966, P.L. 89-810, 80 Stat. 1591
May 27, 1968, P.L. 90-320, 82 Stat. 140
June 30, 1970, P.L. 91-297, 84 Stat. 354
Oct. 10, 1997, P.L. 105-61, 3 U.S. Code § 204 nt.

District of Columbia Police Authorization and Expansion Act of 1989
Dec. 12, 1989, P.L. 101-223, 103 Stat. 1901

District of Columbia Policemen and Firemen's Retirement and Disability Act Amendments of 1970
Oct. 26, 1970, P.L. 91-509, 84 Stat. 1136

District of Columbia Policemen and Firemen's Retirement and Disability Acts
Aug. 21, 1957, P.L. 85-157, 71 Stat. 391
Oct. 23, 1962, P.L. 87-857, 76 Stat. 1133
Oct. 26, 1970, P.L. 91-509, 84 Stat. 1136

Dec. 7, 1970, P.L. 91-532, 84 Stat. 1392

District of Columbia Practical Nurses' Licensing Act
July 29, 1970, P.L. 91-358, 84 Stat. 585

District of Columbia Practice of Psychology Act
Jan. 8, 1971, P.L. 91-657, 84 Stat. 1955

District of Columbia Procurement Practices Act of 1985
April 17, 1995, P.L. 104-8, 109 Stat. 149

District of Columbia Prohibition Law
March 3, 1917, Ch. 165, 39 Stat. 1123

District of Columbia Public Assistance Act of 1962
Oct. 15, 1962, P.L. 87-807, 76 Stat. 914
July 29, 1970, P.L. 91-358, 84 Stat. 571
Dec. 7, 1970, P.L. 91-531, 84 Stat. 1391

District of Columbia Public Education Act
Nov. 7, 1966, P.L. 89-791, 80 Stat. 1426
June 20, 1968, P.L. 90-354, 82 Stat. 241
Jan. 5, 1971, P.L. 91-650, 84 Stat. 1935

District of Columbia Public School Food Services Act
Oct. 8, 1951, Ch. 448, 65 Stat. 367
Aug. 5, 1955, Ch. 575, 69 Stat. 536
Sept. 2, 1958, P.L. 85-901, 72 Stat. 1735

District of Columbia Public Space Rental Act
Oct. 17, 1968, P.L. 90-596, 82 Stat. 1156

District of Columbia Public Space Utilization Act
Oct. 17, 1968, P.L. 90-598, 82 Stat. 1166
July 29, 1970, P.L. 91-358, 84 Stat. 571

District of Columbia Public Utility Act
March 4, 1913, Ch. 150, 37 Stat. 938

District of Columbia Public Works Act of 1954
Jan. 5, 1971, P.L. 91-650, 84 Stat. 1930
Nov. 21, 1989, P.L. 101-168, 103 Stat. 1280

District of Columbia Real Estate Deed Recordation Tax Act
July 29, 1970, P.L. 91-358, 84 Stat. 572

District of Columbia Red Light Abatement Act
Feb. 7, 1914, Ch. 16, 38 Stat. 280

District of Columbia Redevelopment Act of 1945
Aug. 2, 1946, Ch. 736, 60 Stat. 790
July 15, 1949, Ch. 338, 63 Stat. 439
Aug. 28, 1958, P.L. 85-854, 72 Stat. 1102
July 29, 1970, P.L. 91-358, 84 Stat. 571

District of Columbia Rents and Food Act
See Ball Act (Rents In District Of Columbia)

District of Columbia Retirement Act
Oct. 12, 1984, P.L. 98-473, 98 Stat. 1975

District of Columbia Retirement Protection Act of 1997
Aug. 5, 1997, P.L. 105-33, Title XI, Subtitle A, 111 Stat. 715

District of Columbia Revenue Act
See Revenue Act (District of Columbia)

District of Columbia Revenue Act of 1937
Aug. 17, 1937, Ch. 690, 50 Stat. 673
July 10, 1940, Ch. 568, 54 Stat. 747
July 29, 1970, P.L. 91-358, 84 Stat. 573

District of Columbia Revenue Act of 1939
July 26, 1939, Ch. 367, 53 Stat. 1085
March 2, 1940, Ch. 37, 54 Stat. 38
April 17, 1995, P.L. 104-8, 109 Stat. 120

District of Columbia Revenue Act of 1947
July 16, 1947, Ch. 258, 61 Stat. 328
May 3, 1948, Ch. 246, 62 Stat. 206
May 27, 1949, Ch. 146, 63 Stat. 129
Jan. 5, 1971, P.L. 91-650, 84 Stat. 1930

District of Columbia Revenue Act of 1949
May 27, 1949, Ch. 146, 63 Stat. 112
Sept. 1, 1950, Ch. 836, 64 Stat. 576
Sept. 8, 1950, Ch. 921, 64 Stat. 791
July 29, 1970, P.L. 91-358, 84 Stat. 573

District of Columbia Revenue Act of 1956
March 31, 1956, Ch. 154, 70 Stat. 68

District of Columbia Revenue Act of 1968
Aug. 2, 1968, P.L. 90-450, 82 Stat. 612

District of Columbia Revenue Act of 1969
Oct. 31, 1969, P.L. 91-106, 83 Stat. 169

District of Columbia Revenue Act of 1970
Jan. 5, 1971, P.L. 91-650, 84 Stat. 1930

District of Columbia Revenue Bond Act of 1985
Feb. 7, 1985, P.L. 99-242, 100 Stat. 4

District of Columbia Revenue Bond Act of 1988
Sept. 20, 1988, P.L. 100-438, 102 Stat. 1718

District of Columbia Revenue Bond Act of 1989
Nov. 17, 1989, P.L. 101-158, 103 Stat. 946

District of Columbia Revenue Bond Act of 1990
Nov. 6, 1990, P.L. 101-526, 104 Stat. 2309

District of Columbia Sales Tax Act
May 27, 1949, Ch. 146, 63 Stat. 112
March 31, 1956, Ch. 154, 70 Stat. 80
July 29, 1970, P.L. 91-358, 84 Stat. 573
Jan. 5, 1971, P.L. 91-650, 84 Stat. 1932

District of Columbia School Reform Act of 1995
April 26, 1996, P.L. 104-134, Title II, 110 Stat. 1321-107

District of Columbia Securities Act
Aug. 30, 1964, P.L. 88-503, 78 Stat. 620
July 29, 1970, P.L. 91-358, 84 Stat. 571

District of Columbia Self-Government and Governmental Reorganization Act of 1973
Dec. 24, 1973, P.L. 93-198, 87 Stat. 774
April 17, 1974, P.L. 93-268, 88 Stat. 86
April 24, 1974, P.L. 93-272, 88 Stat. 93
Nov. 15, 1977, P.L. 95-185, 91 Stat. 1383

Dec. 28, 1977, P.L. 95-218, 91 Stat. 1612
Dec. 28, 1979, P.L. 96-160, 93 Stat. 1232
Aug. 6, 1981, P.L. 97-30, 95 Stat. 150
Aug. 13, 1981, P.L. 97-30, 95 Stat. 150
Aug. 14, 1981, P.L. 97-35, 95 Stat. 441
Aug. 14, 1981, P.L. 97-40, 95 Stat. 944
Oct. 15, 1982, P.L. 97-328, 96 Stat. 1626
June 12, 1984, P.L. 98-315, 98 Stat. 241
June 12, 1984, P.L. 98-316, 98 Stat. 242
Oct. 12, 1984, P.L. 98-473
Nov. 8, 1984, P.L. 98-621, 98 Stat. 3378
Oct. 18, 1986, P.L. 99-500, 100 Stat. 1783
Oct. 28, 1986, P.L. 99-573, 100 Stat. 3231, 3234
Sept. 20, 1988, P.L. 100-438, 102 Stat. 1718
Nov. 21, 1989, P.L. 101-168, 103 Stat. 1279
Dec. 12, 1989, P.L. 101-223, 103 Stat. 1901
Aug. 17, 1991, P.L. 102-102, 105 Stat. 495
Aug. 17, 1991, P.L. 102-106, 105 Stat. 539
Oct. 1, 1991, P.L. 102-111, 105 Stat. 569
Oct. 5, 1992, P.L. 102-382, 106 Stat. 1433
Oct. 19, 1994, P.L. 103-373, 108 Stat. 3488
April 17, 1995, P.L. 104-8, 109 Stat. 106

District of Columbia Snow and Ice Removal Acts
March 2, 1895, Ch. 178, 28 Stat. 809
March 2, 1897, Ch. 361, 29 Stat. 608

District of Columbia Spouse Equity Act of 1988
Oct. 16, 1992, P.L. 102-422, 106 Stat. 2167

District of Columbia Stadium Act of 1957
Oct. 29, 1986, P.L. 99-581, 100 Stat. 3313, 3314

District of Columbia Street Railway Act
May 23, 1908, Ch. 190, 35 Stat. 246

District of Columbia Supplemental Appropriations and Recissions Act, 1994
Sept. 30, 1994, P.L. 103-334, 108 Stat. 2595

District of Columbia Supplemental Appropriations and Rescissions Act, 1991
Oct. 1, 1991, P.L. 102-111, 105 Stat. 575

District of Columbia Supplemental Appropriations and Rescissions Act, 1992

Oct. 5, 1992, P.L. 102-382, 106 Stat. 1447

District of Columbia Supplemental Appropriations and Rescissions Act, 1993

Oct. 29, 1993, P.L. 103-127, 107 Stat. 1350

District of Columbia Tax Act

July 26, 1939, Ch. 367, 53 Stat. 1085
March 2, 1940, Ch. 37, 54 Stat. 38

District of Columbia Teachers' Leave Act of 1949

Aug. 5, 1955, Ch. 569, 69 Stat. 530
May 27, 1968, P.L. 90-319, 82 Stat. 132

District of Columbia Teachers' Retirement Acts

Jan. 15, 1920, Ch. 39, 41 Stat. 387
May 22, 1970, P.L. 91-263, 84 Stat. 257

District of Columbia Teachers' Salary Act of 1945

July 21, 1945, Ch. 321, 59 Stat. 488
July 24, 1945, Ch. 326-A, 59 Stat. 502

District of Columbia Teachers' Salary Act of 1947

July 7, 1947, Ch. 208, 61 Stat. 248
Oct. 8, 1951, Ch. 448, 65 Stat. 368
Oct. 24, 1951, Ch. 541, 65 Stat. 603
March 3, 1952, Ch. 73, 66 Stat. 11

District of Columbia Teachers' Salary Act of 1955

Aug. 5, 1955, Ch. 569, 69 Stat. 521
Aug. 28, 1958, P.L. 85-836, 72 Stat. 1004
Oct. 24, 1962, P.L. 87-881, 76 Stat. 1229
Nov. 13, 1966, P.L. 89-810, 80 Stat. 1594
May 27, 1968, P.L. 90-319, 82 Stat. 132
June 30, 1970, P.L. 91-297, 84 Stat. 358

District of Columbia Tissue Bank Act

Sept. 10, 1962, P.L. 87-656, 76 Stat. 534
May 26, 1970, P.L. 91-268, 84 Stat. 270
July 29, 1970, P.L. 91-358, 84 Stat. 579

District of Columbia Traffic Act, 1925

March 3, 1925, Ch. 443, 43 Stat. 1119
April 20, 1948, Ch. 215, 62 Stat. 173
Aug. 16, 1954, Ch. 741, 68 Stat. 732
July 24, 1956, Ch. 695, 70 Stat. 633
Oct. 3, 1962, P.L. 87-737, 76 Stat. 710
Oct. 3, 1962, P.L. 87-745, 76 Stat. 742
July 29, 1970, P.L. 91-358, 84 Stat. 583

District of Columbia Unemployment Compensation Act

Aug. 28, 1935, Ch. 794, 49 Stat. 946
April 22, 1940, Ch. 127, 54 Stat. 149
July 2, 1940, Ch. 524, 54 Stat. 730
June 4, 1943, Ch. 117, 57 Stat. 100
Aug. 31, 1954, Ch. 1139, 68 Stat. 988
July 25, 1956, Ch. 724, 70 Stat. 643
Nov. 10, 1966, P.L. 89-803, 80 Stat. 1520

District of Columbia Uniform Act on Fresh Pursuit

July 26, 1939, Ch. 375, 53 Stat. 1124
July 29, 1970, P.L. 91-358, 84 Stat. 654

District of Columbia Uniform Commercial Code

Dec. 30, 1963, P.L. 88-243, 77 Stat. 630

District of Columbia Uniform Controlled Substances Act of 1981

Dec. 12, 1989, P.L. 101-223, 103 Stat. 1902

District of Columbia Uniform Fiduciaries Act

Sept. 14, 1965, P.L. 89-183, 79 Stat. 776

District of Columbia Uniform Gifts to Minors Act

Oct. 15, 1962, P.L. 87-821, 76 Stat. 938
Sept. 14, 1965, P.L. 89-183, 79 Stat. 744

District of Columbia Uniform Limited Partnership Act

Sept. 28, 1962, P.L. 87-716, 76 Stat. 655
July 29, 1970, P.L. 91-358, 84 Stat. 589

District of Columbia Uniform Narcotic Drug Act

June 20, 1938, Ch. 532, 52 Stat. 785
Continued

July 29, 1970, P.L. 91-358, 84 Stat. 574

District of Columbia Uniform Partnership Act
Sept. 27, 1962, P.L. 87-709, 76 Stat. 636

District of Columbia Uniform Simultaneous Death Act
Sept. 14, 1965, P.L. 89-183, 79 Stat. 700

District of Columbia Use Tax Act
May 27, 1949, Ch. 146, 63 Stat. 124
March 31, 1956, Ch. 154, 70 Stat. 81
Jan. 5, 1971, P.L. 91-650, 84 Stat. 1932

District of Columbia Water and Sewer Authority Act of 1996
Aug. 6, 1996, P.L. 104-184, 110 Stat. 1696
D.C. Code Ann., §§ 43-1675, 47-301 et seq.

District of Columbia Work Release Act
Nov. 10, 1966, P.L. 89-803, 80 Stat. 1519

District of Columbia Zoning Act
March 1, 1920, Ch. 92, 41 Stat. 500

District Organization Law
Cal. Government Code § 58000 et seq.

District Permanent Care and Improvement Fund Act (Public Cemetery)
Mont. Code Ann., 7-35-2101 et seq.

District Reorganization Act
Cal. Government Code § 56000 et seq.

District Revenue Act (Drainage)
Wash. Rev. Code Ann., 85.32.010 et seq.

Districting Act (Congressional)
See Congressional Districting Act

Districting Act (General Court)
Mass. Gen. Laws Ann., 57:3, 57:4

Districting Act (Legislative)
Conn. Gen. Stat. Ann., § 9-9
Ga. Code Ann., 21-2-4
Ill. Rev. Stat. 1991, Ch. 46, § 801
Iowa Code Ann., 41.1, 41.2
N.H. Rev. Stat. 1955, 662:1

Tenn. Code Ann., 3-1-101 et seq.
Wis. Stat. Ann., 4.001 et seq.

Districts Act (Judicial)
Tex. Government Code, § 24.301 et seq.

Districts Act for Counties (Recreation)
Wash. Rev. Code Ann., 36.69.900

Districts Securities Commission Law
Cal. Water Code § 20000 et seq.

Disturbances Act
Wash. Rev. Code Ann., 9.27.015 et seq.

Disturbing the Peace Act
La. Rev. Stat. Ann., 14:103
Miss. Code Ann. 1972, §§ 97-35-15, 97-35-5, 97-35-3

Ditch Act
Minn. Stat. 1988, 106A.005 et seq.
Wash. Rev. Code Ann., 85.28.010 et seq.

Ditch or Drainage Act
Ohio Rev. Code 1953, 6131.01 et seq.

Diversion Act (Anti-Drug)
Okla. Stat. Ann., Title 63, § 2-309A et seq.

Diversion Loan Act (Worcester)
Mass. Acts 1956, Ch. 15

Diversity Conservation Act (Biological)
Mich. Comp. Laws Ann., 299.231 et seq.

Divestiture Act (Penn's Estate)
Pa. Purdon's Stat., Title 64, § 1 et seq.

Dividend Housing Corporation Act (Limited)
Cal. Health and Safety Code § 34800 et seq.

Dividend Privilege Tax Act
Wis. Laws 1935, Ch. 505, § 3

Dividends in Liquidation Proceedings Act (Secured Creditors)
Wis. Stat. Ann., 128.25

Dividends Tax Act
Haw. Rev. Laws 1955, § 120-1 et seq.

Division Engineers Act (Irrigation)
Colo. Rev. Stat. 1963, 148-12-1 et seq.

Division Fence Act
Mo. Rev. Stat., 272.060 et seq.

Division of Assets Act
Kan. Stat. Ann., 39-785 et seq.

Division of Developmental Disabilities Act
N.J. Stat. Ann., 30:6D-23 et seq., 30:60-1 et seq.

Division of Economic Assistance Act (Department of Honor Services)
N.J. Stat. Ann., 30:4B-1 et seq.

Division of Hospitals Act
Ark. Stat. 1947, 82-301 et seq.

Division of Hospitals and Nursing Homes Act
Ark. Code Ann. 1987, 20-9-201 et seq.

Division of Income for Tax Purposes Act
See also Uniform Division of Income for Tax Purposes Act
Ariz. Rev. Stat. Ann., § 43-1131 et seq.
Mont. Code Ann., 15-31-301 et seq.
N.D. Cent. Code, 57-38.1-01 et seq.
Va. Code 1950, § 58-131.1 et seq.

Division of Legislative Districts Act
Ill. Rev. Stat. 1991, Ch. 46, § 810 et seq.

Division of Occupational and Professional Licensing Act
Utah Code Ann. 1953, 53-1-101 et seq., 58-1-1 et seq.

Division of Travel and Tourism Act
N.J. Stat. Ann. 34:1A-45 et seq.

Division of Trusts Act (Trustee)
Ark. Code 1987, 28-69-701 et seq.

Division of Vocational Rehabilitation Act
S.D. Codified Laws 1967, 28-9-23 et seq.

Division on Alcoholism and Drug Abuse Act
Neb. Rev. Stat. 1943, 83-158.01 et seq.

Division on Deafness Act
Mich. Comp. Laws Ann., 408.201 et seq.

Division on Women Act
N.J. Stat. Ann., 52:27D-43.8 et seq.

Divorce Act
Ala. Code 1975, § 30-2-1 et seq.
Alaska Stat. 1962, § 25.24.010 et seq.
Ariz. Rev. Stat. Ann., § 25-311 et seq.
Cal. Civil Code §§ 4500 et seq., 4425 et seq.
Colo. Rev. Stat., 14-10-101 et seq.
Conn. Gen. Stat. Ann., § 46b-40 et seq.
D.C. Code 1973, § 16-901 et seq.
Fla. Stat. Ann., 61.001 et seq.
Ga. Code Ann., 19-5-1 et seq.
Haw. Rev. Stat. Ann., § 580-41 et seq.
Ill. Rev. Stat. 1991, Ch. 40, § 401 et seq.
Ind. Code Ann., 31-1-23-1 et seq.
Iowa Code 1983, 598.1 et seq.
Kan. Stat. Ann., 60-1601 et seq.
Ky. Rev. Stat. 1971, 403.010 et seq.
La. Rev. Stat. Ann., 9:301 et seq.
Mass. Gen. Laws Ann., 208:1 et seq.
Md. Ann. Code 1974, Art. FL § 7-101 et seq.
Me. Rev. Stat. Ann. 1964, Title 19, § 661 et seq.
Mich. Comp. Laws Ann., 552.1 et seq.
Minn. Stat. Ann., 518.002 et seq.
Miss. Code Ann. 1972, § 93-5-1 et seq.
Mo. Rev. Stat., 452.300 et seq.
Mont. Code Ann., 40-4-101 et seq.
N.C. Gen. Stat. 1943, § 50-2 et seq.
N.D. Cent. Code, 14-05-01 et seq.
Neb. Rev. Stat. 1943, 42-347 et seq.
Nev. Rev. Stat. Ann., 125.005 et seq.
N.H. Rev. Stat. 1955, 458:4 et seq.
N.J. Rev. Stat. 1937, 2A34-1 et seq.
N.M. Stat. Ann., 40-4-1 et seq.
N.Y. Domestic Relations Law (Consol. Laws Ch. 14) § 170 et seq.
Ohio Rev. Code 1953, 3105.01 et seq.
Okla. Stat. Ann., Title 43, § 101 et seq.
Ore. Rev. Stat., 107.010 et seq.
Continued

Pa. Cons. Stat., Title 23, § 3101 et seq.
R.I. Gen. Laws 1956, 15-5-1 et seq.
S.C. Code Ann. 1976, § 20-3-10 et seq.
S.D. Codified Laws 1967, 25-4-1 et seq.
Tenn. Code Ann., 36-4-101 et seq.
Tex. Family Code, § 3.01 et seq.
Utah Code Ann. 1953, 30-3-1 et seq.
Vt. Stat. Ann., Title 15, § 551 et seq.
Wis. Stat. Ann., 767.001 et seq.
W. Va. Code 1966, § 48-2-1 et seq.
Wyo. Stat. Ann., § 20-2-104 et seq.

Divorce Act (Servicemen)
Okla. Stat. Ann., Title 43, § 102
Tex. Family Code, § 3.23

Divorce and Alimony Act
Ark. Code Ann. 1987, 9-12-302 et seq.
Colo. Rev. Stat., 14-10-101

Divorce and Annulment Act
Del. Code of 1974, Title 13, § 1501 et seq.

Divorce and Marriage Act
Ariz. Rev. Stat. Ann., § 25-311 et seq.
Colo. Rev. Stat. 14-2-101 et seq., 14-10-101
et seq.
D.C. Code Ann., § 16-901 et seq.
Ill. Rev. Stat. 1991, Ch. 40, § 101 et seq.
Ky. Rev. Stat. 1971, 403.010, 403.110 et seq.

Divorce and Separation Act
R.I. Gen. Laws 1956, 15-5-1 et seq.

Divorce Cooling Off Act
Cal. Civil Code § 5000

Divorce for Divorce Act
Fla. Stat. 1965, 65.04, Subsec. 8

Divorce Injunction Act
Ill. Rev. Stat. 1991, Ch. 40, § 701

Divorce Investigation Act
Ohio Civ. Rule 75(D)

Divorce Lien Act
Ariz. Rev. Stat. Ann., § 25-318

Divorce Partition Act (Property)
Pa. Purdon's Stat., Title 68, § 501 et seq.

Divorce Proctor Act
Tenn. Acts 1915, Ch. 121

Divorce Recognition Act
See also Uniform Divorce Recognition Act.
La. Acts 1952, No. 241
Wash. Rev. Code 1951, 26.08.200,
26.08.210 et seq.

Divorce Reform Act
N.Y. Domestic Relations Law (Consol. Laws
Ch. 14), §§ 170, Subd. 5, 6, 210, 211, 230,
235
Wis. Stat. Ann., 767.001 et seq.

Divorce Registry Act
Cal. Civil Code § 4100 et seq.
Ill. Rev. Stat. 1991, Ch. 40, § 900 et seq.

Divorce Statute (Military Personnel)
N.M. Stat. Ann., 40-4-5

Divorced Spouse Act (Probate)
Fla. Stat. Ann., 732.507

Dixon-Zenovich-Maddy California Arts Act
Cal. Government Code § 8750 et seq.

DNA and Genetic Marker Database Act
Ida. Code 1947, 19-5501 et seq.

DNA Database and Databank Act
Me. Rev. Stat. Ann. 1964, Title 25, § 1571 et
seq.
N.J. Stat. Ann., 53:1-20.17 et seq.
W. Va. Code 1966, § 15-2B-1 et seq.

**DNA Detection of Sexual and Violent
Offenders Act**
Ark. Code 1987, 12-12-1101 et seq.
Neb. Rev. Stat. 1943, 29-4101 to 29-4115
Pa. Purdon's Stat., Title 35, § 7651.101 et
seq.

DNA Identification Act
N.M. Stat. Ann., 29-16-1 to 29-16-13

DNA Identification Act of 1994
Sept. 13, 1994, P.L. 103-322, 42 U.S. Code §§ 3751, 3753, 3793, 3796kk et seq., 3797, 13701 nt., 14131 et seq.

DNA Identification Profiling System Act
Mich. Comp. Laws Ann., 28.171 et seq.

Do-It-Yourself School Funding Fund
Ill. Comp. Stat. 1992, Ch. 30, §§ 105/5.449, 105/6z-42; Ch. 35, § 5/245

Do Not Resuscitate Act
W. Va. Code 1966 § 16-30C-1 et seq.

Do Not Resuscitate Order Act (General Medical Services)
S.C. Code Ann. 1976, § 44-78-10 et seq.

Dock and Harbor Acts
P.R. Laws Ann. 1954, Title 23, §§ 381 et seq., 2101 et seq.

Dock Seizure Act
Haw. Session Laws 1951, Act 209

Dockery Act (Accounting)
July 31, 1894, Ch. 174, 28 Stat. 205, 22 U.S. Code § 1191; 25 U.S. Code §§ 96, 97; 31 U.S. Code §§ 48, 50, 72, 74 to 76, 78, 84, 86 to 88, 93, 147, 150, 162, 496, 506, 514; 41 U.S. Code §§ 20, 21; 42 U.S . Code § 112; 43 U.S. Code § 14

Docks Act
Ala. Code 1975, § 33-2-1 et seq.

Docks Acts
Ala. Code 1975, 33-2-30 et seq., 33-2-60 et seq., 33-2-90 et seq.

Doctor Bill Filante California Winegrape Local Commission Act
Cal. Statutes 1989, Ch. 854
Cal. Statutes 1992, Ch. 998

Doctor Good Samaritan Law
N.Y. Education Law 1947 (Consol. Laws Ch. 16) § 6527, Subd. 2

Doctoral Assistance Act (Minority)
N.M. Stat. Ann., 21-21I-1 et seq.

Doctors Draft Act
Sept. 9, 1950, Ch. 939, 64 Stat. 826, 50 U.S. Code Appx. §§ 454, 454a, 454b
June 29, 1953, Ch. 158, 67 Stat. 87, 50 U.S. Code Appx. § 454a
June 18, 1954, Ch. 307, 68 Stat. 254, 50 U.S. Code Appx. § 454a

Doctors Immunity Act
Conn. Gen. Stat. Ann., § 52-557b

Doctors Lien Act
Ill. Rev. Stat. 1991, Ch. 82, § 101.1 et seq.

Doctor's Title Act
Okla. Stat. Ann., Title 59, § 725.1 et seq.

Doctrine of Worthier Title Abolishment Act
Ill. Rev. Stat. 1991, Ch. 30, § 187.9 et seq.

Documentary Heritage Act
N.Y. Education Law 1947 (Consol. Laws Ch. 16) § 140

Documentary Letters of Credit Act
Pa. Cons. Stat., Title 13, § 5101 et seq.

Documentary Stamp Act
Neb. Rev. Stat. 1943, 76-901 et seq.

Documentary Stamp Act (Minerals)
Miss. Code Ann. 1972, § 27-31-71 et seq.

Documentary Stamp Tax Act
Cal. Revenue and Taxation Code § 11901 et seq.
Fla. Stat. Ann., 201.01 et seq.
Haw. Session Laws 1876, Ch. 55
Mich. Comp. Laws Ann., 207.501 et seq.
N.Y. Tax Law (Consol. Laws Ch. 60) § 270 et seq.
Pa. 1935 Pamph. Laws 203, No. 90
S.C. Code Ann. 1976, § 12-21-310 et seq.

Documentary Transfer Tax Act
Cal. Revenue and Taxation Code § 11901 et seq.

Documents Act
D.C. Code Ann., §§ 1-1531 et seq., 1-1611, 1-1612
Md. Ann. Code 1974, Art. SG, § 7-201 et seq.
Pa. Purdon's Stat., Title 45, § 1101 et seq.

Documents Act (Government)
Ga. Code Ann., 50-18-50 et seq.

Documents Inspection Act
Cal. Code of Civil Procedure § 2031

Documents of Title Act
See also Uniform Commercial Code-Documents of Title
La. Rev. Stat. Ann., 10:7-101 et seq.
Mass. Gen. Laws, 1990, 106:7-101 et seq.
Pa. Cons. Stat., Title 13, § 7101 et seq.
S.C. Code Ann. 1976, § 36-7-101 et seq.

Dodd Act (Taxation)
Ohio Laws Vol. 112, p. 501

Dodge Act (Settlement of Estates)
Mich. Comp. Laws Ann., 701.1 et seq.

Dog Act
Cal. Food and Agricultural Code § 30501 et seq.
Cal. Health and Safety Code § 25970 et seq.
Conn. Gen. Stat. Ann., § 22-327 et seq.
Mass. Gen. Laws Ann., 140:136A et seq.
Mich. Comp. Laws Ann., 287.261 et seq.
Ohio Rev. Code 1953, 955.01 et seq.
Pa. Purdon's Stat., Title 3, § 459-101 et seq.
R.I. Gen. Laws 1956, 4-13-1 et seq.
Tenn. Code Ann., 70-4-122
Va. Code 1950, § 29-213.5 et seq.

Dog Act (Personal Injuries)
Ill. Rev. Stat. 1991, Ch. 8, § 366

Dog Act (Rabies Control)
W. Va. Code 1966, § 19-20A-1 et seq.

Dog Act (Research Laboratories)
Ill. Rev. Stat. 1991, Ch. 111 1/2, § 128 et seq.

Dog and Cat Humane Death Act
Tenn. Code Ann., 44-17-301 et seq.

Dog and Cat Sterilization Act
Okla. Stat. Ann., Title 4, § 499 et seq.

Dog and Horse Lien Act
S.C. Code Ann. 1976, § 29-15-60

Dog Bite Act (Liability)
Ariz. Rev. Stat. Ann., § 24-521 et seq.
Cal. Civil Code § 3342
Ky. Rev. Stat. 1971, 258.275
Mass. Gen. Laws Ann., 140:155
N.J. Stat. Ann., 4:19-16

Dog Collar and Tag Act
N.C. Gen. Stat. 1943, § 67-6

Dog Game and Inland Fish Act
Ga. Code Ann., 4-8-20 et seq.
Va. Code 1950, § 29-1 et seq.

Dog Injury Act
Conn. Gen. Stat. Ann., 22-355 et seq.

Dog Inoculation Act
S.C. Code Ann. 1976, § 47-5-60 et seq.

Dog Licensing Act
Ky. Rev. Stat. 1971, 258.135 et seq.
Md. Ann. Code 1957, Art. 56, § 191 et seq.
Me. Rev. Stat. Ann. 1964, Title 7, § 3942 et seq., § 3921
N.H. Rev. Stat. 1955, 466:1 et seq.
N.Y. Agriculture and Markets Law (Consol. Laws, Ch. 69) § 106 et seq.
Ore. Rev. Stat. 1953, 609.100 et seq.

Dog or Horse Racing Act
Fla. Stat. Ann., 550.011 et seq.
Vt. Stat. Ann., Title 31, § 601 et seq.

Dog Racing Act
Ariz. Rev. Stat. Ann., § 5-101 et seq.
N.H. Rev. Stat. 1955, 284:1 et seq.
Vt. Stat. Ann., Title 31, § 601 et seq.

Dog Registration Act
Tex. Health and Safety, § 822.027
W. Va. Code 1966, § 19-20-1 et seq.

Dog Tax Act
Ala. General Acts 1919, p. 1077, No. 728
D.C. Code 1973, § 47-2001 et seq.
S.C. Code Ann. 1976, § 12-37-890

Dog Tax and Liability Act
N.J. Stat. Ann., 4:19-1 et seq.

Doing Business Act (Corporations)
Ga. Code Ann., 14-2-230 et seq.
Kan. Stat. Ann., 17-7303 et seq.
Ky. Rev. Stat. 1971, 271.610

Doing Business Act (Foreign Corporations)
Ariz. Rev. Stat. Ann., § 10-106 et seq.
N.Y. Business Corporation Law (Consol.
  Laws Ch. 4) § 1301 et seq
Okla. Stat. 1971, Title 18, § 1135

Doing Business Act (Process)
Ala. Code 1975, § 10-2A-235 et seq.
Cal. Corporations Code § 2100 et seq.
Fla. Stat. Ann., 48.181 et seq.
N.H. Rev. Stat. 1955, 293-A:119
Ohio Rev. Code 1953, 1703.19 et seq.
Vt. Stat. Ann., Title 12, § 855 et seq.

Doing Business Service Act (Venue, Nonresidents)
Miss. Code Ann. 1972, §§ 11-11-11, 13-3-57

DOJAA
See Department Of Justice Appropriation
  Act, 1987

Dollar-a-Day Act
Ark. Code Ann. 1987, 14-55-603

Dollar Adjustment Act
S.C. Code Ann. 1976, § 37-1-109 et seq.

Dollar and Half Tax Act
Ind. Burns' 1933, 64-307 et seq.

Dollinger Act (Food and Drugs)
See Federal Food, Drug, and Cosmetic Act

Aug. 31, 1957, P.L. 85-250, 71 Stat. 567

Dolphin Protection Consumer Information Act
Nov. 28, 1990, P.L. 101-627, 16 U.S. Code
  § 1385
Aug. 15, 1997, P.L. 105-42, 16 U.S. Code
  § 1385

Dolwig Act (San Francisco Bay)
Cal. Streets and Highways Code § 30651 et
  seq.

Dolwig-Davis Act (Water Projects)
Cal. Water Code § 11900 et seq.

Dolwig-Porter Ground Water Basin Protection Law
Cal. Water Code § 12920 et seq.

Domain Act (Eminent)
N.Y. Highway Law (Consol. Laws Ch. 25),
  § 29

Domestic Abuse Act
Ark. Acts 1989, No. 636
Iowa Code 1983, 236.1 et seq.
Minn. Stat. Ann., 518B.01
Neb. Rev. Stat. 1943, 42-901
S.C. Code Ann. 1976, § 16-25-10 et seq.

Domestic Abuse and Neglect of Adults with Disabilities Study and Demonstration Program Act
Ill. Rev. Stat. 1991, Ch. 23, § 3381 et seq.

Domestic Abuse Insurance Protection Act
N.M. Stat. Ann., 59A-16B-1 to 59A-16B-10

Domestic Abuse Prevention and Intervention Act
P.R. Acts 1989, No. 54

Domestic Abuse Protection Act
Miss. Code Ann. 1972, § 93-21-1 et seq.
Neb. Rev. Stat. 1943, 42-901 et seq.
Okla. Stat. Ann., Title 22, § 60 et seq.
S.D. Codified Laws 1967, 25-10-1 et seq.

Domestic Abuse Reporting Act
Okla. Stat. Ann., Title 22, § 40.5 et seq.

Domestic and Foreign Investment Improved Disclosure Act
Dec. 19, 1977, P.L. 95-213, 15 U.S. Code §§ 78a nt., 78m et seq.

Domestic and Juvenile Relations Courts Act
S.C. Code Ann. 1976, § 14-21-10 et seq.

Domestic Animal and Poultry Disease Act
Ind. Code Ann., 15-2.1-1-1 et seq.

Domestic Animal Fund Act
Iowa Code 1983, 352.1 et seq.

Domestic Animals and Wildlife Act (Rabies Prevention and Control)
Pa. Purdon's Stat., Title 3, § 455.1 et seq.

Domestic Animals Disease Act
Neb. Rev. Stat. 1943, 54-701 et seq.

Domestic Animals Poisoning Act
Ohio Rev. Code 1953, 959.03

Domestic Chemical Diversion Control Act of 1993
Dec. 17, 1993, P.L. 103-200, 21 U.S. Code § 801 nt.
Sept. 13, 1994, P.L. 103-322, 21 U.S. Code §§ 802, 960, 971

Domestic Commerce Act
N.Y. General Business Law (Consol. Laws Ch. 20)

Domestic Corporations Act
Ind. Code Ann., 23-1-17-3, 23-7-1.1-1 et seq.

Domestic Housing and International Recovery and Financial Stability Act
Nov. 30, 1983, P.L. 98-181, 12 U.S. Code § 1701 nt.

Domestic International Banking Facility Act
Ga. Code Ann., 7-1-730 et seq.

Domestic Minerals Program Extension Act of 1953
Aug. 7, 1953, Ch. 339, 67 Stat. 417, 50 U.S. Code Appx. §§ 2181 to 2183

Domestic Products Preference Law
Iowa Code Ann., 73.1 et seq.

Domestic Products Procurement Act
Mo. Rev. Stat., 34.350 et seq.

Domestic Public Corporation Takeover Act
S.D. Codified Laws 1967 Miscellaneous Superseded, 47-32-1 et seq.

Domestic Relations Act
D.C. Code 1973, § 30-101 et seq.
N.Y. Consol. Laws Ch. 14
Ohio Rev. Code 1953, 3101.01 et seq.
Pa. Cons. Stat., Title 23, § 101 et seq.

Domestic Relations and Juvenile Court Act
N.J. Rev. Stat. 2A:4A-20 et seq.
Va. Code 1950, § 16.1-226 et seq.

Domestic Relations and Juvenile Court Act (Nashville)
Tenn. Private Acts 1947, Ch. 246, Art. 51

Domestic Relations Court Act
Ill. Rev. Stat. 1977, Ch. 37, § 105.19 et seq.
N.C. Gen. Stat. 1943, § 7-101 et seq.

Domestic Relations Court Act of the City of New York
N.Y. Laws 1933, Ch. 482

Domestic Relations Mediation Act
N.M. Stat. Ann., 40-12-1 et seq.

Domestic Relations Order Act (Eligible)
Mich. Comp. Laws Ann., 38.1701 et seq.

Domestic Tungsten, Asbestos, Fluorspar, and Columbium-Tantalum Production and Purchase Act of 1956
July 19, 1956, Ch. 638, 70 Stat. 579

Domestic Violence Act
Ill. Rev. Stat. 1991, Ch. 40, § 2311-1 et seq.
Ohio Rev. Code 1953, 3113.31 et seq.
W. Va. Code, § 48-2C-1 et seq.

Domestic Violence Act (Law Enforcement Response to)

Cal. Penal Code § 13700

Domestic Violence Act of 1989

W. Va. Code 1966, § 48-2C-1 et seq.

Domestic Violence and Family Protection Intervention Act

N.Y. Criminal Procedure Law (Consol. Laws Ch. 11A) §§ 30.30, 60.46, 100.07, 140.10, 170.55, 530.11, 530.12

N.Y. Domestic Relations Law (Consol. Laws Ch. 14) § 252

N.Y. Executive Law 1951 (Consol. Laws Ch. 18) §§ 214b, 837, 840

N.Y. Family Court Act, §§ 115, 154b, 155, 812 to 815, 821a, 826 to 828, 841, 842, 845 to 847

N.Y. Judiciary Law (Consol. Laws Ch. 30) §§ 212, 216, 254a

N.Y. Penal Law 1965 (Consol. Laws Ch. 40) §§ 120.14, 215.51

N.Y. Public Health Law 1953 (Consol. Laws Ch. 45)§ 2803

Domestic Violence Crime Prevention Act

Ida. Code 1947, 39-6301 et seq.

Domestic Violence Prevention Act

Cal. Code of Civil Procedure § 540 et seq.

Cal. Family Code § 6200 et seq.

N.J. Stat. Ann. 2C:25-1 et seq.

N.Y. Social Services Law (Consol. Laws Ch. 55), § 459a et seq.

Wash. Rev. Code Ann., 10.99.010 et seq., 26.50.010 et seq.

Domestic Violence Prevention and Victim Protection Act

Alaska Stat. 1962, § 18.66.010 et seq.

Domestic Violence Shelters Act

Ill. Rev. Stat. 1991, Ch. 40, § 2400 et seq.

Domestic Violence Victim Shelter Act

Ohio Rev. Code 1953, 3113.33 et seq.

Domestic Volunteer Service Act Amendments of 1979

Dec. 13, 1979, P.L. 96-143, 42 U.S. Code §§ 4951 nt., 4953, 4955, 4958, 4973, 4974, 4992, 5043, 5044, 5050, 5051, 5055, 5057, 5058, 5060, 5063, 5064, 5081, 5084

Domestic Volunteer Service Act Amendments of 1984

May 21, 1984, P.L. 98-288, 42 U.S. Code § 6951 nt.

Oct. 27, 1986, P.L. 99-551, 42 U.S. Code § 5024

Domestic Volunteer Service Act Amendments of 1986

Oct. 27, 1986, P.L. 99-551, 42 U.S. Code § 4950 nt.

Domestic Volunteer Service Act Amendments of 1989

Dec. 7, 1989, P.L. 101-204, 42 U.S. Code § 4950 nt.

Sept. 21, 1993, P.L. 103-82, 42 U.S. Code § 4954 nt.

Domestic Volunteer Service Act Amendments of 1993

Sept. 21, 1993, P.L. 103-82, 42 U.S. Code §§ 4950 nt.; 4951 et seq.

Domestic Volunteer Service Act of 1973

Oct. 1, 1973, P.L. 93-113, 87 Stat. 394, 5 U.S. Code § 8332; 42 U.S. Code §§ 3067, 4951 to 4957, 4971 to 4974, 4991, 4992, 5001, 5011, 5012, 5021 to 5023, 5031, 5032, 5041 to 5062, 5081 to 5085

July 12, 1974, P.L. 93-351, 88 Stat. 357, 42 U.S. Code § 5001

Oct. 18, 1978, P.L. 95-478, 42 U.S. Code §§ 5001, 5011, 5012, 5082

Dec. 13, 1979, P.L. 96-143, 42 U.S. Code §§ 4953, 4955, 4958, 4973, 4974, 4992, 5043, 5044, 5050, 5051, 5055, 5057, 5058, 5060, 5063, 5064, 5081

May 21, 1984, P.L. 98-288, 42 U.S. Code §§ 4951 to 4956, 5041, 5042, 5081, 5082

Oct. 27, 1986, P.L. 99-551, 42 U.S. Code §§ 4950, 5011 nt., 5013, 5056

Oct. 27, 1986, P.L. 99-570, 42 U.S. Code § 4994

Continued

Nov. 18, 1988, P.L. 100-690, 42 U.S. Code
§ 4994, 5081

Dec. 7, 1989, P.L. 101-204, generally 42
U.S. Code § 4951 et seq.

Nov. 16, 1990, P.L. 101-610, 42 U.S. Code
§§ 5091, 5091a to 5091n

March 12, 1991, P.L. 102-10, 42 U.S. Code
§ 5091m

July 25, 1991, P.L. 102-73, 42 U.S. Code
§§ 4995, 5081

Sept. 21, 1993, P.L. 103-82, 42 U.S. Code
§§ 5041, 5042

Aug. 23, 1994, P.L. 103-304, 42 U.S. Code
§§ 4953, 5024

Dec. 21, 1995, P.L. 104-66, 42 U.S. Code
§ 5026

Aug. 7, 1998, P.L. 105-220, 42 U.S. Code
§ 5061

Oct. 21, 1998, P.L. 105-277, 42 U.S. Code
§§ 4953, 4959

**Domestic Water System Revenue Bond Act
(Irrigation District)**
Ida. Code 1947, 43-1907 et seq.

Domestic Wine Act
Ga. Code Ann., 3-6-1, 3-6-2, 3-6-3
N.M. Stat. 1978, 60-6A-21 et seq.

Domestic Winery and Small Brewery Act
N.M. Stat. Ann., 60-6A-21 et seq.

Domesticated Wild Animals Act
Ill. Rev. Stat. 1991, Ch. 8, § 23y et seq.

Domestication Act (Foreign Corporations)
Va. Code 1950, § 13.1-102 et seq.

Domestication Act (Foreign Railroads)
S.C. Acts 1896, p. 114, No. 50

Domicile Act
Mont. Code Ann., 1-1-215

Domiciliary Home Act (Veterans')
Fla. Stat. Ann., 296.01 et seq.

Dominick Act (Motor Carriers)
Ala. Code 1975, § 37-3-1 et seq.

Dominion Statute (Adverse Possession)
Tex. Rev. Civ. Stat., Art. 5519a

Donahoe Higher Education Act
Cal. Education Code 1976, § 66000 et seq.

Donated Food Limited Liability Act
Pa. Purdon's Stat., Title 10, § 351 et seq.

Donation Act
Ark. Stat. 1947, 10-905 et seq.

Donation Acts (Public Lands)
Sept. 27, 1850, Ch. 76, 9 Stat. 496
Feb. 14, 1853, Ch. 69, 10 Stat. 158
July 17, 1854, Ch. 84, 10 Stat. 305

Donation of Medical Devices Act
Tex. Civil Practice and Remedies Code,
§§ 88.001 to 88.003

Donation Solicitation Law
Iowa Code Ann., 122.1 et seq.

Donee Act
Miss. Code Ann. 1972, § 89-1-15

Donlan Act (White Slavery)
Mont. Rev. Code 1947, 94-4109 et seq.

Donnelly Amendment.
Oct. 7, 1980, P.L. 96-387, 46 U.S. Code
Appx. 1121-1

Donnelly Antimonopoly Act
N.Y. General Business Law (Consol. Laws,
Ch. 20) § 340 et seq.

Donnelly Antitrust Act
N.Y. General Business Law (Consol. Laws,
Ch. 20) § 340 et seq.

Donnelly-Baginsky Act (Municipal Courts)
Mich. Comp. Laws Ann., 725.7, 725.23 et
seq.

Donnelly Conspiracy Act
N.Y. General Business Law (Consol. Laws,
Ch. 20) § 340 et seq.

Donner Summit Public Utility District Act
Cal. Water Code, Appendix, § 58-1 et seq.

Donohue-Lockwood Law (Teachers' Salaries)
N.Y. Education Law 1947 (Consol. Laws Ch. 16) § 3101 et seq.

Donor Act (Bone Marrow)
S.C. Code Ann. 1976, § 44-43-60 et seq.

Donor Act (Good Faith)
Tex. Civil Practice and Remedies Code, § 76.002

Donor and Donee Act (Good Faith)
D.C. Code Ann., §§ 33-801, 33-802

Donors Act
Mont. Code Ann. 1987, 27-1-716

Door Closing Act (Deficiency Judgments)
N.C. Gen. Stat. 1943, § 45-21.38

Door Closing Act (Foreign Corporations)
Miss. Code Ann. 1972, § 79-11-363 et seq.

Door Closing Act (Venue)
S.C. Code Ann. 1976, § 15-5-150

Door to Door Home Repair Sales Act
N.J. Stat. Ann., 17:16C-95 et seq.

Door to Door Retail Installment Sales Act
N.J. Stat. Ann., 17:16C-61.1 et seq.

Door to Door Sales Act
Iowa Code Ann., 82.1 et seq.
Md. Ann. Code 1974, Art. CL, § 14-301 et seq.
N.M. Stat. Ann., 57-12-21, 57-12-22
N.Y. Personal Property Law (Consol. Laws Ch. 41) § 425 et seq.
R.I. Gen. Laws 1956, 6-28-1 et seq.

Dorchester County Assessors Act
S.C. Code Ann. 1962, § 65-1811

Dormancy Act (Judgment Executions)
Okla. Stat. Ann., Title 12, § 735

Dormant Judgments Act
Ga. Code Ann., 9-12-60 et seq.
Kan. Stat. Ann., 60-2403
Neb. Rev. Stat. 1943, 25-1515
Ohio Rev. Code 1953, 2329.07
Okla. Stat. Ann., Title 12, § 735
Wash. Rev. Code Ann., 4.56.050 et seq.

Dormant Mineral Interests Act
Conn. Public Acts 1991, No. 283

Dormant Minerals Act
Mich. Comp. Laws Ann., 554.291 et seq.

Dormitory Authority Act
N.Y. Public Authorities Law (Consol. Laws Ch. 43A) § 1675 et seq.

Dormitory Bond Refunding Act
Okla. Stat. Ann., Title 70, § 1946.1 et seq.

Dormitory Revenue Bond Act
Cal. Education Code 1976, § 92400 et seq.

Dortch Ballot Law
Tenn. Code Ann., Superseded Vol., 2-1201 et seq.

Dothan Civil Service Act
Ala. Local Acts 1947, p. 196, No. 273

Dothan Pension Act
Ala. Acts 1953, p. 145

Double Damage Act
Ark. Code Ann. 1987, 723-12-908

Double Damage Act (Fires)
Ark. Code Ann. 1987, 20-22-304, 18-60-103.

Double Damage Act (Railroads)
Mo. Rev. Stat., 389.650, 537.270 et seq.

Double-Damage Act (Tenants)
Iowa Code Ann., 562.2

Double Dipping Act (Dual Offices)
La. Rev. Stat. Ann., 14:137

Double Election Board Act
Iowa Code Ann., 51.1 et seq.
Kan. Laws 1915, Ch. 205

Double Jeopardy Act
Ark. Code Ann. 1987, 5-1-112 et seq.
Cal. Penal Code §§ 687, 1023
Ida. Code 1947, 19-107, 19-1719
La. Code of Crim. Proc. 1966, Art. 591 et seq.
Mont. Code Ann., 46-11-501 et seq.
Nev. Rev. Stat. Ann., 174.085, 178.391
N.Y. Penal Law 1965 (Consol. Laws, Ch. 40) § 70.25, 75.10, 80.15
Vt. Stat. Ann., Title 13, § 6556 et seq.
Wash. Rev. Code Ann., 10.43.020 et seq.

Double Liability Act (Bank Stockholders)
Ky. Rev. Stat. 1971, 287.360
Miss. Code Ann. 1972, § 81-5-27
N.Y. Banking Law (Consol. Laws, Ch. 2) §§ 113a, 113b
Ohio Laws Vol. 108, p. 80 § 75

Double Punishment Act
Ariz. Rev. Stat. Ann., § 13-116

Double Rent Act
Ill. Rev. Stat. 1991, Ch. 110, § 9-203

Double-Time Act (Service by Mail)
S.C. Code Ann. 1976, § 15-9-950

Double Venue Act (Criminal)
Mont. Code Ann., 46-3-111 et seq.

Double Verdict Act (Homicide)
Pa. Cons. Stat., Title 42, § 9711

Doug Barnard, Jr. to 1996 Atlanta Centennial Olympic Games Commemorative Coin Act
Oct. 6, 1992, P.L. 102-390, 31 U.S. Code § 5112 nt.
Dec. 26, 1995, P.L. 104-74, 31 U.S. Code § 5112 nt.

Dougherty County School System Act
Ga. Laws 1951, p. 2233

Doughton Bond Limitation Act
See Second Liberty Bond Act

Doughton Current Tax Payment Act of 1943
See Current Tax Payment Act Of 1943

Doughton Unemployment Compensation Act
April 19, 1939, Ch. 73, 53 Stat. 581, 42 U.S. Code § 501

Douglas County Civil Service Act
Ga. Laws 1967, p. 2579

Douglas County Community Improvements Districts Act
Ga. Laws 1991, p. 3709

Douglas County-Douglasville Charter Commission Act
Ga. Laws 1991, p. 4297

Douglas County Emergency Communications Service District Act
Ga. Laws 1991, Ex. Sess., p. 46

Douglas County Lodgers Tax Law
Nev. Stat. 1969, Ch. 639, p. 1250

Douglasville-Douglas County Water and Sewer Authority Act
Ga. Laws 1985, p. 3584

Douglasville-Douglas County Water Authority Act
Ga. Laws 1974, p. 3376

Dower Act
Ark. Code Ann. 1987, 2-11-101 et seq.
Del. Code of 1974, Title 12, § 901 et seq.
Fla. Stat. 1973, 731.34 et seq.
Ga. Code 1933, 31-101 et seq.
Ill. Rev. Stat. 1991, Ch. 110 1/2, § 2-9 et seq.
Iowa Code Ann., 633.211 et seq.
Md. Ann. Code 1957, Art. 45, §§ 6,7
Mich. Comp. Laws Ann., 558.1 et seq.
Mont. Rev. Code 1947, 22-101 et seq.
N.C. Gen. Stat. 1943, §§ 30-4 to 30-14
N.H. Rev. Stat. 1955, 560:3 et seq.
N.J. Stat. Ann. 3B:28-1 et seq.

Ohio Rev. Code 1953, 5305.01 et seq.
Ore. Rev. Stat. 1953, 113.010
R.I. Gen. Laws 1956, 33-4-1 et seq.
Va. Code 1950, § 64.1-19 et seq.

Dower and Curtesy Law
Ky. Rev. Stat. 1971, 392.010 et seq.

Dower Renunciation Act
S.C. Code Ann. 1976, Superseded Vols.,
§ 21-5-110 et seq.

Dower Statute of Limitations
N.Y. Real Property Actions and Proceedings
Law (Consol. Laws Ch. 81) § 1001 et seq.

**Down-Payment System for Government
Purveyors of Goods and Services Act**
P.R. Acts 1989, No. 25

Downed Aircraft Search and Location Act
Cal. Public Utilities Code § 21500 et seq.

Downing Act (County Racing Commission)
Ala. Code 1958, App. 609 (147) et seq.

Downing Dram Shop Act
Mo. Laws 1883, p. 86

**Downing, Engel and Fite Act (Navigable
Waterway and Flood Control)**
Ala. Code 1975, § 33-17-1 et seq.

Downstate Forest Preserve District Act
Ill. Rev. Stat. 1991, Ch. 96 1/2, § 6300 et seq.

Downstate Public Transportation Act
Ill. Rev. Stat. 1991, Ch. 111 2/3, § 661 et seq.

Downtown Development Authorities Law
Colo. Rev. Stat., 31-25-801 et seq.
Ga. Code Ann., 36-42-1 et seq.

**Downtown Development Authority Act
(Bradenton)**
Fla. Special Laws 1974, Ch. 74-425

**Downtown Development Authority Act
(Delray Beach)**
Fla. Special Laws 1971, Ch. 71-604

**Downtown Development Authority Act
(Johnson City)**
Tenn. Private Acts 1985, Ch. 52

**Downtown Development Authority Act
(Lake Worth)**
Fla. Special Laws 1972, Ch. 72-592

**Downtown Development Authority Act
(Lakeland)**
Fla. Special Laws 1977, Ch. 77-588

**Downtown Development Authority Act
(Marianna)**
Fla. Special Laws 1973, Ch. 73-548

**Downtown Development Authority Act
(West Palm Beach)**
Fla. Special Laws 1967, Ch. 67-2170

**Downtown Development Board Act
(Clearwater)**
Fla. Special Laws 1970, Ch. 70-635

**Downtown Development Board Act (Winter
Haven)**
Fla. Special Laws 1970, Ch. 70-987

**Downtown Development Corporation Act
(Sanford)**
Fla. Special Laws 1976, Ch. 76-483

**Downtown Improvement and Parking
District Act**
Neb. Rev. Stat. 1943, 19-3401 et seq.

**Downtown Improvement Authority Act (St.
Petersburg)**
Fla. Special Laws 1974, Ch. 74-603

**Downtown Improvement Authority Act
(Tallahassee)**
Fla. Special Laws 1971, Ch. 71-935

**Downtown Improvement Board Act
(Panama City)**
Fla. Special Laws 1973, Ch. 73-585
Fla. Special Laws 1974, Ch. 74-571

Downtown Improvement Board Act (Pensacola)
Fla. Special Laws 1972, Ch. 72-655

Downtown Smyrma Development Authority Act
Ga. Laws 1991, p. 4382

Doyle Act (State Bondholders Committee)
Mich. Comp. Laws 1948, 451.351 et seq.

Doyle-Dernham Act (Hunting Licenses and Permits)
Mich. Comp. Laws Ann., 314.7 et seq.

Doyle-Neustein State Labor Relations Act
N.Y. Labor Law (Consol. Laws Ch. 31) § 700 et seq.

Doyle-Ployhar Act (Constitutional Amendments)
N.D. Laws 1911, Ch. 94

Doyle-Rees Health and Welfare Program Supervision Act
Cal. Insurance Code § 10640 et seq.

Doyle-Short Act (Community Mental Health Services)
Cal. Welfare and Institutions Code § 5600 et seq.

Dr. King's Birthday Act
D.C. Code Ann., §§ 1-504, 28-2701

Draft Act of 1942
See National Service Life Insurance Act Of 1940 and Selective Training and Service Act Of 1940

Draft Card Destruction Act
Ill. Rev. Stat. 1991, Ch. 38, §§ 90-10, 90-11

Draft Sales Act
P.R. Laws Ann. 1954, Title 10, § 111 et seq.

Drafted Persons Act (Municipal Liability)
Mich. Comp. Laws Ann., 123.401 et seq.

Drag Racing Act
Ohio Code 1953, 4511.251

Dragonetti Civil Proceedings Act
Pa. Cons. Stat., Title 42, § 8351 et seq.

Drainage Act
Ala. Code 1975, § 9-9-1 et seq.
Ark. Code Ann. 1987, 14-121-101, 14-121-201 et seq.
Conn. Gen. Stat. Ann., § 52-456 et seq.
Del. Code of 1974, Title 7, § 4101 et seq.
Ill. Rev. Stat. 1991, Ch. 42, § 1-1 et seq.
Kan. Stat. Ann., 24-101a et seq.
Mich. Comp. Laws Ann., 280.1 et seq.
Minn. Stat. 1988, 106A.005 et seq.
N.D. Cent. Code, 61-21-01 et seq.
Neb. Rev. Stat. 1943, 31-101 et seq.
Okla. Stat. Ann., Title 82, § 281 et seq.
S.C. Code Ann. 1976, § 49-11-10 et seq.
Vt. Stat. Ann., Title 10, § 851 et seq.
Wash. Rev. Code Ann., 85.28.010 et seq.

Drainage Act (Circuit Court)
Ind. Code Ann., 19-4-1-1 et seq.
Ky. Rev. Stat. 1971, 267.010 et seq.
Md. Ann. Code 1957, Art. 25, § 52 et seq.
Mo. Rev. Stat., 242.010 et seq.
N.C. Gen. Stat. 1943, §§ 156-1 to 156-141
N.J. Stat. Ann. 4:30-1 et seq.
N.Y. Environmental Conservation Law 1972, (Consol. Laws Ch. 43B) § 15-1903 et seq.

Drainage Act (Counties)
Neb. Rev. Stat. 1943, 31-901 et seq.

Drainage Act (County Court)
Mo. Rev. Stat., 243.010 et seq.

Drainage Act (Farm)
Wis. Stat. Ann., 88.01 et seq.

Drainage Act (Interstate)
S.D. Codified Laws 1967, 46A-13-1 et seq.

Drainage Act (Intrastate)
S.D. Codified Laws 1967, 46A-10-1 et seq.

Drainage Act (Mutual License)
Ill. Rev. Stat. 1953, Ch. 42, § 193 et seq.

Drainage and Conservancy Act
Minn. Stat. 1986, 111.01 et seq.

Drainage and Flood Act (Urban)
Miss. Code Ann. 1972, § 51-35-301 et seq.

Drainage and Flood Control Act
Mass. Acts 1955, Ch. 574 (Linden), (Spot Pond), (Townline Brooks)
Mass. Acts 1955, Ch. 743 (Neponset River)

Drainage and Flood Control Act (Urban)
Colo. Rev. Stat., 32-11-101 et seq.
Miss. Code Ann., § 51-35-301 et seq.

Drainage and Flood Control Loan Act
Mass. Acts 1963, Ch. 595

Drainage and Flood Planning Assessments Act (Joint)
N.M. Stat. Ann., 73-24-1 et seq.

Drainage and Stream Improvement Loan Act (Weymouth)
Mass. Acts 1958, Ch. 481
N.Y. Local Laws 1973, Town of Lewi

Drainage Corporation Act
Ind. Burns' 1933, 27-901 et seq.

Drainage District Act
Cal. Statutes 1885, p. 204
Cal. Statutes 1903, p. 291
Cal. Statutes 1919, p. 731
Cal. Statutes 1923, Ch. 102, p. 196
Cal. Water Code, Appx., §§ 5-1 et seq., 8-1 et seq., 31-1 et seq.
Colo. Rev. Stat., 37-20-101 et seq.
Fla. Stat. Ann., 298.01 et seq.
Ga. Code 1933, 23-2501 et seq.
Ida. Code 1947, 42-2901 et seq.
Ill. Rev. Stat. 1991, Ch. 42, § 1 et seq.
Iowa Code Ann., 468.1 et seq.
Md. Ann. Code 1957, Art. 25, § 52 et seq.
Mich. Comp. Laws Ann., 280.1 et seq.
Minn. Stat. 1988, 106A.005 et seq.
Miss. Code Ann. 1972, § 51-31-7 et seq.
Mo. Rev. Stat., 242.010 et seq.
Mont. Code Ann., 85-8-101 et seq.

N.C. Gen. Stat. 1943, § 156-1 et seq.
N.D. Cent. Code, 61-21-01 et seq.
Neb. Rev. Stat. 1943, 31-101 et seq.
N.J. Stat. Ann., 4:30-1 et seq., 58:11A-1 et seq.
N.Y. Environmental Conservation Law 1972 (Consol. Laws Ch. 43B) § 15-1903 et seq.
Okla. Stat. 1971, Title 82, §§ 281 et seq., 301 et seq.
Ore. Rev. Stat. 1953, 547.005 et seq.
S.C. Code Ann. 1976, § 49-11-10 et seq.
Tenn. Code Ann., 69-6-101 et seq.
Va. Code 1950, § 21-292 et seq.
Vt. Stat. Ann., Title 10, § 851 et seq.
Wash. Rev. Code Ann., 85.06.010 et seq.
Wis. Stat. Ann., 88.27 et seq.
W. Va. Code 1966, § 19-21-1 et seq.

Drainage District Act (Chicago)
Ill. Comp. Stat. 1992, Ch. 70, § 615/0.01 et seq.

Drainage District Act (Colusa Basin)
Cal. Statutes 1987, Ch. 1399, p. 5698

Drainage District Act (Everglades)
Fla. Laws 1913, Ch. 6456

Drainage District Act (Irrigation District)
Cal. Water Code § 22095 et seq.

Drainage District Act (Knights' Landing Ridge)
Cal. Statutes 1913, Ch. 99, p. 109

Drainage District Act (Sacramento and San Joaquin)
Cal. Water Code § 8500 et seq.

Drainage District Act (Storm Drain Maintenance)
Cal. Statutes 1937, Ch. 265, p. 566
Cal. Statutes 1939, p. 3029

Drainage District Improvement Act
Cal. Water Code, Appendix, § 31-1 et seq.

Drainage District Improvement Act of 1919
Cal. Statutes 1919, Ch. 354, p. 371

Drainage District Pollution Abatement Act
Ill. Rev. Stat. 1991, Ch. 42, §§ 472.9, 473

Drainage District Reorganization Act
Wash. Rev. Code Ann., 85.20.010 et seq.

Drainage District Revenue Act
Wash. Rev. Code Ann., 85.32.010 et seq.

Drainage Facilities and Minor Construction Act
June 13, 1956, Ch. 382, 70 Stat. 274; 43 U.S. Code § 505

Drainage Improvement Act
Minn. Stat. 1986, 106A.201 et seq.

Drainage Improvement District Act
Wash. Rev. Code Ann., 85.08.010 et seq.

Drainage Improvement District Maintenance Act
Wash. Rev. Code Ann., 85.16.010 et seq.

Drainage Intercounty District Act
Wash. Rev. Code Ann., 85.24.010 et seq.

Drainage, Irrigation and Watershed Improvement District Act
Ark. Code Ann. 1987, 14-117-101 et seq.

Drainage Law
Ind. Code Ann., 36-9-27-1 et seq.

Drainage Loan Act (Spruce Pond Brook of Franklin)
Mass. Acts 1958, Ch. 387

Drainage Maintenance Act
Ark. Code Ann. 1987, 14-121-412

Drainage of Lands Act
Wis. Stat. Ann., 88.01 et seq.

Drainage Relief Act (San Joaquin Valley)
Cal. Water Code § 14900 et seq.

Drainage Rights Act
Mo. Rev. Stat., 244.010

Drainage Utility Systems Act
Tex. Government Code, § 402.041 et seq.

Drainage Utility Systems Act (Municipal)
Tex. Local Gov. Code, § 402.041 et seq.

Drake Amendment
Mont. Code Ann., 1-2-112

Dram Shop Act
Ala. Code 1975, §§ 6-5-70, 6-5-71
Ark. Acts 1879, p. 33, No. 31, §§ 10 to 14
Colo. Rev. Stat., 13-21-103
Conn. Gen. Stat. Ann., § 30-102
Del. Code of 1953, Title 4, § 716
Ill. Rev. Stat. 1991, Ch. 43
Iowa Code Ann., 123.92 et seq.
Mass. Gen. Laws Ann., 138:69
Me. Rev. Stat. Ann. 1964, Title 17, § 2001 et seq.
Mich. Comp. Laws Ann., 436.22 et seq.
Minn. Stat. Ann., 340A.801
Miss. Code Ann. 1972, § 67-1-83
Mo. Rev. Stat., 537.053
Mont. Code Ann., 27-1-710
N.C. Gen. Stat. 1943, § 14-332
N.D. Cent. Code, 5-01-6.1
Nev. Rev. Stat. 1967 Reprint, Replaced Pages, 202.070
N.J. Laws 1922, Ch. 257
N.J. Stat. Ann. 2A:22A-1 et seq.
N.M. Stat. Ann., 41-11-1
N.Y. General Obligations Law (Consol. Laws, Ch. 24A) § 11-101
Ohio Rev. Code 1953, 4399.01
Ore. Rev. Stat., 30.730
Pa. Purdon's Stat., Title 47, § 4-493
R.I. Gen. Laws 1956, 3-11-1, 3-11-2
S.D. Codified Laws 1967, 35-4-38
Tenn. Code Ann., 57-10-101, 57-10-102
Utah Code Ann. 1953, 32A-14-101, 32A-14-102
Vt. Stat. Ann., Title 7, § 501 et seq.
Wash. Rev. Code 1951, 71.08.080
Wis. Stat. 1979, 176.35
Wyo. Stat. Ann., § 12-5-502

Dram Shop Liability Act
N.C. Gen. Stat. 1943, § 18B-305, Subsec. a

Draw Poker Option Act
Cal. Penal Code § 337s

Draw Poker Video Machine Control Law
Mont. Laws 1985, Ch. 720

**Dream Project (Dare to Reach for
Educational Aspirations and Marks)**
Wash. Rev. Code, 1989, 28A.630.750 et seq.

Dredge and Placer Mining Protection Act
Ida. Code 1947, 47-1312 et seq.

Dredge Materials Act
Tex. Rev. Civ. Stat., Art. 5415e-4

**Dredge Mining Regulation and Land
Preservation Act**
Mont. Rev. Code 1947, 50-1101 et seq.

Driftnet Act Amendments of 1990
Nov. 28, 1990, P.L. 101-627, 16 U.S. Code
§ 1826

**Driftnet Impact Monitoring, Assessment,
and Control Act of 1987**
Dec. 29, 1987, P.L. 100-220, 16 U.S. Code
§ 1822 nt.

Drill Hole Act (Lode and Placer Claims)
Wyo. Stat. Ann., §§ 30-1-106, 30-1-107

Drillers Act (Water Well)
Mo. Rev. Stat. 1978, 256.600 et seq.

Drilling Code (Well)
Conn. Gen. Stat. Ann., § 25-126 et seq.

Drilling Operations Act
Ill. Rev. Stat. 1991, Ch. 96 1/2, § 9651 et seq.

Drinking Cup Law
Ky. Rev. Stat. 1971, Superseded Vol.,
438.090

Drinking Water Act
N.C. Gen. Stat. 1943, § 130A-311 et seq.
S.C. Code Ann. 1976, § 40-23-150 et seq.

Drinking Water Act (Safe)
Cal. Health and Safety Code §§ 1040.9, 4010
et seq., 4010.8, 4011 et seq., 4018, 4019,
4021 et seq., 4023.5, 4024, 4026 et seq.,
4027, 4027.5, 4028, 4032, 4036.5 et seq.,
4039, 4039.1, 4039.6
Wash. Rev. Code Ann., 70.119A.900

Drinking Water Bond Law (Safe)
Cal. Water Code § 13810 et seq.

Drinking Water Protection Act
R.I. Gen. Laws 1956, 46-15.3-1 et seq.

Drinking Water Protection Act (Local)
Cal. Health and Safety Code §§ 116610,
116612

Drinking Water Purity Act
P.R. Laws Ann. 1954, Title 12, § 1551 et seq.

Drinking Water Quality Act
Ore. Rev. Stat. 1953, 448.119 et seq.,
454.235, 454.255, 757.005

**Drinking Water State Revolving Loan Fund
Act**
Neb. Rev. Stat. 1943, 71-5314 to 71-5327
N.M. Stat. Ann., 6-21A-1 to 6-21A-9

Drive-By Shooting Prevention Act of 1994
Sept. 13, 1994, P.L. 103-322, 18 U.S. Code
§§ 36 nt., 36

Drive for Teen Employment Act
Oct. 31, 1998, P.L. 105-334, 112 Stat. 3137,
29 U.S. Code § 201 nt.

Driver and Traffic Safety Education Act
Tex. Rev. Civ. Stat., Art. 4413(29c)

Driver Education Act
Ill. Rev. Stat. 1991, Ch. 122, § 27-24 et seq.

Driver Education Program Act
Md. Ann. Code 1974, Art. TR, § 16-501 et
seq.

Driver Improvement Act
Ga. Code Ann., 40-5-80 et seq.
Va. Code 1950, § 46.1-514.1 et seq.

Driver Improvement and Motor Vehicle Safety Responsibility Act
Ind. Code Ann., 9-2-1-1 et seq.

Driver License Medical Review Act
Ill. Rev. Stat. 1991, Ch. 95 1/2, § 506-1 et seq.

Driver Responsibility Act (Teenage and Adult)
Ga. Laws 1997, p. 760

Driver Safety Act
Cal. Vehicle Code 1959, § 23240 et seq.

Driver School Licensing Act
Ala. Code 1975, § 32-14-1 et seq.
Ga. Code Ann., 43-13-1 et seq.
N.M. Stat. Ann., 66-10-1 et seq.

Driver Training Act
Ariz. Rev. Stat. Ann., § 32-2351 et seq.

Driver Training Schools Act
Ala. Code 1975, § 32-14-1 et seq.
Kan. Stat. Ann., 8-273 et seq.
Neb. Rev. Stat. 1943, 60-409.06 et seq.
Utah Code Ann. 41-2-301 et seq.

Driver Training Schools Act (Commercial)
Utah Code Ann. 1953, 53-3-501 et seq.

Drivers' and Chauffeurs' License Act
Wyo. Stat. Ann., § 31-7-101 et seq.

Drivers' Financial Responsibility Act
See Financial Responsibility Act

Drivers' License Act
See also Uniform Driver's License Act
Ala. Code 1975, § 32-6-1 et seq.
Alaska Stat. 1962, § 28.15.011 et seq.
Ariz. Rev. Stat. Ann., § 28-401 et seq.
Cal. Vehicle Code 1959, § 12500 et seq.
D.C. Code Ann., § 40-301 et seq.
Fla. Stat. Ann., 322.01 et seq.
Ga. Code Ann., 40-5-1 et seq.
Ind. Code Ann., 9-1-4-26 et seq.
Iowa Code Ann., 321.174 et seq.

Kan. Stat. Ann., 8-234a et seq.
Ky. Rev. Stat. 1971, 186.400 et seq.
La. Rev. Stat. Ann., 32:401 et seq.
Md. Ann. Code 1974, Art. TR, § 16-701 et seq.
Minn. Stat. Ann., 171.01 et seq.
Miss. Code Ann. 1972, § 63-1-1 et seq.
Mo. Rev. Stat., 302.010 et seq.
N.C. Gen. Stat. 1943, § 20-5 et seq.
N.D. Cent. Code, 39-06-01 et seq.
Neb. Rev. Stat. 1943, 60-401 et seq.
Nev. Rev. Stat. Ann., 483.010 et seq.
Ohio Rev. Code 1953, 4507.01 et seq.
S.D. Codified Laws 1967, 32-12-1 et seq.
Tenn. Code Ann., 55-7-101 et seq.
Tex. Rev. Civ. Stat., Art. 6687b
Utah Code Ann. 1953, 41-2-101 et seq.
Utah Code Ann. 1953, 53-3-201 et seq.
Vt. Stat. Ann., Title 23, § 601 et seq.
Wis. Stat. Ann., 343.01 et seq.
Wyo. Stat. Ann., § 31-7-101 et seq.

Drivers License Act (Commercial)
See also Uniform Commercial Driver's License Act
Ark. Code Ann. 1987, 27-23-101 et seq.
Colo. Rev. Stat., 42-2-501 et seq.
Fla. Stat. Ann., 322.01 et seq.
Ga. Code Ann., 40-5-140 et seq.
Md. Ann. Code 1974, Art. TR, § 16-801 et seq.
Mo. Rev. Stat., 302.700 et seq.
N.J. Stat. Ann., 39:3-10.9 et seq.
N.M. Stat. Ann., 66-5-52 et seq.
Pa. Cons. Stat., Title 75, § 1601 et seq.
R.I. Gen. Laws 1956, 31-10.3-1 et seq.
S.C. Code Ann. 1976, § 56-1-2010 et seq.
Tex. Rev. Civ. Stat., Art. 6687b-2
Tex. Transportation Code, § 522.001 et seq.
Utah Code Ann. 1953, 41-2-701 et seq.
Va. Code 1950, § 46.1-372.1 et seq.
Va. Code 1950, § 46.2-341.1
Wash. Rev. Code Ann., 46.25.001
Wyo. Stat. Ann., § 31-17-101 et seq.

Drivers License Compact Act
Ala. Code 1975, § 32-6-30 et seq.

Ariz. Rev. Stat. Ann., § 28-1601 et seq.

Ark. Code Ann. 1987, 27-17-101 et seq.

Cal. Vehicle Code § 15000 et seq.

Del. Code of 1974, Title 21, § 8101 et seq.

Fla. Stat. Ann., 322.43 et seq.

Haw. Rev. Stat. Ann., § 286C-1 et seq.

Ida. Code 1947, 49-2101 et seq.

Ill. Rev. Stat. 1991, Ch. 95 1/2, § 6-700 et seq.

Ind. Code Ann., 9-5-1-1 et seq.

Iowa Code Ann., 321C.1, 321C.2

Kan. Stat. Ann., 8-1212 et seq.

La. Rev. Stat. Ann., 32:1420 et seq.

Md. Ann. Code 1974, Art. TR, § 16-701 et seq.

Me. Rev. Stat. Ann. 1964, Title 29, § 631 et seq.

Me. Rev. Stat. Ann. 1964, Title 29-A, § 1451 et seq.

Minn. Stat. Ann., 171.50 et seq.

Miss. Code Ann. 1972, § 63-1-101 et seq.

Mo. Rev. Stat., 302.600

Mont. Code Ann., 61-5-401 et seq.

Nev. Rev. Stat. Ann. 483.640 et seq.

N.J. Stat. Ann., 39:5D-1 et seq.

N.M. Stat. Ann., 66-5-49 et seq.

Okla. Stat. Ann., Title 47, § 781 et seq.

Ore. Rev. Stat., 802.540 et seq.

S.C. Code Ann. 1976, § 56-1-610 et seq.

S.C. Code Ann. 1976, § 56-1-610 et seq.

Tenn. Code Ann., 55-7-201 et seq.

Tex. Transportation Code, § 23.001 et seq.

Utah Code Ann. 1953, 41-17-1 et seq.

Utah Code Ann. 1953, 53-3-601 et seq.

Va. Code 1950, § 46.2-483 et seq.

Vt. Stat. Ann., Title 23, § 3901 et seq.

Wash. Rev. Code Ann., 46.21.010 et seq.

W. Va. Code 1966, §§ 17B-1A-1, 17B-1A-2

Wyo. Stat. Ann., § 31-7-20

Driver's License Suspension Law
N.D. Cent. Code, 39-06-32 et seq.

Driver's Permit Law
S.D. Codified Laws 1967, 32-12-1 et seq.

Driver's Privacy Protection Act of 1994
Sept. 13, 1994, P.L. 103-322, 18 U.S. Code §§ 2721 nt., 2721 et seq.

Driver's Responsibility Act
Ga. Code Ann., 40-9-1 et seq.

Drivers' Training School License Act
Kan. Stat. Ann., 8-1212 et seq.

Driving While Intoxicated Act
See Drunken Driving Act

Driving While Under the Influence Act
Ga. Code Ann., 40-6-391

Driving with Permission Act
Cal. Vehicle Code 1959, § 17150 et seq.

Dropout Prevention Act
Fla. Stat. Ann., 230.2316
Tenn. Code Ann., 49-1-501 et seq.

Dropout Prevention Act (School)
Fla. Stat. Ann., 230.2316
Pa. Purdon's Stat., Title 24, § 6601 et seq.

Dropout Prevention Technical Correction Amendment of 1991
Nov. 13, 1991, P.L. 102-155, 20 U.S. Code §§ 236 nt., 240

Drought Aid Act
April 6, 1949, Ch. 49, 63 Stat. 43

Drought Assistance Act (Reclamation States)
Aug. 11, 1988, P.L. 100-387, 43 U.S. Code § 502 nt.

Drought Disaster Relief Act
Cal. Water Code, § 20300 et seq.

Drought, Flood and Hurricane Disaster Act (Farmers)
Va. Code 1950 § 3.1-22.13 et seq.

Drought Relief Act
Dec. 20, 1930, Ch. 21, 46 Stat. 1032

Drought Relief and Safe Drinking Water Act
Cal. Water Code § 15125 et seq.

Drought Response Act
S.C. Code Ann. 1976, § 49-23-10 et seq.

Drovers and Freighters Act
Kan. Stat. Ann., 47-104, 47-120

Drug Abatement Act
Ark. Code 1987, 16-105-401 et seq.

Drug Abuse Act
Fla. Stat. Ann., 893.01 et seq.
Md. Ann. Code 1974, Art. HG, § 8-101 et seq.
N.M. Stat. Ann., 26-2-1 et seq.
Utah Code Ann. 1953, 58-37-1 et seq.

Drug Abuse Act (Student Organization Responsibilities)
Ga. Code Ann., 20-3-90 et seq.

Drug Abuse Advisory Council Act
N.J. Stat. Ann. 26:2G-4.1 et seq.

Drug Abuse, Alcohol, and Mental Health Services Act
Fla. Stat. Ann., 394.65 et seq.

Drug Abuse and Alcohol Prevention and Life Skills Educational Act
Okla. Stat. Ann., Title 70, § 1210.229-1 et seq.

Drug Abuse and Alcohol Services Act
Okla. Stat. Ann., Title 63, § 2100 et seq.
Tex. Health and Safety Code, § 461.001 et seq.

Drug Abuse and Alcoholism Act
Me. Rev. Stat. Ann. 1964, Title 22, § 7101 et seq.

Drug Abuse and Alcoholism Division Act.
Neb. Rev. Stat. 1943, 83-158.01 et seq.

Drug Abuse and Dependency Act (Alcoholism)
Ill. Comp. Stat. 1992, Ch. 20, § 301/1-1 et seq.

Drug Abuse Control Act
Ark. Code Ann. 1987, 20-64-301 et seq.
Cal. Health and Safety Code § 11900 et seq.
Ga. Code Ann., 26-5-1 et seq.
Haw. Rev. Stat. Ann., §§ 321-191, 329-1 et seq.
Ill. Rev. Stat. 1969, Ch. 111 1/2, § 801 et seq.
Md. Ann. Code 1974, Art. HG, § 9-101 et seq.
N.J. Stat. Ann., 26:2G-1 et seq.
R.I. Gen. Laws 1956, 21-28.2-1 et seq.
S.D. Codified Laws 1967, 34-20B-1 et seq.
Va. Code 1950, § 54-446.3 et seq.

Drug Abuse Control Amendments
July 15, 1965, P.L. 89-74, 79 Stat. 226, 18 U.S. Code § 1114; 21 U.S. Code §§ 321, 331, 334, 360, 360a, 372

Drug Abuse Education Act
Ala. Code 1975, § 16-41-1 et seq.
Del. Code of 1974, Title 16, § 4801 et seq.
Fla. Stat. Ann., 233.067
Okla. Stat. Ann., Title 70, § 1210.221 et seq.

Drug Abuse Education Act of 1970
Dec. 3, 1970, P.L. 91-527, 84 Stat. 1385, 21 U.S. Code §§ 1001 to 1007
Sept. 21, 1974, P.L. 93-422, 88 Stat. 1154, 21 U.S. Code §§ 1001 to 1004, 1007

Drug Abuse Office and Treatment Act of 1972
March 21, 1972, P.L. 92-255, 86 Stat. 65, 5 U.S. Code §§ 5313, 5315, 5316; 21 U.S. Code §§ 1101 to 1104, 1111 to 1123, 1131 to 1143, 1151 to 1155, 1161 to 1165, 1171 to 1180, 1191; 42 U.S. Code §§ 218, 246, 257, 2684, 2688a, 2688k, 2688n-1, 2688t
May 14, 1974, P.L. 93-282, 88 Stat. 136, 21 U.S. Code §§ 1175, 1191
March 19, 1976, P.L. 94-237, 21 U.S. Code § 1174 et seq.
Aug. 1, 1977, P.L. 95-83, 21 U.S. Code § 1112 et seq.
Oct. 4, 1979, P.L. 96-79, 21 U.S. Code § 1176

Jan. 2, 1980, P.L. 96-181, 21 U.S. Code
§§ 1101 et seq., 1101 nt. , 1118 to 1120,
1131 to 1133 repealed, 1162, 1164, 1176,
1177, 1180, 1181, 1191 to 1193

Drug Abuse Prevention and Control Act
Fla. Stat. Ann., 893.01 et seq.

**Drug Abuse Prevention, Intervention and
Treatment Law (Alcohol and Other)**
Ky. Acts 1994, Ch. 901

**Drug Abuse Prevention, Treatment and
Rehabilitation Act**
Oct. 12, 1984, P.L. 98-473, 21 U.S. Code
§ 1111
Nov. 18, 1988, P.L. 100-690, 21 U.S. Code
§§ 1103, 1111 to 1116

**Drug Abuse Prevention, Treatment, and
Rehabilitation, Amendments of 1979**
Jan. 2, 1980, P.L. 96-181, 21 U.S. Code
§§ 1101 et seq., 1101 nt. , 1162, 1164, 1176,
1177, 1180, 1181, 1191 to 1193; 42 U.S.
Code §§ 300l-2, 300m-3, 3733

**Drug Abuse Professional Practice Act
(Alcohol and Other)**
N.H. Rev. Stat. 1955, 330-C:1 et seq.

Drug Abuse Resistance Education Act
Fla. Stat. Ann., 233.0661 et seq.
Tenn. Code Ann., 49-1-401 et seq.

Drug Abuse Treatment Act
Cal. Statutes 1972, Ch. 1255, p. 2464
Kan. Stat. Ann., 65-5201 et seq.

Drug Abuse Treatment and Education Act
Ga. Code Ann., 26-5-1 et seq.

**Drug Abuse Treatment Technical
Corrections Act of 1989**
Aug. 16, 1989, P.L. 101-93, 42 U.S. Code
§ 201 nt., generally 42 U.S. Code § 201 et
seq.

**Drug Abuse Treatment Waiting Period
Reduction Amendments of 1990**
Aug. 15, 1990, P.L. 101-374, 42 U.S. Code
§ 201 nt.

Drug Act
D.C. Code 1973, § 33-501 et seq.
Del. Code of 1974, Title 16, § 4701 et seq.
Ind. Code 1971, 16-13-7.5-1 et seq.
Md. Ann. Code 1957, Art. 27, § 276 et seq.
Minn. Stat. Ann., 151.01 et seq.
N.H. Rev. Stat. 1955, 146:1 et seq., 318-B:1
et seq.
Pa. 1897 Pamph. Laws 85, No. 68
Pa. 1917 Pamph. Laws 758, No. 282
P.R. Laws Ann. 1954, Title 24, § 711 et seq.
R.I. Gen. Laws 1956, 21-28-1.01 et seq.
S.C. Code Ann. 1976, § 39-23-10 et seq.
W. Va. Code 1966, § 16-7-1 et seq.

Drug Act (Dangerous)
N.M. Stat. Ann. 1953, 54-6-20 et seq.

Drug Act (Emergency Box)
Neb. Rev. Stat. 1943, 71-2410 et seq.

Drug Act (Narcotic)
See also Uniform Controlled Substances Act
Vt. Stat. Ann., Title 18, § 4201 et seq.

Drug Act (Omnibus)
N.C. Gen. Stat. 1943, § 90-86 et seq.

Drug Act (Pure)
R.I. Gen. Laws 1956, 21-31-1 et seq.

Drug Addiction Act
Cal. Welfare and Institutions Code § 3000 et
seq.
Ill. Rev. Stat. 1983, Ch. 91 1/2, § 120.1 et
seq.
Mass. Gen Laws 1932, Ch. 123, § 38 et seq.
Ore. Rev. Stat., 475.005 et seq.

**Drug Addiction and Alcoholism Intervenor
and Reporter Immunity Act**
Ill. Rev. Stat. 1991, Ch. 70, § 651 et seq.

**Drug Addiction and Alcoholism Treatment
and Support Act**
Wash. Rev. Code, 1989, 74.50.010 et seq.

Drug Addicts Care and Treatment Act (District of Columbia)
D.C. Code 1973, § 24-613 et seq.

Drug Addicts Hospital Treatment Act
D.C. Code 1973, § 24-601 et seq.

Drug Addicts Treatment Act
Mich. Comp. Laws Ann., 330.1116 et seq.

Drug Adulteration Act
Wash. Rev. Code Ann., 69.04.001 et seq.

Drug Amendments of 1962
Oct. 10, 1962, P.L. 87-781, 76 Stat. 780, 21 U.S. Code §§ 321, 331, 332, 348, 351 to 353, 355, 357 to 360, 372, 374, 376, 381

Drug and Alcohol Abuse Act
Ind. Code Ann., 16-13-6.1-1 et seq.

Drug and Alcohol Abuse Commitment Act
S.C. Code Ann. 1976, § 44-52-10 et seq.

Drug and Alcohol Abuse Control Act
Pa. Purdon's Stat., Title 71, § 1690.101 et seq.

Drug and Alcohol Abuse Policy Board Act
Okla. Stat. Ann., Title 74, § 30 et seq.

Drug and Alcohol Abuse Services Act
Okla. Stat. Ann., Title 43A, § 3-401 et seq.

Drug and Alcohol Dependent Offenders Treatment Act of 1986
Oct. 27, 1986, P.L. 99-570, 18 U.S. Code § 3661 nt.

Drug and Alcohol Dependent Offenders Treatment Act of 1989
Oct. 12, 1990, P.L. 101-421, 18 U.S. Code § 3661 nt.

Drug and Alcohol Testing Act (Standards for Workplace)
Okla. Stat. Ann., Title 40, § 551 et seq.

Drug and Alcohol Testing Act (Workforce)
Mont. Code Ann., 39-2-205 et seq.

Drug and Cosmetic Act
Alaska Stat. 1962, § 17.20.010 et seq.
Ark. Code Ann. 1987, 20-56-201 et seq.
Fla. Stat. Ann., 499.001 et seq.
Ga. Code Ann., 26-3-1 et seq.
Haw. Rev. Stat. Ann., § 328-1 et seq.
Iowa Code Ann., 203A.1 et seq.
N.C. Gen. Stat. 1943, § 106-120 et seq.

Drug and Food Act
See Food and Drug Act

Drug and Household Substance Mailing Act of 1990
Oct. 31, 1990, P.L. 101-493, 39 U.S. Code § 3001 nt.

Drug and Pharmacy Act
Ore. Rev. Stat., 453.001 et seq.

Drug Asset Forfeiture Procedure Act
Ill. Rev. Stat. 1991, Ch. 56 1/2, § 1671 et seq.

Drug Baron's Enforcement Act
Ala. Acts 1986, No. 534

Drug Control Act
Conn. Gen. Stat. Ann., § 21a-240 et seq.
D.C. Code Ann., §§ 24-601 et seq., 33-501 et seq., 33-601 et seq.
Mo. Rev. Stat., 195.005 et seq.
Tenn. Code Ann., 39-6-401 et seq.
Tenn. Code Ann., 39-17-401 to 39-17-427, 53-11-301 to 53-11-308, 53-11-401 to 53-11-414
Va. Code 1950, § 54.1-3400 et seq.
Vt. Stat. Ann., Title 18, § 4201 et seq.
Wyo. Stat. 1957, § 35-371.1 et seq.

Drug Control Act (Retail)
Conn. Gen. Stat. Ann., § 21a-126 et seq.

Drug Cosmetic and Food Act
Cal. Health and Safety Code § 26000 et seq.
Ind. Code Ann., 16-1-28-1 et seq.
N.D. Cent. Code, 19-02.1-01 et seq.
R.I. Gen. Laws 1956, 21-31-1 et seq.

Drug, Cosmetic and Hazardous Substance Labeling Act
Vt. Stat. Ann., Title 18, § 4051 et seq.

Drug Crimes Amendments Act
Ala. Acts 1991, p. 1047 No. 603

Drug Crimes Search Act
Ala. Code 1975, § 15-5-8

Drug, Dairy and Food Act
Wis. Stat. Ann., 97.01 et seq.

Drug Dealer Liability Act
Mich. Comp. Laws Ann., 691.1601 et seq.
Okla. Stat. Ann., Title 63, § 2-421 et seq.

Drug Demand Reduction Act
Oct. 21, 1998, P.L. 105-277, Division D, 112 Stat. 2681, 21 U.S. Code § 1801 nt.

Drug Dependent Federal Offenders Act of 1978
Nov. 18, 1988, P.L. 100-690, 18 U.S. Code § 4255 nt.

Drug, Device and Cosmetic Act
Iowa Code Ann., 126.1 et seq.
N.M. Stat. Ann., 26-1-1 et seq.
Okla. Stat. Ann., Title 63, § 1-1401 et seq.
Pa. Purdon's Stat., Title 35, § 780-101 et seq.
Tex. Health and Safety Code, § 432.001 et seq.

Drug Device Cosmetic and Food Salvage Act
Tex. Rev. Civ. Stat. 1974, Art. 4476-5e

Drug Distribution Licencing Act (Wholesale)
W. Va. Code 1966 § 60A-8-1 et seq.

Drug Distributor Licensing Act (Wholesale)
Minn. Stat. Ann., 151.42 et seq.
N.C. Gen. Stat. 1943, § 106-145.1 et seq.
Neb. Laws 1992, L.B. 1019, §§ 1 to 26
Pa. Purdon's Stat., Title 63, § 391.1 et seq.

Drug Distributors License Act (Wholesale Prescription)
Pa. 1992 Pamph. Laws, No. 145

Drug Diversion Act
Cal. Penal Code § 1000 et seq.

Drug Education Act
Cal. Education Code 1976, § 51260 et seq.
N.J. Stat. Ann., 18A:4-28.4 et seq.
S.D. Codified Laws 1967, 34-3B-1 et seq.

Drug Elimination Act (Public Housing)
N.Y. Public Housing Law (Consol. Laws Ch. 44A) § 301 et seq.

Drug Enforcement Act (Intergovernmental)
Me. Rev. Stat. Ann. 1964, Title 25, § 2951 et seq.
Me. Rev. Stat. Ann. 1964, Title 25, § 2951 et seq.

Drug Enforcement Enhancement Act of 1986
Oct. 27, 1986, P.L. 99-570, 100 Stat. 3248

Drug Export Amendments Act of 1986
Nov. 14, 1986, P.L. 99-660, 21 U.S. Code § 301 nt.

Drug, Food and Cosmetic Act
See Food, Drug and Cosmetic Act

Drug-Free Communities Act of 1997
June 27, 1997, P.L. 105-20, 21 U.S. Code § 1501 nt.

Drug-Free Corrections Act
Fla. Stat. Ann., 944.471 et seq.

Drug-Free Media Campaign Act of 1998
Oct. 21, 1998, P.L. 105-277, Division D, Title I, Subtitle A, 112 Stat. 2681, 21 U.S. Code § 1801 nt.

Drug-Free Postsecondary Education Act
Ga. Code Ann., 20-1-20 et seq.

Drug-Free Prisons and Jails Act of 1998
Oct. 21, 1998, P.L. 105-277, Division D, Title I, Subtitle B, 112 Stat. 2681, 42 U.S. Code § 3751 nt.

Drug-Free Public Housing Act of 1988
Nov. 18, 1988, P.L. 100-690, 42 U.S. Code § 11901 nt.

Drug-Free Public Work Force Act
Ga. Code Ann., 45-23-1 et seq.

Drug Free Public Work Force Act
Mo. Laws 1993, S.B. No. 67

Drug-Free School Act
Del. Code of 1974, Title 14, § 3801 et seq.
Mo. Rev. Stat., 161.500 et seq.

Drug-Free School Zones Act
Tenn. Code Ann., 39-17-432, 40-35-114

Drug-Free Schools and Communities Act Amendments of 1989
Dec. 12, 1989, P.L. 101-226, 20 U.S. Code § 2701 nt.
Nov. 29, 1990, P.L. 101-647, 20 U.S. Code §§ 3181, 3194, 3196, 3224a, 3224b

Drug-Free Schools and Communities Act of 1986
Oct. 27, 1986, P.L. 90-570, 20 U.S. Code § 4601 et seq.
April 28, 1988, P.L. 100-297, 102 Stat. 252, 20 U.S. Code §§ 3171 et seq.
Nov. 18, 1988, P.L. 100-690, 20 U.S. Code §§ 3181, 3191 to 3195, 3197, 3212, 3222
Dec. 12, 1989, P.L. 101-226, 20 U.S. Code §§ 3181, 3182, 3191 to 3197, 3201, 3211, 3212, 3216, 3217, 3221, 3223, 3224a, 3224b, 3227
Nov. 29, 1990, P.L. 101-647, 20 U.S. Code §§ 3181, 3182, 3192, 3194 to 3196, 3201 to 3203, 3212, 3216, 3233

Drug-Free Schools Quality Assurance Act
Oct. 21, 1998, P.L. 105-277, Division D, Title I, Subtitle C, 112 Stat. 2681, 20 U.S. Code § 6301 nt.

Drug Free Truck Stop Act
Sept. 13, 1994, P.L. 103-322, 21 U.S. Code §§ 801 nt., 841, 849; 28 U.S. Code § 994 nt.

Drug-Free Workplace Act
Cal. Government Code § 8350 et seq.

Fla. Stat. Ann., 112.0455
Ga. Code Ann., 50-24-1 et seq.
Ida. Code 1947, 72-1701 et seq.
Ill. Rev. Stat. 1991, Ch. 127, § 132.311 et seq.
S.C. Code Ann. 1976, § 44-107-10 et seq.

Drug-Free Workplace Act of 1988
Nov. 18, 1988, P.L. 100-690, 41 U.S. Code § 701 nt.
Oct. 13, 1994, P.L. 103-355, 41 U.S. Code § 701
Feb. 10, 1996, P.L. 104-106, 41 U.S. Code § 701
Nov. 18, 1997, P.L. 105-85, 41 U.S. Code § 702

Drug-Free Workplace Act of 1998
Oct. 21, 1998, P.L. 105-277, Division C, Title IX, 112 Stat. 2681, 15 U.S. Code § 631 nt.

Drug-Free Workplace Workers' Compensation Premium Reduction Act
Miss. Code Ann., §§ 71-3-201 to 71-3-225

Drug Free Zone Act (Juvenile)
Cal. Health and Safety Code § 11353

Drug Identification Act
Wyo. Stat. Ann., § 33-24-201 et seq.

Drug-Induced Rape Prevention and Punishment Act of 1996
Oct. 13, 1996, P.L. 104-305, 21 U.S. Code § 801 nt.

Drug Intoxication Law (Emergency Commitment)
R.I. Gen. Laws 1956, 40.1-4.1-1 et seq.

Drug Kingpin Law
S.C. Code Ann. 1976, § 44-53-475

Drug Lab Act (Clandestine)
Utah Code Ann. 1953, 58-37d-1 et seq.

Drug Labeling and Adulteration Act
Iowa Code 1983, 203.1 et seq.

Drug Listing Act of 1972
Aug. 16, 1972, P.L. 92-387, 86 Stat. 559, 21 U.S. Code §§ 331, 355, 360

Drug Misbranding Act
Mich. Comp. Laws Ann., 333.7301 et seq.
Wash. Rev. Code Ann., 69.04.001 et seq.

Drug Nuisance Law
Pa. Cons. Stat., Title 42, § 8381 et seq.

Drug Offender School Program Act
Tenn. Public Acts 1990, Ch. 992

Drug Paraphernalia Act
Colo. Rev. Stat., 12-22-501 et seq.
D.C. Code Ann., § 33-601 et seq.
Del. Code of 1974, Title 16, § 4771 et seq.
Minn. Stat. Ann., 152.092 et seq.
Mont. Code Ann., 45-10-101 et seq.
N.C. Gen. Stat. 1943, § 90-113.20 et seq.
S.C. Code Ann. 1976, § 44-53-110 et seq.
Utah Code Ann. 1953, 58-37a-1 et seq.

Drug Paraphernalia Control Act
Ill. Rev. Stat. 1991, Ch. 56 1/2, § 2101 et seq.

Drug Peddlers Act
Mich. Comp. Laws Ann., 446.301 et seq.

Drug Possession Penalty Act of 1986
Oct. 27, 1986, P.L. 99-570, 21 U.S. Code § 801 nt.

Drug Precursor Act
N.M. Stat. Ann., 30-31B-1 et seq.

Drug Predator Control Act
Ala. Acts 1991, p. 1061, No. 612

Drug Prescription by Podiatrists Act
S.C. Code Ann. 1976, § 40-43-150 et seq.

Drug Price Competition and Patent Term Restoration Act of 1984
Sept. 24, 1984, P.L. 98-417, 98 Stat. 1585, 15 U.S. Code §§ 68b, 68c, 70b; 21 U.S. Code §§ 301, 355, 360cc; 28 U.S. Code § 2201; 35 U.S. Code §§ 156, 271, 282

Drug Product Selection Act
Del. Code of 1974, Title 24, § 2589
Mont. Code Ann., 37-7-501 et seq.
Neb. Rev. Stat. 1943, 71-5401 et seq.
S.C. Code Ann. 1976, § 39-24-10 et seq.

Drug Products Law (Generic Equivalent)
Miss. Code Ann., § 73-21-117

Drug Profits Forfeiture Act
Ala. Code 1975, § 20-2-93

Drug Punishment Act
Fla. Stat. Ann., 953.001 et seq.

Drug Racketeering Act
La. Rev. Stat. Ann., 15:1351 et seq.

Drug Reform Act
N.J. Stat Ann., 2A:4A-26, 2C:5-2, 2C:20-2, 2C:35-1 et seq., 2C:36-1 et seq., 2C:36A-1, 2C:39-7, 2C:41-1, 2C:43-1 et seq., 2C:43-6, 2C:43-7, 2C:43-12, 2C:44-2, 2C:52-5, 2C:64-2, 24:21-22 et seq., 24:21-29, 24:21-36

Drug Regulation Act
Mich. Comp. Laws Ann., 333.7101 et seq.
Mo. Rev. Stat., 1983 supp., 195.005 et seq.

Drug Services and Alcohol Act (Hal S. Marchman)
Fla. Stat. Ann., 397.301 et seq.

Drug Stamp Tax Act (Illegal)
Ida. Code 1947, 63-4201 et seq.
Utah Code Ann. 1953, 59-19-101 et seq.

Drug Substitution Act (Generic)
Utah Code Ann. 1953, 58-17-27 et seq.

Drug Tax Act (Dangerous)
Mont. Laws 1991, Ch. 563, § 1 et seq.

Drug Testing for Employment
Mont. Code Ann., 39-2-304

Drug Traffickers Act (Model Expedited Eviction of)
Pa. Purdon's Stat., Title 35, § 780-151 et seq.

Drug Trafficking Amendments Act
Ala. Code 1975, §§ 13A-12-31, 20-2-80, 20-2-81

Drug Trafficking Enterprise Act
Ala. Code 1975, § 13A-12-233 et seq.

Drug Treatment Program Act
Tex. Rev. Civ. Stat. 1974, Art. 4476-15a

Drug Treatment Program Act (McAllister)
Tex. Health and Safety Code, § 465.001 et seq.

Drug Treatment Program Act (R.B. McAllister)
Tex. Health and Safety Code, § 465.001 et seq.

Drug Users Act
D.C. Code 1973, § 24-601 et seq.
Mich. Comp. Laws Ann., 335.201 et seq.

Drug Utilization Review Act
Tenn. Public Acts 1992, Ch. 899

Drug Violations Act (School Reporting of)
Ill. Comp. Stat. 1992, Ch. 105, § 127/1 et seq.

Drug—Alcohol Intervention and Prevention Act (Teen)
Utah Code Ann. 1953, 62A-8-202 et seq.

Druggists Act
Ky. Rev. Stat. 1971, 315.010 et seq.
Mo. Rev. Stat., 338.010 et seq.
N.H. Rev. Stat. 1955, 318:1 et seq.
W. Va. Code 1966, § 30-5-1 et seq.

Druggists Act (Alcohol Sales)
S.C. Code Ann. 1976, § 61-11-10 et seq.

Druggists' Relief Act
Tenn. Acts 1887, Ch. 89

Drugless Healing Act
Wash. Rev. Code Ann., 18.36.035 et seq.

Drugless Practice Act
Ky. Rev. Stat. 1948, 311.070

Drugs Act
See Food and Drug Acts

Drugs Act (Counterfeit)
S.C. Code Ann. 1976, § 44-53-110 et seq.

Drugs Act (Generic)
N.Y. Education Law 1947 (Consol. Laws Ch. 16) §§ 6810, 6816a, 6826
N.Y. Public Health Law 1953 (Consol. Laws Ch. 45) § 206

Drugs and Medical Supplies Manufacturers Act
Pa. 1945 Pamph. Laws 615, No. 261

Drugs and Substances Control Act
S.D. Codified Laws 1967, 34-20B-1 et seq.

Drugs in Schools Law
N.Y. Penal Law 1965 (Consol. Laws Ch. 40), §§ 70.00 Subd. 2, 3, 220.00 Subd. 14, 220.34 Subd. 7, 220.44

Drunk Driver Act (Persistent)
Colo. Rev. Stat., 42-1-102, 42-2-126, 42-3-130.5, 42-4-1301, Subd. 9, 42-7-406, 16-4-103

Drunk Driver Visitation Program Act (Youthful)
Cal. Vehicle Code 1959, § 23509 et seq.

Drunk Driver Visitation Program Act (Youths)
Cal. Vehicle Code 1959, § 23145 et seq.
Fla. Stat. Ann., 233.0602

Drunk Driving Act (Omnibus)
Wash. Laws 1994, Ch. 275

Drunk Driving Child Protection Act of 1994
Sept. 13, 1994, P.L. 103-322, 18 U.S. Code §§ 1 nt., 13

Drunk Driving Death Act
Colo. Rev. Stat. 1963, 40-2-10

Drunk Driving Prevention Act of 1988
Nov. 18, 1988, P.L. 100-690, 23 U.S. Code § 401 nt.

Drunk Driving Protection Act
Okla. Stat. Ann., Title 47, § 6-106.1 et seq.

Drunk Driving Victims' Bill of Rights
N.J. Stat. Ann., 39:4-50.9 et seq.

Drunken Driving Act
Ariz. Rev. Stat. Ann., § 28-691 et seq.
Cal. Vehicle Code 1959, § 23101
Colo. Rev. Stat., 42-4-1202
Conn. Gen. Stat. Ann., § 14-227a
Del. Code of 1974, Title 21, § 4177 et seq.
Ga. Code Ann., 40-6-391 et seq.
Ida. Code 1947, 18-8004, 18-8005
Kan. Stat. Ann., 8-1001 et seq.
Ky. Rev. Stat. 1971, 189A.010 et seq.
La. Rev. Stat. Ann., 14:98
Me. Rev. Stat. Ann. 1964, Title 29, § 1311-A et seq.
Mich. Comp. Laws Ann., 257.625
Mo. Rev. Stat., 577.001 et seq.
N.C. Gen. Stat. 1943, §§ 20-138, 20-139, 20-179
N.H. Rev. Stat. 1955, 265:82
N.J. Stat. Ann. 39:4-50
Ohio Rev. Code 1953, 4511.19
Okla. Stat. Ann., Title 47, § 11-901
Ore. Rev. Stat., 813.010 et seq.
Pa. Cons. Stat., Title 75, § 3731
R.I. Gen. Laws 1956, 31-27-2
Tenn. Code Ann., 55-10-401 et seq.
Tex. Rev. Civ. Stat., Art. 4413(29c), 67011-1
Va. Code 1950, § 54-201 et seq., § 18.2-266
Wash. Rev. Code Ann., 46.61.500 et seq.
Wis. Stat. Ann., 346.63

Drunkenness Act
Cal. Penal Code § 647, Subd. f
Wash. Rev. Code Ann., 70.96A.010 et seq.

Dry Bean Resources Act
Neb. Rev. Stat. 1943, 2-3735 et seq.

Dry Cell Battery Management Act
Cal. Public Resources Code § 15000 et seq.

Dry Cleaners Act
Cal. Business and Professions Code § 9500 et seq.
Del. Laws Vol. 40, p. 414, Ch. 120
N.C. Gen. Stat. 1943, § 105-74
N.M. Stat. Ann., 61-20-1 et seq.
Ohio Rev. Code 1953, 3739.01 et seq.
Okla. Stat. Ann., Title 59, § 741 et seq.
Va. Code 1950, § 54-201 et seq.

Dry Cleaning and Barber Act
Ala. General Acts 1935, p. 746, No. 316

Dry Cleaning and Dyeing Act
Ky. Rev. Stat. 1971, 288.010 et seq.
Mich. Comp. Laws Ann., 29.201 et seq.
Pa. Purdon's Stat., Title 35, § 1269.1 et seq.

Dry Cleaning and Laundry Industry Act
Fla. Laws 1937, Ch. 17894

Dry Cleaning Industry Task Force Act
Cal. Health and Safety Code § 42800 et seq.

Dry Cleaning Law
Pa. Purdon's Stat., Title 35, § 1270.1 et seq.

Dry Dock Facilities Act
R.I. Gen. Laws 1956, 34-46-1 et seq.

Dry Draw Law (Waters)
S.D. Codified Laws 1967, 46-4-1 et seq.

Dry Enforcement Act
D.C. Code 1973, § 25-101 et seq.

Dry Law
Ga. Code Ann., 3-10-1 et seq.

Dry Municipality Law
Mo. Rev. Stat., 311.110 et seq.

Drycleaner Environmental Response and Reimbursement Law
Minn. Stat. Ann., 115B.47 to 115B.51

Drycleaner Environmental Response Trust Fund Act
Ill. Comp. Stat. 1992, Ch. 415, § 135/1 et seq.

Drycleaner's Environmental Response Act
Kan. Stat. Ann., 65-34,141 et seq.
Tenn. Code Ann., 4-29-218, 68-217-101 to
68-217-112

Dual Compensation Act
Aug. 19, 1964, P.L. 88-448, 78 Stat. 484, 2
U.S. Code § 162 (See 5 U.S. Code §§ 3326,
3501 to 3503, 5531 to 5533, 5541, 6101,
6301 to 6305, 6310, 8331, 8701) 13 U.S.
Code § 23; 15 U.S. Code §§ 327, 603 nt.; 20
U.S. Code § 907; 22 U.S. Code §§ 277d-3,
2386, 2512, 2584; 33 U.S. Code § 873; 36
U.S. Code § 426; 38 U.S. Code § 4103 nt.;
42 U.S. Code §§ 2038, 2473, 2474; 50 U.S.
Code § 403f; 50 U.S. Code Appx. § 2253

Dual Job Law
N.Y. Education Law 1947 (Consol. Laws Ch.
16) § 2573, Subd. 14

Dual Office Holding Act
La. Rev. Stat. Ann., 14:137

**Dual Party Relay Service and Telecommuni-
cation Device Distribution Program**
Pa. Purdon's Stat., Title 35, § 6701 et seq.

Dublin City Court Act
Ga. Laws 1900, p. 117

**Dublin-Laurens County Commission on
Children, Youth, and Families Act**
Ga. Laws 1998, H.B. 1763

**Dublin-Laurens County Recreation
Authority Act**
Ga. Laws 1999, H.B. 378

Dubuque Law (Process after Judgment)
Mass. Acts 1898, Ch. 549

Duck Stamp Act
Nov. 7, 1986, P.L. 99-625, 16 U.S. Code
§ 718b
Miss. Code Ann. 1972, § 49-7-161 et seq.

**Dudley-McElhanon Consolidation and
Coordination Law (Revenue
Commission)**
Ark. Stat. 1947, 84-1701 et seq.

Due Care Act (Defamation by Radio)
Mich. Comp. Laws Ann., 484.331

Due Care Statute
Mass. Gen. Laws Ann., 231:85

Due Process Act (Teacher)
Okla. Stat. Ann., Title 70, § 6-101.20 et seq.

**Due Process in Competence Determinations
Act**
Cal. Civil Code § 39
Cal. Probate Code §§ 810 to 814, 1801, 1881,
3201, 3204, 3208

Due Process in Sterilization Act
Me. Rev. Stat. Ann. 1964, Title 34-B, § 7001
et seq.

Dueling Act
Ky. Rev. Stat. 1971, 61.100, 437.030
Miss. Code Ann. 1972, § 97-39-1 et seq.
W. Va. Code 1966, § 61-2-18 et seq.

Dues Act (State Bar)
Ky. Rev. Stat. 1971, Superseded Vols.,
30.170
Ky. Supreme Court Rules, Rule 3.040

Duffey-Buller Act (Highways)
Ind. Laws 1919, Ch. 53, p. 119

Duffield Act (Taxation)
N.J. Stat. Ann., 54:29A-12, 54:29A-9,
54:29A-24, 54:29A-44, 54:29A-45,
54:29A-71

Duffy Act (Installment Sales)
Ky. Rev. Stat. 1971, 371.210 et seq.

Duffy Alzheimer's Disease Institute Act
Cal. Health and Safety Code § 1310 et seq.

**Duffy-Greene-McAlister Unemployment
Benefit Pension Offset Refund Act**
Cal. Statutes 1985, Ch. 1217, §§ 1, 7, 11, 16

**Duffy-Moscone Family Nutrition Education
and Services Act**
Cal. Education Code 1976, § 49510 et seq.

Duffy-Waxman Prepaid Health Plan Act
Cal. Welfare and Institutions Code § 14200 et seq.

Dukes County Airport Loan Act
Mass. Acts 1952, Ch. 429
Mass. Acts 1957, Ch. 201
Mass. Acts 1958, Ch. 504

Dukes County Court House Addition Act
Mass. Acts 1953, Ch. 88

Dukes County Gosnold Airport Assistance Loan Act
Mass. Acts 1956, Ch. 716

Dukes County Harbor Improvement Loan Act
Mass. Acts 1959, Ch. 488

Dukes County Highway Protection Loan Act
Mass. Acts 1954, Ch. 215

Duluth Airport Authority Act
Minn. Laws 1969, Ch. 577

Duluth Conciliation Court Act
Minn. Laws 1927, Ch. 17

Duluth Transit Authority Act
Minn. Laws 1969, Ch. 720

Dumas Act (Churches)
Ala. Code 1958, Title 58, § 104 et seq.

Dumb Act (Judge's Opinion)
Ga. Code Ann., 9-10-7

Dumb Animals Act
Colo. Rev. Stat. 1963, 40-20-24 et seq

Dummy Plates Act
Iowa Code Ann., 18.115, 321.19

Dumping Elimination Act (Ocean Sludge)
N.J. Stat. Ann., 58:10A-44 et seq.

Dumping Enforcement Act (Ocean)
N.J. Stat. Ann., 58:10A-47 et seq.

Dumps Control Act (Illegal)
Ark. Code 1987, 8-6-501 to 8-6-507, 8-6-1002 to 8-6-1004

Dunckel-Burns-Diggs-Hailwood Act (Civil Rights)
Mich. Comp. Laws Ann., 750.146 et seq.

Dune Protection Coastal Erosion, and Beach Access Preservation and Enhancement Coastal Management Plan
Tex. General and Special Laws 1991, Ch. 295
Tex. Natural Resources Code, § 63.001 et seq.

Dunipace-Weir Act (Probate Code)
Ohio Rev. Code 1953, 2101.01 et seq.

Dunlap-Berman-Alatorre-Zenovich Agricultural Labor Relations Act of 1975
Cal. Labor Code § 1140 et seq.

Dunmore Act (Prevailing Rate of Wage)
N.Y. Labor Law (Consol. Laws Ch. 31) § 225 et seq.

Dunn County Court Act
Wis. Laws 1943, Ch. 14

Dunn State Aid Road Act
Minn. Laws 1913, Ch. 323

Dunnigan Act (Registration)
N.Y. Election Law 1976 (Consol. Laws Ch. 17) § 5-210

Dunnigan-Penny Pari-Mutuel Act
N.Y. Laws 1940, Ch. 254

DuPage County Civic Center Act
Ill. Rev. Stat. 1991, Ch. 85, § 3401 et seq.

DuPage County Forest Preserve District Tax Levy Validation Act
Ill. Rev. Stat. 1991, Ch. 96 1/2, § 6360 et seq.

DuPage County, Sterling, Elgin, Orland Park, Centre East, and Schaumburg Civic Centers Act
Ill. Rev. Stat. 1991, Ch. 85, § 3400 et seq.

Duplicate Bond Law
Cal. Government Code § 53460 et seq.

Durable Medical Equipment Coverage Act
Minn. Stat. 1986, 62Q.66, 62Q.67

Durable Power of Attorney Act
See also Uniform Durable Power of Attorney Act
Ill. Rev. Stat. 1991, Ch. 110 1/2, § 802-1 et seq.
Ind. Code Ann., 30-2-11-1 et seq.
Tex. Probate Code, § 481 et seq.

Durable Power of Attorney for Health Care Act
Ga. Code Ann., 31-36-1 et seq.
Miss. Code Ann., § 41-41-151 et seq.
Tex. Civil Practice & Remedies Code, § 135.001

Duress Act
N.Y. Penal Law 1965 (Consol. Laws Ch. 40) § 40.00
Wash. Rev. Code Ann., 9A.16.060

Durham Capital Reserve Act
N.C. Laws 1955, Ch. 1091

Durham County Consolidation Act
N.C. Laws 1974, Ch. 989

Durham-Humphrey Drug Prescriptions Act
See Humphrey-Durham Drug Prescriptions Act

Durham Peace Officers' Relief Fund Act
N.C. Public-Local Laws 1939, Ch. 538

Dust Blowing and Soil Erosion Act
Colo. Rev. Stat., 35-72-101 et seq.

Dust Bowl Act
Okla. Stat. Ann., Title 82, § 455 et seq.

Dust Disease Act
Mich. Comp. Laws Ann., 418.501 et seq.

Duster's and Sprayer's Lien Law
Wash. Rev. Code Ann., 60.14.010 et seq.

Dutch John Federal Property Disposition and Assistance Act of 1998
Oct. 30, 1998, P.L. 105-326, 112 Stat. 3040, 16 U.S. Code § 460v nt.

Dutchess County Resource Recovery Agency Act
N.Y. Public Authorities Law (Consol. Laws Ch. 43A) § 2047a et seq.

Dutchess County Water and Wastewater Authority Act
N.Y. Public Authorities Law (Consol. Laws Ch. 43A) § 1121 et seq.

Duties and Responsibilities of the Advisory Neighborhood Commissions Act
D.C. Code Ann., § 1-261 et seq.

Duties to Disabled Persons Act
See Uniform Duties to Disabled Persons Act

Duty to Aid the Endangered Act
Vt. Stat. Ann., Title 12, § 519

Duval County Bait Shrimp Law
Fla. Special Laws 1970, Ch. 70-678

Duval County Budget Act
Fla. Laws 1961, Ch. 1628

Duval County Civil Service Board Act
Fla. Special Laws 1943, Ch. 22263

Duval County Teachers' Tenure Act
Fla. Special Laws 1941, Ch. 21197

Duval County Water and Sanitary Sewerage Authority Act
Fla. Special Laws 1959, Ch. 59-1248

Duxbury Sea Wall Loan Act
Mass. Acts 1952, Ch. 531

Dwelling House Act
Cal. Health and Safety Code § 17910 et seq.

Dwelling Structure Contract Act
Ill. Rev. Stat. 1991, Ch. 29, § 8.10 et seq.

Dwelling Unit Installment Contract Act
Ill. Rev. Stat. 1991, Ch. 29, § 8.20 et seq.

DWI Act
N.H. Rev. Stat. 1955, 265:82
S.C. Code Ann. 1976, § 56-5-2940 et seq.

DWI Act (Omnibus)
Ark. Code Ann. 1987, 5-65-101 et seq.

DWI Local Grant Program Act
N.M. Stat. Ann., 11-6A-1 et seq.

Dwight D. Eisenhower Leadership Development Act of 1992
July 23, 1992, P.L. 102-325, 20 U.S. Code § 1135f

Dwight D. Eisenhower Mathematics and Science Education Act
April 28, 1988, P.L. 100-297, 102 Stat. 219, 20 U.S. Code §§ 2981 et seq.
Nov. 16, 1990, P.L. 101-589, 20 U.S. Code §§ 237, 240, 240 nt., 2982 nt., 2983 et seq., 2994 et seq., 2996, 5301 et seq. generally; 42 U.S. Code § 1869

Dwight D. Eisenhower Memorial Bicentennial Civil Center Act
Oct. 21, 1972, P.L. 92-520, 40 U.S. Code § 616 nt.

Dwight David Eisenhower Commemorative Coin Act of 1988
Oct. 3, 1988, P.L. 100-467, 102 Stat. 2275, 31 U.S. Code § 5112 nt.
Oct. 6, 1992, P.L. 102-390, 31 U.S. Code § 5112 nt.

Dycus-Linton Act
Ky. Rev. Stat. 1971, 134.300 et seq., 134.990

Dye and Chemical Control Act, 1921
May 27, 1921, Ch. 14, 42 Stat. 18

Dyeing and Dry Cleaning Law
Pa. Purdon's Stat., Title 35, § 1269.1 et seq.

Dyer Act (Motor Vehicles)
See National Motor Vehicle Theft Act

Dyer County Budget Act
Tenn. Private Acts 1972, Ch. 319

Dyer Industrial Stabilization Act
Ind. Laws 1935, Ch. 177, p. 854

Dying Declarations Act
Tex. Code of Criminal Procedure, Art. 38.20

Dykstra Act (Trunk Line Highways)
Mich. Comp. Laws 1948, 250.31, 250.34

Dymally Adoption Act
Cal. Statutes 1971, Ch. 1724, p. 3669

Dymally-Alatorre Bilingual Services Act
Cal. Government Code § 7290 et seq.

Dymally-Sieroty Children's Center Construction Act of 1968
Cal. Education Code 1976, § 16260 et seq.

Dymally-Waxman Campaign Disclosure Act
Cal. Elections Code 1976, § 11500 et seq.
Wyo. Stat. Ann., § 19-5-101 et seq.

Dynamic Capital and Surplus Act
N.J. Stat. Ann., 17B:18-67 et seq.

E

E. Richard Barnes Act (Teachers' Retirement)
Cal. Education Code 1976, § 22000 et seq.

Earl H. Wright School Bus Replacement Act
Fla. Stat. Ann., 236.0835

Earle Act (Workmen's Compensation)
Pa. Purdon's Stat., Title 77, § 1 et seq.

Early Assistance, Early Childhood, and Prevention Act
Fla. Stat. Ann., 411.201 et seq.

Early Childhood and Adult Education Act
Ark. Code Ann. 1987, 6-16-301 et seq.

Early Childhood and Family Development Act
Fla. Stat. 1983, 23.13 et seq.

Early Childhood and Family Education Act
Minn. Stat. 1984, 129B.06 et seq.

Early Childhood Assistance Act
Wash. Rev. Code Ann., 28A.34A.010 et seq.

Early Childhood Development Act
Ga. Code 1933, 32-2101b et seq.

Early Childhood Development and Academic Assistance Act
S.C. Code Ann. 1976, § 59-139-05 et seq.

Early Childhood Education Grant-in-Aid Program Act
Miss. Code Ann. 1972, § 37-21-7

Early Childhood Education Professional Loan Forgiveness Act
Pa. Purdon's Stat., Title 24, § 7101 et seq.

Early Childhood Intervention Services Act
Mass. Gen. Laws Ann., 111F:1 et seq., 111G:1 et seq.

Early High School Graduation Scholarship Program
Tex. Education Code, Art. 56.201 et seq.

Early HOPE Scholarship Act
Ga. Code Ann., 20-2-2080 et seq.

Early Intervention Act
Neb. Rev. Stat. 1943, 43-2501 et seq.
Okla. Stat. Ann., Title 70, § 13-121 et seq.

Early Intervention Act for Infants and Toddlers
Miss. Code Ann. 1972, § 41-87-1 et seq.

Early Intervention Act for Infants and Toddlers with Disabilities
Ala. Code 1975, § 21-3A-1 et seq.

Early Intervention Services Act
Cal. Government Code § 95000 et seq.

Early Intervention Services System Act
Ill. Comp. Stat. 1992, Ch. 325, § 20/1 et seq.
Ill. Rev. Stat. 1991, Ch. 23, § 4151 et seq.
Pa. Purdon's Stat., Title 11, § 875-101 et seq.

Early Investment Act (Children's)
Fla. Stat. Ann., 411.23

Early Mental Health Intervention and Prevention Services for Children Act (School-based)
Cal. Welfare and Institutions Code § 4370 et seq.

Early Mental Health Intervention and Prevention Services for Children Act (School-Based)
Cal. Welfare and Institutions Code § 4370 et seq.

Early Retirement Incentive and Permanent Payroll Reduction Act
La. Rev. Stat. Ann., 42:541 et seq.

Early Retirement Reserve Act
Ill. Rev. Stat. 1991, Ch. 108 1/2, § 201 et seq.

Early Start Project
R.I. Gen. Laws 1956, 42-72.3-1 et seq.

Early Voting Act (Absentee)
N.M. Stat. Ann., 1-6A-1 et seq.

Earned Income Tax Credit Information Act
Del. Laws, Vol. 67, Ch. 443
Ill. Comp. Stat. 1992, Ch. 820, § 170/1 et seq.

Earnings Protection Act
Cal. Code of Civil Procedure § 723.010 et seq.

Earnings Tax on Nonresidents Act (Yonkers)
N.Y. Laws 1987, Ch. 333, § 167

Earthquake Education Act
Cal. Public Resources Code §§ 2800 et seq., 2805 et seq.

Earthquake Fault Zoning Act (Alquist-Priolo)
Cal. Public Resources Code § 2621 et seq.

Earthquake Hazards Reduction Act
Cal. Government Code § 8870 et seq.

Earthquake Hazards Reduction Act of 1977
Oct. 7, 1977, P.L. 95-124, 42 U.S. Code §§ 7701 et seq., 7701 nt.
Nov. 20, 1981, P.L. 97-80, 42 U.S. Code § 7706
Jan. 12, 1983, P.L. 97-464, 42 U.S. Code § 7706
March 22, 1984, P.L. 98-241, 42 U.S. Code § 7706
Sept. 30, 1985, P.L. 99-105, 42 U.S. Code §§ 7704, 7706
Feb. 29, 1988, P.L. 100-252, 102 Stat. 18, 42 U.S. Code §§ 7704, 7706
Nov. 23, 1988, P.L. 100-707, 42 U.S. Code § 7704
Nov. 16, 1990, P.L. 101-614, 42 U.S. Code § 7701 et seq.
Oct. 19, 1994, P.L. 103-374, 42 U.S. Code § 7706
Oct. 1, 1997, P.L. 105-47, 42 U.S. Code §§ 7704, 7705, 7705a, 7706

Earthquake Preparedness Act
Ark. Code Ann. 1987, 12-77-101 et seq.

Earthquake Protection Act (Riley)
Cal. Health and Safety Code § 19100 et seq.

Earthquake Reconstruction and Replacement Bond Law
Cal. Education Code 1976, §§ 17400 et seq., 17500 et seq.

Earthquake Recovery Act (Green, Hill, Areias, Farr)
Cal. Insurance Code § 5000 et seq.

Earthquake Relief and Seismic Retrofit Bond Act
Cal. Government Code § 8879 et seq.

Earthquake Safety Act (Hughes)
Cal. Education Code 1976, §§ 17701, 39141.4, 39250

Earthquake Safety and Housing Rehabilitation Bond Act
Cal. Government Code § 8878.15 et seq.

Earthquake Safety and Public Buildings Rehabilitation Act
Cal. Government Code § 8878.50 et seq.

Earthslide Relief Act
Alaska Stat. 1962, § 09.45.800 et seq.

Easement Act (Land Conservation)
Utah Code Ann. 1953, 57-18-1 et seq.

Easement Act (Land Use)
N.M. Stat. Ann., 47-12-1 et seq.

Easement Act (Open-Space)
Cal. Government Code § 51070 et seq.

Easements Act (Public Lands)
Wash. Rev. Code Ann., 79.36.230 et seq.

Easements Vacation Law (Public Streets, Highways, and Service)
Cal. Streets and Highways Code § 8300 et seq.

East Asia Development Advisory Board Act
Ill. Rev. Stat. 1991, Ch. 127, § 3451 et seq.

East Aurora Sign Law
N.Y. Local Laws 1972, Village of East Aurora, p. 3170

East Bay Commuter Transit Corporation Act
R.I. Gen. Laws 1956, 42-64.2-1 et seq.

East Boston Terminal Facilities Loan Act
Mass. Acts 1952, Ch. 505

East Bridgewater Sewerage Loan Act
Mass. Acts 1964, Ch. 88

East Fork of the Jemez River and the Pecos River Wild and Scenic Rivers Addition Act of 1989
June 6, 1990, P.L. 101-306, 16 U.S. Code § 1271 nt.

East Hudson Parkway Authority Act
N.Y. Public Authorities Law (Consol. Laws Ch. 43A) § 450 et seq.

East Kentucky Economic Development and Job Creation Corporation Act
Ky. Rev. Stat. 1971, 154B.100 et seq.

East Kern-Antelope Valley Water Agency Law
Cal. Statutes 1959, Ch. 2146, p. 5114, § 49 et seq.

East Providence Minimum Nonresidential Standards Act
R.I. Public Laws 1968, Ch. 208

East Providence Minimum Standards Housing Act
R.I. Public Laws 1961, Ch. 66

East Randolph Zoning Local Act
N.Y. Local Laws 1964, Village of East Randolph, p. 818

East River Statute (Navigation)
N.Y. Laws 1848, Ch. 321

East St. Louis Airport Act
Ill. Comp. Stat. 1992, Ch. 620, § 55/1 et seq.
Ill. Rev. Stat. 1991, Ch. 15 1/2, §§ 260, 261

East St. Louis Area Development Act
Ill. Comp. Stat. 1992, Ch. 70, § 505/1 et seq.
Ill. Rev. Stat. 1991, Ch. 85, § 5501 et seq.

East St. Louis Development Act
Ill. Rev. Stat. 1991, Ch. 38, § 5501 et seq.

East-West Center Corporation Act
Haw. Rev. Stat. Ann., § 88-49.7

East-West Expressway Act
La. Rev. Stat. Ann., 48:1451 et seq.

Eastchester Anti-Litter Law
N.Y. Local Laws 1971, Town of Eastchester, p. 1617

Eastchester Minimum Housing Standards Code
N.Y. Local Laws 1971, Town of Eastchester, p. 1637

Eastchester Parade Law
N.Y. Local Laws 1971, Town of Eastchester, p. 1631

Eastern Illinois University Law
Ill. Comp. Stat. 1992, Ch. 110, § 665/10-1 et seq.

Eastern Illinois University Name Change Act
Ill. Rev. Stat. 1991, Ch. 144, §§ 699, 700

Eastern Illinois University Objects Act
Ill. Rev. Stat. 1991, Ch. 144, § 702.01 et seq.

Eastern Illinois University Revenue Bond Law
Ill. Comp. Stat. 1992, Ch. 110, § 666/11-1 et seq.

Eastern Orthodox Church Act
Ind. Burns' 1988, 25-4501 et seq.

Eastern Pacific Tuna Licensing Act of 1984
Oct. 4, 1984, P.L. 98-445, 98 Stat. 1715, 16 U.S. Code §§ 972 et seq., 972 nt.

Eastern Rensselaer County Solid Waste Management Authority Act
N.Y. Public Authorities Law (Consol. Laws Ch. 43A) § 2050aa et seq.

Eastern Will Sanitary District Act
Ill. Comp. Stat. 1992, Ch. 70, § 3020/1 et seq.

Eastpoint Water and Sewer District Act
Fla. Special Laws 1967, Ch. 67-1399

Easy to Read Life and Health Insurance Policy Act
Tenn. Code Ann., 56-7-101, 56-7-1601 et seq., 56-26-106, 56-26-108, 56-26-109

Eaton Foreign Service Act
July 19, 1939, Ch. 330, 53 Stat. 1067

Eatonton-Putman County Charter Commission Act
Ga. Laws 1972, p. 2665

Eau Gallie Urban Renewal Act
Fla. Special Laws 1967, Ch. 67-1362

Eaves-Boatwright Parole Review Act
Cal. Penal Code § 3041.2

Eaves-Felando-Presley Wiretap Act
Cal. Penal Code § 629 et seq.

Eavesdropping Act
Ariz. Rev. Stat. Ann., § 13-3004 et seq.
Colo. Rev. Stat., 16-15-101 et seq.
Ga. Code Ann., 16-11-60 et seq.
Ill. Rev. Stat. 1991, Ch. 38, § 14-1 et seq.
Mass. Gen. Laws Ann., 272:99
N.Y. Criminal Procedure Law (Consol. Laws Ch. 11A) § 700.05 et seq.
N.Y. Penal Law 1965 (Consol. Laws Ch. 40) § 250.00 et seq.
Pa. Cons. Stat., Title 18, § 5701 et seq.

Echols County Water Authority Act
Ga. Laws 1972, p. 2981

Ecologically Harmful Species Law
Minn. Stat. Ann., 84.967 et seq.

Ecology Procedures Simplification Act
Wash. Rev. Code Ann., 43.21B.001 et seq.

Economic Action Plan (Rural)
Okla. Stat. Ann., Title 62, § 2001 et seq.

Economic Adjustment Act (Local)
Tenn. Code Ann., 9-14-101 et seq.

Economic Advancement District Act
N.M. Stat. Ann., 6-19-1 et seq.

Economic and Business Development Act
Cal. Government Code § 15310 et seq.
Utah Code Ann. 1953, 9-2-201 et seq.

Economic and Community Development Act
Tenn. Public Acts 1972, Ch. 852

Economic and Environmental Assistance Act (Underground Storage Tank)
Wyo. Stat. Ann., § 35-11-1401 et seq.

Economic and Environmental Impact Statement Act
N.J. Stat. Ann., 52:13F-1 et seq.

Economic and Fiscal Commission Act
Ill. Rev. Stat. 1991, Ch. 63, § 341 et seq.

Economic and Industrial Development Corporation Act
Okla. Stat. 1981, Title 74, § 1351 et seq.

Economic and Industrial Development Revenue Bond Law
Ark. Code Ann. 1987, 14-164-501 et seq.

Economic and Social Opportunity Act
Mich. Comp. Laws Ann., 400.1101 et seq.

Economic Assistance Act
Wash. Rev. Code Ann., 43.31A.010 et seq.

Economic Assistance Act (Department of Human Services)
N.J. Stat Ann., 30:4B-1 to 30:4B-10

Economic Betterment Program (Community)
Iowa Code Ann., 15.315 et seq.

Economic Competitiveness Act (Workforce and)

Tex. General and Special Laws 1993, p. 2468, Ch. 668

Economic Cooperation Act of 1948

April 3, 1948, Ch. 169, 62 Stat. 137, 7 U.S. Code § 612c nt.; 22 U.S. Code § 286b

April 19, 1949, Ch. 77, 63 Stat. 50

April 5, 1952, Ch. 159, 66 Stat. 43, 22 U.S. Code §§ 272b, 281b, 290a, 1434

June 20, 1952, Ch. 449, 66 Stat. 150, 22 U.S. Code §§ 1510, 1513

July 16, 1953, Ch. 195, 67 Stat. 161, 22 U.S. Code §§ 1509, 1513, 1513 nt.

Economic Cooperation Act of 1950

June 5, 1950, Ch. 220, 64 Stat. 198

Economic Crime Act

Cal. Penal Code § 1203.044

Economic Crimes and Fraud Prosecution Act

Tenn. Public Acts 1984, Ch. 998

Economic Development Act

Ark. Code Ann. 1987, 15-4-101 et seq.

Fla. Laws 1988, Ch. 201

Ill. Rev. Stat. 1983, Ch. 48, § 901 et seq.

Ind. Code Ann., 496B.1 et seq.

Kan. Stat. Ann., 74-5002 et seq.

Ky. Rev. Stat. 1971, Superseded Vols., 152.050 et seq.

La. Rev. Stat. Ann., 51:2301 et seq.

Mich. Comp. Laws 1948, 125.1 et seq.

N.D. Cent. Code, 54-34-01 et seq.

Nev. Rev. Stat. 1979 Reprint, 231.010 et seq.

N.M. Laws 1967, Ch. 89

N.Y. Economic Development Law (Consol. Laws Ch. 15) § 1 et seq.

Okla. Laws 1991, Ch. 222

Okla. Stat. 1971, Title 74, § 671 et seq.

W. Va. Code 1966 § 5B-1-1 et seq.

Economic Development Act (Agricultural)

Fla. Stat. Ann., 570.241 et seq.

Economic Development Act (Ayala-Baca)

Cal. Statutes 1993, 1st Ex. Sess., Ch. 2

Economic Development Act (Baca-Ayala)

Cal. Statutes 1993, 1st Ex. Sess., Ch. 1

Economic Development Act (Business)

Utah Code Ann. 1953, 63-31-1 et seq.

Economic Development Act (Comprehensive)

Fla. Laws 1990, Ch. 201

Economic Development Act (Delaware Bay Area and Port of New Jersey Revitalization, Dredging, Environmental Cleanup, and Lake Restoration)

N.J. Laws 1996, Ch. 70

Economic Development Act (Local Option Municipal)

Neb. Rev. Stat. 1943, 18-2701 to 2723

Economic Development Act (Local)

Ida. Laws 1988, Ch. 210

N.M. Stat. Ann., 5-10-1 et seq.

Economic Development Act (Minority Business)

Ark. Acts 1991, No. 698

Economic Development Act (Municipalities)

Ind. Code 1976, 18-6-4.5-1 et seq.

Vt. Stat. Ann., Title 24, § 2741 et seq.

Economic Development Act (Regional)

Conn. Public Acts 1993, No. 382, §§ 23 to 28

Economic Development Act (Rural Facilities)

Ga. Code Ann., 50-8-210 et seq.

Economic Development Act (Rural)

Cal. Government Code § 15373 et seq.

Ill. Rev. Stat. 1991, Ch. 5, § 2201-1

Economic Development Administration and Appalachian Regional Development Reform Act of 1998

Nov. 13, 1998, P.L. 105-393, 112 Stat. 3596, 42 U.S. Code § 3121 nt.

Economic Development Administration Reform Act of 1998
Nov. 13, 1998, P.L. 105-393, Title I, 112 Stat. 3597, 42 U.S. Code § 3121 nt.

Economic Development Agency, Fiduciary and Lender Environmental Liability Protection Act
Pa. Purdon's Stat., Title 35, § 6027.1 et seq.

Economic Development and Commerce Department Act
N.J. Stat. Ann., 52:27H-1 et seq.

Economic Development and Gaming Control Act (Riverboat)
La. Rev. Stat. Ann., 4:501 et seq.

Economic Development and Job Creation Corporation Act (East Kentucky)
Ky. Rev. Stat. 1971, 154B.100 et seq.

Economic Development and Manufacturing Assistance Act
Conn. Gen. Stat. 1983, § 32-220 et seq.

Economic Development and Manufacturing Assistance Act of 1990
Conn. Public Acts 1991, No. 270

Economic Development and Planning Act
Miss. General Laws 1991, Ch. 484, p. 499

Economic Development and Port Authority Corporation Act
R.I. Gen. Laws 1956, 42-64-1 et seq.

Economic Development and Research Act (University Based)
Ind. Code Ann., 262B.1 et seq.

Economic Development and Tax—Related Job Creation Act
Del. Code of 1974, Title 30, § 1102

Economic Development and Tourism Department Act
N.M. Stat. Ann., 9-15-16 et seq.

Economic Development Area Tax Increment Allocation Act
Ill. Rev. Stat. 1991, Ch. 67 1/2, § 1001 et seq.

Economic Development Assistance Act
N.J. Stat. Ann., 13:16-1 et seq.
R.I. Gen. Laws 1956, 42-64.1-1 et seq.

Economic Development Assistance Corporation Act (Community)
Mass. Gen. Laws 1984, 40H:1 et seq.

Economic Development Authority Act
Ind. Code 1976, 4-23-5-1 et seq.
N.J. Stat. Ann., 34:1B-1 et seq.
W. Va. Code 1966, § 31-15-1 et seq.

Economic Development Authority Act (Burke County)
Ga. Laws 1991, p. 4120

Economic Development Authority Act (Jasper County)
Ga. Laws 1991, p. 4524

Economic Development Authority Act (Rabun County)
Ga. Laws 1992, p. 4912

Economic Development Bond Act
Kan. Stat. Ann., 12-1740 et seq.
Mont. Code Ann., 17-5-1501 et seq.

Economic Development Compact (Chickasaw Trail)
Miss. Code Ann. 1972, § 57-36-1 et seq.

Economic Development Corporations Act
Mich. Comp. Laws Ann., 125.1601 et seq.

Economic Development Credit Enhancement Act
Ark. Acts 1989, No. 945

Economic Development Department Act
N.M. Stat. Ann., 9-15-1 et seq.

Economic Development Financing Act
N.C. Gen. Stat. 1943, § 159-101 et seq.
Pa. Purdon's Stat., Title 73, § 371 et seq.

Economic Development Fund Act
S.C. Code Ann. 1976, § 41-43-10 et seq.

Economic Development Grant Authorization Act (City and County)
Ark. Code Ann. 1987, 14-173-101 et seq.

Economic Development Highway Act
Miss. Code Ann. 1972, § 65-4-1 et seq.

Economic Development Industrial Cluster Act
S.C. Code Ann. 1976, §§ 12-6-3480, 12-10-45, 12-20-105, 38-7-190

Economic Development Innovation Act
Okla. Stat. 1981, Title 74, § 5009.1 et seq.

Economic Development Network Act
Ind. Code Ann., 15.301 et seq.

Economic Development Organization Act
Mich. Comp. Laws Ann., 125.2401 et seq.

Economic Development Partnerships Act
Neb. Rev. Stat. 1943, 81-1288 et seq.

Economic Development Plan for the Northwestern Band of the Shoshoni Nation Act
Sept. 8, 1988, P.L. 100-419, 102 Stat. 1575

Economic Development Planning Act (Statewide)
Miss. Code Ann. 1972, § 57-63-1 et seq.

Economic Development Policy and Planning Act
Mo. Rev. Stat. 1978, 620.600

Economic Development Program Act (Rural)
Pa. Purdon's Stat., Title 73, § 392.101 et seq.

Economic Development Program for Depressed Areas Act
Haw. Rev. Stat. Ann., § 208.1 et seq.

Economic Development Project Area Property Tax Allocation Act (County)
Ill. Comp. Stat. 1992, Ch. 55, § 90/1 et seq.

Economic Development Project Area Tax Increment Allocation Act (County)
Ill. Rev. Stat. 1991, Ch. 34, § 8001 et seq.

Economic Development Promotion Act
N.M. Stat. Ann., 3-58-1, 3-58-2

Economic Development Reform Act
Miss. Code Ann. 1972, § 57-73-1 et seq.

Economic Development Reporting Act
R.I. Gen. Laws 1956, 42-64.4-1 et seq.

Economic Development Revenue Bond Act
Colo. Rev. Stat., 29-3-101 et seq.
Md. Ann. Code 1957, Art.41, § 14-101 et seq.

Economic Development Revenue Bond Act (County)
Nev. Rev. Stat. 1979 Reprint, 244A.669 et seq.

Economic Development Training Act
Del. Code of 1974, Title 29, § 5070 et seq.

Economic Development Zones Act (New York State)
N.Y. General Municipal Law (Consol. Laws Ch. 24) § 955 et seq.

Economic Disaster Act (Farr)
Cal. Government Code § 8695 et seq.

Economic Dislocation and Worker Adjustment Assistance Act
Aug. 23, 1988, P.L. 100-418, 102 Stat. 1524, 29 U.S. Code § 1501 nt.

Economic Diversification and Afforestation Act
Mo. Laws 1990, H.B. No. 1653, §§ 1 to 12
Mo. Rev. Stat. 1978, 252.300

Economic Education Act
Okla. Stat. Ann., Title 70, § 1210.251 et seq.

Economic Espionage Act of 1996
Oct. 11, 1996, P.L. 104-294, 18 U.S. Code § 1 nt.

Dec. 2, 1997, P.L. 105-133, 42 U.S. Code § 13751 nt.

Economic Estimates Commission Act
Ida. Code 1947, 67-6801 et seq.

Economic Growth and Regulatory Paperwork Reduction Act of 1996
Sept. 30, 1996, P.L. 104-208, 12 U.S. Code § 226 nt.

Economic Growth Authority Act
Mich. Comp. Laws Ann., 207.801 et seq.

Economic Impact Act
Wash. Rev. Code Ann., 43.130.010 et seq.

Economic Impact Act (Major)
Miss. Code Ann. 1972, § 57-75-1 et seq.

Economic Impact Disclosure Act
Fla. Laws 1976, Ch. 76-1
Tenn. Code Ann., 4-33-101

Economic Impact Statement Act
Tex. Gov. Code, § 315.001 et seq.

Economic Impact Zone Community Development Act
S.C. Code Ann. 1976, § 12-14-10 et seq.

Economic Land Development Act
Mont. Code Ann., 15-24-1301 et seq.

Economic Opportunity Act
Ill. Rev. Stat. 1991, Ch. 127, § 2601 et seq.

Economic Opportunity Act of 1964
Aug. 20, 1964, P.L. 88-452, 78 Stat. 508, 42 U.S. Code §§ 2701, 2711 to 2720, 2731 to 2736, 2751 to 2756, 2761, 2781 to 2791, 2801 to 2807, 2821, 2822 and others
April 30, 1965, P.L. 89-16, 79 Stat. 108, 42 U.S. Code § 2881
Oct. 9, 1965, P.L. 89-253, 79 Stat. 973, 42 U.S. Code §§ 2713, 2714, 2716, 2720, 2734, and others
Nov. 8, 1965 P.L. 89-329, 79 Stat. 1249, 42 U.S. Code §§ 2751 to 2755, 2761

Nov. 8, 1966, P.L. 89-794, 80 Stat. 1451, 42 U.S. Code §§ 2701, 2713, 2714, 2716, 2721, 2722, 2732 to 2735, 2761, 2762, 2771, 2782, 2783, 2785 to 2788, and others
Sept. 6, 1967, P.L. 90-82, 81 Stat. 194, 42 U.S. Code § 2754
Oct. 11, 1967, P.L. 90-104, 81 Stat. 269, 42 U.S. Code § 2902
Dec. 23, 1967, P.L. 90-222, 81 Stat. 672, 42 U.S. Code §§ 2711 to 2729, 2737 to 2749, 2751 to 2756, 2763 to 2768 and others
Oct. 16, 1968, P.L. 90-575, 82 Stat. 1019, 42 U.S. Code §§ 2741, 2751 to 2756, 2809
Oct. 22, 1968, P.L. 90-623, 82 Stat. 1315, 42 U.S. Code §§ 2727, 2994b
Dec. 30, 1969, P.L. 91-177, 83 Stat. 827, Title 42 U.S. Code §§ 2701, 2769 to 2769f 2771, 2809, 2834, 2837, 2851, 2871, 2907, 2933 and others
Aug. 12, 1970, P.L. 91-375, 84 Stat. 783, 42 U.S. Code § 2942
June 27, 1972, P.L. 92-320, 86 Stat. 382, 42 U.S. Code § 2902
Sept. 19, 1972, P.L. 92-424, 86 Stat. 688, 42 U.S. Code §§ 2720b, 2724, 2742, 2749, 2771, 2791, 2809, 2812 to 2815, 2824, 2827, 2836, 2837, and others
Dec. 28, 1973, P.L. 93-202, 87 Stat. 838, 42 U.S. Code § 2809
July 25, 1974, P.L. 93-355, 88 Stat. 378, 42 U.S. Code §§ 2996 to 2996l
Aug. 23, 1974, P.L. 93-386, 88 Stat. 745, 42 U.S. Code §§ 2855, 2942, 2949, 2982a
Nov. 2, 1978, P.L. 95-568, 42 U.S. Code §§ 2701 nt., 2713, 2716, 2790 et seq.

Economic Opportunity Amendments of 1978
Nov. 2, 1978, P.L. 95-568, 42 U.S. Code §§ 2701 nt., 2713, 2716, 2790 et seq.

Economic Opportunity Programs
W. Va. Code 1966, § 7-13-1 et seq.

Economic Planning and Development Act
Ariz. Rev. Stat. Ann., § 41-1501 et seq.

Economic Poisons Act
Ga. Code Ann., 2-7-20 et seq.
Minn. Stat. 1974, 24.069 et seq.
Miss. Code Ann. 1972, § 69-23-1 et seq.
Continued

N.H. Rev. Stat. 1955, 430:28 et seq.

R.I. Gen. Laws 1956, 2-8-1 et seq.

Wash. Rev. Code Ann., 94.67 et seq.

Economic Poisons Act (Pesticides)

Ariz. Laws 1945, Ch. 93

Cal. Food and Agricultural Code 1967, §§ 11901, 12501 et seq., 12751 et seq.

Ga. Code Ann., 2-7-50 et seq.

Haw. Rev. Stat. Ann., § 149-1 et seq.

Ida. Code 1947, 22-3401 et seq.

Ky. Rev. Stat. 1971, 217.541 et seq.

Me. Rev. Stat. Ann. 1964, Title 7, § 601 et seq.

Mich. Comp. Laws Ann., 286.161 et seq.

Minn. Stat. 1974, § 24.069 et seq.

Miss. Code Ann. 1972, § 69-23-1 et seq.

Mo. Rev. Stat., 263.269 et seq.

Nev. Rev. Stat. 1979 Reprint, 586.010 et seq.

N.H. Rev. Stat. 1955, 430:28 et seq.

N.J. Stat. Ann., 4:8A-1 et seq.

N.M. Stat Ann. 1978, 76-4-1 et seq.

Ore. Rev. Stat., 634.006 et seq.

Pa. 1917 Pamph. Laws 208 No. 119 § 17

P.R. Laws Ann. 1954, Title 10, § 976 et seq.

R.I. Gen. Laws 1956, 2-8-1 et seq.

S.C. Code Ann. 1962, § 3-151 et seq.

Wash. Rev. Code Ann., 94.67 et seq.

Economic Protection Act (Depositors)

R.I. Gen. Laws 1956, 42-116-1 et seq.

Economic Protection Trust Fund Act (Northeast Minnesota)

Minn. Stat. Ann., 298.291 et seq.

Economic Recovery Fund Act

N.J. Laws 1992, Ch. 16

Economic Recovery Program Act (Community)

Pa. Purdon's Stat., Title 73, § 399.1 et seq.

Economic Recovery Tax Act of 1981

Aug. 31, 1981, P.L. 97-34, 26 U.S. Code § 1 nt.

July 18, 1984, P.L. 98-369, 98 Stat. 1042, 1053, 26 U.S. Code §§ 51 nt., 3306 nt.

April 7, 1986, P.L. 99-272, 26 U.S. Code § 3306 nt.

Oct. 22, 1986, P.L. 99-514, 26 U.S. Code §§ 51 nt., 165 nt.

Nov. 10, 1988, P.L. 100-647, 26 U.S. Code §§ 261 nt., 471 nt.

Dec. 19, 1989, P.L. 101-239, 26 U.S. Code § 51 nt.

Nov. 5, 1990, P.L. 101-508, 26 U.S. Code § 51 nt.

Economic Rehabilitation Act

Ga. Code Ann., 49-8-1 et seq.

Economic Revitalization Act

Pa. Purdon's Stat., Title 73, § 392.1 et seq.

Economic Revitalization Act (Distressed Areas)

R.I. Gen. Laws 1956, 42-64.3-1 et seq.

Economic Revitalization Act (West Kentucky)

Ky. Rev. Stat. 1971, 154.85-010c et seq.

Economic Revitalization Fund Appropriation Act

Pa. 1985 Pamph. Laws, No. 10A

Economic Revitalization Tax Assistance Act

Pa. 1977 Pamph. Laws 237 No. 76

Economic Revitalization Tax Assistance Act (Local)

Pa. Purdon's Stat., Title 72, § 4722 et seq.

Economic Revitalization Tax Credit Law

Pa. Cons. Stat., Title 72, § 7217 et seq.

Economic Security Act (Family)

Cal. Welfare and Institutions Code § 11200 et seq.

Economic Stabilization Act

Md. Ann. Code 1957, Art. 41A, § 3-301 et seq.

Economic Stabilization Act of 1970

Aug. 15, 1970, P.L. 91-379, 84 Stat. 799, 12 U.S. Code § 1904 nt.

Dec. 17, 1970, P.L. 91-558, 84 Stat. 1468, 12 U.S. Code § 1904 nt.

March 31, 1971, P.L. 92-8, 85 Stat. 13, 12 U.S. Code § 1904 nt.

May 18, 1971, P.L. 92-15, 85 Stat. 38, 12 U.S. Code § 1904 nt.

Dec. 22, 1971, P.L. 92-210, 85 Stat. 743, 12 U.S. Code § 1904 nt.

Oct. 29, 1992, P.L. 102-572, 12 U.S. Code § 1904 nt.

Economic Support Act (Business)
Ill. Comp. Stat. 1992, Ch. 30, § 760/1 et seq.

Economic Support for Business Act
Ill. Rev. Stat. 1991, Ch. 48, § 2701 et seq.

Economy Act (City of New York)
N.Y. Laws 1932, Ex. Sess., Ch. 637
N.Y. Laws 1934, Ch. 178

Economy Acts
June 30, 1932, Ch. 314, 47 Stat. 382, 15 U.S. Code § 276; 30 U.S. Code § 7; 31 U.S. Code §§ 686, 686b; 40 U.S. Code §§ 267 nt., 303b

March 3, 1933, Ch. 212, 47 Stat. 1489, 31 U.S. Code §§ 227, 767b; 36 U.S. Code § 13; 41 USC §§ 10a to 10c

March 20, 1933, Ch. 3, 48 Stat. 8

Oct. 15, 1982, P.L. 97-332, 31 U.S. Code § 686

Economy in Government Loan Fund Act
N.J. Stat. Ann., 40:8B-10 et seq.

Ector County Independent School District Pilot Project
Tex. Education Code, Art. 29.186

Edge Act
See Mineral Lands Leasing Act

Edge Act (Federal Reserve Banks)
Dec. 24, 1919, Ch. 18, 41 Stat. 378, 12 U.S. Code §§ 611 to 631

Edgewater Utilities Revenue Bond Act
Fla. Special Laws 1947, Ch. 24494

Edible Bean Industry Promotion Act
N.D. Cent. Code, 4-10.3-01 et seq.

Edible Oil Regulatory Reform Act
Nov. 20, 1995, P.L. 104-55, 33 U.S. Code § 2701 nt.

Edmonds Act (Teachers Salaries)
Pa. 1911 Pamph. Laws 309, § 1210

Edmunds Act (Polygamy)
March 22, 1882, Ch. 47, 22 Stat. 30

Edmunds-Tucker Act (Polygamy)
March 3, 1887, Ch. 397, 24 Stat. 635, 48 U.S. Code § 1480a

Educable Mentally Handicapped Children Act
Ill. Rev. Stat. 1991, Ch. 122, § 14-1.01 et seq.

Education Accountability Act
Ga. Code Ann., 20-3-650 et seq.

Education Accountability and Assessment of Performance Act
Miss. Code Ann. 1972, § 37-3-46 et seq.

Education Act
Alaska Stat. 1962, § 14.30.010 et seq.
Cal. Education Code 1976, § 51000 et seq.
Colo. Rev. Stat., 22-2-101 et seq.
Ga. Code Ann., 20-1-1 et seq.
Md. Ann. Code 1974, Art. ED, § 1-101 et seq.
Minn. Stat. Ann., 120.01 et seq.
N.D. Cent. Code, 15-01-01 et seq.
Neb. Rev. Stat. 1943, 79-201 et seq.
N.H. Rev. Stat. 1955, 2-N:1 et seq.
N.J. Stat. Ann., 18A:75-1 et seq.
N.Y. Consol. Laws Ch. 16
Pa. Purdon's Stat., Title 24 § 1-101 et seq.
R.I. Gen. Laws 1956, 16-28-4, 16-33.1-6, 16-57-7, 16-59-1 et seq., 42-6-1, 42-35-18
Tenn. Code Ann., 49-1-101 et seq.
Wyo. Stat. Ann., § 21-1-101 et seq.

Education Act (Alcohol Server)
N.M. Stat. Ann., 60-6D-1 et seq.

Education Act (Alternative)
Mo. Rev. Stat. 1978, 167.320

Education Act (American Indian)
Minn. Stat. Ann., 126.45 et seq.

Education Act (Bilingual)
Mass. Gen. Laws 1984, 71A:1 et seq.

Education Act (Community Hospital)
Fla. Stat. Ann., 381.0403

Education Act (Competency Based)
Ark. Code. Ann. 1987, 6-15-401 et seq.

Education Act (Comprehensive Health)
Colo. Rev. Stat., 22-25-101 et seq.

Education Act (Compulsory)
See Compulsory School Attendance Act

Education Act (Conservation)
Ill. Rev. Stat. 1991, Ch. 122, § 698.01 et seq.

Education Act (Dental Health)
Me. Rev. Stat. Ann. 1964, Title 22, § 2121 et seq.

Education Act (Department of Health)
N.M. Stat. Ann., 24-3B-1 et seq.

Education Act (Driver and Safety)
Tex. Rev. Civ. Stat., Art. 4413 (29c)

Education Act (Drug Abuse Resistance)
Fla. Stat. Ann., 233.0661 et seq.
Tenn. Code Ann., 49-1-401 et seq.

Education Act (Drug-Free Postsecondary)
Ga. Code Ann., 20-1-20 et seq.

Education Act (Environmental)
Mich. Comp. Laws Ann., 229.31 et seq.
Pa. 1993 Pamph. Laws, No. 24

Education Act (Excellence in)
Mo. Rev. Stat. 1978, 160.251 et seq.

Education Act (Exceptional Children)
Colo. Rev. Stat., 22-20-101 et seq.
Ky. Rev. Stat. 1971, 157.200 et seq.

Education Act (Federal Vocational)
Miss. Code Ann. 1972, § 37-33-157

Education Act (Interstate Compact)
Ill. Rev. Stat. 1991, Ch. 122, § 100-0.1 et seq.

Education Act (Motorcycle Rider)
Utah Code Ann. 1953, 41-26-101 et seq.

Education Act (Osteoporosis Prevention and Treatment)
Miss. Code Ann. 1972, § 41-93-1 et seq.

Education Act (Preschool Special)
Ala. Code 1975, § 16-39A-1

Education Act (Public School)
N.J. Stat. Ann., 18A:7A-1 et seq.

Education Act (Quality)
N.J. Stat. Ann., 18A:70-1 et seq.

Education Act (Regional Cooperative)
N.M. Stat. Ann., 22-2B-1 et seq.

Education Act (Remedial)
La. Rev. Stat. Ann., 17:394 et seq.
Miss. Code Ann. 1972, § 37-20-1 et seq.

Education Act (State Department of)
Colo. Rev. Stat., 22-1-109 et seq.

Education Act (Twenty-First Century)
N.M. Stat. Ann., 22-13B-1 et seq.
Ore. Laws 1991, Ch. 693

Education Act (Veterans)
See Veterans' Education Act

Education Act (Vocational)
Ill. Rev. Stat. 1991, Ch. 122, § 693h et seq.

Education Act (Work Force)
Miss. Code Ann. 1972, § 37-153-1 et seq.

Education Act for the 21st Century
Ore. Laws 1991, Ch. 693
Ore. Rev. Stat., 326.705

Education Adequate Program Act

Ga. Code Ann., 20-2-130 et seq.

Education Amendments of 1972

June 23, 1972, P.L. 92-318, 86 Stat. 235, 7 U.S. Code §§ 301 nt., 326a, 329, 331, 343, 349, 361a, 361c, 1626; 12 U.S. Code §§ 24, 84, 1464, 1757; 16 U.S. Code §§ 582a-3, 582a-7; 20 U.S. Code §§ 1 , 2 nts., 240, 241a nt., 241c, 241e, 241aa to 241ff 242 to 244, 331a, 332, 421, 425 nt., 426 nt., 441, 511, 513, 746 nt., 761 nt., 821 nt., 822, 823, 842, 843, 863 , 880b-3a, 887c, 887d, 900 to 900a-5, 1001, 1003, 1005a, 1006 to 1011, 1021 to 1024, 1027, 1031, 1033, 1034, 1041, 1042, 1051 to 1056, 1060 nt., 1061, 1068, 1070 to 1070d-1, 1070e, 1070e-1, 1074, 1075, 1077, 1078, 1078a, 1080, 1083, 1084, 1087, 1087-1, 1087-2, 1087a 1087c, 1087aa to 1087ff, 1088, 1088c to 1088g, 1089, 1091, 1091a, 1091b, 1091c, 1101, 1102, 1108 to 1111, 1115, 1116, 1118, 1119, 1119a, 1119b-2, 1121, 1129, 1132a to 1132a-7, 1132b, 1132b-1, 1132c to 1132c-5, 1132d to 1132d-5, 1132e 1132e-1, 1133a, 1134 to 1134s, 1135 to 1135c-1, 1136, 1136a, 1136b, 1141, 1142a, 1142b, 1144a, 1145a, 1211, 1221, 1221a to 1221h, 1222 to 1227, 1231 to 1231f 1232, 1232c, 1232e, 1233, 1233g, 1242, 1244, 1248, 1302, 1321, 1322, 1323, 1341, 1352, 1371, 1391, 1412, 1601 to 1619, 1651 to 1656, 1681 to 1686; 29 U.S. Code §§ 203, 213; 42 U.S. Code §§ 2000c, 2000c-6, 2000c-9, 2000h-2, 2751, 2752, 2754, 2756a, 3501 nts.

Oct. 23, 1972, P.L. 92-531, 20 U.S. Code § 1070 nt.

May 16, 1973, P.L. 93-35, 20 U.S. Code § 1070 nt.

Aug. 21, 1974, P.L. 99-380, 20 U.S. Code § 1221g

Dec. 31, 1974, P.L. 93-568, 20 U.S. Code § 1681

April 21, 1976, P.L. 94-273, 20 U.S. Code § 1221g

Oct. 12, 1976, P.L. 94-482, 20 U.S. Code § 1681

Oct. 3, 1980, P.L. 96-374, 7 U.S. Code § 301 nt.

March 22, 1988, P.L. 100-259, 102 Stat. 28, 20 U.S. Code §§ 1687, 1688

Oct. 20, 1994, P.L. 103-382, 20 U.S. Code § 1687

Education Amendments of 1974

Aug. 21, 1974, P.L. 93-380, 88 Stat. 484, 20 U.S. Code §§ 237-240 , 241-1, 241a nt., 241b, 241b-1, 241c to 241d, 241d-11, 241e to 241h, 241j to 241l, 241n 241o, 241bb, 244, 246, 351d, 441, 633, 635, 645, 646, 821, 822, 841, 842, 844a, 845, 847a, 861, 862, 866, 866a, 867, 880b, 880b-1, 880b-7 to 880b-13, 884, 887, 887a, 887c to 887e, 900a-1, 900a-5, 1009, 1052, 1071d-1, 1070e-1, 1101, 1103, 1104, 1134r-1, 1135, 1202 to 1205, 1208, 1208-1, 1208b, 1209, 1211, 1211a, 1221 to 1221c, 1221e to 1221e-3, 1221g 1221i, 1223, 1225 to 1228, 1230, 1231, 1231b-1 to 1231f, 1232, 1232c 1232f to 1232i, 1233b, 1233d, 1233f, 1233h, 1242, 1244, 1248, 1262, 1391, 1393 to 1393f, 1402, 1403, 1411 to 1413, 1424a to 1426, 1436, 1444, 1452, 1454, 1461, 1603, 1605, 1607 to 1609, 1615, 1619, 1681 nt., 1701 to 1710, 1712 to 1718, 1720, 1721, 1751 to 1758, 1801 to 1806, 1821, 1831, 1832, 1851 to 1853, 1861 to 1867, 1901, 1921, 1941 to 1944, 1961 to 1963, 1981, 1982

Nov. 29, 1975, P.L. 94-142, 89 Stat. 773, 20 U.S. Code §§ 1411 nt., 1412 nt., 1413 nt.

Dec. 31, 1975, P.L. 94-194, 89 Stat. 1103 to 1107, 20 U.S. Code §§ 1921, 1944, 1961, 1963, 1964, 1965, 1966, 1981, 1982, 1983

April 21, 1976, P.L. 94-273, 90 Stat. 375, 382, 20 U.S. Code §§ 238 nt., 241c nt., 1865, 1867

Oct. 8, 1976, P.L. 94-462, 90 Stat. 1981, 20 U.S. Code § 1867

Oct. 12, 1976, P.L. 94-482, 90 Stat. 2220, 2233, 2235, 2236, 2237, 20 U.S. Code §§ 238 nt., 241a nt., 241c nt., 241d-1, 241d-2, 246, 441 nt., 841 880b-1 nt., 1135, 1209, 1221e nt., 1232c nt., 1233b, 1402 nt., 1607, 1864 to 1866

Dec. 13, 1977, P.L. 95-207, 91 Stat. 1472, 20 U.S. Code § 1865

May 3, 1978, P.L. 95-272, 20 U.S. Code § 1221-1 nt.

May 3, 1978, P.L. 95-272, 92 Stat. 227, 20 U.S. Code § 1221-1

Nov. 1, 1978, P.L. 95-561, 20 U.S. Code §§ 240, 241b-1, 1221-1 nt.
Continued

Nov. 1, 1978, P.L. 95-561, 92 Stat. 2335, 20 U.S. Code § 1221-1 nt.

Sept. 30, 1996, P.L. 104-208, 20 U.S. Code § 1221i

Education Amendments of 1976

Oct. 12, 1976, P.L. 94-482, 90 Stat. 2081, 20 U.S. Code §§ 238, 240, 241a nt., 241c nt., 241c-5, 241d, 241d-1, 241d-2, 241e, 241g, 2410, 244, 246, 403, 441, 442, 512, 512a, 513, 588, 824, 841, 845, 880b-1 nt., 880b-10, 880b-11, 880b-13, 881, 1001 to 1006, 1008, 1008b, 1009 to 1011, 1015 to 1015f, 1021, 1041 to 1046, 1051, 1052, 1070, 1070a, 1070b, 1070b-2, 1070c, 1070c01, 1070c- 2, 1070c-4, 1070d, 1070d-1 to 1070d-3, 1070e-1, 1071 to 1078, 1078-1, 1078a, 1079 to 1087, 1087-1 to 1087-4, 1087aa, 1087cc, 1087dd, 1087ff, 1088b, 1088b-1 to 1088b-3, 1088f, 1088f-1, 1101 to 1104, 1119, 1119a, 1119a-1, 1119c-4, 1121, 1124, 1132a to 1132c, 1132a-1 to 1132a-6, 1132c-1, 1132c-2, 1132c-4, 1132c-5, 1132d-1, 1132d-11, 1132e, 1132e-1, 1133 to 1133b, 1134, 1134a to 1134l, 1134n, 1134p, 1134r-1, 1134r-2, 1135, 1135a, 1135a-1, 1135a-3, 1135a-7, 1136b, 1141, 1142b, 1145b 1145c, 1176, 1206, 1208, 1208b, 1209, 1221c, 1221d, 1221e, 1221e-1, 1225, 1230, 1231a, 1232, 1232-1, 1232a, 1232c, 1232f, 1232i, 1233, 1233b 1242, 1302, 1321, 1393c, 1393f, 1402 nt., 1452, 1603, 1606 to 1609, 1615, 1619, 1681, 1801, 1803, 1806, 1831, 1853, 1864 to 1866, 2301 to 2312, 2330 to 2334, 2350 to 2356, 2370, 2380, 2390 to 2392, 2401, 2402, 2411 to 2421, 2441 to 2444, 2461, 2501 to 2506, 2531 to 2534, 2561 to 2565; 25 U.S. Code § 13; 29 U.S. Code §§ 817, 952, 953; 42 U.S. Code §§ 53, 54, 56a, 2751, 2753, 2754

June 3, 1977, P.L. 95-40, 20 U.S. Code §§ 11 nt., 2563

June 15, 1977, P.L. 95-43, 20 U.S. Code §§ 513 et seq.

Dec. 13, 1977, P.L. 95-207, 20 U.S. Code § 2502

Nov. 1, 1978, P.L. 95-561, 20 U.S. Code § 2532

Education Amendments of 1977

Sept. 24, 1977, P.L. 95-112, 20 U.S. Code §§ 241b et seq., 821 nt.

Education Amendments of 1978

Nov. 1, 1978, P.L. 95-561, 20 U.S. Code §§ 236 et seq., 236 nt., 633 et seq., 887c-1, 887c-2, 921 et seq., 921 nt., 1072, 1072 nt., 1087ee, 1088f-1, 1119, 1119a, 1172 nt., 1201 et seq., 1411, 1411 nt., 1601 nt., 1603, 1851 to 1853, 2003 et seq., 2532, 2701 et seq., 2701 nt.; 22 U.S. Code § 287 nt.; 37 U.S. Code § 429; 42 U.S. Code §§ 1769b, 1773, 1789

Aug. 6, 1979, P.L. 96-46, 20 U.S. Code §§ 236 nt., 930, 1211a, 1211b nt., 1221-1 nt., 1221e nt., 1231a nt., 2701 nt., 3381 to 3386; 25 U.S. Code §§ 13 nt., 2001, 2002, 2006, 2008, 2012

Oct. 3, 1980, P.L. 96-374, 20 U.S. Code § 236 nt.

Dec. 21, 1982, P.L. 97-375, 25 U.S. Code § 2016

Oct. 19, 1984, P.L. 98-511, 25 U.S. Code §§ 2001, 2004, 2006, 2008, 2009, 2011, 2012, 2016, 2018, 2020 to 2023

Aug. 15, 1985, P.L. 99-89, 25 U.S. Code §§ 2001, 2004, 2006, 2008 , 2009, 2016, 2020 to 2023

Oct. 27, 1986, P.L. 99-570, 25 U.S. Code §§ 2001, 2009

April 28, 1988, P.L. 100-297, 102 Stat. 363, 25 U.S. Code §§ 2001 et seq.; 20 U.S. Code §§ 241aa et seq., 1221h et seq., 25 U.S. Code §§ 2019, 2022a, 2022b

Sept. 9, 1988, P.L. 100-427, 25 U.S. Code §§ 2001, 2006, 2008 to 2011

May 24, 1990, P.L. 101-301, 25 U.S. Code §§ 2008a, 2019

Oct. 27, 1992, P.L. 102-531, 25 U.S. Code § 2001

Oct. 20, 1994, P.L. 103-382, 25 U.S. Code § 2001 et seq.

Nov. 2, 1994, P.L. 103-437, 20 U.S. Code § 1226c-1

April 26, 1996, P.L. 104-134, 25 U.S. Code § 2001

Nov. 10, 1998, P.L. 105-362, 25 U.S. Code §§ 2001, 2002, 2012, 2017, 2019

Education Amendments of 1980
Oct. 3, 1980, P.L. 96-374, 20 U.S. Code
§ 1001 nt.
Nov. 28, 1990, P.L. 101-638, 104 Stat. 4599

Education Amendments of 1984
Oct. 19, 1984, P.L. 98-511, 20 U.S. Code
§ 2701 nt.
April 28, 1988, P.L. 100-297, 102 Stat. 293,
20 U.S. Code §§ 4101 et seq.
Oct. 20, 1994, P.L. 103-382, 20 U.S. Code
§ 5240 nt.

Education and Crime Prevention Act (Youth and Adult Offender)
Cal. Statutes 1991, Ch. 1358

Education and Development Act (Community)
Ga. Code Ann., 50-8-170 et seq.

Education and Employment Act (AFDC)
Tex. Rev. Civ. Stat., Art. 6950

Education and Employment Governing Board Act
P.R. Laws Ann. 1954, Title 3, § 2001 et seq.

Education and Literacy Rights Act (Blind Persons')
Fla. Stat. Ann., 233.0561 et seq.
Ga. Code Ann., 30-7-1 et seq.
La. Rev. Stat. Ann., 17:1981 et seq.
S.C. Code Ann. 1976, § 59-34-10 et seq.
Utah Code Ann. 1953, 53A-25a-101 et seq.

Education and Prevention Act (Alcohol Abuse)
Cal. Health and Safety Code § 11802
Cal. Statutes 1986, Ch. 1118
Cal. Vehicle Code 1959, § 23196

Education and Private Sector Partnership Act
Fla. Stat. Ann., 229.602

Education and Public Information Act (Diethylstilbestrol)
Pa. Purdon's Stat., Title 35, § 6211 et seq.

Education and Research Act (Propane)
Mo. Laws 1993, S.B. No. 178, § A, Subsecs.
1 to 10

Education and Safety Inspection Act
Ill. Rev. Stat. 1990, Ch. 48, § 59.01 et seq.

Education and State Employees Group Insurance Act
Okla. Stat. Ann., Title 74, § 1301 et seq.

Education and Technology Enhancement Act (Computer Recycling)
N.Y. Education Law 1947 (Consol. Laws Ch.
16) § 318
N.Y. State Finance Law 1940 (Consol. Laws
Ch. 56) §§ 167, 168

Education and Training Act (Dementia)
Ala. Acts 1993, No. 547

Education and Training Act (High Technology)
Wash. Rev. Code Ann., 28B.65.010 et seq.

Education and Training Act (Primary Care)
N.Y. Public Health Law 1953 (Consol. Laws
Ch. 45) § 900 et seq.

Education and Training for a Competitive America Act of 1988
Aug. 23, 1988, P.L. 100-418, 102 Stat. 1469,
20 U.S. Code § 5001
May 11, 1989, P.L. 101-26, 20 U.S. Code
§ 5122
Oct. 20, 1994, P.L. 103-382, 20 U.S. Code
§§ 2411 nt., 4624 nt. 5001 to 5004, 5011 to
5016, 5021 to 5023, 5031 to 5039, 5051 to
5057, 5061 to 5066, 5071, 5072, 5091 to
5097, 5101 to 5106, 5111, 5121 to 5124; 29
U.S. Code 565, 1501 nt., 1651 nt.

Education and Training Program (High School Coaching)
Cal. Education Code 1976, § 35179.1 et seq.

Education and Work Force Act
Miss. Laws 1994, Ch. 581, §§ 42 to 48

Education Appropriation Act
N.M. Laws 1995, Ch. 13

Education Articulation Act (Post-Secondary)
N.M. Stat. Ann., 21-1B-1 et seq.

Education Assessment Act
Ark. Stat. 1947, 80-151 et seq.

Education Assistance Act
S.C. Code Ann. 1976, § 59-115-10 et seq.

Education Assistance Act (Employee Literacy)
Cal. Labor Code § 1040 et seq.

Education Assistance Act (Equal Opportunity)
La. Rev. Stat. Ann., 17:2990.1 et seq.

Education Assistance and Development Tax Credit Act
R.I. Gen. Laws 1956, 44-42-1 et seq.

Education Authority Act (Schools)
Ga. Code Ann., 20-2-550 et seq.

Education Authority Act (University)
Ga. Code Ann., 20-3-150 et seq.

Education Authorization Act (Postsecondary)
Tenn. Code Ann., 49-7-2001 et seq.

Education Ballot and Bond Validation Act
Ill. Rev. Stat. 1991, Ch. 122, §§ 407.35h, 407.36

Education Board Act (State)
Wash. Rev. Code Ann., 28A.04.010 et seq.

Education Center Act (Labor)
Kan. Stat. Ann.,76-496 et seq.

Education Challenge Act 2000
Okla. Laws 1991, p. 1210

Education Code Law
Miss. Code Ann. 1972, § 23-15-1 et seq.
Tex. Education Code, Art. 1.01 et seq.

Education Code Supplemental Act
Cal. Statutes 1977, Ch. 36

Education Compact (Midwestern Higher)
Mich. Comp. Laws Ann., 390.1531, 390.1532

Education Compact (New England Higher)
Me. Rev. Stat. Ann. 1964, Title 20-A § 11001 et seq.

Education Compact Act
Ala. Code 1975, § 16-44-1 et seq.
Alaska Stat. 1962, § 14.44.050 et seq.
Ariz. Rev. Stat. Ann., § 15-1901
Ark. Code Ann. 1987, 6-4-201 et seq.
Cal. Education Code 1976, § 12510 et seq.
Conn. Gen. Stat. 1983, § 10-374 et seq.
Del. Code of 1974, Title 14, § 8201
Fla. Stat. Ann., 244.06 et seq.
Ga. Code Ann., 20-6-20 et seq.
Haw. Rev. Stat. Ann., § 311-1 et seq.
Ida. Code 1947, 33-4101 et seq.
Ind. Code Ann., 20-11-1-1 et seq.
Ind. Code Ann., 272B.1 et seq.
Kan. Stat. Ann., 72-6011 et seq.
Ky. Rev. Stat. 1971, 156.710
Mass. Acts 1967, Ch. 453
Me. Rev. Stat. Ann. 1964, Title 20A § 601 et seq.
Mich. Comp. Laws Ann., 388.1301 et seq.
Minn. Stat. Ann., 121,81 et seq.
Miss. Code Ann. 1972, § 37-135-11 et seq.
Mo. Rev. Stat., 173.300 et seq.
N.C. Gen. Stat. 1943, § 115C-104
N.D. Cent. Code, 15-64-01, 15-64-02
Neb. Rev. Stat. 1943, 79-2501 et seq.
N.H. Rev. Stat. 1955, 200-G:1 et seq.
N.J. Stat. Ann., 18A:75-1 et seq.
N.M. Stat. Ann., 11-8-1 et seq.
Ohio Rev. Code 1953, 3301.48
Okla. Stat. Ann., Title 70, § 506.1 et seq.
Ore. Laws 1967, Ch. 606
Pa. Purdon's Stat., Title 24, § 5401 et seq.
R.I. Gen. Laws 1956, 16-47-1
S.C. Code Ann. 1976, § 59-11-10 et seq.
S.D. Codified Laws 1967, 13-15-15 et seq.
Tex. Education Code, § 161.01 et seq.
Utah Code Ann. 1953, 63-7-17 et seq.
Va. Code 1950, § 22.1-336 et seq.

Vt. Stat. Ann., Title 16, § 1501 et seq.

Wash. Rev. Code Ann., 28A.92.010 et seq.

Wyo. Stat. Ann., §§ 21-16-301, 21-16-302

Education Compact Act (Midwest)

See Midwest Education Compact Act

Iowa Code Ann., 272B.1 et seq.

Education Compact Act (Regional)

Tex. Educational Code, § 160.01 et seq.

Education Compact Act (Southern Region)

Md. Ann. Code 1974, Art. ED, § 25-501 et seq.

Education Consolidation and Improvement Act of 1981

Aug. 13, 1981, P.L. 97-35, 20 U.S. Code § 3801 nt.

Oct. 14, 1982, P.L. 97-313, 20 U.S. Code § 3842

June 12, 1984, P.L. 98-312, 20 U.S. Code §§ 3804, 3851

April 28, 1988, P.L. 100-297, 102 Stat. 293, 20 U.S. Code §§ 3801 et seq.

Education Control Act of 1991

June 27, 1991, P.L. 102-62, 20 U.S. Code § 1221-1 nt.

Education Cost-Effectiveness Agenda Act

Ill. Rev. Stat. 1991, Ch. 122, § 1950

Education Council Act of 1991

Oct. 20, 1994, P.L. 103-382, 20 U.S. Code § 1221-1 nt.

Education Department Act

Colo. Rev. Stat., 22-2-101 et seq.

Education Employees Group Dental, Health, and Life Insurance Act

Okla. Stat. Ann., Title 70, §§ 25-101 to 25-118

Education Employment Relations Act

Ind. Code Ann., 20-7.5-1-1 et seq.

Education Excellence Act

Wash. Init. Meas. No. 177, § 2, prec. Wash. Rev. Code Ann., 28A.01.010

Education Expense Grant Act

N.C. Gen. Stat. 1943, § 115-274 et seq.

Education Facilities Authority Act (Health and Higher)

Me. Rev. Stat. Ann. 1964, Title 5, § 721 et seq.

Education Facilities Authority Act (Postsecondary)

Colo. Rev. Stat., 23-15-01 et seq.

Ind. Code Ann., 20-12-b3-1 et seq.

Education Facilities Bond Act (Higher)

Cal. Education Code 1976, § 67010

Cal. Education Code 1976, § 67345 et seq.

Education Facilities Finance Corporation Act (Cultural)

Tex. Rev. Civ. Stat., Art. 1528m

Education Facilities Revenue Bond Act

Cal. Education Code 1976, § 67359.6 et seq.

Education Facilities Trust Fund Act (Higher)

N.J. Stat. Ann., 18A:72A-49 et seq.

Education Finance Act

Fla. Stat. Ann., 236.012 et seq.

Minn. Stat. 1986, 124A.697 et seq.

S.C. Code Ann. 1976, § 59-20-10 et seq.

Tenn. Code Ann., 49-3-301 et seq.

Education Financial Assistance Act (Post-Secondary)

Miss. Code Ann. 1972, § 37-106-1 et seq.

Education Flexibility Partnership Act of 1999

April 29, 1999, P.L. 106-25, 113 Stat. 41, 20 U.S. Code § 5801 nt.

Education Flexibility Partnership Demonstration Act

March 31, 1994, P.L. 103-227, 20 U.S. Code § 5891

Education for All Handicapped Children Act of 1975
Nov. 29, 1975, P.L. 94-142, 20 U.S. Code § 1401 et seq.
Oct. 30, 1990, P.L. 101-476, 20 U.S. Code § 1400 nt.
Oct. 16, 1992, P.L. 102-421, 20 U.S. Code §§ 681 to 685, 691 to 691g, 693 to 693b, 695 to 695c, prec. 4301, 4301, 4301 nt., 4303, 4304, 4305, 4311, 4321, 4322, prec. 4331, 4331, 4332, 4341, 4342, 4343, 4344, prec. 4351, 4351 to 4360

Education for Economic Security Act
Aug. 11, 1984, P.L. 98-377, 20 U.S. Code §§ 3901, 3901 nt., 3902, 3911 et seq., 3961 et seq., 3981 et seq., 4001 et seq., 4011 et seq., 4031 et seq. 4051 et seq., 4071 et seq.
Oct. 30, 1984, P.L. 98-558, 20 U.S. Code § 4061
Nov. 22, 1985, P.L. 99-159, 20 U.S. Code §§ 3902, 3911 to 3922, 3963 to 3973, 3982 to 3988, 4003, 4033, 4051, 4053, 4056, 4059
April 28, 1988, P.L. 100-297, 102 Stat. 319, 20 U.S. Code §§ 3961 , 3983, 4001 et seq., 4031 et seq., 4051 et seq., 4081 et seq.
Aug. 23, 1988, P.L. 100-418, 102 Stat. 1471, 20 U.S. Code §§ 3963 , prec. 3981
Dec. 21, 1995, P.L. 104-66, 20 U.S. Code § 3917
Oct. 7, 1998, P.L. 105-244, 20 U.S. Code § 3902

Education for Exception Children Act (Special)
Kan. Stat. Ann., 72-961 et seq.

Education for Handicapped Adults Act (Zollie M. Maunard, Sr.)
Fla. Stat. Ann., 228.0727

Education for Homeless Children Act
Ill. Comp. Stat. 1992, Ch. 105, § 45/1-1

Education for Limited English Proficient Students Act
Minn. Stat. Ann., 126.261 et seq.

Education for the Gifted and Talented Act
Mich. Comp. Laws Ann., 388.1091 et seq.

Minn. Stat. 1986, 124.247

Education Foundation Act (Bank Examiners)
Ill. Comp. Stat. 1992, Ch. 20, § 3210/2

Education Fund Act
Fla. Stat. Ann., 240.498

Education Gift Disclosure Act
Pa. Purdon's's Stat., Title 24, § 6301 et seq.

Education Grants Act (Health Services)
Ill. Rev. Stat. 1991, Ch. 111 1/2, § 821 et seq.

Education Health and Fitness Act (State Employees)
Tex. Government Code, § 664.001 et seq.

Education Improvement Act
Ala. Acts 1991, No. 323
Okla. Laws 1985, H.B. 1466
S.C. Acts 1984, p. 2176, No. 512
Tenn. Public Acts 1992, Ch. 535

Education, Jobs, and Competitiveness Bond Act
N.J. Laws 1988, Ch. 78

Education Law (Gifted)
Miss. Code Ann. 1972, § 37-23-171 et seq.

Education Licensure Commission Act
D.C. Code Ann., § 31-1601 et seq.

Education Literacy Act (Blind Persons')
Fla. Stat. Ann., 233.0561 et seq.

Education Loan Act (Vietnam Veterans)
Neb. Rev. Stat. 1943, 80-801 et seq.

Education Loan Forgiveness Act (Agriculture)
Pa. 1992 Pamph. Laws, No. 64

Education Lottery Act (Public)
Fla. Stat. Ann., 24.101 et seq.

Education Management Improvement Act
Fla. Stat. Ann., 231.087 et seq.

Education Management Training Act
Fla. Stat. Ann., 231.087

Education Minimum Foundation Program Act
See Minimum Foundation Program Act (Education)

Education Now and Babies Later (ENABL) Act
Fla. Stat. Ann., 411.24 et seq.

Education of Blind Acts
March 3, 1879, Ch. 186, 20 Stat. 468, 20 U.S. Code §§ 101, 102, 104
June 25, 1906, Ch. 3536, 34 Stat. 460, 20 U.S. Code §§ 101, 102, 104
March 4, 1913, Ch. 142, 37 Stat. 748, 20 U.S. Code § 105
Aug. 4, 1919, Ch. 31, 41 Stat. 272, 20 U.S. Code § 101
Nov. 4, 1919, Ch. 93, 41 Stat. 332, 20 U.S. Code § 103
Feb. 8, 1927, Ch. 76, 44 Stat. 160, 20 U.S. Code § 101
Aug. 23, 1937, Ch. 736, 50 Stat. 744, 20 U.S. Code § 101
May 22, 1952, Ch. 321, 66 Stat. 89, 20 U.S. Code § 101
Aug. 2, 1956, Ch. 882, 70 Stat. 938, 20 U.S. Code §§ 101, 102
Sept. 22, 1961, P.L. 87-294, 75 Stat. 627, 20 U.S. Code §§ 101, 102
April 13, 1970, P.L. 91-230, 84 Stat. 194, 20 U.S. Code §§ 102, 104

Education of Blind and Deaf Children Act
Kan. Stat. Ann., 72-853 et seq.

Education of Handicapped Children Act (Joint Funding)
Cal. Education Code 1976, § 56875 et seq.

Education of Mentally or Physically Handicapped Children Act
Ida. Code 1947, 33-2001 et seq.

Education of the Deaf Act Amendments of 1993
Aug. 11, 1993, P.L. 103-73, 20 U.S. Code § 4301 nt.

Education of the Deaf Act of 1986
Aug. 4, 1986, P.L. 99-371, 20 U.S. Code §§ 4301 nt., 4301 to 4303, 4311, 4321, 4322, 4331, 4332, 4341 to 4344, 4351 to 4360
Oct. 30, 1990, P.L. 101-476, 20 U.S. Code § 1400 nt.
Aug. 11, 1993, P.L. 103-73, 20 U.S. Code §§ 4301 et seq., 4331 et seq., 4351 et seq., 4359 et seq.
Oct. 7, 1998, P.L. 105-244, 20 U.S. Code §§ 4304, 4305, 4332, 4351, 4353 to 4355, 4357 to 4359, 4359a, 4359b, 4360, 4360a

Education of the Handicapped Act
Jan. 2, 1968, P.L. 90-247, 81 Stat. 804, 20 U.S. Code §§ 871 to 880a
April 13, 1970, P.L. 91-230, 84 Stat. 175, 20 U.S. Code §§ 1401 to 1404, 1411 to 1414, 1421 to 1426, 1431 to 1436, 1441 to 1444, 1451 to 1454, 1461
Nov. 29, 1975, P.L. 94-142, 89 Stat. 773, 20 U.S. Code §§ 1401, 1405, 1406, 1411 to 1420, 1453
June 17, 1977, P.L. 95-49, 20 U.S. Code § 1426 et seq.
Nov. 1, 1978, P.L. 95-561, 20 U.S. Code §§ 1411, 1411 nt.
Dec. 2, 1983, P.L. 98-199, 20 U.S. Code §§ 1401 to 1403, 1406, 1407, 1418, 1419, 1420 to 1427, 1441 to 1444, 1461
Nov. 22, 1985, P.L. 99-159, 20 U.S. Code § 1411
July 9, 1986, P.L. 99-362, 20 U.S. Code § 1411
Aug. 5, 1986, P.L. 99-372, 20 U.S. Code § 1415
Aug. 22, 1986, P.L. 99-386, 20 U.S. Code § 1453
Oct. 8, 1986, P.L. 99-457, 20 U.S. Code §§ 1408, 1411, 1419, 1421, 1422, 1471 to 1485
Nov. 7, 1988, P.L. 100-630, 20 U.S. Code §§ 1401 et seq., 1471 et seq.

Education of the Handicapped Act Amendments of 1983
Dec. 2, 1983, P.L. 98-199, 20 U.S. Code § 1400 nt.

Education of the Handicapped Act Amendments of 1986

Oct. 8, 1986, P.L. 99-457, 20 U.S. Code § 1400 nt.

Education of the Handicapped Act Amendments of 1990

Oct. 30, 1990, P.L. 101-476, 20 U.S. Code §§ 1400 and nt.,

Education of the Handicapped Amendments of 1977

June 17, 1977, P.L. 95-49, 20 U.S. Code §§ 1401 nt., 1426 et seq.

Education Opportunities Act (Inservice)

Kan. Stat. Ann., 72-9601

Education Opportunity Program Act

N.Y. Education Law 1947 (Consol. Laws Ch. 16) § 559 et seq.

Education Partnership Act

Ga. Code Ann., 20-2-1030 et seq.

Education Professional Loan Forgiveness Act (Early Childhood)

Pa. Purdon's Stat., Title 24, § 7101 et seq.

Education Professional Negotiations Act

Tenn. Code Ann., 49-5-601 et seq.

Education Professions Development Act

Nov. 8, 1965, P.L. 89-329, Title V, 79 Stat. 1219, 20 U.S. Code §§ 1091 to 1092, 1101 to 1119c-4

June 29, 1967, P.L. 90-35, 81 Stat. 82, 20 U.S. Code §§ 1091, 1091a to 1091f, 1092

Jan. 2, 1968, P.L. 90-247, 81 Stat. 820, 20 U.S. Code §§ 1111, 1112, 1118, 1119

Oct. 16, 1968, P.L. 90-576, 82 Stat. 1091, 20 U.S. Code §§ 1119c to 1119c-4

April 13, 1970, P.L. 91-230, 84 Stat. 189, 20 U.S. Code §§ 1091a, 1119c-4

Education Program Act (Accountability and Adequate)

Miss. Code Ann. 1972, § 37-151-1 et seq.

Education Program Act (Award for Excellence in)

Wash. Rev. Code 1983, 28A.625.010 et seq.

Education Quality Improvement Act (K through 12 Mathematics, Science, and Computer)

Fla. Stat. Ann., 233.64 et seq.

Education Reform Act

Ala. Acts 1984, p. 1260
Ga. Code Ann., 20-1A-1 et seq.
Ky. Acts 1990, Ch. 476
Mass. Laws 1993, Ch. 71
Miss. Code Ann. 1972, § 37-1-1 et seq.
Tenn. Code Ann., 49-5-5001 et seq.

Education Reform Act (Private Postsecondary and Vocational)

Cal. Education Code 1976, § 94300 et seq.

Education Reorganization Act (Veterans)

Ga. Code Ann., 38-4-30 et seq.

Education Reporting Act (Adult)

Ill. Comp. Stat. 1992, Ch. 105, § 410/0.01 et seq.

Education Research Program Act (Rural)

N.Y. Education Law 1947 (Consol. Laws Ch. 16) § 1201 et seq.

Education Rights and Privacy Act (Family)

Ky. Acts 1994, Ch. 98

Education Savings Act (Baccalaureate)

Tenn. Code Ann., 49-7-901 et seq.

Education Security Information Act (Postsecondary)

Fla. Stat. Ann., 240.2682 et seq.

Education Service Act (Youth)

Kan. Stat. Ann., 74-32-108 et seq.

Education Service Agencies Act (Regional)

Va. Code 1950, § 22-351 et seq.

Education Service Center Act (Regional)

Okla. Stat. Ann., Title 70, § 1210.271 et seq.

Education Services for Visually Impaired, Auditorily Impaired, and Learning Disabled Students Act
N.J. Stat. Ann., 18A:72H-1 et seq.

Education Sponsorship Act (Construction Management)
Cal. Business and Professions Code § 7139 et seq.

Education System Trust Act (Baccalaureate)
Tenn. Code Ann., 49-7-801 to 49-7-806

Education Tax Act
Pa. Purdon's Stat., Title 72, § 7201 et seq.

Education Tax Act (State)
Mich. Comp. Laws Ann., 211.901 et seq.

Education Technology Act
Minn. Stat. Ann., 124C.21 et seq.

Education Technology Equipment Act
N.M. Stat. Ann., 6-15A-1 to 6-15A-16

Education Trust Act
Mich. Comp. Laws Ann., 390.1421 et seq.
N.M. Stat. Ann., 21-21K-1 to 21-21K-7

Education Trust Fund Act
Neb. Rev. Stat. 1943, 79-1330

Education Trust Fund Act (Volunteer Public)
Tenn. Code Ann., 49-3-401 et seq.

Education Truth in Reporting and Employee Protection Act
Tenn. Code Ann., 49-50-1401 et seq.

Education, Welfare and Public Health Tax Act
Conn. Gen. Stat. 1983, § 12-406 et seq.

Educational Accountability Act
Colo. Rev. Stat., 22-7-101 et seq.
Fla. Stat. Ann., 229.55 et seq.

Educational Accountability and Assessment of Performance Act
Miss. Code Ann. 1972, § 37-3-46 et seq.

Educational Accreditation Act
Colo. Rev. Stat., 22-11-101 et seq.

Educational Achievement Act
Colo. Rev. Stat., 22-22-101 et seq.

Educational Act (Veterans)
Ore. Rev. Stat., 408.010 et seq.

Educational Advancement Act
Del. Code of 1974, Title 14, §§ 201 et seq., 1001 et seq.

Educational Agencies Financial Aid Act
Sept. 30, 1950, Ch. 1124, 64 Stat. 1100, 20 U.S. Code §§ 236 to 244
Dec. 18, 1963, P.L. 88-210, 77 Stat. 419, 20 U.S. Code §§ 237 to 239
Oct. 16, 1964, P.L. 88-665, 78 Stat. 1109, 20 U.S. Code §§ 237 to 239, 244
July 21, 1965, P.L. 89-77, 79 Stat. 243, 20 U.S. Code §§ 241, 241c
April 13, 1970, P.L. 91-230, 84 Stat. 154, 20 U.S. Code §§ 237 to 240, 244
Me. Rev. Stat. Ann. 1964, Title 20-A, § 15001 et seq.

Educational Aid to Children of Deceased Veterans Act
Mich. Comp. Laws Ann., 35.111, 35.112

Educational Aid to Soldiers, Sailors, and Marines Act (World War I)
Ore. Laws 1919, Ch. 428

Educational and Cultural Facilities Authority Act
Colo. Rev. Stat., 23-15-101 et seq.

Educational and Health Building Corporation Act
R.I. Gen. Laws 1956, 45-38.1-1 et seq.

Educational and Health Facilities Authority Act
Mass. Gen. Laws 1984, 53:1 et seq.

Educational and Health Facilities Authority Act (Higher)
N.H. Rev. Stat. 1955, 195-D-1 et seq.

Educational Apportionment Act
N.M. Stat. Ann., 22-3-17 et seq.

Educational Appropriation Act
Tenn. Public Acts 1984, Ex. Sess., Ch. 14

Educational Appropriation Budget Act
Ala. Acts 1978, p. 1616

Educational Assistance Act
N.M. Stat. Ann., 21-21A-1 et seq.

Educational Assistance Act (National Guard)
Ala. Acts 1984, p. 498
N.H. Rev. Stat. 1955, 110-B:63a et seq.

Educational Authorization Act (Postsecondary)
Ga. Code Ann., 20-3-100 et seq.

Educational Benefits for Dependents of Blind Parents Act
Ala. Code 1975, § 16-33-1 et seq.

Educational Bond Act
N.M. Laws 1984, Sp. Sess., Ch. 6

Educational Bonus Act (Veterans)
Wis. Stat. 1961, 4539

Educational Capital Improvements Bond Act
N.M. Laws 1986, Ch. 113

Educational Claims Act (Constitutionally Based)
Ida. Code 1947, 6-2201 et seq.

Educational Commission Act (Special)
Tenn. Public Acts 1933, Ch. 104

Educational Construction Fund Act (New York City)
N.Y. Education Law 1947 (Consol. Laws Ch. 16) § 450 et seq.

Educational Construction Fund Act (Yonkers)
N.Y. Education Law 1947 (Consol. Laws Ch. 16) § 475 et seq.

Educational Cooperation Act
La. Rev. Stat. Ann., 17:2801 et seq.
Tenn. Code Ann., 49-2-1301 et seq.

Educational Cooperative Act
Ark. Code Ann. 1987, 6-13-901 et seq.

Educational Corporation Act (German School)
Ill. Rev. Stat. 1991, Ch. 32, §§ 199.90, 199a

Educational Corporations Act
Ill. Rev. Stat. 1991, Ch. 144, § 12.9 et seq.

Educational Development Board Act
Ill. Rev. Stat. 1991, Ch. 122, § 1051 et seq.

Educational Effectiveness and Fiscal Efficiency Act (School Districts)
Ill. Rev. Stat. 1991, Ch. 122, § 870.1 et seq.

Educational Employment Relations Act
Cal. Government Code § 3540 et seq.
Wash. Rev. Code Ann., 41.59.010 et seq.

Educational Endowment Management Act
N.J. Laws 1971, Ch. 256

Educational Enhancement Deposit Act (Student)
Me. Rev. Stat. Ann. 1964, Title 20-A, § 12601 et seq.

Educational Equity Act
Fla. Stat. Ann., 228.2001 et seq.

Educational Excellence Foundation Act
Utah Code Ann. 1953, 53A-4-101 et seq.

Educational Exchange Program
Colo. Rev. Stat., 23-3.3-600.1 et seq.

Educational Extension Act
Fla. Stat. 1963, 239.0100 et seq.

Educational Facilities Act
Fla. Stat. Ann., 235.001 et seq.
N.J. Stat. 1983, 235.001 et seq.

Educational Facilities Asbestos Detection Program
La. Rev. Stat. Ann., 17:3701

Educational Facilities Authorities Act (Higher)
Fla. Stat. Ann., 243.18 et seq.

Educational Facilities Authority Act
Cal. Education Code 1976, § 94100 et seq.
Conn. Gen. Stat. 1983, § 10-335 et seq.
Ill. Rev. Stat. 1991, Ch. 144, § 1301 et seq.
Ind. Code Ann., 20-12-63-1 et seq.
Mass. Acts 1968, Ch. 614
Neb. Rev. Stat. 1943, 79-2901 et seq.
N.J. Stat. Ann., 18A:72A-1 et seq.
S.D. Codified Laws 1967, 1-16A-1 et seq.
Va. Code 1950, § 23-30.39 et seq.

Educational Facilities Authority Act (Postsecondary)
Colo. Rev. Stat., 23-15-101 et seq.

Educational Facilities Authority Act for Private, Nonprofit Institutions of Higher Learning
Miss. Code Ann. 1972, § 37-104-1 et seq.
S.C. Code Ann. 1976, § 59-109-10 et seq.

Educational Facilities Construction and Finance Act
Fla. Stat. Ann. 235.001 et seq.

Educational Facilities Infrastructure Improvement Act
Fla. Stat. Ann., 364.506 et seq.
Pa. Purdon's Stat., Title 24, § 5501 et seq.

Educational Finance Act (Federal)
Neb. Rev. Stat. 1943, 79-1320 et seq.

Educational Finance and Cultural Affairs Department Act
N.M. Stat. Ann., 9-4-1 et seq.

Educational Finance Commission Act
S.C. Code Ann. 1962, § 21-52 et seq.

Educational Financing Authority Act
Mass. Gen. Laws 1984, 15C:2

Educational Funding Accountability Act
Fla. Stat. Ann., 236.685

Educational Grant Act
Ga. Code Ann., 20-2-640 et seq.

Educational Improvement Act
Cal. Education Code 1976, § 54600 et seq.
Ky. Rev. Stat. 1971, 158.650 et seq.

Educational Improvement and Financing Act (Comprehensive)
N.J. Stat. Ann., 18A:7F-1 et seq.

Educational Institution Act (Post-Secondary)
N.M. Stat. Ann., 21-23-1 et seq.

Educational Institution Bond Authorization Act
Ill. Rev. Stat. 1991, Ch. 127, § 306.9 et seq.

Educational Institution Improvement Bond Act
N.M. Laws 1975, 1st Sp. Sess., Ch. 4

Educational Institution Presiding Officer Act
Ill. Rev. Stat. 1991, Ch. 144, §§ 16m, 17

Educational Institutions Act
Ariz. Laws 1934, 3rd Sp. Sess., Ch. 7
Fla. Stat. Ann., 243.01 et seq.
Ida. Code 1947, 33-3801 et seq.
Tenn. Code Ann., 49-3-1101 et seq.

Educational Institutions Act (Nonpublic Postsecondary)
Ga. Code Ann., 20-3-250.1 et seq.

Educational Institutions Bond Act
Va. Acts 1975, Ch. 219
Va. Acts 1977, Ch. 650
Va. Acts 1992, Ch. 894

Educational Labor Relations Act
Ill. Rev. Stat. 1991, Ch. 48, § 1701 et seq.

Educational Leadership Training Act
Fla. Stat. Ann., 229.542 et seq.

Educational Leave Act
Me. Rev. Stat. Ann. 1964, Title 5, § 721 et
seq.

Educational Lending Act
R.I. Gen. Laws 1956, 19-25.1-1 et seq.

Educational Loan Authority Act
Me. Rev. Stat. Ann. 1964, Title 20-A,
§ 11411 et seq.

Educational Loan Default Act
Ill. Rev. Stat. 1991, Ch. 127, § 3550 et seq.

Educational Loan Program Act
Ga. Code Ann., 20-3-260 et seq.

Educational Loan Purchase Program Law
Ill. Rev. Stat. 1991, Ch. 122, § 30-15.14a et
seq.

Educational Mining Act of 1982
Jan. 3, 1983, P.L. 97-406, 96 Stat. 2031
Aug. 22, 1984, P.L. 98-396, 98 Stat. 1385

Educational Oath Statute
N.J. Stat. Ann., 18A:6-7, 18A:26-9

Educational Opportunities Act
N.J. Stat. Ann., 18A:71-28 et seq.
Pa. Purdon's Stat., Title 24, § 5001 et seq.

Educational Opportunities Act (Consortium for)
Ill. Comp. Stat. 1992, Ch. 110, § 930/1 et seq.

Educational Opportunities Support and Tax Equity Act
Neb. Rev. Stat. 1943, 79-3801 et seq.

Educational Opportunity Act (University and Colleges)
Cal. Education Code 1976, § 69620 et seq.

Educational Partnership Act
Ill. Rev. Stat. 1991, Ch. 144, § 2201 et seq.

Educational Partnerships Act of 1988
Aug. 23, 1988, P.L. 100-418, 102 Stat. 1483,
20 U.S. Code § 5031

Oct. 20, 1994, P.L. 103-382, 20 U.S. Code
§§ 5031 to 5039

Educational Personnel Contracts Act (Interstate)
Conn. Gen. Stat. 1983, § 10-146c et seq.

Educational Personnel Qualification Act
Fla. Stat. Ann., 244.09 et seq.
Me. Rev. Stat. Ann. 1964, Title 20-A,
§ 13901
Pa. Purdon's Stat., Title 24, § 2401.1

Educational Personnel Qualification Agreement Act
See Interstate Agreement on Qualifications
of Educational Personnel Act

Educational Personnel Qualifications Act
N.C. Gen. Stat. 1943, §§ 115C-349 to
115C-358

Educational Planning Act
Ark. Code Ann. 1987, 6-15-101
Colo. Rev. Stat., 22-6-101 et seq.

Educational Planning Act (Post-Secondary)
N.M. Stat. Ann., 21-2-1 et seq.

Educational Policies Act (Discrimination)
N.Y. Education Law 1947 (Consol. Laws Ch.
16) § 313

Educational Practices Act
Colo. Rev. Stat., 22-65-101 et seq.

Educational Practices and Policies Act
N.Y. Education Law 1947 (Consol. Laws Ch.
16) § 313

Educational Professional Practices Act
Utah Code Ann. 1953, 53A-7-101 et seq.

Educational Program Act (Correctional)
Colo. Rev. Stat., 17-32-101 et seq.

Educational Programs Act (McAteer)
Cal. Education Code 1976, § 54400 et seq.

Educational Records Bill of Rights Act
R.I. Gen. Laws 1956, 16-71-1 et seq.

Educational Redistricting Act
N.M. Laws 1991, 1st Sp. Sess., Ch. 4

Educational Redistricting Act of 1991
N.M. Laws 1991, 1st Sp. Sess., Ch. 4

Educational Reform Act
Cal. Statutes 1983, Ch. 498
Fla. Stat. Ann., 228.041, 228.085 et seq.,
229.565, 231.531 et seq. 236.02, 236.091,
236.092, 240.4062, 240.4064, 240.541

Educational Reform Act (Hughes-Hart)
Cal. Education Code 1976, § 1296

Educational, Religious or Charitable Corporation Dissolution Act
Ill. Rev. Stat. 1991, Ch. 32, §§ 200.9, 201

Educational, Religious or Charitable Institution Textile Machine Free Importation Act
N.J. Stat. Ann., 18A:73-44 et seq.

Educational Research and Museum Development Act
N.J. Stat. Ann., 18A:73-44 et seq.

Educational Research, Development, Dissemination, and Improvement Act of 1994
March 31, 1994, P.L. 103-227, 20 U.S. Code § 6001
Oct. 20, 1994, P.L. 103-382, 20 U.S. Code §§ 3412, 3423b, 3474, 3481, 6011
Oct. 21, 1998, P.L. 105-277, 20 U.S. Code § 6041

Educational Resource Sharing through Distance Learning Act
Pa. Purdon's Stat., Title 73, § 7001 et seq.

Educational Retirement Act
N.M. Stat. Ann., 22-11-1 et seq.

Educational, Scientific, and Cultural Materials Importation Act of 1966
Oct. 14, 1966, P.L. 89-651, 80 Stat. 897

Educational, Scientific, and Cultural Materials Importation Act of 1982
Jan. 12, 1983, P.L. 97-446, 96 Stat. 2346-2349
Oct. 30, 1984, P.L. 98-573, 98 Stat. 2971
Aug. 23, 1988, P.L. 100-418, 102 Stat. 1138

Educational Service Agencies Act (Cooperative)
Ga. Code Ann., 20-2-200 et seq.

Educational Services Commission Act
N.J. Stat. Ann., 18A:6-51 et seq.

Educational Services Registration Act
Wash. Rev. Code Ann., 28B.05.010 et seq.

Educational Technology Act
Cal. Education Code § 51870 et seq.

Educational Technology Act (Morgan-Farr-Quackenbush)
Cal. Education Code 1976, § 51870 et seq.

Educational Technology Teacher Training Act
N.J. Stat. Ann., 18A:6-103 et seq.

Educational Television Act
Miss. Code Ann. 1972, § 37-63-1 et seq.
Neb. Rev. Stat. 1943, 79-2101 et seq.
Okla. Stat. Ann., Title 70, § 23.101 et seq.
Va. Code 1950, § 22-344.4 et seq.

Educational Television Act of 1962
See Communications Acts
May 1, 1962, P.L. 87-447, 76 Stat. 64

Educational Television and Radio Amendments of 1969
Oct. 27, 1969, P.L. 91-97, 83 Stat. 146, 47 U.S. Code §§ 391, 396
Dec. 31, 1975, P.L. 94-194, 89 Stat. 1103, 20 U.S. Code §§ 1921, 1944, 1961, 1963 to 1966, 1982, 1983

Educational Television Commission Act
Wyo. Stat. Ann., § 9-2-501 et seq.

Educational Television Network Act
Tenn. Code Ann., 49-50-901 et seq.

Educational Trustees Act
Ill. Rev. Stat. 1991, Ch. 144, § 7.9 et seq.

Educator Licensing Act
Colo. Rev. Stat., 22-60.5-101 et seq.

Edwards-Bates Act (Utility Pensions)
Ky. Rev. Stat. 1971, 96.180

Edwards-Norton Act (Highway Code)
Ohio Rev. Code 1953, 5501.02 et seq.

Edwards Snowmobile Law
N.Y. Local Laws 1973, Town of Edwards, p. 1678

Edwin E. Aldrin Commemorative Scholarship Act
N.J. Laws 1969, Ch. 190

EEOC Education, Technical Assistance, and Training Revolving Fund Act of 1992
Oct. 14, 1992, P.L. 102-411, 42 U.S. Code § 2000a

Effect and Form of Conveyances Act
R.I. Gen. Laws 1956, 34-11-1 et seq.

Effective Date of Laws Act
Ill. Rev. Stat. 1991, Ch. 1, § 1200 et seq.

Effective Death Penalty Act
Ark. Code 1987, 16-91-201 et seq.
S.C. Code Ann. 1976, §§ 16-3-21, 17-25-380, 17-27-130, 17-27-150, 17-27-160

Effective Instructional Leadership Act
Ky. Rev. Stat. 1971, 156.101

Effective School Project Act
Ark. Code Ann. 1987, 6-15-301 et seq.

Effective Schools Program Act
N.J. Stat. Ann., 18A:6-33-7 et seq.

Effectiveness of Judgment Act
P.R. Laws Ann. 1954 Title 32, § 1069 et seq.

Efficiency Act (Appellate Court)
Tenn. Public Acts 1991, Ch. 147

Efficiency Act (Transportation)
Fla. Laws 1992, Ch. 152

Efficiency and Conservation Act (Budget)
Fla. Stat. Ann., 366.80 et seq.

Efficiency and Realignment Act (Trial Court)
Cal. Statutues 1991, Ch. 90

Efficiency Program Act (School)
N.J. Stat. Ann., 18A:7E-6 et seq.

Efficiency Standards Act (Appliance)
Mass. Gen. Laws 1984, 25B:1 et seq.

Efficient Water Management Practices Act (Agricultural Water Suppliers)
Cal. Water Code § 10900 et seq.

Effingham Family Connection Commission Act
Ga. Laws 1999, H.B. 771

E.F.I.S. Policy Council Act
Mich. Comp. Laws Ann., 28.151

Egan Bill (Juries)
N.J. Stat. Ann., 2:69-4, 2A:68-1 et seq., 2A:68-13, 2A:70-1 et seq., 2A:71-3, 2A:71-7, 2A:71-9, 2A:72-2, 2A:73-1, 2A:78-1

Egg Act
Kan. Stat. Ann.,2-2501 et seq.

Egg Act (Graded)
Neb. Rev. Stat. 1943, 2-3501 et seq.

Egg Act (Sales)
N.D. Cent. Code, 19-07-01 et seq.

Egg Act (State)
Colo. Rev. Stat., 35-21-101 et seq.
Ind. Code Ann., 16-6-1-1 et seq.
Kan. Stat. Ann., 2-2501 et seq.
Ky. Rev. Stat. 1971, 260.600 et seq.

Md. Ann. Code 1974, Art. AG, § 4-301 et
seq.
Minn. Stat. Ann., 29.21 et seq.
N.C. Gen. Stat. 1943, § 106-245.13 et seq.
Okla. Stat. Ann., Title 2, § 737.1 et seq.
Ore. Rev. Stat., 632.705 et seq.
S.C. Code Ann. 1976, § 39-39-10 et seq.
Tenn. Code Ann., 53-2-101 et seq.
Tex. Agriculture Code, § 132.001 et seq.
Wash. Rev. Code Ann., 69.25.010 et seq.

Egg and Egg Products Act
Ariz. Rev. Stat. Ann., § 3-701 et seq.
Ill. Rev. Stat. 1991, Ch. 56 1/2 § 55-1 et seq.

Egg and Poultry Resources Act
Neb. Rev. Stat. 1943, 2-3401 et seq.

Egg Candling and Grading Act
Ill. Rev. Stat. 1991, Ch. 56 1/2, § 55-6 et seq.
Ind. Code Ann., 196.1 et seq.

Egg Classification Act
Fla. Stat. Ann., 583.01 et seq.

Egg Commission Act
La. Rev. Stat. Ann., 3:551.1 et seq.

Egg Grading Act
N.M. Stat. Ann., 25-6-1 et seq.

Egg Grading and Marketing Law
La. Rev. Stat. Ann., 3:821 et seq.

Egg Labeling Act
Ark. Code Ann. 1987, 20-58-201 et seq.

Egg Market Development Act
Ill. Rev. Stat. 1991, Ch. 5, § 501 et seq.

Egg Marketing Law
Ark. Code Ann. 1987, 20-58-201 et seq.
Ga. Code Ann., 26-2-260 et seq.
Ky. Rev. Stat. 1971, 260.540 et seq.
Miss. Code Ann. 1972, §§ 69-7-251 et seq.
W. Va. Code 1966, § 19-10A-1 et seq.

Egg Placard Act
Haw. Rev. Stat. Ann., § 147-97 et seq.

Egg Placard Act (Foreign Eggs)
Wash. Rev. Code 1974, 69.24.320 et seq.

**Egg, Poultry and Livestock Production
Assistance Act**
Miss. Code 1942, § 4435-51 et seq.

Egg Products Inspection Act
Dec. 29, 1970, P.L. 91-597, 84 Stat. 1620, 15
U.S. Code §§ 633, 636; 21 U.S. Code
§§ 1031 to 1056
Aug. 6, 1971, P.L. 92-67, 85 Stat. 173, 21
U.S. Code § 1044
Dec. 13, 1991, P.L. 102-237, 21 U.S. Code
§§ 1034, 1037, 1041, 1042, 1046, 1052
Oct. 29, 1992, P.L. 102-571, 21 U.S. Code
§ 1033
Nov. 2, 1994, P.L. 103-437, 21 U.S. Code
§ 1054

Egg Products Inspection Law
Cal. Food and Agricultural Code 1967,
§ 27951 et seq.

Egg Refrigeration Law
Pa. Purdon's Stat., Title 31, § 300.1 et seq.

**Egg Research and Consumer Information
Act**
Oct. 1, 1974, P.L. 93-428, 88 Stat. 1171, 7
U.S. Code §§ 2701 to 2718
June 17, 1980, P.L. 96-276, 94 Stat. 541, 7
U.S. Code §§ 2707, 2708, 2714
Oct. 31, 1988, P.L. 100-575, 7 U.S. Code
§§ 2707, 2712
Dec. 12, 1989, P.L. 101-220, 7 U.S. Code
§ 2711
Dec. 14, 1993, P.L. 103-188, 7 U.S. Code
§§ 2707, 2708, 2711

**Egg Research and Consumer Information
Act Amendments of 1980**
June 17, 1980, P.L. 96-276, 7 U.S. Code
§§ 2701 et seq., 2701 nt.

**Egg Research and Consumer Information
Act Amendments of 1988**
Oct. 31, 1988, P.L. 100-575, 7 U.S. Code
§ 2701 nt.

Egg Research and Consumer Information Act Amendments of 1993
Dec. 14, 1993, P.L. 103-188, 7 U.S. Code § 2701 nt.

Egg Standards Act
Mich. Comp. Laws Ann., 289.321 et seq.

Eggs and Baby Chicks Act
S.C. Code Ann. 1976, § 39-39-10 et seq.

Eggs Products and Wholesome Eggs Act
Wash. Rev. Code 1983, 69.25.930

Egress Act (Public Building)
Ill. Rev. Stat. 1991, Ch. 111 1/2, § 3500 et seq.

Eight Hour Act
Wyo. Stat. Ann., §§ 16-6-110, 16-6-111

Eight Hour Act (Government Employees)
Ore. Rev. Stat., 279.334 et seq.

Eight Hour Act (Minors)
Cal. Labor Code § 1390 et seq.

Eight Hour Act (Public Employees)
Mass. Gen. Laws Ann., 149:30 et seq.
Okla. Stat. Ann., Title 61, § 3

Eight Hour Act (Public Works)
Ore. Rev. Stat., 279.338

Eight Hour Act (Retail Stores)
Mont. Code Ann., 39-4-105

Eight Hour Act (Underground Workings)
Alaska Stat. 1962, § 23.10.405 et seq.

Eight Hour Act (Women)
Cal. Labor Code § 1350 et seq.
D.C. Code 1973, § 36-301 et seq.

Eight Hour Employment Law
N.J. Stat. Ann., 30:4-144, 34:10-1 to 34:10-5

Eight Hour Labor Act
Cal. Labor Code § 510 et seq.
Colo. Rev. Stat., 8-13-101 et seq.

Ill. Rev. Stat. 1991, Ch. 48, § 0.01 et seq.
Ind. Code 1976, 22-2-1-1 et seq.
Kan. Stat. Ann., 44-201 et seq.
Minn. Stat. 1971, 181.25, 181.26
Ohio Rev. Code 1953, 4113.01
Pa. 1868 Pamph. Laws 99, No. 60
Pa. 1897 Pamph. Laws 418, No. 379
Tex. Rev. Civ. Stat., Art. 5165 et seq.
Utah Code Ann. 1953, 34-21-2
Wash. Rev. Code Ann., 103.38
Wash. Rev. Code Ann., 49.28.010 et seq.
Wyo. Stat. Ann., §§ 16-6-110, 16-6-111

Eight Hour Labor Act (Public Employees)
Okla. Stat. 1981, Title 61, § 3

Eight-Hour Laws
See Contract Work Hours And Safety Standards Act

Eight Hour Work Day Act
Ill. Rev. Stat. 1991, Ch. 48, § 0.01 et seq.
N.Y. Labor Law (Consol. Laws Ch. 31) §§ 160 Subd. 3; 220 Subd. 1

Eight Months Claim Act (Probate)
Fla. Stat. 1971, 733.16

Eight Percent Act (Unfair Trade Practices)
Minn. Stat. Ann., 325D.08

Eighteen-Year Olds May Donate Blood Act
S.C. Code Ann. 1976, § 44-43-20 et seq.

Eighteenth Amendment
Jan. 28, 1919, 40 Stat. 1941

Eighth Class Counties Act (Officers Salaries)
Pa. Purdon's Stat., Title 16, § 1555

Eighty Cent Gas Law
N.Y. Laws 1906, Ch. 125

Eikenberry Act (Building and Loan Associations)
Ohio Rev. Code 1953, 1157.01 et seq.

Eikenberry Act (Feed Stuffs)
Ohio Rev. Code 1953, 923.41 et seq.

Eisenhower Exchange Fellowship Act of 1990

Oct. 24, 1990, P.L. 101-454, 20 U.S. Code §§ 5201 to 5206

Oct. 25, 1994, P.L. 103-415, 108 Stat. 4302

Dec. 23, 1995, P.L. 104-72, 109 Stat. 776

Ejectment Act

Fla. Stat. Ann., 66.011 et seq.

Ga. Code Ann., 44-11-1 et seq.

Ill. Rev. Stat. 1991, Ch. 110, § 6-101 et seq.

Mich. Comp. Laws Ann., 600.5701 et seq.

N.J. Stat. Ann., Superseded Vol., 2A:35-1 et seq.

Pa. Purdon's Stat., Title 12, § 1511 et seq.

R.I. Gen. Laws 1956, 34-20-2 et seq.

Vt. Stat. Ann., Title 12, § 4761 et seq.

Wash. Rev. Code Ann., 7.28.010 et seq.

El Camino Real de Tierra Adentro Study Act of 1993

Nov. 17, 1993, P.L. 103-144, 16 U.S. Code §§ 1241 nt., 1244

El Camino Real Para Los Texas Study Act of 1993

Nov. 17, 1993, P.L. 103-145, 16 U.S. Code §§ 1241 nt., 1244

El Centro Naval Air Facility Ranges Withdrawal Act

Sept. 23, 1996, P.L. 104-201, Title XXIX, Subtitle B, 110 Stat. 2813

El Dorado County Toll Tunnel Authority Act

Cal. Streets and Highways Code § 31100 et seq.

El Dorado County Water Agency Act

Cal. Statutes 1959, Ch. 2139, p. 5084

El Paso Courts Act

Tex. Government Code, § 30.031 et seq.

El Paso Criminal Law Magistrates Act

Tex. Laws 1987, p. 1711 Ch. 317

El Rio Chama Scenic and Pastoral Act

N.M. Stat. Ann., 16-4-1 et seq.

Elabash, Rosemary, Call before You Dig Act

Ala. Acts 1994, p. 922, No. 489

Elbert County Richard B. Russell Development Authority Act

Ga. Laws 1991, p. 3587

Elbridge Animal Control Law

N.Y. Local Laws 1972, Town of Elbridge, p. 1329

N.Y. Local Laws 1973, Village of Elbridge, p. 3323

Elbridge Electrical Code

N.Y. Local Laws 1973, Town of Eldridge, p. 1687

Elder Abuse and Dependent Adult Civil Protection Act

Cal. Welfare and Institutions Code § 15600 et seq.

Elder Abuse and Neglect Act

Ill. Rev. Stat. 1991, Ch. 23, § 6601 et seq.

Elder Abuse Demonstration Program Act

Ill. Rev. Stat. 1989, Ch. 23, § 6500 et seq.

Elder Abuse Prevention Act

Mont. Code Ann., 52-3801 et seq.

Ore. Rev. Stat., 124.005 et seq.

Elder and Developmentally Disabled Abuse Prevention Act

Mont. Code Ann. 1987, 53-5-501 et seq.

Elder Iowans Act

Iowa Code Ann., 231.1

Elderly Abuse, Exploitation, Neglect and Abandonment Reporting Act

Ida. Code 1947, 39-5301 et seq.

Elderly Act (Community)

Fla. Stat. Ann., 410.021 et seq.

Elderly Act (Office for the Affairs of)

P.R. Laws Ann. 1954, Title 3, § 1951 et seq.

Elderly Act of 1973
Me. Rev. Stat. Ann. 1964, Title 22, § 5101 et seq.

Elderly Adults Act (Public Guardian for)
N.J. Stat. Ann., 52:27G-20 et seq.

Elderly Affairs Department Act
Fla. Stat. Ann., 430.01 et seq.

Elderly All-Inclusive Care Act
Ill. Rev. Stat. 1991, Ch. 23, § 6901 et seq.

Elderly and Disabled Coordinated Public Transportation Assistance Act
Kan. Stat. Ann.,75-5032 et seq.

Elderly and Handicapped Coordinated Public Transportation Assistance Act
Kan. Stat. Ann., 75-5032 et seq.

Elderly and Handicapped Security Assistance Act
Fla. Stat. Ann., 426.001 et seq.

Elderly and Incapacitated Victim's Protection Program
Okla. Stat. Ann., Title 22, § 991a-5 et seq.

Elderly Care Act (AU-Inclusive Program)
Colo. Rev. Stat., 26-16-101 et seq.

Elderly Homeowner Rehabilitation Assistance and Housing Predevelopment Act
Fla. Stat. Ann., 420.303 et seq.

Elderly Householders Tax and Rent Refund Act
Me. Rev. Stat. Ann. 1964, Title 36, § 6101 et seq.

Elderly Housing and Urban Betterment Act
Mass. Acts 1973, Ch. 1215

Elderly Persons Abuse Act
Mass. Gen. Laws Ann., 19A:14 et seq.

Elderly Persons Housing Authority Act
Wash. Rev. Code Ann., 66.395

Elderly Persons Low Rent Housing Bond Act
Cal. Health and Safety Code § 35990 et seq.

Elderly Pharmaceutical Insurance Coverage
N.Y. Executive Law 1951 (Consol. Laws, Ch. 18) § 547 et seq.

Elderly Protective Services Act
Okla. Stat. Ann., Title 43A, § 801 et seq.

Eldorado Valley Development Law
Nev. Rev. Stat. 1979 Reprint, 321.390 et seq.

Elected Assessors Retention Law
N.Y. Local Laws 1971, Town of Skaneateles, p. 3476
N.Y. Local Laws 1971, Town of Spafford, p. 3491

Elected Board of Education Act
D.C. Code 1973, § 31-101 et seq.

Elected Official Remuneration Law
D.C. Code Ann., § 1-1301 et seq.
N.Y. Local Laws 1973, Village of Greenwood Lake, p. 3396

Elected Officials Salaries and Expenses Act
Ind. Code Ann., 4-2-1-1, 4-2-1-2

Election Act
Ala. Code 1975, § 17-1-1 et seq.
Alaska Stat. 1962, § 15.05.010 et seq.
Ariz. Rev. Stat. Ann., § 16-101 et seq.
Ark. Stat. 1947, 7-1-101 et seq.
Cal. Elections Code 1976, § 1 et seq.
Cal. Statutes 1939, § Ch. 26, p. 49
Colo. Rev. Stat., 1-1-101 et seq.
Conn. Gen. Stat. 1983, § 9-1 et seq.
D.C. Code Ann., § 1-1301 et seq.
Del. Code of 1974, Title 15, § 101 et seq.
Fla. Stat. Ann., 97.011 et seq.
Ga. Code Ann., 21-2-1 et seq.
Haw. Rev. Stat. Ann., § 11-1 et seq.
Ida. Code 1947, 34-101 et seq.
Ill. Rev. Stat. 1981, Ch. 46
Ind. Code Ann., 3-5-1-1 et seq., 43.1 et seq.
Kan. Stat. Ann., 25-101 et seq.
Ky. Rev. Stat. 1971, 116.013 et seq.

La. Rev. Stat. Ann., 18.1 et seq.
Mass. Gen. Laws Ann., 54:1 et seq.
Md. Ann. Code 1957, Art. 33
Me. Rev. Stat. Ann. 1964, Title 21, § 1 et seq.
Mich. Comp. Laws Ann., 168.1 et seq.
Minn. Stat. Ann., 200.01 et seq.
Miss. Code Ann. 1972, § 23-15-1 et seq.
Mo. Rev. Stat., 115.001 et seq.
Mont. Code Ann., 13-1-101 et seq.
N.C. Gen. Stat. 1943, § 163,279 et seq.
N.D. Cent. Code, 16.1-01-01 et seq.
Neb. Rev. Stat. 1943, 32-101 et seq.
Nev. Rev. Stat. 1979 Reprint, 293.010 et seq.
N.H. Rev. Stat. 1955, 652:1 et seq.
N.J. Rev. Stat. 1937, 19:1-1 et seq.
N.M. Stat. Ann., 1-1-1 et seq.
N.Y. Consol. Laws, Ch. 17
Ohio Rev. Code 1953, 3501.01 et seq.
Okla. Stat. Ann., Title 26, § 1-101 et seq.
Ore. Rev. Stat. 1953, 246.010 et seq.
Pa. Purdon's Stat., Title 25, § 2600 et seq.
P.R. Laws Ann. 1954, Title 16, § 1 et seq.
S.C. Code Ann. 1976, § 7-1-10 et seq.
S.D. Codified Laws 1967, 12-1-1 et seq.
Tenn. Code Ann., 2-1-101 et seq.
Tex. Election Code 1985, § 1.001 et seq.
Vt. Stat. Ann., Title 17, § 2101 et seq.
Wash. Rev. Code Ann., 29.01.005 et seq.
W. Va. Code 1966, § 3-1-1 et seq.
Wyo. Stat. Ann., § 22-1-101 et seq.

Election Act (Australian Ballot)
See Australian Ballot Act

Election Act (Corrupt Practices)
Alaska Stat. 1962, § 15.56.010 et seq.

Election Act (Decedents Estates)
Ohio Rev. Code 1953, 2107.39 et seq.

Election Act (General)
Ill. Rev. Stat. 1991, Ch. 46, § 17-1 et seq.

Election Act (Mail Ballot)
Colo. Rev. Stat., 1-7.5-101 et seq.
N.M. Stat. Ann., 1-23-1 et seq.

Election Act (Municipal)
See Municipal Election Act

Election Act (Primary)
See Primary Election Act
Me. Rev. Stat. Ann. 1964, Title 21-A, § 331
et seq.

Election Act (Spouse)
Wash. Rev. Code Ann., 861.03

Election Act Amendments of 1976
D.C. Code 1973, § 1-1301 et seq.

Election Betting Act
Mont. Code Ann. 1978, 13-35-212

Election Books Act (County)
Fla. Laws 1935, Ch. 17399

Election Campaign Act
Mass. Gen. Laws 1984, 55:1 et seq.

**Election Campaign Act Amendments
(Federal)**
Mo. Rev. Stat., 115.526 et seq.
Neb. Rev. Stat. 1943, 32-1001 et seq.
N.J. Stat. Ann., 19:29-1 et seq.
N.M. Stat. Ann., 1-14-1 et seq.
Wash. Rev. Code Ann., 29.65.010 et seq.

Election Campaign Disclosure Act
Mass. Gen. Laws Ann., 55:1 et seq.

Election Campaign Finance Disclosure Act
La. Rev. Stat. Ann., 18:1481 et seq.

Election Campaign Financing Act
Fla. Stat. 1983, 106.30 et seq.

Election Campaign Fund Act
Cal. Revenue and Taxation Code § 18701 et
seq.

Election Code
Utah Code Ann. 1953, 20A-1-101 et seq.

**Election Consolidation Implementation Act
of 1978**
Ill. Laws 1978, P.A. 80-1469

Election Contest Act
Cal. Elections Code 1976, § 20000 et seq.
Ida. Code 1947, 34-2101 et seq.
Ind. Code Ann., 3-12-6-1 et seq., 3-12-10-1 et seq., 57.1 et seq.
Minn. Stat. Ann., 209.01 et seq.
Mo. Rev. Stat., 115.526 et seq.
Neb. Rev. Stat. 1943, 32-1001 et seq.
N.J. Stat. Ann., 19:29-1 et seq.
N.M. Stat. Ann., 1-14-1 et seq.
Wash. Rev. Code Ann., 29.65.010 et seq.

Election District Alteration and Data Reporting Act
Pa. Purdon's Stat., Title 25, § 3601 et seq.

Election Expenditures Act (Garfield)
Ohio Rev. Code 1953, 3517.08 et seq.

Election Expense Act (Constitutional Convention)
Ill. Comp. Stat. 1992, Ch. 50, §§ 435/0.01, 435/1

Election Finance Act (Registry)
Tenn. Code Ann., 2-10-201 et seq.

Election Interference Prohibition Act
Ill. Rev. Stat. 1991, Ch. 46, § 101 et seq.

Election Judge Compensation Act
Ill. Rev. Stat. 1991, Ch. 46, § 900 et seq.

Election Law
June 10, 1872, Ch. 415, 17 Stat. 347
N.C. Gen. Stat. 1943, § 163-1 et seq.
P.R. Laws Ann. 1954, Title 16, § 1 et seq.
R.I. Gen. Laws 1956, 17-1-1 et seq.
Vt. Stat. Ann., Title 17, § 1 et seq.

Election Law (School)
N.M. Stat. Ann., 1-22-1 et seq.

Election Law Revision Act
Wyo. Stat. 1957, § 22-118 et seq.

Election of Remedies Act
Ala. Code 1975, § 6-5-440

Election Primary Recount Act
Ga. Code Ann., 21-2-495

Election Proposition Publication Act
Ill. Rev. Stat. 1991, Ch. 46, § 1000 et seq.

Election Recount Act
See Recount Act (Election)

Election Reform Act
Ala. Code 1975, § 17-24-1 et seq.
N.Y. Election Laws 1976 (Consol. Laws Ch. 17) §§ 2-118, 3-102, 3-212, 5-210, 5-211, 6-104, 6-132 et seq., 6-158, 7-104, 9-209, 14-114, 14-120, 16-102
N.Y. Public Service Law (Consol. Laws Ch. 48) § 44
N.Y. Tax Law (Consol. Laws Ch. 60) § 691

Election Registration Act
Fla. Stat. Ann., 97.011 et seq.
Mich. Comp. Laws Ann., 168.491 et seq.
Mont. Code Ann., 13-2-102 et seq.
Nev. Rev. Stat. 1979 Reprint, 293.485 et seq.
R.I. Gen. Laws 1956, 17-9-1 et seq.
Wash. Rev. Code Ann., 29.07.010 et seq.

Election Regulation Law (Campaigns)
Cal. Elections Code 1976, § 11500 et seq.

Election Validating Act (1935)
Ida. Laws 1935, First Extra Session, Ch. 4
Ida. Laws 1937, Ch. 203
Mont. Laws 1935, Ch. 99

Elections Act (Special District)
Wyo. Stat. Ann., § 22-29-101 et seq.

Elections and Latino Community Development Amendments Act of 1976
D.C. Laws 1977, No. 1-126

Elections Bribery Act
Wash. Rev. Code Ann., 12.11 et seq.

Elections District Act (Metropolitan)
N.Y. Election Law 1976 (Consol. Laws Ch. 17) § 4-100

Elections Emergency Act
Fla. Stat. Ann., 101.731 et seq.

Elections Hours Act
Ky. Rev. Stat. 1971, Superseded Vols.,
118.040, 118.350, 118.370
Ky. Rev. Stat. 1971, 117.275, 118.025,
118.035

Elections Organization Act
D.C. Code Ann., §§ 1-1302 to 1-1304,
1-1306, 1-1312

Elective Act (Spouse)
Wyo. Stat. Ann., § 2-4-101

Elective Community Property Act
Okla. Laws 1939, p. 356

Elective Compensation Law
Ala. Code 1975, § 25-5-1 et seq.

**Elective Franchise Act (District of
Columbia)**
Jan. 8, 1867, Ch. 6, 14 Stat. 375

Elective Franchise Act (Territories)
Jan. 25, 1867, Ch. 15, 14 Stat. 379

Electoral Act
P.R. Laws Ann. 1954, Title 16, § 3001 et seq.

Electoral Commission Act
Jan. 29, 1877, Ch. 37, 19 Stat. 227

Electoral Count Act
Feb. 3, 1887, Ch. 90, 24 Stat. 373 (See 3 U.S.
Code §§ 5 to 7, 15 to 18)

Electoral Count Resolution
Feb. 8, 1865, No. 12, 13 Stat. 567

Electoral Votes Exclusion Resolution
July 20, 1868, No. 58, 15 Stat. 257

Electors Act (Absentee)
Ill. Rev. Stat. 1991, Ch. 46, § 19-1 et seq.

Electors Qualifications Act
Ala. Code 1975, § 17-3-9 et seq.

**Electric and Hybrid Vehicle Research,
Development, and Demonstration Act of
1976**
Sept. 17, 1976, P.L. 94-413, 15 U.S. Code
§ 2501 et seq.
Feb. 25, 1978, P.L. 95-238, 15 U.S. Code
§ 2506 et seq.
Jan. 7, 1980, P.L. 96-185, 15 U.S. Code
§ 2512
Dec. 21, 1982, P.L. 97-375, 15 U.S. Code
§ 2506
Nov. 2, 1994, P.L. 103-347, 15 U.S. Code
§§ 2506, 2509
Dec. 21, 1995, P.L. 104-66, 15 U.S. Code
§ 2513

Electric and Telephone Cooperative Act
Alaska Stat. 1962, § 10.25.010 et seq.

Electric Authorities Act
Va. Code 1950, § 15.1-1603 et seq.

Electric Co-operative Corporation Act
Neb. Rev. Stat. 1943, 70-701 et seq.

Electric Companies Act
Mich. Comp. Laws Ann., 486.251 et seq.

Electric Company Act (Municipal)
Wash. Rev. Code Ann., 66.073

Electric Consumers Council Act
S.D. Codified Laws 1967, 49-41A-1 et seq.

Electric Consumers Protection Act of 1986
Oct. 16, 1986, P.L. 99-495, 16 U.S. Code
§ 791a nt.

Electric Cooperative Act (Rural)
Fla. Stat. Ann., 425.01 et seq.
Mont. Code Ann. 1987, 35-18-101 et seq.
N.M. Stat. Ann., 62-15-1 et seq.
Okla. Stat. Ann., Title 18, § 437 et seq.
S.C. Code Ann. 1976, § 33-49-10 et seq.

Electric Cooperatives Act
Ark. Code Ann. 1987, 23-18-301 et seq.
La. Rev. Stat. Ann., 12:401 et seq.
Pa. Cons. Stat., Title 15, § 7301 et seq.

Electric Cooperatives Act (Electricity Generation Choice for Customers of)
Pa. Cons. Stat., Title 15, § 7401 et seq.

Electric Cooperatives Corporation Act
Ala. Code 1975, § 37-6-1 et seq.
Ariz. Rev. Stat. Ann., § 10-751 et seq.
Conn. Gen. Stat. 1983, § 33-218 et seq.
Kan. Stat. Ann., 17-4601 et seq.
La. Rev. Stat. Ann., 12:401 et seq.
Md. Ann. Code 1974, Art. CA, § 5-601 et seq.
N.D. Cent. Code, 10-13-01 et seq.
Neb. Rev. Stat. 1943, 70-701 et seq.
S.D. Codified Laws 1967, 47-21-1 et seq.
Tenn. Code Ann., 65-25-101 et seq.
Tex. Utilities Code, § 161.001 et seq.
Va. Code 1950, § 56-209 et seq.
Vt. Stat. Ann., Title 30, § 3001 et seq.

Electric District Enabling Act (Municipal)
Me. Rev. Stat. Ann. 1964, Title 35-A, § 3901 et seq.

Electric Energy Wholesale Competition and Economic Development Act
Va. Code 1950, §§ 56-576 to 56-591

Electric Equity Act
Ore. Laws 1977, Ch. 888

Electric Facility Need Assessment Act
N.J. Stat. Ann., 48:7-16 et seq.

Electric Generation Facility Siting Act
Kan. Stat. Ann., 66-1, 158 et seq.

Electric Home and Farm Authority Act
March 31, 1936, Ch. 163, 49 Stat. 1186

Electric Industry Restructuring Act
Va. Code 1950, §§ 56-576 to 56-594

Electric Light Loan Act (Braintree)
Mass. Acts 1957, Ch. 674

Electric Loan Act (Hudson)
Mass. Acts 1955, Ch. 19

Electric Loan Act (Peabody)
Mass. Acts 1956, Ch. 648

Electric Loan Act (Taunton)
Mass. Acts 1955, Ch. 201

Electric Membership Corporation Act
Ala. Code 1975, § 37-7-1 et seq.
Ga. Code Ann., 46-3-170 et seq.
N.C. Gen. Stat. 1943, § 117-6 et seq.
Tenn. Code Ann., 65-24-101 et seq.

Electric Meters Act (Tampering)
S.C. Code Ann. 1976, § 16-13-385

Electric Patrol Vehicle Act
Mich. Comp. Laws Ann., 257.1571 to 257.1577

Electric Plant Act
Tenn. Code Ann., 7-52-101 et seq.

Electric Plant Law (Municipal)
Miss. Code Ann. 1972, § 77-5-401 et seq.

Electric Power Act (Fernald)
Me. Rev. Stat. 1954, Ch. 50, § 1

Electric Power and Energy Act (Joint Municipal)
See Joint Municipal Electric Power and Energy Act

Electric Power and Energy Act (Municipal)
S.C. Code Ann. 1976, § 6-23-10 et seq.

Electric Power Association Law
Miss. Code Ann. 1972, § 77-5-701 et seq.

Electric Power Authority Act
P.R. Laws Ann. 1954, Title 22, § 191 et seq.

Electric Power Generation Act (Municipal)
Ark. Code Ann. 1987, 14-202-101 et seq.
N.M. Stat. Ann., 3-24-11 et seq.

Electric Power Planning and Conservation Act (Pacific Northwest)
Wash. Rev. Code 1983, 43.52A.010 et seq.

Electric Power Tax Act
S.C. Code Ann. 1976, § 12-23-10 et seq.

Electric Rate Reform Act
Me. Rev. Stat. Ann. 1964, Title 35-A, § 3151 et seq.

Electric Refunding Revenue Bond Act
Ill. Rev. Stat. 1991, Ch. 111 2/3, § 110 et seq.

Electric Revenue Bond Act (Kissimmee-St. Cloud)
Fla. Special Laws 1970, Ch. 70-767

Electric Service Customer Choice and Rate Relief Law
Ill. Comp. Stat. 1992, Ch. 220, § 5/16-101 et seq.

Electric Supplier Act
Ill. Rev. Stat. 1991, Ch. 111 2/3, § 401 et seq.

Electric Supplier Certified Territory Act (Retail)
Okla. Stat. Ann., Title 17, § 158.21 et seq.

Electric Supplier Stabilization Act
Ida. Code 1947, 61-332 et seq.

Electric Surface Transmission Law
Cal. Public Utilities Code § 8026 et seq.

Electric System Act
Ky. Rev. Stat. 1971, 96.520 et seq.

Electric System Financing Act (Municipal)
Ark. Code Ann. 1987, 14-203-101 et seq.

Electric System Tax Equivalent Law
Tenn. Public Acts 1991, Ch. 84

Electric Systems Bond Act
Ala. Code 1975, 11-81-200 et seq.

Electric Transmission Line Certification Act
Mich. Comp. Laws Ann., 460.561 et seq.

Electric Transmission Siting and Regulatory Act
R.I. Gen. Laws 1956, 39-25-1 et seq.

Electric Underground Transmission Law
Cal. Public Utilities Code § 8051 et seq.

Electric Utility Companies Act
Aug. 26, 1935, Ch. 687, 49 Stat. 847, 16 U.S. Code §§ 824 to 825r

Electric Utility Industry Restructuring and Customer Choice Act
Mont. Code Ann., 69-8-101 et seq.

Electric Utility Transitional Funding Law
Ill. Comp. Stat. 1992, Ch. 220, § 5/18-101 et seq.

Electrical Act
D.C. Code Ann., § 5-1301
Fla. Stat. Ann., 553.15 et seq.
Minn. Stat. Ann., 326.241 et seq.
Neb. Rev. Stat. 1943, 81-2101 et seq.
N.Y. Local Laws 1966, Village of Ossining, p. 2053
N.Y. Local Laws 1972, Village of Baldwinsville, p. 3033
N.Y. Local Laws 1973, Town of Elbridge, p. 1687
N.Y. Local Laws 1973, Village of Jordan, p. 3441

Electrical Administrative Act
Mich. Comp. Laws Ann., 338.881 et seq.

Electrical Code
N.Y. Adm. Code 1985, § 27-3001 et seq.

Electrical Code Authority Act
Ark. Acts 1991, No. 653

Electrical Contractors Act
Ala. Acts 1985, 2d Sp. Sess., No. 921
Ga. Code Ann., 43-14-1 et seq.
N.M. Stat. Ann. 1953, 67-19-1 et seq.

Electrical Contractors Licensing Act
N.J. Stat. Ann., 45:5A-1 et seq.

Electrical District Act
Ariz. Rev. Stat. Ann., § 48-1701 et seq.

Electrical Energy Producers Act
N.H. Rev. Stat. 1955, 362-A:1 et seq.

Electrical Energy Tax Act
N.M. Stat. Ann., 7-18-1 et seq.

Electrical License Act
Okla. Stat. Ann., Title 59, § 1680 et seq.

Electrical Power Plant Siting Act
Fla. Stat. Ann., 403.501 et seq.

Electrical Safety Law
Mont. Code Ann., 37-68-101 et seq.
Ore. Rev. Stat. 1953, 479.510 et seq.

Electrical Subway Act (Overhead Wires)
N.Y. Laws 1884, Ch. 534

Electrical Utilities and Electric Cooperatives Act
S.C. Code Ann. 1976, § 58-27-10 et seq.

Electrical Wiring Code
Ore. Rev. Stat. 1953, 479.510 et seq.

Electricians Act
Mass. Gen. Laws Ann., 141:1 et seq.
Neb. Laws 1969, Ch. 765
R.I. Gen. Laws 1956, 5-6-1 et seq.
Vt. Stat. Ann., Title 26, § 881 et seq.

Electricians Licensing Act
Me. Rev. Stat. Ann. 1964, Title 32, § 1201 et seq.
Utah Code Ann. 1953, 58-55-1 et seq.

Electricity and Gas Joint Ownership Act
Ill. Rev. Stat. 1991, Ch. 76, § 10 et seq.

Electricity Companies Regulation Act
Wash. Rev. Code Ann., 80.28.010 et seq.

Electricity Excise Tax Law
Ill. Comp. Stat. 1992, Ch. 35, § 640/2-1 et seq.

Electricity Generation Choice for Customers of Electric Cooperatives Act
Pa. Cons. Stat., Title 15, § 7401 et seq.

Electricity Generation Customer Choice and Competition Act
Pa. Cons. Stat., Title 66, § 2801 et seq.

Electricity Infrastructure Maintenance Fee Law
Ill. Comp. Stat. 1992, Ch. 35, § 645/5-11 et seq.

Electricity License Tax Act
Ida. Code 1947, 63-2701 et seq.

Electricity Rates Regulation Act
Wash. Rev. Code Ann., 80.28.010 et seq.

Electricity Transmission Act
Mich. Comp. Laws Ann., 460.551 et seq.

Electrification Act (Rural)
N.C. Gen. Stat. 1943, § 117-1 et seq.
S.C. Acts 1933, p. 362, No. 275

Electrification Authority Act
Mont. Laws 1935, Ch. 98

Electrification Authority Act (Rural)
S.C. Code Ann. 1976, § 58-29-10 et seq.

Electrification Cooperative Agency Act (Municipal and Rural)
Me. Rev. Stat. Ann. 1964, Title 35-A, § 4101 et seq.

Electrification Cooperative Enabling Act (Rural)
Me. Rev. Stat. Ann. 1964, Title 35-A, § 3701 et seq.

Electrification Transfer Act (Rural)
S.C. Acts 1940, p. 2059, No. 1030

Electrocution Act
Ga. Code Ann., 17-10-38 et seq.
Neb. Rev. Stat. 1943, 29-2532 et seq.

Electrologist Act (Registered)
Okla. Stat. Ann., Title 59, § 536.1 et seq.

Electrologists Practice Act
Md. Ann. Code 1974, Art. HO, § 6-101 et seq.

Tenn. Code Ann., Superseded Vol., 62-2401 et seq.

Tenn. Code Ann., 62-34-101 et seq., 62-34-201 et seq.

Electrologists' Registration Act

Mass. Gen. Laws Ann., 112:87EEE et seq.

Electrolysis Practice Act

Fla. Stat. Ann., 478.40 et seq.

N.C. Gen. Stat. 1943, § 88A-1 et seq.

Electronic and Appliance Repair Dealer Registration Law

Cal. Business and Professions Code § 9800 et seq.

Electronic Authentication Act

Minn. Stat. Ann., 325K.01 et seq.

Wash. Rev. Code Ann., 19.34.010 et seq.

Electronic Authentication of Documents Act

N.M. Stat. Ann., 14-15-1 et seq.

Electronic Benefits Transfer Act

Cal. Welfare and Institutions Code § 10065 et seq.

Electronic Commerce Act

Cal. Civil Code § 1789 et seq.

Tex. Government Code, § 2177.001 et seq.

Electronic Communications Privacy Act of 1986

Oct. 21, 1986, P.L. 99-508, 18 U.S. Code § 2510 nt.

Electronic Data and Billing Exchange Act

See Uniform Electronic Data and Billing Exchange Act

Electronic Data Processing Act (Broward County)

Fla. Special Laws 1969, Ch. 69-904

Electronic Data Processing Management Act

Fla. Stat. Ann., 23.021 et seq.

Electronic Data Processing Management Act (Escambia County)

Fla. Special Laws 1967, Ch. 67-1373

Electronic Eavesdropping Act

Haw. Rev. Stat. Ann., § 803-41 et seq.

Electronic Filing Act

Ga. Code Ann., 21-5-3, 21-5-6, 21-5-30, 21-5-34, 21-5-50, 21-5-73

Electronic Freedom of Information Act Amendments of 1996

Oct. 2, 1996, P.L. 104-231, 5 U.S. Code § 552 nt.

Electronic Fund Transfer Act

Nov. 10, 1978, P.L. 95-630, 15 U.S. Code § 1693 et seq.

Dec. 21, 1982, P.L. 97-375, 15 U.S. Code § 1693p

Aug. 9, 1989, P.L. 101-73, 15 U.S. Code § 1693o

Dec. 19, 1991, P.L. 102-242, 15 U.S. Code § 1693o

Aug. 22, 1996, P.L. 104-193, 15 U.S. Code § 1693b

Mont. Code Ann., 32-6-101 et seq.

Electronic Fund Transfer Privacy Act

N.J. Stat. Ann., 17-16K-1 et seq.

Electronic Fund Transfer Transmission Facility Act

Ill. Rev. Stat. 1991, Ch. 17, § 1301 et seq.

Electronic Funds Act (Bank)

Colo. Rev. Stat., 11-6.5-101 et seq.

Electronic Funds Transfer Study Act

Ill. Rev. Stat. 1991, Ch. 127, § 39d-101 et seq.

Electronic Home Detention Act

Cal. Penal Code § 1203.016

Ill. Rev. Stat. 1991, Ch. 38, § 1005-8A-1 et seq.

S.C. Code Ann. 1976, § 24-13-1510 et seq.

Electronic Repair Act

Fla. Stat. 1983, 468.150 et seq.

Electronic Repair Dealer Registration Act
Utah Code Ann. 1953, Miscellaneous Superseded Code Provisions, 58-38-1 et seq.

Electronic Signature Act
Fla. Stat. Ann., 282.70 et seq.

Electronic Signature and Filing Act
Ida. Code 1947, 67-2351 to 67-2357

Electronic Signatures and Records Act
Ga. Code Ann., 10-12-1 et seq.
R.I. Gen. Laws 1956, 42-127-1 et seq.

Electronic Superhighway Act
N.J. Stat. Ann., 40A-43 et seq.

Electronic Surveillance Act
La. Rev. Stat. Ann., 15:1301 et seq.
N.J. Stat. Ann., 2A:156A-1 et seq.

Electronic Surveillance and Wiretapping Act
W. Va. Code 1966 § 62-1D-1 et seq.

Electronic Surveillance Control Act
Pa. Cons. Stat., Title 18, § 5701 et seq.

Electronic Tax Return Filing Act
Ala. Code 1975, § 40-30-1 et seq.

Electronic Voting Act
Mass. Gen. Laws Ann., 54:33E et seq.

Electronic Voting Systems Act
Fla. Stat. Ann., 101.5601 et seq.

Electronics Payment Acceptance Act
Conn. Public Acts 1994, May Special Session No. 2, § 193

Eleemosynary Funds Investment Guidlines Law
Mo. Rev. Stat., 402.010 et seq.

Element Enforcement Act (Binding)
Ky. Rev. Stat. 1971, 100.401 to 100.419

Elementary and Secondary Amendments of 1988
April 28, 1988, P.L. 100-297, 102 Stat. 302, 20 U.S. Code §§ 1201 et seq., 1201 nt.

Elementary and Secondary Education Act (Nonpublic)
N.J. Stat. Ann., 18A:58-59 et seq.
Pa. Purdon's Stat., Title 24, § 5601 et seq.

Elementary and Secondary Education Act of 1965
April 11, 1965, P.L. 89-10, 79 Stat. 27, 20 U.S. Code §§ 236 to 244, 331 to 332b 821 to 827, 841 to 848, 861 to 870, 881 to 885

Nov. 3, 1966, P.L. 89-750, 80 Stat. 1196, 20 U.S. Code §§ 821 to 823, 841 to 844, 861 to 864, 867, 871 to 886

Jan. 2, 1968, P.L. 90-247, 81 Stat. 783, 20 U.S. Code §§ 237 to 239, 241-1, 241a to 241m 244, 618, 633, 635 and others

Oct. 16, 1968, P.L. 90-576, 82 Stat. 1097, 20 U.S. Code § 241c

April 13, 1970, P.L. 91-230, 84 Stat. 121, 20 U.S. Code §§ 241a to 241d-2, 241d-11 to 241m, 331a, 821, 822, 824 and others

May 21, 1970, P.L. 91-260, 84 Stat. 254, 20 U.S. Code § 635

Sept. 24, 1977, P.L. 95-112, 20 U.S. Code §§ 241b et seq.

Nov. 1, 1978, P.L. 95-561, 20 U.S. Code §§ 2701 et seq., 2701 nt. , 2881 et seq., 3381, 3384, 3385

Aug. 6, 1979, P.L. 96-46, 20 U.S. Code §§ 2721, 2733 to 2735, 2740, 2762, 2763, 2772, 2782, 2902, 3084, 3163, 3164, 3200, 3289, 3311 et seq.

Oct. 17, 1979, P.L. 96-88, 20 U.S. Code § 2711

Oct. 19, 1984, P.L. 98-524, 20 U.S. Code §§ 3223, 3385

Nov. 22, 1985, P.L. 99-159, 20 U.S. Code § 2763

April 28, 1988, P.L. 100-297, 102 Stat. 140, 20 U.S. Code §§ 1221 , 1232, 2701 et seq.

Oct. 31, 1988, P.L. 100-569, 20 U.S. Code §§ 3156a, 3157 Oct. 31, 1988, P.L. 100-570, 20 U.S. Code §§ prec. 3011, 3011, 3012

Nov. 18, 1988, P.L. 100-690, 20 U.S. Code § 3156a

March 6, 1990, P.L. 101-250, 20 U.S. Code §§ 3243, 3244, 3271

Oct. 30, 1990, P.L. 101-476, 20 U.S. Code § 1400 nt.

Nov. 16, 1990, P.L. 101-600, 20 U.S. Code §§ 2762 to 2765b, 2766, 2767, 2767a, 2768

June 27, 1991, P.L. 102-62, 20 U.S. Code §§ 1211-1 nt., 2965, 3156b, 3157

July 25, 1991, P.L. 102-73, 20 U.S. Code §§ 2711, prec. 2741, 2742 to 2747, 2749, 2941, 2963, 2966, 3142

Aug. 17, 1991, P.L. 102-103, 20 U.S. Code § 2791

Oct. 27, 1992, P.L. 102-545, 20 U.S. Code §§ 3161 to 3161g

March 31, 1994, P.L. 103-227, 20 U.S. Code §§ 3155, 3351 et seq. 3381 to 3384, 3386

May 18, 1994, P.L. 103-252, 20 U.S. Code § 3161 et seq.

Oct. 20, 1994, P.L. 103-382, 20 U.S. Code §§ 2701 et seq., 6301 nt., 6301 et seq.

March 23, 1995, P.L. 104-5, 20 U.S. Code § 7812

Feb. 10, 1996, P.L. 104-106, 20 U.S. Code § 7703

April 26, 1996, P.L. 104-134, 20 U.S. Code §§ 6311, 6317, 6322, 6364, 6365, 6491, 7707, 8001, 8941

Aug. 22, 1996, P.L. 104-193, 20 U.S. Code §§ 6313, 6333, 7233

Sept. 16, 1996, P.L. 104-195, 20 U.S. Code §§ 7702, 7703, 7709

Sept. 23, 1996, P.L. 104-201, 20 U.S. Code § 7703

Sept. 30, 1996, P.L. 104-208, 20 U.S. Code §§ 6621, 6645, 6648, 6649, 6813, 7703, 8091, 8102, 8104

June 12, 1997, P.L. 105-18, 20 U.S. Code §§ 6491, 7702, 7703

Nov. 13, 1997, P.L. 105-78, 20 U.S. Code §§ 7702, 7703, 7714, 8064

Aug. 7, 1998, P.L. 105-220, 20 U.S. Code §§ 6362, 6365, 6366, 6813, 7881

Oct. 7, 1998, P.L. 105-244, 20 U.S. Code §§ 7132, 7601, 8801

Oct. 21, 1998, P.L. 105-277, 20 U.S. Code §§ 6353, 6362, 6363, 6364, 6365, 6368, 6369, 6369a, 6369b, 6370, 6453, 6455, 6493, 6603, 6646, 6661, 6661a to 6661i, 6701, 7144, 7702, 8221 to 8224, 8351, 8371, 8801, 8893

Oct. 22, 1998, P.L. 105-278, 20 U.S. Code §§ 7331, 7351, 8061 8065, 8065a to 8065d, 8066, 8067, 8801

Oct. 31, 1998, P.L. 105-332, 20 U.S. Code §§ 6314, 7815, 8004, 8852, 8857

Elementary and Secondary Education Amendments of 1966

April 28, 1988, P.L. 100-297, 102 Stat. 302, 20 U.S. Code §§ 1201 et seq.

Oct. 20, 1994, P.L. 103-382, 42 U.S. Code § 2000d-5

Elementary and Secondary Education Opportunity Program Act

N.Y. Education Law 1947 (Consol. Laws Ch. 16) § 559 et seq.

Elementary and Secondary Private Education Authorization Act

Nev. Rev. Stat. 1979 Reprint, 394.201 et seq.

Elementary and Secondary School Dropout Prevention Act

Cal. Education Code 1976, § 54660 et seq.

Elementary and Secondary School Finance Authority Act

Neb. Rev. Stat. 1943, 79-1801 to 79-1852

Elementary and Secondary School Reform Act

N.C. Public Laws 1984, Ch. 1103

Elementary and Secondary School Self-Insurance Act

Ark. Code Ann. 1987, 6-20-1501 et seq.

Elevated Highway Act (Park District)

Ill. Rev. Stat. 1991, Ch. 105, § 327c.9 et seq.

Elevated Railroad Approval Act

Ill. Rev. Stat. 1991, Ch. 131 1/4, § 12.9 et seq.

Elevation Act (Estates)

Mich. Comp. Laws 1948, 556.9

Elevation Act (Real Property)

N.Y. Estates, Powers and Trusts Law (Consol. Laws Ch. 17B) § 10-6.3

Elevator Act
D.C. Code Ann., § 1-323
Ind. Code Ann., 89A.1 et seq.
Mich. Comp. Laws Ann., 408.801 et seq.
N.H. Rev. Stat. 1955, 157-B:1 et seq.
Pa. Purdon's Stat., Title 35, § 1341 et seq.
S.C. Code Ann. 1976, § 41-16-10 et seq.

Elevator Air Act (Clean Public)
Ill. Rev. Stat. 1991, Ch. 111 1/2, § 7651 et seq.

Elevator and Boiler Safety Law
Haw. Rev. Stat. Ann., § 397-1 et seq.

Elevator Inspection Act
Neb. Rev. Stat. 1943, 48-418 et seq.
Ohio Rev. Code 1953, 4105.01 et seq.

Elevator Installation Act
Ill. Rev. Stat. 1991, Ch. 111 1/2, § 4000 et seq.

Elevator Loan Act (Essex County)
Mass. Acts 1955, Ch. 287

Elevator Safety Act
Ark. Code Ann. 1987, 20-24-101 et seq.
Fla. Stat. 1965, 399.01 et seq.
Ind. Code Ann., 22-12-1-1 et seq.
N.C. Gen. Stat. 1943, § 595-110.1 et seq.
Ore. Rev. Stat., 460.005 et seq.

Elevator Tactile Identification Act
Ill. Rev. Stat. 1991, Ch. 111 1/2, § 3900 et seq.

Elgin Civic Center Act
Ill. Rev. Stat. 1991, Ch. 85, § 3601 et seq.

Elgin, Orland Park, Centre East, Schaumburg, DuPage County, and Sterling Civic Centers Act
Ill. Rev. Stat. 1991, Ch. 85, § 3400 et seq.

Eligible Domestic Relations Order Act
Mich. Comp. Laws Ann., 38.1701 et seq.

Elimination Act (Asbestos Hazard)
Miss. Code Ann. 1972, § 37-137-1 et seq.

Elimination of the Chest X-Ray Requirement Act
D.C. Code Ann., § 1-319

Elisa's Law Child Protective Services Reform Act
N.Y. Domestic Relations Law (Consol. Laws Ch. 14) § 240
N.Y. Family Court Act, § 651a
N.Y. Mental Hygiene Law 1972 (Consol. Laws Ch. 27) § 45.07
N.Y. Social Services Law (Consol. Laws Ch. 55) §§ 20, 372, 409a, 409f, 419, 422, 422a, 424, 424a, 424c,

Elizabeth River Tunnel Revenue Bond Act
Va. Acts 1942, Ch. 130

Elkins Act (Interstate Commerce)
Feb. 19, 1903, Ch. 708, 32 Stat. 847, 49 U.S. Code §§ 41 to 43

Elko Charter
Nev. Statutes 1971, Ch. 276, p. 474

Elkton Charter of 1972
Tenn. Private Acts 1972, Ch. 296

Ellen Marshall Bennett Act
Ala. Code 1975, § 22-30-4

Ellender Sugar Act
See Sugar Act Of 1937

Ellery Mobile Homes and Mobile Home Parks Regulations
N.Y. Local Laws 1973, Town of Ellery, p. 1690

Ellicott Peddling, Vending and Soliciting Law
N.Y. Local Laws 1972, Town of Ellicott, p. 1337

Ellicottville Zoning Local Act
N.Y. Local Laws 1964, Village of Ellicott-ville, p. 846

Ellijay-Gilmer County Water and Sewerage Authority Act
Ga. Laws 1991, p. 5424

Elliott-Fitzgerald Displaced Homemakers Act
Mich. Comp. Laws Ann., 421.101 et seq.

Elliott-Larson Civil Rights Act
Mich. Comp. Laws Ann., 37.2101 et seq.

Ellis-Engel Act (Engineering and Land Surveying)
Ala. Code 1975, §§ 34-11-1, 34-11-4

Ellis Health Act
Ga. Code Ann., 31-3-1 et seq., 31-5-1 et seq.

Elmira Firemen's Pension Act
N.Y. Local Laws 1925, Elmira, No. 2

Elmira Parking Authority Act
N.Y. Public Authorities Law (Consol. Laws Ch. 43A) § 1450 et seq.

Elmira Policemen's Pension Act
N.Y. Local Laws 1926, Elmira, No. 2
N.Y. Local Laws 1940, Elmira, No. 2

Elmira School Act
N.Y. Laws 1895, Ch. 370

Elmira Unsafe Building Demolition Law
N.Y. Local Laws 1973, Town of Elmira, p. 1706

Elmore County Animal Owner Responsibility Act
Ala. Acts 1995, p. 789, No. 387

Elmsford Gasoline Service Station Act
N.Y. Local Laws 1964, Village of Elmsford, p. 878

Elwell Act (Streets and Parks)
Minn. Stat. Ann., 430.01 et seq.

Elwell Highway Law
Minn. Laws 1911, Ch. 254

Elwha River Ecosystem and Fisheries Restoration Act
Oct. 24, 1992, P.L. 102-495, 106 Stat. 3173

Emancipation Act (Children)
Ga. Code Ann., 19-9-3
La. Rev. Stat. Ann., 9:901

Emancipation Act (Married Women)
Ark. Code Ann. 1987, 9-11-502 et seq.
Fla. Stat. Ann., 708.08 et seq.
Ill. Rev. Stat. 1991, Ch. 40, § 1000 et seq.
La. Rev. Stat. Ann., 9:51 et seq.
N.C. Gen. Stat. 1943, § 52-2
Neb. Rev. Stat. 1943, 42-201 et seq.
Ohio Rev. Code 1953, 3103.01 et seq.
Okla. Stat. Ann., Title 43, § 214
Pa. Purdon's Stat., Title 48, § 64 et seq.
S.C. Code Ann. 1976, § 20-5-10 et seq.
Tenn. Code Ann., 36-3-501 et seq.
Tex. Family Code, § 4.03
W. Va. Code 1966, § 48-3-1 et seq.

Emancipation Juneteenth Cultural and Historical Commission Act
Tex. Government Code, § 448.001 et seq.

Emancipation of Mature Minors Act
Ill. Rev. Stat. 1991, Ch. 40, § 2201 et seq.

Emancipation of Minors Act
Cal. Civil Code § 60 et seq.
Cal. Family Code § 7000 et seq.
N.M. Stat. Ann., 28-6-1 et seq., 32A-21-1 to 32A-21-7

Emancipation Proclamation
Jan. 1, 1863, No. 17, 12 Stat. 1268

Emanuel County Development Authority Act
Ga. Laws 1965, p. 2770

Embalmers and Funeral Directors Act
Ariz. Rev. Stat. Ann., § 32-1301 et seq.
Cal. Business and Professions Code § 7600 et seq.
Colo. Rev. Stat. 1963, 61-1-1 et seq.
Ill. Rev. Stat. 1991, Ch. 111, § 2800 et seq.
Ind. Code Ann., 25-15-2-1 et seq.
Md. Ann. Code 1974, Art. HO, § 7-101 et seq.
Mich. Comp. Laws Ann., 338.861 et seq.
Continued

N.H. Rev. Stat. 1955, 325:1 et seq.
N.M. Stat. Ann. 1953, 67-20-1 et seq.
Ohio Rev. Code 1953, 4717.01 et seq.
Okla. Stat. Ann., Title 59, § 396 et seq.
Ore. Rev. Stat., 692.010 et seq.
Pa. Purdon's Stat., Title 63, § 479.1 et seq.
R.I. Gen. Laws 1956, 5-33-1 et seq.
Tenn. Code Ann., 62-5-101 et seq.
Utah Code Ann. 1953, 58-9-12 et seq.
Va. Code 1950, § 54.1-2800 et seq.
Wash. Rev. Code Ann., 455.01 et seq.
W. Va. Code 1966, § 30-6-1

Embalmers Board Act
P.R. Laws Ann. 1954, Title 20, § 1001 et seq.

Embalming Board Act
Okla. Stat. 1981, Title 59, § 396 et seq.

Embalming Fluid Act
Ill. Rev. Stat. 1991, Ch. 111 1/2, § 280 et seq.

Embarcadero Municipal Improvement District Act
Cal. Statutes 1960, 1st Ex. Sess., Ch. 81

Embargo Acts
March 26, 1794, No. 2, 1 Stat. 400
April 2, 1794, No. 3, 1 Stat. 400
April 18, 1794, No. 4, 1 Stat. 401
May 7, 1794, No. 5, 1 Stat. 401
April 18, 1806, Ch. 29, 2 Stat. 379
Dec. 22, 1807, Ch. 5, 2 Stat. 451
Jan. 9, 1808, Ch. 8, 2 Stat. 453
March 12, 1808, Ch. 33, 2 Stat. 473
April 25, 1808, Ch. 66, 2 Stat. 499
Jan. 9, 1809, Ch. 5, 2 Stat. 506
April 4, 1812, Ch. 49, 2 Stat. 700
April 14, 1812, Ch. 56, 2 Stat. 707
Dec. 17, 1813, Ch. 1, 3 Stat. 88
June 15, 1917, Ch. 30, 40 Stat. 223

Embassy Picketing Act
D.C. Code 1973, §§ 22-1115, 22-1116

Embezzlement Act
Ala. Code 1975, § 13A-8-3 et seq.
Cal. Penal Code § 503 et seq.
Colo. Rev. Stat. 1963, 40-5-15 et seq.

Md. Ann. Code 1957, Art. 27, § 341
Mich. Comp. Laws Ann., 750.174 et seq.
N.H. Rev. Stat. 1955, 555:1 et seq.
Ore. Rev. Stat. 1989, 165.002 et seq.
R.I. Gen. Laws 1956, 11-41-3
Tenn. Code Ann., 39-14-103 et seq.
Vt. Stat. Ann., Title 13, § 2531 et seq.

Embezzlement Act (Banks)
Tex. Penal Code, § 32.71

Embezzlement Act (Public Officers)
Ohio Rev. Code 1953, 2945.64
Okla. Stat. Ann., Title 21, § 341
Tenn. Code Ann., 39-14-103

Embezzlement Act (Tax Collectors)
Pa. 1885 Pamph. Laws 72, No. 45

Emblems and Flags Act
R.I. Gen. Laws 1956, 11-15-1 et seq.

Embracery Act
Ga. Code Ann., 16-10-91

Embry-Robinson Act (Intoxicating Liquors)
Ky. Rev. Stat. 1971, 244.290, 244.480

Emergency Act (Hazardous Materials)
Ill. Rev. Stat. 1991, Ch. 127, § 1250 et seq.

Emergency Act of 1933-1940
Neb. Laws 1933, Ch. 127
Neb. Laws 1935, Ch. 153
Neb. Laws 1937, Ch. 170
Neb. Laws 1939, Ch. 99

Emergency Adjusted Compensation Act, 1931
Feb. 27, 1931, Ch. 318, 46 Stat. 1429

Emergency Agricultural Credit Act of 1984
April 10, 1984, P.L. 98-258, 7 U.S. Code § 1921 nt.

Emergency Agricultural Credit Adjustment Act of 1978
Aug. 4, 1978, P.L. 95-334, 7 U.S. Code prec. § 1961 nt.
March 30, 1980, P.L. 96-220, 7 U.S. Code prec. 1961 nt.

April 10, 1984, P.L. 98-258, 7 U.S. Code prec. § 1961 nt.

Dec. 23, 1985, P.L. 99-198; 7 U.S. Code prec. § 1961 nt.

Nov. 28, 1990, P.L. 101-624, 7 U.S. Code prec. § 1961 nt.

Emergency Agricultural Relief Act
See Agricultural Adjustment Act; Emergency Farm Mortgage Act Of 1933

Emergency Air Mail Act
March 27, 1934, Ch. 100, 48 Stat. 508

Emergency Aircraft Restriction Act (Military)
Ill. Rev. Stat. 1991, Ch. 15 1/2, § 178.9 et seq.

Emergency Ambulance Service Act
W. Va. Code 1966, § 7-15-1 et seq.

Emergency Amusement Revenue Act
Miss. Code Ann. 1972, § 27-11-1 et seq.

Emergency and Disaster Management Compact Act
Ky. Rev. Stat. 1971, 39.450 et seq.

Emergency and Nonemergency Medical Services Act
Fla. Stat. Ann., 401.21 et seq.

Emergency Appropriation Acts
June 19, 1934, Ch. 648, 48 Stat. 1044, 2 U.S. Code §§ 36, 40a, 66, 67; 5 U.S. Code § 248b; 7 U.S. Code §§ 604, 605; 16 U.S. Code § 587a; 40 U.S. Code § 22a

July 3, 1947, Ch. 206, 61 Stat. 243

Emergency Archaeological Property Acquisition Act
Fla. Stat. Ann., 253.027

Emergency Assistance Act
Cal. Government Code § 53100 et seq.

Emergency Assistance Act (Local Government)
N.J. Laws 1979, Ch. 34

Emergency Assistance and Disaster Act
La. Rev. Stat. Ann., 29:721 et seq.

Emergency Assistance for Families with Children at Imminent Risk of Out-of-Home Placement Act
Colo. Rev. Stat., 26-5.3-101 et seq.

Emergency Banking Act
Ind. Code Ann., 524.224 et seq.
Md. Laws 1933, Ch. 46
Me. Rev. Stat. Ann. 1964, Title 9B, §§ 151, 152
Mich. Public Acts 1933, No. 32
N.J. Stat. Ann., 17:9A-23.50 et seq.

Emergency Banking Relief Act
March 9, 1933, Ch. 1, 48 Stat. 1, 12 U.S. Code §§ 51a to 51d, 95 to 95b, 201 to 211, 248, 347b to 347d, 445; 50 U.S. Code Appx. §§ 5, 5a

Emergency Box Drug Act
Neb. Rev. Stat. 1943, 71-2410 et seq.

Emergency Budget Act
Ala. Acts 1991, p. 602, No. 30
Ill. Laws 1982, P.A. 82-1038
Ill. Rev. Stat. 1991, Ch. 127, § 4351 et seq.

Emergency Business Space Rent Control Laws
N.Y. Laws 1945, Ch. 314
N.Y. Laws 1949, Ch. 535
N.Y. Laws 1951, Ch. 430
N.Y. Laws 1952, Ch. 417
N.Y. Laws 1953, Ch. 452

Emergency Capital Improvements Act
Del. Laws Vol. 60, p. 14, Ch. 7

Emergency Capital Outlay Act (Public School)
N.M. Stat. Ann., 22,24,1 et seq.

Emergency Capital Outlay Loan Act
Mass. Acts 1957, Ch. 485

Emergency Care Act (Law Enforcement)
Ill. Rev. Stat. 1991, Ch. 70, § 60, 61

Emergency Cargo-Ship Construction Act
Feb. 6, 1941, Ch. 5, 55 Stat. 5, 46 U.S. Code
§§ 1119a 1119b, 1125a, 1214

Emergency Child Care Centers Act
Pa. 1943 Pamph. Laws 176, No. 89

Emergency City and School District Relief Act
N.Y. Laws 1976, Ch. 349, § 2
N.Y. Unconsolidated Law § 9471 et seq.

Emergency Civil Defense Act
Colo. Laws 1943, p. 435, Ch. 140

Emergency Commercial Space Rent Control Laws
N.Y. Laws 1945, Ch. 3
N.Y. Laws 1945, Ch. 315
N.Y. Laws 1949, Ch. 534
N.Y. Laws 1951, Ch. 431
N.Y. Laws 1952, Ch. 416

Emergency Commitment Act (Mentally Ill)
La. Rev. Stat. Ann., 28:54

Emergency Commitment for Drug Intoxication Law
R.I. Gen. Laws 1956, 40.1-4.1-1 et seq.

Emergency Communications Act
Ark. Acts 1991, No. 554

Emergency Communications District Act
Tenn. Public Acts 1984, Ch. 867
Tex. Health and Safety Code, § 772.201 et seq.

Emergency Communications Service District Act (Decatur County)
Ga. Laws 1990, p. 3982

Emergency Communications Service District Act (Douglas County)
Ga. Laws 1991 Ex. Sess., p. 46

Emergency Communications Service District Act (Gordon County)
Ga. Laws 1990, p. 4310

Emergency Communications Service District Act (Houston County)
Ga. Laws 1990, p. 3517

Emergency Communications Service District Act (Lamar County)
Ga. Laws 1990, p. 4871

Emergency Community Facilities Act
Oct. 6, 1970, P.L. 91-481, 84 Stat. 886, 42
U.S. Code §§ 3102, 3108

Emergency Compensation and Special Unemployment Assistance Extension Act of 1975
June 3, 1975, P.L. 94-45, 89 Stat. 236, 26
U.S. Code §§ 44, 3302, 3304 nt.

Emergency Conflagration Act
Ore. Rev. Stat., 476.510 et seq.

Emergency Copyright Act of 1941
Sept. 25, 1941, Ch. 421, 55 Stat. 732 (See 17
U.S. Code § 9)

Emergency Dairy, Farm and Business Assistance Act
Wis. Laws 1983, Act 92

Emergency Daylight Saving Time Energy Conservation Act of 1973
Dec. 15, 1973, P.L. 93-182, 87 Stat. 707, 15
U.S. Code § 260a nt.

Emergency Debtors' Relief Act
Ind. Code Ann., 654.15

Emergency Defense Act
Ala. General Acts 1943, p. 79
Ala. General Acts 1945, p. 28
Mass. Acts 1941, Ch. 719
N.J. Stat. Ann., App. A:9-33 et seq.
R.I. Gen. Laws 1956, 30-15-1 et seq.

Emergency Dental Act
Nev. Statutes 1943, Ch. 9, p. 9

Emergency Detention Act of 1950
Sept. 23, 1950, Ch. 1024, 64 Stat. 1019, 50
U.S. Code §§ 811 to 826

Aug. 28, 1958, P.L. 85-791, 72 Stat. 950, 50 U.S. Code §§ 820, 821

Oct. 27, 1972, P.L. 92-596, 86 Stat. 1318, 50 U.S. Code § 833

Sept. 23, 1996, P.L. 104-201, 50 U.S. Code § 833

Emergency Drought Relief Act of 1996
Oct. 19, 1996, P.L. 104-318, 110 Stat. 3862

Emergency Employment Act of 1971
July 12, 1971, P.L. 92-54, 85 Stat. 146, 42 U.S. Code § 4871 to 4883

Emergency Employment Development Act
Ill. Rev. Stat. 1991, Ch. 48, § 2401 et seq.
Minn. Stat. Ann., 268.671 et seq.
N.J. Stat. Ann. 1937, App. A:11-1 et seq.

Emergency Employment Intervention Program Act
N.Y. Labor Law (Consol. Laws Ch. 31) § 820 nt.
N.Y. Laws 1983, Ch. 525

Emergency Energy Act
Mich. Comp. Laws Ann., 460.151 et seq.

Emergency Energy Conservation Act
Nov. 8, 1984, P.L. 98-620, 42 U.S. Code § 85

Emergency Energy Conservation Act of 1979
Nov. 5, 1979, P.L. 96-102, 42 U.S. Code §§ 6261, 6261 nt., 6262, 6263, 6422, 8501 et seq., 8501 nt.

Emergency Energy Fair Practices Act
N.J. Stat. Ann., 52:27f-16

Emergency Equipment Act (Township)
Ill. Rev. Stat. 1991, Ch. 139, § 350 et seq.

Emergency Extension Act of 1985
Sept. 30, 1985, P.L. 99-107, 26 U.S. Code § 5702 nt., 42 U.S. Code § 1395ww; 45 U.S. Code § 360

Nov. 14, 1985, P.L. 99-155, 42 U.S. Code § 1395ww nt.

Dec. 13, 1985, P.L. 99-181, 42 U.S. Code § 1395ww nt.

Dec. 18, 1985, P.L. 99-189, 42 U.S. Code § 1395ww nt.

Dec. 23, 1985, P.L. 99-201, 42 U.S. Code § 1395ww nt.

April 7, 1986, P.L. 99-272, 42 U.S. Code §§ 1395ww, 1395ww nt.

Emergency Fair Rent Act
Va. Code 1950, § 44-160 et seq.

Emergency Farm Credit Allocation Act
Ill. Rev. Stat. 1991, Ch. 5, § 1251 et seq.

Emergency Farm Financial Relief Act
Aug. 12, 1998, P.L. 105-228, 7 U.S. Code § 7201 nt.

Emergency Farm Mortgage Act of 1933
May 12, 1933, Ch. 25, 48 Stat. 41, 12 U.S. Code §§ 347, 462b, 636, 637, 723, 771, 781, 810, 821, 823 nt., 963a, 992, 993, 1016 to 1019; 43 U.S. Code §§ 403, 404

Feb. 1, 1940, Ch. 19, 54 Stat. 19, 12 U.S. Code § 1016

June 3, 1942, Ch. 321, 56 Stat. 306, 12 U.S. Code § 1016

June 27, 1942, Ch. 449, 56 Stat. 392, 12 U.S. Code § 1016

June 26, 1943, Ch. 146, 57 Stat. 196, 12 U.S. Code § 1016

June 30, 1944, Ch. 329, 58 Stat. 646, 12 U.S. Code § 1016

June 30, 1945, Ch. 204, 59 Stat. 269, 12 U.S. Code § 1016

July 12, 1946, Ch. 570, 60 Stat. 532, 12 U.S. Code § 1016

Oct. 4, 1961, P.L. 87-353, 75 Stat. 773, 12 U.S. Code § 1016

March 18, 1968, P.L. 90-269, 82 Stat. 50, 31 U.S. Code § 821

Ill. Rev. Stat. 1991, Ch. 122, § 1B-1

Emergency Farm Operating Loans Act
Minn. Laws 1985, Ch. 4, §§ 3 to 10

Emergency Farm Production Act
Cal. Statutes 1943, p. 307

Emergency Fees and Salaries Act
Kan. Laws 1933, Ch. 186

Emergency Finance Act
N.C. Laws 1971, Ch. 108

Emergency Financial Aid to Local Government Act
Tenn. Code Ann., 9-13-201 et seq.

Emergency Financial Aid to Local Government Law
Tenn. Code Ann., 9-13-101 et seq.
Tenn. Public Acts 1984, Ch. 996

Emergency Fiscal Responsibility and Recovery Act
Ida. Laws 1983, Ch. 4

Emergency Flood Control Bond Act
N.J. Laws 1978, Ch. 78

Emergency Flood Relief Law
Cal. Government Code § 54150 et seq.

Emergency Food Access and Food Stamp Act
Cal. Welfare and Institutions Code §§ 18904.3, 18905.1, 18911 et seq., 18914.5

Emergency Food Assistance Act of 1983
Dec. 13, 1991, P.L. 102-237, 7 U.S. Code § 612c nt.
Dec. 21, 1995, P.L. 104-66, 7 U.S. Code § 612c nt.
April 4, 1996, P.L. 104-127, 7 U.S. Code § 612c nt.
Aug. 22, 1996, P.L. 104-193, 7 U.S. Code § 612c nt.

Emergency Food Stamp Vendor Accountability Act of 1976
July 5, 1976, P.L. 94-339, 7 U.S. Code § 2011 et seq.

Emergency Foreclosure Act
Mich. Public Acts 1933, No. 98

Emergency Fuel Oil Delivery Act
N.J. Stat. Ann., 26:3-31.4 et seq.

Emergency Fuel Set-Aside Act
N.Y. Energy Law (Consol. Laws Ch. 17A) § 10-101 et seq.

Emergency Fund Act
P.R. Laws Ann. 1954, Title 3, § 457 et seq.

Emergency Gift Tax Act
Wis. Stat. 1987, 72.75

Emergency Government Act
Wash. Rev. Code Ann., 166.01 et seq.

Emergency Government Relocation Act
Ill. Rev. Stat. 1991, Ch. 85, § 50 et seq.

Emergency Health Personnel Act Amendments of 1972
Oct. 27, 1972, P.L. 92-585, 86 Stat. 1290, 42 U.S. Code §§ 234, 354b, 294a

Emergency Health Personnel Act of 1970
Dec. 31, 1970, P.L. 91-623, 84 Stat. 1868, 42 U.S. Code §§ 233, 254b

Emergency Highway Energy Conservation Act
Jan. 2, 1974, P.L. 93-239, 87 Stat. 1046, 23 U.S. Code § 101 nt., 49 U.S. Code § 1421

Emergency Home Finance Act
July 24, 1970, P.L. 91-351, 84 Stat. 450, 12 U.S. Code §§ 82, 371 , 1430, 1451 to 1459 and others
Oct. 21, 1998, P.L. 105-276, 42 U.S. Code § 1454

Emergency Home Heating Act
Me. Public Laws 1979, Ch. 574

Emergency Home Purchase Assistance Act of 1974
July 2, 1975, P.L. 94-50, 89 Stat. 256, 12 U.S. Code § 1723e nt.
Oct. 12, 1977, P.L. 95-128, 12 U.S. Code § 1723e nt.
Oct. 31, 1978, P.L. 95-557, 12 U.S. Code § 1723e nt.
Sept. 28, 1979, P.L. 96-71, 12 U.S. Code § 1723e nt.

Nov. 8, 1979, P.L. 96-105, 12 U.S. Code
§ 1723e nt.
Dec. 21, 1979, P.L. 96-153, 12 U.S. Code
§ 1723e nt.

Emergency Home Winterization Act
N.M. Laws 1977, Ch. 212

Emergency Homeowners' Relief Act
July 2, 1975, P.L. 94-50, 89 Stat. 249, 12
U.S. Code §§ 2701 et seq.
Oct. 17, 1984, P.L. 98-479, 12 U.S. Code
§§ 2706, 2709

Emergency Hospital Service Act
Ill. Rev. Stat. 1991, Ch. 111 1/2, § 85z et seq.

Emergency Housing Act
Minn. Laws 1949, Ch. 733

Emergency Housing Act (Veterans)
Ohio Rev. Code 1953, 3735.58 et seq.

Emergency Housing Act of 1975
July 2, 1975, P.L. 94-50, 89 Stat. 249, 12
U.S. Code §§ 1723e, 1735b, 2701 et seq.;
42 U.S. Code §§ 1452b, 4106

Emergency Housing Corporation Act
See National Housing Act

Emergency Housing Rent Control Law (New York City)
N.Y. Unconsolidated Law, § 8601 et seq.

Emergency Housing Rent Control Law (New York State)
N.Y. Unconsolidated Law, § 8581 et seq.

Emergency Housing Rent Control Laws
N.Y. Laws 1946, Ch. 274
N.Y. Laws 1949, Ch. 591
N.Y. Laws 1951, Ch. 443
N.Y. Laws 1962, Ch. 21, § 1

Emergency Immigrant Education Act of 1984
April 28, 1984, P.L. 100-297, 102 Stat. 242,
20 U.S. Code §§ 3121 et seq.
Oct. 19, 1984, P.L. 98-511, 20 U.S. Code
§§ 4101 nt., 4101 to 4108

Emergency Immigration Act
May 19, 1921, Ch. 8, 42 Stat. 5

Emergency Insured Student Loan Act of 1969
Oct. 22, 1969, P.L. 91-95, 83 Stat. 141, 20
U.S. Code §§ 421, 1061, 1078a; 42 U.S.
Code § 2751

Emergency Interim Consumer Product Safety Standard Act of 1978
July 11, 1978, P.L. 95-319, 15 U.S. Code
§§ 2051 nt., 2068, 2082, 2082 nt.

Emergency Interim Executive and Judicial Succession Act
Ark. Code Ann. 1987, 21-1-301 et seq.
Del. Code of 1974, Title 10, § 1801 et seq.
Fla. Stat. Ann., 22.01 et seq.
Ida. Code 1947, 59-1401 et seq.
Iowa Code 1971, 38A.1 et seq.
Kan. Stat. Ann., 48-1201 et seq.
Okla. Stat. Ann., Title 63, § 685.1 et seq.
Pa. Purdon's Stat., Title 71, § 779.1 et seq.
S.C. Code Ann. 1976, § 1-9-10 et seq.
S.D. Codified Laws 1967, 1-30-1 et seq.
Utah Code Ann. 1953, Miscellaneous
Superseded Code Provisions, 63-20-1 et
seq.
W. Va. Code 1966, § 6A-1-1 et seq.

Emergency Interim Executive Succession Act
Del. Code of 1974, Title 29, § 7801 et seq.
Ill. Rev. Stat. 1991, Ch. 102, § 101 et seq.
Me. Rev. Stat. Ann. 1964, Title 1, § 651 et
seq.
N.J. Rev. Stat. 1937, 52:14A-1 et seq.
Pa. Purdon's Stat., Title 71, § 779.1 et seq.
Tex. Government Code, § 401.021 et seq.

Emergency Interim Judicial Succession Act
Del. Code of 1974, Title 10, § 1801 et seq.
La. Rev. Stat. Ann., 13:2701 et seq.
Mich. Comp. Laws Ann., 691.971 et seq.

Emergency Interim Legislative Succession Act
Ala. Code 1975, § 29-3-1 et seq.
Continued

Ark. Code Ann. 1987, 10-6-101 et seq.

Del. Code of 1974, Title 29, § 1701 et seq.

Ida. Code 1947, 67-413 et seq.

Kan. Stat. Ann., 48-1301 et seq.

La. Rev. Stat. Ann., 24:61 et seq.

Okla. Stat. Ann., Title 63, § 686.1 et seq.

Pa. Purdon's Stat., Title 46, § 145.1 et seq.

S.C. Code Ann. 1976, § 2-5-10 et seq.

S.D. Codified Laws 1967, 2-3-1 et seq.

Tex. Government Code, § 304.001 et seq.

Emergency Interim Local Executive Succession Act

La. Rev. Stat. Ann., 33:1401 et seq.

Emergency Interim Local Government Executive Succession Act

N.C. Gen. Stat. 1943, § 162B-5 et seq.

Emergency Interim Local Succession Act

Mich. Comp. Laws Ann., 31.101 et seq.

Emergency Interim Public Office Succession Act

Tex. Government Code, § 616.001 et seq.

Emergency Interim Relocation Act

Okla. Stat. 1981, Title 63, § 687.1 et seq.

Emergency Interim State Executive Succession Act

La. Rev. Stat. Ann., 49:851 et seq.

Emergency Interim Succession Act

Ala. Code 1975, 29-3-1 et seq.

N.H. Rev. Stat. 1955, 108-A:1 et seq.

Utah Code Ann. 1953, 63-5b-101 et seq.

Vt. Stat. Ann., Title 20, § 181 et seq.

Emergency Jobs and Unemployment Assistance Act of 1974

June 30, 1975, P.L. 94-45, 89 Stat. 240, 26 U.S. Code § 3304 nt.

Oct. 21, 1998, P.L. 105-277, 26 U.S. Code § 3304 nt.

Emergency Jobs Programs Extension Act of 1976

Oct. 1, 1976, P.L. 94-444, 29 U.S. Code §§ 801 et seq.

Emergency Labor Disputes Act

Mass. Gen. Laws Ann., 150B:1 et seq.

Emergency Legislative Succession and Procedures Act

Neb. Rev. Stat. 1943, 50-501 et seq.

Emergency Livestock Credit Act of 1974

July 25, 1974, P.L. 93-357, 88 Stat. 391, 7 U.S. Code prec. § 1961 nt.

June 16, 1975, P.L. 94-35, 89 Stat. 213, 7 U.S. Code § 1961 nt.

Oct. 15, 1976, P.L. 94-517, 90 Stat. 2446, 7 U.S. Code prec. § 1961 nt.

Aug. 4, 1978, P.L. 95-334, 7 U.S. Code prec. §§ 1961 nt., 2908

Oct. 19, 1980, P.L. 96-470, 94 Stat. 2237, 7 U.S. Code prec. § 1961 nt.

Emergency Loan Fund and Water Pollution Control Revolving Fund Act

Miss. Code Ann. 1972, §§ 49-17-81 to 49-17-89

Emergency Loan Guarantee Act

Aug. 9, 1971, P.L. 92-70, 85 Stat. 178, 15 U.S. Code §§ 1841 to 1852

Emergency Low Income Housing Preservation Act of 1987

See Low-Income Housing Preservation And Resident Homeownership Act Of 1990

February 5, 1988, P.L. 100-242, 12 U.S. Code § 1715l nt.

Dec. 15, 1989, P.L. 101-235, 12 U.S. Code § 1715l nt.

Emergency Management Act

Ala. Code 1975, 31-9-1 et seq.

Fla. Stat. Ann., 252.31 et seq.

Ga. Code Ann., 38-3-1 et seq.

Kan. Stat. Ann.,48-904 et seq.

Mich. Comp. Laws 1988, 30.401 et seq.

Minn. Stat. 1986, 12.01 et seq.

Miss. Code Ann. 1972, § 33-15-1 et seq.

N.C. Gen. Stat. 1943, § 166A-1 et seq.

N.M. Stat. Ann., 74-4B-1 et seq.

Wash. Rev. Code Ann., 38.52.005 et seq.

**Emergency Management Act
(Comprehensive)**
Utah Code Ann. 1953, 53-2-101 et seq.

**Emergency Management Act (Nuclear
Safety)**
Kan. Stat. Ann., 48-940 et seq.

Emergency Management Agency Act
Ill. Rev. Stat. 1991, Ch. 127, § 1051 et seq.
Me. Rev. Stat. Ann. 1964, Title 37-B, § 701

**Emergency Management and Civil Defense
Act**
Md. Ann. Code 1957, Art. 41, § 17-101 et
seq.

**Emergency Management and Disaster
Compact Act**
Ky. Rev. Stat 1971, 39.450

Emergency Management and Disaster Law
Ind. Code Ann., 10-4-1-1 et seq.

**Emergency Management Assistance
Compact**
Ark. Code 1987, 12-49-401, 12-49-402
Del. Code of 1974, Title 20, § 3401 et seq.
Fla. Stat. Ann., 252.921 et seq.
Minn. Stat. 1986, 192.89
Tenn. Code Ann., 58-2-403
Tex. Health and Safety Code, § 778.001 et
seq.

**Emergency Management Compact
(Southern Regional)**
Ga. Code Ann., 38-3-80, 38-3-81
Miss. Code Ann. 1972, §§ 45-18-1, 45-18-3
S.C. Code Ann. 1976, §§ 25-9-410, 25-9-420

Emergency Management Services Code
Pa. Cons. Stat., Title 35, § 7101 et seq.

Emergency Medical Care Act (Access to)
S.C. Code Ann. 1976, § 38-71-1510 et seq.

**Emergency Medical Care Act (Good
Samaritan)**
S.D. Codified Laws 1967, 20-9-3, 20-9-4.2

Emergency Medical Care Liability Act
Ill. Rev. Stat. 1981, Ch. 111 1/2, §§ 87a, 87b

**Emergency Medical Service District Budget
Act**
Okla. Stat. Ann., Title 19, § 1701 et seq.

**Emergency Medical Services (EMS) Systems
Act**
Ill. Comp. Stat. 1992, Ch. 210, § 50/1 et seq.

Emergency Medical Services Act
Ark. Code Ann. 1987, 20-13-201 et seq.
Colo. Rev. Stat., 25-3.5-101 et seq.
Conn. Gen. Stat. 1983, § 19a-175 et seq.
Me. Rev. Stat. Ann. 1964, Title 32, § 81 et
seq.
Miss. Code Ann. 1972, § 41-59-1 et seq.
N.C. Gen. Stat. 1943, § 143-507 et seq.
Neb. Laws 1997, L.B. 138, §§ 1 to 30
Nev. Rev. Stat. 1979, Reprint, 450B.015 et
seq.
N.M. Stat. Ann., 24-10B-1 et seq.
Okla. Stat. 1981, Title 63, § 1-2501 et seq.
Pa. Purdon's Stat., Title 63, § 421.1 et seq.
S.C. Code Ann. 1976, § 44-61-10 et seq.
Tenn. Code Ann., 68-140-101 et seq.
Tex. Health and Safety Code, § 773.001 et
seq.
Tex. Rev. Civ. Stat., Art. 773.001 et seq.
Utah Code Ann. 1953, 26-8-1 et seq.
Wash. Rev. Code Ann., 146.35
W. Va. Code 1966, § 16-4D-1 et seq.,
16-4C-1 et seq.
Wyo. Stat. Ann., § 33-36-101 et seq.

**Emergency Medical Services Act
(Children's)**
S.C. Code Ann. 1976, § 44-61-300 et seq.

**Emergency Medical Services Amendments
of 1976**
July 10, 1979, P.L. 96-32, 42 U.S. Code
§ 295g-9

**Emergency Medical Services and Care
Systems Act**
Okla. Stat. 1981, Title 63, § 330.90 et seq.

Emergency Medical Services and Trauma Care System Act (State-wide)

Wash. Rev. Code Ann., 70.168.010 et seq.

Emergency Medical Services Do Not Resuscitate Order Act

S.C. Code Ann. 1976, § 44-78-10 et seq.

Emergency Medical Services for Children Resource Center Act

Okla. Stat. Ann., Title 63, § 1-706.10 et seq.

Emergency Medical Services Fund Act

N.M. Stat. Ann., 24-10A-1 et seq.

Emergency Medical Services Grant Act

Fla. Stat. Ann., 401.101 et seq.

Emergency Medical Services Personnel Training Act

N.Y. Public Health Law 1953 (Consol. Laws Ch. 45) § 3050 et seq.

Emergency Medical Services Reform Act

N.Y. Public Health Law (Consol. Laws Ch. 45) § 2805b

Emergency Medical Services Revolving Fund Act

Ark. Code Ann. 1987, 20-13-101 et seq.

Emergency Medical Services System and Prehospital Emergency Medical Care Personnel Act

Cal. Health and Safety Code § 1797 et seq.

Emergency Medical Services System Support Act

Minn. Stat. Ann., 144.8093

Emergency Medical Services Systems Act (EMS)

Haw. Rev. Stat. Ann., § 321-221 et seq.

Ill. Rev. Stat. 1991, Ch. 111 1/2, § 5501 et seq.

Mich. Comp. Laws Ann., 325.3001 et seq.

Pa. Purdon's Stat., Title 35, § 6921 et seq.

Emergency Medical Services Systems Act of 1973

Nov. 16, 1973, P.L. 93-154, 87 Stat. 594, 33 U.S. Code § 763c; 42 U.S. Code §§ 201 nts., 211a, 212a, 222 nt., 295f-2, 295f-4, 295f-6, 300d to 300d-9

Emergency Medical Services Systems Amendments of 1979

Dec. 12, 1979, P.L. 96-142, 42 U.S. Code §§ 201 nt., 295g-9, 295g-9 nt., 300d-1 to 300d-3, 300d-6, 300d-8, 300d-21

Emergency Medical Technician-Paramedic Act

Ky. Rev. Stat. 1971, 211.960 et seq., 311.650 et seq.

Neb. Rev. Stat. 1943, 71-5501 et seq.

Emergency Medical Technician Practices Act (Advanced)

Mich. Comp. Laws Ann., 338.1901 et seq.

Emergency Medical Technician Training Fund Act

N.J. Stat. Ann., 26:2K-54 et seq.

Emergency Medical Transportation Services Act

Fla. Stat. Ann., 401.2101 et seq.

Emergency Medical Treatment Act

Ill. Rev. Stat. 1991, Ch. 111 1/2, §§ 852 et seq., 6150, 6151

Emergency Milk Control Act

N.J. Stat.Ann., Superseded Vol., 4:12A-59 et seq.

S.C. Acts 1966, p. 2847, No. 1165

Emergency Milk Price Control Act

R.I. Gen. Laws 1956, 21-4-1 et seq.

Emergency Moratorium Act for New York City

N.Y. Laws 1975, Ex. Sess., Ch. 874

Emergency Moratorium Law (Mortgages)

N.Y. Laws 1936, Ch. 703

Emergency Mortgage Redemption Act
Iowa Laws 1933 (45th G. A.), Ch. 179

Emergency Mosquito Abatement Funding Act
Cal. Statutes 1983, Ch. 1055

Emergency Municipal Finance Board Act
Me. Rev. Stat. Ann. 1964, Title 30, § 5301 et seq.

Emergency Municipal Loan Act
Mich. Comp. Laws Ann., 141.931 et seq.

Emergency Natural Gas Act of 1977
Feb. 2, 1977, P.L. 95-2, 15 U.S. Code § 717 nt.

Emergency Notification Act (Hazardous and Toxic Materials)
Ark. Acts 1991, No. 917

Emergency Number Act (Nine-One-One)
Okla. Stat. Ann., Title 63, § 2811 et seq.
Tex. Health and Safety Code, § 772.101 et seq.

Emergency Nutrition and Temporary Emergency Relief Program
Tex. Government Code, § 2306.651 et seq.

Emergency Officers' Pay Act
July 15, 1940, Ch. 626, 54 Stat. 760

Emergency Officers' Retirement Act
May 24, 1928, Ch. 735, 45 Stat. 735

Emergency Personnel Act
Mich. Comp. Laws Ann., 338.1921 et seq.

Emergency Petroleum Allocation Act of 1973
Nov. 27, 1973, P.L. 93-159, 87 Stat. 627, 15 U.S. Code §§ 751 to 756
Nov. 14, 1975, P.L. 94-133, 89 Stat. 694, 15 U.S. Code § 753
Dec. 22, 1975, P.L. 94-163, 89 Stat. 871, 15 U.S. Code §§ 753 to 755, 757 to 760h

Emergency Petroleum Products Supply Act
N.M. Stat. Ann., 70-8-1 et seq.

Emergency Petroleum Set-Aside Act
Vt. Stat. Ann., Title 9, § 4131 et seq.

Emergency Planning Act (Nuclear)
Me. Rev. Stat. Ann. 1964, Title 37-B, § 951 et seq.

Emergency Planning and Community Right-to-Know Act
Ariz. Rev. Stat. Ann., § 26-341 et seq.
Haw. Session Laws 1993, Act 300
Ill. Rev. Stat. 1991, Ch. 111 1/2, § 7701 et seq.
Kan. Stat. Ann., 65-5701 et seq.
Neb. Rev. Stat. 1943, 81-15,191 to 81-15,235

Emergency Planning and Community Right-to-Know Act of 1986
Oct. 17, 1986, P.L. 99-499, 42 U.S. Code §§ 11001 nt., 11001 to 11005 prec. 11021, 11021 to 11023, prec. 11041, 11041 to 11050

Emergency Planning and Response Act (Hazardous Material)
Pa. Purdon's Stat., Title 35, § 6022.101 et seq.

Emergency Plant Act
Ark. Code Ann. 1987, 2-16-301 et seq.

Emergency Powers Act
Tenn. Code Ann., 41-1-301 et seq.

Emergency Powers Act (Prison Overcrowding)
Miss. Code Ann. 1972, § 47-5-701 et seq.
Okla. Stat. 1981, Title 57, § 570 et seq.

Emergency Powers Continuation Acts
July 3, 1952, Ch. 570, 66 Stat. 330
March 31, 1953, Ch. 13, 67 Stat. 18
June 30, 1953, Ch. 172, 67 Stat. 131

Emergency Pre-Hospital Medical Services Act
Ill. Rev. Stat. 1979, Ch. 111 1/2, § 4101 et seq.

Emergency Preparedness Act
Kan. Stat. Ann., 48-904 et seq.

Emergency Preparedness Act (Civil)
Me. Rev. Stat. Ann. 1964, Title 37-B, § 701
et seq.

Emergency Preparedness Act (Nuclear Safety)
Kan. Stat. Ann.,48-940 et seq.

Emergency Price Control Act of 1942
Jan. 30, 1942, Ch. 26, 56 Stat. 23
Oct. 2, 1942, Ch. 578, 56 Stat. 767
June 30, 1944, Ch. 325, 58 Stat. 632
June 30, 1945, Ch. 214, 59 Stat. 306 to 309
July 25, 1946, Ch. 671, 60 Stat. 664
July 30, 1947, Ch. 361, 61 Stat. 610

Emergency Procedure Act
Tenn. Acts 1935, Ex. Sess., Ch. 30

Emergency Procedure Act (Municipalities)
Pa. 1937 Pamph. Laws 1604, No. 329
S.D. Laws 1935, Ch. 161

Emergency Profits Tax Act
Pa. 1923 Pamph. Laws 876, No. 333

Emergency Public Transportation Assistance Act of 1971
Ill. Rev. Stat. 1977, Ch. 111 2/3, § 611 et seq.

Emergency Public Transportation Loan Act
Ill. Rev. Stat. 1983, Ch. 111 2/3, § 621 et seq.

Emergency Public Works Act
Wash. Rev. Code Ann., 39.28.010 et seq.

Emergency Rail Facilities Restoration Act
Oct. 27, 1972, P.L. 92-591, 86 Stat. 1304

Emergency Rail Services Act of 1970
Jan. 8, 1971, P.L. 91-663, 84 Stat. 1975, 45
U.S. Code §§ 661 to 669
Nov. 6, 1978, P.L. 95-598, 45 U.S. Code
§ 662
Nov. 8, 1978, P.L. 95-611, 45 U.S. Code
§ 662
Nov. 4, 1979, P.L. 96-101, 45 U.S. Code
§ 662
Dec. 21, 1982, P.L. 97-375, 45 U.S. Code
§ 669

Dec. 29, 1995, P.L. 104-88, 45 U.S. Code
§§ 661, 662, 665

Emergency Railroad Transportation Act, 1933
June 16, 1933, Ch. 91, 48 Stat. 211, 49 U.S.
Code §§ 5, 5a, 15a, 15b, 19a

Emergency Relief Act
N.Y. Laws 1931, Ex. Sess., Ch. 798
N.Y. Laws 1932, Chs. 545, 567
N.Y. Laws 1933, Chs. 2, 9, 34, 44, 69, 259,
646
N.Y. Laws 1933, 1st Ex. Sess., Ch. 782
N.Y. Laws 1934, Chs. 15, 65, 71, 273, 303
N.Y. Laws 1935, Chs. 25, 239, 264
N.Y. Laws 1936, Chs. 13, 210

Emergency Relief Act of 1933
See Federal Emergency Relief Act Of 1933

Emergency Relief Administration Act
Ind. Code Ann., 251.1 et seq.

Emergency Relief and Construction Act of 1932
July 21, 1932, Ch. 520, 47 Stat. 709, 12 U.S.
Code § 343; 31 U.S. Code § 767a; 40 U.S.
Code § 258a nt.
June 30, 1947, Ch. 166, 61 Stat. 208, 12 U.S.
Code §§ 1148, 1148a

Emergency Relief Appropriation Acts
April 8, 1935, Ch. 48, 49 Stat. 115
June 22, 1936, Ch. 689, 49 Stat. 1608
June 29, 1937, Ch. 401, 50 Stat. 357
June 21, 1938, Ch. 554, 52 Stat. 809
June 30, 1939, Ch. 252, 53 Stat. 927
June 26, 1940, Ch. 432, 54 Stat. 611, 7 U.S.
Code § 612c nt.; 15 U.S. Code § 609i; 16
U.S. Code §§ 584g-1, 8311; 29 U.S. Code
§§ 205, 206, 208 nt.
July 1, 1941, Ch. 266, 55 Stat. 396, 7 U.S.
Code 612c nt.
July 1, 1941, Ch. 266, 55 Stat. 401
July 2, 1942, Ch. 479, 56 Stat. 634

Emergency Relief Bond Act
Ill. Rev. Stat. 1957, Ch. 23, § 3701 et seq.
Wash. Laws 1933, Ch. 65

Emergency Relief Commission Act
Ill. Rev. Stat. 1965, Ch. 23, § 393 et seq.

Emergency Relief Sales Tax Act
Pa. Purdon's Stat., Title 72, § 3282

Emergency Relocation Act
Ida. Code 1947, 67-102 et seq.

Emergency Rent Act
D.C. Code 1967, § 45-1601 et seq.
N.Y. Laws 1920, Chs. 130 to 139
N.Y. Laws 1920, Ex. Sess., Chs. 942 to 945, 947 to 952
N.Y. Laws 1922, Chs. 663, 664
N.Y. Laws 1923, Ch. 892

Emergency Rent Control Act
Minn. Laws 1947, Ch. 632
Wis. Laws 1947, Ch. 442

Emergency Replacement Revenue Act
N.D. Laws 1933, Ch. 261

Emergency Rescue First Responders Act
Neb. Rev. Stat. 1943, 71-7301 et seq.

Emergency Reserve Fund of Stanly County
N.C. Laws 1963, Ch. 691

Emergency Residential Housing Rent Regulation and Control Act
Alaska Stat. 1962, § 34.06.010 et seq.

Emergency Response Act
Okla. Stat. Ann., Title 27A, § 4-1-101 et seq.

Emergency Response and Community Right-to-Know Act (Hazardous Materials)
Fla. Stat. Ann., 252.81 et seq.
Mich. Comp. Laws Ann., 30.401 et seq.

Emergency Response and Notification Act
Okla. Stat. 1981, Title 63, § 689 et seq.

Emergency Response Hazardous Substances Protection Act
Minn. Stat. 1984, 299F.091 et seq.

Emergency Response Reimbursement Act (Hazardous Material)
Ill. Rev. Stat. 1991, Ch. 127 1/2, § 1001 et seq.

Emergency Retail Sales Tax Act
Ark. Code Ann. 1987, 26-52-101 et seq.
Colo. Rev. Stat., 39-26-101 et seq.

Emergency Revenue Act
Miss. Code Ann. 1972, § 27-65-1 et seq.
N.C. Public Laws 1933, Ch. 445, § 400 et seq.
Utah Code Ann. 1953, Miscellaneous Superseded Code Provisions, 59-15-1 et seq.

Emergency Revenue Act (Sales Tax)
Mo. Rev. Stat., 144.010 et seq.

Emergency Salary Adjustment Act
Wis. Stat. 1975, 66.195

Emergency Sales Tax Act
Wyo. Session Laws 1935, Ch. 74

Emergency School Aid Act
June 23, 1972, P.L. 92-318, 20 U.S. Code § 1601 nt.
June 28, 1975, P.L. 94-43, 89 Stat. 233, 20 U.S. Code § 1615

Emergency School Classroom Law
Cal. Education Code 1976, § 17785 et seq.

Emergency School Leasing Authority Act
Miss. Code Ann. 1972, § 37-7-351

Emergency School Tax Act
N.M. Stat. Ann. 1953, 72-16-1 et seq.

Emergency School Tax Act (Oil and Gas)
N.M. Stat. Ann., 7-31-1 et seq.

Emergency Seat of Government Act
Ill. Rev. Stat. 1991, Ch. 123, § 6.9 et seq.
S.C. Code Ann. 1976, § 1-9-210 et seq.

Emergency Seat of Local Government Act
Neb. Rev. Stat. 1943, 13-701 et seq.

Emergency Seat of State Government Act
Neb. Rev. Stat. 1943, 72-701.01 et seq.

Emergency Seizure Act (Public Utilities)
Mo. Rev. Stat., 295.180

Emergency Service and Law Enforcement Solicitation of Funds Act
Fla. Stat. Ann., 496.20 et seq.

Emergency Services Act
Ark. Code Ann. 1987, 12-75-101 et seq.
Cal. Government Code § 8550 et seq.
N.J. Stat. Ann., 52:14E-1 et seq.
Wash. Rev. Code Ann., 38.52.005 et seq.

Emergency Services Act (Medical)
Tex. Health and Safety Code, § 773.001 et seq.

Emergency Services and Disaster Act
Ill. Rev. Stat. 1991, Ch. 127, § 1051 et seq.
Va. Code 1950, § 44-146.13 et seq.

Emergency Services and Disaster Agency Act
Ill. Rev. Stat. 1987, Ch. 127, § 1101 et seq.

Emergency Services District Act
Tex. Rev. Civ. Stat., Art. 2351a-9

Emergency Services District Act (Supplemental)
Okla. Stat. Ann., Title 63, § 2451 et seq.

Emergency Services Law
Ga. Code Ann., 31-11-80 to 31-11-82

Emergency Services Mutual Aid Act (Interstate)
Mont. Laws 1991, Ch. 5
Wyo. Stat. Ann., § 19-5-201 et seq.

Emergency Services Retirement Act (Statewide)
Tex. Rev. Civ. Stat., Art. 6243e.3 et seq.

Emergency Ship Repair Act
Aug. 20, 1954, Ch. 777, 68 Stat. 754, 50 U.S. Code Appx. §§ 2391 to 2394

Aug. 6, 1956, Ch. 1012, 70 Stat. 1067, 50 U.S. Code Appx. § 2393

Emergency Storm Damage Loan Act
Mass. Acts 1939, Ch. 63

Emergency Student Loan Consolidation Act of 1997
Nov. 13, 1997, P.L. 105-78, § 609, 20 U.S. Code § 1001 nt.

Emergency Succession Act
P.R. Laws Ann. 1954, Title 25, § 161 et seq.

Emergency Succession Act (State Officers)
Neb. Rev. Stat. 1943, 84-1101 et seq.

Emergency Supplemental Appropriation Act, 1940
Feb. 12, 1940, Ch. 27, 54 Stat. 22

Emergency Supplemental Appropriations Act of 1994
Feb. 12, 1994, P.L. 103-211, 108 Stat. 3

Emergency Supplemental Appropriations and Rescissions for the Department of Defense to Preserve and Enhance Military Readiness Act of 1995
April 10, 1995, P.L. 104-6, 109 Stat. 73

Emergency Supplemental Appropriations for Additional Disaster Assistance, for Anti-terrorism Initiatives, for Assistance in the Recovery from the Tragedy that Occurred at Oklahoma City, and Rescissions Act, 1995
July 27, 1995, P.L. 104-19, 109 Stat. 194

Emergency Supplemental Appropriations for Relief From the Major, Widespread Flooding in the Midwest Act of 1993
Aug. 12, 1993, P.L. 103-75, 107 Stat. 739

Emergency Supplemental Assistance for Israel Act of 1991
March 28, 1991, P.L. 102-21, 105 Stat. 70

Emergency Supplemental Persian Gulf Refugee Assistance Act of 1991
May 5, 1991, P.L. 102-45, 105 Stat. 247

Emergency Tariff Act of 1921
May 27, 1921, Ch. 14, 42 Stat. 9

Emergency Tax Relief Act for Interstate Railroads
R.I. Public Laws 1961, Ch. 46

Emergency Technical Provision Act of 1976
June 30, 1976, P.L. 94-328, 20 U.S. Code § 1001 et seq.

Emergency Technical Provisions Act
June 28, 1975, P.L. 94-43, 89 Stat. 233, 20 U.S. Code §§ 1070a nt., 1615; 42 U.S. Code § 2756

Emergency Telecommunications Board Act (Statewide)
Mass. Gen. Laws 1984, 6A:18B et seq.

Emergency Telephone Access Act
Colo. Rev. Stat., 40-3.4-101 et seq.

Emergency Telephone Act (Public Safety)
Fla. Stat. Ann., 365.171
Okla. Stat. Ann., Title 63, § 2801 et seq.
Pa. Cons. Stat., Title 18, § 6902
Pa. Purdon's Stat., Title 35, § 7011 et seq.

Emergency Telephone Number Act (911)
Ga. Code Ann., 46-5-120 et seq.
Mont. Code Ann. 1987, 10-4-101 et seq.
R.I. Gen. Laws 1956, 39-21.1-1 et seq.
Tex. Health and Safety Code, § 772.301 et seq.

Emergency Telephone Number Act (911 Emergency Telephone Number Act)
Cal. Government Code § 53100 et seq.
Mont. Code Ann., 10-4-101 et seq.
Okla. Stat. Ann., Title 63 § 2811 et seq.
R.I. Gen. Laws 1956, 39-21.1-1 et seq.
Tex. Health and Safety Code, § 772.101 et seq.

Emergency Telephone Number Act (Enhanced 911 Emergency Telephone Number Act)
N.M. Stat. Ann., 63-9D-6 et seq.

Emergency Telephone Service Act
Utah Code Ann. 1953, 69-2-1 et seq.
Wyo. Stat. Ann., § 16-9-101 et seq.

Emergency Telephone Service Enabling Act
Mich. Comp. Laws Ann., 484.1101 et seq.

Emergency Telephone System Act
Ill. Rev. Stat. 1991, Ch. 134, § 30.01 et seq. .

Emergency Telephone Users' Bill of Rights
Cal. Revenue and Taxation Code § 41160 et seq.

Emergency Telephone Users Surcharge Act
Cal. Revenue and Taxation Code § 41001 et seq.

Emergency Tenancy Laws
N.Y. Laws 1945, Ch. 3
N.Y. Laws 1945, Ch. 314
N.Y. Laws 1945, Ch. 315
N.Y. Laws 1946, Ch. 274
N.Y. Laws 1949, Ch. 534
N.Y. Laws 1949, Ch. 535
N.Y. Laws 1949, Ch. 591

Emergency Tenant Protection Act
N.Y. Laws 1974, Ch. 576, § 4
N.Y. Unconsolidated Laws, § 8621 et seq.

Emergency Termination of Public Contracts Act
Cal. Government Code § 4400 et seq.
Utah Code Ann. 1953, Miscellaneous Superseded Code Provisions, 63-14-1 et seq.

Emergency Transportation Act
N.M. Stat. Ann., 22-17-1 et seq.
Wash. Laws 1943, Ch. 243

Emergency Transportation Tax Act
N.J. Stat. Ann., 54:8A-1 et seq.

Emergency Treatment Act (Insect Sting)
Ark. Code Ann. 1987, 20-13-401 et seq.
Fla. Stat. Ann., 402.60
S.C. Code Ann. 1976, § 44-99-10 et seq.

Emergency Unemployment Compensation Act of 1971

Dec. 29, 1971, P.L. 92-224, 85 Stat. 810, 26 U.S. Code § 3304 nt.

Emergency Unemployment Compensation Act of 1973

June 30, 1972, P.L. 92-329, 86 Stat. 398, 26 U.S. Code § 3304 nt.

Aug. 7, 1974, P.L. 93-368, 88 Stat. 420, 26 U.S. Code § 3304 nt.

March 29, 1975, P.L. 94-12, 89 Stat. 65, 26 U.S. Code § 3304 nt.

June 30, 1975, P.L. 94-45, 89 Stat. 236, 26 U.S. Code § 3304 nt.

Emergency Unemployment Compensation Act of 1974

April 12, 1977, P.L. 95-19, 26 U.S. Code § 3304 nt.

Emergency Unemployment Compensation Act of 1991

Aug. 17, 1991, P.L. 102-107, 26 U.S. Code § 3304 nt.

Nov. 15, 1991, P.L. 102-164, 26 U.S. Code § 3304 nt.

Dec. 4, 1991, P.L. 102-182, 26 U.S. Code § 3304 nt.; 45 U.S. Code § 352 nt.

Feb. 7, 1992, P.L. 102-244, 26 U.S. Code § 3304 nt., 45 U.S. Code § 352 nt.

July 3, 1992, P.L. 102-318, 26 U.S. Code § 3304 nt.; 42 U.S. Code § 502 nt.; 45 U.S. Code § 352 nt.

March 4, 1993, P.L. 103-6, 26 U.S. Code § 3304 nt.; 45 U.S. Code § 352 nt.

Nov. 24, 1993, P.L. 103-152, 26 U.S. Code § 3304 nt.; 45 U.S. Code § 352 nt.

Emergency Unemployment Compensation Amendments of 1993

March 4, 1993, P.L. 103-6, 2 U.S. Code § 31 nt.; 26 U.S. Code sect§ 1 nt., 3304 nts.; 45 U.S. Code § 352 nt.

Emergency Unemployment Compensation Extension Act of 1977

April 12, 1977, P.L. 95-19, 2 U.S. Code §§ 359 et seq.

Emergency Unemployment Relief Income Tax Act

Wis. Laws 1931-32, Special Session, Ch. 29

Emergency Vehicles Right of Way Act

Wash. Rev. Code Ann., 46.61.210

Emergency Veteran's Housing Act

N.J. Stat. Ann., 55:14G-1 et seq.

Emergency Veterans' Job Training Act of 1983

See Veterans' Job Training Act

Nov. 21, 1983, P.L. 98-160, 29 U.S. Code § 1721 nt.

Emergency War Act

Iowa Laws 1943 (50th G. A.), Ch. 61

Emergency War Powers Act

Mont. Laws 1943, Ch. 155

N.C. Gen. Stat. 1943, § 147-33.1 et seq.

Emergency Wetlands Resources Act of 1986

Nov. 10, 1986, P.L. 99-645, 16 U.S. Code § 3901 nt.

Aug. 23, 1988, P.L. 100-418, 102 Stat. 1156, 16 U.S. Code § 3912

Oct. 23, 1992, P.L. 102-440, 16 U.S. Code § 3931

Nov. 2, 1994, P.L. 103-437, 16 U.S. Code § 3902

Oct. 9, 1996, P.L. 104-253, 16 U.S. Code § 668dd nt.

Emerging Crops Fund Act

Ga. Code Ann., 2-8A-1 et seq.

Emerging Industry Jobs Act (New York State)

N.Y. Laws 1998, Ch. 56, Part A, § 29

Emerging Technologies and Advanced Technology Program Amendments Act of 1991

Feb. 14, 1992, P.L. 102-245, 15 U.S. Code § 271 nt.

Emerging Technology and Biotechnology Financial Assistance Act

N.J. Stat. Ann., 34:1B-7.37 et seq.

Emerson Act (Franchise Taxes)
 N.Y. Tax Law (Consol. Laws Ch. 60) § 208
 et seq.

Emerson Beauchamp Act (Local Fairs)
 Ky. Rev. Stat. 1971, 247.220

Emigrant Agent Act
 Ala. Code 1958, Title 51, §§ 513-521
 Mich. Comp. Laws 1979, 286.651 et seq.
 S.C. Code Ann. 1976, § 16-17-610
 Tex. Rev. Civ. Stat., Art. 5221a-4

Eminent Domain Act
 Ala. Acts 1985, p. 802
 Ala. Code 1975, § 18-1-1 et seq.
 Alaska Stat. 1962, § 09.55.010 et seq.
 Ariz. Rev. Stat. Ann., § 12-1111 et seq.
 Ark. Code Ann. 1987, 18-15-102 et seq.
 Cal. Code of Civil Procedure, § 1230.010 et
 seq.
 Colo. Rev. Stat., 38-1-101 et seq.
 Fla. Stat. Ann., 73.012 et seq.
 Ga. Code Ann., 22-1-1 et seq.
 Haw. Rev. Stat. Ann., § 101-1 et seq.
 Ida. Code 1947, 7-701 et seq.
 Ill. Rev. Stat. 1991, Ch. 110, § 7-101 et seq.
 Ind. Code Ann., 32-11-1-1 et seq.
 Iowa Code Ann., 6A.1 et seq.
 Kan. Stat. Ann., 26-101 et seq.
 Ky. Rev. Stat. 1971, 416.010 et seq.
 La. Rev. Stat. Ann., 19:1 et seq.
 Mass. Gen. Laws Ann., 79:1 et seq.
 Md. Ann. Code 1974, Art. RP, § 12-101 et
 seq.
 Mich. Comp. Laws Ann., 213.21 et seq.
 Minn. Stat. Ann., 117.011 et seq.
 Miss. Code Ann. 1972, § 11-27-1 et seq.
 Mont. Code Ann., 70-30-101 et seq.
 N.C. Gen. Stat. 1943, § 40A-1 et seq.
 N.D. Cent. Code, 32-15-01 et seq.
 Neb. Rev. Stat. 1943, 76-701 et seq.
 Nev. Rev. Stat. 1979 Reprint, 37.009 et seq.
 N.J. Stat. Ann., 20:3-1 et seq.
 N.M. Stat. Ann., 42A-1-1 et seq.
 Ohio Rev. Code 1953, 163.01 et seq.
 Pa. Purdon's Stat., Title 26, § 1-101 et seq.

 P.R. Laws Ann. 1954, Title 32, § 2901 et seq.
 S.C. Code Ann. 1976, § 28-3-10 et seq.
 S.D. Codified Laws 1967, 21-35-1 et seq.
 Tenn. Code Ann., 29-16-101 et seq.
 Tex. Property Code, § 21.001 et seq.
 Utah Code Ann. 1953, 78-34-1 et seq.
 Va. Code 1950, § 25-46.1 et seq.
 Wash. Rev. Code Ann., 32.01 et seq.
 W. Va. Code 1966, § 54-1-1 et seq.
 Wyo. Stat. Ann., § 1-26-101 et seq.

**Eminent Domain Act (Boroughs and
 Incorporated Towns)**
 Pa. Purdon's Stat., Title 53, § 53359 et seq.

Eminent Domain Act (Cities)
 Wash. Rev. Code Ann., 8.12.010 et seq.

Eminent Domain Act (Corporations)
 Wash. Rev. Code Ann., 8.20.010 et seq.

Eminent Domain Act (Counties)
 Wash. Rev. Code Ann., 8.08.010 et seq.

Eminent Domain Act (Damages)
 Pa. Purdon's Stat., Title 26, § 1-701 et seq.

Eminent Domain Act (Highways)
 Me. Rev. Stat. Ann. 1964, Title 23, § 3021 et
 seq.
 N.Y. Highway Law (Consol. Laws Ch. 25)
 § 29

Eminent Domain Act (Public Works)
 N.C. Gen. Stat. 1943, § 40A-40 et seq.
 Nev. Rev. Stat. 1979 Reprint, 340.010 et seq.
 S.C. Code Ann. 1976, Superseded Vols.,
 § 28-5-10 et seq.

Eminent Domain Act (School Districts)
 Wash. Rev. Code Ann., 8.16.010 et seq.

Eminent Domain Act (School Land)
 Me. Rev. Stat. Ann. 1964, Title 20-A,
 § 16101 et seq.

Eminent Domain Act (State Authorities)
 S.C. Code Ann. 1976, § 28-3-20 et seq.

Eminent Domain Act (State)
 Wash. Rev. Code Ann., 8.04.010 et seq.

Eminent Domain Act for First Class Cities
Ind. Code 1971, 18-4-16-1 et seq.

Eminent Domain-Comdemnation Proceedings before a Special Master Act
Ga. Code Ann., 22-2-107

Eminent Domain Condemnation Procedures Act
Mich. Comp. Laws Ann., 213.51 et seq.

Eminent Domain Law (Public Works)
S.C. Code Ann. 1976, § 28-5-10 et seq.

Eminent Domain Procedure Act
Kan. Stat. Ann., 26-501 et seq.
Neb. Rev. Stat. 1943, 76-701 et seq.
N.Y. Consol. Laws, Ch. 73
S.C. Code Ann. 1976, § 28-2-10 et seq.

Eminent Scholars Act
Fla. Stat. Ann., 240.257

Eminent Scholars and Research Equipment Act (Science and Technology)
Okla. Stat. Ann., Title 74, § 2013 et seq.

Emission Control Act (Vehicles)
Ga. Code Ann., 40-8-180 et seq.

Emission Inspection and Maintenance Act (Motor Vehicle)
Ga. Code Ann., 12-9-40 et seq.

Emissions Inspection and Maintenance Program Act (Motor Vehicle)
Mich. Comp. Laws Ann., 257.2051 et seq.

Emissions Testing Program Act (Motor Vehicle)
Mich. Comp. Laws Ann., 257.2001 et seq.

Emotionally Disturbed Children Services Law
R.I. Gen. Laws 1956, 40.1,7,1 et seq.

Emplosives Control Act
S.C. Code Ann. 1976, § 23-36-10 et seq.

Employables Program Act
S.C. Code Ann. 1976, § 43-5-510 et seq.

Employed Electors Act
Nev. Rev. Stat. 1979 Reprint, 293.463

Employee and Community Hazardous Chemical Information Act
Mont. Code Ann., 50-78-101 et seq.

Employee Arbitration Act
Ill. Rev. Stat. 1991, Ch. 10, § 18.9 et seq.

Employee Bargaining Act (Public)
N.M. Stat. Ann., 10-70-1 et seq.

Employee Benefit Contribution Act
Ill. Rev. Stat. 1991, Ch. 48, § 39v.9 et seq.

Employee Benefits Act (Public Safety)
Ill. Comp. Stat. 1992, Ch. 820, § 320/1 et seq.

Employee Bonding Act
Tex. Rev. Civ. Stat., Art. 6003b

Employee Certification Act (Food)
Pa. Cons. Stat., Title 3, § 6501 et seq.

Employee Collective Bargaining Act (Public)
Ore. Rev. Stat., 243.650 et seq.

Employee Combined Charitable Campaign Act
Ala. Code 1975, § 36-1A-1

Employee Commute Options Act
Del. Code of 1974, Title 2, § 1901 et seq.
Ill. Laws 1992, P.A. 87-1275

Employee Commute Options Emissions Reduction Credit Act (Voluntary)
Ill. Comp. Stat. 1992, Ch. 625, § 33/1 et seq.

Employee Commuting Flexibility Act of 1996
Aug. 20, 1996, P.L. 104-188, 29 U.S. Code § 251 nt.

Employee Compensation Act of 1911
Ill. Rev. Stat. 1991, Ch. 48, § 138.1 et seq.

Employee Cooperative Corporations Act
Ala. Acts 1997, 1st Sp. Sess., No. 949

Mass. Gen. Laws Ann., 157A:1 et seq.
Me. Rev. Stat. Ann. 1964, Title 13, § 1971 et seq.
Ore. Rev. Stat., 62.765 et seq.
Wash. Rev. Code Ann., 23.78.010 et seq.

Employee Disability Act
Ill. Rev. Stat. 1991, Ch. 70, §§ 90.9, 91

Employee Equity Act (Railroad)
Me. Rev. Stat. Ann. 1964, Title 26, § 2071 et seq.

Employee Fair Hearing Act (Public School)
Ark. Acts 1991, No. 631

Employee Grievance Procedure Act
S.C. Code Ann. 1976, § 8-17-310 et seq.

Employee Grievance Procedure Act (County and Municipal)
S.C. Code Ann. 1976, § 8-17-110 et seq.

Employee Grievance Procedure Act (State-Local)
S.C. Code Ann. 1976, § 8-17-110 et seq.

Employee Health Care Access Act
Fla. Stat. Ann., 627.6699

Employee Housing Act
Cal. Health and Safety Code § 17000 et seq.

Employee Housing Protection Act
Cal. Statutes 1992, Ch. 1298

Employee Illiteracy Education Assistance Act
Cal. Labor Code § 1040 et seq.

Employee Incentive and Agency Productivity Act
Miss. Laws 1999, H.B. 406

Employee Incentive Plan Act (State)
Tenn. Public Acts 1992, Ch. 908

Employee Leasing Act
N.M. Stat. Ann., 60-13A-1 et seq.
Tenn. Code Ann., 62-43-103 et seq.

Employee Leasing Company Act
Ill. Comp. Stat. 1992, Ch. 215, § 113/1 et seq.

Employee Leasing Company Licensing Act
Utah Code Ann. 1953, 58-59-101 et seq.

Employee Leasing Company Registration Act
Utah Code Ann. 1953, 16-14-1 et seq.

Employee Long-Term Care Plan Act
Fla. Laws 1998, Ch. 400

Employee-Management Cooperation Act (Catham County)
Ga. Laws 1968, p. 2953

Employee-Management Relations Act (Local Government)
Nev. Rev. Stat. 1979 Reprint, 288.010 et seq.

Employee Medical Contribution Act
Ill. Rev. Stat. 1991, Ch. 48, § 35a et seq.

Employee Non-Liability Act
D.C. Code Ann., § 1-1211 et seq.

Employee-Owned Corporation Act
Mich. Comp. Laws Ann., 450.731 et seq.

Employee Ownership Act
Cal. Government Code §§ 15330, 15332
Cal. Statutes 1983, Ch. 998

Employee Ownership Assistance Act
Ill. Rev. Stat. 1991, Ch. 48, § 1301 et seq.
Pa. Purdon's Stat., Title 73, § 396.1 et seq.

Employee Ownership Assistance Program
W. Va. Code 1966, §§ 5B-5-1 to 5B-5-7

Employee Ownership Opportunity Act
Mont. Laws 1991, Ch. 671
Ore. Laws 1991, Ch. 677, § 1

Employee Patent Act
Ill. Rev. Stat. 1991, Ch. 140, § 301 et seq.

Employee Pension Revocation and Reduction Act (Public)
R.I. Gen. Laws 1956, 36-10.1-1 et seq.

Employee Polygraph Protection Act of 1988

Sept. 23, 1996, P.L. 104-201, 29 U.S. Code § 2006

Employee Privacy Act

N.M. Stat. Ann., 50-11-1 et seq.

Employee Protection Act (Conscientious)

N.J. Stat. Ann., 34:19-1 et seq.

Employee Protection Act (State)

Ala. Code 1975, § 36-26A-1 et seq.

Mont. Code Ann., 2-18-1201 et seq.

Employee Protection and Education Truth in Reporting Act

Tenn. Code Ann., 49-50-1401 et seq.

Employee Regulation and Fire Equipment Distributor Act

Ill. Rev. Stat. 1991, Ch. 111, § 8001 et seq.

Employee Relations Act (Municipal)

Mass. Gen. Laws Ann., 150e:1 et seq.

Mich. Comp. Laws Ann., 423.201 et seq.

Employee Retirement Act (Public)

N.M. Stat. Ann., 10-11-1 et seq.

Employee Retirement Income Security Act of 1974

Sept. 2, 1974, P.L. 93-406, 88 Stat. 829, 29 § 1001 nt.

March 29, 1975, P.L. 94-12, 89 Stat. 47, 26 U.S. Code § 410 nt.

Dec. 19, 1977, P.L. 95-214, 29 U.S. Code § 1381

Nov. 6, 1978, P.L. 95-598, 29 U.S. Code § 1342, 1362, 1368

Nov. 8, 1978, P.L. 95-615, 26 U.S. Code § 401 nt.

June 19, 1979, P.L. 96-24, 29 U.S. Code § 1381

April 30, 1980, P.L. 96-239, 29 U.S. Code § 1381

June 28, 1980, P.L. 96-293, 29 U.S. Code § 1381

Jan. 14, 1983, P.L. 97-473, 29 U.S. Code §§ 1002, 1144

July 18, 1984, P.L. 98-369, 29 U.S. Code §§ 1391, 1397, 1399, 1461

Aug. 23, 1984, P.L. 98-397, 29 U.S. Code §§ 1001 nt., 1025, 1052 to 1056, 1144

Oct. 12, 1984, P.L. 98-473, 29 U.S. Code § 1111

Nov. 8, 1984, P.L. 98-620, 29 U.S. Code § 1303

April 7, 1986, P.L. 99-272, 29 U.S. Code §§ 1144, 1161 to 1168

Oct. 21, 1986, P.L. 99-509, 29 U.S. Code §§ 1002, 1052, 1054, 1162, 1163, 1166, 1167

Oct. 22, 1986, P.L. 99-514, 29 U.S. Code §§ 1052 to 1056, 1054 nt., 1108, 1162, 1165 to 1167, 1349, 1416

Dec. 7, 1987, P.L. 100-182, 29 U.S. Code § 1111

Dec. 22, 1987, P.L. 100-203, 29 U.S. Code §§ 1021, 1023, 1024, 1054, 1082 to 1086, 1103, 1107, 1113, 1132, 1201, 1301, 1305 to 1307, 1322, 1341, 1342, 1344, 1349, 1362, 1364, 1367, 1368, 1371

Nov. 10, 1988, P.L. 100-647, 29 U.S. Code § 1167

Dec. 19, 1989, P.L. 101-239, 26 U.S. Code § 411; generally 29 U.S. Code § 1001 et seq.

Nov. 5, 1990, P.L. 101-508, 29 U.S. Code §§ 1002, 1021, 1082, 1103, 1104, 1108, 1132, 1306, 1344

Nov. 8, 1990, P.L. 101-540, 29 U.S. Code § 1107

Aug. 14, 1991, P.L. 102-89, 29 U.S. Code § 1002

Dec. 12, 1991, P.L. 102-229, 29 U.S. Code § 1301

Aug. 10, 1993, P.L. 103-66, 29 U.S. Code §§ 1021, 1132, 1144, prec. 1161, 1169

Oct. 22, 1994, P.L. 103-401, 29 U.S. Code § 1132

Dec. 8, 1994, P.L. 103-465, 29 U.S. Code §§ 1021, 1053, 1054, 1055, 1056, 1082, 1103, 1108, 1132, 1301, 1303, 1305, 1306, 1310, 1311, 1322, 1341, 1342, 1343, 1350

Aug. 20, 1996, P.L. 104-188, 29 U.S. Code §§ 1021, 1053, 1055, 1101, 1104, 1108, 1162

Aug. 21, 1996, P.L. 104-191, 29 U.S. Code §§ 1003, 1021, 1022, 1024, 1132, 1136, prec. 1161, 1166, 1167, prec. 1181, 1181 to 1187

Aug. 22, 1996, P.L. 104-193, 29 U.S. Code § 1169

Sept. 26, 1996, P.L. 104-204, 29 U.S. Code §§ 1003, 1021, 1022, 1024, 1132, 1136, 1144, prec. 1181, 1181, 1185, 1185a, prec. 1191, 1191, 1191a to 1191c

Oct. 11, 1996, P.L. 104-290, 29 U.S. Code § 1002

Aug. 5, 1997, P.L. 105-33, 29 U.S. Code § 1169

Aug. 5, 1997, P.L. 105-34, 29 U.S. Code §§ 1021, 1022, 1024, 1026 to 1028, 1053 to 1056, 1082, 1107, 1108, 1132

Nov. 10, 1997, P.L. 105-72, 29 U.S. Code § 1002

Nov. 19, 1997, P.L. 105-92, 29 U.S. Code §§ 1146, 1147

July 16, 1998, P.L. 105-200, 29 U.S. Code §§ 1021, 1144, 1169

Oct. 21, 1998, P.L. 105-277, 29 U.S. Code §§ 1001 nt., 1185b

Employee Right to Know Act
Mich. Comp. Laws Ann., 423.501 et seq.
Minn. Laws 1983, Ch. 316

Employee Rights Violation Act
Ill. Rev. Stat. 1991, Ch. 127, § 63b100-1 et seq.

Employee Safety Act (Underground Sewer)
Ill. Rev. Stat. 1991, Ch. 48, § 1100 et seq.

Employee Stock Ownership Plan Act
N.J. Stat. Ann., 34:1B-30

Employee Washroom Act
Ill. Rev. Stat. 1991, Ch. 48, § 97.9 et seq.

Employee Welfare Fund Disclosure Act
Mass. Gen. Laws Ann., 151D:1 et seq.
N.Y. Insurance Law 1984 (Consol. Laws Ch. 28) § 4401 et seq.

Employees' Accident Compensation Act
Nev. Rev. Stat. 1979 Reprint, 616.010 et seq.

Employees Act (Supported)
Ill. Rev. Stat. 1991, Ch. 127, § 3901 et seq.

Employees' and Municipal Officers' Ethics Act
Utah Code Ann. 1953, 67-17-1 et seq.

Employees' and Officers' Group Insurance Act
Minn. Stat. Ann., 471.61

Employees' and Officers' Tenure Act (Augusta)
Ga. Laws 1937-38 Ex. Sess., p. 938

Employees and Officials Group Insurance Act (State)
Colo. Rev. Stat., 10-8-201 et seq.

Employees' Annuity and Benefit Fund Act (Municipal)
Ill. Rev. Stat. 1991, Ch. 108, § 8-101 et seq.

Employees' Arbitration Act (911 Employees' Arbitration Act)
R.I. Gen. Laws 1956, 28-9.6-1 et seq.

Employees' Bond Law
Cal. Labor Code § 400 et seq.

Employees' Chemical Right to Know Act (Public)
Ark. Acts 1991, No. 556

Employees' Civil Service Act (Fulton County)
Ga. Laws 1943, p. 971

Employees Collective Bargaining Act (State)
Neb. Rev. Stat. 1943, 81-1369 et seq.

Employees' Compensation Act
D.C. Code Ann., § 36-301 et seq.
Ill. Rev. Stat. 1991, Ch. 48, § 138.1 et seq.
La. Rev. Stat. Ann., 23:1021 et seq.
Tex. Rev. Civ. Stat., Art. 8308-1.01 et seq.

Employees' Compensation Acts
See Workmen's Compensation Acts

Employees' Compensation Commission Appropriation Acts
June 26, 1940, Ch. 428, 54 Stat. 594
July 1, 1941, Ch. 269, 55 Stat. 494
July 2, 1942, Ch. 475, 56 Stat. 588
July 12, 1943, Ch. 221, 57 Stat. 513, 16 U.S. Code § 584m nt.; 41 U.S. Code § 6a nt.
June 28, 1944, Ch. 302, 58 Stat. 566, 16 U.S. Code § 584m nt.; 41 U.S. Code § 6a nt.
July 3, 1945, Ch. 263, 59 Stat. 377, 16 U.S. Code § 584m nt.; 41 U.S. Code § 6a nt.
July 26, 1946, Ch. 672, 60 Stat. 697, 16 U.S. Code § 584m nt.; 41 U.S. Code § 6a nt.

Employees' Contributory Retirement Act
Me. Rev. Stat. Ann. 1964, Title 5, § 17001 et seq.

Employees Contributory Retirement Act (Public)
Mass. Gen. Laws Ann., 32:1 et seq.

Employees Deferred Compensation Plan Act (Government)
Fla. Stat. Ann., 112.215
Tenn. Code Ann. 1955, 8-4301 et seq.
Va. Code 1950, § 51-111.67:14 et seq.

Employees Dental Freedom of Choice Act
Ill. Rev. Stat. 1991, Ch. 32, § 690.71 et seq.

Employees Direct Deposit Act (State)
Okla. Stat. 1981, Title 74, § 292-10 et seq.

Employees Disability Program Act (State)
Okla. Stat. 1981, Title 74, § 1331 et seq.

Employees' Drinking Water Law
Cal. Labor Code § 2441

Employees' Earnings Protection Act
Cal. Code of Civil Procedure § 723.010 et seq.

Employees' Fitness Act (Devine-Corrigan)
Ohio Rev. Code 1953, 124.35

Employees Flexible Benefits Act (State)
Okla. Stat. 1981, Title 74, § 1341 et seq.

Employee's Garnishment Act
D.C. Code Ann., § 1-516

Employees Group Benefits Act (State)
Colo. Rev. Stat., 24-50-601 et seq.

Employees' Group Insurance Act (State)
Ill. Rev. Stat. 1991, Ch. 127, § 521 et seq.
N.H. Rev. Stat. 1955, 21-I:26 et seq.

Employees Labor Relations Act (Judicial)
Me. Rev. Stat. Ann. 1964, Title 26, § 1281 et seq.

Employees' Liability Act
La. Rev. Stat. Ann., 23:1021 et seq.

Employees' Liability Act (Carriers)
Ga. Code Ann., 34-7-41

Employees' Medical and Hospital Care Act
Cal. Government Code § 22751 et seq.

Employees' Medical Examination Act
Ill. Rev. Stat. 1991, Ch. 48, § 172c.9 et seq.

Employees' Merit System Act (State)
Conn. Gen. Stat. 1983, § 5-193 et seq.

Employees Military Active Duty Act (Municipal)
Ill. Rev. Stat. 1991, Ch. 24 1/2, § 149m et seq.

Employees' Minimum Sick Leave Law (School)
Ark. Code Ann. 1987, 6-17-1301 et seq.

Employees' Pension Act (County)
Ga. Laws 1937, p. 738

Employees' Pension Act (Floyd County)
Ga. Laws 1951, p. 2746

Employees' Pension Act (Fulton County)
Ga. Laws 1939, p. 571

Employees' Pension Fund Act (Augusta)
Ga. Laws 1945, p. 813

Employees' Pension Fund Act (Richmond County)
Ga. Laws 1945, p. 748

Employees' Personnel System Act (State)
N.H. Rev. Stat. 1955, 21-I:48 et seq.

Employees Political Activity Act (State)
Ill. Rev. Stat. 1991, Ch. 24 1/2, § 38r.9 et seq.

Employees' Political Rights Act (Local Government)
Ill. Rev. Stat. 1987, Ch. 85, § 7601 et seq.

Employees' Political Rights Law
Cal. Labor Code § 1101 et seq.

Employees Pretax Benefits Program Act (State)
Fla. Stat. Ann., 110.161

Employees Protection Act (State)
Ala. Code 1975, § 36-26A-1 et seq.

Employees' Purchase Law
Cal. Labor Code § 450 et seq.

Employees Relations Act (Municipal)
Mass. Gen. Laws 1984, 150E:1 et seq.

Employees' Retirement Act
Colo. Rev. Stat., 24-51-101 et seq.
N.Y. City Admin. Code 1985, § 13-101 et seq.

Employees Retirement Act (Cities)
Kan. Stat. Ann., 13-1246 et seq.

Employees' Retirement Act (County)
Cal. Government Code, §§ 31250 et seq., 31450 et seq.
Mich. Comp. Laws Ann., 46.12a
N.J. Stat. Ann., 43:10-1 et seq.
Pa. Purdon's Stat., Title 16, § 11501 et seq.

Employees Retirement Act (First Class)
Wash. Rev. Code Ann., 41.28.005 et seq.

Employees' Retirement Act (Municipal-Public Funds)
N.J. Stat. Ann., 43:12-1.12 et seq.

Employees' Retirement Act (Municipal-Trust Funds)
N.J. Rev. Stat. 1937, 43:13-2 to 43:13-54

Employees' Retirement Act (Municipal)
Conn. Gen. Stat. 1983, § 7-425 et seq.
Ill. Rev. Stat. 1981, Ch. 108 1/2, § 7-101 et seq.
Mich. Comp. Laws Ann., 38.601 et seq.
Pa. Purdon's Stat., Title 53, § 881.101
Tex. Rev. Civ. Stat. Arts. 6235a-1, 6243g, 6243h
Wash. Rev. Code Ann., 41.28.005 et seq.

Employees' Retirement Act (Public Employees)
Mass. Gen. Laws 1984, 32:1 et seq.
N.Y. Retirement and Social Security Law (Consol. Laws Ch. 51A) § 2 et seq.
Ore. Rev. Stat., 237.001 et seq.

Employees' Retirement Act (Public Schools)
Mich. Comp. Laws Ann., 38.201 et seq.

Employees' Retirement Act (Public)
Mont. Code Ann., 19-3-101 et seq.

Employees Retirement Act (School)
Neb. Rev. Stat. 1943, 79-1501 to 79-1566

Employees' Retirement Act (State and County)
Fla. Stat. Ann., 112.05, 112.051, 122.01 et seq.
Kan. Stat. Ann., 40-2301 et seq.
Ore. Rev. Stat., 237.001 et seq.

Employees' Retirement Act (State)
See State Employees Retirement Act

Employees' Retirement Act (Third Class Cities)
Conn. Gen. Stat. 1983, § 7-425 et seq.
Mich. Comp. Laws Ann., 38.601 et seq.
Pa. Purdon's Stat., Title 53, § 39371 et seq.
Tex. Rev. Civ. Stat., Arts. 6235a-1, 6243g, 6243h
Wash. Rev. Code Ann., 41.28.005 et seq., 41.44.005 et seq.

Employees' Retirement Acts
Pa. Purdon's Stat., Title 71, § 1731 et seq.

Employees' Retirement Code (State)
Pa. Cons. Stat., Title 71, § 5101 et seq.

Employees' Retirement Fund Act (Fulton County)
Ga. Laws 1945, p. 528

Employees' Retirement Plan Act (Forsyth County)
N.C. Laws 1945, Ch. 298

Employees' Retirement System Act
Ala. Code 1975, 36-27-1 et seq.
Haw. Rev. Stat. Ann., § 88-21 et seq.
N.H. Rev. Stat. 1955, 100-A:1 et seq.
N.J. Stat. Ann., 43:15A-1 et seq.
Wis. Stat. 1979, 41.01 et seq.

Employees' Retirement System Act (Local Governments)
N.C. Gen. Stat. 1943, § 128.21 et seq.

Employees' Retirement System Act (Public)
Okla. Stat. 1981, Title 74, § 901 et seq.

Employees' Retirement System Act (State)
Ga. Code Ann., 47-2-1 et seq.
Mo. Rev. Stat., 104.310 et seq.
N.C. Gen. Stat. 1943, § 135-1 et seq.
Tex. Public Retirement Systems, Title 110B
Vt. Stat. Ann., Title 3, § 455 et seq.

Employees Right to Bargain Act
Mass. Gen. Laws Ann., 150A:3

Employees' Right to Know Act
Wash. Rev. Code Ann., 101.58 et seq.

Employees' Safety Act
Cal. Labor Code §§ 6300 et seq., 6400 et seq.

Employees' Service Letter Act
Mo. Rev. Stat., 290.140

Employees Sick Leave Act (School)
S.C. Code Ann. 1976, §§ 8-11-40 et seq.,
59-1-400 et seq.

Employees Stock Ownership Plan Act
N.J. Stat. Ann., 52:27H-90 et seq.

Employees Unification Act (Judicial)
N.J. Stat. Ann., 2B:11-1 et seq.

Employees Uniform Group Insurance Benefits Act
Tex. Insurance Code, Art. 3.50-2

Employees Vacation Act
See Federal Employees Vacation Act

Employees' Voting Time Act
Ind. Code Ann., 3-5-4-2, 3-5-4-3
Neb. Rev. Stat. 1943, 32-1046

Employees' Wage Act
Kan. Stat. Ann., 44-312 et seq.

Employees' Welfare Fund Disclosure Act
Cal. Insurance Code § 10640 et seq.
Mass. Gen. Laws Ann., 151D:1 et seq.
N.Y. Insurance Law (Consol. Laws Ch. 28) § 4401 et seq.
Wash. Rev. Code Ann., 48.20.020 et seq.

Employees' Welfare Funds Act
Conn. Gen. Stat. 1983, Miscellaneous Superseded Code Provisions, § 31-78 et seq.

Employer as Lessee Bond Act
Ill. Rev. Stat. 1991, Ch. 48, § 39f-1 et seq.

Employer Assistance for Environmental Protection Act
W. Va. Code 1966 § 21-3B-1 et seq.

Employer-Employee Relations Act
Cal. Government Code § 3540 et seq.
Kan. Stat. Ann., 44-801 et seq.
Nev. Rev. Stat. 1979 Reprint, 288.010 et seq.
N.J. Stat. Ann., 34:13A-1 et seq.

Employer-Employee Relations Act (Peace Officer's)
N.M. Stat. Ann., 29-14-1 et seq.

Employer Recognition Act (Professional)
Ida. Code 1947, 44-2401 et seq.

Employer Welfare Arrangement Act
Fla. Stat. Ann., 624.436 et seq.

Employers' Disaster Reinsurance Fund Act
Wyo. Stat. Ann., § 27-12-701

Employers' Hospital Service Law
Cal. Labor Code § 2500 et seq.

Employer's Insurance Act
Mont. Code Ann. 1987, 39-71-101 et seq.

Employers' Insurance Association Act
Tex. Rev. Civ. Stat., Art. 8308

Employers' Liability Act
Ala. Code 1975, § 25-6-1 et seq.
Alaska Stat. 1962, § 23.30.005 et seq.
Ariz. Rev. Stat. Ann., § 23-801 et seq.
Ark. Code Ann. 1987, 11-8-103 et seq.
Cal. Labor Code §§ 2801, 3200 et seq.
Colo. Rev. Stat., 8-2-201 et seq.
Conn. Gen. Stat. 1983, § 31-275 et seq.
Ill. Rev. Stat. 1991, Ch. 48, § 138.1 et seq.
Ind. Code Ann., 22-3-9-1 et seq.
Kan. Stat. Ann., 66-237 et seq.
Mass. Gen. Laws Ann., 153:1 et seq., 229:6C et seq.
Me. Rev. Stat. Ann. 1964, Title 39, § 141 et seq.
Mich. Comp. Laws Ann., 419.51 et seq.
Mo. Rev. Stat., 537.180 et seq.
Neb. Rev. Stat. 1943, 48-101 et seq.
Nev. Rev. Stat. 1979 Reprint, 616.010 et seq.
N.H. Rev. Stat. 1955, 281:1 et seq.
N.Y. Consol. Laws, Ch. 74
Ore. Rev. Stat., 654.305 et seq.
Pa. Purdon's Stat., Title 43, §§ 171, 172
S.C. Code Ann. 1976, § 58-17-3710 et seq.
Wash. Rev. Code Ann., 51.12.080

Employers' Liability Act (Fellow Servant Rule)
Ohio Rev. Code 1953, 4113.03 et seq.

Employers' Liability Act (Hazardous Employment)
Ore. Rev. Stat., 654.305 et seq.

Employers' Liability Act (Railroads)
See also Railroad Employers' Liability Act
Ga. Code Ann., 34-7-40 et seq.
Ky. Rev. Stat. 1971, 277.310, 277.320
Minn. Stat. Ann., 219.77 et seq.
Mont. Code Ann. 1983, 69-14-1006
N.D. Cent. Code, 49-16-02 et seq.
Ore. Rev. Stat., 764.110 et seq.
S.D. Codified Laws 1967, 49-24-7 et seq.
Tex. Rev. Civ. Stat., Art. 6432 et seq.
Va. Code 1950, § 8.01-57 et seq.

Employers' Liability Act (Workmen's Compensation)
Tex. Rev. Civ. Stat., Art. 8306 et seq.

Employers' Liability Acts (Railroads)
June 11, 1906, Ch. 3073, 34 Stat. 232
April 22, 1908, Ch. 149, 35 Stat. 65, 45 U.S. Code §§ 51 to 59
April 5, 1910, Ch. 143, 36 Stat. 291, 45 U.S. Code §§ 56, 59
Aug. 11, 1939, Ch. 685, 53 Stat. 1404, 45 U.S. Code §§ 51, 54, 56, 60

Employers' Liability Insurance Act
N.J. Stat. Ann., 34:15-70 et seq.
Ohio Rev. Code 1953, 4123.01 et seq.

Employers Mutual Company Act
N.M. Stat. Ann., 52-9-1 et seq.

Employers' Mutual Liability Insurance Associations Act
Pa. 1915 Pamph. Laws 771, No. 771

Employers' Retirement Act (Public)
Ore. Rev. Stat., 237.001 et seq.

Employer's Ridesharing Incentive Act
Cal. Statutes 1981, Ch. 844

Employers' Safety Act
Ore. Rev. Stat., 654.001 et seq.

Employment Act
La. Acts 1946, No. 180

Employment Act (Age Discrimination)
Neb. Rev. Stat. 1943, 48-1001 et seq.

Employment Act (First Class Cities)
Ky. Rev. Stat. 1971, 90.110 et seq.

Employment Act (Teacher Quality)
N.J. Stat. Ann., 18A:29-5.1 et seq.

Employment Act (Welfare)
Del. Code of 1974, Title 31, § 1501 et seq.

Employment Act (Wrongful Discharge)
Mont. Code Ann., 39-2-901 et seq.

Employment Act of 1946
Feb. 20, 1946, Ch. 33, 60 Stat. 23, 15 U.S. Code §§ 1021 to 1024
Aug. 2, 1946, Ch. 753, 60 Stat. 838, 15 U.S. Code §§ 1022, 1024
Feb. 2, 1948, Ch. 42, 62 Stat. 16, 15 U.S. Code § 1024
Oct. 6, 1949, Ch. 627, 63 Stat. 721, 15 U.S. Code § 1024
June 18, 1956, Ch. 399, 70 Stat. 289, 15 U.S. Code §§ 1022, 1024; 50 U.S. Code Appx. § 1916
Feb. 17, 1959, P.L. 86-1, 73 Stat. 3, 15 U.S. Code § 1024
Oct. 13, 1964, P.L. 88-661, 78 Stat. 1093, 15 U.S. Code § 1024
Jan. 25, 1967, P.L. 90-2, 81 Stat. 4, 15 U.S. Code § 1024
Oct. 27, 1978, P.L. 95-523, 15 U.S. Code § 1021 et seq.
May 10, 1979, P.L. 96-10, 15 U.S. Code §§ 1022, 1022a
Nov. 2, 1994, P.L. 103-446, 15 U.S. Code § 1022a
Oct. 21, 1998, P.L. 105-277, 15 U.S. Code § 1022a

Employment Agencies Act (Private)
Ga. Code Ann., 34-10-1 et seq.
Ill. Rev. Stat. 1991, Ch. 111, § 900 et seq.
N.D. Cent. Code, 34-13-01 et seq.

Employment Agencies Law (Theatrical)
Colo. Rev. Stat., 12-24-201 et seq.

Employment Agencies Licensing Act
N.Y. General Business Law (Consol. Laws Ch. 20) § 170 et seq.

Employment Agencies Licensing Acts
N.Y. General Business Law (Consol. Laws Ch. 20) § 170 et seq.

Employment Agency Act
See also Private Employment Agency Act
Alaska Stat. 1962, § 23.15.330 et seq.
Ark. Code Ann. 1987, 11-11-201 et seq.
Cal. Labor Code § 1550 et seq.
Fla. Stat. 1979, 449,01 et seq.
Ind. Code Ann., 25-16-1-1 et seq.
Ind. Code Ann., 95.1 et seq.
Kan. Stat. Ann., 44-401 et seq.
Mass. Gen. Laws Ann., 140:46A et seq.
Md. Ann. Code 1974, Art. BR, § 9-601 et seq.
Mont. Code Ann., 39-5-101 et seq.
N.D. Cent. Code, 34-13-01 et seq.
Neb. Rev. Stat. 1943, 48-501.01 et seq.
N.J. Stat. Ann., 34:8-24 et seq.
N.M. Stat. Ann., 61,22,1 et seq.
N.Y. General Business Law (Consol. Laws Ch. 20) § 170 et seq.
Ohio Rev. Code 1953, 4143.01 et seq.
Ore. Rev. Stat., 658.005 et seq.
Pa. Purdon's Stat., Title 43, § 535 et seq.
S.C. Code Ann. 1976, § 41-25-10 et seq.
S.D. Codified Laws 1967, 60-6A-1 et seq.
Wash. Rev.Code 1989, 19.31.010 et seq.

Employment Agency, Employment Counseling and Job Listing Services Act
Cal. Civil Code § 1812.500 et seq.

Employment Agency Law
Colo. Rev. Stat., 12-24-101 et seq.

Employment and Construction Act
Cal. Statutes 1946, 1st Ex. Sess., Ch. 20, p. 30

Employment and Economic Incentive Act
Cal. Government Code § 7080 et seq.

Employment and Education Governing Board Act
P.R. Laws Ann. 1954, Title 3, § 2001 et seq.

Employment and Investment Growth Act
Neb. Rev. Stat. 1943, 77-4101 et seq.

Employment and Labor Agency Law
Tex. Rev. Civ. Stat., Art. 5221a-5

Employment and Training Act
Fla. Stat. 1981, 450.50 et seq.
N.C. Laws 1985, Ch. 543 § 143B-438.1 et seq.

Employment and Training Act of 1973
Cal. Unemployment Insurance Code § 16000 et seq.

Employment and Training for Older Californians Act
Cal. Unemployment Insurance Code § 16000 et seq.

Employment Anti-Discrimination Act
Vt. Stat. Ann., Title 21, § 495 et seq.

Employment Antidiscrimination Act
R.I. Gen. Laws 1956, 28-5-1 et seq.

Employment Assistance and Training Program Act
Alaska Laws 1991, Ch. 95

Employment Bureau Licensing Act (Private)
Mich. Comp. Laws Ann., 338.2001 et seq.

Employment, Compensation, and Dismissal Act (Teacher)
Colo. Rev. Stat., 22-63-101 et seq.

Employment Contract Act
Cal. Labor Code § 430 et seq.
Ill. Rev. Stat. 1991, Ch. 48, §§ 2b, 2b.1

Employment Cooperation Act (State and Federal)
Ill. Rev. Stat. 1991, Ch. 48, § 172a et seq.

Employment Council and Training Act
Mo. Rev. Stat. 1978, 620.521

Employment Demonstration and Personal Responsibility Program Act
Colo. Rev. Stat., 26-2-501 et seq.

Employment Development Act
Cal. Statutes 1973, Chs. 1206, 1207
Ore. Rev. Stat., 657.005 et seq.

Employment Development Act (Emergency)
N.J. Stat. Ann., App. A:11-1 et seq.

Employment Development Commission Act
Ind. Code Ann., 4-4-11-1 et seq.

Employment Discrimination Act (Defense Contract)
Ill. Rev. Stat. 1991, Ch. 29, § 24a.1 et seq.

Employment Discrimination Act (Public Works)
Ill. Rev. Stat. 1991, Ch. 29, § 16.9 et seq.

Employment Discrimination Law
Wash. Rev. Code Ann., 49.60.010 et seq.

Employment Expansion and Investment Incentive Act
Neb. Rev. Stat. 1943, 77-27, 187 et seq.

Employment for Older Californians Act
Cal. Unemployment Insurance Code § 16000 et seq.

Employment Incentive Act
Tex. Rev. Civ. Stat., Art. 695n

Employment, Industrial and Health Resources Development Act
Tex. Rev. Civ. Stat., Art. 5190.1

Employment Intervention Program Act (Emergency)
N.Y. Labor Law (Consol. Laws Ch. 31) § 820 nt.

Employment Labor Relations Act
Wash. Rev. Code Ann., 111.80 et seq.

Employment Labor Relations Act (State Officers and Employees)
Wis. Stat. Ann., 111.80 et seq.

Employment of Detectives by Public Officals Act
Ill. Rev. Stat. 1991, Ch. 111, §§ 2700, 2701

Employment of Illinois Workers on Public Works Act
Ill. Rev. Stat. 1991, Ch. 48, § 2200 et seq.

Employment of Minors Act
D.C. Code Ann., § 36-501 et seq.

Employment of Strikebreakers Act
Ill. Rev. Stat. 1991, Ch. 48, § 2d.9 et seq.

Employment of the Handicapped Act
Okla. Stat. Ann., Title 74, § 9.29 et seq.

Employment Offices and Agencies Act
Ill. Rev. Stat. 1991, Ch. 48, § 172.90 et seq.

Employment Opportunities Act
D.C. Code Ann., § 36-601 et seq.
Pa. Purdon's Stat., Title 62, § 4001 et seq.

Employment Opportunities for Disabled Americans Act
Nov. 10, 1986, P.L. 99-643, 42 U.S. Code § 1305 nt.

Employment Opportunity Act
Fla. Stat. Ann., 409.029

Employment Opportunity Act (Youth)
Colo. Rev. Stat., 8-12-101 et seq.

Employment Peace Act
Wash. Rev. Code Ann., 111.01 et seq.

Employment Pilot Program (Part-Time)
Cal. Government Code § 18030 et seq.

Employment Practices Act
Ga. Code Ann., 45-19-20 et seq.
Haw. Rev. Stat. Ann., § 378-1 et seq.
Ind. Code Ann., 601A.6, 729.4
Mass. Gen. Laws 1984, 151C:1 et seq.

Okla. Stat. 1981, Title 74, § 840.19
R.I. Gen. Laws 1956, 28-5-1 et seq.

Employment Practices Act (Fair)
Okla. Stat. Ann., Title 74, § 840-4.12, Subd. I

Employment Preference Act (Handicapped Persons and Veterans)
Mont. Code Ann., 39-30-101

Employment Preference Act (Veterans)
N.C. Gen. Stat. 1943, § 128-15

Employment Procedures Law (School)
Miss. Code Ann. 1972, § 37-9-101 et seq.

Employment Program (Youth Incentive)
La. Rev. Stat. Ann., 23:1821 et seq.

Employment Record Disclosure Act
Ill. Comp. Stat. 1992, Ch. 745, § 46/1 et seq.

Employment Relations Act
Haw. Rev. Stat. Ann., § 377-1 et seq.
N.Y. Labor Law (Consol. Laws Ch. 31) § 700 et seq.
Wash. Rev. Code Ann., 111.01 et seq.

Employment Relations Act (Educational)
Wash. Rev. Code Ann., 41.59.010 et seq.

Employment Relations Act (Municipal)
Wash. Rev. Code Ann., 111.70, 111.71

Employment Relations Act (Police and Firefighters)
Del. Code of 1974, Title 19, § 1601 et seq.

Employment Relief Act (Forest Industry)
Cal. Public Resources Code § 4650

Employment Representative Act (Veterans')
Ill. Rev. Stat. 1991, Ch. 48, § 186a et seq.

Employment Retraining Act
Okla. Stat. Ann., Title 2, § 2001 et seq.

Employment Revitalization Act
S.C. Code Ann. 1976, § 59-54-10 et seq.

Employment Safety Act
Ind. Code Ann., 88.1 et seq.

Employment Security Act
Ala. Code 1975, § 25-5-30 et seq.

Alaska Stat. 1962, § 23.20.005 et seq.

Ariz. Rev. Stat. Ann., § 23-601 et seq.

Ark. Code Ann. 1987, 11-10-102 et seq.

Colo. Rev. Stat., 8-70-101 et seq.

Ga. Code Ann., 34-8-1 et seq.

Haw. Rev. Stat. Ann., § 383-1 et seq.

Ida. Code 1947, 72-1301 et seq.

Ind. Code Ann., 22-4-1-1 et seq.

Ind. Code Ann., 96.1 et seq.

Kan. Stat. Ann., 44-701 et seq.

La. Rev. Stat. Ann., 23:1471 et seq.

Mass. Gen. Laws Ann., 151A:1 et seq.

Md. Ann. Code 1974, Art. LE, § 8-101 et seq.

Me. Rev. Stat. Ann. 1964, Title 26, § 1041 et seq.

Mich. Comp. Laws Ann., 421.1 et seq.

Minn. Stat. Ann., 268.026 et seq.

Miss. Code Ann. 1972, § 71-5-1 et seq.

Mo. Rev. Stat., 288.010 et seq.

N.C. Gen. Stat. 1943, § 96-1 et seq.

Neb. Rev. Stat. 1943, 48-601 et seq.

Nev. Rev. Stat. 1979 Reprint, 612.010 et seq.

N.J. Stat. Ann., 43:21-1 et seq.

Okla. Stat. Ann., Title 40, § 1-101 et seq.

Pa. Purdon's Stat., Title 43, § 751 et seq.

P.R. Laws Ann. 1954, Title 29, § 701 et seq.

R.I. Gen. Laws 1956, 28-42-1 et seq.

S.C. Code Ann. 1976, § 41-27-10 et seq.

S.D. Codified Laws 1967, 61-1-1 et seq.

Tenn. Code Ann., 50-7-101 et seq.

Utah Code Ann. 1953, 35-4-1 et seq.

Utah Code Ann. 1953, 35-4-101 et seq.

Wash. Rev. Code Ann., 50.01.005 et seq.

W. Va. Code 1966, § 21A-1-1 et seq.

Wyo. Stat. Ann., § 27-3-101 et seq.

Employment Security Act of 1960
Sept. 13, 1960, P.L. 86-778, 74 Stat. 970, 26 U.S. Code §§ 3301, 3302, 3304 nt., 3305, 3306, 3308, 3309; 29 U.S. Code § 49d; 42 U.S. Code §§ 501, 1101 to 1104, 1301, 1321 to 1324, 1361 to 1364, 1367, 1371, 1400c

Aug. 10, 1970, P.L. 91-373, 84 Stat. 695, 26 U.S. Code §§ 1563, 3302 to 3306, 3309 to 3311, 6157; 42 U.S. Code §§ 504, 1106, 1108

Employment Security Administration Enhancement Act
Ala. Acts 1988, 1st Sp. Sess., No. 783

Employment Security Administration Law
Nev. Rev. Stat. 1979 Reprint, 612.205 et seq.

Employment Security Administrative Financing Act of 1954
Aug. 5, 1954, Ch. 657, 68 Stat. 668

Employment Security Department Act
N.M. Stat. Ann., 9-13-1 et seq.

Employment Security Enhancement Act
Ala. Code 1975, §§ 25-4-31, 25-4-32, 25-4-54, 25-4-143

Employment Service Act
Ida. Code 1947, 72-1345
Minn. Stat. Ann., 268.03 et seq.
S.D. Codified Laws 1967, 60-6-1 et seq.

Employment Service Letter Act
Mo. Rev. Stat., 290.140
Okla. Stat. Ann., Title 40, § 171

Employment Services Licensing and Regulation Act
D.C. Code Ann., § 36-1001 et seq.

Employment Services Rights Act (Veteran)
Mich. Comp. Laws Ann., 35.1091 et seq.

Employment Stabilization Act of 1931
Feb. 10, 1931, Ch. 117, 46 Stat. 1084

Employment Standards for Youth Act
Mich. Comp. Laws Ann., 409.101 et seq.

Employment Tax Credit Act (Project Mainstream)
N.M. Stat. Ann., 7-1A-1 et seq.

Employment Tax Increment Financing Act
Me. Rev. Stat. Ann. 1964, Title 36, § 6751 et seq.

Employment Taxpayer's Bill of Rights Act
Cal. Unemployment Insurance Code §§ 650, 1206, 1222, 1231 et seq., 13004.1

Empowerment Zone Development Corporation Act
Mich. Comp. Laws Ann., 125.2561 et seq.

Empson Act (Directed Verdict)
Mich. Comp. Laws 1948, 691.691 et seq.

Emunson-Vander Werp Act (Fishing)
Mich. Comp. Laws 1948, 308.131

ENABL Act (Education Now and Babies Later)
Fla. Stat. Ann., 411.24 et seq.

Enabling Act (City Manager)
Ark. Code 1987, 14-61-101 et seq.

Enabling Act (Interstate Library Compact)
Vt. Stat. Ann., Title 22, § 21 et seq.

Enabling Act (Land Development and Subdivision Review)
R.I. Gen. Laws 1956, 45-23-25 et seq.

Enabling Act (Local Government Comprehensive Planning)
S.C. Code Ann. 1976, § 6-29-310 et seq.

Enabling Act (Municipal Electric District)
Me. Rev. Stat. Ann. 1964, Title 35-A, § 3901 et seq.

Enabling Act (Rural Electrification Cooperative)
Me. Rev. Stat. Ann. 1964, Title 35-A, § 3701 et seq.

Enabling Act for Local Legislation on Cruelty to Domestic Animals and Domestic Animal Control
Ga. Laws 1979, p. 516

Enabling Act for Local Option City Charters
N.H. Rev. Stat. 1955, 49-B:1 et seq.

Enabling Acts (Constitutional Convention)
Mont. Laws 1971, Ch. 296
Mont. Laws 1971, Ex. Sess., Ch. 1

Enabling and Contracting Act (Private Prison)
W. Va. Code 1966 § 25-5-1 et seq.

End-Use Act (Waste of Natural Gas)
Wyo. Stat. Ann., § 30-5-121 et seq.

Endangered Act (Duty to Aid)
Vt. Stat. Ann., Title 12, § 519

Endangered American Wilderness Act of 1978
Feb. 24, 1978, P.L. 95-227, 16 U.S. Code § 1132 nt.

Endangered and Nongame Species Conservation Act
See Nongame and Endangered Species Conservation Act

Endangered or Threatened Wildlife Species and Nongame Conservation Act
Colo. Rev. Stat., 33-2-101 et seq.
Fla. Stat. Ann., 372.072
Tenn. Code Ann., 70-8-101 et seq.

Endangered Plant and Insect Species Act
Fla. Stat. Ann., 581.185 et seq.
N.J. Stat. Ann., 13:1B-15.151 et seq.
Va. Code 1950, § 3.1-1020 et seq.

Endangered Species Act
Cal. Fish and Game Code 1957, § 2050 et seq.
Ga. Code Ann., 27-3-130 et seq.
Haw. Rev. Stat. Ann., § 195D-1 et seq.
Ill. Rev. Stat. 1991, Ch. 8, § 331 et seq.

Mass. Gen. Laws 1984, 131A:1 et seq.

Mich. Comp. Laws Ann., 299.221 et seq.

S.C. Code Ann. 1976, § 50-15-10 et seq.

Vt. Stat. Ann., Title 10, § 5401 et seq.

Endangered Species Act Amendments of 1978

Nov. 10, 1978, P.L. 95-632, 16 U.S. Code §§ 1531 et seq., 1531 nt.

Endangered Species Act of 1973

Dec. 18, 1973, P.L. 93-205, 87 Stat. 884, 7 U.S. Code § 136; 16 U.S. Code §§ 460k-1, 460l-9, 668dd, 715i, 715s, 1362, 1371, 1372, 1402, 1531 to 1543

Dec. 19, 1977, P.L. 95-212, 16 U.S. Code § 1535

Nov. 10, 1978, P.L. 95-632, 16 U.S. Code § 1532 et seq.

Dec. 28, 1979, P.L. 96-159, 16 U.S. Code § 1531 et seq.

May 23, 1980, P.L. 96-246, 16 U.S. Code § 1535

Oct. 13, 1982, P.L. 97-304, 16 U.S. Code §§ 1531 nt., 1532 to 1539, 1539 nt., 1540, 1542

June 25, 1984, P.L. 98-327, 16 U.S. Code §§ 1540, 3375

Nov. 14, 1986, P.L. 99-659, 16 U.S. Code § 1536

Nov. 14, 1988, P.L. 100-653, 16 U.S. Code § 1538

Nov. 23, 1988, P.L. 100-707, 16 U.S. Code § 1536

Endangered Species and Nongame Conservation Law

Kan. Stat. Ann.,32-957

Miss. Code Ann. 1972, § 49-5-101 et seq.

Endangered Species Conservation Act

Dec. 5, 1969, P.L. 91-135, 83 Stat. 283, 16 U.S. Code §§ 668aa to 668cc-5

Mont. Code Ann., 87-5-101 et seq.

Neb. Rev. Stat. 1943, 37-430 et seq.

N.H. Rev. Stat. 1955, 212-A:1 et seq.

Endangered Species of Fish Conservation Act

Md. Ann. Code 1974, Art. NR, § 4-2A01 et seq.

Endicott Parking Authority Act

N.Y. Public Authorities Law (Consol. Laws Ch. 43A) § 1550 et seq.

Endowed Care Cemetery Act

N.M. Stat. Ann., 58-17-1 et seq.

Endowment Act (University)

N.M. Stat. Ann., 21-1A-1 et seq.

Endowment for Vocational Rehabilitation Act

Fla. Stat. Ann., 413.615

Endowment Fund for Higher Education Act

Fla. Stat. Ann., 240.498

Endowment Management Act (Educational)

N.J. Stat. Ann., 15:18-15 et seq.

Endowment Scholarship Act (Legislative)

N.M. Stat. Ann., 21-21J-1 et seq.

Endowment Trust Fund for Eminent Scholars

Fla. Stat. 1983, 240.257

Endowment Trust Fund for Higher Education Act

Fla. Stat. Ann., 240.498

Energy Act

N.Y. Consol. Laws, Ch. 17A

Tenn. Code. Ann., 4-28-101 et seq.

W. Va. Code 1966 § 22-1-1 et seq.

Energy Act (Cost of)

N.Y. Energy Law (Consol. Laws Ch. 17A) § 17-101 et seq.

Energy Act (Emergency)

Mich. Comp. Laws Ann., 460.151 et seq.

Energy Advisory Council Act

Okla. Stat. 1971, Title 74, § 3361 et seq.

Energy and Coal Development Bond Act

Ill. Comp. Stat. 1992, Ch. 20, § 1110/1 et seq.

**Energy and Economic Development
Authority Act**
Minn. Stat. Ann., 116M.01 et seq.

Energy and Electric Power Act (Municipal)
S.C. Code Ann. 1976, § 6-23-10 et seq.

Energy and Minerals Department Act
N.M. Stat. Ann., 9-5A-1 et seq.

Energy and Natural Resources Act
La. Rev. Stat. Ann., 30:501 et seq.

Energy and Power Authority Act
La. Rev. Stat. Ann., 33:4545.1 et seq.

Energy and Transportation Planning Act
Miss. Code Ann. 1972, § 57-39-1 et seq.

**Energy and Water Development Appropri-
ation Act, 1980**
Sept. 25, 1979, P.L. 96-69, 40 U.S. Code
§ 174b-1 nt.

**Energy and Water Development Appropri-
ation Act, 1987**
Oct. 18, 1986, P.L. 99-500, 100 Stat. 3555
Oct. 30, 1986, P.L. 99-591, 100 Stat. 3555

**Energy and Water Development Appropri-
ation Act, 1988**
Dec. 22, 1987, P.L. 100-202, 101 Stat. 1329
Nov. 17, 1988, P.L. 100-676, 102 Stat. 4043
Sept. 29, 1989, P.L. 101-101, 103 Stat. 657
Oct. 24, 1992, P.L. 102-486, 106 Stat. 2944

**Energy and Water Development Appropri-
ation Act, 1990**
Sept. 29, 1989, P.L. 101-101, 103 Stat. 641

**Energy and Water Development Appropria-
tions Act, 1991**
Nov. 5, 1990, P.L. 101-514, 16 U.S. Code
§ 831b nt.; 40 U.S. Code Appx. § 401 nt.;
41 U.S. Code § 10b nt.; 42 U.S. Code
§§ 2061 nt., 7133, 7171 nt.; 43 U.S. Code
§§ 377a, 502 nt., 618d nt.
Nov. 13, 1995, P.L. 104-46, 42 U.S. Code
§ 7133 nt.

**Energy and Water Development Appropria-
tions Act, 1992**
Aug. 17, 1991, P.L. 102-104, 105 Stat. 536
Oct. 24, 1992, P.L. 102-486, 15 U.S. Code
§ 717c nt.

**Energy and Water Development Appropria-
tions Act, 1993**
Oct. 2, 1992, P.L. 102-377, 106 Stat. 1315
Oct. 28, 1993, P.L. 103-126, 107 Stat. 1334

**Energy and Water Development Appropria-
tions Act, 1994**
Oct. 28, 1993, P.L. 103-126, 107 Stat. 1312

**Energy and Water Development Appropria-
tions Act, 1995**
Aug. 26, 1994, P.L. 103-316, 108 Stat. 1707

**Energy and Water Development Appropria-
tions Act, 1996**
Nov. 13, 1995, P.L. 104-46, 109 Stat. 402

**Energy and Water Development Appropria-
tions Act, 1997**
Sept. 30, 1996, P.L. 104-206, 110 Stat. 2984

**Energy and Water Development Appropria-
tions Act, 1998**
Oct. 13, 1997, P.L. 105-62, 111 Stat. 1320

**Energy and Water Development Appropria-
tions Act, 1999**
Oct. 7, 1998, P.L. 105-245, 112 Stat. 1838

Energy Assistance Act
Ill. Rev. Stat. 1991, Ch. 111 2/3, §§ 1301 et
seq., 1401 et seq.

**Energy Assistance and Coastal Resources
Act**
Cal. Public Resources Code § 35000 et seq.

**Energy Assistance and Information
Program Act**
Md. Ann. Code 1957, Art. 41, § 6-401 et seq.
Md. Ann. Code 1974, Governor-Executive
and Administrative Departments, § 6-401 et
seq.

Energy Compact Act (Southern States)
See Southern States Energy Compact Act

Energy Conservation Act
Colo. Rev. Stat., 24-20-401 et seq.
Ill. Rev. Stat. 1991, Ch. 96 1/2, § 7601 et seq.
N.C. Laws 1977, Ch. 792
Ore. Laws 1977, Ch. 887

**Energy Conservation Act (Public
University)**
Ill. Comp. Stat. 1992, Ch. 110, § 62/1 et seq.

**Energy Conservation Act (Residential
Building)**
Colo. Rev. Stat., 6-7-101 et seq.

Energy Conservation Act (Rural)
Ill. Rev. Stat. 1991, Ch. 5, § 2202-1 et seq.

Energy Conservation Act (State Building)
Mont. Code Ann., 90-4-601 et seq.

Energy Conservation and Assistance Act
Pa. Purdon's Stat., Title 62, § 3011

**Energy Conservation and Coal Development
Act**
Ill. Comp. Stat. 1992, Ch. 20, § 1105/13.1 et
seq.

Energy Conservation and Efficiency Act
S.C. Code Ann. 1976, § 48-52-10 et seq.

**Energy Conservation and Home Insulation
Act**
N.Y. Public Service Law (Consol. Laws Ch.
48) § 135a et seq.

Energy Conservation and Policy Act
Ark. Stat. 1947, 5-1301 et seq.

Energy Conservation and Production Act
Aug. 14, 1976, P.L. 94-385, 42 U.S. Code
§ 6801 et seq.
July 21, 1977, P.L. 95-70, 42 U.S. Code
§ 6881
Nov. 9, 1978, P.L. 95-617, 42 U.S. Code
§ 6801 et seq.
Dec. 21, 1982, P.L. 97-375, 42 U.S. Code
§ 6840

Oct. 18, 1990, P.L. 101-440, 42 U.S. Code
§§ 6861 to 6865, 6871, 6872
Oct. 24, 1992, P.L. 102-486, 42 U.S. Code
§§ 6832 to 6840, 6862, 6864a, 6864b
Sept. 21, 1993, P.L. 103-82, 42 U.S. Code
§ 6863
Aug. 7, 1998, P.L. 105-220, 42 U.S. Code
§ 6862
Oct. 21, 1998, P.L. 105-277, 42 U.S. Code
§ 6864
Nov. 13, 1998, P.L. 105-388, 42 U.S. Code
§ 6872
Ore. Laws 1977, Ch. 732, §§ 1 to 21

**Energy Conservation and Renewable
Energy Resource Finance Act**
Ark. Code Ann. 1987, 14-167-201 et seq.

Energy Conservation Assistance Act
Cal. Public Resources Code § 25410 et seq.
Pa. Purdon's Stat., Title 62, § 3011

Energy Conservation Bond Act
N.J. Laws 1980, Ch. 68

Energy Conservation Building Code
Ala. Code 1975, § 41-9-170 et seq.

**Energy Conservation Building Standards
Act**
Ga. Code Ann., 8-2-22
Md. Ann. Code 1974, Art. NR, § 7-401 et
seq.

**Energy Conservation Construction Code
Act**
N.Y. Energy Law (Consol. Laws Ch. 17A)
§ 11-101 et seq.

Energy Conservation Endorsement Act
Ark. Code Ann. 1987, 23-3-401 et seq.

Energy Conservation in Building Act
Fla. Stat. 1983, 225.251 et seq.
Me. Rev. Stat. Ann. 1964, Title 5, § 1761 et
seq.
Miss. Code Ann. 1972, § 29-11-1 et seq.
Tex. Rev. Civ. Stat., Art. 601B, § 5.27 et seq.

Energy Conservation in Existing Buildings Act of 1976

Aug. 14, 1976, P.L. 94-385, 42 U.S. Code § 6801 et seq.

Nov. 9, 1978, P.L. 95-619, 42 U.S. Code §§ 6862, 6863, 6865, 6872

June 30, 1980, P.L. 96-294, 42 U.S. Code § 6863 et seq.

Nov. 30, 1983, P.L. 98-181, 42 U.S. Code § 6872

Oct. 17, 1984, P.L. 98-479, 42 U.S. Code § 6863

Oct. 30, 1984, P.L. 98-558, 42 U.S. Code §§ 6862, 6865

February 5, 1988, P.L. 100-242, 42 U.S. Code § 6862

Oct. 19, 1996, P.L. 104-316, 42 U.S. Code § 6881

Energy Conservation Measures for Local Governments Act

Tex. Local Government Code, § 302.001 et seq.

Energy Conservation Programs Act (Local)

Cal. Public Resources Code § 25390 et seq.

Energy Conservation Reauthorization Act of 1998

Nov. 13, 1998, P.L. 105-388, 112 Stat. 3477, 42 U.S. Code § 6201 nt.

Energy Conservation Revolving Loan Fund Act

W. Va. Code 1966, § 31-18A-1 et seq.

Energy Conservation Standards Act

Fla. Stat. Ann., 553.951 et seq.

Energy Conservation Standards for New Buildings Act of 1976

Aug. 14, 1976, P.L. 94-385, 42 U.S. Code § 6801 et seq.

Nov. 9, 1978, P.L. 95-619, 42 U.S. Code § 6836

February 5, 1988, P.L. 100-242, 42 U.S. Code § 6832

Energy Conservation through Improved Transportation Bond Act

N.Y. Laws 1979, Ch. 369

Energy Conversion and Transmission Facility Siting Act

N.D. Cent. Code, 49-22-01 et seq.

Energy Coordinating Council Act

Colo. Rev. Stat., 2-3-1101 et seq.

Energy Corridors Act

Haw. Rev. Stat. Ann., § 277-1 et seq.

Energy Crisis Management Act

R.I. Gen. Laws 1956, 42-60-1 et seq.

Energy Department Act

Ky. Rev. Stat. 1971, 152A.011 et seq.

N.J. Stat. Ann., 52:27F-1 et seq.

Energy Development Act

Neb. Rev. Stat. 1943, 66-801 et seq.

Tex. Rev. Civ. Stat., Art. 4413(47a), 4413(47b)

Energy Education and Marketing Act

Okla. Stat. Ann., Title 52, § 288.1 et seq.

Energy Efficiency Act (Public Building)

N.M. Stat. Ann., 6-23-1 et seq.

Energy Efficiency and Conservation Act

Fla. Stat. Ann., 366.80 et seq.

Energy Efficiency Building Performance Standards Act

Me. Rev. Stat. Ann. 1964, Title 10, § 1411 et seq.

Energy-Efficiency Rating Act (Building)

Fla. Stat. Ann., 553.990 et seq.

Energy Efficiency Standard Act (Buildings)

S.C. Code Ann. 1976, § 6-10-10 et seq.

Energy Emergency Powers Act

N.M. Stat. Ann., 12-12-1 et seq.

Wyo. Stat. 1957, § 9-32.5 et seq.

Energy Emergency Preparedness Act of 1982

Aug. 8, 1982, P.L. 97-229, 42 U.S. Code §§ 6201 nt., 6234 nt., 6239, 6240, 6247, 6271, 6272, 6281, 6385

Energy Employment Act
Mich. Comp. Laws Ann., 460.801 et seq.

Energy Facility Finance and Resource Recovery Act
N.C. Gen. Stat. 1943, § 159F-1 et seq.

Energy Facility Permit Act
S.D. Codified Laws 1967, 49-41B-1 et seq.

Energy Facility Siting Act
Ore. Rev. Stat., 469.300 et seq.

Energy Fair Practices Act (Emergency)
N.J. Stat. Ann., 52:27F-16

Energy Finance Authorities Act (Municipal)
Colo. Rev. Stat., 35-25-901 et seq.

Energy Financing Act
Md. Ann. Code 1957, Art. 83A, § 6-301 et seq.

Energy Financing Voter Approval Act
Wash. Rev. Code Ann., 80.52.010 et seq.

Energy Impacted Area Assistance Act
La. Rev. Stat. Ann., 30:1351 et seq.

Energy Lifeline Act
Cal. Public Utilities Code § 739

Energy Management Act
La. Rev. Stat. Ann., 39:251 et seq.
Miss. Code Ann. 1972, § 57-39-101 et seq.

Energy Management and Conservation Act
Ala. Code 1975, § 41-6A-1 et seq.

Energy, Minerals and Natural Resources Department Act
N.M. Stat. Ann., 9-5A-1 et seq.

Energy Petroleum Allocation Act of 1973
June 30, 1980, P.L. 96-294, 15 U.S. Code § 753

Energy Policy Act
N.C. Gen. Stat. 1943, §§ 62-2, 113B-1 et seq.

Energy Policy Act of 1992
Oct. 24, 1992, P.L. 102-486, 42 U.S. Code § 13201 nt.
Nov. 2, 1994, P.L. 103-437, 16 U.S. Code § 797 nt.; 25 U.S. Code § 3505
Dec. 21, 1995, P.L. 104-66, 16 U.S. Code § 797 nt.; 42 U.S. Code §§ 6349, 6350, 8262g, 13474
Dec. 29, 1995, P.L. 104-88, 42 U.S. Code § 13369
April 26, 1996, P.L. 104-134, 42 U.S. Code § 2296b-7
Aug. 20, 1996, P.L. 104-188, 26 U.S. Code §§ 142, 468A, 737
Oct. 9, 1996, P.L. 104-259, 42 U.S. Code §§ 2296a, 2296a-2
Oct. 9, 1996, P.L. 104-271, 42 U.S. Code § 13436
July 3, 1997, P.L. 105-23, 42 U.S. Code § 13478
Dec. 2, 1997, P.L. 105-135, 42 U.S. Code § 13556
Oct. 7, 1998, P.L. 105-245, 42 U.S. Code § 13503
Oct. 21, 1998, P.L. 105-277, 42 U.S. Code § 13220
Nov. 10, 1998, P.L. 105-362, 42 U.S. Code §§ 6349, 6350, 13295, 13435, 13451 nt., 13552
Nov. 13, 1998, P.L. 105-388, 25 U.S. Code § 3503; 42 U.S. Code §§ 2296a, 2296a-2, 13218, 13220

Energy Policy and Conservation Act
Dec. 22, 1975, P.L. 94-163, 89 Stat. 871, 12 U.S. Code § 1904 nt., 15 U.S. Code §§ 753 to 755, 757 to 760h, 792, 796, 2001 to 2012; 42 U.S. Code §§ 6201, 6202, 6211 to 6214, 6231 to 6246, 6261 to 6263, 6271 to 6275, 6291 to 6309, 6321 to 6326, 6341 to 6346, 6361 to 6363, 6381 to 6384, 6391 to 6401, 6421, 6422; 50 Appx. U.S. Code § 2071
July 21, 1977, P.L. 95-70, 42 U.S. Code §§ 6246, 6309
Sept. 18, 1978, P.L. 95-372, 42 U.S. Code § 6213
Nov. 9, 1978, P.L. 95-619, 42 U.S. Code §§ 6202, 6215, 6293 to 6296, 6303 et seq., 6325, 6341 et seq., 6361
Continued

Nov. 9, 1978, P.L. 95-620, 42 U.S. Code § 6211

June 30, 1979, P.L. 96-30, 42 U.S. Code § 6272

Sept. 29, 1979, P.L. 96-72, 42 U.S. Code §§ 6212, 6274

Nov. 15, 1979, P.L. 96-102, 42 U.S. Code §§ 6261, 6261 nt., 6262, 6263, 6422

Nov. 30, 1979, P.L. 96-133, 42 U.S. Code § 6272

June 30, 1980, P.L. 96-294, 42 U.S. Code § 6240

April 1, 1982, P.L. 97-163, 42 U.S. Code 6272(j)

June 1, 1982, P.L. 97-190, 42 U.S. Code 6272(j)

July 19, 1982, P.L. 97-217, § 42 U.S. Code § 6272

Aug. 8, 1982, P.L. 97-229, 42 U.S. Code §§ 6201 nt., 6234 nt., 6239, 6240, 6247, 6271, 6272, 6281, 6385

March 20, 1984, P.L. 98-239, 42 U.S. Code § 6272

July 18, 1984, P.L. 98-370, 42 U.S. Code §§ 6276, 6276 nt.

Oct. 5, 1984, P.L. 98-454, 98 Stat. 1736, 42 U.S. Code § 6202

July 2, 1985, P.L. 99-58, 42 U.S. Code §§ 6239, 6240, 6241, 6247, 6251, 6272, 6285

Aug. 15, 1985, P.L. 99-88, 42 U.S. Code § 6240

April 7, 1986, P.L. 99-272, 42 U.S. Code § 6240

Oct. 21, 1986, P.L. 99-509, 42 U.S. Code §§ 6240, 6245, 6341 to 6346

March 3, 1987, P.L. 100-12, 42 U.S. Code §§ 6291 to 6297, 6299, 6302, 6303, 6305, 6306, 6308, 6309

June 28, 1988, P.L. 100-357, 42 U.S. Code §§ 6291 to 6295, 6297 Oct. 14, 1988, P.L. 100-494, 42 U.S. Code §§ prec. 6374, 6374, 6374a to 6374d 6374 nt.

Nov. 5, 1988, P.L. 100-615, 42 U.S. Code § 6361

Dec. 11, 1989, P.L. 101-218, 42 U.S. Code § 6276

March 31, 1990, P.L. 101-262, 42 U.S. Code §§ 6251, 6285; 50 U.S. Code Appx. § 2071 nt.

Aug. 10, 1990, P.L. 101-360, 42 U.S. Code §§ 6251, 6285; 50 U.S. Code Appx. § 2071 nt.

Sept. 15, 1990, P.L. 101-383, 42 U.S. Code §§ 6202, 6232, 6239, 6240, 6241, 6247, 6249 to 6249c, 6251, 6285; 50 Appx. § 2071 nt.

Oct. 18, 1990, P.L. 101-440, 42 U.S. Code §§ 6322 to 6327, 6371, 6371e, 6371f

Nov. 14, 1990, P.L. 101-548, 42 U.S. Code § 6240

Oct. 24, 1992, P.L. 102-486, 42 U.S. Code §§ 6201, 6234, 6237, 6240, 6241, 6247, 6249, 6276, 6291 to 6297, 6307, 6311, 6313 to 6317, 6322, 6323, 6325, 6374 to 6374c

July 5, 1994, P.L. 103-272, 42 U.S. Code § 6362

Oct. 22, 1994, P.L. 103-406, 42 U.S. Code §§ 6251, 6285

Dec. 21, 1995, P.L. 104-66, 42 U.S. Code §§ 6240, 6245, 6272, 6325, 6374

Feb. 10, 1996, P.L. 104-106, 42 U.S. Code § 6392

Oct. 14, 1996, P.L. 104-306, 42 U.S. Code §§ 6246, 6251, 6276, 6285

Oct. 19, 1996, P.L. 104-316, 42 U.S. Code § 6382

Aug. 5, 1997, P.L. 105-33, 42 U.S. Code § 247a

June 1, 1998, P.L. 105-177, 42 U.S. Code §§ 6234, 6246, 6251, 6271, 6272, 6285

Oct. 7, 1998, P.L. 105-244, 42 U.S. Code § 6322. E

Nov. 13, 1998, P.L. 105-388, 42 U.S. Code §§ 6241, 6292, 6294, 6325, 6295, 6306, 6316, 6322, 6371, 6371c, 6371f, 6371i, 6372c, 6372h, 6374, 6383, 6422, 6802; 50 U.S. Code Appx. § 2071 nt.

Energy Policy and Conservation Act Extension Amendment of 1990

March 31, 1990, P.L. 101-262, 42 U.S. Code § 6201 nt.

Oct. 22, 1994, P.L. 103-406, 42 U.S. Code § 6201 nt.

Energy Policy and Conservation Act Short-Term Extension Amendment of 1990

Aug. 10, 1990, P.L. 101-360, 42 U.S. Code § 6201 nt.

Energy Policy and Conservation Amendments Act of 1985

July 2, 1985, P.L. 99-58, 42 U.S. Code §§ 6201 nt., 6239 to 6241, 6247, 6251, 6272, 6285, 7277, 7277 nt., 50 U.S. Code Appx. § 2071 nt.

Energy Policy and Planning Act

Ill. Rev. Stat. 1991, Ch. 96 1/2, § 7801 et seq.

Tex. Rev. Civ. Stat., Art. 4413(47a)

Energy Policy Conservation Act

June 25, 1999, P.L. 106-36, 42 U.S. Code §§ 2296b, 2296b-6

June 25, 1999, P.L. 106-36, 42 U.S. Code § 6374

Energy Producing and Solid Waste Disposal Service Act (Metro East)

Ill. Rev. Stat. 1991, Ch. 111 1/2, § 7101 et seq.

Energy Reorganization Act of 1974

Aug. 9, 1975, P.L. 94-79, 89 Stat. 414, 42 U.S. Code § 5841

June 3, 1977, P.L. 95-39, 42 U.S. Code § 5913 et seq.

Dec. 13, 1977, P.L. 95-209, 42 U.S. Code § 5841 et seq.

Feb. 25, 1978, P.L. 95-238, 42 U.S. Code § 5821

Nov. 6, 1978, P.L. 95-601, 42 U.S. Code § 5849

Aug. 22, 1986, P.L. 99-386, 42 U.S. Code § 5841

Oct. 24, 1992, P.L. 102-486, 42 U.S. Code §§ 5813, prec. 5841, 5851

Nov. 2, 1994, P.L. 103-437, 42 U.S. Code § 5821

Dec. 21, 1995, P.L. 104-66, 42 U.S. Code § 5848

Oct. 17, 1998, P.L. 105-261, 42 U.S. Code § 5842

Ark. Code Ann. 1987, 15-10-201 et seq.

Energy Research and Development Administration Authorization Act for Fiscal year 1977

Feb. 10, 1996, P.L. 104-106, 42 U.S. Code § 5816a

Energy Research and Development Authority Act

N.Y. Public Authorities Law (Consol. Laws Ch. 43A) § 1850 et seq.

Energy Research and Development Institute Act

N.M. Stat. Ann., 71-4-9 et seq.

Energy Research, Demonstration, and Development Program (Local Interest)

Cal. Public Resources Code § 25620 et seq.

Energy Research, Development, Demonstration and Commercialization Act

Cal. Public Resources Code § 25645 et seq.

Energy Resources Act

Me. Rev. Stat. Ann. 1964, Title 5, § 5001 et seq.

N.M. Stat. Ann. 1953, 65-13-1 et seq.

Energy Resources and Conservation Act

Miss. Code Ann. 1972, § 49-2-41 et seq.

Okla. Stat. Ann., Title 52, § 601 et seq.

Energy Resources Conservation and Development Act

Cal. Public Resources Code § 25000 et seq.

Energy Resources Shortages Act

D.C. Code Ann., § 6-1501 et seq.

Energy Resources Surcharge Bill of Rights

Cal. Revenue and Taxation Code § 40200 et seq.

Energy Resources Surcharge Law

Cal. Revenue and Taxation Code § 40001 et seq.

Energy Safety and Environmental Coordination Act of 1974

June 22, 1974, P.L. 93-319, 88 Stat. 246, 15 U.S. Code §§ 791 to 798; 42 U.S. Code §§ 1857b-1, 1857c-5, 1857c-8 to 1857c-10, 1857d-1, 1857f-1, 1857f-6e 1857f-6f, 1857f-7, 1857h-5, 1957l

Energy Savings Act (Guaranteed)
Pa. Cons. Stat., Title 62, § 3751 et seq.

Energy Savings Tax Incentives Act
Ark. Stat. 1947, 84-2093 et seq.

Energy Security Act
June 30, 1980, P.L. 96-294, 42 U.S. Code
§§ 8701 et seq., 8701 nt.
Oct. 24, 1992, P.L. 102-486, 42 U.S. Code
§§ 7361 to 7364
Oct. 28, 1992, P.L. 102-550, 12 U.S. Code
§ 3601 et seq.

**Energy Supply and Environmental
Coordination Act of 1974**
Dec. 22, 1975, P.L. 94-163, 89 Stat. 875, 15
U.S. Code §§ 792, 796
July 21, 1977, P.L. 95-70, 15 U.S. Code
§ 792
Nov. 9, 1978, P.L. 95-620, 15 U.S. Code
§ 796

Energy Tax Act of 1978
Nov. 9, 1978, P.L. 95-618, 26 U.S. Code §§ 1
nt., 39, 44C, 46 to 48, 56, 57, 120 nt., 124,
167, 263, 465, 613, 613A, 614, 1016, 1254,
4041, 4061 4063, 4064 nt., 4081, 4217,
4221, 4222, 4293, 4483, 6096, 6411, 6412,
6421, 6424, 6427, 6504, 6675

**Energy Tax Receipts Property Tax Relief
Act**
N.J. Stat. Ann., 52:27D-438 et seq.

Energy/Fusion Technology Act
Utah Code Ann. 1953, 9-2-801 et seq.

Enforce Payments Act (Actions to)
Ill. Comp. Stat. 1992, Ch. 815, § 115/0.01 et
seq.

Enforcement Act (Commodities)
Miss. Code Ann. 1972, § 75-89-1 et seq.

Enforcement Act (Embargo)
Jan. 9, 1809, Ch. 5, 2 Stat. 506

Enforcement Act (Family Obligations)
W. Va. Code 1966 § 48A-1-1 et seq.

Enforcement Act (Hazardous Waste)
Cal. Health and Safety Code § 25160

**Enforcement Act (Liquid Fuels and Fuel Use
Tax)**
Pa. Cons. Stat., Title 75, § 9401 et seq.

Enforcement Act (Prohibition)
Okla. Stat. Ann., Title 37, § 81 et seq.

Enforcement Act (Software License)
La. Rev. Stat. Ann., 51:1961 et seq.

**Enforcement Act (Support and Parenting
Time)**
Mich. Comp. Laws Ann., 552.601 et seq.

Enforcement Act (Tariff)
Mar 2, 1833, Ch. 57, 4 Stat. 632

Enforcement Acts (Civil Rights)
See Civil Rights Acts

**Enforcement and Establishment of Child
Support Administrative Procedure Act**
Colo. Rev. Stat., 26-13.5-101 et seq.

**Enforcement and Prevention of Street
Terrorism Act**
Fla. Stat. Ann., 874.01 et seq.

**Enforcement of County Codes and
Resolutions Code**
Kan. Stat. Ann., 19-4701 et seq.

Enforcement of Fair Labor Standards Act
Cal. Labor Code § 50.6

**Enforcement of Food Handling Regulation
Act**
Ill. Rev. Stat. 1991, Ch. 56 1/2, § 330 et seq.

Enforcement of Foreign Judgments Act
See also Uniform Enforcement of Foreign
Judgments Act
Ala. Acts 1986, 1st Sp. No. 713
Md. Ann. Code 1974, Art. CJ, § 11-801 et
seq.
Mont. Laws 1991, Ch. 66
W. Va. Code 1966 § 55-14-1 et seq.

Enforcement of Income Withholding for Support Obligations Act
S.C. Code Ann. 1976, § 20-7-1315 et seq.

Enforcement of Judgments Act
Cal. Code of Civil Procedure § 680.010 et seq.

Enforcement of Support Act
Cal. Code of Civil Procedure § 1650 et seq.
Fla. Stat. Ann., 88.011 et seq.
Mass. Gen. Laws Ann., 273A:1 et seq.
Minn. Stat. Ann., 518C.01 et seq.
N.D. Cent. Code, 14-12.1-01 et seq.
N.M. Stat. Ann., 40-4A-1 et seq.
Ohio Rev. Code 1953, 3115.01 et seq.
Pa. Cons. Stat., Title 23, § 4501 et seq.
S.C. Code Ann. 1976, § 20-7-960 et seq.
S.D. Codified Laws 1967, 25-9A-1 et seq.
Tex. Family Code, § 21.01 et seq.

Enforcement of Support Act (Reciprocal, Revised)
See Revised Uniform Reciprocal Enforcement of Support Act

Enforcement of Support Act (Reciprocal)
See Uniform Reciprocal Enforcement of Support Act

Enforcement of Support Act (Revised)
Ill. Rev. Stat. 1991, Ch. 40, § 1201 et seq.
Me. Rev. Stat. Ann. 1964, Title 19, § 331 et seq.
Mich. Comp. Laws Ann., 780.151 et seq.
Nev. Rev. Stat. Ann., 130.010 et seq.
N.M. Stat. Ann., 40-6-1 et seq.

Enforcement Procedure Act (Collegiate Athletic Association Compliance)
Fla. Stat. Ann., 240.5339 et seq.

Enforcement Procedures for Town Planning Board Regulations Law
N.Y. Local Laws 1972, Town of Olive, p. 2249

Enforcement Procedures Law
N.Y. Local Laws 1969, Town of Perinton, p. 1920

Enforcement Tax Act (Intoxicating Liquors)
Ind. Code 1971, 7-4-1-1

Enfranchisement of Ex-Felons Voting Act
D.C. Code Ann., § 1-1302

Engel, Downing and Fite Act (Navigable Waterway and Flood Control)
Ala. Code 1975, § 33-17-1 et seq.

Engel-Ellis Act (Engineering and Land Surveying)
Ala. Code 1975, §§ 34-11-1, 34-11-4

Engine Cab Handrail Law
Cal. Labor Code § 6952

Engine Repair and Aircraft Maintenance Facilites State Financing Act
Minn. Stat. Ann., 116R.01 et seq.

Engine Tender Clearance Law
Cal. Labor Code §§ 6950, 6951

Engineer and Architect Selection Act
N.M. Stat. Ann., 13-1-119 et seq.

Engineer, Land Surveyor and Geologist Registration Law
Pa. 1992 Pamph. Laws, No. 151

Engineered Plants Law (Genetically)
Minn. Stat. Ann., 18F.01 et seq.

Engineering and Architectural Services Act
Md. Ann. Code 1957, Art. 21, § 9-101 et seq. § 9-101 et seq.
Md. Ann. Code 1974, Art. SF, § 13-101 et seq.

Engineering and Land Surveying Practice Act
N.M. Stat. Ann., 61-23-1 et seq.

Engineering, Architectural and Land Surveying Qualifications Based Selection Act
Ill. Rev. Stat 1991, Ch. 127, § 4151-1 et seq.

Engineering, Architectural and Land Surveying Services Procurement Act
Wyo. Stat. Ann., § 9-2-1027 et seq.

Engineering Licensing Act (Structural)
Ill. Rev. Stat. 1991, Ch. 111, § 6601 et seq.

Engineering Practice Act
Colo. Rev. Stat., 12-25-101 et seq.
N.D. Cent. Code, 43-19.1-01 et seq.
Tex. Rev. Civ. Stat., Art. 3271a

Engineering Practice Act (Professional)
Ill. Rev. Stat. 1991, Ch. 111, § 5201 et seq.

Engineering School Equipment Act
Pa. Purdon's Stat., Title 24, § 5901 et seq.

Engineers Act
Cal. Business and Professions Code § 6700 et seq.
Del. Code of 1974, Title 24, § 2801 et seq.
Ky. Rev. Stat. 1971, 322.010 et seq.
Md. Ann. Code 1974, Art. BO, § 14-101 et seq.
Mich. Comp. Laws Ann., 338.551 et seq.
N.H. Rev. Stat. 1955, 310-A:2 et seq.
Okla. Stat. Ann., Title 59, § 475.1 et seq.
Ore. Rev. Stat., 672.002 et seq.
R.I. Gen. Laws 1956, 5-8-1 et seq.
Vt. Stat. Ann., Title 26, § 1161 et seq.

Engineers Act (Professional)
Fla. Stat. Ann., 471.001 et seq.

Engineers and Architects Regulation Act
Neb. Laws 1997, L.B. 622, §§ 1 to 55

Engineers and Highway Superintendent Liability Act (County)
Ill. Comp. Stat. 1992, Ch. 745, § 15/0.01 et seq.

Engineers and Land Surveyors Registration Act
Ind. Code Ann., 25-31-1-1 et seq.
N.C. Gen. Stat. 1943, § 89c-1 et seq.
Ohio Rev. Code 1953, 4733.01 et seq.
Pa. Purdon's Stat., Title 63, § 148 et seq.

Engineers, Architects and Surveyors Examining Board Act
P.R. Laws Ann. 1954, Title 20, § 711 et seq.

Engineers, Land Surveyors and Architects Registration Act
Alaska Stat. 1962, § 08.48.011 et seq.

Engineers Licensing Act
Pa. Purdon's Stat., Title 63, § 148 et seq.

Engineers' Registration Act
Ala. Code 1975, § 34-11-30 et seq.
D.C. Code Ann., § 2-2301 et seq.
Mont. Code Ann., 37-67-101 et seq.
Nev. Rev. Stat. 1979 Reprint, 625.010 et seq.
N.M. Stat. Ann., 61-23-4 et seq.
Tex. Rev. Civ. Stat., Art. 3271a
Wash. Rev. Code Ann., 18.43.010 et seq.

Engineers Registration Act (Professional)
Mass. Gen. Laws Ann., 112:81D et seq.

Engle Act (Minerals)
See Mining Claims Rights Restoration Act Of 1955

Englewood Charter
N.J. Laws 1978, Ch. 123

English Fluency in Higher Education Act
Pa. Purdon's Stat., Title 24., § 6801 et seq.

English Fluency in Higher Learning Act
S.C. Code Ann. 1976, § 59-103-160

English Language Acquisition Program
Cal. Education Code 1976, § 400 et seq.

English Language Proficiency Act
Colo. Rev. Stat., 22-24-101 et seq.

Engstrom-Jenema-Milliken Act (Cherry Production)
Mich. Comp. Laws Ann., 290.501 et seq.

Enhanced Access to Public Records Act
Mich. Comp. Laws Ann., 15.441 et seq.

Enhanced Oil Recovery Act
N.M. Stat. Ann., 7-29A-1 et seq.

Enhanced Penalty Act
Ore. Rev. Stat. 1953, 168.015 et seq.

Enhanced 911 Act
N.M. Stat. Ann., 63-9D-6 et seq.

Enhanced 911 Service District Act (Lowndes County)
Ga. Laws 1991, p. 4842

Enhancement Act (Habitual Criminals)
Tex. Penal Code, §§ 12.42, 12.43

Enhancement and Management of Fish and Wildlife and Their Habitation Private Lands Act
Cal. Fish and Game Code 1957, § 3400 et seq.

Enhancement Deposit Act (Student Educational)
Me. Rev. Stat. Ann. 1964, 20-A, § 12601 et seq.

Enlarged Homestead Acts
Feb. 19, 1909, Ch. 160, 35 Stat. 639, 43 U.S. Code § 218
June 17, 1910, Ch. 298, 36 Stat. 531, 43 U.S. Code § 219
Feb. 11, 1913, Ch. 39, 37 Stat. 666, 43 U.S. Code § 219
Dec. 29, 1916, Ch. 9, 39 Stat. 862, 43 U.S. Code §§ 291 to 301
March 4, 1923, Ch. 245, 42 Stat. 1445, 43 U.S. Code §§ 222, 302

Enlisted Men Status Act
July 14, 1939, Ch. 267, 53 Stat. 1001

Enoch Arden Law
Cal. Civil Code § 61, Subd. 2
N.Y. Domestic Relations Law (Consol. Laws Ch. 14) §§ 7a, 220, 221
Okla. Stat. 1981, Title 58, § 941 et seq.

Enrollment Acts (Civil War)
See Selective Draft Acts

Enrollment of Pupils Act
N.C. Gen. Stat. 1943, § 115C-364 et seq.

Enrollment Options Act (Post-Secondary)
Me. Rev. Stat. Ann. 1964, Title 20-A, § 4751 et seq.

Enrollment Options Act (Postsecondary)
Ind. Code Ann., 261C.1 et seq.
Me. Rev. Stat. Ann. 1964, Title 20-A, § 4751 et seq.
Minn. Stat. Ann., 123.3514

Entails Statute
Ill. Rev. Stat. 1991, Ch. 30, § 5

Enterprise Act (Drug Trafficking)
Ala. Code 1975, § 13A-12-233

Enterprise Act (Heritage)
Mont. Code Ann., 20-26-1401 et seq.

Enterprise Community Development Corporation Act
Mich. Comp. Laws Ann., 125.2601 et seq.

Enterprise Corporation Act
N.C. Gen. Stat. 1943, § 53A-35 et seq.

Enterprise for the Americas Act of 1992
Oct. 28, 1992, P.L. 102-549, 22 U.S. Code § 2151 nt.

Enterprise for the Americas Initiative Act of 1992
Oct. 27, 1992, P.L. 102-532, 7 U.S. Code § 1691 nt.

Enterprise Protection Act (Animal)
Fla. Stat. Ann., 828.40 et seq.

Enterprise Zone Act
Ala. Acts 1991, p. 897
Ark. Code Ann. 1987, 15-4-801 et seq.
Cal. Government Code § 7070 et seq.
Fla. Stat. Ann., 290.001 et seq.
Ill. Rev. Stat. 1991, Ch. 67 1/2, § 601 et seq.
Kan. Stat. Ann.,74-50,113 et seq.
La. Rev. Stat. Ann., 51:1781 et seq.
Mich. Comp. Laws Ann., 125.2101 et seq.
Continued

Miss. Code Ann. 1972, § 57-61-13 et seq.
Neb. Rev. Stat. 1943, 13-2101 to 13-2112
N.M. Stat. Ann., 5-9-1 et seq.
Okla. Stat. Ann., Title 62, § 690.1 et seq.
Ore. Rev. Stat., 284.115 et seq.
S.C. Code Ann. 1976, § 11-11-410 et seq.
S.C. Code Ann. 1976, § 12-10-10 et seq.
Tenn. Public Acts 1984, Ch. 993
Tex. Government Code, § 2303.001 et seq.
Utah Code Ann. 1953, 9-2-401 et seq.
Va. Code 1950, § 59.1-270 et seq.

Enterprise Zone Act (Neighborhood)
Mich. Comp. Laws Ann., 207.771 et seq.

Enterprise Zone Employment Act
Ga. Code Ann., 36-88-1 et seq.

Enterprise Zone Loan Act
Ill. Rev. Stat. 1991, Ch. 67 1/2, § 618 et seq.

Enterprise Zone Municipal Tax Exemption Reimbursement Act
Pa. Purdon's Stat., Title 72, § 4729-1 et seq.

Entire Contract Act (Insurance)
Ore. Rev. Stat. 1989, 742.016

Entomological Commission Act
Kan. Stat. Ann., 74-511 et seq.

Entomologist Act
Colo. Rev. Stat., 35-4-101 et seq.

Entomology Act
Ga. Code Ann., 2-7-1 et seq.

Entrepreneur Development Act
R.I. Gen. Laws 1956, 44-43-1 et seq.

Entrepreneurial Training and Self-Employment Assistance Act
N.J. Stat. Ann., 43:21-67 et seq.

Entry After Notice Act
Ala. Code 1975, § 13A-7-2

Entry and Detainer Act
Colo. Rev. Stat., 13-40-101 et seq.

Entry on Adjoining Land to Accomplish Repairs Act
Ill. Rev. Stat. 1991, Ch. 30, §§ 1050, 1051

Entry or Re-entry Rights Act
Ill. Rev. Stat. 1991, Ch. 30, § 37a.9 et seq.

Environment Cleanup and Responsibility (Comprehensive)
Mont. Code Ann. 1987, 75-10-701 et seq.

Environment Department Act
N.M. Stat. Ann., 9-7A-1 et seq.

Environmental Act (Public Policy)
P.R. Laws Ann. 1954, Title 12, § 1121 et seq.

Environmental Affairs Act
La. Rev. Stat. Ann., 30:2001 et seq.

Environmental Aid Act
N.J. Stat. Ann., 13:1H-1 et seq.

Environmental and Industrial Pollution Control Facilities Financing Authority Act
P.R. Laws Ann. 1954, Title 12, § 1251 et seq.

Environmental and Land Recycling Remediation Standards Act
Pa. Purdon's Stat., Title 35, § 6026.101 et seq.

Environmental and Land Use Dispute Resolution Act
Fla. Stat. Ann., 70.51

Environmental and Natural Resources Protection Act
Mich. Comp. Laws Ann., 324.101 et seq.

Environmental Assessment Act (Industrial Sites)
Pa. Purdon's Stat., Title 35, § 6028.1 et seq.

Environmental Audit Act (Voluntary)
Mont. Code Ann., 75-1-1201 et seq.

Environmental Barriers Act
Ill. Rev. Stat. 1991, Ch. 111 1/2, sect. 3711 et seq.

Environmental Cleanup and Fee Reform Act
Cal. Health and Safety Code § 25143 et seq.
Cal. Revenue and Taxation Code §§ 43053 to 43055, 43101, 43152.16

Environmental Cleanup and Responsibilities Act (Comprehensive)
Mont. Code Ann., 75-10-701 et seq.

Environmental Cleanup Responsibility Act
N.J. Stat. Ann., 13:1K-6 et seq.

Environmental Compact Act (Interstate)
See Interstate Environmental Compact Act

Environmental Compliance Act
N.M. Stat. Ann., 74-7-1 et seq.
S.D. Laws 1988, Ch. 290, § 40 to 66

Environmental Conservation Law
N.Y. Consol. Laws Ch. 43B

Environmental Consortium Act
La. Rev. Stat. Ann., 30:1150.90 et seq.

Environmental Control Act
Ill. Rev. Stat. 1991, Ch. 111 1/2, § 1001 et seq.
Vt. Stat. Ann., Title 10, § 6081 et seq.

Environmental Control Act (Loxahatchee River)
Fla. Special Laws 1971, Ch. 71-822

Environmental Control Act (Martin County)
Fla. Special Laws 1978, Ch. 78-560

Environmental Control Act (Palm Beach County)
Fla. Special Laws 1970, Ch. 70-862
Fla. Special Laws 1977, Ch. 616

Environmental Control Act (St. Lucie County)
Fla. Laws 1983, Ch. 83-511

Environmental Control Compact Act
La. Rev. Stat. Ann., 40:2331

Environmental Coordination Act
Va. Code 1950, § 10-17.31 et seq.

Environmental Coordination Act (Water Project)
Kan. Stat. Ann., 82a-325 et seq.

Environmental Coordination Procedures Act
Minn. Stat. Ann., 116C.22 et seq.
Wash. Rev. Code Ann., 90.62.010 et seq.

Environmental Crimes Act
Okla. Stat. Ann., Title 21, § 1230.1 et seq.

Environmental Disclosure Act
Haw. Rev. Stat. Ann., § 343D-1 et seq.

Environmental Education Act
Oct. 30, 1970, P.L. 91-516, 84 Stat. 1312, 20 U.S. Code §§ 1531 to 1536
May 10, 1974, P.L. 93-278, 88 Stat. 121, 20 U.S. Code §§ 1531, 1532, 1536
Fla. Stat. Ann., 229.8055
Ga. Laws 1974, p. 1113
La. Rev. Stat. Ann., 33:2501 et seq.
Mich. Comp. Laws Ann., 229.31 et seq.
N.C. Gen. Stat. 1943, § 143B-285.20 et seq.
N.J. Stat. Ann., 18A:6-80 et seq.
Pa. Purdon's Stat., Title 35, § 7521 et seq.

Environmental Education Act of 1978
Oct. 17, 1979, P.L. 96-88, 20 U.S. Code § 3012

Environmental Education and Information Act
N.C. Laws 1973, Ch. 619

Environmental Efficiency Act
Fla. Stat. Ann., 403.814 et seq.

Environmental Emergencies Fund Act
P.R. Laws Ann. 1954, Title 12, § 1271 et seq.

Environmental Enforcement Act
Minn. Laws 1991, Ch. 347, Arts. 1, 3
R.I. Public Laws 1991, Ch. 535

Environmental Export Promotion Act of 1994
Oct. 22, 1994, P.L. 103-392, 15 U.S. Code § 4701 nt.

Environmental Facilities Authority Act
Ga. Code Ann., 50-23-1 et seq.

Environmental Facilities Authority Act (Local Government)
La. Rev. Stat. Ann., 33:4548.1 et seq.

Environmental Facilities Corporation Act
N.Y. Public Authorities Law (Consol. Laws Ch. 43A) § 1280 et seq.

Environmental Facilities Financing Act
Ill. Rev. Stat. 1991, Ch. 127, § 721 et seq.

Environmental Farming Act (Cannella)
Cal. Food and Agricultural Code § 560 et seq.

Environmental Fee Accountability Act
N.J. Stat. Ann., 52:27B-20.1 et seq.

Environmental Flexibility Act (Small Community)
Colo. Rev. Stat., 25-19-101 et seq.

Environmental Health Act (County)
N.J. Stat. Ann., 26:3A2-1 et seq.

Environmental Health Act (Public Water and Wastewater)
Tenn. Code Ann., 68-221-101 et seq.

Environmental, Health, and Safety Audit Privilege Act
Tex. Rev. Civ. Stat., Art. 4447cc et seq.

Environmental Hearing Board Act
Pa. Purdon's Stat., Title 35, § 7511 et seq.

Environmental Impact Fee Law
Ill. Comp. Stat. 1992, Ch. 415, § 125/301 et seq.

Environmental Impact Statement Act
N.J. Stat. Ann., 52:13F-1 et seq.

N.Y. Environmental Conservation Law 1972 (Consol. Laws Ch. 43B) §§ 8-0105, 8-0109 et seq.

Environmental Improvement Act
N.M. Stat. Ann., 74-1-1 et seq.

Environmental Improvement Authorities Act
Ala. Code 1975, § 9-6-1 et seq.

Environmental Improvement Compact
Pa. Purdon's Stat., Title 53, § 11400-101 et seq.

Environmental Improvement Compact Act
Pa. Cons. Stat., Title 53, § 2501 et seq.

Environmental Infrastructure Trust Act
N.J. Stat. Ann., 58:11B-1 et seq.

Environmental Justice Act
Ga. Code Ann., 12-17-1 et seq.

Environmental Laboratory Certification Program Act
Ark. Code Ann. 1987, 8-2-201 et seq.

Environmental Laboratory Improvement Act
Cal. Health and Safety Code §§ 1010, 1029

Environmental Land and Water Management Act
Fla. Stat. Ann., 380.012 et seq.

Environmental Law Enforcement Act
N.D. Cent. Code, 32-40-01 et seq.

Environmental Lead Hazard Control Act
Neb. Rev. Stat. 1943, 71-6318

Environmental Leadership Act
Colo. Rev. Stat., 25-6.7-101 et seq.

Environmental Legal Resources Act
Ill. Rev. Stat. 1991, Ch. 14, § 251 et seq.

Environmental Management Act
Ala. Code 1975, § 22-22A-1 et seq.

Environmental Management and Natural Resources Council Law
N.D. Laws. 1961, Ch. 326

Environmental Management Council Law
N.Y. Local Laws 1973, Village at Monticello, p. 3587

Environmental Opportunity Zone Act
N.J. Stat. Ann., 54:4-3.150 et seq.

Environmental Permitting Act
See Uniform Environmental Permitting Act

Environmental Pesticide Control Act
Wyo. Stat. Ann., § 35-7-350 et seq.

Environmental Policy Act
Ga. Code Ann., 12-16-1 et seq.
Mass. Gen. Laws Ann., 30:61, 30:62
Md. Ann. Code 1974, Art. NR, § 1-301 et seq.
Minn. Stat. Ann., 116D.01 et seq.
Mont. Code Ann., 75-1-101 et seq.
N.C. Gen. Stat. 1943, § 113A-1 et seq.
S.D. Codified Laws 1967, 34A-9-1 et seq.
Wash. Rev. Code Ann., 43.21C.010 et seq.

Environmental Policy and Conflict Resolution Act of 1998
Feb. 11, 1998, P.L. 105-156, 20 U.S. Code § 5601 nt.

Environmental Preservation and Oil Spill Cleanup Act
Tenn. Code Ann., 68-216-101 et seq.

Environmental Procedures Coordination Act
Alaska Stat. 1962, § 46.35.010 et seq.

Environmental Programs Assistance Act of 1984
June 12, 1984, P.L. 98-313, 42 U.S. Code § 4368a, 4368a nt.
Oct. 21, 1998, P.L. 105-277, 42 U.S. Code § 4368a

Environmental Protection Act
Conn. Gen. Stat. 1983, § 22a-14 et seq.

Fla. Stat. Ann., 403.412
Ill. Rev. Stat. 1991, Ch. 111 1/2, § 1001 et seq.
Mich. Comp. Laws Ann., 691.1201 et seq.
Neb. Rev. Stat. 1943, 81-1501 et seq.
N.J. Stat. Ann., 13:1D-1 et seq.
N.Y. Environmental Conservation Law 1972 (Consol. Laws Ch. 43B) §§ 27-0109, 54-0101 et seq.
N.Y. Local Laws 1972, Town of Lake George, p. 1964
N.Y. Public Lands Law (Consol. Laws Ch. 46) § 23
N.Y. Real Property Actions and Proceedings Law (Consol. Laws Ch. 81) § 543
N.Y. State Finance Law 1940 (Consol. Laws Ch. 56) § 92s
N.Y. Tax Law (Consol. Laws Ch. 60) §§ 171a, 1421
S.C. Code Ann. 1962, § 58-1801 et seq.
S.D. Codified Laws 1967, 34A-10-1 et seq.

Environmental Protection Act (Employer Assistance)
W. Va. Code 1966 § 21-3B-1 et seq.

Environmental Protection Act (Hillsborough County)
Fla. Special Laws 1967, Ch. 67-1504
Fla. Special Laws 1972, Ch. 72-563
Fla. Special Laws 1984, Ch. 84-446

Environmental Protection Act (Manatee County)
Fla. Laws 1991, Ch. 412

Environmental Protection Act (Second Century)
S.D. Laws 1992, Ch. 254

Environmental Protection Act (Utilities)
Nev. Rev. Stat. 1979 Reprint, 704.820 et seq.

Environmental Protection Act (Utility Facility Siting)
S.C. Code Ann. 1976, § 58-33-10 et seq.

Environmental Protection and Health Act
Ida. Code 1947, 39-101 et seq.

Environmental Protection and Research Act

Cal. Health and Safety Code §§ 39069 to 39074, 39100 et seq.

Cal. Vehicle Code 1959, § 5100 et seq.

Environmental Protection Bond Authorization Act

Mich. Comp. Laws Ann., 299.651 et seq.

Environmental Protection Bond Implementation Act

Mich. Comp. Laws Ann., 299.671 et seq.

Environmental Protection Council Act

Miss. Code Ann. 1972, § 49-21-1 et seq.

Environmental Protection Fund Act

S.C. Code Ann. 1976, § 48-2-10 et seq.

Environmental Protection Fund Act (Taconite)

Minn. Stat. Ann., 298.222 et seq.

Environmental Protection Permit Reform Act

Cal. Public Resources Code § 71000 et seq.

Environmental Protection Trust Fund Act

Ill. Rev. Stat. 1991, Ch. 111 1/2, §§ 1060, 1061

Environmental Quality Act

Ark. Code Ann. 1987, 15-20-301 et seq.

Cal. Public Resources Code § 21000 et seq.

Haw. Rev. Stat. Ann., § 341-1 et seq.

Ind. Code Ann., 455B.101 et seq.

La. Rev. Stat. Ann., 30:1051 et seq.

N.M. Stat. Ann. 1953, 12-20-1 et seq.

Okla. Stat. Ann., Title 27A, § 1-1-101 et seq.

Ore. Rev. Stat., 468.005 et seq.

Va. Code 1950, § 10.1-1200 et seq.

Wyo. Stat. Ann., § 35-11-101 et seq.

Environmental Quality Assessment Act

Cal. Health and Safety Code § 25570 et seq.

Environmental Quality Bond Act

N.Y. Environmental Conservation Law 1972 (Consol. Laws Ch. 43B) §§ 49-0201 et seq., 52-0101 et seq., 54-0101 et seq.

N.Y. Laws 1972, Ch. 658

N.Y. State Finance Law 1940 (Consol. Laws Ch. 56) §§ 61, 97dd

Environmental Quality Bond Implementation Act

N.Y. Environmental Conservation Law 1972 (Consol. Laws Ch. 43B) § 52-0101 et seq.

Environmental Quality Code

Okla. Stat. Ann., Title 27A, § 2-1-101 et seq.

Utah Code Ann. 1953, 19-1-101 et seq.

Environmental Quality Improvement Act

April 3, 1970, P.L. 91-224, 84 Stat. 114, 42 U.S. Code §§ 4371 to 4374

May 18, 1973, P.L. 93-36, 87 Stat. 72, 42 U.S. Code § 4374

July 3, 1975, P.L. 94-52, 89 Stat. 258, 42 U.S. Code § 4374

June 26, 1978, P.L. 95-300, 42 U.S. Code § 4374

Oct. 18, 1982, P.L. 97-350, 42 U.S. Code § 4374

Oct. 30, 1984, P.L. 98-581, 42 U.S. Code §§ 4374, 4375

Environmental Quality Reorganization Act

Wash. Rev. Code Ann., 43.21A.010 et seq.

Environmental Quality Review Act

N.Y. Environmental Conservation Law 1972 (Consol Laws Ch. 43B) § 8-0101 et seq.

Environmental Radiation Protection Act

Pa. Purdon's Stat., Title 35, § 7110.101 et seq.

Environmental Regulatory Fee Law

N.Y. Environmental Conservation Law 1972 (Consol. Laws Ch. 43B) § 72-0101 et seq.

Environmental Reorganization Act

Fla. Laws 1993, Ch. 213

Fla. Stat. Ann., 20.10, 20.25, 20.261, 120.721, 253.1221, 253.76, 258.004, 370.02, 373.073, 373.114, 380.12, 403.5111, 403.801 to 403.813

Environmental Research, Development, and Demonstration Authorization Act of 1976

Oct. 11, 1976, P.L. 94-475, 42 U.S. Code § 4361

Dec. 21, 1995, P.L. 104-66, 42 U.S. Code § 4361

Environmental Research, Development, and Demonstration Authorization Act of 1978

Nov. 8, 1977, P.L. 95-155, 42 U.S. Code §§ 4361a, 300j-3a et seq.

Oct. 18, 1978, P.L. 95-477, 42 U.S. Code §§ 300j-3a, 300j-3a nt.

Nov. 2, 1994, P.L. 103-437, 42 U.S. Code § 4365

Dec. 21, 1995, P.L. 104-66, 42 U.S. Code §§ 4361a, 4365

Environmental Research, Development and Demonstration Authorization Act of 1979

Oct. 18, 1978, P.L. 95-477, 42 U.S. Code §§ 300j-3a, 300j-3b, 4361c, 4363a 4366 et seq.

Nov. 2, 1994, P.L. 103-437, 42 U.S. Code § 4369

Environmental Research Geographic Location Information Act

Nov. 16, 1990, P.L. 101-617, 42 U.S. Code §§ 4366a, 4366a nt.

Environmental Response Act

Kan. Stat. Ann., 65-3452 et seq.

Mich. Comp. Laws Ann., 299.601 et seq.

Environmental Response Act (Drycleaner's)

Kan. Stat. Ann.,39-1801

Tenn. Code Ann., 4-29-218, 68-217-101 to 68-217-112

Environmental Response and Liability Act

Minn. Stat. Ann., 115B.01 et seq.

Environmental Response and Reimbursement Law (Drycleaner)

Minn. Stat. Ann., 115B.47 to 115B.51

Environmental Response Bank Act (Underground Petroleum)

S.C. Code Ann. 1976, § 44-2-10 et seq.

Environmental Response Trust Fund Act (Drycleaner)

Ill. Comp. Stat. 1992, Ch. 415, § 135/1 et seq.

Environmental Responsibility Act (Oil Pipeline)

Cal. Civil Code § 3333.4

Environmental Restoration Jobs Act

Wash. Rev. Code Ann., 43.21J.900

Environmental Revitalization Act

Ky. Rev. Stat. 1971, 224A.290

Environmental Rights Act

Minn. Stat. Ann., 116B.01 et seq.

N.J. Stat. Ann., 2A:35A-1 et seq.

R.I. Gen. Laws 1956, 10-20-1 et seq.

Environmental Rules Analysis Law

Tex. Government Code, § 2001.0225

Environmental Sanitarian Act

Md. Ann. Code 1974, Art. EN, § 11-101 et seq.

Environmental Services Gross Receipts Tax Act (County)

N.M. Stat. Ann., 7-20B-1 et seq.

Environmental Services Gross Receipts Tax Act (Municipal)

N.M. Stat. Ann., 7-19B-1 et seq.

Environmental Specialist and Sanitarian Registration Act

Okla. Stat. Ann., Title 59, § 1150.1 et seq.

Environmental Standards Act (Public Utility)

Conn. Gen. Stat. 1983, § 16-50g et seq.

Environmental Standing Act

Md. Ann. Code 1974, Art. NR, § 1-501 et seq.

Environmental Technology Act
Mich. Comp. Laws Ann., 299.781 et seq.

Environmental Toxicology Act
Ill. Rev. Stat. 1991, Ch. 111 1/2, § 981 et seq.

Environmental Trust Act
Neb. Laws 1992, L.B. 1257, §§ 44 to 53

Environmental Water Act
Cal. Water Code §§ 11913, 12303, 12929.10, 12929.12, 12929.13

Epidemic Diseases Act
March 27, 1890, Ch. 51, 26 Stat. 31

Equal Access Act
Aug. 11, 1984, P.L. 98-377, 20 U.S. Code §§ 4071 et seq., 4071 nt.
Nov. 2, 1994, P.L. 103-437, 20 U.S. Code § 3917
Ark. Code Ann. 1987, 6-21-201 et seq.

Equal Access to Justice Act
Oct. 21, 1980, P.L. 96-481, 5 U.S. Code § 504 nt.
Aug. 5, 1985, P.L. 99-80, 5 U.S. Code § 504 nt.; 28 U.S. Code § 2412 nt.
Fla. Stat. Ann., 57.111
N.Y. Civ. Prac. Laws and Rules (Consol. Laws Ch. 8) § 8600 et seq.
Tenn. Public Acts 1984, Ch. 495

Equal Access to Justice Act (Small Business)
Cal. Code of Civil Procedure § 1028.5
Utah Code Ann. 1953, 78-27a-1 et seq.

Equal Accommodations Act
Mich. Comp. Laws Ann., 750.146

Equal and Civil Rights Enforcement Act
Ill. Rev. Stat. 1991, Ch. 14, §§ 8.9, 9

Equal Consumer Credit Act
Ark. Code Ann. 1987, 4-87-101 et seq.
Tenn. Code Ann., 47-17-101 et seq.

Equal Credit Opportunity Act
March 23, 1976, P.L. 94-239, 15 U.S. Code § 1691 et seq.

Aug. 9, 1989, P.L. 101-73, 15 U.S. Code § 1691c
Dec. 19, 1991, P.L. 102-242, 15 U.S. Code §§ 1691, 1691c, 1691e
Oct. 28, 1992, P.L. 102-550, 15 U.S. Code § 1691c
Dec. 29, 1995, P.L. 104-88, 15 U.S. Code § 1691c
Sept. 30, 1996, P.L. 104-208, 15 U.S. Code § 1691c-1
La. Rev. Stat. Ann., 9:3581 et seq.
Md. Ann. Code 1974, Art. CL, § 12-603 et seq., 12-701 et seq.
Nev. Rev. Stat. 1979 Reprint, 598B.010 et seq.
Va. Code 1950, § 59.1-21.19 et seq.

Equal Education Opportunity Act
Vt. Acts 1997, No. 60

Equal Employment for the Handicapped Code
Ga. Code Ann., 34-6A-1 et seq.

Equal Employment Opportunity Act
Ill. Rev. Stat. 1991, Ch. 68, § 2-101 et seq.
Ind. Code Ann., 20-8.1-2-1 et seq.
Ky. Rev. Stat. 1971, 45.550 et seq.
N.C. Gen. Stat. 1943, §§ 126-16 to 126-39
N.M. Stat. Ann., 28-1-1 et seq.

Equal Employment Opportunity Act of 1972
March 24, 1972, P.L. 92-261, 86 Stat. 103, 5 U.S. Code §§ 5108, 5314, 5315, 5316; 42 U.S. Code §§ 2000e, 2000e-1 to 2000e-6, 2000e-8, 2000e-9, 2000e-13 to 2000e-17

Equal Employment Practices Act
Ariz. Rev. Stat. Ann., § 41-1461 et seq.
N.C. Gen. Stat. 1943, § 143-422.1 et seq.

Equal Export Opportunity Act
Aug. 29, 1972, P.L. 92-412, 86 Stat. 644, 50 U.S. Code Appx. §§ 2401 to 2404, 2413

Equal Health Standard Milk Sanitation Act
Tex. Rev. Civ. Stat., Art. 165-3a

Equal Management Law
La. Civil Code 1972, Art. 2325 et seq.

Equal Nationality Act
May 24, 1934, Ch. 344, 48 Stat. 797

Equal Opportunities Act
Ky. Rev. Stat. 1971, 207.130 et seq.

Equal Opportunities for the Handicapped Act
Ill. Rev. Stat. 1979, Ch. 38, § 65-21 et seq.

Equal Opportunity Act (Higher Education)
Pa. Purdon's Stat., Title 24, § 2510-301 et seq.

Equal Opportunity Education Assistance Act
La. Rev. Stat. Ann., 17:2990.1 et seq.

Equal Opportunity Education Assistance Act (Nonpublic School Aid)
La. Rev. Stat. Ann., 17:2990.1 et seq.

Equal Opportunity for Displaced Homemakers Act
Ark. Stat. 1947, 81-630 et seq.
Neb. Rev. Stat. 1943, 48-1301 et seq.

Equal Opportunity in Education Act
Neb. Rev. Stat. 1943, 79-3001 et seq.

Equal Opportunity in Postsecondary Education Act
Neb. Laws 1996, L.B. 900

Equal Pay Act
Alaska Stat. 1962, § 18.80.220
Ariz. Rev. Stat. Ann., §§ 23-340, 23-341
Ark. Code Ann. 1987, 11-4-607 et seq.
Cal. Labor Code § 1197.5
Colo. Rev. Stat., 8-5-101 et seq.
Haw. Rev. Stat. Ann., § 387-4
Ill. Rev. Stat. 1991, Ch. 48, § 4a
Mass. Gen. Laws Ann., 149:105A et seq.
Me. Rev. Stat. Ann. 1964, Title 26, § 628
Mich. Comp. Laws Ann., 750.556
N.D. Cent. Code, 34-06.1-01 et seq.
N.H. Rev. Stat. 1955, 275:36 et seq.
N.Y. Labor Law (Consol. Laws Ch. 31) § 194
Ohio Rev. Code 1953, 4111.17

Ore. Rev. Stat., 652.220 et seq.
Pa. Purdon's Stat., Title 43, § 336.1 et seq.
R.I. Gen. Laws 1956, 28-6-17 et seq.
Wyo. Stat. Ann., § 27-4-301 et seq.

Equal Pay Act (Teachers' Salaries)
Mass. Gen. Laws Ann., 71:40
N.Y. Education Law 1947 (Consol. Laws Ch. 16) § 3026

Equal Pay Act (Women)
Conn. Gen. Stat. 1983, § 31-75
Mo. Rev. Stat., 290.400 et seq.
Mont. Code Ann., 39-3-104
N.J. Stat. Ann., 34:11-4.1 et seq.

Equal Pay Act of 1963
June 10, 1963, P.L. 88-38, 77 Stat. 56, 29 U.S. Code § 206

Equal Pay for Equal Work Act
Ga. Code Ann., 34-5-1 et seq.
Minn. Stat. Ann., 181.66 et seq.
Ore. Rev. Stat., 652.210 et seq.
S.D. Codified Laws 1967, 60-12-15 et seq.
Wash. Rev. Code Ann., 49.12.175

Equal Public Employment Opportunities Act
Ariz. Rev. Stat. Ann., § 41-1461 et seq.

Equal Retirement Benefits Act
Ga. Laws 1976, p. 3257

Equal Rights Act
Cal. Civil Code §§ 51, 52
Mass. Gen. Laws Ann., 151B:1 et seq.
Pa. Purdon's Stat., Title 18, § 4654
Wis. Stat. 1987, 942.04

Equal Rights Act (District of Columbia)
March 18, 1869, Ch. 3, 16 Stat. 3

Equal Rights Act (Public Accommodations)
S.D. Codified Laws 1967, 20-12-1 et seq.

Equal Rights Amendment (ERA) Ratification Act
D.C. Laws 1978, No. 2-79

Equal Rights Commission Act
Haw. Session Laws 1935, Act 212

Equal Rights Enforcement Act (Civil and)
Ill. Comp. Stat. 1992, Ch. 15, §§ 210/0.01, 210/1

Equal Rights in Business Establishment Act
Cal. Civil Code §§ 51, 52

Equal Time Act
See Communications Acts
June 19, 1934, Ch. 652, 48 Stat. 1088

Equal Treatment Act (Foreign Corporations)
Minn. Stat. Ann., 303.09
N.C. Gen. Stat. 1943, § 55-132

Equal Wage Act
Ill. Rev. Stat. 1991, Ch. 48, § 4a et seq.

Equality Act (Corrections)
Fla. Stat. Ann., 944.24

Equality Act (County Corrections)
Fla. Stat. Ann., 951.175

Equality of Citizenship Act
Ala. Code 1975, §§ 17-1-7, 36-26-38

Equalization Act
N.J. Stat. Ann., 54:1-33 to 54:1-35, 54:2-37, 54:2-38, 54:3-17 to 54:3-19

Equalization Act (Educational Funds)
Ala. General Acts 1927, p. 442, No. 382

Equalization Act (Pensions)
June 6, 1874, Ch. 219, 18 Stat. 61

Equalization Act (School Building)
Utah Code Ann. 1953, 53A-21-101 et seq.

Equalization Act (Taxation)
Mich. Comp. Laws Ann., 209.1 et seq.

Equalization Aid Act (Schools)
Okla. Stat. Ann., Title 70, § 18-4

Equalization and Review Commission Act (Tax)
Neb. Rev. Stat. 1943, 77-5001 to 77-5021

Equalization Fund Law (Schools)
Ark. Stat. 1947, 80-821 et seq.
N.D. Cent. Code, 15-40.1-01 et seq.

Equalization of Assessments Act
Wash. Rev. Code Ann., 84.48.010 et seq.

Equalization of Educational Opportunities Act
Ga. Laws 1937, p. 882

Equalization of Real Property Values Act (Hoffman)
Ohio Rev. Code 1953, 5715.01, 5715.29 et seq.

Equestrian Center Authority Act
Conn. Public Acts 1995, No. 231

Equine Act
Ga. Code Ann., 4-4-110 etseq.

Equine Activity Liability Act
Mich. Comp. Laws Ann., 691.1661 et seq.

Equine Infectious Anemia Control Act
Ill. Rev. Stat. 1991, Ch. 8, § 951 et seq.

Equine Infectious Anemia Eradication Act
Okla. Stat. Ann., Title 2, § 6-281 et seq.

Equine Liability Act
N.M. Stat. Ann., 42-13-1 et seq.

Equine Liability Limitation Act
Utah Laws 1992, Ch. 126

Equine Protection Act
Cal. Food and Agricultural Code 1967, § 24101 et seq.

Equines Humane Care Act
Ga. Code Ann., 4-13-1 et seq.

Equipment and Facilities Authority Act (Hospital)
Miss. Code Ann. 1972, § 41-73-1 et seq.

Equipment Business Regulation Act
Neb. Rev. Stat. 1943, 87-701 et seq.

Equipment Dealer Act (Multiline Heavy)
Ga. Code Ann., 10-1-730 et seq.

Equipment Dealer Contract Act
Md. Ann. Code 1974, Art. Art. CL, § 19-101
et seq.

Equipment Dealership Act (Agriculture)
Kan. Stat. Ann., 16-1201 et seq.
Minn. Stat. Ann., 325E.061 et seq.

Equipment Fair Dealership Law
Ill. Rev. Stat. 1991, Ch. 5, § 1501 et seq.

**Equipment Franchise Act (Tractor, Lawn
and Garden and Light Industrial**
Ala. Code 1975, § 8-21A-1

**Equipment Franchise Act (Tractor, Lawn
and Garden, and Light Industrial)**
Ala. Code 1975, § 8-21A-1 et seq.

**Equipment Identification Defacement Act
(Construction)**
Ill. Comp. Stat. 1992, Ch. 720, §§ 245/0.01,
245/1

**Equipment Lease Purchase Act (Local
Government)**
La. Rev. Stat. Ann., 38:2319 et seq.

**Equipment Leasing Fund Act (Higher
Education)**
N.J. Stat. Ann., 18A:72A-40 et seq.

**Equipment Loan Authority Act (Higher
Education)**
Ala. Code 1975, § 16-18B-1 et seq.

Equipment Loan Fund for the Disabled
N.Y. Social Services Law (Consol. Laws Ch.
55) § 326a et seq.

**Equipment Manufacturers and Dealers Act
(Farm)**
Fla. Stat. Ann., 686.40 et seq.

Equipment Safety Act (Playground)
Mich. Comp. Laws Ann., 408.681 et seq.

Equipment Safety Compact (Vehicle)
Ind. Code Ann., 9-28-6-1 et seq.

**Equitable and Extrordinary Remedies
Procedures Act**
Ga. Code Ann., 23-13-1 et seq.

**Equitable Distribution Law (Marital
Property)**
N.Y. Domestic Relations Law (Consol. Laws
Ch. 14) § 236
N.Y. General Obligations Law (Consol.
Laws Ch. 24A) § 5-311
N.Y. Laws 1980, Ch. 281

Equitable Proration Tax Act
Pa. 1937 Pamph. Laws 2762, No. 565

Equitable Restrooms Act
Ill. Rev. Stat. 1991, Ch. 111 1/2, § 3751-1 et
seq.

Equity Act
Haw. Rev. Stat. Ann. 1985, § 603-21.6 et
seq.
Me. Rev. Stat. 1954, Ch. 113, § 15 et seq.
Mich. Comp. Laws 1948, 606.4

**Equity Act (Stacey, Bennett and Randall
Shareholders)**
Mich. Comp. Laws Ann., 450.1790 et seq.

Equity Act (Tax)
Colo. Rev. Stat., 39-22-101 et seq.

Equity Conversion Act (Home)
Fla. Stat. Ann., 697.20 et seq.

Equity in Athletics Disclosure Act
Oct. 20, 1994, P.L. 103-382, 20 U.S. Code
§ 1001 nt.

**Equity in Educational Land-Grant Status
Act of 1994**
Oct. 20, 1994, P.L. 103-382, 7 U.S. Code
§§ 301 nt., 343
April 4, 1996, P.L. 104-127, 7 U.S. Code
§ 301 nt.
Continued

759

June 23, 1998, P.L. 105-185, 7 U.S. Code
§ 301 nt.

Oct. 31, 1998, P.L. 105-332, 7 U.S. Code
§ 301 nt.

Eradication Act (Boll Weevil)
Ga. Code Ann., 2-7-150 et seq.
Okla. Stat. Ann., Title 2, §§ 3-50.1 to 3-50.20

Eradication and Pseudorabies Control Act
S.C. Code Ann. 1976, § 47-6-10 et seq.

Erdman Acts (Labor Disputes)
June 1, 1898, Ch. 370, 30 Stat. 424
July 15, 1913, Ch. 6, 38 Stat. 103

Erie County Act
N.Y. Laws 1884, Ch. 135

Erie County Administrative Code
N.Y. Local Laws 1960, Erie County, No. 1

Erie County Budget Act
N.Y. Laws 1944, Ch. 383

Erie County Highway Improvement Act
N.Y. Laws 1927, Ch. 190

Erie County Tax Act
N.Y. Laws 1942, Ch. 812

Erie County Water Authority Act
N.Y. Public Authorities Law (Consol. Laws
Ch. 43A) § 1050 et seq.

Erie Extension Act (Pennsylvania Turnpike)
Pa. 1949 Pamph. Laws 1037, No. 301

**Erin Act (Childbirth, Health Insurance
Benefits)**
Wash. Rev. Code Ann., 48.43.115

Erin Mobile Home Park Law
N.Y. Local Laws 1968, Town of Erin, p.
2312

Erin Snowmobile Law
N.Y. Local Laws 1972, Town of Erin, p.
1342

ERISA
See Employee Retirement Income Security
Act Of 1974, supra

Ernestina Commission Act
Mass. Gen. Laws Ann., 6:182A to 6:182C

Erosion and Sediment Control Act
Del. Code of 1974, Title 7, § 4001 et seq.
Ga. Code Ann., 12-7-1 et seq.
Neb. Rev. Stat. 1943, 2-4601 et seq.
S.C. Code Ann. 1976, § 48-18-40 et seq.
Va. Code 1950, § 21-89.1 et seq.

Erosion Control Act (Wind)
Ala. Code 1975, § 41-6A-1 et seq.
Colo. Rev. Stat., 35-72-101 et seq.
Okla. Stat. Ann., Title 2, § 841 et seq.

Erosion District Act (Brevard County)
Fla. Special Laws 1970, Ch. 70-603

Erosion District Act (Broward County)
Fla. Special Laws 1961, Ch. 61-1967

Erosion District Act (St. Lucie County)
Fla. Special Laws 1967, Ch. 67-2001

Erosion Law (Coastal)
Tex. Natural Resources Code, § 33.601 et
seq.

**Erosion Loan Act (Metropolitan District
Beach)**
Mass. Acts 1956, Ch. 736

Erosion Management Act (Coastal)
N.Y. Environmental Conservation Law 1972
(Consol. Laws Ch. 43B) §§ 34-0101 et seq.,
70-0107, 70-0117

**Erosion Prevention District Act (Broward
County)**
Fla. Special Laws 1959, Ch. 59-1159

Errors Act
N.J. Revised Stat. 1937, 2:27-344 to
2:27-363

Erwin Act (Political Contributions)
Cal. Government Code § 9900 et seq.

Erwin Law (Highway Aid)
N.Y. Laws 1950, Ch. 824

Erwin Planning Board Land Subdivision Rules and Regulations
N.Y. Local Laws 1972, Town of Erwin, p. 1352

Erwin Snowmobile Local Law
N.Y. Local Laws 1971, Town of Erwin, p. 1731

Erwin Town Zoning Act
N.Y. Local Laws 1967, Town of Erwin, p. 1483

Erwin Underground Services Law
N.Y. Local Laws 1969, Town of Erwin, p. 1202

Escambia County Agriculture Extension Council Act
Fla. Special Laws 1947, Ch. 24501

Escambia County Bridge Revenue Bond Act
Fla. Special Laws 1941, Ch. 21216

Escambia County Civil Service Act
Fla. Special Laws 1951, Ch. 27537

Escambia County Extension Council Act
Fla. Special Laws 1967, Ch. 67-1366

Escambia County Gaseous Fuels and Equipment Act
Fla. Special Laws 1963, Ch. 63-1326

Escambia County-Pensacola Promotion and Development Commission Act
Fla. Special Laws 1967, Ch. 67-1365

Escambia County Permanent Registration Act
Fla. Laws 1947, Ch. 23903

Escambia County Utility Act
Fla. Special Laws 1957, Ch. 57-1313

Escambia County Water and Sewer Act
Fla. Special Laws 1971, Ch. 71-629

Escambia-Pensacola Charter
Fla. Special Laws 1970, Ch. 70-681

Escape Act
Cal. Penal Code § 4530 et seq.
Ill. Rev. Stat. 1991, Ch. 38, § 31-6
Mich. Comp. Laws Ann., 750.183 et seq.
N.M. Stat. Ann., 30-22-8 et seq.
Wash. Rev. Code Ann., 9A.76.110 et seq.

Escaped Inmate Damages Act
Ill. Rev. Stat. 1991, Ch. 23, §§ 4040, 4041

Esch Act (Hours of Service on Railroads)
March 4, 1907, Ch. 2939, 34 Stat. 1415, 45 U.S. Code §§ 61 to 64

Esch Car Service Act
May 29, 1917, Ch. 23, 40 Stat. 101, 49 U.S. Code § 1 (11)

Esch-Cummings Act (Railroads)
See Transportation Acts

Esch Water Power Act
See Federal Water Power Act

Escheat Act
Alaska Stat. 1962, § 09.50.070 et seq.
Ariz. Rev. Stat. Ann., § 12-881 et seq.
Cal. Code of Civil Procedure § 1410 et seq.
Conn. Gen. Stat. 1983, § 3-56a et seq.
Fla. Stat. Ann., 716.01 et seq.
Ida. Code 1947, 14-501 et seq.
Ill. Rev. Stat. 1991, Ch. 49, § 0.01
Ind. Code Ann., 633.543 et seq.
Ky. Rev. Stat. 1971, 393.010 et seq.
Md. Ann. Code 1974, Art. ET, § 3-105
Mich. Comp. Laws Ann., 567.11 et seq.
Mo. Rev. Stat., 470.010 et seq.
Mont. Rev. Code 1947, 91-501 et seq.
N.C. Gen. Stat. 1943, § 116B-1 et seq.
Neb. Rev. Stat. 1943, 76-401 et seq.
N.Y. Abandoned Property Law (Consol. Laws Ch. 1) § 200 et seq.
Okla. Stat. Ann., Title 84, § 271 et seq.
Continued

Ore. Rev. Stat., 116.193 et seq.
Pa. Cons. Stat., Title 20, § 3540
Pa. Purdon's Stat., Title 72, § 1301.1 et seq.
S.C. Code Ann. 1976, § 27-19-10 et seq.
Tex. Property Code, § 71.001 et seq.
Vt. Stat. Ann., Title 14, § 681 et seq.
Wash. Rev. Code Ann., 177.01 et seq.
Wash. Rev. Code Ann., 11.08.101 et seq.
Wyo. Stat. Ann., § 9-5-201 et seq.

Escheat Act (Abandoned Property)
Mass. Gen. Laws Ann., 200A:1 et seq.

Escheat Act (Bank Deposits)
N.J. Stat. Ann., 17:9-18 et seq.

Escheat Act (Insurance)
Mo. Rev. Stat. 1969, 379.395

Escheat Act (Personal Property)
N.J. Stat. Ann., 2A:37-11 et seq.

Escheat Act (Real Property)
N.J. Stat. Ann., 2A:37-1 et seq.
N.Y. Abandoned Property Law (Consol.
Laws Ch. 1) § 200 et seq.

Escheat Act (State Warrants)
Ill. Rev. Stat. 1991, Ch. 15, § 210.14 et seq.

**Escheat of Postal Savings System Accounts
Act**
Ark. Stat. 1947, 50-613 et seq.
Iowa Code 1983, 556.30 et seq.
Md. Ann. Code 1957, Art. 95C, § 27 et seq.
N.D. Laws 1971, Ch. 518
Nev. Rev. Stat. 1979 Reprint, 40.500 et seq.
Okla. Stat. Ann., Title 60, § 701 et seq.
R.I. Gen. Laws 1956, 33-21A-1 et seq.

Escheated Estates Act
Mont. Code Ann., 72-14-101 et seq.

Escheated Property Act
Mont. Code Ann., 72-14-101 et seq.

Escort Service Code
Colo. Rev. Stat., 12-25.5-101 et seq.

Escrow Account Act (Mortgage)
Ill. Rev. Stat. 1991, Ch. 17, § 4901 et seq.

**Escrow Accounts Act (Interest on Real
Estate Brokers' IREBEA)**
Miss. Code Ann. 1972, § 73-35-101 et seq.

Escrow Agent Registration Act
Wash. Rev. Code Ann., 18.44.010 et seq.

Escrow Agents Act
Ariz. Rev. Stat. Ann., § 6-801 et seq.

Escrow Businesses Regulation Act
Mont. Laws 1989, Ch. 651

Escrow Company Act
N.M. Stat. Ann., 58-22-1 et seq.

Escrow Law
Cal. Financial Code § 17000 et seq.
Ore. Rev. Stat., 696.505 et seq.

Esopus Unsafe Building Demolition Law
N.Y. Local Laws 1973, Towns of Esopus, p.
1711

Espionage Act
June 15, 1917, Ch. 30, 40 Stat. 217 (See 18
U.S. Code §§ 11, 791 to 794, 2388, 3241)
22 U.S. Code §§ 213, 220 to 222, 401 to
408; 50 U.S. Code §§ 191, 192, 194
March 28, 1940, Ch. 72, 54 Stat. 79
Aug. 13, 1953, Ch. 434, 67 Stat. 577, 22 U.S.
Code § 401

Espionage and Sabotage Act of 1954
Sept. 3, 1954, Ch. 1261, 68 Stat. 1216, 18
U.S. Code §§ 794, 2151, 2153 to 2156

Esquirol Act (Slot Machines)
N.Y. Penal Law 1965 (Consol. Laws Ch. 40)
§ 225.30

**Essential Health Provider Recruitment
Strategy Act**
Mich. Comp. Laws Ann., 333.2701 et seq.

Essential Insurance Act
Mich. Comp. Laws Ann., 500.2101 et seq.

Essential Insurance Coverage Act
W. Va. Code 1966 § 33-20A-1 et seq.

Essential Records Preservation Act
Tex. Government Code, § 441.051 et seq.
W. Va. Code 1966, § 5-8-1 et seq.

Essential Services Buildings Seismic Safety Act
Cal. Health and Safety Code § 16000 et seq.

Essex Agricultural and Technical Institute Building Loan Act
Mass. Acts 1963, Ch. 516

Essex County Agricultural School Building Loan Act
Mass. Acts 1961, Ch. 387

Essex County Budget Act (Cash Basis)
N.Y. Laws 1946, Ch. 883

Essex County Court House Loan Act
Mass. Acts 1963, Ch. 140

Essex County Elevator Loan Act
Mass. Acts 1955, Ch. 287

Essex-Franklin Counties Solid Waste Management Authority Act
N.Y. Public Authorities Law (Consol. Laws Ch. 43A) § 2051a et seq.

Establishment and Enforcement of Child Support Administrative Procedure Act
Colo. Rev. Stat., 26-13.5-101 et seq.

Establishments for Handicapped Persons Licensing Law
Cal. Health and Safety Code § 1500 et seq.

Establishments for the Aged Act
Okla. Stat. 1961, Title 68, § 1571 et seq.
P.R. Laws Ann. 1954, Title 8, § 351 et seq.

Estate Administration Act
Ill. Rev. Stat. 1991, Ch. 110 1/2, § 9-1 et seq.
Tenn. Code Ann., 30-2-306 et seq.

Estate Administration Act (Independent)
Cal. Probate Code §§ 591 et seq., 10400

Estate and Generation-Skipping Transfer Tax Act
Ill. Comp. Stat. 1992, Ch. 35, § 405/1 et seq.
Ill. Rev. Stat. 1991, Ch. 120, § 405A-1 et seq.

Estate and Gift Tax Act
P.R. Laws Ann. 1954, Title 13, § 5001 et seq.
Vt. Stat. Ann., Title 32, § 7401 et seq.

Estate and Inheritance Tax Act
Pa. Cons. Stat., Title 72, § 1701 et seq.

Estate and Transfer Tax Reform Act
Haw. Rev. Stat. Ann., § 236D-1 et seq.
Ida. Code 1947, 14-401 et seq.
Wash. Rev. Code Ann., 83.100.010 et seq.

Estate Claims Act
Colo. Rev. Stat., 15-12-805
Ohio Rev. Code 1953, 2117.06 et seq.
Wash. Rev. Code Ann., 11.40.010 et seq.

Estate Mortgage Act
N.H. Rev. Stat. 1955, 554:30 et seq.

Estate Recovery Act (Medicaid
N.M. Stat. Ann., 27-2A-1 et seq.

Estate Tax Act
Ala. Code 1975, § 40-15-1 et seq.
Alaska Stat. 1962, Replaced Titles, § 43.31.011 et seq.
Ariz. Rev. Stat. Ann., § 42-1501 et seq.
Ark. Code Ann. 1987, 63-101 et seq.
Ark. Stat. 1947, 26-59-101 et seq.
Colo. Rev. Stat. 1973, 39-23.5-101 et seq.
Conn. Gen. Stat. 1983, § 12-391 et seq.
D.C. Code Ann., § 47-3701 et seq.
Del. Code of 1974, Title 30, § 1501 et seq.
Fla. Stat. Ann., 198.01 et seq.
Ga. Code Ann., 48-12-1 et seq.
Haw. Rev. Stat. Ann., § 236-1 et seq.
Ill. Rev. Stat. 1991, Ch. 120, § 405A-1 et seq.
Ind. Code Ann., 451.1 et seq.
Kan. Stat. Ann., 79-1501 et seq., 79-1537 et seq.
Mass. Gen. Laws Ann., 65A:1 et seq.
Md. Ann. Code 1957, Art. 62A
Continued

Me. Rev. Stat. Ann. 1964, Title 36, § 3741 et seq.

Mich. Comp. Laws Ann., 205.231 et seq.

Minn. Stat. Ann., 291.005 et seq.

Miss. Code Ann. 1972, § 27-9-1 et seq.

Mont. Code Ann., 72-16-901 et seq.

N.D. Cent. Code, 57-37.1-01 et seq.

Neb. Rev. Stat. 1943, 77-2101.01 et seq.

N.J. Stat. Ann., 54:38-1 to 54:38-16

N.M. Stat. Ann., 7-7-1 et seq.

N.Y. Tax Law (Consol. Laws Ch. 60) § 249m et seq.

Ohio Rev. Code 1953, 3115.01 et seq., 5731.01 et seq.

Okla. Stat. Ann., Title 68, § 801 et seq.

Pa. Purdon's Stat., Title 72, § 2301 et seq.

R.I. Gen. Gen. Laws 1956, 44-22-1 et seq.

S.C. Code Ann. 1976, §§ 12-15-10 et seq., 12-16-10 et seq.

S.D. Codified Laws 1967, 10-40A-1 et seq.

Tenn. Code Ann., 67-8-201 et seq.

Va. Code 1950, §§ 58-238.1 et seq., 58.1-900 et seq.

Vt. Stat. Ann., Title 32, § 7401 et seq.

Wash. Rev. Code Ann., 72.60 et seq.

W. Va. Code 1966 § 11-11-1 et seq.

Estate Tax Act (Credit Difference)
Pa. Purdon's Stat., Title 72, § 2303

Estate Tax Act (Nonresident)
Pa. Purdon's Stat., Title 72, § 2303

Estate Tax Acts
Sept. 8, 1916, Ch. 463, 39 Stat. 777
March 3, 1917, Ch. 159, 39 Stat. 1002
Oct. 3, 1917, Ch. 63, 40 Stat. 324
Feb. 24, 1919, Ch. 18, 40 Stat. 1096
Nov. 23, 1921, Ch. 136, 42 Stat. 277
June 2, 1924, Ch. 234, 43 Stat. 303
Feb. 26, 1926, Ch. 27, 44 Stat. 69
Aug. 30, 1935, Ch. 829, 49 Stat. 1014
May 28, 1938, Ch. 289, 52 Stat. 564, 11 U.S. Code §§ 421, 422, 490, 537, 553

Estate Tax Apportionment Act
See also Uniform Estate Tax Apportionment Act
Miss. Code Ann. 1972, § 27-10-1 et seq.

Okla. Stat. Ann., Title 58, § 2001 et seq.

Pa. Cons. Stat., Title 23, § 4501 et seq.

Estate Tax Apportionment Act (Revised Uniform)
Haw. Rev. Stat. Ann., § 236A-1 et seq.

Estate Tax Exemption Law
N.Y. Tax Law (Consol. Laws Ch. 60) § 249q

Estate Tax Proration Act
Pa. 1937 Pamph. Laws 2762, No. 565

Estate Transfer Tax Act
La. Rev. Stat. Ann., 47:2431 et seq.

Estates Act
Pa. Cons. Stat., Title 20, § 6101 et seq.

Estates Administration Act (Independent)
Cal. Probate Code § 10400 et seq.

Estates and Wills Act
Colo. Rev. Stat., 15-10-201 et seq.

Estates, Powers, and Trusts Law
N.Y. Consol. Laws, Ch. 17B

Estates Procedures Act
Colo. Rev. Stat., 15-14-401 et seq.

Estates Settlement Act
Wash. Rev. Code Ann., 11.76.010 et seq.

Estero Municipal Improvement District Act
Cal. Statutes 1960, 1st Ex. Sess., Ch. 82, p. 459

Estes-Campbell-Martin Act
Ala. Code 1972, §§ 32-6-150, 32-6-156

Estes Fee Bill
Tenn. Code Ann., 8-22-101 et seq.

Esthetics, Barber and Cosmetology Act
Ill. Rev. Stat. Ch. 111, § 1701-1 et seq.

Estoppel Act (Workmen's Compensation)
Okla. Stat. Ann., Title 85, § 65.2

Estrays Act
Iowa Code Ann., 169B.1 et seq.

Estrays Act (Animals)

Ark. Code Ann. 1987, 2-38-101 et seq.

Cal. Food and Agricultural Code 1967, § 17001 et seq.

Ind. Code Ann., 32-9-3-1 et seq.

Md. Ann. Code 1957, Art. 34, § 1 et seq.

Mich. Comp. Laws Ann., 434.3 et seq.

Mont. Code Ann., 81-4-601 et seq.

N.C. Gen. Stat. 1943, § 68-15 et seq.

Neb. Rev. Stat. 1943, 54-401 et seq.

N.H. Rev. Stat. 1955, 471:1 et seq.

Ohio Rev. Code 1953, 951.01 et seq.

Okla. Stat. Ann., Title 4, § 85.2 et seq.

Ore. Rev. Stat., 607.300 et seq.

R.I. Gen. Laws 1956, 4-16-1 et seq.

S.C. Code Ann. 1976, § 47-7-10 et seq.

Tenn. Code Ann., Superseded Vol., 44-1501 et seq.

Tex. Agriculture Code, § 142.001 et seq.

Wash. Rev. Code Ann., 16.28.010 et seq.

Estrays and Lost Property Act

Ill. Rev. Stat. 1991, Ch. 50, § 0.01 et seq.

Estuarine Waters Dredge or Fill Act

N.C. Gen. Stat. 1943, § 113.229

Estuary Management Act (Hudson River)

N.Y. Laws 1991, Ch. 612

Ethanol Authority and Development Act

Neb. Rev. Stat. 1943, 66-1301 et seq.

Ethanol Production Law (Agricultural)

La. Rev. Stat. Ann., 3:3701 et seq.

Ethics Act

Pa. Purdon's Stat., Title 65, § 401 et seq.

Ethics Act (Municipal Officers' and Employees')

Utah Code Ann. 1953, 67-17-1 et seq.

Ethics Act (Public Officials and Employees)

Ala. Code 1975, § 36-25-1 et seq.

Ethics and Efficiency in Government Act

Ga. Code Ann., 28-11-1 et seq.

Ethics Code (Governmental)

La. Rev. Stat. Ann., 42:1101 et seq.

Ethics Commission Act

Okla. Stat. Ann., Title 74, § 4200 et seq.

Ethics, Government Accountability and Campaign Reform Act

S.C. Code Ann. 1976, § 8-13-100 et seq.

Ethics in Government Act

Cal. Government Code § 89500 et seq.

Ga. Code Ann., 21-5-1 et seq.

Ida. Code 1947, 59-701 et seq.

N.Y. Executive Law 1951 (Consol. Laws Ch. 18) §§ 94, 166

N.Y. General Municipal Law (Consol. Laws Ch. 24) §§ 805a, 806, 808, 810 to 813

N.Y. Judiciary Law (Consol. Laws Ch. 30) § 211

N.Y. Laws 1987, Ch. 813

N.Y. Legislative Law (Consol. Laws Ch. 32) § 80

N.Y. Public Officers Law (Consol. Laws Ch. 47), §§ 73, 73a, 76, 78, 88

P.R. Laws Ann. 1954, Title 3, § 1801 et seq.

Ethics in Government Act Amendments of 1982

Jan. 3, 1983, P.L. 97-409, 28 U.S. Code § 1 nt.

Ethics in Government Act Amendments of 1985

Dec. 19, 1985, P.L. 99-190, 5 U.S. Code Appx. §§ 201, 207

Ethics in Government Act Amendments of 1990

July 16, 1990, P.L. 101-334, 5 U.S. Code Appx. § 101 nt.

Ethics in Government Act of 1978

Oct. 26, 1978, P.L. 95-521, 2 U.S. Code §§ 118a, 288 nt., 288d et seq. 701 et seq., 701 nt.; 5 U.S. Code § 6316; 5 U.S. Code Appx.; 18 U.S. Code § 207; 28 U.S. Code §§ 49, 528, 529, 591 et seq., 1364; 39 U.S. Code §§ 3210, 3216, 3219

Continued

June 13, 1979, P.L. 96-19, 2 U.S. Code
§§ 701 to 704, 707, 708; 5 U.S. Code Appx.
§§ 201 to 207, 209, 402; 28 U.S. Code
Appx. §§ 301 to 303, 305, 308

June 22, 1979, P.L. 96-28, 18 U.S. Code
§ 207

Jan. 3, 1983, P.L. 97-409, 28 U.S. Code
§§ 591, 591 nt., 592, 594 , 596, 598

Nov. 11, 1983, P.L. 98-150, 2 U.S. Code
§ 702; 5 U.S. Code Appx. § 201, 210 to
212, 401 to 405, 407; 28 U.S. Code Appx.
§ 302

June 19, 1986, P.L. 99-336, 2 U.S. Code
§ 288d

Dec. 15, 1987, P.L. 100-187, 5 U.S. Code
Appx. §§ 203, 205; 28 U.S. Code 591 nt.

Nov. 30, 1989, P.L. 101-194, 5 U.S. Code
Appx. §§ 101 to 112, 201 to 212, 501 to
505; 28 U.S. Code Appx. §§ 301 to 309

Dec. 18, 1989, P.L. 101-237, 28 U.S. Code
Appx. § 308

May 4, 1990, P.L. 101-280, 5 U.S. Code
Appx. §§ 101, 103, 104, 105, 106, 109, 110,
111, 112, 501, 502, 503

July 16, 1990, P.L. 101-334, 5 U.S. Code
Appx. § 405

Dec. 1, 1990, P.L. 101-650, 5 U.S. Code
Appx. §§ 104, 502

April 6, 1991, P.L. 102-25, 5 U.S. Code
Appx. § 101

Aug. 14, 1991, P.L. 102-90, 5 U.S. Code
Appx. §§ 102, 103, 105, 503, 505

Dec. 9, 1991, P.L. 102-198, 5 U.S. Code
Appx. § 502

Oct. 2, 1992, P.L. 102-378, 5 U.S. Code
Appx. §§ 101, 109, 501, 502

Oct. 24, 1992, P.L. 102-506, 5 U.S. Code
Appx. § 405

Dec. 19, 1995, P.L. 104-65, 5 U.S. Code
Appx. § 102

Aug. 6, 1996, P.L. 104-179, 5 U.S. Code
Appx. §§ 401, 403, 405, 408

Aug. 20, 1996, P.L. 104-186, 5 U.S. Code
Appx. § 103, 109

Sept. 23, 1996, P.L. 104-201, 5 U.S. Code
Appx. § 105

Oct. 30, 1998, P.L. 105-318, 5 U.S. Code
Appx. § 105

Ethics in Government Law
Nev. Rev. Stat. 1979 Reprint, 281.411 et seq.

Ethics Law (Public)
Md. Ann. Code 1974, Art. SG, § 15-101 et
seq.

Ethics Law of the Town of Stanford
N.Y. Local Laws 1970, Town of Stanford, p.
2749

Ethics Reform Act of 1989
Nov. 30, 1989, P.L. 101-194, 5 U.S. Code
Appx. § 101 nt.

May 4, 1990, P.L. 101-280, 2 U.S. Code
§ 31-2; 5 U.S. Code §§ 3393, 7701; 5 U.S.
Code Appx. §§ 101 nt., 501, 502, 503; 18
U.S. Code §§ 207 nt., 208 nt.; 31 U.S. Code
§ 1344 nt.

Aug. 14, 1991, P.L. 102-90, 2 U.S. Code
§ 31-2

Aug. 20, 1996, P.L. 104-186, 31 U.S. Code
§ 1344 nt.

Ethnic Harrassment Act
R.I. Gen. Laws 1956, 42-80-1 et seq.

Ethnic Minority Fellowship Program
Kan. Laws 1993, Ch. 47

Ethnic Reference Repeal Act
D.C. Laws 1975, No. 1-26 § 31-2207

Etowah County Bingo Act
Ala. Acts 1991, p. 942

Etowah-Forsyth Water Authority Act
Ga. Laws 1984, p. 4779

Etowah Water and Sewer Act
Ga. Laws 1980, p. 3407

Eugenical Sterilization Act
Mont. Code Ann. 1981, 53-23-101 et seq.
Ore. Rev. Stat., 436.205 et seq.
Va. Code 1950, § 37.1-171.1

Eugenics Act
Iowa Code 1977, 145.1 et seq.
Pa. 1939 Pamph. Laws 148, No. 76

EURATOM Co-operation Act of 1958
Aug. 28, 1958, P.L. 85-846, 72 Stat. 1084, 42
U.S. Code §§ 2291 to 2296

Eve

Sept. 6, 1961, P.L. 87-206, 75 Stat. 479, 42
U.S. Code §§ 2293, 2294, 2296

Aug. 1, 1964, P.L. 88-394, 78 Stat. 376, 42
U.S. Code § 2294

Dec. 14, 1967, P.L. 90-190, 81 Stat. 578, 42
U.S. Code § 2994

Aug. 14, 1973, P.L. 93-88, 87 Stat. 296, 42
U.S. Code § 2294

Eureka Charter
Nev. Statutes 1877, Ch. 60, p. 99

Euro Conservation Act
Ill. Comp. Stat. 1992, Ch. 815, § 617/1 et seq.

**European Bank for Reconstruction and
Development Act**
Nov. 5, 1990, P.L. 101-513, 22 U.S. Code
§ 2901 nt.

European Corn Borer Law
N.J. Stat. Ann., 4:7-43, 4:7-44

European Recovery Program
See Foreign Assistance Act Of 1948

European Security Act of 1998
Oct. 21, 1998, P.L. 105-277, Division G,
Subdivision B, Title XXVII, 112 Stat. 2681,
22 U.S. Code § 1928 nt.

Eustis Revenue Bond Act
Fla. Special Laws 1949, Ch. 25822

Euthanasia for Animals Act
S.C. Code Ann. 1976, § 47-3-410 et seq.

Evacuation Authority Act
N.M. Stat. Ann. 1953, Superseded Vols.,
9-14-1, 9-14-2

Evaluation Act (Job Training)
Ill. Comp. Stat. 1992, Ch. 20, §§ 2220/5-1,
2220/5-5

**Evaluation and Justification Act (State
Government)**
Me. Rev. Stat. Ann. 1964, Title 3, §§ 921 et
seq., 951 et seq.

**Evangeline Parish Solid Waste Disposal Act
of 1984**
La. Rev. Stat. Ann., 33:8001

**Evans Cable, Allen Law (State Board of
Education-Negro Member)**
Ind. Laws 1939, Ch. 82, p. 474

**Evans County Industrial Development
Authority Act**
Ga. Laws 1971, p. 2341

**Evans Dangerous Buildings and Structures
Law**
N.Y. Local Laws 1973, Town of Evans, p.
1716

Evans Junk Car Disposal Law
N.Y. Local Laws 1967, Town of Evans, p.
1551

Evans Mobile Home Development Law
N.Y. Local Laws 1972, Town of Evans, p.
1369

Evans Public Improvement Law
N.Y. Local Laws 1972, Town of Evans, p.
1380

**Evans Rental or Unoccupied Premises
Standards Law**
N.Y. Local Laws 1967, Town of Evans, p.
1532

Evans Vehicle and Traffic Law
N.Y. Local Laws 1969, Town of Evans, p.
1208

Evarts Act (Circuit Courts of Appeals)
See Circuit Court Of Appeals Act

Evasion Act
Ill. Rev. Stat. 1991, Ch. 40, § 216 et seq.

Evasion Act (Marriage)
See Marriage Evasion Act

Everett-Sample Act (Optometry)
Ky. Rev. Stat. 1971, 320.200 et seq.

Everglades Drainage District Act

Fla. Laws 1913, Ch. 6456

Everglades Forever Act

Fla. Stat. Ann., 373.4592

Everglades National Park Acts

May 30, 1934, Ch. 371, 48 Stat. 816, 16 U.S. Code §§ 410 to 410c

Aug. 21, 1937, Ch. 732, 50 Stat. 742, 16 U.S. Code § 410b

Dec. 6, 1944, Ch. 508, 58 Stat. 794, 16 U.S. Code § 410d

Oct. 10, 1949, Ch. 659, 63 Stat. 733, 16 U.S. Code §§ 410e to 410h

July 2, 1958, P.L. 85-482, 72 Stat. 280, 16 U.S. Code §§ 410i to 410p

Sept. 14, 1959, P.L. 86-269, 73 Stat. 553, 16 U.S. Code §§ 410q, 410r

Sept. 2, 1960, P.L. 86-681, 74 Stat. 577, 16 U.S. Code §§ 410r-1, 410r-2

Sept. 12, 1964, P.L. 88-588, 78 Stat. 933, 16 U.S. Code §§ 410r-3 , 410r-4

Oct. 17, 1969, P.L. 91-88, 83 Stat. 134, 16 U.S. Code § 410p

Sept. 26, 1970, P.L. 91-428, 84 Stat. 885, 16 U.S. Code §§ 410j, 410p

Everglades National Park Protection and Expansion Act of 1989

Dec. 13, 1989, P.L. 101-229, 16 U.S. Code § 410r-5 nt.

March 9, 1994, 16 U.S. Code § 410r-8

Nov. 2, 1994, P.L. 103-437, 16 U.S. Code § 410r-8

Nov. 13, 1997, P.L. 105-82, 16 U.S. Code § 410r-7

Everglades Protection Act (Marjory Stoneman Douglas)

Fla. Stat. Ann., 373.4592

Evergreen Underground Water Conservation District Act

Tex. General and Special Laws 59th Leg., 1965, p. 398, Ch. 197

Eviction Act (Retaliatory)

Ill. Rev. Stat. 1991, Ch. 80, §§ 70, 71

N.Y. Real Property Law (Consol. Laws Ch. 50), § 223b

Eviction Law

N.Y. City Admin. Code 1938, Ch. 51, § Y51-6.0

Eviction of Tenants Act

La. Code of Civil Procedure Art. 4701 et seq.

Evidence Act

Cal. Statutes 1965, Ch. 299, p. 1297

Fla. Stat. Ann., 90.101 et seq.

Ga. Code Ann., 24-1-1 et seq., 24-5-26

Ill. Rev. Stat. 1991, Ch. 110, § 8-101 et seq.

Md. Ann. Code 1974, Art. CJ, § 10-101 et seq.

Mo. Rev. Stat., 490.010 et seq.

Neb. Rev. Stat. 1943, 25-1209 et seq.

N.J. Stat. Ann., 2A:81-1 et seq., 2A:84A-1 et seq.

Ohio Rev. Code 1953, 2317.36 et seq.

Okla. Stat. Ann., Title 12, § 2101 et seq.

Ore. Rev. Stat. 1953, 40.010 et seq.

Pa. Cons. Stat., Title 42, § 6101 et seq.

P.R. Laws Ann. 1954, Title 32, § 1621 et seq.

Wash. Rev. Code Ann., 5.24.010 et seq.

Evidence Act (Business and Public Records as)

Me. Rev. Stat. Ann. 1964, Title 16, § 451 et seq.

Evidence Act (Business Records)

See Uniform Business Records as Evidence Act

Evidence Act (Foreign Law)

Minn. Stat. Ann., 599.02

Pa. Cons. Stat., Title 42, § 5327

Evidence Act (Photographic Copies of Business and Public Records)

See Uniform Photographic Copies of Business and Public Records as

Evidence Act (Public Records)

N.Y. Civil Practice Laws and Rules (Consol. Laws Ch. 8) § 4518

Evidence Law
Cal. Code of Civil Procedure § 1823 et seq.

Evidence of Death and Absentees' Property Act
Wash. Rev. Code Ann., 813.22 et seq.

Evidence of Indebtedness Act (Mutilated)
Ill. Rev. Stat. 1991, Ch. 130, §§ 42.9, 43

Evidence Perpetuation Act
Neb. Rev. Stat. 1943, 25-1267.08 et seq.
Wash. Rev. Code Ann., Rules of Court, Rule 26a, Rule 696

Evidence Rules
Neb. Rev. Stat. 1943, 27-101 et seq.
Wis. Stat. Ann., 901.01 et seq.

Ex-Servicemen's Unemployment Compensation Act of 1958
Aug. 28, 1958, P.L. 85-848, 72 Stat. 1087 (See 5 U.S. Code §§ 8501, 8506, 8521 to 8525)

Examination before Trial Act
N.C. Rules of Civil Procedure, Rules 26 to 37

Examination Forty-Eight Hours after Arrest Act
Haw. Rev. Stat. Ann., § 803-9 et seq.

Examination Law
N.C. Gen. Stat. 1943, § 58-2-131 et seq.

Examination of Injured Claimant Act
Wash. Rev. Code Ann., Rules of Court, Rule 35

Examination Parity and Year 2000 Readiness for Financial Institutions Act
March 20, 1998, P.L. 105-164, 12 U.S. Code § 1461 nt.

Examiners Act (Deception Detection)
Utah Code Ann. 1953, 53-5-301 et seq.

Examiners Act (Detection of Deception)
Ill. Rev. Stat. 1991, Ch. 111, § 2400 et seq.

Examining Act (Insurance Companies)
Tex. Insurance Code, Art. 1.15 et seq.

Excavation Fence Act
Ill. Rev. Stat. 1991, Ch. 54, §§ 25.9, 26

Excavation Law
N.Y. Local Laws 1971, Town of Wheatland, p. 3708
N.Y. Local Laws 1972, Town of Perinton, p. 2541
N.Y. Local Laws 1973, Village of Ardsley, p. 3165

Excavation Protection Act (Adjacent Landowner)
Ill. Comp. Stat. 1992, Ch. 765, §§ 410/0.01, 410/1
Ill. Rev. Stat. 1991, Ch. 111 1/2, §§ 3300, 3301

Excavations Near Underground Utility Facilities Act
Miss. Code Ann. 1972, § 77-13-1 et seq.

Excellence in Academic Medicine Act
Ill. Comp. Stat. 1992, Ch. 30, § 775/1 et seq.

Excellence in Education Act
Aug. 11, 1984, P.L. 98-377, 20 U.S. Code §§ 4031 et seq., 4031 nt.
Sept. 30, 1986, P.L. 99-425, 20 U.S. Code § 4033
Mo. Rev. Stat. 1978, 160.251 et seq.

Excellence in Education Bond Issue Act (Pete Turnham)
Ala. Acts 1998, No. 374

Excellence in Education Program Act (Award for)
Wash. Rev. Code 1983, 28A.625.010 et seq.

Excellence in Higher Education Act
Tex. Education Code, § 62.001 et seq.

Excellence in Local Education Act
Ala. Code 1975, § 16-13-60 et seq.

Excellence in Mathematics, Science and Engineering Education Act of 1990

Nov. 16, 1990, P.L. 101-589, 20 U.S. Code §§ 5301, 5301, 5311

Aug. 17, 1991, P.L. 102-103, 20 U.S. Code §§ 5381, 5411

July 23, 1992, P.L. 102-325, 20 U.S. Code §§ 5381, 5411

Oct. 20, 1994, P.L. 103-382, 20 U.S. Code §§ 240 nt., 2982 nt., 5301, 5301 nt., 5311, 5321, 5331, 5341 to 5343, 5351, 5361 to 5364, 5371 to 5373, 5381 to 5386, 5401, 5411, 5421, 5422, 5431, 5441

Excellence in Minority Health Education and Care Act

Aug. 18, 1987, P.L. 100-97, 42 U.S. Code §§ 201 nt., 295g-8a

Excellence in Teacher Preparation Act (Award for)

Wash. Rev. Code 1983, 28A.625.350 et seq.

Excelsior Linked Deposit Act

N.Y. State Finance Law 1940 (Consol. Laws Ch. 56) § 212 et seq.

Exceptional Child Education Act

Ala. Code 1975, § 16-39-1 et seq.

Colo. Rev. Stat., 22-20-101 et seq.

Exceptional Children Special Education Act

Kan. Stat. Ann., 72-961 et seq.

Ky. Rev. Stat. 1971, 157.200 et seq.

Exceptional Children's Act (Handicapped)

La. Rev. Stat. 1950, 40:2121 et seq.

Exceptions Act

Wash. Rev. Code Ann., 4.80.010 et seq.

Excess Insurance Agents Act

Ga. Code Ann., 33-5-20 et seq.

Excess Profits Tax Acts

March 3, 1917, Ch. 159, 39 Stat. 1000

Oct. 3, 1917, Ch. 63, 40 Stat. 302

Feb. 24, 1919, Ch. 18, 40 Stat. 1088

Nov. 23, 1921, Ch. 136, 42 Stat. 271

Oct. 8, 1940, Ch. 757, 54 Stat. 974

March 7, 1941, Ch. 10, 55 Stat. 27, 26 U.S. Code § 23

Jan. 3, 1951, Ch. 1199, 64 Stat. 1137

Excessive Sentence Act

Mich. Comp. Laws Ann., 769.24

Exchange Facilitation Fund Act (Land)

Mich. Comp. Laws Ann., 322.461 et seq.

Exchange Law (Telephone Companies)

Ky. Rev. Stat. 1971, 278.520, 278.530, 278.990

Exchange of Insurance Securities Act

Colo. Rev. Stat., 10-3-601 et seq.

Exchange or Reciprocal Insurance Act

Tenn. Code Ann., 56-16-201 et seq.

Exchange Rates and International Economic Policy Coordination Act of 1988

Aug. 23, 1988, P.L. 100-418, 22 U.S. Code § 5301

Exchange Statutes (Water Rights)

Wyo. Stat. Ann., § 41-3-106

Excise Act

P.R. Laws Ann. 1954, Title 13, § 4001 et seq.

Excise Act (Motor Vehicle)

Mass. Gen. Laws 1984, 60A:1 et seq.

Excise Act of the Commonwealth of Puerto Rico

P.R. Laws Ann. 1954, Title 13, § 7001 et seq.

Excise and Use Tax Act

Tex. Tax Code, § 151.001 et seq.

Excise, Estate, and Gift Tax Adjustment Act of 1970

Dec. 31, 1970, P.L. 91-614, 84 Stat. 1836, 15 U.S. Code § 1232a; 26 U.S. Code §§ 56, 1015, 1223, 2012, 2032, 2055, 2204, 2501 to 2504, 2512, 2513, 2515 and others; 31 U.S. Code § 1033

Excise Tax (Gasoline and Special Fuel)

W. Va. Code 1966, § 11-14-1 et seq.

Excise Tax Act
Ariz. Rev. Stat. Ann., § 42-1301 et seq.
Ark. Code Ann. 1987, 18-47-201 et seq.
Haw. Rev. Stat. Ann., § 237-1 et seq.
P.R. Laws Ann. 1954, Title 13, § 4001 et seq.
Tenn. Code Ann., 67-4-801 et seq.
Wash. Rev. Code Ann., 82.01.050 et seq.

Excise Tax Act (Aircraft)
Ind. Code Ann., 6-6-6.5-1 et seq.

Excise Tax Act (Automobile Rental)
Iowa Code Ann., 422C.1 et seq.

Excise Tax Act (Banks)
Haw. Rev. Stat. Ann., § 241-1 et seq.

Excise Tax Act (Boat and Motor)
Okla. Stat. Ann., Title 63, § 828 et seq.

Excise Tax Act (Corporations)
Mass. Gen. Laws Ann., 63:30 et seq.
Ore. Rev. Stat., 317.005 et seq.

Excise Tax Act (County Fire Protection)
N.M. Stat. Ann., 7-20A-1 et seq.

Excise Tax Act (Foreign Corporations)
Pa. Purdon's Stat., Title 72, § 8001 et seq.

Excise Tax Act (Liquor)
N.M. Stat. Ann., 7-17-1 et seq.

Excise Tax Act (Local Liquor)
N.M. Stat. Ann., 7-24-1 et seq.

Excise Tax Act (Motor Fuel)
Colo. Rev. Stat., 39-27-101 et seq.
Okla. Stat. Ann., Title 68, § 501 et seq.

Excise Tax Act (Motor Vehicles)
Ind. Code Ann., 6-6-5-1 et seq.
N.M. Stat. Ann., 7-14-1 et seq.
Okla. Stat. Ann., Title 68, § 2101 et seq.

Excise Tax Act (Petroleum)
Okla. Stat. Ann., Title 68, § 1101 et seq.

Excise Tax Act (Resources)
N.M. Stat. Ann., 7-25-1 et seq.

Excise Tax Act (Telecommunications)
Ill. Comp. Stat. 1992, Ch. 35, § 630/1 et seq.

Excise Tax Act (Vessel and Motor)
Okla. Stat. 1981, Title 63, § 4101 et seq.

Excise Tax Acts
Oct. 3, 1917, Ch. 63, 40 Stat. 316
Feb. 24, 1919, Ch. 18, 40 Stat. 1122
Nov. 23, 1921, Ch. 136, 42 Stat. 291
June 2, 1924, Ch. 234, 43 Stat. 322
March 11, 1947, Ch. 17, 61 Stat. 12

Excise Tax Administration Act
Wash. Rev. Code Ann., 82.32.010 et seq.

Excise Tax on Financial Institutions Law
Ala. Code 1975, § 40-16-1 et seq.

Excise-Tax Rate Extension Act of 1964
June 30, 1964, P.L. 88-348, 78 Stat. 237, 26
U.S. Code §§ 165, 4061, 4251, 4261, 5001,
5022, 5041, 5051, 5063, 5701, 5707, 6412

Excise Tax Reduction Acts
March 31, 1954, Ch. 126, 68 Stat. 37
June 21, 1965, P.L. 89-44, 79 Stat. 136, 23
U.S. Code § 120 nt.; 26 U.S. Code §§ 39,
40, 72, 501 nt., 874, 1314, 1481, 4041,
4055, 4057, 4061, 4063 and others

Excise Tax Refund Act (Federal)
Ill. Comp. Stat. 1992, Ch. 35, § 730/1
Ill. Rev. Stat. 1991, Ch. 127, §§ 39d-1,
39d-1.1

Excise Tax Technical Changes Acts
Sept. 2, 1958, P.L. 85-859, 72 Stat. 1275, 26
U.S. Code §§ 4001, 4003, 4031, 4041,
4053, 4057, 4058, 4121, 4141 to 4143,
4192, 4216 to 4218, 4221 to 4225 and
others
Sept. 21, 1959, P.L. 86-344, 73 Stat. 617, 26
U.S. Code §§ 4001, 4057, 4221, 4233,
4241, 4243, 4253, 4294, 4321, 4323, 4461

Excise Tax Warrant Law
Wash. Rev. Code Ann., 82.32.210 et seq.

Exclusion Act (Chinese)
Haw. Session Laws 1887, Special Session, Ch. 28

Exclusion Program Act (Homestead Property)
Pa. Cons. Stat., Title 53, § 8581 et seq.

Exclusionary Rule
Mont. Code Ann. 1987, 46-13-301, 46-13-302

Exclusive Fisheries Zone Act
Nev. Rev. Stat. 1979 Reprint, 645.320

Exclusive Listing Act
Nev. Rev. Stat. 1979 Reprint, 645.320

Excuse Act (Homicide)
Wash. Rev. Code Ann., 9A.16.030

Execution Act (Judgments)
Ky. Rev. Stat. 1971, 426.010 et seq.
Neb. Rev. Stat. 1943, 25-1501 et seq.
N.J. Stat. Ann., 2A:17-1 et seq.
N.M. Stat. Ann., 39-4-1 et seq.
N.Y. Civil Practice Law and Rules (Consol. Laws Ch. 8) § 5230 et seq.
Wash. Rev. Code Ann., 815.01 et seq.
Wash. Rev. Code Ann., 6.17.010 et seq.

Execution Act (Property)
Ohio Rev. Code 1953, 2329.01 et seq.

Execution and Attachment Act
Haw. Rev. Stat. Ann., § 651-1 et seq.

Execution Law
Neb. Rev. Stat. 1943, 25-1501 et seq.

Execution Methods Reform Act
Ala. Acts 1997, H.B. 64

Execution Methods Reform Act of 1998
Ala. Acts 1997, H.B. 64

Execution of Wills Act
Tenn. Code Ann., 32-1-101 et seq.

Execution Sales and Redemption Law
Wash. Rev. Code Ann., 6.21.010 et seq., 6.24.010 et seq.

Execution Supplemental Proceedings Act
Wash. Rev. Code Ann., 6.32.010 et seq.

Executions Act (Stay)
Pa. 1861 Pamph. Laws 770, No. 696

Executions Against Spendthrift Trusts Act
Pa. Cons. Stat., Title 23, § 4301 et seq.

Executions, Judgments and Decrees Act
Ill. Rev. Stat. 1991, Ch. 110

Executive Accountant Act
S.D. Laws 1913, Ch. 206

Executive Agencies Reorganization Act
Mich. Comp. Laws 1948, 16.1 et seq.

Executive Agents Act
Mass. Gen. Laws Ann., 3:39 et seq.

Executive and Administrative Departments Act
Haw. Rev. Stat. Ann., § 226-1 et seq.

Executive and Judicial Salary Act
Utah Code Ann. 1953, 67-8-1 et seq.

Executive and Judicial Succession Act
Okla. Stat. Ann., Title 63, § 685.1 et seq.

Executive and Judicial Succession Act (Emergency)
See Emergency Interim Executive and Judicial Succession Act

Executive and Professional Liability Fund Act
Md. Ann. Code 1957, Art. 48A. § 557 et seq.

Executive Branch Code of Ethics
Ky. Rev. Stat. 1971, 11A.001 et seq.

Executive Branch Reform Act
Okla. Stat. Ann., Title 74, §§ 10.1 to 10.3

Executive Branch Reorganization Act
N.H. Rev. Stat. 1955, 21-G:1 et seq.

Executive Budget Act
Alaska Stat. 1962, § 37.07.010 et seq.
Colo. Rev. Stat., 24-37-401 et seq.
Haw. Rev. Stat. Ann., § 37-61 et seq.
N.C. Gen. Stat. 1943, § 143-1 et seq.

Executive Clemency Act
Mont. Code Ann., 46-23-101 et seq.

Executive Conflict of Interest Act
Wash. Rev. Code Ann., 42.18.010 et seq.

Executive Department Law
N.Y. Local Laws 1972, Town of Oyster Bay.
p. 2483

Executive Exchange Program Voluntary Services Act of 1986
Sept. 30, 1986, P.L. 99-424, 5 U.S. Code § 4103 nt.
Aug. 16, 1989, P.L. 101-87, 5 U.S. Code § 4103 nt.

Executive Law
N.Y. Consol. Laws Ch. 18

Executive Mansion Fine Arts Commission Act
N.C. Gen. Stat. 1943, §§ 143B-79, 143B-80

Executive Mansion Trust Act
N.Y. Arts and Cultural Affairs Law (Consol. Laws Ch. 11C) § 54.01 et seq.

Executive Office Appropriation Acts
Aug. 6, 1962, P.L. 87-575, 76 Stat. 315
June 13, 1963, P.L. 88-39, 77 Stat. 63
Aug. 1, 1964, P.L. 88-392, 78 Stat. 373
June 30, 1965, P.L. 89-57, 79 Stat. 201
June 29, 1966, P.L. 89-474, 80 Stat. 227, 3 U.S. Code § 102 nt.
July 7, 1967, P.L. 90-47, 81 Stat. 117, 3 U.S. Code § 102 nt.
June 19, 1968, P.L. 90-350, 82 Stat. 194, 3 U.S. Code § 102 nt.
Sept. 29, 1969, P.L. 91-74, 83 Stat. 121, 3 U.S. Code § 102 nt.

Sept. 26, 1970, P.L. 91-422, 84 Stat. 877, 3 U.S. Code § 102 nt.
July 9, 1971, P.L. 92-49, 85 Stat. 113, 3 U.S. Code § 102 nt.
July 13, 1972, P.L. 92-351, 86 Stat. 477, 3 U.S. Code § 102 nt.
Oct. 30, 1973, P.L. 93-143, 87 Stat. 510, 26 U.S. Code § 7443 nt.; 31 U.S. Code § 638c; 33 U.S. Code § 776
Aug. 9, 1975, P.L. 94-91, 89 Stat. 447, 26 U.S. Code § 7443 nt.; 31 U.S. Code §§ 638c nt., 699b; 33 U.S. Code § 776; 40 U.S. Code § 490
Dec. 22, 1987, P.L. 100-202, 101 Stat. 1329
Nov. 3, 1989, P.L. 101-136, 103 Stat. 790

Executive Office Appropriations Act, 1991
Nov. 5, 1990, P.L. 101-509, 3 U.S. Code § 102 nt.; 28 U.S. Code § 524

Executive Office Appropriations Act, 1992
Oct. 28, 1991, P.L. 102-141, 105 Stat. 844

Executive Office Appropriations Act, 1993
Oct. 6, 1992, P.L. 102-393, 3 U.S. Code § 102 nt.

Executive Office Appropriations Act, 1994
Oct. 28, 1993, P.L. 103-123, 107 Stat. 1235

Executive Office Appropriations Act, 1995
Sept. 30, 1994, P.L. 103-329, 108 Stat. 2392

Executive Office Appropriations Act, 1996
Nov. 19, 1995, P.L. 104-52, Title III, 109 Stat. 477

Executive Office Appropriations Act, 1998
Oct. 10, 1997, P.L. 105-61, Title III, 111 Stat. 1290

Executive Office Appropriations Act, 1999
Oct. 21, 1998, P.L. 105-277, 101(h), Title III, 112 Stat. 2681

Executive Organization Act
Mich. Comp. Laws Ann., 16.101 et seq.
N.C. Gen. Stat. 1943, §§ 143A-1 et seq., 143B-1 et seq.

Executive Pay Act of 1949
Oct. 15, 1949, Ch. 695, 63 Stat. 880

Executive Planning Act
N.M. Stat. Ann., 9-14-1 et seq.

Executive Reorganization Act
Fla. Stat. Ann., 20.01 et seq.
Ga. Code Ann., 50-4-1 et seq.
Haw. Rev. Stat. Ann., 1985, § 26-1 et seq.
La. Rev. Stat. Ann., 36:1 et seq.
Miss. Code Ann. 1972, § 7-17-1 et seq.
Mont. Code Ann., 2-15-101 et seq.
N.J. Stat. Ann., 52:14C-1 et seq.
N.M. Stat. Ann., 9-1-1 et seq.
P.R. Laws Ann. 1954, Title 3, § 1551 et seq.

Executive Reorganization Implementation Act
Ill. Rev. Stat. 1991, Ch. 127, § 1801 et seq.

Executive Reorganization Orders
S.D. Codified Laws 1967, 1-32-1 et seq.
S.D. Laws 1974, Ch. 3
S.D. Laws 1975,Ch. 5
S.D. Laws 1979, Ch. 351 et seq.
S.D. Laws 1980, Ch. 366 et seq.
S.D. Laws 1980, Ch. 370 et seq.
S.D. Laws 1980, Ch. 379
S.D. Laws 1980, Ch. 380
S.D. Laws 1981, Ch. 374 et seq.
S.D. Laws 1983, Ch. 388 et seq.
S.D. Laws 1984, Ch. 343
S.D. Laws 1985, Ch. 399 et seq.
S.D. Laws 1987, Ch. 390 et seq.
S.D. Laws 1988, Ch. 439
S.D. Laws 1988, Ch. 440
S.D. Laws 1991, Ch. 6
S.D. Laws 1991, Ch. 17
S.D. Laws 1991, Ch. 19
S.D. Laws 1991, Ch. 20

Executive Salary Cost-of-Living Adjustment Act
Aug. 9, 1975, P.L. 94-82, 89 Stat. 419, 2 U.S. Code §§ 31, 60a nt., 136a, 136a-1, 356; 3 U.S. Code § 104; 5 U.S. Code §§ 5305, 5312 to 5316, 5318; 11 U.S. Code § 68; 28 U.S. Code §§ 5, 44, 135, 173, 213, 252, 461, 792; 31 U.S. Code §§ 42a, 51a; 40 U.S. Code §§ 162a, 166b; 44 U.S. Code § 303

Executive Statutory Suspension Act
Del. Laws Vol. 44, p. 239, Ch. 62

Executive Succession Act (Emergency Interim)
Tex. Government Code, § 401.021 et seq.

Executive Succession Act (Emergency)
See Emergency Interim Executive Succession Act

Executive Sucession Act
Ida. Code 1947, 59-1401 et seq.
Kan. Stat. Ann., 48-1201 et seq.
S.C. Code Ann. 1976, § 1-9-10 et seq.
S.D. Codified Laws 1967, 1-30-1 et seq.

Executors Act
Md. Ann. Code 1974, Art. ET, 36-101 et seq.

Executors and Administrators Act
Del. Code of 1974, Title 12, § 1501 et seq.
N.J. Stat. Ann., 3B:10-1 et seq.
Wash. Rev. Code Ann., 11.36.010, 11.48.010 et seq.

Executors and Administrators Disqualification Act
Wash. Rev. Code Ann., 11.36.010

Executors and Trustees—Investments Authorized Act
Ga. Code Ann., 53-8-1 et seq.

Exemplary Damage Act
Colo. Rev. Stat., 13-21-102

Exemplary Teacher Training Act (Wildman-Keeley-Solis)
Cal. Education Code 1976, § 44391 et seq.

Exempt Estates Act (Administration)
Neb. Rev. Stat. 1943, 30-24,127; 30-24.128

Exempt Firemen Act
N.J. Stat. Ann., Superseded Vol., 15:7-1 to 15:7-12

Exemption Act
Tex. Property Code, § 41.001 et seq.

Exemption Act (Agent Orange Award)
  Mich. Comp. Laws Ann., 35.1071, 35.1072

Exemption Act (Execution)
  Ala. Code 1975, § 6-10-1 et seq.
  Alaska Stat. 1962, § 09.38.010 et seq.
  Cal. Code of Civil Procedure § 690 et seq.
  Colo. Rev. Stat., 13-54-102 et seq.
  D.C. Code 1973, § 15-501 et seq.
  Ind. Code Ann., 34-2-28-0.5 et seq.
  Ind. Code Ann., 627.2 et seq.
  Kan. Stat. Ann., 60-2301 et seq.
  Ky. Rev. Stat. 1971, 427.010 et seq.
  Md. Ann. Code 1974, Art. CJ, § 11-504 et
    seq.
  Mich. Comp. Laws Ann., 600.6021 et seq.
  Minn. Stat. Ann., 550.37 et seq.
  Miss. Code Ann. 1972, § 85-3-1 et seq.
  Mont. Code Ann., 25-13-601 et seq.
  N.H. Rev. Stat. 1955, 511:2
  Ohio Rev. Code 1953, 2329.62 et seq.
  Okla. Stat. Ann., Title 31, § 1 et seq.
  Ore. Rev. Stat., 23.160 et seq.
  Pa. Cons. Stat., Title 42, § 8123 et seq.
  R.I. Gen. Laws 1956, 9-26-4
  Tenn. Code Ann., 26-2-101 et seq.
  Tex. Education Code, § 23.61 et seq.
  Utah Code Ann. 1953, 78-23-1
  Vt. Stat. Ann., Title 12, § 2740
  Wash. Rev. Code Ann., 815.18
  Wash. Rev. Code Ann., 6.15.010 et seq.
  W. Va. Code 1966, § 38-8-1 et seq.

Exemption Act (Family)
  Pa. Cons. Stat., Title 20, § 3121 et seq.

Exemption Act (Home Municipal)
  Miss. Code Ann. 1972, § 27-33-1 et seq.

Exemption Act (Homesteads)
  See Homestead Exemption Act

Exemption Act (Insurance)
  Wash. Rev. Code Ann., 48.18.400 et seq.

Exemption Act (Judgements)
  Wash. Rev. Code Ann., 6.15.010 et seq.

Exemption Act (Jury)
  See Jury Exemption Act

Exemption Act (Life Insurance)
  N.Y. Insurance Law 1984 (Consol. Laws Ch.
    28) § 3212
  Pa. 1868 Pamph. Laws 103, No. 64

Exemption Act (Personal Property)
  Ill. Rev. Stat. 1991, Ch. 110, § 12-901 et seq.
  S.D. Codified Laws 1967, 43-45-1 et seq.
  Tenn. Code Ann. 1955, 26-201 et seq.

Exemption Act (Property Tax)
  S.C. Code Ann. 1976, § 12-37-220

Exemption Act (Taxation)
  Ala. Code 1975, § 40-23-62
  Ariz. Rev. Stat. Ann., § 42-271
  Conn. Gen. Stat. 1983, § 12-88 et seq.
  D.C. Code Ann., § 47-1002 et seq.
  Fla. Stat. Ann., 212.08
  Ga. Code Ann., 48-5-40 et seq.
  Ida. Code 1947, 63-105
  Ind. Code Ann., 6-1.1-10-1 et seq.
  Ind. Code Ann., 427.1 et seq.
  Mass. Gen. Laws Ann., 59:5
  Me. Rev. Stat. Ann. 1964, Title 36, § 651 et
    seq.
  Mich. Comp. Laws Ann., 205.94
  Miss. Code Ann. 1972, § 27-31-1 et seq.
  Neb. Rev. Stat. 1943, 77-202
  N.H. Rev. Stat. 1955, 72:22 et seq.
  N.J. Stat. Ann., 54:4-3.3 et seq.
  Ohio Rev. Code 1953, 5709.01 et seq.
  Pa. Purdon's Stat., Title 72, § 5020-204
  S.C. Code Ann. 1976, § 12-37-220 et seq.
  S.D. Codified Laws 1967, 10-4-7 et seq.
  Wash. Rev. Code Ann., 84.36.005 et seq.

Exemption Act (Wage Garnishment)
  Fla. Stat. Ann., 222.11

Exemption Act (Wages)
  Md. Ann. Code 1974, Art. CL, §§ 15-602,
    15-603

Exemption Act (Widows)
Pa. Cons. Stat., Title 20, § 3121 et seq.

Exemption and Abatement Law (Five-Year)
N.J. Stat. Ann., 40A:21-1 et seq.

Exemption and Refund of Taxes on Petroleum Products Act
Tenn. Code Ann., 67-3-201 et seq.

Exemption of Domestic Servants and Agricultural Workers Act (Workmen's Compensation)
Pa. 1915 Pamph. Laws 777, No. 343

Exercise of Power of Appointment Act
Ill. Rev. Stat. 1991, Ch. 30, §§ 176.50, 176.51

Exeter School Development Act
R.I. Public Laws 1958, Ch. 160

Exhaust Emission Standards Act
D.C. Laws 1977, No. 1-132

Exhibitions and Shows License Act
R.I. Gen. Laws 1956, 5-22-1 et seq.

Exhibitors Safety Act (Aerial)
Ill. Comp. Stat. 1992, Ch. 720, § 530/0.01 et seq.

Existing Industry Training Act
Colo. Rev. Stat., 23-60-307

Exotic Livestock and Exotic Livestock Products Inspection Act
Okla. Stat. Ann., Title 2, § 6-290.1 et seq.

Exotic Weed Act
Ill. Rev. Stat. 1991, Ch. 5, § 931 et seq.

Expanded Health Care Coverage Act
N.Y. Laws 1988, Ch. 703

Expansion Act (Capital)
Neb. Rev. Stat. 1943, 72-1261 et seq.

Expansion Act (Home Care)
N.J. Stat. Ann., 30:4E-5 et seq.

Expansion Act (Navy)
See Naval Expansion Act

Expansion Act (State Capitol)
N.M. Stat. Ann. 1953, 6-2-14 et seq.

Expatriation Act
See Citizenship Act
Ky. Rev. Stat. 1971, 2.010

Expatriation Act (Civil War)
Ky. Acts 1861-62 (Feb., Public) Ch. 509

Expatriation Act of 1954
Sept. 3, 1954, Ch. 1256, 68 Stat. 1146, 8 U.S. Code § 1481

Expedited Child Support Act
Ill. Rev. Stat. 1991, Ch. 40, § 2701 et seq.

Expedited Eviction of Drug Traffickers Act (Model)
Pa. Purdon's Stat., Title 35, § 780-151 et seq.

Expedited Funds Availability Act
Aug. 10, 1987, P.L. 100-86, 12 U.S. Code §§ 248a, 24a nt., 4001 nt., 4001 to 4010
Aug. 9, 1989, P.L. 101-73, 12 U.S. Code § 4009
Nov. 28, 1990, P.L. 101-625, 12 U.S. Code § 4002
Dec. 19, 1991, P.L. 102-242, 12 U.S. Code §§ 4002, 4003, 4009

Expedited Permit Process
R.I. Gen. Laws 1956, 42-117-1 et seq.

Expedited Remedial Action Reform Act
Cal. Health and Safety Code § 25396.1 et seq.

Expediting Act (Revenue Collections)
Ky. Rev. Stat. 1971, 132.330, 132.340, 135.060, 135.070

Expediting Acts (Trusts and Interstate Commerce)
Feb. 11, 1903, Ch. 544, 32 Stat. 823, 15 U.S. Code §§ 28, 29; 49 U.S. Code §§ 44, 45
Feb. 19, 1903, Ch. 708, 32 Stat. 847, 49 U.S. Code §§ 41 to 43

June 25, 1910, Ch. 428, 36 Stat. 854, 15 U.S. Code § 28; 49 U.S. Code § 44

April 6, 1942, Ch. 210, 56 Stat. 198, 15 U.S. Code § 28, 28 nt.; 49 U.S . Code §§ 44, 44 nt.

June 9, 1944, Ch. 239, 58 Stat. 272, 15 U.S. Code § 29; 49 U.S. Code § 45

Nov. 8, 1984, P.L. 98-620, 15 U.S. Code § 28

Expeditions and Economical Tax Appeals Act
Ala. Code 40-3-25

Expenditures and Appropriations Review Act
Neb. Rev. Stat. 1943, 50-701.01 et seq.

Expenses of Audit or Appraisal Statute
Mich. Comp. Laws Ann., 460.401 et seq.

Experimental Air Mail Act
Aug. 23, 1958, P.L. 85-726, 72 Stat. 808

Experimental Cancer Treatment Act
Ill. Rev. Stat. 1991, Ch. 111 1/2, § 6001 et seq.

Experimental Organ Transplantation Procedures Act
Ill. Rev. Stat. 1991, Ch. 111 1/2, § 6601 et seq.

Experimental Program to Stimulate Competitive Research on Space and Aeronautics Act
Nov. 4, 1992, P.L. 102-588, 42 U.S. Code § 2467b

Expert Testimony Act
La. Rev. Stat. Ann., 15:464 et seq.
S.D. Codified Laws 1967, 19-6-1 et seq.
S.D. Codified Laws 1967, 19-15-1 et seq.
Vt. Stat. Ann. 1959, Title 12, § 1643

Expert Witnesses Act
S.D. Codified Laws 1967, 19-15-1 et seq.

Exploitation Act (Adult Abuse and Neglect)
Ida. Code 1947, 39-5301 et seq.

Exploitation of Children Act (Sexual)
N.M. Stat. Ann., 30-6A-1 et seq.

Exploited, Abused, or Neglected Disabled Adult Protection Act
N.C. Gen. Stat. 1943, §§ 108-102 et seq., 108A-99 et seq.

Explosives Act
Oct. 6, 1917, Ch. 83, 40 Stat. 385, 50 U.S. Code §§ 121 to 133, 135 to 144
Nov. 24, 1942, Ch. 641, 56 Stat. 1022, 50 U.S. Code § 123
Cal. Health and Safety Code § 12000 et seq.
Colo. Rev. Stat., 9-7-101 et seq.
Del. Code of 1974, Title 16, § 7101 et seq.
Fla. Stat. Ann., 552.081 et seq.
Ill. Rev. Stat. 1987, Ch. 96 1/2, § 4801 et seq.
Ill. Rev. Stat. 1991, Ch. 96 1/2, § 1-1001 et seq.
Mich. Comp. Laws Ann., 750.200 et seq., 29.41 et seq.
Mont. Code Ann. 1985, 50-38-101 et seq.
N.H. Rev. Stat. 1955, 158:9 et seq.
N.J. Rev. Stat. 1937, 21:1A-128 et seq.
N.M. Stat. Ann., 30-7-17 et seq.
P.R. Laws Ann. 1954, Title 25, § 561 et seq.
R.I. Gen. Laws 1956, 23-28.28-1 et seq.
Utah Laws 1941, 2d Sp. Sess., Ch. 37
Vt. Stat. Ann., Title 20, § 3061 et seq.
Wash. Rev. Code Ann., 70.74.010 et seq.

Explosives and Fireworks Act
Miss. Code Ann. 1972, § 45-13-101 et seq.

Explosives Control Act
Md. Ann. Code 1957, Art. 38A, § 26 et seq.
S.C. Code Ann. 1976, § 23-36-10 et seq.

Explosives Licensing Act
Ill. Rev. Stat. 1987, Ch. 96 1/2, § 4811 et seq.

Explosives Regulation Act
S.D. Codified Laws 1967, 34-36-3 et seq.

Explosives Safety Act
Ala. Code 1975, § 8-17-240 et seq.

Explosives Sales Records Law
Cal. Health and Safety Code § 12100 et seq.

Explosives Transportation Acts

May 30, 1908, Ch. 234, 35 Stat. 554

March 4, 1909, Ch. 331, 35 Stat. 1134 (See 18 U.S. Code §§ 831 to 835)

March 4, 1921, Ch. 172, 41 Stat. 1444 (See 18 U.S. Code §§ 831 to 835)

Export Act (Farm)

Mich. Comp. Laws Ann. 447.201 et seq.

Export Administration Act of 1979

Dec. 16, 1980, P.L. 96-533, 50 U.S. Code Appx. § 2405

Dec. 29, 1981, P.L. 97-145, 50 U.S. Code Appx. §§ 2405, 2410, 2411, 2417

Oct. 1, 1983, P.L. 98-108, 50 U.S. Code Appx. 2149

July 12, 1985, P.L. 99-64, 50 U.S. Code Appx. § 2401 et seq.

Aug. 27, 1986, P.L. 99-399, 50 U.S. Code Appx. § 2405

Nov. 7, 1986, P.L. 99-633, 50 U.S. Code Appx. § 2417

Dec. 4, 1987, P.L. 100-180, 50 U.S. Code Appx. § 2406

Aug. 23, 1988, P.L. 100-418, 50 U.S. Code Appx. § 2403 et seq.

Sept. 28, 1988, P.L. 100-449, 50 U.S. Code Appx. § 2406

Nov. 5, 1990, P.L. 101-510, 50 U.S. Code Appx. §§ 2405, 2410b

Oct. 28, 1991, P.L. 102-138, 50 U.S. Code Appx. §§ 2405, 2410c

Dec. 4, 1991, P.L. 102-182, 50 U.S. Code Appx. §§ 2405, 2410c

March 27, 1993, P.L. 103-10, 50 U.S. Code Appx. §§ 2417, 2419

April 30, 1994, P.L. 103-236, 50 U.S. Code Appx. § 2405

July 5, 1994, P.L. 103-277, 50 U.S. Code Appx. § 2419

Oct. 19, 1996, P.L. 104-316, 50 U.S. Code Appx. § 2405

Oct. 21, 1998, P.L. 105-277, 50 U.S. Code Appx. § 2405

Export Administration Acts

Dec. 30, 1969, P.L. 91-184, 83 Stat. 841, 50 U.S. Code Appx. §§ 2401 to 2413

June 30, 1971, P.L. 92-37, 85 Stat. 89, 50 U.S. Code Appx. § 2413

Oct. 30, 1971, P.L. 92-150, 85 Stat. 416, 50 U.S. Code Appx. § 2413

April 29, 1972, P.L. 92-284, 86 Stat. 133, 50 U.S. Code Appx. § 2413

Aug. 29, 1972, P.L. 92-412, 86 Stat. 644, 50 U.S. Code Appx. §§ 2401 to 2404, 2413

June 30, 1974, P.L. 93-327, 88 Stat. 287, 50 U.S. Code Appx. § 2413

Aug. 14, 1974, P.L. 93-372, 88 Stat. 444, 50 U.S. Code Appx. § 2413

June 22, 1977, P.L. 95-52, 50 U.S. Code Appx. § 2402 et seq.

Dec. 28, 1977, P.L. 95-223, 50 U.S. Code Appx. § 2402 et seq.

Sept. 21, 1979, P.L. 96-67, 50 U.S. Code Appx. § 2403

Sept. 29, 1979, P.L. 96-72, 7 U.S. Code § 1732; 22 U.S. Code §§ 3108, 3108 nt., 2778; 26 U.S. Code § 993; 42 U.S. Code §§ 6212, 6274; 50 U.S. Code Appx. §§ 2401 et seq., 2401 nt.

Dec. 5, 1983, P.L. 98-207, 50 U.S. Code Appx. § 2419

Feb. 29, 1984, P.L. 98-222, 50 U.S. Code Appx. § 2419

July 12, 1985, P.L. 99-64, 50 U.S. Code Appx. § 2401 et seq.

Aug. 27, 1986, P.L. 99-399, 22 U.S. Code § 2780

Nov. 7, 1986, P.L. 99-633, 50 U.S. Code Appx. § 2417

Aug. 23, 1988, P.L. 100-418, 102 Stat. 1347, 50 U.S. Code Appx. §§ 2403 to 2406, 2409 to 2414, 2417, 2419

Dec. 12, 1989, P.L. 101-222, 50 U.S. Code Appx. § 2405

Export Administration Amendments Act of 1981

Dec. 29, 1981, P.L. 97-145, 50 U.S. Code Appx. 2401 nt.

Export Administration Amendments Act of 1985

July 12, 1985, P.L. 99-64, 5 U.S. Code §§ 5314, 5315; 15 U.S. Code § 4051 et seq.; 42 U.S. Code §§ 2153, 2159; 50 U.S. Code Appx. § 2401 et seq.

Oct. 3, 1986, P.L. 99-441, 5 U.S. Code § 5314 nt.

Nov. 7, 1986, P.L. 99-633, 15 U.S. Code § 4052

Aug. 23, 1988, P.L. 100-418, 102 Stat. 1344, 15 U.S. Code §§ 4051 , 4052

Oct. 21, 1992, P.L. 102-429, 15 U.S. Code § 4052

Oct. 22, 1994, P.L. 103-392, 15 U.S. Code § 4052

Export Administration Amendments of 1977

June 22, 1977, P.L. 95-52, 50 U.S. Code Appx. § 2401 et seq., 2401 nt.

Export and Import Trade Development Act

La. Rev. Stat. Ann., 6:81 et seq.

Export Apple and Pear Act

June 10, 1933, 48 Stat. 123, 7 U.S. Code §§ 581 to 589

Oct. 1, 1962, P.L. 87, 725, 76 Stat. 676, 7 U.S. Code § 590

Export Control Act of 1949

Feb. 26, 1949, Ch. 11, 63 Stat. 7, 50 U.S. Code Appx. §§ 2021 to 2032

May 16, 1951, Ch. 83, 65 Stat. 43, 50 U.S. Code Appx. § 2032

June 16, 1953, Ch. 116, 67 Stat. 62, 50 U.S. Code Appx. § 2032

June 29, 1956, Ch. 473, 70 Stat. 407, 50 U.S. Code Appx. §§ 2024 nt., 2032

June 25, 1958, P.L. 85-466, 72 Stat. 220, 50 U.S. Code Appx. § 2032

May 13, 1960, P.L. 86-464, 74 Stat. 130, 50 U.S. Code Appx. § 2030

July 1, 1962, P.L. 87-515, 76 Stat. 127, 50 U.S. Code Appx. §§ 2021, 2022, 2023, 2025, 2032

June 30, 1965, P.L. 89-63, 79 Stat. 209, 50 U.S. Code Appx. §§ 2022 to 2025, 2032

June 30, 1969, P.L. 91-35, 83 Stat. 42, 50 U.S. Code Appx. § 2032

Aug. 18, 1969, P.L. 91-59, 83 Stat. 101, 50 U.S. Code Appx. § 2032

Oct. 31, 1969, P.L. 91-105, 83 Stat. 169, 50 U.S. Code Appx. § 2032

Oct. 15, 1970, P.L. 91-452, 84 Stat. 931, 50 U.S. Code Appx. § 2026

Export Control Extension Act

See Army Reorganization Acts

Export Council Act

Ill. Rev. Stat. 1991, Ch. 127, § 2401 et seq.

Export Development Act

Ill. Rev. Stat. 1991, Ch. 127, § 2501 et seq.

Mich. Comp. Laws Ann., 447.151 et seq.

Tenn. Code Ann., 13-27-101 et seq.

Export Development and International Trade for Agricultural Products Act

Tenn. Code Ann., 13-27-202 et seq.

Export Development Authority Act

W. Va. Code 1966, §§ 5B-3-1 to 5B-3-18

Export Development Office Act

Mo. Rev. Stat. 1978, 620.170 et seq.

Export Enhancement Act of 1988

Aug. 23, 1988, P.L. 100-418, 102 Stat. 1325, 15 U.S. Code §§ 4701 nt., 4701 et seq.

Oct. 21, 1992, P.L. 102-429, 5 U.S. Code § 5315; 15 U.S. Code §§ 4721, 4727, 4728, 4729

Oct. 22, 1994, P.L. 103-392, 15 U.S. Code § 4728

Dec. 21, 1995, P.L. 104-66, 15 U.S. Code §§ 4727, 4729

Aug. 20, 1996, P.L. 104-188, 15 U.S. Code § 4711

Oct. 11, 1996, P.L. 104-288, 15 U.S. Code § 4727

Export Enhancement Act of 1992

Oct. 21, 1992, P.L. 102-429, 12 U.S. Code § 635 nt.

Export Enhancement Program Amendments of 1994

Dec. 8, 1994, P.L. 103-465, 7 U.S. Code § 5601 nt.

Export Expansion Finance Act of 1971

Aug. 17, 1971, P.L. 92-126, 85 Stat. 345, 12 U.S. Code §§ 95a nt. , 635, 635e, 635f

Export Finance Act

Kan. Stat. Ann., 74-5069 et seq.

Export Finance Awareness Program Act (New York State)
N.Y. Banking Law (Consol. Laws Ch. 2) § 45
N.Y. Education Law 1947 (Consol. Laws Ch. 16) § 305, Subd. 18

Export Finance Corporation Act
Fla. Stat. Ann., 288.771 et seq.

Export Finance Program Act
Cal. Government Code § 15390 et seq.
N.Y. Banking Law (Consol. Laws Ch. 2) § 45 et seq.
N.Y. Commerce Law (Consol. Laws Ch. 7a) § 100
N.Y. Education Law 1947 (Consol. Laws Ch. 16) § 305

Export Financing Opportunities Act
N.J. Stat. Ann., 34:1B-93 et seq.

Export Grape and Plum Act
Sept. 2, 1960, P.L. 86-687, 74 Stat. 734, 7 U.S. Code §§ 591 to 599
July 26, 1961, P.L. 87-105, 75 Stat. 220, 7 U.S. Code §§ 591, 594

Export-Import Bank Act Amendments of 1978
Nov. 10, 1978, P.L. 95-630, 12 U.S. Code §§ 635 et seq.

Export-Import Bank Act Amendments of 1983
Nov. 30, 1983, P.L. 98-181, 12 U.S. Code § 635 nt.

Export-Import Bank Act Amendments of 1986
Oct. 15, 1986, P.L. 99-472, 12 U.S. Code § 635 nt.

Export-Import Bank Act of 1945
July 31, 1945, Ch. 341, 59 Stat. 526, 12 U.S. Code §§ 635-635h
Dec. 28, 1945, Ch. 602, 59 Stat. 666, 12 U.S. Code § 635
June 9, 1947, Ch. 101, 61 Stat. 130, 12 U.S. Code §§ 635, 635d, 635f, 635i

Oct. 3, 1951, Ch. 445, 65 Stat. 367, 12 U.S. Code §§ 635d, 635e, 635f
May 21, 1953, Ch. 64, 67 Stat. 28, 12 U.S. Code §§ 635, 635e
Aug. 9, 1954, Ch. 660, 68 Stat. 677, 12 U.S. Code §§ 635a, 635d
June 17, 1957, P.L. 85-55, 71 Stat. 82, 12 U.S. Code § 635f
May 22, 1958, P.L. 85-424, 72 Stat. 133, 12 U.S. Code §§ 635d, 635e
Sept. 26, 1961, P.L. 87-311, 75 Stat. 673, 12 U.S. Code § 635
Aug. 20, 1963, P.L. 88-101, 77 Stat. 128, 12 U.S. Code §§ 635, 635e, 635f
March 13, 1968, P.L. 90-267, 82 Stat. 47, 12 U.S. Code §§ 635 to 635b, 635d to 635i
Aug. 17, 1971, P.L. 92-126, 85 Stat. 345, 12 U.S. Code §§ 635, 635e, 635f
July 4, 1974, P.L. 93-331, 88 Stat. 289, 12 U.S. Code § 635f
Aug. 14, 1974, P.L. 93-374, 88 Stat. 445, 12 U.S. Code § 635f
Sept. 30, 1974, P.L. 93-425, 88 Stat. 1166, 12 U.S. Code § 635f
Oct. 26, 1977, P.L. 95-143, 12 U.S. Code §§ 635, 635f
Nov. 1, 1983, P.L. 98-143, 12 U.S. Code § 635f
Nov. 30, 1983, P.L. 98-181, 12 U.S. Code §§ 635-635b, 635f, 635g, 635o to 635t
Oct. 2, 1986, P.L. 99-440, 12 U.S. Code § 635
Oct. 15, 1986, P.L. 99-472, 12 U.S. Code §§ 635, 635a-2, 635f
Oct. 21, 1986, P.L. 99-509, 12 U.S. Code § 635i-4
Dec. 29, 1987, P.L. 100-217, 12 U.S. Code § 635i-3
Aug. 23, 1988, P.L. 100-418, 12 U.S. Code §§ 635, 635i-3
Nov. 18, 1988, P.L. 100-690, 12 U.S. Code § 635
Dec. 19, 1989, P.L. 101-240, 12 U.S. Code §§ 635, 635i-3
Nov. 5, 1990, P.L. 101-513, 12 U.S. Code §§ 635, 635i-3
Nov. 21, 1990, P.L. 101-623, 12 U.S. Code § 635
April 1, 1992, P.L. 102-266, 12 U.S. Code §§ 635, 635e

Oct. 21, 1992, P.L. 102-429, 12 U.S. Code §§ 635, 635a, 635b to 635h, 635i-1 to 635i-7

Nov. 2, 1992, P.L. 102-583, 12 U.S. Code § 635

Sept. 30, 1993, P.L. 103-87, 12 U.S. Code § 635i-8

Nov. 23, 1993, P.L. 103-149, 12 U.S. Code § 635

April 30, 1994, P.L. 103-236, 12 U.S. Code § 635

Oct. 31, 1994, P.L. 103-428, 12 U.S. Code §§ 635, 635i-5, 635i-8

Nov. 2, 1994, P.L. 103-447, 12 U.S. Code § 635

Jan. 11, 1996, P.L. 104-97, 12 U.S. Code § 635i-3

Feb. 12, 1996, P.L. 104-107, 12 U.S. Code § 635i-3

Sept. 23, 1996, P.L. 104-201, 12 U.S. Code § 635

Sept. 30, 1997, P.L. 105-46, 12 U.S. Code § 635f

Nov. 26, 1997, P.L. 105-121, 12 U.S. Code §§ 635, 635a, 635f, 635i-3

Export-Import Bank and Tied Aid Credit Amendments of 1988

Aug. 23, 1988, P.L. 100-418, 102 Stat. 1383, 11 U.S. Code § 635 nt.

Export-Import Bank Extension Act

March 4, 1939, Ch. 5, 53 Stat. 510, 15 U.S. Code §§ 713, 713a-4, 713c

March 2, 1940, Ch. 34, 54 Stat. 38

Export-Import Bank of Washington Appropriation Acts

Aug. 11, 1951, Ch. 301, 65 Stat. 182

June 30, 1952, Ch. 523, 66 Stat. 293

Export-Import Bank Reauthorization Act of 1997

Nov. 26, 1997, P.L. 105-121, 12 U.S. Code § 635 nt.

Export-Import Bank Reconstruction Finance Corporation Appropriation Acts

June 30, 1949, Ch. 286, 63 Stat. 374, 15 U.S. Code §§ 603b, 603c

May 28, 1954, Ch. 242, 68 Stat. 149

Export-Import Treaty (United States Reciprocity)

Haw. Session Laws 1876, p. 161, Jan. 30, 1875

Export Network Act (Global)

N.J. Stat. Ann., 34:1B-62 et seq.

Export Partnership Act

Pa. Purdon's Stat., Title 73, § 399.71 et seq.

Export Promotion Act (Environmental)

Ill. Comp. Stat. 1992, Ch. 20, § 225/1 et seq.

Export Trade Act

April 10, 1918, Ch. 50, 40 Stat. 516, 15 U.S. Code §§ 61 to 65

Export Trade Development Act

Miss. Code Ann. 1972, § 57-57-1 et seq.

Export Trading Company Act

Del. Code of 1974, Title 5, § 1201

Del. Code of 1974, Title 6, § 7401 et seq.

Ill. Rev. Stat. 1991, Ch. 127, § 3601 et seq.

Okla. Stat. Ann., Title 74, § 2101 et seq.

Export Trading Company Act Amendments of 1988

Aug. 23, 1988, P.L. 100-418, 102 Stat. 1384, 12 U.S. Code § 1841 nt.

Export Trading Company Act of 1982

Oct. 8, 1982, P.L. 97-290, 15 U.S. Code 4001 et seq.

Aug. 23, 1988, P.L. 100-418, 102 Stat. 1346, 15 U.S. Code § 4003

Exporting Infrastructure Funding Act (Economic Development)

Mo. Rev. Stat. 1978, 100.250 et seq.

Exposition and Auditorium Authority Act (Metropolitan)

Ill. Rev. Stat. 1991, Ch. 85, § 1391 et seq.

Exposition and Fair Law

Cal. Food and Agricultural Code 1967, § 3551 et seq.

Exposition and Fair Transfer of Funds Act
Ill. Rev. Stat. 1991, Ch. 127, §§ 167f1.9,
167f2

Exposition and Fairgrounds Act
Mich. Comp. Laws Ann., 285.161 et seq.

**Exposition and Performing Arts Authority
Act (Metro-East)**
Ill. Rev. Stat. 1977, Ch. 85, § 1501 et seq.

Exposition Authority Act
N.J. Laws 1971, Ch. 137

Exposition Authority Incorporation Act
Ill. Rev. Stat. 1991, Ch. 32, § 503a90 et seq.

**Exposition Authority Lease Act (Park
District)**
Ill. Rev. Stat. 1991, Ch. 105, § 327v5.9 et
seq.

Express Companies Gross Receipts Tax Act
Minn. Stat. 1967, 295.15,

Express Companies' License Tax Act
Mont. Code Ann. 1989, 15-54-101 et seq.

Express Highway Act
Wash. Rev. Code Ann., 47.52.001 et seq.

Express Powers Act (Counties)
Md. Ann. Code 1957, Art. 25A § 5 et seq.

Expressway Act
Conn. Gen. Stat. 1983, § 13a-20 et seq.
Ill. Rev. Stat. 1991, Ch. 121, § 8-101 et seq.
La. Rev. Stat. Ann., 48:1251 et seq.

Expressway Authority Act
Fla. Stat. Ann., 348.0001 et seq.
N.J. Stat. Ann., 27:12C-1 et seq.

**Expressway Authority Act (Brevard
County)**
Fla. Stat. Ann., 348.216 et seq.

**Expressway Authority Act (Broward
County)**
Fla. Stat. Ann., 348.24 et seq.

Expressway Authority Act (Jacksonville)
Fla. Stat. Ann., 348.9401 et seq.

**Expressway Authority Act (Orlando-
Orange County)**
Fla. Stat. Ann., 348.751 et seq.

Expressway Authority Act (Palm Beach)
Fla. Stat. Ann., 348.77 et seq.

Expressway Authority Act (Pasco County)
Fla. Stat. Ann., 348.80 et seq.

Expressway Authority Act (Pinellas County)
Fla. Stat. 1975, 348.012 et seq.

**Expressway Authority Act (Saint Lucie
County)**
Fla. Stat. Ann., 348.9401 et seq.

**Expressway Authority Act (Seminole
County)**
Fla. Stat. Ann., 348.95 et seq.

**Expressway Authority Act (St. Lucie
County)**
Fla. Stat. Ann., 348.9401 et seq.

Expressway Authority Act (St. Petersburg)
Fla. Stat. 1965, 348.011 et seq.

**Expressway Authority Act
(Tampa-Hillsborough County)**
Fla. Stat. Ann., 348.50 et seq.

Expropriation Act
La. Rev. Stat. Ann., 19:1 et seq.
P.R. Laws Ann. 1954, Title 32, § 2901 et seq.

Expropriation Act (Highways)
La. Rev. Stat. Ann., 48:441 et seq.

Expulsion Act (Pupils)
Kan. Stat. Ann., 72-8901 et seq.

Expungement Act (Criminal Record)
N.J. Stat. Ann., 2C:52-1 et seq.

**Extended Benefits Law (Unemployment
Compensation)**
N.J. Stat. Ann., 43:21-24.11 et seq.

Extended Day Child Care Program Act
Mo. Rev. Stat. 1978, 167.290 et seq.

Extended Jurisdiction Prosecution Act
Mont. Laws 1995, Ch. 438

Extended Manufacturer's Liability Doctrine
Ala. Code 1975, § 6-5-226

Extended Schoolday Activities and Violence Reduction Act
Cal. Education Code 1976, § 58750 et seq.

Extended Unemployment Compensation Act
Cal. Unemployment Insurance Code § 3501 et seq.

Extension Act (Dalton City Limits)
Ga. Laws 1946, p. 477, No. 2

Extension Act (Highway Employees' Merit System)
Ga. Code 1933, 40-2210 et seq.

Extension Act (Limitations)
Mo. Rev. Stat., 516.230

Extension Act of 1991
Dec. 11, 1991, P.L. 102-227, 26 U.S. Code § 1 nt.

Extension Limitation Act (Property Tax)
Ill. Comp. Stat. 1992, Ch. 35, § 245/1 et seq.

Extension of Partial Exemption from Real Property Taxation (Village of Spring Valley)
N.Y. Local Laws 1970, Village of Spring Valley, p. 4178

Extortion Act
Cal. Penal Code § 518 et seq.
Fla. Stat. Ann., 836.05
La. Rev. Stat. Ann., 14:66
Mich. Comp. Laws Ann., 750.213, 750.214
Mont. Rev. Code 1947, 94-1601 et seq.
N.J. Stat. Ann., 2C:20-5
N.Y. Penal Law 1965 (Consol. Laws Ch. 40) § 155.05
R.I. Gen. Laws 1956, 11-42-2

Tenn. Code Ann., 39-14-112
Vt. Stat. Ann., Title 13, § 1701
Wash. Rev. Code Ann., 9A.56.110 et seq.

Extortion Act (Officials)
Tex. Penal Code, § 39.01

Extortion by Public Officer Act
Wash. Rev. Code 1974, 9.33.040

Extra Long Staple Cotton Act of 1983
Aug. 26, 1983, P.L. 98-88, 97 Stat. 494, 7 U.S. Code §§ 1308, 1342 nt., 1347, 1421 nt., 1427, 1441, 1444

Extra Municipal Sewer District Law
Cal. Health and Safety Code § 4659 et seq.

Extra-Territorial Airports Act
Neb. Rev. Stat. 1943, 3-240 et seq.

Extra-Territorial Jurisdiction Act (Workmen's Compensation)
Okla. Stat. Ann., Title 85, § 4

Extra-Territorial Personal Jurisdiction Act
Ore. Rev. Stat. 1953, 14.035

Extradition Act
See Uniform Extradition Act
March 3, 1869, Ch. 141, 15 Stat. 337

Extradition Act (Criminal)
See Criminal Extradition Act and Uniform Criminal Extradition Act

Extradition Act (Insane Persons)
Haw. Rev. Stat. Ann., § 337-1 et seq.

Extradition Act (Persons of Unsound Mind)
Md. Ann. Code 1957, Art. 41, § 2-301 et seq.
Wash. Rev. Code Ann., 51.81 et seq.

Extradition Compact Act
Ind. Code Ann., 818.1 et seq.

Extradition of Criminals Act (Interstate)
See also Uniform Extradition Act
Mich. Comp. Laws Ann., 780.1 et seq.

Extradition of Persons of Unsound Mind Act
See Uniform Act for Extradition of Persons of Unsound Mind

Extradition of Prisoners as Witnesses Act
See Uniform Act for the Extradition of Prisoners as Witnesses

Extradition of Witnesses Act
Fla. Stat. Ann., 942.01 et seq.
Utah Code Ann. 1953, 77-33-1 et seq.

Extradition of Witnesses in Criminal Actions Act
See Uniform Act for the Extradition of Witnesses in Criminal Actions

Extradition Treaties Interpretation Act of 1998
Oct. 30, 1998, P.L. 105-323, Title II, 112 Stat. 3033, 18 U.S. Code § 3181 nt.

Extraordinary and Equitable Remedies Act
Ga. Code Ann., 23-3-1 et seq.

Extraordinary Repairs Loan Act (Boston)
Mass. Acts 1958, Ch. 668

Extraordinary School Repairs Loan Act
Mass. Acts 1959, Ch. 429

Extraterritorial Airports Section
N.D. Cent. Code, 2-06-20

Extraterritorial Service Act
Tex. Rev. Civ. Stat., Art. 2031b

Extremely Hazardous Substances Risk Management Act
Del. Code of 1974, Title 7, § 7701 et seq.

Eye and Ear Infirmary Act
Ill. Rev. Stat. 1991, Ch. 127, § 167m et seq.

Eye Care Access Act
N.J. Stat. Ann., 45:12-1

Eye Care Act (Patient Access to)
Ga. Code Ann., 31-1-20 et seq.

Eye Care for the Homeless Program in Washington
Wash. Laws 1993, Ch. 96

Eye Care Services Act
S.C. Code Ann. 1976, § 38-71-440

Eye Disease Act (Infant)
Ill. Rev. Stat. 1991, Ch. 111 1/2, § 4700 et seq.

Eye Exam Advertising Act
Ill. Rev. Stat. 1991, Ch. 121 1/2, § 340 et seq.

Eye Protection in School Act
Ill. Rev. Stat. 1991, Ch. 122, §§ 698.10, 698.11

Eyeglass Frame and Lens Act
Ill. Rev. Stat. 1991, Ch. 121 1/2, § 344 et seq.

F

FAA Civil Penalty Administrative Assessment Act of 1992
Aug. 26, 1992, P.L. 102-345, 49 U.S. Code Appx. § 1301 nt.

FAA Research Engineering, and Development Authorization Act of 1998
Feb. 11, 1998, P.L. 105-155, 49 U.S. Code § 40101 nt.

FAA Research, Engineering, and Development Management Reform Act of 1996
Oct. 9, 1996, P.L. 104-264, Title XI, 49 U.S. Code § 40101 nt.

Fabrics Act
Colo. Stat. Ann. 1935, Ch. 178

Facade and Conservation Easements Act
Ga. Code Ann., 44-10-1 et seq.

Facilitative Technology Act (Warranties for)
Colo. Rev. Stat., 6-1-501 et seq.

Facilities Act
Fla. Stat. Ann., 235.001

Facilities Act (Animal Care)
Mo. Laws 1992, S.B. No. 636, §§ 1 to 6

Facilities Construction Act (Mental Retardation)
Wis. Stat. Ann., 140.65 et seq.

Facilities Development Act (Federal)
Okla. Stat. Ann., Title 68, § 3501 et seq.

Facilities Development Corporation Act
N.Y. Unconsolidated Laws § 4401 et seq.

Facilities Education Act
N.J. Laws 1979, Ch. 207

Facilities for Child Day Care Act
S.C. Code Ann. 1976, § 20-7-2700 et seq.

Facilities for the Handicapped Act
Ill. Rev. Stat. 1983, Ch. 111 1/2, § 3701 et seq.
Md. Ann. Code 1974, Art. SF, § 2-501 et seq.

Facilities Improvement Act (Coastal)
Mass. Gen. Laws Ann., 21F:1 et seq.

Facilities Law (Health Care)
Iowa Code Ann., 135C.1 et seq.

Facilities Licensing Act (Child Care)
Okla. Stat. Ann., Title 10, § 401 et seq.

Facilities Licensing Act (Personal Care)
Tex. Health and Safety Code, § 247.001

Facilities Requiring Smoke Detectors Act
Ill. Comp. Stat. 1992, Ch. 425, § 10/0.01 et seq.
Ill. Rev. Stat. 1991, Ch. 127 1/2, § 820 et seq.

Facilities Trust Fund Act (Higher Education)
N.J. Stat. Ann., 18A:72A-49 et seq.

Facility Act (Self-Storage)
Fla. Stat. Ann., 83.801 et seq.

Facility Administrators Licensure Act (Nursing)
Tex. Rev. Civ. Stat., Art. 4512q

Facility Alternatives for Schools to Expedite Replacement Act
N.Y. Laws 1996, Ch. 512

Facility Development Act (Federal)
Mich. Comp. Laws Ann., 3.931 et seq.

Facility Development Act (Former Military)
Okla. Stat. Ann., Title 63, § 3801 et seq.

Facility Liability Act (Baseball)
Ill. Comp. Stat. 1992, Ch. 745, § 38/1 et seq.

Facility Protection Act (Underground)
N.J. Stat. Ann., 48:2-73 et seq.

Facility Receivership Law (Long-Term Care)
Ark. Code 1987, 20-10-901 et seq.

Facility Siting Act
Mont. Code Ann., 75-20-101 et seq.

Facsimile Seals and Signatures Act
Wyo. Stat. Ann., § 16-2-101 et seq.

Facsimile Signature Act (Securities)
Tenn. Code Ann., 9-3-101 et seq.

Facsimile Signature of Public Officials Act
See Uniform Facsimile Signature of Public Officials Act

FACT Act
See Food, Agriculture, Conservation, And Trade Act Of 1990

Fact Finders' Act
Dec. 5, 1924, Ch. 4, 43 Stat. 704, 21 U.S. Code § 129; 31 U.S. Code § 532; 43 U.S. Code §§ 371, 376, 377, 396, 412, 417, 433, 438, 462, 463, 466, 467, 472 to 474 and others
April 19, 1945, Ch. 80, 59 Stat. 54, 43 U.S. Code § 377

Fact Finders Act (Reclamation Projects)
Ga. Code Ann., 45-19-20 et seq., § 4, Subsec. B

Factories Act (Butter and Cheese)
Ill. Comp. Stat. 1992, Ch. 410, § 610/0.01 et seq.

Factories Registration Law
Cal. Labor Code § 2600 et seq.

Factors Act
Cal. Civil Code §§ 2026 et seq., 2367 et seq.
Conn. Gen. Stat. Ann., § 42a-9-101 et seq.
Mass. Gen. Laws Ann., 104:1 et seq.
Mont. Code Ann., 30-11-601 et seq.
N.D. Cent. Code, 3-06-01 et seq.
N.J. Stat. Ann., 12A:9-101 et seq.
N.Y. Uniform Commercial Code (Consol. Laws, Ch. 38), § 9-101 et seq.

Ohio Rev. Code 1953, 1302.44
Pa. Purdon's Stat., Title 6, §§ 201, 202
S.D. Codified Laws 1967, 59-9-1 et seq.
Tenn. Code 1932, § 6676 et seq.
Tex. Rev. Civ. Stat., Art. 1274 et seq.

Factors Act (Sign)
Va. Code 1950, § 55-152

Factors Lien Act
Ala. Code 1958, Title 47, § 132 (1) et seq.
Cal. Civil Code § 3053
Del. Code of 1953, Title 25, § 3301 et seq.
Fla. Stat. 1963, 85.29 et seq.
Ga. Code Ann., 44-14-400 et seq.
Ill. Rev. Stat. 1961, Ch. 82, § 102 et seq.
Ind. Laws 1955, Ch. 167, p. 337
Mass. Gen. Laws 1932, Ch. 255, § 40 et seq.
Md. Ann. Code 1974, Art. CL, § 9-101 et seq.
Me. Rev. Stat. Ann. 1964, Title 11, § 9-101 et seq.
Mich. Comp. Laws 1948, 570.501 et seq.
Minn. Stat. 1961, 514.80 et seq.
Miss. Code 1942, § 382-11 et seq.
Mo. Rev. Stat. 1959, 430.260 et seq.
Mont. Code Ann., 71-3-1501
N.C. Gen. Stat. 1943, § 44-70 et seq.
N.D. Cent. Code, 35-20-06
N.H. Rev. Stat. 1955, 446:1 et seq.
N.J. Stat. Ann., 2A:44-179
N.Y. Uniform Commerical Code (Consol. Laws, Ch. 38) § 9-101 et seq.
Ohio Rev. Code 1953, 1309.07 et seq.
Pa. 1947 Pamph. Laws 529, No. 241
P.R. Laws Ann. 1954, Title 10, § 551 et seq.
R.I. Public Laws 1938, Ch. 2568
S.C. Code Ann. 1962, § 45-401 et seq.
S.D. Code Supp. 1960, 39.1901 et seq.
Tenn. Code Ann., Superseded Vol., 64-1801 et seq.
Tex. Business and Commerce Code, § 9.101 et seq.
Va. Code 1950, § 55-143 et seq.
Vt. Acts 1947, No. 37
Wash. Rev. Code Ann., 60.60.010
Wis. Stat. Ann., 779.45
W. Va. Acts 1945, Ch. 82

Factory Act
Conn. Gen. Stat. Ann., § 31-1 et seq.
Ind. Code 1971, 22-1-2-1 et seq.
Kan. Stat. Ann., 44-101 et seq.
Mich. Comp. Laws 1948, 408.51 et seq.
Minn. Stat. 1971, 182.01 et seq.
Mo. Rev. Stat., 292.010 et seq.
N.J. Rev. Stat. 1937, 34:6-1 et seq.
N.Y. Labor Law (Consol. Laws Ch. 31)
§ 255 et seq.
Ohio Rev. Code 1953, 4107.01 et seq.
Pa. Purdon's Stat., Title 43, § 25-1 et seq.
Wash. Rev. Code Ann., 49.17.010 et seq.

Factory Act (Accident Reports)
Ill. Rev. Stat. 1937, Ch. 48, § 103 et seq.

Factory Act (Child and Female Labor)
N.J. Stat. Ann., 34:2-1 et seq.
Va. Code 1950, § 40-52 et seq.

Factory-Built Housing Act
Cal. Health and Safety Code § 19960 et seq.
Fla. Laws 1971, Ch. 71-172
Haw. Rev. Stat. Ann., § 360-1 et seq.
Nev. Rev. Stat. 1979 Reprint, 461.020 et seq.

Factory for the Blind Act
Ga. Code Ann., 30-2-1 et seq.

Factory Inspection Act
Colo. Rev. Stat., 8-11-105 et seq.
Mo. Rev. Stat., 291.010 et seq.
N.J. Stat. Ann., 34:6-1 et seq.
Okla. Stat. 1971, Title 40, § 111 et seq.
Ore. Rev. Stat., 654.202 et seq.
Pa. 1909 Pamph. Laws 417, No. 233
Tenn. Code Ann., 50-3-301 et seq.

Factory Inspection Act (Education and Safety)
Ill. Rev. Stat. 1991, Ch. 48, § 59.01 et seq.

Factory Law (Safety Regulations)
Neb. Rev. Stat. 1943, 48-401 et seq.

Factory Manufactured Mobile Homes Standards Act
See Uniform Standards Code for Factory Manufactured Mobile Homes Act

Factory Manufactured Movable Homes Act
Miss. Code Ann. 1972, § 75-49-1 et seq.

Factory-Manufactured Structures and Recreational Vehicles Standards Code
Tenn. Code Ann., 68-126-101 et seq.

Factory Medical Chest Law
Cal. Labor Code § 2440

Factory Sanitation Law
Cal. Labor Code § 2350 et seq.

Faculty Research and Consulting Act (University)
Ill. Rev. Stat. 1991, Ch. 144, § 215.9 et seq.

Faddis Machine Tool Act
Oct. 10, 1940, Ch. 836, 54 Stat. 1090, 50 U.S. Code § 99 nt.

Failed Banks Act (Public Funds)
Ill. Rev. Stat. 1991, Ch. 102, §§ 18.9, 19

Failure to Support Act
Okla. Stat. Ann., Title 12, § 1600.1 et seq.

Fair Access to Insurance Requirements Act
Ga. Code Ann., 33-33-1 et seq.
Minn. Stat. Ann., 65A.31 et seq.
N.M. Stat. Ann., 59A-29-1 et seq.

Fair and Exposition Authority Reconstruction Act
Ill. Comp. Stat. 1992, Ch. 70, § 215/1 et seq.

Fair and Exposition Transfer of Funds Act
Ill. Comp. Stat. 1992, Ch. 30, §§ 135/0.01, 135/1
Ill. Rev. Stat. 1991, Ch. 127, §§ 167f1.9, 167f2

Fair Automobile Insurance Reform Act
N.J. Stat. Ann., 17:33B-1 et seq.

Fair Bidding Act (Motion Picture)
Utah Code Ann. 1953, 13-13-1 et seq.

Fair Board Act
Okla. Stat. Ann., Title 2, § 156 et seq.

Fair Business Practices Act
Ga. Code Ann., 10-1-390 et seq.
Vt. Stat. Ann., Title 9, § 2451 et seq.

Fair Campaign Financing Act
Md. Ann. Code 1957, Art. 33, § 31-1 et seq.

Fair Campaign Practices Act
Ala. Acts 1988, 1st Sp. Sess., No. 873
Ala. Code 1975, § 17-22A-1 et seq.
Ill. Rev. Stat. 1991, Ch. 46, § 1101 et seq.
Minn. Stat. 1988, 210A.01 et seq.
Mont. Code Ann., 13-35-301 et seq.
N.J. Stat. Ann., 19:34-64 et seq.
Tex. Election Code, 1985, § 258.001 et seq.
Wash. Rev. Code Ann., 42.17.955

Fair Competition Law (Bituminous Coal)
Colo. Stat. Ann. 1935, Ch. 110 § 167(1) et seq.

Fair Credit and Charge Card Disclosure Act of 1988
Nov. 3, 1988, P.L. 100-583, 15 U.S. Code § 1601 nt.

Fair Credit Billing Act
Oct. 28, 1974, P.L. 93-495, 15 U.S. Code §§ 1601, 1602, 1610, 1631, 1632, 1637, 1666 to 1666j

Fair Credit Extension Act
Haw. Rev. Stat. Ann., § 477E-1 et seq.

Fair Credit Reporting Act
Oct. 26, 1970, P.L. 91-508, 84 Stat. 1128, 15 U.S. Code §§ 1681 to 1681t
Sept. 19, 1972, P.L. 92-424, 42 U.S. Code § 2701 nt.
Nov. 6, 1978, P.L. 95-598, 15 U.S. Code § 1681
Aug. 9, 1989, P.L. 101-73, 15 U.S. Code §§ 1681b, 1681s

Dec. 19, 1991, P.L. 102-242, 15 U.S. Code § 1681s
Oct. 27, 1992, P.L. 102-537, 15 U.S. Code §§ 1681a, 1681s-1, 1681t
Oct. 28, 1992, P.L. 102-550, 15 U.S. Code § 1681s
Sept. 23, 1994, P.L. 103-325, 12 U.S. Code § 1681q
Dec. 29, 1995, P.L. 104-88, 15 U.S. Code § 1681s
Jan. 6, 1996, P.L. 104-93, 15 U.S. Code § 1681u
Aug. 22, 1996, P.L. 104-193, 15 U.S. Code § 1681b
Sept. 30, 1996, P.L. 104-208, 15 U.S. Code §§ 1681a to 1681e, 1681g to 1681j, 1681m to 1681o, 1681q to 1681s, 1681s-2, 1681t, 1681u
Nov. 20, 1997, P.L. 105-107, 15 U.S. Code §§ 1681b, 1681e
Nov. 2, 1998, P.L. 105-347, 15 U.S. Code §§ 1681a to 1681c, 1681g, 1681i, 1681k, 1681s
Kan. Stat. Ann., 50-701 et seq.
Me. Rev. Stat. Ann. 1964, Title 10, § 1311 et seq.
N.H. Rev. Stat. 1955, 359-B:1 et seq.
N.J. Stat. Ann., 56:11-28 et seq.
N.Y. General Business Law (Consol. Laws Ch. 20) § 380 et seq.
Wash. Rev. Code Ann., 19.182.900

Fair Deal Dealership Act (Motor Vehicles)
Cal. Civil Code § 80 et seq.
La. Rev. Stat. Ann., 32:1251 et seq.
Pa. Purdon's Stat., Title 73, § 205-1 et seq.
Wis. Stat. Ann., 135.01 et seq.

Fair Dealership Farm Equipment Law
Ill. Rev. Stat. 1991, Ch. 5, § 1501 et seq.

Fair Dealership Law
Wis. Stat. Ann., 135.01 et seq.

Fair Dealing Act (Beer Franchise)
Md. Ann. Code 1957, Art. 2B, § 203A et seq.

Fair Dealing Act (Beer Industry)
Ill. Comp. Stat. 1992, Ch. 815, § 720/1 et seq.
Miss. Code Ann. 1972, § 67-7-1 et seq.

Fair Debt Collection Practices Act

Sept. 20, 1977, P.L. 95-109, 15 U.S. Code §§ 1601 nt., 1692 et seq.

July 8, 1986, P.L. 99-361, 15 U.S. Code § 1692a

Aug. 9, 1989, P.L. 101-73, 15 U.S. Code § 1692l

Dec. 19, 1991, P.L. 102-242, 15 U.S. Code § 1692 1

Oct. 28, 1992, P.L. 102-550, 15 U.S. Code § 1692 1

Dec. 29, 1995, P.L. 104-88, 15 U.S. Code § 1692

Sept. 30, 1996, P.L. 104-208, 15 U.S. Code § 1692e

Cal. Civil Code § 1788 et seq.

Colo. Rev. Stat., 12-14-101 et seq.

Me. Rev. Stat. Ann. 1964, Title 12, § 11001 et seq.

Fair Dismissal Act

Ala. Code 1975, § 36-26-100 et seq.

Fair Dismissal Act (Teacher)

Ark. Stat. 1947, 80-1264 et seq., 80-1266 et seq.

Fair Dismissal Act of 1983 (Teachers)

Ark. Stat. 1947, 6-17-501 et seq.

Fair Dismissal Law (Public School)

Ore. Rev. Stat., 342.805 et seq.

Fair Educational Opportunities Act

Pa. Purdon's Stat., Title 24, § 5001 et seq.

Fair Educational Practices Act

Ind. Code Ann., 20-8.1-2-1 et seq.

Mass. Gen. Laws Ann., 151C:1 et seq.

Fair Educational Practices and Policies Act

N.Y. Education Law 1947 (Consol. Laws Ch. 16) § 313

Fair Employment Act (Public Employees)

N.Y. Civil Service Law 1958 (Consol. Laws Ch. 7) § 200 et seq.

Fair Employment and Dismissal Practices Act (Public School)

Ark. Stat. 1947, 80-1243 et seq.

Fair Employment and Housing Act

Cal. Government Code § 12900 et seq.

Fair Employment Contracting Act

Va. Code 1950, § 2.1-374 et seq.

Fair Employment Practices Act

Alaska Stat. 1962, § 18.80.220

Colo. Rev. Stat., 24-34-301 et seq.

Conn. Gen. Stat. Ann., § 46a-51 et seq.

Del. Code of 1974, Title 19, § 710 et seq.

Ga. Code Ann., 45-19-20 et seq.

Haw. Rev. Stat. Ann., § 378-1 et seq.

Ida. Code 1947, 18-7301 et seq.

Ill. Rev. Stat. 1991, Ch. 68, § 2-101 et seq.

Ind. Code Ann., 22-9-1-1 et seq.

Iowa Code Ann., 601A.6, 729.4

Kan. Stat. Ann., 44-1001 et seq.

Ky. Rev. Stat. 1971, 344.200 et seq.

Mass. Gen. Laws Ann., 151C:1 et seq.

Me. Rev. Stat. Ann. 1964, Title 5, § 4571 et seq.

Mich. Comp. Laws Ann., 423.301 et seq.

Minn. Stat. Ann., 363.01 et seq.

Mo. Rev. Stat., 213.055 et seq.

Neb. Rev. Stat. 1943, 48-1101 et seq.

N.J. Stat. Ann., 10:5-1 et seq.

N.M. Stat. Ann., 28-1-1 et seq.

N.Y. Executive Law 1951 (Consol. Laws Ch. 18) § 290 et seq.

Ohio Rev. Code 1953, 4112.01 et seq.

Okla. Stat. Ann., Title 74, §§ 840.19, 840-4.12, Subd. I

Ore. Rev. Stat., 659.010 et seq.

Pa. Purdon's Stat., Title 43, § 951 et seq.

R.I. Gen. Laws 1956, 28-5-1 et seq.

Utah Code Ann. 1953, 34-35-1 et seq.

Vt. Stat. Ann., Title 21, § 495 et seq.

Wash. Rev. Code Ann., 49.60.010 et seq.

Wis. Stat. Ann., 111.31 et seq.

W. Va. Code 1966, § 5-11-1 et seq.

Wyo. Stat. Ann., § 27-9-101 et seq.

Fair Eviction Notice Act
  N.J. Stat. Ann., 2A:42-10.15, 2A:42-10.16

Fair Ground Donation Law
  Cal. Government Code § 50332

Fair Housing Act
  April 11, 1968, P.L. 90-284, 42 U.S. Code § 3601 et seq.
  Aug. 22, 1974, P.L. 93-383, 42 U.S. Code §§ 3604 to 3606
  March 27, 1978, P.L. 95-251, 5 U.S. Code § 3105
  Oct. 13, 1978, P.L. 95-454, 15 U.S. Code § 1715; 42 U.S. Code § 3608
  Nov. 6, 1978, P.L. 95-598, 42 U.S. Code § 3602
  Sept. 13, 1988, P.L. 100-430, 42 U.S. Code § 3601 et seq.
  Sept. 13, 1994, P.L. 103-322, 42 U.S. Code § 3631
  Dec. 28, 1995, P.L. 104-76, 42 U.S. Code § 3607
  Sept. 30, 1996, P.L. 104-208, 42 U.S. Code § 3614-1
  Ala. Code 1975, § 24-8-1 et seq.
  Ariz. Rev. Stat. Ann., § 41-1491 et seq.
  Cal. Statutes 1992, Ch. 182
  Colo. Rev. Stat., 24-34-501 et seq.
  Conn. Gen. Stat. Ann., § 46a-64
  Del. Code of 1974, Title 6, § 4600 et seq.
  Fla. Stat. Ann., 760.20 et seq.
  Ill. Rev. Stat. 1981, Ch. 24, § 11-11.1-1
  Ind. Code Ann., 35-15-2-1
  Kan. Stat. Ann., 44-1015 et seq.
  Mass. Gen. Laws Ann., 151B:1 et seq.
  Mich. Comp. Laws Ann., 564.101 et seq.
  Minn. Stat. Ann., 363.01 et seq.
  N.C. Gen. Stat. 1943, § 41A-1 et seq.
  Nev. Rev. Stat. 1979 Reprint, 118.010 et seq.
  N.J. Stat. Ann., 2A:42-10.16, 10:5-4, 52:27D-301 et seq., 55:14A-7.5 et seq.
  Ohio Rev. Code 1953, 4112.01 et seq.
  Ore. Rev. Stat., 659.031 et seq.
  Pa. Purdon's Stat., Title 43, § 951 et seq.
  S.C. Code Ann. 1976, § 31-21-10 et seq.
  Tex. Property Code, § 301.001 et seq.
  Utah Code Ann. 1953, 57-21-1 et seq.
  Va. Code 1950, § 36-86 et seq.
  Wash. Rev. Code Ann., 49.60.222 et seq.
  W. Va. Code 1966, § 5-11A-1 et seq.

Fair Housing Act (Public School Employee)
  Ark. Acts 1991, No. 631

Fair Housing Act (Rumford)
  Cal. Health and Safety Code § 35700 et seq.

Fair Housing Amendments Act of 1988
  Sept. 13, 1988, P.L. 100-430, 102 Stat. 1619, 28 U.S. Code §§ 2341, 2342; 42 U.S. Code §§ 3601 nt., 3602, 3602 nt., 3604, 3605, 3607,3608, 3610 to 3619

Fair Housing Practices Act
  R.I. Gen. Laws 1956, 34-37-1 et seq.

Fair Housing Practices Act (Urban Redevelopment)
  Wis. Stat. Ann., 66.405 Subsec. 2m

Fair Information Practices Act
  Iowa Code Ann., 22.11
  Mass. Gen. Laws Ann., 66A:1 et seq.

Fair Information Reporting Act (Insurance)
  Minn. Stat. Ann., 72A.49 et seq.

Fair Invention Development Standards Act
  Ill. Comp. Stat. 1992, Ch. 815, § 620/10 et seq.
  Ill. Rev. Stat. 1991, Ch. 29, § 101 et seq.

Fair Labor Practices Act
  Ariz. Rev. Stat. Ann., § 23-1321 et seq.

Fair Labor Standards Act
  La. Rev. Stat. Ann., 23:1 et seq.
  Minn. Stat. Ann., 177.21 et seq.

Fair Labor Standards Act, 1938
  June 25, 1938, Ch. 676, 52 Stat. 1060, 29 U.S. Code §§ 201 to 219
  Oct. 29, 1941, Ch. 461, 55 Stat. 756, 29 U.S. Code § 207 (b) (2)
  May 14, 1947, Ch. 52, 61 Stat. 84, 29 U.S. Code § 216
  July 20, 1949, Ch. 352, 63 Stat. 446, 29 U.S. Code § 207

Oct. 26, 1949, Ch. 736, 63 Stat. 910, 29 U.S.
Code §§ 202 to 207, 208, 211 to 216, 216b,
217

Aug. 12, 1955, Ch. 867, 69 Stat. 711, 29 U.S.
Code §§ 204 to 206, 208, 210

Aug. 8, 1956, Ch. 1035, 70 Stat. 1118, 29
U.S. Code §§ 206, 213, 216

Aug. 30, 1957, P.L. 85-231, 71 Stat. 514, 29
U.S. Code §§ 213, 216, 217

Aug. 25, 1958, P.L. 85-750, 72 Stat. 844, 29
U.S. Code § 208

Aug. 28, 1958, P.L. 85-791, 72 Stat. 948, 29
U.S. Code § 210

July 12, 1960, P.L. 86-624, 74 Stat. 417, 29
U.S. Code §§ 213, 217

May 5, 1961, P.L. 87-30, 75 Stat. 65, 29 U.S.
Code §§ 203 to 208, 212 to 214, 216, 217

June 10, 1963, P.L. 88-38, 77 Stat. 56, 29
U.S. Code § 206

Sept. 23, 1966, P.L. 89-601, 80 Stat. 830, (29
U.S. Code §§ 203, 206, 207, 213, 214, 216,
218)

Oct. 15, 1966, P.L. 89-670, 80 Stat. 943, 29
U.S. Code § 213

June 22, 1972, P.L. 92-318, 86 Stat. 375, 29
U.S. Code §§ 208, 213

April 8, 1974, P.L. 93-259, 88 Stat. 55, 29
U.S. Code §§ 201 et seq.

April 8, 1974, P.L. 93-259, 88 Stat. 55, 29
U.S. Code §§ 202 to 208, 210, 212 to 214,
216, 255, 260

Nov. 1, 1977, P.L. 95-151, 29 U.S. Code
§§ 203 et seq., 206

Sept. 27, 1979, P.L. 96-70, 29 U.S. Code
§ 213

Nov. 13, 1985, P.L. 99-150, 29 U.S. Code
§§ 203, 203 nt., 207, 207 nt., 211, 215, 216
nt.

Oct. 16, 1986, P.L. 99-486, 29 U.S. Code
§ 214

Nov. 17, 1989, P.L. 101-157, 29 U.S. Code
§§ 203, 205 to 208, 213, 214, 216

Nov. 5, 1990, P.L. 101-508, 29 U.S. Code
§ 216

Sept. 30, 1994, P.L. 103-329, 29 U.S. Code
§ 213

Jan. 23, 1995, P.L. 104-1, 29 U.S. Code
§ 203 Sept. 6, 1995, P.L. 104-26, 29 U.S.
Code § 207

Dec. 21, 1995, P.L. 104-66, 29 U.S. Code
§ 204

Dec. 29, 1995, P.L. 104-88, 29 U.S. Code
§ 213

Aug. 6, 1996, P.L. 104-174, 29 U.S. Code
§§ 213, 216

Aug. 20, 1996, P.L. 104-188, 29 U.S. Code
§§ 203, 206, 213

Aug. 7, 1998, P.L. 105-221, 29 U.S. Code
§ 203

Oct. 31, 1998, P.L. 105-334, 29 U.S. Code
§ 213

Fair Labor Standards Amendments of 1977
Nov. 1, 1977, P.L. 95-151, 29 U.S. Code
§§ 201 nt., 206 et seq.

Fair Labor Standards Amendments of 1985
Nov. 13, 1985, P.L. 99-150, 29 U.S. Code
§§ 201 nt., 203, 207, 211, 215 nt., 216 nt.

Fair Labor Standards Amendments of 1989
Nov. 17, 1989, P.L. 101-157, 29 U.S. Code
§ 201 nt.

Fair Liability Act (Licensed Alcoholic Beverage Server)
N.J. Stat. Ann., 2A:22A-1 et seq.

Fair Liability and Roller Skating Rink Safety Act
N.J. Stat. Ann., 5:14-1 to 5:14-7

Fair Packaging and Labeling Act
Nov. 3, 1966, P.L. 89-755, 80 Stat. 1296, 15
U.S. Code §§ 1451 to 1461

Oct. 22, 1968, P.L. 90-628, 82 Stat. 1320, 15
U.S. Code § 1459

Dec. 21, 1982, P.L. 97-375, 15 U.S. Code
§ 1457

Feb. 14, 1992, P.L. 102-245, 15 U.S. Code
§§ 1453, 1454

Aug. 3, 1992, P.L. 102-329, 15 U.S. Code
§§ 1453, 1454

Cal. Business and Professions Code § 12601
et seq.

Me. Rev. Stat. Ann. 1964, Title 7, § 521 et
seq.

FAIR Plan Act (Fair Access to Insurance Requirements)
Minn. Stat. Ann., 65A.31 et seq.
N.M. Stat. Ann., 59A-29.1 et seq.
Continued

N.M. Stat. Ann., 59-10-1 et seq.

Pa. Purdon's Stat., Title 40, § 1600.101 et seq.

Tex. Insurance Code, Art. 21.49A

Fair Practices Act
La. Rev. Stat. Ann., 51:521 et seq.
Mont. Code Ann., 49-3-101 et seq.

Fair Practices Act (Catfish Processor)
Miss. Code Ann. 1972, § 69-7-651 et seq.

Fair Practices Act (Home Energy)
N.Y. Public Service Law (Consol. Laws Ch. 48) § 30 et seq.

Fair Practices Act (Insurance)
N.M. Stat. Ann., 59-11-9 et seq.

Fair Practices Act (Mail and Telephone Consumer Product Promotion)
Ark. Acts 1991, No. 680

Fair Practices Act (Motor Vehicle)
Ga. Code Ann., 10-1-660 et seq.

Fair Practices Act (Subcontractors)
N.M. Stat. Ann., 13-4-31 et seq.

Fair Practices Act (Subletting and Subcontracting)
Cal. Public Contract Code § 4100 et seq.

Fair Practices in the Distribution and Showing of Cinematographic Films Act
P.R. Laws Ann. 1954, Title 10, § 2101 et seq.

Fair Price Act
Md. Ann. Code 1974, Art. CL, § 11-401 et seq.

Fair Procedure Code (Investigating Agencies)
N.J. Stat. Ann., 52:13E-1 et seq.

Fair Rent Act
Va. Code 1950, § 44-160 et seq.

Fair Sales Act
Cal. Business and Professions Code § 17000 et seq.
Conn. Gen. Stat. Ann., § 42a-2-101 et seq.

N.J. Rev. Stat. 1937, 56:4-1 et seq.
Pa. 1937 Pamph. Laws 2672, No. 533
W. Va. Code 1966, § 47-11A-1 et seq.

Fair Share Fee Law (Public Employee)
Pa. Purdon's Stat., Title 43, § 1102.1 et seq.

Fair Share Refugee Act
July 14, 1960, P.L. 86-648, 74 Stat. 504, 8 U.S. Code §§ 1182, 1205, 1251, 1255

Fair Share Tax Act
N.C. Laws 1991, Ch. 557

Fair Teachers Dismissal Act
Miss. Code Ann. 1972, § 37-9-101 et seq.

Fair Trade Act
Aug. 17, 1937, Ch. 690, 50 Stat. 693, 15 U.S. Code § 1
Ariz. Rev. Stat. Ann., § 44-1421 et seq.
Ark. Stat. 1947, 70-201 et seq.
Cal. Business and Professions Code § 16900 et seq.
Colo. Rev. Stat., 6-3-101 et seq.
Conn. Gen. Stat. Ann., § 42a-2-101 et seq.
Del. Code of 1974, Title 6, § 1901 et seq.
Fla. Stat. 1973, 541.001 et seq.
Ga. Code 1933, 106-401 et seq.
Haw. Rev. Laws 1955, § 205-20 et seq.
Ida. Code 1947, 48-301 et seq.
Ill. Rev. Stat. 1991, Ch. 140 § 7.9 et seq.
Ind. Code Ann., 24-1-1-1 et seq.
Iowa Code 1975, 550.1 et seq.
Kan. Laws 1937, Ch. 165
Ky. Rev. Stat. 1971, Superseded Vols., 365.080, 365.090
La. Rev. Stat. Ann., 51:421 et seq.
Mass. Gen. Laws Ann., 93:14E et seq.
Md. Ann. Code 1974, Art. CL, § 11-101 et seq.
Me. Rev. Stat. Ann. 1964, Title 10, § 1151 et seq.
Mich. Comp. Laws Ann., 445.151 et seq.
Minn. Stat. Ann., 325D.01 et seq.
Miss. Code Ann. 1972, § 75-23-1 et seq.
Mont. Laws 1937, Ch. 42
N.C. Gen. Stat. 1943, § 66-50 et seq.

Neb. Rev. Stat. 1943, Superseded Vol., 59-1101 et seq.

Nev. Rev. Stat. 1957, 599.010 et seq.

N.H. Rev. Stat. 1955, 357:1 et seq.

N.J. Rev. Stat. 1937, 56:4-1 to 56:4-6

N.M. Stat. Ann. 1953, 49-2-1 et seq.

N.Y. General Business Law (Consol. Laws Ch. 20) § 369a et seq.

Ohio Rev. Code 1953, 1333.05 et seq., 1333.27 et seq.

Okla. Stat. Ann., Title 78, § 41 et seq.

Ore. Rev. Stat., 646.605 et seq.

Pa. Purdon's Stat., Title 73, § 7 et seq.

P.R. Laws Ann. 1954, Title 10, § 281 et seq.

R.I. Gen. Laws 1956, 6-12-1 et seq.

S.C. Code Ann. 1976, § 39-7-10 et seq.

S.D. Codified Laws 1967, Superseded Vol., 37-9-1 et seq.

Tenn. Code Ann., 47-25-101

Utah Code Ann. 1953, Miscellaneous Superseded Code Provisions, 13-4-1 et seq.

Va. Code 1950, § 59.1-1 et seq.

Wash. Rev. Code Ann., 19.86.010 et seq.

Wis. Stat. 1975, 133.25

W. Va. Acts 1937, Ch. 123

Wyo. Stat. 1957, § 40-8 et seq.

Fair Trade Act (Agricultural)
Utah Code Ann. 1953, 4-8-1 et seq.

Fair Trade Act (Intoxicating Liquors)
Minn. Stat. Ann., 340A.301 et seq.

Fair Trade in Auto Parts Act of 1988
Aug. 23, 1988, P.L. 100-418, 102 Stat. 1325, 15 U.S. Code § 4701 nt., generally § 4701 et seq.

April 30, 1994, P.L. 103-236, 15 U.S. Code § 4704

Fair Trade in Automotive Parts Act of 1998
Oct. 17, 1998, P.L. 105-261, Title XXXVIII, 112 Stat. 2275, 15 U.S. Code § 4701 nt.

Fair Trade Practices Act
Cal. Business and Professions Code § 17000 et seq.

Minn. Stat. Ann., 325D.01 et seq.

Fair Trade Practices Act (Cigarette)
N.M. Stat. Ann., 57-2-1 et seq.

Fair Trade Practices Act (Insurance)
Md. Ann. Code 1957, Art. 48A, § 212 et seq.

Mo. Rev. Stat., 375.930 et seq.

Fair Trade Practices Act (Motion Pictures)
Mont. Code Ann., 30-14-301 et seq.

Fair Trade Practices Act (Petroleum Products)
N.M. Stat. Ann., 57-19A-1 et seq.

Fair Trade Regulations Act
Ala. Code 1958, Title 57, § 77 et seq.

Fair Treatment Standards for Crime Victims' Act
Also known as the Crime Victims' Bill of Rights

N.Y. Executive Law 1951 (Consol. Laws Ch. 18) § 640 et seq.

Fair Trial Act
Mont. Code Ann., 3-2-204

Fair Wage Act
Conn. Gen. Stat. Ann., § 31-58 et seq.

Mass. Gen. Laws Ann., 151:1 et seq.

Fairfax-Kaw City Authority Act
Okla. Stat. Ann., Title 82, § 951 et seq.

Fairfax Parking Authority Act
Va. Acts 1958, Ch. 536

Fairfield County Convention Authority Act
Conn. Gen. Stat. Ann., § 32-200 et seq.

Fairfield-Suisun Sewer District Act
Cal. Statutes 1951, Ch. 303, p. 553

Fairgrounds and Exposition Act
Mich. Comp. Laws Ann., 285.161 et seq.

Fairness Act (Regulatory)
Wash. Rev. Code Ann., 19.85.010 et seq.

Fairness in Health Care Act
Ga. Code Ann., 33-24-59.12 to 33-24-59.16

Fairness in Lending Act
Ill. Comp. Stat. 1992, Ch. 815, § 120/1 et seq.
Ill. Rev. Stat. 1991, Ch. 17, § 851 et seq.
Wash. Rev. Code Ann., 30.04.500 et seq.

Fairness In Music Licensing Act of 1998
Oct. 27, 1998, P.L. 105-298, Title II, 112
Stat. 2830, 17 U.S. Code § 101 nt.

Fairness in Retail Sales Taxation Act
Cal. Code of Civil Procedure § 318
Fla. Stat. Ann., 212.215

Faith-Based Chemical Dependency Treatment Program Act
Tex. Health and Safety Code, § 464.051 et seq.

Faith Donor Act (Good)
Tex. Civil Practice and Remedies Code, § 76.002

Fake Sales Act
Ore. Rev. Stat. 1953, 646.210 et seq.

Fall River Water Users District Rural Water System Act of 1998
Nov. 3, 1998, P.L. 105-352, 112 Stat. 3222

Fallon Paiute Shoshone Indian Tribes Water Rights Settlement Act of 1990
Nov. 16, 1990, P.L. 101-618, 104 Stat. 3289, 16 U.S. Code § 668dd nt.

Falls of the Ohio Interstate Park Compact
Ind. Code Ann., 14-6-24-1 et seq.
Ky. Rev. Stat. 1971, 148.241

Falmouth Selectmen-Manager Administration Act
Mass. Acts 1960, Ch. 254

Falmouth Sewer Loan Act
Mass. Acts 1928, Ch. 288, § 6

Falmouth Town Meeting Act
Mass. Acts 1935, Ch. 349

False Advertising Act
Ga. Code Ann., 10-1-420 et seq.
Haw. Rev. Stat. Ann., § 708-871 et seq.

Ill. Rev. Stat. 1991, Ch. 121 1/2, § 157.21a et seq.
Mass. Gen. Laws Ann., 266:91
Md. Ann. Code 1957, Art. 27, § 195
Minn. Stat. Ann., 325F.67
Mo. Rev. Stat. 1969, 561.660
Mont. Code Ann., 45-6-318
N.C. Gen. Stat. 1943, § 358 et seq.
N.J. Stat. Ann., 2C:21-7
N.Y. Penal Law 1965 (Consol. Laws Ch. 40) § 190.20
Ohio Rev. Code 1953, 4165.01 et seq.
Tex. Business and Commerce Code § 17.12
Tex. Penal Code, § 32.42
Wash. Rev. Code Ann., 9.04.010

False Advertising and Anti-Deceptive Practices Act
Wis. Stat. Ann., 100.18

False Advertising Process Act (Unauthorized Insurers)
See Unauthorized Insurers False Advertising Process Act

False Advertising Process Act (Unauthorized)
Md. Ann. Code 1974, Art. IN, § 27-701 et seq.

False and Misleading Advertising Act
Pa. Cons. Stat., Title 18, § 4107

False Branding or Marking Act
July 1, 1902, Ch. 1357, 32 Stat. 632, 21 U.S. Code §§ 16, 17

False Check Act
Iowa Code Ann., 714.1

False Claim Act (Medicaid)
Mich. Comp. Laws Ann., 400.601 et seq.
Tenn. Code Ann., 71-5-181 et seq.

False Claims Act
March 2, 1893, Ch. 67, 12 Stat. 698, 31 U.S. Code § 231 et seq.
Cal. Government Code § 12650 et seq.
Fla. Stat. Ann., 68.081 et seq.

False Claims Act (Health Care)
Conn. Gen Stat. 1989, § 53-440 et seq.
Tenn. Code Ann., 56-26-401 et seq.
Utah Code Ann. 1953, 26-20-1 et seq.
Wash. Rev. Code 1983, 48.80.010 et seq.

False Claims Amendments Act of 1986
Oct. 27, 1986, P.L. 99-562, 31 U.S. Code § 3701 nt.

False Entries Act (Accounts)
Tex. Penal Code, § 32.21

False Entries Act (Horse Racing)
Ill. Rev. Stat. 1991, Ch. 8, § 33.90 et seq.

False Identification Crime Control Act of 1982
Dec. 31, 1982, P.L. 97-398, 18 U.S. Code § 1001 nt.

False Impersonation Act
Wash. Rev. Code Ann., 9A.60.040

False Imprisonment Act
Tex. Penal Code, § 20.02

False Medicaid Claims Act
Neb. Rev. Stat. 1943, 68-1037.01 to 68-1037.05

False Pretenses Act
Ala. Code 1975, § 13A-8-3 et seq.
Cal. Penal Code § 484
Conn. Gen. Stat. Ann., § 53a-119
Ga. Code Ann., 16-8-3
Kan. Stat. Ann., 21-3701
Ky. Rev. Stat. 1971, Superseded Vols., 434.050 et seq.
Ky. Rev. Stat. 1971, 514.040
Md. Ann. Code 1957, Art. 27, § 150
Me. Rev. Stat. Ann. 1964, Title 17A, § 351 et seq.
Mich. Comp. Laws Ann., 750.218 et seq.
Mont. Rev. Code 1947, 94-1805
N.H. Rev. Stat. 1955, 637:1 et seq.
N.J. Stat. Ann., 2C:20-4
Okla. Stat. Ann., Title 21, § 1541.1 et seq.
Ore. Rev. Stat. 1953, 165.002 et seq.

Pa. Cons. Stat., Title 18, §§ 3922, 4114
R.I. Gen. Laws 1956, 11-41-4
Tenn. Code Ann., 39-14-103 et seq.
Tex. Penal Code, §§ 31.03, 31.04
Vt. Stat. Ann., Title 13, § 2002
Wash. Rev. Code Ann., 9A.60.030 et seq.

False Representations Act
Wash. Rev. Code Ann., 9.38.010 et seq.

False Statement Act (Bail Bond)
Ill. Comp. Stat. 1992, Ch. 720, §§ 540/0.01, 540/1
Ill. Rev. Stat. 1991, Ch. 16, §§ 25.9, 26

False Statement Act (Securities)
Fla. Stat. Ann., 517.301

False Statements Accountability Act of 1996
Oct. 11, 1996, P.L. 104-292, 18 U.S. Code § 1001 nt.

False Statements Act
Ky. Rev. Stat 1971, Superseded Vols., 404.090
Ky. Rev. Stat. 1971, 517.090

False Token Act
Ore. Rev. Stat. 1953, 136.560

False Weights and Measures Act
Wash. Rev. Code Ann., 9.45.122 et seq.

Families and Children Act
Ore. Rev. Stat., 417.300 et seq.

Families and Children, Youth Department Act
N.M. Stat. Ann., 9-2A-1 et seq.

Families Assistance Act (Homeless)
Haw. Rev. Stat. Ann., § 358D-1 et seq.

Families of Children with Disabilities Support Act of 1994
Oct. 20, 1994, P.L. 103-382, 20 U.S. Code § 1491 et seq.

Families of the Working Poor Assistance Act
N.J. Laws 1971, Ch. 209

Family Abuse Prevention Act
Ore. Rev. Stat., 107.700 et seq.

Family Allowance in the Settlement of Small Estates Act
D.C. Code 1973, § 19-101 et seq.

Family and Child Services and Child Protection Act
Me. Rev. Stat. 1964, Title 22, § 4001 et seq.

Family and Child Services Resources Act
Miss. Code Ann. 1972, § 43-1-59

Family and Children Community Protection Act
Ill. Rev. Stat. 1991, Ch. 122, § 2051 et seq.

Family and Children Services Act
Ill. Comp. Stat. 1992, Ch. 20, § 505/1 et seq.
Wash. Rev. Code Ann., 74.14A.010 et seq.

Family and Children Trust Fund Act
N.Y. Executive Law (Consol. Laws, Ch. 18) § 171 et seq.

Family and Children Trust Fund Act (William B. Hoyt Memorial)
N.Y. Social Services Law (Consol. Laws Ch. 55) § 481a et seq.

Family and Community Endeavor Schools Act
Sept. 13, 1994, P.L. 103-322, 42 U.S. Code § 13792
Oct. 21, 1998, P.L. 105-277, 42 U.S. Code § 13792

Family and Disabled Persons Support Act
Neb. Rev. Stat. 1943, 68-1501 et seq.

Family and Marital Therapist, Professional Counselor, and Associate Counselor Licensing Act
Ga. Code Ann., 43-10A-1 et seq.
Ill. Rev. Stat. 1991, Ch. 111, § 8351-1 et seq.
Kan. Stat. Ann., 65-6401 et seq.
N.C. Gen. Stat. 1943, § 90-270.45 et seq.
Okla. Stat. Ann., Title 59, § 1925.1 et seq.
S.C. Code Ann. 1976, § 40-75-10 et seq.

Tex. Rev. Civ. Stat., Art. 4512c-1

Family and Marriage Therapist Licensing Act
Utah Code Ann. 1953, 58-60-301 et seq.

Family and Marriage Therapy Licensure Act
Ala. Code 1975, § 34-44-1
Miss. General Laws 1997, Ch. 516

Family and Medical Leave Act of 1993
Feb. 5, 1993, P.L. 103-3, 2 U.S. Code §§ 60m, 60n; 5 U.S. Code §§ 2105, 6381 to 6387; 29 U.S. Code § 2601 et seq.
Oct. 20, 1994, P.L. 103-382, 29 U.S. Code § 2618
Jan. 23, 1995, P.L. 104-1, 2 U.S. Code §§ 60m, 60n; 29 U.S. Code §§ 2611, 2617

Family and Runaway Youth Act
Fla. Stat. Ann., 409.441

Family and Small Business Act
Cal. Unemployment Insurance Code § 1118

Family Assessment Intervention and Resource Act
Cal. Welfare and Institutions Code § 1400 et seq.

Family Assistance Law for Mentally Disabled Children
Ill. Rev. Stat. 1991, Ch. 91 1/2, § 1803-1 et seq.

Family Assistance Law for Mentally Disturbed Children
Ill. Comp. Stat. 1992, Ch. 405, § 80/3-1 et seq.

Family Car Act
Conn. Gen. Stat. Ann., § 52-182

Family Car Doctrine
N.Y. Vehicle and Traffic Law 1959 (Consol. Laws Ch. 71) § 388

Family-Care Home Act (Adult)
Fla. Stat. Ann., 400.616 et seq.

Family Care Safety Act
Mo. Laws 1999, H.B. No. 308, §§ 3 to 15

Family Caregiver Support Act
Ga. Code Ann., 49-6-70 et seq.
Pa. Purdon's Stat., Title 62, § 3061 et seq.

Family Code
Cal. Statutes 1992, Ch. 162
Wis. Stat. Ann., 765.001 et seq.

Family Conciliation Court Law
Cal. Code of Civil Procedure § 1731 et seq.
Cal. Family Code § 1800 et seq.

Family Conflict Act
Wash. Rev. Code Ann., 13.32A.010 et seq.

Family Connection Authority Act (Haralson County)
Ga. Laws 1999, H.B. 920

Family Connection Commission Act (Effingham)
Ga. Laws 1999, H.B. 771

Family Connection Commission Act (Gilmer County)
Ga. Laws 1999, H.B. 403

Family Connection Commission Act (Union County)
Ga. Laws 1999, S.B. 151

Family Counseling Services Act (Circuit Court)
Mich. Comp. Laws Ann., 551-331 et seq.

Family Court Act
Del. Code of 1974, Title 10, § 901 et seq.
Haw. Rev. Stat. Ann., § 571-1 et seq.
Ill. Rev. Stat. 1991, Ch. 37, § 805-1 et seq.
N.J. Stat. Ann., 2A:4A-1 et seq.
N.Y. Laws 1962, Ch. 686
Pa. 1937 Pamph. Laws 460, No. 107
R.I. Gen. Laws 1956, 8-10-1 et seq., 14-1-1 et seq.
S.C. Code Ann. 1976, § 14-21-10 et seq.
Utah Code Ann. 1953, 30-3-1 et seq.
Wash. Rev. Code Ann., 26.12.010 et seq.

Wis. Stat. Ann., 753.016 Subsec. 3, 767.13 et seq.

Family Day Care Home Act
R.I. Gen. Laws 1956, 42-72.1-1 et seq.

Family Day Care Provider Registration Act
N.J. Stat. Ann., 30:5B-16 et seq.

Family Desertion and Nonsupport Act
Wash. Rev. Code Ann., 26.20.030 et seq.

Family Development Account Program
Mo. Laws 1999, H.B. No. 349, §§ 1 to 6

Family Development Act
Fla. Stat. Ann., 23.13 et seq.

Family Disability Insurance Continuity of Coverage Act
Mont. Code Ann., 33-22-305 et seq.

Family District Court Act
Tex. Government Code, § 24.601 et seq.

Family Economic Security Act
Cal. Welfare and Institutions Code § 11200 et seq.

Family Education Rights and Privacy Act
Ky. Acts 1994, Ch. 98

Family Education Savings Act
Mont. Code Ann., 15-62-101 et seq.

Family Educational Rights and Privacy Act of 1974
Aug. 21, 1974, P.L. 93-380, 20 U.S. Code §§ 1221 nt., 1232g

Family Exemption Act
Pa. Cons. Stat., Title 20, § 3121 et seq.

Family Expense Act
Colo. Rev. Stat., 39-22-127
Conn. Gen. Stat. Ann., § 46b-37
Ill. Rev. Stat. 1991, Ch. 40, § 1015
Ore. Rev. Stat., 108.040
Wash. Rev. Code Ann., 26.16.205

Family Expense Law
Ill. Comp. Stat. 1992, Ch. 750, § 65/15

Family Farm Act
S.D. Codified Laws 1967, 47-9A-1 et seq.

Family Farm Credit Program Act
La. Rev. Stat. Ann., 3:251 et seq.

Family Farm Development Act
Iowa Code Ann., 175.1 et seq.
Mich. Comp. Laws Ann., 285.251 et seq.
S.C. Code Ann. 1976, § 46-47-10

Family Farm Rehabilitation Act
Kan. Stat. Ann., 2-3401 et seq.

Family Farm Survival Act
N.D. Laws 1985, Ch. 136

Family Farm Water Act
Wash. Rev. Code Ann., 90.66.010 et seq.

Family Housing Demonstration Program
Cal. Health and Safety Code § 50880 et seq.

Family in Need of Services Act
N.M. Stat. Ann., 32-3-1 et seq.

Family Income Tax Credit Law (Working)
Minn. Stat. Ann., 290.0671

Family Independence Act
S.C. Laws 1995, p. 642, No. 102

Family Independence Program
Wash. Rev. Code Ann., 74.21.010 et seq.

Family Insurance Act
Ore. Laws 1991, Ch. 674
Tenn. Code Ann., 68-1-115, 4-3-1404, 50-7-3-4

Family Investment Plan
Minn. Stat. Ann., 256.031 et seq.

Family Investment Program-Statewide
Minn. Stat. 1986, 256J.01 et seq., 256K.01 et seq.

Family Law Act
Cal. Civil Code, § 4000 et seq.

Family Leave Act
Alaska Laws 1992, Ch. 96
N.J. Stat. Ann., 34:11B-1 et seq.

Family, Marriage, and Child Counselors Act
Cal. Health and Safety Code § 309.100 et seq.

Family Nutrition Education and Service Act
Cal. Education Code 1976, § 49510 et seq.

Family Obligations Enforcement Act
W. Va. Code 1966 § 48A-1-1 et seq.

Family Physician Training Act (Song-Brown)
Cal. Education Code 1976, § 69270 et seq.

Family Placement Act (Homeless)
Ill. Comp. Stat. 1992, Ch. 310, § 85/1 et seq.

Family Planning Act
Ark. Code Ann. 1987, 20-16-301 et seq.
Fla. Stat. Ann., 381.382
Miss. Code Ann. 1972, § 41-42-1 et seq.
N.M. Stat. Ann., 24-8-1 et seq.
Tenn. Code Ann., 68-34-101 et seq.
Wyo. Stat. Ann., § 35-14-101 et seq.

Family Planning Act (Comprehensive)
Fla. Stat. Ann., 381.0051

Family Planning Services Act
Ga. Code Ann., 49-7-1 et seq.
Iowa Code Ann., 234.21 et seq.

Family Planning Services and Population Research Act
Nev. Rev. Stat. 1967 reprint, 439.273 et seq.

Family Planning Services and Population Research Act of 1970
Dec. 24, 1970, P.L. 91-572, 84 Stat. 1504, 33 U.S. Code § 763c; 42 U.S. Code §§ 211a, 212a, 300 to 300a-6, 3505a to 3505c

Family Policy Act
Fla. Stat. Ann., 409.801 et seq.
Mont. Code Ann., 41-7-101 et seq.

Family Practice Residency Act
Ill. Rev. Stat. 1991, Ch. 144, § 1451 et seq.

Family Practice Training Act
Mont. Code Ann., 50-5-421 et seq.

Family Preservation Act
Colo. Rev. Stat., 26-5.5-101 et seq.
Minn. Stat. Ann., 256F.01 et seq.
Miss. Code Ann. 1972, § 43-51-1 et seq.
N.M. Stat. Ann., 32A-17-1 et seq.
Pa. Purdon's Stat., Title 62, § 2171 et seq.

Family Preservation Act (Indian)
Minn. Stat. Ann., 257.35 et seq.

Family Preservation and Child Protection Reform Act
Ga. Code Ann., 49-5-200 et seq.

Family Preservation Services Act
La. Rev. Stat. Ann., 46:287.1 et seq.

Family Protection Act
Cal. Statutes 1976, Ch. 977

Family Protection and Domestic Violence Intervention Act
N.Y. Criminal Procedure Law (Consol. Laws Ch. 11A) § 30.30 et seq.
N.Y. Domestic Relations Law (Consol. Laws Ch. 14) § 252
N.Y. Executive Law 1951 (Consol. Laws Ch. 18) § 214b et seq.
N.Y. Family Court Act, § 115 et seq.
N.Y. Judiciary Law (Consol. Laws Ch. 30) § 212 et seq.
N.Y. Penal Law 1965 (Consol. Laws Ch. 40) §§ 120.14, 120.15
N.Y. Public Health Law 1953 (Consol. Laws Ch. 45) § 2803

Family Protection Shelter Support Act
W. Va. Code 1966, § 48-2C-1 et seq.

Family Reconciliation Act
Wash. Rev. Code Ann., 13.32A.010 et seq.

Family Relations Sessions Act
Conn. Gen. Stat. Ann., § 46b-1 et seq.

Family Resource Act
Nov. 3, 1990, P.L. 101-501, 42 U.S. Code §§ 12301 nt., 12351 to 12355

Family Responsibility Act
Cal. Civil Code § 4700
Cal. Code of Civil Procedure §§ 395, 1681

Family Responsibility Act (Expenses)
Colo. Rev. Stat., 14-6-110

Family Responsibility Act (Poor Law)
Mich. Comp. Laws Ann., 401.1 et seq.

Family Responsibility and Abortion Prevention Act
Wis. Laws 1985, Act 56
Wis. Stat. Ann., 46.24, 46.245, 46.93, 940.13, 940.15, 943.145

Family Rights Act
Cal. Statutes 1991, Ch. 462

Family Rights Act (Moore-Brown-Roberti)
Cal. Government Code §§ 12945.1, 12945.2, 19702.3

Family-School Partnership Act
La. Rev. Stat. Ann., 17:406 et seq.

Family Service System and Children with Disabilities Act
Neb. Rev. Stat. 1943, 79-3901 et seq.

Family Services and Child Protection Act
Me. Rev. Stat. Ann. 1964, Title 22, § 4001 et seq.

Family Support Act
See also Uniform Interstate Family Support Act
See also Uniform Intrastate Family Support Act
Colo. Rev. Stat., 14-5-101 et seq.
N.J. Stat. Ann., 30:6D-33 et seq.

Family Support Act of 1988

    Oct. 13, 1988, P.L. 100-485, 42 U.S. Code § 1305 nt.

    Nov. 10, 1988, P.L. 100-647, 42 U.S. Code § 607

    Dec. 19, 1989, P.L. 101-239, 42 U.S. Code § 602 nt.

    Nov. 5, 1990, P.L. 101-508, 42 U.S. Code §§ 666 nt., 1315 nt.

    July 3, 1992, P.L. 102-318, 42 U.S. Code § 666 nt.

    Oct. 31, 1994, P.L. 103-432, 42 U.S. Code §§ 602 nt., 1315 nt.

    Aug. 22, 1996, P.L. 104-193, 42 U.S. Code §§ 602 nt., 655, 1315 nt.

Family Support Demonstration Project Act

    Ill. Rev. Stat. 1991, Ch. 23, § 4101 et seq.

Family Support for Persons with a Serious Mental Illness Act

    N.J. Stat. Ann., 30:177-43 et seq.

Family Support Law

    Mich. Comp. Laws Ann., 552.451 et seq.

    N.Y. Domestic Relations Law (Consol. Laws Ch. 14) § 30

    N.Y. Family Court Act § 411 et seq.

Family Support Law (Estates)

    Wash. Rev. Code Ann., 11.52.010 et seq.

Family Support Magistrates Act

    Conn. Gen. Stat. 1983, § 46b-231 et seq.

Family Support Personnel Polices Act

    Fla. Stat. Ann., 110.1521 et seq.

Family Therapist and Marital Licensure Act

    S.C. Code Ann. 1976, § 40-75-10 et seq.

Family Therapy and Practicing Marriage Act

    N.J. Stat. Ann., 45:8B-1 et seq.

Family Transition Act

    Fla. Stat. Ann., 409.921 et seq.

Family Unity Demonstration Project Act

    Sept. 13, 1994, P.L. 103-322, 42 U.S. Code §§ 13701 nt., 13881 et seq., 13901, 13902

Family Violence Prevention and Services Act

    Oct. 9, 1984, P.L. 98-457, 98 Stat. 1757, 42 U.S. Code §§ 10401 et seq., 10401 nt.

    April 25, 1988, P.L. 100-294, 102 Stat. 124, 42 U.S. Code §§ 10402, 10409 to 10411, 10413

    May 28, 1992, P.L. 102-295, 42 U.S. Code §§ 10401 to 10403, 10405, 10407 to 10410, 10412 to 10415

    Sept. 13, 1994, P.L. 103-322, 42 U.S. Code §§ 10402, 10407 et seq., 10416 et seq.

    Sept. 30, 1996, P.L. 104-208, 42 U.S. Code § 10403

    Oct. 3, 1996, P.L. 104-235, 42 U.S. Code §§ 10402, 10403, 10409

    Nov. 13, 1998, P.L. 105-392, 42 U.S. Code § 10418

Family Violence Protection Act

    La. Rev. Stat. Ann., 46:2121 et seq.

    N.M. Stat. Ann., 40-13-1 et seq.

    Wyo. Stat. Ann., § 35-21-101 et seq.

Family Violence Protection Order Enforcement Act

    Ala. Code 1975, § 30-5A-1 et seq.

Family Violence Relief Act (Post Separation)

    La. Rev. Stat. Ann., 9:361 et seq.

Family Week in South Carolina Act

    S.C. Code Ann. 1976, § 53-3-10 et seq.

Far Eastern Economic Assistance Act of 1950

    Feb. 14, 1950, Ch. 16, 64 Stat. 5

Farm Agricultural Warehouse Act

    Ky. Rev. Stat. 1971, 251.010 et seq.

Farm and Equipment Act

    Mich. Comp. Laws Ann., 125.2401 et seq.

Farm and Home Purchase Act (Veterans)

    Cal. Military and Veterans Code § 987.50 et seq.

Miss. Code Ann. 1972, § 35-7-1 et seq.

Farm and Open Space Tax Law
Me. Rev. Stat. Ann. 1964, Title 36, § 1101 et seq.

Farm and Ranch Heritage Museum Act
N.M. Stat. Ann., 18-11-1 et seq.

Farm and Road Camp Act
Cal. Penal Code § 4100 et seq.

Farm and Utility Equipment Franchise Act
Mich. Comp. Laws Ann., 445.1451

Farm Animal and Research Facilities Protection Act
Ga. Code Ann., 4-11-30 et seq.
Kan. Stat. Ann., 47-1825 et seq.
Mont. Laws 1991, Ch. 205
S.C. Code Ann. 1976, § 47-21-10 et seq.
Tenn. Public Acts 1992, Ch. 782

Farm Assessment Act
Md. Ann. Code 1974, Art. TP, § 8-209

Farm Bankruptcy Act
See Frazier-Lemke Farm Mortgage Act

Farm Bill of 1938
See Agricultural Adjustment Act Of 1938

Farm Bureau Act
Kan. Laws 1915, Ch. 166
Ky. Rev. Stat. 1971, 247.240 et seq.
P.R. Laws Ann. 1954, Title 5, § 941 et seq.
R.I. Gen. Laws 1956, 2-3-1 et seq.

Farm Chattel Lien Act
Va. Code 1950, § 43-44

Farm Credit Act Amendments of 1980
Dec. 24, 1980, P.L. 96-592, 12 U.S. Code § 2001 nt.

Farm Credit Act Amendments of 1986
Oct. 21, 1986, P.L. 99-509, 12 U.S. Code § 2001 nt.

Farm Credit Act of 1933
June 16, 1933, Ch. 98, 48 Stat. 257, 12 U.S. Code § 1131 et seq.
Oct. 28, 1949, Ch. 782, 63 Stat. 972, 12 U.S. Code § 1138f
Oct. 31, 1949, Ch. 792, 63 Stat. 1058, 12 U.S. Code §§ 1134c, 1134j
Oct. 24, 1951, Ch. 554, 65 Stat. 614, 12 U.S. Code § 1138f
Aug. 6, 1953, Ch. 335, 67 Stat. 395, 12 U.S. Code § 1131c
Aug. 23, 1954, Ch. 834, 68 Stat. 770, 12 U.S. Code § 2234m
Aug. 11, 1955, Ch. 785, 69 Stat. 655, 12 U.S. Code §§ 65, 1131e to1131g, 1134c, 1134d, 1134g to 1134l nt., 1138c, 1138e
July 26, 1956, Ch. 741, 70 Stat. 664, 12 U.S. Code §§ 1131c to 1131g, 1131i, 1134, 1134a, 1134c, 1134j, 1138 to 1138c, 1138e
June 11, 1960, P.L. 86-503, 74 Stat. 197, 12 U.S. Code § 1134g
Oct. 3, 1961, P.L. 87-343, 75 Stat. 758, 12 U.S. Code §§ 1131f, 1131i
Oct. 4, 1961, P.L. 87-353, 75 Stat. 774, 12 U.S. Code § 1138b
Aug. 31, 1964, P.L. 88-528, 78 Stat. 736, 12 U.S. Code § 1134l
Oct. 4, 1965, P.L. 89-237, 79 Stat. 924, 12 U.S. Code §§ 1131f, 1131g
Aug. 2, 1966, P.L. 89-525, 80 Stat. 334, 12 U.S. Code §§ 1134c, 1134j
Dec. 15, 1967, P.L. 90-204, 81 Stat. 612, 12 U.S. Code §§ 1131g, 1134c, 1134j
June 18, 1968, P.L. 90-345, 82 Stat. 183, 12 U.S. Code § 1131g
Oct. 17, 1968, P.L. 90-582, 3, 82 Stat. 1145, 12 U.S. Code §§ 1131c, 1134e

Farm Credit Act of 1937
Aug. 19, 1937, Ch. 704, 50 Stat. 703, 12 U.S. Code §§ 640a to 640l, 656a 671, 677a, 682a, 712, 719, 723, 724, 732, 745 to 747, 761, 771, 781, 823, 831 and others
Oct. 29, 1949, Ch. 786, 63 Stat. 986, 12 U.S. Code § 640a
Aug. 6, 1953, Ch. 335, 67 Stat. 396, 12 U.S. Code §§ 640b, 640d
Aug. 11, 1955, Ch. 785, 69 Stat. 666, 12 U.S. Code § 640b

Continued

July 26, 1956, Ch. 741, 70 Stat. 666, 12 U.S. Code §§ 640d, 640h, 640l

Aug. 18, 1959, P.L. 86-168, 73 Stat. 387, 12 U.S. Code § 640l

Aug. 2, 1966, P.L. 89-525, 80 Stat. 334, 12 U.S. Code §§ 640e, 640f

Farm Credit Act of 1953

Aug. 6, 1953, Ch. 335, 67 Stat. 390, 7 U.S. Code § 452; 12 U.S. Code §§ 636a nt., 636a to 636h, 640b, 640d, 903, 1131c, 1131e-1, 1134d, 1134l

Aug. 11, 1955, Ch. 785, 69 Stat. 666, 12 U.S. Code §§ 636 nt., 636c

July 26, 1956, Ch. 741, 70 Stat. 666, 12 U.S. Code §§ 636g, 1131e- 1

Aug. 18, 1959, P.L. 86-168, 73 Stat. 387, 12 U.S. Code § 636d

Oct. 4, 1961, P.L. 87-353, 75 Stat. 774, 12 U.S. Code § 636f

Oct. 4, 1961, P.L. 87-367, 75 Stat. 793, 12 U.S. Code 636d

Aug. 2, 1966, P.L. 89-525, 80 Stat. 335, 12 U.S. Code § 636c

Oct. 17, 1968, P.L. 90-582, 82 Stat. 1145, 12 U.S. Code 1131e-1

Farm Credit Act of 1955

Aug. 11, 1955, Ch. 785, 69 Stat. 655, 12 U.S. Code §§ 636 nt., 636c, 636f, 640b, 640d, 663, 665, 714, 734, 757, 771, 781, 832, 901, 902 and others

Farm Credit Act of 1956

July 26, 1956, Ch. 741, 70 Stat. 659, 12 U.S. Code §§ 24, 636g, 640d, 640h, 640l 781, 832, 1022 and others 18 U.S. Code §§ 658, 1014; 31 U.S. Code §§ 846, 856, 867, 868

Farm Credit Act of 1959

Aug. 18, 1959, P.L. 86-168, 73 Stat. 384, 12 U.S. Code §§ 636a nt., 636d, 640l 656, 662, 742, 751 to 757, 771, 861, 864, 901, 911, 967, 1033, 1093; 26 U.S. Code 26 § 3121; 28 U.S. Code § 2680; 42 U.S. Code § 410

Farm Credit Act of 1971

Dec. 1, 1971, P.L. 92-181, 85 Stat. 583, 12 U.S. Code § 2001 nt. Dec. 23, 1985, P.L. 99-198, 12 U.S. Code § 2129

Dec. 23, 1985, P.L. 99-205, 5 U.S. Code §§ 5314, 5315; 12 U.S. Code §§ 393 nt., 2001 et seq., 2151 et seq., 2205 et seq., 2216 et seq.

Oct. 21, 1986, P.L. 99-509, 12 U.S. Code §§ 2015, 2075, 2131, 2159, 2205, 2252, 2254

Jan, 6, 1988, P.L. 100-233, 7 U.S. Code §§ 2006, 5101 to 5106, 12 U.S. Code §§ 2001 et seq., prec. . 2279aa, 2279aa to 2279aa-14

Oct. 1, 1988, P.L. 100-460, 12 U.S. Code §§ 2278b-9, 2278b-9 nt.

Aug. 9, 1989, P.L. 101-73, 12 U.S. Code § 2245

Dec. 12, 1989, P.L. 101-220, 12 U.S. Code §§ 2020, 2277a-4, 2277a-8, 2277a-10

Nov. 28, 1990, P.L. 101-624, 12 U.S. Code §§ 2019, 2075, 2076a, 2077, 2128, 2129, 2218, 2252, 2254, 2255, 2277a-5, 2277a-9, 2277a-10, 2277a-14, 2278a-6, 2279aa, 2279aa-11

Dec. 13, 1991, P.L. 102-237, 12 U.S. Code §§ 2019, 2071, 2072, 2092, 2128, 2129, 2214, 2252, 2271, 2277a-7, 2277a-14, 2278a-2, 2278b-3, 2279e, prec. 2279aa-1, 2279aa-3, 2279aa-6, 2279aa-11, prec. 2279bb, 2279bb to 2279bb-6

Oct. 28, 1992, P.L. 102-552, 12 U.S. Code §§ 2074, 2122, 2123, 2154a, 2160, 2204, 2209, 2242, 2250, 2252, 2254, 2271, 2277a-2, 2277a-4 nt., 2277a-7, 2277a-8, 2278a-9, 2278b-1, 2278b-6, 2278b-8, 2278b-11, 2279aa-3, 2279aa-11, 2279bb-1

Oct. 13, 1994, P.L. 103-354, 12 U.S. Code §§ 2122, 2128, 2129, 2202e, 2206a

Oct. 19, 1994, P.L. 103-376, 12 U.S. Code §§ 2122, 2128, 2129, 2206a

Feb. 10, 1996, P.L. 104-105, 12 U.S. Code §§ 2013, 2018, 2129, 2154a, 2199, 2202a, 2214a, 2252, 2254, 2277a et seq., 2279aa et seq., 2279bb-1 et seq., 2279cc

Oct. 19, 1996, P.L. 104-316, 12 U.S. Code § 2279aa-10

Farm Credit Administration Appropriation Acts

June 29, 1937, Ch. 404, 50 Stat. 433

June 16, 1938, Ch. 464, 52 Stat. 750

June 30, 1939, Ch. 253, 53 Stat. 939

Farm Credit Allocation Act (Emergency)
Ill. Rev. Stat. 1981, Ch. 5, § 1251 et seq.

Farm Credit Amendments Act of 1985
Dec. 23, 1985, P.L. 99-205, 12 U.S. Code
§ 2001 nt.

Farm Credit Banks and Associations Safety and Soundness Act of 1992
Oct. 28, 1992, P.L. 102-552, 12 U.S. Code
§§ 950aaa-5, 2001 nt.
Oct. 19, 1996, P.L. 104-316, 12 U.S. Code
§ 2277a-4

Farm Credit Program Act (Family)
La. Rev. Stat. Ann., 3:251 et seq.

Farm Credit Security Act
P.R. Laws Ann. 1954, Title 5, § 181 et seq.

Farm Credit System Agricultural Export and Risk Management Act
Oct. 19, 1994, P.L. 103-376, 12 U.S. Code
§ 2001 nt.

Farm Credit System Reform Act of 1996
Feb. 10, 1996, P.L. 104-105, 12 U.S. Code
§ 2001 nt.

Farm Credits Act
See Agricultural Credits Act Of 1923

Farm Crossing Act
Ill. Rev. Stat. 1991, Ch. 95 1/2, § 18c-7504

Farm Debt Adjustment Commission Law
Cal. Statutes 1935, Ch. 704, p. 1905

Farm Development Act
Ill. Rev. Stat. 1991, Ch. 5, § 1201 et seq.

Farm Development Authority Act (Family)
S.C. Code Ann. 1976, § 46-47-10 et seq.

Farm Disaster Assistance Act of 1987
May 27, 1987, P.L. 100-45, 7 U.S. Code
§§ 1444-1, 1444-3, 1445b-3, 1446; 16 U.S.
Code § 3835 nt.; 33 U.S. Code § 701 n
Aug. 18, 1987, P.L. 100-100, 101 Stat. 717

Farm Drainage Act
Ill. Rev. Stat. 1953, Ch. 42, § 82 et seq.
Wis. Stat. Ann., 88.01 et seq.

Farm Equipment Dealer Contract Act
W. Va. Code 1966 § 47-11F-1 et seq.

Farm Equipment Fair Dealership Act
Colo. Rev. Stat., 35-38-101 et seq.
Ill. Rev. Stat. 1991, Ch. 5, § 1501 et seq.

Farm Equipment Manufacturers and Dealers Act
Fla. Stat. Ann., 686.40 et seq.

Farm Export Act
Mich. Comp. Laws Ann., 447.201 et seq.

Farm Finance Act of 1939
Cal. Statutes 1939, Ch. 929, p. 2624

Farm Homestead Protection Act
Neb. Rev. Stat. 1943, 76-1901 et seq.

Farm Implement Buyer Protection Act
Ill. Rev. Stat. 1991, Ch. 5, § 1551 et seq.

Farm Implements Act
Wash. Rev. Code Ann., 19.98.010 et seq.

Farm, Industrial, and Construction Equipment Fair Dealership Law
Ill. Rev. Stat. 1991, Ch. 5, § 1501 et seq.

Farm Insurance Act
P.R. Laws Ann. 1954, Title 5, § 1401 et seq.

Farm Interest Act
June 16, 1938, Ch. 462, 52 Stat. 709, 12 U.S.
Code §§ 771, 1016

Farm Labor Act
Ariz. Rev. Stat. Ann., § 23-1381 et seq.

Farm Labor Center Law
Cal. Health and Safety Code § 36050 et seq.

Farm Labor Contractor Certification Act
Ill. Rev. Stat. 1991, Ch. 111, § 801 et seq.

Farm Labor Contractor Registration Act of 1963

Sept. 7, 1964, P.L. 88-582, 78 Stat. 920, 7 U.S. Code §§ 2041 to 2053

Nov. 1, 1978, P.L. 95-562, 7 U.S. Code § 2042

Jan. 14, 1983, P.L. 97-470, 7 U.S. Code §§ 2041 nt., 2041 to 2050 2050a to 2050c, 2051 to 2055

Farm Labor Contractors Act

Neb. Rev. Stat. 1943, 48-1701 et seq.

Farm Labor Registration Law

Fla. Stat. Ann., 450.27 et seq.

Farm Labor Supply Appropriation Act, 1944

Feb. 14, 1944, Ch. 16, 58 Stat. 11, 50 U.S. Code Appx. §§ 1351 to 1355

Dec. 28, 1945, Ch. 589, 59 Stat. 632

June 30, 1947, Ch. 165, 61 Stat. 202, 50 U.S. Code Appx. §§ 1351 nt., 1355

Farm Laborer's Lien Act

N.D. Cent. Code, 35-30-01 et seq.

Wash. Rev. Code Ann., 60.12.010 et seq.

Farm Land and Forest Land Assessment Act

Pa. Purdon's Stat., Title 72, § 5490.1 et seq.

Farm Legal Assistance Act

Ill. Rev. Stat. 1991, Ch. 5, § 2050-1 et seq.

Farm Loan Act

Mont. Laws 1915, Ch. 28

Wyo. Stat. Ann., § 11-34-101 et seq.

Farm Loan Acts

See Federal Farm Loan Acts

Farm Machine Safety Act

Ill. Rev. Stat. 1991, Ch. 70, § 2.9 et seq.

Farm Machinery Construction Equipment and Motor Vehicle Franchise Practice Act

Ga. Code 1933, 84-6601 et seq.

Farm Machinery Dealerships Act

Va. Code 1950, § 59.1-344 et seq.

Farm Markets Regulation and Inspection Act

P.R. Laws Ann. 1954, Title 5, § 121 et seq.

Farm Mediation Act

Ark. Code 1987, 2-7-101 et seq.

Neb. Rev. Stat. 1943, 2-4801 et seq.

Farm Milk Tank Law

Miss. Code Ann. 1972, § 75-31-201

Farm Mortgage Act

See Frazier-Lemke Farm Mortgage Act

Farm Mortgage Foreclosure Act

June 11, 1934, Ch. 446, 48 Stat. 929, 12 U.S. Code § 1016

Farm Mutual Insurance Company Act

Ill. Rev. Stat. 1991, Ch. 73, § 1251 et seq.

Farm Names Act

Ill. Rev. Stat. 1991, Ch. 5. § 56.9 et seq.

Farm Nuisance Suit Act

Ill. Rev. Stat. 1991, Ch. 5, § 1100 et seq.

Farm Operating Loans Act (Emergency)

Minn. Laws 1985, Ch. 4, §§ 3 to 10

Farm Picketing Act

Ida. Laws 1943, Ch. 76

Farm Pond Act

Md. Ann. Code 1974, Art. NR, § 9-202 et seq.

Farm Poundage Quota Revisions Act of 1990

Nov. 15, 1990, P.L. 101-577, 7 U.S. Code § 1281 nt.

Farm Produce Commission Merchants Act

Ill. Rev. Stat. 1991, Ch. 111, § 100 et seq.

Farm Produce Storage Act

Mich. Comp. Laws Ann., 285.61 et seq.

Farm Productivity and Open Space Land Law

Me. Rev. Stat. Ann. 1964, Title 36, § 1101 et seq.

Farm Products Authority Act
Ga. Laws 1988, p. 4947

Farm Products Inspection Act
Ill. Rev. Stat. 1991, Ch. 5, § 91.9 et seq.

Farm Products Marketing Act
Cal. Food and Agricultural Code 1967,
§§ 56801 et seq., 58001
Colo. Rev. Stat., 12-16-101 et seq.
Ill. Rev. Stat. 1991, Ch. 5, §§ 90z, 91

Farm Products Marketing Facilities Act
La. Rev. Stat. Ann., 3:521 et seq.

Farm Products Secured Interest Act
N.M. Stat. Ann., 56-13-1 et seq.

Farm Reform Act
Miss. Code Ann. 1972, 69-2-1 et seq.

Farm Rehabilitation Act (Family)
Kan. Stat. Ann., 2-3401 et seq.

Farm Research Act
June 29, 1935, Ch. 338, 49 Stat. 438, 7 U.S.
Code §§ 427 to 427g

Farm Safety and Occupational Health Act
Pa. Purdon's Stat., Title 3, § 1901 et seq.

Farm Standards Act
Pa. Purdon's Stat., Title 3, § 21 et seq.

Farm Storage Act (Grain)
Kan. Laws 1935, Ch. 184
S.D. Code 1939, 60.0601 et seq.

Farm Tenant Act
See Bankhead-Jones Farm Tenant Act
Iowa Code 1979, 234.15 et seq.

Farm to Market Road Act
Ala. Code 1958, Title 23, § 78(1) et seq.
Iowa Code Ann., 310.1 et seq.

Farm Tractor Fuel Act
Tenn. Code Ann., 67-3-301 et seq.

Farm Tractor Gasoline Tax Refund Act
Ga. Code 1933, 92-1403, Subd. I

Farm Tractor Warranty Act
Ga. Code Ann., 10-1-810 et seq.

Farm Warehouse Act (Grain)
Mo. Rev. Stat. 1959, 411.580 et seq.

Farm Warehouse and Depository Act
Ind. Code 1971, 26-3-6-1 et seq.

Farm Warehousing Act
Neb. Rev. Stat. 1943, 88-601 et seq.

Farm Winery Act
Ida. Code 1947, 23-1301 et seq.

Farm Woodlot Tax Exemption Act
Wis. Laws 1989, 70.113 Subsec. 2

Farm Youth Loan Program Act
La. Rev. Stat. Ann., 3:541 et seq.

Farmer-Lender Mediation Act
Minn. Stat. Ann., 583.20 et seq.

Farmer Major Drought, Flood and Hurricane Disaster Act
Va. Code 1950, § 3.1-22.13 et seq.

Farmer-to-Consumer Direct Marketing Act of 1976
Oct. 8, 1976, P.L. 94-463, 7 U.S. Code
§ 3001 et seq.
Nov. 2, 1994, P.L. 103-437, 7 U.S. Code
§ 3005
Nov. 10, 1998, P.L. 105-362, 7 U.S. Code
§§ 3005, 3006

Farmers Act (Tractor Registration)
N.Y. Vehicle and Traffic Law 1959 (Consol.
Laws Ch. 71) § 401

Farmers Bill (Commercial Vehicle Registration)
N.Y. Vehicle and Traffic Law 1959 (Consol.
Laws Ch. 71) § 401, Subd. 7, § E

Farmers' Credit Association Law
Miss. Code Ann. 1972, § 81-17-1

Farmers' Home Administration Act of 1946

Aug. 14, 1946, Ch. 964, 60 Stat. 1062, 7 U.S. Code §§ 451 nt., 1010 nt.; 12 U.S. Code §§ 371, 1702 nt.; 31 U.S. Code § 82h

April 28, 1947, Ch. 43, 61 Stat. 55

April 20, 1950, Ch. 94, 64 Stat. 73

Farmers Home Administration Improvement Act of 1994

May 11, 1994, P.L. 103-248, 7 U.S. Code §§ 1921 nt., 1981

Farmers' Moratorium Act

Ill. Rev. Stat. 1991, Ch. 5, § 91

Farmers' Pooling Act

Ky. Rev. Stat. 1971, 272.010 et seq.

Farmers' Produce Market Act

D.C. Code 1967, § 10-137

Farmer's Protection and Farm Preservation Act

N.Y. Real Property Tax Law (Consol. Laws Ch. 50A) § 483b

N.Y. Tax Law (Consol. Laws Ch. 60) §§ 208, 210, 606, 612

Farmers' Warehouse Act (State Regulated)

La. Rev. Stat. Ann., 54:241 et seq.

Farming and Organic Food Law

Fla. Stat. Ann., 504.21 et seq.

Farmington Code of Ethics

N.Y. Local Laws 1970, Town of Farmington, p. 1516

Farmington Dangerous Buildings and Structures Local Law

N.Y. Local Laws 1968, Town of Farmington, p. 2386

Farmington Partial Exemption from Taxation of Certain Real Property Owned by Persons Sixty-five Years of Age or Over Local Law

N.Y. Local Laws 1971, Town of Farmington, p. 1750

Farmington Retention of Assessors Local Law

N.Y. Local Laws 1971, Town of Farmington, p. 1751

Farmington Sewer Use Local Law

N.Y. Local Laws 1967, Town of Farmington, p. 1554

Farmington Water Rules and Regulations Local Law

N.Y. Local Laws 1968, Town of Farmington, p. 2381

Farmington Wild and Scenic River Study Act

Oct. 30, 1986, P.L. 99-590, 16 U.S. Code § 1271 nt.

Aug. 26, 1994, P.L. 103-313, 16 U.S. Code § 1671 nt.

Farmland and Agricultural District Preservation Act

Tenn. Code Ann., 43-34-101 et seq.

Farmland and Forest Land Assessment Act (Clean and Green)

Pa. Purdon's Stat., Title 72, § 5490.1 et seq.

Farmland and Open Space Preservation Act

Mich. Comp. Laws Ann., 554.701 et seq.

Farmland Assessment Act

N.J. Stat. Ann., 54:4-23.1 et seq.

Utah Code Ann. 1953, 59-2-501 et seq.

Farmland, Green Acres, Clean Water and Historic Preservation Bond Act

N.J. Laws 1992, Ch. 88

Farmland Preservation Act

Ill. Rev. Stat. 1991, Ch. 5, § 1301 et seq.

R.I. Gen. Laws 1956, 42-82-1 et seq.

Farmland Preservation Bond Act

N.J. Laws 1981, Ch. 276

Farmland Preservation Enabling Act

N.C. Gen. Stat. 1943, § 106-735 et seq.

Farmland Protection Policy Act
Dec. 22, 1981, P.L. 97-98, 7 U.S. Code
§ 4201 nt.
Dec. 23, 1985, P.L. 99-198, 7 U.S. Code
§§ 4207, 4209
Nov. 28, 1990, P.L. 101-624, 7 U.S. Code
§§ 4202, 4208

Farmland Tax Stabilization Act (Preserved)
Pa. Purdon's Stat., Title 72, § 5491.1 et seq.

Farms for the Future Act of 1990
Nov. 28, 1990, P.L. 101-624, 7 U.S. Code
§ 4201 nt.
Dec. 13, 1991, P.L. 102-237, 7 U.S. Code
§ 4201 nt.

Farmworker Housing Assistance Act
Fla. Stat. Ann., 420.801 et seq.

Farnsworth Act (Abandoned State Lands, State Parks)
Ohio Laws Vol. 114, p. 518

Farr-Davis Driver Safety Act
Cal. Vehicle Code 1959, § 23240 et seq.

Farr Economic Disaster Act
Cal. Government Code § 8695 et seq.

Farr-Morgan-Quackenbush Educational Technology Act
Cal. Education Code 1976, § 51870 et seq.

Fascell Fellowship Act
Aug. 27, 1986, P.L. 99-399, 22 U.S. Code
§§ 4901 nt., 4901 to 4904
Dec. 22, 1987, P.L. 100-204, 22 U.S. Code
§ 4904
Dec. 17, 1993, P.L. 103-199, 22 U.S. Code
§ 4901
Oct. 21, 1998, P.L. 105-277, 22 U.S. Code
§ 4902

Fascell Fellowship Amendments Act of 1990
Oct. 24, 1990, P.L. 101-454, 22 U.S. Code
§§ 4901, 4901 nt., 4902, 4902 nt., 4904

Fastener Quality Act
Nov. 16, 1990, P.L. 101-592, 15 U.S. Code
§§ 5401 nt., 5401 to 5414

March 7, 1996, P.L. 104-113, 15 U.S. Code
§ 5401 et seq.
Aug. 14, 1998, P.L. 105-234, 15 U.S. Code
§ 5414
June 8, 1999, P.L. 106-34, 15 U.S. Code
§§ 5401 to 5411, 5411a, 5411b, 5412, 5414

Fastener Quality Act Amendments Act of 1999
June 8, 1999, P.L. 106-34, 113 Stat. 118, 15
U.S. Code § 5401 nt.

Fatherhood Initiative
Conn. Public Acts 1999, No. 193

Fatherhood Responsibility Act
Ga. Code Ann., 19-11-14.1

Father's Day Act
April 24, 1972, P.L. 92-278, 86 Stat. 124, 36
U.S. Code § 142a

Fathers Day and Mothers Day Act
Ill. Rev. Stat. 1991, Ch. 1, § 3051-40,
3051-70

Faulkner Act (Optional Municipal Charters)
N.J. Rev. Stat. 1937, 40:69A-1 et seq.

Faxon-McNamee Art in Public Places Act
Mich. Comp. Laws Ann., 18.71 et seq.

Fay Kirtland Retirement Act
Fla. Stat. Ann., 112.363

Fayette County Public Facilities Authority Act
Ga. Laws 1978, p. 3377

Fayette County Public Works Act
Tenn. Private Acts 1974, Ch. 234

Fayette County Road Act
Tenn. Private Acts 1941, Ch. 454

Fayette County Water Authority Act
Ga. Laws 1991, p. 4026

FBI Files Act
See Jencks Act

FDA Export Reform and Enhancement Act of 1996

April 26, 1996, P.L. 104-134, 21 U.S. Code § 301 nt.

FDIC Assessment Rate Act of 1990

Nov. 5, 1990, P.L. 101-508, 12 U.S. Code § 1811 nt.

Feasibility Study Act (Hazardous Waste)

N.M. Stat. Ann., 74-4C-1 et seq.

Featherstone Act (Railroads)

Va. Code 1950, §§ 56-426, 56-428

Feature Motion Picture Fair Business Practices Law

Pa. Purdon's Stat., Title 73, § 203-1 et seq.

Federal Acquisition of Land Act

W. Va. Code 1966, § 1-1-3

Federal Acquisition Reform Act of 1996

Feb. 10, 1996, P.L. 104-106, Division D, 41 U.S. Code § 251 nt.

Federal Acquisition Streamlining Act of 1994

Oct. 13, 1994, P.L. 103-355, 41 U.S. Code § 251 nt.

Feb. 10, 1996, P.L. 104-106, 5 U.S. Code Appx. § 5 nt.; 10 U.S. Code §§ 2306a, 2324, 2409, 2539b; 41 U.S. Code §§ 10a nt., 2531, 254b nt., 255, 413 nt., 418b, 605

Nov. 18, 1997, P.L. 105-85, 41 U.S. Code §§ 413 nt., 426a nt.

Federal Activities Inventory Reform Act of 1998

Oct. 19, 1998, P.L. 105-270, 112 Stat. 2382, 31 U.S. Code § 501 nt.

Federal Advisory Committee Act

Oct. 6, 1972, P.L. 92-463, 5 U.S. Code Appx. I

Dec. 17, 1997, P.L. 105-153, 5 U.S. Code Appx. (FACA) §§ 3, 15, 16

Federal Advisory Committee Act Amendments of 1997

Dec. 17, 1997, P.L. 105-153, 5 U.S. Code Appx. (FACA) § 1 nt.

Federal Affairs Administration of the Government Act

P.R. Laws Ann. 1954, Title 7, § 851 et seq.

Federal Agriculture Improvement and Reform Act of 1996

April 4, 1996, P.L. 104-127, 7 U.S. Code § 7201 nt.

Aug. 6, 1996, P.L. 104-180, 7 U.S. Code § 1932

June 23, 1998, P.L. 105-185, 7 U.S. Code §§ 2204f, 3224, 3224 nt., 3319d, 3319d nt.

Oct. 7, 1998, P.L. 105-244, 7 U.S. Code § 2279c

Oct. 21, 1998, P.L. 105-277, 7 U.S. Code § 2204f

Federal Aid Act (Assent)

Tenn. Code Ann., 54-3-101 et seq.

Federal Aid Acts

July 11, 1916, Ch. 241, 39 Stat. 355

Feb. 28, 1919, Ch. 69, 40 Stat. 1200

Sept. 5, 1940, Ch. 715, 54 Stat. 867

Dec. 31, 1970, P.L. 91-605, 84 Stat. 1725

Federal-Aid Combined Road Plan Act

Cal. Streets and Highways Code § 2220 et seq.

Federal Aid for Highway Safety Improvements Act

Cal. Streets and Highways Code, § 2330 et seq.

Federal Aid for Metropolitan Transportation Planning Act

Cal. Streets and Highways Code, § 2230 et seq.

Federal Aid for Safer Off-System Roads Act

Cal. Streets and Highways Code, § 2520 et seq.

Federal Aid for Urban Systems Act

Cal. Streets and Highways Code § 2350 et seq.

Federal Aid Highway Act

June 16, 1936, Ch. 582, 49 Stat. 1519 (See 23 U.S. Code §§ 101, 104, 105, 114, 118)

Utah Code Ann. 1953, 27-12-121 et seq.

Federal-Aid Highway Act of 1944

Dec. 20, 1944, Ch. 626, 58 Stat. 838 (See 23 U.S. Code §§ 109, 307, 318)

June 29, 1948, Ch. 732, 62 Stat. 1107 (See 23 U.S. Code § 104)

June 29, 1956, Ch. 462, 70 Stat. 381 (See 23 U.S. Code §§ 103, 124)

Federal-Aid Highway Act of 1948

June 29, 1948, Ch. 732, 62 Stat. 1105 (See 23 U.S. Code §§ 101, 104, 202, 204, 205)

Federal-Aid Highway Act of 1950

Sept. 7, 1950, Ch. 912, 64 Stat. 785

Oct. 15, 1951, Ch. 501, 65 Stat. 421

Oct. 16, 1951, Ch. 507, 65 Stat. 422

Federal-Aid Highway Act of 1952

June 25, 1952, Ch. 462, 66 Stat. 158

June 29, 1956, Ch. 462, 70 Stat. 386

Federal-Aid Highway Act of 1954

May 6, 1954, Ch. 181, 68 Stat. 70, 16 U.S. Code §§ 8-1 nt., 460c nt.; 18 U.S. Code § 1020; See 23 U.S. Code §§ 101, 103, 104 to 106, 112, 114, 118, 307, 310

Oct. 13, 1964, P.L. 88-660, 78 Stat. 1092

Federal-Aid Highway Act of 1956

June 29, 1956, Ch. 462, 70 Stat. 374 (See 23 U.S. Code §§ 101, 103, 104, 107 to 109, 113, 115, 118, 120, 123, 128, 129, 304 to 306)

April 16, 1958, P.L. 85-381, 72 Stat. 93 (See 23 U.S. Code §§ 101, 104, 123, 128, 304)

Aug. 6, 1958, P.L. 85-597, 72 Stat. 513 (See 23 U.S. Code § 108)

Aug. 28, 1958, P.L. 85-823, 72 Stat. 983, 23 U.S. Code § 307 nt.

Sept. 2, 1958, P.L. 85-899, 72 Stat. 1725, 23 U.S. Code § 104 nt.

Sept. 21, 1959, P.L. 86-342, 73 Stat. 611, 23 U.S. Code § 101 nt.

June 29, 1961, P.L. 87-61, 75 Stat. 122, 23 U.S. Code § 101 nt.

Aug. 28, 1965, P.L. 89-139, 79 Stat. 578, 23 U.S. Code §§ 101 nt., 104 nt.

Sept. 16, 1966, P.L. 89-574, 80 Stat. 766, 23 U.S. Code § 101 nt.

Aug. 23, 1968, P.L. 90-495, 82 Stat. 815, 23 U.S. Code § 101 nt.

Dec. 31, 1970, P.L. 91-605, 84 Stat. 1714, 23 U.S. Code § 101 nt.

Nov. 6, 1978, P.L. 95-599, 23 U.S. Code § 101 nt.

Jan. 6, 1983, P.L. 97-424, 23 U.S. Code § 101 nt.

Sept. 30, 1985, P.L. 99-104, 23 U.S. Code § 104 nt.

April 2, 1987, P.L. 100-17, 23 U.S. Code § 101 nt.

Federal-Aid Highway Act of 1958

April 16, 1958, P.L. 85-831, 72 Stat. 89 (See 23 U.S. Code §§ 101, 104, 117, 118, 121, 123, 128, 203, 304)

Sept. 2, 1958, P.L. 85-899, 72 Stat. 1725, 23 U.S. Code § 104 nt.

Sept. 21, 1959, P.L. 86-342, 73 Stat. 611, 23 U.S. Code § 104 nt.

Federal-Aid Highway Act of 1959

Sept. 21, 1959, P.L. 86-342, 73 Stat. 611, 23 U.S. Code §§ 101 nt., 120, 125, 131, 307 nt., 320; 26 U.S. Code §§ 4041, 4081, 4082, 4226, 6412, 6416, 6421

Federal-Aid Highway Act of 1961

June 29, 1961, P.L. 87-61, 75 Stat. 122, 23 U.S. Code §§ 111, 120 nt., 131, 210; 26 U.S. Code §§ 4041, 4061, 4071, 4081, 4218, 4221, 4226, 4481, 4482, 6156, 6157, 6412, 6416, 6421, 6601

Federal-Aid Highway Act of 1962

Oct. 23, 1962, P.L. 87-866, 76 Stat. 1145, 23 U.S. Code §§ 101, 103, 104, 133, 134, 203, 214, 307

Federal-Aid Highway Act of 1963

Oct. 24, 1963, P.L. 88-157, 77 Stat. 276, 23 U.S. Code §§ 104, 106, 109, 121, 131, 307

Federal-Aid Highway Act of 1964

Aug. 13, 1964, P.L. 88-423, 78 Stat. 397, 23 U.S. Code §§ 101, 104, 205, 209, 320

Sept. 13, 1966, P.L. 89-574, 80 Stat. 766, 23 U.S. Code §§ 101, 104, 106 nt., 108 nt., 109, 118, 120, 125, 131, 136 to 138, 302, 319

Federal-Aid Highway Act of 1966

Sept. 13, 1966, P.L. 89-574, 80 Stat. 766, 23 U.S. Code §§ 101, 104, 106 nt., 108 nt., 109, 118, 120, 125, 131, 136 to 138, 302, 319

Federal-Aid Highway Act of 1970

Dec. 31, 1970, P.L. 91-605, 84 Stat. 1713, 23 U.S. Code §§ 101, 103 to 106, 109, 120, 125, 128, 129 and others; 33 U.S. Code § 517

Federal-Aid Highway Act of 1973

Aug. 13, 1973, P.L. 93-87, 87 Stat. 253, 23 U.S. Code §§ 101, 103 to 105, 108, 109, 114, 117, 121, 126, 129, 135, 140, 142, 143, 145 to 150, 207, 217, 218, 303, 307 to 310, 312, 314, 320, 323, 324; 33 U.S. Code § 526a; 49 U.S. Code § 1602a

Nov. 6, 1978, P.L. 95-599, 23 U.S. Code §§ 130 nt., 142 nt.

Jan. 6, 1983, P.L. 97-424, 23 U.S. Code § 130 nt.

April 2, 1987, P.L. 100-17, 23 U.S. Code § 130 nt.; 101 Stat. p. 205

Dec. 22, 1987, P.L. 100-202, 23 U.S. Code § 130 nt.

Dec. 18, 1991, P.L. 102-240, 23 U.S. Code § 130 nt.

Dec. 21, 1995, P.L. 104-66, 23 U.S. Code § 130 nt.

Federal-Aid Highway Act of 1976

May 5, 1976, P.L. 94-280, 49 U.S. Code § 1605 et seq.

Nov. 6, 1978, P.L. 95-599, 23 U.S. Code §§ 101 nt., 124 nt.

Federal-Aid Highway Act of 1978

Nov. 6, 1978, P.L. 95-599, 23 U.S. Code §§ 101 to 105, 109, 111, 116 et seq. 215, 217, 219c, 307 nt., 320, 406; 40 Appx. § 201; 42 U.S. Code § 5904; 46 U.S. Code § 883 nt.; 49 U.S. Code §§ 303, 1605 nt., 1653 nt.

Nov. 9, 1979, P.L. 96-106, 23 U.S. Code §§ 103, 103 nt., 109 nt., 129 nt., 141 nt., 144 nt.

Jan. 6, 1983, P.L. 97-424, 23 U.S. Code §§ 103 nt., 307 nt.

April 7, 1986, P.L. 99-272, 23 U.S. Code § 144 nt.

April 2, 1987, P.L. 100-17, 23 U.S. Code §§ 109, 141 nt., 217, 217 nt.; 101 Stat. p. 155

Dec. 18, 1991, P.L. 102-240, 23 U.S. Code § 109 nt.

Federal-Aid Highway Act of 1981

Dec. 29, 1981, P.L. 97-134, 23 U.S. Code § 101 nt.

Federal-Aid Highway Act of 1982

Oct. 15, 1982, P.L. 97-327, 23 U.S. Code §§ 101 nt., 104 nt., 130 nt., 144

Jan. 6, 1983, P.L. 97-424, 23 U.S. Code § 104 nt.

Federal-Aid Highway Act of 1987

April 2, 1987, P.L. 100-17, 23 U.S. Code §§ 101 nt., 103 nt.

Sept. 30, 1988, P.L. 100-457, 102 Stat. 2157

Federal-Aid Highway Amendments of 1974

April 2, 1987, P.L. 100-17, 23 U.S. Code §§ 109, 217, 217 nt.

Federal Aid in Fish Restoration Act of 1950

See Fish Restoration And Management Projects Act

Federal Aid in Wildlife Restoration Act

See Wildlife Restoration Act

Federal Aid Road Act

See Federal Highway Act

Federal Aid Secondary Highways Act
Cal. Streets and Highways Code § 2200 et seq.

Federal Aid to Aviation Channeling Act
Ind. Code Ann., 8-21-8-1

Federal Aid to Wildlife Restoration Act
See Wild Life Restoration Act

Federal Airport Act
May 13, 1946, Ch. 251, 60 Stat. 170, 49 U.S. Code §§ 1101 to 1119

April 17, 1948, Ch. 192, 62 Stat. 173, 49 U.S. Code §§ 1101, 1102,1106, 1108, 1109

June 29, 1948, Ch. 738, 62 Stat. 1111, 49 U.S. Code 1116

July 25, 1949, Ch. 359, 63 Stat. 478, 49 U.S. Code § 1111

July 26, 1949, Ch. 363, 63 Stat. 480, 49 U.S. Code § 1114

Aug. 12, 1949, Ch. 423, 63 Stat. 603, 49 U.S. Code § 1113

Aug. 15, 1949, Ch. 426, 63 Stat. 605, 49 U.S. Code § 1109

Oct. 25, 1949, Ch. 724, 63 Stat. 903, 49 U.S. Code §§ 1105

Oct. 26, 1949, Ch. 751, 63 Stat. 925, 49 U.S. Code § 1104

Feb. 9, 1950, Ch. 5, 64 Stat. 4, 49 U.S. Code § 1107

March 18, 1950, Ch. 72, 64 Stat. 28, 49 U.S. Code §§ 1102, 1108

Sept. 27, 1950, Ch. 1055, 64 Stat. 1074, 49 U.S. Code § 1104

Jan. 9, 1951, Ch. 1214, 64 Stat. 1237, 49 U.S. Code § 1109

July 8, 1953, Ch. 181, 67 Stat. 140, 49 U.S. Code § 1116

Aug. 3, 1955, Ch. 494, 69 Stat. 441, 49 U.S. Code §§ 1101 to 1104,1105, 1108, 1111

Aug. 23, 1958, P.L. 85-726, 72 Stat. 806, Title 49 U.S. Code §§ 1101, 1102, 1103, 1105, 1108, 1111, 1116

June 29, 1959, P.L. 86-72, 73 Stat. 155, 49 U.S. Code §§ 1101, 1102, 1104, 1106, 1108, 1109, 1112

Sept. 21, 1959, P.L. 86-295, 73 Stat. 572, 49 U.S. Code § 1105

Sept. 20, 1961, P.L. 87-255, 75 Stat. 523, 49 U.S. Code §§ 1101 to 1103, 1104 to 1106, 1108 to 1110, 1112

March 11, 1964, P.L. 88-280, 78 Stat. 158, 49 U.S. Code §§ 1101 to 1103, 1104 to 1106, 1107a to 1111, 1113, 1120

July 2, 1964, P.L. 88-349, 78 Stat. 239, 49 U.S. Code § 1114

Oct. 13, 1966, P.L. 89-647, 80 Stat. 894, 49 U.S. Code §§ 1104, 1105

Va. Code 1950, §§ 5.1-47, 5.1-48

Federal Airport Funds Act
Utah Code Ann. 1953, 2-3-1 et seq.

Federal Alcohol Administration Act
Aug. 29, 1935, Ch. 814, 49 Stat. 977, 27 U.S. Code §§ 201 to 211

April 20, 1942, Ch. 244, 56 Stat. 219, 27 U.S. Code § 205 (f) (2)

Aug. 7, 1946, Ch. 770, 60 Stat. 870, 27 U.S. Code § 202

Aug. 28, 1958, P.L. 85-791, 72 Stat. 946, 27 U.S. Code § 204

Nov. 18, 1988, P.L. 100-690, 27 U.S. Code § 201

Federal and Other Funds Oversight Act
S.C. Acts 1983, p. 424, No. 151

Federal and State Apportionment Act
N.Y. Estate, Powers and Trust Law (Consol. Laws Ch. 17B) § 2-1.8

Federal and State Employment Cooperation Act
Ill. Rev. Stat. 1991, Ch. 48, § 172a et seq.

Federal and State Land Jurisdiction Act
Ill. Rev. Stat. 1991, Ch. 1, § 7151 et seq.

Federal Anti-Injunction Act
March 23, 1932, Ch. 90, 47 Stat. 70, 29 U.S. Code §§ 101 to 115

Federal Assistance Management Act
Mont. Code Ann., 17-3-101 et seq.

Federal Augmentation Appropriation Act
Pa. 1976 Pamph. Laws 1383, No. 17A
Pa. 1977 Pamph. Laws 452, No. 12A
Continued

Pa. 1978 Pamph. Laws 1598 No. 56A

Pa. 1979 Pamph. Laws 665, No. 10-A

Pa. 1980 Pamph. Laws 1445, No. 23-A

Pa. 1981 Pamph. Laws 776, No. 56A

Federal Aviation Act of 1958

Aug. 23, 1958, P.L. 85-726, 72 Stat. 731, 14 U.S. Code §§ 81, 82, 90; 15 U.S. Code § 45; 16 U.S. Code § 7a; 31 U.S. Code § 686; 48 U.S. Code §§ 485 to 485d; 49 U.S. Code §§ 212, 486 nt., 1101 1102, 1103, 1105, 1108, 1111, 1116, 1151, 1152 and others; 50 U.S. Code § 123; 50 U.S. Code Appx. §§ 1622 to 1622c

July 8, 1959, P.L. 86-81, 73 Stat. 180, 49 U.S. Code §§ 1403, 1404

Aug. 25, 1959, P.L. 86-199, 73 Stat. 427, 49 U.S. Code § 1485

June 29, 1960, P.L. 86-546, 74 Stat. 255, 49 U.S. Code § 1486

July 12, 1960, P.L. 86-627, 74 Stat. 445, 49 U.S. Code § 1373

Sept. 13, 1960, P.L. 86-758, 74 Stat. 901, 49 U.S. Code § 1378

July 20, 1961, P.L. 87-89, 75 Stat. 210, 49 U.S. Code § 1542

Sept. 5, 1961, P.L. 87-197, 75 Stat. 466, 49 U.S. Code §§ 1301, 1472, 1473, 1511

Sept. 13, 1961, P.L. 87-225, 75 Stat. 497, 49 U.S. Code § 1486

Sept. 20, 1961, P.L. 87-255, 75 Stat. 527, 49 U.S. Code § 1509

Oct. 4, 1961, P.L. 87-367, 75 Stat. 787, 49 U.S. Code §§ 1322, 1343

July 10, 1962, P.L. 87-528, 76 Stat. 143, 49 U.S. Code §§ 1301, 1371, 1376, 1387, 1471, 1472

Oct. 11, 1962, P.L. 87-793, 76 Stat. 864, 49 U.S. Code § 1343

Oct. 15, 1962, P.L. 87-810, 76 Stat. 921, 49 U.S. Code §§ 1323, 1441, 1472, 1505

Oct. 15, 1962, P.L. 87-820, 76 Stat. 936, 49 U.S. Code § 1380

June 30, 1964, P.L. 88-346, 78 Stat. 236, 49 U.S. Code §§ 1403, 1406

Aug. 14, 1964, P.L. 88-426, 78 Stat. 424, 49 U.S. Code §§ 1321, 1341, 1342

June 13, 1966, P.L. 89-447, 80 Stat. 199, 49 U.S. Code 1542

Oct. 15, 1966, P.L. 89-670, 80 Stat. 942, 42 U.S. Code § 1376

July 21, 1968, P.L. 90-411, 82 Stat. 395, 49 U.S. Code § 1431

Sept. 26, 1968, P.L. 90-514, 82 Stat. 867, 49 U.S. Code §§ 1301, 1371

Aug. 20, 1969, P.L. 91-62, 83 Stat. 103, 49 U.S. Code §§ 1377, 1378

May 21, 1970, P.L. 91-248, 84 Stat. 235, 49 U.S. Code §§ 1354, 1509

May 21, 1970, P.L. 91-258, 84 Stat. 234, 49 U.S. Code §§ 1344, 1430

Sept. 8, 1970, P.L. 91-399, 84 Stat. 837

Oct. 14, 1970, P.L. 91-449, 84 Stat. 921, 49 U.S. Code §§ 1301, 1472

Oct. 15, 1970, P.L. 91-452, 84 Stat. 931, 49 U.S. Code § 1484

Dec. 23, 1970, P.L. 91-569, 84 Stat. 1502, 49 U.S. Code § 1512

Dec. 29, 1970, P.L. 91-596, 84 Stat. 1619, 49 U.S. Code § 1421

Dec. 31, 1970, P.L. 91-604, 84 Stat. 1705, 49 U.S. Code §§ 1421, 1430

Nov. 18, 1971, P.L. 92-159, 85 Stat. 481, 49 U.S. Code § 1429

Nov. 27, 1971, P.L. 92-174, 85 Stat. 492, 49 U.S. Code §§ 1429, 1432

March 22, 1972, P.L. 92-259, 86 Stat. 95, 49 U.S. Code §§ 1374, 1461, 1482

Oct. 27, 1972, P.L. 92-574, 86 Stat. 1239, 49 U.S. Code § 1431

June 18, 1973, P.L. 93-44, 87 Stat. 90, 49 U.S. Code § 1513

Jan. 2, 1974, P.L. 93-239, 87 Stat. 1048, 49 U.S. Code § 1421

Aug, 5, 1974, P.L. 93-366, 88 Stat. 409, 49 U.S. Code §§ 1301, 1471 to 1473, 1487, 1514, 1515

Aug. 9, 1975, P.L. 94-90, 89 Stat. 439, 49 U.S. Code §§ 1531 nt., 1536, 1542

Sept. 20, 1977, P.L. 95-109, 15 U.S. Code § 1692l

Nov. 9, 1977, P.L. 95-163, 49 U.S. Code §§ 1531 to 1533, 1535 et seq.

March 8, 1978, P.L. 95-241, 49 U.S. Code § 1401

March 14, 1978, P.L. 95-245, 49 U.S. Code § 1388

Oct. 24, 1978, P.L. 95-504, 49 U.S. Code § 1301 et seq., 1324 nt., 1341 nt., 1371 et seq., 1461, 1471 et seq., 1504, 1551, 1552, 1711, 1729

Feb. 15, 1980, P.L. 96-192, 49 U.S. Code § 1371 et seq.

Feb. 18, 1980, P.L. 96-193, 49 U.S. Code §§ 1472, 1512

Oct. 14, 1982, P.L. 97-309, 49 U.S. Code §§ 1542, 1551

Oct. 4, 1984, P.L. 98-443, 98 Stat. 1703

Oct. 12, 1984, P.L. 98-473, 49 U.S. Code Appx. §§ 1301, 1471, 1472

Oct. 19, 1984, P.L. 98-499, 49 U.S. Code Appx. § 1429 et seq.

Aug. 8, 1985, P.L. 99-83, 49 U.S. Code Appx. §§ 1356, 1471, 1514, 1515a

Dec. 19, 1985, P.L. 99-190, 49 U.S. Code Appx. § 1519

Aug. 22, 1986, P.L. 99-386, 49 Appx., § 1307

Oct. 2, 1986, P.L. 99-435, 49 Appx. U.S. Code § 1374

Oct. 27, 1986, P.L. 99-570, 49 U.S. Code Appx. §§ 1401, 1472, 1474, 1509

Nov. 10, 1986, P.L. 99-646, 49 U.S. Code Appx. § 1472

Sept. 30, 1987, P.L. 100-121, 49 U.S. Code Appx. § 1472

Oct. 30, 1987, P.L. 100-147, 49 U.S. Code Appx. § 1542

Dec. 22, 1987, P.L. 100-202, 49 Appx. U.S. Code § 1374

Dec. 30, 1987, P.L. 100-223, 101 Stat. 1507; 49 U.S. Code Appx. §§ 1301, 1354, 1389, 1389 nt., 1421 nt., 1421, 1461, 1472, 1475, 1475 nt., 1501

Sept. 30, 1988, P.L. 100-457, 102 Stat. 2155, 49 U.S. Code Appx. §§ 1551, 1553

Nov. 3, 1988, P.L. 100-591, 49 U.S. Code Appx. § 1353

Nov. 18, 1988, P.L. 100-690, 49 U.S. Code Appx. §§ 1303, 1354, 1401, 1422, 1425, 1429, 1471, 1472

Nov. 21, 1989, P.L. 101-164, 49 U.S. Code Appx. § 1374

Dec. 15, 1989, P.L. 101-236, 49 U.S. Code Appx. §§ 1421, 1475

May 4, 1990, P.L. 101-281, 49 U.S. Code Appx. § 1475

Aug. 15, 1990, P.L. 101-370, 49 U.S. Code Appx. §§ 1357, 1475, 1482 nt.

Nov. 5, 1990, P.L. 101-508, 49 U.S. Code Appx. §§ 1307, 1344, 1353, 1357, 1371, 1389, 1433, 1513

Nov. 16, 1990, P.L. 101-604, 49 U.S. Code Appx. §§ 1356, 1357, 1357 nt., 1358a to 1358d, 1358d nt., 1380, 1380 nt., 1432, 1515

Oct. 28, 1991, P.L. 102-143, 49 U.S. Code Appx. § 1434

Aug. 26, 1992, P.L. 102-345, 49 U.S. Code Appx. §§ 1422, 1429, 1471, 1475

Oct. 31, 1992, P.L. 102-581, 49 U.S. Code Appx. §§ 1302, 1344, 1348, 1357, 1471, 1501, 1513, 1534, 1542

Federal Aviation Administration Authorization Act of 1994

Dec. 18, 1991, P.L. 102-240, 23 U.S. Code § 101, 101 nt.

Aug. 23, 1994, P.L. 103 to 305, 49 U.S. Code § 40101 nt.

Sept. 30, 1994, P.L. 103-331, 23 U.S. Code § 101 nt.

Dec. 29, 1995, P.L. 104-88, 49 U.S. Code § 10521 nt.

Federal Aviation Administration Drug Enforcement Assistance Act of 1988

Nov. 18, 1988, P.L. 100-690, 49 U.S. Code Appx. § 1301 nt.

Federal Aviation Administration Research, Engineering, and Development Authorization Act of 1990

Nov. 5, 1990, P.L. 101-508, 49 U.S. Code Appx. §§ 2201 nt., 2226d

Federal Aviation Administration Research, Engineering, and Development Authorization Act of 1992

Oct. 31, 1992, P.L. 102-581, 49 U.S. Code Appx. § 2201 nt.

Federal Aviation Administration Research, Engineering, and Development Authorization Act of 1994

Aug. 23, 1994, P.L. 103-305, 49 U.S. Code §§ 40101 nt.

Federal Aviation Reauthorization Act of 1996

Oct. 9, 1996, P.L. 104-264, 49 U.S. Code § 40101 nt.

Nov. 20, 1997, P.L. 105-102, 49 U.S. Code §§ 106, 46301, 47117

Continued

813

Oct. 21, 1998, P.L. 105-277, 49 U.S. Code § 47114

March 31, 1999, P.L. 106-6, 49 U.S. Code § 47117

Federal Banking Agency Audit Act

July 21, 1978, P.L. 95-320, 31 U.S. Code §§ 65 nt., 67e; 18 U.S. Code § 1906

Nov. 10, 1978, P.L. 95-630, 31 U.S. Code § 67

Federal Boat Safety Act of 1971

Aug. 10, 1971, P.L. 92-75, 85 Stat. 213, 46 U.S. Code § 1451 et seq., 1451 nt.

June 30, 1978, P.L. 95-308, 46 U.S. Code § 1479

Oct. 15, 1982, P.L. 97-322, 46 U.S. Code §§ 1482 to 1484

Jan. 6, 1983, P.L. 97-424, 46 U.S. Code §§ 1474, 1475, 1479

Federal Boating Act of 1958

Sept. 2, 1958, P.L. 85-911, 72 Stat. 1754, 46 U.S. Code §§ 288 nt., 526l, 626o, 626t nt., 526u, 527 to 527h

March 28, 1960, P.L. 86-396, 74 Stat. 10, 46 U.S. Code § 526u

Aug. 30, 1961, P.L. 87-171, 75 Stat. 408, 46 U.S. Code §§ 527, 527a, 527e, 527h

Federal Capital Investment Program Information Act of 1984

Oct. 19, 1984, P.L. 98-501, 31 U.S. Code § 1105

Federal Caustic Poison Act

March 4, 1927, Ch. 489, 44 Stat. 1406, 15 U.S. Code §§ 401 to 411

July 12, 1943, Ch. 221, 57 Stat. 498

March 5, 1952, Ch. 78, 66 Stat. 13, 50 U.S. Code Appx. §§ 2255, 2281

June 25, 1952, Ch. 461, 66 Stat. 158, 50 U.S. Code Appx. § 2281

Federal Cave Resources Protection Act of 1988

Nov. 18, 1988, P.L. 100-691, 16 U.S. Code §§ 4301 et seq., 4301 nt.

Federal Cigarette Labeling and Advertising Act

July 27, 1965, P.L. 89-92, 79 Stat. 282, 15 U.S. Code §§ 1331 to 1339

April 1, 1970, P.L. 91-222, 84 Stat. 87, 15 U.S. Code §§ 1331 et seq., 1331 nt.

Sept. 21, 1973, P.L. 93-109, 87 Stat. 352, 15 U.S. Code §§ 1332, 1335

Aug. 16, 1985, P.L. 99-92, 15 U.S. Code §§ 1332, 1333 and nt., 1336

Oct. 7, 1985, P.L. 99-117, 15 U.S. Code § 1333

Oct. 12, 1986, P.L. 98-474, 15 U.S. Code §§ 1331, 1331 nt., 1333, 1335, 1335a nt., 1336 to 1340

Federal Civil Defense Act of 1950

Jan. 12, 1951, Ch. 1228, 64 Stat. 1245, 50 U.S. Code Appx. §§ 2251 to 2297

June 3, 1954, Ch. 253, 68 Stat. 170, 50 U.S. Code Appx. § 2297

Aug. 2, 1956, Ch. 888, 70 Stat. 949, 50 U.S. Code Appx. § 2281

July 11, 1958, P.L. 85-514, 72 Stat. 356, 50 U.S. Code Appx. § 2297

Aug. 8, 1958, P.L. 85-606, 72 Stat. 532, 50 U.S. Code Appx. §§ 2251, 2253, 2260, 2281, 2286

Oct. 4, 1961, P.L. 87-390, 75 Stat. 820, 50 U.S. Code Appx. § 2281

June 27, 1962, P.L. 87-501, 76 Stat. 111, 50 U.S. Code Appx. § 2297

June 30, 1964, P.L. 88-335, 78 Stat. 231, 50 U.S. Code Appx. §§ 2281, 2286

Aug. 19, 1964, P.L. 88-448, 78 Stat. 494, 50 U.S. Code Appx. § 2253

June 30, 1966, P.L. 89-483, 80 Stat. 235, 50 U.S. Code Appx. § 2297

June 10, 1968, P.L. 90-336, 82 Stat. 175, 50 U.S. Code Appx. §§ 2281, 2286

June 30, 1970, P.L. 91-299, 84 Stat. 367, 50 U.S. Code Appx. § 2297

Aug. 2, 1972, P.L. 92-360, 86 Stat. 503, 50 U.S. Code Appx. §§ 2260, 2281, 2286

Nov. 9, 1979, P.L. 96-107, 50 U.S. Code Appx. § 2260

Sept. 8, 1980, P.L. 96-342, 50 U.S. Code Appx. § 2281 et seq.

Nov. 1, 1993, P.L. 103-160, 50 U.S. Code Appx. §§ 2251, 2251 nt., 2252, 2281, 2286, 2289, 2301 et seq.

Oct. 5, 1994, P.L. 103-337, 50 U.S. Code Appx. §§ 2251 nt., 2251 to 2263, 2271, 2272, 2281 to 2284, 2276, 2288, 2289, 2291 to 2297

Federal Civil Penalties Inflation Adjustment Act of 1990

Oct. 5, 1990, P.L. 101-410, 28 U.S. Code § 2461 nt.

April 26, 1996, P.L. 104-134, 28 U.S. Code § 2461 nt.

Nov. 10, 1998, P.L. 105-362, 28 U.S. Code § 2461 nt.

Federal Civilian Employee and Contractor Travel Expenses Act of 1985

Jan, 2, 1986, P.L. 99-234, 2 U.S. Code § 476; 5 U.S. Code §§ 5701, 5702, 5706a, 5707, 5724a, 5734; 22 U.S. Code § 2396; 26 U.S. Code § 4941; 28 U.S. Code § 456; 31 U.S. Code § 326; 41 U.S. Code § 420; 42 U.S. Code § 2477

Federal Claims Collection Act of 1966

July 19, 1966, P.L. 89-508, 80 Stat. 308, 31 U.S. Code §§ 951 to 953

Oct. 25, 1982, P.L. 97-365, 31 U.S. Code §§ 951 nt., 952, 954, 955

Federal Clean Air Mandate Act

N.J. Stat. Ann., 39:8-41 et seq.

Federal Coal Leasing Amendments Act of 1975

Aug. 4, 1976, P.L. 94-377, 30 U.S. Code §§ 181 et seq.

Federal Coal Mine Health and Safety Act of 1969

Dec. 30, 1969, P.L. 91-173, 83 Stat. 742, 15 U.S. Code §§ 633, 636; 30 U.S. Code §§ 801 to 804, 811 to 821, 841 to 846, 861 to 878, 901, 902, 921 to 924, 931 to 936, 951 to 960

May 19, 1972, P.L. 92-303, 86 Stat. 150, 30 U.S. Code §§ 902, 921 to 924, 931 to 934, 936 to 940, 951

Nov. 9, 1977, P.L. 95-164, 30 U.S. Code §§ 801 et seq., 801 nt.

March 27, 1978, P.L. 95-251, 30 U.S. Code §§ 804, 938

Nov. 8, 1984 P.L. 98-620, 30 U.S. Code § 816

Federal Coal Mine Safety Act

May 7, 1941, Ch. 87, 55 Stat. 177, 30 U.S. Code §§ 451 to 460

July 16, 1952, Ch. 877, 66 Stat. 692, 30 U.S. Code §§ 451 to 460, 471 to 483

June 11, 1960, P.L. 86-507, 74 Stat. 201, 30 U.S. Code §§ 477, 478

March 26, 1966, P.L. 89-376, 80 Stat. 85, 30 U.S. Code §§ 471 to 473, 475 to 477, 480, 482

Federal Coal Mine Safety Act Amendments of 1965

March 26, 1966, P.L. 89-376, 80 Stat. 84, 30 U.S. Code §§ 471 to 473, 475 to 477, 479 nt., 480, 482

Federal Commodity Disbursement Act

Ill. Rev. Stat. 1991, Ch. 127, § 176a9 et seq.

Federal Communications Commission Authorization Act of 1983

Dec. 8, 1983, P.L. 98-214, 47 U.S. Code § 609 nt.

Federal Communications Commission Authorization Act of 1988

Nov. 3, 1988, P.L. 100-594, 47 U.S. Code § 609 nt.

Oct. 27, 1992, P.L. 102-538, 47 U.S. Code § 154 nt.

Federal Communications Commission Authorization Act of 1990

Sept. 28, 1990, P.L. 101-396, 47 U.S. Code §§ 154 nt., 609 nt.

Federal Comprehensive Environmental Response, Compensation, and Liability

Mont. Code Ann., 75-10-601 et seq.

Federal Condemnation Act

Va. Code 1950, § 25-56 et seq.

Federal Conformity Income Tax Act

Kan. Stat. Ann., 79-32,109 et seq.

Federal Contested Election Act

Dec. 5, 1969, P.L. 91-138, 82 Stat. 284, 2 U.S. Code §§ 381 to 396

Aug. 20, 1996, P.L. 104-186, 2 U.S. Code § 381, 382, 396

Federal Control Act (Transportation System)

March 21, 1918, Ch. 25, 40 Stat. 451

June 30, 1919, Ch. 5, 41 Stat. 34

Federal Control of Telegraphs and Telephones Acts

July 16, 1918, Ch. 154, 40 Stat. 904

Oct. 29, 1918, Ch. 197, 40 Stat. 1017

July 11, 1919, Ch. 10, 41 Stat. 157

Federal Cooperation Act (Irrigation Districts)

Cal. Water Code § 23175 et seq.

Federal Correctional Institutions Cession Law (Pekin and Greenville)

Ill. Comp. Stat. 1992, Ch. 5, § 517/10-1

Federal Corrupt Practices Acts

Jan. 26, 1907, Ch. 420, 34 Stat. 864

June 25, 1910, Ch. 392, 36 Stat. 822

Aug. 19, 1911, Ch. 33, 37 Stat. 25

Aug. 23, 1912, Ch. 349, 37 Stat. 360

Oct. 16, 1918, Ch. 187, 40 Stat. 1013

Feb. 28, 1925, Ch. 368, 43 Stat. 1070 (See 18 U.S. Code § 602)

June 23, 1947, Ch. 120, 61 Stat. 159

Dec. 23, 1971, P.L. 92-220, 85 Stat. 795, 2 U.S. Code § 241

Federal Court Local Law Certificate Procedure Act

Wash. Rev. Code Ann., 2.60.010 et seq.

Federal Court State Law Certificate Procedure Act

Wyo. Stat. Ann., § 1-13-104 et seq.

Federal Courts Administration Act of 1992

Oct. 29, 1992, P.L. 102-572, 28 U.S. Code § 1 nt.

Federal Courts Improvement Act of 1982

April 2, 1982, P.L. 97-164, 28 U.S. Code §§ 171 et seq., 1494 to 1497, 1499 to 1503

Federal Courts Improvement Act of 1996

Oct. 19, 1996, P.L. 104-317, 28 U.S. Code § 1 nt.

Federal Courts Study Act

Nov. 19, 1988, P.L. 100-702, 102 Stat. 4644

Federal Courts Study Committee Implementation Act of 1990

Dec. 1, 1990, P.L. 101-650, 5 U.S. Code § 8331 et seq. generally, 8402; 9 U.S. Code § 15; 11 U.S. Code § 305; 18 U.S. Code §§ 3006A nt., 3551 nt.; 28 U.S. Code §§ 1 nt., 108 et seq. generally, 332, 333, 375-377, 601 et seq. generally, 995, 996, 1330, 1334 et seq. generally, 1441 et seq. generally, 1605 et seq. generally, 1821, 1871, 2072

Federal Credit Reform Act of 1990

Nov. 5, 1990, P.L. 101-508, 2 U.S. Code §§ 621 nt., 661-661f

Aug. 5, 1997, P.L. 105-33, 2 U.S. Code §§ 661a, 661c to 661e

Federal Credit Union Acts

June 26, 1934, Ch. 750, 48 Stat. 1216, 12 U.S. Code §§ 1751 to 1770

July 9, 1937, Ch. 471, 50 Stat. 487, 12 U.S. Code § 1771

June 15, 1940, Ch. 366, 54 Stat. 398, 12 U.S. Code § 1761

July 31, 1946, Ch. 711, 60 Stat. 744, 12 U.S. Code §§ 1757, 1759, 1761, 1766, 1772

Oct. 25, 1949, Ch. 713, 63 Stat. 890, 12 U.S. Code §§ 1757, 1761, 1762

April 17, 1952, Ch. 214, 66 Stat. 62, 12 U.S. Code § 1755

May 8, 1952, Ch. 245, 66 Stat. 66, 12 U.S. Code § 1772

May 13, 1952, Ch. 264, 66 Stat. 70, 12 U.S. Code § 1757

Aug. 24, 1954, Ch. 905, 68 Stat. 792, 12 U.S. Code §§ 1761, 1766

Sept. 22, 1959, P.L. 86-354, 73 Stat. 628, 12 U.S. Code §§ 1751, 1752 to 1756, 1757 to 1772

Oct. 17, 1963, P.L. 88-150, 77 Stat. 270, 12 U.S. Code §§ 1760, 1761a

July 2, 1964, P.L. 88-353, 78 Stat. 269, 12 U.S. Code §§ 1757, 1761, 1761b, 1761c

May 24, 1966, P.L. 89-429, 80 Stat. 167, 12 U.S. Code § 1757

July 3, 1967, P.L. 90-44, 81 Stat. 110, 12 U.S. Code § 1757

Dec. 13, 1967, P.L. 90-188, 81 Stat. 567, 12 U.S. Code §§ 1761c, 1763

July 5, 1968, P.L. 90-375, 82 Stat. 284, 285, 12 U.S. Code §§ 1757, 1761b to 1761d 1766, 1772a

Aug. 1, 1968, P.L. 90-448, 82 Stat. 545, 12 U.S. Code § 1757

Mar 10, 1970, P.L. 91-206, 84 Stat. 49-51, 12 U.S. Code §§ 1752, 1752a 1753 to 1759, 1761, 1761a to 1761d, 1762, 1766, 1767, 1771, 1772a

Oct. 19, 1970, P.L. 91-468, 84 Stat. 994 to 1017, 12 U.S. Code §§ 1752 to 1772a 1781 to 1790

Dec. 23, 1971, P.L. 92-221, 85 Stat. 796, 12 U.S. Code §§ 1781, 1788

April 19, 1977, P.L. 95-22, 12 U.S. Code § 1752 et seq.

Sept. 20, 1977, P.L. 95-109, 15 U.S. Code § 1692l

Oct. 28, 1977, P.L. 95-147, 12 U.S. Code §§ 1789a, 1790

Nov. 10, 1978, P.L. 95-630, 12 U.S. Code §§ 1752a, 1755 to 1757, 1781, 1782, 1786, 1787, 1795 et seq.

Dec. 21, 1979, P.L. 96-153, 12 U.S. Code §§ 1757, 1787

Dec. 28, 1979, P.L. 96-161, 12 U.S. Code §§ 1752, 1757

March 31, 1980, P.L. 96-221, 12 U.S. Code § 1751 et seq.

Oct. 15, 1982, P.L. 97-320, 12 U.S. Code §§ 1752 to 1753, 1755, 1757, 1760 to 1761b 1763, 1764, 1766, 1771, 1782, 1795f, 1795j

Jan. 12, 1983, P.L. 97-457, 12 U.S. Code §§ 1757, 1761b, 1770, 1782

July 18, 1984, P.L. 98-369, 98 Stat. 1203, 12 U.S. Code § 1781 et seq.

Oct. 3, 1984, P.L. 98-440, 98 Stat. 1691, 12 U.S. Code § 1757

Oct. 17, 1984, P.L. 98-479, 12 U.S. Code § 1757

Oct. 27, 1986, P.L. 99-570, 12 U.S. Code § 1786

Aug. 10, 1987, P.L. 100-86, 12 U.S. Code §§ 1757, 1761a, 1761b, 1764, 1766, 1767, 1772b, 1772c, 1786, 1787, 1788

Aug. 9, 1989, P.L. 101-73, 12 U.S. Code §§ 1766, 1872, 1784, 1786, 1787, 1790b, 1790c

Aug. 9, 1989, P.L. 101-73, 12 U.S. Code § 1790a

Nov. 9, 1989, P.L. 101-144, 12 U.S. Code § 1766

Nov. 28, 1989, P.L. 101-179, 12 U.S. Code § 1757

Nov. 29, 1990, P.L. 101-647, 12 U.S. Code §§ 1786, 1787

Dec. 19, 1991, P.L. 102-242, 12 U.S. Code §§ 1782, 1790b

Oct. 28, 1992, P.L. 102-550, 12 U.S. Code §§ 1772d, 1782, 1786, 1790b

Nov. 30, 1993, P.L. 103-160, 12 U.S. Code § 1770

Sept. 13, 1994, P.L. 103-322, 12 U.S. Code § 1785

Sept. 23, 1994, P.L. 103-325, 12 U.S. Code §§ 1757, 1766, 1772c- 1, 1784

Oct. 22, 1994, P.L. 103-394, 12 U.S. Code § 1787

Sept. 30, 1996, P.L. 104-208, 12 U.S. Code §§ 1757, 1781

March 20, 1998, P.L. 105-164, 12 U.S. Code § 1786a

Aug. 7, 1998, P.L. 105-219, 12 U.S. Code §§ 1752a, 1757a, 1759, 1762, 1782, 1784 to 1787, 1790d

Federal Crime Reporting Act of 1988
See Uniform Federal Crime Reporting Act of 1988

Federal Crop Insurance Act
Feb. 16, 1938, Ch. 30, 52 Stat. 72, 7 U.S. Code §§ 1501 to 1518

Dec. 23, 1944, Ch. 713, 58 Stat. 918, 7 U.S. Code §§ 1302 nt., 1508, 1516 nt., 1518

Aug. 1, 1947, Ch. 440, 61 Stat. 718, 7 U.S. Code §§ 1502, 1505 to 1508

Aug. 25, 1949, Ch. 512, 63 Stat. 663, 7 U.S. Code §§ 1504 to 1508, 1518

Aug. 13, 1953, Ch. 431, 67 Stat. 575, 7 U.S. Code § 1508
Continued

Aug. 3, 1956, Ch. 950, 70 Stat. 1034, 7 U.S.
Code § 1516

July 23, 1957, P.L. 85-111, 71 Stat. 309, 7
U.S. Code § 1508

Aug. 4, 1959, P.L. 86-131, 73 Stat. 278, 7
U.S. Code § 1508

Sept. 12, 1964, P.L. 88-589, 78 Stat. 933, 7
U.S. Code § 1508

June 6, 1972, P.L. 92-310, 86 Stat. 205, 7
U.S. Code § 1507

July 23, 1972, P.L. 92-357, 86 Stat. 501, 7
U.S. Code § 1520

June 16, 1977, P.L. 95-47, 7 U.S. Code
§ 1504

Nov. 15, 1977, P.L. 95-181, 7 U.S. Code
§§ 1504, 1508 nt.

Dec. 23, 1985, P.L. 99-198, 7 U.S. Code
§ 1516

Aug. 11, 1988, P.L. 100-387, 102 Stat. 941, 7
U.S. Code §§ 1421 nt., 1508

Aug. 14, 1989, P.L. 101-82, 7 U.S. Code
§ 1508a

Nov. 28, 1990, P.L. 101-624, 7 U.S. Code
§§ 1506, 1508

Dec. 13, 1991, P.L. 102-237, 7 U.S. Code
§§ 1506 to 1508, 1518

Aug. 10, 1993, P.L. 103-66, 7 U.S. Code
§§ 1506, 1508, 1508a

April 4, 1996, P.L. 104-127, 7 U.S. Code
§§ 1508, 1516, 1519

June 23, 1998, P.L. 105-185, 7 U.S. Code
§§ 1506, 1508, 1516

Oct. 21, 1998, P.L. 105-277, 7 U.S. Code
§ 1508

Federal Crop Insurance Act of 1980

Sept. 26, 1980, P.L. 96-365, 94 Stat. 1312, 7
U.S. Code §§ 1441, 1444, 1444c, 1445b,
1501 nt., 1504, 1504 nt., 1505 to 1508,
1508 nt., 1515, 1516,1516 nt., 1518

Federal Crop Insurance Commission Act of 1988

Oct. 28, 1988, P.L. 100-546, 102 Stat. 2730

Federal Crop Insurance Reform Act of 1994

Oct. 13, 1994, P.L. 103-354, 7 U.S. Code
§§ 1501 nt., 1502 et seq.

Federal Crop Insurance Reform and Department of Agriculture Reorganization Act of 1994

Oct. 13, 1994, P.L. 103-354, 7 U.S. Code
§ 6901 nt.

Oct. 21, 1998, P.L. 105-277, 7 U.S. Code
§§ 5314, 6918, 6919, 7005, 7014

Federal Data Facility Act

Mich. Comp. Laws Ann., 3.951

Federal Death Penalty Act of 1994

Sept. 13, 1994, P.L. 103-322, 18 U.S. Code
§ 3591 nt.

Federal Debt Collection Procedures Act of 1990

Nov. 29, 1990, P.L. 101-647, 11 U.S. Code
§ 523; 18 U.S. Code §§ 3142, 3552; 28 U.S.
Code §§ 1 nt., 550, 1962, 1963, 2044, 2410,
3001 nt., 3001 to 3015, 3101 to 3105, 3201
to 3206, 3301 to 3308

Federal Debt Recovery Act

April 26, 1996, P.L. 104-134, 31 U.S. Code
§ 1718 nt.

Federal Deposit Insurance Act

Sept. 21, 1950, Ch. 967, 64 Stat. 873, 12 U.S.
Code §§ 264, 1728, 1811 to 1831

July 14, 1952, Ch. 725, 66 Stat. 605, 12 U.S.
Code § 1813

Aug. 1, 1956, Ch. 852, 70 Stat. 908, 12 U.S.
Code § 1813

Sept. 8, 1959, P.L. 86-230, 73 Stat. 460, 12
U.S. Code § 1812

May 13, 1960, P.L. 86-463, 74 Stat. 129, 12
U.S. Code § 1828

July 14, 1960, P.L. 86-671, 74 Stat. 546, 12
U.S. Code §§ 1813, 1817, 1820

Oct. 15, 1962, P.L. 87-827, 76 Stat. 953, 12
U.S. Code § 1828

Sept. 12, 1964, Pub S 88-593, 78 Stat. 940,
12 U.S. Code § 1817

July 21, 1965, P.L. 89-79, 79 Stat. 244, 12
U.S. Code § 1828

Feb. 21, 1966, P.L. 89-356, 80 Stat. 7, 12
U.S. Code § 1828

Aug. 16, 1973, P.L. 93-100, 87 Stat. 342, 12
U.S. Code § 1828

Sept. 20, 1977, P.L. 95-109, 15 U.S. Code § 1692l

Sept. 17, 1978, P.L. 95-369, 12 U.S. Code § 1811 et seq.

Nov. 10, 1978, P.L. 95-630, 12 U.S. Code §§ 1813, 1817 et seq., 1828, 1831c

Nov. 5, 1979, P.L. 96-104, 12 U.S. Code §§ 1828, 1831a

Dec. 21, 1979, P.L. 96-153, 12 U.S. Code § 1821

Dec. 28, 1979, P.L. 96-161, 12 U.S. Code §§ 1828, 1831a

March 31, 1980, P.L. 96-221, 12 U.S. Code §§ 1828, 1831d

Oct. 15, 1982, P.L. 97-320, 12 U.S. Code §§ 1813 to 1815, 1817, nt., 1817, 1818, 1820 to 1823, 1828, 1831c

Nov. 30, 1982, P.L. 98-181, 12 U.S. Code § 1812

Jan. 12, 1983, P.L. 97-457, 12 U.S. Code §§ 1823, 1831

Oct. 27, 1986, P.L. 99-570, 12 U.S. Code §§ 1817, 1818

Aug. 10, 1987, P.L. 100-86, 12 U.S. Code §§ 1813, 1817, 1821, 1823, 1828, 1831

Nov. 18, 1988, P.L. 100-690, 12 U.S. Code § 1829b

Aug. 9, 1989, P.L. 101-73, generally 12 U.S. Code § 1811 et seq.

Oct. 16, 1990, P.L. 101-432, 12 U.S. Code § 1831l

Nov. 5, 1990, P.L. 101-508, 12 U.S. Code §§ 1817, 1824

Nov. 29, 1990, P.L. 101-647, 12 U.S. Code §§ 1818, 1821, 1828, 1829, 1831k

March 23, 1991, P.L. 102-18, 12 U.S. Code § 1812

Dec. 12, 1991, P.L. 102-233, 12 U.S. Code § 1821

Dec. 19, 1991, P.L. 102-242, 12 U.S. Code §§ 191, 1464, 1813 to 1815, 1817 to 1820, 1820 nt., 1821, 1821a, 1823 to 1825, 1827, 1828, 1831a, 1831e, 1831f, 1831f-1, 1831j, 1831m to 1831o, 1831s, 1831t, 3105, 3305 nt.

Oct. 6, 1992, P.L. 102-389, 12 U.S. Code § 1831q

Oct. 28, 1992, P.L. 102-550, 12 U.S. Code §§ 1813, 1815 to 1818, 1820 to 1824, 1829, 1829b, 1831a, 1831f, 1831m, 1831o, 1831p to 1831r-1, 1831t

Oct. 28, 1992, P.L. 102-558, 12 U.S. Code §§ 1817, 1817 nt., 1820

June 28, 1993, P.L. 103-44, 12 U.S. Code § 1822

Aug. 10, 1993, P.L. 103-66, 12 U.S. Code § 1821

Dec. 17, 1993, P.L. 103-204, 12 U.S. Code §§ 1811, 1813, 1815, 1817, 1818, 1821, 1822, 1824, 1831j, 1831q

Sept. 13, 1994, P.L. 103-322, 12 U.S. Code §§ 1829, 1831m

Sept. 23, 1994, P.L. 103-325, 12 U.S. Code §§ 1441a, 1813, 1815, 1817, 1820, 1821, 1823, 1828, 1829b, 1831b, 1831e, 1831f, 1831j, 1831k, 1831m, 1831p-1, 1831t

Sept. 29, 1994, P.L. 103-328, 12 U.S. Code §§ 1820, 1821, 1828, 1831a, 1831r-1, 1831u

Oct. 22, 1994, P.L. 103-394, 12 U.S. Code § 1821

Aug. 6, 1996, P.L. 104-179, 12 U.S. Code § 1822

Sept. 30, 1996, P.L. 104-208, 12 U.S. Code §§ 1812, 1813, 1815 to 1817, 1820, 1821, 1821a, 1823 to 1825, 1827, 1828, 1831a, 1831e, 1831h, 1831i, 1831m, 1831o, 1831r-1

Oct. 19, 1996, P.L. 104-316, 12 U.S. Code §§ 1821, 1831o

July 3, 1997, P.L. 105-24, 12 U.S. Code § 1831a

March 20, 1998, P.L. 105-164, 12 U.S. Code § 1818

Oct. 21, 1998, P.L. 105-277, 12 U.S. Code § 1828

Nov. 10, 1998, P.L. 105-362, 12 U.S. Code § 1818

Federal Deposit Insurance Corporation Act

June 16, 1933, Ch. 89, 48 Stat. 162, 12 U.S. Code §§ 462a-1, 1811 to 1831

Federal Deposit Insurance Corporation Improvement Act of 1991

Dec. 19, 1991, P.L. 102-242, 12 U.S. Code § 1811 nt. Oct. 28, 1992, P.L. 102-550, 106 Stat. 4081, 4088, 4089; 12 U.S. Code §§ 191, 251, 1467a, 1811 nt., 1813 to 1815, 1817, 1817 nt., 1818, 1820, 1821 nt., 1831m nt., 1831q nt., 1831t nt., 1834, 1834a, 1843, 2808, 3102 nt., 3105, 4304 to 4306, 4309 to 4312, 4402

Continued

Oct. 28, 1992, P.L. 102-558, 12 U.S. Code
§§ 1815, 1817, 1818, 1834, 1834a

Sept. 23, 1994, P.L. 103-325, 12 U.S. Code
§§ 1825 nt., 1828 nt.

Dec. 21, 1995, P.L. 104-66, 12 U.S. Code
§ 1825 nt.

Sept. 30, 1996, P.L. 104-208, 12 U.S. Code
§ 251

Oct. 19, 1996, P.L. 104-316, 12 U.S. Code
§§ 1823 nt., 1825 nt.

Federal Deposit Insurance Protection Act

Tex. Rev. Civ. Stat., Art. 489b

Federal District Court Organization Act of 1978

March 30, 1979, P.L. 96-4, 28 U.S. Code
§ 93 nt.

Federal District Court Organization Act of 1980

Oct. 15, 1980, P.L. 96-462, 28 U.S. Code § 1
nt.

Federal Drivers Act

Sept. 21, 1961, P.L. 87-258, 75 Stat. 539, 28
U.S. Code § 2679(b) to 2679(e)

July 18, 1966, P.L. 89-506, 80 Stat. 307, 28
U.S. Code § 2679(b)

Federal Drug Law Enforcement Agent Protection Act of 1986

Oct. 27, 1986, P.L. 99-570, 21 U.S. Code
§ 801 nt.

Federal Educational Finance Act

Neb. Rev. Stat. 1943, 79-1320 et seq.

Federal Election Absentee Voting Act (Overseas Residents)

N.J. Stat. Ann., 19:59-1 et seq.

Federal Election Campaign Act Amendments of 1979

Jan. 8, 1980, P.L. 96-187, 2 U.S. Code
§§ 431, 431 nt., 432 to 434, 437, 437c, 437d
to 437g, 437k to 439a, 441b, 441d; 5 U.S.
Code § 3132;18 U.S. Code §§ 591, 602,
603, 607; 22 U.S. Code § 901a; 26 U.S.
Code § 9008; 42 U.S. Code § 5043

Federal Election Campaign Act of 1971

Feb. 7, 1972, P.L. 92-225, 86 Stat. 3, 2 U.S.
Code §§ 431 to 441, 451 to 454; 18 U.S.
Code §§ 591, 600, 608, 610, 611; 47 U.S.
Code §§ 312, 315, 802 to 805

Oct. 15, 1974, P.L. 93-443, 88 Stat. 1277, 2
U.S. Code §§ 431 et seq., 441, 455, 456,
490a, 490b, 490c

May 11, 1976, P.L. 94-283, 90 Stat. 475, 2
U.S. Code §§ 431, 432, 434, 436, 437b to
437h, 438, 439c, 441 to 441-j, 455

Oct. 12, 1977, P.L. 95-127, 2 U.S. Code
§ 439c

Dec. 20, 1977, P.L. 95-216, 2 U.S. Code
§§ 441, 441 nt.

Jan. 8, 1980, P.L. 96-187, 93 Stat. 1339, 2
U.S. Code §§ 431 to 434, 437, 437c, 437d,
437f, 437g, 437h, 438, 439, 439a, 439c,
441a to 441i

May 29, 1980, P.L. 96-253, 2 U.S. Code
§ 439c

Oct. 1, 1981, P.L. 97-51, 95 Stat. 966, 2 U.S.
Code § 441i

June 27, 1988, P.L. 100-352, 102 Stat. 663, 2
U.S. Code § 437h

Nov. 30, 1989, P.L. 101-194, 2 U.S. Code
§§ 439a, 441i

May 4, 1990, P.L. 101-280, 2 U.S. Code
§ 441i

Aug. 14, 1991, P.L. 102-90, 2 U.S. Code
§ 441i

July 5, 1994, P.L. 103-272, 2 U.S. Code
§ 451

Dec. 28, 1995, P.L. 104-79, 2 U.S. Code
§§ 432, 434, 438, 439

Dec. 29, 1995, P.L. 104-88, 2 U.S. Code
§ 451

Oct. 11, 1996, P.L. 104-287, 2 U.S. Code
§ 251

Oct. 10, 1997, P.L. 105-61, 2 U.S. Code
§§ 432, 437c

Federal Emergency Relief Act of 1933

May 12, 1933, Ch. 30, 48 Stat. 55

Federal Employee Representation Improvement Act of 1996

Aug. 6, 1996, P.L. 104-177, 18 U.S. Code
§ 201 nt.

Federal Employee Substance Abuse Education and Treatment Act of 1986

Oct. 27, 1986, P.L. 99-570, 5 U.S. Code § 7301 nt.

Federal Employee Travel Reform Act of 1996

Sept. 23, 1996, P.L. 104-201, Title XVII, 5 U.S. Code § 5701 nt.

Federal Employees Benefits Improvement Act of 1986

Feb. 27, 1986, P.L. 99-251, 5 U.S. Code § 8901 nt.

July 2, 1986, P.L. 99-349, 100 Stat. 748

Federal Employees Clean Air Incentives Act

Dec. 2, 1993, P.L. 103-172, 5 U.S. Code §§ 7901 nt., 7905, 7905 nt.

Federal Employees' Compensation Act

See Workmen's Compensation Acts

Sept. 7, 1916, Ch. 458, 39 Stat. 742 (See 1 U.S. Code § 1, 5 U.S. Code §§ 7902, 8101 to 8103, 8105 to 8107, 8110, 8114 to 8124, 8126, 8128 to 8135, 8138, 8145 to 8149; See 18 U.S. Code § 1920)

Oct. 14, 1949, Ch. 691, 63 Stat. 855 (See 5 U.S. Code §§ 7902, 8101, 8103 to 8118, 8120, 8123, 8125 to 8127, 8129, 8133, 8134, 8145, 8150; See 18 U.S. Code §§ 1, 292, 1921)

Sept. 26, 1950, Ch. 1049, 64 Stat. 1038 (See 5 U.S. Code § 5342)

Aug. 1, 1956, Ch. 837, 70 Stat. 883 (See 5 U.S. Code § 8101)

June 29, 1957, P.L. 85-71, 71 Stat. 242 (See 5 U.S. Code § 8102)

Aug. 8, 1958, P.L. 85-608, 72 Stat. 538 (See 5 U.S. Code §§ 8101, 8102)

Sept. 13, 1960, P.L. 86-767, 74 Stat. 906 (See 5 U.S. Code §§ 8101, 8103, 8107, 8111, 8112, 8115, 8116, 8122, 8131, 8133, 8134, 8138, 8147; See18 U.S. Code §§ 1, 1922)

Aug. 30, 1964, P.L. 88-508, 78 Stat. 666 (See 5 U.S. Code § 8146)

July 4, 1966, P.L. 89-488, 80 Stat. 252 to 256 (See 5 U.S. Code §§ 3315a, 8101, 8103, 8107 to 8112, 8116, 8122, 8124, 8131 to 8133, 8135, 8146a, 8147, 8149)

Federal Employees Family Friendly Leave Act

Oct. 22, 1994, P.L. 103-388, 5 U.S. Code §§ 6301 nt., 6307

Federal Employees Flexible and Compressed Work Schedules Act of 1978

Oct. 12, 1978, P.L. 95-454, 5 U.S. Code § 6101 et seq.

March 26, 1982, P.L. 97-160, 5 U.S. Code § 6101 nt.

Federal Employees Flexible and Compressed Work Schedules Act of 1982

July 23, 1982, P.L. 97-221, 5 U.S. Code § 6120 et seq.

July 22, 1985, P.L. 99-69, 5 U.S. Code § 6101 nt.

Sept. 30, 1985, P.L. 99-109, 5 U.S. Code § 6101 nt.

Oct. 31, 1985, P.L. 99-140, 5 U.S. Code § 6101 nt.

Dec. 19, 1985, P.L. 99-190, 5 U.S. Code § 6101 nt.

Dec. 23, 1985, P.L. 99-196, 5 U.S. Code § 6101 nt.

Federal Employees' Group Life Insurance Act of 1954

Aug. 17, 1954, Ch. 752, 68 Stat. 736 (See 5 U.S. Code §§ 1308, 8701 to 8716)

Aug. 11, 1955, Ch. 794, 69 Stat. 676 (See 5 U.S. Code §§ 8706, 8710, 8714)

May 28, 1956, Ch. 328, 70 Stat. 213 (See 5 U.S. Code § 8706)

Aug. 1, 1956, Ch. 901, 70 Stat. 955 (See 5 U.S. Code § 8701)

Aug. 2, 1956, Ch. 901, 70 Stat. 955 (See 5 U.S. Code § 8701)

April 11, 1958, P.L. 85-377, 72 Stat. 87 (See 5 U.S. Code § 8714)

Sept. 23, 1959, P.L. 86-377, 73 Stat. 701 (See 5 U.S. Code §§ 8706, 8707)

July 1, 1960, P.L. 86-568, 74 Stat. 302 (See 5 U.S. Code § 8706)

Aug. 28, 1962, P.L. 87-611, 76 Stat. 406 (See 5 U.S. Code § 8705)

Aug. 31, 1964, P.L. 88-531, 78 Stat. 737 (See 5 U.S. Code § 8704)

Continued

Oct. 6, 1964, P.L. 88-631, 78 Stat. 1007 (See 5 U.S. Code § 8704)

March 23, 1966, P.L. 89-373, 80 Stat. 78 (See 5 U.S. Code § 8705)

July 18, 1966, P.L. 89-504, 80 Stat. 298 (See 5 U.S. Code § 8706)

Federal Employee's Group Life Insurance Act of 1980

Oct. 10, 1980, P.L. 96-427, 5 U.S. Code § 8701, 8701 nt., 8704, 8704 nt., 8706, 8707, 8709, 8713, 8714a, 8714a nt., 8714b, 8714c

Federal Employees Health Benefits Act of 1959

Sept. 28, 1959, P.L. 86-382, 73 Stat. 708 (See 5 U.S. Code §§ 1104, 1308, 5109, 5316, 8901 to 8913)

July 1, 1960, P.L. 86-568, 74 Stat. 303 (See 5 U.S. Code §§ 8901, 8913)

July 8, 1963, P.L. 88-59, 77 Stat. 76 (See 5 U.S. Code §§ 8901, 8903)

March 17, 1964, P.L. 88-284, 78 Stat. 164 (See 5 U.S. Code §§ 8901, 8902, 8906, 8908, 8909, 8913)

Aug. 14, 1964, P.L. 88-426, 78 Stat. 426 (See 5 U.S. Code § 5316(99))

Aug. 31, 1964, P.L. 88-531, 78 Stat. 747 (See 5 U.S. Code § 8901)

Oct. 6, 1964, P.L. 88-631, 78 Stat. 1007 (See 5 U.S. Code § 8913)

July 18, 1966, P.L. 89-504, 80 Stat. 298, (See 5 U.S. Code §§ 8901, 8906)

Federal Employees Health Benefits Amendments Act of 1988

Nov. 14, 1988, P.L. 100-654, 5 U.S. Code § 8901 nt.

Federal Employees Health Care Protection Act of 1998

Oct. 19, 1998, P.L. 105-266, 112 Stat. 2363, 5 U.S. Code § 8901 nt.

Federal Employees' International Organization Service Act

Aug. 28, 1958, P.L. 85-795, 72 Stat. 959

Federal Employees Leave Sharing Act of 1988

Oct. 31, 1988, P.L. 100-566, 5 U.S. Code § 6301 nt.

Oct. 8, 1993, P.L. 103-103, 5 U.S. Code § 6331 et seq. nts.

Federal Employees Leave Sharing Amendments Act of 1993

Oct. 8, 1993, P.L. 103-103, 5 U.S. Code §§ 6301 nt., 6331 et seq., 6361 et seq.

Federal Employees Liability Reform and Tort Compensation Act of 1988

Nov. 18, 1988, P.L. 100-694, 28 U.S. Code § 1 nt.

Federal Employees Life Insurance Improvement Act

Oct. 30, 1998, P.L. 105-311, 112 Stat. 2950, 5 U.S. Code § 8701 nt.

Federal Employees Pay Act of 1945

June 30, 1945, Ch. 212, 59 Stat. 295, 2 U.S. Code §§ 60e-2, 60e-2b, 60e-3, 60e-4; See 5 U.S. Code §§ 5342, 5504, 5505, 5541 to 5549, 6101; See 28 U.S. Code § 604 and nt.

May 24, 1946, Ch. 270, 14, 60 Stat. 217, 2 U.S. Code §§ 60e-3, 60e-4; See 5 U.S. Code §§ 5342, 5541, 5543, 5545 to 5547)

Aug. 4, 1947, Ch. 452, 61 Stat. 727 (See 5 U.S. Code § 5541)

July 3, 1948, Ch. 830, 62 Stat. 1268 (See 5 U.S. Code § 5547)

June 23, 1949, Ch. 238, 63 Stat. 265, 2 U.S. Code § 60e-3

Oct. 28, 1949, Ch. 782, 63 Stat. 973 (See 5 U.S. Code § 5504)

Sept. 26, 1950, Ch. 1049, 64 Stat. 1038 (See 5 U.S. Code §§ 305, 5102, 5342)

June 17, 1957, P.L. 85-56

June 20, 1958, P.L. 85-462, 72 Stat. 214 (See 5 U.S. Code § 5504)

July 18, 1958, P.L. 85-525, 72 Stat. 363 (See 5 U.S. Code § 5545)

July 18, 1958, P.L. 85-533, 72 Stat. 377 (See 5 U.S. Code § 5546)

Sept. 2, 1958, P.L. 85-857, 72 Stat. 1265

July 31, 1959, P.L. 86-122, 73 Stat. 268 (See 5 U.S. Code § 5504)

Aug. 18, 1959, P.L. 86-168, 73 Stat. 389 (See Title 5 U.S. Code § 5541)

Aug. 29, 1959, P.L. 86-211, 73 Stat. 436

Aug. 14, 1964, P.L. 88-426, 78 Stat. 402 (See 5 U.S. Code § 5504)

Oct. 29, 1965, P.L. 89-301, 79 Stat. 1123 (See 5 U.S. Code § 6101)

June 29, 1966, P.L. 89-478, 80 Stat. 231 (See 5 U.S. Code § 6101)

July 18, 1966 P.L. 89-504, §§ 404, 405(b) to (e), 80 Stat. 297 (See 5 U.S. Code §§ 5542, 5543, 5545, 5546; 39 U.S. Code § 3573)

Federal Employees Pay Act of 1946

July 3, 1948, Ch. 830, 62 Stat. 1268 (See 5 U.S. Code § 5547)

Sept. 1, 1954, Ch. 1208, 68 Stat. 1109 (See 5 U.S. Code §§ 5541 to 5547, 6101)

Feb. 15, 1980, P.L. 96-191, 31 U.S. Code § 46A

Federal Employees Pay Comparability Act of 1990

Nov. 5, 1990, P.L. 101-509, 2 U.S. Code § 60a-2; 3 U.S. Code § 104; 5 U.S. Code §§ 3132, 3304a, 3324, 3326, 3405, 3594, 4502, 4505a, 5102, 5104, 5108, 5109, 5301 et seq. generally, 5403, 5405, 5524a, 5532, 5542 to 5545, 5547, 5595, 5706b, 5723, 5753 to 5755, 5901 to 5903, 8344, 8431, 8468, 8476; 10 U.S. Code § 9314; 18 U.S. Code §§ 207, 207 nt.; 20 U.S. Code § 3404 nt.; 28 U.S. Code §§ 461, 586, 586 nt., 31 U.S. Code §§ 325, 732; 42 U.S. Code § 3501 nt.

Oct. 2, 1992, P.L. 102-378, 5 U.S. Code §§ 5304 nt., 5305 nt., 5378 nt., 5545

Sept. 30, 1993, P.L. 103-89, 5 U.S. Code § 5304 nt.

Oct. 28, 1993, P.L. 103-123, 5 U.S. Code § 5305 nt.

Dec. 3, 1993, P.L. 103-178. 5 U.S. Code § 5305

Federal Employees' Retirement Contribution Temporary Adjustment Act of 1983

Nov. 29, 1983, P.L. 98-168, 5 U.S. Code § 8331 nt.

Dec. 19, 1985, P.L. 99-190, 5 U.S. Code § 8331 nt.

June 6, 1986, P.L. 99-335, 5 U.S. Code § 8331 nt.

Federal Employees' Retirement System Act of 1986

June 6, 1986, P.L. 99-335, 5 U.S. Code §§ 5102, 5314, 6301, 6303, 8116, 8331, 8331 nt., 8332, 8334, 8343a, 8347 to 8351, 8401 et seq., 8701, 8714a- 8714c, 8901, 8905; 10 U.S. Code § 1065; 22 U.S. Code §§ 3901 nt., 4041 et seq., 4071 et seq.; 26 U.S. Code §§ 3121, 6103; 39 U.S. Code § 1005; 42 U.S. Code § 410, 50 U.S. Code § 403

Oct. 21, 1986, P.L. 99-509, 5 U.S. Code § 8351 nt.

Oct. 27, 1986, P.L. 99-556, 5 U.S. Code §§ 6301, 8331 nt.

April 7, 1987, P.L. 100-20, 5 U.S. Code § 8331 nt.

Jan. 8, 1988, P.L. 100-238, 5 U.S. Code § 8331 nt.

Federal Employees' Retirement System Open Enrollment Act of 1997

Oct. 10, 1997, P.L. 105-61, § 642, 5 U.S. Code § 8331

Federal Employees' Retirement System Technical Corrections Act of 1986

Oct. 27, 1986, P.L. 99-556, 5 U.S. Code § 8401 nt.

Federal Employees Salary Act of 1964

Aug. 14, 1964, P.L. 88-426, 78 Stat. 400, 3 U.S. Code § 102 nt.; See 5 U.S. Code §§ 5108, 5303, 5332, 5333, 5504; 16 U.S. Code § 590h nt.; 22 U.S. Code §§ 867, 870; 38 U.S. Code §§ 4103, 4107; 39 U.S. Code §§ 1, 702, 704, 2009, 2102, 3501, 3513, 3516 to 3530, 3542 to 3544, 3552, 3560, 6007

Oct. 29, 1965, P.L. 89-301, 79 Stat. 1111, 2 U.S. Code §§ 31, 60a nt., 60e-12, 60f nt., 293a; See 5 U.S. Code 5332, 5335, 5595, 5901, 6101, 8331; 16 U.S. Code § 590h nt.; 22 U.S. Code §§ 867, 870; 28 U.S. Code §§ 508 nt., 603 nt., 604 nt., 753 nt.; 38 U.S. Code § 4107

July 18, 1966, P.L. 89-504, 80 Stat. 288 (See 5 U.S. Code §§ 5332, 5545; 16 U.S. Code § 590h nt.; 22 U.S. Code §§ 867, 870; 28 U.S. Code § 548 nt.; 38 U.S. Code § 4107

Continued

April 15, 1970, P.L. 91-231, 84 Stat. 195, 3 U.S. Code § 102 nt., 5 U.S. Code §§ 5332 nt., 5545

Federal Employees Salary Increase Act of 1955

June 28, 1955, Ch. 189, 69 Stat. 172, 2 U.S. Code §§ 60a nt., 60e-5, 60e-6, 60e-7, 60f, 60f nts.; See 5 U.S. Code §§ 5108, 5316(25) to 5316(28), 5332, 5335, 5336, 8331; 7 U.S. Code §§ 1762, 2213; 12 U.S. Code § 1138f; 22 U.S. Code §§ 867 nt., 1461 nt.; 28 U.S. Code §§ 603 nt., 604 nt., 753; 50 U.S. Code Appx. §§ 2160, 2253

June 27, 1956, Ch. 453, 70 Stat. 363, 2 U.S. Code § 60e-7

Aug. 21, 1959, P.L. 86-176, 73 Stat. 401, 2 U.S. Code § 60f nt.

Aug. 20, 1964, P.L. 88-454, 78 Stat. 538, 2 U.S. Code § 60f nt.

Aug. 27, 1966, P.L. 89-545, 80 Stat. 357, 2 U.S. Code § 60f nt.

July 28, 1967, P.L. 90-57, 81 Stat. 144, 2 U.S. Code § 60f nt.

Federal Employees Salary Increase Act of 1958

June 20, 1958, P.L. 85-462, 72 Stat. 203, 2 U.S. Code §§ 60a nt., 60e-8, 60f nt., 61b nt., 72a, 74a nt., 273 nt.; See 5 U.S. Code §§ 3104, 3324, 3325, 5104, 5108, 5332, 5361, 5504, 8331; 28 U.S. Code §§ 603 nt., 604 nt., 753; 40 U.S. Code § 166b-2; 42 U.S. Code § 210

May 29, 1959, P.L. 86-36, 73 Stat. 63, 10 U.S. Code § 1581

Sept. 23, 1959, P.L. 86-370, 73 Stat. 651 (See 5 U.S. Code §§ 3104, 3325, 5361)

Federal Employees Salary Increase Act of 1960

July 1, 1960, P.L. 86-568, 74 Stat. 298, 2 U.S. Code §§ 60a nt., 60e-9, 60f nt.; See 5 U.S. Code §§ 5332, 8331, 8332, 8347, 8701, 8716, 8901, 8913; 16 U.S. Code §§ 590h nt.; 22 U.S. Code §§ 867, 870; 28 U.S. Code §§ 603 nt., 604 nt., 753; 38 U.S. Code §§ 4103, 4107, 4108

Federal Employees Uniform Allowance Act

Sept. 1, 1954, Ch. 1208, 68 Stat. 1114 (See 5 U.S. Code §§ 5901, 8331)

May 13, 1955, Ch. 40, 69 Stat. 49 (See 5 U.S. Code § 5901)

Oct. 29, 1965, P.L. 89-301, 79 Stat. 1122 (See 5 U.S. Code § 5901)

July 18, 1966, P.L. 89-504, 80 Stat. 299 (See 5 U.S. Code §§ 5901, 5902)

Federal Employees Vacation Act

March 14, 1936, Ch. 140, 49 Stat. 1161 (See 5 U.S. Code Ch. 63)

Federal Employers' Liability Act (Railroads)

See Employers' Liability Act (Railroads)

Federal Employment Pay Act of 1946

May 24, 1946, Ch. 270, 60 Stat. 210, 2 U.S. Code §§ 60e-2, 60e-3, 60e-4; See 5 U.S. Code §§ 5342, 5351, 5541, 5543, 5545 to 5547, 8331; See 28 U.S. Code § 604, 604 nt.; 31 U.S. Code § 46a

Federal Employment Service Act

June 6, 1933, Ch. 49, 48 Stat. 113, 29 U.S. Code §§ 49 to 49l

Federal Energy Administration Act of 1974

May 7, 1974, P.L. 93-275, 88 Stat. 96, 15 U.S. Code §§ 761 to 786

June 30, 1976, P.L. 94-332, 15 U.S. Code § 761 et seq.

July 21, 1977, P.L. 95-70, 15 U.S. Code § 761 et seq.

Dec. 21, 1995, P.L. 104-66, 15 U.S. Code § 790d

Feb. 10, 1996, P.L. 104-106, 15 U.S. Code § 789

July 18, 1997, P.L. 105-28, 15 U.S. Code § 776

Federal Energy Administration Authorization Act of 1977

July 21, 1977, P.L. 95-70, 15 U.S. Code § 761 et seq.; 42 U.S. Code § 6246 et seq.

Federal Energy Management Improvement Act of 1988

Nov. 5, 1988, P.L. 100-615, 42 U.S. Code § 8201 nt.

Oct. 24, 1992, P.L. 102-486, 42 U.S. Code § 8253 nt.

Federal Energy Regulatory Commission Member Term Act of 1990

April 11, 1990, P.L. 101-271, 42 U.S. Code § 7101 nt.

Federal Environmental Pesticide Control Act of 1972

Oct. 21, 1972, P.L. 92-516, 86 Stat. 973, 7 U.S. Code §§ 136 to 136y; 15 U.S. Code §§ 1261, 1371; 21 U.S. Code §§ 321 to 346a

Dec. 28, 1973, P.L. 93-205, 87 Stat. 903, 7 U.S. Code § 136

Federal Escape Act

May 14, 1930, Ch. 274, 46 Stat. 327, 18 U.S. Code §§ 751, 752, 1072, 1791

Aug. 3, 1935, Ch. 432, 49 Stat. 513, 18 U.S. Code § 751

Federal Estate Tax Apportionment Law

Nev. Rev. Stat. 1979 Reprint, 150.290 et seq.

Federal Excise Tax Refund Act

Ill. Comp. Stat. 1992, Ch. 35, § 730/1

Ill. Rev. Stat. 1991, Ch. 127, §§ 39d-1, 39d-1.1

Federal Executive Pay Act of 1956

July 31, 1956, Ch. 804, 70 Stat. 736, 3 U.S. Code § 105; See 5 U.S. Code §§ 1102, 1103, 1308, 3323, 5108, 5114, 8331 to 8348; 21 U.S. Code § 113a; 22 U.S. Code §§ 387n, 1787; 42 U.S. Code §§ 210, 3504; 50 U.S. Code § 158

July 18, 1958, P.L. 85-524, 72 Stat. 363

Sept. 23, 1959, P.L. 86-370, 73 Stat. 651

July 1, 1960, P.L. 86-568, 74 Stat. 304

July 7, 1960, P.L. 86-599, 74 Stat. 336

Aug. 11, 1961, P.L. 87-137, 75 Stat. 338

Sept. 26, 1961, P.L. 87-322, 75 Stat. 685

Oct. 4, 1961, P.L. 87-367, 75 Stat. 792

Oct. 4, 1961, P.L. 87-392, 75 Stat. 822

July 2, 1964, P.L. 88-352, 78 Stat. 258

Federal Executive Salary Act of 1964

Aug. 14, 1964, P.L. 88-426, 78 Stat. 415, 3 U.S. Code §§ 104, 105; See 5 U.S. Code §§ 5311 to 5317, 5363, 5364; 8 U.S. Code § 1104; 10 U.S. Code §§ 135 nt., 137, 3012, 3013, 5031, 5033, 5034 nt. 8012, 8013; 15 U.S. Code § 78d; 21 U.S. Code § 113a; 22 U.S. Code §§ 287n, 866, 2124, 2384, 2503, 2562 to 2564, 2653; 23 U.S. Code § 303; 26 U.S. Code § 7801; See 28 U.S. Code §§ 504 nt., 505 nt., 508; 35 U.S. Code § 3; 38 U.S. Code § 210; 40 U.S. Code § 661; 42 U.S. Code §§ 210 nt., 1861 nt., 2032, 2034, 2035, 2037, 2038, 2471 to 2473, 2474, 2502, 3502; 46 U.S. Code § 1111 nt.; 49 U.S. Code §§ 1321, 1341, 1342; 50 U.S. Code §§ 402 nt., 1506; 50 U.S. Code Appx. §§ 1217, 2271 nt.

Oct. 6, 1964, P.L. 88-631, 78 Stat. 1008 (See 5 U.S. Code § 5363; 28 U.S. Code § 508 nt.)

Aug. 9, 1965, P.L. 89-115, 79 Stat. 449 (See 5 U.S. Code §§ 5315, 5316)

Aug. 26, 1965, P.L. 89-136, 79 Stat. 569, 570 (See 5 U.S. Code §§ 5315, 5316)

Sept. 9, 1965, P.L. 89-174, 79 Stat. 669 (See 5 U.S. Code § 5316)

Oct. 2, 1965, P.L. 89-234, 79 Stat. 903 (See 5 U.S. Code § 5315)

July 5, 1966, P.L. 89-492, 80 Stat. 262 (See 5 U.S. Code §§ 5315, 5316)

July 18, 1966, P.L. 89-504, 80 Stat. 299 (See 5 U.S. Code §§ 5314, 5315)

Federal Explosives Act

Oct. 6, 1917, Ch. 83, 40 Stat. 385, 50 U.S. Code §§ 121 to 133, 135 to 142, 143 nt.

Nov. 24, 1942, Ch. 641, 56 Stat. 1022, 50 U.S. Code § 123

Aug. 23, 1958, P.L. 85-726, 72 Stat. 808, 50 U.S. Code § 123

Oct. 15, 1966, P.L. 89-670, 80 Stat. 943, 50 U.S. Code § 123

Oct. 15, 1970, P.L. 91-452, 84 Stat. 960, 50 U.S. Code § 121 to 144

Federal Facilities Development Act

Okla. Stat. Ann., Title 68, § 3501 et seq.

Federal Facilities Reserve Fund Act

Mass. Gen. Laws Ann., 29:2X

Federal Facility Compliance Act of 1992

Oct. 6, 1992, P.L. 102-386, 42 U.S. Code
§§ 6901 nt., 6908, 6939c nt., 6961 nt., 6965

Federal Facility Development Act

Mich. Comp. Laws Ann., 3.931 et seq.

Federal Farm Board Act

June 15, 1929, Ch. 24, 46 Stat. 11, 12 U.S.
Code §§ 1141 to 1141j

Federal Farm Loan Acts

July 17, 1916, Ch. 245, 39 Stat. 360, 12 U.S.
Code §§ 641, 642, 651 to 664, 671 to 683,
691 to 697, 701, 711 to 722, 731 to 734, 741
to 745, 751 to 756, 761 and others

April 20, 1920, Ch. 154, 41 Stat. 570, 12 U.S.
Code §§ 656, 751, 761, 771, 864, 874

Feb. 27, 1921, Ch. 78, 41 Stat. 1148, 12 U.S.
Code § 672

July 1, 1921, Ch. 39, 42 Stat. 105

Aug. 13, 1921, Ch. 63, 42 Stat. 159, 12 U.S.
Code § 861

March 4, 1923, Ch. 252, 42 Stat. 1454,
(Generally dispersed throughout 12 U.S.
Code)

June 29, 1940, Ch. 441, §§ 1, 2, 54 Stat. 684,
12 U.S. Code §§ 771, 1016

June 27, 1942, Ch. 449, 56 Stat. 391, 12 U.S.
Code § 771 par 12

June 30, 1945, Ch. 204, 59 Stat. 265, 12 U.S.
Code §§ 672, 712, 745, 751 to 753, 771,
781, 857, 861, 874, 880, 1016, 1020b,
1020d

Oct. 29, 1949, Ch. 786, 63 Stat. 985, 12 U.S.
Code §§ 672, 723, 771, 781 nt., 891

Aug. 6, 1953, Ch. 335, 67 Stat. 395, 12 U.S.
Code §§ 903, 1131c, 1134d, 1134e, 1134l

June 1, 1955, Ch. 117, 69 Stat. 81, 12 U.S.
Code § 781 par 20

Aug. 11, 1955, Ch. 785, 69 Stat. 664, 12 U.S.
Code §§ 663, 734, 757, 771, 781, 901, 902,
911

July 26, 1956, Ch. 741, 70 Stat. 660, 12 U.S.
Code §§ 781, 1022, 1031, 1033, 1041,
1044, 1045, 1051, 1061, 1072

Aug. 18, 1959, P.L. 86-168, 73 Stat. 384, 12
U.S. Code § 636a nt., 636c, 636g, 640b,
640d to 640f, 656 and others

Oct. 3, 1961, P.L. 87-343, 75 Stat. 758, 12
U.S. Code §§ 771, 1033

Oct. 4, 1961, P.L. 87-353, 75 Stat. 774, 12
U.S. Code §§ 723, 772, 781, 897

Oct. 4, 1965, P.L. 89-237, 79 Stat. 922, 12
U.S. Code §§ 1031, 1041, 1061, 1072

Aug. 2, 1966, P.L. 89-525, 80 Stat. 334, 12
U.S. Code §§ 771, 781, 1031, 1092

Sept. 20, 1966, P.L. 89-595, 80 Stat. 821, 12
U.S. Code § 1042

Dec. 15, 1967, P.L. 90-204, 81 Stat. 612, 12
U.S. Code § 771

June 18, 1968, P.L. 90-345, 82 Stat. 182, 12
U.S. Code §§ 1041, 1061, 1072

Oct. 17, 1968, P.L. 90-582, 82 Stat. 1145, 12
U.S. Code § 1061

Federal Farm Mortgage Corporation Act

Jan. 31, 1934, Ch. 7, 48 Stat. 344, 12 U.S.
Code §§ 347, 355, 723, 772, 781, 897, 1016,
1131i, 1138b

June 30, 1945, Ch. 204, 59 Stat. 269

July 12, 1946, Ch. 580, 60 Stat. 532

Oct. 4, 1961, P.L. 87-353, 75 Stat. 773, 12
U.S. Code § 723

**Federal Financial Institutions Examination
Council Act of 1978**

Nov. 10, 1978, P.L. 95-630, 12 U.S. Code
§ 3301 et seq.

Oct. 15, 1982, P.L. 97-320, 12 U.S. Code
§ 3305

Aug. 9, 1989, P.L. 101-73, 12 U.S. Code
§§ 3302, 3303, 3305, 3309, 3310

Sept. 23, 1994, P.L. 103-325, 12 U.S. Code
§ 3305

**Federal Financial Institutions Reform,
Recovery, and Enforcement Act of 1989**

Sept. 30, 1996, P.L. 104-208, 12 U.S. Code
§ 3337

Federal Financial Management Act of 1994

Oct. 13, 1994, P.L. 103-356, 31 U.S. Code
§ 3301 nt.

April 26, 1996, P.L. 104-134, 31 U.S. Code
§ 3332

Federal Financial Management Improvement Act of 1996

Sept. 30, 1996, P.L. 104-208, 31 U.S. Code § 3512 nt.

Federal Financing Bank Act of 1973

Dec. 29, 1973, P.L. 93-224, 87 Stat. 937, 12 U.S. Code § 2281 et seq.

Federal Fire Prevention and Control Act of 1974

Oct. 29, 1974, P.L. 93-498, 15 U.S. Code §§ 278f, 1511, 2201 et seq.

Nov. 16, 1979, P.L. 96-121, 15 U.S. Code §§ 278f, 2216, 2218, 2222, 2223

Nov. 20, 1981, P.L. 97-80, 15 U.S. Code § 2216

March 22, 1984, P.L. 98-241, 15 U.S. Code §§ 2214, 2216

Sept. 26, 1985, P.L. 99-97, 15 U.S. Code § 2216

July 8, 1986, P.L. 99-359, 15 U.S. Code § 2216

Sept. 25, 1990, P.L. 101-391, 15 U.S. Code §§ 2203, 2224 to 2226

Oct. 26, 1992, P.L. 102-522, 15 U.S. Code §§ 2216, 2224, 2225, 2227

May 26, 1994, P.L. 103-254, 15 U.S. Code §§ 2216, 2220, 2227, 2228

Oct. 19, 1996, P.L. 104-316, 15 U.S. Code § 2227

Nov. 20, 1997, P.L. 105-108, 15 U.S. Code §§ 2216, 2225, 2227

Federal Firearms Act

June 30, 1938, Ch. 850, 52 Stat. 1250

Feb. 7, 1950, Ch. 2, 64 Stat. 3

Oct. 3, 1961, P.L. 87-342, 75 Stat. 757

Sept. 15, 1965, P.L. 89-184, 79 Stat. 788 (See 18 U.S. Code § 921 et seq.)

Federal Firearms License Reform Act of 1993

Nov. 11, 1993, P.L. 103-159, 18 U.S. Code §§ 921 nt., 922 et seq.

Federal Flood Insurance Acts

Aug. 7, 1956, Ch. 1025, 70 Stat. 1078, 42 U.S. Code §§ 2401 to 2421

Aug. 1, 1968, P.L. 90-448, 82 Stat. 573, 42 U.S. Code § 2414

Nov. 30, 1983, P.L. 98-181, 42 U.S. Code § 2414

Oct. 17, 1984, P.L. 98-479, 42 U.S. Code § 2414

February 5, 1988, P.L. 100-242, 42 U.S. Code § 2414

Federal Food, Drug, and Cosmetic Act

June 25, 1938, Ch. 675, 52 Stat. 1040, 21 U.S. Code §§ 301 to 392

Dec. 22, 1941, Ch. 613, 55 Stat. 851, 21 U.S. Code §§ 333, 352, 356

July 12, 1943, Ch. 221, 57 Stat. 498

July 6, 1945, Ch. 281, 59 Stat. 463, 21 U.S. Code §§ 331, 352, 357

March 10, 1947, Ch. 16, 61 Stat. 11, 21 U.S. Code §§ 331, 352, 357

June 24, 1948, Ch. 613, 62 Stat. 582, 21 U.S. Code §§ 331, 334

July 13, 1949, Ch. 305, 63 Stat. 409, 21 U.S. Code §§ 352, 357

Oct. 18, 1949, Ch. 696, 63 Stat. 882, 21 U.S. Code § 381

March 16, 1950, Ch. 61, 64 Stat. 20, 21 U.S. Code §§ 331, 342, 347

Oct. 26, 1951, Ch. 578, 65 Stat. 648, 21 U.S. Code §§ 333, 333 nt., 353

Aug. 5, 1953, Ch. 334, 67 Stat. 389, 21 U.S. Code § 352

Aug. 7, 1953, Ch. 350, 67 Stat. 476, 21 U.S. Code §§ 331, 334, 374

Apr 15, 1954, Ch. 143, 68 Stat. 54, 21 U.S. Code §§ 341, 371

July 22, 1954, Ch. 559, 68 Stat. 511, 21 U.S. Code §§ 321, 342, 346a, 346b

Sept. 3, 1954, Ch. 1263, § 37, 68 Stat. 1239, 21 U.S. Code § 337

Aug. 1, 1956, Ch. 861, 70 Stat. 919, 21 U.S. Code §§ 341, 371

Aug. 31, 1957, P.L. 85-250, 71 Stat. 567, 21 U.S. Code § 334

Aug. 28, 1958, P.L. 85-791, 72 Stat. 947, 21 U.S. Code §§ 346a, 371

Sept. 6, 1958, P.L. 85-929, 72 Stat. 1784, 21 U.S. Code §§ 321, 331, 342, 346, 348

March 17, 1959, P.L. 86-2, 73 Stat. 3, 21 U.S. Code § 342

Continued

827

June 11, 1960, P.L. 86-507, 74 Stat. 201, 21 U.S. Code § 355

June 29, 1960, P.L. 86-537, 74 Stat. 251, 21 U.S. Code § 343

June 29, 1960, P.L. 86-546, 74 Stat. 255, 21 U.S. Code § 348

July 12, 1960, P.L. 86-618, 74 Stat. 397, 21 U.S. Code §§ 321, 331, 333, 342, 343, 346, 351, 361, 362, 371, 376

Oct. 10, 1962, P.L. 87-781, 76 Stat. 780, 21 U.S. Code §§ 321, 331, 332, 348, 351 to 353, 355, 357 to 360, 372, 374, 376, 381

July 15, 1965, P.L. 89-74, 79 Stat. 226, 21 U.S. Code §§ 321, 331, 333, 334, 360, 360a, 372

June 29, 1966, P.L. 89-477, 80 Stat. 231, 21 U.S. Code § 342

July 13, 1968, P.L. 90-399, 82 Stat. 342, 21 U.S. Code §§ 321, 331, 342, 351, 352, 357, 360b, 381, 392

Oct. 24, 1968, P.L. 90-639, 82 Stat. 1361, 1362, 21 U.S. Code §§ 321, 331, 333, 334, 360a

Oct. 15, 1970, P.L. 91-452, 84 Stat. 930, 21 U.S. Code § 373

Oct. 27, 1970, P.L. 91-513, 84 Stat. 1281, 21 U.S. Code §§ 321, 333, 334, 360, 372, 381

Oct. 30, 1970, P.L. 91-515, 84 Stat. 1311, 21 U.S. Code § 346, 376

Dec. 30, 1970, P.L. 91-601, 84 Stat. 1673, 21 U.S. Code §§ 343, 352, 353, 362

Aug. 16, 1972, P.L. 92-387, 86 Stat. 500, 21 U.S. Code §§ 331, 355, 360

Oct. 21, 1972, P.L. 92-516, 21 U.S. Code §§ 321, 346a

Nov. 18, 1972, P.L. 92-157, 85 Stat. 404, 21 U.S. Code § 346a

Nov. 23, 1977, P.L. 95-203, 21 U.S. Code § 321 et seq.

Nov. 10, 1978, P.L. 95-633, 21 U.S. Code § 352

Jan. 4, 1983, P.L. 97-414, 21 U.S. Code § 360aa et seq.

Sept. 24, 1984, P.L. 98-417, 98 Stat. 1585, 21 U.S. Code §§ 355, 360cc

Oct. 30, 1984, P.L. 98-551, 21 U.S. Code § 360bb

Nov. 8, 1984, P.L. 98-620, 21 U.S. Code §§ 346a, 348

Aug. 15, 1985, P.L. 99-91, 21 U.S. Code §§ 360aa to 360cc

Feb. 27, 1986, P.L. 99-252, 21 U.S. Code § 342

Oct. 27, 1986, P.L. 99-570, 21 U.S. Code §§ 331, 350a

Nov. 14, 1986, P.L. 99-660, 100 Stat. 3743 et seq.

April 18, 1988, 102 Stat. 90, P.L. 100-290, 21 U.S. Code § 360bb

Nov. 4, 1988, P.L. 100-607, 21 U.S. Code § 293

Nov. 18, 1988, P.L. 100-690, 21 U.S. Code §§ 333, 393

Nov. 3, 1990, P.L. 101-502, 21 U.S. Code § 331

Nov. 5, 1990, P.L. 101-508, 21 U.S. Code § 331

Nov. 28, 1990, P.L. 101-629, 21 U.S. Code §§ 321, 333, 333 nt., 351, 353, 360c, 360c nt., 360e to 360j, 360i nt., 360j nt., 360hh nt., 361i nt., 361j, 383, 383 nt.

Nov. 28, 1990, P.L. 101-635, 21 U.S. Code §§ 379b to 379d, 394

Nov. 29, 1990, P.L. 101-647, 21 U.S. Code § 333

Aug. 17, 1991, P.L. 102-108, 21 U.S. Code §§ 343, 343-1, 353, 360b

May 13, 1992, P.L. 102-282, 21 U.S. Code §§ 321, 335a to 335c, 336, 337

June 16, 1992, P.L. 102-300, 21 U.S. Code §§ 321, 331, 334, 346a, 352, 353, 357, 360c, 360g to 360i, 3601, 360mm, 372, 372a

Aug. 26, 1992, P.L. 102-353, 21 U.S. Code §§ 333, 353, 353 nt., 381

Oct. 29, 1992, P.L. 102-571, 21 U.S. Code §§ 321, 331, 342, 343, 346a, 351, 360j, 361, 362, 372, 376, 379 to 379h

June 10, 1993, P.L. 103-43, 21 U.S. Code §§ 394, 395

Aug. 13, 1993, P.L. 103-80, 21 U.S. Code §§ 321, 331 et seq., 341 et seq., 346a, 350a, 355 et seq., 360b, 360c, 360e, 360i, 360cc, 360kk, 361, 371 et seq., 376, 379e, 381

May 26, 1994, P.L. 103-261, 21 U.S. Code § 343 nt.

Oct. 22, 1994, P.L. 103-396, 21 U.S. Code §§ 331, 343-1, 360b

Oct. 25, 1994, P.L. 103-417, 21 U.S. Code § 350b

April 1, 1996, P.L. 104-124, 21 U.S. Code § 343

Aug. 6, 1996, P.L. 104-180, 21 U.S. Code §§ 349, 381, 382

Oct. 9, 1996, P.L. 104-250, 21 U.S. Code § 354

Nov. 21, 1997, P.L. 105-115, 21 U.S. Code §§ 321, 331, 334, 343, 343-3, 348, 335a, 351, 352, 353, 353a, 355, 355a, 356, 356a, 356b, 356c, 357, 360, 360b, 360c, 360d, 360g, 360e, 360i, 360j, 360l, 360m, 360aa, 360bb, 360cc, 360ee, 360aaa, 360aaa-1 to 360aaa-6, 360bbb, 360bbb-1, 360bbb-2, 371, 374, 379g, 379h, 379k, 379l, 379o, 379r, 379s, 379v, 381, 382, 393, 396, 397

Oct. 21, 1998, P.L. 105-277, 21 U.S. Code § 360b

Oct. 30, 1998, P.L. 105-324, 21 U.S. Code §§ 321, 346a

Nov. 10, 1998, P.L. 105-362, 21 U.S. Code § 360qq

La. Rev. Stat. Ann., 40:601 et seq.

Federal Government Conveyance Act (Park Commissioners)

Ill. Rev. Stat. 1991, Ch. 105, §§ 325a.9, 325b

Federal Grant Act (Miscellaneous)

Ark. Code Ann. 1987, 19-7-501 et seq.

Federal Grant and Cooperative Agreement Act of 1977

Feb. 3, 1978, P.L. 95-224, 41 U.S. Code §§ 501 et seq., 501 nt.

April 1, 1982, P.L. 97-162, 41 U.S. Code § 501 nt.

Federal Grant Review Act

La. Rev. Stat. Ann., 49:661 et seq.

Federal Grant Tax and Bond Act (Municipal)

Ill. Rev. Stat. 1991, Ch. 24, § 808.01 et seq.

Federal Hazardous Substances Act

July 12, 1960, P.L. 86-613, 74 Stat. 372, 15 U.S. Code §§ 1261 to 1273

Nov. 3, 1966, P.L. 89-756, 80 Stat. 1303, 15 U.S. Code §§ 1261 to 1265, 1273

Nov. 6, 1969, P.L. 91-113, 83 Stat. 187, 189, 15 U.S. Code §§ 1261, 1262, 1274

Oct. 15, 1970, P.L. 91-452, 84 Stat. 929, 15 U.S. Code § 1271

Dec. 30, 1970, P.L. 91-601, 84 Stat. 1673, 15 U.S. Code § 1261

Oct. 21, 1972, P.L. 92-516, 86 Stat. 998, 15 U.S. Code § 1261

Nov. 10, 1978, P.L. 95-631, 15 U.S. Code §§ 1261, 1263, 1264, 1273, 1275

Jan. 4, 1983, P.L. 97-414, 15 U.S. Code § 1274

Oct. 17, 1984, P.L. 98-491, 15 U.S. Code § 1274

June 19, 1986, P.L. 99-339, 15 U.S. Code §§ 1261, 1263

Aug. 23, 1988, P.L. 100-418, 102 Stat. 1156, 15 U.S. Code § 1274

Nov. 18, 1988, P.L. 100-695, 15 U.S. Code § 1277

Nov. 16, 1990, P.L. 101-608, 15 U.S. Code §§ 1262, 1264, 1274

June 16, 1994, P.L. 103-267, 15 U.S. Code § 1278

Federal Highway Act of 1938

June 8, 1938, Ch. 328, 52 Stat. 633 (See 23 U.S. Code §§ 101, 103, 109, 112, 126)

Federal Highway Act of 1960

July 14, 1960, P.L. 86-657, 74 Stat. 522 (See 23 U.S. Code §§ 104, 114, 120, 129, 132, 203, 205, 210, 305)

Federal Highway Acts

July 11, 1916, Ch. 241, 39 Stat. 355

Nov. 9, 1921, Ch. 119, 42 Stat. 212

June 16, 1936, Ch. 582, 49 Stat. 1519, 4 U.S. Code § 12 (See 23 U.S. Code § 101); 25 U.S. Code § 318b

Sept. 5, 1940, Ch. 715, 54 Stat. 867, 16 U.S. Code §§ 8-1, 460b, 460c; (See 23 U.S. Code §§ 105, 126, 311); 25 U.S. Code § 318b

July 13, 1943, Ch. 236, § 1, 57 Stat. 560 (See 23 U.S. Code § 101)

Sept. 7, 1950, Ch. 912, 64 Stat. 788

Aug. 30, 1954, Ch. 1076, 68 Stat. 966

June 29, 1956, Ch. 462, 70 Stat. 376 (See 23 U.S. Code §§ 101, 202, 204, 205)

April 16, 1958, P.L. 85-381, 72 Stat. 94 (See 23 U.S. Code § 121)

Federal Highway Safety Act

Ariz. Rev. Stat. Ann., § 28-611

Federal Home Loan Bank Act

July 22, 1932, Ch. 522, 47 Stat. 725, 12 U.S. Code §§ 1421 to 1449

Aug. 1, 1947, Ch. 431, 61 Stat. 714, 12 U.S. Code § 1430

July 3, 1948, Ch. 825, 62 Stat. 1240, 12 U.S. Code § 1439

April 20, 1950, Ch. 94, 64 Stat. 80, 12 U.S. Code § 1430

June 27, 1950, Ch. 369, 64 Stat. 256, 12 U.S. Code §§ 1425a, 1426, 1431, 1440

Sept. 1, 1951, Ch. 378, 65 Stat. 303, 12 U.S. Code § 1430

July 14, 1952, Ch. 723, 66 Stat. 604, 12 U.S. Code §§ 1422, 1423

Aug. 2, 1954, Ch. 649, 68 Stat. 622, 12 U.S. Code §§ 1430, 1431, 1436

Aug. 11, 1956, Ch. 783, 70 Stat. 640, 12 U.S. Code § 1426, 1427, 1437

Sept. 2, 1958, P.L. 85-857, 72 Stat. 1264, 12 U.S. Code § 1430

June 25, 1959, P.L. 86-70, 73 Stat. 142, 12 U.S. Code § 1422

Sept. 22, 1959, P.L. 86-349, 73 Stat. 625, 12 U.S. Code § 1427

July 12, 1960, P.L. 86-624, 74 Stat. 411, 12 U.S. Code § 1422

Sept. 8, 1961, P.L. 87-210, 75 Stat. 482, 483, 12 U.S. Code § 1426

Sept. 8, 1961, P.L. 87-211, 75 Stat. 486, 12 U.S. Code § 1427

Sept. 19, 1962, P.L. 87-676, 76 Stat. 559, 12 U.S. Code § 1427

Oct. 9, 1962, P.L. 87-779, 76 Stat. 779, 12 U.S. Code §§ 1422, 1430

Sept. 2, 1964, P.L. 88-560, 78 Stat. 800, 805, 12 U.S. Code §§ 1430, 1431, 1436

Sept. 21, 1966, P.L. 89-597, 80 Stat. 824, 12 U.S. Code § 1425b

Nov. 3, 1966, P.L. 89-754, 80 Stat. 1293, 12 U.S. Code §§ 1432, 1438

Aug. 1, 1968, P.L. 90-448, 82 Stat. 545, 12 U.S. Code §§ 1431, 1432, 1436

Sept. 21, 1968, P.L. 90-505, 82 Stat. 856, 12 U.S. Code §§ 1425a, 1425b

Dec. 23, 1969, P.L. 91-151, 83 Stat. 372, 12 U.S. Code §§ 1425b, 1431

Dec. 24, 1969, P.L. 91-152, 83 Stat. 401, 12 U.S. Code § 1425

Dec. 31, 1970, P.L. 91-609, 84 Stat. 1811, 12 U.S. Code §§ 1431, 1432

June 29, 1977, P.L. 95-56, 12 U.S. Code § 1437 et seq.

Aug. 4, 1977, P.L. 95-90, 12 U.S. Code § 1437

Sept. 20, 1977, P.L. 95-109, 15 U.S. Code § 1692l

Oct. 12, 1977, P.L. 95-128, 12 U.S. Code § 1430

Nov. 5, 1979, P.L. 96-104, 12 U.S. Code § 1425b

Dec. 21, 1979, P.L. 96-153, 12 U.S. Code §§ 1426, 1431

Dec. 28, 1979, P.L. 96-161, 12 U.S. Code § 1425b

March 31, 1980, P.L. 96-221, 12 U.S. Code § 1425a

Oct. 15, 1982, P.L. 97-320, 12 U.S. Code §§ 1425, 1426, 1428, 1430, 1431, 1436, 1437

Jan. 12, 1983, P.L. 97-457, 12 U.S. Code §§ 1426, 1430, 1437

Nov. 30, 1983, P.L. 98-181, 12 U.S. Code § 1437

Oct. 17, 1984, P.L. 98-479, 12 U.S. Code § 1425

Aug. 10, 1987, P.L. 100-86, 12 U.S. Code §§ 1430, 1436, 1439-1, 1441, 1442a

Aug. 9, 1989, P.L. 101-73, generally 12 U.S. Code § 1422 et seq.

Nov. 28, 1990, P.L. 101-625, 12 U.S. Code § 1441a

March 23, 1991, P.L. 102-18, 12 U.S. Code § 1441a

Oct. 28, 1991, P.L. 102-139, 12 U.S. Code § 1441a

Dec. 12, 1991, P.L. 102-233, 12 U.S. Code §§ 1441, 1441a, 1441a nt.

Dec. 19, 1991, P.L. 102-242, 12 U.S. Code § 1441a

Oct. 2, 1992, P.L. 102-378, 12 U.S. Code § 1441a

Oct. 28, 1992, P.L. 102-550, 12 U.S. Code §§ 1441, 1441a, 1441b, 1422, 1422a, 1430, 1430b

Dec. 17, 1993, P.L. 103-204, 12 U.S. Code §§ 1441a, 1447

Feb. 12, 1994, P.L. 103-211, 12 U.S. Code § 1441a

Sept. 29, 1994, P.L. 103-328, 12 U.S. Code § 1441a

Dec. 21, 1995, P.L. 104-66, 12 U.S. Code §§ 1438, 1441a

Sept. 30, 1996, P.L. 104-208, 12 U.S. Code §§ 1431, 1441, 1441a, 1441b

Dec. 2, 1997, P.L. 105-135, 12 U.S. Code § 1441a

Federal Home Loan Mortgage Corporation Act

July 24, 1970, P.L. 91-351, 84 Stat. 451, 12 U.S. Code §§ 1451 to 1459

Oct. 12, 1977, P.L. 95-128, 12 U.S. Code § 1454

Oct. 31, 1978, P.L. 95-557, 12 U.S. Code § 1454

Nov. 9, 1978, P.L. 95-619, 12 U.S. Code § 1451

Nov. 10, 1978, P.L. 95-630, 12 U.S. Code § 1451

June 30, 1980, P.L. 96-294, 12 U.S. Code §§ 1451, 1454

Oct. 6, 1982, P.L. 97-289, 12 U.S. Code § 1455(f)

Oct. 3, 1984, P.L. 98-440, 98 Stat. 1693, 12 U.S. Code §§ 1451, 1454

Sept. 30, 1987, P.L. 100-122, 12 U.S. Code § 1454

Feb. 5, 1988, P.L. 100-242, 12 U.S. Code §§ 1454, 1455, 1718, 1723a

Aug. 9, 1989, P.L. 101-73, 12 U.S. Code §§ 1451 nt., 1452 to 1457, 1459

Oct. 28, 1992, 12 U.S. Code §§ 1451, 1451 nt., 1452, 1453 to 1456

Oct. 21, 1998, P.L. 105-276, 12 U.S. Code § 1454

Federal Housing Act

See National Housing Act

Federal Housing Enterprise Financial Safety and Soundness Act of 1992

Oct. 28, 1992, P.L. 102-550, 12 U.S. Code §§ 4501 et. seq., 4501 nt.

Sept. 23, 1994, P.L. 103-325, 12 U.S. Code § 4521

Oct. 27, 1997, P.L. 105-65, 12 U.S. Code § 4565

Oct. 21, 1998, P.L. 105-276, 12 U.S. Code § 4513

Federal Impoundment and Information Act

Oct. 27, 1972, P.L. 92-599, 86 Stat. 1325, 31 U.S. Code § 581c-1

March 8, 1973, P.L. 93-9, 87 Stat. 7, 31 U.S. Code § 581c-1

Federal Information Centers Act

Oct. 20, 1978, P.L. 95-491, 40 U.S. Code §§ 751 nt., 760

Federal Insecticide, Fungicide and Rodenticide Act

Miss. Code Ann. 1972, §§ 69-23-3, 69-23-107

Federal Insecticide, Fungicide, and Rodenticide Act

June 25, 1947, Ch. 125, 61 Stat. 163, 7 U.S. Code §§ 121 nt., 135, 135a, 135b to 135f, 135f nt., 135g, 135h, 135i, 135j, 135k

Aug. 7, 1959, P.L. 86-139, 73 Stat. 286, 7 U.S. Code § 135

May 12, 1964, P.L. 88-305, 78 Stat. 190 to 193, 7 U.S. Code §§ 135 to 135b, 135f, 135g

Oct. 15, 1970, P.L. 91-452, 84 Stat. 928, 7 U.S. Code § 135c

Dec. 30, 1970, P.L. 91-601, 84 Stat. 1673, 7 U.S. Code § 135

Oct. 21, 1972, P.L. 92-516, 86 Stat. 973, 7 U.S. Code §§ 136 to 136y

Oct. 10, 1975, P.L. 94-109, 89 Stat. 571, 7 U.S. Code § 136y

Nov. 28, 1975, P.L. 94-140, 89 Stat. 751, 7 U.S. Code §§ 136 to 136b, 136p, 136s, 136w, 136y

March 27, 1978, P.L. 95-251, 7 U.S. Code § 136d

Dec. 2, 1983, P.L. 98-201, 7 U.S. Code §§ 136w, 136y

Dec. 23, 1985, P.L. 99-198, 7 U.S. Code § 136y

June 27, 1988, P.L. 100-352, 102 Stat. 664, 7 U.S. Code § 136w

Nov. 28, 1990, P.L. 101-624, 7 U.S. Code §§ 136a, 136a-1, 136d, 136w-3

Dec. 13, 1991, P.L. 102-237, 7 U.S. Code §§ 136, 136a, 136a-1, 136c, 136d, 136e, 136f, 136g, 136h, 136i, 136j, 136 l, 136n, 136 o, 136p, 136r, 136s, 136w, 136w-1

Continued

April 4, 1996, P.L. 104-127, 7 U.S. Code § 136w-3

Aug. 3, 1996, P.L. 104-170, 7 U.S. Code §§ 136w-5 to 136w-7, 136x, 136y

Federal Insecticide, Fungicide, and Rodenticide Act Amendments of 1988

Oct. 25, 1988, P.L. 100-532, 7 U.S. Code § 136 nt.

Federal Insurance Contributions Act (1939)

Feb. 10, 1939, Ch. 2, 53 Stat. 175 (See 26 U.S. Code §§ 3101 to 3125)

Aug. 10, 1939, Ch. 666, 53 Stat. 1387

Dec. 22, 1943, Ch. 375, 57 Stat. 607

Dec. 16, 1944, Ch. 600, 58 Stat. 812

Nov. 8, 1945, Ch. 453, 59 Stat. 576

Dec. 29, 1945, Ch. 652, 59 Stat. 670

Aug. 10, 1946, Ch. 951, 60 Stat. 978

Aug. 6, 1947, Ch. 510, 61 Stat. 793

Federal Insurance Contributions Act of 1954

Aug. 16, 1954, Ch. 736, 68A Stat. 415, 26 U.S. Code §§ 3101, 3102,3111, 3112, 3121 to 3125

Sept. 1, 1954, Ch. 1206, 68 Stat. 1090, 26 U.S. Code §§ 3101, 3102, 3111, 3121, 3122, 3124

Aug. 1, 1956, Ch. 836, 70 Stat. 824, 26 U.S. Code §§ 3101, 3111, 3113, 3121

Aug. 1, 1956, Ch. 837, 70 Stat. 878, 26 U.S. Code § 3121

Sept. 2, 1958, P.L. 85-866, 72 Stat. 1606, 26 U.S. Code §§ 3121, 3122

July 30, 1965, P.L. 89-97, 79 Stat. 342, 26 U.S. Code §§ 3101, 3111

Federal Insurance Interpleader Act

May 8, 1926, Ch. 273, 44 Stat. 416 (See 28 U.S. Code §§ 1335, 1397, 2361)

Federal Judgeship Act of 1984

July 2, 1986, P.L. 99-349, 28 U.S. Code § 152 nt.

Federal Judgeship Act of 1990

Dec. 1, 1990, P.L. 101-650, 28 U.S. Code §§ 1 nt., 44, 44 nt., 133, 133 nt., 331 nt.

Federal Judicial Salary Acts

Aug. 14, 1964, P.L. 88-426, 78 Stat. 433, 10 U.S. Code § 867; 11 U.S. Code § 68; 26 U.S. Code § 7443; 28 U.S. Code §§ 5, 44, 135, 173, 213, 252, 603, 604 nt., 753 nt., 792

July 18, 1966, P.L. 89-504, 80 Stat. 293, 28 U.S. Code §§ 603 nt., 604 nt., 753 nt.

Federal Juvenile Delinquency Act

June 16, 1938, Ch. 486, 52 Stat. 764, (See 18 U.S. Code §§ 5031 to 5037)

Sept. 7, 1974, P.L. 93-415, 88 Stat. 1133, 18 U.S. Code §§ 5031 to 5042

March 15, 1976, P.L. 94-233, 90 Stat. 233, 18 U.S. Code § 5041

Federal Laboratory Animal Welfare Act

Aug. 24, 1966, P.L. 89-544, 80 Stat. 350, 7 U.S. Code §§ 2131 to 2154

Federal Land Exchange Facilitation Act of 1988

Aug. 20, 1988, P.L. 100-409, 102 Stat. 1086, 16 U.S. Code §§ 505a, 505b, 521b; 43 U.S. Code §§ 751 nt., 1701 nt., 1716, 1716 nt., 1723

Federal Land Policy and Management Act of 1976

Oct. 21, 1976, P.L. 94-579, 43 U.S. Code § 1701 et seq.

Aug. 20, 1978, P.L. 95-352, 43 U.S. Code § 1747

Oct. 25, 1978, P.L. 95-514, 43 U.S. Code §§ 1739, 1751 to 1753

May 25, 1984, P.L. 98-300, 43 U.S. Code § 1764

Oct. 24, 1984, P.L. 98-540, 43 U.S. Code § 1737(d) to 1737(g)

Oct. 27, 1986, P.L. 99-545, 100 Stat. 3047

Oct. 27, 1986, P.L. 99-548, 100 Stat. 3061

Nov. 7, 1986, P.L. 99-632, 43 U.S. Code § 1715

Aug. 20, 1988, P.L. 100-409, 102 Stat. 1087, 43 U.S. Code §§ 1716, 1723

Nov. 3, 1988, P.L. 100-586, 43 U.S. Code § 1732

May 9, 1990, P.L. 101-286, 43 U.S. Code § 1737

Oct. 24, 1992, P.L. 102-486, 43 U.S. Code
§ 1761

Nov. 2, 1994, P.L. 103-437, 43 U.S. Code
§§ 1714, 1723, 1741

Nov. 12, 1996, P.L. 104-333, 43 U.S. Code
§§ 1748, 1764

Federal Lands Act (Rights-of-Way Across)
Utah Code Ann. 1953, 27-16-101 et seq.

Federal Lands Cession Act
S.C. Code Ann. 1976, § 3-1-110 et seq.

Federal Lands Cleanup Act of 1985
Aug. 27, 1986, P.L. 99-402, 36 U.S. Code
§§ 169i nt., 169i, 169i- 1

Nov. 12, 1996, P.L. 104-333, 36 U.S. Code
§§ 169i, 169i-1

**Federal Law Enforcement Dependents
Assistance Act of 1996**
Oct. 3, 1996, P.L. 104-238, 42 U.S. Code
§ 3711 nt.

**Federal Law Enforcement Officer Immunity
Act**
Ill. Comp. Stat. 1992, Ch. 745, § 22/1

**Federal Law Enforcement Pay Reform Act
of 1990**
Nov. 5, 1990, P.L. 101-509, 5 U.S. Code
§§ 4521 to 4523, 5305 nt., 5541, 5542,
5547, 8335, 8335 nt., 8425

Oct. 10, 1997, P.L. 105-61, 5 U.S. Code
§ 5305 nt.

Federal Legislative Salary Act of 1964
Aug. 14, 1964, P.L. 88-426, 78 Stat. 413, 2
U.S. Code §§ 31, 60a nt., 60e-11, 60f nt.,
61a, 61a-2, 61d, 61e, 72a, 84-2, 136a,
136a-1, 273a; 31 U.S. Code §§ 42a, 51a; 40
U.S. Code §§ 162a, 166b, 166b-1; See 44
U.S. Code § 303

Dec. 16, 1967, P.L. 90-206, 81 Stat. 639, 2
U.S. Code §§ 136a, 136a-1; 31 U.S. Code
§§ 42a, 51a; 40 U.S. Code §§ 162a, 166b,
166b-1; See 44 U.S. Code § 303

Aug. 5, 1977, P.L. 95-94, 2 U.S. Code
§ 61a-2

Federal Legislative Salary Act of 1966
July 18, 1966, P.L. 89-504, 80 Stat. 294, 2
U.S. Code §§ 60f nt., 293b

Federal Lien Registration Act
See also Uniform Federal Lien Registration
Act
Pa. Cons. Stat., Title 42, § 4306
Pa. Purdon's Stat., Title 74, § 157-1
Tenn. Code Ann., 26-6-101 et seq.

**Federal Loan Agency Appropriation Act,
1946**
May 21, 1945, Ch. 129, 59 Stat. 169

**Federal Low-Income Housing Tax Credit
Program Act**
Miss. Code Ann. 1972, § 7-1-255

Federal Magistrate Act of 1979
Oct. 10, 1979, P.L. 96-82, 18 U.S. Code
§ 3401; 28 U.S. Code §§ 604, 631, 631 nt.,
633 to 636

Federal Magistrates Act
Oct. 17, 1968, P.L. 90-578, 82 Stat. 1107, 18
U.S. Code §§ 202, 3006A, 3041, 3043,
3045, 3060, 3102 and others; 28 U.S. Code
§§ 604, 631 to 639

Federal Mandates Act
Mont. Code Ann., 2-1-401 et seq.

**Federal Maritime Commission Authori-
zation Act of 1990**
Nov. 16, 1990, P.L. 101-595, 104 Stat. 2979

**Federal Maritime Commission Authori-
zation Act of 1991**
Aug. 17, 1991, P.L. 102-100, 105 Stat. 491

Federal Marshals Act
June 15, 1935, Ch. 259, 49 Stat. 377 (See 18
U.S. Code § 3053; See 28 U.S. Code § 567)

Federal Mass Transportation Act of 1987
April 2, 1987, P.L. 100-17, 49 U.S. Code
Appx. § 1601 nt.

Federal Meat Inspection Act

Dec. 15, 1967, P.L. 90-201, 81 Stat. 584, 19 U.S. Code § 1306; 21 U.S. Code §§ 601 to 623, 641 to 645, 661, 671 to 680, 691

July 18, 1970, P.L. 91-342, 84 Stat. 438, 21 U.S. Code § 623

Oct. 17, 1984, P.L. 98-487, 21 U.S. Code § 661

Dec. 23, 1985, P.L. 99-198, 21 U.S. Code § 620

Nov. 10, 1986, P.L. 99-641, 21 U.S. Code §§ 606 nt., 606, 609 nt., 609, 621 nt., 621, 671 nt., 671, 676 nt., 676

Aug. 23, 1988, P.L. 100-418, 102 Stat. 1408, 21 U.S. Code § 620

Dec. 7, 1989, P.L. 101-205, 21 U.S. Code § 673

Dec. 13, 1991, P.L. 102-237, 21 U.S. Code § 623

Oct. 29, 1992, P.L. 102-571, 21 U.S. Code § 601

Dec. 8, 1993, P.L. 103-182, 21 U.S. Code § 620

Nov. 2, 1994, P.L. 103-437, 21 U.S. Code §§ 620, 661

Dec. 8, 1994, P.L. 103-465, 7 U.S. Code § 620

April 4, 1996, P.L. 104-127, 21 U.S. Code §§ 471, 607, 679a, 680

Federal Mediation and Conciliation Service Appropriation Acts

June 14, 1948, Ch. 465, 62 Stat. 406

Aug. 31, 1951, Ch. 373, 65 Stat. 222

July 5, 1952, Ch. 575, 66 Stat. 372

July 31, 1953, Ch. 296, 67 Stat. 258

Federal Metal and Nonmetallic Mine Safety Act

Sept. 16, 1966, P.L. 89-577, 80 Stat. 772, 30 U.S. Code §§ 721 to 740

Federal Mine Safety and Health Act of 1977

Nov. 9, 1977, P.L. 95-164, 91 Stat. 1290, 5 U.S. Code §§ 5314, 5315; 29 U.S. Code § 557a; 30 U.S. Code §§ 801 et seq., 801 nt.; 31 U.S. Code § 11 nt.; 43 U.S. Code § 1456a

March 1, 1978, P.L. 95-239, 30 U.S. Code §§ 801 nt., 901 nt., 902 et seq., 4121

June 30, 1980, P.L. 96-294, 12 U.S. Code § 1723g et seq.

Nov. 5, 1990, P.L. 101-508, 30 U.S. Code § 820

Federal National Mortgage Association Act

July 1, 1948, Ch. 784, 62 Stat. 1206, 12 U.S. Code §§ 1716 to 1721

Dec. 29, 1973, P.L. 93-222, 87 Stat. 936, 12 U.S. Code § 1721

Federal National Mortgage Association Charter Act

Aug. 2, 1954, Ch. 649, 68 Stat. 612, 12 U.S. Code §§ 1716 to 1723c

Sept. 2, 1958, P.L. 85-857, 72 Stat. 1265, 12 U.S. Code § 1717

Sept. 9, 1965, P.L. 89-174, 79 Stat. 669, 12 U.S. Code § 1723

May 24, 1966, P.L. 89-429, 80 Stat. 164 to 166, 12 U.S. Code §§ 1717, 1720

Nov. 3, 1966, P.L. 89-751, 80 Stat. 1236, 12 U.S. Code § 1717

June 30, 1970, P.L. 91-296, 84 Stat. 350, 12 U.S. Code § 1717

Nov. 9, 1978, P.L. 95-619, 12 U.S. Code §§ 1717, 1723f to 1723h

Oct. 15, 1982, P.L. 97-320, 12 U.S. Code §§ 1718, 1719

Nov. 30, 1983, P.L. 98-181, 12 U.S. Code §§ 1720, 1721, 1723a, 1723e nt.

Oct. 3, 1984, P.L. 98-440, 98 Stat. 1692, 12 U.S. Code § 1717

Oct. 17, 1984, P.L. 98-479, 12 U.S. Code § 1717

Sept. 30, 1987, P.L. 100-122, 12 U.S. Code § 1717

Feb. 5, 1988, P.L. 100-242, 12 U.S. Code §§ 1717, 1719

Nov. 7, 1988, P.L. 100-628, 12 U.S. Code §§ 1454, 1717

Aug. 9, 1989, P.L. 101-73, 12 U.S. Code §§ 1716, 1717, 1719, 1723a

Nov. 28, 1990, P.L. 101-625, 12 U.S. Code § 1721

Oct. 28, 1992, P.L. 102-550, 12 U.S. Code §§ 1716 to 1719, 1721, 1723, 1723 nt., 1723a, 1723c, 1723g, 1723h

March 28, 1996, P.L. 104-120, 12 U.S. Code § 1721

Oct. 26, 1996, P.L. 104-330, 12 U.S. Code
§ 1721

Federal Naturalization Act
See Naturalization Act

**Federal Nonnuclear Energy Research and
Development Act of 1974**
Dec. 31, 1975, P.L. 94-187, 89 Stat. 1075, 42
U.S. Code §§ 5916, 5197
June 3, 1977, P.L. 95-39, 42 U.S. Code
§ 5912 et seq.
Feb. 25, 1978, P.L. 95-238, 42 U.S. Code
§ 5905 et seq.
Aug. 22, 1986, P.L. 99-386, 42 U.S. Code
§ 5906
Oct. 24, 1992, P.L. 102-486, 42 U.S. Code
§ 5905
Nov. 2, 1994, P.L. 103-437, 42 U.S. Code
§§ 5919, 5920
Dec. 21, 1995, P.L. 104-66, 42 U.S. Code
§ 5910
Feb. 10, 1996, P.L. 104-106, 42 U.S. Code
§ 5918
Oct. 19, 1996, P.L. 104-316, 42 U.S. Code
§ 5919

Federal Noxious Weed Act of 1974
Jan. 3, 1975, P.L. 93-629, 88 Stat. 2148, 7
U.S. Code §§ 2801 to 2813
Nov. 28, 1990, P.L. 101-624, 7 U.S. Code
§ 2814
Nov. 2, 1994, P.L. 103-437, 30 U.S. Code
§ 1752
Dec. 8, 1994, P.L. 103-465, 7 U.S. Code
§ 2803
Nov. 18, 1997, P.L. 105-86, 7 U.S. Code
§ 2802

Federal Official Records Act
Pa. Cons. Stat., Title 42, § 6104

**Federal Oil and Gas Royalty Management
Act of 1982**
Jan. 12, 1983, P.L. 97-451, 30 U.S. Code
§§ 188, 191, 1701 et seq., 1701 nt.
Aug. 13, 1996, P.L. 104-185, 30 U.S. Code
§§ 1702, 1712, 1721, 1721a, 1724, 1725,
1726, 1735
Sept. 22, 1996, P.L. 104-200, 30 U.S. Code
§§ 1702, 1721, 1724, 1726

Nov. 10, 1998, P.L. 105-362, 30 U.S. Code
§§ 1752, 1753

**Federal Oil and Gas Royalty Simplification
and Fairness Act of 1996**
Aug. 13, 1996, P.L. 104-185, 30 U.S. Code
§ 1701 nt.

**Federal Onshore Oil and Gas Leasing
Reform Act of 1987**
Dec. 22, 1987, P.L. 100-203, 30 U.S. Code
§ 181 nt.

Federal Overseas Voting Rights Act
Va. Code 1950, § 24.1-72.10 et seq.

Federal Pay Comparability Act of 1970
Aug. 19, 60a 1972, P.L. 92-392, 86 Stat. 575,
2 U.S. Code §§ 60a, 60a nt.
Jan. 8, 1971, P.L. 91-656, 84 Stat. 1946, 5
U.S. Code §§ 5108, 5301, 5305 to 5308,
5942, 5947; 39 U.S. Code § 410
Aug. 9, 1975, P.L. 94-82, 89 Stat. 422, 2 U.S.
Code § 60a nt.
Nov. 5, 1990, P.L. 101-509, 2 U.S. Code
§§ 60a-1, 60a-2
Oct. 2, 1992, P.L. 102-378, 2 U.S. Code
§ 60a-2
Aug. 20, 1996, P.L. 104-186, 2 U.S. Code
§ 60a-2

**Federal Payment Reauthorization act of
1994**
Oct. 19, 1994, P.L. 103-373, 108 Stat. 3488
D.C. Code Ann., § 47-3406.1

Federal Photovoltaic Utilization Act
Nov. 9, 1978, P.L. 95-619, 42 U.S. Code
§ 8271 et seq.
June 30, 1980, P.L. 96-294, 42 U.S. Code
§ 8721 et seq.

**Federal Physicians Comparability
Allowance Act of 1978**
Nov. 6, 1978, P.L. 95-603, 5 U.S. Code
§ 5948
Oct. 26, 1993, P.L. 103-114, 5 U.S. Code
§ 5948 nt.
Oct. 10, 1997, P.L. 105-61, 5 U.S. Code
§ 5948 nt.

Federal Physicians Comparability Allowance Amendments of 1979

Dec. 29, 1979, P.L. 96-166, 5 U.S. Code §§ 5383, 5948, 5948 nt.

Federal Physicians Comparability Allowance Amendments of 1981

Dec. 29, 1981, P.L. 97-141, 5 U.S. Code § 5948 nt.

Federal Physicians Comparability Allowance Amendments of 1983

Nov. 29, 1983, P.L. 98-168, 5 U.S. Code § 5948 nt.

Federal Plant Pest Act

May 23, 1957, P.L. 85-36, 71 Stat. 31, 7 U.S. Code §§ 147a, 149, 150aa to 150jj

Dec. 8, 1994, P.L. 103-465, 7 U.S. Code §§ 150bb, 150cc, 154, 156, 281

Federal Portability and Accountability Act (Insurance-Public Health)

N.Y. Laws 1997, Ch. 661

Federal Possession and Control Act (Railroads in War)

Aug. 29, 1916, Ch. 418, 39 Stat. 645 (See 10 U.S. Code §§ 4742, 9742)

Federal Power Act

See also Federal Water Power Act

June 10, 1920, Ch. 285, 41 Stat. 1063, 16 U.S. Code §§ 791a to 825r

Aug. 26, 1935, Ch. 687, 49 Stat. 838, 16 U.S. Code §§ 791, 791a, 796 to 800, 803, 807, 810 and others

May 28, 1948, Ch. 351, 62 Stat. 275, 16 U.S. Code § 818

Aug. 7, 1953, Ch. 343, 87 Stat. 461, 16 U.S. Code § 824a

June 4, 1956, Ch. 351, 70 Stat. 226, 16 U.S. Code § 811

Aug. 28, 1958, P.L. 85-791, 72 Stat. 947, 16 U.S. Code § 825l

July 12, 1960, P.L. 86-619, 74 Stat. 407, 16 U.S. Code § 792

Sept. 7, 1962, P.L. 87-647, 76 Stat. 447, 16 U.S. Code § 803

Aug. 3, 1968, P.L. 90-451, 82 Stat. 616, 16 U.S. Code §§ 800, 803, 807, 808

Oct. 15, 1970, P.L. 91-452, 84 Stat. 929, 16 U.S. Code § 825f

Nov. 9, 1978, P.L. 95-617, 16 U.S. Code §§ 796, 823a et seq.

June 30, 1980, P.L. 96-294, 16 U.S. Code §§ 796, 824i

Dec. 21, 1982, P.L. 97-375, 16 U.S. Code § 797

Oct. 16, 1986, P.L. 99-498, 16 U.S. Code §§ 797, 803, 808, 817, 823a, 832b

Oct. 27, 1986, P.L. 99-546, 16 U.S. Code § 803

Nov. 15, 1990, P.L. 101-575, 16 U.S. Code § 796

May 17, 1991, P.L. 102-46, 16 U.S. Code § 796

Oct. 24, 1992, P.L. 102-486, 16 U.S. Code §§ 796, 803, 814, 824, 824j to 824m, 825n, 825o, 825o-1

Feb. 10, 1996, P.L. 104-106, 16 U.S. Code § 799

Oct. 19, 1996, P.L. 104-316, 16 U.S. Code § 799

July 14, 1998, P.L. 105-192, 16 U.S. Code § 799

Federal Prison Industries, Incorporated, and The Institute of Inter- American Affairs Appropriation Acts

July 20, 1949, Ch. 354, 63 Stat. 474

Sept. 6, 1950, Ch. 896, 64 Stat. 633

Federal Prisoner Production Expense Act

Ill. Rev. Stat. 1991, Ch. 38, §§ 156-10, 156-11

Federal Procurement Policy Act

Oct. 30, 1984, P.L. 98-577, 10 U.S. Code §§ 2320, 2320a; 41 U.S. Code §§ 416, 416 nt., 418a, 418b, 419

Federal Procurement Policy Act Amendments of 1988

May 15, 1989, P.L. 101-28, 41 U.S. Code § 423 nt.

Federal Program Information Act

Dec. 28, 1977, P.L. 95-220, 31 U.S. Code §§ 1701 et seq., 1701 nt.

Federal Property and Administrative Procedures Act of 1979

Nov. 18, 1988, P.L. 100-690, 40 U.S. Code § 484

Federal Property and Administrative Services Act of 1949

June 30, 1949, Ch. 288, 63 Stat. 377, 40 U.S. Code §§ 471 to 475, 481, 483, 484 to 492, 751 to 758; 41 U.S. Code §§ 5, 251 to 255, 257 to 260; 50 U.S. Code Appx. §§ 1622, 1641

Oct. 31, 1951, Ch. 652, 65 Stat. 700, 41 U.S. Code § 254

July 12, 1952, Ch. 703, 66 Stat. 593, 40 U.S. Code §§ 472, 483, 484, 487, 490, 756; 41 U.S. Code §§ 251 to 255, 259, 260

July 14, 1954, Ch. 481, 68 Stat. 474, 40 U.S. Code § 484

Aug. 31, 1954, Ch. 1178, 68 Stat. 1051, 40 U.S. Code § 485

Sept. 1, 1954, Ch. 1211, 68 Stat. 1126, 40 U.S. Code §§ 471, 472, 490, 491

June 3, 1955, Ch. 130, 69 Stat. 83, 40 U.S. Code § 484

July 12, 1955, Ch. 329, 69 Stat. 297 (See 44 U.S. Code §§ 2101 to 2110)

Aug. 1, 1955, Ch. 442, 69 Stat. 430, 40 U.S. Code § 484

Aug. 12, 1955, Ch. 859, 69 Stat. 695 (See 44 U.S. Code §§ 2101 to 2110)

Aug. 12, 1955, Ch. 874, 69 Stat. 721, 40 U.S. Code §§ 472, 521 to 524

July 3, 1956, Ch. 513, 70 Stat. 493, 40 U.S. Code § 484; See 44 U.S. Code §§ 2101 to 2110

Aug. 3, 1956, Ch. 942, 70 Stat. 1020, 40 U.S. Code § 484

June 13, 1957, P.L. 85-51, 71 Stat. 69 (See 44 U.S. Code §§ 2101 to 2110)

Feb. 28, 1958, P.L. 85-337, 72 Stat. 29, 40 U.S. Code § 472

March 15, 1958, P.L. 85-341, 72 Stat. 34 (See 44 U.S. Code §§ 2101 to 2110)

July 2, 1958, P.L. 85-486, 72 Stat. 288, 40 U.S. Code § 484

July 2, 1958, P.L. 85-493, 72 Stat. 294, 40 U.S. Code § 490

Aug. 1, 1958, P.L. 85-579, 72 Stat. 456, 40 U.S. Code §§ 523, 524

Aug. 19, 1958, P.L. 85-680, 72 Stat. 631, 40 U.S. Code § 488

Aug. 23, 1958, P.L. 85-726, 72 Stat. 808, 40 U.S. Code § 474

Aug. 27, 1958, P.L. 85-781, 72 Stat. 936, 40 U.S. Code § 481

Aug. 28, 1958, P.L. 85-800, 72 Stat. 966, 41 U.S. Code §§ 252, 255, 257, 260

Sept. 2, 1958, P.L. 85-886, 72 Stat. 1709, 40 U.S. Code § 490

June 25, 1959, P.L. 86-70, 73 Stat. 148, 40 U.S. Code §§ 472, 522

Sept. 1, 1959, P.L. 86-215, 73 Stat. 446, 40 U.S. Code § 485

Sept. 9, 1959, P.L. 86-249, 713 Stat. 482, 40 U.S. Code § 490

June 8, 1960, P.L. 86-498, 74 Stat. 165, 40 U.S. Code §§ 523, 524

July 5, 1960, P.L. 86-591, 74 Stat. 330, 40 U.S. Code § 756

July 12, 1960, P.L. 86-624, 74 Stat. 418, 40 U.S. Code §§ 472, 491, 514, 522

July 20, 1961, P.L. 87-94, 75 Stat. 213, 40 U.S. Code § 484

Oct. 4, 1961, P.L. 87-372, 75 Stat. 802, 40 U.S. Code § 756

Aug. 24, 1962, P.L. 87-600, 76 Stat. 401, 40 U.S. Code § 756

Aug. 31, 1962, P.L. 87-619, 76 Stat. 414, 40 U.S. Code § 486

Oct. 10, 1962, P.L. 87-786, 76 Stat. 805, 40 U.S. Code § 484

Oct. 10, 1962, P.L. 87-787, 76 Stat. 805, 40 U.S. Code §§ 523, 524

Oct. 23, 1962, P.L. 87-847, 76 Stat. 1117, 40 U.S. Code § 757

Feb. 5, 1964, P.L. 88-265, 78 Stat. 8 (See 44 U.S. Code §§ 3101 to 3107)

June 29, 1964, P.L. 88-330, 78 Stat. 226, 40 U.S. Code §§ 523, 524

July 28, 1964, P.L. 88-383, 78 Stat. 335 (See 44 U.S. Code §§ 2501 to 2507

Oct. 20, 1965, P.L. 89-276, 79 Stat. 1010, 40 U.S. Code § 490

Oct. 30, 1965, P.L. 89-306, 79 Stat. 1127, 40 U.S. Code § 759

Nov. 8, 1965, P.L. 89-343, 79 Stat. 1303, 40 U.S. Code § 474; 41 U.S. Code §§ 252, 257, 260

Continued

Nov. 8, 1965, P.L. 89-344, 79 Stat. 1034, 40 U.S. Code § 490

Sept. 27, 1966, P.L. 89-607, 80 Stat. 850, 41 U.S. Code § 254

May 25, 1967, P.L. 90-19, 81 Stat. 22, 40 U.S. Code § 474

July 7, 1967, P.L. 90-50, 81 Stat. 119, 40 U.S. Code §§ 523, 524

March 16, 1968, P.L. 90-268, 82 Stat. 49, 41 U.S. Code §§ 252, 253

Aug. 8, 1968, P.L. 90-461, 82 Stat. 638 (See 44 U.S. Code §§ 2501 to 2507

Oct. 16, 1968, P.L. 90-577, 82 Stat. 1104, 40 U.S. Code §§ 531 to 535

Oct. 22, 1968, P.L. 90-626, 82 Stat. 1319, 40 U.S. Code § 490

Aug. 12, 1970, P.L. 91-375, 84 Stat. 782, 40 U.S. Code § 474

Sept. 26, 1970, P.L. 91-426, 84 Stat. 883, 40 U.S. Code §§ 481, 512

Oct. 17, 1970, P.L. 91-466, 84 Stat. 990, 40 U.S. Code §§ 523, 524

Oct. 22, 1970, P.L. 91-485, 84 Stat. 1084, 40 U.S. Code § 484

June 16, 1972, P.L. 92-313, 86 Stat. 218, 40 U.S. Code § 490

Aug. 4, 1972, P.L. 92-362, 86 Stat. 503, 40 U.S. Code § 484

Oct. 27, 1972, P.L. 92-582, 86 Stat. 1278, 40 U.S. Code §§ 541 to 544

July 25, 1974, P.L. 93-356, 88 Stat. 390, 41 U.S. Code § 252

Aug. 30, 1974, P.L. 93-400, 40 U.S. Code §§ 474, 481, 487

Oct. 20, 1978, P.L. 95-491, 40 U.S. Code § 760

Oct. 24, 1978, P.L. 95-506, 40 U.S. Code § 491

July 30, 1979, P.L. 96-41, 40 U.S. Code § 485

Aug. 15, 1979, P.L. 96-60, 40 U.S. Code § 474

Oct. 10, 1979, P.L. 96-83, 40 U.S. Code §§ 481, 487

Dec. 1, 1983, P.L. 98-191, 41 U.S. Code §§ 252, 474, 481, 487

July 18, 1984, P.L. 98-369, 98 Stat. 1175 et seq., 40 U.S. Code § 759; 41 U.S. Code § 251 et seq.

Oct. 12, 1984, P.L. 98-473, 40 U.S. Code § 484

Oct. 30, 1984, P.L. 98-577, 41 U.S. Code §§ 253b, 253c, 253c nt., 253d to 243f, 253f nt.

Nov. 8, 1985, P.L. 99-145, 40 U.S. Code § 759; 41 U.S. Code §§ 253, 253c to 253g, 759

Oct. 18, 1986, P.L. 99-500, 40 U.S. Code §§ 751, 757, 759; 44 U.S. Code § 3504

July 22, 1987, P.L. 100-77, 40 U.S. Code § 484

Dec. 22, 1987, P.L. 100-202, 40 U.S. Code § 756

Jan. 8, 1988, P.L. 100-235, 40 U.S. Code § 759

Nov. 5, 1988, P.L. 100-612, 40 U.S. Code §§ 481, 484, 485, 488

Nov. 15, 1988, P.L. 100-656, 40 U.S. Code § 541

Nov. 17, 1988, P.L. 100-679, 40 U.S. Code § 541

Nov. 19, 1988, P.L. 100-700, 41 U.S. Code § 256

Aug. 9, 1989, P.L. 101-73, 40 U.S. Code § 474

Nov. 3, 1989, P.L. 101-136, 40 U.S. Code § 757

Nov. 5, 1990, P.L. 101-510, 40 U.S. Code § 485; 41 U.S. Code § 253

Oct. 24, 1992, P.L. 102-486, 40 U.S. Code § 490

Sept. 21, 1993, P.L. 103-82, 40 U.S. Code § 484

Oct. 28, 1993, P.L. 103-123, 40 U.S. Code § 485

Nov. 1, 1993, P.L. 103-160, 40 U.S. Code § 484

Oct. 13, 1994, P.L. 103-355, 40 U.S. Code §§ 759, 481, 541 nt.; 41 U.S. Code §§ 252a, 252b, 252c, 253, 253a, 253b, 253e, 253g, 253h, 253i, 253j, 253k, 253l, 254, 254b, 254c, 254d, 255, 256, 258, 259, 261, 262, 263, 264, 264a, 264b, 265, 266

Dec. 21, 1995, P.L. 104-66, 40 U.S. Code § 484

Feb. 10, 1996, P.L. 104-106, 40 U.S. Code §§ 485, 759; 41 U.S. Code §§ 253, 253a, 253b, 253m, 254b, 254d, 257, 264a, 265, 266

Sept. 23, 1996, P.L. 104-201, 40 U.S. Code § 490; 41 U.S. Code §§ 253b, 254d

Sept. 30, 1996, P.L. 104-208, 40 U.S. Code § 490

Oct. 19, 1996, P.L. 104-316, 40 U.S. Code § 490; 41 U.S. Code § 257

Oct. 19, 1996, P.L. 104-320, 41 U.S. Code § 253

July 18, 1997, P.L. 105-27, 40 U.S. Code § 484

Oct. 6, 1997, P.L. 105-50, 40 U.S. Code § 484

Oct. 10, 1997, P.L. 105-61, 40 U.S. Code § 481

Nov. 18, 1997, P.L. 105-85, 41 U.S. Code §§ 252c, 253, 256, 259, 263

Nov. 26, 1997, P.L. 105-119, 40 U.S. Code § 484

Oct. 17, 1998, P.L. 105-261, 41 U.S. Code §§ 254b, 256

Federal Property for Schools Act (Surplus)

Ill. Rev. Stat. 1991, Ch. 122, §§ 737.9, 738

Federal Property Management Improvement Act of 1988

Nov. 5, 1988, P.L. 100-612, 40 U.S. Code § 471 nt.

Federal Public Buildings Appropriation Act of 1938

June 21, 1938, Ch. 554, 52 Stat. 818

Federal Public Transportation Act of 1978

Nov. 6, 1978, P.L. 95-599, 15 U.S. Code § 1418; 49 U.S. Code §§ 1601 nt., 1062 et seq.

Federal Public Transportation Act of 1982

Jan. 6, 1983, P.L. 97-424, 49 U.S. Code §§ 1601 nt., 1601c, 1602, 1603, 1604, 1604a, 1607a, 1607a-1, 1607c, 1608, 1611, 1612, 1614, 1617, 1618

Federal Question Jurisdictional Amendments Act of 1980

Dec. 1, 1980, P.L. 96-486, 28 U.S. Code § 1 nt.

Federal Railroad Control Act

See Railroad Control Act

Federal Railroad Safety Act of 1970

Oct. 16, 1970, P.L. 91-458, 84 Stat. 971, 45 U.S. Code §§ 431 to 441

Aug. 14, 1973, P.L. 93-90, 87 Stat. 305, 45 U.S. Code § 441

Jan. 3, 1975, P.L. 93-633, 88 Stat. 2164 to 2166

July 19, 1975, P.L. 94-56, 89 Stat. 263, 45 U.S. Code §§ 440, 441

July 8, 1976, P.L. 94-348, 90 Stat. 817, 819

Nov. 2, 1978, P.L. 95-574, 45 U.S. Code §§ 436, 437, 441

Oct. 10, 1980, P.L. 96-423, 94 Stat. 1811 to 1817

Oct. 19, 1980, P.L. 96-470, 94 Stat. 2245

Aug. 13, 1981, P.L. 97-35, 95 Stat. 702

Jan. 14, 1983, P.L. 97-468, 96 Stat. 2580, 2581

June 22, 1988, P.L. 100-342, 102 Stat. 624, 45 U.S. Code §§ 431, 437, 438, 438 nt., 440, 441, 444, 445

Nov. 5, 1990, P.L. 101-508, 45 U.S. Code §§ 444, 447

Nov. 16, 1990, P.L. 101-615, 45 U.S. Code §§ 435, 436, 439

Oct. 28, 1991, P.L. 102-143, 45 U.S. Code § 431

Sept. 3, 1992, P.L. 102-365, 45 U.S. Code §§ 431, 438, 441, 444

Oct. 27, 1992, P.L. 102-533, 45 U.S. Code § 431

Federal Railroad Safety Authorization Act of 1973

Aug. 14, 1973, P.L. 93-90, 87 Stat. 305, 45 U.S. Code § 441; 49 U.S. Code § 1762

July 19, 1975, P.L. 94-56, 89 Stat. 263, 45 U.S. Code §§ 440, 441; 49 U.S. Code § 1812

Federal Railroad Safety Authorization Act of 1976

July 7, 1976, P.L. 94-348, 45 U.S. Code § 421 et seq.

Federal Railroad Safety Authorization Act of 1978

Nov. 2, 1978, P.L. 95-574, 45 U.S. Code §§ 6, 13, 34, 61, 63a, 63a nt., 421 nt., 436, 437, 440 nt., 441, 442; 49 U.S. Code § 26

Federal Railroad Safety Authorization Act of 1980

Oct. 10, 1980, P.L. 96-423, 43 U.S. Code § 975; 45 U.S. Code §§ 6, 29, 34, 64a, 421 nt., 431, 432, 435-439, 441, 443, 444; 49 U.S. Code Appx. § 26

Federal Railroad Safety Authorization Act of 1982

Jan. 14, 1983, P.L. 94-468, 45 U.S. Code §§ 13, 17 to 21, 421 nt., 431, 438, 444

Federal Railroad Safety Authorization Act of 1994

Nov. 2, 1994, P.L. 103-440, 49 U.S. Code § 20101 nt.

Federal Records Act of 1950

Sept. 5, 1950, Ch. 849, 64 Stat. 583 (See 44 U.S. Code Chs. 21, 25, 27, 29, 31)

Federal Register Act

July 26, 1935, Ch. 417, 49 Stat. 500 (See 44 U.S. Code §§ 1501 to 1511)

June 19, 1937, Ch. 369, 50 Stat. 304 (See 44 U.S. Code § 1510)

Dec. 10, 1942, Ch. 717, 56 Stat. 1045 (See 44 U.S. Code § 1510)

Aug. 5, 1953, Ch. 333, 67 Stat. 388 (See 44 U.S. Code § 1510)

Aug. 15, 1953, Ch. 510, 67 Stat. 614, 12 U.S. Code § 371

June 29, 1954, Ch. 422, 68 Stat. 329, 12 U.S. Code § 355

June 30, 1954, Ch. 434, 68 Stat. 358, 12 U.S. Code §§ 371c, 371d

July 19, 1954, Ch. 547, 68 Stat. 495, 12 U.S. Code § 413

July 22, 1954, Ch. 561, 68 Stat. 525, 12 U.S. Code § 371

Aug. 17, 1954, Ch. 751, 68 Stat. 736, 12 U.S. Code § 371

Aug. 11, 1955, Ch. 781, 69 Stat. 633, 12 U.S. Code § 371

June 25, 1956, Ch. 447, 70 Stat. 339, 12 U.S. Code § 355

June 25, 1959, P.L. 86-70, 73 Stat. 149 (See 44 U.S. Code § 1508)

July 12, 1960, P.L. 86-624, 74 Stat. 421 (See 44 U.S. Code § 1508)

Dec. 2, 1963, P.L. 88-190, 77 Stat. 343 (See 44 U.S. Code § 1510)

Federal Regulation of Lobbying Act

Aug. 2, 1946, Ch. 753, 60 Stat. 839, 2 U.S. Code §§ 261, 262 to 270

Dec. 19, 1995, P.L. 104-65, 2 U.S. Code §§ 261, 262, 270

Federal Removal Act (Suits)

See Removal of Causes Act

Federal Reports Act of 1942

Dec. 24, 1942, Ch. 811, 56 Stat. 1078 (See 44 U.S. Code §§ 3501 to 3511)

Federal Reports Elimination Act of 1998

Nov. 10, 1998, P.L. 105-362, 112 Stat. 3280

Federal Reports Elimination and Sunset Act of 1995

Dec. 21, 1995, P.L. 104-66, 109 Stat. 707

Federal Research Committee Act

Utah Code Ann. 1953, Miscellaneous Superseded Code Provisions, 63-33-9 et seq.

Federal Reserve Acts

Dec. 23, 1913, Ch. 6, 38 Stat. 251, (See 12 U.S. Code generally); 31 U.S. Code § 409

Aug. 15, 1914, Ch. 252, 38 Stat. 691, 12 U.S. Code §§ 142, 374, 463 to 466

March 3, 1915, Ch. 93, 38 Stat. 958, 12 U.S. Code §§ 345 to 347, 372

Sept. 7, 1916, Ch. 461, 39 Stat. 752, 12 U.S. Code §§ 82, 92, 342, 343, 345 to 347, 358, 361, 371 to 373, 412, 601 to 605

June 21, 1917, Ch. 32, 40 Stat. 232, 12 U.S. Code §§ 142, 305, 306, 321 to 331, 358, 372, 374 to 376, 412 to 416, 461 to 467, 503, 521, 593 to 595

March 3, 1919, Ch. 101, 40 Stat. 1314, 12 U.S. Code §§ 104, 242, 531

Dec. 24, 1919, Ch. 18, 41 Stat. 378, 12 U.S. Code §§ 611 to 631

April 13, 1920, Ch. 128, 41 Stat. 550, 12 U.S. Code § 357

Feb. 27, 1921, Ch. 73, 41 Stat. 1145, 12 U.S. Code § 611

June 14, 1921, Ch. 22, 42 Stat. 28, 12 U.S. Code § 618

March 4, 1923, Ch. 252, 42 Stat. 1478, 12 U.S. Code §§ 329, 343, 344, 346 to 352, 357, 359, 393

March 1, 1937, Ch. 20, 50 Stat. 23, 12 U.S. Code § 412 nt.

April 25, 1938, Ch. 173, 52 Stat. 223, 12 U.S. Code § 375a

May 25, 1938, Ch. 276, 52 Stat. 442, 12 U.S. Code § 2641 (7)

April 7, 1941, Ch. 43, 55 Stat. 131, 12 U.S. Code §§ 358, 632

June 30, 1941, Ch. 264, 55 Stat. 395, 12 U.S. Code § 412

March 27, 1942, Ch. 199, 56 Stat. 180, 12 U.S. Code § 355; 50 U.S. Code Appx. prec. § 634)

July 7, 1942, Ch. 488, 56 Stat. 647, 12 U.S. Code §§ 263 (a), 462b, 464

April 13, 1943, Ch. 62, 57 Stat. 65, 12 U.S. Code §§ 264 (h) (1), 462a-1

May 25, 1943, Ch. 102, 57 Stat. 85, 12 U.S. Code § 412

June 12, 1945, Ch. 186, §§ 1 to 3, 59 Stat. 237, 12 U.S. Code §§ 248, 412 to 414

Aug. 14, 1946, Ch. 964, 60 Stat. 1072, 12 U.S. Code § 371

April 28, 1947, Ch. 44, 61 Stat. 56, 12 U.S. Code § 355

July 30, 1947, Ch. 352, 61 Stat. 520, 12 U.S. Code § 522

Aug. 5, 1947, Ch. 492, 61 Stat. 773, 12 U.S. Code § 264

May 25, 1948, Ch. 334, 62 Stat. 265, 12 U.S. Code § 371

Aug. 16, 1948, Ch. 836, 62 Stat. 1291, 12 U.S. Code § 462c

Oct. 25, 1949, Ch. 729, 63 Stat. 906, 12 U.S. Code § 371

April 20, 1950, Ch. 94, 64 Stat. 80, 12 U.S. Code § 371

June 30, 1950, Ch. 425, 64 Stat. 307, 12 U.S. Code § 355

Aug. 17, 1950, Ch. 729, 64 Stat. 307, 12 U.S. Code §§ 264, 321

Sept. 1, 1951, Ch. 378, 65 Stat. 303, 12 U.S. Code § 371

June 23, 1952, Ch. 454, 66 Stat. 154, 12 U.S. Code § 355

July 15, 1952, Ch. 753, 66 Stat. 633, 12 U.S. Code §§ 36, 321, 329

May 29, 1953, Ch. 87, 67 Stat. 41, 12 U.S. Code § 522

June 30, 1958, P.L. 85-476, 72 Stat. 261, 12 U.S. Code § 355

July 7, 1958, P.L. 85-508, 72 Stat. 350, 12 U.S. Code § 222

July 18, 1958, P.L. 85-536, 72 Stat. 396, 12 U.S. Code § 371

Mar 18, 1959, P.L. 86-3, 73 Stat. 12, 12 U.S. Code § 222

June 25, 1959, P.L. 86-70, 73 Stat. 142, 12 U.S. Code §§ 221, 466

July 28, 1959, P.L. 86-114, 73 Stat. 263, 12 U.S. Code §§ 462, 462b

Sept. 8, 1959, P.L. 86-230, 73 Stat. 457, 12 U.S. Code § 371c

Sept. 9, 1959, P.L. 86-251, 73 Stat. 488, 12 U.S. Code §§ 248, 371

July 1, 1960, P.L. 86-567, 74 Stat. 295, 12 U.S. Code § 355

June 30, 1961, P.L. 87-66, 75 Stat. 147, 12 U.S. Code §§ 415, 416

June 30, 1961, P.L. 87-70, 75 Stat. 188, 12 U.S. Code § 371

Oct. 4, 1961, P.L. 87-353, 75 Stat. 773, 12 U.S. Code §§ 347, 355

June 28, 1962, P.L. 87-506, 75 Stat. 112, 12 U.S. Code § 355

Aug. 15, 1962, P.L. 87-588, 76 Stat. 388, 12 U.S. Code § 604a

Aug. 31, 1962, P.L. 87-622, 76 Stat. 418, 12 U.S. Code §§ 521, 522

Sept. 28, 1962, P.L. 87-717, 76 Stat. 662, 12 U.S. Code § 371

Sept. 28, 1962, P.L. 87-722, 76 Stat. 670, 12 U.S. Code § 248

Oct. 15, 1962, P.L. 87-827, 76 Stat. 953, 12 U.S. Code § 371b

June 4, 1963, P.L. 88-36, 77 Stat. 54, 12 U.S. Code § 418

June 30, 1964, P.L. 88-341, 78 Stat. 233, 12 U.S. Code § 371

June 30, 1964, P.L. 88-344, 78 Stat. 235, 12 U.S. Code § 355

Sept. 2, 1964, P.L. 88-560, 78 Stat. 807, 12 U.S. Code § 371

March 3, 1965, P.L. 89-3, 79 Stat. 5, 12 U.S. Code §§ 413, 467

July 21, 1965, P.L. 89-79, 79 Stat. 244, 12 U.S. Code § 371b

Continued

Aug. 10, 1965, P.L. 89-117, 79 Stat. 461, 12 U.S. Code § 371

May 20, 1966, P.L. 89-427, 80 Stat. 161, 12 U.S. Code §§ 248, 413

June 30, 1966, P.L. 89-484, 80 Stat. 235, 12 U.S. Code § 355

July 1, 1966, P.L. 89-485, 80 Stat. 241, 12 U.S. Code §§ 304, 334, 371c, 601

Sept. 21, 1966, P.L. 89-597, 80 Stat. 823, 12 U.S. Code §§ 355, 371a, 371b, 374, 374a, 461, 463 to 466

Nov. 3, 1966, P.L. 89-754, 80 Stat. 1277, 12 U.S. Code § 371

Nov. 5, 1966, P.L. 89-765, 80 Stat. 1314, 12 U.S. Code § 248

May 25, 1967, P.L. 90-19, 81 Stat. 28, 12 U.S. Code § 371

July 3, 1967, P.L. 90-44, 81 Stat. 109, 12 U.S. Code § 375a

Dec. 15, 1967, P.L. 90-203, 81 Stat. 609, 12 U.S. Code § 339

March 18, 1968, P.L. 90-269, 82 Stat. 50, 12 U.S. Code §§ 248, 391, 413 to 416, 467

May 4, 1968, P.L. 90-300, 82 Stat. 113, 12 U.S. Code § 355

June 19, 1968, P.L. 90-349, 82 Stat. 189, 12 U.S. Code §§ 412, 415, 417, 467

Aug. 1, 1968, P.L. 90-448, 82 Stat. 518, 12 U.S. Code § 371

Sept. 21, 1968, P.L. 90-505, 82 Stat. 856, 12 U.S. Code §§ 347, 347c, 371b

Dec. 23, 1969, P.L. 91-151, 83 Stat. 374, 12 U.S. Code § 461

July 24, 1970, P.L. 91-351, 84 Stat. 462, 12 U.S. Code § 371

July 31, 1970, P.L. 91-360, 84 Stat. 668, 12 U.S. Code § 355

Dec. 31, 1970, P.L. 91-609, 84 Stat. 1803, 12 U.S. Code § 371

July 2, 1971, P.L. 92-45, 85 Stat. 100, 12 U.S. Code § 355

Nov. 12, 1975, P.L. 94-125, 89 Stat. 678, 12 U.S. Code § 355

April 19, 1977, P.L. 95-22, 12 U.S. Code § 355

Oct. 12, 1977, P.L. 95-128, 12 U.S. Code § 355

Nov. 7, 1977, P.L. 95-154, 12 U.S. Code § 355

Nov. 16, 1977, P.L. 95-188, 12 U.S. Code § 225a et seq.

March 27, 1978, P.L. 95-251, 12 U.S. Code § 248

Sept. 17, 1978, P.L. 95-369, 12 U.S. Code §§ 347d, 611a, 611a nt., 614 et seq.

Oct. 27, 1978, P.L. 95-523, 12 U.S. Code §§ 225a, 225a nt.

Oct. 27, 1978, P.L. 95-534, 12 U.S. Code § 355

Nov. 10, 1978, P.L. 95-630, 12 U.S. Code §§ 226 nt., 375a, 375b, 412, 504, 505

June 8, 1979, P.L. 96-18, 12 U.S. Code §§ 355, 355 nt., 359a

Nov. 5, 1979, P.L. 96-104, 12 U.S. Code § 371b-1

Dec. 28, 1979, P.L. 96-161, 12 U.S. Code §§ 371a, 371b-1

March 31, 1980, P.L. 96-221, 12 U.S. Code §§ 226 nt., 248, 461

Oct. 8, 1982, P.L. 97-290, 12 U.S. Code § 372

Oct. 15, 1982, P.L. 97-320, 12 U.S. Code §§ 371, 371 nt., 375a, 375b, 461, 501, 504, 505

Jan. 12, 1983, P.L. 97-457, 12 U.S. Code §§ 248, 371c

Aug. 10, 1987, P.L. 100-86, 12 U.S. Code §§ 248a, 248a nt., 371c-1, 619, 619 nt.

Aug. 23, 1988, P.L. 100-418, 102 Stat. 1375, 12 U.S. Code § 225a

Aug. 9, 1989, P.L. 101-73, 12 U.S. Code §§ 248, 324, 461, 504, 505, 506

Dec. 19, 1991, P.L. 102-242, 12 U.S. Code §§ 191, 248, 330, 343, 347a, 347b, 348-352, 371b-2, 375b, 611 et seq.

Oct. 23, 1992, P.L. 102-485, 12 U.S. Code § 338a

Oct. 24, 1992, P.L. 102-491, 12 U.S. Code § 522

Oct. 28, 1992, P.L. 102-550, 12 U.S. Code § 375b

Aug. 10, 1993, P.L. 103-66, 12 U.S. Code §§ 289, 290, 531

Sept. 23, 1994, P.L. 103-325, 12 U.S. Code §§ 248, 289, 341, 375a, 375b, 418, 419, 420, 421, 445, 633

Sept. 30, 1996, P.L. 104-208, 12 U.S. Code §§ 338a, 347b, 371d, 375b, 618

Federal Reserve Bank Branch Modernization Act

Oct. 24, 1992, P.L. 102-491, 12 U.S. Code § 226 nt., 522

Federal Reserve Note Security Act

March 6, 1934, Ch. 47, 48 Stat. 398, 12 U.S. Code § 412

Federal Reserve Reform Act of 1977

Nov. 16, 1977, P.L. 95-188, 12 U.S. Code § 225a et seq.; 18 U.S. Code § 208

Federal Retiree Refund Act

Ga. Code Ann., 48-2-101 et seq.

Federal Revenue Sharing Act (National Forest Revenues for National Forest Road and Trail Expenditures)

March 4, 1913, Ch. 145, 37 Stat. 845, 16 U.S. Code § 501

Sept. 21, 1944, Ch. 412, 58 Stat. 737, 16 U.S. Code § 501

Federal Revenue Sharing Act (National Forest Revenues for Public School and Road Expenditures)

May 23, 1908, Ch. 192, 35 Stat. 260, 16 U.S. Code § 500

March 1, 1911, Ch. 186, 36 Stat. 963, 16 U.S. Code § 500

June 30, 1914, Ch. 131, 38 Stat. 441, 16 U.S. Code § 500

Sept. 21, 1944, Ch. 412, 58 Stat. 737, 16 U.S. Code § 500

April 24, 1950, Ch. 97, 64 Stat. 87, 16 U.S. Code § 500

Federal Revenue Sharing Trust Fund Supplement to the General Appropriation Acts

Pa. 1974 Pamph. Laws 1334, No. 4A

Pa. 1974 Pamph. Laws 1418, No. 25A

Pa. 1975 Pamph. Laws 648, No. 7A

Pa. 1976 Pamph. Laws 1327, No. 6A

Pa. 1978 Pamph. Laws 1444, No. 6-A

Pa. 1978 Pamph. Laws 1581, No. 48-A

Pa. 1979 Pamph. Laws 722, No. 13-A

Federal Rules of Civil Procedure Amendments Act of 1982

Jan. 12, 1983, P.L. 97-462, 28 U.S. Code § 2071 nt.

Federal Rules of Evidence

Oct. 16, 1975, P.L. 94-113, 89 Stat. 576, 28 U.S. Code Appx. Rule 801

Federal Rules of Evidence and Criminal Procedure Amendments

Dec. 12, 1975, P.L. 94-149, 89 Stat. 805, 18 U.S. Code §§ 3491, 3492, 3771 nt.; 28 U.S. Code § 2076; 28 U.S. Code Appx. Rule 410, 606, 893 804, 1101

Federal Safety Appliance Act

See Safety Appliance Act (Interstate Commerce)

Federal Salary Act of 1967

Dec. 16, 1967, P.L. 90-206, 81 Stat. 624, 2 U.S. Code §§ 60e-14, 60j, 61-1, 61-2, 74a-2, 136a, 136a-1, 293c, 351 to 361; 3 U.S. Code § 102 nt.; 5 U.S. Code §§ 3110, 4101, 5303, 5304 nt., 5314 to 5316, 5332, 5345, 5533, 5542, 5544, 5545, 5733, 8339, 8704 nt.; 16 U.S. Code § 590h nt.;22 U.S. Code §§ 867, 870; 28 U.S. Code §§ 548 nt., 603, 604 nt., 753 nt., 792; 31 U.S. Code §§ 42a, 51a; 38 U.S. Code § 4107; 40 U.S. Code §§ 162a, 166b, 166b-1, 166b-3

Nov. 6, 1978, P.L. 95-598, 2 U.S. Code § 356

Dec. 23, 1985, P.L. 99-190, 2 U.S. Code §§ 352, 356, 357-360

July 2, 1986, P.L. 99-349, 100 Stat. 749

Aug. 22, 1986, P.L. 99-386, 40 U.S. Code § 484

Oct. 30, 1986, P.L. 99-591, 40 U.S. Code §§ 751, 757, 759; 44 U.S. Code § 3504

Nov. 7, 1986, P.L. 99-627, 40 U.S. Code § 512

Dec. 22, 1987, P.L. 100-202, 2 U.S. Code § 356

Nov. 30, 1989, P.L. 101-194, 2 U.S. Code §§ 351-353, 356-360, 362-364

Federal Salary and Fringe Benefits Act of 1966

July 18, 1966, P.L. 89-504, 80 Stat. 288, 2 U.S. Code §§ 60a nt. 60f nt., 293b; 16 U.S. Code § 590h nt.; 22 U.S. Code §§ 867, 870; 28 U.S. Code §§ 548 nt., 603 nt., 604 nt., 753 nt.; 38 U.S. Code § 4107

Federal Salary Reform Act of 1962

Oct. 11, 1962, P.L. 87-793, 76 Stat. 841, 2 U.S. Code §§ 60a nt., 60e-10, 60f nt.; See 5 U.S. Code §§ 3104, 3325, 5108, 5301 to 5304, 5332 to 5338, 5361, 8331; 7 U.S. Code § 1857; 10 U.S. Code §§ 1581,3535 nt.; 16 U.S. Code §§ 590h nt., 742b; 21 U.S. Code § 113a; 22 U.S. Code §§ 290a, 867, 870, 1017, 2385, 2454, 2506; 28 U.S. Code §§ 508, 603 nt., 604 nt., 753 nt.; 38 U.S. Code §§ 4103, 4107, 4108, 4111; 42 U.S. Code §§ 210, 2201, 2473, 2521; 49 U.S. Code § 1343; 50 U.S. Code § 402 nt.

Aug. 14, 1964, P.L. 88-426, 78 Stat. 412 (See 5 U.S. Code § 5303)

Federal Savings and Loan Insurance Corporation Recapitalization Act of 1987

Aug. 10, 1987, P.L. 100-86, 12 U.S. Code §§ 226 nt., 1430, 1436, 1441, 1725, 1727, 1730 nt.; 31 U.S. Code § 9101

Federal Security Agency Appropriation Acts

June 26, 1940, Ch. 428, 54 Stat. 580; 16 U.S. Code §§ 584h-1, 584n-1; 29 U.S. Code § 31; 42 U.S. Code. § 1301a

July 1, 1941, Ch. 269, 55 Stat. 471, 16 U.S. Code §§ 584f-1, 584n- 1; 21 U.S. Code § 46a; 24 U.S. Code § 169

July 2, 1942, Ch. 475, 56 Stat. 569, 16 U.S. Code §§ 584 nt., 584nnt.; 24 U.S. Code § 169

July 12, 1943, Ch. 221, 57 Stat. 498

June 28, 1944, Ch. 302, 58 Stat. 552, 24 U.S. Code § 169, 41 U.S. Code § 6a nt.; 42 U.S. Code § 207 nt.

July 3, 1945, Ch. 263, 59 Stat. 365, 24 U.S. Code § 169; 41 U.S. Code § 6a nt.; 42 U.S. Code §§ 209c, 231

July 26, 1946, Ch. 672, 60 Stat. 687, 24 U.S. Code § 169; 41 U.S. Code § 6a nt.

July 8, 1947, Ch. 210, 61 Stat. 260, 24 U.S. Code § 169; 41 U.S. Code § 6a nts.; 42 U.S. Code §§ 703a, 704a

June 14, 1948, Ch. 465, 62 Stat. 396, 41 U.S. Code § 6a nt.

June 29, 1949, Ch. 275, 63 Stat. 284, 41 U.S. Code § 6a nt.; 42 U.S. Code §§ 703a, 704a

Oct. 26, 1949, Ch. 722, 63 Stat. 898

Sept. 6, 1950, Ch. 896, 64 Stat. 645, 42 U.S. Code §§ 703a, 704a

Aug. 31, 1951, Ch. 373, 65 Stat. 212, 42 U.S. Code § 703a

July 5, 1952, Ch. 575, 66 Stat. 361, 42 U.S. Code §§ 703a, 704a, 704b, 905

Sept. 2, 1960, P.L. 86-703, 74 Stat. 773, 42 U.S. Code § 905

Jan. 4, 1983, P.L. 97-414, 42 U.S. Code § 231

Federal Seed Act

Aug. 9, 1939, Ch. 615, 53 Stat. 1275, 7 U.S. Code §§ 1551 to 1618

Sept. 21, 1944, Ch. 412, 58 Stat. 741, 7 U.S. Code § 1605

July 9, 1956, Ch. 520; 70 Stat. 508, 7 U.S. Code §§ 1574, 1596, 1602

Aug. 1, 1956, Ch. 852, 70 Stat. 908, 7 U.S. Code § 1561

Aug. 1, 1958, P.L. 85-581, 72 Stat. 476, 7 U.S. Code §§ 1561, 1562, 1571 to 1574, 1581, 1582, 1586

Aug. 28, 1958, P.L. 85-791, 72 Stat. 949, 7 U.S. Code § 1599 to 1601

June 11, 1960, P.L. 86-507, 74 Stat. 200, 7 U.S. Code § 1599

Oct. 15, 1966, P.L. 89-686, 80 Stat. 975, 7 U.S. Code §§ 1561, 1571 to 1573, 1581, 1582, 1584

Oct. 17, 1969, P.L. 91-89, 83 Stat. 134, 7 U.S. Code §§ 1561, 1562

Dec. 24, 1970, P.L. 91-577, 84 Stat. 1558, 7 U.S. Code §§ 1562, 1611

Dec. 22, 1981, P.L. 97-98, 95 Stat. 1272, 7 U.S. Code § 1611

Jan. 8, 1983, P.L. 97-439, 96 Stat. 2287, 7 U.S. Code §§ 1561, 1571, 1581 to 1586

Dec. 8, 1993, P.L. 103-182, 7 U.S. Code § 1582

Dec. 8, 1994, P.L. 103-465, 7 U.S. Code §§ 1581, 1582, 1585, 1586

Federal Seed Act Amendments of 1982

Jan. 8, 1983, P.L. 97-439, 7 U.S. Code §§ 1551 nt., 1561, 1571, 1581, 1583 to 1586

Federal Ship Financing Act of 1972
Oct. 10, 1972, P.L. 92-507, 86 Stat. 909, 46 U.S. Code §§ 1177 nt., 1271 to 1276

Federal Ship Mortgage Insurance Act
Sept. 28, 1950, Ch. 1093, 64 Stat. 1078, 46 U.S. Code § 1274

Federal Sick Leave Act
March 14, 1936, Ch. 141, 49 Stat. 1162 (See 5 U.S. Code Ch. 63)
March 2, 1940, Ch. 33, 54 Stat. 38 (See 5 U.S. Code § 6302)

Federal Social Security Enabling Act
Iowa Code Ann., 97C.1 et seq.

Federal-State Communications Joint Board Act
Sept. 30, 1971, P.L. 92-131, 85 Stat. 363, 47 U.S. Code § 410(c)

Federal-State Extended Unemployment Compensation Act of 1970
Aug. 10, 1970, P.L. 91-373, 84 Stat. 708, 26 U.S. Code § 3304
Oct. 27, 1972, P.L. 92-599, 86 Stat. 1326, 26 U.S. Code §§ 3504, 3504 nt.
July 1, 1973, P.L. 93-53, 87 Stat. 137, 26 U.S. Code § 3304 nt.
Dec. 31, 1973, P.L. 93-233, 87 Stat. 974, 26 U.S. Code § 3304 nt.
March 28, 1974, P.L. 93-256, 88 Stat. 53, 26 U.S. Code § 3384 nt.
June 30, 1974, P.L. 93-329, 88 Stat. 288, 26 U.S. Code § 3304 nt.
Aug. 7, 1974, P.L. 93-368, 88 Stat. 420, 26 U.S. Code § 3304 nt.
July 3, 1992, P.L. 102-318, 26 U.S. Code § 3304 nt.

Federal-State Tax Collection Act of 1972
Oct. 20, 1972, P.L. 92-512, 86 Stat. 936, 26 U.S. Code §§ 6361 to 6365, 6405, 7463

Federal Supplemental Appropriation Act
Pa. 1978 Pamph. Laws 1664, No. 62-A

Federal Supplemental Compensation Act of 1982
Oct. 24, 1983, P.L. 98-135, 26 U.S. Code § 3304 nt.
April 4, 1985, P.L. 99-15, 26 U.S. Code § 3304 nt.

Federal Supplemental Compensation Amendments of 1983
Oct. 24, 1983, P.L. 98-135, 26 U.S. Code § 3304 nt.

Federal Surplus Property Acquisition Act
Cal. Government Code § 54140 et seq.

Federal Surplus Property Act
Ill. Rev. Stat. 1991, Ch. 127, § 176d et seq.

Federal Tax Lien Act of 1966
Nov. 2, 1966, P.L. 89-719, 80 Stat. 1125, 26 U.S. Code §§ 545, 3505, 6322 to 6325, 6331, 6332, 6334, 6335, 6337, 6338, 6339, 6342, 6343, 6502, 6503 and others; 28 U.S. Code §§ 1346, 1402, 2410; 40 U.S. Code § 270a

Federal Tax Lien Registration Act
See also Revised Uniform Federal Tax Lien Registration Act
See also Uniform Federal Tax Lien Registration Act
Cal. Government Code § 7200 et seq., § 27330 et seq.
Haw. Rev. Stat. Ann., § 505-1 et seq.
Ind. Code Ann., 36-2-11-21 et seq.
Mich. Comp. Laws Ann., 211.671 et seq.
Mo. Rev. Stat., 14.010 et seq.
N.Y. Lien Law (Consol. Laws Ch. 33) § 240 et seq.
Ore. Rev. Stat., 87.806 et seq.

Federal Tax Lien Registration Act (Revised)
See Revised Uniform Federal Tax Lien Registration Act

Federal Tea Tasters Repeal Act of 1996
April 9, 1996, P.L. 104-128, 21 U.S. Code § 41 nt.

Federal Technology Transfer Act of 1986

Oct. 20, 1986, P.L. 99-502, 15 U.S. Code § 3701 nt.

Federal Timber Contract Payment Modification Act

Oct. 16, 1984, P.L. 98-478, 16 U.S. Code §§ 539, 618, 619

Federal Tort Claims Act

See Tort Claims Act

Aug. 2, 1946, Ch. 753, 60 Stat. 842 (See 28 U.S. Code §§ 1291, 1346(b), (c), 1402(b), 1504, 3110, 2401(b), 2402, 2411(b), 2412(c), 2671 to 2680

Aug. 1, 1947, Ch. 446, 61 Stat. 722 (See 28 U.S. Code §§ 1346, 1402, 2402, 2411, 2412, 2674, 2675, 2676)

June 25, 1948, Ch. 646, 62 Stat. 929, 28 U.S. Code §§ 1291, 1346(b), (c), 1402(b), 1504, 2110, 2401(b), 2402, 2411(b), 2412(c), 2671 to 2680

April 25, 1949, Ch. 92, 63 Stat. 62, 28 U.S. Code §§ 1346(b), 2401(b), 2672

May 24, 1949, Ch. 139, 63 Stat. 101, 28 U.S. Code §§ 1346(b), 2110, 2671, 2672, 2675

July 16, 1949, Ch. 340, 63 Stat. 444, 28 U.S. Code § 2680

Sept. 23, 1950, Ch. 1010, 64 Stat. 987, 28 U.S. Code § 2672

Sept. 26, 1950, Ch. 1049, 64 Stat. 1038, 28 U.S. Code § 2680

July 7, 1958, P.L. 85-508, 72 Stat. 348, 28 U.S. Code § 1346(b)

Aug. 18, 1959, P.L. 86-168, 73 Stat. 389, 28 U.S. Code § 2680

Sept. 8, 1959, P.L. 86-238, 73 Stat. 471, 28 U.S. Code §§ 2672, 2401(b)

Sept. 21, 1961, P.L. 87-258, 75 Stat. 539, 28 U.S. Code § 2679

July 18, 1966, P.L. 89-506, 80 Stat. 306-308

March 16, 1974, P.L. 93-252, 88 Stat. 50

Dec. 29, 1981, P.L. 97-124, 95 Stat. 1666

Federal Trade Commission Act

Sept. 26, 1914, Ch. 311, 38 Stat. 717, 15 U.S. Code §§ 41 to 51

May 12, 1933, Ch. 25, 48 Stat. 31, 7 U.S. Code § 610

March 21, 1938, Ch. 49, 52 Stat. 111, 15 U.S. Code §§ 41, 44, 45, 52 to 58

March 16, 1950, Ch. 61, 64 Stat. 21, 15 U.S. Code §§ 45, 55

July 14, 1952, Ch. 745, 66 Stat. 632, 15 U.S. Code §§ 45, 45 nt.

Aug. 23, 1958, P.L. 85-726, 72 Stat. 809, 15 U.S. Code § 45

Aug. 28, 1958, P.L. 85-791, 72 Stat. 942, 15 U.S. Code § 45

Sept. 2, 1958, P.L. 85-909, 72 Stat. 1750, 15 U.S. Code § 45

June 11, 1960, P.L. 86-507, 74 Stat. 200, 15 U.S. Code § 45

Oct. 15, 1970, P.L. 91-452, 84 Stat. 929, 15 U.S. Code § 49

Nov. 16, 1973, P.L. 93-153,

Sept. 20, 1977, P.L. 95-109, 15 U.S. Code § 1692l

July 23, 1979, P.L. 96-37, 15 U.S. Code §§ 45, 46, 57a

May 28, 1980, P.L. 96-252, 15 U.S. Code § 45 et seq.

Oct. 6, 1982, P.L. 97-290, 15 U.S. Code § 45(a)(3)

Nov. 8, 1984, P.L. 98-620, 15 U.S. Code § 45

Aug. 10, 1987, P.L. 100-86, 15 U.S. Code §§ 45, 46, 57a

Aug. 9, 1989, P.L. 101-73, 15 U.S. Code § 57a

Dec. 19, 1991, P.L. 102-242, 15 U.S. Code §§ 44, 57a

Oct. 28, 1992, P.L. 102-550, 15 U.S. Code § 57a

Aug. 26, 1994, P.L. 103-312, 15 U.S. Code §§ 45, 53, 57a, 57b-1, 57b-2, 57c, 58

Nov. 2, 1994, P.L. 103-437, 15 U.S. Code §§ 46, 57a

Nov. 2, 1994, P.L. 103-438, 15 U.S. Code §§ 46, 57b-1

Oct. 1, 1996, P.L. 104-216, 15 U.S. Code § 57c

Federal Trade Commission Act Amendments of 1994

Aug. 26, 1994, P.L. 103-312, 15 U.S. Code § 58 nt.

Federal Trade Commission Improvements Act of 1980

May 28, 1980, P.L. 96-252, 15 U.S. Code § 45 et seq.

Nov. 8, 1984, P.L. 98-620, 15 U.S. Code § 57a-1

Federal Trade Commission Reauthorization Act of 1996

Oct. 1, 1996, P.L. 104-216, 15 U.S. Code § 58 nt.

Federal Trademark Dilution Act of 1995

Jan. 16, 1996, P.L. 104-98, 15 U.S. Code § 1051 nt.

Federal Transit Act

See also Urban Mass Transportation Act of 1964

Dec. 18, 1991, P.L. 102-240, 49 U.S. Code Appx. § 1601 nt.

Sept. 23, 1992, P.L. 102-368, 49 U.S. Code Appx. § 1607c

Oct. 6, 1992, P.L. 102-388, 49 U.S. Code Appx. §§ 1602, 1607, 1608, 1612, 1614, 1617, 1622

Federal Transit Act Amendments of 1991

Dec. 18, 1991, P.L. 102-240, 49 U.S. Code Appx. §§ 1601 et seq., 1601 nt.

Federal Transit Act of 1998

June 9, 1998, P.L. 105-178, Title III, 49 U.S. Code § 5101 nt.

July 22, 1998, P.L. 105-206, 23 U.S. Code §§ 138 nt., 322 nt.; 49 U.S. Code §§ 5301 nt., 5302, 5303, 5304, 5305, 5307, 5307 nt., 5308, 5309, 5309 nt., 5310 nt., 5315, 5320, 5325, 5328, 5337, 5338, 5338 nt.

Federal Triangle Development Act

Aug. 21, 1987, P.L. 100-113, 40 U.S. Code §§ 1101 nt., 1101 to 1109

Oct. 21, 1998, P.L. 105-277, 40 U.S. Code § 1106

Federal Unemployment Tax Act

Oct. 22, 1986, P.L. 99-514, 26 U.S. Code §§ 3302, 3306

Federal Unemployment Tax Act of 1939

Feb. 10, 1939, Ch. 2, 53 Stat. 183 (See 26 U.S. Code §§ 3301 to 3308)

Aug. 10, 1939, Ch. 666, 53 Stat. 1381

Feb. 25, 1944, Ch. 63, 58 Stat. 76

Dec. 29, 1945, Ch. 652, 59 Stat. 670

Aug. 10, 1946, Ch. 951, 60 Stat. 989

July 24, 1947, Ch. 309, 61 Stat. 416

Aug. 5, 1954, Ch. 657, § 4, 68 Stat. 672

Federal Unemployment Tax Act of 1954

Aug. 16, 1954, Ch. 736, 68A Stat. 439, 26 U.S. Code §§ 3301 to 3308

Sept. 1, 1954, Ch. 1212, 68 Stat. 1130, 26 U.S. Code §§ 3303, 3305, 3306

May 29, 1963, P.L. 88-31, 77 Stat. 51, 26 U.S. Code §§ 3301, 3302

Dec. 20, 1977, P.L. 95-246, 26 U.S. Code § 3304

Federal Unfunded Mandates Act

Miss. Code Ann. 1972, §§ 5-3-73, 5-3-79

Federal Urban Land-Use Act

Oct. 16, 1968, P.L. 90-577, 82 Stat. 1104, 40 U.S. Code §§ 531 to 535

Federal Vacancies Reform Act of 1998

Oct. 21, 1998, P.L. 105-277, Division C, § 151, 112 Stat. 2681, 5 U.S. Code § 3301 nt.

Federal Vocational Education Act

Miss. Code Ann. 1972, § 37-33-157

Federal Voting Assistance Act of 1955

Aug. 9, 1955, Ch. 656, 69 Stat. 584

June 18, 1968, P.L. 90-343, 82 Stat. 180, 50 U.S. Code §§ 1451, 1464

June 18, 1968, P.L. 90-344, 82 Stat. 181, 50 U.S. Code §§ 1452, 1454, 1463, 1464

Nov. 4, 1978, P.L. 95-593, 42 U.S. Code §§ 1973cc, 1973cc-12 to 1973cc-14

Dec. 21, 1982, P.L. 97-375, 42 U.S. Code § 1973cc-11

Aug. 28, 1986, P.L. 99-410, 42 U.S. Code § 1973cc et seq.

Federal Voting Rights Compliance Act

See Uniform Federal Voting Rights Compliance Act

Federal Water Pollution Control Act

June 30, 1948, Ch. 758, 33 U.S. Code § 1251 et seq.

July 17, 1952, Ch. 927, 66 Stat. 755

June 25, 1959, P.L. 86-70, 73 Stat. 148, 33 U.S. Code §§ 1157, 1173

July 12, 1960, P.L. 86-624, 74 Stat. 417, 33 U.S. Code §§ 1157, 1173

July 20, 1961, P.L. 87-88, 75 Stat. 204 (See 33 U.S. Code §§ 1151 et seq.)

July 9, 1965, Ch. 518, 70 Stat. 498 (See 33 U.S. Code § 1151 et seq.)

Oct. 2, 1965, P.L. 89-234, 79 Stat. 903 (See 33 U.S. Code §§ 1151 et seq.)

Nov. 3, 1966, P.L. 89-753, 80 Stat. 1246 (See 33 U.S. Code § 1151 et seq.)

Apr 3, 1970, P.L. 91-224, 84 Stat. 91, 33 U.S. Code §§ 1152, 1155, 1156, 1158, 1160 to 1175

Dec. 31, 1970, P.L. 91-611, 84 Stat. 1823, 33 U.S. Code § 1161

July 9, 1971, P.L. 92-50, 85 Stat. 124, 33 U.S. Code §§ 1157, 1158

March 1, 1972, P.L. 92-240, 86 Stat. 47, 33 U.S. Code §§ 1155, 1157, 1158

Oct. 18, 1972, P.L. 92-240, 86 Stat. 816, 33 U.S. Code §§ 1151 nt., 1251 to 1265, 1281 to 1292, 1311 to 1328, 1341 to 1345, 1361 to 1376

Dec. 28, 1973, P.L. 93-207, 87 Stat. 906, 33 U.S. Code §§ 1254, 1286, 1287, 1321, 1325, 1369

Jan. 2, 1974, P.L. 93-243, 87 Stat. 1069, 33 U.S. Code §§ 1283, 1285, 1371, 1375

Dec. 27, 1977, P.L. 95-217, 33 U.S. Code §§ 1251 nt., 1254 et seq.

Nov. 2, 1978, P.L. 95-576, 33 U.S. Code §§ 1254, 1321

Oct. 19, 1982, P.L. 97-357, 33 U.S. Code § 1282

Jan. 8, 1983, P.L. 97-440, 33 U.S. Code § 1311

July 2, 1986, P.L. 99-349, 100 Stat. 728

Feb. 4, 1987, P.L. 100-4, 33 U.S. Code § 1251 et seq.

Dec. 22, 1987, P.L. 100-202, 33 U.S. Code § 1330

Jan. 8, 1988, P.L. 100-236, 33 U.S. Code § 1369

Nov. 1, 1988, P.L. 100-581, 33 U.S. Code § 1377

Nov. 11, 1988, P.L. 100-688, 33 U.S. Code §§ 1268, 1311, 1330, 1362

Nov. 14, 1988, P.L. 100-653, 33 U.S. Code § 1330

Aug. 18, 1990, P.L. 101-380, 33 U.S. Code §§ 1319, 1321, 1321 nt.

Nov. 16, 1990, P.L. 101-596, 33 U.S. Code §§ 1268 to 1270, 1270 nt., 1324

Oct. 6, 1992, P.L. 102-388, 33 U.S. Code § 1321

Oct. 31, 1992, P.L. 102-580, 33 U.S. Code § 1342

Oct. 13, 1994, P.L. 103-355, 33 U.S. Code § 1368

Oct. 31, 1994, P.L. 103-431, 33 U.S. Code § 1311

Dec. 21, 1995, P.L. 104-66, 33 U.S. Code §§ 1252, 1311, 1324, 1375

Feb. 10, 1996, P.L. 104-106, 33 U.S. Code §§ 1322, 1362

Oct. 12, 1996, P.L. 104-303, 33 U.S. Code § 1269

Oct. 19, 1996, P.L. 104-324, 33 U.S. Code § 1321

Oct. 7, 1998, P.L. 105-244, 30 U.S. Code § 1262

Nov. 10, 1998, P.L. 105-362, 33 U.S. Code §§ 1254, 1266, 1285, 1290, 1324, 1329, 1330, 1375

Nov. 13, 1998, P.L. 105-383, 33 U.S. Code § 1321

Federal Water Power Act

See also Federal Power Act

June 10, 1920, Ch. 285, 41 Stat. 1063, 16 U.S. Code §§ 791 to 823

March 3, 1921, Ch. 129, 41 Stat. 1353, 16 U.S. Code § 797

June 23, 1930, Ch. 572, 46 Stat. 797., 16 U.S. Code §§ 792, 793, 797

Aug. 26, 1935, Ch. 687, 49 Stat. 803, 16 U.S. Code §§ 791a, 796 to 800, 803, 807, 810, 811, 816 to 818, 824 to 825r

June 4, 1956, Ch. 351, 70 Stat. 226, 16 U.S. Code § 811

Federal Water Project Recreation Act

July 9, 1965, P.L. 89-72, 79 Stat. 213, 16 U.S. Code §§ 460l-5, 460l-12 to 460l-21, 662

March 7, 1974, P.L. 93-251, 88 Stat. 33, 16 U.S. Code §§ 460l-13, 406l-14

Oct. 2, 1992, P.L. 102-377, 16 U.S. Code § 4601-18

Oct. 30, 1992, P.L. 102-575, 16 U.S. Code §§ 460l-13, 460l-14, 460l-15, 460l-18

Federal Water Resources Development Act

N.C. Gen. Stat. 1943, § 143-215.38 et seq.

Federal Workforce Restructuring Act of 1994

March 30, 1994, P.L. 103-226, 5 U.S. Code § 2101 nt.

Nov. 19, 1995, P.L. 104-52, 5 U.S. Code § 8331 nt.

Federal Youth Corrections Act

Sept. 30, 1950, Ch. 1115, 64 Stat. 1085, 18 U.S. Code §§ 5005 to 5024

March 8, 1952, Ch. 162, 66 Stat. 45, 18 U.S. Code §§ 5023 to 5026

Federal—State Cash Exchange Act

Utah Code Ann. 1953, 67-4-2 et seq.

Federalizing Act (Income Tax Return)

N.D. Cent. Code, 57-38-31, Subsec. 7

Federally Aided State Program Coordination Act

S.D. Codified Laws 1967, 4-8B-1 et seq.

Federally Recognized Indian Tribe List Act of 1994

Nov. 2, 1994, P.L. 103-454, 25 U.S. Code §§ 479a, 479a et seq.

Federally Subsidized Housing Preservation Act

Ill. Rev. Stat. 1991, Ch. 67 1/2, § 1151 et seq.

Federally Subsidized Mortgage Act (Notice of Prepayment)

Ill. Rev. Stat. 1991, Ch. 67 1/2, § 901 et seq.

Federally Supported Health Centers Assistance Act of 1992

Oct. 24, 1992, P.L. 102-501, 42 U.S. Code § 201 nt.

Federally Supported Health Centers Assistance Act of 1995

Dec. 26, 1995, P.L. 104-73, 42 U.S. Code § 201 nt.

Fee-Based Practicing Pastoral Counselor Certification Act

N.C. Gen. Stat. 1943, § 90-350 et seq.

Fee Bill Act

Ill. Rev. Stat. 1991, Ch. 25, §§ 27.9, 28

Pa. Mar. 28, 1814, 6 Sm. L. 228, Ch. 3994

Tenn. Code Ann., 8-22-101 et seq.

Tex. Rev. Civ. Stat., Art. 3882 et seq.

Fee Bill Act (Constables)

Pa. Purdon's Stat., Title 13, § 61 et seq.

Fee Bill Act (Magistrates of Cities of First Class)

Pa. Purdon's Stat., Title 42, § 231

Fee Bill Act (Minor Judiciary)

Pa. Purdon's Stat., Title 42, § 216

Fee Bill Act (Recorders)

Pa. 1929 Pamph. Laws 127, No. 128

Fee Bill Act (Sheriffs)

Pa. Purdon's Stat., Title 16, § 7861 et seq.

Fee Collection Procedures Law

Cal. Revenue and Taxation Code § 55001 et seq.

Fee Deposit Act

Ill. Rev. Stat. 1991, Ch. 85, § 720 et seq.

Wis. Stat. Ann., 94.72

Fee in Lieu of Tax Simplification Act

S.C. Code Ann. 1976, § 12-44-10 et seq.

Fee Law

N.J. Stat. Ann., 22A:1-1 et seq.

Fee Tail Act
Ark. Code Ann. 1987, 18-12-301
Colo. Rev. Stat., 38-30-106 et seq.
Mo. Rev. Stat., 442.470, 474.470

Feeble-minded Law
Pa. 1907 Pamph. Laws 292, No. 222

Feed Act
Haw. Rev. Stat. Ann., § 144-1 et seq.
La. Rev. Stat. Ann. 3:1891 et seq.
Wash. Rev. Code Ann., 15.53.010 et seq.

Feed Act (Commercial)
See also Commercial Feed Act
Fla. Stat. Ann., 580.011 et seq.
Ill. Comp. Stat. 1992, Ch. 505, § 30/1 et seq.
Ind. Code Ann., 15-5-13-1 et seq.
Iowa Code Ann., 198.1 et seq.
Md. Ann. Code 1974, Art. AG, § 6-101 et seq.
Me. Rev. Stat. Ann. 1964, Title 7, § 711 et seq.
Mich. Comp. Laws Ann., 287.521 et seq.
Miss. Code Ann. 1972, § 75-45-151 et seq.
Neb. Laws 1984, L.B. 322
N.H. Rev. Stat. 1955, 435:17 et seq.
Okla. Stat. Ann., Title 2, § 8-41 et seq.
S.C. Code Ann. 1976, § 46-27-10 et seq.
S.D. Codified Laws 1967, 39-14-39 et seq.
Utah Code Ann. 1953, 4-12-1
Vt. Stat. Ann., Title 6, § 321 et seq.

Feed Fertilizer and Livestock Remedy Act
Wash. Rev. Code Ann., 15.52.010

Feed Grain Act of 1963
May 20, 1963, P.L. 88-26, 77 Stat. 44, 7 U.S. Code §§ 1339a, 1441 nt.; 16 U.S. Code § 590p

Feed Yards Act
Okla. Stat. Ann., Title 2, § 9-201 et seq.

Feeder Pig Act
Ind. Code Ann., 15-2.1-12-1 et seq.

Feeder Road Act - Pilot Program
Miss. Code Ann. 1972, § 65-10-1 et seq.

Feeder Swine Act
Ill. Rev. Stat. 1991, Ch. 8, § 501 et seq.

Feeder Swine Dealer Act
Ill. Rev. Stat. 1985, Ch. 111, § 201 et seq.

Feeder Swine Dealer Licensing Act
Ill. Rev. Stat. 1991, Ch. 111, § 219 et seq.

Feeding Garbage to Animals Act
Ill. Rev. Stat. 1991, Ch. 8, § 210 et seq.

Feedlot Certification Act
Colo. Rev. Stat., 35-53.5-101 et seq.

Feedstuffs Act
Ind. Code Ann., 15-5-13-1 et seq.
Ky. Rev. Stat. 1962, 250.240 et seq.
Ohio Rev. Code 1953, 923.41 et seq.
Ore. Rev. Stat., 633.006 et seq.
Pa. 1907 Pamph. Laws 273, No. 211
S.C. Code Ann. 1976, § 46-27-10 et seq.

Fees Allowances and Costs Act
W. Va. Code 1966, § 59-1-1 et seq.

Fees and Costs Act
N.J. Stat. Ann., 2A:15-59 et seq.

Fees and Salaries Act
Ill. Rev. Stat. 1991, Ch. 53

Fees and Salaries Act (County Officers)
Ind. Code Ann., 36-3-6-2 et seq.

Fees and Salaries Act (Emergency)
Kan. Laws 1933, Ch. 186

Fees and Salaries Act (State Officers)
Ind. Code Ann., 4-2-1-1, 4-2-1-2

FEGLI Living Benefits Act
Oct. 25, 1994, P.L. 103-409, 5 U.S. Code § 8701 nt.

Fehling-Morley-Fitzgerald Act (Holidays)
Mich. Comp. Laws Ann., 435.101 et seq.

Feignbaum Act (Water Appropriation)
Cal. Water Code § 10500 et seq.

Feinberg Act (Incompetents)
N.Y. Mental Hygiene Law 1972 (Consol. Laws Ch. 27) § 78.03

Feinberg Law (Subversive Teachers)
N.Y. Civil Service Law 1958 (Consol. Laws, Ch. 7) § 105

Felando-Polanco Fisheries Act
Cal. Statutes 1986, Ch. 1049

Felando-Presley-Eaves Wiretap Act
Cal. Penal Code § 629 et seq.

Feld-Crawford Act (Fair Trade)
N.Y. General Business Law (Consol. Laws Ch. 20) § 369a et seq.

Feld-Hamilton Career Act
N.Y. Civil Service Law 1958 (Consol. Laws Ch. 7) § 40 et seq.

Feld-McGrath Tenure Law (Teachers)
N.Y. Education Law 1947 (Consol. Laws Ch. 16) § 6206 et seq.

Fellow Servant Act
Ark. Code Ann. 1987, 11-8-109
Colo. Rev. Stat., 8-2-201
Conn. Public Acts 1913, p. 1735, Ch. 138
Mo. Rev. Stat., 537.180 et seq.

Fellow Servant Act (Railroads)
Minn. Stat. Ann., 219.77
N.C. Gen. Stat. 1943, § 62-242
Tex. Rev. Civ. Stat., Arts. 6432 et seq.

Fellow Servant Act (Workmen's Compensation)
Kan. Stat. Ann., 44-545

Fellow Servant Rule Abrogation Act
Ohio Rev. Code 1953, 4113.03 et seq.

Felon Registration Act
Ala. Code 1975, § 13A-11-180 et seq.

Felon with a Gun Act
Colo. Rev. Stat., 18-12-108

Felonious Driving Act
Mich. Comp. Laws Ann., 752.191, 752.192

Felony Arrest Act
Conn. Gen. Stat. Ann., § 54-1f
N.Y. Criminal Procedure Law (Consol. Laws Ch. 11A) § 140.10

Felony-Firearm Statute
Mich. Comp. Laws Ann., 750.316

Felony Manslaughter Act
La. Rev. Stat. Ann., 14:31

Felony Murder Act
Cal. Penal Code § 189
Colo. Rev. Stat., 18-3-101 et seq.
Fla. Stat. Ann., 782.04
Kan. Stat. Ann., 21-3401 et seq.
Mass. Gen. Laws Ann., 265:17, 265:18, 265:21
Mich. Comp. Laws Ann., 750.316
Mo. Rev. Stat., 565.021, Subsec. 1, Subd. 2
Mont. Code Ann., 45-5-102
N.J. Stat. Ann., 2C:11-3
N.Y. Penal Law 1965 (Consol. Laws Ch. 40) § 125.25, Subd. 3
Pa. Cons. Stat., Title 18, §§ 1102, 2502

Felony Offender Act (Habitual)
Ala. Code 1975, § 13A-5-9

Felony Offender Law (Fourth)
N.Y. Penal Law 1965 (Consol. Law Ch. 40) § 70.10

Female and Minority Business Enterprise Act
Ill. Rev. Stat. 1991, Ch. 127, § 132.600

Female and Minority Small Business Procurement Act
Iowa Laws 1991, 220.1(28)

Female Eight Hour Act
D.C. Code 1973, § 36-301 et seq.
N.M. Stat. Ann., 50-5-1

Female Employees' Protection Law
Cal. Labor Code § 1250 et seq.

851

Female Genital Mutilation Act
Cal. Health and Safety Code § 124170
Cal. Penal Code § 273.4
N.Y. Laws 1997, Ch. 618

Female Hour Law
Wyo. Stat. Ann., § 27-6-101 et seq.

Female Labor Act
D.C. Code Ann., §§ 36-901, 36-902
Del. Code of 1953, Title 19, § 301 et seq.
Ill. Rev. Stat. 1991, Ch. 48, § 4a et seq.
Neb. Rev. Stat. 1943, 48-212, 48-21
Pa. Purdon's Stat., Title 43, § 101 et seq.
Wash. Rev. Code Ann., 49.12.200 et seq.

Female Labor Act (Maximum Hours)
N.J. Stat. Ann., 34:2-24 et seq.

Female Ten Hour Law
Ore. Rev. Stat. 1953, 653.255

Feme Sole Traders Act
Pa. Purdon's Stat., Title 48, § 41 et seq.

Fence Act
Cal. Statutes 1850, Ch. 49, p. 131
Ill. Rev. Stat. 1991, Ch. 54, § 0.01 et seq.
Kan. Stat. Ann., 29-101 et seq.
Mich. Comp. Laws Ann., 43.51 et seq.
Mo. Rev. Stat., 272.210 et seq.
Mont. Code Ann., 81-4-101 et seq.
Neb. Rev. Stat. 1943, 34-101 et seq.
N.H. Rev. Stat. 1955, 473:1 et seq.
N.J. Stat. Ann., 4:20-1 to 4:20-32
N.M. Stat. Ann., 77-16-1 et seq.
N.Y. Town Law (Consol. Laws Ch. 62)
    § 300 et seq.
Ohio Rev. Code 1953, 971.01 et seq.
Pa. Mar. 27, 1784, 1 Sm. L. 96, Ch. 1078
R.I. Gen. Laws 1956, 34-10-1 et seq.
Tenn. Code Ann., 44-8-101 et seq.
Vt. Stat. Ann. Title 24, § 3801 et seq.
Wash. Rev. Code Ann., 16.60.010 et seq.

Fence Act (Excavation)
Ill. Rev. Stat. 1991, Ch. 54, §§ 25.9, 26

Fence Act (Livestock)
Colo. Rev. Stat., 35-46-101 et seq.

Fence Act (Spite)
Ky. Rev. Stat. 1971, Superseded Vol.,
    433.860
Mass. Gen. Laws Ann., 49:21 et seq.
Vt. Stat. Ann. Title 24, § 3817

Fence and Stock Act
N.C. Gen. Stat. 1943, § 68-1 et seq.

Fence Viewers Act
Ill. Rev. Stat. 1991, Ch. 54, § 0.01 et seq.
Pa. Purdon's Stat., Title 29, § 1 et seq.

Fences Act (Boundaries)
Mont. Rev. Code 1947, 67-802 et seq.

Fencing Act
Haw. Rev. Stat. Ann., § 664-21 et seq.

Fencing Act (Farms)
Ky. Rev. Stat. 1971, 256.010 et seq.

Fencing Act (Public Lands)
Feb. 25, 1885, Ch. 149, 23 Stat. 321, 43 U.S.
    Code §§ 1061 to 1066

Fencing and Grazing Law
Okla. Stat. Ann., Title 69, § 281 et seq.

Fencing and Operating of Railroads Act
Ill. Rev. Stat. 1991, Ch. 95 1/2, § 18c-7504 et
    seq.

Fencing District Act
Ark. Code Ann. 1987, 14-386-104 et seq.

**Fenner Law (Military Leave for Civil
Employees)**
N.Y. Military Law (Consol. Laws Ch. 36)
    § 242

FEPCA
See Federal Employees Pay Comparability
    Act Of 1990

Ferguson Act (Strikes by Public Employees)
Ohio Rev. Code 1953, 4117.15 et seq.

Ferguson-Polanco Anti-Child Pornography Act
Cal. Penal Code § 311.11

Ferguson-Polanco Housing Assistance Act
Cal. Health and Safety Code §§ 33080.7, 33334.10, 33334.12, 34312.5

Fermented Malt Beverage Act
Colo. Rev. Stat., 12-46-101 et seq.

Fernald Act (Electric Power)
Me. Rev. Stat. 1954, Ch. 50, § 1

Ferriday, Louisiana Redevelopment Agency Act
La. Acts 1972, No. 762

Ferries Act
Ill. Rev. Stat. 1991, Ch. 121, § 700 et seq.

Ferries, Bridges and Highways Act
S.C. Code Ann. 1976, § 57-1-10 et seq.

Ferris Institute Act
Mich. Comp. Laws Ann., 390.801 et seq.

Ferris Law (Billboards in Adirondack Park)
N.Y. Environmental Conservation Law (Consol. Laws, Ch. 438) §§ 13, 9-0305, 9-1305

Ferry Act
Mich. Comp. Laws Ann., 255.1 et seq.
Wash. Rev. Code Ann., 36.53.010 et seq.

Ferry Act (Cape May County)
N.J. Stat. Ann., Superseded Vol., 32:13B-1 et seq.

Ferry District Act
Wash. Rev. Code Ann., 47.57.230 et seq.

Ferry Seizure Act
Va. Code 1950, § 33-202 et seq.

Ferry System Act (Puget Sound)
Wash. Rev. Code Ann., 47.60.010 et seq.

Ferry Transportation Act
Alaska Stat. 1962, Replaced Titles, § 42.25.010 et seq.

Fertility Clinic Success Rate and Certification Act of 1992
Oct. 24, 1992, P.L. 102-493, 42 U.S. Code §§ 201 nt., 263a-1 et seq.

Fertilizer Act
Ala. Code 1975, § 2-22-1 et seq.
Cal. Food and Agricultural Code 1967, § 14501 et seq.
Colo. Rev. Stat., 35-12-101 et seq.
Conn. Gen. Stat. Ann., § 22-111a et seq.
Del. Code of 1974, Title 3, § 2101 et seq.
Ga. Code Ann., 2-12-1 et seq.
Ida. Code 1947, 22-601 et seq.
Ill. Rev. Stat. 1991, Ch. 5, § 55.1 et seq.
Ind. Code Ann., 15-3-3-1 et seq.
Iowa Code Ann., 200.1 et seq.
Ky. Rev. Stat. 1971, 250.360 et seq.
La. Rev. Stat. Ann., 3:1311 et seq.
Mass. Gen. Laws Ann., 128:64 et seq.
Md. Ann. Code 1974, Art. AG, § 6-201 et seq.
Me. Rev. Stat. Ann. 1964, Title 7, § 741 et seq.
Mich. Comp. Laws Ann., 286.751 et seq.
Minn. Stat. 1986, 17.711 et seq.
Miss. Code Ann. 1972, § 75-47-1 et seq.
Mont. Code Ann., 80-10-101 et seq.
N.C. Gen. Stat. 1943, § 106-655 et seq.
N.D. Cent. Code, 19-20.1-01 et seq.
Neb. Rev. Stat. 1943, 81-2, 162.01 et seq.
N.H. Rev. Stat. 1955, 431:1 et seq.
N.M. Stat. Ann., 76-11-1 et seq.
Ore. Rev. Stat., 633.310 et seq.
Pa. Purdon's Stat., Title 3, § 68.1 et seq.
P.R. Laws Ann. 1954 Title 5, § 519 et seq.
R.I. Gen. Laws 1956, 2-7-1 et seq.
S.C. Code Ann. 1976, § 46-25-10 et seq.
S.D. Codified Laws 1967, 38-19-1 et seq.
Tenn. Code Ann., 43-11-101 et seq.
Utah Code Ann. 1953, 4-13-1 et seq.
Va. Code 1950, § 3.1-74 et seq.
Wash. Rev. Code Ann., 15.54.270 et seq.
Continued

W. Va. Code 1966, § 19-15-1 et seq.
Wyo. Stat. Ann., § 11-14-101 et seq.

Fertilizer Act (Commercial)
N.M. Stat. Ann. 1953, 45-13-1 et seq.

Fertilizer Act (Open Formula)
S.C. Code Ann. 1976, Superseded Vols.,
§ 46-25-220

Fertilizer and Lime Act
S.D. Codified Laws 1967, 38-19-1 et seq.
Vt. Stat. Ann., Title 6, § 411 et seq.

Fertilizer and Soil Conditioner Act
Colo. Rev. Stat., 35-12-101 et seq.
Minn. Stat. 1988, 17.711 et seq.
N.D. Cent. Code, 19-20.1-01 et seq.
Neb. Rev. Stat. 1943, 81-2, 162.01 et seq.
N.J. Stat. Ann., 4:9-15.1 et seq.

Fertilizer Control Act
Tex. Agriculture Code, § 63.001 et seq.

Fertilizer Inspection Act
Fla. Stat. Ann., 576.011 et seq.
Mich. Comp. Laws Ann., 286.761, 286.762

Fertilizer Materials Act
Minn. Stat. Ann., 18C.001 et seq.

Fertilizer Soil Act
Pa. Purdon's Stat., Title 3, § 68.1 et seq.

Fess-Kenyon Act (Vocational Rehabilitation)
June 2, 1920, Ch. 219, 41 Stat. 735, 29 U.S.
Code §§ 31 to 44

Fetal Alcohol Syndrome and Fetal Alcohol Effect Prevention and Services Act
Nov. 13, 1998, P.L. 105-392, § 419, 42 U.S.
Code § 201 nt.

Fetal and Infant Experimentation Act
N.M. Stat. Ann., 24-9A-1 et seq.

Fetal Infant and Child Mortality Prevention Act
Mont. Code Ann., 50-19-401 et seq.

FGB Act
Oct. 11, 1996, P.L. 104-297, 16 U.S. Code
§§ 1362, 1857

Fiberglass Recycled Content Act
Cal. Public Resources Code § 19500 et seq.

Fictitious Business Name Act
Cal. Business and Professions Code, § 17900
et seq.

Fictitious Corporate Name Act
Pa. Purdon's Stat., Title 15, § 51 et seq.
Pa. Purdon's Stat., Title 54, § 81 et seq.

Fictitious Groups Act (Insurance)
Okla. Stat. Ann., Title 36, § 6001.1

Fictitious Name Act
Fla. Stat. Ann., 865.09
Mass. Gen. Laws Ann., 110:5, 110:6
Mich. Comp. Laws Ann., 445.1 et seq.
Mo. Rev. Stat., 417.200 et seq.
N.C. Gen. Stat. 1943, § 66-68 et seq.
N.Y. General Business Law (Consol. Laws
Ch. 20) § 130
Pa. Cons. Stat. Title 54, § 301 et seq.
R.I. Gen. Laws 1956, 6-1-1 et seq.
S.D. Codified Laws 1967, 37-11-1 et seq.
Va. Code 1950, § 59.1-69
W. Va. Code 1966, § 47-8-2 et seq.

Fictitious Names Act (Partnership)
Ohio Rev. Code 1953, 1777.01 et seq.

Fictitious Partnership Act
Okla. Stat. Ann., Title 54, § 81 et seq.

Fictitious Party Act
Ala. Code 1958, Title 7, § 136

Fictitious Payee Act
Ark. Stat. 1947, 68-109, Subd. 3
Cal. Civil Code § 3090, Subd. 3 § 1725
Ga. Code 1933, 14-209, Subd. 3
Ida. Code 1947, Superseded Vol., 27-109
La. Rev. Stat. Ann., 7:9
Md. Ann. Code 1974, Art. CL, § 3-405
Minn. Stat. 1961, 335.052, Subd. 3

Mont. Rev. Code 1947, 55-209, Subsec. 3
Va. Code 1950, § 6-361, Subsec. 3
W. Va. Code 1931, § 46-1-9
Wyo. Stat. 1957, § 13-295, Subsec. 3

Fictitious Payee Act (Negotiable Instruments)
N.Y. Uniform Commercial Code (Consol. Laws Ch. 38) § 3-405

Fiducial and Judicial Sales of Real Estate Act
Ky. Rev. Stat. 1971, 389A.010 et seq.

Fiduciaries Accounting Act
Conn. Gen. Stat. Ann., § 45a-175 et seq.

Fiduciaries Act
See also Uniform Fiduciaries Act
Mich. Comp. Laws Ann., 700.501 et seq.
N.D. Cent. Code, 35-29-01 et seq.
N.H. Stat. Ann. 1978, 48-1-1 et seq.
Okla. Stat. Ann., Title 68, § 24300 et seq.
S.C. Code Ann. 1976, § 12-57-10 et seq.
Tex. Tax Code, § 113.201 et seq.
Va. Code 1950, § 55-142.1 et seq.
Wash. Rev. Code Ann., 60.68.005 et seq.

Fiduciaries Act of 1924
La. Rev. Stat. Ann., 9:3801 et seq.

Fiduciaries Code (Probate Estates)
Pa. Cons. Stat., Title 20, § 101 et seq.

Fiduciaries Compensation and Allowances Act
Pa. 1953 Pamph. Laws 190, No. 10

Fiduciaries' Emergency Act
Neb. Laws 1943, Ch. 237
R.I. Gen. Laws 1956, 18-3-1 et seq.

Fiduciaries in Military Service Act
Pa. Cons. Stat., Title 20, § 4301 et seq.

Fiduciaries Investment Act
Ala. Code 1975, § 19-3-120
N.J. Stat. Ann., 3B:20-1 et seq.
N.M. Stat. Ann. 1953, 33-1-14 et seq.
Ohio Rev. Code 1953, 2109.37

Pa. Cons. Stat., Title 20, § 7301 et seq.
S.C. Code Ann. 1976, § 21-11-10 et seq.
Tenn. Code Ann., 35-3-117

Fiduciaries Legal List Act
Wis. Stat. Ann., 881.01 et seq.

Fiduciaries Powers Act
Colo. Rev. Stat., 15-1-801 et seq.
Conn. Gen. Stat. Ann., § 45a-233 et seq.
N.Y. Estates, Powers and Trusts Law (Consol. Laws Ch. 17B) § 11-1.1 et seq.

Fiduciaries' Securities Transfer Act
Del. Code of 1974, Title 12, § 4301 et seq.

Fiduciaries' Wartime Substitutions Law
Cal. Probate Code, § 350 et seq.

Fiduciary and Lender Environmental Liability Protection Act (Economic Development Agency)
Pa. Purdon's Stat., Title 35, § 6027.1 et seq.

Fiduciary Depository Act
Fla. Stat. Ann., 69.031

Fiduciary Investment Company Act
Ga. Code Ann., 7-1-330 et seq.
Ky. Rev. Stat. 1971, 386.510 et seq.
Ohio Rev. Code 1953, 1109.32 et seq.

Fiduciary Obligations Act
Ill. Rev. Stat. 1991, Ch. 17, § 2001 et seq.

Fiduciary Security Transfers Act
Fla. Stat. Ann., 610.011 et seq.
Haw. Session Laws 1965, Act 44
Ill. Rev. Stat. 1991, Ch. 32, § 439.49 et seq.
La. Rev. Stat. Ann., 9:3831 et seq.
Me. Rev. Stat. Ann. 1964, Title 13, § 641 et seq.
Mich. Comp. Laws Ann., 441.101 et seq.
Minn. Stat. Ann., 520.21 et seq.
Miss. Code Ann. 1972, § 91-11-1 et seq.
S.C. Code Ann. 1976, § 35-7-10 et seq.
Tex. Bus and Com Code, § 33.01 et seq.
Wash. Rev. Code Ann., 21.17.010 et seq.
W. Va. Code 1966, § 31-40-1 et seq.

Fiduciary Security Transfers Simplification Act

See Uniform Simplification of Fiduciary Security Transfers Act

Fiduciary Surety Release Act

Ill. Rev. Stat. 1991, Ch. 103, § 17.9 et seq.

Field Act (School Architecture)

Cal. Education Code 1959, §§ 15451 et seq., 39140, 81130

Field Archaeology Act

Minn. Stat. Ann., 138.31 et seq.

Wis. Stat. 1985, 27.012

Field Code

Kan. Stat. Ann., 60-101 et seq.

Field Crops Inspection Law

Cal. Food and Agricultural Code 1967, §§ 52001 et seq., 52061

Field Sanitation Act

Ill. Rev. Stat. 1991, Ch. 111 1/2, § 5901 et seq.

Field Seed Act

Mo. Rev. Stat., 266.011 et seq.

Fielder Act (Juries)

N.J. Stat. Ann., 2A:70-1, 2A:70-2

Fielder Grade Crossing Law

N.J. Stat. Ann., 48:12-61 et seq.

Fielding Act (District Courts)

Mass. Gen. Laws Ann., 218:19 et seq., 223:2

Fields Act (Workers Compensation)

Ky. Rev. Stat. 1971, 342.012 et seq.

FIFRA

See Federal Insecticide, Fungicide, And Rodentcide Act

Fifteen Year Statute of Limitations (Color of Title)

Ark. Code Ann. 1987, 18-11-103

Fifteen Year Statute of Limitations (Estate Tax Liens)

N.Y. Tax Law (Consol. Law, Ch. 60) § 24911

Fifteenth Amendment

March 30, 1870, No. 10, 16 Stat. 1131

Fifth Circuit Court of Appeals Reorganization Act of 1980

Oct. 14, 1980, P.L. 96-452, 28 U.S. Code § 1 nt.

Fifth Class Cities (Flood Control)

Ind. Burns' 1933, 48-5001 et seq.

Fifth Class County Retirement Act

Pa. Purdon's Stat., Title 16, § 11652 et seq.

Fifth Supplemental National Defense Appropriation Act of 1941

April 5, 1941, Ch. 41, 55 Stat. 123

Fifth Supplemental National Defense Appropriation Act of 1942

March 5, 1942, Ch. 141, 56 Stat. 128, 22 U.S. Code § 412 nt.

Fifty-Fifty Act (State Forests)

Minn. Stat. Ann., 89.034

Fifty-Five Alive Mature Driving Program

Mont. Code Ann., 33-16-203, 33-16-221 et seq.

Fifty States Commemorative Coin Program Act

Oct. 20, 1996, P.L. 104-329, Title III, 31 U.S. Code § 5101 nt.

Dec. 1, 1997, P.L. 105-124, 31 U.S. Code § 5101 nt.

Fifty Ward Act

Ill. Rev. Stat. 1991, Ch. 24, § 21-36 et seq.

Fifty Year Abstract Act

Ind. Code Ann., 32-1-5-1 et seq.

Fifty Year Mortgage Foreclosure Act

Mass. Gen. Laws Ann., 260:33.

Fighting and Baiting Act (Animal)
S.C. Code Ann. 1976, § 16-27-10 et seq.

File and Use Act (Casualty Insurance)
Ohio Rev. Code 1953, 3937.01 et seq.

File and Use Act (Insurance Rates)
Del. Code of 1974, Title 18, § 2301 et seq.
Mass. Gen. Laws Ann., 174A:1 et seq.

Filiante-Johnston Hazardous Substance Cleanup Financing Authority Act
Cal. Health and Safety Code § 25392 et seq.

Filiante Tanning Facility Act
Cal. Business and Professions Code § 22700 et seq.

Filiation Act
Ore. Rev. Stat. 1953, 109.110 et seq.

Filiation Law (New York City)
N.Y. City Crim. Courts Act § 60 et seq.

Filing Act
N.Y. Uniform Commercial Code (Consol. Laws Ch. 38) § 9-401

Filing Act (Chattel Mortgages)
Okla. Stat. Ann., Title 46, § 57

Filing Act (Conditional Sales)
N.Y. Uniform Commercial Code (Consol. Laws Ch. 38) §§ 9-103(3), 9-401, 9-403

Filing Act (Health Insurance Claim)
Ill. Rev. Stat. 1991, Ch. 73, § 1350 et seq.

Filing and Corner Perpetuation Act
Ida. Code 1947, 55-1601 et seq.

Filing of Copies Act
Ill. Rev. Stat. 1991, Ch. 116, § 100 et seq.

Filing Reform Act (Accident and Health)
Pa. Purdon's Stat., Title 40, § 3801 et seq.

Filled Cheese Act
June 6, 1896, Ch. 337, 29 Stat. 253

Filled Dairy Products Act
Kan. Stat. Ann., 65-725 et seq.
Minn. Stat. Ann., 32.529 et seq.
N.M. Stat. Ann. 1953, 52-2-5 et seq.
Wash. Rev. Code Ann., 15.38.001 et seq.

Filled Milk Act
March 4, 1923, Ch. 262, 42 Stat. 1486, 21 U.S. Code §§ 61 to 63
July 12, 1943, Ch. 221, 57 Stat. 498
Ill. Rev. Stat. 1981, Ch. 56 1/2, § 19(c) et seq.
Kan. Stat. Ann., 65-707
Mass. Gen. Laws Ann., 94:17A
Mich. Comp. Laws Ann., 288.171 et seq.
Neb. Laws 1923, Ch. 12
Pa. Purdon's Stat., Title 31, § 520-1.1 et seq.

Filled Milk Act (Voight)
Wis. Stat. Ann., 97.48

Film and Television Investment Act
Fla. Stat. Ann., 288.051 et seq.

Film Censorship Act
Md. Ann. Code 1957, Art. 66A, § 1 et seq.
Ohio Rev. Code 1953, 2907.31 et seq.
Pa. Cons. Stat., Title 18, § 5903

Film Permit Act
See Uniform Film Permit Act

Filmed Records Certification Act
Ill. Rev. Stat. 1991, Ch. 116, § 34.2, 34.3

Filmed Records Destruction Act
Ill. Rev. Stat. 1991, Ch. 116, §§ 47.01, 47.1

Filmed Records Reproduction Act
Ill. Rev. Stat. 1991, Ch. 116, § 34.9 et seq.

Filmmaker's Credit Act
N.M. Stat. Ann., 7-9B-1 et seq.

Finance Act
Ariz. Rev. Stat. Ann., § 35-101 et seq.
Cal. Statutes 1951, Ch. 364, p. 829
Ill. Rev. Stat. 1985, Ch. 127, § 137 et seq.
Pa. 1947 Pamph. Laws 1110, No. 476

Finance Act (Agricultural)
N.C. Gen. Stat. 1943, § 122D-1 et seq.
Tex. Agriculture Code, § 58.001 et seq.

Finance Act (Asbestos Abatement)
Ill. Rev. Stat. 1991, Ch. 111 1/2, § 8100 et
seq.

Finance Act (Consumer)
Md. Ann. Code 1974, Art. CL, § 14-101 et
seq.

Finance Act (County)
N.C. Gen. Stat. 1943, § 153-69 et seq.

Finance Act (Education)
Minn. Stat. 1986, 124A.697 et seq.

Finance Act (Export)
Kan. Stat. Ann., 74-5069 et seq.

Finance Act (Federal Educational)
Neb. Rev. Stat. 1943, 79-1320 et seq.

Finance Act (Higher Educational Facilities)
N.C. Laws 1985, Ch. 794

Finance Act (Housing Incentive)
N.J. Stat. Ann., 55:14K-45 et seq.

Finance Act (Housing)
La. Rev. Stat. Ann., 40:600.1 et seq.

Finance Act (Industrial)
Md. Ann. Code 1974, Art. FI, § 11-201 et
seq.

Finance Act (Installment)
Fla. Stat. Ann., 520.50 et seq.

Finance Act (Motor Vehicle Retail Installment Sales
Vt. Stat. Ann., Title 9, § 2351 et seq.

Finance Act (Motor Vehicle Sales)
Me. Rev. Stat. Ann. 1964, Title 9, § 3401 et
seq.
Mich. Comp. Laws Ann., 492.101 et seq.

Finance Act (Municipal)
See Municipal Finance Act

Mass. Gen. Laws Ann., 44:1 et seq.

Finance Act (Providence)
R.I. Public Laws 1945, Ch. 1665

Finance Act (Public School)
Colo. Rev. Stat., 22-54-101 et seq.

Finance Act (Public Works)
Ill. Rev. Stat. 1991, Ch. 29, § 33a.1 et seq.

Finance Administration Act (Rural)
Minn. Stat. Ann., 41B.01 et seq.

Finance Agency Act (Housing)
Utah Code Ann. 1953, 9-4-901 et seq.
Vt. Stat. Ann., Title 10, § 381 et seq.

Finance and Administration Act (Property Assessment)
Fla. Stat. Ann., 195.0011 et seq.

Finance and Administration Department Act
N.M. Stat. Ann., 9-6-1 et seq.

Finance and Housing Authority Act
Ga. Code Ann., 50-26-1 et seq.

Finance and Quality Performance Act (School District)
Kan. Stat. Ann., 72-6405 et seq.

Finance and Unitary Residence Responsibility Act
Minn. Stat. Ann., 256G.01 et seq.

Finance Authorities Act for Large Municipalities (Urban Residential)
Ga. Code Ann., 36-41-1 et seq.

Finance Authority Act
Me. Rev. Stat. Ann. 1964, Title 10, § 961 et
seq.
N.M. Stat. Ann., 6-21-1 et seq.
Tex. Rev. Civ. Stat., Art. 601c

Finance Authority Act (Community Development)
N.H. Rev. Stat. 1955, 162-L:1 et seq.

Finance Authority Act (Development)
Kan. Stat. Ann., 74-8901

Finance Authority Act (Forest)
Mich. Comp. Laws Ann., 320.2001 et seq.

Finance Authority Act (Public)
Tex. Rev. Civ. Stat., Art. 601c, 601d

Finance Awareness Program Act (Export)
N.Y. Banking Law (Consol. Laws Ch. 2) § 45
N.Y. Education Law 1947 (Consol. Laws Ch. 16) § 305, Subd. 18

Finance Charges and Related Provisions (Consumer Credit Code)
Iowa Code Ann., 537.2101 et seq.
Me. Rev. Stat. Ann. 1964, Title 9-A, § 2-101 et seq.

Finance Charges and Related Provisions (Revised Uniform Consumer Credit Code)
See Revised Uniform Consumer Credit Code—Finance Charges and Related Provisions

Finance Charges and Related Provisions (Uniformed Consumer Credit Code)
Kan. Stat. Ann., 10a-2-101 et seq.

Finance Charges Disclosure Act
Conn. Gen. Stat. Ann., § 36-393 et seq.
N.H. Rev. Stat. 1955, 399-B:1 et seq.

Finance Commission Act
N.J. Stat. Ann., 52:27-1 et seq.

Finance Commission Act (Education)
S.C. Code Ann. 1962, § 21-52 et seq.

Finance Companies Act
Md. Ann. Code 1974, Art. FI, § 11-401 et seq.
Mich. Comp. Laws 1948, 492.1 et seq.

Finance Company Act (Insurance Premium)
Me. Rev. Stat. Ann. 1964, Title 9, § 4051 et seq.
Mich. Comp. Laws Ann., 500.1500 et seq.

Minn. Stat. Ann., 59A.01 et seq.

Finance Company Privilege Tax Act
Miss. Code Ann. 1972, § 27-21-1 et seq.

Finance Corporation Act (Community Development)
Ill. Comp. Stat. 1992, Ch. 315, § 15/1 et seq.

Finance Corporation Act (Cultural Education Facilities)
Tex. Rev. Civ. Stat., Act. 1528m

Finance Corporation Act (Development)
Fla. Laws 1993, Ch. 187, §§ 25 to 45

Finance Corporation Act (Export)
Fla. Stat. Ann., 288.771 et seq.

Finance Corporation Act (Housing and Mortgage)
R.I. Gen. Laws 1956, 42-55-1 et seq.

Finance Corporation Act (Housing)
Fla. Stat. Ann., 420.501 et seq.

Finance Corporation Act (Industrial)
Tenn. Code Ann., 4-17-401 et seq.

Finance Corporation Act (John Dempsey Hospital)
Conn. Gen. Stat. Ann., § 10a-250 et seq.

Finance Corporation Act (Technology)
Utah Code Ann. 1953, 9-2-701 et seq.

Finance Council Act
Kan. Stat. Ann., 75-3708 et seq.

Finance Fund Act (Mortgage)
Neb. Rev. Stat. 1943, 76-1601 et seq.

Finance Lenders Law (Commercial)
Cal. Financial Code § 26000 et seq.

Finance Modification Act (Governmental)
Okla. Laws 1999, H.B. 1008

Finance Reorganization Act
Mass. Gen. Laws Ann., 7:2 et seq.

Financial Administration Act
Ariz. Rev. Stat. Ann., § 35-101 et seq.

Financial Aid to Local Government Act (Emergency)
Tenn. Code Ann., 9-13-201 et seq.

Financial and Safety Responsibility Act
Iowa Code Ann., 321A.1 et seq.

Financial Assistance Act (Emerging Technology and Biotechnology)
N.J. Stat. Ann., 34:1B-7.37 et seq.

Financial Assistance Act (Post-Secondary Education)
Miss. Code Ann. 1972, § 37-106-1 et seq.

Financial Assistance Act (Student)
Tex. Education Code, Art. 56.001 et seq.

Financial Assistance Act for Nonpublic Institutions of Higher Learning
Ill. Rev. Stat. 1991, Ch. 144, § 1331 et seq.

Financial Assistance for Community Services Act
Fla. Stat. Ann., 409.501 et seq.

Financial Business Tax Act
N.J. Stat. Ann., 54:10B-1 et seq.

Financial Capital Act
Conn. Gen. Stat. Ann., § 32-11a et seq.

Financial Center Development Act
Del. Code of 1974, Title 5, § 801 et seq.

Financial Control Act
Ala. Code 1975, § 41-4-80 et seq.

Financial Control Act (Counties)
Ala. Code 1975, § 11-8-1 et seq.

Financial Control Act (Higher Education)
Okla. Stat. Ann., Title 70, § 3906 et seq.

Financial Coordination Act (Local-State)
Cal. Government Code § 53980 et seq.
Cal. Government Code § 65591 et seq.

Financial Corporations Tax Act
N.M. Stat. Ann., 7-2A-1 et seq.

Financial Disclosure Act
Fla. Stat. Ann., 112.311 et seq.
N.M. Stat. Ann., 10-16A-1 et seq.

Financial Disclosure Act (Good Government)
Mich. Comp. Laws Ann., 15.421 et seq.

Financial Disclosure Act (Public Officers)
Cal. Government Code § 3700 et seq.

Financial Emergencies Act (Local Government)
Fla. Stat. Ann., 218.50 et seq.

Financial Emergency Act for the City of New York
N.Y. Laws 1975, Ex. Sess., Ch. 868, § 2

Financial Emergency Act for the City of Yonkers
N.Y. Laws 1975, Ex. Sess., Ch. 871, § 2
N.Y. Laws 1984, Ch. 103, § 2

Financial Emergency and Accountability Act (Local Government)
Fla. Stat. 1983, 11.45, 75.05, 112.61,
112.625 to 112.665, 121.135, 165.091,
189.001 to 189.009, 218.31, 218.32,
218.37, 218.38, 218.50 et seq.

Financial Frauds Prevention Act
N.Y. Banking Law (Consol. Laws Ch. 2),
§ 76 et seq.

Financial Guaranty Insurance Act
Conn. Public Acts 1993, p. 292, No. 136

Financial Institution Acquisition Act
Ida. Code 1947, 26-2601 et seq.

Financial Institution Activity Reporting Act
Ill. Rev. Stat. 1991, Ch. 17, § 7401-1 et seq.

Financial Institution Individual Account Deposit Act
Wash. Rev. Code Ann., 30.22.010 et seq.

Financial Institutions Act

Ga. Code Ann., 7-1-1 et seq.

Ill. Rev. Stat. 1991, Ch. 17, § 101 et seq.

Ind. Code Ann., 28-1-1-1 et seq.

Mich. Comp. Laws Ann., 487.301 et seq.

Mont. Code Ann., 32-1-101

Utah Code Ann. 1953, 7-1-101 et seq.

Financial Institutions Act (Control of Money Laundering in)

Fla. Stat. Ann., 655.50

Financial Institutions Act (State Board)

S.C. Code Ann. 1976, § 34-1-10 et seq.

Financial Institutions Anti-Fraud Enforcement Act of 1990

Nov. 29, 1990, P.L. 101-647, 12 U.S. Code §§ 4201 to 4213, 4201 nt., 4221 to 4230, 4241 to 4247; 18 U.S. Code § 3059A

Financial Institutions Board Act

S.C. Code Ann. 1976, § 34-1-10 et seq.

Financial Institutions Commissioner's Office Act

P.R. Laws Ann. 1954, Title 7, § 2001 et seq.

Financial Institutions Conversion Act

Tenn. Code Ann., 45-11-101 et seq.

Financial Institutions Digital Signature Act

Ill. Comp. Stat. 1992, Ch. 205, § 705/1 et seq.

Financial Institutions Disclosure Act

Ill. Rev. Stat. 1991, Ch. 17, §§ 360.2, 503

Wash. Rev. Code Ann., 19.106.010 et seq.

Financial Institutions Emergency Acquisitions Amendments of 1987

Aug. 10, 1987, P.L. 100-86, 2 U.S. Code §§ 905, 906; 12 U.S. Code §§ 481, 1439-1, 1464, 1464 nt., 1726, 1727, 1729, 1730a, 1772b, 1785, 1786, 1811 nt., 1813, 1817, 1821, 1823, 1828, 1842, 1843, 1849

Financial Institutions Excise Tax Act

Ala. Code 1975, 40-16-1 et seq.

Financial Institutions Franchise Act

P.R. Laws Ann. 1954, Title 7, § 1171 et seq.

Financial Institutions Insurance Sales Law

Ill. Comp. Stat. 1992, Ch. 215, §§ 5/1400 to 5/1416

Financial Institutions Reform, Recovery, and Enforcement Act of 1989

Aug. 9, 1989, P.L. 101-73, 12 U.S. Code § 1811 nt.

Nov. 29, 1990, P.L. 101-647, 12 U.S. Code § 1833a

Dec. 12, 1991, P.L. 102-233, 12 U.S. Code §§ 1437 nt., 3345, 3348

Dec. 19, 1991, P.L. 102-242, 12 U.S. Code §§ 1818 nt., 1833d; 3345, 3348

Oct. 23, 1992, P.L. 102-485, 12 U.S. Code § 3352

Oct. 28, 1992, P.L. 102-550, 12 U.S. Code § 3341

Sept. 23, 1994, P.L. 103-325, 12 U.S. Code § 3351

Sept. 29, 1994, P.L. 103-328, 12 U.S. Code § 1811 nt.

Sept. 30, 1996, P.L. 104-208, 12 U.S. Code §§ 1811, 1833, 1833a, 3341

Oct. 11, 1996, P.L. 104-294, 18 U.S. Code § 1014

Oct. 19, 1996, P.L. 104-316, 12 U.S. Code § 3341

Financial Institutions Regulatory and Interest Rate Control Act of 1978

Nov. 10, 1978, P.L. 95-630, 5 U.S. Code §§ 5108, 5314, 5315; 12 U.S. Code §§ 27, 93, 226 nt., 375b, 412, 461, 504, 505, 601 nt., 635 et seq. 1114, 1464, 1729 et seq., 1752 et seq., 1771, 1772a, 1781 et seq. 1813, et seq., 1828, 1843, 1844, 1847, 1972, 3106a, 3201 et seq., 3301 et seq.; 15 U.S. Code §§ 1601 nt., 1666f nt., 1693 to 1693r; 18 U.S. Code § 709; 31 U.S. Code §§ 67, 856; 42 U.S. Code § 2153e-1

Financial Institutions Supervisory Act of 1966

Oct. 16, 1966, P.L. 89-695, 80 Stat. 1028, 12 U.S. Code §§ 1464, 1724, 1728, 1730, 1730a, 1813, 1817 to 1821

Financial Integrity Act

Tenn. Code Ann., 9-18-101 et seq.

Financial Integrity and Accountability Act
R.I. Gen. Laws 1956, 35-14-1 et seq.

Financial Integrity and Accountability Act (Public Corporation)
R.I. Gen. Laws 1956, 35-20-1 et seq.

Financial Integrity and State Manager's Accountability Act
Cal. Government Code § 13400 et seq.

Financial Management and Reporting Act (Local Government)
Fla. Stat. Ann., 218.30 et seq.

Financial Planning and Management Service Act
Ill. Rev. Stat. 1991, Ch. 17, § 5301 et seq.
La. Rev. Stat. Ann., 37:2581 et seq.

Financial Planning and Supervision Act (Local Government)
Ill. Rev. Stat. 1991, Ch. 85, § 7201 et seq.

Financial Policies and Procedures Act
Colo. Rev. Stat., 22-44-201 et seq.

Financial Privacy Act
Cal. Government Code § 7460 et seq.
Mo. Rev. Stat. 1978, 408.675 et seq.
N.C. Gen. Stat. 1943, § 53B-1 et seq.
Okla. Stat. Ann., Title 6, § 2201 et seq.

Financial Privacy Act (Motor Vehicles)
Cal. Vehicle Code § 16000 et seq.

Financial Privacy Act (Operation of Vehicles by Private Owners)
Cal. Vehicle Code § 17150 et seq.

Financial Privacy Act (Operation of Vehicles by State and Governmental Agencies)
Cal. Vehicle Code § 17000 et seq.

Financial Records Privacy Act
Tenn. Code Ann., 45-10-101 et seq.

Financial Recovery Act (Municipalities)
Pa. Purdon's Stat., Title 53, § 11701.101 et seq.

Financial Recovery Act (Small Business)
Conn. Public Acts 1993, No. 382, §§ 39, 40, 42 to 49

Financial Regulation Simplification Act of 1980
March 31, 1980, P.L. 96-221, 12 U.S. Code §§ 3501 nt., 3521 et seq.

Financial Reorganization Act
Ind. Code Ann., 4-13-2-1 et seq.

Financial Reporting and Budget Accountability Reform Act
N.Y. Education Law 1947 (Consol. Laws Ch. 16) §§ 355, 2575, 6202, 6221, 6230, 6231
N.Y. Labor Law (Consol. Laws Ch. 31) § 530
N.Y. Public Lands Law (Consol. Laws Ch. 46) § 2
N.Y. State Finance Law 1940 (Consol. Laws Ch. 56) §§ 2, 3, 8, 8a, 22, 22a, 23, 40a, 49, 51, 53, 53b, 54, 57, 70 to 72, 75, 92, 93, 122a, 200 to 207, 210, 211

Financial Reports Act of 1988
Aug. 23, 1988, P.L. 100-418, 102 Stat. 1387, 22 U.S. Code § 5351

Financial Reports Law (Audited)
La. Rev. Stat. Ann., 22:1321 et seq.

Financial Responsibility Act (Aircraft)
Cal. Public Utilities Code § 24230 et seq.
Conn. Gen. Stat. Ann., § 15-102 et seq.
Ind. Code Ann., 8-21-3-1 et seq.
Mass. Gen. Laws Ann., 90:49B et seq.
Mich. Comp. Laws Ann., 259.671 et seq.
N.H. Rev. Stat. 1955, 422-A:1 et seq.
S.C. Code Ann. 1976, § 55-8-10 et seq.

Financial Responsibility Act (Common Carriers)
Wis. Stat. Ann., 194.41 et seq.

Financial Responsibility Act (Livestock Dealers)
Ala. Code 1975, § 2-15-130 et seq.

Financial Responsibility Act (Motor Vehicles)

Ala. Code 1975, § 32-7-11 et seq.

Alaska Stat. 1962, § 28.20.010 et seq.

Ariz. Rev. Stat. Ann., § 28-1101 et seq.

Ark. Code Ann. 1987, 27-19-201 et seq.

Cal. Vehicle Code 1959, § 16000 et seq.

Colo. Rev. Stat., 42-7-101 et seq.

Conn. Gen. Stat. Ann., § 14-112 et seq.

D.C. Code Ann., § 40-401 et seq.

Del. Code of 1974, Title 21, § 2901 et seq.

Fla. Stat. Ann., 324.011 et seq., 324.28 et seq.

Ga. Code Ann., 40-9-1 et seq.

Haw. Rev. Stat. Ann., § 287-1 et seq.

Ida. Code 1947, 49-1201 et seq.

Ill. Rev. Stat. 1991, Ch. 95 1/2, § 7-100 et seq.

Ind. Code Ann., 9-2-1-1 et seq.

Iowa Code Ann., 321A.1 et seq.

Kan. Laws 1939, Ch. 86

Ky. Rev. Stat. 1971, 187.290 et seq.

La. Rev. Stat. Ann., 32:891 et seq.

Mass. Gen. Laws Ann., 90:34A et seq., 175:113A et seq.

Md. Ann. Code 1974, Art. TR, § 17-101 et seq.

Me. Rev. Stat. Ann. 1964, Title 29, § 781 et seq.

Mich. Comp. Laws Ann., 257.501 et seq.

Minn. Stat. Ann., 65B.001 et seq.

Miss. Code Ann. 1972, § 63-15-1 et seq.

Mo. Rev. Stat., 303.010 et seq.

Mont. Code Ann., 61-6-101 et seq.

N.C. Gen. Stat. 1943, §§ 20-279.1 et seq., 20-309 et seq.

N.D. Cent. Code, 39-16-01 et seq.

Neb. Rev. Stat. 1943, 60-501 et seq.

N.H. Rev. Stat. 1955, 264:1 et seq.

N.J. Stat. Ann., 39:6-23 et seq.

N.M. Stat. Ann., 66-5-201 et seq.

N.Y. Vehicle and Traffic Law 1959 (Consol. Laws, Ch. 71) § 330 et seq.

Ohio Rev. Code 1953, 4509.01 et seq.

Okla. Stat. Ann., Title 47, § 7-101 et seq.

Ore. Rev. Stat., 806.010

Pa. Cons. Stat., Title 75, § 1701 et seq.

R.I. Gen. Laws 1956, 31-31-1 et seq.

S.C. Code Ann. 1976, § 56-9-10 et seq.

S.D. Codified Laws 1967, 32-35-1 et seq.

Tenn. Code Ann., 55-12-101 et seq.

Tex. Rev. Civ. Stat., Art. 6701h

Va. Code 1950, § 46.1-388 et seq.

Vt. Stat. Ann., Title 23, § 801 et seq.

Wash. Rev. Code Ann., 46.29.010 et seq.

Wis. Stat. Ann., 344.01 et seq.

W. Va. Code 1966, § 17D-1-1 et seq.

Wyo. Stat. Ann., § 31-9-101 et seq.

Financial Responsibility Act (Robbins-McAlister)

Cal. Statutes 1991, Ch. 946

Financial Responsibility Act (Underground Storage Tank)

R.I. Gen. Laws 1956, 46-12.9-1 et seq.

Financial Responsibility Act (Workmen's Compensation)

Ky. Rev. Stat. 1971, Superseded Vols. 342.016, 342.017

Financial Responsibility and Accountability Act (State Department)

Colo. Rev. Stat., 24-17-101 et seq.

Financial Responsibility and Management Assistance Act (District of Columbia)

Ill. Comp. Stat. 1992, Ch. 625, § 27/1 et seq.

Financial Responsibility of Motor Vehicle Owners and Operators Act

Utah Code Ann. 1953, 41-12A-101 et seq.

Financial Right of Privacy Act

Mo. Rev. Stat 1986, 408.675 et seq.

Financial Security Act

N.M. Stat. Ann., 66-5-201 et seq.

Financial Security Act (Motor Vehicles)

N.Y. Vehicle and Traffic Law 1959 (Consol. Laws Ch. 71) § 310 et seq.

Financial Services and Banking Industry Act

Del. Laws Vol. 71, Ch. 25

Financial Services Loan Companies Act
Haw. Rev. Stat. Ann., § 408-1 et seq.

Financial Statement Act (Local Goverment)
Ill. Rev. Stat. 1991, Ch. 85, §§ 600, 601

Financial Statements Act (Fraud)
Tex. Penal Code, §§ 31.03, 32.03

Financial Transaction Card Crime Act
S.C. Code Ann. 1976, § 16-14-10 et seq.

Financial Transaction Device Crime Act
Colo. Rev. Stat., 18-5-701 et seq.

Financially Disadvantaged Municipalities Matching Assistance Act
Pa. Purdon's Stat. Title 73, § 398.1 et seq.

Financially Distressed City Law
Ill. Rev. Stat. 1991, Ch. 24, § 8-12-1 et seq.

Financially Distressed Municipalities Act
Pa. Purdon's Stat., Title 53, § 11701.101 et seq.

Financially Distressed Municipalities, Counties, Utility Districts and Education Agencies Act
Tenn. Code Ann., 9-13-301 et seq.

Financing Act (Child Care Facilities)
Cal. Health and Safety Code § 1499 et seq.

Financing Act (District Library)
Mich. Comp. Laws Ann., 397.281 et seq.

Financing Act (Economic Development)
N.C. Gen. Stat. 1943, § 159-101 et seq.

Financing Act (Industrial Development)
Fla. Stat. Ann., 159.44 et seq.

Financing Act (Local Development)
Mich. Comp. Laws Ann., 125.2151 et seq.

Financing Act (Multicounty Airport and Riverport)
Ark. Acts 1991, No. 738

Financing Act (Nuclear Decommissioning)
Me. Rev. Stat. Ann. 1964, Title 35-A, § 4351 et seq.

Financing Act (School Corporations)
Ind. Code Ann., 21-2-12-1 et seq.

Financing Act (Tax Increment)
N.J. Stat. Ann., 52:27D-250 et seq.
Tex. Tax Code, § 311.001 et seq.

Financing and Investment Commission Act
Ga. Official Ann., 50-17-20 et seq.

Financing and State Health Care Policy Act
Colo. Rev. Stat., 25.5-1-102 et seq.

Financing Authority Act (Cambean Basin Projects)
P.R. Acts 1989, First Special Session, No. 9

Financing Authority Act (Educational)
Mass. Gen. Laws Ann., 15C:2

Financing Authority Act (Infrastructure)
P.R. Laws Ann. 1954, Title 3, § 1901 et seq.

Financing Authority Act for Industrial and Environmental Pollution Control Facilities
P.R. Laws Ann. 1954, Title 12, § 1251 et seq.

Financing Bank Act (Public Utilities)
Me. Rev. Stat. Ann. 1964, Title 35-A, § 2901 et seq.

Financing Community Improvement Districts Act (Sumter County)
Ga. Laws 1991, p. 3592

Financing Institution Licensing Act
Mo. Rev. Stat., 364.010 et seq.

Financing Opportunities Act (Export)
N.J. Stat. Ann., 34:1B-93 et seq.

Financing Statement Act (Central Filing)
Colo. Rev. Stat., 4-9.5-101 et seq.

Finders Act
Mich. Comp. Laws Ann., 434.1 et seq.

Fine Arts Act
Fla. Stat. Ann., 265.281 et seq.

Fine Arts Commission Act
May 17, 1910, Ch. 243, 36 Stat. 371, 40 U.S. Code §§ 104, 106

Fine Arts Committee Act (Executive Mansion)
N.C. Gen. Stat. 1943, §§ 143B-79, 143B-80

Fine Arts Endowment Program
Fla. Stat. Ann., 265.601 et seq.

Fine Arts Preservation Act
Pa. Purdon's Stat., Title 72, § 2101 et seq.

Fine Print Disclosure Act
Cal. Civil Code § 1740 et seq.
Ill. Rev. Stat. 1991, Ch. 121 1/2, § 360 et seq.

Fines Paid to Societies Act
Ill. Rev. Stat. 1991, Ch. 23, § 2410 et seq.

Fingerprint Identification System Policy Council Act (Automated)
Mich. Comp. Laws Ann., 28.151 et seq.

Fingold Act (Defective Delinquents)
Mass. Act 1953, Ch. 645

Finland War Debt Act
June 15, 1940, Ch. 371, 54 Stat. 398

Finnish Loan Act
March 2, 1940, Ch. 34, 54 Stat. 38

Fire Academy Act
Ga. Code Ann., 25-7-1 et seq.

Fire Act (Arson)
Iowa Code Ann., 712.1 et seq.

Fire Act (Railroads)
Colo. Rev. Stat., 40-30-101 et seq.
S.C. Code Ann. 1976, § 58-17-3920

Fire Administration Authorization Act of 1992
Oct. 26, 1992, P.L. 102-522, 106 Stat. 3410

Fire and Arson Training Act
Cal. Health and Safety Code §§ 13159.7 to 13159.10

Fire and Casualty Act
D.C. Code Ann., § 35-1501 et seq.

Fire and Inland Marine Insurance Rate Regulatory Act
Minn. Stat. 1967, 70.60 et seq.

Fire and Panic Act
Pa. Purdon's Stat., Title 35, § 1221 et seq.

Fire and Police Civil Service Law for Small Municipalities and for Parishes and Fire Protection Districts
La. Rev. Stat. Ann., 33:2531 et seq.

Fire and Police Commissioners Act
Ill. Rev. Stat. 1991, Ch. 24, § 10-2.1-1 et seq.
Wis. Stat. Ann., 62.13

Fire and Police Department Organization Act (Dalton)
Ga. Laws 1945, p. 593

Fire and Police Departments Act
Ky. Rev. Stat. 1971, 95.010 et seq.

Fire and Police Employee Relations Act
Tex. Local Government Code, § 174.001 et seq.

Fire and Police Retirement System Act
Ark. Code Ann. 1987, 24-10-101 et seq.

Fire and Tornado Insurance Act
N.D. Cent. Code, 26.1-22-01 et seq.

Fire Claim Act
Haw. Session Laws 1901, Act 15

Fire Codes of Montana
Mont. Code Ann., 2-15-2011

Fire Commissioner Act
Ga. Code Ann., 25-2-1

Fire Commissioner Act (State)
Pa. Purdon's Stat., Title 71, § 1199.21 et seq.

Fire Company, Ambulance Service and Rescue Squad Assistance Act (Volunteer)
Pa. Purdon's Stat., Title 72, § 3943.1 et seq.

Fire Damage Representation Agreement Act
Ill. Rev. Stat. 1991, Ch. 29, §§ 80, 81

Fire Defense Mobilization Act
Ga. Code 1933, 86-1701 et seq.
Ind. Laws 1943, Ch. 123, p. 376
Tenn. Public Acts 1943, Ch. 13
Wash. Laws 1943, Ch. 96

Fire Defense Mobilization Act (Municipal)
D.C. Code Ann., § 35-1601 et seq.
Fla. Laws 1943, Ch. 21763

Fire Department Act
D.C. Code Ann., § 4-301 et seq.

Fire Department Aid Act
Ky. Rev. Stat. 1971, 17.210 et seq.

Fire Department Civil Service Act (Second Class Cities)
Mo. Rev. Stat. 1969, 85.360 et seq.

Fire Department Operations Act
D.C. Code Ann., § 4-301 et seq.

Fire Department Salary Act
D.C. Code Ann., § 4-406 et seq.

Fire Department Work Hours Act
Mich. Comp. Laws Ann., 123.841 et seq.

Fire Departments Nomenclature Act (Municipal, County, and Volunteer)
Ga. Code Ann., 25-13-1 et seq.

Fire District Act
Mo. Rev. Stat., 321.010 et seq.
Neb. Rev. Stat. 1943, 35-501 et seq.

Fire District Bond Act
N.M. Stat. Ann., 5-7-1 et seq.

Fire District Disincorporation Act
Cal. Health and Safety Code § 14800 et seq.

Fire District Law (Bergeson)
Cal. Health and Safety Code § 13800 et seq.

Fire Drill Act
Ill. Rev. Stat. 1991, Ch. 122, § 840 et seq.
N.J. Stat. Ann., 18A:41-1 et seq.

Fire Equipment Distributor and Employee Regulation Act
Ill. Rev. Stat. 1991, Ch. 111, § 8001 et seq.

Fire Equipment Standardization Law
Cal. Health and Safety Code § 13025 et seq.

Fire Escapes Act
Conn. Gen. Stat. Ann., § 29-389 et seq.
D.C. Code Ann., § 5-501 et seq.
Ill. Rev. Stat. 1991, Ch. 55 1/2, § 0.01 et seq.
Mont. Code Ann., 50-61-101 et seq.
R.I. Gen. Laws 1956, 23-28.8-1 et seq.

Fire Extinguisher Law (Portable)
Cal. Health and Safety Code § 13109.1 et seq.

Fire Extinguisher Service Act
Ill. Rev. Stat. 1991, Ch. 127 1/2, §§ 60, 61

Fire Fighters Arbitration Act
Me. Rev. Stat. Ann. 1964, Title 26, § 965 et seq.
R.I. Gen. Laws 1956, 28-9.1-1 et seq.

Fire Fighting and Law Enforcement Medal of Honor Act
Ill. Rev. Stat. 1991, Ch. 127, § 3851-1 et seq.

Fire Hazards Act
Va. Code 1950, § 27-63 et seq.

Fire Hydrant Act
Ill. Rev. Stat. 1991, Ch. 127 1/2, §§ 850, 851

Fire Hydrant Act (Parking)
Iowa Code Ann., 321.358

Fire Instruction Act (Apartment)
Ill. Comp. Stat. 1992, Ch. 425, § 5/0.01 et seq.

Ill. Rev. Stat. 1991, Ch. 127 1/2, § 71.9 et seq.

Fire Insurance Act

Ill. Rev. Stat. 1991, Ch. 73, § 1005 et seq.

Mich. Comp. Laws Ann., 500.2804 et seq.

N.Y. Insurance Law 1984 (Consol. Laws Ch. 28) § 3404

Ore. Rev. Stat. 1953, 744.005 et seq.

S.D. Codified Laws 1967, 58-24-1 et seq.

Fire Insurance Act (Patrol Associations)

La. Rev. Stat. Ann., 22:1551 et seq.

Fire Insurance Act (Policy Provisions)

N.Y. Insurance Law (Consol. Laws Ch. 28) § 3404

Fire Insurance Application Act

Md. Ann. Code 1957, Art. 48A, § 575 et seq.

Fire Insurance Commission Act

Tex. Insurance Code, Art. 5.25 et seq.

Fire Insurance Corporations Guaranty Surplus and Special Reserve Funds and Limited Liability Act

Cal. Insurance Code § 3030 et seq.

Fire Insurance Rating Act

Ark. Stat. 1947, 66-3101 et seq.

D.C. Code Ann., § 35-1601 et seq.

Miss. Code Ann. 1972, § 83-3-1 et seq.

Okla. Stat. Ann., Title 36, § 921 et seq.

S.D. Codified Laws 1967, 58-24-1 et seq.

Va. Code 1950, Misc. Superseded Code Provisions, § 38-19 et seq.

Wis. Stat. 1975, 203.32

Fire Investigation Act

Ill. Rev. Stat. 1991, Ch. 127 1/2, § 5.9 et seq.

Fire Investigation Act (Peace Officer)

Ill. Rev. Stat. 1991, Ch. 127 1/2, §§ 500, 501

Fire Island National Seashore Act

Sept. 11, 1964, P.L. 88-587, 78 Stat. 928, 16 U.S. Code §§ 459e to 459e-9

Fire Island National Seashore Amendments Act of 1984

Oct. 17, 1984, P.L. 98-482, 16 U.S. Code §§ 459e nt., 459e-1, 459e-2

Fire Lanes and Fire Hydrants Act

D.C. Code Ann., § 1-319

Fire Liability Law (Failure to Control)

Cal. Health and Safety Code § 13007 et seq.

Fire Lookout Purchase Law

Cal. Public Resources Code § 4031

Fire Loss Act

Ill. Rev. Stat. 1991, Ch. 73, §§ 1152.1, 1153

Fire, Marine and Inland Marine Rate Regulatory Act

Mass. Gen. Laws Ann., 174A:1 et seq.

Pa. Purdon's Stat., Title 40, § 1221 et seq.

Fire, Marine and Inland Navigation Act

Ill. Rev. Stat. 1991, Ch. 73, § 1065.18-1 et seq.

Fire Marshal Act

Cal. Health and Safety Code § 13100 et seq.

Ill. Rev. Stat. 1991, Ch. 127 1/2, §§ 0.01 et seq., 5.9 et seq.

Ind. Code Ann., 22-14-2-1 et seq.

N.Y. Laws 1912, Ch. 453

Ore. Rev. Stat., 476.005 et seq.

Fire Marshal's Act (Explosives)

Tenn. Code Ann., 68-102-101 et seq.

Fire Patrol Act

Ore. Rev. Stat., 477.062 et seq.

Fire Platoon System Act

Minn. Stat. 1965, 65.011

N.Y. Laws 1941, Ch. 626

Fire Policy Act (Standard)

Minn. Stat. Ann., 65A.01 et seq.

Fire Prevention Act

Ark. Code Ann. 1987, 12-13-101 et seq.

Mass. Gen. Laws Ann., 148:1 et seq.

Continued

Md. Ann. Code 1957, Art. 25, § 11
Mich. Comp. Laws Ann., 29.1 et seq.
Mont. Code Ann., 50-62-101 et seq.
R.I. Gen. Laws 1956, 23-28-1 et seq.
Utah Code Ann. 1953, 63-27-101 et seq.,
   63-29-1 et seq.

Fire Prevention Act (Watson-O'Connell)
Cal. Health and Safety Code § 13132.7

Fire Prevention and Building Code Act
N.Y. Executive Law 1951 (Consol. Laws Ch.
   18) § 370 et seq.

Fire Prevention and Control Act
W. Va. Code 1966, § 29-3-1 et seq.

Fire Prevention and Fireworks Act
Utah Code Ann. 1953, 53-7-201 et seq.

**Fire Prevention Code (Adoption by Second
Class Townships)**
Pa. Purdon's Stat., Title 53, § 65732

Fire Prevention Code (Schools)
N.D. Cent. Code, 18-12-01 et seq.

Fire Prevention Code Act
Miss. Code Ann. 1972, § 45-11-107
N.Y. Adm. Code '85, § 27-4001 et seq.
Va. Code 1950, § 27-94 et seq.

Fire Protection Act
Kan. Stat. Ann., 31-132 et seq.
Vt. Stat. Ann., Title 20, § 2981 et seq.

Fire Protection Act (Forests)
S.C. Code Ann. 1976, § 48-33-10 et seq.

Fire Protection Act (Land)
Haw. Rev. Stat. Ann., § 185-1 et seq.

Fire Protection Act (Township)
Mich. Comp. Laws Ann., 41.801 et seq.

**Fire Protection and Resources Management
Act (Wildland)**
Cal. Public Resources Code § 4461 et seq.

**Fire Protection Compact (Northeastern
Forest Fire)**
Vt. Stat. Ann., Title 10, § 2501 et seq.

Fire Protection Contracts Law
Cal. Health and Safety Code § 13052.5

Fire Protection District Act (Forest)
Ill. Rev. Stat. 1991, Ch. 96 1/2, § 7000 et seq.

Fire Protection District Budget Act
Okla. Stat. Ann., Title 19, § 901.31 et seq.

Fire Protection District Validation Act
Ill. Rev. Stat. 1991, Ch. 127 1/2, §§ 45.3a,
   45.4

Fire Protection Districts Act
Cal. Health and Safety Code §§ 13800 et
   seq., 14001 et seq.
Ida. Code 1947, 31-1401 et seq.
Ill. Rev. Stat. 1991, Ch. 127 1/2, § 20.9 et
   seq.
N.D. Cent. Code, 18-10-01 et seq.
S.D. Codified Laws 1967, 34-31A-2 et seq.
Wash. Rev. Code Ann., 52.02.020 et seq.

Fire Protection Excise Tax Act (County)
N.M. Stat. Ann., 7-20A-1 et seq.

Fire Protection Fund Law
N.M. Stat. Ann., 59A-53-1 et seq.

Fire Protection of Unprotected Area Act
Ill. Rev. Stat. 1991, Ch. 127 1/2, § 300 et seq.

Fire Protection Program Fund Act (Rural)
Okla. Stat. Ann., Title 19, § 901.55 et seq.

Fire Protection Sprinkler Systems Act
S.C. Code Ann. 1976, § 23-45-10 et seq.

Fire Protection Tax Act
Ill. Rev. Stat. 1991, Ch. 24, §§ 11-7-1, 11-7-3

Fire Protection Training Act
Ark. Acts 1975, p. 1321, No. 483
Ill. Rev. Stat. 1991, Ch. 85, § 531 et seq.

Fire Rating Act
  Miss. Code Ann. 1972, § 83-3-1 et seq.

Fire Regulations Act
  Ky. Rev. Stat. 1971, 227.200 et seq.
  R.I. Gen. Laws 1956, 23-29-1 et seq.

Fire Research and Safety Act of 1968
  March 1, 1968, P.L. 90-259, 82 Stat. 34, 15
    U.S. Code §§ 278f, 278g

Fire Safe Cigarette Act of 1990
  Aug. 10, 1990, P.L. 101-352, 15 U.S. Code
    § 2054 nt.

Fire Safety Act
  Cal. Health and Safety Code § 13143.2
  D.C. Code Ann., § 1-319
  Mass. Gen. Laws Ann., 143:3 et seq.
  N.J. Stat. Ann., 52:27D-192 et seq.
  R.I. Gen. Laws 1956, 23-28.1-1 et seq.
  Tenn. Code Ann., 68-120-101 et seq.
  Va. Code 1950, § 27-63 et seq.

Fire Safety Act (Furniture)
  Ill. Rev. Stat. 1991, Ch. 127 1/2, § 951-1 et
    seq.
  Minn. Stat. Ann., 299F.840 et seq.

Fire Safety Act (Green-Hansen)
  Cal. Health and Safety Code §§ 13143.2,
    13143.5, 13146, 13869.7, 17958.5

Fire Safety Act (Truss Construction)
  Ill. Comp. Stat. 1992, Ch. 425, § 68/1 et seq.

Fire Service Act
  P.R. Laws Ann. 1954, Title 25, § 311 et seq.

Fire Service Extension Law
  Cal. Health and Safety Code § 13050 et seq.

Fire Service Institute Act
  Ill. Rev. Stat. 1991, Ch. 127 1/2, § 401 et seq.
  Iowa Code Ann., 266.40

Fire Service Retirement Law (County)
  Cal. Government Code § 32200 et seq.

**Fire Service Training and Education
    Program Act**
  Cal. Health and Safety Code § 13155 et seq.

Fire Sprinkler Act
  Ga. Code Ann., 25-11-1 et seq.

Fire Station Loan Act (Pembroke)
  Mass. Acts 1959, Ch. 258

**Firearm Accident Prevention Act
    (Children's)**
  Cal. Statutes 1991, Ch. 956

Firearm Act (McClintock)
  Cal. Penal Code §§ 1170.1, 1192.7, 12021,
    12021.1, 12022.5

**Firearm Education and Training Law
    (County Probation and Parole Officers')**
  Pa. Purdon's Stat., Title 61, § 332.1 et seq.

Firearm Owners Identification Card Act
  Ill. Rev. Stat. 1991, Ch. 38, § 83-0.1 et seq.

Firearm Safety Act (Minors)
  Minn. Stat. Ann., 97B.021

Firearm Seizure Act
  Ill. Rev. Stat. 1991, Ch. 38, § 161 et seq.

Firearm Training Act (Peace Officer)
  Ill. Rev. Stat. 1991, Ch. 85, § 514 et seq.

Firearms Act
  See also Uniform Firearms Act
  N.Y. Penal Law 1965 (Consol. Laws Ch. 40)
    § 265.00 et seq.

Firearms and Weapons Act
  Ga. Code Ann., 16-11-120 et seq.

Firearms Control Regulations Act
  D.C. Code Ann., § 6-2301 et seq.

Firearms Owners' Protection Act
  May 19, 1986, P.L. 99-308, 18 U.S. Code
    § 921 nt.
  July 8, 1986, P.L. 99-360, 18 U.S. Code
    § 921 nt.

Firearms Regulatory Act
Ore. Rev. Stat. 1953, 744.005 et seq.

Firearms Safety Act
Minn. Stat. Ann., 97B.015 et seq.

Firearms Silencer Act
Cal. Penal Code § 12500 et seq.

Firearms Training Act
Ill. Rev. Stat. 1991, Ch. 127, § 63b60 et seq.

Firefighter and Peace Officer Survivors Scholarship Act
N.M. Stat. Ann., 21-21F-5 et seq.

Firefighter and Police Postretirement Adjustment Act (Special Ad Hoc Municipal)
Pa. Purdon's Stat., Title 53, § 896.101 et seq.

Firefighter and Rescue Squad Worker Protection Act (Volunteer)
Del. Code of 1974, Title 19, § 1621 et seq.

Firefighter Liability Act
Ill. Rev. Stat. 1991, Ch. 127 1/2, §§ 45.9, 46

Firefighter Standards and Training Act
Ga. Code Ann., 25-4-1 et seq.

Firefighters and Law Enforcement Officers Death Benefit Act
Fla. Stat. Ann., 112.1904, 112.1914

Firefighters and Police Officers Retirement Act
Mich. Comp. Laws Ann., 38.551 et seq.

Firefighters and Police Officer's Survivors Educational Assistance
Ala. Acts 1991, p. 1058 Act

Firefighters and Policemens Arbitration Law
Mich. Comp. Laws Ann., 423.231 et seq.
Okla. Stat. Ann., Title 11, § 51-101 et seq.

Firefighters and State Peace Officers Retirement Act
Cal. Government Code § 21252.02

Firefighters Bargaining Act
Fla. Stat. 1973, 447.20 et seq.

Firefighters' Benefit Law (Volunteer)
N.Y. Consol. Laws, Ch. 64A

Firefighters' Bill of Rights Act
Fla. Stat. Ann., 112.80 et seq.

Firefighters Collective Bargaining Act
Ky. Rev. Stat. 1971, 345.010 et seq.

Firefighters Collective Bargaining Act (Palm Beach County)
Fla. Special Laws 1970, Ch. 70-1004

Firefighters Corps Act
P.R. Laws Ann. 1954, Title 25, § 331 et seq.

Firefighters Mediation Act
Ga. Code Ann., 25-5-1 et seq.

Firefighters Negotiations Act
Utah Code Ann. 1953, 34-20a-1 et seq.

Firefighters Pension and Retirement System Modification Act
Okla. Laws 1999, H.B. 1045

Firefighters Pension Law
Iowa Code Ann., 410.1 et seq.

Firefighters Relief Act
Kan. Stat. Ann., 40-1701 et seq.

Firefighters Relief Association Act (Volunteer)
Pa. Purdon's Stat., Title 53, § 8501 et seq.

Firefighters' Retirement Act
Utah Code Ann. 1953, 49-5-101 et seq.

Firefighters Retirement Act (Statewide Volunteer)
Tex. Rev. Civ. Stat., Art. 6243e.3

Firefighters Retirement System Act
Wash. Rev. Code Ann., 41.26.005 et seq.

Firefighters' Safety Study Act
Oct. 22, 1990, P.L. 101-446, 5 U.S. Code
§§ 2223a, 2223a nt., 2223b to 2223e

Firefighters Training Council Act
Mich. Comp. Laws Ann., 29.361 et seq.

Firefighters Unified Retirement Act
Mont. Code Ann., 19-13-101 et seq.

**Firefighting Rescue Unit Use Act
(Volunteer)**
Ill. Rev. Stat. 1991, Ch. 127, § 288.9 et seq.

Fireman's Relief Fund Act
N.H. Rev. Stat. 1955, 402:66 et seq.

Fireman's Rule
N.Y. General Municipal Law (Consol. Laws
Ch. 24) § 205e

Firemen and Police Pension Act (Dalton)
Ga. Laws 1945, p. 593, § 15 et seq.

Firemen and Police Pension Act (Tampa)
Fla. Special Laws 1941, Ch. 21590

**Firemen and Police Pension Fund Act
(Macon)**
Ga. Laws 1939, p. 1149

**Firemen and Policemen Arbitration Act
(Labor Disputes)**
Pa. Purdon's Stat., Title 43, § 217.1 et seq.

Firemen and Policemen Pension Act
Colo. Rev. Stat. 31-30-501 et seq.
Mass. Gen. Laws Ann., 32:80 et seq.
Minn. Stat. Ann., 69.011 et seq., 424.01 et
seq.
Miss. Code Ann. 1972, § 21-29-101 et seq.
Wyo. Stat. Ann., § 15-5-201 et seq.

Firemen and Policemen Salary Act
D.C. Code Ann., § 4-406 et seq.

Firemen and Policemen Tenure Act
Ind. Code Ann., 36-8-3.5-1 et seq.

Firemen and Policemen's Civil Service Act
Mich. Comp. Laws Ann., 38.501 et seq.

Pa. 1947 Pamph. Laws 1621, No. 568, § 39
Tex. Local Government Code, § 143.001 et
seq.

**Firemen and Policemen's Heart and Lung
Act**
Pa. Purdon's Stat., Title 53, § 637

**Firemen and Policemen's Retirement and
Disability Act Amendments of 1957
(District of Columbia)**
D.C. Code Ann., § 4-607 et seq.

**Firemen and Policemen's Special
Compensation Act (Disability)**
Pa. Purdon's Stat., Title 53, §§ 637, 638

Firemen Compensation Act
Ill. Rev. Stat. 1991, Ch. 48, § 281 et seq.

**Firemen, Law Enforcement Officers, Civil
Defense Workers, Civil Air Patrol
Members and Paramedics Compensation
Act**
Ill. Rev. Stat. 1991, Ch. 48, § 281 et seq.

**Firemen's and Police Relief Association
Guidelines Act**
Minn. Stat. Ann., 69.77

Firemen's and Policemen's Pension Act
Ill. Rev. Stat. 1961, Ch. 24, § 931 et seq.
Ind. Code Ann., 36-8-8-1 et seq.
Miss. Code Ann. 1972, § 21-29-101 et seq.
N.J. Rev. Stat. 1937, 43:16-1 et seq.
Ohio Rev. Code 1953, 741.02 et seq.
Okla. Stat. Ann., Title 11, § 49-103 et seq.
S.C. Code Ann. 1976, § 9-13-10 et seq.
Tex. Rev. Civ. Stat. Arts. 6243a-1, 6243b,
6243f

**Firemen's and Policemen's Pension Reform
Act**
Colo. Rev. Stat., 31-30-801 et seq.

Firemen's and Policemen's Relief Act
Minn. Stat. Ann., 69.011 et seq.

**Firemen's and Policemen's Retirement
System Act**
N.J. Stat. Ann., 43:16A-1 et seq.
Continued

871

N.Y. Retirement and Social Security Law
(Consol. Laws Ch. 51A) § 290 et seq.

**Firemen's and Rescue Worker's Pension
Fund Act**
Ind. Code Ann., 18-1-12-1 et seq.
N.C. Gen. Stat. 1943, § 58-86-1 et seq.

**Firemen's Annuity and Benefit Fund Act
(Cities over 500,000)**
Ill. Rev. Stat. 1985, Ch. 108 1/2, § 6-101 et
seq.

Firemen's Civil Service Act
Minn. Stat. Ann., 420.01 et seq.
Ore. Rev. Stat., 242.702 et seq.
Pa. Purdon's Stat., Title 53, § 39861 et seq.
Wash. Rev. Code Ann., 41.08.010 et seq.
W. Va. Code 8-15-11 et seq.

Firemen's Civil Service Act (Asheville)
N.C. Laws 1947, Ch. 83

Firemen's Civil Service Act (Removal)
Ind. Code Ann., 36-8-3.5-17 et seq.

Firemen's Compensation Act (Volunteer)
Mont. Code Ann., 19-12-101 et seq.

Firemen's Dependents Act
Ohio Rev. Code 1953, 146.01 et seq.

Firemen's Disciplinary Act
Ill. Rev. Stat. 1991, Ch. 85, § 2501 et seq.

Firemen's Fund Act
Ill. Rev. Stat. 1961, Ch. 24, § 918 et seq.

Firemen's Immunity Act
Ill. Rev. Stat. 1991, Ch. 85, § 1-101 et seq.

Firemen's Minimum Wage Act
Ill. Rev. Stat. 1991, Ch. 24, § 10-3-2 et seq.

Firemen's Pension Account Reform Act
Wyo. Stat. Ann., § 15-5-401 et seq.

Firemen's Pension Act
Colo. Rev. Stat., 31-30-501 et seq.
Fla. Special Laws 1945, Ch. 2344
Ga. Laws 1924, p. 167

Iowa Code Ann., 410.1 et seq.
Mass. Gen. Laws Ann., 32:80 et seq.
Minn. Stat. Ann., 69.011 et seq., 424.01 et
seq.
Okla. Stat. Ann., Title 11, § 49-101 et seq.
S.C. Code Ann. 1976, § 9-13-10 et seq.
Wash. Rev. Code Ann., 41.16.010 et seq.
Wyo. Stat. Ann., § 15-5-201 et seq.

Firemen's Pension Act (Augusta)
Ga. Laws 1925, p. 867

Firemen's Pension Act (Elmira)
N.Y. Local Laws 1925, Elmira, No. 2

Firemen's Pension Act (New Orleans)
La. Rev. Stat. Ann., 33:2101 et seq.

Firemen's Pension Act (Wilmington)
Del. Laws Vol. 33, p. 303, Ch. 118
Del. Laws Vol. 45, p. 634, Ch. 168

**Firemen's Pension and Relief Fund Act
(Birmingham)**
Ala. Code 1958, Appx., § 1467 et seq.

**Firemen's Pension and Relief Fund Act
(Lake Charles)**
La. Acts 1944, No. 186

Firemen's Pension Fund Act
Ill. Rev. Stat. 1991, Ch. 108 1/2, §§ 4-101 et
seq., 6-101 et seq.

Firemen's Pension Funds in Cities Act
S.C. Code Ann. 1976, § 9-13-10 et seq.

Firemen's Pension Law (First Class Cities)
Neb. Rev. Stat. 1943, 35-201 et seq.

Firemen's Relief and Pension Act
Ark. Code Ann. 1987, 24-11-801, 24-11-804
Cal. Government Code § 50800 et seq.
Fla. Stat. Ann., 75.021 et seq.
Ohio Rev. Code 1953, 741.01 et seq.
Okla. Stat. Ann., Title 11, § 49-103 et seq.
Pa. Purdon's Stat., Title 53, § 23601 et seq.
Tex. Rev. Civ. Stat., Arts. 6243e, 6243e.1
Wash. Rev. Code Ann., 41.16.010 et seq.

Firemen's Relief and Pension Fund Act (Panama City)
Fla. Special Laws 1973, Ch. 73-587

Firemen's Relief Association Act (Volunteer)
Pa. Purdon's Stat., Title 53, § 8501 et seq.

Firemen's Relief Associations Act
N.D. Cent. Code, 18-05-01 et seq., 18-11-01 et seq.

Firemen's Relief Fund Act
Ill. Laws 1887, p. 117, No. 2
Minn. Laws 1949, Ch. 87
N.H. Rev. Stat. 1955, 402:66 et seq.

Firemen's Retirement Act
Ida. Code 1947, 72-1401 et seq.
Iowa Code Ann., 411.1 et seq.
N.H. Rev. Stat. 1955, 102:1 et seq.
Utah Code Ann. 1953, 49-5-101 et seq.

Firemen's Tenure Act
Ky. Rev. Stat. 1971, 95.440

Firemen's Wages and Hours Act
La. Rev. Stat. Ann., 33:1991 et seq.

Fires and Arson Act
R.I. Gen. Laws 1956, 11-4-1 et seq.

Firescope Act
Cal. Health and Safety Code § 13070 et seq.

Fireworks Act
Cal. Health and Safety Code § 12500 et seq.
Ida. Code 1947, 39-2601 et seq.
Mass. Gen. Laws Ann., 148:39
N.H. Rev. Stat. 1955, 160-A:1 et seq.
Ore. Rev. Stat., 480.110 et seq.
R.I. Gen. Laws 1956, 11-13-1
Utah Code Ann. 1953, 53-7-220 et seq.
Wash. Rev. Code Ann., 70.77.120 et seq.
Wis. Stat. Ann., 167.10

Fireworks Act (County and Municipal)
Utah Code Ann. 1953, 11-3-1 et seq.

Fireworks and Explosives Act
Miss. Code Ann. 1972, § 45-13-101 et seq.

Fireworks Control Act
Ga. Code Ann., 25-10-1 et seq.

Fireworks Licensing and Safety Act
N.M. Stat. Ann., 60-2C-1 et seq.

Fireworks Regulatory Act
Colo. Rev. Stat., 12-28-101 et seq.
Ga. Code Ann., 25-10-1 et seq.
Ill. Rev. Stat. 1991, Ch. 127 1/2, § 101 et seq.
Ind. Code Ann., 22-11-14-1 et seq.
Iowa Code Ann., 727.2
Ky. Rev. Stat. 1971, 227.700 et seq.
Mass. Gen. Laws Ann., 148:39 et seq.
Mich. Comp. Laws Ann., 750.243 et seq.
Mont. Code Ann., 50-37-101 et seq.
N.H. Rev. Stat. 1955, 1601 et seq.
N.J. Stat. Ann., 21:2-1 et seq.
Ohio Rev. Code 1953, 3743.27 et seq.
Ore. Rev. Stat., 480.110 et seq.
Pa. Purdon's Stat., Title 35, § 1271 et seq.
R.I. Gen. Laws 1956, 11-13-1 et seq.
Utah Code Ann. 1953, 11-3-1 et seq.
Vt. Stat. Ann., Title 20, § 3131 et seq.

Fireworks Use Act
Ill. Rev. Stat. 1991, Ch. 127 1/2, § 126.9 et seq.

Firm Name Act
S.C. Code Ann. 1976, § 39-13-10 et seq.

First Aid Equipment Law
Cal. Education Code 1976, § 32040 et seq.

First Aid Task Force Act
Ill. Comp. Stat. 1992, Ch. 20, § 3937/1 et seq.

First Amendment to the Citrus County Hospital and Medical Nursing and Convalescent Home Act
Fla. Special Laws 1970, Ch. 70-1001

First and Second Class Cities and Villages Combined Improvement
Neb. Rev. Stat. 1943, 19-2408 et seq. Act

First and Second Class County Property Tax Relief Act
Pa. Purdon's Stat., Title 72, § 4749.1 et seq.

First Bite Act (Motor Vehicles)
Conn. Gen. Stat. Ann., § 14-112 et seq.
Kan. Laws 1939, Ch. 86

First Bond Issue Act (Roads)
Ill. Rev. Stat. 1957, Ch. 121, § 266 et seq.

First Budget Adjustment Act
Vt. Acts 1984, No. 253

First Bus Act
Ky. Acts 1924, Ch. 81

First Class Cities Act
Ind. Code 1971, 18-4-16-1 et seq.
Kan. Stat. Ann., 13-101 et seq.
Wash. Rev. Code Ann., 35.22.010 et seq.

First Class Cities and Counties Act
Ind. Code Ann., 36-3-1-1 et seq.

First Class Cities Employees' Retirement System Law
Wash. Rev. Code Ann., 41.28.005 et seq.

First Class Cities Housing Authorities Law
Neb. Laws 1937, Ch. 90

First Class Cities Intergovernmental Cooperation Authority Act
Pa. Purdon's Stat., Title 53, § 12720.101 et seq.

First Class Cities Off-Street Parking Act
Ind. Code Ann., 36-1-3.5-2 et seq.

First Class Cities Plumbing Code
Pa. Purdon's Stat., Title 53, § 14791 et seq.

First Class City and School District Corporate Net Income Tax Act
Pa. Purdon's Stat., Title 53, § 16111 et seq.

First Class City Building Code
Pa. 1929 Pamph. Laws 1063, No. 413

First Class City Business Tax Reform Act
Pa. Purdon's Stat., Title 53, § 16181 et seq.

First Class City Charter Act
Pa. Purdon's Stat., Title 53, § 12101 et seq.

First Class City Civil Service Act
Pa. Cons. Stat., Title 42, § 4322

First Class City Home Rule Act
Pa. Purdon's Stat., Title 53, § 13157 et seq.

First Class City Hotel Room Rental Tax Act
Pa. Purdon's Stat., Title 53, § 16171 et seq.

First Class City Housing Act
Kan. Stat. Ann., 17-2336

First Class City Park Act
Ind. Code Ann., 36-10-2-2 et seq.

First Class City Pension Fund Act
Pa. Purdon's Stat., Title 53, § 13431 et seq.

First Class City Permanent Registration Act
Pa. Purdon's Stat., Title 25, § 623-1 et seq.

First Class City Public Education Home Rule Act
Pa. Purdon's Stat., Title 53, § 13201 et seq.

First Class City Revenue Bond Act
Pa. Purdon's Stat. Title 53, § 15901 et seq.

First Class City Zoning Act
Mo. Rev. Stat., 89.150 et seq.
Pa. Purdon's Stat., Title 53, § 14751 et seq.

First Class Corporation Charter Act
Pa. 1923 Pamph. Laws 246, No. 160

First Class County Recreation Authority Act
N.J. Rev. Stat. 1937, 40:37B-1 et seq.

First Class County Register of Wills Fee Bill Act
Pa. 1982 Pamph. Laws 11, No. 5

First Class School District Liquor Sales Tax Act
Pa. Purdon's Stat., Title 53, § 16131 et seq.

First Class School District Mercantile License Tax Act
Pa. Purdon's Stat., Title 24, § 582.1 et seq.

First Class School District Tax Act
Pa. Purdon's Stat., Title 24, § 584.1 et seq.

First Class School Districts Act (Personal Property Tax)
Pa. Purdon's Stat., Title 24, § 581.1 et seq.

First Class Township Law
Pa. Purdon's Stat., Title 53, § 55101 et seq.

First Class Township Zoning Enabling Act
Pa. Purdon's Stat., Title 53, § 10101 et seq.

First Colony Management District Act
Tex. Local Government Code, § 376.111 et seq.

First Decontrol Act of 1947
March 31, 1947, Ch. 29, 61 Stat. 34, 50 U.S. Code Appx. § 645

First Deficiency Appropriation Act
Aug. 9, 1989, P.L. 101-73, 15 U.S. Code § 712a

First Deficiency Appropriation Act of 1926
March 3, 1926, Ch. 44, 44 Stat. 162, 2 U.S. Code §§ 64a, 96, 196
Oct. 31, 1969, P.L. 91-105, 83 Stat. 169, 2 U.S. Code § 64a
Aug. 18, 1970, P.L. 91-382, 84 Stat. 810, 2 U.S. Code § 64a
July 17, 1984, P.L. 98-367, 2 U.S. Code § 64a

First Deficiency Appropriation Act of 1936
June 22, 1936, Ch. 689, 49 Stat. 1634, 15 U.S. Code § 712a; 22 U.S. Code § 275
Oct. 4, 1961, P.L. 87-353, 75 Stat. 774, 15 U.S. Code § 712a

First Deficiency Appropriation Act of 1939
March 15, 1939, Ch. 10, 53 Stat. 512

First Deficiency Appropriation Act of 1940
April 6, 1940, Ch. 77, 54 Stat. 82

First Deficiency Appropriation Act of 1941
April 1, 1941, Ch. 32, 55 Stat. 62

First Deficiency Appropriation Act of 1942
Feb. 21, 1942, Ch. 108, 56 Stat. 98

First Deficiency Appropriation Act of 1943
March 18, 1943, Ch. 17, 57 Stat. 21, 22 U.S. Code § 412a; 31 U.S. Code § 317e-1

First Deficiency Appropriation Act of 1945
April 25, 1945, Ch. 95, 59 Stat. 77, 2 U.S. Code § 60g-1; 12 U.S. Code § 1805; 31 U.S. Code § 690; 42 U.S. Code §§ 1523, 1534 nt.
July 3, 1945, Ch. 264, 59 Stat. 383, 42 U.S. Code § 1534 nt.
July 5, 1945, Ch. 271, 59 Stat. 412, 42 U.S. Code § 1523 nt.

First Deficiency Appropriation Act of 1946
Dec. 28, 1945, Ch. 589, 59 Stat. 632, 2 U.S. Code §§ 46a, 46b nts.; 24 U.S. Code § 45 nt.
June 28, 1949, Ch. 266, 63 Stat. 279
April 20, 1960, P.L. 86-426, 74 Stat. 54, 2 U.S. Code § 60e-1

First Deficiency Appropriation Act of 1947
May 1, 1947, Ch. 49, 61 Stat. 58, 2 U.S. Code §§ 46a, 46b nts.

First Deficiency Appropriation Act of 1948
May 10, 1948, Ch. 270, 62 Stat. 213, 2 U.S. Code § 46a nt.

First Deficiency Appropriation Act of 1949
May 24, 1949, Ch. 138, 63 Stat. 76, 2 U.S. Code § 46d-1; 49 U.S. Code § 305 nt.

First Degree Assault Act
N.Y. Penal Law 1965 (Consol. Laws, Ch. 40) § 120.10

First Degree Burglary Law
Ala. Code 1975, § 13A-7-5

First Import Law (Motor Fuel Tax)
N.Y. Laws 1985, Ch. 44

First Liberty Bond Act

 April 24, 1917, Ch. 4, 40 Stat. 35, 31 U.S. Code §§ 746, 755, 759,764, 768, 774, 804

 Feb. 19, 1941, Ch. 7, 55 Stat. 7, 31 U.S. Code § 755 nt.

First National Mortgage Association Charter Act

 February 5, 1988, P.L. 100-242, 12 U.S. Code § 1721

First Offender Act

 Ga. Code Ann., 42-8-60 et seq.

First Program

 Colo. Rev. Stat., 2-3-1401

First Responders Emergency Rescue Act

 Neb. Laws 1992, L.B. 1138, §§ 1 to 18

First Revisory Act

 Ill. Laws 1987, P.A. 85-293

 Ill. Laws 1989, P.A. 85-1440

 Ill. Laws 1990, P.A. 86-1028

 Ill. Laws 1991, P.A. 87-435

First School Bond Validating Act of 1952

 Cal. Statutes 1952, 2nd Ex. Sess., Ch. 23, p. 466

First Special Service Force Memorial Monument Permanent Trust Act

 Mont. Code Ann., 35-21-901 to 35-21-903

First Supplemental Appropriation Act of 1945

 Dec. 22, 1944, Ch. 660, 58 Stat. 853

 March 31, 1945, Ch. 47, 59 Stat. 46

First Supplemental Appropriation Act of 1947

 Aug. 8, 1946, Ch. 870, 60 Stat. 910

First Supplemental Capital Budget Project Itemization Act of 1994-1995

 Pa. 1994 Pamph. Laws, No. 136

First Supplemental Civil Functions Appropriation Act of 1941

 Oct. 9, 1940, Ch. 780, 54 Stat. 1030, 31 U.S. Code § 671a

 Aug. 20, 1996, P.L. 104-186, 2 U.S. Code § 174k nt.

First Supplemental General Appropriation Act

 Pa. 1984 Pamph. 1549 No. 59A

 Pa. 1986 Pamph. Laws, 1754, No. 2A

 Pa. 1988 Pamph. Laws, No. 55A

 Pa. 1991 Pamph. Laws, 432, No. 2A

First Supplemental National Defense Appropriation Act

 June 26, 1940, Ch. 430, 54 Stat. 599

 Aug. 25, 1941, Ch. 409, 55 Stat. 669, 16 U.S. Code § 584f-1; 46 U.S. Code § 119a nt.

 July 25, 1942, Ch. 524, 56 Stat. 704, 31 U.S. Code §§ 215a, 529 nt., 655 nt., 761a; 41 U.S. Code § 6a nts.

 Dec. 23, 1943, Ch. 380, 57 Stat. 611, 42 U.S. Code §§ 46, 1523 nt., 1701, 1705; 46 U.S. Code § 1241 nt.

 July 1, 1966, P.L. 89-485, 80 Stat. 242, 12 U.S. Code § 1828

 Sept. 21, 1966, P.L. 89-597, 80 Stat. 824, 12 U.S. Code § 1828

 Oct. 16, 1966, P.L. 89-695, 80 Stat. 1046, 1055, 1056, 12 U.S. Code §§ 1813, 1817 to 1821

 Dec. 15, 1967, P.L. 90-203, 81 Stat. 610, 12 U.S. Code §§ 1829a, 1830, 1831

 Sept. 21, 1968, P.L. 90-505, 82 Stat. 856, 12 U.S. Code § 1828

 Dec. 23, 1969, P.L. 91-151, 83 Stat. 372, 12 U.S. Code §§ 1813, 1817, 1821, 1828

 Oct. 15, 1970, P.L. 91-452, 84 Stat. 929, 12 U.S. Code § 1820

 Oct. 26, 1970, P.L. 91-508, 84 Stat. 1114, 12 U.S. Code §§ 1829b, 1830, 1831

 Dec. 31, 1970, P.L. 91-609, 84 Stat. 1811, 12 U.S. Code §§ 1813, 1817

First Supplemental Surplus Appropriation Rescission Act of 1946

 Feb. 18, 1946, Ch. 30, 60 Stat. 6, 42 U.S. Code § 1543

 Aug. 8, 1946, Ch. 870, 60 Stat. 915

 July 25, 1947, Ch. 329, 61 Stat. 455

 Aug. 1, 1956, Ch. 837, 70 Stat. 884

First-Time Home Buyer Savings Account Act

Mont. Code Ann., 15-63-101 et seq.

First Time Home Buyers Bond Act

Cal. Health and Safety Code § 52525 et seq.

First Unification Act

Kan. Stat. Ann., 72-6734 et seq.

First Validating Act

Cal. Statutes 1951, Ch. 675, p. 1882

Cal. Statutes 1952, 2nd Ex. Sess., Ch. 31, p. 505

Cal. Statutes 1953, Ch. 1151, p. 2655

Cal. Statutes 1955, Ch. 11, p. 454

Cal. Statutes 1956, 1st Ex. Sess., Ch. 15, p. 302

Cal. Statutes 1957, Ch. 133, p. 719

Cal. Statutes 1958, 1st Ex. Sess., Ch. 10, p. 191

Cal. Statutes 1959, Ch. 12, p. 1857; Ch. 30, p. 1875

Cal. Statutes 1960, 1st Ex. Sess., Ch. 6

Cal. Statutes 1961, Ch. 405

Cal. Statutes 1963, Ch. 7, p. 613

Cal. Statutes 1964, 1st Ex. Sess., Ch. 11, p. 114

Cal. Statutes 1965, Ch. 95, p. 1035

Cal. Statutes 1967, Ch. 2, p. 4

Cal. Statutes 1968, Ch. 6, p. 145

Cal. Statutes 1970, Ch. 4, p. 6

Cal. Statutes 1971, Ch. 12, p. 17

Cal. Statutes 1972, Ch. 41, p. 53

Cal. Statutes 1973, Ch. 38

Cal. Statutes 1974, Ch. 258

Cal. Statutes 1975, Ch. 12

Cal. Statutes 1976, Ch. 114

Cal. Statutes 1977, Ch. 33

Cal. Statutes 1978, Ch. 135

Cal. Statutes 1979, Ch. 54

Cal. Statutes 1980, Ch. 980

Cal. Statutes 1981, Ch. 51

Cal. Statutes 1982, Ch. 617

Cal. Statutes 1983, Ch. 9

Cal. Statutes 1984, Ch. 91

Cal. Statutes 1986, Ch. 75

Cal. Statutes 1988, Ch. 95

Cal. Statutes 1990, Ch. 87

Cal. Statutes 1991, Ch. 17

Cal. Statutes 1991, Ch. 18

Cal. Statutes 1991, Ch. 22

First Validating Act of 1992

Cal. Statutes 1992, Ch. 62

First Validating Act of 1993

Cal. Statutes 1993, Ch. 10

First Validating Act of 1997

Cal. Statutes 1997, Ch. 126

First Validating Act of 1998

Cal. Statutes 1998, Ch. 102

First Validating Act of 1999

Cal. Statutes 1999, Ch. 19

First War Powers Act of 1941

Dec. 18, 1941, Ch. 593, 55 Stat. 838, 12 U.S. Code § 95a; 50 U.S. Code Appx. § 5

March 8, 1946, Ch. 83, 60 Stat. 50

Aug. 8, 1946, Ch. 878, 60 Stat. 925, 50 U.S. Code Appx. §§ 32 to 37

Jan. 12, 1951, Ch. 1230, 64 Stat. 1257

June 1, 1955, Ch. 120, 69 Stat. 82

First Whitney Act (Drug Maintenance Treatment)

N.Y. Laws 1917, Ch. 431

First 84th General Assembly Combining Revisory Act

Ill. Laws 1986, P.A. 84-1308, § 3, Art. II

First 1993 General Revisory Act

Ill. Laws 1993, P.A. 88-45

First 1996 General Revisory Act

Ill. Laws 1996, P.A. 89-626

First 1997 General Revisory Act

Ill. Laws 1997, P.A. 90-14

Fiscal Accountability and Financial Reform Act

N.Y. Education Law 1947 (Consol. Laws Ch. 16) §§ 355, 2575, 6202, 6221, 6230, 6231

Continued

N.Y. Labor Law (Consol. Laws Ch. 31) § 530

N.Y. Public Lands Law (Consol. Laws Ch. 46) § 2

N.Y. State Finance Law 1940 (Consol. Law Ch. 56) §§ 2, 3, 8, 8a, 22, 22a, 23, 40a, 49, 51, 53, 53b, 54, 57, 70 to 72, 75, 92, 93, 122a, 200 to 207, 210, 211

Fiscal Accounting Management Information System Act
Fla. Stat. Ann., 215.90 et seq.

Fiscal Affairs Office Act
N.J. Stat. Ann., 52:11-43

Fiscal Agency Act
Kan. Stat. Ann., 10-501 et seq.

Fiscal Agency Act (Municipal)
N.C. Gen. Stat. 1943, §§ 160-404, 160-405

Fiscal Agency Act (State)
Cal. Government Code § 16670 et seq.

Fiscal Agent Designation Act
Ill. Rev. Stat. 1991, Ch. 127, §§ 320.9, 321

Fiscal Code
Ark. Stat. 1947, 13-202 et seq.
Pa. Purdon's Stat., Title 72, § 1 et seq.

Fiscal Control Act (County)
N.C. Gen. Stat. 1943, § 159-7 et seq.

Fiscal Control and Internal Auditing Act
Ill. Rev. Stat. 1991, Ch. 15, § 1001 et seq.

Fiscal Disclosure and Property Tax Law
R.I. Gen. Laws 1956, 44-35-1 et seq.

Fiscal Disparities Act
Minn. Stat. Ann., 473F.01 et seq.

Fiscal Impact Statement Act
S.C. Code Ann. 1976, § 2-7-70 et seq.

Fiscal Information Act (Local Government)
N.C. Gen. Stat. 1943, § 120-30.41 et seq.

Fiscal Management Responsibility Act (Local)
Ark. Acts 1991, No. 724

Fiscal Note Act
Ga. Code Ann., 28-5-40 et seq.
Ill. Rev. Stat. 1990, Ch. 63, § 42.30 et seq.

Fiscal Notes Act (Local Government Impact)
Ga. Code Ann., 28-5-47 et seq.

Fiscal Procedures Act
Alaska Stat. 1962, § 37.05.010 et seq.

Fiscal Procedures Act for Cities and Counties
Utah Code Ann. 1953, 10-6-101 et seq., 17-36-1 et seq.

Fiscal Procedures Act for Towns (Uniform)
Utah Code Ann. 1953, 10-5-101 et seq.

Fiscal Procedures for Special Districts Act
See Uniform Fiscal Procedures for Special Districts Act

Fiscal Reorganization Act
Ind. Code Ann., 4-13-2-1 et seq.

Fiscal Responsibility Accounting Act (Public Works)
Colo. Rev. Stat., 24-16-101 et seq.

Fiscal Responsibility Act
S.C. Code Ann. 1976, § 1-1-970 et seq.

Fiscal Responsibility Act (Local Government)
Mich. Comp. Laws Ann., 141.1201 et seq.

Fiscal Responsibility and Accounting Act (State)
Mich. Comp. Laws Ann., 21.421 et seq.

Fiscal Responsibility and Recovery Act (Emergency)
Ida. Laws 1983, Ch. 4

Fiscal Responsibility Report Card Act
Ill. Rev. Stat. 1989, Ch. 120, § 2651 et seq.

Fiscal Stabilization Act
Mich. Comp. Laws Ann., 141.1001 et seq.

Fiscal Year Adjustment Act
April 21, 1976, P.L. 94-273, 31 U.S. Code §§ 701 et seq., 1020 et seq.

Fiscal Year Transition Act
April 21, 1976, P.L. 94-274, 31 U.S. Code §§ 701 et seq., 1020 et seq.

Fiscal Year 1981 Airport Development Authorization Act
Aug. 13, 1981, P.L. 97-35, 49 U.S. Code § 1701 nt.

Fiscal Year 1991 General Appropriation Act
Tex. Laws 1986, Ch. 13, Arts. 1 to 9

Fiscal Year 1993 Omnibus Appropriations Act—Big Bill
Vt. Acts 1991, No. 245

Fiscal Year 1994-Budget Adjustment Act
Vt. Acts 1993, No. 140

Fiscal Year 1995 Appropriations Act—Big Bill
Vt. Acts 1993, No. 210

Fiscal Year 1995 Deficit Reduction Act
Vt. Acts 1995, No. 74

Fiscal Year 1996 Bond and Capital Improvements Act
Del. Laws Vol. 70, Ch. 210

Fiscal Year 1997 Bond and Capital Improvements Act
Del. Laws Vol. 70, Ch. 473

Fischel Act (Minimum Wage)
N.Y. Labor Law (Consol. Laws Ch. 31) § 650 et seq.

Fish Act
Ala. Code 1975, § 9-2-60 et seq.
Ill. Rev. Stat. 1991, Ch. 56, § 1.1 et seq.
La. Rev. Stat. Ann., 56:311 et seq.
Md. Ann. Code 1974, Art. NR, § 4-101 et seq.
Pa. Purdon's Stat., Title 30, § 1 et seq.
Va. Code 1950, § 28.1-47 et seq.

Fish Act (Game and Fresh Water)
Md. Ann. Code 1974, Art. NR, § 4-601 et seq.

Fish Act (Leases)
N.J. Revised Stat. 1937, 2:58-32

Fish and Aquatic Life Act
Ill. Rev. Stat. 1989, Ch. 56, § 1.1 et seq.

Fish and Boat Code
Pa. Cons. Stat., Title 30, § 101 et seq.

Fish and Game Act
Alaska Stat. 1962, § 16.05.010 et seq.
Ariz. Rev. Stat. Ann., § 17-101 et seq.
Ark. Stat. 1947, 47-101 et seq.
Cal. Fish and Game Code 1957, § 1 et seq.
Colo. Rev. Stat., 33-1-101 et seq.
Conn. Gen. Stat. Ann., § 26-1 et seq.
D.C. Code Ann., § 22-1628 et seq.
D.C. Code 1973, § 22-1628 et seq.
Del. Code of 1974, Title 7, § 101 et seq.
Fla. Stat. Ann., 372.001 et seq.
Ga. Code Ann., 27-1-1 et seq.
Haw. Rev. Stat. Ann., § 187-1 et seq.
Ida. Code 1947, 36-101 et seq.
Kan. Stat. Ann., 32-101 et seq.
Ky. Rev. Stat. 1971, 150.010 et seq.
Mass. Gen. Laws Ann., 131:1 et seq.
Mich. Comp. Laws Ann., 300.1 et seq., 311.1 et seq.
Minn. Stat. Ann., 97A.011 et seq.
Miss. Code Ann. 1972, § 49-1-1 et seq.
Mo. Rev. Stat., 252.010 et seq.
Mont. Rev. Code 1947, 26-101 et seq.
Mont. Rev. Code 1991, 87-1-101 et seq.
N.D. Cent. Code, 20.1-01-01 et seq.
Neb. Rev. Stat. 1943, 37-101 et seq.
Nev. Rev. Stat. 1979 Reprint, 501.010 et seq.
N.H. Rev. Stat. 1955, 206:1 et seq.
N.J. Stat. Ann., 23:1-1 et seq.
N.M. Stat. Ann., 7-1-1 et seq.
N.Y. Environmental Conservation Law 1972 (Consol. Laws Ch. 43B) § 11-0101 et seq., 13-0101
Ohio Rev. Code 1953, 1531.01 et seq., 1533.01 et seq.
Continued

Okla. Stat. Ann., Title 29, § 101 et seq.
Ore. Rev. Stat., 496.002 et seq.
Pa. 1901 Pamph. Laws 302, No. 203
S.C. Code Ann. 1976, § 50-1-10 et seq.
S.D. Codified Laws 1967, 41-1-1 et seq.
Tenn. Code Ann., 70-1-101 et seq.
Utah Code Ann. 1953, 23-13-1 et seq.
Vt. Stat. Ann., Title 10, § 4001 et seq.
Wash. Rev. Code Ann., 77.04.010 et seq.
Wis. Stat. Ann., 29.01 et seq.
Wyo. Stat. Ann., § 23-1-101 et seq.

Fish and Game Act (Inland)
Me. Rev. Stat. Ann. 1964, Title 12, § 7001 et seq.

Fish and Game Bond Act
N.M. Stat. Ann., 17-1-16 et seq.

Fish and Game Conservation Law
Iowa Code Ann., 109.1 et seq.

Fish and Game District Act (Klamath River)
Cal. Fish and Game Code § 11036

Fish and Game Enforcement Act
Mich. Comp. Laws Ann., 300.11 et seq.

Fish and Game Federal Loan Act
Kan. Laws 1933, Sp. Sess., Ch. 107

Fish and Game Free Permit Act
Ind. Code Ann., 14-2-7-19 et seq.

Fish and Game Lifetime License Trust Fund
Mich. Comp. Laws Ann., 316.1001 et seq.

Fish and Game Point System Act
S.C. Code Ann. 1976, § 50-9-1010 et seq.

Fish and Game Protection Trust Fund Act
Mich. Comp. Laws Ann., 300.211 et seq.

Fish and Game Refuge Law
Cal. Fish and Game Code 1957, § 10500 et seq.

Fish and Game Reorganization Act (Charles Brown)
Cal. Statutes 1951, Ch. 715, p. 1979

Fish and Game Sanctuary Act
March 10, 1934, Ch. 54, 48 Stat. 400, 16 U.S. Code §§ 694 to 694b

Fish and Game Warden Retirement Act
Wyo. Stat. Ann., § 9-3-601 et seq.

Fish and Seafood Promotion Act of 1986
Nov. 14, 1986, P.L. 99-659, 16 U.S. Code § 4001 nt.
June 27, 1988, P.L. 100-350, 102 Stat. 660, 16 U.S. Code § 4004
Nov. 28, 1990, P.L. 101-627, 16 U.S. Code §§ 4004 nt., 4005, 4005 nt., 4006, 4008

Fish and Wildlife Act
Ind. Code Ann., 14-2-1-1 et seq.
Mont. Code Ann., 87-1-101 et seq.
N.Y. Environmental Conservation Law 1972 (Consol. Laws Ch. 43B) 11-0101 et seq.

Fish and Wildlife Act of 1956
Aug. 8, 1956, Ch. 1036, 70 Stat. 1119, 15 U.S. Code §§ 713c-3, 713c-3 nt.; 16 U.S. Code §§ 742a to 742j
Sept. 2, 1958, P.L. 85-888, 72 Stat. 1710, 16 U.S. Code § 742c
Oct. 4, 1961, P.L. 87-367, 75 Stat. 788, 16 U.S. Code § 742b
May 20, 1964, P.L. 88-309, 78 Stat. 199, 16 U.S. Code § 742c
July 24, 1965, P.L. 89-85, 79 Stat. 262, 16 U.S. Code §§ 742c, 742c nt.
June 12, 1970, P.L. 91-279, 84 Stat. 309, 16 U.S. Code § 742
Aug. 24, 1970, P.L. 91-387, 84 Stat. 829, 16 U.S. Code § 742c
Nov. 18, 1971, P.L. 92-159, 85 Stat. 480, 16 U.S. Code § 724j-1
Oct. 18, 1972, P.L. 92-502, 86 Stat. 905, 16 U.S. Code § 742j-1
April 22, 1974, P.L. 93-271, 88 Stat. 92, 16 U.S. Code § 742b
Nov. 8, 1978, P.L. 95-616, 16 U.S. Code § 742f
Oct. 18, 1982, P.L. 97-347, 16 U.S. Code §§ 742c, 742f
Oct. 19, 1984, P.L. 98-498, 16 U.S. Code §§ 742 et seq.

Nov. 14, 1986, P.L. 99-659, 16 U.S. Code
§ 742c

Oct. 5, 1998, P.L. 105-242, 16 U.S. Code
§ 742f

Fish and Wildlife and Their Habitation on Private Lands Act (Enhancement and Management of)

Cal. Fish and Game Code § 3400 et seq.

Fish and Wildlife Conservation Act of 1980

Sept. 29, 1980, P.L. 96-366, 16 U.S. Code
§ 2901 et seq., 2901 nt.

Dec. 31, 1982, P.L. 97-396, 16 U.S. Code
§ 2911

Aug. 7, 1986, P.L. 99-375, 16 U.S. Code
§ 2810

Nov. 14, 1988, P.L. 100-653, 16 U.S. Code
§§ 2910, 2912

Nov. 16, 1990, P.L. 101-593, 16 U.S. Code
§§ 668dd nt., 2910

Oct. 23, 1992, P.L. 102-440, 16 U.S. Code
§ 2910

Fish and Wildlife Coordination Act

March 10, 1934, Ch. 55, 48 Stat. 401, 16 U.S.
Code §§ 661 to 666c

Aug. 14, 1946, Ch. 965, 60 Stat. 1080, 16
U.S. Code 661 to 666c

June 19, 1948, Ch. 528, 62 Stat. 497, 16 U.S.
Code § 665a

Aug. 12, 1958, P.L. 85-624, 72 Stat. 563, 16
U.S. Code §§ 661 to 664

July 9, 1965, P.L. 89-72, 79 Stat. 216, 16
U.S. Code § 662

Fish and Wildlife Crimestoppers Act

Mont. Code Ann., 87-5-601 et seq.

Fish and Wildlife Habitat Enhancement Act

Cal. Fish and Game Code 1957, § 2600 et
seq.

Fish and Wildlife Improvement Act of 1978

Nov. 8, 1978, P.L. 95-616, 16 U.S. Code
§§ 460k-3, 666g, 668a, 668dd, 690e et seq.;
18 U.S. Code §§ 1114, 3112

Dec. 31, 1982, P.L. 97-396, 16 U.S. Code
§ 742l

Oct. 30, 1998, P.L. 105-328, 16 U.S. Code
§ 742l

Fish and Wildlife Revenue Enhancement Act of 1998

Oct. 30, 1998, P.L. 105-328, 112 Stat. 3057,
16 U.S. Code § 742a nt.

Fish and Wildlife Trust Fund Act (Nongame)

Mich. Comp. Laws Ann., 299.151 et seq.

Fish Canners' License Law

Cal. Fish and Game Code 1957, § 8040

Fish, Dog and Game Act

Va. Code 1950, § 29-1 et seq.

Fish Enhancement Bond Act

Cal. Water Code, § 11922 et seq.

Fish Farming Act

Tex. Agriculture Code, § 134.001 et seq.

Fish Fund Hatchery Improvement Capital Budget Act

Pa. 1990 Pamph. Laws, No. 162

Fish, Game and Forestry Act

Cal. Water Code § 11922 et seq.

N.Y. Environmental Conservation Law 1972
(Consol. Laws Ch. 43B)

W. Va. Code 1966, § 20-1-1 et seq.

Fish, Game and Watercraft Law

S.C. Code Ann. 1976, § 50-1-10 et seq.

Fish Health Protection Law

Cal. Fish and Game Code 1957, § 6300 et
seq.

Fish Marketing Act

Cal. Corporations Code § 13200 et seq.

Cal. Statutes 1933, p. 2161

Haw. Rev. Stat. Ann., § 422-1 et seq.

Me. Rev. Stat. Ann. 1964, Title 13, § 2001 et
seq.

Wash. Rev. Code Ann., 24.36.010 et seq.

Fish Poundage Fee Act

Ore. Rev. Stat., 508.505 et seq.

Fish Products Inspection Act
Me. Rev. Stat. Ann. 1964, Title 12, § 4681 et seq.

Fish Propagators' Regulation Law
Cal. Fish and Game Code 1957, § 6450 et seq.

Fish Protection Act
Ind. Code Ann., 14-2-5-9

Fish Restoration and Management Projects Act
Aug. 9, 1950, Ch. 658, 64 Stat. 430, 16 U.S. Code §§ 777 to 777k
July 2, 1956, Ch. 489, 70 Stat. 473, 16 U.S. Code §§ 777a, 777k
Aug. 1, 1956, Ch. 852, 70 Stat. 908, 16 U.S. Code § 777k
Oct. 23, 1970, P.L. 91-503, 84 Stat. 1101, 16 U.S. Code §§ 777c, 777e to 777g, 777k

Fish Restoration Project Law
Ill. Rev. Stat. 1989, Ch. 56, § 249, 250

Fish Sanctuary Act
Wash. Rev. Code Ann., 75.20.110 et seq.

Fish Trap Act
Alaska Stat. 1962, § 16.10.060 et seq.

Fisher Act (Forest Lands)
N.Y. Real Property Tax Law (Consol. Laws Ch. 50A) § 480

Fisher Act (Grade Crossings)
Ohio Rev. Code 1953, 5561.01 et seq.

Fisheries Act
Alaska Stat. 1962, § 16.10.060 et seq.
Ga. Code Ann., 27-1-1 et seq.
N.C. Gen. Stat. 1943, § 113-127 et seq.
P.R. Laws Ann. 1954, Title 12, § 41 et seq.
Wash. Rev. Code Ann., 75.08.010 et seq.

Fisheries Act (Atlantic States Marine Commission)
Md. Ann. Code 1974, Art. NR, § 4-301 et seq.

Fisheries Act (Bristol Bay)
Alaska Comp. Laws Ann. 1949, § 39-2-4

Fisheries Act (Coastal)
Me. Rev. Stat. Ann. 1964, Title 12, § 6001 et seq.
S.C. Code Ann. 1976, § 50-17-10 et seq.

Fisheries Act (Commercial)
Alaska Comp. Laws Ann. 1949, § 39-2-13 et seq.
S.C. Code Ann. 1976, § 50-17-10 et seq.

Fisheries Act (Felando-Polanco)
Cal. Statutes 1986, Ch. 1049

Fisheries Act (Potomac River)
Md. Ann. Code 1974, Art. NR, § 4-306 et seq.

Fisheries Act (Tidewater)
Md. Ann. Code 1974, Art. NR, § 4-701 et seq.

Fisheries Act of 1995
Nov. 3, 1995, P.L. 104-43, 16 U.S. Code § 5501 nt.
Oct. 11, 1996, P.L. 104-297, 16 U.S. Code § 971c nt.

Fisheries Amendments of 1982
Dec. 29, 1982, P.L. 97-389, 16 U.S. Code § 779 nt.

Fisheries and Wildlife Management Act
Miss. Code Ann. 1972, § 49-3-1 et seq.

Fisheries Compact (Atlantic States)
Me. Rev. Stat. Ann. 1964, Title 12, § 4601 et seq.

Fisheries Compact Act
Wash. Rev. Code Ann., 75.40.010 et seq.

Fisheries Compact Act (Atlantic States Marine)
See Atlantic States Marine Fisheries Compact Act

Fisheries Compact Act (Gulf States Marine)
See Gulf States Marine Fisheries Compact Act

Fisheries Compact Act (Pacific Marine)
See Pacific Marine Fisheries Compact Act

Fisheries Financing Act
Oct. 11, 1996, P.L. 104-297, Title II, 46 U.S. Code Appx. § 1245 nt.
Oct. 21, 1998, P.L. 105-277, 46 U.S. Code Appx. § 1274 nt.

Fisheries Restoration Act
Cal. Fish and Game Code 1957, § 2760 et seq.
Mich. Comp. Laws Ann., 300.151

Fisheries Restoration and Enhancement Act
Ore. Laws 1991, Ch. 512

Fisherman's Right-to-Know Act
Ala. Acts 1998, H.B. 72

Fishermen's Economic Development Act
N.C. Gen. Stat. 1943, § 113-315.15 et seq.

Fishermen's Hull Commercial Insurance, and Protection and Indemnity Club Act
N.C. Gen. Stat. 1943, § 58-340.1 et seq.

Fishermen's License Act (Commercial)
Tex. Parks and Wildlife Code, § 47.001 et seq.

Fishermen's License Act (Nonresident Commercial)
Tex. Penal Code 1925, Art. 934b-1

Fishermen's Protective Act
Nov. 3, 1987, P.L. 100-151, 22 U.S. Code § 1977
June 27, 1988, P.L. 100-350, 102 Stat. 660, 22 U.S. Code § 1977

Fishermen's Protective Act of 1967
Aug. 27, 1954, P.L. 680, Ch. 1018, 68 Stat. 883, 22 U.S. Code §§ 1971 to 1976
Aug. 12, 1968, P.L. 90-482, 82 Stat. 729, 22 U.S. Code §§ 1971 nt., 1973, 1975, 1977

Dec. 23, 1971, P.L. 92-219, 85 Stat. 786, 22 U.S. Code § 1978
Oct. 26, 1972, P.L. 92-569, 86 Stat. 1182, 22 U.S. Code §§ 1972, 1973, 1975, 1977, 1979
Oct. 27, 1972, P.L. 92-594, 86 Stat. 1313, 22 U.S. Code § 1977
Nov. 18, 1977, P.L. 95-194, 22 U.S. Code §§ 1977, 1980
Oct. 28, 1978, P.L. 95-541, 22 U.S. Code §§ 1971 and nt.
Aug. 15, 1979, P.L. 96-61, 22 U.S. Code § 1978
July 17, 1984, P.L. 98-364, 22 U.S. Code §§ 1972, 1972 nt., 1973 to 1975, 1977, 1979
Nov. 14, 1986, P.L. 99-659, 22 U.S. Code §§ 1977 nt., 1977
Nov. 23, 1988, P.L. 100-711, 22 U.S. Code § 1978
Nov. 28, 1990, P.L. 101-627, 22 U.S. Code § 1977
Nov. 2, 1992, P.L. 102-582, 22 U.S. Code § 1978
Nov. 3, 1995, P.L. 104-43, 22 U.S. Code §§ 19777, 1980a, 1980b
June 25, 1999, P.L. 106-36, 22 U.S. Code § 1978

Fishermen's Vocational Regulation Law
Cal. Fish and Game Code 1957, §§ 1050 et seq., 7850

Fishery Act
Haw. Rev. Stat. Ann., § 187A-21 et seq.

Fishery Conservation Amendments of 1990
Nov. 28, 1990, P.L. 101-627, 16 U.S. Code §§ 1373 nt., 1801 nt., 1802, 1802 nt., 1822 nt.

Fishery Conservation and Management Act of 1976
April 13, 1976, P.L. 94-265, 16 U.S. Code § 1801 et seq.
April 28, 1978, P.L. 95-354, 16 U.S. Code § 1801 et seq.
Aug. 15, 1979, P.L. 96-61, 16 U.S. Code §§ 1821, 1883
Nov. 16, 1979, P.L. 96-118, 16 U.S. Code § 1821
April 30, 1994, P.L. 103-236, 16 U.S. Code § 1821

Fishery Conservation Zone Transition Act
Feb. 21, 1977, P.L. 95-6, 16 U.S. Code
§§ 981 nt., 1801 nt., 1823 nt., 1826
March 3, 1977, P.L. 95-8, 16 U.S. Code
§ 1823 nt.
July 26, 1977, P.L. 95-73, 16 U.S. Code
§ 1823 nt.
Dec. 28, 1977, P.L. 95-219, 16 U.S. Code
§§ 1801 nt.
July 1, 1978, P.L. 95-314, 16 U.S. Code
§ 1823 nt.
July 17, 1984, P.L. 98-364, 16 U.S. Code
§ 1823

Fishery Conservation Zone Transition Act Amendments of 1977
March 3, 1977, P.L. 95-8, 16 U.S. Code
§ 1823 nt.

Fishing Act
Fla. Stat. Ann., 372.001 et seq.

Fishing Act (Sportsmen)
Mich. Comp. Laws Ann., 301.1 et seq.

Fishing and Fisheries Act (Commercial)
Mich. Comp. Laws Ann., 308.1 et seq.
Ore. Rev. Stat., 506.001 et seq.

Fishing and Hunting Act
Me. Rev. Stat. Ann. 1964, Title 12, § 7001 et seq.

Fishing and Hunting License Law
Cal. Fish and Game Code 1957, § 1050 et seq.

Fishing Control Act
Cal. Fish and Game Code 1957, § 7891

Fishing Enhancement Act
La. Rev. Stat. Ann., 639.1 et seq.

Fishing Guide Licensing Act
Ark. Code Ann. 1987, 15-42-109 et seq.,
15-43-239, 47-208

Fishing Law (Salt Water-Pinellas County)
Fla. Special Laws 1953, Ch. 29432

Fishing License Act
Alaska Stat. 1962, § 16.05.330 et seq.
Ky. Rev. Stat. 1971, 150.170 et seq.
Mich. Comp. Laws Ann., 316.101 et seq.
Wash. Rev. Code Ann., 75.32.001 et seq.

Fishing License Act (Commercial)
Wash. Rev. Code Ann., 75.28.010 et seq.

Fishing Loan Act (Commercial)
Alaska Stat. 1962, § 16.10.300 et seq.

Fishing Season Act (Newberry County)
S.C. Acts 1933, p. 387, No. 282

Fishlake National Forest Enlargement Act
May 26, 1992, P.L. 102-292, 106 Stat. 181

Fit Premises Act
Utah Code Ann. 1953, 57-22-1 et seq.

Fitchburg Off-Street Parking Garage Act
Mass. Acts 1954, Ch. 608

Fitchburg Water Loan Act
Mass. Acts 1951, Ch. 732

Fite, Engel and Downing Act (Navigable Waterways and Flood Control)
Ala. Code 1975, § 33-17-1 et seq.

Fite Law (Classified Service)
N.Y. Civil Service Law 1958 (Consol. Laws Ch. 7) § 10, 11a, 23 et seq.

Fitting and Selling of Hearing Aids Act
Fla. Stat. Ann., 484.0401 et seq.
S.C. Code Ann. 1976, § 40-25-10 et seq.

Fitzgerald Act (Apprentice Labor)
See National Apprenticeship Act

Fitzgerald Act (Erie County Supplies)
N.Y. Laws 1938, Ch. 331

Fitzgerald and Ben Hill County Development Authority Act
Ga. Laws 1963, p. 2003

Fitzgerald-Ben Hill County Charter Commission Act
Ga. Laws 1999, H.B. 896

Fitzgerald-Elliott Displaced Homemakers Act
Mich. Comp. Laws Ann., 421.101 et seq.

Fitzgerald-Fehling-Morley Act (Holidays)
Mich. Comp. Laws Ann., 435.101 et seq.

Fitzgerald-Tyson Act
See Emergency Officers' Retirement Act

Fitzhugh-Robertson Liquor Law
Tex. Bus. and Commerce Code, § 15.01 et seq.
Tex. Penal Code 1911, Art. 611 et seq.

Fitzpatrick-Lowman-Rayburn-Ray Act (Teachers' Retirement)
Ky. Rev. Stat. 1971, 161.220, 161.260, 161.290, 161.340, 161.400, 161.430, 161.470, 161.515, 161.540, 161.550, 161.600, 161.620

Five Acre Homestead Act (Alaska)
Alaska Comp. Laws Ann. 1949, § 47-2-71

Five Civilized Tribes Act (Disposition of Affairs)
April 26, 1906, Ch. 1876, 34 Stat. 137

Five Commissioners Bill
Del. Laws Vol. 19, Part 1, p. 58, Ch. 26

Five Counties Act
Ky. Acts 1883-84 (Local and Private) Ch. 598

Five Day Act (Marriage License)
Mass. Gen. Laws 1932, Ch. 207, § 19 et seq.
Mich. Comp. Laws Ann., 551.103a

Five-Day Bank Week Act
Ind. Code 1971, 28-2-10-1 et seq.

Five-gallon Act (Intoxicating Liquors)
Ala. Code 1975, § 28-4-115

Five Mile Act (Dramshops)
Mo. Laws 1907, p. 257, No. 1

Five Percent Preference Act (Public Works)
Ariz. Rev. Stat. 1956, § 34-241

Five Percent Reserved Fund Act
S.C. Constitution, Article III, § 36

Five-Sixths Jury Verdict Act
Minn. Stat. Ann., 546.17
N.Y. Civil Practice Law and Rules (Consol. Laws Ch. 8) § 4113
Wis. Stat. Ann., 805.09

Five-Year Exemption and Abatement Law
N.J. Stat. Ann., 40A:21-1 et seq.

Five Year School Building Program Act
D.C. Code Ann., §§ 31-203, 47-203

Five-Year School Building Program Act (D. C.)
Feb. 26, 1925, Ch. 342, 43 Stat. 986

Five Year Statute of Limitations
Cal. Code of Civil Procedure § 318
Mo. Rev. Stat., 516.120

Five Year Statute of Limitations (Written Instruments)
Ark. Code Ann. 1987, 16-56-111

Fixed Charges Loan Act
R.I. Public Laws 1939, Ch. 680

Fixed Guideway Authority Act (Intermountain)
Colo. Rev. Stat., 32-16-101 et seq.

Flag Act
Ariz. Rev. Stat. Ann., § 41-853
Cal. Government Code § 430 et seq.
Conn. Gen. Stat. Ann., § 53-258a
Del. Code of 1974 Title 11, § 1331
La. Rev. Stat. Ann., 14:116, 14:117
Md. Ann. Code 1957, Art. 27, § 81 et seq.
Me. Rev. Stat. Ann. 1964, Title 1, § 251 et seq.
Mich. Comp. Laws Ann., 750.244 et seq.
Continued

Miss. Code Ann. 1972, § 97-7-39

Mont. Code Ann., 45-8-215

N.H. Rev. Stat. 1955, 646:1, 646:2

Ohio Rev. Code 1953, 2927.11(A)(1)

Okla. Stat. Ann., Title 21, § 371 et seq.

Pa. Cons. Stat., Title 18, § 2101 et seq.

S.D. Codified Laws 1967, 22-9-1

Tenn. Code Ann., 39-5-841 et seq.

Va. Code 1950, § 18.2-486 et seq.

Vt. Stat. Ann., Title 13, § 1901 et seq.

Wash. Rev. Code Ann., 9.86.010 et seq.

Wis. Stat. Ann., 946.05, 946.06

Flag and Emblems Act

R.I. Gen. Laws 1956, 11-15-1 et seq.

Flag and Seal, Seat of Government, and the States

July 30, 1947, Ch. 389, 61 Stat. 641, 4 U.S. Code §§ 1 to 110

May 24, 1949, Ch. 139, 63 Stat. 107, 4 U.S. Code § 111

Oct. 31, 1951, Ch. 655, 65 Stat. 712, 4 U.S. Code §§ 141 to 146

Sept. 3, 1954, Ch. 1263, 68 Stat. 1227, 4 U.S. Code § 107

Aug. 1, 1956, Ch. 827, 70 Stat. 799, 4 U.S. Code § 104

Aug. 3, 1956, Ch. 941, 70 Stat. 1020, 4 U.S. Code § 111

Feb. 16, 1962, P.L. 87-406, 76 Stat. 9, 4 U.S. Code § 111

Sept. 6, 1966, P.L. 89-554, 80 Stat. 608, 4 U.S. Code §§ 42, 111, 112

Nov. 7, 1966, P.L. 89-789, 80 Stat. 1422, 33 U.S. Code § 709a

July 5, 1968, P.L. 90-381, 82 Stat. 291, 4 U.S. Code § 3

Flag Day Act

Ill. Rev. Stat. 1991, Ch. 1, §§ 3051-45

Flag Desecration Act

D.C. Code 1967, § 22-3414

Ill. Rev. Stat. 1991, Ch. 1, § 3350 et seq.

Mass. Gen. Laws Ann., 264:1 et seq.

N.Y. General Business Law (Consol. Laws Ch. 20) § 136

Flag Desecration Law

Iowa Code Ann., 718A.1 et seq.

Flag Display Act

D.C. Code Ann., § 1-121 et seq.

Ill. Rev. Stat. 1991, Ch. 1, § 3300 et seq.

Flag Protection Act of 1989

Oct. 28, 1989, P.L. 101-131, 18 U.S. Code §§ 700, 700 nt.

Flag Salute Act

Mass. Gen. Laws Ann., 71:69

N.J. Stat. Ann., 18A:36-3

N.Y. Education Law 1947 (Consol. Laws Ch. 16) § 802

Pa. Purdon's Stat., Title 24, § 7-771

Flagship of Pennsylvania Act

Pa. 1988 Pamph. Laws, No. 61

Flameproof Decorations Act

Ohio Rev. Code 1953, 3743.44 et seq.

Flammable and Combustible Liquids Act

Pa. 1998 Pamph. Laws, No. 15

Flammable Articles Act

Md. Ann. Code 1974, Art. EN, § 6-201 et seq.

Flammable Fabrics Act

June 30, 1953, Ch. 164, 67 Stat. 111, 15 U.S. Code §§ 1191 to 1200

Aug. 23, 1954, Ch. 833, 68 Stat. 770, 15 U.S. Code § 1193

Dec. 14, 1967, P.L. 90-189, 81 Stat. 568, 15 U.S. Code §§ 1191 to 1195, 1197, 1198, 1200 to 1204

Oct. 25, 1972, P.L. 92-542, 86 Stat. 1108, 15 U.S. Code § 1191 nt.

Nov. 10, 1978, P.L. 95-631, 15 U.S. Code §§ 1196, 1202

Nov. 16, 1990, P.L. 101-608, 15 U.S. Code §§ 1193, 1194

N.J. Stat. Ann., 2A:123-3 et seq.

R.I. Gen. Laws 1956, 23-24.2-1 et seq.

Wash. Rev. Code Ann., 70.110.010 et seq.

Flanagan Act (Slot Machines)
N.C. Gen. Stat. 1943, § 14-304 et seq.

Flare Act (Motor Vehicles)
Del. Code of 1974, Title 21, § 4357
Ind. Code Ann., 9-8-6-41, 9-8-6-42
La. Rev. Stat. Ann., 32:367 et seq.
Minn. Stat. Ann., 169.75
N.H. Rev. Stat. 1955, 265:113

Flat Grant Law (Schools)
Ind. Code Ann., 21-3-4.5-1 et seq.

Flat Salary Law
Ore. Rev. Stat., 204.116 et seq.

Flathead Basin Commission Act
Mont. Code Ann., 75-7-301 et seq.

Fleming Act (Lake Erie)
Ohio Rev. Code 1953, 1506.10 et seq.,
721.04 et seq.

Fletcher Budget and Financial Control Act
Ala. Code 1975, § 41-4-80 et seq.

Fletcher-Rayburn Securities Act of 1933
See Securities Act Of 1933

Flexibility Act (University of Medicine and Dentistry)
N.J. Stat. Ann., 18A:64G-1 et seq.

Flexible Benefits Act (State Employees)
Okla. Stat. Ann., Title 74, § 1341 et seq.

Flexible Tariff Act
June 17, 1930, Ch. 497, 46 Stat. 590, 19 U.S. Code § 1336

Flight Hazard Act
N.Y. General Municipal Law (Consol. Laws Ch. 24) § 355 et seq.

Flight Obstruction Easement Act
Neb. Rev. Stat. 1943, 3-204

Flight Officer Act
July 8, 1942, Ch. 493, 56 Stat. 649

Flint Act (Municipal Courts)
Mich. Comp. Laws Ann., 730.101 et seq.

Flirting Act
N.C. Gen. Stat. 1943, § 14-274

Floating Home Residency Law
Cal. Civil Code § 800 et seq.

Floating Homes Residency Act
Ida. Code 1947, 55-2701 et seq.

Flood and Drainage Control Act (Urban)
Miss. Code Ann. 1972, § 51-35-301 et seq.

Flood and Drainage Planning Assessments Act (Joint)
N.M. Stat. Ann., 73-24-1 et seq.

Flood Control Act
July 2, 1986, P.L. 99-349, 100 Stat. 724
Ariz. Rev. Stat. Ann., § 45-1441 et seq.
Cal. Water Code § 8000 et seq., 15100 et seq.
Ill. Rev. Stat. 1981, Ch. 17, § 126a et seq.
Ind. Code Ann., 13-2-22-1 et seq.
Miss. Code Ann. 1972, § 51-35-101 et seq.
N.Y. Laws 1936, Ch. 862
Ore. Rev. Stat., 549.010 et seq.
Pa. Purdon's Stat., Title 32, § 653 et seq.

Flood Control Act (Arroyo)
N.M. Stat. Ann., 72-16-1 et seq.

Flood Control Act (Blue Waters Ditch)
Ill. Comp. Stat. 1992, Ch. 615, § 85/0.01 et seq.
Ill. Rev. Stat. 1991, Ch. 19, § 1150 et seq.

Flood Control Act (Charles River)
Mass. Acts 1955, Ch. 768

Flood Control Act (Counties)
Wash. Rev. Code Ann., 86.12.010 et seq.

Flood Control Act (Fresno Metropolitan)
Cal. Water Code, Appendix, § 73-1 et seq.

Flood Control Act (Las Cruces Arroyo)
N.M. Ann. 1978, 72-17-1 et seq.

Flood Control Act (Orange County)
Cal. Statutes 1927, Ch. 723, p. 1325
Cal. Water Code, Appendix, § 36-1 et seq.

Flood Control Act (San Bernardino County)
Cal. Statutes 1939, Ch. 73, p. 1011
Cal. Water Code, Appendix, § 43-1 et seq.

Flood Control Act (Southern Sandoval County Arroyo)
N.M. Stat. Ann., 72-19-1 et seq.

Flood Control Act (Urban)
Colo. Rev. Stat., 32-11-101 et seq.

Flood Control Act (Vallejo County)
Cal. Statutes 1952, 1st Ex. Sess., Ch. 17, p. 351

Flood Control Act (Ventura County)
Cal. Water Code, Appendix, § 46-1 et seq.

Flood Control Act (Westfield)
Mass. Acts 1939, Ch. 278

Flood Control Act of Fifth Class Cities
Ind. Burns' 1933, 48-5001 et seq.

Flood Control Act of 1937
Sept. 3, 1954, Ch. 1264, 68 Stat. 1266, 33 U.S. Code § 701g

Flood Control Act of 1938
Sept. 3, 1954, Ch. 1264, 68 Stat. 1266, 33 U.S. Code § 706

Flood Control Act of 1944
Dec. 22, 1944, Ch. 665, 58 Stat. 887, 16 U.S. Code §§ 460d, 825s; 33 U.S. Code §§ 701-1, 701a-1, 701b-1, 701c nt., 708, 709; 43 U.S. Code § 390

Flood Control Act of 1946
July 24, 1946, Ch. 596, 60 Stat. 641 (See 10 U.S. Code § 3296 et seq.;16 U.S. Code § 460d; 33 U.S. Code §§ 701c-3, 701f-1 nt., 701g, 701n to 701r; See 40 U.S. Code § 483; 43 U.S. Code § 931b)
Oct. 30, 1951, Ch. 636, 65 Stat. 693
March 7, 1974, P.L. 93-254, 88 Stat. 20, 33 U.S. Code § 701r

Nov. 28, 1990, P.L. 101-640, 104 Stat. 4617

Flood Control Act of 1948
June 30, 1948, Ch. 771, 62 Stat. 1175, 33 U.S. Code §§ 701c nt., 701n, 701o, 701s, 701t
July 11, 1956, Ch. 558, 70 Stat. 522, 33 U.S. Code § 701s
Oct. 23, 1962, P.L. 87-874, 76 Stat. 1194, 33 U.S. Code § 701s
March 7, 1974, P.L. 93-254, 88 Stat. 29, 33 U.S. Code § 701s

Flood Control Act of 1950
May 17, 1950, Ch. 188, 64 Stat. 170, 33 U.S. Code §§ 701-1 nt., 701b-1, 701b-8, 701c nt. and others
June 28, 1955, Ch. 194, 69 Stat. 186, 33 U.S. Code § 701n
Oct. 12, 1996, P.L. 104-303, 33 U.S. Code § 701u

Flood Control Act of 1954
Sept. 3, 1954, Ch. 1264, 68 Stat. 1256, 16 U.S. Code § 460d; 33 U.S. Code §§ 701b-8, 701c nt., 701c-3, 701-1 nt., 701g, 702a-12 nt., 706
March 7, 1974, P.L. 93-251, 88 Stat. 20, 33 U.S. Code § 701g

Flood Control Act of 1958
July 3, 1958, P.L. 85-500, 72 Stat. 319, 33 U.S. Code § 701b-8a

Flood Control Act of 1960
July 14, 1960, P.L. 86-645, 74 Stat. 488, 33 U.S. Code §§ 701r-1, 709a
Oct. 23, 1962, P.L. 87-874, 76 Stat. 1196, 33 U.S. Code § 701r-1
Oct. 27, 1965, P.L. 89-298, 79 Stat. 1089, 33 U.S. Code § 709a
Nov. 7, 1966, P.L. 89-789, 80 Stat. 1422, 33 U.S. Code §§ 642, 709a
Dec. 31, 1970, P.L. 91-611, 84 Stat. 1832, 33 U.S. Code § 709a
March 7, 1974, P.L. 93-251, 88 Stat. 17, 33 U.S. Code § 701r-1, 709a
Nov. 28, 1990, P.L. 101-640, 33 U.S. Code § 709a

Flood Control Act of 1962

Oct. 23, 1962, P.L. 87-874, 76 Stat. 1180, 16 U.S. Code § 460d; 33 U.S. Code §§ 701n, 701r-1, 701s

Dec. 31, 1970, P.L. 91-611, 84 Stat. 1833, 16 U.S. Code § 460d

Aug. 11, 1988, P.L. 100-387, 102 Stat. 959, 43 U.S. Code § 502 nt.

Nov. 28, 1995, P.L. 104-58, 109 Stat. 560

Flood Control Act of 1965

Oct. 27, 1965, P.L. 89-298, 79 Stat. 1073, 10 U.S. Code § 3036 nt.; 16 U.S. Code § 460d-1; 33 U.S. Code §§ 701-1 nt., 701c-1 nt., 709a; 42 U.S. Code §§ 1962d-5, 3142a

Nov. 2, 1994, P.L. 103-437, 42 U.S. Code § 1962d-5

Cal. Structures 1944, 4th Es. Sess., Ch. 44, p. 168

Flood Control Act of 1966

Nov. 7, 1966, P.L. 89-789, 80 Stat. 1418, 33 U.S. Code §§ 642, 701-1 nt., 701c nt., 709a

Flood Control Act of 1968

Aug. 13, 1968, P.L. 90-483, 82 Stat. 739, 16 U.S. Code § 460d-3; 33 U.S. Code §§ 598, 701-1 nt., 701c nt.; 42 U.S. Code § 1962d-5a

Nov. 17, 1988, P.L. 100-676, 42 U.S. Code § 1962d-5a

Aug. 10, 1993, P.L. 103-66, 16 U.S. Code § 460d-3

Oct. 12, 1996, P.L. 104-303, 16 U.S. Code § 460d-3; 42 U.S. Code § 1962d-5a

Flood Control Act of 1970

Dec. 31, 1970, P.L. 91-611, 84 Stat. 1824, 5 U.S. Code § 5315; 10 U.S. Code § 3013; 16 U.S. Code § 460d; 33 U.S. Code §§ 426e, 709a; 42 U.S. Code §§ 1962-2, 1962d-5b; 43 U.S. Code § 1511a

Dec. 23, 1971, P.L. 92-222, 85 Stat. 799, 42 U.S. Code § 1962d-5b

Feb. 10, 1996, P.L. 104-106, 42 U.S. Code § 1962d-5b

Oct. 12, 1996, P.L. 104-303, 42 U.S. Code §§ 1962-2, 1962d-5b

Flood Control Acts

See Mississippi River Flood Control Act

March 1, 1917, Ch. 144, 39 Stat. 948, 33 U.S. Code §§ 643, 701 to 703

June 22, 1936, Ch. 688, 49 Stat. 1570, 33 U.S. Code §§ 701a to 701f, 701h

Aug. 28, 1937 Ch. 877, 50 Stat. 877, 33 U.S. Code § 706b-6

June 28, 1938, Ch. 795, 52 Stat. 1215, 33 U.S. Code §§ 701b, 701b-1, 701b-2, 701c, 701c-1, 701f, 701f-1, 701i, 701j, 702a-11, 706

Aug. 18, 1941, Ch. 377, 55 Stat. 639, 33 U.S. Code § 702a-12

July 24, 1946, Ch. 596, 60 Stat. 642, 16 U.S. Code § 460d; 33 U.S. Code §§ 701c-3, 701g, 701n

Jan. 19, 1948, Ch. 2, 62 Stat. 4, 33 U.S. Code §§ 701b-6, 701b-7

June 30, 1948, Ch. 771, 62 Stat. 1175

June 30, 1948, Ch. 771, 62 Stat. 1182, 33 U.S. Code § 701n

June 16, 1953, Ch. 114, 67 Stat. 61, 33 U.S. Code § 701c-3

Oct. 23, 1962, P.L. 87-874, 76 Stat. 1194, 33 U.S. Code § 701n

March 7, 1974, P.L. 93-251, 88 Stat. 34, 33 U.S. Code § 701a

June 20, 1977, P.L. 95-51, 33 U.S. Code § 701n

Flood Control Agency Act (Sacramento Area)

Cal. Statutes 1990, Ch. 510, p. 2421

Flood Control and Insurance Act

Tex. Water Code, § 16.311 et seq.

Flood Control and Urban Drainage Act

Miss. Code Ann. 1972, § 51-35-301 et seq.

Flood Control and Water Conservation Agency Act (Madera County)

Cal. Water Code, Appendix, § 110-100 et seq.

Flood Control and Water Conservation District Act

Cal. Statutes 1931, Ch. 641, p. 1369
Continued

Cal. Statutes 1945, Ch. 1122, p. 2131 (Riverside County)

Cal. Statutes 1947, Ch. 699, p. 1739 (Monterey County)

Cal. Statutes 1949, Ch. 994, p. 1793 (Sonoma County)

Cal. Statutes 1949, Ch. 995, p. 1810 (Mendocino County)

Cal. Statutes 1949, Ch. 1275, p. 2240 (Alameda County)

Cal. Statutes 1951, Ch. 1405, p. 3336 (Santa Clara County)

Cal. Statutes 1951, Ch. 1449, p. 3411 (Napa County)

Cal. Statutes 1951, Ch. 1544, p. 3522 (Lake County)

Cal. Statutes 1951, Ch. 1617, p. 3638 (Contra Costa County)

Cal. Statutes 1951, Ch. 1656, p. 3748 (Solano County)

Cal. Statutes 1951, Ch. 1657, p. 3772 (Yolo County)

Cal. Statutes 1953, Ch. 666, p. 1915 (Marin County)

Cal. Statutes 1955, Ch. 1057, p. 2006 (Santa Barbara County)

Cal. Statutes 1955, Ch. 1489, p. 2701 (Santa Cruz County)

Cal. Statutes 1956, 1st Ex. Sess., Ch. 46, p. 387 (San Joaquin County)

Cal. Statutes 1957, Ch. 1280, p. 2581 (Tehama County)

Cal. Statutes 1959, Ch. 2114, p. 4912 (Plumas County)

Cal. Statutes 1959, Ch. 2121, p. 4946 (Siskiyou County)

Cal. Statutes 1959, Ch. 2123, p. 4979 (Sierra County)

Cal. Statutes 1959, Ch. 2127, p. 5009 (Lassen-Modoc County)

Cal. Statutes 1983, Ch. 926 (Colusa County)

Flood Control and Water Conservation District Act (Alameda County)
Cal. Water Code, Appendix, § 55-1 et seq.

Flood Control and Water Conservation District Act (Contra Costa County)
Cal. Water Code, Appendix, § 63-1 et seq.

Flood Control and Water Conservation District Act (Lake County)
Cal. Water Code, Appendix, § 62-1 et seq.

Flood Control and Water Conservation District Act (Marin County)
Cal. Water Code, Appendix, § 68-1 et seq.

Flood Control and Water Conservation District Act (Mendocino County)
Cal. Water Code, Appendix, § 54-1 et seq.

Flood Control and Water Conservation District Act (Napa County)
Cal. Water Code, Appendix, § 61-1 et seq.

Flood Control and Water Conservation District Act (Placer County)
Cal. Water Code, Appendix, § 126-1 et seq.

Flood Control and Water Conservation District Act (Riverside County)
Cal. Water Code, Appendix, § 48-1 et seq.

Flood Control and Water Conservation District Act (San Joaquin County)
Cal. Water Code, Appendix, § 79-1 et seq.

Flood Control and Water Conservation District Act (San Louis Obispo County)
Cal. Water Code, Appendix, § 49-1 et seq.

Flood Control and Water Conservation District Act (Santa Barbara County)
Cal. Water Code, Appendix, § 74-1 et seq.

Flood Control and Water Conservation District Act (Santa Cruz County)
Cal. Water Code, Appendix, § 77-1 et seq.

Flood Control and Water Conservation District Act (Sonoma County)
Cal. Water Code, Appendix, § 53-1 et seq.

Flood Control and Water Conservation District Act (Sutter County)
Cal. Water Code, Appendix, § 125-1 et seq.

Flood Control and Water Conservation District Act (Tehoma County)
Cal. Water Code, Appendix, § 82-1 et seq.

Flood Control and Water Conservation District Act (Yolo County)
Cal. Water Code, Appendix, § 65-1 et seq.

Flood Control Bond Act (Emergency)
N.J. Laws 1978, Ch. 78

Flood Control Compact Act (Connecticut River)
Conn. Gen. Stat. Ann., § 25-99 et seq.
N.H. Rev. Stat. 1955, 484:1 et seq.
Vt. Stat. Ann., Title 10, § 1151 et seq.

Flood Control Compact Act (Merrimack River)
N.H. Rev. Stat. 1955, 484:7 et seq.

Flood Control District Act
Cal. Statutes 1945, Ch. 939, p. 1754 (Humbolt County)
Cal. Statutes 1953, Ch. 1771, p. 3528 (Morrison Creek)
Cal. Statutes 1955, Ch. 166, p. 613 (Del Norte County)
Cal. Statutes 1959, Ch. 2108, p. 4885, (San Mateo County)
Ida. Code 1947, 42-3101 et seq.
N.D. Cent. Code, 61-16-05 et seq., 61-16.1-01 et seq.
Nev. Rev. Stat. 1979 Reprint, 543.160 et seq.
Nev. Statutes 1947, Ch. 174, p. 610 (Lincoln County)
N.M. Stat. Ann., 72-18-1 et seq.

Flood Control District Act (American River)
Cal. Water Code, Appendix, § 37-1 et seq.

Flood Control District Act (Del Norte County)
Cal. Water Code, Appendix, § 72-1 et seq.

Flood Control District Act (Humbolt County)
Cal. Water Code, Appendix, § 47-1 et seq.

Flood Control District Act (Los Angeles County)
Cal. Water Code, Appendix, § 28-1 et seq.

Flood Control District Act (Merced County)
Cal. Water Code, Appendix, § 54-1 et seq.

Flood Control District Act (San Diego County)
Cal. Water Code, Appendix, § 105-1.5 et seq.

Flood Control District Act (San Mateo County)
Cal. Water Code, Appendix, § 87-1 et seq.

Flood Control District Bond Validation Laws
Cal. Statutes 1933, Ch. 120, p. 574
Cal. Statutes 1935, Ch. 116, p. 466

Flood Control Facilities Act
N.J. Stat. Ann., 58:16A-1 et seq.
Wash. Rev. Code Ann., 86.05.010 et seq.

Flood Control Financing Act (Municipal and County)
N.J. Stat. Ann., 40:23-34 et seq.
N.J. Stat. Ann., 40A:27-1 et seq.

Flood Control Fund Act
Cal. Water Code § 12800 et seq.

Flood Control Zones Act
Wash. Rev. Code Ann., 86.16.010 et seq.

Flood Damage Prevention Act
Ill. Rev. Stat. 1991, Ch. 85, § 1710 et seq.

Flood Damage Reduction Act
Va. Code 1950, § 62.1-44.108 et seq.

Flood Disaster Protection Act of 1973
Dec. 31, 1973, P.L. 93-234, 87 Stat. 975, 12 U.S. Code §§ 24, 1709-1; 42 U.S. Code §§ 4001 to 4003, 4012a, 4013 to 4016, 4026, 4054, 4056, 4101, 4104 to 4107, 4121, 4128
July 2, 1975, P.L. 94-50, 89 Stat. 256, 42 U.S. Code § 4106
Dec. 31, 1975, P.L. 94-198, 89 Stat. 1116, 42 U.S. Code § 4106
Oct. 12, 1977, P.L. 95-128, 42 U.S. Code § 4106 et seq.
Nov. 30, 1983, P.L. 98-181, 42 U.S. Code §§ 4003, 4012, 4105 to 4107
Continued

Nov. 23, 1988, P.L. 100-707, 42 U.S. Code
§ 4003
Sept. 23, 1994, P.L. 103-325, 42 U.S. Code
§§ 4003, 4012a, 4029, 4106, 4121

**Flood, Drought and Hurricane Disaster Act
(Farmers)**
Va. Code 1950, § 3.1-22.13 et seq.

Flood Hazard Area Control Act
N.J. Stat. Ann., 58:16A-50 et seq.

Flood Hazard Management Act
Md. Ann. Code 1974, Art. NR, § 8-9A-01 et
seq.

Flood Plain Management Act
Minn. Stat. 1988, 104.01 et seq.
Pa. Purdon's Stat., Title 32, § 679.101 et seq.

**Flood Plain Management Act
(Cobey-Alquist)**
Cal. Water Code § 8400 et seq.

Flood Plain Management Law
Minn. Stat. 1986, 103F.101 et seq.

Flood Plains Hatch Act
Mass. Gen. Laws Ann., 131:40

Flood Prevention Act
Ind. Code Ann., 36-3-1-6
Vt. Stat. Ann., Title 10, § 951 et seq.

**Flood Prevention and Control Compact
(Kansas-Missouri)**
Mo. Laws 1985, S.B. No. 26

**Flood Prevention District Act (Watershed
Protection)**
Nev. Rev. Stat. 1973 Reprint, Replaced
Pages, 542.010 et seq.

Flood Protection Act (Delta)
Cal. Water Code §§ 12300, 12301, 12310 to
12316, 12912.5, 12986, 12987, 12987.5,
12992, 12993

Flood Protection Loan Act
Mass. Acts 1956, Ch. 235
Mass. Acts 1962, Ch. 552
Mass. Acts 1962, Ch. 638

Flood Rehabilitation Act of 1952
Oct. 24, 1951, Ch. 555, 65 Stat. 615

Flood Relief Act (Emergency)
Cal. Government Code § 54150 et seq.

Flood Relief Loan Act (General)
Mass. Acts 1955, Ch. 699

Flood Relief Loan Act (Highway)
Mass. Acts 1955, Ch. 698

Flood Victims Tax Relief Act
Ky. Rev. Stat. 1971, 141.011

Floodable Zone Building Control Act
P.R. Laws Ann. 1954, Title 23, § 225 et seq.

Flooding Disaster Law
Miss. Code Ann. 1972, § 27-107-151 et seq.

Floodplain Management Act
Minn. Stat. Ann., 103F.101 et seq.
N.D. Cent. Code, 61-16.2-01 et seq.
Okla. Stat. Ann., Title 82, § 1601 et seq.

Floodway Management Act
Mont. Code Ann., 76-5-101 et seq.

Floodway Obstruction Act
Neb. Laws 1967, Ch. 1

Floor Plan Act (Chattel Mortgages)
Okla. Stat. Ann., Title 46, § 91 et seq.

**Floral Research and Consumer Information
Act**
Dec. 22, 1981, P.L. 97-98, 7 U.S. Code
§ 4301 nt.

Florence Agreement
See Educational, Scientific, And Cultural
Materials Importation Act Of 1966

Florence County Memorial Commission Act
S.C. Acts 1946, p. 2102, No. 711

Florida Canal-Pipe Line Act
July 23, 1942, Ch. 520, 56 Stat. 703, 15 U.S.
Code prec. § 715 nt.

Florida Indian Land Claims Settlement Act of 1982
Dec. 31, 1982, P.L. 97-399, 25 U.S. Code §§ 1741 nt., 1741 et seq.

Florida Keys Area Protection Act
Fla. Stat. Ann., 500.01 et seq.

Florida Keys National Marine Sanctuary and Protection Act
Nov. 16, 1990, P.L. 101-605, 16 U.S. Code § 1433 nt.
Nov. 4, 1992, P.L. 102-587, 16 U.S. Code § 1433 nt.

Florida Nuclear Code and Southern Interstate Nuclear Compact Law
Fla. Stat. Ann., 377.711
Fla. Stat. Ann., 404.011 et seq.

Florida Supplemental Retirement Act
Fla. Stat. Ann., 112.361

Florida Wilderness Act of 1983
Sept. 28, 1984, P.L. 98-430, 98 Stat. 1665, 16 U.S. Code § 1132 nt.

Flour, Bread and Corn Meal Enrichment Act
Ala. Code 1975, 20-1-70 et seq.
Ark. Code Ann. 1987, 20-57-301 et seq.
N.C. Gen. Stat. 1943, § 106-219.1 et seq.
N.J. Stat. Ann., 24:11A-1 et seq.
N.M. Stat. Ann., 25-5-1 et seq.

Flour Content Act
Wash. Rev. Code Ann., 69.08.010 et seq.

Flour Label Act
S.D. Codified Laws 1967, Superseded Vol., 39-12-1 et seq.

Flovilla, City of Jackson, and City of Jenkinsburg Water and Sewer Authority Act
Ga. Laws 1986, p. 5457

Flower and Tree Act
Ill. Rev. Stat. 1991, Ch. 1, §§ 2901-40, 3009

Floyd County Employees' Pension Code
Ga. Laws 1951, p. 2746

Floyd County Merit System Act
Ga. Laws 1967, p. 2253
Ga. Laws 1969, p. 2505

Flu Vaccine for Elderly (Thurman Act)
Cal. Welfare and Institutions Code § 9310

Flue Cured Tobacco Act
Ga. Code Ann., 10-4-100 et seq.

Flue-Cured Tobacco Marketing Act
Fla. Stat. Ann., 573.857 et seq.

Fluid Milk Act
Mich. Comp. Laws Ann., 288.21 et seq.
Ore. Rev. Stat., 621.005 et seq.
Wash. Rev. Code Ann., 15.36.005 et seq.

Fluid Milk and Cream Stabilization and Marketing Act
Cal. Food and Agricultural Code 1967, §§ 61801, 62730 et seq.

Fluid Milk Promotion Act of 1990
Nov. 28, 1990, P.L. 101-624, 7 U.S. Code §§ 6401, 6401 nt., 6402 to 6417
Dec. 13, 1991, P.L. 102-237, 7 U.S. Code § 6411
Aug. 11, 1993, P.L. 103-72, 7 U.S. Code §§ 6402, 6409
April 4, 1996, P.L. 104-127, 7 U.S. Code §§ 6401, 6402, 6413, 6414

Fluid Milk Promotion Amendments Act of 1993
Aug. 11, 1993, P.L. 103-72, 7 U.S. Code § 6401 nt.

Fluoridation Act (Water Supply)
S.D. Codified Laws 1967, 34-24A-1 et seq.

Foley Act (Decedent's Estates)
N.Y. Estates, Powers and Trusts Law (Consol. Laws Ch. 178) §§ 1.25, 2-1.13, 2-1.5, 4-1.1 et seq., 5-1.1 et seq., 5-4.4, 11.1(b), 13-1.4

Foley-Walker Law (Workmen's Compensation)
N.Y. Laws 1913, Ch. 816
N.Y. Laws 1914, Ch. 41

Foliage Plant Marketing Act
Fla. Stat. Ann., 573.50 et seq.

Folk Dance Act
Ill. Rev. Stat. 1991, Ch. 1, § 2901-65.

Folklife Preservation Act
Minn. Stat. Ann., 138.81 et seq.
Mont. Code Ann., 22-2-201 et seq.

Folkston-Charlton County Airport Authority Act
Ga. Laws 1970, p. 3253

Follis Bill (Cooperative Insurance)
Ky. Rev. Stat. 1977, 299.010 et seq.

Follow Through Act
Aug. 13, 1981, P.L. 97-35, 42 U.S. Code § 9801 nt.
Oct. 30, 1984, P.L. 98-558, 42 U.S. Code §§ 9861, 9862
Sept. 30, 1986, P.L. 99-425, 42 U.S. Code §§ 9862, 9867
Nov. 3, 1990, P.L. 101-501, 42 U.S. Code §§ 9861 to 9867, 9869
Oct. 7, 1991, P.L. 102-119, 42 U.S. Code § 9862
Oct. 20, 1994, P.L. 103-382, 42 U.S. Code §§ 9801 nt., 9861 et seq.

Folsom Lake Bridge Authority Act
Cal. Streets and Highways Code § 30910 et seq.

Folsom-Wallace Prepaid College Tuition Act
Ala. Acts 1991, p. 1717

Food Act
Ga. Code Ann., 26-2-20 et seq.
Ill. Rev. Stat. 1991, Ch. 56 1/2, § 401 et seq.
Me. Rev. Stat. Ann. 1964, Title 22, § 2151 et seq.
Mich. Comp. Laws Ann., 289.701 et seq.

Minn. Stat. Ann., 31.001 et seq.
Neb. Rev. Stat. 1943, 81-217.11 et seq.
N.M. Stat. Ann., 25-2-1 et seq.
Okla. Stat. Ann., Title 63, § 180.1 et seq.
Ore. Rev. Stat., 616.005 et seq.
Pa. Purdon's Stat., Title 31, §§ 1 et seq., 20.1 et seq.
Va. Code 1950, § 3.1-386 et seq.

Food Act (Organic)
Okla. Stat. Ann., Title 2, § 5-301 et seq.

Food Act (Pure)
Minn. Stat. Ann., 31.01 et seq.

Food Additives Amendment of 1958
Sept. 6, 1958, P.L. 85-929, 72 Stat. 1784, 21 U.S. Code §§ 321, 331, 342, 346, 348, 348 nt.; 42 U.S. Code § 210
April 7, 1961, P.L. 87-19, 75 Stat. 42, 21 U.S. Code § 342 nt.
Oct. 3, 1964, P.L. 88-625, 78 Stat. 1002, 21 U.S. Code § 342 nt.

Food Additives Transitional Provisions Amendment of 1961
April 7, 1961, P.L. 87-19, 75 Stat. 42, 7 U.S. Code § 135 nt.; 21 U.S. Code § 342 nt.

Food Additives Transitional Provisions Amendment of 1964
Oct. 3, 1964, P.L. 88-625, 78 Stat. 1002, 7 U.S. Code § 135 nt.; 21 U.S. Code § 342 nts.

Food Adulteration Act
Ind. Code Ann., 16-1-29-1 et seq.
Iowa Code Ann., 190.1 et seq.
N.Y. Agriculture and Markets Law (Consol. Laws Ch. 69) § 198 et seq.
Wash. Rev. Code Ann., 69.04.001 et seq.
Wis. Stat. Ann., 97.01 et seq.

Food, Agriculture, Conservation, and Trade Act Amendments of 1991
Dec. 13, 1991, P.L. 102-237, 7 U.S. Code § 1421 nt.
Oct. 28, 1992, P.L. 102-552, 7 U.S. Code §§ 1942, 1985, 1991 nt.; 16 U.S. Code § 3821

April 1, 1993, P.L. 103-11, 7 U.S. Code
§§ 2015 nt., 2016 nt.

Dec. 17, 1993, P.L. 103-205, 7 U.S. Code
§§ 2015 nt., 2016 nt.

March 25, 1994, P.L. 103-225, 7 U.S. Code
§§ 2015 nt., 2016 nt.

Food, Agriculture, Conservation, and Trade Act of 1990

Nov. 5, 1990, P.L. 101-508, 7 U.S. Code
§§ 1421 nt., 5822; 21 U.S. Code § 136a

Nov. 28, 1990, P.L. 101-624, 5 U.S. Code
§ 3132; 7 U.S. Code §§ 138, 144b nt., 147a,
361c, 411a, 450i, 450l, 499a nt., 608c nts.,
1301 et seq. generally, 1421 et seq.
generally, 1622 nt., 2011 nt., 2242, 2244,
2279, 5801, 5901 et seq. generally; 12 U.S.
Code § 2001 nt.; 15 U.S. Code § 714 nt.; 21
U.S. Code §§ 113a, 114a, 114b, 114i, 136,
136a; 22 U.S. Code § 2151x-2; 25 U.S.
Code §§ 492, 494; 42 U.S. Code §
sect1751 nt., 5177a

Dec. 13, 1991, P.L. 102-237, 7 U.S. Code
§§ 136i-1, 138f, 450i, 612c nt., 950aaa-1,
1421 nt., 1422 nt., 1431, 1444f-1, 1445e nt.,
1446e-1, 1601 nt., 1736bb-6, 1748, 1749,
1926-1, 1981, 1981e, 1991, 1994, 2006f nt.,
2007a, 2007c, 2007d, 2007e, 2101 nt.,
2106a, 2112 nt., 2279, 3122, 3293, 4201 nt.,
5403, 5503, 5505, 5506, 5622 nt., 5801,
5814, 5822, 5831, 5832, 5842, 5843, 5852,
5853, 5883, 5921, 5923, 5925, 5926, 5927,
5928, 5930, 5931, 5934, 6001 nt., 6002,
6005, 6010, 6104, 6107, 6108, 6204, 6207,
6208, 6304, 6305, 6309, 6504, 6509, 6510,
6511, 6515, 6517, 6518, 6519, 6520; 21
U.S. Code § 136a

Oct. 24, 1992, P.L. 102-511, 7 U.S. Code
§ 3293

Oct. 28, 1992, P.L. 102-551, 7 U.S. Code
§§ 950aaa-4, 950aaa-5

Oct. 28, 1992, P.L. 102-552, 7 U.S. Code
§ 1942

Oct. 26, 1993, P.L. 103-115, 7 U.S. Code
§ 6612

Dec. 8, 1993, P.L. 103-182, 7 U.S. Code
§ 5622 nt.

Oct. 13, 1994, P.L. 103-354, 7 U.S. Code
§§ 950aaa-2, 950aaa-3, 1421 nt.

Dec. 21, 1995, P.L. 104-66, 7 U.S. Code
§§ 958, 1421 nt., 1421b, 1421c, 5505, 5924;
15 U.S. Code § 714 nt.

April 4, 1996, P.L. 104-127, 7 U.S. Code
§§ 624 nt., prec. 950aaa nt., 950aaa,
950aaa-1 to 950aaa-4, 950aaa-4 nt.,
950aaa-5, 1446e-1, 1706, 1761 nt., 1926
nt., 1926-1, 1932, 2007, 2007a to 2007e,
2106a, 2662, 2662 nt., 2662a, 3125b,
3125c, 3130, 3293, 5501, 5506, 5622 nt.,
5694 nt., 5801, 5811, 5812, 5821,
5831,5832, 5841, 5844, 5855, 5871 to
5874, 5881 to 5885, 5901 to 5909, 5923 to
5933, 6613, 6703, 6704, 6710; 13 U.S.
Code §§ 141 nt., 142; 15 U.S. Code
§ 714nt.; 21 U.S. Code §§ 114i, 136a

Aug. 22, 1996, P.L. 104-193, 7 U.S. Code
§ 612c nt.

June 23, 1998, P.L. 105-185, 7 U.S. Code
§§ 3125b, 5501 to 5505, 5832, 5844, 5923,
5924, 5925, 5925a, 5925b, 5926, 5928,
5933

Food, Agriculture, Conservation, and Trade Act of 1991

April 4, 1996, P.L. 104-127, 7 U.S. Code
§ 5930 nt.

Food and Agricultural Code

Cal. Food and Agricultural Code § 1 et seq.

Food and Agriculture Act of 1962

Sept. 27, 1962, P.L. 87-703, 76 Stat. 605, 7
U.S. Code §§ 608c, 1010, 1011, 1301, 1301
nt., 1331 to 1334, 1334 nt., 1334b to 1337,
1339 to 1339c and others; 15 U.S. Code
§§ 713a-13; 16 U.S. Code §§ 590g, 590h,
590p, 1004, 1005

May 20, 1963, P.L. 88-26, 77 Stat. 47, 7 U.S.
Code § 1339a

Nov. 3, 1965, P.L. 89-321, 79 Stat. 1192, 7
U.S. Code §§ 1339a, 1339c

Nov. 28, 1990, P.L. 101-624, 7 U.S. Code
§ 1339a

Dec. 13, 1991, P.L. 102-237, 7 U.S. Code
§ 1339a

Food and Agriculture Act of 1965

Nov. 3, 1965, P.L. 89-321, 79 Stat. 1187, 7
U.S. Code §§ 608c, 1282 nt., 1301, 1305,
1306, 1314b, 1316, 1332 to 1335, 1339,
1339a, 1339c, 1340 and others; 16 U.S.
Code § 590p

Nov. 11, 1966, P.L. 89-808, 80 Stat. 1538, 7
U.S. Code § 1446a-1

Continued

895

Dec. 18, 1967, P.L. 90-210, 81 Stat. 657, 7 U.S. Code § 1838

Oct. 11, 1968, P.L. 90-559, 82 Stat. 996, 7 U.S. Code §§ 608c nt., 1314b, 1332, 1339, 1344b, 1346, and others; 16 U.S. Code § 590p

June 19, 1970, P.L. 91-284, 84 Stat. 314, 7 U.S. Code § 1316

Food and Agriculture Act of 1977

Sept. 29, 1977, P.L. 95-113, 7 U.S. Code §§ 1281 nt., 1308 et seq.; 15 U.S. Code §§ 7146, 7146 nt.; 42 U.S. Code §§ 1328e nt., 6651; 16 U.S. Code §§ 590h, 590o et seq.

May 15, 1978, P.L. 95-279, 7 U.S. Code § 1309

Aug. 4, 1978, P.L. 95-334, 7 U.S. Code §§ 1309, 1309 nt.

Oct. 28, 1978, P.L. 95-547, 7 U.S. Code § 3222

March 18, 1980, P.L. 96-213, 7 U.S. Code §§ 1308, 1309

June 30, 1980, P.L. 96-294, 7 U.S. Code § 1435 et seq.

Dec. 21, 1982, P.L. 97-375, 7 U.S. Code § 2011 nt.

Dec. 23, 1985, P.L. 99-198, 7 U.S. Code §§ 1309, 2266, 2267

Aug. 11, 1988, P.L. 100-387, 102 Stat. 931, 7 U.S. Code § 2267

Nov. 28, 1990, P.L. 101-624, 7 U.S. Code §§ 3109, 3705, 3714, 3716, 3720, 3724, 3728

Nov. 10, 1998, P.L. 105-362, 7 U.S. Code § 2284

Food and Animal Drug Act (Wholesome)
Utah Code Ann. 1953, 4-5-1 et seq.

Food and Coal Commission Act
Ind. Laws 1920, Special Session, Ch. 44, p. 143

Food and Cosmetic Act
S.C. Code Ann. 1976, § 39-25-10 et seq.

Food and Dairy Inspection Act
Mich. Comp. Laws Ann., 289.35 et seq.

Food and Drink Act
Mich. Comp. Laws Ann., 289.81 et seq.

Food and Drug Act
Ala. Code 1975, § 20-1-1 et seq.
Ark. Code Ann. 1987, 20-57-101 et seq.
Colo. Rev. Stat., 25-5-401 et seq.
D.C. Code 1973, § 33-101 et seq.
Iowa Code Ann., 189.1 et seq.
Mo. Rev. Stat., 196.010 et seq.
N.D. Cent. Code, 19-02.1-01 et seq.
Neb. Rev. Stat. 1943, 81-217.11 et seq.
N.J. Stat. Ann., 24:1-1 et seq.
Ohio Rev. Code 1953, 3715.01 et seq.
R.I. Gen. Laws 1956, 21-1-1 et seq.
S.C. Code Ann. 1976, § 44-53-10 et seq.
S.D. Codified Laws 1967, 39-1-1 et seq.
Tex. Rev. Civ. Stat., Art. 4465a et seq.
Utah Code Ann. 1953, 4-5-1 et seq.
W. Va. Code 1966, § 16-7-1 et seq.
Wyo. Stat. Ann., § 35-7-101 et seq.

Food and Drug Acts
See Federal Food, Drug, And Cosmetic Act
June 30, 1906, Ch. 3915, 34 Stat. 768
Aug. 23, 1912, Ch. 352, 37 Stat. 416

Food and Drug Administration Act of 1988
Nov. 4, 1988, P.L. 100-607, 21 U.S. Code § 301 nt.

Food and Drug Administration Modernization Act of 1997
Nov. 21, 1997, P.L. 105-115, 21 U.S. Code § 301 nt.

Food and Drug Administration Revitalization Act
Nov. 28, 1990, P.L. 101-635, 21 U.S. Code § 301 nt.

Food and Drug Enforcement Act
Mich. Comp. Laws Ann., 289.2 et seq.

Food and Fiber Production Act
Cal. Statutes 1943, 2d Ex. Sess., p. 3397

Food and Housing Assistance Act
Ill. Rev. Stat. 1991, Ch. 23, § 6401 et seq.

Food and Nutrition Access Act
Mont. Laws 1991, Ch. 569

Food Authority Act
Md. Ann. Code 1957, Art. 41, § 13-101 et seq.

Food Bank Act
Cal. Food and Agricultural Code 1967, § 58501 et seq.

Food Bank Good Samaritan Act
N.J. Stat. Ann., 24:4A-1 et seq.

Food Center Act (New Orleans)
La. Rev. Stat. Ann., 3:431 et seq.

Food Center Authority Act
Md. Ann. Code 1957, Art. 41A, § 6-101 et seq.

Food Conservation Acts
Aug. 10, 1917, Ch. 52, 40 Stat. 273
Aug. 10, 1917, Ch. 53, 40 Stat. 276

Food Control Act
Oct. 22, 1919, Ch. 80, 41 Stat. 297

Food, Dairy and Drug Act
Wis. Stat. Ann., 97.01 et seq.

Food Distribution Authorities Law (County)
N.J. Stat. Ann., 40:37D-1 et seq.

Food Distribution Authority Law (South Jersey)
N.J. Stat. Ann., 4:26-1 et seq.

Food Distribution Center Commission Law (Hackensack Meadowlands)
N.J. Stat. Ann., 13:17A-1 et seq.

Food Distributors Law
Mont. Rev. Code 1947, 27-301 et seq.

Food Donation Act (Good Samaritan)
Ill. Rev. Stat. 1991, Ch. 56 1/2, § 2001 et seq.
Wash. Rev. Code Ann., 69.80.031

Food Donors Liability Act
N.M. Stat. Ann., 41-10-1 et seq.

Food, Drug, and Cosmetic Act
See Federal Food, Drug, And Cosmetic Act

Food, Drug and Cosmetic Act
Alaska Stat. 1962, § 17.20.010 et seq.
Ark. Code Ann. 1987, 20-56-201 et seq.
Cal. Health and Safety Code § 26000 et seq.
Conn. Gen. Stat. Ann., § 21a-91 et seq.
Fla. Stat. Ann., 500.01 et seq.
Ga. Code Ann., 26-1-1 et seq.
Haw. Rev. Stat. Ann., § 328-1 et seq.
Ida. Code 1947, 37-113 et seq.
Ill. Rev. Stat. 1991, Ch. 56 1/2, § 501 et seq.
Ill. Rev. Stat. 1991, Ch. 56 1/2, § 2101 et seq.
Ind. Code Ann., 16-1-28-1 et seq.
Kan. Stat. Ann., 65-655 et seq.
Ky. Rev. Stat. 1971, 217.005 et seq.
La. Rev. Stat. Ann., 40:601 et seq.
Md. Ann. Code 1974, Art. HG, § 21-201 et seq.
Mont. Code Ann., 50-31-101 et seq.
N.C. Gen. Stat. 1943, § 106-120 et seq.
N.D. Cent. Code, 19-02.1-01 et seq.
N.H. Rev. Stat. 1955, 146:1 et seq.
P.R. Laws Ann. 1954, Title 24, § 711 et seq.
R.I. Gen. Laws 1956, 21-31-1 et seq.
Tenn. Code Ann., 53-1-101 et seq.
Tex. Health and Safety Code, § 431.001 et seq.
Wash. Rev. Code Ann., 69.04.001 et seq.

Food, Drug, Cosmetic and Hazardous Substance Labeling Act
Vt. Stat. Ann., Title 18, § 4051 et seq.

Food, Drug, Device, and Cosmetic Salvage Act
Tex. Health and Safety Code, § 432.001 et seq.

Food Employee Certification Act
Pa. Cons. Stat., Title 3, § 6501 et seq.

Food Establishment Grading Act
N.M. Stat. Ann. 1953, 54-3-1 et seq.

Food Establishment Law
Iowa Code Ann., 137A.1 et seq.

Food Establishments Law (Home)
Iowa Code Ann., 137D.1 et seq.
N.J. Stat. Ann., 40:37D-1 et seq.

Food for Peace Act of 1966
Nov. 11, 1966, P.L. 89-808, 80 Stat. 1526, 7
U.S. Code §§ 1427, 1431, 1431b, 1446a-1,
1691, 1701 to 1710, 1721 to 1725, 1731 to
1736d
Oct. 21, 1978, P.L. 95-501, 7 U.S. Code
§ 1707a et seq.
Nov. 8, 1984, P.L. 98-623, 7 U.S. Code
§ 1707a
Dec. 23, 1985, P.L. 99-198, 7 U.S. Code
§ 1701a
Aug. 23, 1988, P.L. 100-418, 102 Stat. 1400,
7 U.S. Code § 1707a
Nov. 28, 1990, P.L. 101-624, 7 U.S. Code
§ 1707a

Food for Progress Act of 1985
Dec. 23, 1985, P.L. 99-198, 7 U.S. Code
§ 1736o
Nov. 28, 1990, P.L. 101-624, 7 U.S. Code
§ 1736o
Dec. 13, 1991, P.L. 102-237, 7 U.S. Code
§ 1736o
April 4, 1996, P.L. 104-127, 7 U.S. Code
§ 1736o
Oct. 21, 1998, P.L. 105-277, 7 U.S. Code
§ 1736o

Food Garden Act (Community)
Ill. Comp. Stat. 1992, Ch. 20, § 3923/1 et seq.

Food Handlers License Act
Minn. Stat. 1969, 31.411 et seq.

Food Handling Regulation Enforcement Act
Ill. Rev. Stat. 1991, Ch. 56 1/2, § 330 et seq.

Food Inspection Law
Ill. Rev. Stat. 1991, Ch. 56 1/2, § 66.90 et
seq.

Food Labeling Act
See Labeling Act (Food)

Food Locker Plant Act
Miss. Code Ann. 1972, § 75-37-1 et seq.

Food Misbranding Act
Wash. Rev. Code Ann., 69.04.001 et seq.

Food or Drugs Act (Tampering)
S.C. Code of Law 1976, §§ 16-1-10, 16-3-75
et seq.

Food Preparation Act (Sanitary)
Ill. Rev. Stat. 1991, Ch. 56 1/2, § 66.90 et
seq.

Food Processing Act
Mich. Comp. Laws Ann., 289.801 et seq.
Wash. Rev. Code Ann., 69.07.005 et seq.

Food Production Stimulation Act
Nov. 21, 1918, Ch. 212, 40 Stat. 1045

Food Products Delivery Guarantee Act
N.M. Stat. Ann., 57-24-1 et seq.

Food Products Standards Act (Organic)
Pa. Cons. Stat., Title 3, § 5901 et seq.

Food Purchase Program Act (State)
Pa. Purdon's Stat., Title 62, § 4041 et seq.

Food Quality Protection Act of 1996
Aug. 3, 1996, P.L. 104-170, 7 U.S. Code
§ 136 nt., Title IV, 21 U.S. Code § 301 nt.

Food Regulation Law
Wis. Stat. Ann., 97.01 et seq.

Food Safety Act
Fla. Stat. Ann., 500.01 et seq.

Food Safety Act (Lauren Beth Rudolph)
Cal. Health and Safety Code § 113996 et seq.

Food Safety Transportation Act
Ill. Rev. Stat. 1991, Ch. 56 1/2, § 2401 et seq.

Food Sanitation Act
Cal. Health and Safety Code § 28280 et seq.

Food Security Act of 1985
Dec. 23, 1985, P.L. 99-198, 7 U.S. Code
§ 1281 nt.
March 20, 1986, P.L. 99-260, 7 U.S. Code
§§ 1736-1, 1736s, 1736v, 2025 nt.

Sept. 30, 1986, P.L. 99-524, 7 U.S. Code
§ 1932 nt.

Oct. 18, 1986, P.L. 99-500, 7 U.S. Code
§§ 1308 nt., 1308, 1932 nt.; 16 U.S. Code
§ 3831

Oct. 30, 1986, P.L. 99-591, 7 U.S. Code
§§ 1308 nt., 1308, 1932 nt., 16 U.S. Code
§ 3831

Nov. 10, 1986, P.L. 99-641, 16 U.S. Code
§ 3831

Jan. 6, 1987, P.L. 100-233, 16 U.S. Code
§ 3835

April 24, 1987, P.L. 100-28, 7 U.S. Code
§ 1446; 16 U.S. Code § 3812

July 11, 1987, P.L. 100-71, 7 U.S. Code
§§ 1308, 5001, 5001 nt., 5002

Dec. 22, 1987, P.L. 100-202, 7 U.S. Code
§ 1932; P.L. 100-203, 7 U.S. Code §§ 1308,
1308 nt., 1308-1 nt., 1308-2 nt., 1308-3 nt.,
1421

April 4, 1988, P.L. 100-277, 102 Stat. 67, 7
U.S. Code § 1736 nt.

Aug. 11, 1988, P.L. 100-387, 102 Stat. 950,
16 U.S. Code § 3834 nt.

Aug. 23, 1988, P.L. 100-418, 102 Stat. 1397,
7 U.S. Code §§ 1736o, 1736s, 1736t,
1736v, 1736x; 15 U.S. Code § 713a-14

Sept. 19, 1988, P.L. 100-435, 102 Stat. 1651,
7 U.S. Code § 1731 nt.; 15 U.S. Code
§ 713a-14

Oct. 30, 1989, P.L. 101-134, 7 U.S. Code
§ 1308a

Dec. 11, 1989, P.L. 101-217, 7 U.S. Code
§ 1308

Dec. 19, 1989, P.L. 101-239, 7 U.S. Code
§ 1736s

Nov. 5, 1990, P.L. 101-508, 7 U.S. Code
§ 1999 nt.

Nov. 28, 1990, P.L. 101-624, 7 U.S. Code
§ 1308 et seq. generally, 1310a, 1385 nt.,
1441 et seq. generally, 1446 et seq.
generally, 1736et seq. generally, 3175e,
3224; 15 U.S. Code § 713a-14; 16 U.S.
Code § 3801 et seq. generally

Nov. 29, 1990, P.L. 101-647, 21 U.S. Code
§ 881a

Dec. 13, 1991, P.L. 102-237, 7 U.S. Code
§§ 1308, 1308-1, 3811, 3812, 3821, 3823,
3832, 3837, 3839, 3847

July 22, 1992, P.L. 102-324, 16 U.S. Code
§§ 3831, 3835a

Oct. 24, 1992, P.L. 102-511, 7 U.S. Code
§ 1736o

Oct. 28, 1992, P.L. 102-552, 16 U.S. Code
§ 3845

Aug. 10, 1993, P.L. 103-66, 7 U.S. Code
§§ 1308, 1308-3; 16 U.S. Code §§ 3830,
3831, 3837

Dec. 8, 1994, P.L. 103-465, 7 U.S. Code
§§ 713a-14, 1731 nt.

Dec. 21, 1995, P.L. 104-66, 7 U.S. Code
§ 499n nt.; 16 U.S. Code § 3846

March 12, 1996, P.L. 104-114, 7 U.S. Code
§ 1446g nt.

April 4, 1996, P.L. 104-127, 7 U.S. Code
§§ 1308, 1308-1, 1308-3, 1631, 1736p to
1736r; 15 U.S. Code § 713a-14; 16 U.S.
Code §§ 2005a, 2101 nt., 3801, 3811, 3812,
3812a, 3813, 3814, 3821 to 3823, 3830 to
3832, 3835, 3837, 3837a, 3837c, 3838 to
3838f, prec. 3839aa, 3839aa, 3839aa-1 et
seq., prec. 3839bb, 3839bb, prec. 3841,
3841 to 3847, 3861, 3862

Nov. 21, 1997, P.L. 105-113, 7 U.S. Code
§ 2276

Oct. 21, 1998, P.L. 105-277, 16 U.S. Code
§§ 3837, 3837d

**Food Security Commodity Reserve Act of
1996**

April 4, 1996, P.L. 104-127, 7 U.S. Code
§§ 1736f-1, 1736f-1 nt.

Food Security Wheat Reserve Act of 1980

Dec. 3, 1980, P.L. 96-494, 7 U.S. Code
§ 1736f-1 nt.

Dec. 23, 1985, P.L. 99-198, 7 U.S. Code
§ 1736f-1

Nov. 28, 1990, P.L. 101-624, 7 U.S. Code
§ 1736f-1

Food Service and Lodging Act

Kan. Stat. Ann., 36-501 et seq.

Food Service Licensure Act

N.H. Rev. Stat. 1955, 143-A:1 et seq.

Food Service Sales Plan Act (Home)

Del. Code of 1974, Title 6, § 2590 et seq.

Food Service Sanitation Act

Iowa Code Ann., 137B-1 et seq.

N.M. Stat. Ann., 25-1-1 et seq.

Food Stamp Act
Tenn. Code Ann., 71-5-301 et seq.

Food Stamp Act Amendments of 1980
May 26, 1980, P.L. 96-249, 7 U.S. Code § 2012 et seq., 26 U.S. Code § 6103; 42 U.S. Code §§ 503, 504

Food Stamp Act Amendments of 1982
Sept. 8, 1982, P.L. 97-253, 7 U.S. Code §§ 1624 nt., 2011 nt., 2012, 2014, 2015 to 2018, 2020 to 2023, 2025 to 2028, 2028 nt., 2029

Food Stamp Act of 1964
Aug. 31, 1964, P.L. 88-525, 78 Stat. 703, 7 U.S. Code §§ 2011 to 2025

Sept. 27, 1967, P.L. 90-91, 81 Stat. 228, 7 U.S. Code § 2025

Oct. 8, 1968, P.L. 90-552, 82 Stat. 958, 7 U.S. Code § 2025

Nov. 13, 1969, P.L. 91-116, 83 Stat. 191, 7 U.S. Code § 2025

Jan. 11, 1971, P.L. 91-671, 84 Stat. 2048, 7 U.S. Code §§ 2011 to 2014, 2016, 2019, 2023 to 2025

Oct. 30, 1972, P.L. 92-603, 86 Stat. 1491, 7 U.S. Code §§ 2012, 2019, 2023

Aug. 10, 1973, P.L. 93-86, 87 Stat. 246, 7 U.S. Code §§ 2012, 2014, 2016, 2019, 2025, 2026

Oct. 18, 1973, P.L. 93-125, 87 Stat. 450, 7 U.S. Code §§ 2012, 2016, 2019

Dec. 31, 1973, P.L. 93-233, 87 Stat. 956, 7 U.S. Code §§ 612c nt., 1431 nt., 2012 nts.

July 8, 1974, P.L. 93-335, 88 Stat. 291, 7 U.S. Code §§ 612c nts., 1431 nt., 2012 nts.; 42 U.S. Code § 1382e nt.

July 12, 1974, P.L. 93-347, 88 Stat. 341, 7 U.S. Code § 2024

Sept. 29, 1977, P.L. 95-113, 7 U.S. Code §§ 2011 et seq., 2011 nt.

Food Stamp Act of 1977
Sept. 29, 1977, P.L. 95-113, 7 U.S. Code §§ 2011 et seq., 2011 nt.

Aug. 14, 1979, P.L. 96-58, 7 U.S. Code §§ 2012, 2014, 2015, 2019, 2025, 2027

April 2, 1980, P.L. 96-223, 7 U.S. Code § 2014

May 26, 1980, P.L. 96-249, 7 U.S. Code § 2012 et seq.

July 18, 1984, P.L. 98-369, 98 Stat. 1150, 7 U.S. Code § 2020

Oct. 1, 1985, P.L. 99-114, 7 U.S. Code §§ 2026, 2028

Nov. 15, 1985, P.L. 99-157, 7 U.S. Code §§ 2026, 2028, 2028 nt.

Dec. 13, 1985, P.L. 99-182, 7 U.S. Code §§ 2026, 2028

Dec. 23, 1985, P.L. 99-198, 7 U.S. Code §§ 2012 to 2023, 2025 to 2028, 2029

Oct. 18, 1986, P.L. 99-500, 7 U.S. Code § 2014

Oct. 27, 1986, P.L. 99-570, 7 U.S. Code §§ 2012, 2018, 2019

Oct. 30, 1986, P.L. 99-591, 7 U.S. Code § 2014

Nov. 6, 1986, P.L. 99-603, 7 U.S. Code § 2025

July 22, 1987, P.L. 100-77, 7 U.S. Code §§ 2012, 2014, 2020, 2025

Dec. 22, 1987, P.L. 100-203, 7 U.S. Code § 2030

Jan. 5, 1988, P.L. 100-232, 7 U.S. Code §§ 2014, 2014 nt.

Aug. 11, 1988, P.L. 100-387, 102 Stat. 960, 7 U.S. Code §§ 2014, 2014 nt., 2017, 2017 nt.

Sept. 19, 1988, P.L. 100-435, 7 U.S. Code §§ 2012, 2014 to 2017, 2020 to 2023, 2025, 2026

Nov. 23, 1988, P.L. 100-707, 7 U.S. Code § 2014

Dec. 6, 1989, P.L. 101-202, 7 U.S. Code § 2031

Nov. 28, 1990, P.L. 101-624, 7 U.S. Code §§ 2012, 2012 nt., 2014 to 2018, 2020 to 2022, 2024 to 2028 nt., 2032

Dec. 13, 1991, P.L. 102-237, 7 U.S. Code §§ 2012, 2014, 2015, 2017, 2018, 2020, 2022, 2025, 2026, 2028, 2029, 2031

March 26, 1992, P.L. 102-265, 7 U.S. Code § 2014

Aug. 26, 1992, P.L. 102-351, 7 U.S. Code § 2012

Sept. 7, 1992, P.L. 102-367, 7 U.S. Code § 2014

Aug. 10, 1993, P.L. 103-66, 7 U.S. Code §§ 2012, 2014, 2015, 2017, 2020 et seq.

March 25, 1994, P.L. 103-225, 7 U.S. Code §§ 2012, 2015, 2016, 2018, 2026

Oct. 13, 1994, P.L. 103-354, 7 U.S. Code § 2012

Nov. 2, 1994, P.L. 103-448, 7 U.S. Code § 2018

Dec. 21, 1995, P.L. 104-66, 7 U.S. Code §§ 2020, 2025

April 4, 1996, P.L. 104-127, 7 U.S. Code §§ 2021, 2025 to 2028, 2033, 2034

Aug. 22, 1996, P.L. 104-193, 7 U.S. Code §§ 2012, 2014 to 2018, 2020 to 2027, 2029, 2035, 3036

Sept. 30, 1996, P.L. 104-208, 7 U.S. Code § 2015

Oct. 19, 1996, P.L. 104-316, 7 U.S. Code § 2030

June 12, 1997, P.L. 105-18, 7 U.S. Code §§ 2016, 2026

Aug. 5, 1997, P.L. 105-33, 7 U.S. Code §§ 2015, 2020, 2025

June 23, 1998, P.L. 105-185, 7 U.S. Code § 2025

Oct. 21, 1998, P.L. 105-277, 7 U.S. Code §§ 2014, 2015, 2026

Nov. 10, 1998, P.L. 105-362, 7 U.S. Code § 2027

Nov. 12, 1998, P.L. 105-379, 7 U.S. Code § 2020

Food Stamp and Commodity Distribution Amendments of 1981

Dec. 22, 1981, P.L. 97-98, 7 U.S. Code § 2011 nt.

Food Stamp and Emergency Food Access Act

Cal. Welfare and Institutions Code §§ 18904.3, 18905.1, 18911 to 18914, 18914.5

Food Stamp Distribution Act

Mich. Comp. Laws Ann., 400.751 et seq.

Food Stamp Plan Act

Miss. Code Ann. 1972, 41-1-27, 97-7-42, 97-19-71, 21-19-41, 27-65-111

Food Stamp Program Improvements Act of 1994

March 25, 1994, P.L. 103-225, 7 U.S. Code §§ 2011 nt., 2012, 2012 nt., 2014, 2015, 2015 nt., 2016, 2016 nt., 2018, 2026

Food Stamp Program Information Act

Cal. Welfare and Institutions Code §§ 18904.2, 18904.3, 18904.25, 18911

Food Stamp Trafficking Control Act

Del. Code of 1974, Title 31, § 610 et seq.

Food Stamp Vendor Accountability Act (Emergency)

Mich. Comp. Laws Ann., 338.971 et seq.

Food Survey Act

See Food Conservation Acts

Food Technology Laboratory Act

Miss. Code Ann. 1972, § 57-19-1 et seq.

Food Transport Act (Clean)

Cal. Public Utilities Code §§ 215.6, 215.7, 1071.5, 3558, 3587, 3588, 3595, 3595.5, 4848.5

Cal. Statutes 1990, Ch. 1685

Cal. Vehicle Code 1959, § 34516

Food Warehousemen Act

Cal. Public Utilities Code § 2501 et seq.

Foot-and-Mouth Disease Act (Mexico)

Feb. 28, 1947, Ch. 8, 61 Stat. 7, 21 U.S. Code §§ 114b, 114c

July 27, 1966, P.L. 89-521, 80 Stat. 330, 21 U.S. Code §§ 114b, 114d-1

Foot and Mouth Disease Quarantine Act

Tex. Agriculture Code, § 161.141

Tex. Rev. Civ. Stat., Art. 7014f-14

Foot and Mouth Emergency Act

Ind. Burns' 1933, 16-701 et seq.

Football Stadium District Act (Metropolitan)

Colo. Rev. Stat., 32-15-101 et seq.

Footpath and Bicycle Trail Act

Mont. Code Ann., 60-3-301 et seq.

For Hire Landscapers Law

Ore. Rev. Stat., 671.510 et seq.

For Hire Vehicle Act
Wash. Rev. Code Ann., 46.72.010 et seq.

For Hire Vessel Act
Cal. Statutes 1933, p. 723

Forage Crop Certification Act (Weed-Free)
Colo. Rev. Stat., 35-275-101 to 35-275-108

Foraker Act (Puerto Rico)
See Puerto Rico Civil Code

Foran-Collier Act
Cal. Streets and Highways Code § 135.3 et
seq.

Foran-Collier Act (Relocation Assistance)
Cal. Government Code § 15950 et seq.

**Foran-Marks Residential Rehabilitation Act
of 1973**
Cal. Health and Safety Code § 37910 et seq.

Forbes Mechanical Contractors Act
Mich. Comp. Laws Ann., 338.971 et seq.

Force Act
May 31, 1870, Ch. 114, 16 Stat. 140

Force Act (State Defense)
Colo. Rev. Stat., 28-4-101 et seq.
Haw. Rev. Stat. Ann., § 122A-1 et seq.

Force Act (Suits against Revenue Officers)
March 2, 1833, Ch. 57, 4 Stat. 633

Forced Heir Act
La. Civil Code Art. 1493
Okla. Stat. Ann., Title 84, § 44

Forced Pooling Law (Oil and Gas)
Okla. Stat. Ann., Title 52, § 87.1

Forced Share Act
Ala. Code 1975, § 43-1-15
Ark. Code Ann. 1987, 28-9-214
Colo. Rev. Stat., 15-11-201
Conn. Gen. Stat. Ann., § 45a-436
Del. Code of 1974, Title 12, § 901
Ill. Rev. Stat. 1991, Ch. 110 1/2, § 2-8

Mass. Gen. Laws Ann., 191:15
Mo. Rev. Stat., 474.160
N.H. Rev. Stat. 1955, 560:10
N.Y. Estates, Powers and Trusts Law
(Consol. Laws Ch. 17B) § 5-1.1
Pa. Cons. Stat., Title 20, § 2201
Tenn. Code Ann., 31-4-101 et seq.

Forcible Entry and Detainer Act
Ala. Code 1975, § 6-6-310 et seq.
Alaska Stat. 1962, § 09.45.060 et seq.
Ariz. Rev. Stat. Ann., § 12-1171 et seq.
Cal. Code of Civil Procedure § 1159 et seq.
Colo. Rev. Stat., 13-40-101 et seq.
Ill. Rev. Stat. 1991, Ch. 110, § 9-101 et seq.
Kan. Stat. Ann., 61-2301 et seq.
Me. Rev. Stat. Ann. 1964, Title 14, § 6001 et
seq.
Mich. Comp. Laws Ann., 600.5701 et seq.
Minn. Stat. Ann., 566.01 et seq.
Mont. Code Ann., 70-27-101 et seq.
Neb. Rev. Stat. 1943, 25-21, 219 et seq.
Ohio Rev. Code 1953, 1923.01 et seq.
Okla. Stat. Ann., Title 12, § 1148.1 et seq.
Ore. Rev. Stat., 105.105 et seq.
R.I. Gen. Laws 1956, 34-19-1 et seq.
S.C. Code Ann. 1976, § 15-67-410 et seq.
S.D. Codified Laws 1967, 21-16-1 et seq.
Tex. Property Code, § 24.001 et seq.
Utah Code Ann. 1953, 78-36-1 et seq.
Vt. Stat. Ann., Title 12, § 4911 et seq.
Wash. Rev. Code Ann., 59.12.010 et seq.
Wis. Stat. Ann., 799.40 et seq.

**Ford-DeMarcus-Buckman College
Scholarship Act**
Ky. Rev. Stat. 1971, 164.740 et seq.

Fordney-McCumber Act (Tariff)
Sept. 21, 1922, Ch. 356, 42 Stat. 858, 19 U.S.
Code §§ 5, 257, 258, 261, 1333; 31 U.S.
Code §§ 521, 549; 46 U.S. Code §§ 11, 58,
321, 333

Foreclosure Act (Emergency)
Mich. Public Acts 1933, No. 98

Foreclosure Act (Fifty Year Mortgage)
Mass. Gen. Laws Ann., 260.33

Foreclosure Act (Mortgages)
Haw. Rev. Stat. Ann., § 667-1 et seq.

Foreclosure Act (Real Property)
Alaska Stat. 1962, § 09.45.170 et seq.
Ga. Code Ann., 44-14-180 et seq.
Ga. Code 1933, 67-201 et seq.
S.D. Codified Laws 1967, 21-50-1 et seq.
Wash. Rev. Code Ann., 61.12.020 et seq.

Foreclosure Act (Tax Liens)
N.C. Gen. Stat. 1943, § 105-374 et seq.

Foreclosure Act (Taxes)
Fla. Stat. 1967, 194.01 et seq.
Kan. Stat. Ann., 79-2801 et seq.

Foreclosure Fee Law (Attorneys)
Cal. Code of Civil Procedure § 730

Foreclosure Moratorium Act
Neb. Laws 1933, Ch. 65

Foreclosure Validating Act of 1974
Minn. Laws 1974, Ch. 226

Foreign Accounts Bank Act
See Federal Reserve Act

Foreign Acknowledgments Act
La. Rev. Stat. Ann., 35:551 et seq.
Tenn. Code Ann., 66-22-104
Wis. Stat. Ann., 706.07

Foreign Affairs Agencies Consolidation Act of 1998
Oct. 21, 1998, P.L. 105-277, Division G, Subdivision A, Title XI, 112 Stat. 2681, 22 U.S. Code § 6501 nt.

Foreign Affairs Reform and Restructuring Act of 1998
Oct. 21, 1998, P.L. 105-277, Division G, 112 Stat. 2681, 22 U.S. Code § 6501 nt.

Foreign Agencies Act
Mich. Comp. Laws Ann., 14.201 et seq.

Foreign Agents Registration Act of 1938
June 8, 1938, Ch. 327, 52 Stat. 631, 22 U.S. Code §§ 611 to 617
April 29, 1942, Ch. 263, 56 Stat. 248, 22 U.S. Code §§ 611, 612 to 621
Oct. 4, 1961, P.L. 87-366, 75 Stat. 784, 22 U.S. Code §§ 611, 613
July 4, 1966, P.L. 89-486, 80 Stat. 244 to 248, 22 U.S. Code §§ 611 to 616, 618
Aug. 12, 1970, P.L. 91-375, 84 Stat. 782, 22 U.S. Code § 611
Nov. 8, 1984, P.L. 98-620, 22 U.S. Code § 618
Dec. 19, 1995, P.L. 104-65, 22 U.S. Code §§ 611, 613, 614, 616, 618, 621
Sept. 30, 1996, P.L. 104-208, 22 U.S. Code § 618
April 6, 1998, P.L. 105-166, 22 U.S. Code § 613

Foreign Agricultural Investment Disclosure Act
Va. Code 1950, § 3.1-22.22 et seq.

Foreign Aid Act of 1947
Dec. 17, 1947, Ch. 520, 61 Stat. 934

Foreign Aid and Related Agencies Appropriation Acts
Oct. 23, 1962, P.L. 87-872, 76 Stat. 1163, 22 U.S. Code §§ 2151 nt., 2370 nts.
Jan. 6, 1964, P.L. 88-258, 77 Stat. 857, 2 U.S. Code §§ 46a, 46c; 22 U.S. Code §§ 2151 nt., 2370 nts.

Foreign Aid Appropriation Acts
Oct. 6, 1949, Ch. 621, 63 Stat. 709
Sept. 6, 1950, Ch. 896, 64 Stat. 757

Foreign Animal Diseases Act
Okla. Stat. Ann., Title 2, § 6-131 et seq.

Foreign Assistance Act of 1948
April 3, 1948, Ch. 169, 62 Stat. 137, 7 U.S. Code § 612c nt.; 22 U.S. Code § 286b

Foreign Assistance Act of 1961
Sept. 4, 1961, P.L. 87-195, 75 Stat. 424, 22 U.S. Code §§ 276, 279a, 1041, 1112, 1136, 1148, 1157, 1613d, 1753 nt., 1783, 1785 nt., 1811 nt. and others
Continued

Sept. 30, 1961, P.L. 87-329, 75 Stat. 719, 22 U.S. Code § 2151 nt.

Aug. 1, 1962, P.L. 87-565, 76 Stat. 255, 22 U.S. Code §§ 276, 2151, 2161, 2171, 2172, 2181, 2182, 2184, 2192, 2211 to 2213, 2222 and others

Oct. 11, 1962, P.L. 87-793, 76 Stat. 865, 22 U.S. Code § 2385

Dec. 16, 1963, P.L. 88-205, 77 Stat. 379, 22 U.S. Code §§ 2151, 2161, 2162, 2172, 2174, 2181, 2182, 2184, 2201, 2211 to 2213, 2216 and others

Aug. 14, 1964, P.L. 88-426, 78 Stat. 426, 22 U.S. Code § 2384

Aug. 19, 1964, P.L. 88-448, 78 Stat. 495, 22 U.S. Code § 2386

Oct. 7, 1964, P.L. 88-633, 78 Stat. 1009, 22 U.S. Code §§ 2161, 2172, 2174, 2176, 2177, 2181, 2184, 2192, 2212, 2222, 2242, 2261 and others

Sept. 6, 1965, P.L. 89-171, 79 Stat. 653 to 661, 22 U.S. Code §§ 2151, 2165, 2166, 2172, 2174, 2181 to 2184, 2212, 2221, 2222, 2242, 2261, 2311 to 2313, 2315 to 2320, 2355, 2362, 2363, 2370, 2382, 2384 to 2386, 2390, 2391, 2395 to 2399a, 2403, 2404, 2408

March 18, 1966, P.L. 89-371, 80 Stat. 74, 22 U.S. Code §§ 2242, 2261, 2360

Sept. 19, 1966, P.L. 89-583, 80 Stat. 796, 22 U.S. Code §§ 2151, 2161, 2162, 2165, 2171, 2172, 2174, 2181, 2182, 2184, 2211, 2212, 2217 to 2218, 2221 and others

Nov. 14, 1967, P.L. 90-137, 81 Stat. 445, 22 U.S. Code §§ 2151, 2161, 2162, 2165, 2167 to 2169, 2171, 2172, 2174, 2178 and others

Oct. 8, 1968, P.L. 90-554, 82 Stat. 960, 22 U.S. Code §§ 2151 nt., 2161, 2162, 2171, 2172, 2174, 2181 and others

Oct. 22, 1968, P.L. 90-629, 82 Stat. 1327, 22 U.S. Code §§ 2344, 2382, 2392, 2394, 2403

Dec. 30, 1969, P.L. 91-175, 83 Stat. 805, 22 U.S. Code §§ 2162, 2163, 2172, 2174, 2179 to 2183, 2191 to 2200a, 2212, 2219a, 2221 and others

Jan. 5, 1971, P.L. 91-652, 84 Stat. 1942, 22 U.S. Code §§ 2242, 2261, 2411

Feb. 7, 1972, P.L. 92-226, 86 Stat. 21, 22 U.S. Code §§ 2162, 2169, 2172, 2174, 2180a, 2181, 2183, 2198 to 2200, 2212, 2219a, 2222, 2261, 2291, 2292, 2312

June 6, 1972, P.L. 92-310, 86 Stat. 207, 22 U.S. Code § 2199

July 13, 1972, P.L. 92-352, 86 Stat. 496, 22 U.S. Code § 2291

Dec. 17, 1973, P.L. 93-189, 87 Stat. 714, 22 U.S. Code §§ 2151, 2151l, 2163, 2174, 2181, 2183, 2195, 2200, 2212, 2219a

July 8, 1974, P.L. 93-333, 88 Stat. 290, 22 U.S. Code §§ 2262, 2399-1a

Aug. 27, 1974, P.L. 93-390, 88 Stat. 763, 22 U.S. Code §§ 2191, 2194, 2195, 2197, 2199, 2200, 2200a

Nov. 29, 1975, P.L. 94-141, 89 Stat. 760, 22 U.S. Code § 2321

Dec. 20, 1975, P.L. 94-161, 89 Stat. 849, 22 U.S. Code §§ 2151 to 2151e, 2151h to 2151k, 2151n, 2169, 2174, 2181 to 2183, 2201, 2220a to 2220e 2221, 2222, 2225, 2292 to 2292f, 2293, 2357, 2399-1a, 2399-1b 2399h, 2421, 2425 to 2427

April 18, 1977, P.L. 95-21, 22 U.S. Code § 2292j

July 20, 1977, P.L. 96-35, 22 U.S. Code §§ 2349 to 2349b

Aug. 3, 1977, P.L. 95-88, 22 U.S. Code § 2151 et seq.

Aug. 4, 1977, P.L. 95-92, 22 U.S. Code § 2261 et seq.

Aug. 17, 1977, P.L. 95-105, 22 U.S. Code § 2151n et seq.

April 24, 1978, P.L. 95-268, 22 U.S. Code § 2191 et seq.

Nov. 6, 1978, P.L. 95-598, 22 U.S. Code § 2199

Aug. 14, 1979, P.L. 96-53, 22 U.S. Code § 2151-1 et seq.

Oct. 29, 1979, P.L. 96-92, 22 U.S. Code §§ 2261, 2291, 2291a, 2304, 2312, 2318, 2321h to 2321j, 2346, 2346c, 2346d, 2347a, 2348, 2348a, 2403

Nov. 9, 1979, P.L. 96-109, 22 U.S. Code § 2292m

Nov. 13, 1979, P.L. 96-110, 22 U.S. Code § 2292n

May 31, 1980, P.L. 96-257, 22 U.S. Code § 2346e

Aug. 8, 1980, P.L. 96-327, 22 U.S. Code § 2199

June 30, 1982, P.L. 97-208, 22 U.S. Code § 2292p

Dec. 21, 1982, P.L. 97-377, 22 U.S. Code §§ 2151z, 2151z nt.

Jan. 8, 1983, P.L. 97-438, 22 U.S. Code § 2182a

Nov. 14, 1983, P.L. 97-151, 22 U.S. Code §§ 2346a, 2349aa-4

Nov. 22, 1983, P.L. 98-164, 22 U.S. Code §§ 2151n, 2151q, 2291, 2384

April 2, 1985, P.L. 99-8, 22 U.S. Code § 2292q

July 12, 1985, P.L. 99-64, 22 U.S. Code § 2304

Aug. 8, 1985, P.L. 99-83, 22 U.S. Code §§ 2151-1 et seq., 2174, 2182, 2222, 2227, 2271 et seq., 2291 et seq. 2311 et seq., 2321, 2346 et seq. 2349aa-2 et seq., 2394, 2411, 2413, 2420, 2421

Aug. 16, 1985, P.L. 99-93, 22 U.S. Code § 2357

Dec. 19, 1985, P.L. 99-190, 22 U.S. Code § 2371

Dec. 23, 1985, P.L. 99-204, 22 U.S. Code §§ 2151 nt., 2191, 2191a, 2194, 2194b, 2195, 2197, 2199, 2200a, 2200a nt.

Jan. 2, 1986, P.L. 99-234, 22 U.S. Code § 2396

July 2, 1986, P.L. 99-349, 100 Stat. 749

Aug. 27, 1986, P.L. 99-399; 22 U.S. Code §§ 2151a, 2349aa-2, 2349aa-4

Oct. 2, 1986, P.L. 99-440, 22 U.S. Code §§ 2151n, 2151o, 2346d

Oct. 24, 1986, P.L. 99-529, 22 U.S. Code §§ 2151b, 2151p, 2151p- 1, 2151q, 2222, 2291a, 2427

Oct. 27, 1986, P.L. 99-550, 22 U.S. Code § 2396

Oct. 27, 1986, P.L. 99-570, 22 U.S. Code §§ 2291, 2291 nt., 2291a, 2291c

Nov. 7, 1986, P.L. 99-631, 22 U.S. Code §§ 2151c, 2151n, 2346d, 5001 nt.

Nov. 14, 1986, P.L. 99-661, 22 U.S. Code § 2321j

Dec. 22, 1987, P.L. 100-202, 22 U.S. Code §§ 2151u nt., 2183, 2182, 2291, 2291 nt., 2321, 2321h, 2346c, 2373, 2375, 2396, 2398, 2398 nt.

Dec. 22, 1987, P.L. 100-204, 22 U.S. Code §§ 2151n, 2291, 2304

Aug. 23, 1988, P.L. 100-418, 102 Stat. 1328, 22 U.S. Code §§ 2151f, 2191a, 2195, 2421

Oct. 1, 1988, P.L. 100-461, 22 U.S. Code §§ 2191, 2194, 2194b, 2195, 2197, 2199, 2200a, 2291, 2311, 2321h

Oct. 25, 1988, P.L. 100-530, 22 U.S. Code § 2151q nt.

Nov. 18, 1988, P.L. 100-690, 22 U.S. Code §§ 2222, 2291, 2291a, 2291e to 2291h, 2321i, 2392

Nov. 21, 1989, P.L. 101-165, 22 U.S. Code §§ 2321i, 2392

Nov. 21, 1989, P.L. 101-167, 22 U.S. Code §§ 2621, 2151q, 2182, 2184, 2199, 2318, 2321h, 2321i, 2346c, 2375, 2396

Nov. 28, 1989, P.L. 101-179, 22 U.S. Code §§ 2184, 2185, 2199

Nov. 29, 1989, P.L. 101-189, 22 U.S. Code § 2321j

Dec. 11, 1989, P.L. 101-218, 22 U.S. Code § 2194

Dec. 12, 1989, P.L. 101-222, 22 U.S. Code §§ 2364, 2371

Dec. 13, 1989, P.L. 101-231, 22 U.S. Code §§ 2291, 2291a, 2321k

Dec. 19, 1989, P.L. 101-240, 22 U.S. Code §§ 2281 to 2286

May 25, 1990, P.L. 101-302, 22 U.S. Code § 2182

Nov. 5, 1990, P.L. 101-513, 22 U.S. Code §§ 2151, 2151c, 2151k, 2151n, 2151p, 2151s, 2151u, 2151x, 2182, 2184, 2199, 2261, 2294, 2314, 2321h, 2321j, 2321l, 2321m, 2346c, 2347, 2375, 2420

Nov. 16, 1990, P.L. 101-604, 22 U.S. Code §§ 2321h, 2349aa-2

Nov. 21, 1990, P.L. 101-623, 22 U.S. Code §§ 2321k, 2291c, 2346c, 2360, 2360 nt.

Aug. 14, 1991, P.L. 102-88, 22 U.S. Code § 2422

Dec. 5, 1991, P.L. 102-190, 22 U.S. Code § 2321j

April 1, 1992, P.L. 102-266, 22 U.S. Code § 2375

Oct. 6, 1992, P.L. 102-391, 22 U.S. Code § 42186, prec. 2296, 2296, 2321, 2321h, 2321i, 2321j, 2354, 2375, 2376

Oct. 23, 1992, P.L. 102-484, 22 U.S. Code § 2321j

Oct. 24, 1992, P.L. 102-511, 22 U.S. Code §§ 2370, prec. 2295, 2295 et seq.

Continued

Oct. 28, 1992, P.L. 102-549, 22 U.S. Code §§ 2191, 2191a, 2194, 2195, 2197, 2198, 2199, 2200a, 2200b, 2421, 2430 to 2430i

Oct. 28, 1992, P.L. 102-550, 22 U.S. Code § 2291

Nov. 2, 1992, P.L. 102-583, 22 U.S. Code §§ 2291, 2291a, 2291c- 2291h, 2321k, 2347

Sept. 30, 1993, P.L. 103-87, 22 U.S. Code §§ 2321h, 2375

Nov. 23, 1993, P.L. 103-149, 22 U.S. Code §§ 2151n, 2151o, 2346d, 5001

Nov. 30, 1993, P.L. 103-160, 22 U.S. Code § 2321j

Dec. 17, 1993, P.L. 103-199, 22 U.S. Code §§ 2301, 2364, 2370

April 30, 1994, P.L. 103-236, 22 U.S. Code §§ 2151n, 2227, 2291a, 2304, 2314, 2321j et seq., 2349aa-2, 2375, 2429, 2429, 2761, 2776 et seq.

Aug. 23, 1994, P.L. 103-306, 22 U.S. Code §§ 2321h, 2370

Nov. 2, 1994, P.L. 103-437, 22 U.S. Code §§ 2151n, 2304, 2314, 2394-1

Nov. 2, 1994, P.L. 103-447, 22 U.S. Code §§ 2291, 2291a, 2291e, 2291f, 2291h, 2291i, 2291j, 2291k

Dec. 21, 1995, P.L. 104-66, 22 U.S. Code §§ 2291h, 2291i, 2291j, 2291k

Feb. 10, 1996, P.L. 104-106, 22 U.S. Code §§ 2321j, 2415

Feb. 12, 1996, P.L. 104-107, 22 U.S. Code §§ 2321h, 2375, 2420

March 12, 1996, P.L. 104-114, 22 U.S. Code §§ 2295a, 2295b, 2370

April 24, 1996, P.L. 104-132, 22 U.S. Code §§ 2349aa-2, 2377, 2378

July 21, 1996, P.L. 104-164, 22 U.S. Code §§ 2291, 2291a, 2303, 2318, 2321i to 2321n, 2347, 2347c, 2347e, 2349aa, 2349aa-2 to 2349aa-5, 2378a, 2403, 2411, 2415

Aug. 20, 1996, P.L. 104-188, 22 U.S. Code § 2191a

Sept. 30, 1996, P.L. 104-208, 22 U.S. Code §§ 2195, 2378-1

Oct. 19, 1996, P.L. 104-319, 22 U.S. Code §§ 2151n, 2304

Nov. 26, 1997, P.L. 105-118, 22 U.S. Code §§ 2195, 2199, 2318, 2321h

July 29, 1998, P.L. 105-214, 22 U.S. Code §§ prec. 2431, 2431, 2431a to 2431k

Oct. 21, 1998, P.L. 105-277, 22 U.S. Code §§ 2151n, 2151aa, 2227, 2321d, 2321h, 2346, 2359, 2370, 2370 nt., 2376

Oct. 27, 1998, P.L. 105-292, 22 U.S. Code §§ 2151n, 2304

Oct. 30, 1998, P.L. 105-320, 22 U.S. Code § 2152

Nov. 10, 1998, P.L. 105-362, 22 U.S. Code § 2226

May 21, 1999, P.L. 106-31, 22 U.S. Code § 2194

Foreign Assistance Act of 1962

Aug. 1, 1962, P.L. 87-565, 76 Stat. 255, 22 U.S. Code §§ 276, 2151, 2161, 2171, 2172, 2181, 2182, 2184, 2192, 2211 to 2213, 2222, 2242, 2261, 2271 and others

Foreign Assistance Act of 1963

Dec. 16, 1963, P.L. 88-205, 77 Stat. 379, 7 U.S. Code §§ 1701, 1705, 1706, 1722; 19 U.S. Code § 1861; 22 U.S. Code §§ 816, 961, 1136, 1138a, 1139, 1928a, 1942 nt., 1943, 2151, 2161, 2162, 2172, 2174 and others

Foreign Assistance Act of 1964

Oct. 7, 1964, P.L. 88-633, 78 Stat. 1009, 22 U.S. Code §§ 276, 1754, 2151 nts., 2161, 2172, 2174, 2176, 2177, 2181, 2184, 2192, 2212, 2222, 2242and others

Foreign Assistance Act of 1965

Sept. 6, 1965, P.L. 89-171, 79 Stat. 653, 7 U.S. Code § 1707; 22 U.S. Code §§ 2151, 2165, 2166, 2172, 2174, 2181 to 2184, 2212, 2222, 2242, 2261, 2311 to 2313 and others

Foreign Assistance Act of 1966

Sept. 19, 1966, P.L. 89-583, 80 Stat. 795, 22 U.S. Code §§ 2151, 2161, 2162, 2165, 2171, 2172, 2174, 2181, 2182, 2184, 2211, 2212, 2217 to 2218, 2221 and others

Foreign Assistance Act of 1967

Nov. 14, 1967, P.L. 90-137, 81 Stat. 445, 22 U.S. Code §§ 276c, 276c-1, 1928b to 1928d, 1934, 2151, 2161, 2162, 2165, 2167 to 2169, 2171, 2172, 2174 and others

Foreign Assistance Act of 1968

Oct. 8, 1968, P.L. 90-554, 82 Stat. 960, 16 U.S. Code § 617; 22 U.S. Code §§ 2151 nt., 2161, 2162, 2171, 2172, 2174, 2181, 2184, 2212, 2218, 2219a and others

Foreign Assistance Act of 1969

Dec. 30, 1969, P.L. 91-175, 83 Stat. 805, 5 U.S. Code §§ 3343, 3581, 3582, 5314 to 5316; 22 U.S. Code §§ 290f, 2162, 2163, 2172, 2174, 2179 to 2183 and others; 31 U.S. Code § 846

Aug. 17, 1977, P.L. 95-105, 22 U.S. Code § 290f

Aug. 24, 1982, P.L. 97-241, 22 U.S. Code § 290f

Nov. 22, 1983, P.L. 98-164, 22 U.S. Code § 290f

Aug. 8, 1985, P.L. 99-83, 22 U.S. Code § 290f

Oct. 24, 1986, P.L. 99-529, 22 U.S. Code § 290f

Oct. 28, 1991, P.L. 102-138, 22 U.S. Code § 290f

Foreign Assistance Act of 1980

Nov. 21, 1989, P.L. 101-167, 22 U.S. Code §§ 4010, 4136

Foreign Assistance and Related Agencies Appropriation Acts

Sept. 30, 1961, P.L. 87-329, 75 Stat. 717, 22 U.S. Code §§ 2151 nt., 2366 nt.

Oct. 7, 1964, P.L. 88-634, 78 Stat. 1015, 22 U.S. Code §§ 2151 nt., 2370 nt., 2601

Oct. 20, 1965, P.L. 89-273, 79 Stat. 1002, 22 U.S. Code §§ 2151 nt., 2370 nt.

Oct. 15, 1966, P.L. 89-691, 80 Stat. 1018, 2 U.S. Code § 61g-1; 22 U.S. Code §§ 2151 nt., 2221 nt., 2370 nts.

Jan. 2, 1968, P.L. 90-249, 81 Stat. 936, 22 U.S. Code §§ 2151 nt., 2181 nt., 2221 nt., 2344 nts., 2370 nts.

Oct. 17, 1968, P.L. 90-581, 82 Stat. 1137, 22 U.S. Code §§ 2151 nt., 2221 nt., 2344 nt., 2370 nt.

Feb. 9, 1970, P.L. 91-194, 84 Stat. 5, 22 U.S. Code §§ 2151 nt., 2221 nt., 2344 nts., 2370 nts.

Dec. 31, 1970, P.L. 91-619, 84 Stat. 1856

June 30, 1976, P.L. 94-330, 22 U.S. Code § 2292a-1

Oct. 12, 1984, P.L. 98-473, 98 Stat. 1884-1903

Dec. 19, 1985, P.L. 99-190, 19 U.S. Code § 2423 nt., 22 U.S. Code §§ 262h, 262l, 282j, 284q, 286e-1j, 290g-13, 2151u nt., 2371, 2414a 2423 nt.

Oct. 18, 1986, P.L. 99-500, 100 Stat. 3584

Oct. 30, 1986, P.L. 99-591, 100 Stat. 3584

Dec. 22, 1987, P.L. 100-202, 22 U.S. Code § 2151u nt.

Nov. 21, 1989, P.L. 101-167, 22 U.S. Code § 2414a

Feb. 16, 1990, P.L. 101-246, 22 U.S. Code 2414a

Foreign Bank Office Act

N.H. Rev. Stat. 1955, 384-F:8

Foreign Bank Supervision Enhancement Act of 1991

Dec. 19, 1991, P.L. 102-242, 12 U.S. Code § 3101 nt.

Foreign Banking Developments Act

Del. Laws Vol. 65, p. 856, Ch. 444

Foreign Business Trusts Act (Registration of)

Miss. Code Ann. 1972, § 79-16-1 et seq.

Foreign Capital Depository Act

Mont. Code Ann., 15-31-801 et seq.

Foreign Claims Act

Jan. 2, 1942, Ch. 645, 55 Stat. 880

April 22, 1943, Ch. 67, 57 Stat. 66

July 31, 1945, Ch. 338, 59 Stat. 511

Foreign Claims Limitations Act

Mich. Comp. Laws Ann., 600.5861

Okla. Stat. Ann., Title 12, § 104 et seq.

Foreign Corporation Act

Mass. Gen. Laws Ann., 181:1 et seq.

Foreign Corporation Registration Act (Doing Business)

N.Y. Business Corporation Law (Consol. Laws Ch. 4) § 1301 et seq.

Foreign Corporations Equal Treatment Act
N.C. Gen. Stat. 1943, § 55-132

Foreign Corporations Substituted Service Act
Mass. Gen. Laws Ann., 181:4, 181:15

Foreign Corrupt Practices Act Amendments of 1988
Aug. 23, 1988, P.L. 100-418, 102 Stat. 1415, 15 U.S. Code § 78a nt.

Foreign Corrupt Practices Act of 1977
Dec. 19, 1977, P.L. 95-213, 15 U.S. Code §§ 78a nt., 78m et seq.
Aug. 23, 1988, P.L. 100-418, 102 Stat. 1419, 15 U.S. Code § 78dd-2
Sept. 13, 1994, P.L. 103-322, 15 U.S. Code § 78dd-2
Nov. 10, 1998, P.L. 105-366, 15 U.S. Code §§ 78dd-2, 78dd-3

Foreign Country Money Judgments Recognition Act
See also Foreign-Money Judgments Recognition Act;
See also Uniform Foreign-Money Judgments Recognition Act
N.J. Stat. Ann., 2A:49A-16 et seq.

Foreign Currency Exchange and Check Cashing Act
Fla. Stat. Ann., 560.301 to 560.310
Me. Rev. Stat. Ann. 1964, Title 36, § 6751 et seq.

Foreign Debt Reserving Act of 1989
Dec. 19, 1989, P.L. 101-240, 12 U.S. Code § 3901 nt.

Foreign Decrees Act
Colo. Rev. Stat., 14-11-101

Foreign Depositions Act
See also Uniform Foreign Depositions Act
See Uniform Foreign Depositions Act
Ala. Code 1958, Title 7, § 464
Alaska Laws 1923, Ch. 13
Okla. Stat. Ann., Title 12, § 461 et seq.
Wyo. Stat. Ann., § 1-12-115

Foreign Depositions Act (Canal Zone)
See Uniform Foreign Depositions Act (Canal Zone)

Foreign Direct Investment and International Financial Data Improvements Act of 1990
Nov. 7, 1990, P.L. 101-533, 22 U.S. Code §§ 3141 to 3146
Oct. 19, 1996, P.L. 104-316, 22 U.S. Code § 3143

Foreign Discriminatory Boycotts Act
Md. Ann. Code 1974, Art. CL, § 11-101 et seq.

Foreign Dividends Taxation Act
Ala. Code 1975, § 40-18-35

Foreign Earned Income Act of 1978
Nov. 8, 1978, P.L. 95-615, 26 U.S. Code § 1 nt.
April 1, 1980, P.L. 96-222, 26 U.S. Code §§ 43 et seq.
Nov. 5, 1990, P.L. 101-508, 26 U.S. Code § 911 nt.

Foreign Economic Administration Appropriation Act of 1945
June 30, 1944, Ch. 324, 58 Stat. 627

Foreign Economic Assistance Act of 1950
June 5, 1950, Ch. 220, 64 Stat. 198

Foreign Egg Law
Wash. Rev. Code 1974, 69.24.320 et seq.

Foreign Exchange License Act
Ill. Rev. Stat. 1991, Ch. 17, § 2601 et seq.

Foreign Executed Wills Act
Alaska Stat. 1962, Replaced Titles, § 13.05.100
Kan. Stat. Ann., 59-609
La. Rev. Stat. Ann., 9:2401
Mass. Gen. Laws Ann., 191:5
Mich. Comp. Laws Ann., 702.27 et seq.
Minn. Stat. 1974, 525.183
Nev. Rev. Stat. 1979 Reprint, 133.080

N.Y. Estates, Powers and Trusts Law
(Consol. Laws Ch. 17B) § 3-5.1, Subd. c

Wis. Stat. Ann., 853.05

Wis. Stat. 1969, 238.07

**Foreign Fire Insurance Tax Distribution
Law**

Pa. Purdon's Stat., Title 53, § 895.701 et seq.

Foreign Franchise Tax Reform Act

Ala. Code 1975, § 40-14-41

Foreign Gifts and Decorations Act of 1966

Oct. 15, 1966, P.L. 89-673, 80 Stat. 952, 22
U.S. Code §§ 804, 2621 to 2626

Foreign Heirs Reciprocal Rights Act

Cal. Probate Code § 259 et seq.

Iowa Code Ann., 567.8

Mont. Rev. Code 1947, 91-520, 91-521

Ore. Rev. Stat. 1953, 111.070

Foreign Insurance Companies Act

Ill. Rev. Stat. 1991, Ch. 73, § 720 et seq.

N.C. Gen. Stat. 1943, § 58-16-1 et seq.

N.H. Stat. 1955, 405:1 et seq.

R.I. Gen. Laws 1956, 27-2-1 et seq.

Foreign Intelligence Surveillance Act of 1978

Oct. 25, 1978, P.L. 95-511, 18 U.S. Code
§§ 2511, 2518, 2519; 50 U.S. Code § 1801
et seq., 1801 nt.

Oct. 14, 1994, P.L. 103-359, 50 U.S. Code
§§ 1801 nt., 1821 et seq.

Oct. 20, 1998, P.L. 105-272, 50 U.S. Code
§§ 1801 nt., 1841 to 1846, 1861 to 1863

**Foreign Investment Disclosure Act (Agricul-
tural)**

Ill. Comp. Stat. 1992, Ch. 765, § 50/1 et seq.

Ill. Rev. Stat. 1991, Ch. 5, § 601 et seq.

**Foreign Investment in Real Property Tax
Act of 1980**

Dec. 5, 1980, P.L. 96-499, 26 U.S. Code § 1
nt.

Foreign Investors Tax Act of 1966

Nov. 13, 1966, P.L. 89-809, 80 Stat. 1541, 26
U.S. Code §§ 1, 116, 154, 245, 301, 512,
542, 543, 545, 821, 822, 831, 832, 841, 842,
861, 864, 871 to 875 and others

Foreign Judgments Act

Tex. Civil Practice and Remedies Code,
§ 35.002

**Foreign Judgments Enforcement Act
(Uniform)**

See Uniform Enforcement of Foreign
Judgments Act

Foreign Land Sales Practices Act

Mont. Code Ann., 76-4-1201 et seq.

Foreign Language Assistance Act of 1988

April 28, 1988, P.L. 100-297, 102 Stat. 228,
20 U.S. Code § 3001 et seq.

Aug. 23, 1988, P.L. 100-418, 102 Stat. 1476,
20 U.S. Code § 5011

Foreign Language School Act

Haw. Session Laws 1920, Sp. Sess., Act 30

**Foreign Language Teacher Exchange and
Recruitment Law**

Cal. Education Code 1976, § 44610 et seq.

Foreign Law Act (Judicial Notice)

Ark. Code Ann. 1987, 16-40-104

Me. Rev. Stat. Ann. 1964, Title 16, § 401 et
seq.

Mo. Rev. Stat., 490.070 et seq.

Neb. Rev. Stat. 1943, 25-12.101 et seq.

R.I. Gen. Laws 1956, 9-19-2 et seq.

Foreign Law Ascertainment Act

Ill. Rev. Stat. 1991, Ch. 110, § 8-1003 et seq.

Foreign Law Consultants Act

N.M. Stat. Ann., 36-3-1 et seq.

Foreign Law Evidence Act

Pa. Cons. Stat., Title 42, § 5327

Foreign Law Judicial Notice Act

See Uniform Judicial Notice of Foreign Law
Act

Foreign Legatees Benefit Rule Act
Md. Ann. Code 1974, Art. ET, § 9-108

Foreign Legation Act
D.C. Code Ann., § 45-1302

Foreign Limited Liability Companies Act (Registration of)
Miss. Code Ann. 1972, § 79-6-1 et seq.

Foreign Limited Liability Partnerships Act (Registration of)
Miss. Laws 1994, Ch. 390
Tex. Rev. Civ. Stat., Art. 6132b-10.01 et seq.

Foreign Limited Partnership Act
Ala. Code 1975, § 10-9-140 et seq.
N.Y. Partnership Law (Consol. Laws Ch. 39) § 120 et seq.

Foreign Market Development Export Incentive Program for California Agricultural Act (Waters-Nielsen-Vuich-Berryhill)
Cal. Food and Agricultural Code 1967, § 58551 et seq.

Foreign Military Sales Act
Oct. 22, 1968, P.L. 90-629, 82 Stat. 1320, 22 U.S. Code §§ 2341 nt., 2344, 2382, 2392, 2394, 2403, 2751 to 2754, 2761 to 2764, 2771 to 2777, 2791 to 2793
Jan. 12, 1971, P.L. 91-672, 84 Stat. 2053, 22 U.S. Code §§ 2751, 2753, 2771, 2773
Feb. 7, 1972, P.L. 92-226, 86 Stat. 32, 22 U.S. Code §§ 2321b, 2771, 2773, 2791
Dec. 17, 1973, P.L. 93-189, 87 Stat. 729, 22 U.S. Code §§ 2321b, 2751, 2753, 2762, 2764, 2771, 2773, 2776, 2777, 2794
Nov. 29, 1975, P.L. 94-141, 89 Stat. 760, 22 U.S. Code § 2791

Foreign Missions Act
See State Department Basic Authorities Acts Of 1956
Aug. 24, 1982, P.L. 97-241, 22 U.S. Code § 4301 et seq.
Dec. 22, 1987, P.L. 100-204, 22 U.S. Code § 4302

Foreign Missions Amendments Act of 1983
Nov. 22, 1983, P.L. 98-164, 22 U.S. Code § 4301 nt.
Aug. 16, 1985, P.L. 99-93, 99 Stat. 418

Foreign Money Claims Act
See Uniform Foreign Money Claims Act

Foreign-Money Claims Act
See also Uniform Foreign-Money Claims Act
See Uniform Foreign-Money Claims Act
N.C. Gen. Stat. 1943, § 1C-1820 et seq.

Foreign-Money Judgments Recognition Act
See also Uniform Foreign-Money Judgments Recognition Act
Mont. Code Ann., 25-9-601 et seq.
N.C. Gen. Stat. 1943, §§ 1C-1800, 25-4A-101 et seq.

Foreign Money Judgments Recognition Act
See Uniform Foreign Money Judgments Recognition Act

Foreign Nonprofit Corporations Act
S.D. Codified Laws 1967, 47-28-1 et seq.

Foreign Operations, Export Financing, and Related Programs Appropriations Act, 1988
Dec. 22, 1987, P.L. 100-202, 101 Stat. 1329
Oct. 1, 1988, P.L. 100-461, 22 U.S. Code § 2291 nt.
Nov. 18, 1988, P.L. 100-690, 22 U.S. Code § 2291 nt.
Nov. 21, 1989, P.L. 101-167, 8 U.S. Code § 1101 nt.; 22 U.S. Code §§ 2414a, 2764 nt.
Dec. 19, 1989, P.L. 101-240, 22 U.S. Code § 2621 nt.
Feb. 16, 1990, P.L. 101-246, 22 U.S. Code § 2414a
Nov. 5, 1990, P.L. 101-513, 8 U.S. Code § 1101 nt.
Nov. 29, 1990, P.L. 101-649, 8 U.S. Code § 1101 nt.
Dec. 12, 1991, P.L. 102-232, 8 U.S. Code § 1101 nt.
April 1, 1992, P.L. 102-266, 22 U.S. Code § 2764 nt.

Foreign Operations, Export Financing, and Related Programs Appropriations Act, 1989

Oct. 1, 1988, P.L. 100-461, 102 Stat. 2268-53

Nov. 18, 1988, P.L. 100-690, 102 Stat. 4269

Nov. 21, 1989, P.L. 101-167, 8 U.S. Code § 1101 nt.; 22 U.S. Code § 2414a

Feb. 16, 1990, P.L. 101-246, 22 U.S. Code § 2414a

Nov. 5, 1990, P.L. 101-513, 8 U.S. Code § 1101 nt.

Foreign Operations, Export Financing, and Related Programs Appropriations Act, 1990

Nov. 21, 1989, P.L. 101-167, 103 Stat. 1195

May 25, 1990, P.L. 101-302, 8 U.S. Code § 1101 nt.

Nov. 5, 1990, P.L. 101-513, 8 U.S. Code §§ 1157 nt., 1255 nt.

Nov. 29, 1990, P.L. 101-649, 8 U.S. Code § 1255 nt.

Oct. 28, 1991, P.L. 102-138, 22 U.S. Code § 4010 nt.

Dec. 12, 1991, P.L. 102-232, 8 U.S. Code § 1255 nt.

Oct. 6, 1992, P.L. 102-391, 8 U.S. Code §§ 157 nt., 1255 nt., 22 U.S. Code § 2321j nt.

Oct. 24, 1992, P.L. 102-511, 8 U.S. Code §§ 1157 nt., 1255 nt.

April 30, 1994, P.L. 103-236, 8 U.S. Code §§ 1157, 1255

Oct. 25, 1994, P.L. 103-416, 8 U.S. Code § 1255 nt.

Sept. 30, 1996, P.L. 104-208, 8 U.S. Code §§ 1157 nt., 1255 nt.

Oct. 19, 1996, P.L. 104-319, 8 U.S. Code §§ 1157 nt., 1255 nt.

Nov. 26, 1997, P.L. 105-118, 8 U.S. Code §§ 1157 nt., 1255 nt.

Oct. 21, 1998, P.L. 105-277, 8 U.S. Code §§ 1157 nt., 1255 nt.

Foreign Operations, Export Financing, and Related Programs Appropriations Act, 1991

Nov. 5, 1990, P.L. 101-513, 104 Stat. 1979

April 10, 1991, P.L. 102-27, 22 U.S. Code § 2621

Oct. 28, 1991, P.L. 102-138, 5 U.S. Code § 5561 nt.; 22 U.S. Code § 2075

Oct. 6, 1992, P.L. 102-391, 106 Stat. 1685

Oct. 24, 1992, P.L. 102-499, 5 U.S. Code § 5561 nt.

Sept. 30, 1993, P.L. 103-87, 107 Stat. 958

Aug. 23, 1994, P.L. 103-306, 108 Stat. 1640

Foreign Operations, Export Financing, and Related Programs Appropriations Act, 1992

April 1, 1992, P.L. 102-266, 106 Stat. 93

Foreign Operations, Export Financing, and Related Programs Appropriations Act, 1993

Oct. 6, 1992, P.L. 102-391, 106 Stat. 1633

Foreign Operations, Export Financing, and Related Programs Appropriations Act, 1994

Sept. 30, 1993, P.L. 103-87, 107 Stat. 931

Aug. 23, 1994, P.L. 103-306, 108 Stat. 1656

Foreign Operations, Export Financing, and Related Programs Appropriations Act, 1995

Aug. 23, 1994, P.L. 103-306, 108 Stat. 1608

Foreign Operations, Export Financing, and Related Programs Appropriations Act, 1996

Feb. 12, 1996, P.L. 104-107, 110 Stat. 704

Foreign Operations, Export Financing, and Related Programs Appropriations Act, 1997

Sept. 30, 1996, P.L. 104-208, Title I to Title V, 110 Stat. 3009

Nov. 26, 1997, P.L. 105-118, 22 U.S. Code § 262k-1

Foreign Operations, Export Financing, and Related Programs Appropriations Act, 1998

Nov. 26, 1997, P.L. 105-118, 111 Stat. 2386

Oct. 21, 1998, P.L. 105-277, 101(e), 112 Stat. 2681

Foreign Operations, Export Financing, and Related Programs Appropriations Act, 1999

May 21, 1999, P.L. 106-31, 22 U.S. Code § 2381 nt., 2753 nt.

Foreign Probate Act

See Uniform Foreign Probate Act

Foreign Probated Wills Act

La. Rev. Stat. Ann., 9:2421 et seq.

Nev. Rev. Stat. Ann., 136.260 et seq.

Foreign Railroads (Domestication Act)

S.C. Acts 1896, p. 114, No. 50

Foreign Relations Authorization Act, Fiscal Year 1978

April 30, 1994, P.L. 103-236, 22 U.S. Code §§ 2151n-1, 2428a

Foreign Relations Authorization Act, Fiscal Years 1986 and 1987

Oct. 28, 1991, P.L. 102-138, 22 U.S. Code §§ 287e nt., 4021 nt.

Nov. 23, 1993, P.L. 103-149, 107 Stat. 1505

Dec. 17, 1993, P.L. 103-199, 22 U.S. Code § 4702

April 30, 1994, P.L. 103-236, 22 U.S. Code §§ 1461-1a, 1928 nt., 4711

Nov. 26, 1997, P.L. 105-119, 22 U.S. Code § 2291 nt.

Oct. 7, 1998, P.L. 105-244, 22 U.S. Code § 4703

Oct. 21, 1998, P.L. 105-277, 22 U.S. Code § 4021 nt.

Foreign Relations Authorization Act, Fiscal Years 1988 and 1989

Nov. 29, 1990, P.L. 101-649, 8 U.S. Code § 1182 nt.

Oct. 28, 1991, P.L. 102-138, 22 U.S. Code §§ 287e, 1461 nt., 2656 nt., 2680 nt.

Nov. 23, 1993, P.L. 103-149, 107 Stat. 1505

Dec. 17, 1993, P.L. 103-199, 22 U.S. Code § 4301 nt.

April 30, 1994, P.L. 103-236, 22 U.S. Code §§ 2656f, 4301 nt.

Sept. 30, 1996, P.L. 104-208, 22 U.S. Code § 2656f

Oct. 21, 1998, P.L. 105-277, 22 U.S. Code § 1464a nt.

Foreign Relations Authorization Act, Fiscal Years 1990 and 1991

Oct. 28, 1991, P.L. 102-138, 22 U.S. Code § 287e nt.

Oct. 24, 1992, P.L. 102-499, 106 Stat. 3264

Oct. 24, 1992, P.L. 102-511, 106 Stat. 3353

Dec. 17, 1993, P.L. 103-199, 22 U.S. Code § 4301 nt.

April 30, 1994, P.L. 103-236, 22 U.S. Code §§ 4001 nt., 4864

Oct. 21, 1998, P.L. 105-277, 22 U.S. Code §§ 4171 nt., 4864

Foreign Relations Authorization Act, Fiscal Years 1992 and 1993

Oct. 28, 1991, P.L. 102-138, 22 U.S. Code § 2651 nt.

Dec. 4, 1991, P.L. 102-182, 22 U.S. Code §§ 2798, 5601 et seq., 5601 nt.; 50 U.S. Code Appx. §§ 2405, 2410c

Oct. 24, 1992, P.L. 102-511, 22 U.S. Code § 2452 nt.

Nov. 23, 1993, P.L. 103-149, 107 Stat. 1505

Dec. 17, 1993, P.L. 103-199, 107 Stat. 2326

April 30, 1994, P.L. 103-236, 22 U.S. Code §§ 287e nt., 2452 nt., 2652b, 2656g

Sept. 30, 1996, P.L. 104-208, 8 U.S. Code § 1182 nt.

Oct. 21, 1998, P.L. 105-277, 22 U.S. Code §§ 1475h, 2452 nt.

May 21, 1999, P.L. 106-29, 22 U.S. Code § 2075.

Foreign Relations Authorization Act, Fiscal Years 1994 and 1995

April 30, 1994, P.L. 103-236, 22 U.S. Code § 2651 nt. Oct. 25, 1994, P.L. 103-415, 8 U.S. Code §§ 1182 nt., 1351; 10 U.S. Code § 1058 nt.; 22 U.S. Code §§ 287e, 292 nt., 2605, 2651a nt., 2655a, 2705 nt., 2751 nt., 3926 nt., 3965 nt., 4010a nt., 4105, 4304, 4858, 6202, 6204, 6208, 6214

July 2, 1995, P.L. 104-17, 109 Stat. 191

Aug. 14, 1995, P.L. 104-22, 109 Stat. 260

Sept. 30, 1995, P.L. 104-30, 109 Stat. 277

Nov. 13, 1995, P.L. 104-47, 109 Stat. 423

Jan. 4, 1996, P.L. 104-89, 109 Stat. 960

Sept. 30, 1996, P.L. 104-208, 8 U.S. Code
§ 1182 nt.

Nov. 26, 1997, P.L. 105-119, 8 U.S. Code
§ 1182 nt.

Oct. 7, 1998, P.L. 105-244, 22 U.S. Code
§ 2452 nt.

Oct. 21, 1998, P.L. 105-277, 22 U.S. Code
§§ 2651a nt., 2684a

**Foreign Relations Authorization Act, Fiscal
Years 1998 and 1999**

Oct. 21, 1998, P.L. 105-277, Division G,
Subdivision B, Title XX, 112 Stat. 2681, 22
U.S. Code § 2651 nt.

Foreign Relations Authorization Act of 1972

Oct. 21, 1998, P.L. 105-277, 2 U.S. Code
§ 194a

Foreign Relations Authorization Acts

July 13, 1972, P.L. 92-352, 86 Stat. 489, 5
U.S. Code §§ 5313 to 5315, 8331; 22 U.S.
Code §§ 194a, 901, 1461, 1474 to 1476,
2291, 2291a,2501, 2502, 2511 nt., 2571,
2589, 2652, 2653, 2680, 2821 to 2826; 31
U.S. Code § 3721

Oct. 18, 1973, P.L. 93-126, 87 Stat. 452, 2
U.S. Code § 194a; 22 U.S. Code § 2823

Nov. 29, 1975, P.L. 94-141, 89 Stat. 756, 5
U.S. Code § 5924; 22 U.S. Code §§ 276,
276a-1, 276c, 287e, 966, 991, 995, 1037 to
1037c, 1934, 2321d, 2551, 2562, 2576,
2585, 2589, 2590, 2601, 2666, 2679a, 2687,
2688, 2791

July 12, 1976, P.L. 94-350, 22 U.S. Code
§ 2689 et seq.

Aug. 15, 1979, P.L. 96-60, 22 U.S. Code
§ 1731 nt.

Aug. 24, 1982, P.L. 97-241, 22 U.S. Code
§§ 1741 nt., 2151 nt., 2370 nt., 2384 nt.,
2680 nt., 2871 nt., 4021 nt., 4195 nt.

Nov. 22, 1983, P.L. 98-164, 22 U.S. Code
§§ 2384 nt., 2691 nt.

Aug. 16, 1985, P.L. 99-93, 5 U.S. Code
§§ 5314, 5315, 22 U.S. Code §§ 1461-1a,
2651 nt., 4701 et seq.

Aug. 27, 1986, P.L. 99-399, 22 U.S. Code
§ 3929a

Dec. 22, 1987, P.L. 100-202, 22 U.S. Code
§§ 1641 nt., 2291 nt., 2656 nt.; P.L.
100-204, 22 U.S. Code §§ 287e nt., 2651
nt., 3922, 4021 nt.

Aug. 23, 1988, P.L. 100-418, 102 Stat. 1452,
22 U.S. Code §§ 2656 to 2656d

Oct. 1, 1988, P.L. 100-461, 8 U.S. Code
§ 1182 nt.

Feb. 16, 1990, P.L. 101-246, 8 U.S. Code
§ 1182 nt.; 22 U.S. Code §§ 287 nt., 2651
nt., 2656 nt., 2656f, 4851 nt.

May 25, 1990, P.L. 101-302, 22 U.S. Code
§§ 2656 nt., 2877a, 4177 nt.

**Foreign Relations Persian Gulf Conflict
Emergency Supplemental Authorization
Act, Fiscal Year 1991**

March 27, 1991, P.L. 102-20, 105 Stat. 68

Foreign Securities Act

April 13, 1934, Ch. 112, 48 Stat. 574 (See 18
U.S. Code § 955)

Foreign Service Act

May 24, 1924, Ch. 182, 43 Stat. 140, 31 U.S.
Code § 72

Feb. 23, 1931, Ch. 276, 46 Stat. 1207, 22
U.S. Code §§ 2654, 2664

April 20, 1940, Ch. 118, 54 Stat. 143

Dec. 22, 1987, P.L. 100-204, 22 U.S. Code
§§ 3905, 3927, 3941, 3941 nt., 3942, 3942
nt., 3946, 3946 nt., 3949, 3961, 3965, 4001,
4010, 4023, 4069a to 4069c 4137, 4173

Oct. 21, 1998, P.L. 105-277, 22 U.S. Code
§ 4064

Foreign Service Act of 1946

Aug. 13, 1946, Ch. 957, 60 Stat. 999, 22 U.S.
Code §§ 801, 801 nts., 802 to 811, 821 to
890, 901 to 1139, 1146 to 1158; See 26 U.S.
Code §§ 115, 121, 526, 892, 893, 911, 912,
933, 943

July 6, 1949, Ch. 300, 63 Stat. 407, 22 U.S.
Code §§ 867, 870

Aug. 31, 1954, Ch. 1177, 68 Stat. 1051, 22
U.S. Code § 868

April 5, 1955, Ch. 23, 69 Stat. 24, 22 U.S.
Code §§ 868, 882, 888,912, 922, 961, 1003,
1004, 1064, 1092 and others

May 1, 1956, Ch. 229, 70 Stat. 125, 22 U.S.
Code §§ 1079 to 1079f

July 18, 1956, Ch. 627, 70 Stat. 563, 22 U.S.
Code § 1148

Continued

913

July 28, 1956, Ch. 770, 70 Stat. 704, 22 U.S.
Code §§ 866, 867, 869, 911, 912, 1004,
1005, 1007, 1076, 1111, 1132, 1139, 1151,
1156, 1157, 1158

June 20, 1958, P.L. 85-462, 72 Stat. 211, 22
U.S. Code §§ 867, 870

June 30, 1958, P.L. 85-477, 72 Stat. 273, 22
U.S. Code § 961

July 24, 1959, P.L. 86-108, 73 Stat. 257, 22
U.S. Code § 922

July 1, 1960, P.L. 86-568, 74 Stat. 299, 22
U.S. Code §§ 867, 870

Sept. 6, 1960, P.L. 86-707, 74 Stat. 795, 22
U.S. Code §§ 1131, 1136, 1138

Sept. 8, 1960, P.L. 86-723, 74 Stat. 831, 22
U.S. Code §§ 809, 842 nt., 871, 872, 881,
886, 889, 900, 911, 912, 915, 928, 936, 937,
961, 965, 968 and others

Sept. 4, 1961, P.L. 87-195, 75 Stat. 464, 22
U.S. Code §§ 1041, 1112, 1136, 1148, 1157

Oct. 11, 1962, P.L. 87-793, 76 Stat. 861, 22
U.S. Code §§ 867, 870, 1017

Dec. 16, 1963, P.L. 88-205, 77 Stat. 391, 22
U.S. Code §§ 816, 961, 1136, 1138a, 1139

Aug. 14, 1964, P.L. 88-426, 78 Stat. 411, 22
U.S. Code §§ 866, 867, 870

Oct. 29, 1965, P.L. 89-301, 79 Stat. 1118, 22
U.S. Code §§ 867, 870

Oct. 31, 1965, P.L. 89-308, 79 Stat. 1131, 22
U.S. Code §§ 1076, 1082, 1121

July 18, 1966, P.L. 89-504, 80 Stat. 292, 22
U.S. Code §§ 867, 870

Oct. 15, 1966, P.L. 89-673, 80 Stat. 953, 22
U.S. Code § 804

Dec. 16, 1967, P.L. 90-206, 81 Stat. 632, 22
U.S. Code §§ 867, 870

Dec. 23, 1967, P.L. 90-221, 81 Stat. 671, 22
U.S. Code §§ 1136, 1159

Aug. 20, 1968, P.L. 90-494, 82 Stat. 814, 22
U.S. Code § 922

Feb. 28, 1970, P.L. 91-201, 84 Stat. 17, 22
U.S. Code §§ 1064, 1071, 1076, 1082,
1091, 1092, 1105, 1106, 1121

Oct. 18, 1973, P.L. 93-126, 87 Stat. 453, 22
U.S. Code § 993

Nov. 29, 1975, P.L. 94-141, 89 Stat. 763, 22
U.S. Code §§ 966, 991, 995, 1037 et seq.

Aug. 17, 1977, P.L. 95-105, 22 U.S. Code
§ 881 et seq.

Aug. 15, 1979, P.L. 96-60, 22 U.S. Code
§ 889

Foreign Service Act of 1980

Oct. 17, 1980, P.L. 96-465, 22 U.S. Code
§ 3901 nt.

Aug. 24, 1982, P.L. 97-241, 22 U.S. Code
§§ 3927, 3962, 4024, 4054

Nov. 22, 1983, P.L. 98-164, 22 U.S. Code
§§ 3968, 4021, 4086, 4153

Aug. 16, 1985, P.L. 99-93, 22 U.S. Code
§§ 3901 nt., 3930, 4084

Aug. 27, 1986, P.L. 99-529, 22 U.S. Code
§ 3929

Jan. 8, 1988, P.L. 100-238, 22 U.S. Code
§§ 4044, 4045, 4046 nt., 4046, 4048, 4049,
4051, 4054, 4054 nt., 4055, 4066, 4069-1,
4069a-1 to 4069c-1 4071a, 4071c, 4084

April 10, 1989, P.L. 101-12, 22 U.S. Code
§ 4139

Nov. 30, 1989, P.L. 101-194, 22 U.S. Code
§ 3945

Feb. 16, 1990, P.L. 101-246, 22 U.S. Code
§§ 3905, 3968, 4002, 4010, 4027, 4056,
4057, 4069a to 4069c, 4081, 4141 to 4141c

Nov. 5, 1990, P.L. 101-509, 22 U.S. Code
§ 3963

Nov. 5, 1990, P.L. 101-513, 22 U.S. Code
§§ 4046, 4052

Oct. 28, 1991, P.L. 102-138, 22 U.S. Code
§§ 3942, 3961, 3968, 4010, 4053, 4081,
4115, 4131, 4134, 4136, 4137, 4139, 4140

Oct. 24, 1992, P.L. 102-499, 22 U.S. Code
§§ 4045, 4046, 4052

Aug. 10, 1993, P.L. 103-66, 22 U.S. Code
§ 4047

Dec. 3, 1993, P.L. 103-178, 22 U.S. Code
§§ 4071b, 4071c

April 30, 1994, P.L. 103-236, 22 U.S. Code
§§ 3928, 3948, 3951, 3964, 3965, 3968,
3972, 3984, 4001, 4009, 4010a, 4011 et
seq., 4021 et seq., 4053, 4083, 4102, 4105,
4117, 4131, 4136, 4140, 4171

Oct. 25, 1994, P.L. 103-415, 22 U.S. Code
§§ 3949, 3951, 4010, 4010a, 4021

Dec. 19, 1995, P.L. 104-65, 22 U.S. Code
§ 4002

Aug. 5, 1997, P.L. 105-33, 22 U.S. Code
§§ 4045, 4071c, 4071e

Oct. 21, 1998, P.L. 105-277, 22 U.S. Code
§§ 3922, 3929, 3930, 3965, 4009, 4010,
4021, 4024, 4026, 4071d, 4103, 4117, 4131

Oct. 27, 1998, P.L. 105-292, 22 U.S. Code §§ 3965, 4013, 4028

Nov. 13, 1998, P.L. 105-382, 22 U.S. Code §§ 4044 to 4046, 4052, 4071a, 4071d

Foreign Service Annuity Adjustment Act of 1965

Oct. 31, 1965, P.L. 89-308, 79 Stat. 1129, 22 U.S. Code §§ 1076, 1079m to 1079s, 1082, 1121

Foreign Service Appointment Act

June 29, 1935, Ch. 337, 49 Stat. 436 (See 22 U.S. Code § 906, 907)

June 19, 1952, Ch. 446, 66 Stat. 140, 22 U.S. Code §§ 293, 295 to 297

Foreign Service Building Act, 1986

Aug. 27, 1986, P.L. 99-399, 22 U.S. Code § 300

Foreign Service Buildings Act of 1926

May 7, 1926, Ch. 250, 44 Stat. 403, 22 U.S. Code §§ 292 to 299

May 25, 1938, Ch. 275, 52 Stat. 441, 22 U.S. Code § 295a

Apr 19, 1945, Ch. 78, 59 Stat. 53, 22 U.S. Code § 300

Sept. 8, 1960, P.L. 86-723, 74 Stat. 847, 22 U.S. Code § 295

Aug. 12, 1963, P.L. 88-94, 77 Stat. 121, 22 U.S. Code §§ 292, 294, 295, 300

Aug. 10, 1964, P.L. 88-414, 78 Stat. 387, 22 U.S. Code § 295

May 21, 1965, P.L. 89-22, 79 Stat. 112, 22 U.S. Code § 295

Oct. 10, 1966, P.L. 89-636, 80 Stat. 881, 22 U.S. Code §§ 292, 295, 300, 301

July 30, 1968, P.L. 90-442, 82 Stat. 461, 22 U.S. Code § 295

Dec. 24, 1970, P.L. 91-586, 84 Stat. 1578, 22 U.S. Code § 295

June 22, 1973, P.L. 93-47, 87 Stat. 98, 22 U.S. Code § 295

April 12, 1974, P.L. 93-263, 88 Stat. 83, 22 U.S. Code § 993

Nov. 29, 1975, P.L. 94-141, 89 Stat. 760, 22 U.S. Code § 295

June 15, 1977, P.L. 95-45, 22 U.S. Code § 295

Nov. 22, 1983, P.L. 98-164, 22 U.S. Code § 302

Feb. 16, 1990, P.L. 101-246, 22 U.S. Code § 300

Oct. 28, 1991, P.L. 102-138, 22 U.S. Code §§ 294, 301

Dec. 17, 1993, P.L. 103-199, 22 U.S. Code § 295

Oct. 21, 1998, P.L. 105-277, 22 U.S. Code § 303

Foreign Service Pension System Act of 1986

June 6, 1986, P.L. 99-335, 22 U.S. Code §§ 3901 nt., 4041 et seq., 4071 et seq.

Foreign Service Personnel Act

April 24, 1939, Ch. 84, 53 Stat. 583

Foreign Service Salary Reform Act of 1962

Oct. 11, 1962, P.L. 87-793, 76 Stat. 861, 22 U.S. Code §§ 867, 870, 1017

Foreign Shipping Practices Act

Aug. 23, 1988, P.L. 100-418, 102 Stat. 1570, 46 U.S. Code Appx. § 1701nt.

Oct. 14, 1998, P.L. 105-258, 46 U.S. Code Appx. § 1710a

Foreign Sovereign Immunities Act of 1976

Oct. 21, 1976, P.L. 94-583, 28 U.S. Code §§ 1330, 1332, 1391, 1441, 1602 et seq.

Foreign Stations Act

May 29, 1934, Ch. 370, 48 Stat. 816

Foreign Statute Act (Evidence)

Conn. Gen. Stat. Ann., § 52-163

Foreign Statute of Limitations

Okla. Stat. Ann., Title 12, § 99

Foreign Statute of Limitations (Judgments)

Tex. Civil Practice and Remedies Code, § 36.001 et seq.

Foreign Trade Antitrust Improvements Act of 1982

Oct. 8, 1982, P.L. 97-290, 15 U.S. Code §§ 1 nt., 6a, 45(a)(3)

Foreign Trade Zone Act

Cal. Government Code § 6300 et seq.

Continued

Colo. Rev. Stat., 7-49.5-101 et seq.

Ill. Rev. Stat. 1991, Ch. 24, § 1360 et seq.

Tenn. Code Ann., 7-85-101 et seq.

Foreign Trade Zones Act
June 18, 1934, Ch. 590, 48 Stat. 998, 19 U.S. Code § 81a et seq.

Oct. 30, 1984, P.L. 98-573, 19 U.S. Code § 81c

Aug. 23, 1988, P.L. 100-418, 102 Stat. 1300, 19 U.S. Code § 81c

Aug. 20, 1990, P.L. 101-382, 19 U.S. Code § 81c

Dec. 8, 1993, P.L. 103-182, 19 U.S. Code § 81c

Oct. 11, 1996, P.L. 104-295, 19 U.S. Code § 81c

June 25, 1999, P.L. 106-36, 19 U.S. Code §§ 81c, 81i

Foreign Warehouse Receipts Law
Cal. Civil Code § 1858.90 et seq.

Foreign Watercraft Act (Process)
La. Rev. Stat. Ann., 13:3479 et seq.

Foreign Wills Act (Probate)
Ala. Code 1975, § 43-1-52

Alaska Stat. 1962, Replaced Titles, § 13.15.120

Colo. Rev. Stat. 1963, 153-6-1 et seq.

La. Rev. Stat. Ann., 9:2421 et seq.

Mich. Comp. Laws Ann., 702.27 et seq.

Minn. Stat. Ann., 524.4-101 et seq.

Ohio Rev. Code 1953, 2129.05 et seq.

Tenn. Code Ann., 32-5-101 et seq.

Tex. Probate Code, § 100 et seq.

Wis. Stat. Ann., 853.05

Wyo. Stat. Ann., § 2-4-220

Foreign Witness Attendance Law
S.D. Codified Laws 1967, 23-40-14 et seq.

Forensic Client Services Act
Fla. Stat. Ann., 916.10 et seq.

Forensic Laboratory Funding Act
Mich. Comp. Laws Ann., 12.201 et seq.

Forensic Medicine Institute Act
P.R. Laws Ann. 1954, Title 18, § 851 et seq.

Forensic Polygraph Examiners Act
Mich. Comp. Laws Ann., 338.1701 et seq.

Forensic Psychiatry Act
Mich. Comp. Laws Ann., 330.2020 et seq.

Forensic Psychiatry Institute Act
P.R. Laws Ann. 1954, Title 24, § 6171

Forensic Science Laboratory Enhancement Program
Cal. Penal Code § 13890 et seq.

Forensic Science System Act
Mont. Code Ann., 44-3-101 et seq.

Forensic Sciences Act
Ga. Code Ann., 35-3-14 to 35-3-16, 35-3-150 to 35-3-155, 45-16-21 et seq.

Forensic Sciences Institute Act
P.R. Laws Ann. 1954, Title 34, § 3001 et seq.

Forest Act
Ill. Rev. Stat. 1991, Ch. 96 1/2, § 5900 et seq.

P.R. Laws Ann. 1954, Title 12, § 191 et seq.

Forest Act (County)
Wis. Stat. Ann., 28.10, 28.11

Forest Act (Municipal)
Mich. Comp. Laws Ann., 320.201 et seq.

Forest and Mineral Resource Development Fund Act
Mich. Comp. Laws Ann., 299.251 et seq.

Forest and Rangeland Renewable Resources Planning Act of 1974
Aug. 17, 1974, P.L. 93-378, 88 Stat. 476, 16 U.S. Code §§ 581h, 1601 to 1610

Nov. 28, 1990, P.L. 101-624, 16 U.S. Code §§ 1601, 1602

Forest and Rangeland Renewable Resources Research Act of 1978
June 30, 1978, P.L. 95-307, 16 U.S. Code §§ 1600 nt., 1641 et seq.

Oct. 24, 1988, P.L. 100-521, 16 U.S. Code
§ 1642

Nov. 5, 1990, P.L. 101-513, 16 U.S. Code
§§ 1641, 1643

Nov. 28, 1990, P.L. 101-624, 16 U.S. Code
§§ 1642, 1648, 1649

June 23, 1998, P.L. 105-185, 16 U.S. Code
§§ 1641, 1642, 1644

Oct. 21, 1998, P.L. 105-277, 16 U.S. Code
§ 1642

**Forest and Rangeland Resources
Assessment and Policy Act**
Cal. Public Resources Code § 4789 et seq.

Forest Authority Act
Me. Rev. Stat. Ann. 1964, Title 12, § 1701 et
seq.

Forest Best Management Practices Act
S.C. Code Ann. 1976, §§ 48-36-10 to
48-36-30

Forest Closure Act
Va. Code 1950, § 27-54.1 et seq.

Forest Commission Act
N.Y. Laws 1885, Ch. 283

Forest Conservation and Taxation Act
Mont. Code Ann., 76-13-101 et seq.
N.H. Rev. Stat. 1955, 79:1 et seq.
N.M. Stat. Ann., 68-2-1 et seq.
Ore. Rev. Stat., 527.610 et seq.
Wash. Rev. Code Ann., 76.09.010 et seq.

Forest Conservation Districts Act
Md. Ann. Code 1974, Art. NR, § 5-601 et
seq.

Forest Crop Act
Wis. Stat. Ann., 77.01 et seq.

Forest Development Act
N.C. Gen. Stat. 1943, § 113A-176 et seq.

Forest Development Corporations Law
Cal. Public Resources Code §§ 4731 et seq.,
4601

**Forest Ecosystems and Atmospheric
Pollution Research Act of 1988**
Oct. 24, 1988, P.L. 100-521, 16 U.S. Code
§ 1600 nt.

Forest Exchange Act
March 20, 1922, Ch. 105, 42 Stat. 465, 16
U.S. Code §§ 485, 486
June 17, 1940, Ch. 392, 54 Stat. 402
Nev. Statutes 1937, Ch. 208, p. 471

Forest Fee and Yield Tax Act
Ore. Rev. Stat., 321.257 et seq.

Forest Finance Authority Act
Mich. Comp. Laws Ann., 320.2001 et seq.

Forest Fire Act
N.J. Stat. Ann., 13:9-1 et seq.
Ore. Rev. Stat., 477.001 et seq.
Va. Code 1950, § 10.1-1135 et seq.

Forest Fire Control Law
Cal. Public Resources Code § 4101 et seq.

**Forest Fire Control Organization Act
(Horry County)**
S.C. Code Ann. 1976, § 48-25-10 et seq.

Forest Fire Emergency Committee Act
Ga. Code 1933, 43-244 et seq.

Forest Fire Hazards Act
Wash. Rev. Code Ann., 76.04.370

Forest Fire Prevention and Control Act
See also South Central Interstate Forest Fire
Protection Compact
Ky. Rev. Stat. 1971, 149.080 et seq.
N.J. Stat. Ann., 13:9-44.1 et seq.
N.M. Stat. Ann. 1953, 62-2-1 et seq.
Wis. Stat. Ann., 26.12

Forest Fire Protection Compact
Conn. Gen. Stat. 1983, § 23-53 et seq.

**Forest Fire Protection Compact (South
Central Interstate)**
Tex. Education Code, § 88.116 et seq.

Forest Fire Protection Compact Act
Ga. Code Ann., 12-6-80 et seq.
S.C. Code Ann. 1976, §§ 48-33-10 et seq.,
48-37-10 et seq.

Forest Fire Protection Compact Act (Middle Atlantic Interstate)
Md. Ann. Code 1974, Art. NR, § 5-801 et seq.
N.C. Gen. Stat. 1943, § 113-60.11 et seq.
N.J. Stat. Ann., 32:24-1 et seq.
Okla. Stat. Ann., Title 2, § 1301-215
Pa. Purdon's Stat., Title 32, § 422 et seq.
S.C. Code Laws 1976, § 48-37-10 et seq.

Forest Fire Protection Compact Act (Northeastern)
See also Northeastern Interstate Forest Fire Protection Compact Act
Conn. Gen. Stat. Ann., § 23-53 et seq.
N.H. Rev. Stat. 1955, 226:1 et seq.
Vt. Stat. Ann., Title 10, § 2501 et seq.

Forest Fire Protection Compact Act (Regional)
Ga. Code Ann., 12-10-60 et seq.

Forest Fire Protection Compact Act (Southeastern)
See Southeastern Interstate Forest Fire Protection Compact Act

Forest Fire Protection District Act
Ill. Rev. Stat. 1991, Ch. 96 1/2, § 7000 et seq.

Forest Fire Protection Tax Act
Ark. Code Ann. 1987, 26-61-103 et seq.

Forest, Fish and Game Act
N.Y. Laws 1900, Ch. 20

Forest Harvesting Law
Miss. Code Ann. 1972, § 49-19-51 et seq.

Forest Improvement Act
Cal. Public Resources Code § 4790 et seq.
Cal. Statutes 1978, Ch. 1181
Mich. Comp. Laws Ann., 320.1101 et seq.

Forest Industries Industrial Foundation Act
W. Va. Code 1966, § 31-16-1 et seq.

Forest Industry Employment Relief Act
Cal. Public Resources Code § 4650

Forest Insect and Disease Control Act
Wash. Rev. Code Ann., 76.06.010 et seq.

Forest Land and Farm Land Assessment Act
Pa. Purdon's Stat., Title 72, § 5490.1 et seq.

Forest Land and Timber Tax Law
Ida. Code 1947, 63-324 et seq.

Forest Land Classification and Reforestation Act
Ore. Rev. Stat. 1953, 321.257 et seq.

Forest Land Donations Law
Cal. Public Resources Code §§ 4701, 4326 et seq.

Forest Land Exchange Act
Ill. Rev. Stat. 1991, Ch. 96 1/2, §§ 6200, 6201

Forest Lands Exemption Act (Fisher)
N.Y. Real Property Tax Law (Consol. Laws Ch. 50A) § 480

Forest Lands Prospecting Act
Pa. Purdon's Stat., Title 32, § 141 et seq.

Forest Lands Tax Act
Mont. Laws 1991, Ch. 783, § 1 et seq.

Forest Lands Tax Exemption Act
N.Y. Real Property Tax Law (Consol. Laws Ch. 50A) § 480

Forest Lieu Lands Act
See Forest Reserve Acts (General)

Forest Management Services Act
Wash. Rev. Code 1991, 76.52.010 et seq.

Forest, Open Space and Agricultural Land Act
Tenn. Code Ann., 11-14-201, 11-15-107, 11-15-108, 67-5-1001 et seq.

Forest Park Civic Center Law
Ill. Rev. Stat. 1991, Ch. 85, § 7401 et seq.

Forest Pest Control Act
June 25, 1947, Ch. 141, 61 Stat. 177, 16 U.S. Code §§ 594-1, 594- 1nt., 594-2 to 594-5
Vt. Stat. Ann., Title 10, § 2401 et seq.

Forest Practice Act
Cal. Public Resources Code § 4511 et seq.

Forest Practices Act
Cal. Public Resources Code §§ 4511 et seq., 4901 et seq.
Ida. Code 1947, 38-1301 et seq.
Nev. Rev. Stat. 1979 Reprint, 528.010 et seq.
Ore. Rev. Stat., 527.610 et seq.
Wash. Rev. Code Ann., 76.09.010 et seq.

Forest Practices Study Committee Act
N.C. Laws 1974, Ch. 1029

Forest Preservation Act
Mich. Comp. Laws Ann., 320.21 et seq.
N.Y. Environmental Conservation Law 1972 (Consol. Laws Ch. 43B) § 9-0101 et seq.

Forest Preserve Botanic Gardens Act
Ill. Rev. Stat. 1991, Ch. 96 1/2, § 6700 et seq.

Forest Preserve District Act
Ill. Rev. Stat. 1991, Ch. 96 1/2, § 6300 et seq. (Downstate)

Forest Preserve District Act (Cook County)
Ill. Comp. Stat. 1992, Ch. 70, § 810/0.01 et seq.

Forest Preserve District Corporate Powers Affirmation Act
Ill. Rev. Stat. 1991, Ch. 96 1/2, §§ 6602.9, 6603

Forest Preserve District Refunding Bond Act
Ill. Rev. Stat. 1991, Ch. 96 1/2, § 6550 et seq.

Forest Preserve District Tax Levy Validation Act of 1986
Ill. Rev. Stat. 1991, Ch. 96 1/2, § 6350 et seq.

Forest Preserve Zoological Parks Act
Ill. Rev. Stat. 1991, Ch. 96 1/2, § 6800 et seq.

Forest Preserves District Defective Bond Repayment Act
Ill. Rev. Stat. 1991, Ch. 96 1/2, § 6500 et seq.

Forest Product Assessment Act (Primary)
N.C. Gen. Stat. 1943, § 113A-189 et seq.

Forest Products Act
May 22, 1928, Ch. 678, 45 Stat. 699, 16 U.S. Code §§ 581, 581a, 581b to 581i
June 15, 1936, Ch. 553, 49 Stat. 1515, 16 U.S. Code § 581a
June 15, 1936, Ch. 558, 40 Stat. 1515, 16 U.S. Code § 581a
May 31, 1944, Ch. 217, 58 Stat. 265, 16 U.S. Code § 581h
June 25, 1949, Ch. 245, 63 Stat. 271, 16 U.S. Code § 581h
Aug. 8, 1953, Ch. 378, 67 Stat. 489, 16 U.S. Code § 581h
Aug. 17, 1974, P.L. 93-378, 88 Stat. 476, 16 U.S. Code § 581h

Forest Products Harvest Tax Act
Ore. Rev. Stat., 321.005 et seq.

Forest Products Industry Recovery Act
Wash. Rev. Code Ann., 79.01.1331 et seq.

Forest Products Marks and Brands Act
Wash. Rev. Code Ann., 76.36.010 et seq.

Forest Products Severance Tax Act
Ala. Code 1975, § 9-13-80 et seq.

Forest Products Tax Act
Va. Code 1950, § 58.1-1600 et seq.

Forest Products Transportation Act
Ill. Rev. Stat. 1991, Ch. 96 1/2, § 6901 et seq.

Forest Products Utilization Act
Miss. Code Ann. 1972, § 57-17-1 et seq.

Forest Protection Act
Fla. Stat. Ann., 590.01 et seq.
Ore. Rev. Stat., 526.009 et seq.
Continued

Wash. Rev. Code Ann., 76.04.010 et seq.

Forest Re-Leaf Act
N.M. Stat. Ann., 68-2-29 et seq.

Forest Rehabilitation Act
Ore. Rev. Stat., 530.210 et seq.

Forest Renewal Act
S.C. Code Ann. 1976, 48-28-10 et

Forest Research and Experimental Tax Act
Ore. Rev. Stat., 321.185

Forest Research, Experiment and Emergency Fire Suppression Act
Ore. Rev. Stat. 1953, 321.165

Forest Reserve Act
Mich. Comp. Laws Ann., 320.101 et seq.

Forest Reserve Act (California)
Oct. 1, 1890, Ch. 1263, 26 Stat. 650, 16 U.S. Code §§ 55, 61, 471c, 471d

Forest Reserve Act (Commercial)
Mich. Comp. Laws Ann., 320.301 et seq.

Forest Reserve Acts (General)
March 3, 1891, Ch. 561, 26 Stat. 1095, 1103, 16 U.S. Code §§ 471, 607 to 610; 25 U.S. Code §§ 426, 495; 30 U.S. Code §§ 35, 44, 45, 48; 43 U.S. Code §§ 161, 162, 165, 173, 174, 202, 212, 235, 254, 261, 277, 321, 323 and others
June 4, 1897, Ch. 2, 30 Stat. 11, 5 U.S. Code § 460; 16 U.S. Code §§ 424, 430g 473 to 482, 551; 24 U.S. Code § 58; 31 U.S. Code §§ 171 to 178, 346, 583 par 8, 604; See 44 U.S. Code §§ 732, 1318, 1324

Forest Reserve Homestead Act
June 11, 1906, Ch. 3074, 34 Stat. 233, 16 U.S. Code §§ 506 to 509

Forest Resource Advisory Council Act
Vt. Stat. Ann., Title 10, § 2221 et seq.

Forest Resource Assessment and Development Act
Vt. Stat. Ann., Title 10, § 2221 et seq.

Forest Resource Development Law
Miss. Code Ann. 1972, § 49-19-201 et seq.

Forest Resource Management Act
Minn. Stat. Ann., 89.001 et seq.

Forest Resources and Practices Act
Alaska Stat. 1962, § 41.17.116 et seq.

Forest Resources Assessment and Policy Act
Cal. Public Resources Code §§ 4800 et seq., 4789

Forest Resources Conservation and Shortage Relief Act of 1990
Aug. 20, 1990, P.L. 101-382, 16 U.S. Code §§ 620, 620 nt., 620a- 620j
July 1, 1993, P.L. 103-45, 16 U.S. Code §§ 620c, 620d
Nov. 14, 1997, P.L. 105-83, 16 U.S. Code §§ 620b, 620c, 620d, 620e, 620f
June 25, 1999, P.L. 106-36, 16 U.S. Code §§ 620, 620c

Forest Resources Conservation and Shortage Relief Act of 1997
Nov. 14, 1997, P.L. 105-83, Title VI, 16 U.S. Code § 620 nt.

Forest Resources Conservation and Shortage Relief Amendments Act of 1993
July 1, 1993, P.L. 103-45, 16 U.S. Code §§ 620 nt., 620c, 620c nt., 620d, 620d nt.

Forest Stewardship Act of 1990
Nov. 28, 1990, P.L. 101-624, 16 U.S. Code §§ 582 nt., 582a-8, 1601 nt., 1642 nt., 2101 nt., 2106a, 2112 nt.

Forest Sustained Yield Act
Wash. Rev. Code Ann., 79.56.010 et seq.

Forest Tax Act
Wash. Rev. Code Ann., 84.33.010 et seq.

Forest Taxation Reform Act
Cal. Statutes 1976, Ch. 176

Forest Test Control Act
June 20, 1975, P.L. 94-40, 89 Stat. 224, 16 U.S. Code § 594-5

Forest Transfer Act
Feb. 1, 1905, Ch. 288, 33 Stat. 628, 16 U.S. Code §§ 472, 476, 495, 551, 554, 615b

Forest Tree Seedling Act
Pa. Purdon's Stat., Title 32, § 451 et seq.

Forest Wildfire Emergency Pay Equity Act of 1988
Oct. 24, 1988, P.L. 100-523, 5 U.S. Code § 5547 nt.

Forestal and Agricultural Districts Act
Va. Code 1950, § 15.1-1506 et seq.

Foresters Act
Cal. Public Resources Code § 750 et seq.
Md. Ann. Code 1974, Art. BO, § 7-101 et seq.
Mich. Comp. Laws Ann., 338.721 et seq.
Ore. Rev. Stat., 321.257 et seq.

Foresters Registration Act
Ark. Code Ann. 1987, 17-28-101 et seq.
Miss. Code Ann. 1972, § 73-36-1 et seq.

Forestry Act
Cal. Public Resources Code § 4001 et seq.
Del. Code of 1974, Title 7, § 2901 et seq.
Fla. Stat. Ann., 589.01 et seq.
Ida. Code 1947, 38-101 et seq.
Ill. Rev. Stat. 1991, Ch. 96 1/2
Ky. Rev. Stat. 1971, 149.010 et seq.
Mass. Gen. Laws Ann., 132:1 et seq.
Md. Ann. Code 1974, Art. NR, § 5-101 et seq.
Minn. Stat. Ann., 88.02 et seq.
Mo. Rev. Stat., 254.010 et seq.
N.H. Rev. Stat. 1955, 218:5 et seq., 219:1 et seq.
Okla. Stat. Ann., Title 2, § 1301-101 et seq.
Ore. Rev. Stat., 526.005 et seq.
Pa. Purdon's Stat., Title 32, § 161 et seq.
S.D. Codified Laws 1967, 41-20-1 et seq.
Tenn. Code Ann., 11-4-101 et seq.
W. Va. Code 1966, § 20-3-1 et seq.

Forestry Act (Community and Urban)
Mont. Code Ann., 77-5-401 et seq.

Forestry Act (Urban)
Cal. Public Resources Code § 4799.06 et seq.

Forestry and Agricultural Activity Act
Miss. Code Ann. 1972, § 49-33-1 et seq.

Forestry and Shade Tree Assistance Act (Community)
N.J. Stat. Ann., 13:1L-17.1 et seq.

Forestry Bank Act
Miss. Code 1942, § 6046-61 et seq.

Forestry Cooperative Agreement Act
Ill. Rev. Stat. 1991, Ch. 96 1/2, § 6100 et seq.

Forestry Development Act
Ill. Rev. Stat. 1991. Ch. 96 1/2, § 9101 et seq.
W. Va. Code 1966 § 5-24-1 et seq.

Forestry Promotion Act
Ill. Rev. Stat. 1991, Ch. 96 1/2, §§ 6000, 6001

Forestry Resources and State Park Act
N.J. Stat. Ann., 13:1L-1 et seq.

Forestry Study Act
N.C. Gen. Stat. 1943, § 113-44.3 et seq.

Forfeited Lands Redemption Act
Ohio Rev. Code 1953, 5723.03

Forfeiture Act
Ky. Stat. 1936, §§ 4076b to 4076k
N.H. Rev. Stat. 1955, 617:1 et seq.
S.D. Codified Laws 1967, 21-9-11

Forfeiture Act (Criminal Activity)
Mo. Rev. Stat 1986, 513.600 et seq.

Forfeiture Act (Criminal)
Haw. Rev. Stat. Ann., § 712A-1 et seq.

Forfeiture Act (Intoxicating Liquors)
Tenn. Code Ann., 57-3-411

Forfeiture Act (Narcotic Drugs)
Ill. Rev. Stat. 1991, Ch. 38, § 1651 et seq.

Forfeiture Act (Omnibus Criminal)
Haw. Rev. Stat. Ann., § 712A-1 et seq.

Forfeiture Act (Railroad Land Grants)
See Railroad Land Grant Forfeiture Act

Forfeiture Act (Real Estate Contract)
Wash. Rev. Code Ann., 61.30.010 et seq.

Forfeiture Act (Uncontested)
Ark. Acts 1991, No. 859

Forfeiture Act (Usury)
Fla. Stat. Ann., 687.04

Forfeiture Act (Vehicles)
Cal. Health and Safety Code § 11610 et seq.

Forfeiture of Drug Profits Act
Del. Code of 1974, Title 16, § 4784

Forfeiture of Office Act
N.J. Stat. Ann., 2C:51-2 et seq.

Forfeiture Reform Act
Iowa Code 1983, 809A.1 et seq.

Forged or Raised Check Act
Conn. Gen. Stat. Ann., § 42a-4-406

Forgery Act
Ala. Code 1975, § 13A-9-1 et seq.
Cal. Penal Code § 470 et seq.
Ga. Code Ann., 16-9-1 et seq.
Ill. Rev. Stat. 1991, Ch. 38, § 17-3
Me. Rev. Stat. Ann. 1964, Title 17-A, § 701 et seq.
Mich. Comp. Laws Ann., 750.248 et seq.
Mont. Code Ann., 45-6-325
N.H. Rev. Stat. 1955, 638:1 et seq.
Va. Code 1950, § 18.2-168 et seq.
Vt. Stat. Ann., Title 13, § 1801 et seq.
Wash. Rev. Code Ann., 9A.60.020 et seq.
Wis. Stat. Ann., 943.38

Forgery and Counterfeiting Act
Mich. Comp. Laws Ann., 750.248 et seq.
R.I. Gen. Laws 1956, 11-17-1 et seq.

Forgotten Man Act
Okla. Stat. Ann., Title 57, § 332.7

Form and Effect of Conveyances Act
R.I. Gen. Laws 1956, 34-11-1 et seq.

Form of Council-Manager Government Act
S.C. Code Ann. 1976, § 5-13-10 et seq.

Forma Pauperis Act
July 20, 1892, Ch. 209, 27 Stat. 252, 28 U.S. Code § 1915
La. Code Civil Procedure Art. 5181 et seq.
Md. Ann. Code 1957, Art. 27, § 645E

Formation of Local Governments Act
Fla. Stat. Ann., 165.011 et seq.

Former Military Facility Development Act
Okla. Stat. Ann., Title 68, § 3801 et seq.

Former Presidents Act of 1958
Aug. 25, 1958, P.L. 85-745, 72 Stat. 838, 3 U.S. Code § 102 nt.
Sept. 2, 1960, P.L. 86-682, 74 Stat. 730, 3 U.S. Code § 102 nt.
Aug. 14, 1964, P.L. 88-426, 78 Stat. 412, 3 U.S. Code § 102 nt.
Sept. 6, 1966, P.L. 89-554, 80 Stat. 660, 3 U.S. Code § 102 nt.
Dec. 16, 1967, P.L. 90-206, 81 Stat. 642, 3 U.S. Code § 102 nt.
Jan. 8, 1971, P.L. 91-658, 84 Stat. 1963, 3 U.S. Code § 102 nt.

Former Soviet Union Demilitarization Act of 1992
Oct. 23, 1992, P.L. 102-484, 22 U.S. Code § 5901 et seq.

Forms and Publications Management Act
Pa. Purdon's Stat., Title 71, § 2011 et seq.

Forms Management Center Act
R.I. Gen. Laws 1956, 42-84-1 et seq.

Forms Management Program Act
Ill. Rev. Stat. 1991, Ch. 127, § 1401 et seq.
Neb. Rev. Stat. 1943, 81-1162 et seq.

Forms Reduction Act
Wash. Rev. Code Ann., 43.41.200 et seq.

Fornication Act
Wis. Stat. 1989, 944.15

Forsyth County Airport Authority Act
Ga. Laws 1978, p. 3490

Forsyth County Civil Service System Act
Ga. Laws 1978, p. 3572

Forsyth County Employees Retirement Plan Act
N.C. Laws 1945, Ch. 298

Forsyth County Water and Sewerage Authority Act
Ga. Laws 1975, p. 3767
Ga. Laws 1996, p. 4084

Forsyth-Cumming County Unification Commission Act
Ga. Laws 1991, p. 3611

Forsyth-Etowah Water Authority Act
Ga. Laws 1984, p. 4779

Fort Carson-Pinon Canyon Military Lands Withdrawal Act
Sept. 23, 1996, P.L. 104-201, Title XXIX, Subtitle A, 110 Stat. 2807

Fort Donelson National Battlefield Act
Sept. 8, 1960, P.L. 86-738, 74 Stat. 875, 16 U.S. Code §§ 428k to 428o

Fort Hall Indian Reservation Act
June 6, 1900, Ch. 813, 31 Stat. 672

Fort Hall Indian Water Rights Act of 1990
Nov. 16, 1990, P.L. 101-602, 104 Stat. 3059

Fort Lauderdale Downtown Development Authority Law
Fla. Special Laws 1969, Ch. 69-1056

Fort Lauderdale Urban Renewal Law
Fla. Special Laws 1961, Ch. 61-2165

Fort Leavenworth Act of Cession
Kan. Stat. Ann., 27-104

Fort McDowell Indian Community Water Rights Settlement Act of 1990
Nov. 28, 1990, P.L. 101-628, 43 U.S. Code § 1522 nt.

Fort Mohave Valley Development Law
Nev. Rev. Stat. 1979 Reprint, 321.480 et seq.

Fort Myers Sewer Revenue Bond Act
Fla. Special Laws 1945, Ch. 23284, Fla. Laws 1945, Ch. 23293

Fort Ord Reuse Authority Act
Cal. Government Code § 67650 et seq.

Fort Peck-Montana Compact
Mont. Code Ann., 85-20-201 et seq.

Fort Peck Rural County Water Supply System Act of 1996
Oct. 11, 1996, P.L. 104-300, 110 Stat. 3646

Fort Phoenix Beach Improvement Loan Act
Mass. Acts 1962, Ch. 637

Fort Pierce and St. Lucie County Consolidated Government Charter Act
Fla. Special Laws 1972, Ch. 72-543

Fort Pierce Port and Airport Authority Act
Fla. Special Laws 1961, Ch. 61-2754

Fort Pierce Urban Renewal Act
Fla. Special Laws 1967, Ch. 67-1392

Fort Sheridan Retrocession Act
Ill. Rev. Stat. 1989, Ch. 1, §§ 4350, 4351

Fort Valley-Perry Airport Authority Act
Ga. Laws 1971, p. 2589

Fort Vancouver National Historic Site Act
June 19, 1948, Ch. 546, 62 Stat. 532, 16 U.S. Code §§ 450ff to 450ff-2
June 30, 1961, P.L. 87-78, 75 Stat. 196, 16 U.S. Code §§ 450ff-3 to 450ff-6

Fortification of Wine Acts
Oct. 1, 1890, Ch. 1244, 26 Stat. 621
June 7, 1906, Ch. 3046, 34 Stat. 215

Fortified Wine Control Act
N.C. Gen. Stat. 1943, § 18-94 et seq.

Fortune Telling Act
Mont. Rev. Code 1947, 94-3585 et seq.
Vt. Acts 1937, No., 34

Forty-Acre Law
Mont. Code Ann., 76-2-101 to 76-2-228

Forty-Eight Hour Act (Examination after Arrest)
Haw. Rev. Stat. Ann., § 803-9

Forty-eight Hour Act (Women and Children)
Mass. Gen. Laws Ann., 149:56
R.I. Gen. Laws 1956, 28-3-11

Forty-five Dollar Old Age Pension Act
Colo. Rev. Stat. 1963, 101-1-1 et seq.

Forty Four Hour Wage Law
Pa. 1937 Pamph. Laws 2766, No. 567

Forty Mill Tax Limit Law
Wash. Rev. Code Ann., 84.52.050

Forty Mill Tax Referendum Law
Wash. Rev. Code. 1989, 84.52.052

Forty Year Marketable Title Act
Iowa Code Ann., 614.29 et seq.
Mich. Comp. Laws Ann., 565.101 et seq.

Forum Act (Choice of)
N.H. Rev. Stat. 1955, 508-A:1 et seq.

Foshee-Onderdonk Act
Ala. Code 1975, §§ 40-20-1, 40-20-2

Foster Care and Adoption Services Act
Mich. Comp. Laws Ann., 722.951 et seq.

Foster Care and Out of Home Placement Act
Okla. Stat. Ann., Title 10, § 7201 et seq.

Foster Care Custody Act (Long-Term)
N.J. Stat. Ann., 30:4C-26.10 et seq.

Foster Care Facility Licensing Act (Adult)
Mich. Comp. Laws Ann., 400.701 et seq.

Foster-Care Licensing Act
Ida. Code 1947, 39-1208 et seq.

Foster Care of Children Act
Mich. Comp. Laws Ann., 400.18c et seq.

Foster Care Review Act
Neb. Rev. Stat. 1943, 43-1301 et seq.

Foster Child Review Act
Del. Code of 1974, Title 31, § 3801 et seq.

Foster Homes Act
Alaska Stat. 1962, § 47.35.010 et seq.
Nev. Rev. Stat. 1979 Reprint, 424.010 et seq.

Foundation Act (Conservation)
Ill. Comp. Stat. 1992, Ch. 20, § 880/1

Foundation Act (State Parks)
Mich. Comp. Laws Ann., 318.331 et seq.

Foundation Act (Student Loan)
Conn. Gem. Stat. 1983, § 10a-201 et seq.

Foundation for Educational Excellence Act
Utah Code Ann. 1953, 53A-4-101 et seq.

Foundation or Holding Company Act
Ind. Code 1971, 23-7-2-1 et seq.

Foundation Program Act (Public Schools)
Wyo. Stat. Ann., § 21-13-101 et seq.

Foundation Program Act (Schools)
Colo. Rev. Stat. 1963, 123-6-1 et seq.
Fla. Stat. 1971, 236.01 et seq.
Ohio Rev. Code 1953, 3317.01 et seq.
Okla. Stat. Ann., Title 70, § 5-145 et seq.
S.D. Codified Laws 1967, 13-13-10 et seq.
Tex. Education Code, §§ 16.001 et seq., 21.161 et seq.
Wyo. Stat. Ann., § 21-13-305 et seq.

Foundation Program for Local Law Enforcement Officers Act (Minimum)
Fla. Stat. 1971, 163.550 et seq.

Foundlings Act
Ill. Rev. Stat. 1991, Ch. 40, § 1101 et seq.

Foundry Sanitation Law
Cal. Labor Code § 2330 et seq.

Four Mile Law (Intoxicating Liquors)
Tenn. Acts 1877, Ch. 23
Tenn. Acts 1885, Ch. 123
Tenn. Acts 1887, Ch. 167
Tenn. Acts 1905, Ch. 422
Tenn. Acts 1909, Ch. 1

Four Mill Tax Act (Personal Property)
Pa. Purdon's Stat., Title 72, § 4821 et seq.

Four Month Statute of Limitations (Administrative Review)
N.Y. Civ. Prac. Law and Rules (Consol. Laws, Ch. 8) § 217

Four Months Act (Criminal Prosecution)
Ill. Rev. Stat. 1981, Ch. 38, § 103-5

Four Months Statute (Rehearings)
Ala. Code 1958, Title 7, § 279

Four Rod Act (Highways)
Minn. Stat. Ann., 160.05

Four Term Act (Prosecutions)
Ill. Rev. Stat. 1981, Ch. 38, § 103-5

Four Year Catch All Act (Statute of Limitations)
Ohio Rev. Code 1953, 2305.09, Subd. D

Four Year Statute of Limitations
Ga. Code Ann., 9-3-25, 9-3-30 et seq.
Miss. Code Ann. 1972, § 15-1-25
N.M. Stat. Ann., 37-1-4

Four Year Statute of Limitations (Contracts for Sale)
Ill. Rev. Stat. 1991, Ch. 26, § 2-725

Four Year Statute of Limitations (Personal Actions)
Cal. Code of Civil Procedures § 337

Four Year Statute of Limitations (Trespass)
R.I. Gen. Laws 1956, 9-1-15

Four Years Act (Taxation)
Ohio Rev. Code 1953, 5721.01 et seq.

Fourteen Days Act
N.Y. Debtor and Creditor Law (Consol. Laws Ch. 12) § 120 et seq.

Fourteen Year Personal Property Escheat Act
N.J. Rev. Stat. 1937, 2A:37-11 et seq.

Fourteenth Amendment
July 27, 1868, No. 12, 15 Stat. 708

Fourteenth Census Act
March 3, 1919, Ch. 97, 40 Stat. 1291

Fourth Class Cities Act
Mich. Comp. Laws Ann., 81.1 et seq.

Fourth Class County Retirement Law
Pa. Purdon's Stat., Title 16, § 11651 et seq.

Fourth Felony Offender Law
N.Y. Penal Law 1965 (Consol. Laws Ch. 40) § 70.10

Fourth Liberty Bond Act
July 9, 1918, Ch. 142, 40 Stat. 844, 31 U.S. Code §§ 750, 752, 772, 774

Fourth Offender Act
Fla. Stat. 1969, 775.084
Mich. Comp. Laws Ann., 769.12
N.Y. Penal Law 1965 (Consol. Laws Ch. 40) § 70.10
Pa. Cons. Stat., Title 18, § 1103 et seq.

Fourth Supplemental Appropriation Act of 1961
June 30, 1961, P.L. 87-74, 75 Stat. 195

Fourth Supplemental National Defense Appropriation Act of 1941
March 17, 1941, Ch. 16, 55 Stat. 34

Fourth Term Act (Criminal Prosecutions)
Ill. Rev. Stat. 1981, Ch. 38, § 103-5

Fourth to Eighth Class County Assessment Law
Pa. Purdon's Stat., Title 72, § 5453.101 et seq.

Fouts-Busby Act (Highways)
Ohio Laws Vol. 108, p. 478

Fowls and Hatching Eggs Act
P.R. Laws Ann. 1954, Title 5, § 815 et seq.

Fox Canyon Groundwater Management Agency Act
Cal. Statutes 1982, Ch. 1023

Fox-Lance-Crane Act (Urban Development)
N.J. Stat. Ann., 40:55C-40 et seq.

Fox River Waterway—Chain O Lakes Management Agency Act
Ill. Rev. Stat. 1991, Ch. 19, § 1201 et seq.

Foxborough School Addition Loan Act
Mass. Acts 1949, Ch. 16

Franchise Act (Automobiles)
See also Automobile Franchise Act
Cal. Public Utilities Code § 6201 et seq.
Conn. Gen. Stat. Ann., § 42-133e et seq.
Kan. Stat. Ann., 12-2001 et seq.
Utah Code Ann. 1953, 13-14-1 et seq.
Wyo. Stat. Ann., § 40-15-101 et seq.

Franchise Act (Motorcycle Dealers)
Wash. Rev. Code Ann., 46.94.001 et seq.

Franchise Act (Petroleum Products)
Va. Code 1950, § 59.1-21.8 et seq.

Franchise Act (Public Utilities)
R.I. Gen. Laws. 1956, 39-17-1 et seq.

Franchise Act (Tractor, Lawn and Garden, and Light Industrial Equipment)
Ala. Code 1975, § 8-21A-1

Franchise and Distributorship Investment Regulations Act
R.I. Gen. Laws 1956, 19-28-1 et seq.

Franchise and Income Tax Act (Corporate)
N.M. Stat. Ann., 7-2A-1 et seq.

Franchise and Privilege Fee Act (Corporations)
Mich. Comp. Laws Ann., 450.2062 et seq.

Franchise and Privilege Tax Act (Corporations)
Utah Code Ann. 1953, 59-13-1 et seq.

Franchise Bond Change Law
Cal. Public Utilities Code § 6066 et seq.

Franchise Continuation and Succession Act (Motor Vehicle)
Ga. Code Ann., 10-1-650 et seq.

Franchise Dealers Fair Practices Act (Petroleum Dealers)
Cal. Business and Professions Code § 21140 et seq.

Franchise Disclosure Act
Ill. Rev. Stat. 1991, Ch. 121 1/2, § 701 et seq.

Franchise Investment Act
R.I. Gen. Laws 1956, 19-28.1-1 et seq.

Franchise Investment Law
Cal. Corporations Code § 31000 et seq.
Haw. Rev. Stat. Ann., § 482E-1 et seq.
Mich. Comp. Laws Ann., 445.1501 et seq.
N.D. Cent. Code, 51-19-01 et seq.
Wis. Stat. Ann., 553.01 et seq.

Franchise Investment Protection Act
Wash. Rev. Code Ann., 19.100.010 et seq.

Franchise or Wholesale Insurance Act
Cal. Insurance Code § 10200.5

Franchise Practices Act
Ark. Code Ann. 1987, 4-72-201 et seq.
Neb. Rev. Stat. 1943, 87-401 et seq.
N.J. Stat. Ann., 56:10-1 et seq.

Franchise Practices Act (Motor Vehicle)
Ga. Code Ann., 10-1-620 et seq.

Franchise Protection Act (Motor Vehicles)
S.D. Codified Laws 1967, 32-6A-1 et seq.

Franchise Registration Tax Act (Business)
W. Va. Code 1966, § 11-12-1 et seq.

Franchise Relations Act
Cal. Business and Professions Code § 20000
et seq.

Franchise Resettlement Law
Cal. Public Utilities Code § 6451 et seq.

Franchise Sales Act
Md. Ann. Code 1974, Art. BR, § 14-233 et
seq.
N.Y. General Business Law (Consol. Laws
Ch. 20) § 680 et seq.

Franchise Sales Act (Public Utilities)
Cal. Public Utilities Code § 6001 et seq.

Franchise Security Act
Del. Code of 1974, Title 6, § 2551 et seq.

Franchise Tax Act
Ala. Code 1975, § 40-14-40 et seq.
Cal. Revenue and Taxation Code § 23181 et
seq.
D.C. Code Ann., § 47-1801.1 et seq
Del. Code of 1974, Title 8, § 501 et seq.
Ill. Rev. Stat. 1991, Ch. 32, § 15.05 et seq.
Md. Ann. Code 1974, Art. TG, § 8-101 et
seq.
Minn. Stat. Ann., 290.02 et seq.
N.C. Gen. Stat. 1943, § 105-114 et seq.
N.H. Rev. Stat. 1955, 83-C:1 et seq.
N.J. Stat. Ann., 54:38-16 et seq.
N.M. Stat. Ann., 53-3-11 et seq.
N.Y. Tax Law (Consol. Laws Ch. 60) § 180
et seq.

Okla. Stat. Ann., Title 68, § 1201 et seq.
Tenn. Code Ann., 67-4-901 et seq.
Tex. Tax Code, § 171.001 et seq., 12.01 et
seq.
Vt. Stat. Ann., Title 32, § 5811 et seq.

Franchise Tax Act (Business)
W. Va. Code 1966 § 11-23-1 et seq.

Franchise Tax Act (Corporate)
Ark. Code Ann. 1987, 26-54-101 et seq.

Franchise Tax Act (Corporations)
Ga. Code Ann., 48-5-420 et seq.
La. Rev. Stat. Ann., 47:601 et seq.
Miss. Code Ann. 1972, § 27-31-1 et seq.
Mo. Rev. Stat., 147.010 et seq.
Ohio Rev. Code 1953, 5725.18 et seq.,
5733.01 et seq.
Pa. 1879 Pamph. Laws 112, No. 122
Pa. 1889 Pamph. Laws 420, No. 332
R.I. Gen. Laws 1956, 44-12-1 et seq.

Franchise Tax Act (Foreign Corporations)
Pa. Purdon's Stat., Title 72, § 7601 et seq.

Franchise Tax Act (Income Tax)
N.Y. Tax Law (Consol. Laws Ch. 60) § 208
et seq.

Franchise Tax Act (Insurance Companies)
Ida. Code 1947, Superseded Vol., 41-401 et
seq.
Ohio Rev. Code 1953, 5725.18 et seq.

Franchise Tax Act (Public Utilities)
Ky. Rev. Stat. 1971, 136.120

Franchise Tax Board Act
Cal. Government Code § 15700 et seq.

Franchise Termination Act
N.M. Stat. Ann., 57-23-1 et seq.

Franchised Automobile Dealers Act
N.Y. Vehicle and Traffic Law 1959 (Consol.
Laws Ch. 71) § 460 et seq.

**Franchising Practices Act (Motor Vehicle
Dealers and Distributors)**
Vt. Stat. Ann., Title 32, § 5931 et seq.

Frank Annunzio Act
See also Christopher Columbus
Quincentenary Coin Act
May 13, 1992, P.L. 102-281, 20 U.S. Code
§ 5701 nt.
Oct. 6, 1992, P.L. 102-390, 31 U.S. Code
§ 5112 nt.

Franklin County Court Act
Ala. Local Acts 1923, p. 272

**Franklin County Public Building Authority
Act**
Ga. Laws 1997, H.B. 904

Franklin County Recreation Authority Act
Ga. Laws 1998, H.B. 4033

Franklin County Revenue Board Act (Oden)
Ala. General Acts 1951, p. 1288, No. 735

**Franklin County Road and Bridge Repair
Act (Todd)**
Ala. General Acts 1951, p. 378, No. 143

**Franklin County Water and Sewerage
Authority Act**
Ga. Laws 1980, p. 4388

**Franklin-Essex Counties Solid Waste
Management Authority Act**
N.Y. Public Authorities Law (Consol. Laws
Ch. 43A) §§ 2051a to 2051x

Franklin-Hart Airport Authority Act
Ga. Laws 1996, p. 3927

**Franklin-Heard County Water Authority
Act**
Ga. Laws 1984, p. 4613

Franklin Wood Law (Security)
N.Y. Business Corporation Law (Consol.
Laws Ch. 4) § 627, 720b

Fraternal Benefit Societies Act
Ala. Code 1975, § 27-34-1 et seq.
Ariz. Rev. Stat. Ann., § 20-861 et seq.
Ark. Code Ann. 1987, 23-74-101 et seq.
Cal. Insurance Code § 10970 et seq.
Colo. Rev. Stat., 10-14-101 et seq.

D.C. Code Ann., § 35-1201 et seq.
Ga. Code Ann., 33-15-1 et seq.
Ill. Rev. Stat. 1981, Ch. 73, § 894.1 et seq.
Ind. Code Ann., 27-11-1-1 et seq.
Iowa Code 1989, 512.1 et seq.
Kan. Stat. Ann., 40-701 et seq.
Mass. Gen. Laws Ann., 176:1 et seq.
Me. Rev. Stat. Ann. 1964, Title 13, § 2341 et
seq.
Mich. Comp. Laws Ann., 500.8000 et seq.
Mo. Rev. Stat., 378.010 et seq.
Neb. Rev. Stat. 1943, 44-1001 et seq.
N.H. Rev. Stat. 1955, 418:1 et seq.
Okla. Stat. Ann., Title 36, § 2701 et seq.
Ore. Rev. Stat. 1953, 748.105 et seq.
Pa. Cons. Stat., Title 40, § 6501 et seq.
Pa. 1992 Pamph. Laws, No. 134
S.D. Codified Laws 1967, 58-37-1 et seq.
Tex. Insurance Code, Art. 10.01 et seq.
Vt. Stat. Ann., Title 8, § 4461 et seq.
Wash. Rev. Code Ann., 48.36A.010 et seq.

Fraternal Code
R.I. Gen. Laws 1956, 27-25-1 et seq.

**Fraternal Corporation Property and
Borrowing Powers Act**
Ill. Rev. Stat. 1991, Ch. 32, §§ 388.9, 389

Fraternal Insignia Registration Act
Ore. Rev. Stat., 649.010 et seq.

Fraternal Insurance Act
Ill. Rev. Stat. 1935, Ch. 73, § 404

Fraternal Societies Act
Neb. Rev. Stat. 1943, 44-1001 et seq.
Wash. Rev. Code Ann., 24.20.010 et seq.

Fraternity Act
Miss. Code Ann. 1972, § 37-111-1 et seq.

Fraud Act (Criminal)
Vt. Stat. Ann., Title 13, § 2001 et seq.

Fraud Act (Medicaid)
N.M. Stat. Ann., 30-44-1 et seq.

Fraud Act (Securities)
Pa. Purdon's Stat., Title 70, §§ 1-101 et seq.

Fraud Act (Telephone Charge)
Ill. Rev. Stat. 1991, Ch. 134, §§ 15b.9, 15c

Fraud and Economic Crimes Prosecution Act
Tenn. Public Acts 1984, Ch. 998

Fraud by Bailee of Animal Act
Wash. Rev. Code 1974, 9.08.040

Fraud by Check Act
Colo. Rev. Stat., 18-5-205

Fraud by Larceny Act
Okla. Stat. Ann., Title 21, § 1701

Fraud Control Act (Medicaid)
Miss. Code Ann. 1972, § 43-13-201 et seq.

Fraud Prevention Act (Auto Repair)
Del. Code of 1974, Title 6, § 4901A et seq.

Fraud Prevention Act (Insurance)
Cal. Insurance Code § 1871 et seq.
Del. Code of 1974, Title 18, § 2401 et seq.
Pa. Purdon's Stat., Title 40, § 3501-101 et seq.

Fraud Prevention Act (Telephone)
Utah Code Ann. 1953, 13-2-1 et seq.

Fraud Prevention and Detection Act (Odometer)
Fla. Stat. Ann., 319.001 et seq.

Fraud Protection Act (Insurance)
Mont. Code Ann., 33-1-1201 et seq.

Fraud Reporting Immunity Act (Insurance)
N.M. Stat. Ann., 59A-16A-1 et seq.
Wash. Rev. Code Ann., 48.50.010 et seq.

Fraudelent Transactions Act
Fla. Stat. Ann., 517.301

Frauds Act
Ga. Code Ann., 13-5-30

Ill. Rev. Stat. 1988, Ch. 59, § 0.01 et seq.
Wyo. Stat. Ann., § 1-23-105

Frauds and Perjuries Act
Ill. Rev. Stat. 1991, Ch. 59

Frauds and Swindles Act
Wash. Rev. Code Ann., 9.45.020 et seq.

Frauds Prevention Act (Financial)
N.Y. Banking Law (Consol. Laws Ch. 2), § 76 et seq.

Frauds Prevention Act (Insurance)
N.Y. Criminal Procedure Law (Consol. Laws Ch. 11A) § 2.10
N.Y. Executive Law 1951 (Consol. Laws Ch. 18) § 835
N.Y. Insurance Law 1984 (Consol. Laws Ch. 28) § 401 et seq.
N.Y. Penal Law 1965 (Consol. Laws Ch. 40) § 176.00 et seq.

Fraudulent Advertising Act
D.C. Code 1973, § 22-1411 et seq.
Ill. Rev. Stat. 1991, Ch. 121 1/2, § 157.21a et seq.
Tenn. Code Ann., 39-14-127

Fraudulent Advertising Act (D. C.)
May 29, 1916, Ch. 130, 39 Stat. 165

Fraudulent Advertising Act (Printers' Ink)
Wis. Stat. Ann., 100.18

Fraudulent and Corrupt Practices Act
Ill. Rev. Stat. 1991, Ch. 102, § 1 et seq.

Fraudulent Auctions Act
D.C. Code Ann., § 47-2701 et seq.

Fraudulent Breach of Trust Act
Tenn. Code Ann., 39-14-103

Fraudulent Check Act
Ind. Burns' 1933, 10-2104, 10-2105
N.H. Rev. Stat. 1955, 638:4, 507:7
R.I. Gen. Laws 1956, 19-19-2 et seq.
Tex. Penal Code, §§ 31.06, 32.41

Fraudulent Claims and Arson Information Reporting Act
Colo. Rev. Stat., 10-4-1001 et seq.

Fraudulent Concealment Act (Limitation of Actions)
Mich. Comp. Laws Ann., 600.5855

Fraudulent Conversion Act
Pa. Cons. Stat., Title 18, § 4113

Fraudulent Conveyance Act
See Uniform Fraudulent Conveyance Act

Fraudulent Debtors Act
Ga. Code Ann., 18-2-20 et seq.
Mich. Comp. Laws 1948, 644.1 et seq.

Fraudulent Degree Law (Medical)
Cal. Business and Professions Code § 580 et seq.

Fraudulent Marriages Act
Ind. Code 1971, 34-4-5-1 et seq.

Fraudulent Practice Law
Colo. Rev. Stat., 11-51-101 et seq.

Fraudulent Practices with Securities Act
N.Y. General Business Law (Consol. Laws Ch. 20) § 352 et seq.

Fraudulent Sales Act
Ill. Rev. Stat. 1991, Ch. 121 1/2, § 157.01 et seq.

Fraudulent Securities Act
N.J. Stat. Ann., 49:3-47 et seq.

Fraudulent Telemarketing Act
N.M. Stat. Ann., 30-50-1 et seq.

Fraudulent Transfer Act
See Uniform Fraudulent Conveyance Act

Fraudulent Transfers Act
See also Uniform Fraudulent Conveyance Act
See also Uniform Fraudulent Transfer Act
Tex. Business and Commerce Code, § 24.001 et seq.

Frawley Boxing Law
N.Y. Laws 1920, Ch. 912
N.Y. Unconsolidated Law, § 8901 et seq.

Frazier-Lemke Farm-Mortgage Act
June 28, 1934, Ch. 869, 48 Stat. 1289
Aug. 28, 1935, Ch. 792, 49 Stat. 942
March 4, 1940., Ch. 39, 54 Stat. 40

Fred Bishop Act (Teacher's Retirement)
Ky. Rev. Stat. 1971, Superseded Vol., 161.715

Fredericksburg and Spotsylvania County Battlefields Memorial National Military Park Expansion Act of 1989
Dec. 11, 1989, P.L. 101-214, 16 U.S. Code §§ 425k to 425o

Fredericksburg Parking Authority Act
Va. Acts 1978, Ch. 691

Free Care Act (Tuberculosis)
Wis. Laws 1945, Ch. 104, § 4

Free Coinage of Gold Act
See Specie Payment Resumption Act

Free County Libraries Act
N.J. Stat. Ann., 40:33-1 et seq.

Free Cuba Act
Fla. Laws 1993, Ch. 218

Free Cuba Act of 1993
Fla. Laws 1993, Ch. 218

Free Dealer Act (Married Woman)
Cal. Code of Civil Procedure § 1811 et seq.
Fla. Stat. 1965, 62.38 et seq.
Nev. Rev. Stat. 1973 Reprint, Replaced Pages, 124.010 et seq.
Pa. Purdon's Stat. Title 48, § 41 et seq.
Tex. Family Code, § 4.04

Free Design Barrier Act
S.C. Code Ann. 1976, § 10-5-240 et seq.

Free Employment Agency Act
Ill. Rev. Stat. 1985, Ch. 48, § 172.90 et seq.

Free Enterprise and Antitrust Act
Tex. Business and Commerce Code § 15.01 et seq.

Free Enterprise and Consumer Education Act
Fla. Stat. Ann., 233.0641

Free Enterprise Encouragement Act
Ga. Code Ann., 36-89-1 et seq.

Free Fair Law
Okla. Stat. Ann., Title 2, § 104 et seq.

Free-flow Milk Act
Kan. Stat. Ann., 65-737 et seq.

Free Flow of Information Act
Minn. Stat. Ann., 595.021 et seq.
Neb. Rev. Stat. 1943, 20-144 et seq.

Free Gift Advertising Act
Fla. Stat. Ann., 817.415

Free Homestead Act
May 17, 1900, Ch. 479, 31 Stat. 179, 43 U.S. Code § 179

Free Lunch Act
Ohio Laws Vol. 101, p. 357, No. 1

Free Lunch Program Act (School)
Ill. Rev. Stat. 1991, Ch. 122, § 712.01 et seq.

Free Pass Act (Railroads)
Ky. Rev. Stat. 1971, 276.240 et seq.

Free Permit Act (Fish and Game)
Ind. Code Ann., 14-2-7-19 et seq.

Free Port Act
Neb. Rev. Stat. 1943, 77-1226.01 et seq.
Ore. Rev. Stat., 307.810 et seq.

Free Port Act (Property in Transit)
Nev. Rev. Stat. 1979 Reprint, 361.160 et seq.

Free Public Library Act
D.C. Code 1973, § 37-101 et seq.

Free Public Library Act (Manatee County)
Fla. Special Laws 1971, Ch. 71-760

Free Scholarship Act
Ore. General Laws 1885, p. 10, No. 2, § 8

Free Television Act
Cal. Statutes 1965, Vol. 1, p. A-132

Free Textbook Act
Ala. Code 1975, § 16-36-1 et seq.
Ark. Code Ann. 1987, 6-21-401 et seq.
Cal. Education Code 1959, §§ 10051 et seq., 60000 et seq.
Ga. Code Ann., 20-2-1010 et seq.
Ind. Code Ann., 20-10.1-11-1 et seq.
Ky. Rev. Stat. 1971, 157.100 et seq.
N.Y. Education Law 1947 (Consol. Laws Ch. 16) § 703
Okla. Stat. Ann., Title 70, § 16-20
Ore. Rev. Stat., 337.150
Tex. Education Code, § 12.01 et seq.

Free Textbook Act (High School)
Ark. Stat. 1947, 80-1752 et seq.

Free Textbook Act (Knox County)
Tenn. Private Acts 1925, Ch. 625

Free Trade Zone Act
June 18, 1934, Ch. 590, 48 Stat. 998, 19 U.S. Code §§ 81a-81u
June 2, 1970, P.L. 91-271, 84 Stat. 292, 19 U.S. Code § 81c

Free Transcript Act (Indigent Accused)
W. Va. Code 1966, § 51-7-7

Free Transportation Act (Private Schools)
Conn. Gen. Stat. Ann., § 10-281

Free Tuition Act (Nonresidents)
N.Y. Laws 1903, Ch. 542

Free Turnpike Act
Ky. Stat. 1936, §§ 4748b-1 to 4748b-16

Freedman's Bureau Bills
March 3, 1865, Ch. 90, 13 Stat. 507
July 16, 1866, Ch. 200, 14 Stat. 173
Continued

931

July 6, 1868, Ch. 135, 15 Stat. 83

Freedman's Saving and Trust Company Acts
June 20, 1874, Ch. 349, 18 Stat. 131
Feb. 13, 1877, Ch. 57, 19 Stat. 231
Feb. 21, 1881, Ch. 64, 21 Stat. 326
Feb. 17, 1883, Ch. 48, 22 Stat. 420
March 3, 1899, Ch. 440, 30 Stat. 1353

Freedom Act (Religious)
Mass. Gen. Laws Ann., 119:33

Freedom for Russia and Emerging Eurasian Democracies and Open Markets Support Act of 1992
Oct. 24, 1992, P.L. 102-511, 22 U.S. Code §§ 5801, 5801 nt., 5811 to 5814
Dec. 21, 1995, P.L. 104-66, 22 U.S. Code § 5825
April 4, 1996, P.L. 104-127, 7 U.S. Code § 5621 nt.
Oct. 21, 1998, P.L. 105-277, 22 U.S. Code § 5855

Freedom from Parental Custody and Control Act
Cal. Civil Code § 232 et seq.

Freedom of Access Law
Me. Rev. Stat. Ann. 1964, Title 1, § 401 et seq.

Freedom of Access Law (Public Record)
Me. Rev. Stat. Ann. 1964, Title 13, § 401 et seq.

Freedom of Access to Clinic Entrances Act of 1994
May 26, 1994, P.L. 103-259, 18 U.S. Code §§ 248, 248 nt.

Freedom of Choice Act (Health Care)
Okla. Stat. Ann., Title 36, § 6053 et seq.

Freedom of Choice and Cost Containment Act (Automobile Insurance)
N.J. Stat. Ann., 17:28-1.1 et seq.

Freedom of Choice in Denture Services Act
Me. Rev. Stat. Ann. 1964, Title 1, § 401 et seq.

Mont. Code Ann., 37-29-101 et seq.

Freedom of Choice School Assignment Law (Savannah-Chatham County)
Ga. Laws 1971 Ex. Sess., p. 2198

Freedom of Financial Choice Act
Cal. Government Code § 19993.05

Freedom of Information Act
July 4, 1966, P.L. 89-487, 80 Stat. 250 (See 5 U.S. Code § 552)
June 5, 1967, P.L. 90-23, 81 Stat. 54, 5 U.S. Code § 552
Nov. 21, 1974, P.L. 93-502, 88 Stat. 1561, 5 U.S. Code § 552
Ark. Code Ann. 1987, 25-19-101 et seq.
Cal. Government Code § 6250 et seq.
D.C. Code Ann., § 1-1521 et seq.
Del. Code of 1974, Title 29, § 10001 et seq.
Ill. Rev. Stat. 1991, Ch. 116, § 201 et seq.
Iowa Code Ann., 22.1 et seq.
Mich. Comp. Laws Ann., 15.231 et seq.
N.Y. Public Officers Law (Consol. Laws Ch. 47) § 84 et seq.
S.C. Code Ann. 1976, §§ 30-4-10 et seq., 30-3-10 et seq.
Va. Code 1950, § 2.1-340 et seq.

Freedom of Information Act (Charles County)
Md. Ann. Code 1957, Art. 24, § 5-101

Freedom of Information Act (Open Records)
Kan. Stat. Ann., 45-215 et seq.

Freedom of Information Reform Act of 1986
Oct. 27, 1986, P.L. 99-570, 5 U.S. Code § 552 nt.

Freedom of Religion Act
Tenn. Code Ann., 39-17-309 et seq.

Freedom Restoration Act (Religious)
Nov. 16, 1993, P.L. 103-141, 107 Stat. 1488
Fla. Stat. Ann., 761.01 et seq.
R.I. Gen. Laws 1956, 42-80.1-1 et seq.

FREEDOM Support Act
See Freedom For Russia And Emerging Eurasian Democracies And Open Markets Support Act Of 1992

Freedom to Work Act
Ark. Code Ann. 1987, 6-13-613 et seq.

Freedom Trail Program Act (New York State)
N.Y. Laws 1997, Ch. 574

Freeholders Act
N.J. Stat. Ann., 40:21-1 et seq.

Freeport Law
Kan. Stat. Ann., 79-201f
Tenn. Code Ann., 67-5-217

Freeport Public Employees Fair Employment Act
N.Y. Local Laws 1969, Village of Freeport, p. 2510

Freeway Act
Cal. Streets and Highways Code § 100.1 et seq.
Colo. Rev. Stat., 43-3-101 et seq.
Ill. Rev. Stat. 1991, Ch. 121, §§ 2-212, 8-101 et seq.
R.I. Gen. Laws 1956, 24-10-1 et seq.

Freeway Service Patrol Act
Cal. Streets and Highways Code § 2560 et seq.

Freeze Act (Tax Assessments)
N.J. Stat. Ann., 54:2-43, 54:3-26

Freiberg-Dickey Act (Narcotics)
N.Y. Laws 1927, Ch. 672

Freight Car Tax Act
Okla. Stat. Ann., Title 68, § 805 et seq.

Freight Carriers Act (Motor)
R.I. Gen. Laws 1956, 39-12-1 et seq.

Freight Forwarding Act
Fla. Stat. Ann., 323.51 et seq.

Freight Motor Vehicle Act
Md. Ann. Code 1957, Art. 56, § 181 et seq.

Freight Rate Act
Iowa Code Ann., 327D.1 et seq.

Freight Terminal Act
N.Y. Transportation Corporations Law (Consol. Laws Ch. 63) § 100 et seq.

Freighters and Drovers Act
Kan. Stat. Ann., 47-104, 47-120

French Creek Scenic Rivers Act
Pa. Purdon's Stat., Title 32, § 820.51 et seq.
Pa. 1982 Pamph. 351 No. 97

French Friendship Treaty
Haw. Session Laws Vol. 2, p. 101, March 26, 1846
Haw. Session Laws 1858-59, p. 489, Sept. 8, 1858

French Spoliation Claims Act
Jan. 20, 1885, Ch. 25, 23 Stat. 283

Frequenter Act
Ohio Rev. Code 1953, 4101.11 et seq.

Fresh Cut Flowers and Fresh Cut Greens Promotion and Information Act of 1993
Dec. 14, 1993, P.L. 103-190, 7 U.S. Code §§ 6801 nt., 6801 et seq.

Fresh Fruit Act
Mich. Comp. Laws Ann., 286.341 et seq.

Fresh Fruit and Vegetable Marketing Act
Ill. Rev. Stat. 1991, Ch. 5, § 138.z et seq.

Fresh Fruit Sales Limitation Act
Wash. Rev. Code Ann., 15.21.010 et seq.

Fresh Pursuit Act
See also Uniform Act on Fresh Pursuit
See Uniform Act on Fresh Pursuit
Fla. Stat. Ann., 941.31 et seq.
Wash. Rev. Code Ann., 10.89.010 et seq.

Fresh Pursuit Act (Intrastate)
See Uniform Act on Intrastate Fresh Pursuit

Fresh Pursuit by Military Forces Act
Pa. Cons. Stat., Title 51, § 4701 et seq.

Fresh Strawberry Marketing Law
La. Rev. Stat. Ann., 3:481 et seq.

Fresh Water Fishing Act
Fla. Stat. Ann., 372.001 et seq.
Md. Ann. Code 1974, Art. NR, § 4-101 et
seq.

Fresh Water Supply Districts Act
Tex. Water Code, § 53.001 et seq.

**Freshwater and Groundwater Protection
Act**
Mich. Comp. Laws Ann., 286.851 et seq.

Freshwater Lands Protection Act (Geneva)
Fla. Stat. Ann., 373.4597

Freshwater Wetlands Protection Act
N.J. Stat. Ann., 13:9B-1 et seq.
N.Y. Environmental Conservation Law 1972
(Consol. Laws Ch. 43B) § 24-0101 et seq.
R.I. Gen. Laws 1956, 2-1-18 et seq.

**Fresno County Transportation
Improvement Act**
Cal. Public Utilities Code § 142000 et seq.

Fresno Metropolitan Flood Control Act
Cal. Statutes 1955, Ch. 503, p. 971
Cal. Water Code, Appendix, § 73-1 et seq.

Fresno Metropolitan Transit District Act
Cal. Public Utilities Code, Appendix §§ 1.1,
2

Frey-Munshaw Act (Prison Industries)
Mich. Comp. Laws 1948, 800.301 et seq.

Friend Memorial Act
Cal. Vehicle Code § 23109

Friend of the Court Act
Ky. Rev. Stat. 1971, 403.090

Mich. Comp. Laws Ann., 552.251 et seq.

FRIENDSHIP ACT
See Act For Reform In Emerging New
Democracies And Support And Help For
Improved Partnership With Russia,
Ukraine, And Other New Independent
States

**Fringe Benefit Security Act (Construction
Workers')**
N.J. Stat. Ann., 34:11A-1 et seq.

Frisk Law
Ore. Rev. Stat., 131.605 et seq.

Frivolous Civil Proceedings Sanctions Act
S.C. Code Ann. 1976, § 15-36-10 et seq.

Frivolous Lawsuits Act
N.J. Stat. Ann., 2A:15-59.1 et seq.

Frog-blocking Act
Colo. Rev. Stat., 40-29-104, 40-29-105

Front Foot Assessment Act
Tenn. Code Ann., 7-32-101 et seq.

Front Royal Parking Authority Act
Va. Acts 1970, Ch. 413

Frontage Consent Act
Ill. Rev. Stat. 1991, Ch. 24, § 11-90-2

Frontage Tax Act
Haw. Rev. Stat. Ann., §§ 67-2, 67-4

Frontier Authority Act (Niagara)
N.Y. Public Authorities Law (Consol. Laws
Ch. 43A) § 500 et seq.

Fronton Law
Fla. Stat. Ann., 551.01 et seq.

Frozen Dairy Products Act
Me. Rev. Stat. Ann. 1964, Title 7, § 831 et
seq.

Frozen Dessert Manufacturer Licensing Act
Tex. Health and Safety Code, § 440.001 et
seq.

Frozen Desserts Act
Colo. Rev. Stat., 25-5.5-301 et seq.,
   35-34-101 et seq.
Fla. Stat. Ann., 503.011 et seq.
Ill. Rev. Stat. 1973, Ch. 56 1/2, § 258 et seq.
Iowa Code Ann., 190A.1 et seq.
Mich. Comp. Laws Ann., 288.321 et seq.
Miss. Code Ann. 1972, § 75-31-125 et seq.
Okla. Laws 1953, p. 5
Ore. Rev. Stat., 621.305 et seq.
Pa. Purdon's Stat., Title 31, § 417-1 et seq.
S.D. Codified Laws 1967, 39-8-1 et seq.

Frozen Food Locker Plant Act
Cal. Health and Safety Code § 28700 et seq.
Iowa Code Ann., 172.1 et seq.
Miss. Code Ann. 1972, § 75-37-1 et seq.
Mo. Rev. Stat., 196.450 et seq.
N.M. Stat. Ann. 1953, 54-4-1 et seq.
Okla. Stat. Ann., Title 63, § 1-101 et seq.

Frozen Food Products Act
R.I. Gen. Laws 1956, 21-1-1 et seq.

Frozen Food Provisioner's Law
Colo. Rev. Stat., 35-33-101 et seq.

Fruit and Vegetable Container Act
Ind. Code Ann., 24-6-6-1 et seq.

Fruit and Vegetable Labeling Act
Ark. Code Ann. 1987, 2-20-301 et seq.

Fruit and Vegetable Law (Certification)
Cal. Food and Agricultural Code 1967,
   §§ 40531 et seq., 42681 et seq.

Fruit and Vegetable Standardization Act
Ariz. Rev. Stat. Ann., § 3-481 et seq.
Cal. Food and Agricultural Code 1967,
   § 42501 et seq.
N.M. Stat. Ann., 76-15-1 et seq.

Fruit Grading Act
Wash. Rev. Code Ann., 15.17.010 et seq.

Fruit, Nut and Vegetable Law (Standards)
Cal. Food and Agricultural Code 1967,
   § 42501 et seq.

Fruit Policy Act (Tropical)
Fla. Stat. Ann., 603.201 et seq.

Fruit Sulphur Sales Law
Cal. Health and Safety Code § 28500 et seq.

**Fruits and Vegetables Standardization and
   Inspection Act**
Fla. Stat. Ann., 603.11 et seq.

Frye Acts (Shipping)
See Shipping Acts

**Frymeier, Nichols, Hahn, Ashby, Hale,
   Render Act (Mosquito Control)**
Ky. Rev. Stat. 1971, 249.510 et seq.

Fuel Act (Solid)
Md. Ann. Code 1974, Art. AG, § 11-501 et
   seq.

Fuel Administration Law
N.Y. Laws 1922, Ex. Sess., Ch. 673

Fuel Alcohol Act
Okla. Stat. Ann., Title 2, § 1901 et seq.
Okla. Stat. Ann., Title 37, § 504

Fuel Conservation Act (Motor Vehicle)
Cal. Public Resources Code § 25370 et seq.

Fuel Conversion Act (Alternative)
N.M. Stat. Ann., 13-1B-1 et seq.

Fuel Distribution Act
Sept. 22, 1922, Ch. 413, 42 Stat. 1025

Fuel Distribution Act (Motor)
Mich. Comp. Laws Ann., 445.1801 et seq.

Fuel Immunization Act
Cal. Statutes 1990, Ch. 600, p. 2655

Fuel Inspection Act
Utah Code Ann. 1953, 4-33-1 et seq.

Fuel Marketing Act
Ala. Acts 1984, p. 433

Fuel Oil Act
Mich. Comp. Laws Ann., 125.551 et seq.

Fuel Oil Delivery Act (Emergency)
N.J. Stat. Ann., 26:3-31.4 et seq.

Fuel Oil Tax Acts
Wash. Laws 1935, Ch. 180, § 78 et seq.
Wash. Laws 1939, Ch. 186

Fuel Protection Act
La. Rev. Stat. Ann., 51:1600 et seq.

Fuel Quality Act (Motor)
Wash. Rev. Code Ann., 19.112.005 et seq.

Fuel Reporting Act (Petroleum)
Mass. Gen. Laws Ann., 94:295C et seq.

Fuel Set-Aside Act (Emergency)
N.Y. Energy Law (Consol. Laws Ch. 17A)
§ 10-101 et seq.

Fuel Tax Act
Haw. Rev. Stat. Ann., § 243-1 et seq.
Ida. Code 1947, 63-2401 et seq.
Me. Rev. Stat. Ann. 1964, Title 36, § 3201 et seq.

Fuel Tax Act (Alternative)
N.M. Stat. Ann., 7-16B-1 et seq.

Fuel Tax Act (Compressed)
Neb. Rev. Stat. 1943, 66-697 et seq.

Fuel Tax Act (Diesel)
Tex. Tax. Code, § 153.201 et seq.

Fuel Tax Act (Gasoline and Liquid)
Pa. Purdon's Stat., Title 72, § 2611a et seq.

Fuel Tax Act (Motor Carrier)
Ark. Code Ann. 1987, 26-55-201, 26-55-203
Mich. Comp. Laws Ann., 207.211 et seq.

Fuel Tax Act (Motor Vehicles)
See also Motor Vehicle Fuel Tax Act
Ky. Rev. Stat. 1971, 138.210 et seq.
Md. Ann. Code 1957, Art. 56, § 135 et seq.
Mo. Rev. Stat., 142.010 et seq.
N.D. Cent. Code, 57-43.1-01 et seq.
Neb. Rev. Stat. 1943, 66-401 et seq.
N.J. Stat. Ann., 54:39-1 et seq.

Ohio Rev. Code 1953, 5735.01 et seq.

Fuel Tax Act (Special)
See also Special Fuel Tax Act
Ky. Rev. Stat. 1971, 138.210 et seq.
Me. Rev. Stat. Ann. 1964, Title 36, § 3201 et seq.
Mont. Code Ann., 15-70-301 et seq.
N.C. Gen. Stat. 1943, § 105-449.1 et seq.
Neb. Rev. Stat. 1943, 66-601 et seq.
Nev. Rev. Stat. 1979 Reprint, 366.010 et seq.
Wash. Rev. Code, 82.38.010 et seq.

Fuel Tax Agreement Act (Regional)
N.H. Rev. Stat. 1955, 260:65-b to 260:65-d

Fuel Use and Liquid Fuel Tax Enforcement Act
Pa. Cons. Stat., Title 75, § 9401 et seq.

Fuel Use Reporting Law
R.I. Gen. Laws 1956, 31-36.1-1 et seq.

Fuel Use Tax Act
Ariz. Rev. Stat. Ann., § 28-1551 et seq.
Ind. Code Ann., 6-6-2-1 et seq.
La. Rev. Stat. Ann., 47:801 et seq.
Me. Rev. Stat. Ann. 1964, Title 36, § 3040
Okla. Stat. Ann., Title 68, § 701 et seq.
Ore. Rev. Stat., 319.510 et seq.
Pa. Purdon's Stat., Title 72, § 2614.1 et seq.
Tenn. Code Ann., 67-3-801 et seq.
Wash. Rev. Code, 82.38.010 et seq.

Fuel Use Tax Act (Interstate)
Iowa Code Ann., 452A.50 et seq.

Fuel Use Tax Act (Truckers)
N.C. Gen. Stat. 1943, § 105-449.37 et seq.

Fuels Conversion Act (Alternative)
Okla. Stat. Ann., Title 74, § 130.1 et seq.

Fuels Conversion Program Act (Clean)
Utah Code Ann. 1953, 9-1-701 et seq.

Fuels Loan Program (Alternative)
Kan. Stat. Ann., 75-37,116

Fuels Supplier Tax Act (Special)
N.M. Stat. Ann., 7-16A-1 et seq.

Fugitive Apprehension Reward Act
Ill. Rev. Stat. 1991, Ch. 60, § 11.9 et seq.

Fugitive Bail Act
Colo. Rev. Stat., 16-19-116 et seq.

Fugitive Felon Act
June 22, 1932, Ch. 271, 47 Stat. 326 (See 18 U.S. Code § 1073)
May 18, 1934, Ch. 301, 48 Stat. 301 (See 18 U.S. Code § 1073)

Fugitive Husbands Act
Ala. Code 1975, § 30-4-80 et seq.
Conn. Gen. Stat. Ann., 46b-180 et seq.
N.C. Gen. Stat. 1943, § 52A-1 et seq.

Fugitive Slave Laws
Sept. 18, 1850, Ch. 60, 9 Stat. 462
June 28, 1864, Ch. 166, 13 Stat. 200

Fugitives from Justice Act
D.C. Code Ann., § 23-701 et seq.
Ill. Rev. Stat. 1991, Ch. 60, § 11.9 et seq.
P.R. Laws Ann. 1954, Title 34, § 1881 et seq.

Full Coverage Act (Workmen's Compensation Insurance)
La. Rev. Stat. Ann., 23:1162

Full Crew Act (Railroads)
Ariz. Rev. Stat. Ann., § 40-881 et seq.
Ark. Stat. 1947, 73-720 et seq.
Cal. Labor Code § 6901 et seq.
Ind. Code Ann., 8-9-2-1 et seq.
Mass. Gen. Laws Ann., 160:185
Miss. Code 1942, § 7759 et seq.
Neb. Rev. Stat. 1943, 74-532 et seq.
Nev. Rev. Stat. 1979 Reprint, 705.390 et seq.
N.J. Stat. Ann., 48:12-155
N.Y. Railroad Law (Consol. Laws Ch. 49) § 54a et seq.
Ohio Rev. Code 1953, 4999.06
Ore. Rev. Stat., 764.110 et seq.
Pa. 1911 Pamph. Laws 1053
Pa. 1937 Pamph. Laws 1120, No. 287

Tex. Rev. Civ. Stat., Art. 6380
Wash. Rev. Code Ann., 81.40.010 et seq.
Wis. Stat. Ann., 192.25

Full Disclosure Act (Credit Card)
Cal. Civil Code § 1748.10 et seq.

Full Disclosure Act (Land Sales)
N.H. Rev. Stat. 1955, 356-A:1 et seq.
N.J. Stat. Ann., 45:15-16.3 et seq.

Full Disclosure Act (Planned Real Estate Development)
N.J. Stat. Ann., 45:22A-21 et seq.

Full Disclosure Act (Real Estate Sales)
N.J. Stat. Ann., 45:15-16.27 et seq.

Full Employment Act
Conn. Gen. Stat. Ann., § 31-356 et seq.

Full Employment and Balanced Growth Act of 1978
Oct. 27, 1978, P.L. 95-523, 12 U.S. Code § 225a; 15 U.S. Code §§ 1021 et seq., 1021 nt., 3101 et seq., 3101 nt., 3111 et seq.; 31 U.S. Code §§ 1322, 1326
Nov. 5, 1990, P.L. 101-508, 15 U.S. Code § 1022
Oct. 21, 1998, P.L. 105-277, 15 U.S. Code §§ 3116, 3151

Full Employment Planning Act
Mich. Comp. Laws Ann., 408.901 et seq.

Full Faith and Credit Act (Divorce)
Kan. Stat. Ann., 60-1611

Full Faith and Credit for Child Support Orders Act
Oct. 20, 1994, P.L. 103-383, 28 U.S. Code §§ 1 nt., 1738B nt., 1738B

Full Immunization Act
Cal. Health and Safety Code § 322.8

Full Political Participation Act
D.C. Laws 1978, No. 2-101

Fuller Act (Intoxicating Liquor)
Ala. Code 1958, Title 29, § 104 et seq.

Fuller Act (Pensions, Civil War, War with Mexico)
May 1, 1920, Ch. 165, 41 Stat. 585

Fuller-Plank Act (Town Highways)
N.Y. Laws 1898, Ch. 351

Fulton County and Atlanta Recreation Authority Act
Ga. Laws 1960, p. 2810

Fulton County Civil Service Act
Ga. Laws 1943, p. 971

Fulton County Community Improvement Districts Act
Ga. Laws 1991, p. 5460

Fulton County Local Improvement Assessment Act
Ga. Laws 1949, p. 1423

Fulton County Pension Act
Ga. Laws 1939, p. 571

Fulton County Teachers' Pension and Retirement Act
Ga. Laws 1937, p. 892

Fulton Mall Special Assessment Act
N.Y. Laws 1976, Ch. 911

Fulton Parking Authority Act
N.Y. Public Authorities Law (Consol. Laws Ch. 43A) § 1525 et seq

Fund Act (Insurers Insolvency)
Mass. Gen. Laws Ann., 175D:1 et seq

Fund Depository Act
Nev. Rev. Stat. 1979 Reprint, 365.010 et seq.

Fund Disclosure Act (Welfare)
N.Y. Insurance Law 1984 (Consol. Laws Ch. 28) § 4401 et seq.

Fund for Economic Development Act
S.C. Code Ann. 1976, § 41-43-10 et seq.

Fund for the Improvement and Reform of Schools and Teaching Act
April 28, 1988, P.L. 100-297, 102 Stat. 338, 20 U.S. Code §§ 4801 and nt., 4811 et seq.
Oct. 20, 1994, P.L. 103-382, 20 U.S. Code §§ 4801, 4801 nt., 4811, 4812, 4821 to 4823, 4831 to 4833, 4841 to 4843

Fund Investments Act (Twenty-First Century)
Del. Code of 1974, Title 29, § 6102A

Fund-Raising Act (Public Employee)
N.J. Stat. Ann., 52:14-15.9cl et seq.

Fund Transfer Privacy Act (Electronic)
N.J. Stat. Ann., 17:16K-1 et seq.

Fund Transfer Transmission Facility Act (Electronic)
Ill. Rev. Stat. 1991, Ch. 17, § 1301 et seq.

Fund Transfers (Uniform Commercial Code)
See Uniform Commercial Code-Funds Transfers

Fundamental Sciences Act
Ore. Rev. Stat., 676.010 et seq.

Funding Act
Kan. Stat. Ann., 10-116

Funding Act (Lincoln County)
Nev. Rev. Stat. 1873, Ch. 13, p. 54

Funding Act (Public School Facilities)
Tex. Rev. Civ. Stat., Art. 717t

Funding Act (Sports Authorities)
Tenn. Code Ann., 67-6-103, 67-6-601, 67-6-712

Funding Acts
Aug. 4, 1790, Ch. 34, 1 Stat. 138
April 12, 1866, Ch. 39, 14 Stat. 31

Funding and Improvement Bond Act
N.C. Public Laws 1933, Ch. 330

Funding and Tax Administration Act (Motor Carrier)
Tenn. Code Ann., 55-4-113

Funding Bond Act
Colo. Rev. Stat., 30-26-401 et seq.

Funding Bond Act (Municipal)
Okla. Stat. Ann., Title 62, §§ 391 et seq., 411 et seq.
Wash. Rev. Code Ann., 39.52.010 et seq.

Funding Bond Act (State)
Okla. Stat. Ann., Title 62, § 133 et seq.

Funding Loan Act (Boston)
Mass. Acts 1957, Ch. 717

Funding Loan Act (Malden)
Mass. Acts 1956, Ch. 25
Mass. Acts 1958, Ch. 451
Mass. Acts 1960, Ch. 280

Funding Loan Act (Revere)
Mass. Acts 1955, Ch. 543

Funding of Public Schools Act (60/40)
R.I. Gen. Laws 1956, 16-69-1 et seq.

Funding of State Debt Law
Tenn. Code Ann., 9-9-101 et seq.

Funding Pilot Program (Mixed)
Mont. Laws 1995, Ch. 584

Funds Act (Solicitation of Charitable)
Conn. Gen. Stat. Ann., § 17-21a et seq.

Funds Act (State)
Wash. Rev. Code Ann., 43.79.010 et seq.

Funds Collateral Act (Public)
Tex. Rev. Civ. Stat., Art. 2529d

Funds Consolidation Act
Ida. Code 1947, 57-801 et seq.
Nev. Rev. Stat. 1967 Reprint, Replaced Pages, 353.290 et seq.
Utah Code Ann. 1953, 51-5-1 et seq.
Wyo. Stat. Ann., § 9-4-201 et seq.

Funds Deposit Act (Banks)
Cal. Government Code § 16500 et seq.

Funds for Guidance Centers Act (Township)
Ill. Rev. Stat. 1991, Ch. 139, § 167.20 et seq.

Funds for Historical Societies Act (Township)
Ill. Rev. Stat. 1991, Ch. 139, § 167.30 et seq.

Funds for Schools Act (Township)
Ill. Rev. Stat. 1991, Ch. 139, § 167.3m et seq.

Funds for Securing Loans to Eligible Businesses Act
P.R. Laws Ann. 1954, Title 23, § 263 et seq.

Funds Investment Act (Public)
Tex. Rev. Civ. Stat., Art. 842a-2

Funds Law (Professional Liability)
Ore. Rev. Stat., 752.055 et seq.

Funds Management Act
Colo. Rev. Stat., 24-75-901 et seq.

Funds Reform Act (State)
Tex. Government Code, § 404.091 et seq.

Funds Soliciation Act (Charitable)
Mass. Gen. Laws Ann., 68:18 et seq.

Funds Transfer Facilities Act (Consumer)
See Uniform Management of Institutional Funds Act

Funds Transfer Study Act (Electronic)
Ill. Rev. Stat. 1991, Ch. 127, § 39d-101 et seq.

Funds Transfers
See Uniform Commercial Code-Funds Transfers

Funds Transfers (Uniform Commercial Code)
See Uniform Commercial Code-Funds Transfers

Funds Transmission and Payment Instruments Act
Fla. Stat. Ann., 560.200 to 560.213

Funeral and Cemetery Services Act
Fla. Stat. Ann., 497.001 et seq.

Funeral Arrangement Act (Preneed)
Utah Code Ann. 1953, 58-58-1 et seq.

Funeral Consumer Protection Act (Preneed)
N.Y. General Business Law (Consol. Laws Ch. 20) § 453
N.Y. Public Health Law 1953 (Consol. Laws Ch. 45) §§ 3428, 3442, 3450

Funeral Directors Act
Md. Ann. Code 1974, Art. HO, § 7-101 et seq.
Mich. Comp. Laws Ann., 338.861 et seq.
N.H. Rev. Stat. 1955, 325:1 et seq.
Pa. Purdon's Stat., Title 63, § 479.1 et seq.
Vt. Stat. Ann., Title 26, § 1211 et seq.
Wis. Stat. Ann., 445.01 et seq.
W. Va. Code 1966, § 30-6-1 et seq.

Funeral Directors and Embalmers Act
See also Embalmers and Funeral Directors Act
Ariz. Rev. Stat. Ann., § 32-1301 et seq.
Cal. Business and Professions Code, § 7600 et seq.
Colo. Rev. Stat. 1963, 61-1-1 et seq.
Ill. Rev. Stat. 1991, Ch. 111, § 2800 et seq.
Ind. Code Ann., 25-15-1-1 et seq.
N.M. Stat. Ann. 1953, 67-20-1 et seq.
Ore. Rev. Stat., 692.010 et seq.
R.I. Gen. Laws 1956, 5-33-1 et seq.

Funeral Directors' Board Act
Okla. Stat. Ann., Title 59, § 396 et seq.

Funeral Directors' Licensing Act
N.M. Stat. Ann. 1953, 67-20-1 et seq.

Funeral Establishment Licensing Act
Ariz. Rev. Stat. Ann., § 32-1381 et seq.

Funeral Insurance Regulatory Act (Prearranged)
N.M. Stat. Ann., 59A-49-1 et seq.

Funeral or Burial Funds Act
Ill. Rev. Stat. 1991, Ch. 111 1/2, § 73.101 et seq.

Funeral Picketing Act
Kan. Laws 1992, Ch. 210

Funeral Service Act
Ga. Code Ann., 43-18-1 et seq.

Funeral Service Contract Act (Pre-need)
Ga. Code Ann., 43-18-90 et seq.

Funeral Service Contracts Act
R.I. Gen. Laws 1955, 5-33.1-1 et seq.

Funeral Services Licensing Act
Okla. Stat. Ann., Title 59, § 395.1 et seq.
Utah Code Ann. 1953, 58-9-1 et seq.

Funeral Transportation and Living Expenses Benefits Act of 1974
March 29, 1974, P.L. 93-257, 88 Stat. 53, 37 U.S. Code § 406 nt.

Fungicide, Insecticide and Rodenticide Act
Colo. Rev. Stat., 35-9-101 et seq.
Iowa Code Ann., 206.1 et seq.
Mich. Comp. Laws Ann., 286.201 et seq.
Mont. Rev. Code 1947, 27-201 et seq.
N.C. Gen. Stat. 1943, §§ 106-65.1 et seq., 143-434 et seq.
N.D. Cent. Code, 19-18-01 et seq.
S.D. Codified Laws 1967, 38-20A-1 et seq.
Tenn. Code Ann., 43-8-101 et seq.
Tex. Agriculture Code, § 76.001 et seq.
Utah Code Ann. 1953, 4-14-1 et seq.
Va. Code 1950, § 3.1-189 et seq.
Vt. Stat. Ann., Title 6, § 911 et seq.

Fungicide, Rodenticide and Insecticide Act (Federal)
Miss. Code Ann. 1972, §§ 69-23-3, 69-23-107

Fur-bearing Mammals Protection Law
Cal. Fish and Game Code 1957, § 4000 et seq.

Fur Buyers License Act
Ind. Code Ann., 14-2-7-7
Minn. Stat. 1984, 98.46, 98-51

Fur Dealers Act
Utah Code Ann. 1953, 23-19-1 et seq.

Fur Farming Act
Alaska Comp. Laws Ann. 1949, § 47-2-76 et seq.

Fur Products Labeling Act
Aug. 8, 1951, Ch. 298, 65 Stat. 175, 15 U.S. Code §§ 69 to 69j

Fur Seal Act of 1966
Nov. 2, 1966, P.L. 89-702, 80 Stat. 1091, 16 U.S. Code §§ 1151 to 1159, 1161 to 1168, 1171, 1172, 1181 to 1187
Oct. 14, 1983, P.L. 98-129, 16 U.S. Code § 1151 nt.
Oct. 14, 1983, P.L. 98-129, 16 U.S. Code § 1161 et seq.
July 18, 1984, P.L. 98-369, 98 Stat. 1061, 16 U.S. Code § 1169a
Nov. 23, 1988, P.L. 100-711, 16 U.S. Code § 1166
March 9, 1992, P.L. 102-251, 16 U.S. Code § 1151
Dec. 17, 1993, P.L. 103-199, 16 U.S. Code §§ 1151, 1152

Fur Trappers and Dealers License Act
Tex. Parks and Wildlife Code, § 71.001 et seq.

Furlough Compact (Interstate)
Tenn. Public Acts 1991, Ch. 231

Furlough Compact Act
Utah Code Ann. 1953, 77-34-1 et seq.

Furnisher's Lien Act
Tenn. Code Ann., 66-11-112 et seq.

Furniture and Bedding Inspection Act
Cal. Business and Professions Code § 19000 et seq.
Mass. Gen. Laws Ann., 94:270 et seq.

Furniture and Bedding Label Law
Cal. Business and Professions Code § 19080 et seq.
Mass. Gen. Laws Ann., 94:270 et seq.

Furniture Fire Safety Act
Ill. Rev. Stat. 1991, Ch. 127 1/2, § 951-1 et seq.
Minn. Stat. Ann., 299F.840 et seq.

Fusion—Energy Technology Act
Utah Code Ann. 1953, 9-2-801 et seq.
Utah Code 1953, 63-76-1 et seq.

Futch Act (Taxation)
Fla. Laws 1933, Ch. 16252,
Fla. Laws 1941, Ch. 20981

Future Interests Act
Ill. Rev. Stat. 1991, Ch. 30, § 39.9, 40

Future Trading Act
Aug. 24, 1921, Ch. 86, 42 Stat. 187

Futures Trading Act of 1978
Jan. 11, 1983, P.L. 97-444, 7 U.S. Code § 16a

Futures Trading Act of 1982
Jan. 11, 1983, P.L. 97-444, 7 U.S. Code § 1 nt.

Futures Trading Act of 1986
Nov. 10, 1986, P.L. 99-641, 7 U.S. Code 1 nt.
Dec. 21, 1995, P.L. 104-66, 7 U.S. Code § 76 nt.

Futures Trading Practices Act of 1992
Oct. 28, 1992, P.L. 102-546, 7 U.S. Code § 1 nt.

G

G. I. Bill of Rights
See Servicemens Readjustment Act of 1944

GAA Amendments Act
Pa. 1992 Pamph. Laws, No. 169

Gag Act (Obscene Literature)
Minn. Stat. Ann., 617.241

Gage-Mullan Act (Prohibition Enforcement)
N.Y. Laws 1921, Chs. 155, 156

Gain Time for Good Conduct Act (County Prisoners)
Fla. Stat. Ann., 951.21

Gain Time for Good Conduct Act (State Prisoners)
Fla. Stat. Ann., 944.275

Gaines-Gilbert Act (Taxation)
Ky. Rev. Stat. 1971, 132.020

Gaines-Myers Compulsory Primary Law
Ky. Acts 1935 (Ex. Sess.) Ch. 1

Gainesville and Alachua County Unified Government Charter Act
Fla. Special Laws 1975, Ch. 75-376

Gainesville Area Park Commission Act
Ga. Laws 1980, p. 4054

Gainesville Civil Service Act
Ga. Laws 1960, p. 2240

Gainesville Pension Act
Ga. Laws 1941, p. 1453

Gainesville Redevelopment Act
Fla. Special Laws 1972, Ch. 72-549
Fla. Special Laws 1973, Ch. 73-475

Gainesville Urban Renewal Law
Fla. Laws 1961, Ch. 61-2195

Gains Tax Act (Real Property)
N.Y. Tax Laws (Consol. Laws Ch. 60) § 1440 et seq.

Gallagher Act (Refunding Bonds)
Ohio Rev. Code 1953, 133.58, 133.61, 133.64

Gallatin Land Consolidation Act of 1998
Oct. 19, 1998, P.L. 105-267, 112 Stat. 2371

Gallatin Range Consolidation and Protection Act of 1993
Oct. 1, 1993, P.L. 103-91, 107 Stat. 987

Galveston County Pilots Licensing and Regulatory Act
Tex. Transportation Code, § 67.001 et seq.

Gambling Act
Ala. Code 1975, § 13A-12-21 et seq.
Alaska Stat.1962, § 11.66.200 et seq.
Cal. Penal Code § 330 et seq.
Colo. Rev. Stat., 18-10-101
D.C. Code 1973, § 22-1501 et seq.
Del. Code of 1974, Title 11, § 1401 et seq.
Fla. Stat. Ann., 849.01 et seq.
Ga. Code Ann., 16-12-20 et seq.
Haw. Rev. Stat. Ann., § 712-1220 et seq.
Ida. Code 1947, 18-3801 et seq.
Ill. Rev. Stat. 1991, Ch. 38, § 28-1 et seq.
Ind. Code Ann., 35-45-5-1 et seq.
Iowa Code Ann., 725.5 et seq.
Kan. Stat. Ann., 21-4302 et seq.
Ky. Rev. Stat. 1971, Superseded Vols., 436.200 et seq.
Ky. Rev. Stat. 1971, 372.010 et seq., 528.010 et seq.
La. Rev. Stat. Ann., 14:90
Md. Ann. Code 1957, Art. 27, § 237 et seq.
Mich. Comp. Laws Ann., 750.301 et seq.
Mont. Code Ann., 23-5-112 et seq.
N.C. Gen. Stat. 1943, § 14-292 et seq.
Nev. Rev. Stat. 1979 Reprint, 463.010 et seq.
N.H. Rev. Stat. 1955, 647:2
N.M. Stat. Ann., 30-19-1 et seq.
Ohio Rev. Code 1953, 2915.01 et seq.
Okla. Stat. Ann., Title 21, § 941 et seq.

Ore. Rev. Stat., 167.117 et seq.

Pa. Cons. Stat., Title 18, § 5512 et seq.

R.I. Gen. Laws 1956, 11-19-1 et seq.

Tenn. Code Ann., 39-17-501 et seq.

Vt. Stat. Ann., Title 13, §§ 2132 et seq., 2101 et seq.

Wash. Rev. Code Ann., 9.46.010 et seq.

Wis. Stat. Ann., 945.01 et seq.

Gambling Act (Bingo)
Alaska Stat. 1962, § 05.15.010 et seq.

Gambling Act (Johnson)
Tenn. Code Ann., 39-17-502 et seq.

Gambling and Raffle Act (Charitable)
Tex. Rev. Civ. Stat., Art. 179f

Gambling Contracts Act
Vt. Stat. Ann., Title 9, § 3981 et seq.

Gambling Control Act
Cal. Business and Professions Code § 19800 et seq.

Gambling Devices Act (Possession)
Wash. Rev. Code Ann., 9.46.030

Gambling Devices Act of 1962
Oct. 18, 1962, P.L. 87-840, 76 Stat. 1075, 15 U.S. Code §§ 1171, 1172, 1173, 1178

Gambling Devices Transportation Act
Jan. 2, 1951, Ch. 1194, 64 Stat. 1134, 15 U.S. Code §§ 1171 to 1177

Gambling Establishment Act
Ky. Rev. Stat. 1971, Superseded Vol., 436.440 et seq.
Ky. Rev. Stat. 1971, 528.030, 528.070

Gambling in Futures Act
Ill. Rev. Stat. 1991, Ch. 38, § 28-1 et seq.

Gambling Losses Recovery Act
Mont. Code Ann., 23-5-131 et seq.
Wash. Rev. Code Ann., 4.24.070

Gambling Machines Act
Vt. Stat. Ann. Title 13, § 2135 et seq.

Gambling, Pari-Mutuel Wagering Act
Fla. Stat. Ann., 550.001 et seq.

Gambling Ships Control Law
Cal. Penal Code § 11300 et seq.

Game Act
P.R. Laws Ann. 1954, Title 12, § 1 et seq.

Game Act (Wildlife and Forestry)
Ala. Code 1975, § 9-11-230 et seq.
Alaska Comp. Laws Ann. 1949, § 39-6-1 et seq.
Ill. Rev. Stat. 1991, Ch. 61, § 1-1 et seq.
Ind. Code Ann., 14-2-4-1 et seq.
La. Rev. Stat. Ann., 56:1 et seq.
Md. Ann. Code 1974, Art. NR, § 10-101 et seq.
Mich. Comp. Laws Ann., 311.1 et seq.
Mo. Rev. Stat., 252.010 et seq.
N.C. Gen. Stat. 1943, § 113-82 et seq.
N.H. Rev. Stat. 1955, 206:1
N.J. Stat. Ann., 23:1-1 et seq.
N.Y. Environmental Conservation Law 1972 (Consol. Laws Ch. 43B) § 11-0101 et seq.
Ore. Rev. Stat., 496.002 et seq.
Pa. Purdon's Stat., Title 34, § 1311.1 et seq.
P.R. Laws Ann. 1954, Title 12, § 1 et seq.
Wash. Rev. Code Ann., 77.04.010 et seq.
Wis. Stat. Ann., 29.01 et seq.

Game and Fish Act
See Fish and Game Act

Game and Fish Act (Inland)
Me. Rev. Stat. Ann. 1964, Title 12, § 7001 et seq.

Game and Fish Bond Act
N.M. Stat. Ann., 17-1-16 et seq.

Game and Fish Enforcement Act
Mich. Comp. Laws Ann., 300.11 et seq.

Game and Fish Lifetime License Trust Fund
Mich. Comp. Laws Ann., 316.1001 et seq.

Game and Fish Point System Act
S.C. Code Ann. 1976, § 50-9-1010 et seq.

Game and Fish Protection Trust Fund Act
Mich. Comp. Laws Ann., 300.211 et seq.

Game and Fish Warden Retirement Act
Wyo. Stat. Ann., § 9-3-601 et seq.

Game and Fresh Water Fish Act
Fla. Stat. Ann., 372.001 et seq.
Md. Ann. Code 1974, Art. NR, § 4-101 et seq.

Game and Parks Commission State Headquarters Construction Act
Neb. Rev. Stat. 1943, 81-805.04 et seq.

Game and Wild Life Act
June 15, 1935, Ch. 261, 49 Stat. 378, 16 U.S. Code §§ 141b, 715d- 1, 715d-2, 715e, 715e-1, 715k-1, 715s, 718b to 718e; See 18 U.S. Code §§ 42, 44, 3054, 3112
Oct. 31, 1951, Ch. 654, 65 Stat. 707, 16 U.S. Code § 715s
Aug. 30, 1964, P.L. 88-523, 78 Stat. 701, 16 U.S. Code § 715s
Oct. 15, 1966, P.L. 89-669, 80 Stat. 930, 16 U.S. Code § 715s

Game and Wildlife Code
Pa. Cons. Stat., Title 34, § 101 et seq.

Game Bag Limit Act
Mich. Comp. Laws Ann., 312.12

Game Breeder's License Act
Tex. Parks and Wildlife Code, § 44.001 et seq.

Game Farmers Act
Wash. Rev. Code Ann., 77.12.095, 77.12.200, 77.12.220, 77.12.570 et seq.

Game, Fish and Forestry Act
W. Va. Code 1966, § 20-1-1 et seq.

Game, Fish and Oyster Commission Act
Tex. Penal Code 1925, Art. 978f

Game, Fish and Sea Food Act
Ala. Code 1975, § 9-2-60 et seq.

Game, Fish and Watercraft Law
S.C. Code Ann. 1976, § 50-1-10 et seq.

Game Fund Capital Budget Act
Pa. 1983 Pamph. Laws 141, No. 38
Pa. 1984 Pamph. Laws 581, No. 116
Pa. 1986 Pamph. Laws, No. 94
Pa. 1990 Pamph. Laws, No. 5
Pa. 1991 Pamph. Laws, No. 93

Game Fund Capital Budget Act for 1992-1993
Pa. 1992 Pamph. Laws, No. 171

Game Fund Capital Budget Act for 1995-1196
Pa. 1995 Pamph. Laws, No. 32

Game, Inland Fish and Dog Act
Va. Code 1950, § 29-1 et seq.

Game Licenses Act
Wash. Rev. Code Ann., 77.32.005 et seq.

Game Permit Act (Balloon Dart)
Ill. Rev. Stat. 1991, Ch. 111 1/2, § 4091-1 et seq.

Game Propagation District Law (Refuge)
Cal. Fish and Game Code 1957, § 10500 et seq.

Game Trapping Act
Fla. Stat. Ann., 372.001 et seq.

Game Wardens' Retirement Act
Mont. Code Ann., 19-8-105 et seq.

Games of Chance Licensing Law
N.Y. General Municipal Law (Consol. Laws Ch. 24) § 185 et seq.

Games of Chance Licensing Law (City of New York)
N.Y. Adm. Code '85, § 20-433 et seq.

Gaming Act
Ark. Code Ann. 1987, 5-66-103 et seq.
Cal. Penal Code § 330 et seq.
Conn. Gen. Stat. Ann., § 53-278a et seq.

Haw. Rev. Stat. Ann., § 712-1220 et seq.

Ky. Rev. Stat. 1971, Superseded Vols.,
436.200 et seq.

Ky. Rev. Stat. 1971, 372.010 et seq., 528.010
et seq.

Mass. Gen. Laws Ann., 271:1 et seq.

Nev. Rev. Stat. 1979 Reprint, 463.010 et seq.

N.J. Stat. Ann., 2C:37-1 et seq.

P.R. Laws Ann. 1954, Title 15, § 71 et seq.

Tenn. Code Ann., 39-17-501 et seq.

Tex. Penal Code, § 47.01 et seq.

W. Va. Code 1966, § 61-10-1 et seq.

Wyo. Stat. Ann., § 6-7-101 et seq.

Gaming Act (Limited)
Colo. Rev. Stat., 12-47.1-101 et seq.

Gaming Control Act
Miss. Code Ann. 1972, § 75-76-1 et seq.
N.M. Stat. Ann., 60-2E-1 to 60-2E-61

Gaming Reform Act
Alaska Stat. 1962, § 05.15.010 et seq.

Gaming Registration Act
Cal. Business and Professions Code § 19800
et seq.

Gananda School District Act
N.Y. Laws 1972, Ch. 928

**Gang and Juvenile Delinquency Prevention
Act**
Fla. Stat. Ann., 39.025
Fla. Stat. Ann., 39.025 et seq.
La. Rev. Stat. Ann., 15:1421 et seq.

Gang Control Grant Act
Ill. Rev. Stat. 1991, Ch. 127, § 3300 et seq.

**Gang, Crime, and Violence Prevention
Partnership Program**
Cal. Penal Code § 13825.1 et seq.

Gang Crime Witness Protection Act
Ill. Comp. Stat. 1992, Ch. 725, § 172/5-1 et
seq.

Gangster Act
N.J. Stat. Ann., 2:136-1 to 2:136-5

Gann, Paul, Blood Safety Act
Cal. Health and Safety Code § 1645

Garage Keepers and Liverymen's Lien Act
D.C. Code Ann., § 38-201 et seq.

Garagemens Lien Act
Ill. Rev. Stat. 1991, Ch. 82, § 39.9 et seq.
La. Rev. Stat. Ann., 9:4501
Md. Ann. Code 1974, Art. CL, § 16-201 et
seq.
Mich. Comp. Laws Ann., 570.301 et seq.
Nev. Rev. Stat. 1979 Reprint, 108.270,
108.360
N.J. Stat. Ann., 2A:44-20 et seq.

Garbage Collection Act
N.M. Stat. Ann., 4-56-1 et seq.

Garbage Disposal Act (New Castle County)
Del. Code of 1974, Title 9, § 2401 et seq.
Ill. Rev. Stat. 1991, Ch. 34, § 5-8001 et seq.
Mich. Comp. Laws Ann., 123.361 et seq.

Garbage Disposal District Act
Cal. Health and Safety Code § 4100 et seq.
Colo. Rev. Stat., 30-20-201 et seq.
Wash. Rev. Code 1951, 55.04.010 et seq.

Garbage Disposal Franchise Law
Cal. Health and Safety Code § 4200 et seq.

Garbage Feeding Act (Swine)
Ind. Code Ann., 15-2.1-18-20 et seq.
Okla. Stat. Ann., Title 2, § 6-21 et seq.
Tenn. Code Ann., 44-2-401 et seq.

Garbage Incinerators Act
D.C. Code 1973, § 6-505 et seq.

Garden and Zoological Park District Act
Miss. Code Ann. 1972, § 55-21-1 et seq.

Garden State Scholarship Act
N.J. Stat. Ann., 18A:71-26.1 et seq.

**Garden, Tractor and Lawn and Light
Industrial Equipment Franchise Act**
Ala. Code 1975, § 8-21A-1

Gardner Act (Sinking Fund Levies)
Ohio Laws Vol. 108, p. 1199

Gardner Building Alteration Loan Act
Mass. Acts 1955, Ch. 53

Garfield Act (Compulsory Railway Connection)
June 15, 1866., Ch. 124, 14 Stat. 66

Garfield Act (Election Expenditures)
Ohio Rev. Code 1953, 3517.08 et seq.

Garland County Salary Act
Ark. Acts 1957, p. 976, No. 339

Garment Industry Job Retention Act
N.Y. Labor Law (Consol. Laws Ch. 31) § 358a
N.Y. Laws 1981, Ch. 624

Garment Industry Law (Apparel Industry)
N.Y. Labor Law (Consol. Laws Ch. 31) § 340 et seq.

Garn-St Germain Depository Institutions Act of 1982
Oct. 15, 1982, P.L. 97-320, 12 U.S. Code § 226 nt.
Oct. 8, 1985, P.L. 99-120, 12 U.S. Code § 1464 nt., 1729, 1823
April 24, 1986, P.L. 99-278, 12 U.S. Code §§ 1464 nt., 1729 nt., 1823
Aug. 27, 1986, P.L. 99-400, 12 U.S. Code § 1464 nt.
Oct. 8, 1986, P.L. 99-452, 12 U.S. Code §§ 1464 nt., 1729 and nt., 1823
Aug. 10, 1987, P.L. 100-86, 12 U.S. Code §§ 1729 nt., 1730a, 1785, 1786, 1823, 1842, 1843

Garnett-Mayer Act
Ky. Acts 1936, Ch. 19

Garnishment and Attachment Act
Ala. Code 1975, § 6-6-370 et seq.
Ariz. Rev. Stat. Ann., § 12-1571 et seq.
Colo. Rev. Stat., 79-9-1 et seq.
Conn. Gen. Stat. Ann., § 52-329 et seq.
Fla. Stat. Ann., 77.01 et seq.

Ga. Code Ann., 18-4-60 et seq.
Haw. Rev. Stat. Ann., § 652-1 et seq.
Ill. Rev. Stat. 1991, Ch. 110, § 12-701 et seq.
Ind. Code Ann., 34-1-11-1 et seq.
Iowa Code Ann., 642.1 et seq.
Kan. Stat. Ann., 60-714 et seq.
Mass. Gen. Laws Ann., 246:1 et seq.
Md. Ann. Code 1974, Art. CJ, § 3-30-1 et seq.
Md. Rules of Procedure, Rule 2-645, 3-645 et seq.
Mich. Comp. Laws Ann., 600.4001 et seq., 600.4011 et seq.
Minn. Stat. Ann., 571.41 et seq.
Mo. Rev. Stat., 525.010 et seq.
N.D. Cent. Code, 32.09.1-01 et seq.
N.M. Stat. Ann. 1953, 26-2-1 et seq.
N.Y. Personal Property Law (Consol. Laws Ch. 41) § 46 et seq.
Ohio Rev. Code 1953, 2716.01 et seq.
Okla. Stat. Ann., Title 12, § 1171 et seq.
R.I. Gen. Laws 1956, 10-5-7 et seq.
S.C. Code Ann. 1976, § 15-39-410
S.D. Codified Laws 1967, 21-18-1 et seq.
Tex. Civil Practice and Remedies Code § 63.001 et seq.
Utah Rules of Civil Procedure 1950, Rule 64D
Wash. Rev. Code Ann., 6.26.010 et seq., 6.27.010 et seq.
Wis. Stat. Ann., 812.01 et seq.
Wyo. Stat. Ann., § 1-15-101 et seq.

Garnishment and Personal Property Owner's Rights Act
Tenn. Code Ann., 26-2-101

Garnishment Reform Act
Minn. Stat. Ann., 181.041, 550.141, 550.142, 550.37, 571.41, 571.471, 571.495, 571.55, 571.61, 571.67, 571.68, 671.69

Garrett Act (Elections)
Ala. Acts 1967, Sp. Sess., p. 323, No. 243

Garrett Quail and Squirrel Act
Ark. Special Acts 1923, p. 565, No. 267

Garrigus-Lagomarsino Act (Conservation Schools)
Cal. Education Code 1976, § 1790 et seq.

Garrison Diversion Unit Reformulation Act of 1986
May 12, 1986, P.L. 99-294, 100 Stat. 426

Gary Corbin-Quincy Hoffman Act
Mich. Comp. Laws Ann., 205.202 et seq.

Gas Act
La. Rev. Stat. Ann., 40:1841 et seq.

Gas Act (Liquefied Petroleum)
N.M. Stat. Ann., 70-5-1 et seq.
Okla. Stat. Ann., Title 52, § 420.1 et seq.
Utah Code Ann. 1953, 53-7-301 et seq.

Gas and Coal Resource Coordination Act
Pa. Purdon's Stat., Title 58, § 501 et seq.

Gas and Electric Company Act
Mass. Gen. Laws Ann., 164:1 et seq.

Gas and Electric Consumers Council Act
S.D. Laws 1969, Ch. 231

Gas and Electric Loan Act (Holyoke)
Mass. Acts 1951, Ch. 436

Gas and Electricity Joint Ownership Act
Ill. Rev. Stat. 1991, Ch. 76, § 10 et seq.

Gas and Oil Act
Md. Ann. Code 1974, Art. NR, § 6-101 et seq.
N.M. Stat. Ann., 70-2-1 et seq.
Pa. Purdon's Stat., Title 58, § 601.101 et seq.
Va. Code 1950, § 45.1-286 et seq.

Gas and Oil Act (Offshore)
Ore. Rev. Stat., 274.705 et seq.

Gas and Oil Compact Act
N.Y. Environmental Conservation Law 1972, (Consol. Laws Ch. 43B) § 23-2101

Gas and Oil Compulsory Pooling Act
Miss. Code Ann. 1972, § 53-3-7

Gas and Oil Conservation Act
See also Oil and Gas Conservation Act
Ala. Code 1975, 9-17-1 et seq.
Alaska Stat. 1962, § 31.05.005 et seq.
Ark. Code Ann. 1987, 15-72-101 et seq.
Ida. Code 1947, 47-315 et seq.
Iowa Code Ann., 84.1 et seq.
Ky. Rev. Stat. 1971, 353.500 et seq.
Me. Rev. Stat. Ann. 1964, Title 10, § 2151 et seq.
Mich. Comp. Laws Ann., 319.1 et seq.
Miss. Code Ann. 1972, § 53-1-1 et seq.
Mont. Code Ann., 82-11-101 et seq.
Neb. Rev. Stat. 1943, 57-901 et seq.
Ohio Rev. Code 1953, 1509.01 et seq.
Pa. Purdon's Stat., Title 58, § 401 et seq.
S.D. Codified Laws 1967, 45-9-1 et seq.
Utah Code Ann. 1953, 40-6-1 et seq.
Utah Stat. Ann., Title 29, § 501 et seq.
Vt. Stat. Ann., Title 29, § 501 et seq.
Wash. Rev. Code Ann., 78.52.001 et seq.
Wyo. Stat. Ann., § 30-5-101 et seq.

Gas and Oil Conservation Compact Act
See Interstate Compact to Conserve Oil and Gas Act

Gas and Oil Conservation Compact Act (Extension)
See Interstate Compact to Conserve Oil and Gas (Extension)

Gas and Oil Deep Drilling Act
Ga. Code Ann., 12-4-40 et seq.

Gas and Oil Emergency School Tax Act
N.M. Stat. Ann., 7-31-1 et seq.

Gas and Oil Interstate Compact Act
Md. Ann. Code 1974, Art. NR, § 6-401 et seq.
Mich. Comp. Laws Ann., 319.301 et seq.

Gas and Oil Lands Leasing Act
See Oil and Gas Lands Leasing Act

Gas and Oil Lease Release Act
Ill. Rev. Stat. 1989, Ch. 80, § 38.9 et seq.

Gas and Oil Leasing Act
Ariz. Rev. Stat. Ann., § 27-551 et seq.

Gas and Oil Lien Act
See Oil and Gas Lien Act

Gas and Oil Manufacturers Privilege Tax Act
N.M. Stat. Ann., 7-33-1 et seq.

Gas and Oil Proceeds Payment Act
N.M. Stat. Ann., 70-10-1 et seq.

Gas and Oil Production Equipment Ad Valorem Tax Act
N.M. Stat. Ann., 7-34-1 et seq.

Gas and Oil Recovery Act
Ill. Rev. Stat. 1991, Ch. 96 1/2, § 5100 et seq.

Gas and Oil Rights Act
Ill. Rev. Stat. 1991, Ch. 96 1/2, § 4900 et seq.

Gas and Oil Severance Tax Act
Kan. Laws 1957, Ch. 516
Mich. Comp. Laws Ann., 205.301 et seq.

Gas and Oil Surface Owners Compensation Act
Tenn. Code Ann., 60-1-601 et seq.

Gas and Oil Unitization Act
Neb. Rev. Stat. 1943, 57-910 et seq.

Gas and Oil Waste Haulers Act
Tex. Water Code, § 29.001 et seq.

Gas and Oil Well Safety Regulation Act
W. Va. Code 1966, § 22B-1-1

Gas and Oil Well Spacing Act
Cal. Public Resources Code §§ 3000, 3600 et seq.

Gas and Oil Wells on Public Lands Act
Ill. Rev. Stat. 1991, Ch. 96 1/2, § 5000 et seq.

Gas Appliance Act
Ariz. Rev. Stat. Ann., § 36-1621 et seq.

Gas Authority Law (Municipal)
Miss. Code Ann. 1972, § 77-6-1 et seq.

Gas Chamber Act
Miss. Code Ann. 1972, § 99-19-51 et seq.

Gas Commission Act
N.Y. Laws 1905, Ch. 737

Gas Companies Regulation Act
Mich. Comp. Laws Ann., 486.251 et seq.
N.J. Stat. Ann., 48:9-1 to 48:9-32
Wash. Rev. Code Ann., 80.28.010 et seq.

Gas Company Property Act
Ill. Rev. Stat. 1991, Ch. 32, § 398-9 et seq.

Gas Conservation Act
Kan. Stat. Ann., 55-701 et seq.
N.C. Gen. Stat. 1943, § 113-381 et seq.
Okla. Stat. Ann., Title 52, § 231 et seq.

Gas Container Act (Liquefied Petroleum)
Ill. Rev. Stat. 1991, Ch. 96 1/2, § 5700 et seq.

Gas Education, Safety, and Research Act (Propane)
Fla. Stat. Ann., 527.20 to 527.23

Gas Facility Cost Allocation Act
N.Y. Laws 1988, Ch. 357
N.Y. Public Service Law (Consol. Laws Ch. 48) § 66

Gas Gathering Tax Act
La. Rev. Stat. Ann., 47:671 et seq.
Tex. Rev. Civ. Stat., Art. 7057f

Gas Gross Production Tax Act
Tex. Tax Code, § 201.051 et seq.

Gas Guzzler Tax
Nov. 9, 1978, P.L. 95-618, 26 U.S. Code § 4064

Gas Measurement Act
Ark. Code Ann. 1987, 15-74-301 et seq.
La. Rev. Stat. Ann., 55:151 et seq.
Okla. Stat. Ann., Title 52, § 471 et seq.

Tex. Natural Resources Code, § 91.051 et seq.

Gas, Oil and Solution Mining Law
N.Y. Environmental Conservation Law 1972 (Consol. Laws Ch. 43B) § 23-0101 et seq.

Gas Operation, Well-Drilling, Petroleum and Coal Mining Act
Pa. Purdon's Stat., Title 58, § 601.101 et seq.

Gas Pipe Line Act
Mich. Comp. Laws Ann., 483.101 et seq.

Gas Pipe Line Safety Act
Ill. Rev. Stat. 1991, Ch. 111 2/3, § 551 et seq.

Gas Pipelines Act (Interstate)
Miss. Code Ann. 1972, § 77-11-301 et seq.

Gas Policy Act
Cal. Public Utilities Code § 785

Gas Pricing Act
N.M. Stat. Ann., 62-7-1 et seq.

Gas Procurement Act
Ky. Acts 1958, Ch. 38

Gas Production and Transportation Act
Okla. Stat. Ann., Title 52, § 21 et seq.

Gas Rates Regulation Act
Wash. Rev. Code Ann., 80.28.010 et seq.

Gas Regulation Act (Liquefied Petroleum)
Ill. Rev. Stat. 1991, Ch. 96 1/2, § 5600 et seq.

Gas Related Activities Act of 1990
Nov. 15, 1990, P.L. 101-572, 15 U.S. Code § 79k nt.

Gas Research, Marketing and Safety Act (Liquefied Petroleum)
Okla. Stat. 1981, Title 52, § 420.20 et seq.

Gas Revenue Tax Act
Ill. Comp. Stat. 1992, Ch. 35, § 615/1 et seq.
Ill. Rev. Stat. 1991, Ch. 120, § 467-16 et seq.

Gas Safety Act
Fla. Stat. Ann., 368.01 et seq.

S.C. Code Ann. 1976, § 58-5-910 et seq.

Gas Safety Appliance Act
Ill. Laws 1911, p. 146

Gas, Sewer and Solid Waste Management Districts Act (Rural)
Okla. Stat. Ann., Title 82, § 1324.1 et seq.

Gas Storage Act
Ark. Code Ann. 1987, 15-72-601 et seq.
Ill. Rev. Stat. 1991, Ch. 96 1/2, § 5500 et seq.
Mich. Comp. Laws Ann., 486.252
Mo. Rev. Stat., 393.410 et seq.

Gas System Tax Equivalent Law
Tenn. Public Acts 1991, Ch. 220

Gas Tax Act
S.C. Code Ann. 1976, § 12-27-10 et seq.

Gas Tax Act (Liquefied Gas)
Tex. Taxation-General 1959, Art. 10.51 et seq.

Gas Tax Act (Off-Highway)
Cal. Statutes 1972, Ch. 1382, p. 2870
Cal. Statutes 1972, Ch. 1405, p. 2928

Gas Transmission and Distribution Piping Systems Safety Code
Fla. Stat. Ann., 368.01 et seq.

Gas Transmission Facilities Act
Ill. Rev. Stat. 1991, Ch. 111 2/3, § 570 et seq.

Gas Users Act (Agriculture)
Tex. Rev. Civ. Stat., Art. 6066g
Tex. Utilities Code, § 123.021 et seq.

Gas Utilities Act
Tex. Rev. Civ. Stat., Art. 6050 et seq.

Gas Utility Regulatory Act
Tex. Utilities Code, § 101.001 et seq.

Gas Wastage Law
Cal. Public Resources Code § 3500 et seq.

Gas Well Law
Iowa Code Ann., 84.1 et seq.

Gas Well Plugging Fund Act (Coalbed Methane)
Ala. Code 1975, § 9-17-130 et seq.

Gaseous Fuels and Equipment Act (Escambia County)
Fla. Special Laws 1963, Ch. 63-1326

Gasohol Act
La. Rev. Stat. Ann., 30:1301 et seq.

Gasohol and Energy Development Act
Neb. Rev. Stat. 1943, 66-801 et seq.

Gasohol and Gasoline Products Marketing Act
Md. Ann. Code 1974, Art. CL, § 11-301 et seq.

Gasohol Competition Act of 1980
Dec. 2, 1980, P.L. 96-493, 15 U.S. Code § 1 nt.

Gasohol Fuels Tax Abatement Act
Ill. Comp. Stat. 1992, Ch. 35, §§ 125/1 to 125/3, 125/10
Ill. Rev. Stat. 1991, Ch. 5, § 1751 et seq.

Gasohol Use Act (State Colleges and Universities)
Ill. Rev. Stat. 1991, Ch. 144, § 2851 et seq.

Gasoline Act
Ala. Code 1975, § 8-17-150 et seq.

Gasoline Act (Retail Sales)
N.J. Stat. Ann., 56:6-1 et seq.

Gasoline and Liquid Fuels Tax Act
Pa. Purdon's Stat., Title 72, § 2611a et seq.

Gasoline and Oil Excise Tax Act
Miss. Code 1942, § 10013-01 et seq.

Gasoline and Oil Inspection Act
N.C. Gen. Stat. 1943, § 119-14 et seq.

Gasoline and Special Fuel Excise Tax Act
W. Va. Code 1966, § 11-14-1 et seq.

Gasoline Container Act
Mich. Comp. Laws Ann., 750.502

Gasoline Dealer Bill of Rights Act
Wash. Rev. Code Ann., 19.120.010 et seq.

Gasoline Dealers Franchise Act
Conn. Gen. Stat. Ann., § 42-133j et seq.
Wash. Rev. Code Ann., 19.120.010 et seq.

Gasoline Filling Station Act (Location)
Conn. Gen. Stat. Ann., § 14-318 et seq.

Gasoline Inspection Act
Fla. Stat. Ann., 525.01 et seq.

Gasoline License Tax Act
Cal. Revenue and Taxation Code § 7301 et seq.
Mont. Code Ann., 15-70-201 et seq.

Gasoline License Tax Refund Act
Mont. Code Ann., 15-70-225 et seq.

Gasoline Marketing Practices Act
Ga. Code Ann., 10-1-230 et seq.

Gasoline Pipeline Law
Iowa Code Ann., 479.1 et seq.

Gasoline Price Advertising Act
Ill. Rev. Stat. 1991, Ch. 121 1/2, § 860 et seq.

Gasoline Price Fixing Act
Tenn. Public Acts 1927, Ch. 22

Gasoline Price Posting Act
Wis. Stat. Ann., 100.18, Subsec. 8

Gasoline Products Leasing Act
Alaska Stat. 1962, § 45.50.800 et seq.

Gasoline Products Marketing Act
Md. Ann. Code 1974, Art. CL, § 11-301 et seq.
Utah Code Ann. 1953, 13-12-1 et seq.

Gasoline Pump License Act
Iowa Code Ann., 214.1 et seq.

Gasoline Receptacle Labeling Act
Ill. Rev. Stat. 1991, Ch. 127 1/2, § 150 et seq.

Gasoline Sale Sign Act
Nev. Rev. Stat. 1979 Reprint, 590.160 et seq.

Gasoline Sales Licensing Act
Conn. Gen. Stat. Ann., § 14-318 et seq.

Gasoline Service Station Act
N.Y. Local Laws 1964, Village of Elmsford, p. 878

Gasoline Stations Licensing Act
N.Y. Tax Law (Consol. Laws Ch. 60) § 283a

Gasoline Storage Act
Ill. Rev. Stat. 1991, Ch. 127 1/2, § 152-9 et seq.

Gasoline Tax Act
Ala. Code 1975, § 40-17-30 et seq.
Ark. Code Ann. 1987, 26-55-201, 26-55-203 et seq.
Colo. Rev. Stat., 39-27-101 et seq.
Conn. Gen. Stat. Ann., § 12-455a et seq.
D.C. Code Ann., § 47-2301 et seq.
Fla. Stat. Ann., 206.01 et seq.
Haw. Rev. Stat. Ann., § 243-1 et seq.
Ida. Code 1947, 63-2401 et seq.
Ind. Code Ann., 6-6-1.1-101 et seq.
Kan. Stat. Ann., 79-3401 et seq.
Ky. Rev. Stat. 1971, 138.210 et seq.
La. Rev. Stat. Ann., 47:711 et seq.
Mass. Gen Laws 1984, 64A:1 et seq.
Me. Rev. Stat. Ann. 1964, Title 36, § 2901 et seq.
Mich. Comp. Laws Ann., 207.101 et seq.
Minn. Stat. Ann., 296.01 et seq.
Mont. Code Ann., 15-70-201 et seq.
N.C. Gen. Stat. 1943, § 105-430 et seq.
N.D. Cent. Code, 57-43.1-01 et seq.
Nev. Rev. Stat. 1979 Reprint, 365.010 et seq.
N.H. Rev. Stat. 1955, 260:30 et seq.
N.M. Stat. Ann., 7-13-1 et seq.
Ohio Rev. Code 1953, 5735.01 et seq.
Ore. Rev. Stat., 319.010 et seq.
R.I. Gen. Laws 1956, 31-36-1 et seq.

S.C. Code Ann. 1976, § 12-27-10 et seq.
Tenn. Code Ann., 67-3-601 et seq.
Tex. Tax Code, § 153.001 et seq.
Vt. Stat. Ann., Title 32, § 8801 et seq.
Wash. Rev. Code Ann., 82.36.010 et seq.
W. Va. Code 1931, Miscellaneous Superseded Code Provisions, § 11-14-1
Wyo. Stat. Ann., § 39-6-201 et seq.

Gasoline Tax Act (Horton)
Mich. Comp. Laws 1948, 207.119 et seq.

Gasoline Tax Act (Municipal and County)
N.M. Stat. Ann., 7-24A-1 et seq.

Gasoline Tax Act (Special County Hospital)
N.M. Stat. Ann., 7-24B-1 et seq.

Gasoline Tax and Postage Rate Act
June 16, 1933, Ch. 96, 48 Stat. 254

Gasoline Tax Appropriation Act
Ala. Code 1958, Title 23, § 124 (11s)

Gasoline Tax Distribution Act
Neb. Laws 1943, Ch. 138, § 1

Gasoline Tax Refund Act
Ga. Code 1933, 92-1403, Subd. I

Gasparilla Island Conservation District Act
Fla. Special Laws 1980, Ch. 80-473

Gasparilla Island Historic and Conservation District Act
Fla. Special Laws 1979, Ch. 79-490

Gasque Spanish War Pensions Act
May 24, 1938, Ch. 268, 52 Stat. 440

Gateway Amendment
Ill. Const. 1870, Art. 14, § 2

Gateway National Recreation Area Act
Oct. 27, 1972, P.L. 92-592, 86 Stat. 1308, 16 U.S. Code §§ 460cc to 460cc-4

Gateway Roads Program
Mass. Gen. Laws Ann., 90H:1 et seq.

Gathering Line Land Acquisition Act
N.M. Stat. Ann., 70-3A-1 et seq.

Gatlinburg Development Impact Fee Act
Tenn. Private Acts 1990, Ch. 167

GATT
See Uruguay Round Agreements Act

Gay Act (Public Lands in Louisiana)
March 2, 1889, Ch. 395, 25 Stat. 877

Gay-Shattuck Act (Intoxicating Liquor)
La. Acts 1908, No. 176

Geak-R. Hood-McNeely Malpractice Arbitration Act
Mich. Comp. Laws Ann., 600.5040 et seq.

Gearhart Act (Armistice Day Act)
May 13, 1938, Ch. 210, 52 Stat. 351 (See 5 U.S. Code § 6103)

Geary Act (Chinese Exclusion)
May 5, 1892, Ch. 60, 27 Stat. 25

Geddes-Meyers State Employees' Medical and Hospital Care Act
Cal. Government Code § 22751 et seq.

Geerlings-Derenzinski Job Development Authority Act
Mich. Comp. Laws Ann., 125.1701 et seq.

Gem and Precious Metal Dealer Act
Mich. Comp. Laws Ann., 445.481 et seq.

Gender Balanced Appointments Act
Ill. Rev. Stat. 1991, Ch. 127, § 4301 et seq.

Gender Tax Repeal Act
Cal. Civil Code § 51.6

Gene Chappie Heritage Network Act
Cal. Vehicle Code 1959, § 5066

General Absentee Voters' Law
Ore. Rev. Stat., 253.005 et seq.

General Accessory Act
Ill. Rev. Stat. 1961, Ch. 38, § 5-1 et seq.

General Accounting and Budgetary Procedures Law
Ark. Code Ann. 1987, 19-4-101 et seq.

General Accounting Office Act of 1980
April 3, 1980, P.L. 96-226, 31 U.S. Code §§ 1 nt., 42 et seq., 42 U.S. Code §§ 3523, 7148

General Accounting Office Act of 1996
Oct. 19, 1996, P.L. 104-316, 31 U.S. Code § 701 nt.

General Accounting Office Personnel Act of 1980
Feb. 15, 1980, P.L. 96-191, 31 U.S. Code §§ 52-1 et seq.

General Accounting Office Personnel Amendments Act of 1988
Sept. 9, 1988, P.L. 100-426, 5 U.S. Code § 5349; 31 U.S. Code §§ 701 nt., 703, 732, 751, 752, 755, 755 nt., 771, 772, 772 nt., 773, 774, 776, 777

General Administrative Agencies Act (Commissions, Boards and Institutions)
Va. Code 1950, § 9-6.1 et seq.

General Agents Act (Managing)
Colo. Rev. Stat., 10-2-401 et seq., 10-2-1001 et seq.
Del. Code of 1974, Title 18, § 1801 et seq.
Ida. Code 1947, 41-1501 et seq.
Mass. Gen. Laws Ann., 175:177F to 175:177L
Me. Rev. Stat. Ann. 1964, Title 24-A, § 1881 et seq.
Mo. Rev. Stat., 375.147 et seq.
Okla. Stat. Ann., Title 36, § 1471 et seq.
S.C. Code Ann. 1976, § 38-44-10 et seq.
Wash. Rev. Laws 1993, Ch. 462, §§ 34 to 42

General Agricultural Marketing Act
Ala. Code 1975, § 2-10-20 et seq.

General Allotment Act (Indians)
See Indian General Allotment Act

General and Business Corporation Act
Mo. Rev. Stat., 351.010 et seq.

General Appropriation Act

Fla. Stat. 1971, 282.01

Haw. Session Laws 1971, Act 68

Haw. Session Laws 1973, Act 218

Haw. Session Laws 1975, Act 195

Haw. Session Laws 1977, First Special Session, Act 10

Haw. Session Laws 1979, Act 214

Haw. Session Laws 1981, First Special Session, Act 1

Haw. Session Laws 1983, Act 301

Haw. Session Laws 1984, Act 287

Haw. Session Laws 1985, Act 300

Haw. Session Laws 1986, Act 347

Haw. Session Laws 1987, Act 216

Haw. Session Laws 1988, Act 314

Haw. Session Laws 1989, Act 316

Haw. Session Laws 1990, Act 300

Haw. Session Laws 1991, Act 216

Haw. Session Laws 1991, Act 296

Haw. Session Laws 1991, Act 316

Haw. Session Laws 1991, Act 317

Mont. Laws 1977, p. 1981

Mont. Laws 1979, p. 2001

Mont. Laws 1981, p. 1458

Mont. Laws 1983, p. 1783

Mont. Laws 1985, p. 1772

Mont. Laws 1987, p. 1896

Mont. Laws 1989, p. 2043

Mont. Laws 1991, p. 3223

N.M. Laws 1972, Ch. 98

N.M. Laws 1973, Ch. 403

N.M. Laws 1974, Special Session, Ch. 3

N.M. Laws 1975, Special Session, Ch. 17

N.M. Laws 1976, Special Session, Ch. 58

N.M. Laws 1977, Ch. 50

N.M. Laws 1978, Sp. Sess., Ch. 4

N.M. Laws 1979, Ch. 404

N.M. Laws 1980, Ch. 155

N.M. Laws 1981, Ch. 38

N.M. Laws 1982, Ch. 4

N.M. Laws 1983, Ch. 46

N.M. Laws 1984, Sp. Sess., Ch. 7

N.M. Laws 1985, Ch. 22

N.M. Laws 1986, Ch. 19

N.M. Laws 1986, Special Session, Ch. 2

N.M. Laws 1987, Ch. 355

N.M. Laws 1988, Ch. 13

N.M. Laws 1989, Ch. 107

N.M. Laws 1990, Ch. 131

N.M. Laws 1991, Ch. 10

Pa. 1931 App. 16, No. 15A

Pa. 1933 App. 169, No. 300A

Pa. 1935 App. 71, No. 77A

Pa. 1937 App. 74, No. 103A

Pa. 1939 App. 60, No. 69A

Pa. 1941 App. 13, No. 12A

Pa. 1943 App. 59, No. 77A

Pa. 1945 App. 63, No. 87A

Pa. 1947 App. 72, No. 94A

Pa. 1949 App. 62, No. 89A

Pa. 1951 App. 87, No. 134A

Pa. 1953 App. 54, No. 78A

Pa. 1959 App. 34, No. 38-A

Pa. 1961 App. 38, No. 5-A

Pa. 1963 App. 33, No. 45-A

Pa. 1964 App. 36, No. 50-A

Pa. 1967 App. 29, No. 31-A

Pa. 1968 App. Laws 55, No. 72-A

Pa. 1969 App. Laws 14, No. 12-A

Pa. 1971 Pamph. Laws 809, No. 3-A

Pa. 1971 Pamph. Laws 878, No. 27-A

Pa. 1972 Pamph. Laws 1849, No. 17-A

Pa. 1973 Pamph. Laws 489, No. 11-A

Pa. 1974 Pamph. Laws 1371, No. 21-A

Pa. 1975 Pamph. Laws 650, No. 8-A

Pa. 1976 Pamph. Laws 1331, No. 7-A

Pa. 1977 Pamph. Laws 411, No. 11-A

Pa. 1978 Pamph. Laws 1485, No. 16-A

Pa. 1979 Pamph. Laws 626, No. 9-A

Pa. 1980 Pamph. Laws 1391 No. 17-A

Pa. 1981 Pamph. Laws 628, No. 5-A

Pa. 1982 Pamph. Laws 1488, No. 2-A

Pa. 1983 Pamph. Laws, 422, No. 2A

Pa. 1984 Pamph. Laws 1360, No. 7-A

Pa. 1985 Pamph. Laws, 592, No. 5-A

Pa. 1986 Pamph. Laws, 1776, No. 5A

Pa. 1988 Pamph. Laws, No. 5A

Pa. 1990 Pamph. Laws, No. 7A

Pa. 1991 Pamph. Laws, No. 7A

Pa. 1991 Pamph. Laws, No. 9A

Pa. 1991 Pamph. Laws, 801, No. 3A

General Appropriation Act (First Supplement)
Pa. 1986 Pamph. Laws, 1754, No. 2A

General Appropriation Act (First Supplemental Appropriation Act)
Pa. 1988 Pamph. Laws, No. 55A
Tex. Laws 69th Leg. 1986, p. 95, Ch. 13, Arts. 1 et seq.

General Appropriation Act (Motor License Fund Supplement)
Pa. 1981 Pamph. Laws 621, No. 2-A
Vt. Acts 1969, No. 300
Vt. Acts 1971, No. 260
Vt. Acts 1973, No. 77

General Appropriation Act Supplement (Motor License Fund)
Pa. 1971 Pamph. Laws 805, No. 2A
Pa. 1976 Pamph. Laws 1378, No. 15-A

General Appropriation Act, 1951
Sept. 6, 1950, Ch. 896, 64 Stat. 595, 2 U.S. Code §§ 46b nt., 52, 65a; 3 U.S. Code § 201 nt.; 7 U.S. Code §§ 367, 414, 435; 12 U.S. Code §§ 362, 1020a-2, 1020c-1, 1023a, 1131a-1, 1749d; 15 U.S. Code §§ 283, 284, 327 nt., 329, 713a-10; 16 U.S. Code §§ 571a, 571b, 579, 590e-1; 21 U.S. Code § 129; 22 U.S. Code §§ 269a, 269b, 275, 276, 277, 278, 280b, 280i, 287e nts., 287f, 287r nt., 297a, 1382 nt.; 24 U.S. Code § 290; 29 U.S. Code § 49d nt.; 31 U.S. Code §§ 543 nt. 649a, 665, 686-1, 760 nt.; 33 U.S. Code §§ 574, 851, 872; 36 U.S. Code § 122; 41 U.S. Code §§ 6a nt. 6b, 219 nt.; 42 U.S. Code §§ 703a, 704a, 1431, 1576; 43 U.S. Code §§ 50, 377a; 46 U.S. Code § 1241 nt.; 48 U.S. Code §§ 1401f, 1423l; 49 U.S. Code § 305a, 50 U.S. Code §§ 157, 160; 50 U.S. Code Appx. 6b, 1738b, 2012a

General Appropriations Act
Fla. Stat. Ann., 216.053, 216.178
Ga. Laws 1995, p. 1082
Haw. Session Laws 1993, Act 289
Haw. Session Laws 1997, Act 328
Mont. Laws 1992 Spec. Sess., Ch. 13, § 1
Mont. Laws 1993, Ch. 623, § 1
Mont. Laws 1995, Ch. 593

Mont. Laws 1997, Ch. 551
N.M. Laws 1992, Ch. 94
N.M. Laws 1993, Ch. 365
N.M. Laws 1994, Ch. 6
N.M. Laws 1995, Ch. 30
N.M. Laws 1996, Ch. 12
Pa. 1992 Pamph. Laws, No. 8A

General Arbitration Act
N.J. Stat. Ann., 2A:24-1 et seq.
Tex. Rev. Civ. Stat., Art. 224 et seq.

General Assembly Act
Colo. Rev. Stat. 1963, 63-1-1 et seq.

General Assembly Appointing Authority Act
Ill. Rev. Stat. 1991, Ch. 85, § 40 et seq.

General Assembly Appointments Act
Ill. Rev. Stat. 1991, Ch. 63, §§ 160, 161

General Assembly Apportionment Act
Ga. Code Ann., 28-1-1 et seq.
Ill. Rev. Stat. 1991, Ch. 46, § 158-1 et seq.
N.C. Gen. Stat. 1943, §§ 120-1, 120-2
N.J. Stat. Ann., 54:4A-5
Tenn. Code Ann., 3-1-101 et seq.

General Assembly Combining Revisory Act (First 84th)
Ill. Laws 1986, P.A. 84-1308, § 3, Art. II

General Assembly Compensation Act
Ill. Rev. Stat. 1991, Ch. 63, § 13-9 et seq.

General Assembly Integrity Act
Ga. Code Ann., 21-5-74

General Assembly Operations Act
Ill. Rev. Stat. 1991, Ch. 63, § 23-01 et seq.

General Assembly Organization Act
Ill. Rev. Stat. 1991, Ch. 63, § 0-01 et seq.

General Assembly Retirement System Act
Ill. Rev. Stat. 1991, Ch. 108 1/2, § 2-101 et seq.

General Assembly Staff Assistants Act
Ill. Rev. Stat. 1991, Ch. 63, § 131-01 et seq.

General Assessment Act (Taxes)
Tenn. Code Ann. 1955, 9-201 et seq.

General Assignment Act
Ill. Rev. Stat. 1937, Ch. 10 3/4
Ill. Rev. Stat. 1991, Ch. 111

General Assignments for Benefit of Creditors Act
N.Y. Debtor and Creditor Law (Consol. Laws Ch. 12) § 2 et seq.

General Assistance Act
Minn. Stat. Ann., 245A.01 et seq.

General Assistance Article
Minn. Stat. Ann., 256D.01 et seq.

General Assistance Law (Poor Relief)
S.D. Codified Laws 1967, 28-13-1 et seq.

General Assistance Tax Act
Ill. Rev. Stat. 1991, Ch. 107, §§ 36-9, 36a

General Association Act
N.Y. Consol. Laws, Ch. 29
Pa. Cons. Stat., Unconsol. Stat., Title 15, § 20101 et seq.

General Attachment Act
Ark. Code Ann. 1987, 16-110-101 et seq.
Me. Rev. Stat. Ann. 1964, Title 14, § 4101 et seq.
S.C. Code Ann. 1976, § 15-19-10 et seq.

General Attempt Act (Crimes)
Ill. Rev. Stat. 1991, Ch. 38, § 8-4
Wis. Stat. Ann., 939.32

General Automobile Registration Law
Ark. Code Ann. 1987, 27-14-201 et seq.

General Aviation Revitalization Act of 1994
Aug. 17, 1994, P.L. 103-298, 49 U.S. Code § 40101 nt.
Nov. 20, 1997, P.L. 105-102, 49 U.S. Code § 40101 nt.

General Banking Act
Ill. Rev. Stat. 1991, Ch. 17

Ky. Rev. Stat. 1971, 287.010

General Bond Act (Counties or Road Districts)
S.C. Acts 1926, p. 1001, No. 559

General Bond Law
Kan. Stat. Ann., 10-101 et seq.

General Borough Act
Pa. Purdon's Stat., Title 53, § 45101 et seq.

General Bridge Act of 1946
Aug. 2, 1946, Ch. 753, 60 Stat. 847, 33 U.S. Code §§ 525, 525 nt., 526 to 533
May 25, 1948, Ch. 336, 62 Stat. 267, 33 U.S. Code § 529
Oct. 15, 1982, P.L. 97-322, 33 U.S. Code §§ 525, 533
Oct. 30, 1984, P.L. 98-557, 33 U.S. Code § 525
April 2, 1987, P.L. 100-17, 33 U.S. Code §§ 508, 526, 529

General Budget Joint Resolution
P.R. Acts 1986, J.R. No. 145

General Building Corporations Law
N.Y. Laws 1853, Ch. 117

General Business and Financial Tax Law (New York City)
N.Y.C. Adm. Code 1938, Ch. 46, § B46-1.0 et seq.

General Business Corporation Act
Ark. Code Ann. 1987, 4-26-101 et seq.
Ill. Rev. Stat. 1991, Ch. 32, § 1-01 et seq.

General Business Law
N.Y. Consol. Laws, Ch. 20

General Business Tax Act
Pa. Purdon's Stat., Title 24, § 584.1 et seq.

General Cemetery Act
Ind. Code Ann., 23-14-1-1 et seq.
Tenn. Code Ann., 46-1-101 et seq.
Vt. Stat. Ann., Title 18, § 5301 et seq.
Wash. Rev. Code Ann., 68.04.020 et seq.

General City Law
N.Y. Consol. Laws, Ch. 21

General Civil Service Act
N.J. Stat. Ann., 11A:2-1 et seq.

General Competency Act
Ariz. Rev. Stat. Ann., § 12-2201

General Competency Act (Witnesses)
Mont. Code Ann. 1947, 94-8801 et seq.

General Condemnation Act (Public Buildings)
N.J. Stat. Ann., 20:3-1 et seq.

General Condemnation Procedure Act
Ore. Rev. Stat. 1953, 35.205 et seq.

General Consolidated Public Utility System Improvement District Law
Ark. Code Ann. 1987, 14-217-101 et seq.

General Construction Act
N.Y. Consol. Laws, Ch. 22

General Construction Loan Act
Md. Laws 1960, Ch. 86

General Cooperative Associations Act
P.R. Laws Ann. 1954, Title 5, § 881 et seq.

General Corporation Act
Ala. Code 1975, § 10-1-1 et seq.
Ariz. Rev. Stat. Ann., § 10-002 et seq.
Cal. Corporations Code § 100 et seq.
Del. Code of 1974, Title 8, § 101 et seq.
Fla. Stat. Ann., 607.0101 et seq.
Haw. Rev. Stat. Ann., § 416-1 et seq.
Ind. Code Ann., 23-1-17-1 et seq.
Iowa Code Ann., 491.1 et seq.
Kan. Stat. Ann., 17-6001 et seq.
Md. Ann. Code 1974, Art. CA, § 1-101 et seq.
Mich. Comp. Laws Ann., 450.1101 et seq.
Neb. Rev. Stat. 1943, 21-2001 et seq.
N.J. Stat. Ann., 14A:1-1 et seq.
N.Y. Consol. Laws, Ch. 23
Ohio Rev. Code 1953, 1701.01 et seq.

Okla. Stat. Ann., Title 18, § 1001 et seq.
Ore. Rev. Stat., 56.005 et seq.
Pa. Cons. Stat., Title 15, § 1101 et seq.
P.R. Laws Ann. 1954, Title 14, § 1101 et seq.
R.I. Gen. Laws 1956, 7-1.1-1 et seq.
Tenn. Code Ann., 48-1-101 et seq.
Vt. Stat. Ann. 1959, Title 11, § 1 et seq.
W. Va. Code 1966, § 31-1-1 et seq.
Wyo. Stat. Ann., § 17-1-101 et seq.

General Corporation Fee Act
Ind. Code Ann., 23-1-18-3 et seq.

General Costs Act
Alaska Stat. 1962, § 09.60.010 et seq.

General County Airport and Landing Field Act
Ill. Rev. Stat. 1991, Ch. 15 1/2, § 68-90 et seq.

General County Assessment Law
Pa. Purdon's Stat., Title 72, § 5020-1 et seq.

General County Law
Pa. Purdon's Stat., Title 16, § 101 et seq.

General County Rural Highway System Act
Kan. Stat. Ann., 68-591 et seq.

General Court Districting Act
Mass. Gen. Laws Ann., 57:1 et seq.

General Debt Policy Law and Procedures Act (State)
La. Rev. Stat. Ann., 39:1361 et seq.

General District Law
N.Y. Laws 1926, Ch. 470
N.Y. Unconsolidated Law, § 5651 et seq.

General Dividend Act
Pa. 1913 Pamph. Laws 336, No. 222

General Drainage Act
Fla. Stat. Ann., 298.01 et seq.
N.Y. Environmental Conservation Laws (Consol. Laws, Ch. 43B) § 15-1903 et seq.

General Education Provisions Act

Jan. 2, 1968, P.L. 90-247, 20 U.S. Code §§ 1221, 1221 nt., 1222- 1226, 1231 to 1231f, 1232 to 1232e, 1233 to 1233g

April 13, 1970, P.L. 91-230, 84 Stat. 164, 20 U.S. Code §§ 241 to 243, 332a, 355c, 561, 581, 636, 642, 643, 752, 870, 880b-5, 883, 886, 1001 and others

June 23, 1972, P.L. 92-318, 20 U.S. Code §§ 1221, 1221a to 1221e, 1222 to 1226, 1227, 1231 to 1231f, 1232 to 1232e, 1233 to 1233g

Aug. 21, 1974, P.L. 93-380, 20 U.S. Code §§ 1221, 1221a to 1221c, 1221e to 1221e-3, 1223, 1225, 1226, 1226a to 1226d, 1227, 1228, 1230, 1231, 1231b-1, 1231b-2, 1231c to 1231f, 1232, 1232c, 1232f to 1232i, 1233b, 1233d, 1233f, 1233h

Dec. 31, 1974, P.L. 93-568, 20 U.S. Code § 1232g

Nov. 29, 1975, P.L. 94-142, 89 Stat. 796, 20 U.S. Code § 1232

April 21, 1976, P.L. 94-273, 20 U.S. Code §§ 1221e-1, 1225, 1232f

Oct. 12, 1976, P.L. 94-482, 20 U.S. Code §§ 1221, 1221c, 1221d, 1221e, 1221e-1, 1225 nt., 1230, 1231a, 1232, 1232-1, 1232c, 1232f, 1232i, 1233b

June 15, 1977, P.L. 94-482, 20 U.S. Code § 1233g

Sept. 24, 1977, P.L. 95-112, 20 U.S. Code § 1225

Nov. 1, 1978, P.L. 95-561, 20 U.S. Code §§ 1221e-1, 1221e-3, 1231c-1, 1225, 1226c, 1226d, 1231b-2, 1231c, 1232-1, 1232c et seq.

Aug. 6, 1979, P.L. 96-46, 20 U.S. Code §§ 1221-3, 1226, 1232

Aug. 13, 1979, P.L. 96-49, 20 U.S. Code §§ 1221d to 1221e

Oct. 3, 1980, P.L. 96-374, 20 U.S. Code §§ 1221e, 1221e-1b, 1221e-4, 1226a, 1226c, 1232

Oct. 19, 1980, P.L. 96-470, 20 U.S. Code §§ 1221c, 1226d

Dec. 11, 1980, P.L. 96-511, 20 U.S. Code § 1221-3

Aug. 13, 1981, P.L. 97-35, 20 U.S. Code § 1232

Oct. 19, 1984, P.L. 98-511, 20 U.S. Code §§ 1221e, 1221e-1, 1226c, 1232d, 1232e

Nov. 22, 1985, P.L. 99-159, 20 U.S. Code §§ 1221e-1b, 1221e-1c

June 3, 1987, P.L. 100-50, 20 U.S. Code §§ 1221e, 1221e-1

April 28, 1988, P.L. 100-297, 102 Stat. 331, 20 U.S. Code §§ 236 et seq., 236 nt. 1221e-1, 1232, 1234 et seq., 3306 et seq., 25 U.S. Code § 2642

Nov. 16, 1989, P.L. 101-589, 20 U.S. Code § 1221e-1

Nov. 8, 1990, P.L. 101-542, 20 U.S. Code § 1232g

July 23, 1992, P.L. 102-325, 20 U.S. Code §§ 1221e-1, 1232g

May 25, 1993, P.L. 103-33, 20 U.S. Code § 1221e, 1221e-1

March 31, 1994, P.L. 103-227, 20 U.S. Code §§ 1221e, 1221e-1, 1232h

May 18, 1994, P.L. 103-252, 20 U.S. Code § 1235 et seq.

Oct. 20, 1994, P.L. 103-382, 20 U.S. Code §§ 1221 et seq., 1226 et seq.

Nov. 2, 1994, P.L. 103-437, 20 U.S. Code §§ 1221e-1, 1221e-1a, 1232, 1233g, 1226c

April 26, 1996, P.L. 104-134, 20 U.S. Code § 1228b

Oct. 7, 1998, P.L. 105-244, 20 U.S. Code §§ 1228c, 1232g

Oct. 21, 1998, P.L. 105-277, 20 U.S. Code § 1232j

General Election Act

See Election Act

General Election Contest Act

Ind. Code Ann., 3-12-6-1 et seq., 3-12-10-1 et seq.

General Election Law

Ark. Code Ann. 1987, 7-1-101 et seq.

Ore. Rev. Stat. 1953, 246.012 et seq.

General Election Recount Law

Okla. Stat. Ann., Title 26, § 8-101 et seq.

General Emergency Succession Act

Neb. Rev. Stat. 1943, 84-1101 et seq.

General Enabling Act (Claims against Counties)

Mich. Comp. Laws Ann., 46.71 et seq.

General Escheat Act
Pa. Purdon's Stat., Title 72, § 1301.1 et seq.

General Excise Tax Act
Haw. Rev. Stat. Ann., § 237-1 et seq.

General Fee and Deposit Law
N.Y. Local Laws 1972, Village of
Lattingtown, p. 3561
N.Y. Local Laws 1972, Village of Old
Brookville, p. 3680

General Food Law
Pa. Purdon's Stat., Title 31, § 1 et seq.

General Foreclosure Act (Taxes)
Fla. Stat. 1967, 194.01 et seq.

General Fund Bond Sinking Fund Act
N.C. Gen. Stat. 1943, § 142-50 et seq.

General Fund Stabilization Act
Miss. Code Ann. 1972, § 27-103-77 et seq.

**General Funding and Improvement Bond
Act**
N.C. Public Laws 1933, Ch. 330

General Game and Fresh Water Fish Act
Fla. Stat. Ann., 372.001 et seq.

**General Government Matters Appropri-
ation Acts**
June 29, 1955, Ch. 226, 69 Stat. 192, 31 U.S.
Code § 638c; 36 U.S. Code §§ 121b, 122,
122a; 40 U.S. Code § 33a; 50 U.S. Code
Appx. § 2012a
June 13, 1956, Ch. 385, 70 Stat. 281, 31 U.S.
Code § 638c; 36 U.S. Code §§ 121b, 122,
122a; 40 U.S. Code § 33a
June 5, 1957, P.L. 85-48, 71 Stat. 49, 31 U.S.
Code §§ 638c, 665a; 36 U.S. Code §§ 121b,
122, 122a; 40 U.S. Code § 33a
June 25, 1958, P.L. 85-468, 72 Stat. 220, 31
U.S. Code § 638c; 36 U.S. Code §§ 121b,
122, 122a; 40 U.S. Code § 33a
July 8, 1959, P.L. 86-79, 73 Stat. 161, 31
U.S. Code §§ 200, 638c, 701; 36 U.S. Code
§§ 121b, 122, 122a; 40 U.S. Code § 33a

July 12, 1960, P.L. 86-642, 74 Stat. 473, 31
U.S. Code § 638c; 36 U.S. Code §§ 121b,
122, 122a; 40 U.S. Code § 33a

**General Government Matters, Department
of Commerce, and Related Agencies
Appropriation Act, 1962**
Aug. 3, 1961, P.L. 87-125, 75 Stat. 268, 15
U.S. Code §§ 278e nt., 633 nt.; 31 U.S.
Code § 638c; 33 U.S. Code § 851; 36 U.S.
Code §§ 121b, 122, 122a; 40 U.S. Code
§ 33a; 41 U.S. Code § 6b; 50 U.S. Code
Appx. § 1738b

General Gross Receipts Tax Act
Ga. Laws 1929, p. 103

General Guardianship Act
Tex. Probate Code, § 108 et seq.

General Herd Act (Running at Large)
N.D. Cent. Code, 36-11-01 et seq.

General Highway Act
See Highway Act

General Hospital Act
Minn. Stat. Ann., 261.21 et seq.

General Hospital Assistance Act (Public)
N.J. Stat. Ann., 30:9-12.29 et seq.

General Hospital Commission Act
D.C. Code Ann., § 32-201 et seq.

**General Hospital Commission Act
Amendments**
D.C. Code Ann., §§ 32-220, 32-243, 32-251

General Improvement and Assessment Act
Cal. Statutes 1901, Ch. 32, p. 27
Kan. Stat. Ann., 12-6a01 et seq.

General Improvement Distribution Act
Ark. Acts 1997, No. 1356

General Improvement District Law
Nev. Rev. Stat. 1979 Reprint, 318.010 et seq.

General Improvements Act
Haw. Session Laws 1971, Act 197
Haw. Session Laws 1972, Act 176

Haw. Session Laws 1977, First Special
Session, Act 9
Haw. Session Laws 1978, Act 244
Haw. Session Laws 1984, Act 287
Haw. Session Laws 1986, Act 347
Haw. Session Laws 1988, Act 314
Haw. Session Laws 1990, Act 300
Haw. Session Laws 1991, Act 317

General Income Tax Act
Tenn. Public Acts 1931, 2nd Ex. Sess., Ch. 21

General Incorporation Act
Ill. Rev. Stat. 1991, Ch. 32, § 1.01 et seq.

General Insolvent Law
Del. Code of 1974, Title 10, § 7301 et seq.

General Insurance Act
Ariz. Rev. Stat. Ann., § 20-101 et seq.
Miss. Code Ann. 1972, § 83-1-1 et seq.
N.J. Stat. Ann., 17:1-1 to 17:3-3, 17:17-1 to 17:47-13
Ore. Rev. Stat. 1953, 731.004

General Irrigation District Law
Cal. Water Code § 20500 et seq.

General Land Office Act
April 25, 1812, Ch. 68, 2 Stat. 716

General Law Village Act
Mich. Comp. Laws Ann., 74.1 et seq.

General Leasing Act
June 27, 1930, Ch. 642, 46 Stat. 822, 43 U.S. Code § 98a

General Legislative Procedures Act
D.C. Code Ann., § 1-230 et seq.

General License Law
D.C. Code Ann., § 47-2801 et seq.

General Lines Agent and Broker Law
Me. Rev. Stat. Ann. 1964, Title 24-A, § 1601 et seq.

General Lines Agents Law
Fla. Stat. Ann., 626.726 et seq.

General Local Government Code
Pa. Cons. Stat., Title 53, § 101 et seq.

General Manufacturing Corporation Act
N.Y. Laws 1811, Ch. 67
N.Y. Laws 1848, Ch. 40

General Medical Law
N.Y. Education Law 1971 (Consol. Laws, Ch. 16) § 6521 et seq.

General Medical Law (Profession)
N.Y. Education Law 1947 (Consol. Laws Ch. 16) § 6520

General Military Act
Fla. Stat. Ann., 250.01 et seq.

General Mill Act
Ill. Rev. Stat. 1939, Ch. 92, § 1 et seq.

General Municipal Corporations Act
Cal. Government Code §§ 34300 et seq., 35000 et seq.

General Municipal Election Act
Ala. Code 1975, 11-46-20 et seq.

General Municipal Employees' Retirement Law
Miss. Code Ann. 1972, § 21-29-1 et seq.

General Municipal Incorporation Act
Ill. Rev. Stat. 1991, Ch. 24, § 2-2-1 et seq.

General Municipal Law
N.Y. Consol. Laws, Ch. 24

General Municipal Plant Enabling Act
Vt. Stat. Ann. 1959, Title 30, § 2901 et seq.

General Noncontributory Pension Act
N.J. Stat. Ann., 43:8B-1 et seq.

General Nonprofit Corporation Act
See Nonprofit Corporation Act

General Obligation Bond Act
Cal. Government Code § 16720 et seq.
Ill. Rev. Stat. 1991, Ch. 127, § 651 et seq.

General Obligation Bond Act (Capital Projects)
N.M. Laws 1992, Ch. 103
N.M. Laws 1994, Ch. 142

General Obligation Bond Investment Act
Ill. Rev. Stat. 1991, Ch. 127, § 330 et seq.

General Obligation Bond Procedure Act
Conn. Gen. Stat. Ann., § 3-20

General Obligation Non-debt Bond Act
Pa. 1970 Pamph. Laws 145, No. 58

General Obligation Public Securities Refunding Act
Okla. Stat. Ann., Title 62, § 751 et seq.
S.D. Codified Laws 1967, 6-8A-1 et seq.
Wyo. Stat. Ann., § 16-5-101 et seq.

General Obligations Law
N.Y. Consol. Laws, Ch. 24A

General Park District Code
Ill. Rev. Stat. 1991, Ch. 105, § 1-1 et seq.

General Partnership Act
Utah Code Ann. 1953, 48-1-1 et seq.

General Pension Act
Fla. Stat. Ann., 291.02 et seq.

General Poor Relief Act
Pa. 1925 Pamph. Laws 762, No. 413

General Primary Election Act
Cal. Election Code 1976, § 6400 et seq.
Ill. Rev. Stat. 1985, Ch. 46, § 7-1 et seq.
Ky. Rev. Stat. 1971, 118.015
N.D. Cent. Code, 16.1-11-01 et seq.

General Prohibition Act
Ore. Rev. Stat. 1953, 471.405 et seq.

General Property Tax Act
Haw. Session Laws 1896, Act 51
Mich. Comp. Laws Ann., 211.1 et seq.

General Provisions
July 30, 1947, Ch. 388, 61 Stat. 633, 1 U.S. Code §§ 1 to 213
Sept. 23, 1950, Ch. 1001, 64 Stat. 979, 1 U.S. Code §§ 112, 112a
Oct. 31, 1951, Ch. 655, 65 Stat. 710, 1 U.S. Code §§ 106a, 106b, 112
Sept. 3, 1954, Ch. 1263, 68 Stat. 1226, 1 U.S. Code §§ 201, 209
July 8, 1966, P.L. 89-497, 80 Stat. 271, 1 U.S. Code § 113

General Public Assistance Act
N.J. Stat. Ann., 44:8-107 et seq.

General Public Assistance for Unemployables (G-U) Benefits Limitation Act
D.C. Code Ann., § 3-211

General Public Notice Act (Public Meetings)
Wash. Rev. Code 1989, 42.32.030

General Railroad Act
Haw. Rev. Stat. Ann., § 273-1 et seq.
N.J. Stat. Ann., 48:12-1 to 48:12-167

General Railroad Incorporation Act
Ill. Rev. Stat. 1991, Ch. 114, § 0.01 et seq.

General Recording Act (Real Property)
N.Y. Real Property Law (Consol. Laws Ch. 50) § 290 et seq.

General Refunding Act
Fla. Stat. Ann., 132.01 et seq.
Miss. Code Ann. 1972, § 31-15-1 et seq.

General Registration Act
Ill. Rev. Stat. 1941, Ch. 46, § 139 et seq.
P.R. Laws Ann. 1954, Title 16, § 391 et seq.

General Registration Act (Elections)
P.R. Laws Ann. 1954, Title 16 § 391 et seq.

General Reimbursement Act (Highways)
S.C. Acts 1926, p. 1001, No. 559

General Religious Society Act
N.J. Stat. Ann., 16:1-1 to 16:19-9

General Replevin Act
N.J. Stat. Ann., 2A:59-1 et seq.

General Reserve Fund Act
S.C. Const. Art. 3, § 36

General Reserve Fund Act (Port of New York Authority)
N.Y. Laws 1931, Ch. 48

General Retirement Act
Ariz. Rev. Stat. Ann., § 38-741 et seq.

General Revenue Act
Ala. Code 1975, 40-1-1 et seq.
Ill. Rev. Stat. 1991, Ch. 120, § 482 et seq.

General Revisory Act (First 1993)
Ill. Laws 1993, P.A. 88-45

General Revisory Act of 1980
Ill. Laws 1979, P.A. 81-1050, Art. 2
Ill. Laws 1980, P.A. 81-1509, Art. 3

General Riparian Act
N.J. Stat. Ann., 12:3-2 et seq.

General Road Act
Ill. Rev. Stat. 1991, Ch. 121, § 1-101 et seq.
Pa. Purdon's Stat., Title 36, § 1781 et seq.
Tenn. Code Ann., 54-10-101 et seq.

General Road Law (County)
Pa. 1911 Pamph. Laws 244

General Safety Act
Ore. Rev. Stat. 1953, 654.001 et seq.

General Safety Act (Employees)
Pa. Purdon's Stat., Title 43, § 25-1-et seq.

General Sales Tax Act
Ala. Code 1975, § 40-23-1 et seq.
Mich. Comp. Laws Ann., 205.51 et seq.

General Saving Act
Alaska Stat. 1962, § 01.10.100
Ill. Rev. Stat. 1991, Ch. 1, § 1103
La. Rev. Stat. Ann., 24:171

General Savings Bank Act
N.J. Stat. Ann., 17:9A-7 et seq.

General School Act
See School Act

General School Powers Act
Ind. Code Ann., 20-5-1-1 et seq.

General Seed Act
See Seed Act

General Services Administration Act
N.J. Stat. Ann., 52:18A-178 et seq.
P.R. Laws Ann. 1954, Title 3, § 931 et seq.

General Services Administration Act of 1984
N.J. Stat. Ann., 52:18A-178

General Services and State Purchasing Act
Tex. Government Code, § 2151.001 et seq.

General Services Department Act
N.M. Stat. Ann., 9-17-1 et seq.
Tenn. Public Acts 1972, Ch. 543

General Services Law
N.Y. Local Laws 1972, Town of Oyster Bay, p. 2480

General Sessions Court Act
Tenn. Code Ann., 16-15-101 et seq.

General Sessions Court Act (Davidson County)
Tenn. Private Acts 1937, Ch. 12

General Sessions Court Reform Act
Tenn. Public Acts 1993, Ch. 241

General Sewer Financing Act
Fla. Stat. 1971, 184.01 et seq.

General Solicitors Act
Ala. Code 1975, § 12-17-180 et seq.

General Stage Coach Corporation Law
N.Y. Transportation Corporations Law (Consol. Laws, Ch. 63) § 60 et seq.

General State Aid Continuing Appropriation Law
Ill. Comp. Stat. 1992, Ch. 105, § 235/15-5 et seq.

General State Authority Act
Pa. Purdon's Stat., Title 71, § 1707.1 et seq.

General Stock Act
Miss. Code Ann. 1972, § 69-13-1 et seq.
S.C. Code Ann. 1976, § 47-7-110 et seq.
W. Va. Code 1966, § 19-18-1 et seq.

General Stock Company Act (Insurance)
Ind. Code Ann., 27-1-6-1 et seq.

General Street Surface Railroad Law
N.Y. Railroad Law (Consol. Laws, Ch. 49) § 170 et seq.

General Survival of Tort Actions Act
D.C. Code Ann., § 12-101

General Taxing Acts
Ill. Rev. Stat. 1991, Ch. 120, § 499.1 et seq.
N.J. Stat. Ann., 54:4-1 to 54:8-16

General Township Act
Pa. Purdon's Stat., Title 53, § 54101 et seq.

General Travel Act
Okla. Stat. Ann., Title 74, § 500.1 et seq.

General Using Authorities Procurement of Architectural and Engineering Services Act
Md. Ann. Code 1974, Art. SF, § 13-101 et seq.

General Warrant Act
Ill. Rev. Stat. 1991, Ch. 146 1/2, § 0.01 et seq.

General Welfare Act
Ind. Code Ann., 12-1-1-1 et seq.

General Welfare Corporation Law
Tenn. Code Ann. 1955, 48-1101 et seq.

General Welfare Law (Municipal Corporations)
Ark. Code Ann. 1987, 14-54-105

Generation-Skipping and Estate Transfer Tax Act
Ill. Rev. Stat. 1991, Ch. 120, § 405A-1 et seq.

Generation Skipping Transfer Tax Act
Cal. Revenue and Taxation Code § 16700 et seq.
R.I. Gen. Laws 1956, 44-40-1 et seq.
Tenn. Code Ann., 67-8-601 et seq.

Generic Animal Drug and Patent Term Restoration Act
Nov. 16, 1988, P.L. 100-670, 21 U.S. Code § 301 nt.

Generic Drug Enforcement Act of 1992
May 13, 1992, P.L. 102-282, 21 U.S. Code § 301 nt.

Generic Drug Substitution Act
Utah Code Ann. 1953, 58-17-27 et seq.
Wyo. Stat. Ann., § 33-24-146 et seq.

Generic Drugs Act
N.M. Stat. Ann., 26-3-1 et seq.
N.Y. Education Law 1947 (Consol. Laws Ch. 16) §§ 6810, 6816a, 6826
N.Y. Public Health Laws 1953 (Consol. Laws Ch. 45) § 206

Generic Equivalent Drug Products Law
Miss. Code Ann. 1972, § 73-21-117

Genesee River Protection Act of 1989
Nov. 27, 1989, P.L. 101-175, 16 U.S. Code § 1276 nt.

Genesee-Rochester Regional Transportation Authority Act
N.Y. Public Authorities Law (Consol. Laws Ch. 43A) § 1299aa et seq.

Genesee Valley Regional Market Authority Act
N.Y. Public Authorities Law (Consol. Laws Ch. 43A) § 875 et seq.

Geneseo Subdivision Regulations
N.Y. Local Laws 1972, Village of Geneseo, p. 3305

Geneseo Zoning Law
N.Y. Local Laws 1972, Village of Geneseo, p. 3276

Genetic Counseling and Education and Newborn Screening Act
Colo. Rev. Stat. 25-4-1001 et seq.

Genetic Discrimination Act
Minn. Stat. 1986, 72A.139

Genetic Information Nondiscrimination in Health Insurance Act
Miss. Laws 1999, H.B. 347

Genetic Information Privacy Act
Ill. Comp. Stat. 1992, Ch. 410, § 513/1 et seq.
N.M. Stat. Ann., 24-21-1 to 24-21-7

Genetic Privacy Act
N.J. Laws 1996, Ch. 126, §§ 1 to 10

Genetic Testing to Determine Paternity Act
Okla. Stat. Ann., Title 10, § 501 et seq.

Genetically Engineered Organisms Release Act
Ill. Rev. Stat. 1991, Ch. 111 1/2, § 7600 et seq.

Genetically Engineered Plants Law
Minn. Stat. Ann., 18F.01 et seq.

Genetically Handicapped Person's Act
Neb. Rev. Stat. 1943, 68-1401 et seq.

Geneva City Charter
N.Y. Local Laws 1973, City of Geneva, p. 69

Geneva Freshwater Lands Protection Act
Fla. Stat. Ann., 373.4597

Genocide Convention Implementation Act of 1987 (the Proxmire Act)
Nov. 4, 1988, P.L. 100-606, 18 U.S. Code § 1091 nt.

Geo. L. Smith II Georgia World Congress Center Act
Ga. Code Ann., 10-9-1 et seq.

Geodetic and Coast Survey Act
Ill. Rev. Stat. 1991, Ch. 1, § 3500 et seq.

Geodetic Survey Monumentation Law
N.Y. Local Laws 1971, County of Monroe, p. 716
N.Y. Local Laws 1973, County of Saratoga, p. 1203

Geologic Hazard Zones Act (Alquist-Priolo)
Cal. Public Resources Code § 2621 et seq.

Geological Survey Act
Wyo. Stat. Ann., § 9-2-804 et seq.

Geologist Act
Cal. Business and Professions Code § 7800 et seq.

Geologist and Geophysicist Act
Cal. Business and Professions Code § 7800 et seq.

Geologist, Engineer and Land Surveyor Registration Law
Pa. 1992 Pamph. Laws, No. 151

Geologist Licensing Act (Professional)
Ala. Code 1975, § 34-41-1 et seq. Gift and Prizes Act
S.C. Code Ann. 1976, § 37-15-10 et seq.

Geologists and Soil Scientists Certification Act
Me. Rev. Stat. Ann. 1964, Title 32, § 4901 et seq.

Geologists Practice Act
Ark. Code Ann. 1987, 17-45-101 et seq.
Del. Code of 1974, Title 24, § 3601 et seq.
Ga. Code Ann., 43-19-1 et seq.
N.C. Gen. Stat. 1943, § 89E-1 et seq.
Wyo. Stat. Ann., § 33-41-101 et seq.

Geophysical Exploration Act
Mont. Code Ann., 82-1-101 et seq.

Geopressure and Geothermal Energy Research and Development Act
La. Rev. Stat. Ann., 30:681.1 et seq.

George Act (Police)
N.J. Stat. Ann., 40:174-202

George-Barden Act
See Vocational Education Act Of 1946

George Bill
Feb. 24, 1945, Ch. 4, 59 Stat. 5, 12 U.S. Code §§ 1801 to 1804

George Bush School of Government and Public Service Act
Oct. 19, 1996, P.L. 104-319, Title IV, 110 Stat. 3867

George-Deen Vocational Education Act
See Vocational Education Act Of 1936

George Miller, Jr., Education Act
Cal. Education Code 1976, § 51000 et seq.

George Montgomery Railroad Act
Mich. Comp. Laws Ann., 207.13

George-Murray Contract Settlement Act of 1944
See Contract Settlement Act Of 1944

George Rogers Clark National Historical Park Act
July 23, 1966, P.L. 89-517, 80 Stat. 325, 16 U.S. Code §§ 291 to 291b

George Washington Bridge Second Deck Act
N.J. Stat. Ann., 32:1-83.1

George Washington Commemorative Coin Act
Dec. 23, 1981, P.L. 97-104, 31 U.S. Code § 391 nt.

George Washington National Forest Mount Pleasant Scenic Area Act
Aug. 26, 1994, P.L. 103-314, 16 U.S. Code §§ 545, 545a, 545a nt.
April 4, 1996, P.L. 104-127, 16 U.S. Code §§ 545, 545 nt., 545a

Georgia M. Davis, Mae Street Kidd, H H Hughes McGill Civil Rights Act
Ky. Rev. Stat. 1971, 344.010 et seq.

Georgia Wilderness Act of 1984
Oct. 19, 1984, P.L. 98-514

Geothermal Act of 1970
Dec. 24, 1970, P.L. 91-581, 84 Stat. 1566, 30 U.S. Code §§ 1001 to 1025

Geothermal and Cable System Development Permitting Act
Haw. Rev. Stat. Ann., § 196D-1 et seq.

Geothermal and Geopressure Energy Research and Development Act
La. Rev. Stat. Ann., 30:681.1 et seq.

Geothermal Energy Act of 1980
June 30, 1980, P.L. 96-294, 30 U.S. Code § 1501 et seq., 1501 nt.

Geothermal Energy Research, Development, and Demonstration Act of 1974
Sept. 3, 1974, P.L. 93-410, 88 Stat. 1079, 30 U.S. Code §§ 1101, 1102, 1121 to 1126, 1141 to 1144, 1161 to 1164
Feb. 25, 1978, P.L. 95-238, 30 U.S. Code § 1121 et seq.
June 30, 1980, P.L. 96-294, 30 U.S. Code § 1141 et seq.
Oct. 28, 1992, P.L. 102-558, 30 U.S. Code § 1143
Nov. 2, 1994, P.L. 103-437, 30 U.S. Code § 1141

Geothermal Heat Suppliers Act
Colo. Rev. Stat. 40-40-101 et seq.

Geothermal Resource Conservation Act
N.M. Stat. Ann., 71-5-1 et seq.
Utah Code Ann. 1953, 73-22-1 et seq.
Va. Code 1950, § 45.1-179.1 et seq.

Geothermal Resources Act
Alaska Stat. 1962, § 38.05.181
Cal. Public Resources Code § 6901 et seq.
Colo. Rev. Stat. 37-90.5-101 et seq.
Ida. Code 1947, 42-4001 et seq.

Md. Ann. Code 1974, Art. NR, § 8-8A-01 et seq.

N.M. Stat. Ann., 19-13-1 et seq.

Tex. Natural Resources Code, § 141.001 et seq.

Wash. Rev. Code Ann., 79.76.010 et seq.

Geothermal Steam Act Amendments of 1988

Sept. 22, 1988, P.L. 100-443, 30 U.S. Code §§ 191, 226-3, 1001, 1001 nt., 1005, 1005 nt., 1017, 1019, 1026, 1026 nt., 1027

Geothermal Steam Act of 1970

Dec. 24, 1970, P.L. 91-581, 84 Stat. 1566, 30 U.S. Code §§ 1001 et seq.

Sept. 22, 1988, P.L. 100-443, 30 U.S. Code §§ 1001, 1005, 1017, 1019, 1026, 1027

Aug. 10, 1993, P.L. 103-66, 30 U.S. Code § 1019

GEPA

See General Education Provisions Act

Geran Act (Elections)

N.J. Laws 1911, p. 276

Gerhardt Law (Public Improvements under New York City Charter)

N.Y. Laws 1901, Ch. 466, § 247

N.Y. Laws 1911, Ch. 679

Geriatric Medicine Assistance Act

Ill. Rev. Stat. 1991, Ch. 144, §§ 2001, 2002

German School Educational Corporation Act

Ill. Rev. Stat. 1991, Ch. 32, §§ 199.90, 199a

Gerontological Committee Act (University of Illinois)

Ill. Rev. Stat. 1991, Ch. 144, § 54.01 et seq.

Gerry Act (Corrupt Practices)

Oct. 16, 1918, Ch. 187, 40 Stat. 1013

Get Statute (Removal of Barriers to Remarriage)

N.Y. Domestic Relations Law (Consol. Laws Ch. 14) § 253

Gettysburg Extension Act (Pennsylvania Turnpike)

Pa. Purdon's Stat., Title 36, § 667.1 et seq.

Ghost Candidates Law

S.C. Code Ann. 1976, § 7-11-50 et seq.

GI Bill Improvement Act of 1977

Nov. 23, 1977, P.L. 95-202, 38 U.S. Code §§ 101 nt., 1504 et seq.

Aug. 4, 1978, P.L. 95-336, 38 U.S. Code § 246

Aug. 6, 1991, P.L. 102-83, 38 U.S. Code § 106 nt.

G.I. Bill of Rights Act (Infants)

Ky. Rev. Stat. 1971, 384.090

Okla. Stat. Ann., Title 72 § 301 et seq.

Gibbens Amendment (Initiative Petitions)

N.D. Laws 1911, Ch. 89

N.D. Laws 1913, Ch. 98

Gibson-Waldie-Lanterman Act (Legislative Organization)

Cal. Government Code § 8900 et seq.

Gift Acceptance Act (Counties and Municipalities)

Cal. Government Code §§ 37354, 37355

Gift Act

Ariz. Rev. Stat. Ann., § 33-601

Pa. 1939 Pamph. Laws 141, No. 70

Tex. Bus. and Commerce Code, § 6.101 et seq.

Gift Act (Anotomical)

Me. Rev. Stat. Ann. 1964, Title 22, § 2901 et seq.

N.H. Rev. Stat. 1955, 291-A:1 et seq.

Wash. Rev. Code Ann., 68.50.340 et seq.

Gift Act (Corporations)

Md. Ann. Code 1974, Art. CA, § 2-103, Subd. 13

Gift Act (Personal Property)

W. Va. Code 1966, § 36-1-5

Gift and Contests Giveaway Act
Tex. Rev. Civ. Stat., Art. 5069-17.01

Gift and Estate Tax Act
P.R. Laws Ann. 1954, Title 13, § 5001 et seq.
Vt. Stat. Ann., Title 32, § 7401 et seq.

Gift Annuity Act (Charitable)
Neb. Rev. Stat. 1943, 59-1801 to 59-1803

Gift Ban Act (State)
Ill. Comp. Stat. 1992, Ch. 5, § 425/1 et seq.

Gift Enterprise Act
Iowa Code 1975, 553.15 et seq.
Mass. Gen. Laws Ann., 271:29
Md. Ann. Code 1957, Art. 27, § 369
Minn. Stat. 1961, 623.25

Gift Giveaway and Contests Act
Tex. Rev. Civ. Stat., Art. 5069-17.01

Gift of Life Act (Bobbie Green McDowell)
Ala. Code 1975, §§ 22-19-70 to 22-19-74

Gift of Life Organ and Tissue Procurement Act
S.C. Code Ann. 1976, §§ 12-6-5065,
44-13-1310 et seq.

Gift Tax Act
Cal. Revenue and Taxation Code § 15101 et seq.
Colo. Rev. Stat., 39-25-101 et seq.
La. Rev. Stat. Ann., 47:1201 et seq.
Minn. Stat. 1978, 292.01 et seq.
N.C. Gen. Stat. 1943, § 105-188 et seq.
Okla. Stat. Ann., Title 68, § 808 et seq.
Ore. Rev. Stat., 119.005 et seq.
P.R. Laws Ann. 1954, Title 13, §§ 881 et seq.
R.I. Gen. Laws 1956, 44-24-1 et seq.
S.C. Code Ann. 1976, § 12-17-10 et seq.
Tenn. Code Ann., 67-8-101 et seq.
Tenn. Code Ann. 1955, 67-2501 et seq.
Va. Code 1950, § 58-218.1 et seq.
Vt. Acts 1969, No. 269
Wash. Rev. Code 1981, 83.58.010 et seq.
Wis. Stat. Ann., 72.75 et seq.

Gift Tax Acts
June 2, 1924, Ch. 234, 43 Stat. 313
June 6, 1932, Ch. 209, 47 Stat. 245
May 10, 1934, Ch. 277, 48 Stat. 761
Aug. 30, 1935, Ch. 829, 49 Stat. 1014
May 28, 1938, Ch. 289, 52 Stat. 564

Gifted and Talented Children's Education Act of 1978
Nov. 1, 1978, P.L. 95-561, 20 U.S. Code § 3311 et seq.

Gifted and Talented Education Act
Miss. Code Ann. 1972, § 37-23-171 et seq.
Ore. Laws 1991, Ch. 337

Gifted and/or Academically Talented Education Act
Mich. Comp. Laws Ann., 388.1091 et seq.

Gifted Child Development Act
N.J. Laws 1979, Ch. 192

Gifts and Grants to Government Act
Ill. Rev. Stat. 1991, Ch. 127, § 168-80 et seq.

Gifts and Prizes Act
Va. Code 1950, § 59.1-415 et seq.
W. Va. Code 1966, § 46A-6D-1 et seq.

Gifts of Securities to Minors Act
Alaska Stat. 1962, § 45.60.010 et seq.
Cal. Civic Code § 1154 et seq.
Mich. Comp. Laws Ann., 554.451 et seq.
Ohio Rev. Code 1953, 1339.31 et seq.
S.C. Code Ann. 1976, Superseded Vols., § 35-3-30
Wis. Stat. Ann., 880.61 et seq.
Wyo. Stat. 1957, § 34-127 et seq.

Gifts to State for Charitable Use Act
Ill. Rev. Stat. 1991, Ch. 23, §§ 4000, 4001

Gila Bend Indian Reservation Land Replacement Act
Oct. 20, 1986, P.L. 99-503, 100 Stat. p. 1798

Gilbert-Brock Election Law
Ky. Stat. 1936, §§ 1468, 1472, 1481 et seq.

Gilbert E. Bursley School District Equalization Act
Mich. Comp. Laws Ann., 388.1101 et seq.

Gilbert-Gaines Act (Taxation)
Ky. Rev. Stat. 1971, 132.020

Gilbert-Wells Tobacco Control Act
Ky. Rev. Stat. 1971, 248.010, 248.280 et seq.

Gillen-Cramer Act (Habitual Criminals)
Ohio Rev. Code 1953, 2929.11 et seq.

Gillen-Roberts Act (State Insurance Fund)
Ohio Laws Vol. 114, p. 26

Gillen-Ward Act (Criminal Courts)
Ohio Rev. Code 1953, 2931.01 et seq.

Gillespie-Tillman Resolution (Transportation of Coal and Oil)
March 7, 1906, No. 8, 34 Stat. 823

Gillmore Act (Railroads)
Ohio Rev. Code 1953, 4907.02 et seq.

Gilmer-Aiken Act (School Administration)
Tex. Education Code, § 11.01 et seq.

Gilmer-Aiken Act (School Program)
Tex. Education Code, § 16.001 et seq.

Gilmer-Aiken Act (Teachers' Retirement)
Tex. Education Code, § 3.01 et seq.

Gilmer County Family Connection Commission Act
Ga. Laws 1999, H.B. 403

Gilmer County Water and Sewerage Authority Act
Ga. Laws 1984, p. 5215

Gin Act
Miss. Code Ann. 1972, § 75-41-1 et seq.

Gin Wedding Law
N.Y. Domestic Relations Law (Consol. Laws, Ch. 14) § 13 et seq.

Ginseng Act
Mich. Comp. Laws Ann., 290.751 et seq.

Ginseng Harvest Season Act
Tenn. Code Ann., 70-8-201 et seq.

Ginseng Harvesting Act
Ill. Rev. Stat. 1991, Ch. 61, § 500 et seq.

Ginseng Protection Act
Ga. Code Ann., 12-6-150 et seq.

Girls' and Boys' Homes Act
N.J. Stat. Ann., 30:4-156 et seq.

Girls' Term Court Act
N.Y. Laws 1951, Ch. 716

Girrbach-Goulette-Cloon Act (City Charter Amendments-Primaries)
Mich. Comp. Laws 1948, 117.21, 168.322

Giveaway Act (Contests and Gifts)
Tex. Rev. Civ. Stat., Art. 5069-17.01

Glacier Bay National Park Boundary Adjustment Act of 1998
Oct. 30, 1998, P.L. 105-317, 112 Stat. 3002, 16 U.S. Code § 410hh-1 nt.

Glacier National Park Act
Aug. 22, 1914, Ch. 264, 38 Stat. 699, 16 U.S. Code §§ 163, 168 to 177

Glasgow Vocational-Technical High School Construction Act
Del. Laws Vol. 59, p. 891, Ch. 259

Glaspie Act (Interurban Railroad Fare)
Mich. Comp. Laws Ann., 468.31 et seq.

Glass Bank Official Loan Act
April 25, 1938, Ch. 173, 52 Stat. 223, 12 U.S. Code § 375a

Glass Ceiling Act of 1991
Nov. 21, 1991, P.L. 102-166, 42 U.S. Code § 2000e nt.

Glass Federal Reserve Nt. Act
June 30, 1939, Ch. 256, 53 Stat. 991, 12 U.S. Code § 412

Glass Reserve Nt. Act
See Federal Reserve Act

Glass R.F.C. Recovery Loan Act
See Reconstruction Finance Corporation Act

Glass-Steagall Act, 1932
Feb. 27, 1932, Ch. 58, 47 Stat. 56, 12 U.S. Code §§ 347a, 347b, 412

Glass-Steagall Act, 1933
See Banking Act Of 1933

Glasscock-Burgess Act (Water Uses)
Tex. Water Code, § 11.021 et seq.

Glen Canyon National Recreation Area Act
Oct. 27, 1972, P.L. 92-593, 86 Stat. 1311, 16 U.S. Code §§ 460dd to 460dd-9

Glenn Cold Check Act
Ky. Rev. Stat. 1971, 514.040

Glenn Falls Center Authority Act
N.Y. Public Authorities Law (Consol. Laws Ch. 43A) § 1930 et seq.

Glens Falls City Court Act
N.Y. Laws 1961, Ch. 425

Glenview Naval Air Station Tax Exemption Act
Ill. Comp. Stat. 1992, Ch. 35, § 805/1
Ill. Rev. Stat. 1991, Ch. 1, §§ 3400, 3401

Glenville Fire Prevention Code
N.Y. Local Laws 1967, Town of Glenville, p. 1573

Global Change Research Act of 1990
Nov. 16, 1990, P.L. 101-606, 15 U.S. Code § 2921 et seq.

Global Climate Change Prevention Act of 1990
Nov. 28, 1990, P.L. 101-624, 7 U.S. Code §§ 6701 to 6710

Global Climate Protection Act of 1987
Dec. 22, 1987, P.L. 100-204, 15 U.S. Code § 2901 nt.
Dec. 17, 1993, P.L. 103-199, 15 U.S. Code § 2901 nt.

Global Environmental Protection Assistance Act of 1989
Dec. 19, 1989, P.L. 101-240, 22 U.S. Code § 2151 nt.

Global Export Network Act
N.J. Stat. Ann., 34:1B-62 et seq.

Glocester Non-partisan School Committee Act
R.I. Public Laws 1976, Ch. 101

Gloucester County Tunnel Law
N.J. Stat. Ann., 32:13A-1 to 32:13A-20

Gloucester Playgrounds Loan Act
Mass. Acts 1956, Ch. 627

Glouchester High School Grounds Loan Act
Mass. Acts 1953, Ch. 625

Glue Sniffing Act
N.C. Gen. Stat. 1943, § 90-113.8A et seq.
R.I. Gen. Laws 1956, 11-48-1 et seq.

Glynn County-Brunswick Charter Commission Act
Ga. Laws 1968, p. 2914

Goals 2000: Educate America Act
March 31, 1994, P.L. 103-227, 20 U.S. Code § 5801 nt.
Oct. 20, 1994, P.L. 103-382, 20 U.S. Code §§ 5802, 5824, 5845, 5861 to 5864, 5889, 5890, 5891, 5895, 5897
April 26, 1996, P.L. 104-134, 20 U.S. Code §§ 5801, 5802, 5821 to 5824, 5841 to 5851, prec. 5861, prec. 5871, 5871, 5884 to 5889, 5892, 5894 to 5897, 5900, 5933, 5934
Oct. 21, 1998, P.L. 105-277, 20 U.S. Code § 5951

Gober Municipal Utility District Act
Tex. General and Special Laws 1997, Ch. 756

Goebel Election Law

Ky. Acts 1898, Ch. 13

Goemaere-Anderson Wetland Protection Act

Mich. Comp. Laws Ann., 281.701 et seq.

Goff-May Act (Jefferson Davis Day)

Ky. Rev. Stat. 1971, 2.110

Going Act (Liquor Licenses)

Ark. Acts 1913, p. 180, No. 59

Going Out of Business Sales

N.Y. General Business Law (Consol. Laws Ch. 20) § 580 et seq. bfe Golden State Scholarshare Trust Act

Gold Bullion Coin Act of 1985

Dec. 17, 1985, P.L. 99-185, 31 U.S. Code §§ 5112, 5112 nt., 5113, 5116, 5118, 5132

Oct. 6, 1992, P.L. 102-390, 31 U.S. Code § 5112 nt.

Gold Clause Act

Aug. 27, 1935, Ch. 780, 49 Stat. 938, 31 U.S. Code §§ 773a to 773d

Gold Diggers Act

Mich. Comp. Laws Ann., 551.301 et seq.

Gold Hoarding Act

March 9, 1933, Ch. 1, 48 Stat. 1, 12 U.S. Code § 248

Gold Labeling Act of 1976

Oct. 1, 1976, P.L. 94-450, 15 U.S. Code §§ 294 et seq.

Gold Repeal Joint Resolution

June 5, 1933, Ch. 48, 48 Stat. 113, 31 U.S. Code §§ 462, 463, 821

Gold Reserve Act of 1934

Jan. 30, 1934, Ch. 6, 48 Stat. 337, 12 U.S. Code §§ 212, 411 to 415, 417, 467; 31 U.S. Code §§ 315b, 408a, 408b, 440 to 446, 733, 734, 752, 753, 754a, 754b and others

Jan. 23, 1937, Ch. 5, 50 Stat. 4, 31 U.S. Code §§ 821, 822a

June 30, 1941, Ch. 265, 55 Stat. 395, 31 U.S. Code §§ 821(b)(2), 822a(c)

April 29, 1943, Ch. 76, 57 Stat. 68, 31 U.S. Code § 822a

June 25, 1959, P.L. 86-70, 73 Stat. 147, 31 U.S. Code § 444

March 18, 1968, P.L. 90-269, 82 Stat. 50, 31 U.S. Code §§ 405b, 408a, 408b

Dec. 30, 1970, P.L. 91-599, 84 Stat. 1659, 31 U.S. Code § 822a

Oct. 28, 1977, P.L. 95-147, 31 U.S. Code § 822a

Nov. 8, 1978, P.L. 95-612, 31 U.S. Code § 822a

Gold Rush Parkway Authority Act

Cal. Streets and Highways Code § 30910 et seq.

Gold Standard Act

March 14, 1900, Ch. 41, 31 Stat. 45

Gold Star Mothers Act

Aug. 16, 1937, Ch. 659, 50 Stat. 660

Gold Star Mothers' Day Act

Ill. Rev. Stat. 1991, Ch. 1, § 3051-50

Goldberg Bill (Dual Jobs)

N.Y. Education Law 1947 (Consol. Laws Ch. 16) § 2573, Subd. 14

Golden Eagle Protection Act

See also Bald Eagle Protection Act

Oct. 24, 1962, P.L. 87-884, 76 Stat. 1246

Golden Empire Transit District Act

Cal. Public Utilities Code § 101000 et seq.

Golden Gate National Recreation Area Act

Oct. 27, 1972, P.L. 92-589, 86 Stat. 1299, 16 U.S. Code §§ 460bb to 460bb-5

Dec. 26, 1974, P.L. 93-544, 88 Stat. 1741, 16 U.S. Code §§ 460bb- 1

Golden Gate National Recreation Area Addition Act of 1992

June 9, 1992, P.L. 102-299, 16 U.S. Code §§ 460bb-1, 460bb-1 nt.

Golden Gimmick Act (Income Tax)
Colo. Rev. Stat., 39-22-303

Golden-Helton Act (Attendance of Witnesses)
Ky. Rev. Stat. 1971, 421.230 et seq.

Golden Meadow, Louisiana Redevelopment Agency Act
La. Acts 1968, No. 439

Golden Nematode Act
June 15, 1948, Ch. 471, 62 Stat. 442, 7 U.S. Code §§ 150 to 150g

Golden Nematode Act (Potato Disease)
N.Y. Laws 1947, Ch. 663

Goldwater-Nichols Department of Defense Reorganization Act of 1986
Oct. 1, 1986, P.L. 99-433, 10 U.S. Code §§ 111 et seq., 111 nt.
Oct. 31, 1986, P.L. 99-591, 10 U.S. Code §§ 133, 133a, 134, 135, 138
Nov. 14, 1986, P.L. 99-661, 10 U.S. Code §§ 133-135, 138
April 21, 1987, P.L. 100-26, 10 U.S. Code § 3033 nt.
Dec. 4, 1987, P.L. 100-180, 10 U.S. Code §§ 194 nt., 743, 2431- 2434
Sept. 29, 1988, P.L. 100-456, 102 Stat. 1971, 10 U.S. Code § 661 nt.
Nov. 29, 1989, P.L. 101-189, 10 U.S. Code § 11 nt.
Nov. 5, 1990, P.L. 101-510, 10 U.S. Code § 111 nt.

Golf Course Commission Act (Springbrook)
Ga. Laws 1999, H.B. 1021

Golf Course Loan Act (Dennis)
Mass. Acts 1963, Ch. 599

Golf Hall of Fame Act
Ga. Code Ann., 50-12-64 et seq.

Golf Hall of Fame Authority Act
Ga. Code Ann., 12-3-580 to 12-3-582

Gomez Clause (Public Officers-Salaries)
Fla. Stat. 1953, 111.01, Subsec. 4

Gonsalves-Deukmejian-Petris Senior Citizens Property Tax Assistance Law
Cal. Revenue and Taxation Code § 20501 et seq.

Gonsalves Milk Pooling Act
Cal. Food and Agricultural Code 1967, § 62700 et seq.

Good Behavior (Prison Sentences)
Ala. Code 1975, § 14-9-40 et seq.
Conn. Gen. Stat. Ann., § 18-7
Ind. Code Ann., 11-7-6.1-1 et seq.
Iowa Code 1983, 246.38, 246.39, 246.43
Ky. Rev. Stat. 1971, 197.045
La. Rev. Stat. Ann., 15:571.3 et seq.
Mass. Gen. Laws Ann., 127:129
Mich. Comp. Laws Ann., 800.33
Minn. Stat. Ann., 643.29
N.M. Stat. Ann. 1953, 42-1-54
Ore. Rev. Stat., 421.120
Pa. Purdon's Stat., Title 61, § 271 et seq.
R.I. Gen. Laws 1956, 42-56-24
S.C. Code Ann. 1976, § 24-13-210 et seq.
Tex. Rev. Civ. Stat., Art. 6181-1
Utah Code Ann. 1953, Miscellaneous Superseded Code Provisions, 77-62-10
Wash. Rev. Code Ann., 9.95.070
Wis. Stat. 1987, 53.11

Good Behavior Commutation Act
Pa. Purdon's Stat., Title 61, § 271 et seq.

Good Conduct Act (Prisoners)
Tex. Rev. Civ. Stat., Art. 6184-1

Good Driver Protection Act
N.J. Stat. Ann., 34:1B-21.1 et seq.

Good Faith Act
Del. Code of 1974, Title 6, § 8-406

Good Faith Donor and Donee Act
D.C. Code Ann., §§ 33-801, 33-802
Mont. Code Ann., 27-1-716
Tex. Civil Practice and Remedies Code, § 76.002 et seq.

Good Faith Improver of Property Law
Cal. Code of Civil Procedure § 871.1 et seq.

Good Government Financial Disclosure Act
Mich. Comp. Laws Ann., 15.421 et seq.

Good-McCormick Act (Budget)
See Budget and Accounting Act Of 1921

Good Road Districts Act
Ida. Code 1947, 40-1501 et seq.

Good Roads Act
July 11, 1916, Ch. 433, 39 Stat. 699
Conn. Gen. Stat. 1958, § 13-87
N.Y. Laws 1898, Ch. 115
Pa. 1905 Pamph. Laws 318, No. 220

Good Samaritan Act
Ala. Code 1975, § 6-5-332
Alaska Stat. 1962, § 09.65.090
Ariz. Rev. Stat. Ann., §§ 32-1471, 32-1472
Ark. Code Ann. 1987, 17-93-101
Cal. Business and Professions Code § 2144
Colo. Rev. Stat., 13-21-108, 13-21-108.5, 13-21-114
Conn. Gen. Stat. Ann., § 52-557b
Fla. Stat. Ann., 768.13
Ga. Code Ann., 51-1-29
Ill. Comp. Stat. 1992, Ch. 745, § 49/1 et seq.
Ill. Rev. Stat. 1985, Ch. 111, § 4404
Ind. Code Ann., 34-4-12-1, 34-4-12-2
Iowa Code Ann., 613.17
Kan. Stat. Ann., 65-2891
La. Rev. Stat. Ann., 37:1731 et seq.
Mass. Gen. Laws Ann., 112:12B
Md. Ann. Code 1957, Art. 27, § 12A
Md. Ann. Code 1974, Art. CJ, § 5-309 et seq.
Me. Rev. Stat. Ann. 1964, Title 14, § 164, Title 32, §§ 2594, 3151
Mich. Comp. Laws 1948, 691.1501
Miss. Code Ann. 1972, § 73-25-37
Mont. Code Ann., 27-1-714
N.D. Cent. Code, 32-03.1-01 et seq.
Neb. Rev. Stat. 1943, 25-1152
N.H. Rev. Stat. 1955, 329:25
N.J. Rev. Stat. 1937, 2A:62A-1, 2A:62A-2
N.M. Stat. Ann., 24-10-3

Ohio Rev. Code 1953, 2305.23
Okla. Stat. Ann., Title 59, § 518
Okla. Stat. Ann., Title 76, § 5
Pa. Cons. Stat., Title 42, § 8331 et seq.
R.I. Gen. Laws 1956, 5-37-14
S.C. Code Ann. 1976, § 15-1-310
S.D. Codified Laws 1967, 20-9-3, 20-9-4.2
Tenn. Code Ann., 63-6-218
Tex. Civil Practice and Remedies Code, § 74.001 et seq.
Utah Code Ann. 1953, 58-12-23
Va. Code 1950, § 54-276.9
Wis. Stat. Ann., 895.48
Wyo. Stat. Ann., § 33-26-143

Good Samaritan Act (Food Bank)
N.J. Stat. Ann., 24:4A-1 et seq.

Good Samaritan Act (Physicians)
Alaska Stat. 1962, § 08.64.365
Mass. Gen. Laws 1984, 112:12B
N.D. Cent. Code, 32-03.1-04 et seq.

Good Samaritan Act (Veterinary)
N.J. Stat. Ann., 45:16-9.10, 45:16-9.11

Good Samaritan Food Donation Act
Nov. 16, 1990, P.L. 101-610, 42 U.S. Code § 12672
Ill. Rev. Stat. 1991, Ch. 56 1/2, § 2001 et seq.
Wash. Rev. Code Ann., 69.80.031

Good Samaritan Hazardous Waste Cleanup Act
N.Y. Environmental Conservation Law 1972 (Consol. Laws Ch. 43B) § 27-1321
R.I. Gen. Laws 1956, 23-19.8-1 et seq.

Good Samaritan Law (Accident Involving Compressed Gas)
N.Y. Civil Rights Law (Consol. Laws Ch. 6) § 79k

Good Samaritan Law (Dentist)
N.Y. Education Law 1947 (Consol. Laws Ch. 16) § 6611, Subd. 6

Good Samaritan Law (Doctor)
N.Y. Education Law 1947 (Consol. Laws Ch. 16) § 6527, Subd. 2

Good Samaritan Law (Injury While Acting to Prevent a Crime)
N.Y. Executive Law 1951 (Consol. Laws Ch. 18) § 621, Subd. 7
N.Y. Executive Law 1991 (Consol. Laws Ch. 18) § 631, Subd. 5

Good Samaritan Law (Nurse)
N.Y. Education Law 1947 (Consol. Laws Ch. 16) § 6909, Subd. 1

Good Samaritan Law (Physical Therapist)
N.Y. Education Law 1947 (Consol. Laws Ch. 16) § 6737

Good Samaritan Law (Physician's Assistant)
N.Y. Education Law 1947 (Consol. Laws Ch. 16) § 6547

Good Samaritan Law (Podiatrist)
N.Y. Education Law 1947 (Consol. Laws Ch. 16) § 7006, Subd. 3

Good Samaritan Law (Public Transportation Employee Helping Victim of Crime)
N.Y. Transportation Law (Consol. Laws Ch. 61a) § 105a

Good Samaritan Law (Ski Patrol Member)
N.Y. Unconsolidated Law, § 7310

Good Samaritan Law (Universal)
N.Y. Public Health Law 1953 (Consol. Laws Ch. 45) § 3000a

Good Time Act (Prison Sentences)
Ala. Code. 1975, § 14-19-40 et seq.
Conn. Gen. Stat. Ann., §§ 18-7, 18-7a
Ind. Code 1976, 11-7-6.1-1 et seq.
Ky. Rev. Stat. 1971, 197.045
Mass. Gen. Laws Ann., 127:129
Mich. Comp. Laws Ann., 800.33
Minn. Stat. Ann., 643.29
N.M. Stat. Ann., 33-2-34
Ore. Rev. Stat., 421.120
R.I. Gen. Laws 1956, 42-56-24 et seq.
S.C. Code Ann. 1976, § 24-13-210 et seq.

Utah Code Ann. 1953, Miscellaneous Superseded Code Provisions, 77-62-10
Wis. Stat. 1987, 53.11

Good Time Act (State Farm Prisoners)
Ind. Code 1976, 11-7-5-1 et seq.

Goode Law (County Roads)
Ala. General Acts 1915, p. 573

Goodman-Stavisky Law (New York City Funding)
N.Y. Education Law 1947 (Consol. Laws Ch. 16) § 2576, Subd. 5

Goodrich Act (Sexual Psychopaths)
Mich. Comp. Laws 1948, 780.501 et seq.

Goods and Services Installment Sales Act
Pa. Purdon's Stat., Title 69, § 1101 et seq.

Goodwin-Roberts Act (Gasoline Tax)
Ohio Rev. Code 1953, 4501.04, 5735.23

Goodwyn Act (Sewage)
Ala. General Acts 1932, Ex. Sess., p. 254

Goodwyn Act (Waterworks)
Ala. General Acts 1932, Ex. Sess., p. 264

Gordon County-Calhoun Airport Authority Act
Ga. Laws 1971, p. 2861

Gordon County Emergency Communications Service District Act
Ga. Laws 1990, p. 4310

Gordon Rockwell, Thomas J. Anderson Environmental Protection Act
Mich. Comp. Laws Ann., 691.1201 et seq.

Gordonsville Charter
Va. Acts 1975, Ch. 346

Goshen Town Zoning Law
N.Y. Local Laws 1973, Town of Goshen, p. 1785

Gosnold Airport Assistance Loan Act (Dukes County)
Mass. Acts 1956, Ch. 716

Gould Amendment (Food and Drugs)
March 3, 1913, Ch. 117, 37 Stat. 732

Goulette-Cloon-Girrbach Act (City Charter Amendments-Primaries)
Mich. Comp. Laws 1948, 117.21, 168.322

Goulette-Heath-Carroll Act (Liquor Purchases by Minors)
Mich. Comp. Laws Ann., 436, 33b et seq.

Gourmet Restaurant Enjoyment Act of Tennessee (GREAT)
Tenn. Public Acts 1992, Ch. 675

Governance Parity Act (Corporate)
Cal. Corporations Code § 318

Government Accountability Act
Mont. Code Ann., 2-11-101 et seq.

Government Accountability and Reform Act
S.C. Code Ann. 1976, §§ 2-47-50 et seq., 8-1-15 et seq., 11-35-310

Government Accountability, Ethics and Campaign Reform Act
S.C. Code Ann. 1976, § 8-13-100 et seq.

Government Accounting Act
P.R. Laws Ann. 1954, Title 3, § 283 et seq.

Government Act
Alaska Comp. Laws Ann. 1949, §§ 1-1-1 et seq., 66-3-1
Cal. Stat. 1943, Ch. 134, p. 896
Pa. 1915 Pamph. Laws 661, No. 293

Government Act (County)
Nev. Rev. Stat. 1979 Reprint, 244.010 et seq.

Government Act (Emergency Seat of State)
Neb. Rev. Stat. 1943, 72-701.D1

Government Act (Local)
N.C. Gen. Stat. 1943, § 159-1 et seq.

Government Act (Municipal)
N.C. Gen. Stat. 1943, § 160A-1 et seq.
S.C. Code Ann. 1976, § 5-1-10 et seq.

Government Act (York County)
S.C. Code Ann. 1962, § 14-3601 et seq.

Government Administrative Procedure Act (Washington County)
Md. Ann. Code 1957, Art. § 237 et seq.

Government Agencies Reorganization Act
See Reorganization Act (Government Agencies)

Government-Aided Railroad and Telegraph Act
Aug. 7, 1888, Ch. 772, 25 Stat. 382, 47 U.S. Code §§ 9 to 15

Government Authorities Registration Act (Local)
Ga. Code Ann., 36-80-16

Government Center Loan Act
Mass. Acts 1960, Ch. 635

Government Comprehensive Merit Personnel Act
D.C. Code Ann., § 1-601.1 et seq.

Government Comprehensive Planning Act (Local)
Fla. Stat. Ann., 163.3161 et seq.

Government Comprehensive Planning Enabling Act (Local)
S.C. Code Ann. 1976, § 6-29-310 et seq.

Government Continuity Cause
Wash. Rev. Code Ann., 42.14.010 et seq.

Government Convention, Sports Facility, Meeting and Tourism Act (State and Local)
Mo. Laws 1991, S.B. Nos. 295, 312, §§ 21 to 31

Government Cooperation Act
Fla. Stat. Ann., 164.101 et seq.

Government Corporation Control Act
Dec. 6, 1945, Ch. 557, 59 Stat. 597, 31 U.S. Code §§ 841 to 869
Continued

July 30, 1947, Ch. 358, 61 Stat. 574, 31 U.S. Code § 849

Aug. 10, 1948, Ch. 832, 62 Stat. 1283, 31 U.S. Code § 846

June 30, 1949, Ch. 285, 63 Stat. 356, 31 U.S. Code § 846

Sept. 12, 1950, Ch. 946, 64 Stat. 832, 31 U.S. Code § 847

Sept. 26, 1950, Ch. 1049, 64 Stat. 1038, 31 U.S. Code § 846

May 13, 1954, Ch. 201, 68 Stat. 95, 31 U.S. Code § 846

July 26, 1956, Ch. 741, 70 Stat. 667, 31 U.S. Code §§ 846, 856, 867, 868

June 30, 1958, P.L. 85-477, 72 Stat. 272, 31 U.S. Code § 846

Oct. 4, 1961, P.L. 87-353, 75 Stat. 774, 31 U.S. Code § 846

Aug. 30, 1964, P.L. 88-518, 78 Stat. 698, 31 U.S. Code §§ 850, 851, 857, 858

May 25, 1967, P.L. 90-19, 81 Stat. 20, 31 U.S. Code § 846

Aug. 1, 1968, P.L. 90-448, 82 Stat. 544, 31 U.S. Code § 846

Dec. 30, 1969, P.L. 91-175, 83 Stat. 825, 31 U.S. Code § 846

May 7, 1971, P.L. 92-12, 85 Stat. 37, 31 U.S. Code §§ 856, 868

Oct. 27, 1972, P.L. 92-578, 86 Stat. 1274, 31 U.S. Code § 846

Aug. 20, 1978, P.L. 95-351, 31 U.S. Code §§ 856, 867, 868

Government Corporations Appropriation Acts

July 20, 1946, Ch. 589, 60 Stat. 586, 40 U.S. Code § 351; 42 U.S. Code §§ 1431, 1702 nt.

July 30, 1947, Ch. 358, 61 Stat. 574, 16 U.S. Code § 831h-2; 31 U.S. Code § 849; 40 U.S. Code §§ 1 nt., 33a, 129; 42 U.S. Code § 1431

June 30, 1948, Ch. 773, 62 Stat. 1183, 12 U.S. Code §§ 1020c-1 nt.; 40 U.S. Code § 33a; 42 U.S. Code § 1431

July 15, 1949, Ch. 338, 63 Stat. 440

Government Council Act

Ariz. Laws 1967, Ch. 109

Government Data Practices Act

Minn. Stat. Ann., 13.01 et seq.

Government Documents Act

Ga. Code Ann., 50-18-50 et seq.

Government Effectiveness Act (State)

Neb. Rev. Stat. 1943, 81-2701 et seq.

Government Electronics Payment Acceptance Act

N.J. Stat. Ann., 40A:5-43 et seq.

Government Employee Rights Act of 1991

Nov. 21, 1991, P.L. 102-166, 2 U.S. Code § 1201 et seq.

Jan. 23, 1995, P.L. 104-1, 2 U.S. Code §§ 1201, 1202, 1219, 1220

Oct. 26, 1996, P.L. 104-331, 2 U.S. Code § 1219

Government Employees' Compensation Act

See Workmen's Compensation Acts

Government Employees Deferred Compensation Plan Act

Fla. Stat. Ann., 112.215

Miss. Code Ann. 1972, § 25-14-1 et seq.

Tenn. Code Ann., 8-25-101 et seq.

Va. Code 1950, § 51-111.67:14 et seq.

Government Employees Incentive Awards Act

Sept. 1, 1954, Ch. 1208, 68 Stat. 1112 (See 5 U.S. Code §§ 1308, 3362, 4501 to 4506)

Aug. 18, 1959, P.L. 86-168, 73 Stat. 389 (See 5 U.S. Code §§ 3362, 4501)

Government Employees Interchange Act

Me. Rev. Stat. Ann. 1964, Title 5, § 3001 et seq.

N.C. Gen. Stat. 1943, § 126-51 et seq.

N.J. Stat. Ann., 52:14-6.10 et seq.

S.C. Code Ann. 1976, § 8-12-10 et seq.

Government Employees Retirement System Act

P.R. Laws Ann. 1954, Title 3, § 761 et seq.

Government Employees Salary Reform Act of 1964

Aug. 14, 1964, P.L. 88-426, 78 Stat. 400, 2 U.S. Code §§ 31, 60a nt., 60e-11, 60f nt., 61a, 61a-2, 61d, 61e, 72a, 84-2, 136a, 136a-1, 273a; 3 U.S. Code §§ 102 nt., 104, 105; See 5 U.S. Code §§ 5108, 5303, 5311 to 5317, 5332, 5333, 5363, 5364, 5504, 8331; 8 U.S. Code § 1104; 10 U.S. Code §§ 135 nt., 137, 867, 3012, 3013, 5031, 5033, 5034 nt., 8012, 8013; 11 U.S. Code § 68; 15 U.S. Code § 78d; 16 U.S. Code § 590h nt.; 21 U.S. Code § 113a; 22 U.S. Code §§ 287n, 866, 867, 870, 2124, 2384, 2503, 2562 to 2564, 2653; 23 U.S. Code § 303; 26 U.S. Code §§ 7443, 7801; 28 U.S. Code §§ 5, 44, 135, 173, 213, 252, 504 nt., 505 nt., 508, 603, 604 nt. 753 nt., 792; 31 U.S. Code §§ 42a, 51a; 35 U.S. Code § 3; 38 U.S. Code §§ 210, 4103, 4107; 40 U.S. Code §§ 162a, 166b, 166b-1, 661; 42 U.S. Code §§ 210 nt., 1861 nt., 2032, 2034, 2035, 2037, 2038, 2471 to 2473, 2474, 2502, 3502; 46 U.S. Code § 1111 nt.; 49 U.S. Code §§ 1321, 1341, 1342; 50 U.S. Code § 402 nt.; 50 U.S. Code Appx. §§ 1217, 2271 nt.

Oct. 6, 1964, P.L. 88-631, 78 Stat. 1008 (See 5 U.S. Code § 5363; 28 U.S. Code § 508 nt.)

Government Employees Tort Immunity Act

Ill. Rev. Stat. 1991, Ch. 85, § 1-101 et seq.

Government Employees Training Act

July 7, 1958, P.L. 85-507, 72 Stat. 327 (See 5 U.S. Code §§ 1308, 4001, 4101 to 4118; See 38 U.S. Code § 4113; 42 U.S. Code § 2201; 46 U.S. Code § 1111; See 49 U.S. Code §§ 1353, 1354, 1463; 50 U.S. Code §§ 403a nts., 403e to 403h, 403j)

May 26, 1959, P.L. 86-33, 73 Stat. 62 (See 5 U.S. Code § 4102)

Aug. 2, 1962, P.L. 87-566, 76 Stat. 264 (See 5 U.S. Code § 4102)

Government Employers' Liability Act

See Workmen's Compensation Acts
May 30, 1908, Ch. 236, 35 Stat. 556

Government Ethics Act

Cal. Government Code § 89500 et seq.

Ga. Code Ann., 21-5-1 et seq.
Ida. Code 1947, 59-701 et seq.
N.J. Stat. Ann., 40A:9-22.1 to 40A:9-22.25
P.R. Laws Ann. 1954, Title 3, § 1801 et seq.

Government Evaluation and Justification Act (State)

Me. Rev. Stat. Ann. 1964, Title 3, § 921 et seq.

Government Formation Act (Local)

Fla. Stat. Ann., 165.011 et seq.

Government Health Care Information Act

Mont. Code Ann., 50-16-601 et seq.

Government Health Facilities Act (Administration, Operation and Regulation of Contracting between Government and Private Interests)

P.R. Laws Ann. 1954, Title 24, § 338 et seq.

Government Immunity Act

Colo. Rev. Stat., 24-10-101 et seq.
Fla. Stat. Ann., 286.011
Utah Code Ann. 1953, 63-30-1 et seq.

Government in the Sunshine Act

Sept. 13, 1976, P.L. 94-409, 5 U.S. Code §§ 552b et seq.
Fla. Stat. Ann., 286.011

Government Infrastructure Commitment Act

Fla. Laws 1991, Ch. 239

Government Liability Act

N.Y. Court of Claims Act § 8

Government Losses in Shipment Act

July 8, 1937, Ch. 444, 50 Stat. 479, 31 U.S. Code §§ 528, 738a; 40 U.S. Code §§ 721 to 729, 721 nts.

Aug. 10, 1939, Ch. 665, 53 Stat. 1358, 31 U.S. Code §§ 528, 738a; 40 U.S. Code §§ 723 to 725, 729

Nov. 8, 1945, Ch. 453, 59 Stat. 574, 31 U.S. Code § 738a

Dec. 3, 1945, Ch. 515, 59 Stat. 592, 31 U.S. Code § 528

Continued

Aug. 12, 1970, P.L. 91-375, 84 Stat. 782, 40 U.S. Code §§ 723, 724

May 27, 1971, P.L. 92-19, 85 Stat. 74, 31 U.S. Code § 738a

Government Management Reform Act of 1994

Oct. 13, 1994, P.L. 103-356, 31 U.S. Code § 3301 nt.

Government Miscellaneous Expenditure Act (Local)

Neb. Rev. Stat. 1943, 13-2201 et seq.

Government of the County Act

S.C. Code Ann. 1976, § 4-9-10 et seq.

Government Omnibus Act (Local)

Cal. Statutes 1991, Ch. 1226

Government Organization and Employees

Sept. 6, 1966, P.L. 89-554, 80 Stat. 378, 5 U.S. Code §§ 101 to 8913

Oct. 8, 1966, P.L. 89-632, 80 Stat. 878, 5 U.S. Code § 5108

Oct. 15, 1966, P.L. 89-670, 80 Stat. 948, 5 U.S. Code §§ 101, 5312 to 5317

Nov. 2, 1966, P.L. 89-734, 80 Stat. 1163, 5 U.S. Code §§ 5315, 5316

Nov. 2, 1966, P.L. 89-737, 80 Stat. 1164, 5 U.S. Code §§ 8114, 8331, 8704

Nov. 2, 1966, P.L. 89-747, 80 Stat. 1179, 5 U.S. Code § 6305

Nov. 6, 1966, P.L. 89-779, 80 Stat. 1364, 5 U.S. Code §§ 5315, 5316

April 10, 1967, P.L. 90-9, 81 Stat. 12, 5 U.S. Code § 5316

June 5, 1967, P.L. 90-23, 81 Stat. 54, 5 U.S. Code § 552

July 28, 1967, P.L. 90-57, 81 Stat. 143, 5 U.S. Code § 5533

Sept. 11, 1967, P.L. 90-83, 81 Stat. 195, 5 U.S. Code §§ 500, 902, 903, 1104, 1305, 2101, 2107, 2108 and others

Oct. 11, 1967, P.L. 90-103, 81 Stat. 258, 5 U.S. Code § 5334

Oct. 11, 1967, P.L. 90-105, 81 Stat. 273, 5 U.S. Code §§ 3101 nt., 3304a

Dec. 16, 1967, P.L. 90-206, 81 Stat. 624, 5 U.S. Code §§ 3110, 4101, 5303, 5314 to 5316, 5332, 5345, 5533, 5542, 5544, 5545, 5733, 8339, 8704, 8707, 8708, 8714a

Dec. 23, 1967, P.L. 90-221, 81 Stat. 671, 5 U.S. Code § 6325

April 19, 1968, P.L. 90-291, 82 Stat. 98, 5 U.S. Code §§ 8191 to 8193

June 19, 1968, P.L. 90-351, 82 Stat. 205, 5 U.S. Code §§ 5315, 5316, 7313

June 28, 1968, P.L. 90-363, 82 Stat. 250, 5 U.S. Code § 6103

June 29, 1968, P.L. 90-367, 82 Stat. 277, 5 U.S. Code §§ 3502, 5334, 6312

July 18, 1968, P.L. 90-407, 82 Stat. 366, 5 U.S. Code §§ 5313, 5314, 5316

Aug. 1, 1968, P.L. 90-448, 82 Stat. 567, 5 U.S. Code § 5315

Aug. 13, 1968, P.L. 90-486, 82 Stat. 757, 5 U.S. Code §§ 2105, 8332, 8334, 8339

Aug. 17, 1968, P.L. 90-491, 82 Stat. 791, 5 U.S. Code § 3551

Oct. 10, 1968, P.L. 90-556, 82 Stat. 969, 5 U.S. Code §§ 5542, 5545

Oct. 12, 1968, P.L. 90-560, 82 Stat. 997, 5 U.S. Code § 5341

Oct. 17, 1968, P.L. 90-588, 82 Stat. 1151, 5 U.S. Code §§ 5519, 6323, 6326

Oct. 21, 1968, P.L. 90-610, 82 Stat. 1201, 5 U.S. Code § 5102

Oct. 21, 1968, P.L. 90-616, 82 Stat. 1212, 5 U.S. Code § 5584

Oct. 22, 1968, P.L. 90-623, 82 Stat. 1312, 5 U.S. Code §§ 559, 2108, 3102, 3502, 5314 to 5316. and others

March 27, 1969, P.L. 91-5, 83 Stat. 6, 5 U.S. Code § 905

June 30, 1969, P.L. 91-34, 83 Stat. 41, 5 U.S. Code §§ 5102, 5109, 5365

Oct. 20, 1969, P.L. 91-93, 83 Stat. 136, 5 U.S. Code §§ 1308, 8331, 8333, 8334, 8339 to 8341, 8348

Nov. 10, 1969, P.L. 91-114, 83 Stat. 190, 5 U.S. Code §§ 5702, 5703

Nov. 19, 1969, P.L. 91-121, 83 Stat. 207, 5 U.S. Code § 5315

Dec. 24, 1969, P.L. 91-164, 83 Stat. 446, 5 U.S. Code § 576

Dec. 30, 1969, P.L. 91-175, 83 Stat. 825, 5 U.S. Code §§ 3343, 3581, 3582, 5314 to 5316

Dec. 30, 1969, P.L. 91-177, 83 Stat. 831, 5 U.S. Code § 8322

Dec. 30, 1969, P.L. 91-187, 83 Stat. 850, 5 U.S. Code § 5108; 50 U.S. Code § 402 nt.

Dec. 30, 1969, P.L. 91-189, 83 Stat. 851, 5 U.S. Code § 1304

March 10, 1970, P.L. 91-206, 84 Stat. 51, 5 U.S. Code §§ 5108, 5315

April 15, 1970, P.L. 91-231, 84 Stat. 198, 5 U.S. Code § 5545

July 29, 1970, P.L. 91-358, 84 Stat. 591, 5 U.S. Code § 5102

Aug. 10, 1970, P.L. 91-373, 84 Stat. 701, 5 U.S. Code § 8524

Aug. 12, 1970, P.L. 91-375, 84 Stat. 775, 5 U.S. Code §§ 2104, 2105, 3104, 4301, 5102 to 5104, 5312, 5314 to 5316, 5541, 6301, 6323, 7101, 8344

Sept. 22, 1970, P.L. 91-405, 84 Stat. 852, 5 U.S. Code § 2106

Sept. 25, 1970, P.L. 91-418, 84 Stat. 869, 5 U.S. Code §§ 8701, 8901, 8906

Oct. 21, 1970, P.L. 91-477, 84 Stat. 1073, 5 U.S. Code § 5315

Oct. 21, 1970, P.L. 91-481, 84 Stat. 1081, 5 U.S. Code § 5709

Oct. 21, 1970, P.L. 91-496, 84 Stat. 1038, 5 U.S. Code § 5315

Oct. 26, 1970, P.L. 91-510, 84 Stat. 1191, 5 U.S. Code §§ 2107, 8332

Dec. 19, 1970, P.L. 91-563, 84 Stat. 1476, 5 U.S. Code §§ 5515, 5537, 5751, 6322

Dec. 29, 1970, P.L. 91-596, 84 Stat. 1604, 5 U.S. Code §§ 5108, 5314, 5315, 7902

Dec. 31, 1970, P.L. 91-611, 84 Stat. 1829, 5 U.S. Code § 5315

Jan. 2, 1971, P.L. 91-644, 84 Stat. 1887, 5 U.S. Code §§ 5108, 5313, 5314, 5315, 5316

Jan. 5, 1971, P.L. 91-648, 84 Stat. 1920, 5 U.S. Code §§ 3371 to 3376

Jan. 8, 1971, P.L. 91-656, 84 Stat. 1946, 5 U.S. Code §§ 5108, 5301, 5305 to 5308, 5942, 5947

Jan. 8, 1971, P.L. 91-658, 84 Stat. 1961, 5 U.S. Code §§ 8332, 8339, 8341, 8344

June 1, 1971, P.L. 92-22, 85 Stat. 76, 5 U.S. Code § 5315

Government Paperwork Elimination Act

Oct. 21, 1998, P.L. 105-277, Division C, Title XVII, 112 Stat. 2681, 44 U.S. Code § 3504 nt.

Government Parking Citation Enforcement Act (Local)

Ky. Rev. Stat. 1971, 82.600 et seq.

Government Partnership Act (State and Local)

Ga. Code Ann., 28-5-47 to 28-5-54

Government Performance and Account-ability Act

Fla. Laws 1994, Ch. 249

Government Performance and Results Act of 1993

Aug. 3, 1993, P.L. 103-62, 31 U.S. Code § 1101 nt.

Government Personnel Compensation Act

P.R. Laws Ann. 1954, Title 3, § 760 et seq.

Government Preference Procurement Policy Act

June 8, 1993, P.L. 103-40, 107 Stat. 112

P.R. Acts 1989, No. 42

Government Printing Office Electronic Information Access Enhancement Act of 1993

June 8, 1993, P.L. 103-40, 44 U.S. Code §§ 101 nt., prec. 4101, 4101 to 4104

Government Printing Office Inspector General Act of 1988

Oct. 18, 1988, P.L. 100-504, 102 Stat. 2530, 44 U.S. Code § 101 nt.

Government Property Transfer Act (Local)

Ill. Rev. Stat. 1991, Ch. 30, § 155h et seq.

Government Purveyors of Goods and Services Act (Down-Payment System)

P.R. Acts 1989, Second Session, No. 25

Government Quality Improvement Act (State)

Tenn. Public Acts 1992, Ch. 774

Government Records Access and Management Act
Utah Code Ann. 1953, 63-2-101 et seq.

Government Records Act (Local)
Me. Rev. Stat. Ann. 1964, Title 30-A, § 1701 et seq.
Tex. Local Government Code, § 201.001 et seq.

Government Records Law (Local)
Me. Rev. Stat. Ann. 1964, Title 30-A, § 1701 et seq.

Government Records Preservation Act
Kan. Stat. Ann., 45-401 et seq.

Government Relocation Act (Emergency)
Ill. Rev. Stat. 1991, Ch. 85, § 50 et seq.

Government Reorganization Act
See also Reorganization Act Of 1939
Fla. Stat. Ann., 20.02 et seq.
Haw. Rev. Stat. Ann., § 26-1 et seq.
Ky. Rev. Stat. 1971, 12.010 et seq.
Wyo. Stat. Ann., § 9-2-1701 et seq.

Government Reorganization Act (New York City)
N.Y. Laws 1870, Ch. 137

Government Revenue Bond Act (State and Local)
N.C. Gen. Stat. 1943, § 159-80 et seq.

Government Salary Withholding Act
Ill. Rev. Stat. 1991, Ch. 85, § 470 et seq.

Government Sale of Merchandise Act
N.C. Gen. Stat. 1943, § 66-58

Government Sales and Use Tax Act (Local)
Colo. Rev. Stat., 29-1-501 et seq.

Government Securities Act Amendments of 1993
Dec. 17, 1993, P.L. 103-202, 15 U.S. Code § 78a nt.

Government Securities Act of 1986
Oct. 28, 1986, P.L. 99-571, 15 U.S. Code § 78a nt.

Government Service Sharing and Combination Incentives Law (Local)
Minn. Stat. Ann., 465.80 et seq.

Government Surplus Airports and Equipment Act
Aug. 23, 1958, P.L. 85-726, 72 Stat. 807, 50 U.S. Code Appx. §§ 1622 to 1622c

Government Tort Liability Act
Cal. Government Code § 810 et seq.
Okla. Stat. Ann., Title 51, § 151 et seq.
Ore. Rev. Stat., 30.260 et seq.

Government Training Act (Local)
Ala. Code 1975, § 11-3-40 et seq.

Government Transportation Assistance Act (Local)
Fla. Stat. Ann., 335.20

Government Unit Debt Act (Local)
Pa. Cons. Stat., Title 53, § 8001 et seq.

Government Volunteer Act
Cal. Government Code § 3110 et seq.
S.C. Code Ann. 1976, § 8-25-10 et seq.

Government Volunteers Act
Cal. Government Code § 3110 et seq.

Governmental Account Audit Act
Ill. Rev. Stat. 1991, Ch. 85, § 700 et seq.

Governmental Accountability Act
Del. Code of 1974, Title 29, § 10501 et seq.

Governmental, Accountability, Audit and Internal Control Act
N.Y. Laws 1987, Ch. 814

Governmental Accountability, Audit and Internal Control Act (New York State)
N.Y. Executive Law 1951 (Consol. Laws Ch. 18) §§ 950 to 954
N.Y. Judiciary Law (Consol. Laws Ch. 30) §§ 211, 249 to 249c

N.Y. Legislative Law (Consol. Laws Ch. 32)
§§ 89 to 92

N.Y. Public Authorities Law (Consol. Laws
Ch. 43A) §§ 2930 to 2932

N.Y. Public Officers Law (Consol. Laws Ch.
47) §§ 87, 88

N.Y. State Finance Law 1940 (Consol. Laws
Ch. 56) §§ 2a, 8, 112

**Governmental Activities Act (Improper
Reporting of)**
Cal. Government Code § 8547 et seq.

**Governmental Agencies Liability Law
(Operation of Motor Vehicles)**
Cal. Vehicle Code 1959, § 17000 et seq.

Governmental Claims Act
Wyo. Stat. Ann., § 1-39-101 et seq.

Governmental Conduct Act
N.M. Stat. Ann., 10-16-2 et seq.

**Governmental Conflict of Interests and
Disclosure Act**
Cal. Government Code §§ 3600, 3601 et seq.

Governmental Cooperation Act
Fla. Stat. Ann., 164.101 et seq.

Governmental Dispute Resolution Act
Tex. Government Code, § 2008.001 et seq.

Governmental Efficiency Act
Fla. Laws 1992, Ch. 316

Governmental Entity Review Law
Tenn. Code Ann., 4-29-101 et seq.

Governmental Ethics Act
Ill. Rev. Stat. 1991, Ch. 127, § 601-101 et
seq.
W. Va. Code 1966, § 6B-1-1 et seq.

Governmental Ethics Act (State)
Kan. Stat. Ann., 46-215 et seq.

Governmental Ethics Code
La. Rev. Stat. Ann., 42:1101 et seq.

Governmental Facilities Authority Act
Me. Rev. Stat. Ann. 1964, Title 4, § 1601 et
seq.

Governmental Finance Modification Act
Okla. Laws 1999, H.B. 1008

Governmental Frauds Act
Va. Code 1950, § 18.2-498.1 et seq.

Governmental Immunity Act
Colo. Rev. Stat., 24-10-101 et seq.
Kan. Laws 1970, Ch. 200
Utah Code Ann. 1953, 63-30-1 et seq.

Governmental Joint Purchasing Act
Ill. Rev. Stat. 1991, Ch. 85, § 1600 et seq.

Governmental Leasing Act
Ala. Code 1975, § 41-16A-1 et seq.
Ky. Rev. Stat. 1971, 65.940 et seq.

**Governmental Motor Vehicle Tort Claims
Act**
S.C. Code Ann. 1976, § 15-77-210 et seq.

**Governmental Operations Accountability
Law (K-Goal)**
Kan. Stat. Ann., 74-7283 et seq.

**Governmental Reorganization and
Termination from Employment Act**
Ga. Code Ann., 45-24-1 et seq.

**Governmental Reorganization of the
Twentieth Legislature Act**
Alaska Laws 1951, Ch. 133

**Governmental Reorganization Procedures
Act**
D.C. Code Ann., § 1-299.1 et seq.

Governmental Services Payment Act
Ill. Rev. Stat. 1991, Ch. 102, § 36 et seq.

Governmental Tort Claims Act
Okla. Stat. Ann., Title 51, § 151 et seq.
Ore. Rev. Stat., 30.260 et seq.

Governmental Tort Claims and Insurance Reform Act
W. Va. Code 1966, § 29-12A-1 et seq.

Governmental Tort Liability Act
Tenn. Code Ann., 29-20-101 et seq.

Governmental Uneconomic Practices Act
Ill. Rev. Stat. 1991, Ch. 121 1/2, § 205.9 et seq.

Governmental Unit Deposit Protection Act
N.J. Stat. Ann., 17:9-41 et seq.

Governmental Units Immunity Act
Cal. Civil Code § 22.3

Governor Act
Wash. Rev. Code Ann., 43.06.010 et seq.

Governor Square Act
Mass. Acts 1925, Ch. 341

Governor Succession Act
Ill. Rev. Stat. 1991, Ch. 127, §§ 63b121.9, 63b122

Governor Transition Act
Ill. Rev. Stat. 1991, Ch. 127, §§ 63b120.9, 63b121

Governor's Advocacy Council on Children and Youth Act
N.C. Gen. Stat. 1943, § 143B-414 et seq.

Governors' and Legislative Service Pension Act
Utah Code Ann. 1953, 49-7-101 et seq.

Governors Annual Teacher Recognition Act
N.J. Stat. Ann., 18A:29A-1 et seq.

Governor's Appointment Proclamation (Alabama)
June 21, 1865, No. 43, 13 Stat. 767

Governor's Appointment Proclamation (Florida)
July 13, 1865, No. 47, 13 Stat. 771

Governor's Appointment Proclamation (Georgia)
June 17, 1865, No. 41, 13 Stat. 764

Governor's Appointment Proclamation (Mississippi)
June 13, 1865, No. 39, 13 Stat. 761

Governor's Appointment Proclamation (North Carolina)
May 29, 1865, No. 38, 13 Stat. 760

Governor's Appointment Proclamation (South Carolina)
June 30, 1865, No. 46, 13 Stat. 769

Governor's Appointment Proclamation (Texas)
June 17, 1865, No. 42, 13 Stat. 765

Governor's Bill Action Report Act
Ill. Rev. Stat. 1991, Ch. 63, § 330 et seq.

Governors Board Act
Ill. Rev. Stat. 1991, Ch. 144, § 1000 et seq.

Governor's Committee on Employment of the Handicapped Act
Iowa Code 1985, 601 F.1 et seq.
Okla. Stat. Ann., Title 74, § 9.29 et seq.

Governors Conference Act
Ill. Rev. Stat. 1991, Ch. 127, §§ 185.01, 185.1

Governor's Council on Employment of the Handicapped Act
N.C. Gen. Stat. 1943, § 143-283.1 et seq.

Governors Council on Health and Physical Fitness
Ill. Comp. Stat. 1992, Ch. 20, § 3950/1 et seq.

Governor's Emergency Fund Act
Neb. Laws 1949, Ch. 306

Governor's Justice Commission Act
R.I. Gen. Laws 1956, 42-26-1 et seq.

Governors Office of Voluntary Action Act
Ill. Rev. Stat. 1991, Ch. 127, § 3800 et seq.

Governor's Portraits Law
Cal. Government Code §§ 13072, 14623

Governor's Powers Act
Mont. Laws 1937, Ch. 5

Governors Scholars Board of Sponsors Act
Ill. Rev. Stat. 1991, Ch. 127, § 63b130 et seq.

Governor's Scholars Program Act
Ark. Code Ann. 1987, 6-82-301, 6-82-301

Governors State University Law
Ill. Comp. Stat. 1992, Ch. 110, § 670/15-1 et
seq.

**Governors State University Revenue Bond
Law**
Ill. Comp. Stat. 1992, Ch. 110, § 671/16-1 et
seq.

**Grace H. Kenyon Prostrate Cancer
Detection Act**
Cal. Business and Professions Code § 2248

**Grade "A" Condensed and Dry Milk
Products Act**
Neb. Laws 1973, L.B. 497

Grade "A" Milk Inspection Law
Iowa Code 1977, 192.1 et seq.

**Grade "A" Pasteurized Milk and Milk
Products Act**
Ark. Code Ann. 1987, 20-59-401 et seq.
Fla. Stat. Ann., 502.091, 502.191
Ill. Rev. Stat. 1991, 56 1/2, § 2201 et seq.
Okla. Stat. Ann., Title 63, § 1-1301.1 et seq.

Grade A Inspection Law
Iowa Code Ann., 192.101 et seq.

Grade A Milk and Milk Products Act
Mich. Comp. Laws Ann., 288.21 et seq.

Grade Crossing Act
Ind. Code Ann., 8-6-1-1 et seq.
N.J. Rev. Stat. 1937, 48:12-61 et seq.
Ohio Rev. Code 1953, 4957.01 et seq.

Grade Crossing Act (County Road)
Ohio Rev. Code 1953, 5561.01 et seq.

Grade Crossing Act (New Construction)
N.Y. Railroad Law (Consol. Laws Ch. 49)
§ 89 et seq.

Grade Crossing Act (Signals)
Va. Code 1950, § 56-414 et seq.

Grade Crossing Commission Act (Buffalo)
N.Y. Laws 1888, Ch. 345

Grade Crossing Elimination Act
Ga. Code Ann., 32-6-193 et seq.
Ky. Rev. Stat. 1971, Superseded Vol., 94.550
et seq.
N.Y. Transportation Law (Consol. Laws Ch.
61a) § 220 et seq.

Grade Crossing Elimination Act (Buffalo)
N.Y. Laws 1923, Ch. 231
N.Y. Laws 1928, Ch. 679

**Grade Crossing Elimination Act (City of
New York)**
N.Y. Laws 1928, Ch. 677

**Grade Crossing Elimination Act (Outside
Cities of New York, Buffalo, and
Syracuse)**
N.Y. Laws 1926, Ch. 233
N.Y. Laws 1928, Ch. 678

Grade Crossing Elimination Act (Syracuse)
N.Y. Laws 1926, Ch. 439

Grade District Separation Act
Cal. Streets and Highways Code § 8100 et
seq.

Grade Separation Act (Highways)
Mich. Comp. Laws Ann., 253.51 et seq.,
253.51 et seq.

Grade Separation Districts Act
Cal. Streets and Highways Code § 8100 et
seq.

Graded Egg Act
Neb. Rev. Stat. 1943, 2-3501 et seq.

Graded Milk Act
Neb. Rev. Stat. 1943, 81-229 et seq.

Graded School Act
Ky. Acts 1891-93, Ch. 260, § 100 et seq.

Grading Act (Apples)
Me. Rev. Stat. Ann. 1964, Title 7, § 531 et seq.

Grading Act (Swiss Cheese)
Wis. Laws 1933, Ch. 405

Grading Law for Milk Used for Manufacturing Purposes
Iowa Code Ann., 194.1 et seq.

Graduate Fellowship Act
N.M. Stat. Ann., 21-21G-1 et seq.

Graduate Public Health Training Act of 1964
Aug. 27, 1964, P.L. 88-497, 78 Stat. 613, 42 U.S. Code §§ 242d, 242g

Graduated Gross Sales Tax Law
Ky. Acts 1930, Ch. 149

Graduated Income Tax Law
Wash. Laws 1933, Ch. 5

Graduation Act of 1854 (Public Lands)
Aug. 4, 1854, Ch. 244, 10 Stat. 574

Grady Law (Retirement, Department of Finance Employees, New York City)
N.Y. Laws 1905, Ch. 583

Graft Law
Wash. Rev. Code Ann., 9A.68.010 et seq.

Grafton Snowmobile Local Law
N.Y. Local Laws 1971, Town of Grafton, p. 1833

Graham Act (Retirement)
Mass. Gen. Laws Ann., 32:1 et seq.

Grain and Storage Act
Kan. Stat. Ann., 34-101 et seq.

Grain and Warehouse Act
Minn. Stat. Ann., 232.20 et seq.

Grain Buyer Act
Minn. Stat. Ann., 223.15 et seq.
Neb. Rev. Stat. 1943, 75-901 et seq.

Grain Coloration Act
Ill. Rev. Stat. 1991, Ch. 5, § 210 et seq.
Mich. Comp. Laws Ann., 289.611 et seq.

Grain Dealers Act
Ala. Code 1975, 2-31-1 et seq.
Ill. Rev. Stat. 1991, Ch. 111, § 301.1 et seq.
Iowa Code Ann., 203.1 et seq.
Mich. Comp. Laws Ann., 285.61
Miss. Code Ann. 1972, § 75-45-301 et seq.
Neb. Rev. Stat. 1943, 75-901 et seq.

Grain Futures Act
See Commodity Exchange Act
Sept. 21, 1922, Ch. 369, 42 Stat. 998, 7 U.S. Code §§ 1 to 17

Grain Grading and Inspection Act
N.D. Laws 1917, Ch. 56
N.D. Laws 1919, Ch. 138
N.D. Laws 1923, p. 549

Grain Inspection Act
See United States Grain Standards Act
Ore. Rev. Stat., 586.570 et seq.
Wash. Rev. Code Ann., 22.09.011 et seq.

Grain Inspection Act (Warehouse)
Minn. Stat. Ann., 233.07

Grain Inspection, Weighing, Sampling, and Analysis Act
Minn. Stat. Ann., 17B.01 et seq.

Grain Insurance Act
Ill. Rev. Stat. 1991, Ch. 114, § 701 et seq.
Ky. Rev. Stat. 1971, 251.600 et seq.

Grain Marketing Compact Act
See also Interstate Compact on Agricultural Grain Marketing Act
Colo. Rev. Stat., 24-60-2001 et seq.

Kan. Stat. Ann., 2-3101

Grain Marketing Compact Act (Interstate)
S.D. Codified Laws 1967, 38-28-1

Grain Quality Improvement Act of 1986
Nov. 10, 1986, P.L. 99-641, 7 U.S. Code § 71 nt.
Mich. Comp. Laws Ann., 285.61 et seq.
Miss. Code Ann. 1972, § 75-45-301 et seq.

Grain Quality Incentives Act of 1990
Nov. 28, 1990, P.L. 101-624, 7 U.S. Code §§ 71 nt., 75b, 76 nt., 1593a, 1622a

Grain Quality Program Act
Ill. Rev. Stat. 1991, Ch. 5, § 2451 et seq.

Grain Sorghum Resources Act
Neb. Rev. Stat. 1943, 2-4001 et seq.

Grain Standards Act
See United States Grain Standards Act
Cal. Food and Agricultural Code 1967, § 52001 et seq.
Mont. Code Ann., 80-4-101 et seq.

Grain Standards, Warehouse, and Commodity Dealer Act (Agricultural)
Mont. Code Ann., 80-4-401 et seq.

Grain Storage Act
Ill. Rev. Stat. 1965, Ch. 114, § 293 et seq.
Kan. Stat. Ann., 34-101 et seq.
Minn. Stat. Ann., 232.20 et seq.
Mont. Code Ann., 80-4-201 et seq.
Nev. Rev. Stat. 1957, 103.010 et seq.
Okla. Stat. Ann., Title 2, § 9-41 et seq.
Ore. Rev. Stat., 587.010 et seq.

Grain Storage Warning Sign Act
Ill. Rev. Stat. 1991, Ch. 114, § 333.01 et seq.

Grain Warehouse Act
Cal. Food and Agricultural Code 1967, §§ 5501 et seq., 14006.6 et seq.
Ill. Rev. Stat. 1991, Ch. 114, § 214.1 et seq.
Kan. Stat. Ann., 34-223 et seq.
Ky. Rev. Stat. 1971, 251.010 et seq.
Minn. Stat. 1980, 232.01 et seq.

Miss. Code Ann. 1972, § 75-44-1 et seq.
Mo. Rev. Stat., 411.010 et seq.
Mont. Code Ann., 80-4-501 et seq.
Neb. Rev. Stat. 1943, 88-525 et seq.
S.D. Codified Laws 1967, 49-43-1 et seq.
Tex. Agriculture Code, § 14.001 et seq.
Wash. Rev. Code Ann., 22.09.011 et seq.

Grainger County Road Act
Tenn. Private Acts 1945, Ch. 476

Grainger School Bus Safety Act
Ala. Code 1975, § 16-27-1 et seq.

Grainger Water Pollution Act
Ala. Code 1975, § 22-22-1 et seq.

Grand Canyon National Park Enlargement Act
Nov. 2, 1994, P.L. 103-437, 16 U.S. Code § 228i

Grand Canyon Protection Act of 1992
Oct. 30, 1992, P.L. 102-575, 106 Stat. 4669

Grand Juror Qualification Act
Va. Code 1950, § 19.2-195

Grand Jury Act
Ariz. Rev. Stat. Ann., § 21-401 et seq.
Cal. Penal Code § 888 et seq.
Fla. Stat. Ann., 905.31 et seq.
Ill. Rev. Stat. 1991, Ch. 38, § 1701 et seq.
Mich. Comp. Laws Ann., 767.1 et seq.
Mont. Code Ann. 1987, 3-15-601 et seq.
N.J. Stat. Ann., 2A:73A-1 et seq.
N.M. Stat. Ann., 31-6-1 et seq.
P.R. Laws Ann. 1954, Title 34, § 521 et seq.
R.I. Gen. Laws 1956, 12-11-1 et seq.
Wash. Rev. Code Ann., 10.27.010 et seq.

Grand Jury Act (Multicounty)
Okla. Stat. Ann., Title 22, § 350 et seq.

Grand Jury Act (One-Man)
Mich. Comp. Laws Ann., 767.3 et seq.

Grand Jury Act (State)
Miss. Code Ann. 1972, § 13-7-1 et seq.
S.C. Code Ann. 1976, § 14-7-1600 et seq.

Grand Jury Investigation Act
Pa. Cons. Stat., Title, 42, § 4541

Grand Jury Training, Communication, and Efficiency Act
Cal. Penal Code §§ 914, 933, 933.05, 938.4

Grand Larceny Act
Ala. Code 1975, § 13A-8-3
Minn. Stat. Ann., 609.52

Grand Rapids Police Court Act
Mich. Comp. Laws Ann., 729.1 et seq.

Grand River Dam Authority Act
Okla. Stat. Ann., Title 82, § 861 et seq.

Grand Ronde Restoration Act
Nov. 22, 1983, P.L. 98-165, 25 U.S. Code §§ 713 et seq.

Grand Theft Law
Cal. Penal Code § 487 et seq.

Grand Water Act
Colo. Rev. Stat., 37-90-101 et seq.

Grandfather Clause (Elections)
N.C. Gen. Stat. 1943, § 163-28

Grandfather Clause (Motor Carriers)
Ky. Rev. Stat. 1971, 281.665
Miss. Code Ann. 1972, § 77-7-41
Neb. Laws 1937, Ch. 142, § 7(a)

Grandmothers Day Act
Ill. Rev. Stat. 1991, Ch. 1, § 3051-55

Grandparents as Foster Parents Program
Mo. Rev. Stat., 208.029

Grandparents Visitation Act
Me. Rev. Stat. Ann. 1964, Title 19, § 1001 et seq.
S.C. Code Ann. 1976, § 20-7-420 et seq.

Grandparents Visitation Privileges Act
Me. Rev. Stat. Ann. 1964, Title 19-A, § 1801 et seq.
N.M. Stat. Ann., 40-9-1 et seq.

Grandparents' Visitation Rights Act
Miss. Code Ann. 1972, § 93-16-1 et seq.
Tenn. Code Ann., 36-6-301

Grange Act
Mich. Comp. Laws Ann., 453.1 et seq.

Grange Power Law
Wash. Rev. Code Ann., 54.04.010 et seq.

Granger Act (Public Works Program)
Utah Code Ann. 1953, 55-3-1 et seq.

Granger-Thye Act
Oct. 21, 1998, P.L. 105-277, 16 U.S. Code § 580d

Granite City Depot Retrocession Act
Ill. Rev. Stat. 1991, Ch. 1, §§ 4601.9, 4602

Granite Watershed Enhancement and Protection Act of 1998
Oct. 26, 1998, P.L. 105-281, 112 Stat. 2695

Grant Act (Cooperative Secondary Facilities)
Minn. Stat. Ann., 124.491 et seq.

Grant Act (Desegregation Capital Improvement)
Minn. Stat. Ann., 124C.55 et seq.

Grant Act (Instructional Technology)
Fla. Stat. Ann., 229.603

Grant Act (Pollution Control and Sewage Treatment Plant)
Fla. Stat. Ann., 403.1821 et seq.

Grant Act (Student-to-Student)
Ill. Rev. Stat. 1991, Ch. 144, § 270 et seq.

Grant Act (Water Pollution Control and Sewage Treatment Plant)
Fla. Stat. Ann., 403.1821 et seq.

Grant and Contract Management Act
See Uniform Grant and Contrant Management Act

Grant and Loan Act (Tuition Assistance)
Va. Code 1950, § 23-38.11 et seq.

Grant and Scholarship Program (Mental Health Therapist)
Utah Code Ann. 1953, 62A-13-101 et seq.

Grant and Scholarship Program (Physicians and Physicians Assistants)
Utah Code Ann. 1953, 26-9-201 et seq.

Grant Consortium Act (Sea)
S.C. Code Ann. 1976, § 48-45-10 et seq.

Grant Funds Recovery Act
Ill. Rev. Stat. 1991, Ch. 127, § 2301 et seq.

Grant-in-Aid Act
Ala. Code 1958, Title 52, § 61 (17)

Grant-in-Aid Act (Bicentennial)
N.M. Stat. Ann., 11-5-1 et seq.

Grant-Kohrs Ranch National Historic Site Boundary Adjustment Act of 1998
Nov. 10, 1998, P.L. 105-365, 112 Stat. 3301, 16 U.S. Code § 461 nt.

Grant Park Act
Ill. Rev. Stat. 1991, Ch. 105, §§ 451.9, 452, 453

Grant Park Boundary Act
Ill. Rev. Stat. 1991, Ch. 105, § 800 et seq.

Grants and Gifts to Government Act
Ill. Rev. Stat. 1991, Ch. 127, § 168-80 et seq.

Grants for Education Act
Ga. Code Ann., 20-2-640 et seq.

Grants to Counties for Regional Jail Capital Expenditures Act
Ga. Code Ann., 42-4-120 et seq.

Grape and Wine Law
Tenn. Code Ann., 57-3-207

Grape Herbicides Act
Pa. Purdon's Stat., Title 3, § 214-51 et seq.

Grape Standards Act
Mich. Comp. Laws Ann., 290.141 et seq.

Grape/Wine Foundation Act
N.Y. Laws 1985, Ch. 80, § 1 et seq.

Grapefruit Advertising Act
Fla. Stat. Ann., 601.15

Grapefruit Offshore Export Indemnity Act
Fla. Stat. Ann., 601.1515

Grass Conservation Act
Mont. Code Ann., 76-16-101 et seq.

Grasshopper and Other Range Pest Control Act
N.M. Stat. Ann., 76-5-2 et seq.
Wyo. Sessions Law 1951, Ch. 120

Grasshopper Control Act
Neb. Rev. Stat. 1943, 2-1066 et seq.

Gratuities Law
Cal. Labor Code § 350 et seq.

Grave and Cemetery Restoration Act
Ill. Rev. Stat. 1991, Ch. 21, § 60.9 et seq.

Grave Protection Act
Ida. Code 1947, 27-501 et seq.

Grave Protection and Repatriation Act (Native American)
Utah Code Ann. 1953, 9-9-401 et seq.

Gravel and Sand Removal Act
Conn. Gen. Stat. Ann., § 22a-383 et seq.

Graves Act (Speed Limits)
N.Y. Vehicle and Traffic Law 1959, (Consol. Laws Ch. 71) § 1180

Graveyards Act (Public)
Ill. Rev. Stat. 1991, Ch. 21, § 12.9 et seq.

Gray-Percy Racing Act
N.Y. Laws 1895, Ch. 570

Grayson County Airport Authority Act
Tex. Laws 62nd Leg., 1971, p. 1087, Ch. 237

Grayson Water Quality Act
Ga. Laws 1991, p. 4195

Grazing Act
Alaska Stat. 1962, § 03.35.010 et seq.
Colo. Rev. Stat., 35-45-101 et seq.
Mont. Code Ann., 76-16-101 et seq.
Nev. Rev. Stat. 1979 Reprint, 568.010 et seq.
Okla. Stat. Ann., Title 69, § 281 et seq.
Ore. Code 1991, §§ 20-2101 to 20-111

Grazing Land Cooperation Law
Cal. Public Resources Code § 8551 et seq.

Great Basin National Park Act of 1986
Oct. 27, 1986, P.L. 99-565, 16 U.S. Code § 410mm nt.
April 26, 1996, P.L. 104-134, 16 U.S. Code § 410mm-1

Great Lakes Basin Compact
Ill. Rev. Stat. 1991, Ch. 127, § 192.01 et seq.
Ind. Code Ann., 13-5-3-1 et seq.
Mich. Comp. Laws Ann., 3.651 et seq.
Minn. Stat. Ann., 138.81 et seq.
Ohio Rev. Code 1953, 6161.01 et seq.
Pa. Purdon's Stat., Title 32, § 817.1 et seq.

Great Lakes Coastal Barrier Act of 1988
Nov. 23, 1988, P.L. 100-707, 16 U.S. Code § 3501 nt.

Great Lakes Conservation Act
Mich. Comp. Laws Ann., 323.51 et seq.

Great Lakes Critical Programs Act of 1990
Nov. 16, 1990, P.L. 101-596, 33 U.S. Code § 1251 nt.

Great Lakes Fish and Wildlife Restoration Act of 1990
Nov. 8, 1990, P.L. 101-537, 16 U.S. Code §§ 941 nt., 941, 941a- 941g
Nov. 29, 1990, P.L. 101-646, 16 U.S. Code §§ 941 et seq.
Oct. 19, 1998, P.L. 105-265, 112 Stat. 2358, 16 U.S. Code §§ 941, 941 nt., 941a to 941g

Great Lakes Fish and Wildlife Restoration Act of 1998
Oct. 19, 1998, P.L. 105-265, 112 Stat. 2358, 16 U.S. Code § 941 nt.

Great Lakes Fish and Wildlife Tissue Bank Act
Oct. 23, 1992, P.L. 102-440, 16 U.S. Code §§ 943, 943 nt., 943a, 943b, 943c

Great Lakes Fishery Act of 1956
June 4, 1956, Ch. 358, 70 Stat. 242, 16 U.S. Code §§ 931 to 939c
Nov. 14, 1986, P.L. 99-659, 16 U.S. Code § 932

Great Lakes Naval Station Tax Exemption Act
Ill. Comp. Stat. 1992, Ch. 35, § 810/1
Ill. Rev. Stat. 1991, Ch. 1, §§ 3450, 3451

Great Lakes Oil Pollution Research and Development Act
Nov. 8, 1990, P.L. 101-537, 33 U.S. Code § 2701 nt.
Nov. 29, 1990, P.L. 101-646, 33 U.S. Code § 2701 nt.

Great Lakes Pilotage Act of 1960
June 30, 1960, P.L. 86-555, 74 Stat. 259, 46 U.S. Code §§ 216 to 216i

Great Lakes Planning Assistance Act of 1988
Nov. 23, 1988, P.L. 100-707, 102 Stat. 4711

Great Lakes Preservation Act
Mich. Comp. Laws Ann., 323.71 et seq.

Great Lakes Protection Act
Mich. Comp. Laws Ann., 323.31 et seq.

Great Lakes Protection Fund Act
Pa. Purdon's Stat., Title 32, § 817.11

Great Lakes Protection Fund Authorization Act
Mich. Comp. Laws Ann., 3.671 et seq.

Great Lakes Shoreline Mapping Act of 1987
Dec. 29, 1987, P.L. 100-220, 33 U.S. Code § 883a nt.

Great Lakes Submerged Lands Act
Mich. Comp. Laws Ann., 322.701 et seq.

Great Neck North Water Authority Act
N.Y. Public Authorities Law (Consol. Laws Ch. 43A) § 1197a et seq.

Great Neck Plaza Housing Code
N.Y. Local Laws 1972, Village of Great Neck Plaza, p. 3396

Great Neck Water Authority Act
N.Y. Public Authority Law (Consol. Laws Ch. 43A), § 1250 et seq.

Great Outdoors Colorado Program
Colo. Rev. Stat., 33-60-101 et seq.

Great Park Authority Act
Ga. Code Ann., 12-3-390 et seq.
Ga. Laws 1980, p. 328

Great Ponds Act
Mass. Gen. Laws Ann., 91:1 et seq.

Great River Bridge Construction Compact (Arkansas-Mississippi)
Miss. Code Ann. 1972, § 65-25-121 et seq.

Great River Road Act
Ark. Code Ann. 1987, 27-69-102 et seq.
Iowa Code Ann., 308.1 et seq.
Minn. Stat. Ann., 161.1419 et seq.
Miss. Code Ann. 1972, § 55-5-1 et seq.
Mo. Rev. Stat., 226.280 et seq.
Wis. Stat. Ann., 84.105

Great Salt Lake Authority Act
Utah Code Ann. 1953, 65-8-1 et seq.

Great Salt Lake Development Authority Act
Utah Code Ann. 1953, 17A-2-1601 et seq.

Great Salt Lake Land Act
Utah Code Ann. 1953, 65-9-1 et seq.

Great Smoky Mountain National Park Act
Tenn. Public Acts 1927, Ch. 54

Greater Arizona Development Authority Act
Ariz. Rev. Stat. Ann., §§ 41-1554 et seq., 42-1341, 43-206

Greater Avenues for Independence Act
Cal. Welfare and Institutions Code § 11320 et seq.

Greater Bakersfield Metropolitan Transit District Act
Cal. Public Utilities Code § 101000 et seq.

Greater Baltimore Consolidated Wholesale Food Market Authority Act
Md. Ann. Code 1957, Art. 41, § 13-104 et seq.

Greater Knoxville Act
Tenn. Private Acts 1917, Ch. 97

Greater Mobile Act
Ala. General Acts 1956, 2nd Sp. Sess., p. 279

Greater Montgomery Act
Ala. Acts 1978, p. 358

Greater Municipality Parking Law
N.M. Stat. Ann., 3-51-1 et seq.

Greater Orlando Aviation Authority Act
Fla. Special Laws 1957, Ch. 57-1658, 1975, Ch. 75-464

Greater Orlando Port Authority Act
Fla. Special Laws 1957, Ch. 57-1658

Greater Troy Area Solid Waste Management Authority Act
N.Y. Public Authorities Law (Consol. Laws Ch. 43A), § 2052a et seq.

Greater Utica Area Water Purification Finance Authority Act
N.Y. Public Authorities Law (Consol. Laws Ch. 43A) § 1226 et seq.

Greathouse Moratorium Act (Real Estate Liens)
Tex. General Laws 43rd Leg., 1933, p. 225, Ch. 102

Greece Removal of Brush, Grass, Rubbish or Weeds and Spraying of Poisonous Shrubs or Weeds Law
N.Y. Local Laws 1971, Town of Greece, p. 1847

Greek and Turkish Assistance Acts
May 27, 1947, Ch. 81, 61 Stat. 103
April 3, 1948, Ch. 169, 62 Stat. 157

Greek Loan of 1929 Settlement Act
Nov. 5, 1966, P.L. 89-766, 80 Stat. 1314

Greek Orthodox Church Act
Ind. Burns' 1933, 25-4501 et seq.

Green Acres and Recreation Opportunities Bond Act
N.J. Laws 1974, Ch. 102

Green Acres Bond Act
N.J. Laws 1961, Ch. 46
N.J. Laws 1971, Ch. 165
N.J. Laws 1978, Ch. 118
N.J. Laws 1983, Ch. 354

Green Acres, Clean Water, Farmland and Historic Preservation Bond Act
N.J. Laws 1992, Ch. 88

Green Acres Cultural Center and Historic Preservations Bond Act
N.J. Laws 1991, Ch. 265

Green Acres, Farmland and Historic Preservation, and Blue Acres Bond Act
N.J. Laws 1995, Ch. 204

Green Acres Land Acquisition Act
N.J. Stat. Ann., 13:8A-19 et seq.
R.I. Gen. Laws 1956, 32-4-1 et seq.

Green Acres Land Acquisition and Recreation Opportunities Act
N.J. Stat. Ann., 13:8A-35 et seq.

Green Acres Law
Minn. Stat. Ann., 276.111

Green Acres Library Services Act
N.Y. Laws 1975, Ch. 593

Green Act (Highways)
Ohio Rev. Code 1953, 5541.01 et seq.

Green County Development Authority Act
Ga. Laws 1963, p. 3005

Green-Hansen Fire Safety Act
Cal. Health and Safety Code §§ 13143.2, 13143.5, 13146, 13869.7, 17958.5

Green, Hill, Areias, Farr California Residential Earthquake Recovery Act
Cal. Insurance Code § 5000 et seq.

Green Island Power Authority Act
N.Y. Public Authorities Law (Consol. Laws Ch. 43A) § 1020 et seq.

Green Light-Green Thumb Programs Act
Cal. Welfare and Institutions Code § 18310 et seq.

Greenbelt Act
Fla. Stat. Ann., 193.461, 193.501
Mont. Code Ann., 15-7-201 et seq.
Tenn. Code Ann., 67-5-1001

Greenbelt Act (Open Spaces)
Cal. Government Code § 6950 et seq.

Greene County Airport Authority Act
Ga. Laws 1978, p. 3223

Greene County Vacancies Filling Law
N.Y. Local Laws 1973, County of Greene, p. 1075

Greene-Harmer Motor Vehicle Damage Control Act
Cal. Vehicle Code 1959, §§ 34700, 34710, 34715, 34725

Greene-Hughes School Building Lease-Purchase Bond Law
Cal. Education Code 1976, §§ 17700, 17696 et seq.

Greene-Hughes School Facilities Act
Cal. Statutes 1986, Ch. 886

Greene-McAlister-Duffy Unemployment Benefit Pension Offset Refund Act
Cal. Statutes 1985, Ch. 1217, §§ 1, 7, 11, 16

Greene Refuse Disposal Law
N.Y. Local Laws 1972, Town of Greene, p. 1574

Greenfield Mobile Home Parks and Trailer Camps Local Law
N.Y. Local Laws 1972, Town of Greenfield, p. 1580

Greenfield New Senior High School Building Loan Act
Mass. Acts 1959, Ch. 359

Greenmail Act
Tenn. Code Ann., 48-35-501 et seq.

Greenport Demolition Law
N.Y. Local Laws 1972, Village of Greenport, p. 3424

Greens Creek Land Exchange Act of 1995
April 1, 1996, P.L. 104-123, 16 U.S. Code § 431 nt.

Greensboro Municipal-County Court Act
N.C. Laws 1949, Ch. 693
N.C. Public Laws 1909, Ch. 651

Greensboro Public School Code
N.C. Laws 1949, Ch. 385

Greensboro Zoning and Street Improvement Act
N.C. Private Laws 1921, Extra Session, Ch. 130

Greenstein Act (Mental Examinations of Defendants)
Pa. 1933 Pamph. Laws 224, No. 78

Greenville County Bond Act
S.C. Acts 1926, p. 1534, No. 782

Greenville County Comptroller Act
S.C. Acts 1930, p. 1244, No. 729

Greenway Act (Hudson River Valley)
N.Y. Laws 1991, Ch. 748

Greenways Act
R.I. Gen. Laws 1956, 42-125-1 et seq.

Greenways and Trails Act
Fla. Stat. Ann., 260.011 et seq.

Greenwood Lake Animal Control Law
N.Y. Local Laws 1972, Village of Greenwood Lake, p. 3436

Greenwood Lake Antilittering Law
N.Y. Local Laws 1972, Village of Greenwood Lake, p. 3430

Greenwood Lake Comprehensive Zoning Act
N.Y. Local Laws 1964, Village of Greenwood Lake, p. 912

Greenwood Lake Demolition Law
N.Y. Local Laws 1972, Village of Greenwood Lake, p. 3427

Greenwood Lake Elected Official Renumeration Law
N.Y. Local Laws 1973, Village of Greenwood Lake, p. 3396

Greenwood Lake Fire Prevention Code
N.Y. Local Laws 1964, Village of Greenwood Lake, p. 892

Greenwood Lake Health and Sanitation Law
N.Y. Local Laws 1972, Village of Greenwood Lake, p. 3431

Greenwood Lake Interim Zoning Act
N.Y. Local Laws 1964, Village of Greenwood Lake, p. 912

Greenwood Lake Nonpublication Local Act
N.Y. Local Laws 1964, Village of Greenwood Lake, p. 911

Greer Spring Acquisition and Protection Act of 1991
Dec. 11, 1991, P.L. 102-220, 16 U.S. Code § 539h nt.

Gregorio-Chappie Off-Highway Gas Tax Act
Cal. Statutes 1972, Chs. 1382, p. 2870; 1405, p. 2928

Grey Markets Merchandise Act (Warranty Disclosure)
N.Y. General Business Law (Consol. Laws Ch. 20) § 218aa

Greyhound Racing Law
Ark. Code Ann. 1987, 23-111-101 et seq.

Grievance Procedure Act (County and Municipal Employees)
S.C. Code Ann. 1976, § 8-17-110 et seq.

Grievance Procedure Act (State Employees)
S.C. Code Ann. 1976, § 8-17-310 et seq.

Griffin-Landrum Act
See Labor-Management Reporting and Disclosure Act Of 1959

Griffin Law (Intoxicating Liquors)
Tenn. Acts 1899, Ch. 221

Griffin Pensions Act
Ga. Laws 1941, p. 1474

Griffin-Spalding County Anti-Drug Commission Act
Ga. Laws 1988, p. 4053

Griffin-Spalding County Charter and Unification Commission Act
Ga. Laws 1995, p. 4429

Griffin-Spalding County Charter Commission Act
Ga. Laws 1991, p. 3802

Griffin-Spalding County Personal Care Health Board Act
Ga. Laws 1991, p. 4609

Griggs Bills (Taxation)
N.J. Stat. Ann., 54:19-1 to 54:29-7

Grinding, Buffing and Polishing Equipment Sanitation Act
Ill. Rev. Stat. 1937, Ch. 48, § 52.1 et seq.

Grisham-Davis Missing Children Act
Cal. Statutes 1986, Ch. 249

Griswold-Hughes Act (Health Districts)
Ohio Rev. Code 1953, 3709.01 et seq., 3709.05 et seq.

Griswoldville Water District Loan Act
Mass. Acts 1962, Ch. 470

Grogan-Harrison Act (Dividends)
Ky. Rev. Stat. 1971, 287.350

Gross Earnings Tax Act
Minn. Stat. Ann., 294.01 et seq.

Gross Income Tax Act
Del. Laws Vol. 47, p. 225, Ch. 147
Haw. Rev. Stat. Ann., § 235-1 et seq.
Ind. Code Ann., 6-2.1-1-1 et seq.
N.J. Stat. Ann., 54A:1-1 et seq.
S.D. Laws 1933, Ch. 184

Gross Income Tax Act (Adjusted)
Ind. Code Ann., 6-3-1-1 et seq.

Gross Premium Tax Act (Insurance Companies)
Cal. Revenue and Taxation Code § 12201 et seq.
Pa. 1951 Pamph. Laws 1799, No. 478
Pa. 1961 Pamph. Laws 33, No. 15

Gross Production Statute (Oil)
Ky. Rev. Stat. 1971, 137.120 et seq., 137.990

Gross Production Tax Act (Gas)
Tex. Tax Code, § 201.051 et seq.

Gross Production Tax Code (Minerals)
Okla. Stat. Ann., Title 68, § 1001 et seq.

Gross Receipts and Compensating Tax Act
N.M. Stat. Ann., 7-9-1 et seq.

Gross Receipts Franchise Tax Act
N.J. Stat. Ann., 54:30A-16 et seq.

Gross Receipts Road Tax Act
Va. Code 1950, § 58-638 et seq.

Gross Receipts Tax Act
Utah Code Ann. 1953, 59-17-1 et seq.

Gross Receipts Tax Act (County Correctional Facility)
N.M. Stat. Ann., 7-20F-1 et seq.

Gross Receipts Tax Act (County Environmental Services)
N.M. Stat. Ann., 7-20B-1 et seq.

Gross Receipts Tax Act (County Health Care)
N.M. Stat. Ann., 7-20D-1 et seq.

Gross Receipts Tax Act (County)
N.M. Stat. Ann., 7-20-1 et seq.

Gross Receipts Tax Act (General)
Ga. Laws 1929, p. 103
Md. Ann. Code 1957, Art. 24, § 9-202
Minn. Stat. Ann., 295.01 et seq.
Tex. Tax Code, § 182.001 et seq.

Gross Receipts Tax Act (Income)
Ind. Code Ann., 6-2-1-1 et seq.

Gross Receipts Tax Act (Interstate Telecommunications)
N.M. Stat. Ann., 7-9C-1 et seq.

Gross Receipts Tax Act (Leased Vehicle)
N.M. Stat. Ann., 7-14A-1 et seq.

Gross Receipts Tax Act (Local Hospital)
N.M. Stat. Ann., 7-20C-1 et seq.

Gross Receipts Tax Act (Medical)
Ark. Code 1987, 26-52-1101 et seq.

Gross Receipts Tax Act (Municipal Environmental Services)
N.M. Stat. Ann., 7-19B-1 et seq.

Gross Receipts Tax Act (Municipal Infrastructure)
N.M. Stat. Ann., 7-19C-1 et seq.

Gross Receipts Tax Act (Municipal)
N.M. Stat. Ann., 7-19-1 et seq.

Gross Receipts Tax Act (Petroleum Products)
N.J. Stat. Ann., 54:15B-1 et seq.

Gross Receipts Tax Act (Public Transportation)
Pa. Purdon's Stat., Title 72, § 8101 et seq.

Gross Receipts Tax Act (Public Utilities)
N.J. Rev. Stat. 1937, 54:30A-16 et seq.

Gross Receipts Tax Act (Retail Sales)
Ala. Code 1958, Title 51, § 752 et seq.
Ark. Code Ann. 1987, 26-52-101
Cal. Revenue and Taxation Code § 6051 et seq.
Ky. Acts 1934 (Ex. Sess.) Ch. 25
N.J. Stat. Ann., 54:11C-1 et seq.

Gross Receipts Tax Act (Special County Hospital)
N.M. Stat. Ann., 7-20-19 et seq.

Gross Receipts Tax Act (Special Municipal)
N.M. Stat. Ann., 7-19A-1 et seq.

Gross Receipts Tax Registration Act
N.M. Stat. Ann., 7-10-1 et seq.

Gross Sales and Income Tax Act
W. Va. Code 1966, § 11-13-1 et seq.

Gross Sales Tax Law
Ky. Acts 1930, Ch. 149

Ground Absorption Sewage Treatment and Disposal Act
N.C. Gen. Stat. 1943, § 130-166.62 et seq.

Ground and Surface Water Drainage Act
Md. Laws 1971, Ch. 344

Ground Hog Bounties Act
Ill. Rev. Stat. 1991, Ch. 8, § 120 et seq.

Ground Water Act
Ariz. Rev. Stat. Ann. 1956, §§ 45-101 et seq., 45-301 et seq.
Colo. Rev. Stat., 37-90-101 et seq.
Ida. Code 1947, 42-226 et seq.
Continued

Mont. Code Ann., 85-2-501 et seq.

Nev. Rev. Stat. 1979 Reprint, 534.010 et seq.

N.M. Stat. Ann., 72-12-1 et seq.

Okla. Stat. Ann., Title 82, § 1020.1 et seq.

Ore. Rev. Stat., 537.505

Va. Code 1950, § 62.1-44.83 et seq.

Wash. Rev. Code Ann., 90.44.020 et seq.

Ground Water and Wells Act

S.D. Codified Laws 1967, 46-6-1 et seq.

Ground Water Appropriation Act

Wyo. Stat. Ann., § 41-3-901 et seq.

Ground Water Assessment Act

Mont. Laws 1991, Ch. 769, §§ 1 to 7

Ground Water Basin Protection Act (Porter-Dolwig)

Cal. Water Code § 12920 et seq.

Ground Water Conservation Act

Ind. Code Ann., 13-2-2-1 et seq.

Neb. Rev. Stat. 1943, 46-614 et seq.

Ground Water District Act

Tex. Water Code § 52.001 et seq.

Ground Water Districts Act

Ida. Code 1947, 42-5201 et seq.

Ground Water Exploration and Protection Act

Kan. Stat. Ann., 82a-1201 et seq.

Ground Water Management Act

Ariz. Rev. Stat. Ann., § 45-401 et seq.

Colo. Rev. Stat., 37-90-101 et seq.

Ground Water Management and Protection Act

Neb. Rev. Stat. 1943, 46-656 et seq.

Ground Water Permit Act (Cities Villages and Municipal Corporation)

Neb. Rev. Stat. 1943, 46-638 et seq.

Ground-Water Protection Act

S.C. Code Ann. 1976, § 40-23-10 et seq.

Ground Water Quality Protection Act

Ida. Code 1947, 39-120 et seq.

Ground Water Recordation Act

Cal. Water Code § 4999 et seq.

Ground Water Transfers Permit Act (Municipal and Rural)

Neb. Rev. Stat. 1943, 46-638 et seq.

Ground Water Use Act

Ga. Code Ann., 12-5-90 et seq.

Haw. Rev. Stat. Ann., § 177-1 et seq.

S.C. Code Ann. 1976, § 49-5-10 et seq.

Groundwater and Freshwater Protection Act

Mich. Comp. Laws Ann., 286.851 et seq.

Groundwater Basin Act (Honey Lake Valley)

Cal. Statutes 1991, Ch. 1392

Groundwater Basin Act (Sierra Valley)

Cal. Water Code Appendix, § 119-101 et seq.

Groundwater Basin Act (Surprise Valley)

Cal. Statutes 1995, Ch. 698

Groundwater Basin Act (Willow Creek Valley)

Cal. Water Code Appendix, § 135-101 et seq.

Groundwater Management Agency Act (Ojai Basin)

Cal. Water Code Appendix § 131-101 et seq.

Groundwater Management District Act (Mono County Tri-Valley)

Cal. Statutes 1991, Ch. 844

Groundwater Protection Act

Ill. Rev. Stat. 1991, Ch. 111 1/2, § 7451 et seq.

Iowa Code Ann., 455E.1 et seq.

N.M. Stat. Ann., 74-6B-1 et seq.

R.I. Gen. Laws 1956, 46-13.1-1 et seq.

S.C. Code Ann. 1976, § 40-23-10 et seq.

W. Va. Code 1966, § 22-12-1 et seq.

Groundwater Protection Act (Agricultural Chemical)
Mont. Laws 1989, Ch. 668

Groundwater Recharge and Recovery Act
Utah Code Ann. 1953, 73-3b-101 et seq.

Groundwater Recharge Facilities Financing Act
Cal. Water Code § 12925 et seq.

Groundwater Use Act
S.C. Code Ann. 1976, § 49-5-10 et seq.

Group Benefits Act
N.M. Stat. Ann., 10-7B-1 et seq.

Group Benefits Act (Political Subdivision Employees)
See Uniform Group Benefits Act (Political Subdivision Employees)

Group Benefits Act (State Employees)
Colo. Rev. Stat., 24-50-601 et seq.

Group Credit Life Insurance Act
Tex. Insurance Code, Art. 3.50 et seq.

Group Disability Insurance Act
Wash. Rev. Code Ann., 48.21.010 et seq.

Group Disability Insurance Coordination of Benefits Act
Mich. Comp. Laws Ann., 550.251

Group-Funded Pool Act (Municipal)
Kan. Stat. Ann., 12-2616 et seq.

Group Health Coverage Reform Act (Small Employer)
N.C. Gen. Stat. 1943, § 58-50-100 et seq.
Tenn. Public Acts 1992, Ch. 808

Group Health Insurance Act (State Employees and Officials)
Colo. Rev. Stat., 10-8-201 et seq.

Group Health Insurance Act (State Employees)
Okla. Stat. Ann., Title 74, § 1301 et seq.
Wyo. Stat. Ann., § 9-3-202 et seq.

Group Health Insurance Program Act
Fla. Stat. Ann., 216.235 et seq.

Group Health Plan Act
Mich. Comp. Laws Ann., 550.1801 et seq.

Group Home for Handicapped Persons Act
La. Rev. Stat. Ann., 28:475 et seq.

Group Homes for Persons with Developmental Disabilities Act
Okla. Stat. Ann., Title 63, § 1-818.1 et seq.

Group Homes for Persons with Developmental or Physical Disabilities Act
Okla. Stat. Ann., Title 10, § 1430.1 et seq.

Group Hospital Service Act
Tex. Insurance Code, Art. 20.01 et seq.

Group Insurance Act
Iowa Code Ann., 509.1 et seq.

Group Insurance Act (Long-Term Care)
Cal. Government Code §§ 31696.1 to 31696.5

Group Insurance Act (Many Employees)
Mass. Gen. Laws Ann., 32B:1 et seq.

Group Insurance Act (Municipal Employees)
Mass. Gen. Laws Ann., 32B:1 et seq.

Group Insurance Act (Officers and Employees)
Minn. Stat. Ann., 471.61

Group Insurance Act (State Employees)
Colo. Rev. Stat., 10-8-201 et seq.
Ill. Rev. Stat. 1991, Ch. 127, § 521 et seq.
Mass. Gen. Laws Ann., 32A:1 et seq.
N.H. Rev. Stat. 1955, 21-I:26 et seq.

Group Insurance Board Authority Act (Atlanta)
Ga. Laws 1979, p. 4037

Group Insurance Program Act
Utah Code Ann. 1953, 49-8-101 et seq.

Group Libel Act
Ill. Rev. Stat. 1961, Ch. 38, § 471
Mass. Gen. Laws Ann., 272:98C

Group Life Insurance Law
Ark. Code Ann. 1987, 23-83-101 et seq.
Cal. Insurance Code § 10200 et seq.
Del. Code of 1974, Title 18, § 3101 et seq.
Fla. Stat. Ann., 627.551 et seq.
Ida. Code 1947, 41-2001 et seq.
Ky. Rev. Stat. 1971, 304.16-010 et seq.
Me. Rev. Stat. Ann. 1964, Title 24-A, § 2601 et seq.
N.C. Gen. Stat. 1943, § 58-58-135 et seq.
Neb. Rev. Stat. 1943, 44-1601 et seq.
Nev. Rev. Stat. 1979 Reprint, 688B.010 et seq.
N.M. Stat. Ann., 59A-21-1 et seq.
Ohio Rev. Code 1953, 3917.01 et seq.
Pa. Purdon's Stat., Title 40, § 532.1 et seq.
Vt. Stat. Ann., Title 8, § 3801 et seq.
Wash. Rev. Code Ann., 48.24.010 et seq.
Wyo. Stat. Ann., § 26-17-101 et seq.

Group Life Insurance Law (State Employees)
Pa. Purdon's Stat., Title 71, § 780.1 et seq.

Group or Blanket Disability Insurance Act
Ida. Code 1947, 41-2201 et seq.
Wyo. Stat. Ann., § 26-19-101 et seq.

Group or Blanket Health Insurance Law
Del. Code of 1974, Title 18, § 3501 et seq.
Ky. Rev. Stat. 1971, 304.18.010 et seq.
Me. Rev. Stat. Ann. 1964, Title 24-A, § 2801 et seq.
Nev. Rev. Stat. 1979 Reprint, 689B.010 et seq.

Group Residential Housing Act
Minn. Stat. Ann., 256I.01 to 256I.06

Group Self-Insurance Act
N.M. Stat. Ann., 52-6-1 et seq.

Groups, Organizations and Professional Employers Licensing Act
Mont. Code Ann. 39-8-101 et seq.

Grove Act (Quiet Title)
Ala. Code 1975, § 6-6-540 et seq.

Growen Act (Municipal Home Rules)
Ga. Code Ann., 36-35-1 et seq.

Growers Cost Guarantee Act
Fla. Laws 1935, Ch. 16862

Growing Media Act (Agricultural)
Ga. Code Ann., 2-12-100 et seq.

Growing Media Act (Horticultural)
N.H. Rev. Stat. 1955, 433-A:1 et seq.

Growth and Development Act
Ga. Code Ann., 12-5-41, 20-2-553, 32-10-4, 45-12-170

Growth Authority Act (Economic)
Mich. Comp. Laws Ann., 207.801 et seq.

Growth Management Act
Wash. Rev. Code Ann., 36.70A.010 et seq.

Growth Policies Agreement Act (Southern)
See Southern Growth Policies Act
Ala. Code 1975, 41-18-1 et seq.
Ark. Code Ann. 1987, 5-2-101
La. Rev. Stat. Ann., 49:61
Okla. Stat. Ann., Title 74, § 3501, 3502

Growth Policy Development Act
Mass. Acts 1975, Ch. 807

Growth through Agriculture Act
Mont. Laws 1987, Ch. 665, §§ 2 to 13

Grubstake Act
Alaska Stat. 1962, § 27.10.020, 27.15.10

Grubstake Contract Law (Recordation)
Cal. Public Resources Code § 2606

Grunsky-Burton Open Meeting Act
Cal. Government Code § 9027 et seq.

Grunsky-Davis Act
Cal. Water Code § 12880 et seq.

Grunsky-McBride Insurance Regulatory Act
Cal. Insurance Code §§ 754, 1850 et seq.

GSP Renewal Act of 1996
Aug. 20, 1996, P.L. 104-188, 19 U.S. Code
§ 2101 nt.

Guadalupe-Blanco River Authority Act
Tex. General and Special Laws 44th Leg.,
1935, 1st C.S., p. 1615, Ch. 410

Guadalupe Mountains National Park Act
Oct. 15, 1966, P.L. 89-667, 80 Stat. 920, 16
U.S. Code §§ 283 to 283e

**Guadalupe Valley Municipal Improvement
District Act**
Cal. Statutes 1959, Ch. 2037, p. 4703

Guam Development Fund Act of 1968
Oct. 17, 1968, P.L. 90-601, 82 Stat. 1172, 48
U.S. Code §§ 1428 to 1428e

Guam Elective Governor Act
Sept. 11, 1968, P.L. 90-497, 82 Stat. 842, 10
U.S. Code § 335; 48 U.S. Code §§ 1421a to
1421d, 1421f, 1422 to 1422d, 1423b,
1423h, 1423i

Guam Excess Lands Act
Oct. 6, 1994, P.L. 103-339, 108 Stat. 3116

Guam Organic Act Amendments of 1998
Oct. 27, 1998, P.L. 105-291, 112 Stat. 2785,
48 U.S. Code § 1421 nt.

Guarantee Act (Local Improvements)
Ida. Code 1947, 50-1762 et seq.

Guarantee Authority Act
Me. Rev. Stat. Ann. 1964, Title 10, § 701 et
seq.

**Guarantee Authority Revenue Obligation
Securities Act**
Me. Rev. Stat. Ann. 1964, Title 10, § 861 et
seq.

**Guarantee Fund Act (Community Facilities
Project)**
N.Y. Unconsolidated Law § 8721 et seq.

Guarantee Fund Act (Self-Insurers')
N.M. Stat. Ann., 52-8-1 et seq.

**Guarantee Fund of New York Act (Urban
Development)**
N.Y. Unconsolidated Law § 6341 et seq.

**Guaranteed Energy Cost Savings Contract
Act**
Mo. Laws 1997, S.B. No. 408

Guaranteed Energy Savings Act
Pa. Cons. Stat., Title 62, § 3751 et seq.

Guaranteed Loan Program
Iowa Code Ann., 261.35 et seq.

**Guaranteed Return Trip Demonstration
Project**
Cal. Government Code §§ 14170, 14925

Guaranteed Student Loan Act
W. Va. Acts 1968, Ch.54
W. Va. Code 1966, § 18-22D-1 et seq.

Guaranteed Student Loan Program Act
Iowa Code Ann., 261.35 et seq.

Guaranteed Work Force Program
W. Va. Code 1966, § 5B-2D-1 et seq.

Guaranty Act
Mont. Code Ann., 28-11-101 et seq.

Guaranty Act (Industrial Bank Savings)
Colo. Rev. Stat., 11-22-701 et seq.

Guaranty Act (Life Insurance)
N.M. Stat. Ann., 59A-42-1 et seq.

Guaranty Act (Savings and Loan)
Colo. Rev. Stat., 11-47.5-101 et seq.

**Guaranty Association Act (Casualty
Insurance)**
N.D. Cent. Code, 26.1-38.1-01 et seq.
Utah Code Ann. 1953, 31A-28-201 et seq.

**Guaranty Association Act (Health and Life
Insurance)**
Kan. Stat. Ann., 40-2901 et seq.
Continued

N.C. Gen. Stat. 1943, § 58-62-2 et seq.

Ohio Rev. Code 1953, 3956.01 et seq.

Guaranty Association Act (Insurance)

See Insurance Guaranty Association Act

Guaranty Association Act (Life, Accident, Health and Hospital Service Insurance)

Tex. Insurance Code, Art. 21.28-D0

Guaranty Association Act (Life and Disability)

Utah Code Ann. 1953, 31A-28-101 et seq.

Guaranty Association Act (Life and Health Insurance)

See Life and Health Insurance Guaranty Association Act

Minn. Stat. Ann., 61B.18 to 61B.32

N.H. Rev. Stat. 1955, 408:B-1 et seq.

Guaranty Association Act (Property and Casualty Insurance)

Ohio Rev. Code 1953, 3955.01 et seq.

Vt. Stat. Ann., Title 8, § 3611 et seq.

Guaranty Association Act (Self-Insurance Fund)

Fla. Stat. Ann., 631.90 et seq.

Guaranty Capital Savings and Loan Association Act

Wyo. Stat. Ann., § 13-6-101 et seq.

Guaranty Corporations Rehabilitation Law

N.J. Stat. Ann., 17:30C-1

Guaranty Fund Act

N.D. Laws 1917, Ch. 126

N.D. Laws 1923, Ch. 200

Guaranty Fund Act (Bank Deposits)

Neb. Laws 1909, Ch. 10, §§ 44-47

S.D. Laws 1915, Ch. 102, Art. 3

Tex. Rev. Civ. Stat. 1925, Arts. 437, 440 to 449

Guaranty Fund Act (Self-Insurers)

Mont. Laws 1989, Ch. 244

Guaranty Fund Act (Surplus Lines Insurance)

N.J. Stat. Ann., 17:22-6.70 et seq.

Guaranty Insurance Act (Financial)

Conn. Public Acts 1993, p. 292, No. 136

Guaranty Loan and Savings Associations Act

Ind. Code Ann., 28-7-6-1 et seq.

Guaranty Surplus and Special Reserve Funds Act (Fire Insurance Corporations)

Cal. Insurance Code § 3030 et seq.

Guard Act

Ill. Rev. Stat. 1991, Ch. 129, § 228h et seq.

Guard Act (Soldiers' Relief)

Ohio Rev. Code 1953, 5901.08

Guard Act (State Militia)

Ala. Code 1958, Title 35, § 203 et seq.

Cal. Military and Veterans Code § 210 et seq.

Del. Code of 1974, Title 20, § 301 et seq.

N.M. Stat. Ann., 20-10-1 et seq.

P.R. Laws Ann. 1954, Title 25, § 2201 et seq.

W. Va. Code 1966, § 15-4-1 et seq.

Guard Act (State)

Neb. Rev. Stat. 1943, 55-201 et seq.

Guard and Reserve Forces Facilities Authorization Act, 1976

Oct. 7, 1975, P.L. 94-107, 89 Stat. 568, 10 U.S. Code § 2233a

Guardian and Ward Act

Cal. Probate Code § 1400 et seq.

Haw. Rev. Stat. Ann., § 551-1 et seq.

Ill. Rev. Stat. 1991, Ch. 110 1/2, § 11-1 et seq.

Md. Ann. Code 1974, Art. ET, § 13-101 et seq.

Mich. Comp. Laws. 1970, 703.1 et seq.

N.H. Rev. Stat. 1955, 464-A:1 et seq.

N.J. Stat. Ann., 3B:12-12 et seq.

Ohio Rev. Code 1953, 2111.01 et seq.

R.I. Gen. Laws 1956, 33-15-1 et seq.

Vt. Stat. Ann., Title 14, § 2601 et seq.

Guardian or Conservator, Act for Obtaining
Kan. Stat. Ann., 59-3001 et seq.

Guardianship Act
Fla. Stat. Ann., 744.101 et seq.
Ga. Code Ann., 29-4-1 et seq.
Mo. Rev. Stat., 475.010 et seq.
Mont. Code Ann., 72-5-101 et seq.
Okla. Stat. Ann., Title 30, § 1-101 et seq.
Ore. Rev. Stat. 1953, 126.003 et seq.
Tenn. Code Ann., 34-1-101 et seq.
Tex. Probate Code, § 108 et seq.
Utah Code Ann. 1953, 75-5-301 et seq.
Wash. Rev. Code Ann., 11.88.005 et seq.

Guardianship Act (Joint)
Conn. Gen. Stat. Ann., § 45a-606

Guardianship Act (Keterans)
Vt. Stat. Ann., Title 14, § 1301 et seq.

Guardianship Act (Minors)
Iowa Code Ann., 633.552 et seq.

Guardianship Act (Public)
Fla. Stat. 1983, 744.701 et seq.
Wyo. Stat. Ann., § 3-7-101 et seq.

Guardianship Act (Standby)
N.J. Stat. Ann., 3B:12-67 et seq.

Guardianship Act (Veterans)
Fla. Stat. Ann., 744.701 et seq.
Iowa Code Ann., 633.614 et seq.
Kan. Stat. Ann., 73-501 et seq.
Md. Ann. Code 1957, Art. 96 1/2, § 19 et seq.
Me. Rev. Stat. Ann. 1964, Title 18-A,
§ 5-101 et seq.
Mich. Comp. Laws Ann., 35.71 et seq.
Mont. Code Ann. 1947, 91-4801 et seq.
N.C. Gen. Stat. 1943, § 34-1 et seq.
Nev. Rev. Stat. Ann., 160.010 et seq.
N.H. Rev. Stat. 1955, 465:1 et seq.
R.I. Gen. Laws 1956, 33-16-1 et seq.
Wash. Rev. Code Ann., 73.36.010 et seq.
Wis. Stat. Ann., 880.60
W. Va. Code 1966, § 44-15-1 et seq.
Wyo. Stat. Ann., § 3-6-101 et seq.

Guardianship Act (Veterans')
See also Uniform Veterans'Guardianship
Act
N.Y. Mental Hygiene Law 1972 (Consol.
Laws Ch. 27) § 79.01 et seq.

Guardianship and Advocacy Act
Ill. Rev. Stat. 1991, Ch. 91 1/2, § 701 et seq.

Guardianship and Conservatorship Act
W. Va. Code 1966, § 44A-1-1 et seq.

Guardianship and Conservatorship Law
Okla. Stat. Ann., Title 30, § 1-101 et seq.

**Guardianship and Protective Proceedings
Act**
See Uniform Guardianship and Protective
Proceedings Act

Guardianship-Conservatorship Law
Cal. Probate Code § 1400 et seq.

**Guardianship for Adults with Mental
Retardation Act (Public)**
Minn. Stat. Ann., 252A.01 et seq.

Guardianship for Disabled Adults Act
Ill. Rev. Stat. 1991, Ch. 110 1/2, § 11a-1 et
seq.

Guardianship of Infants Act
Ky. Rev. Stat. 1971, Superseded Vol.,
403.070

Guardianship Program Act
Kan. Stat. Ann., 74-9601 et seq.

Guardianship Veterans Act
Iowa Code Ann., 633.614 et seq.

Guards Act (Security)
Me. Rev. Stat. Ann. 1964, Title 32, § 9401 et
seq.

**Guatemala Relief and Rehabilitation Act of
1976**
April 21, 1976, P.L. 94-276, 22 U.S. Code
§§ 2292g et seq.

Guayule Rubber Act
March 5, 1942, Ch. 140, 56 Stat. 126, 7 U.S. Code §§ 171 to 173
Oct. 20, 1942, Ch. 617, 56 Stat. 796, 7 U.S. Code §§ 171, 172

Gubernatorial Appointee Oath Act
Ill. Rev. Stat. 1991, Ch. 101, §§ 100, 101

Gubernatorial Transition Act
Ga. Code Ann., 45-12-190 et seq.
Md. Ann. Code 1974, Art. SG, § 3-201 et seq.
N.J. Stat. Ann., 52:15A-1 et seq.

Guertin Act (Insurance Nonforfeiture)
Va. Code 1950, § 38.2-3200 et seq.

Guertin Act (Standard Valuation)
Minn. Stat. Ann., 61A.25

Guest Act
Wyo. Stat. Replacement Titles 1977, § 31-5-1116

Guest Act (Airplanes)
Cal. Public Utilities Code § 21406
Ill. Rev. Stat. 1975, Ch. 15 1/2, § 22.83

Guest Act (Motor Vehicles)
Neb. Rev. Stat. 1991, Ch. 32, § 12.35 et seq.

Guest Act (Motorboats)
Cal. Harbors and Navigation Code § 661.1

Guest Passenger Act
Nev. Rev. Stat. 1979 Reprint, Replaced Pages, 41.180

Guest Registration Act (Hotels)
N.H. Rev. Stat. 1955, 353:3

Guest Statute (Motor Vehicles)
Ala. Code 1975, § 32-1-2
Ark. Stat. 1947, 75-913 et seq.
Cal. Vehicle Code 1959, § 17158
Colo. Rev. Stat., 42-9-101
Conn. Public Acts, 1991, p. 4404, Ch. 308
Del. Code of 1974, Title 21, § 6101
Fla. Stat. 1971, 320.59

Ga. Code 1933, 68-301
Ida. Code 1947, 49-2415
Ill. Rev. Stat. 1991, Ch. 95 1/2, §§ 10-201, 10-202
Ind. Code Ann., 9-3-3-1, 9-3-3-2
Iowa Code Ann., 321.494
Kan. Laws 1931, Ch. 81
Ky. Stat. 1936, § 12-7
Mich. Comp. Laws Ann., 257.401
Mont. Rev. Code 1947, 32-1113 et seq.
N.D. Cent. Code, Superseded Volume, 39-15-01 et seq.
Neb. Rev. Stat. 1943, 39-6,191
Nev. Rev. Stat. (1979 Reprint), 41.180
Nev. Rev. Stat. 1979 Reprint, Replaced Pages, 41.180
N.M. Stat. Ann. 1953, 64-24-1, 64-24-2
Ohio Rev. Code 1953, 4515.02
Ore. Rev. Stat., 30.115
S.C. Code Ann. 1976, § 15-1-290
S.D. Codified Laws 1967, 32-34-1, 32-34-2
Tex. Civ. Practice and Remedies Code, § 72.001 et seq.
Utah Code Ann. 1953, Miscellaneous Superseded Code Provisions, 41-9-1, 41-9-2
Va. Code 1950, § 8.01-63
Vt. Acts 1929, No. 78
Wash. Rev. Code Ann., 46.08.070
Wyo. Stat. Replacement Titles 1977, § 31-5-1116

Guffey-Snyder Coal Act
Aug. 30, 1935, Ch. 824, 49 Stat. 991

Guffey-Vinson Act
See Bituminous Coal Act of 1937

Guggisberg-Nichols-Higgins Act (Tax Exemptions)
Mich. Comp. Laws Ann., 211.7, 211.9

Guide Dogs Act
Ill. Rev. Stat. 1991, Ch. 38, § 65, 65-1
N.M. Stat. Ann., 28-11-1 et seq.

Guidelines Act (Parole)
Fla. Stat. Ann., 947.001 et seq.

Guidelines Act (Sentencing)
Kan. Laws 1992, Ch. 239

Guides and Outfitters Act
Colo. Rev. Stat. 1963, 62-22-1 et seq.
Mont. Code Ann. 1985, 87-4-101 et seq.

Guilderland Zoning Law
N.Y. Local Laws 1971, Town of
Guilderland, p. 2055

Guilford County Public Morals Act
N.C. Public-Local Laws 1913, Ch. 761

Guilford Municipal-County Court Act
N.C. Laws 1955, Ch. 971
N.C. Public Laws 1909, Ch. 651

Gulf Coast Regional Wastewater Authority Act
Miss. Code Ann. 1972, § 49-17-301 et seq.

Gulf Coast Waste Disposal Authority Act
Tex. Rev. Civ. Stat. 1948, Art. 7621d-2

Gulf Islands National Seashore Act
Jan. 8, 1971, P.L. 91-660, 84 Stat. 1967, 16
U.S. Code §§ 459h to 459h-10

Gulf Regional District Act
Miss. Code Ann. 1972, § 17-11-1 et seq.

Gulf States Marine Fisheries Compact Act
Ala. Code 1975, § 9-12-180 et seq.
La. Rev. Stat. Ann., 56:71 et seq.
Miss. Code Ann. 1972, § 49-15-101 et seq.
Tex. Parks and Wildlife Code, § 91.001 et
seq.

Gulf War Syndrome Registry Act
Colo. Rev. Stat., 25-4-1901 et seq.

Gulledge-Cates Banking Reform Act
Ala. Code 1975, § 5-1A-1 et seq.

Gun Control Act
D.C. Code Ann., § 6-2301 et seq.
Kan. Stat. Ann., 48-1901
Mass. Gen. Laws Ann., 140:121 et seq.
N.J. Stat. Ann., 2C:39-1 et seq.

N.Y. Criminal Procedure Law (Consol. Laws
Ch. 11A) §§ 220.10, 220.30
N.Y. Penal Law 1965 (Consol. Laws Ch. 40)
§§ 60.05, 60.11, 70.02, 70.04, 70.15,
120.11, 265.02, 265.08 et seq., 400.00

Gun Control Act (New York City)
N.Y. City Adm. Code 1938, Ch. 18,
§ 436-6.0 et seq.

Gun Control Act of 1968
Oct. 22, 1968, P.L. 90-618, 82 Stat. 1213, 18
U.S. Code §§ 921 to 928; 18 U.S. Code
Appx. 26 U.S. Code §§ 5801, 5802, 5811,
5812, 5821, 5822, 5841 to 5849, 5851 to
5854, 5871, 5872, 6806, 7273

Gun Control Law (Bartley-Fox)
Mass. Gen. Laws 1984, 269:10

Gun-Free School Zone Act
Cal. Penal Code § 626.9

Gun-Free School Zone Act of 1990
Nov. 29, 1990, P.L. 101-647, 18 U.S. Code
§§ 921-922 nt., 924

Gun-Free Schools Act of 1994
March 31, 1994, P.L. 103-227, 20 U.S. Code
§ 2701 nt.

Guns Act (Zero Tolerance for)
N.J. Stat. Ann., 18A:37-7 et seq.

Gunshot Wound Act
Ohio Rev. Code 1953, 2917.44

Gwinnett County Airport Authority Act
Ga. Laws 1971, p. 3668

Gwinnett County Public Facilities Authority Act
Ga. Laws 1975, p. 4463

Gwinnett County Recreation Authority Act
Ga. Laws 1975, p. 3108

Gwinnett County Water and Sewerage Authority Act
Ga. Laws 1970, p. 2827

Gwynne Act (Portal to Portal)
   May 14, 1947, Ch. 52, 61 Stat. 84, 29 U.S.
      Code §§ 216, 251 to 262

Gymnasium and Village Library Tax Act
   Ill. Rev. Stat. 1991, Ch. 81, § 73.9 et seq.

Gypsy Moth Act
   Conn. Gen. Stat. 1953, § 22-91a et seq.